HANDBOOK

WRTH

THE DIRECTORY OF GLOBAL BROADCASTING

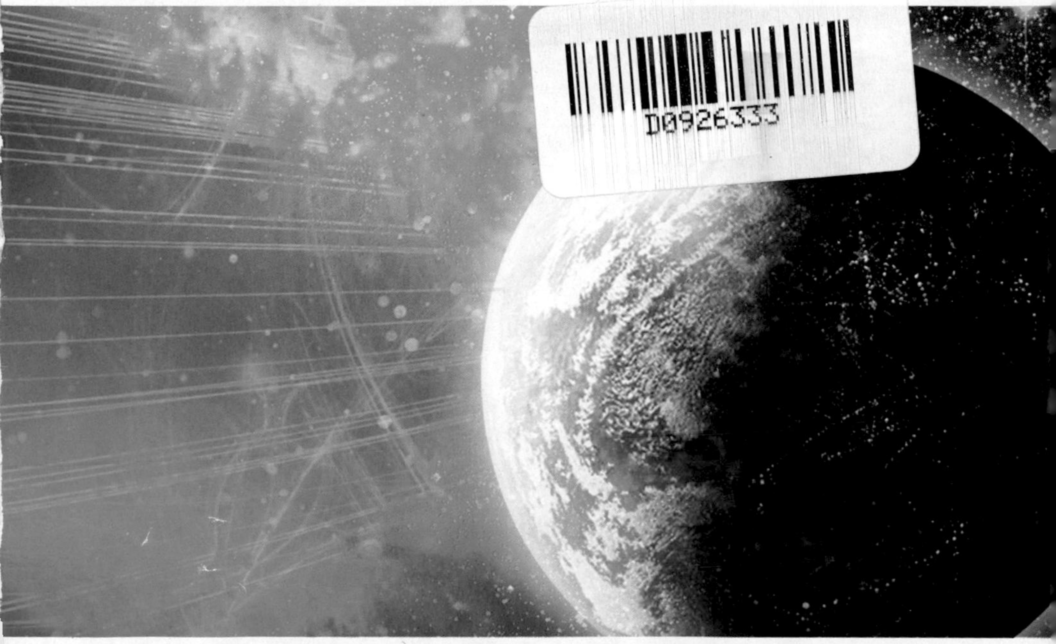

2021

Never stop asking

QQQQQ
QQQQQ
QQQQQ
QQQQQ
QQQ&A

Plus how and why from the BBC's international news teams

VOLUME 75 – 2021

Publisher
Nicholas Hardyman

International Editor
Sean Gilbert

'A' Schedule & Web Updates Editor
Mauno Ritola

Television Editor
Bernd Trutenau

Equiment Reviews
Keith Rawlings

Contributing Editors
George Jacobs *Editor Emeritus*
Bengt Ericson *Editor Emeritus*
Dave Kenny
Mauno Ritola
Bernd Trutenau
Torgeir Woxen

Cover Design
Richard Boxall Design Associates

WRTH Publications Limited
PO Box 290
Oxford OX2 7FT
United Kingdom
Tel: +44 (0) 1865 339355
Fax: +44 (0) 1865 339301
Email: wrth@wrth.com
Web: www.wrth.com
ISBN 978-1-9998300-3-8

Printed and bound in the UK by CPI William Clowes, Beccles NR34 7TL

WORLD RADIO TV HANDBOOK

CONTENTS

Section Contents

Features & Reviews

Editorial

THE 75TH EDITION OF *WRTH*

This edition is dedicated to the *WRTH* readers and all radio enthusiasts who have lost their lives as a result of the Covid-19 pandemic.

We are delighted to welcome you to *WRTH* 2021, and to provide you once again with the most comprehensive and up-to-date information on global broadcasting available anywhere in the world. This book is the result of the hard work and endurance of our team of editors and contributors without whom the compilation of such a large volume of data would not be possible.

It was with great sadness that we heard that Swedish DXer and member of the Arctic Radio Club, Olle Alm, had passed away in December 2019. Olle was for many years the contributor responsible for the US and Canadian entries in *WRTH*. A civil engineer by profession, Olle's hobby was listening to North American stations, and he spent a few weeks in January every year in the far north of Sweden monitoring the bands.

We were also very sorry to hear that Dario Monferini, long-term *WRTH* contributor for Italy, had suffered a serious stroke and we wish him all the best in his recovery.

NEW WAVES

We are pleased this year finally to be able to review the latest tabletop receiver from AOR, the AR5700D, and to begin to investigate the extraordinary range of modes it is able to receive. We have also delighted in the impressive and very well designed IC-7610 transceiver from Icom, and it was also very good to get a view of the long-awaited Tecsun PL-990. With a wealth of new SDRs on the market we chose the new RSPdx from SDRPlay and were happy in our choice as this company contines to innovate and produce exceptional receivers. Lastly, we have belatedly had a look at the KiwiSDR, with which many readers will be familiar. This very effective 'kit' SDR has the added feature of being able to be put online from any location with a network connection, to the benefit of DXers everywhere.

Given the decline in some DX Club activity we were glad to hear that the Indian DX Club International is resurrecting their *Asian DX Review* publication. It will be issued monthly as an online pdf, and it will surely be a worthy successor to the paper version last seen in 1990.

It is heartening to read surveys showing that more people than for many years are listening to radio of all kinds. A fascinating visualisation of the wealth of available transmissions is provided by *Radio Garden*. For those who don't know it, this program from the Netherlands Institute for Sound & Vision, shows a globe with green dots spread across it representing worldwide broadcast radio stations. Drag the globe to listen to broadcasts from Bermuda to New Calendonia and everywhere in between. Whether accessed via a receiver, or using more recent technology, radio broadcasting is thriving.

***WRTH* FREQUENCY BARGRAPH**

The bargraph frequency CDs proved once again to be very popular, and we will be producing them for the B20 and A21 seasons. There will also be the facility to download a file containing all the data on the CD. The CDs and downloads will again only be available from our website.

WEBSITE UPDATES

We will as usual be uploading free pdf updates to our website. Updates to the B20 season will be available in February 2021. The full schedules for the A21 season will be posted in May 2021 with an update in July 2021. We will also continue to provide updates to the National Radio section on the *WRTHmonitor* page on our website.

PRIZE DRAW RESULTS

These winners were again drawn by members of the British DX Club. The Reader's Questionnaire will once more be on an online form which can be accessed from a link on the website. Please do fill in the form. We greatly value your feedback and you will also be entered into a Prize Draw with the chance to win a copy of *WRTH* 2022.

RESULTS OF THE
***WRTH* 2020 PRIZE DRAW**

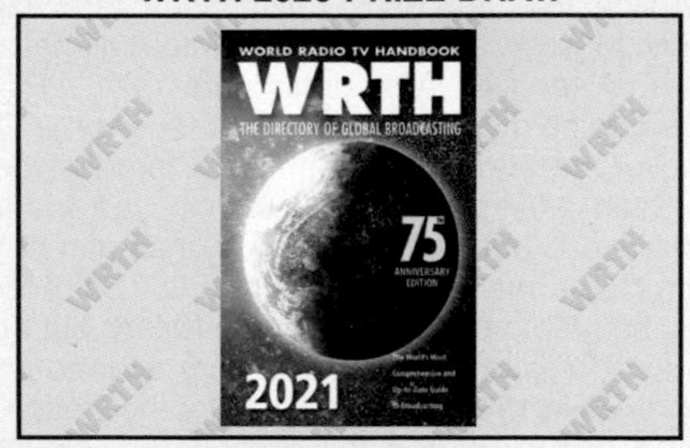

5 WINNERS will receive a copy of *WRTH* 2021

Gigi Nadali, Italy
Mogire Machuki, Kenya
Paul Lewis, UK
Dominic Fongemie, USA
Pedro Cunha, Portugal

I hope you will enjoy reading and using this new edition of *WRTH*

Nicholas Hardyman
Publisher

WRTH Contributors 2021

***WRTH* contributors & editors come from all walks of life, yet share a common fascination with all aspects of global broadcasting. Each year we profile one of the people whose dedicated work makes possible the enormous task of updating *WRTH* each year. This year it is the turn of Stig Hartvig Nielsen to give us an insight into what makes a *WRTH* Contributor.**

Stig Hartvig Nielsen

My interest in radio started around 1970 when I was tall enough to reach the radio tuning knob and tune away from dull Radio Denmark. There would often be fewer than 60 minutes of poorly presented pop music on this station, and the news and current affairs programmes were in favour of the Vietnam War and anti-socialist. Therefore I was thrilled to listen to music from stations such as Radio Caroline, RNI, and Radio Luxembourg, and excited to hear different views about the Vietnam War on Radio Moscow and Radio Berlin International, which at that time carried Danish programmes on their external services. After getting the 1971 WRTH, which opened an amazing new world for me, and after buying my first full coverage receiver, a GE BRT400, I started chasing shortwave stations from all over the world. My favourite DX targets were Latin America, The Caribbean, and the pirates.

Soon after starting the DX hobby, a friend and I founded Dansk DX Lytter Klub (Danish DX Listeners' Club) and I have been chairman of the club for most of the years since. Besides DDXLK, I am also a member of the British DX Club, Medium Wave Circle and Malmoe Shortwave Club. Not only has radio been my favourite hobby, but I have also worked with radio for most of my life.

After private local stations were allowed in Denmark an application to launch Radio Viborg was approved in 1984. My inspiration for the station was the formats, programming and presentation I had heard, especially from the Netherlands, the UK and Latin America. It was a full-service station with popular music and newscasts during prime time and specialized programming in the evenings. It became hugely popular and was the number one private station in Denmark for several years.

After leaving Radio Viborg I was General Manager of Radio ABC in Randers – a CHR format radio station targeting younger listeners – and launched Radio Alfa, catering to a more adult audience. We were the first private station in Denmark to offer two formats for our target area. Shortly before leaving these stations, I began weekly broadcasts in English on shortwave via Kaliningrad. I also worked for the Danish public service station, DR (Radio Denmark), as controller for regional stations and head of programming at P4. Later I was a member of the Board of Directors at DR.

But life as a broadcaster has taken me to other places. I was a presenter on pirate Radio Viking (1977-78) and ran the 50W transmitter on 6240kHz for the last months before it was raided by the Danish authorities. For six months in 1990 I transmitted pirate Q-AM Quality Radio on 9985kHz with 500W on Sundays. My later shortwave activities were legal. I joined World Music Radio (WMR) as a presenter in 1982 when it was being heard via Radio Dublin and Radio Milan International. I took over the name in 1997 and began broadcasting on SW from Denmark in 2004. Later I also started Radio208 on SW and MW from Copenhagen. It is great to be a MW/SW-broadcaster and fight the decline in MW broadcasting in Europe and in SW broadcasting in general.

For many years I published a handbook covering radio and TV stations in Denmark, Faroe Islands and Greenland. It was modelled on WRTH but with more details on the stations. The handbook was published 34 times until 2008. Around this time, I also ran a website for the Danish radio industry with daily news coverage on the broadcasting scene in Denmark and abroad.

Over the years I have travelled a lot, almost always with radio in my mind and a radio in my luggage. In 1980-81 I travelled to the Caribbean and South America with my beloved SPR4 and 30m of longwire, and have been to many other countries, often visiting radio stations and writing articles about them for DX magazines. More recently I travelled the countries in the southern part of South America with my Perseus receiver and an ALA1530 loop aerial cut into three pieces so as to fit in my luggage. In 1996 I was the proud winner of the Nordic DX Championship.

Besides the GE400, SPR4, and the Perseus, I have used a Ten-Tec RX340 and a Sony ICF2001 for DXing, but for the past few years I have preferred using my AOR AR7030+. FM DXing has also been an area of activity, but for me transatlantic MW DX is the best part of the hobby.

I feel pretty sure that DXing is going to live on for at least the rest of my lifetime, so rest assured that I will still be tuning the bands in the years to come.

Stig Hartvig Nielsen

Official WRTH Contributor for Anguilla, Antigua, Bahamas, Barbados, Bermuda, Cayman Is, Denmark, Dominica, Faroe I., Greenland, Grenada, Jamaica, Martinique, Montserrat, St Kitts, St Lucia, St Vincent, Trinidad & Tobago, Turks & Caicos, Virgin Is (British & US)

A large project such as *WRTH* could not be produced without the help of many people from all over the world. The following organisations and publications give invaluable help:

Asian Broadcasting Institute, Australian Radio DX Club, BC-DX Top News, British DX Club, Club Diexistas de la Amistad Internacional, DX-Listening Digest, DX Re Mix News, Grupo Radioescucha Argentino, International Radio Club of America, National Radio Club Inc (USA listings), World SW Radio Association

our Country Contributors provide us with updated entries for the countries for which they are responsible:

Herman Boel, Luís Carvalho, Swopan Chakroborty, Bryan Clark, Svetomir Cuckovic, Alan Davies, Alok Dasgupta, Barry Hartley, Stuart Forsyth, David Foster, Christian Ghibaudo, Martin Hadlow, Stig Hartvig Nielsen, Kevin Hand, István Hegedüs, Karel Honzík, Richard Jary, Jose Jacob, Dave Kenny, Tetsuya Kondo, Vashek Korinek, Kai Ludwig, Dario Monferini, Paul Rawdon, Andy Reid, Mauno Ritola, Francisco Rubio Cubo, Roberto Scaglione, Mike Smith, Bernd Trutenau, Max van Arnhem, Thierry Vignaud, Tore B Vik, Torgeir Woxen

they and we are greatly aided by our other major contributors:

Ian Baxter, Erich Bergmann, Hansjörg Biener, Dino Bloise, Héctor García Bojorge, Wolfgang Büschel, Mustafa Cancurt, Alfredo Cañote, Julio Pineda Cordón, Marcelo Cornachioni, Fredrik Dourén, Amine Ferhane, Claudio Galaz, Santiago San Gil, Dan Goldfarb, Victor Goonetilleke, Noel Green, Chris Greenway, Rudolf Walter Grimm, Rawad Hamwi, Glenn Hauser, Tetsuya Hirahara, Dave Kernick, Anatoly Klepov, Rubén Medina, Humberto Molina, Don Moore, Adán Mur, Michael Nevradakis, Horacio Nigro, Anker Petersen, Mieczyslaw Pietruski, Arnulf Piontek, Rimantas Pleikys, Patrick Robic, Enric Roca, Victor Rutkovsky, Zhang ShiFeng, Berny Solano, Mohammad Hassan Soltani, David Stanley, Luis Toranzo, Tarek Zeidan

We thank them, and also all our readers who have written or emailed us with useful ideas and information. Please keep sending your thoughts and updates to:

wrth@wrth.com

AOR AR5700D

US$5840 £4595 €5010

OVERVIEW

The AR5700D is a high-performance wide-band communications receiver. As well as resolving the common modes of AM, SAM, FM, WFM(S), SSB and CW it also decodes the TETRA (including Direct Mode, Traffic Channel and GSSI user group filtering), DMR, NXDN, D-STAR, DPMR, APCO 25, YAESU and Alinco EJ-47 digital voice modes. It sports a backlit LCD main display with a frequency span of up to 10MHz. It has provision for computer control, and free software is provided along with the required USB to PC leads. With a frequency coverage of 9kHz to 3.7GHz and multi-mode reception, the AR5700D has all the makings of an extremely capable receiver.

FEATURES

The AR5700D comes in a smart looking case not dissimilar to the AR5000, AR5001 and AR6000. The front panel markings appear prominent with the buttons, controls and display standing out well. The unit is reasonably weighty at around 5kg and measures approximately 225mm x 110mm x 330mm. It has a carry handle on one side and four feet on the opposite with a retractable tilt bail on the underside. The overall black finish contrasts with the grey trim and white lettering to give a very neat appearance. The characters on the dot matrix LCD display, while looking pixelated, stand out well. The analogue signal strength meter is on the small side but easily readable and has a pleasant amber backlight. Signal strengths are repeated in dBm or dBu on the LCD display.

The front panel controls are good quality and consist of three rotary encoders – one volume, one squelch and one acting as a sub dial – and the main tuning control, which is free running. The front panel also has a selection of push buttons, all having more than one function, there is a 3.5mm phones socket, an SD card port and also an 8-pin mini DIN accessory socket.

On the rear panel there are two Type N sockets for aerial inputs. Ant 1 is for frequencies over 25MHz and Ant 2 is used for the full coverage of the radio, although please note that this changes when using the software (see below).

There are sockets for IF out (BNC with 15MHz bandwidth), 10MHz external reference clock input (SMA), video out (phono/RCA), USB (type B) for I/Q and Computer Control, 9-pin D for receiver serial control or an optional Ethernet controller, Aux 2 8-pin Mini DIN (provided for 'future applications'), and two 3.5mm jacks for speaker and line output. 12V DC power to the set is taken from the supplied external mains unit which plugs into a 2.5mm socket. The main DC power-off switch is located on the rear panel.

We found little information available on the inner workings of the set but the sales literature states that the radio is fitted with four Renesas SH2 CPU's, three Analogue Devices Blackfin DSPs, one Analogue Devices ADSP-2185 DSP, and four Intel Altera Cyclon FPGAs. These devices providing signal processing, demodulation and decoding. It is claimed that 63/65MHz sampling frequencies are used for the analogue to digital converters. Clearly, the AR5700D benefits from some advanced technology. There are 33 RF bandpass filters and AOR claim IP_3 figures of +20dBm at 14.1MHz Preselector off, +6dBm at 50MHz and +5dBm at 620MHz Preamp off.

There is provision for instant recording and playback to the supplied 16Gb SD Card.

Two thousand memory channels are provided in 50x40 banks and these can be customised to hold between 5 to 95 channels per bank in a form of 'dynamic memory', allowing banks with only a few entries to be set aside for specific uses. There are also 40 search banks, and 1230 pass or priority channels can be set. The supplied manual describes the basic operations.

EVALUATION

We are grateful to Frederic Collin of AOR Japan for supplying the review unit, which came with firmware version Main-007A DON7B P007A installed. Updates to the AR5007D firmware can only be installed at AOR dealers. Aerials used in the evaluation were a 66ft inverted L and home made Active Loop for HF, and a Diamond V2000 and discone for VHF. These were connected to the rear panel with ANT1 for VHF and ANT2 for HF. The AR5007D is a complex radio and only the main features will be discussed.

Having experience of an AR5000+3 it soon became apparent that operating the AR50007D is very similar. The rotary controls for AF Gain, Squelch and Sub Dial are of the detent type, giving a positive click as they were rotated and the main tuning control is free-running and smooth enough. Mode and step size – tuning steps from 1Hz to 999.999kHz are available – may be altered by a short press of the red Mode and Step buttons next to the main tuning control. Settings are then selected by stepping through the options with the sub dial and pressing the red MHz/ENT button to select. A long press on the Mode or Step button will select default settings. There are five variable frequency oscillators (VFO) on the AR57000D and each may be stepped through by continually pressing the red VFO button. Each VFO retains its main settings and can be used as a quick and convenient form of memory channel. IF bandwidths can be changed by pressing the Func button and then the 3/IF BW button. Again selection is by the sub dial. The radio is restricted to fixed filter bandwidths when not under computer control. The narrowest setting for SSB is 3kHz which can be considered slightly wide for use on Amateur bands but in the past has been common on receivers for the commercial market. AGC can be selected in a similar fashion but this time using the Func Step/AGC button. Settings are Fast, Medium, Slow and Off with RF gain being selected with button 6; the Squelch control thus becoming the RF Gain control, indicated by two small parallel bars on the LCD display. Direct frequency entry is made using the front panel keypad and can be entered as either kHz or MHz.

An interesting inclusion is a 10-0.4MHz wide Band Scope (or spectrum display) on the LCD. This gives an effective indication of activity either side of the frequency being monitored. The bandwidth is adjusted using the Func-tuning wheel.

The AR57000D is capable of dual band reception where one receiver operates on frequencies below 25MHz (Main) and the second on frequencies above 25MHz (Sub). The 'up' and 'down' buttons being used to toggle between the control of the main and sub receivers. Volume balance can be adjusted between the two and it is possible to tune the radio while in this mode. An Offset and Triple receive mode is also provided.

During the evaluation it was noticed that with the attenuator there was a delay before the set reached full gain when switching from either the 10dB or 20dB settings directly back to Auto.

Noise reduction has three settings, with Low and Medium giving the best results; the High setting sounding rather 'watery'.

Sensitivity was checked against published figures over the broadcast bands up to 108MHz and it was found that these were broadly met.

Operation on the VHF broadcast bands produced clean and crisp audio and the IF filter setting of 100kHz rejected adjacent channel interference from strong stations while still providing good-quality audio. Stereo reproduction through PC speakers when using the software was good.

LW and MW reception quality was again good and the 6kHz IF filter setting was just right for busy bands. There was some interference noted from the supplied PSU between 621-931kHz.

On HF the receiver showed it had good strong-signal handling capability with no signs of overload. Synchronous AM was effective on noisy broadcast stations, taking the edge off fading signals, and IF shift worked well to remove interference. CW reception is limited to the 500kHz filter so reasonably careful tuning is needed when looking for signals, this is easy enough with 10Hz steps selected and once tuned the filter is effective at rejecting adjacent signals. General SSB reception is good but the 3kHz filter, while providing good audio quality, was found to be a touch too wide on the amateur bands, however this ceases to be a problem when under PC control.

A quick evaluation was made of the digital voice modes DMR, D-STAR and NXDN. Signals were decoded fairly easily, both manually and with the 'DALL' automatic setting, although the signals had to be moderately strong and clear.

Overall the set coped very well and returned a good signal to noise ratio on some noisy bands.

AR-IQ-III SOFTWARE

This accompanying software for the radio is supplied on a USB dongle. Installation is reasonably straightforward and full details are given in the manual. The software considerably enhances operation and, as Microtelecom make it under licence, it will be familiar to Perseus users.

When under software control the AR5700D shows 'Remote' on the display and all control is undertaken by the software.The software screen is dominated by a spectrum display that can also be set as a waterfall – but not both. Here the spectrum may be viewed up to a maximum of 900kHz bandwidth. Signal amplitude can be read on the vertical axis as dBm with a scale at the left side of the window. Mode selection is below this, and there is a 'User' button. When the User demodulator is selected the Virtual Audio Cable output is fed with zero-IF IQ samples, which is useful when a third party application wishes to process this data stream at the selected frequency. It seems that automatic frequency control does not function on WFM and there are no digital mode settings when using the software.

When the radio is in 'local control' and is being used as a normal receiver the antenna inputs are ANT1 25MHz to 3.7GHz and ANT2 9kHz to 3.7GHz, but under computer control these are reversed. This means that if both local and PC control is required, users will either have to swap the connections or supply a reversing switch. Incidentally this also applies when using the IF output as the inputs are reversed for this as well.

There is a smaller 'secondary' spectrum window where the receiver's IF bandwidth range can be selected and varied. A right click drags the entire bandwidth and the upper and lower bandwidth edges can also be dragged independently with a left click and drag.

There are sliders for Pass Band Tuning, Notch, Auto Notch, CW Peak, spectrum display averaging and a fully variable Noise Blanker. To the far right of this box is another slider with AGC settings, Marker Select, Memory Bank, an S Meter calibrated in dBm and S Units, and a Database selector. The database selector, used for example with EIDB, looks up the frequency the radio is tuned to and if there is an entry found, displays station information. To the right of this box are sliders for AF Volume and also Variable Noise Reduction. At the bottom of the screen are settings for recording and playback of the whole 900kHz spectrum of the receiver. We found that on our system the software would not save to the hard drive of the PC but happily saved to other drives. This may be connected to our setup as the feature worked well on another Windows 10 PC.

With the USB dongle plugged into the computer it is possible to run multiple instances of AR-IQ-III, thus the radio can be simultaneously controlled and recordings made in one instance, while playing back saved files for analysis in others. As well as the dongle, there need to be two further free USB ports on the computer one for the I/Q line and another for computer control.

MEMORY MANAGER

Also available for our evaluation was a small memory management utility, the AR57000D Editing Software v.1.1.1.0, which facilitates the editing of memory banks and channels, scan groups, search banks and search groups. This is a useful addition as while it is possible to edit these details directly into the receiver the process can be tedious. Using this utility to set up two new search banks took mere seconds. Memory editing is a little slower but still much quicker than doing so from the keypad. Data is not saved to a hard drive but sent directly to the radio. A 'save to disk' feature would be a useful addition.

CONCLUSION

The AOR AR5700D sales brochure states, 'Your wide-band signal detection, monitoring, voice decoding, recording and playback solution' and this is certainly true. The radio is reasonably intuitive to use and any previous owner of an AR5000-6000 would be immediately at home. The front panel controls are nice and positive and with multiple VFOs set up for different frequencies and reception modes it is a breeze to step between the many different operating modes the set provides. The AR5700D is in some ways two different receivers, because the AR-IQ-III software significantly extends the versatility of the receiver and adds features that are not available in standalone mode, all of which were found to be effective. The software also allows the spectrum to be visually monitored and recorded when searching for signals. What sets the AR5700D apart from most other radios is the inclusion of all the popular VHF/UHF digital voice modes.

Taking everything into account the AR57000D is an exceptionally versatile tool for spectrum searching or monitoring as well as surveillance or unattended operation.

Its performance on all the broadcast bands was excellent, coping well under various conditions. It covers all modes; has admirable computer control; and has a discriminator output, so that whatever the AR5700 cannot do itself, can be sent to external devices or software that can. In short, it offers users just about everything they would ever need in a receiver.

Rating table for AOR AR5700D

Constructional quality	★★★★★
Sensitivity	★★★★★
Dynamic range	★★★★★
RF intermodulation	★★★★★
Versatility	★★★★★
VFM	★★★★
Overall rating	**★★★★★**

Key:
★ = Poor ★★ = Fair ★★★ = Average
★★★★ = Very Good ★★★★★ = Excellent
VFM = Value for money

The reviews in this section have been prepared in the main by **Keith Rawlings** (G4MIU). Keith writes extensively on radio matters and currently has a monthly column in *RadioUser* magazine. First licensed in 1976 under the call G8MCK, and with a life-long interest in radio and electronics, he has been involved with telecommunications professionally for many years.

Bonito NTi MegaDipol MD300DX

US$555 £430 €469

The MegaDipol is a broadband active dipole operating from 9kHz to 300MHz. It has an external head unit containing a high performance amplifier, with two detachable 2.5-metre PVC-coated steel wire dipole elements, and a Bias-T power inserter to power the head unit via a coaxial cable. The inserter can be powered from a 10-15V DC supply, or from a 5V supply such as a USB power bank. Both inputs are protected against electrostatic discharge up to 8kV. All components appear to be of the highest quality.

The MegaDipol is versatile and can be mounted as a horizontal or vertical dipole, a V or inverted V, a sloper, or an L or inverted L. The element length can be increased to up to 4m for more gain, and there is a jumper inside where gain can be increased by 3dB within 9kHz to 150MHz. Its small size makes it a good choice for those who are bound by rules governing aerials or don't have the space for a full-sized array.The MegaDipol however, is best used in an electrically quiet environment because the aerial reacts to the electrical field and is prone to picking up locally-generated electrical interference. With its very high gain, receivers should have a good dynamic range to be used successfully with the MegaDipol.

Comparison aerials for the evaluation were a 66ft Inverted L end fed with the top at 20ft and a home made PA0RDT Mini Whip with good grounding located at 15ft. The Megadipol was mounted vertically with the amplifier box central at 13ft. It is recommended that good quality coaxial cable is fitted to the amplifier and we used a 25ft run Antennax ANT-240 that was to hand.

In the first instance the Megadipol was used in an electrically noisy urban environment. On the LW and MW bands we found that it produced better signal strengths and signal-to-noise ratio (SNR) readings than the Mini Whip, and there was also an improvement in the overall noise floor between approximately 150 to 1700kHz. On the HF bands we compared it to the Inverted L and here results varied. On some signals the L returned better SNR figures and on others it was the reverse, but in every case the overall noise floor was better on the L throughout the HF range. On the VHF broadcast bands and mounted horizontally the MegaDipol produced entirely satisfactory signal levels for general listening.

Heeding Bonito's advice we then took the MegaDipol to a relatively quiet RF environment and here the change was remarkable. We found signal strength levels similar to what we would expect from a full-size dipole, yet the noise floor was low with relative s-meter readings of no more than 3 S points. Over the range of 9kHz to 30MHz the Dipol provided excellent reception and VHF reception was also noticeably improved.

CONCLUSION

The Megadipol is clearly very effective. It has high gain with a low noise factor coupled with good dynamic range, and returns an SNR performance which is comparable to a full sized dipole.

Being so small it is ideal for portable operation or for those with limited space, although they may well be in built up areas where there is likely to be a lot of locally generated noise, and this needs to be taken into account. However it may be possible to experiment with placing and orientating the aerial in such a way as to minimise noise pick-up.

In locations which lack space for an efficient aerial for lower frequencies, the MegaDipol is a great choice as it is capable of returning excellent results down to the lowest frequencies, and in the right environment it works exceptionally well.

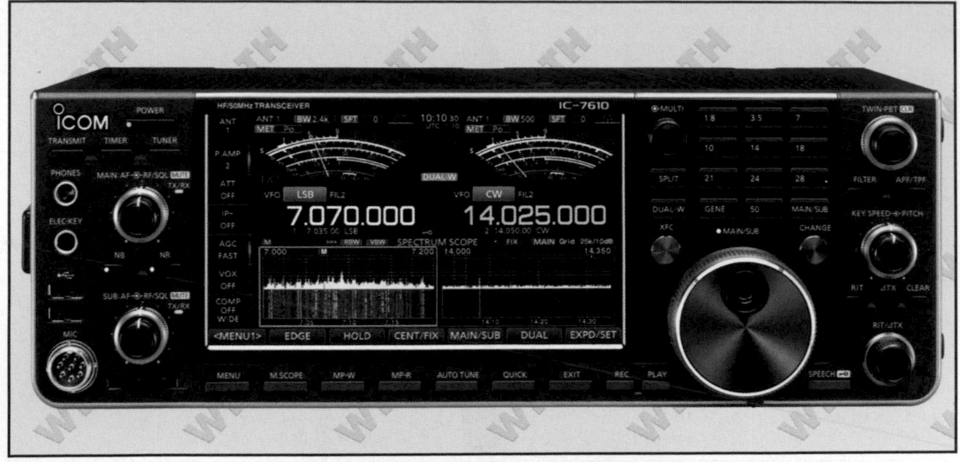

Icom IC-7610

US$3840 £3000 €3240

Overview

The IC-7610 is a smart looking HF+50MHz transceiver from Icom, and we are grateful to Icom UK for the loan of this unit. From the outside it appears to be a conventional radio with knobs and buttons but, on the inside, it employs advanced and powerful direct sampling SDR technology and can therefore be operated without recourse to a separate computer.

This inbuilt technology brings many advantages including the provision of two totally separate receivers which can be tuned to anywhere within the range of 30kHz to 60MHz, each receiver being completely independent of the other, and providing genuine dual-receive capability.

A large and eye-catching 7-inch (178mm) 800x480px colour touch-screen display provides the user with all the operating details, and the means to make changes to the radio's settings with a simple sequence of screen 'touches'.

The IC-7610 looks stylish, is packed with many advanced features, and promises excellent performance. In this evaluation we will concentrate primarily on the receiver side of the set.

FEATURES

Each receiver incorporates direct sampling up-conversion SDR techniques. Signals from the aerial are fed to a 16-bit Analogue to Digital Converter (ADC) via a two stage pre-selector which protects the ADC from strong out of band signals; the first stage being Icom's DigiSel tracking pre-selector. A Field Programmable Gate Array performs all of the signal processing functions such as demodulation and delivers a 12kHz IF to the Digital to Analogue Converter (DAC).

In addition to the display, the front panel has its share of controls and buttons.The main tuning knob runs smoothly and the mechanical buttons have a pleasing 'click' when pressed.The concentric controls feel a little 'light' to operate but are positive enough and function well.

Two USB sockets are provided on the front panel for such things as I/Q output, which can be fed to a PC for data decoding, or a flash drive which may be used for firmware updates, saving of screen images, memory channels, transmitted or received audio and so on. An SD card slot is also provided for storing data. Two 6mm jack sockets, one for headphones and the other for an electronic keyer, are located above the USB ports and below these is the 8-pin microphone socket.

The main item that dominates the front panel is the colour LCD touch screen display and it is this that really brings this radio alive. A bar graph or analogue-styled 'swing' type Signal Meter may be selected and a dual (or single) band Spectrum Scope can also be displayed with a bandwidth of up to 1Mhz (+/-500kHz).

Signals can be seen visually in real time and are easily tuned to with a couple of finger touches on the display. Parameters for filter bandwidths, Mode, Notch Filter selection, and many others are clearly visible, enabling the operator to instantly see the status of the radio. The display can also present received (and transmitted) audio waveforms graphically in order to monitor the AF characteristics.

On the rear panel there are a number of connectors, amongst which are two main aerial connections utilising SO239 sockets and also two BNC receiving aerial sockets. The IC-7610 can save various combinations of antenna settings to memory. An external BNC 10MHz precision reference frequency input is provided, and located next to this is a BNC transverter port. There are two separate speaker outputs, and a DVI-D display connector for an external video monitor.

A LAN (Ethernet) connection enables the IC-7610 to be connected directly to a network, without the need for a PC, for local and worldwide remote access. Optional RS-BA1v2 software is available for remote operation and is compatible with the RC28 USB remote control encoder wheel. A good quality speaker is located at the top front of the radio on the right hand side.

As already mentioned, the receiver covers the range of 30kHz to 60MHz (performance guaranteed from 500kHz-30MHz and 50-54MHz), while the transmitter covers all the amateur bands, depending on the regional version, with an output power of 1-100W (1-25W AM).

The IC-7610 has good strong signal handling capabilities and Icom quote the 'reciprocal mixing dynamic range' as 110dB. Frequency stability is quoted as being less than +/- 0.5 ppm at 0-50 deg C. Operating Modes are USB, LSB, AM, CW, RTTY, PSK31/63 and FM. There is sadly no Synchronous AM capability.

Two pre-amplifier settings are provided. Pre-Amp one has 12dB of gain with wide dynamic range and is recommended for low HF operation. Pre-Amp two has 20dB of gain and is for use on the higher HF bands.There is a 3-45dB variable attenuator and a selectable IP+ feature which improves the receiver's third-order intercept point.

Three pre-set ACG settings for each mode are provided but are menu-adjustable with delay settings from 0.1 to 6 seconds (8 seconds for AM) and Off. For FM the AGC is fixed.

Digital Twin Passband Tuning (T-PBT) enables the IC-7610 to eliminate adjacent channel interference by electronically shifting the IF above or below the IF centre frequency, and a Notch filter can be selected with both manual or automatic operation. There are three pre-set IF filter settings for each mode but these bandwidths can be varied by the operator. There are 99 memory channels for saving favourite frequencies.

Power consumption is 23A at 100W on transmit and 3-3.5A on receive with a 13.8V DC supply. There is no inbuilt PSU so a DC lead, complete with a large in-line EMC filter, is supplied. An inbuilt ATU is provided which can match an impedance range of 16.7-150 Ohms.

The IC-7610 sits in the 'Mid' size of amateur transceivers measuring 340x118x277mm and weighs in at 8.5kg. The review model came with an MH-219 hand-held microphone.

A basic operators manual is supplied with the radio and an advanced manual can be downloaded from the internet. Both manuals are comprehensive, informative and concise.

EVALUATION

Aerials used for reception were a 66ft inverted L end fed at 30ft with a 20:1 BALUN providing a DC path to ground, and a home made Active Magnetic Loop of 1m diameter. A 100ft top doublet at 30ft fed with 450 Ohm ladder line was used with an external ATU for both receiver and transmitter evaluation.The radio was initially evaluated without reference to the manual and it was found that operation was intuitive to the extent that the manual was only needed for those aspects of operation that were less commonly used.

On power-up the operator is presented with a splash screen (where a user-defined message may be displayed) the set will then continue with the same configuration as at power off.

Dual receiver operation is termed 'Dual Watch' and is selected via the 'Dual-W' button.

The operator can use the 'Main/Sub' button to select the 'focus' of the Main or Sub band and this can also be achieved with a press on the meter section of the display of each receiver. On doing this the selected band's display is brightly lit and the non-selected band's display is grey. The Change button toggles receivers between the left and right displays. Pressing either the Main or Sub volume controls quickly mutes that receiver, and both receivers have separate concentric Volume and RF Gain/Squelch controls. When set to the 12 o'clock position, rotating the RF Gain/Squelch to the left adjusts the RF gain, and rotating to the right adjusts the squelch level. The squelch was usable on SSB signals where the background noise was reasonably quiet.

There is no actual keypad on the front panel. Direct frequency entry is easily achieved: a long press on the leading digit on the frequency display causes a keypad to appear on the screen.

Pressing the screen Mode caption brings up the mode selection menu. A one-second press on the Noise Blanker, Noise Reduction, Filter and APF/TPF buttons brings up a menu for the rapid setting of these features. On the left-hand side of the screen is the Multi Function Key Group which gives access to items such as Ant 1&2 switching, Pre-amp, Attenuator, IP+ and AGC.

Strong signal performance was found to be very good throughout the range 30kHz-30MHz, and there were no warnings of receiver overflow except when the pre-amplifiers were deliberately used inappropriately. When this occurred there was a sign of slight distortion on the signal and "OVF" flashed on the display.

We found that the pre-amplifers were generally not needed during the review period.The preset parameters for SSB and CW are about right, but are easily adjusted to suit the user's preferences. The IC-7610's APF proved to be very effective on CW.

AM reception was likewise very good and the ability to adjust the audio response by means of High Pass and Low Pass filters, and also the bass and treble, was much appreciated (this is also available in other modes).

An experiment was made using the two receive sections together for diversity reception on the broadcast bands. This was undertaken by using either a single aerial to listen to a station which was on two different bands at the same time, or by listening to a station with each receiver on the same frequency but utilising different aerials. While the aerial types used were not necessarily ideal for this sort of operating it was found that in the limited testing we were able to undertake this feature looked very promising. While performing this function audio out was split between L and R headphones. There is also a tracking function whereby the Sub receiver can have its operating mode and frequency synchronised with the Main receiver.

QRM sources, such as the power line communications system PLT can be a nuisance on the HF bands but the Noise Blanker in the IC-7610 was able to nullify the type that emit 'ignition pulse' noise quite well, although very careful adjustment was needed to avoid distortion on the received signal. This was tried on the 22m, 19m and 16m bands with good results.

The ability to tailor the bandwidths of the IF filters was of great use on the amateur bands and the pre-sets for AM worked very well for most broadcast band listening.

Filter bandwidths are adjustable from 50Hz to 10kHz depending on the mode employed, with the filter shape graphically demonstrated during adjustment. The filter shape can be set at any point between Sharp and Soft.

Another useful feature on AM is 'Quick Tune'. If, for example, you have tuned to a signal directly by a double press of the Spectrum Scope and found that you are a couple of kHz off the signal, the use of Quick Tune will bring the receiver to the dead centre of the signal.

The digital T-PBT was found to give excellent results in shifting QRM off a signal. This worked particularly well with AM stations that were suffering from local QRM, caused by switch mode power supplies and plasma TV buzz, which were having a noticeable effect on reception. As with the IF filter adjustment, using the graphical display when adjusting T-PBT was very useful in helping us to understand what the adjustments were doing. A long press on the T-PBT knob will instantly revert settings to normal.

To test the ability of the T-PBT, an AM signal modulated at 60% with a 1kHz tone was injected at 912kHz at a level deliberately designed to produce an annoying heterodyne on a target signal on 909kHz. Using T-PBT the heterodyne could be completely eliminated with practically no disturbance to the wanted signal.

The IC-7610 received well on the long and medium waves where it performed admirably. The noise reduction capability built into the receiver was very effective, with its ability to take the edge off a noisy band making long sessions of operating much less tiring.

A brief sensitivity check was made and compared with the available published data. On FM, for example, at 29.6MHz for 12dB signal-to-noise and distortion ratio (SINAD) a figure of .516μV was measured. And for AM at 15MHz, figures of less than 2μV for 10dB SINAD were recorded which were very close to the published figures.

CONCLUSIONS.

The Icom IC-7610 stands out as a very impressive and capable radio. It has an excellent set of features, feels solidly constructed and has stylish looks. The touch screen is very responsive and, with its vibrant colours, clarity, and the wealth of information presented on the screen, provides the operator with a full awareness of what is going on in the bands, especially when used with the Dual Spectrum Scopes.

Although somewhat menu driven, the functions which are used most often are available at a single button press, and where changes do need to be made this can be done with a minimum of fuss and clearly displayed on the screen.

Audio quality from the internal speaker was good with little distortion or 'rattling' even at maximum volume. Audio quality naturally improved when using an external speaker unit, in our case a Yaesu SP6 that was to hand.

The IC-7610's ergonomics are excellent throughout and difficult to fault; clearly a huge amount of effort has been put into the design. Most operators should get to grips with this radio very quickly. The provision of dual independent receivers adds to the versatility and with excellent strong signal capability the IC-7610 will appeal to the serious amateur, whether their interest is in DXing, contesting, PSK/RTTY, or just 'rag chewing', even on the most crowded of bands.

For the DXer or SWL this receiver offers great performance on the broadcast bands, and all users will appreciate the excellent IF filtering, and the admirable noise reduction and noise blanking capabilities which can cope with all but the most severe levels of QRM.

In short, the IC-7610 is thoroughly recommended and can be summed up in just one word, which is: superb.

Rating table for Icom IC-7610

Constructional quality	★★★★★
Sensitivity	★★★★★
Dynamic range	★★★★★
RF intermodulation	★★★★★
Versatility	★★★★★
VFM	★★★★

Overall rating ★★★★★

Key:
★ = Poor ★★ = Fair ★★★ = Average
★★★★ = Very Good ★★★★★ = Excellent
VFM = Value for money

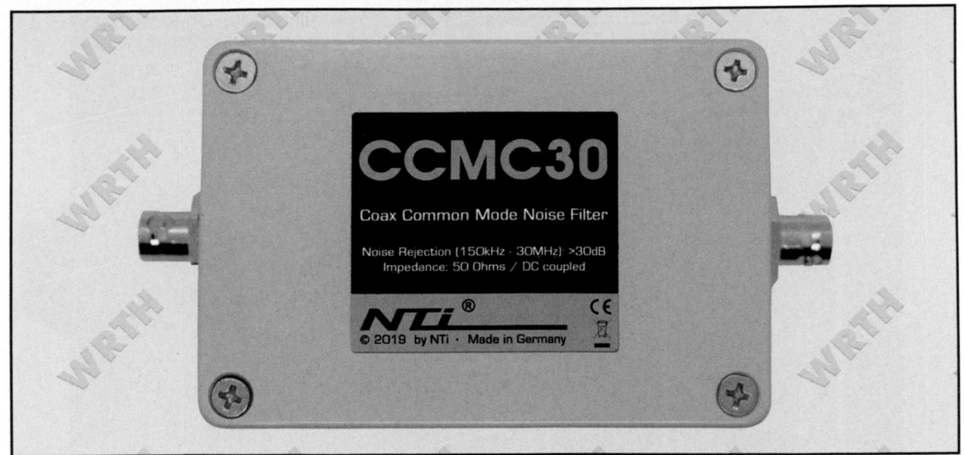

Bonito NTi CCMC30

US$115 £87 €99

It is commonly known that RF current flows down the centre conductor of a coaxial cable on the outside surface, and then returns on the inner surface of the outer braided shield. If there is an imbalance introduced somewhere in the system however, and there often is, this can change and currents can flow on the outer braided shield of the cable. These are called *common mode currents* and are made up of the unbalanced currents not returning along the intended route on the inside of the outer braid.

As these currents have nowhere to go they tend to radiate off the cable, and the level of radiation is proportional to the common mode current flowing on the cable. Even a small amount of extaneous radiation can cause serious problems and can lead to RF hot spots on the equipment when transmitting and, on receiving equipment, common mode currents can cause annoying noise pick up and a reduction in the all-important signal-to-noise ratio.

One solution to this problem is to incorporate an RF *choke* into the system which presents a high impedance to current flowing on the outside of the coaxial cable.

The Bonito NTi CCMC30 is one such choke which has been designed specifically to be used with receivers of any kind.

In use the choke is inserted in the aerial line immediately before the receiver, and after items such as ATU's, Pre-selectors and Bias-T power inserters. It is essential that there are no ground paths that bypass the choke and for this reason the choke is built into a plastic case.

The CCMC30 has a guaranteed frequency range of 150kHz to 30MHz. Common Mode rejection is quoted as >30dB: 150kHz to 30MHz (>20dB: 30kHz to 60MHz) with an Insertion loss of <1dB up to 150MHz. It is fitted with two BNC sockets, allowing quick connect/disconnect of the coaxial cable, and is built into a box which measures 100 x 68 x 50mm and weighs 320g.

EVALUATION

We initially examined the choke's specifications by assessing it on the test bench. Common mode attenuation was measured as -38dB at 150kHz rising to -46dB over the longwave band and -45dB over the mediumwave band. On the HF band we measured -30dB at 17MHz and -31dB at 30MHz. Insertion loss measured .03dB at 150kHz rising to .45 dB at 30MHz which is certainly well within the quoted specification.

The aerial system that the CCMC30 was evaluated on already has considerable measures implemented to reduce noise so we rigged up a temporary set up bypassing these measures as far as was possible and were able to find some noise around 650kHz. This was clearly visible on a waterfall display. We froze the trace with the filter out of circuit, and then restarted it with the filter in place and could see that the filter had been effective at removing all the noise.

CONCLUSION

With the increase of locally generated interference from modern day devices, especially in urban areas, a listener can sometimes need every tool they can muster to make listening more pleasurable or even possible. The CCM30 is one such tool. Where there is a common mode noise problem, and when used correctly, it should be effective at completely removing it.

In fact, interference or not, serious operators may wish to install such a choke in the system as a matter of course as it will help to ensure that the receiving station has as clean a signal as possible, and for this the CCM30 is a good choice.

SDRPlay RSPdx

US$200 £190 €210

OVERVIEW

The SDRplay RSPdx is a 14-bit single tuner SDR capable of receiving the entire RF spectrum from 1kHz to 2GHz. With its accompanying software, SDRuno, it can display and record a spectrum of up to 10MHz anywhere within that range. Powered from the USB port of a host computer it now replaces the well established RSP2 & Pro models, promising better strong signal handling capabilities and a more flexible antenna connection.

From the beginning SDRplay has opened the door to reasonably priced and high quality SDR reception while the team behind it have continually supported and upgraded both the hardware and accompanying software.

Naturally we were keen to try out the new model and compare it, side by side, with the RSP2 it has superseded. Our review unit was kindly loaned to us by Jon Hudson at SDRPlay.

FEATURES

A number of improvements have been incorporated into this redesigned model. Overall, performance has been enhanced by an increase from 12 to 14-bit architecture and the refinement of the Pre-Selection filters. The low pass filters are now operational on all three aerial ports, and a new 500kHz low pass filter has been added, improving reception below 500kHz. There are two software selectable hardware notches for AM/FM and DAB filters, which also work on all input ports.

When using SDRuno, the software for use with the entire SDRPlay range, the RSPdx is supported by a new High Dynamic Range (HDR) mode for framed bands below 2MHz. This feature increases dynamic range, improves intermodulation and reduces spurious responses.

The RSPdx has two 50 Ohm SMA aerial inputs, Ant A & B, but whereas these operated from 1.5-2GHz on the RSP2, they now cover the entire spectrum of 1kHz to 2GHz.

The three-pin 900 Ohm Hi Z input port fitted on the RSP2 which operated from 1kHz to 30MHz has been replaced by a 50 Ohm BNC connector, and now operates from 1kHz to 200MHz. Better isolation between aerial ports has been achieved and all inputs are software selectable.

The RSPdx still has the capability to accept an external 24MHz reference input via a female MCX connector to an external frequency standard such as a GPSDO. The reference output has been deleted. Bias-T output is still available on Ant B.

Supplied in a 95x90x30mm metal case, from the outside the RSPdx looks little different from the RPS2 Pro – the BNC socket being the only real give away from a distance – and the same could be said of SDRuno. However, a closer look at the Main panel in SDRuno now displays a DAB Notch Filter selection box and the Hi Z input selection box now reads 'ANT C'. By selecting the Bands button in the RX control panel the new HDR modes can be selected and it is here that the improvements become noticeable. The 'Framed' frequency ranges in HDR mode are, approximately: LW 150-290kHz, MW 550-1700kHz, NDB-H 486-546kHz, NDB-L 180-500kHz, LFER 144-205kHz, FULL 50-1700kHz and Low 0-520kHz. Each can be selected or deselected by a click on the appropriate button.

Incidentally existing users of SDRplay devices using SDRuno will be pleased to know that upgrading to the RSPdx merely requires pluging the new device into a USB port. SDRuno (v.1.33 and above) will recognise the device and set itself up, there being no further setting up required, and all previous settings are retained. Indeed two instances of SDRuno can be run if owners decide to keep their previous RSP unit. For new users the installation of SDRuno is straightforward and should present no problems.

EVALUATION

We used SDRuno v. 1.33 running under Windows 10 on an elderly Dell Inspiron Athlon IIx 4 630 with 16gb RAM and with the operating system and SDRuno software installed on a solid state drive. Other third party software is available.

Aerials used for HF were a 66ft inverted L end fed at 30ft with a 20:1 transformer providing a DC path to ground and a home made Active Magnetic Loop of 1m diameter. No ATU was used for the evaluation. At VHF and above a diamond V2000 and simple discone at 20ft were used.

FM implementation works very well. WFM or WFM Stereo may be selected by software and there are four pre-set IF filter bandwidths which can all be varied. 50µs and 75µs de-emphasis may be selected or set to Off. There is also an effective variable noise reduction filter that works on stereo FM to reduce 'hiss' on marginal signals. Station RDS info may also be displayed.

Turning to the lower frequencies we found that this is where the improvements are more immediately noticeable. As an example, for good reception below 500kHz using the RSP2, an external 500kHz Low Pass Filter was helpful in rejecting out-of-band signals. On the RSPdx with its internal filter this is no longer needed, demonstrating a marked improvement with no spurious signals present. We found the same on the LW and MW broadcast bands where some spurious signals on the RSP2 were not present on the RSPdx.

The individual HDR band frames for MW and LW work really well. The RSPdx's ability to pick out weak signals, sandwiched between much stronger ones on MW, was impressive and narrowing the IF filters efficiently removed any splatter. The HDR band frame Full which covers the spectrum up to 1700kHz will appeal to those keen to explore this part of the spectrum in one chunk. Outside the HDR modes, on HF the RSPdx produces very good results and is a great performer on the broadcast bands. It is even possible to try out a form of diversity reception when simultaneous transmissions can be received on different bands that are within the selected spectrum bandwidth of the RSPdx. A brief check of the new DAB Notch filter demonstrated that it effectively prevented DAB breakthrough on the receiver above 230MHz.

Naturally all of the versatile facilities provided by the SDRuno software are available with the RSPdx. Synchronous AM with selectable sidebands is effective when noise or interference affects a weak broadcast station. In this mode it is also possible to make accurate frequency measurements of a station; the frequency offset being displayed in the RX Control panel.

IF filters have sharp skirts and bandwidths may be fully varied by dragging the vertical bars on the Aux SP Panel, IF shift can also be implemented to avoid interference. SDRuno also provides good noise reduction facilities and fully variable wide and narrow noise blanking which, when used carefully, helps to reduce a surprising amount of noise found on the bands. A click of the mouse will access four variable notch filters.

Audio playback quality will depend on the host computer system. When using a pair of reasonable quality outboard Yamaha PC speakers, we found the dx capable of good audio reproduction.

There are no limits on memories or memory banks and memory channel scanning is possible. A calibrated RSSI allows accurate signal measurements to be made.

The RDS feature on broadcast FM is a nice touch for quick station identification and, with the introduction of software version 1.4, it should be possible to obtain a plug-in for DAB reception, and a very useful FRAN (Frequency Annotation) plug-in which can read SWSKEDS or users own .s1b files to display stations relative to frequency on the main spectrum window. Also noted was that the RF gain control has more refined steps. Another excellent feature of SDRuno is the ability to run multiple virtual receivers anywhere within the selected bandwidth. We also found that the recording and playback feature makes instant or unattended recording a very simple matter.

SDRuno certainly makes the RSPdx a very versatile receiver and it is worth investing time to learn its many features and 'quirks'.

Another great plus for any SDRplay user is the free Spectrum Analyser software available from the SDRplay website. Owners of the RSPdx can have an accurate 1kHz to 2GHz spectrum analyser for just the cost of the SDRplay device.

CONCLUSION

The SDRplay RSPdx certainly offers improved performance over the RSP2. This is not overly obvious on the higher bands but where the upgrades have really made a difference is on the lower bands. There were no spurious signals found on the MW band and there is no longer a need for an external low pass filter for work below 500kHz. HDR works effectively, improving the strong signal handling capability of the RSPdx and the DAB notch filter stops the DAB multiplex breakthrough. The aerial input arrangements are a great improvement, being a lot more flexible.

This receiver excels at all types of monitoring whether it be broadcast, amateur, utility, L-Band and more. With decent aerials there is not much out there than can escape the SDRplay RSPdx. It impresses with its good overall performance, wide band coverage, small footprint, all mode reception, and powerful free software; it is also so reasonably priced that it's hard to think what's not to like about this great little receiver.

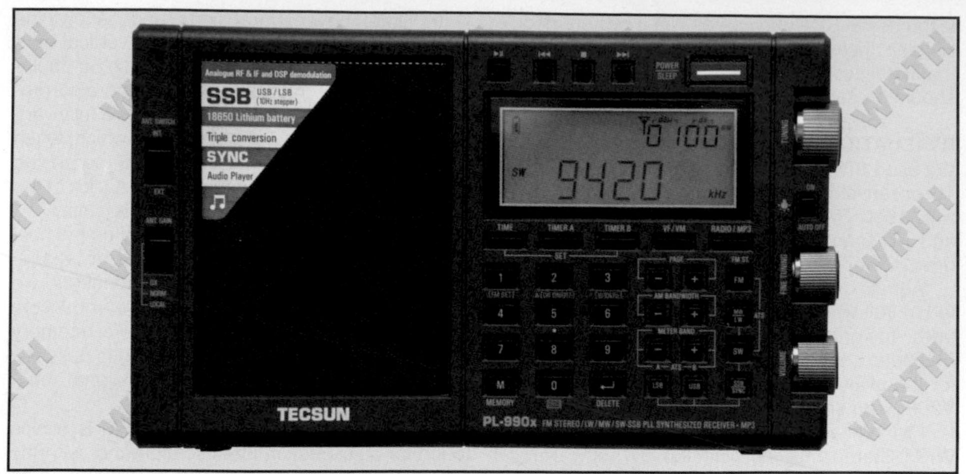

Tecsun PL-990

US$235 £180 €195

OVERVIEW

In the summer of 2019 we learned that the China-based radio manufacturer Tecsun was planning to introduce three new models to the market in honor of the company's anniversary. Tecsun had an ambitious production schedule for the new PL-990, H-501, and PL-330, and produced early pilot and domestic production runs to meet their anniversary deadline. These models, however, were simplified versions with reduced features.

The number of pilot and early production runs on the market caused confusion in radio enthusiast communities across the globe. To add to the confusion, some of these initial units appeared on global online retailers such as AliExpress and eBay, usually at inflated prices.

The PL-990 was the first radio to be released and reviewed online by China-based radio enthusiasts but, by the time those reviews had been posted, Tecsun had already released firmware upgrades, which made keeping track of the various versions of the PL-990 very complicated. We learnt that one way to distinguish the final 'export' model of the PL-990 from previous models was a series of three buttons on the front panel: the first version of the radio had Time, Alarm, and Display buttons, while on the export version the buttons were to be labeled Time, Timer A, and Timer B.

To make the situation even more complicated, we learned there were to be at least two versions of the export model: the PL-990 and PL-990x. Performance was meant be identical in the two models, but the PL-990x would offer the radio enthusiast slightly more flexibility with the possibility of expanded ranges on LW (50-522kHz v 100-519kHz) and SW (1621-29999kHz), and finer FM tuning steps when the 87.5-108MHZ range was selected (50kHz v 100kHz steps).

Tecsun anticipated shipping export versions of the Tecsun PL-990/PL-990x in February 2020. However, they were forced to close their factories in mid-January due to COVID-19, which rapidly crippled production among most consumer electronic manufacturers across the globe.

Finally, and thanks to our contact Anna at the Hong Kong-based Tecsun distributor Anon-Co, I received a Tecsun PL-990x pre-production model for evaluation in August 2020. In general, we do not review pre-production models, but made an exception in light of the pandemic. Moreover, Tecsun Radios Australia very kindly sent me a production unit of the PL-990. I am most grateful to them for expediting shipment of this unit so that we could confirm that performance is identical to the PL-990x pre-production unit, although this version does have the expanded ranges.

OVERVIEW

The Tecsun PL-990 is very much in keeping with the Tecsun design aesthetic. Button layout and labels are clear, spaced appropriately, and intuitive. If you've used a Tecsun portable in the past, you'll feel at home holding the PL-990. All but the hidden functions are obvious and didn't require referencing the owner's manual. The buttons have a nice feel and tactile response and, as in previous Tecsun models, keying in the frequency directly is merely a matter of typing the frequency in kHz or MHz. To listen to the Voice of Greece on the 31 meter band, for example, simply type '9420' – there is no need to indicate direct frequency entry, nor to confirm entry.

The PL-990 is powered by one 18650 lithium battery that can be charged internally via the radio's smart charging function. Through Tecsun's use of a speaker and acoustic chamber, which give its small speaker more depth and range, the PL-990's audio fidelity is impressive.

FEATURES

The PL-990 is a triple conversion receiver with DSP demodulation and it is evidently an high-grade portable. The PL-990 has both SSB and synchronous detection, both with USB/LSB-selectable sidebands. It also features multiple selectable bandwidths for AM, SSB, and synchronous detection modes as well.

The PL-990 has a digital audio player which plays files from an included removable MicroSD card found on the bottom of the radio. When I first discovered the PL-990 had removable digital storage I hoped this meant it could make off-air recordings natively and store them on the card. But unfortunately there is no recording function, only playback. That said, this does make the PL-990 a versatile audio device, and it can also be used as an external PC speaker via USB.

HIDDEN FEATURES

As with the PL-880, the PL-990 has a number of 'hidden features' that are not documented in early versions of the manuals, but are built into the radio and accessible with specific key presses.

One of the most surprising of these features is that the PL-990 can be used as a Bluetooth speaker. Why this wasn't added as a documented or labeled feature is unclear. There is also a Dynamic Noise Reduction (DNR) feature which auto-adjusts the filter bandwidth. I'm not a great fan of DNR as I like to be in control of the bandwidth and would much rather switch it manually but, if you like it, you'll be pleased. Other hidden features allow control and adjustment of muting thresholds, FM de-emphasis, line output levels, and display settings, and there is also a hidden feature to calibrate SSB mode. There's even a procedure to toggle use of the internal ferrite bar and telescoping whip on the MW and LW bands.

PERFORMANCE

My initial impression of the PL-990 was that it is a solid receiver. I found no obvious unfavorable characteristics and it seemed to perform well using the built-in telescoping whip antenna and/or an external wire antenna (either clipped to the whip antenna, or using the external antenna port on the left side of the radio). To evaluate receiver performance I spent a great deal of time comparing the PL-990 with the venerable PL-880 in the field, far removed from urban noise or RFI.

In general, enthusiasts will be pleased with the PL-990's performance on the shortwave bands. When comparing directly with the PL-880, I found that the PL-880 has a slight edge on the PL-990 in terms of sensitivity; selectivity seems comparable. The PL-880 did a better job of bringing weak stations out of the noise with better overall stability, but performance was identical with strong stations. Audio fidelity is also slightly better on the PL-880 with deeper bass tones and higher treble; less noticeable in AM mode, most noticeable in FM mode. Although we did not disassemble the PL-990x, I suspect this may be due to a slightly smaller internal speaker than that incorporated in the PL-880.

One welcome addition on the PL-990 is a proper synchronous detector. While the PL-880 has an undocumented 'hidden' sync detector feature, it is very poorly implemented and ineffective. You engage the sync detector on the PL-990 by pressing and holding the SSB/Sync button. Once engaged, the user can select the sideband by pressing either the LSB or USB buttons. I was initially pleased with the sync detector in that it engaged and worked as I would expect, but with further testing I found that the sync lock is not quite as stable as in previous Tecsun models such as the PL-660 and PL-680. In addition, the AM filter can only be widened to 4kHz in sync mode as opposed to 6kHz in normal AM mode.

I found the PL-990 to be slightly more sensitive than the PL-880 on the mediumwave band. My distant benchmark stations were slightly more intelligible and stable using the PL-990 in normal AM mode. On both shortwave and mediumwave, I found the AM filters helped greatly in eliminating the edge of adjacent signals.

As expected with a DSP portable, there are a number of annoying 'birdies' (internally-generated noises) throughout the bands but fortunately few of these birdies appear in the vicinity of recognized broadcasting frequencies.

On the FM band, I found the PL-990 and PL-880 comparable in terms of sensitivity, which is to say that they have superb FM sensitivity. Again, the PL-880's speaker gives it slightly better audio fidelity. Like the PL-880, the PL-990 does not have an RDS (Radio Data System) function, thus cannot display station information on the display.

CONCLUSION

All in all, I've been pleased with the PL-990. While it might not be an upgrade in terms of raw performance, it does offer features like synchronous detection, digital audio playback, and even Bluetooth, all of which certainly give the PL-990 more versatility in our digital/mobile world. While I've commented on audio fidelity in comparison with the PL-880, until I compared it I was very pleased with the audio. It's certainly among one of the best for audio in the portable shortwave radio market. Like all Tecsuns, the PL-990 is a pleasure to use, and caters well to the radio enthusiast with its versatility, tuning controls, and overall intuitive ergonomics.

We are very grateful to **Thomas Witherspoon** (K4SWL) for providing this review. An active radio enthusiast, Thomas is the owner of *The SWLing Post*, curator of the Shortwave Radio Audio Archive and founder of the Radio Spectrum Archive.

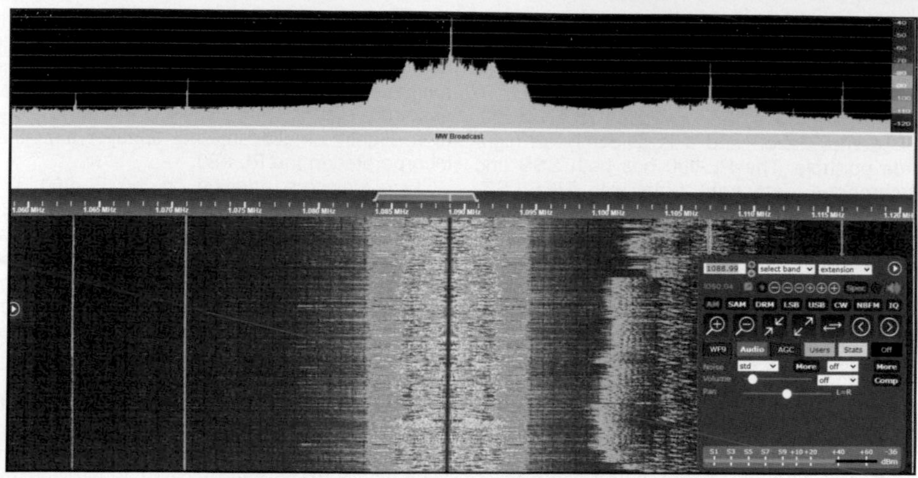

Valent F(x) KiwiSDR

US$300 £250 €270

OVERVIEW

The KiwiSDR is a 14-bit receive-only wideband HF Software Defined Radio which is capable of receiving the entire 10kHz to 32MHz VLF/LW/MW/HF spectrum in one chunk. Unlike other SDRs that connect directly to a personal computer, the KiwiSDR is a 'cape' or add-on board, for a BeagleBone computing platform, which is similar in many ways to the well known Raspberry Pi. The KiwiSDR can therefore be left running continuously, as a standalone unit, autonomously sharing your 10kHz-32MHz receive spectrum over a network or the internet. All of the processing is performed by the KiwiSDR itself before being sent over the network and the 'data', that is audio and waterfall, is accessed via a web browser which produces very little load on the PC, tablet or even mobile phone it is being used on.

FEATURES

The KiwiSDR comes in two main parts the BeagleBone and the KiwiSDR PCB which plugs into the expansion ports of the BeagleBone. The KiwiSDR board has an on-board Xilinx Artix-7 A35 FPGA which handles the DSP processing and an LTC2248 14-bit 65MHZ ADC. A non-Temperature Compensated Crystal Oscillator (TCXO) is used, and accurate timekeeping and frequency stability is achieved using GPS; a Patch Antenna being supplied for this purpose.

There are actually two receivers, one for the main HF receiver and the other for the GPS, with 2 SMA sockets for the aerials, an Ethernet port, and a 2.1mm 5V DC power socket. Also on the board is a terminal block for connecting a long wire aerial and ground. As the KiwiSDR is network based it connects directly to a network. This is done using an Ethernet connection to a router. We believe it may also be possible to use a wireless adaptor although we did not test this.

The kit comes with an enclosure made of acrylic plastic which has metal side plates. There is an element of self assembly required as the case has to be fitted onto the two boards and pinned into place with plastic rivets. A separate 5V DC power supply is required.

EVALUATION

We found the assembly of the kit parts straightforward but realised after assembly that we should not have added the case until setup had been completed, as the Kiwi board covers the reset button on the BeagleBone. The case having been removed to get to the button, we hooked up an Ethernet cable, the GPS, and an aerial. On first powering up the KiwiSDR looks to the Internet for an update and we found this took quite some time; in fact over an hour on a 70mb/s line. At one point we thought it had 'hung' however all was well, and we were able to access the Open-WebRX interface on the PC by entering kiwisdr.local:8073 into our browser. Adding '/admin' to the address allowed us to access the setup page which is where the receiver's parameters, including networking, are set.

The OpenWebRX interface is where the radio is controlled. A 'Welcome' inset window opens up on the left had side of the screen offering the user tips on operating the interface. This can be dismissed by clicking the arrow on the top right of the box. To the right users will see another box and most of the features they will use to control the radio will be found here.

There are a lot of features built into the KiwiSDR and we only have space to consider the main ones here. Direct frequency entry may be entered, in kHz, at the top left of this window or alternately there is a band selection box located to its right and the user can then click on the main waterfall display to select a station in that band. There are controls for zooming the waterfall in and out and also for stepping along the band. Mode is selected by clicking the relevant button, such as AM, SAM, DRM. Double clicking on most buttons will step through different pre-set bandwidths.

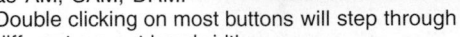

At the top of the waterfall display is a marker called 'Pass Band' and this can be dragged to select a different frequency, or dragged to open up or reduce the IF filter bandwidth. There are also buttons to select settings for the Waterfall, Audio, AGC, information on how many users are accessing the receiver, and system statistics. Below this is a bar style S Meter reading S units and dBm. The KiwiSDR has a number of noise reduction options which we found needed some experimentation for best results, as did the AGC and Autonotch settings. Even on a local network there is a slight delay for these adjustments to become apparent so they need to be done carefully otherwise the optimal setting may be missed. IF filtering has quite steep skirts which effectively reject adjacent signals and, because the pass band marker at the top of the display can have its edges dragged, the upper or lower pass band may be expanded or reduced as required, as may the receiver's IF bandwidth.

It is possible to select a spectrum display in addition to the waterfall. This is located above the waterfall and tracks the spectrum bandwidth of the waterfall as it is adjusted. By left clicking and dragging the waterfall the spectrum may be moved up or down in frequency.

At the top right of the inset control panel there is a selection box named 'Extensions' and here the user can find added features. One of the most useful is probably TDoA, or 'Timed Distance of Arrival'. This extremely interesting option uses other KiwiSDRs on the global network to bracket an area in order to locate a transmitter site. It does require a bit of practise and a steady signal to achieve effective results, so sites may not always be located to 'pin point' accuracy but it is great fun to use and often a 'ball park' figure is enough to identify a transmitting site.

Also in the Extensions are CW, Navtex, DRM and other decoders. Instant audio recording is available at the click of a button, and files may be saved to the computer for later use.

Right clicking a point on the waterfall display brings up a dialogue box that has a number of selections, two of them being database look-ups for known stations on that frequency.

As stated, the KiwiSDR may be configured for multiple users. The standard setting is for four users. This can be increased to eight users although this does lead to reduced bandwidth. Alternatively, three receivers may be set, resulting in increased bandwidth. These and other settings are accessed by logging on to the Admin Interface which is done in a similar way to accessing a home network's router settings.

By opening up further Web SDR windows the KiwiSDR may be run with multiple instances up to the limits set in the Admin Interface. Assuming there are no other users, then up to eight receive instances may be run from a single Kiwi receiver at any frequency in its 10kHz to 32MHz range.

We found the performance of the KiwiSDR good over its operating range and on HF the wide bandwidth waterfall screen clearly displayed what bands were open. Needless to say, with the GPS, frequency accuracy and stability were excellent.

Some Kiwi hosts with long-wire or Beverage antennas, or with preamplifiers, have reported problems with strong signals causing overloading or clipping as a result of poor dynamic range. We understand that RF attenuation cannot be implemented effectively without significantly increasing the Kiwi's price, and such users need to connect an external attenuator.

CONCLUSION

The KiwiSDR is not a plug-and-play unit and some basic networking skills will be needed to get it working on the internet. Clearly the receiver is aimed at those who wish to stream over a network, either for their own private access or for others to use. The web interface is comprehensive and presents many features which may well be enhanced in the future.

The receiver itself works well and displayed no overloading or imaging problems.

We very much liked the KiwiSDR both as a receiver and also as a concept of users world wide who make their receivers available to others, and are to be congratulated for doing so.

The Kiwi receiver with its many features would be an asset to any listening post in its own right, and when combined with the global network of shared receivers it produces an excellent means for world-wide monitoring.

WRTH HF Receiver Guide 2021

Hand-held, Portables & Budget

Maker	Model	Size	SEL	DR	OV	US$	£	€
AOR	AR8200D	H	***	***	***	900	660	730
Icom	IC-R30	H	****	***	****	750	570	630
Reuter	RDR51 'Pocket'	H	*****	*****	*****	†1775	1290	1445
C. Crane	CC Skywave	S	****	****	****	170	130	145
Degen (Kaito)	DE-1103	S	***	***	**	70	80	90
Sangean	ATS-909X	S	****	****	****	225	250	220
Tecsun	PL-310ET	S	****	***	****	45	36	40
Tecsun	PL-380	S	****	****	*****	46	45	50
Tecsun	PL-600	S	****	***	****	100	80	100
Tecsun	PL-660	S	***	****	****	130	140	150
Tecsun	PL-680	S	***	***	***	150	150	170
Tecsun	PL-880	S	***	****	****	160	190	230
Tecsun	PL-990	S	***	****	****	235	180	195
Tecsun	S-8800	S	***	***	***	260	280	360
XHDATA	D-808	S	***	***	***	95	70	80

† prices quoted are the middle of the variant price spread

SDRs, Serious Shortwave & Semi-pro Receivers

Maker	Model	Size	SEL	DR	OV	US$	£	€
Airspy	HF+ Discovery	C	*****	*****	*****	169	199	219
Alinco	DX-R8E	M	****	****	****	600	470	530
AOR	AR5001D	M	*****	****	****	4450	3000	3300
AOR	AR5700D	L	*****	*****	*****	5840	4595	5010
AOR	AR6000	L	****	*****	****	6600	4700	5200
AOR	AR8600	L	**	***	***	1050	640	800
AOR	AR-DV1	M	****	****	****	1300	1200	1300
Elad	FDM-DUOr	C	*****	*****	*****	1000	775	900
Expert Electronics	ColibriNano	C	****	****	****	320	250	270
FunCube Dongle	Pro+	C	****	***	****	190	150	165
Icom	IC-718	L	***	****	****	585	700	770
Icom	IC-7300	L	****	****	****	1050	1200	1345
Icom	IC-7610	L	*****	*****	*****	3840	3000	3240
Icom	IC-8600	L	*****	****	****	2400	2500	2750
Icom	IC-R9500	L	*****	*****	*****	12500	10700	11800
Icom	IC-R9500	L	*****	*****	*****	12500	10700	11800
Microtelecom	Perseus	C	*****	*****	*****	900	700	750
Palstar	R30	M	*****	*****	****	900	1000	1100
Reuter	RDR55D	L	*****	*****	*****	5500	4000	4500
SDRplay	SDRplay RSPdx	C	****	****	*****	200	190	210
Ten-Tec	RX340	L	*****	*****	*****	7495	4500	5000
Valent F(x)	KiwiSDR	C	****	***	****	300	250	270
WinRadio	G31 Excalibur	C	*****	****	*****	970	700	795
WinRadio	G33 Excalibur Pro	C	*****	*****	*****	1900	1600	1800
WinRadio	G35 Excalibur Ultra	C	*****	*****	*****	5000	3800	4200
WinRadio	G65 Excalibur Sigma	C	*****	*****	*****	8500	6200	6950
WinRadio	G313i	C	*****	****	*****	1420	1100	1210
WinRadio	G313e	C	*****	*****	*****	1450	1120	1235

KEY: SEL = Selectivity, DR = Dynamic Range, OV = Overall Value. C = SDR, H = Hand-held, L = Large, table top use, M = Medium, suitcase size, S = Small, easily portable. * = Avoid ** = Poor *** = Fair **** = Very Good ***** = Outstanding.

NOTE: Prices vary due to exchange rate fluctuations. Some models may be unavailable in certain markets.

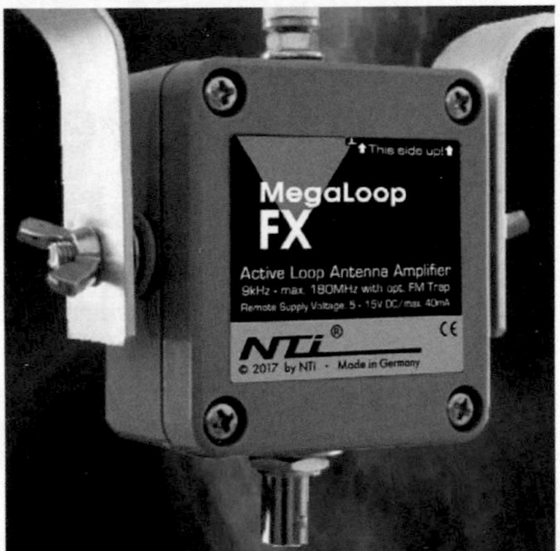

The Development of HF Broadcast Transmitters

*Former BBC Senior Transmitter Engineer, **Dave Porter** G4OYX, outlines the history and development of HF high power broadcast transmitters*

Sender 1, an STC 10/15kW transmitter, at Daventry in 1932

The development of HF broadcast transmitters had slow beginnings. Compared to the rapidly expanding government VLF and LF Morse services, and the commercial and government LF and MF 'Amplitude Modulated' (AM) broadcast services in the early 1920s, the HF spectrum was largely ignored. It was left to enthusiastic radio amateurs to discover exactly what could be achieved on HF for 'Carrier Wave' (CW), used for Morse code, and AM services in terms of transmission and propagation.

To begin with, as high power valves were yet to appear, HF transmitters often just had tens or hundreds of Watts of power. The trend from the 1920s was to try to increase transmitter power. By the late 1920s G5SW at Chelmsford in the UK was running an HF transmitter at 8kW, Deutschlandsender at Zeesen in Germany had a Telefunken shortwave transmitter at 8/12kW in August 1929, AWA's VK3ME station at Pennant Hills in Australia was at 20kW (from where they made their first 'Empire Broadcast in September 1927), and W8XK had a transmitter at 40kW at Forest Hills in the USA. By the mid 1930s the United States had a growing audience in Europe for relayed commercial programmes using HF via, for example, W2XAF and W2XAD owned by General Electric, W2XDV owned by the Atlantic Broadcasting Corporation and the National Broadcasting Company's W3XAL.

The international coverage of HF had not gone unnoticed by governments, nor had its potential as a propaganda tool. The result was that almost limitless state funding for HF broadcasting became available causing a large increase in the number of manufacturers making transmitters and a significant effort to improve the performance of the valves which were one of the key elements in achieving more powerful transmitters and therefore stronger signals.

The valves (or 'tubes') were used to generate a low-level carrier wave on the required frequency and then amplify this in further tuned stages to the required output power. CW transmitters were the simplest, as the carrier wave was just keyed on and off for the Morse characters. All transmitters employed a series of Radio Frequency (RF) stages, often composed of multiple valves, to amplify the power and achieve the required power output from a Final RF (FRF) stage.

For broadcasting it is necessary to apply modulation to the amplified power. Modulation entails adding an information-bearing modulation wave, for example an audio signal, to the carrier wave which, having a much higher frequency than the sound modulation wave, carries the information. In AM, the amplitude of the carrier wave is varied. For example, a continuous wave RF signal (a sinusoidal carrier wave) has its amplitude modulated by an audio waveform before transmission.

One of the first ways of producing AM with valve transmitters for LF, MF and HF was to employ Heising anode, or 'Class A', modulation. Here the current to the FRF valve is fed through a high-value inductor (or 'choke'). The audio amplifier (or modulator) valve anode is fed through the same inductor, which makes the modulator valve divert current from the RF amplifier. The choke acts as a constant current source in the audio range. The Heising modulator had a power efficiency of only around 30%.

The modulator stage was composed of low-level amplifiers which raised the programme signal to a level sufficient to drive the modulator output valve, typically around 75W output. The FRF output would normally be about 100-125W and could then be amplified linearly (to preserve the modulated waveform) by more stages to reach the desired power output.

The BBC's experience is typical and by 1932, after some low-power tests, Senders 1 and 2 – both STC 10/15kW transmitters – had been installed at the newly-built Empire Station at Daventry; Sender 3 at Daventry was the relocated G5SW from Chelmsford, now upgraded to 12kW. They employed Heising modulation and then linearly amplified it up to the full RF output power. The disadvantage with linear amplification is that its overall efficiency is at best only up to 20%. Overall efficiency also suffered as the electrical power source at the RF stage was low-powered motor generator sets. This poor efficiency limited the amount of power that could be obtained from the valves and components, and created a problem over the removal of the waste heat generated by the process.

The valves needed to be cooled and two means of cooling them were used in the early transmitters. These were air cooling by natural radiation or forced draught, and water cooling. Later developments included vapour steam cooling and Hypervapotron cooling.

Valves with water-cooled anodes soon appeared. Unfortunately, the way they operated in the HF bands generally meant that it was not possible to obtain as much output power at, say, 21MHz as at 6MHz. This was mainly caused by the extra heat generated at the glass-to-metal seals in the valves by the higher RF currents as the frequency increased.

This problem was addressed by using a technique developed in 1919. In that year W. G. Houskeeper from Coatesville in the USA, and then working for Western Electric, devised a technique using thin copper sheets to achieve a knife-edge seal where effectively the expansion and contraction coefficients of the metal matched that of the glass. Valves using this technology were gradually introduced to HF broadcast transmitters, making them significantly more efficient.

An STC CS8 at Skelton

Six BD272 Senders at Woofferton in 1963. (the late Lee Davison)

A second cause of extra heat gain were the valve filaments. Originally these were made of pure tungsten and had to be heated to 2550°K to produce an emission of 7mA/W. These filaments consumed a significant proportion of the total input power to the transmitter. A considerable improvement was obtained from a tungsten filament which contained just 2% of thorium oxide. Even at a reduced temperature of 2000°K this produced an emission of 70-100mA/W, reducing the energy needed to light the tube or, on the other hand, allowing much more power to be extracted from the same tube.

With international tensions increasing, governments requested higher RF power in order to increase global reach. To this end Daventry acquired two STC C50 transmitters at 50-80kW which had the new Class B audio modulation system. This employed a modulator with two or more valves in push-pull in the output stage, increasing the power available from the supply voltage, and helping to increase power efficiency to 55% . This increase was also partly because motor generator sets had been replaced by transformer power supplies, and also because efficient mercury-arc rectifiers (invented in 1902 by Peter Cooper Hewitt in the USA to provide reliable power for industrial motors) were used to supply the high voltage current, typically 11kV DC, that was required along with other high-power components to make this system work. These continued to be used until the advent of solid state semiconductor rectifiers in the 1970s.

Sender 6, an SWB14 by Marconi's Wireless Telegraph (MWT) and installed at Daventry in 1938, was the exception in that it had a 'series modulator'. Series modulation dispensed with the modulation transformer and instead had a Class A modulator with one large valve, It was not very

A BY1144L triode valve in the LH modulator position in an MWT BD272 transmitter (Neale Bateman)

The MWT BD272 at Woofferton showing (L to R) Modulator and Control, RF stages and 5kW driver transmitter (Neale Bateman)

efficient and needed a high voltage supply of 22kV. It did, however, have the energy-saving feature of 'floating carrier' where the 100kW output could be reduced to about 30kW when no modulation was present. This concept was later used by AEG-Telefunken from the late 1970s.

For Class B systems it was convenient to use four identical high-power tubes; two to generate the RF output carrier wave and two in the modulator. The days of multi-tubed stages with small valves in parallel were over.

Sender 7 at Daventry was a dual channel STC type CS7, which went on air in 1940. This transmitter had the innovation of four RF channels. Up to two channels could be in use at a time with a common Class B modulator, so the same programme could go out on the two channels at 70kW on each or 100kW on a single one. As the schedule changes rolled round over 24 hours the spare channels could be set ready to go to the next frequency as soon as the previous channel ended, with no time lost changing wavelengths. Two additional MWT 100kW SWB18 transmitters were installed as Senders 8 and 9 in 1939 and a further pair as Senders 10 and 11 in 1940.

Skelton B was equipped with six dual-channel STC CS8 100kW transmitters making the Skelton complex the biggest HF site in the World by mid-1943, and in the same year six RCA MI-7730 50kW transmitters were installed at Woofferton. All of these were Class B modulated.

In 1962, Senders 4, 5 and 6 were replaced by MWT BD253 100kW dual-channel transmitters. These were some of the first HF transmitters in the BBC with 'vapour steam cooling'. Vapour steam cooling, or 'vapour cooling' as it came to be known was effected by the valve anode being immersed in a water tank or boiler. The heat from the valve made the water boil which meant, in effect, that the heat was removed by evaporation. This was an ingenious solution as 170kW will evaporate one gallon (or 4.5 litres) of water per minute at 100°C. The resultant steam rises naturally to a heat exchanger where it condenses and is returned by gravity to the boiler.

From 1963 the MWT 250kW BD272/B6122 was to become, and remain for many years, the standard workhorse at all the BBC sites, replacing ageing equipment. It was again Class B modulated and about 50% power efficient overall. It had just two RF output type BY1144L vapour steam cooled valves for the 250kW, with two more in the modulator. The first six of these transmitters were installed at Woofferton in 1963 for the Voice of America relays, and in 1964 Continental Electronics in the USA produced a Doherty version Type 420A at 500kW for Radio Free Europe/Radio Liberty and Voice of America sites. This transmitter used eight tubes in the output, cleverly configured to produce AM.

The evolution of valves continued until the introduction of solid state components for broadcast transmitters in the late 1970s. But for the moment these Class B modulated analogue all-valved units marked the apogee of High Frequency transmitter development.

Radio in Bhutan

Manfred Rippich tells the story of the introduction and expansion of radio in the Land of the Thunder Dragon

A Farm in the Eastern Mountains near Trashigang (Ulysse Pixel)

The mountainous and landlocked Kingdom of Bhutan in the Eastern Himalayas, or *Druk Yul* ('Land of the Thunder Dragon') as it is known in Dzongkha, has changed vastly in the past 60 years. 'Bhutan is jumping from the feudal age to the modern age. It's bypassing the industrial age', says newspaper editor Tenzing Lamsang. He is absolutely right. Today, there are about as many cellular phone subscribers as there are inhabitants, but less than 60 years ago there were no postage stamps, no currency, no hotels, no telephones, and certainly no radio stations.

There were also no roads accessible by motor vehicles. Despite this, in 1958, the great statesman Nehru made the long and difficult journey via Sikkim to Bhutan, travelling by jeep and on horseback, and arriving at the town of Paro on a yak. He was greeted by King Jigme Dorji Wangchuck and a crowd of his loyal subjects. Bhutan was, and still is, important as a buffer between China and India, 'which saved us billions of dollars in defence spending', as an Indian Congressman pointed out decades later. Nehru held long discussions with the King about mutual concerns and also persuaded the King to abolish serfdom and introduce land reforms.

This visit may have sparked the construction of a metalled road from the border town of Phuntsholing to Thimphu, which had just become the official capital. After this, things happened relatively quickly. The first post office opened in 1962 and a set of seven stamps was issued. The first phones were installed a year later in government offices. The first hotels were built in 1974 in preparation for the coronation of the fourth *Druk Gyalpo* or Dragon King. That year also saw the introduction of Bhutan's own currency, the Ngultrum, which was issued in July 1974 to replace the Rupee. Seven months earlier the first radio voices made their way through the ether in Bhutan: the birth of what is now the Bhutan Broadcasting Corporation.

In 1964 the King asked the Swiss Fritz von Schulthess, a friend of the Royal family, to look for a radio expert. He needed a quick and reliable connection between his border posts in the north and the capital. Messages brought by runners to Thimphu took many days, so a radio connection would represent great progress. The King could have asked India for assistance but that might have led to interference with the information transmitted. A Swiss technician finally arrived in April 1965 and quickly installed the desired connections between Thimphu and the border posts. Unfortunately he had to work with obsolete transmitters and receivers that had been used by the US army in World War Two.

Possibly the first radio seen and listened to in Bhutan was brought to the country in 1952 by Burt Kerr Todd – an American who later produced for Bhutan most of the 'World Firsts' in postage stamp design: 3-D, steel-foil, silk, and above all the talking stamps – who had trekked through the country with a portable radio set. Years later, in the early 1960s, some foreigners working on the construction of the highway from the Indian border to Thimphu were given radio sets by the then Prime Minister. One of them later recalled how, learning that the men missed listening to music from their native lands, the Prime Minister immediately ordered Sony transistors from Japan for them.

The next and most important achievement came eight years later when, on 11 November 1973, on the occasion of the 18th birthday of the new King, a group of young Bhutanese started broadcasting to the general public. Most of the youngsters were members of the National Youth Association of Bhutan and so they called the station Radio NYAB. They used a borrowed BEL transmitter which a contemporary witness described as '. . . a military piece made of pure iron that would give electric shocks from all its parts when it was ON'. Broadcasts were made only on Sundays, and then for just half an hour. 'I was the first voice', recalls Paljor Jigme Dorji. The news on his sheet was mainly composed of gruesome details from the war in Vietnam, so he decided to talk about more pleasant things. During the programme he occasionally announced the time, 'By the way guys, it's 3:30 Bhutan Standard Time'.

Radio NYAB soon became so popular that broadcasting hours were extended, languages such as Sharchopkha and Lhotsamkha added and broadcasts extended to Wednesdays. Paljor Dorji, who was perhaps the most remarkable of the bunch of youngsters, was later awarded the honorific title of *Dasho.* He is known in Bhutan as Dasho Benji and is still active in the national media, doing broadcasts on Radio Valley. A cousin of the fourth king, he studied in India and Britain and was Bhutan's ambassador at the UN in Geneva. He married a British woman, Louise Major, who is listed in some past issues of *WRTH* as Louise Dorji.

Louise Dorji stayed with NYAB and joined the management team when Radio NYAB was taken over by the government on 2 June 1986. On that day the station put into service a 5kW Croatian RIZ transmitter. Mrs Dorji later became deputy director of the Bhutan Broadcasting Service (BBS), when it was inaugurated under its new name in the early 1990s.

Dorji Wangdi who for 30 years was the major voice of the Sharchopkha programmes at BBS

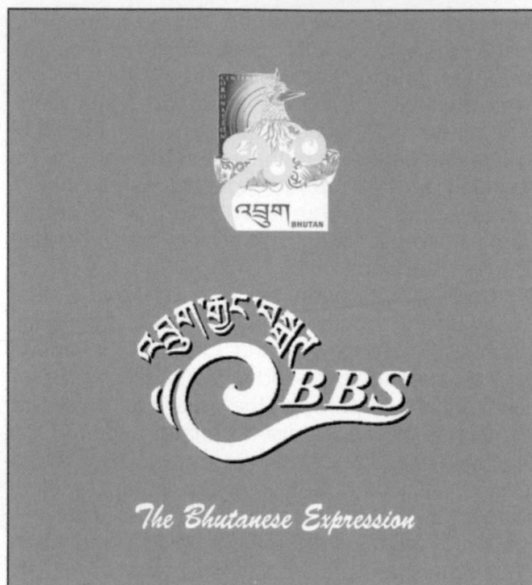

BBS Annual Report cover

In 1991, the BBS moved into a new studio and administrative complex, which was built by Bhutan's greatest benefactor, India. All the technical equipment was also provided by India. In December 1994 I was lucky enough to pay a visit to the studios, and had the opportunity of talking to the director, Mr Sonam Tshong. Initially he was not amused to find a foreigner within the walls of BBS without prior appointment, and without his permision, but after this initial difficulty we had a friendly talk for about an hour before he had to leave. Little did either Mr Tshong or I imagine that 18 years later he would become Bhutan's ambassador to the European Union.

On the 21st day of the seventh month of the Year of the Water Monkey, or October 1st 1992, the King ordered that the Bhutan Broadcasting Service become an independent body, being no more under the umbrella of the Ministry of Communication. The BBS remained, however, the sole provider of broadcasting in the kingdom until the media scene changed in 2006 and Kuzoo FM, the first commercial radio station in Bhutan, was set up in Thimphu. Other stations followed: Radio Valley in 2007, Centennial Radio a year later, and in 2009 came the launch of Sherubtse FM. This station, with its admittedly short schedule and low power, became the first radio station outside the capital, and was situated in the rather remote area of Kanglung in Eastern Bhutan. There were more to come – Radio High on 92.7MHz and Radio Wave on 88.8MHz were both inaugurated in 2010.

The last addition to the capital's radio scene was Yiga Radio which was inaugurated on Bhutan's national day, December 17th, in 2013. All these stations were more or less of a commercial nature. But it was recognised that there was also a need to educate and inform those in rural areas with poor access to district headquarters, schools and hospitals. It was therefore decided to establish community radio stations, usually with foreign aid and assistance. There are three of them, in villages in the districts of Samtse, Sarpang and Pema Gatshel. These districts are in the south of the country, bordering India.

One of them, Lhop Community Radio, was inaugurated by Her Majesty the Queen Mother, Dorji Wangmo Wangchuck in March 2016. Anothe station called KYD Community Radio – short for the villages of Khotakpa, Yalang and Denchi – was inaugurated by communications minister Dhungyel, also in March 2016.

'My work as a *tshogpa* will become much easier now, as we would be able to use radio to inform people about various meetings and disseminate other important messages immediately', said village leader Bopo Drukpa. 'I am really happy, the radio station will both inform and entertain us', he added.

One of the villagers, Namgay Wangdi, added that the community could reap a lot of benefit from the newly established radio station: 'Ours is a very remote village. I see the radio airing important agricultural and health-related information. Because it is coming from our own local station it will be helpful to us.'

Reflecting the part the Swiss played in the installation of the first radio communications in Bhutan, the establishment of all these stations was partly funded by a Swiss NGO.

BBS tx antenna at Sangaygang high above Thimphu

Coastwatchers & the AWA Teleradio 3BZ

WRTH *contributor and military historian,* **Dr Martin Hadlow**, *explains why an early 'portable' radio was of fundamental importance in the Pacific War*

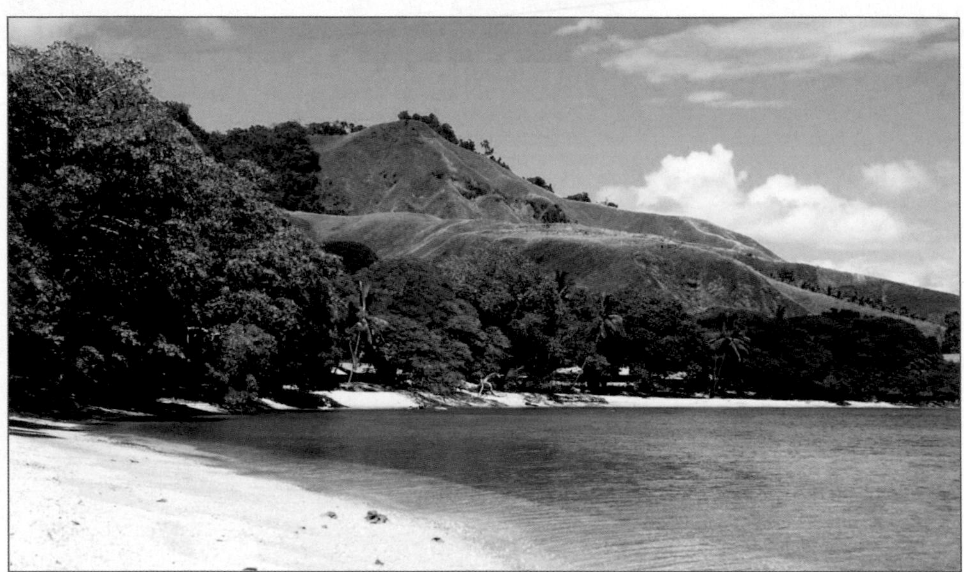

Visale, Solomon Islands (StewyOz CC BY-SA httpscreativecommons.orglicensesby-sa4.0)

While it took the personal courage of resourceful Allied Coastwatchers and their loyal Scouts to gather intelligence in the enemy-occupied islands of the South Pacific during World War Two, at the technical heart of the Coastwatching operation was a wireless set, the AWA 3B model Teleradio. Without a radio to transmit vital information from hidden jungle locations to the military authorities in Australia, the secret intelligence gathered under dangerous conditions would never have reached the ears of those who needed it most and could act upon the information.

Early models of the AWA Teleradio 3B were developed by Amalgamated Wireless Australasia Pty Ltd (AWA) at its radio factories and testing laboratories in Australia in the 1930s. The sets were originally designed for commercial use in remote locations in northern Australia, by planters and traders living in the then Australian Mandated Territory of Papua and New Guinea, and in the neighbouring British Solomon Islands. The initial 3A and 3B models were very popular as they were relatively easy for a non-specialist radio operator to use and could transmit messages through both voice and Morse code.

The name of the 3BZ model was used generically for the Teleradio across the Coastwatching network although, depending on circumstances, a typical Coastwatcher's set-up could include items of equipment from the 3A, 3B and 3BZ range, or in fact whatever was procurable. AWA developed the Teleradio 3BZ in 1942. While the 3BZ was similar to the 3B, this later version had a slightly modified receiver, a redesigned transmitter with six crystal channels and, importantly, the equipment was tropicalized to minimise mildew, rot and fungus. Surprisingly, given the hundreds of sets manufactured during World War Two, few good examples remain in museums or in the hands of private collectors.

The receiver for the 3BZ had five tunable frequency bands or four plus one crystal. The valve lineup of the receiver was a 1C4 RF amplifier, 1C6 oscillator/mixer, 1C4 IF, 1K6 detector/AVC/AF, a 1D4 audio output and a 1K4 BFO. The IF frequency was 535kHz. The receiver was not actually called '3BZ' but was the 'Superhetrodyne Receiver Type *C6770' where the '*' was replaced by a version number.

The 3BZ transmitter (Type J50062) was a new design with the antenna (aerial) tuner built in and six crystal channels, and was identified as the 'Teleradio 3BZ Transmitter' on the name plate. The valve complement included a 6V6 crystal

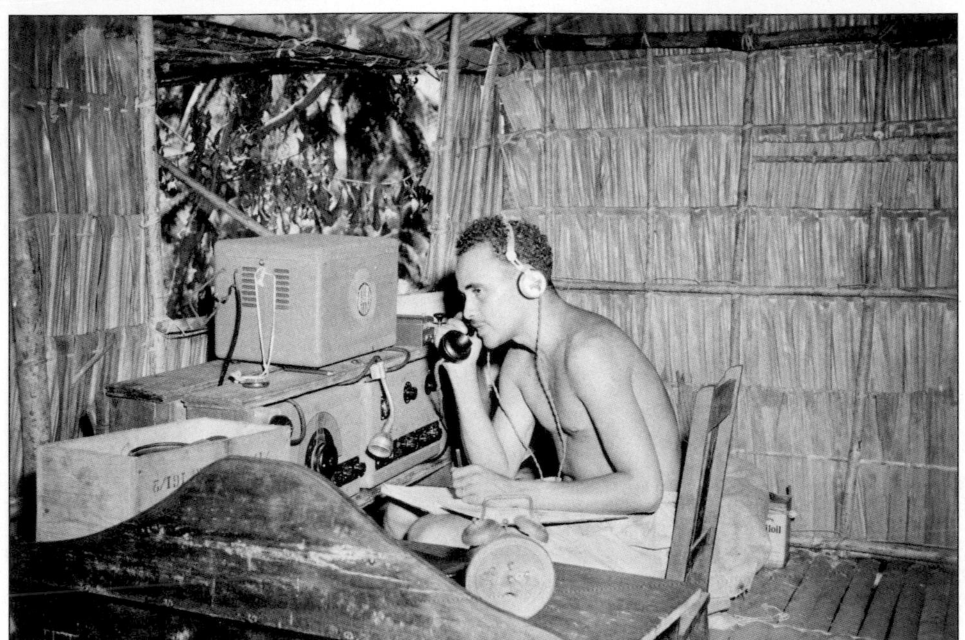

A wireless telegraphist, Sergeant William 'Billy' Bennett, MM, of the British Solomon Islands Protectorate Defence Force (BSIPDF), operating an AWA Teleradio at Seghe Coastwatchers' station ZGJ5 in 1943 (AWA 306814)

oscillator, with a 6V6 microphone amplifier driving two 6V6's in push-pull to modulate an 807 RF amplifier. A heavy duty vibrator was included on the chassis, and operation was from 12 Volt DC only. The frequency coverage of the 3BZ transmitter was 10 to 2.5 Mc/s (30 to 120 metres) with a power output of around 12 Watts on CW and 15 Watts on speech. Power consumption was 7.5 amps during operation and 1.5 amps on standby. Crystals in the range from 2.5 to 5 Mc/s could be fitted. When operating in the 5-10 Mc/s range part of the 807 power amplifier loading coil was shorted by the crystal switch, allowing it to be tuned to the second harmonic of the crystal frequency.

There was a low impedance antenna terminal to suit a ¼ wave Marconi antenna – used for less than 160km (100 miles) communications – and a separate 600 Ohm high impedance terminal to allow a single wire feed half-wave Hertz aerial, for 130 to 800km (80 to 500 miles) distances.

Once operational, the Teleradio set had a transmitting range of some 650km (400 miles) when used in voice mode and a longer reach, about 1,000km (625 miles), when Morse code signals were being sent. The Coastwatching stations used a secret frequency of 6675 kc/s and messages were sent either *en clair* or in simple Playfair code. Essential repairs to the equipment had to be undertaken by the Coastwatchers themselves; the biggest problem being moisture from heat and humidity which affected the electrical circuits, valves and other operating parts.

With Imperial Japan becoming a potential strategic threat to the northern approaches of Australia, the Royal Australian Navy developed a Coastwatching and Signals Intelligence Network, code-named *Ferdinand*, throughout the islands of the Pacific. The network was activated in 1939, when war broke out in Europe, only reaching its full potential when the War spread to the Pacific following the Imperial Japanese attack on Pearl Harbor on 7 December 1941.

Once Imperial Japanese ground forces invaded New Guinea and then Guadalcanal in the British Solomon Islands, the information flow through the Teleradio network gained increased importance. Coastwatchers hidden on the island of Bougainville would watch squadrons of Japanese aircraft flying overhead towards Guadalcanal from Rabaul, and send urgent messages such as, "24 torpedo-bombers headed yours", thus giving Allied fighter aircraft time to take off before the attackers arrived.

The AWA Teleradio 3BZ was the most efficient and effective 'portable' radio of its type and its time. The whole set was comprised of a transmitter, a receiver, a loudspeaker, a Morse key, a microphone, headphones, aerials, large batteries, a petrol engine to charge the batteries, and drums of fuel for the engine. All-up, the set weighed over 200kgs (440lbs) and, packed in steel boxes, it took 14 to 16 men to carry it into the jungle and up the hills. The carriers, men from local villages, had to be particularly careful to hold the batteries upright so that the acid did not leak out. The Teleradio often had to be moved

An AWA Teleradio 3BZ transmitter from 1942, now in a modern collection (Martin Hadlow)

hurriedly and in dangerous situations, such as when Japanese army patrols, often with tracker dogs, came looking for the Coastwatching stations that were causing so many military losses.

The Teleradio also played a vital role in ensuring that reports on Allied aircrew and sailors rescued by Coastwatchers were quickly relayed so that they could be picked up by patrolling seaplanes. Lt John F. Kennedy, later to become US President, was one such sailor saved by Coastwatchers in the British Solomon Islands.

Without the AWA Teleradio 3BZ, US Navy Admiral William 'Bull' Halsey would never have been able to say at the end of the War that, "The Coastwatchers saved Guadalcanal, and Guadalcanal saved the South Pacific".

Sgt Bennett, a Solomon Islander, joined the Solomon Islands Broadcasting Service as an announcer and producer after the War. He later became Chairman of the Board of the Solomon Islands Broadcasting Corporation.

We are grateful to the late Colin MacKinnon for technical information about the 3BZ which comes, with permission, from his excellent article *The 3BZ Coast Watchers Wireless Set.*

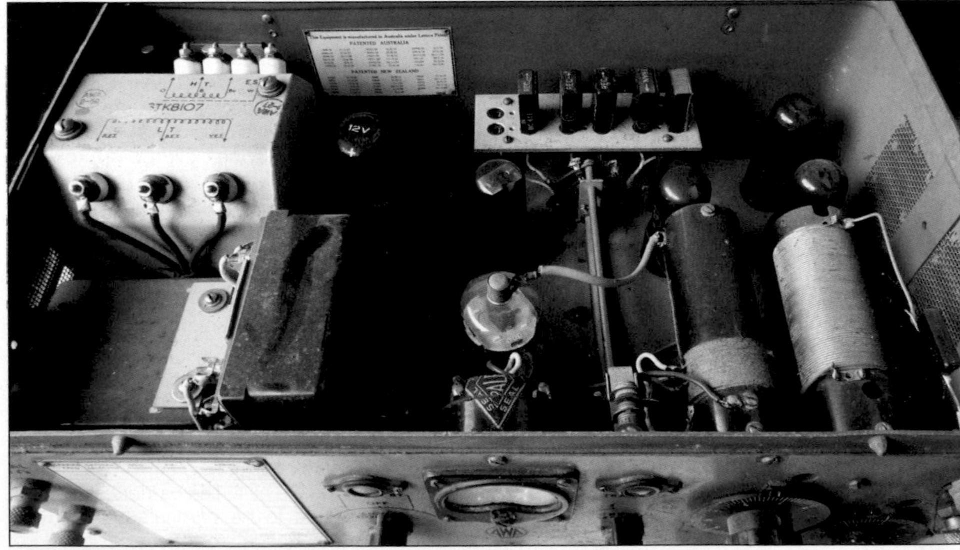

Inside the AWA Teleradio 3BZ transmitter (Martin Hadlow)

THE PREMIER
CLUB FOR
BROADCAST
BAND DXERS
INTERNATIONAL
IRCA
RADIO CLUB
ONLINE MEMBERSHIP:
$5.00 TO JOIN,
$0/YEAR THEREAFTER
ircamember@ircaonline.org
50 years of reprints for FREE download from our website, plus TIS/HAR, Slogans and the IRCA Mexican Log. Books also available.
www.ircaonline.org
P.O. Box 60241, Lafayette LA 70596
Search for "International Radio Club of America"

RadioVisión
M
BCN
ADXB
desde1979, expertos
en radiodifusión
MUNDI
MEDIA
CTK
CHECOSLOVAQUIA
Viendo y
escuchando
Radio historia
en Onda Corta
MCV87
editor
http://www.mundodx.net
info@mundodx.net

Scandinavian Weekend Radio

Alan Pennington, of the British DX Club, visited Scandinavian Weekend Radio and saw for himself the home of the station which celebrated 20 years on the air in 2020

The Scandinavian Weekend Radio crew and some former colleagues in July 2020 (SWR)

Shortwave broadcasts from Finland's state broadcaster, Yleisradio (YLE), ceased on 31 December 2006. However, Finland can still be heard on shortwave thanks to the regular transmissions of Scandinavian Weekend Radio (SWR), although these are not as easy to hear as YLE's were. In the summer of 2020, SWR celebrated 20 years of broadcasting.

In complete contrast to YLE, Scandinavian Weekend Radio is run solely by volunteers, who are members of a non-profit association set up to run the station: Vaihtoehtoisen Radiotoiminnan Tukiyhdistys ry (or Association to Support Alternative Radio). The original nine members of the Association all had a passion for radio through various hobby pursuits such as DXing, Amateur radio (it also operates amateur radio call OH6SWR), pirate radio, electronics and CB radio. Only Finnish citizens can be members of the Association and the station is funded by fees and donations from members as well as sales of merchandise from their online shop. Although a voluntary organisation, SWR still has to pay broadcasting licence fees to licencing authority Traficom and copyright fees for broadcasting music.

The Association was founded in December 1999 and by the following summer Scandinavian Weekend Radio was ready to make its first shortwave broadcast. The studio, transmitters and antennas were built on the site of a disused chicken farm near the village of Liedenpohja, on the northern tip of Lake Toisvesi in Western Finland (N 62°22', E 23°37'). It's a two-hour drive north from the city of Tampere, down a small track off Route 66, hidden amongst birch and pine trees in a landscape of fields and forest. SWR's first antenna tower was transported there by road, with snow still on the ground, in the spring of 2000. Their first transmitter was for the 25-metre band, designated ESATX25 as it was constructed by SWR's engineer Esa Saunamäki. It was tested and approved by the Finnish communications agency, FICORA (now Traficom) in June 2000.

Scandinavian Weekend Radio's first 24-hour broadcast started at 2100 UTC on 30 June 2000 (midnight local summer time, 1 July in Finland), initially on 11690kHz with transmitter RF output of just 50 Watts. The frequency changed later that day to 11720kHz. Both these 25 metre band frequencies are still used to this day. SWR switches

Drone view of the SWR studio, transmitter hut, SW mast and accomodation block in 2018 (SWR)

between the two frequencies to try and avoid interference. The antenna was a single half-wave dipole 20 metres high on the newly erected tower. Much stronger stations could, of course, make reception of low-powered SWR difficult – in 2000, for example, Radio Jordan and Voice of Turkey used 11690kHz and Radio New Zealand 11720 kHz – but some reception reports from around Europe did arrive at the station's Jyväskylä address. Not for nothing is one of SWR's slogans

SWR 25m and 48m SW transmitters (Alan Pennington)

'Hardest DX in the World'. The first programme was presented by DJ Tex Willer in Finnish and English, though ironically his picture was missing from the Crew photo on the station's first QSL card. Part of the first SWR show (along with others since) can be heard again online on the station's website at: www.swradio.net/sounds

The 25mb frequencies give the best chance of more distant reception of SWR and in 2001 they received their first QSL report from the USA. Transmitter power was increased to 100 Watts in 2003 and, in 2004, a new 3-element beam was installed for this band. This antenna's azimuth is usually 230 degrees although it can be re-directed for DX tests. However, one of the SWR crew has to climb the tower to do this, so the operation is heavily dependent on weather conditions.

In the summer of 2001, SWR's second shortwave transmitter launched in the 48-metre band, in parallel to their 25-metre band frequency. Their renewed licence now included the additional frequencies of 5980, 5990 and 6170kHz. The 24-hour transmission signed on at 2100 UTC on Friday 1 June. The home-built transmitter had an RF output power of 100 Watts and could be switched between each of the licensed frequencies. The antenna for 48 metres is a half-wave cage dipole strung about 12 metres above the ground. Currently two 48-metre band frequencies are used: 5980 and 6170kHz.

As volunteers travel from all over Finland, sleeping quarters were needed at the site from the outset. Other essentials have been added over the years: a sauna hut, hot tub and BBQ grill house plus a big woodburning stove in the studio.

In 2004, SWR's MW transmitter came on air on 1602kHz, this transmitter was also built by Esa

Saunamäki. This now runs at 400 Watts output power. A recycled telecoms mast was erected in 2006 in a forest clearing 250m away to support the MW antenna which is a quarter-wave vertical about 44m high. As YLE's last MW transmitter (on 558kHz) closed in 2007, SWR is keeping the medium wave band alive in Finland!

In May 2012, FM transmissions were added, initially on 104.2MHz. In 2013 a new FM transmitter was installed, now on 94.9MHz with 1kW ERP. A 4-element stacked dipole, on top of the tower used for the 25m band SW antenna, radiates the FM signal up to 40-50km around Virrat.

SWR operate with short-term licences, each for just a three-month period. The licence fixes the broadcasts dates and frequencies in advance. The frequencies are proposed by SWR, and the SW frequencies have remained the same, as the transmitters use frequency-specific crystal oscillators. As there has to be a 60-day gap between each licence period, there are three months with no broadcasts. SWR's regular 24-hour broadcasts are on the first Saturday of the month (starting at 2200 UTC Friday in winter, 2100 UTC in summer). Special broadcasts have also aired on Christmas Day and at Midsummer. There have also been special broadcasts in conjunction with like-minded radio enthusiasts at the

SWR studio and SW 25m/FM tower (Alan Pennington)

Sounds too free to be legal...
2000 2020
SCANDINAVIAN WEEKENDRADIO
The hardest DX in the world !

SWR 20 years of the Hardest DX in the World logo

Finnish DX Association (SDXL) summer meetings, and when European DX Council (EDXC) conferences are held in Finland.

SWR's programmes from the outset have been mainly live and 'free format', so DJs play their own choice of tracks according to their diverse tastes. Around half the music played is from Finland. Live music has also featured regularly, with a separate studio in a renovated barn which also houses SWR's transmitter room. Another of the station's slogans is 'Sounds too free to be legal' and, indeed, in the early years some DXers had to be reminded that SWR was a licensed broadcaster and not a pirate! As well as music, SWR also has programmes such as DJ Häkä's 'Virrat Tänään' (Virrat Today) covering local current affairs. Around three-quarters of programmes are in Finnish; the rest in English. Sometimes SWR carries programmes from other stations, for example Radio Marabu and, recently, the UK-based Radio Emma Toc.

SWR involves the local community with, for example, students from the local college visiting the station for training and, in 2014, a visit from a 'Youngsters on the Air' radio group. There are also open-days, music gigs and even an outside broadcast from a boat on Lake Toisvesi.

As radio enthusiasts themselves, SWR have always verified listeners' reception reports provided programme details cover at least 15 minutes of the broadcast. QSL verifications are numbered: more than 864 have been issued by the station in the past 20 years. Until 2012, only reports submitted by post received QSL cards. Since then, reports sent via the webform or email receive an e-QSL letter. So far 282 of these have been issued. Distant reports have been received from the USA, Canada, Japan and Argentina, although most reports are from Europe, especially Finland, Germany and Sweden.

In early July 2020, the crew of SWR celebrated 20 years on air with a live 48-hour broadcast. Still possibly the 'Hardest DX in the world', check out their website or Facebook page for details of their next broadcasts from Finland.

HF BROADCASTING RECEPTION CONDITIONS EXPECTED DURING 2021

Likely listening conditions in the coming year by **Ulf-Peter Hoppe**

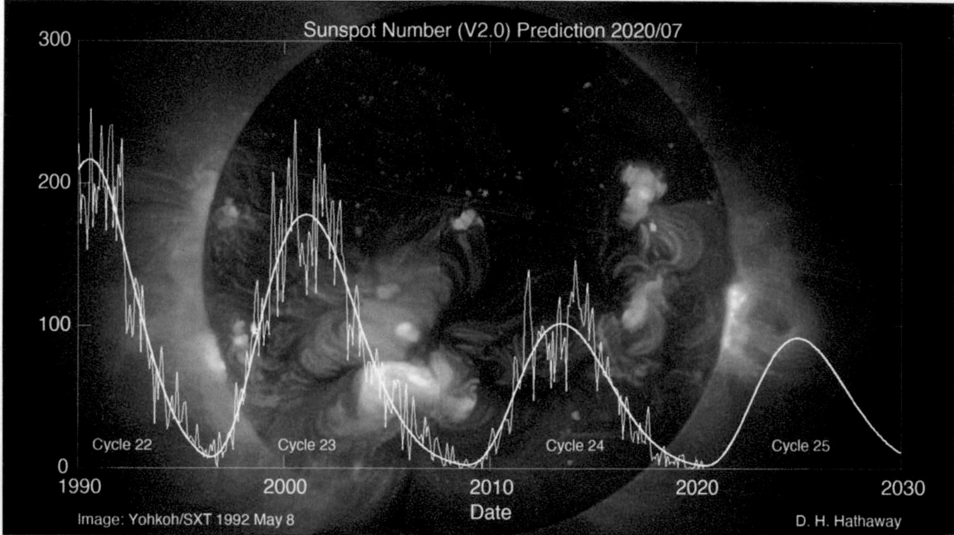

Fig. 1 Sunspot Cycles 22, 23, 24 and 25 (D H Hathaway and Yohkoh/SXT)

NEW SOLAR CYCLE 25

Solar minimum was reached in December 2019. This minimum marks the beginning of solar cycle 25. We can expect good conditions due to a slowly increasing ionosphere in the coming year.

Solar Cycles, also called sunspot cycles, have been counted since 1756. During the 75 years of WRTH, we have experienced seven of them. Fig. 1 charts the last 30 years of sunspot numbers.

Solar scientists estimate that the smoothed sunspot number will increase from about 9 in Jan-Apr 2021 to about 15 in May-Aug and rise to around 26 in Sept-Dec. This is slower than the international group of experts thought a year ago.

Solar ultraviolet radiation creates the ionosphere, the ionized fraction of the earth's atmosphere. The F-region of the ionosphere starts about 150 km (93 miles) above the ground and constitutes the most important reflector for HF radio waves. The E-region at 100 to 120 km (62 to 74 miles) is weaker, but sometimes also plays a role in HF radio communication. The flux of ultraviolet light from the sun is smallest when the solar cycle is near its minimum, and increases with increasing sunspot activity. The electron density in the ionosphere will therefore generally increase during the course of 2021. The actual number of sunspots will vary, reaching up to 20 more than average on some individual days. The best reception conditions on a given day can occur in a shortwave band neighbouring the ones given in the prediction table.

The ionospheric conditions at the reflection point halfway along the great circle from transmitter to receiver have the greatest influence on the best frequency to use, except for the rarer two-hop circuits and the even rarer circuits taking the opposite direction, along the longest part of the great circle. When the reflection point is in daylight, the 17, 19, and 21 MHz bands often give the most stable reception conditions. When the reflection point is on the night side, the 11, 9, 7, 6, and 5 MHz bands give the best results.

Reception conditions in 2021 will be at least as good as last year, and day-to-day changes will be small. In the years close to solar minimum, there are fewer than average solar flares or coronal mass ejections, which are giant explosions on the surface of the sun. These can spew light, energy and solar material into space. When such an ejection hits our planet, it can upset HF radiowave propagation.

We still observe little interference between stations, so we can expect a good year of reception on the HF broadcasting bands.

2021 will be a very good year for newcomers to start shortwave listening, and equally good for all the experienced radio enthusiasts.

We wish WRTH and its readers a happy eighth solar cycle!

ABOUT THE AUTHOR

Ulf-Peter Hoppe is an adjunct professor of physics at the Arctic University of Norway.

Most Suitable Frequencies 2021

Prepared by Prof. Dr. rer. nat. Ulf-Peter Hoppe, Chief Scientist
E-mail: ulf-peter.hoppe@tveco.net
Web: http://tinyurl.com/pg46arx

TRANSMITTING STATION LOCATION

LISTENER'S AREA	LOCAL TIME	APPROX. UTC TIME	JAN/FEB & NOV/DEC								MAR/APR & SEPT/OCT								MAY-AUGUST							
			EUR/NAF	N.AM(E)	N.AM(W)	C/S.AM	C/S.AF	ME/S.AS	E.AS	AUS/NZ	EUR/NAF	N.AM(E)	N.AM(W)	C/S.AM	C/S.AF	ME/S.AS	E.AS	AUS/NZ	EUR/NAF	N.AM(E)	N.AM(W)	C/S.AM	C/S.AF	ME/S.AS	E.AS	AUS/NZ
EUROPE AND NORTH AFRICA	00:00-04:00	23:00-03:00	7	9	7	11	9	7	9	-	7	9	9	11	9	9	9	-	9	9	11	9	7	9	11	-
	04:00-08:00	03:00-07:00	6	7	7	9	9	13	15	17	7	7	11	9	11	15	17	17	11	7	13	9	11	15	17	15
	08:00-12:00	07:00-11:00	13	9	9	11	17	17	17	21	13	9	9	11	17	17	17	25	17	11	11	13	15	21	17	21
	12:00-16:00	11:00-15:00	15	15	6	17	17	15	13	17	17	15	9	21	21	17	17	15	17	15	9	17	13	17	15	-
	16:00-20:00	15:00-19:00	9	17	13	21	15	7	9	13	9	17	13	21	15	9	15	15	9	15	13	17	13	11	11	15
	20:00-00:00	19:00-23:00	6	9	11	13	11	9	9	11	7	13	13	17	11	9	11	13	9	11	15	15	9	9	9	13
NORTH AMERICA (EAST)	22:00-02:00	03:00-07:00	7	6	6	7	9	-	-	-	9	6	7	7	11	-	-	11	9	7	9	7	9	-	-	13
	02:00-06:00	07:00-11:00	9	6	6	7	-	-	9	13	9	6	6	6	-	-	9	11	11	6	7	7	-	-	11	9
	06:00-10:00	11:00-15:00	15	11	7	13	21	15	13	11	15	11	9	13	17	15	15	15	15	11	9	11	17	15	15	13
	10:00-14:00	15:00-19:00	15	13	13	17	21	11	9	-	15	13	11	17	21	17	-	-	15	15	15	17	17	17	-	-
	14:00-18:00	19:00-23:00	9	13	15	15	17	11	11	15	15	13	13	17	21	13	15	17	13	11	13	15	15	15	15	21
	18:00-22:00	23:00-03:00	6	7	9	7	11	13	13	-	9	9	11	9	15	15	15	21	11	11	11	11	11	17	17	21
NORTH AMERICA (WEST)	00:00-04:00	08:00-12:00	9	7	6	7	-	9	9	11	9	6	6	9	-	-	9	11	11	7	7	9	-	-	11	9
	04:00-08:00	12:00-16:00	13	11	7	15	17	9	9	9	15	11	9	15	17	11	11	11	13	13	11	15	15	13	11	11
	08:00-12:00	16:00-20:00	15	15	13	21	21	11	13	15	15	15	15	17	17	15	13	15	15	17	15	17	17	17	13	-
	12:00-16:00	20:00-00:00	9	15	13	17	21	11	13	17	11	13	11	17	17	-	15	17	15	13	13	17	15	17	15	17
	16:00-20:00	00:00-04:00	9	7	9	9	11	15	15	17	7	9	9	9	13	15	15	21	11	11	11	11	9	15	17	17
	20:00-00:00	04:00-08:00	7	7	6	9	9	-	-	11	9	6	7	9	9	-	15	13	11	7	7	9	11	-	15	13
CENTRAL AND SOUTH AMERICA	00:00-04:00	04:00-08:00	7	7	9	9	11	-	17	15	9	7	11	9	11	-	17	17	9	7	11	9	9	-	-	11
	04:00-08:00	08:00-12:00	15	7	9	7	17	15	11	11	15	7	9	7	17	21	15	9	13	9	9	6	17	17	15	-
	08:00-12:00	12:00-16:00	21	17	13	17	25	21	-	-	21	17	15	17	21	25	-	-	17	15	15	17	17	21	17	-
	12:00-16:00	16:00-20:00	17	17	21	21	25	-	-	-	25	17	15	21	21	-	-	-	15	15	17	21	15	17	-	-
	16:00-20:00	20:00-00:00	9	13	21	17	21	11	11	21	11	13	17	17	13	13	15	21	11	13	17	15	9	13	15	17
	20:00-00:00	00:00-04:00	9	7	9	11	9	13	15	21	11	7	13	11	13	17	17	17	9	9	13	9	11	15	17	15
CENTRAL AND SOUTH AFRICA	00:00-04:00	22:00-02:00	11	13	17	13	7	9	13	-	13	15	15	11	7	9	15	-	9	11	-	9	7	7	11	-
	04:00-08:00	02:00-06:00	7	9	9	9	7	15	17	17	9	9	11	9	7	15	17	17	9	7	11	7	7	13	17	-
	08:00-12:00	06:00-10:00	17	-	-	13	15	21	21	21	17	-	-	-	17	25	25	21	17	-	-	-	15	21	17	17
	12:00-16:00	10:00-14:00	17	21	-	21	21	21	21	17	21	17	-	25	21	21	25	-	21	17	-	21	15	17	25	-
	16:00-20:00	14:00-18:00	17	21	13	25	15	15	11	11	21	21	13	25	15	11	15	13	17	21	15	17	11	11	11	9
	20:00-00:00	18:00-22:00	9	15	17	21	11	9	11	11	13	17	17	17	9	9	13	11	9	17	17	11	7	7	13	9
MIDDLE EAST AND SOUTH ASIA	00:00-04:00	21:00-01:00	7	11	11	11	9	7	7	-	7	13	13	15	9	9	9	9	9	13	-	13	9	9	11	-
	04:00-08:00	01:00-05:00	7	9	15	9	7	13	17	25	9	11	15	13	9	15	17	25	9	13	15	15	9	17	17	21
	08:00-12:00	05:00-09:00	17	-	-	-	15	17	21	25	15	-	-	17	17	25	21	25	15	-	15	-	13	21	21	21
	12:00-16:00	09:00-13:00	17	-	9	21	17	17	13	17	17	-	-	21	17	21	17	17	15	15	13	17	17	21	17	15
	16:00-20:00	13:00-17:00	13	15	9	25	17	9	9	15	13	17	11	25	17	11	11	11	13	17	13	25	15	13	15	11
	20:00-00:00	17:00-21:00	7	-	11	15	11	7	7	11	9	17	13	17	11	11	9	13	11	17	15	17	9	9	11	11
EAST ASIA AND FAR EAST	00:00-04:00	16:00-20:00	9	15	17	17	13	9	6	13	11	17	13	21	13	11	7	15	11	15	15	17	13	9	11	13
	04:00-08:00	20:00-00:00	7	7	11	9	11	11	7	11	7	9	15	9	11	11	9	15	9	15	15	11	9	9	9	15
	08:00-12:00	00:00-04:00	7	6	9	7	9	9	17	-	7	7	9	9	9	11	17	-	7	7	11	9	7	11	11	-
	12:00-16:00	04:00-08:00	7	6	6	7	9	13	17	-	9	6	9	7	11	17	25	15	9	7	9	7	11	17	17	13
	16:00-20:00	08:00-12:00	13	7	9	11	17	15	7	21	13	9	9	13	17	17	11	17	13	11	11	11	17	17	13	-
	20:00-00:00	12:00-16:00	13	15	11	25	17	17	6	17	15	15	13	25	17	17	9	-	13	17	15	17	13	15	11	-
AUSTRALIA AND NEW ZEALAND	00:00-04:00	14:00-18:00	15	15	9	-	11	11	9	6	15	-	11	-	11	9	9	6	13	-	9	-	9	11	7	6
	04:00-08:00	18:00-22:00	11	21	15	17	11	9	7	6	11	21	17	15	11	11	7	6	11	-	15	-	9	9	9	6
	08:00-12:00	22:00-02:00	-	25	25	21	15	15	21	7	-	25	25	21	13	17	17	7	-	-	17	17	-	15	15	7
	12:00-16:00	02:00-06:00	-	-	15	17	-	21	25	11	17	-	21	21	-	21	25	9	17	15	17	15	-	21	21	6
	16:00-20:00	06:00-10:00	25	13	9	13	17	17	15	9	17	11	9	13	21	17	17	9	21	9	13	9	17	17	15	7
	20:00-00:00	10:00-14:00	17	11	11	15	17	11	13	7	17	11	11	11	-	9	11	6	-	11	9	11	-	11	7	6

Band selections have been made according to predicted propagation conditions. Also check neighbouring bands of the most suitable bands shown here. A '-' means there is no reliable propagation in any frequency band.

How to use *WRTH*

ORGANISATION OF THE BOOK

The book consists of three main areas: **Features**, consisting of equipment reviews, broadcasting predictions and informative radio-related articles; **Directory**, which is further divided into *National Radio*, *International Radio* (including Clandestine and Other Target Broadcasts), *Frequency Lists* (which includes Mediumwave lists by region, Shortwave Stations of the World, International Broadcasts in selected languages and International DRM broadcasts), and *Terrestrial Television*; and finally **Reference** where a full country index, abbreviations used in WRTH and transmitter site location tables, as well as other useful information related to the world of radio broadcasting can be found.

Each section is identified by a unique 'side-bar', which can be found both on the main contents page and on each individual page throughout the book. Each section starts with an alphabetical country listing.

In the Directory, countries are listed alphabetically within each section so that they may be easily located by flicking forward to the relevant location. Alternatively, the index in the Reference section may be used to find the exact page number for a specific country of interest.

Under each country in the National Radio section, state broadcasters are listed first followed by major networks and then other stations. Armed forces stations and local relays of international stations are at the end of the entry. For all stations, mediumwave is listed first, followed by shortwave and finally FM. Many stations now only broadcast on FM. Details are given of digital radio multiplexes where appropriate.

OPERATING TECHNIQUES

When operating their receivers, the majority of listeners tend to operate in one of two main modes, switching between them as and when they deem appropriate. One method is to 'target' a given station or country by monitoring known frequencies and the other is simply to 'cruise' a specific band and identify each station as they occur (known as 'band scanning'). We have designed WRTH in such a way that either of these methods can be accommodated.

When operating in the targeting mode there are two ways to find a particular country. The first option is to go to the main contents page and use the section 'side-bars' to direct you to the right area of the book. Once there, you then only have to flick forward a few pages to locate the country of interest. Alternatively you can use the country index at the back of the book, which will tell you the precise page number. As you develop a 'feel' for the book and get used to the alphabetical layout, you will probably find that the side-bar method is simpler and quicker than using the country index.

Should you prefer to use band-scanning, there are listings of both medium wave and international short-wave broadcasts available in the Frequency Listings. These can also be useful for casual listening, but in either case can help to identify a station by frequency – whereupon further details can be obtained using the country entry to identify alternative frequencies for the station of interest.

UTC

UTC (Coordinated Universal Time) is the current time standard used throughout the world by broadcasters and many other organisations. UTC replaced Greenwich Mean Time, GMT, as the world time standard some years ago. UTC, like its predecessor, is based on the Greenwich meridian at 0 degrees longitude (in London, England). To find out how many hours ahead or behind UTC your location is, refer to the World Time Table elsewhere in this section. If your location is ahead of UTC (indicated by a '+' sign in the table), you will need to add that number of hours to the time shown in the schedules. Likewise, if your location is behind UTC (indicated by '-'), you will need to subtract that many hours from the time shown in the schedules in order to find out at what time the broadcast can be heard at your location.

RECEPTION REPORTS

When requesting a verification of the reception report you sent (commonly referred to as a QSL-card), it is important that you include details of the programming heard (over a period of time, usually at least 15 minutes wherever possible); The date and time, in UTC (as explained above); how well you heard the broadcast and what receiver/antenna you were using. Where possible, try to use the language of the broadcast, rather than English, as there may be no English speakers available at the station. Be polite and do not demand a QSL card – stations on a tight budget may not have the resources to print QSL cards, but may send you promotional items and a verification letter instead.

It is courteous to enclose return postage when writing to small domestic broadcasters. This can be in the form of an International Reply Coupon (IRC) available from post offices. In all cases, when writing to radio stations you must write clearly. Remember, if the station cannot read your address, then you cannot expect to receive a reply!

NB: Not all entries are in the same format, example above is given for guidance and should cover most entries. If a country observes Daylight Savings Time/Summer Time, the effective dates are shown after the local time (**L.T**).

Indian DX Club International
ASIAN DX REVIEW
DX Newsletter from IDXCI
an online publication distributed free
DXC
DXING A SCIENTIFIC HOBBY
GPO Box 646, Kolkata 700001, India.
www.idxci.in
idxcidxpedition.blogspot.com
fb.com/groups/idxcintl
t.me/IDXCI
For free membership, ADXR subscription write to
idxc.international@gmail.com

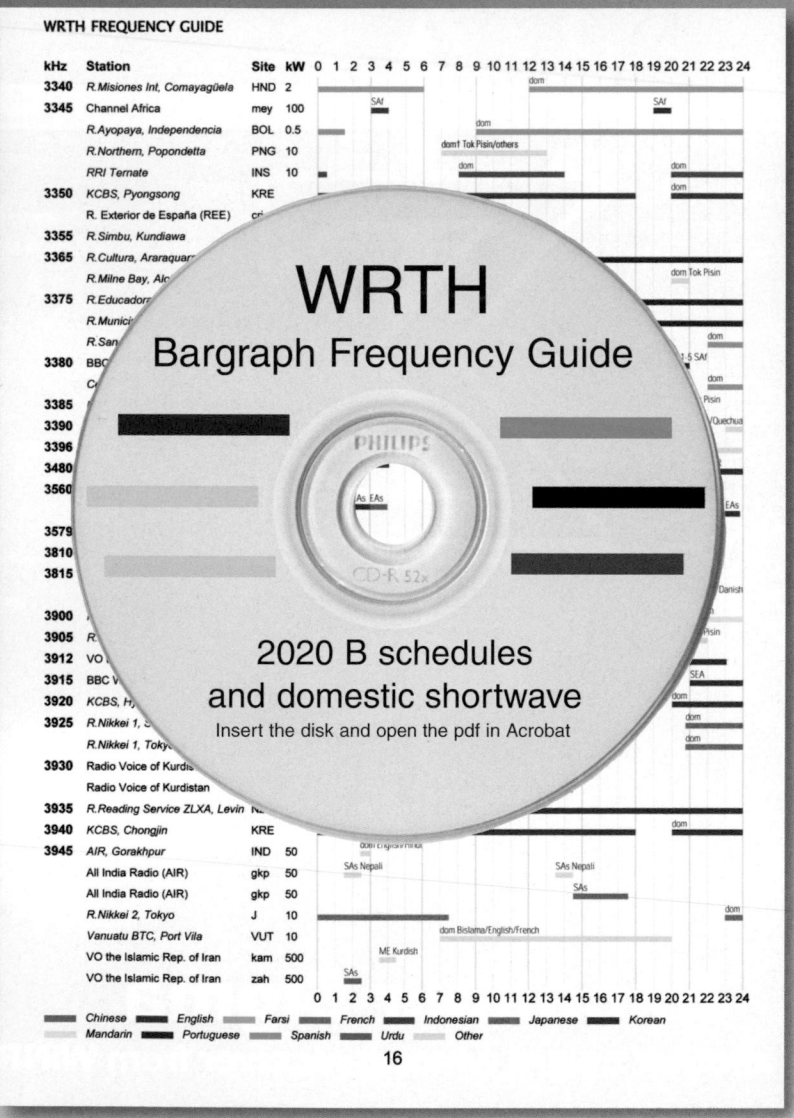

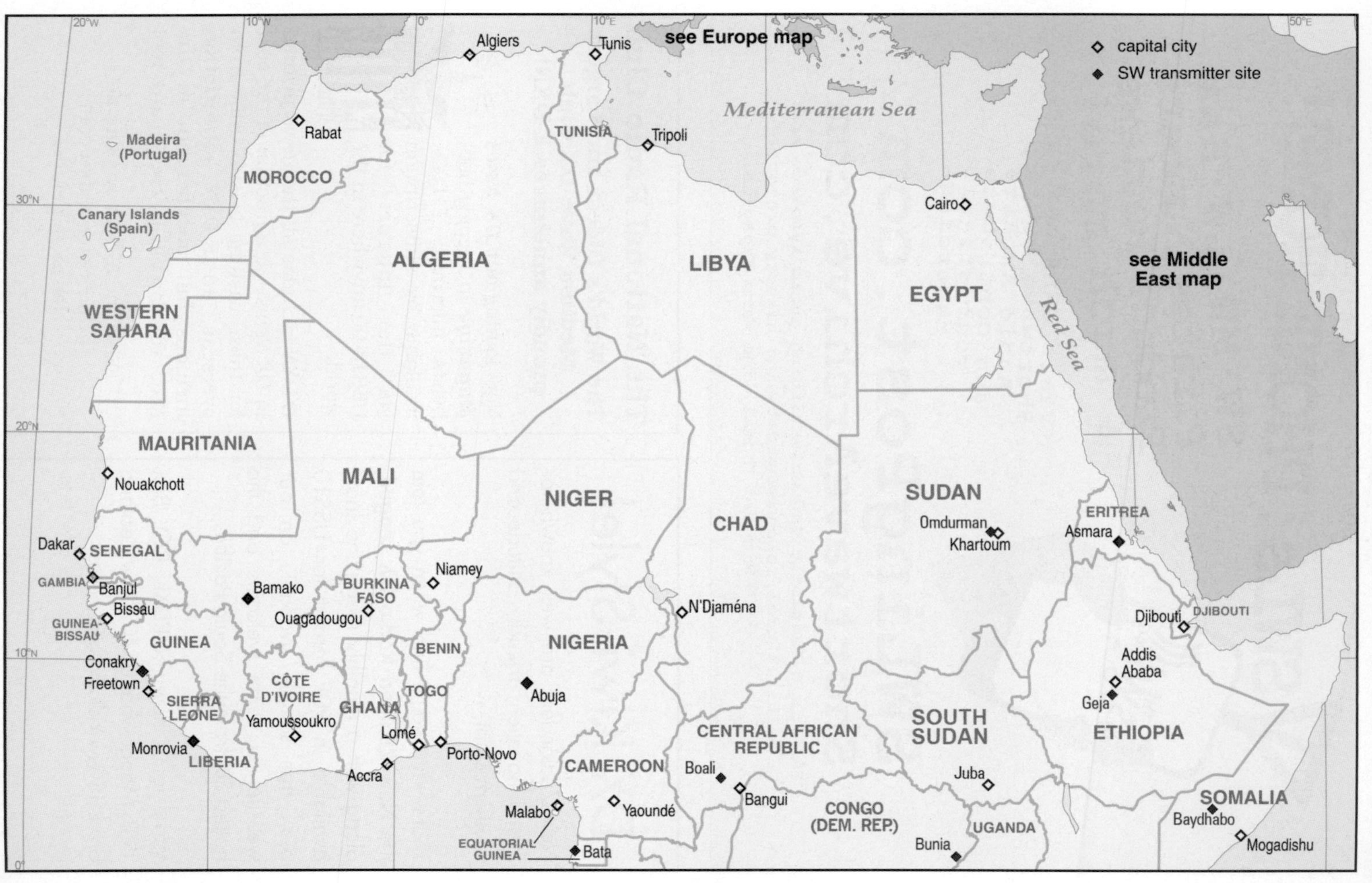
capital city
SW transmitter site
see Europe map
see Middle East map
Mediterranean Sea
Red Sea
Madeira (Portugal)
Canary Islands (Spain)
WESTERN SAHARA
MOROCCO
Rabat
ALGERIA
Algiers
TUNISIA
Tunis
LIBYA
Tripoli
EGYPT
Cairo
SUDAN
Omdurman
Khartoum
SOUTH SUDAN
Juba
ERITREA
Asmara
DJIBOUTI
Djibouti
ETHIOPIA
Addis Ababa
Geja
SOMALIA
Baydhabo
Mogadishu
UGANDA
Bunia
CONGO (DEM. REP.)
CENTRAL AFRICAN REPUBLIC
Bangui
Boali
CHAD
N'Djaména
NIGER
Niamey
NIGERIA
Abuja
CAMEROON
Yaoundé
Bata
Malabo
EQUATORIAL GUINEA
BENIN
Porto-Novo
TOGO
Lomé
GHANA
Accra
BURKINA FASO
Ouagadougou
CÔTE D'IVOIRE
Yamoussoukro
MALI
Bamako
MAURITANIA
Nouakchott
SENEGAL
Dakar
GAMBIA
Banjul
GUINEA-BISSAU
Bissau
GUINEA
Conakry
SIERRA LEONE
Freetown
LIBERIA
Monrovia
30°N
20°N
10°N
0°
20°W
10°W
0°
10°E
50°E

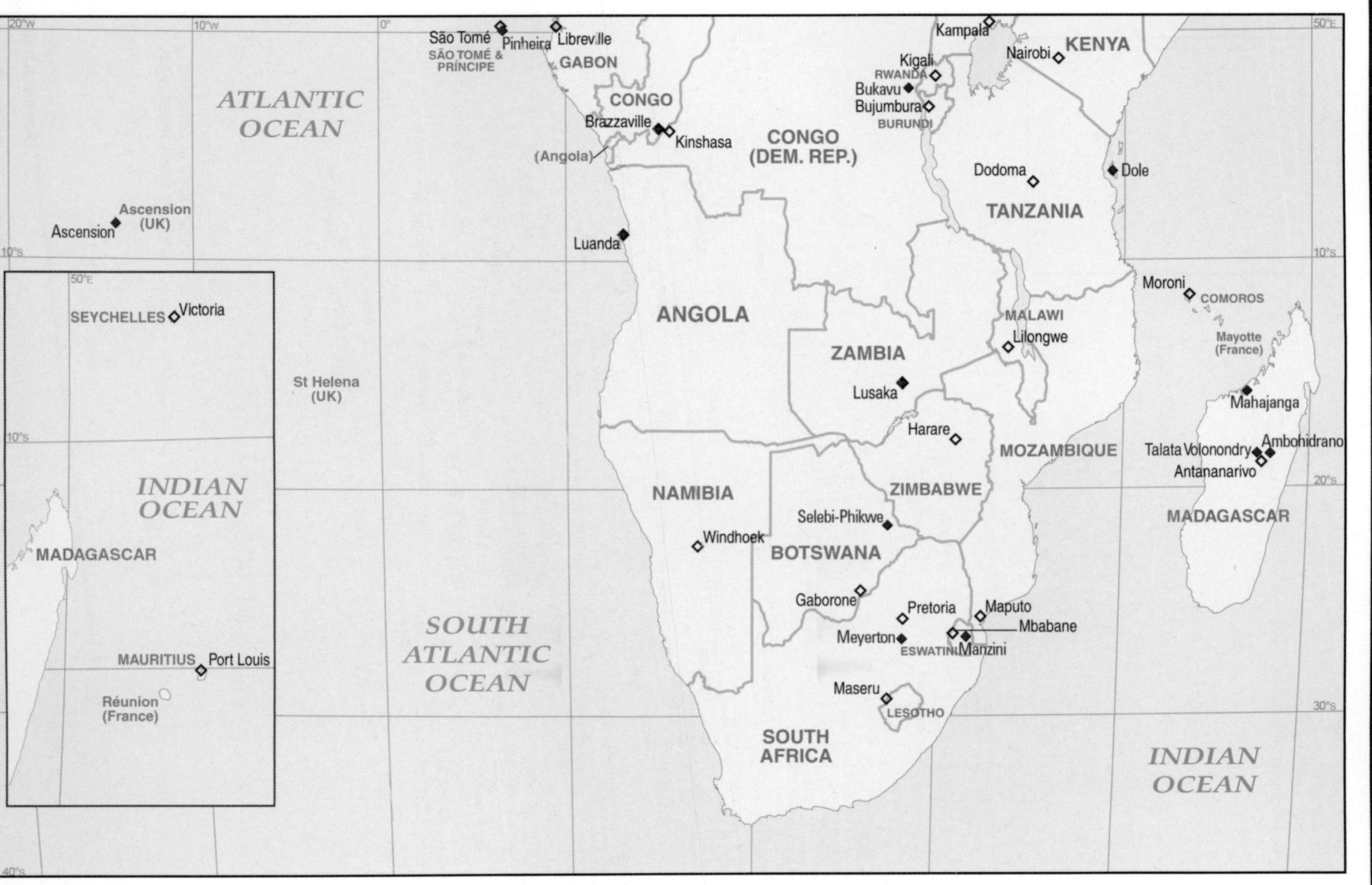

ATLANTIC OCEAN
Ascension (UK)
Ascension
São Tomé
Pinheira
SÃO TOMÉ & PRÍNCIPE
Libreville
GABON
CONGO
Brazzaville
Kinshasa
(Angola)
Luanda
CONGO (DEM. REP.)
Kampala
Nairobi
KENYA
Kigali
RWANDA
Bukavu
Bujumbura
BURUNDI
Dodoma
Dole
TANZANIA
Moroni
COMOROS
Mayotte (France)
Mahajanga
Talata Volonondry
Ambohidrano
Antananarivo
MADAGASCAR
ANGOLA
ZAMBIA
Lusaka
MALAWI
Lilongwe
Harare
MOZAMBIQUE
ZIMBABWE
NAMIBIA
Windhoek
Selebi-Phikwe
BOTSWANA
Gaborone
Pretoria
Maputo
Mbabane
Meyerton
ESWATINI
Manzini
Maseru
LESOTHO
SOUTH AFRICA
St Helena (UK)
SOUTH ATLANTIC OCEAN
INDIAN OCEAN
SEYCHELLES
Victoria
INDIAN OCEAN
MADAGASCAR
MAURITIUS
Port Louis
Réunion (France)
20°W
10°W
0°
50°E
10°S
20°S
30°S
40°S

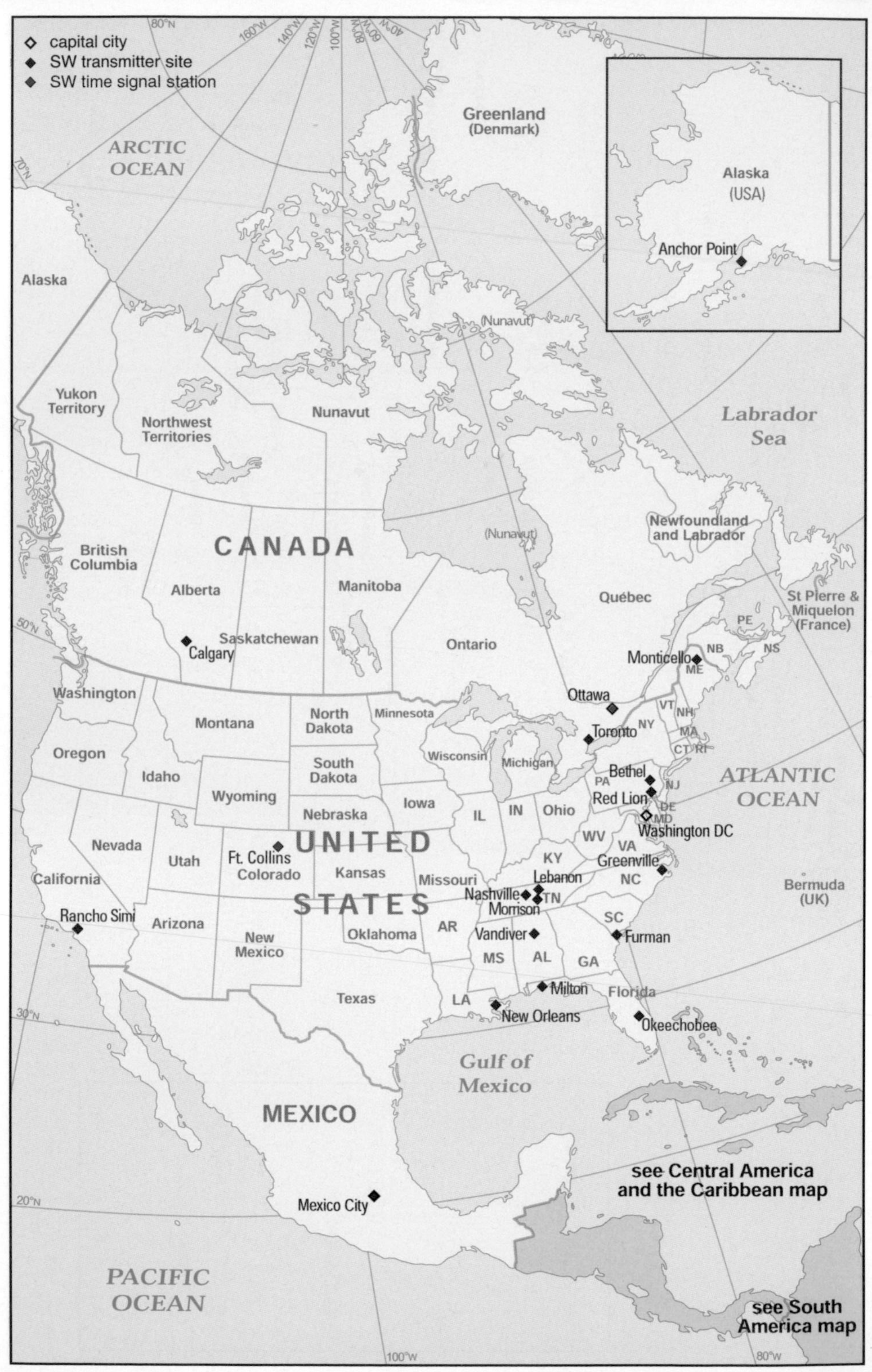
capital city
SW transmitter site
SW time signal station
ARCTIC OCEAN
Greenland (Denmark)
Alaska (USA)
Anchor Point
Alaska
Yukon Territory
Northwest Territories
Nunavut
(Nunavut)
Labrador Sea
British Columbia
CANADA
Alberta
Manitoba
Saskatchewan
Calgary
Ontario
Québec
Newfoundland and Labrador
St Pierre & Miquelon (France)
PE
NB
NS
Monticello
ME
Ottawa
Toronto
VT
NH
NY
MA
CT
RI
Washington
Montana
North Dakota
Minnesota
Oregon
Idaho
South Dakota
Wisconsin
Michigan
Wyoming
Iowa
Nebraska
PA
Bethel
NJ
Red Lion
DE
MD
Washington DC
ATLANTIC OCEAN
IL
IN
Ohio
WV
VA
Nevada
Utah
Ft. Collins
Colorado
UNITED STATES
Kansas
Missouri
KY
Greenville
NC
California
Lebanon
Nashville
TN
Morrison
Bermuda (UK)
Rancho Simi
Arizona
New Mexico
Oklahoma
AR
Vandiver
SC
Furman
MS
AL
GA
Milton
Florida
Texas
LA
New Orleans
Okeechobee
Gulf of Mexico
MEXICO
see Central America and the Caribbean map
Mexico City
PACIFIC OCEAN
see South America map
80°N
70°N
50°N
30°N
20°N
160°W
140°W
120°W
100°W
80°W
60°W
40°W

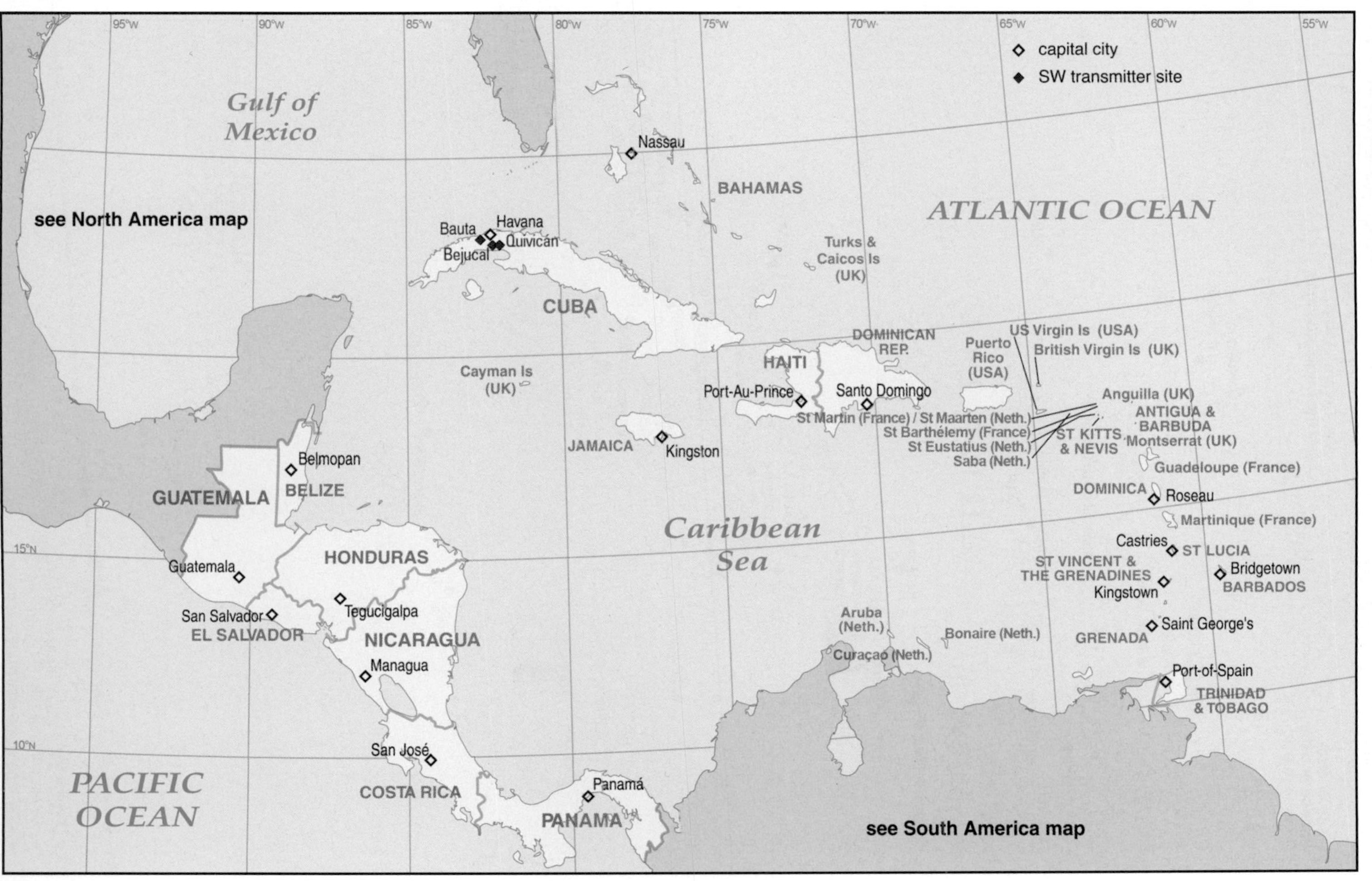
capital city
SW transmitter site
ATLANTIC OCEAN
Gulf of Mexico
see North America map
Caribbean Sea
PACIFIC OCEAN
see South America map
95°W
90°W
85°W
80°W
75°W
70°W
65°W
60°W
55°W
15°N
10°N
BAHAMAS
Nassau
Turks & Caicos Is (UK)
CUBA
Havana
Bauta
Bejucal
Quivicán
Cayman Is (UK)
JAMAICA
Kingston
HAITI
Port-Au-Prince
DOMINICAN REP.
Santo Domingo
Puerto Rico (USA)
US Virgin Is (USA)
British Virgin Is (UK)
Anguilla (UK)
ANTIGUA & BARBUDA
ST KITTS & NEVIS
Montserrat (UK)
Guadeloupe (France)
St Martin (France) / St Maarten (Neth.)
St Barthélemy (France)
St Eustatius (Neth.)
Saba (Neth.)
DOMINICA
Roseau
Martinique (France)
ST LUCIA
Castries
Bridgetown
BARBADOS
ST VINCENT & THE GRENADINES
Kingstown
GRENADA
Saint George's
Port-of-Spain
TRINIDAD & TOBAGO
Aruba (Neth.)
Curaçao (Neth.)
Bonaire (Neth.)
GUATEMALA
Guatemala
BELIZE
Belmopan
HONDURAS
Tegucigalpa
EL SALVADOR
San Salvador
NICARAGUA
Managua
COSTA RICA
San José
PANAMA
Panamá

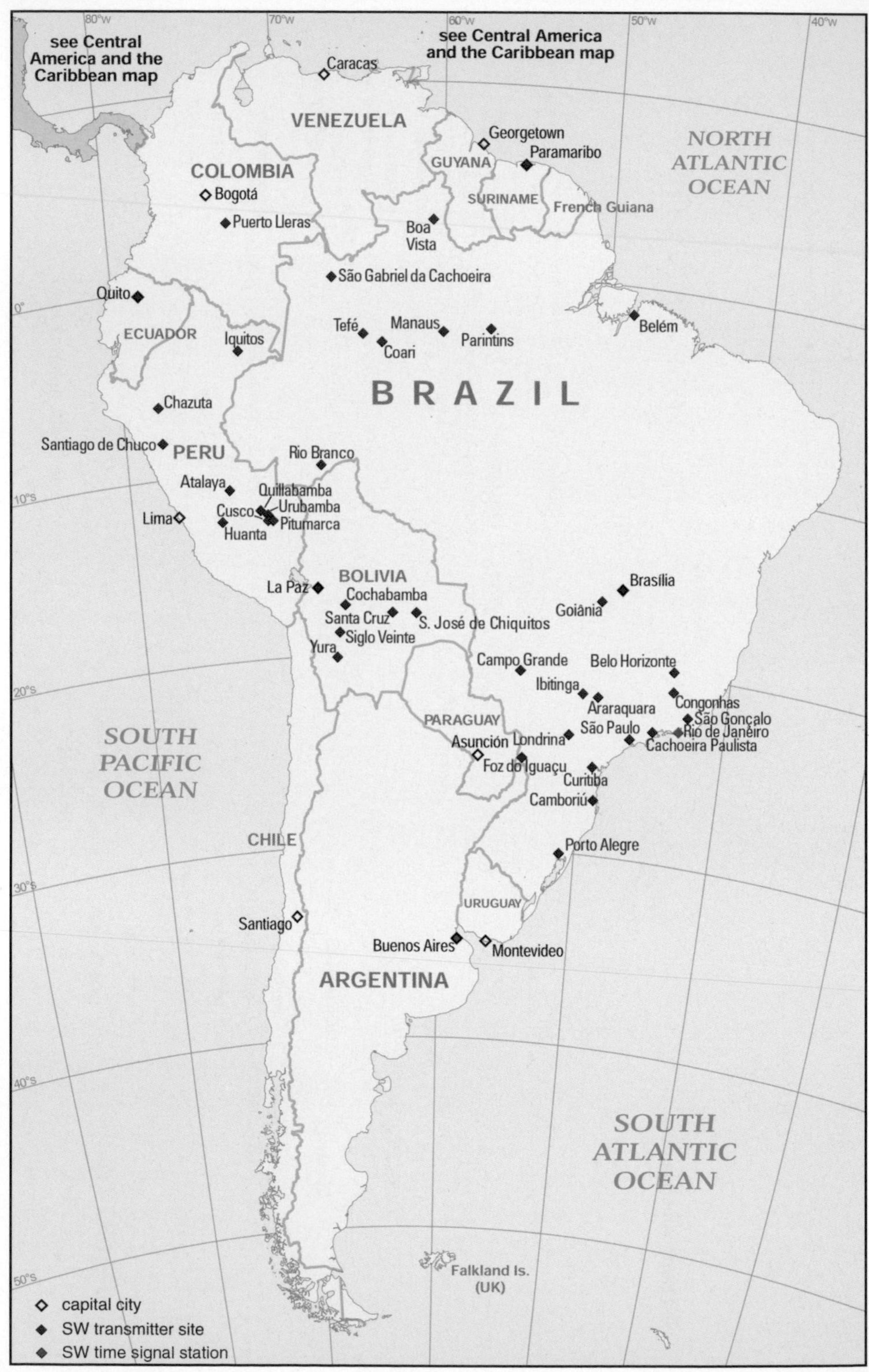

see Central America and the Caribbean map
see Central America and the Caribbean map
NORTH ATLANTIC OCEAN
SOUTH PACIFIC OCEAN
SOUTH ATLANTIC OCEAN
VENEZUELA
COLOMBIA
GUYANA
SURINAME
French Guiana
ECUADOR
PERU
BRAZIL
BOLIVIA
PARAGUAY
CHILE
URUGUAY
ARGENTINA
Falkland Is. (UK)
Caracas
Georgetown
Paramaribo
Bogotá
Puerto Lleras
Boa Vista
São Gabriel da Cachoeira
Quito
Tefé
Manaus
Parintins
Belém
Iquitos
Coari
Chazuta
Santiago de Chuco
Rio Branco
Atalaya
Quillabamba
Cusco
Urubamba
Pitumarca
Lima
Huanta
La Paz
Cochabamba
Santa Cruz
S. José de Chiquitos
Siglo Veinte
Yura
Brasília
Goiânia
Campo Grande
Belo Horizonte
Ibitinga
Araraquara
Congonhas
São Gonçalo
Rio de Janeiro
Cachoeira Paulista
São Paulo
Londrina
Asunción
Foz do Iguaçu
Curitiba
Camboriú
Porto Alegre
Santiago
Buenos Aires
Montevideo
capital city
SW transmitter site
SW time signal station

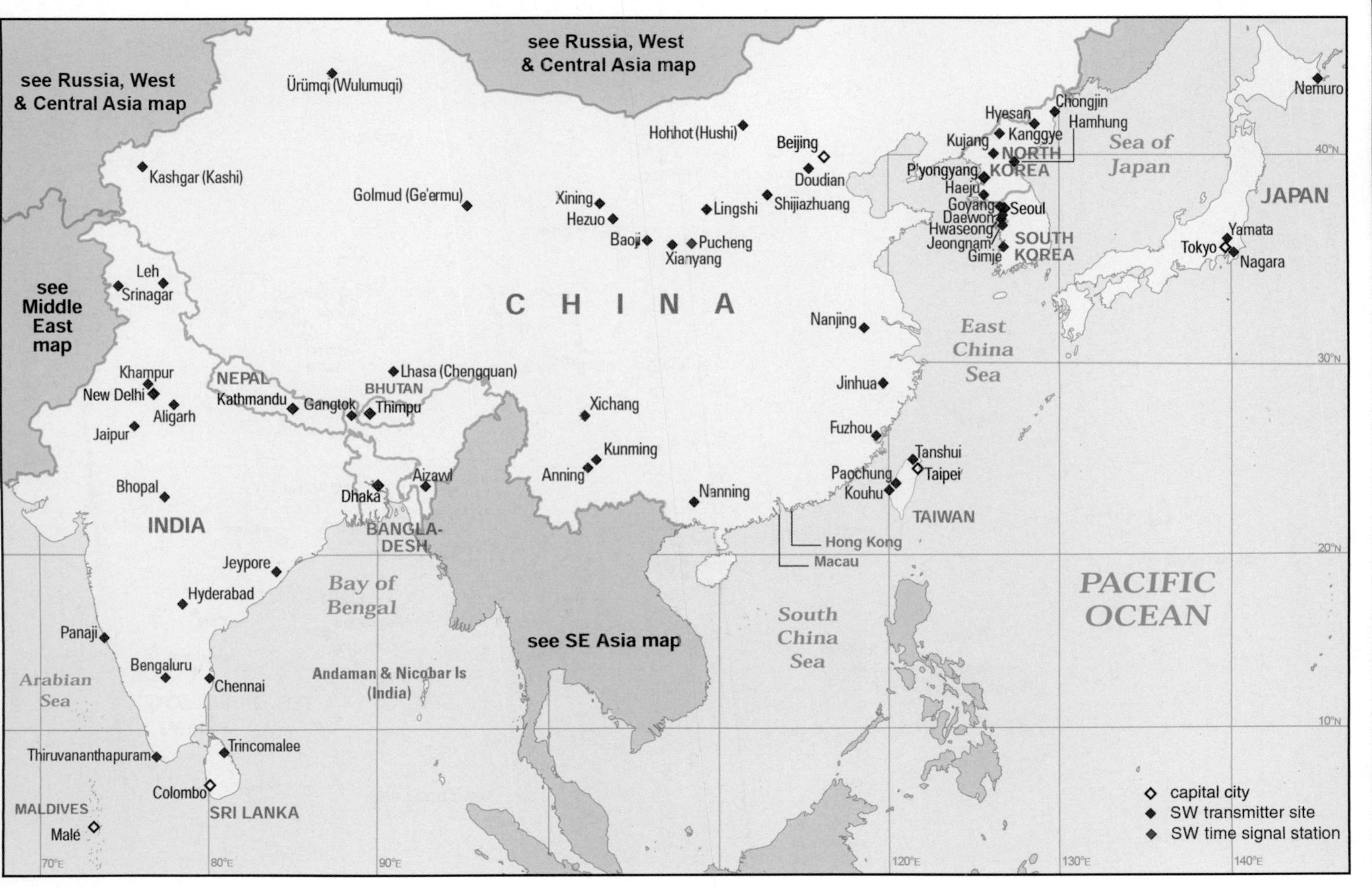
see Russia, West & Central Asia map
see Russia, West & Central Asia map
see Middle East map
see SE Asia map
Ürümqi (Wulumuqi)
Kashgar (Kashi)
Golmud (Ge'ermu)
Hohhot (Hushi)
Beijing
Doudian
Shijiazhuang
Lingshi
Xining
Hezuo
Baoji
Pucheng
Xianyang
CHINA
Leh
Srinagar
Khampur
New Delhi
Aligarh
Jaipur
NEPAL
Kathmandu
Gangtok
BHUTAN
Thimpu
Lhasa (Chengguan)
Xichang
Kunming
Anning
Nanning
Nanjing
Jinhua
Fuzhou
Tanshui
Taipei
Paochung
Kouhu
TAIWAN
Hong Kong
Macau
Hyesan
Chongjin
Hamhung
Kanggye
Kujang
NORTH KOREA
P'yongyang
Haeju
Goyang
Seoul
Daewon
Hwaseong
Jeongnam
Gimje
SOUTH KOREA
Sea of Japan
JAPAN
Tokyo
Yamata
Nagara
Nemuro
East China Sea
Bhopal
INDIA
Dhaka
Aizawl
BANGLA-DESH
Jeypore
Hyderabad
Bay of Bengal
Panaji
Bengaluru
Chennai
Arabian Sea
Andaman & Nicobar Is (India)
South China Sea
PACIFIC OCEAN
Thiruvananthapuram
Trincomalee
Colombo
SRI LANKA
MALDIVES
Malé
capital city
SW transmitter site
SW time signal station
40°N
30°N
20°N
10°N
70°E
80°E
90°E
120°E
130°E
140°E

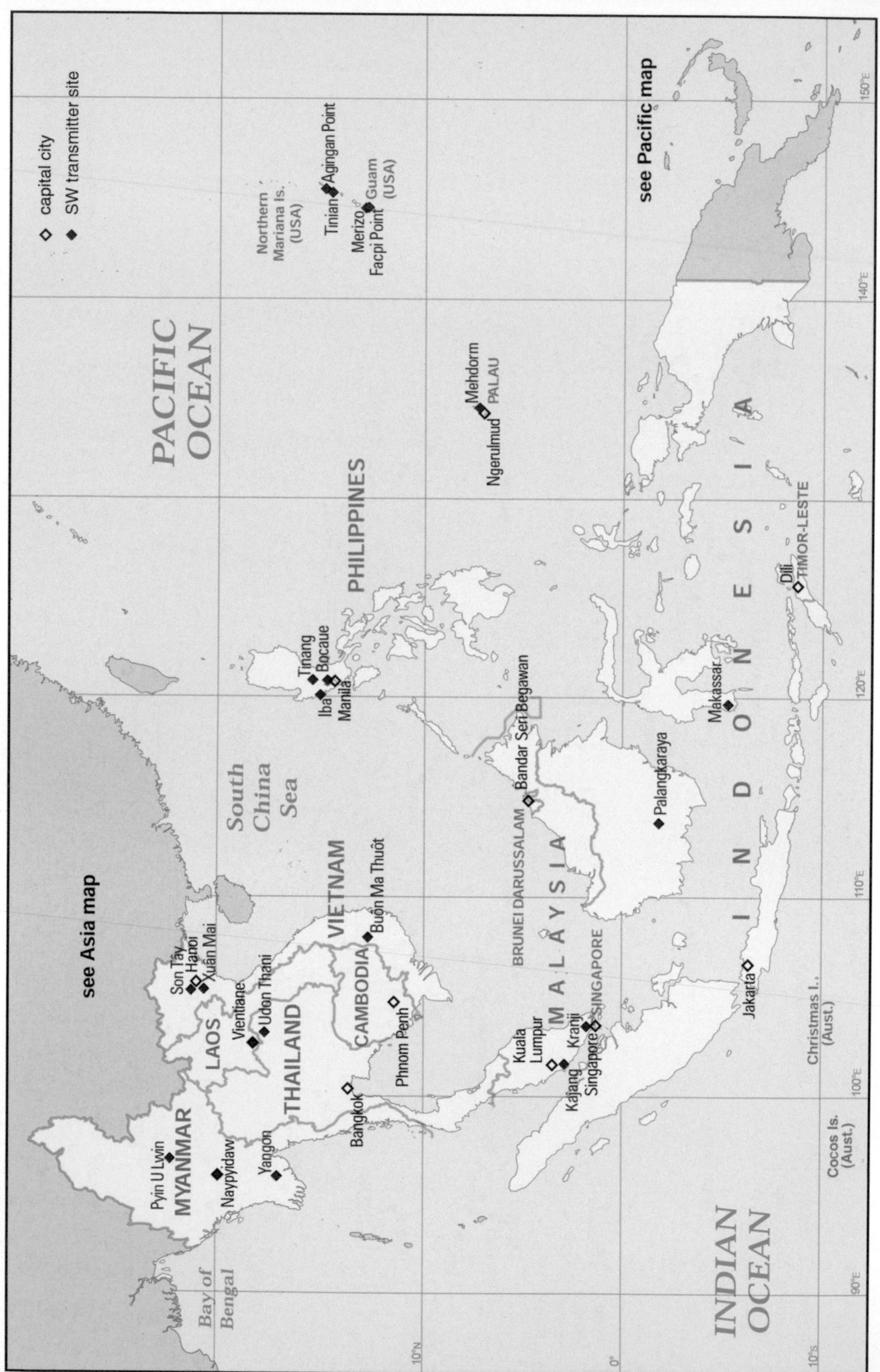
capital city
SW transmitter site
see Asia map
see Pacific map
PACIFIC OCEAN
INDIAN OCEAN
South China Sea
Bay of Bengal
MYANMAR
Pyin U Lwin
Naypyidaw
Yangon
LAOS
Vientiane
THAILAND
Udon Thani
Bangkok
CAMBODIA
Phnom Penh
VIETNAM
Hanoi
Son Tay
Xuân Mai
Buôn Ma Thuôt
PHILIPPINES
Tinang
Bocaue
Iba
Manila
MALAYSIA
Kuala Lumpur
Kajang
Kranji
SINGAPORE
Singapore
BRUNEI DARUSSALAM
Bandar Seri Begawan
INDONESIA
Jakarta
Palangkaraya
Makassar
Dili
TIMOR-LESTE
Christmas I. (Aust.)
Cocos Is. (Aust.)
PALAU
Mehdorm
Ngerulmud
Northern Mariana Is. (USA)
Tinian
Agingan Point
Guam (USA)
Merizo
Facpi Point
10°N
0°
10°S
90°E
100°E
110°E
120°E
140°E
150°E

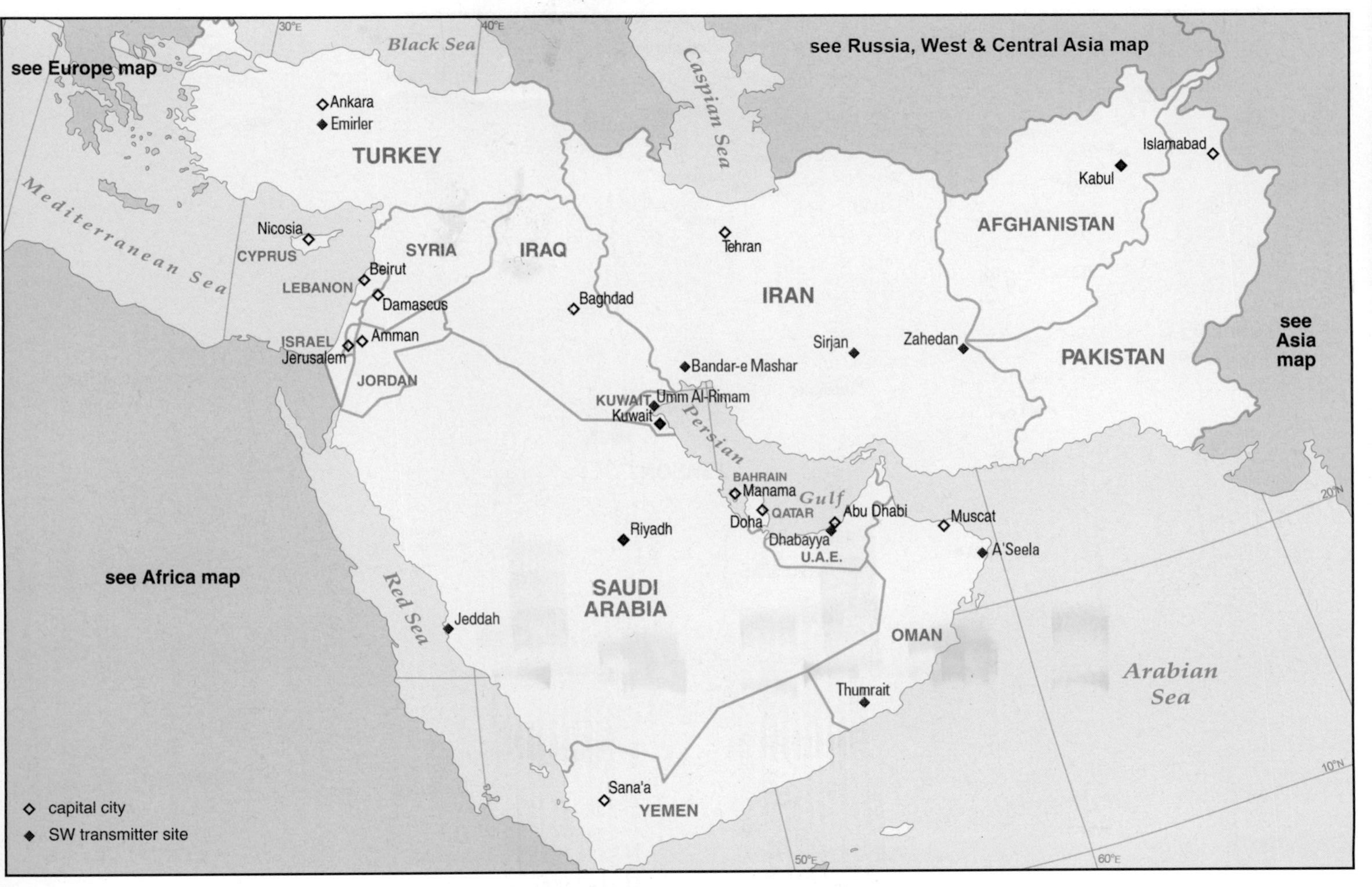
see Europe map
see Russia, West & Central Asia map
see Asia map
see Africa map
Black Sea
Caspian Sea
Mediterranean Sea
Red Sea
Persian Gulf
Arabian Sea
TURKEY
CYPRUS
SYRIA
IRAQ
IRAN
AFGHANISTAN
PAKISTAN
LEBANON
ISRAEL
JORDAN
KUWAIT
BAHRAIN
QATAR
U.A.E.
SAUDI ARABIA
OMAN
YEMEN
Ankara
Emirler
Nicosia
Beirut
Damascus
Amman
Jerusalem
Baghdad
Tehran
Bandar-e Mashar
Sirjan
Zahedan
Kabul
Islamabad
Umm Al-Rimam
Kuwait
Manama
Doha
Abu Dhabi
Dhabayya
Muscat
A'Seela
Riyadh
Jeddah
Thumrait
Sana'a
30°E
40°E
50°E
60°E
20°N
10°N
capital city
SW transmitter site

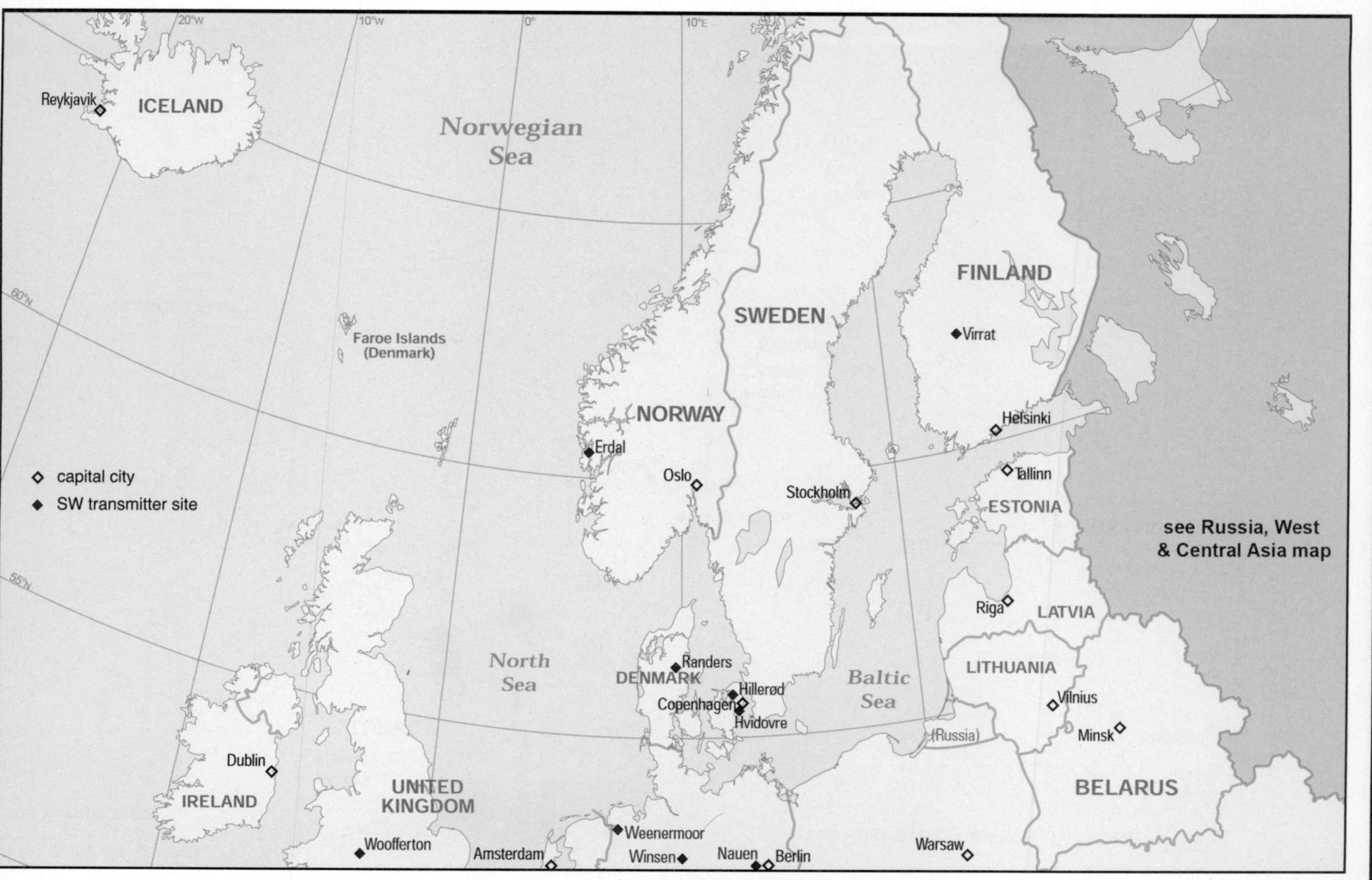
Reykjavik
ICELAND
Norwegian
Sea
20°W
10°W
0°
10°E
60°N
55°N
Faroe Islands
(Denmark)
NORWAY
Erdal
Oslo
SWEDEN
Stockholm
FINLAND
Virrat
Helsinki
Tallinn
ESTONIA
see Russia, West
& Central Asia map
Riga
LATVIA
LITHUANIA
Vilnius
Minsk
(Russia)
BELARUS
Warsaw
Baltic
Sea
North
Sea
DENMARK
Randers
Hillerød
Copenhagen
Hvidovre
Weenermoor
Winsen
Nauen
Berlin
Amsterdam
UNITED
KINGDOM
Woofferton
Dublin
IRELAND
capital city
SW transmitter site

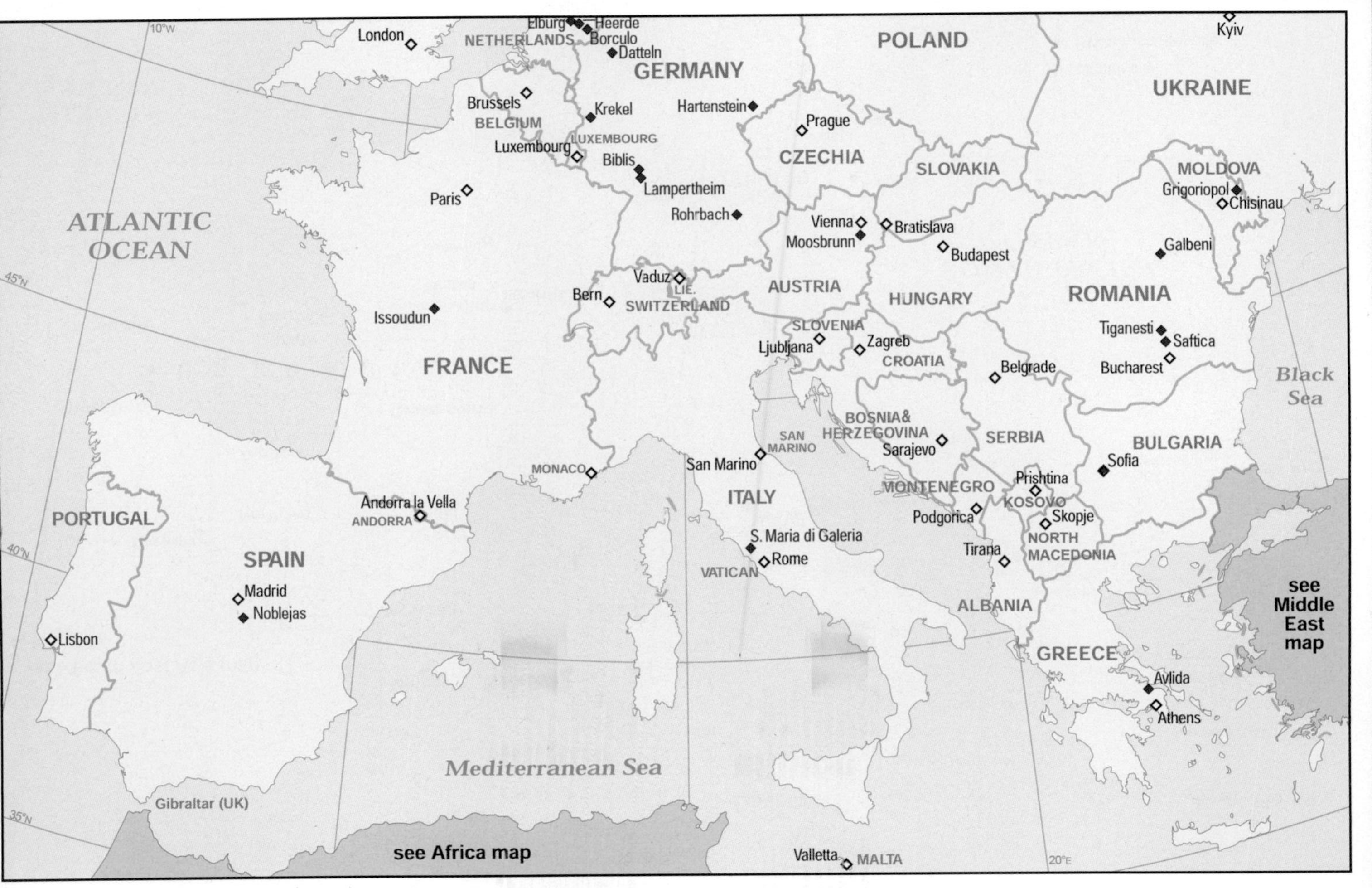

London
Elburg
Heerde
Borculo
NETHERLANDS
Datteln
GERMANY
POLAND
UKRAINE
Kyiv
Brussels
BELGIUM
Krekel
Hartenstein
Prague
LUXEMBOURG
Luxembourg
Biblis
Lampertheim
CZECHIA
SLOVAKIA
MOLDOVA
Grigoriopol
Chisinau
Paris
Rohrbach
Vienna
Moosbrunn
Bratislava
Budapest
Galbeni
ATLANTIC OCEAN
Vaduz
LIE.
Bern
SWITZERLAND
AUSTRIA
HUNGARY
ROMANIA
Issoudun
SLOVENIA
Ljubljana
Zagreb
CROATIA
Tiganesti
Saftica
Bucharest
FRANCE
Belgrade
Black Sea
BOSNIA& HERZEGOVINA
Sarajevo
SAN MARINO
San Marino
SERBIA
BULGARIA
Sofia
MONACO
MONTENEGRO
Prishtina
KOSOVO
ITALY
Andorra la Vella
ANDORRA
Podgorica
Skopje
PORTUGAL
NORTH MACEDONIA
S. Maria di Galeria
Rome
VATICAN
Tirana
SPAIN
Madrid
Noblejas
ALBANIA
see Middle East map
Lisbon
GREECE
Avlida
Athens
Mediterranean Sea
Gibraltar (UK)
see Africa map
Valletta
MALTA
10°W
45°N
40°N
35°N
20°E

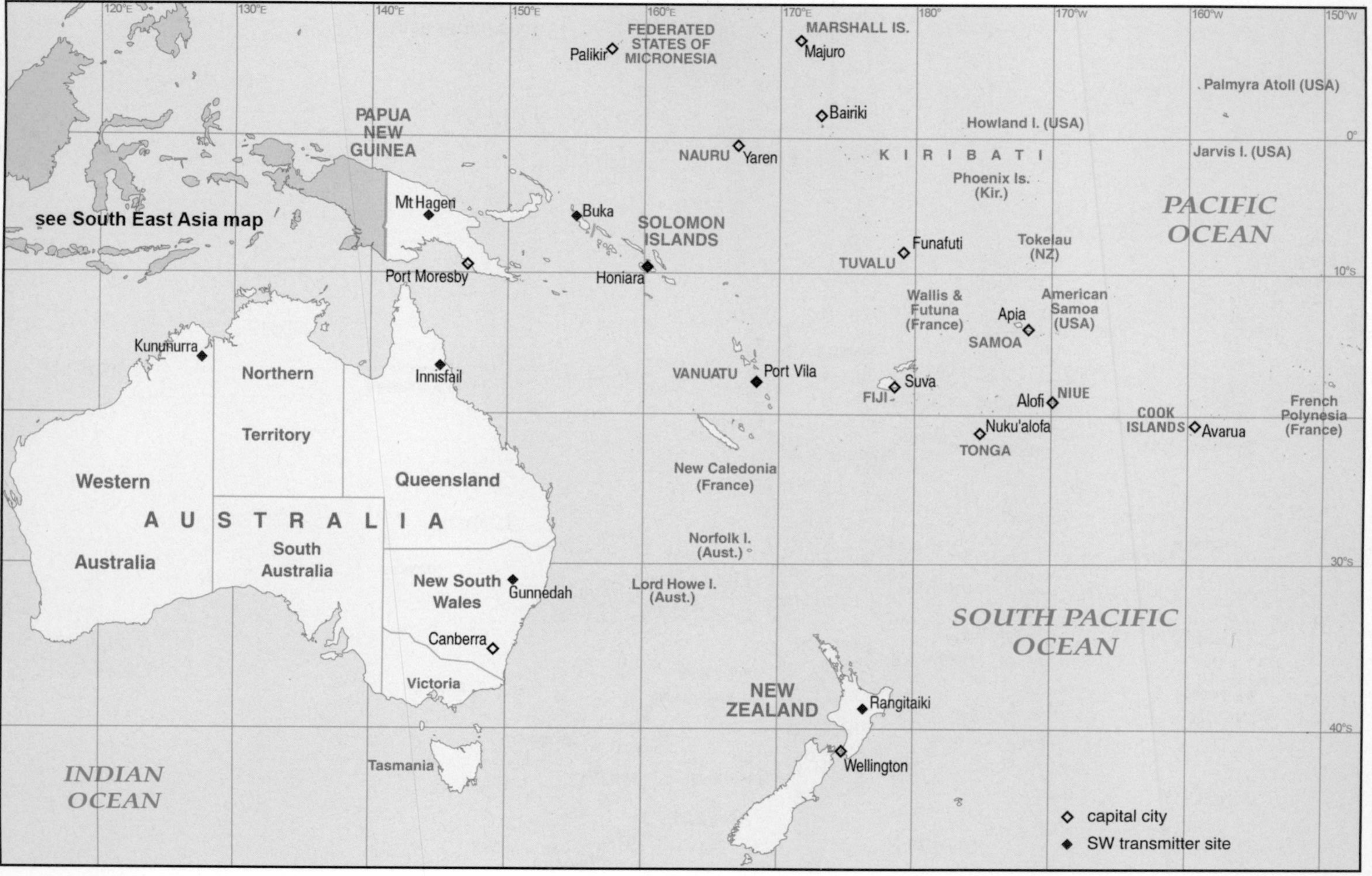

FEDERATED STATES OF MICRONESIA
Palikir
MARSHALL IS.
Majuro
Palmyra Atoll (USA)
Bairiki
Howland I. (USA)
PAPUA NEW GUINEA
NAURU
Yaren
K I R I B A T I
Jarvis I. (USA)
Phoenix Is. (Kir.)
Mt Hagen
Buka
see South East Asia map
SOLOMON ISLANDS
PACIFIC OCEAN
Funafuti
Tokelau (NZ)
TUVALU
Port Moresby
Honiara
Wallis & Futuna (France)
American Samoa (USA)
Apia
SAMOA
Kununurra
Northern
Innisfail
VANUATU
Port Vila
Suva
FIJI
Alofi
NIUE
French Polynesia (France)
COOK ISLANDS
Avarua
Nuku'alofa
Territory
TONGA
New Caledonia (France)
Western
Queensland
A U S T R A L I A
Norfolk I. (Aust.)
South Australia
Australia
New South Wales
Gunnedah
Lord Howe I. (Aust.)
SOUTH PACIFIC OCEAN
Canberra
Victoria
NEW ZEALAND
Rangitaiki
Tasmania
Wellington
INDIAN OCEAN
capital city
SW transmitter site

ARCTIC OCEAN
Barents Sea
Kara Sea
Laptev Sea
East Siberian Sea
Baltic Sea
see Europe map
Taldom
Moscow
RUSSIA
UKRAINE
Sea of Okhotsk
Tbilisskaya
Komsomolsk-na-Amure
GEORGIA
Tbilisi
Caspian Sea
Aral Sea
Nur-Sultan
ARMENIA
Yerevan
Gavar
KAZAKHSTAN
Hailar
Baku
Mörön
AZERBAIJAN
UZBEKISTAN
Ulaanbaatar
TURKMENISTAN
Altai
MONGOLIA
Sea of Japan
Bishkek
Tashkent
Ashgabat
KYRGYZSTAN
capital city
SW transmitter site
SW time signal station
see Middle East map
Dushanbe
Orzu
TAJIKISTAN
see Asia map

NATIONAL RADIO

Section Contents

Initial entries for each letter, see Main Index for full details

AFGHANISTAN

L.T: UTC +4½h — **Pop:** 37 million — **Pr.L:** Dari (official), Pashto (official), Turkmen, Uzbek — **E.C:** 230V/50Hz — **ITU:** AFG

AFGHANISTANTELECOM REGULATORY AUTHORITY (ARTA)

✉ Moh. Jaan Khan Watt St, 10th floor MoCIT Building, Kabul ☎+93 20 2105361 **W:** atra.gov.af **E:** media@atra.gov.af

RADIO TELEVISION AFGHANISTAN (RTA, Gov.)

✉ PO Box 544, Street No. 13, near Wazir Mohammad Akbar Khan Hospital, Kabul ☎+93 20 2102487 **W:** rta.org.af **E:** info@rta.org.af
L.P: DG: Zarin Anzor. DG Radio: Abdul Ghaney Mudaqiq.
MW: Kabul (Pol-e-Charkhi) 1107kHz 400kW.
FM: Kabul 93.0 1kW, 105.2MHz 30W.
D.Prgr: 0030-1930 on 1107kHz and 105.2MHz. 93.0MHz carries R. Kabul local sce 0130-1530 and Ext. Sce 1530-1730. Main **N:** Pashto 1430, Dari 1530. **Ann:** "Radyo Afghanistan, Kabul".

EXTERNAL SERVICE: see International Radio section.

PROVINCIAL STATIONS
R. Badakhshan, Faizabad: 105.1MHz 30W – **R. Badghis,** Qalay-e Naw: 91.4MHz 250W – **R. Baghlan,** Pol-e-Khomri 103.0MHz, Baghlan: 106.6MHz 250W – **R. Balkh,** Mazar-e-Sharif: 105.1MHz 0.1kW. – **R. Bamyan:** 88.0MHz – **R. Day Kundi:** Nili 103.2MHz 30W, Qalat 99.0MHz 0.5kW – **R. Farah,** Farah: 88.5MHz 1kW – **R. Faryab,** Maimana: 104.3MHz 30W – **R. Ghazni**: 92.4MHz 30W – **R. Ghor,** Chaghcharan: 93.4MHz – **R. Helmand,** Lashkar Ga: 96.1MHz 1kW. – **R. Herat**: 95.5MHz 250W – **R. Jowzjan,** Sheberghan 106.6MHz 250W – **R. Kandahar**: 1305kHz 10kW, 90.6MHz 1kW. 0230-1430 **W:** kandahar-tv.com – **R. Kapisa,** Mahmud-e-Raqi: 101.1MHz 600W – **R. Khost**: 91.2MHz 1kW – **R. Kunar,** Asadabad: 1575kHz 2kW, 100.5MHz 1kW – **R. Kunduz**: 94.4MHz 250W – **R. Laghman,** Mehtarlam: 88.2MHz‡ 0.5kW – **R. Logar,** Pol-e-Alam: 92.7MHz – **R. Nangarhar**, Jalalabad: 93.5MHz 250W – **R. Nimroz,** Zaranj: 90.0MHz 1kW – **R. Nuristan,** Nuristan: 88.5MHz 300W – **R. Paktia,** Gardez: 104.2MHz 0.5kW – **R. Paktika,** Zareh Sharan: 93.2MHz – **R. Panjshir,** Bazarak: 88.0MHz 0.1kW – **R. Parwan,** Charikar: 88.9MHz – **R. Samangan,** Aybak: 90.4MHz 150W – **R. Sar-e-Pol**: 89.9MHz – **R. Takhar**, Taloqan: 91.2MHz 30W – **R. Uruzgan,** Tarin Kowt: 93.0MHz 50W – **R. Wardak,** Meydan Shahr: 88.9MHz – **R. Zabul,** 88.7MHz.

R. AZADI/R. MASHAL/VOA ASHNA & DEEWA R.(US Gov.)

R. Azadi & VOA Ashna R:
MW: Kabul (Pol-e-Charkhi) 1296kHz 400kW 0030-1730. **FM**: Ghazni/Herat/Jalalabad/Kabul/Kandahar/Lashkar Gah/Mazar-e-Sharif/Mehtar Lam/Nuristan/Pil-Alam/Qalat/Sharan 100.5MHz. 24h in Dari/Pashto/English.
R. Mashal & VOA Deewa R: MW: Khost 621kHz 0100-1900.
FM: Asadabad/Gardez/Khost 100.5MHz.
For SW broadcasts & more details see International R. section (USA).

Other stations, main networks:
Radio Talwasa ✉ Daud Khan Sqaure, Ahmad Shak Baba, District 12 Kabul / Sherana, Paktika **W:** talwasa.af **E:** talwasa@talwasa.af **L.P:** Dir: Sulaiman Faisal **MW:** Sharana 945kHz 10/2.5kW **FM:** Sharana 87.9MHz 6kW. **D.Prgr:** 0130-1730.
Arakozia FM W: arakozia.fm Laghman/Nangarhar 90.3, Khost/Paktia/Zabul 90.4, Ghazni/Helmand/Kunar 94.6, Kandahar 94.9, Logar 103.4MHz
Ariana FM ✉ Darlaman St. (near Ministry of Trade), Kabul **W:** ariana.fm **FM:** about 50 transmitters on 93.5, Khost 96.4, Kabul 100.2MHz.
Arman FM ✉ P.O. Box 1045, Central PO, Kabul **W:** arman.fm **FM:** 12 transmitters on 98.1, Zabul 98.3 MHz.
Eslah Voice R. W: eslahonline.net **FM:** Kabul/Kunduz/Nangarhar 104.3, Balkh 104.6MHz.
Khurshid FM W: khurshidfm.com **FM:** Kabul 98.6, Balkh/Herat/Kandahar/Nangarhar 98.7 MHz
R. Jawanan W: jawanan.fm **FM:** Balkh/Helmand/Herat/Kabul/Kandahar/Khost/Kunduz/Nangarhar 97.5MHz
R. Killid ✉ The Killid Group, House No. 442, Street No. 6, Chardehi Watt, Near to Uzbekha Mosque, Karta-e-sea, Kabul 442 **W:** tkg.af **FM:** Kabul 88.0 4kW, Herat 88.0 2kW, Nangarhar 88.0, Khost 88.2, Nimroz 88.8, Kandahar 89.4, Balkh 89.5, Ghazni 89.6, Baghlan 91.3, Kunduz 92.0MHz.
R. Nawa FM W: sabacent.org/nawa **FM:** 103.1MHz (13 locations)
R. Watandar: Balkh/Herat/Kabul/Kandahar/Kunduz/Nangarhar 87.5 0.5/1kW
Royan FM W: facebook.com/royan.radio **FM:** Jowzjan 90.8, Kunduz 91.7, 6 locations on 103.1MHz.
Shamshad FM W: facebook.com/ShamshadRadio **FM:** Nangarhar 88.3, 8 locations on 95.2, 4 locations on 103.4MHz, Parwan 104.6MHz
Sheba Radio W: shebaradio.com **FM:** Kabul 99.9 8kW, Kunduz 101.7, 12 locations on 104.3MHz 1kW
Talimi FM: 33 locations on 96.1-96.8MHz
Talimul Islam R. W: taleemulislam.net **FM:** Urozgan 88.2, Zabul 89.3, Helmand 89.5, Farah 89.6, Kandahar 89.7, Nimroz 90.3, Nangarhar 91.0MHz
Zhwandoon FM W: zhwandoon.tv **FM:** Balkh 101.3, Herat/Kandahar/Nangarhar 101.4, Kabul 107.0MHz

Relays of international stations:
BBC World Sce: in English/Pashto/Dari/Uzbek/Farsi: Kunar 87.5, Gardez 87.9, Imam Sahib/Konduz 88.1, Ghazni/Taloqan 88.3, Fayzabad 88.4, Bamian/Farah/Jalalabad/Kabul/Mazar-e-Sharif/Qalat/Rustaq/Uruzgan/Zareh Sharan 89.0, Jabal Saraj/Sar-e Pul 89.1, Chaghcharan/Herat/Lashkar-Ga/Shindand 89.2, Kandahar 90.0, Khost 90.1, Maidan Shahr 90.2, Shebergan 91.0, Maimana 92.1, Pul-e Khomri 99.6, Kabul 101.6 (English), Pul-e Alam 105.7MHz.
R. France Int: Kabul 89.5 0.2kW.
BFBS Radio: FM: HKIA, HQRS & Qargha: 104.0MHz, R. 2 105.8MHz, R. Gurkha 107.5MHz **W:** forces.net/radio

ALASKA (USA)

L.T: UTC -9h (14 Mar-7 Nov: -8h); Aleutian Is: -10h (14 Mar-7 Nov: -9h) — **Pop:** 735,000 — **Pr.L:** Official languages: English & 20 indigenous languages — **E.C:** 120V/60Hz — **ITU:** ALS

FEDERAL COMMUNICATIONS COMMISSION (FCC)

see main entry under USA

ALASKA BROADCASTERS ASSOCIATION

✉ 700 W 41st Ave #102, Anchorage 99503 ☎+1 907 258 2424 **W:** alaskabroadcasters.org

MW	kHz	Call	kW	N	City of License	h of tr
2)	550	KTZN	3.1/5		Anchorage	
3)	560	KVOK	1		Kodiak	
5)	590	KHAR	5		Anchorage	
6)	620	KGTL	5		Homer	
7)	630	KIAM	10/3.1		Nenana	2000-1200
8)	630	KJNO	5/1		Juneau	
9)	640	KYUK	10		Bethal	1900-1300
10)	650	KENI	50		Anchorage	
11)	660	KFAR	10		Fairbanks	
12)	670	KDLG	10		Dillingham	1900-1300
13)	680	KBRW	10		Barrow	
14)	700	KBYR	10		Anchorage	
15)	720	KOTZ	10		Kotzebue	1800-1300
16)	750	KFQD	50		Anchorage	
17)	770	KCHU	9.7		Valdez	1800-1300
18)	780	KNOM	25/14		Nome	1855-1510
19)	790	KCAM	5		Glennallen	
20)	800	KINY	10/7.6		Juneau	
21)	820	KCBF	10		Fairbanks	
22)	830	KSDP	1		Sand Point	
24)	850	KICY	50	*	Nome	
26)	890	KBBI	10		Homer	1900-1300
27)	900	KZPA	5	r	Fort Yukon	
28)	910	KIYU	5		Galena	
29)	920	KSRM	5		Soldotna	
12)	930	KNSA	4.2	r	Unalakleet	
30)	930	KTKN	5/1		Ketchikan	
33)	970	KFBX	10		Fairbanks	
34)	1020	KVNT	10	d	Eagle River	
36)	1080	KOAN	10		Anchorage	
35)	1110	KAGV	10		Big Lake	
29)	1140	KSLD	10		Soldotna	
37)	1170	KJNP	50/21	#	North Pole	
38)	1230	KIFW	1		Sitka	1800-1300
39)	1230	KVAK	1		Valdez	
40)	1330	KXXJ	10/3		Juneau	
41)	1430	KVHZ	1		Wasilla	

MW kHz	Call	kW	N	City of License	h of tr
42) 1450	KLAM	0.25		Cordova	

d=directional *=directional 0800-1200 (Summer -1h) r=relay #=April-Oct: M-F 1337-0813, Sat. 1455-0813, Sun. 1555-0813

FM	Call	MHz	kW	City of License
	KAKL	88.5	11	Anchorage
	KATB	89.3	14.5	Anchorage
	KNBA	90.3	100	Anchorage
	KSKA	91.1	100	Anchorage
	KFAT	92.9	10	Anchorage
	KAFC	93.7	27	Anchorage
	KEAG	97.3	55	Anchorage
	KLEF	98.1	25	Anchorage
2)	KYMG	98.9	100	Anchorage
2)	KBFX	100.5	25	Anchorage
2)	KGOT	101.3	26	Anchorage
	KTMB	102.1	23	Anchorage
	KMXS	103.1	100	Anchorage
5)	KBRJ	104.1	55	Anchorage
	KMVN	105.7	51	Anchorage
5)	KWHL	106.5	100	Anchorage
2)	KASH-FM	107.5	100	Anchorage
	KJNR	91.9	3	Bethel
7)	KYKD	100.1	12	Bethel
	KCUK	88.1	6	Chevak
	KTDZ	103.9	28	College
42)	KCDV	100.9	1.2	Cordova
	KRUP	99.1	6	Dillingham
	KDJF	93.5	15.5	Ester
	KZVV	88.3	3.2	Fairbanks
	KRFF	89.1	10	Fairbanks
	KUAC	89.9	38	Fairbanks
	KSUA	91.5	3	Fairbanks
	KQHE	92.7	2	Fairbanks
	KWDD	94.3	28	Fairbanks
	KXLR	95.9	28	Fairbanks
	KYSC	96.9	15.5	Fairbanks
	KWLF	98.1	28	Fairbanks
33)	KAKQ-FM	101.1	50	Fairbanks
33)	KIAK-FM	102.5	100	Fairbanks
33)	KKED	104.7	50	Fairbanks
	KEUL	88.9	1.4	Girdwood
19)	KCAM-FM	88.7	1.7	Glennallan
17)	KXGA	90.5	3.2	Glennallen
	KHNS	102.3	3	Haines
6)	KWVV-FM	103.5	25	Homer
	KBBO-FM	92.1	10	Houston
34)	KZND-FM	94.7	15	Houston
	KXLW	96.3	10	Houston
	KAKI	88.1	1.7	Juneau
	KLSF	89.7	1.7	Juneau
	KXLL	100.7	6	Juneau
	KRNN	102.7	6	Juneau
	KTOO	104.3	1.4	Juneau
20)	KTKU	105.1	3.8	Juneau
	KSUP	106.3	10	Juneau
29)	KFSE	106.9	8	Kasilof
	KOGJ	88.1	1.1	Kenai
	KDLL	91.9	4.9	Kenai
	KWHQ-FM	100.1	25	Kenai
	KRBD	105.3	3.4	Ketchikan
	KVOK-FM	101.1	3.1	Kodiak
	KYKA	104.9	19	Meadow Lakes
	KAKN	100.9	3	Naknek
	KXBA	93.3	50	Nikiski
18)	KNOM-FM	96.1	1	Nome
24)	KICY-FM	100.3	1	Nome
37)	KJNP-FM	100.3	25	North Pole #
	KNLT	95.5	64	Palmer
	KFSK	100.9	2	Petersburg
	KIBH-FM	91.7	1	Seward
	KSBZ	103.1	3.1	Sitka
	KCAW	104.7	3.6	Sitka
29)	KKIS-FM	96.5	10	Soldotna
6)	KPEN-FM	101.7	25	Soldotna
	KKNI-FM	105.3	25	Sterling
	KTNA	88.9	7.2	Talkeetna
	K220AD	91.9	1.1	Valdez
39)	KVAK-FM	93.3	1.2	Valdez
	KMBQ-FM	99.7	51	Wasilla
	KAYO	100.9	50	Wasilla
	KSTK	101.7	3	Wrangell

+ txs below 1kW

NB: FM reference numbers for mailing addr only

Addresses & other information (add AK before zip code):
2) 800 E Dimond Blvd, Suite #3-370, Anchorage 99515-2058 **W:** 550thezone.com – **3)** Box 708, Kodiak 99615-0708 **W:** kvok.com – **5)** 301 Arctic Slope Ave #200, Anchorage 99518-3035 **W:** khar590.com – **6)** Box 109, Homer 99603-0109 **W:** facebook.com/am620theanswer – **7)** Box 474, Nenana 99760-0474 **W:** vfcm.org – **9)** Box 468, Bethel 99559-0468 **W:** kyuk.org – **8)** as 20) – **10)** as 2) **W:** 650keni.com – **11)** as 21) **W:** kfarradio.com – **12)** Box 670, Dillingham 99576-0670 **W:** kdlg.org – **13)** Box 109, Barrow 99723-0109 **W:** kbrw.org – **14)** 1399 West 34th Ave #202, Anchorage 99503-3659 **W:** kbyr.com – **15)** Box 78, Kotzebue 99752-0078 **W:** kotz.org – **16)** as 5) **W:** kfqd.com – **17)** Box 467, Valdez 99686-0467 **W:** kchu.org – **18)** Box 988, Nome 99762-0988 **W:** knom.org – **19)** Box 249, Glennallen 99588-0249 **W:** kcam.org – **20)** 3161 Channel Dr Suite 2, Juneau 99801-7855 **W:** kinyradio.com – **21)** 819 1st Ave #A, Fairbanks 99701-4449 **W:** espnradiofairbanks.com – **22)** Box 328, Sand Point 99661 **W:** apradio.org – **24)** Box 820, Nome 99762-0820 **W:** kicy.org. Russian 0800-1200 (Summer -1h) – **26)** 3913 Kachemak Way, Homer 99603-7618 **W:** kbbi.org – **27)** Box 50, Fort Yukon 99740-0050 **W:** kzparadio.com – **28)** Box 165, Galena 99741-0165 **W:** kiyu.com – **29)** 40960 Kalifornsky Beach Rd, Kenai 99611-6445 **W:** radiokenai.net – **30)** 526 Stedman St, Ketchikan 99901-6629 **W:** ketchikanradio.com – **33)** 546 9th Ave, Fairbanks 99701-4902 **W:** 970kfbx.com – **34)** 2709 Boniface Pkwy, Anchorage 99504 **W:** 1020kvnt.com – **35)** 4723 King David St, Houston Park 99694-ND **W:** as 7) – **36)** 814 W Northern Lights, Anchorage 99503 **W:** koanfm.com – **37)** Box 56359, North Pole 99705-1359 **W:** mosquitonet.com/~kjnp – **38)** 611 Lake St, Sitka 99835-7402 **W:** sitkaradio.com – **39)** Box 367, Valdez 99686-0367 **W:** kvakradio.com **40)** as 20) **W:** kxjradio.com – **41)** 9915 Hermond Rd, Wasilla 99654 **W:** khitz.com – **42)** Box 60, Cordova 99574-0060 **W:** cordovaradio.com

EXTERNAL SERVICE: Radio Station KNLS
See International Broadcasting section.

ALBANIA

L.T: UTC +1h (28 Mar-31 Oct: +2h) — **Pop:** 2.9 million — **Pr.L:** Albanian — **E.C:** 230V/50Hz — **ITU:** ALB

AUTORITETI I MEDIAVE AUDIOVIZIVE (AMA) (Audiovisual Media Authority)

Rr. Abdi Toptani, 1001 Tiranë ☎ +355 42226288 **E:** info@ama.gov.al **W:** ama.gov.al **L.P:** Chmn: Gentian Sala

RADIO TELEVIZIONI SHQIPTAR (RTSH) (Pub)

Rr. Ismail Qemali nr. 11, 1001 Tiranë ☎ +355 42230842 **E:** marketing@rtsh.al **W:** rtsh.al **L.P:** DG: Thoma Gëllçi

FM (MHz)	1	2	3	kW	FM	1	2	3	kW
Delvinë	107.0	-	-	1	Midë	96.0	-	-	5
Elbasan	95.4	-	-	1	Pogradec	99.1	-	-	3
Gllavë	97.0	-	-	1.6	Shkodër	91.0	-	-	1.3
Llogarë	88.3	-	-	1.6	Tiranë	99.5	95.8	101.2	25/2.3/38
Lurth	91.5	-	-	1	Vlorë	99.8	-	-	3

+ sites with only txs below 1kW.

D.Prgr: Prgr 1 (R. Tirana): 24h – **Prgr 2 (R. Tirana 2):** 24h – **Prgr 3 (R. Tirana Klasik):** 24h.

RTSH Regional Stations
Radio Televizioni Gjirokastra (RTGJ): 6001-2 Gjirokastër. On 102.5MHz (0.3kW). Incl. prgrs in Greek, Macedonian. – **Radio Televizioni Korça (RTK):** Rr. Don Gjon Buzuku, 7001-4 Korçë. On 89.5MHz (0.9kW). Incl. prgrs in Macedonian, Montenegrin, Romany, Vlakh – **R. Kukësi:** Rr. Gjalica nr. 13, 8501-3 Kukësi. On 100.4MHz (0.9kW) – **R. Shkodra:** Sheshi Demokracia, 4001 Shkodër. On 92.0MHz (1.6kW).

OTHER STATIONS

FM	MHz	kW	Location	Station
32)	88.1	1	Shkodër	Vintage R.
24)	88.5	6	Tiranë	R. Ngjallja
21)	89.3	1.6	Tiranë	R. Kontakt
9)	89.5	1	Shkodër	R. 1

FM	MHz	kW	Location	Station
5)	89.6	1	Fier	R. Klan
6)	89.8	60	Tiranë	Best R.
2B)	90.3	1	Fier	Top Gold R.
4)	90.7	1.6	Tiranë	Love R.
9)	92.2	5	Midë	R. 1
2A)	93.0	1.6	Gjirokastër	Top Albania R.
9)	93.2	5	Tiranë	R. 1
2A)	94.1	3	Shkodër	Top Albania R.
33)	94.3	1	Elbasan	R. Hit FM
18)	94.4	1.6	Tiranë	R. EuroStar
2)	95.0	3	Cardhak	Top Albania R.
23)	95.2	4	Tiranë	R. Maria Shqiptare
17)	95.7	4	Korçë	R. Emanuel
2A)	96.0	31	Gllavë	Top Albania R.
28)	96.4	1.6	Tiranë	R. Spektrum
25)	96.7	1	Tiranë	R. Ora News
27)	97.0	3	Tiranë	R. RASH
8)	97.3	3	Tiranë	My Music R.
11)	97.5	1	Shkodër	R. 7
20)	97.5	1	Vlorë	R. Albania News
11)	97.7	6	Tiranë	R. 7
16)	98.2	3	Tiranë	R. DJ 98.2
2A)	98.5	5	Pogradec	Top Albania R.
13)	98.7	1.6	Tiranë	Super Star R.
2A)	99.0	1.6	Durrës	Top Albania R.
2B)	99.3	1	Shkodër	R. Top Gold
2A)	100.0	50	Tiranë	Top Albania R.
12)	100.1	2	Korçë	R. ABC
15A)	100.4	12.5	Tiranë	R. Club FM
2A)	100.6	28	Sarandë	Top Albania R.
2B)	100.8	56	Tiranë	Top Gold R.
2A)	101.3	22.4	Midë	Top Albania R.
15B)	101.6	28	Tirane	Big FM
C)	102.0	1	Tiranë	RFI relay
2A)	102.2	3	Vlorë	Top Albania R.
3)	102.6	6.3	Tiranë	Alfa dhe Omega R.
14)	103.1	3	Tiranë	MCN R.
26)	103.3	2	Vlorë	R. Val'e Kaltër
2A)	103.5	3	Fier	Top Albania R.
A)	103.9	2	Tiranë	BBCWS relay
2A)	104.0	14	Delvinë	Top Albania R.
2A)	104.3	7	Prezë	Top Albania R.
31)	104.6	25	Tiranë	R. Travel
1)	105.0	1	Tiranë	ABC News R.
30)	105.5	1.6	Fier	R. Star
7)	105.7	1	Tiranë	IN R. 105.7
B)	106.0	2	Tiranë	R. Ejani (CRI relay)
19)	106.3	1	Tiranë	Alsion R.
10)	106.6	1.6	Tiranë	NRG
22)	107.0	3.5	Korçë	R. Magic Star

+ txs below 1kW.

Addresses & other information:
1) Rr. Aleksandër Moisiu, 1001 Tiranë – **2A,B)** Rr. 5 Dëshmorët nr. 20, Mëzez, 1050 Tiranë – **3)** Rr. Vaso Pasha, 1000 Tiranë – **4)** Rr. Abdyl Frashëri, EGT Tower, 1000 Tiranë – **5)** Rr. Aleksandër Moisiu nr. 97, 1007 Tiranë – **6)** Asim Vokshi, pranë Arkivit të Shtetit, 1000 Tiranë – **7)** Rr. Dhaskal Tod'hri nr. 26, Kashar, 1051 Tiranë – **8)** Bvd. Dëshmorët e Kombit, Qendra Ndërkombëtare e Kulturëse "Arbnori", 1000 Tiranë – **9)** Kashar, Mëzes, pranë shkollës "Kasem Shima", 1050 Tiranë **E:** info@radio1.al – **10)** Rr. Faik Konica nr. 1, 1010 Tiranë – **11)** Rr. Sefer Kondi nr. 35, 1000 Tiranë – **12)** Bvd. Shën Gjergji, Qendra Baze, 7000 Korçë – **13)** Rr. Naim Frashëri, 1001 Tiranë – **14)** Rr. Ismail Qemali nr. 11, 1001 Tiranë – **15)** Rogner Hotel, Bvd. Dëshmorët e Kombit, 1000 Tiranë – **16)** Rr. Abdyl Frashëri, EGT Tower, 1000 Tiranë – **17)** Rr. Thimi Mitko nr. 13, 7000 Korçë – **18)** Rr. Hamdi Pepa, Qyteti i Nxënësve, 1000 Tiranë – **19)** Lagjja "Hekurudha", Rr. Syrja Dylgjeri, 3000 Elbasan – **20)** Bvd. Dëshmorët e Kombit, Kullat Binjake, Kati 12, Hyrja 1, 1000 Tiranë – **21)** Rr. Fadil Rada, pranë ATSH, 1000 Tiranë – **22)** Rr. e Xhamisë së Re, 7000 Korçë – **23)** Rr. Papa Gjon Pali II nr. 4, 1047 Fushë e Kërçikëve – **24)** Rr. Dritan Hoxha, Pallati Komfort, 1000 Tiranë – **25)** Rr. Aleksandër Moisiu nr. 76, 1001 Tiranë – **26)** Lagjja 24 Maji, 9400 Vlorë – **27)** Rr. Ali Demi, Ish Kombinati i Autotraktorëve, Zyrat e Administratës, 1000 Tiranë – **28)** Rr. Jordan Misja, Kompleksi Usluga, 1000 Tiranë – **29)** Rr. 5 Dëshmorët nr. 20, Mëzez, 1050 Tiranë – **30)** Lagjja "Apolonia", 9300 Fier – **31)** Rr. Ibrahim Rugova nr. 28, 1000 Tiranë – **32)** Rr. Karakacej, 4000 Shkodër – **33)** L. "Vullnetari", Pll. 648/1, Kati 4, 3000 Elbasan – **A)** Rel. BBCWS (UK) – **B)** Rel. CRI (P.R. China) – **C)** Rel. RFI (France)

ALGERIA

L.T: UTC +1h — **Pop:** 44 million — **Pr.L:** Arabic (official), Tamazight (official), French — **E.C:** 230V/50Hz — **ITU:** ALG

TÉLÉDIFFUSION D'ALGERIE (Transmitter Operator)

✉ Direction Générale, B.P. 50, Bouzaréah, Route de Baïnam, 16340 Algér ☎+213 21 901717 🖷 +213 21 902424 **W:** tda.dz **E:** contact@tda.dz

RADIO ALGÉRIENNE (RA, Pub.)

✉ 21 Boulevard des Martyrs, El Mouradia, Algér (Jil FM: DCRR, 12 Rue Shakespeare, El Mouradia, Algér) ☎+213 21 230805 🖷 +213 21 694620 **W:** radioalgerie.dz **E:** radionet@radioalgerie.dz

	LW/MW	kHz	kW	Pr.	Hrs.
	Tipaza	252	*1500	3	24h
	F'Kirina	531	600	J	24h
	Sidi Hamadouche	549	600	J	24h
20)	Touggourt	558	10	1/L	24h
4)	Béchar	576	*400	L	24h
30)	Tindouf	666	10	1/L	24h
	Aboudid (Ain el H.) ‡	693	5	2	24h
1)	Reggane	693	10	1/L	24h
14)	Laghouat	702	25	3/L	24h
12)	In Amenas	738	5	1/L	24h
12)	Djanet	783	5	1/L	24h
24)	El Oued	783	10	1/L	24h
10)	Ghardaïa	873	10	1/L	24h
	Ouled Fayet (Algér) †	891	*600	1	24h
	Tamanrasset	909	10	1	24h
1)	Timimoun	927	10	1/L	24h
	Ouled Fayet (Algér)	981	100	2	24h
20)	Hassi Messaoud	1026	10	1/L	24h
	Illizi	1071	5	1	24h
1)	Adrar	1089	10	1/L	24h
27)	In Salah	1161	5	1/L	24h
	Ouled Fayet	1422	50	M	24h

*) half-power 1900-0600

FM (MHz)	1	2	3	I	M	J	kW(TRP)
Abadla	90.8	100.8	94.0	97.3	-	104.9	
Adrar	-	-	98.0	105.0	-	90.0	2.5
Aflou	90.7	93.9	97.2	-	-	-	10
Aïn N'Sour	94.0	100.8	97.3	-	104.4	-	10
Aïn Oussera	89.8	92.9	99.4	-	-	-	1
Aïn Tagourait	99.0	-	89.4	102.5	106.1	-	0.1
Akfadou	101.8	91.8	105.4	95.0	98.3	-	10
Aneb	90.3	93.4	96.6	103.4	107.0	-	2.5
Béchar	92.4	-	98.8	90.5	-	103.5	5
Beni Abess	89.1	-	96.1	91.5	-	105.3	
Beni Ounif	105.1	102.4	88.5	94.6	-	95.6	10
Bordj El Bahri	91.0	104.2	89.2	-	100.5	-	2.5
Bordj Omar Driss	101.6	105.2	-	-	-	-	0.1
Bouachoui	102.4	-	-	-	-	-	0.1
Bouzaréah	-	100.0	-	95.6	-	-	0.1
Bouzizi	89.7	102.8	92.8	-	106.4	-	0.1
Chenachene	95.6	-	-	-	-	102.4	0.1
Chréa	98.0	-	88.4	101.5	105.1	94.7	10
Debdeb	103.5	90.4	93.5	-	-	-	0.1
Dellys	102.9	106.5	-	-	-	-	
Dirah	90.2	96.5	-	-	-	-	2.5
Djanet	89.6	-	-	-	-	-	
Djelfa	88.0	97.9	94.3	95.9	-	-	10
Doukhane	94.2	97.5	91.0	-	-	-	2.5
El Bayadh	98.6	89.0	92.1	102.1	105.7	-	2.5
El Hadjira	88.7	95.0	98.3	105.4	101.8	-	10
El Oued	-	-	-	-	102.8	94.7	0.1
Filfila	96.1	98.1	101.6	-	-	-	2.5
Gara Djebilet	98.0	-	-	-	-	-	0.1
Ghardaïa	93.2	96.4	-	-	-	94.7	2.5
Hassi Messaoud	104.4	94.0	97.3	100.8	-	-	0.2
Ifri	100.7	-	-	-	-	-	0.1
Illizi	95.9	89.6	99.2	-	-	94.7	0.1
In Amenas	91.7	94.9	98.2	-	-	-	
In Guezzam	92.6	-	89.5	-	95.8	-	
Kef El Akhal	90.7	97.2	87.6	104.3	100.7	-	10
Kerzaz	92.0	95.2	98.9	105.3	-	107.9	0.1

FM (MHz)	1	2	3	I	M	J	kW(TRP)
Khar	107.2	-	-	-	-	-	2.5
Ksar Chellala	97.5	88.9	94.2	-	-	-	0.1
Laghouat	-	-	92.0	-	106.0	101.1	
Mahouna	94.3	-	91.1	-	-	-	2.5
M'Cid	91.9	101.9	105.5	98.4	-	-	10
Mécheria	87.8	100.9	97.4	94.1	104.5	-	10
Meghriss	93.5	96.7	100.0	107.1	103.5	-	10
Metlili	94.4	101.2	97.7	-	104.8	-	10
Mihoub	104.6	-	-	-	-	-	0.1
Nador	98.0	88.4	91.5	101.5	105.1	-	10
Ouargla	98.6	95.3	105.7	-	98.0	94.7	0.2
Oum Ali	97.9	-	91.4	-	-	-	2.5
Puits des Zouaves	98.9	96.1	102.4	-	-	92.4	0.1
Regheiss	98.9	-	-	-	-	-	0.5
Riyad el Fath	-	-	-	-	93.6	-	
Rosfa Taiba	93.6	96.8	100.1	103.6	-	-	0.1
Sidi Abdelkrim	97.8	88.2	91.3	-	-	-	2.5
Sidi Ahmed	93.3	-	90.2	-	-	-	0.1
Tabelbada	91.7	89.3	105.3	104.7	-	-	
Tamanrasset	92.6	-	89.5	-	95.8	94.7	2.5
Tessala	102.7	89.6	106.3	-	-	-	2.5
Thar	93.0	96.2	99.5	-	-	-	2.5
Tiaret	89.4	-	-	-	-	-	2.5
Timimoun	90.9	-	103.0	101.0	-	102.0	
Tindouf	91.4	94.6	97.9	101.4	-	102.9	
Tinzaouten	92.9	-	-	96.1	-	-	0.1
Tizi Ouzou	96.2	88.0	-	-	-	-	0.1
Zarga	95.3	-	-	-	-	-	2.5
Zouggara	90.6	-	93.7	-	96.9	103.7	2.5

Regional Stations:

FM	Station, location	MHz	kW(TRP)
14)	R. Laghouat, Aflou	87.6	10
4)	R. Béchar, Abadla	87.7	
5)	R. Chlef, Ain N'sour	87.7	10
1)	R. Adrar, Timimoun	87.8	
28)	R. Tébessa, Doukhane	87.9	2.5
32)	R. Tlemcen, Marsa BEn M'hidi	88.0	0.1
3)	R. Batna, Metlili	88.1	10
11)	R. El Tarf, Oum Ali	88.3	2.5
30)	R. Tindouf, Tindouf	88.3	
26)	R. Soummam, Akfadou	88.7	10
2)	R. Annaba, M'Cid	88.8	10
46)	R. Blida, Oued Jer	89.0	0.1
3)	R. Batna, Regheiss	89.3	0.5
4)	R. Béchar	89.3	5
39)	R. Tipaza	89.9	
9)	R. Setif, Meghriss	90.4	10
4)	R. Béchar, Rosfa Taiba	90.5	
19)	R. Oran, Khar	90.5	2.5
39)	R. Tipaza, Chrea	90.6	
21)	R. Rélizane, Ain N'sour	90.8	10
18)	R. Naama, Mecheria	90.9	10
30)	R. Tindouf, Chenachene	92.4	0.1
16)	R. Djelfa, Sbaa Mokrane	91.1	2.5
32)	R. Biskra, Metlili	91.2	10
7)	R. El Bahdja, Chréa	91.5	10
20)	R. Ouargla	91.8	
1)	R. Adrar	91.9	2.5
20)	R. Ouargla	92.1	2.5
29)	R. Tiaret	92.5	2.5
35)	R. Khenchela, Regheiss	92.4	0.5
19)	R. Oran, Tessala	92.7	10
43)	R. Aïn Defla, Djendel	93.0	
44)	R. Tizi Ouzou, Belloua	93.0	0.25
40)	R. Médéa, Dirah	93.3	2.5
12)	R. Illizi	93.5	0.1
6)	R. Constantine, Kef El Akhal	93.9	10
7)	R. El Bahdja, Bordj el Bahri	94.2	2
41)	R. Saïda, Sidi Abdelkrim	94.5	2
32)	R. Tlemcen, Nador	94.7	10
23)	R. Skikda, Filfila	94.8	2
25)	R. Souk Ahras, M'cid	95.1	10
43)	R. Aïn Defla, Anneb	95.2	0.25
45)	R. Oum el Bouaghi, Regheiss	95.6	0.5
36)	R. Aïn Témouchent, Tessala	95.9	10
45)	R. Oum el Bouaghi, Chettaia	96.4	2.5
41)	R. Saida, Sidi Ahmed	96.5	0.1
12)	R. Illizi, Debdeb	96.7	0.1
17)	R. Mostanagem, Mostanagem	96.8	0.1
21)	R. Rélizane, Oued es Salam	97.0	0.2
46)	R. Blida, Bordj el Bahri	97.5	2.5
20)	R. Ouargla, El Borma	98.0	0.1
12)	R. Illizi, Bordj Omar Driss	98.1	0.1
4)	R. Béchar, Tabelbala	98.2	
47)	R. Guelma, Mahouna	97.6	2.5
10)	R. Ghardaïa, El Golea	98.0	2.5
14)	R. Laghouat, Hassi R'Mel	98.0	2.5
24)	R. El Oued, 3 locations	98.0	
27)	R. Tamanrasset, 2 locations	98.0	1
30)	R. Tindouf	98.0	0.1
4)	R. Béchar, Kerzaz	98.5	0.1
15)	R. Mascara, Chareb Rih	98.5	2.5
37)	R. Bordj Bou Arreridj, Tafartas	98.7	2.5
27)	R.Tamanrasset, In Guezzam/Taman.	99.1	0.2
27)	R. Tamanrasset, Tinzaouten	99.4	0.1
22)	R. Sidi Bel Abbés, Tessala	99.2	10
28)	R. Tébessa, Ain Zerga	99.6	0.1
34)	R. Bouira, Dirah	99.8	2.5
43)	R. Aïn Defla, Anneb	99.9	1
8)	R. El Bayadh	100.1	0.1
40)	R. Médéa, Médéa	100.7	0.1
46)	R. Blida, Chréa/Dirah	100.9	0.2
41)	R. Saïda, Saïda	101.3	0.1
42)	R. Boumerdes	102.6	0.1
38)	R. Mila, Kef Bouderga	102.7	2.5
13)	R. Jijel, Kern	103.0	2.5
33)	R. Tissemsilt	103.2	0.1
32)	R. Tlemcen, Bab el Assa	103.9	0.1
17)	R. Mostaganem	104.0	2.5
32)	R. Tlemcen, Sidi Boudjenane	104.5	0.1
48)	R. M'Sila	104.5	1.5
35)	R. Khenchela, Chettaia	105.7	2.5
7)	R. El Badhja, Puits des Zouaves	106.0	2.5
32)	R. Tlemcen, El Abed	106.0	0.1
32)	R. Tlemcen, Hounaine	106.0	0.1
43)	R. Aïn Defla, Tacheta Zougagha	107.3	0.1
43)	R. Aïn Defla, Tariq Ibn Ziad	107.7	0.1

+tens of more low power transmitters.

D.Prgr: 1=Chaîne 1 in Arabic: 24h. 2=Chaîne 2 in Tamazight: 24h. 3=Chaîne **3** in French: 24h. **Int=R. Algérie Internationale** in Arabic, French, English & Spanish: 24h. **M= Radio Multichaine** consists of **R. Culture** in Arabic: 1400-2300 & **R. Quran** 2300-1400. 1422kHz carries also Radio UFC 1200-1600 and may carry Ch. 2 in the evening. **J: Jil FM:** youth channel in Algerian Arabic: 24h.

L=Local stations: times of local prgrs vary slightly by stn, but mostly between 0800-1900 (R. Bahdja and R. Oran 24h). Most local stns transmit Chaîne 1/2, Culture or R. Algérie Int. after 1900. At 2300 many stations switch to relaying R. Quran. Most local stns carry news from Chaîne 1 at 0600, 1200, 1630 & 1830.

Addresses & other information:

Audio feeds for local stations: **W:** radioalgerie.dz/player/fr

1) B.P. 309, Adrar – **2)** 7, Boulevard Radji Mokhtar, Quartier Annasr, Annaba – **3)** B.P. 453, Batna **W:** radio-batna.dz – **4)** Cité Badr, B.P. 330, Béchar **W:** radiobechar.com – **5)** Ain N'sour – **6)** B.P. 28B El Koudia, Constantine **W:** radio-constantine.dz – **7) W:** facebook.com/pages/Radio-El-Bahdja-FM/239397829331 – **8)** B.P. 195, El Bayadh – **9)** B.P. 54, Ain Tbinet, Sétif **W:** radio-setif.com – **10)** B.P. 17, Ghardaïa – **11)** El Tarf **W:** radio-eltarf.com – **12)** Route de l'aéroport, B.P. 230, Illizi **W:** facebook.com/radioillizi.dz – **13)** B.P. 48, Jijel – **14)** B.P. 1410, Bd. de l'Indépendance Mamourah, El Maqam, Laghouat **W:** radiolagh.voila.net – **15)** Place Mostfa Ben Touhami, Mascara – **16)** Djelfa – **17)** Place El Matemar, B.P. 1014, Mostaganem 027000 **W:** radiomostaganem.net – **18)** Av. du 1 Novembre, BP 223, Naama **W:** radionaamafm.com – **19)** 4 place Aîssa Messaoudi, Oran – **20)** Ruissat, B.P. 83, Ouargla – **21)** 15 Rue Ismail Mustapha, Maison de Culture, Rélizane **W:** radiorelizane.net – **22)** Ex Gare de l´État, Sidi Bel Abbés 022000 – **23)** Porte des Aurès, B.P. 55, Skikda **W:** facebook.com/radio.skikda – **24)** Cité Reml El Oued, B.P. 172, El Oued – **25)** Blvd. Messous Hamid, Souk Ahras – **26)** Boulevard Youcef Bouchebah, Béjaia – **27)** B.P. 1080, Tamanrasset – **28)** Unité de Tébéssa, Parc des Loisirs, Tébéssa – **29)** Rue des Fréres Saim Tiaret, B.P. 671, Tiaret **W:** radiotiaret.dz – **30)** B.P. 213, Agence Enasr, Tindouf – **31)** B.P. 44K, Tlemcen – **32)** Av. Idriss Mohamed, Biskra **W:** radiobiskra.com – **33)** Tissemsilt – **34)** Bouira – **35)** Khenchela – **36)** Aïn Témouchent **W:** radioaintemouchent.com – **37)** Bordj Bou Arreridj **W:** facebook.com/radio.bordj – **38)** Mila – **39)**

Tipaza – **40)** Médéa – **41)** Saïda **W:** saidafm.com – **42)** Boumerdes – **43)** Aïn Defla – **44)** Tizi Ouzou – **45)** Boulevard Houari Boumédiène, 0400 Oum el Bouaghi **W:** facebook.com/radio.oeb – **46)** Blida – **47)** Guelma **W:** facebook.com/radio.guelma.fm – **48)** M'Sila
Ann: Chaîne 1: "Al Kanet al Oula min Idha'at al-Djazairiyah.", 2: "Radio Tisnath", 3: "Algérie Chaîne trois", C: "Idha'atul-Thaqafiyah", K:"Idha'atul-Koran al Karim".

DAB: Algér channel 5B 176.64MHz 600W: Chaîne 1-3, Jil FM

ANDORRA

L.T: UTC + 1h (28 Mar-31 Oct: + 2h) — **Pop:** 76.100 — **Pr.L:** Catalan, French, Spanish — **E.C:** 230V/50Hz — **ITU:** AND

ANDORRA TELECOM (Gov)

✉ Mn. Lluís Pujol 8-14, AD500 Santa Coloma (Admin.) ✉Av. Meritxell 112, AD500 Andorra la Vella (Comm.) ☎+376 875000 🖷 +376 821414 **E:** comunicacio@andorratelecom.ad **W:** andorratelecom.ad **L.P:** Admin Dir: Jordi Nadal Bentadé

RNA RÀDIO NACIONAL D'ANDORRA (Pub)

✉ RTVA Ràdio i Televisió d'Andorra S.A., Baixada del Molí 24, AD500 Andorra la Vella ☎+376 873777 🖷 +376 863242 **E:** rtva@rtva.ad **W:** andorradifusio.ad **L.P:** DG: Xavier Mujal Closa

CADENA PIRENAICA DE RÀDIO I TELEVISIÓ (Comm.)

✉ Cadena Pirenaica de Ràdio i Televisió, SA, Av. Príncep Benlloch 24, AD200 Encamp ☎+376 732000 🖷 +376 834831 - Av. Pau Claris 8, ES-25700 Seu d'Urgell, Spain **E:** info@cadenapirenaica.com **W:** cadenapirenaica.com

GRUP FLAIX ANDORRA (Comm.)

✉ Ràdio i Televisió de les Valls S.A., (GRUP FLAIX ANDORRA), Av. del Fener 11-13, 1r 3a - Edifici Eland-Unió, AD500 Andorra la Vella ☎+376 862288 **W:** flaixfmandorra.com **E:** publicitat@flaixandorra.com

COPE- AD RÀDIO (Comm.)

✉ Avda. Bonaventura Riberaygua, 39, 5è Pis, Edifici Alexandre, AD500 Andorra la Vella ☎+376 877477 **W:** diariandorra.ad **E:** laradio@adradio.ad

SER PRINCIPAT D'ANDORRA (Comm.)

✉ C. Prat de la Creu, 32, AD500 Andorra la Vella ☎+376 808300 🖷 +376 828301 **E:** msfuentes@prisaradio.com **W:** cadenaser.ad

FM	MHz	kW	Location	Station
2)	87.8	0.3	La Comella	Gestiona R.
1)	88.1	0.3	Pic de Carroi	Cadena Dial
2)	89.0	0.3	Pic de Carroi	R7P - RAC1
2)	89.5	0.3	Pic de Carroi	Europa FM
2)	90.1	0.3	Valls Valira	R. Tele Taxi
7)	90.7	0.1	Pas de la Casa	Pyrénées FM
8)	90.9	0.1	Valls Valira	iCat
6)	91.4	0.1	Pic de Maià	R. Nacional d'Andorra
1)	92.1	1	Pic de Carroi	SER Catalunya
1)	92.6	1	Pic de Carroi	Los 40 classic
2)	93.3	0.3	Pic de Carroi	R. Valira - Onda Cero
10)	93.8	0.3	Pic de Carroi/Pic de Maià	Flaix FM Andorra
6)	94.2	1	Pic de Carroi/Pic de Maià	R. Nacional d'Andorra
2)	94.6	0.3	Encamp	Pròxima FM
2)	95.0	0.3	Pic de Carroi	Pròxima FM
8)	95.6	0.1	Valls Valira	Catalunya Informació
10)	96.0	1	Pic de Carroi/Pic de Maià	R. Flaixbac
8)	96.5	0.1	Valls Valira	Catalunya Música
6)	97.0	1	Pic de Carroi/Pic de Maià	Andorra Música
3)	97.7	0.1	Sant Julià de Lòria	R. Festa Major
2)	98.1	0.1	Valls Valira	RAC 105
2)	98.5	0.1	La Comella	R. Valira - Onda Cero
2)	98.9	1	Pic de Carroi	Kiss FM
2)	100.2	0.1	Valls Valira	RAC 105
4)	100.6	0.3	Pic de Carroi	NRJ
9)	101.5	1	Pic de Carroi/Pic de Maià	COPE - AD R.
4)	101.8	1	Pic de Carroi/Pic de Maià	France Inter
1)	102.3	1	Pic de Carroi/Pic de Maià	R. SER Principat d'Andorra
4)	102.6	1	Pic de Carroi/Pic de Maià	France Musique
1)	103.3	1	Pic de Carroi/Pic de Maià	Los 40 Andorra
4)	104.0	1	Pic de Carroi/Pic de Maià	France Culture
8)	104.6	1	Pic de Carroi/Pic de Maià	Catalunya R.
4)	106.0	1.2	Pic de Carroi/Pic de Maià	RNE R. 4
4)	106.8	1.2	Pic de Carroi/Pic de Maià	RNE R. 1
5)	107.5	1.2	Valls Valira	R. Principat - R. Estel
4)	107.9	1.2	Pic de Carroi/Pic de Maià	RNE R. 3

Addresses & other information:
1) SER Principat d'Andorra ✉ C. Prat de la Creu, 32, AD500 Andorra la Vella ☎+376 808300 🖷 +376 828301 **E:** informatiusserandorra@prisaradio.com **W:** cadenaser.ad
2) Cadena Pirenaica de Ràdio i Televisió, SA, ✉ Av. Príncep Benlloch 24, AD200 Encamp ☎+376 732000 🖷 +376 834831 **E:** info@cadenapirenaica.com **W:** cadenapirenaica.com
3) R. Festa Major, ✉ Plaça Major, 3, AD600 Sant Julià de Lòria ☎+376 842601 (temporary station only last week of July) **E:** joventut@commusantjulia.ad
4) Andorra Telecom ✉ Mn. Lluís Pujol 8-14, AD500 Santa Coloma (Admin.) ☎+376 875000 🖷 +376 821414 **E:** comunicacio@andorratelecom.ad **W:** andorratelecom.ad
5) R. Principat - R. Estel ✉ Comtes de Bell-lloc, 67-69 ES-08014 Barcelona, Spain. ☎+973 354400 **E:** radioestel@radioestel.cat
6) RTVA Ràdio i Televisió d'Andorra S.A., ✉ Baixada del Molí 24, AD500 Andorra la Vella **W:** andorradifusio.ad – **7)** Pyrénées FM ✉ Le Barry d'en Fort 09110 Montaillou Cedex – 16 boulevard de l'Europe F-31520 Ramonville-Saint Agne, France **W:** pyreneesfm.com **E:** contact@pyrenesfm.com ☎ +33 561440000
8) CCMA ✉ Av. Diagonal 614-616, ES-08021 Barcelona, Spain ☎+34 933069200 **W:** catradio.cat
9) COPE - AD RÀDIO ✉ Avda. Bonaventura Riberaygua, 39, 5 Pis, Edifici Alexandre, AD500 Andorra la Vella ☎+376 877477 **W:** diariandorra.ad **E:** laradio@adradio.ad
10) GRUP FLAIX ANDORRA ✉ Av. del Fener, 11-13, 1r 3a - Edifici Eland-Unió, AD500 Andorra la Vella ☎ +376 862288 **E:** publicitat@flaixandorra.com **W:** flaixandorra.com

ANGOLA

L.T: UTC +1h — **Pop:** 33 million — **Pr.L:** Portuguese (official), indigenous languages — **E.C:** 220V/50Hz — **ITU:** AGL

MINISTÉRIO DA COMUNICAÇÃO SOCIAL (MCS)

✉ Av. Comandante Valódia 1°& 2° amdar , CP. 2608, Luanda ☎+244 22 2443495 🖷 +244 22 2392649 **W:** www.mcs.gov.ao **L.P:** Min: Carolina Cerqueiro.

RÁDIO NACIONAL DE ANGOLA (RNA, Pub.)

✉ Av. Comandante Gika, CP. 1329, Luanda ☎+244 22 2323172 🖷 +244 22 2324647 **W:** rna.ao

MW	kHz	kW	Prgr.	H of tr
Mulenvos	‡945	25	N	24h
SW	**kHz**	**kW**	**Prgr.**	**H of tr.**
Mulenvos	4950	25	A	24h

Ann: "Rádio Nacional de Angola".

Prgrs: A=Canal A in Portuguese (general coverage): 24h. **N:** on the h.
N=Rádio N'Gola Yetu (ethnic languages): 24h. **N:** rel. Canal A.
International service: relayed on Rádio N'Gola Yetu's fqs 2000-2400 in Lingala, French, English and Portuguese.
RFM=Rádio FM Estéreo (music): 1000-2400.
5=Rádio 5 (sports): 0500-2300.
P=Emissora Provincial: 0400-2300, rel. A at night.

Provincial MW transmitters:

MW	Location	kHz	kW	Pr
18)	Soyo	v1290‡	5	P

FM	Location	A	N	5	RFM	P	kW
1)	Luanda	93.5	101.4	94.5	96.5	99.9	4
1)	Viana	90.0	101.0	94.2	-	92.8	
2)	Caxito	91.5	-	88.2	-	87.9	4
3)	Lobito	93.5	104.9	101.0	98.5	89.1	1
3)	Benguela	91.5	90.4	-	92.3	92.9	2
3)	Bocoio	93.3	-	-	-	98.3	
3)	Ganda	90.0	-	93.1	-	95.1	
3)	Cubal	91.3	-	88.2	-	94.4	
3)	Canjala	100.0	-	-	-	98.0	
3)	Caimbambo	88.1	-	-	-	99.1	
3)	Balombo	95.3	-	-	-	93.1	
3)	Dombe Grande	88.5	-	98.0	-	-	
4)	Kuito	92.0	91.0	94.5	-	106.7	4

Prov.	Location	A	N	5	RFM	P	kW
4)	Chinguar	101.8	-	88.9	-	98.5	
5)	Cabinda	-	98.8	95.0	-	88.2/91.3	4
5)	Malembo	97.7	-	-	-	90.8	
5)	Belize	102.5	-	-	-	100.0	
6)	Ondjiva	92.2	101.0	91.8	-	88.7	5
6)	Xangongo	98.9	-	-	-	94.7	
7)	Huambo	99.2	89.0	91.6	-	88.5/98.7	4
7)	Bailundo	95.9	-	-	-	99.2	
7)	Caála	-	-	-	-	94.8	
8)	Lubango	95.8	90.2	99.1	92.8	96.6	4
9)	Menongue	91.4	92.0	94.6	96.5	88.3	
9)	Kuito Kuanavale	91.1	-	88.0	-	-	
10)	N'dalatando	95.5	95.0	91.8	-	92.3/98.8	1
10)	Dondo	92.7	-	-	-	88.2	
10)	Golungo Alto	97.2	-	105.4	-	-	
10)	Camabatela	100.0	-	98.0	-	-	
11)	Sumbe	101.1	104.7	91.7	-	97.6	4
11)	Waco Cungo	100.7	-	97.2	-	-	
11)	Gabela	95.7	-	-	-	100.7	
11)	Porto Ambuim	90.0	-	-	-	93.3	
11)	Liholo	92.7	-	90.2	-	-	
11)	Kibala	94.7	-	91.7	-	-	
12)	Dundo	94.4	-	93.3	-	90.3/97.7	4
12)	Lucapa	88.7	-	-	-	91.7	
12)	Cafunfo	90.2	-	99.9	-	-	
13)	Saurimo	103.7	106.2	90.3	-	100.2	
14)	Malanje	92.0	93.7	90.9	94.8	100.7	4
15)	Luena	90.7	107.3	103.7	-	97.2	2
15)	Cazombo	87.9	-	90.3	-	-	
15)	Luau	90.2	-	93.3	-	-	
16)	Namibe	88.5	92.5	91.6	97.7	95.2	4
16)	Bibala	88.5	-	92.6	-	-	
16)	Camucuio	90.3	-	93.4	-	-	
16)	Tômbwa	87.7	-	-	-	95.9	
17)	Uíge	99.8	106.3	92.5	-	89.6/91.0	4
17)	Negage	94.4	-	88.0	-	103.0	
17)	Quitexi	99.3	-	-	-	92.4	
17)	Bungo	-	-	-	-	97.3	
18)	Mbanza Congo	101.9	97.1	92.7	-	95.1	2
18)	Soyo	103.7	-	88.7	-	92.3	

+50 more low power transmitters.

Provincial & local stations:
1) R. Luanda & R. Cacuaco 105.0MHz, R. Cazenga 102.1MHz – **2)** R. Bengo, Caxito – **3)** R. Benguela, R. Lobito. R. Ganda & R. Kubal are carried daytime on R. 5 fqs. – **4)** R. Bié, Kuito – **5)** R. Cabinda **W:** facebook.com/radiocabinda – **6)** R. Cunene, Ondjiva & R. Xangongo – **7)** R. Huambo & R. Caála – **8)** R. Huíla, Lubango – **9)** R. Cuando Cubango, Menongue – **10)** Cuanza Norte: R. N'dalatando & R. Dondo – **11)** Cuanza Sul: R. Sumbe – **12)** R. Lunda Norte, Lucapa – **13)** Lunda Sul: R. Saurimo – **14)** R. Malanje – **15)** R. Moxico, Luena – **16)** R. Namibe, R. Tombwa – **17)** R. Uíge, R. Negage, R. Quitexi, R. Bungo – **18)** R. Zaire, Mbanza Congo & R. Soyo.
Affiliated community stations on FM in Buco Zau, Camabatela, Golungo Alto, Tombwa, Viana and Virei.

Other stations:
Luanda Antena Comercial: Luanda 95.5MHz 5kW **W:** lacluanda.blogspot.com
R. Ecclesia (Rlg.): Luanda 97.5MHz 5kW **W:** radioecclesia.org
R. Escola: Luanda 88.5MHz 1kW **W:** cefojor.co.ao/sobre-a-radio
R. Kairos: Luanda 98.4MHz **W:** fb.com/radiometodistakairos98.4
R. Mais: Huambo 89.9MHz, Huila 91.3MHz, Benguela 96.3MHz, Luanda 99.1MHz **W:** radiomais.co.ao

ANGUILLA (UK)

L.T: UTC -4h — **Pop**: 15,000 — **Pr.L**: English — **E.C**: 110V/60Hz — **ITU**: AIA

RADIO ANGUILLA (Gov. Comm.)

PO Box 60, AI-2640 The Valley AI-2640 ☎ +1 264 497 2218 **E:** radioaxa@anguillanet.com **W:** radioaxa.com **L.P**: Dir.: Farrah Banks. PM: Keith Stone Greaves. Eng.: Lester Richardson
FM: 95.5MHz (3kW), Crocus Hill.

THE CARIBBEAN BEACON (Rlg.)

PO Box 690, AI-2640 The Valley
☎+1 264 497 4348 🖷 +1 264 497 4311
FM: 100.1MHz 20kW – F.pl.: change to 89.5MHz
F.pl.: Reactivation of 690, 1610, 6090, and 11775 kHz
D.Prgr: University Network, 24h. No local programming.
Owned by University Network (see under USA for SW schedule)

PRIVATE FM STATIONS (FM in MHz):
FUSION RADIO, PO Box 805, AI-2640 The Valley ☎ +1 264 235 6425 **W:** fusionradioanguilla.com **FM:** 89.1 - **KLASS FM**, Wilmot Estate Rock Farm, PO Box 339, AI-2640 The Valley ☎ +1 264 581 6208 **W:** klass929.com **FM:** 92.9 – **KOOL FM**, North Side, AI-2640 The Valley ☎ +1 264 497 0103 **W:** koolfm103.com **FM:** 103.3. Format: Urban Caribbean – **NEW BEGINNING RADIO/GRACE FM**, Shoal Bay Village, PO Box 1122, AI-2640 The Valley **FM:** 99.3 - **UP BEAT RADIO**, Cedar Av., Rey Hill, PO Box 5045, AI-2640 The Valley ☎ +1 264 498 3354 **W:** hbr1075.com **FM:** 97.7 – **VOICE OF CREATION RADIO**, Sachasses, South Hill, AI-2640 The Valley ☎ +1 264 497 0106 **FM:** 106.7 Format: Gospel – **Z105.1**, 2nd Floor, Express Blg, Simpson Bay, St.Maarten ☎ +1 721 544 3377 **W:** www.z1051.com **FM:** 105.1

ANTARCTICA

L.T: Antártida Argentina: UTC -3h; Antártida Chilena: UTC -4h (6 Aug 20-4 Apr 21, 5 Sep 21-3 Apr 22: -3h); Ross Dependency (NZL): UTC +12h (27 Sep 20-4 Apr 21, 26 Sep 21-3 Apr 22: +13h). **NB:** UTC times in schedules refer to DST period — **Pop:** (non-permanent) c. 5,000 (local summer), c. 1,000 (local winter) — **ITU:** ATA

RADIO NACIONAL "ARCANGEL SAN GABRIEL" (LRA36) (Pub)
LRA36 Radio Nacional Arcangel San Gabriel, Base de Ejercito Esperanza, CP 9411-Antártida Argentina, Argentina. ☎+54 2974 44 5304, 810 222 0776 (from Argentina) **E**: esperanzaantar@infovia.com.ar, lra36esperanza@yahoo.com.ar **L.P:** Dir: Guillermo Bolger, Op.: Pablo González
SW: see international section. **FM:** 96.7MHz 24h.

SOBERANIA FM, Villa Las Estrellas, Antartica Chilena, Chile. **FM:** 90.5MHz 0.1kW.
ICE FM, McMurdo Station, Ross Dependency. **FM:** 104.5MHz 0.05kW. Rel AFRTS exc. some local prgrs
KOLD, South Pole Station, Ross Dependency. **FM:** 87.5MHz
88.7 FM, McMurdo Station, Ross Dependency. **FM:** 88.7MHz
SCOTT BASE R., Scott Base, Ross Dependency. **FM:** 97.0MHz
AMERICAN FORCES ANTARCTIC NETWORK, AFAN McMurdo, US Naval Support Force Antarctica, 651 Lyons Str, Port Hueneme, CA 93043-4345, USA. **FM:** 93.9MHz 0.03kW. **D.Prgr:** 24h.

ANTIGUA & BARBUDA

L.T: UTC -4h — **Pop:** 98,000 — **Pr.L:** English — **E.C:** 230V/60Hz — **ITU:** ATG

ANTIGUA & BARBUDA BROADCASTING SERVICE (Gov. Comm.)

Cecil Charles Bldg, Cross Street, St. John's ☎ +1 268 462 0821 **E:** info.abs@ab.gov.ag **W:** abstvradio.com **L.P:** PM: Blondell Anthony. CEN: Denis Leandro
FM: 90.5/101.5MHz **D.Prgr: ABS Radio** 24h

CARIBBEAN RADIO LIGHTHOUSE (Rlg.)

Jolly Hill, PO Box 1057, St. John's ☎ +1 268 462 1454 **E:** lighthouseBIMI@gmail.com **W:** radiolighthouse.website **L.P:** SM & CE: Nathan Owens. Owned by Baptist Int. Missions Inc.
MW: 1160kHz 10kW **FM:** 92.3MHz 1kW **D.Prgr:** MW & FM: 24h

OBSERVER MEDIA GROUP (Comm.)

ABI, Redcliffe Street, PO Box 1318, St. John's ☎ +1 268 481 9100 **W:** antiguaobserver.com
FM: Observer Radio 91.1MHz (News/talk) – **Hitz 91.9:** 91.9MHz

FAMILY FM LTD. (Rlg.)

1st Floor Belmont School of Business Building, All Saints Rd, St. John's ☎ +1 268 560 7578/9 **E:** info@familyfm.ltd **W:** familyfm.ltd **L.P:** MD John Silcott
FM: Vibz FM 92.9MHz – **English Harbour Radio:** 93.5MHz

OTHER FM STATIONS (FM in MHz):
ABUNDANT LIFE RADIO, Codrington Village, Barbuda ☎ +1 268 562 4821 **W:** abundantliferadioag.com **L.P:** MD: Clifton Francois

FM: Barbuda: 103.1 (1kW) & Antigua 103.9 (1kW) Format: Gospel – **BBC** relay **FM** 89.1 – **CATHOLIC RADIO,** Michaels Mount, PO Box 836, St. John's ☎ +1 268 562 6868 **E:** catholicradio@candw.ag **W:** thecatholicradio.com **FM** 89.7 – **CRUSADOR RADIO,** Newgate/Popesheard Str, St. John's ☎ +1 268 562 1075 **FM** 107.3 – **GOD FIRST RADIO,** Ford Rd, St. John's ☎ +1 268 720 3120 **E:** godfirstradioag@gmail.com **W:** godfirstradio.com **L.P.**: William Dorset **FM** 102.9 Format: Gospel – **HEALTY CHOICE FM,** Ramco Bldg, Independence Ave, PO Box 1296, St. John's ☎ +1 268 462 2273 🖷 +1 268 462 2275 **W:** healtychoicefm.com **L.P:** CEO: Lester Storm **FM** 94.9 – **JUMP FM**, St. Mary's Str., St. John's ☎ +1 268 720 9529 **W:** jump268.com **FM** 100.1 – **NICE FM**, All Saints Rd, Clarkes Hill ☎ +1 268 728 8738 **W:** nicefmradio.com **FM** 104.3 – **POINTE FM**, The Point ☎ +1 268 562 4989 **E:** pointefm991@gmail.com **W:** pointville.ag **FM** 99.1 – **RED HOT RADIO**, Carlisle Estate, St. John's ☎ +1 268 701 1581 **E:** redhotfm@hotmail.com **W:** redhotflames.com **FM** 98.5 – **SECOND ADVENT RADIO**, America Rd, PO Box 109, St. John's ☎ +1 268 562 1015 **L.P.:** SM Necole Caleb. **W**: secondadventradio.org **FM** 101.5. Format: Rlg. – **ZDK LIBERTY RADIO**, Grenville Radio Ltd., Bird & All Saints Rd, St. John's ☎ +1 268 462 1100 **L.P.:** Sean Bird **FM** 97.1 (1kW) – **ZOOM RADIO**, Blackburn St. 5, Villa, St. John's ☎ +1 268 463 0043 **W:** zoomradiofm.com **FM** 95.7 Format: Classic soul and jazz

ARGENTINA

L.T: UTC -3h — **Pop:** 45 million — **Pr.L:** Spanish — **E.C.:** 220V/50Hz — **ITU:** ARG — **Int. dialling code:** +54

ENTE NACIONAL DE COMUNICACIONES (ENaCom)

🖃 Perú 103, 1067 CA Buenos Aires ☎ 11 4347-9850 **E:** contacto@enacom.gob.ar **W:** www.enacom.gob.ar **L.P:** Presidente: Claudio Julio Ambrosini

SECRETARIA DE MEDIOS Y COMUNICACIONES PUBLICA

🖃 Balcarce 50, 1064CA Buenos Aires ☎ 11 4344-3600 **W:** argentina.gob.ar/comunicacionpublica **L.P:** Francisco Meritello

ASOCIACIÓN DE RADIODIFUSORAS PRIVADAS ARGENTINAS (ARPA)

🖃 Juan Domingo Perón 1561, Piso 3, C1037ACB Buenos Aires ☎ 11 43715999 **E:** arpaorg@arpa.org.ar **W:** www.arpa.org.ar **L.P:** Pres: Jose Alberto Ponzoni
NB: ARPA is an association of privately owned commercial stns.

° = on-air stn name not confirmed, ‡ = inactive, ± = varying freq.

MW	Call	kHz	kW	Station, location and h of tr
CF34)		530	1/0.25	Somos R. AM 530, Buenos Aires
CF53)		540	1	R. Pasión, Buenos Aires
BA119)		540		R. Italia, Villa Martelli (nf 1620)
SF01)	LRA14	540	25/1	R. Nacional, Santa Fé
SA01)	LRA25	540	10/5	R. Nacional,Tartagal
CB04)	LU17	540	10/5	R. Golfo Nuevo, Pto. Madryn
TF03)		‡540	25/5	Ushuaia (F.Pl)
NE11)	LRG206	550	2.5/0.5	La Primera, Neuquen
CB01)	LRA9	560	25/1	R. Nacional, Esquel
BA01)	LRA13	560	25/5	R. Nacional, Bahia Blanca
ER01)	LT15	560	10/3	R. del Litoral, Concordia
SJ01)	LV1	560	25/5	R. Colón, San Juan
JU01)	LRA16	560	25/1	R. Nacional, La Quiaca
CF30)		570	5	R. Argentina, Buenos Aires
CB02)	LU20	580	20	R. Chubut, Trelew
CO01)	LW1	580	25/5	R. Univ. Nal. de Córdoba, Córdoba
ME12)		580	3	R. Andina, San Rafael
CF01)	LS4	590	100	R. Continental, Buenos Aires
RN01)	LRA30	590	25/1	R. Nacional, San Carlos de Bariloche
TU01)	LV12	590	25/10	R. Independencia, San Miguel de Tucumán
NE04)	LU5	600	25/1	R. Neuquén, Neuquén: 24h (retrs Cadena tres 03:00-09:00)
SE03)	LRK201	610	1	R. Solidaridad, Añatuya
BA91)		610	5	R. General San Martin - "La Buena R." San Martin
ME07)	LV4	620	25/5	R. Nacional, San Rafael: 24h
LR01)	LRA28	620	25/5	R. Nacional, La Rioja
SC01)	LRA18	620	25/5	R. Nacional, Río Turbio
MS01)	LT17	620	25/5	R. Provincia de Misiones, Posadas
CH03)	LRA26	620	25/5	R. Nacional. Resistencia
CF02)	LS5	630	50/5	R. Rivadavia, Buenos Aires
JU03)	LW8	630	25/5	R. San Salvador de Jujuy
CB05)	LRF201	630	25/5	R. Nacional Patagonia – R. Patagonia, Comodoro Rivadavia
TF01)	LRA24	640	25/5	R. Nacional, Río Grande
RN02)	LU18	640	10/5	R. El Valle, General Roca
SL01)	LV15	640	10/5	R. Villa Mercedes, Villa Mercedes
CF38)		650	3	Belgrano AM 650, Buenos Aires
ER04)	LT41	660	1/0.25	R. LV del Sur Entrerriano, Gualeguaychú
BA36)		660	1	Amplitud 660, Ciudad Evita
BA172)		670	4	R. Republica, Ciudad Evita
CB03)	LRA11	670	25/5	R. Nacional, Comodoro Rivadavia
LR04)		‡670	5/1	R. Universidad, La Rioja (F.pl)
NE01)	LRA52	670	10/3	R. Nacional, Chos Malal
MS02)	LT4	670	1	R. LT4 Digital, Posadas - CNN
BA02)	LRI209	670	25/5	R. Mar del Plata, Mar del Plata
BA173)		680	2	R. Magna, Villa Martelli
SF07)	LT3	680	10/5	R. Cerealista, Rosario
SC02)	LU12	680	25/5	R. Río Gallegos, Río Gallegos
ME01)	LV6	680	25/5	R. Nihuil, Mendoza
CF45)		690	2	K-24 en R., Virrey del Pino
SA02)	LRA4	690	50/5	R. Nacional, Salta
RN03)	LU19	690	10/5	R. LV de Comahue, Cipolletti
CO05)	LV3	700	25/5	Cadena 3 - R. Córdoba
NE02)	LRA17	710	25/1	R. Nacional, Zapala: 24h
MS03)	LRA19	710	25/5	R. Nacional, Pto. Iguazú: 24h
CF13)	LRL202	710	50	R. Diez, Buenos Aires
SC03)	LRA59	720	1	R. Nacional, Gobernador Gregores
ME02)	LV10	720	50/5	R.de Cuyo – LV Diez, Mendoza:
LP01)	LRA3	730	25/5	R. Nacional, Santa Rosa: 24h
SC04)	LU23	730	20/1	R. Nal - R. Lago Argentino, El Calafate:
CA01)	LRA27	730	25/5	R. Nacional, Catamarca
CF27)		730	10/5	R. Concepto (BBN-R.), Gonzáles Catán
CB07)	LRA55	740	1	R. Nacional, Alto Río Senguer: 2h
CF48)		740	5	R. Rebelde, Valentin Alsina
SC05)	LRI200	740	3	R. Municipal, Puerto Deseado
CH05)	LRH251	740	5/1	R. Provincia del Chaco, Resistencia
RN13)		740	10	AM 740 La Carretera, Allen
CF51)	LRL203	750	1/0.5	R. AM 7-50, Llavallol
CO02)	LRA7	750	100	R. Nacional, Córdoba:
BA09)	LU6	760	18/4	Emisora Atlántica, Mar del Plata
CF21)		770	5/1	R. Cooperativa, Tapiales
TF02)	LRA10	780	25/5	R.Nacional, Ushuaia
CS01)	LRA12	780	25/5	R. Nacional, Santo Tomé
ME03)	LV8	780	25/5	R. Libertador (R. Nacional), Mendoza
CB06)	LRF210	780	10/5	R. Tres "Cadene Patagoni", Trelew
ME06)	LV19	790	5	R. Malargüe
CF04)	LR6	790	100	R. Mitre "AM 80," Buenos Aires
JU02)	LRA22	790	25/5	R. Nacional, San Salvador de Jujuy
RN04)	LU15	800	25/2	R. Viedma, Viedma
ME04)	LV23	800	1/0.25	R. Andina – R. Rio Atuel, General Alvear
CH01)	LT43	800	5	R. Mocoví, General Pinedo
CF52)		810	5/1	R. Federal, CF Buenos Aires
CO16)		810	10/1	R. Mitre AM 810, Córdoba
FO01)	LRA8	820	25/5	R. Nacional, Formosa: 24h
BA04)	LU24	820	5/1	R. Tres Arroyos, Tres Arroyos
BA33)	LRI208	820	2/0.5	Estacion 820, Glew (R.Maria)
CF24)		830	5	R. Del Pueblo, Villa Luzuriaga
SF02)	LT8	830	10/5	La Ocho AM 830, Rosario
ME08)	LV18	830	10/1	R. Municipal, San Rafael
SC06)	LU14	830	25/5	R. Provincia de Santa Cruz,Río Gallegos:
CS05)	LT21	830	1/0.5	R. Municipal, Alvear
CS02)	LT12	840	10/5	R. General Madariaga - R.Nal, Paso de los Libres
BA05)	LU2	840	25/10	R. Bahía Blanca, Bahía Blanca
SA03)	LV9	840	25/5	R. Salta AM 840, Salta
CF18)		840	5	R. General Belgrano, Ciudad Evita
BA182)		850	1	AM 850 La Gauchita, Merlo
BA139)		‡860	0.5	R. Digital, Lanus
SC07)	LRA56	860	1	R. Nacional, Perito Moreno
RN14)		860		San Carlos de Bariloche – F.Pl
CF05)	LRA1	870	100	R. Nacional, Buenos Aires
RN12)		880	1/0.25	R. Provincial de Sierra Colorada, Sierra Colorada
SC06)	LU14	‡880	10/5	R. Provincia de Santa Cruz, Las Heras (//LU14 830)
BA183)		890	10	R. Libre, Villa Caraza

MW	Call	kHz	kW	Station, location and h of tr
LP02)	LU33	890	20/1	Emisora Pampeana, Santa Rosa
SE01)	LV11	890	25/5	Em. Santiago del Estero, Rubia Moreno
CS03)	LT7	900	25/2.5	R. Provincia de Corrientes, Corrientes
LP05)		900	10/1	R. Municipal, 25 de Mayo
SJ02)	LRA23	910	25/5	R. Nacional, San Juan
CF06)	LR5	910	150	R. La Red, Ituzaingó
TU02)	LV7	930	25/1	R. Tucumán, San Miguel de Tucumán
CO09)	LV28	930	5/0.5	R. Villa María, Villa María
BA138)		930	5	R. Nativa, Ciudad Evita
SL03)	LRJ241	940	20/5	R. Dimensión, San Luís
ER07)	LRH200	940	3/0.5	R. Chajarí, Chajarí
CF07)	LR3	950	25/5	CNN – R.Argentina, Buenos Aires
CH04)	LT16	950	25/5	RSP - R. Sáenz Peña, Roque Saénz Peña
ME05)	LRA6	960	25/5	R. Nacional,Mendoza
BA06)	LU13	960	10/1	R. Necochea, Necochea
CF35)		970	3	R. Génesis, Valentin Alsina
CS07)	LT25	970	5/1	R. Guaraní, Curuzú Cuatiá
NE12)	LRA43	‡970	25	R. Nacional, Neuquén (F.Pl)
LP03)	LU37	980	3/1	R. General Pico "Radio37"
ER06)	LT39	980	5/1	R. Victoria, Victoria
JU06)		‡980	5/1	San Salvador de Jujuy (F.Pl.)
RN11)		980	25/1	R. Luján Valcheta, Valcheta
SC08)		‡980	25/5	Rio Gallegos (F.Pl.
CF12)	LR4	990	25/5	AM 990 - R. de Verdad, Villa Dominico
SJ03)	LRJ201	990	1	R. Calingasta, Tamberías
FO03)	LRH203	990	25/5	R. AM 990, Formosa
BA120)		1000	1	R. Sintonia, José C.Paz
LR03)		‡1000	10/1	La Rioja (FPl.)
RN05)	LU16	1000	5/1	R. Río Negro, Villa Regina
CS06)	LT42	1000	1/0.25	R. Del Iberá, Mercedes
CH09)		‡1000	5/1	Comodoro Rivadavia (FPl.)
CO04)	LV16	1010	20/5	R. Rio Cuarto, Rio Cuarto
CF15)		1010	4	R. Onda Latina, Valentin Alsina
SJ07)	LRJ214	1020	25/2.5	AM Mil 20, San Juan
SF03)	LT10	1020	10/5	R. Univ. Nal. del Litoral, Santa Fé
CH02)	LRA58	1020	1/0.5	R. Nacional, Río Mayo
CF08)	LS10	1030	100	R. del Plata, Buenos Aires
LP06)	LRG203	1040	10/1	R. Capital "Antena 10", Santa Rosa
CF50)		1050	1.3	R. General Güemes, Villa Lynch
CO08)	LV27	1050	10/1	R. San Francisco, San Francisco
BA56		1060	1.5	R. Excelsior, Monte Grande
CB11)		‡1070	2 5/1	Paseo de Indios (FPl)
BA08)	LU3	1080	25/5	Ondas del Sur, Bahía Blanca:
CO21)		1080	10/1	AM 1080, Paso de los Libres (FPl)
SA06)	LW4	‡1080	0.25	R. Orán, Argentina
BA141)		1090	3	R. Décadas, José León Suárez
SF17)		1090	1	AM Libertad , Rosario
BA66)		1100	1	R. Estilo, Glew
CO17)		1100	10/0.5	R. Mitre, Corrientes
LP08)	LRG204	1100	5/0.5	Red Pampeana, General Pico
CF03)	LS1	1110	25/5	R. de la Ciudad, Dique Luján
BA184)		1120	1	R. Sudamericana, San Andrés
BA198)		1120	1	Em. Santiago y Copla, Ciudad Evita
SJ04)	LV5	1120	25/5	R. Sarmiento, San Juan
TU04)	LRK204	1120	1/0.5	R. 21, San Miguel
BA229)		1130	5	R. Show, Francisco Alvarez
SE02)	LRA21	1130	25/5	R. Nacional, Santiago del Estero
BA12)	LU22	‡1140	10/1	R. Tandil, Tandil
BA208)		1140	1	R. La Luna, El Palomar
RN06)	LRA2	1150	25/5	R. Nacional, Viedma
SJ05)	LRA51	1150	5/1	R. Nacional, Jáchal
SF04)	LT9	1150	10/1	R. Brigadier López, Santa Fé
MS07)	LRH202	1150	50/5	R. Tupámbaé, Posadas
BA154)		1150	0.1	R. Sagrada Familia (R. Maria), Ciudad Madero
RN07)	LRA57	1160	5/1	R. Nacional, El Bolsón
MS04)	LRH253	1160	5/0.5	R. Cataratas (CNN), Pto. Iguazú:
BA10)	LU32	1160	5/2.5	R. Coronel Olavarría, Olavarría
BA185)		1160	1	R. Independencia, Remedios de Escalada
SA07)		‡1160	5/1	Salta (FPl.)
SL02)	LRA29	1170	10/5	R. Nacional, San Luis
BA77)		1170	5	La R. de Mi País, Hurlingham
BA155)	LRI230	1180	1/0.5	R. de la Sierra, Tandil (R.Maria)
BA253)		1180	0.25	AM San Ponciano, Abasto
BA232)		1190		R. La Más Santiagueña, Gregorio de Laferrere: 0900-0300
TU03)	LRA15	1190	50/5	R. Nacional, San Miguel de Tucumán
CF10)	LR9	‡1190		R. Perfil, Buenos Aires (F.Pl)
BA241)		1200		R.Juventud, Florencia Varela
CB09)	LRF203	1200	5/1	R. 3 Andina "Cad. Patagonia", Esquel
CS04)	LT6	1200	5/1.5	R. Goya, Goya
ME05a)		1200	1/0.5	Uspallata
TF04)		‡1200	5/1	Rio Grande (F.Pl)
BA29)	LRI229	1210	1/0.5	R. Las Flores, Las Flores
BA200)		1210	1.5	R. Mailin, Gregorio de Laferrere (nf 1330)
BA233)		1210		R. del Promesero, José C. Paz
BA83)	LRI224	1220	10/5	R. Onda Marina, Mar del Plata (Cad. Eco)
CF16)		1220	5/1	Eco R. AM 1210, Buenos Aires
CH06)		‡1220	1	Precidencia Roque Sáenz Peña - fpl
SF05)	LT2	1230	25/5	R. Gen. San Martín "R.Dos", Rosario
JU05)	LW5	1230	5/1	R. Libertador, General San Martin
BA89)		1230	1	R. Litoral, Isidro Casanova
CF44)		‡1230	1	R. Creativa, Lanus
BA127)		‡1230		R. Claridad, Monte Grande (nf 1080)
BA230)	LRI218	1240	10/1	R. Universidad Nal. del Sur, Bahia Blanca
CF31)		1240	1	R. Cadena Uno, Ciudadela
BA31)		‡1250	10	R. Estirpe Nacional, San Justo
BA131)		1260	0.5	R. Amor, Villa Tesel
BA269)		1260		AM 1260-Somos Parte de Tu Vida, Temperly
ER02)	LT14	1260	10/5	R. Nacional General Urquiza, Paraná
NE10)		‡1260		R. y Television del Neuquén, Neuquén (F.Pl)
FO02)	LRA20	1270	25/5	R. Nacional, Las Lomitas
BA11)	LS11	1270	100/25	R. Provincia de Buenos Aires, La Plata
BA15)	LU11	1280	7/1.5	R. Trenque Lauquén, Tr. Lauquén
CF17)		‡1280	6	R. Cadena. Eco, CA Buenos Aires (nf 1530)
BA244)		1280	5	AM 1280 La R.,Gregorio de Laferrere
SF11)	LRI371	1290	1/0.5	R. Amanecer, Reconquista
BA53)		1290	1	R. Interactiva, Ciudad Madero
ME10)	LRJ212	1290	5/1	R. Murialdo, Villa Nueva de Guaymallén
SF06)	LRA5	1300	10/1	R. Nacional, Rosario
BA72)		1290	1	R. Provinciana, San Miguel (nf 1290)
CF26)		1300	2	R. La Salada - RLS, Buenos Aires
ME17)		1300	5/1	R. Mitre, San Rafael
BA90)		1310		R. Imagen, Castelar
BA199)		1310	0.25	Gesell Radio, Villa Gesell
BA205)		1310	0.8	AM Renecar,Moreno (nf 1340)
ER03)	LRA42	1310	10/5	R. Nacional, Gualeguaychú
NE06)		1310	0.5	R. Dr. Gregorio Alvarez Piedra del Aguila
BA13)	LU10	1320	5/3	R. Azul, Azul
BA63)		‡1320		Plus R., Lanús
BA187)		1320	1	R. Máster, Luján
BA209)		‡1320		R. Area Uno, Caseros
BA261)		‡1320	0.5	R. Sintonia, Canning
BA275)		1320		R.Santa Catalina, José C. Paz
ME09)	LV24	1320	5/1	R. Andina, Tunuyán
SF19)	LRI237	1330	10/1	AM Rosario, Rosario
BA205)		1340	0.8	R. Renacer, Moreno
CS08)		‡1340	1/0.25	Goya (F.Pl.)
ER13)		1340	1	R. Mediterránea, Rosario del Tala
CF11)	LS6	1350	25/5	R. Buenos Aires, Burzaco
CH07)		‡1350	1/0.25	Juan José Castelli, Chaco (F.Pl.)
CO13)		‡1350	5/1	R. Sucesos, Villa Carlos Paz
BA38)		1360	0.4	R. Nuestra Señore de Itatí, Morón
ER15)		1360	0.25	AM 1360 - R. Cooperativa Estirpe Entrerriana, Maria Grande
RN08)	LRA54	1370	10/5	R. Nacional, Ingeniero Jacobacci
BA76)		1370	3	AM Trece-70, González Catan
BA226)		‡1370	0.25	Junin (F.Pl.)
SF20)		1370	1/0.25	ADN Radio, Rafaela
BA144)		1380	2	R. Buenas Nuevas, Merlo
BA179)		1380	0.5	R. AM Súper Sport, Temperley
BA190)	LRI231	1380	5/1	AM 1380 R.Necochea, Necochea
BA14)	LR11	1390	12/3	R. Univ. Nacional, La Plata
BA216)		1390		R.General Paz,José C Paz
BA254)		‡1390		La Rocha Azul AM 1390, Libertad
ME18)	LRJ217	1390	1/0.25	R.Municipal. Malargü (F.Pl)
BA266)		‡1400	1	R. Carandá, Gregorio de Laferrerè
BA276)		1400		R.Salavina, Moron
CO22)	LRI216	1400	1/0.25	Universidad de Villa Maria
NE07)	LRG202	1400	5/1	R. Cumbre, Neuquén
CH08)	LRH207	1400	1/0.25	AM del NEA, Charata
BA42)		1410	5/1	R. Folclorismo, José León Suárez
BA214)		1410	0.5	R. Fundacion, Rafael Calzada
BA218)		1410	1	La Mil 1410, Chivilcoy
ME15)		1410	1/0.25	Godoy Cruz – (F.Pl)

MW	Call	kHz	kW	Station, location and h of tr
SL04)		1410	0.5	R. María de La Paz, Villa Mercedes
BA108)		1420	1	R. General Conesa, General Conesa
CF28)	LRI220	1420	1/0.25	AM 1420 Con Vos, Villa Martelli
JU04)	LRK221	1420	1/0.25	R. Ciudad Perico, Perico
SL05)		1420		R. Grandero Puntanos, San Luis
BA16)	LT24	1430	1/0.25	R. San Nicolas, San Nicolás
CA02)		‡1430	5/1	San Fernando del Valle (F.PI)
CO06)	LV26	1430	1/0.25	R. Rio Tercero, Río Tercero
BA212)		1430	1	R. Cunumi Guasú, Rafael Castillo
BA257)		1440		R. AM 1440 "La R. Cooperativa", Mar de Ajó
NE03)	LRA53	1440	5/1	R. Nacional San Martín de los Andes
BA18)	LU36	1440	0.25	R. Coronel Suárez, Coronel Suárez
CO07)	LV20	1440	1/0.25	R. Laboulaye, Laboulaye
BA52)		1440	2	R. Impacto, Ciudad Madero
BA234)		‡1440	0.25	Villa Gesell (F.PI)
SE04)		‡1440	5/1	Santiago del Estero (F.PI)
SF12)	LRI221	1440	1/0.25	R. General Obligado, Reconquista
BA235)		1450	5	AM Banderas, Moreno
CF37)	LRI213	1450	5/1	R. El Sol, Don Bosco
CS09)		‡1450	5/1	R. Epoca, Corrientes (F.PI)
LP09)		‡1450	1/0.25	General Acha (F.PI)
SF26)		‡1450	1/0.25	Ceres (F.PI)
SJ06)	LRJ211	1450	1/0.25	R. AM Las 40, Villa Aberastain
SF08)	LT29	1460	1/0.25	R. Venado Tuerto, Venado Tuerto
BA19)	LU30	1460	0.25	R. Maipú (Cad. Eco), Maipú
BA20)	LU34	1460	0.1	R. Pigüé, Pigüé
BA41)		1460	1	R. Contacto, San Antonio de Padua
BA191)		1460	0,25	R. Jerusalén, Monte Grande
BA21)	LT20	±1470	1/0.25	R. Junín, Junin
BA22)	LU26	1470	1/0.5	La Dorrego AM 1470, Coronel Dorrego (r. 1468)
BA174)		‡1470		R. Lider, Mariano Acosta
BA84)		1470	0.7	R. Cad. AM 1470, Remedios de Escalada
ER05)	LT26	1470	1/0.5	R. Nuevo Mundo, San José
RN09)		1470	1	R. Municipal, Luis Beltrán
SF09)	LT28	1470	2/0.5	R. Rafaela, Rafaela
BA147)		1480	1	Tu Voz En R., Tapiales
CO15)	LV22	1490	1/0.25	R. Huinca Renancó, Huinca Renancó:
BA69)		1490	1.5	R. Gama, Lanús
BA169)		1490		R. Dif. Emanuel, Partido de Ezieza (nf 1600)
BA246)		1490		R. Ciudad de Caá Cati, Maquinista Savio
CO18)		1490	1	R. AM Vida, Córdoba
SJ08)		‡1490	1/0.25	Rivadavia (F.PI.)
BA23)	LT34	±1500	0.25	R. Nuclear, Zárate
BA178)		1500	0.25	R. Olivera, General Rodriguez (nf 1590)
BA237)		1500		AM Entre Mares, San Clemente del Tuyú
BA270)		1500		R. Tres Fronteras, Isidro Casanova
CO20)		‡1500		R. Vida, Río Cuarto
ME16)		1500	5/1	Mendoza (F.PI)
BA34)		‡1510		LV del Oeste, Libertad
BA220)		‡1510	1	R. RBN "R. de las Buenas Nuevas", Banfield Oeste
BA74)		‡1510	1	R. Alabanza, Guernica
CH11)		‡1510	2/0.25	Villa Angela (F.PI)
SF14)	LRI253	1510	1/0.25	R. Belgrano, Suardi
ER08)	LT38	1520	0.25	R. Gualeguay, Gualeguay
BA47)		1520	3	R. Cielo Nuevo, Isidro Casanova (nf 1490)
BA92)		1520	5/0.5	R. Chascomus – LV Regional, Chascomús
BA145)		1520	2	R. Norteña, Los Polvorines
BA258)		1520	2	LV del Sur, Luis Guillón
BA274)		1520		R. Palabra de Vida, La Matanza
BA192)		1530	1.5	R. Esencia "LV del Litoral", San Miguel Oeste
BA238)		1530	5	LV del Futuro, Merlo
CO12)	LRJ200	1530	0.25	R. Centro Morteros, Morteros
BA25)	LT35	1540	0.25	R. Mon, Pergamino
BA26)	LU28	1540	0.25	R. Tuyú
BA100)		‡1540	1	R. AM Lider, Benavidez
BA231)		1540		R. Zorobabel, Monte Grande
BA277)		1540		R. Luminares al Mundo, Maximo Paz
SC09)		‡1540		Rio Gallegos (F.PI)
BA251)		1550	1	Estacion Quince Cincuenta, Villa Florito
SF10)	LT23	1550	5/0.25	R. Regional, San Genaro
BA27)	LT32	1550	0.25	R. Chivilcoy, Chivilcoy
BA259)		1550		R. La Amistad, José C. Paz
BA278)		1560		R. Antena, Lobos
ER10)	LT11	1560	10/5	R. Gral. Francisco Ramírez, Concepción del Uruguay
BA28)	LT33	1560	0.25	Cadena Nueve, 9 de Julio
BA44)		1560	1.5	R. Castañares, Ituzaingó
BA194)		1560	0.5/0.25	LV de Tandil, Tandil
ME13)		‡1560	1/0.25	Mendoza (F.PI)
BA55)		1570	2.5	R. Melody, Remedios de Escalada: 1200-0300
BA71)		1570	1	R. AM Rocha, Tolosa
BA163)		‡1570		R. La Morena de Itati, Grand Bourg
BA267)		1570	0.5	R. Eben-Ezer, Ezeiza
BA264)	LRI223	‡1570	5/1	Lomas de Zamora (F.PI)
SF22)		1570		R. La Region, Luis Palacio
ER11)	LT27	1580	0.25	R. LV del Montiel, Villaguay
BA48)		1580	2	AM Tradición, San Martín
BA135)		1580	1	R. 26. de Julio, Longchamps
BA176)	LT36	1580	0.25	R. Chacabuco, Chacabuco
BA247)		1580		R. Cóndor, Moreno
CH10)		‡1580		Charata (F.PI)
MS08)		1580	1	R. La Cueva, 25 de Mayo
BA223)		1590	1	R. Dolores, Dolores
BA271)		1590		R. Americana, Villa Fiorito
CF49)		‡1590		R. Stentor, Buenos Aires
BA37)		1600	1	R. Armonia, Caseros
SF21)		‡1600	0.25	R. EME Centro, Montes de Oca
BA51)		1610	1	R. Luz del Mundo, Rafael Calzada
CO14)		1610	0.5	R. Magica, Laboulaye
BA180)		1620	10/1	AM 16-20 La Radio, Mar del Plata
BA224)		1620		R. Sentires,Merlo
BA279		1620	5/1	Universidad de Buenos Aires (F.PI)
SF25)		1620		R. Mitre, Cañada de Gómez //790
BA219)		‡1630	1	R. Unidad, Alejandro Korn
ER12)	LRI222	1630	10/1	R. America, San José
BA177)		1640	1	R. Hosanna 1640, Isidro Casanova
BA268)		‡1640		General Madariaga (F.PI)
BA239)		‡1650		R. Estrellas, Longchamps
BA156)		1660	1	R. Revivir, Gregorio de la Ferrere
BA265)		‡1660	0.25	Junin (F.PI)
ER14)	LRI232	1660	5/0.25	R. Ciudad de Nogoyá, Nogoyá
CO19)		‡1660	1/0.25	Paso de los Libres (F.PI.)
BA273)		‡1680	0.2	R. G, Quilmes
BA280)		1680	1/0.5	Universidad Tecnlógica Nacional (F.PI)
BA263)		1710		R. Selva, Gonzáles Catán

Addresses & other information:

BA00) BUENOS AIRES (PROV.):

BA01) Moreno 30, 1° Piso, 8000 Bahía Blanca ☎ 291 453 2700 **W:** radionacional.com.ar **E:** administracionlra13@radionacional.gov.ar - **FM**: 95.1 MHz – **BA02)** Hipólito Yrigoyen 2641, 7600Mar del Plata ☎223 494-1039 **W:** lu9mardelplata.com.ar **E:** lu9-adm@lacapitalnet.com.ar - **FM:** 103.3MHz FM 103 Universo – **BA04)** Av. Belgrano 457, 7500 Tres Arroyos ☎2983 42 3504 **W:** lu24.com.ar **E:** noticias@lu24.com.ar - **FM**: 95.3MHz FM Ilusiones – **BA05)** Martiniano Rodriguez 55 8000 Bahía Blanca ☎291 459 0040 **W:** lu2.com.ar **E:** radio@lu2.com.ar - **FM**: 94.7MHz FM Ciudad – **BA06)** Calle 64 Nº 2946, Gran Galería Central, EP, 7630 Necochea ☎2262 42-0100 **E:** administracion@lu13radionecochea.com.ar - **FM**: 88.1MHz FM Oceánica – **BA08)** Av. Lamadrid 116, 8000 Bahía Blanca ☎291 452 0382 **W:** www.lu3ondas.com.ar **E:** radiolu3@yahoo.com.ar - **FM:** 94.3MHz FM Ondas – **BA09)** Córdoba 1865, 7600 Mar del Plata ☎223 491-7047 **W:** lu6.com.ar **E:** radioa@lu6.com.ar - **FM:** 93.3MHz – **BA10)** Alsina 3377, 7400 Olavarría ☎2284 41 0911 **W:** lu32.com.ar **E:** administracion@lu32.com.ar - **FM:** 98.7MHz FM Cristal – **BA11)** Calle 53 Nº. 810, 1900 La Plata ☎221 609 7890 **W:** radioprovincia.gba.gob.ar **E:** radioprovinciarrss@gmail.com - **FM:** 97.1MHz FM Provincia – **BA12)** Gral. Rodriguez 762, PA, 7000 Tandil ☎249 442-4353 **W:**radiotandil.com **E:** contacto@radiotandil.com - **FM:** 97.1MHz Galática FM – **BA13)** Av. Bartolomé Mitre 819, 7300 Azul ☎2281 57-0587 **W:** lu10radioazul.com **E:** lu10radioazul@hotmail.com - **FM:** 89.5MHz FM Más Rock – **BA14)** Calle 48 Nro 566, Piso 8 Edifico Karakachoff, 1900 La Plata ☎221 644-7202 **W:** radiouniversidad.unlp.edu.ar/am-1390 **E:** administracion@radiouniversidad.unlp.edu.ar - **FM:** 107.5MHz – **BA15)** Kienast 7200, 6400 Trenque Lauquen ☎2392 51-6157 **W:** facebook.com/pages/category/Radio-Station/Radio-Rec-Trenque-Lauquen-105140210947891 **E:** am1280radiotrenquelauquen@gmail.com - **FM:** 88.5MHz FM Proyección – **BA16)** Av. Moreno 124, 2900 San Nicolás de los Arroyos ☎336 452-6744 **W:**diariolaciudad.com.ar - **FM:** 88.3MHz FM 88 – **BA18)** Garibaldi 71, 7540 Coronel Suárez ☎2926 43-2706 **W:** radiocoronelsuarez.com.ar **E:** hdukartproductora@hotmail.com - **FM:** 100.5MHz "Frecuencia 36" – **BA19)** Lavalle Sud 312, 7160 Maipú ☎2268 42-1774 **W:** lu30radiomaipu.com.ar **E:** lu30rm@yahoo.com.ar - **FM:** 104.1 FM Cristal – **BA20)** Lavalle 210, 8170 Pigüé ☎2923 4 2205 **W:** radiopigue.com.ar **E:** radiolu34@

s8.coopenet.com.ar - **FM:** 96.3MHz FM Serrana – **BA21)** Roque Sáenz Peña 167, 6000 Junín ☎236 463 3610 **W:** radiojunin.com **E:** mensajes.radio@grupolaverdad.com - **FM:** 89.1MHz Nova Retro – **BA22)** Maciel 282, 8150 Coronel Dorrego ☎2921 40 6576 **W:** ladorrego.com.ar **E:** ladorrego@yahoo.com.ar – **BA23)** Independencia 501, 2800 Zárate ☎3487 42-3116 **W:** radionuclear.com.ar **E:** radionuclear@gmail.com - **FM:** 90.1MHz FM Top – **BA25)** Dr. Alem 340, 2700 Pergamino ☎2477 42 4022 **W:** lt35radiomon.com.ar **E:** lt35radiomon@speedy.com.ar - **FM:** 90.3MHz FM Mágica – **BA26)** Av. San Martín 366, 7163 General Madariaga ☎ 2267 55-1540 **W:**radiotuyu.blogspot.com **E:** radiotuyu@telpin.com.ar - **FM:** 92.5MHz FM Tuy – **BA27)** Av. Mitre 924. 6620 Chivilcoy ☎2346 58-3073 **W:** laradiodechivilcoy.com.ar **E:** radiochivilcoy@gmail.com- **FM:** 101.1MHz FM Sónica – **BA28)** Pte. Hipólito Yrigoyen 969, 6500 9 de Julio ☎2317 52-1333 **W:** cadenanueve.com **E:** lt33@cadenanueve.com - **FM:** 89.9MHz Maxima FM – **BA29)** Av. Avellaneda 773, 7200 Las Flores ☎2244 45 2320 **W:** radiolasflores.com **E:** am1210@hotmail.com - **FM:** 89.7MHz FM Condor – **BA31)** Juan Florio 3573, 1754 San Justo ☎11 4441-1400 **W:** facebook.com/LRI208ESTACION820 **E:** estirpe1250@yahoo.com.ar – **BA33)** Antonio Sáenz 572, 2° piso, 1832 Lomas de Zamora ☎11 4243 7891 **W:** radioestacion820.com.ar **E:** administracion@estacion820.com.ar - **FM:**90.3 FM Familia – **BA34)** Isla Soledad 2510, 1716 Libertad ☎220 497-4623 **W:** lavozdeloesteam1510.com **E:** lavozdeloesteam1510@hotmail.com – **BA36)** Avenida Dr. Ignacio Ariota 3950 1754 San Justo ☎11 4651-0193 **W:** am660.com.ar **E:** am660khz@gmail.com – **BA37)** Wenceslao Paunero 2915, 1678 Caseros ☎11 4716-2279 **W:** am1600armonia.com **E:** armoniaam1600@gmail.com – **BA38)** San Luís 991, 1708 Morón ☎11 4627-7439 **W:** radioitati.com.ar – **BA41)** Agustin Zárate 154, 1718 San Antonio de Padua ☎220 482-4526 **W:** amcontacto.blogspot.com **E:** contacto1460@gmail.com – **BA42)** Lacroze 7277 (Ex 1871), 1655 José León Suárez ☎11 4720 2688 **W:** radiofolclorisimo.com.ar **E:** folclorísimo@hotmail.com – **BA44)** Treinta y Tres 1033, Villa Ariza, 1714 Ituzaingó ☎11 4623-7773 **W:** emisoraam1560.blogspot.com.ar **E:** am1560castanares@gmail.com – **BA47)** Juan Jofré 4243, 1765 Isidro Casanova ☎11 4694-8131 **W:** emisoracielonuevo.weebly.com **E:** radio.cielonuevo@hotmail.com – **BA48)** Pueyrredón 3846, 1650 San Martín ☎11 4754 8784 **W:** amtradicion.com.ar **E:** amtradicion@gmail.com – **BA51)** Catamarca 2560, 1847 Rafael Calzada ☎11 4219-1150 **W:** facebook.com/luzdelmundo610 **E:** radioluzdelmundo@gmail.com –**BA52)** Juncal 12, 1° Piso, Of. "3", 1770 Tapiales ☎11 4442-6333 **W:** am-1440.com.ar **E:** impactoam@hotmail.com – **BA53)** Mariquita Sánches de Thompson 1850, 1768 Ciudad Madero ☎11 4622-1570 **W:** radiointeractiva1290.com **E:** radiointeractiva1290@hotmail.com – **BA55)** Las Piedras 2447, 1824 Lanus Este ☎11 4249-6047 **W:** radiomelody1570.com.ar **E:** melody1570@hotmail.es – **BA56)** Andrés Berasain 659, 1842 Monte Grande ☎11 4281-3740 **W:** amexcelsior.com.ar **E:**amexcelsior@gmail.com - **FM:** 91.5MHz FM Malvinas – **BA63)** Eva Perón 1169, 1824 Lanús ☎11 4247-3106 **W:** amplusradio.com **E:** plusradio1300@hotmail.com – **BA66)** Florencio Sánchez 119, Bo Los Alamos, 1856 Glew ☎11-4233 1323 **W:** am1100estilo.blogspot.com **E:** amestilo@hotmail.com – **BA69)** Choele Choel 1233, 1822 Valentín Alsina ☎11 4218-5333 **W:** radiogamaeninternet.com **E:** radiogama@hotmail.com – **BA71)** Calle 39 Nº 256 1902 La Plata ☎221 427-3360 **W:** radiorocha.com **E:** rocha1570@yahoo.com.ar – **BA72)** Domingo F.Sarmiento 2220, 1663 San Miguel ☎11 4667-4460 **W:** radioprovinciana.com **E:** radioprovincianaam1290@hotmail.com – **BA74)** Santiago del Estero 73, 1862 Guernica ☎2224 47-6963 **W:** facebook.com/Radio-Alabanzas-AM-1510-132987926726234 **E:** radioalabanzas@hotmail.com – **BA76)**Av. Cristianía 3747, 1765 Isidro Casanova ☎11 4069-5434 **W:**la1370.com.ar - **FM:** 92.1MHz R. Cosmos – **BA77)** Jauretche 1052, 1° Piso "B", 1686 Hurlingham ☎11 4662 5016 **W:** laradiodemipais.com.ar **E:** info@laradiodemipais.com.ar – **BA83)** Av. Pedro Luro 2237, 16° Piso "A", 7600 Mar del Plata - **FM:** 89.1MHz – **BA84)** Carlos Gardel 1133. 1824 Lanús ☎11 4225-7304 **W:** cadenaam1470.com **E:** info@cadenaam1470.com – **BA89)** Francisco Beazley 1209 1755 Rafael Castillo ☎11 4697-7333 **W:** am1230radiolitoral.com **E:** litoral1230@gmail.com – **BA90)** Madrid 3987, Barrio San Juan, 1712 Castelar ☎11 4692-4412 **W:** amimagen.com.ar **E:** amimagen@gmail.com – **BA91)** Av. General Paz 3755, 1672 Villa Lynch ☎11 4755-9061 **W:** radioam610.com.ar **E:** radioam610@gmail.com – **BA92)** Juárez 250, 7130 Chascomús ☎2241 770-222 **W:** lavozregional.com **E:**radiochascomusam1520@gmail.com - **FM:** 90.9MHz – **BA100)** Pte Hipólito Yrigoyen 51, Oficina 303, 1640 Martinez ☎11 4793-7471 **W:** amlider.com.ar **E:** amlider@gmail.com - **FM:** 99.3MHz – **BA108)** Cnl. Manuel Dorrego 292, 7101 General Conesa ☎2245 49-2180 **W:** am1420.com.ar **E:** am1420radioconesa@hotmail.com – **BA119)** Gral. Martín Miguel de Güemez 5025, 1603 Villa Martelli ☎11 4709-1172 **W:** amitalia.com.ar **E:** radioitalia.am@gmail.com – **BA120)** Domingo F.Sarmiento 4154, 1665 José C.Paz ☎2320 42 3306 **E:** sintonia1000@yahoo.com.ar – **BA127)** Vicente López 235 2º Piso, 1842 Monte Grande ☎11 4284-3192 **W:** radioclaridad.com.ar **E:** radioclaridad@hotmail.com.ar – **BA131)** Cnl. Brandsen 1175, 1646 San Fernando ☎11 4746-6856 **W:** radiooasis92.com **E:** angelbonarrico@yahoo.com.ar - **FM:** 92.5MHz FM Sencacion – **BA135)** Francisco Beiró 567, Glew, Almirante Brown ☎ 22 2443-4726 **W:** radio26dejulio.com **E:** radio26dejulio@gmail.com – **BA138)** Juan Florio 3573, 1754, San Justo ☎11 4482 0419 **W:**amnativa.com.ar **E:** radionativa930@gmail.com – **BA139)** Fray Mamerto Esquiú 1161, 1824 Lanús ☎11 4225-2256 **W:** digital860.blogspot.com – **BA141)** Jauretche 1052, 1° Piso "C", 1686 Hurlingham ☎11 4452-5153 4452 8688 **W:** radiodecadas.com.ar **E:** info@radiodecadas.com.ar – **BA144)** Santa Fe 2540, 1722 Merlo ☎220 485 6696 **W:**radiobuenasnuevas1.wixsite.com/buenasnuevasam1380 **E:** radiobuenasnuevasam1380@yahoo.com.ar - **FM:** 92.5MHz – **BA145)** Ex. Combatientes de Malvinas 2053, 1613 Los Polvorines ☎2320 44-7711 **W:** radionorteña.com.ar **E:** radionortena@hotmail.com – **BA147)** Donovan 1433, 1770 Tapiales ☎11 6088-3980 **W:** am1480.com.ar **E:** info@1480.com.ar – **BA154)** Salta 2641, 1754 San Justo ☎11 4441-8196 - **FM:** 104.5MHz FM Sintonia – **BA155)** Gral. Belgrano 531, 7000 Tandil ☎249 444-6383 **W:** am1180.com.ar **E:** contacto@am1180.com.ar - **FM:** 99.5MHz – **BA156)** Av Bdier. Juan Manuel de Rocas Nº 10840, 1757 Gregorio de Laferrere ☎11 4640-1021 **W:** radiorevivir.net **E:** radiorevivir@gmail.com - **FM:** 89.7MHz – **BA163)** Juan F.Segui 895, 1615 Grand Bourg ☎2320 68-6565 **W:** lamorenadeitati.com – **BA169)** Yatay 628,Bo Lamadrid, 1804 Ezeiza ☎11 4232-7070 **W:** radiodifusoraemanuel.jimdo.com **E:** radiodifusoraemanuel@hotmail.com – **BA172)** Juan Florio 3573, 1754 San Justo ☎11 4482-3393 **W:** radiorepublica670.com.ar – **BA173)** Belgrano 4033, 1650 San Martin ☎11 4713-8808 **W:** facebook.com/Magna.AM680 **E:** radiomagna680@gmail.com – **BA174)** Heredia 920, Augstín Ferrari, 1724 Mariano Acosta ☎220 498-1498 **W:** radiolider1470.blogspot.com **E:** informesam1470@gmail.com – **BA176)** Remedios de Escalada San Martin 76, 6740 Chacabuco ☎2352 42-6156 **W:**lt36radiochacabuco.com.ar **E:** lt36radio_chacabuco@yahoo.com.ar - **FM:** 91.7 MHz FM Universal – **BA177)** Zufriategui 871, 1765 Isidro Casanova ☎11 4467-2468 **W:** radiohosannaam1640.com - **E:** hosannaam1640@hotmail.com – **BA178)** Pedro Laurenz 237, Las Malvinas 1748, General Rodríguez ☎11 3363-3927 **W:** radioolivera.es.tl **E:** radioolivera@yahoo.com.ar – **BA179)** Bombero Ariño 1150, 1834 Temperley ☎11 2098-8508 **W:**lasupersport.com **E:** lasuper@lasupersport.com – **BA180)** Hipólito. Yrigoyen 2629, 7600 Mar del Plata ☎223 494-1428 **E:** am1620@yahoo.com.ar – **BA182)** Salta 138, 2° Piso "C", 1708 Morón ☎11 4489-5240 **E:** lagauchita810@hotmail.com – **BA183)** Av Cnel Ramón L. Falcón 6219 14085 CA Buenos Aires ☎11 4641-2821 **W:** facebook.com/Am890RadioLibre **E:** operadores890@gmail.com – **BA184)** Santa Rosalía (Diagonal 78) 1465 1650 San Andrés ☎11 4839-8145 **W:** sudamericana1120.com.ar **E:** info@sudamericana1120.com.ar – **BA185)** Fray Mamerto Esquiú 2855, 1826 Remedios de Escalada ☎11 4225-3198 **W:** radioindependencia.com.ar **E:** radioindependencia@hotmail.com - **FM:** 99.3MHz Radio G – **BA187)** Las Heras 1478, 6700 Luján ☎2323 42-9595 **W:** radiomasterlujan.com.ar **E:** master1310@ciudad.com.ar – **BA190)** Avenida 59 N° 2465, PA, 7630 Necochea ☎2262 52-0003 - **FM:** 103.9MHz – **BA191)** Guatemala 1856, 1838 Luis Gullión ☎11 4272 9005 **W:** jerusalenradio.com **E:** info@jerusalenradio.com – **BA192)** Paula Albarracin 3957, Barrio Sarmiento 1663 San Miguel Oeste ☎2320 46-0649 **W:** amesencia.com.ar **E:** radioesencia@live.com.ar – **BA194)** Av. Aristóbulo del Valle 1202, 7000 Tandil ☎249 444-8008 **W:**lavozdetandil.com.ar **E:** 1560@lavozdetandil.com.ar – **BA198)** Luis Vernet 6654, 1757 Gregorio de Laferrere ☎11 6863-1120 **W:** santiagoycopla.com.ar **E:**info@santiagoycopla.com.ar – **BA199)** Av. Buenos Aires 735, Galeria Pinar, Local 11, 7165 Villa Gesell ☎2255 47-6749 **E:** am1310gesell@hotmail.com - **FM:** 89.9MHz – **BA200)** Calle Carabobo 5493, 1753 Villa Luzuraga ☎11 4466-4294 **W:** radiomailin.com.ar **E:** radiomailinam1330@gmail.com – **BA205)** Ottone de Asconape 371, 1742 Paso del Rey ☎237 460-0878 **W:**amrenacer.com.ar **E:** radiorenaceram1340@hotmail.com – **BA208)** Ramón L.Falcón 2193, 1685 El Palomar ☎11 4443 7424 **W:** radiolaluna.com.ar **E:**am1140radiolaluna@gmail.com - **FM:** 90.7MHz – **BA209)** Dr. Rebizzo- (Calle 626) - Nº 3917 1678 Caseros ☎11 4578-5130 **E:** radioarea1@gmail.com – **BA212)** Marcelo T.de Alvear 548 1755 Rafael Castillo ☎11 4697-4919 **W:** cunumiguasu.com.ar **E:** cunumiquasu@hotmail.com – **BA214)** Juan Lavalle 2307, 1847 Rafael

Calzada ☎11 4219-1903 **W:** radiofundacion.org.ar **E:**radiofundacion@gmail.com – **BA216)** Andrés Blanqui 4233, 1666 José C. Paz ☎2320 59-9321 **E:** generalpazam1390@hotmail.com – **BA218)** General Pinto 230,6620 Chivilcoy ☎2346 42-4532 **W:** lagacetadeloeste.com.ar **E:** cope1410@gmail.com - **FM:** 101.5 MHz – **BA219)** Juan Manuel de Rosas 1053, 1852 Glew ☎2225 42-6063 **W:** radiounidadam1630.com **E:** radiounidad941@yahoo.com.ar - **FM:** 94.1MHz – **BA220)** Ejército de los Andes 5, 1821 Villa Florito ☎11 4276-2423 **W:** rbn1510am.com.ar **E:** rbn_am1510@hotmail.com – **BA223)** Faustino Brughetti 1392, 7100 Dolores ☎2245 42-4280 **W:** radiodolores.com.ar **E:** radiodolores@hotmail.com - **FM:** 94.9MHz Red 94 – **BA224)** Mozart 1015, 1721 Parque San Martin, Merlo ☎220 470-4265 **W:** amsentires.com.ar **E:** sentires1620@hotmail.com – **BA226)** Bernardo de Irigoyen 423, 6000 Junin ☎236 442 2299 **W:** dimarcomedios.com **E:** condor@dimarcointernacional.com - **FM:** 96.5MHz – **BA229)** Lavalle 1625. P.B., Oficina 4 1048 CA Buenos Aires ☎11-4372 1548 **W:** am1130.com.ar **E:** am1130radio@gmail.com – **BA230)** San Andrés 800, Barrio Altos de Palihue, 8000 Bahia Blanca ☎291 459-5190 **W:** radio.uns.edu.ar **E:** radio@uns.edu.ar – **BA231)** Carmen d Areco 406, Barrio Santa Lucia, 1841 Monte Grande ☎11 4263-4108 **W:** radiojcb.com.ar/player-zorobabel – **BA232)** Hilario Ascasubi 4446 1757 Gregorio de Laferrere ☎11 2766-4041 **W:** lamasantiagueña.com **E:** amoncenoventa@gmail.com – **BA233)** Dr. Carlos Saavedra Lamas 3636, 1666 José C. Paz ☎2320 45-3200 **W:** facebook.com/groups/383600008327857 - **FM:** 91.3MHz – **BA234)** Villa Gesell – **BA235)** Av Gaona 6589, Colectora Norte - 1743 Moreno ☎237 468-7766 **W:** ambanderas.com.ar **E:** banderas@gmail.com – **BA237)** Calle 51 N° 559, 7105 San Clemente del Tuyú ☎15 3889-4419 **W:** amentremares.com.ar **E:** amentremares@hotmail.com - **FM:** 101.7 MHz Cadena Virtual – **BA238)** Patricias Argentinas 456, Parque San Martin, 1721 Merlo ☎220 480-2134 **W:** am1530.com.ar **E:** info@am1530.com.ar – **BA239)** Carlos Diehl 2196, 1854 Longchamps ☎11 2119-9094 W: radiolasestrellas.com.ar **E:**radio@radiolasestrellas.com.ar – **BA241)** Cjal. José Dans Rey, Calle 26 - N° 742, 1887 Florencia Varela ☎11 4255-0739 – **BA244)** Soberania Nacional 2945, 1757 Gregorio de Laferrere ☎11 4457 3674 **W:** elsonidodelagente.com.ar – **BA246)** Chaco 67 1620 Maquinista Savio ☎348 448-3825 **E:**radioam1490caacati@gmail.com – **BA247)** Sófocles 4825, 1743 Moreno ☎237 468-7195 **W:** facebook.com/Radio-condor-am-1580 **E:** radiocondoram1580@hotmail.com – **BA251)** Traful 3836, PA, 1437 Buenos Aires ☎11 4911-0270 **W:** am1550.com.ar **E:** estacion1550@gmail.com – **BA253)** Call 515 s/n, e /Calles 203 y 204, 1903 Abasto, La Plata ☎221 491-6476 **W:** fmsanponciano.com.ar **E:** fmsanponciamo@yahoo.com.ar - **FM:** 99.7MHz – **BA254)** Aconquija 1053 1716 Libertad ☎220 494-2303 **W:** facebook.com/wwwlarocaazulam1390 **E:** dijitalradio@hotmail.com.ar – **BA257)** Azopardo 186, 7109 Mar de Ajó ☎2257 60-4540 **W:** radioam1440.com.ar **E:** radioam1440@gmail.com – **BA258)** Robertson 1249, 1° Piso "B", 1838 Luis Guillón ☎11 4290-2892 **W:** lavozdelsur.com.ar **E:** amlavozdelsur@gmail.com – **BA259)** General Arenales 2154, 1666José C. Paz **W:** radiolaamistad.com **E:** radiolaamistad@hotmail.com – **BA261)** Alvarez de Toledo 3150, 1847 Monte Grande ☎11 4235-1510 **W:** fmsintonia977.blogspot.com.ar **E:** fmsintonia977@hotmail.com - **FM:** 97.7 MHz – **BA263)** General Villegas 2157, 1714 Ituzaingó ☎11 6088-8991 **W:** facebook.com/amselva1710 **E:** amselva1710@gmail.com – **BA264)** Laprida 1166, 1832 Lomas de Zamora – **BA265)** Junin – **BA266)** Calle Soberania Nacional 2945,1757 Gregorio de Laferrère ☎11 4457-8712 – **BA267)** Catamarca 445, Villa Golf, 1803 La Union-Ezeiza ☎11 4295-2246 **W:** radiodediosebenezer.org **E:** radio@radiodediosebenezer.org – **BA268)** General Madariaga – **BA269)** El Mirasol 2921, 1834 Temperly ☎11 4264-3088 **W:** 1260am.com.ar **E:** info@1260am.com.ar - **FM:** 94.5 R.JCB – **BA270)**Isidor Casanova ☎11 2069-2380 **W.:** radiotresfronteras.com **E:**info@radiotresfronteras.com – **BA271)** Ejército de los Andes 501 1821 Villa Fiorito ☎11 4276-2396 **W:** radiofmlitoral.com.ar – **BA273)**844 Avenue 899, 1855 Villa la Florida, Quilmes ☎11 4280-0212 **E:** benza3039@gmail.com – **BA274)** Calle Octavio Massotti 5850, Virry del Pino, La Matanza ☎2202 49-9792 **W:**Facebook.com/iglesia.palabravida.39 – **BA275)** Ca Nueva Granada 222 escuina Martin Coronado, Parade La Sonia, José C.Paz ☎2320 45-5318 **W:** facebook.com/pages/category/Festival/Salon-Albertito-1712544718854826 – **BA276)**Calle 14 de Julio 3384, Barrio Marina, Mérlo Gómez Castelar ☎11 7398-8791 – **BA277)** Maximo Paz **W:** reproface.com.ar/luminaries.html – **BA278)** Aristóbulo del Valle 23, 7240 Lobos ☎2227 42-1211 **W:** amradioantena.com **E:** arielgardenal@hotmail.com – **BA279)** Buenos Aires – **BA280)** Av. Ramón France 5050, 1874 Villa Dominico ☎11 4227-0037 **W:** fra.utn.edu.ar - **FM:** 88.3 MHz FM La Tecnica

CA00) CATAMARCA:
CA01) Chacabuco 762, 4700 S.F. del Valle de Catamarca ☎383 442-4223 **W:** radionacional.com.ar **E:** nacionalcatamarca@gmail.com - **FM:** 103.5MHz – **CA02)** San Fernando del Valle, Catamatca

CB00) CHUBUT:
CB01) Av. Alvear 1180, 9200 Esquel ☎2945 45-1900 **W:** radionacional.com.ar **E:** esquel@radionacional.gov.ar - **FM:** 88.7MHz – **CB02)** Av. Hipólito Yrigoyen 1735, 9102 Trelew ☎280 443-0580 **W:** radiochubut.com **E:** info@radiochubut.com - **FM:** 95.7MHz Galaxia – **CB03)** 25 de Mayo 453, 9000 Comodoro Rivadavia ☎297 447-2125 **W:** radionacional.com.ar **E:** nacionalcomodoro@hotmail.com - **FM:** 94.7MHz – **CB04)** Estivariz 226, 9120 Puerto Madryn ☎280 445-9200 **W:** lu17.com **E:** lu17@lu17.com - **FM:** 96.1MHz Paraiso FM – **CB05)** Av. Rivadavia 198, 9000 Comodoro Rivadavia ☎297 447 -6570 **W:** lu4radio.com.ar **E:** direccion@lu4radio.com.ar - **FM:** 101.7MHz FM Alfa – **CB06)** 25 de Mayo 740, 9100 Trelew ☎280 443-5221 **W:** radio3cadenapatagonia.com **E:** radio3noticias@gmail.com – **CB07)**. Patagonia Argentina y Mariano Moreno, 9033 Alto Rio Senguer ☎2945 49-7050 **W:** radionacional.com.ar **E:** lra_55@hotmail.com - **FM:** 93.5MHz – **CB09)** 25 de Mayo 740 9100 Trelew ☎280 443-5221 **W:** radio3cadenapatagonia.com.ar **E:** radio3noticias@gmail.com – **CB11)** Paseo de Indioas

CF00) CIUDAD AUTÓNOMA DE BUENOS AIRES (BUENOS AIRES):
CF01) Calle Gorriti 5995, Barrio de Palemero, 1414 CA Buenos Aires ☎11 4338-4250 **W:** continental.com.ar – **CF02)** Arenales 2467, 1124 CA Buenos Aires ☎11 5219-4744 **W:** rivadavia.com.ar **E:** info@rivadavia.com.ar - **FM:** 103.1 R.Uno – **CF03)** Sarmiento 1551, 8° Piso, 1042 CA Buenos Aires ☎11 5371 -4638 **W:** buenosaires.gob.ar/medios/radio-ciudad-am-1110 **E:** laoncediez@gmail.com – **CF04)** Gral. Mansilla 2668, 1° piso 1425 CA Buenos Aires ☎11 5777-1500 **W:** radiomitre.cienradios.com **E:** info@radiomitre.com.ar – **CF05)** Maipú 555, 1006 CA Buenos Aires ☎11 4327-3021**W:** radionacional.com.ar **E:** redesosiales@radionacional.goc.ar - **External Sce:** see Int. Broadc. section – **CF06)** Angel Justiano Carranza 1441 1414 CA Buenos Aires ☎11 4535-2011 **W:** lared.am **E:** info@radiolared.com.ar – **CF07)** Av Pueyrredón 1080, 2° Piso, 1118 CA Buenos Aires ☎11 5239- 2000 **W:** cnnespanol.cnn.com/seccion/cnn-radio-argentina **E:** socialmedia@cnnradio.com.ar – **CF08)** José Ignacio Gottiti 5963, 1414 CA Buenos Aires ☎11 4532-2222 **W:** facebook.com/radiodelplata1030/**E:** radiodelplata@hotmail.com – **CF10)** California 2715 1289 CA Buenos Aires ☎11 5985-4000 – **CF11)** Av. Entre Ríos 1931, 1133 CA Buenos Aires ☎11 4307-2200 **W:** radiobuenosaires.com.ar - **FM:** 106.3 R.Aleluya – **CF12)** Conde 935, 1426 CA Buenos Aires ☎11 3828-0990 **W:** la990.com.ar **E:** la990radio@gmail.com – **CF13)** Olleros 3551, 1414 CA Buenos Aires ☎11 4535 4000 **W:** minutouno.com/radio10 **E:** info@minutouno.com – **CF15)** Sarmiento 1586, 6° Piso "E", 2° Cuerpo, 1042 CA Buenos Aires ☎11 4199-5346 **W:** am1010ondalatina.com.ar **E:** contactoam1010@yahoo.com.ar – **CF16)** Lavalle 900, 9° Piso B, 1047 CA Buenos Aires ☎11 4325 1220 **W:** ecomedios.com **E:**contacto@ecomedios.com – **CF18)** Traful 3834, Pompeya 1437 CA Buenos Aires ☎11 4912-0497 **W:** am840generalbelgrano.com **E:** am840generalbelgrano@hotmail.com – **CF21)** Austria 1873 1 "B", 1425 Recoleta, CA Buenos Aires ☎11 5275 0770 **W:** radiocooperativa.com.ar **E:** contacto@radiocooperativa.com.ar – **CF24)** Lavalle 1625, P.B., Oficina 4, 1048 CA Buenos Aires ☎11 4371-2597 **W:** radiodelpueblo.com.ar **E:** gerencia@radiodelpueblo.com.ar – **CF26)** Bonpland 1114, 1414 CA Buenos Aires ☎11 4856 8043 **W:** am1300lasalada.com **E:** info@am1300lasalada.com – **CF27)** Maipu 267 7° Piso, 1084 CA Buenos Aires ☎11 4136-1050 **W:** conceptoam.com.ar **E:** radio@conceptoam.com.ar – **CF28)** Humboldt 1477, 1414 CA Buenos Aires ☎11 4778-8200 **W:** amconvos.com.ar **E:**info@amconvos.com.ar - **FM:** 89.9 MHz– **CF30)** San Martin 569 2° Piso "7", 1004 CA Buenos Aires ☎11 4535-5707 **W:** am570radioargentina.com.ar **E:** info@am570radioargentina.com.ar – **CF31)** Cerrito 228, Piso 2 Oficina "A", 1010 CA Buenos Aires ☎11 4541-0303 **W:** cadenauno1240.com.ar **E:** info@cadenauno1240.com.ar – **CF34)** Pte. Luis Sàenz Peña 210 1110 CA Buenos Aires ☎11 5277-3533 **W:** am530somosradio.com **E:** radio530somos@gmail.com – **CF35)** Santander 970, 1424 CA Buenos Aires ☎11 4926-1622 **W:** radiogenesis970.com **E:** radiogenesis970@gmail.com – **CF37)** Avenida Alicia Moreau de Justo 2050, 1°P, Of. "132", 1107 CA Buenos Aires ☎11 4893-7555 **W:** radioelsol.com.ar **E:** radio@radioelsol.com.ar – **CF38)** San Martín 569, 2° Piso "6", 1004 CA Buenos Aires ☎11 4893-1701 **W:** belgrano650.com.ar **E:** info@belgrano650.com.ar – **CF44)** Av. Callao 441, 17° Piso "G", 1022 CA Buenos Aires ☎11 4372-5863 **W:** am1230creativa.com.ar **E:** am1230creativa@yahoo.com.ar – **CF45)** Ulrico Schmidt 6057, 4° Piso, 1440 CA Buenos Aires

☎11 4642-5533 **W:** am690.com.ar **E:** radioam690@yahoo.com.ar – **CF48)** Av.Pueyrrdeón 19, 2° Piso, 1032 CA Buenos Aires ☎11 4524-7816 **W:** rebelde740.com.ar **E:** rebelde740@gmail.com – **CF49)** Libertad 434, 1° Subsuelo, Of. 5, 1012 CA Buenos Aires ☎15 6565 2476 **W:** facebook.com/Am1590Stentor – **CF50)** Diagonal Roque Saenz Pena 124, 1010 Buenos Aires ☎11 5943-6804 **W:** facebook.com/guemesam/**E:** guemes1050am@gmail.com – **CF51)** Venezuela 370, 2° piso, 1095 CA Buenos Aires ☎11 5354-6651 **W:** radioam750.com.ar **E:** contacto@radioam750.co.ar - **FM.** 89.1 Octubre FM – **CF52)** Ramón L Falcón 6219, Linieres, 1408 CA Buenos Aires ☎11 4641-3920 **W:** 810am.com.ar **E** operadores810@gmail.com – **CF53)** Ca Ulrico Schmidt 6057, 4° Piso, 1440CA Buenos Aires ☎5411 4641-0359 **W:** am540.com.ar **E:** radioam540@yahoo.com

CH00) CHACO:

CH01) Av. General Güemes 1103, 3370 Charata ☎3731 42 0226 **W:** mocovi.com.ar **E:**publicidadmocovi@yahoo.com.ar - **FM:** 95.7MHz FM Lider – **CH02)** Acceso Ruta Nacional N° 40 s/n, Bo Gendarmería, 9030 Río Mayo ☎2903 42-0099 **W:** radionacional.com.ar **E:** direccionlra58@radionacional.gov.ar - **FM:** 88.1MHz – **CH03)** Av. Sarmiento 1202, 3502 Resistencia ☎362 443-2920 **W:** radionacional.com.ar **E:** larijoa@gmail.com **Guaraní**: Sat. 1800 - **FM:** 96.7MHz – **CH04)** Hermana Hortensia - Calle 19 - N° 151, 3700 Presidencia Roque Sáenz Peña ☎364 442-8047 **W:** radiorsp.com.ar **E:** lt16am950@yahoo.com.ar - **FM:** 93.3MHz FM Sentimientos – **CH05)** Casa de las Culturas, Marcelo T. de Alvear 90, 4° Piso,3500 Resistencia ☎362 441-9319 **W:** chaco.tv/radiochaco - **FM:** 101.5MHz – **CH06)** Av 25 de Mayo 775,3700 Presidencia Roque Sáenz Peña – **CH07)** Ruta Provincial N°5, Charca 3, Circ. 8, Juan José Castelli – **CH08)** Maipú 550 3730 Charata ☎3731 42-1869 **W:** amdelnea.com.ar **E:** nuevaeracharate@gmail.com - **FM:** 92.1 MHz – **CH09)** Comodoro Rivadavia – **CH10)** Santiago de Linieres 46, 3730 Charata – **CH11)** Villa Angela – **CH12)** Domingo Faustino Sarmiento s/n Planta Urbana, Mision Nueva Pompeya

CO00) CORDOBA:

CO01) Fray Miguel de Mojica 1600, Bo Marquez de Sobremonte, 5008 Córdoba ☎351 410-5000 **W:** cba24n.com.ar **E:** am580@srt.com - **FM:** 102.3MHz Más que Musica – **CO02)** Santa Rosa 241, 5000 Córdoba ☎351 422-5663 **W:** radionacional.com.ar **E:**ccnk@radionacional.gov.ar - **FM:** 100.1 MHz – **CO04)** Constitución 399, 5800 Río Cuarto ☎358 463-8255 **W:** lv16.com **E:** lv16@lv16.com - **FM:** 93.9, 106.9MHz – **CO05)** Alvear 139, 5000 Córdoba ☎351 526-0597 **W:** cadena3.com.ar **E**: info@cadena3.com.ar - **FM:** 92.3, 100.5, 106.9MHz – **CO06)** Libertad 455 2° Piso, 5850 Río Tercero ☎3571 42-1019 **W:**facebook.com/lv26radiotiotercero/ **E:** lv26@itc.com.ar - **FM:** 94.5MHz FM Libra – **CO07)** 1 de Mayo 14, 6120 Laboulaye ☎3385 42 0110 **W:** radiolv20.com **E:** info@radiolv20.com - **FM:** 89.9MHz Stereo Atlántica – **CO08)** Córdoba 50,"Edifico Reggio II", 2400San Francisco ☎3564 42-2186 **W:** radiosanfrancisco.com.ar **E:** am1050radio@gmail.com - **FM:** 88.7MHz FM Galaxia – **CO09)** Av Santa Fe 1490, 5900 Villa María ☎353 45-23754 **W:** radiovillamaria.com **E:** contame.radiovillsmaria@gmail.com - **FM:** 98.5MHz FM Record – **CO12)** Blvd. 25 de Mayo 133, PB, 2421 Morteros ☎3562 42-2148 **W:** radiomorteros.com.ar **E:** info@radiomorteros.com.ar - **FM:** 90.3MHz FM Selección – **CO13)** Av. Concepción Arenal 1174, 5004 Córdoba ☎351 460-1010 **W:** radiosucesos.com **E**: radiosucesos@yahoo.com.ar - **FM:** 104.7MHz – **CO14)** Pte.Gral. Julio A. Roca 32, 6120 Laboulaye ☎3385 45-5199 **W:** radiomagicalaboulaye.blogspot.com **E:** radiomagicalaboulaye@gmail.com - **FM:** 106.1 Magica FM – **CO15)** Santa Fé y La Pampa, 6270 Huinca Renancó ☎2336 44-2007 **W:** lv22.com.ar **E:** lv22_1490@yahoo.com.ar – **CO16)** Av. Fernando Fader 3469, Barrio Cerro de Las Rosas, 5009 Córdoba ☎351 526-1330 **W:** radiomitre.cienradios.com/mitre-cordoba **E:** comercial@radiomitre.com - **FM:** 97.9MHz – **CO17)** La Rioja 995, 3400 Corrientes ☎379 442-6600 **W:** mitrecorrientes.com **E:** mitrecorrientes@gmail.com – **FM:** 92.9MHz R.Ciudad – **CO18)** Tolosa 2379, Bo Maipú, 5014 Córdoba ☎351 411-9190 **W:** facebook.com/radioamvida1490 **E:** radioamvida@gmail.com – **CO19)** Paso de los Libres – **CO20)** Muñiz y Colombia, 5800 Río Cuarto ☎358 462-8179 **W:** misiomvida.com.ar **E:** misionvidariocuarto@gmail.com - **FM:** 89.3 MHz – **CO21) Colón 1030,**3230 Paso delos Libres ☎3772 12-3456 – **FM:** Radio 3 93.3 MHz – **CO22)**Blvb. España 210, 5900 Villa Maria ☎353 461-0048 **W:** //fmuniversidadcom.ar/la-radio/ **E:** info@fmuniversidad.com.ar - **FM:** 106.9 MHz

CS00) CORRIENTES:

CS01) Av. General Gervasio Artigas s/n,Chacra 46,La Tablada, 3340 Santo Tomé ☎3756 42-0090 **W:** radionacional.com.ar **E:** santotomelra12@radionacional.gov.ar - **FM:** 100.5MHz – **CS02)** Juan Sitja Nin 941, 3230 Paso de los Libres ☎3772 42-4332 **W:** radiolt12.com.ar **E:** contacto@radiolt12.com.ar - **FM:** 92.7MHz FM Confluencia – **CS03)** La Rioja 743, 3400 Corrientes ☎379 442-3560 **W:** radiolt7.com **E:**radiolt7corrientes@gmail.com - **FM:** 95.3MHz FM Capital – **CS04)** Mariano I. Loza 231, 3450 Goya ☎3777 43-3002 **W:** facebook.com/lt6am1200radiogoya **E:** lt6radiogoya@hotmail.com - **FM:** 98.3MHz FM Splendida – **CS05)** Av.Isaco Abitbol y General Paz 903, 3344 Alvear ☎3772 52-1701 **W:** radiolt21.blogspot.com.ar **E:** radiomunicipalalvear@hotmail.com – **CS06)** Av. Atanaico Aguirre Km 2, 3470 Mercedes ☎3773 420-087 **W:** radiodelibera.com.ar **E:** radiodelibera@hotmail.com - **FM:** 93.5MHz – **CS07)** San Martín 1380, 3460 Curuzú Cuatiá ☎3774 42-3536 **W:** lt25.com.ar **E:** am970administracion@hotmail.com - **FM:** FM Guarani 107.1MHz – **CS08)** Goya – **CS09)** Hipólito Yrigoyen 835, 3400Corrientes ☎379 443-4333

ER00) ENTRE RIOS:

ER01) San Martín 371, 3202 Concordia ☎345 421-5506 **W:** lt15concordia.com.ar **E:** gerencia@lt15concordia.com.ar - **FM:** 89.3MHz – **ER02)** Almeda de la Federacion 126, E3100 Paraná ☎343 423-0101 **W:** radionacional.com.ar **E:** lt14web@gmail.com - **FM:** 93.1MHz Baxada del Paraná – **ER03)**Urquiza 3840 (Parade 12), 2820 Gualeguaychú ☎3446 43 1646 **W:** radionacional.com.ar **E:** gualeguaychu@radionacional.gov.ar - **FM:** 98.7MHz – **ER04)** Montiel 29, 2820 Gualeguaychú ☎3446 42-1471 **W:** radiolt41.com.ar **E**: lt14web@gmail.com - **FM:** 90.3 FM Sur – **ER05)** Av. Pte. Juan D. Perón 117, 3280 Colón ☎3447 42-1067 **W:** nuevomundodigital.com.ar **E:** radionmundo@colonred.com.ar - **FM:** 93.7MHz FM Palmares – **ER06)** Blvd. Eva Peron - Ex Sarmiento - 474, 3153 Victoria ☎3436 42 6520 **W:** lt39noticias.com.ar **E:** gerencia@lt39am980.com.ar - **FM:**90.3MHz FM Victoria – **ER07)** Pablo Stampa 2430, 3228 Chajarí ☎3456 42-0002 **W:** chajarialdia.com.ar **E:** info@multimedioschajari.com - **FM** 107.7MHz – **ER08)** Presidente Hipólito Yrigoyen 322, 2840 Gualeguay ☎3444 42 3038 **W:** radiogualeguay.com **E:** info@radiogualeguay.com.ar - **FM:** 104.9MHz – **ER10)** Onésimo Leguizamón 269, 3260 Concepción del Uruguay ☎3442 43 -2843 **W:** radionacional.com.ar **E:** lt11@live.com.ar - **FM:** 92.9MHz FM Arena – **ER11)** Av. Vélez Sársfield 1111, 3240 Villaguay ☎3455 42-1717 **W:** lt27lavozdelmontiel.com.ar **E:** lt27lavozdelmontiel@gmail.com - **FM:** 88.7MHz – R.Urbans – **ER12)** Chacabuco 1514, 3283 San José ☎3447 47-0998 **W:** 10tv.com.ar **E:** danycanal@hotmail.com - **FM:** 105.3 MHz R.Melody – **ER13)** Dr. Rozados 533, 3174 Rosario del Tala ☎344 542-3009 **W:** radiomediterranea.com.ar **E:** frecuenciamediterranea@gmail.com - **FM:** 102.5MHz – **ER14)** Ca.Urquiza 1115, 3150 Nogoya ☎343 511-429 **W:** Facebook **E:** radioam1660@gmail.com - **FM:** 96.1 MHz – **ER15)** Av.Libertador Gral. San Martin 359, 3133 Maria Grande ☎343 494-0486 **E:** comercialam1360@hotmail.com.ar

FO00) FORMOSA:

FO01) Junín 655, 3600 Formosa ☎370 442-6197 **W:** radionacional.com.ar **E:** radionacionalformosa@yahoo.com.ar - **FM:** 94.1MHz – **FO02)** Ruta Nacional 81 y Ruta Provincial 32, 3630 Las Lomitas ☎3715 43-2167 **W:** radionacional.com.ar **E:** laslomitas@radionacional.gov.ar - **FM:** 93.5MHz – **FO03)** Av. 9 de Julio 165, 3600 Formosa ☎370 461-9790 **W:** am990formosa.com **E:** info@produccionesyprogramas.com - **FM:** 98.9MHz FM Unica

JU00) JUJUY:

JU01) Av. España (Sur) 700, 4650 La Quiaca ☎3885 47-8095 **W:** radionacional.com.ar **E:** lra16radionacionallaquiaca@gmail.com - **FM:** 92.5MHz – **JU02)** Rio Bermejo y Olavarria, 4600 San Salvador de Jujuy ☎388 422-2781 **W:** radionacional.com.ar **E:**radionacionaljujuy@gmail.com - **FM:** 94.1MHz – **JU03)** Dr. Horacio Guzmán 496, 4607 San Salvador de Jujuy ☎388 423-0035 **W:** radiovisionjujuy.com.ar **E:** info@radiovisionjujuy.com.ar - **FM:** 97.7MHz FM Tropico – **JU04)** Av. Chile – Ex Villafane y Guatemala, 4608 Perico ☎388 491-1465 **W:** radiovisionjujuy.com.ar **E:** radiociudadperico@gmail.com – **JU05)** Av San Antonio y Los Ceibos, 4512 Libertador General San Martin ☎3886 42-6440 **W:** radiovisionjujuy.com.ar **E:** gerencia@radiovisionjujuy.com.ar – **JU06)** San Salvador de Jujuy - **FM:** 92.1MHz

LP00) LA PAMPA:

LP01) Av. Dr.Alfredo Palacios 950, 6304 Santa Rosa ☎2954 41-3600 **W:** radionacional.com.ar **E:** santarosa@radionacional.gov.ar - **FM:** 95.9MHz – **LP02)** Lisandro de la Torre 474, 6300 Santa Rosa ☎2954 41-4015 **W:** radiospampeanas.com.ar **E:**lu33am890contacto@gmail.com - **FM:** 103.7MHz FM Power – **LP03)** Calle 40 esquina 29, 6360 General Pico ☎2302 58-7157 **W:** radio37.com.ar **E:** danieldepa@hotmail.com - **FM:** 97.3 – **LP05)** General Pico 610, 8201 25 de Mayo ☎299 494 8086 **W:**am900.com.ar **E:**radiomunicipal25@gmail.com - **FM:** 91.1MHz FM Rio – **LP06)** Pasaje Rabinad 545, 6304 Santa Rosa ☎2954 42-7545 **W:** lu100.com.ar **E:** radioantena10@gmail.com - **FM:** 102.5MHz R.10 – **LP08)** Ca 105 Bis (Oeste) N° 546, 6360 General

Pico ☎2302 43-2331 **W:** laredpampeana.com.ar **E** laredpampeana@yahoo.com.ar - **FM:** 89.7 MHz – **LP09)** General Acha

LR00) LA RIOJA:

LR01) Hipólito Yrigoyen 318, 5300 La Rioja ☎380 442-5396 **W:** radionacional.com.ar **E:** larijo@radionacional.gov.ar - **FM:** 102.5MHz – **LR03)** La Rioja – **LR04)** Av Dr. Luis Maria de la Fuente y Av Laprida, 9° Piso 5300 La Rioja ☎380 445-7038 **W:** radiounlar.com.ar **E:** unlarfm@gmail.com - **FM:** 90.9 MHz

ME00) MENDOZA:

ME01) Manuel A.Sáez 2421, 5593 Las Heras ☎261 462- 3604 **W:** radionihuil.com.ar **E:** radionihuil@radionihuil.com.ar - **FM:** 98.9MHz – **ME02)** Rioja 1093, 5500 Mendoza ☎261 691-3078 **W:** lvdiez.com.ar **E:** alberto.moles@lvdiez.com.ar - **FM:** 104.1MHz – **ME03)** Rioja 1484, 5500 Mendoza ☎261 423-8872 **W:** radionacional.com.ar **E:** direccionlv8@radionacional.gov.ar - **FM:** 92.7MHz – **ME04)** Bernado de Irigoyen 17, PA 5620 General Alvear ☎2625 42-6566 **W:** facebook.com/LV-23-Radio-Río-Atuel-1221509851194781 **E:** admlv23@yahoo.com.ar - **FM:** 88.9MHz FM Paraiso – **ME05)** Emilio Civit 460, 5502 Mendoza ☎261 420-4385 **W:** radionacional.com.ar **E:** mendozalra6@radionacional.gov.ar - **FM:** 97.1 MHz – **ME05a)** Relay at Uspallata of R.Nacional, Mendoza at 960 kHz – **ME06)** Esquivel Aldao 350, 5613 Malargüe ☎260 447-0254 **W:** radionacional.com.ar **E:** radiomalargue@gmail.com - **FM:** 88.1MHz – **ME07)** Av. Hipólito Yrigoyen 223, 5602 San Rafael ☎260 443-0065 **W:** radionacional.com.ar - **FM:** 97.3MHz – **ME08)** Comandante Salas 150 1° Piso Of. 6, 5600 San Rafael ☎260 442-6057 **W:** lv18radio.com.ar **E:** lv18@sanrafael.gov.ar - **FM:** 101.5MHz – **ME09)** Av. Pellegrini 692, 5560 Tunuyán ☎261 396-3033 **W:** radioandina.com.ar **E:**radioandinamza@gmail.com - **FM:** 104.5MHz – **ME10)** Av. Bandera de los Andes 4420, 5521 Villa Nueva de Guaymallén ☎261 421-3992 **W:** radiomurialdo.com.ar **E:** mensajes@radiomurialdo.com.ar - **FM:** 90.5MHz FM Familia – **ME12)** Comandante Salas 200, 5602 San Rafael ☎260 442-4265 **W:** radioandina.com.ar **E:** andinasr@gmail.com - **FM:** 104.5 MHz FM Andina – **ME13)** Mendoza – **ME15)** Godoy Cruz – **ME16)** Mendoza – **ME17)**Calle Bernardo de Irigoyen 139, 5600 San Rafael **W:** radiomitremendoza.com.ar - **FM:** 91.1 MHz – **ME18)**Fray Francisco Inalicán 94 este, 5631 Malargü ☎260447-0506 **W:** malargue.gov.ar

MS00) MISIONES:

MS01) Cristóbal Colón 1452, 3300 Posadas ☎376 443-8727 **W:** radiolt17.com.ar **E:** info@radiolt17.com.ar - **FM:** 107.3MHz FM Provincia – **MS02)** Cl 93 –Las Araucarias - No 2289, 3300 Posadas ☎376 446-1603 **W:** lt4digital.com **E:** produccion@lt4digital.com - **FM:** 104.5MHz – **MS03)** Av. Victoria Aguirre Sur 809, 3370 Puerto Iguazú ☎3757 42-0099 **W:** radionacional.com.ar **E:** direccionlra19@radionacional.gov.ar - **FM:** 99.1MHz – **MS04)** Av. Las Calandrias y Las Golondrinas, Bo IPRODHA, 3370 Puerto Iguazú ☎3757 42-0060 **W:** radiocataratas.com **E:** info@radiocataratas.com - **FM:** 94.7MHz – **MS07)** Domingo F.Sarmiento 1847, 7° Piso, 3300 Posadas ☎376 442 0203 **W:** radiotupambae.com.ar **E:** administracion@radiotupambae.com.ar - **FM:** 105.9MHz – **MS08)** Calle Manantial (Ruta Proncial N°8) s/n 3363 25 de Mayo ☎3755 49-3084 **W:** radiolacueva1580.com **E:** radiolacueva.sinai@gmail.com - **FM:** 106.5 MHz R.Sinaí

NE00) NEUQUÉN:

NE01) Gral. Paz 536, 8353 Chos Malal ☎2948 42-1198 **W:** radionacional.com.ar **E:** chosmalal@radionacional.gov.ar - **FM:** 92.3MHz – **NE02)** Av. San Martín y Chaneton, 8340 Zapala ☎2942 42-1403 **W:** radionacional.com.ar **E:** direccionlra17@radionacional.gov.ar - **FM:** 93.9MHz – **NE03)** Gral. Villegas 1375, 8370 San Martín de los Andes ☎2972 42-7766 **E:** radionacional.com.ar **E:** lra53@smandes.com.ar - **FM:** 92.5MHz – **NE04)** Fotheringham 445, 8300 Neuquén ☎299 449-0485 **W:** lu5am.com.ar **E:** info@lu5am.com.ar - **FM:** 94.7 MHz FM 5 – **NE06)** Las Rosas 81, Bo Jardín, 8315 Piedra del Aguila ☎2942 49-3216 **W:** radiogregorioalvarez.net **E:** equiporga@gmail.com - **FM:** 99.5MHz – **NE07)** Pte. Bernardino Rivadavia 609, 8300 Neuquén ☎299 443-0249 **W:** amcumbre.com **E:**info@amcumbre@gmail.com - **FM:** 89.9MHz FM Cumbre – **NE10)** Santa Cruz 679, 8300 Neuquén ☎299 449-5109 🖷299 442 1568 **W:** rtnweb.gob.ar **E:** rtnweb@neuquen.gov.ar - **FM:** 104.9MHz – **NE11)** Montevideo 605 8300 Neuquen ☎299 443-4472 **W:** am550laprimera.com **E:** info@am550laprimera.com - **FM:** 90.7MHz – **NE12)** Maestro Thames Alderete 560, 8300 Neuquén ☎299 448-5788 **W:** radionacional.com.ar - **FM:** 103.3MHz

RN00) RIO NEGRO:

RN01) Av. 12 de Octubre 2421, 8403 San Carlos de Bariloche ☎294 443-1856 **W:** radionaconal.com.ar **E:** administracionlra30@radionacional.gov.ar - **FM:** 95.5MHz – **RN02)** Tucumán 1074, 8332 General Roca ☎298 443-6640 **W:** radioelvalle.com **E:** publicidad@radioelvalle.com - **FM:** 99.3MHz FM Color – **RN03)** Gral. Roca 365, 2° piso, 8324 Cipolletti ☎299 477-6800 **W:** lu19.com.ar **E:** publicidadradiolu19@yahoo.com.ar - **FM:** 102.9MHz FM Comanhue – **RN04)** Av. Alvaro Barros 1148, 8500 Viedma ☎2920 42-7700 **W:** lu15am.com.ar **E:** lu15radioam@gmail.com - **Italian:** Sat 1500-1600. - **FM:** 94.3MHz FM Rio – **RN05)** Remedios de Escalada 52, 8336 Villa Regina ☎298 446-1102 **W:** lu16radiorn.com.ar **E:** administracion@lu16radio.com.ar - **FM:** 92.7MHz FM Rio Negro – **RN06)** Gral. Manuel Belgrano 710, 8500 Viedma ☎2920 42-3226 **W:** radionacional.com.ar **E:** viedma@radionacional.gov.ar - **FM:** 93.5MHz – **RN07)** Av. San Martín (sur) y Salta, 8430 El Bolsón ☎294 449-2350 **W:** radionacional.com.ar **E:** lra57@elbolson.com - **FM:** 92.3MHz – **RN08)** José Hernández 326, 8418 Ingeniero Jacobacci ☎2940 43-2032 **W:** radionacional.com.ar - **FM:** 93.5MHz – **RN09)** Casa de Tucumán 481, 8361 Luis Beltrán ☎2946 41-3090 - **FM:** 96.5 MHz – **RN11)** Hipólito Yrigoyen y Remedios de Escalada, 8536 Valcheta ☎2934 49-3283 **E:** aznarezmarco@hotmail.com - **FM:** 105.3MHz FM Luján – **RN12)** Hipólito Yrigoyen 402, 8534 Sierra Colorada ☎298 460 2122 **W:** facebook.com/AM1580SierraColorada **E:** radiolujan@hotmail.com – **RN13)** Ruta Nacional Nº 22, Km 1200 y Acceso Martin Fierro, 8328 Allen ☎299 504 3266 **W:** radioam740.com.ar **E:** radioam740@gmail.com – **RN14)** San Carlos de Bariloche

SA00) SALTA:

SA01) Ruta Nal. 34, Km. 1433, 4560 Tartagal ☎3875 42-1600 **W:** radionacional.com.ar **E:** tartagal@radionacional.gov.ar - **FM:** 92.3MHz – **SA02)** Av Dr.Carlos Pellegrini 715, 1° piso, 4402 Salta ☎387 426-0245 **W:** radionacional.com.ar - **FM:** 102.9MHz – **SA03)** Av Ex Combatientes de Malvinas 3890, 4412 Salta ☎387 424-62226234 **W:** radiosalta.com prensaradiosalta@gmail.com - **FM:** 96.9MHz FM Genesis – **SA06)** 9 de Julio 163, 4530 San Ramón de la Nueva Orán ☎3878 42 1026 **E:** oranradio@yahoo.com - **FM:** 90.9MHz FM Orán – **SA07)** Salta

SC00) SANTA CRUZ:

SC01) Comodoro Py 342, Casa 16, Dept. 1, Barrio Las Lengas 9407 Río Turbio ☎2902 42-1131 **W:** radionacional.com.ar **E:**lra18radionacional620@gmail.com - **FM:** 90.3MHz – **SC02)** Zapiola 25, 9400 Río Gallegos ☎2966 42-0023 **W:** lu12.com.ar **E:** lu12_am680@speedy.com.ar - **FM:** 92.9MHz FM Laser – **SC03)** Av. San Martín 324, 9311 Gobernador Gregores ☎2962 43 3468 **W.** radionacional.com.ar **E:** direccionlra59@radionacional.gov.ar - **FM:** 99.9MHz – **SC04)** Hermanos Vidal 127, 9405 El Calafate **W:** radionacional.com.ar **E:** lu23@cotecal.com.ar ☎2902 49-5696. - **FM:** 88.1MHz Glaciar FM – **SC05)** Ramón Lista 36, 9050 Puerto Deseado ☎297 487-1211 **E:** lri200@deseado.gob.ar – **FM:** 99.3 MHz – **SC06)** Av. Néstor Kirchner - 823, 1°piso, 9400 Río Gallegos **W:** lu14.com.ar **E:** oyenteslu14@gmail.com ☎2966 42-2315 - **FM:** 96.3MHz – **SC07)** Saavedra 1318, 9040 Perito Moreno ☎2963 43-2233 **W:** radionacional.com.ar **E:** administracionlra56@radionacional.gov.ar - **FM:** 93.5MHz – **SC08)** Rio Gallegos – **SC09)** Rio Gallegos

SE00) SANTIAGO DEL ESTERO:

SE01) 9 de Julio 390, 4200 Santiago del Estero ☎385 403-0080 **W:** facebook.com/radiolv11 **E:** radiolv11sde@gmail.com - **FM:** 88.1, 89.5MHz FM Total – **SE02)** Urquiza 332, 1° Piso, 4200 Santiago del Estero ☎385 421-2565 **W:** radionacional.com.ar **E:** nacionalsantiago@hotmail.com **FM:** 98.5MHz – **SE03)** Av. 25 de Mayo sur 69, 3760 Añatuya ☎3844 42-1661 **W:** radiosolidaridad.com.ar **E:** amsolidaridad@yahoo.com.ar – **SE04)** Misiones 541, 4202 Santiago del Estero

SF00) SANTA FE:

SF01) Juan de Gary 2960, 3000 Santa Fé ☎342 483-5327 **W:** radionacional.com.ar **E:** administracionlra14@radionacional.gov.ar - **FM:** 102.9MHz – **SF02)** Sarmiento 763, 2000 Rosario ☎341 422-9500 **W:** lt8.com.ar **E:** info@lt8.com.ar - **FM:** 99.5MHz – **SF03)** 9 de Julio 3560, 3000 Santa Fé ☎342 452-1200 **W:** lt10.com.ar **E:** noticiaslt10@gmail.com - **FM:** 103.5MHz FM X – **SF04)** 4 de Enero 2153, 3000 Santa Fé ☎342 410-9999 **W:** lt9.com.ar **E:** info@lt9.com.ar - **FM:** 92.5MHz – **SF05)** Av. Pte. Juan Domingo Perón 8101, 2010 Rosario ☎341 457-7000 **W:** rosario3.com **E:** radio2@rosario3.com - **FM:** 97.9MHz – **SF06)** Córdoba 1331, Planta Alta, 2000 Rosario ☎341 421-8149 **W:** radionacional.com.ar **E:** rosario@radionacional.gov.ar - **FM:** 104.5MHz – **SF07)** Corrientes y Mendoza, 2000 Rosario ☎ 9341 330-3333 **W:** lt3.com.ar **E:** digital@lt3.com.ar - **FM:** 102.7MHz – **SF08)** Av. Casey 642, 2600 Venado Tuerto ☎346 242-1526 **W:** radiovenadotuerto.com **E:** lt29@radiovenadotuerto.com - **FM:** 88.9MHz – **SF09)** Cornelia Saavedra 52, 1° piso, 2300 Rafaela ☎3492 45-0300 **W:** radiorafaela.com.ar **E:** lt28radiorafaela@gmail.com - **FM:** 107.5MHz – **SF10)** Juan Chavarri 452, 2147 San Genaro ☎3401 49-3069 **W:** lt23.com.ar **E:** gerencialt23@co19set.com.ar - **FM:** 92.1MHz FM Concierto – **SF11)** Lucas Funes 1258, 3560 Reconquista ☎3482 42-8945 **W:** radioamanecer.com.ar **E:** radioamanecer@radioamanecer.com.ar - **FM:** 92.7MHz FM

Amanecer – **SF12)** Calle 107 N° 55, 3561 Reconquista ☎3482 48-2716 **E:** am1440rqta@yahoo.com.ar - **FM:** 95.7MHz – **SF14)** Belgrano 470, 2349 Suardi ☎3562 47-7612 **W:** radiobelgranosuardi.com.ar **E:** belgrano@suardi.com.ar - **FM:** 104.9MHz – **SF17)** San Luis 935, Oficina 7, 2000 Rosario ☎341 558-1090 **W:** amlibertad.com.ar **E:** contacto@amlibertad.com.ar - **FM:** FM Latina 94.5MHz – **SF19)** Av Carlos Pellegrini 168, 2000 Rosario ☎341 424-5259 **W:** am1330rosario.com.ar **E:** am1330rosario@gmail.com - **FM:** 105.9 MHz – **SF20)** Calle Ciudad Esperanza 583, Rafaela ☎3492 42-3979 **W:** adn979.com **E:** contacto@adn979.com - **FM:** 97.9MHz – **SF21)** Eva Peron 2240, 3000 Santa Fe ☎342 456-1719 **W:** radioeme.com **E:** contacto@radioeme.com - **FM:** 102.7MHz FM La Red – **SF22)** Juan Pablo Ravena 524, 2142 Luis Palacios ☎3476 49-9729 **W:** portaldelaregion.com **E:** radioalegriaregional@hotmail.com.ar - **FM:** 100.9MHz – **SF25)** Ruta Nacional N° 9,Km 380, Cañada de Gómez ☎3471 68-4175 **W:** mitrecanadadegomez.com.ar **E:**gvaschetto@icloud.com – **SF26)** Ceres

SJ00) SAN JUAN:

SJ01) Av José Ignacio de la Rozo 247 oeste 5402 San Juan ☎264 422 2344 **W:** radiocolon.com.ar **E:** radiocolon@gmail.com - **FM:** 106.3MHz – **SJ02)** Av. Ignacio de la Roza 293 Este, 2° Piso, 5402 San Juan ☎264 421-4149 **W:** radionacional.com.ar - **FM:** 101.9MHz – **SJ03)** General Soler y Rio Colorado, 5405 Barreal ☎2648 44-1260 **W:** facebook.com/Radio-Calingasta-FM-Nuestra-704584983027761/ **E:** radiocalingasta@gmail.com - **FM:** FM Nuestra 103.5MHz – **SJ04)** Mendoza Sur 454, 5420 San Juan ☎264 420-4028 **W:** lv5sarmiento.com.ar **E:** contacto@lv5sarmiento.com.ar - **FM:** 102.3, 103.7, 104.3, 104.7MHz Sarmiento FM – **SJ05)** General Paz 631, 5460 San José de Jáchal ☎2647 42 0028. **W:** radionacional.com.ar **E:** lra51nacionaljachal@gmail.com - **FM:** 102.1MHz – **SJ06)** Mitre 11 este, 5402 San Juan ☎264 427-2740 **E:** amlas40@yahoo.com.ar - **FM**: 105.1 – **SJ07)** Santa Fe 668 oeste, 5402 San Juan ☎264 6265-5995 **W:** facebook.com/radiolagente **E:** am1020sj@gmail.com - **FM:** 96.3 – **SJ08)** Rivadavia

SL00) SAN LUIS:

SL01) Juan Wenceslao 383, 5730 Villa Mercedes ☎2657 42-4406 **W:** radiolv15.com.ar **E:** info@radiolv15.com.ar - **FM:** 95.5MHz FM Unica – **SL02)** Av. Lafinur 488, 5700 San Luís ☎266 487-1444 **W:** radionacional.com.ar **E:** administracionlra29@radionacional.gov.ar - **FM:** 96.7MHz – **SL03)** Belgrano 927, 1° piso, 5700 San Luís ☎266 465-3965 **W:** cadenadimension.com.ar **E:** noticiasam940@hotmail.com - **FM:** 102.7MHz – **SL04)** General Paz 1078, 5732 Villa Mercedes ☎2657 43-7734 **W:** radiomariadelapaz.com.ar **E:**radiomariadelapaz@gmail.com - **FM:** 105.3MHz – **SL05)**Junin 565, 5700 San Luis ☎266 442-5050 **W:** radiopopularsanluis.com.ar **E:** publicidad@radiopopularsanluis.com.ar - **FM:** 98.5 MHz

TU00) TUCUMAN:

TU01) Lapride 530, 4000 San Miguel de Tucmán ☎381 431-3800 **W:** lv12.com.ar **E:** contacto@lv12.com.ar - **FM:** 99.1 MHz FM Independencia – **TU02)** Mendoza 273, 4000 San Miguel de Tucumán ☎381 497 5080 **W:** lv7.com.ar **E:** comercial.lv7@gmail.com - **FM:** 102.7MHz – **TU03)** San Martín 251, 4° Piso, 4000 San Miguel de Tucumán ☎381 431-0131 **W:** radionacional.com.ar **E:** tucuman@radionacional.gov.ar - **FM:** 98.7MHz – **TU04)** San Martin 610 – Piso 6 – Of 6,4000 San Miguel de Tucum ☎381 454-4739 **W:** radio21tucuman.com.ar **E:** radio21tucuman@yahoo.com.ar

TF00) TIERRA DEL FUEGO:

TF01) Leonardo Rosales 490, 9420Río Grande ☎2964 42-2176 **W:** radionacional.com.ar **E:** lra24radionacional@yahoo.com.ar - **FM:** 88.1MHz – **TF02)** Av. San Martin 331 (9410) Ushuaia ☎2901 42-1670 **W.:** radionacional.com.ar **E:** ushuaia@radionacional.gov.ar - **FM:** 92.1 MHz **TF03)** Ushuaia – **TF04)** Rio Grande

Capital Federal: CF16) 90.3 MHz Delta FM – **CF05)** 93.7 R.Pop Nac – 96.7 FM Clásica Nacional – 98.7 Folclórica FM – **CF22)** 89.1 – **CF28)** 89.9 FM Con Vos – **CF16)** 90.3 Eco Radio, 91.1 R.Abierta, 92.1 Mambo, 92.3 La Radio – **CF03)** 92.7 La Ciudad – **CF37)** 93.1 R.Late – 93.7, FM Federal – **CF09)** 94.3 Disney – **CF23)** 94.3 R.Nueva Bolivia 94.7 FM Palermo – **CF08)** 95.1 La Metro – **CF12)** 95.9 Rock & Pop, 96.3 R.Jai – **CF05)** 96.7 Clásica, 97.1 FM Europa, 97.3 Contacto FM, 97.9 R.Cultura – **CF13)** 98.3 Mega – **CF05)** 98.7 FM Folklorica, 99.1 Cadena 3 Argentina – **CF04)** 99.9 Cadena 100, 100.3 FM Cultural Musical – **CF07)** 100.7 Blue FM, 101.1 La Ciento Uno – **CF06)** 101.5 Pop Radio – **CF10)** 102.3 Aspen Classic – **CF02)** 103.1 R. Uno, 103.7 Amadadeus FM – **CF01)** 104.3 – **CF01)** 105.5 FM Hit – **CF11)** 106.3 R.Aleluya, 106.7 X4, 107.3 Milenium, 107.9 Kabul Rock.

In the city area there are over 150 unlicensed LP FM stns; about 900 in the rest of the country.

ARMENIA

L.T: UTC +4h — **Pop:** 3 million — **Pr.L:** Armenian — **E.C:** 220V/50Hz — **ITU:** ARM

HERUSTATESUTYAN YEV RADIOYI AZGAYIN HANDZNAZHOGHOV (HRAH)

(National Commission on Radio & TV)

✉ Isahakyan St. 28, 0009 Yerevan ☎ +374 10 528370 **E:** nctr@tvradio.am **W:** tvradio.am **L.P:** Chmn: Tigran Hakobyan

HAYASTANI HANRAYIN RADIOYNKERUTYUN PBY (Pub) (Public R. Company of Armenia CJSC)

✉ A.Manoogian St. 5, 0025 Yerevan ☎ +374 10 551143 **E:** info@armradio.am **W:** armradio.am **L.P:** CEO: Garegin Khumaryan

FM	1	2	kW	FM	1	2	kW
Jermuk	100.3	-	1	Vanadzor	103.7	-	1
Noyemberyan	101.7	-	5	Yerevan	107.7	103.8	1
Pushkini Lernantsk	101.1	-	5	Zovashen	104.0	-	1

+ sites with only txs below 1kW.

D.Prgr: Prgr 1 (Arajin tsragir): 24h. – **Prgr 2 (Im R.):** 24h.

OTHER STATIONS

FM	MHz	kW	Location	Station
14)	88.3	4	Yerevan	Kiss FM
15)	89.3	4	Yerevan	Pop FM
2B)	89.7	4	Yerevan	Autoradio
4)	90.1	1	Yerevan	R. Shanson
5)	90.7	1	Yerevan	R. Jan
13)	91.1	1	Yerevan	R. Vem
16)	93.7	1	Yerevan	R. Mir Relay
1A)	100.2	10	Dilijan	R. Hay
1A)	100.4	5	Armavir	R. Hay
1A)	100.4	5	Ashtarak	R. Hay
8)	100.7	1	Yerevan	R. Aurora
11)	101.1	10	Amasia	R. Shirak
2A)	101.9	2	Yerevan	R. Yerevan
9)	102.4	1	Yerevan	RFI Relay
3)	103.5	1	Yerevan	R. Marshal
1A)	103.6	10	Noyemberyan	R. Hay
12)	104.1	1	Gyumri	R. Shant
2A)	104.4	1	Charentsavan	R. Yerevan
2A)	104.6	1	Vedi	R. Yerevan
7)	104.9	1	Yerevan	Russkoye R.
2A)	105.4	10	Pushkini Lernantsk	R. Yerevan
2A)	105.2	1	Talin	R. Yerevan
1B)	105.5	1	Yerevan	FM 105.5
10)	106.0	1	Yerevan	R. Sputnik Relay
2A)	106.1	10	Noyemberyan	R. Yerevan
2)	106.8	1	Zovashen	R. Yerevan
6)	106.9	1	Yerevan	Lav R. 106.9
2A)	107.2	1	Vanadzor	R. Yerevan
2A)	107.3	1	Jermuk	R. Yerevan

+ txs below 1kW

Addresses & other information:

1A,B) Pavstos Buzandi St. 1/3, 0010 Yerevan – **2A,B)** A.Manoogian St. 5, 0025 Yerevan – **3)** Armeniak Armenakyan St. 250, 0047 Yerevan – **4)** A.Manoogian St. 5, 0025 Yerevan. Rel. R. Shanson (Russia) – **5)** Acharyan St. 42, 0040 Yerevan – **6)** Hyusisain Ave. 1, 0001 Yerevan. Rel. R. Sputnik (Russia) – **7)** Khandjyan St. 13a, 0010 Yerevan. Rel. Russkoye R. (Russia) – **8)** Nairi Zaryan St. 22, 0051 Yerevan – **9)** Ovsepyan St. 95, 0047 Yerevan. Rel. RFI (France) – **10)** Yerevan – **11)** Abovyan St. 248, 3104 Gyumri – **12)** Kievyan St. 16, 0028 Yerevan – **13)** Pavstos Buzandi St. 1/3, 0010 Yerevan – **14)** Nairi Zaryan St. 22a, 0051 Yerevan – **15)** Hrazdan Gorge St. 4/2, 0082 Yerevan – **16)** Arshakunyats Ave. 4, 0023 Yerevan . Rel. R. Mir (Russia

ARUBA (Netherlands)

L.T: UTC -4h — **Pop:** 106,000 — **Pr.L:** Papiamentu (official), Dutch (official), English, Spanish — **E.C:** 127V/60HZ — **ITU:** ABW

DIRECTIE TELECOMMUNICATIE ZAKEN

✉ Rumbastraat 19, Oranjestad ☎ +297-582-6069 🖷 +297-582-5307 **E:** dirtelza@setarnet.aw **W:** dtz.aw

FM	MHz	kW	Station, location
12)	88.1	1	Mega 88FM, Ponton
11)	88.9	0.1	Bo Guia, Jaburibari
3)	89.9	0.25	Canal 90FM, Bo Superstation Ponton

FM	MHz	kW	Station, location
14)	90.7	0.45	Caliente FM, Hooiberg
7)	91.5	0.3	R. Aruba 91.5FM, Hooiberg
10)	92.3	0.1	Latina Tu FM, Hooiberg
1)	93.1	0.66	R. Victoria, Hooiberg (Rlg.)
12)	94.1	1	Hit 94 FM, Ponton
7)	95.1	0.5	Top 95 FM, Hooiberg
8)	96.5	0.2	Magic 96.5 FM, Hooiberg
6)	97.9	0.2	Easy FM ,Hooiberg
13)	98.9	0.75	Cool FM 98.9, Hooiberg
9)	99.9	0.5	GFM Galactica 99.9 ,Urataka
16)	100.9	0.85	Hits 100.9 FM, Simeon Antonio
17)	101.7	0.7	Power 101.7 FM, Jaburibari
18)	104.3	0.6	Fresh FM
19)	106.7	0.6	Heart Radio, Oranjestad
2)	107.5	0.2	Blue FM 107.5

Addresses & other information:
1) Washington 23A Noord, Oranjestad ☎ +297 587 3444 Mngr: Nico J. Arts. Rlg: 24h in English, Spanish, Papiamentu, Dutch, Creole, Tagalog and Cantonese **W:** srv931fm.org **E:srv931aw@gmail.com and** radiovictoria@setarnet.aw – **2)** Rotonde di Paradera, Oranjestad ☎ +297 588 2488 🖷 +297 588 2438 Manager : Humerto Benito – **3)** Van Leeuwenhoekstraat 26, PO Box 219, Oranjestad ☎+297 582 8952 and 297 582 1601 🖷 +297 583 7340 Dir: Mr. Elton Arends Programs: 24h in English, Papiamentu, Dutch, Creole and Spanish **W:** canal90fm.aw **E:** canal90fmaruba@gmail.com and canal90fm@gmail.com –**6)** Sabana Basora 31-D, Pos Chiquito ☎+297 593 3637 🖷 +297 585 2639 GM: Wouter Gesterkamp 24h easy listening modern hits in English, Papiamentu, Spanish and Dutch **E:** info@easyfm.aw **W:** easyfm.aw – **7)** Santa Cruz 110, Oranjestad ☎+297 585 9500 🖷+297 585 0951 **W:** top95fm.aw; **E:**solodipueblo@gmail.com Radio 91.5 FM in Papiamentu with the slogan: Voz di pueblo Dir. Edmond Croes – **8)** South Beach Centre, Palm Beach ☎+297 586 0965 🖷 +297 586 5350 24h **E:** magicarubapromo@gmail.com **W:** magic96-5.com – **9)** Macapruimstraat 1-I, Oranjestad +297 588 2536 Man. Dir: Richard A. Arends Stn Man.: Maikel Oduber 24h in Papiamentu, English and Dutch **E:** gfmgalactica@gmail.com and awecugalactica@hotmail.com – **10)** La Nueva Latina**,** Tanki Leendert 8 ☎ +297 582 6608 Pop Latino **E:** info@latinatufm.com and latinatufm@gmail.com– **11)** Tanki Flip 26B ☎+297 587 7889 🖷 +297 587 5889 Dir. Francisco Rosel **W:** boguiafm.com **E:** radio.boguia@gmail.com ; 24 h in Papiamentu, Christian Gospel and cultural programmes – **12)** Caya Ernesto Petronia 68-A, Oranjestad. Mega 88 FM ☎ +297 582 6888 🖷 +297 582 0494 **W:** mega88fm.com E: mail@mega88fm.com 24h in Papiamentu, Spanish and English: Latin Caribbean R **W**: hit94.com **E:** hit94fm@gmail.com ☎ +297 582 0694 and +297 583 9494 🖷 +297 582 0494 24h in Papiamentu, Spanish and English. Dir: John A. Habibe – **13)** Cumana 1A ☎ + 297 583 3111 Dir. Alexander Ponson 24 prgr in Papiamentu **W:** coolaruba.com **E:** info@coolaruba.com – **14)** Windstraat 29, Oranjestad +297 560 7212 🖷+ 297 583 1515 **W:** calientefmaruba.com **E:** calientefmaruba@gmail.com –**16)** Kolibristraat 2, Oranjestad, Dir. Aldrich F. Croes. Prgr 24 hrs in Papiamentu ☎+297 588 6100 **W:** hits100fm.com **E:** hits100fm.aruba@gmail.com – **17)** Piedra Plat 44 C-D, Lok 12, Paradera, Oranjestad ☎+297 585 2021 Dir. Ralph Maduro, 10hrs live program and the rest of the program: computer Prgrs in Papiamentu, Spanish,English and Dutch **W:** powerfmaruba.com and powerfm1017.com **E:** power101fm@gmail.com – **18)** Cumana 1A, Oranjestad ☎ +297 583 2220; Dir. Alexander Ponson 24 prgr in Dutch, **E:** info@fresharuba.com **W:** fresharuba.com – **19)** Caya Taratata 15, Oranjestad☎ +297 593 4493 **W:** heartradioaruba.com **E:**info@heartradioaruba.com

ASCENSION ISLAND (UK)

L.T: UTC — **Pop:** 800 — **Pr.L:** English — **E.C:** 230V/50Hz — **ITU:** ASC

VOLCANO RADIO (USAF) (Mil)

🖃 Ascension Radio Station, Ascension AAF, P.O. Box 4235, Patrick AFB, FL 32925-0235, USA.
FM: AFN, 98.7MHz 0.4kW 24h.

BBC ATLANTIC RELAY STATION

🖃 English Bay, Ascension Island, So. Atlantic.
Local Sce: FM: 93.2MHz 15W (24h relay of BBCWS in English plus occ. local prgrs). See International section for details of SW relays.

BRITISH FORCES BROADC. SCE: W: forces.net/radio

FM(MHz): Travellers Hill: Forces Radio BFBS 100.9, BFBS Radio 2 97.3, Green Mt: Forces Radio BFBS 107.3, BFBS Radio 2 105.3.

SAINT FM: Jamestown, St Helena. Green Mt.:91.4 & Georgetown: 95.5MHz 25W *(see main entry under St. Helena)*

AUSTRALIA

L.T: See World Time Table. (DST where applicable: 4 Oct 20-4 Apr 21, 3 Oct 21-3 Apr 22 — **Pop:** 25.1 million — **Pr.L:** English — **E.C:** 230V/50Hz — **ITU:** AUS

DEPT. OF COMMUNICATIONS AND THE ARTS (DoCA)

🖃 38 Sydney Ave, Forrest ACT 2603 (🖃 GPO Box 2154, Canberra ACT 2601) ☎+61 2 6271 1000 **W**: communications.gov.au **E**: communications.gov.au/who-we-are/contact-us/form The Australian Government's lead advisor on Communications and the Arts. Works to promote innovative cultural and communications sectors through policy advice, prgr. implementation and sce delivery to the benefit of all Australians. Regulates radio, television, internet, phone, post and spectrum.

AUSTRALIAN COMMUNICATIONS AND MEDIA AUTHORITY (ACMA)

🖃 Level 5 The Bay Centre, 65 Pirrama Road, Pyrmont NSW 2009 (🖃 PO Box Q500, Queen Victoria Building NSW 1230) ☎+61 2 9334 7700 **W**: acma.gov.au **E**: info@acma.gov.au Government agency responsible for regulation of broadcasting, the internet, radiocommunications and telecommunications.

COMMERCIAL RADIO AUSTRALIA (CRA)

🖃 Lvl 5, 88 Foveaux St, Surry Hills NSW 2010 ☎+61 2 9281 6577 **W**: commercialradio.com.au **E**: commercialradio.com.au/contact-us Peak body representing most commercial radio services.

COMMUNITY BROADCASTING ASSOCIATION OF AUSTRALIA (CBAA)

🖃 Suite One, Level Three, 44-54 Botany Rd. Alexandria, NSW 2015 (🖃 POB 564, Alexandria, NSW 1435) ☎+61 2 9310 2999 **W**: cbaa.org.au **E**: office@cbaa.org.au Peak body representing most community radio services.

AUSTRALIAN NARROWCAST RADIO ASSOCIATION (ANRA)

🖃 PO Box 299, Lane Cove NSW 1595 ☎+61 2 4295 6740 **W**: anra.org.au **E**: secretary@anra.org.au Peak body representing most High Power Open Narrowcast and Low Power Open Narrowcast services.

FIRST NATIONS MEDIA AUSTRALIA

🖃 2/70 Elder St, Alice Springs NT 0870 (🖃 PO Box 2731, Alice Springs NT 0871) ☎+61 8 8952 6465 **W**: irca.net.au **E**: info@irca.net.au Peak body representing remote indigenous media organisations.

AUSTRALIAN BROADCASTING CORP. (ABC)

HQ: 🖃 Ultimo Centre, 700 Harris Str, Ultimo, NSW 2007(🖃 GPO Box 9994, Sydney NSW 2001) ☎+61 2 9333 1500
Networks: N=Radio National, L=Local Radio, FM=Classic FM, JJJ=Triple J Network (alternative), PNN=Parliamentary/News R
Digital-only Networks: Double J (AC Music), ABC Country, ABC Jazz, ABC Grandstand (sport), ABC Extra (special events), Triple J Unearthed (independent music)
Callsigns typically N = xRN, xABCRN, L = xABCRR,, FM = xABCFM, JJJ = xJJJ, PNN = xPB, xPNN - some are localised. **Call letters:** 1 = A.C.T., 2 = NSW (some A.C.T.), 3 = Victoria, 4 = Queensland, 5 = So. Australia, 6 = We. Australia, 7 = Tasmania, 8 = Northern Territory.

MW	Call	kHz	kW	Netw	Location
46)	6DL	531	10	L	Dalwallinu
29)	4QL	540	10	L	Longreach
11)	2CR	549	50	L	Orange (Cumnock)
44)	6WA	558	50	L	Wagin
25)	4JK	567	10(d)	L	Julia Creek
47)	6MN	567	0.1	L	Newman
47)	6PN	567	0.1	L	Pannawonica
47)	6PU	567	0.1	L	Paraburdoo
47)	6TP	567	0.1	L	Tom Price
2)	2RN	576	50	N	Sydney
6)	6PB	585	10	P	Perth
7)	7RN	585	10	N	Hobart
42)	3WV	594	50	L	Horsham

MW	Call	kHz	kW	Netw	Location
2)	2RN	603	10(d)	N	Nowra
26)	4CH	603	10(d)	L	Charleville
47)	6PH	603	2	L	Port Hedland
4)	4QR	612	50	L	Brisbane
6)	6RN	612	10	N	Dalwallinu
3)	3RN	621	50	N	Melbourne
2)	2PB	630	10	P	Sydney
24)	4QN	630	50	L	Townsville (Brandon)
48)	6AL	630	5	L	Albany
7)	7RN	630	0.4	N	Queenstown
23)	4MS	639	1	L	Mossman
31)	5CK	639	10	L	Port Pirie (Crystal Brook)
8)	8RN	639	2	N	Katherine
14)	2NU	648	10	L	Tamworth (Manilla)
43)	6GF	648	2	L	Kalgoorlie
19)	2BY	657	10(d)	L	Byrock
8)	8RN	657	2	N	Darwin
1)	2CN	666	5	L	Canberra ACT
9)	2CO	675	10	L	Albury (Corowa)
45)	6BE	675	5	L	Broome
13)	2KP	684	10	L	Kempsey (Smithtown)
49)	6BS	684	5	L	Busselton
8)	8RN	684	1	N	Tennant Creek
34)	5SY	693	2(d)	L	Streaky Bay
2)	2BL	702	50	L	Sydney
47)	6KP	702	10	L	Karratha
26)	4QW	711	10(d)	L	Roma/St.George
16)	2ML	720	0.4	L	Murwillumbah
2)	2RN	720	0.05	N	Armidale
38)	3MT	720	2(d)	L	Omeo
23)	4AT	720	4	L	Atherton
6)	6WF	720	50	L	Perth
5)	5RN	729	50	N	Adelaide
16)	2NR	738	50	L	Grafton
49)	6MJ	738	5(d)	L	Manjimup
26)	4QS	747	10	L	Toowoomba (Dalby)
7)	7PB	747	3.5	P	Hobart
8)	8JB	747	0.2	L	Jabiru
13)	2TR	756	2(d)	L	Taree
3)	3RN	756	10(d)	N	Wangaratta
3)	3LO	774	50	L	Melbourne
20)	8AL	783	2	L	Alice Springs
4)	4RN	792	25	N	Brisbane
23)	4QY	801	2	L	Cairns
17)	2BA	810	10	L	Bega
6)	6RN	810	20	N	Perth
14)	2GL	819	10	L	Glen Innes
45)	6KW	819	5	L	Kununurra
38)	3GI	828	10	L	Sale (Longford)
46)	6GN	828	10	L	Geraldton
21)	4RK	837	10	L	Rockhampton (Gracemere)
43)	6ED	837	1	L	Esperance
1)	2RN	846	10	N	Canberra
47)	6CA	846	2.5	L	Carnarvon
30)	4QB	855	10(d)	L	Pialba
30)	4QO	855	10	L	Eidsvold
45)	6DB	873	2	L	Derby
5)	5AN	891	50	L	Adelaide
4)	4PB	936	10	P	Brisbane
7)	7ZR	936	10(d)	L	Hobart
5)	5PB	972	2	P	Adelaide
3)	3RN	990	0.5	N	Albury-Wodonga
8)	8GO	990	0.5	L	Nhulunbuy (Gove)
10)	2NB	999	2	L	Broken Hill
45)	6WH	1017	0.5	L	Wyndham
3)	3PB	1026	14.5	P	Melbourne
18)	2UH	1044	2(d)	L	Muswellbrook
23)	4WP	1044	0.5	L	Weipa
49)	6BR	1044	1	L	Bridgetown
23)	4TI	1062	2	L	Thursday Island
32)	5MV	1062	2	L	Renmark/Loxton
2)	2RN	1098	0.2	N	Goulburn
6)	6PB	1152	10(d)	P	Busselton
33)	5PA	1161	10(d)	L	Naracoorte
35)	7FG	1161	1(d)	L	Fingal
47)	6XM	1188	2	L	Exmouth
46)	6NM	1215	0.5	L	Northam
15)	2NC	1233	10	L	Newcastle
6)	6RN	1269	5	N	Busselton
6)	6RN	1296	10	N	Wagin
5)	5RN	1305	2	N	Renmark/Loxton
11)	2LG	1395	0.2	L	Lithgow
2)	2RN	1431	2	N	Wollongong
2)	2PB	1458	2	P	Newcastle
33)	5MG	1476	1(d)	L	Mt. Gambier
2)	2RN	1485	0.1	N	Wilcannia
24)	4HU	1485	0.05	L	Hughenden
34)	5LN	1485	0.2	L	Port Lincoln
2)	2RN	1512	10	N	Newcastle
21)	4QD	1548	50	L	Emerald
30)	4GM	1566	0.2	L	Gympie
10)	2WA	1584	0.1	L	Wilcannia
31)	5WM	1584	0.05	L	Woomera
7)	7SH	1584	0.1	L	St. Helens
17)	2CP	1602	0.4	L	Cooma
41)	3WL	1602	0.25	L	Warrnambool
31)	5LC	1602	0.2	L	Leigh Creek South

FM	Area	State	N	L	FM	JJJ
5)	Adelaide	SA	-	-	103.9	105.5
5)	Adel. Foothills	SA	-	-	97.5	95.9
39)	Alexandra	VIC	104.5	102.9	-	-
14)	Armidale	NSW		101.9	103.5	101.1
3)	Bairnsdale	VIC	106.3	-	-	-
36)	Ballarat	VIC	-	107.9	105.5	107.1
17)	Batemans Bay	NSW	105.1	103.5	101.9	-
2)	Bega/Cooma	NSW	100.9	-	99.3	100.1
37)	Bendigo	VIC	-	91.1	02.7	90.3
17)	Bombala	NSW	-	94.1	-	-
2)	Bourke	NSW	101.1	-	-	-
4)	Brisbane	QLD	-	-	106.1	107.7
5)	Broken Hill	NSW	102.9	-	103.7	102.1
6)	Broome	WA	107.7	-	-	-
6)	Bunbury	WA	-	-	93.3	94.1
35)	Burnie	TAS	-	102.5	-	-
23)	Cairns	QLD	105.1	106.7	105.9	107.5
23)	Cairns North	QLD	93.9	95.5	94.7	97.1
6)	Camballin	WA	-	102.1	-	-
1)	Canberra	ACT	-	-	102.3	101.5
4)	Cardwell QLD	-	100.1	-	-	
6)	Cen.Agricult	WA	-	-	98.9	98.1
2)	Cen.Table'nds	NSW	104.3	-	102.7	101.9
11)	Cen. West. Sl.	NSW	107.9	107.1	105.5	102.3
4)	Darling Downs	QLD	105.7	-	107.3	104.1
8)	Darwin	NT	-	105.7	107.3	103.3
2)	Deniliquin	NSW	99.3	-	-	-
19)	Dubbo (City)	NSW	-	95.9	-	-
35)	E. Devonport	TAS	-	100.5		-
4)	Emerald	QLD	93.9	-	90.7	-
6)	Esperance	WA	106.3	-	104.7	-
6)	Geraldton	WA	99.7	-	94.9	98.9
2)	Glen Innes	NSW	105.1	-	-	-
22)	Gold Coast	QLD	90.1	91.7	88.5	97.7
39)	Goulburn V.	VIC	-	97.7	96.1	94.5
13)	Grafton/Kemp.	NSW	99.5	92.3	97.9	91.5
30)	Gympie	QLD	96.9	95.3	93.7	-
9)	Hay	NSW	88.9	88.1	-	-
7)	Hobart	TAS	-	-	93.9	92.9
12)	Illawarra	NSW	-	97.3	95.7	98.9
2)	Jerilderie	NSW	94.1	-	-	-
6)	Kalgoorlie	WA	97.1	-	95.5	98.7
50)	Katherine	NT	-	106.1	-	-
5)	Keith	SA	96.9	-	-	-
35)	King Island	TAS	-	88.5	-	-
38)	Latrobe Valley	VIC	-	100.7	101.5	96.7
35)	Lileah	TAS	89.7	91.3	-	-
16)	Lismore	NSW	96.9	94.5	95.3	96.1
4)	Longreach	QLD	99.1	-	-	-
28)	Mackay	QLD	102.7	101.1	97.9	99.5
13)	Manning River	NSW	97.1	95.5	98.7	96.3
35)	Maydena	TAS	-	89.7	-	-
4)	Meandarra	QLD	104.3	-	-	-
3)	Melbourne	VIC	-	-	105.9	107.5
40)	Mildura	VIC	105.9	104.3	102.7	101.1
23)	Mission Beach	QLD	90.9	89.3	-	-
4)	Monto	QLD	101.9	-	-	-
28)	Moranbah	QLD	106.5	104.9	-	-
4)	Mossman	QLD	90.1	-	-	-
5)	Mount Gambier	SA	103.3	-	104.1	102.5
25)	Mount Isa	QLD	107.3	106.5	101.7	104.1
39)	Murray Valley	VIC	-	102.1	103.7	105.3

FM	Area	State	N	L	FM	JJJ
9)	Murrumbidgee	NSW	98.9	100.5	97.3	96.5
18)	Muswellbrook	NSW	-	105.7	-	-
27)	Nambour	QLD	-	90.3	88.7	89.5
6)	Narrogin	WA	-	-	92.5	-
35)	NE Tas.	TAS	94.1	91.7	93.3	90.9
2)	Newcastle	NSW	-	-	106.1	102.1
3)	Nhill	VIC	95.7	-	-	-
6)	Perth	WA	-	-	97.7	99.3
6)	Port Hedland	WA	95.7	-	-	-
41)	Portland	VIC	98.5	96.9	-	-
5)	Renmark	SA	-	-	105.1	101.9
4)	Rockhampton	QLD	103.1	-	106.3	104.7
6)	Roebourne	WA	107.5	-	-	-
4)	Rolleston Mine	QLD	-	-	98.5	-
26)	Roma	QLD	107.3	105.7	97.7	-
31)	Roxby Downs	SA	101.9	102.7	103.5	-
6)	Salmon Gums	WA	100.7	-	-	-
6)	S. Agricultural	WA	96.9	-	94.5	92.9
46)	South'n Cross	WA	107.9	106.3	-	-
26)	South'n Downs	QLD	106.5	104.9	101.7	103.3
5)	Spencer Gulf N	SA	106.7	-	104.3	103.5
5)	Streaky Bay	SA	100.9	-	-	103.3
9)	SW Slopes	NSW	89.1	89.9	88.3	90.7
2)	Sydney	NSW	-	-	92.9	105.7
2)	Tamworth	NSW	93.9	-	103.1	94.7
4)	Townsville	QLD	104.7	91.1	101.5	105.5
5)	Tumby Bay	SA	101.9	-	-	-
39)	Upper Murray	VIC	-	106.5	104.1	103.3
14)	Upper Namoi	NSW	100.7	99.1	96.7	99.9
3)	Warrnambool	VIC	101.7	-	92.1	89.7
42)	Western Vic.	VIC	92.5	94.1	93.3	94.9
30)	Wide Bay	QLD	100.9	100.1	98.5	99.3
4)	Winton	QLD	107.9	-	-	-
5)	Wirrulla	SA	107.3	-	-	-
5)	Wudinna	SA	107.7	-	-	105.3
6)	Wyndham	WA	-	-	-	98.9

NB: Txs 1kW and higher

Parliamentary/News Radio Network (MHz): 89.1 Emerald QLD (8d), 89.3 Horsham VIC (20), 89.5 Bendigo VIC (10), 89.7 Bega/Cooma NSW (112d), 90.5 Burnie TAS (1d), 90.7 Grafton/Kemspey NSW (20d), 90.9 Illawarra NSW (150d), 91.3 Warrnambool VIC (3.2d), 91.5 SW Slopes/E Riverina NSW (80), 91.5 Tumby Bay SA (2), 91.7 Tamworth NSW (10), 91.7 Western Victoria (80d), 91.9 Central Tablelands NSW (5d), 92.1 Southern Agricultural WA (80), 92.5 NE Tasmania (192d), 93.5 Inverell NSW (10), 93.9 Renmark SA (150d), 94.3 Ballarat VIC (5d), 94.3 Townsville QLD (92d), 94.5 Gympie QLD (20d), 94.5 Nambour QLD (20d), 94.7 Manning River NSW (5), 94.9 Port Hedland WA (2), 95.1 Latrobe Valley VIC (200d), 95.7 Gold Coast (26d), 95.9 Murray Valley VIC (20), 96.3 Cairns North QLD (10d), 96.3 Warwick QLD (2), 96.3 Wagin WA (5), 96.7 Toowoomba QLD (2.5d), 97.7 Portland VIC (2.6d), 97.7 Wide Bay QLD (10d), 98.1 Murrumbidgee I.A. NSW (100), 98.5 Lismore NSW (100d), 99.7 Central Agricultural WA (80), 100.3 Mildura VIC (150d), 100.3 Kalgoorlie WA (6), 100.5 Batemans Bay NSW (40d), 100.9 Deniliquin NSW (2d), 100.9 Upper Murray VIC (2), 101.1 Cairns QLD (100), 101.3 Geraldton WA (10), 101.5 Upper Namoi NSW (20d), 102.1 E.. Devonport TAS (1.2), 102.5 Darwin (32d), 102.7 Armidale NSW (4), 102.7 Spencer Gulf North SA (70), 103.1 Esperance WA (5), 103.9 Canberra ACT (80), 104.1 Alice Springs NT (1), 104.3 Mackay QLD (100d), 104.5 Broken Hill NSW (4), 104.7 Colac VIC (10d), 104.9 Muswellbrook NSW (16), 104.9 Mount Isa QLD (1), 105.3 Katherine NT (1), 105.5 Rockhampton QLD (80), 105.7 Mt Gambier SA (240d), 106.3 Central West. Slopes NSW (220d), 106.9 Broome WA (2), 107.7 Goulburn Valley VIC (5d), 107.9 Bairnsdale VIC (2d)

Digital Radio

	DAB+	Call	Ch	MHz	kW
1)	Canberra ACT	DAB9C	9C	206.352	20
1)	Sydney NSW	DAB9C	9C	206.352	50
2)	Melbourne VIC	DAB9C	9C	206.352	50(d)
1)	Brisbane QLD	DAB9C	9C	206.352	50
1)	Adelaide SA	DAB9C	9C	206.352	50
1)	Perth WA	DAB9C	9C	206.352	50(d)
1)	Darwin NT	DAB9C	9C	206.352	20

All permanent digital multiplexes shared with SBS and carry all ABC radio networks. Several digital on-channel repeaters provide in-fill coverage (ERP 300-1000W). All programming at **W:** digitalradioplus.com.au/listen. Reports to originating stns.

ABC Addresses:
NB: Reports for R. National, Parliament/News, ABC-FM, Triple J and DAB+ only channels should go to the capital city ABC office in that state (Addresses 1-8).
1) ABC Canberra, GPO Box 9994, Canberra ACT 2601 – **2)** ABC Sydney, GPO Box 9994, Sydney NSW 2001 – **3)** ABC Melbourne, GPO Box 9994, Melbourne VIC 3001 – **4)** ABC Brisbane, GPO Box 9994, Brisbane QLD 4001 – **5)** ABC Adelaide, GPO Box 9994, Adelaide SA 5001 – **6)** ABC Perth, GPO Box 9994, Perth WA 6848 – **7)** ABC Hobart, GPO Box 9994, Hobart TAS 7001 – **8)** ABC Darwin, PO Box 9994, Darwin NT 0801 – **9)** ABC Riverina, 100 Fitzmaurice St, Wagga Wagga NSW 2650 – **10)** ABC Broken Hill, PO Box 315, Broken Hill NSW 2880 – **11)** ABC Central West, PO Box 8549, East Orange NSW 2800 – **12)** ABC Illawarra, PO Box 973, Wollongong NSW 2520 – **13)** ABC Mid North Coast, PO Box 42, Port Macquarie NSW 2444 – **14)** ABC New England / North West, PO Box 558, Tamworth NSW 2340 – **15)** ABC Newcastle, PO Box 2205, Dangar NSW 2309 – **16)** ABC North Coast, PO Box 908, Lismore NSW 2480 – **17)** ABC South East NSW, PO Box 336, Bega NSW 2550 – **18)** ABC Upper Hunter, PO Box 400, Muswellbrook NSW 2333 – **19)** ABC Western Plains, PO Box 985, Mudgee NSW 2830 – **20)** ABC Alice Springs, PO Box 1144, Alice Springs NT 0871 – **21)** ABC Capricornia, GPO Box 911, Rockhampton QLD 4700 - **22)** ABC Gold Coast, PO Box 217, Mermaid Beach QLD 4218 – **23)** ABC Far North, PO Box 932, Cairns QLD 4810 – **24)** ABC North Queensland, PO Box 694, Townsville QLD 4810 – **25)** ABC North West Queensland, 114 Camooweal St, Mount Isa QLD 4825 – **26)** ABC Southern Queensland, PO Box 358, Toowoomba QLD 4350 – **27)** ABC Sunshine Coast, PO Box 1212, Maroochydore QLD 4558 – **28)** ABC Tropical Queensland, PO Box 127, Mackay QLD 4740 – **29)** ABC Western Queensland, PO Box 318, Longreach QLD 4730 – **30)** ABC Wide Bay, PPO Box 1152, Bundaberg QLD 4670 – **31)** ABC North and West South Australia, PO Box 289, Port Pirie SA 5540 – **32)** ABC Riverland, PO Box 20, Renmark SA 5341 – **33)** ABC Southeast, PO Box 1448, Mount Gambier SA 5290 – **34)** ABC Eyre Peninsula, PO Box 679, Port Lincoln SA 5606 – **35)** ABC Northern Tasmania, PO Box 201, Launceston TAS 7250 – **36)** ABC Ballarat, PO Box 7, Ballarat VIC 3353 – **37)** ABC Central Victoria, PO Box 637, Bendigo VIC 3550 – **38)** ABC Gippsland, PO Box 330, Sale VIC 3850 – **39)** ABC Goulburn Murray, PO Box 1063, Wodonga VIC 3690 – **40)** ABC Mildura / Swan Hill, PO Box 10083, Mildura VIC 3502 – **41)** ABC South West Victoria, PO Box 310, Warrnambool VIC 3280 – **42)** ABC Western Victoria, PO Box 506, Horsham VIC 3402 – **43)** ABC Goldfields / Esperance, PO Box 125, Kalgoorlie WA 6430 – **44)** ABC Great Southern, 58 Tudhoe St, Wagin WA 6315 – **45)** ABC Kimberley, PO Box 217, Broome WA 6725 – **46)** ABC Mid West & Wheatbelt, PO Box 211, Geraldton WA 6530 – **47)** ABC North West, PO Box 994, Karratha WA 6714 – **48)** ABC South Coast, 2 St Emilie Way, Albany WA 6330 – **49)** ABC South West, PO Box 242, Bunbury WA 6231 – **50)** PO Box 1240, Katherine NT 0851

EXTERNAL SERVICE: Radio Australia
No shortwave broadcasts. Available via satellite, internet, and some local retransmissions.

SPECIAL BROADCASTING SERVICE (SBS)

HQ: ✉ 14 Herbert St, Artarmon, NSW 2064 (✉ Locked Bag 028, Crow's Nest, NSW 1585) ☎+61 (02) 9430 2828
Networks: **Radio 1** (Syd/Mlb AM), **Radio 2** (Syd/Mlb FM), **National Radio Network** (NRN, mix of Radio 1 & 2 for regional areas), **Radio 3** (digital only), **Radio 4** (BBS WS & special events, digital only), **Arabic24** (digital only), **Chill** (digital only), **PopAsia** (digital only), **PopDesi** (digital only). Non-music networks time-shifted to accord local time in each State.
NB: (t) translator stn licensed to SBS. (rt) retransmission sce licensed to self-help groups such as local councils.

	MW	Call	kHz	kW	Service
1)	Wollongong	2EA(t)	1035	2	R. 2
1)	Sydney	2EA	1107	5	R. 1
2)	Melbourne	3EA	1224	5(d)	R. 1
1)	Newcastle	2EA(t)	1413	5(d)	NRN
1)	Canberra	1EA(t)	1440	2	R. 1
1)	Wollongong	2EA(t)	1485	0.15	R. 1
	FM	**Call**	**MHz**	**kW**	**Service**
1)	Cairns	4SBSFM(rt)	90.5	1(d)	NRN
2)	Melbourne	3SBSFM	93.1	100	R. 2
1)	Brisbane	4SBSFM	93.3	100(d)	NRN
1)	Adel. Hills	5SBSFM(t)	95.1	2(d)	NRN
2)	Ballarat	3SBSFM(rt)	95.9	1	NRN
1)	Perth	6SBSFM	96.9	100	NRN

FM	Call	MHz	kW	Service
1) Sydney	2SBSFM	97.7	150(d)	R. 2
1) Lismore	2SBSFM(rt)	98.9	1	NRN
1) Wondai	4SBS(rt)	98.9	2	NRN
1) Darwin	8SBSFM	100.9	18(d)	NRN
1) Sapphire	4SBS(rt)	103.5	1	NRN
1) Canberra	2SBS	105.5	80	R. 2
1) Hobart	7SBS	105.7	56	NRN
1) Adelaide	5SBS	106.3	32	NRN

DAB+	Call	Ch	MHz	kW
1) Canberra ACT	DAB9C	9C	206.352	20
1) Sydney NSW	DAB9C	9C	206.352	50
2) Melbourne VIC	DAB9C	9C	206.352	50(d)
1) Brisbane QLD	DAB9C	9C	206.352	50
1) Adelaide SA	DAB9C	9C	206.352	50
1) Perth WA	DAB9C	9C	206.352	50(d)
1) Darwin NT	DAB9C	9C	206.352	20

NB: Txs 1kW and higher

All permanent digital multiplexes shared with ABC and carry all SBS radio networks excepting NRN. Several digital on-channel repeaters provide infill coverage (ERP 300-1000W). All prgr at **W:** digitalradioplus.com.au/listen

Addresses: 1) Locked Bag 028, Crows Nest, NSW 158 – **2)** PO Box 294, South Melbourne, Vic 3205

COMMERCIAL RADIO SERVICES

NB: (t) is a designated translator stn which may carry local content.

News: Additional newscasts are often carried during breakfast and drive times.

MW	Call	kHz	kW	Location
1)	2PM	531	5(d)	Kempsey
2)	3GG	531	5(d)	Warragul
3)	4KZ	531	5(d)	Innisfail
4)	7SD	540	5(d)	Scottsdale
5)	4AM	558	5(d)	Atherton
6)	4GY	558	5(d)	Gympie
8)	2BH	567	0.5	Broken Hill
164)	6EL	621	2	Bunbury
133)	2HC	639	5(d)	Coffs Harbour
33)	4CC(t)	666	2(d)	Biloola
103)	4LM	666	2	Mount Isa
160)	6LN	666	1	Carnarvon (F.PI FM)
105)	3AW	693	5(d)	Melbourne
9)	4KQ	693	10/5(d)	Brisbane
3)	4KZ(t)	693	0.5	Tully
103)	4LM(t)	693	1	Cloncurry
131)	6SE	747	5(d)	Esperance (F.PI FM)
166)	6TZ	756	2	Margaret River
10)	2EC	765	5(d)	Bega
73)	4GC(t)	765	0.5	Hughenden
134)	5CC	765	5(d)	Port Lincoln
147)	8HOT(t)	765	0.5	Katherine
13)	6VA	783	2	Albany (F.PI FM)
14)	5RM	801	2	Berri
73)	4GC	828	1	Charters Towers
17)	4EL	846	5(d)	Cairns
18)	4GR	864	2	Toowoomba
19)	6AM	864	2	Northam
21)	2GB	873	6	Sydney
24)	4BH	882	5(d)	Brisbane
23)	6PR	882	10	Perth
25)	2LM	900	5(d)	Lismore (F.PI FM)
107)	2LT	900	5(d)	Lithgow (F.PI FM)
58)	6BY	900	2	Bridgetown
28)	8HA	900	2	Alice Springs
153)	4VL	918	2/2.5	Charleville
164)	6NA	918	2	Narrogin
32)	3UZ	927	5	Melbourne
33)	4CC	927	5(d)	Gladstone
69)	4HI(t)	945	1(d)	Dysart
21)	2UE	954	5	Sydney
17)	4EL(t)	954	0.35	Gordonvale
38)	2RG	963	5(d)	Griffith
37)	4WK	963	5(d)	Warwick
93)	5SE	963	5(d)	Mt. Gambier
164)	6TZ	963	2	Bunbury
86)	2DU(t)	972	0.3	Cobar
39)	2MW	972	5(d)	Murwillumbah
112)	2NM	981	5(d)	Muswellbrook
41)	3HA	981	2	Hamilton
42)	6KG	981	2	Kalgoorlie
43)	4RO	990	5(d)	Rockhampton
45)	2ST	999	5(d)	Nowra (F.PI FM)
46)	4TAB	1008	10(d)	Brisbane
49)	2KY	1017	5	Sydney
139)	4AA	1026	5(d)	Mackay
53)	5AU(t)	1044	2	Port Pirie
54)	2CA	1053	5(d)	Canberra
55)	3EL	1071	5(d)	Maryborough
56)	4SB	1071	2	Kingaroy
151)	6WB	1071	2	Katanning
57)	2MO	1080	2	Gunnedah
167)	6IX	1080	2	Perth
59)	2EL	1089	5(d)	Orange
60)	3WM	1089	5(d)	Horsham
61)	4LG	1098	2	Longreach
62)	6MD	1098	2	Merredin
156)	3AK	1116	5(d)	Melbourne
65)	4BC	1116	6.3/17(d)	Brisbane
113)	5MU	1125	5(d)	Murray Bridge
66)	2AD	1134	2(d)	Armidale (F.PI FM)
67)	3CS	1134	5(d)	Colac
164)	6TZ(t)	1134	2	Collie
68)	2HD	1143	2	Newcastle
69)	4HI	1143	5(d)	Emerald
70)	2WG	1152	2	Wagga Wagga
30)	4FC	1161	2	Maryborough
72)	2CH	1170	10	Sydney
75)	2NZ	1188	2	Inverell
80)	2CC	1206	5/5(d)	Canberra
78)	2GF	1206	5(d)	Grafton
69)	4HI(t)	1215	0.25	Moranbah
82)	3GV	1242	5(d)	Sale
85)	4AK	1242	2	Toowoomba/Oakey
84)	5AU	1242	2(d)	Port Augusta
86)	2DU	1251	2	Dubbo
32)	3SR	1260	2	Shepparton
89)	2SM	1269	5	Sydney
90)	3EE	1278	5	Melbourne
91)	2TM	1287	2	Tamworth (F.PI FM)
32)	3BT	1314	5(d)	Ballarat
40)	5DN	1323	3.3(d)	Adelaide
98)	3SH	1332	2	Swan Hill
99)	4BU	1332	5(d)	Bundaberg
102)	2LF	1350	5(d)	Young
104)	2GN	1368	2	Goulburn (F.PI FM)
105)	3MP	1377	5(d)	Melbourne
106)	5AA	1395	5(d)	Adelaide
108)	2PK	1404	2	Parkes/Forbes
5)	4AM(t)	1422	1	Port Douglas
111)	2MG	1449	5	Mudgee
32)	3ML	1467	2	Mildura
115)	4ZR	1476	2	Roma
116)	2AY	1494	2	Albury
119)	2QN	1521	2	Deniliquin
120)	2VM	1530	2	Moree
121)	2RE	1557	2	Taree (F.PI FM)
122)	3NE	1566	5(d)	Wangaratta
10)	2EC(t)	1584	0.2	Narooma
33)	4CC(t)	1584	0.5	Rockhampton
153)	4VL(t)	1584	0.2	Cunnamulla

FM	Call	MHz	kW	Location
117)	2BS(t)	88.1	2(d)	Burraga NSW
3)	4KZ(t)	88.5	1(d)	Mission Beach QLD
165)	4RGC	88.5	1	Mossman QLD
170)	8SAT	88.7	4(d)	Urana NSW
170)	8SAT	88.7	1	Hawker SA
41)	3HFM	88.9	20(d)	Hamilton VIC
56)	4KRY	89.1	15	Kingaroy QLD
117)	2BS(t)	89.3	1(d)	Blayney NS
63)	7LAA	89.3	5(d)	Launceston TAS
46)	4TAB	89.7	5(d)	Beaudesert QLD
71)	5CCC	89.9	6(d)	Port Lincoln SA
48)	7EXX	90.1	5(d)	Launceston TAS
69)	4HIT(t)	90.3	1	Blackwater QLD
130)	5SSA (t)	90.3	2(d)	Adelaide Foothills SA
69)	4HI	90.5	2(d)	Moranbah QLD
154)	4SEA	90.9	25(d)	Gold Coast QLD
170)	8SAT	90.9	4(d)	Maitland SA

FM	Call	MHz	kW	Location
168)	4MCY	91.1	10(d)	Nambour QLD
123)	2MAC	91.3	1	Campbelltown NSW
120)	2NOW(t)	91.3	1	Lightning Ridge NSW
96)	4HIT	91.3	5	Moranbah QLD
148)	3PTV	91.5	56(d)	Melbourne VIC
29)	2SKI(t)	91.7	1	Bombala NSW
45)	2ST(t)	91.7	1(d)	St Georges Basin NSW
17)	4HOT(t)	91.7	1	Mossman QLD
52)	6HED	91.7	5(d)	Port Hedland WA
135)	6MM	91.7	5(d)	Mandurah WA
55)	3BDG	91.9	120(d)	Bendigo VIC
18)	4RGD	91.9	2	Warwick QLD
15)	4SEE	91.9	10(d)	Nambour QLD
169)	5ADL	91.9	20(d)	Adelaide SA
16)	7XS	92.1	1(d)	Queenstown/Zeehan TAS
11)	4TOO(t)	92.3	1	Ayr/Home Hill QLD
29)	2XXL(t)	92.5	1	Bombala NSW
96)	4CCA(t)	92.5	1	Mossman QLD
155)	4GLD	92.5	25(d)	Gold Coast QLD
86)	2ZOO	92.7	10	Dubbo NSW
15)	4SSS	92.7	10(d)	Nambour QLD
29)	2SKI(t)	92.9	1	Thredbo NSW
91)	2TTT	92.9	20(d)	Tamworth NSW
120)	2VM(t)	92.9	1	Lightning Ridge NSW
41)	3HA/t	92.9	1(d)	Portland VIC
44)	6PPM	92.9	40(d)	Perth WA
143)	2GEE	93.1	10	Mudgee NSW
70)	2WZD	93.1	80	Wagga Wagga NSW
150)	4BRZ	93.1	1(d)	Bulahdelah NSW
154)	4RGB	93.1	3(d)	Bundaberg QLD
34)	4TSV	93.1	1	Ayr/Home Hill QLD
14)	5RIV	93.1	10(d)	Renmark/Loxton SA
163)	2DBO	93.5	10	Dubbo NSW
1)	2PM(t)	93.5	3(d)	Port Macquarie NSW
104)	2SNO	93.5	40	Goulburn NSW
35)	3BBO	93.5	120(d)	Bendigo VIC
43)	4ROK	93.5	1(d)	Gladstone QLD
41)	3HFM(t)	93.7	2(d)	Portland VIC
87)	3SUN(t)	93.7	1	Alexandra/Eildon VIC
87)	3SUN(t)	93.7	1(d)	Yea VIC
150)	4RBL	93.7	4	Tenterfield NSW
47)	6PER	93.7	40(d)	Perth WA
102)	2LFF	93.9	40	Young NSW
101)	3BAY	93.9	56(d)	Geelong VIC
99)	4RUM	93.9	3.2(d)	Bundaberg QLD
170)	8SAT	93.9	3	Bunnaloo NSW
150)	4RBL	94.1	1(d)	Bulahdelah NSW
83)	2BDR	94.1	1(d)	Falls Creek VIC
52)	6NW	94.1	5(d)	Port Hedland WA
2)	3SEA(t)	94.3	7(d)	Warragul VIIC
60)	3WWM(t)	94.5	2	Nhill/Lawloit VIC
22)	3YB	94.5	20(d)	Warrnambool VIC
79)	6MIX	94.5	40(d)	Perth WA
29)	2SKI(t)	94.7	2	Jindabyne NSW
69)	4HIT	94.7	5	Emerald QLD
45)	2WSK	94.9	50(d)	Nowra NSW
141)	4MIX	94.9	50(d)	Ipswich QLD
88)	6KAN	94.9	5(d)	Katanning WA
117)	2BS	95.1	8(d)	Bathurst NSW
75)	2GEM	95.1	10	Inverell NSW
43)	4RGK	95.1	1(d)	Gladstone QLD
115)	4ROM	95.1	1	Roma QLD
145)	2PTV	95.3	150(d)	Sydney NSW
32)	3SRR	95.3	100(d)	Shepparton VIC
162)	3YFM	95.3	20(d)	Warrnambool VIC
13)	6AAY	95.3	50(d)	Albany WA
16)	7AUS	95.3	1(d)	Queenstown/Zeehan TAS
170)	8SAT	95.3	5	Speed VIC
170)	8SAT	95.3	2(d)	Karoonda SA
108)	2ROK	95.5	10	Parkes/Forbes NSW
101)	3CAT	95.5	56(d)	Geelong VIC
170)	8SAT	95.5	3(d)	Kingscote SA
151)	6BUN	95.7	55(d)	Bunbury WA
4)	7SD	95.7	5	Scottsale TAS
73)	4CHT	95.9	1.5	Charters Towers QLD
12)	2ONE	96.1	5	Katoomba NSW
29)	2XXL	96.1	45(d)	Cooma NSW
6)	4NNN	96.1	5(d)	Gympie QLD
150)	4RBL	96.1	1	Weipa QLD
93)	5SEF	96.1	20	Mount Gambier SA
125)	6NOW	96.1	40(d)	Perth WA
113)	5MU	96.3	20(d)	Murray Bridge SA
8)	2HIL	96.5	4	Broken Hill NSW
95)	2UUL	96.5	40(d)	Wollongong NSW
142)	6GGG	96.5	30(d)	Geraldton WA
19)	6NAM	96.5	10	Northam WA
170)	8SAT	96.5	4(d)	Pinnaroo SA
40)	5ADD(t)	96.7	2(d)	Adelaide Foothills SA
161)	2SYD	96.9	150(d)	Sydney NSW
118)	3SUN	96.9	100(d)	Shepparton VIC
170)	8SAT	96.9	5	Meringur VIC
14)	5RIV	97.1	2.5(d)	Waikerie SA
159)	4BFM	97.3	12	Brisbane QLD
135)	6CST	97.3	5(d)	Mandurah WA
57)	2GGG	97.5	20(d)	Gunnedah NSW
29)	2SKI	97.7	50(d)	Cooma NSW
170)	8SAT	97.7	3(d)	Coonalpyn SA
136)	3RMR	97.9	12(d)	Mildura VIC
5)	4AMM	97.9	5(d)	Atherton QLD
42)	6KAR	97.9	4(d)	Kalgoorlie WA
170)	8SAT	97.9	1.3(d)	Roxby Downs SA
112)	2VLY	98.1	20(d)	Muswellbrook NSW
123)	2WIN	98.1	40(d)	Wollongong NSW
142)	6BAY	98.1	30(d)	Geraldton WA
147)	8HOT	98.1	1	Katherine NT
120)	2NOW	98.3	100(d)	Moree NSW
82)	3GV	98.3	5(d)	Bainsdale VIC
11)	4TOO	98.3	2(d)	Bowen QLD
3)	4ZKZ	98.3	20(d)	Innisfail QLD
77)	5MMM(t)	98.3	2(d)	Adelaide Foothills SA
60)	3WWM(t)	98.5	1(d)	Ararat VIC
98)	3SHI(t)	98.7	1(d)	Kerang VIC
158)	4RGM	98.7	90(d)	Mackay QLD
113)	5EZY	98.7	20(d)	Murray Bridge SA
27)	7AD	98.9	7(d)	Devonport TAS
170)	8SAT	98.9	10(d)	Minlaton SA
169)	5ADL(t)	99.1	2(d)	Adelaide Foothills SA
117)	2BXS	99.3	10	Bathurst NSW
170)	8SAT	99.3	4	Streaky Bay SA
150)	4RBL	99.4	2(d)	Mt. Tamborine QLD
107)	2ICE	99.5	1(d)	Katoomba NSW
114)	3MDA	99.5	20(d)	Mildura VIC
82)	3TFM	99.5	20(d)	Sale VIC
157)	4RGC	99.5	10(d)	Cairns QLD
170)	8SAT	99.5	1(d)	Kapunda SA
38)	2RGF	99.7	50	Griffith NSW
113)	5EZY	99.7	1	Victor Harbour SA
132)	6CAR	99.7	5	Carnarvon WA
154)	7RGS	99.7	5(d)	Scottsdale TAS
82)	3TFM(t)	99.9	5(d)	Bairnsdale VIC
69)	4HI(t)	100.1	1(d)	Rolleston Mine QLD
147)	8HOT	100.1	17(d)	Darwin NT
66)	2NEB	100.3	10	Armidale NSW
121)	2RE(t)	100.3	1.6(d)	Forster NSW
36)	3MEL	100.3	56(d)	Melbourne VIC
51)	4MKY	100.3	90(d)	Mackay QLD
113)	5EZY(t)	100.3	1	Mount Barker SA
170)	8SAT	100.3	5(d)	Padthaway East SA
116)	2AAY(t)	100.5	1(d)	Falls Creek VIC
88)	6BET	100.5	5	Bridgetown WA
164)	6NAN	100.5	5	Narrogin WA
150)	4BRZ	100.6	2(d)	Mt. Tamborine QLD
1)	2PQQ	100.7	20(d)	Port Macquarie NSW
18)	4RGD	100.7	10(d)	Toowoomba QLD
11)	4RGR	100.7	100(d)	Townsville QLD
25)	2ZZZ	100.9	32(d)	Lismore NSW
7)	7BU	100.9	20(d)	Burnie/Wynyard TAS
144)	7TTT	100.9	36	Hobart TAS
107)	2LT(t)	101.1	1(d)	Katoomba NSW
50)	3TTT	101.1	56(d)	Melbourne VIC
140)	2CFM	101.3	16	Gosford NSW
60)	3WWM	101.3	20(d)	Horsham VIC
52)	6HED	101.3	2	Broome WA
170)	8SAT	101.5	5(d)	Lake Cargellico NSW
43)	4RGK	101.5	10	Rockhampton QLD
81)	2UUS	101.7	150(d)	Sydney NSW
33)	4CCC	101.7	2	Charleville QLD
20)	7HHO	101.7	36	Hobart TAS
27)	7SEA(t)	101.7	20(d)	Burnie TAS
120)	2NOW(t)	101.9	1	Collarenebri NSW

FM	Call	MHz	kW	Location
126)	3FOX	101.9	56(d)	Melbourne VIC
149)	4CEE	101.9	10(d)	Maryborough QLD
139)	4MMK	101.9	90(d)	Mackay QLD
122)	3NNN	102.1	25(d)	Wangaratta VIC
1)	2ROX	102.3	20	Port Macquarie NSW
94)	3RBA	102.3	20(d)	Ballarat VIC
11)	4TOO	102.3	100(d)	Townsville QLD
40)	5ADD	102.3	20(d)	Adelaide SA
131)	6SEA	102.3	2.5(d)	Esperance WA
10)	2EEE	102.5	5	Bega NSW
119)	2MOR	102.5	50	Deniliquin NSW
150)	4BRZ	102.5	4	Tenterfield NSW
150)	4BRZ	102.5	1	Childers QLD
88)	6KA	102.5	1(d)	Karratha WA
170)	8SAT	102.5	3	Bourke NSW
96)	4CCA	102.7	10(d)	Cairns QLD
75)	2GEM	102.9	2	Warialda NSW
109)	2KKO	102.9	8(d)	Newcastle NSW
45)	2ST	102.9	2	Bowral NSW
76)	4HTB	102.9	25(d)	Gold Coast QLD
52)	6NW	102.9	2(d)	Broome WA
94)	3BBA	103.1	20(d)	Ballarat VIC
34)	4TSV	103.1	100(d)	Townsville QLD
120)	2VM(t)	103.5	1	Collarenebri NSW
96)	4HOT	103.5	10(d)	Cairns QLD
149)	4MBB	103.5	10(d)	Maryborough QLD
78)	2GF(t)	103.9	5(d)	Maclean NSW
128)	2DAY	104.1	150(d)	Sydney NSW
39)	2MW(t)	104.1	1(d)	Gold Coast QLD
10)	2EEE	104.3	20(d)	Batemans Bay/Moruya NSW
25)	2LM(t)	104.3	1(d)	Kyogle NSW
74)	3KKZ	104.3	56(d)	Melbourne VIC
171)	2GOS	104.5	16	Gosford NSW
61)	4LRE	104.5	1(d)	Longreach QLD
127)	4MMM	104.5	12	Brisbane QLD
78)	2CLR	104.7	20(d)	Grafton NSW
138)	2ROC	104.7	20	Canberra ACT
77)	5MMM	104.7	20(d)	Adelaide SA
116)	2AAY	104.9	100(d)	Albury NSW
129)	2MMM	104.9	150(d)	Sydney NSW
150)	4RBL	104.9	3	Bourke NSW
146)	8MIX	104.9	17(d)	Darwin NT
120)	2NOW(t)	105.1	1(d)	Walgett NSW
59)	2OAG	105.1	5	Orange NSW
1)	2ROX	105.1	10(d)	Kempsey NSW
124)	3MMM	105.1	56(d)	Melbourne VIC
62)	6MER	105.1	6(d)	Merredin WA
139)	2NEW	105.3	20(d)	Newcastle NSW
92)	4BBB	105.3	12	Brisbane QLD
133)	2CSF	105.5	15	Coffs Harbour NSW
10)	2EC(t)	105.5	1	Eden NSW
120)	2VM(t)	105.5	1	Mungindi NSW
83)	2BDR	105.7	100(d)	Albury NSW
167)	6IX(t)	105.7	4(d)	Wanneroo WA
10)	2EC(t)	105.9	20(d)	Batemans Bay/Moruya NSW
59)	2GZF	105.9	5	Orange NSW
84)	5AUU	105.9	20	Spencer Gulf North SA
170)	8SAT	106.1	3	Ceduna/Smoky Bay SA
137)	1CBR	106.3	20	Canberra ACT
133)	2CFS	106.3	15(d)	Coffs Harbour NSW
67)	3CCS	106.3	10(d)	Colac VIC
11)	4RGT	106.3	100(d)	Townsville QLD
64)	2WFM	106.5	150(d)	Sydney NSW
170)	8SAT	106.5	5(d)	Birchip VIC
88)	6RED	106.5	1(d)	Karratha WA
1)	2PQQ	106.7	10(d)	Kempsey NSW
45)	2ST(t)	106.7	1.6	Ulladulla NSW
120)	2VM(t)	106.7	1	Walgett NSW
150)	4RBL	106.7	1	Childers QLD
100)	2XXX	106.9	20(d)	Newcastle NSW
26)	4BNE	106.9	12	Brisbane QLD
170)	8SAT	106.9	2	Minnipa SA
146)	8MIX	106.9	1	Katherine NT
120)	2NOW(t)	107.1	1	Mungindi NSW
130)	5SSA	107.1	20(d)	Adelaide SA
121)	2MVB	107.3	10(d)	Taree NSW
29)	2XXL(t)	107.3	2	Jindabyne NSW
150)	4BRZ	107.3	1	Bourke NSW
152)	7XXX	107.3	36	Hobart TAS
170)	8SAT	107.3	2(d)	Kingston SE SA
97)	2GGO	107.7	10(d)	Gosford NSW
104)	2GN	107.7	35	Goulburn NSW
98)	3SHI	107.7	10	Swan Hill VIC
27)	7DDD	107.7	7(d)	Devonport TAS
107)	2ICE	107.9	10(d)	Lithgow NSW
43)	4ROK	107.9	10	Rockhampton QLD
34)	4TSV(t)	107.9	2(d)	Bowen QLD

NB: Txs 1kW and higher

Digital Services

DAB+	Call	Ch	MHz	kW
Canberra	DAB8D	8D	201.072	20
Sydney	DAB9A	9A	202.928	50(d)
Sydney	DAB9B	9B	204.64	50(d)
Melbourne	DAB9A	9A	202.928	50(d)
Melbourne	DAB9B	9B	204.64	50(d)
Brisbane	DAB9A	9A	202.928	50(d)
Brisbane	DAB9B	9B	204.64	50(d)
Adelaide	DAB9B	9B	204.64	50(d)
Perth	DAB9B	9B	204.64	50(d)
Mandurah	DAB8C	8C	199.36	10(d)
Darwin	DAB9A	9A	202.928	20

All permanent digital multiplexes carry simulcasts of all local wide-coverage commercial services, are shared with Community services, and carry additional digital only content. Several digital on-channel repeaters provido infill coverage (ERP 300-500W). Canberra is a trial shared with ABC & SBS. Darwin is a trial shared with ABC. Both trials have more limited content. All prgr at **W:** digitalradioplus.com.au

Commercial Addresses & other information:

NB: ARN=Australian Radio Network The term midnight-to-dawn refers to local time. Exact hrs vary from stn to stn

1) PO Box 1161, Port Macquarie NSW 2444 (DMG). Supplementary stn. on 102.3MHz and 105.1MHz – **2)** PO Box 253, Warragul Vic. 3820. – **3)** PO Box 19, Innisfail, Qld. 4860 **E:** zedamfm@4kz.com.au Translators: Tully 693kHz 0.5kW, Dunk Island 88.5MHz 0.5kW – **4)** PO Box 189, Scottsdale, TAS. 7254. Part of TASmanian Broadcasting Network – **5)** PO Box 177, Mareeba, QLD 4880 Translators: Port Douglas 1422kHz, Weipa 97.7MHz – **6)** PO Box 42, Gympie QLD 4370 – **7)** PO Box 120, Burnie, TAS. 7320 – **8)** 25 Garnet St, Broken Hill, NSW 2880 . Supplementary stn on 106.9MHz – **9)** PO Box 693, Newstead, QLD 4006 – **10)** PO Box 471, Bega, NSW 2550. Translators: 1584=Narooma, 105.9MHz = Batemans Bay – **11)** PO Box 986, Townsville, QLD 4810 **E:** fourto@ultra.net.au **W:** ozemail.com.au/~asichter (N-1:) – **12)** PO Box 145, Penrith, NSW 2750 – **13)** PO Box 293, Albany, WA 6330. – **14)** PO Box 321, Berri SA 5343 **E:** fiverm@riverland.net.au **W:** riverland.net.au /~fiverm/ – **15)** PO Box 828, Nambour, QLD 4560 – **16)** 29 Cutten St, Queenstown, TAS 7467. Translators at Strahan 105.1MHz 25w & Rosebery 107.1MHz 0.3kW – **17)** PO Box 6110, Cairns, QLD 4870. (N-1:Sky Radio) – **18)** PO Box 111, Toowoomba, QLD 4350 – **19)** PO Box 256 Northam, WA 6401 – **20)** GPO Box 542F, Hobart, TAS 7001 – **21)** PO Box 27, Willoughby NSW 2068 – **22)** PO Box 485, Warrnambool, Vic. 3280 – **23)** GPO Box 6072, Perth, W.A. 6000 – **24)** GPO Box 906, Brisbane, QLD 4001 – **25)** PO Box 44, Lismore, NSW 2480. – **26)** Locked Bag 1069, Fortitude Value BC, QLD 4006 – **27)** PO Box 635, Launceston TAS 7310 – **28)** PO Box 2106, Alice Springs 0871 .Translator at Yulara on 100.5MHz with 100w. Supplementary st. 8SUN on 96.9MHz with 300w at Alice Springs – **29)** PO Box 651, Cooma, NSW 2630 Relays 2UE 9:00-10:00 and AUSTEREO 16:00-18:00. Translators: Thredbo 92.1MHz 1kW, Jindabyne 96.3MHz 2kW and Perisher 98.7MHz 1kW – **30)** 625 Wyndham St, Shepparton, VIC 3630 – **31)** PO Box 665, Carnarvon WA 6701 – **32)** 3UZ Pty Ltd, PO Box 927, Carlton, VIC 3053 ID's as "Sport 927" – **33)** PO Box 420, Gladstone, QLD 4680. . Translator at Rockhampton on 1584 with 500w and at Biloela on 666kHz with 2.5 Kw – **34)** PO Box 986, Townsville, QLD 4810 (FM **E:** hotfm@ultra.net.au) . 4RR: Racing format, prgrs 8.00-24.00, also relays 4TAB 1008. 4RAM: Translator at Mt Stuart 107.9MHz 1kW, ID's as "103.1 Hot FM" – **35)** PO Box 108, Golden Square, Vic. 3555 – **36)** Level 2, 678 Victoria Street, Richmond, Vic, 3121 – **37)** PO Box 195, Warwick, QLD 4370 Rel 2TM 1287 7:00pm to 6:00am. Translator: Toowoomba 1359kHz 0.3kW – **38)** PO Box 493, Griffith, NSW 2680 (N-10) – **39)** PO Box 97, Coolangatta, QLD 4225 . Ids as "Radio 97" – **40)** 201 Tynte St, Nth Adelaide SA 5006. **W:** 5dn.com.au – **41)** PO Box 981, Hamilton, VIC 3300 – **42)** PO Box 440, Kalgoorlie, WA 6430 – **43)** PO Box 159, Rockhampton, QLD 4700 – **44)** PO Box 157, Subiaco, WA 6008 – **45)** PO Box 540, Nowra 2540 . Translators: Uladulla 106.7MHz. Supplementary St. on 94.9MHz. – **46)** Radio 4TAB, PO Box 275, Albion, QLD 4010. Racing format – **47)** Level 1, 464 Hay St, Subiaco, WA 6008 – **48)** G.PO

Box 572F, Hobart, TAS 7001 on 1008kHz & 1080kHz, 87.6MHz 1W narrowcast throughout Queenstown, Strahan, Zeehan, Roseberry, Tullah, Stanley& Smithton (N-1:Sky Radio). Racing format. Rel 2UE M-F – **49)** 79 Frenchs Forest Rd., Frenchs Forest NSW 2086 (N-3: Sky Sports) Provides relays to over 100 NSW stns carrying racing: – **50)** Private Bag 1011, Richmond Vic. 3121 – **51)** PO Box 183, Mackay, QLD 4740 . Airlie Beach on 94.7MHz. Bowen on 107.9MHz – **52)** PO Box 2216, South Hedland, WA 6722 – **53)** PO Box 481, Pt. Pirie, SA 5540 – **54)** PO Box 163, Canberra City, ACT 2601 **W:** 2ca.village.com.au – **55)** PO Box 178, Bendigo VIC 3550 – **56)** PO Box 305, Kingaroy, QLD 4610 ID's as "1071AM" and "Classic Gold" – **57)** PO Box 62, Gunnedah 2380 – **58)** 3 Gommes Lane, Yornup WA 6256 – **59)** PO Box 88, Orange, NSW 2800. (N-1:Sky Radio) – **60)** PO Box 606, Horsham, VIC 3400. – **61)** PO Box 20, Longreach, QLD 4730 – **62)** PO Box 264, Merredin, WA 6415. – **63)** PO Box 835G, Launceston, TAS 7250 – **64)** PO Box 1107, Neutral Bay NSW 2089 ID's as "Mix 106.5 FM" – **65)** G.PO Box 95, Brisbane, QLD 4001 – **66)** PO Box 270, Armidale, NSW 2350. **E:** 2AD@mpx.com.au (N-1 – **67)** PO Box 63, Colac, Vic. 3250 – **68)** PO Box 19, Mayfield, NSW 2304 – **69)** PO Box 267, Emerald, QLD 4720. . Translators: 945kHz 1kW, 1215kHz 0.1kW, 88.1MHz 30W, 92.5MHz 10W, 98.2MHz 0.1kW, 102.1MHz 0.25kW. Rel 4AM 558kHz, 4ZR 1476kHz, 4CC 927kHz – **70)** PO Box 480, Wagga Wagga, NSW 2650. Translator at Tumut on 107.9MHz with 10w. Supplementary St. on 93.1MHz. Both stns – **71)** PO Box 143, Maryborough, QLD 4650. – **72)** GPO Box 2516, Nth Sydney, NSW 2001 – **73)** PO Box 381, Charters Towers, QLD 4820 Translator: Hughenden 765kHz 0.5kW – **74)** Private Bag 1043, Richmond Vic. 3121 ID's as "Gold FM" – **75)** PO Box 770, Inverell, NSW 2360. – **76)** PO Box 10290, Southport BC, QLD 4215 – **77)** PO Box 1047, Unley, SA 5061 Translator in Adelaide city on 98.3MHz 0.5kW – **78)** PO Box 276, Grafton, NSW 2460. – **79)** PO Box 945, Subiaco, WA 6008 (N-1: BBC) – **80)** PO Box 1499, Canberra City, ACT 2601 – **81)** PO Box 234, Seven Hills, NSW 2147 (N-1 – **82)** PO Box 160, Sale, Vic. 3850 – **83)** 490 David Street, Albury NSW 2640 – **84)** PO Box 496, Port Augusta, SA 5700 – **85)** PO Box 783, Toowoomba, QLD 4350 – **86)** PO Box 1221, Dubbo, NSW 2830 **E:** 2du@lisp.com.au. FM station "ZOO FM" Dubbo 92.7MHz, Cobar 103.7MHz – **88)** PO Box 153, Karratha, WA 6714. – **89)** 8 Jones Bay Road, Pyrmont NSW 2009 **E:** contact@kick-am.com.au. **W:** kick-am.com.au/ ID's as "Kick AM" – **90)** GPO Box 369F, Melbourne 3001 **W:** 3aw.com.au/ – **91)** PO Box 497, Tamworth, NSW 2340 . Supplementary stn. on 92.9MHz – **92)** PO Box 105, Albion, QLD 4010 ID's as "B105" – **93)** PO Box 500, Mt. Gambier, SA 5290 – **94)** PO Box 360, Ballarat, VIC 3350. – **95)** PO Box 1234, Wollongong, NSW 2500 **E:** mike@w151.aone.net.au – **96)** 68 Abbott St Cairns QLD 4870 – **97)** PO Box 564, Gosford, NSW 2250 – **98)** PO Box 504, Swan Hill, VIC 3585 – **99)** PO Box 1059, Bundaberg, QLD 4670 – **100)** PO Box 97, Charlestown, NSW 2290 – **101)** PO Box 9550, Geelong, VIC 3220 **E:** krock@slanreach.au . ID's as "K-Rock" – **102)** PO Box 31, Young, NSW 2594 – **103)** PO Box 780, Mount Isa, QLD 4825 .Relays to 4GC 828. Translator: Cloncurry 693kHz. Supplementary FM license at Mt. Isa. – **04)** PO Box 115, Goulburn, NSW 2580 (N-1: Sky Radio) – **105)** PO Box 75, Frankston, Vic. 3199 **E:** magic@magic.com.au .3EE ID's as "Magic" – **106)** GPO Box 5AA, Adelaide SA 5001 – **107)** Mailbag 90, Lithgow, NSW 2790 **E:** 2lt@lisp.com.au. (for QSL'ing purposes) c/o John Wright, 15 Olive Cres, Peakhurst NSW 2210 – **108)** PO Box 295, Parkes, NSW 2870. – **109)** PO Box 606, Charlestown, NSW 2290. – **111)** PO Box 17, Mudgee, NSW 2850 – **112)** PO Box 600, Muswelbrook, NSW 2333 2VLY 98.1 ID's as "Power FM" – **113)** PO Box 470, Murray Bridge, SA 5253 Serves Murray Bridge, The Coorong and Meningie – **114)** PO Box 539, Mildura, VIC 3500 . 3MA 99.5 ID's as "Today's Music 99.5FM" – **115)** PO Box 22, Roma, QLD 4455. (N-1:Sky Radio) – **116)** PO Box 670, Albury, NSW 2640 **W:** albury.net.au/radio.albury.wodonga/2ay.html . Supplementary stn. on FM – **117)** PO Box 310, Bathurst, NSW 2795 **E:** stereo@2bs.ix.net.au or 2bs@csu.edu.au **W:** 2bs.ix.net.au FM service on 99.3MHz – **118)** PO Box 195, Shepparton, Vic. 3630 – **119)** PO Box 312, Deniliquin, NSW 2710. 2MOR 102.5 ID's as "Edge FM" – **120)** PO Box 389, Moree, NSW 2400. . Supplementary license on 98.3MHz. Translator on 88.7MHz with 250w r. – **121)** PO Box 275, Taree, NSW 2430. Translator: Gloucester 100.1MHz and Forster on 100.3MHz – **122)** PO Box 449, Wangaratta, VIC 3677 .3NE Translators: Mt. Hotham 89.3MHz 0.02kW, Mt. Buffalo 105.3MHz 0.2kW, Mt. Beauty 90.3MHz 10w. 3NNN ID's as "Edge FM" – **123)** Locked Bag 6198 Sth Coast Mail Centre NSW 2521 ID's as "98FM" – **124)** GPO Box 105, Melbourne, VIC – **125)** 111 Wellington Str, East Perth, WA 6004. – **126)** PO Box 1019, St. Kilda, Vic. 3182 – **127)** GPO Box 1041, Brisbane, QLD 4001. – **128)** Level 15, 50 Goulburn Street, Sydney, NSW 2000 **W:** 2dayfm.com.au – **129)** Level 14, 50 Goulburn Street, Sydney, NSW 2000 **W:** triplem.com.au – **130)** PO Box 1071, Unley, SA 5061.24h Translator South Tce, Adelaide on 91.1MHz 1kW. ID's as "SAFM" – **131)** PO Box 527, Esperance, WA 6450. N-1. Rel. 6PPM-FM 1000-2200 – **132)** PO Box 665, Carnarvon, WA 6701. 2200-1500 Translator: Exmouth – **133)** PO Box 1950, Coffs Harbour, NSW 2450 .Rp – **134)** PO Box 483, Port Lincoln, SA 5606. – **135)** 141 Mandurah Tce, Mandurah, WA 6210 – **136)** GPO Box 163, Canberra, ACT 2601. Belongs to 54). **F.PI:** translator for Tuggeranong area – **137)** PO Box 106, Dickson, ACT 2602. ID's as "Mix 106.3" – **138)** GPO Box 163, Canberra, A.C.T. 2601 – **139)** PO Box 185, Mackay QLD 4740 – **140)** PO Box 2101, Gosford, NSW 2250 – **141)** PO Box 7, Ipswich, QLD 4305 ID's as "Mix 106.9 QFM" – **142)** PO Box 128 Geraldton, WA 6530. 24h – **143)** 15 Puttabucca Rd, Mudgee NSW 2850 – **144)** G.PO Box 1800, Hobart, TAS. 7001 – **145)** Locked Bag 5000, Broadway NSW 2007 – **146)** GPO Box 2510, Darwin NT 0801 – **147)** 4 Peary St., Darwin, NT 0800 Translators: Katherine 765kHz 0.5kW – **148)** 678 Victoria St, Richmond VIC 3121 – **149)** 403 The Esplanade, Torquay QLD 4655 – **150)** PO Box 332, Beaudesert QLD 4285 – **151)** PO Box 148, Bunbury WA 6231 – **152)** GPO Box 1345, Hobart TAS 7001 – **153)** PO Box 84, Charleville, QLD 4470 ID's as "Outback Radio". Translator: Cunnamulla 1584kHz 0.2kW – **154)** PO Box 5910 Gold Coast Mail Centre Bundall QLD 4217 r. – **155)** Private Bag 925 Gold Coast Mail Centre QLD 4215. – **156)** Level 5, 111 Coventry Street, Southbank VIC 3006 – **157)** Sea FM, 320 Sheridan St Cairns QLD 4870 – **158)** Sea FM, Suncorp/Metway Building Suite 3, Level 3, 123 Victoria St, Mackay QLD 4740 – **159)** 444 Logan Rd, Stones Corner QLD 4120 – **160)** PO Box 665 Carnarvon WA 6701 – **161)** 33 Saunders Road, Pyrmont NSW 2009 – **162)** Regional Communications Pty Ltd, PO Box 7515, St Kilda Road VIC 3004 – **163)** 47 Wingewarra St Dubbo NSW 2830 – **164)** DMG Regional Radio, Locked Bag 5000, Broadway NSW 2007 – **165)** 68 Aboott St, Cairns QLD 4870 – **166)** PO Box 112, Bunbury WA 6230 – **167)** PO Box 33, Tuart Hill WA 6060 **168)** cnr Plaza Pde & Carnaby St, Maroochydore QLD 4558 – **169)** Locked Bag 919, Adelaide SA 5001 – **170)** PO Box 579, Lilydale VIC 3140 – **171)** PO Box 3535, Erina NSW 2250.

COMMUNITY RADIO SERVICES

MW	Call	Location	kHz	kW
1)	2WEB	Bourke	585	10(d)
2)	6WR	Kununurra	693	5
3)	3CR	Melbourne	855	3.5(d)
4)	7RPH	Hobart	864	2
9)	3RPH	Warrnambool	882	2(d)
15)	6FX	Fitzroy Crossing	936	5
9)	6RPH	Perth	990	5.5
7)	1RPH	Canberra	1125	2(d)
9)	3RPH	Melbourne	1179	5
8)	4YB	Brisbane	1197	0.5
10)	5RPH	Adelaide	1197	2
11)	2RPH	Sydney	1224	5(d)
6)	4MW	Thursday Is.	1260	2
18)	4RPH	Brisbane	1296	5(d)
193)	3KND	Melbourne	1503	5(d)

FM	Call	MHz	kW	Location
151)	3MFM	88.1	2(d)	Leongatha
9)	3BPH	88.7	6.6	Bendigo
176)	3RUM	88.7	1	Walwa/Jingellic
240)	2BRW	88.9	2	Braidwood
13)	2RBR	88.9	1(d)	Coraki
14)	2YOU	88.9	1	Tamworth
217)	4CCR	89.1	2(d)	Cairns
148)	5BBB	89.1	1	Barossa Valley
239)	5UMA	89.1	4(d)	Port Augusta
17)	4CRB	89.3	25(d)	Gold Coast
16)	4SDB	89.3	2	Warwick
149)	5EFM	89.3	1	Victor Harbour
150)	5GFM	89.3	5(d)	Arthurton
151)	3MFM	89.5	1(d)	Foster
218)	2HIM	89.7	1	Tamworth
19)	2TEN	89.7	4	Tenterfield
147)	5TCB(t)	89.7	1.5	Naracoorte
158)	6TCR	89.7	2(d)	Wanneroo
238)	3TSC	89.9	56(d)	Melbourne
20)	4DDD	89.9	2	Dalby
152)	5GSFM	90.1	1	Victor Harbour
153)	3SYN	90.7	35(d)	Melbourne
21)	4CSB	90.7	5(d)	Wondai
22)	5KIX	90.7	3(d)	Kangaroo Island
23)	1CMS	91.1	20	Canberra
24)	2CBD	91.1	5	Deepwater
1)	2WEB(t)	91.1	1(d)	Coonamble
25)	2MAX	91.3	10(d)	Narrabri
241)	2BJG	91.5	1(d)	Wellington

FM	Call	MHz	kW	Location
102)	4BRR	91.5	1	Gayndah
26)	4GCR	91.5	1	Gympie
27)	1WAY	91.9	20	Canberra
198)	2STA	91.9	1(d)	Inverell
28)	4RGL	91.9	1	Gladstone
37)	2ARM	92.1	2	Armidale
30)	2MFM	92.1	15(d)	Sydney
31)	6RTR	92.1	16(d)	Perth
33)	2MCE	92.3	1	Bathurst
34)	3ZZZ	92.3	56(d)	Melbourne
35)	1ART	92.7	20	Canberra
155)	5FBI	92.7	20(d)	Adelaide
36)	2NCR	92.9	6	Lismore
147)	5TCB	92.9	2	Kingston SE
38)	2BBB	93.3	3.2	Dorrigo
156)	2MNO	93.3	2	Monaro
157)	2SNR	93.3	2(d)	Gosford
9)	3RPH	93.5	1	Warragul
39)	2BAR	93.7	1(d)	Bega
212)	2LND	93.7	50(d)	Sydney
40)	5DDD	93.7	6.3	Adelaide
226)	2CCM	94.1	2(d)	Gosford
41)	2LIV	94.1	4(d)	Wollongong/Nowra
43)	2DCB	94.3	2	Dubbo
213)	2FBI	94.5	150(d)	Sydney
45)	8KNB	94.5	15	Darwin
33)	2MCE	94.7	1	Orange
228)	3PLS	94.7	56(d)	Geelong
47)	4BCR	94.7	3(d)	Bundaberg
194)	2GCB	94.9	2	Gosford
70)	3MCR	94.9	1	Castlemaine
160)	2MIA	95.1	3.5(d)	Griffith
229)	2TRR	95.3	2	Coolah
161)	6EBA	95.3	16(d)	Perth
229)	2TRR	96.1	1	Dunedoo
11)	7RPH	96.1	3.2	Devonport
32)	7THE	96.1	3(d)	Hobart
48)	2CCC	96.3	2(d)	Gosford
49)	3GGR	96.3	56(d)	Geelong
137)	6PAC	96.3	6	Kalgoorlie
50)	2CHR	96.5	2(d)	Cessnock/Maitland
51)	3EON	96.5	1(d)	Bendigo
52)	4FRB	96.5	12	Brisbane
46)	4RFM	96.9	4	Moranbah
168)	7MID	97.1	2	Oatlands
159)	2OLD	97.3	1	Lake Macquarie
54)	3HCR	97.3	1	Omeo
165)	7TAS	97.7	1	Tasman Peninsula
55)	8GGG	97.7	15	Darwin
56)	2LVR	97.9	4.2(d)	Parkes/Forbes
57)	6DBY	97.9	2	Derby
58)	4EB	98.1	12	Brisbane
59)	1XXR	98.3	20	Canberra
60)	6MKA	98.3	1	Meekatharra
61)	2OOO	98.5	25(d)	Sydney
62)	3ONE	98.5	10(d)	Shepparton
167)	4YOU	98.5	1	Rockhampton
63)	6SON	98.5	16(d)	Perth
64)	2KRR	98.7	1	Kandos
65)	4CIM	98.7	10(d)	Cairns
66)	4AAA	98.9	12	Brisbane
29)	3SFM	99.1	1	Swan Hill
67)	3RPC	99.3	2(d)	Portland
68)	2RFM	99.7	10(d)	Newcastle
70)	3MCR	99.7	1	Mansfield
215)	4ACR	99.7	1	Woorabinda
169)	4RED	99.7	2(d)	Redcliffe
71)	6GME	99.7	2	Broome
170)	2BAY	99.9	3	Byron Bay
72)	2PMQ	99.9	3(d)	Port Macquarie
73)	3BBB	99.9	3	Ballarat
74)	4TCB	99.9	20(d)	Townsville
171)	5MBS	99.9	2.5	Adelaide Foothills
75)	2BCB	100.1	10	Bathurst
9)	3SPH	100.1	10(d)	Shepparton
172)	4RIM	100.1	1	Boonah
214)	5GTR	100.1	1	Mt. Gambier
5)	6NR	100.1	6.5(d)	Perth
216)	2YAS	100.3	1.5	Yass
77)	4BAY	100.3	3(d)	Wynnum/Redlands
11)	2RPH(t)	100.5	4	Newcastle
11)	2RPH(t)	100.5	1(d)	Sydney Eastern Suburbs
78)	3CH	100.7	1(d)	Kyneton
79)	4US	100.7	1	Rockhampton
76)	5LFM	100.7	5(d)	Renmark
211)	2PSR	100.9	1(d)	Port Stephens
80)	6CRA	100.9	8(d)	Albany
166)	6NME	100.9	16(d)	Perth
81)	4CBL	101.1	4(d)	Logan
82)	3WPR	101.3	1	Wangaratta
85)	8KTR	101.3	1	Katherine
83)	2GLA	101.5	10(d)	Forster
230)	3BBS	101.5	1	Bendigo
174)	4BSR	101.5	1	Beaudesert
84)	4OUR	101.5	3(d)	Caboolture
185)	5UV	101.5	20(d)	Adelaide
9)	2APH	101.7	2	Albury
231)	6SEN	101.7	8(d)	Perth
177)	2PAR	101.9	1	Ballina
86)	4ZZZ	102.1	12	Brisbane
87)	6WR	102.1	1	Wyndham
88)	2NIM	102.3	1	Nimbin
89)	2MBS	102.5	50(d)	Sydney
90)	3RRR	102.7	56(d)	Melbourne
178)	4DDB	102.7	4	Toowoomba
91)	2CVC	103.1	1(d)	Grafton
92)	2WET	103.1	1	Kempsey
210)	3BBR	103.1	1	Warragul
93)	5EBI	103.1	20(d)	Adelaide
94)	2CBA	103.2	50(d)	Sydney
95)	2TLP	103.3	3(d)	Taree
97)	2CCB	103.5	1.5	Orange
98)	3MBR	103.5	4.8	Murrayville
99)	3MBS	103.5	56(d)	Melbourne
100)	2NUR	103.7	10(d)	Newcastle
53)	3WAY	103.7	5	Warrnambool
101)	4MBS	103.7	12	Brisbane
179)	7LTN	103.7	2(d)	Launceston
103)	2WAY	103.9	3	Port Macquarie
104)	3BGR	103.9	3	Ballarat
209)	3GCB	103.9	10(d)	Latrobe Valley
105)	4TTT	103.9	20	Townsville
106)	6ESP	103.9	1.4(d)	Esperance
107)	2CHY	104.1	5	Coffs Harbour
44)	8TFM	104.1	15	Darwin
69)	2UUU	104.5	2(d)	Nowra
147)	5TCB	104.5	1.6	Keith
109)	2BOB	104.7	5	Taree
110)	3GCR	104.7	4	Latrobe Valley
111)	3GRR	104.7	5(d)	Echuca
112)	7DBS	104.7	2	Devonport
181)	4SFM	104.9	3	Nambour
182)	5RCB	104.9	20(d)	Mt. Gambier
113)	4WBR	105.1	10(d)	Maryborough
201)	5TRX	105.1	5	Port Pirie
114)	7WAY	105.3	3.2	Launceston
115)	4MET	105.7	10(d)	Gold Coast
24)	2CBD	105.9	3	Glen Innes
116)	2NVR	105.9	2(d)	Nambucca Heads
175)	4MUR	105.9	1	Mackay
147)	5TCB	106.1	1.6	Bordertown
112)	7DBS	106.1	10(d)	Wynyard
117)	2CUZ	106.5	10	Bourke
183)	4CLG	106.5	2(d)	Nambour
96)	7HFC	106.5	18	Hobart
227)	3HOT	106.7	1	Mildura
118)	3PBS	106.7	56(d)	Melbourne
119)	2VOX	106.9	2(d)	Wollongong
120)	3UGE	106.9	1	Alexandra/Eildon
4)	7RPH	106.9	3.2	Launceston
121)	4KIG	107.1	16	Townsville
122)	2REM	107.3	2	Albury
123)	2SER	107.3	14	Sydney
124)	4CAB	107.3	10(d)	Gold Coast
125)	2EAR	107.5	1.6(d)	Moruya
173)	2OCB	107.5	5	Orange
9)	3MPH	107.5	1	Mildura
126)	4CRM	107.5	1	Mackay
176)	3RUM	107.7	1	Tumbarumba
127)	2AIR	107.9	1(d)	Coffs Harbour

FM	Call	MHz	kW	Location
128)	2COW	107.9	1	Casino
129)	5RAM	107.9	20(d)	Adelaide
130)	6CCR	107.9	1(d)	Fremantle

NB: Txs 1kW and higher

Digital Community Radio

DAB+	Call	Ch	MHz	kW
Sydney	DAB9A	9A	202.928	50(d)
Sydney	DAB9B	9B	204.64	50(d)
Melbourne	DAB9A	9A	202.928	50(d)
Melbourne	DAB9B	9B	204.64	50(d)
Brisbane	DAB9A	9A	202.928	50(d)
Brisbane	DAB9B	9B	204.64	50(d)
Adelaide	DAB9B	9B	204.64	50(d)
Perth	DAB9B	9B	204.64	50(d)

Digital multiplexes carry simulcasts of many local wide coverage community services.

HIGH POWER OPEN NARROWCAST SERVICES (HPON)

NB: These stns are licenced in the usual MW & FM broadcast bands. Programming is narrowcast. Official callsigns are issued but not used on-air, actual on-air identifiers may resemble normal callsigns. Many stns not using full licensed tx power/ERP.

MW	Station	kHz	kW	Location
188)	R. Italiana 531		0.5	Adelaide SA
244)	SEN Track	657	2	Perth WA
244)	SEN Track	801	5	Gosford NSW
189)	4AY	873	2	Innisfail QLD
138)	R. TAB	891	5(d)	Townsville QLD
146)	RSN	945	2	Bendigo VIC
139)	Sky Sports R.	1008	0.3	Canberra ACT
132)	TAB R. (WA)	1008	2	Geraldton WA
138)	R. TAB	1008	5(d)	Launceston TAS
164)	Vision Christian R.	1017	1	Bunbury WA
244)	SEN Track	1053	0.5	Brisbane QLD
138)	R. TAB	1080	5(d)	Hobart TAS
132)	TAB R. (WA)	1206	2	Perth WA
138)	R. TAB	1242	2	Darwin NT
139)	Sky Sports R.	1314	5(d)	Wollongong NSW
144)	Star AM	1323	0.4(d)	Canberra ACT
139)	Sky Sports R.	1341	5(d)	Newcastle NSW
192)	3CW 1341	1341	5(d)	Geelong VIC
146)	RSN	1359	0.2	Mildura VIC
132)	TAB R. (WA)	1404	4	Busselton WA
164)	Vision Christian R.	1413	0.5(d)	Shepparton VIC
195)	3XY R. Hellas	1422	5	Melbourne VIC
200)	R. Great Southern	1422	2	Wagin WA
164)	Vision Christian R.	1431	2	Kalgoorlie WA
132)	TAB R. (WA)	1449	2	Mandurah WA
141)	Niche R. Network	1539	1	Sydney NSW
138)	R. TAB	1539	5(d)	Adelaide SA
136)	KIX Country	1557	0.5(d)	Renmark/Loxton SA
244)	SEN Track	1575	5	Wollongong NSW
139)	Sky Sports R.	1593	0.2	Murwillumbah NSW
244)	SEN Track	1593	5(d)	Melbourne VIC

FM	Station	MHz	kW	Location
197)	KIK FM	88.7	2(d)	Atherton QLD
132)	TAB R. (WA)	89.5	1.2	Esperance WA
136)	KIX Country	90.5	1(d)	Barossa Valley SA
139)	Sky Sports R.	90.5	1(d)	Tamworth NSW
242)	Perth Chinese R.	90.5	5	Perth WA
243)	FAB FM	90.9	1	Mossman QLD
139)	Sky Sports R.	90.9	1	Mudgee NSW
135)	Triple M Country	91.5	1	Toowoomba QLD
135)	Kids FM	91.9	1(d)	Latrobe Valley VIC
136)	KIX Country	92.3	10(d)	Maryborough QLD
139)	Sky Sports R.	92.7	1	Inverell NSW
139)	Sky Sports R.	92.7	3(d)	Port Macquarie NSW
164)	Vision Christian R.	93.7	5	Albany WA
139)	Sky Sports R.	94.3	1	Goulburn NSW
164)	Vision Christian R.	94.9	4	Broken Hill NSW
139)	Sky Sports R.	95.5	10(d)	Wagga Wagga NSW
138)	R. TAB	95.5	3(d)	Bundaberg QLD
138)	R. TAB	95.5	4.5(d)	Emerald QLD
138)	R. TAB	95.5	5(d)	Renmark/Loxton SA
139)	Sky Sports R.	95.9	20(d)	Gunnedah NSW
138)	R. TAB	95.9	1	Alice Springs NT
139)	Sky Sports R.	96.9	1(d)	Cooma NSW
164)	Vision Christian R.	97.5	2(d)	Bairnsdale VIC
138)	R. TAB	97.5	1	Blackwater QLD
138)	R. TAB	97.7	1(d)	Burnie TAS
136)	KIX Country	98.1	1	Inglewood QLD
184)	Tourist Gold 98.7 FM	98.7	1	Alice Springs NT
139)	Sky Sports R.	99.9	10	Parkes/Forbes NSW
138)	R. TAB	99.9	1	Rockhampton QLD
139)	Sky Sports R.	100.5	4	Broken Hill NSW
132)	TAB R. (WA)	100.5	1	Wyndham WA
139)	Sky Sports R.	100.9	10	Bathurst NSW
136)	KIX Country	101.1	10(d)	Nowra NSW
138)	R. TAB	101.3	2	Devonport TAS
139)	Sky Sports R.	101.5	1	Grafton NSW
139)	Sky Sports R.	101.5	1	Kempsey NSW
132)	TAB R. (WA)	101.7	1	Karratha WA
164)	Vision Christian R.	102.1	1	Hamilton VIC
139)	Sky Sports R.	102.7	2(d)	Jindabyne NSW
164)	Vision Christian R.	102.9	2	Horsham VIC
139)	Sky Sports R.	103.3	1	Muswellbrook NSW
138)	R. TAB	103.5	100(d)	Mackay QLD
139)	Sky Sports R.	103.7	1	Moree NSW
139)	Sky Sports R.	103.7	2(d)	Nowra NSW
138)	R. TAB	103.7	1	Katherine NT
139)	Sky Sports R.	104.3	10	Armidale NSW
138)	R. TAB	104.3	10(d)	Cairns QLD
164)	Vision Christian R.	105.3	1	Portland VIC
136)	KIX Country	105.3	2(d)	Wollongong NSW
139)	Sky Sports R.	105.7	5	Taree NSW
249)	2QN	106.1	1	Deniliquin NSW
139)	Sky Sports R.	106.7	5	Orange NSW
146)	RSN	106.9	10	Swan Hill VIC
139)	Sky Sports R.	107.1	1	Eden NSW
139)	Sky Sports R.	107.5	3	Glen Innes NSW

NB: Txs 1kW and higher

MEDIUM FREQUENCY-NARROWBAND AREA SERVICES (MF-NAS)

NB: These stns are licenced to channels 1611-1701kHz. Programming is narrowcast except for earlier services which may be commercial format. Official callsigns are issued but not used on-air, on-air identifiers may resemble normal callsigns. Many stns are licensed but not operational. Many stns not using full licensed tx power of 400W.

MW	Station	kHz	kW	Location
246)	Station X	1611	0.4	Wee Waa NSW
164)	Vision Christian R.	1611	0.4	Grafton NSW
164)	Vision Christian R.	1611	0.4	Sydney [West] NSW
164)	Vision Christian R.	1611	0.4	Tamworth NSW
199)	Old Gold 1611AM	1611	0.4	Mildura VIC
164)	Vision Christian R.	1611	0.4	Chiltern VIC
164)	Vision Christian R.	1611	0.4	Melbourne [West] VIC
189)	4KZ	1611	0.4	Karumba QLD
145)	Hot Country	1611	0.4	Emerald QLD
145)	Hot Country	1611	0.4	Goondiwindi QLD
145)	Hot Country	1611	0.4	Roma QLD
145)	Hot Country	1611	0.4	St George QLD
164)	Vision Christian R.	1611	0.4	Adelaide SA
164)	Vision Christian R.	1611	0.4	Margaret River WA
200)	Easy Listening 1611	1611	0.4	Wagin WA
237)	Gold MX	1611	0.4	Albany WA
SBS)	SBS PopDesi	1611	0.4	Launceston TAS
250)	Canb.Chinese R.	1620	0.4	Canberra ACT
190)	R. 2MORO	1620	0.4	Sydney NSW
141)	Rete Italia	‡1620	0.4	Wangaratta VIC
247)	4BRZ	1620	0.4	Toowoomba QLD
164)	Vision Christian R.	1620	0.4	Brisbane QLD
244)	SEN Track	1620	0.4	Gold Coast QLD
141)	Rete Italia	1620	0.4	Sunshine Coast QLD
164)	Vision Christian R	1620	0.4	Taylors Beach QLD
203)	R. 1629AM	1629	0.1	Newcastle NSW
164)	Vision Christian R.	1629	0.4	Bathurst NSW
164)	Vision Christian R.	1629	0.4	Dubbo NSW
248)	ACR Huaxia	1629	0.4	Melbourne VIC
202)	Radio Nostalgia	1629	0.4	Melbourne VIC
141)	Rete Italia	1629	0.4	Shepparton VIC
145)	Hot Country	1629	0.4	Dalby QLD
244)	SEN 1629 SA	1629	0.4	Adelaide SA
244)	SEN 1629 SA	1629	0.4	Mt.Gambier SA
234)	3ABN	1629	0.4	Busselton WA
164)	Vision Christian R.	1638	0.4	Armidale NSW
222)	2ME	1638	0.4	Sydney NSW
222)	2ME	1638	0.4	Melbourne VIC
245)	Kerinvale Comaudio	1638	0.4	Biloela QLD

MW	Station	kHz	kW	Location
245)	Kerinvale Comaudio‡	1647	0.4	Dixalea QLD
164)	Vision Christian R.	1647	0.4	Mackay QLD
140)	R. Rhythm	1656	0.4	Melbourne VIC
140)	R. Rhythm†	1656	0.4	Brisbane QLD
164)	Vision Christian R.	1656	0.4	Bundaberg QLD
204)	2MM	1656	0.4	Darwin NT
204)	2MM	1665	0.4	Sydney NSW
164)	Vision Christian R.	1665	0.4	Melbourne VIC
225)	R. Haanji	1674	0.4	Sydney NSW
225)	R. Haanji	1674	0.4	Melbourne VIC
207)	R. Club AM	1683	0.4	Sydney NSW
207)	R. Club AM	1683	0.4	Melbourne VIC
133)	R. Symban	1692	0.4	Campbelltown NSW
140)	R. Rhythm (F.PI)	1692	0.4	Cairns QLD
164)	Vision Christian R.	1692	0.06	Nanango QLD
140)	R. Rhythm (F.PI)	1692	0.4	Adelaide SA
140)	R. Rhythm	†1692	0.4	Perth WA
235)	Voice of Charity	1701	0.4	Sydney NSW
224)	Islamic Voice R.	1701	0.4	Somerton VIC
208)	R. Brisvaani	1701	0.1	Brisbane QLD

†=irregular ‡=inactive

Community, HPON & MF-NAS addresses & other information

1) Western Region Educational Broadc. Co. Ltd, PO Box 426, Bourke NSW 2840. Plus 5 FM translators. – **2)** Radio Station 6WR., PO Box 162 Kununurra WA 6743. (N-1:CBAA) Aboriginal prgrs from National Indigenous Radio Service – **3)** Community R. Federation Ltd, PO Box 277, Collingwood VIC 3066. Various foreign languages – **4)** Radio 7RPH Broadcasting Services for Handicapped Inc., 136 Davey St, Hobart TAS. 7000. Information and reading service format. Relays BBCWS 11:00pm to 10:00am Mon-Sat, Sunday – **5)** Curtin Univ of Technology, GPO Box U1987, Perth WA 6001. Rel. CBAA Network at times and BBCWS overnight – **6)** PO Box 385, Thursday Island QLD 4875 – **7)** Print-Handicapped Radio of ACT Inc, Barton Highway, Gungahlin, ACT 2912 – relays BBCWS Mon-Fri 1:00pm to 6:00pm SA noon to Su 9:30am – **8)** Brisbane Youth Radio, PO Box 5130, West End QLD, 4101 – **9)** Vision Australia, 454 Glenferrie Rd, Kooyong 3144. Relays BBCWS overnight – **10)** Radio 5RPH, 231 Morphett St. Adelaide SA 5000. Relays BBCWS overnight – **11)** R. for the Print-Handicapped (NSW) Co-op Ltd, 7/184 Glebe Point Rd, Glebe NSW 2037 – **12)** PO Box 148, Toogoolawah QLD 4313 – **13)** 50 Houghwood Rd, Bora Ridge NSW 2471 – **14)** PO Box 998, Tamworth NSW 2340 – **15)** PO Box 52, Fitzroy Crossing WA 6765 – **16)** Rainbow FM, PO Box 473, Warwick QLD 4370 – **17)** PO Box 86, Burleigh Heads QLD 4220 – **18)** Unit 3/17 Henry Street, Spring Hill QLD 4000 – **19)** PO Box 93, Tenterfield NSW 2372 – **20)** PO Box 483, Dalby QLD 4405 – **21)** Crow FM, PO Box 171, Emerald QLD 4606 – **22)** PO Box 90, Kingscote SA 5223 – **23)** PO Box 3882, Weston ACT 2611 (Ethnic) – **24)** Gough St, Deepwater NSW 2371 – **25)** PO Box 94, Narrabri NSW 2390 – **26)** The Positive Alternative, PO Box 774, Gympie QLD 4570 (Christian) – **27)** Canberra Christian Radio, PO Box 927, Fyshwick ACT 2609 (Christian) – **28)** 257 Goondoon St Warwick QLD 4680 (Christian) – **29)** PO Box 998, Swan Hill VIC 3585 – **30)** Muslim Community Radio, PO Box 969, Bankstown NSW 1885 (Ethnic) – **31)** Arts Radio, PO Box 949, Nedlands WA 6009 – **32)** GPO Box 1324, Hobart TAS 7001 – **33)** Charles Sturt University, Locked Bag 30, Bathurst NSW 2795 – **34)** PO Box 1106, Collingwood VIC 3066 (Ethnic) – **35)** Artsound, PO Box 87, Curtin ACT 2605 – **36)** PO Box 5123, East Lismore NSW 2480 – **37)** PO Box 707, Armidale NSW 2350 – **38)** PO Box 304, Dorrigo NSW 2454 – **39)** Edge FM, PO Box 771, Bega NSW 2550 – **40)** 48 Nelson St, Stepney SA 5069 – **41)** Living Sound Broadcasters, PO Box 7, Coniston NSW 2500 (Christian) – **42)** Radio Hope Island, PO Box 16, Sanctuary Cove QLD 4212 – **43)** Radio Rhema, PO Box 1502, Dubbo NSW 2830 (Christian) – **44)** 1041 Territory FM, Charles Darwin University NT 0909 – **45)** Radio Larrakia, Shop 2, Alawa Shops, Alawa NT 0810 (Aboriginal) – **46)** PO Box 597, Moranbah QLD 4744 – **47)** PO Box 2678, Bundaberg QLD 4670 – **48)** PO Box 19, Gosford NSW 2250 – **49)** Rhema FM, PO Box 886, Belmont VIC 3216 (Christian) – **50)** PO Box 421, Cessnock NSW 2325 – **51)** Radio KLFM, PO Box 2997, Bendigo Delivery Centre VIC 3554 – **52)** Family Radio, PO Box 1700, Milton QLD 4064 – **53)** PO Box 752, Warrnambool VIC 3280 – **54)** PO Box 86, Omeo VIC 3898 – **55)** Darwin Christian Broadcasters, PO Box 43146, Casaurina NT 0810 (Christian) – **56)** Parkes Road, Forbes NSW 2871 – **57)** PO Box 655, Derby WA 6728 – **58)** 140 Main St, Kangaroo Point QLD 4169 – **59)** 2XX, GPO Box 812, Canberra ACT 2601 – **60)** PO Box 259, Meekatharra WA 6642 – **61)** Radio 2000, 2/25 Belmore Rd, Burwood NSW 2134 (Ethnic) – **62)** PO Box 6824, Shepparton VIC 3630 – **63)** Sonshine FM, PO Box 6340, Morley WA 6062 (Christian) – **64)** PO Box 99, Kandos NSW 2848 – **65)** PO Box 1856, Cairns QLD 4870 (Aboriginal) – **66)** Box 6229, Fairfield Gardens QLD 4103 (Aboriginal) – **67)** PO Box 450, Portland VIC 3305 – **68)** Rhema FM, PO Box 2000, Dangar NSW 2309 (Christian) – **69)** PO Box 884, Nowra NSW 2541 – **70)** PO Box 667, Mansfield VIC 3724 – **71)** PMB Turkey Creek, via Kununurra WA 6743 (Aboriginal) – **72)** Radio Rhema, PO Box 1537, Port Macquarie NSW 2444 (Christian) – **73)** Voice FM, PO Box 149, Ballarat VIC 3350 – **74)** Live FM, PO Box 332, Aitkenvale QLD 4814 (Christian) – **75)** Radio Rhema, PO Box 615, Bathurst NSW 2795 (Christian) – **76)** PO Box 1680, Loxton SA 5333 – **77)** PO Box 1003, Cleveland QLD 4163 – **78)** Central Highlands Broadc. Inc, PO Box 966, Woodend VIC 3442 – **79)** PO Box 663, Rockhampton QLD 4700 (Aboriginal) – **80)** 211-217 North Road, Albany WA 6330 – **81)** PO Box 2101, Logan City DC QLD 4114 – **82)** PO Box 605, Wangaratta VIC 3676 – **83)** PO Box 1015, Tuncurry NSW 2428 – **84)** PO Box 418, Caboolture QLD 4510 – **85)** PO Box 889, Katherine NT 0851 – **86)** PO Box 509, Fortitude Valley QLD 4006 – **87)** PO Box 815, Kununurra WA 6743 (Aboriginal) – **88)** PO Box 522, Nimbin NSW 2480 – **89)** 76 Chandos St, St Leonards NSW 2065 – **90)** PO Box 304, Fitzroy VIC 3065 – **91)** PO Box 115, Grafton NSW 2460 (Christian) – **92)** PO Box 200, West Kempsey NSW 2440 – **93)** 10 Byron Pl, Adelaide SA 5000 (Ethnic) – **94)** PO Box 54, Five Dock NSW 2046 – **95)** Ngarralinyi, The Listening Place, PO Box 657, Taree NSW 2430 (Aboriginal) – **96)** PO Box 1033, New Town TAS 7008 – **97)** Radio Rhema, PO Box 974, Orange NSW 2800 – **98)** PO Box 139, Murrayville VIC 3512 – **99)** 146 Cotham Road, Kew VIC 3101 – **100)** University Dr, Callaghan NSW 2308 – **101)** 384 Old Cleveland Rd, Coorparoo QLD 4151 – **102)** PO Box 915, Gayndah QLD 4625 – **103)** PO Box 603, Port Macquarie 2446 – **104)** Good News Radio, PO Box 312, Ballarat VIC 3350 – **105)** PO Box 1033, Townsville QLD 4810 – **106)** PO Box 2154, Esperance WA 6450 – **107)** PO Box J233, Coffs Harbour NSW 2450 – **108)** PO Box 40146, Casaurina NT 0810 – **109)** PO Box 400, Taree NSW 2430 – **110)** PO Box 579, Morwell VIC 3840 – **111)** 1/15 Matong Rd, Echuca VIC 3564 – **112)** PO Box 333, Wynyard TAS 7325 – **113)** Rhema FM, PO Box 384, Hervey Bay QLD 4655 (Christian) – **114)** 93 Reatta Rd, Trevallyn TAS 7250 (Christian) – **115)** Radio Metro, PO Box 6530, GCMC QLD 9726 – **116)** PO Box 69, Bowraville NSW 2449 – **117)** PO Box 363, Bourke NSW 2840 (Aboriginal) – **118)** PO Box 2917, Fitzroy VIC 3065 – **119)** PO Box 1663, Wollongong NSW 2500 – **120)** PO Box 270, Alexandra VIC 3714 – **121)** PO Box 5483, Townsville QLD 4810 (Aboriginal) – **122)** Garland Ave, North Albury NSW 2640 – **123)** PO Box 123, Broadway NSW 2007 – **124)** Life FM, PO Box 948, Southport QLD 4125 (Christian) – **125)** PO Box 86, Moruya NSW 2537 – **126)** PO Box 1075, Mackay QLD 4740 – **127)** PO Box 2028, Coffs Harbour NSW 2450 – **128)** PO Box 1149, Casino NSW 2470 – **129)** Radio Alta Mira, PO Box 1079, North Adelaide SA 5006 (Christian) – **130)** Unit 4, 153 Rockingham Rd, Hamilton Hill WA 6163 – **131)** Aboriginal Resource and Development Services, 64 Winnellie Rd, Winnellie NT 0820 – **132)** TAB WA, 14 Hasler Rd, Osborne Park WA 6017 – **133)** 867 New Canterbury Rd, Hurlstone Park NSW 2193 – **133)** 867 New Canterbury Rd, Hurlstone Park NSW 2193 – **134)** PO Box 403, Murgon QLD 4605 –**135)** PO Box 111, Toowoomba QLD 4350 – **136)** Program Manager, KIX Country, PO Box 1059, Bundaberg QLD 4670 – **137)** PO Box 1049, Kalgoorlie WA 6433 –**138)** Radio TAB, PO Box 275, Albion QLD 4010 – **139)** 79 Frenchs Forest Rd, Frenchs Forest NSW 2086 – **140)** 2/110 Logan Rd, Wooloongabba QLD 4102 – **141)** PO Box 250, Brunswick West VIC 3068. Broadcasts the Rete Italia program until 1500LT then Asian language programs until 2200LT – **142)** Ambersky, PO Box 540, Nowra NSW 2541 – **143)** PO Box 5109, GCMC, Bundall QLD 9726 – **144)** Suite 14, 3 Jamison Centre, Macquarie ACT 2614 – **145)** PO Box 1172, Kingaroy QLD 4610 – **146)** PO Box 927, Carlton VIC 3053 – **147)** PO Box 526, Bordertown SA 5268 – **148)** PO Box 654, Tanunda SA 5352 – **149)** PO Box 591 Victor Harbour SA 5211 – **150)** PO Box 390, Kadina SA 5554 – **151)** PO Box 144, Inverloch VIC 3996 – **152)** PO Box 999, Victor Harbour SA 5211 – **153)** PO Box 12013, A'Beckett St, Melbourne VIC 8006 – **154)** 7/60 West Terrace, Adelaide SA 5000 –**155)** Level 2, 230-232 Angas St, Adelaide SA 5000 – **156)** PO Box 28, Nimmitabel NSW 2631 – **157)** PO Box 2050, Gosford NSW 2250 – **158)** PO Box 281, Wanneroo WA 6946 – **159)** PO Box 205, Budgewoi NSW 2262 – **160)** PO Box 2122, Griffith NSW 2680 – **161)** PO Box 1005, Subiaco WA 6904 – **162)** c/- PO, Gordon St, Poatina TAS 7302 – **163)** PO Box 79, Earlwood NSW 2206 – **164)** Locked Bag 3, Springwood QLD 4127 (Christian) – **165)** GPO Box 1345, Hobart TAS 7001 – **166)** PO Box 105, Bentley WA 6102 – **167)** PO Box 5035, North Rockhampton MC QLD 4701 – **168)** 33 Esplanade, Oatlands TAS 7120 – **169)** PO Box 139, Redcliffe QLD 4020 – **170)** PO Box 440, Byron Bay NSW 2481 – **171)** PO Box 7016, Hutt St, Adelaide SA 5000 – **172)** PO Box 243, Boonah QLD 4310 – **173)** PO Box 1031, Orange NSW 2800

– **174)** PO Box 235, Beaudesert QLD 4285 – **175)** PO Box 5337, Mackay MC QLD 4741 – **176)** 55 Main St, Walwa VIC 3709 – **177)** PO Box 612, Ballina NSW 2478 – **178)** PO Box 400, Toowoomba QLD 4350 – **179)** 43 Tamar St, Launceston TAS 7250 – **180)** CAAMA, PO Box 2608, Alice Springs NT 0871 – **181)** 5 Desiree Cl, Buderim QLD 4556 – **182)** Radio Rhema, PO Box 1465, Mt. Gambier SA 5290 – **183)** Radio Rhema, PO Box 200, Woombye QLD 4559 – **184)** PO Box 2106, Alice Springs NT 0871 – **185)** 3 Cinema Pl, Adelaide SA 5000 – **186)** 8/12 Mulloon St, Queanbeyan East NSW 2620 – **187)** c/- John Wright, 29 Milford Rd, Peakhurst NSW 2210 – **188)** GPO Box 1329, Adelaide SA 5001 (Italian) – **189)** PO Box 19, Innisfail QLD 4860 – **190)** 2MORO, Suite 1B, 9 Burwood Rd, Burwood NSW 2134 – **191)** GPO Box 572F, Hobart TAS 7001 – **192)** Suite 3, 15-29 Bank St, South Melbourne VIC 3205 – **193)** 48 Mary Street, Preston VIC 3072 –**194)** Radio Rhema, Suite 4, 162 The Entrance Road, Erina NSW 2250 – **195)** Level 2, 280 William St, Melbourne VIC 3000 – **196)** 5 Phoenix St, Castle Hill NSW 2154 – **197)** 175A Byrnes St, Mareeba QLD 4880 – **198)** PO Box 866, Inverell NSW 2360 – **199)** PO Box 2181, Mildura VIC 3501 – **200)** PO Box 280, Wagin WA 6315 – **201)** PO Box 887, Port Pirie SA 5540 – **202)** 12 Freshwater Point, Point Cook VIC 3030 – **203)** 70 Dawson St, Cooks Hill NSW 2300 – **204)** PO Box 163, Dulwich Hill NSW 2203 – **205)** 1 Woodley Close, Kariong NSW 2250 – **206)** Locked Bag 888, St. Peters NSW 2044 – **207)** 1546A Canterbury Rd, Punchbowl NSW 2196 – **208)** PO Box 1187, Oxley QLD 4075 – **209)** PO Box 124, Sale VIC 3853 – **210)** PO Box 995, Drouin VIC 3818 – **211)** PO Box 22 Salamander Bay NSW 2317 – **212)** PO Box 966, Strawberry Hills NSW 2012 – **213)** PO Box 1962, Strawberry Hills NSW 2012 – **214)** PO Box 2161, Mt Gambier SA 5290 – **215)** Rankin St, Woorabinda QLD 4702 – **216)** PO Box 51, Yass NSW 2582 – **217)** PO Box 891, Manunda QLD 4870 – **218)** PO Box 1527, Tamworth NSW – **219)** PO Box 866, Inverell NSW 2360 – **220)** Vision Australia, 454 Glenferrie Rd, Kooyong VIC 3144 – **221)** 12 Pickering Close, Hoppers Crossing VIC 3029 – **222)** 5 Macquarie St, Parramatta NSW 2150 – **223)** Level 5, 189 Gray St, South Brisbane QLD 4101 – **224)** 44 Kyabram St, Coolaroo VIC 3048 – **225)** 1/203 William Street, St Albans VIC 3021 – **226)** PO Box 1042, Gosford NSW 2250 (country format) – **227)** PO Box 1067, Mildura VIC 3502 – **228)** 68-70 Little Ryrie Street, Geelong VIC 3220 – **229)** PO Box 1000, Dunedoo NSW 2844 – **230)** PO Box 1206, Bendigo Central VIC 3552 – **231)** PO Box 1388, Booragoon WA 6954 – **232)** 395 William St, Perth WA 6000 – **233)** PO Box 1921, Southport BC QLD 4125 – **234)** PO Box 752, Morrisset NSW 2264 – **235)** 22 Frank St, Mt. Druitt NSW 2770 – **236)** Level 2, 31-33 London Circuit, Canberra City ACT 2601 – **237)** 36 Stead Road, Albany WA 6330 – **238)** Locked Bag 899, Mitcham VIC 3132 – **239)** PO Box 2192, Port Augusta SA 5700 – **240)** PO Box 230, Braidwood NSW 2622 – **241)** PO Box 502, Wellington NSW 2820 – **242)** Level 4, 158 City Rd, Southbank VIC 3006 – **243)** PO Box 212, Port Douglas QLD 4877 – **244)** Level 5, 111 Coventry Street, Southbank VIC 3006 – **245)** 3A Murchison St, Biloela QLD - **246)** thexradionetwork@gmail.com – **247)** PO Box 332, Beaudesert QLD 4285 - **248)** E3, 350 Ingles Street, Port Melbourne VIC Broadcasts in Mandarin from 12-15hrs LT via Radio Nostalgia. **249)** PO Box 312, Deniliquin, NSW 2710 **250)** Level 2, 31-33 London Circuit, Canberra City ACT 2601

HF DOMESTIC SHORTWAVE

4KZ / Coastal Broadcasters P/L
✉ PO Box 19, Innisfail QLD 4860 **W**: 4kz.com.au **E**: reception@4kz.com.au **SW:** Innisfail QLD 5055kHz 1kW 2000-1000. F.PI 2485.

Unique Radio
✉ PO Box 814, Gunnedah NSW 2880 **W**: www.uniqueradio.biz **E:** nri3@yahoo.com.au
SW: Gunnedah NSW 3210kHz (USB) 1kW, 5045kHz (USB) 1kW. Schedule on website. Off air from August 2020, expected to return from another QTH in the region in future.

AUSTRIA

L.T: UTC +1h (28 Mar-31 Oct: +2h) — **Pop:** 8.8 million — **Pr.L:** German — **E.C:** 230V/50Hz, — **ITU:** AUT

RUNDFUNK UND TELEKOM REGULIERUNGS-GMBH

✉ Mariahilfer Str. 77-79, 1060 Wien ☎ +43 1 580580 🖷 +43 1 580589191 **E:** rtr@rtr.at **W:** www.rtr.at **L.P:** Chmn: Klaus M. Steinmaurer

ORF - ÖSTERREICHISCHER RUNDFUNK (Pub)

✉ ORF-Funkhaus, Argentinierstr. 30A, 1040 Wien ☎+43 1 50101 18699 🖷 +43 1 50101 82500 **W:** orf.at
L.P: DG: Dr. Alexander Wrabetz PD: Kathrin Zechner MD: Monika Eigensperger Tech. Dir.: Michael Götzhaber

FM (MHz)	Ö-1	Ö-Reg	Ö-3	FM4	kW
Bad Gleichen	-	94.9a	-	-	6
Bludenz	87.6	96.0h	98.8		4
Bregenz	93.3	98.2h	89.6	102.1	50
Bruck/Mur	87.6	93.2f	98.7	102.1	20
Graz	91.2	95.4f	89.2	101.7	67
Innsbruck	92.5	96.4g	88.5	101.4	45
Klagenfurt	92.8	97.8b	90.4	102.9	100
Kufstein	97.5	95.4g	103.9	99.9	5
Lienz	89.3	93.8b	99.3	101.0	2.6
	-	95.9g	-	-	2.6
Linz	97.5	95.2d	88.8	104.0	100
	-	90.1c	-	-	10
Mattersburg	89.0	96.2a	100.9		0.6/3/0.6
Rechnitz	90.6	93.5a	87.9	97.4	6
	-	100.1f	-	-	3
Salzburg	90.9	94.8e	99.0	104.6	100
	-	101.2d	-	-	7
St. Pölten	97.0	91.5c	89.4	98.8	100
Schärding	92.5	99.5d	88.2	-	3/4/3
Schladming	94.3	96.3f	101.3	103.3	3
Semmering	90.3	95.8c	88.2	92.4	9
Spittal/Drau	91.6	100.4b	87.9	103.6	3
Weitra	92.7	95.7c	98.1	101.4	2
Wolfsberg	96.7	94.5b	99.5	102.3	1.5
Wien	92.0	89.9i	99.9	103.8	100
	-	97.9c	-	-	100
Wien	-	94.7a	-	-	2.4

+ more than 500 low power txs

Österreich-1 (Ö1): 24h **N:** on the h
Österreich 2 (Ö2): Regional services
a) Burgenland – Buchgraben 51, 7001 Eisenstadt **W:** burgenland.orf.at **b)** Kärnten – Sponheimerstr. 13, 9010 Klagenfurt **W:** kaernten.orf.at **c)** Niederösterreich – Radioplatz 1, 3100 St. Pölten **W:** noe.orf.at **d)** Oberösterreich – Europaplatz 3, 4010 Linz **W:** ooe.orf.at **e)** Salzburg – Nonntaler-Hauptstr. 49d, 5020 Salzburg **W:** salzburg.orf.at **f)** Steiermark – Marburgerstr. 20, 8042 Graz **W:** steiermark.orf.at **g)** Tirol – Rennweg 14, 6010 Innsbruck **W:** tirol.orf.at **h)** Vorarlberg – Höchsterstrasse 38, 6851 Dornbirn **W:** vorarlberg.orf.at **i)** Wien – Argentinierstr. 30a, 1040 Wien **W:** wien.orf.at
Österreich 3 (Ö3): 24h **N:** on the h
FM4: Prgrs in English (0000-1200), otherwise in German (0500-0900 block is bilingual English/German, and on weekends the prgrs are almost all in German.) **W:** fm4.orf.at
Ann: "Österreich 1", "Ö2 (Wien, Niederösterreich, Tirol)", "Ö3"
IS: Österreich 1: composition by Werner Pirchner. Ö2: Composition by Bert Breit. Ö3: Electronic Music

EXTERNAL SERVICES: Relay of Ö1 on SW: see international radio section

PRIVATE STATIONS:
MUSEUMSRADIO AM

✉ Reinhard Pirnbacher, Golfstraße 1a, 4820 Bad Ischl ☎ +43 664 7396 2755 **E:** postmaster@plattenkiste.radio **W:** https://www.plattenkiste.radio/
MW: Bad Ischl 1476kHz 0.4kW (1500-2100)

KRONEHIT

Nationwide network with regional news windows.
✉ Daumegasse 1, A-1100 Wien **W:** kronehit.at

FM	MHz	kW	FM	MHz	kW
Weitra	90.2	3	Schärding	104.9	8
Linz	92.6	14	St. Pölten	105.3	100
Semmering	102.9	8	Schladming	105.6	2
Bad Gleichenberg	103.2	1.5	Wien	105.8	100
Mattersburg	103.4	1	Innsbruck	106.5	32
Klagenfurt	103.7	2	Lienz	107.1	1
Rechnitz	104.1	6	Graz	107.5	1

+ 40 txs below 1kW

RADIO AUSTRIA

Nationwide network
✉ Friedrichstrasse 10, A-1010 Wien **W:** radioaustria.at

FM	MHz	kW	FM	MHz	kW
Linz	89.2	0.2	St.Pölten	96.3	1
Graz	89.6	1	Bregenz	96.8	0.1
Klagenfurt	93.4	0.1	Salzburg	101.8	10

FM	MHz	kW	FM	MHz	kW
Wien	102.5	20	Innsbruck	105.1	0.2
Eisenstadt	102.5	0.1			

+ 50 low power txs

Other Private Stations by Area - FM (MHz):
BURGENLAND: 88.6 Radio Live Stream, 106.3 Mattersburg, 1kW; 105.5 Rechnitz, 2.5kW + 1rly

KÄRNTEN (Carinthia): Antenne Kärnten, 104.9 Klagenfurt, 100kW; 107.4 Spittal a.d.Drau, 3kW; 104.3 Wolfsberg, 2kW + 4rly – **R. Dva (ORF)-Agora**, (German/Slovenian progr), 105.5 Klagenfurt, 10kW; 106.8 Wolfsberg, 1kW + 7rly – **Welle 1 Kärnten**, 95.2 Klagenfurt, 2kW + 4rly – **R. Maria**, 99.3 Spittal a.d. Drau, 0.2kW – **Lokalradio Spittal a.d.Drau**, 101.6 Spittal a.d.Drau, 1kW (F.Pl.)

NIEDERÖSTERREICH (Lower Austria): **88.6 Radio Live Stream**, 104.9 Weitra/Nebelstein, 3kW; 103.3 Melk, 3kW; 100.8 St. Pölten, 2kW; 106.7 Hornstein, 1kW; 101.6 Horn 1kW; 96.0 Oed 1kW + 9rly – **Campus & City R. St. Pölten**, 94.4 St. Pölten, 0.4kW – **R. Ypsilon Live**, 94.5 Hollabrunn, 0.1kW; 93.7 Mistelbach, 0.3kW + 2rly – **R. Maria**, 95.5 St. Pölten, 0.2kW; 104.7 Waidhofen a.d.Ybbs, 0.5kW; 93.4 Baden-Tattendorf, 0.4kW – **R. Arabella Wien Live,** 99.4 Tulln-Judenau, 1kW; 96.5 Ybbs a.d. Donau, 2kW + 3rly

OBERÖSTERREICH (Upper Austria): Life R., 100.5 Linz, 100kW; 102.6 Schärding, 3kW; 102.2 Bad Ischl, 0.4kW + 7rly – **Welle 1 Linz**, 91.8 Linz, 0.3kW, 102.6 Steyr, 1.4kW; 107.5 Kirchdorf b. Krems, 0.3kW + 3 rly – **R. Arabella OÖ Live**, 96.7 Linz, 4kW – **R. FRO Stream**, 105.0 Linz, 0.3kW – **LoungeFM OOE**, 102.0 Linz, 2kW; 95.8 Wels, 0.3kW; + 2rly – **Freies R. Salzkammergut**, 100.2 Bad Ischl, 1kW; 107.3 Gmunden, 0.1kW + 4rly – **Freies R. Freistadt**, 107.1 Freistadt, 0.6kW + 1rly

SALZBURG: Antenne Salzburg, 95.2 Salzburg/Gaisberg, 2kW; 106.6 Hallwang, 0.5kW – **Welle 1 Salzburg**, 106.2 Salzburg/Gaisberg, 10kW; 107.1 Zell am See, 0.3kW; 107.5 St. Johann Pongau, 0.2kW – **Radiofabrik Livestream**, 107.5 Salzburg/Hochgitzen, 0.5kW – **Klassik R. - Live,** 102.5 Salzburg/Wartberg, 0.5kW – **Energy Salzburg**, 94.0 Salzburg/Gaisberg, 0.3kW – **Radio Maria**, 107.9 Salzburg/Wartberg, 0.3kW

STEIERMARK (Styria): Antenne Steiermark, 99.1 Graz/Schöckl, 80kW; 105.7 Bruck a.d. Mur, 20kW; 92.0 Schladming, 2kW; 106.1 Rechnitz, 3kW + 17rly – **R. Soundportal,** 89.6 Bruck a.d. Mur 8kW, 97.9 Graz, 2kW, 100.4 Bad Gleichenberg 1.3kW + 5rly – **R. Helsinki**, 92.6 Graz, 1kW – **R. Grün-Weiss**, 106.3 Schladming 2kW, 106.6 Bruck a.d.Mur 2.5kW + 3rly – **R. Freequenns**, 100.8 Liezen/Salberg, 0.6kW – **Welle 1 Graz,** 104.6 Graz, 0.5kW – **R. Klassik Stephansdom**, 94.2 Graz, 0.5kW

TIROL (Tyrol): Life R. Tirol, 103.4 Inzing 8kW; 101.8 Innsbruck 1kW; 104.4 Lienz 2kW; 105.4 Haiming 1kW; 106.0 Landeck 1kW; 106.8 Kufstein 1kW + 8rly – **R. U1 Tirol**, 97.0 Innsbruck 1kW; 89.2 Jenbach 0.4kW; 101.6 Landeck 0.5kW; 106.8 Haiming 0.5kW + 8rly – **FREIRAD - Freises R. Innsbruck**, 105.9 Innsbruck 1kW – **R. Osttirol**, 101.7 Matrei-Hopfgarten 1kW; 107.8 Lienz 0.4kW; + 6rly – **Energy Innsbruck**, 99.9 Innsbruck 0.3kW – **Klassik R. - Live**, 95.5 Innsbruck 0.3kW – **R. Maria**, 91.1 Innsbruck 0.4kW; 107.9 Jenbach 0.2kW; 96.0 Mayrhofen 0.2kW – **T-Rock**, 103.8 Inzing 0.5kW – **Antenne Südtirol**, 100.8 Zirog 1kW

VORARLBERG: Antenne Vorarlberg, 106.5 Bregenz/Pfänder, 50kW; 101.1 Bludenz, 0.5kW; 105.1 Feldkirch 0.2kW + 2rly – **R. Proton**, 104.6 Bludenz, 0.5kW; 95.9 Bregenz, 0.3kW; 104.3 Feldkirch 0.2kW – **Lokalradio Bregenz**, 103.2 Bregenz/Pfänder, 1kW (F.Pl.)

WIEN (Vienna): 88.6 Radio Live Stream, 88.6 Wien/Kahlenberg, 10kW – **R. Arabella Wien Live**, 92.9 Wien-Donauturm, 3kW – **R. Energy Wien**, 104.2 Wien/RiFu-Arsenal, 1kW – **R. Klassik Stephansdom**, 107.3 Wien-Donauturm, 2kW – **Orange 94.0**, 94.0 Wien/Donauturm, 0.4kW; **98.3 Superfly**, 98.3 Wien/Donauturm, 1.4kW – **Mein Kinderradio**, 103.2 Wien – Reiffeisenhaus 0.3kW; **LoungeFM,** 102.1 Wien, 0.1kW

DIGITAL RADIO (DAB+)
5B DAB+ Austria (Salzburg 6kW, Bregenz 10kW, Innsbruck 10kW, 12 private stns)
5D DAB+ Austria (Sankt Pölten 6kW, Wien-1 11kW, Wien-9 7kW, Wien-8 10kW, Semmering 6kW, Bruck (Mur) 10kW, 12 private stns)
6A DAB+ Austria (Wolfsberg 2,5kW, Klagenfurt 5kW, 12 private stns)
6D DAB+ Austria (Linz 10kW, 12 private stns)
8A DAB+ Austria (Rechnitz 6kW, Graz 10 kW, 12 private stns)
11C CityMUX Wien II (Wien, 13kW, 14 private stns)

AZERBAIJAN

L.T: UTC +4h — **Pop:** 10 million — **Pr.L:** Azeri (official), Armenian — **E.C:** 220V/50Hz — **ITU:** AZE

MILLI TELEVIZIYA VÄ RADIO SURASI (MTRS) (National TV & Radio Council)

Nizami küç. 145, AZ 1000 Bakı ☎ +994 12 5983659 🖷 +994 12 4987668 **E:** office@ntrc.gov.az **W:** www.ntrc.gov.az
L.P: Chmn: Nuşirävan Mähärrämov

AZÄRBAYCAN TELEVIZIYA VÄ RADIO VERILISLÄRI QSC (Gov) (Azerbaijan TV and Radio Broadcasting CJSC)

Mehdi Hüseyn küç. 1, AZ 1011 Bakı ☎ +994 12 5370299 **E:** umumi.shobe@aztv.az **W:** www.aztv.az **L.P:** Chmn: Rövşän Mämmädov

FM	MHz	kW	FM	MHz	kW
Gülüstan	88.0	5	Danaçi	103.0	2
Astara	90.0	1	Ordubad*	103.0	1
Poylu	90.0	5	Şäki	104.0	1
Daşkäsän	101.5	2	Babäk*	104.5	1.5
Lerik	101.5	2	Şärur*	105.0	1
Yergüc	101.5	2	Bakı	105.0	5

+ sites txs below 1kW. *) situated in Naxçıvan (autonomous republic)
D.Prgr: Azärbaycan Radiosu 24h. For ethnic minorities: N. in Russian 1100-1105 (W).

ASAN RADIO (Gov)

Şärifzadä küç. 157, AZ 1138 Bakı ☎ +994 12 4474448 **E:** info@asanradio.az **W:** asanradio.az **L.P:** Dir: Emin Musävi

FM	MHz	kW	FM	MHz	kW
Lerik	92.7	-	Bakı	100.0	5
Gäncä	96.5	-			

D.Prgr: ASAN R. 24h.

ICTIMAI TELEVIZIYA VÄ RADIO YAYIMLARI SIRKÄTI (Pub) (Public TV and Radio Broadcasting Co.)

Şärifzadä küç. 241, AZ 1012 Bakı ☎ +994 12 4313968 **E:** info@itv.az **W:** itv.az **L.P:** DG: Balakişi Qasımov

FM	MHz	kW	FM	MHz	kW
Daşkäsän	88.3	1	Danaçı	100.6	1
Lerik	88.3	1	Gülüstan	102.5	5
Yergüc	88.3	1	Poylu	103.0	5
Bakı	90.0	5	Babäk*	103.0	1
Şäki	91.6	1			

+ txs below 1kW. *) situated in Naxçıvan (autonomous republic)
D.Prgr: Ictimai R. 24h.

OTHER STATIONS

FM	MHz	kW	Location	Station
1)	88.6	1	Danaçı	R. 105 FM
7)	89.0	1	Gäncä	Xäzär FM
7)	89.0	1	Lerik	Xäzär FM
7)	89.6	5	Gülüstan	Xäzär FM
1)	91.0	1	Gülüstan	R. 105 FM
2)	100.0	1	Poylu	R. Antenn
2)	100.0	1	Lerik	R. Antenn
1)	100.7	1	Quba	R. 105 FM
2)	101.0	1	Bakı	R. Antenn
2)	101.2	1	Gülüstan	R. Antenn
3)	102.7	1	Poylu	Käpäz FM
1)	102.8	1	Lerik	R. 105 FM
7)	103.0	2	Bakı	Xäzär FM
10)	103.3	4	Bakı	Araz FM
4)	104.0	2	Bakı	R. Space
6)	105.0	1	Gäncä	Lider Jazz R.
2)	105.3	2	Daşkäsän	R. Antenn
8)	105.5	2.5	Bakı	Media FM
5)	106.3	2	Bakı	106.3 FM
6)	107.0	1	Bakı	Lider Jazz R.
6)	107.0	1	İmişli	Lider Jazz R.
9)	107.7	1	Bakı	Avto FM

+ txs below 1kW

Addresses & other information:
1) Atatürk pr. 28, AZ 1069 Bakı – **2)** Azadlıq pr. 189, AZ 1130 Bakı – **3)** C.Räfibäyli küç 66, AZ 2007 Gäncä – **4)** C.Cabbarlı küç. 33, AZ 1009 Bakı – **5)** Şärifzadä küç. 10, AZ 1100 Baki – **6)** Ş.Mehdiyev küç. 83/23, AZ 1141 Bakı – **7)** Atatürk pr. 28, AZ 1069 Bakı – **8)** Teymur Äliyev küç. 25A, AZ 1130 Bakı – **9)** Mämmäd Araz küç. 43, AZ 1106 Bakı – **10)** Mätbuat pr. 23M, AZ 1100 Bakı. Incl. rel. R. Sputnik (Russia).

DAB Transmitter (DAB+) (Trial)
Tx Operator: Teleradio **M:** 106FM, R. Antenn, Araz FM, ASAN R., Avto FM, Azärbaycan Radiosu, Färqli R., Ictimai R., Lider Jazz R., Media FM, Space R., Xäzär FM **Tx:** Block 11B (Bakı)

NAKHCHIVAN
(Autonomous republic)

NAXÇIVAN MUXTAR RESPUBLIKASI DÖVLÄT TELEVIYIZA VÄ RADIO VERILISLÄRI KOMITÄSI

(State TV-Radio Committee of the Autonomous Republic of Nakhchivan)
✉ İstiqlaliyyät küç, 82, AZ 7000 Naxçıvan ☎ +994 136 440711 **E:** ntv@nakhchivan.az **W:** naxcivantv.az **L.P:** Chmn: Sahil Tahirli
FM: Naxçıvan 104.1MHz. **D.Prgr: Naxçivan Dövlät Radiosu** 24h.

OTHER STATIONS

FM	MHz	kW	Location	Station
11)	96.0	1	Sädäräk	Naxçıvanin säsi
11)	100.6	1	Naxçıvan	Naxçıvanin säsi
11)	106.0	1	Babäk	Naxçıvanin säsi
11)	106.0	1	Ordubad	Naxçıvanin säsi

+ txs below 1kW.
Addresses & other information:
11) Çänlibel mähallási 11, AZ 7000 Naxçıvan.

MOUNTAINOUS KARABAGH
(Self-proclaimed "Nagorno-Karabakh Republic")

LERNAYIN GHARABAGH HANRAYIN HERUSTARADIOYIN KERUTYUN (Pub*)

(Public Radio & TV Co. of Mountainous Karabagh)
(* Run by the administration of the "Nagorno-Karabakh Republic")
✉ Tigran Mets St. 23a, 375000 Stepanakert, Mountainous Karabagh ☎ +374 47 945261 **L.P:** Chmn: Norek Gasparyan
FM: Stepanakert 102.3MHz. **D.Prgr:** in Armenian.

OTHER STATIONS

FM	MHz	kW	Location	Station
3A)	87.5		Stepanakert	R. Mix 1
4)	91.1		Stepanakert	R. Vem
5)	101.8		Stepanakert	Ekho Moskvy
3C)	103.0		Stepanakert	R. Mix 3
2)	104.3		Stepanakert	R. Pace
3B)	105.0		Stepanakert	R. Mix 2
1)	105.5		Stepanakert	R. Hay
B)	106.0		Stepanakert	R. Sputnik relay
A)	106.3		Stepanakert	Armenian Public R. relay
3D	106.6		Stepanakert	R. Mix 4
6)	107.5		Stepanakert	R. Sevan

Addresses & other information:
1) Azatamartikneri St. 18a, 375000 Stepanakert. Rel. Hay FM (Armenia) – **2)** Vazgen Sarkisyan St. 25, 375000 Stepanakert – **3A-D)** Azatamartikneri St. 18a, 375000 Stepanakert – **4)** Stepanakert. Rel. R. Vem (Armenia) – **5)** 375000 Stepanakert. Rel. Ekho Moskvy (Russia) – **6)** 375000 Stepanakert. Rel. R. Sevan (Lebanon) – **A)** Rel. Armenian Public R. (Armenia) – **B)** Rel. R. Sputnik (Russia)

AZORES (Portugal)

L.T: UTC -1h (28 Mar-31 Oct: UTC) — **Pop:** 246,000 — **Pr.L:** Portuguese — **E.C:** 230V/50Hz — **ITU:** AZR

ANACOM-Autoridade Nacional de Comunicações, Delegação dos Açores

✉ Rua dos Valados 18, 9500-652 Relva (São Miguel) ☎+351 296 30 20 40 🖷 +351 296 30 20 41

RÁDIO E TELEVISÃO DE PORTUGAL, S.A. (RTP) (Pub) - Centro Regional da RDP-Açores

✉ Rua de Castelo Branco, 9500-062 Ponta Delgada ☎+351 296 201100 🖷 +351 296 201120 **E:** rdp.acores@rtp.pt, rtpa@rtp.pt **W:** rtp.pt **L.P:** Lorina Amaral
RDP Antena 1 Açores

MW	kHz	kW	Island
Monte das Cruzes	828	1	Flores

FM (MHz)	Ant. 1	Ant. 2	Ant. 3	kW
Arrife	94.5	97.5	-	0.3
Cabeço Gordo	88.9	105.8	99.2	9.1
Cabeço Verde	98.1	92.9	-	1
Cascalho Negro	92.2	103.3	104.2	1
Espalamaca	93.8	101.4	102.7	0.03/0.5/1
Fajãzinha	100.4	103.7	-	1
Furnas	93.6	-	-	0.5
Lajes das Flores	102.6	97.0	-	0.2/0.5
Lajes do Pico	96.5	93.5	98.6	1
Macela	87.6	93.2	-	1
Monte das Cruzes	99.8	97.4	102.0	1
Morro Alto	93.5	91.9	95.6	1
Mosteiros	95.5	105.2	107.0	0.1
Nordeste	104.6	-	-	0.1
Nordestinho	103.7	91.8	-	1
Pico Alto Santa Maria	96.7	-	-	10
Pico Bartolomeu	92.7	89.9	99.1	0.5/1
Pico da Barrosa	97.9	101.7	87.7	33/33/30
Pico das Éguas	89.5	-	-	10
Pico do Geraldo	103.7	107.5	-	1
Pico do Jardim	97.0	-	-	0.9
Pico São Mateus	103.4	-	-	0.1
Ponta Delgada	94.1	100.8	-	0.3/1.3
Ponta Ruiva	87.6	-	-	1
Povoação	102.8	97.2	94.2	0.5
Santa Bárbara	90.5	98.9	103.0	35/35/30
Serra do Cume	99.7	89.2	103.9	0.9

D.Prgrs: all networks 24h
V: by QSL card via RTP in Lisboa
Prgr: Antena 1 Açores carries its own prgrs M-F 0630-0000, Sat. 0700-0100, Sun. 0700-0000 LT; Antena 2 & Antena 3 relay Lisboa 24h

DAB: RTP halted T-DAB broadcasts in June 2011. There are no current plans to reactivate this service but it may be restored in future.

COMMERCIAL STATIONS:
RÁDIO RENASCENÇA – Em. Católica Portuguesa (Rlg/Comm)
✉ (see Portugal) - **FM**: Pico da Barrosa 95.2MHz 50kW (RR), 100.0MHz 50kW (RFM)

PRIVATE STATIONS:
RÁDIO CLUBE DE ANGRA – "A VOZ DA TERCEIRA" (Comm.)
✉ Av. Tenente Coronel José Agostinho, 4, 9700-108 Angra do Heroísmo ☎+351 295 213101 🖷 +351 295 213102 **E:** direccao@rcangra.pt **W:** rcangra.pt
FM: Santa Bárbara 101.1MHz 0.4kW, Serra do Cume 94.7MHz 0.05kW & Pico Matias Simão 89.6 MHz 0.05 kW (all in Terceira island)

ESTAÇÃO EMISSORA DO CLUBE ASAS DO ATLÂNTICO (Comm.)
✉ Aeroporto de Santa Maria, Apartado 545, 9580-908 Vila do Porto ☎+351 296 820720/1/2 🖷+351 296 820725 **E:** geral@asasdoatlantico.pt radio@asasdoatlantico.pt **W:** asasdoatlantico.pt
FM: Pico Alto, 103.2MHz, 2kW **D.Prgr**: 24h
NB: R. Clube de Angra & R. Clube Asas do Atlântico own also MW licenses although they have been broadcasting only on VHF-FM.

Private stations owning only FM licences:
CANAL FM (Comm.)
✉Rua Manuel Augusto Amaral, 1-D 2-Direito, 9500-222 Ponta Delgada ☎+351 296 307470 & +351 919 261 002🖷+351 296 307479 **E:** radio@canal.fm, mariotravanca@canal.fm **W:** canal.fm
FM: S. Miguel island: 91.0 MHz 0.5 kW Pico da Barrosa, 91.5 & 94.5 MHz Povoação (both 0.05 kW); S. Jorge island: 100.5 MHz 0.5 kW Calheta (Macelinha); Pico island: 92.7 MHz 0.05 kW Madalena; Flores Island: 104.5 MHz 0.5 kW Santa Cruz das Flores
Local FM stn relaying prgs from Canal FM: R. Graciosa 107.9 MHz 0.5 kW Santa Cruz da Graciosa (Graciosa Island - see below)

ANTENA 9 (Comm.)
✉Rua de São João, 38-B, 9900-129 Horta ☎+351 292 29 33 90 & +315 961 714 118 🖷 +351 292 391 602 **E:** radioantenanove@sapo.pt **W:** antenanove.com

FM: Faial island: txs at Cabeço Gordo 91.3 MHz 0.5 kW, Cabeço Verde 94.9 MHz 0.050 kW, Espalhafatos 95.9 MHz 0.050 kW & Espalamaca 102.2 MHz 0.05 kW

MY TOP FM (Comm.)
Rua Serpa Pinto, 66, 9760-438 Praia da Vitória ☎+351 295 701 657 **E:** mytopfm@gmail.com & geral@mytopfm.pt **W:** mytopfm.pt
FM: S. Miguel island: txs at Pico da Barrosa (Ponta Delgada) 102.4 MHz 0.5 kW & 98.4 MHz 0.05 kW Sete Cidades (Ponta Delgada; both inactive); Terceira island: Santa Bárbara (Praia da Vitória) 106.6 MHz 1 kW, Serra do Cume (Praia da Vitória) 92.4 MHz 0.05 kW & Quatro Ribeiras (Praia da Vitória) 96.6 MHz 0.05 kW

RÁDIO CLUBE DAS LAJES DO PICO - "A voz da montanha" (Comm.)
Rua de S. Pedro, 9, 9930-129 Lajes do Pico ☎292-672076 **E:** radiomontanha@gmail.com **W:** radiomontanha.com
FM: Pico island: 104.7 MHz 0.5 Lajes do Pico, 88.3 MHz 0.05 kW Lajes do Pico & Piedade 105.3 MHz 0.05 kW; São Jorge island: Urzelina 91.9 MHz 0.05 kW
NB: Also relays "RFM"

RÁDIO HORIZONTE AÇORES (Comm.)
Caminho do Meio, nº 51, S. Carlos, 9700 Angra do Heroísmo ☎295 332 161 & 962 296 789 🖷295 216 015 **E:** gerencia@horizonteacores.com comercial@horizonteacores.com **W:** horizonteacores.com
FM: Terceira island: 104.4 MHz 1 kW Serra de Stª Bárbara (Angra do Heroísmo) & 98.1 MHz 0.05 kW Serra do Cume (Praia da Vitória)

RÁDIO LUMENA (Comm.)
Rua Cunha da Silveira, 25, 9800-531 Velas ☎295 412575 🖷295 412810 **E:** radiolumena@gmail.com **W:** radiolumena.com
FM: São Jorge island: 107.1 0.5 kW Pico de Stº Amaro (Velas) & 90.0 0.05 kW Manadas; Graciosa island: 92.2 MHz 0.05 kW Luz

RÁDIO PICO (Comm.)
Av. Machado Serpa, 57, 9950-321 Madalena do Pico
☎292 622 727 & 917 840 877 🖷292 622 874 **E:** geral@radiopico.com **W:** radiopico.com
FM: Faial island: 100.2 MHz 0.5 kW Cabeço Gordo; Pico island: 90.2 MHz 0.05 kW São Mateus; São Jorge island: 107.7 MHz 0.05 kW Macela

OTHER STATIONS:

FM	Island	MHz	kW	Station, location
3)	São Miguel	88.5	3	R. Atlântida, Pico da Barrosa
2)	São Miguel	90.2	0.5	R80 R., Pico da Barrosa
4)	São Miguel	99.4	3	TSF - Rádio Açores, Pico da Barrosa
3)	Pico	100.2	0.5	R. Pico, Madalena do Pico
8)	São Miguel	105.0	0.5	105 FM, Pico da Barrosa
5)	São Miguel	105.5	2	R. Nova Cidade, Pico da Barrosa
7)	Pico	106.1	0.5	R. Cais, São Roque do Pico
1)	São Miguel	107.2	1	R. Insular, Pico da Barrosa
6)	Graciosa	107.9	0.5	R. Graciosa, Serra Branca

+ 4 relays of 50W used by 3 stns
Addresses & other information (add +351 to tel/fax nos):
1) Caminho do Meio, 51, São Carlos, 9700-222 Angra do Heroísmo ☎296 653 911/2/3/4 – **2)** Rua Bento José Morais, 23 - 5º Esqº, 9500-772 Ponta Delgada ☎296- 201 919 **E:** r80.superonda@gmail.com **W:** r80.pt – **3)** Rua Bento José Morais, 23 - 5º Sul, 9500-772 Ponta Delgada ☎296 201 910 & 917 209 720 & 963 232 222 🖷296 629 856 **E:** geral@radioatlantida.net, director@radioatlantida.net **W:** radioatlantida.net – **4)** (also relays TSF Lisboa) Rua Dr. Bruno Tavares Carreiro, 34-2.º, 9500-055 Ponta Delgada ☎ 296 202 800 🖷 296 202 825 **E:** radioacores@acorianooriental.pt **W:** acorianooriental.pt/pagina/acores-tsf – **5)** Rua Adolfo Coutinho de Medeiros, 24, 9600-516 Ribeira Grande ☎296 472738/296 & 961 326 134 🖷296 472654 **E:** radionovacidade@gmail.com **W:** radionovacidade.pt – **6)** Rua do Corpo Santo, 37, 9880-368 Santa Cruz da Graciosa ☎295-732536 & 919 204 526 🖷295 712768 **E:** radiograciosa@sapo.pt – **7)** Pct. dos Baleeiros, Cais do Pico, 9940-301 São Roque do Pico ☎292642930 **E:** radiocais@sapo.pt – **8)** Solmar Avenida Center, Av. Infante D. Henrique, 71 - 1º Piso, Loja 129, 9504-529 Ponta Delgada ☎296 654 112 /277 & 927 501 853 **E:** geral@105fm.pt **W:** 105fm.pt

Military Stations:
RÁDIO LAJES – A VOZ DA FAP-FORÇA AÉREA PORTUGUESA (The Voice of the Portuguese Air Force)
Comando da Zona Aérea dos Açores, 9760-290 Lajes, Terceira ☎+351 295 540891/2/3 🖷 +351 295 540791 **E:** radiolajes@radiolajes.pt **W:** radiolajes.pt **LP:** Dir.: Major Paulo Roda
FM 93.5MHz 150W **F.Pl.:** 500W 24h
N.B. R. Lajes owns also a MW licence, although the stn. has been broadcasting only on FM.

UNITED STATES AFRTS
Lajes, Terceira, 9760 Praia da Vitoria ☎+351 295 57 34 97
MW 1503kHz 100W (1kW nominal). **FM** 96.1MHz 150W
D.Prgr: Relays 24h/day international AFRTS signal

BAHAMAS

L.T: UTC -5h (14 Mar-7 Nov: -4h) — **Pop:** 390,000 — **Pr.L:** English — **E.C:** 120V/60Hz — **ITU:** BAH

UTILITIES REGULATION & COMPETITION AUTHORITY (URCA)
Frederick House, Frederick Str, PO Box N-4860, Nassau ☎ +1 242 3930234 🖷 +1 242 3930153
E: info@urcabahamas.bs **W:** www.urcabahamas.bs
L.P: Chmn: Neville B. Wilchcombe II. CEO: Shevonn Cambridge (acting)

ZNS – THE BROADCASTING CORPORATION OF THE BAHAMAS (Comm., Gov.)
Harcourt 'Rusty' Bethel Drive, Third Terrace, Centreville, PO Box N-1347, Nassau
☎ +1 242 502 3800 🖷 +1 242 322 6598 **W:** znsbahamas.com **E:** info@znsbahamas.com
L.P: GM: Kayleaser Deveaux-Isaacs
MW: The National Voice: Nassau: 1540kHz 50kW **The Light**: Freeport 810kHz 10kW
FM: The National Voice: Nassau: 104.5MHz 5kW **Inspiration 107.9**: Alice Town 107.1MHz 0.3kW & Nassau 107.9MHz 10kW **Power FM 104.5**: Freeport 104.5MHz 10kW. All four channels are on the air 24h.

TRIBUNE RADIO LTD (Comm.)
Radio House, Shirley St- & School Lane, PO Box N-3207, Nassau & Media House, Yellow Pine Street, PO Box F-40773, Freeport ☎ +1 242 328 0950 **W:** 100jamz.com **L.P:** COO: Ollie Ferguson
100 Jamz: FM: Nassau 100.3 & Freeport 100.3. Format: Urban Contemporary
Kiss FM: FM: Freeport 96.1MHz. Format: Urban AC
Y98.7: FM: Nassau 98.7MHz. Format: AC
Joy FM, Dowdeswell St., PO Box N-3207, Nassau ☎ +1 242 356 5112 FM: Nassau 101.9MHz. Format: All gospel and inspirational
Classical 98.1: FM: Nassau 98.1MHz. Format: Easy listening

THE NASSAU GUARDIAN (Comm.)
Carter St, PO Box N-3011, Nassau ☎ +1 242 302 2300/328 6868 🖷 +1 242 328 5311 **W:** guardiantalkradio.com / hot917fm.com / star106fm.com
Guardian Radio: FM 96.9MHz – **Hot 91.7:** FM 91.7MHz – **Star 106.5:** FM 106.5MHz

OTHER STATIONS (FM IN MHZ):
Bahamian or Nuttin, Rum Cay Media Group, PO Box SP-64038, Nassau ☎ +1 242 361 5535 **W:** bahamianornuttin.com **FM:** Nassau: 92.5 – **Dove 103**, 8 Oak Str, PO Box F-44008, Freeport, Grand Bahama ☎ +1 242 351 3683 **W:** dove103fm.com **FM:** Freeport 103.7 – **Gems Radio**, 51 Sears Hill, Mt Rose Ave, PO Box SS-6094, Nassau ☎ +1 242 326 4381 **FM:** Nassau: 105.9 – **Global 99.5 FM**, Elizabeth Ave, PO Box EE 15884, Nassau ☎ +1 242 326 0270 **W:** global995fm.com **FM:** Nassau: 99.5 – **Glory FM**, 14 Warwich St, PO Box N-9178, Nassau ☎ +1 242 393 0012 **W:** thelifeexperience.com **FM:** Nassau 93.9 – **Gospel 107**, 30 Thompson Blvd, Nassau ☎ +1 242 612 4574 **E:** info@gospel107.com **W:** gospel107.cc **FM:** Nassau: 107.1 – **Infoflights 90.1,** Bahamas National Library, PO Box N-3913, Nassau ☎ +1 242 322 4973 **FM:** Nassau 90.1 – **Island FM**, Edmark House, Dowdeswell St, PO Box N-1807, Nassau ☎ +1 242 332 8826 **FM:** Nassau 102.9 – **Love-97 FM**, East St North, PO Box N-3909, Nassau ☎ +1 242 326 8255 🖷 +1 242 356 7256 **FM:** Nassau 97.5 – **Love-97 FM North**, Regent Centre West, PO Box F-40399, Freeport ☎ +1 242 351 6175 **FM:** Freeport 97.5 – **Mix 102.1**, Bishop's Place 31, PO Box F-44008, Freeport ☎ +1 242 373 2275 **FM:** Freeport 102.1 (5kW) – **More 94 FM**, Carmichael Rd, PO Box CR54245, Nassau ☎

+1 242 361 2447 **W:** more94fm.com **FM:** Nassau 94.9 – **Peace 107**, McKinney Media Group Ltd., Gibbs Lane 6, Fort Charlotte, PO Box N-1220, Nassau ☎ +1 242 325 0235 **W:** peace107.5.com **FM:** Nassau 107.5 – **SNL RADIO**, Kort Wright St, PO Box NT-532, Matthew Town, Great Inagua ☎ +1 242 453 1502 **FM:** 98.3 – **Splash FM**, #12 Str, PO Box EL-27495, Spanish Wells, Eleuthera ☎ +1 242 333 4638 🖷 +1 242 333 4693 **FM:** Eleuthera: 89.9, Abaco 95.5, South Eleuthera 98.5 – **The Beat**, 21 University Drive, Nassau ☎ +1 242 323 7775 **W:** 103beat.com **FM:** Nassau 103.5 – **The Blaze**, Alternative Venture Holdings Ltd, 11 Hoopers Bay, 242 Farmer's Hill ☎ +1 242 828 0983 FM: Exuma 98.3 – **Turning Point Radio (BBN)**, PO Box N-8993, Nassau ☎ +1 242 322 6273 **W:** tprb1023fm.com **FM:** Nassau: 102.3 – **Word SBS 88.3 FM**, South Bahamas Conference of Seven-day Adventists, Tonique Williams-Darling Highway, PO Box N-356, Nassau **W:** soencouragement.com **FM:** 88.3 (1.4kW)

BAHRAIN

L.T: UTC +3h — **Pop:** 1.7 million — **Pr.L:** Arabic — **E.C:** 230V/50Hz — **ITU:** BHR

MINISTRY OF INFORMATION AFFAIRS (MIA)

✉ P.O. Box 33766, Al Esteglal Highway, Manama ☎+973 17 684222 🖷 +973 17 781400 **W:** mia.gov.bh **E:** info@mia.gov.bh

BAHRAIN RADIO & TV CORPORATION (BRTC, Gov.)

✉ P.O.Box 33766, Manama ☎+973 17 686000 🖷 +973 17 687567 **E:** btw@brtc.gov.bh
General Prgr. in Arabic: 24h **MW:** ‡801kHz 100kW **FM:** 102.3MHz 5kW – **Quran Prgr:** 24h **MW:** 612kHz 100kW. **FM:** 106.1MHz 5kW – **Bahrain TV audio**: **MW:** 1521kHz 10kW, **FM:** 89.8MHz 5kW – **English Sce (R. Bahrain)**: 24h **MW:** (0300-2100) 1584kHz 1kW **FM:** 96.5MHz 10kW, 99.5MHz 0.5kW, – **Bahrain FM in Arabic** : 24h **FM:** 93.3MHz 10kW – **Shabab FM** (Youth prgr.): **FM:** 98.4MHz 4kW – **Traditional channel: FM:** 95.0MHz 5kW – **Classical music channel: FM:** 96.9MHz 5kW
Ann: A: "Idha'atul-Bahrain". E: "Radio Bahrain".
IS: Local composition on guitar and violin.

OTHER STATIONS:
Arabian Gulf R., W: twitter.com/argulf_radio Manama: 103.0MHz
Emarat FM, Manama: 92.3MHz 5kW. See main entry under UAE.
AFN, Manama: 106.3MHz 250W.
BBC World Sce: English 101.0MHz 2kW, Arabic 103.8MHz 2kW.
Monte Carlo Doualiya, Manama: 90.9MHz 1kW.
R. Sawa, Manama: 89.3MHz
F.PI: BFBS Radio on FM

BANGLADESH

L.T: UTC +6h — **Pop:** 168 million — **Pr.L:** Bengali — **E.C:** 220V/50Hz — **ITU:** BGD

BANGLADESH TELECOMMUNICATIONS REGULATORY COMMISSION

✉ IEB Bhaban, Ramna, Dhaka-1000 ☎ +880 2 9611111 🖷 +880 2 9556677 **E:** btrc@btrc.gov.bd **W:** www.btrc.gov.bd
L.P: Chmn: Md. Jahurul Haque

BANGLADESH BETAR (Gov.)

✉ National Broadcasting Authority, NBA House, 121 Kazi Nazrul Islam Ave, Dhaka-1000 ☎ +880 2 ,8625538 8625904 🖷 +880 2 8612021 **E:** rrc@dhaka.net **W:** betar.gov.bd betarprogram.org
L.P: DG: Hosne Ara Talukdar DDG (News): ASM Zahid: Chief Engr: Ahmed Kamruzzaman Sr. Engr.: Md. Towhidur Rahman: Stn. Engr : Md. Kamal Hossain, Md. Azizul Islam: Dy. Stn. Engr.: Nusrat Zahan Ruma Asst. Radio Engr: Asif Mehedi

MW	kHz	kW	H. of Tr.
Khulna	558	100	0030-0400, 0600-1710
Dhaka	630	100	0300-1300
Dhaka-A	693	1000	0030-0600, 0815-1730
Rajshahi	846	100	0030-0400, 0600-1710
Chittagong	873	100	0030-0400, 0600-1710
Dhaka B	819	100	0030-0610, 0815-1710, 1830-2100
Sylhet	963	20	0030-0400, 0600-1710
Thakurgaon	999	10	0950-1710
Rangpur	1053	10	0030-0400, 0800-1710
Rajshahi	1080	10	0030-0400 0600-1710
Rangamati	1161	10	0530-1030
Dhaka-C	1170	20	0900-1100
Barishal	1287	10	0030-0510, 1030-1710
Cox's Bazar	1314	10	0545-1045
Comilla	1413	10	1000-1710
Bandorban	1431	10	0530-1030 Inactive

SW	kHz	kW	H. of Tr.
Shavar	4750	100	0600-1715

NB: Rel. Dhaka A prog. Sign on/off varies due to special prgr rel.

FM	MHz	kW	Rel	H. of Tr.
Chittagong	105.4	5	c	Test trs
Chittagong	88.8	10	j, b	0030-0400 0600-1710
Chittagong	90.0	5	c	0000-1800
Comilla	101.2	2	j	1500-1545
Comilla	103.6	10	b	0030-0200 1200-1710
Dhaka	97.6	5		0030-0600 0800-1730
Dhaka	104.0	10	j	1500-1545
Dhaka	90.0	5	a	0100-0400, 1230-2000
Dhaka	103.2	5		1330-1600
Dhaka	102.0	10	c	0000-1830
Dhaka	100.0	3	b	0000-0600, 0700-0900 1100-1700
Dhaka	106.0	10		0300-0600 1200-1730
Khulna	102.0	1		0000-0400, 0830-1715
Khulna	88.8	10	j, b	0030-0700 1300-1715
Khulna	90.0	5		0415-0515 1330-1700
Rajshahi	104.0	5		0030-0400 0600-1710
Rajshahi	88.8	10	j, b	0030-0400 1000-1710
Rajshahi	90.0	5		0400-0500 1330-1700
Rajshahi	105.0	1		0030-0400 1200-1710 (Test trs)
Rangpur	104.6	1	j	1110-1235 1500-1545
Rangpur	88.8	10	b	0030-0300 0800-1710 1300-1600
Rangpur	90.0	5		0330-0420
Sylhet	105.0	1	j	0030-0400 1300-1700
Sylhet	88.8	10	b	0030-0400 0500-1710
Sylhet	90.0	5		1330-1700
Thakurgaon	92.0	5	b	0030-0200 1330-1700
Traffic Channel	88.8	10		0100-1500
Barisal	105.2	10	b	0030-0200 0445-1115 1330-1700
Coxsbazar	100.8	10	b	0030-0200 0545-1045 1330-1700
Rangamati	103.2	5		0530-1030
Bandorban	104.0	10		0530-1030
Mymensingh	92.0	10		0150-0530 1130-1430
Gopalganj	92.0	10		0200-0500 1100-1400
Jessore	100.8	10		Test trs

a) Rel. Ext. Sce 12:30-20:00 b) Rel. BBC World Service Dhaka 100 MHz 0000-0600, 1100-1700, other cities 0030-0100 0130-0200, 1330-1400, 1630-1700 c) China R Int. 1300-1400 j) Radio Japan 1500-1545
N. in English: 0200, 1100, 1530, 1805. **N. in Bengali:** 0100, 0300, 0400, 0500, 0600, , 0900, 1000, 1200, 1430, 1600, 1700 **SAARC N. in Bengali:** 1235 **SAARC N. in English:** 1250 Every Mon
F.PI: 100kW tx at Chittagong to be replaced. Replacement of 100kW tx at Dhaka B. One standby 100kW tx for Dhaka B. Digitisation and modernisation of transmitters, Modernisation and shifting of Shahbag office to Agargaon

EXTERNAL SERVICE: BANGLADESH BETAR
See International Radio section.

OTHER STATIONS:
RADIO TODAY ✉ Radio Broadcasting FM (Bangladesh) Co. Ltd Awal Centre (13th & 19th floors), Kamal Atraturk Avenue, Banani, Dhaka 1213 ☎ +880 2 982 0370-4 🖷 +880 2 9821486 **E:** wm@radiotodaybd.fm **W:** radiotodaybd.fm - **FM:** 89.6MHz 10kW Dhaka, Khulna, Chittagong, Cox's Bazar, Sylhet, Rajshahi, Barishal, Mymensingh
RADIO FOORTI ✉ Radio Foorti Limited Landmark (8th floor), 12-14 Gulshan-2 North C/A, Dhaka 1212 ☎ +880 2 8835747 8835748 **E:** info@radiofoorti.fm **W:** radiofoorti.fm - **FM:** 88.0MHz 20kW Dhaka, Chittagong, Sylhet, Mymensingh, Rajshahi, Barishal, Khulna, Cox's Bazar
RADIO AAMAR ✉ Uniwave Broadcasting Company Limited, Silver Tower (12th floor), 52, Gulshan Avenue, Gulshan- 1, Dhaka- 1212 ☎ +880 2 9886800, 9861133, 8832989 **E:** info@radioaamar.com **W:** radioaamar.com **LP:** CEO: Zulfiker Ahmed - **FM:** 88.4MHz 24h Dhaka
ABC RADIO ✉ Ayena Broadcasting Corporation, Dhaka Trade Centre, 99 Kazi Nazrul Islam Avenue, Kawran Bazar, Dhaka 1215 ☎ +880 2 8142038 8189307 🖷 +880 2 9128141 **E:** program@abcradiobd.

fm **W:** abcradiobd.fm **LP:** Man. Dir.: Matiur Rahman Choudhury - **FM:** 89.2MHz 24h Dhaka, Chittagong, Cox's Bazar

DHAKA FM Navana Tower (15th floor), 45, Gulshan South, Circle-1 Dhaka-1212 ☎ +880 2 8811720-21 +880 2 8811722 **E:** admin90.4@dhakafm904.com **W:** dhakafm904.com **FM:** 90.4MHz 10kW 24h Dhaka, Rajshahi, Bogra, Barishal, Chittagong, Cox's Bazar, Sylhet, Khulna, Rangpur, Mymensignh

PEOPLES RADIO 41, Samsuddin Mashon, 5th floor, Gulshan-2 Dhaka 1212 ☎ +880 2 9890952-3 +880 2 9570757 **E:** info@peoplesradio.fm **W:** peoplesradio.fm **LP:** Man. Dir.: Abdul Awal - **FM:** 91.6MHz 24h Dhaka

RADIO SHADHIN Asiatic Centre, House 63, Block H, Road 7B, Banani, Dhaka 1213 ☎+880 9666924924 **E:** info@radioshadhin.fm **W:** radioshadhin.fm - **FM** 92.4MHz Dhaka

RADIO BHUMI 40, Shahid Tajuddin Ahmed Sarani Tejgaon, Dhaka 1208 ☎ +880 2 8891939 **E:** radiobhumi@gmail.com **W:** radiobhumi.fm - **FM:** 92.8MHz 24h Dhaka

CITY FM Hasan Holdings Building, 14th floor, New Eskaton Road, Banglamotor, Dhaka 1000,☎ +880 2 9341828-9, **E:** info@cityfm96bd.com **W:** cityfm96bd.com **LP:** Man. Dir.: Syedur Aftab - **FM:** 96MHz 5kW 24h Dhaka

ASIAN RADIO Ka-34 Chowdhury Bari, South Badda Gulshan, Dhaka 1212 ☎ +880 2 9854475-78 **E:** info@asianradiofm.com **W:** asianradiofm.com **LP:** Chmn: Alhaj Harun Ur Rashid - **FM:** ‡90.8MHz 24h Dhaka (currently inactive).

COLOURS FM 67/4, Pioneer Road, Kakrail, Dhaka 1000, Dhaka, Bangladesh ☎ +880 961016016 **E:** info@colours.fm **W:** colours.fm - **FM:** 101.6MHz 24h Dhaka

JAGO FM Pran RFL Centre, 105 Middle Badda, Dhaka 1212 ☎ +880 2 9881792 **E:** info@jago.fm **W:** jago.fm - **FM:** 94.4MHz 24h Dhaka

RADIO EDGE 7th Floor, 84 Skylark Mark, Road-11, Dhaka 1213 ☎ +880 2 9820971 **E:** info@radioedge.rocks **W:** radioedge.rocks - **FM:** ‡95.6MHz Dhaka (currently inactive)

RADIO CAPITAL East West Media Group Ltd. 371/A, Block-D, Bashundhara R/A, 1229 Dhaka ☎ +880 2 8432370 Ext 3184 **E:** info@radiocapital.fm **W:** radiocapital.fm - **FM:** Capital FM 94.8MHz 23h30 Dhaka

RADIO DHONI Wega Zone Ltd. 80/A, Siddheswari Circular Road, Hazrat Shahjalal Tower (15th floor), Dhaka ☎ +880 2 9361430 **E:** info@radiodhoni.fm **W:** radiodhoni.fm - **FM:** 91.2MHz Dhaka

RADIO NEXT 17 Bir Uttam AK Khandakar Rd, Mohakhali, Dhaka ☎ +8809636100932 **W:** radionext.fm - **FM:** ‡93.2MHz Dhaka (currently inactive)

RADIO DIN RAAT 2 Bir Uttor Ziaur Rahman Road, (New Airport Road) Banani, Dhaka 1213 **E:** radiodinraat93.6@gmail.com **W:** radiodinraat.fm **FM:** 93.6MHz Dhaka

RADIO DHOL LK Tower -2 (Level 16) 59 & 61 Gulshan South Avenue Gulshan-1, Dhaka 1212 ☎ +880 2 9889494 **E:** info@radiodhol.fm **W:** radiodhol.fm **LP:** CEO: Silvia Pervin Leni - **FM:** 94.0MHz Dhaka

BANGLA RADIO Reza Group, Shwadesh Tower 16th floor 41/6 Box Culvert Road, Purana Paltan, Dhaka 1000 ☎ +880 2 9513765-67 **E:** info@banglaradio.fm **W:** banglaradio.fm **LP:** Chrmn: A.K.M. Shaheed Reza - **FM:** 95.2MHz Dhaka

SPICE FM Radio Masala Limited, MG Tower,13th floor, 389/B West Rampura, Dhaka 1219 ☎ +880 2 58315184-85 1841964000 **E:** info@spicefmbd.com **W:** spicefmbd.com **LP:** CEO: Tasnim Borsha Islam - **FM:** 96.4MHz 24h Dhaka

RADIO EKATTOR Radio Ekattor, Reaz Motors, 63 Kakrail, Ramna, Dhaka 1000 ☎ +88 01617167171 **E:** info@ekattor.fm; radioekattor@outlook.com **W:** ekattor.fm **LP:** Man. Dir. & CEO: Reaz Rahman - **FM:** 98.4MHz 24h Dhaka

RADIO AMBER Radio Amber, Navana Tower (13th floor), 45 Gulshan South C/A, Circle 1, Dhaka 1212 ☎ +88 09611000333 **E:** info@radioamber.com **W:** radioamber.com - **FM:** 102.4MHz 24h Dhaka

SUFI FM: Test 102.8MHz

FM Community Stations (all MHz):
R. Chilmari, Kurigram 99.2 – **R. Mukti**, Bogra 99.2 – **Barendra R.**, Naogaon 99.2 – **R. Mahananda**, Chapai Nawabganj 98.8 – **R. Padma**, Rajshahi 99.2 – **R. Jhenuk**, Jhenidah 99.2 – **R. Nalta**, Satkhira 99.2 – **R. Sundarban**, Khulna 98.8 – **Loko Betar**, Barguna 99.2 – **Krishi R.**, Barguna 98.8 – **R. Naf**, Cox's Bazar 99.2 – **R. Sagor Giri**, Chittagong 99.2 – **R. Bikrampur**, Munsiganj 99.2 – **R. Pallikantho**, Moulavi Bazar 99.2 – **R. Boral**, Charghat-Bagha, Rajshai 99.0 – **R. Sarabela**, Gaibandha 98.8 – **R. Meghna**, Bhola 99.0

F.Pl: Licence to be issued for one community stn in each district.

BARBADOS

L.T: UTC -4h — **Pop:** 290,000 — **Pr.L:** English (official), Bajan Creole — **E.C:** 115V/50Hz — **ITU:** BRB

FAIR TRADING COMMISSION

Good Hope, Green Hill, St. Michael ☎ +1 246 4240260 Ext 222 +1 246 4240300 **E:** info@ftc.gov.bb **W:** www.ftc.gov.bb **L.P:** CEO: Sandra Sealy

CARIBBEAN BROADCASTING CORP. (Gov. Comm.)

The Pine, Wildey, St.Michael ☎ +1 246 467 5400 **W:** cbc.bb, 947fm.bb, theone.bb & qfm.bb **L.P:** Chrmn: David Leacock, CEO: Sanka Price, Head of R.: Pearson Bowen

MW: CBC Radio 94.7: 900kHz 5kW: 24h (// 94.7)

FM: CBC Radio 94.7: 94.7MHz 5kW: 24h – **98.1 The One:** 98.1MHz 5kW: 24h – **Q 100.7 FM:** 100.7MHz 5kW – **Government Emergency Broadcast Station:** 91.1MHz 1kW

BARBADOS BROADCASTING SERVICE (Comm.)

Astoria House, St George, BB 19190 ☎ +1 246 437 9550 +1 246 437 9203

L.P: MD: Anthony T. Brian. GM: Gail Sherry Anne Padmore

FM: BBS-FM 90.7MHz 5kW: 24h – **Faith FM** (Rlg.) 102.1MHz 1kW: 24h

STARCOM NETWORK INC. (Comm.)

River Road, PO Box 1267, Bridgetown ☎ +1 246 430 7300 **W:** starcomnetwork.net, life975.com, vob929.com, hott953.com & thebeat104.com **L.P:** GM: David Ellis

FM: Life 97.5: 97.5MHz 1kW – **VOB Voice of Barbados:** 92.9MHz 5kW – **Hott 95.3 FM:** 95.3MHz 3kW – **The Beat 104.1 FM:** 104.1MHz 3kW

POWER BROADCASTING INC. (Comm.)

Haggatt Hall, Bridgetown ☎ +1 246 434 1011 +1 246 437 7526 **W:** slam101fm.com & y103fm.com. **L.P:** COO Marian Elias.

FM: Slam FM: 101.1MHz 5kW – **Y103:** 103.3MHz 5kW

OTHER STATIONS (FM in MHz):

BBC: Bridgetown 92.1 5kW. 24h relay of BBC World Service – **CAPITAL MEDIA HD** The Loft, Limegrove, Lifestyle Centre, Holetown ☎ +1 246 629 0991. L.P: CEO: Vic Fernandes FM 99.3 – **CITA RADIO (CHRIST IS THE ANSWER)** Bishop's Court Hill, BB46307, St. Michael ☎ +1 246 430 3599 **W:** citaradio.com FM 90.1 (5kW) – **MIX 96.9** (Comm./rlg.) First Floor, Sheraton Mall, Christ Church, St. Michael ☎ +1 246 228 4183 +1 246 228 3550 L.P: MD: Scott Weatherhead FM 96.9 (4kW) – **NBG RADIO** (Rlg.): Ryden Ave, Brittons Hill, Bridgetown ☎ +1 246 537 6489 **W:** nbglive.com FM 104.7 – **RADIO GED** (Educ.) Barbados Community College, Eyrie Howells Cross Rd, St. Michael ☎ +1 246 426 3312 **W:** bcc.edu.bb/Divisions/GEDRadio/ FM 106.1 (20W). D.Prgr: 1500-1900MF during school terms only

BELARUS

L.T: UTC +3h — **Pop:** 9.5 million — **Pr.L:** Belarusian (official), Russian (official) — **E.C:** 230V/50Hz — **ITU:** BLR

MINISTERSTVA KULTURY (Ministry of Culture)

pr. Peramožcaŭ 11, 220004 Minsk ☎ +375 17 2037574 **E:** ministerstvo@kultura.by **W:** www.kultura.by **L.P:** Minister: Jurij Bondar

NACYJANALNAJA DZIARŽAUNAJA TELERADYJOKAMPANIJA RESPUBLIKI BELARUS (Gov)

vul. Makajonka 9, 220807 Minsk ☎ +375 17 3896352 **E:** pr@tvr.by **W:** tvr.by **Radio studios:** vul. Čyrvonaja 4, 220807 Minsk; exc. **Radyus FM:** vul. Čyhunačnaja 27/2, 220014 Minsk.

L.P: Chmn: Ivan Ejsmant

FM (MHz)	**1**	**2**	**3**	**4**	**°1**	**°2**	**kW**
Asipovičy	91.0	107.7	72.47	104.9	67.46	71.69	1/3x2/2x4
Asvieja	103.5	106.0	-	-	-	-	4
Babrujsk	101.6	106.0	73.01	104.1	71.45	68.96	2x2/4/2/2x4
Bierazino	94.7	107.4	67.07	100.7	70.79	-	1/0.25/3x1
Brahin	103.3	105.8	69.11	100.8	67.37	68.30	2/2x4/2/2x4
Braslaŭ	105.7	107.7	73.49	102.3	69.08	71.99	2/2x4/2/2x4
Brest	100.0	88.5	72.47	103.7	70.91	71.69	2x1/4x4
Drahičyn	101.8	-	69.80	102.4	72.14	-	0.5/1/0.5/1

FM (MHz)	1	2	3	4	°1	°2	kW
Hieraniony	105.8	102.2	69.26	103.3	72.32	68.39	2/1/4/2/2x4
Homiel	105.1	91.5	66.20	100.1	67.76	69.26	2x1/2/1/2x2
Hrodna	103.0	95.0	68.90	100.5	66.98	66.20	4/1/4/2/2x4
Kapyl	102.3	101.6	73.22	103.9	-	70.97	4/0.5/3x0.1
Kasciukovičy	104.7	107.2	69.38	102.2	66.47	68.03	2/1/4/2/2x4
Krupki	103.8	106.3	-	-	-	-	4
Luki	90.6	94.7	-	104.3	-	-	1
Mahilioŭ	105.9	99.1	71.18	100.9	72.74	71.96	2/1/4/1/2x4
Miadziel	106.4	104.9	66.86	103.9	68.69	70.31	2x2/4x4
Minsk	106.2	102.9	105.1	103.7	71.33	70.43	2/1/1/3x4
Minsk	-	-	72.89	72.11	-	-	4
Mscislaŭl	106.7	101.7	73.73	102.9	66.89	-	1/0.25/3x1
Pinsk	104.5	106.8	67.88	102.0	66.32	67.10	2/5x4
Salihorsk	100.3	106.7	68.57	102.8	70.22	72.23	4/2/1/4/2x1
Slonim	106.5	97.3	-	104.0	66.56	67.34	4/1/3x4
Smarhon	103.6	-	66.38	101.4	67.97	70.13	3x1/2x2
Smiataničy	106.3	104.6	70.28	103.8	67.22	68.00	4
Staryja Darohi	100.6	103.1	-	-	-	-	1
Svislač	105.9	98.9	68.72	96.7	-	66.08	0.5/4/0.1/2x4
Trokieniki	104.5	-	-	-	-	70.76	1/0.5
Ušačy	106.7	101.7	70.94	102.7	72.65	66.74	4/1/4x4
Vasilievičy	102.0	106.5	73.19	-	-	-	1
Viciebsk	100.5	99.3	72.26	105.5	70.67	69.92	2x2/4x4
Vorša	107.0	105.0	73.82	100.2	67.85	69.14	3x1/2x2/4
Žlobin	105.5	101.0	71.81	100.5	69.68	71.03	2/1/4x2

+ sites with only txs below 1kW. °) Prgr 1+2 freqs in the OIRT FM band, are to be phased out

D.Prgr: Prgr 1 (Peršy kanal): 24h in Belarusian, Russian – **Prgr 2 (Kanal Kultura)**: 24h in Belarusian, Russian – **Prgr 3 (Radyjo Stalica):** 24h in Belarusian – **Prgr 4 (Radyus FM):** 24h in Russian – **Prgr 5 (R. Belarus):** 24h in Belarusian, Polish, Russian on (MHz) 96.4 (Brest 0.5kW), 96.9 (Hrodna 1kW), 99.9 (Hieraniony 1kW), 100.8 (Svislač 1kW), 102.0 (Miadziel 4kW), 106.6 (Braslaŭ 1kW).

Belteleradyjokampanija Regional Stations

D.Prgr: all stns 24h in Belarusian, Russian. **TRK "Brest"**, vul. Kujbyšava 64, 224030 Brest. **E:** radiobrestgosti@tut.by. Prgr 1 ("R. Brest") on (MHz) 69.08 (Pinsk 4kW), 69.44 (Slonim 4kW), 69.68 (Brest 4kW), 94.6 (Pinsk 1kW), 101.1 (Baranavičy 0.5kW), 102.5 (Stolin 0.5kW), 104.2 (Drahičyn 2kW), 104.8 (Brest 2kW), 105.6 (Pružany 0.1kW); Prgr 2 ("Horod FM") on 97.7MHz (Brest 0.1kW). – **TRK "Homiel"**, vul. Puškina 8, 246050 Homiel. **E:** radio@tvrgomel.by. Prgr 1 ("Homiel FM") on (MHz) 66.44 (Smiataničy 4kW), 66.98 (Homiel 2kW), 68.45 (Žlobin 2kW), 69.92 (Brahin 4kW), 101.3 (Homiel 1kW), 103.0 (Žlobin 2kW), 103.3 (Smiataničy 2kW), 105.3 (Brahin 1kW), 105.4 (Mazyr 0.5kW), 107.8 (Vasilievičy 1kW); Prgr 2 ("Homiel Plus"): on Homiel 103.7MHz (0.5kW). – **TRK "Hrodna"**, vul. Horkaha 85, 230015 Hrodna. **E:** radio@tvr.grodno.by. "R. Hrodna" on (MHz) 67.76 (Hrodna 4kW), 68.12 (Slonim 4kW), 68.48 (Masty 0.5kW), 71.54 (Hieraniony 4kW), 72.80 (Trokieniki 0.5kW), 101.2 (Hrodna 1kW), 101.8 (Luki 1kW), 102.5 (Slonim 1kW), 102.8 (Smarhon 1kW), 104.4 (Svislač 4kW), 107.8 (Hieraniony 1kW). – **TRK "Mahilioú"**, vul. Peršamajskaja 83, 212030 Mahilioŭ. **E:** radiomogilev@tut.by. "R. Mahilioŭ" on (MHz) 66.02 (Babrujsk 4kW), 67.25 (Kasciukovičy 4kW), 70.10 (Mahilioŭ 4kW), 70.91 (Asipovičy 2kW), 96.4 (Mahilioŭ 1kW), 99.4 (Kasciukovičy 1kW), 100.0 (Kryčaŭ 0.5kW), 100.4 (Mscislaŭl 0.25kW), 102.3 (Asipovičy 1kW), 102.7 (Slavharad 0.25kW), 106.6 (Babrujsk 1kW), 106.8 (Ciachcin 0.25kW). – **TRK "Viciebsk"**, vul. Kamunistyčnaja 8, 210602 Viciebsk. **E:** info@radio.vitebsk.by. "R. Viciebsk" on (MHz) 67.64 (Miadziel 4kW), 68.30 (Ušacy 4kW), 71.48 (Viciebsk 4kW), 91.2 (Viciebsk 2kW), 100.6 (Hara 1kW), 102.0 (Asvieja 1kW), 102.4 (Vorša 2kW), 104.0 (Byčycha 0.5kW), 104.6 (Braslaŭ 1kW), 105.2 (Sianno 1kW), 107.8 (Ušačy 4kW).

OTHER STATIONS

FM	MHz	kW	Location	Station
11A)	87.5	1	Minsk	Relax FM
11B)	87.5	2	Brest	Yumor FM
9B)	87.5	1	Hrodna	Narodnoye R.
20)	88.1	4	Smiataničy	Pravda R.
18)	88.2	1	Hrodna	Dushevnoye R.
7)	88.4	1	Braslaŭ	Evropa plus
23)	89.2	1	Maladziečna	Molodechno FM
11B)	89.9	1	Hrodna	Yumor FM
6)	90.0	1	Mahilioŭ	R. Unistar
8)	90.6	1	Vorša	R. Mir Belarus
1A)	91.0	1	Homiel	R. BA
11B)	91.2	1	Slonim	Yumor FM
7)	91.4	2	Ušačy	Evropa plus
11B)	91.9	1	Mahilioŭ	Yumor FM
5)	92.2	1	Viciebsk	Pilot FM
15)	92.4	2	Minsk	R. Minsk
11C)	92.7	2	Slonim	Avtoradio
11B)	93.7	2	Minsk	Yumor FM
22)	94.1	1	Minsk	Legendy FM
1A)	95.7	1	Hrodna	R. BA
1B)	96.2	1	Minsk	Melodii veka
22)	96.8	1	Žlobin	Legendy FM
11B)	97.0	1	Baranavičy	Yumor FM
21)	97.4	2	Minsk	MV-Radyjo
7)	97.8	1	Viciebsk	Evropa plus
22)	98.3	1	Salihorsk	Legendy FM
9A)	98.4	1	Minsk	Novoye R.
3)	98.6	1	Mahilioŭ	Russkoye R.
22)	98.7	1	Hieraniony	Legendy FM
9A)	98.7	1	Viciebsk	Novoye R.
3)	98.9	2	Minsk	Russkoye R.
20)	99.3	1	Žlobin	Pravda R.
6)	99.5	2	Minsk	R. Unistar
6)	99.8	1	Homiel	R. Unistar
19)	100.0	1	Baranavičy	Baranavičy FM
13)	100.4	1.5	Minsk	Energy FM
15)	100.4	1	Brest	R. Minsk
4)	100.8	2	Brest	Alfa-Radio
2)	101.2	1	Brest	R. ROKS
5)	101.2	2	Minsk	Pilot FM
1A)	101.5	1	Slonim	R. BA
14)	101.7	2	Minsk	Tsentr FM
8)	101.8	1	Viciebsk	R. Mir Belarus
2)	102.1	1	Minsk	R. ROKS
5)	102.1	1	Hrodna	Pilot FM
6)	102.3	1	Brest	R. Unistar
21)	102.4	1	Miadziel	MV-Radyjo
9B)	102.5	1	Minsk	Narodnoye R.
5)	102.9	1	Brest	Pilot FM
2)	103.0	1	Viciebsk	R. ROKS
2)	103.4	1	Mahilioŭ	R. ROKS
8)	103.6	1	Babrujsk	R. Mir Belarus
8)	104.3	2	Salihorsk	R. Mir Belarus
1A)	104.5	1	Mahilioŭ	R. BA
12)	104.6	1	Viciebsk	Retro FM
1A)	104.6	4	Minsk	R. BA
12)	104.7	1	Palack	Retro FM
21)	104.8	1	Kapyl	MV-Radyjo
16)	105.0	1	Hrodna	MFM
21)	105.3	1	Salihorsk	MV-Radyjo
21)	105.5	1	Bierazino	MV-Radyjo
21)	105.6	1	St. Darohi	MV-Radyjo
18)	105.7	2	Minsk	Dushevnoye R.
18)	106.0	1	Homiel	Dushevnoye R.
10)	106.1	1	Pinsk	Svaje R.
1A)	106.2	4	Brest	R. BA
15)	106.4	1	Viciebsk	R. Minsk
8)	106.6	1	Brest	R. Mir Belarus
9A)	106.7	1	Homiel	Novoye R.
2)	106.9	1	Hrodna	R. ROKS
8)	107.1	4	Minsk	R. Mir Belarus
17)	107.4	1	Homiel	R. 107.4 FM
21)	107.4	2	Maladziečna	MV-Radyjo
17)	107.6	1	Žlobin	R. 107.4 FM
4)	107.6	1	Viciebsk	Alfa-Radio
8)	107.8	1	Mahilioŭ	R. Mir Belarus
4)	107.9	2	Minsk	Alfa-Radio

+ txs below 1kW.

Addresses & other information:

1A,B) vul. Surhanova 26, 220010 Minsk – **2)** vul. Staražoŭskaja 8a, 220002 Minsk. In Russian – **3)** vul. Staražoŭskaja 8a, 220002 Minsk. In Russian – **4)** pr. Niezaliežnasci 181, 220125 Minsk. In Russian – **5)** vul. K.Marksa 40, 220030 Minsk – **6)** pr. Niezaliežnasci 4, 220050 Minsk. In Russian – **7)** Minsk. In Russian – **8)** vul. Kamunistyčny 17, 220029 Minsk. In Russian – **9A,B)** pr. Puškina 39, 220092 Minsk. In Russian – **10)** vul. Karasiova 6, 225710 Pinsk. In Russian – **11A-C)** vul. Uschodniaja 131, 220113 Minsk. 20A) in Russian – **12)** vul. Hoholia 11, 210601 Viciebsk. Rel. Retro FM (Russia) – **13)** vul. Kamunistyčny 6a, 220029 Minsk. Rel. Hit FM (Russia) – **14)** vul. Kamunistyčny 6, 220029 Minsk – **15)** zav. Kaliningradski 20a, 220012 Minsk. In Russian – **16)** pl. Savieckaja 6, 230025 Hrodna – **17)** vul. Šašejnaja 41, 246004 Homiel. In Russian – **18)** vul. K.Marksa 40, 220030 Minsk. In Russian – **19)**

vul. Haharina 40, 225409 Baranavičy. In Russian – **20)** Palieskaja vul. 17, 246003 Homiel – **21)** vul. Čkalova 5, 220039 Minsk – **22)** Lahojski trakt 22a, 220090 Minsk – **23)** vul. Budaŭnikoŭ 1, 222307 Maladziečna. In Russian.

Radio via DTT: see National TV section

DAB Transmitter (DAB+) (Trial)
Tx Operator: Beltelekom **M:** various tests **Tx:** Block 5B (Minsk 1kW)

BELGIUM

L.T: UTC +1h (28 Mar-31 Oct: +2h) — **Pop:** 11.5 million — **Pr.L:** Official languages: Flemish, French, German — **E.C:** 230V/50Hz — **ITU:** BEL

FLANDERS

Pop: 6.5 million — **Pr.L.:** Flemish

VLAAMSE REGULATOR VOOR MEDIA (VRM)

Koning Albert II-laan 20, 1000 Brussel ☎ +32 2 5534504 🖹 +32 2 5534506 **E:** vrm@vlaanderen.be **W:** www.vlaamseregulatormedia.be
L.P: Chmn: Matthias Storme

VLAAMSE RADIO EN TELEVISIEOMROEP (VRT) (Pub) Flemish (Dutch) Language Network

Public Sce grants by Flemish government.
VRT, August Reyerslaan 52, B-1043 Brussels ☎+32 2 741 3111 🖹 +32 2 734 9351 **W:** vrt.be **E:** info@vrt.be **L.P:** General Director Media: Frederik Delaplace; Radiomanager: Els Van de Sijpe
Regional Centres Radio 2:
Antwerpen: Jan Van Rijswijcklaan 157, 2018 Antwerpen ☎+32 3 2479111🖹 +32 3 2378282 **E:** redactieantwerpen@radio2.be
Vlaams-Brabant: Dikke Lindelaan 2, 1020 Brussels ☎+32 2 7414111 🖹 +32 2 4780800 **E:** redactievlaamsbrabant@radio2.be
Oost-Vlaanderen: Martelaarslaan 232, 9000 Gent ☎+32 9 2247256 🖹 +32 9 2254903 **E:** redactieoostvlaanderen@radio2.be
West-Vlaanderen: Doorniksesteenweg 241B, 8500 Kortrijk ☎+32 56 247311 🖹 +32 56 221358 **E:** redactiewestvlaanderen@radio2.be
Limburg: Via Media 2, 3500 Hasselt ☎+32 11 249611 🖹 +32 11 242436 **E:** redactielimburg@radio2.be

FM (MHz)	R1	R2	RK	SB	M	kW
Antwerpen	-	-	92.0	-	-	1
Brussegem	-	90.7	-	-	-	2
Brussels	-	-	-	-	88.3	1
Diest	-	92.4	-	-	-	1
Egem O.+W.-Vl.	95.7	-	90.4	102.1	101.5	50/50/50/40
Egem O.-Vl	-	98.6	-	-	-	50
Egem W.-Vl.	-	-	-	100.1	-	50
Genk	99.9	97.9	89.9	101.4	102.0	20/20/20/40/40
	-	-	-	-	93.0	3
Gent	-	-	-	94.5	-	0.5
Leuven	98.5	-	-	88.0	-	0.5/0.5
N'kerken Waas	-	89.8	-	-	-	1
Schoten	94.2	97.5	96.4	100.9	89.0	20/20/3/40/20
St-Pieters-Leeuw	91.7	93.7	89.5	100.6	97.0	50/50/50/50/2
Veltem	-	88.7	-	-	94.8	1/1

+3 txs under 1kW
R1=Radio Een (information and music), **R2**=Radio Twee (light & popular music), **RK**=Radio Klara (classical music), **SB**=Studio Brussel (youth stn), **M**=MNM (hit music stn)
Radio 2 Regional prgrs: 0500-0700 (M-F), 1100-1200 (M-F), 1500-1700 (daily) on FM
Sporza: replaces normal R.1 prgrs during sports events **W:** sporza.be
D.Prgr: Night prgr on all frequencies.
DAB: 223.936 MHz 12A. All services plus all regional Radio 2 outlets, Sporza, MNM hits, Klara continuo, and VRT NWS (news repeat).
Ann: R1:"Radio Een", R2: "Radio Twee", RK: "Klara", SB: "Studio Brussel", M: "MNM"

COMMERCIAL NETWORKS:

FM	Mhz	kW	Location	Station
1)	87.6	5	Oostende	Nostalgie
1)	88.0	8	Kortrijk	Nostalgie
1)	88.1	1	Brugge	Nostalgie
2)	88.3	1	Oost-Vleteren	QMusic
2)	88.6	3	Gent	Qmusic
3)	88.8	1	Lummen	Joe
6)	88.9	1	Diksmuide	VBRO
3)	89.1	3	Tongeren	Joe
3)	89.2	1	Sint-Truiden	Joe
6)	89.6	2	Brugge	VBRO
3)	90.6	5	Turnhout	Joe
3)	90.9	4	Herzele	Joe
5)	91.3	3	Brugge	NRJ
3)	92.2	3	Dendermonde	Joe
2)	92.2	2	Herentals	Qmusic
7)	92.7	2	Kortrijk	TOP R.
3)	92.8	1	Gent	Joe
1)	92.8	1.5	Beringen	Nostalgie
3)	93.5	2	Sint-Niklaas	Joe
3)	93.5	2.5	Meeuwen	Joe
3)	93.5	2	Westerlo	Joe
8)	93.6	20	Ardooie	Stadsradio Vlaanderen
7)	94.0	6	Ardooie	TOP R.
1)	94.7	1	Genk	Nostalgie
1)	94.8	1	Tongeren	Nostalgie
5)	95.1	1	Turnhout	NRJ
3)	95.5	1	StPietersLeeuw	Joe
3)	95.6	1	Brussegem	Joe
2)	95.8	1	Veltem	Qmusic
6)	96.3	2	Gent	VBRO
1)	96.5	1.2	Hamont-Achel	Nostalgie
3)	96.7	2	Mechelen	Joe
1)	96.9	1	Sint-Truiden	Nostalgie
9)	98.0	1	Antwerpen	R. Minerva
1)	98.1	4	Brussel	Nostalgie
1)	98.2	15	Egem	Nostalgie
4)	98.8	3	Brussel	Bruzz
1)	98.2	1	Scherpenheuvel	Nostalgie
6)	99.0	1	Mechelen	VBRO
2)	99.2	10	Antwerpen	Qmusic
10)	99.3	1	Bree	FM Goud Noordoost-Limburg
5)	99.4	3	Gent	NRJ
2)	100.0	1	Wuustwezel	Qmusic
6)	100.2	2	Antwerpen	VBRO
1)	101.0	20	Ieper	Nostalgie
2)	102.5	1	Brussel	QMusic
2)	102.5	50	Genk	Qmusic
7)	102.6	2	Leuven	TOP R.
11)	102.6	1	Eeklo	R. Tamboer
7)	102.7	2	Aalst	TOP R.
12)	102.7	3	Brugge	R. Brugs Ommeland
7)	102.8	1	Brussel	TOP R.
1)	102.9	100	Schoten	Nostalgie
2)	103.0	20	Egem	Qmusic
1)	103.0	2	Bree	Nostalgie
2)	103.1	50	StPietersLeeuw	Qmusic
3)	103.3	1	Diest	Joe
2)	103.3	1	Brugge	Qmusic
3)	103.4	31	Brussel	Joe
3)	103.4	5	Antwerpen	Joe
3)	103.4	20	Genk	Joe
1)	103.5	20	Gent	Nostalgie
5)	103.6	1	Oostende	VBRO
3)	103.7	2	Wuustwezel	Joe
3)	103.7	2	Lommel	Joe
1)	103.7	2	Sint-Niklaas	Nostalgie
1)	103.8	3	Leuven	Nostalgie
8)	103.8	2	Gent	Stadsradio Vlaanderen
5)	103.8	1	Geel	NRJ
5)	103.8	1	Hasselt	VBRO
3)	104.1	50	Egem	Joe
5)	104.1	2	Hasselt	NRJ
5)	104.2	3	Leuven	NRJ
3)	104.2	1	Aalst	Joe
7)	104.2	2	Antwerpen	TOP R.
13)	104.5	1	Gent	Zen FM
8)	104.5	1	Oostende	Stadsradio Vlaanderen
5)	104.5	1	Poperinge	NRJ
1)	104.5	1	Mechelen	Nostalgie
1)	104.5	1	Oud-Turnhout	Nostalgie
1)	104.6	2	Geel	Nostalgie
5)	104.6	2	Antwerpen	NRJ
8)	104.7	1	Hasselt	Stadsradio Vlaanderen
1)	104.8	3	Aalst	Nostalgie

+ many stns below 1kW
Addresses & other information:
1) Katwilgweg 2, 2050 Antwerpen **W:** nostalgie.eu – **2)** Medialaan 1,

1800 Vilvoorde **W:** qmusic.be – **3)** Medialaan 1, 1800 Vilvoorde **W:** joe.be – **4)** Eugène Flageyplein 18 bus 18, 1050 Elsene **W:** bruzz.be – **6)** Vlamingstraat 35, 8000 Brugge **W:** vbro.be – **7)** Nekkerputstraat 150, 9000 Gent **W:** topradio.be – **8)** P. Cuyperstraat 3, 1040 Brussel **W:** stadsradiovlaanderen.be – **9)** Wandeldijk 20, 2050 Antwerpen **W:** minerva.be – **10)** Peerderbaan 84, 3990 Peer **W:** fmgoud.be – **13)** Overpoortstraat 70, 9000 Gent **W:** zenfm.be

DAB+: Operator Norkring 11A, 5A and 5D on 174.928, 180.064 and 216.928 MHz: TOPradio, Radio Maria, Evergreen, BBC World Service, Joe, Qmusic, Q Maximum Hits, Q Foute Radio, Willy, Joe 60s&70s, Joe 80s, Joe 90s, Joe Easy, Joe Best of BE, Radio Nostalgie, NRJ, Stadsradio Vlaanderen, RTBF Mix

WALLONIA

Pop: 3.6 million — **Pr.L.:** French, German

CONSEIL SUPERIEUR DE L'AUDIOVISUEL (CSA)

✉ Rue Royale 89, 1000 Bruxelles ☎ +32 2 3495880 🖷 +32 2 3495897 **E:** info@csa.be **W:** www.csa.be **L.P:** DG: Karim Ibourki

MEDIENRAT DER DEUTSCHSPRACHIGEN GEMEINSCHAFT BELGIENS

✉ Gospertstr. 42 4700, Eupen ☎ +32 87 596300 🖷 +32 87 552891 **E:** info@medienrat.be **W:** www.medienrat.be **L.P:** Pres: Oswald Weber

RADIO-TÉLÉVISION BELGE DE LA COMMUNAUTÉ FRANCAISE (RTBF) (Pub.)

French Language Network

Public sce. Grants by French Parliament.

✉ Cité de la Radio-Television, B-1044 Brussels ☎+32 2 737 2111 🖷 +32 2 737 4357 **W:** rtbf.be

L.P: Admin. Gen: Jean-Paul Philippot. Dir. Médias: Xavier Huberland

Regional & Local Centres: Bruxelles: Boulevard Auguste Reyers 52, 1044 Bruxelles **Charleroi:** Place de la Digue 8, 6000 Charleroi **Liège:** Boulevard Raymond Poincaré 15, 4020 Liège **Hainaut:** Rue du Gouvernement 15, 7000 Mons **Namur-Brabant-Wallon:** Av. Golenvaux 8, 5000 Namur

FM (MHz)	1	2	3	4	5	kW
Anderlues	93.4	92.3	-	99.1	96.6	0.6/40/40/40
Bruxelles	-	99.3	91.2	93.2	88.8	3/40/1/0.5
Léglise	96.4	91.5	94.1	87.6	-	10/10/10/10
Liège	96.4	90.5	99.5	95.6	92.5	5/40/40/13/0.1
Malmédy	89.2	91.6	-	-	-	1/0.1
Marche	93.3	95.2	-	-	-	0.5/4
Profondeville	102.7	-	92.8	90.8		25/10/10
Tournai	106.0	101.8	102.6	104.6	90.6	25/30/30/30/?
Verviers	91.3	103.0	-	-	87.9	1/3/0.1
Wavre	96.1	97.3	-	-	101.1	10/35/50

+ many txs under 1kW

Network 1 (Première – information & musique)
Network 2 (Vivacité – light music) - **Reg. Prgrs:** W 0500-0700
Network 3 (Musique 3 – classical music)
Network 4 (Classic 21 – oldies & rock classics)
Network 5 (Pure FM – youth stn)

DAB: 225.648MHz 12B - all services plus Tarmac (Belgian hip hop) and BRF 1. **Provincial MUXs:** 5B, 5C, 6A, 6B, 6C, 6D, 8D, and 11D carry both RTBF and network radio stations such as: Bel RTL, BRF1, BRF2, Classic 21, DAB Info, DH Radio, Fun Radio, La 1ère (+ regional stations), Maximum, Musiq3, Must FM, Nostalgie, NRJ, Pure, Radio Contact, Chérie FM, Sud Radio, TARMAC, Test RTBF, Jam, Viva+, Classic21, Test RTBF Musiq3, Vivacité regional stations. More stations to be added.

Ann: "Vous écoutez La Première, Vivacité, Musique trois, Radio 21, Pure FM, Classic 21"

BELGISCHES RUNDFUNK-UND FERNSEHZENTRUM DER DEUTSCHSPRACHIGEN GEMEINSCHAFT (BRF)

German Language Network (Pub)

Grants by RDG-Rat (German speaking community council)

✉ Kehrweg 11, B-4700 Eupen ☎+32 87 59 1111 🖷+32 87 591199 **W:** brf.be **E:** info@brf.be

Regional: ✉ Blvd. Reyers 52, B-1044 Brussels – Vennbahnstraße 4/3, B-4780 St. Vith **L.P:** Dir.: Toni Wimmer

FM	MHz	kW	Ch.	FM	MHz	kW	Ch.
Lüttich	88.5	50	1	Lüttich	91.0	0.5	2
Bernister	88.8	0.1	1	Auel	92.2	0.16	1
Lontzen	89.0	0.4	1	Lontzen	93.2	5	2
Recht	94.9	5	1	Namur	97.7	0.5	1
Eupen	94.9	0.05	1	Eupen	98.4	1	2
Brussel*	95.2	2	1	Recht	104.1	20	2
Bernister	97.6	0.1	2	Raeren	105.9	0.1	2

*: broadcasts joined prgrs of Deutschlandfunk and BRF

DAB: BRF1 and BRF2 on Muxs 6B – 6C – 6D for Brussels and Wallonia

Ann: "Hier ist der Belgischer Rundfunk"

COMMERCIAL NETWORKS:

FM	Mhz	kW	Location	Station
14)	87.6	1	Ath	Sud R.
14)	88.2	1	Charleroi	Sud R.
11)	88.7	1	Sambreville	NRJ
1)	88.9	1	Ronquières	Bel RTL
14)	90.0	1	Tournai	Sud R
17)	90.2	2	Bruxelles	R. Judaica
11)	91.9	1	Charleroi	NRJ
10)	92.3	1	Verviers	R. Nostalgie
11)	92.7	1	Malmédy	NRJ
7)	92.9	1	Bastogne	Fun R.
3)	94.1	1	Louvain-la-Neuve	R. Antipode
2)	94.4	1	Bütgenbach	100.5 Das Hitradio
9)	94.7	5	Bouillon	Must FM
10)	95.0	1	Liège	R. Nostalgie
15)	95.6	1	Houdeng	DH R.
8)	97.1	1	Liège	Maximum FM
7)	97.4	1	Mont-St-Aubert	Fun R.
14)	97.6	1	Braine-le-cte	Sud R.
18)	97.8	1.2	Bruxelles	R. Kif
8)	98.6	1	Esneux	Maximum FM
12)	98.8	1	Ciney	R. Contact
1)	99.0	2.5	Bouillon	Bel RTL
7)	99.0	1	Liège	Fun R.
16)	99.9	1	Quevaucamps	Beloeil FM
10)	100.0	5	Brussel	R. Nostalgie
4)	100.1	1	Liège	Equinoxe FM
1)	100.2	1	Limal	Bel RTL
10)	100.2	4	Saint-Hubert	R. Nostalgie
10)	100.4	4	Namur	R. Nostalgie
2)	100.5	20	Eupen	100.5 Das Hitradio
10)	100.5	2	Couvin	R. Nostalgie
10)	100.6	5	Bouillon	R. Nostalgie
10)	100.7	1	Dinant	R. Nostalgie
8)	100.9	2	Liège	Maximum FM
15)	101.4	1	Bruxelles	DH R.
1)	101.6	5	Marche-en-F	Bel RTL
12)	101.6	1	Verviers	R. Contact
1)	101.7	2	Namur	Bel RTL
1)	101.7	1	Couvin	Bel RTL
12)	101.8	1	Meix-le-Tige	R. Contact
14)	102.0	2	Mons	Sud R
12)	102.2	10	Brussel	R. Contact
12)	102.2	5	Charleroi	R. Contact
12)	102.2	2	Liège	R. Contact
12)	102.3	2	Mons	R. Contact
10)	102.4	1	Arlon	R. Nostalgie
12)	102.5	1	Houffalize	R. Contact
11)	103.2	10	Vlessart	NRJ
15)	103.2	2	Liège	DH R.
1)	103.4	5	Mons	Bel RTL
1)	103.6	5	Liège	Bel RTL
11)	103.7	5	Brussel	NRJ
1)	104.0	15	Brussel	Bel RTL
1)	104.0	2	Charleroi	Bel RTL
6)	104.3	1	Brussel	BXFM
11)	104.5	5	Liège	NRJ
12)	104.5	1	Bièrges	R. Contact
12)	104.6	1	Marche	R. Contact
7)	104.7	5	Brussel	Fun R.
12)	104.7	1	Malmédy	R. Contact
12)	104.7	5	Namur	R. Contact
2)	104.8	3	Sankt Vith	100.5 Das Hitradio
12)	104.8	2	Virton	R. Contact
12)	105.1	1	Ath	R. Contact
7)	105.5	1	Wavre	Fun R.
8)	106.0	1	Verviers	Maximum FM
12)	106.2	1	Florzé	R. Ourthe Amblève
3)	106.3	2	Tubize	R. Antipode
5)	106.8	1	Malmédy	Impact FM
10)	100.2	50	Saint-Hubert	R. Nostalgie

FM	Mhz	kW	Location	Station
11)	104.5	5	Liège	NRJ
12)	107.0	1	Eupen	R. Contact (DE)
19)	107.2	1.5	Bruxelles	Vibration FM
7)	107.5	1	Arlon	Fun R.
2)	107.6	1	Honsfeld	100.5 Das Hitradio
11)	107.6	1	Mons-St-Aubert	NRJ
12)	107.8	1	Libramont	R. Contact

+ many stns below 1kW

Addresses & other information:
1) Avenue Georgin 2, 1030 Bruxelles +32 2 3376911 **W:** belrtl.be – **2)** Kehrweg 11, B-4700 Eupen +32 87 591259 🖷 +32 87 591249 **W:** hitradioworld.fm – **3)** Boîte postale 2, 1348 Louvain-La-Neuve ☎ +32 10 451110 🖷 +32 10 451717 **W:** antipode.be – **4)** Rue Montagne St Walburge, 261, 4000 Liège **W:** equinoxefm.be – **5)** Malmédy **W:** impact-fm.be – **6) W:** bxfm.be – **7)** Av. Telemaque 33, 1190 Bruxelles ☎ +32 2 3457575 **W:** funradio.be – **8)** 22 Rue de la Chaudronnerie, 4030 Grivegnée **W:** maximumfm.be – **9)** BP20, 1360 Perwez ☎ +32 81 655469 **W:** mustfm.be – **10)** Quai au Foin 55, 1010 Bruxelles ☎ +32 2 2270450 🖷 02-2231455 **W:** nostalgie.eu – **11)** Chaussèe de Louvain 467, 1030 Bruxelles ☎ +32 2 5137575 🖷 +32 2 5114859 **W:** nrj.be – **12)** Avenue des Croix de Guerre 94, 1120 Bruxelles ☎ +32 2 2442711 🖷 +32 2 2442710 **W:** radiocontact.be and derbestemix.be (DE) – **13)** Rue Armand Binet 35B, 4140 Rouvreux (Sprimont) – **14)** 42, rue de la chaussée de Mons, 7000 Mons ☎ +32 65 401010 🖷 +32 65 401011 **W:** sudradio.net – **15)** Rue des Francs, 79, 1040 Bruxelles **W:** dhnet.be/medias/dh-radio – **16) W:** beloeil-fm.be – **17) W:** radiojudaica.be – **18) W:** radiokif.be – **19) W:** vibration.fm

DAB+: Many local (up to 216) expected on MUX 11B and 12B, no concrete dates

Military Stations:
AMERICAN FORCES NETWORK BENELUX
🖃 Bldg 318, Room 101, B-7000 Mons. ☎+32 65 44 36 09 **E:** dma.afnbenelux@mail.mil
L.P: Officer-in-charge: Cpt. G. Martel. Broadc. Supcrv: SFC C. Kubicek. Chief Eng: René Libre
Stations: Kleine Brogel 106.2MHz 0.1kW, Brussels 101.7MHz 0.9kW, 106.5MHz 4kW, Chievres 107.9MHz 0.1kW
D.Prgr: 24h - All txs carry AFN Europe's "The Eagle" channel.

BRITISH FORCES BROADCASTING SERVICE
Stations: BFBS 1 Casteau 107.7MHz 0.04kW
🖃 Otto-Hahn-Strasse 20, 33104 Paderborn, Sennelager **W:** forces.net/radio **D.Prgr:** rel. BFBS Germany

BELIZE

L.T: UTC -6h — **Pop:** 400,000 — **Pr.L:** English (official), Belize Creole, Spanish — **E.C:** 110V/60Hz — **ITU:** BLZ

PUBLIC UTILITIES COMMISSION (PUC)
🖃 PO Box 300, 41 Gabourel Lane, Belize City ☎+501 2234938 🖷 +501 2236818 **W:** puc.bz **E:** info@puc.bz

FM	MHz	kW	Station, location
5)	88.1	4	Love FM, Punta Gorda
5)	88.9	4	Love FM, Ladyville
1)	90.5	0.25	Positive Vibes R, Belize City
6)	91.1	13	Krem FM, Ladyville
2)	92.3	1	Reef R, San Pedro
8)	93.7	1	My Refuge Christian R, Roaring Creek
15)	94.3		BFBS Radio
11)	94.1	1	Faith FM, Pine Ridge
5)	95.1	1	Love FM, Belize City
17)	95.5		Power FM, Orange Walk
5)	95.9	1	Estéreo Amor, Belmopan
15)	96.3		BFBS R. 2, Belize
6)	96.5	6	Krem FM, Belize/Carmelita/Cattle Landing
7)	97.1	1	Integrity R, Belize City
4)	97.5		Estéreo Amor, Belize City
5)	98.1		Love FM, 4 sites
15)	98.3		BFBS R. Gurkha, Belize
17)	98.9		Power FM, Belize City
16)	99.5	1	More FM, Belize City
14)	99.7	1	R. Bahia, Corozal
8)	100.5	0.2	My Refuge Christian R, Belize City
6)	101.1	1	Krem FM, Dangriga
9)	101.3		Lighthouse Christian R, San Pedro
1)	102.9		Positive Vibes R, Belmopan
10)	103.1	1	Sugar City R. Station, Orange Walk
11)	104.5		Faith FM, Punta Gorda
13)	106.7		Fiesta FM, Orange Walk
16)	107.1		More FM, Belmopan

NB: H of Tr: usually 24h

Addresses & other information:
1) W: facebook.com/vibesradiobz – **2) W:** facebook.com/Reef-Radio-100202586796704 – **4)** 5 more txs **W:** estereoamor.com – **5)** 9 more txs **W:** lovefm.com – **6) W:** krembz.com – **7) W:** facebook.com/IntegrityRadio97.1FM – **8) W:** myrefugebelize.com – **9) W:** lighthouseradio.org – **10) W:** scrs.bz – **11) W:** faithfmbelize.com – **13) W:** fiestafmbz.com – **14) W:** facebook.com/rabahia99.7 – **15) W:** forces.net/radio – **16) W:** facebook.com/morefm – **17) W:** powerfm955belize.com

BENIN

L.T: UTC +1h — **Pop:** 12 million — **Pr.L:** French (official), Baatonum, Fon, Yom, Yoruba — **E.C:** 220V/50Hz — **ITU:** BEN

HAUTE AUTORITÉ DE L'AUDIOVISUEL ET DE LA COMMUNICATION (HAAC)
🖃 BP 3567, Ave. de la Marina, Face Hôtel du Port, 01 Cotonou ☎+229 21311743 🖷 +229 21311742 **W:** www.facebook.com/haacbenin

OFFICE DE RADIODIFFUSION ET TÉLÉVISION DU BENIN (ORTB, Gov.)
🖃 01 B.P. 366, Cotonou ☎+229 21360047 **W:** ortb.bj **E:** ortb@intnet.bj
FM: Cotonou 94.7 10kW, Parakou 89.4/92.5MHz 2kW.
Radio Benin: Yaoui 92.7MHz 0.5kW, Cotonou Centre 94.7 10kW, Cotonou 98.2MHz 2kW, Dassa-Zoumè 105.7MHz 2kW.
Atlantic FM: Cotonou 92.2MHz 5kW.
R. Regionale: Tanguiéta 90.0MHz 1kW, Parakou 92.5MHz 2kW, Bembèrèkè 94.0MHz 0.5kW, Kandi 96.1MHz, 2kW, Abomey 102.9MHz 1kW, Malanville 103.8MHz 0.5kW, Natitingou 106.7MHz 2kW.

OTHER STATIONS, main networks:
R. Adja Ouèrè: Bohicon 90.4MHz, Cotonou 92.6MHz, Sakété 95.3/100.6MHz, Porto Novo 100.0MHz, Zagnanado 107.6MHz.
R. Immaculee Conception (Rlg.): Djougou 89.1MHz, Natitingou 93.1MHz, Parakou 93.3MHz, Cotonou 98.7MHz, Bembèrèkè 100.8MHz, Bohicon 100.9MHz, Allada 101.3MHz, Dassa-Zoum 107.3MHz ric.immacolata.com
R. MJR-Maranatha Jesus Revient: Cotonou 103.1MHz, Parakou 103.3MHz, both 0.5kW **W:** maranathabenin.org
R. Wekê, Cotonou: 107MHz –
R. Rurale stns in Tanguiéta 94.5, Ouessè 97.7, Dogbo 100.0, Ouaké 101.0 & Banikoara 104.2MHz
BBC African Service: Cotonou 101.7MHz.
RFI Afrique: Cotonou 90.0MHz, Parakou 106.1MHz.
Trans World R, Parakou (Serarou): 1566kHz 100kW 0315-0545, 1725-2230 & 1476kHz 100kW 0320-0550, 1725-2050 beamed to Nigeria. For details see International Radio section.

BERMUDA (UK)

L.T: UTC -4h (14 Mar-7 Nov: -3h) — **Pop:** 62,000 — **Pr.L:** English — **E.C:** 120V/60Hz— **ITU:** BER

BERMUDA BROADCASTING CO. LTD. (Comm.)
🖃 4 Fort Hill Road, Prospect, Devonshire DV 02, PO Box HM 452, Hamilton HM BX ☎ +1 441 295 2828 **W:** bermudabroadcasting.com **L.P:** Owner: Chris Perry. CEO: Patrick Singleton, News Dir.: Gary Moreno, CEN: Earlston Chapman
FM: Ocean 89: 89.1MHz 1kW – **Power 95 FM:** 94.9MHz 2kW – **Inspire 105** (Rlg.): 105.1MHz 2kW

DEPARTMENT OF EMERGENCY MEASURES ORGANIZATION
🖃 Global House, 43 Church Street, Hamilton HM 12 ☎ +1 441 295 5151 **L.P:** Coordinator Steve Cosham **Gov. Emergency Broadcasting Station:** Prospect, Devonshire 100.1MHz 1kW

INTER-ISLAND COMMUNICATIONS LTD. (Comm.)
✉ 49 Union Square Mall, Hamilton ☎ +1 441 297 1076 📠 +1 441 296 7680 **E:** feedback@hott1075bermuda.bm **W:** hott1075bermuda.bm **L.P:** Owner & CEO: Glenn A. Blakeney. **FM: Magic 102.7:** 102.7MHz – **Hott 107.5** 107.5MHz

LTT BROADCASTING LTD. (Comm.)
✉ P.O. Box 1564 HMGX, Hamilton HMEX ☎ +1 441 700 9810 📠 +1 441 292 9492 **E:** iriebermuda@gmail.com **W:** irie.bm
FM: Irie FM: 98.3MHz

HARPER DIGITAL ENTERTAINMENT LTD. (Comm.)
✉ 12 Whale Bay Rd, Southhampton SB03 ☎ +1 441 232 0699 **E:** info@vibe103.com **W:** vibe103.com **L.P:** Owner: Zarah Harper
FM: Vibe 103 FM: 103.3MHz

BHUTAN

L.T: UTC +6h — **Pop:** 830,000 — **Pr.L:** Dzongkha (official), Lhot-am (Nepali), Sharchhop, English — **E.C:** 230V/50Hz — **ITU:** BTN

BHUTAN INFOCOMM AND MEDIA AUTHORITY
✉ Olakha, Expressway Road, Thimphu ☎ +975 2 321506 📠 +975 2 326909 **E:** bicma@bicma.bt **W:** www.bicma.gov.bt
L.P: Chmn: Dasho Karma W. Penjore

BHUTAN BROADCASTING SERVICE (Gov)
✉ P.O. Box 101, Thimphu ☎ +975 2 322866/322533/323071 📠 +975 2 323073 **W:** bbs.bt **E:** request@bbs.com.bt
L.P: Exec. Dir: Sonam Tshong.Tech. MD: Pema Choden, Dir: Dorji Wangchuk. Prgr. Dir: Tashi Dhendup. News Dir: Thinley Tobgye

SW(kHz)	**kW**	**Location & other information**
6035	†100	Thimpu (tx running at 30/100kW)

FM(MHz)	**Main**	**R.Dz**	**FM**(MHz)	**Main**	**R.Dz**
Bangtar	90.0	96.0	Samtse-Saurani	98.0	96.0
Bumthang	90.0	92.0	Samtse-Tendu	93.0	90.0
Chukha-Dala	98.0	96.0	Sarpang	98.0	96.0
Chukha-Pachu	90.0	93.0	Thimphu	88.1	90.0
Dagana	90.0	88.1	Thimphu	96.0	98.0
Haa	98.0	90.0	Thonphu	96.0	98.0
Lamsorong	90.0	93.0	Trashigang	90.0	88.1
Mongar	90.0	88.1	Trongsa	93.0	96.0
Ngalamdung	98.0	93.0	Tsirang	92.0	88.1
Panbang	90.0	93.0	Wangdue	98.0	96.0
Paro	92.0	93.0	Zhemgang	88.1	90.0
Phuentsholing	92.0	-	Zorchen Tranhiyangtse	98.0	96.0

NB: R.Dz = R. Dzongkha 24h on FM only.
Main D.Prgr: on SW: S/on s/off varies but usually 0100-1200), **on FM** 24h **English:** Daily 0800-1200, 1800-2100 English Music/Repeat broadcast **N:** Daily: 0800,1100; **English Request Show:**Sun 0900-1000, **English Live Call In:** Mon-Sat 0900-1000; **UN Radio Prgr:** Thurs 0815; **NHK Prog** Mon 1015; **Bhutan This week** Fri 1015; **Sharchhop:** 0000-0400,1200-1400 (**N:**0100,0200,0300,1200,1300), 2100-2400 Music/Repeat broadcast; **Lhotsam** (Nepali): Daily 0400-0800, 1400-1800 (**N:**0400,0700,1400,1500 inc. 1600-1800 Music/ Repeat broadcast.
V. by QSL card. 15 min prgr details req. Rp. (2 IRCs)

Other FM Stations
Kuzoo FM, ✉ P.O. Box 419, Thimphu **W:** kuzoo.net **DPrgr:** 24h in English on 105.0MHz and Dzongkha on 104.0MHz – **Radio Valley,** ✉ P.O. Box 224/225, Thimphu **W:** radiovalley.bt **DPrgr:** 0200-1630 in E on 99.9MHz – **Yiga Radio** Thimpu 94.7 MHz 0000-1600 in English and Dzongkha

BOLIVIA

L.T: UTC -4h — **Pop:** 11.4 million — **Pr.L:** Official languages: Spanish & 36 indigenious languages — **E.C:** 220V/50Hz (exc. some older buildings in La Paz which may still have 110V/50Hz) — **ITU:** BOL — **Int. dialling code:** +591

AUTORIDAD DE REGULACIÓN Y FISCALIZACIÓN DE TELECOMUNICACIONES Y TRANSPORTES (ATT)
✉ Calle 13 de Calacoto, entre Av. Los Sauces y Av. Costanera, N° 8260, La Paz ☎ 2 2772266 📠 2 2772299 **W:** att.gob.bo
L.P: CEO: Roque Roy Méndez Soleto

ASOCIACIÓN BOLIVIANA DE RADIODIFUSORAS (ASBORA)
✉ La Paz **W:** www.facebook.com/Asbora-Asociaci%C3%B3n-Boliviana-de-Radiodifusoras-495938463944689

NB: ‡ = inactive, ± = varying freq., † = irregular, RPO – Radioemisoras de los Pueblos Originarios

MW	**kHz**	**kW**	**Station, location, h of tr**
LP77)	540		Radiodifusora Victoria, La Paz
LP03)	560	15	R. El Mundo, La Paz
LP01)	580	10	R. Panamericana, La Paz: 1000-0300 (Sun 1100-0100)
CH01)	600	10	R. ACLO, Sucre: 0800-0200
LP35)	600	1	Radioemisoras del Recobro, La Paz
SC55)	600		R. Familiar, Santa Cruz
LP02)	620	10	R. San Gabriel, El Alto: 0800-0100
TA12)	640		R. ACLO, Tarija: 0850-0130
LP11)	650	15	R. Dif. Integración, El Alto: 0930-0200
LP150)	660		R. Taller de Historia Oral Andina, La Paz
SC10)	660	1	R. ABC, Santa Cruz: 0900-0100
LP147)	670		R. Comunitaria Cadena Provincial, Jihuacuta
PO28)	680		R. ACLO, Potosi: 0850-0130
LP27)	680	5	R. Andina, La Paz: 0900-0300
LP155)	680	10	R. Jallalla Coca, Chulumani
LP116)	700		R. Pacha Kamasa, El Alto (RPO): 0955-0100 (Sat -1805, Sun -1615)
PO40)	710	10	R. Pío XII, Siglo Veinte: 0830-0230
LP06)	720	10	R. La Cruz del Sur, La Paz: Sat 1300(Sun 1200)-2100
LP05)	730	2.5	R. Yungas, Chulumani: 0900-1700, 2000-0100
LP151)	740		R. Pueblo de Dios, La Paz
LP07)	760	50	R. Fides, La Paz: 1045-0100
CO02)	770	5	R. Cosmos, Cochabamba: 1100-0300
LP08)	800	5	R. Play, La Paz
LP10)	820	10	R. Altiplano Advenir, La Paz: 24h
LP75)	840	3	R. Atipiri, El Alto: 1045-0030 (Sun: 2300)
SC03)	850	5	R. María, Montero: 0900-0100
LP12)	860	10	R. Nueva America, La Paz
CO86)	860		R. FM Colores, Cochabamba
LP42)	880		R. Inca, El Alto: -0200
SC39)	880		Rdif. Oriente, Santa Cruz
CH31)	900		R. Tomina la Frontera, Villa Tomina
TA01)	900	0.25	R. LV Nacional, Tarija: 0100-2300
LP36)	900	5/0.1	La Popular, La Paz: 1000-0100
PO39)	900		R. Dios es Amor Universal, Potosi
CO33)	‡900	1	R. Central Misionera, Cochabamba:1100-0100
CO85)	920		R. Dios es Amor Universal, Cochabamba
CH11)	920	3	R. Encuentro, Sucre: 0900-0100, Sat: 2300-0200, Sun: 1000-2200
LP65)	920	1	R. San Andres de Topohoco, Topohoco: 0900-0330
LP88)	920		R. Bartolina Sisa, El Alto
CH13)	940	1	R. Chuquisaca XXI, Sucre
LP13)	940		R. Metropolitana, La Paz: 0930-0430, Sat: 1100-0530 Sun: 1000-0400
SC53)	940		R. Pan de de Vida, Santa Cruz
PO02)	960	1	R. Kollasuyo, Potosí: 1000-0400(Sun -0200)
SC04)	960	10	R. Santa Cruz (Fe y Alegria), Santa Cruz
LP43)	960	1	R. Huayna Potosí, Milluni
CO04)	980	3	R. Esperanza, Aiquile: 0900-0100(Fri -0400), Sat 1000-0300(Sun -2230)
LP14)	980	2.5	R. Mar, La Paz: 1000-0200
OR41)	980		R.dif. Concordia, Oruro
CH26)	980		R. La Bohemia, Sucre
PO30)	990		R. Municipal de Colcha "K"
CO84)	1000		FM Unica, Cochabamba
SC33)	1000	1	Rdif. del Oriente, Santa Cruz: 0930-0400, Sat: 0900-0330, Sun: 1130-0430
LP115)	1000		R. LV del Arrebatamiento, Guaqui
LP44)	1000	1	R. Taypi, La Paz: 1000-0400
OR03)	1010	10	R. Bahá'í de Bolivia, Oruro
LP15)	1020	10	R. Illimani - R. Patria Nueva, La Paz: 0900-0400
CO57)	1020		R. Illimani - R. Patria Nueva, Cochabamba
CO59)	1020		R. Illimani - R. Patria Nueva, Valle Alto
CO60)	1020		R. Illimani - R. Patria Nueva. Tarata
CO61)	1020		R. Illimani - R. Patria Nueva, Chapare
CO70)	1020		R. Illimani - R. Patria Nueva, Colomi
CO87)	1020		R. Illimani - R. Patria Nueva, Tiraque
BE21)	1020		R. Illimani - R. Patria Nueva, Trinidad
BE22)	1020		R. Illimani - R. Patria Nueva, San Borja
BE24)	1020		R. Illimani - R. Patria Nueva, Riberalta
PA10)	1020		R. Illimani - R. Patria Nueva, Cobija

MW	kHz	kW	Station, location, h of tr
PO07)	1020		R. Illimani - R. Patria Nueva, Potosi
PO08)	1020		R. Illimani - R. Patria Nueva, Catavi
PO32)	1020		R. Illimani - R. Patria Nueva, Unica
PO33)	1020		R. Illimani - R. Patria Nueva, Villazon
PO34)	1020		R. Illimani - R. Patria Nueva, Llica
PO35)	1020		R. Illimani - R. Patria Nueva, Tupiza
PO35)	1020		R. Illimani - R. Patria Nueva, Uyuni
SC40)	1020		R. Illimani - R. Patria Nueva, Santa Cruz
SC41)	1020		R. Illimani - R. Patria Nueva, Vallegrande
SC42)	1020		R. Illimani - R. Patria Nueva, Camiri
SC43)	1020		R. Illimani - R. Patria Nueva, Yapacani
SC56)	1020		R. Illimani - R. Patria Nueva, Puerto Quijarro
CO62)	1020		R. Illimani - R. Patria Nueva, Kami
CO68)	1020		R. Illimani - R. Patria Nueva, Independencia
CH21)	1020		R. Illimani - R. Patria Nueva, Sucre
CH32)	1020		R. Illimani - R. Patria Nueva, Sopachuy
CH35)	1020		R. Illimani - R. Patria Nueva, Azurduy
CH36)	1020		R. Illimani - R. Patria Nueva, Machareti
TA13)	1020		R. Illimani - R. Patria Nueva, Tarija
TA14)	1020		R. Illimani - R. Patria Nueva, Bermejo
TA16)	1020		R. Illimani - R. Patria Nueva, Villamontes
TA18)	1020		R. Illimani - R. Patria Nueva, Yacuiba
TA19)	1020		R. Illimani - R. Patria Nueva, Entre Rios
OR29)	1020		R. Illimani - R. Patria Nueva, Oruro
OR36)	1020		R. Illimani - R. Patria Nueva, Caracolla
OR37)	1020		R. Illimani - R. Patria Nueva, Huanuni
OR44)	1020		R. Illimani - R. Patria Nueva, Challapata
LP89)	1020		R. Illimani - R. Patria Nueva, Ichoca-Quime
LP90)	1020		R. Illimani - R. Patria Nueva, Pucarani
LP91)	1020		R. Illimani - R. Patria Nueva, Copacabana
LP92)	1020		R. Illimani - R. Patria Nueva, Caranavi
LP93)	1020		R. Illimani - R. Patria Nueva, Chulumani
LP94)	1020		R. Illimani - R. Patria Nueva, Guaqui
LP126)	1020		R. Illimani - R. Patria Nueva, Topohoco
LP127)	1020		R. Illimani - R. Patria Nueva, Vilaque
LP128)	1020		R. Illimani - R. Patria Nueva, Taraco
LP129)	1020		R. Illimani - R. Patria Nueva, Tapichullo
LP130)	1020		R. Illimani - R. Patria Nueva, Tiawanaku
LP132)	1020		R. Illimani - R. Patria Nueva, Qhurpa
LP133)	1020		R. Illimani - R. Patria Nueva, La Asunta
LP135)	1020		R. Illimani - R. Patria Nueva, Escoma
LP136)	1020		R. Illimani - R. Patria Nueva, Desaguadero
LP140)	1020		R. Illimani - R. Patria Nueva, Coro Coro
CH19)	1030		R. Mojocoya AM (RPO), Mojocoya:1000-0200
LP156)	1030		R. Illimani - R. Patria Nueva, Coripata
LP157)	1030		R. Illimani - R. Patria Nueva, Coroico
OR26)	1030	3	R. de los Pueblos Originarios (RPO), Orinaca
PO)41	1030		R. Illimani - R. Patria Nueva, San Pablo de Lipez
CO48)	1030	3	R. Independencia (RPO), Independencia
CO51)	1030		R. 24 de Junio (RPO) Totora
BE20)	1030	3	R. Comunitaria Riberalte (RPO), Riberalta
CH41)	1030		R. Illimani – R.Patria Nueva, Camargo
CH18	1040		R. 12 de Marzo (RPO), Tarabuco
SC38)	1040		R. San Julián (RPO), San Julián
LP45)	1040	1	R. Bolivianíssima, La Paz
OR14)	1040	0.25	R. Atlántida, Oruro: 1100-2400
CH33)	1050		R. Comunitaria, Huacaya
OR27)	1050	3	R. Sabaya (RPO) Sabaya
PO26)	1050		R. Caiza D (RPO), Caiza D
LP95)	1060		R. Qhana Amazonía, Caranavi
OR01)	1060	1.5	R. Noticias, Oruro: 1000-2200, 0200-0600
CH02)	1060	1	R. Dif. Colosal, Sucre: 0900-0300
CH30)	1080		R. Comunitaria, Sopachuy
CH34)	1080		R. Comunitaria, Juana Azurduy
CH40)	1080		R. Comunitario Carama, Sucre
LP158)	1080		R. Comunitario Carama, Machareti
LP159)	1080		R. Espiritu Santo, La Paz
LP110)	1090		R. Comunitaria Pachakuti, Achocalla
OR06)	1100	1	R. Universidad de Oruro: 1100(Sun 1200)-2300
LP29)	1100		R. Chaka, Pucarani: 0900-1300, 2030-0130
LP153)	1100		Universal R. Concienia, El Alto
CO76)	1110		R. Raqaypampa (RPO), Raqaypampa
CO53)	1120		R. El Porvenir, Tiquipaya
LP96)	1120		R. Celestial el Milagro, El Alto
LP97)	1120		R. Wiñay Khantatt, Tiawuanaku
LP124)	1120		R. Illimani - R. Patria Nueva, Huarina
SC57)	1130		R. Illimani - R. Patria Nueva, Montero
CO69)	1140		R. San Isidro, Colomi
LP23)	1140		R. Sol Poder de Dios, La Paz: 0930-0300
LP23)	1140		R. Sol Poder de Dios, Huancane: 0930-0300
LP50)	1150	0.3	R. Guaqui, Puerto de Guaqui
SC11)	1160	5	R. Centenario "La Nueva", Sta. Cruz
CO08)	1160	3/1	R. RTC Deportiva, Cochabamba: 10454-2330
CH03)	1160	1	R. Nuevo Mundo, Sucre: 1000-0300
LP33)	1160	10	R. Continental, La Paz: 0930-2400
LP18)	1180	1	R. Ingavi, Viacha: 1000-0200 (Sun 1100-2400)
OR40)	1180		R. Sajama Estero, Oruro
LP122	1190		R. Comunitaria, Guaqui
LP100)	1200		Cuarzo Comunicaciones, La Paz
SC12)	1200	5	R. Oriental, Santa Cruz
CO10)	1200	0.25	R. 24 de Noviembre, Valle Alto
OR31)	1200		R. Capital, Oruro
CO80)	1220		R. Progreso La Luz del Alba, Cochabamba
LP19)	1220	1	R. Splendid, La Paz: 0800-0200
LP134)	1220		R. La Asunta, Asunta
LP143)	1220		R. La Voz Cristiana, Achacachi
OR09)	1220	1	R. Batallión Topátar, Oruro 1055-0100
TA03)	1240	2	R. Los Andes, Tarija: 1000-2200
LP131)	1240		R. Nueva Generación, Qhurpa
LP154)	1240		R. Lider Zaráte Willka, La Paz
CH04)	1250	2.5	R. La Plata, Sucre: 1430-2400
LP51)	1250		Rdif. Achocalla, Achocalla
LP146)	1250		R. Comunitaria Compi, Capilaya
PO29)	1250		R. Indoamerica, Potosi
SC52)	1250		R. Amboro, Santa Cruz
SC54)	1250		R. Sararenda, Camiri
CO54)	1260		R. LV de la Esperanca, Quillacollo
LP137)	1260		R. SERVIR, Caranavi
LP160)	1260		Red de Com. Nueva Imagen Para Bolivia
OR20)	1260	10	R. Nacional de Huanuni, Hunanuni: 0930-0200, Sat 1100-1800(Sun -1600)
TA21)	1260		R. Dios es Amor Universal, Tarija
CO65)	1280		R. Cristiana Comunidad del Sur, Cochabamba
LP68)	1280		R. Comunitaria Ondas del Titicaca, Huarina
LP142)	1280		R. Altar de Dios, Achacachi
TA17)	1280		R. Fronera, Yacuiba
LP148)	1290		R. Comunitaria Alaxpacha, Canaviri
OR12)	1290	1	Radiodifusoras Minería, Oruro
PO31)	1290		R. Tomas Katari de America, Ocuri
CH05)	1300	2.5	R. Loyola, Sucre: 1000-2400, Sun 1015-0200
CO72)	1300		R. Voz de Dios y No del Hombre, Cochabamba
SC16)	1300	1	R. Fuerzas Armadas, Sta. Cruz
LP23)	1300	15/6	R. Sol Poder de Diós, El Alto: 0930-0300
BE18)	1300	5	R. Bandera Beniana, Trinidad
OR39)	1300		Sistem de Cumuncacion "Perez", Oruro
CO14)	1320	10	R. San Rafael, Cochabamba: 0900-0200
CH25)	1320		R. Sucre, Sucre
LP53)	1320		R. Comunitaria Tawantinsuyo, Taraco
LP111)	1320		R. Em. Septima Voz, Achocalla
LP121)	1320	3	R. Comunitaria La Lumbrera, La Paz
CO79)	1340		TV Sist. de Comunicacione Mundial, Cochabama
LP39)	1340	0.5	R. Copacabana, Copacabana: 1000(Sun 1100)-0200
LP40)	1340	0.5	R. Comunitaria Jach'a Suyu, Corocoro: 1000-1630, 2000-0100
LP145)	1340		R. Comunitaria La Voz de Valle, Sococoni
LP152)	1340		R. La Mision, La Paz
CH06)	1350		R. America, Sucre: 1000-0400
LP113)	1350		R. Comunitario Inti, Contorno/Viacha
LP123)	1350		R. Llacxa, Achocalla
SC49)	1350		R. TV Salesiana, Yapacani
CO15)	±1355	0.25	R. Armonía, Cliza (n.f.: 1350)
CO05)	1360	2.5	R. Cochabamba "CBA", Cochabamba: 1030-0200
PO37)	1360		R. La Cruz del Sur, Potosi
SC47)	1360		R. 24 de Septiembre, Santa Cruz
CO16)	1370	0.15	R. Libertad, Cliza
OR32)	1370		R. Coral, Oruro
CH22)	1380		R. Global, Sucre
LP104)	1380		R. Maria, La Paz
LP141)	1380		R. TV Minera Matilde, Carabuco
LP161)	1380		R. Em. Tunupa, Tianawaku
LP162)	1380		LV del Espiritu Santo, El Alto
SC51)	1380		R. Maria, Santa Cruz
CO34)	1380	1.5	R. Bandera Tricolor, Cochabamba: 1100-0300
OR33)	1380		R. Horizontes, Huanuni
TA06)	1380	0.5	R. Luis de Fuentes, Tarija: 0930-0400
CO50)	1390		R. Andina (RPO), Pongo Khasa
CH20)	1400		R. Antena 2000, Sucre
LP25)	‡1400	5	R. Nacional de Bolivia, La Paz: 0900-0200

MW	kHz	kW	Station, location, h of tr
OR38)	1410	0.25	R. Atlantida, Oruro
LP105)	1420		R. Omasuyos Andina, Achacachi
LP114)	1420		R. Creo en Milagros, Murillo
TA05)	1420	1.5	R. Guadalquivir, Tarija: 0900-0100
CO18)	1420	1	R. Centro, Cochabamba: 1030-2300 (Sun 1100-0000)
CH15)	1420	1	R. Real Audiencia, Sucre: 0900-0200
SC50)	1420		R. Comunitaria, José Ballivian
SC58)	‡1420		R. Luz del Mundo, Santa Cruc (F.Pl.)
CH39)	1440		Sistema de Comunicaciones Horizontes, Sucre
LP26)	1440	1	R. Batallón Colorados, La Paz: 1000-0400(Sun 1100-)
LP139)	1440		R. Comunitaria Eco Saywani, Carabuco
SC21)	1440	2/1	R. Yaguary, Vallegrande: 1000- 0200
CO42)	‡1440	0.25	R. Bolivia, Cochabamba
CO74)	1440		LV de Juno (RPO), Tiraque
BE02)	1440		R. Dif. Tropico, Trinidad
CO39)	1450	0.5	R. Magnal, Capinota
OR13)	1450	1	R. Em. Bolivia, Oruro
LP106)	1460		R. Plenitud de Vida, El Alto
LP138)	1460		R. Jiwasa, Carabuco
CO78)	1460		R. Canal de Television Quillacollo
CH29)	1470	1	R. Integración, Padilla
LP109)	1470		R. Em. Ayni, Corapata
CH24)	1480		R. Charcas-Mundial, Sucre
LP108)	1480		LV de los Andes, Carabuco
PO12)	1480	0.1	R. Cadena Sur, Potosi
CO32)	1480	1/0.8	R. Chiwalakii, Vacas: 0900-1400, 2100-0100
CO40)	1480		R. Domingo Savio, Independencia
CO66)	1480		R. Bendita Trinidad y Espirito Santo, Cochabamba
PA09)	1480		R. Bendita Trinidad y Espirito Santo, Cobija
SC48)	1480		R. Bendita Trinidad y Espirito Santo, Santa Cruz
LP58)	1480		R. Amor de Diós, El Alto
LP107)	1480		R. Comunitaria Waley, Desaguadero
OR15)	1490	1	R. Jacinto Rodriguez, San José, Oruro
CO77)	1500		R. Litoral, Cochabamba
LP101)	1500	2	R. Comunitaria Tawantinsuyo, Laja: 0800-0100
SC25)	1500	1	R. Sagrado Corazón, Mineros
TA15)	1500		R. Universidad Juan Misael Saracho, Villamontes
LP144)	1510		R. Wiñay Jatha, El Alto
CH38)	1520		R. Universidad Juan Misael Saracho, Sucre
CO64)	1520	1	R. la Chiwana, Cochabamba
CO73)	1520		R. Rural, Tarata
LP59)	1520		R. La Luz del Tiempo, El Alto
LP120)	1520		R. San Pedro, Tiawuanaku
CO67)	1530		R. Salesiana, Kami
PO10)	1530	0.25	R. Litoral, Llica
CH37)	1540		R. Comunitaria Rio Chico, Sucre
LP34)	1540	0.8	R. Sariri, Escoma: 1000-1300, 2200-0200
LP112)	1540		R. Comunitario Tutuka, Vilaque
LP67)	1540		R. Bendita Trinidad y Espirito Santo, El Alto
LP28)	1550	10	R. Caranavi, Caranavi: 0930-1800, 2200-0200
LP149)	1560	15	R. Luz del Mundo, La Paz
OR19)	1560	1	R. Occidental, Oruro
CO27)	1560	0.5	R. Urkupiña, Quillacollo: 1000-2400
BE23)	1570		R. Pedro Ignacio Muiba
CH28)	1580		R. Contacto, Sucre: 0830-2300, Sat/Sun.: 1800
CO75)	1580		LV del Valle, Valle Alto
OR35)	1580		R. Comunitaria Jacinto Rodrìguez, Caracolla
SC29)	1580	1	R. Adonai, Santa Cruz: 1000-0300
LP62)	1580		R. El Fuego del Espíritu Santo, El Alto: 1000-2400
TA07)	1580	3	R. Bermejo, Bermejo
TA20)	1580		R. Magazine Tarija, Tarija
CO24)	1590	1	R. Wayana Songo, Pongo K´asa
LP61)	1590		R. Kollasuyo Marka, Tiawanaku
CO28)	1600	0.5	R. P.C.A., Valle Alto
CO88)	1600		LV del Campesino, Cochabamba
SW	**kHz**	**kW**	**Station, location, h of tr**
CO29)	3310	10	R. Mosoj Chaski, Cochabamba: 0900-1300, 2100-0100
SC30)	†5580	0.25	R. San José, San José de Chiquitos
PO15)	5935		R. Yura, Yura
PO40)	±5952	5	R. Pío XII, Siglo Veinte: (n. 5955)
LP15)	6025	10	R. Illimani - Red Patria Nueva, La Paz: 0930-0300
LP01)	±6105	10	R. Panamericana, La Paz
SC04)	6135	10	R. Santa Cruz, Santa Cruz: 1100-0200

Addresses and other information:

NB: Whenever listed, Casilla addresses should preferably be used for mailing purposes.

ERBOL (Educación Radiofónica de Bolivia), Calle Ballivián 1323, 4° piso (Cas. 5946), La Paz ☎ 2 2324606, 232 4768 🖷 2 2391985 **W:** erbol.combo – Pte.: Jorge Trias S.J. Secr. Ejecutivo: Jorge Aliaga Murillo

UNESBO (Unión de Emisoras Sindicales de Bolivia), Yanacocha 689, La Paz ☎1 2341881 Pte: Jorge Bustillo Burgos

BE00 (BENI)

BE02) Avenida Panamericana Carretera a Santa Crtuz km 2½ - EPARU, Trinidad ☎3 4635300 **W:** Facebook: Radio Tropico **E:** radiodifusorastropico@yahoo.com - **FM:** 92.2 MHz – **BE06)** Sucre 320, Guayaramerín – **BE09)** Av Selim Majuli (Correo Central), San Borja, Pcia BalliviáN – **BE12)** Calle Nicanor Gonzalo Salvatierra 249, Riberalta - **FM:** 91.1MHz – **BE13)** Ballivián s/n, San Ignacio de Moxos – **BE14)** Cas 395, Guayaramerín – **BE15)** Calle Beni s/n, Guayaramerín – **BE16)** Plaza Fr Martín Baltasar de Espinosa, Santa Ana del Yacuma – **BE18)** Calle Santa Cruz esq Mamoré s/n, Trinidad – **BE19)** Avenida Primero de Mayo esquina Loreto, Guayaramerin **E:** ninafelima@hotmail.com – **BE20)** Riberalta, Prov Vaca Diez – **BE21)** Trinidad – **BE22)** San Borja – **BE23)** Calle Isiboro esquina Machupo, Trinidad **W:** apcbolivia.org/Medios/muiba.aspx - **FM:** 89.5 MHz – **BE24)** Riberalta

CH00 (CHUQUISACA)

CH01) Calle Guillermo Loayza Nº 274 esq Vecente Donoso (Zona Mercado Campesino), (Cas 538), Sucre ☎4 64-39597 Prgrs in **Quechua** except **Spanish** 1330-2030 0900-0200 **W:** aclo.org.bo/radio-aclo-chuquisaca **E:** aclochuquisaca@aclo.org.bo – **FM:** 101.5 MHz – **CHO2)** Calle San Alberto Nº 19 (Cas 335), Sucre ☎4 6442888 🖷4 6444433 **W:** colosal.com.bo **E:** fundacionradiotv@colosal.com.bo - **FM:** 90.7MHz – **CH03)** Junin Nª 841 (Cas 25), Sucre – **CHO4)**) Avaroa 422 Zona Central, Cas 276, Sucre ☎4 6461616 **W:** radiolaplata.com.bo/ **E:** info@laplata.com.bo- **FM:** 99.7MHz – **CH05)** Calle Ayacucho 161, Sucre ☎4 6453677 🖷4 6442555 **E:** loyola@radiofides.com - **FM:** 98.3MHz "Onda Joven" – **CH06)** Calle Guillermo Loayza 377, Mercado Campesino, Sucre ☎4 46446574 🖷4 46444445 – **W:** radioamericatk.com.bo **E:** info@radioamericatk.com.bo – **FM:** 97.5 MHz – **CH09)** Alcaldía Municipal, Padilla **CH11)** Calle Loa No 41, Sucre ☎6 441300 **W:** encuentroradio.com – **FM:** 95.9MHz – **CH13)** Calle Kantuta 3 Ed. Canal 15, Barrio Ferroviario, Zona San Matias, Sucre ☎6 461157 🖷6 458321 **E:** pulsartv@bolivia.com– **CH15)** Calle Avarioa 537, Sucre – **CH16)** Sucre – **CH17)** Sucre – **CH18)** Comunidad de Tarabco, Prov Yamparáez – **CH19)** Comunida de Mojocoya, Prov Zudáñez – **CH20)** Calle Lima Pampa 72, Esq. Elidora Ayllón, Sucre ☎6 440 606 **E:** contacto@radioantena2000.com - **FM:** 89.1 MHz – **CH21)** Sucre – **CH22)** Barrio Petrolero, Sucre ☎🖷6 442900 **W:** radioglobalbolivia.com - **FM:** 106.7 MHz – **CH23)** Calle Eduardo Berdecio 568, Sucre. **W:** radiohorizonte.boliviastreaming.com - **FM:** 91.1 MHz – **CH24)** Calle Eduardo Berdecio Nº 522, Sucre ☎6 461 112 **W:** facebook.com - Radio Charcas-Mundial **E:** radiocharcasam1480@hotmail.com - **FM:** 96.4 MHz – **CH25)** Sucre **W:** radiosucre1320.com - **FM:** 105.9 MHz – **CH26)** Sucre – **CH28)** Calle Bustillos Nº 322, Sucre ☎4 6435205 **W:** radiocontactosucre.com **E:** direccion@radiocontactosucre.com – **CH29)** Padilla - **FM:** 98.5 MHz – **CH30)** Sopachuy – **CH31)** Villa Tomina – **CH32)** Sopachuy – **CH33)** Huacaya – **CH34)** Azurduy – **CH35)** Azurduy – **CH36)** Machareti – **CH37)** Sucre – **CH39)** Sucre – **CH40)** Sucre – **CH41)** Camargo

CO00 (COCHABAMBA)

CO02) Av Heroinas O-0467, Centro Nor Oeste, (Cas 1092), Cochabamba ☎4 4250422 🖷4 4251173 **Quechua:** 0930-1030, 0000-0200 1100-0300 - **FM:** 95.1MHz "Fides" – **CO04)** Calle Loa Final s/n, Ivirganzama, (Cas 5716), Cochabamba. ☎4 4343044 **W:** Facebook: R.Esperanza **E:** radioesperanza.aiquile@gmail.com **Quechua:** 8 hours daily - **FM:** 100.3MHz – **CO05)** Calle 25 de Mayo 230 entre Bolívar y Sucre (Cas 5500), Cochabamba ☎4 4251504 🖷4 4251561 **E:** ragarobol@yahoo.es - **FM:** 104.3MHz "Gaviota" – **CO07)** Cochabamba – **CO08)** Lanza esq Ecuador N-0261 (Cas 846), Cochabamba ☎4 4257289 🖷4 4241414 **W:** web.supernet.com.bo/radiortc **E:** radiortc@yahoo.com – **CO10)** Valle Alto – **CO14)** Calle Calama E-0315 (Cas 546), Cochabamba ☎4 4256563 🖷4 250 522 **Quechua/Aymara:** 0900-0200 - **FM:** 92.1MHz – **CO15)** Calle 6 de Agosto 11, Cliza – **CO16)** Calle Santa Cruz 4, Cliza – **CO18)** Calle Ecuador casi Avenida Ayacucho No 115 (Cas 839), Cochabamba ☎4 4251434 **W:** grupocentro.com.bo **E:** contactos@grupocentro.com.bo - **FM:** 96.3 & 106.7 MHz – **CO24)** Cas 1151, Cochabamba ☎🖷4 8119295 **W:** sdb.bo **E:** japaricio@sdb.bo – **CO27)** A. Suarez Miranda final s/n, Zona Norte, Cochabamba ☎4 260 661 **E:** radioam1560@hotmail.com – **CO28)** Ayacucho 138, Punata – **CO29)** Calle Abaroa 254 (Cas 4493), Cochabamba **W:** mosochaski.org **E:** radiomosojchaski@hotmail.com – **CO32)** Misuk'ani (Cas 80), Vacas ☎4 223089 🖷4 255390 **E:** chiwalak@entelnet.bo Prgrs mainly in **Quechua** 0900-1400, 2100-0100 – **CO33)** Av Petrolera Km 0.5, Cochabamba – **CO34)** Av. Oquendo No 560 entre Paccieri y Federeico

Blanco (Cas 3655), Zona Muyurina, Cochabamba ☎4 520202 **E:** latripple999@yahoo.com **Quechua:** 1000-1200 - **FM:** 99.9MHz "La Triple" – **CO39)** Augusto Larrain, Capinota. – **CO40)** Independencia, Prov. Ayopaya (Av. Papa Paulo No 0982, Muyurina, Cochabamba) **W:** radiosavio.galeon.com **E:** radiosavio@hotmail.com - **FM:** 98.1 MHz – **CO42)** Calle Calama 0-0135, Cochabamba – **CO43)** Calle Junín 309, Tiraque, Prov Arani – **CO48)** Independencia – **CO50)** Calle Tumusla esquina Ecuador No 310, Plazuela Cobija, area Oeste (Cas. 1986) Cochabamba ☎4 589366 📠4 589377 **W:** ceprabolivia.org **E:** cepra@supernet.com.bo - **FM:** 101.1 MHz – **CO51)** Totora, Prov Carrasco – **CO53)** Calle Pablo Jaimes 188, Tiquipaya, Prov Quillacollo - **FM:** 90.5MHz – **CO54)** Calle Montenegro N° 234 Zona: Villa Paraiso, Cochabamba ☎4 448647– **CO57)** Cochabamba – **CO59)** Valle Alto – **CO60)** Tarata – **CO61)** Chapare – **CO62)** Kami – **CO64)** Junin casi Aroma, Edif. De la Federacion de Campesinos - 5° piso, Cochabamba ☎4 4584389 **W:** radiolachiwana.org **E:** radiolachiwana@gmail.com - **FM:** 107.9 MHz – **CO65)** MNPPD Ira. Avanzada, Huayana Kápac, Pasaje B, Cochabamba ☎4 661203 **W:** http//radiocomunitariadelsur.com **E:** info@radiocomunitariadelsur.com – **CO66)** Av. Circunbalacion, Calle Atahuallpa, Cochabamba ☎7 9361282 **FB:** - Radio Bendita Trinidad Bolivia – **CO67)** Kami – **CO68)** Independencia – **CO69)** Colomi – **CO70)** Colomi – **CO72)** Cochabamba – **CO73)** Tarata – **CO74)** Tiraque – **CO75)** Valle Alto – **CO76)** Raqay Pampa – **CO77)** Cochabamba – **CO78)** Cochabamba – **CO79)** Cochabamba – **CO80)** Cochabamba – **CO84)** Cochabamba – **CO85)** Cochabamba – **CO86)** Cochabamba – **CO87)** Tiraque – **CO88)** Cochabamba

LP00 (LA PAZ)

LP01) Edificio 16 de Julio, P.9, Of 902, El Prado, La Paz **W:** panamericana.bo ☎2 2334271 **E:** socialpanamericana@gmail.com **N:** «El Panamericano» relayed by many stns – **LP02)** Pza de la Cruz N° 100 – Av.Bolivia, Comunidad Charapaqui Colpani Villa Adela, (C.P. 4792) El Alto ☎2 2832544 **W:** radiosangabriel.org.bo **E:** info@radiosangabriel.org.bo Prgrs in **Aymara** exc Sp & Quechua 1400-1430, Sat 2100-2130 – **FM:** 98.2 MHz – **LP03)** Av. La Bandera No 1462, V.Pabón, La Paz – **LP05)** Calle Nuñez del Prado s/n esquina Calle Santa Cruz, Chulumani (Cas 4535, La Paz) ☎2 896031 **W:** radioyungas.com.bo **E:** radio.yungas@hotmail.com - **FM:** 92.1MHz – **LP06)** Calle Nicaragua 1759(Cas 1408), La Paz ☎2 220541 📠2 243337 **W:** radiocruzdelsur.com **E:** contactos@radiocruzdelsur.com – **LP07)** Av Sucre Esq. Genaro Sanjines N° 799, 9143La Paz ☎2 2406363 **W:** radiofides.com **E:** contactos@radiofides.com - **N:** «La hora del país», relayed by many stns, at 1100, 1630, 2230, 0130 – **LP08)** Calle 24 de Calacoto, Edif. TorreCesur, Piso 4 Of 402,La Paz ☎ 2 790743 📠 2 770292 **W:** radioplaybolibvia.com **E:** info@radioplaybolivia.com – **LP10)** Calle Abdon Saavedra N° 2110 casi esquina Fernando Guachalla, (Cas 8631), Sopocachi) La Paz ☎2 426742 redadvenir.org/proyectos/radio-altiplano – **LP11)** Calle 2 No 95 P.3 entre Av. 6 de Marzo y Jorge Carrasco, Ceja, El Alto (Cas. 312472, La Paz) ☎2 810048 📠2 810048 **W:** radiointegracion.com **E:** integracionam@yahoo.es **Aymara:** 0830-1200 0900-0130 – **LP12)** Calle Abdón Saavedra 1990 (or Cas 2431), La Paz ☎2 2356622 – **LP13)** Juan de la Riva 1527 (Cas 8704), Zona Central, La Paz ☎2 203339 **E:** metropolitana940@gmail.com – **LP14)** Calle Jenaro Sanjinés 799 esqquina Calle Sucre, Centro, La Paz ☎2 406 590 📠2 406740 **E:** editor@radiofides.com – **LP15)** Avenida Camacho 1485, Edifico la Urbana Piso 5, La Paz ☎2 2200390 **W:**radioillimani.bo **E:** radioillimani.bo@gmail.com – **LP18)** Calle General Lanza 93, Viacha, Provincia Ingavi – **LP19)**Av. 16 de Julio "El Prado" Nâ 1490, Edifico Avenida, Piso 12, Of. 12B La Paz. ☎2 319885 Prgr. in Aymara 0800-0200 **W:** cercacomunicaciones.com **E:**cercacomunicaciones@yahaoo.es – **LP23)** Calle Calama s/n entre Humahuca y Montenegro, Zona Norte, La Paz ☎2 286983 - **FM:** 90.1 MHz – **LP25)** Av. Tumusla No 639, 2° piso (or Cas 2532), Zona 14 de Septiembre, La Paz. ☎2 453945 📠 2 454 211 **W:** lafolklorisima1035.com.ar - **FM:** 103.5/107.7 MHz – **LP26)** Av. Saavedra del Ejército, Zona Miraflores, La Paz ☎2 149439 **Aymara:** 1100-1200 **W:** radiobatalloncolorados.com – **LP27)** Calle Francisco de Chirino No 1080, Miraflores (Cas. 12413), La Paz– **LP28)** Liga de Oración en Misión Mundial, Av Civica S/N, Caranavi, (Cas. 266, La Paz) ☎📠2 823 2239 **W:** Facebook: Radio Television Caranavi **E:** rtc@hotmail.com - **FM:** 92.1 MHz – **LP29)** Casilla 204, Colegio Don Bosco, Pucarani Prgrs mainly in **Aymara**, but also in Spanish 0900-1300, 2030-0130 **W:** Facebook – **LP33)** Av República 870 Esq. Quintanilla Zuazo, Zona Pura Pura, La Paz ☎2 463470 – **LP34)** Colegio Don Bosco, Parroquia Escoma, Escoma (Cas 204, La Paz) **E:** escoma@caoba.entelnet.bo ☎📠2 135336 - **FM:** 104.7MHz – **LP35)** Calle Murillo 1379, La Paz ☎2 350588 – **LP36)** Calle Panama N° 1153 Shopping Miraflores Pido 4 Oficina 1, Zona Miraflores sobre la Plaza Uyuni, La Paz ☎2 222368 **W:** radiogentebolivia.com **E:** sistemapopular@hotmail.com - **FM:** 88.9 MHz – **LP39)** Ca Gral. Hugo Ballivián No 11 Copacabana, Prov. Manco Capac ☎2 341920 **W:** apcbolivia.org/Medios/copacabana.aspx - **FM:** 95.7 MHz – **LP40)** Plaza 15 de Agosto, Corocoro, Prov Pacajes **E:** tricolor-jachasuyu@hotmail.com ☎2 830192 Prgr In **Aymara & Sp** 1000-1630, 2000-0100 – **LP42)** Av. Patriótica # 3048 entre c.Topáter y Héroes del Acre Z. Bolívar Municipal P.1, El Alto ☎📠2 821675 – **LP43)** Avenida del Ejercito No 30, Viacha ☎2 800208 – **FM:** 101.9 MHz – **LP44)** Ca Policarpio Eyzaguirre N° 1156 entre Padre L. Bertonio y Calatayod, Zona Callampaya (Cementerio), La Paz ☎2 2461224 📠2455319 **W:** radiotaypi.com **E:** radio-taypi@hotmail.com – **LP45)** Calle Viacha # 360 e/ Avenida Manco Kapac y Av. América, Barrio Churubamba , La Paz – **LP46)** Comunidad Contorno Letania, Camino a Collana 30, Letania, Prov IngavI – **LP47)** Av Manco Kapac 50, Tiawanaku, Prov Ingavi – **LP50)** Calle Costa Rica No 1229, Miraflores, La Paz ☎2 220401 – **LP51)** Av. Franco Valle No 87, Achocalla, Prov. de Murillo – **LP53)** Plaza 16 de Julio s/n, Cantón Taraco, Taraco ☎8 114157 - **FM:** 105.3 MHz – **LP54)** Calle Noel Kempf 140, El Alto, La Paz – **LP55)** Tiawanaku, Prov Ingavi – **LP56)** Calle Yanacocha 70, Achacachi – **LP57)** Plaza 4 de Octubre, Rosario, Corapata, Prov Los Andes – **LP58)** Calle Noaviri 2105, Zona Amor de Dios, El Alto ☎2 223916 – **LP59)** Raúl Salmón 92 entre Calle 4 y 5, Zona Ceja, El Alto (Cas. 8631, Murillo, La Paz) ☎2 2825169 **E:** radiomisionglobal@yahoo.es– **LP60)** Plaza Principal, Cantón Villa Iquiaca, Vilaque, Prov Los Andes – **LP61)** Tihuanaco Provincia Ingavi S/N, Comunidad Achaca, Tiahuanacu ☎2 822470 – **LP62)** Avenida Panoramica No. 5018, Zona Faro Murillo , El Alto ☎2 2813504 **W:** cesi.pastoralcl – **LP64)** Calle Topater 830, La Paz – **LP65)** Plaza Principal, Topohoco, Prov. Pacajes – **LP66)** Ca Jotan Save 3132 entre Bluniel, Zona 16 de Julio, La Paz – **LP67)** Calle Pascoe N° 2614-B, Zona 16 de Julio, El Alto ☎77444761 **FB:** Radio Bendita Trinidad Bolivia **E:** radio_bendita_trinidad_bolivia@hotmail.com – **LP68)** Ca Batalla de Huarina No 255, Huarina ☎71977644 – **LP74)** Tumupasa, Prov de Iturralde – **LP75)** Av. Grigota N° 1514, Urb. Atipiris 8 Sector Ex-Tranca Senkata, La Paz – El Alto ☎2 2882066 **FB:** Radio-Atipiri-Oficial **E:** radioatipiri@gmail.com – **LP77)** Calle 11 de Calacote No 7837, La Paz. – **LP88)** Calle S.Rodriguez No 1155, Zona 16 de Febrero, Distrito 4 Carretera a Laja antes del Puente Seke, Zona 16 de Febrero ☎73700079 **E:** bartolinasisa920am@gmail.com – **LP89)** Ichoca-Quime – **LP90)** Pucarani – **LP91)** Copacabana – **LP92)** Caranavi – **LP93)** Chulumani – **LP94)** Guaqui – **LP95)** Av Cíivica frente Estadio Orlando Quiroga, Caranavi ☎2 8243810 **W:** qhana.org.bo **E:** rqamazonia@qhana.org.bo **LP96)** Pza. Ballivian No 525, 16 de Julio, El Alto ☎2 844344 – **LP97)** Av.Manco Kapaca No 50, Tiawuanacu ☎2 597 357 – **LP98)** Calle Calama s/n entre Humahuca y Montenegro, Zona Norte, La Paz ☎2 286983 – **LP99)** Calle Calama s/n entre Humahuca y Montenegro, Zona Norte, La Paz ☎2 286983 – **LP100)** Calle Topáter # 830, Zona Norte, La Paz – **LP101)** Laja, Calle Carrasco No 16, entre Hermani y Av. La Paz, El Alto ☎2 847197 **W:** facebook.com/red.tawantinsuyo **E:** redtawantinsuyo@hotmail.com – **LP104)** Lanza N° 844, Cochabamba ☎4 520313 **W:** radiomaria.org.bo **E.** info.bol@radiomaria.org – **LP105)** Calle Bolivar No 249, Achacachi – **LP106)** Av. Chacaltaya, calle Tiquina N° 6580 Alto Lima primera sección (Cas.8628), El Alto ☎📠2 2842492 **W:** plenituddevida.net **E:** info@plenituddevida.net – **LP107)** Ave. Cornelio Saavedra No 2875 esq. Kantuta, Desaguadero ☎2 730 628 – **LP108)** Batallas, ☎71580034 – **LP109)** Corapata, Prov. De Los Andes – **LP110)** Letania, Prov. de Ingavi – **LP111)** Achocalla, Prov. de Murillo – **LP112)** Villa Iquiaca, Prov. de Los Andes – **LP113)** Contorno/Viacha, Prov. de Ingavi – **LP114)** Av.Eduardo 1168, Zona Los Andes, Murillo ☎2 2458567 **E:** jorgetito@redcotel.bo – **LP116)** Plaza Avaroa N° 105, Carr. Viacha, El Alto. ☎2 825504 📠2 821007 **E:** pachaqamasa700@yahoo.es – **LP120)** Unidad Académica Campesina de Tiahuanacu, Tiawuanaku ☎2 898542 – **LP121)** Diócesis de El Alto, Zona Ferropetrol, Plaza Boris Banzer, El Alto 2 ☎28444264 – **LP122)** Ca Cochabamba N° 102, Puerto de Guaqui ☎77592170 **W:** http//1190radioguaqui.blogspot.no **E:** radio1190guaqui@hotmail.com – **LP123)** Achocalla – **LP124)** Huarina – **LP126)** Topohoco – **LP127)** Vilaque – **LP128)** Taraco – **LP129)** Tapichullo – **LP130)** Tiawanaku – **LP131)** Qhurpa – **LP132)** Qhurpa – **LP133)** Asunta – **LP134)** Asunta – **LP135)** Escoma – **LP136)** Desaguadero – **LP137)** Caranavi – **LP138)** Carabuco – **LP139)** Corocoro – **LP140)** Carabuco – **LP141)** Carabuco – **LP142)** Achacachi – **LP143)** Achacachi – **LP144)** El Alto – **LP145)** Sococoni – **LP146)** Capilaya – **LP147)** Jihuacuta – **LP148)** Canaviri – **LP149)** Calle Jorge Carrasco N°12 entre calle 1 y calle 2 - Zona 12 de Octubre, El Alto ☎22 821473 **W:** radioluzdelmundobolivia.com **E:** luzdelmundo.bolivia@hotmail.com – **LP150)** León M. Loza No. 1199, Esquina Ascencio Padilla Alto San Pedro, La Paz ☎2-483395 – **LP151)** Ca 140 N° 140, Zona Villa Avaros, El Alto ☎2 115472 –

LP152) La Paz – **LP153)** 3er piso, Edifico Las Delicias, frente a la linea roja del Teleférico, Av. Panorámica, El Alto – **LP154)** La Paz – **LP155)** Chulumani **W:** radiojallallacoca.com - **FM:** 100.1MHz – **LP156)** Coripata – **LP157)** Coroico – **LP158)** Machareti – **LP159)** La Paz – **LP160)** La Paz – **LP161)** Tianawaku – **LP162)** Cl 6#777 esq. Moscoso, Zona Villa Dolores **W:** radiolavozdelespiritusantobolivia.com **E:** jorgenriveros.bo@gmail.com

OR00 (ORURO)

OR01) Calle Ayacucho 785 (Alto) (Cas 670), Oruro ☎2 5253500 🖷2 5252500 **E:** cpi@coteor.net.bo **Aymara & Quechua:** 1000-2200, 0200-0600 – **OR03)** Cas 1019, Oruro ☎2 5112259 **W:** bahai.org.bo **E:** servicio@bahai.org.bo **Aymara & Quechua:** 11 hours daily – **OR05)** Oruro – **OR06)** Calle Cochabamba esquiina 6 de Octubre (Cas 49), Oruro ☎2 525 0004 🖷2 524 2215 – **OR09)** Calle Junín y 6 de Agosto, Oruro ☎2 5260200 **W:** radiobatallontopater.com **Aymara & Quechua:** 1000-1100 - **FM:** 98.2MHz – **OR12)** San Felipe 493 entre Tarapacá y Tejerina (Cas 247), Oruro **Aymara:** 2200-2400 - **FM:** 107.7MHz – **OR13)** Av. Velasco Galvarro entre León y Rodriguez 1551, Oruro - **FM:** 105.1 MHz – **OR14)** Linares 1160 entre Cochabamba y Caro, Oruro – **OR15)** Calle SoriaGalvarro entre Murgio y Aldana No 1810, Oruro ☎2 525 9714 **W:** radiojacintorodriguez.org **E:** radiojacintorodriguez@gmail.com – **OR19)** Av Bakovic 1027 entre Caro y Montecinos, (Cas 326), Oruro **Aymara & Quechua:** 0930-1030 - **FM:** 93.1MHz – **OR20)** Calle Sucre, Huanuni (Cas 681), Oruro ☎2 5520421 **W:** nacionaldehuanuni.com **E:** nacionaldehuanuni@gmail.com – **OR24)** Calle Adolfo Mier 1231, Oruro – **OR25)** Huanuni – **OR26)** Orinoca, Prov Sud Carangas – **OR27)** Sabaya, Prov Sabaya – **OR29)** Oruro – **OR31)** Calle 6 de Octubre # 6160, Oruro ☎5 275344 **E:** radiocapitaloruro@hotmail.com - **FM:** 102.7 MHz – **OR32)** Avenida 6 de Octubre y Montecinos 1042, Oruro ☎5 25143 🖷5 276 645 - **FM:** 97.1 MHz **E:** Davidglg@hotmail.com – **OR33)** Calle Sucre 503, Plaza Fermin López, Zona Central (✉ Casilla 147) , Huanuni ☎50020040 **W:** caephorizontes.com **E:** radiohorizontes.caep@gmail.com – **FM:** 93.5MHz – **OR34)** Oruro – **OR35)** Caracollo – **OR36)** Caracolla – **OR37)** Huanuni – **OR38)** Oruro – **OR39)** Oruro – **OR40)** Oruro – **OR41)** Oruro - **FM:** 98.7 MHz – **OR44)** Challapata

PA00 (PANDO)

PA09) Barrio Paraiso, Calle Margarita, Esquina Jazmin, Cobija **W:** FB.com – Radio Bendita Trinidad Bolivia ☎76510837 – **PA10)** Cobija

PO00 (POTOSI)

PO02) Calle Cobija 15, Zona Central, Potosí ☎6 222680 🖷6 226210 **W:** radiokollasuyo.net - **FM:** 105.1MHz – **PO07)** Potosi – **PO08)** Catavi – **PO10)** Llica, Pcia Daniel Campos – **PO12)** Potosi - **FM:** 107.5 MHz – **PO14)** Campamento Minero Tazna, Pcia Nor Chichas – **PO15)** Cas 326, Yura, Prov Antonio Quijarro **E:** radioyura@hotmail.com – **PO16)** Dtto Minero de Animas – **PO19)** Calle Final Uruguay s/n (Cas 16), Uyuni, Prov Antonio Quijarro ☎2 693 2145 **E:** max_nelson_t@hotmail.com – **PO26)** Comunidad de Caiza, Prov Chayanta – **PO28)** Av. Cívica 739 (Cas. 538), Potosi. ☎🖷2 62236660 **W:** aclo.org.bo **E:** aclopotosi@aclo.org.bo - **FM:** 106.7 MHz – **PO29)** Calle Matos No 107 (Cas.472), Potosi. ☎6 223 936 **W:** indoamericafm.com **E:** info@indoamericafm.com – **PO30)** Colcha "K" – **PO31)** Ocuri – **PO32)** Unica – **PO33)** Villazon – **PO34)** Llica – **PO35)** Tupiza – **PU36)** Uyuni – **PO37)** Potosi **W:** radiocruzdelsur.com **E:** contactos@radiocruzdelsur.com – **PO39)** Potosi – **PO40)** Campamento Siglo XX, Llallagua (or Cas 434, Oruro) **W:** radiopio12.com.bo **E:** rpiodoce@entelnet.bo ☎2 5820250 🖷 2 5820554 **Aymara** & **Quechua** 6 hrs daily - **FM:** MHz – **PO41)** San Pablo de Lipez

SC00 (SANTA CRUZ)

SC02) Plaza 31 de Julio, San Ignacio de Velasco ☎3 962 2188 **W:** sanignacio-diocesis.com/ **E:** radiojuan@hotmail.com - **FM:** 100.3MHz – **SC03)** Calle Potosí s/n entre calles German Bush y Rafael Terrazas, Barrio la Floresta (or Cas 38), Montero ☎3 9220237 **W:** radiomariaauxiliadora.sdb.bo **E:** ramacon@cotas.com.br - **FM:** 105.5MHz "Concierto" – **SC04)** Calle Mariano Saucedo Sevilla esquina Güendá No 20, Santa Cruz **W:** irfabolivia.org **E:** juanpablo.sejas@irfabolivia.org ☎3 3531817 **Guaraní:** 1830-1900 - **FM:** 92.2MHz – **SC10)** Warnes 334 (Cas 629), Santa Cruz ☎3 3363990 🖷3 3363992 - **FM:** 92.7MHz – **SC11)** Av. Grigota s/n, B.Matpetrol (2Cdra. Antes del 4to Anillo) Cas 818), Santa Cruz ☎3 3529265 🖷3 3524747 **E:** mision.eplabol@scbbs-bo.com **Quechua & Guarani:** 0900-0945 - **FM:** 90.7MHz "R Super Color" – **SC12)** Independencia 372 (Cas 186), Santa Cruz ☎3 3337194 🖷3 3335778 - **FM:** 96.3MHz – **SC16)** Av Charcas 1051 lado octava División del Ejército, Santa Cruz ☎3 3360447 🖷3 3372242 - **FM:** 98.1MHz – **SC21)** Florida esq Montes Claros 143, Vallegrande ☎3 9422033 – **SC25)** Cas 507, Santa Cruz - **FM:** 89.5MHz. Prgrs also in **Quechua** – **SC29)** Calle España 572, 2°piso, Santa Cruz - **FM:** 97.9MHz – **SC30)** San José de Chiquitos ☎71090545 **W:** facebook.com/Parroquiasjchi **E:** radiosanjose103.9@gmail.com – **FM:** 103.9MHz – **SC33)** Cas 1766, Santa Cruz **W:** difusorasdeloriente.mex.tl **E:** verdeyblanco5@hotmail.com – **SC35)** Calle Quijarro 74 esq Av Uruguay, Santa Cruz - **FM:** 105.5MHz – **SC38)** Comunidad de San Julián, Prov Nuflo de Chávez – **SC39)** Santa Cruz – **SC40)** Santa Cruz – **SC41)** Vallegrande – **SC42)** Camiri – **SC43)** Yapacani – **SC45)** Calle Lanza No 84 entre La Paz y Oruro, Santa Cruz ☎4 4526100 🖷4 4681178 **W:** radiomaria.org.bo **E:** info.bol@radiomaria.org – **SC47)** Santa Cruz – **SC48)** Zona Plan 3000 Av. Paurito Frente al Mercado Guapurú, Santa Cruz ☎3 3318829 **W:** facebook.com/Radio.Bendita.Trinidad.Bolivia.OFFICIAL – **SC49)** Yapacani – **SC50)** José Ballivian – **SC51)** Calle Lanza 844 (entre C La Paz y C Oruro) Santa Cruz **W:** radiomaria.org.bo **E:** web@radiomaria.org.bo - **FM:** 97.5 MHz – **SC52)** Santa Cruz ☎3 33346299 **W:** facebook.com- Radio Amboro - **FM:** 98.5 MHz – **SC53)** Santa Cruz – **SC54)** Camiri – **SC55)** Tercer Anillo Externo Av. Radial13 y Av. Santos Dumont, Lado FELCC, Santa Cruz ☎3353 4400 **W:** Facebook: RadioFamiliar925FmY600KhzAm - **FM:** 92.5 MHz – **SC56)** Puerto Quijarro – **SC57)** Montero – **SC58)** Santa Cruz

TA00 (TARIJA) TA01)

Calle Virginio Lema 788 (Cas 404), Tarija ☎4 6643890 – **TA03)** Av Las Américas 9630, Edif Radiofónico Los Andes (Cas 344), Tarija ☎6 642800 - **FM:** 103.1MHz – **TA05)** Calle Bolivar esq. Méndez Nº 327 piso 1 Tarija ☎4 6634444 🖷4 6635555 **W:** facebook.com – Radio Guadalquivir **E:** radioguadalquivir@entelnet.com.bo - **FM:** 91.5MHz – **TA06)** Bolívar 376, Edificio Borda (Cas 125), Tarija - **FM:** 93.1MHz – **TA07)** Av Barrientos esq Ameller, Bermejo ☎🖷4 6961584 - **FM:** 99.1MHz – **TA10)** Av Bolívar 608, Bermejo – **TA12)** Av Cnl Carlos Diaz Sossa, Entre Av. Panamericana, Zona Aeropuerto, Tarija ☎4 6643425 **W:** aclo.org.bo/radio-aclo-tarija **E:** aclotarija@aclo.org.bo - **FM:** 101.5 MHz – **TA13)** Tarija – **TA14)** Bermejo – **TA15)** Villamontes – **TA16)** Villamontes – **TA17)** Yacuiba – **TA18)** Ycuiba – **TA19)** Entre Rios – **TA20)** Ca Cochabamba Nº 1403, Tarija ☎4 6664141 - **FM:** 101.5 MHz – **TA21)** Tarija

FM in La Paz (MHz): 87.7 87.7FM – 88.5 Doble 8 Latina – 88.9 Gente – 89.3 Sistema Cristiano de Comunicaciones – 89.7 Salesiana – **LP23)** 90.1 R.Sol Poder de Dios – 90.5 Panamericana Classica – 90.9 PCM – 91.3 Ciudad – 91.7 El Comercio – 92.1 Estudio 92 FM – 92.5 Estelar – 92.9 Galáctica – 93.3 Melodia – 93.7 Chacaltaya – 94.1 R La Voz de Bolivia – 94.5 Red Nuevo Tiempo – 94.9 Gigante – **LP06)** 95.3 – 95.7 Digital Sur – 96.1 – 96.5 R.Panamericana – 96.9 Diferente – 97.3 Stereo 97 – 97.7 – 98.1 Láser – 98.5 Andina – 98.9 Restauración – 99.3 Melodía – 99.7 Cristo Viene – 100.1 FM Cien – 100.5 Constelación – 100.9 R. Color – **LP07)** 101.3 – 101.7 Graffitti – 102.1 RRB – 102.5 Sintonia – 102.9 Cristal – 103.3 R. Deseo – **LP25)** 103.5 - 103.7 San Francisco de Asis – 104.1 Cadena CNT – 104.5 RCN – **LP26)** 104,8 - 104.9 Fantástica – 105.3 Nuevo Amanacer – 105.7 Majestad – 106.1 Pachamama – 106.5 – 106.9 Paris-La Paz – 107.3 Nueva Cosmos – **LP08)** 107.5 R.Play – 107.7 Central FM

BONAIRE (Netherlands)

L.T: UTC -4h — **Pop:** 20,100 — **Pr.L:** Dutch (official), Papiamentu, English — **E.C:** 230V/50Hz — **ITU:** BES

AGENTSCHAP TELECOM (Bonaire, Saba, Sint Eustatius)

✉ Kaya Grandi 69, P.O. Box 791, Bonaire ☎ + 599 717 3140 🖷 +599 717 3554 **W:** agentschaptelecom.nl **E:** bes@agentschaptelecom.nl

MW	Call	kHz	kW	Station, location
1)	PJB	800	440	Trans World R., Kralendijk

FM	MHz	kW	Station, location
1)	89.5	0.5	Trans World R., Kralendijk
9)	91.1		R. Adventista Boneiru, Kralendijk
2)	93.1	0.5	Alpha FM 93.1, Kralendijk
10)	93.5		R. BròKès, Kralendijk
2)	94.7	0.5	Voz di Bonaire, Kralendijk
3)	97.1		Play FM, Kralendijk
4)	97.5	0.5	Dolfijn FM, Kralendijk
2)	99.5	0.5	MegaClassics
8)	99.9		Live 99.9 FM, Kralendijk
2)	101.1	0.5	Mega Hit FM, Kralendijk
6)	102.7		Bon FM, Kralendijk
7)	107.5		Rumbera Network, Kralendijk

Addresses & other information:

1) Kaya Gobernador N. Debrot 64, Kralendijk, Bonaire ☎ +599 717 8800 🖷 +599 717 8808 Dir.Jason Helmholdt **MW DPrgr**:

800kW 00:00-03:00 440kW North West pattern, Spanish; 03:00-05:00, 200kW Caribbean pattern, Spanish; 08:00-10:00, 440kW South East pattern, Portuguese; 10:00-11:30, 100kW Caribbean pattern, Spanish; 23:00-00:00, 225kW Caribbean pattern, English. **FM DPrgr**: The Voice of Hope 24h mostly music with English news and occasional Bible based prgrs in English, Spanish, Dutch and Papiamentu **W:** twrbonaire.com **E:** 800am@twr.org and bonaire@twr.org – **2)** Radiodifucion Boneriano NV, Kaya Gobernador N. Debrot 2, Kralendijk, ☎ +599 717 5947 🖷 +599 717 8820, Dir: Feliciano da Silva Piloto **W:** vozdibonaire.com **E:** vozdibonaire@gmail.com **Prgrs**: **Voz di Bonaire**: Papiamentu and Dutch, music and information 24h **Mega Hit FM**: Dutch and English, music and information 24h **Alpha FM**: Spanish, music and information 24h**Mega Classics** : Music 24 h and news in Dutch on top of the hour – **3)** Kaya Grandi 8, Kralendijk ☎ +599 717 9710 – **4)** Kaya Amsterdam 27, Kralendijk ☎ +599 9 465 9975 🖷 +599 9 461 9975 Stn Manager: Egon Sybrandy **DPrgr.** 24h in Dutch **E:** info@dolfijnfm.com **W:** dolfijnfm.com –**6)** Kaya Irlandia 11, Kralendijk ☎ +599 717 2102 🖷 +599 717 2002 GM: Carmo R. Cecilia. 24h in Papiamentu **W:** bonfm.com **E:** bonfm@hotmail.com – **7)** Kaya Grandi, Kralendijk ☎ +599 9 683 7074 **W:** rumberanetworkbonaire.com– **8)** Kaya Atom 33, Kralendijk ☎+599 717 0999 CEO: Aimed Ayubi; 24 h in Papiamentu **W:** live99fm.com **E:** info@live99fm.com – **9)** Kaya Pos di Amor #1, Kralendijk ☎+599 796 0911 **W:** rabonaire.interamerica.org **E:** bonaire@awr.org GM : Ashley Thomas, **Prgrs**: 24 hrs in Papiamentu (main language), Spanish, Dutch and English – **10)** Kaya Bamba 8b, Nikiboko ☎ +599 796 9133, Dir. Ethel Leoneta, 24 hours in Papiamentu, with music in mostly Papiamentu, Spanish and Dutch **E:** 93.5boneiru@gmail.com

TRANS WORLD RADIO (Rlg. Cult. Educ.)
see International Broadcasting section

BOSNIA & HERZEGOVINA

L.T: UTC +1h (28 Mar-31 Oct: +2h) — **Pop:** 3.3 million — **Pr.L:** Bosnian, Croatian, Serbian — **E.C:** 230V/50Hz — **ITU:** BIH

REGULATORNA AGENCIJA ZA KOMUNIKACIJE BIH (RAK) (Communications Regulatory Agency BH)

🖃 Mehmeda Spahe 1, 71000 Sarajevo ☎ +387 33 250600 🖷 +387 33 713080 **E:** info@rak.ba **W:** rak.ba **L.P:** DG: Draško Milinović

RADIO-TELEVIZIJA BOSNE I HERCEGOVINE (BHRT)(Pub)

🖃 Bulevar Meše Selimovica 12, 71000 Sarajevo ☎ +387 33 461101 **E:** pitajte@bhrt.ba **W:** bhrt.ba **L.P:** DG: Belmin Karamehmedović

FM	MHz	kW	FM	MHz	kW
Tušnica	88.1	30	Vlašić	97.0	100
V. Gomila	88.8	30	Lisin	100.3	30
Lipik	93.7	30	Hum	100.7	10
Leotar	94.1	30	Kozara	103.1	30
Drvar	94.7	5	Trebević	103.7	10

+ txs below 1kW.
D.Prgr: BHR1 in Bosnian, Croatian, Serbian: 24h.

FEDERACIJA BOSNE I HERCEGOVINE

RADIO-TELEVIZIJA FEDERACIJE BOSNE I HERCEGOVINE (RTV FBiH) (Pub)

🖃 Bulevar Meše Selimovica 12, 71000 Sarajevo ☎ +387 33 461539 **E:** press@rtvfbih.ba **W:** rtvfbih.ba **L.P:** DG: Džemal Šabić

FM	MHz	kW	FM	MHz	kW
Tuzla	88.5	10	V. Gomila	95.7	30
Čapljina	89.1	1	Hum	95.7	10
Vlašić	89.3	100	Lipik	98.9	30
Fortica	91.7	5	Hadžića Brdo	99.5	5
Tušnica	92.5	30	Gradačac	103.5	5
Lisin	94.5	30	+ txs below 1kW.		

D.Prgr: Radio FBiH in Bosnian, Croatian: 24h.

OTHER STATIONS

MW	kHz	kW	Location	Station
42)	‡ 792	1	Banovići	R. Banovići
43)	1503	1	Zavidovići	R. 1503 Zavidovići

‡) Stn has licenses for MW+FM, but has been using only FM in recent years

FM	MHz	kW	Location	Station
12)	88.1	1	Mostar	R. Mostarska Panorama
4)	88.6	1	Mostar	R. Gradska Mreža
15)	88.7	1	Trebačko Brdo	R. Antena
26)	88.8	1	Makljen	R. Rama
33)	89.5	2	Drvar	R. Drvar
37)	89.9	1	Cazin	R. Cazin
22)	90.0	2	Mostar	R. Kalman
23)	90.3	1	Radovanj	R. Plus
27)	90.5	1	Kupres	Kupreški Radio
14)	90.5	1	Sarajevo	R. Mix
38)	90.9	5	Mostar	R. Grude
5)	90.9	1	Sarajevo	Antena Sarajevo
22)	91.2	2	Lisin	R. Kalman
39)	91.3	1	Čapljina	R. Postaja Čapljina
22)	91.5	1	Sarajevo	R. Kalman
7)	91.5	1	Livno	R. Livno
7)	91.5	5	Bos. Grahovo	R. Livno
34)	91.6	1	Velika Kladuša	Trend R.
41)	91.8	3	Srebrenik	R. TK
2)	93.1	5	Grude	R. Široki Brijeg
19)	94.3	2.5	Majevica	Obiteljski R. Valentino
32)	94.3	3.5	Radovanj	R. Herceg-Bosne
18)	94.7	1	Bihać	R. Bihać
35)	95.0	1	Lisin	R. Konjic
30)	95.1	2	Tomislavgrad	R. Tomislavgrad
3)	95.2	1	Sarajevo	R. Miljacka
38)	95.5	5	Grude	R. Grude
6)	95.6	5	Gradačac	R. Kameleon
30)	95.9	1	Duvno	R. Tomislavgrad
11)	96.2	1	Mostar	R. Dobre Vibracija
20)	96.5	5	Sarajevo	R. BIR
13)	97.5	5	Zenica	RSG R.
28)	97.6	1	Livno	R. Studio N
32)	98.1	30	Fojnica	R. Herceg-Bosne
20)	98.1	2	Bužim	R. BIR
8)	98.7	1	Trebević*	R. M
40)	99.1	1	Ključ	R. Ključ
32)	99.3	2.5	Lisac	R. Herceg-Bosne
1)	99.5	1.5	Sanski Most	R. USK
25)	99.9	1	Gradačac	R. Bet Fratello
17)	100.0	1	Mostar	R. Mir Međugorje
20)	100.1	1	Bugojno	R. BIR
7)	100.9	1	Livno	R. Livno
9)	101.2	1	Sarajevo	TNT R.
16)	101.5	1.2	Goražde	R. BPK
17)	101.5	5	Biokovo	R. Mir Međugorje
17)	101.8	1	Bugojno	R. Mir Međugorje
A)	102.0	1	Sarajevo	Forces R. BFBS (UK) relay
24)	102.9	1	Radovanj	R. Posušje
30)	103.3	5	Livno	R. Tomislavgrad
29)	103.4	5	Mostar	R. Oscar C
10)	103.7	2	Lokveni Vrh*	R. Sana
32)	103.9	5	Hrgud*	R. Herceg-Bosne
13)	104.3	16	Lisin	RSG R.
13)	104.3	1	Čapljina	RSG R.
17)	104.7	1	Makljen	R. Mir Međugorje
1)	105.1	30	Velika Gomila	R. USK
36)	105.2	1	Tuzla	R. Glas Drine
32)	106.0	5	Motajica*	R. Herceg-Bosne
32)	106.3	1	Vranic	R. Herceg-Bosne
21)	106.6	10	Lisac	R. Zenica
17)	106.7	3	Kozara*	R. Mir Međugorje
A)	106.9	1	Sarajevo	BFBS R.2 (UK) relay
31)	107.0	5	Pećigrad	R. Velkaton
17)	107.8	50	Licka Plješivica**	R. Mir Međugorje
22)	107.8	1	Bugojno	R. Kalman
22)	107.8	1	Zenica	R. Kalman
22)	107.8	2	Trebačko Brdo	R. Kalman
22)	107.8	1	Tuzla	R. Kalman

+ txs below 1kW.
*) Located in Republika Srpska **) Located in Croatia

Addresses & other information:
1) Kulturni centar bb, 77000 Bihać – **2)** Trg Gojka Šuška 5c, 88220 Široki Brijeg – **3)** Kujundžija 6, 71000 Sarajevo – **4)** Rade Bitange 13, 88104 Mostar – **5)** Urijan Dedina 7, 71000 Sarajevo – **6)** Dr. Milana Jovanovića 6, 75000 Tuzla – **7)** Kneza Mutimira 29, 80101 Livno – **8)** Fra Anđela Zvizdovića 1, 71000 Sarajevo – **9)** Zenjak 9D, 72270 Travnik – **10)** Banjalučka 2, 75260 Sanski Most – **11)** Kralja Petra Krešimira IV bb, 88000 Mostar – **12)** Trg hrvatskih velikana bb, 88000 Mostar – **13)** Urijan Dedina 7, 71000 Sarajevo – **14)** Urijan Dedina 7, 71000 Sarajevo – **15)** Titova bb, 74264 Jelah – **16)** Marka Oreškovića

42, 80260 Drvar – **17)** Gospin Trg 1, 88266 Međugorje – **18)** Krupska bb, 77000 Bihac – **19)** Kolodvorska 108a, 76204 Bijela – **20)** Reisa Džemaludina Čauševića 2, 71000 Sarajevo – **21)** Bulevar Kralja Tvrtka I bb, 72000 Zenica – **22)** Varaždinska 18, 71000 Sarajevo – **23)** Fra Grge Martica bb, 88240 Posušje – **24)** Kraljice Jelene 2, 88240 Posušje – **25)** 1. maja 1, 76250 Gradacac – **26)** Kralja Tomislava bb, 88440 Prozor-Rama – **27)** Mate Bobana 1, 80320 Kupres – **28)** Splitska bb, 80101 Livno – **29)** Smrčenjaci bb, 88000 Mostar – **30)** Mijata Tomića bb, 80240 Tomislavgrad – **31)** Kulište 2, 77230 Velika Kladuša – **32)** Kralja Petra Krešimira IV. bb, 88000 Mostar – **33)** Marka Oreškovića 42, 80260 Drvar – **34)** Fadila Šerica bb, 77230 Velika Kladuša – **35)** Trg državnosti "Alija Izetbegović" 1, 88400 Konjic – **36)** Srebrenickog odreda bb, 75430 Srebrenica – **37)** Cazinskih brigada 12, 77220 Cazin – **38)** Viteza Ranka Bobana, 88340 Grude – **39)** Ruđera Boškovića 4, 88340 Čapljina – **40)** Branilaca BiH bb, 79280 Ključ – **41)** Mije Keroševica 20, 75000 Tuzla – **42)** 7. novembra 4, 75290 Banovići **E:** radiobanovici@yahoo.com – **43)** Maršala Tita 3, 72220 Zavidovići **E:** dadozavi@zona.ba. Incl. rel. BHR1 and/or R. FBiH at times – **A)** Rel. BFBS (UK).

REPUBLIKA SRPSKA

RADIO TELEVIZIJA REPUBLIKE SRPSKE (RTRS) (Pub)

Trg Republike Srpske 9, 78000 Banja Luka ☎ +387 51 339900 **E:** radiodesk@rtrs.tv **W:** rtrs.tv **L.P:** DG: Mladen Branković

FM	MHz	kW	FM	MHz	kW
Kmur	87.8	1	Duge Njive	90.7	10
Trebević	88.7	10	Kozara	92.7	30
Udrigovo	89.9	30	Leotar	92.8	30
Veliki Žep	90.3	30			

+ txs below 1kW. *) Located in Federacija Bosne i Hercegovine.
D.Prgr: Radio RS in Serbian: 24h.

OTHER STATIONS

FM	MHz	kW	Location	Station
9)	87.7	5	Hum*	Nes R.
1)	87.9	4	Doboj	K3 R.
12B)	88.3	1	Gacko	BIG R. 2
5)	88.4	6	Bijeljina	R. Slobomir
11)	88.9	1	Kmur	Bobar R.
7)	88.9	1	Prnjavor	R. Ljubić
17)	89.6	1	Udrigovo	R. HIT
6)	89.6	1	Kostreš	Vikom R.
13)	89.9	2.2	Kozara	R. Kozara
16)	90.0	1	Gacko	R. Gacko
4)	90.5	5	Hrgud	BN R.
12B)	91.5	1	Banja Luka	BIG R. 2
21)	92.0	2	Lipovac	R. Džungla
4)	92.0	1.4	Trebević	BN R.
8)	92.5	1	Kmur	R. Foca
4)	93.1	1	Busija	BN R.
12B)	93.2	1	Trebević	BIG R. 2
12A)	93.6	1	Banja Luka	BIG R. 1
3)	94.7	2	Kozarska Dubica	R. Feniks
4)	95.3	1	Bileca	BN R.
11)	95.3	23	Kozara	Bobar R.
10)	95.9	1	Leotar	R. Trebinje
2)	96.3	2	Doboj	R. Doboj
24)	96.3	2.5	Udrigovo	R. Slobomir
12B)	96.4	1	Foča	BIG R. 2
12C)	96.5	1	Banja Luka	BIG R. 3
15)	96.7	1	Kozarska Dubica	Dub R.
12B)	97.9	5	Hrgud	BIG R. 2
25)	98.3	10	Kozara	Free R.
4)	99.9	9	Banja Luka	BN R.
23)	100.7	2	Lipovac	R. Studio M
11)	100.9	10	Busija	Bobar R.
14)	101.9	1	Gacko	Korona R. 2
4)	102.4	30	Vlašić*	BN R.
18)	102.7	2.2	Banja Luka	Hard Rock R.
11)	102.8	8	Trebević	Bobar R.
19)	104.0	1	Višegrad	R. Višegrad
4)	104.1	2	Modriča	BN R.
11)	104.7	30	Vlašić*	Bobar R.
20)	105.3	3	Banja Luka	Plavi R.
4)	105.4	10	Livno*	BN R.
11)	105.5	22	Leotar	Bobar R.
26)	105.5	30	Udrigovo	R. Daš
4)	105.7	1	Kozara	BN R.
11)	105.9	40	Hrgud	Bobar R.
9)	106.4	22.5	Kozara	Nes R.
22)	107.5	1	Banja Luka	R. Uno

+ txs below 1kW. *) Located in Federacija Bosne i Hercegovine.

Addresses & other information:
1) Svetog Save 25, 78430 Prnjavor – **2)** Kneza Lazara 8, 74000 Doboj – **3)** Svetosavska bb, 79240 Kozarska Dubica – **4)** Laze Kostića 146, 76320 Bijeljina – **5)** Tržni centar bb, 76300 Bijeljina – **6)** Srpska 2/II, 78000 Banja Luka – **7)** Trg Srpskih Boraca bb, 78430 Prnjavor – **8)** Njegoševa 1, 73300 Foča – **9)** Braće Pišteljić 1, 78000 Banja Luka – **10)** Svetosavska 21, 79240 Kozarska Dubica – **11)** Filipa Višnjića 211, 76320 Bijeljina – **12A-C)** Vuka Karadžića 6, 78000 Banja Luka – **13)** Vidovdanska 2, 78400 Gradiška – **14)** Preobraženska bb, 89000 Trebinje – **15)** Svetosavska 21, 79240 Kozarska Dubica – **16)** Solunskih Dobrovoljaca 2, 89240 Gacko – **17)** Miroslava Krleže 48, 76100 Brčko – **18)** 78000 Banja Luka – **19)** Vuka Karadžića bb, 73240 Višegrad – **20)** Branka Popovića 92a, 78000 Banja Luka – **21)** Nikole Pašica bb, 74000 Doboj – **22)** Veselina Masleše 1/12, 78000 Banja Luka – **23)** Stevana Mokranjca 10, 74270 Teslić – **24)** Slobomir bb, 76300 Bijeljina – **25)** Žarka Zgonjanina 15, 79101 Prijedor – **26)** Stevana Krnjića 18, 76300 Bijeljina.

BRCKO DISTRICT

OTHER STATIONS

FM	MHz	kW	Location	Station
1)	94.8	1	Brčko	R. Brčko

Addresses & other information:
1) Klosterska 20, 76100 Brčko.

BOTSWANA

L.T: UTC +2h — **Pop:** 2.2 million — **Pr.L:** Setswana (official), English (official) — **E.C:** 230V/50Hz — **ITU:** BOT

BOTSWANA COMMUNICATIONS REGULATORY AUTHORITY (BOCRA)

Plot 50671, Independence Ave., Gaborone ☎ +267 3957755 🖷 +267 3957976 **E:** info@bocra.org.bw **W:** www.bocra.org.bw

RADIO BOTSWANA (Pub, Comm.)

Private Bag 0060, Gaborone ☎+267 3653000

MW	kHz	kW	MW	kHz	kW
Maun	531	50	Shakawe	693	25
Muchenje	558	50	Sebele	972	50
Selebi-Phikwe	621	100	Mahalapye	1215	50
Mopipi	648	50	Tshapong	†1350	50

FM(MHz)	RB1	RB2	kW	FM(MHz)	RB1	RB2	kW
Bobonong	95.9	102.7	0.5	Mabule	92.3	105.9	
Charleshill	93.5	103.5		Mabutsane	94.2	104.6	
Francistown	103.6	90.5	3	Mahalapye	96.6	107.0	2.5
Gaborone	89.9	103.0	5	Maun	94.2	104.6	0.5
Gantsi	94.0	100.8	0.1	Olifant's Drift	88.0	104.7	
Good Hope	94.6	101.6	0.5	Orapa	89.9	98.6	0.1
Hukuntsi	89.9	96.2	0.5	Palapye	91.5	101.5	0.5
Jwaneng	99.2	106.3	0.5	Sekakangwe Hill	91.9	101.9	2
Kanye	89.0	95.3	0.5	Selebi-Phikwe	94.2	104.6	0.1
Kang	89.3	98.9		Serowe	99.4	92.9	1
Kasane	94.4	104.8	0.5	Sojwe	87.7	90.7	
Lobatse	98.6	105.7	1	Tsabong	96.6	107.0	0.5

National Sce (RB1) in Setswana/English on MW/FM: 24h.
N. in English: on the hour exc. **in Setswana:** 1100, 1600, 1900.
Commercial Sce (RB2): 24h. **N:** rel. RB1.
Ann: E: "This is R. Botswana broadcasting from Gaborone", "RB", "RB1", "RB2". Setswana: "Se Ke Seromamowa Sa Botswana mo Gaborone".
IS: RB1: Bird chirps and first bars of the National Anthem.

Other stations (all MHz):
Duma FM: Hebron 92.5, Gaborone 93.0, Francistown 93.6, Kanye 94.5, Lobatse 100.9 **W:** dumafm.co.bw – **Gabz FM**: **FM:** Tsabong 90.3, Ghanzi 90.8, Maun/Selebi-Phikwe 91.0, Mahalapye 93.4, Palapye 94.7, Serowe 96.1, Gaborone 96.2, Francistown 96.8, Kasane 97.7, Hukuntsi 102.9 **W:** gabzfm.com – **Yarona FM:** Francistown 100.1, Gaborone 106.6 **W:** yaronafm.co.bw
Voice of America relay station:
Selebi-Phikwe, Moepeng Hill: 909kHz 600kW 0300-0700, 1600-2200 & SW. For further details see International Radio section (USA)

BRAZIL

L.T: PE (Fernando de Noronha only): UTC -2h. AL, AP, BA, CE, DF, ES, GO, MA, MG, PA, PB, PE, PI, PR, RJ, RN, RS, SC, SP, TO: UTC -3h. AC, AM, MS, MT, RO, RR: UTC -4h — **Pop:** 212 million — **Pr.L:** Portuguese — **E.C:** 127V/60Hz, 220V/60Hz — **ITU:** B — **Int. dialling code:** +55

AGÊNCIA NACIONAL DE TELECOMUNICAÇAOES (ANATEL)

SAUS Quadra 06, Blocos C, E, F, e H, CEP 70070-940 Brasília/DF ☎ 61 23122000 **W:** www.anatel.gov.br **Pres:** Leonardo Euler de Morais

ASSOCIAÇÃO BRASILEIRA DE EMISSORAS DE RÁDIO E TELEVISÃO (ABERT)

SAF Sul Quadra 02, Ed. Via Esplanada Sala 101, - 70.070-600 - Brasília - DF ☎ 61 21044600 **E:** abert@abert.org.br **W:** abert.org.br **L.P:** Pres: Paulo Tonet Camargo

Callsign For the full callsign add ZY to the front of the calls shown. The letters preceding the stn number indicate the state or territory. ‡ = inactive ± = varying freq † = irregular * stn may migrate to FM during 2020/2021

N.B: all stns carry «A Voz do Brasil» (official prgr.). Main tr. M F 2200-2300 but stns may also transmit at other times during the day.

MW	Call	kHz	kW	Station, location, h. of tr.
CE01)	H610	540	1/0.25	R. Jornal, Canindé
GO01)	H755	540	10/1	R. Riviera, Goiânia
MA01)	H894	540	1/0.25	R. Guajajara, Barra do Corda
MG151)	L331	540	1/0.5	R. Ipanema, Ipanema
PI31)	I914	540	1/0.25	R. Primeiro de Julho, Agua Branca
PR110)	J322	*540	1/0.25	R. Nova Era, Borrazópolis
RJ01)	J450	540	10/2.5	Feliz FM, Niterói
RS02)	K322	540	10/1	R. Sepé, Santo Ângelo
SC01)	J778	540	10/1	R. Mirador, Rio do Sul
SP02)	K734	540	1/0.25	R. Wolf Sumaré, Sumaré
CE59)	H644	550	1/0.25	R. Vale do Quincoê, Acopiara
MG01)	L225	550	5/0.5	R. Cataguases, Cataguases
MG02)	L263	550	20/5	Super Rede Boa Vontade
MT29)	I429	550	10/5	R. Mais, Sinop (RB)
PE01)	I796	550	5/1	R. Aleluia, Garanhuns
PI01)	I902	550	1/0.25	R. Serra da Capivara, São Raimundo Nonato
PR139)	J331	550	10/0.5	R. Banda B, Curitiba
RS03)	K287	550	2.5/0.25	R. Santa Cruz, Santa Cruz do Sul
SP03)	K578	550	5/0.5	R. Mantiqueira, Cruzeiro
SP04)	K700	550	5/0.5	Super Rede Boa Vontade, Sertãozinho
AM09)	H289	560	1/0.25	R. Coari, Coari
BA02)	H456	560	5/1	R. Jornal, Itabuna
CE41)	H604	560	1/0.25	R. Educ. Jaguaribana, Limoeiro do Nte.
GO25)	H769	560	5/0.25	R. Sul Goiana, Quirinópolis
MA02)	H887	560	25/5	R. Educadora do Maranhão, São Luís
PR01)	J214	560	1/0,5	R. Londrina Londrina
RS04)	K231	560	5/1	Tua Rádio São Francisco, Caxias do Sul
SP213)	K761	560	35/1	R. Paulista, Santa Isabel
CE02)	H613	570	5/0.25	R. Verde Vale, Juazeiro do Norte
CE03)	H614	570	1/0.25	R. Uirapuru, Itapipoca
MG03)	L261	570	25/5	R. Capital, Belo Horizonte
MT30)	N407	570	1/0.25	R. Jornal, São José dos Quatro Marcos
PR146)	J349	570	1/0.5	R. Continental, Palotina
RS05)	K267	570	1/0.5	R. Diario Gospel 570, Passo Fundo
SC02)	J735	570	5/0.5	R. Eldorado, Criciúma (RB)
SC99)	J794	570	1/0.25	R. Fronteira, Dionísio Cerqueira
SP06)	K672	570	5/1	R.Difusora, Taubaté
SP195)	K698	570	1/0.25	R. Jornal, Nhandeara
SP150)	K717	570	1/0.25	Bariri R. Clube, Bariri
GO44)	H799	580	1/0.25	R. Serra Azul, Caiapônia
MG04)	L328	580	7/0.5	R. América, Uberlândia
MS01)	I387	580	25/1	R. Imaculada Conceição, Campo Grande
PE02)	I776	580	20/10	R. Rede Brasil, Recife
PR105)	J327	580	2/0.25	R. Pitanga, Pitanga
PR03)	J330	580	2.5/0.25	R. Grande Lago, Santa Helena
RJ03)	J465	580	50/5	R. Relógio, Sao Gonçalo
RS06)	K299	580	2/0.5	R. Thê São Gabriel, São Gabriel: 0900-0300
SP07)	K540	580	1/0.25	R. Clube, Americana
SP08)	K724	580	1/0.25	R. Regional, Palmital
BA04)	H445	590	10/5	R. Cruzeiro da Bahia, Salvador
PB25)	I692	590	5/0.25	R. Serrana, Araruna
PR04)	J234	590	10/5	R. Difusora AM 590, Curitiba
PR38)	J240	590	2.7/0.75	R. Dif. Regional, Cruzeiro do Oeste
RR01)	O700	590	10	R. Dif. de Roraima, Boa Vista
RS08)	K210	590	5/0.5	R. Alegrete, Alegrete
SC03)	J901	590	2/1	R. Progresso, Descanso
SP09)	K534	590	10/1	R. Atlântica, Santos
SP10)	K612	590	1/0.25	R. Clube, Mirandópolis
SP11)	K643	590	5/1	R. 79, Ribeirão Preto
AM02)	H287	600	10	R. Municipal, São Gabriel da Cachoeira
BA05)	H486	600	10/1	R. Vale do Rio Grande, Barreiras
BA64)	H…	600	1/0.25	R. Dif.de Rio Real, Rio Real
CE38)	H627	600	1/0.25	R. Cultura, Aracati
MA38)	H920	600	10/1	R. Mirante, São Luís
RS09)	K278	600	100	R. Gaúcha, Porto Alegre
AL10)	H249	610	10/2	R. Imperial, Marechal Deodoro
AM18)	H321	610	10	Super Rede Boa Vontade, Manaus
MG06)	L268	610	100/25	R. Itatiaia, Belo Horizonte
PB01)	I678	610	1/0.25	R. Progresso, Sousa
SC04)	J746	610	10/0.5	R. Super Condá, Chapecó
SP12)	K532	‡610	1/0.25	R. Transertaneja, Mogi Mirim
CE05)	H590	620	10	R. Assunção Cearense, Fortaleza (RB)
PR05)	J332	620	2.5/0.25	R. Jandaia, Jandaia do Sul
RS10)	K270	620	10/1	R. Pelotense, Pelotas
RS11)	K315	620	1/0.25	R. Municipal, Tenente Portela
SC05)	J779	620	5/0.25	Super-R. Dif., Rio do Sul
SP16)	K521	620	50/10	R. Jovem Pan, São Paulo
AP01)	H422	630	25/10	R. Dif. de Macapá, Macapá
CE58)	H636	630	1/0.5	R. Cidade, Campos Sales
MA16)	H924	630	10/0.5	R. Macaru, Viana
MT05)	I384	630	10/5	R. Dif. Bom Jesús, Cuiabá
PI03)	I904	630	1/0.5	R. Dif., Barras
PR06)	J284	630	10/0.5	R. Parana Educativa, Curitiba
PR07)	J300	630	5/0.25	R. Educadora, Marechal Cândido Rondón
RS13)	K289	630	1/0.25	R. Santamariense, Santa Maria
SC06)	J800	630	1/0.25	R. Doze de Maio, São Lourenço d'Oeste
SE02)	J920	630	10/5	R. Aperlpe, Aracaju
SP18)	K635	‡630	5/0.25	R. Cidade, Presidente Prudente
BA12)	H458	640	10/0.5	R. Dif. Sul da Bahia, Itabuna
GO05)	H757	640	50/5	R. Dif. Pai Eterno. Goiânia, Goiânia
MG125)	L320	640	10/0.25	R. Educadora, Porteirinha
MT18)	I424	640	10/1	R. Tangará, Tangará da Serra
PR08)	J262	640	20/1	Super R. Deus é Amor, Londrina (IPDA)
RS14)	K277	640	50/10	R. Bandeirantes, Porto Alegre
BA06)	H462	650	5/0.5	R. Clube, Valença
GO06)	H790	650	1/0.25	R. Kompleta, Jussara
MG09)	L200	650	10/0.5	R. Vitoriosa, Lagoa Formosa
MG85)	L309	650	5/0.5	R. Veredas, Unaí
PA20)	I540	650	10/1	R. Tropical, Santarém
PB02)	I672	650	5/0.5	R. Alto Piranhas, Cajazeiras
PI26)	I925	650	1/0.25	R. Tapuio, Miguel Alves
PR09)	J202	650	1/0.5	R. Banda B Norte Pioneiro, Cambará
PR91)	J250	650	8/1	R. Colméia, Cascavel: 24h
RS15)	K238	650	5/0.5	R. Difusão Sul Riograndense, Erechim
SP20)	K508	650	1/0.25	R. Andradina, Andradina
SP22)	K518	650	5/1	R. da Cidade, Santos
SP21)	K524	650	5/0.8	R. Dif., Piracicaba (RB)
BA07)	H465	660	5/0.25	R. Nova Jornal, Itapetinga
BA65)	H518	660	1/0.25	R. Planalto, Euclides da Cunha
MG11)	L206	660	10/0.25	R. Clube, Curvelo
PA21)	I552	660	1/0.25	R. Xinguara, Xinguara
PE04)	I787	660	5/1	R. Jornal, Limoeiro
PI34)	I925	660	1/0.25	R. Tacarijus, São Miguel do Tapuio
RJ06)	J472	660	5/1	R. Friburgo, Nova Friburgo
RO01)	J673	*660	10/5	R. Boas Novas AM, Porto Velho
RS16)	K286	660	1/0.25	R. Marajá, Rosário do Sul
RS17)	K319	660	1/0.25	R. Canção Nova, Vacaria
SP23)	K639	660	10/0.5	R. Clube 1, Ribeirão Preto (RB)
SP112)	K777	660	20/0.5	R. Mundial, São Paulo
AC11)	H208	670	0.25	R. Dif., Sena Madureira
AM04)	H288	670	1	R. Nac. do Alto Solimões, Tabatinga
AM03)	H297	670	1/0.25	R. Vale do Rio Madeira R-VRM, Humaitá
AP02)	H420	670	10/1	R. Jovem Pan News - Equatorial, Macapá

MW	Call	kHz	kW	Station, location, h. of tr.
MG126)	L347	670	1/0.25	R. Montanhesa, Ponte Nova
MG123)	L361	670	5/0.25	R. Vitoriosa, Uberaba
-MT16)	I422	670	6/1	R. Transpantaneira, Poconé
PA02)	I537	670	1/0.25	R. Rural, Altamira
PA22)	I539	670	5/0.25	R. Atalaia, Óbidos
PI32)	I927	670	1/0.25	R. Livramento, José de Freitas
PR10)	J231	670	3/0.25	R. Canção Nova Esperança, Nova Esperança
PR11)	J248	670	10/2	R. Cidade, Curitiba
RS18)	K296	670	2.5/0.25	R. Cult. Jaguarão, Santa. Vitória do Palmar
RS19)	K370	670	10/0.5	R. Gazeta, Carazinho
SE03)	J921	670	10/5	R. Cultura de Sergipe, Aracaju (RA)
SP26)	K598	670	1/0.5	R. Convenção, Itu
GO09)	H765	680	10/0.5	R. Difusora, Jataí
MG13)	L326	680	1/0.25	R. União, João Pinheiro
MG196)	L348	680	1/0.25	R. Futura, Ibiá
PE06)	I793	680	10/1	R. Grande Rio, Petrolina
PR155)	J362	*680	5/0.25	R. Poema, Pitanga
RJ07)	J452	680	20/5	R. Copacabana, Rio de Janeiro (Rede Aleluia)
RS69)	K275	680	50	R. Farroupilha, Porto Alegre
BA96)	H453	690	10/1	R. Cultura, Ilhéus
CE08)	H587	690	25/10	R. Shalom, Fortaleza
ES10)	I201	690	10/1	R. América, Vitoria
GO48)	H780	690	50/1	R. Sociedade Ceres, Ceres
MG14)	L228	690	50/5	R. Mineira, Belo Horizonte
PA03)	I532	690	20/5	R. Clube do Pará, Belém (RB)
PR13)	J229	690	5/1	R. Dif. de Londrina, Londrina
SP30)	K588	690	1/0.25	R. Clube, Guaratinguetá
SP31)	K625	690	1/0.25	R. Cidade, Pereira Barreto
SP220)	K646	690	1/0.25	R. Brasil, Santa Bárbara d'Oeste
GO47)	H801	700	25/0.5	R. Pouso Alto, Piracanjuba
RJ56)	J507	700	5/0.4	R. Aliança, Italva
RS22)	K356	700	1/0.25	R. Batovi, São Gabriel
SP32)	K686	700	50	Nossa Radio, São Paulo
AL02)	H240	710	5/1	R. Jornal, Maceió
BA46)	H490	710	10/0.25	R. 21 News, Eunápolis
DF07)	H710	710	10/2.5	R. Aliança, Brasília
MA27)	H910	710	1/0.5	R. Verdes Vales, Grajaú
MG79)	L219	710	10/0.5	R. Cancella, Ituiutaba
MG15)	L258	710	20/0.5	R. Manhuaçu, Manhuaçu (RA)
MG80)	L319	710	2/0.25	R. Planeta, Carmo do Paranaíba
MG16)	L333	710	2/0.25	R. Dif. HD, Pouso Alegre
PA04)	I534	710	25/5	R. Rural, Santarém
PI19)	I901	‡710	1/0.25	R. Alvorada do Sertão, São João do Piauí
PI23)	I933	710	1/0.5	R. Clube, Barras
PR141)	J328	710	1/0.25	R. Alternativa, Cândido de Abreu
RJ09)	J451	710	10	R. Sucesso AM, Rio de Janeiro
SP33)	K559	710	10/0.25	R. 710, Bauru
AC01)	H202	720	10	R. Integração, Cruzeiro do Sul
AM05)	H281	720	1	CBN, Itacoatiara
MS04)	I390	720	5/1	R. Clube, Dourados
PE07)	I770	720	100	R. Cl de Pernambuco, Recife
RS23)	K276	720	100	R. Guaíba, Porto Alegre
SP34)	K575	720	1/0.25	R. Difusora, Casa Branca
SP35)	K701	*720	1/0.25	R. Sentinela, Ourinhos
SP36)	K718	720	1/0.25	R. RC Vale, Cruzeiro
SP37)	K722	720	1/0.25	R. Espaço Livre, Olímpia
ES16)	I217	730	10/0.5	R. Novo Tempo, Vitória
GO31)	H759	730	50/5	R. Sagres 730 AM, Goiânia
MA04)	H896	730	1/0.25	R. Eldorado, Codó
MG17)	L287	730	5/1	R. JM 730, Uberaba
MG18)	L297	730	10/1	R. Manchester, Juiz de Fora
MT09)	I410	730	10/2.5	R. Jornal, Cáceres
PR15)	J208	730	7/0.6	R. Marumby, Curitiba
PR16)	J323	730	1/0.25	R. Objetiva, Campo Mourão
PR147)	J353	730	5/0.25	R. Integração Metropolitana, Corbélia
SC09)	J787	730	5/1	R. Tubá, Tubarão (RA)
SP38)	K523	730	10/0.25	R. Cidade, Jundiaí
SP39)	K610	730	10/1	R. Dirceu, Marília
BA11)	H446	740	100	R. Soc. da Bahia, Salvador
RS25)	K265	740	2.5/0.25	R. Palmeira, Palmeira das Missões
RS26)	K283	740	5/0.25	R. Cultura Riograndina, Rio Grande
SC10)	J753	740	10/1	CBN Diário, Florianópolis: 24h
SP40)	K553	740	1/0.25	R. Cultura, Bariri
SP41)	K650	740	25/0.5	R. Trianon, São Paulo
DF01)	H709	750	50/25	R. Jovem Pan, Brasília
MG19)	L213	750	100/5	R. América, Belo Horizonte (Rede Aparecida)
PA28)	I541	750	1/0.25	R. Ximango, Alenquer
PI05)	I897	750	1/0.25	R. Liberdade, Campo Maior
SC11)	J815	750	5/0.25	R. Aliança, Concórdia
SP42)	K516	*750	1/0.25	R. Clube, Osvaldo Cruz
SP43)	K642	750	12/0.5	R. CMN, Ribeirão Preto
SP44)	K661	750	1.5/0.25	R. Super Piratininga, São José dos Campos
SP283	K696	750	5/0.5	R. Atual, Registro
TO03)	H792	750	1/0.25	R. Tocantins, Tocantinópolis
AL12)	H252	760	1/0.25	R. Delmiro, Delmiro Gouveia
BA44)	H461	760	5/0.5	R. Cidade, Vitória da Conquista (F.PI. 1550)
CE10)	H588	760	25/10	R. Uirapuru, Fortaleza
MG83)	L257	760	2.5/0.25	R. Difusora, Machado
MG137)	L360	760	10/0.5	R. Terra, Monte Claros
RJ11)	J478	760	25/1	R. Manchete AM, Niterói
SC12)	J742	*760	25/2	R. Nereu Ramos, Blumenau
SP149)	K541	760	1/0.25	R. Urubupungá, Andradina
MA28)	H922	770	1/0.25	R. Vitória, Coelho Neto
MG20)	L209	770	2.5/0.25	R. Cultura d'Oeste, Lavras
MG22)	L337	770	1/0.25	R. Itabira, Itabira
MS11)	I412	770	5/0.5	R. Caiuás, Dourados
PA29)	I560	770	10/0.25	R. Clube, Marabá
PR131)	J344	770	5/0.25	R. Cidade, Cambé (RB)
SP46)	K506	770	5/0.5	R. Mix, Limeira
MA24)	H919	780	10/5	R. Alvorada, Zé Doca
MG103)	L259	780	10/1	R. Manhumirim, Manhumirim
PE09)	I771	780	30/10	R. Jornal do Comércio, Recife
RS30)	K229	780	5/2	R. Diário da Manhã, Carazinho
RS31)	K279	780	25	R. Princesa AM, Porto Alegre
SP158)	K691	780	50/25	R. America, Sao Paulo
BA14)	H505	790	1/0.25	R. Regional, Serrinha
MA30)	H899	790	1/0.25	R. Rio Flores, Tuntum
PI36)	I931	790	1/0.25	R. Mafrense, Simplício Mendes
PR130)	J316	790	2.5/0.25	R. Clube, Faxinal
PR20)	J337	790	10/0.25	R. RCC, Curitiba
SC14)	J789	790	1/0.25	R. Videira, Videira
SP162)	K674	790	5/0.25	R. Cultura, Taubaté
DF02)	H705	800	10/1	R. MEC, Brasília (EBC)
PI08)	I921	800	10	R. Antares, Teresina
RJ12)	J457	800	100	R. MEC, Rio de Janeiro
RS33)	K292	800	10	R. Universidade, Santa Maria
CE13)	H589	810	50/5	R. Verdes Mares, Fortaleza
MG92)	L252	810	1/0.25	R. Educadora, Ubá
MG138)	L354	810	1/0.25	R. Cidade, Capinópolis
PR49)	J261	810	2/0.25	Rede Terra Nativa, Cornélio Procópio
PR111)	J336	810	5/0.5	R. Esperança, Prudentópolis
RS136)	K324	810	1.9/0.25	R. Cinderela, Campo Bom
SP50)	K604	810	5/0.25	R. Dif. Jundiaiense, Jundiaí
SP89)	K655	810	1/0.5	R. Universal, Santos
SP51)	K732	810	5/0.5	R. Canção Nova do Coração de Maria, São José do Rio Preto
AC03)	H...	820	1/0.25	R. Educ. 6 de Agosto, Xapuri
AC12)	H207	820	0.25	R. Dif. de Tarauacá, Tarauacá
BA15)	H534	820	20/1	R. Cultura, Utinga
GO16)	H752	820	50/5	R. Bandeirantes, Goiânia
MG30)	L291	820	1/0.25	R. da Familia, São Sebastião do Paraíso
PE10)	I775	820	5/1	R. Paulo Frei, Recife
PI06)	I912	820	5/0.25	R. Cacique Bruenque, Regeneração
PR21)	J238	820	10/5	R. Cultura, Foz do Iguaçu
PR150)	J357	820	1/0.25	R. Princesa, Roncador
RS34)	K241	820	5/1	R. do Vale, Estrela: 0900-0200
SC15)	J738	820	10/5	CBN, Blumenau: 24h
SP53)	K602	820	1/0.25	R. Jauense, Jaú
SP54)	K622	820	0.5/0.25	R. Clube, Ourinhos
BA67)	H506	*830	5/0.25	R. Extremo Sul da Bahia, Itamaraju:
CE65)	H659	830	1/0.25	R. Pioneira, Forquilha
MA26)	H905	830	10/1	R. Mirante do Maranhão, Imperatriz
MA21)	H925	830	1/0.25	R. Boa Esperança, Esperantinópolis
MG31)	L244	830	15/5	R. Cultura, Belo Horizonte
PA24)	I556	830	10/1	R. Guarany de Marajó, Soure
PI07)	I906	830	1/0.25	R. Primeira Capital, Oeiras
PR22)	J224	830	7.5/0.75	R. Iguassu, Araucária
PR23)	J311	830	1/0.25	R. Progresso, Clevelândia
RJ39)	J488	830	10/0.5	R. Tropical AM, Rio de Janeiro
RS35)	K332	830	5/0.25	R. Independente, Cruz Alta

MW	Call	kHz	kW	Station, location, h. of tr.
RS132)	K346	830	5/0.6	R. Cassino, Rio Grande
SE06)	J926	830	20/1	R. Princesa da Serra, Itabaiana
SP227)	K746	830	5/1	R. Novo Tempo, Nova Odessa
AL13)	H253	840	10/0.25	R. Canaviero, União dos Palmares
AM07)	H298	840	1/0.25	R. Rio Madeira, Manicoré
BA16)	H447	840	25/5	R. Excelsior da Bahia, Salvador (RA)
CE51)	H648	840	1/0.5	R. Campo Maior, Quixeramobim:
PI39)	I937	‡840	1/0.25	R. Vitória, Batalha
PR75)	J320	840	10/1.2	R. Inconfidência, Umuarama
RS36)	K248	840	10	R. Cultura, Porto Alegre
SC17)	J750	840	10/1	R. Rural, Concórdia
SP57)	K687	840	100/50	R. Bandeirantes, São Paulo
BA17)	H474	850	5/0.25	R. Caraiba, Senhor do Bonfim
GO17)	H776	850	5/1	R.Tropical, Porangatu
PA06)	I555	*850	1/0.25	R. Tocantins, Cametá
PB22)	I693	850	5/1	R. Rural, Guarabira
PI30)	I909	850	1/0.25	R. Grande Picos, Picos
RJ31)	J470	850		R. Campos Difusora,Campos dos Goytacazes
SC20)	J808	850	2.5/0.25	R. Cidade, Brusque
SC102)	J807	850	1/0.25	R. Atalaia, Campo Erê
SP58)	K644	850	2.5/0.25	R. Clube AM, Rio Claro
CE16)	H592	860	25/10	R. Cidade de Fortaleza, Maracanaú
RS37)	K288	860	10/1	R. Guarathan, Santa Maria
BA18)	H457	870	12/0.25	R. Nacional, Itabuna
BA84)	H499	870	5/1	R. Cidade, Juazeiro
CE17)	H591	870	1/0.25	R. Liberdade, Iguatu
GO18)	H749	870	5/0.5	R. Lago Dourado, Uruaçu
GO32)	H754	870	10/0.5	R. Universitária, Goiânia
MA05)	H906	870	10/0.5	R. Mirante, Codó
MG38)	L318	870	1/0.5	R. Cultura, Diamantina
MG128)	L349	870	5/0.25	R. Atividade, Muriaé
MT35)	N409	870	1/0.5	R. Garça Branca, Guiratinga
PA11)	I547	870	1/0.25	R. Marajó, Breves
PR25)	J243	*870	5/0.25	R. Nova Ingá, Maringá (RB)
SC96)	J784	870	12/0.25	R. São Francisco, São Francisco do Sul (RB)
SP61)	K705	870	5/1	R. Central, Campinas
MG35)	L275	880	100	AM 880 R. Inconfidência, Belo Horizonte
PB18)	I680	880	1/0.25	R. Maringá, Pombal
RS38)	K249	880	25/2.5	R. Itaí, Porto AlegreIPDA)
RS87)	K317	880	2.5/0.25	R. São Miguel, Uruguaiana
RS20)	K363	880	8/0.25	R. Seberi, Seberirel (Rede Gaucha)
CE46)	H642	890	1/0.25	R. Itatiaia, Santa Quitéria
DF03)	H706	890	50/2.5	R. Planalto, Brasília
MG36)	L250	890	10/1	R. Santa Cruz, Almenara
MG154)	L370	890	5/0.25	R. Clube, Inhapim
MS33)	I453	890	10/0.5	R. Guaicurus, Fátima do Sul
PA13)	I536	*890	5/1	R. Ponta Negra, Santarém
PE11)	I772	890	20/10	R. Tamandaré, Olinda
PR117)	J287	890	2.5/0.25	R. Ubá, Ivaiporã
PR26)	J338	890	5/0.25	R. Itapuã, Pato Branco
RS39)	K215	890	5/0.25	R. Difusora, Bento Gonçalves
SC18)	J755	890	1/0.25	R. Santa Catarina, Florianópolis (IPDA)
SP178)	K562	890	1/0.25	R. Imaculada Conceição, Bilac
BA19)	H488	900	1	R. Sisal, Conceição do Coité
MG148)	L311	900	2.5/0.25	Rede Gerais, Carangola
MG124)	L338	900	1/0.25	R. Vinícola, Andradas (RA)
MT36)	I455	900	10/2.5	R. Dif. Arco-Íris, Araputanga
PA10)	I533	900	25/5	R. Liberal, Belém
PR28)	J295	900	5/0.25	R. União, Toledo
RJ15)	J454	900	50/10	R. Tamoio, Rio de Janeiro
RS41)	K211	900	2.5/0.5	R. Aratiba, Aratiba
RS179)	K263	*900	5/0.5	R. ABC 900, Nôvo Hamburgo
RS164)	K301	900	1/0.25	R. Municipal, São Pedro do Sul
SP63)	K511	900	5/0.25	R. Difusora, Presidente Prudente
SP64)	K664	900	10/0.8	R. Jovem Pan, São José do Rio Preto
SP65)	K742	900	1/0.25	R. Clube de Itapetininga, Itapetininga
GO23)	H804	910	10/0.5	R. Cidade, Jaraguá
MG37)	L292	910	1/0.25	R. Teófilo Otoni, Teófilo Otoni: 24h
MG149)	N206	910	5/1	R. Play Hits, Juiz de Fora
PR29)	J207	910	1/0.25	R. Nova AM, Apucarana
RS43)	K320	910	5/0.5	R. Venâncio Aires, Venâncio Aires:
SP66)	K536	910	7.5/0.25	R. Jovem Pan News, Piracicaba
BA57)	H519	920	25/2	R. Novo Tempo, Salvador
GO33)	H788	920	5/1	R. Vale da Serra, São Luís de Monte Belos
MG39)	L271	920	5/0.5	R. Cultura, Visconde do Rio Branco
PB31)	I697	‡920	5/0.5	João Pessoa
PI09)	I895	920	1/0.25	R. Dif. Grande, Picos
PI11)	I893	920	10/0.5	R. Educadora, Parnaíba
RS44)	K348	920	20/2	R.Tramandaí, Tramandaí
SP67)	K584	920	10/0.25	R. Imperador, Franca (RA)
SP221)	K775	920	40/1	R. Nacional Gospel, Cotia
CE52)	H646	930	7/0.25	R. Metropolitana, Caucaia
MG42)	L229	930	10/5	R. Vitoriosa, Araguari
MT12)	I423	930	10/0.5	R. Clube, Rondonópolis
PR30)	J227	930	1/0.25	R. Cultura, Rolândia
PR31)	J232	930	10/1	R. Cultura, Curitiba
PR69)	J235	930	10/1	R. Princesa, Francisco Beltrão
RS45)	K230	930	20/2.5	R. Caxias, Caxias do Sul
RS46)	K298	930	10/0.5	R. Santo Ângelo, Santo Ângelo
SP68)	K503	930	1/0.25	R. Clube, Itapira
RJ16)	J453	940	100	Super Rede Boa Vontade, Rio de Janeiro
CE19)	H593	950	10/1	R. Educadora do Nordeste, Sobral
MA17)	H916	950	10/0.25	R. Dif. Karajás, João Lisboa
MG43)	L212	950	25/10	R. Atalaia, Belo Horizonte
MG44)	L281	950	7/0.5	R. Indy, Bueno Brandão (RB)
PB17)	I681	950	1/0.25	R. Jornal, Sousa
PE13)	I782	950	25/5	R. Planalto, Carpina
PI20)	I932	950	10/0.25	R. São José dos Altos, Altos
PI42)	I923	950	1/0.25	R. Boa Esperança, Padre Marcos
RS47)	K260	950	10/0.25	R. Independente, Lajeado
SC21)	J736	950	1/0.25	R. Vale, Tijucas
SP72)	K510	950	5/0.25	Super R. 950, Vera Cruz
AL04)	H241	960	10	R. Difusora de Alagôas, Maceió
CE37)	H618	960	1/0.25	R. Cultura dos Inhamuns, Tauá
GO45)	H802	960	50/1	R. Caraiba, Aparecida de Goiânia (IPDA)
PA26)	I551	960	1/0.25	R. Clube, Itaituba
PR32)	J257	*960	1/0.25	R. Mais, Maringá
SC22)	J733	960	5/0.25	R. Guarujá, Orleans
SC23)	J813	960	8/0.25	R. Super Difusora, Xanxerê
SP73)	K689	960	50/10	R. São Paulo, São Paulo
CE20)	H612	970	5/0.25	R. Monólitos, Quixadá
MG45)	L243	970	5/0.25	R. Caratinga, Caratinga
MG46)	L264	970		R. São João del Rei, São João del Rei
PR33)	J260	970	7.5/1	R. Alvorada, Londrina (RA)
PR34)	J277	970	10/0.25	R. Difusora do Paraná, Marechal Cândido Rondón
RS49)	K201	970	50/10	R. Liberdade, Porto Alegre
SC24)	J730	970	5/0.25	R. Araguaia, Brusque
SP75)	K529	970	1/0.25	R. Piratininga, São João da Boa Vista
SP76)	K684	970	5/0.25	R. Hertz, Franca
DF04)	H707	980	50/300	R. Nacional, Brasília (EBC)
PI44)	I922	990	1/0.25	R. Vale do Canindé, Oeiras
RJ53)	J461	990	100/10	R. Contemporânea, Rio de Janeiro
RN05)	J596	990	10/1	R. Rural, Mossoró
RS154)	K360	990	1/0.25	R. Clube, Pedro Osório
SC25)	J763	990	2/0.25	R. Itapiranga, Itapiranga
SP239)	K579	990	10/0.25	R. Cultura Regional, Dois Córregos
PB30)	I698	1000	2.5/0.5	R. Oeste da Paraíba, Cajazeiras
PE14)	I791	1000	1/0.25	R. Princesa Serrana, Timbaúba
SP77)	K522	1000	200	R. Record, São Paulo
BA22)	H448	1010	25/5	R. Bahia, Salvador
CE21)	H625	1010	12.5/2.5	R. O´Povo CBN, Fortaleza
GO39)	H772	1010	10/0.5	R. Santelenense, Sta. Helena de Goiás
MG50)	L230	1010	10/1	R. Educadora, Coronel Fabriciano (RA)
PR35)	J263	1010	25/5	R. Celinauta, Pato Branco
RS53)	K232	1010	7/0.75	R. Tua Voz, Caxias do Sul
RS54)	K344	1010	3/1	R. Missioneira, São Luiz Gonzaga
SP151)	K507	1010	5/0.5	R. Dif., Lençóis Paulista
SP79)	K611	1010	5/0.25	R. Diário, Martinópolis
AL05)	H247	1020	25/1	R. Maceio, Rio Largo
AP04)	H423	1020	1/0.25	R. Porto, Santana
CE79)	H664	1020	1/0.25	R. Macambira, Ipueiras
GO52)	H781	1020	10/0.5	R. Boas Novas, Firminópolis
PR36)	J244	1020	10/0.25	R. Colombo, Curitiba
PR37)	J307	1020	1/0.25	R. Independência, Medianeira
RS49)	K202	1020	25/5	R. Eldorado, Porto Alegre
SP81)	K515	1020	5/0,25	R. Cultura, Assis
SP82)	K531	1020	2.5/0.5	R. Educadora, Limeira
MA07)	H892	1030	10/1	R. Jainara, Bacabal
MA66)	I441	1030		R. Itai do Rio Claro, Rondonopolis (IPDA)
PE15)	I777	*1030	20/5	R. Olinda, Olinda
PR39)	J271	1030	5/0.25	R. Atalaia, Londrina
PR120)	J312	1030	2.5/0.25	R. Clube, Realeza

MW	Call	kHz	kW	Station, location, h. of tr.
RJ18)	J467	1030	100/5	R. Capital, Rio de Janeiro (IPDA)
RO10)	J683	1030	5/1	R. Rondônia, Ariquemes
RS129)	K224	1030	1/0.25	R. Cultura, Canguçu
SP84)	K525	1030	5/0.25	R. Difusora, Franca
SP85)	K554	1030	1/0.25	R. Em. da Barra, Barra Bonita (RB)
TO05)	H791	1030	1/0.25	R. Colinas, Colinas do Tocantins
SP87)	K537	1040	200/100	R. Capital, São Paulo
ES07)	I203	1050	100/1	R. Capixaba, Vitória (IPDA)
MG52)	L236	1050	1/0.25	R. Rural, Tupaciguara
RJ19)	J497	1050	10/0.5	R. Angra, Angra dos Reis
SP160)	K601	1050	10/0.5	R. Show Jardinópolis
BA23)	H460	1060	5/1	R. Cl. de Conquista, Vitória da Conquista
GO54)	H807	1060	5	R. Serra Dourada, Minacu:
MG53)	L278	1060	25	R. 880, Belo Horizonte (IPDA)
MS39)	N604	1060	5/1	R. Imaculada Conceição, Dourados
PR42)	J246	1060	10/0.5	R. Evangelizar, Curitiba
PR44)	J306	1060	10/0.5	R. Educadora, Francisco Beltrão
RJ20)	J495	1060	30/1	R. Canção Nova, Nova Iguaçu
RN06)	J597	1060	5	R. Tapuyo, Mossoró (RPC)
RS56)	K220	1060	5/0.25	R. Camaqüense, Camaquã
RS57)	K302	*1060	2/0.25	R. São Luiz, São Luiz Gonzaga
SC103)	J830	1060	2/0.4	R. Mais Alegria, Florianópolis
SP88)	K533	1060	5/0.25	R. Educadora, Piracicaba
SP229)	K765	1060	5/0.25	R. Universitária, Garça
BA48)	H492	1070	5/0.5	R. Rural 'R. Tropical', Ipiaú
MG56)	L316	1070	1/0.25	R. do Povo, Muzambinho
PB08)	I673	1070	20/2.5	R. Cajazeiras, Cajazeiras
RS58)	K218	1070	2/0.25	R. Caçapava, Caçapava do Sul
RS59)	K343	1070	1/0.25	R. Metrópole, Crissiumal
RS60)	K357	1070	2/0.25	R. Serrana, Bento Gonçalves
SP91)	K603	1070	1/0.25	R. Piratininga de Jaú, Jaú (RB)
SP145)	K615	1070	10/0.25	R. Metropolitana, Mogi das Cruzes
SP92)	K633	1070	10/1	Prudente AM, Presidente Prudente
SP212)	K758	1070	1/0.25	R. Jornal, Barretos
BA24)	H470	1080	10/0.5	R. Subaé, Feira de Santana
BA25)	H485	1080	1/0.25	R. Fascinação, Itapetinga
DF05)	H708	1080	25/5	R. Capital – Rede Aleliua, Brasília
MG109)	L232	1080	2.5/0.5	R. Cultura, Dores do Indaiá
MG57)	L251	1080	25/0.7	R. Capital, Juiz de Fora (IPDA)
PA32)	I540	1080	15/5	R. Novo Tempo, Belém
PE16)	I784	1080	10/0.5	R. Jornal do Comercio, Caruaru
RS61)	K254	1080	3/0.25	R. Marabá, Iraí
RS62)	K280	1080	10	R. da Universidade, Porto Alegre
SP94)	K557	1080	5/1	R. Difusora, Batatais
SP96)	K669	1080	10/1	R. Boa Nova, Sorocaba
SP97)	K704	1080	1/0.25	R. Monumental, Aparecida
AL15)	H254	1090	5/0.5	R. Gazeta, Pão de Açucar
BA26)	H455	1090	1/0.25	R. Santa Cruz, Ilhéus
GO24)	H758	1090	25/1	R. Aliança, Aparecida de Goiânia
MA08)	H893	1090	10	R. Rio Balsas, Balsas
MG145)	L357	1090	5/0.25	R. Catuaí, Manhuaçu
PR51)	J283	*1090	2.5/0.25	R. Vicente Palotti, Coronel Vivida
PR171)	J345	1090	1/0.25	R. Banda 1, Sarandi
RJ22)	J468	1090	50/5	R. Metropolitana, Rio de Janeiro
RS64)	K262	*1090	1/0.25	R. Salette, Marcelino Ramos
RS65)	K341	1090	1/0.25	R. Giruá, Giruá
SC30)	J732	1090	1/0.25	R. Colón, Joinville
SC31)	J786	1090	5/0.5	R. Bandeirantes, Tubarão
SP98)	K609	1090	3/0.5	R. Clube, Marília
SP99)	K618	1090	3/0.25	R. Cultura, Monte Alto
SP233)	K768	1090	1/0.25	R. Canção Nova, Paulina
CE67)	H638	1100	1/0.25	R. Dif. dos Inhamuns, Tauá
RN18)	J607	1100	1/0.25	R. Seridó, Caicó
BA100)	H464	1110	1	R. Vox, Muritiba
GO46)	H782	1110	25/2	R. Redentor, Sto. Antônio do Escoberto
MG58)	L205	1110	1/0.25	R. Planalto, Araguari
MG59)	L267	1110	1	R. Aurilândia, Nova Lima
MS08)	I392	1110	1	R. Transamérica, Ponta Porã
PB09)	I689	1110	20/10	R. Tabajara, João Pessoa
RS66)	K257	1110	2.5/0.25	R. Cultura Jaguarão, Jaguarão
RS67)	K306	1110	2/0,25	R. Sobradinho, Sobradinho
RS68)	K325	1110	2.5/0.25	R. Cruzeiro do Sul, Itaqui
SC32)	J752	1110	1/0.5	R. Cultura, Florianópolis
SP103)	K617	1110	1/0,25	Transamérica Hits, Mogi Mirim (RB)
BA72)	H513	1120	5/0.5	R. Belo Campo, Belo Campo
BA79)	H511	1120	0.3	R. Jornal, Souto Soares
BA98)	H257	1120	10	R. Estrela, Valenta
PE17)	I778	1120	5/1	R. Relógio, Paulista
PR53)	J253	1120	25/1	R. Mais, São José dos Pinhais
SP105)	K660	1120	10/1	R. Cidade, São José dos Campos
SP106)	K671	1120	1/0.25	R. Clube Imperial, Taquaritinga
CE72)	H667	1130	10/0.25	R. Patu, Senador Pompeu
PA08)	I531	1130	10	R. Marajoara, Belém
PE18)	I783	*1130	5/1	R. Cultura do Nordeste, Caruaru
PR54)	J333	1130	5/0.25	R. Ingamar, Marialva
RJ17)	J460	1130	100/50	R. Nacional, Rio de Janeiro (EBC)
SC34)	J790	1130	5/1	R. Princesa d'Oeste, Xanxerê
BA81)	H449	1140	10	R. Cultura da Bahia, Salvador
CE24)	H607	1140	10/1	R. Progresso, Russas
MG63)	L248	1140	1/0.25	R. Doicesana, Campanha
MS22)	I398	1140	10/0.5	R. Regional, Fátima do Sul
PR144)	J352	1140	1/0.25	R. Dif. América, Chopinzinho: 24h
RS71)	K228	1140	2/0.25	R. Cruz Alta, Cruz Alta
RS72)	K316	1140	5/0.7	R. Charrua, Uruguaiana
RS73)	K330	1140	2/0.5	R. Jornal Sobral, Butiá
SP108)	K550	1140	10/0.5	R. Difusora, Assis
SP110)	K645	1140	1/0.25	R. Cultura, Rio Claro (RB)
SP111)	K709	1140	5/0.25	R. Costa Azul, Ubatuba
SP273)	K708	1140	1/0.25	R. Nova Regional, Registro
AL11)	H250	1150	20/1	R. Cultura, Arapiraca
RJ24)	J456	1150	10/0.5	R. Três Rios, Três Rios
RN25)	J617	1150	5/0.5	R. Cabugi do Seridó, Jardim do Seridó
SP232)	K656	1150	100/50	Super Radio, São Paulo
AM24)	H323	*1160	1/0.25	R. Soc. TV Manauara, Boca do Acre
CE62)	H652	1160	1/0.25	R. Vale do Coreaú, Granja
CE80)	H660	1160	1/0.25	R. Montevidéo, Cedro
DF09)	H714	‡1160	30/0.5	Brasília
ES08)	I202	1160	50/10	R. Espírito Santo, Vitória
MT15)	I385	1160	10/5	R. A Voz Do Oeste, Cuiabá
PA30)	I558	*1160	5/1	R. Guamá, São Miguel do Guamá
RS74)	K242	1160	9/1	R. Miriam, Farroupilha
RS75)	K245	1160	5/1	R. Luz e Alegria, Frederico Westphalen
RS77)	K273	1160	2.5/1	R. Universidade Católica, Pelotas
SC36)	J741	1160	9/0.7	R. Itaberá, Blumenau (RB)
SP114)	K517	1160	5/0.5	R. Cacique, Sorocaba
SP124)	K558	1160	2.5/1	R. Bandeirantes, Bauru
SP115)	K582	1160	5/0.25	R. Difusora, Fernandópolis (RB)
SP237)	K673	1160	4/0.25	R. Cacique, Taubaté
AC15)	H205	1170	1/0.25	R. Dif. de Feijó, Feijó
AM08)	H284	1170	5/2.5	R. Guaranópolis, Maués
BA27)	H473	*1170	5/0.25	R. Jornal, Eunápolis
MG75)	L327	1170	10/0.25	R. Vanguarda, Ipatinga
PR57)	J273	1170	20/10	R. Aleluia, Curitiba
PR90)	J334	1170	2.5/0.45	R. Entre Rios, Sto. Antônio do Sudoeste
RJ49)	J498	1170	5/0.25	R. Bom Jesus, Bom Jesus de Itabapoana
RN08)	J598	1170	10/1	R. Difusora, Mossoró
RS78)	K207	1170	1/0.25	R. Itapuí, Santo Antônio da Patrulha
RS155)	K380	1170	1.5	R. Pitangueira, Itaqui
SP117)	K569	1170	10/5	R. Bandeirantes, Campinas
AL06)	H248	*1180	1/0.25	R. Correio do Sertão, Santana do Ipanema
MA09)	H889	1180	10/5	R. Capital, São Luís
MG118)	L203	1180	10/0.25	R. Cultura, Alfenas:
PE19)	I797	1180	1/0.25	R. Jornal, Vitória de Sto. Antão
PR58)	J237	1180	10/0.5	R. Guaçu, Toledo
PR81)	J314	1180	2.5/0.25	R. Educadora, São João do Ivaí
RJ25)	J463	1180	50/10	R. Mundial, Rio de Janeiro (IPDA)
SC39)	J737	1180	5/0.25	R. Integração d'Oeste, São José do Cedro
SP217)	K749	1180	5/0.25	R. Nova, Bebedouro
BA28)	H459	1190	10/1	R. Juazeiro, Juazeiro
MG68)	L221	1190	50/1	R. Guarani, Belo Horizonte
RS82)	K234	1190	5/0.5	R. Cerro Azul, Cerro Largo
RS102)	K301	1190	2.5/0.25	R. São Lourenço, São Lourenço do Sul
SP199)	K512	1190	2.5/0.25	R. Marconi, Paraguaçu Paulista
SP119)	K729	1190	10/0.25	R. 31 de Março, Sta. Cruz das Palmeiras
SP120)	K741	1190	1/0.5	R. Regional, Taquarituba
AL14)	H251	1200	50/1	R. Correio, Pilar
BA29)	H482	1200	10/0.5	R. Clube Rio do Ouro, Jacobina
CE26)	H585	1200	10	R. Clube AM 1200, Fortaleza //R. Super Tupi
RS84)	K239	1200	5/1	R. Erechim, Erechim
RS85)	K342	1200	1/0.5	R. Fundação Cotrisel, São Sepé
SP121)	K520	1200	100/20	R. Cultura Brasil, São Paulo
BA58)	H498	*1210	10/0.25	R. Canção Nova, Vitória da Conquista

MW	Call	kHz	kW	Station, location, h. of tr.
CE50)	H637	1210	5/0.25	R. Principe Imperial, Crateús
DF08)	H711	1210	50/2.5	Super Rede Boa Vontade (RBV), Brasília
PE20)	I786	1210	10/1	R. Jornal, Garanhuns
PR60)	J219	1210	25/5	Super R. Deus é Amor, Curitiba (IPDA)
RN29)	J620	1210	5/0.5	R. Potengi, São Paulo do Potengi
RS86)	K240	1210	10/5	R. Transcontinental, Porto Alegre
SC42)	J785	*1210	10/0.5	R. Super Santa, Tubarão
SP122)	K509	1210	10/1	R. Vida Nova, Jaboticabal
SP125)	K668	1210	5/0.25	R. Vanguarda, Sorocaba
BA59)	H532	*1230	1/0.25	R. Povo, Ubatã
GO27)	H756	1230	10/2.5	R. Daqui, Goiânia
MA23)	H...	1230	1/0.25	R. Veneza, Caxias
MG105)	L208	1230	5/0.25	R. Correio da Serra, Barbacena
MG176)	N203	1230	10/0.7	R. Estrela de Ibiúna, Campina Verde
PB12)	I670	1230	10/1	R. Correio Jovem Pan, João Pessoa
RS89)	K326	*1230	2/0.25	R. Clube Nonoai, Nonoai
RS90)	K333	1230	2.3/0.35	R. Prata, Nova Prata
RS91)	K352	1230	1/0.25	R. Encruzilhadense, Encruzilhada do Sul
SC38)	J776	1230	5/0.65	R. Dif. Colméia, Porto União
SP126)	K573	1230	1/0.25	R. Cacique, Capão Bonito
SP258)	K637	1230	10/0.25	R. Difusora, Rancharia
SP128)	K716	1230	5/0.5	Jovem Pan News, Campinas
SP266)	R699	1230	50/10	Super Rede Boa Vontade, São Paulo
CE49)	H654	1240	1/0.25	R. São Francisco, Canindé
MG97)	L294	1240	5/0.25	R. Três Pontas, Três Pontas
MG72)	L303	1240	10/0.35	R. Platina/Jovem Pan News, Ituiutaba
MG116)	L317	*1240	5/0.25	R. Pirapora AM, Pirapora
PE21)	I774	1240	5	R. Capibaribe, Recife
PR112)	J215	*1240	1/0.25	R. Arapongas, Arapongas
PR61)	J280	1240	2/0.25	R. Matelândia, Matelândia
RS92)	K200	1240	1/0.25	R. Aparados da Serra, Bom Jesus
RS93)	K251	1240	5/0.25	R. Ibirubá, Ibirubá
RS94)	K355	1240	1/0.25	R. São Jerônimo, São Jerônimo
SC44)	J810	1240	2.2	R. Iracema, Cunhae Porã
SP129)	K565	1240	10/0.25	R. Municipalista, Botucatu
SP130)	K621	1240	5/0.25	Orlândia R. Clube, Orlândia
SP131)	K653	1240	10/2.5	R. Clube, Santos
CE27)	H594	1250	1	R. Educadora, Crateús
MG153)	L367	1250	50	Nossa Radio, Belo Horizonte
MS11)	I412	1250	5/0.5	R. Caiuás, Dourados
PB27)	I701	1250	1/0.25	R. Sociedade de Soledade, Soledade
PR64)	J313	1250	2.5/0.25	R. Danúbio Azul, Sta. Isabel do Oeste
RJ50)	J500	1250	15/0.5	R. Litoral, Casimiro de Abreu
RS95)	K233	1250	15/0.5	R. Dif. Caxiense, Caxias do Sul
RS96)	K272	1250	1	R. Tupanci, Pelotas
SC45)	J766	1250	5/0.25	R. Jovem Pan News, Joinville
RS97)	K204	1260	1/0.25	R. Cultura, São Borja
SC46)	J740	1260	10/0.5	R. Arca da Aliança, Blumenau (RA)
SP257)	K629	1260	1/0.25	Pirajau R. Clube, Pirajuí
SP134)	K688	1260	100/40	R. Morada do Sol, São Paulo
GO30)	H753	1270	100/10	R. Brasil Central, Goiânia
MG107)	L300	1270	2.5/0.5	R. Estância, São Lourenço
PA09)	I530	1270	10/2.5	R. Boas Novas, Belém
PR65)	J222	1270	5/0.5	R. Guairacá, Mandaguari
PR67)	J236	1270	10/1	R. Capital, Curitiba
RN10)	J593	1270	5/0.5	R. Clube AM 1270, Natal
RS131)	K206	1270	5/0.5	R. América, Montenegro
RS101)	K250	1270	5/0.5	R. Vera Cruz, Horizontina
SP136)	K678	1270	5/0.5	R. Brasil, Campinas
SP274)	K640	1270	2/0.5	R. Bandeirantes, Ribeirão Preto
PB21)	I688	1280	10/5	R. Sanhauá, Bayeux
RJ27)	J455	1280	100	R. Tupi, Rio de Janeiro: 0900-2300
BA32)	H450	1290	10/1	R. Metropole, Salvador
MA10)	H888	±1290	10/5	R. Timbira, São Luís
PR73)	J310	1290	25/0.5	R. Brasil Sul, Londrina
SC81)	J734	1290	5/1	R. Araranguá, Araranguá (RB)
SC49)	J804	1290	5/1	R. Camboriú, Balneário Camboriú
SP137)	K663	1290	5/1	R. Novo Tempo, São José do Rio Preto
SP216)	K745	1290	1/0.5	R. Estadão, São José dos Campos
CE29)	H586	1300	10	R. Iracema, Fortaleza
MG143)	L339	1300	5/1	R. Eldorado, Sete Lagoas
PE22)	I799	1300	1/0.25	R. Guarany, Camaragibe
PR127)	J288	1300	5/0.25	R. Educadora, Dois Vizinhos
RS104)	K203	1300	80/13	Super Rede Boa Vontade, Porto Alegre
RS105)	K337	1300	1/0.25	R. Regional, Santo Cristo
SP138)	K535	1300	50/1	R. Universo, São Paulo (IPDA)
SP252)	K649	1300	30/0.25	R. Onda Viva, Santo Anastácio
SP226)	K762	1300	2/0.25	R. Real AM 1300, São Carlos (RB)
AP05)	H422	1310	1/0.25	R. Nova Mazagão, Mazagão
BA33)	H454	1310	1/0.25	R. Bahiana, Ilhéus
CE63)	H656	1310	1/0.25	R. Liberdade, Boa Viagem
MG168)	L351	1310	10/0.25	R. Difusora, Salinas
PB23)	I691	1310	10/0.5	R. Cidade Esperança, Esperança
PR70)	J274	1310	10/0.5	R. Atalaia, Maringá
RJ28)	J504	1310	1/0.25	R. Coroados, São Fidélis
RS107)	K305	1310	10/1	R. Sarandi, Sarandi
SP141)	K566	1310	5/0.25	Bragança AM, Bragança Paulista
SP139)	K596	1310	2/1	R. Difusora, Itápolis
GO55)	H809	1320		R. Liberdade, Uruaçu
MG136)	L322	1320	5/0.25	R. Mucuri, Teófilo Otoni
PE31)	I823	1320	1/0.25	R. Cultura, São José do Egito
PR72)	J255	1320	12/0.5	R. Tropical Gospel, Curitiba
PR145)	J351	1320	5/0.5	R. RCI, Foz do Iguaçu (RB)
RJ29)	J475	1320	50/5	R. Boas Novas, Petropôlis
RS108)	K223	1320	1/0.25	R. Clube, Canela
RS109)	K266	1320	3/0.25	R. Sulbrasileira, Panambi
RS110)	K271	1320	5/1	R. Cultura, Pelotas
SC104)		1320	5/0.45	R. Vitôria, Videira
BA34)	H468	1330	1	R. Continental, Serrinha
PR74)	J264	1330	10/0.5	R. Jaguariaíva, Jaguariaiva
RN27)	J621	1330	10/0.5	R. Eldorado, Natal
RS111)	K236	1330	1/0.25	R. Upacaraí, Dom Pedrito
SC50)	J739	1330	10/0.5	R. Clube, Blumenau
SC51)	J749	1330	5/1	R. Chapecó, Chapecó
SP142)	K638	1330	30/0.25	R. Paulista, Regente Feijó
SP143)	K641	1330	5/1	R. Terra, Ribeirão Preto (rel: SP187)
SP187)	K736	1330	50/10	R. Terra, Osasco
CE71)	H661	1340	2.5/0.25	R. Pitaguary, Maracanaú
MA11)	H886	1340	10/2	R. São Luís, São Luís
MG81)	L241	1340	10/5	R. Cultura, Itabirito
PB13)	I671	1340	5/1	R. Correio, João Pessoa
PR76)	J205	1340	2.5/0.25	R. Difusora, Rio Negro
PR77)	J249	1340	5/0.25	R. Cultura, Arapongas (RB)
PR41)	J368	1340	20/0.25	R. Nacional News, Cascavel
RJ40)	J490	1340	5/0.5	R. Jornal, Rio Bonito
RS113)	K227	1340	25/4	CBN, Porto Alegre
RS173)	K374	1340	10/4	R. Journal da Manhã, Ijui
AC05)	H201	1350	50/5	R. Capital, Rio Branco (IPDA)
BA70)	H520	1350	50/10	Super Rede Boa Vontade, Salvador
CE56)	H662	1350	1/0.25	R. Liberal Jagoaribana, Morada Nova
RS115)	K313	1350	5/1	R. Difusora, Três Passos
SC53)	J760	1350	1/0.25	R. Bandeirantes, Itajaí
SP265)	K692	1350	50/0.25	RBC AM, Ibiuna
BA35)	H469	1360	10/1	R. Cultura, Paulo Afonso
CE57)	H650	1360	5/0.25	R. Iracema, Ipu
PR165)	J265	1360	10/0.25	R. Cidade, Pato Branco
PR78)	J268	1360	1/0.25	Rede Terra Nativa, Assaí
RJ30)	J464	1360	50/10	R. Bandeirantes, Rio de Janeiro
RS151)	K281	1360	3/0.25	R. Navegantes, Porto Lucena
SP148)	K739	1360	1/0.25	R. Regional, Dracena
SP235)	K759	1360	1/0.25	R. Luzes da Ribalta, Santa Bárbara d'Oeste
BA82)	H555	1370	0.25	R. Jornal Grande, Monte Santo:
CE81)	H628	1370	1/0.25	R. Vanguarda, Caridade
PI13)	I892	1370	2.5	R. Difusora, Teresina (RB)
PR80)	J267	1370	50/7	R. Canção Nova, Curitiba
RN28)	J618	1370	2.5/0.25	R. Dif.,São Miguel
RS118)	K243	1370	25/0.5	R. Mãe de Deus, Flores da Cunha
RS119)	K334	1370	1/0.25	R. Gazeta, Alegrete
AM12)	H283	1380	5/1	R. Alvorada, Parintins
BA83)	H495	‡1380	5/0.25	R. União, Gandu
ES21)	I…	1380	10/1	R. Itaí de Rio Claro, Iúna
MA40)	H909	1380	1/0.25	R. Tropical, Caixas
MG172)	L218	1380	1/0.25	Rede Gerais, Brasópolis
MG130)	L323	1380	1/0.25	R. Gorutubana, Janaúba
PE23)	I773	1380	10/5	R. Continental - IPDA, Recife
PR152)	J367	1380	1/0.25	R. Integração, Toledo
RS120)	K293	1380	1/0.25	R. Cultura, Sant´Aana do Livramento
RS121)	K350	1380	6/0.25	R. Cultura, Tapera
RS165)	K372	1380	6/0.25	R. Chiru, Palmitinho
SC93)	J827	1380	6/0.25	R. Barriga Verde, Capinzal
SC105)	J831	1380	1/0.25	R. Freguencia, Garopaba
SP152)	K616	1380	1/0.5	R. Difusora, Mogi Guaçu
SP224)	K751	1380	5/0.25	R. Fronteira, Presidente Prudente
PA12)	I535	1390	10/1	R. Educadora, Bragança
PR82)	J242	1390	10/1	R. Cultura, Maringá (IPDA)

MW	Call	kHz	kW	Station, location, h. of tr.
RJ32)	J473	1390	5/0.5	R. Sul Fluminense AM, Barra Mansa
RN32)	J599	1390	5/0.25	R. Farol, Touros
RR02)	O701	1390	10/5	R. Roraima, Caracaraí
RS122)	K209	1390	25	R. Esperança, Porto Alegre
SP153)	K570	1390	25	Campinas
SP2859	K594	1390	2.5	R. Anchieta, Itanhaém
AC06)	H200	1400	10/1	R. Dif. Acreana, Rio Branco
PI27)	I926	1400	1/0.25	R. Cantagalo, Jaicós
PR119)	J339	1400	10/1	R. Ágape, Balsa Nova
PR148)	J346	1400	2/0.45	R. Jornal São Miguel, São Miguel do Iguaçu
RJ33)	J462	1400	50/5	R. Rio de Janeiro, Rio de Janeiro
SC58)	J775	1400	5/0.35	R. Entre Rios, Palmitos
SP157)	K682	1400	5/0.25	R. Metrópole, São José do Rio Preto
TO08)	N660	1400	1	Radiodifusão Guaraí, Guaraí
BA37)	H467	1410	10/0.5	R. Planeta, São Gonçalo dos Campos
GO19)	H803	1410	30/0.85	R. JK AM, Sto Antônio do Descoberto
MS14)	I382	1410	5/1	Nova R. Clube, Corumbá
RN21)	J614	1410	5/0.5	R. Santa Cruz, Santa Cruz
RS137)	K246	1410	5/1	R. Garibaldi, Garibaldi
RS125)	K284	1410	1/0.25	R. Minuano, Rio Grande
RS126)	K294	1410	5	R. Santa Rosa, Santa Rosa
SP264	K683	1410	1/0.25	Jovem Pan News, Rio Claro
MG89)	L288	1420	5/1	R. Cultura, Sete Lagoas
MG90)	L313	1420	1/0.25	R. Montanhês Botelhos, Botelhos
PR88)	J269	1420	5/0.25	R. Cultura, Umuarama
RN12)	J609	1420	1/0.25	R. Farol, Alexandria
RS171)	K308	1420	3	R. Tapense, Tapes
SC59)	J754	1420	10/2.5	R. Guarujá, Florianópolis (RB)
SP159)	K597	1420	2.5/0.5	C.R.N., Itatiba
SP163)	K733	1420	1/0.25	R. Nova, São Manuel
PE32)	I826	1430	5/0.25	R. Independência, Goiana
PR42)	J200	1430	50/10	R. Evangelizar, Curitiba
RS167)	K366	1430	1/0.25	R. Guarita, Coronel Bicaco
RS198)	K379	1430	5	Estação Portão, Portão
SP164)	K666	1430	1/0.25	R. Serra Negra, Serra Negra
SP275)	K707	1430	25/0.25	R. Imaculada Conceição, São Roque
BA38)	H466	1440	50/1	R. Independência, Santo Amaro (IPDA)
RJ35)	J469	1440	20/5	R. Livre, Rio de Janeiro
RS168)	K221	1440	2.5/0.5	R. Ceres, Naõ Me Toque
RS130)	K328	1440	5/0.3	R. Excelsior, Gramado
SP253)	K568	1440	1/0.25	R. Eldorado Centro Norte Paulista, Cajuru
SP165)	K634	1440	10/0.25	R. Comercial, Presidente Prudente (RB)
SP218)	K752	1440	1/0.25	R. Azul, Americana (RB)
SP284)		1440	2.5/0.5	R. Clarim AM, Itai
BA73)	H531	1450	1/0.25	R. Ipirá, Ipirá – (IPDA)
CE34)	H601	1450	1/0.25	R. Difusora Cristal, Quixeramobim
CE35)	H623	1450	1/0.25	R. Pinto Martins, Camocim
MA32)	H900	1450	1/0.25	R. Boa Esperança, São João dos Patos
MA13)	H901	1450	1/0.25	R. Cultura, Pedreiras
MG94)	L312	1450	3/0.25	R. Diamante, Coromandel
PA33)	I559	1450	1/0.25	R. Juruá, São Felix do Xingu
PB29)	I699	1450	1/0.25	R. Certão, Patos
PE25)	I794	1450	1/0.25	R. Cultura, Palmares
PI21)	I908	1450	1/0.25	R. Cultura do Gurguéia, Bom Jesus
PR93)	J279	1450	1/0.25	R. Cabiúna, Bandeirantes
PR95)	J317	1450	1/0.25	R. Rainha de Altônia, Altônia
PR179)	J301	*1450	1/0.25	R. Dif. Ubiratanense, Ubiratã
RO12)	J674	1450	1/0.25	R. Vilhena, Vilhena
RR03)	O701	1450	1/0.25	R. Transamérca Hits, Alto Alegre
RS177)	K338	1450	1/0.25	R. Cultura, Arvorezinha
SC63)	J822	1450	10/0.25	Jovem Pan News AM, Criciúma
SP238)	K526	1450	2.5/0.25	R. Cultura, Ituverava
SP167)	K591	1450	50/5	R. Boa Nova, Guarulhos
SP168)	K657	1450	1/0.25	R. São Carlos, São Carlos do Pinhal
BA85)	H523	1460	1/0.25	R. Ferro Doido, Morro do Chapéu
CE53)	H595	1460	1/0.25	R. Ressurreição, Massapé
CE36)	H616	1460	1/0.25	R. Uirapuru, Morada Nova
MA33)	H917	1460	1/0.25	R. Vanguarda, Santa Luzia
MG95)	L201	*1460	1/0.25	R. Cul. do Porto Novo, Além Paraíba
MG131)	L363	1460	1/0.25	R. Gerais AM, Raul Soares
PI14)	I903	1460	1/0.25	R. Cultura, Amarante
PR97)	J228	1460	1/0.25	R. Central do Paraná, Ponta Grossa
PR101)	J308	1460	5/0.25	R. Ampere, Ampere
RN20)	J615	1460	10/0,25	R. Agreste, Santo Antônio
RS133)	K214	1460	1/0.25	R. Cultura, Bagé
RS175)	K373	1460	1/0.25	R. Campinas, Campinas do Sul
SC64)	J756	1460	2.5	R. Sentinela do Vale, Gaspar
SE12)	J932	1460	10/0.5	TransBRasil AM, Estância
SP242)	K548	1460	5/0.5	R. Clube Ararense, Araras
TO02)	H774	1460	1/0.25	R. Independência do Tocantins, Paraíso do Tocantins
BA86)	H509	1470	0.25	R. Morro Verde, Mairi
CE64)	H665	1470	1/0.25	R. Guanancés de Itapajé, Itapajé:
GO37)	H779	1470	1/0.25	R. Cidade, Goiás
MA34)	H908	1470	1/0.25	R. Paranoá, Presidente Dutra
MA39)	H901	1470	1/0.25	R. Urbano Santos,Urbano Santos
MA43)		1470	1	R. Cidade, Turiaçu
MG96)	L247	1470	1/0,25	R. Dif., Ituiutaba
MS29)	I413	1470	1/0.25	R. Alvorada, Itaporã
PI15)	I900	1470	1/0.25	R. Difusora Vale do Uruçuí, Uruçuí
PI24)	I913	1470	1/0.25	R. Ingazeira, Paulistana
PR173)	ZYJ374	1470	3/0.25	R. Tradição, Rio Branco de Sul
RJ08)	J476	1470	1/0.25	R. Absoluta, Campos dos Goytacazes
RJ38)	J481	1470	1/0.25	R. Barra do Pirai, Barra do Piraí
RN23)	J616	1470	1/0.25	R. Rural de Parelhas, Parelhas
RO05)	J676	1470	1/0.25	R. Rondônia, Cacoal
SC66)	J798	1470	3/0.25	R. Nova Líder, Herval d'Oeste
SP173)	K599	1470	5/0.25	R. Mensagem, Jacareí
SP174)	K632	1470	1/0.25	R. Primavera, Porto Ferreira
SP175)	K712	1470	1/0.25	R. Jornal, Indaiatuba
SP243)	K771	1470	1/0.25	R. Bastos AM, Bastos
BA75)	H524	1480	1/0.25	R. Santana, Santana
CE74)	H671	1480	1/0.25	R. Princesa do Norte, Morrinhos
MA14)	H897	1480	10	R. Itapecuru, Colinas
MG99)	L265	1480	5/0.25	R. Difusora, Nanuque
PR174)	J370	1480	1/0.25	R. Pérola, Pérola d'Oeste
RJ55)	J485	1480	10/0.5	R. Popular, Duque de Caxias
RO15)	J681	1480	1/0.25	R. Rondônia, Pimenta Bueno
SC67)	J731	1480	1/0.25	R. Arca da Aliança, Joinville (RA)
SP177)	K551	1480	1/0.25	R. Atibaia, Atibaia
SP255)	K767	1480	0.5	R. Boituva, Boituva
TO06)	H795	1480	1/0.25	R. Cultura, Miracema do Tocantins
AL09)	H246	1490	5/1	Em. Rio São Francisco, Penedo
BA87)	H512	1490	0.25	R. Planalto d'Oeste, Correntina
MG162)	L231	1490	0.25	R. Onda Viva, Araguari
MG163)	L274	*1490	1/0.25	R. Paraisópolis, Paraisópolis
MG165)	L353	1490	1/0.25	R. Pirapetinga, Pirapetinga
PR108)	J210	1490	1/0.25	R. Cornélio, Cornélio Procópio
RS138)	K208	1490	25/0.25	R. Assisense, São Francisco de Assis
RS140)	K309	1490	3/0.25	R. Taquara, Taquara
SC70)	J791	1490	2.5/0.25	R. Cultura, Xaxim
SP180)	K530	1490	1/0.25	R. Difusora, Olímpia (RB)
SP182)	K583	1490	1/0.25	R. Educadora, Fernandópolis
SP244)	K680	1490	1/0.25	R. Cult., Vargem Grande do Sul
SP183)	K764	1490	25/0.5	R. Imaculada Conceição, Mauá
BA49)	H487	1500	0.5	R. Jacuípe, Riachão do Jacuípe
MG140)	L340	1500	1/0.25	R. Aparecida do Sul, Ilicínea
PI46)	I919	1500	1/0.25	R. Voz do Longa, Esperantina
RS139)	K225	1500	5/0.25	R. Liberdade, Canguçu
SP184)	K549	1500	2.5/0.25	R. Cidade das Arvores, Araras
SP186)	K706	1500	1/0.25	R. Vale do Rio Grande, Miguelópolis
SP211)	K773	1500	1/0.25	R. Cumbica, Guarulhos
BA52)	H493	1510	5/0.5	R. Dif. do Descobrimento, Porto Seguro
CE40)	H608	1510	1/0.25	R. Planalto, São Benedito
CE84)	H630	1510	0.25	R. Trapiá, Pedra Branca
PA01)	I544	‡1510	10/0.25	R. Oriente de Redenção, Redenção
PI17)	I896	‡1510	1/0.25	R. Progresso, Corrente
PI49)	I936	1510	1/0.25	R. Nordeste, Picos
RJ43)	J492	1510	1/0.25	R. Teresópolis, Teresópolis
RN15)	J602	1510	1/0.25	R. Centenário, Caraúbas
RO24)		1510	0.25	R. Central, Jaru
SP188)	K654	1510	10/1	R. Cacique, Santos
SP189)	K665	1510	1/0.25	R. Cl. Regional, São Manuel (RB)
SP256)	K770	1510	0.5/0.25	R. Vale - Aleluia Musica, Salto
SP230)	K...	1510	1/0.25	R. Rural, Rinópolis
SP269)	K719	1510	1/0.25	R. Athenas Paulista, Jaboticabal
CE75)	H635	1520	1/0.25	R. Regional, Ipu
CE83)	H653	1520	1/0.25	R. Cachoeira, Solonópole
GO53)	H806	1520	1/0.25	R. Nova RCB, Campos Belos
MA15)	H899	1520	1/0.25	R. Mirante, Pindaré-Mirim
MA35)	H928	1520	1/0.25	R. Mirante AM, Chapadinha
PE28)	I801	1520	1/0.25	R. Surubim, Surubim
PR118)	J292	1520	1/0.25	R. Nova Cultura, Palotina
RJ44)	J491	1520	10/0.5	R. Continental, São João do Meriti
SE13)	J931	1520	10/0.5	R. Ilha AM, Tobias Barreto
SP191)	K614	1520	10/1	R. da Cidade, Mogi das Cruzes

MW	Call	kHz	kW	Station, location, h. of tr.
SP192)	K627	1520	1/0.25	Pinhal R. Cl., Espírito Sto. do Pinhal
SP225)	K760	1520	1/0.25	R. Catedral, Sorocaba
SP286)	K...	1520	0.25	R. Legal, Viradouro
TO07)	H797	1520	1/0.25	R. Cristal, Cristalândia
CE76)	H666	1530	1/0.25	R. Tres Fronteiras, Campos Sales: 0800-2300
MG175)	L262	1530	0.25	R. Progresso, Monte Santo de Minas
MG110)	L280	1530	1/0.25	R. Clube, Pouso Alegre
RS143)	K235	1530	1/0.25	R. Sulina, Dom Pedrito
RS144)	K300	1530	5/0.25	R. Progresso, São Leopoldo
SC77)	J761	1530	1/0.25	R. Dif., Itajaí
SC79)	J796	1530	2.5	R. Porto Feliz, Mondaí
SP231)	K755	1530	1/0.25	R. Universal, Teodoro Sampaio
BA89)	H...	1540	0.25	R. Sociedade, Itiruçu
MA36)	H921	1540	1/0.25	R. Santa Maura, Lago da Pedra
MG111)	L217	1540	1/0.25	Super Difusora Bomdespachense, Bom Despacho
PA14)	I545	1540	1/0.25	R. Boa Vista, São Sebastião da Boa Vista
RJ54)	J508	1540	1/0.25	R. Clube, Paraíba do Sul
RN30)	J611	‡1540	1/0,25	R. Baixa Verde, João Câmara
RS157)	K282	1540	1/0.25	R. Quaraí, Quaraí
SC80)	J803	1540	5/0.25	R. Capinzal, Capinzal
SP245)	K514	1540	1/0.25	R. Cultura, Leme (RB)
SP196)	K564	1540	2/0.5	Jovem Pan News, Botucatu
SP197)	K723	1540	50/1	R. Nova Difusora, Usasco
SP288)		1540		R. Novo Milenio, Ribeirão Preto (IPDA)
BA80)	H518	1550	5/0.25	R. Independencia do São Francisco, Juazeiro
MA37)	H926	1550	10/1	Sist. Janaina de Rdif, Vargem Grande
MG114)	L211	1550	1/0.25	R. Cultura, Monte Carmelo
MG169)	L222	1550	1/0.25	R. Difusora, Carmo do Rio Claro
PA34)	I550	1550	1/0.25	R. Cabano, Maracanã
PB32)	I700	1550	10/0.25	R. Jardim da Borborema, Areia
RJ46)	J479	1550	1/0.25	R. Imperial, Petrópolis
RN19)	J606	1550	1/0.25	R. Ivipanin, Areia Branca (RPC)
RS162)	K377	1550	1/0.25	R. Cidade AM, Capão do Leão
RS159)	K375	1550	1/0.25	R. Soledad, Soledade
SP198)	K501	1550	1/0.25	R. Clube, Itararé
SP200)	K572	1550	1/0.25	R. Cacique, Capivari
SP201)	K590	1550	10/1	R. Guarujá AM, Guarujá
CE43)	H622	1560	1/0.25	R. Difusora Vale de Curu, Pentecoste
MA18)	H903	1560	1/0.25	R. Agua Branca, Vitorino Freire
MG117)	L256	1560	1/0.25	R. Jornal, Leopoldina
MT56)	I...	1560	1/0.25	R. Paranaita, Paranaita
PR161)	J361	1560	0.25	R. Cultura Serpin, Ribeirão do Pinhal
PR184)		1560	10/0.25	R. Barigui, Almirante Tamandaré
PR162)	J364	1560	1/0.25	R. Clube, Mallet
RJ47)	J501	1560	5/0.25	R. Grande Rio, Itaguaí
RS158)	K310	1560	2.5/0.25	R. Açoriana, Taquari
SP261)	K593	1560	1/0.25	R. Show, Igarapava
SP249)	K725	‡1560	0.25	R. Cidade, Pedreira
CE44)	H621	1570	1/0.25	R. Sertão Central,Senador Pompeu
MA22)	H907	1570	10/0.5	R. Cultura do Rio Jordão, Coroatá
MG146)	L242	1570	0.25	R. Unifei, Itajubá
PR137)	J341	1570	1/0.25	R. Clube, Nova Aurora
RJ48)	J493	1570	1/0.25	R. Cultura, Valença
RS147)	K358	1570	5/0.25	R. Metrópole, Gravataí
SC107)	J832	1570	1/0.25	R. Tanagrá, Tangará
SP204)	K552	*1570	1/0.25	R. Avaré, Avaré
SP205)	K605	1570	1/0.25	R. Junqueirópolis, Junqueirópolis
SP262)	K648	1570	1/0.25	R. Zequinha de Abreu, Santa Rita do Passa Quatro
SP206)	K651	1570	10/0.25	R. ABC, Santo André
SP207)	K667	1570	1/0.25	R. Socorro, Socorro
TO10)	N665	1570	1/0.25	R. Nossa R., Gurupi
BA53)	H497	1580	2.5/0.25	R. Barra de Mendes, Barra do Mendes
BA62)	H502	1580	1/0.25	R. Atalaia, Canavieiras
MG119)	L210	1580	1/0.25	R. Liberdade, Itapecirica
MG121)	L290	1580	1/0.25	R. Cultura, Santos Dumont
MG122)	L329	1580	1/0.25	R. Educadora, Espinosa
MG133)	L335	1580	1/0.25	R. Nova Guaranésia, Guaranésia
MS43)	N611	1580	1/0.25	R. Difusora, Ivinhema
PI18)	I898	1580	1/0.25	R. Santa Clara, Floriano
PR164)	J342	1580	2.5/0.25	R. São João do Sudoeste, São João
RJ51)	J487	1580	1/0.5	R. Popular Fluminense, Conceição de Macabu
RJ52)	J506	1580	5/0.25	R. Resende AM, Resende
RJ58)	J505	1580	0.25	R. Geração 2000, Teresópolis
RN24)	J613	1580	1/0.25	R. Novos Tempos, Ceará Mirim
RS148)	K237	1580	9/0.25	R. Encantado AM, Encantado
SP251)	K504	1580	1/0.25	R. Difusora, Amparo
SP209)	K743	1580	0.25	R. São João Batista, Itaporanga
SP289)		1580	0.25	R. Grande Vale, Paraibuna
BA55)	H...	1590	0.3	R. Vale do Jiquiriçá, Jiquiriça
CE100)	H...	1590	1	R. Veneza, Eusébio
MG171)	L368	1590	1/0.25	R. Cidade Carinho, Ubá
MG134)	L369	1590	10/1	R. Guaicuí, Várzea da Palma
MG193)	N207	1590	0,25	Lambari
MS26)	I403	1590	1/0.25	R. Independência, Eldorado
PB34)	I703	1590	1/0.25	R. Correio do Vale, Itaporanga
PE41)	ZYI802	1590	1	R. Restauração, Bezerros
PR129)	J290	1590	1/0.25	R. Cultura, Andirá
SC101)	J823	1590	10/0.5	R. Clube, Joinville
SP254)	K774	1590	10/0.5	R. Japi, Cabreúva
SP263)	K779	1600	100/20	R. Nove de Julho, São Paulo (RA)

SW	Call	kHz	kW	Station, location, h. of tr.
SP49)	G855	3365	1	R. Cultura, Araraquara
AM02)	F276	3375	3.5	R. Municipal, São Gabriel da Cachoeira: 0700-1200; 2200-0200
MG55)	G207	4775	1	R. Congonhas, Congonhas: 0800-0100
SP287)	G869	4845	1	R. Meteorologia Paulista, Ibitinga: (rel. R. Ternura FM)
PR33)	G641	4865	5	R. Alvorada, Londrina
RR01)	G810	4875	10	R. Roraima, Boa Vista: 0800-0300
AC06)	F201	4885	5	R. Dif. Acreana, Rio Branco: 0900-0400
PA03)	G362	4885	10	R. Clube do Pará, Belém: 24h
MS32)	R200	4895	5	R. Novo Tempo, Campo Grande
RJ03)	G683	4905	5	R. Relógio Federal, São Gonçalo
GO27)	F691	4915	10	R. Daqui, Goiânia
AM10)	F282	4925	5	R. Educação Rural, Tefé: 1000-1600, 2000-0200
GO30)	F690	4985	10	R. Brasil Central, Goiânia
AM09)	F272	†5035	5	R. Educação Rural, Coari
SP52)	G853	5035	10	R. Aparecida, Aparecida
SC86)		5940	10	R. Voz Missionária, Camboriú
MG06)	E523	‡5970	10	R. Itatiaia, Belo Horizonte
MG35)	E521	6010	5	R. Inconfidência, Belo Horizonte
PR42)	E275	6040	7.5	R. Evangelizar, Curitiba
PR15)	E726	6080	10	R. Marumby, Curitiba
PR138)	F728	6105	10	R. Cultura Filadélfia, Foz do Iguaçu
SP52)	E954	6135	10	R. Aparecida, Aparecida (RA)
AM11)	E245	6160	7.5	R. Rio Mar, Manaus
RS104)	E854	6160	1	Super Rede Boa Vontade, Porto Alegre
DF06)	E365	6180	250	R. Nal. da Amazônia, Brasília (EBC)
RS104)	E855	9550	10	Super Rede Boa Vontade, Porto Alegre
SP52)	E954	9630	10	R. Aparecida, Aparecida(RA)
SC86)	E890	9665	10	R. Voz Missionária, Camboriú
SP80)	E971	9675	10	R. Canção Nova, Cachoeira Paulista
AM11)	E245	9695	7.5	R. Rio Mar, Manaus
PR42)	E725	9725	7.5	R. Evangelizar, Curitiba
SP263)	E971	9820	10	R. Nove de Julho, São Paulo
DF06)	E365	11780	250	R. Nal. da Amazônia, Brasília (EBC)
GO30)	E440	11815	7.5	R. Brasil Central, Goiânia
SP52)	E954	11855	10	R. Aparecida, Aparecida
RS104)	E856	11895	10	Super Rede Boa Vontade, Porto Alegre
RS09)	E851	11915	10	R. Gaucha, Porto Alegre
PR42)	E725	11935	7.5	R. Evangelizar, Curitiba
MG35)	E521	15190	5	R. Inconfidência, Belo Horizonte

RADIO NETWORKS

There are several radio networks. Below are listed just some of them. The affiliated outlets are often subject to alteration.

CBN - CENTRAL BRASILEIRA DE NOTICIAS: W: radioclick.globo.com/cbn

EBC - EMPRESA BRASIL DE COMUNICAÇÃO: W: ebc.com.br/

IPDA - IGREJA PENTECOSTAL DEUS È AMOR: W: ipda.com.br

IURD - IGREJA UNIVERSAL DO REINO DE DEUS: W: igrejauniversal.org.br

Rede JOVEM PAN ✉ Av. Paulista 807, 24° andar, 01311-915 São Paulo, SP **W:** jovempan.uol.com.br

RB - RADIO BANDEIRANTES: W: radiobandeirantes com.br

RA – Rede Aparecida – a12.com.radio

REDE BOA VONTADE - LBV ✉ Legião da Boa Vontade, Rua Doraci 90, Bairro Bom Retiro, 01134-020 São Paulo, SP **W:** boavontade.com**REDE BOAS NOVAS – RBN: W:** rbn.org.br

REDE CANÇÃO NOVA DE RÁDIO ✉ Rua João Paulo II s/, Alto da Bela Vista, 12630-000 Cachoeira Paulista, SP **W:** cancaonova.com **E:**

radio@cancaonova.com
REDE CATÓLICA DE RÁDIO – RCR: ✉ União de Radiodifusão Católica, Rua Vergueiro 3086, Conj. 91, Vila Mariana, 04102-001 São Paulo, SP **W:** rcrunda.com.br **E:** rcr@rcrunda.com.br
REDE GAÚCHA SAT ✉ Av. Erico Veríssimo 400, Edificio Maurício Sirotsky Sobrinho, 90169-900 Porto Alegre, RS **W:** rbs.clicrbs.com.br
REDE ESPERANCA: W: redeesperança.com
REDE ITATIAIA: W: itatiaia.com.br/rede
REDE MILICIA SAT: W: milicia.org.br
REDE MINERIA DE RADIO; W: redemineiraderadio.com.br
REDE NOVO TEMPO: W: novotempo.org.br
REDE PAULUS SAT: ✉ Rua Doutor Pinto Ferraz 183, Vila Mariana, 04117-900 São Paulo, SP **W:** radioamericasp.com.br/paulussat.htm
REDE POTGUAR DE COMUNICAÇÃO (RPC): W: redepotiguar.com
REDE SUL DE RÁDIO: W: saofrancisco.am.br
REDE TRANSAMÉRICA DE RÁDIO: W: transanet.uol.com.br
SISTEMA GUAÍBA SAT: ✉ Rua Caldas Jr. 219, 2° andar, 90019-900 Porto Alegre, RS **W:** guaiba.com.br
REDE SOMZOOM SAT: ✉ Av. Herois do Acre 590, Passaré, 60743-760 Fortaleza, CE **W:** somzoom.com.br **E:** somzoomsat@somzoom.com.br

AC00) ACRE
AC01) Rua de Alagoas, 270, Colégio, 69980-000 Cruzeiro do Sul ☎68 3322 4637 **W:** radioetvintegracao.com.br **E:** radiointegracao@hotmail.com - **FM:** 99.9MHz – **AC03)** Rua Coronel Brandão, 1665, Bairro Aeroporto, 69930-000 Xapuri ☎68 3542 2830 **E:** raimari.cardoso@gmail.com – **AC05)** Rua Epaminondas Jacome, 3121, Base, 69900-280 Rio Branco ☎68 3224 0505 – **AC06)** Rua Benjamin Constant 1232, 69900-161 Rio Branco ☎68 3223 9696 **W:** difusora.ac.gov.br **E:** difusoraacreana@gmail.com – **AC11)** Rua Maria Glória Farias, 1 qd 3 c 4, Cannisio Brasil, 69940-000 Sena Madureira ☎68 3612 3733 **E:** rivaldosevero@hotmail.com - **FM:** 105.9MHz – **AC12)** Rua Nilo Freire de Albuquerqe, s/n, Novo, 69970-000 Tarauacá ☎68 3462 1416 **E:** railtonrodrigues@ac.gov.br – **AC15)** Travasse Posto, 168, Cidade Novo, 69960-000 Feijo ☎68 3463 3310 **E:** jocivaldogomes@bol.com.br
AL00) ALAGOAS
AL02) Av Siqueira 494, Prado, 57010-000 Maceió ☎82 3223 1710 **W:** Facebook: Rádio-Jornal **E:** comercial@jornalam710.com.br – **AL04)** Av Fernandes Lima,1047, Farol, 57050-000 Maceió ☎82 3315 9927 **W:** izp.al.gov.br **E:** ascom@izp.al.gov.ar – **AL05)** Rua Miguel Palmeira 1513, 7° andar, Farol, 57055-330 Maceió ☎82 9980 88516 **W:** maceioam1020.com.br **E:** contato@maceioam1020.com.br – **AL06)** Praça Senador Eneas Araújo 61, 57500-000 Santana do Ipanema **W:** radiocorreiodosertao.com.br – **AL09)** Cj São José s/n, gdC, Dom Constantino, 57200-000 Penedo ☎82 3551 2215 – **AL10)** Loteamento Cidade Imperia,l 4 lt 3, Pedras, 57160-000 Taperagua ☎82 3263 7298 **W:** jovempanam1020.com.br/afiliadas.html – **AL11)** Rua Miguel Palmeira, 1513 7° andar, Farol, 57055-330 Maceió **W:** jovempanam1020.com.br/afiliadas.html – **AL12)** Praça Manoel Monteiro 72, 57480-000 Delmiro Gouveia ☎82 3641 2007 📠82 3641 4047 **W:** radiodelmiro.com.br **E:** radiodelmiro@gclnet.com.br - **FM:** 89.9MHz – **AL13)** BR-104 Km 36, Roberto Correia de Arajuó, 57800-000 União dos Palmares – **AL14)** Rua Pedro Oliverio Rocha 784, 3 AND SL 01, Farol, 57075-560 Maceió ☎82 4009 0009 **W:** radiocorreio.com.br - **FM:** 91.7 MHz – **AL15)** Rua Aristeu de Andrade, 355, Farol, 57021-050 Maceio ☎82 3624 1157
AM00) AMAZONAS
AM02) Av Alvaro Maia s/n, 69750-000 São Gabriel da Cachoeira (📠97 3471 1109 – **AM03)** Rua Júlio de Oliveira, 1323, São Pedro, 69800-000 Humaitá (📠97 3373 3946 **W:** radiovrm.com **E:** radiovrm@bol.com.br – **AM04)** A/C Prefeitura Municipal de Tabatinga (✉C.P 31), 69640-000 Tabatinga (📠97 3412 2829 **W:** radios.ebc.com.br/nacionalaltosolimo **E:** altossolimoes@ebc.com.br - **FM:** 96.1 MHz – **AM05)** Rua Solimões 809, 69100-000 Itacoatiara (📠92 3521 1635 **W:** facebook.com/cbnitacoatiara **E:** radiodifusora_ita@hotmail.com - **FM:** 94.5MHz – **AM07)** Av Major Santana 2502, 69280-000 Manicoré – **AM08)** Rua Guaranópolis 533, 69190-000 Maués.☎92 3542 1254 **E:** radioguaranopolis@hotmail.com – **AM09)** Praça São Sebastião 263, 69460-000 Coari ☎97 3561 2383 **W:** radiocoariamot.blogspot.no **E:** radiocoari@hotmail.com – **AM10)**Rua Benjamin Constant 283, 69470-000 Tefe ☎97 3343-3017 **W:**radioruraltefe.com.br **E:** radioruralam1270@hotmail.com – **FM:** 93.9 MHz – **AM11)** Rua José Clemente, 500, Centro, 69010-070 Manaus ☎92 9142-5676 **W:** radioriomarfm.com.br **E:** contato@radioriomarfm.com.br - **FM:** 103.5 MHz – **AM12)** Rua Governador Leopoldo Neves (✉ C.P. 004)503, 69151-460 Parintins ☎92 3533 2002 **W:** alvoradaparintins.com.br **E:**radioalvoradapin@gmail.com - **FM:** 100.1MHz – **AM18)** Rodovia Manoel Urbano, km 2, 69405-000 Iranduba **W:** boavontade.com/radio – **AM24)** Av Eduardo Ribeiro 520, 2 andar sala 201/215, 69010-690 Manaus ☎92 3633 2345
AP00) AMAPÁ
AP01) Av. Padre Júlio Maria Lombeard, 1614, Santa Rita, 68901-283 Macapá ☎96 3312 1000 **W:** difusora.ap.gov.br **E:** rdm@rdm.ap.gov.br – **AP02)** Rua Eliezer Levy 684, 68901-016 Macapá ☎96 3222 3111 **W:**jovempan.com.br/afiliada/macapa – **AP04)** Av. Rio Branco 3748, Fonte Nova, 68925-000 Santana ☎96 3281 5649 **W:** radioporto.xpg.com.br – **AP05)** Rua Hildemar Maia 1000, 68940-000 Mazagão ☎96 3271 1227 **W:** facebook.com/radionova.mazagao
BA00) BAHIA
BA02) Av. Itajuipe, 1789, Santo Antonio, 45602-380 Itabuna. ☎73 3211 2385 **W:** radiojornaldeitabuna.com.br **E:** radiojornaldeitabuna@hotmail.com – **BA04)** Rua Lord Cochrane, 66, Barra, 40140-070 Salvador ☎71 3264 1244 **W:** sistemacruzeiro.com.br **E.** cruzeiro@veloxmail.com.br – **BA05)** Rua Dom Pedro II, 306 2° andar, Primavera, 47804-510 Barreiras ☎77 3611 3570 **W:** radiovale.com.br **E:** radiovale@radiovale.com.br – **BA06)** R Jorge Antonio Menezes Silva, 220, Dendezeiros, 45400-000 Valença ☎75 3641 0660 **W:** radioclubedevalenca.com.br – **BA07)** Alamaeda Rui Barbosa 42, 45700-000 Itapetinga ☎77 3261 1010 **W:** novajornal.net – **BA11)** Rua Jardim Federacão, 81, 40231-0900 Salvador ☎71 3486 3201 **W:** radiosociedadeam.com.br **E:** comercial@radiosociedadeam.com.br **FM:** 102.5 MHz – **BA12)** Av. Cinquenteário 1429, 45600-006 Itabuna ☎73 3215 2271 **W:** difusorabahia.com.br – **BA14)** Praça Luiz Nogueira 385, 48700-000 Serrinha **W:** grupoolmos.com.br **E:** grupolomes@grupolomes.com.br– **BA15)** Rua Antonio Neto 27, 46810-000 Utinga ☎75 3337 1011 **W:** radiocultura820.com.br **E:** comercial@radiocultura820.com.br – **BA16)** Fundação Dom Avelar Brandão, Rua Martin Afonso de Souza, 270, Garcia, 40100-050 Salvador ☎71 3114 5088 **W:** am840.com.br **E:** excelsiorcomercial@gmail.com – **BA17)** Av Visconde do Rio Branco 68, 48970-000 Senhor do Bonfim ☎74 3541 4617 **W:** radiocaraiba.com.br **E:** caraiba@radiocaraiba.com.br – **BA18)** Travessa da Catedral s/n, 45600-000 Itabuna ☎73 3215 0909 – **BA19)** Rua Wercelêncio da Mota 81, 48730-000 Conceição do Coité (📠75 3262 1010 **W:** radiosisal.com **E:** comercial@radiosisal.com – **BA22)** Rua Gabriel Soares, 23, Ladeira dos Aflitos, 40060-040 Salvador – **BA23)** Praça Barão do Rio Branco 42, 45100-000 Vitória da Conquista **W:** radioclubeconquista.com.br – **BA24)** Av Maria Quitéria, 223, Serraria Brasil, 44062-630 Feira de Santana ☎75 3623 8927 📠75 3623 2851 **W:** radiosubaeam.com.br - **FM:** 95.3MHz Nordeste FM – **BA25)** Rua José Bonifacio, 17 2° andar , 45700-000 Itapetinga (📠77 3261 2610 **W:** radiofascinacao.com.br **E:** comercial@radiofascinacao.com.br – **BA26)** Rua Marquês de Paranagua, 259 - Centro 45660-000 ☎73 3231 3612 **W:** santacruzam.com.br – **BA27)** Av. Dq de Caxias, 491 S 301(C.P 29), 45820-000 Eunápolis ☎73 3281 5370 – **BA28)** Rua Cel. Aprigio Duarte N 05, 48903-410 Juazeiro ☎76 3611 7435 **W:** radiojuazeiro.com.br **E:** radiojuazeiro@gmail.com br – **BA29)** Rua Senador Pedro Lago 54, 44700-000 Jacobina ☎74 3621 3636 **W:** radiocluberiodooruro.com.br **E:** radio@radiocluberiodoouro.com.br – **BA32)** Rua Conde Pereire Carneiro, 226 -Pernambúes, 41100-010 Salvador ☎71 3460 8500 **W:** radiometropole.com.br - **FM:** 101.3MHz – **BA33)** Av. Itabuna , 45653-160 Ilhéus ☎73 3231 5462 **W:** radionovabahianaam1310.blogspot.com.br **E:** clinton.alves@hotmail.com – **BA34)** Praça Luiz Nogueira 99 1° andar, 48700-000 Serrinha **W:** continentalam.com.br – **BA35)** Rua São Francisco 159-163A, 48601-070 Paulo Afonso ☎75 3281 5588 **W:** redecultura.com.br **E:** redecultura@redecultura.com.br - **FM:** 92.7MHz – **BA37)** Av Getúlio Vargas 394 44330-000 São Gonçalo dos Campos ☎77 3481 6161 **W:**planeta1410.com.br – **BA38)** Av Barros Reis 295, 40353-100 Salvador ☎71 3383 5283 **W:** radioindependenciabahia.com.br – **BA44)** Av Ascendino Melo 297, 267, Sis 106/107, Shopping Itatiaia, Recreio, 45020-908 Vitória da Conquista ☎77 3472 0760 **W:** clubenet.com.br **E:** radiocidade@clubenet.com.br – **BA45)** Tv Virgillo Gonzalves Pereira 196, 44340-000 Muritiba ☎73 3424 2048 – **BA46)** Av Porto Seguro, 718 1° andar, 45820-006 Eunápolis. ☎73 3281 5594 **W:** facebook.com/radio21news – **BA49)** Rua Padre Argemiro Guimarães 32, 44640-000 Riachão do Jacuípe ☎75 3264 2189 **W:** radiojacuipe.com.br – **BA52)** Rua Saldanha Marinho, 30 Sala 23/24, Mesmo, 45810-000 Porto Seguro ☎73 3288 2136 **E:** radioguadalupeam@yahoo.com.br – **BA53)** Rua Alvaro Campos 83, 44990-000 Barra do Mendes **W:** facebook.com: Radio Barra do Mendes – **BA55)** Rua Coronel Vicente s/n, 45470-000 Jiquiriça – **BA57)** Rua Gamboa de Cima 18, Campo Grande, 40060-008 Salvador ☎71 3337 3216 **W:** novotemposalvador.com.br – **BA58)** Av Regis Pacheco 534, 45100-

000 Vitória da Conquista **W:** blog.cancaonova.com/conquista **E:** radioconquista@cancaonova.com – **BA59)** Rua Lauro de Freitas, 1176, Alto da Bela Vista, 45550-000 Ubatã ☎73 3245 1233 **W:** radiopovo.com.br **E:** admpovoubata@gmail.com – **BA62)** Rua Virgilio Brasil, 175, Cidade Nova, 45860-000 Canavieiras ☎73 9823 0453 **W:** atalaiaamba.webnode.pt **E:** radioatalaia_am@hotmail.com – **BA64)** Rua Farias Goes 164, 48330-000 Rio Real **W:** radiodifusora600.com.br – **BA65)** Rua Manoel Conselho Campos 135, 48500-000 Euclides da Cunha ☎75 3271 1652 – **BA67)** Rua Jose de Anchita, 128 2º andar, 45836-000 Itamaraju. ☎73 3294-5455 **W:** radioextremosulam.com.br **E:** radioam830@gmail.com – **BA70)** Terreiro de Jesus 13 - Centro Histórico, Pelourinho, 40025-010 Salvador ☎71 3421 6300 📠71 3234 9324 **W:** radio.boavontade.com **E:** radiocristal@uol.com.br – **BA72)** Rua 2 de Julho s/n, 45160-000 Belo Campo (📠77 3437 2122 – **BA73)** Praça São José 279, 44600-000 Ipirá – **BA75)** Rua Teixeira de Freitas s/n, 47700-000 Santana – **BA79)** Av Luis Eduardo Magalhães, s/n - Centro, 46990-000 Souto Soares ☎75 3339 2328 **W:** radiojornal1120.com.br **E:** radiojornal@bol.com.br – **BA80)** Rua Jvencio Alves, 01, 1 andar - Centro, 48930-480 Juazeiro – **BA81)** Largo do Campo Grande, 14-1º Pavimento, Campao Grande, 40110-005 Salvador ☎71 3565-2452 – **BA82)** Rua Élcio Cardoso de Matos s/n, 48800-000 Monte Santo ☎75 3275 1212 – **BA83)** Praça Simões Filho 54, 45450-000 Gandu – **BA84)** Praça Sta Terezinha, 3, Piranga, 48900-130 Juazeiro ☎74 3611 5533 **W:** radiocidadeam870.com.br **E:** cidade870@yahoo.com.br – **BA85)** Rua Coronel Dias Coelho 240, 44850-000 Morro do Chapéu – **BA86)** Travessa Juracy Magalhães 4, 2° andar, 44630-000 Mairi – **BA87)** Praça Raimundo Sales, 94 - Centro, 1° andar, 47650-000 Correntina ☎77 3488 2827 **W:** radioplanaltodooeste.com.br **E:** radioplanaltoba@yahoo.com.br – **BA96)** Rua Juana Angélica, 125, Conquista, 45650-023 Ilhéus ☎73 3634 7020 **W:** radioculturadeilheus.com.br **E:** radiocultura@radioculturadeilheus.com.br - **FM:** 97.9 MHz – **BA98)** Rua Padroeira de Brasil 100, 48890-970 Valente ☎71 8727 8216 **W:** radioestreladovale.com **E:** radioestreladoval@hotmail,com – **BA100)** Travessa Virigilio Pereira 196, 44340 Muritiba **W:** radiovoxbahia.com

CE00) CEARÁ

CE01) Rua Romeu Martins - Centro S/N, Ed 29 de Julho, 62700-000 Canindé ☎85 3343 2233 **W:** radiojornal540.com **E:** radiojornal540@hotmail.com – **CE02)** Rua Monsenhor Lima, 227, Lagoa Seca, 63050-020 Juazeiro do Norte ☎88 3512 5557 **W:** radioverdevale570.com.br **E:** contato@radioverdevale570.com.br – **CE03)** Av Monsenhor Tabosa, 2514 - Centro, 62500-000 Itapipoca ☎88 3631 2173 **W:** radiouirapurudeitapipoca.com.br **E:** ribamar.p@bol.com.br – **CE05)** Av.Rui Barbosa, 1901, Aldeota, 60115-221 Fortaleza ☎88 3264 5500 **W:** 620am.com.br – **CE08)** Shalom da Paz, Rua Maria Tomásia, 72, Aldeota, 60150-170 Fortaleza ☎85 3261 4444 **W:** shalom690.com**E:** benfeitordapaz@comshalom.org **FM:** 89.1 MHz – **CE10)** Rua Uirapuru, 500, Jardim Cearence, 60711-790 Fortaleza ☎88 3298 2655 Facebook: Rádio Uirapuru de Fortaleza – **CE13)** Av. Desembargador Moreira, 2430, Dionísio Torres, 60170-002 Fortaleza ☎85 3261 2323 **W:** verdinha.com.br **E:** radios@verdesmares.com.br – **CE16)** Av Desembargador Moreira, 2565, Dionísio Torres, 60170-002 Fortaleza ☎85 3261 7000 **W:**grupocidade.com.br/cidadeam/ **E:** amcidade@grupocidadece.com.br – **CE17)** Rua Floriano Peixoto 358, 63500-000 Iguatu **W:** radioliberdadeam.com – **CE19)** Praça Quirino Rodrigues 76/3, 62011-260 Sobral ☎88 3611 2496 📠88 3611 1550 **W:** radioeducadora950.com.br **E:** radioeducadora@gmail.com – **CE20)** Rua Tabelião Enéas 495 2º Andar, (✉ C.P 87, 63901-970) 63900-000 Quixadá ☎88 3414 5970 📠88 3412 0554 **W:** sistemamonolitos.com.br/radiomonolitosam **E:** contato@sistemamonolitos.com.br - **FM:** 105.9 MHz – **CE21)** Av. Aguanambi, 282, José Bonifácio, 60060-200 Fortaleza ☎85 3066 4000 **W:** radios.opovo.com.br/opovocbn - **FM:** 95.5 MHz CBN – **CE24)** Av Francisco R Oliveira 643, Alto Bela Vista, 62900-000 Russas ☎88 3411 0320 **W:** radioprogresso1140.com.br – – **CE26)** Rua Tiburcio Frota 905, 60130-301 Fortaleza.☎85 3121 1200 **W:** radioclube1200.com.br **E:** comercial@radioclube1200.com.br – **CE27)** Rua Coronel Zezé 1158, 63700-000 Crateús – **CE29)** Av General Osóri Paiva, 7235, Canindezinho, 60731-335 Fortaleza ☎ 85 3498 4796 **W:** ipda.com.br/nova/vozlibertacao/nr/iracema.html – **CE34)** Rua Monsenhor Salviano Pinto 71, 63800-000 Quixeramobim ☎88 3441 1516 **W:** difusoracristal.com.br **E:** contato@difusoracristal.com.br – **CE35)** Praça Pinto Martins 260, 62400-000 Camocim – **CE36)** Av Manoel Castro 815, 62940-000 Morada Nova ☎88 3422 1198 – **CE37)** Av. Moacir Pereira Gondim, 333, Planalto dos Colibris, 63660-000 Tauá (📠88 3437 1345 **W:** cultura960am.com.br **E:** cultura960am@hotmail.com – **CE38)** Travessa São Pedro, 62800-000 Aracati ☎88 3421 1805 – **CE40)** Rua Italiano Júlio Filisola, 512, 62370-000 São Benedito ☎88 3626 2142 – **CE41)** Rua Coronel Antônio Joaquim 2143, 62930-000 Limoeiro do Norte ☎88 3423 4225 **W:** radioeducadora.com.br **E:** educadora560@yahoo.com.br – **CE43)** Rua João Verçosa s/n, 62640-000 Pentecoste ☎85 3352 2554 **W:** difusoravaledocuru.com.br – **CE44)** Av Francisco Franca 414, 63600-000 Senador Pompeu ☎88 3449 0206 **W:** radiosertaocentralam.com.br **E:** radiosertaocentral@hotmail.com – **CE46)** Rua Doutor Otávio Lobo, 198, Santa Quitéria, 62280-000 Santa Quitéria ☎88 3628 0033 **W:** itataia890.com.br – **CE49)** Rua Simão Barbosa,1209, São Mateus, 62700-000 Canindé ☎ 85 3343 1597 **W:** sistemadecomunicacao.net – **CE50)** Rua Coronel Lucio 489, 63700-000 Crateús ☎88 3691 5155 – **CE51)** Rua Monsenhor Salviano Pinto 507, 63800-000 Quixeramobim ☎88 3441 0263 📠88 3441 1209 **W:** sistemamaior.com.br/radio_campomaior **E:** contatomaior@sistemamaior.com.br – **CE52)** Rua Engenheiro João Alfredo, 1554 - Centro, 61600-050 Caucaia ☎85 3342 3677 – **CE53)** Av da Ressurreiçao, 926, Pe Ibiapina, 62000-000 Sobral ☎88 3111 3121 **W:** radioressurreicao.com.br – **CE56)** Rua Raimundo Nonato 81, 62940-000 Morada Nova ☎88 3422 2561 – **CE57)** Rua Dr Chagas Pinto 351, 62250-000 Ipu ☎88 3683 2186 **W:** radioiracemadeipu.com.br **E:** recados1360@hotmail.com – **CE58)** Rua Francisco Gomes de Souza 198, 63150-000 Campos Sales. ☎88 3533 1188 **W:** cidadeam630.com.br – **CE59)** Av Cazuzinha Marques 87, 63560-000 Acopiara ☎88 3565 0063 **W:** radiovaleacopiara.am.br **E:** radiovaleacopiara@gmail.com – **CE62)** Av. Senador Esmerino Arruda s/n, 62430-000 Granja ☎88 3624 1106 **W:** Facebook:Rádio Vale do Coreaú Am **E:** radiovaleam@hotmail.com – **CE63)** Rua Antônio Queiroz 343, 63870-000 Boa Viagem ☎88 3427 1064 **W:** radioamliberdade.blogspot.no**E:** deadator@gmail.com – **CE64)** Rua Major Barreto 3000, 62600-000 Itapajé (📠85 9104 5447 **W:** radioguanaces.com.br **E:** kekpubli@hotmail.com – **CE65)** Rua Padre Fialho 265, 62010-970 Sobral ☎88 3613 2749 **W:** pioneiraam830.com.br **E:** gerardoneto@pioneiraam830.com.br – **CE67)** Rua Monsenhor Jovinano Baretto 22 2º andar, 63660-000 Tauá ☎88 3437 1509 **W:** difusorataua.com.br **E:** contato@difusorataua.com.br – **CE71)** Av. Maria Hosana Matos Lima (Parque Leste) 90, Ditrito Industrial, 61939-130 Maracanaú ☎85 3382 2222 **W:** radiopitaguary.com.br **E:** radiopitaguary@yahoo.com.br – **CE72)** Rodovia BR-226 km 20, Distrito de Bonfim, 63600-000 Senador Pompeu **W:** facebook.com/AMPATU1130 – **CE74)** Avenida Alcides Rocha, s/n, São Luis, 62550-000 Morrinhos ☎88 3665 1422 **W:** princesaam.com **E:** princesaam@outlook.com – **CE75)** Rua Cel. José Lourenço, 97, Altos, (C.P. 063) 62250-000 Ipu ☎88 3683 1204 **W:** radioregionaldeipu.com.br **E:** radioregional1520am@hotmail.com – **CE76)** Rua Joaquim Távora 333, 63150-000 Campos Sales ☎88 3533 1530 **W:** tresfronteirasam.com.br **E:** tresfronteirasam@gmail.com – **CE79)** Rua Raul Catunda Fontenele 61, 62230-000 Ipueiras ☎88 3685 1368 **W:** radiomacambira.com.br – **CE80)** Rua Raimundo Guedes Martins 25, 63400-000 Cedro ☎88 3564 1075 **W:** radiomontevideoam.com.br – **CE81)** Ro BR 020, s/n, Zona Rural, 62730-000 Caridade ☎85 3324 1292 – **CE83)** Av. Rabelo, s/n, Alto Vistoso, 63620- 000 Solonópole ☎88 3518 1520 **W:** radiocachoeiraam.com.br MSN: radio.cachoeira.am@hotmail.com – **CE84)** Rua Augusto Vieira 32, 63630-000 Pedro Branca ☎88 3515 2121 **W:** amtrapia1510.com.br **E:** contato@amtrapia1510.com.br – **CE100)** Rua Mário Perdigão 130, 61760-000 Eusébio ☎85 3361 2755

DF00) DISTRITO FEDERAL

DF01) SRTS, Qd 701, Ed Assis Chateaubriand, Bl 2, salas 701 a 716, 70340-906 Brasília ☎61 3039 8771 **W:** brasilia.jovempanfm.virgula.uol.com.br **E:** jovempan@jovempadf.com.br - **FM:** 107.9 MHz – **DF02)** SCS Q 08, Bloco B-60, 1° Subsolo, Ed. Venâncio, 70333-900 Brasília ☎61 3799 5700 **W:** radiomec.com.br – **DF03)** Sig Quadra.02 Lt 340 Bl.02, 1° andar,(✉ C.P. 8042, 70673-1080) 70610-901 Brasília ☎61 3342 1080 **W:** radioplanalto.com.br **E:** contato@clube.fm – **DF04)** SCRN 702/03, B1 «B», Edificio Radiobrás, (CP 259) 70710-750 Brasília ☎61 3799 5474 **W:** radios.ebc.com.br/nacionalbrasiliaam **E:** centraldoouvinte@ebc.com.br – **DF05)** Rádio Antena9, Setor de Rádio e Televisão Sul Q.2, 70340-000 Brasília ☎61 2103-4019 **W:** facebook.com/redealeluiabrasilia – **DF06)** C.P 259, 70710-750 Brasília **W:** radios.ebc.com.br/nacionalamazonia **E:** amazoniabrasileira@ebc.com.br – **DF07)** SGAS 601 Módulos 3/4, Av L2 Sul, 70340-902 Brasília ☎61 2103 0710 **W:** novaalianca.org.br **E:** contato@novaalianca.org.br - **FM:** 103.6 MHz – **DF08)** SGAS 915 lt 75, 70390-150 Asa Sul ☎61 3114 1010 **W:** redeboavontade.com.br **E:** superrbv@boavontade.com – **DF09)** C-01, Lotes 1/12, Ed. Taguatinga Trade Center, Sala 1025, 72010-010 Taguatinga ☎61 3451 3700 – **DF10)** Senado Federal, Praça dos Tres Poderes, Anexo II, Bloco B, Térreo, 70165-900 Brasília ☎61 3303 4691 **W:** senado.gov.br/radio **E:** radio@senado.gov.br

ES00) ESPÍRITO SANTO

ES07) Av Santo Antônio, 366 al Caratoira, 29025-645 Vitória ☎27 3222 4376 📠27 3222 7747 **W:** radiocapixaba.com.br – **ES08)** Av

NS da Penha, 2141, Santa Luzia, 29045-403 Vitória ☎227 3137 2900 **W:** rtv.es.gov.br **E:** radiojornalismo@rtv.es.gov.br – **ES10)** Rua Alberto de Oliveira Santos 42, Edifico Ames 19° andar, salas 1916-1920 - Centro, 29010-901 Vitória ☎27 3198 0850 📠27 3222 4960 **W:** redeamericaes.com.br - **FM:** 101.5MHz "Cidade" – **ES16)** Rua Graciano Neves 250, 29156-050 Cariacica ☎27 3331 8300 **W:** novotemponet.com.br **E:** recepcaonovotempo@gmail.com - **FM:** 95.9 MHz – **ES21)** Rodovia Mickel Chequer, s/n, Zona Rural, 293900-000 Iúna ☎28 3545 1205

GO00) GOIÁS

GO01) Av. Goiás Q 10 1449, 74010-010 Goiânia ☎62 3212 0735 **W:** radioriviera.webnode.com **E:** radioam.riviera@gmail.com – **GO05)** Av 24 de Outobro, 1854, Campinas, 74505-011 Goiânia ☎62 3233 4000 **W:** difusorapaieterno.com.br **E:** difusorapaieterno@grupotd1.com.br – **GO06)** Av Marechal Rondón, 1088, 76270-000 Jussara ☎62 3373 1739 **W:** kompletafm.net **E:** komletafm@gmail.com **FM:** 96.7 MHz – **GO09)** Rua José de Carvalho Bastos 542, 75800-447 Jataí ☎64 3631 1521 **W:** difusoradejatai.com.br/ **E:** contato@difusoraonline.com.br – **GO16)** Av. C-255, 400 – St. Nova Suica, Edifico eldorado Business Tower, 74835-180 Goiânia ☎62 3945 3820 **W:** radiobandeirantesgoiania.com.br **E:** administrativo@radiobandeirantesgoiania.com.br – **GO17)** Av. Brasilia, Nº 10, 76550-000 Porantagatú ☎ 62 3362-4085 **W:** radiotropical850am.com.br **E:** tropical.go@uol.com.br – **FM:** 90.9 MHz – **GO18)** Av Tocantins N° 65 1° andar, 76400-000 Uruaçu ☎62 3357 6626 **W:** radiolagodourado.com.br **E:** contato@radiolagodourado.com.br – **GO19)** SBS Qd 2, s/n Bl Q lt 03 Ed João Carlos Saad. Asa Sul, 70070-120 Brasilia ☎61 3325 1499 – **GO23)** Rua Diógenes de Castro Ribeirao, 223, Central, 76330-000 Jaraguá ☎62 3326 4020 **W:** portalradiocidade.com.br **E:** comercialradiocidade910am@gmail.com – **GO24)** Rua F-52 Qd. 164 Lt 5/18 No 120, Faiçalville IV, 74350-450 Goiânia ☎62 3254-1090 **W:** aliancaredefonte.com **E:** adm@redefonte.com – **GO25)** Rua Freio João Batista 76, 75860-000 Quirinópolis. ☎64 3651 1452 **W:** sulgoiana.com.br **E:** quirinopolis@hotmail.com – **GO27)** Rua Thomaz Edson Qd 07, St. Serrinha, 74820-250 Goiânia ☎62 3250 1230 **W:** Facebook.com/daquigoiania **E:** marketing.radio@gjccorp.com.br – **GO30)** Rua SC-01, N° 299, Parque Santa Cruz, 74860-270 Goiânia ☎62 3201 7667 **W:**abc.go.gov.br/tv-radio-imprensa-oficial/ao-vivo-rbc-am.htm **E:**radiobrasilcentral@goias.gov.br – **GO31)** Rua Monsenhor Celso, Quadra Área, Lote 2, s/n, Vila Santa, 74912-590 Aparecidsa de Goiania, ☎62 3216 0730 **W:** sagresonline.com.br **E:** jornalismo@sistemasagres.com.br – **GO32)** Alameda das Rosas, 2.200, Setor Oeste, 74126-010 Goiânia ☎62 3521 1937 **W:** radio.ufg.br **E:** radiouniversitaria@ufg.br – **GO33)** Av Amazonas, 356, Central, 76100-000 São Luís de Montes Belos ☎64 3671 1621 **W:**. redediocesanaderadio.com **E:** radiovaleamfm@hotmail.com – **GO37)** Rua 15 Novembro Q ,1 36 lt 1, 76600-000 Goiás ☎62 3371 1575 – **GO39)** Praça Pres Médici, s/n, Central, 75920-000 Santa Helena de Goiás ☎63 3641 1555 **W:** radiosantelenense.com.br **E:** radiosantelenense@globo.com – **GO44)** Rua 23 Q 1 s/n lt 3, Andrade, 75850-000 Caiapônia ☎64 3363 1219 – **GO45)** Rua Lazer Q82, s/n lt 2, Res Village Garavelo, 74900-000 Aparecida de Goiânia ☎62 3283 1040 – **GO46)** QS 03 lotes 3,5,7 e 9 salas 1513/1515, Ed. Pátio Capital. Aguas Claros, 71953-000 Brasilia DF (C.P 06-799, 71701-970 Brasília, DF) ☎61 3039 1162 **W:** radioredentor.com.br **E:** contato@radioredentor.com.br – **GO47)** Rua 22, 150, St.Aeroporto, 75640-000 Piracanjuba ☎64 3405 1919 **W:** radiopousoalto.com.br – **GO48)** Rua 49, Q 53 218, Nova Vila, 76300-000 Ceres ☎62 3307 3042 – **GO52)** Av Joaquim David Ferreira 1390, 76105-000 Firminópolis ☎62 3239-1020 **W:** radioboasnovas1020am.com.br – **GO53)** Av Santana, Qd 55, lote 01, Sector Vila Baiana, 73840-000 Campas Belos ☎62 3451 1209 **W:** novarcbam.websom.net – **GO54)** Rua 73, 349-Bloco A Térreo, Jardim Goiás, 74810-370 Minacu ☎62 8401 0530 **W:** reedeserradourada.com.br/emissora/minacu – **GO55)** Rua Anapoils, 53, Quadra 15 Lote 14-A, 76400-000 Uruaçu ☎62 3357 3696 W: radiolibrtdadegoias.com.br **E:** radioliberdadeuruacu@gmail.com

MA00) MARANHÃO

MA01) Av Eliézer Moreira s/n, 65950-000 Barra do Corda – **MA02)** Rua Frei Querubim, 57, Apicum Centro, 65025-420 São Luís ☎98 3878 5709 **W:** educadora560.com.br – **MA04)** Pc Pallmeiro Cantanhede 1524, 65400-000 Codó ☎99 3661 1944 **W:** eldoradoam.com.br **E:** radioeldoradoam@hotmail.com – **MA05)** Av São Benedito, 1075, Bairo São Benedito, 65400-000 Codó – **MA07)** Rua Manoel Alves de Abreu 373, 65700-000 Bacabal ☎99 3621 1510 **W:** Facebook: R.Jainari – **MA08)** Av Coronel Fonseca 200, 65800-000 Balsas ☎99 3541 2458 – **MA09)** Av Cel Colares Moreira, 1000 sala 12- Marcus Center, Sao francisco, 65075-440 São Luís ☎98 3235 7676 **W:** http//radio.capital118+.com.brt **E:** radio@capital1180.com.br – **MA10)** Rua Beira Mar 276, 65010-400 Sao Luis ☎98 2108 6329 **W:** ma.gov.br/timbira **E:** timbira@secom.ma.gov.br – **MA11)** Av President Media, 77, Areinha, 65032-075 São Luís ☎98 2109 7777 **W:** grupozildenifalcao.com.br **E:** edjandejesus@yahoo.com.br – **MA13)** Av Rio Branco, 670, 65725-000 Pedreiras – **MA14)** Av Kennedy 353, 65690-000 Colinas ☎99 3552 1411 – **MA15)** Av. Ana Jansen 200, 65076-902 São Luis ☎98 3235 3013 – **MA16)** Rua Antônio Lopes 971, 65215-000 Viana ☎98 3351 1353 – **MA17)** Rua Guarani, s/n QD 03 LOTE 09, Caicara, 65922-000 João Lisboa – **MA18)** Rua João Castelo s/n, 65320-000 Vitorino Freire ☎98 3655 1240 **W:** sistemaaguabranca.com – **MA21)** Rua Cláudio Carneiro 177, 65750-000 Esperantinópolis ☎99 3645 1403 – **MA22)** Alexandre Trovao 338, 65415-000 Coroatá ☎99 3641 0931 – **MA23)** Rua Aarão Reis, 1963, Morro Alecrim, 65604-060 Caxias ☎93 3521 0047 – **MA24)** Rua Tiradente 134, 65365-000 Zê Doca ☎98 3655 3972 – **MA26)** Rua Alagoas 497, 65917-010 Imperatriz ☎99 3523 3779 **W:** imirante.globo.com**E:** imirante@mirante.com.br - **FM:** 96.1 MHz – **MA27)** Av Amaral Raposo s/n, 65940-000 Grajaú ☎99 3532 6165 – **MA28)** Rua Rui Barbosa s/n, 65620-000 Coelho Neto – **MA30)** Rua Frederico Coelho esquina com Av Frei Aniceto, 65763-000 Tuntum **W:** imirante.globo.com **E:** imirante@mirante.com.br – **MA32)** Parque da Bandeira, 222, Edificio Ariana, 65665-000 São João dos Patos ☎95 3551 2418 – **MA33)** Praça do Guarim s/n, 65390-000 Santa Luzia – **MA34)** Rua Terra esquina com Rua Jupiter s/n, 65760-0000 Presidente Dutra – **MA35)** Praça Coronel Luis Vieira 26, 65500-000 Chapadinha ☎98 3471 1337 **W:** imirante.globo.com **E:** imirante@mirante.com.br – **MA36)** Rua Senador Vitorino Freira 85, 65715-000 Lago da Pedra ☎99 3644 1220 **W:** radiosantamaura.com.br – **MA37)** Rua Hemeterio Leitão 103, 65430-00 Vargem Grande – **MA38)** Av Ana Jansen 200, 65076-902 São Luís ☎98 3230 3013 **W:** imirante.globo.com – **MA39)** Rua Monsenhor Gentil s/n, 65530-000 Urbano Santos – **MA40)** Rua Bela Vista 1894, Castelo Branco, 65604-160 Caxias ☎99 3521 033 – **MA42)** Belo Horizonte, s/n, Formosa, 65634-080 Timon ☎89 2107 3000 – **MA43)** Rua Principal, Turiaçu

MG00) MINAS GERAIS

MG01) Rua Rabelo Horta 39, 36770-064 Cataguases ☎32 3422 1724 **W:** radiocataguases.com **E:** contato@radiocataguases.com - **FM:** 89.5MHz – **MG02)** Rua General Carneiro 10, Edificio Milinardo s 200 à 305, 39400-095 Montes Claros – **MG03)** Rua Serrinha, 1200, Vale do Jacobá, 30668-250 Belo Horizonte ☎31 3322 1945 – **MG04)** Praça Nossa Senhora Aparecida, 134, Aparecida, 38400-726 Uberlândia ☎34 3292 0401 **W:** radioamerica.com.br **E:** america@radioamerica.com.br – **MG06)** Rua Itatiaia, 117, Bonfim, 31210-170 Belo Horizonte ☎31 2105 3588 📠31 2105 3613 **W:** itatiaia.com.br **E:** itatiaia@itatiaia.com.br - **FM:** 95.7MHz – **MG09)** Rua Euripides Ribeiro 739, 38720-000 Lagoa Formosa ☎34 3824 9980 **W:** radiovitoriosa.com.br – **MG11)** Avenida Juscelino Kubitschek, 30, Passaginha, 35790-000 Curvelo ☎38 3721 2300 **W:** radioclubecurvelo.com.br - **FM:** 95.5 MHz – **MG13)** Rua Geraldo Rios 98, 38770-000 João Pinheiro ☎38 3561 1381 – **MG14)** Rua Entre Rios, 33, Carlos Prates, 30710-080 Belo Horizonte ☎31 8406 0673 **W:** radiomineiro.com **E:** radiomineiro@radiominerio.com – **MG15)** Praça 15 de Novembro 339 5° andar, 36900-000 Manhuaçu ☎33 3332 4080 **W:** radiomanhuacu.com.br **E:** contato@radiomanhuacu.com.br - **FM:** 88 MHz – **MG16)** Rua Cel. José Inácio 96, 37550-000 Pouso Alegre ☎35 3423 1488 **W:** difusorahd.com.br **E:** contato@difusorahd.com.br.com.br – **MG17)** Av Dr Fidélis Reis 810, 38010-030 Uberaba ☎34 3331 7999 **W:** radiojm730.com.br – **MG18)** Av Barão do Rio Branco 3231 Sl 1004 , 36010-012 Juiz de Fora ☎32 3231 1388 – **MG19)** Av Itaú, 515 Sl 1013, Dom Cabral, 34692-500 Belo Horizonte ☎31 3469 2549 **W:** radioamerica.arquidiocesebh.org – **MG20)** Praça Leonardo Venerando Pereira 200, 37200-000 Lavras ☎35 3822 5000 **W:** radiocultura770.com.br – **MG22)** Rua dos Cravos, 467, Bairro São Pedro, 35900-125 Itabira ☎31 3831 2928 **W:** radioitabira.com.br **E:** euclideseder@yahoo.com.br – **MG30)** Rua Dos Antunes 1175 Ed São Sebastião, 37950-000 São Sebastião do Paraíso ☎35 3531 2396 **W:** radiodafamilia.com.br **E:** contato@radiofamilia.com.br – **MG31)** Av. Itú, 515 – barrio Dom Cabral, 30535-910 Belo Horizonte ☎31 3565 6289 **W:** redegeraisderadio.com.br/am830.php **E:** contato@redegeraisradio.com.br – **MG35)** Av Raja Gabáglia, 1666, Santa Lúcia, 30350-540 Belo Horizonte ☎31 3298 3401 📠31 3298 3400 **W:** inconfidencia.com.br **E:** inconfidencia@inconfidencia.com.br Eng.: gleisonferreira@inconfidencia.com - **FM:** 100.9 MHz – **MG36)** Rua Dr Olinto Martins 207, 39960-000 Jequitinhonha ☎33 3741 1521 **W:** santacruz890.com.br – **MG37)** Av Getúlio Vargas 420, 39800-015 Teófilo Otoni ☎33 3522 3635 **W:** radioteofilotoni.com.br **E:** vanessa@radioteofilotoni.com.br – **MG38)** Largo Dom João 122, 39100-000 Diamantina ☎38 3531 1408 – **MG39)** Praça 28 de Setembro, 95 -

Centro, 36520-000 Visconde do Rio Branco ☎32 3551 1877 **W:** radioculturariobranco.com **E:** radioculturavrb @gmail.com or radiocultura920@hotmail.com – **MG43)** Rua Santa Catarina, 610 3° andar, Lourdes, 30170-081 Belo Horizonte ☎31 3349 7308 **W:** radioatalaiabh.com.br – **MG44)** Av Bom Jesus, 330 - Centro, (CP 10) 37578-000 Bueno Brandão ☎35 3463 1006 **W:** radioindy.com.br **E:** indyamcomercial@gmail.com – **MG45)** Rua Radialista Hamilton Macedo, 204, Limoero, 35300-121 Caratinga ☎33 3321 2800 – **MG46)** Rua Santa Tereza, 97 – Centro, 36300-114 São João del-Rei ☎32 3371-7777 W:radiosaojoaodelrei.com.br **E:**radiosaojoaodelrei@hotmail.com **MG50)** Rua Manoel Joaquim Pires 63, 35170-082 Coronel Fabriciano ☎31 3842 1400 **W:** educadoramg.com.br - **FM:** 107.1MHz – **MG52)** Rua Duque de Caixas 258, Primavera, 38430-000 Tupaciguara ☎34 3281 5800 **W:** rural1050.com – **MG53)** Av. Alvares Cabral, 1030 s 206, Lourdes, 30170.001 Belo Horizonte ☎31 3453 3989 **W:** ipda.com.br – **MG56)** Av Dr Américo Luz, 153, Sala 105 - Centro, 37890-000 Muzambinho ☎35 3571 1145 **W:** radiodopovo.com.br **E:** radiodopovoam@yahoo.com.br – **MG57)** Rua Halfeld 744 Sl 401,36010-003 Juiz de Fora ☎32 3215 4477 – **MG58)** Av Bahia 720, 38440-000 Araguari ☎34 3241 3131 **W:** radioplanaltoaraguari.com **E:** ouvintes@radioplanaltoaraguari.com – **MG59)** Rua Areião do Matadouro, 1281, Matadouro, 34000-000 Nova Lima ☎31 3541 1823 – **MG63)** Rua João Bressane 1, 37400-000 Campanha ☎35 3261 1229 **W:** radiodiocesanaam.com.br **E:** radiocesana@yahoo.com.br – **MG68)** Av Assis Chateaubriand, 499, Floresta, 30150-101 Belo Horizonte ☎31 3237 6000 **W:** guarani.com.br **E:** guarani@guarani.com - **FM:** 96.5 MHz – **MG72)** Av. Treze, 658 6° andar, Edifico Ituiutaba - Centro, 38300-140 Ituiutaba ☎34 3271 7440 **W:** platinaam.com.br **E:** redacao@sistemacancella.com.br - **FM:** 97.3 MHz – **MG75)** Rua Itajubá 62, 35160-035 Ipatinga ☎31 3801 4300 **W:** vanguardaam.com.br **E:** comercial@radio95fm.com.br - **FM:** 95 MHz – **MG79)** Av Treze, 658, 6° andar, Edifício Ituiutaba 6° andar, 38300-140 Ituiutaba ☎34 3271 7400 **W:** cancelaam.com - **FM:** 97.3MHz – **MG80)** Av Costa Junior 467, 38840-000 Carmo do Paranaíba ☎34 3851 2066 **W:** sistemaplaneta.net **E:** rplaneta@sistemaplaneta.net – **MG81)** Rua Mariana, 178 -Monte Sinai, 35450-000 Itabirito ☎31 3561 3499 **W:** redegeraisderadio.com.br/am1340.php **E:** rgr1340amitabirito@redegeraisderadio.com.br – **MG83)** Rua Col José Paulino, 261 - Centro, 37750-000 Machado ☎35 3295 1361 **W:** difusoramachado.com.br **E:** gilson0408@gmail.com – **MG85)** Rua Calixto Martins de Melo 391, 38610-000 Unaí ☎38 3676 1490 **W:** radioveredas.com.br **E:** contato@radioveredas.com.br - **FM:** 98.0MHz – **MG89)** Rua Niquel, 457, Industrial, 35701-107 Sete Lagoas ☎31 3773 3694 **W:** culturasl.com.br - **FM:** 92.1MHz «Musirama» – **MG90)** Av Major Antônio Alberto Fernandes 178, 37720-000 Botelhos ☎35 3741 1277 – **MG92)** Rua XV de Novembro 62, 36500-000 Ubá ☎32 3531 1830 **W:** educadora.com.br - **FM:** 94.5MHz – **MG94)** Av Governador Israel Pinheiro 651, 38550-000 Coromandel ☎34 8855 2288 **W:** Facebook: R.Diamante **E:** locutoresdiamanteam@gmail.com – **MG95)** Rua Juliano Marques Duarte, 110, Iha Gama Cerqueira, 36660-000 Além Paraíba ☎32 3462 7400 **W:** Facebook: R.Cultura de Porto Novo **E:** sistemahf@gmail.com – **MG96)** Av 15 895, 10° andar Sala 1002 e 1005, Edifico Executivo, 38300-000 Ituiutaba ☎34 3261 7118 **W:** difusoraituiutaba.com.br **E:** administracao@difusoraituiutaba.com.br – **MG97)** Av. Iparanga, 198 - Centro, 37190-000 Três Pontas ☎35 3265 2252 – **MG99)** Av Belo Horizonte 108, 39860-000 Nanuque – **MG103)** Rua Nunes da Rosa 70, 36970-000 Manhumirim ☎33 3341 1491 **W:** radiomanhumirim.com **E:** radiomanhumirimfinanceiro@gmail.com – **MG105)** Rua João Ribeiro Navarro 285, 36200-000 Barbacena ☎32 3331 7988 **W:** correiosat.com.br - **FM:** 100.3 MHZ – **MG107)** Alameda Monteiro Lobato, Solar dos Lagos, 37470-000 São Lourenço ☎35 3332 4333 **W:** radioestancia.com.br **E:** estancia@radioestancia.com.br - **FM:** 94.3MHz – **MG109)** Av Magalhães Pinto, 829, São Sebastião, 35610-000 Dores do Indaiá ☎37 3551 1402 – **MG110)** Rua Comendador José Garcia, 27, sala 1202, 37550-000 Pouso Alegre ☎35 3423 6566 **W:** radioclubepousoalegre.com.br/ **E:** radioclubedepousealegre@outlook.com – **MG111)** Rua Dr José Gonçalves 17 sl 17, 35600-000 Bom Despacho ☎37 3522 4111 – **MG114)** Praça Nossa Senhora do Carmo 224, 38500-000 Monte Carmelo ☎34 3842 1361 **W:** difusorabd.com.br **E:** contato@difusorbd.com.br – **MG115)** Rua Sancho Vilela, 19, Radio, 37540-000 Santa Rita do Sapucaí ☎35 3473 4400 **W:** difusora1550.com.br **E:** comercial@difusora1550.com.br - **FM:** 95.3MHz – **MG116)** Av Brasil 508, 39270-000 Pirapora ☎38 3741 1400 **E:** radiopirapora@hotmail.com – **MG117)** Praça João XXIII 15, Sala 15, 36700-000 Leopoldina ☎32 3441 4260 **W:** radiojornal.net **E:** radiojornalleopoldina@gmail.com – **MG118)** Rua Bias Fortes 191, 37130-000 Alfenas ☎35 3299 3886 **W:** radioculturaalfenas.com.br **E:** radiocultura@unifenas.br – **MG119)** Av JK 108, 35500-000 Itapecerica ☎37 3341 8533 **FM:** 101.3MHz – **MG121)** Rua Sérgio Neves, 63/Sala 303, 36240-000 Santos Dumont ☎32 3251 1580 **W:** radioculturasd.com.br **E:** contato@radioculturasd.com.br – **MG122)** Av Minas Gerais 584, 39510-000 Espinosa ☎38 3812 1299 – **MG123)** Rua Pepino Laterza, 920, Independência, 38304-216 Uberaba ☎34 3269 0255 🖷34 3269 0244 **W:** redevitoriosa.com.br **E:** comercial@redevitoriosa.com.br – **MG124)** Av Hermenegildo Donatti, 199, Jd. Nova Andradas, 37795-000 Andradas ☎35 3731 2291 **W:** radiovinicola.com.br **E:** vinicola@andradas-net.com.br - **FM:** 94.9MHz – **MG125)** Praça Coronel Odilon Coelho 123, 39520-000 Porteirinha. ☎38 3831 1228 **W:** educadoraam640.com.br – **MG126)** Av. Dr. Otávo Soares 108, Palmeiras, 35430-229 Ponte Nova ☎31 3881 6700 **W:** montanhesa.am.br/pontenova/ **E:** montanhesapontenova@montanhesa.am.br – **MG128)** Rua Benedito Valadares 433, Barra, 36880-000 Muriaé ☎32 3729 4800 **W:** redeatividade.com/radioam - **FM:** 94.7MHz – **MG130)** Rua José Teotônio 87-b,, 39440-000 Janaúba ☎38 3821 2000 🖷38 3821 2263 **W:** radiogorutubanaam.com **E:** radiogorutubanaam@gmail.com – **MG131)** Av Afonso Pena, 726, Conj. 1000 10° andar, 30130-003 Belo Horizonte **W:** redegeraisderadio.com.br/am1460.php **E:** contato@redegeraisderadio.com.br – **MG133)** Av. Deputada Humborta de Almeida, 60 - Centro, 37810-000 Guaranésia ☎35 3555 1350 **W:** radioam1580guaranesia.com.br **E:** radioam1580@guaranesia.com.br – **MG134)** BR-496 Km 33, 39260-000 Várzea da Palma – **MG136)** Rua Jair Werneck, 330, Cidade Alta, 39800-000 Teófilo Otoni ☎33 3522 2000 **W:** radiomucuri.com.br – **MG137)** Rua Major Honor Sarmento, 393, São João, 39400-533 Montes Claros ☎38 3223 5666 🖷38 3221 5590 **W:** radioterraam.com.br – **MG138)** Av 119 N° 122, Brasilia, 38360- 000 Capinópolis ☎34 3263 1095 – **MG140)** Rua Tiradentes, 784, Nova Horizonte, 37175-000 Ilicínea ☎35 3854 1342 **W:** radioaparecidadosulam.com **E:** apdosulam@gmail.com – **MG143)** Rua Dr Pena 35, 35700-032 Sete Lagoas ☎31 3772 0244 **W:** eldorado1300.com.br **E:** contato@eldorado1300.com.br – **MG145)** Pc Cordovil Pinto Coelho, 165, Sala 1003, 36900-000 Manhuaçu – **MG146)** Av BPS, 1303, Pinheirinho, 37500-000 Itajubá ☎35 3622 1008 **W:** unifei.edu.br/radio **E:** radiounifei@unifei.edu.br – **MG148)** Praça Getúlio Vargas 108, 36800-000 Carangola ☎32 3741 1770 **W:** redegeraisderadio.com.br/am900.php br **E:** rgr900amcarangola@redegeraisderadio.com.br - **FM:** 102.7MHz «Caparaó» – **MG149)** Rua Oscar Vidal 307, 36016-290 Juiz de Fora ☎32 3213-6652 **W:** radioglobojf.com.br **E:** atendimento@radioglobojf.com.br – **MG151)** Av 7 de Setembro 55-A, 36950-000 Ipanema **W:** radioipanemaam.com.br – **MG153)**Rua dos Tamoios, 200, 21° andar, Centro 30120-050 Belo Horizonte ☎31 3271-0971 **W:** nossaradiobh.com **E:**ouvinte@nossaradiofm.com.br - **FM:** 97.3 MHz – **MG154)** Rua Padre Vigilato 230, 35330-000 Inhapim ☎33 3315 1299 **W:** Facebook: Radio Clube de Inhapim – **MG162)** Rua Silvino Brandão, 164, Aeroporto, 38440-170 Araguari ☎34 3246 0103 **W:** ondavivaaraguari.com.br **E:** comercialmaisfm@yahoo.com.br - **FM:** 93.5 MHz – **MG163)** Travessa Cônego Benedito Profício, 95, 37660-000 Paraisópolis ☎35 3651 1119 **W:** paraisopolis.com.br **W:** contato@radioparaisopolis.com.br – **MG165)** Rua Antônio Ribeiro da Costa Junior 16, 36730-000 Pirapetinga ☎32 3465 1233 **W:** radiopirapetinga.com.br – **MG168)** Rua Marcos Vinícius Ferreira, 226, São Miguel, 39560-000 Salinas ☎38 341 1060 **W:** radiodifusoradesalinas.com.br **E:** programacao@radiodifusoradesalinas.com.br – **MG169)** Av Rondón Pacheco, 450, Santo Antônio, 37150-000 Carmo do Rio Claro ☎35 3561 1967 – **MG171)** Rua Coronel Carlos Brandão 98, sala 07/08, 36500-000 Ubá ☎32 3532 3122 – **MG172)** Av Dr Pedro Rosa s/n, 37530-000 Brasópolis ☎35 3641 1317 **W:** redegeraisderadio.com.br/am1380.php **E:** contato@redegeraisderadio.com.br – **MG175)** Praça Coronel Silverio de Melo 172, 37958-000 Monte Santo de Minas ☎35 3591-1175 **W:** radioprogresso1530.com.br **E:**radioprogressoam@hotmail.com – **MG176)** Rua 18, 1974, Industrial, 38270-000 Campina Verde ☎34 3412 1504 – **MG193)** Rua Coronel Ferraz 135, 37470-000 São Loureço ☎35 3332 6646 – **MG196)** Rua 20, 2080, Santa Cruz,38950-000 Ibiá ☎34 9981 7016 **W:** maximafm.com.br **E:** futura@ibiamg.com.br - **FM:** 87.9 MHz

MS00) MATO GROSSO DO SUL

MS01) Av Mato Grosso 530, 79002-233 Campo Grande **W:** miliciadaimaculada.org.br/v2/Rural580.asp **E:** 580am@miliciadaimaculada.org.br – **MS04)** Rua Ciro Melo 2045, 79805-000 Dourados ☎67 3421 1540 – **MS08)** Rua Jorge Roberto Salomão, 1301, Vila Industrial, 79904-170 Ponta Porã – **MS11)** Av Marcelino Pires 1404, 79801-002 Dourados ☎67 3423 0498 – **MS14)** Rua Dom Pedro II, 26, Previsul, 79300-000 Corumbá ☎67 3231 7397 **W:** novaclubeam.com **E:** novaclube1410am@gmail.com – **MS22)**Av 9 de Julho 1557, 79700-000 Fátima do Sul ☎67 7467 1258 – **MS26)** Rua Ponta Porã, s/n, Jardim das Grevileas, 79970-000 Eldorado ☎67 3473 2022 – **MS29)** Pedro Celestino C Costa 687, 79890-000 Itapora ☎67 3421 1104 **W:** radioalvorada1470.com.br – **MS33)** Rua Severino de Araujo Ferreira, 1375, Marta Rocha, 79700-000 Fátima do Sul ☎67 3467 1833 **W:** radioguaicurus.com.br **E:** radioguaicurus@uol.com.br – **MS39)** Rua Ipiranga, 556, Jardim Itaipu, 79824-190 Dourados ☎67 3426 9261 **W:** facebook.com/ric1060 **E:** 1060am@miliciadaimaculada.org.br – **MS43)** Av Reinaldo Massi 2144, 79740-000 Ivinhema

MT00) MATO GROSSO

MT05) Praça do Seminário 239, 78015-140 Cuiabá ☎65 3055 3182 **W:** radiodifusoracuiaba.com.br **E:** radiodifusoracba@gmail.com – **MT09)** Rua São Pedro 806, 78200-000 Cáceres – **MT12)** Av Cuiabá 829, Edifício Mikerinos, 12° andar, 78700-090 Rondonópolis ☎66 3425 1070 **W:** radioclubemt.com.br – **MT15)** Rua Zulmira Canavarros 285, 78005-390 Cuiabá ☎85 3121-1200 **W:** rvonews.com.br **E:** contato@rvonews.com.br – **MT16)** Rua 2 No 32, 78175-000 Poconé – **MT18)** av Brasil 765-N, 78300-000 Tangará da Serra ☎65 3326-2080 **W:** radiotangara.com.br **E:** comercial@radiotangara.com.br – **MT29)** Rua das Aroeiras 1589, (✉ C.P. 509) 78550-114 Sinop ☎66 3517 3550 **W:** radiomaissinop.com.br **E:**contato@radiomaissinope.com.br – **MT30)** Avenida Luiz Barbosa esq. c/ Sete de Setembro No 477, 78285-000 São José dos Quatro Marcos ☎65 3251 1062 **W:** radiojornalam570.com.br – **MT35)** Rua Generoso Ponce, 478 78760-000 Guiratinga ☎66 3431 1842 **W:** rgbgga.blogspot.com.br **E:** radiorgb@gmail.com – **MT36)** Rua Limiro Rosa Pereira, 690, 78260-000 Araputanga ☎65 9944-2419 **W:** rdadifusoraarcoiris.com.br **E:** contato@rdadifusoraarcoiris.com.br – **MT66)**200 Travess Araçatuba, 78700-310 Rondonopolis ☎11 3347-4700

PA00) PARÁ

PA01) Av Araguaia 247, 68551-000 Redenção – **PA02)** Manoel Umbuzeiro, 1456 -Altos Centro, 68371-180 Altamira ☎93 9171 0908 **W:** radioruralaltamira.no.comunidades.net **E:** radioruralaltamira@hotmail.com – **PA03)** Av Almirante Barroso, 2190 3° andar, Marco, 66095-000 Belém (🖷91 3084 0112 **W:** radioclubedopara.com.br **E:** timaocampeao@radioclubedopara.com.br – **PA04)** Av São Sebastião 622-A Bloco A, 68005-090 Santarém ☎93 3523 1066 🖷93 3523 2685 **W:** radioruraldesantarem.com.br **E:** edilrural@gmail.com.br – **PA06)** Praça dos Notáveis 1006, 68400-000 Cametá ☎91 3781 1495 – **PA08)** Travessa Campos Sales 370, 66015-080 Belém ☎91 4005 4400 **W:** supermarajoara.com.br **E:** contato@supermarajoara.com.br - **FM:** 100.9MHz – **PA09)** Travessa Vileta 2193, 66093-380 Belém ☎91 3344 4718 **W:** boasnovas.net **E:** marketing@boasnovas.net – **PA10)** Av Brás de Aguiar, 351, Nazaré, 66035-395 Belém ☎91 3213 1540 **W:** radioliberal.com.br – **PA11)** Tv. Cap 75, 68801-970 Breves ☎91 3783 1269 – **PA12)** Rua 13 de Mayo s/n, 68600-000 Bragança ☎91 3425 1774 **W:** fundacaoeducadora.com.br - **FM:** 106.7MHz – **PA13)** Av Mendonça Furtado, 1481, Santa Clara, 68005-100 Santarém **W:** rtvpontanegra.com.br **E:** am890@rtvpontanegra.com.br ☎93 3523 3348 – **PA14)** Av Coronel Monfredo 42, 68820-000 São Sebastião da Boa Vista – **PA16)** Av Almirante Barroso 735, 66093-020 Belém ☎91 4005 7700 **W:** portalcultura.com.br - **FM:** 93.7MHz – **PA20)** Av Afonso Pena, 25, Aeroporto Velho, 68005-390 Santarém ☎93 3523 5114 **E:** tvsantarem@hotmail.com – **PA21)** Av Xingu s/n, 68555-010 Xinguara ☎94 3426 1008 **W:** radioxinguaraam.com.br **E:** radioxinguara@hotmail.com – **PA22)** Travessa Dom Floriano 330, 68250-000 Óbidos ☎93 3547 1966 – **PA24)** Travessa 18 No 1863, entre 4 e 5 ruas, 68870-000 Soure ☎91 3741 1248 **W:** Facebook: R.Guarany do Marajó – **PA26)** Av.Fernando Guilhon, 358 Bela Vista, 68180-000 Itaituba ☎93 3518 4169 **W:** radioclubedeitaituba.com.br **E:** radioclube@hotmail.com – **PA28)** Travessa sete de setembro com a Rua Visconde do Rio Branco, 68200-000 Alenquer ☎93 9175 6458 **W:** radioximango.com.br **E:** radioximango@hotmail.com – **PA29)** Rodovia Transamazônica s/n Km 04, 68502-290 Marabá ☎94 3322 4838 **W:** radioclubemaraba.com.br – **PA30)** Rodovia BR-010 Km 1409, Industrial, 68660-000 São Miguel do Guamá ☎91 8022 0000 **W:** http//radioguama.com **E:** direcao.radioguama@gmail.com – **PA32)** Rodovia BR-316 KM 11 3528, São João, 67200-000 Marituba ☎91 3323 3059 **W:** novotempobelem.org.br **E:** belemnovotempo@hotmail.com – **PA33)** Av Antonio Marques Ribeiro 242, 68380-000 São Felix do Xingu ☎91 4351 1243 – **PA34)** Av Bertoldo Costa, 68710-000 Maracanã

PB00) PARAÍBA

PB01) Rua Pres. João Pessoa 07,Centro, 58800-000 Sousa ☎83 3521 2197 **W:** portalprogresso.com – **PB02)** Rua Justino Bezerra 41, 58900-000 Cajazeiras ☎83 3531 1236 **W:** radioaltopiranhas.com.br **E:** altopiranhas@uol.com.br – **PB08)** Rua Coronel Juvêncio Cameiro 160, (CP 20) 58900-000 Cajazeiras ☎88 3531 4530 **W:**radios.diariodosertao.com.br/?radioid=4614**E:** radiocajazeiras@gmail.com - **FM:** 94.5 MHz – **PB09)** Av D.Pedro II s/n, Torre, (C.P 1089, 58001-970) 58040-440 João Pessoa ☎83 3218 7900 **W:** radiotabajara.pb.gov.br **E:** redacaotabajara@gmail.com - **FM:** 105.5 MHz – **PB12)** Av Pedro II 523, 58013-420 João Pessoa ☎83 3216 5044 **W:** correiosat.com.br – **PB13)** Rua das Trincheiras 198, 58011-000 João Pessoa ☎83 3216 5015 – **PB17)** Rua Dr Carlos Pires 17, São José, 58804-200 Sousa ☎83 3522 1796 **W:** Facebook: R.Jornal 950 AM Sousa – **PB18)** Rua Monsenhor Valeriano s/n, 58840-000 Pombal ☎83 3431 2277 **W:** maringa98fm.com.br **E:** maringa98fm@hotmail.com - **FM:** 98.7 MHz – **PB21)** Rua Conselheiro Henrique 17, 58000-000 João Pessoa ☎83 3249 2020 **W:** portalsanhaua.com.br **E:** radioshanua@hotmail.com – **PB22)** Rua Epitácio Pessoa 8, 58200-000 Guarabira ☎83 3271 1000 **W:** radioruralam850.com.br **E:** contato@radioruralam850.com.br – **PB23)** Rua Monsenhor Palmeira 471, 58135-000 Esperança ☎83 3361 2452 **W:** redeesperanca.com.br – **PB25)** Rua Coronel Pedro Targino s/n, 58233-000 Araruna ☎83 3373 1102 **W:** radioserranadeararuna.com.br **E:** radioserrana@gmail.com or radioserranaam@hotmail.com – **PB27)** Rua Gouveia Nobrega 34, 58155-000 Soledade ☎83 3383 1229 – **PB29)** Praça Frei Martinho s/n, 1° andar, 58700-100 Patos ☎83 3421 3704 **W:** radiosertaoam.com.br **E:** marketing@radiosertaoam.com.br - **FM:** 102.9MHz – **PB30)** Rua Cel Guimarães 56, 58900-000 Cajazeiras ☎83 3531 3715 **W:** oeste1000.com.br **E:** radiooesteam@hotmail.com – **PB31)** Joao Pessoa – **PB32)** Rua Epitácio Pessoa 184, 58397-000 Areia ☎63 3362 2423 **W:** Facebook: Radio Jardim Da Borborema Am **E:** germanosoaresbrasil@hotmail.com – **PB34)** Av Ananias Conserva 18, 58780-000 Itaporanga ☎83 3451 3879 **W:** correiosat.com.br

PE00) PERNAMBUCO

PE01) Av. Radialista Flauberto de Elias, s/n, 55290-000 Garanhuns ☎87 3762 2211 **W:** redealeluia.com – **PE02)** Rua Caramuru, 72, Santo Amaro, 81 3221-000 Recife ☎81 3221 6767 **W:** am.redebrasiloficial.com.br**E:**onlineredebrasil@gmail.com – **PE04)** Rua Vigário Joaquim Pinto 721 al 12, 55700-000 Limoeiro ☎81 3628 9733 **W:** radiojornal.com.br **E:** programacao@radiojornal.com.br – **PE06)** Av Sete de Setembro, s/n, Km 02, 56302-060 Petrolina ☎87 3861 4744 **W:** granderioam.com.br **E:** granderioam@uol.com.br – **PE07)** Rua do Veiga, 600, Santo Amaro, 50040-915 Recife ☎81 3412 4432 **W:** radioclubepe.com.br – **PE09)** Rua Capitão Lima, 250, Santo Amaro, 50040-080 Recife ☎81 3413 6110 **W:** radiojornal.com.br **E:** programacao@radiojornal.com.br – **PE10)** Av.Norte, 68, Santo Amaro, 50040-200 Recife ☎81 3879 5427 **W:** upe.br – **PE11)** Av Pres Kennedy, 3092, Peixinhos, 53260-640 Olinda ☎81 3423 0033 **W:** radiotamandare.com.br **E:** pastores@radiotamandares.com.br – **PE13)** Av Padre Rocha s/n, 55810-000 Carpina – **PE14)** Av Maria Emília Cavalcanti, 570, Bairro, 55870-000 Timbaúba ☎81 3631 2229 **W:** princesaserrana.com.br **E:** contato@princesaserrana.com.br – **PE15)** Rua Duarte Coelho, 240, Santa Tereza, 53010-010 Olinda ☎81 3444 7855 **W:** radioolindaam.com.br **E:** comercial@radioolindaam.com.br – **PE16)** C.P 88, 55001-970 Caruaru **W:** radiojornal.com.br **E:** programacao@radiojornal.com.br – **PE17)** Av Presidente Kennedy, 3092, Peixinhos, 53260-640 Olinda ☎81 3444 9499 **W:** radiorelogio1120am.com.br **E:** contato@radiorelogio1120am.com.br – **PE18)** Rua Rádio Cultura Nordeste. 1130, Indianópolis, 55026-690 Caruaru ☎81 37211130 **W:** radiocultura1130.com.br **E:** jornalismo@radiocultura1130.com.br – **PE19)** Rua Prefeito José Joaquim Silva, 50 an 2, Livramento, 55602-150 Vitória de Santo Antão ☎81 3523 2003 – **PE20)** Av. Rui Barbosa, 1236, Heliopólis 55293-300 Garanhuns ☎87 3762 7244 **W:** radiojornal.ne10.uol.com.br – **PE21)** Rua Coronel Urbano Ribeiro de Sena, 956, Água Fria, 52221-000 Recife ☎55 3444 2562 **W:** radiocapibaribe.com.br **E:** contato@radiocapibaribe.com.br – **PE22)** Rua Radio Guarany, Nova Tiúma, 54727-160 Sao Lourenço da Mata ☎81 3485 1322 **W:** radioguarany.com.br **E:** falecom@radioguarany.com.br – **PE23)** Rua Pajussara, 225, Tejipio, 50920-120 Recife ☎81 3252 5868 **W:** radionovasdepaz.com.br/novasdepaz – **PE25)** Rodovia BR101 Sul, s/n km 117, Newton Cameiro, 55540-000 Palmares ☎81 3662 1288 **W:**rcpalmares.com.br **E:** rcpalmares@yahoo.com.br – **PE28)** Rua Agamenom Magalhães 271, 55750-000 Surubim ☎81 3634 1448 **W:** radiosurubimam.com.br – **PE31)** Tv José Paulo 16, 56700-999 São José do Egito ☎87 3844 1081 **W:** radiocultura1320.com.br**E;** radiocultura1320@yahoo.com.br – **PE32)** Praça Duque de Caxias 818, 55900-000 Goiana – **PE41)** Comunidade Restauração Casa-Mae, 55000-000 Caruaru ☎81 3728 8255 **W:** comunidadecr.blogspot.no **E:** radiorestauracao_am1590@hotmail.com

PI00) PIAUÍ

PI01) Av Professor João Menezea, 64770-000 São Raimundo Nonato ☎89 3582 1497 🖷89 3582 1649 **W:** radioserradacapivara.com.br **E:** capivara550@yahoo.com.br – **PI03)** Rua Taumaturgo de Azevedo

995, 64100-000 Barras – **PI07)** Praça Coronel Orlando Carvalho 400, 64500-000 Oeiras 89 3462 1200 – **PI08)** Av Valter Alencar, 2021, Monte Castelo, 64019-625 Teresina ☎86 3216 5056 **W:** fundacaoantares.org **E:** antres@fundacaoantares.org – **PI09)** Rua Coronel Joaquim Balduino, 40, Bomba, 64600-000 Picos ☎89 3422 1989 – **PI13)** Rua Professor Magalhães, 4190, Recanto das Palmares, 64045-750 Teresina ☎86 3232 5411 **W:** portaldifusora.com – **PI14)** Av Mathias Olimpico s/n, 64400-000 Amarante ☎86 3292 1129 – **PI15)** Rua Barão Rio Branco 314, 64860-000 Uruçuí ☎89 3544 1328 – **PI17)** Av Des Amaral. 2616, 64980-000 Corrente – **PI18)** Rua Clementino Ribeiro, 187, Sambaida Veklha, 64800-000 Floriano ☎89 3522 1504 **W:** radiosantaclara.com.br **E:** radiosantaclara@veloxmail.com.br – **PI19)** Rua Sabino Paulo 696, 64760-000 São João do Piauí ☎89 3483 1317 – **PI21)** Rua Arcenio Santos 555, 64900-000 Bom Jesus ☎89 3562 1525 – **PI23)** Rua Leonidas Melo 867, 64100-000 Barras ☎86 3242 1590 – **PI24)** Pc Presidente Castelo Branco 161, 64750-000 Paulistana ☎89 3487 1373 **W:** http//radioingazeira.com.br – **PI26)** Av José de Deus Lacerda 584, 64130-000 Miguel Alves – **PI27)** Tv Benedito da C Alencar, 78 - Centro, 64575-000 Jaicós ☎89 3457 1610 – **PI30)** Rua Joaqium Baldoíno, 48, Bomba, 64600-000 Picos ☎89 3422 2512 – **PI31)** Av João Ferreira 199, 64460-000 Agua Branca ☎86 3282 1344 **W:** radio1dejulho.blogspot.com.br **E:** radio1dejulho@hotmail.com – **PI32)** Rua Hugo Napoleão 940, 64110-000 José de Freitas ☎86 3264 1407 – **PI34)** Rua Pedro II, 249, 64330-000 São Miguel do Tapuio ☎86 3249 1101 – **PI36)** Rua Matias Gomes 510, 64700-000 Simplício Mendes ☎89 3482 1105 – **PI39)** Rua Coronel Messeas Melo 430, 64190-000 Batalha ☎86 3347 1314 – **PI42)** Rua Joaquim Rodrigues Macedo 245, 64680-000 Padre Marcos ☎89 3431 1137 – **PI44)** Praça da Bandeira 91, 64500-000 Oeiras ☎89 3462 1482 – **PI46)** Rua Coronel José Fortes 549, 64180-000 Esperantina ☎86 3383 1245 – **PI49)** Rua Padre Madeira 191,64600-000 Picos ☎89 3422 1900

PR00) PARANÁ

PR01) Rua Quintino Bocaiuva 41, 86020-100 Londrina ☎43 3344 2038 **W:** radiolondrina.com.br **E:** radiolondrina@onda.com.br – **PR03)** Av Brasil, 1720(✉C.P 10, 85892-970), 85892-000 Santa Helena ☎45 3268 1212 **W:** radiograndelago.com.br **E:** grandelago@rgl.com.br – **PR04)** Rua Humberto de Alencar Castelo Branco, 590, Cristo Rei, 82530-195 Curitiba ☎41 3263 3311 **W:** difusoraam590.com.br **E:** jornalismo@difusoraam590.com.br - **FM:** 102.3 MHz – **PR05)** Praça de Café N° 1100, 86900-000 Jandaia do Sul ☎43 3432 9797 **W:** radiojandaia.com.br - **FM:** 103.3MHz – **PR06)** Rua Julio Perneta, 695, Mercês, 80810-110 Curitiba ☎41 3331 7400 **W:** paranaeducativa.pr.gov.br - **FM:** 97.1 MHz – **PR07)** Rua 7 de Setembro 520, 85960-000 Marechal Cândido Rondón ☎45 3284 1212 **W:** radioeducadora.com **E:** educadora@rondonet.com.br – **PR08)** Rod João Carlos Strass, s/n, Heimtal, 86084-610 Londrina ☎43 3339 6244 **W:** superradiodeuseamor.com.br – **PR09)** Rua António Costa, 529, Bela Vista Alegre, 80820-020 ☎41 3240 7500 **W:** radiobandab.com.br **E:** portal@radiobandab.com.br – **PR10)** Rua Lord Lovat 497, 87600-000 Nova Esperança ☎44 3252 4533 **W:** cancaonova.com **E:** rede@cancaonova.com – **PR11)** Rua Oyapock, 649, Cristo Rei, 80050-450 Curitiba ☎41 3218 5860 **W:** radiocidade670.com.br – **PR13)** Rua Sergipe, 843, sala 05, 86010-360 Londrina ☎43 3306 1105 **W:** radiodifusoradelondrina.com.br **E:** contato@radiodifusoralondrina.com.br – **PR15)** Av Paraná, 1885, Boa Vista, 82510-000 Curitiba ☎41 3251 2410 **W:**radioevangelismo.com **E:** marumby@terra.com.br – **PR16)** Av. Capitão Índio Bandeira, 1400 5° Andar - Centro Empresarial Antares, 87300-005 Campo Mourão ☎44 3017 0013 **W:** Facebook: R.Objetiva – **PR20)** rua Ephigenio Pereira da Cruz 1404, 83820-000 Rio Grande ☎43 3627 1131 **W:** redecartario.com.br – **PR21)** Rua Francisco Rosa e Silva, 28, Parque Presidente, 85852-250 Foz do Iguaçu ☎45 3026 8020 **W:** radioculturafoz.com.br **E:** jornalismocultura@foz.net – **PR22)** Rodovia do Xisto BR 476 Km 20 No 2018, 83700-000 Araucária ☎41 3642 1010 **W:** radioiguassu.com.br **E:** radioiguassu@radioiguassu.com.br – **PR23)** Rua Coronel Manoel Ferreira Bello 64, 85530-000 Clevelândia ☎46 3252 1286 **W:** rdprogresso.com.br **E:** redacao@rdprogreso.com.br – **PR25)** Av. Euclides Cunha 455, Zona 04, 87015-180 Maringá ☎44 3225 8050 **W:**novainga.com.br **E:**comercial@pingafogo.com.br – **PR27)** Praça Marechal Floriano Peixoto 581, 3° andar, (C.P 090 84001-970) 84010-910 Ponta Grossa ☎42 3028 0042 📠42 3222 3566 **W:** radiosantana.com.br **E:** comercial@radiosantana.com.br – **PR28)** Av Largo São Vicente de Paulo 1085, 85900-215 Toledo ☎45 3055 2841 **W:** radiouniaodetoledo.com.br **E:** radiouniaoatendimento@uol.com.br – **PR29)** Rua Sao Paulo 910, 86808-070 Apucarana ☎43 3423 1100 **W:** novaam.com.br **E:** novaam@uol.com.br – **PR30)** Av Aylton Rodrigues Alves 1189, 86600-000 43 3255 2276 Rolândia **W:** Facebook: R.Cultura de Rolândia **E:** radioculturaderolandia@gmail – **PR31)** Rua Robero Vichinheski, 242, Pilarzinh, 82530-130 Curitiba ☎41 3013 3280 **W:** Facebook: R.Cultura AM 930 – **PR32)** Av Brasil 4312, 10° andae, 87013-000 Maringá ☎44 3041 4960 **W:** radiomaisfmpr.com.br **E:** oppec@gruporadiomais.com.br – **PR33)** Rua Dom Bosco, 145, Jd Dom Bosco, 86060-340 Londrina **W:** facebook.com/radioalvoradalondrina/ **E:** radioalvoradalondrina@gmail.com ☎43 3347 0303 – **PR34)** Rua Santa Catarina 970, 85960-000 Marechal Cândido Rondón ☎45 3284 8080 **W:** radiodifusora.com.br **E:** comercial@radiodifusora.net - **FM:** 95.1 MHz – **PR35)** Rua Araribóia, 1909, Parque Santa Clara,(CP 540) 85505-030 Pato Branco ☎46 2101 2244 **W:** radiocelinauta.com.br **E:** comercial@redecelinauta.com.br – **PR36)** Praça Generoso Marques 90, Galeria Andrade, Ed Claudia 1° andar, 80020-230 Curitiba ☎41 3322 8483 **W:** radiocolombo.com.br **E:** comercial@radiocolombo.com.br – **PR37)** Av Pedro Soccol 542, 85884-000 Medianeira ☎45 3264 1713 **W:** independenciaam.com.br – **PR38)** Rua Paraná 650, 874-000 Cruzeiro do Oeste ☎44 3676 1184 **W:** difusoraregional.com.br – **PR39)** Rua Visconde de Mauá, 123, Jardim Shangrilá, 86070-540 Londrina ☎43 3328 1030 – **PR41)** Rua Maranhão, 2955, Alto Alegre, 85805-220 Cascavel ☎45 3321 7000 **W:** nacionalnews.com.br **E:** cantini@cbncascavel.com.br – **PR42)** Praça Senador Corrêa 55 (✉ CP 20548, 80010-210 Curitiba, ☎41 3221 6070 **W:** padrereginaldomanzotti.org.br **E:** sas@evangelizarepreciso.com.br - **FM:** 90.9 & 99.5 MHz – **PR44)** Rua Porto Alegre 21, Edifico Scala 1° andar, 85601-480 Francisco Beltrão ☎46 3055 2255 **W:** radioeducadorafb.com.br **E:** contato@radioeducadorefb.com.br – **PR49)** Rua João Carlos Farias 85, 86300-000 Cornélio Procópio ☎43 3524 2333 **W:** terranativaam.com.br – **PR51)** Rua das Américas 255, 85550-000 Coronel Vivida ☎46 3232 1142 **W:** portalrvp.com.br **E:** atendimento@radiovicentepallotti.com.br – **PR53)** Rua Quince de Novembro 2175, 8° andar, 83005-000 São José dos Pinhais ☎40 3058 7404 **W:** radiomais.am.br **E:**opec@gruporadiomais.com.br – **PR54)** Av Cristóvão Colombo 1055, 86990-000 Marialva ☎44 3232 1115 – **PR57)** Av. Sete de Setembro, 3341, Cristo Rei, 80050-315 Curitiba ☎41 3025 5770 **W:** radioatalaiacuritiba.com.br - **FM:** 88.5 MHz – **PR58)** Rua Raimundo Leonardi 1301, 85900-110 Toledo ☎45 3378 3161 **W:** radioguacu.com.br **E:** radioguacu@uol.com.br – **PR60)** Rua João Negrão 595, 80010-200 Curitiba ☎41 3324 3849 **W:** superradiodeuseamor.com.br – **PR61)** Av Paraná 596, 85887-000 Matelândia ☎45 3262 1140 **W:** radiomatelandia.com.br **E:** radiomatelandia@matelnet.com.br – **PR64)** Rua Cedro 418, 85650-000 Santa Isabel do Oeste ☎46 3542 1239 **W:** radiodanubioazul.com.br **E:** contato@radiodanubioazul.com.br – **PR65)** Rua José Ferreira "Nhô Belo" 262, 86975-000 Mandaguari ☎44 3233 1180 **W:** radioguairaca.com.br **E:** guairaca@bwnet.com.br – **PR67)** Rua Julio Perneta, 570 – Mercês, 80810-110 Curitiba ☎41 3082 3476 **W:**capital.grpcom.com.br **E:** isaquemenezes@hotmail.com – **PR69)** Rua Ponta Grossa 1982 1° Andar (✉ C.P. 71), 85601-600 Francisco Beltrão ☎46 3524 2676 **W:** seleski.com.br/princesa.html **E:** princesaam@seleski.com.br – **PR70)** Av Pedro Taques, 1864, Jd Alvorada 87033-000 Maringá ☎44 3267 3000 **W:** radioatalaia.com.br **E:** radioatalaiamaringa@hotmail.com – **PR72)** Rua Ana Berta Rosekamp, 940, Jardim Rosekamp, 81530-250 Curitiba ☎41 3266 1320 **W:** radiotropicalgospel.com.br – **PR73)** Rua João Batista de Oloveira Filho 255, 86030-550 Londrina ☎43 3378 2100 **W:** radiobrasilsul.com.br **E:** comercial@radiobrasilsul.com.br – **PR74)** Rua TV Silvério Carneiro, 3 - Centro, 84220-000 Cidade Sengés ☎43 3535 1144 – **PR75)** Rua Doutor Camargo 5152, 87502-010 Umuarama ☎44 3622 5033 **W:** radioinconfidenciaam.com.br **E:**nova@radioinconfidenciaam.com.br – **PR76)** Rua Exp Adir Jorge 511, 83880-000 Rio Negro ☎47 3642 3969 – **PR77)** Rua Flamingos 357, 86701-390 Arapongas ☎42 3252 0570 **W:** cultura1340.com.br – **PR78)** Av Paul Harris, 50, Conjunto Paraiso, 86220-000 Assaí ☎43 3262 1367 **W:** redeterranativa.com **E:** radiolideram@hotmail.com.br – **PR80)** Av. Marechal Floriano Peixa, 4809, Vila Hauer, 81610-150 Curitiba ☎41 3091 1370 **W:** blog.cancaonova.com/curitiba **E:** radiocuritiba@cancaonova.com – **PR81)** Rua Paraiba 168, 86930-000 São João do Ivaí ☎43 3477 1117 **E:** radioeducadora1180@gmail.com – **PR82)** Av.Pedro Taques 1901, 87033-190 Maringa ☎44 3220 8061 **W:**facebook.com/ipdmaringa/ - **FM:** 102.5MHz – **PR88)** Rua Nicanor do Santos Silva 4465, 87501-120 Umuarama ☎44 3624 4664 **W:** culturaumuarama.com.br – **PR90)** Rua Dom Pedro I 420, 85710-000 Santo Antônio do Sudoeste ☎46 3563 1541 **W:** radioentrerios1170.com.br **E:** contato@radioentrerios1170.com.br – **PR91)** Rua Mato Grosso 2229, 85812-020 Cascavel ☎45 3220 1717 **W:** radiocolmeia.com.br **E:** radiocolmeia@brturbo.com – **PR93)** Rua Vicente Inácio Filho 241, 86360-000 Bandeirantes ☎43 3542 3233 **W:** radiocabiuna.com.br – **PR95)** Rua Mal Deodoro da Fonseca 717, 87550-000 Altônia

☎44 3659 3444 **W:** radiorainha.com.br – **PR97)** Rua Coronel Dulcido 1101, 84010-908 Ponta Grossa ☎42 3225 2144 23222 7115 **W:** centraldoparana.com.br **E:** central@centraldoparana.com.br – **PR101)** Rua dos Andradas 249, 85640-000 Ampére ☎46 3547 1236 **W:** radioampere.com.br **E:** radioampere@ampernet.com.br – **PR105)** Rua Arthor Mehl 390, 85200-000 Pitanga ☎43 3641 1739 **W:** radiopitanga.com.br **E:** radiopitanga@radiopitanga.com.br – **PR108)** Rua João Carlos Farias 85, 86300-000 Cornélio Procópio ☎43 3524 2333 **W:** rc1490.com/ **E:** radiocornelio@uol.com.br – **PR110)** Avenida Paraná,540, 86925-000 Borrazópolis ☎43 3425 1233 **W:** radionovaera.com.br – **PR111)** Av, São João No. 1952 (✉C.P 121, 84400-970) 84400-000 Prudentópolis ☎📠42 3446 1547 **W:** radioesperancaam.com.br **E:** radioesperanca810@hotmail.yahoo.com.br – **PR112)** Rua Rouxinol 752, 86703-150 Arapongas ☎43 3055 2133 **W:** radioarapongas.com.br **E:** radioarapongas@uol.com.br – **PR115 PR117)** Av Souza Naves 890, 86870-000 Ivaiporã ☎43 3472 4366 **W:** radiouba.com.br – **PR118)** Rua 1° de Maio 694, 85950-000 Palotina ☎44 3649 5266 **W:** vivaoeste.com.br **E:** vivaoeste@novaradiocultura.com.br – **PR119)** Rua Dom Pedro II, 1889, Vila Dom Pedro II, 834608-380 Campo Largo ☎41 3392 1111 **W:**radioagapeam.com.br **E:**radioagapeam@brturbo.com.br – **PR120)** Rua Mauá 2518, 85770-000 Realeza ☎46 3543 1030 **W:** radiocluberza.com **E:** radioclube@wln.com.br – **PR127)** Rua do Comércio 654, 85660-000 Dois Vizinhos ☎46 3536 3131 **W:** educadoradv.com.br **E:** radio@educadoradv.com.br – **PR129)** Rua Sao Paulo 180, 86380-000 Andirá ☎43 3538 3522 **W:** culturaandira.com.br **E:** comercial@culturaandira.com.br – **PR130)** Rua São Paulo 489, 86840-000 Faxinal ☎📠43 3461 1291 **W:** radioclubdefaxinal.com.br – **PR131)** Rua Noruega 98, 86182-000 Cambé ☎43 3154 1772 **W:** cidadeam770.com.br – **PR137)** Rua Melissa 520, 85410-000 Nova Aurora ☎45 3243 1233 **W:** clubamnovaaurora.com.br **E:** comercial@clubamnovaaurora.com.br – **PR138)** Avenida Brasil 531, 85851-000 Foz do Iguaçu ☎45 3572 2410 **W:** radiofiladelfia.com.br **E:** radioculturamorenafiladelfia@gmail.com – **PR139)** Rua Antônio Costa, 529, Vista Alegere das Mercês, 80820-020 Curitiba ☎41 3240 7000 **W:** radiobandab.com.br **E:** bandabad@radiobandab.com.br – **PR141)** Av Paraná, 220 - Centro, 84470-000 Cândido de Abreu (📠43 3476 1244 **W:** alternativa710.com.br **E:** ralternativa@onda.com.br – **PR144)** Rua Cet San Tiago Dantas 159 , 85560-000 Chopinzinho ☎46 3242 1435 **W:** radiodifusoraamerica.com.br – **PR145)** Av Paraná, 201,, 85852-000 Foz do Iguaçu ☎45 3523 2211 **W:** semprerci.com.br **E:** administrativo@cbnfoz.com.br – **PR146)** Av Presidente Kennedy, 170, Norte, 85950-000 Palotina ☎44 3649 0570 **W:** Facebook: R.Continental Palotina **E:** radiocontinentalam@hotmail.com – **PR147)** Av. Minas Gerais 31, 85420-000 Corbélia ☎45 3242 1799 **W:** radiointegracao.net – **PR148)** Rua Farroupilha 80, 2° andar, 85877-000 São Miguel do Iguaçu ☎43 3565 1033 **W:** radiojornalsaomiguel.com.br **E:** artistico@gmail – **PR150)** Av Sao Paulo 440, 87320-000 Roncador ☎44 3575 1341 **W:** princesa820.com.br - **FM:** 87.9 MHz – **PR152)** Rua Dom Pedro II 1581, 85901-270 Toledo. ☎45 3055 2240 **W:** radiointegracaoam.com.br **E:** radiointegracao@uol.com.br – **PR155)** Rua Rosalvo Petrechem 551, 85200-000 Pitanga ☎42 3646 3366.**W:** radiopoema.com.br **E:** radiopoema@radiopoema.com.br – **PR161)** Rua Antonio Rosa 1170, 86490-000 Ribeirão do Pinhal ☎43 3551 1438 **W:** culturapinhal.com **E:** contat@culturapinhal.com – **PR162)** Rua Vicente Machado, 84570-000 Mallet ☎42 3542 2004 – **PR164)** Rua São Miguel 922, 85570-000 São João ☎46 3533 1474 **W:** radiosaojoao.com.br **E:** radio@radiosaojoao.com.br – **PR165)** Rua Guarani 829, 85501-140 Pato Branco ☎46 3225 4000 **W:** radiopatobranco.com.br **E:** ouvinte@radiopatobranco.com.br – **PR171)** Av Londrina 523, 87111-220 Sarandi ☎44 3042 1090 **W:** banda1am.com.br – **PR173)** Rua Paraná 21, 83540-000 Rio Branco do Sul ☎41 3652 7070 **W:** radiotradicaoam.com.br **E:** comercial@radiotradicaoam.com.br – **PR174)** Rua Parigot de Souza 47, 86740-000 Pérola d´Oeste ☎46 3556 1048 **W:** radioperola.com.br **E:** contato@radioperola.com.br – **PR179)** Rua Pedro de Oliveira 938, 85440-000 Ubiratã ☎📠44 3543 1717 **W:** radiodifusoraubirata.com.br **E:** rdifusora@gmail.com – **PR184)** Rua José Carlos Colodel, 306 cj 5, Vila Santa Terezina, 83501-140 Almirante Tamandaré ☎41 3699 6622 **W:** radiobarigui.com.br

RJ00) RIO DE JANEIRO

RJ01) Rua Visconde Itaboraí, 184, Guaratiba, 23032-500 Niterói ☎11 2985 8596 **W:** felizfm.fm - **FM:** 94.9 MHz – **RJ03)** Estrada dos Bandeirantes, 1000, Taquara, 22710-112 Rio de Janeiro ☎21 3412 1175 **W:** radiorelogiofederal.blogspot.no **E:** nossaradiorio@gmail.com – **RJ06)** Praça Demerval Barbosa Moreira 28, 28610-160 Nova Friburgo ☎22 2523 3034 **W:** radiofriburgoam.com.br **E:** contato@novafriburgoam.com.br – **RJ07)** Rua General Gustavo Cordeiro de Farias, 84, Benfica, 20910-220 Rio de Janeiro ☎21 2567-2000 **W:**radiocopacabanaam.com **E:** copacabana680@gmail.com – **RJ08)** Rua Vinte e Um de Abril, 272 An 4 Sl 413, 28010-170 Campos dos Goytacazes ☎22 2723 8080 **W:** radioabsoluta.com.br – **RJ09)** Rua México 111 slj, 20031-145 Rio de Janeiro ☎21 2220 3656 **W:** redesucesso.com – **RJ11)** Rua Abilio José de Mattos, 3745 - Portoda Pedra São Gonçalo, 24436-000 Rio de Janeiro ☎21 2215-1768 **W:** radiomanchete.com.br **E:** contato@radiomanchete.com.br – **RJ12)** Rua da Relação, 18, 12° andar, 20231-110 Rio de Janeiro ☎21 2117-6202 221 2117 6235 **W:** radios.ebc.com.br – **RJ15)** Rua Av. Portugal 96, 22291-050 Rio de Janeiro ☎21 4002 4190 **W:** radiotamoio.com.br – **RJ16)** Av. Marchal Floriano 114, 20080-002 Rio de Janeiro **W:** boavontade.com.br **E:** superrbv@boavontade.com – **RJ17)** Rua de Relação, 18, 12° andar, 20231 110 Rio de Janeiro ☎21 2117 6202 **W:** radios.ebc.com.br/nacionalrioam – **RJ18)** Rua Senador Pompeu, 27, 20008-010 Rio de Janeiro ☎21 2263 7521 **W:** radiocapitalrio.com.br – **RJ19)** Travessa Santa Luiza 91, 23900-900 Angra dos Reis ☎21 2295 8770 – **RJ20)** Rua Buenos Aires, 68, 19° andar, 20070-020 Rio de Janeiro ☎21 3171 1060 **W:** blog.cancaonova.com/riodejaneiro **E:** radioespiritosanto@cancaonova.com – **RJ22)** Estrada Adhemar Bebiano (ex-Estr. Velha da Pavuna), 3517, Inhaúma, 20765-170 Rio de Janeiro ☎21 2176 8276 **W:** metropolitana1090.com.br **E:** contato@metropolitana1090.com.br – **RJ24)** Rua Presidente Vargas, 541 - Centro, 25802-220 Três Rios ☎24 2252 0720 **W:** Facebook: Radio 3 Rios **E:** rtr@radiotresrios.com.br - **FM:** 89.7MHz – **RJ25)** Rua da Assembléia, 10, Sala 1201,20011-901 Rio de Janeiro ☎21 3799 1180 **W:** radiomundialamrj.com – **RJ27)** Rua do Livramento, 189 8°andar, Gamboa, 20221-194 Rio de Janeiro ☎21 2126 2421 **W:** tupi.am - **FM:** 96.5 MHz – **RJ28)** Rua Alberto Torres, 410 an3°, 28400-000 São Fidelis ☎22 2758 1275 **W:** radiocoroadosam.com **E:** radiocoroadosam1310@hotmail.com – **RJ29)** Av 28 de Setembro, 258, Loja 01, Vila Isabel, 20551-031 Rio de Janeiro ☎21 2576 9737 **W:** radioboasnovas.com.br **E:** comercial@radioboasnovas.com.br – **RJ30)** Rua Alvaro Ramos, 350, Botafogo, 22280-110 Rio de Janeiro ☎21 2543 1360 – **RJ31)** Rua Carlos Lacerda, 52-2° Andar – Centro, 28010-242 Campos dos Goytacazes ☎9827-9797 **W:** Facebook.com/radiocamposdifusiora/ **E:** angeladifusora@yahoo.com.br – **RJ32)** Av. Domingos Mariano No 291, 27345-310 Barra Mansa ☎24 3401-0724 **W:**novasulfluminenseam.com.br **E:**faturamento@radiosulfluminense.fm- **FM:** 96.1MHz – **RJ33)** Estrada do Dendê, 659-Tauá, Ilha do Governador, 21920-000 Rio de Janeiro ☎21 3386 1400 **W:** radioriodejaneiro.am.br **E:** marketing@radioriodejaneiro.am.br – **RJ35)** Rua do Mercado, 34-Sala 802, 20010-120 Rio de Janeiro ☎21 2233 8822 **W:** radiolivream.com.br **E:** falecom@radiolivream.com.br – **RJ38)** Rua Ana Nery, 120 9° andar, 27123-150 Barra do Piraí ☎24 2443 1470 224 2401 8367 **W:** gruporbp.com.br **E:** radiobpfm@gmail.com - **FM:** 89.9MHz – **RJ39)** Rua Senador Dantas 117, cob 02, Nova Iguaçú ☎21 2767 3333 **W:** tropicalam830.com **E:** tropical@tropicalam830.com – **RJ40)** Rod Br 101 Km 270 No 220 Basilio, 28800-000 Rio Bonito ☎21 2635 2263 **W:** facebook.com/radiojornal1340/**E:** sintoniadoforro@gmail.com – **RJ43)** Rua Emile Ducumunn,No 77 – Vázea, 25953-050 Teresópolis ☎21 2643 5555 **W:** portalgrpcom.com.br **E:** radioteresopolisam@gmail.com – **RJ44)** Rua Carvalho de Souza, 20 an 3°, Madureira, 21350-180 Rio de Janeiro ☎21 3390 1422 **W:** continental1520.com.br **E:** contato@continental1520.com.br – **RJ46)** Rua Marechal Deodoro, 46 an 9°salas 905, 25620-150 Petrópolis ☎24 2237 6161 📠24 2237 6161 **W:** http//radioimperiala.com.br **E:** imperialam@compuland.com.br – **RJ47)** Rua Francisco Belisário, 439, Santa Cruz, 23570-510 Rio de Janeiro ☎21 3395 1560 **W:** granderioam.com **E:**granderio1560am@gmail.com– **RJ48)** Rua Carneiro de Mendonça. 29-A, 27600-000 Valença ☎24 2453 4418 **W:** radioculturadovale.com.br – **RJ49)** Rua Tenente José Teixeira, 147-an 1°, 28360-000 Bom Jesus do Itabapoana ☎22 3831 1570 **W:** bomjesusam.com.br – **RJ50)** Rodovia Barão 101, s/n Km 206, 28860-000 Casimiro de Abreu ☎22 2778 5101 – **RJ51)** Rua Frei Valerio 58, 28740-00 Conceição de Macabu ☎22 2779 2100 **W:** popularfluminens.com **E:** frpfluminense@yahoo.com.br – **RJ52)** Rua São Marcos No 9 – Bairro Paraiso, 27536-050 Resende ☎24 3355 2266 **W:** r1r2.com.br **FM:** 90.5 MHz – **RJ53)** Rua Gal.Gustavo C.Farias, 84, Benfica, 20910-220 Rio de Janeiro ☎21 2582 0990 **W:** radiocontemporanea.com.br – **RJ54)** Rua Barão Piabanha, 107 Anexo 1 Mini Shopping, 25850-000 Paraíba do Sul ☎24 2263 2343 **W:** radioclube1540.com.br **E:** radioclube1540@hotmail.com – **RJ55)** Rua Gal Dionísio, 327, Guaratiba, 23025-330 Duque de Caxias ☎21 3652 1480 – **RJ56)** Rua Berlindo Figueiras de Barros 100, 28250-000 Italva ☎22 2783 1777 **W:** aliancaam.com.br **E:** superaliancaam@yahoo.com.br – **RJ58)** Rua Coronel Santiago, 250, Agriões, 25963-220 Teresópolis ☎21 2642 2000 **W:**

radiogeracao2000.com.br
RN00) RIO GRANDE DO NORTE
RN05) Praça Vigário Antonio Joaquim 39, 59600-520 Mossoró ☎84 8723 7993 **W:** ruraldemossoro.com.br **E:** gerencial@ruraldemossoro.com.br – **RN06)** Rua Augusto da Escossia Nogueira Neto, 2141, 59625-750 Mossoró ☎84 3312 4618 **W:** redepotiguar.com.br – **RN08)** Av Dr Cunha Mota, s/n, Pereiros, 59600-160 Mossoró (🖷84 3317 6167 **W:** portaldifusoramossoro.com**E:** difusora@difusoramossore.com.br – **RN10)** Av Deodoro, 245, 59012-600 Natal **W:** redeclubebrasil.blogspot.no – **RN12)** Rua Francisca Delfina 30, 59860-620 Alexandria ☎84 3381 2321 **W:** redepotiguar.com.br **E:** comercial@rederpc.com.br – **RN15)** Rua Nero Nazareno Fernandes, 250, Alto de Liberdade, 59780-0100 Caraúbas ☎🖷84 3337 2297 **W:** rpccentenario.com.br/ **E:** rpccentenario@hotmail.com – **RN18)** Rua Major Lula, 59300-000 Caicó ☎84 3421 2500 **W:** radioserido.com.br **E:** daguisoares@hotmail.com – **RN19)** Rua Avinida Rio Branco 173, 59655-000 Areia Branca ☎🖷84 3312 4618 **W:** redepotiguar.com.br **E:** comecial@rederpc.com.br – **RN20)** Rua Ana de Pontes, 419, 59255-000 Santo Antônio ☎84 3282 2347 – **RN21)** Rua Odorico Férreira de Souza, 70, Bairro DNER, 59200-000 Santa Cruz ☎84 3291 2300 **W:** radiosantacruzam.com.br **E:** radiosantacruzam@yahoo.com.br – **RN23)** Rua Cícero Tomáz de Azevedo, 1052, Cruz do Monte, 59360-000 Parelhas ☎🖷84 3471 2401 **W:** ruralam.com.br **E:** ruraldeparelhas@hotmail.com – **RN24)** Rua Heráclito Vilar, 59570-000 Ceará Mirim ☎84 3274 2794 – **RN25)** Rua Sebastião Guilherme Caldas, s/n, Baixa da Beleza, 59343-000 Jardim do Seridó (🖷84 3472 2587 **W:** radiocabugidoserido.com **E:** cabugidoserido@yahoo.com.br – **RN27)** Rua Presidente Quaresma, 708, Alecrim, 59031-150 Natal ☎84 3213 8911 – **RN28)** Rua Deputado Hésiquio Fernandes, 59930-000 São Miguel ☎84 3353 2112 **W:** radiodifusoradesaomiguel.blogspot.com.br – **RN29)** Av Ouro Branco, 430, 59460-000 São Paulo do Potengi 84 3251 2381**W:** radiopotengi.com.br – **RN30)** Av 21 de Abril 460, BR-460, 59550-000 João Câmara ☎ 🖷84 3262 2189 – **RN32)** Rua do Chafariz 1390, Bairro Novo Horizonte, 59584-000 Touros ☎84 3263 2121 **W:** R.Farol AM 1390 **E:** radiofarolgerencia@hotmail.com
RO00) RONDÔNIA
RO01) Rua José Bonifácio, 787, Olaria, 78902-280 Porto Velho ☎69 3224 1887 **W:** rbn-pvh.com.br – **RO05)** Rua Rui Barbosa 3375, Floresta, 76965 736 Cacoal ☎69 3441 2122 **W:** portalradiorondonia.com.br – **RO10)** Rua Dourados 4, Setor Industriales, 78930-000 Ariquemes ☎69 3535 3000 **W:** portalradiorondonia.com.br – **RO12)** Rua Princesa Isabel, 128, 78995-000 Vilhena ☎69 3321 3309 **W:** radiovilhena.com.br **E:** radiovilhena@brturbo.com.br – **RO15)** Rua Carlos Doneje 1304, Ctg, 78984-000 Pimenta Bueno ☎69 3222 5308 **W:** radiorondonia.com **E:** comercialpb@radiorondonia.com – **RO24)** Rua Jorge Texteira No 2005 Setor 07, 78940-000 Jaru ☎69 3521 4320 **W:** radiocentraljaru.com.br **E:** contato@radiocentraljaru.com.br
RR00) RORAIMA
RR01) Av Capitão Ene Garcez, 888, São Francisco, 69304-000 Boa Vista ☎95 3224 1651 **W:** radiororaima.com.br – **RR02)** Rua Sebastião Diniz, 363 - Centro, 69360-000 Caracaraí – **RR03)** 69350-000 Alto Alegre
RS00) RIO GRANDE DO SUL
RS02) Rua Antunes Ribas, 1535-an 3°, 98801-630 Santo Angelo ☎55 3313 3666 **W:** radiosepe.com.br **E:** contato@radiosepe.com.br – **RS03)** Rua Ramiro Barcelos 737, 96810-054 Santa Cruz ☎51 3715 5958 **W:** radiosantacruz.com.br **E:** gerencia@radiosantacruz.com.br – **RS04)** Rua General Sampaio, 161, Rio Branco, 95097-000 Caxias do Sul ☎54 3220 9400 **W:** tuaradio.com.br **E:** jornalismo@tuaradio.com.br - **FM:** 98.5MHz – **RS05)** Av. Sete de Setembro 509, 99010-121 Passo Fundo ☎54 3316 4800 **E:** diretoria@diariodamanha.net - **FM:** 98.7 MHz – **RS06)** Av Mascarenhas de Morães 586, 97300-000 São Gabriel ☎🖷55 3232 9335 **W:** redetche.com.br – **RS08)** Praça Oswaldo Aranha 39, 97541-540 Alegrete ☎55 3422 1600 **W:** redetche.com.br/alegrete **E:** joaoulisses@radioalegrete.com.br – **RS09)** Av Ipiranga, 1075-an3°, Azenha, 90160-093 Porto Alegre ☎51 3218 6600 **W:** clicrbs.com.br **E:** gaucha@rdgaucha.com.br - **FM:** 93.7 MHz – **RS10)** Rua Alberto Soveral, 64 – Barrio Treptow, 96020-120 Pelotas ☎53 3222 4334 **W:** radiopelotense.com.br **E:** radiopelot@terra.com.br – **RS11)** Rua Suécia 255, 98500-000 Tenente Portela ☎55 3551 1395 **W:** radiomunicipalam.com **E:** sec@radiomunicipalam.com – **RS13)** Rua Paul Harris 02, 97015-480 Santa Maria ☎55 3220 2131 **W:** radiosantamariense.com.br **E:** radiosantamariense@terra.com.br – **RS14)** Rua Delfino Riet, 183, Santo Antonio, 90660-120 Porto Alegre ☎51 3218 2100 **W:** band.com.br/rs – **RS15)** Av Mauricio Cardoso, 88 1° andar, 99700-000 Erechim ☎54 3321 2243 **W:**facebook.com.radiodifusaosul **E:** jornalismo@radiodifusaosul.com.br - **FM:** 94.9 MHz – **RS16)** Rua Voluntários da Patria 1432 , 97590-000 Rosário do Sul ☎55 3231 2533 **W:** radiomaraja.com **E:** contacto@radiomaraja.com – **RS17)** Rua Ramiro Barcelos 800, 95200-000 Vacaria ☎54 3232 4014 **W:** radio.cancaonova.com.vacari **E:** radiovacaria@hotmail.com - **FM:** 93.1MHz – **RS18)** Rua Neita Ramos 217, 96230-000 Santa Vitória do Palmar ☎53 3263 1660 **W:** redemeridional.com/sta.html **E:** culturasantavitoria@redemeridional.com – **RS19)** Rua Domingos Secchi 35, Boa Vista, 99500-000 Carazinho **W:** gazeta670.com.br **E:** comercial@gazeta670.com.br ☎54 3330 3143 – **RS20)** Travessa 4 de Junho 84, 98380-000 Seberi ☎55 3746 1040 🖷55 3746 1033 **W:** radioseberiam.com.br **E:** gerencia@radioseberi.com.br – **RS22)** Rua Mascarenhas de Morães 298, 97300-000 São Gabriel ☎55 3232 2244 **W:** radiobatovi.com.br **E:** radiobatovi@terra.com.br – **RS23)** Rua Caldas Jr. 219, 90019-900 Porto Alegre ☎51 3215 6320 **W:** radioguaiba.com.br **E:** guaibeiro@radioguaiba.com.br - **FM:** 101.3MHz – **RS25)** Av Júlio de Castilhos, 435, Vila Vista Alegre, 98300-000 Palmeira das Missões **W:** radiopalmeira.com.br **E:** am740@radiopalmeira.com.br ☎55 3742 2255 - **FM:** 101.7MHz – **RS26)** República do Libano 240, 96200-340 Rio Grande ☎53 3232 2303 **W:** radioculturariograndina.com.br **E:** radioculturariograndina@vetorial.net – **RS30)** Rua Pedro Vargas 846, 99500-000 Carazinho ☎54 3331 5250 **W:** diarioam780.com.br **E:** radio2@dariodamanha.net – **RS31)** Rua Orfanatrófio, 711, Alto Teresópolis , 90840-440 Porto Alegre ☎51 3218 2625 **W:** pampa.com.br/caicara **E:** ouvintrcaicara@pampa.com.br – **RS33)** Av Roraima, 1000-Cidade Universitária, Bairro Camboi, 97105-900 Santa Maria ☎55 3220 8377 **W:** ufsm.br/radio/ **E:** rd.universidade@gmail.com – **FM:** 107.9MHz – **RS34)** Rua Max Henrique Erichsen, 38 sala 101, Oriental, 95880-000 Estrela ☎51 3712 1259 **W:** 820dovale.com.br **E:** ouvinte@820dovale.com.br – **RS35)** Av Presidente Vargas 892, 98005-160 Cruz Alta ☎55 3322 1803 **W:** radioindependente.am.br – **RS36)** Av Julio de Castilhos, 607 - Centro Historico, 90030-131 Porto Alegre ☎51 3228 0191 **W:** radiocapital.net **E:** contato@radiocapital.net – **RS37)** Caladão Salvador Isaia, 1330, 3° andar, 97010-902 Santa Maria – **RS38)** Rua Álvaro Guaspari, 80, Marcilio Dias, 90035-020 Porto Alegre ☎51 3060 8008 **W:** radioitai.com.br **E:** radioitairs@gmail.com – **RS39)** Rua Osvaldo Aranha, 808 Sala 102B, Juventud, 95700-000 Bento Gonçalves ☎54 3452 7777 **W:**difusora890.com.br **E:** contato@difusora890.com.br – **RS41)** Rua XV de Novembro 336, 99770-000 Aratiba ☎54 3376 1138 **W:** radioaratiba.com.br **E:** am.900@hotmail.com – **RS43)** Rua 7 de Setembro, 1441 - Centro, 95800-000 Venâncio Aires ☎51 3741 2000 **W:** radiovenancioaires.com.br **E:** rva@radiovenancioaires.com.br – **RS44)** Av.Fernandes Bastos, 1683, Sobreloja, 95590-000 Tramandai ☎🖷51 3661 5657 **W:** Facebook: Radio Tramandaí AM 920 **E:** radiotramandai@hotmail.com - **FM:** 97.1 MHz – **RS45)** Rua Garibaldi, 789-21° andar, Ed. Estrela, 95084-900 Caxias do Sul ☎54 3289 3000 **W:** radiocaxias.am.br **E:** radiocaxias@radiocaxias.am.br - **FM:** 93.5 MHz – **RS46)** Av. Brasil 523, 98801-590 Santo Ângelo (🖷55 3313 2440 **W:** radiosantoangelo.com.br **E:** radiosan@radiosantoangelo.com.br – **RS47)** Av Alberto Müller, 242, Alto do Parque, 95900-000 Lajeado ☎51 3710 4900 **W:** independente.com.br **E:** recepcao@independente.com.br – **RS49)** Rua Orfanatrófio, 711, Alto Teresópolis, 90840-440 Porto Alegre ☎51 3218 2525 **W:** facebook.com/rdeldorado **E:** liberdade@pampa.com.br - **FM:** 99.7 MHz – **RS53)** Rua Garibaldi, 789 21° andar, 95084-900 Caxias do Sul ☎54 3289 3067 **W:** tuavoz.com.br **E:** ti@radiocaxias.com.br – **RS54)** Rua Julio de Castilhos, 2236, 97800-000 São Luís Gonzaga ☎55 3352 4141 **W:** radiomissioneira.com **E:** atendimento@radiomissioneira.com – **RS56)** Rua General Zeca Netto 1396, 96180-000 Camaquã. ☎51 3671 0962 **W:** redemeridional.com **E:** radiocamaquense@redemeridional.com – **RS57)** Rua São João, 1894, 97800-000 São Luís Gonzaga ☎55 3352 4444 **W:** radiosaoluiz.com **E:** redacao@radiosaoluiz.com – **RS58)** Rua General Osório 625, 96570-000 Caçapava do Sul ☎55 3281 1495 **W:** redemeridional.com/cacapava.html **E:** radiocacapava@redemeridional.com – **RS59)** Rua Tucunduva 758, 98640-000 Crissiumal ☎55 3524 1212 **W:** metropole1070.com.br – **RS60)** Rua Irmão José Sion, 370, 95720-000 Garibaldi ☎54 3462-4504 **W:** radioserrano.net **E:** geral@radioserrana.net – **RS61)** Rua João Carlos Machado 645, 98460-000 Iraí ☎55 3745 1444 **W:** radiomaraba.com.br **E:** maraba@speedrs.com.br – **RS62)** Rua Sarmento Leite, 426 - Centro, 90046-900 Porto Alegre ☎51 3308 3435 **W:** ufrgs.br/radio **E:** radiodir@ufrgs.br – **RS64)** Praça Padre Basso, 95, 99800-000 Marcelino Ramos ☎54 3372 1389 **W:** radiosalette.com.br **E:** radiosalette@terra.com.br – **RS65)** Av Bento Gonçalves, 733 - Centro, 98870-000 Giruá ☎55 3361 2020 **W:** radiogirua.com **E:** radiogirua@terra.com.br – **RS66)** Av Odilo Gonçalves 633, 96300-000 Jaguarão ☎53 3261 2933 **W:** redemeridional.com/jaguarao.html **E:** culturajaguarao@redemeridional.com – **RS67)** Rua Padre Oswaldo Stracke 56, 96900-

000 Sobradinho ☎51 3742 1089 **W:** radiosobradinho.com.br **E:** recepcao@radiosobradinho.com.br - **FM:** 97.3MHz "R.Jacuí" – **RS68)** Rua Borges do Canto, 1056, 97650-000 Itaqui ☎55 3433 8181 **W:** radiocruzeirodosul.com.br **E:** radiocruzeirodosul@terra.com.br – **RS69)** Rua Corrêa Lima, 1960, Morro Santa Tereza, 90850-250 Porto Alegre ☎51 3218 5781 🖷51 3218 5789 **W:** radiofarroupilha.com.br **E:** farroupilha@rdfarroupilha.com.br – **RS71)** Rua João Manoel 628, 98005-000 Cruz Alta ☎55 3322 7222 **W:** facebook.com/radiocruzalta**E:** jornalismo@grupopilau.com.br - **FM:** 105.1MHz – **RS72)** Rua Domingos de Almeida 2194, 97501-690 Uruguaiana ☎55 3412 1731 **W:** radiocharruaamfm.com.br **E:** amfm@radiocharrua.com.br - **FM:** 97.7MHz – **RS73)** Travess Victor Hugo Demaman Tomé 02, 96750-000 Butiá, **W:** radiojornalsobral.com.br **E:** contato@radiojornalsobral.com.br ☎51 3652 1140 – **RS74)** Rua Rui Barbosa 96, 95170-440 Farroupilha ☎54 3261 2121 **W:** miriamcaravaggio.com.br **E:** comercial@radiomiriam.com.br – **RS75)** Rua Tenente Lira 950 (C.P. 74), 98400-000 Frederico Westphalen ☎🖷55 3744 3500 **W:** luzealegria.com.br **E:** direcao@luzealegria.com.br - **FM:** 95.9MHz – **RS77)** Rua Félix da Cunha, 412, 96010-000 Pelotas ☎53 3225 1160 **W:** radiouniversidadeam.com.br – **RS78)** Av Coronel Victor Villa Verde, 491, Pitangueiras, 95500-000 Santo Antônio da Patrulha (🖷51 3662 1255 **W:** radioitapui.com.br **E:** itapui@radioitapui.com.br — **RS82)** Rua Anunciação, 480, Morro do Convento, 97900-000 Cerro Largo ☎55 3359 2022 **W:** radiocerroazul.com.br **E:** radiocerroazul@via-rs.net - **FM:** 105.9MHz 'Shamballa' – **RS84)** Av Comandantedt Kraemer, 97, 99700-000 Erechim ☎54 3522 1389 **W:** redetche.com.br **E:** administracao@radioerechim.com.br – **RS85)** BR 392, Km 232(✉ C.P. 130), 97340-000 São Sepé ☎55 3233 1113 🖷55 3233 1163 **W:** radiocotrisel.com.br **E:** radiocotrisel@radiocotirsel.com.br – **RS86)** Av Júlio de Castilho 607, 90030-131 Porto Alegre ☎51 3284 0778 **W:** radiotranscontinental.net **E:** radiorec@terra.com.br – **RS87)** Rua General Canabarro, 1450, Francisca Tarragaô, 97503-384 Uruguaiana ☎55 3412 1217 **W:** radiosaomiguel.com.br **E:** contato@radiosaomiguel.com.br – **RS89)** Rua Rui Barbosa 373, 99600-000 Nonoai ☎54 3362 1384 **W:** cluberadio.com.br - **FM:** 89.7 MHz – **RS90)** Av Adolfo Schneider,85 2° andar, 95320-000 Nova Prata ☎🖷54 3242 1648 **W:** radioprata.com.br **E:** radioprata@radioprata.com.br – **RS91)** Praça Silvestre Corréa 77, 96610-000 Encruzilhada do Sul ☎51 3733 1157**W:** radioencruzilhadense.com.br – **RS92)** Rua Júlio de Castilhos 605 2° andar, 95290-000 Bom Jesus ☎54 3237 1247 **W:** bomjesus.rs.gov.br/radio_aparados.php **E:** radioaparados@bomjesus.rs.gov.br – **RS93)** Rua General Osório 1134, 98200-000 Ibirubá ☎54 3324 1758 **W:** sistemaepu.com.br **E:** atendimento@sistemaepu.com.br - **FM:** 96.6MHz – **RS94)** Rua Ponciano Ramos 74, 96700-000 São Jerônimo ☎51 3651 1113 **W:** radiosaojeronimo.com.br **E:** am.1240@hotmail.com – **RS95)** Av Júlio de Castilhos, 1511-8° andar, salas 81/84, 95010-003 Caxias do Sul ☎54 3223 6788 **W:** radiodifusoracaxiense.com.br **E:** radio@ radiodifusoracaxiense.com.br – **RS96)** Rua 15 de Novembro 717, 96015-000 Pelotas **W:** radiotupanci.com.br **E:** tupanci@terra.com.br ☎53 3222 7263 – **RS97)** Rua Riachuelo 928, 97670-000 São Borja ☎55 3431 2479 **W:** radioculturaam1260.com.br **E:** contato@radioculturaam1260.com.br – **RS101)** Rua Balduíno Schneider 254, 98920-000 Horizontina (🖷55 3537 1212 **W:** radioveracruz.com.br **E:** recepcao@radioveracruz.com.br – **RS102)** Rua Dr Pio Ferreira 453, 96170-000 São Lourenço do Sul ☎53 3251 1303 **W:** radiosaolourenco.com.br **E:** radio.sls@vetorial.net – **RS104)** Av São Paulo, 722, 3° andar, São Geraldo, 90230-160 Porto Alegre **W:** boavontade.com/radio/ **E:** superrbv@bosvontade.com ☎51 3325 7000 – **RS105)** Rua 25 de Julho 39, 98960-000 Santo Cristo ☎55 3541 1188 **W:** radioregional1300.com.br – **RS107)** Av Duque de Caxias 1320, 99560-000 Sarandi ☎54 3361 5656 **W:** tuaradio.com.br/sarand-am **E:** conteudo@redescalabriniana.org – **RS108)** Av Júlio de Castilhos 232, 95680-000 Canela ☎54 3282 8822 **W:** radioclubedecanela.com.br **E:** radioclube@pdh.com.br - **FM:** 88.5MHz – **RS109)** Rua General Osório, 1276, 98280-000 Panambi ☎55 3375 8200 **W:** grupopilau.com.br **E:** panambi@grupopilau.com.br – **RS110)** Av Bento Goncalves 3361, 96015-145 Pelotas ☎53 3027 2175 **W:** radioculturapelotas.com.br **E:** estudio@radioculturapelotas.com.br – **RS111)** Av Rio Branco 401, 96450-000 Dom Pedrito ☎53 3243 4000 **W:** radioupacarai.com.br **E:** comercial.upacarai@hotmail.com – **RS113)** Av. Ipiranga, 1075, Azena, 90160-093 Porto Alegre ☎51 3218 6754 **W:** cbn.com.br **E:** cbn@rbsradios.com.br – **RS115)** Av Santos Dumont 240, 98600-000 Três Passos ☎55 3522 1011 **W:** rd3.net.br **E:** radiodifusoratrespassos@yahoo.com – **RS118)** Rua John Kennedy 2220 sala 18, 95270-000 Flores da Cunha ☎54 3028 3888 **W:** http:/comunidadeoasis.org.br **E:** oasis@comunidadeoasis.org.br - **FM:** 107.9 MHz – **RS119)** Rua Gaspar Martins 55-3° andar, 97542-000 Alegrete ☎55 3422 1236 **W:** gazetadealegrete.com**E:** rgta@ig.com.br – **RS120)** Rua Conde de Porto Alegre 521, 97573-581 Sant´Ana do Livramento ☎55 3242 3066 **W:** culturalivramento.com.br **E:** culturalivramento@brturbo.com.br – **RS121)** Rua Presidente Getúlio Vargas 153, 99490-000 Tapera ☎54 3385 1166 **W:** sistemaepu.com.br **E:** cultura@sistemaepu.com.br – **RS122)** Rua Chaves Barcellos, 36, conj 1205 - Centro Historico, 90030-120 Porto Alegre ☎🖷51 3226 1390 **W:** radioesperanca.com.br **E:** adm@radioesperanca.com.br – **RS125)** Rua Marechal Floriano, 373, Cassino, 96205-190 Rio Grande ☎53 3201 5054 **W:** radiominuano.adcast.com.br **E:** minuanorg@gmail.com – **RS126)** Rua São Francisco 246, 98900-970 Santa Rosa ☎55 3312 4060 **W:** radiosantarosa.com.br – **RS129)** Rua Teófilo Conrado de Matos 135, 96600-000 Canguçu br ☎53 3252 1144 **W:** radiocultura1030am.com.br **E:** cultura1030@brturbo.com.br – **RS130)** Av das Hortencias 78, 95670-000 Gramado ☎54 3286 2323 **W:** radioexcelsior.com.br **E:** excelsioram@serragaucha.com.br – **RS131)** Rua São João 1637, 95780-000 Montenegro ☎51 3632 6496 **W:** radioamerica-am.com.br **E..** radio@radioamerica-com.br – **RS132)** Rua Republica de Líbano 135, 96200-360 Rio Grande ☎53 3035 3060 **W:** radiocassino.com.br **E:** diretor@radiocassino.com.br – **RS133)** Av Sete de Setembro 672, 96400-003 Bagé ☎53 3242 1471 **W:** radioculturabage.com.br **E:** radioculturabage@hotmail.com – **RS136)** Rua Santos Inacio de Loiola 253, sl 203, 93700-000 Campo Bom ☎51 3585 1470 **E:** radiocinderela@gmail.com.br – **RS137)** Rua Julio de Castilhos 325, 95720-000 Garibaldi ☎54 3464 7500 **W:** radsiogaribaldi.com.br **E:** jornalismo@radiogaribaldi.com.br – **RS138)** Rua Gabriel Machado, 1590, 3° andar, 97610-000 São Francisco de Assis **E:** radiodifusao@terra.com.br ☎55 3252 1166 – **RS139)** Rua General Osorio 943, 96600-000 Canguçu (🖷53 3252 1515 **W:** radioliberdadeam.com.br **E:** atendimento@radioliberdadeam.com.br – **RS140)** Rua Rio Branco 1006, 95600-000 Taquara **W:** jornalpanorama.com.br **E:** radiotaquara@faccat.br ☎51 3542 2288 – **RS143)** Rua José Bonafácio 1128, (✉ C.P. 144) 96450-970 Dom Pedrito ☎53 3243 1434 **W:** modulosite.tecnologia.ws/modulo-am/SULINA **E:** **radio**sulina@hotmail.com – **RS144)** Rua Quitino Bocaiuva 100, 93135-030 São Leopoldo ☎51 3554 2894 **W:** redetche.com.br – **RS147)** Av Flores da Cunha 4283, 949150-004 Cachoeirinha ☎51 3421 1922 **W:** radiometropoleam.com.br **E:** radiometropoleam@terra.com.br – **RS148)** Rua 7 de Setembro 792, 95960-970 Encantado ☎51 3751 1580 **W:** rdencantado.com.br **E:** comercial@rdencantado.com.br - **FM:** 97.7 MHz – **RS151)** Rua Paraguai 42, 98980-000 Porto Lucena ☎55 3565 1200 **W:** portalfunave.com.br **E:** radionavegantes@san.psi.br – **RS154)** Rua Tiradentes 2839 Sala 5, 96360-970 Pedro Osório ☎53 3254 1239 **W:** radioclube990.com.br **E:** comercial@radioclube990.com.br – **RS155)** Av Borges de Medeiros, 1462, Chacara, 97650-000 Itaqui ☎56 3433 2301 **W:** radiopitangueira.com.br **E:** radio@pintagueira.com.br - **FM:** 94.5 MHz – **RS157)** Rua Baltazar Brum, 343, 97560-000 Quaraí ☎55 3423 1065 – **RS158)** Rua Sete de Setembro, 1835 - Centro, 95860-000 Taquari ☎51 3653 4033 **W:** jornaloacoriano.com **E:** contato@jornaloacoriano.com – **RS159)** Av Maurício Cardoso 761, 99300-000 Soledade ☎54 3381 1550 **W:** radiosoledade.com.br **E:** radiosoledade@terra.com.br – **RS162)** Av. Narciso Silva 1791, 96160-000 Capão do Leão ☎53 3227 4252 **W:** facebook.com/redecidaders **E:** redecidaders@gmail.com – **RS164)** Rua Floriano Peixoto 222, 97400-000 São Pedro do Sul ☎55 3276 1311 **W:** radiomunicipalsaopedrense.com.br **E:** contato@radiomunicipalsaopedrense.com.br – **RS165)** Rua Duque de Caxias 375, Sala 302, 98430-000 Palmitinho ☎55 3791 1175 **W:** radiochiru.com.br **E:** radiochiru@radiochiru.com.br - **FM:** 107.9 MHz – **RS167)** Rua Francisco Gobbi 545, 98580-970 Coronel Bicaco ☎55 3557 1195 🖷55 3557 1220 **W:** radioguarita.com.br **E:** radioguarita@yahoo.com.br – **RS168)** Av Alto Jacuí, 435, 99470-000 Não Me Toque ☎54 3332 1488 **W:** radioceres.com.br **E:** radioceres@radioceres.com.br – **RS171)** Rua Luiz Vieira 525, 96760-970 Tapes ☎51 3672 1031 **W:** radiotapense.com **E:** rt@conectsul.com.br – **RS173)** Rua Albino Brendler, 122 - Centro, 98700-000 Ijuí ☎55 3332 7090 **W:** jmijui.com.br **E:** radiojmijui@gmail.com – **RS175)** Rua Pedro Alvares Cabral 164, 99660-000 Campinas do Sul ☎51 3366 1266 **W:** radiocampinasdosul.com.br **E:** radiocampinas@tolrs.com.br – **RS177)** Av Barão do Triunfo 584 2° andar, 95995-000 Arvorezinha ☎51 3772 2443 **W:** redeculturaderadio.com.br **E:** admcultura@msbnet.com.br - **FM:** 92.3MHz – **RS179)** Rua Jornal NH, 99, Ideal, 93334-350 Novo Hamburgo ☎51 3593 9000 **W:** radioabc900.com.br **E:** diretorabc@gruposinos.com.br – **RS198)** Av. Brasil, 385 sala 202, 93180-000 Portão ☎55 3562 5300 **W:** radioestacaoportao.com.br **E.:** radioam1430@hotmail.com – **RS201)** Rua Orfanotrófio, 711, Santa Tereza, 90840-440 Porto Alegre ☎51 3218 2525 **W:** redepampa.com.br/rdgenral **E:** grenal@rdgrenal.com.br - **FM:** 95.9 MHz

SC00) SANTA CATARINA

SC01) Almeda Aristiliano Ramos 36, 89160-000 Rio do Sul **W:** radiomirador.com.br **E:** am540@radiomirador.com.br ☎47 3531 2100 📠47 3531 2102 – **SC02)** Av Centenario, 6050, Próspera, 88815-000 Criciúma ☎48 3461 5700 **W:** am570.com.br **E:** jornalismo@radioeldorado.net - **FM:** 89.5 MHz – **SC03)** Av Martin Piaseski 25, 89910-970 Descanso. ☎49 3623 0307 **W:**progresso.am.br **E:** comerical@progresso.am.br – **SC04)** Rua Benjamin Constant, 286-D 3 e 4 andares, 89801-970 Chapecó ☎49 3323 5177 📠49 3323 0526 **W:** superconda.com.br **E:** jornalismoconda@zipway.com.br – **SC05)** Rua Carlos Gomes 12, 89160-051 Rio do Sul (📠47 3521 1155 **W:** superdifusora.am.br/?pg=2Vale **E:** difusora@superdifusora.am.br - **FM**: 94.9 «Amanda FM» – **SC06)** Rua João Beux Sobredinho 350, 89990-000 São Lourenço d'Oeste **W:** radiodoze.com.br **E:** contato@radiodoze.com.br ☎49 3344 1544 – **SC09)** Rua Gustavo Richard 90, 88701-220 Tubarão ☎48 3626 4633 **W:** radiotuba.com.br **E:** radiotuba@radiotuba.com – **SC10)** Rua General Vieira da Rosa 1570, 88020-420 Florianópolis ☎48 3216 2550 **W:** cbndiario.com.br **E:** cbndiario@gmail.com – **SC11)** Rua Guilherme Helmut Arent 277, 89700-970 Concórdia ☎49 3441 2800 **W:** radioalianca.com.br – **SC12)** Rua Buenos Aires, 145, Ponta Aguda, 89051-050 Blumenau ☎47 3222-9004 **W:** radionereuramos.com.br **E:** nereu@radionereuramos.com.br – **SC14)** Rua Veneriano dos Passos 385, 89560-000 Videira 49 3533 4000 **W:** radiovideira.com.br – **SC15)** Rua Ângelo Dias 207, Cj 61/62/63, 89010-020 Blumenau ☎47 3041-9699 **W:**facebook.com/radiogloboblumenau **E:** rfc@rfc.com.br – **SC17)** Rua João Suzin Marini 64, 89700-000 Concórdia ☎49 3441 3838 **W:** radiorural.com.br – **SC18)** Av do Adão 1784, Morro da Cruz, 88025-150 Florianópolis **SC20)** Rua Conselheiro Rui Barbosa, 50 1° andar, 88350-320 Brusque ☎47 3351 4611 **W:** radiocidadeam.com.br **E:** diretoria@radiocidadeam.com.br – **SC21)** Rua Santa Catarina 93 Sala 2, 88200-000 Tijucas ☎48 3263 0303 **W:** radiovaletj.com.br **E:** contato@radiovaletj.com.br – **SC22)** Rua João Ramiro Machado, 321 Edificio Cidade das Colinas, 88870-000 Orleãns ☎48 3466 0533 **W:** guarujaam.com.br **E:** guarujadirecao@terra.com.br – **SC23)** Av Brasil, 260 Centro Comercial Tiradentes-3° andar, 89820-970 Xanxerê ☎49 3433 0171 **W:** superdifusora.com.br **E:** difusora@superdifusora.com.br – **SC24)** Centro Comercial Geschäfthaus, sala 20/21, 88353-120 Brusque ☎47 3351 1744 **W:** araguaia970am.com.br **E:** fale@araguaia970am.com.br – **SC25)** Rua São Bonifacio 280, 89896-000 Itapiranga ☎49 3677 0362 **W:**facebook.com/radioitapiranga– **SC30)** Alameda Rolf Colin, 80, America, 89204-070 Joinville ☎47 3422 2325 **W:**radiocolon.com.br – **SC31)** Rua Vidal Ramos 519, 88701-160 Tubarão ☎48 3632 9009 **W:** bandeirantes1090.com.br – **SC32)** Largo São Sebastião, 88-Centro, 88015-530 Florianópolis ☎48 3224-6470 **W:**divinooleiro.com.br/radio/cultura-am1110 **E:** direcao@radiocultura1110am.com.br – **SC34)** Travessa João Winkler 15, 89820-000 Xanxerê ☎49 3433 1110 **W:** redeprincesa.com.br **E:** ademir@redeprincesa.com.br - **FM:** 101.3 MHz – **SC36)** Rua 15 de Novembro, 600-sala 401, Edifico Visconde de Mauá, 89010-000 Blumenau ☎47 3322 9773 **W:** radioitabera.com **E:** contato@radioitabera.com – **SC38)** Rua Siqueira Campos 33, 89400-970 Porto União ☎📠42 3522 2245 **W:** colmeia.am.br **E:** colmeia@colmeia.am.br – **SC39)** Rua Padre Aurélio 240, 89930-970 São José do Cedro ☎49 3643 0211 **W:** radiointegracaoam1180.com.br **E:** comercial@radiointegracaoam1180.com.br – **SC42)** Bruno Pedro dal Bó, 3073 Humaitá de Cima, 88708-197 Tubarão ☎48 3628 0658 📠48 3628 1356 **W:** radiosc.com.br **E:** radiosc@radiosc.com.br – **SC44)** Av Canal 130, 89890-000 Cunha Porã ☎49 3646 0157 **W:** http//iracema.radio.br – **SC45)** Rua Nove de Março, 737-Ed.Turim 8° andar, 89201-400 Joinville ☎47 3026 1000 **W:** jovempanjoinville.com.br**E:** jornalismo@jovempanjoinville.com.br - **FM:** 91.1MHz – **SC46)** Rua Dr. Amadeu da Luz 31-sala 03 , 89010-160 Bluemau ☎47 3340 1260 **W:** arcadaalianca.com.br **E:** fale@radioblumenau.com.br – **SC49)** Av Alvin Bauer 585, 88330-643 Balneário Camboriú ☎47 3405 1644 📠47 3405 1609 **W:** radiocamboriu.com.br **E:** radiocamboriu@radiocamboriu.com.br – **SC50)** Rua Buenos Aires, 145, Ponta Aguda, 89051-050 Blumenau ☎47 3222 9070 **W:** radioclubeblumenau.com.br **E:**comercial@radioclubeblumenau.com.br – **SC51)** Rua Marechal Floriano Peixoto 161, 89802-010 Chapecó ☎49 3322 0688 **W:** radiochapeco.com.br **E:** comercial@radiochapeco.com.br - **FM:** 107.1MHz – **SC53)** Rua Imbituba, 190, Dom Bosco, 88303-570 Itajaí ☎47 3241 0092 **W:** bandamitajai.com.br**E:** contato@bandamitajai.com.br – **SC58)** Rua Visconde do Rio Branco 1028, 89887-000 Palmitos ☎49 3647 0292 **W:** radioentrerios.com.br **E:** entrerios@futurasc.net – **SC59)** Rua Nunes Machado 94, Edifico Tiradentes-10° andar, 88010-460 Florianópolis (📠48 2108 5555 **W:**radioguaruja.com.br - **FM:** 92.1 MHz – **SC63)** Rodovia Luiz Lazzarin 2601, Maria Céu, 88801-660 Criciúma ☎48 3413 7971 **W:** radiohulhanegra.com.br **E:** euquero@radiohulhanegra.com.br - **FM:** 104.3 MHz – **SC64)** Rua São Pedro 245, 89110-000 Gaspar ☎47 3332 0783 **W:** radiosentinela.com.br **E:** ouvinte@radiosentinela.com.br – **SC66)** Rua Santos Dumont 204, 89610-000 Herval d'Oeste ☎49 3527 9013 **W:** radiolider.am.br **E:** gerencia@radiolider.am.br – **SC67)** Av Coronel Procópio Gomes, 1155, Bucarein, 89202-300 Joinville ☎47 3026 1480 **W:** arcadaalianca.com.br **E:** contato@radioarcadaalianca.com.br – **SC70)** Av Plínio Arlindo de Nes 476, 89825-000 Xaxim ☎49 3353 2425 **W:** radioculturaxaxim.com.br **E:** cultura@radioculturaxaxim.com.br – **SC77)** Rua Manoel Vieira Garcao 3-Edif. Catarinense 14° andar, 88301-050 Itajaí ☎47 3348-2992 **W:** difusoraitajai.com.br **E:**contato@difusoraitajai.com.br – **SC79)** Av Porto Feliz 188, 89893-000 Mondaí ☎49 3674 0122 **W:** portofeliz.am.br **E:** jornalismo2@portofeliz.am.br – **SC80)** Rua Carmello Zocolli 205, 89600-000 Capinzal ☎49 3555 1333 📠49 3555 1333 **W:** radiocapinzal.am.br **E:** contato@radiocapinzal.am.br – **SC81)** Av Getúlio Vargas 429, 88900-000 Araranguá (📠48 3524 0137 **W:** radioararangua.com.br **E:** radioararangua @radioararangua.com.br - **FM:** 92.5MHz – **SC86)** Rua Joaquim Nuns 244, (C.P. 2008) 888340-000 Camboriú ☎47 3404 8722 **W:** radiovozmissionaria.com.br **E:** radiovozmissionaria.co@gmail.com – **SC93)** Rua AV XV de Novembro 6-sala 2, 89665-000 Capinzal ☎49 3555 1799 **W:** radiobarrigaverde.am.br – **SC96)** Rua Rafael Pardinho 249, 89240-000 São Francisco do Sul ☎47 3444 2733 📠47 3444 0450 **W:** radiosaofranciscosc.com.br **E:** ouvintes@radiosaofranciscosc.com.br – **SC99)** Rua 7 de Setembro 496, 89950-000 Dionísio Cerqueira ☎49 3644 1042 **W:** radiofronteira.com.br - **FM:** 94.3 – **SC101)** Av Dr Albano Schultz, 925 2° andar, 89201-220 Joinville (📠47 3481 3030 **W:** radioclubejoinville.com.br **E:** contato@radioclubejoinville.com.br - **FM:** 103.1MHz – **SC102)** Rua Maranhão 700, sala 02, 89980-000 Campo Erê ☎ 49 3655 2100 **W:** peperi.com.br **E:** atalaia@peperi.com.br – **SC103)** Rua Pref.Dib Cherem 3440 Salas 02/03, Capoeiras, 88090-001 Florianopolsi ☎48 3028 1240 **W:** radiomaisalegria.com.br - **FM:** 106.5 MHz – **SC104)** Rua XV de Novembro 495, 89560-000 Videira ☎49 3566 25000 **W:** radiovitoriaam.com.br **E:** adm@vitoriaam.com.br – **SC105)** Rua João Lino da Silva Neto 621, 88495-000 Garopaba ☎48 3254 3055 **W:** radiofrequencia.net **E:** frequencia@radiofrequencia.net

SE00) SERGIPE

SE02) Rua Laranjeiras, 1837, Getúlio Vargas, 49055-380 Aracaju ☎79 3198 2700 **W:** aperipe.com.br - **FM:** 104.9MHz – **SE03)** Rua Simão Dias 643, 49010-430 Aracaju ☎79 3226 8710 **W:** cultura670.com.br **E:** cultura@cultura670.com.br – **SE06)** Rua 13 de Maio 119, 49500-000 Itabaiana ☎79 3431 1762 **W:** radioprincesadaserra.com.br ☎79 3431 5036 – **SE12)** Av Raimundo Silveira, 3996-01 Andar Sala 02, Alagoas, 49200-000 Estância ☎79 3522 4804 **W:** radioabaisam.com.br **E:** radioabaisamcomercial@hotmail.com – **SE13)** Travessa Santa Luzia, 69 - Centro, 49300-000 Tobias Barreto ☎79 3541 1548 **W:** redeilha.com.br **E:** am1520@redeilha.com

SP00) SÃO PAULO

SP02) Rua Antônio do Vale Mello, 807, 13170-011 Sumaré ☎18 3873 1407 **W:** radiowolf.com.br **E:** sac@radiowolf.com.br – **SP03)** Rua Dom Bosco, 573, 12700-000 Cruzeiro ☎12 3144 1364 **W:** radiomantiqueira.com **E:** atendimento@mantiqueira.com - **FM:** 100.7MHz – **SP04)** Rua José Bonini, 1415, 14160-000 Sertãozinho **W:** boavontade.com/radio/?cdgEms=6 **E:** superrbv@boavontade.com – **SP06)** Rua Dr Sousa Alves 960, 12020-030 Taubaté ☎12 3632 8122 **W:** rededifusora.com.br **E:** midia@rededifusora.com.br – **SP07)** Rua Tamoio, 875, Vila Santa Catarina, 13465-250 Americana ☎19 3475 8801 **W:** radiovoce.com.br **E:** radiovoce@radiovoce.com.br – **SP08)** Av Rotary 85, 19970-000 Palmital ☎18 3351 2601 **W:** radioregionalpalmital.com.br – **SP09)** Rua Pedro Lessa 1640, sala 809, Embaré, 11025-002 Santos ☎13 3273 6900 **W:** radioatlantica.com.br **E:** radioatlantica@radioatlantica.com.br – **SP10)** Rua das Nações Unidas 127, 16800-000 Mirandópolis ☎18 3701 4084 **W:** clubeam590.com.br – **SP11)** Av Maurilio Biagi, 2103, Ribeirânia, 14096-170 Ribeirão Preto ☎16 3968 7000 **W:** radio79.com.br **E:** natocampos@thathi.com.br – **SP12)**Avenida Luiz Gonzaga de Amoedo Campos, 28-Centro Mogi Mirim ☎19 3814-1237 **W:**transertaneja.com – **SP16)** Av Paulista, 807-24° andar, Bela Vista, 01311-941 São Paulo ☎11 2870 9700 **E:** info@jovempan.com.br **W:** jovempan.com.br **E:** jovempanonline@jovempan.com.br – **SP18)** Rua Casemiro Dias, 785, Vila Ocidental, 19015-250 Presidente Prudente – **SP20)** Rua Homero Rodrigues Silva 1072, 16901-025 Andradina ☎18 3722 2352 – **SP21)** Praça José Bonifácio 815, 13400-340 Piracicaba ☎19 2105 6622 **W:** portaldifusora.com.br **E:** atendimento@portaldifusora.com.br - **FM:** 102.3MHz – **SP22)** Rua Tolentino Figueiras, 119 7° andar, cj 71/72, Gonzaga, 11060-471 Santos ☎13 3289 4727 **W:** radiodacidadesantos.com.br - **FM:** 105.5MHz – **SP23)** Av Nove de

Julho, 606, Higienópolis, 14025-000 Ribeirão Preto ☎16 2101-3500 **W:** radioclube1.com.br - **FM:** 100.5MHz – **SP26)** Rua Quintino Bocaiúva 37, 13300-135 Itu.- ☎℻11 4023 2363 **W:** radioconvencao.com.br **E:** radioconvencao@hotmail.com – **SP30)** Praça Conselheiro Rodrigues Alves 170, 12500-020 Guaratinguetá ☎12 3122 3611 **W:** radioclube97fm.com.br **E:** rclube97@uol.com.br - **FM:** 97.1MHz – **SP31)** Av Humberto Liedtke 1936, 15370-970 Pereira Barreto ☎18 3704 2121 **W:** radiocidadeam690.com.br **E:** contato@radiocidadeam690.com.br **MSN:** radiocidadeampb@hotmail.com – **SP32)** Av.Eng Caetano Alvares, 55, Limão, 02598-900 Sao Paulo ☎11 2108 6700 **W:** radio.estado.com.br - **FM:** 92.9MHz – **SP33)** Rua 1 de Agosto 927, 17010-011 Bauru – **SP34)** Rua dos Pelegrinis 11, Desterro, 13700-000 Casa Branca ☎19 3671 2101 **W:** radiodifusoracasabranca.com.br **E:** contato@radiodifusoracasabranca.com.br – **SP35)** Rua Antonio Carlos Mori 288, 19900 080 Ourinhos ☎14 3322 5758 **W:** sentinelaam.com.br – **SP36)** Rua Dr Carlos Varela 104, Cruzeiro ☎12 3143 6894 **W:** rcvale.com.br – **SP37)** Rua Washington Luis 576, 15400-000 Olímpia ☎17 3281 3044 **W:** espaciolivream.com.br **E:** adm@espaciolivream.com.br – **SP38)** Rua Siqueira de Morães, 578 10° andar, 13201-900 Jundiaí ☎11 4586 0969 **W:** cidadeam.com **W:** radiocidadejundai.com.br **E:** diretoria@radiocidadejundai.com – **SP39)** Rua Coronel Galdino de Almeida 55, 17500-100 Marília ☎14 3402 5128 **W:** dirceu.am.br – **SP40)** Av. João Lemos 578, 17250-000 Bariri ☎14 3662 9191 **W:** radioculturadebariri.com.br **E:** comercial@radioculturadobariri.com.br – **SP41)** Av Paulista, 900, Bela Vista, 01310-100 São Paulo ☎11 3289 3755 ℻11 3280 3768 **W:** new.radiotrianon.com.br **E:** contato@radiotrianon.com.br – **SP42)** Rua Itapura 6, 17700-970 Osvaldo Cruz ☎18 3528 1089 **W:** radioosvaldocruz.com.br **E:** contato@radioosvaldocruz.com.br - **FM:** 97.3MHz 'California FM' – **SP43)** Rua Ramos de Azevedo, 622, Jardim Paulista, 14090-180 Ribeirão Preto ☎16 3624 2622 **W:** radiocmn.com.br – **SP44)** Rua Euclides Miragaia 394, 18° andar, 12245-820 São José dos Campos ☎12 3909 8000 **W:** radiopiratininga.com.br **E:** jornalismo@radiopiratininga.com.br - **FM:** 99.7MHz – **SP46)** Av Lauro Correia da Silva, 3230, 13481-598 Limeira ☎19 3404 4000 **W:** radiomixlimeira.com.br **E:** manoelmixregional@gmail.com – **SP49)** Av Bento de Abreu, 889, Jardim Primavera, 14802-3986 Araraquara ☎16 3303 3622 **W:** radiocultura.net **E:** comercial@radiocultura.net DX-reports to: Daneielnx18@gmail.com - **FM:** 97.3MHz – **SP50)** Rua Barão de Jundiaí 1041-9° andar, 13201-906 Jundiaí ☎11 4586 2020 **W:** radiodifusorajundiai.com.br **E:** radio@radiodifusorajundiai.com.br – **SP51)** Rua Quince de Novembro 3131, 15015-110 São José do Rio Preto ☎17 3233 4600 **W:** blog.cancaonova.com/riopreto **E:** radioriopreto@cancaonova.com – **SP52)** Av Julio Prestes, s/n – 12570 000 Aparecida ☎12 310402590 **W:** A12.com/radio-aparecida contato@a12.com – **SP53)** Rua Tenente Lopes 191, (C.P.3) 17201-460 Jaú ☎14 3622 2800 ℻14 3622 4376 **W:** radiojauense.com.br **E:** radiojauense@netsite.com.br - **FM:** 101.1MHz – **SP54)** Rua José Galvão, 359, Vila Moraes, (C.P 94) 19900-260 Ourinhos ☎14 3322 2997 ℻14 3322 6255 **W:** radioclube820.com.br – **SP57)** Rua Radiantes, 13, Jardim Leonor, 05614-900 São Paulo **W:** radiobandeirantes.band.uol.com.br**E:** rbnoar@band.com.br - **FM:** 90.9MHz – **SP58)** Avenida 2, 1420, Jardim Claret, 13502-240 Rio Claro ☎19 3533 2307 **W:** radioclubeam.am.br **E:** comercial@radioclubefm.fm.br - **FM:** 94.3 MHz – **SP61)** Rua Romualdo Andreazzi, 516, Jd Leonor, 13041-030 Campinas ☎19 3772 1750 ℻19 3772 1766 **W:** radiocentral.com.br **E:** radiocentral@radiocentral.com.br – **SP63)** Rua Rui Barbosa 723, 19015-000 Presidente Prudente ☎18 222 2500 – **SP64)** Rua Siqueira Campos 3223, 15010-040 São José do Rio Preto - **FM:** 102.1MHz «R Onda Nova FM» – **SP65)** Rua Miguel Janez, 295, Vila Arlindo Luz, 18212-480 Itapetininga ☎15 3373 7301 – **SP66)** Av Independencia,350 Edifico Primus Center 11° andar, Vila Areão, 13414-018 Piracicaba ☎19 3436 6300 **W:** facebook.com/jovempannewspiracicaba/ - **FM:** 105.3 – **SP67)** Rua Monsenhor Rosa 1561, 14400-670 Franca ☎16 3713 3977 **W:** radioimperador.com.br **E:** contato@radioimperador.com.br – **SP68)** Av Brasil, 31, Parque de Felicidade, 13973-255 Itapira ☎19 3863 0138 **W:** radioclubeitapira.com.br **E:** radioclube@dglnet.com.br – **SP72)** Av Sampaio Vidal, 185, Barbosa, 17500-441 Marília ☎14 3301 4341 **W:** radio950.com.br – **SP73)** Av João Dias, 1800, Santo Amaro, 04724-002 São Paulo ☎11 3442 2660 – **SP75)** Rua Floriano Peixoto 64, 13870-060 São João da Boa Vista ☎19 3631 5853 **W:** piratininga970am.com.br **E:** radio970@dglnet.com.br – **SP76)** Rua Luis Pires, 250, Jardim Redentor, 14409-283 Franca ☎16 3704 0888 **W:** hertzam.com.br - **FM:** 96.5MHz – **SP77)** Rua da Várzea, 240, Várzea da Brra Funda, 01140-080 São Paulo ☎11 3661 6727 **W:** radiosetvs.com/radiorecord_sp **E:** radiorecordamsp@r7.com – **SP79)** Rua Kametaro Morishita, 95, 3°andar, Cidade Universitaria, 19050-700 Presidente Prudente **W:** diario1010.com.br – **SP81)** Rua Benjamin Constant 33 10° andar, 19806-130 Assis ☎18 3322 8811 **W:** culturadeassis.com.br **E:** cultura@culturadeassis.com.br – **SP82)** Rua Profa Aparecida M. Faveri, 988, Parque Egisto Ragazzo, 13485-316 Limeira ☎19 3441 3760 **W:** educadoraam.com.br **E:** radio@educadoraam.com.br – **SP84)** Av Eliz Verzola Gosuen, 3103, Jardim Angela Rosa, , 14403-605 Franca ☎16 3713 8899 **W:** difusora.com.br **E:** difusora@gcn.net.br – **SP85)** Av Industrial José E Ortigosa, 570 an 1, Dis Industrial 1 - Centro, 17340-970 Barra Bonita ☎14 3641 0131 – **SP87)** Praça Rodrigues de Abreu, 228, Paraiso, 04040-080 São Paulo ☎11 3053 1040 **W:** capitalcomvoce.com.br **E:** faleconosco@capitalcomvoce.com.br – **SP88)** Rua Boa Morte 1122, 13400-140 Piracicaba ☎19 3422 1060 **W:** educadora1060.com.br **E:** ouvinte@educadora1060.com.br – **SP89)** Av Rangel Pestana, 147, Vila Matias, 11031-551 Santos ☎13 3224 3098 – **SP91)** Rua Marechal Bitencourt 346, 17201-430 Jaú ☎14 9961 2747 **W:** radiopiratiningajau.com **E:** contato@radiopiratiningajau.com – **SP92)** Av Washington Luiz 1250, 19015-150 Presidente Prudente ☎81 2104 6000 **W:** prudente.am.br **E:** ouvinte@fm101fm.com.br - **FM** 101.1MHz – **SP94)** Rua Santos Dumont 239, 14300-000 Batatais **W:** difusoraam.com.br **E:** diretoria@difusoraam.com.br ☎16 3761 3600 – **SP96)** Av André Luiz, 723, Picanco, 07082-050 Sorocaba ☎11 2457 7000 **W:** radioboanova.com.br **E:** rede@radioboanova.com.br – **SP97)** Av Zezé Valadão 359, 12570-970 Aparecida ☎12 3105 0754 **W:** radiomonumental.com.br **E:** radio_monumental@hotmail.com – **SP98)** Av Carlos Artêncio 117, 17519-255 Marília ☎14 3414 1794 **W:** radioclubemarilia.com **E:** gerencia@emissorascoligadas.com.br – **SP99)** Av 15 de Maio 455, 15910-970 Monte Alto ☎16 3242 1258 **W:** radioculturamontealto.com.br **E:** contato@radioculturamontealto.com.br – **SP103)** Av Luíz Gonzaga de Amoêdo Campos, 28, Vila Áurea, 13800-908 Mogi Mirim ☎19 3814 1234 **W:** hitstransamerica.com.br - **FM:** 91.1MHz – **SP105)** Rua Euclides Miragaia, 548 12245-820 São José dos Campos ☎11 3941 4114 **W:** cidadeam1120.com.br **E:** radio@cidadeam1120.com.br – **SP106)** Rua Duque de Caxias, 260 cj 22 an 2, 15900-970 Taquaritinga ☎16 3252 2999 **W:** radioimperial.com.br – **SP108)** Rua Gonçalves Dias 208, 19800-110 Assis ☎18 3302 3833 **W:** difusoraassis.com.br **E:** difusora@difusoraassis.com.br – **SP110)** Av. 2 N° 1420, Jardim Claret, 13502-240 Rio Claro ☎19 3522 4741 **W:** cultura.am.br **E:** comercial@cultura.am.br – **SP111)** Rua Dr. Esteves da Silva 100, 11680-000 Ubatuba ☎12 3832 2993 **W:** radiocostaazul.com.br **E:** comercial@radiocostaazul.com.br – **SP112)** Av Paulista, 2200Cerquira Cesar, 01310-300, Sao Paulo ☎11 3016 5999 **W:** radiomundial.com.br - **FM:** 95.7MHz – **SP114)** Rua Saldanha de Gama 184, 18035-040 Sorocaba ☎15 3232 3207 **W:** radiocacique.com.br **E:** contato@radiocacique.com.br - **FM:** 96.5MHz – **SP115)** Av. Manoel Marques Rosa, 1075-Ed. Atlântis, 15600-000 Fernandópolis ☎17 3442 2666 **W:** radiodifusorafernandopolis.com.br - **FM:** 99.0MHz – **SP117)** Av Eng Antonio Francisco de Paula Souz, 2799 – jd São Bagriel, V 13045-541 Campinas ☎19 3779 7400 **W:** rb1170.com.br **E:** jcoimbra@band.com.br ~ **SP119)** Av XV de Novembro 715, 13650-000 Santa Cruz das Palmeiras ☎19 3672 6976 – **SP120)** Rodovia Taquarituba Avare, s/n km 384, 18740-000 Taquarituba ☎14 3762 1487 **W:** radioregional1190.com.br **E:** regionalam@yahoo.com.br – **SP121)** Rua Vladimir Herzog, 75, Agua Branca, 05036-900 São Paulo **W:** culturabrasil.com.br ☎11 2182 3080 – **SP122)** Rua Rui Barbosa 546-4° andar, 14870-300 Jaboticabal ☎16 3202 0266 **W:** radiovidanova.com.br **E:** falecom@diovidanovaam.com.br – **SP124)** Av Dr Nunu de Assis 5050, Jardim Bela Vista, 17010-120 Bauru ☎14 3232 3571 **W:** radiobandeirantesbauru.com.br – **SP125)** Av. Roberto Simonsen, 280, Jd. Santa Rosalia,18090-000 Sorocaba ☎15 3224 5300 **W:** radiovanguarda.com.br **E:** comercial@radiovanguardia.com.br - **FM:** 94.9MHz – **SP126)**Rua Floriano Peixoto, 777 B B, 18300-250 Capão Bonito ☎15 3542 2811 – **SP128)** Rua Dr Miguel Penteado 585, Jardim Chapadão, 13073-180 Santos – **SP129)** Praça Emilio Peduti 28, 18600-410 Botucatu ☎14 3882 0236 **W:** radiomunicipalista.com.br – **SP130)** Rua 8 472, 14620-000 Orlândia ☎16 3826 3000 ℻16 3826 3006 **W:** orc.com.br **E:** orc@orc.com.br – **SP131)** Rua Julia Conceicão,510, Encruzilhada 11055-320 Santos **W:** Facebook: Rádio Clube de Santos 1240AM – **SP134)** Av Bento Abreu 889, 1408-396 Araraquara ☎16 3303 3622 **W:** radiomorada.com.br **E:** radiomorada@uol.com.br – **SP136)** Rua Irmã Serafina, 88, Bosque, 13026-066 Campinas ☎19 3231 7860 **W:** brasilcampinas.com.br **E:** radio@brasilcampinas.com.br – **SP137)** Rua dos Radialistas Riopretense, 650 – Andar N° 1, Nova Redentora, 15090-070 São José do Rio Preto ☎17 3016 3222 **W:** novotempoam.com/radiosaojosedoriopreto **E:** mailradio@novotempo.com.br – **SP138)** Av do Estado, 4568, Cambuchi, 01516-901 Sao Paulo **W:** ipda.com.br **E:** webmaster@ipda.com.br – **SP139)** Rua Barao do Rio Branco 559, 14900-000 Itápolis

☎16 3262 3063 – **SP141)** Rua Coronel Osório 84, 12900-150 Bragança Paulista ☎11 4034-1467 **W:** radiobraganca.com.br – **SP142)** Rua Siqueira Campos 633, 19010-061 Presidente Prudente ☎18 3222 6021 **W**: radiopaulista1330.com.br **E:** contato@radiopaulista1330.com.br – **SP143)** Rua Batatais, 36-Jardim Paulista, 14090-160 Ribeirão Preto ☎16 3967 6002 – **SP145)** Rua Barão de Jaceguai 468, 08710-905 Mogi das Cruzes ☎11 4799 2888 **W:** redemetropolitana.com.br – **SP148)** Av Orlando Fruchi, 97, Distrito Industrial, 17900-000 Dracena ☎18 3821 2593 **W:** radioregionaljp.com.br **E:** contato@radioregionaljp.com – **SP149)** Rua Cuiabá 361, 16901-200 Andradina ☎18 3722 2729 – **SP150)** Av Vice-Pref. Sérgio Forcin, 230, 17250-000 Bariri ☎14 3662 4000 **W:** baririradioclube.com.br **E:** contato@baririradioclube.com.br – **SP151)** Rua Pedro Natalia Lorenzetti 172, 18680-110 Lençóis Paulista ☎14 3264 8100 **W:** difusora1010.com.br **E:** administracao@difusora1010.com.br – **SP152)** Rua Vereador Eugênio Mazon, Jardim Centenário, 13845-197 Mogi Guaçu ☎19 3861 0098 – **SP153)** Av. Benjamin Constant 1214-3° andar, 13010-141 Campinas ☎19 3731 5100 – **SP157)** Rua Voluntários de Sao Paulo 3066-10 andar conjunto 1003, 15015-200 São José do Rio Preto ☎17 3212 7012 **W:** radiometropole1400am.blogspot.com.br **E:** metropoleam@terra.com.br – **SP158)** Rua Dona Inácia 62, 04110-020 São Paulo ☎11 2039 1410 **W:** radio.cancaonova.com/radio-america – **SP159)** Ladeira Prof Irineu Lopes de Lima 418, 13250-241 Itatiba ☎11 4524 0003 **W:** crnitatiba.com.br **E:** crnitatiba@terra.com.br – **SP160)** Rua Cerqueira Cesar 481, 14010-130 Ribeirão Preto – **SP162)** Praça Barão do Rio Branco 30, 12010-090 Taubaté ☎12 3622 1866 **W:** diocesedetaubate.org.br/radio – **SP163)** –Rua Cel. Joaquim Floriano, 344, 18650-000 São Manuel ☎14 3841 3133 **W:** novasaomanuel.com.br **E:** radionova@uol.com.br – **SP164)** Rua Juca Cintra 85, 13930-000 Serra Negra ☎19 389 1125 **W:** Facebook: Rádio Serra Negra AM 1430 **E:** radio.serranegra@terra.com.br – **SP165)** Av Manoel Goulart, 291 1° andar, 19010-270 Presidente Prudente ☎18 3221 2900 **W:** comercialam.com.br **E:**contato@comercialam.com.br – **SP167)** Av André Luís, 723, Picanço, 07082-050 Guarulhos. ☎11 2457 7000 **W:** radioboanova.com.br **E:** rede@radioboanova.com.br – **SP168)** Rua 9 de Julho 1801, 13560-042 Sao Carlos do Pinhal ☎16 3371 3724 **W:** saocarlosam.com.br **E:** comercial@saocarlosam.com.br – **SP173)** Av Rui Barbosa 229, 12308-520 Jacareí ☎12 3954 3000 📠12 3954 3009 **W:** radiomensagem.am.br **E:** mensagem@radiomensagem.am.br – **SP174)** Rua Sao Sebastiao 33, 13660-013 Porto Ferreira ☎19 3581-2921 – **SP175)** Rua 13 de Maio, 2680, Vila Georgina, 13333-080 Indaiatuba ☎19 3875 9141 **W:** radiojornalindaiatuba.com.br **E:** contato@radiojornalindaiatuba.com.br – **SP177)** Av Brigadeiro José Vicente Faria Lima 54, 12940-284 Atibaia ☎11 4411 8773 – **SP178)** Rua Conceiçao 596, 16210-000 Bilac ☎18 3659 1854 **W:** miliciadaimaculada.org.br **E:** 890am@miliciadaimaculada.org.br – **SP180)** Av Governador Ademar Pereira de Barros, 134, Lotamente Canterville, 15400-000 Olímpia ☎17 3281 1097 **W:** difusoraolimpia.com.br – **SP182)** Av Brasil, 1712, 15600-970 Fernandópolis ☎217 3462 1112 **W:** educadorafernandopolis.com.br **E:** ouvinteeducadora@terra.com.br – **SP183)** Rua Padre Moro Grande, 870, Dos Finco, 09831-250 São Bernardo do Campo ☎11 4397 6500 **W:** miliciadaimaculada.org.br **E:** sam@miliciadaimaculada.org.br – **SP184)** Av Guerino Turatti, 200, DistritoIndustrial III, 13602- 100 Araras ☎📠19 3543 7990 **W:** radiocidadedasarvores.com.br **E:** contato@radiocidadedasarvores.com.br - **FM:** 97.9MHz – **SP186)** Av Leopoldo Carlos de Oliveira 1038, 14530-000 Miguelópolis ☎16 3835 1500 **W:** radiofmvale.com.br - **FM:** 87.9 MHz – **SP187)** Av.Paulista, 2200 13° andar, Cerqueira Cesar, 01310-300 Osasco ☎11 3266 6880 **W:** radioterra.am.br – **SP188)** Rua Silva Jardim, 480, Macuco, 11015-020 Santos ☎13 3221 9500 📠13 3327 7643 **W:** radiocacique1510.com.br **E:** radio.cacique@hotmail.com – **SP189)** Rua Coronel Rodrigues Simõs 69 , 18650-000 São Manuel ☎14 3841 2555 **W:** cluberegional.com.br **E:** jornalismo@cluberegional.com.br – **SP191)** Rua Princesa Isabel de Braganca 235, 08710-460 Mogi das Cruzes ☎11 4796 1478 **W:** radiodacidadeam.com.br – **SP192)** Rua Vereador Rosas 171, 13990-000 Espírito Santo do Pinhal ☎19 3651 1755 **W:** pinhalradioclube.com.br **E:** radiopinhal@dglnet.com.br - **FM:** 102.7MHz – **SP195)** Rua Benedito Carlos dos Reis 700, 15190-970 Nhandeara ☎17 3472 1668 – **SP196)** Rua Marechal Deodoro 320, 18600-320 Botucatu ☎14 3882 1535 **W:** radiof8.com.br **E:** gravadorf8@hotmail.com – **SP197)** Av Diogo Antonio Feijo, 1185, Jardim das Flores, 06114-029 Osasco ☎11 3681 6753 **W:**Facebook.com/novadifusoraam1540/ – **SP198)** Rua Dom José Carlos Aguirre 567, 18460-000 Itararé ☎15 3532 4055 **W:** radioclube.cjb.net **E:** falecom@radioclubeam.net – **SP199)** Rua Pedro de Toledo 205, 19700-000 Paraguaçu Paulista ☎18 3361 1203 📠18 3362 2306 **W:** radiomarconi.com.br **E:** marconi@radiomarconi.com.br – **SP200)** Rua Lino Dorelli 120, 13360-000 Capivari ☎19 3492 1550 **W:** caciqueam.com.br **E:** matheus@caciqueam.com.br – **SP201)** Rua José Vaz de Porto, 175, Vila Santa Rosa, 11431-190 Guarujá ☎13 3269 1010 **W:** radioguarujaam.com.br **E:** radioguarujaam@radioguarujaam.com.br - **FM:** 104.5MHz – **SP204)** Rua Rio Grande do Sul, 2165, Braz I 18701-190 Avaré ☎14 3732 1564 **W:** radioavare.com.br **E:** radioavare@yahoo.com.br – **SP205)** Rua Belo Horizonte Nº930 17890-000 Junqueirópolis ☎18 3841 1465 **W:** radiojunqueiropolis.com **E:** contato@radiojunqueiropolis.com – **SP206)** Av Pereira Barreto, 1200, Vila Gilda, 09190-210 Santo André ☎11 4435 9000 📠11 4435 9001 **W:** radioabc.com.br **E:** faleconosco@radioabc.com.br – **SP207)** Rua Dr Vicente D´Anna 473, 13960-970 Socorro ☎19 3895 1444 **W:** radiosocorro.com.br **E:** radiosocorro@gmail.com – **SP209)** Rua Dr Felipe Vita 1616, 18480-000 Itaporanga ☎15 3565 3525 **W:** radiosaojoaobatista.com.br **E:** radiosaojoaobatista@yahoo.com – **SP211)** Rua Joaquim Moreira, 12, Parque São Miguel, 07260-220 Guarulhos ☎11 2496 1542 **W:** radiocumbica.org **E:** moacyrcustodio@radiocumbica.com.br – **SP212)** Av 17 560, 14780-000 Barretos ☎17 3324 1000 **W:** radiojornaldebarretos.com.br **E:** radiojornal@jornalbarretos.com.br - **FM:** 101.1 MHz – **SP213)** Av Paulista 2202, 8° andar, Conj 81/82, 01310-300 São Paulo ☎11 5543 0762 – **SP216)** Rua Rubião Junior, 84 sl.89, Shopping Centro, 12210-180 São José dos Campos ☎17 3343-1051 **W:** radionovabebdouro.com.br **E:** radionovacomercial@terre.com.br – **SP217)** Rua Coronel João Manoel 604 sl, 14700-000 Bebedouro ☎17 3343 6528 **W:** radionovaamaovlvo.com.br – **SP218)**Rua 12 de Novembro, 551 – Centro – 13465-490 Americana ☎19 3604-1899 **W:**radioazul.net.br**E:**falecom@radioazul.net.br – **SP220)** A Monte Castelo 225, 13450-285 Santa Bárbara d'Oeste ☎19 3463 5255 **W:** radiobrasilsbo.com.br **E:** radiobrasil@radibrasilsbo.com.br – **SP221)** Rua Maximo Ribeiro Nunes, 75, Jardim Peri Peri, 05535-000 Sao Paulo ☎11 3723 7575 **W:** nacionalgospel.com.br **E:** radio@nacionalgospel.com.br - **FM:** 100.5 MHz – **SP224)** Rua Kametaro Morishita, 95, 19050-700 Presidente Prudente ☎18 3229-0364 **W:** radiofronteiraapp.com.br **E**:contato@radiofronteiraapp.com.br - **FM:** 106.7MHz – **SP225)** Rua Imperatriz Leopoldina, 41, Vila Delgado Romano, 18044-010 Sorocaba ☎15 3222 5740 – **SP226)** Rua Bento Carlos 61, 13560-660 São Carlos ☎16 3362 3322 **W:** portalrealidade.com.br – **FM:** 88.9 MHz – **SP227)** Rua Duque de Caxais 33, 13460-000 Nova Odessa ☎19 3466 5026 **W:** novotempocampinas.com.br **E:** comercial@novotempocampinas.com.br – **SP229)** Av Dr Labiano da Costa Machado, 1735, Hilmar Machado, 17400-000 Garça ☎14 3471 0700 **W:** uniradio.com.br – **SP231)** Francisco Troani 1211, 19280-000 Teodoro Sampaio ☎18 3282 1534 – **SP232)** Av Paulista, 2200-17 andar, Bela Vista, 01310-300 São Paulo ☎11 3284 9184 **W:** superradio1150.com.br – **SP233)** Av. Pref. José Lozano Araújo. 102 – Jardim America, 13140-711 Paulínia ☎19 3844 8500 **W:** radio.cancaonova.com/paulinia **E:** cnpaulinia@cancaonova.com – **SP235)** Rua Joaquim de Oliveira 586, 13450-038 Santa Bárbara d'Oeste ☎19 3464 1300 **W:** radioluzes.com.br **E:** radioluzes@uol.com.br – **SP237)** Rua Marechal Rondon, 170, Alto São Pedro, 12082-420 Taubaté ☎12 3632 0555 – **SP238)** Av Dr Soares de Oliveira 2070, 14500-970 Ituverava ☎16 3839 7739 **W:** radiocultura1450.com.br **E:** radiocultura@netsite.com.br – **SP239)** Av Frederico Ozanan, 554, 17300-000 Dois Córregos ☎14 3652 2949 **W:** radioculturaregional.com.br – **SP242)** Av Washington Luíz 214, 13600-720 Araras ☎19 3541-3714 **W:** facebook.com/RadioClubeArarense **E:** comercial@radioclube.com.br – **SP243)** Rua Dom Pedro I 65, 17690-970 Bastos ☎14 3478 2525 – **SP244)** Rua Santana 440, 13880-000 Vargem Grande do Sul ☎219 3641 5646 **W:** http//radioculturaam.com **E:** r.cultura@itelefonica.com.br – **SP245)** R. Rafael de Barros 126, 13610-120 Lemé ☎ 19 3571 4288 **W:** radioculturadeleme.com.br **E:** ouvinte@radioculturadeleme.com.br – **SP249)** Rua 15 de Novembro 52, 13920-000 Pedreira – **SP251)** Rua Comendador Guimarães 25 sl 402, 13900-470 Amparo ☎19 3807 2237 **W:** difusoradeamparo.com.br **E:** radio@difusoradeamparo.com.br – **SP252)** Rua Padre João Goetz, 370, Jardim Esplanada, 19061-460 Presidete Prudente ☎218 3918 5300 **W:** ondaviva.com.br **E:** radioondaviva@stetnet.com.br – **SP253)** Rua 7 de Setembro 911, 14240-000 Cajuru – **SP254)** Av São Paulo, 100, Jacaré, 13318-000 Cabreúva **W:** radiojapi.radio.br – **SP255)** Alameda dos Lírios 111, 18550-000 Boituva ☎15 3363 2590 **W:** rboituva.com.br **E.:** contato@rboituva.com.br – **SP256)** Rua Roque Lazazera, 136 – Nossa Sra. Monte Serrat, 13323-300 Salto ☎19 98254 0890 **W:** www.radioaleluiamusica.com.br **E:** contato@radioaleluiamusica.com.br – **SP257)** Rua 9 de Julho 666, 16600-000 Pirajui ☎14 3572 1352 **W:** pirajuiradioclube.net.br **E:** contato@pirajuiradioclube.net.br – **SP258)** Rua dos Operários, 1441, Vila Rigueti, 19600-000 Rancharia ☎18

3265 1528 – **SP261)** Rua Nicalau Nassif, 523, Jardim Imperial, 14540-000 Igarapava ☎16 3172 2570 **W:** radioshowam.blogspot.no/ **E:** radioshowigarapava@gmail.com – **SP262)** Rua Inácio Ribeiro 592, 13670-000 Santa Rita do Passa Quatro ☎🖷19 3582 1278 **W:** radiozequinhadeabreu.com.br **E:** contato@radiozequinhadeabreu.com.br – **SP263)** Rua Manoel de Arzão, 85, Vila Albertina, 02730-030 São Paulo ☎11 3932 3393 **W:** radio9dejulho.com.br **E:** radio@radio9dejulho.com.br – **SP264)** Av 04 882, 13500-030 Rio Claro ☎19 3526 1055 **W:** jornalcidade.net/radio/ **E:** radio@jcrioclaro.com.br – **SP265)**Av.São Sebastião, 192 piso 3, 18150-000 Ibiuna – **SP266)** Legião da Boa Vontade (LBV), Rua Doraci, 90, Bom Retiro, 01134-050 Sao Paulo **W:** redeboavontade.com.br **E:** superrbv@boavontade.com – **SP269)** Rua 24 de Maio, 690, 14870-350 Jaboticabal ☎16 3203 5355 **W:** radioathenas.com.br **E:** adm@radioathenas.com.br – **SP273)** Av Clara Gianotti de Suza 1124, 11900-970 Registro ☎13 3821 1606 **W:** radionovaregionalam.blogspot.com.br **E:** radionovaregionalam1140@gmail.com – **SP274)** Rdv. Anel Viário Contorno Sul, 99, City, 14021-800 Ribeirao Preto ☎16 3621 2337 **W:** radiobandeirantes.com.br – **SP275)** Rua Honório Mendes de Moraes, 23, Esplanada Mendes Moares, 18130-760 São Roque ☎11 4712 4976 **W:** miliciadaimaculada.org.br **E:** 1430am@miliciadaiimaculada.org.bra – **SP280)** Rua Épiró, 110, Vila Alexandria, (C.P 80761, 04646-970) 04635-030 São Paulo **W:** transmundial.org.br **E:** rtm@transmundial.org.br Rec. Rpts to: qsl@transmundial.com.br – **SP283)** Praca Osvaldo Cruz, 124, Conjuto 116, 11900-000 Registro – **SP284)** Rua Aristides Pires 1397, 18370-970 Itai ☎14 3761 2753 – **SP285)** Rua Luiza Bechelli, 284, Jardim Sabaúna, 11740-000 Itanhaém ☎13 3422 1177 **W:** Facebook: Rádio Anchiete AM 1390 kHz – **SP286)** Rua Tiradentes 31,14740-000 Viradouro ☎17 3392 3008 **W:** cliqueradiolegal.com **E:** contato@ cliqueradiolegal.com – **SP287)** Rua Gabriel Hadad 283,14940-970 Ibatinga ☎16 3341 9900 **W:** radioibitinga.com.br **E:** radio.ibatinga@ibinet.com.br - **FM:** 99.3MHz «Ternura FM» – **SP288)** IPDA, Rua Saldanha Marinho 740, Ribeirao Preto ☎16 3636 6111 – **SP289)** Rua Coronel Nabor Nogueira Santos 258, 3º andar, 12260-000 Paraibuna **W:** radiograndevale.com.br **E.** ouvinte@radiograndevale.com.br

TO00) TOCANTINS

TO02) Praça José Tôrres 3, 77600-000 Paraíso do Tocantins (🖷63 3602 1135 – **TO03)** Av Nossa Senhora de Fátima 894, 77900-000 Tocantinópolis ☎63 3471 1572 – **TO05)** Rua Raul do Espírito Santo 1334,77760-000 Colinas do Tocantins ☎63 3476 1180 – **TO06)** Rua Justianio Borpa, Q.3, Setor Santa Filomena, 77650-000 Miracema do Tocantins ☎63 3366 1264 **W:** radioojornal.com.br **E:** radiocultura1480@hotmail.com – **TO07)** Almeda João Pires Querido 827, 77490-000 Cristalândia ☎63 3354 1600 – **TO08)** Av Bernardo Sayão 2201, 77700-000 Guaraí **W:** Facebook: Rádio Guaraí Am 1400 kHz **E:** gersonnk@hotmail.com – **TO10)** Av Piaui entre Ruas 3 e 4, 77402-970 Gurupi **W:** nossaradioto.com.br **E:** nossaradioto@outlook.com

BRITISH INDIAN OCEAN TERRITORY

L.T: UTC + 6h — **Pop:** c.2,000 on the Diego Garcia atoll (US & British military personnel and contractors). Original population of c. 2,300 was removed to Mauritius and the Seychelles between 1967 and 1973 — **Pr.L:** English — **E.C:** 110V/60Hz — **ITU:** BIO **Diego Garcia ITU:** DGA

DIEGO GARCIA

ARMED FORCES RADIO AND TELEVISION SCE (U.S. Mil.)
🖃 Naval Media Center Detachment-Diego Garcia, PSC 466 Box 14, FPO, AP 96595-0014. ☎+246 370 3680/3685 🖷+246 370 3681
E: dgar@mediacen.navy.mil
FM: Power 99, 99.1MHz 0.25kW, weekdays 0600-1400, rock & roll, live DJ. **Island Variety,** 101.9MHz 250W, mixture of rock, alternative, urban & country. **D.Prgr:** 24h **V.** by letter.

BRITISH FORCES BROADCASTING SERVICE
W: forces.net/radio **FM:** Diego Garcia 90.7MHz

BRUNEI DARUSSALAM

L.T: UTC +8h — **Pop:** 440,000 — **Pr.L:** Malay (official), English, Chinese — **E.C:** 240V/50Hz — **ITU:** BRU

AUTHORITY FOR INFO-COMMUNICATIONS TECHNOLOGY INDUSTRY OF BRUNEI DARUSSALAM - AITI (Regulatory Body)
🖃 Block B14, Simpang 32-5, Kampung Anggerek Desa, Jalan Berakas BB3713 ☎ +673 2323232 🖷 +673 2382447 **E:** info@aiti.gov.bn **W:** aiti.gov.bn **L.P:** Chmn: Yang Mulia Dato Seri Paduka Awang Haji Matsatejo Bin Sokiaw

RADIO TELEVISION BRUNEI - RTB (Gov)
🖃 Bangunan Sekretariat, Jalan Elizabeth II, Bandar Seri Begawan BA8610 ☎ +673 2242296-7 🖷 +673 2241882 **E:** rtbipro@brunet.bn **W:** rtb.gov.bn
L.P: Acting Dir Gen: Haji Azman bin Haji Abdul Rahim. Acting Dep. Dir: Development: Cheong Chee Keong. Acting Dep. Dir. Operation: Pg Haji Ismail bin Pg Hj Muhammad Kifli. Acting Head R. Prgrs: Koh Thian Chan

FM	Na	Pi	Pe	Ha	NI	kW
1) Andulau	93.8	96.9	91.0	97.7	94.9	5
2) Bukit Subok	92.3	95.9	91.4	94.1	93.3	5/0.5

DAB: on 225.648MHz
1) Kuala Belait & Tutong areas. **2)** Bandar Seri Begawan (BSB) area. Na = Nasional FM in Malay: 24h Pi = Pilihan FM. English: 0300-0800 (Sat 0300-0700), 1200-0100. Chinese: 0100-0300, 0800-1100. Gurkha: daily 1100-1200, Sat 0700-0800. Pe = Pelangi FM (prgrs for young people in English & Malay): 24h Additional FM freqs: 88.5MHz in BSB area, 96.3MHz in Kuala Belait area. Ha = Harmoni FM (music sce.): 24h NI = Rangkaian Nur Islam (rlg. talk channel): 24h

KRISTAL MEDIA SDN. BHD. (subsidiary of DST Group, DataStream Technology Sdn Bhd) (Comm.)
🖃 2nd Fl, Building 4, DST Headquarters, Jalan Tungku Link, Bandar Seri Begawan BE 3619 ☎ +673 2456828 🖷 +673 2420682 **W:** kristal.fm **L.P:** Radio Operations Manager: Azmi Ghazali

FM	KFM	RQ	FM (MHz)	KFM	RQ
Andulau	98.7	99.7	Bukit Subok	90.7	89.1

KFM=Kristal FM. RQ=Recital of Al-Quran
D.Prgr: Kristal FM: 24h in English/Malay. RQ: 24h in Arabic
N: (Kristal FM) rel. RTB 0500 (Fri 0545), 0600, 0930, 1100, 1200, 1300, 2300

BRITISH FORCES BROADCASTING SERVICE
🖃 BFBS Brunei, BFPO 11 ☎ +673 3223424 🖷 +673 3224113 **E:** bfbsbrunei@bfbs.com **W:** radio.bfbs.com/stations/bfbs-brunei **Prgr:** 24h in English on 101.7MHz 0.25kW, in Nepali (Gurkha) on 89.5MHz 0.25kW. Location: Brunei Garrison HQ, Tuker Lines, Seria, Belait District

BULGARIA

L.T: UTC +2h (28 Mar-31 Oct: +3h) — **Pop:** 7 million — **Pr.L:** Bulgarian (official), Turkish — **E.C:** 230V/50Hz — **ITU:** BUL

SAVET ZA ELEKTRONNI MEDII
(Council for Electronic Media)
🖃 bul. Shipchenski prohod 69, 1574 Sofia ☎ +359 29708810 🖷+359 29733769 **E:** office@cem.bg **W:** www.cem.bg
L.P: Chair: Betina Zhoteva

BALGARSKO NATSIONALNO RADIO (BNR) (Pub)
🖃 bul. Dragan Tsankov 4, 1040 Sofia ☎ +359 29336330 **E:** bnr@bnr.bg **W:** bnr.bg **L.P:** DG: Andon Baltakov

MW	kHz	kW	Prgr
Vidin	576	200	1

FM	1	2	kW	FM	1	2	kW
Babyak	87.6	-	1	M.Tarnovo	90.2	106.1	1
Belogradchik	102.3	88.2	10/1	Momchilgrad	105.0	99.2	10/1
Berkovitsa	101.4	99.5	10/7	Montana	100.4	-	1
Bistritsa	91.8	-	1	Nesebar	102.5	99.3	10
Botev vrah	100.9	92.2	10	Varna	100.9	104.8	5/1
Burgas	90.2	96.1	1	V. Tarnovo	96.0	99.6	1
Dobrich	104.3	102.3	3/1	Nikopol	96.4	98.2	0.1/1
Dupnitsa	104.1	87.8	1	Oryahovo	99.8	101.7	1
Dzhebel	102.1	88.4	1	Pleven	102.7	100.2	1
Gabrovo	103.2	95.4	1	Plovdiv	88.1	91.7	1
G.Delchev	100.3	98.5	10/1	Popovo	103.5	95.7	0.5/1
Ivailovgrad	91.6	96.4	0.1/1	Provadiya	88.9	102.9	3
Karnobat	103.2	95.0	1	Razgrad	103.5	99.4	1
Kavarna	88.1	90.1	10/1	Roman	94.7	-	1
Kresna	88.8	89.7	1	Ruse	103.0	95.7	10/1
Kyustendil	102.1	99.3	10	Silistra	103.3	107.2	3/1

FM	1	2	kW	FM	1	2	kW
Sliven	87.8	98.7	1	Shumen (a)	94.5	100.4	0.25/1
Smolyan	101.6	96.0	5/1	Targovishte	92.8	95.4	1/0.5
Sofia	103.0	92.9	10	Tran	97.6	90.0	1
St.Zagora	-	98.3	1	Tsarevo	102.2	90.8	1
Svilengrad	99.7	94.9	3	Vratsa	103.4	97.8	1/0.45
Shumen	102.0	-	10	Yablanitsa	89.2	95.0	1
Shumen	*90.1	-	1	(a) Shumen City			

+ sites with only txs below 1kW. *) incl. T

D.Prgr: Prgr 1 (Horizont): 24h – **Prgr 2 (Hristo Botev):** 24h – **Service for Turkish ethnic minority (T):** 0600-0700, 1300-1400, 1830-1930 in Turkish.

BNR Regional Stations

D.Prgr: all stns: 24h – **BNR R. Blagoevgrad:** ul. Ivan Mihaylov 56, 2700 Blagoevgrad **E:** koordinacia.blg@bnr.bg. On (MHz) 90.9 (Yakoruda 1kW), 102.3 (Gotse Delchev 1kW), 103.2 (Blagoevgrad 1kW), 105.2 (Kresna 0.5kW), 106.6 (Kyustendil 1kW) – **BNR R. Burgas:** ul. Filip Kutev 2, 8000 Burgas **E:** radioburgas@bnr.bg. On (MHz) 91.7 (Tsarevo 1kW), 91.9 (Yambol 1kW), 92.5 (Burgas 1kW), 98.9 (M.Tarnovo 1kW), 106.0 (Elhovo 0.5kW): own prgrs 0400-1900; rel. BNR Prgr 1 (Horizont) at other times – **BNR R. Kardzhali:** bul. Balgariya 74, 6600 Kardzhali. On 90.0MHz (Momchilgrad 1kW): own prgrs 0700-1000; rel. BNR Prgr 1 (Horizont) & BNR Service for the Turkish ethnic minority at other times – **BNR R. Plovdiv:** ul. Dondukov korsakov 2, 4000 Plovdiv **E:** director@radioplovdiv.bg. On (MHz) 88.3 (Panagyurishte 0.25kW), 94.0 (Plovdiv 3kW), 100.1 (Velingrad 0.1kW), 100.6 (Dospat 0.2kW), 103.1 (Smolyan 1kW) – **BNR R. Sofia:** bul. Dragan Tsankov 4, 1040 Sofia **E:** sofia@bnr.bg. On (MHz) 90.4 (Svoge 0.15kW), 94.5 (Sofia 1kW), 100.0 (Samokov 0.2kW), 104.6 (Ihtiman 0.3kW) – **BNR R. Stara Zagora:** ul. Knyaz Boris 75, 6000 Stara Zagora **E:** rsz@radio-sz.net. On (MHz) 88.3 (Stara Zagora 1kW), 97.2 (Sliven 1kW), 107.8 (Svilengrad 1kW) – **BNR R. Shumen:** ul. Dobro Voynikov 7, 9700 Shumen **E:** admin@radioshumen.net. On (MHz) 87.6 (Shumen 10kW), 90.3 (Silistra 3kW), 93.4 (Shumen/City 1kW), 94.0 (Targovishte 0.5kW), 97.0 (Razgrad 0.5kW), 98.6 (Ruse 1kW) – **BNR R. Varna:** bul. Primorski 22, 9000 Varna **E:** bnr@radiovarna.com. On (MHz) 88.5 (Nesebar 1kW), 88.7 (Dobrich 1kW), 98.2 (Kavarna 0.5kW), 103.4 (Varna 1kW), 105.3 (Provadiya 1kW) – **BNR R. Vidin:** ul. Gradinska 1, 3700 Vidin **E:** office@radiovidin.com. On (MHz) 94.4 (Vratsa 0.3kW), 97.1 (Vidin 0.25kW), 103.9 (Berkovitsa 1.5kW), 106.8 (Belogradchik 1kW).

OTHER STATIONS

FM	MHz	kW	Location	Station
2B)	87.6	1	Nesebar	R. Fresh
1)	87.9	1	Sandanski	Darik R.
5C)	88.2	1	Smolyan	The Voice
7)	89.5	1	Varna	R. Fokus
1)	89.7	2	Samokov	Darik R.
14)	89.9	1	Rusne	BTV R.
10)	90.2	1	Petrich	R. Bella
4)	90.6	1	Belogradchik	R. NRJ
5B)	90.9	1	Smolyan	R. Vitosha
1)	91.0	1	Belogradchik	Darik R.
8)	91.1	1	Burgas	Power FM
1)	91.4	1	Shumen	Darik R.
1)	91.6	1	Ruse	Darik R.
3A)	91.9	1	Petrich	R. Vega+
1)	93.2	1	Momchilgrad	Darik R.
7)	93.4	1	Primorsko	R. Fokus
2B)	94.1	1	Burgas	R. Fresh
5A)	94.3	1	Smolyan	R. Veselina
5A)	94.8	1	Burgas	R. Veselina
4)	95.5	1	Kozloduy	R. NRJ
9)	95.7	1	Burgas	BG R.
6)	96.0	1	Tutrakan	R. N-Joy
1)	96.7	1	Yablanitsa	Darik R.
5B)	96.7	1	Burgas	R. Vitosha
5A)	97.1	1	Momchilgrad	R. Veselina
11)	97.3	1	Sandanski	R. Gea
12)	98.3	1	Burgas	Glast na Burgas
1)	99.3	1	Varna	Darik R.
7)	99.7	1	Ruse	R. Fokus
4)	99.9	1	Burgas	R. NRJ
1)	100.6	1	Kyustendil	Darik R.
6)	100.6	1	Primorsko	R. N-Joy
1)	100.7	1	Silistra	Darik R.
4)	101.1	1	Primorsko	R. NRJ
1)	101.2	1	Sliven	Darik R.
13)	101.3	1	Momchilgrad	R. Nova News
6)	101.8	1	Burgas	R. N-Joy
7)	102.8	1	Momchilgrad	R. Fokus
5A)	103.2	1	Vidin	R. Veselina
3B)	103.4	1	Sandanski	R. Ultra
1)	104.0	1	Svilengrad	Darik R.
1)	104.5	2	Burgas	Darik R.
7)	104.5	1	Tutrakan	R. Fokus
1)	105.0	2	Sofia	Darik R.
1)	105.4	3	Plovdiv	Darik R.
5A)	105.7	1	Sandanski	R. Veselina
1)	106.2	1	Gotse Delchev	Darik R.
1)	106.6	1	V.Tarnovo	Darik R.
1)	106.8	1	Kavarna	Darik R.
1)	107.0	1	Smolyan	Darik R.
1)	107.2	1	Blagoevgrad	Darik R.
7)	107.5	1	Nesebar	R. Fokus
1)	107.7	1	Dobrich	Darik R.
7)	107.7	1	Vidin	R. Fokus

+ txs below 1kW.

Addresses & other information:

1) bul. Knyaz A.Dondukov 82, 1504 Sofia – **2A,B)** ul. Yerusalim 51, 1784 Sofia – **3A,B)** pl. Balgaria 2, 2800 Sandanski – **4)** bul. Tsar Boris III 23, 1612 Sofia – **5A-C)** ul. Srebarna 21, 1407 Sofia – **6)** ul. Panayot Volov 3, 1504 Sofia – **7)** ul. Filip Stanislavov 6, 1404 Sofia – **8)** ul. A.Bogoridi 16, 8000 Burgas – **9)** ul.Rikardo Vakarini 6b, 1612 Sofia – **10)** pl. Makedonia 10, 2850 Petrich – **11)** bul. Svoboda 13, 2800 Sandanski – **12)** ul. Gladston 47, 8000 Burgas – **13)** bul. Hristov Kolumb 41, 1592 Sofia – **14)** bul. Panayot Volov 3, 1504 Sofia.

DAB Transmitter (DAB+) (Trial)

Tx Operator: Digitalno Audio Balgaria EOOD **M:** Test prgrs **Tx:** Block 12B (Sofia 0.03kW)

BURKINA FASO

L.T: UTC — **Pop:** 21 million — **Pr.L:** French (official), Fulfulde, Jula, Mòoré — **E.C:** 220V/50Hz — **ITU:** BFA

AUTORITÉ DE RÉGULATION DE LA COMMANDE PUBLIQUE (ARCOP)

Avenue de l'Europe, Ouagadougou ☎ +226 25331167 **E:** arcop@arcop.bf **W:** arcop.bf

RADIODIFFUSION TÉLÉVISION DU BURKINA (Pub)

BP 7029, Ouagadougou 01 ☎+226 50324302 🖷 +226 50310441 **W:** rtb.bf **E:** radio@rtb.bf

FM (MHz): Banfora 101.5, Bobo-Dioulasso 90.6, Bogande 91.5, Boromo 91.4, Boulsa 88.9, Dedougou 90.5/93.6, Diapaga 89.5/92.6, Djibo 89.0, Dori 91.0, Fada N'Gourma 89.2/92.3, Gaoua 103.2, Hounde 98.3, Kaya 89.8/103.2, Kompienga 91.4, Koudougou 89.1, Manga 92.5, Mangodara 101.5, Nouna 98.4, Orodara 88.1, Ouagadougou 88.5/99.9, Ouahigouya 89.5/95.5, Pô 89.8, Tenkodogo 91.1, Tougan 88.3.

D.Prgr in French/Ethnic: 24h. **N. in French:** 0630MF, 1000SS + Thurs, 1245 (regional), 1300, 1900, 2200. **N. in English:** W1920 (approx). **Ann:** "RTV Burkina", "RTB". **IS:** Balafon.

Canal Arc-en-Ciel, 03 BP 7045, Ouagadougou **FM:** Ouagadougou 96.6MHz, Bobo-Dioulasso 89.8MHz.

REGIONAL STATIONS:

Radio Bobo, BP 392, Bobo-Dioulasso **FM:** 92.0MHz 0.02kW **D.Prgr:** MF 0600-0800, 1200-1400, 1600-2400, SS 0800-2400 – **R. Gaoua**, Gaoua. **FM**: 90.1MHz – **R. Rurale**: FM txs in Diapaga, Djibasso, Gassan, Kongoussi, Orodara & Poura.

Other Stations (MHz):

Al Houda FM, Ouagadougou: 98.5 – **Bankuy FM**, Dédougou: 107.7 – **Hit R**, Ouagadougou 87.7, Dori 104.6 **W:** hitradio.ma – **Horizon FM**: Tenkodogo 97.6, Banfora 98, Koudougou 98.7, Ouayigouya 100.4, Dédougou 102.7, Ouagadougou 104.4, Dori 104.6 – **Ouaga FM**: Bobo-Dioulasso 101.1, Ouagadougou 105.2 **W:** ouagafm-bf.com – **R. Ahmadiya**, Dori: 104.6 – **R. de l'Alliance Chrétienne**, Bobo-Dioulasso: 95.9 – **R. Balafon**, Bobo-Dioulasso: 102.7 – **R. Buayaba**, Diapaga 96.2MHz – **R. FM Boulgou,** Garango: 101.1 – **R. Cascade**, Banfora: 98 – **R. Catholique Teriya**, Banfora 94.7 – **R.**

Djawoampo, Bogandé 98.0 – **R. Djongo**, Pô: 106.4 – **Echo des Cotonniers**, Solenzo: 95.1 – **R. Djibasso:** 94.6 – **R. Energie**: Kaya 92.2, Yako 94.9, Fada N'Gourma 98.8 – **R. de l'Espoir**, Réo: 102.8 – **R. Évangile Développement**: Ouagadougou 93.4, Houndé 95.5, Léo 97.8, Koudougou 101.0, Ouahigouya 104.0, Yako 105.3, Bobo-Dioulasso 106.3. **W:** red-burkina.org – **R. Evangile du Sud-Ouest**, Gaoua: 99.7 – **R. Eveil**, Bogandé 101.0 – **R. Fréquence Espoir**: Dédougou 96.8 1kW, Tougan 101.4 0.1kW – **R. Frontière**, Tenkodogo: 97.6 – **R. Gambidi**, Ouagadougou: 97.7 – **R. Gassan:** 105.5 – **R. Gayeri**: 91.8 – **R. Goulou**, Po 99.5 – **R. du Grand Nord**, Dori: 97.5 – **R. Kadoadb**, Ziniare: 107.7 – **R. Kantigya**, Nouna 88.8 – **R. Kongoussi:** 93.2 – **R. Kouritta**, Koupela: 93.7 – **R. La Voix des Bales**, Boromo 103.6 – **R. La Voix du Soum**, Djibo 92.1 – **R. Lotamu**, Solenzo 101.9 – **R. LCD,** Djibo 98.6 – **R. Loudon**, Sapouy 104.9 – **R. Lumière:** Ouagoudougou: 98.1 – **R. Manegda**, Kaya: 99.4 – **R. Maria**: Ouagadougou 91.6 1kW, Kaya 99.4, Koupêla 96.9 1kW. **W:** radiomaria.org – **Media Star**, Bobo-Dioulasso: 96.7 – **R. Munyu FM**, Banfora: 94.7 – **R. Naboswende**, Pouytenga: 103.7 – **R. Natigmeb Zanga**, Yako: 98.2 – **R. Nemaro,** Cassou 94.2 – **R. Nerwaya,** Kongoussi 99.7 – **R. Notre Dame de la Réconciliation**, Koudougou 105.8 – **R. Nostalgie,** Ouagadougou, 94.4 – **R. Notre Dame:** Kaya 102.9, Kouhougou 105.8, Ouahigouya 102.6 – **R. Omega**: Ouagadougou 103.9, Bobo-Dioulasso 104.7 **W:** omegabf.net – **R. Paglayiri**, Zabré 94.3 – **R. Palabre**, B.P. 196, Kougougou: 92.2 – **R. Pog-Neere**, Pouytenga 100.2MHz – **R. Poura:** 98.2 – **R. Pulsar**, Ouagadougou: 94.8 0.4kW – **R. Salaki,** Dedougou 101.1 – **R. Salankoloto**, Ouagadougou: 97.3 – **R. Sanmentenga**, Kaya: 96.1 – **R. Tin-Taani**, Kantchari 100.0 – **La Voix du Sud-Ouest**, Diébougou: 101.5 – **R. Taanba**, Fada N'Gourma: 98.8 1kW **W:** radioafricanetwork.org.za/RadioTaanba.html – **R. Tapao**, Diapaga: 95.8 – **R. Unitas**, Diébougou: 94.7 – **R. Vive le Paysan**, Saponé: 107.0 – **R. la Voix du Passoré**, Yako: 105.3 – **R. la Voix du Paysan**, Ouahigouya: 97.0 – **R. La Voix du Verger**, Orodara: 91.2 – **R. Zoodo**, Ouahigouya: 100.4 **R. Savane**, Ouagadougou: 103.4 **W:** savanefm.bf
BBC African Sce: Ouagadougou 99.2 4kW.
RFI Afrique: Banfora 91.5, Koudougou 93.0, Ouagadougou 94.0, Ouahigouya 94.3, Bobo-Dioulasso 99.4.
Voice of America: Ouagadougou 102.4MHz

BURUNDI

L.T: UTC +2h — **Pop:** 12 million — **Pr.L:** Kirundi (official), French (official), English (official), Swahili — **E.C:** 220V/50Hz — **ITU:** BDI

CONSEIL NATIONAL DE LA COMMUNICATION (CNC)

✉ Blvd de l'Uprona, Immeuble Nyogozi-Marcoil, BP 1398, Bujumbura ☎ +257 22259064 **E:** cncburundi@yahoo.fr **W:** cnc-burundi.bi

RADIO-TÉLÉVISION NATIONALE DU BURUNDI (RTNB, Pub)

✉ B.P. 1900, Bujumbura ☎+257 22223742 🖷 +257 22226547 **W:** rtnbdi.bi **E:** rtnb@cbinf.com

FM(MHz)	**RTNB1**	**RTNB2**	**FM**(MHz)	**RTNB1**	**RTNB2**
Birime	94.2	98.9	Kaberenge	94.7	98.0
Bujumbura	102.9	92.9	Manga	95.6	98.9
Inanzerwe	88.4	91.4	Mutumba	88.8	91.9

D.Prgr: W 0300-0700 & 0900-2100, Sun 0300-2100. (RTNB1 in Kirundi, RTNB2 in French/Swahili/English). **N.** in French: 0530, 1200, 1500, 1900. **N.** in Swahili: 0630, 1245, 1800. **N.** in Kirundi: 0500, 0700, 1130, 1800, 2000. **N.** in English: 0445, 1230, 1600, 1845.
Ann: "Ici Bujumbura, Radio-Télévision Nationale du Burundi". **IS:** Drums.

Other stations (FM MHz):
Buja FM, Bujumbura 87.6 **W:** bujafm.com – **Hit R**, Bujumbura 91.4 **W:** hitradio.ma – **R. CCIB FM,** Bujumbura: 99.4, nationwide 102.4 – **R. Culture**, Bujumbura: 88.2/99.9 – **R. Isanganiro:** Bujumbura 89.7, Bururi 93.3/95.1, Kirundo 90.6, Ruyigi 90.7, Manga 101.0. **W:** web-africa.org/isanganiro – **R. Ivyizigiro**, Bujumbura: 90.9/104.8 – **R. Publique Africaine:** Bugesera 89.4, Birime 92.6, Bujumbura 93.7, Manga 107.1 **W:** rpa.bi – **R. Renaissance,** Bujumbura 101.4 – **R. Scolaire Nderagakura**, Bujumbura 87.9 – **Rema FM**, Bujumbura: 88.6/103.6/107.5. **W:** remafm.com

BBC African Sce: Bujumbura 90.2, Mount Manga 105.6MHz.
China R. Int, Bujumbura 89.2MHz
RFI Afrique: Bujumbura 96.1, Mutemba 99.5, Mt. Manga 103.7MHz.
VOA African Sce: Bujumbura 94.9, Mount Manga 95.2MHz

CABO VERDE

L.T: UTC -1h — **Pop:** 560,000 — **Pr.L:** Portuguese (official), Cabo Verdian Creole — **E.C:** 220V/50Hz — **ITU:** CPV

AGÊNCIA NACIONAL DAS COMUNICAÇÕES (ANAC)

✉ C.P. 892, Edifício MIT, Ponta Belém, Praia ☎+238 2604400 🖷 +238 2613069 **W:** anac.cv **E:** info.anac@anac.cv

RÁDIOTELEVISÃO DE CABO VERDE (RCV, Pub)

✉ Rua 13 de Janeiro 1-A, Achada de Santo António, Praia ✉C.P. 29, Av. Marginal, Mindelo, São Vicente ✉ C.P. 40, Espargos, Ilha do Sal ☎🖷+238 2411444 **W:** rtc.cv **E:** rtc@cvtelecom.cv
FM: Monte Verde 87.6MHz 1kW, Morro Curral 89.7MHz 0.25kW, Monte Tchota 91.6MHz 1kW, Mindelo 95.6MHz 0.5kW, Praia 98.1MHz 0.1kW + 12 relays below 0.1kW. **D.Prgr:** 24h.

Other stations (FM MHz):
R. Nova (Rlg.): Pinhão 91.8, Monte Vermelho 94.1, Cachaço 95.1, Sal Rei 97.0, Monte Tropetona 99.1, Pedra Rachada 99.9, M. Tchota 101.6 0.25kW, Mindelo 102.3, M. Verde 104.3 0.5kW, Morro do Curral 106.4 **W:** radionova.cv – **R. Comercial**: Santiago 92.9 1kW, Ponta Rachada 96.1MHz, Praia/M. Verde 99.9 **W:** facebook.com/radiocomercial.cv – **R. Crioula:** M. Tchota, M. Barro/M. Verde 89.6, Praia 94.9, Morro Curral 98.9 **W:** crioulafm.cv – **R. Educativa:** Monte Verde 101.5, M. Tchota 102.3, Praia & 4 sites 103.1 **W:** radioeducativa.cv – **Mosteiros FM**: M. Chota 96.1, São Filipe/Mosteiros 97.3 **W:** radiomosteirosfm.com

RDP África: Monte Verde 93.9MHz 3kW, Monte Tchota/Pedra Rachada 105.2MHz 3/1kW, Pedra Rachada 105.2MHz 1kW + 4 trs under 1kW.
RFI Afrique: Praia 99.3MHz 1kW, Mindelo 100.7MHz 0.25kW in French and Portuguese

CAMBODIA

L.T: UTC +7h — **Pop:** 17 million — **Pr.L:** Khmer (Cambodian) — **E.C:** 230V/50Hz — **ITU:** CBG

MINISTRY OF INFORMATION

✉ 62, Preah Monivong, Phnom Penh ☎ +855 23 430514 🖷 +855 23 430514 **W:** www.info.gov.kh **L.P:** Minister: Mr Khieu Kanharith

NATIONAL RADIO OF KAMPUCHEA (RNK) (Gov)

✉ No 6 Street 19 (Corner Street 102), Sangkat Wat Phnom, Khan Daun Penh, Phnom Penh 12202 ☎ +855 23 725522 🖷 +855 23 427319 **W:** rnk.gov.kh **L.P:** Dir. Gen: HE Tun Sarath
MW: AM 918, Phnom Penh (Kandal Steung) 918kHz 600kW: 2200-1700
Wat Phnom FM: Phnom Penh 105.7MHz 10kW
N. in English & French: 0600 & 1200-on 918kHz & 105.7MHz.
FM-96 (comm.): ✉ Steung Meanchey, Phnom Penh 12352 **FM:** 96.0MHz 20kW
Cambodia-China Friendship Radio (joint service with China Radio International): 2300-1700 in Chaozhou, English, Khmer and Mandarin **FM:** Phnom Penh 96.5MHz 10kW, Siem Reap 105.0MHz
Provincial sces: ✉ via the Information Department of the relevant provincial govt. Banteay Meanchey (Sisophon) 94.0MHz 5kW, Battambang (R. Chamka Chek) 92.7MHz 2kW, Kampong Cham (R. Phnom Pros Phnom Srey) 92.5MHz 2kW, Kampong Chhnang (R. Phnom Krang Dey Meas) 92.3MHz, Kampong Speu (R. Kirirom, Chbar Mon) 89.3MHz, Kampot (R. 9 Makhara) 99.7MHz 2kW, Kampong Thom 98.3MHz, Kep (R. Chhner Kep) 99.0MHz, Kratie 98.5MHz 2kW, Mondulkiri (Sen Monorom) 97.0MHz, Oddar Meanchey (R. Prasat Ta Mean, Samraong) 91.5MHz, Pailin 90.5MHz 2kW. Pursat 98.5MHz 2kW, Preah Vihear (R. Phnom Tbeng) 97.0MHz, Prey Veng (R. Baray Andet) 97.3MHz, Ratanakiri (Ban Lung) 89.5MHz 2kW, Siem Reap (R. Nokor Phnom) 103.0MHz, Sihanoukville (R. Kampong Som) 93.0MHz 2kW, Stung Treng (R. Sekong) 99.0MHz, Svay Rieng (R. Romdoul) 98.7MHz 2kW, Takeo (R. Kork Thlok) 92.5MHz 2kW, Tbong Khmum (Ponhea Kraek) 88.1MHz.
Ann: (Khmer): 'Thini Sathani Vithyu Cheat Kampuchea'

PHNOM PENH MUNICIPAL RADIO STATION

✉ No 29, Street 335 / 1005 National Road 2, Phnom Penh 12312 ☎ +855 23 982265
Sweet FM: Phnom Penh 88.0MHz 10kW. **Sweet FM stations in provinces:** Banteay Meanchey (Sisophon) 103.5MHz 2.5kW

Battambang 103.3MHz 1kW, Kampong Cham 100.5MHz 1kW, Kampong Chhnang 104.7MHz, Kampong Thom 103.5MHz 1kW, Kampot 93.3MHz, Koh Kong 103.5MHz, Kratie 103.5MHz, Preah Vihear (Chamksan) 99.5MHz, Pursat 100.5MHz 1kW, Siem Reap 100.5MHz 2kW, Sihanoukville 100.5MHz 1kW,, Stung Treng 100.5MHz, Svay Rieng 103.7MHz 10kW, Takeo 100.5MHz
Love FM: Phnom Penh 97.5MHz 1kW, Siem Reap 97.5MHz 1kW in English and Khmer
Municipality R.: Phnom Penh 103.0MHz, 10kW

RADIO BAYON FM
✉ Russei Sros Village, Sangkat Niroth, Khan Meanchey, Phnom Penh 12410 ☎ +855 23 333795
FM: Kandal (Phnom Penh area) 95.0MHz 24kW. Rel. stns: Banteay Meanchay (Mongkol Borey) 97.5MHz 5kW, Battambang 104.0MHz 2kW, Kampong Cham 91.5MHz 10kW, Kampong Thom 91.0MHz 2kW, Kampot 91.0MHz 2kW, Koh Kong 95.5MHz 2kW, Kratie (Chhloung) 91.0MHz 2kW, Mondulkiri (Sen Monorom) 93.0MHz 2kW, Oddar Meanchey 94.0MHz 2kW, Preah Vihear (Chamksan) 95.0MHz 2.5kW, Pursat 91.5MHz 2kW, Ratanakiri (Ban Lung) 94.0MHz 1kW, Siem Reap 93.0MHz 10kW, Sihanoukville 92.0MHz 3kW, Stung Treng 92.0MHz 2kW, Svay Rieng 95.5MHz 2kW

Other Stations:

FM Location	MHz	kW	Station
1) Battambang	87.5		PSN R.
2) Phnom Penh	87.5		Daun Penh EFM
1) Suong (t)	87.5		PSN R.
2) Kampong Cham	87.7	1	Daun Penh EFM
3) Sen Monorom (m)	87.7		Sok San Monorom
4) Phnom Penh	87.7		Fresh FM
2) Siem Reap	87.7	1	Daun Penh EFM
5) Siem Reap	88.0		Vayo FM
1) Sihanoukville	88.0		PSN R.
6) Stoung (kt)	88.0		V. of Buddhism of Cambodia (R. Prek Rolok)
30) Takeo	88.0		Vithyu Setthi Seiha
7) Kampong Chhnang	88.3		KC FM
8) Phnom Penh	88.3		R. Meanchey FM
9) Pursat	88.3		Angel FM
10) Siem Reap	88.3	2	R. Mahanakor Khemara
11) Sisophon (m)	88.3		Stung Khiev Thmey (Samleng Ek)
12) Battambang	88.5		Kolyanmet R.
31) Takeo	88.5		Vithyu Li Sali Na
3) Ban Lung (r)	88.5		Sok San Monorom
14) Kampong Cham	88.7	10	Mongkulsavann FM
15) Kratie	88.7		Vithyu Mekong
16) Phnom Penh	88.7		R. Kong Meas
16) Prey Veng	88.7		R. Kong Meas
16) Pursat	88.7		R. Kong Meas
17) Siem Reap	88.7		Friends FM
18) Sisophon (m)	88.7		Cam TV
19) Sihanoukville	88.8		V. of People with Disabilities (VOD, Samleng Chun Pikear)
20) Battambang	89.0		NRG 89 FM
20) Kampong Thom	89.0		NRG 89 FM
20) Phnom Penh	89.0		NRG 89 FM
20) Siem Reap	89.0		NRG 89 FM
20) Sihanoukville	89.0		NRG 89 FM
21) Battambang	89.3		Vithyu Sek Meas
22) Kampong Chhnang	89.3		Samleng Kolbot Khmai (Voice of Khmer Youth)
23) Phnom Penh	89.3		FM 89.25
24) Takeo	89.3		Sokha FM
25) Battambang	89.5		ABC R.
26) Kratie	89.5		Voice of Women (Samleng Strey)
27) Phnom Penh	89.5	10	VO New Life R. (Samleng Chivit Thmey)
28) Siem Reap	89.5		ABC Cambodia R. (R. Krong Angkor)
29) Banteay Meanchey	89.7		Wellness FM (Vithyu Pha Sokhpheap)
29) Phnom Penh	89.7		Wellness FM (Vithyu Pha Sokhpheap)
29) Siem Reap	89.7		Wellness FM (Vithyu Pha Sokhpheap)
29) Suong (t)	89.7		Wellness FM (Vithyu Pha Sokhpheap)
14) Kampong Thom	90.0		R. Mongkulsovann
133) Phnom Penh	90.0		R. Solida (Soft FM)
32) Poipet (m)	90.0		My FM
31) Battambang	90.3	1	R. Khlaing Meoung
33) Kampong Chhnang	90.3		R, Sovannara
31) Prey Veng	90.3		Vithyu Li Sali Na
34) Siem Reap	90.3		Voice of Entrak Tevy (PSN R.)
19) Svay Rieng	90.3		V. of People with Disabilities (VOD, Samleng Chun Pikear)
31) Kampong Speu	90.7		Vithyu Li Sali Na
35) Koh Kong	90.7		South East Asia FM
35) Pursat	90.7		South East Asia FM
35) Sisophon (m)	90.7		South East Asia FM
37) Battambang	91.0	5	R. FM Khemara
38) Phnom Penh	91.0		People R. (Pracheachon)
39) Pursat	91.0		Metta R.
40) Siem Reap	91.0		Vithyu Changrit Meas (CMD FM, Golden Cricket)
41) Kampong Cham	91.1		One FM
42) Kampong Chhnang	91.3		Ratanak Kampong Chhnang
43) Phnom Penh	91.3		Star FM
44) Pursat	91.3		R. Sompov Meas
48) Sispohon (m)	91.5	3	Solika FM
45) Phnom Penh	91.5		VOY FM (Voice of Youth)
46) Stung Treng	91.5		Stung Treng FM
133) Phnom Penh	91.7		R. Solida (Soft FM)
14) Sispohon (m)	91.9		R. Mongkulsavann
45) Kampong Thom	92.0		VOY FM (Voice of Youth)
45) Suong (t)	92.0		VOY FM (Voice of Youth)
45) Battambang	92.1		VOY FM (Voice of Youth)
14) Kampot	92.3		R. Mongkulsavann
49) Phnom Penh	92.3	5	Top FM
19) Siem Reap	92.3		V. of People with Disabilities (VOD, Samleng Chun Pikear)
37) Battambang	92.5		People R. (Pracheachon)
50) Phnom Penh	92.5		Khmer FM
9) Sihanoukville	92.5		Angel FM
25) Kampong Cham	92.7		R. ABC
25) Kampong Thom	92.7		R. ABC
25) Phnom Penh	92.7		R. Ambel Prajok (ABC)
51) Pursat	92.7		R. Sophal
38) Kampong Cham	93.1		Metta R.
32) Battambang	93.2		My FM
27) Kampong Chhnang	93.2		VO New Life R. (Samlang Chivit Thmey)
17) Phnom Penh	93.3		Friends FM – News R.
52) Poipet (m)	93.3		Seven FM
53) Suong (t)	93.3		Peanichakam FM
14) Batttambang	93.5		R. Mongkulsavann
54) Siem Reap	93.5		R. Sela Angkor
55) Stung Treng	93.5		Stung Treng FM
56) Memot (t)	93.7		ORM TV
57) Phnom Penh	93.7		Vithyu Ekreach (Independent R.)
58) Siem Reap	93.7		R. Ratanak Angkor
9) Sisophon (m)	93.7		Angel FM
59) Kampong Cham	94.0		R. Kontreum Asean
45) Kampot	94.0		VOY FM (Voice of Youth)
60) Phnom Penh	94.0		Phnom Penh R.
45) Siem Reap	94.1		VOY FM (Voice of Youth)
45) Sihanoukville	94.0		VOY FM (Voice of Youth)
61) Kampong Chhnang	94.3		DP FM
9) Siem Reap	94.3		Angel FM
62) Takeo	94.3		Bayong FM
63) Kampong Thom	94.5		Metrey R.
64) Koh Kong	94.5		Sako Koh Kong
66) Svay Rieng	94.5		R. Mohachun
67) Mongkol Borey (m)	94.7		Luong FM
50) Phnom Penh	94.7		V. of Dharma Buddhist R.
50) Siem Reap	94.7		V. of Dharma Buddhist R.
50) Svay Rieng	94.7		V. of Dharma Buddhist R.
68) Battambang	95.0		R. Bopha
69) Battambang	95.3		R. Dewey FM
70) Kampong Cham	95.3		Voice of the Blind (VOB, Samleng Chun Pikear Phnek)
66) Phnom Penh	95.3		R. Mohachun
57) Kampong Chnnang	95.5		Vithyu Ekreach (Independent R.)
57) Kampot	95.5		Vithyu Ekreach (Independent R.)
57) Phnom Penh	95.5		Vithyu Ekreach (Independent R.)
71) Poipet (m)	95.5		Music FM (Dontreay)
73) Battambang	95.7		Town FM
74) Memot (t)	95.7		Sopheak Mongkul
75) Phnom Penh	95.7	5	Reasmey Hang Meas FM
76) Kampong Cham	96.3		R. Nakor Bachey
77) Kampong Thom	96.3		Phnom Santuk R.
66) Siem Reap	96.3		R. Mohachun
66) Stung Treng	96.5		R. Mohachun
78) Sisopohon (m)	96.5	10	Banteay Meanchey Provincial R.

FM	Location	MHz	kW	Station
16)	Kampong Cham	96.7		Kong Meas
38)	Kampong Thom	96.7		Metta R.
38)	Phnom Penh	96.7		Metta R.
68)	Pursat	96.7		R. Bopha
38)	Siem Reap	96.7		Metta R.
38)	Sihanoukville	96.7		Metta R.
79)	Phnom Penh	97.0	10	R Apsara
80)	Kompong Cham	97.1		New Style
70)	Banteay Meanchey	97.3		Voice of the Blind (VOB, Samleng Chun Pikear Phnek)
16)	Kampong Chhnang	97.3		Kong Meas
81)	Kampong Speu	97.3		Rithy Sen
9)	Kampot	97.3		Angel FM
82)	Phnom Penh	97.3		Khemony Panya
83)	Takeo	97.3		R. Ponletrayroth
68)	Ban Lung (r)	97.5		Vithyu Khmer Isan
46)	Kampong Cham	97.5		DP FM
16)	Kampong Thom	97.5		Kong Meas
84)	Pailin	97.5		R O Torng Pailin
68)	Ratanakiri	97.5		R. Bopha
85)	Svay Rieng	97.8		Mohasal FM
79)	Svay Rieng	97.8		R. Apsara
86)	Battambang	97.8		Koltoteng R.
86)	Phnom Penh	97.8		Koltoteng R.
86)	Siem Reap	97.8		Koltoteng R.
57)	Kampong Cham	98.0		Vithyu Ekreach (Independent R.)
87)	Phnom Penh	98.0	10	FM98 (Armed Forces R., Khemark Phomin)
88)	Battambang	98.1		R. Ratanak
89)	Kampot	98.3		Soren Mountain Top FM
90)	Phnom Penh	98.3		R. Ponleu Thom Preaphut
91)	Poipet (m)	98.3		FM98.3
90)	Siem Reap	98.3		R. Ponleu Thom Preaphut
57)	Sihanoukville	98.3		Vithyu Ekreach (Independent R.)
93)	Kampong Thom	98.5		R. Kong San
57)	Phnom Penh	98.5		Vithyu Ekreach (Independent R.)
92)	Siem Reap	98.5		Tourist R. (Tesachar)
25)	Sisophon (m)	98.5		ABC Cambodia R.
86)	Svay Rieng	98.5		Koltoteng R.
95)	Battambang	98.7		R. Steung Khiev (VSK)
96)	Kampong Cham	98.7		Tonle Om
32)	Kampong Chhnang	98.7		My FM
35)	Kampong Thom	98.7		South East Asia FM
97)	Siem Reap	98.8		Preah Neareay R.
66)	Kampong Chhnang	99.0		R. Mohachun
98)	Phnom Penh	99.0	10	FM99
68)	Pursat	99.0		Vithyu Khmer Isan
99)	Siem Reap	99.0	0.5	Kiss FM
8)	Sisophon (m)	99.0	2	Meanchey FM
100)	Phnom Penh	99.3		Vithyu Somaleu
85)	Prey Veng	99.3		Mohasal FM
83)	Suong (t)	99.3		R. Ponletrayroth
32)	Kampong Cham	99.5		My FM
32)	Oddar Meanchey	99.5		My FM
101)	Phnom Penh	99.5	10	KRUSA FM (FEBC/Family FM)
32)	Pursat	99.5	1	My FM
32)	Sisophon (m)	99.5	1	My FM
102)	Kampong Cham	99.7		Kampong Cham R. Station
81)	Kampong Chhnang	99.7		Rithy Sen
46)	Phnom Penh	99.7		DP FM
103)	Takeo	99.7		Angkor Sunly FM
101)	Kampong Thom	99.8	0.5	KRUSA FM (FEBC/Family FM)
105)	Battambang	100.0		VO Dombang Kronhoung
13)	Kampong Thom	100.0	1	Steung Sen R.
106)	Ponhea Kraek (t)	100.1		Neak Poun
107)	Prey Veng	100.1		Vithyu Kdei Sangkhum (Hope R.)
33)	Battambang	100.3		Sovannara
108)	Kampong Chhnang	100.3		Nokor Chum
1)	Phnom Penh	100.3	5	PSN R.
57)	Siem Reap	100.3		Vithyu Ekreach (Independent R.)
109)	Phnom Penh	100.5		Lotus R. (Phka Chhouk)
110)	Poipet (m)	100.5		Vithyu Chokchai
103)	Kampong Chhnang	100.7		Angkor Sunly FM
111)	Kampot	100.7		Vithyu Yuvochon (Youth R.)
112)	Phnom Penh	100.7		Cool FM
113)	Phnom Penh	101.3		EVO FM
114)	Srey Santhor (kc)	101.5		Mongkol Panha
63)	Takeo	101.5		Metrey R.
115)	Ban Lung (r)	101.7		Wildflower R. (Phka Prei)
46)	Battambang	101.7		DP FM
106)	Kampong Cham	101.7		Neak Poun
46)	Phnom Penh	101.7		DP FM
14)	Pursat	101.7		Mongkulsavann FM
89)	Siem Reap	101.7		Soren Mountain Top FM
116)	Kampong Cham	102.0		FM 102
116)	Kampong Thom	102.0	1	FM 102
116)	Kratie	102.0	1	FM 102 (Kratie FM)
116)	Moung Roussei (b)	102.0		FM 102
36)	Phnom Penh	102.0	10	FM 102
36)	Svay Rieng	102.0	1	FM 102
9)	Battambang	102.3		Angel FM
46)	Kampong Thom	102.3		DP FM
73)	Phnom Penh	102.3	5	Town FM
59)	Siem Reap	102.3		Kontreum Siem Reap
17)	Kampong Cham	102.5		R. Tonle FM (River FM)
17)	Phnom Penh	102.5	2	R. Tonle FM (River FM)
117)	Siem Reap	102.5	1	Sathani Vithyu Krom Siem Reap, Tonle FM (Siem Reap City R. Stn)
5)	Sihanoukville	102.5		Vayo FM
50)	Battambang	102.7		V. of Dharma Buddhist R.
50)	Kampong Thom	102.7		V. of Dharma Buddhist R.
50)	Pursat	102.7		V. of Dharma Buddhist R.
50)	Phnom Penh	102.8		V. of Dharma Buddhist R., Vat Than
50)	Sihanoukville	102.8		V. of Dharma Buddhist R.
50)	Kampong Cham	102.9		V. of Dharma Buddhist R.
57)	Phnom Penh	103.3		Vithyu Ekreach (Independent R.)
116)	Phnom Penh	103.5	10	R. WMC
119)	Battambang	103.7		R. Phnom Sampov
120)	Kampong Chhnang	103.7		R. Chhnang Meas
130)	Takeo	103.7		R. Phnom Borey
90)	Sihanoukville	103.7		Ponleu Thom Preaphut
131)	Phnom Penh	104.0	10	R. Sovann Phum
132)	Sihanoukville	104.0	2	Sung Meas FM
133)	Phnom Penh	104.3		R. Solida (Soft FM)
85)	Battambang	104.5		Mohasal FM (Sangke FM)
134)	Phnom Penh	104.5	5	R. Hang Meas FM
135)	Preah Vihear	104.5		Krong Preah Vihear
136)	Kampong Cham	104.7		Kizuna FM
90)	Kampot	104.7		Ponleu Thom Preaphut
137)	Phnom Penh	104.7		FM 104.7
138)	Takeo	104.7		FM 104.7
9)	Battambang	105.0		R. Steung Khiev Thmey
68)	Kratie	105.0		R. Bopha
139)	Phnom Penh	105.0	5	Sombok Ka Mum (R. Beehive)
106)	Ban Lung (mk)	105.1		Neak Poun
18)	Kampong Cham	105.1		Cam TV
71)	Kampong Thom	105.3		Music FM (Dontreay)
96)	Memot (t)	105.3		Tonle Om
121)	Phnom Penh	105.3		Vithyu Ponleu Poutthochak
57)	Pursat	105.3		Vithyu Ekreach (Independent R.)
6)	Samraong (om)	105.3		V. of Buddhism of Cambodia
73)	Siem Reap	105.3		Town FM
88)	Sisophon (m)	105.3		R. Ratanak
5)	Phnom Penh	105.5		Vayo FM
14)	Siem Reap	105.5		Mongkulsovann FM
14)	Sihanoukville	105.5		Mongkulsovann FM
65)	Sisophon (m)	105.7		Vithyu Rikreay Banteay Meanchey (Joy for You R,)
97)	Battambang	105.7		Preah Neareay R. (PNR FM)
94)	Battambang	106.0		Sovann Angkor FM
35)	Phnom Penh	106.0	10	South East Asia FM
83)	Sihanoukville	106.0		R. Ponletrayroth
141)	Phnom Penh	106.3		Vong Kamha Slek Meas
6)	Siem Reap	106.3	5	V. of Buddhism of Cambodia
143)	Sisophon (m)	106.5	1	U FM
66)	Battambang	106.7		R. Mohachun
59)	Kampong Cham	106.7		Kontreum Kampong Cham
131)	Kampong Chhnang	106.7		R. Sovann Phum
145)	Phnom Penh	106.7		Vithyu Aoveat Preahpout
146)	Siem Reap	106.7		Mekea
147)	Battambang	107.0		Lotus Flower R. (Phka Chhouk)
148)	Phnom Penh	107.0	10	FM107
70)	Battambang	107.3		Voice of the Blind (VOB, Samleng Chun Pikear Phnek)
25)	Kampong Cham	107.3		ABC Cambodia R.
63)	Phnom Penh	107.3		Metrey R.
25)	Ban Lung (mk)	107.5		ABC Cambodia R.
25)	Battambang	107.5		ABC Cambodia R.
25)	Kampong Chhnang	107.5		ABC Cambodia R.

FM	Location	MHz	kW	Station
25)	Kampong Thom	107.5		ABC Cambodia R.
25)	Kampot	107.5		ABC Cambodia R.
25)	Koh Kong	107.5		ABC Cambodia R.
25)	Kratie	107.5		ABC Cambodia R.
25)	Phnom Penh	107.5	5	ABC Cambodia R.
25)	Pailin	107.5		ABC Cambodia R.
25)	Pursat	107.5		ABC Cambodia R.
25)	Ratanakiri	107.5		ABC Cambodia R.
25)	Svay Rieng	107.5		ABC Cambodia R.
149)	Siem Reap	107.5		Krong Kampuchea
25)	Sihanoukville	107.5		ABC Cambodia R.
25)	Stung Treng	107.5		ABC Cambodia R.
150)	Kampong Cham	107.7		Samleng Yeung (Our Voice)
4)	Takeo	107.7		Fresh FM
151)	Phnom Penh	107.7	5	Sky R.
141)	Siem Reap	107.7	5	Vong Kamha Slek Meas
133)	Battambang	108.0		R. Solida (Soft FM)
133)	Kampong Thom	108.0		R. Solida (Soft FM)
133)	Phnom Penh	108.0	10	R. Solida (Soft FM)
133)	Siem Reap	108.0		R. Solida (Soft FM)

(b)=Battambang Prov. (kc)=Kampong Cham Prov. (kt)=Kampong Thom Prov. (m)=Banteay Meanchey Prov. (mk)=Mondulkiri Prov (om)=Oddar Meanchey Prov. (r)=Ratanakiri Prov. (t)=Tbong Khmoum Prov.

Addresses & other information:
1) 87 Street 16BT, Sangkat Boeng Tompong, Meanchey District, Phnom Penh – **2)** No 25B, Street 320, Sangkat Boeng Keng Kang 3, Chamkar Mon District, Phnom Penh 12304 – **3)** 7 Makara Village, Sangkat Labansiek, Ban Lung City, Ratanakiri– **5)** No 13B Street 70, Phnom Penh **W:** vayofm.com – **6)** Vat Preah Neang, Stoung District, Kampong Thom – **8)** Thmey Village, Chamkar Dong, Phnom Penh 12410 – **9)** Romchek IV Village, Sangkat Rotanak, Battambang – **10)** Phum Wattamem, Khum O Dombong I, Sangkae District, Battambang Province. – **11)** Street 208, Romchek IV Village, Sangkat Rotanak, Battambang. Roung Masin Village, Sangkat O'Ambel, Sispohon – **12)** Vat Ta Meum Village, O Dombong Commune I, Sangkae District, Battambang – **13)** Slaket Village, Prey Tahou Commune, Steung Sen District, Kompong Thom – **14)**.National Highway 6, Tavean Village, Sala Kamkreuk, Siem Reap – **17)**Trasak Phum Street (Street 63) no 246, Sangkat Boong Keng 1, Chamkar Mon District, Phnom Penh – **18)** No. 627 Street 69, Sala Kanseng Village, Svay Dangkum Commune, Siem Reap – **20)** No 131B, Street 271, Boeung Salang, Toul Kork, Phnom Penh – **25)** No 73 Street 271 (Yothapol Khemarek Phoumin), Phnom Penh 12160 **W:** abccambodia.com – **27)** PO Box 1426 Phnom Penh. Operated by Final Frontiers Foundation – **28)** Chong Kaosou Village, Slor Kram Commune, Siem Reap – **29)** No 37 Street 87BT, Phnom Penh 12351 —**32)** Wat Thmey Street, Palelay Village, Poipet, Banteay Meanchey. Romchek III Village, Sangkat Rotanak, Battambang – **33)** Phsar Dam Rong Street, Mong Barang Village, Sangkat Boer, Kampong Chhnang – **35)** Slaeng Roleung Village, Sangkat Tuek Thla, Sen Sok District, Phnom Penh – **37)** Prek Mohatep Village, Sangkat Svay Por, Battambang – **38)** Vat Koltoteng, Kaoh Krabei Village, Sangkat Prey Thmey, Chbar Ambov District, Phnom Penh – **40)** Vat Damnak Village, Sangkat Salakamreuk, Siem Reap – **41)** Former National Route 7, Boeng Kok Village, Sangkat Boeng Kok, Kampong Cham – **45)** 15A, Street 371, Sangkat Tuek Thla, Sen Sok District, Phnom Penh – **49)** Lot 35, Street 1709, Sangkat KmNo 6, Russey Keo District, Phnom Penh 12401 —**54)** Chong Kao Sou Village, Slorkram Commune, Siem Reap – **57)** Borey New Town #L14, Street 113KF, Sangkat Chaom Chao, Pou Senchey District, Phnom Penh – **62)** Chork Village, Sangkat Roka Knong, Doun Kaev City, Takeo – **63)** Vat Sankor, Sankor Commune, Kampong Svay District, Kompong Thom –**66)** Romchek IV Village, Sangkat Rotanak, Battambang – **67)** Wat Luong, Mongkul Borey, Banteay Meanchey – **68)** Romchek IV Village, Sangkat Rotanak, Battambang – **69)** Dewey International University, Street 207, Battambang – **70)** Group 10, Chong Kaosou Village, Slorkram Commune, Siem Reap – **73)** No 20 Street 592, Sangkat Tuol Sangke, Russei Keo District, Phnom Penh – **75)** No 33, Street 115, Phnom Penh 12258 – **78)** Kou Than Village, Sangkat O'Ambel, Sisophon, Banteay Meanchey Province – **79)** No 69, Street No 57 (Corner Street No 370), Phnom Penh – **80)** Boeng Kok II Village, Sangkat Boeng Kok, Kampong Cham – **81)** National Highway 4, Chbar Mon City, Kampong Speu– **82)** Vat Pothivan, Sangkat Snaor, Pou Senchey District, Phnom Penh – **83)** Vat Prasat Nengkmoa, Rovieng Commune, Samraong District, Takeo. Khnar Village, Sralab Commune, Suong, Tbong Khmum District – **84)** Chamkar Cafe Village, Sangkat Tuol Lvea, Pailin – **85)** Romchek IV Village, Sangkat Rotanak, Battambang – **87)** Rue de Tchechoslovaquie (Street 164), Phnom Penh – **89)** National Road 6, Chong Kaosou Village, Slorkram Commune, Siem Reap – **90)** Sangkat I, Sihanoukville – **91)** Km 4, Poipet, Banteay Meanchey Province – **94)** Romchek IV Village, Sangkat Ratana, Battambang. Chong Kaosou Village, Sangkat Slor Kram, Siem Reap **W:** sovannangkorfm106.com – **97)** Phum Otakam II, Sangkat Toul Ta Ek, Battambang – **98)** No 41 Street 360, Phnom Penh – **101)** No 8D Street 355, Sangkat Tuol Sangkei, Russei Keo District, Phnom Penh 12105 – **103)** Kleang Prak Village, Sangkat Boer, Kampong Chhnang. Chork Village, Sangkat Roka Knong, Doun Kaev City, Takeo – **105)** Wat Leap, Wat Leap Village, Battambang **W:** vodfm.com – **106)** Boeng Kok II Village, Kampong Cham – **108)** see 33) – **109)** 597, National Road 1, Daeum Slaeng Village, Chbar Ampov District, Phnom Penh – **112)** No 150 Street 516, Phnom Penh – **113)** Evocam Freedom International Cambodia, No 507J Tuol Kok Village, Tuol Kok District, Phnom Penh – **114)** Vat Phteah Kandal, Phteah Kandal Commune, Srey Santhor District, Kampong Cham – **115)** Tay Seng Building, Phumi 4 Village, Sangkat Kachanh, Ban Lung City, Ratanakiri – **116)** Women's Media Center of Cambodia, 19A Street 564, Sangkat Boeng Kok, Tuol Kok District, Phnom Penh **W:** wmc.org.kh – **117)** No. 627, Street 99, Sala Kanseng Village, Sangkat Svay Dangkum, Siem Reap – **119)** Phum Otakam II, Sangkat Toul Ta Ek, Battambang – **120)** see 33) –**130)** Psar Takeo Village, Sangkat Roka Knong, Doun Kaev City, Takeo – **131)** No 29, Street 210, Phnom Penh 12158 – **133)** 69 Choeng Ek Village, Sangkat Choeng Ek, Dangkao District, Phnom Penh 12415 – **134)** No 33, Street 115, Phnom Penh 12258 – **139)** No 33, Street 26BT, Thnort Chrum Village, Sangkat Boeng Thumpon, Meanchey District, Phnom Penh 12351 **W:** sbk.com.kh – **141)** No 45A, Boulevard Federation de Russie, Phnom Penh – **142)** Wat Bo, Sangkat Sala Kamroek, Siem Reap – **147)** Wat Po Veal, Battambang – **148)** No 18, Rd. 562, Phnom Penh 12151 – **149)** National Road 6, Borey Seang Nam, Khnar Thmey Village, Sangkat Chreav, Siem Reap – **150)** Old National Highway 7, Veal Vong Village, Sangkat Veal Vong, Kampong Cham – **151)** Damnak Thom Village, Steung Meanchey Commune, Meanchey District, Phnom Penh 12352

Relays of International Broadcasters
BBC World Service: Phnom Penh 100.0MHz 1kW in English.
Radio France Internationale. RFI Cambodge: Battambang 94.5MHz 0.25kW, Kampong Cham 94.5MHz 0.25kW, Phnom Penh 92.0MHz 10kW, Siem Reap 92.0MHz 1kW, Sihanoukville 94.5MHz 0.5kW 24h n French and Khmer. **RFI Monde:** Phnom Penh 88.5MHz 24h in French

CAMEROON

L.T: UTC +1h — **Pop:** 27 million — **Pr.L:** French (official), English (official), Cameroon Pidgin — **E.C:** 220V/50Hz — **ITU:** CME

NATIONAL COMMUNICATIONS COUNCIL (CNC)
Siège CNC Yaoundé, Quartier Bastos, B.P. 12 535, Yaoundé Centre 237 ☎+237 22 210309 🖷 +237 22 210308 **W:** cnc.gov.cm **E:** contact@cnc.gov.cm

CAMEROON RADIO TELEVISION (CRTV, Gov.)
B.P. 1634, Yaoundé +237 22214077 🖷 +237 22204340
W: crtv.cm **E:** infos@crtv.cm
FM (MHz):
CRTV R. Nationale: Yaoundé 88.8 10kW, Douala 89.2 10kW, Bertoua 89.8 10kW, Bafoussam 91.1 10kW, Ngaoundéré 92.5. Buéa 98.6.
Regional stations:
CRTV Yaoundé FM: 94.0, **CRTV Centre,** Yaoundé: 101.9 – **CRTV Littoral,** B.P. 986, Douala: 91.3, **Suelaba FM**: 104.9 10kW – **CRTV Sud-Ouest,** Buea 94.5, **CRTV Mont Cameroun,** Buea 98.0 – **CRTV Nord,** B.P. 103, Garoua: 101.2 10kW – **CRTV Est,** B.P. 230, Bertoua: 92.9 10kW – **CRTV Ouest,** B.P. 970, Bafoussam: 93.5 10kW, Pouala FM 104.5 – **CRTV Nord-Ouest,** B.P. 4049, Bamenda: 93.5 10kW – **CRTV Sud,** Ebolowa 97.6 10kW, **Kaze FM** 91.1 – **CRTV Adamaoua,** Ngaoundéré: 102.5 10kW – **CRTV Extrême-Nord,** Maroua 94.8, Kousseri 95.5.

Other FM Stations (MHz):
Dynamic FM, Douala: 103.9 – **Kalak FM,** Yaoundé: 94.5 **W:** facebook.com/KalakOnline – **Magic FM,** Yaoundé: 100.1 – **R. Bon Berger,** Kaélé 99.0 – **R. Bonne Nouvelle**: Yaoundé 97.7, Ngaoundére 98.5, Douala 102.5, Ebolowa 102.7 – **R. Campus,** Ngaoundéré: 99.0 – **R. Environnement,** Yaoundé: 107.7 – **R. Equinoxe,** Douala: 93 **W:** lanouvelleexpression.net – **R. Le Lauréat,** Douala: 90.5 – **R. Lumière,** Yaoundé: 91.9 – **R. Noor,** Ngaoundéré: 106.1 – **R. Nostalgie,** Douala: 96.0 **W:** facebook.com/nostalgie.cm – **R. Reine**: Yaoundé 103.7 1kW, Buéa 97.7 1kW – **R. Salaaman,** Garoua: 89.0 – **R. Sawtu Linjiila,** Ngaoundéré: 95.7 1kW (SW relays see Target Broadcasts Section)

– **R. Siantou**, Yaoundé: 90.5 – **R. Venus**, Yaoundé: 95.4 – **R. Veritas**, Douala: 96.8 – **R. Vie Nouvelle**, Douala: 100.5 – **Real Time Music**, Douala: 103.5, Yaoundé 106.0 – **Sky One R**, Yaoundé: 104.5, Douala 100.1. **W:** skyonecameroun.com– **Sweet FM**, Douala: 88.7 – **TBC FM**, Yaoundé: 93.0.
BBC African Sce: Garoua 94.4, Bamenda 95.7, Yaoundé 98.4, Douala 101.3.
Medi 1 Afrique Internationale: Yaoundé 96.2
RFI Afrique: Douala 97.8, Bafoussam 101.1, Maroua 101.6, Garoua 104.8, Yaoundé 105.5, Bamenda 105.8MHz

CANADA

L.T: See World Time Table (DST where applicable: 14 Mar-7 Nov) — **Pop:** 37 million — **Pr.L:** English (official), French (official) — **E.C:** 120V/60Hz — **ITU:** CAN

CANADIAN RADIO-TELEVISION AND TELECOMMUNICATIONS COMMISSION - CRTC

✉ Ottawa, ON K1A 0N2 ☎+1 819 997 0313 📠+1 819 994 0218 **W:** crtc.gc.ca **L.P:** Chair and CEO: Ian Scott. Vice-Chair, Broadcasting: Dr. Caroline J. Simard
The CRTC is an independent public organisation that regulates and supervises Canadian broadcasting and telecommunications systems.

Provinces & Territories: AB=Alberta, BC=British Columbia, MB=Manitoba, NB=New Brunswick, NL=Newfoundland & Labrador, NS=Nova Scotia, NT=Northwest Territories, NU=Nunavut, ON=Ontario, PE=Prince Edward Island, QC=Québec, SK=Saskatchewan, YT=Yukon

CANADIAN BROADCASTING CORPORATION/ RADIO-CANADA (Pub)

✉ Box 3220 Stn C, Ottawa ON K1Y 1E4 ☎+1 613 288 6033 **W:** cbc.radio-canada.ca **L.P:** Chair, Board of Dir: Michael Goldbloom. Pres. and CEO: Catherine Tait. Exec. VP, Media Technology and Infrastructure Sces: Daniel Boudreau. VP, Legal Sces. General Counsel and Corp. Secretary: Sylvie Gadoury. Exec. VP and CFO: Judith Purves. VP, People and Culture: Marco Dubé
English Networks: ✉ Box 500 Stn A, Toronto ON M5W 1E6 ☎+1 416 205 3311 **W:** cbc.ca
French Networks: ✉ 1400 boul René-Lévesque Est 21e étage, Montréal PQ H2L 2M2 ☎+1 514 597 6000 **W:** ici.radio-canada.ca **L.P:** Exec. VP, Radio-Canada: Michel Bissonnette

English Radio

CBC Radio One

MW	Location	Prov	kHz	kW	Call
4)	Grand Falls-Windsor	NL	540	10	CBT
2)	Watrous	SK	540	50	CBK
4)	St. John's	NL	640	10	CBN
5)	Vancouver	BC	690	25	CBU
7)	Edmonton	AB	740	50	CBX
4)	Bonavista Bay	NL	750	10	CBGY
10)	Prince Rupert	BC	860	10/2.5	CFPR
11)	Inuvik	NT	860	1	CHAK
15)	Winnipeg	MB	990	50/46	CBW
4)	Corner Brook	NL	990	10	CBY
17)	Calgary	AB	1010	50	CBR
9)	Sydney	NS	1140	10	CBI
21)	Iqaluit	NU	1230	1	CFFB
4)	Gander	NL	1400	4	CBG

FM	Location	Prov	MHz	kW	Call
7)	Bonnyville	AB	92.9	55.5	CBX-1-FM
17)	Calgary	AB	99.1	7	CBR-1-FM
7)	Edmonton	AB	93.9	3.9	CBX-2-FM
7)	Grand Prairie	AB	102.5	100	CBXP-FM
17)	Lethbridge	AB	100.1	100	CBRL-FM
28)	Kamloops	BC	94.1	4.8	CBYK-FM
30)	Kelowna	BC	88.9	5.2	CBTK-FM
33)	Prince George	BC	91.5	59.6	CBYG-FM
5)	Vancouver	BC	88.1	97.6	CBU-2-FM
31)	Victoria	BC	90.5	6.3	CBCV-FM
15)	Brandon	MB	97.9	90	CBWV-FM
15)	Dauphin/Baldy Mountain	MB	105.3	95	CBWW-FM
15)	Winnipeg	MB	89.3	2.8	CBW-1-FM
18)	Allardville	NB	97.9	100	CBAA-FM
14)	Bon Accord	NB	103.3	38.5	CBZC-FM
32)	Edmundston	NB	99.5	24	CBAN-FM
14)	Fredericton	NB	99.5	3.2	CBZF-FM
18)	Moncton	NB	106.1	69.5	CBAM-FM
32)	Saint John	NB	91.3	89	CBD-FM
22)	Happy Valley-Goose Bay	NL	89.5	4.5	CFGB-FM
4)	Marystown	NL	90.3	100	CBNM-FM
4)	St. John's	NL	88.5	3.6	CBN-1-FM
9)	Halifax	NS	90.5	91	CBHA-FM
9)	Middleton	NS	106.5	93.4	CBHM-FM
9)	Mulgrave	NS	106.7	100	CBHB-FM
9)	Sydney	NS	92.1	8.2	CBIS-FM
9)	Yarmouth	NS	92.1	100	CBHY-FM
11)	Yellowknife	NT	98.9	4.1	CFYK-FM
6)	Huntsville	ON	94.3	70	CBLU-FM
6)	Kingston	ON	107.5	100	CBCK-FM
34)	Kitchener/Brantford	ON	89.1	10.4	CBLA-FM-2
39)	London	ON	93.5	100	CBCL-FM
20)	North Bay	ON	96.1	100	CBCN-FM
12)	Ottawa	ON	91.5	84	CBO-FM
6)	Owen Sound	ON	98.7	100	CBCB-FM
12)	Pembroke	ON	92.5	100	CBCD-FM
6)	Peterborough	ON	98.7	12.4	CBCP-FM
20)	Sault Ste. Marie	ON	89.5	46	CBSM-FM
20)	Sudbury	ON	99.9	50	CBCS-FM
8)	Thunder Bay	ON	88.3	23.7	CBQT-FM
6)	Toronto	ON	99.1	98	CBLA-FM
25)	Windsor	ON	97.5	19	CBEW-FM
23)	Charlottetown	PE	96.1	100	CBCT-FM
13)	Montréal	QC	88.5	25	CBME-FM
13)	Québec	QC	104.7	65.8	CBVE-FM
29)	Saguenay	QC	102.7	30	CBJE-FM
13)	Sherbrooke	QC	91.7	15.9	CBMB-FM
13)	Val-d'Or/Amos	QC	101.1	50	CBMN-FM
2)	Regina	SK	102.5	2.7	CBKR-FM
35)	Saskatoon	SK	94.1	4.1	CBK-1-FM
3)	Whitehorse	YT	94.5	6.3	CFWH-FM

+ 383 mono relay txs **NB:** calls not announced

CBC Music

FM	Location	Prov	MHz	kW	Call
17)	Calgary	AB	102.1	100	CBR-FM
7)	Edmonton	AB	90.9	100	CBX-FM
17)	Lethbridge	AB	91.7	100	CBBC-FM
17)	Red Deer	AB	99.9	71.5	CBR-FM-1
5)	Kamloops	BC	105.3	4.8	CBU-FM-4
5)	Kelowna	BC	89.7	5	CBU-FM-3
5)	Vancouver	BC	105.7	95.8	CBU-FM
31)	Victoria	BC	92.1	88.5	CBU-FM-1
15)	Brandon	MB	92.7	90	CBWS-FM
15)	Winnipeg	MB	98.3	160	CBW-FM
18)	Moncton	NB	95.5	68	CBA-FM
32)	Saint John/Fredericton	NB	101.5	86.9	CBZ-FM
4)	Baie Verte	NL	95.5	49	CBN-FM-6
4)	Grand Falls-Windsor	NL	90.7	100	CBN-FM-1
4)	Marystown	NL	91.7	100	CBN-FM-5
4)	St. John's	NL	106.9	100	CBN-FM
9)	Halifax	NS	102.7	92	CBH-FM
9)	Mulgrave	NS	103.1	81.7	CBH-FM-2
9)	Sydney	NS	105.1	68	CBI-FM
11)	Yellowknife	NT	95.3	0.1	CBNY-FM
6)	Huntsville	ON	106.9	70	CBL-FM-1
6)	Kitchener/Brantford	ON	90.7	8.2	CBL-FM-2
6)	London	ON	100.5	15.3	CBBL-FM
12)	Ottawa	ON	103.3	84	CBOQ-FM
6)	Peterborough	ON	103.9	12.4	CBBP-FM
20)	Sudbury	ON	90.1	50	CBBS-FM
8)	Thunder Bay	ON	101.7	25	CBQ-FM
6)	Toronto	ON	94.1	38	CBL-FM
25)	Windsor	ON	89.9	100	CBE-FM
23)	Charlottetown	PE	104.7	100	CBCH-FM
13)	Montréal	QC	93.5	100	CBM-FM
13)	Québec	QC	96.1	0.8	CBM-FM-2
13)	Sherbrooke	QC	89.7	16.9	CBM-FM-1
2)	Regina	SK	96.9	100	CBK-FM
2)	Saskatoon	SK	105.5	98	CBKS-FM
2)	Warmley	SK	101.5	100	CBK-FM-2
2)	Yorkton	SK	91.7	57	CBK-FM-3
3)	Whitehorse	YT	104.5	0.5	CBU-FM-8

+ 16 relay txs **NB:** calls not announced

French Radio – Ici Radio-Canada

Ici Radio-Canada Première

MW	Location	Prov	kHz	kW	Call
2)	Gravelbourg	SK	690	5	CBKF-1

MW	Location	Prov	kHz	kW	Call
6)	Toronto	ON	860	50	CJBC
2)	Saskatoon	SK	860	10	CBKF-2
25)	Windsor	ON	1550	10	CBEF

FM	Location	Prov	MHz	kW	Call
7)	Calgary	AB	103.9	22	CBRF-FM
7)	Edmonton	AB	90.1	100	CHFA-10-FM
5)	Vancouver	BC	97.7	95.8	CBUF-FM
5)	Victoria	BC	99.7	1.2	CBUF-FM-9
15)	Winnipeg	MB	88.1	100	CKSB-10-FM
18)	Allardville	NB	105.7	100	CBAF-FM-2
18)	Bon Accord	NB	91.7	60.2	CBAF-FM-21
18)	Edmundston	NB	100.3	20.9	CBAF-FM-4
18)	Grande-Anse/Caraquet	NB	90.3	100	CBAF-FM-18
18)	Moncton	NB	88.5	50	CBAF-FM
18)	Saint John/Fredericton	NB	102.3	93.1	CBAF-FM-1
4)	St. John's	NL	105.9	45.6	CBAF-FM-17
9)	Halifax	NS	92.3	91	CBAF-FM-5
9)	Mulgrave	NS	107.5	100	CBAF-FM-11
20)	North Bay	ON	95.1	100	CBON-FM-17
12)	Ottawa	ON	90.7	84	CBOF-FM
20)	Sudbury	ON	98.1	50	CBON-FM
23)	Charlottetown	PE	88.1	88	CBAF-FM-15
24)	Gaspé	QC	89.3	4.3	CBGA-10-FM
40)	Harve-Saint-Pierre	QC	92.5	50	CBSI-FM-7
24)	Matane	QC	102.1	42.9	CBGA-FM
13)	Mont-Laurier	QC	91.9	40.4	CBF-FM-9
13)	Montréal	QC	95.1	100	CBF-FM
27)	Québec	QC	106.3	52.5	CBV-FM
26)	Rimouski	QC	89.1	38.8	CJBR-FM
26)	Rivière-du-Loup	QC	89.5	100	CJBR-FM-1
36)	Rouyn-Noranda	QC	90.7	11.4	CHLM-FM
29)	Saguenay	QC	93.7	50	CBJ-FM
24)	Sainte-Anne-des-Monts	QC	101.1	91	CBGA-FM-7
40)	Sept îles	QC	98.1	96.8	CBSI-FM
38)	Sherbrooke	QC	101.1	31.4	CBF-FM-10
37)	Trois-Rivières	QC	96.5	100	CBF-FM-8
36)	Val-d'Or/Amos	QC	91.5	100	CHLM-FM-1
36)	Ville-Marie	QC	89.1	66.4	CBFY-FM
2)	Regina	SK	97.7	22.3	CBKF-FM

+ 158 mono relay txs

Ici musique

FM	Location	Prov	MHz	kW	Call
7)	Calgary	AB	89.7	10	CBCX-FM
7)	Edmonton	AB	101.1	3.9	CBCX-FM-1
5)	Vancouver	BC	90.9	2.8	CBUX-FM
5)	Victoria	BC	88.9	6.7	CBUX-FM-1
15)	Winnipeg	MB	89.9	61	CKSB-FM
18)	Allardville	NB	101.9	100	CBAL-FM-1
18)	Edmundston	NB	94.3	100	CBAL-FM-5
18)	Grande-Anse/Caraquet	NB	88.3	100	CBAL-FM-2
18)	Moncton	NB	98.3	67.6	CBAL-FM
18)	Saint John/Fredericton	NB	88.1	76.7	CBAL-FM-4
9)	St. John's	NL	101.9	90.2	CBAX-FM-2
9)	Halifax	NS	91.5	77.5	CBAX-FM
12)	Ottawa	ON	102.5	84	CBOX-FM
20)	Sudbury	ON	90.9	50	CBBX-FM
6)	Toronto	ON	90.3	10	CJBC-FM
9)	Charlottetown	PE	88.9	88	CBAX-FM-1
24)	Gaspé	QC	90.1	6.2	CBFX-FM-5
24)	Matane	QC	107.5	31.7	CBRX-FM-1
13)	Mont-Laurier	QC	91.1	82.8	CBFX-FM-6
13)	Montréal	QC	100.7	100	CBFX-FM
27)	Québec	QC	95.3	64.6	CBVX-FM
26)	Rimouski	QC	101.5	100	CBRX-FM
26)	Rivière-du-Loup	QC	90.7	100	CBRX-FM-3
36)	Rouyn-Noranda	QC	89.9	10.9	CBFX-FM-4
29)	Saguenay	QC	100.9	50	CBJX-FM
40)	Sept îles	QC	96.1	84.8	CBRX-FM-2
38)	Sherbrooke	QC	90.7	33.2	CBFX-FM-2
37)	Trois-Rivières	QC	104.3	100	CBFX-FM-1
36)	Val-d'Or/Amos	QC	88.3	100	CBFX-FM-3
2)	Regina	SK	88.9	96.4	CKSB-FM-1
2)	Saskatoon	SK	88.7	100	CKSB-FM-2

+ 7 relay txs

NB: Full list of E and F freqs at **W:** cbc.ca/frequency

Addresses & other information:

2) Box 540, Regina SK S4P 4A1 **W:** cbc.ca/sask **W: (F):** ici.radio-canada.ca/saskatchewan – **3)** 3103 3rd Ave, Whitehorse YT Y1A 1E5 **W:** cbc.ca/north – **4)** Box 12010 Stn A, St. John's NL A1B 3T8 **W:** cbc.ca/nl **W: (F):** ici.radio-canada.ca/terre-neuve-et-labrador – **5)** 700 Hamilton St, Vancouver BC V6B 4A2 **W:** cbc.ca/bc **W: (F):** ici.radio-canada.ca/colombie-britannique-et-yukon – **6)** Box 500 Stn A, Toronto ON M5W 1E6 **W:** cbc.ca/toronto **W: (F):** ici.radio-canada.ca/toronto – **7)** 123 Edmonton City Centre 10062-102 Ave, Edmonton AB T5J 2Y8 **W:** cbc.ca/edmonton **W: (F):** ici.radio-canada.ca/alberta – **8)** 213 Miles St E, Thunder Bay ON P7C 1J5 **W:** cbc.ca/thunderbay **W: (F):** as 20) – **9)** 6940 Mumford Rd Suite 100, Halifax NS B3L 0B7 **W:** cbc.ca/ns **W: (F):** ici.radio-canada.ca/nouvelle-ecosse – **10)** Unit 1 222 3rd Ave W, Prince Rupert BC V8J 1L1 **W:** cbc.ca/daybreaknorth – **11)** 5002 Forrest Dr, Yellowknife NT X1A 2A9 **W:** as 3) – **12)** Box 3220 Stn C, Ottawa ON K1Y 1E4 **W:**. cbc.ca/ottawa **W: (F):** ici.radio-canada.ca/ottawa-gatineau – **13)** Box 6000, Montréal QC H3C 3A8 **W:** cbc.ca/montreal **W: (F):** ici.radio-canada.ca/montreal – **14) W:** cbc.ca/informationmorningfredericton **W: (F):** as 18) – **15)** 541 Portage Ave, Winnipeg MB R3C 2H1 **W:** cbc.ca/manitoba **W: (F):** ici.radio-canada.ca/manitoba – **17)** Box 2640, Calgary AB T2P 2M7 **W:** cbc.ca/calgary **W: (F):** as 7) – **18) W:** cbc.ca/informationmorningmoncton **W: (F):** ici.radio-canada.ca/nouveau-brunswick – **20)** 43 Elm St Unit 120, Sudbury ON P3C 1S4 **W:** cbc.ca/sudbury **W: (F):** ici.radio-canada.ca/nordontario – **21)** Box 490, Iqaluit NU X0A 0H0 **W:** as 3) – **22)** as 4) **W:** cbc.ca/labradormorning – **23)** Box 2230, Charlottetown PE C1A 8B9 **W:** cbc.ca/pei **W: (F):** ici.radio-canada.ca/ile-du-prince-edouard – **24)** 303 avenue Saint-Jérôme, Matane QC G4W 3A8 **W:** ici.radio-canada.ca/gaspesie-iles-de-la-madeleine – **25)** 825 Riverside Dr W, Windsor ON N9A 5K9 **W:** cbc.ca/windsor **W: (F):** ici.radio-canada.ca/windsor – **26)** 185 boul René-Lepage Est, Rimouski QC G5L 1P2 **W: (F):** ici.radio-canada.ca/bas-saint-laurent – **27)** 888 rue Saint-Jean, Québec QC G1R 5H6 **W: (F):** ici.radio-canada.ca/quebec – **28)** 218 Victoria St, Kamloops BC V2C 2A2 **W:** cbc.ca/kamloops – **29)** 500 rue des Sagenéens, Chicoutimi QC G7H 6N4 **W: (F):** ici.radio-canada.ca/saguenay-lac-saint-jean – **30)** 243 Lawrence Ave, Kelowna BC V1Y 6L2 **W:** cbc.ca/daybreaksouth – **31)** CHEK Media Centre 780 Kings Rd, Victoria BC V8T 5A2 **W:** cbc.ca/ontheisland – **32) W:** cbc.ca/informationmorningsaintjohn **W: (F):** as 18) – **33)** Unit 1 890 Victoria St, Prince George BC V2L 5P1 **W:** as 10) – **34)** 117 King St W, Kitchener ON N2G 1A7 **W:** cbc.ca/kitchener-waterloo – **35)** 100 128 4th Ave S, Saskatoon SK S7K 1M8 **W:** cbc.ca/saskatoon – **36)** 70 avenue Principale, Rouyn-Noranda QC J9X 4P2 **W: (F):** ici.radio-canada.ca/abitibi-temiscamingue – **37)** 225 des Forges bureau 101, Trois-Rivières QC G9A 2G7 **W: (F):** ici.radio-canada.ca/mauricie – **38)** 1335 rue King Ouest, Sherbrooke QC J1J 2B8 **W: (F):** ici.radio-canada.ca/estrie – **39)** 251 Dundas St, London ON N6A 6H9 **W:** cbc.ca/london – **40)** 350 rue Smith Bureau 30, Sept îles QC G4R 3X2 **W: (F):** ici.radio-canada.ca/cote-nord

PRIVATE STATIONS

MW	kHz	Call	kW	N	Location	Prov
705)	530	CHLO	1/0.25	m	Brampton	ON
701)	560	CFOS	7.5/1		Owen Sound	ON
204)	570	CKWL	1		Williams Lake	BC
500)	570	CFCB	10/1		Corner Brook	NL
702)	570	CKGL	10		Kitchener	ON
912)	570	CKSW	10		Swift Current	SK
101)	580	CHAH	10	m	Edmonton	AB
703)	580	CFRA	50/30		Ottawa	ON
706)	580	CKWW	0.5		Windsor	ON
207)	590	CFTK	1		Terrace	BC
302)	590	CFAR	10/1		Flin Flon	MB
402)	590	CJCW	1/0.25		Sussex	NB
501)	590	VOCM	20		St. John's	NL
707)	590	CJCL	50		Toronto	ON
203)	600	CKSP	50/20	m	Vancouver	BC
708)	600	CKAT	10/5		North Bay	ON
803)	600	CFQR	10/5		Montréal	QC
900)	600	CJWW	25/8		Saskatoon	SK
209)	610	CHNL	25/5		Kamloops	BC
303)	610	CHTM	1		Thompson	MB
709)	610	CKTB	10/5		St. Catharines	ON
501b)	620	CKCM	10	r	Grand Falls-Windsor	NL
901)	620	CKRM	10		Regina	SK
102)	630	CHED	50		Edmonton	AB
711)	630	CFCO	10/6		Chatham-Kent	ON
712)	640	CFMJ	50		Toronto	ON
208)	650	CISL	20/4		Vancouver	BC
501d)	650	CKGA	5		Gander	NL
908)	650	CKOM	10		Saskatoon	SK
108)	660	CFFR	50		Calgary	AB
305)	680	CJOB	50		Winnipeg	MB
714)	680	CFTR	50		Toronto	ON
810)	690	CKGM	50		Montréal	QC

MW	kHz	Call	kW	N	Location	Prov
105)	700	CJLI	50/20		Calgary	AB
501e)	710	CKVO	10		Clarenville	NL
213)	730	CHMJ	50		Vancouver	BC
306)	730	CKDM	10/5		Dauphin	MB
804)	730	CKAC	50	F	Montréal	QC
501a)	740	CHCM	10	c r	Marystown	NL
717)	740	CFZM	50		Toronto	ON
911)	750	CKJH	25		Melfort	SK
224a)	760	CFLD	1	r	Burns Lake	BC
103)	770	CHQR	50		Calgary	AB
206)	800	CKOR	10/0.5		Penticton	BC
502)	800	VOWR	10/2.5		St. John's	NL
704)	800	CJBQ	10		Belleville	ON
713)	800	CKLW	50		Windsor	ON
811)	800	CJAD	50/10		Montréal	QC
902)	800	CHAB	10		Moose Jaw	SK
307)	810	CKJS	10	c m	Winnipeg	MB
723)	820	CHAM	50/10		Hamilton	ON
104)	840	CFCW	50/40		Camrose	AB
205)	840	CKBX	1/0.5		100 Mile House	BC
206c)	870	CKIR	1/0.25	r	Invermere	BC
224)	870	CFBV	1/0.5		Smithers	BC
500a)	870	CFSX	0.5	r	Stephenville	NL
114)	880	CHQT	50		Edmonton	AB
312)	880	CKLQ	10		Brandon	MB
230)	890	CJDC	10		Dawson Creek	BC
725)	900	CHML	50		Hamilton	ON
903)	900	CKBI	10/2.8		Prince Albert	SK
106)	910	CKDQ	50		Drumheller	AB
308)	920	CFRY	25/15		Portage la Prairie	MB
728)	920	CKNX	10/1		Wingham	ON
107)	930	CJCA	50		Edmonton	AB
405)	930	CFBC	2/0.15		Saint John	NB
503)	930	CJYQ	25/3.5		St. John's	NL
805)	940	CFNV	50	F	Montréal	QC
904)	940	CJGX	50/10		Yorkton	SK
309)	950	CFAM	10		Altona	MB
406)	950	CKNB	10/1		Campbellton	NB
109)	960	CFAC	50		Calgary	AB
726)	960	CKNT	2/0.28		Mississauga	ON
214)	980	CKNW	50		Vancouver	BC
731)	980	CFPL	10/5		London	ON
905)	980	CJME	10/5		Regina	SK
733)	1010	CFRB	50	*	Toronto	ON
215)	1040	CKST	50		Vancouver	BC
734)	1050	CHUM	50		Toronto	ON
906)	1050	CJNB	10		North Battleford	SK
111)	1060	CKMX	50	*	Calgary	AB
220)	1070	CFAX	10		Victoria	BC
736)	1070	CHOK	10		Sarnia	ON
221)	1130	CKWX	50		Vancouver	BC
122)	1140	CHRB	50/46		High River	AB
222)	1150	CKFR	10		Kelowna	BC
724)	1150	CKOC	50/20		Hamilton	ON
909)	1150	CJSL	10		Estevan	SK
907)	1190	CFSL	10/5		Weyburn	SK
225)	1200	CJRJ	25	m	Vancouver	BC
710)	1200	CFGO	50		Ottawa	ON
910a)	1210	CFYM	1/0.25	r	Kindersley	SK
313)	1220	CJRB	10		Boissevain	MB
742)	1220	CFAJ	10		St. Catharines	ON
223)	1240	CKMK	1	r	Mackenzie	BC
206b)	1240	CJOR	1		Osoyoos	BC
233)	1240	CFNI	1		Port Hardy	BC
304)	1240	CJAR	1		The Pas	MB
501c)	1240	CKIM	1	r	Baie Verte	NL
310)	1250	CHSM	10		Steinbach	MB
721)	1250	CJYE	10		Oakville	ON
119)	1260	CFRN	50		Edmonton	AB
410)	1260	CKHJ	10/0.032		Fredericton	NB
605)	1270	CJCB	10/1.35		Sydney	NS
807)	1280	CFMB	50	m	Montréal	QC
311)	1290	CFRW	10		Winnipeg	MB
751)	1290	CJBK	10		London	ON
753)	1310	CIWW	50		Ottawa	ON
229)	1320	CHMB	50	m	Vancouver	BC
722)	1320	CJMR	10	m	Oakville	ON
910)	1330	CJYM	10		Rosetown	SK
209a)	1340	CINL	1	r	Ashcroft	BC
210)	1340	CFKC	0.25	r	Creston	BC
612)	1350	CKAD	1/0.4		Middleton	NS
755)	1350	CIRF	1/0.45	m	Brampton	ON
758)	1380	CKPC	25		Brantford	ON
209b)	1400	CHNL-1	1	r	Clearwater	BC
206a)	1400	CIOR	1	r	Princeton	BC
216)	1410	CFTE	50		Vancouver	BC
836)	1410	CJWI	10	F	Montréal	QC
764)	1430	CHKT	50	m	Toronto	ON
121)	1440	CKJR	10		Wetaskiwin	AB
607)	1450	CFAB	1		Windsor	NS
834)	1450	CHOU	2/1	m	Montréal	QC
768)	1460	CJOY	10		Guelph	ON
234)	1470	CJVB	50	m	Vancouver	BC
912a)	1490	CJSN	1		Shaunavon	SK
773)	1540	CHIN	50/30	m	Toronto	ON
835)	1570	CJLV	10	F	Laval/Montréal	QC
756)	1580	CKDO	10		Oshawa	ON
774)	1610	CHHA	6.25	m	Toronto	ON
825)	1610	CHRN	1	m	Montréal	QC
729)	1650	CINA	5/0.68	m	Mississauga	ON
837)	1650	CKZW	1	F	Montréal	QC
823)	1670	CJEU	1	F	Gatineau	QC
720)	1690	CHTO	6/1	m	Toronto	ON
831)	1690	CJLO	1		Montréal	QC

+ txs below 0.1kW

SW	kHz	Call	kW	Location	Prov	Relays
111)	6030	CFVP	0.1	Calgary	AB	CKMX
733)	6070	CFRX	1	Toronto	ON	CFRB

NB: Stns that broadcast a common prgr during part of the day have a letter as part of the reference number

Addresses & other information:

Alberta

101) 5119 22 Ave S W, Edmonton T6X 2N4 **W:** myradio580.com – **102)** 5204 84th St NW, Edmonton T6E 5N8 **W:** 630ched.com – **103)** 200-3320 17th Ave SW, Calgary T3E 0B4 **W:** newstalk770.com – **104)** 5708-48 Ave, Camrose T4V 0K1 **W:** cfcw.com – **105)** 100-4510 MacLeod Trail S, Calgary T2G 0A4 **W:** cjli.ca – **106)** Box 1480, Drumheller T0J 0Y0 **W:** realcountry910.ca – **107)** 5316 Calgary Trail NW, Edmonton T6H 4J8 **W:** cjca.ca – **108)** 535 7th Ave SW, Calgary T2P 0Y4 **W:** 660news.com – **109)** 240-2723 37th Ave NE, Calgary T1Y 5R8 **W:** sportsnet.ca/960 – **111)** 300-1110 Centre St NE, Calgary T2E 2R2 **W:** funny1060.com Rpt: qslcalgary@gmail.com – **114)** as 102) **W:** 880edmonton.ca – **119)** 100-18520 Stony Plain Rd NW, Edmonton T5S 2E2 **W:** tsn.ca/radio – **121)** 5214A-50th Ave, Wetaskiwin T9A 0S8 **W:** w1440.com – **122)** 11-5th Ave SE, High River T1V 1G2 **W:** highriveronline.com

British Columbia

203) 1228-20800 Westminster Hwy, Richmond V6V 2W3 **W:** sherepunjabradio.ca – **204)** 83 First Ave S, Williams Lake V2G 1H4 **W:** mycariboonow.com – **205)** Box 1834, 100 Mile House V0K 2E0 **W:** as 204) – **206)** 33 Carmi Ave, Penticton V2A 3G4 **W:** penticton.myezrock.com – **206a)** Box 1400, Princeton V0X 1W0 – **206b)** 203 – 8309 Main St, Osoyoos V0H 1V0 – **206c)** Box 1403, Golden V0A 1H0 – **207)** 4625 Lazelle Ave, Terrace V8G 1S4 **W:** terrace.myezrock.com – **208)** as 221) **W:** sportsnet.ca/650 – **209)** 611 Lansdowne St, Kamloops V2C 1Y6 **W:** radionl.com – **209a)** Ashcroft – **209b)** Clearwater – **210)** Box 310, Creston V1R 1M4 **W:** kootenays.myezrock.com – **213)** as 214) **W:** am730.ca – **214)** 2000-700 W Georgia St, Vancouver V7Y 1K9 **W:** cknw.com – **215)** 500-969 Robson St, Vancouver V6Z 1X5 **W:** tsn.ca/radio – **216)** as 215) **W:** bnnbloomberg.ca – **220)** 1420 Broad St, Victoria V8W 2B1 **W:** cfax1070.com – **221)** 2440 Ash St, Vancouver V5Z 4J6 **W:** news1130.com – **222)** 300-435 Bernard Ave, Kelowna V1Y 6N8 **W:** am1150.ca – **223)** 2nd flr – 1810 3rd Ave, Prince George V2M 1G4 **W:** 993thedrive.com – **224)** Box 335, Smithers V0J 2N0 **W:** mybulkeylakesnow.com – **224a)** Burns Lake – **225)** 110-3060 Norland Ave, Burnaby V5B 3A6 **W:** spiceradio1200am.com. Mostly langs – **229)** 100-1200 73rd Ave W, Vancouver V6P 6G5 **W:** am1320.ca Mostly Chinese – **230)** 901 102nd Ave, Dawson Creek V1G 2B6 **W:** purecountry890.ca – **233)** 7035A Market St, Port Hardy V0N 2P0 **W:** mytriportnow.com – **234)** 2090 Aberdeen Centre 4151 Hazelbridge Way, Richmond V6X 4J7 **W:** am1470.com Mostly langs

Manitoba

302) Box 430 Stn Main, Flin Flon R8A 1N3 **W:** flinflononline.com – **303)** 103 Cree Rd, Thompson R8N 0B9 **W:** thompsononline.ca – **304)** Box 2980 Stn Main, The Pas R9A 1R7 **W:** thepasonline.com – **305)** 200-1440 Jack Blick Ave, Winnipeg R3G 0L4 **W:** cjob.com – **306)** 1735 Main St S, Dauphin R7N 2V4 **W:** 730ckdm.com – **307)** 520 Corydon Ave, Winnipeg R3L 0P1 **W:** ckjs.com Mostly langs – **308)** 2390

Sissons Dr, Portage la Prairie R1N 0G5 **W:** portageonline.com – **309)** Box 950, Altona R0G 0B0 **W:** pembinavalleyonline.com – **310)** 105-32 Brandt St, Steinbach R5G 2J7 **W:** steinbachonline.com – **311)** 1445 Pembina Hwy, Winnipeg R3T 5C2 **W:** tsn.ca/radio – **312)** 624 14th St E, Brandon R7A 7E1 **W:** qcountryfm.ca – **313)** 420 S Railway St, Boissevain R0K 0E0 **W:** discoverwestman.com

New Brunswick

402) 6 Marble St, Sussex E4E 5M2 **W:** 590cjcw.com – **405)** 226 Union St, Saint John E2L 1B1 **W:** cfbcradio.com – **406)** 74 Water St, Campbellton E3N 1B1 **W:** 95cknb.ca – **410)** 206 Rookwood Ave, Fredericton E3B 2M2 **W:** purecountry1035.ca

Newfoundland & Labrador

500) Box 570 Stn Main, Corner Brook A2H 6H5 **W:** vocm.com – **500a)** 60 West St, Stephenville A2N 1C6 – **501)** Box 8590 Stn A, St. John's A1B 3P5 **W:** as 500) – **501a)** Box 560, Marystown A0E 2M0 – **501b)** Box 620 Stn Main, Grand Falls-Windsor A2A 2K2 – **501c)** Baie Verte – **501d)** Box 650 Stn Main, Gander A1V 1X2 – **501e)** Gen. Delivery, Clarenville A5A 2C1 – **502)** 101 Patrick St, St. John's A1E 3Y5 **W:** vowr.org – **503)** as 501) **W:** 930kixxcountry.ca – **505)** 1041 Topsail Rd, Mt. Pearl A1N 5E9 **W:** voar.org

Nova Scotia

605) Box 1270 Stn A, Sydney B1P 6K2 **W:** cjcbradio.com – **607)** 169-A Water St, Windsor B0N 2T0 **W:** avrnetwork.com – **612)** Box 550, Middleton B0S 1P0 **W:** as 607)

Ontario

701) Box 280 Stn Main, Owen Sound N4K 5P5 **W:** 560cfos.ca – **702)** 230 The Boardwalk 2nd flr, Kitchener N2N 0B1 **W:** 570news.com – **703)** 87 George St, Ottawa K1N 9H7 **W:** cfra.com – **704)** Box 488 Stn Main, Belleville K8N 5B2 **W:** cjbq.com – **705)** 5312 Dundas St W, Toronto M9B 1B3 **W:** am530.ca Mostly langs – **706)** as 713) **W:** am580radio.com – **707)** 1 Ted Rogers Way 5th flr, Toronto M4Y 3B7 **W:** sportsnet.ca/590 – **708)** Box 3000, North Bay P1B 8K8 **W:** country600.com – **709)** Box 977 Stn Main, St. Catharines L2R 6Z4 **W:** 610cktb.com – **710)** as 703) **W:** tsn.ca/radio – **711)** Box 100 Stn Main, Chatham-Kent N7M 5K1 **W:** country929.com – **712)** Corus Quay 25 Dockside Dr, Toronto M5A 0B5 **W:** 640toronto.com – **713)** 1640 Ouellette Ave, Windsor N8X 1L1 **W:** am800cklw.com – **714)** as 707) **W:** 680news.com – **717)** 70 Jefferson Ave, Toronto M6K 1Y4 **W:** zoomerradio.ca – **720)** 437 Danforth Ave Suite 300, Toronto M4K 1P1 **W:** am1690.ca Mostly Greek – **721)** 284 Church St, Oakville L6J 7N2 **W:** joy1250.com – **722)** as 721) **W:** cjmr1320.ca Mostly langs – **723)** 883 Upper Wentworth St Suite 401, Hamilton L9A 4Y6 **W:** funny820.com – **724)** as 723) **W:** tsn.ca/radio – **725)** 875 Main St W #900, Hamilton L8S 4R1 **W:** 900chml.com – **726)** 130 Westmore Dr #2, Etobicoke M9V 3Y6 **W:** sauga960am.ca – **728)** 215 Carling Terrace, Wingham N0G 2W0 **W:** cknx.ca – **729)** 200-65 International Blvd, Toronto M9W 6L9 **W:** cinaradio.com Mostly langs – **731)** Box 2580 Stn B, London N6A 4H3 **W:** am980.ca – **733)** 250 Richmond St W 3rd flr, Toronto M5V 1W4 **W:** newstalk1010.com Rpt: cfrbcfrxreport@gmail.com – **734)** as 733) **W:** tsn.ca/radio – **736)** 1415 London Rd, Sarnia N7A 1P9 **W:** chok.com – **742)** 5823 Ferry St, Niagara Falls L2G 1S8 **W:** facebook.com/1220CFAJ – **751)** 743 Wellington Rd S, London N6C 4R5 **W:** cjbk.com – **753)** 2001 Thurston Dr, Ottawa K1G 6C9 **W:** 1310news.com – **755)** as 825) **W:** 1350.ca – **756)** 207-1200 Airport Blvd, Oshawa L1J 8P5 **W:** ckdo.ca – **758)** 571 West St, Brantford N3R 7C5 **W:** arisebrantford.ca – **764)** 8-135 East Beaver Creek Rd, Richmond Hill L4B 1E2 **W:** am1430.com. Mostly Chinese – **768)** 75 Speedvale Ave E, Guelph N1E 6M3 **W:** cjoy.com – **773)** 622 College St, Toronto M6G 1B6 **W:** chinradio.com Mostly Italian – **774)** 22 Wenderly Dr, Toronto M6B 2N9 **W:** chha1610am.ca Mostly langs

Québec

803) 6322 Jean-Talon St E, Montréal H1M 1S8 – **804)** 800 rue de la Gauchetière Ouest Bureau 1100, Montréal H5A 1M1 **W:** radiocirculation.net – **805)** as 803) **W:** cfnv940.com – **807)** 5877 ave Papineau, Montréal H2G 2W3 **W:** cfmbradio.com Mostly langs – **810)** as 811) **W:** tsn.ca/radio – **811)** 1717 boul René-Lévesque Est, Montréal H2L 4T9 **W:** cjad.com – **823)** 855 boul de Gappe pièce 310, Gatineau J8T 8H9 **W:** radiojeunesse.ca – **825)** 7655 rue Cordner, LaSalle H8N 2X2 **W:** radiohumsafar.com Mostly langs – **831)** 7141 Sherbrooke St Ouest Room CC430, Montréal H4B 1R6 **W:** cjlo.com – **834)** 11876 rue de Meulles, Montréal H4J 2E6 **W:** meradio.ca Mostly Arabic – **835)** as 825) **W:** radiomieuxetre.com – **836)** 3390 blvd Crémazie est, Montréal H2A 1A4 **W:** cpam1410.com – **837)** 4835 Côte St. Catherine Rd #2, Montréal H3W 1M4 **W:** laradiogospel.ca

Saskatchewan

900) 366 3rd Ave S, Saskatoon S7K 1M5 **W:** cjwwradio.com – **901)** 1900 Rose St, Regina S4P 0A9 **W:** 620ckrm.com – **902)** Box 800 Stn Main, Moose Jaw S6H 4P5 **W:** discovermoosejaw.com – **903)** 1316 Central Ave, Prince Albert S6V 6P5 **W:** 900ckbi.com – **904)** Broadc Place 120 Smith St E, Yorkton S3N 3V3 **W:** gx94radio.com – **905)** 210-2401 Saskatchewan Dr, Regina S4P 4H8 **W:** cjme.com – **906)** Box 1460 Stn Main, North Battleford S9A 2Z5 **W:** cjnb.com – **907)** Box 340 Stn Main, Weyburn S4H 2K2 **W:** discoverweyburn.com – **908)** 715 Saskatchewan Cres W, Saskatoon S7M 5V7 **W:** ckom.com – **909)** Box 1280 Stn Main, Estevan S4A 2H8 **W:** discoverestevan.com – **910)** Box 490, Rosetown S0L 2V0 **W:** westcentralonline.com – **910a)** Box 1330, Kindersley S0L 1S1 – **911)** Box 750, Melfort S0E 1A0 **W:** beachradiosk.ca – **912)** 300 - 198 1st Ave, Swift Current S9H 2B2 **W:** swiftcurrentonline.com – **912a)** Box 1176, Shaunavon S0N 2M0

FM	Prov	MHz	kW	N	Call
Airdrie	AB	106.1	6		CFIT-FM
Athabasca	AB	94.1	9		CKBA-FM
Bonnyville	AB	98.7	12.3	F	CHFB-FM
Bonnyville	AB	99.7	50		CFNA-FM
Bonnyville	AB	101.3	27		CJEG-FM
Brooks	AB	101.1	8.6		CIXF-FM
Brooks	AB	105.7	14		CIBQ-FM
Calgary	AB	88.1	100	m	CJWE-FM
Calgary	AB	88.9	100		CJSI-FM
Calgary	AB	90.3	100		CKMP-FM
Calgary	AB	90.9	18		CJSW-FM
Calgary	AB	92.1	100		CJAY-FM
Calgary	AB	92.9	100		CFEX-FM
Calgary	AB	93.7	100		CKUA-FM-1
Calgary	AB	94.7	53		CHKF-FM
Calgary	AB	95.3	100		CKWD-FM
Calgary	AB	95.9	100		CHFM-FM
Calgary	AB	96.9	100		CJAQ-FM
Calgary	AB	97.7	100		CHUP-FM
Calgary	AB	98.5	100		CIBK-FM
Calgary	AB	101.5	100		CKCE-FM
Calgary	AB	103.1	100		CFXL-FM
Calgary	AB	105.1	100		CKRY-FM
Calgary	AB	106.7	8	m	CKYR-FM
Calgary	AB	107.3	100		CFGQ-FM
Camrose	AB	98.1	50		CFCW-FM
Cochrane	AB	91.5	10		CKXY-FM
Cold Lake	AB	95.3	100		CJXK-FM
Drayton Valley	AB	92.9	50		CIBW-FM
Drumheller	AB	91.3	100		CKUA-FM-13
Edmonton	AB	91.7	96		CHBN-FM
Edmonton	AB	92.5	97		CKNG-FM
Edmonton	AB	94.9	100		CKUA-FM
Edmonton	AB	95.7	100		CKEA-FM
Edmonton	AB	96.3	100		CKRA-FM
Edmonton	AB	97.3	100		CIRK-FM
Edmonton/Spruce Grove	AB	98.5	100	m	CFWE-FM-4
Edmonton	AB	99.3	100		CIUP-FM
Edmonton	AB	100.3	97		CFBR-FM
Edmonton	AB	101.7	100	m	CKER-FM
Edmonton	AB	102.3	100		CKNO-FM
Edmonton	AB	102.9	100		CHDI-FM
Edmonton	AB	103.9	98		CISN-FM
Edmonton	AB	104.9	100		CFMG-FM
Edmonton	AB	105.9	100		CJRY-FM
Edmonton	AB	107.1	40		CKPW-FM
Edson	AB	94.3	20		CFXE-FM
Fort McMurray	AB	91.1	25		CKOS-FM
Fort McMurray	AB	93.3	43.5		CJOK-FM
Fort McMurray	AB	94.5	23.5	m	CFWE-FM-5
Fort McMurray	AB	97.9	43.5		CKYX-FM
Fort McMurray	AB	100.5	50		CHFT-FM
Fort McMurray	AB	103.7	50		CFVR-FM
Fort Saskatchewan	AB	107.9	20		CKFT-FM
Grande Prairie	AB	93.1	100		CJXX-FM
Grande Prairie	AB	96.3	70		CJGY-FM
Grande Prairie	AB	97.7	100		CFGP-FM
Grande Prairie	AB	98.9	100		CIKT-FM
Grande Prairie	AB	100.9	100		CKUA-FM-4
Grande Prairie	AB	104.7	100		CFRI-FM
Grande Prairie	AB	105.7	100	m	CFWE-FM-7
High Level	AB	102.1	29		CKHL-FM
High Level	AB	106.1	29		CFKX-FM
High Prairie	AB	93.5	29		CKVH-FM
High River/Okotoks	AB	99.7	16		CFXO-FM
High River/Okotoks	AB	100.9	100		CKUV-FM
Joussard	AB	91.7	4.2	m	CFWE-FM-1
Lac La Biche	AB	90.5	19.6	m	CFWE-FM-6

FM	Prov	MHz	kW	N	Call
Lacombe	AB	94.1	55		CJUV-FM
Leduc	AB	93.1	5.6		CJLD-FM
Lethbridge	AB	94.1	100		CJOC-FM
Lethbridge	AB	95.5	100		CHLB-FM
Lethbridge	AB	98.1	20		CKBD-FM
Lethbridge	AB	99.3	100		CKUA-FM-2
Lethbridge/Taber	AB	106.7	100		CJRX-FM
Lethbridge	AB	107.7	100		CFRV-FM
Lloydminster	AB	95.9	100		CKSA-FM
Lloydminster	AB	106.1	100		CKLM-FM
Medicine Hat	AB	94.5	100		CHAT-FM
Medicine Hat	AB	96.1	100		CFMY-FM
Medicine Hat	AB	97.3	100		CKUA-FM-3
Medicine Hat	AB	102.1	40		CJCY-FM
Medicine Hat	AB	105.3	100		CKMH-FM
Moose Hills	AB	96.7	100	m	CFWE-FM-3
Olds	AB	96.5	35		CKLJ-FM
Olds	AB	104.5	35		CKJX-FM
Peace River	AB	94.9	100		CKYL-FM
Peace River	AB	96.9	22		CKUA-FM-5
Peace River	AB	106.1	50		CKKX-FM
Piikani/Blood First Nation	AB	89.3	10.2	m	CFWE-FM-2
Pincher Creek	AB	92.7	6		CJPV-FM
Red Deer	AB	90.5	38		CKRD-FM
Red Deer	AB	95.5	100		CKGY-FM
Red Deer	AB	98.9	100		CIZZ-FM
Red Deer	AB	100.7	100		CKEX-FM
Red Deer	AB	101.3	50		CKIK-FM
Red Deer	AB	105.5	100		CHUB-FM
Red Deer	AB	106.7	100		CFDV-FM
Red Deer	AB	107.7	100		CKUA-FM-6
Slave Lake	AB	92.7	5		CHSL-FM
St. Paul	AB	97.7	45		CHSP-FM
Stettler	AB	93.3	23		CKSQ-FM
Strathmore	AB	104.5	7		CKOV-FM
Suffield	AB	104.1	4.3		CKBF-FM
Taber	AB	93.3	100		CJBZ-FM
Vegreville	AB	106.5	13		CKVG-FM
Wabasca-Desmarais	AB	94.3	6		CHSL-FM-1
Wainwright	AB	93.7	50		CKWY-FM
Wainwright	AB	101.9	50		CKKY-FM
Westlock	AB	97.9	48		CKWB-FM
Whitecourt	AB	96.7	9		CFXW-FM
Whitecourt	AB	105.3	42.3		CIXM-FM
Campbell River	BC	99.7	6		CIQC-FM
Campbell River	BC	100.7	8		CKCC-FM
Chilliwack	BC	98.3	5		CKSR-FM
Courtenay	BC	97.3	11.6		CKLR-FM
Courtenay	BC	98.9	5		CFCP-FM
Duncan	BC	89.7	3.5		CJSU-FM
Fort St. John	BC	98.5	50		CHRX-FM
Fort St. John	BC	101.5	40		CKNL-FM
Gibsons	BC	107.5	4.6		CISC-FM
Houston	BC	105.5	3.5		CJFW-FM-7
Kamloops	BC	97.5	4.3		CKRV-FM
Kamloops	BC	98.3	4.3		CIFM-FM
Kamloops	BC	100.1	3.5		CKBZ-FM
Kamloops	BC	103.1	5		CJKC-FM
Kelowna	BC	96.3	31		CKKO-FM
Kelowna	BC	99.9	35		CHSU-FM
Kelowna	BC	101.5	33.3		CILK-FM
Kelowna	BC	103.1	35		CKQQ-FM
Kelowna	BC	104.7	36		CKLZ-FM
Nanaimo	BC	101.7	3		CHLY-FM
Nanaimo	BC	102.3	3		CKWV-FM
Nanaimo	BC	106.9	3		CHWF-FM
Penticton	BC	100.7	14.1		CIGV-FM
Port Alberni	BC	93.3	6		CJAV-FM
Powell River	BC	95.7	5.8		CFPW-FM
Prince George	BC	94.3	11.5		CIRX-FM
Prince George	BC	97.3	12		CJCI-FM
Prince George	BC	99.3	9.3		CKDV-FM
Prince George	BC	101.3	9.1		CKKN-FM
Quesnel	BC	94.9	3.5		CFFM-FM-2
Quesnel	BC	100.3	3.5		CKCQ-FM
Squamish	BC	107.1	30		CISQ-FM
Terrace	BC	103.1	3.2		CJFW-FM
Trail	BC	95.7	14		CJAT-FM
Vancouver	BC	93.1	8	m	CKYE-FM
Vancouver	BC	93.7	71		CJJR-FM

FM	Prov	MHz	kW	N	Call
Vancouver	BC	94.5	90		CFBT-FM
Vancouver	BC	95.3	57		CKZZ-FM
Vancouver	BC	96.1	100	m	CHKG-FM
Vancouver	BC	96.9	70		CJAX-FM
Vancouver	BC	99.3	100		CFOX-FM
Vancouver	BC	100.5	11		CFRO-FM
Vancouver	BC	101.1	100		CFMI-FM
Vancouver	BC	102.7	95		CKPK-FM
Vancouver	BC	103.5	100		CHQM-FM
Vancouver	BC	104.3	9.1		CHLG-FM
Vancouver	BC	104.9	31		CKKS-FM-2
Vernon	BC	105.7	100		CICF-FM
Vernon	BC	107.5	100		CJIB-FM
Victoria	BC	91.3	3.5		CJZN-FM
Victoria	BC	98.5	100		CIOC-FM
Victoria	BC	100.3	100		CKKQ-FM
Victoria	BC	103.1	20		CHTT-FM
Victoria	BC	107.3	20		CHBE-FM
Brandon	MB	91.5	100		CKLQ-FM
Brandon	MB	94.7	100		CKLF-FM
Brandon	MB	96.1	100		CKX-FM
Brandon	MB	101.1	100		CKXA-FM
Nepawa	MB	97.1	3.2		CJBP-FM
Portage la Prairie	MB	93.1	27		CHPO-FM
Portage la Prairie	MB	96.5	24		CJPG-FM
Steinbach	MB	96.7	100		CILT-FM
Steinbach	MB	107.7	27		CJXR-FM
Winkler	MB	88.9	100		CKMW-FM
Winkler/Morden	MB	93.5	100		CJEL-FM
Winnipeg	MB	91.1	61	F	CKXL-FM
Winnipeg	MB	92.1	140		CITI-FM
Winnipeg	MB	94.3	100		CHIQ-FM
Winnipeg	MB	95.1	100		CHVN-FM
Winnipeg	MB	97.5	310		CJKR-FM
Winnipeg	MB	99.1	100		CFPG-FM
Winnipeg	MB	99.9	100		CFWM-FM
Winnipeg	MB	100.5	100		CFJL-FM
Winnipeg	MB	102.3	100		CKY-FM
Winnipeg	MB	103.1	100		CKMM-FM
Winnipeg	MB	104.1	100		CFQX-FM
Winnipeg	MB	104.7	3		CIUR-FM
Winnipeg/Selkirk	MB	105.5	100		CICY-FM
Winnipeg	MB	106.1	40		CHWE-FM
Winnipeg	MB	107.1	100		CKCL-FM
Bathurst	NB	92.9	100	F	CKLE-FM
Bathurst	NB	104.9	33.5		CKBC-FM
Campbellton	NB	103.9	11.3	F	CIMS-FM
Edmundston	NB	92.7	40.8	F	CJEM-FM
Fredericton	NB	92.3	100		CFRK-FM
Fredericton	NB	93.1	100		CIHI-FM
Fredericton	NB	105.3	78		CFXY-FM
Fredericton	NB	106.9	78		CIBX-FM
Grand Falls/Grand-Sault	NB	93.5	5.3		CIKX-FM
Grand Falls/Grand-Sault	NB	105.1	3	F	CFAI-FM-1
Grande-Anse/Caraquet	NB	94.1	100	F	CJVA-FM
Inkerman/Pokemouche	NB	97.1	44.4	F	CKRO-FM
Kedgwick	NB	90.1	3	F	CFJU-FM
Miramichi	NB	93.7	11	F	CKMA-FM
Miramichi	NB	95.9	25		CHHI-FM
Miramichi	NB	99.3	17.8		CFAN-FM
Moncton	NB	90.7	30	F	CFBO-FM
Moncton	NB	91.9	70		CKNI-FM
Moncton	NB	94.5	19		CKCW-FM
Moncton	NB	96.9	100		CJXL-FM
Moncton	NB	99.9	9.5	F	CHOY-FM
Moncton	NB	103.1	46.8		CJMO-FM
Moncton	NB	103.9	70		CFQM-FM
Saint John	NB	88.9	25		CHNI-FM
Saint John	NB	94.1	100		CHSJ-FM
Saint John	NB	97.3	100		CHWV-FM
Saint John	NB	98.9	12		CJYC-FM
Saint John	NB	100.5	100		CIOK-FM
Shediac	NB	89.5	38	F	CJSE-FM
St. Stephen	NB	98.1	40		CHTD-FM
Woodstock	NB	104.1	10		CJCJ-FM
Argentia	NL	100.3	3.7		CFOZ-FM
Bonavista	NL	92.1	6.7		CJOZ-FM
Carbonear	NL	103.9	30		CHVO-FM
Clarenville	NL	100.7	4.1		VOCM-FM-1
Clarenville	NL	105.3	4.7		CJMY-FM

FM	Prov	MHz	kW	N	Call
Clarenville	NL	107.5	25.5		CKSJ-FM-1
Corner Brook	NL	92.3	7.7		CKOZ-FM
Corner Brook	NL	103.9	35.6		CKXX-FM
Gander	NL	97.7	3.1		CFAZ-FM
Gander	NL	98.7	6		CKXD-FM
Grand Falls-Windsor	NL	95.9	46.6		CKMY-FM
Grand Falls-Windsor	NL	102.3	36		CKXG-FM
Marystown	NL	96.3	27		CIOZ-FM
Port au Choix	NL	96.7	4.3		CFNW-FM
St. John's	NL	94.7	100		CHOZ-FM
St. John's	NL	96.7	100		VOAR-FM
St. John's	NL	97.5	100		VOCM-FM
St. John's	NL	99.1	100		CKIX-FM
St. John's	NL	101.1	20		CKSJ-FM
Stephenville	NL	98.5	3		CIOS-FM
Amherst	NS	101.7	50		CKDH-FM
Amherst	NS	107.9	6.5		CFTA-FM
Antigonish	NS	98.9	75.4		CJFX-FM
Barrington	NS	96.3	5.5		CJLS-FM-2
Bridgewater	NS	98.1	32		CKBW-FM
Bridgewater	NS	100.7	10		CJHK-FM
Chéticamp	NS	106.1	3	F	CKJM-FM
Glace Bay	NS	89.7	6		CKOA-FM
Halifax	NS	89.9	100		CHNS-FM
Halifax	NS	92.9	100		CFLT-FM
Halifax	NS	93.9	3.1		CJLU-FM
Halifax	NS	95.7	65		CJNI-FM
Halifax	NS	96.5	100		CKUL-FM
Halifax	NS	100.1	100		CIOO-FM
Halifax	NS	101.3	100		CJCH-FM
Halifax	NS	101.9	91		CHFX-FM
Halifax	NS	103.5	100		CKHZ-FM
Halifax	NS	104.3	100		CFRQ-FM
Halifax	NS	105.1	100		CKHY-FM
Inverness	NS	102.5	10		CJFX-FM-1
Kentville	NS	89.3	30		CIJK-FM
Kentville	NS	94.9	100		CKWM-FM
Kentville	NS	97.7	18		CKEN-FM
Liverpool	NS	94.5	8.7		CKBW-1-FM
New Glasgow	NS	94.1	80		CKEC-FM
New Tusket	NS	93.5	3		CJLS-FM-1
Petit-de-Grat	NS	104.1	5.8	F	CITU-FM
Pictou	NS	97.9	100		CKEZ-FM
Port Hawkesbury	NS	101.5	38.1		CIGO-FM
Shelburne	NS	93.1	8.6		CKBW-2-FM
Sydney	NS	94.9	61		CKPE-FM
Sydney	NS	98.3	100		CHER-FM
Sydney	NS	101.9	58		CHRK-FM
Sydney	NS	103.5	26.5		CKCH-FM
Truro	NS	99.5	16.8		CKTY-FM
Truro	NS	100.9	50		CKTO-FM
Weymouth	NS	103.3	3		CKDY-1-FM
Yarmouth	NS	95.5	18		CJLS-FM
Yarmouth	NS	104.1	23.7	F	CIFA-FM
Ajax	ON	95.9	50		CJKX-FM
Bancroft	ON	97.7	50		CHMS-FM
Barrie	ON	93.1	100		CHAY-FM
Barrie	ON	95.7	100		CFJB-FM
Barrie	ON	100.3	32.8		CJLF-FM
Barrie	ON	101.1	7.5		CIQB-FM
Barrie	ON	107.5	50		CKMB-FM
Barry's Bay	ON	106.5	12		CHBY-FM
Belleville	ON	91.3	3.2		CJLX-FM
Belleville	ON	95.5	35		CJOJ-FM
Belleville	ON	97.1	50		CIGL-FM
Belleville	ON	100.1	32		CHCQ-FM
Belleville	ON	102.3	15		CKJJ-FM
Bluewater	ON	91.7	6		CIBU-FM-1
Bracebridge	ON	99.5	12		CFBG-FM
Bracebridge/Gravenhurst	ON	102.3	23		CJMU-FM
Brantford	ON	92.1	80		CKPC-FM
Brantford	ON	93.9	3		CFWC-FM
Brockville	ON	103.7	100		CJPT-FM
Brockville	ON	104.9	7.7		CFJR-FM
Cambridge	ON	107.5	6		CJDV-FM
Chatham-Kent	ON	89.3	18.7		CKGW-FM
Chatham-Kent	ON	94.3	50		CKSY-FM
Chatham-Kent	ON	95.1	42		CKUE-FM
Cobourg	ON	93.3	15.5		CKSG-FM
Cobourg	ON	103.1	86.7		CFMX-FM
Cobourg	ON	107.9	20		CHUC-FM
Collingwood	ON	102.9	23		CFMO-FM
Cornwall	ON	101.9	3.2		CJSS-FM
Cornwall	ON	104.5	28.2		CFLG-FM
Dryden	ON	92.7	39		CKDR-FM
Dunvegan	ON	92.1	20.5	F	CHOD-FM-1
Englehart	ON	105.7	3.3		CJTK-FM-7
Fort Erie	ON	101.1	50		CFLZ-FM
Fort Frances	ON	93.1	21		CFOB-FM
Gananoque	ON	99.9	4.5		CJGM-FM
Georgina	ON	93.7	39		CKOU-FM
Goderich	ON	104.9	12.6		CHWC-FM
Guelph	ON	106.1	50		CIMJ-FM
Haldimand	ON	92.9	10		CHTG-FM
Haliburton	ON	93.5	6		CFZN-FM
Haliburton	ON	100.9	3.4		CKHA-FM
Hamilton/Burlington	ON	94.7	100		CHKX-FM
Hamilton	ON	95.3	100		CING-FM
Hamilton	ON	102.9	40.3		CKLH-FM
Hamilton/Burlington	ON	107.9	26.1		CJXY-FM
Hearst	ON	91.1	5.5	F	CINN-FM
Huntsville	ON	88.7	5.7		CKAR-FM
Huntsville	ON	105.5	43.4		CFBK-FM
Kapuskasing	ON	89.7	3	F	CKGN-FM
Kapuskasing	ON	100.9	12		CKAP-FM
Kawartha Lakes	ON	91.9	11.4		CKLY-FM
Kenora	ON	89.5	50		CJRL-FM
Kincardine	ON	95.5	5.7		CIYN-FM
Kingston	ON	93.5	7.5		CKXC-FM
Kingston	ON	96.3	28		CFMK-FM
Kingston	ON	98.3	95.5		CFLY-FM
Kingston	ON	98.9	15		CKLC-FM
Kingston	ON	101.9	3		CFRC-FM
Kingston	ON	104.3	8		CKWS-FM
Kingston	ON	105.7	50		CIKR-FM
Kirkland Lake	ON	101.5	23		CJKL-FM
Kitchener/Waterloo	ON	88.3	8.2		CJIQ-FM
Kitchener/Waterloo	ON	91.5	10		CKBT-FM
Kitchener	ON	96.7	80		CHYM-FM
Kitchener	ON	99.5	4.3		CKKW-FM
Kitchener	ON	105.3	100		CFCA-FM
Kitchener/Waterloo	ON	106.7	5		CIKZ-FM
Leamington	ON	92.7	4		CJSP-FM
Leamington	ON	96.7	27		CHYR-FM
London	ON	92.7	50		CJBX-FM
London	ON	94.9	6		CHRW-FM
London	ON	95.9	300		CFPL-FM
London	ON	97.5	50		CIQM-FM
London	ON	98.1	40		CKLO-FM
London	ON	102.3	100		CHST-FM
London	ON	106.9	3		CIXX-FM
Manitoulin Island	ON	94.1	90		CKNR-FM
Manitoulin Island	ON	100.7	15		CFRM-FM
Manitoulin Island	ON	103.1	24.8		CHAW-FM
Marathon	ON	93.1	50		CFNO-FM
Markham	ON	105.9	3	m	CFMS-FM
Midland	ON	104.1	20		CICZ-FM
Napanee	ON	88.7	11.1		CKYM-FM
New Tecumseth	ON	92.1	3.8		CIMA-FM
Newmarket	ON	88.5	30		CKDX-FM
Niagara Falls	ON	105.1	15		CJED-FM
North Bay	ON	100.5	100		CHUR-FM
North Bay	ON	101.9	100		CKFX-FM
North Bay	ON	106.3	10		CFXN-FM
North Perth	ON	100.1	8		CHLP-FM
Ohsweken	ON	100.3	5		CKRZ-FM
Orangeville	ON	103.5	30.7		CIDC-FM
Orillia	ON	105.9	20		CICX-FM
Oshawa	ON	94.9	50		CKGE-FM
Ottawa	ON	88.5	90		CILV-FM
Ottawa	ON	89.1	18.1		CHUO-FM
Ottawa	ON	89.9	27		CIHT-FM
Ottawa	ON	93.1	12		CKCU-FM
Ottawa	ON	93.9	95		CKKL-FM
Ottawa	ON	95.7	9.1	m	CFPO-FM
Ottawa	ON	97.9	6.8	m	CJLL-FM
Ottawa	ON	99.1	66		CHRI-FM
Ottawa	ON	99.7	100		CJOT-FM
Ottawa	ON	100.3	100		CJMJ-FM
Ottawa	ON	101.7	21		CIDG-FM

FM	Prov	MHz	kW	N	Call
Ottawa	ON	105.3	84		CISS-FM
Ottawa	ON	106.1	100		CHEZ-FM
Ottawa	ON	106.9	84		CKQB-FM
Owen Sound	ON	92.3	9.4		CJOS-FM
Owen Sound	ON	93.7	22		CKYC-FM
Owen Sound	ON	106.5	28		CIXK-FM
Parry Sound	ON	103.3	46.6		CKLP-FM
Pembroke	ON	96.7	100		CHVR-FM
Pembroke	ON	99.9	7.5		CKQB-FM-1
Pembroke	ON	104.9	34		CIMY-FM
Penetanguishene	ON	88.1	40	F	CFRH-FM
Perth	ON	88.1	5.4		CHLK-FM
Peterborough	ON	96.7	7		CJWV-FM
Peterborough	ON	99.7	11		CKPT-FM
Peterborough	ON	100.5	15		CKRU-FM
Peterborough	ON	101.5	15.2		CKWF-FM
Peterborough	ON	105.1	7.5		CKQM-FM
Prescott	ON	107.9	4.2		CKPP-FM
Prince Edward County	ON	99.3	3		CJPE-FM
Quinte West	ON	107.1	15		CJTN-FM
Renfrew	ON	96.1	7.1		CHMY-FM
Renfrew	ON	98.7	20		CJHR-FM
Sarnia	ON	99.9	26		CFGX-FM
Sarnia	ON	106.3	50		CHKS-FM
Saugeen Shores	ON	90.9	3.1		CIYN-FM-2
Saugeen Shores	ON	97.9	8.3		CFPS-FM
Sault Ste. Marie	ON	100.5	13.9		CHAS-FM
Sault Ste. Marie	ON	104.3	100		CJQM-FM
Shelburne	ON	104.9	36.2		CFDC-FM
Simcoe	ON	98.9	50		CHCD-FM
Simcoe	ON	99.7	18		CKNC-FM
Smiths Falls	ON	92.3	17		CJET-FM
Smiths Falls	ON	101.1	100		CKBY-FM
St. Catharines	ON	97.7	50		CHTZ-FM
St. Catharines	ON	105.7	50		CHRE-FM
St. Thomas	ON	94.1	4.4		CKZM-FM
St. Thomas	ON	103.1	60		CFHK-FM
Stratford	ON	107.1	4		CJCS-FM
Stratford	ON	107.7	6		CHGK-FM
Sudbury	ON	91.7	50		CICS-FM
Sudbury	ON	92.7	100		CJRQ-FM
Sudbury	ON	93.5	100		CIGM-FM
Sudbury	ON	95.5	8.1		CJTK-FM
Sudbury	ON	98.9	3.8	F	CHYC-FM
Sudbury	ON	103.9	100		CHNO-FM
Sudbury	ON	105.3	100		CJMX-FM
Sunderland	ON	89.9	5		CJKX-FM-1
Tamiskaming Shores	ON	104.5	10		CJTT-FM
Thunder Bay	ON	91.5	100		CKPR-FM
Thunder Bay	ON	94.3	93		CJSD-FM
Thunder Bay	ON	105.3	100		CKTG-FM
Tillsonburg	ON	101.3	26		CKOT-FM
Tillsonburg	ON	107.3	7.8		CJDL-FM
Timmins	ON	92.1	40		CJQQ-FM
Timmins	ON	93.1	16.4		CHMT-FM
Timmins	ON	99.3	40		CKGB-FM
Toronto	ON	88.1	12		CIND-FM
Toronto	ON	88.9	4.2	m	CIRV-FM
Toronto	ON	89.5	15		CIUT-FM
Toronto	ON	91.1	40		CJRT-FM
Toronto	ON	91.9	5	m	CHIN-1-FM
Toronto	ON	92.5	13		CKIS-FM
Toronto	ON	93.5	3.7		CFXJ-FM
Toronto	ON	96.3	60		CFMZ-FM
Toronto	ON	97.3	28.9		CHBM-FM
Toronto	ON	98.1	44		CHFI-FM
Toronto	ON	99.9	40		CKFM-FM
Toronto	ON	100.7	8.5	m	CHIN-FM
Toronto	ON	102.1	35.4		CFNY-FM
Toronto	ON	104.5	40		CHUM-FM
Toronto	ON	107.1	40		CILQ-FM
Wallaceburg	ON	99.1	3		CKXS-FM
Welland	ON	89.1	4.3		CKYY-FM
Welland	ON	91.7	50		CIXL-FM
West Nipissing	ON	97.1	6.5	F	CHYQ-FM
Windsor	ON	88.7	100		CIMX-FM
Windsor	ON	90.5	7.5		CJAH-FM
Windsor	ON	93.9	100		CIDR-FM
Windsor	ON	95.9	11.8		CJWF-FM
Windsor	ON	100.7	9		CKUE-FM-1

FM	Prov	MHz	kW	N	Call
Windsor	ON	102.3	5	m	CINA-FM
Wingham	ON	94.5	75		CIBU-FM
Wingham	ON	101.7	100		CKNX-FM
Woodstock	ON	103.9	51		CKDK-FM
Woodstock	ON	104.7	20		CIHR-FM
Charlottetown	PE	93.1	75		CHLQ-FM
Charlottetown	PE	95.1	100		CFCY-FM
Charlottetown	PE	100.3	88		CHTN-FM
Charlottetown	PE	105.5	88		CKQK-FM
Elmira	PE	99.9	3.4		CHTN-FM-1
Elmira	PE	103.7	3.4		CKQK-FM-1
St. Edward	PE	89.9	5		CHTN-FM-2
St. Edward	PE	91.1	5		CKQK-FM-2
Summerside	PE	102.1	50		CJRW-FM
Alma	QC	95.7	100	F	CKYK-FM
Alma	QC	104.5	20	F	CFGT-FM
Amos	QC	105.3	32.2	F	CHOW-FM
Amqui	QC	99.9	23.8	F	CFVM-FM
Baie-Comeau	QC	97.1	4.2	F	CHLC-FM
Bécancour	QC	90.5	60	F	CKBN-FM
Cap-aux-Meules	QC	92.7	6.3	F	CFIM-FM
Carleton-sur-Mer	QC	94.9	37.6	F	CIEU-FM
Chandler	QC	96.3	22.9	F	CFMV-FM
Chibougamau	QC	93.5	56.2	F	CKXO-FM
Chisasibi	QC	101.1	3	m	CHFG-FM
Dégelis	QC	95.5	12.5	F	CFVD-FM
Dolbeau-Mistassini	QC	100.3	50	F	CHVD-FM
Drummondville	QC	92.1	3	F	CJDM-FM
Drummondville	QC	105.3	5.3	F	CHRD-FM
Eastmain	QC	104.1	38.1	m	CJEQ-FM-1
Forestville	QC	100.5	6	F	CFRP-FM
Fort-Coulonge	QC	101.9	11.9	F	CHIP-FM
Gaspé	QC	94.5	6	F	CJRG-FM
Gatineau	QC	94.9	84	F	CIMF-FM
Gatineau	QC	97.1	11.2	F	CHLX-FM
Gatineau	QC	104.1	19	F	CKTF-FM
Gatineau	QC	104.7	100	F	CKOF-FM
Granby	QC	104.9	4.3	F	CFXM-FM
Joliette	QC	103.5	4.5	F	CJLM-FM
Kebaowek	QC	104.1	6		CKFF-FM
La Pocatière	QC	97.5	25.2	F	CHOX-FM
La Sarre	QC	92.5	6	F	CJMM-FM-1
La Sarre	QC	102.1	4.1	F	CJGO-FM
La Tuque	QC	97.1	28.4	F	CFLM-FM
Lac-Etchemin	QC	100.5	8.6	F	CFIN-FM
Lachute	QC	104.9	3	F	CJLA-FM
Lac-Mégantic	QC	106.7	4.3	F	CJIT-FM
Les Escoumins	QC	94.9	4.7	F	CHME-FM
Louisville	QC	103.1	4.2	F	CHHO-FM
Maliotenam	QC	104.5	6	m	CKAU-FM
Maniwaki	QC	97.3	16.9	F	CHGA-FM
Matane	QC	95.3	14.6	F	CHOE-FM
Matane	QC	105.3	30	F	CHRM-FM
Mistissini	QC	95.3	50	m	CINI-FM
Mont-Laurier	QC	104.7	16.9	F	CFLO-FM
Montmagny	QC	90.3	40.7	F	CIQI-FM
Montréal	QC	89.3	10	F	CISM-FM
Montréal	QC	90.3	5		CKUT-FM
Montréal	QC	91.3	36.2	F	CIRA-FM
Montréal	QC	91.9	4.7	F	CKLX-FM
Montréal	QC	92.5	100		CKBE-FM
Montréal	QC	94.3	41.4	F	CKMF-FM
Montréal	QC	95.9	41.2		CJFM-FM
Montréal	QC	96.9	148	F	CKOI-FM
Montréal	QC	97.7	41.2		CHOM-FM
Montréal	QC	98.5	100	F	CHMP-FM
Montréal	QC	99.5	8.7	F	CJPX-FM
Montréal	QC	105.7	48	F	CFGL-FM
Montréal	QC	107.3	42.9	F	CITE-FM
Natashquan	QC	104.1	6.6	F	CKNA-FM
Nemaska	QC	103.1	18.5		CJNM-FM
New Carlisle	QC	107.1	5.6	F	CHNC-FM
Oujé-Bougoumou	QC	103.9	48.5	m	CKOJ-FM
Oujé-Bougoumou	QC	106.9	48.4	m	CHIU-FM
Pikogan	QC	100.1	3.7	m	CKAG-FM
Port-Cartier	QC	99.1	45	F	CIPC-FM
Québec	QC	90.9	5.7	F	CION-FM
Québec	QC	91.9	31	F	CJEC-FM
Québec	QC	93.3	33	F	CJMF-FM
Québec/Sainte-Foy	QC	94.3	6	F	CHYZ-FM

FM	Prov	MHz	kW	N	Call
Québec	QC	98.1	40	F	CHOI-FM
Québec	QC	98.9	41	F	CHIK-FM
Québec/Lévis	QC	102.1	33.9	F	CFEL-FM
Québec/Lévis	QC	102.9	32.8	F	CFOM-FM
Québec	QC	107.5	37	F	CITF-FM
Rimouski/Mont-Joli	QC	93.3	27.3	F	CFYX-FM
Rimouski/Mont-Joli	QC	96.5	5.8	F	CKMN-FM
Rimouski	QC	98.7	100	F	CIKI-FM
Rimouski	QC	102.9	33.6	F	CJOI-FM
Rivière-du-Loup	QC	103.7	60	F	CIEL-FM
Rivière-du-Loup	QC	107.1	100	F	CIBM-FM
Roberval	QC	99.5	50	F	CHRL-FM
Rouyn-Noranda	QC	88.7	3.4	F	CHIC-FM
Rouyn-Noranda	QC	95.7	44	F	CJGO-FM-1
Rouyn-Noranda	QC	96.5	61.1	F	CHOA-FM
Rouyn-Noranda	QC	99.1	3	F	CJMM-FM
Saguenay	QC	92.5	14.2	F	CKAJ-FM
Saguenay	QC	94.5	100	F	CJAB-FM
Saguenay	QC	96.9	100	F	CFIX-FM
Saguenay	QC	98.3	100	F	CILM-FM
Sagueney	QC	105.5	6	F	CKGS-FM
Saguenay	QC	106.7	46.2	F	CION-FM-2
Sainte-Marie	QC	101.5	72	F	CHEQ-FM
Saint-Fabien-de-Panet	QC	92.5	20	F	CIQI-FM-1
Saint-Georges	QC	99.7	100	F	CHJM-FM
Saint-Georges	QC	103.5	15	F	CKRB-FM
Saint-Hyacinthe	QC	106.5	3	F	CFEI-FM
Saint-Jérôme	QC	103.9	36.5	F	CIME-FM
Saint-Marie	QC	105.3	4.5	F	CHCT-FM
Salaberry-de-Valleyfield	QC	103.1	3	F	CKOD-FM
Sept-Îles	QC	94.1	11.3	F	CKCN-FM
Shawinigan	QC	92.9	3.8	F	CFUT-FM
Sherbrooke	QC	93.7	25.5	F	CFGE-FM
Sherbrooke	QC	102.7	92	F	CITE-FM-1
Sherbrooke	QC	107.7	25	F	CKOY-FM
Sorel-Tracy	QC	101.7	3	F	CJSO-FM
St-Gabriel-de-Brandon	QC	99.1	9.8	F	CFNJ-FM
Témiscouata-sur-le-Lac	QC	98.3	3	F	CIEL-FM-3
Thetford Mines	QC	97.3	100	F	CFJO-FM
Thetford Mines	QC	105.5	6	F	CKLD-FM
Trois-Rivières	QC	89.1	3	F	CFOU-FM
Trois-Rivières	QC	89.9	3.2	F	CIRA-FM-2
Trois-Rivières	QC	94.7	100	F	CHEY-FM
Trois-Rivières	QC	100.1	64.1	F	CJEB-FM
Trois-Rivières	QC	102.3	5.8	F	CIGB-FM
Trois-Rivières	QC	106.9	100	F	CKOB-FM
Val-des-Sources	QC	99.3	11.1	F	CJAN-FM
Val-d'Or	QC	102.7	96	F	CJMV-FM
Val-d'Or/Amos	QC	103.5	100	F	CHOA-FM-1
Val-d'Or/Amos	QC	104.3	94	F	CHGO-FM
Ville-Marie	QC	93.1	34	F	CKVM-FM
Waskaganish	QC	92.5	38	m	CJRH-FM
Waswanipi	QC	93.9	6.2	m	CFNE-FM
Wemindji	QC	99.7	24.7	m	CHPH-FM
Assiniboia	SK	98.1	29		CIAT-FM
Buffalo Narrows	SK	89.3	6	m	CIBN-FM
Dafoe	SK	100.3	100		CJVR-FM-1
Estevan	SK	102.3	100		CHSN-FM
Estevan	SK	106.1	100		CKSE-FM
Gravelbourg	SK	107.1	97		CJME-2-FM
Humboldt	SK	107.5	100		CHBO-FM
Kindersley	SK	104.9	100		CKVX-FM
Meadow Lake	SK	102.3	45		CJNS-FM
Meadow Lake	SK	104.5	45		CJCQ-FM-1
Melfort	SK	105.1	100		CJVR-FM
Moose Jaw	SK	100.7	100		CILG-FM
Moose Jaw	SK	103.9	100		CJAW-FM
Nipawin	SK	94.7	14.8		CJNE-FM
North Battleford	SK	93.3	100		CJHD-FM
North Battleford	SK	95.5	28	m	CJLR-FM-6
North Battleford	SK	97.9	100		CJCQ-FM
Okanese First Nation	SK	95.3	50		CHXL-FM
Prince Albert	SK	88.1	49	m	CJLR-FM-3
Prince Albert	SK	99.1	100		CFMM-FM
Prince Albert	SK	101.5	100		CHQX-FM
Regina	SK	90.3	43	m	CJLR-FM-4
Regina	SK	92.1	100		CHMX-FM
Regina	SK	92.7	100		CHBD-FM
Regina	SK	94.5	100		CKCK-FM
Regina	SK	98.9	100		CIZL-FM
Regina	SK	104.9	100		CFWF-FM
Saskatoon	SK	92.9	100		CKBL-FM
Saskatoon	SK	95.1	100		CFMC-FM
Saskatoon	SK	96.3	100		CFWD-FM
Saskatoon	SK	98.3	100		CJMK-FM
Saskatoon	SK	102.1	100		CJDJ-FM
Swift Current	SK	94.1	100		CIMG-FM
Swift Current	SK	97.1	100		CKFI-FM
Swift Current	SK	101.7	100		CJME-1-FM
Wapella	SK	102.9	14		CFGW-FM-2
Warmley	SK	107.3	87		CJME-3-FM
Waskesiu Lake	SK	106.3	11		CJVR-FM-2
Weyburn	SK	103.5	100		CKRC-FM
Weyburn	SK	106.7	100		CHWY-FM
Yorkton	SK	94.1	100		CFGW-FM
Yorkton	SK	98.5	50		CJJC-FM
Whitehorse	YT	96.1	4.4		CKRW-FM

+ txs below 3kW

NB: c=moving to FM F=French m=ethnic/multilingual r=relay *=also on SW +=**F.Pl.** Most FM stns identify using a name rather than calls. FM stns with calls containing numbers are relays.

Innovation, Science and Economic Development Canada Department stn list database available at **W:** sms-sgs.ic.gc.ca/eic/site/sms-sgs-prod.nsf/eng/h_00015.html. Stn history & info at: **W:** broadcasting-history.ca

BRITISH FORCES BROADCASTING SERVICE

✉ BFBS Canada BFPO 14 BATUS, Suffield AB ☎+1 403 544 4104 **W:** radio.bfbs.com **BFBS Canada**: **FM:** 104.1, 107.1 CKBF-FM

CANARY ISLANDS (Spain)

L.T: UTC (28 Mar-31 Oct: +1h) — **Pop:** 2.2 million — **Pr.L:** Spanish — **E.C:** 230V/50Hz — **ITU:** CNR

MW	kHz	kW	Net	Location	Island
1)	576	20	RNE-1	Las Palmas	GC
2)	621	300	RNE-1	Santa Cruz	TF
2)	720	10	RNE-5	Santa Cruz	TF
1)	747	25	RNE-5	Las Palmas	GC
3)	837	10	COPE	Las Palmas	GC
4)	882	20	COPE	Santa Cruz	TF
5)	*1008	10	Grupo R.	Las Palmas	GC
6)	1179	25	SER	R. Clube Tenerife	

*=MW only used for special events

Addresses & other information

Abbreviations: GC=Gran Canaria, GCF=Fuerteventura, GCL=Lanzarote, TF=Tenerife, TFP=Isla de la Palma, TFG=Isla de la Gomera, TFH=Hierro. (For network abbreviations refer to Spain)

1) R. Nacional de España, Av. Escaleritas 300-340, prolongacion Pedro Infinito, 35013 Las Palmas ☎ +34 928 364 088 🖷 +34 928 362 754 – **2)** R. Nacional de España, San Martín 1, 38001 Sta. Cruz de Tenerife ☎ +34 (922) 288400 🖷 +34 922 283363 **R.1:** 24h on 621kHz **N:** On the h. **R.2:** (classical music) 24h. **R.3:** 24h. **R.5:** 24h – **3)** R. Popular de Las Palmas, Av. Escaleritas 60-1°, Las Palmas 35011 ☎ +34 928 286970 **E:** direccion.laspalmas@cadenacope.net Dir: Antonio Miguel Díaz **D.Prgr:** 24h. **FM** :99.1MHz – **4)** R. Popular de Tenerife, Darías y Padron, 1-2º-38003 Santa Cruz de Tenerife ☎ +34 922 236900/05/09 🖷 +34 922 2369121 **E:** tenerife@cadenacope.net Dir: José Carlos Marrero Gonzales. **D.Prgr:** 24h FM 97.1 MHZ and COPE MAS in FM: 93.7 MHZ, 99.0 MHZ and 105.1 MHZ – **5)** GRUPO Radio Las Palmas, C/ Profesor Lozano 5, 2°, Urb. Industrial El Sebadal, 35008 Las Palmas de Gran Canaria **W:** radiolaspalmas.com **FM** :97.3 MHZ and 104.4 MHZ **E:** informacion@radiolaspalmas.com ☎ +34 928 462052 🖷 +34 928 462057 Dir:María Enma Hernández Martín. **D.Prgr:** 24h – **6)** R. Club Tenerife, Av. de Anaga 35, Santa Cruz de Tenerife 38001 ☎ +34 922 270400 🖷 +34 922 281043 **E:** radioclubtenerife@unionradio.es Dir:Juan Ramon Hernandez. **FM** 101.1MHz – **7)** Av. Escaleritas 64 1°, 35011 Las Palmas de Gran Canaria **W:** radioecca.org **E:** info@radioecca.org **FM**: 99.5MHz

Dial FM Networks:

Gran Canaria Las Palmas (MHz): Cope Más Las Palmas 87.6 - R.T.I. Insular 87.7 – R. Maria 87.9 – R. Marca 88.2 – RNE5 INF.88.6 – Hit FM 88.9 –FUN R 89.9 – ECCA 90.4 – R.ECCA 90.7– COPE 91.0 – esRadio 91.1 – Canaras R. 91.4 – C100 91.8 – R. Top 21 92.0 –RNE1 92.8 – Aire Radio 93.4– R. Juventud 94.1 – Los 40 94.4 – RNE2 95.1

– Inolvidable FM 95.8 – Tamaran FM Formula Hits 96.2 – R.Las Palmas 97.3 – Europa FM 98.0 – RNE3 98.5 – COPE FM 99.1 – Infierno FM 99.5 – SER Las Palmas 100.3 – Global FM 100.6 – Canarias R. 100.8 – Cadena Dial 101.7 – Los 40 Dance 102.7 – Cope Más Las Palmas 103.0 – UD Radio 103.4 – R.Univerdance 103.8 – R. Faycan 104.2 – Los 40 Classic 105.4 – R. Guiniguada 105.9 – OCR 106.8
Gran Canaria Maspalomas Playa del Ingles (MHz): 9 Radio 87.9 –RNE1 88.5 - R.Arguineguin 89.4 – 7,7 Radio 89.6 – COPE FM 90.7 – ECCA Sur 91.4 – R.TOP 21 92.0 – R.Faro 92.5 – Onda Islena 93.8 – R.Sol 94.8 – esRadio 95.3 – R.Faro Sur 97.2 – R.Rondo 98.2 –RNE2 99.1 - SER Maspalomas 99.6 –RNE3 100.9 - R.Maria 102.7 – R.Abrisajac 103.5 – RNE5 INF. 106.5 – R.Dunas 107.6
Fuerteventura (MHz): RNE2 87.7 – R.Sintonia 88.2 – RNE5 89.8 - Nueve R. OCR 90.7 – COPE 91.2 – COPE 91.6 – R.Maxorata 92.1 – RNE1 92.6 - ECCA 93.0 – Atlantica FM 94.2 – Dunas FM 94.4 – RNE1 94.6 – Europa FM 95.6 –RNE2 96.0 - Canarias R. 96.9 – Nueve R. 97.7 – Q FM Corralejo 98.0 – R.Agua Cabra 99.6 Morro Jable – RNE3 100.6- Canarias R. 104.4 – RNE5 INF. 104.8 – R.Archipielago 105.0 – C.100 Puerto del Rosario 105.3 – MCM Mision Cristiana Moderna Radio 106.9
Lanzarote (MHz): O2 Radio 88.5 – esRadio 89.0 - SER 89.7 – Alo FM 90.1 – OCR 90.7 – OCR 91.1 – R.Cristal 92.0 – RNE1 92.5 – ECCA 93.0 – R.Marca 93.6 – R.Maria 93.9 – RNE2 94.9 – O2 Radio 96.4 – R.Insular 96.7 – COPE 98.3 – R. Las Arenas 98.6 – RNE5 99.0 - Onda Conejera 99.1 – RNE1 99.6 - RNE5 INF. 100.2 – Guapa FM 100.9 – Canarias R. 101.2 – RNE3 102.3 - RNE3 102.8 – Mi Tierra FM 103.1 – Los 40 104.0 – Cronicas R. 105.5 – Europa FM 106.5 – Latina Stereo 107.7
Tenerife Norte (MHz): R.Decibelios FM 87.5 – Cadena Dial 87.8 – MM Radio La Laguna 88.1 – Onda CIT 88.5 – RNE5 INF. 88.8 – Cadena Dial Sur 88.9 – ROCK FM 89.1 – C100 89.4 – ECCA La Laguna 89.6 – Marcha FM 89.8 – RNE3 90.0 – Onda 7 90.2 – R.El Dia La Laguna 90.8 – Los 40 Dance 91.1 –Gestiona R. Tenerife 91.3 - R.Marca Tenerife 91.5 – R.Atlantida 91.9 – RNE1 92.3 — Los 40 Tenerife 93.2 – Antena de Canarias 93.5 – Marcha FM La Laguna 93.8 – Teide OCR 94.0 R.Marca La Laguna 94.5 – RNE1 94.8 – Onda CIT R. Turismo La Laguna 95.2 – Gente R. 95.6 –Fun FM La Laguna 95.8 – RNE2 96.2 – Inter Magica FM 96.8 – COPE La Laguna 97.1 – Gestiona R. Tenerife 97.2 - R.Maria 97.5 – R.Marca 97.7 – Onda 7 La Laguna 97.9 – RNE5 INF. 98.1 – Onda Tenerife 98.5 – Canal 4 98.8 – Los 40 99.1 – Kiss FM 99.4 – esRadio 99.5 - SER R.Club Norte 99.8 – Los 40 Classic 100.1 – R.Pimienta La Orotava 100.3 – Orquestras del Atlantico La Laguna R. 100.5 – R.Taoro 100.7 – SER R.Club Tenerife 101.1 – COPE 101.4 – R.Majuelos La Laguna 101.7 – RNE2 102.1 – esRadio 102.3 – Kiss FM 102.5 – R.Maria La Laguna 103.2 – R.ECCA Los Cristianos 103.4 – RKM R. 103.8 – RNE5 INF.104.0 – Canarias R. 104.2 – La Mega Latina La Laguna 104.5 – Canarias R. 104.7 – esRadio 104.9 – Gestiona R. Valle Güimar 104.9 - Cope Más Tenerife 105.1 - R.Union Tenerife 105.3 – RNE3 105.7 – Canal 4 R. 106.1 – ECCA 106.6 – Exito R. 107.0 – R.La Guancha 107.2 – R.Realejos Los Realejos 107.9
Tenerife Sur (MHz): R. Gigante 87.7 – El Faro FM 87.9 – Canarias R. 88.1 – Cadena Dial Playa de las Americas 88.9 – R.ECCA 90.4 – RNE2 92.6 - Inter Magica FM 91.1 – RNE 2 92.6 – Los 40 Playa de las Americas 93.3 – R.Costa 93.8 – Gestiona R. 94.0 - Canal 4 R. 94.8 – esRadio 94.9 - RNE3 95.4 – SER R.Club Sur Playa de las Americas 95.9 – Fun R. 96.2 – Fun Radio 96.8 – Atlantico FM 97.1 – R.Marca 97.7 – Onda Nueva 99.7 – Onda Tenerife Arona 100.1 – Astrovision Magica FM 101.9 – Bomba FM R. 102.4 – Hit R. S.Miguel de Abona 103.0 – RNE1 105.7 – Teide OCR S.Miguel de Abona 106.3 – R.Decibelios FM Arona 107.5
Isla de la Palma (MHz): RNE5 88.4 - RNE5 INF. 89.6 – RNE1 90.8 – R.Murion 91.0 – R.Isla Bonita OCR 92.7 – RNE1 92.9 - Canarias R. 93.0 – COPE 95.1 – C100 95.6 – RNE2 96.1 -RNE2 96.7 – Gestiona R. 97.2 - Los 40 97.4 – Canarias R. 97.5 – R.21 Musica 98.0 – RNE5 INF.98.4 –RNE3 98.7 - ECCA 99.5 – Canarias R. 100.5 – SER R.La Palma 101.6 – RNE1 102.7 – R.Maria 103.1 – RNED3 103.8 - Cadena Dial 104.1 – RNE2 104.5 – RNE3 106.1 – R.Isla Bonita OCR 106.4 – Radio LUZ Garafia 107.0 Onda Taburiente El Paso 107.0
La Gomera (MHz): Intersur R. 88.0 – Onda Tagoror Gomera R. 88.5 – R.CLM 90.2 – RNE5 91.7 – R.Insular de la Gomera 92.2 – R.Insular de la Gomera 92.2 – RNE1 94.3 – R.Cantera 94.7 – R.Atlantico Sur 95.6 – Canarias R. 96.7 – Gestiona R. 98.0 - SER R.Garoè 98.8 – RNE2 101.8 – R.Gigante 102.2 – R.Garajonay 102.6 – ECCA 103.4 –Gestiona R. 103.5 - Formula Hit 103.7 – RNE3 105.2 – R.Insular de la Gomera 105.9 – R.Vallehermoso 107.4 – R.Agulo 107.6 – R.Ipalan 107.7
El Hierro (MHz): RNE5 89.8 – ECCA Valverde 90.6 – SER R.Garoè La Frontera 92.0 – RNE1 92.5 – RNE2 93.9 – RNE3 96.4 – RNE2 97.0 – RNE5 98.2 – Onda Herrena Valverde100.8 – RNE1 101.2 – Canarias R. Frontrera 102.3 – Canarias R. Valverde 103.2 – RNE3 104.9 – R.Tajaraste Valverde 105.2 – Onda Herrena Frontera 107.0
NB: For LPFM stns on all islands: **W:** lalistadelafm.com/canarias.htm and Guiadelaradio.com

Tourist Radio FM Stations
These stns broadcast in German, English and other languages to tourists visiting the Canary Islands. Most operate 24h
Atlantis FM (GCF) 98.0 (GCL) 101.7MHz **W:** atlantisfm.de – **Buzz FM** (GCL) 88.6, 88.8MHz **W:** buzzfm.fm – **Coast FM** (GC)102.0, 102.3 MHZ –(TF) 102.5, 102.8 MHz and Coast FM, in SW 6230 KHz irregular. **W:** coastfmtenerife.com – **Energy FM** (TFG) 89.2, 95.7MHz **W:** dancemusicradio.net **Express FM** (TFG) 105.3, 94.6MHz **W:** express-fm.net – **Hola FM** (GCF) 95.1MHz **W:** holafm.de – **Holiday FM** (GC, TF) 95.3, 98.2, 99.0, 100.0MHz **W:** holidayfm.com – **Holland FM** (GC) 90.7MHz **W:** hollandfm906.nl – **Horizon FM** (TFG) 89.9, 104.5MHz **W:** horizon.fm – **Mix 101 FM R.** (GC) 101.0, 104.8MHz **W:** mix-radio.net – **Oasis FM** (TFG) 101.0, 101.2 (TF) 91.3, 98.1MHz **W:** oasisfm.com – **On Life FM** (TF) ,90-5,99.7 **W:** onlifefm.tenerife.com – **QFM** (TF) 94.3MHz **W:** qmusica.com – **R. Europa FM (TF)** 100.6 (GCL) 102.5 **W:** radio-europa.fm **R. Mega Welle** (TF) 88.3, 102.0, 104.7MHz (GC) 88.3, 102.0MHz **W:** megawelle.radio.de – **Russkoe R.** 105 FM (TF) 105.0MHz **W:** russkoe-105fm.ru **Spectrum FM** (TF) 105.3MHz **W:** canaries.spectrumfm.net – **R. Syd** (TF) 90.0, 100.6MHz **W:** radiosyd.net – **UK Away FM** (GCL) 99.4, 99.9MHz **W:** ukawayfm.uk – **Vaughan R.** (GC) 96.7 **W:** vaughanradio.com – **Volna FM** (TF) 102.9MHz **W:** volnafm.ru – **Yumbo FM** (GC) 105.1MHz **W:** yumbofm.com

DAB+: TEST in **Channel 7D**, **Tenerife**, Los Cristianos and **Channel 5A Las Palmas, GC**. Stations: Activos; Atlantis; Coast FM; Energy FM; Flow; La Fresca; Mágica FM; Radio 4G.
Channel 9C Arona, Tenerife and **Channel 5C Mogan, GC**. Stations: Loca FM; Loca Latino; Axel 24; Europa FM; Coast FM; Energy FM; Boggie Bunker Radio; Son FM La Salsera.

CAPE VERDE

See CABO VERDE

CAYMAN ISLANDS (UK)

L.T: UTC -5h — **Pop:** 66,000 — **Pr.L:** English — **E.C:** 120V/60Hz — **ITU:** CYM

THE UTILITY REGULATION AND COMPETITION OFFICE (OFREG)
3rd Floor, Alissta Towers, 85 North Sound Rd, Grand Cayman ☎ +1 345 9464282 Fax +1 345 9458284 **E:** info@ofreg.ky **W:** www.ofreg.ky **L.P:** Chair: Linford Pierson

RADIO CAYMAN (Gov., Comm.)
71B Elgin Ave, PO Box 1110, George Town, Grand Cayman KY1-1102 ☎ +1 345 949 7799 Fax +1 345 949 6536 **W:** radiocayman.gov.ky **L.P:** Dir: Norma McField
FM: R. Cayman One: Grand Cayman 89.9MHz 5kW Cayman Brac: 91.9MHz 0.3kW music, current affairs, news: 24h Relays BBCWS 0500-1100 – **Breeze FM:** Grand Cayman 105.3MHz 5kW Cayman Brac: 93.9MHz 0.3kW music and news

CAYMAN ISLANDS NATIONAL WEATHER SERVICE (Gov.)
Cayman Islands Gov't, 88A Owen Roberts Drive, PO Box 10022 APO, Grand Cayman KY1-1001 ☎+1 345 945 5773 **E:** met.office@gov.ky **L.P:** DG John Tibbetts
FM: Cayman Weather Radio: 107.9MHz 1kW

HURLEYS MEDIA LTD. (Comm.)
18 Forum Lane, Camana Bay, PO Box 30110, KY1-1201 Red Bay, Grand Cayman ☎ +1 345 233 9898/9494/9999/1019 **E:** info@hurleysmedia.ky **W:** z99.ky, rooster101.ky, bobfm.ky & iriefm.ky. **L.P:** Pres. & GM: Randy Merren. PD: Jason Howard **FM: Z99:** George Town 99.9MHz 5kW CHR – **Rooster 101.9:** 101.9MHz 5kW Cayman Brac 101.9MHz 1kW country – **Bob 94.9:** George Town 94.9MHz 1kW oldies – **Irie 98.9:** George Town 98.9MHz 2kW Cayman Brac 98.9MHz 0.3kW reggae

ICCI-FM (Educ.)
International College of the Cayman Islands, Newlands, 595 Hirst

Rd, PO Box 136, Grand Cayman KY1-1501. College ☎ +1 345 947 1100 **E:** radio@icci.edu.ky **W:** icci.edu.ky/icci-fm-101-1-radio/ **L.P:** Robert Lynch **FM:** 101.1MHz 0.5kW **D.Prgr:** 24h locally prod. prgrs for residents, or continuous jazz, classical and easy listening music, acc. to availability of student volunteers.

DMS BROADCASTING LTD. (Comm.)
✉ 38 Godfrey Nixon Way, PO Box 31910, Grand Cayman KY1-1208 ☎ + 1 345 943 1367 **E:** info@dmsbroadcasting.ky **W:** dmsbroadcasting.ky **L.P:** MD: Don Seymour. GM: Dan Charleston
FM: CayRock George Town: 96.5MHz (1kW) Cayman Brac: 96.5MHz (0.3kW) – **HOT FM** George Town: 104.1MHz – **KISS FM** George Town 106.1MHz – **X 107.1** George Town 107.1MHz

PRAISE 87.9 RADIO (Rlg.)
✉ 209 Walkers Rd, PO Box 515, George Town, Grand Cayman KY1-1106 ☎ + 1 345 640 2647 **W:** caymanadventist.org **FM:** 87.9MHz Adventist

INTERACTIVE BROADCASTING & MEDIA LTD. (Comm.)
✉ 42 Edward Str, Unit #2, PO Box 976, George Town KY-1102 ☎ + 1 345 943 3600 **W:** star927cayman.ky **L.P:** John Watler.
FM: Star FM 92.7MHz 2.5kW Urban

BIG FISH (Rlg.)
✉ PO Box 1408, Savannah KY-1501 ☎ + 1 345 925 9550 **E:** pam@bigfish955.ky **W:** bigfish955.ky **L.P:** Pamela Norton. **FM:** 95.5MHz 3kW Contemp. Christian

THE VOICE (Rlg.)
✉ Fairbanks Rd, PO Box 12099, George Town KY1-1010 ☎ + 1 345 746 9797 **E:** info@thevoicefm.ky **W:** thevoicefm.ky **FM:** 97.7MHz Gospel

CENTRAL AFRICAN REPUBLIC

L.T: UTC +1h — **Pop:** 4.9 million — **Pr.L:** French (official), Sango (official) — **E.C:** 220V/50Hz — **ITU:** CAF

HAUT CONSEIL DE LA COMMUNICATION (HCC)
✉ BP 2889, Bangui ☎ +236 21616320 **E:** infohcc_centrafrique@yahoo.fr **W:** hcccentrafrique.wordpress.com; www.facebook.com/Haut-Conseil-de-la-Communication-Centrafrique-719150691590785
L.P: Pres: José Richard Pouambi

RADIO CENTRAFRIQUE (Gov.)
✉ B.P. 940, Bangui ☎+236 75503632 **E:** radio.centrafrique@yahoo.fr
L.P: DG: Aimé-Christian Ndotah. PD: Mrs. Pauline Gbianza.
FM: Bangui 106.9MHz 10kW. **D.Prgr in French/Sango:** 24h.

RADIO WATER FOR GOOD (Rlg.)
✉ B.P. 1035, PK 11 Route de Damara, Bangui **W:** waterforgood.org/radio-programs **E:** info@waterforgood.org **L.P:** Dir: Wilfried Ouilibona, Coordinator: Mr. Farel Ndango Zekewane.
SW: Boali 6030 1kW. **D.Prgr.** in French, Sango, Bayaka and Fulfulde: Mon-Sat 0600-1100, daily 1300-1500 on 6030kHz.

RADIO NDEKE LUKA
(joint initiative between the UN Development Programme, CAF government and Hirondelle Foundation)
✉ c/o PNUD, Av. de l'Indépendance, B.P. 872, Bangui ☎+236 72295252. **W:** radiondekeluka.org **L.P:** Dir: Martin Faye.
FM: Bambari/Bangui/Bouar 100.9MHz 1kW. **D.Prgr:** 24h in Sango/French. Also relayed by R. Water for Good, Boali on 6030 kHz between 1500-1700.

Hirondelle-aided community radios (MHz):
R. Barangbaké, Bria: 100.1 – **R. Be Oko,** Bambari: 103.5 – **R. Kuli Ndounga,** Nola: 98.0 – **R. Linga,** Bangui: 96.5 – **R. Magbadja,** Alindao – **R. Maïgaro,** Bouar: 108.0 – **R. Voix de la Pende,** Paoua: 102.6 – **R. Zoukpana,** Berbérati: 105.9 – **Voix de l'Ouham,** Bossangoa: 99.7.

Other Stations (MHz):
Bangui FM: 96.9 **W:** facebook.com/Bangui-FM-1983104095339364
Fréquence RJDH, Bangui: 100.5 **W:** rjdh.org – **Guira FM,** Bangui/others: 93.3 **W:** minusca.unmissions.org/en/guira-fm – **Hit R,** Bangui: 96.1 **W:** facebook.com/hitradiorca – **R. ESCA - Voix de la Grâce,** Bangui: 98.5 **W:** Facebook – **R. La Voix de L'Évangile,** Bangui: 92.1 **W:** facebook.com/radiovoixdelevangile – **R. Life/Alt. FM,** Bangui: 88.5 – **R. Maria**: Bangui 90.9, Bossangoa 103.4 **W:** radiomariacentrafrique.org – **R. Notre Dame,** Bangui: 103.3 1kW **W:** facebook.com/rndbangui – **R. Operation Jericho,** Bangui: 91.7 **W:** facebook.com/Radio-Operation-Jericho-396464763841342 – **R. Sewa,** Bangui: 100.1 **W:** facebook.com/Radiosewa – **R. Siriri,** Bouar: 103.6 **W:** facebook.com/RadioSiriri – **RTN-Radio-Télévision Néhémie,** Bangui: 104.4 **W:** facebook.com/cosolation – **R. Zereda,** Obo: 100.6 **W:** facebook.com/Radio-Zereda- 453484071414186 – **R. Lengo Songo,** Bangui/Bambari/Bria/Bouar: 98.9 **W:** twitter.com/lengosongo

BBC African Sce, Bangui: 90.2MHz.
China R. Int, Bangui: 97.6MHz
RFI Afrique, Bangui: 99.8MHz.
VOA Afrique, Bangui: 102.4MHz

CHAD

L.T: UTC +1h — **Pop:** 17 million — **Pr.L:** Arabic (official), French (official) — **E.C:** 220V/50Hz — **ITU:** TCD

HAUT AUTORITÉ DES MÉDIAS ET DE L'AUDIOVISUEL (HAMA)
✉ BP 1316, N'Djamena ☎ +235 22523151 **E:** hcc.tchad@yahoo.fr

OFFICE NATIONAL DE RADIO ET TÉLÉVISION DU TCHAD (ONRTV, Gov.)
✉ B.P. 892, Av. Mobutu, N'Djamena. ☎+235 22521513 🖷 +235 22521517 **W:** onrtv.td **L.P:** DG: Doubaye Kieoutuin.
Station: N'Djamena-Gredia.
SW: ‡6165kHz 100kW 0430-1900 (inactive).

FM: 94.5MHz 0.1kW. **D.Prgr:** in French/Arabic/others:24h. Local prgr. for N'djamena on 92.5MHz. **Ann:** "Ici N'Djamena, Office National de Radio et Télévision du Tchad".

REGIONAL FM STATIONS
R. Moundou, B.P. 122, Moundou: 94.05/98.3MHz 200/450W – **R. Sarh,** B.P. 270, Sarh: 94.0MHz – **R. Abéché,** B.P. 105, Abéché: 101.0MHz – **R. Faya-Largeau:** 99.1MHz.
F.Pl: 13 more regional stations.

RADIO NDARASON INTERNATIONALE
✉ N'Djamena ☎+235 62935528 **W:** ndarason.com **E:** info@ndarason.com **L.P:** MD: David Smith. Deputu Pr. Dir: Francis Holt.
FM: Liwa 96.0, Bol 98.8, N'Djamena 107.1MHz, all 1kW.
D.Prgr. 24h in Kanuri, Kanembu & others.
Relays on shortwave: see International Radio section.

Other stations:
Al-Bayan FM, N'Djamena: 93.7MHz – **Al-Nasr,** N'Djamena: 102.1MHz – **Dja FM,** N'Djamena: 96.9MHz 0.5kW – **R. Al-Quran,** N'Djamena: 91.0MHz – **R. Arc en Ciel,** N'Djamena: 107.7MHz – **R. Duji Lokar,** Moundou: 101.8MHz 0.5kW – **R. Effata,** Lai: 98.0MHz **W:** dioceselai.com – **R. Évangile Développement,** Pala: 88.5MHz – **FM Liberté,** N'Djamena: 105.3MHz – **R. Harmonie FM,** N'Djamena: 106.3MHz 0.5kW – **R. Lotiko:** Koumra 100.1MHz, Sarh 97.6MHz 0.5kW **W:** sarh.info/membres/nangadoumbaye/Lotiko Radio.html – **R. Terre Nouvelle,** Bangor 99.4MHz 1kW – **La Voix du Paysan,** Doba: 96.2MHz 1kW.

BBC African Sce: N'Djamena 90.6MHz
RFI Afrique: N'Djamena 100.2, Moundou 100.3, Sarh 100.4, Abéché 100.5MHz 1kW.
R. Sawa/VOA: N'Djamena 93.1MHz

CHILE

L.T: UTC -4h (6 Aug 20-4 Apr 21, 5 Sep 21-3 Apr 22: -3h). **NB:** UTC times in schedules refer to DST period — **Pop:** 18.3 million — **Pr.L:** Spanish — **E.C:** 220V/50Hz — **ITU:** CHL — **Int. dialling code:** +56

SUBSECRETARÍA DE TELECOMUNICACIONES
Offices: Amunátegui 139, Santiago ✉ Clasificador 120, Correo 21, Santiago ☎ 2 24213500 🖷 2 26995138 **W:** subtel.cl

ASOCIACIÓN DE RADIODIFUSORES DE CHILE (ARCHI)

Pasaje Matte 966, Piso 8. Of. 801 Santiago ☎2 28898900 🖷2 26394205 **W:** archi.cl

° = on-air stn name not confirmed ‡ = inactive ± = varying freq.

MW	Call	kHz	kW	Station, location, h of tr
MS01)	CB54	540	1	R. Serrano, Melipilla
BB01)	CC55	550	2	R. Corporación, Concepción
AR02)	CD55	550	1	R. Voz de la Tierra, Angol:1000-0200
MS02)	CB57	570		R. Salud 570, Santiago
BB26)	CC59	590	1	CARACOL 590, Concepción: 24h
MC01)	CD59	590	10	R. Pingüino, Punta Arenas
MS03)	CB60	600	10	R. Vida Nueva, Santiago: 1100-0500
CO01)	CA62	620	1	R. Norte Verde, Ovalle
BB03)	CC62	620	10	R. Bío-Bío, Concepción: 24h
VA01)	CB63	630	10	R. Stela Maris, Valparaíso
AR03)	CD64	640	1	R. Cooperativa, Temuco: 24h
MA13)	CC64	640	0.25	R. Portales, Curico
MS26)	CB66	660	50	R. Colo Colo, Santiago
BB04)	CC68	680	10	R. Cooperativa, Concepción: 24h
MS05)	CB69	690	10	R. Santiago, Santiago
LL02)	CD69	‡690	10	R. Estrella del Mar (R.Maria), Ancud: 24h
LR01)	CD70	700	1	Nueva R. Valdivia, Valdivia
MC02)	CD70A	700	5	R. Magallanes, Punta Arenas: 24h
BB07)	CC72	720	1	R. Interamericana, Concepción
TA09)	CA72	720	1	R. Portales, Iquique
VA02)	CB73	730	10	R. Cooperativa AM, Valparaíso: 24h
BB19)	CD73	730	1	R. Angelina, Los Angeles
MS06)	CB76	760	50	R. Cooperativa, Santiago: 24h
AR10)	CD127	770	5	R. Agricultura, Temuco: 24h
LL04)	CD77	770	1	R. Cooperativa, Castro: 24h
LL05)	CD78	780	10	R. Sago, Osorno
VA03)	CB80	800	5/1	R. Maria, Viña del Mar: 24h
CO02)	CA82B	‡820	10/1	R. La Serena, La Serena
BB05)	CC82	‡820	1	R. UCSC, Concepción
LR02)	CD82	820	1	R. Concordia, La Unión: 24h
MS07)	CB82	820		R. Carabineros, Santiago
VA04)	CB84	840	10	R. Portales, Valparaíso
AS03)	CD84	840	10	R. Santa María, Coyhaique
BB06)	CC86	860	10	R. Inés de Suárez, Concepción: 24h
BB27)	CC89	890	1	R. Nuevo Mundo, Concepcion
MS08)	CB88	880	10	R. Universal, Santiago: 24h
BB08)	CC90	‡900	1	R. Nuble, Chillán: 1100-0400
LL07)	CD90	900	1	R. LV de la Costa, Osorno:0930-0300
VA21)	CB90	900	1	R. Corporacion, Viña del Mar
MA14)	CC91	910	1	R. Tropical Latina (RTL), Talca
AR04)	CD92	920	1	R. 920, Temuco: 1000-0300
MS09)	CB93	±930	10	R. Nuevo Mundo, Santiago: 24h
LL08)	CD93	930	10	R. Reloncaví (R. Cooperativa), Puerto Montt: 24h
VA06)	CB94	940	1	R. Valentín Letelier, Valparaíso
MS10)	CB96	960	10	Dossil Radio Chile, Santiago
MC04)	CD96	960	10	R. Polar, Punta Arenas
MA01)	CC97	970	1	R. Lautaro, Talca: 1000-0500
AS04)	CD97A	970	1	R. Patagonia Chilena, Coyhaique
LR03)	CD97	970	1	R. Austral, Valdivia
VA07)	CB98	980	10	R. Corporacion, Valparaíso
MS11)	CB100	1000	10	BBN R., Santiago
AR22)	CD101	‡1010	10	R. Nielol, Temuco
MA02)	CC102	1020	5	R. Amiga,Talca
BB25)	CC103	1030	10	R. Chilena, Concepción: 1000-0300
MS12)	CB103	1030	1	R. Progreso, Talagante
LL10)	CD103	1030	1	R. Chiloé, Castro:1100-0330
MC05)	CD103A	1030	1	R. Payne AM, Puerto Natales
MS13)	CB106	1060	100	R. Inolvidable, Santiago: 24h
CO03)	CA108	‡1080	1	Vicuña
AR07)	CD108	1080	1	R. Los Confines, Angol
LL23)	CD109	1090	5	Castro
MA11)	CC109	1090	5/1	R. Chilena del Maule, Talca: 1000-0300
VA08	CB110	1100	10	BBN R. Viña del Mar
AR08)	CD111	1110	10	R. La Frontera, Temuco: 0900-0400
MS14)	CB114	1140	100	R. Nacional, Santiago
MA04)	CC116	‡1160	1	R. Ancoa, Linares
AR01)	CD116A	1160	1	R. Baha'i, Temuco: 0930-0130
MC06)	CD117	1170	5	R. Natales, Puerto Natales: 24
MS15)	CB118	±1180	50	R. Portales, Santiago: 24h
BB20)	CD120	1200	10	R. Agricultura, Los Angeles
LL12)	CD121	‡1210	1	Puerto Montt
MA05)	CC121	1210	1	R. Universidad de Talca, Talca: 24h
VA20)	CB121	1210		R. Valparaiso, Valparaiso
AR09)	CD122	1220	10	R. Maria, Temuco
AN08)	CA124	1240	0.25	R. Club Chuquicamate, Calma
MS16)	CB124	1240	25	R. Universidad de Santiago, Santiago
LR04)	CD125	1250	10	R. Pilmaiquen, Valdivia: 24h
MA06)	CC126	1260	1	R. Condell, Curicó
MC07)	CD126	‡1260	10	R. Maria, Punta Arenas
AR24)	CD134A	1270		R.Mirador, Temuco
VA09)	CB127	±1270	5	R. Festival, Viña del Mar: 1000-0400
LL14)	CD128	1280	1	R. la Palabra, Osorno
AN07)	CA129	‡1290	0.25	R. Coya, Los Angeles
MS25)	CB130	1300	1	R. Conexiones, Santiago: 1200-0300
BB21)	CD132	‡1320	1	R. Lincoyan, Mulchén
MS17)	CB133	1330	3	R. Romance, Santiago: 24h
LL16)	CD133	1330	3/1.5	R. Vicente Pérez Rosales, Puerto Montt
VA10)	CB134	1340	10	R. Colo Colo, Valparaíso: 24h
BB11)	CC134	±1340	1	R. La Discusión, Chillán: 24h
LR06)	CD134	1340	1	R. Vida Nueva, Panguipulli
CO06)	CA135	1350	1	R. Riquelme, Coquimbo: 1030-0430
LL24)	CD135	‡1350	0.02	Puerto Montt
BB12)	CC136	1360	5	R. Universidad Bio Bio, Concepcion: 24h
AR11)	CD137	1370	1	R. Vida Nueva, Temuco: 1100-0500
MS18)	CB138	1380	50	R. Plenitud, Santiago: 24h
BB22)	CD140	1400	5	R. La Amistad, Los Angeles
LL18)	CD140A	1400	5	R. Maria, Puerto Montt
VA11)	CB141	1410	5	R. Amor, Valparaiso
AR12)	CD141	1410	1	R. Loncoche, Loncoche
MS19)	CB142	±1420	1	R. Panamericana, Santiago: 1000-0200
GB06)	CC143	‡1430	1	R. Rumbos,Rancagua
BB13)	CC144	1440	1	R. El Sembrador, Chillán: 1000-0230
CO07)	C144A	1440	1	Tu Radio Popular, La Serene: 24h
VA12)	CB145	1450	1	R. Universidad Técnica "Federico Santa María, Valparaíso
MA08)	CC145	1450	4	R. Tropical Latina – RTL, Curicó: 24h
MS20)	CB146	1460	1	R. Palabra Viva, Santiago
BB14)	CC146	1460	1	R. Armonía, Talcahuano
MC09)	CD146B	1460		R. Ona Porvinir
VA13)	CB147	1470	1	R. Sargento Aldea, San Antonio
BB15)	CC148	1480	1	R. La Amistad de Tomé, Tomé
CO08)	CA148	1480	1	R. Comunicativa, Ovalle
AT06)	CA149	‡1490	1	R. Alicanto, El Salvador
MS21)	CB149	1490	0.25	La Mexicana, San Bernardo
MC08)	CD150	1500	1	R. Tierra del Fuego, Porvenir
VA14)	CB150	1500	1	R. Trasandina, Los Andes: 24h, Sun 2000-2200
CO09)	CA151	1510	1/0.5	R. Luís Alvarez Sierra, Illapel: 1000-0100 (Sat: -0400), Sun 1100-0100
GB02)	CC151	1510	1	R. Rancagua, Rancagua: 24h
MA10)	CC152	1520	1	R. Soberanía, Linares: 0930-0005
VA15)	CB152	‡1520	1	R. Integración, San Antonio
AT05)	CA153	1530	1	R. Vida Nueva, Copiapó: 1100-0500
BB16)	CC153	1530	1	R.Patagual, Coronel
VA16)	CB153	1530	1	R. Nexo, Quillota: 1000-0300
BB17)	CC154	‡1540	1	R. Portales, Chillán
LR05)	CD154	±1540	1	R. San José de Alcudia, Río Bueno:
MS22)	CB144	1540		R. Sudamerica, Santiago
VA17)	CB155	1550	1	R. Provincial AM, Putaendo
GB03)	CC155	±1550	1	R. Manuel Rodríguez, San Fernando:
MS23)	CB156	1560	1	R. Manantial, Talagante: 1000-0300 (Sat.: -0500)
AR16)	CD156	1560	1	R. Parque, Villarrica
GB04)	CC157	±1570	1	R. Cristo Llama Al Pecador, Rancagua: 24h
MA11)	CC157A	1570	1	R. Familia del Maule, Talca: 1000-0300
GB05)	CC158	1580	1	R. Colchagua, Santa Cruz
VA18)	CB159	±1590	1	R. Aconcagua, San Felipe: 1000-2300
MA15)	CC159A	‡1590	0.1	Parral
MS24)	CB160	1600	0.25	R. Nuevo Tiempo, Santiago: 24h
VA19)	CB160A	1600	0.25	R. Fe, Viña del Mar
BB18)	CC160	±1600	0.25	R. Llacolén, Concepción
AR23)	CD160	1600	0.25	R. Alternativa, Temuco: 1000-0100

SW	kHz	kW	Station, location, h of tr
MS27)	5825	0.1	R. Triunfal Evangelica, Talagante: 2200-0000 exc. Thu.

Addresses & other information:

AN00 (ANTOFAGASTA – Region II):

AN07) Av Ignacio Carrera Pinto No 401-A, María Elena ☎55 641176 **E:** contacto@radiocoya.cl - **FM:** 92.5 MHz – **AN08)** P.O.Box 13630, Calama **W:** ce1rch.cl **E:** contacto@ce1rch.cl

AR00 (ARAUCANIA – Region IX):
AR01) Cl 1Norte 0684, Labranza, Temuco ☎45 2375142 **W:** radio.bahai.cl – **AR02)** Av. Bernardo O'Higgins 297, piso 2, Angol ☎45 2712331 **E:** radiovozdelatierra@gmail.com – **AR03)** Temuco **W:** cooperativa.cl **E:** internet@cooperativa.cl - **FM:** 103.1 MHz – **AR04)** Portales 527, Temuco ☎45 2277148 **W:** radionueveveinte.com **E:** radionueveveinte@gmail.com – **AR07)** Lautaro 124 Piso 2, Angol ☎45 2413647 **W:** losconfines.cl - **FM:** 94.9MHz – **AR08)** Av Caupolicán 110 Of 2003 Piso 20, Temuco ☎45 213166 **W:** araucanayfrontera.cl **E:** araucanaradio@gmail.com - **FM:** 95.9MHz «La Araucana» – **AR09)** Temuco **W:** radiomaria.cl **E:** contacto@radiomaria.cl – **AR10)** Lynch 6464, Temuco ☎45 213854 **W:** radioagricultura.cl – **AR11)** Av. Maquehue 1115 - Padre las Casas, Temuco ☎452 734948 **W:** radiovidanuevaencristojesus.cl – **AR12)** Ignacio Serrano 264, Loncoche 📠45 2471052 **W:** radioloncoche.cl **E:** radiocd141@gmail.com - **FM:** 105.9MHz «Vibración» – **AR16)** Vicente Reyes 528, Villarrica ☎45 411567 **W:** radioparque.cl **E:** radiopnacional@gmail.com – **AR22)** Temuco. – **AR23)** Manuel Montt 381-C, Temuco ☎45 2483356 **W:** radioalternativa.cl – **AR24)** Temuco ☎45 232-3100 **W:** mirador.FM **E:** radiomirador@gmail.com
AS00) (AISÉN – Region XI)
AS03) Francisco Bilbao 691, Coyhaique ☎67 2232398 📠67 2231306 **W:** radiosantamaria.cl **E:** contacto@radiosantamaria.cl – **FM:** 102.3MHz – **AS04)** Av Francisco Bilboa 457 ☎67 245632 **W:** radiopatagoniachilena.cl **E:** radiopatagoniachilena@gmail.com - **FM:** 99.3MHz «Acro Iris»
AT00 (ATACAMA – Region III):
AT05) Colipi 371, Copiapo ☎52 212031 **W:** radiovidanuevaencristojesus.com – **AT06)** Av. El Tofo 535, Diego de Almagro ☎52 2475023
BB00 (BIO BIO – Region VIII): 648, 2° piso, Concepción ☎41 2738650 **W:** radio-corpora
BB01) Angol cion.cl **E:** contacto@radio-corporacion.cl – **BB03)** O'Higgins 680, Piso 3, Concepción ☎41 2620620 **W:** radiobiobio.cl **E:** biobio@laradio.cl - **FM:** 98.1MHz – **BB04)** Paicavi 119, 2° piso, (Plaza Peru) (or Cas. 2337), Concepción **W:** cooperativa.cl **E:** internet@cooperativa.cl – **FM:** 93.3 MHz– **BB05)** Campus San Andres, Alonso de Ribera 2850, Concepción ☎41 2345000 📠41 2345001**W:** ucsc.cl/ucsc-radio – **BB06)** Castellón 477, 3° piso, 4030000 Concepción ☎41 246 0486 **W:** Facebook.com/radioines **E:** inesdesuarez860am@gmail.com – **BB07)** Calle Barros Arana 871, 5° piso, Of. 51, Concepción ☎41 2214450 **W:** radiointeramericana.cl **E:** contacto@radiointeramericana.cl – **BB08)** 5 de Abril 655, Chillán ☎42 2215530 **W:** radionuble.cl/ **E:** radiocontigo@gmail.com - **FM:** 89.7MHz "R.Nuble" – **BB11)** 18 de Septiembre 721, 3780000 Chillán ☎9 8888 7859 **W:** ladiscusion.cl **E:** radiotv@ladiscusion.cl - **FM:** 94.7MHz – **BB12)** Avd Collao 1202, Casilla 5-C, Concepción ☎📠41 3111 1040 **W:** radioubb.cl E: ubb@ubiobio.cl – **BB13)** Arauco 447, Chillán ☎📠42 2224603 **W:** radioelsembrador.cl **E:** administracion@radioelsembrador.cl - **FM:** 104.7MHz «Aurora FM» – **BB14)** Av.Los Carrera N° 464, Concepcion ☎41 2854594 **W:** armonia.cl **E:** concepcion@armonia.cl - **FM:** 99.5 MHz – **BB15)** Sotomayor 1184 2° piso of 203, Tomé ☎41 2650657 **W:** radiolaamistaddetome.cl **E:** radio@laamistad.tie.cl – **BB16)** Calle Vilumilla 689-B, Coronel ☎**44 289 5074 W:** radiopatagual.cl **E:**radiopatagual@gmail.com – **B17)** Chillán – **BB18)** Calle Barros Arana, Concepción ☎41 2244354 **W:** radiollacolen.com **E:** radiollacolen@gmail.com – **BB19)** Colo-Colo 451 Of. 120, Nivel 2, Los Angeles ☎43 2349920 **E:** contacto@radiocamila.cl - **FM:** 98.3 MHz – **BB20)** Calle Janequeo 615, Los Angeles ☎43 324212 **W:** radioagricultura.cl – **BB21)** Mulchén – **BB22)** Lautaro 279, Departemento 301, Los Angeles 📠43 2329834 **W:** radiolaamistad.cl **E:** radiolaamistad@gmail.com – **BB25)** Arzobispado de la Santísima Concepción, Barros Arana 544, 3° piso, Concepción ☎41 2626167 **W:** radiochilenaconcepcion.cl **E:** contacto@radiochilenaconcepcion.cl – **BB26)** Castellón 746, 2° piso, Concepcion ☎41 2460193 **W:** radiocaracol590.cl– **BB27)** Perez Valenzuela 1620, Cncepcion **W.:** radionuevomundo.cl
CO00 (COQUIMBO – Region IV):
CO01) Ca Santiago 355, Ovalle ☎53 2620359 **W:** radionorteverde.cl **E:** radionorteverde@gmail.com – **CO02)** Av. Trancisco de Aguirre 337 of. 6, La Serena ☎51 2674414 **W:** radiolaserena.cl **E:** laserena@gmail.com – **CO03)** Vicuña – **CO06)** Aldunate 1619, Coquimbo ☎51 2321051 **W:** radioriquelme.cl – **CO07)**Merceds Alvarez 3140 Sindempar , La Serena ☎6353 6299 **W:** radiolaserena.cl – **CO08)** Pedro Montt 181, Ovalle **W:** radiocomunicativa.cl **E:** radiocomunicativa@gmail.com - **FM:** 93.7 MHz – **CO09)** Constitución 060, Illapel ☎53 2521295 **W:** juanpabloylas.cl **E:** lradios@gmail.com - **FM:** 100.9MHz

GB00 (O'HIGGINS – Region VI):
GB02) Pasaje Hoffman 061, 2841046 Rancagua ☎72 2243538 **W:** radiorancagua.cl – **GB03)** Altos Mercado, calle Chacabuco esq. España, San Fernando ☎📠72 714267 **E:** cc155laradio@hotmail.com – **GB04)** Ca Santa Maria 126, Rancagua ☎72 2242741 **W:** https//radio1570.wixsite.com/cristollamaalpecador **E:** radio_1570@hotmail.com – **GB05)** Av Gonzalo Bulnes 45, Santa Cruz ☎📠72 2822193 **E:** radiolunasantacruzana@gmail.com - **FM:** 88.1 MHz «Ensueño» – **GB06)**O`carrol 535, Rancagua ☎72 2334515 **W.:** radiorumbos.cl **E.:** comunicaciones.rancagua@iglesia.cl**LL00**
(LOS LAGOS – Region X):
LL02) Elutero Ramírez 207, Ancud ☎56 65622722 **W:** radioestrelladelmar.cl – **LL04)** Thompson 255 (Cas. 174), Castro **W:** cooperativa.cl **E:** internet@cooperativa.cl – **LL05)** Juan Mckenna 904, Osorno ☎64 2321601 **W:** radiosago.cl **E:** mcifuentes@radiosago.cl - **FM:** 94.5 MHz – **LL07)** Cochrane 746, Osorno ☎64 312525 **W:** radiovozdelacosta.cl **E:** radiolavozdelacosta@hotmail.com – **LL08)** Egana 29, Puerto Montt ☎65 2252234 **W:** radioreloncavi.cl – **LL10)** Bernardo O'Higgins 486 (Cas. 106), Castro ☎ 65 2632260 **W:** radiochiloe.cl **E:** contacto@radiochiloe.cl - **FM:** 90.1MHz «Martin Ruiz de Gamboa» – **LL12)** Av Presidente Ibañez No 872 Piso 2, Puerto Montt ☎65 383290 **W.** armonia.cl **E:** puertomontt@armonia.cl – **LL14)** Eleuterio Ramírez 1050 Dpto.41,, Osorno ☎64 2237440 **W:** radiolapalabra.cl **E:** tuprogramas@radiolapalabra.cl - **FM:** 101.5MHz «La Palabra» – **LL16)** Talca 72 piso2, Puerto Montt ☎65 258439 – **LL18)** Puerto Montt **W:** radiomaria.cl **E:** contacto@radiomaria.cl - **FM:** 103.5 MHz – **LL22)** Pedro Lagos 295, Río Bueno ☎64 2341531 **W:** radiosanjosedealcudia.cl **E:** radio@radiosanjosedealcudia.cl – **LL23)** Castro – **LL24)** Puerto Montt – **LL25)**Lord Cochrane No 746, Puerto Montt W.: radionuevomundo.cl
LR00 (LOS RIOS – Region XIV):
LR01) Arauco 340 Piso 3 Of. 307, Valdivia **W:** FB: Radio Nueva Valdivia – **LR02)** Arturo Prat 466, La Unión ☎64 2322275 **W:** radioconcordia.cl – **LR03)** Arauco 363 3° piso, Valdivia ☎63 2202642 **W:** radioaustralvaldivia. **E:** radioaustral@surnet.cl – **LR04)** Arauco No 340 4 Piso, Valdiva ☎63 2202642 **W:** radiopilmaiquen.cl - **FM:** 98.9 MHz – **LR05)** Pedro Lagos 295, Río Bueno ☎64 2341531 **W:** radiosanjosedealcudia.cl **E:** radio@radiosanjosedealcudia.cl – **LR06)** Bernard O'Higgins 793, Panguipulli. ☎63 2310796 **W:** radiovidanuevaencristojesus.com
MA00 (MAULE – Region VII):
MA01) Tres Sur 767 1 Ote y Pte., Talca ☎71 2970758 **W:** Facebook.com/RadioLautaro **E:** radiolautaro@gmail.com – **MA02)** Avenida Diagonal Isidoro Del Solar 237, Talca ☎71 224333 **W:** facebook.com/pages/category/Radio-Station/Radio-Amiga-de-Talca-451473828270400/ – **MA04)** Independencia 631, Linares ☎76 2612320**W:** radioancoa.cl - **FM:** 103.5MHz – **MA05)** Casa 2 Norte 685, Talca ☎71 200160 **W:** radioemisoras.utalca.cl **E:** storres@utalca.cl - **FM:** 102., 93.7MHz – **MA06)** Carmen 714, Curicó. ☎75 2543520 **W:** radiocondell.cl **E:** direccion@radiocondell.cl - **FM:** 92.7MHz – **MA08)** Maule CL Manuel Montt 198, Curicó ☎75 2328021 **W:** radiortl.cl **E:** publicidadrtl@gmail.com - **FM:** 95.5MHz – **MA10)** Diputado Dario Dueñas 777, Linares ☎73 2210277 **W:** radiosoberania.es.tl **E:** soberania@hotmail.com – **MA11)** 2 Poniente No 1150, 1240000 Talca ☎71 268 6120 **W:** radiochilenadelmaule.cl **E:** contacto@radiochilenadelmaule.cl **FM:** 90.9 MHz – **MA13)** Villouta N° 558, Curico **W:** radiocorporacioncurico.cl – **MA14)** Manuel Montt 198, Curico ☎75 328021 **W:** radiortl.cl **E:** publicidadrtl@gmail.com – **MA15)** Parral
MC00 (MAGALLANES Y DE LA ANTARCTICA CHILENA – Region XII):
MC01) Av España 959, 6200 623 Punta Arenas ☎61 2292900 **W:** elpinguino.com **E:** secretaria@elpinguino.com - **FM:** 95.3MHz – **MC02)** José Nogueira 1370, Punta Arenas ☎61 2243551 **W:** radiomagallanes.cl **E:** prensa@radiomagallanes.cl – **MC04)** Bories 871 Piso 2, Punta Arenas ☎61 2241417 **W:** radiopolar.com **E:** secretaria@radiopolar.com - **FM:** 96.5-98.5-105.7MHz «Finísima» – **MC05)** Cl Bulnes 819, Puerto Natales ☎61 2411450 **E:** famm1605@hotmail.com - **FM:** 89.5 MHz – **MC06)** Eberhard 212, Puerto Natales ☎61 2413034 **W:** radionatales.cl **E:** radionatales@yahoo.es – **MC07)** Punta Arenas **W:** radiomaria.cl - **FM:** 88.9 MHz – **MC08)** Bulnes 449, Porvenir ☎61 2580100 **W:** radiotierradelfuego.cl **E:** director@radiotierradelfuego.cl – **MC09)** Sampaio, Porvinir ☎61 258-0258 **W:** radioona.cl **E:** fmporvinir@gmail.com
MS00 (METROPOLITANA DE SANTIAGO – Region RM):
MS01) Cla Ortuzar 935, 9580000 Melipilla ☎ 2 28323440 **W:** radioserrano.cl **E:** radio.claudia@gmail.com - **FM:** 104.5MHz R.Carica – **MS02)** Santiago ☎32 3172827 **W:** radiosalud.cl **E:**

contacto@radiosalud.cl – **MS03)** Los Jazmines 6065, Estación Central, Santiago ☎2 3269 1181 **W:** radiovidanuevaencristojesus.cl **E:** contato@radiovidanuevaencristojesus.cl - **FM:** 106.7 MHz – **MS05)** Triana 868, Providencia, Santiago. ☎2 2236 0096 **W:** radiosantiago.cl **E:** contacto@radiosantiago.cl – **MS06)** Maipú 525, Santiago 8350372 **W:** cooperativa.cl **E:** internet@cooperativa.cl ☎2 32648000 – **FM:** 93.3 MHz – **MS07)** Av. Bernardo O´Higgins 1196 **W:** carabineros.cl **E:** radioemisora@carabineros.cl – **FM:** 98.1 MHz – **MS08)** Alameda 4263, Estación Central ☎2 277 97261 **W:** radiocolocolo.cl **E:** contacto@radiocolocolo.cl – **MS09)** San Pablo 2271, Santiago ☎2 26883175 **W:** radionuevomundo.cl **E:** info@radionuevomundo.cl – **MS10)** Avenida BrasilSantiago ☎9 4006 6027 **W:** panamericanachile.cl **E:** rpanamericanachile@gmail.com – **MS11)** Paseo Bulnes 120, Oficina 72, Santiago Centro a metros de la Alameda ☎2 26718602 **W:** bbnradio.org **E:** red@bbnmedia.org – **MS12)** Enrique Alcalde 1081, Talagante ☎2 8153279 **W:** Facebook.com/radioprogresotalagante/ – **MS13)** Santiago ☎2 22258544 **W:** radiomaria.cl **E:** contacto@radiomaria.cl – **MS14)** Dardignac 196 Oficina 22, Bellavista-Patronato, Santiago ☎2 17370101 **W:** nacionaldechile.cl **F.** radio@nacionaldechile.cl – **MS15)** Fanor Velasco 11, Santiago ☎2 26960628 **W:** radioportales.cl **E:** administracion@radioportales.cl. – **MS16)** Alameda 3363, Estación Central, Santiago ☎2 7181722 **W:** radiousach.cl **E:** radio@usach.cl – **MS17)** Los Leones 668, Providencia, Santiago ☎2 25836602 **W:** radioromance.cl – **FM:** 92.9 MHz – **MS18)** Alcalde Jorge Monckeberg 2398, Macul, Santiago ☎41 313 5871 **W:** radioplenitude.cl **E.:** contacto@radioplenitude.cl – **MS19)** Gran Avenida Jose Miguel Carrera 5848, 4° piso, San Miguel, Santiago ☎2 22 4160725 **W:** panamericanachile.cl – **MS20)** Ubicado en Carmen No 1436, Santiago Central ☎2 25511378 **W:** radiopalabraviva.cl **E:** contacto@radiopalabraviva.cl – **MS21)** Av. Portales 3020 – Casilla 380, San Bernardo ☎2 2841 4135 – **MS22)** Santiago ☎22 527 3999 **W:** radiosudamerica.cl **E:** contacto@radiosudamerica.cl – **MS23)** Av. Bernardo O'Higgins 854, Talagante ☎2 28151374 **W:** radiomanantial.cl **E:** radiomanantialtalagante@gmail.com - **FM:** 102.9 MHz «Embrujo FM» – **MS24)** Los Cerezos No 6251, Peñalolén, Santiago ☎2 22844921 **W:** nuevotiempo.cl **E:** contactos@nuevotiempo.cl – **MS25)** Purisima 251, Recoleta, Santiago ☎22 7233757 **W:** radioconexiones.tk **E:** radioconexiones1300am@gmail.com – **MS26)** Santiago – **MS27)** Barraza Baja, Talagante ☎ 2 28154375 **W:** FB **E.:** radiotriunfal@gmail.com

TA00 (TARAPACA – Region I):
TA09) Iquique **W:** radioportales.cl

VA00 (VALPARAISO – Region V):
VA01) Pedro Montt 1766 (Cas. 3304), 234000 Valparaíso ☎32 259 5325 **W:** radiostellamaris.cl **E:** contacto@radiostellamaris.cl – **VA02)** Morris No 106, Depto. 155, Piso 15, Valparaiso **W:** cooperativa.cl **E:** internet@cooperativa.cl – **VA03)** Viña del Mar **W:** radiomaria.cl **E:** contacto@radiomaria.cl – **VA04)** Condell 1190 Of 21, Valparaíso. Machupe language Mo/We/Fri – 1200-1300 ☎32 32 225 1543 **W:** portalesfm.cl **E:** contacto@portalesfm.cl - **FM:** 89.5MHz – **VA06)** Av. Errazuriz 2120, Valparaíso ☎32 2507657 **W:** rvl.uv.cl **E:** radio@uv.cl - **FM:** 97.3MHz – **VA07)** Av. Pedro Montt 1868, Valparaíso ☎32 336 9260 **W.:** radiocorporacionvalparaiso.cl **E.:** radiocorporacionvalparaiso@gmail.com – **VA08)** Calle 9 Norte 761, oficina 408 ☎32 3356067 **W:** bbnradio.org **E:** red@bbnmedia.org – **VA09)** Ca Quinta 124 Segundo Nivel Oficina A, Viña del Mar ☎32 2684251 **W:** radiofestival.cl **E:** servicios@festival.cl – **VA10)** Plaza de la Justicia 45, Piso 7 Of. 704, Valparaíso ☎32 2566664 **W:**facebook.com/radiocolcolovalparaiso/?rf=1467497243468037 **E:** radiocolocolovapo@gmail.com – **VA11)** 1 ½ Poniente #443 (Entre 4 y 5, Viña del Mar ☎32 3172827 **W:** radioamor.cl – **FM:** 99.3 MHz – **VA12)** Av. España 1680, Valparaíso ☎🖷32 2797511 **W:** radio.utfsm.cl - **FM:** 99.7MHz – **VA13)** Av. Barros Luco 1678 (✉ Cas. 68,Correo 2) San Antonio ☎35 211321 - **FM:** 90.9 MHz – **VA14)** Papudo 155, Los Andes ☎34 2421425 **W:** Facebook.com/radiotrasandina **E:** publicidadtrasandina@gmail.com – **VA15)** San Antonio – **VA16)** Blanco 185, Quillota ☎33 2268001 **W:** radiolibra.cl **E:** gerencia@radiolibra.cl - **FM:** 104.7MHz «Libra Stereo FM» – **VA17)** Arturo Prat Poniente no 565, Of 5 Piso 2, Putaendo ☎34 502762 **W:** radioprovincialdeputaendo.cl – **VA18)** Santo Domigo 99 - oficina 4, San Felipe ☎34 2510198 **W:** radioaconcagua.cl **E:** ecornejo@radioaconcagua.cl - **FM:** 91.7MHz – **VA19)** Calle Chacabuco 2370, Valparaiso ☎32 3195694 **W:** radiofe.cl/radio/ – **VA20)** Eusebio Lillo 520, local 12, edifico Torre Valparaiso, Valparaiso ☎32 3148080 **W:** radiovalparaiso.cl **E:** prensa@radiovalparaiso.cl - **FM:** 97.7 & 102.5 MHz – **VA21)**Valparaiso 1233, Viña del Mar ☎32 211-5966 **W:** radiocorporacionvinadelmar.cl **E:** corporacionvdelmar@gmail.com

FM in Santiago (all MHz, 1-10kW) **Slogans:** Name + «FM»:MS26) 88.1 Aurora – 88.5 Concierto – **MS14)** 88.9 R. Futuro – **MS13)** 89.3 R. Maria – **MS26)** 89.7 Duna – 90.5 Pudahuel – 91.3 El Conquistador – 91.7 Amistad – 92.5 Radioactiva – 92.9 Romance – 93.3 La Cooperativa – 93.7 Universo – **VA02)** 94.1 Rock & Pop – 95.3 40 principales – **MS25)** 95.9 Tiempo – 96.5 Beethoven – 97.1 Caracol – 97.7 Zero – 98.5 FM 2 – **MS08)** 99.3 Carolina – 99.7 Bío Bío – **MS25)** 100.1 Infinita – **MS26)** 100.9 – 101.3 Corazón – 101.7 FM Hit – 102.1 Oasis – 102.5 Univ. de Chile – 103.3 Horizonte – **MS12)** 103.9 R. Contacto – 104.1 Romantica – **MS03)** 104.5 Monumental – 104.9 Nina – 105.7 Para ti – 106.3 Armonía – **MS11)** 106.9 Sintonía – 107.5 Fantasía

CHINA (People's Rep. of)

L.T: UTC +8h — **Pop:** 1,434 million — **Pr.L:** Standard Chinese (official), Chinese dialects (Amoy, Cantonese, Chaozhou, Hakka, Mandarin), Kazakh, Korean, Mongolian, Tibetan, Uighur, Zhuang — **E.C:** 220V/50Hz — **ITU:** CHN

MINISTRY OF INDUSTRY AND INFORMATION TECHNOLOGY

🖃 13 Xi Chang'an Jie, Beijing 100804 **W:** miit.gov.cn **L.P:** Minister: Miao Wei

NATIONAL RADIO AND TELEVISION ADMINISTRATION (STATE ADMINISTRATION OF RADIO AND TELEVISION) (Gov)

🖃 2 Fuxingmenwai Dajie, Beijing 100866 or PO.Box 4501, Beijing ☎ +86 10 6809 2707 🖷 +86 10 6851 2174
W: www.nrta.gov.cn **L.P:** Dir: Nie Chenxi

CHINA MEDIA GROUP (Gov.)

(Zhongyang Guangbo Dianshi Zongdai, Central Radio Television General Station)
🖃 11 Fuxing Lu, Beijing 100859, Beijing. **L.P:** Dir: Shen Haixiong
Founded in 2018 as the administrator of China National Radio (CNR), China Central Television and China Radio International (see International radio section).

Official P.R.C. Abbreviations: The 31 regions of the People's Republic of China, with their abbreviations and names in Pinyin (Chinese Phonetic Alphabet) version followed by the old spelling in brackets:
AH: Anhui (Anhwei) – BJ: Beijing M. (Peking) – CQ: Chongqing M. (Chungking) – EB: Hebei (Hopeh) – EN: Henan (Honan) – FJ: Fujian (Fukien) – GD: Guangdong (Kwangtung) – GS: Gansu (Kansu) – GX: Guangxi Zhuang A.R. (Kwangsi) – GZ: Guizhou (Kweichow) – HAN: Hainan (Hainan) – HB: Hubei (Hupeh) – HL: Heilongjiang (Heilungkiang) – HN: Hunan (Hunan) – JL: Jilin (Kirin) – JS: Jiangsu (Kiangsu) – JX: Jiangxi (Kiangsi) – LN: Liaoning (Liaoning) – NM: Nei Menggu A.R. (Inner Mongolia) – NX: Ningxia Hui A.R. (Ningsia) – QH: Qinghai (Tsinghai) – SC: Sichuan (Szechwan) – SD: Shandong (Shantung) – SH: Shanghai M. (Shanghai) – SN: Shaanxi (Shensi) – SX: Shanxi (Shansi) – TJ: Tianjin M. (Tientsin) – XJ: Xinjiang Uighur A.R. (Sinkiang) – XZ: Xizang A.R.(Tibet) – YN: Yunnan (Yunnan) – ZJ: Zhejiang (Chekiang).

Regional Services: Add "Renmin Guangbo Diantai" (People's Broadcasting Station) to the stn name shown in the table below to obtain the full name in Standard Chinese.
Abbreviations: 1 = 1st prgr, 2 = 2nd prgr, 3 = 3rd prgr; EBS = Economic Broadcasting Station.
Languages: Standard Chinese (Putonghua), based on the Beijing dialect, is used in broadcasts throughout China. Various dialects and minority languages are included in the relevant regional services and in broadcasts to Taiwan.
Abbreviations: Ch = Standard Chinese, Kg = Kirghiz, Ko = Korean, Kz = Kazakh, Mo = Mongolian, Tb = Tibetan, Ug = Uighur.

MW	kHz	kW	Station	Tx Location
ZJ1)	531	10	Zhejiang	Jinhua
1)	540	50	CNR 1	Shenyang/Hefei
QH4)	540	10	Haixi	Da Qaidam
1)	549	1200	CNR 5	Putian, FJ
EN2)	549	25	Zhengzhou	
EB1)	558	3	Hebei	Shijiazhuang

MW	kHz	kW	Station	Tx Location
FJ1)	558	50	Fujian	Jianyang
FJ1)	558	10	Fujian	Longyan
FJ1)	558	10	Fujian	Pingtan
FJ1)	558	10	Fujian	Putian
FJ1)	558	10	Fujian	Xiamen
FJ1)	558	10	Fujian	Xiapu
NM17)	558	1	Zalantun	
XJ1)	558	120	Xinjiang	Hutubi
YN16)	558	10	Nujiang	Lushui
1)	567	10	CNR 1	Lianyungang, JS
EN17)	567	10	Zhoukou	
TJ1)	567	20	Tianjin	
EN4)	576	10	Luoyang	
FJ5)	576	3	Quanzhou	
YN1)	576	200	Yunnan	Kunming
ZJ1)	±576	1	Zhejiang	Linhai
14)	585	200	Southeast BC	Fuzhou, FJ
EB11)	585	10	Langfang	
EN14)	585	10	Nanyang	
GS3)	585	3	Jinchang	
HB8)	585	10	Jingzhou	
HL3)	585	10	Qiqihar	
JL2)	585	10	Changchun	
JL10)	585	1	Yanbian	Hunchun
JS1)	585	50	Jiangsu	Nanjing
JX5)	585	10	Xinyu	
LN1)	585		Liaoning	Suizhong
LN16)	585	1	Chaoyang	Beipiao
SX6)	585	10	Jincheng	
SD1)	594	50	Shandong	Jinan/Yantai
XZ1)	594	300	Xizang	Lhasa
1)	603	10	CNR 1	Zhanjiang, GD
13)	603	10	VO Pujiang	SH
AH1)	603	10	Anhui	Hefei
BJ1)	603	25	Beijing	
EB1)	603	1	Hebei	Shijiazhuang
EB6)	603		Zhangjiakou	
EN13)	603	10	Sanmenxia	
EN1A)	603	100	Henan	Zhengzhou
GZ1)	603	10	Guizhou	Guiyang
HB3)	603	10	Wuhan	
HL5)	603		Shuangyashan	
JL1)	603		Jilin	Songyuan
JL10)	603		Yanbian	Dunhua
JL3A)	603		Jilin-shi EBS	
JS1)	603		Jiangsu	Yangzhou
JS12)	603		VO Jiangnan	
JS16)	603	5	Suzhou	
JS9)	603	5	Nantong	
JX9)	603	10	Ji'an	
LN1)	603		Liaoning	
LN10)	603		Yingkou	
LN7)	603	10	Dandong	
NM19)	603		Morin Dawa	
SD1)	603	1	Shandong	Zibo
SD3)	603	10	Qingdao	
SD10)	603	10	Jining	
SD5)	603	10	Zaozhuang	
SH1)	603	10	Shanghai	
SN1)	603	25	Shaanxi	Xi'an
SN7)	603		Yan'an	
SX1)	603	50	Shanxi	Taiyuan
SX4)	603	1	Yangquan	
XJ10)	603	1	Shihezi	
XJ9)	603	1	Ili	Yining
YN1)	603	1	Yunnan	Zhaotong/Gejiu
ZJ1)	603	1	Zhejiang	Hangzhou/Wenzhou
ZJ4)	603	10	Ningbo	
FJ1)	612	100	Fujian	Ningde
GD1	612	3	Guangdong	Raoping
GD6)	612	2	Zhuhai	
LN1)	612	10	Liaoning	Chaoyang/Dandong
SC1)	612	10	Sichuan	Neijiang/Yibin
HB9)	621	10	Yichang	
HL1)	621	200	Heilongjiang	Harbin
QH4)	621	20	Haixi	Da Qaidam
SC9)	621	3	Guangyuan	
SD1)	621	10	Shandong	Liaocheng
1)	630	200	CNR 2	Nanchang, JX
1)	630	100	CNR 2	Xingyang, EN
1)	630		CNR 2	XJ
1)	639	200/400	CNR 1	BJ
1)	639	100	CNR 1	Chengdu, SC
AH3)	648	1	Huainan	
GD1)	648	50	Guangdong	Guangzhou
LN16)	648	3	Chaoyang	
SH1)	648	10	Shanghai	
XJ7)	648		Kashi	
1)	657	5	CNR 1	Nanping, FJ
EN1)	657	300	Henan	Zhengzhou
JL7)	657	1	Baishan	
ZJ6)	657		Jiaxing	
11)	666	600	VO Strait	Fuzhou, FJ
AH2)	666	10	Hefei	
GZ5)	666	1	Anshun	
HL10)	666	10	Jiamusi	
JL4)	666	10	Siping	
LN8)	666	2	Jinzhou	
QH1)	666	200	Qinghai	Xining
SD10)	666	1	Jining	
TJ1)	666	50	Tianjin	
ZJ5)	666	10	Wenzhou	
NM1)	675	200	Nei Menggu	Hohhot
XJ1)	675	1	Xinjiang	Altay
YN12)	675	1	Gejiu	
YN15)	675	10	Diqing	Shangri-la
ZJ9)	675	1	Jinhua	
1)	684	1200	CNR 6	Putian, FJ
AH1)	684		Anhui	Xuancheng
AH13)	684		Suzhou	
EB8)	684	10	Tangshan	
GS1)	684	200	Gansu	Lanzhou
HB1)	684	10	Hubei	Jingmen
HB1)	684	10	Hubei Chutian	Huangsh
HL9)	684	10	Mudanjiang	
LN5)	684	10	Fushun	
XJ1)	684	10	Xinjiang	Hotan
ZJ11)	684	10	Zhoushan	
HL3)	693	10	Qiqihar	
SN1)	693	300	Shaanxi	Xianyang
2)	702		CRI DS	Zhuhai, GD
JL3)	702	10	Jilin-shi	
JS1)	702	200	Jiangsu	Nanjing
LN16)	702	3	Chaoyang	Lingyuan
NM15)	702	1	Manzhouli	
SC11)	702	1	Neijiang	
XJ1)	702	10	Xinjiang	Urumqi
YN5)	702	10	Honghe	Gejiu
AH12)	711	3	Fuyang	
EN2)	711	10	Zhengzhou	
QH1)	711	10	Qinghai	Golmud
GZ3)	711	1	Liupanshui	
SC5)	711	1	Panzhihua	
SC8)	711	1	Mianyang	
ZJ10)	711	3	Quzhou	
ZJ12)	711	1	Lishui	
1)	720	10	CNR 2	Minhou, FJ
1)	720	50	CNR 2	Xiamen, FJ
1)	720	10	CNR 8	Yanji, JL
1)	720	10	CNR 13	Yining/Kashi, XJ
1)	720	200	CNR 16	BJ
AH1)	720		Anhui	Hefei/Chuzhou
SC7)	720	1	Deyang	
EN16)	729	10	Shangqiu	
JX1)	729	200	Jiangxi	Nanchang
EB12)	738	10	Hengshui	
EN1)	738		Henan	Anyang
HN1)	738	200	Hunan	Changsha
JL1)	738	150	Jilin	Changchun
XJ1)	738	120	Xinjiang	Hutubi
ZJ8)	738	5	Shaoxing	
1)	747	10	CNR 1	Haifeng,
GD1)	747	10	CNR 12	
BJAH2)	747	1	Hefei	
EB1)	747	25	Hebei	Yincun Zhen
EB5)	747	10	Baoding	
EN5)	747	10	Pingdingshan	
FJ6)	747		Longyan	
GD2)	747	3	Zhujiang EBS	Chenghai
HB1)	747	30	Hubei	Qichun

MW	kHz	kW	Station	Tx Location
JS11)	747	3	Changzhou	
JS6)	747		Yancheng	
JX8)	747		Ganzhou	
LN1)	747		Liaoning	Dandong
LN10)	747		Yingkou	
LN12)	747		Fuxin	
LN16)	747	3	Chaoyang	Jianping
LN5)	747		Fushun	
NM3)	747	10	Baotou	
NM4)	747	1	Wuhai	
NM5)	747	10	Chifeng	
NM6)	747	10	Ulanqab	Jining
NM9)	747	10	Tongliao	
NM13)	747	10	Hinggan	Ulanhot
NX1)	747	10	Ningxia	Yinchuan
SC1)	747	200	Sichuan	Chengdu
SC13)	747	1	Nanchong	
SD11)	747	10	Rizhao	
SD13)	747	10	Linyi	
SN1)	747	50	Shaanxi	Xianyang
SN6)	747	1	Weinan	
SX1)	747	10	Shanxi	Luliang
TJ1)	747	50	Tianjin	
YN6)	747	100	Xishuangbanna	Jinghong
ZJ4)	747		Ningbo	
SX8)	750	1	Xinzhou	
1)	756	50	CNR 1	Guangzhou, GD
1)	756	10	CNR 1	Jieyang, GD
1)	756	50	CNR 1	Zhuhai, GD
1)	756	150	CNR 1	Harbin, HL
1)	756		CNR-1	SD
1)	765	600	CNR 5	Fuzhou, FJ
AH7)	765	1	Bengbu	
EN23)	765	10	Gongyi	
GD8)	765	10	Shaoguan	Wujian
GZ1)	765	10	Guizhou	Zunyi
HB1)	774	200	Hubei	Wuhan
LN8)	774	2	Jinzhou	
SX2)	774		Taiyuan	
XJ6)	774	10	Hotan	
11)	783	600	VO Strait	Zhangpu, FJ
EB1)	783	100	Hebei	Baoding
EB1)	783	10	Hebei	Chengde
EB1)	783		Hebei	Langfang/Handan
GD10)	783	20	guangdong	Meizhou
EN2)	792	1	Zhengzhou	
GS5)	792	1	Jiayuguan	
GX1)	792	1	Guangxi	Chongzuo/ Fangcheng/Hechi
GX1)	792	200	Guangxi	Nanning
LN2)	792	10	Shenyang	
XJ2)	792	10	Urumqi	
SC3)	792	10	Chengdu	
SH1)	792	50	Shanghai	
XJ2)	792		Urumqi	
AH1)	801	10	Anhui	Hefei
AH12)	801	3	Fuyang	
AH15)	801	1	Chizhou	
EB10)	801	25	Cangzhou	
EB8)	801	10	Tangshan	
EN8)	801		Xinxiang	
FJ3)	801	10	Xiamen	Jimei
GD2)	801	50	Zhujiang EBS	Maoming
GS1)	801		Gansu	Lanzhou
HB1)	801	10	Hubei	Jingmen/Macheng
JS1)	801	1	Jiangsu	Zhenjiang
JS3)	801		Xuzhou	
JS5)	801	10	Huai'an	
JS7)	801		Yangzhou	
LN1)	801		Liaoning	Dandong/Gaizhou
LN16)	801	1	Chaoyang	Lingyuan
NX2)	801	10	Yinchuan	
SD10)	801	10	Jining	
SD14)	801	10	Liaocheng	
SD4)	801	10	Zibo	
SD8)	801	10	Yantai	
SD13)	801	10	Linyi	
SN1)	801	1	Shaanxi	Weinan
SN2)	801		Xi'an	
XJ7)	801	1	Kashi	
ZJ5)	801	10	Wenzhou	
EN18)	810	25	Zhumadian	
JL5)	810	10	Liaoyuan	
LN1)	810	5	Liaoning	Panjin
LN15)	810		Tieling	
LN16)	810	10	Chaoyang	
SN2)	810	50	Xi'an	
ZJ1)	810	200	Zhejiang	Hangzhou
SD3)	819		Qingdao	
SX1)	819	200	Shanxi	Yuci
XJ11)	819	1	Kuytun	
XJ12)	819		Bayingolin	Korla
1)	828	10	CNR 2	Shuangyashan, HL
BJ1)	828	50	Beijing	
EN1)	828	10	Henan	
EN17)	±828	10	Zhoukou	
EN6)	828	10	Jiaozuo	
GD1)	828	40	Guangdong	Meizhou
GD1)	828	50	Guangdong	Dongyuan
HB23)	±828	1	Xiantao	
HB8)	828	10	Jingzhou	
1)	837	1000	CNR 5	Quanzhou, FJ
AH1)	837		Anhui	Bengbu
EN15)	837	25	Xinyang	
F1)	837	3	Fujian	Fuding
HL2)	837	50	Harbin	
LN14)	837	10	Liaoyang	
2)	846	10	CRI DS 4	BJ
AH1)	846	10	Anhui	Suzhou
AH2)	846	1	Hefei	Chaohu
EB1)	846		Hebei	Hengshui/Tangshan
EB10)	846	10	Cangzhou	
EB11)	846	10	Langfang	
EB3)	846		Handan	
EN5)	846	3	Pingdingshan	
EN7)	846		Hebi	
GD1)	846	10	Guangdong	Raoping
GD1)	846	10	Guangdong	Yangjiang
GD1)	846	10	Guangdong	Zhaoqing
GX1)	846	10	Guangxi	Nanning/Qinzhou
HB1)	846	30	Hubei	Qichun
HB1)	846	10	Hubei	Xianning/Yichang
JL1)	846	10	Jilin	Changchun
JS1)	846	5	Jiangsu	Nanjing
JS11)	846	10	Changzhou	
JS13)	846	5	Suzhou	
LN13)	846	10	Fuxin Mo BS	
LN8)	846		Jinzhou	
SD2)	846	10	Jinan	
SD7)	846	5	Weifang	
SD9)	846	10	Weihai	
SX1)	846	20	Shanxi	Changzhi
XJ1)	846	3	Xinjiang	Hotan
XZ1)	846	10	Xizang	Lhasa
YN1)	846	1	Yunnan	Longchuan/Fugong
YN1)	846	10	Yunnan	Gejiu
YN11)	846	1	Zhaotong	
1)	855	50	CNR 2	Anning, YN
XJ1)	855		Xinjiang	
AH1)	864	50	Anhui	Hefei
EB20)	864		Renqiu	
EN19)	864		Qinyang	
SD15)	864	10	Binzhou	
ZJ1)	864	1	Zhejiang	Ninghai
ZJ15)	864	1	Jiangshan	
15)	873	200	China Huayi BC	Xiamen, FJ
EB13)	±873		Xinji	
EN3)	±873	10	Kaifeng	
GS1)	873	50	Gansu	Linxia
HB3)	873	50	Wuhan	
HL1)	873	100	Heilongjiang	Harbin
SD13)	873	10	Linyi	
XJ8)	873	1	Changji	
ZJ7)	873		Huzhou	
EB2)	882	20	Shijiazhuang	
EN22)	882		Ruzhou	
EN9)	882		Anyang	
FJ1)	882	10	Fujian	Fu'an
FJ1)	882	200	Fujian	Minhou
FJ1)	882	10	Fujian	Sanming

MW	kHz	kW	Station	Tx Location
FJ1)	882	200	Fujian	Shaowu
GZ6)	882	1	Qiannan	Duyun
LN1)	882	10	Liaoning	Shenyang
LN3)	882	50	Dalian	
QH3)	882	10	Yushu	
XJ4)	882		Karamay	
XJ9)	882	1	Ili	Yining
LN7)	891	10	Dandong	
NX1)	891	200	Ningxia	Yinchuan
SD1)	891	10	Shandong	Dongying
XJ10)	891	10	Shihezi	
1)	900	10	CNR 2	Golmud, QH
2)	900		CRI DS 5	BJ
AH1)	900		Anhui	Lu'an/Bengbu/Haungshan
EB1)	900		Hebei	Shijiazhuang
EB6)	900	10	Zhangjiakou	
EB7)	900	1	Chengde	
EB8)	900		Tangshan	
EB9)	900		Qinhuangdao	
EN1)	900	25	Henan	Zhoukou/Yima
EN12A)	900		Luohe EBS	
GD5)	900	11	Shenzhen	Bao'an
HB1)	900	10	Hubei	Enshi
HB1)	900	10	Hubei	Xiangyang
HL1)	900	50	Heilongjiang	Boi'an/Jiamusi
HN1)	900		Hunan	Changsha
JL16)	900	1	Yanji	
JL2)	900	10	Changchun	
JL4)	900	1	Siping	
JS10)	900	1	Zhenjiang	
JS12)	900		Wuxi	
JS2)	900	10	Nanjing	
JS4)	900	10	Lianyungang	
JS6)	900		Yancheng	
LN1)	900		Liaoning	Chaoyang/Huludao
LN12)	900		Fuxin	
LN19)	900	1	Haicheng	
NM5)	900	10	Chifeng	
SD3)	900	10	Qingdao	
SD4)	900	10	Zibo	
SN1)	900	30	Shaanxi	Xi'an
SN4)	900	1	Baoji	
SX1)	900	10	Shanxi	Jincheng
SX3)	900	10	Datong	
YN9)	900	100	Dehong	Luxi
ZJ1)	900	1	Zhejiang	Jinhua
ZJ11)	900		Zhoushan	
1)	909	300	CNR 6	Quanzhou, FJ
CQ1)	909	10	Chongqing	Fuling
HL8)	909	7.5	Yichun	
JL6)	909	10	Tonghua	
QH1)	909	10	Qinghai	Xining
SC1)	909	50	Sichuan	Xichang
TJ1)	909	50	Tianjin	
XJ1)	909	10	Xinjiang	Bortala
SD1)	918	200	Shandong	Jinan
1)	927	100	CNR 6	Xiamen, FJ
BJ1)	927	50	Beijing	
EB4)	927	12.5	Xingtai	
EN11)	927		Xuchang	
EN14)	927	10	Nanyang	
EN16)	927	10	Shangqiu	
GD1)	927	10	Guangdong	Guangzhou
GD1)	927	3	Zhujiang EBS	Jieyang
GD1)	927	2	Zhujiang EBS	Huizhou
GD2)	927	10	Zhujiang EBS	Zhanjiang
GZ1)	927	200	Guizhou	Kaili
HB1)	927	10	Hubei	Suizhou
HB1)	927	10	Hubei	Xianning
HB10)	927		Jingmen	
HB12)	927	3	Xiaogan	
HL1)	927	10	Heilongjiang	Shuangyashan
HL2)	927	1	Harbin	Hulan
JL19)	927	1	Hunchun	
JL3)	927	10	Jilin-shi	
JS11)	927	3	Changzhou	
JS16)	927	1	Changshu	
JS8)	927		Taizhou	
JX1)	927	10	Jiangxi	Ji'an
LN1)	927	50	Liaoning	Shenyang
SH1)	927	1	Shanghai	
XJ2)	927	10	Urumqi	
YN1)	927	10	Yunnan	Kaiyuan
YN17)	927	1	Lufeng	
ZJ7)	927	10	Huzhou	
ZJ1)	930		Zhejiang	
AH1)	936	200	Anhui	Hefei
1)	945	400	CNR 1	Jiaohe, JL
1)	945	10	CNR 13	Hami/Kuqa, XJ
HB1)	945	10	Hubei	Qichun
HB1)	945	10	Hubei	Jingzhou
HL1)	945	50	Heilongjiang	Harbin/Fujin
NM2)	945	10	Hohhot	
NM7)	945	10	Xilingol	Xilinhot
NM10)	945	10	Ordos	Dongsheng
NM10)	945	10	Ordos	Otog
NM12)	945	10	Alxa	Bayanhot
EB12)	954	10	Hengshui	
GS2)	954	10	Lanzhou	
HA1)	954	30	Hainan	Haikou
LN4)	954	10	Anshan	
NM8)	954	50	Hulun Buir	Hailar
NM9)	954	1	Tongliao	
SC1)	954	10	Sichuan	Chengdu
SC6)	954	1	Luzhou	
ZJ2)	954	25	Hangzhou	
EB3)	963	10	Handan	
HB5)	963	10	Huangshi	
LN1)	963	50	Liaoning	Dalian
XJ1)	963	10	Xinjiang	Qoqek/Gulja
EN1)	972	150	Henan	Xingyang
HL2)	972	10	Harbin	
XJ1)	972	10	Xinjiang	Altay
1)	981	200	CNR 1	Changchun, JL
1)	981	50	CNR 1	Heyuan, GD
1)	981	50	CNR 1	Maoming, GD
1)	981	200	CNR 1	Nanchang, JX
1)	981	10	CNR 1	Shenzhen, GD
1)	981		CNR 1	Urumqi, XJ
SD7)	981	5	Weifang	
EB9)	990	1	Qinhuangdao	
SH1)	990	100	Shanghai	
YN1)	990	10	Yunnan	Hekou/Gejiu/Lincang/Luchun
AH19)	999	1	Bozhou	
GD1)	999	10	Guangdong	Guangzhou
GZ2)	999	10	Guiyang	
HL15)	999		Aihui	
LN1)	999	200	Liaoning	Shenyang
SD1)	999	10	Shandong	Jining
XJ1)	999	10	Xinjiang	Hami/Bortala
XZ1)	999	10	Xizang	Lhasa
1)	1008	200	CNR 1	Anning, YN
1)	1008	1	CNR13	Urumqi, XJ
2)	1008	1	CNR DS 3	BJ
AH1)	1008		Anhui	Suzhou/Fuyang
EB11)	1008		Langfang	
EB3)	1008	10	Handan	
EN13)	1008		Sanmenxia	
EN5)	1008	1	Pingdingshan	
EN2)	1008	25	Zhengzhou	
GJ3)	1008	10	Xiamen	Haicang
GD1)	1008	10	Guangdong	Zhongshan
GD2)	1008	3	Zhujiang EBS	Xinhui
GS1)	1008		Gansu	
HB1)	1008	50	Hubei	Jingmen
HB1)	1008	10	Hubei	Huangshi
HB22)	1008	10	Suizhou	
HN7)	±1008	1	Yueyang	
JS12)	1008		Wuxi	
JS2)	1008	10	Nanjing	
NX1)	1008	1	Ningxia	Guyuan
SD12)	1008	10	Dezhou	
SD3)	1008	10	Qingdao	
SN1)	1008	10	Shaanxi	Hanzhong/Yan'an
SN1)	1008		Shannxi	Xi'an
SX1)	1008	10	Shanxi	Xinzhou
TJ1)	1008	50	Tianjin	
1)	1017	1	CNR 1	Dongtou, ZJ

MW	kHz	kW	Station	Tx Location
EB5)	1017	10	Baoding	
GD1)	1017	10	Guangdong	Jieyang
GD1)	1017	50	Guangdong	Shaoguan
QH1)	1017	1	Qinghai	Gonghe
BJ1)	1026	50	Beijing	
GZ1)	1026	200	Guizhou	Guiyang
JS14)	1026	1	Yizheng	
JS6)	1026	10	Yancheng	
LN10)	1026	2	Yingkou	
XJ6)	1026	10	Hotan	
1)	1035	50	CNR 1	Dalian/Wuhan
NM1)	1044	10	Nei Menggu	Hohhot
XJ1)	1044	10	Xinjiang	Urumqi/Korla
YN8)	1044	1	Dali	
ZJ1)	1050		Zhejiang	
1)	1053	10	CNR 10	BJ
AH2)	1053	1	Hefei	
EB10)	1053	10	Cangzhou	
EB15)	1053	1	Shahe	
EB17)	1053	1	Zhuozhou	
EN18)	1053	10	Zhumadian	
EN3)	1053	10	Kaifeng	
EN4)	1053	10	Luoyang	
HB1)	1053	50	Hubei	Qianjiang
HN7)	1053		Yueyang	
HN9)	1053		Yiyang	
JL10)	1053	20	Yanbian	Yanji
JS1)	1053	10	Jiangsu	Nanjing
LN1)	1053	50	Liaoning	Shenyang
SD2)	1053	10	Jinan	
YN1)	1053	1	Yunnan	Zhaotong
YN4)	1053	10	Wenshan	
GD2)	1062	150	Zhujiang EBS	Huadu
GD2)	1062	50	Zhujiang	Zhuhai
HL11)	1062	1	Qitaihe	
GX1)	1071	1	Guangxi	Napo
GX1)	1071	10	Guangxi	Ningming
HN5)	1071	10	Hengyang	
LN4)	1071	2	Anshan	
SD16)	1071	10	Heze	
SN4)	1071	10	Baoji	
TJ1)	1071	50	Tianjin	
XJ2)	1071	100	Urumqi	
ZJ1)	1071	10	Zhejiang	Hangzhou
GD7)	1080	5	Shantou	
HL7)	1080	1	Daqing	
HL12)	1080	1	Suihua	
JS13)	1080	10	Suzhou	
ZJ1)	±1080	1	Zhejiang	Xiangshan
1)	1089	600	CNR 6	Fuzhou, FJ
HN3)	1089	1	Zhuzhou	
LN1)	1089	200	Liaoning	Shenyang
1)	1098	1000	CNR 1/11	Golmud, QH
AH1)	1098		Anhui	Hefei/Wuhu
AH18)	1098		Dangtu Xian	
AH7)	±1098	1	Bengbu	
EB1)	1098	1	Hebei	Zhangjiakou
EB12)	1098		Hengshui	
EN1)	1098		Henan	Zhoukou
EN5)	1098		Pingdingshan	
GD3)	1098	10	Guangzhou	
GD22)	1098	1	Jieyang	
GX1)	1098	1	Guangxi	Hechi/Liuzhou/ Nanning
HB1)	1098	10	Hubei	Jingzhou/Suizhou
HB8)	1098	10	Xiangyang	
JS1)	1098	1	Jiangsu	Zhenjiang
JS17)	1098	1	Zhangjiagang	
JS3)	1098		Xuzhou	
LN8)	1098		Jinzhou	
LN12)	1098		Fuxin	
SD12)	1098	10	Dezhou	
SX1)	1098		Shanxi	Yangzhou/Changzhi
TJ1)	1098	50	Tianjin	
XJ5)	1098	1	Hami	
YN1)	1098	1	Yunnan	Kaiyuan
ZJ11)	1098	10	Zhoushan	
AH6)	1107	3	Tongling	
EN7)	1107	10	Hebi	
FJ3)	1107	10	Xiamen	Jimei
HA1)	1107	10	Hainan	Tongshi
JL1)	1107	10	Jilin	Yushu/Hunchun
JX4)	1107	1	Pingxiang	
XJ1)	1107	100	Xinjiang	Hutubi
ZJ6)	1107	10	Jiaxing	
1)	1116	120	CNR 2	Harbin, HL
1)	1116	600	CNR 5	Shaowu, FJ
AH12)	1116	10	Fuyang	
HA1)	1116	30	Hainan	Ledong
SC1)	1116	200	Sichuan	Chengdu
SD10)	1116	1	Jining	
EB1)	1125	10	Hebei	Shijiazhuang
HB1)	1125	10	Hubei	Xiantao
HB3)	1125	50	Wuhan	
GS9)	1134	1	Yumen	
SN3)	1134	10	Tongchuan	
XJ9)	1134	1	Ili	Yining
ZJ1)	1134	10	Zhejiang	Wenzhou/Ningbo
1)	1143	10	CNR 8	BJ
EB18)	1143	1	Dingzhou	
EB8)	1143		Tangshan	
EN1)	1143	50	Henan	Zhengzhou
GS4)	1143	10	Tianshui	
GZ5)	1143		Anshun	
HA1)	1143		Hainan	Haikou
HB1)	1143	10	Hubei	Shiyan
HL10)	1143	1	Jiamusi	
JL1)	1143	1	Jilin	Liaoyuan
JL17)	1143	1	Tumen	
JL3)	1143	10	Jilin-shi	
JL8)	1143		Songyuan	
JS11)	1143	3	Changzhou	
JS9)	1143		Nantong	
LN10)	1143		Yingkou	
LN14)	1143	1	Liaoyang	
LN5)	1143		Fushun	
NM16)	1143	1	Yakeshi	
QH1)	1143		Qinghai	Xining
SC11)	1143		Neijiang	
SC15)	1143	1	Dazhou	
SC9)	1143		Guangyuan	
SD13)	1143	10	Linyi	
SD14)	1143	10	Liaocheng	
SD4)	1143	10	Zibo	
SN1)	1143	1	Shaanxi	Baoji/Weinan
SN9)	1143	1	Yulin	
XJ1)	1143	10	Xinjiang	Altay
YN1)	1143	1	Yunnan	Kunming
YN1)	1143	1	Yunnan	Gejiu
ZJ1)	1143	1	Zhejiang	Yuhuan
HN1)	1152	150	Hunan	Changde
LN3)	1152	10	Dalian	
1)	1161		CNR 1	
GX1)	1161	1	Guangxi	Bose/Beihai
HB10)	1161	10	Jingmen	
JS12)	1161	10	Wuxi	
SD7)	1161	10	Weifang	
1)	1170	10	CNR 1	Huizhou, GD
1)	1170	600	CNR 1	Ji'an, JX
AH16)	1170	1	Lu'an	
AH17)	1170	3	Xuancheng	
AH2)	1170	10	Hefei	
GD3)	1170	10	Guangzhou	
GS1)	1170	10	Gansu	Zhangye
JS2)	1170	10	Nanjing	
JS9)	1170	10	Nantong	
NM5)	1170	50	Chifeng	
NM6)	1170	10	Ulanqab	Jining
NM7)	1170	10	Xilingol	Xilinhot
NM8)	1170	50	Hulun Buir	Hailar
NM9)	1170	50	Tongliao	
NM11)	1170	10	Bayannur	Linhe
NM12)	1170	10	Alxa	Bayanhot
NM13)	1170	10	Hinggan	Ulanhot
SD15)	1170	10	Binzhou	
SD5)	1170	10	Zaozhuang	
HB1)	1179	100	Hubei	Wuhan
HL5)	1179	10	Shuangyashan	
JS7)	1179	10	Yangzhou	
XJ4)	1179	10	Karamay	

MW	kHz	kW	Station	Tx Location
EB19)	1188	1	Botou	
EB4)	1188	10	Xingtai	
JL10)	1188		Yanbian	Longjing
FJ5)	1197		Quanzhou	
HL3)	1197	10	Qiqihar	
SD16)	1197	10	Heze	
SH1)	1197	10	Shanghai	
1)	1206	10	CNR 2	Sanming, FJ
EB10)	1206	25	Cangzhou	
EB3)	1206	10	Handan	
EN20)	1206	1	Huixian	
GD1)	1206	50	Guangdong	Bao'an
GD15)	1206	10	Jiangmen	Xinhui
HN1)	1206	10	Hubei	Xiangyang
JL10)	1206	200	Yanbian	Longjing
JS1)	1206	1	Jiangsu	Nanjing
NX1)	1206	1	Ningxia	Zhongning
SD9)	1206	10	Weihai	
SX1)	1206	10	Shanxi	Shuozhou
QH1)	1206	1	Qinghai	Dulan
1)	1215	20	CNR 2	Shenyang, LN
1)	1215	50	CNR 7	Zhuhai, GD
HB1)	1215	10	Hubei	Yichang
HB26)	1215	1	Enshi	
HL14)	1215	50	Heihe	
1)	1224	100	CNR 6	Xiamen, FJ
GX1)	1224	1	Guangxi	Bose/Wuzhou
GX1)	1224	100	Guangxi	Nanning
GX1)	1224	50	Guangxi	yulin
JS10)	1224	10	Zhenjiang	
HN1)	1233	10	Hunan	Yueyang/Shaoyang
JS9)	1233	25	Nantong	
XJ1)	1233	120	Xinjiang	Hutubi
XJ1)	1233	10	Xinjiang	Bortala
XJ1)	1233	10	Xinjiang	Urumqi
HB20)	1242	1	Macheng	
HB24)	1242	1	Qianjiang	
JX9)	1242		Ji'an	
LN9)	1242	1	Huludao	
YN1)	1242	100	Yunnan	Kunming
ZJ10)	1250	1	Quzhou	
2)	1251		CRI DS 1	BJ
AH13)	1251	1	Suzhou	
EB1)	1251		Hebei	Qinhuangdao
EB2)	1251	25	Shijiazhuang	
EN10)	1251	10	Puyang	
EN12)	1251	10	Luohe	
EN21)	1251	1	Yima	
EN6)	1251		Jiaozuo	
EN9)	±1251		Anyang	
HB1)	1251	5	Hubei	Jingmen
JL3A)	1251		Jilin-shi EBS	
JS12)	1251	10	Wuxi	
JS2)	1251		Nanjing	
JS4)	1251		Lianyungang	
JS5)	1251	10	Huai'an	
LN4)	1251		Anshan	
QH1)	1251	200	Qinghai	Xining
SD1)	1251	10	Shandong	Jinan/Zibo
SD13)	1251	10	Linyi	
SD18)	1251		Longkou	
SD3)	1251	10	Qingdao	
SD7)	1251		Weifang	
SN8)	1251	10	Hanzhong	
YN1)	1251	1	Yunnan	Kaiyuan
YN14)	1251		Yuxi	
ZJ1)	1251	1	Zhejiang	Jinhua
ZJ4)	1251		Ningbo	
ZJ7)	1251		Huzhou	
HN8)	1260	1	Changde	
LN1)	1260	10	Liaoning	Fengcheng
XZ3)	1260	1	Shannan	Nedong
JL18)	1269	1	Dunhua	
JS3)	1269	10	Xuzhou	
SX1)	1269	10	Shanxi	Taiyuan/Xinzhou
EB1)	1278	100	Hebei	Shijiazhuang/ Tangshan
FJ3)	1278	10	Xiamen	Jimei
HL13)	1278	7.5	Daxing'anling	Jagdaqi
JX2)	1278	10	Nanchang	
1)	1287	10	CNR 1	Ningde, FJ
EB20)	1287	1	Renqiu	
EN11)	1287	1	Xuchang	
GD5)	1287	25	Shenzhen	Bao'an
JS12)	1287		Wuxi	
LN12)	1287	20	Fuxin	
NX1)	1287	10	Ningxia	Guyuan
SD7)	1287	5	Weifang	
YN7)	1287	10	Chuxiong	
ZJ1)	1287	1	Zhejiang	Dongtou
EB16)	1296	1	Qinghe	
LN20)	1296	1	Xingcheng	
LN6)	1296	20	Benxi	
SC10)	1296	1	Suining	
SH1)	1296	25	Shanghai	
SN5)	1296	10	Xianyang	
1)	1305	10	CNR 2	Xining, QH
1)	1305		CNR8	Ulanhot,NM
SD2)	1305	10	Jinan	
CQ1)	1314	50	Chongqing	
HB14)	1314	3	Xianning	
HB6)	1314	10	Xiangyang	
JS1)	1314	10	Jiangsu	Suzhou/Huai'an
SD8)	1314	10	Yantai	
ZJ1)	1314		Zhejiang	
HN2)	1323	10	Changsha	
JL9)	1323	10	Baicheng	
LN17)	1323	1	Wafangdian	
SD16A)	1323	10	Mudan	Heze
SN1)	1323	10	Shaanxi	Xi'an
ZJ4)	1323	10	Ningbo	
EN1)	1332	10	Henan	Zhengzhou
EN1)	1332	10	Henan	Hebi/Luoyang
EN1)	1332	10	Henan	Anyang
FJ1)	1332	10	Fujian	Yunxiao
FJ2)	1332	10	Fuzhou	Minhou
GS6)	1332	10	Gannan	Hezuo
JL2)	1332	10	Changchun	
1)	1341	100	CNR 1	GD
HB19)	1341	1	Yingcheng	
HB21)	1341	1	Chibi	
HL1)	1341	100	Heilongjiang	Heihe
JS8)	1341	10	Taizhou	
LN1)	1341	10	Liaoning	Shenyang
SD12)	1341	1	Dezhou	
SD19)	1341	1	Qufu	
JX1)	1350	50	Jiangxi	Ji'an
JX1)	1350	10	Jiangxi	Shangrao/Pingxiang
JX1)	1350	1	Jiangxi	Jiujiang
LN19)	1350		Haicheng	
YN2)	1350	50	Kunming	
1)	1359	10	CNR 1	Xiamen/Sanming, FJ
1)	1359	10	CNR 1	Nanjing, JS
FJ1)	±1368	3	Fujian	Changting
HB8)	1368		Jingzhou	
HB18)	1368	1	Guangshui	
HL6)	1368	10	Jixi	
1)	1377	600	CNR 1	Xingyang, EN
AH11)	1377	1	Chuzhou	
FJ1)	1377	5	Fujian	Nanping
NX5)	1377	1	Qingtongxia	
QH1)	1377		Qinghai	Xining
SD3)	1377	10	Qingdao	
XZ1)	1377	100	Xizang	Lhasa
FJ1)	1386	10	Fujian	Quanzhou
GX3)	1386	5	Liuzhou	
HB11)	1386	1	Ezhou	
HB17)	1386	1	Shishou	
JS15)	1386	1	Jiangyin	
SD10)	1386	1	Jining	
TJ1)	1386	50	Tianjin	
AH1)	1395	50	Anhui	Hefei
AH1)	1395	10	Anhui	Fuyang/Chizhou
FJ1)	1395	3	Fujian	Hui'an
YN1)	1395	1	Yunnan	Pu'er
FJ1)	1404	3	Fujian	Shunchang
FJ1)	1404	3	Fujian	Zhangpu
FJ1)	1404	3	Fujian	Zhao'an
FJ1)	1404	1	Fujian EBS	Changle
FJ1)	1404	50	Fujian EBS	Minhou

MW	kHz	kW	Station	Tx Location
HB1)	1404	50	Hubei	Jingzhou
HB1)	1404	10	Hubei	Suizhou/Chongyang
LN7)	1404	10	Dandong	
HL4)	1413	1	Hegang	
JS1)	1413	10	Jiangsu	Yancheng/Wuxi
LN15)	1413	1	Tieling	
NX4)	1413	1	Wuzhong	
XJ1)	1413	10	Xinjiang	Hami/Bortala
1)	1422	600	CNR 1/13	Kashi, XJ
13)	1422	20	VO Pujiang	SH
FJ1)	1422	3	Fujian	Jimei
FJ1)	1422	3	Fujian	Longyan
SC4)	1422	10	Zigong	
SX1)	1422	10	Shanxi	Linfen
SX2)	1422	10	Taiyuan	
AH10)	1431	2	Huangshan	
AH4)	1431	10	Huaibei	
EB2)	1431	10	Shijiazhuang	
FJ1)	1431	3	Fujian	Fuqing
HB16)	1431	1	Danjiangkou	
HN10)	1431	1	Jinshi	
JL8)	1431	2	Songyuan	
NM14)	1431	1	Fengzhen	
1)	1440	10	CNR1	Putian
GX1)	1440	50	Guangxi	Bose
GX1)	1440	1	Guangxi	Chengzuo/Shangsi
GX1)	1440	3	Guangxi	Mengshan
LN18)	1440	10	Zhuanghe	
SD11)	1449	10	Rizhao	
SD6)	1449	10	Dongying	
EN2)	1458	5	Zhengzhou	
JS4)	1458	10	Lianyungang	
LN4)	1458		Anshan	
NM1)	1458	200	Nei Menggu	Hohhot
EB5)	1467	10	Baoding	
FJ1)	1467	3	Fujian EBS	Longhai
JX3)	1467	7.5	Jingdezhen	
SD1)	1467	5	Shandong	Dezhou
HB15)	1476	1	Laohekou	
HL1)	1476	50	Heilongjiang	Qiqihar/Fujin
HL9)	1476		Mudanjiang	
JL14)	1476	1	Qian Gorlos	
LN7)	1476		Dandong	
QH2)	1476	10	Xining	
SC12)	1476	1	Leshan	
SD4)	1476	10	Zibo	
ZJ1)	1476	1	Zhejiang	Leqing
GS1)	1485		Gansu	
GX1)	1485	1	Guangxi	Lingshan
GX4)	1485	1	Guilin	
GX5)	1485	3	Wuzhou	
HB7)	1485	10	Shiyan	
HL6)	1485	1	Jixi	
JL11)	1485	1	Gongzhuling	
JX6)	1485	1	Jiujiang	
LN11)	1485	1	Panjin	
SC3)	1485	1	Chengdu	
SD1)	1485	1	Shandong	Weihai/Liaocheng
SX10)	1485	1	Shuozhou	
XJ11)	1485	1	Kuytun	
XJ5)	1485	1	Hami	
YN13)	1485	1	Chuxiong	
YN5)	1485	1	Honghe	Jinping
AH5)	1494	1	Wuhu	
FJ1)	1494	1	Fujian	Lianjiang
XJ1)	1494	10	Xinjiang	Yining/Tacheng
AH12)	1503	1	Fuyang	
HN4)	1503	10	Xiangtan	
SX1)	1503	10	Shanxi	Datong/Jincheng
GS7)	1512	10	Linxia	
SD2)	1512	10	Jinan	
EB1)	1521	10	Hebei	Xingtai
EB11)	1521	25	Langfang	
EN5)	1521	3	Pingdingshan	
EN8)	1521	10	Xinxiang	
FJ3)	1521	3	Xiamen	
GZ5)	1521		Anshun	
HB25)	1521	10	Xiangzhou	
HL1)	1521	1	Heilongjiang	Jingbohu
JL1)	1521	1	Jilin	Taonan
JS11)	1521	3	Changzhou	
JS12)	1521		Wuxi	
JS13)	1521	5	Suzhou	
JS17)	1521		Zhangjiagang	
JS5)	1521	10	Huai'an	
JS7)	1521		Yangzhou	
SD2)	1521		Jinan	
SN1)	1521	1	Shaanxi	Shangluo
SX5)	1521	1	Changzhi	Qinxian
YN3)	1521	1	Qujing	
YN5)	1521	1	Honghe	Gejiu
ZJ1)	1521	1	Zhejiang	
ZJ7)	1521		Huzhou	
JL1)	1530	10	Jilin	Yanji/Fuyuan
SX7)	1530	1	Jinzhong	
ZJ1)	1530	50	Zhejiang	Hangzhou
1)	1539	100/300	CNR 1	Golmud, QH
QH1)	1539	1	Qinghai	Maqin
SD1)	1548	200	Shandong	Linyi
EB10)	1557	25	Cangzhou	
EB14)	1557	1	Nangong	
EB6)	1566	10	Zhangjiakou	
JL10)	1566	1	Yanbian	Longjing
GS8)	1566	1	Pingliang	
HB1)	1566	10	Hubei	Jingmen
SD14)	1566	1	Liaocheng	
SX9)	1566	1	Yuncheng	
GX1)	1575	1	Guangxi	Daxin/Hechi/Nanning/Chongzuo/Wuzhou
JL12)	1575		Lishu	
LN3)	1575	2	Dalian	
AH8)	1584	1	Ma'anshan	
AH9)	1584	1	Anqing	
EB7)	1584	1	Chengde	
GZ4)	1584	1	Zunyi	
JL13)	1584	1	Meihekou	
SX1)	1584		Shanxi	Taiyuan
SX3)	1584		Datong	
SX5)	1584	10	Changzhi	
YN1)	1584	1	Yunnan	Gongshan
ZJ14)	1584	1	Rui'an	
1)	1593	600	CNR 1	Changzhou, JS
HL1)	1593	10	Heilongjiang	
XJ1)	1593	10	Xinjiang	Korla
JS1)	1602	1	Jiangsu	Hongze

SW	kHz	kW	Station	Tx Loc.	Times (see * below)
NM8)	3900	10	Hulun Buir	Hailar	2130-0700, 0900-1440
XJ1)	3950	100	Xinjiang	Urumqi	Nov-Apr only
1)	3985	100	CNR 2	Golmud	1200-1605
GS6)	3990	15	Gannan	Hezuo	2250-0120, 0345-0625, 1025-1345
XJ1)	3990	100	Xinjiang	Urumqi	Nov-Apr only
XJ1)	4500	50	Xinjiang	Urumqi	Nov-Apr only
1)	4750	10	CNR 1	Hailar	2000-1730, Tu5
1)	4800	100	CNR 1	Golmud	2025-1805, Tu5
XZ1)	4820	100	Xizang	Lhasa	2000(Tu2100)-1800, Tu8
XJ1)	4850	100	Xinjiang	Urumqi	Nov-Apr only
11)	4900	50	VO Strait	Fuzhou	2230-0100, 0930-1600
XZ1)	4905	50	Xizang	Lhasa	2050(Tu2100)-1805, Tu7
XZ1)	4920	50	Xizang	Lhasa	2050(Tu2100)-1805, Tu7
11)	4940	50	VO Strait	Fuzhou	0930-1600
XJ1)	4980	100	Xinjiang	Urumqi	Nov-Apr only
HN1)	4990	10	Hunan	Changsha	2030-0100, 0900-1700
XJ1)	5060	100	Xinjiang	Urumqi	Nov-Apr only
1)	5925	100	CNR 5	Beijing	2055-2400, 1000-1705
XZ1)	5935	100	Xizang	Lhasa	2000(Tu2100)-1800, Tu8
1)	5945	100	CNR 1	Beijing	2025-2300, 1300-1805
XJ1)	5960	100	Xinjiang	Urumqi	2300-0300, 1200-1800
GS6)	5970	15	Gannan	Hezuo	2250-0120, 0345-0625, 1025-1345
1)	5975	100	CNR 8	Beijing	0600(W0900)-1505
QH1)	5990	50	Qinghai	Xining	2250-1600, Tu5
1)	6000	100	CNR 1	Beijing	2025-2330, 1100-1805
1)	6010	100	CNR 11	Baoji-Sif.	2155-2400, 1300-1605
XJ1)	6015	100	Xinjiang	Urumqi	2310-0345, 1150-1800
XZ1)	6025	100	Xizang	Lhasa	2050(Tu2100)-1805, Tu7
1)	d6030	30	CNR 1	Beijing	2025-1805, Tu

SW	kHz	kW	Station	Tx Loc.	Times (see * below)
51)	6040	150	CNR 2	Beijing	2055-2300
NM1)	6040	50	Nei Menggu	Hohhot	2150-1605, Tu2
XZ1)	6050	100	Xizang	Lhasa	2000(Tu2100)-1800, Tu8
SC1)	6060	50	Sichuan	Xichang	2155-0135, 1000-1515
1)	6065	150	CNR 2	Beijing	2055-2230, 1200-1605
1)	6075	10	CNR1	Yushu	0000-1600
1)	6080	100	CNR 1	Golmud	2025-2400, 1100-1805
NM8)	6080	10	Hulun Buir	Hailar	2150-0530, 0935-1600
1)	6090	100	CNR 2	Golmud	2055-0100, 1100-1605
XZ1)	6110	100	Xizang	Lhasa	2050(Tu2100)-1805, Tu7
XJ1)	6120	100	Xinjiang	Urumqi	2300-0245, 1200-1800
1)	6125	100	CNR 1	Beijing	2025-2300, 1000-1805
1)	6125	100	CNR 1	Shijiazhuang	2025-2300, 1100-1805
XZ1)	6130	100	Xizang	Lhasa	2050(Tu2100)-1805, Tu7
QH1)	6145	50	Qinghai	Xining	2140-1600, Tu5
1)	6155	150	CNR 2	Beijing	2055-2300, 1000-1605
1)	6165	100	CNR 6	Beijing	2155-0100, 0900-1605
1)	6175	100	CNR 1	Beijing	2025-2400, 0900-1805
15)	6185	15	China Huayi BC	Fuzhou	0945-1600
1)	6190	100	CNR 2	Golmud	2055-2400
XJ1)	6190	50	Xinjiang	Urumqi	2310-0330, 1210-1800
XZ1)	6200	100	Xizang	Lhasa	2050(Tu2100)-1805, Tu7
12)	6200	100	VO Jinling	Nanjing	1200-1500
XJ1)	7205	100	Xinjiang	Urumqi	2300-0200, 1400-1800
YN1)	7210	20	Yunnan	Kunming	0600-1000, 1100-1500, 2245-0300
1)	7215	100	CNR 1	Shijiazhuang	2025-2400
1)	7220	100	CNR 2	Golmud	0000-1200, W2
SC1)	7225	50	Sichuan	Xichang	2155-0135, 1000-1515
1)	7230	150	CNR 1	Xianyang	2025-1805, Tu5
XJ1)	7230	50	Xinjiang	Urumqi	2300-0330, 0510-1030, 1150-1800
XZ1)	7240	100	Xizang	Lhasa	2000(Tu2100)-0300, 0900(Tu1000)-1800
1)	7245	150	CNR 2	Beijing	2055-2300, 1300-1605
XZ1)	7255	100	Xizang	Lhasa	2050(Tu 2100)-0200, 1000-1805
XJ1)	7260	100	Xinjiang	Urumqi	2300-1800, Tu1
1)	7265	100	CNR 2	Baoji-Sif	2055-0100, 1230-1605
NM1)	7270	50	Nei Menggu	Hohhot	2150-1605, Tu2
1)	7275	100	CNR 1	Beijing	2025-2300, 1100-1805
XJ1)	7275	100	Xinjiang	Urumqi	2300-1800, Tu1
GZ1)	7275	10	Guizhou	Guiyang	0135-1530 Tu6
1)	7290	100	CNR 1	Beijing	2025-0100, 1000-1805
XJ1)	7295	50	Xinjang	Urumqi	Nov-Apr only
1)	7305	100	CNR 1	Shijiazhuang	2025-2200, 1000-1805
XJ1)	7310	100	Xinjiang	Urumqi	2300-0130, 1400-1800
1)	7315	150	CNR 2	Xianyang	2055-0100, 1100-1605
1)	7335	100	CNR 2	Baoji-Sif.	2055-0030, 1300-1605
XJ1)	7340	100	Xinjiang	Urumqi	2310-1800, Tu1
1)	7345	100	CNR 1	Beijing	2025-2400, 1100-1805
1)	7350	100	CNR 11	Baoji-Sif.	2155-2400, 1300-1605
1)	7365	100	CNR 1	Shijiazhuang	1200-1805
1)	7370	150	CNR 2	Beijing	2055-2300, 1300-1605
1)	7375	150	CNR 2	Beijing	1200-1605
1)	7385	100	CNR 5	Beijing	2055-2300, 0900-1705
XZ1)	7385	100	Xizang	Lhasa	2050(Tu2100)-0200, 0930-1805
1)	7395	150	CNR 2	Xianyang	2055-2400
NM1)	7420	50	Nei Menggu	Hohhot	2150-1605, Tu2
1)	7425	150	CNR 2	Xianyang	1300-1605
XZ1)	7450	100	Xizang	Lhasa	2000(Tu2100)-0300, 0900(Tu1000)-1800
1)	9420	100	CNR 6	Beijing	2155-0100, 0900-1605
1)	9420	100	CNR 13	Lingshi	1100-1805
XJ1)	9470	100	Xinjiang	Urumqi	0345-1150, Tu1
1)	9480	100	CNR 11	Baoji-Sif.	2155-2400, 1100-1605
XZ1)	9490	100	Xizang	Lhasa	0200-1000(Tu0600)
1)	9500	100	CNR 1	Shijiazhuang	2025-1805, Tu5
XJ1)	9510	50	Xinjiang	Urumqi	0510-1030
1)	9515	100	CNR 2	Beijing	2055-2400, 0900-1605
NM1)	9520	50	Nei Menggu	Hohhot	2150-1605, Tu2
1)	9530	100	CNR 11	Baoji-Sif.	0000-1300, Tu5
XJ1)	9560	100	Xinjiang	Urumqi	0245-1200, Tu3
1)	9570	100	CNR 2	Golmud	May-Oct 0100-1100, Tu6
XZ1)	9580	100	Xizang	Lhasa	0200-0930(Tu0700)
XJ1)	9600	100	Xinjiang	Urumqi	0130-1400, Tu1
1)	9610	100	CNR 8	Beijing	2055-0600
1)	9620	150	CNR 2	Beijing	May-Oct 2300-1300
1)	9630	100	CNR 1	Golmud	0000-1100, Tu5
1)	9630	100	CNR 17	Lingshi	1200-1805
1)	9645	100	CNR 1	Beijing	2330-1100, Tu5
1)	d9655	30	CNR1	Urumqi	2200-0100, 0800-1200
1)	9665	100	CNR 5	Beijing	2055-2400, 1000-1705
1)	9675	100	CNR 1	Beijing	2300-1000, Tu5
1)	9685	100	CNR 5	Beijing	0000-1000, Tu5
XJ1)	9705	100	Xinjiang	Urumqi	0305-0530, 1005-1230
1)	9710	100	CNR 1	Shijiazhuang	2025-2330, 1100-1805
1)	9720	150	CNR 2	Baoji-Xinjie	0000-1000, Tu5
NM1)	9750	50	Nei Menggu	Hohhot	2150-1605, Tu2
1)	9755	100	CNR 2	Baoji-Sif.	2055-2400, 1000-1605
1)	9775	150	CNR 2	Beijing	2055-0100, 0900-1605
QH1)	9780	50	Qinghai	Xining	2200-1600, Tu5
1)	9785	100	CNR 8	Beijing	0600-1505, Tu5
1)	9810	150	CNR 1	Nanning	2025-2300, 1300-1805
1)	9810	100	CNR 2	Baoji-Sif.	0100-1230, W2
1)	9820	150	CNR 2	Xianyang	2055-2400, 1100-1605
1)	9830	100	CNR 1	Beijing	2025-0100, 0730-1805, Tu10
XJ1)	9835	100	Xinjiang	Urumqi	May-Oct 0300-1200, Tu1
1)	9845	100	CNR 1	Beijing	May-Oct 2025-2400, 1200-1805
QH1)	9850	50	Qinghai	Xining	2250-1600, Tu6
1)	9860	100	CNR 1	Beijing	2025-2300, 1200-1805
1)	d9870	30	CNR1	Qiqihar	1000-1200
1)	9890	100	CNR 13	Lingshi	1400-1805
1)	11610	150	CNR 2	Beijing	May-Oct 2300-1300, We 0600-0900
1)	11620	100	CNR 5	Beijing	0000-1000, W2
1)	11630	100	CNR 17	Lingshi	May-Oct 2355-1805, Tu5
1)	11660	150	CNR 2	Xianyang	May-Oct 0100-1100, W2
1)	11670	100	CNR 2	Beijing	May-Oct 2230-1200, W2
1)	11685	100	CNR 11	Baoji-Sif.	0000-1300, W2
1)	11710	100	CNR 1	Beijing	2025-0030, 1000-1805
1)	11720	100	CNR 1	Shijiazhuang	2330-1100, Tu5
1)	11740	100	CNR 2	Lingshi	2055-0100, 1100-1605
1)	11750	100	CNR 1	Shijiazhuang	2200-1000, Tu5
1)	11760	100	CNR 1	Shijiazhuang	0000-1200, Tu5
XJ1)	11770	100	Xinjiang	Urumqi	2300 1800, Tu1
1)	11800	150	CNR 2	Beijing	May-Oct 2300-1200, W2
1)	11810	100	CNR 8	Beijing	2055-0600
1)	11835	150	CNR 2	Xianyang	0000-1300, W2
1)	11845	150	CNR 2	Xianyang	0000-1100, W2
XZ1)	11860	100	Xizang	Lhasa	0300-0900(Tu0500)
XJ1)	11885	100	Xinjiang	Urumqi	2300-1800, Tu1
1)	11905	100	CNR 6	Beijing	0100-0900(W0600)
1)	11915	100	CNR 2	Baoji-Sif.	0030-1300, W2
1)	11925	100	CNR 1	Lingshi	2025-2330, 1200-1805
1)	11935	100	CNR 5	Beijing	2300-0900(W0600)
XZ1)	11950	100	Xizang	Lhasa	0300-0900(Tu0500)
1)	11960	100	CNR 1	Beijing	0000-0900(Tu0600)
XJ1)	11975	100	Xinjiang	Urumqi	May-Oct 0305-0530, 1005-1230
1)	d11995	30	CNR1	Qiqihar	0100-1000
1)	12045	100	CNR 1	Beijing	2300-1200, Tu5
1)	12055	100	CNR 17	Lingshi	2355-1200, Tu5
1)	12080	100	CNR 2	Baoji-Sif.	0000-1000, W2
1)	13610	150	CNR 1	Nanning	2300-1300, Tu5
XJ1)	13670	100	Xinjiang	Urumqi	0230-1400, Tu1
1)	13700	100	CNR 13	Lingshi	May-Oct 2355-1400, Tu5
1)	d13810	30	CNR1	Qiqihar	0400-1100
1)	d13825	30	CNR1	Beijing	0050-0900
1)	d15180	30	CNR1	Kunming	0050-0400
1)	15270	150	CNR 2	Beijing	0100-0900(W0600)
1)	15370	100	CNR 1	Shijiazhuang	0100-1100, Tu5
1)	15380	100	CNR 1	Beijing	2300-1100, Tu5
1)	15390	100	CNR 13	Lingshi	2355-1100, Tu5
1)	15480	100	CNR 1	Beijing	May-Oct 2300-1300, Tu5
1)	15500	150	CNR 2	Beijing	May-Oct 2300-1000, W2
1)	15540	100	CNR 2	Lingshi	0100-1100, W2
1)	15550	100	CNR 1	Beijing	0000-1100, Tu5
1)	15570	100	CNR 11	Baoji-Sif.	0000-1100, W2
1)	15710	100	CNR 6	Beijing	0100-0900(W0600)
1)	17550	100	CNR 1	Beijing	0000-1200, Tu5

SW	kHz	kW	Station	Tx Loc.	Times (see * below)
1)	17565	100	CNR 1	Beijing	0100-0730(Tu -0600)
1)	17580	100	CNR 1	Lingshi	2330-1200, Tu5
1)	17595	100	CNR 1	Shijiazhuang	2300-1100, Tu5
1)	17605	100	CNR 1	Beijing	0030-1000, Tu5
1)	17625	150	CNR 2	Beijing	0000-0900(W0600)
1)	d17770	30	CNR1	Dongfang	0050-0900
1)	d17830	30	CNR1	Urumqi	0100-0800
1)	17890	100	CNR 1	Beijing	0100-1000, Tu5

NB: Baoji-Sif. = Baoji-Sifangshan. ‡=inactive, .±=variable, d=DRM,
Times: Tu#/W#=excluding time slot for tx maintenance as follows: Tu1= Tuesdays 0800-1100, Tu2=0600-0950, Tu3=0630-1100, Tu4= 0700-0800, Tu5= 0600-0900, Tu6= 0600-0855, Tu7=0700-1000, Tu8=0600-1000, Tu9=0900-1100, Tu10=0730-0900.
W1=Wednesdays 0400-0945, W2= 0600-0900, W3=0600-1200.

FM(MHz)	CNR 1	CNR 2	CNR 3	Prov.T	Prov.M	City.T	City.M
Anshan	101.0	105.1	98.3	97.5	-	99.5	93.6
Baoding	98.3	89.7	105.3	99.2	106.4	104.8	-
Baotou	96.9	99.3	-	95.7	107.4	89.2	100.1
Beihai	102.5	-	97.1	100.3	95.5	99.1	-
Beijing	106.1	96.6	90.0	-	-	103.9	97.4
Benxi	87.2	100.3	-	97.5	98.6	107.4	-
Changchun	99.1	104.7	94.3	103.8	92.7	96.8	106.3
Changde	94.7	102.9	-	89.5	102.1	97.1	98.5
Changsha	95.0	87.6	107.7	91.8	89.3	106.1a	102.2
Chengdu	103.7	-	107.6	101.7	95.5	91.4	105.6
Chifeng	101.2	107.1	88.5	105.6	94.5	101.8	-
Chongqing	102.9	100.0	90.6	-	-	95.5	88.1
Dalian	89.1	104.3	107.8	97.5	-	100.8	106.7
Daqing	97.3	-	102.3	99.8	102.9	95.0	106.0
Fuzhou	93.5	-	92.6	100.7	91.3	87.6	89.3
Guangzhou	89.3	106.6	87.4	105.2	99.3	106.1	102.7
Guilin	89.8	94.1	-	100.3	95.0	88.3a	-
Guiyang	93.6	105.6	107.3	95.2	91.6	102.7	90.9
Haikou	105.8	87.8	89.8	100.0	94.5	-	91.6
Handan	88.7	-	93.9	99.2	102.4	106.8	102.8
Hangzhou	90.2	97.9	103.2	93.0	96.8	91.8	105.4
Harbin	89.9	88.1	100.9	99.8	95.8	92.5	90.9
Hefei	93.5	104.7	91.1	90.8	89.5	102.6	87.6
Hengyang	95.0	105.9	-	100.3	96.9	101.8	-
Hohhot	97.1	-	99.1	105.6	93.6	107.3	-
Jiamusi	94.4	-	-	99.8	105.8	98.0	-
Jilin-shi	98.0	-	104.5	103.8	93.4	105.3	91.3
Jinan	89.8	96.5	95.5	101.1	99.1	103.1	88.7
Jinzhou	104.9	101.2	106.0	97.5	-	100.3	-
Jiujiang	102.4	-	-	105.4	107.9	88.4	91.6
Kaifeng	106.3	100.8	-	104.1	88.1	105.1	-
Kunming	-107.0	88.7	93.0	91.8	97.0	-	-
Lanzhou	94.8	90.3	88.3	103.5	-	-	99.5
Lhasa	89.2	104.3	96.1	-	-	-	-
Lianyungang	93.6	97.2	-	101.1	-	102.1	-
Lijiang	95.1	-	107.2	93.1	100.7	-	-
Nanchang	89.1	93.8	87.2	105.4	103.4	95.1	90.6
Nanjing	95.8	107.5	98.9	101.1	89.7	102.4	105.8
Nanning	106.2	93.6	99.0	100.3	95.0	107.4a	-
Ningbo	95.7	101.2	107.7	93.0	103.2	97.4	93.9
Qingdao	96.7	104.1	98.0	106.0	106.6	89.7	91.5
Qinhuangdao	96.5	-	-	99.3	106.4	100.4	97.3
Qiqihar	97.7	101.8	-	99.8	90.4	94.1	-
Quanzhou	96.9	98.3	102.5	100.7	-	90.4	92.3
Rizhao	89.4	106.9	-	106.0	-	88.1	-
Shanghai	99.0	91.4	107.7	-	-	105.7	101.7
Shenyang	94.8	93.5	99.8	97.5	98.6	-	-
Shenzhen	95.8	-	101.2	105.2	93.9	106.2	97.1
Shijiazhuang	95.6	97.2	105.1	99.2	102.4	94.6	106.7
Suzhou	100.0	98.7	-	101.1	89.7	104.8	94.8
Taiyuan	97.0	99.0	89.3	88.0	94.0	107.0	102.6
Tangshan	93.2	107.4	-	99.3	89.5	96.8	94.0
Tianjin	102.9	98.0	92.5	-	-	106.8	99.0
Urumqi	88.7	90.6	-	94.9	103.9	97.4	106.5
Weifang	96.7	-	-	106.0	106.6	95.9	88.7
Wenzhou	103.1	-	92.1	93.0	104.7	103.9	100.3
Wuhan	95.6	97.8	90.7	92.7	105.8	89.6	101.8
Wuhu	103.8	-	-	90.8	91.8	96.3	98.2
Wuxi	89.4	98.7	-	101.1	89.7	106.9	91.4
Xiamen	102.6	87.5	105.2	100.7	-	107.0	90.9
Xi'an	96.4	103.0	95.5	91.6	98.8	104.3	93.1
Xining	91.6	105.6	100.6	97.2a	-	-	104.3
Yantai	98.8	98.1	-	106.9	107.8	103.0	91.2
Yinchuan	96.4	107.8	99.7	98.4	-	100.6a	-
Yueyang	103.2	87.6	107.7	91.8	-	104.1	106.1
Zhangjiakou	88.9	-	-	101.6	93.9	-	98.6
Zhangzhou	102.6	98.3	100.2	100.7	-	96.6	99.1
Zhengzhou	101.2	96.7		104.1	88.1	91.8	94.4
Zhuhai	99.1	--	104.9	105.2	93.9	87.5a	91.5

Prov.T=Provincial traffic stn **Prov.M**=Provincial music stn **City.T**=City traffic stn **City.M**=City music stn a) Traffic music stn
NB: Official FM band 87.0-108.0MHz. Low power college stns exist 60-87MHz, some spread over 50-108MHz

Addresses & other information:

1) CHINA NATIONAL RADIO (CNR)

(Zhongyang Renmin Guangbo Diantai, which means Central People's Broadcasting Station)

✉ 2 Fuxingmenwai Dajie, Xicheng Qu, Beijing 100866 ☎ +86 10 8609 2636 **W:** cnr.cn **L.P:** Gen. Dir: Yan Xiaoming. CE: Qian Yuelin
V.O. China (1st Prgr News R.): MW/SW/FM 24h (exc. Mon 1805-2025). MW/SW mostly 2025-1805 exc. Tues 0600-0850. SW detail see list. **V.O. the Economy (2nd Prgr China Business R.):** MW/SW/FM 24h (exc. Mon 1600-2100). MW/SW mostly 2055-1605 exc. Wed 0600-0900. SW detail see list. **V.O. the Music (3rd Prgr Music R.):** 2155-1605 (exc. Tue 0600-0900) on FM. **Scripture Music Sce (4th Prgr Golden R.):** 2055-1705 (exc. Tue 0500-0900) on 101.8MHz **V.O. Zhonghua (5th Prgr Zhonghua News R.)**: 2055-1705 on MW/SW/102.3(Fuzhou/Mazu)/94.9MHz (Xiamen/Jinmen). **V.O. Shenzhou (6th Prgr Shenzhou Easy R.)** in Ch, Amoy and Hakka: 2200-1600 on MW/SW/106.2(Fuzhou/Mazu)/107.9MHz (Xiamen/Jinmen). **V.O. the Greater Bay Area (7th Prgr CMG R. the Greater Bay)** for the Guangdong-Hong Kong-Macao Greater Bay Area (GBA): Ch. on 1215kHz/93.2(Foshan)/101.2(Zhongshan)/105.4(Zhuhai)MHz 2055-1805(exc. Tues 0600-0900) in Ch, Cantonese, Chaozhou, Hakka etc. **V.O. the Literary (9th Prgr Story R.):** 2100-1800 (exc. Tues 0500-0900) on 106.6MHz. **V.O. Old Age (10th Prgr Senior Citizen R.):** 2025-1805 (exc. Tue 0600-0900) on 1053kHz. **V.O. Reading (12th Prgr):** 2100-1800 (exc. Tue 0500-0900) on 747kHz. **V.O. Hong Kong (14th Prgr)** for Hong Kong Special Administrative Region: 24h (exc. Mon 1600-2100) in Ch and Cantonese see Hong Kong RTHK Radio 6
China Traffic Sce (15th Prgr): on FM 87.5 (Jiangsu and Zhejiang Provinces), 87.7 (Sichuan Provice), 88.7 (Guangxi Zhuang Autonomous Region) 90.5(Hunan/Jilin Provinces), 91.7(Xinjiang Uighur Autonomous Region/Gansu Province), 94.1 (Shandong Province), 94.8 (Hubei Province), 95.5(Shanghai), 98.8(Hebei Province), 99.6(Beijing-Tianjin-Tanggu Area), 100.4 (Anhui Province), 100.6(Nei Menggu Autonomous Region) and 101.2 (Hebei Province), 101.4 (Heilongjiang Province), 101.9 (Ningxia Hui Autonomous Region), 103.5 (Shaanxi Provice), 104.7 (Henan Province), 106.5 (Shanxi Province) 24h (exc. Mon 1600-2100). **V.O. China Country (16th Prgr):** on 720kHz (Beijing) 24h (exc. Mon 1600-2100). **China National Emergency Broadcasting:** in an emergency including a wide range earthquake on 9800/12000kHz/FM 24h.
V.O. Minorities (8th Prgr Ethnic Minority R.) 2055-1505 on MW/SW (exc. Wed 0600-0900)/104.5MHz (Hohhot), 106.5MHz (Yanji)

Korean	**kHz**
0600-1000	9785, 5975, 1143, 720
1000-1100+JL	9785, 5975, 1143, 720
1100-1505	9785, 5975,1143,720

Mongolian	**kHz**
2100-2330	11810, 9610, 1143
2330-0030+ MN	11810, 9610, 1143
0030-0600	11810, 9610, 1143

11th Prgr. Tibetan Service 2155-1605 on MW/SW (exc. Wed 0600-0855)/105.7MHz (Lhasa)

Tibetan	**kHz**
2155-2300	9480, 7350, 6010, 1098
2300-2400+XZ	9480, 7350, 6010, 1098
0000-0900	15570, 11685, 9530, 1098
0900-1100	15570, 11685, 9530, 1098
1100-1300	11685, 9530, 9480, 1098
1300-1605	9480, 7350, 6010, 1098

13th Prgr. Uighur Service 2355-1805 on MW/SW (exc. Tues 0600-0855) /FM

Uighur	**kHz**
2355-0600	15390, 13700, 1008, 945, 720
0600-0630+XJ	15390, 13700, 1422, 1008, 945, 720

Uighur	kHz
0630-0900	15390, 13700, 1422, 1008, 945, 720
0900-1100	15390, 13700, 1008, 945, 720
1100-1400	13700, 9420, 1008, 945, 720
1400-1430+XJ	9890, 9420, 1008, 945, 720
1430-1805	9890, 9420, 1008, 945, 720

17th Prgr.Kazakh Service 2355-1805 on SW (exc. Tues 0600-0855)

Kazakh	kHz
2355-0900	12055, 11630
0900-0930+XJ	12055, 11630
0930-1200	12055, 11630
1200-1400	11630, 9630
1400-1430+XJ	11630, 9630
1430-1805	11630, 9630

NB +) relayed by regional stns

2) CHINA RADIO INTERNATIONAL (CRI)

(Zhongguo Guoji Guangbo Diantai)
✉ Jia 16, Shijingshan Lu, Shijingshan Qu, Beijing 100040 ☎ +86 10 6889 1001 **W:** cri.cn **L.P:** Gen. Dir: Wang Gengnian

Domestic Sce:
Beijing 1 Easy FM (1251kHz/91.5MHz): 24h in English – **Beijing 2 Hit FM** (88.7MHz): 24h in English – **Beijing 3 Round the Clock** (1008kHz): 24h in English – **Beijing 4 News Plus** (846kHz) 24h in English – **Beijing 5 News R.** (900kHz/90.5MHz): 24h in Chinese – **Tianjin News R.** (105.4MHz): 24h in Chinese – **Shijiazhuang News R.** (92.2MHz): 24h – **Shanghai 1 Hit FM** (87.9MHz): 2200-2400, 0300-1730 – **Shanghai 2 Easy FM** (100.1MHz): 24h – **Shanghai 3 News R.** (102.5MHz): 24h – **Hefei 1 Easy FM** (92.4MHz): 2200-1700 – **Hefei 2 News R.** (90.1MHz): 2200-1700 – **Chizhou News R.** (101.9MHz) – **Xinzhou News R.** (98.1MHz) – **Wuhu News R.** (89.4MHz): 2200-1700 – **Xiamen 1 Hit FM**(90.1MHz): 24h in English – **Xiamen 2 Easy FM** (95.8MHz): 2200-1700 – **Xiamen 3 News R.** (90.1MHz): 24h – **Qingdao News R.** (89.8MHz):24h – **Yantai News R.** (88.4MHz): 2300-2400, 0400-0430, 0900-1000 – **Wuhan News R.** (98.6MHz): 24h – **Changsha News R.** (99.5MHz): 24h – **Guangzhou 1 Hit FM** (88.5MHz): 24h – **Guangzhou 2 News R.** (107.1MHz): 24h – **Guangzhou 3 Easy FM** (98.0MHz) – **Shenzhen News R.** (107.1MHz):24h – **Zhuhai News R.** (702kHz): 24h – **Haikou News R.** (104.4MHz): 24h – **Chengdu News R.** (88.9MHz) – **Chongqing 1 Easy FM** (89.8MHz): 2200-1600 – **Chongqing 2 News R.** (91.7MHz): 24h – **Lhasa Easy FM** (100.0MHz): 1930-1600 – **Guiyang News R.** (102.1MHz): 24h – **Lanzhou Easy FM** (98.5MHz): 2200-1600

DAB: China Digital Multimedia Broadcasting (CDMB), Beijing on 208.720, 210.432, 212.144, 213.856MHz 2200-1600 (exc. Tues 0400-1000). Each freq. contains 5 audio ch and 3 video ch at maximum. Currently there are only one regular regional mux, one trial regional mux and four regular local mux on air.

EXTERNAL SERVICES: China Radio International, Voice of Beibu Bay Radio, Yunnan Broadcasting Station, China Xinjiang Radio and TV Station
See International Broadcasting section

BROADCASTS TO TAIWAN
11) Voice of the Strait (Haixia zhi Sheng), 15 Yuandang Jie, Gulou Qu, Fuzhou, Fujian 350025. Operated by the People's Liberation Army of China **W:** vos.com.cn News Sce in Ch and Amoy on 666/4940kHz/90.6MHz (Fuzhou) 2225-1600 (exc. Wed 0400-0955) where 4940kHz 0930-1600. - Dialect Sce in Amoy on 783/4900kHz/97.9MHz(Xiamen/Jinmen) 2230-1600 (exc. Wed 0400-0955) where 4900kHz 2230-0100, 0930-1600 - Culture & Life Sce on 99.6MHz(Fuzhou) 24h (exc. Wed 0400-0955) – **12) Voice of Jinling** (Jinling zhi Sheng), 132 Zhongshan Donglu, Nanjing, Jiangsu 210002 **W:** vojs.cn/2014new/c/h/ On 6200kHz 1200-1500 On 99.7MHz 24h – **13) Voice of Pujiang** (Pujiang zhi Sheng), Shanghai Media Group(SMG), 11F, 1376 Hongqiao Lu, Changning Qu, Shanghai 200051 or P.O.Box 518, Shanghai 200051 **W:** smg.cn/review/channel/channel_24/index.html. On 1422kHz 24h (exc. Thu 1600-2200) including "Cross-strait this week"prgr in Ch at 1100-1200 & 2300-2400 and relay of SMG First Financial and Ecomonic Sce at 0000-1100 & 1200-2300. **NB:** All SW and FM services have closed since 1 May 2013 – **14) Southeast Broadcasting Company**, Fujian Radio & TV Network, B-10F, Fujian Radio & TV Center, 28 Xihuan Nan Lu, Fuzhou, Fujian350004 **W:** sebc.com.cn/ On 585kHz/97.6/106.2MHz 2155-1600 in Ch and Amoy – **15) China Huayi Broadcasting Corporation**, 15 Yuandang Jie, Baima Bei Lu Xiaoliu, Gulou Qu, Fuzhou 350001 or P.O.Box 251, Fuzhou, Fujian 350001 **W:** chbcnet.com On 873/6185kHz/107.1MHz(Fuzhou) for Taiwan, Hong Kong, Macao and Southeast Asia. 24hexc. Wed 0400-0953, where 6185kHz 0945-1600.

ANHUI PROVINCE
AH1) Anhui Radio and TV St, 666 Longtu Lu, Hefei, Anhui 230071 **W:** ahrtv.cn News General Sce "V.O. Anhui": on 936/846kHz/103.6MHz 2000-1800(Tues 1500) - Economic Sce on 864kHz/97.1MHz 24h (exc. Mon 1500-2100) - Travel Sce "FM1065 Anhui Private Car Sce"on 1098/837/900kHz/96.1/106.5MHz 24h exc. Tues 1500-2000) - Traffic Sce "Automobile 908": on 90.8MHz 24h (exc. Tues 1500-2150) - Life Sce on 603kHz/105.5MHz 2100-1600 - Farm Sce on 720/1008kHz/95.5MHz on 2000-1600(Mon 1500) - Music Sce "Changxiang 895": on 89.5MHz 24h - Novel and Storytelling Sce on 1395kHz/102.9/107.4MHz 2000-1800(Tues 1500) - Chinese Opera Sce on 801kHz/99.5MHz 24h (exc. Tues 1500-2000) "Hefei My FM": on 96.1MHz 24h – **AH2)** Hefei Radio and TV St, 558 Tian'ehu Lu, Hefei, Anhui 230011. News General Sce on 666kHz/91.5MHz 2050-1700 - Traffic Sce on 1053kHz/102.6MHz 24h (exc. Tues 0600-0850) - Automobile Music Sce "Hot FM": on 747kHz/87.6MHz 2200-1700 - Story Sce on 1170kHz/98.8MHz 2100-1700 - Hui Merchant Sce on 100.3MHz 2200-1800 - Xincheng Information Sce on 846kHz/88.1MHz 2125-1500 - Xincheng Traffic and Music Sce on 93.8MHz 2200-1600 – **AH2A)** 327 Jinzhai Lu, Luyang Qu, Hefei, Anhui 230061. Charm Music Sce on 88.6MHz 24h – **AH3)** 11 Dongshan Zhonglu, Huainan, Anhui 232001. News General Sce on 648kHz/103.7MHz 2125-1500 - Traffic and Literary Sce on 97.9MHz 2140-1500 - Music and Story Sce on 104.9MHz 24h(exc. Tues 0600-0900) – **AH4)** Huaibei Radio and TV St, 316 Renmin Zhonglu, Xiangshan Qu, Huaibei, Anhui 235000. News Sce on 1431kHz/94.9MHz 2155-1600 - Traffic Sce on 100.4MHz 2150-1600 (exc. Tues 0630-0900) - Music Sce on 89.3MHz 2150-1600 – **AH5)** 197 Beijing Donglu, Wuhu, Anhui 241000. News General Sce on 100.4MHz 2100-1600 - Life Sce on 1494kHz - Traffic and Economic Sce on 96.3MHz 2128-1630 (Sun -1600) - Music and Story Sce on 98.2MHz 2200-1600 – **AH6)** Tongling Radio and TV St, Yi'an Beilu, Tongling, Anhui 244000. News General Sce on 1107kHz/95.9MHz 2155-1505 - Traffic and Life Sce on 88.7MHz 2230-1500 - Music and Story Sce on 92.4MHz 2225-1505 – **AH7)** Bengbu Radio and TV St, Xuehua Shan, Shengli Donglu, Bengbu, Anhui 233000. News General Sce on 765kHz/107.9MHz 2200-1400 - Economic Sce on 1098kHz/104.2MHz 2150-1430 - Traffic and Literary Sce on 98.4MHz 2200-1500 **AH8)** Ma'anshan Radio and TV St, 46 Yushan Zhonglu, Ma'anshan, Anhui 243011. News Sce on 1584kHz/105.1MHz 2150-1500 (exc. Tues 0600-0850) - Traffic Sce on 92.8MHz 2130-1500 (exc. Tues 0600-0850) - Music FM "Xindong (Heart) 954": on 95.4MHz 2130-1500 – **AH9)** Anqing Radio and TV St, 23 Guanyue Miao, Anqing, Anhui 246004. News General Sce on 1584kHz/90.3MHz 2200-1500 - Traffic and Music Sce on 97.7MHz 2200-1500 (exc. Tues 0600-0925) - Story Sce on 93.7MHz 2200-1500 (exc. Tues 0600-0925) – **AH10)** Huangshan Radio and TV St, 9 Tiandu Dadao, Tunxi Qu, Huangshan, Anhui 245000. News General Sce on 1431kHz/93.3MHz 2200-1500 - Traffic and Travel Sce on 100.4MHz 2200-1500 – **AH11)** 225 Langxie Lu, Chuzhou, Anhui 239000. News General Sce on 95.0/97.3MHz 2125-1440 (exc. Tues 0500-0930) - Traffic and Music Sce on 105.4MHz 2125-1530 - Literary and Story Sce on 1377kHz/97.0MHz 2100-1500 – **AH12)** Nan 2 Huan Lu, Fuyang, Anhui 236034. News Sce on 1116kHz/91.6MHz 2130-1610 - Economic Sce on 711/801/1503kHz 2145-1550 (exc. Tues 0700-0830) - Traffic Sce on 90.0/103.5MHz 2130-1530 - Story Sce on 94.1MHz 2120-1530 – **AH13)** Suzhou Radio and TV St, Baihuiyuan, Huaihai Lu, Suzhou, Anhui 234000. News General Sce on 1251kHz/100.8/100.2MHz 2155-1450 (exc. Tues 0600-0850) - Traffic Sce, on 96.1MHz/95.1MHz 24h - City Music Sce on 97.1/107.3MHz 2130-1600 - Story Sce on 102.3MHz 2200-1600 – **AH15)** Changjiang Nanlu, Guichi Qu, Chizhou, Anhui 247100. News General Sce on 801kHz/98.1MHz 2200-1405 - Traffic and Travel Sce on 96.6MHz – **AH16)** Meishan Nanlu, Lu'an, Anhui 237001. News General Sce on 1170kHz/102.1MHz 2155-1505 - Traffic and Music Sce on 96.4MHz 2155-1505 - Music Ch. on 92.4MHz – **AH17)** 10 Zhuangyuan Lu, Xuancheng, Anhui 242000. News General Sce on 1170kHz/100.6MHz 2155-1500 - Traffic and Literary Sce on 106.1MHz 2155-1500 – **AH18)** 8 Chengguan Ximen, Dangtu Xian, Anhui 243100. Automobile Music BS: on 1098kHz/90.1MHz 2155-1400 (exc. Wed 0600-0900) – **AH19)** 62 Renmin Zhonglu, Bozhou, Anhui 236800 - News General Sce on 999kHz/88.2MHz 2130-1530 - Traffic and Music Sce on 107.2MHz 2130-1530

BEIJING MUNICIPALITY
BJ1) Beijing Radio and TV St.(Beijing Media Network), 14 Jianguomenwai Dajie, Chaoyang Qu, Beijing 100022 **W:** bmn.net.cn/ News Sce on 828kHz/100.6MHz 24h exc. Mon 1600-2200 - Public

Sce on 1026kHz/107.3MHz 2100-1600 - Sports Sce on 102.5MHz 24h - Traffic Sce on 103.9MHz 24h exc. Mon 1600-2100 - Story Sce on 603kHz/95.4MHz 2200-1600 - Foreign Language Sce "Radio Beijing International": on 92.3MHz 2200-1600 - Literary Sce "Joy FM" on 87.6MHz 24h exc. Mon 1630-2100 - Music Sce on 97.4MHz 24h exc. Mon 1600-2100 – Mobile Sce "Metro Radio": on 94.5MHz 24h – Young Sce on 2200-1600 on 927kHz/98.2MHz.

CHONGQING MUNICIPALITY

CQ1) 159 Zhongshan 3 Lu, Yuzhong Qu, Chongqing 400015 **W:** cbg.cn News Sce "V. O. Chongqing" on 909/1314kHz/96.8MHz 24h - Economic Sce on 101.5MHz 24h - Traffic Sce on 95.5MHz 24h - Private Car Sce on 93.8MHz 2200-1600 - Music Sce on 88.1MHz 24h - Literary Sce on 103.5MHz 24h

HEBEI PROVINCE

EB1) Hebei Radio and TV St, 63 Yuhua Donglu, Shijiazhuang, Hebei 050012 **W:** hebradio.com News Sce on 1278/783kHz 2030-1700; on 104.3MHz/FM 24h - Economic Sce on 846kHz/FM 24h - Life Sce on 747/783kHz/89.0/91.0MHz 24h (exc. Tues 1700-2030) - Traffic Sce on 99.2/101.6MHz 24h - Literary Sce "Private Car 907": on 900kHz/90.7/94.8MHz 24h - Music Sce on 102.4MHz/FM 24h (exc. Tues 1700-2015) - Farmer Sce on 558/1251kHz/98.1/88.3MHz 24h (exc. Tues 1700-2030) - Travel Culture Sce "Top Radio": on 603/1521kHz/100.3/88.1MHz 24h - Storytelling Ch on 1125/1521kHz - "Shijiazhuang My FM": on 102.9MHz 24h – **EB2)** Shijiazhuang Radio and TV St, 302 Tiyu Nan Dajie, Shijiazhuang, Hebei 050021. General Sce on 882kHz/88.2MHz 2125-1700 - Economic Sce "V.O. the City" on 1431kHz/100.9MHz 2125-1600 (exc. Tues 0600-0825) - Farm Sce on 1251kHz/96.1MHz 2100-1600 - Traffic Sce on 94.6MHz 2130-1700 - Taxi Sce on 92.2MHz 2230-1600 - Music Sce "NuStar Radio": on 106.7MHz 24h - Pinwei (Taste) Music Sce on 87.6MHz 24h – **EB3)** 246 Renmin Lu, Handan, Hebei 056002. News General Sce on 963kHz/96.4MHz 2100-1600 - Life Sce on 1206kHz 2100-1600 - Traffic Sce on 1008kHz/106.8MHz 2100-1600 - Music Sce on 102.8MHz 2100-1600 - Chinese Opera and Storytelling Sce on 846kHz/104.8MHz 2100-1600 – **EB4)** 15 Yejin Lu, Xingtai, Hebei 054000. News General Sce on 1188kHz/89.6/90.3MHz 2125-1600 (exc. Tues 0530-0930) - Economic Life Sce on 927kHz/102.0MHz 2120-1500 (exc. Tues 0530-0930) - Traffic and Music Sce on 91.8/101.2MHz 2225-1500 (exc. Tues 0630-0930) - Kuaile (Happy) Sce on 96.8MHz – **EB5)** 1620 Yangguang Bei Dajie, Baoding, Hebei 071051. News Sce on 1467kHz/93.7MHz 24h (exc. Tues 0600-0855) - Private Car Sce on 1017kHz/99.7MHz 2145-1600 (exc. Tues 0600-0930) - Traffic Sce on 747kHz/104.8MHz 1850-1600 (exc. Tues 0600-0900) - City Service Sce on 101.6MHz 2200-1400 - City and Country Alliance Sce on 101.3/103.2/105.6MHz - News General Sce on 90.9/92.6MHz– **EB6)** 17 Jianguo Lu, Qiaodong Qu, Zhangjiakou, Hebei 075000. News General Sce on 1566kHz/101.0/107.4MHz 2155-1505 - Traffic Sce on 900kHz/100.0MHz 2130-1600 - Private Car Sce on 603kHz/104.3MHz 2130-1300 (exc. Tues 0500-0900) - Pinwei (Taste) Music Sce on 98.6MHz 2130-1530 (exc. Tues 0600-0900) – **EB7)** 120 Guangdian Lu, Shuangqiao Qu, Chengde, Hebei 067000. News General Ch. on 1584kHz/89.1MHz 2155-0540, 0950-1400 - Traffic and Literary Ch. on 900kHz/97.6MHz 2155-1600 (exc. Tues 0600-0900) - Travel Life Ch. on 100.6MHz 2225-1600 – **EB8)** 1 Guangda Jie, Wenhua Lu, Tangshan, Hebei 063000. News General Sce on 684kHz/91.7MHz 2030-1605 (exc. Tues 0705-0855) - Economic Life Sce on 801kHz/95.5MHz 2130-1530 (exc. Tues 0700-0830) - Traffic and Literary Sce on 1143kHz/96.8MHz 2135-1505 - Music Sce "NuStar Radio": on 94.0MHz 2200-1600 (exc. Tues 0700-0900) - "V.O. Cao Jidian" Novel Sce on 900kHz 2200-1600 (exc. Tues 0630-0900) - Cultural and Entertainment Sce on 105.9MHz – **EB9)** 9 Yingbin Lu, Haigang Qu, Qinhuangdao, Hebei 066000. News General Sce on 990kHz/89.1MHz 24h - Private Car Sce on 900kHz/103.8MHz 24h - Traffic Sce on 100.4MHz 24h (exc. Tues 0700-0800) - Sports and Music Sce on 97.3MHz 24h - Farm Sce "Huanle (Joy) FM": on 92.4/89.9MHz 24h – **EB10)** 12 Jiefang Xilu, Cangzhou, Hebei 061001. News General Sce on 1557kHz/97.0MHz 2057-1500 - Agricultural Economic Sce on 1053kHz/91.7MHz - Traffic and Music Sce on 1206kHz/93.8MHz 2200-1600 - Automobile Music Sce on 105.8MHz 24h - Music Sce on 846kHz/103.6MHz 2200-1500 - Storytelling Sce on 801kHz 2200-1500 – **EB11)** 8 Yongfeng Dao, Langfang, Hebei 065000. News General Sce on 1008/846kHz/95.1MHz 2055-1700 - Storytelling Sce on 585kHz/100.3MHz 24h - Chinese Opera Sce on 1521kHz/105.0MHz 2055-1700 – **EB12)** 693 Hongqi Dajie, Taocheng Qu, Hengshui, Hebei 053000. News General Sce on 954kHz/101.9MHz 2225-0535, 0825-1630 - Traffic Sce on 1098kHz/105.3MHz 2125-1500 - Literary Sce on 738kHz/96.1MHz 2230-1400 – **EB13)** 167, Bei Duan, Xinghua Lu, Xinji, Hebei 052360. 2225-2355, 0255-0500, 1025-1250 – **EB14)** Xitou, Shengli Dajie, Nangong, Hebei 055750. 2225-0045, 1005-1400 – **EB15)** 36 Yingxin Dajie, Shahe, Hebei 054100. 2200-1600 – **EB16)** Sanyang Dongjie, Qinghe Xian, Hebei 054800. 2100-1550 – **EB17)** Beiguan, Zhuozhou, Hebei 072750 – **EB18)** Zhongshan Xilu, Dingzhou, Hebei 073000. 2200-1500 – **EB19)** 393 Xiguan Xijie, Botou, Hebei 062150. 2225-2355, 0345-0450, 1025-1230 – **EB20)** 12-1 Xihuan Lu, Renqiu, Hebei 062550. General Ch. on 1287kHz/92.8MHz 2225-1600 - Storytelling Ch. on 864kHz 2255-1400

HENAN PROVINCE

EN1) Henan Radio and TV St.2 Wei Yilu, Jinshui Qu, Zhengzhou, Henan 450003 **W:** hndt.com News Sce on 657kHz/95.5MHz/FM. 24h - Economic Sce on 738/972kHz/103.2MHz 24h - Traffic Sce on 104.1MHz 24h - Farm Sce "Green Ch.": on 900/107.4MHz 24h – Travel Sce "Private Car 999" on 99.9MHz 24h - Music Sce: on 88.1MHz/FM 24h - Visual Sce "My Radio": on 90.0MHz 24h - Entertainment Sce : on 1143kHz/97.6MHz 24h - Education Sce "UpRadio 1066": on 1332kHz/106.6MHz 24h - Leling (Senior Citizen) Sce on 603/1098kHz/105.6MHz 24h - Tianlai (Sounds of nature) Sce on 93.6MHz 24h– **EN2)** 17 Shangwu Neihuan Lu, Zhengzhou, Henan 450018. News Sce on 549kHz/98.6MHz 24h (exc. Tues 0600-1000, Thurs 1600-2200) - Economic Sce "Chedao (Lane) 931": on 711kHz/93.1MHz 24h - "FM889": on 1008/792kHz/88.9MHz 24h - City Sce "Automobile 912": on 91.2MHz 24h - Music Sce "Huoli (Vitality) 944": on 94.4MHz 24h - Private Car Sce on 1458kHz/91.8MHz 24h - "Classic 1079": on 107.9MHz 24h – **EN3)** 78 Songcheng Lu, Kaifeng, Henan 475004. General Sce on 873kHz/98.6MHz 24h - News Sce on 101.4MHz 2200-1530 - Economic Sce on 100.2MHz 2155-1530 - Traffic Sce on 105.1MHz - New Farm Sce on 1053kHz/96.6MHz 2200-1530 (exc. Tues 0630-0955) – **EN4)** 67, Jiudu Lu, Luoyang, Henan 471009. News Sce "V.O. Heluo": on 576kHz/88.1MHz 2150-1600 - Economic Sce on 1053kHz/106.5MHz 2155-1600 - Traffic Sce on 92.7MHz 2155-1600 - Private Car Sce on 102.1MHz 2200-1600 – **EN5)** Zhong Duan, Jianshe Lu, Pingdingshan, Henan 467000. News Ch. on 747kHz/98.9MHz 2055-1500 - Private Car Sceon 1008kHz/105.8MHz 2155-1600 - Literary Ch. on 846kHz 2200-1600, on 99.6MHz 24h - Traffic Sce on 1521kHz/96.4MHz 24h – **EN6)** 217 Jiefang Zhonglu, Jiaozuo, Henan 454002. News General Sce on 828kHz/103.0MHz 2200-1700 - Traffic and Travel Sce on 99.5MHz - Life and Literary Sce on 1251kHz/89.4MHz 2200-1700 (exc. Tues 0600-0955) – **EN7)** Zhong Duan, Huashan Lu, Hebi, Henan 458030. On 1107kHz/100.3MHz 2155-0535, 0955-1430 - Economic Ch. on 846kHz 2155-0535, 0955-1330 – **EN8)** 173 Renmin Lu, Weibin Qu, Xinxiang, Henan 453000. News General Sce on 801kHz/92.9MHz 2125-1600 (exc. Tues 0530-0955) - Traffic Sce on 1521kHz/99.1MHz 2155-1500 (exc. Tues 0500-0955) - Music Sce on 89.2MHz 24h - Private Car Sce on 90.3MHz 2200-1600 – **EN9)** Zhong Duan, Wenfeng Dadao, Anyang, Henan 455000. News Sce on 882kHz/94.2MHz 2155-1530 - Traffic Sce on 1251kHz/89.0MHz 2200-1400. - Automobile Music Sce "i Radio": on 100.8MHz 2155-1600 – **EN10)** Puyang Radio and TV St, 379 Zhongyuan Lu, Puyang, Henan 457000. News General Sce on 1251kHz/100.1MHz 2130-1535 (exc. Tues 0600-0900) - Economic Life Sce on 91.0MHz 2130-1530 - Traffic Sce on 89.5MHz 2100-1600 – **EN11)** 72 Balong Lu, Xiao Nanhai, Xuchang, Henan 461000. News Sce on 1287kHz/102.0MHz 2200-1500 - Traffic Sce on 92.6MHz 2130-1800 - Farm Sce on 927kHz 2150-1500 - Automobile Music Sce on 93.8MHz 2130-1800 – **EN12)** 152 Daxue Lu, Luohe, Henan 462000. News Sce on 1251kHz/89.0MHz 2055-1620 - Traffic and Music Sce on 106.7MHz 2155-1600 - City Sce "Car Radio": on 98.1MHz 2155-1600 – **EN12A)** 243 Haihe Lu, Luohe, Henan 462000 – **EN12B)** Luohe FM BS, 215 Shuanghui Lu, Luohe, Henan 462000. Life and Literary Sce on 93.6MHz 2230-1400 - Story Sce on 87.5MHz 2155-1430 – **EN13)** Zhong Duan, Jianshe Lu, Sanmenxia, Henan 472000. News General Ch. on 603kHz/90.8MHz 2155-1605 (exc. Tues 0530-0955) - Literary and Traffic Ch. on 1008kHz/104.0MHz 2255-1500 (exc. Tues 0530-1000) - Story Sce on 100.0MHz 24h - New Farm Sce on 98.9MHz – **EN14)** Zhong Duan, Funiu Lu, Nanyang, Henan 473000. News Sce on 104.2MHz 2130-1605 - General Sce on 585kHz/93.6MHz 2130-1605 - Literary Sce on 927kHz/106.0MHz 2130-1605 - Traffic Sce on 97.7/101.0MHz 2155-1605 - Story Sce on 106.0MHz 2130-1605 – **EN15)** Xinyang Radio and TV St, 19 Dongfanghong Dadao, Xinyang, Henan 464000. General Sce on 837kHz 2155-1500 - News Sce on 99.8MHz 2155-1600 - Economic Sce on 106.8MHz 2155-1600 - Traffic Sce on 94.8MHz 2155-1600 - Automobile Sce on 105.8MHz 2300-1600 - Music Sce on 88.8MHz – **EN16)** 35 Xinjian Nanlu, Shangqiu, Henan 476000. News Sce on 729kHz/89.0MHz 2100-1500 - City Sce on 927kHz/100.7MHz 2155-1605 - Traffic Sce on 94.5MHz 2200-1700 - Music Sce on 91.4MHz – **EN17)** 10, Dong Duan, Jianshe Lu, Zhoukou, Henan 466000. News Sce on 828kHz 2050-1515 - Economic

Life Sce on 567kHz 2050-1600 - Traffic Sce on 89.3MHz - Music Sce on 96.0MHz – **EN18)** 209 Wenhua Lu, Zhumadian, Henan 463000. News Sce on 810kHz 2125-? - Traffic and Travel Sce on 102.4MHz 2200-1600 - City Sce on 97.2MHz - Literary Sce on 1053kHz – **EN19)** Lianmeng Xiaoqu, Chengguan Zhen, Qinyang, Henan 454550 – **EN20)** 25 Xi Dajie, Huixian, Henan 453600 – **EN21)** 10 Qianqiu Lu, Yima, Henan 472300 – **EN22)** 30 Guangyu Lu, Ruzhou 467500 – **EN23)** Dufu Lu. Gongyi, Henan 451200. On 765kHz/98.2MHz 2155-1600 - Sunshine Ch. on 107.5MHz 2155-1530

FUJIAN PROVINCE

FJ1)128 Xihuan Nan Lu, Fuzhou, Fujian 350004 **W:** fjrtv.net News General Sce "Vanguard 944": on 558/612/882/1332/1368/1377/ 138 6/1395/1404/1422/1431/1467/1449/1494kHz/91.0/94.4/96.5/ 96.7/ 103.6/103.7/103.9/105.1/106.7MHz 24h in Ch and Amoy - City Life Sce "Private Car Radio" on 98.7/101.5MHz 24h - Traffic Sce on 87.6/100.7MHz 24h (exc. Tues 0600-0850) - Automobile Music FM on 91.3/101.5/103.2MHz 24h (exc. Tues 0600-0900) - Fujian EBS "Caijing 961": on 1404/1467kHz/89.5/89.6/94.2/95.5/96.1/ 98.6/98.9/103.1/1 04.8/104.9/105.4/107.3MHz 24h in Ch and Amoy – **FJ2)** 1 Yuanyang Lu, Fuzhou, Fujian 350004. News Sce on 1332kHz/94.4MHz 24h (exc. Wed 0605-0925) in Ch and Fuzhou dialect — Music Sce "Beauty 893/ Favor Radio"on 89.3MHz 24h (exc. Thurs 0600-0900) - Traffic Sce "Smooth 876" on 87.6MHz 24h (exc. Tues 0600-0900) - V.O. Zuohai "Happy 901" : on 90.1MHz 24h in Fuzhou dialect – **FJ3)** 121 Hubin Beilu, Xiamen, Fujian 361012. News Sce on 1107kHz/99.6MHz 2130-1700 (exc. Tues 0600-0900) in Ch and Amoy - Economic and Traffic Sce on 1278kHz/107.0MHz 2200-1700 (exc. Tues 0800-0900) - V.O. Minnan: on 801kHz/101.2MHz 2200-1600 in Amoy - Music Sce on 90.9MHz 24h (exc. Tues 0600-0830) - Travel Sce on 1008kHz/94.0MHz 2200-1600 – **FJ4)** 95 Dongzhen Lu, Licheng Qu, Putian, Fujian 351100. News General Sce on 93.7MHz 2130-1800 in Ch and Puxian dialect - Music and Traffic Sce on 103.0MHz 2130-1800 – **FJ5)** Quanzhou Radio and TV St, 1 Guangdian Lu, Quanzhou, Fujian 362000. News Sce on 576kHz/88.9MHz 24h - Economic and Life Sce on 92.3MHz 24h - Traffic Sce on 90.4MHz 24h (exc. Tues 0500-0900) V.O.the Music on 88.1MHz 24h - V.O. Citong: on 105.9MHz 24h in Quanzhou dialect– **FJ6)** Longyan Dadao, Longyan, Fujian 364000. News General Ch. on 92.5/106.0MHz 2158-1650 (exc. Tues 0630-0900) - V.O. the Travel: on 94.6MHz 2158-1600 (exc. Tues 0600-0900) – **FJ7)** 1199, Jiulong Dadao, Xiangcheng District, Zhangzhou, Fujian 363000. News General Sce on 89.6/96.2MHz 2200-1700 in Ch and Amoy - Traffic Sce on 96.6/92.7MHz 2200-1700 (exc. Tues 0600-1000) – **FJ8)** 32 Zhuang, Liedong Shuangyuan Xincun, Sanming, Fujian 365000. News General Ch. on 97.5/103.4MHz 2155-1600 - Traffic and Music Sce on 105.6MHz

GUANGDONG PROVINCE

GD1) Guangdong Radio and TV St, 686 Renmin Beilu, Guangzhou, Guangdong 510012 **W:** gdtv.cn News Sce on 648/828/846/1017/ 1206kHz/89.5/90.7/91.0/91.4/91.8/92.1/92.8/ 93.2/94.0/96.4/97.7/ 98.5/99.8/100.3/100.4/103.8/104.2/107.3MHz 24h - V.O. the City: on 103.6MHz 24h in Ch and Cantonese - Yangcheng Traffic St. on 105.2MHz 24h in Ch and Cantonese - Southern Life Sce on 999kHz/93.6/101.6/107.3MHz 24h in Ch and Cantonese - Stock Sce on 927kHz/95.3MHz 24h in Ch and Cantonese - V.O. the Music: on 1008kHz/ 93.9/96.8/96.9/99.2/99.3/MHz 24h - Literary and Sports Sce on 102.0/107.7MHz 24h – **GD2)** Zhujiang EBS, 686 Renmin Beilu, Guangzhou, Guangdong 510012. **W:** gdtv.cn/tv/fm974 on 747/801/927/1008/1062kHz/ 92.0/92.4/97.4/98.7/103.0/103.8/104. 2MHz 24h in Cantonese – **GD3)** Guangzhou Radio and TV St, 231 Huanshi Zhonglu, Guangzhou, Guangdong 510010 **W:** gztv.com News Information Sce on 96.2MHz 24h in Ch and Cantonese- Automobile and Music Sce "Golden Melody": on 102.7MHz 24h in Ch and Cantonese – Economy and Traffic Sce on 1098kHz/106.1MHz 24h in Ch and Cantonese - Youth Sce "My FM":on 1170kHz/88.0MHz 24hin Ch and Cantonese – **GD4)** 18F, Block 1, Phoenix Building 2008 Shennan Road, Futian Qu, Shenzhen, Guangdong 518026 **W:** uradio.cc U Radio on 105.7MHz 24h in Ch and Cantonese –**GD5)** 1 Pengcheng 1 Lu, Futian Qu, Shenzhen, Guangdong 518026 **W:** szmg.com.cn News Ch. on 900kHz/89.8MHz 24h (exc. Tues 0530-0930) in Ch - Life Sce on 94.2MHz 24h in Ch and Cantonese - – Music Sce "Feiyang 971": on 97.1MHz 24h in Ch - Traffic Ch. "Happy 1062" on 1287kHz/106.2MHz 2230-1900 – **GD6)** 1129 Dong, Jiuzhou Dadao, Xiangzhou Qu, Zhuhai, Guangdong 519015. News and Consulting Sce "Xianfeng 951": on 95.1MHz 24h in Ch and Cantonese - Traffic and Literature Sce "Jiaotong 875" on 87.5MHz 24h in Ch and Cantonese Music Sce "Vitality 915": on 612kHz/91.5MHz 24h – **GD7)** Shantou Radio and TV St, 48 Chaoshan Lu, Shantou, Guangdong 515021. Economy Sce on 1080kHz/90.0/102.0MHz 24h in Ch and Chaozhou dialect - Music Sce "Automobile ch.": on 102.5MHz 24h – General Sce "V.O. the Traffic": on 107.2MHz 24h (exc. Wed 0600-0900) in Ch and Chaozhou dialect – **GD8)** 57 Huimin Beilu, Shaoguan, Guangdong 512026. General Sce on 105.7MHz 2230-1600 in Ch - Traffic and Travel Sce on 765kHz/97.5MHz 2230-1600 in Ch and Cantonese – **GD9)** Heyuan PBS, 1 Xingyuan Donglu, Yuancheng Qu, Heyuan, Guangdong 517000. General Sce on 91.1MHz in Ch and Cantonese - Travel and Traffic Sce on 97.8MHz – **GD10)** Meizhou PBS, 42 Dong Jiaochang Bei, Meizhou, Guangdong 514011. News St. on 94.8MHz 2200-1600 in Ch and Hakka - Traffic St. on 105.8MHz 2200-1600 in Ch and Hakka – One Radio on 103.9MHz – **GD11)** Huizhou Radio and TV St, 13 Nantan Beilu, Huicheng Qu, Huizhou, Guangdong 516001. News and General- Ch.: on 100.0MHz 24h (exc. Tues 0030-0830) in Ch and Cantonese - Traffic St. on 98.8MHz 24h - Music St. on 90.7MHz 2230-1730 – **GD12)** Shanwei PBS, Zhong Duan, Shanwei Dadao, Shanwei, Guangdong 516600. General Sce on 103.5MHz 2225-1600 in Ch and Hakka - Farm Sce on 91.3MHz 2225-1600 in Ch and Hakka – **GD13)** Dongguan PBS, 35 Xizheng Lu, Cheng Qu, Dongguan, Guangdong 523000. General Ch."Sunshine 1008": on 100.8MHz 24h in Ch and Cantonese - Traffic Ch. on 107.5MHz 24h in Ch and Cantonese – Music Ch."Sound Power 104": on 104.0MHz 2300-1600– **GD14)** Zhongshan Radio and TV station, 4 Xingzhong Dao, Dong Qu, Zhongshan, Guangdong 528403."New and vigorous 967": on 96.7MHz 2200-1800 in Ch and Cantonese - "Happy 888": on 88.8MHz 2200-1800 in Ch and Cantonese – GD15) 178 Fazhan Dadao, Jiangmen, Guangdong 529000. News General St. on 100.2MHz 2300-1630 in Ch and Cantonese Travel and Music St. on 1206kHz/93.3MHz 2200 1500 in Ch and Cantonese – **GD16)** Foshan PBS, Jihua 6 Lu, Chancheng Qu, Foshan, Guangdong 528000. "FM946": on 94.6MHz 24h in Cantonese - "FM985" on 98.5MHz 24h (exc. Sun 1500-2400) in Cantonese - "FM924": on 92.4MHz 24h in Cantonese - "FM906": on 90.6MHz 24h in Cantonese - "FM901": on 90.1MHz 2225-1600 in Cantonese- "FM883": on 88.3MHz 24h – **GD17)** Yangjiang PBS, 114 Mojiang Lu, Jiangcheng Qu, Yangjiang, Guangdong 529500. General and Consulting Sce: on 91.6MHz 2200-1600 in Ch and Cantonese –Travel and Environmental Protection Sce: on 89.5MHz 2200-1600 in Ch and Cantonese – **GD18)** Zhanjiang Radio and TV St, 123 Haibin Dadao Bei, Chikan Qu, Zhanjiang, Guangdong 524044. News Sce on 98.1MHz 2220-1700 in Ch, Cantonese and Leizhou dialect - Economic Sce on 95.1MHz 2220-1700 – **GD19)** Maoming Radio and TV St, 1 Yingbin 4lu, Maoming, Guangdong. General Sce. on 101.1MHz 2250-1600 in Ch and Cantonese - VO Farming Area on 106.1MHz 2220-1600 – Traffic Sce on 93.5MHz 2245-1600 – **GD20)** Zhaoqing PBS, Xinghu Dadao, Zhaoqing, Guangdong 526060. General Sce on 92.9MHz 2250-1600 in Ch and Cantonese - Traffic and Music Sce on 94.9MHz 2200-1600 in Ch and Cantonese – **GD21)** Qingyuan PBS, 18 Yinquan Lu, Qingcheng District, Qingyuan, Guangdong 511515. General Sce on 88.7MHz 2225-1600 in Ch and Cantonese – Traffic and Travel Sce on 97.8MHz 2225-1600 in Ch and Cantonese –**GD22)** Jinxianmen Dadao, Jieyang, Guangdong 522000.General Sce: on 103.9MHz 2230-1700 in Ch and Jieyang dialect- Agricultural Sce: on 106.5MHz 2330-1600 in Jieyang dialect - Traffic and Travel Sce: on 1098kHz/95.2MHz – **GD23)** Jiedong PBS, Zhongxin Dadao, Jiedong, Guangdong 515500. On 100.2MHz 2220-1700 – **GD24)** Yunfu PBS, Baoma Lu, Yunfu, Guangdong 527300. General Sce on 100.6MHz 2220-1600 – Traffic and Music Sce on 96.4MHz 2220-1600

GANSU PROVINCE

GS1) 561 Zhangsutan, Chengguan Qu, Lanzhou, Gansu 730010. **W:** gstv.com.cn News General Sce on 684/873/1008kHz/96.0MHz 2150-1605 (exc. Tues 0600-0850) - City FM "Happy Radio" on 106.6MHz 24h –City FM "Heart FM 102.2" on 102.2MHz 2200-1700 - Economic Sce "U Radio": on 801kHz/93.4MHz 2255-1700 - Traffic Sce on 103.5/104.8MHz 24h - Youth FM: on 104.8MHz 2250-1600 - Farm Sce "Gansu Rural Radio" on 1170kHz/92.2MHz 2225-1700 (exc. Tues 0600-0850) – **GS2)** 92 Qingyang Lu, Lanzhou, Gansu 730030. General Sce on 954kHz/97.3MHz 2225-1600 - Traffic and Music Sce on 99.5MHz 2200-1900 (exc. Mon 0600-1000) - Private Car Sce "Happy FM 1008" on 100.8MHz 2055-1630 – **GS3)** 6 Yan'an Xilu, Jinchang, Gansu 737100. News General Sce on 585kHz/101.4MHz 2150-1600 - Traffic and Literary Sce on 103.8MHz – **GS4)** Tianshui Radio and TV St, 11-5 Huancheng Zhonglu, Qincheng Qu, Tianshui, Gansu 741000. News General Sce on 1143kHz/98.2MHz 2220-1600 - Music and Literary Sce on 93.7MHz 2225-1600 – **GS5)** 10 Fuqiang Xilu, Jiayuguan, Gansu 735100 – **GS6)** Gannan Radio and TV St, 49 Xi 2 Lu, Hezuo, Gansu 747000. On 1332/3990/5970kHz/97.2MHz 2250-0120, 0345-0625, 1025-1345 in Ch and Tb – **GS7)** 45 Tuanjie Lu, Linxia, Gansu 731100. 2255-0130(Sun 0230) – **GS8)** 45 Hongqi Jie, Kongtong Qu, Pingliang, Gansu 744000. 2200-1500 – **GS9)** Gongyuan Lu, Zhongping Qu, Yumen, Gansu 735200

GUANGXI ZHUANG AUTONOMOUS REGION

GX1) 73 Minzu Dadao, Nanning, Guangxi 530022. **W:** gxtv.cn General Sce "News 910" on 792/1071/1440/1485/kHz/. 91.1/91.4/91.9MHz 24h (exc. Tues 0500-0930) – Economic Sce "Anchorwomen BS" : on 846/1098/1161/1224/1575kHz/97.0/97.4/105.1MHz 24h (exc. Tues 0500-0830) in Ch and Guangxi dialect – Educational Sce "Private Car 930": on 93.0/88.5/90.1/92.3/96.9MHz 2200-1700 (exc. Tues 0500-0930) in Ch and Zhuang - Traffic St. on 100.3/106.3MHz (exc. Tues 0500-0930) 24h- Literary Sce "Music st."on 95.0/105.0MHz 24h (exc. Tues 0500-0930) – Travel Sce "Modern 104": on 104.0MHz 24h – **GX2)** Nanning Radio and TV St. 25 Gecun Lu, Nanning, Guangxi 530012. General Sce "990 News st." on 99.0MHz 24h in Ch and Guangxi dialect - Country Life Sce "Classic 1049" on 104.9MHz 24h - Traffic Sce on 107.4MHz 2300-1600 - Story Sce "Dynamic" on 89.5MHz 24h – **GX3)** 1 Guizhong Dadao, Liuzhou, Guangxi 545006. News Sce on 1386kHz/102.9MHz 2200-1700 in Ch and Liuzhou dialect - Traffic Sce "Love Radio": on 99.1MHz 2200-1700 - Country Life Sce on 105.9MHz 2200-1700 – **GX4)** 1 Anxin Beilu, Xiangshan Qu, Guilin, Guangxi 541002." V.O. the City" on 1485kHz/97.7MHz 2200-1600, - "Take off FM" on 88.3MHz 2200-1600 – Beloved 912 on 91.2MHz 2200-1600 – **GX5)** 69 Xinxing 3 Lu, Wuzhou, Guangxi 543002. News Sce on 1485kHz/100.8MHz 2200-1630 in Ch and Guangxi dialect - V.O. the Music and Traffic: on 107.5MHz 2200-1300 (exc. Mon) – **GX6)** Beihai PBS, 36 Guizhou Nanlu, Beihai, Guangxi 536000. News General Sce on 93.5/88.4MHz 2200-1700 (exc. Tues 0500-0930) in Ch and Guangxi dialect - Economic Music and Traffic Sce on 99.1MHz 2200-1700 (exc. Tues 0500-0930) – **GX7)** Qinzhou PBS, 18 Liqiao Jie, Qinzhou, Guangxi 535000. News General Sce on 98.6MHz 2220-1645 (exc. Tues 0500-0930) - Music Sce on 88.9MHz 2220-1645 (exc. Tues 0500-0930) – **GX8)** Yulin PBS, 1 Guangdian Lu, Yulin, Guangxi 537000. News Sce on 97.8MHz 2200-1700 (exc. Tues 0600-0900) - Traffic and Music St. on 99.2MHz 2200-1700 – **GX9)** Bose PBS, Huochezhan Jinzhan Dadao, Bose, Guangxi 533000. News and General Sce on 105.2MHz 2200-1700 – Music Sce on 87.6MHz 2200-1700 – **GX10)** Hechi PBS, 457 Jincheng Zhong Lu, Hechi, Guangxi 547000. News and General Sce on 98.7MHz – **GX11)** Fangchenggang PBS, Xianren Shanding, Fangchenggang, Guangxi 538001. General Sce on 101.9MHz in Ch Vietnamese and Zhuang

GUIZHOU PROVINCE

GZ1) Guizhou Radio and TV St, 302 Qingyun Lu, Guiyang, Guizhou 550002 **W:** gzstv.com General Sce on 765/927/1026kHz/7275kHz/94.6MHz/FM 24h - Economic Sce on 603kHz/98.9MHz 24h - Travel Sce on 97.2MHz 24h - Traffic Sce on 95.2MHz 24h - City Sce on 106.2MHz 24h - Music Sce on 91.6MHz 24h - Story Sce on 90.0MHz 24h – **GZ2)** 15 Zunyi Lu, Nanming Qu, Guiyang, Guizhou 550002. **W:** qguiyang.cn General Sce on 999kHz/88.9MHz 24h - Female Sce on 104.0MHz 24h - Traffic Sce on 102.7MHz 24h - Music Sce "Dynamic 909" on 90.9MHz 24h – **GZ3)** 31 Minghu Lu, Zhongshan Qu, Liupanshui, Guizhou 553001. News General Ch. on 711kHz/99.8MHz 2225-1800 - Traffic Ch. on 93.8MHz - Music Ch. on 102.1MHz 2225-1800 – **GZ4)** 11 Daxing Lu, Honghuagang Qu, Zunyi, Guizhou 563000. General Sce, on 1584kHz/98.2MHz 2227-1600 - Traffic and Literary Sce on 94.1MHz 2225-1805 - Travel Life Sce on 88.0MHz 2230-1800 – **GZ5)** 34 Guihuang Xilu, Anshun, Guizhou 561000. News General Sce, on 666kHz/105.9MHz - Traffic Sce on 102.9MHz – **GZ6)** Qiannan PBS, 267 Huandong Zhonglu, Duyun, Guizhou 558000. News General Ch. on 882kHz/98.0MHz 2200-1530 - Traffic and Travel Ch. on 93.3/92.2MHz 2225-1600 – **GZ7)** Qiandongnan PBS, 34 Beijing Donglu, Kaili, Guizhou 556000, On 104.9MHz/FM 2230-1600 – **GZ8)** Qianxinan PBS, Xingyi Guangchang Pang, Xingyi, Guizhou 562400. News General Sce on 107.9MHz 2225-1700(Sun 1600) in Ch, Buyi and Miao - Traffic and Travel Sce on 88.3MHz 2225-1700 (Sun 1600)

HAINAN PROVINCE

HA1) Hainan Radio and TV General St, 61 Nansha Lu, Haikou, Hainan 570206 **W:** bluehn.com News Sce on 954/1107/1116kHz/88.6/94.8MHz/FM 24h in Ch and Hainan dialect- International Tourism Radio: on 103.8/95.0/99.0/102.7/103.0/106.8MHz 2200-1700 - Traffic Sce on 1143kHz/100.0/89.3/90.3/98.5/100.3MHz 24h - Music Sce "Coconut FM": on 94.5/91.3/91.4/91.6/107.0MHz 2200-1700 - People Life Sce on 92.2/101.0/107.6MHz 2200-1700 in Ch and Hainan dialect – **HA2)** Haikou Radio and TV St, 15 Zhongsha Lu, Haikou, Hainan 570206. General Sce on 101.8MHz 2155-1800 in Ch and Hainan dialect – Travel and Traffic Sce on 95.4MHz 2200-1800 - Music Sce: on 91.6MHz 2200-1800 – **HA3)** Sanya Radio and TV St, Jiefang 4 Lu, Sanya, Hainan 572000. V.O. Tianya: on 104.6MHz 2200-1700 - Traffic Ch. on 100.3MHz

HUBEI PROVINCE

HB1) Hubei Radio and TV st, 1237 Jiefang Dadao, Jianghan District, Wuhan, Hubei 430022 **W:** hbgbdst.com News General Sce "V.O. Hubei": on 774/1566kHz/104.6MHz/FM 24h (exc. Tues 0700-0850) – Economic and Information Sce on 1179/927/945/1008/1053/1251kHz/99.8/105.2MHz/FM 24h (exc. Tues 0700-0850) – Life Sce (Number One Life Radio): on 801/846/900/927/1098/1143/1215kHz/96.6MHz 24h - Farm Sce on 684/846/900/945/1125kHz/91.2MHz/FM 24h (exc. Tues 0630-0855) - Private Car (Sports and Travel) Sce on 107.8/88.0/90.4MHz 24h - Women and Children Sce "Sunny Radio" on 747/1206kHz/97.1/102.6MHz 24h - Classic Music (Literature) Sce on 103.8MHz 24h - Chutian Traffic Sce on 92.7MHz 24h (exc. Tues 0700-0850) - Chutian Music Sce on684kHz/105.8/96.0/98.6/106.8MHz 24h (exc. Tues 1700-0850) - – **HB3)** Wuhan Radio and TV st, 620 Jianshe Dadao, Jianghan, Wuhan, Hubei 430015. **W:** whbc.com.cn/ General Sce on 873kHz/88.4MHz 24h - Economic Sce on 1125kHz/100.6MHz 2100 -1700 - Traffic Sce on 603kHz/89.6MHz 24h in Ch and Wuhan dialect - Music Sce "Classic 1018" on 101.8MHz 24h - Youth Sce "M-Radio 936": on 93.6MHz 24h – **HB5)** Guanghui Lu, Huangshi, Hubei 435000. News Sce on 963kHz/101.2MHz 2200-1600 - Traffic Sce on 103.3MHz 2200-1600 - Automobile Sce on 106.8MHz 2000-1800 – **HB6)** 200 Tanxi Lu, Fancheng Qu, Xiangyang, Hubei 441021. V.O. Xiangyang (News Sce): on 1098kHz/104.0MHz 2120-1635 (exc. Tues 0700-0830) - Music Sce on 1314kHz/90.9MHz 2130-1600. - Automobile Sce on 105.3MHz 2155-1635 (exc. Tues 0700-0830) - Traffic Sce "Dongli (Power) 890": on 89.0MHz 2155-1635 (exc. Tues 0700-0830) – **HB7)** 4 Renmin Beilu, Shiyan, Hubei 442000. News St. on 1485kHz/94.1MHz 2100-1600 - V.O. Checheng (Mobile City): on 99.1MHz 2200-1600 - Music and Traffic St. on 101.9MHz 2200-1700 (exc. Tues 0600-1000) – **HB8)** 266 Jiangjin Xilu, Shashi Qu, Jingzhou, Hubei 434000. V.O. Jingzhou: on 585kHz/97.2MHz 2200-1600 - General Sce on 828/1368kHz/98.4MHz 2030-1630 - 963 Beauty Music Sce on 96.3MHz 2200-1700 (exc. Tues 0700-0900) - 901 Automobile Sce on 90.1MHz 2130-1600. – **HB9)** 2 Guoyuan 1 Lu, Yichang, Hubei 443000. News General St. on 621kHz/95.6MHz 2100-1615 (exc. Tues 0600-0700) - Automobile St. on 100.6MHz 2130-1600 (exc. Tues 0600-0700) - Traffic and Music St. on 105.9MHz 2225-1645 (exc. Tues 0600-0700) – **HB10)** 100 Xiangshan Dadao, Dongbao Qu, Jingmen, Hubei 448000. News General Sce on 927kHz/96.6MHz 2150-1500 (exc. Tues 0600-1000) - City Life Sce on 1161kHz/89.7MHz 2130-1600 (exc. Tues 0600-1000) - Traffic and Music Sce on 99.3MHz 2200-1500 (exc. Tues 0600-1000) – **HB11)** 157 Binhu Lu, Ezhou, Hubei 436000. 2100-1600 – **HB12)** 116 Changzheng Lu, Xiaogan, Hubei 432100. News General Ch. on 927kHz/91.8MHz 2155-1530 (exc. Tues 0500-1000) - Traffic and Music Sce on 87.7MHz 2255-1505 – **HB13)** Huanggan PBS, 169 Dongmen Lu, Huangzhou Qu, Huanggang, Hubei 438000. News St. on 91.4MHz 2220-1600 - Traffic Sce on 107.6MHz 2220-1530 – **HB14)** 38 Wenquan Lu, Xianning, Hubei 437100. News Sce on 1314kHz/88.1MHz 2150-1505 (exc. Tues 0705-0905) - Traffic Sce on 95.9MHz 2220-1505 (exc. Tues 0705-0905) – **HB15)** 32 Xuefu Lu, Laohekou, Hubei 441800. 2220-0500, 0800-1400 – **HB16)** 4 Renmin Lu, Danjiangkou, Hubei 441900. News General Ch. on 1431kHz 2220-1600 – **HB17)** 2 Shannan Xiaoqu, Shishou, Hubei 434400. 2200-0005, 0955-1235 – **HB18)** 56 Guang'an Lu, Yingshan Zhen, Guangshui, Hubei 432700. 2155-0115, 0955-1305 – **HB19)** 146 Puyang Dadao, Yingcheng, Hubei 432400. 2200-0600, 0900-1305 – **HB20)** 199 Nanhuan Lu, Macheng, Hubei 436100. Educational and Music St. on 1242kHz/92.5/105.0MHz 2155-1430 – **HB21)** 50 Chunchuan Daqiao Lu, Chibi, Hubei 437300. 0950-1340 – **HB22)** 359 Lieshan Dadao, Suizhou, Hubei 441300. News St. on 1008kHz 2150-1600 - Traffic and Economic St. on 96.2MHz 2150-1600 – **HB23)** 117 Mianyang Dadao, Xiantao, Hubei 433000. 2130-1600 – **HB24)** 42 Zhanghua Nanlu, Yuanlin Zhen, Qianjiang, Hubei 433100. On 1242kHz/100.0MHz 2205-0445, 0930-1600 – **HB25)** 201 Hangkong Lu, Xiangzhou Qu, Xiangyang, Hubei 441104. On 1521kHz/96.5MHz 2155-1600 – **HB26)** 278 Dongfeng Dadao, Enshi, Hubei 445000. News General Sec on 1215kHz/99.0MHz- Traffic and Music Sce on 94.0MHz

HEILONGJIANG PROVINCE

HL1) Heilongjiang Radio and TV St., 333 Hanshui Lu, Nangang Qu, Harbin, Heilongjiang 150090 **W:** hljradio.com News St. on 621/900/927/1341/94.6MHz 24h - Private Car Ch. (Life Sce) on 104.5MHz/FM 24h - Traffic Sce on 99.8MHz/FM 24h - City Women Sce on 102.1MHz 24h - Favorite Home Ch. (Children Sce) on 97.0MHz/FM 24h - Music St. on 95.8MHz 24h - Country Sce on 945kHz/103.5MHz/FM 24h - University St. "Radio Young": on 99.3MHz/FM 2200-1600 - - Korean Sce on 873/1476kHz/FM 2100-2400, 1300-1500 in Ko - V.O. Beidahuang (Great Northern Wilderness): on 1476kHz/FM 2055-1600 – **HL2)** Harbin Radio and TV St, 1 Huashan Lu, Xiangyang Qu, Harbin, Heilongjiang 150036. News Sce on 837kHz/94.1/105.6MHz 24h - Literary Sce on 98.4/97.8MHz 24h - Economic Sce on 972kHz.

24h (exc. Tues 0500-0900) - Traffic Sce on 92.5/95.3MHz 24h - Music Sce on 927kHz/90.9/103.0MHz 24h - Automobile FM "Kuaile (Happy) 973": on 97.3/88.8MHz 24h – **HL3)** 99 Yong'an Dajie, Longsha Qu, Qiqihar, Heilongjiang 161005. News Sce on 1197kHz/87.8MHz 2000-1600(Tues 1405) - Life and Literary Sce on 693kHz/89.4/90.0MHz 2020-1505 - Traffic Sce on 94.1/98.0MHz 2050-1605 - Country Sce on 585kHz/103.4/87.5MHz – **HL4)** Jiuma Lu, Xiangyang Qu, Hegang, Heilongjiang 154100. News Sce on 1413kHz/97.2/101.4/107.6MHz 2055-1400 - Traffic and Literary Sce on 106.1MHz 2145-1400 - Life Sce on 93.3MHz – **HL5)** Shuangyashan Radio and TV St, 240 Xinxing Dajie, Jianshan Qu, Shuangyashan, Heilongjiang 155100. News Sce on 1179kHz/103.2/101.5MHz 2120-1230 - Traffic and Literary Sce on 99.5/98.1MHz - Country Life Sce on 98.6/104.2MHz - Storytelling Sce on 603kHz/88.6/94.6MHz – **HL6)** 11 Diantai Lu, Jiguan Qu, Jixi, Heilongjiang 158100. News General Sce on 1368kHz/94.5MHz 2130-0600, 0850-1350 - Traffic Sce on 1485kHz/95.9MHz - Literary and Life Sce on 1143kHz/98.6MHz - Storytelling Sce on 103.9MHz 2055-1500 – **HL7)** Jia 1, Dongfeng Lu, Sa'ertu Qu, Daqing, Heilongjiang 163311. General Sce on 1080kHz/96.7/97.5MHz 24h - Traffic Sce on 95.0MHz 24h - Music Sce on 106.0MHz 1955-1600.- Storytelling Sce on 90.9MHz 24h - V.O. Baihu: on 91.9MHz 2000-1600 – **HL8)** 16 Linshan Lu, Yichun Qu, Yichun, Heilongjiang 153000. News General Sce on 909kHz/92.4/102.1MHz 2130-0810 (exc. Mon 0725-1000) - Traffic and Life Sce on 98.5MHz 2200-1400 – **HL9)** 138 Taiping Lu, Mudanjiang, Heilongjiang 157000. News Sce on 684kHz/87.9MHz 2105-1400 (exc. Tues 0800-0855) - Life and Story Sce on 1476kHz/91.6MHz 2200-1530 - Traffic and Literary Sce on 98.2MHz 2300-1300 – **HL10)** 35 Shunhe Lu, Jiamusi, Heilongjiang 154002. News General Sce on 666kHz/101.7MHz 2055-0530, 0855-1400 - Economic Sce on 1143kHz/95.0MHz 2055-1600 - Traffic and Literary Sce on 98.0/93.8MHz 2225-1600 – **HL11)** 2 Shanhu Dajie, Taoshan Qu, Qitaihe, Heilongjiang 154600. News General Ch. on 1062kHz/89.9MHz 2300-1545 - Traffic Ch. on 98.8MHz – **HL12)** 255 Huanghe Beilu, Suihua, Heilongjiang 152054, Traffic Sce on 90.7MHz 2155-1400 - Farm Sce on 101.1MHz 2150-? - Music Sce on 1080kHz/97.4MHz - Storytelling Sce on 107.0MHz – **HL13)** 2 Xing'an Dajie, Jagdaqi Zhen, Heilongjiang 165000. Peoples Sce on 1278kHz/100.1MHz 2125-1400 (exc. Tues 0600-0955) – **HL14)** 310 Shengdao, Aihui Qu, Heihe, Heilongjiang 164300. General Sce on 1215kHz/103.8/107.3MHz 2100-1400 – **HL15)** 89 Xing'an Jie, Aihui Qu, Heihe, Heilongjiang 164300. V.O.Ai-Guang: on 999kHz/91.2MHz 2220-1500 (exc. Tues 0600-0850)

HUNAN PROVINCE

HN1) 455 Sanyi Dadao, Kaifu District, Changsha, Hunan 410003 **W:** hnradio.com News General Ch. on 738/1152/1233/4990kHz/102.8MHz 24h (exc. 0700-0900) - V.O. Xiaoxiang "News 938" on 93.8/100.7MHz 24h - Economic Sce on 900kHz/90.1/91.0/94.6/95.7MHz24h - literature Sce "Modern Music BS": on 97.5/87.5/90.8/95.7/96.9MHz 24h - Traffic Ch. on 91.8/100.3MHz 24h - V.O. Music on 89.3/89.7/102.1MHz 24h - Travel Ch."Time Music BS" on 87.9/92.1/96.1/99.1/106.9MHz 24h - Jinying (Golden Hawk) 955 BS "V.O. Jinying" on 95.5/91.3/100.5MHz 24h – **HN2)** 989 1duan Xiangfu Donglu, Changsha, Hunan 410016. City News Sce on 1323kHz/105.0MHz 24h (exc. 0600-0900) - Economic Sce on 88.6MHz 24h - Traffic Sce on 106.1MHz 24h - Sound of City on 101.7MHz 24h – **HN2A)** Changsha Pinwei (Taste) Music BS 52 Xiangjiang Zhonglu, Changsha, Hunan 410008. On 102.2MHz 24h – **HN2B)** Changsha 925 Yue BS "U Radio", 3 Laodong Zhonglu, Changsha, Hunan 410007. On 92.5MHz 24h – **HN3)** Zhuzhou Radio and TV St, 658 Taishan Lu, Tianyuan Qu, Zhuzhou, Hunan 412000. News Ch. on 1089kHz/101.2MHz 24h - Traffic Ch. on 98.4MHz 24h – **HN4)** Xiangtan Radio and TV St, Donghu Lu, Xiangtan, Hunan 411104. Mango Radio "V.O. Xiangtan": on 1503kHz/98.6MHz 24h - Traffic Ch. on 104.2MHz 2200-1600 - Da Yanjing (Big Eye) BS: on 106.5MHz 24h - Le Shenghuo (Happy Life) FM on 97.8MHz – **HN5)** 114 Xianfeng Lu, Hengyang, Hunan 421001. News Ch. on 1071kHz/98.9MHz 24h - Traffic Ch. on 101.8MHz 24h – **HN6)** Shaoyang Radio and TV St, 373 Zhangshulong, Baoqing Xilu, Daxiang Qu, Shaoyang, Hunan 422000. Traffic Ch. on 95.4/87.7MHz 2200-1700 - Music Ch. "Feiyang 928": on 92.8MHz 2300-1700 – **HN7)** Yueyang Radio and TV St, 421 Nanhu Dadao, Yueyang, Hunan 414000. News General Ch. on 1053kHz/104.1MHz 2120-1700 – Traffic and Music Ch. on 1008kHz/106.1/104.5MHz 2155-1700 – **HN8)** Changde Radio and TV St, 267 Wuling Dadao, Changde, Hunan 415000. News Ch. on 1260kHz/105.6MHz 2225-1705 - Traffic Ch. on 97.1MHz 2200-1600 - City Traffic and Music Sce on 98.5MHz – **HN9)** Chaoyang Lu, Yiyang, Hunan 413000. Mango Radio "V.O. Yiyang": on 1053kHz/99.7MHz 2200-1600 (exc. Wed 0800-1000) - Traffic Ch. on 88.1MHz 2200-1600 – **HN10)** 51 Renmin Lu, Jinshi, Hunan 415400 – **HN11)** Chenzhou PBS, 7 Li Dadao, Chenzhou, Hunan 423000. Automobile and Music Ch. on 99.2/89.9MHz 2200-1730 - Traffic Ch. on 102.8MHz 2200-1730 - Private Car Ch on 105.5MHz 24h - "Chenzhou My FM": on 88.3MHz – **HN12)** Huaihua PBS, Tianxing Lu, Huaihua, Hunan 418000. City Control Sce on 97.2/107.6MHz 2230-1600 (exc. Tues 0400-0900) - Traffic Ch. on 103.8MHz 2220-1600

JILIN PROVINCE

JL1) Jilin Radio & TV Stn, 2066 Weixing Lu, 118 Shengtai Dajie, Changchun, Jilin 130033 **W:** jlradio.cn News General Sce on 738/1107/1521/1530kHz/91.6MHz 24h (exc. Tues 0500-0900) - Economic Sce on 603/846/1143kHz/93.3MHz 24h - Health and Entertainment Sce on 101.9MHz 24h (exc Tues 1500-1800) - Traffic Sce on 103.8MHz 24h - Information Sce on 100.1MHz 24h (exc. Tues 1500-1800) - Music Sce on 92.7MHz 24h (exc. Tues 1500-1800) - Country Sce on 97.6MHz/FM 24h - Travel Sce on 103.3/94.7/107.7MHz 24h - Educational Sce "Gushi (Story) 963": on 96.3MHz 24h – **JL2)** 149 Baicao Lu, Chaoyang Qu, Changchun, Jilin 130061. News Sce on 900kHz/88.9MHz 24h - Life and Story Sce on 1332kHz/90.0MHz 24h "Changchung My FM": on 88.0MHz 24h (exc. SS1600-2200) - V.O. the Traffic: on 96.8/100.6MHz 24h - City Music Sce "Private Car Radio": on 106.3MHz 24h - City Elite Sce "Top Radio": on 585kHz/99.6MHz 24h– **JL3)** Nanjing Lu, Chuanying Qu, Jilin-shi, Jilin 132011. News Ch. on 927kHz/102.6MHz 24h - V.O. Old Age: on 702kHz/97.0MHz 24h - Traffic Ch. on 105.3MHz 24h - Music and Story St. on 1143kHz/94.0MHz 24h - Automobile Life St. on 88.3MHz 24h – **JL3A)** Jilin-shi EBS, 2 Nanjing Lu, Chuanying Qu, Jilin-shi, Jilin 132011. Dushi (city) 110: on 1494kHz/90.3MHz 24h - V.O. the Health: on 603kHz/92.6MHz 24h - City Life Sce on 89.3MHz 2030-1700 - V.O. Jiangcheng Music: on 1251kHz/91.3MHz 24h – **JL4)** 39 Nan Xinhua Dajie, Siping, Jilin 136000. News General Ch. on 666kHz/93.9MHz 2100-1600 - Traffic and Literary St. on 99.5MHz 24h - Public Storytelling St. on 900kHz/90.5MHz 2100-1500 – **JL5)** Liaoyuan Radio and TV St, 20 Hebin Lu, Longshan Qu, Liaoyuan, Jilin 136200. General Ch. on 810kHz/99.2MHz - Traffic and Literary Sce on 96.2MHz 2125-1500 – **JL6)** Radio St Tong Hua, 199 Cuiquan Lu, Longquan Jie, Tonghua, Jilin 134001. **W:** 909radio.com News Sce on 909kHz/102.8MHz 2100-1500 (exc. Tues 0705-0855) - City Sce on 90.9MHz 2200-1400 - Traffic Sce on 104.7MHz 2140-1700 - Story Sce on 97.9MHz 2150-1400 – **JL7)** 36 Hunjiang Dajie, Badaojiang Qu, Baishan, Jilin 134302. News General Sce on 657kHz/107.7/95.8MHz 2100-1530 - Traffic Sce on 98.4MHz 2100-1500 – **JL8)** 1295 Linjiang Donglu, Ningjiang Qu, Songyuan, Jilin 138000. News General Sce on 1431kHz/89.9MHz 2100-1500 - Traffic and Literary Sce on 1143kHz/100.0MHz 24h - Public Life Sce on 98.6/96.8MHz 24h - Story Sce on 102.5MHz 24h – **JL9)** Baicheng Radio and TV St, 86 Xingfu Nan Dajie, Baicheng, Jilin 137000. News General Sce on 1323kHz/103.0MHz 24h (exc. Tues 0630-0940) - Traffic Sce on 96.5MHz - Literary Sce on 105.8MHz - Storytelling Sce on 98.5MHz – **JL10)** 166 Juzi Jie, Yanji, Jilin 133000. **W:** cn.iybtv.com Ch Satellite Sce on 1053/603/1566kHz/FM 2130-1630 in Ch & Ko - Ch News Sce on 88.2/91.7/92.2/98.3MHz in Ch - Ko News General Sce on 1206kHz/94.9MHz 2040-1600 (exc. Tues 0540-0900) in Ko & Ch - Ko Cultural Life Sce on 585/1188kHz/104.6MHz in Ko 2130-1510 - Traffic and Literary Sce on 105.9MHz 2130-1600 in Ch – **JL11)** 45 Dong Huancheng Lu, Gongzhuling, Jilin 136100. V.O. the Public: on 1485kHz 2050-1420 - V.O. the Traffic: on 101.3MHz – **JL12)** 18 Nan Dalu, Lishu Xian, Jilin 136500. V.O. the Northern Traffic: on 1575kHz/102.4MHz – **JL13)** 70 Henan Jie, Meihekou, Jilin 135000. V.O. the Traffic: on 1584kHz/95.7MHz 2155-1130 – **JL14)** 628 Qingzhen Jie, Qian Gorlos, Jilin 131100. On 1476kHz/91.0MHz 2125-2330, 0325-0500, 0955-1230 in Ch and Mo – **JL15)** Taonan PBS, 298 Tuanjie Xilu, Taonan, Jilin 137100 On 104.6MHz 2055-1500 – **JL16)** 7 Yongle Jie, Yanji, Jilin 133000. Ko Prgr. "Arirang Radio": on 900kHz/88.0MHz 2030-1600 - Yanji V.O. the Traffic BS: on 93.5MHz – **JL17)** 75 Yingchun Lu, Tumen, Jilin. 2155-1230 in Ch and Ko – **JL18)** 1-8 Xinhua Xilu, Dunhua, Jilin 133700. 2130-1500 in Ch and Ko – **JL19)** Jinghe Jie, Hunchun, Jilin 133300. Storytelling St. on 927kHz 2030-1530 in Ch and Ko - North East Asia V.O. Hunchun on 101.0MHz

JIANGSU PROVINCE

JS1) 132 Zhongshan Donglu, Nanjing, Jiangsu 210002 **W:** vojs.cn News General Ch. on 702/801/1314/1413/1602kHz 2000-1700 (exc. Tues/Thurs 0600-0850) - News Sce on 93.7MHz/FM 2100-1600 - Health Sce on 846/603/1098kHz/100.5MHz 24h (exc. Tues 0600-0900) - Financial and Economic Sce on 585kHz/95.2MHz 2000-1800 - Traffic Sce on 101.1MHz 24h (exc. Tues 1800-2000) - Story Sce on 1206kHz/104.9MHz 24h - Music St. "Play FM": on 89.7/107.8MHz 24h (exc. Tues 0600-0900) - Classic Music St. on 97.5MHz 24h - Literary Sce on 1053kHz/91.4MHz 2100-1600 – **JS2)** 358 Baixia Lu, Nanjing,

Jiangsu 210001. News General Sce on 1008kHz/106.9MHz 1900-1700 (exc. Tues 0600-0800) - Economic Sce on 900kHz/98.1MHz 24h - City Control Sce on 1170kHz/96.6MHz 2200-1600 - Traffic Sce on 102.4MHz 24h - Music Sce on 105.8MHz 24h - Sports Sce on 1251kHz/104.3MHz 24h – **JS2A)** 359 Hongwu Lu, Baixia Qu, Nanjing, Jiangsu 210002. "Nanjing My FM": on 103.5MHz 24h – **JS3)** 223 Zhongshan Nanlu, Xuzhou, Jiangsu 221003. News Sce on 1269kHz/93.0/89.3MHz 2000-1730 - Life Sce on 801kHz/91.6MHz 2025-1730 - Traffic Sce on 103.3MHz 2030-1700 - Literary Sceon 1098kHz/89.6MHz 2015-1600 - Music Sce on 99.6MHz 24h – **JS4)** 221 Jiefang Xilu, Xinpu Qu, Lianyungang, Jiangsu 222003. News Sce on 1458kHz/93.6/98.3MHz 2100-1600 (exc. Tues 0600-0855) - Economic Sce on 1251kHz/90.7MHz 2045-1600 - Traffic Sce on 92.7/96.0MHz 2155-1600 - V.O. the Music: on 90.2MHz 2050-1600 - Story Sce on 900kHz/104.8MHz 2200-1600 – **JS5)** 6 Dazhi Lu, Huai'an, Jiangsu 223001. News General Sce on 801kHz/94.1MHz 2000-1600 (exc. Tues 0600-0900) - Economic Life Sce on 1251kHz/105.0MHz 2000-1600 (exc. Tues 0600-0840) - Traffic and Literary Sce on 1521kHz/94.9MHz 2100-1600 - Public (Chengshi Guanli) Sce on 106.7MHz 2055-1600 - Automobile Music Sce on 104.2MHz 2100-1600 – **JS6)** Yancheng Radio and TV St, 4 Shengyuan Lu, Yancheng, Jiangsu 224001. News Sce on 1026kHz/91.5MHz 2100-1600 - Traffic Sce on 747kHz/105.3MHz 2200-1700 - Private Car Sce on 900kHz/88.2MHz 2100-1600 - V.O. the Music "Hi FM": on 98.0MHz – **JS7)** Yangzhou Radio and TV Media Group, 168 Weiyang Lu, Yangzhou, Jiangsu 225009. News Sce on 98.5/105.5MHz 2120-1800 (exc. Tues 0600-0930) - Traffic Sce on 103.5MHz 2120-1800 - Music Sce "Yes FM": on 94.9MHz 2100-1600 (exc. Tues 0645-0800) - Health Life Sce on 1179kHz/96.7MHz 2100-1600 - Classic Music Sce on 801/1521kHz – **JS8)** 20 Qingnian Lu, Taizhou, Jiangsu 225300. News Sce on 1341kHz/103.7/106.2MHz 2120-1525 (exc. Tues 0530-0855) - Music Sce on 927kHz/97.3MHz 2145-1600 - Traffic Sce on 92.1MHz 2200-1600 – **JS9)** 100 Renmin Zhonglu, Nantong, Jiangsu 226001. News Sce on 1233kHz/97.0MHz 2130-1600 - Private Car Sce on 603kHz/103.0/102.6MHz 2130-1600 - Traffic Sce on 1170kHz/92.9MHz 2200-1600 - Xingfu (Happy) Sce on 88.5/88.3MHz 2130-1600 - Music Sce on 91.8MHz 2130-1600 – **JS10)** 94 Zhongshan Xilu, Zhenjiang, Jiangsu 212004. News Sce on 104.0MHz 2055-1600. - Health Life Ch. on 1224kHz/94.0MHz 2000-1800 - Traffic Sce on 88.8MHz 2130-1600 - Music Sce "V.O. Jinshan Lake Music": on 96.3MHz 2100-1800 - City Sce on 90.5MHz 2030-1800 - Private Car BS "Donggan (Dynamic) 102.7": on 900kHz/102.7MHz 2130-1600 – **JS11)** Changzhou Radio and TV St, 10 Xiheng Jie, Changzhou, Jiangsu 213003. News General Sce on 846kHz 24h (exc. Tues 0600-0850) - News Sce on 103.4MHz 24h - Xi Opera Sce on 1143kHz 24h - Fortune Life Sce on 105.2MHz 24h - Traffic Sce on 90.0MHz 24h - Chinese Opera Sce on 747kHz 24h (exc. Tues 0600-0900) - Music Sce "Aiting 935": on 93.5MHz 24h - Classic Music Sce on 927kHz 24h - Literary St. (First Popular Ch): on 1521kHz/100.1MHz 2100-1600 – **JS12)** Wuxi Radio and TV Group, 4 Hubin Lu, Wuxi, Jiangsu 214061. News General Sce on 1161kHz/89.4MHz 2020-1600 (exc. Tues 0500-0900) - News Sce on 93.7MHz 2020-1600 - Economic Sce on 1251kHz/104.0MHz 2020-1600 - Story and Chinese Opera Sce on 1008kHz 24h - Traffic Sce on 106.9MHz 24h - Automobile Music Sce on 900kHz/91.4MHz 2130-1600 - City Life Sce on 1521kHz/98.7/88.1MHz 2130-1600 - V.O. Liangxi: on 603kHz/92.6MHz 2100-1600 – **JS13)** Suzhou Radio and TV Headquarters, 4 Gongyuan Lu, Suzhou, Jiangsu 215006. News General Sce on 1080kHz 2030-1600 (exc. Tues 0600-0730) in Ch and Suzhou dialect - V.O. the City "My Radio": on 91.1MHz 2030-1630 - Traffic Sce on 1521kHz/104.8MHz 2130-1600 - V.O. Old Age: on 603kHz - Life Sce on 96.5MHz 2130-1600(Tues 1525) - Music Sce "Dongting 948": on 94.8MHz 24h (exc. Tues 0600-1000) - Chinese Opera Sce on 846kHz - Automobile Sce on 102.8MHz 2200-1600 – **JS14)** 43 Gongnong Lu, Yizheng, Jiangsu 211400. On 1026kHz/94.3MHz 2155-0535, 0725-1350 – **JS15)** 79 Zhongshan Nanlu, Jiangyin, Jiangsu 214400. Happy Life Ch. on 1386kHz/106.0MHz 2200-1530 - T Automobile Ch. on 90.7MHz 2200-1500 – **JS16)** 29 Haiyu Beilu, Changshu, Jiangsu 215500. News Sce on 1116kHz/99.6MHz 2130-1405 (exc. Sat 0630-0830) - Qinchuan Music Sce on 927kHz 2155-1400 (exc. Sat 0630-0830) - Traffic Sce on 747kHz/100.8MHz 2130-1405 (exc. Sat 0600-0800) – **JS17)** Zhangjiagang Radio and TV St, Chenjiachang Nong, Yangshe Zhen, Zhangjiagang, Jiangsu 215600. News Sce on 1098kHz 2140-1455 (exc. Wed 0600-0830) - Traffic Sce on 102.0MHz 2155-1500 (exc. Wed 0530-0955) - Music Sce on 1521kHz 2155-1500 – **JS18)** 7 Fazhan Dadao, Sucheng Qu, Suqian, Jiangsu 223800. News Sce on 92.1MHz 2110-1600 - Traffic Sce on 101.9MHz 2150-1700 - Aixin Netw. "Love Radio": on 106.3MHz

JIANGXI PROVINCE

JX1) Jiangxi Radio & TV st, 207 Hongdu Zhong Dadao, Nanchang, Jiangxi 330046 **W:** jxntv.cn News Sce on 729/1350kHz/104.4MHz/FM 2000-1600 - City Sce on 106.5MHz/FM 24h - "Financial and Economic 992": on 99.2MHz 2200-1600 - People Life Sce on 927kHz/101.9MHz/FM 24h - Rural Sce "Green 985": on 1350kHz/98.5MHz/FM 2200-1600 - Traffic Sce on 105.4MHz 24h – Number one Music Sce "Classic 1034": on 103.4MHz/FM 24h - Travel Sce "i FM": on 97.4MHz 24h -Story sce on 96.9MHz 24h– **JX2)** Nanchang Radio & TV st, 1 Luyin Lu, Honggutan New District, Nanchang, Jiangxi 330038. News General Ch. on 1278kHz/91.7MHz 2100-1600 - Traffic & Music Sce on 95.1MHz 24h - Economic and Life Ch."Big Eye st": on 89.7MHz 24h – **JX3)** 1073 Cidu Dadao, Jingdezhen, Jiangxi 333000. News General Sce on 1467kHz/96.5/107.3MHz 2200-1600 - Private Car and Gourmet Sce on 99.9MHz 0000-1600 – The Porcelain City's Traffic and Music Sce on 106.2MHz 2300-1600 – **JX4)** Jiangwan Li, Binhe Xilu, Pingxiang, Jiangxi 337005. General Ch. V.O. the City: on 1107kHz/96.8/106.8MHz 2230-1600 - Traffic and Literary Ch. on 99.3MHz 24h – **JX5)** 49 Xianlai Zhong Dadao, Xinyu, Jiangxi 338000. News Sce on 585kHz/94.0MHz 2200-1600 - Traffic Sce on 96.2MHz 24h – "953 Private Car St": on 95.3MHz 24h – **JX6)** 84 Changhong Dadao, Jiujiang, Jiangxi 332000. News Sce on 1485kHz/90.0MHz 24h - Traffic Sce on 88.4/88.9MHz 200-1600 (exc. Tues 0530-0855) - Private Car Sce on 94.5MHz 24h - Culture and Travel Sce on 101.7MHz 24h – **JX7)** Yingtan PBS, 3 Jianshe Lu, Yingtan, Jiangxi 335200. News and General Sce on 104.8MHz 24h - Traffic and Music Sce on 103.2MHz 2200-1400 – **JX8)** Zhong Duan, Ganjiang Yuan Dadao, Ganzhou, Jiangxi 341000. General Sce on 747kHz/93.7MHz 2200-1700 (exc. Tues 0600-0830) in Ch and Hakka - Music Sce on 94.5/103.4MHz 24h - Traffic Sce on 99.2/97.5MHz 2200-1700 – V.O. Ganzhou: on 92.3MHz 2230-1600 – **JX9)** Ji'an Radio and TV St, 19 Beimen Jie, Ji'an, Jiangxi 343000. News Sce on 603/1242kHz/95.6/102.1MHz 2125-1430 - Traffic Sce on 100.6/94.3MHz 2200-1600 – **JX10)** Shangrao PBS, 51 Qingfeng Lu, Shangrao, Jiangxi 334000. News General Ch. on 93.4MHz 2230-1600 - Traffic and Music Ch. on 96.6/95.9MHz 2230-1600

LIAONING PROVINCE

LN1) Liaoning Radio and TV St, 10 Guangrong Jie, Heping Qu, Shenyang, Liaoning 110003 **W:** lntv.com.cn or lntv.cn General Sce on 1089/603/612/963/1260kHz/102.9MHz 24h (exc. Tues 0605-0855). - Economic Sce on 999/585/801/900kHz/88.4/88.8MHz/FM 24h (exc. Tues 0540-0855) - Country Sce on 927kHz/96.9/103.4/107.1MHz 24h (exc. Tues 0500-0800) - Traffic Sce on 97.5MHz 24h - Classic Music on 1053/747/801/810kHz/95.9/99.5/101.8MHz 24h - Life Sce on 882kHz/103.4/90.4MHz 24h (exc. Tues 0500-0855) - City Sce on 1341kHz/92.1MHz 24h - Music Sce on 98.6MHz 24h (exc. Thurs 0500-0855) - Information Sce (Dalian Blanch): on 90.6/90.4MHz 24h – **LN2)** Shenyang Radio and TV St, 89 Sanhao Jie, Heping Qu, Shenyang, Liaoning 110004. News Sce on 792kHz/104.5/107.0MHz 24h – **LN3)** Dalian Radio and TV St, 162 Minquan Jie, Shahekou Qu, Dalian, Liaoning 116022. News Sce on 882kHz/103.3MHz 1955-1605 (exc. Tues 0600-0800) - Financial Sce on 1152kHz/93.1MHz 24h (exc. Tues 0630-0800) - Automobile Sce "V.O. the City": on 99.1MHz 2025-1605 (exc. Tues 0630-0800) - Traffic Sce on 100.8MHz 24h (exc. Tues 0600-0800) - Sports Sce on 105.7MHz 2025-1605 (exc. Tues 0600-0800) - New City and Country Sce "Xingfu (Happy) 956": on 1575kHz/95.6MHz 2025-1600 (exc. Tues 0600-0800) - Music Sce on 106.7MHz 24h (exc. Tues 0600-0800) – **LN4)** Anshan Radio and TV St, 3, 219 Lu, Tiedong Qu, Anshan, Liaoning 114002. News Sce on 954kHz/95.3MHz 24h - Economic Sce on 89.7MHz 24h - Old Age Sce on 1071kHz/88.5MHz - Traffic Sce on 1458kHz/99.5MHz 24h - Music Sce on 93.8MHz 2100-1600 - Storytelling Sce on 1251kHz/87.9MHz – **LN5)** Fushun Radio and TV St, 2 Hunhe Beilu, Shuncheng Qu, Fushun, Liaoning 113006. News Sce on 684kHz/93.0/93.8MHz 2000-1500 - Traffic Sce "i Radio": on 747kHz/106.1MHz 24h - Music Sce "U Radio": on 100.6MHz 2030-1600 - Storytelling Sce on 1143kHz/88.2MHz – **LN6)** 36, Huacheng Lu, Mingshan Qu, Benxi, Liaoning 117000. News General St. on 1296kHz/94.0MHz 2030-1605 - Traffic and Economic St. on 107.4MHz 24h (exc. Tues 0700-0900) - Life St. on 98.0MHz 2000-1600 – **LN7)** Dandong Radio and TV St, 1 Shanshang Jie, Zhenxing Qu, Dandong, Liaoning 118000. **W:** 10001723438.qymgc.com News Sce on 1404kHz/103.6MHz 24h - Traffic Sce on 891kHz/101.7MHz 2000-1600 - City Sce on 1476kHz/104.3MHz 2000-1500 in Ch and Korean - Entertainment Sce (Story Sce) on 603kHz/88.0MHz 2128-1600 – **LN8)** 3, 4 Duan, Beijing Lu, Jinzhou, Liaoning 121000. News Sce Shiyuan (World Park) Ch. on 666kHz/92.7MHz 2125-1500 (exc. Tues 0530-0855) - Economic Sce on 774kHz/96.6MHz 2125-1500 (exc. Tues 0530-0855) - People Life Sce on 1098kHz/90.9/97.7MHz 2125-1500 (exc. Tues 0530-0855) - Traffic Sce on 846kHz/100.3MHz 2125-1500 (exc. Tues 0530-0855) – **LN9)** Huludao Radio and TV St, 23 Haixing Lu, Longwan Dajie, Huludao, Liaoning 125000. News General

Sce on 1242kHz/93.1/95.2MHz 2130-1535 - Traffic and Literary Sce on 87.8MHz 2150-1330 (exc. Tues 0540-0955) – **LN10)** Yingkou Radio and TV St, 10, Dong, Bohai Dajie, Zhanqian Qu, Yingkou, Liaoning 115000. News General Sce on 1026kHz/88.4/106.2MHz 2055-1500 - Economic Life Sce on 747kHz/89.0/92.8MHz 2100-1500 - Traffic and Literary Sce on 1143kHz/95.1MHz 2130-1600 - Storytelling and Entertainment Sce on 603kHz/94.1MHz 2125-1500 – **LN11)** Panjin Radio and TV St, 7 Shifu Dajie, Xinglongtai Qu, Panjin, Liaoning 124010. News General Sce on 1485kHz/104.2MHz 2100-1600 - Traffic and Literary Sce on 90.1MHz 2100-1500 - Economic Life Sce on 97.1MHz 2100-1600 - Storytelling and Chinese Opera Sce on 101.8MHz 2100-1550 - Music Sce "V.O. Hexiang": on 95.3MHz – **LN12)** 61 Zhonghua Lu, Haizhou Qu, Fuxin, Liaoning 123000. News General Sce on 1287kHz/89.3MHz 2100-1510 - Economic and Storytelling Sce on 747kHz 2100-1600 - Literary Sce on 900kHz/105.3MHz 24h - Traffic Sce on 1098kHz/88.7MHz 2100-1600 – **LN13)** Fuxin Mongolian BS, 84 Shanbei Jie, Haizhou Qu, Fuxin, Liaoning 123000. 2155-0610, 1040-1300 in Mo – **LN14)** Liaoyang Radio and TV St, 59 Qingnian Dajie, Taizihe Qu, Liaoyang, Liaoning 111000. News General Sce on 837kHz/106.0MHz 2030-1530 (exc. Tues 0600-0800) - Economic Sce on 1143kHz/102.0MHz 2025-1530 – **LN15)** Tieling Radio and TV St, 45 Gongren Jie, Yinzhou Qu, Tieling, Liaoning 112000. V.O. Tieling: on 1413kHz/101.2MHz 2150-1300 - Traffic Sce on 102.8MHz 2200-1300 - Country Sce on 810kHz/90.8MHz 2130-1430 - Literary Sce on 95.9MHz – **LN16)** Chaoyang Radio and TV St, 88, 1 Duan, Xinhua Lu, Shuangta Qu, Chaoyang, Liaoning 122000. News General Sce on 585kHz/96.1/106.0MHz 2125-1600 - New Farm Sce on 810/702/747kHz/99.5MHz 1955-1600 (exc. Tues 0600-0900) - Traffic and Entertainment Sce on 93.8/103.1MHz 1955-1600 (exc. Tues 0600-0900) - Feiyang FM on 648/801kHz/106.5MHz 1955-1600 – **LN17)** 67 Jinluan Lu, Wafangdian, Liaoning 116300. News General Sce on 1323kHz/89.8/106.2MHz 2125-1345 – **LN18)** 385, 1 Duan, Huanghai Dajie, Zhuanghe, Liaoning 116400. 2100-0100, 0855-1200 – **LN19)** Haicheng Radio and TV St, 14 Huancheng Xilu, Haicheng, Liaoning 114200. News General Sce on 900kHz/90.4MHz 2135-1500 - Traffic and Entertainment Sce on 1350kHz/106.9MHz 2135-1500 – **LN20)** 18, 2 Duan, Xinghai Beilu, Xingcheng, Liaoning 121600 – **LN21)** 6 Qingnian Lu, Nanshan Jie, Beipiao, Liaoning 122100. V.O. Beipiao: on 91.2MHz 2125-1500 (exc. Tues 0500-0930) – **LN22)** Donggang PBS, 122 Huanghai Dajie, Dongguang, Liaoning. News Sce on 93.3/94.3MHz - Traffic and Life Sce on 98.0MHz - New Country Sce on 107.9MHz

NEI MENGGU AUTONOMOUS REGION

NM1) Nei Menggu Radio and TV St. "V.O. Chinese Grassland", 55 Xinhua Dajie, Hohhot, Nei Menggu 010058 **W:**nmtv.cn Ch News General Sce on 675/7420/9520kHz/89.0MHz 2150-1605 (exc. Tues 0600-0950) - Ch News Sce on 95.0MHz/FM 2150-1605 - Mongolian News General Sce on 1458/6040/7270/9750kHz/FM 2150-1605 (exc. Tues 0600-0950) - Economic Life Sce on 101.4/103.8MHz 2100-1700 - V.O. the Traffic: on 105.6MHz/FM 24h - V.O. the Music: on 93.6MHz/FM 2150-1600 - Storytelling and Folk Art Sce on 102.8MHz 24h - Farm and Pastoral Sce "V.O. the Green Field": on 1044/91.9MHz/FM 2150-1605 (exc. Tues 0600-0950) - "V.O. the Grassland": on 105.0MHz – **NM2)** Hohhot Radio and TV St, 159 Gongyuan Xilu, Hohhot, Nei Menggu 010035. Ch General Sce on 945kHz/92.9MHz 24h- Mo General Sce on 105.1MHz 2225-1530 - Traffic Sce on 107.4MHz 2250-1600 - City Life Sce on 90.1MHz 24h - Literary Sce on 99.8MHz 24h - Favorite Car Information Sce "Happy Radio": on 103.9/98.5MHz 24h – **NM3)** Baotou Radio and TV St, 12 Gangtie Dajie, Hondlon Qu, Baotou, Nei Menggu 014030. General Sce on 747kHz/94.9MHz 2040-1600 - Mongolian Sce on 105.9MHz 1955-1605 - Traffic Sce on 89.2MHz 24h - Urban and Rural Sce "Automobile Music 100.1": on 100.1MHz 24h - Literary Sce on 98.1MHz 2055-1800 – **NM4)** Wuhai Radio and TV St, Huanghe Lu, Haibowan Qu, Wuhai, Nei Menggu 016000. General Sce on 747kHz/94.4MHz 2125-1600 - Mo General Sce on 104.2MHz 2125-1600 -Traffic and Music Sce on 99.2MHz 2125-1600 – **NM5)** Chifeng Radio and TV St, 12, Xi Duan, Gangtie Xijie, Hongshan Qu, Chifeng, Nei Menggu 024001. Ch General Sce on 747kHz/96.3MHz 2030-1600 - Mo General Sce on 1170kHz/89.4MHz 2130-1800 - Traffic Sce on 101.8MHz 24h (exc. Tues 0700-1000) - Farm and Pastoral Area Sce on 900kHz/102.4MHz 2100-1600 – **NM6)** 86 Qiaoxi Shahe Lu, Jining Qu, Ulanqab, Nei Menggu 012000. Ch News General Sce on 747kHz99.9MHz 2200-1600 - Mo Sce on 1170kHz/105.3MHz 2230-1210 - Traffic Sce on 92.3MHz in Ch 2155-1700 - Literary Sce on 94.3MHz in Ch 2155-1600 – **NM7)** 89 Xilin Dajie, Xilinhot, Nei Menggu 026000. Ch General Sce on 945kHz/99.4MHz 2225-1455 - Mo General Sce on 1170kHz/ 102.1MHz 2220-1505 - General Literary Sce on 106.9MHz 2255-1505 - Traffic and Literary Sce on 97.5MHz 2225-1455 – **NM8)** 43 Manzhouli Lu, Hailar Qu, Hulun Buir, Nei Menggu 021008. Ch General Ch. on 1170/3900kHz/99.9MHz 2130-1600 - Mo General Ch. on 954/6080kHz/97.3MHz 2140-1430 – Trafiic and Literary Sce on 104.6MHz 2200-1600 – **NM9)** Tongliao Radio and TV St, 29 Heping Lu, Horqin Qu, Tongliao, Nei Menggu 028001. V.O. Tongliao: on 747kHz/97.2/87.8MHz 2110-1730 (exc. Tues?-0855) - Traffic and Literary Sce on 954kHz/91.3MHz 2110-1530 (exc. Tues 0600-0855) - Mo Prgr. "V.O. Horqin": on 1170kHz/93.7/94.4/100.3MHz 2110-1730 – **NM10)** Ordos Radio and TV St, Manduhai Xiang, Dongsheng Qu, Ordos, Nei Menggu 017000. Ch News General Sce on 1170kHz/89.6MHz 2115-1600 - Mo News General Sce on 945kHz/93.5MHz 2220-1430 - Traffic Literary and Sports Sce on 100.8/ 87.9/90.7MHz 2130-1600 - Variety Sce on 97.3/95.3MHz 2155-1600 – **NM11)** 26 Xinhua Xijie, Linhe Qu, Bayannur, Nei Menggu 015000. News General Sce (V.O. Hetao): on 1170kHz/107.0MHz 2000-1600 - Traffic and Literary Sce (V.O. the Yellow River): on 97.7MHz 2200-1600 - V.O. the Traffic: on 95.8MHz 2200-1600 – **NM12)** Alxa Radio and TV St, 1 Elute Donglu, Bayanhot Zhen, Alxa Zuoqi, Nei Menggu 750306. Ch General Sce on 1170kHz/91.0MHz2225-1500 - Mo General Sce on 945kHz/88.8MHz 2220-1500 – **NM13)** 73 Hinggan Bei Dalu, Ulanhot, Nei Menggu 137400. V.O. Hinggan: on 747kHz/89.1MHz 2125-1430 in Ch - V.O. Alateng Hinggan: on 1170kHz/94.7/96.4/96.6/97.7/103.3/107.0MHz 2200-1600 in Ch (0600-0655 in Mo) - V.O. the Traffic: on 99.0MHz 2125-1500 (exc. Tues 0600-0800) - V.O. the City: on 106.8MHz 2200-1500 – **NM14)** Xuegang Shan, Xinchengwan Xiang, Fengzhen, Nei Menggu 012100. 2225-0020, 0355-0505, 0955-1215 – **NM15)** 1 Dianshi Jie, Manzhouli, Nei Menggu 021400. On 702kHz/94.9MHz 2225-1600 in Ch, Mo and Russian – **NM16)** 1 Xing'an Dongjie, Yakeshi, Nei Menggu 022150 **NM17)** 3 Shengli Lu, Shiqiao Jie, Zalantun, Nei Menggu 162650. On 558kHz/98.6/102.7MHz 2155-1400 –**NM19)** 129 Nawenxi Dajie, Nirji Zhen, Morin Dawa, Nei Menggu 162850

NINGXIA HUI AUTONOMOUS REGION

NX1) Ningxia Radio and TV St, 66 Beijing Zhonglu, Jinfeng Qu, Yinchuan, Ningxia 750002 **W:**nxtv.cn/radio/ News Sce on 891/1206/1287kHz/106.1MHz/FM 2100-1700 (exc. Tues 0600-0955) - Economic Sce on 747kHz/92.8MHz 24h - Travel Sce on 103.7MHz 2215-1605 - Traffic Sce on 98.4MHz 24h - Music Sce on 104.7MHz 24h – **NX2)** Yinchuan Radio and TV St, 11 Zhongshan Beijie, Xingqing Qu, Yinchuan, Ningxia 750004. News General Ch. on 801kHz/90.5MHz 2300-1600 - City Economy Sce "Pinwei 950": on 95.0MHz 24h - Traffic and Music Sce on 100.6MHz 2200-1800– **NX3)** Shizuishan PBS, 363 Youyi Xijie, Dawukou Qu, Shizuishan, Ningxia 753000. General Sce on 95.4MHz 24h – **NX4)** 54 Yumin Dongjie, Litong Qu, Wuzhong, Ningxia 751100. On 1413kHz/89.3MHz 2230-1600 – **NX5)** Wenhua Jie, Xiaoba Zhen, Qingtongxia, Ningxia 751600

QINGHAI PROVINCE

QH1) Qinghai Radio and TV St, 81 Xiguan Dajie, Xining, Qinghai 810008 **W:** qhradio.com News General Sce. (Satellite Sce) on 666/711/909/1017/6145/9780kHz/91.6MHz 2200-1600 (exc. Tues 0600-0900) - Tibetan Sce on 1206/1251/1539/5990/9850kHz/98.3MHz 2250-1600 - Economic Sce on 1143kHz/107.5MHz 2255-1600 (exc. Tues 0600-0855) - Traffic and Music Sce on 1377kHz/97.2MHz 2255-1600 - Life Sce on 90.3MHz in Ch and Qinghai dialect – **QH2)** Xining Radio and TV St, 43 Nanguan Jie, Xining, Qinghai 810000. News General Sce on 1476kHz/95.6MHz 2200-1630 - Traffic and Literary Sce on 104.3MHz 2230-1905 - City Life Sce "Easy FM": on 101.3MHz - City Service and Control Sce "Sunshine FM": on 102.7MHz – **QH3)** 139 Hongwei Lu, Jiegu Zhen, Yushu Xian, Qinghai 815000. On 882kHz 2255-0100, 1025-1230 in Ch and Tb. Rel. CNR 1: 1135-1230 – **QH4)** Haixi PBS, 7 Changjiang Lu, Delingha, Qinghai 817000. Ch Prgr. on 621kHz - Mo/Tb Prgr. on 540kHz

SHANDONG PROVINCE

SD1) Shandong Radio and TV St, 81 Jing 10 Lu, Lixia Qu, Jinan, Shandong 250062 **W:** v.iqilu.com General Sce on 603/891/918/1467/1485/ 1548kHz/95.0MHz/FM 1940-1700 - Economic Sce on 594kHz/98.6MHz/FM 24h - "FM96" on 96.0MHz 24h - Life Information Sce on 105.0/88.6/104.7/104.9/107.8MHz 24h - Traffic Sce on 101.1/106.0/106.9MHz 24h - Literary Sce on 97.5MHz/FM 24h - Country Sce on 1251/621/999kHz/91.9MHz/FM 2100-1700 - Music Sce "City FM": on 99.1/92.9/96.9/106.6/107.8MHz 24h - Sports and Leisure Sce on 102.1MHz 24h – **SD2)** Jinan Radio and TV St, 32 Jing 11 Lu, Lixia Qu, Jinan, Shandong 250014. News Sce on 1053kHz/89.3/106.6MHz 24h (exc. Tues 0410-0850) - Economic Sce on 846kHz/90.9/95.7MHz 24h - Traffic Sce on 103.1/91.2MHz 24h (exc. Tues 0400-0850) - Music Sce on 88.7/105.8MHz 24h - Literary Sce "Xingfu (Happy) FM": on 1305kHz/100.5MHz 24h (exc. Tues 0400-0900) - Story Sce on 1512kHz/104.3/87.8MHz 24h - Private Car Sce on 93.6MHz 24h – **SD3)** 200 Ningxia Lu, Qingdao, Shandong 266071.

W: guangdian.qtv.com.cn/ News General Sce on 1377kHz/107.6MHz 1950-1600 – News & Life Sce 819, 97.3MHz Economic Sce Automobile Life Ch. on 1251kHz/102.9MHz 24h - Economic Sce Storytelling Ch. "Happy 603": on 603kHz/100.7MHz 24h - Traffic Sce on 900kHz/89.7MHz 24h - Private Car BS: on 1008kHz/96.4MHz 24h - Music and Sports Sce "Simul Radio": on 91.5MHz 24h - Story Sce on 95.2MHz 24h – **SD4)** Zibo Radio and TV Headquarters, 52 Huaguang Lu, Zhangdian Qu, Zibo, Shandong 255047. **W:** zbradio.com/General Sce on 89.0MHz 2100-1700 - News Sce Story Ch. on 1143kHz - Economy Sce on 801kHz/106.7MHz 2155-1700 - Traffic and Literary Sce on 1476kHz/100.0MHz 2145-1700 - Music Sce "i Radio":on 92.6MHz 2145-1700 - Private Car Sce "Yuedong 106.7" on 106.7MHz 2045-1700 Life Sce 900kHz/89.7MHz – **SD5)** Zaozhuang Radio and TV St, 88 Guangming Xilu, Zaozhuang, Shandong 277102. News Sce on 1170kHz/99.0MHz 2155-1600 - Life and Entertainment Sce on 603kHz/101.4MHz 2200-1600 - Traffic and Literary Sce on 105.2MHz 2200-1600 - Music Sce on 100.6MHz 2200-1600 – **SD6)** 1229 Dongcheng Nan 1 Lu, Dongying, Shandong 257091. News Sce on 1449kHz/91.0MHz 2155-1430 - General Sce on 105.3MHz 2150-1435 - Traffic and Music Sce on 88.1/98.4MHz 2150-1435 – **SD7)** Weifang Radio and TV St, 85 Shengli Dongjie, Kuiwen Qu, Weifang, Shandong 261061. **W:** radio.wfcmw.cn News Sce on 1161kHz/100.2/88.1MHz 2055-1600 - Private Car Sce on 1287kHz/93.3MHz 2100-1600 - Traffic Sce on 846kHz/95.9MHz 2100-1600 - Beloved Home Sce on 98.3MHz 2055-1700 - Music Sce on 90.8MHz 24h - Story Sce on 981kHz/107.1MHz 2055-1600 - Huanle (Joy) FM "New Radio": on 89.9MHz 2200-1300 - Music Sce "Simul Radio": on 88.7MHz 24h – **SD8)** Yantai Radio and TV St, 32 Wenhua Xiang, Zhifu Qu, Yantai, Shandong 264000. General Sce on 1314kHz/101.0/94.3/98.6MHz 2000-1600 - Private Car Sce on 801kHz/105.9/92.8/102.7MHz 2000-1600 - Traffic Sce on 103.0/89.0/95.3MHz 2000-1600 - Music Sce "i Radio": on 91.2/90.5MHz 24h Global Sce on 88.4/96.6/102.4MHz 24h. Rel. CRI "News Radio": 2300-2400, 0400-0430, 0900-1000 – **SD9)** 66 Wenhua Zhonglu, Weihai, Shandong 264200. News General Ch. on 1206kHz/99.6/105.1MHz 2100-1600 (exc. Tues 0600-0825). Ko Prgr: 0530-0600, 1430-1500 - Traffic and Literary Ch. on 846kHz/95.0/102.2MHz 2125-1500 (exc. Tues 0600-0855) - Story Ch. on 96.1MHz 2100-1600 - Music Fashion Sce on 90.7MHz – **SD10)** 11 Hongxing Zhonglu, Jining, Shandong 272037. **W:** jnnews.tv News Sce on 666kHz/101.8MHz 2200-1700 – Private Car Sce on 1116kHz/107.0MHz 2200-1700 - Traffic Sce on 801kHz/104.2MHz 2200-1700 - Music Sce on 1386kHz/103.1MHz 2200-1700 - Scripture Music Sce on 89.0MHz 24h – **SD11)** Rizhao Radio and TV St, Beishou, Yantai Lu, Rizhao, Shandong 276826. News General Ch. on 1449kHz/95.0MHz 2130-1600 (exc. Tues ?-0945) - Traffic and Life Ch. on 747kHz/88.1MHz 2130-1530 - Music Ch. on 104.0MHz 2130-1530 - City Ch. on 103.5MHz 2130-1530 – **SD12)** Dezhou Radio and TV St, 1288 Dongfanghong Xilu, Dezhou, Shandong 253012. News Sce on 1098kHz/104.1MHz 2150-1600 - Traffic and Music Sce on 1341kHz/94.1MHz 2150-1600 - Literary and Life Sce on 1008kHz/92.9MHz 2150-1600 - Private Car Sce on 98.9MHz 2150-1600 - Music FM on 97.9MHz – **SD13)** Linyi Radio and TV St, 21 Jinqueshan Lu, Lanshan Qu, Linyi, Shandong 276004. News General Sce on 873kHz/97.6MHz 2105-1600 (exc. Tues 0530-1020) – Fortune Ch on 1143kHz/93.2MHz 2125-1600 - V.O. the City: on 747kHz/101.0MHz 2130-1600 - Traffic Sce on 801kHz/89.9MHz 2125-1600 (exc. Tues 0600-0950) - Music Sce on 1251kHz/104.5MHz 2155-1600 – **SD14)** Liaocheng Radio and TV Headquaters, 41 Liuyuan Beilu, Liaocheng, Shandong 252000. News Sce on 1143kHz/96.8MHz 2125-1600 - Traffic Sce on 1566kHz/98.9MHz 2200-1600 - Music Sce "I Music": on 801kHz/92.4MHz 2300-1600 – **SD15)** Binzhou Radio and TV St, 358 Huanghe 5 Lu, Binzhou, Shandong 256603. News Sce on 864kHz/107.6MHz 2155-1600 - Life Sce on 1170kHz/99.4MHz 2155-1530 - Traffic Sce on 93.1MHz 2150-1600 - Music Sce on 87.8MHz 2200-1400 Private Car Sce 106.9MHz 24h – **SD16)** 28 Zhonghua Donglu, Heze, Shandong 274033. News Ch. on 1197kHz/93.9MHz 2055-1600 - Traffic Ch. on 94.8MHz 2055-1600 - Private Car Ch. on 1071kHz/96.8MHz 2055-1500 Music Ch. on 89.1MHz – **SD16A)** Mudan PBS, 2093 Changjiang Lu, Heze, Shandong 274000. V.O. Heze on 1323kHz/97.2MHz 2155-1700 - Heze V.O. the City: on 104.0MHz 2155-1700 - Story Sce on 88.0MHz 2300-1800 – **SD17)** Qingzhou PBS, 21 Fangongting Xilu, Qingzhou, Shandong 262500. On 95.4MHz 2125-1600 – **SD18)** Huangcheng Xihuan Lu, Longkou, Shandong 265701. On 101.6MHz - Yantai Longkou Economic and Literary BS: on 1251kHz 2228-0200, 0500-0700 – **SD19)** 4 Gulou Beijie, Qufu, Shandong 273100. On 1341kHz/98.4MHz 2155-0510(SS0450), 0955-1430(SS1410) – **SD20)** Tai'an PBS, 200 Yingxuan Dajie, Taishan Qu, Tai'an, Shandong 271000. News St. on 93.2MHz 2125-1600 - Economic St. on 90.1MHz 2130-1600 (exc. Tues 0600-1000) - Story Sce on 91.6MHz 2130-1600 - Traffic Information Sce on 106.2MHz 2125-1600 (exc. Tues 0600-1000) - V.O. City Music: on 104.4MHz

SHANGHAI MUNICIPALITY

SH1) Shanghai Radio and TV St (SMG), 1376 Hongqiao Lu, Shanghai 200051 **W:** smg.cn, smgradio.cn News Sce on 990kHz/93.4MHz 24h - Traffic Sce on 648kHz/105.7MHz 24h - Chinese Opera and Folk Art Sce on 1197kHz/97.2MHz 2100-1500 in Ch and Shanghai dialect - Story Sce on 927kHz/107.2MHz 2200-1600– Wuxing (Five Stars) Sports Sce on 94.0MHz 2200-1600 - Dong-Guang News St. (Yangtze River Delta FM) on 1296kHz/90.9MHz 24h - Dongfang (Eastern) City Sce on 792kHz/89.9MHz 24h - First Financial and Ecomonic Sce on 603kHz/97.7MHz 24h (exc. Thurs 1600-2200) including relay of Classical Music Sce at 1600-2200 - Popular Music Sce "Donggan101": on 101.7MHz 2200-1800 - Popular Music Sce "Love Radio": on 103.7MHz 24h - Classical Music Sce on 94.7MHz 24h(exc. Thurs 1600-2200) - Contemporary Hit Music Sce "KFM 98.1" on 98.1MHz 24h(exc. Thurs 1700-2200)

SHAANXI PROVINCE

SN1) Shaanxi Radio and TV St, 336 Chang'an Nanlu, Xi'an, Shaanxi 710061 **W:** sxtvs.com News Sce on 693/1008/1143/1521/6176kHz/106.6MHz/FM 24h (exc. Tues 0600-0900) - News Prgr. (City Sce) on 1008kHz/101.8MHz 2058-1630 - Automobile FM on 89.6MHz 24h - Traffic Sce on 801/1323kHz/91.6MHz 24h - Farm Sce on 900kHz 24h - Youth Sce "Hi Radio": on 105.5MHz 24h - Chinese Opera Sce on 747kHz/107.8MHz 24h - Music Sce on 98.8/94.8/97.5MHz 24h - Story Sce on 603kHz 24h (exc. Tues 1700-2000) - Qin Melody Sce on 101.1MHz 2300-1600 - City Express Sce 99.9MHz 24h – **SN2)**Xi`an Radio and TV St, 100, Zhenxing Lu, Xi'an, Shaanxi 710068. News Sce on 810kHz/90.4MHz 2055-1700 - Private Car Sce on 106.1MHz 24h - Traffic and Travel Sce on 104.3MHz 24h - Music Sce on "i Radio":801kHz/93.1MHz 24h - Variety Sce on 102.4MHz 2155-1710 – **SN3)** Miaopu Lu, Hongqi Jie, Tongchuan, Shaanxi 727000. News General Sce on 1134kHz/103.7MHz 2210-0015, 0330-0515, 0915-1405 – **SN4)** 47 Hongqi Lu, Baoji, Shaanxi 721000. News Sce on 1071kHz 2055-1700 - Music Sce on 105.3MHz 2155-1700 - Economic Sce on 900kHz/102.8MHz 2155-1700 - Traffic and Travel Sce on 99.7MHz 2230-1400 – **SN5)** Nan Duan, Fu'an Lu, Xianyang, Shaanxi 712000. News General Sce on 1296kHz/100.7/107.6MHz 2150-1740 - City Music Sce on 99.9MHz 2200-1740 – **SN6)** Xi Duan, Dongfeng Jie, Weinan, Shaanxi 714000. News Sce on 747kHz/101.3/102.6MHz 2100-1600 (exc. Tues 0430-0700) - Life Sce on 96.4MHz 2250-1400 (exc. Tues 0500-0850) - Traffic Sce on 90.9MHz 2157-1600 – **SN7)** Dongguan Jie, Yan'an, Shaanxi 716000. News Sce on 603kHz/100.1/104.6MHz 2210-1500 (exc. Wed 0630-0910) - Traffic Sce on 98.7MHz – **SN8)** 14 Dong Jianshe Xiang, Hanzhong, Shaanxi 723000. News Sce on 1251kHz/95.6MHz 2130-1620 - Music St. on 97.1/99.5MHz 24h (exc. Wed 0700-0930) - Traffic and Travel Sce on 93.0/94.3/101.8MHz – **SN9)** 7 Zhonglou Xiang, Yulin, Shaanxi 719000. News Sce on 1143kHz/99.4MHz - Traffic and Literary Sce on 95.9MHz – **SN10)** Ankang PBS, 113 Bashan Zhonglu, Ankang, Shaanxi 725000. News Sce on 89.7MHz - Traffic Travel and Music Sce on 95.9MHz 2155-1600

SHANXI PROVINCE

SX1) Shanxi Radio and TV St, 318 Yingze Dajie, Taiyuan, Shanxi 030001 **W:** sxrtv.com General Sce on 819/846/900/1269kHz/90.4MHz/FM 2100-1600 (exc. Tues 0600-0900) - Economic Sce on 95.8MHz 24h (exc. Tues 0600-0900) - V.O. the Health: on 1584kHz/105.9MHz 24h (exc. Mon 0600-0900) - Traffic Sce on 88.0MHz 24h - Farm Sce on 603/747/1008/1098/1206/1422/1503kHz /100.9MHz 24h - Music Sce on 94.0MHz 24h - Entertainment Sce on 101.5MHz 24h - Story Sce on 88.6MHz 24h – **SX2)** Taiyuan Radio and TV St, 2 Yifen Jie, Taiyuan, Shanxi 030024. News Sce on 91.2MHz 24h - V.O. Old Age: on 1422kHz/97.5MHz 2155-1600 - Private Car Sce on 774kHz/104.4MHz 24h - Traffic Sce on 107.0MHz 24h - Music Sce "i Radio": on 102.6MHz 24h – **SX3)** Datong Radio and TV St, 178 Yingbin Xilu, Datong, Shanxi 037006. News General Sce on 1584kHz/103.5MHz 2200-1805 - Music Sce on 91.1MHz 2200-1605 - Traffic Sce on 99.6MHz 2200-1805 - Variety Sce 900kHz/88.5MHz 24h – **SX4)** Yangquan Radio and TV St, Ningbo Lu, Yangquan, Shanxi 045000. News General Sce on 603kHz/102.7MHz 2150-1355 - Traffic Sce on 90.1MHz 2200-1600 – **SX5)** 87 Yingxiong Zhonglu, Changzhi, Shanxi 046000. News General Sce on 1584kHz/98.8MHz 2120-0600, 0915-1530 - Traffic Sce on 94.9/101.1MHz 2225-1600 (exc. Tues 0500-0900) – **SX6)** Fengtai Xijie, Jincheng, Shanxi 048000. News General Sce on 585kHz/89.8MHz 2155-1600 - Traffic Sce on 93.5MHz 2155-1600 – **SX7)** 3 Xiaoyuan Lu, Yuci Qu, Jinzhong, Shanxi 030600. News General Sce on 1530kHz/103.4MHz 2200-1600 - Traffic and

Literary Sce on 92.1MHz 2300-1500 – **SX8)** Cangcheng Xijie, Xinzhou, Shanxi 034000 – **SX9)** 233 Hongqi Dongjie, Yuncheng, Shanxi 044000. News General Sce on 1566kHz/93.2MHz 2200-1600 - Traffic and Literary Sce on 101.9MHz 2200-1600 – **SX10)** Shuozhou Radio and TV St, 1 Minfu Xijie, Shuozhou, Shanxi 036002. News General Sce on 1485kHz/100.9MHz - Traffic and Literary Sce on 93.7MHz – **SX11)** Linfen Radio and TV St, 10 Guangxuan Jie, Linfen, Shanxi 041000. News General Sce on 95.1MHz 2200-1600 - Traffic and Literary Sce on 88.9MHz 2200-1600

SICHUAN PROVINCE

SC1) 66 Shijicheng Lu, Wuhou District, Chengdu, Sichuan 610096 **W:** sctv.com General Sce " V.O. Sichuan": on 612/909/1116kHz/98.1/90.0/93.7/ 95.7/103.9/106.6MHz 24h - News Sce on 106.1MHz 24h - Economic Sce on 89.4/94.0MHz 24h - - Traffic Sce on 101.7MHz 24h - - Private Car Sce "V.O. Tianfu": on 92.5MHz 2200-1600 in Ch and Chengdu dialect - Minority Sce on 954/6060/7225kHz 2155-1700 in Ch, Tb, Kham (Tb dialect) and Yi -Pleasure Sce : on 747kHz/90.0MHz 24h - Minjiang Music Sce "i Radio": on 95.5MHz 24h - Sound of City "City FM": on 102.6MHz 24h –**SC3)** 2 Gaopeng Dadao, Chengdu, Sichuan610093. News Sce "Information 998": on 792kHz/99.8MHz24h - Traffic Sce on 1485kHz/91.4MHz 24h - Economic Sce on 105.6MHz 24h in Ch and Chengdu dialect - Cultural and Leisure Sce on 94.6MHz 24h –"Only Music Radio""FM103.2": on 103.2MHz 24h – Signboard Chengdu Music Sce "Billboard Radio Chengdu": on 105.1MHz 24h — Story Sce on 88.2MHz 24h – **SC4)** Zigong Radio and TV St, 122 Dangui Dajie, Huidong Xinqu, Zigong, Sichuan 643000. News General Sce on 1422kHz/97.7MHz 2100-1500 - Cultural and Travel Sce on 90.8MHz 2300-1700 – **SC5)** Panzhihua Radio and TV St, 43, Zhong Duan, Jinshajiang Dadao, Dong Qu, Panzhihua, Sichuan 617000. Gerenal Sce on 711kHz/88.5MHz 2120-1700 - Farm Sce (Automobile St) on 91.0MHz 2230-1700 – **SC6)** Datong Lu, Chengbei Xinqu, Luzhou, Sichuan 646000. News General Sce on 954kHz/89.8/97.0MHz 2155-1600 - Traffic and Music Sce on 96.0/100.6MHz 2155-1600 – **SC7)** 63, 1 Duan, Taishan Nanlu, Deyang, Sichuan 618000. News Sce on 720kHz/95.9MHz 2200-1600 - Music and Traffic Sce on 107.8MHz 2300-1600 – **SC8)** Mianyang Radio and TV St, 232, Nan Duan, 1 Huan Lu, Fucheng Qu, Mianyang, Sichuan 621000. News Sce "V.O. Fujiang": on 711kHz/96.7/102.0MHz 2200-1600 - Traffic Sce on 103.3MHz 2200-1600 - Music Sce on 91.2/92.6MHz 2200-1600 – **SC9)** 585, Xi Duan, Hezhou Donglu, Guangyuan, Sichuan 628017. News General Ch. on 621/1143kHz/102.7MHz 2200-1700 - City and Country Ch. on 104.8MHz 2220-1600 – **SC10)** Suining Radio and TV St, 686 Suizhou Zhonglu, Chuanshan Qu, Suining, Sichuan 629000. News and Story Sce on 1260kHz/99.7MHz 2150-1800 - Traffic and Music Sce on 87.8MHz 2150-1800 – **SC11)** 33, 1 Xiang, Xianglong Lu, Neijiang, Sichuan 641000. Economic Sce on 1143kHz/101.4MHz – **SC12)** 639, Nan Duan, Chunhua Lu, Shizhong Qu, Leshan, Sichuan 614000. News General Ch. on 1476kHz/102.8MHz 2225-1800 - Music and Traffic Ch. "Big Eye": on 100.5MHz 2300(SS 2330)-1700 – **SC13)** 12 Sichou Lu, Nanchong, Sichuan 637000. News Information Sce on 747kHz/100.4/97.5MHz 2130-1630 - Traffic and Music Sce "915 Traveler" on 91.5MHz 2330-1730 – **SC14)** Yibin Radio and TV St, 7, Zhong Duan, Nan'an Changjiang Dadao, Cuiping Qu, Yibin, Sichuan 644000. News Sce on 92.8/97.0/101.4MHz 2200-1700 - Traffic Sce on 94.2/105.9MHz 2200-1700 - Jiudu (Wine City) Music Sce on 104.2MHz 2100-1600 – **SC15)** 92 Zhangjiawan, Tongchuan Qu, Dazhou, Sichuan 635000. News General Ch. on 1143kHz 2200-1600

TIANJIN MUNICIPALITY

TJ1) Tianjin Radio and TV Stn, 143 Weijin Lu, Heping Qu, Tianjin 300070 **W:** radiotj.com News Sce on 909kHz/89.0MHz, 97.2MHz 2100-1800(FM 24h) - Economic Sce on 1071kHz/101.4MHz 2100-1600 - Crosstalk Sce on 567kHz/92.1MHz 2200-1600 - Traffic Sce on 106.8MHz 24h - Life Sce on 1386kHz/91.1MHz 2100-1700 - Literary Sce on 1098kHz/104.6MHz 2100-1800 - Music Sce "Nice Radio": on 99.0MHz 24h - Music Health Sce on 1008kHz 2300-1800 - Binhai Sce "Radio BH": on 747kHz/87.8MHz 2055-1600 - "Dongting 885" 24h on 88.5MHz - Novel Sce on 666kHz 2200-1700

XINJIANG UIGHUR AUTONOMOUS REGION

XJ1) Xinjiang Radio and TV Stn, 830 Tuanjie Lu, Urumqi, Xinjiang 830044 **W:** xjbs.com.cn Ch General Sce on 702/738/999/1494/3950wi/5060wi/ 5960/7260/7310/9600/9835su/ 11770kHz/89.5MHz 2300-1800 (SW exc. Tues 0800-1100) - Ug General Sce on 558/855/1044/1413/1494/ 3990wi/4980wi./6120/7205/7275/9560/11885/13670kHz/101.7MHz 2300-1800 (SW exc. Tues 0800-1100) - Kz Prgr. on 963/1233/1107/ 4850wi/6015/7340/9470kHz 2300-1800 (SW exc. Tue and Thu 0800-1100) - Mo Prgr. on 909/1233/1593/ 4500wi./6190/7230/9510kHz 2300-1800 (SW:exc. Tues 0800-1100) - Kg Prgr. on 1233/7295wi./9705/ 11975su.kHz/98.2MHz 2300-1800 (SW: exc. Tues and Thu 0800-1100) also see International Broadcasting section - Ch News Sce "Pioneer 961" on 96.1MHz 2300-1800 - Ch Private Car Sce (City Sce) on 92.9MHz 2300-1800 - Ch Traffic Sce on 94.9/101.8MHz 2300-1800 Ch Music Sce "MY FM": on 103.9MHz 2300-1800 - Ch Story Sce on 102.8MHz 2300-1800 Ch People Life Sce "WIFI Radio" on 92.4MHz 2300-1800 - Ug Traffic and Literary Sce on 107.4MHz 2300-1800 (exc. Tues 0800-1100) **NB:** wi.:Nov-Apr only, su.:May-Oct only – **XJ2)** 54, Bei 4 Xiang, Hongshan Lu, Urumqi, Xinjiang 830092. **W:** wlmqradio.com News Sce on 100.7MHz 2300-1800 - Economic Sce on 927kHz 2330-1700 - General Sce: on 792kHz 2300-1800 - Traffic Sce on 97.4MHz 2300-1800 - Taste (Travel and Music) Sce on 106.5MHz 2345-1725 - Ug General Sce on 1071kHz/104.6MHz2145-1400. – **XJ3)** Xinjiang Production and Construction Corps Radio and TV Stn (Media Network Bing Tuan), 775 Qingnian Lu, Urumqi, Xinjiang **W:** btzx.com.cn General Sce on 88.2MHz 24h. – **XJ4)** 100 Tianshan Lu, Karamay, Xinjiang 834000. Ch News General Sce on 1179kHz 2355-1800 (exc. Tues 0800-0930) - Ug Sce on 882kHz 2355-1800 - City Sce on 92.6MHz 2355-2000 (exc. Tues 0830-0930) – **XJ5)** 2 Hongxing Xilu, Hami, Xinjiang 839000. Ch News and Traffic Sce "V.O. Hami": on 1485kHz/103.5MHz 2300-1800 - Ug FM on 1098kHz/107.9MHz 2300-1600 - V.O. Tianmi (Honey): on 98.1MHz 2300-1800 - Legend Story Sce "Green Ch": on 91.1MHz 2255-1800 - Music Sce "Touch Radio": on 99.9MHz 24h – **XJ6)** 13 Urumqi Nanlu, Hotan, Xinjiang 848000. Ch Prgr. on 1026kHz - Ug Prgr. on 774kHz/92.2MHz 2300-1800 – **XJ7)** Tiyu Lu, Kashi, Xinjiang 844000. Ch Sce on 648kHz/101.2MHz 2355-0215, 0455-0710, ?-1335 - Ug Sce on 801kHz/103.0MHz 2355-? – **XJ8)** 66 Shangcheng Lu, Changji, Xinjiang 831100. General Sce on 873kHz 2300-1700 - Traffic Sce on 96.9MHz - Story Sce on 107.4MHz 2330-1800 - Legal Sce on 105.3MHz - Music Sce on 103.3MHz – **XJ9)** Ili PBS, 1 Hongqi Lu, Yining, Xinjiang 835000. News General Sce on 1134kHz/96.3/105.9/107.4MHz2255-1805 – Economic Sce on 90.5MHz 2325-1835 - Traffic and Music Sce on 100.8MHz - Ug Prgr. on 882kHz/88.4MHz 2350-0200, 0550-0700, 1150-1600 - Kz Prgr. on 603kHz/93.4MHz 2350-0200, 0550-0700, 1220-1500 – **XJ10)** 184 Bei 2 Lu, Shihezi, Xinjiang 832000. News Ch. on 891kHz/103.5MHz 0030-0730, 1130-1600 - Literary Ch. on 603kHz/89.3MHz – **XJ11)** 8 Kashi Xilu, Kuytun, Xinjiang 833200. Ch Prgr. on 1485kHz W2355-0230, Sun0025-0335, Sun0528-0720, W0558-0740, D1123-1425 - Kz Prgr. on 819kHz – **XJ12)** Bayingolin PBS, 1 Jianguo Nanlu, Korla, Xinjiang 841000. News Sce on 819kHz/96.6MHz - Music Sce on 92.2MHz 2300-1800 - Story Sce on 89.5MHz - Mo Sce on 104.7MHz - Traffic and Literary Sce on 107.7MHz 2330-1700

XIZANG AUTONOMOUS REGION

XZ1) Xizang Radio and TV Stn, 41 Beijing Zhonglu, Lhasa, Xizang 850000 **W:** tibet.cn Ch Sce on 999/1377/4820/5935/6050 /7240/7450/11860/11950kHz/93.3MHz 2000(Tues 2100)-1800 (SW exc. Tues 0600-1000) - Tibetan Sce on 594/846/4905/4920/6025/ 6110/6130/ 6200/7255/7385/9490/9580kHz/101.6MHz 2050 (Tues 2100)-1805 (SW exc. Tues 0600-1000). English Prgr. "Holy Tibet": 0700-0800, 1600-1700 - Kham (Tibetan dialect) General Sce on 594kHz/91.4MHz 2200-1605 - City Life Sce on 98.0MHz 2300-1700 (exc. Tues 0600-1000) Tibetan Science Education Sce on 106.3MHz 2330-0530, 1000-1400 – **XZ2)** Lhasa PBS, Lhasa, Xizang 850000. General Ch. on 91.4MHz 2350-1410 in Tb and Ch – **XZ3)** 25 Nedong Lu, Zetang Zhen, Nedong, Xizang 856000. 2335-0135, 0405-0535, 1005-1340 in Ch and Tb

YUNNAN PROVINCE

YN1) 182 Renmin Xilu, Kunming, Yunnan 650031. **W:** ynradio.com News Sce on 576/846/990/927/1098/1395/1584kHz/105.8MHz 24h – "V.O. Shangri-La": on 99.0MHz 24h - Economic Sce "Private Car Radio": on 1143/88.7MHz 2150-1600 - Minority Sce on 7210kHz/101.4MHz 2245-0300, 0600-1000, 1100-1500 in Ch, Lahu, Jingpo, Lisu, Dehong Dai, Xishuangbanna Dai - V.O. the Traffic: on 603/1098kHz/91.8MHz 24h - Music Sce on 846/1053/1251kHz/97.0MHz 2300-1700 – Educational Sce on 100.0MHz24h - Children Sce on 101.7MHz24h - Farm Sce on 1242kHz/98.9MHz 0000-1600 (exc. Tues 0600-0800) - Int Sce see International Broadcasting section – **YN2)** Kunming Radio and TV St. 198 Danxia Lu, Kunming, Yunnan 650118 **W.** kunmingbc.com General Sce on 1350kHz/100.8MHz 24h - Literature and Travel Sce "FM 1028": on 102.8MHz 24h - City Administration Sce on 95.4MHz 24h - City Information Sce "Elderly BS"on 105.0MHz 24h – **YN3)** 225 Qilin Xilu, Qilin Qu, Qujing, Yunnan 655000. V.O. Zhujiang Yuan: on 1521kHz/104.0MHz 2225-1600 - V.O. the Traffic: on 91.0MHz 2250-1600 – **YN4)** 32 Xinwen Lu, Wenshan, Yunnan 663000. Minority Language Ch. on 1053kHz/105.3MHz 2225-0030, 0355-0530, 0955-1400 in Ch, Zhuang, Miao and Yao - News General Ch. on 103.0/102.2MHz 2220-1500 - Qihua FM on 97.3MHz

2220-1600 – **YN5)** Jinhua Lu, Gejiu, Yunnan 661000. News Sce on 1521/1485kHz/101.4MHz 2200-1700 - Traffic Sce on 99.7MHz 2200-1730 - Minorities Sce on 702kHz/97.5MHz 2225-1830 in Ch, Hani and Yi – **YN6)** 4 Guangdian Lu, Jinghong, Yunnan 666100. Ch Prgr. on 98.9MHz 2225-1620 - Minority Language Prgr. on 747kHz/90.6MHz 2225-1625 in Ch, Xishuangbanna Dai and Hani – **YN7)** 144 Lucheng Donglu, Chuxiong, Yunnan 675000. General Sce on 1287kHz/106.1MHz 2225-1605 in Ch and Yi - Music Sce on 90.6/96.3MHz 2225-1605 – **YN8)** Wanhua Lu, Xiaguan Zhen, Dali, Yunnan 671000. News General Sce on 1044kHz/102.7MHz 2230-1500 - Traffic Sce on 99.9MHz 2230-1600 - Cang'er FM on 105.5MHz 2200-1600 – **YN9)** Dehong Radio and TV St, 51 Nanbeng Lu, Mang Shi, Yunnan 678400. Minority Language Sce on 900kHz/106.1MHz 2230-0110, 0330-0700, 1030-1530 in Ch, Dehong Dai, Jingpo and Zaiwa - General Sce on 104.3MHz 2215-1600 –**YN11)** 6 Longquan Lu, Zhaotong, Yunnan 657000. News General Sce "V.O. Wumeng": on 846kHz/97.5MHz 2225-1600 (exc. Tues 0710-0900) - Traffic and Travel Sce "V.O. Hedu (Crane City)": 2225-1600 – **YN12)** Baohua Lu, Gejiu, Yunnan 661400. V.O. Jinhu (Golden Lake): on 675kHz/102.7MHz – **YN13)** 38 Xueqiao Jie, Chuxiong, Yunnan 675000. W2225-2400, Sun2325-0200, D0325-0600, D0955-1405 – **YN14)** 29 Guihua Lu, Yuxi, Yunnan 653100. Green FM on 1251kHz/102.4MHz 2225-1600 – **YN15)** 67 Changzheng Dadao, Jiantang Zhen, Shangri-la Xian, Yunnan 674400. On 675kHz/104.7MHz in Ch and Tb – **YN16)** Nujiang Radio and TV St, 5 Weiyuan Xiang, Liuku Zhen, Lushui Xian, Yunnan 673100. On 558kHz/105.6MHz in Ch and Lisu – **YN17)** Longcheng Lu, Jinshan Zhen, Lufeng Xian, Yunnan 651200. 2225-1230

ZHEJIANG PROVINCE

ZJ1) Zhejiang Radio & TV Group, 111 Moganshan Lu, Hangzhou, Zhejiang 310005 **W:** zrtg.com V.O. Zhejiang: on 810kHz/88.0/101.6MHz 24h (exc. Tues 0600-0800) - News Sce "Xinrui 988": on 1530kHz/98.8MHz 24h - Economic Sce on 95.0MHz 24h - V.O. the City: on 107.0/88.6/89.4/92.5/98.2/100.7/101.7MHz 24h – V.O. the Traffic: on 93.0/93.6MHz 24h - Music FM: on 1071kHz/96./89.8/94.5/96.8/102.5/106.4/107.8MHz 24h (exc. Tues 0600-0800) - Life Sce "Minsheng 996": on 900/930/1050/1314kHz/99.6/92.3/93.6/104.2/ 104.7MHz 24h - Anchorwomen BS: on 603/1251/1521kHz/104.5MHz 24h – **ZJ2)** 888 Zhijiang Lu, Hangzhou, Zhejiang 310016. **W:** radiohz.com "AM 954" Old Friends R. on 954kHz/69.0MHz 2000-1600 - V.O. Hangzhou "News 89": on 89.0MHz 24h – **ZJ2A)** Hangzhou Traffic and Economic Sce, 5 Qingchun Donglu, Hangzhou, Zhejiang 310016. On 91.8MHz 24h – **ZJ3)** City Music "V.O. Xihu", 86 Moganshan Lu, Hangzhou, Zhejiang 310005. On 105.4MHz 24h in Ch and Hangzhou dialect – **ZJ4)** Ningbo Radio and TV Group, 109 Heyi Lu, Ningbo, Zhejiang 315000. News Sce "V.O. Ningbo": on 1323kHz/92.0MHz 2055-1610. English N: D1600-1610 - "Yangguang (Sunshine) 904": on 1251kHz/90.4MHz 2155-1605 - Economic Sce "i Radio": on 747kHz/102.9MHz 2100-1600 (exc. Tues 0600-0730) - Traffic Sce on 603kHz/93.9MHz 24h - Music Sce "Private Car 986": on 98.6MHz 2300-1600 – **ZJ4A)** 36 Nan Dajie, Zhenhai Qu, Ningbo, Zhejiang 315200. Ningbo Private Car Music St. on 104.7MHz 24h (exc. Mon 0500-0830) - V.O. Yong River: on 100.1MHz – **ZJ5)** Wenzhou Radio and TV Media Group, Xincheng Dadao, Lucheng Qu, Wenzhou, Zhejiang 325027. News General Sce "V.O. Wenzhou": on 666kHz/94.9/102.6MHz 24h (exc. Tues 0600-0900) in Ch and Wenzhou dialect - Economic Life Sce "Xingyun (Fortunate) 888": on 801kHz/88.8MHz 24h - Traffic Sce "Automobile FM": on 97.2/103.9MHz 24h - Private Car Music Sce "i Radio":on 100.3MHz 24h (exc. Tues 0600-0900) - V.O. Green: on 93.8MHz 24h – **ZJ6)** Jiaxing Radio and TV Group, 6 Dongsheng Lu, Jiaxing, Zhejiang 314001. News Sce on 1107kHz/104.1MHz 2125-1505 - Traffic Sce on 657kHz/92.2MHz 2130-1505 (exc. Tues 0530-0700) - Life Sce "Kuaile (Happy) 882" on 88.2MHz 2130-1500 (exc. Tues 0500-0700) – **ZJ7)** Huzhou Radio and TV Headquarters, 628 Xinhua Lu, Huzhou, Zhejiang 313000. News Sce on 873kHz/105.0MHz 2155-1600 (exc. Tues 0600-0730) - Traffic Sce on 927/1521kHz/103.5MHz 2155-1600 - Music Sce on 1251kHz/98.5MHz 2200-1600 – **ZJ8)** Shaoxing Radio and TV Headquarters, 508 Yan'an Donglu, Shaoxing, Zhejiang 312000. News General Sce on 738kHz/93.6MHz 2100-1600 - Traffic Sce on 94.1MHz 2130-1600 (exc. Tues 0600-0830) - Chinese Opera Sce on 102.5MHz 2130-0300 - Music Sce "i Music": on 103.5MHz 2100-1500 (exc. Tues 0600-0900) – **ZJ9)** 238 Renmin Xilu, Jinhua, Zhejiang 321000. News Sce on 675kHz/104.4MHz 2100-1600 (exc. Tues 0600-0900) - Economic Sce "Private Car 101": on 101.4MHz 2200-1700 - Traffic Sce on 94.2MHz 24h – **ZJ10)** Quzhou Radio and TV Headquarters, 35 Nanjie, Quzhou, Zhejiang 324000. News Sce "V.O. Quzhou": on 711kHz/105.3MHz 2155-1600 (exc. Tues 0500-0725) - Traffic and Music Sce on 1250kHz/97.5MHz 2200-1700 – **ZJ11)** Zhoushan Radio and TV Headquarters, 137 Changguo Lu, Dinghai Qu, Zhoushan, Zhejiang 316000. News General Ch. "V.O. Dinghai": on 684kHz/99.8MHz 2130-1500 (exc. Tues 0530-0855) - Traffic and Economic Sce on 1098kHz/97.0MHz 2155-1500 (exc. Tues 0500-0900) - Automobile Music FM "V.O. the City": on 900kHz/91.0/102.6MHz 2155-1500 (exc. Tues 0530-0855) – **ZJ12)** Lishui Radio and TV Headquarters, 2 Huayuan Lu, Liandu Qu, Lishui, Zhejiang 323000. News General Ch. on 711kHz/94.0/96.4MHz 2155-1600 - Traffic and Music Ch. on 106.9MHz 2155-1600 - New Farm Sce on 88.3MHz 24h – **ZJ13)** Xiaoshan PBS, Nanduan, Yucai Lu, Xiaoshan Qu, Hangzhou, Zhejiang 311200. On 107.9MHz 2155-1400 – **ZJ14)** Xishan, Chengguan, Rui'an, Zhejiang 325200. On 1584kHz/91.0MHz ?-1305 – **ZJ15)** 121 Zhongshan Lu, Jiangshan, Zhejiang 324100 – **ZJ16)** Taizhou PBS, 315 Zhongxin Dadao, Jiaojiang Qu, Taizhou, Zhejiang 318000. News Sce "987 Ch.": on 98.7/87.5/90.0MHz 24h - Traffic Sce on 102.7MHz - Music Sce on 100.1MHz.

CHRISTMAS ISLAND (Australia)

L.T: UTC +7h — **Pop:** 1,843 — **Pr.L:** English (official), Malay, Chinese (Amoy, Cantonese, Mandarin) — **E.C:** 240V/50Hz — **ITU:** CHR

MW kHz		Call	kW	Network, location
1)	1422	6ABCRN	0.5	ABC R. National, Phosphate Hill
FM MHz		**Call**	**kW**	**Network, location**
1)	89.3	6ABCRR	0.02	ABC Local R. (Kimberley), Phosphate Hill
1)	90.1	6ABCRN	0.02	ABC R. National, Rocky Point
2)	90.9	6FMS	0.02	Red FM, Phosphate Hill
1)	91.7	6JJJ	0.02	ABC Triple J, Rocky Point
3)	92.5	6RCI	0.02	Christmas Island Cmty R., Phosphate Hill
1)	93.3	6ABCRR	0.02	ABC Local R. (Kimberley), Rocky Point
1)	94.1	6ABCRN	0.02	ABC R. National, Phosphate Hill
1)	95.7	6ABCRR	0.1	ABC Local R. (Kimberley), Drumsite
1)	97.3	6ABCRN	0.02	ABC Radio National, Drumsite
2)	98.9	6FMS	0.02	Red FM, Drumsite
1)	100.5	6JJJ	0.02	ABC Triple J, Drumsite
3)	102.1	6RCI	0.02	Christmas Island Cmty R., Drumsite
1)	103.7	6JJJ	0.02	ABC Triple J, Phosphate Hill
3)	105.3	6RCI	0.02	Christmas Island Cmty R., Rocky Point
2)	106.9	6FMS	0.02	Red FM, Rocky Point

Addresses & other information:

All ABC and RedFM services are 24hr retransmissions via VAST satellite platform – **1)** Dept Infrastructure & Regional Development (Policy Section, Territories Reform & Service Delivery), 111 Alinga St, Canberra ACT 2601 (GPO Box 594, Canberra ACT 2601) ☎ +61 2 2674 7111 **E:** clientservice@infrastructure.gov.au – **2)** RedFM, 50 Hasler Rd, Osborne Park WA 6017 ☎ +61 8 9482 9500 🖷 +61 8 9482 9454 **E:** admin@redfm.com.au **W:** redfm.com.au – **3)** Broadcast House, Nursery Road, Drumsite (PO Box 474) Christmas Island WA 6798 ☎ +61 8 9164 7121 🖷 +61 8 9164 8615 **E:** 6rci@pulau.cx **W:** facebook.com/6RCIradio Local community stn. AKA VLU2-FM

COCOS (KEELING) ISLANDS (Australia)

L.T: UTC +6½h — **Pop:** 544 — **Pr.L:** English, Cocos Malay — **E.C:** 240V/50Hz — **ITU:** ICO

FM	MHz	Call	kW	Network (West Island)
3)	96.6	6CKI	0.1	Voice of the Cocos (Keeling) Isl.
1)	98.9	6JJJ	0.1	Triple J
2)	100.5	6FMS	0.1	Red FM
1)	102.1	6ABCRR	0.1	ABC Local R. Kimberley
FM	**MHz**	**Call**	**kW**	**Network (Home Island)**
3)	102.7	6CKI	0.02	Voice of the Cocos (Keeling) Isl.
1)	105.7	6ABCRR	0.02	ABC Local R. Kimberley

Addresses & other information:

All ABC and Red FM services are 24hr retransmissions via VAST satellite platform **1)** Dept Infrastructure & Regional Development (Policy Section, Territories Reform & Service Delivery), 111 Alinga St, Canberra ACT 2601 (GPO Box 594, Canberra ACT 2601) ☎ +61 2 2674 7111 **E:** clientservice@infrastructure.gov.au **2)** Red FM, 50 Hasler Rd, Osborne Park WA 6017 ☎ +61 8 9482 9500 🖷 +61 8 9482 9454 **E:** admin@redfm.com.au **W:** redfm.com.au **3)** PO Box 1093, Cocos (Keeling) Islands WA 6799 ☎+61 8 9162 6666 **E:** 6cki@cki.cc **W:** facebook.com/6CKI-Voice-of-the-Cocos-Keeling-Islands-570321973012338/ **Prgr:** 24h with local news 0700 UTC M-F local community stn.

COLOMBIA

L.T: UTC -5h — **Pop:** 50 million — **Pr.L:** Spanish — **E.C:** 120V/60Hz — **ITU:** CLM

COMISIÓN DE REGULACIÓN DE COMUNICACIONES (CRC)

Calle 59 A bis No. 5- 53, Edificio Link Siete Sesenta, Piso 9, Bogotá 110231 ☎ +57 1 3198300 +57 1 3198301 **E:** atencioncliente@crcom.gov.co **W:** www.crcom.gov.co **L.P:** CEO: Carlos Lugo Silva

ASOCIACIÓN NACIONAL DE MEDIOS DE COMUNICACIÓN (ASOMEDIA)

Cra 16 No. 93 A 36, of. 504, Barrio Chicó, Bogotá D.C. ☎ +57 1 6111300 **E:** asomedios@asomedios.com **W:** www.asomedios.com **L.P:** Pres: Tulio Angel

Call HJ-, ‡ = inactive, †=irregular, ± = varying freq. The letters preceding the stn number indicate the departamento. Addresses are listed by departamento in alphabetical order.
Hr of tr. usually 24h – see address section for variations.

MW	Call	kHz	kW	Station, location
DC01)	KA	540	10	R. Auténtica, Bogotá
DC02)	HF	550	50	R. Nac. de Colombia, Medellín (Marinilla)
DC02)	GS	560	10	R. Nac. de Colombia, Tunja (Oicatá)
DC02)	ND	570	100	R. Nac. de Colombia, Bogotá (El Rosal)
DC02)	HP	580	50/10	R. Nac. de Colombia, Cali (Jamundí)
AN01)	CR	590	50	Impacto Radio, Medellín
AT01)	HJ	600	50	R. Libertad, Barranquilla
DC02)	D90	‡610	50	R. Nac. de Colombia, Riohacha (Uribia)
DC03)	KL	610	30	La Cariñosa, Bogotá
BO01)	VP	620	10	Colmundo Radio, Cartagena
VA01)	EL	620	50/20	Colmundo Radio, Cali
MA01)	BJ	640	10	RCN Radio, Santa Marta
DC03)	KH	650	50	Antena 2, Bogotá
VA02)	EZ	660	10	R. Auténtica, Cali
AN02)	PL	670	25	Antena 2, Medellín
SS28)	R33	670	10	UIS AM "La Nueva Radio", Bucaramanga
DC02)	ZO	680	50	R. Nac. de Colombia, Barranquilla
DC04)	CZ	690	35	W Radio, Bogotá (r. 99.9)
VA03)	CX	700	30	W Radio, Cali
AN03)	NX	710	10	R. Red RCN, Medellín
BY14)	YD	710	1	R. La Paz, Paipa
QU01)	VO	720	25	Transmisora Quindío, Armenia
DC05)	CU	730	10	Melodía Estéreo, Bogotá
CE01)	NS	740	50	R. Guatapurí, Valledupar
NA01)	HB	740	10	Ecos de Pasto, Pasto
AN01)	DK	750	50	Caracol Radio, Medellín (r. 90.3)
CS01)	LH	750	5	LV de Yopal, Yopal
AT02)	AJ	760	25	RCN Radio, Barranquilla
DC03)	JX	770	100	RCN Radio, Bogotá (r. 93.9)
NA12)	FV	780	5	R. Viva, Pasto
VA04)	ZG	780	10	LV de Dios, Cali
AN25)	DC	790	15	Múnera Eastman R, Medellín
TO01)	NC	790	1	Ecos del Combeima, Ibagué
SS01)	BW	800	100	RCN Radio, Bucaramanga
DC04)	CY	810	60	Caracol R., Bogotá (r. 100.9)
VA03)	ED	820	50	Caracol R., Cali
AN01)	DM	830	15	Q'hubo Radio AM/R. Reloj, Medellín
HU01)	KK	840	30	HJ Doble K Sistema INRAI, Neiva
VA24)	NA	840	5	R. Robledo, Cartago
DC04)	KC	850	35	Candela 8-50, Bogotá
CE02)	NJ	860	50	LV del Cañaguate/W Radio, Valledupar
VA05)	DV	860	10	Voces de Occidente, Buga
AN09)	ZH	870	5	R. Verdad y Vida, Medellín
BY16)	GD	870	1	Em. Reina de Colombia, Chiquinquirá
TO02)	LA	870	10	Uniminuto R. Tolima, Ibagué
SS02)	GE	880	20	Caracol R., Bucaramanga (r. 99.2)
DC06)	CE	890	10	Vida 890, Bogotá
MA03)	PM	890	20	R. Galeón/Caracol R., Santa Marta
NS02)	DD	900	10	RCN Fiesta, Cúcuta
VA04)	EY	900	10	LV de Cali, Cali
AN04)	DO	910	10	LV del Río Grande, Medellín
BY12)	TT	910	1	Ondas del Porvenir, Samacá
IS01)	MY	910	30	RCN Radio, San Andrés
BO03)	AA	920	10	Em. Fuentes, Cartagena
NA02)	JN	920	10	HSB Radio, Pasto
TO03)	SJ	920	10	LV del Pueblo/R. María, Ibagué
CL01)	IA	930	5	Bésame/ W R., Manizales (r. 91.7/101.7)
DC07)	CS	930	10	LV de Bogotá, Bogotá
AN59)	A76	940	5	Frecuencia U, Medellín
NS03)	TL	940	25	RCN Radio, Cúcuta
VA04)	GB	940	10	R. Calima, Cali
BY18)	UJ	950	5	Armonias Boyacenses, Tunja
RI01)	FN	950	15	Caracol Radio, Pereira
BO08)	HN	960	10	Caracol Radio, Magangué
SS23)	HX	960	5	Blu Radio, Bucaramanga
CA01)	VK	970	15	Armonías del Caquetá, Florencia
DC08)	CI	970	10	R. Red RCN, Bogotá
QU02)	HKX59	970	1	Ecos del Cacique, Calarcá
NS04)	JV	980	15	Tropicana, Cúcuta (r. 89.7)
VA06)	ES	980	100	RCN Radio, Cali
AN02)	CH	990	50	RCN Radio, Medellín
BY07)	HI	990	5	LV de Garagoa, Garagoa
BO04)	AQ	1000	15	RCN Radio, Cartagena
DC02)	JG	1000	10	R. Nac. de Colombia, Manizales(La Enea)
AT04)	OP	1010	10	Sistema Cardenal, Barranquilla
CO01)	ZD	†1010	5	R. Panzenú, Montería
DC04)	CC	1010	10	Acuario Estéreo, Bogotá
HU02)	JR	1010	15	Caracol R., Neiva
NA03)	BN	1010	10/5	LV del Galeras, Pasto
AN04)	DQ	1020	10	Emisora Claridad, Medellín
ME01	KS	1020	10	La Cariñosa, Villavicencio
RI02)	FQ	1020	10	RCN Radio, Pereira
SS04)	DZ	1020	15	R. Primavera, Bucaramanga
TO04)	FT	1020	10	La FM, Ibagué
BY01)	DJ	1030	10	La Cariñosa, Duitama
CE03)	RF	‡1030	15	Ondas del Cesar, Aguachica
CO02)	GX	1030	5	RPC Lorica Radio, Lorica
VA06)	DT	1030	30	Antena 2, Cali
AT01)	AI	1040	15	R. Tropical, Barranquilla
CC01)	SY	1040	10	R. 1040, Popayán
DC09)	CJ	1040	15	Colmundo Radio, Bogotá
NA04)	UB	1040	15	Colmundo Radio, Pasto
NS05)	BF	1040	15	LV del Norte/Blu Radio, Cúcuta
QU03)	FM	1040	15	LV de Armenia, Armenia
AR01)	E73	1050	10	LV del Cinaruco/Caracol, Arauca
CE04)	BB	1050	10	Sistema Cardenal, Valledupar
CO04)	AW	1050	10	RCN Radio, Montería
SS05)	GU	‡1050	10	R. Bucarica, Bucaramanga
TO05)	FZ	1050	10	La Cariñosa Voz del Centro, Espinal
VA07)	NG	1050	5	R. Palmira, Palmira
AN05)	MG	1060	1	R. Litoral, Turbo
BY02)	MV	1060	10	R. Furatena, Chiquinquirá
CL02)	FJ	1060	15	RCN Radio, Manizales
GU01)	LY	1060	10	R. Delfín, Riohacha
HU03)	OV	1060	15	R. Surcolombiana, Neiva
SU01)	YX	†1060	1	R. Caracolí, Sincelejo
AT06)	AH	1070	20	Em. Atlántico, Barranquilla
CC02)	VR	1070	15	R. Súper, Popayán
DC11)	CG	1070	30	R. Santa Fe/R. Reloj, Bogotá
AN01)	AX	1080	10	LV de Antioquia, Medellín
CO04)	AW	†1080	10	LV de Montería, Montería
ME03)	KT	1080	10	R. Auténtica, Villavicencio
SS06)	MH	1080	10	R. Melodía, Bucaramanga
VA08)	JF	‡1080	10	Cadena Radial Vida, Cali
BO05)	OM	1090	5	Blu Radio, Cartagena
BY03)	IH	1090	8	R. Reloj Boyacá, Sogamoso
NS06)	BC	1090	15	Caracol R., Cúcuta
TO06)	JB	1090	10	Click Radio/Blu Radio, Guamo
AN06)	GQ	1100	5	Transmisora Surandes/Todelar, Andes
AT04)	AT	1100	15	Caracol R., Barranquilla
DC27)	CN	1100	10	Emisora BBN, Bogotá
HU04)	YZ	1100	15	La FM, Neiva
SS07)	GI	1100	5	Em. José Antonio Galán, Socorro
AN07)	DI	1110	9	R. Bolivariana AM, Medellín
AR02)	GP	1110	5	LV del Río Arauca, Arauca
ME04)	JP	1110	10	RCN Radio, Villavicencio
VA03)	EW	1110	10	R. Reloj, Cali
BY04)	KQ	1120	10	Tropicana Boyacá, Tunja (r. 88.6)
NS01)	TI	1120	10	Emisora Vox Dei, Cúcuta
SS02)	GH	1120	15	R. Reloj, Bucaramanga
DC06)	VA	1130	15	Cadena Radial Vida, Bogotá
NA05)	QQ	1130	10	R. Reloj, Pasto

MW	Call	kHz	kW	Station, location
AN02)	DL	1140	10	R. Paisa/RCN La Cariñosa, Medellín
BO06)	KO	1140	10	R. Esperanza, Cartagena
CU01)	CL	1140	10	R. Panamericana/Blu Radio, Girardot
ME05)	E67	1140	10	LV de los Centauros/Caracol, Villavicencio
SS08)	RN	1140	10	RCN Radio, Barbosa
BY05)	GJ	1150	1	W Radio, Duitama
CH01)	TE	1150	1	LV del Chocó/RCN Radio, Quibdó
HU05)	FP	1150	10	RCN Radio, Neiva
NS07)	BT	1150	10	R. Catatumbo/Blu Radio, Ocaña
QU04)	FI	1150	15	Caracol Radio, Armenia
CA03)	AU	1160	15	Ondas del Orteguaza, Florencia
CO06)	AZ	1160	5	Em. Frecuencia Bolivariana, Montería
DC13)	OC	1160	15	Fuego AM, Bogotá
NA06)	ZV	1160	5	RCN Radio Las Lajas, Ipiales
NS08)	EC	1160	10	R. San José de Cúcuta, Cúcuta
VA04)	EV	1160	10	R. Eco, Cali
AN04)	FW	1170	10	R. Nutibara, Medellín
AR03)	E74	1170	10	Meridiano 70, Arauca
BO07)	NW	1170	10	Caracol Radio, Cartagena
BY05)	GA	1170	10	Lluvias Radio, Tunja (r. 1260)
ME06)	BX	1170	10	Ondas del Meta, Villavicencio
VA09)	JE	1170	1	RCN Radio, Tuluá
CL05)	FX	1180	15	Caracol Radio, Manizales
SS10)	GK	1180	20	La Cariñosa, Bucaramanga
TO07)	JT	1180	10/5	RCN Radio, Ibagué
AT05)	CT	1190	1	LV de la Costa, Barranquilla
DC07)	CV	1190	10	R. Cordillera, Bogotá
NA07)	KG	1190	10	R. Mira, Tumaco
AN49)	IJ	1200	15	LV de la Raza, Medellín
BO08)	BV	1200	10	Radio Principe, Cartagena
BY06)	GC	1200	10	RCN Radio, Sogamoso
CU02)	CD	1200	1	Em. Nueva Época, Fusagasugá
VA10)	NF	1200	10	R. Red RCN, Cali
HU02)	FR	1210	10	Bésame / W Radio, Neiva
NS03)	E65	1210	10	La Cariñosa, Cúcuta
RI02)	BQ	1210	10	La Cariñosa, Pereira
CO07)	AV	1220	10	RCN R. Uno, Montería
DC13)	KR	1220	10	R. María Colombia, Bogotá
NA08)	NM	1220	10	R. Viva, Ipiales
SS11)	MT	1220	10	RCN Radio, San Gil
AN10)	IL	1230	10	Em. Minuto de Dios, Medellín
BY04a)	BR	1230	6	Em. Radio Recuerdos, Tunja
CU03)	TP	1230	1	R. Colina Caracol, Girardot
SS12)	EH	1230	15	Colmundo Radio, Bucaramanga
VA06)	LK	1230	10	R. Calidad, Cali
QU05)	FG	1240	10	RCN Radio, Armenia (Calarcá)
VA11)	JA	1240	3	R. Buenaventura, Buenaventura
AT07)	OK	1250	10	Em. ABC, Barranquilla
DC14)	CA	1250	10	Capital Radio, Bogotá
NS06)	HS	1250	15	W Radio, Cúcuta (r. 99.9)
AN11)	DA	1260	5	R. Auténtica, Medellín
BY05)	NO	1260	5	Lluvias Radio, Duitama
CE05)	OH	1260	5	RCN Radio, Valledupar
IS03)	HU	1260	1	Caracol R., San Andrés (r. Bogotá)
ME07)	LX	1260	5	Emisora Lux Dei, Villavicencio
NS10)	TM	1260	5	R. Sonar, Ocaña
TO08)	CO	1260	5	Caracol R., Ibagué
VA28)	ET	1260	5	R. María Colombia, Cali
BO04)	AR	1270	2	La Cariñosa, Cartagena
CU04)	XQ	1270	1	Radio Auténtica, Ubaté
RI05)	IM	1270	1	Colmundo Radio, Pereira
SS02)	TX	1270	5	W Radio, Bucaramanga
AN12)	MB	1280	5	R. Suroeste, Concordia
DC20)	KN	1280	5	Aviva2, Bogotá
GU02)	HO	1280	5	Impacto Popular, San Juan del Cesar
HU06)	CM	1280	5	HJ Doble K Sistema INRAI, Pitalito
NA05)	LR	1280	5	Caracol R., Pasto
SS14)	NQ	‡1280	1	LV del Río Suárez, Barbosa
AN13)	TH	1290	5	LV de las Estrellas, Medellín
CU05)	KY	1290	5	RCN Radio, Girardot
SU04)	OI	1290	5	ConecZión Radio, Sampués
VA13)	MC	1290	5	R. Viva 12-90, Cali
BO09)	OG	1300	5	Aviva2, Cartagena
BY08)	RB	1300	5	CRB-Cadena Radial Boyacense, Tunja
RI01)	LD	1300	5	R. Reloj, Pereira
SS02)	NB	1300	5	Onda 5, Bucaramanga
TO09)	EA	1300	5	R. Lumbí, Mariquita
AN14)	LM	1310	5	R. Santa Bárbara, Santa Bárbara
AT08)	AK	1310	5	Voz de la Patria Celestial, Barranquilla
CO08)	DG	1310	5	Caracol Radio, Montería
DC23)	JZ	1310	5	Radio 3:16, Bogotá
AN16)	TA	1320	5	R. María, Medellín
BY09)	HT	1320	5	R. Guateque Stereo, Guateque
CU06)	NV	1320	5	La Cariñosa, Girardot
SS15)	MS	1320	5	La Cariñosa, Barrancabarmeja
VA14)	NK	1320	5	Hope Radio, Palmira
AN17)	RD	1330	1	R. Fénix, El Peñol
BO02)	AP	1330	5	R. Auténtica, Cartagena
CC04)	LS	1330	5	Caracol Radio, Popayán
SS16)	NR	1330	5	La Caliente 13-30, San Gil
AN18)	NP	‡1340	1	LV de Nariño, Nariño
AT03)	FA	1340	5	LV del Caribe, Barranquilla
DC03)	FB	1340	5	Amor "Años Maravillosos", Bogotá
HU05)	KD	1340	5	La Cariñosa, Neiva
NA09)	HA	1340	5	RCN Radio, Pasto
NS04)	PY	1340	5	R. Lemas, Cúcuta
SU05)	HY	1340	5	RCN Radio, Sincelejo
VA15)	IS	1340	5	RCN Radio, Buenaventura
AN19)	DS	1350	5	Ondas de la Montaña, Medellín
MA01)	OA	1350	5	RCN R. Uno, Santa Marta
TO10)	HL	1350	5	Bésame, Ibagué
VA16)	EN	1350	5	R. Armonía, Cali
BO08)	UO	1360	5	Sistema Cardenal, Cartagena
RI06)	RA	1360	5	Ecos 1360 R./R. María, Pereira
SS17)	KV	1360	1	R. Zapatoca, Zapatoca
AN23)	NU	1370	2.5	RCN Radio, Rionegro
AT09)	BO	1370	5	Em. Minuto de Dios, Barranquilla
CC05)	EQ	1370	5	RCN Radio, Popayán
DC01)	KI	1370	5	R. Mundial, Bogotá
NS15)	BD	1370	1	Frecuencia F, Cúcuta
SU14)	NI	†1370	1	R. Sabanas/Blu Radio, Sincelejo
AN57)	JD	1380	3	NSE Radio, Medellín
BY11)	EE	1380	5	RCN Radio, Tunja
CE07)	MM	‡1380	5	La Nota, Valledupar
CL06)	LG	1380	3	LV de La Dorada, La Dorada
HU08)	ID	1380	5	Em. Potencia Latina, La Plata
VA18)	EJ	1380	1	Armonías del Palmar, Palmira
CL07)	FO	1390	5	LV de los Andes, Manizales
CU07)	YW	‡1390	5	R. Auténtica, Pacho
SS18)	ZY	1390	1	R. María Colombia, Bucaramanga
TO11)	FY	1390	5	Olímpica Espinal, El Espinal
AT02)	AS	1400	5	La Cariñosa, Barranquilla
CH02)	ER	1400	1	Ecos del Atrato/W Radio, Quibdó
DC16)	KM	1400	5	Em. Mariana, Bogotá
NA10)	JJ	1400	1	Caracol R. Ipiales, Ipiales
NS16)	BK	1400	1	LV de la Gran Colombia, Cúcuta
QU04)	HM	1400	5	La Cariñosa Armenia, Calarcá
AN27)	DU	1410	5	Em. Cultural Univ. de Antioquia, Medellín
SS20)	TY	1410	1	LV del Carare, Vélez
VA19)	EI	1410	5	R. Guadalajara, Buga
AN28)	D23	1420	1	Ecos de Frontino, Frontino
CL05)	HK	‡1420	5	Cadena Radial Vida, Manizales
MA06)	BH	1420	5	R. Magdalena, Santa Marta
SS21)	SN	1420	2	R. Lenguerke, Zapatoca
TO06)	LE	1420	1	La Cariñosa, Ibagué
AN29)	CK	1430	1	R. Sensación, Yarumal
AT10)	PW	1430	5	Radio Ya, Barranquilla
DC17)	KU	1430	5	Uniminuto Radio, Bogotá
SU07)	QX	1430	5	R. Majagual, Sincelejo
AN46)	NZ	1440	5	Colmundo Radio, Medellín
VA20)	EK	1440	5	R. Tuluá, Tuluá
AN31)	E20	1450	1	R. María Colombia, Urrao
CL02)	NL	1450	5	Antena 2/La Cariñosa, Manizales
SS22)	HH	1450	5	R. Católica Metropolitana, Bucaramanga
TO13)	BY	1450	5	Olímpica Girardot, Flandes
AN33)	TN	1460	5	R. María Colombia, Turbo
AN34)	MU	1460	1	LV de Amalfi (Caracol aff.), Amalfi
AN45)	E26	1460	1	R. Capiro, La Ceja
DC18)	JW	1460	5	ENC R. (Em. Nuevo Continente), Bogotá
NA09)	ZU	1460	5	La Cariñosa, Pasto
SU08)	AL	1460	1	R. Sincelejo, Sincelejo
AN04)	II	1470	5	Esperanza Colombia R., Medellín
CU09)	HQ	1470	5	R. Futurama, Pacho
TO14)	TB	1470	5	Ondas de Ibagué, Ibagué
VA26)	NT	1470	5	R. Huellas, Cali
MA07)	OD	1480	5	R. Rodadero, Santa Marta

MW	Call	kHz	kW	Station, location
AN35)	TC	1480	1	R. Sonsón, Sonsón
AT11)	AY	1490	5	R. Vida Nueva, Barranquilla
DC19)	BS	1490	4	Em. Punto Cinco, Bogotá
VA21)	ZB	1490	5	LV de los Robles, Tuluá
CL09)	UW	1500	5	R. María Colombia, Manizales
CU10)	TW	1500	5	Kirios R, Fusagasugá
VA22)	LJ	1500	5	Sonora 1500 AM, Cali
AN37)	D24	1510	5	LV de La Unión, La Unión
BY15)	A22	1510	1	LV de San Luis, San Luis de Gaceno
AN39)	MA	1520	1	LV del Suroeste, Jericó
AT03)	LQ	1520	5	La Radio del Príncipe de Paz, Barranquilla
DC09)	LI	1520	5	Su Presencia Radio, Bogotá
RI07)	RL	1520	1	Antena de los Andes/Reloj, Sta Rosa de Cabal
AN58)	DN	1530	5	Yeshu'a LV de Jesucristo, Medellín
GU03)	OZ	‡1530	5	LV de la Prov. de Padilla, San Juan del Cesar
VA23)	EU	1530	1	Caracol Radio Sevilla, Sevilla
AN41)	A26	1540	1	Em. Brisas del Río Chico, Belmira
CL10)	ZF	1540	5	R. Cóndor, Manizales
SS25)	HD	1540	1	LV del Petróleo/Caracol, Barrancabermeja
DC21)	ZI	1550	5	G12 Radio, Bogotá
QU03)	QD	1550	5	Radio Auténtica, Calarcá
VA31)	LT	1550	5	Em. Revivir en Cristo, Cali
AN52)	XZ	1560	5	Santa María de la Paz, Medellín
SS26)	HE	1560	5	Voces Rovirenses, Málaga
VA08)	LP	1560	5	La Cariñosa, Tuluá
CL11)	E70	1570	1	R. Auténtica, Manizales
AT12)	QZ	1580	5	R. María Colombia, Barranquilla
DC25)	QT	1580	5	Candela 8-50, Bogotá
SU01)	RM	1580	5	Sistema Cardenal, Sincelejo
AN44)	IP	1590	5	Emisora BBN, Envigado
SS27)	WB	1590	5	R. Nuestra Señora/R. María, Socorro
AN51)	HKO63	1600	0.25	R. Jardín, Jardín
SW	**Call**	**kHz**	**kW**	**Name and h of tr**
DC26)		4940	1	La Montana Colombia, Maicao

Major Networks:
RADIO NACIONAL DE COLOMBIA (Pub)
✉ Av. El Dorado Cr. 45 # 26 - 33 Bogotá, D.C. ☎ +571 2200727 🖷 +571 2200700/230 **W:** radionacional.co **E:** info@rtvc.gov.co
CARACOL (Primera Cadena Radial Colombiana)
✉ Calle 67 N° 7-37, Bogotá, DC ☎ +57 1 348 7600 🖷 +57 1 337 7126 **W:** caracol.com.co **E:** caracolcolombia@caracol.com.co - **Regional prgr:** weekdays 1045-1100, 1130-1200, 1600-1700, 1730-1800.
RCN (Radio Cadena Nacional)
✉ Cra. 13A N° 37-32, Bogotá, DC ☎ +57 1 314 7070 🖷 +57 1 314 7070 **W:** rcnmundo.com
All "La Cariñosa" stations relay sport trs regularly from Antena 2.
TODELAR (Circuito Todelar de Colombia)
✉ Ap. 27344 (Av. Cra 20, N° 83-64), Bogotá, DC ☎ +57 1 621 6621 🖷 +57 1 616 0056 **W:** todelar.com **E:** todelar@telesat.com.co
COLMUNDO RADIO
✉ Cruzada Estudiantil y Profesional de Colombia, Diagonal 58 N° 26A-29, Bogotá, DC ☎ +57 1 217 8911 🖷 +57 1 348 2746 **W:** colmundoradio.com.co **E:** correo@colmundoradio.com
SISTEMA VIDA INTERNACIONAL (Rlg)
✉ Avenida Calle 13 No 79-70, Bogotá, DC ☎ +57 1 294 8300 **W:** sistemavida.net
CADENA RADIAL AUTENTICA DE COLOMBIA (Rlg)
✉ Ap. 18350, (Calle 32 N° 16-12), Bogotá, DC. Carrera 38D # 1-52, Barrio Santa Isabel, Cali ☎ +57 1 285 3360 🖷 +57 1 285 2505 **W:** cmb.org.co

State abbreviations: (Departamentos) AM = Amazonas, AN = Antioquia, AR = Arauca, AT = Atlántico, BO = Bolívar, BY = Boyacá, CA = Caquetá, CC = Cauca, CE = Cesar, CH = Chocó, CL = Caldas, CO = Córdoba, CS = Casanare, CU = Cundinamarca, DC = Distrito Capital, GN = Guainía, GU = Guajira, GV = Guaviare, HU = Huila, IS = Islas San Andrés y Providencia, MA = Magdalena, ME = Meta, NA = Nariño, NS = Norte de Santander, PU = Putumayo, QU = Quindío, RI = Risaralda, SS = Santander del Sur, SU = Sucre, TO = Todelar, VA = Valle del Cauca, VI = Vichada, VP = Vaupés.
N.B: These abbreviations are not officially recognized by the Colombian Post Office. Letters should therefore carry full name.

Addresses & other information:
AN00) ANTIOQUIA
AN01) Cl. 35 Sur # 40-48, Br. Obrero, Envigado / Cr. 79A (Av. Nutibara) # 39-45, Br. Laureles / Cra. 81 No. 48A-39, Medellín **W:** impactoradio.co caracol.com.co/emisora/medellin qhuboradio.com cadenaradialjupiter.com – **AN02)** Edificio Coltejer, Calle 52 #47-42, Medellín **W:** rcnmundo.com/antena2/medellin rcnmundo.com facebook.com/RadioPaisa1140 – **AN03)** Calle 50 Colomb N° 67-144, Medellín **W:** radiored.com.co – **AN04)** Av.13 N° 84-42 (or Ap. 1431), Medellín **W:** todelarmedellin.com avivamiento.com/aviva2.php – **AN05)** Cra. 19 N° 20-66, Turbo **W:** 1060radiolitoral.com – **AN06)** Ap. 1431, Andes **W:** todelarmedellin.com - 1000-0200 – **AN07)** Circular 1a N° 70-01, Bloque 6, P7 U.P.B. Laureles, Medellín **W:** radiobolivarianavirtual.com - **FM:** 92.4MHz – **AN09)** Cra. 77B N° 48-144, Medellín **W:** radioverdadyvida.com/Verdadyvida – **AN10)** Calle 56 N° 41-57, Medellín **W:** minutodedios.fm – **AN11)** Calle 41 N° 80B-46, P2, Medellín – **AN12)** Cra. 3 Calles 2 y 3, Concordia **W:** radiosuroeste.com – **AN13)** Ap. 4300, Medellín **W:** lavozdelasestrellas.com – **AN14)** Cra. 51 N° 51-38 (or Ap. 3854), Medellín **W:** radiosantabarbara.com.co - 1000-0500 – **AN16)** Calle 50 N° 67-141 (or Ap. 65103), Medellín **W:** radiomariacol.org – **AN17)** Centro Cooperativo, Parque Principal, El Peñol **W:** radiofenixcolombia.com – **AN18)** Cra. 11 N° 10-34, Nariño **W:** asenred.com/voz-narino - 1100-0100 – **AN19)** Calle 44 N° 94-15, P3, Medellín. **W:** ondasdelamontana.net**AN23)** Cra. 51 N° 49-09, Rionegro **W:** rcnradio.com – **AN24)** Calle 48B N° 79-38, Medellín – **AN25)** Carrera 79A N° 39-63, 057 Medellín **W:** radiomunera.com – **AN27)** Ap. 1226 (or Cra. 44 N° 48-72), Medellín - 1100-0500 **W:** facebook.com/EmisoraCulturalUdeA - **FM:** 101.9MHz – **AN28)** Cra. 32 N° 30-05, Frontino **W:** ecosdefrontino.es.tl - 1000-2300 – **AN29)** Cra. 20 N° 20-21, Yarumal **W:** radiosensacion1430am.com – **AN31)** Urrao **W:** radiomariacol.org - 0900-0300 – **AN33)** Ap. 1289, Medellín **W:** radiomariacol.org - 1000-0400 – **AN34)** Cra. 19 Restrepo N° 19-61, Amalfi **W:** lavozdeamalfi.com - 1000-0300 – **AN35)** Calle 8 N° 6-60, Sonsón **W:** servicoops.com/radiosonson-2 – **AN37)** Calle 10 N° 9-37, La Unión (or Ap. 4897, Medellín) **W:** asenred.com/voz-union - 1000-0200 – **AN39)** Calle 7, Cras. 3 y 4, Jericó **W:** lavozdelsuroeste.co - 1000-0500 – **AN41)** Cra. 20 N° 20-14, Belmira **W:** brisasdelriochico.com – **AN44)** Ap. 81095 (or Cra. 44A N° 31 Sur-16, Barrio San Marcos), Envigado **W:** bbn1.bbnradio.org/spanish/medellin-colombia-1590-am – **AN45)** Calle 20 N° 27-20, La Ceja - 1100-0300 (Sun -0100) **W:** radiocapiro.com – **AN46)** Cra. 80 N° 46-74, Medellín **W:** colmundoradio.com.co – **AN49)** Cra.73 N° 47-35, Medellín **W:** facebook.com/larazadeportes – **AN51)** Palacio Municipal, Jardín **W:** facebook.com/radiojardin1600 – **AN52)** Calle 10 N° 42-22, Medellín **W:** santamariadelapaz.org – **AN57)** Calle 43 No. 67a-16, Barrio San Joaquín, Medellín. **W:** nseradio.com – **AN58)** Cra 81A No. 48-B – 71, Barrio Calasanz, Medellín **W:** ebcyeshua.org/la-voz-de-jesucristo – **AN59)** Cra 87 No. 65, Univ. de Medellín, Medellín. **W:** www.frecuenciau.com

AR00) ARAUCA
AR01) Calle 19 N° 19-62 P2, Arauca **W:** lavozdelcinaruco.com – **AR02)** Cra. 20 N° 19-09, P5, Arauca (or Ap. 16555, Bogotá) **W:** facebook.com/lavozdelrioarauca.co – **AR03)** Cra 20 N° 17-57, P3, Arauca **W:** meridiano70.co

AT00) ATLÁNTICO
AT01) Cra. 53 N° 55-166,Edificio Diario La Libertad, Barranquilla **W:** cadenaradiallalibertad.com.co – **AT02)** Cr 52 84-78 Alto Prado, Barranquilla **W:** rcnradio.com lacarinosa.rcnradio.com/?city=Barranquilla – **AT03)** Calle 82 N° 42H-54, 2do piso, Barranquilla **W:** lavozdelcaribe.com.co principedepaz.com – **AT04)** Cra. 53 # 74 - 56, Edificio Torre Banco de Occidente, Oficina 905, Barranquilla **W:** facebook.com/SistemaCardenal – **AT05)** Cra. 53 N° 82-132, Barranquilla 1030-0200 **W:** emisora.jesbol.co – **AT06)** Organización Radial Olímpica, Calle 72 No 48-37, Barranquilla **W:** emisoraatlantico.com.co - 1000-0500 – **AT07)** Cra. 48 N° 72-25, Ofc. 306, (or Ap. 2010), Barranquilla **W:** emisorasabc.com – **AT08)** Cra. 45 No. 76-125, Barranquilla - 0900-0500 **W:** vozdelapatriacelestial1310.com – **AT09)** Calle 53 N° 50-11, P2, Barranquilla **W:** minutodedios.fm – **AT10)** Cr. 43 # 79B-127 Local 2k P.2, Barranquilla **W:** noticiasya.co – **AT11)** Cra. 26, No 75B-07, Barranquilla **W:** radiovidanueva.net - 1100-0500 – **AT12)** Calle 60 N° 47-70, Centro Cultural Santa Catalina, Barranquilla **W:** radiomariacol.org

BO00) BOLÍVAR
BO01) Av. Venezuela, Edif. Banco Internacional, La Matuna 8B-05, Cartagena **W:** colmundoradio.com.co – **BO02)** Calle Real 20-217, Cartagena **W:** facebook.com/autentica1330 – **BO03)** Calle Mayor N° 6-34 (or Ap. 1771), Cartagena **W:** cadenaradiallalibertad.com.co – **BO04)** Ap. 246, Cartagena **W:** rcnradio.com lacarinosa.rcnradio.com/?city=Cartagena – **BO05) W:** bluradio.com – **BO06)** Calle Sta Fe, N° 13-113, Torices, Cartagena **W:** radioesperanza1140.com – **BO07)** Matuna, Calle 32 No. 8-21, Of. 1106, Edificio Banco Popular, Cartagena **W:** caracol.com.co facebook.com/SistemaCardenal – **BO08)** Barrio

Consolata Mzna. H Lote 20, Cartagena **W:** radioprincipe.com – **BO09)** Cra. 21 N° 29B-10, Cartagena **W:** avivamiento.com/aviva2.php

BY00) BOYACÁ

BY01) Calle 16 N° 15-21, P8, Edif.Camara de Comercio, Duitama **W:** lacarinosa.rcnradio.com/?city=Duitama – **BY02)** Cra. 10 N° 16-36, Chiquinquirá **W:** radiofuratena.com - 0900-0600 – **BY03)** Ap. 282, Sogamoso **W:** facebook.com/Radio-Reloj-Boyacá-1090AM-113020053775156 – **BY04)** Av. Calle 13 No. 79 – 70, Tunja **W:** tropicanafm.com **BY04a)** Calle 20 10-64 ofi. 306, 3piso Banco Bogotá, Tunja **W:** emisoraradiorecuerdos.com – **BY05)** Cr. 13 # 13-23, Duitama **W:** wradio.com.co lluviasradio.co – **BY06)** Ap. 019, Sogamoso **W:** rcnradio.com – **BY07)** Cra. 9 No. 8-65, Garagoa **W:** lavozdegaragoa.com - 1000-0330 – **BY08)** Calle 20 N° 10-64, Tunja **W:** crbradio.net – **BY09)** Cra. 7 N° 9-57, Guateque (or Ap. 17387, Bogotá) **W:** radioguatequestereo1320.com - 1000-0300 – **BY11)** Cra. 10 N° 17-50, P5, Tunja **W:** rcnradio.com – **BY12)** Calle 5,N° 5-25, P2, Parque Santander, Samacá **W:** ondasdelporvenir.com - 0900-0300 – **BY14)** Cra. 6 N° 6-93, Paipa **W:** facebook.com/Radio-La-Paz-710-Am-Paipa-412499012105378 - 1000-0400 – **BY15)** Calle 6 N° 5-42, San Luis de Gaceno **W:** lavozdesanluis.com - 0900-0300 – **BY16)** Calle 18 N° 12-81, P2, Chiquinquirá **W:** emisorasreinadecolombia.com - **FM:** Reina Estéreo 92.6MHz – **BY18)** Calle 20 N° 10-64, Ofc. 307, Tunja **W:** armoniasboyacenses.com

CA00) CAQUETÁ

CA01) Cra.14 N° 12-129, Casa Episcobal, P2 (Ap. 285), Florencia - 1000-0300 – **CA03)** Calle 17 N° 10-40, P2, (Ap. 209), Florencia **W:** ondasdelorteguaza.com - 1100-2300

CC00) CAUCA

CC01) Cra 8 N° 3-17 (or Ap. 1321), Popayán **W:** radio1040am.com - 1000-0400 – **CC02)** Cra. 8 N° 5-41, Popayán **W:** radiosuperpopayan.com – **CC04)** Calle 5A N° 11-25, Popayán **W:** caracol.com.co – **CC05)** Ap. 535, Popayán **W:** rcnradio.com

CE00) CESAR

CE01) Calle 17 N° 15-67, Valledupar - 0900-0200 **W:** radioguatapuri.com – **CE02)** Cra. 5 N° 13-52, Br. Cañaguate, Valledupar **W:** facebook.com/VozDelCanaguate wradio.com.co - 0830-0100 – **CE03)** Calle 5 N° 1-76, Local 210, Aguachica **W:** buturamastereo.com - 1000-0200 – **CE04)** Cl. 15 # 11A-56,, Valledupar **W:** facebook.com/SistemaCardenal - 0900-0500 – **CE05)** Ap. 250, Valledupar **W:** rcnradio.com – **CE07)** Valledupar **W:** facebook.com/La-Nota-1380-AM-103578094337450

CH00) CHOCÓ

CH01) Calle 28 N° 1-04, P2 (or Ap. 482), Quibdó – **CH02)** Cra. 4 N° 25-18, P2, (or Ap. 196), Quibdó - 1000-0400 **W:** ecosdelatrato-8396.m.letio.com

CL00) CALDAS

CL01) Cr. 23 # 25-61, P.4 y 5, Edif. Don Pedro, Manizales **W:** besame.fm wradio.com.co – **CL02)** Ap. 244, Manizales **W:** rcnradio.com lacarinosa.rcnradio.com/?city=Manizales – **CL05)** Ap. 2000, Manizales **W:** caracol.com.co cadenaradialvida.com – **CL06)** Calle 11 N° 3-58 (or Ap. 34), La Dorada **W:** vozdeladorada.co - 0930-0500 – **CL07)** Calle 22 N° 21-40, Plaza Bolívar, Manizales **W:** redsonoraam.com – **CL09)** Cra. 23 N° 71-03 (or Ap. 990), Manizales **W:** radiomariacol.org – **CL10)** Antigua Estación del Ferrocaril, Manizales **W:** facebook.com/radiocondor1540 - 1200-0400 – **CL11)** Cra. 23 N° 71-03, Av. Sant, Manizales **W:** radioautenticamanizales.org

CO00) CÓRDOBA

CO01) Cra. 3A N° 30-12, P2, Montería **W:** colombiaemite.com/emisoras/cordoba/monteria/radio-panzenu - 1000-0400 – **CO02)** Cr. 20 # 3-39, Lorica **W:** sites.google.com/view/rpcradiolorica1030am - Mon-Fri 1100-2200 only – **CO04)** Cra 2 N° 28-53, P2, (or Ap. 497), Montería **W:** rcnradio.com vozdemonteria.com – **CO06)** Ap. 148, Montería **W:** frecuenciabolivariana.com.co – **CO07)** Calle 27 N° 8-25, Montería **W:** radio1.rcnradio.com – **CO08)** Ap. 364, Montería **W:** caracol.com.co

CS00) CASANARE

CS01) Calle 9 N° 22-63, Edif. Cine Casanare, P2, Yopal **W:** lavozdeyopal.co - 1000-0500 - **FM:** 105.3MHz

CU00) CUNDINAMARCA

CU01) Calle 14 N° 11-23, P2, Ofc. 202, Girardot **W:** radiopanamericanadecolombia.com – **CU02)** Av. Las Palmas N° 5-08, P5, Fusagasugá **W:** emisoranuevaepoca.com - 0900-0400 – **CU03)** Terminal de Transportes, Girardot **W:** radiocolina.com – **CU04)** Cra. 6 N° 6-38, Ubaté **W:** facebook.com/autenticaubate – **CU05)** Ap. 416, Girardot **W:** rcnradio.com – **CU06)** Calle 16 N° 10-38, P3, Girardot **W:** lacarinosa.rcnradio.com/?city=Girardot – **CU07)** Calle 7 N° 14-83, Pacho **W:** facebook.com/cadenaradialpacho1390am – **CU09)** Calle 3 N° 16-39, Pacho **W:** radiofuturama.com - 0930-0400 – **CU10)** Calle 8 N° 5-59, Fasagasugá **W:** facebook.com/kirios-radio-102082222235 - 0900-0300

DC00) DISTRITO CAPITAL

DC01) Calle 32 N° 16-12, Bogotá **W:** radioautenticabogota.com radiomundialbogota.com elsiaradio.com/la-empresa – **DC02)** Av. El Dorado, Cra. 45 No. 26-33, Bogotá **W:** radionacional.co – **DC03)** Cra. 13A N° 37-32, Bogotá **W:** lacarinosa.rcnradio.com/?city=Bogota antena2.com.co rcnradio.com rcnmundo.com/anosmaravillosos – **DC04)** Calle 67 No. 7-37, Bogotá **W:** wradio.com.co caracol.com.co candelaestereo.com radiopolis.fm acuarioestereo.com – **DC05)** Calle 45 N° 13-70 , Ap. 19823, Bogotá **W:** cadenamelodia.com – **DC06)** Calle 48 N° 18-77, Bogotá **W:** cadenaradialvida.com Different prgr. on 890 vs. 1130kHz – **DC07)** Av. 13 N° 84-42, Bogotá **W:** todelar.com – **DC08)** Calle 39A N° 18-12, Bogotá **W:** radiored.com.co – **DC09)** Diagonal 58 N° 26A-29, Bogotá **W:** colmundoradio.com.co supresenciaradio.com – **DC10)** Calle 95 Bis No. 50-36, Bogotá, DC **W:** cadenaradialvida.co supresencia.com/su-presencia-radio – **DC11)** Calle 57 N° 17-48, Bogotá **W:** radiosantafe.com – **DC12)** Calle 25ª No. 32, 46 Barrio Gran América, Ap. 2086350, Bogotá D.C. **W:** fuegoam.com.co – **DC13)** Carrera 21A, No. 151-23, Bogotá **W:** radiomariacol.org – **DC14)** Cra. 30 N° 91-84 (or Ap. 250649), Bogotá **W:** 1250amcapitalradio.com – **DC15)** Ap. 9291, Bogotá – **DC16)** Calle 6 N° 7-22, (or Ap. 3201), Bogotá. (alt.address: Calle 385 N° 75-31, Cd. Kennedy, Bogotá) **W:** emisoramariana.org - 1100-0130 – **DC17)** Calle 81B Nº 72 B - 70, Barrio Minuto de Dios, Bogotá **W:** uniminutoradio.com.co - 1100-2300 – **DC18)** Cra. 27 N° 49-48, Bogotá **W:** nuevocontinente.org – **DC19)** Av. 15 N° 123-61, Of. 408, Bogotá **W:** emisorapunto5.com.co - 1100-2300 – **DC20)** Cra 68 # 13-80, Bogotá **W:** aviva2.com – **DC21)** Calle 22C N° 31-01, Bogotá **W:** g12radio.com – **DC23)** Carrera 49, No. 127d-59, Bogotá **W:** radio316.com.co – **DC25)** Diagonal 46A Sur 51-40, Centro Comercial Venecia Plaza 2do piso, Bogotá **W:** candelaestereo.com – **DC26)** (Reports c/o Rafael Rodríguez R., Apartado Aéreo 67751, (oficina Red 4-72 Unicentro), Bogotá, DC. Return postage required for QSL reply) **W:** lamontanacolombia.com **E:** (for reports) rafaelcoldx@yahoo.com – **DC27)** Av. Boyacá 48 A 11, Edificio Castillo Dorado, Of. 301, Bogotá **W:** bbn1.bbnradio.org/spanish/bogota-colombia-1100-am

GU00) GUAJIRA

GU01) Calle 15, Salida a Maicao, Riohacha **W:** radiodelfin.com.co - 0930-0400 – **GU02)** Cra. 6 N° 6-60, San Juan del Cesar **W:** radioimpactopopular.com – **GU03)** Calle 1 N° 5-63, San Juan del Cesar **W:** vozdelaprovinciadepadilla.blogspot.com

HU00) HUILA

HU01) Calle 7 N° 10-36, Neiva **W:** sistemainrai.net - 1000-0300 – **HU02)** Ap. 150, Neiva **W:** wradio.com.co – **HU03)** Ap. 496 (or Cra. 7, Calles 21 y 22), Neiva **W:** radiosurcolombiana.com - 1000-0530 – **HU04)** Cra. 13 N° 3A-24, Neiva **W:** lafm.com.co – **HU05)** Cra. 4 N° 2-21, Of. 501-502, Neiva **W:** rcnradio.com lacarinosa.rcnradio.com/?city=Neiva – **HU06)** Calle 6 N° 1A-31, Pitalito **W:** sistemainrai.net - 0900-0400 – **HU08)** Calle 4a N° 5-59, La Plata **W:** emisorapotencialatina.com - 1000-0100

IS00) ISLAS SAN ANDRÉS Y PROVIDENCIA

IS01) Ap. 354, San Andrés Isla **W:** rcnradio.com – **IS03)** Edif. Bermuda, P2, Av. de las Américas, San Andrés Isla **W:** caracol.com.co

MA00) MAGDALENA

MA01) Av. Libertadores 27-101, Santa Marta **W:** rcnradio.com radio1.rcnradio.com – **MA03)** Calle 17 N° 5-83 (or Ap. 103), Santa Marta **W:** caracol.com.co/emisora/santa_marta – **MA06)** Ap. 1240, Santa Marta **W:** radiomagdalena1420am.com – **MA07)** Calle 11 C N° 18a-34, Santa Marta **W:** radiomagdalena1420am.com/categoria/radio-rodadero

ME00) META

ME01) Calle 38 30 A-106 Centro, Villavicencio **W:** lacarinosa.rcnradio.com/?city=Villavicencio – **ME03)** Calle 38 N° 32-41, P7, Edif. Prollano, Ofc 702, Villavicencio **W:** autentica1080am.com – **ME04)** Cra. 30 N° 36-14, P4, Villavicencio **W:** rcnradio.com – **ME05)** Cra. 31 N° 37-71, Of.1001, (Ap. 2472), Villavicencio **W:** lavozdeloscentauros.com - 0900-0500 – **ME06)** Calle 41B N° 30-11, Barrio La Grama, Villavicencio **W:** ondasdelmeta.com – **ME07)** Cl. 34 # 39-32, Br. Barzal, Villavicencio **W:** facebook.com/luxdei.emisoravillavicencio

NA00) NARIÑO

NA01) Calle 18 No. 28-87, Pasto **W:** emisoraecosdepasto740.com - 1000-0300 – **NA02)** Calle 20 N° 22-82, Pasto **W:** hsbradio.com.co – **NA03)** Ap. 454, Pasto – **NA04)** Calle 20 N° 24-73, Of 603, P6, Pasto **W:** colmundoradio.com.co - 0900-0500 – **NA05)** Cra. 27 N° 19-30, Pasto. **W:** caracol.com.co – **NA06)** Ap. 1005, Ipiales **W:** rcnipiales.com.co/rcn-radio-las-lajas – **NA07)** Cl.15(Cl. Márquez) entre Crs. 8 y 9, Edif. Catedral San Andrés P.3, Parque Colón, Tumaco **W:** actiweb.es/radiomira - 1100-0400 – **NA08)** Cra. 8 N° 4-48, Ipiales **W:**

radiovivafenix.com - 1100-0200 – **NA09)** Ap. 516, Pasto **W:** rcnradio.com lacarinosa.rcnradio.com/?city=Pasto – **NA10)** Cra. 6A N° 9-14, P2, Ipiales **W:** radioipiales.co – **NA12)** Calle 15 N° 14-24 , Pasto **W:** radiovivafenix.com - 1100-0500

NS00) NORTE DE SANTANDER

NS01) Calle 5 N° 3-26 (or Ap. 1650), Cúcuta **W:** emisoravoxdei.com – **NS02)** Centro Comercial Bolívar, Local E4 y E5, Cúcuta **W:** rcnmundo.com/fiestacucuta - 1000-0400 – **NS03)** Ap. 400, Cúcuta **W:** rcnradio.com lacarinosa.rcnradio.com/?city=Cucuta – **NS04)** Calle 5A N° 0-45, Cúcuta **W:** tropicanafm.com **W:** facebook.com/EMISORA1340AM – **NS05)** Av. O. N° 10-54, P2 (or Ap. 624), Cúcuta **W:** lavozdelnorte1040am.com – **NS06)** Ap. 519, Cúcuta **W:** caracol.com.co wradio.com.co – **NS07)** Cra. 13 N° 9-10, P7, Ocaña **W:** catatumboradio.com – **NS08)** Calle 7N N° 4-117 (or Ap. 2284), Cúcuta **W:** unipamplona.edu.co/unipamplona/portalIG/home_24/recursos/areas/radio_sanjose/22102010/radio_sanjose.jsp – **NS10)** Calle 11 N° 15-24, Ocaña **W:** radiosonar.co - 1030-0300 – **NS15)** Calle 12 N° 4-19, Ofc. 214, (or Ap. 2582), Cúcuta **W:** frecuenciaf.com – **NS16)** Av. 0A N° 12-75, Ofc. 101 (or Ap. 1303), Cúcuta **W:** lavozdelagrancolom.wixsite.com/lavoz1400am

QU00) QUINDÍO

QU01) Cra 16 N° 19-23, P10, Armenia **W:** transmisoraquindio.com – **QU02)** Alcaldía Municipal de Calarcá, Cra.24 N° 38-57, Calarcá **W:** ecosdelcacique.blogspot.com – **QU03)** Calle 9 N° 13-50 (or Ap. 2361), Armenia **W:** lavozdearmenia1040am.com – **QU04)** Ap. 2481, Armenia **W:** caracol.com.co – **QU05)** Cr. 14 # 23-27 P. 11, Edif. Cámara de Comercio **W:** rcnradio.com/colombia/eje-cafetero lacarinosa.rcnradio.com/?city=Armenia

RI00) RISARALDA

RI01) Ap. 354, Pereira **W:** caracol.com.co radiopolis.fm – **RI02)** Ap. 045, Pereira **W:** rcnradio.com lacarinosa.rcnradio.com/?city=Pereira – **RI05)** Crra. 7a N° 18-80, Of. 705, Edificio Centro Financiero, Pereira **W:** colmundoradio.com.co – **RI06)** Cra. 6a N° 16-42, Ofic. 205A, C.Cial. Los Arcos (or Ap. 1262), Pereira. R. Maria 0000-1100 **W:** ecos1360.com – **RI07)** Cra. 15 N° 11-80, Santa Rosa de Cabal (or Calle 19 N° 8-74, Pereira) **W:** antenadelosandes.com.co - 1000-0300

SS00) SANTANDER

SS01) Ap. 915, Bucaramanga **W:** rcnradio.com – **SS02)** Cl. 35 # 16-24 P. 8, Edif. José Acevedo y Gómez, Bucaramanga **W:** caracol.com.co wradio.com.co emisoraonda5.com – **SS04)** Cra. 27 N° 45-80, Bucaramanga **W:** radioprimavera.com - 0900-0400 – **SS05)** Ap. 007, Bucaramanga **W:** radiobucarica.com.co – **SS06)** Calle 36 N° 14, 58 Piso 7, Bucaramanga **W:** melodiaenlinea.com – **SS07)** Calle 16 N° 15-01, Esquina, Socorro **W:** emisorajoseantoniogalan.com - 0930-0300 – **SS08)** Transv. 6 N° 9-56, Barbosa – **SS09)** Batallón de Artillcría de Defensa Aerea N° 2 "Nueva Granada" (or Ap. 036), Barrancabermeja – **SS10)** Ap. 1100, Bucaramanga **W:** lacarinosa.rcnradio.com/?city=Bucaramanga – **SS11)** Calle 11 N° 9-80, p. 3, San Gil **W:** rcnradio.com.co – **SS12)** Calle 48 N° 35A-25, Bucaramanga **W:** colmundoradio.com.co – **SS14)** Calle 7 N° 17-44, Barbosa **W:** facebook.com/lavozdelriosuarez – **SS15)** Ap. 578, Barrancabermeja **W:** lacarinosa.rcnradio.com/?city=Barrancabermeja – **SS16)** Calle 12 N° 10-30, Centro, San Gil **W:** lacaliente1330.com - 0900-0300 – **SS17)** Cr. 8 # 18-53, Zapatoca **W:** radiozapatoca.com – **SS18)** Calle 35 N° 20-39 (or Ap. 3104), Bucaramanga **W:** radiomariacol.org – **SS20)** Calle 9 N° 3-21 2° Piso, Vélez **W:** lavozdelcarare.com – **SS21)** Calle 20 N° 6-36, Zapatoca – **SS22)** Av. 36, No. 19-76, Piso 9, Bucaramanga **W:** rcm1450.com - 1100-0300 – **SS23)** Calle 41 N° 19-87, Bucaramanga **W:** bluradio.com – **SS25)** Calle 12 N° 17-10, Ofc.302 (or Ap. 250), Barrancabermeja **W:** emisoralavozdelpetroleo.com - 1000-0400 – **SS26)** Calle 11 N° 6A-11, Edif. San Gabriel, P2, Málaga **W:** vocesrovirenses.com.co - 1000-0200 – **SS27)** Diócesis del Socorro y San Gil, Cra. 13 N° 34, Esquina Socorro **W:** diocesisdesocorroysangil.org/emisora-diocesana.html - 0500-2300 Also r. María – **SS28)** Cra.27, Calle 9, Televis, Bucaramanga **W:** emisoras.uis.edu.co

SU00) SUCRE

SU01) Cra. 20 N° 25-92, P2, Sincelejo **W:** radiocaracoli.com facebook.com/SistemaCardenal – **SU04)** Calle 27 N° 21 - 69 Barrio La María, 40007 Sincelejo **W:** conezcionradio.com – **SU05)** Calle 20 N° 24-93, Av. las Penitas, Sincelejo **W:** rcnradio.com – **SU07)** Cra. 20 N° 25-92 piso 2, Sincelejo **W:** radiomajagual.com – **SU08)** Cra. 20 N° 21-46 (or Ap. 303), Sincelejo **W:** facebook.com/radiosincelejo1460 - 1000-0400 – **SU13)** Ap. 167, Sincelejo **W:** facebook.com/SistemaCardenal – **SU14)** Calle 24 No 18-31, Sincelejo **W:** radiosabanas.com.co

TO00) TOLIMA

TO01) Calle 10 No. 3-76, Edificio Cámara de Comercio, oficinas 304 y 401, Ibagué **W:** ecosdelcombeima.com – **TO02)** Calle 12 N° 1-17, P5, Ibagué **W:** lavozdeltolima.com – **TO03)** Calle 14 N° 2A-14, P2, Ibagué **W:** lavozdelpueblo920am.com Relays María overnight – **TO04)** Parque Murillo Toro N° 3-29, P4, Ibagué **W:** lafm.com.co - 1000-0400 – **TO05)** Cra 7 con Calle 10, Espinal **W:** lacarinosa.rcnradio.com/?city=Espinal – **TO06)** Calle 9 # 12-02, Guamo **W:** clickradio1090am.com lacarinosa.rcnradio.com/?city=Ibague – **TO07)** Ap. 2419, Ibagué **W:** rcnradio.com – **TO08)** Ap. 1094, Ibagué **FM:** 93.9MHz – **TO09)** Calle 5 N° 6-25, Mariquita **W:** radiolumbi.co – **TO10)** Calle 9 N° 1-124, P3, Ibagué. **W:** besame.fm – **TO11)** Calle 11 N° 4-26 (or Ap. 64), El Espinal **W:** olimpicaespinal.com – **TO13)** Cra. 2 N° 11-27, Flandes **W:** olimpicagirardot.com – **TO14)** Cra 3 N° 12-76, Ofc.801 (or Ap. 589), Ibagué **W:** ondasdeibague.com - 1000-0000

VA00) VALLE DEL CAUCA

VA01) Cra. 26 N° 5C-25, San Fernando, Cali **W:** colmundoradio.com.co - 1100-0300 – **VA02)** Cra. 38D Diagonal 37A-52B/Santa Isabel, Cali **W:** autenticacali.com – **VA03)** Cl. 10 # 23A-12, Cali **W:** wradio.com.co caracol.com.co radiorelojcali.com – **VA04)** Ap. 4666, Cali **W:** todelarcali.com – **VA05)** Cra. 14 N° 2-25, P2 (or Ap. 96), Buga **W:** vocesdeoccidente.com - 1100-0500 – **VA06)** Av. 5B Norte N° 21-02, Cali **W:** rcnmundo.com/calidadcali – **VA07)** Cra. 33 N° 28-51 (Ap. 280), Palmira **W:** radiopalmira.com - 1000-0500 – **VA08)** Calle 43 # 6 n 21, Cali **W:** crvradio.com.co lacarinosa.rcnradio.com/?city=Tulua – **VA09)** Ap. 126, Tuluá **W:** rcnradio.com - 1000-0300 – **VA10)** Calle 21 Nte N° 3N-49, P5, Cali **W:** radiored.com.co – **VA11)** Calle 12-39, Ofc 301, Edif.R.Buenaventura (Ap 383), Buenaventura 1030-0500. Rel. R. Maria 0200-1000 **W:** radiobuenaventura.com – **VA13)** Cra 19 N° 2N-29, Ofc 21B, Cali **W:** radiovivafenix.com – **VA14)** Cra. 30 N° 29-09, Palmira **W:** hoperadio1320am.com – **VA15)** Cra 6 N° 54-08, Av. Simon Bolívar, Buenaventura **W:** rcnradio.com – **VA16)** Carrera 66B, No. 6-68, Barrio El Limonar, Cali **W:** armoniacali.com – **VA18)** Cra. 29 N° 32-88/90 (or Ap. 201), Palmira **W:** armoniasdelpalmar.wixsite.com/armoniasdelpalmar - 1130-0300 – **VA19)** Cra. 14 N° 5-77, Buga – **VA20)** Cra. 26 N° 28-72, Tuluá **W:** radiotulua.com – **VA21)** Calle 27 N° 33-35, Tuluá **W:** radiovidanueva.net - 1100-0500 – **VA22)** Av. Roosevelt N° 34-37, Cali **W:** sonora1500am.com – **VA23)** Cra. 51 N° 49-21, Sevilla **W:** caracolradiosevilla.com – **VA24)** Calle 10 N° 6-87, P3, Cartago **W:** radiorobledo.com - 1100-0500 – **VA26)** Calle 13, No. 19-59, Barrio Guayaquil, Cali **W:** radiohuellascali.com - 1100-0500 – **VA28)** Av.Roosevelt N° 28, Cali (Or: Transversal 34 N° 149-23, Cedro Golf, Bogotá) **W:** radiomariacol.org – **VA31)** Cra. 13 N° 10-62, Cali **W:** revivirencristo.com - 1100-0400

FM in Bogotá (MHz):): 88.9 R. Uno (RCN) – 89.9 Blu Radio – 90.4 La UD (University) – 90.9 La Mega (RCN) – 91.9 Javeriana Estereo (University) – 92.4 Policía Nacional (Police) – 92.9 La 92 (Todelar) – 93.4 Colombia Estéreo (Colombian Army) – 93.9 RCN La Radio (rel. 770) – 94.9 La FM (RCN) – 95.9 R. Nac. de Colombia – 96.9 La Kalle. – 97.4 Bésame (Caracol) – 97.9 Radioactiva (Caracol) – 98.5 Universidad Nacional (University) – 99.1 Radionica (RTVC) – 99.9 W Radio (Caracol) – 100.4 Oxígeno by Los 40 (Caracol) – 100.9 Caracol R (rel. 810kHz) – 101.9 Candela Estereó – 102.9 Tropicana (Caracol) – 103.9 La X (Todelar) – 104.4 Fantástica (RCN) – 104.9 Vibra Bogotá (W Radio) – 105.4 EL Sol (RCN) – 105.9 Olímpica – 106.9 Universidad Jorge Tadeo Lozano (University) – 107.9 Minuto de Dios (Rlg)

COMOROS

L.T: UTC +3h — **Pop:** 880,000 — **Pr.L:** Official languages: Comorian, Arabic, French — **E.C:** 220V/50Hz — **ITU:** COM

AUTORITÉ NATIONALE DE RÉGULATION DES TECHNOLOGIES DE L'INFORMATION ET DE LA COMMUNICATION (ANRTIC)

✉ BP 6540, Moroni, Grand Comoro ☎+269 7738761 🖷 +269 7738762 **W:** anrtic.km **E:** contact@anrtic.km

OFFICE DE RADIO TÉLÉVISION DES COMORES (ORTC, Gov)

✉ BP 452, Moroni, Grand Comoro ☎+269 7732531 🖷 +269 7730303 **W:** www.ortc.fr
FM: Moroni 101.2MHz

Other stations:
Hayba FM, Moroni: 91.7MHz **W:** haybafm.webcomores.com
R. Domoni Inter, Anjouan: 102.0MHz **W:** domoni-inter.org
R. KAZ, Mkazi: 107.0MHz **W:** facebook.com/radiokaz.107
RCM 13, Moroni: 107.5MHz **W:** rcm13.fr
RTMC-Radio Télévision Mbéni, Mbéni: 106.0MHz **W:** rtmc.fr
RTS-Radio Télévision Sud, Dembeni Badjini: 106.5MHz **W:** rts269.com

China Radio Int, Moroni: 94.9MHz
RFI Afrique, Moroni 103.0MHz, Mitsamiouli/Moheli/Mutsamundu 103.2MHz

CONGO (Dem. Rep.)

L.T: Kinshasa & western part: UTC +1h, eastern part: UTC +2h — **Pop:** 90 million — **Pr.L:** French (official), Lingala, Kikongo, Swahili, Tshiluba — **E.C:** 220V/50Hz — **ITU:** COD

CONSEIL SUPÉRIEUR DE L'AUDIOVISUEL ET DE LA COMMUNICATION (CSAC)

✉ Kinshasa **W:** www.facebook.com/Conseil-Sup%C3%A9rieur-de-lAudiovisuel-et-de-la-Communication-Csac--307940212929383

RADIO-TÉLÉVISION NATIONALE CONGOLAISE (RTNC, Gov.)

✉ B.P. 3164, Kinshasa-Gombe ☎+243 81 9970699 🖷+243 81 123 7691 **W:** rtnc.cd **E:** info@rtnc-rdc.com
FM: Kinshasa: **RTNC1 Radio Nationale:** 100.0MHz, **RTNC2 Radio Kinshasa:** 91.8MHz, **Channel for national languages:** 97.0MHz.
D.Prgr: 24h in French/Swahili/Lingala/Tshiluba/Kikongo. Also relayed by other stns. **Ann:** "RTNC, Radio-Télévision Nationale Congolaise, émettant de Kinshasa".

Provincial Stations:
FM (MHz): 2) 94.5 3kW – **3)** 88.9/92.0 1.5kW – **4)** 93.3 1.5kW/90.0 0.05kW – **5)** 93.5/98.5 – **6)** 89.1 50kW – **7)** 90.0 – **8)** 92.5 1kW – **9)** 94.8 – **10)** 90.1 – **11)** 93.7
Addresses: 2) B.P. 7296, Lubumbashi – **3)** RTNC Kivu, B.P. 475, Bukavu – **4)** B.P. 1061, Mbandaka – **5)** B.P. 1232, Mbuji-Mayi – **6)** B.P. 708, Kananga, Western Kasai – **7)** B.P. 704, Matadi – **8)** B.P. 1745, Kisangani – **9)** Butembo, Nord-Kivu – **10)** Goma, Nord-Kivu. **E:** rtncnordkivu@yahoo.fr – **11)** Uvira, Sud-Kivu.

BEST RADIO/RADIO KAHUZI (Rlg.)

(operated by Believers Express Service, Inc (BESI))
✉ 2 Ave. Masikita/Muhumba Ave, Bukavu or B.P. 42, Cyangugu, Rwanda. **W:** radiokahuzi.blogspot.com radiokahuzi.com **E:** radiokahuzi@gmail.com **L.P:** Dir: Richard McDonald. National Dir: Kalangwa Dieudone. St. Mgr: Barbara Smith.
SW: Bukavu 6210kHz 0.8kW (irregular). **FM:** 91.1/102.1MHz 0.2kW. **D.Prgr:** 0600-1500 (irr- 1800) in French, English, Kikongo, Kinyarwanda, Lingala, Mashi, Swahili and Tshiluba.

RADIO OKAPI

(joint initiative between the UN Mission in the DRC [MONUC] and Hirondelle Foundation)
✉ QG Monuc, 12 Av. des Aviateurs, Kinshasa-Gombe ☎+243-81-890-6747 **W:** radiookapi.net **E:** info@hirondelle.org
FM (MHz): (powers 1-5kW): Isiro 90.1, Beni 92.0, Butembo 92.9, Gbadolite/Kananga/Lisala 93.0, Mbuji-Mayi 93.8, Kisangani 94.8, Bukavu 95.3, Gemena 95.4, Lubumbashi 95.8, Kanyabayonga/Mahagi 96.0, Aru 98.0, Bundundu 99.0, Matadi 102.0, Baraka/Kindu/Mbandaka 103.0, Kikwit/Kinshasa/Mbuji Mayi 103.5, Kamina 104.3, Manono 104.5, Bunia/Walikale 104.9, Kalemie 105.0, Goma/Uvira 105.2, Shabunda 105.4, Tshomo Ini 106.5.
Prgr. in French/Lingala/Swahili/Tshiluba.

Other stations (all MHz):
Business R. Africa, Kinshasa: 98.6. **W:** brt-africa.com – **Canal Congo pour Christ**, Bukavu: 97.3 – **Canal Futur,** Kinshasa-Gombe: 107.4 – **CEBS,** Kinshasa: 93.7 – **RATELKI,** Kinshasa: 90.2 – **R. Artemis,** Bunia: 90.2 – **R. Boboto,** Isiro: 100.6 100W – **R. Butembo:** 100 – **R. Canal CVV,** Kinshasa: 102.3 – **R. Canal Révélation,** Bunia: 100.7 0.3kW – **R. Congo FM,** Kinshasa: 96.4 – **R. ECC,** Kinshasa: 104.0 – **R. Elikya**, Kinshasa: 97.5 – **R. Lwenge,** Baraki-Fizi: 88.9 150W – **R. Liberté Kinshasa (RALIK),** 96.8 – **R. Maendeleo:** Bukavu 88.7 1kW, Chomuhini 91.7 1kW **W:** radiomaendeleo.info – **R. Malebo Broadcast Channel** (MBC), Kinshasa: 98.3 – **R. Maria Malkia wa Amani** (Rlg.): Bukavu 94.0 & 97.0. **W:** pamojanakakaluigi.org/radio_maria.htm – **R. Méthodiste Lokole,** Kinshasa-Gombe: 100.8 – **R. Moto** (Rlg.): Kivu 103 1.2kW, Butembo 106.0 – **R. Neno la Uzima,** Bukavu: 100.2 – **R. Parole Eternelle,** Kinshasa: 103.8 **W:** facebook.com/rpe2004 – **R. Raga FM**: Kinshasa-Binza 90.5 4kW. **W:** raga.cd – **R. Rehema:** Chamuhini 89.5 0.25kW, Bukavu 99.7 1kW – **R. Réveil FM**, Kinshasa-Gombe: 105.4 **W:** reveilfm.itgo.com – **R. Sango Malamu:** Boma 102.5, Kinshasa 104.5 – **R. Tangazeni Kristo** (Rlg.): Bunia 88.6, Aru/Kwandruma 90.0 **E:** buero@diguna.de – **R. Télé Armée de l'Eternel,** Kinshasa: 94.5 – **R. Télé Amani,** Kisangani; 100.1 25W, 103.1 0.5kW. – **R. Téle Boma** (RTB), Boma: 98.0 – **R. Télé Graben,** Beni/Butembo 98 – **R. Télé Groupe l'Avenir (RTGA)**, Kinshasa 88.1 – **R. Télé Kin Malebo** (RTKM): Kinshasa 95.1, Kananga 97.5 – **R. Télé Kintuadi** (RTK): Boma 91.1, Kinshasa 97.1, Mbanza Ngungu 103.4, Matadi 107.5 – **R. Télé Message de Vie,** Kinshasa: 88.7 – **R. Télé Mosaïque,** Likasi: 88.5 – **R. Télé Puissance**, Kinshasa 101.0 – **RTV Bukavu Liberté,** Ibanda 107.3 – **RTV Mulangane,** Bukavu: 100.1 0.25kW – **R. Sentinelle,** Kinshasa: 97.1 – **R. Tomisa,** Kikwit: 97.5 0.5kW – **R. Veritas** (Rlg.), Kabinda: 105.0 – **R. Vuvu Kietu,** Mbanza Ngungu: 101.0 – **RCLS,** Kirumba: 91.0 – **REB,** Butembo: 90.7 – **RTIV,** Kisangani: 89.4 0.5kW – **Sauti ya Mkaaji,** Makongo: 87.85 – **Top Congo,** Kinshasa: 88.4.

BBC African Sce: Mbandaka/Mbuji-Mayi 90.5, Kisangani/Lubumbashi 92.0, Kinshasa 92.6, Goma 93.8, Kolwezi 95.9, Kananga 96.8, Bunia 100.7, Bukavu 102.2
RFI Afrique: Bunia 90.2, Bukavu/Goma/Lubumbashi/Matadi 98.0, Mbandaka/Mbuji-Mayi 104.9, Kinshasa/Kisangani 105.0MHz.
VOA African Sce: Kananga/Matadi/Mbuji-Mayi 93.5, Goma 96.2, Bukavu 97.4, Kisangani 97.7, Lubumbashi 102.8MHz

CONGO (Rep.)

L.T: UTC +1h — **Pop:** 6 million — **Pr.L:** French (official), Lingala, Kikongo — **E.C:** 220V/50Hz — **ITU:** COG

CONSEIL SUPÉRIEUR DE LA LIBERTÉ DE LA COMMUNICATION (CSLC)

✉ Rte de l'Auberge de Gascogne, Brazzaville ☎+242 06 9159898 **E:** cslccongobz@gmail.com

RADIO CONGO (Gov.)

✉ Direction Générale, B.P. 2241, Brazzaville ☎+242 22 2810608
SW: Brazzaville 6115kHz 50kW 0500-1900 (irreg.)
FM: Dolisie 90.1MHz, Djambala 94.0MHz, Brazzaville 96.4MHz, Pointe-Noire 98.9MHz.
National Network: 0420-2300 in French & ethnic except Pointe-Noire carrying regional programme. **N. in English:** 1900 (approx.)

Other stations:
Canal FM, Brazzaville: 99.3MHz – **Hit R:** Brazzaville 89.0MHz, Pointe Noire 97.7MHz **W:** hitradio.ma – **R. Maria,** Pointe-noire: 88.7MHz **W:** radiomaria.cg/home.aspx – **R. Mucodec,** Brazzaville: 100.3MHz **W:** mucodec.com – **R. Liberté,** Brazzaville: 106.0MHz
Africa Radio, Brazzaville 94.5MHz **W:** africaradio.com
China R. Int, Brazzaville 90.1MHz
RFI Afrique: Brazzaville/Pointe-Noire 93.2MHz
VOA Africa: Pointe-Noire 98.3MHz, Brazzaville 104.3MHz

COOK ISLANDS

L.T: UTC-10h — **Pop:** 17,500 — **Pr.L:** Cook Islands Maori (official), English (official) — **E.C:** 240V/50Hz — **ITU:** CKH

MW	kHz	kW	Station	Location
1)	630	1	R. Cook Islands AM	Rarotonga
FM	**MHz**	**kW**	**Station**	**Location**
2)	88.0		Araura FM.	Aitutaki
3)	88.0		88 FM boomboom baby	Rarotonga
4)	88.7		Adventist World R.	Rarotonga
1)	89.0		R. Cook Islands	Mitiaro
1)	89.0		R. Cook Islands	Pukapuka
5)	89.0		Matariki FM	Muri Ngatangiia, Takitumu (Rarotonga)
5)	89.0		Matariki FM	Maraerenga, Avarua (Rarotonga)
5)	89.0		Matariki FM	Kavera, Puaikura (Rarotonga)
6)	89.5		Kia Orana FM	Rarotonga
7)	‡90.3		Life FM	Rarotonga (r. inactive)
1)	90.6		R. Cook Islands	Mangaia
1)	90.6		R. Cook Islands	Rakahanga
1)	90.6		R. Cook Islands	Palmerston
1)	92.2		R. Cook Islands	Atiu
1)	92.2		R. Cook Islands	Penrhyn
1)	93.8		R. Cook Islands	Mauke
1)	93.8		R. Cook Islands	Nassau
1)	95.4		R. Cook Islands	Manihiki

FM	MHz	kW	Station	Location
8)	‡97.9		Maranatha FM	Rarotonga
9)	100.0		Enuamanu 100 FM	Atiu
1)	101.0		R. Cook Islands	Avarua (Rarotonga)
1)	101.0		R. Cook Islands	Aroa (Rarotonga)
1)	101.0		R. Cook Islands AM	Muri (Rarotonga)

Addresses & other information

1) The Voice of the Nation, Elijah Communications, PO Box 126, Avarua, Rarotonga ☎+682 20100 🖷+682 21907 **W:** www.radio.co.ck. facebook.com/radio-cook-islands-the-voice-of-the-nation **E:** tunein@radio.co.ck On Air M-F 1600-0900 [Fri 1000] Sat 1600-1000 Su 1700-0900 **N:** Local news hourly M-F 1700-0200 RNZP 1600, 1700, 1800 M-F Prgr: Talkback, news, rlg services and music in English and Cook I. Maori. **LP:** CEO Jeanne Matenga. Outer Island Network: Txs outside Rarotonga owned by the Cook Islands govt rel. R. Cook Islands and sometimes originate prgrs as local community stns – **2)** Aitutaki. **E:** Araura88fm@gmail.com – **3)** The Digital Factory, Avarua, Rarotonga ☎+682 23633 **W:** 88fmcookislands.com **E:** 88fmradio@gmail.com **LP:** George (GDub) Williams Prgr: 24h – **4)** PO Box 31, Avarua, Rarotonga ☎+682 22851 **E:** office@adventist.org.ck **LP:** Gen. Man.: Eric Toleafoa Prgr: Rlg – **5)** Matariki FM Ltd, PO Box 511, Avarua, Rarotonga ☎ +682 25997 **W:** matarikifm.co.ck and streaming: matarikifm.radio.net & https://onlineradiobox.com/ck/matariki/ **E:** matarikifm@gmail.com **LP:** William Framhein Format: Polynesian music, predominately Cook Islands and Tahitian. – **6)** Kia Orana Country R., PO Box 521, Avarua, Rarotonga ☎+682 23203 – **7)** United Christian Broadcasters, Matavera, Rarotonga. Prgr: Religious – **8)** Avarua, Rarotonga. Prgr: Religious. – **9)** Enuamanu School, Mapumai, Atiu. Format: local talkback, community affairs, music and school news

COSTA RICA

L.T: UTC -6h — **Pop:** 5.1 million — **Pr.L:** Spanish — **E.C:** 120V/60Hz — **ITU:** CTR

SUPERINTENDENCIA DE TELECOMUNICACIONES (SUTEL)

🖂 Guachipelín de Escazú, Oficentro Multipark, edificio Tapantí, 3er piso, 1000 San José ☎ +506 40000000 🖷 +506 22156821 **E:** info@sutel.go.cr **W:** sutel.go.cr

CÁMARA NACIONAL DE RADIODIFUSIÓN

🖂 De la casa de Matute Gomez, 100m Este, 50m Sur, San José ☎ +506 22562338 **E:** info@canara.org **W:** www.canara.org

Call: TI–, ‡ = inactive, r. = relay, ± = varying freq

MW	Call	kHz	kW	Station, location and h. of tr
1)	SCL	550	5	R. Santa Clara, Cd. Quesada: 1100-0130
2)	ELR	570	5	R. Libertad, San José: 1200-0400
3)	JC	700	10	R. Sonora, San José
4)	LX	†760	5	R. Columbia, San José
5)	RA	780	10	R. América, San José
6)	SD	800	3	R. La Gigante, San José
7)	RDR	‡850	2	R. Cartago, Cartago
8)	UCR	870	10	R. 870 UCR, San Pedro Montes de Oca
9)	UM	910	10	BBN Radio 9-10, San José/Quesada
10)	RCR	†930	5	R. Costa Rica, San José
11)	CS	960	5	R. Actual, San José
12)	TNT	980	10	R. Managua, San José (nf. 670 kHz)
13)	MIL	‡1000	1	R. 2 Rock, San José
14)		1020		R. Metrópoli, Cartago
15)	FC	1080	1	Faro del Caribe, San José
16)	SCR	1100	5	R. Chorotega, Santa Cruz: 1315-0000
17)	ACE	1120	1	R. Alajuela, Alajuela: 1100-0300
18)	DKN	‡1140	5	R. Nueva, Guápiles
19)	PJ	1180	5	R. Victoria, Heredia: 1100-0400
20)	TQ	1200	5	R. Cucu, San José: 1000-0600
21)	Q	‡1220	1	R. Fe y Poder, Limón
22)	DIO	†1260	5	R. Emaús, San Vito de Coto Brus:1100-0300
23)	GL	1300	1	R. La Fuente Musical, Cartago
24)	HR	1340	5	R. Sideral, San Ramón: 1000-0400
25)	CA	†1360		R. Tica, San José
26)	MS	‡1380	1	R. Guanacaste, Liberia
27)	RPN	1420	1	R. Pampa, Liberia: 1100-0100
28)	RDVC	1430	3	R. San Carlos, Cd. Quesada: 1200-2400
29)	RC	1500	1	R. Cima, Ciudad Quesada: 1100-0100
30)	OAR	†1560	5	R. Nicoya, Nicoya: 1000-0300
31)	LGJ	1590	1.5	R. 16, Grecia: 1100-0400
32)	CH	†1600	2	2 R. Buenísima, Golfito
33)	MQ	1600	1.5	R. Pococí, Guápiles: 1100-0400

Hrs of tr.: 24h except where shown.

Addresses & other information:

1) Ap. 221, 4400 Edificio Cenco, Cd. Quesada, San Carlos, Alajuela **W:** radiosantaclara.cr – **2)** Cadena Radial Costarricense, 100m oeste de Taca, La Uruca, 1000 San José or Ap. 301-2400, Desamparados **W:** libertadcr.com – **3)** San José **W:** radiosonoracr.com – **4)** De Casa Presidencial 400 metros oeste, Zapote, San Jose, 1000 San José **W:** columbia.co.cr - **FM:** 98.7MHz – **5)** Edificio de la Prensa Libre, Calle 4, Avenida 4 (or Ap. 177-1009) San José **W:** 780america.com – **6)** Calles 15-13, Av. 11, Barrio Aranjuez (or Ap. 1735) 1000 San José **W:** radiolagigante800am.com – **7)** Altos de Apolo, frente al Palacio Municipal, Cartago **W:** radiocartago.org – **8)** Cd. Universitaria Rodrigo Facio, San Pedro Montes de Oca, 2060-1000 San José **W:** radios.ucr.ac.cr – **9)** De la Municipalidad de Tibas 100 mtrs al Norte y 75 metrs al Oeste, casa blanca a mano derecha (Ap. 2006), 1100 San José **W:** bbnradio.org – **10)** Barrio Córdoba, Autos Bohío 100 sur y 100 este, 894-2200 Coronado **W:** radiocr.net – **11)** De la antigua entrada de emergencias del Calderón Guardia100 mts al norte y 25 al oeste, San José **W:** radioactualfm.com - **FM:** 101.7MHz – **12)** Ap. 800-1000 (or Costado Oeste del Puente Juan Pablo II), 1000 San José **W:** cdrcomercial.cr/radio/radio-managua-670-am – **13)** San José **W:** rock2.am – **14)** Cartago **W:** facebook.com/radio.metropoli – **15)** Ap. 2710, 1000 San José **W:** farodelcaribe.org - **FM:** 97.1MHz – **16)** 700 mts este de Almacén Jiménez y Chaverrí, (or Ap. 92), 5175 Santa Cruz **W:** radiochorotega.com – **17)** 300 metros Norte y 50 Oeste del Antiguo Hospital de Alajuela, Alajuela (or Ap. 233-4060, Moll International, Alajuela) **W:** radioalajuela.com – **18)** Limón, Pococí, Guápiles, 50 metros norte de Correos de CR – **19)** Universidad Nacional, 100 metros norte y 100 metros oeste, Heredia **W:** facebook.com/RadioVictoria1180AM – **20)** Ap. 1128, 1000 San José **W:** radiocucucr.com – **21)** Iglesia Maranatha, 7300 Puerto Limón **W:** feypoderradio.com – **22)** Ap.262, 8257 San Vito de Coto Brus **W:** emaus1260.com – **23)** 1 km este de la Basilica de los Angeles, Carr. a Paraíso, 7050 Cartago **W:** lafuentemusical.com – **24)** Ap. 73, 4250 San Ramón **W:** facebook.com/radiosideral – **25)** San José **W:** radiotica.com – **26)** Residencial Las Brisas, Casa #11A, Buscando la quebrada (Ap. 27), 5600 Liberia, (or Ap. 6462, 1000 San José) – **27)** Ap. 248, 5000 Liberia **W:** radiolapampa.net – **28)** 500 Sur 25 Este del Parque de Ciudad Quesada (Ap. 25), 4400 Cd. Quesada **W:** radiosancarlos.co.cr – **29)** Ciudad Quesada **W:** radiocimacr.com – **30)** Ap. 50, 5200 Nicoya **W:** facebook.com/radionicoya1560 – **31)** 200 mtrs Sur de la Bomba Alvarado y Molina en Grecia Centro (or Ap. 16), 4100 Grecia, Alajuela **W:** radio16.com – **32)** Barrio Laboratorio, Pérez Zeledón, 11901 San José **W:** 88stereo.com/grupo-88 – **33)** Costado Oeste del Estadio de Guápiles (or Ap. 160), 7210 Guápiles **W:** facebook.com/Radio-Pococi-647397988634486

FM in San José and vicinity (MHz): 88.7 Lira – 89.1 La Super Estación – 89.9 R. 899 – 89.5 Life FM Una Senda de Vida – 90.3 Sinfonola – 90.7 R. Ritmo 90.7 – 91.1 911 La Radio – 91.5 R. 915 – 91.9 Puntarenas – 92.3 Onda Radial – 92.7 Columbia Stereo – 93.1 R. Fides – 93.5 Monumental – 93.9 Sonido Latino – 94.3 Reloj – 94.7 R. 94.7 – 95.1 Z-FM – 95.5 R. 95 Cinco Jazz – 95.9 R. Romance – 96.3 Centro – 96.7 Universidad – 97.1 Faro del Caribe – 97.5 R. Musical – 97.9 R. 979 – 98.3 Stéreo Visión – 98.7 Columbia – 99.1 La Mejor FM – 99.5 R. Dos – 99.9 R. Azul – 100.3 FM Globo – 100.7 R. María – 101.1 R. Disney – 101.5 R. Nacional FM – 101.9 "U" – 102.3 La Super – 102.7 Exa FM – 103.1 Cientotres – 103.5 Best FM – 103.9 Sinai – 104.3 Oxígeno – 104.7 R. Hit – 105.1 Omega – 105.5 Ten Fifty-Five/Omega – 105.9 Beatz 106 – 106.3 R. Peninsular – 106.7 Premium – 107.1 R. Actual FM – 107.5 R. 107.5 Real Rock

CÔTE D'IVOIRE

LT: UTC — **Pop:** 27 million — **Pr.L:** French (official), Anyin, Baoulé, Jula — **E.C:** 220V/50Hz — **ITU:** CTI

HAUTE AUTORITÉ DE LA COMMUNICATION AUDIOVISUELLE (HACA)

🖂 2 Plateaux Vallons, Rue J93, lot n°2460, B.P. V56, Abidjan ☎+225 22 419658 🖷 +225 22 411455 **W:** haca.ci **E:** infos@haca.ci **L.P:** Chmn: Ibrahim Sy Savane.

RADIODIFFUSION-TÉLÉVISION IVOIRIENNE (RTI, Gov.)

🖂 B.P. 191, Abidjan ☎+225 20 214800 🖷 +225 20 215038 **W:** rti.ci **L.P:** Acting DG: Lazare Saye Aka. Deputy DG for Radio: Jean-Claude Bayala.

FM (MHz)	1	2	kW	FM (MHz)	1	2	kW
Abobo-Abidjan	88.0	92.0	5	Koun Fao	94.2	101.0	
Bouaflé	99.0	102.6		Man	96.9	100.2	
Bouaké	92.1	98.6		Naingbo	93.0	103.0	
Dabakala	91.0	101.0		Niangue	93.0	95.9	
Dimbokro	99.0	102.9		Séguéla	89.0	95.0	
Divo	88.0	90.8	10	Tengréla	96.3	99.6	
Grabo	88.0	91.0	0.5	Tiémé	88.0	91.0	5/1
Kouakoussikro	89.3	92.4		Touba	94.7	101.5	

R. Côte d'Ivoire (1): 0500-2400. **Fréquence Deux (2):** 24h.
Ann: "R. Côte d'Ivoire" or "Fréquence Deux". **IS:** s/on with clock chimes.

Other Stations:
Alpha Blondy FM, Abidjan: 97.9MHz **W:** alphablondyfm.net – **Bassam FM,** Grand Bassam: 104.2MHz **W:** bassamfm.com – **CNews FM,** Abidjan: 88.6MHz **W:** radiocnews.com – **Cocody FM,** Abidjan: 98.5MHz 1kW **W:** facebook.com/radio-cocody-fm-380951067163 – **Fréquence Vie**: Abidjan 89.4 1kW, Bouaké 94.5, Man 99.2, Abengourou 100.2, Yamoussoukro 103.1MHz **W:** radiofrequencevie.com – **Hit R**, Abidjan: 93.3MHz. **W:** hitradio.ci – **Ivoire FM**, Abidjan: 103.4MHz **W:** ivoirefm.ci – **La Voix de l'Esperance**, Abidjan: 101.6MHz **W:** lavoixdelesperance.org – **Life R**, Yamoussoukro: 107.1MHz **W:** lavoixdelesperance.org – **Onuci FM**: Yamoussoukro 94.4MHz, Bouaké 95.3MHz, Abidjan 96.0MHz & 19 other sites **W:** onucifm.net – **R. Ado FM,** Bouaké: 97.9MHz – **R. Al Bayane,** Gagnoa 88.6, Seguela 89.6, Yamoussoukro 91.2, Abidjan 95.7, Bouna 96.0, Bouaké 100.7, Korhogo 102.2, Daloa 102.6, San-Pédro 102.7MHz. **W:** radio-albayane.com – **R. Arc-en-ciel,** Abidjan: 102.0MHz **W:** facebook.com/RadioArcEnCiel22 – **R. City FM,** Abidjan: 106.1MHz **W:** radiocityfm.ci – **R. Jam:** Yamoussokro 88.1 1kW, Korhogo 92.2, San-Pédro 94.0, Man 95.5, Abengourou 96.9, Abidjan 99.3 3kW, Bouaké 104.3, Gagnoa 105.3MHz **W:** radiojam.biz – **R. Maria,** Yamoussoukro: 104.8MHz. **W:** radiomaria.ci – **R. N'Gowa FM**, Abidjan: 89.7MHz **W:** facebook.com/Radio-NGowa-897FM-172371509804556 – **R. Nationale Catolique:** Aboisso 89.2, Man 96.7, Abengourou 99.0, San-Pédro 99.2, Yamoussoukro 101.2, Abidjan 102.5, Gagnoa 104.7, Daloa 105.0, Bondoukou 107.2MHz **W:** rnc-ci.net – **R. Nostalgie:** Abidjan 101.1, Bouaké 106.5MHz. **W:** nostalgie.ci – **Trace R**, Abidjan 95.0MHz **W:** trace.ci – **Vibe R**, Abidjan 94.6MHz **W:** viberadio.ci – **Zenith FM**, Abidjan: 92.8MHz **W:** facebook.com/Zenith-FM-221020288020468

Africa Radio, Abidjan 91.1MHz **W:** africaradio.com
BBC African Sce: Man 89.2, Bouaké 93.9, Abidjan 94.3, Yamoussoukro 97.7, San Pedro 103.1MHz.
Medi 1 Afrique Internationale: Abidjan 97.2MHz.
RFI Afrique: San Pedro 94.4, Yamoussoukro 96.0, Abidjan/Bouaké/Korhogo 97.6MHz.
Voice of America, Abidjan: 99.0MHz

CROATIA

L.T: UTC +2h (28 Mar-31 Oct: +3h) — **Pop:** 4.1 million — **Pr.L:** Croatian — **E.C:** 230V/50Hz — **ITU:** HRV

HRVATSKA REGULATORNA AGENCIJA ZA MREŽNE DJELATNOSTI (HAKOM) (Croatian Regulatory Authority for Network Industries)

✉ Roberta Frangeša Mihanovića 9, 10010 Zagreb ☎ +385 1 7007007 🖷 +385 1 7007070 **E:** ravnatelj_hakom@hakom.hr **W:** www.hakom.hr
L.P: DG: Miran Gosta

HRVATSKA RADIOTELEVIZIJA (HRT) (Pub)

✉ Prisavlje 3, 10000 Zagreb ☎ +385 1 6342634 **E:** hrt@hrt.hr **W:** www.hrt.hr **L.P:** DG: Kazimir Bačić

FM (MHz)	1	2	3	kW
Belje	93.3	98.1	-	50
Biokovo	89.7	98.9	-	80
Borinci	88.3	96.1	-	3
Brač	99.8	-	88.8	3
Buje	91.3	103.7	93.2	1
Čelevac	95.1	98.1	-	80
Drenovci	92.1	104.4	-	3
Gruda	101.7	106.1	-	2
Ivanšćica	102.4	106.4	96.1	2x15/30
Kalnik	90.8	105.8	107.8	15
Labinštica	91.3	96.1	100.4	30
Lička Plješivica	87.7	90.5	100.3	50
Limski kanal	90.2	102.6	-	1
Mirkovica	91.3	93.3	-	30
Murter	92.7	99.4	104.1	1
Pag	98.5	103.4	-	3
Papuk	94.9	106.8	97.7	10
Psunj	97.3	99.7	-	80
Pula	91.4	94.4	102.1	5
Slavonski Brod	91.3	105.1	107.9	15
Sljeme	92.1	98.5	-	120
Srđ	88.9	98.5	-	30
Štipanov Grič	102.3	97.5	89.7	15
Šubićevac	94.0	90.0	102.3	1
Učka	99.3	105.3	100.5	80
Ugljan	91.6	87.6	-	5
Uljenje	95.1	89.3	105.6	3
Zagreb	-	-	94.3	1

+ txs below 1kW.
D.Prgr: Prgr 1 (HR1): 24h – **Prgr 2 (HR2):** 24h – **Prgr 3 (HR3):** 24h.

Hrvatski Radio (HR) Regional Stations
D.Prgr: all stns 24h (incl. rel. of HR Prgr 1). **HR R. Dubrovnik:** Branitelja Dubrovnika 21, 20000 Dubrovnik. **E:** radiodubrovnik@hrt.hr. On (MHz) 88.2 (Rota 1.7kW), 89.5 (Ilija 1.7kW), 97.2 (Blato 0.3kW), 101.1 (Vela Luka 0.3kW), 103.7 (Slano 0.05kW), 103.8 (Korčula 0.2kW), 105.0 (Srđ 30kW), 106.2 (Lastovo 2.7kW & Ston 0.05kW), 106.5 (Lopud 0.03kW) – **HR R. Knin:** Krešimirova 30, 23300 Knin. **E:** radio.knin@hrt.hr. On (MHz) 88.1 (Šubićevac 0.1kW), 90.2 (Knin 0.6kW), 94.4 (Promina 5kW) – **HR R. Osijek:** Šamačka 13, 31000 Osijek. **E:** radioosijek@hrt.hr. On (MHz) 99.3 (Drenovci 3kW), 102.0 (Psunj 80kW), 102.4 (Osijek), 102.8 (Beli Manastir 50kW), 105.3 (Borinci 3kW), 105.6 (Zlatarevac 0.1kW), 105.8 (Ilok). For ethnic minorities: Hungarian ("Eszéki Rádió"): 1805-1830 – **HR R. Pula:** Riva 10, 52100 Pula. **E:** radiopula@hrt.hr. On (MHz) 93.8 (Novigrad 0.15kW), 93.9 (Limski kanal 1kW), 94.2 (Vrsar 0.16kW), 96.3 (Koromačno 0.3kW), 96.4 (Buje 1kW), 100.0 (Pula 5kW), 101.3 (Učka 80kW), 103.8 (Raša 0.1kW). For ethnic minorities: Italian ("R. Pola"): MF 1000-1003, 1300-1303, 1530-1555 (Sun 1645) – **HR R. Rijeka:** Korzo 24, 51000 Rijeka. **E:** redakcija@radio-rijeka.com. On (MHz) 94.5 (Brgud 0.1kW), 95.1 (Pulac 0.5kW), 97.9 (Cres 0.3kW & Kupjački Vrh 0.3kW), 101.7 (Prezid 0.06kW), 102.7 (Mirkovica 30kW), 104.0 (Fužine 0.3kW), 104.7 (Učka 80kW), 107.4 (Mali Lošinj 0.1kW), 107.5 (Mrkopalj 0.03kW). For ethnic minorities: Italian ("R. Fiume"): W 0930-0935, W 1130-1135, W 1330-1335, W 1500-1510 – **HR R. Sljeme:** Prisavlje 3, 10000 Zagreb. **E:** radio_sljeme@hrt.hr. On 88.1MHz (Sljeme 5kW). – **HR R. Split:** Mažuranićevo šetalište 24a, 21000 Split. **E:** radio.split@hrt.hr. On (MHz) 88.4 (Komiža 0.5kW), 100.2 (Hvar 0.05kW), 101.0 (Labinštica 30kW), 102.0 (Biokovo 80kW), 104.5 (Brač 3kW), 105.3 (Orlovača 0.1kW), 105.8 (Vrlika 0.3kW) – **HR R. Zadar:** Poljana Šime Budinića 3, 23000 Zadar. **E:** radio_zadar@hrt.hr. On (MHz) 101.8 (Ugljan 5kW), 103.0 (Celevac 80kW), 105.9 (Pag 3kW).

OTHER STATIONS

FM	MHz	kW	Location	Station
4)	87.5	1	Krk	Laganini FM
13)	87.8	10	Brač	R. Dalmacija
17)	88.0	10	Rovinj	R. Istra
7)	88.0	3	Beli Manastir	R. Baranja
21)	88.3	3	Virovitica	R. Marija
13)	88.5	2	Čelevac	R. Dalmacija
52)	88.5	10	Rovinj	Rovinj FM
16)	88.6	4	Velika Gorica	City R.
26)	88.6	5	Slavonski Brod	R. Slavonija
38)	88.6	1	Šibenik	R. Šibenik
21)	88.8	2	Veprinac	R. Marija
26)	89.1	2	Nova Gradiška	R. Slavonija
4)	89.1	2.5	Zagreb	Laganini FM
30)	89.3	3	Ugljan	Novi R.
51)	89.4	2	Sisak	R. Sisak
11)	89.6	7	Poreč	R. Centar Poreč
5)	89.7	4.7	Sljeme	Antena Zagreb
49)	89.9	1	Koprivnica	R. Kraj
1)	90.1	1	Buzet	Narodni R.
42)	90.1	3	Martinšćak	Prvi Karlovacki R.
28)	90.2	1	Požega	R. Vallis Aurea
34)	90.2	1	Vinkovci	Radio Postaja Vincovci
1)	90.4	1	Slatina	Narodni R.
3)	90.4	3	Kuna Pelješka	Hrvatski Katolicki R.
1)	90.5	1	Slavonski Brod	Narodni R.
41)	90.5	1	Komiža	Nautic R. Vis
1)	90.6	1	Buje	Narodni R.

FM	MHz	kW	Location	Station
2)	90.6	1	Cres	Otvoreni R.
2)	90.8	1	Šibenik	Otvoreni R.
35)	91.0	1	Đakovo	Slavonski R.
4)	91.0	1	Veprinac	Laganini FM
2)	91.1	1	Moslavačka Gora	Otvoreni R.
19)	91.7	5	Koprivnica	R. Koprivnica
50)	91.7	5	Moslavačka Gora	R. Quirinus
9)	91.8	1	Brač	R. Brač
1)	92.0	5	Čelevac	Narodni R.
1)	92.3	5	Ugljan	Narodni R.
4)	92.4	2	Požega	Laganini FM
2)	92.6	1	Zagreb	Otvoreni R.
32)	92.9	1.9	Virovitica	R. Virovitica
37)	93.0	1	Samobor	R. Samobor
2)	93.2	1.7	Gruda	Otvoreni R.
31)	93.2	1	Velika Gorica	R. Banovina
11)	93.6	7	Poreč	R. Centar Poreč
12)	93.6	1	Sveta Nedelja	Extra FM
6)	93.6	30	Labinština	Ultra FM
1)	93.7	13	Otočac	Narodni R.
32)	93.7	1	Slatina	R. Virovitica
18)	93.8	1	Jastrebarsko	R. Jaska
10)	93.9	3	Bjelovar	R. Terezija
1)	94.5	3	Rijeka	Narodni R.
57)	94.7	1	Hvar	Megamix R. Hvar
52)	94.8	1	Rovinj	Rovinj FM
54)	94.8	1	Krapina	R. Kraj
20)	94.9	5	Velika Gorica	Gold FM
58)	95.2	1	Slunj	R. Slunj
1)	95.3	3	Osijek	Narodni R.
23)	95.4	1	Duga Resa	R. Mrežnica
45)	95.4	5	Drenovci	Hrvatski R. Vukovar
1)	95.5	1	Virovitica	Narodni R.
3)	95.5	1	Ugljan	Hrvatski Katolicki R.
27)	95.6	2	Donja Stubica	R. Stubica
59)	95.6	1	Trogir	Gradski R. Trogir
1)	95.8	1	Hvar	Narodni R.
1)	95.9	1	Pula	Narodni R.
32)	96.3	1	Pitomača	R. Virovitica
40)	96.3	3	Lastovo	Soundset Ragusa
13)	96.4	1	Ugljan	R. Dalmacija
21)	96.4	1	Zagreb	R. Marija
31)	96.8	5	Petrova Gora	R. Banovina
6)	96.8	10	Brač	Ultra FM
17)	96.9	80	Učka	R. Istra
55)	97.1	4	Gospić	R. Gospić
60)	97.3	1	Primošten	R. Ritam
2)	97.3	1	Pula	Otvoreni R.
60)	97.5	1	Dubrovnik	UNIDU R.
56)	97.6	4	Hvar	R. Makarska Rivijera
2)	97.7	3	Pag	Otvoreni R.
17)	98.0	5	Pula	R. Istra
4)	98.0	5	Zagreb	Laganini FM
47)	98.0	1.5	Čakovec	Hrvatski R. Čakovec
43)	98.1	1	Nova Gradiška	R. Nova Gradiška
56)	98.4	2	Makarska	R. Makarska Rivijera
3)	98.6	1	Osijek	Hrvatski Katolicki R.
4)	99.1	1	Osijek	Laganini FM
15)	99.3	1	Maruševec	R. Max
33)	99.5	1	Zaprešić	Z FM
61)	99.7	1	Skitača	R. Labin
13)	100.0	3	Žuljana	R. Dalmacija
3)	100.0	15	Promina	Hrvatski Katolicki R.
39)	100.1	5	Moslavacka Gora	Alfa R.
4)	100.1	1	Delnice	Laganini FM
38)	100.7	3	Žirje	R. Šibenik
44)	101.0	120	Sljeme	R. 101
1)	101.2	3	Metković	Narodni R.
4)	101.3	1	Slavonski Brod	Laganini FM
48)	101.3	1	Ilok	R. Ilok
46)	101.4	1.5	Kutina	R. Moslavina Kutina
36)	101.5	1	Vukovar	R. Dunav
25)	101.7	5	Buje	R. Eurostar
22)	101.8	1	Zagreb	Zabavni R.
29)	102.1	6	Lović	Trend R.
53)	102.5	5	Zagreb	Yammat FM
2)	102.6	1.5	Mali Lošinj	Otvoreni R.
9)	102.7	1	Brač	R. Brač
49)	103.1	1	Lepoglava	R. Kraj
49)	103.2	1	Jazbina	R. Kraj
2)	103.3	13	Otočac	Otvoreni R.
1)	103.5	30	Labinštica	Narodni R.
3)	103.5	120	Sljeme	Hrvatski Katolicki R.
2)	103.6	1	Krk	Otvoreni R.
30)	103.7	1	Starigrad Paklenica	Novi R.
3)	103.9	80	Psunj	Hrvatski Katolicki R.
3)	104.1	50	Lička Plješivica	Hrvatski Katolicki R.
2)	104.2	1	Komor	Otvoreni R.
1)	104.3	3.5	Petrova Gora	Narodni R.
2)	104.4	10	Papuk	Otvoreni R.
12)	104.5	1	Zagreb	Extra FM
3)	104.5	5	Otočac	Hrvatski Katolicki R.
24)	104.9	1	Vidovec	R. Megaton
38)	104.9	5	Šibenik	R. Šibenik
13)	105.5	5	Promina	R. Dalmacija
8)	105.5	1	Okučani	R. Bljesak
14)	105.6	1.5	Čakovec	R. 1
2)	105.6	2	Zagreb	Otvoreni R.
55)	105.7	1.5	Otočac	R. Gospić
1)	106.1	30	Mirkovica	Narodni R.
35)	106.2	50	Beli Manastir	Slavonski R.
60)	106.4	5	Šibenik	R. Ritam
2)	106.5	3	Brač	Otvoreni R.
3)	106.7	80	Učka	Hrvatski Katolicki R.
13)	106.9	4	Labinštica	R. Dalmacija
27)	106.9	2	Marija Bistrica	R. Stubica
29)	106.9	2	Karlovac	Trend R.
40)	107.0	30	Srđ	Soundset Ragusa
45)	107.2	5	Vinkovci	Hrvatski R. Vukovar
1)	107.3	1	Kutina	Narodni R.
13)	107.3	1	Komiža	R. Dalmacija
2)	107.3	80	Čelevac	Otvoreni R.
2)	107.3	1	Buzet	Otvoreni R.
1)	107.5	2	Zagreb	Narodni R.
2)	107.5	1	Slavonski Brod	Otvoreni R.
62)	107.6	2	Senj	Hrvatski R. Otočac
1)	107.9	3	Pag	Narodni R.
3)	107.9	80	Biokovo	Hrvatski Katolicki R.
3)	107.9	1	Slatina	Hrvatski Katolicki R.

+ txs below 1kW.

Addresses & other information:
1) Avenija Većeslava Holjevca 29, 10000 Zagreb – **2)** Cebini 28/III, 10000 Zagreb – **3)** Voćarska cesta 106, 10000 Zagreb – **4)** Slavonska avenija 2, 10000 Zagreb – **5)** Avenija Većeslava Holjevca 29, 10000 Zagreb – **6)** Kralja Zvonimira 14/III, 21000 Split – **7)** Trg slobode 32/3, 31300 Beli Manastir – **8)** Blaženog kardinala A. Stepinca 24, 35430 Okučani – **9)** Mladena Vodanovića 3, 21400 Supetar – **10)** Jurja Haulika 23, 43000 Bjelovar – **11)** Vitomira Širole Paje 18, 52440 Porec – **12)** Avenija Većeslava Holjevca 29, 10000 Zagreb – **13)** Kralja Zvonimira 14/2, 21000 Split – **14)** Nova ulica 7, 40305 Nedelišće – **15)** Cerje Nebojse 151, 42243 Maruševec – **16)** Zagrebačka 19, 10410 Velika Gorica – **17)** Jurja Dobrile 6, 52000 Pazin – **18)** Trg Strossmayerov 5, 10450 Jastrebarsko – **19)** Zagrebačka bb, 48000 Koprivnica – **20)** Zagrebačka 6, 10410 Velika Gorica – **21)** Jordanovac 110, 10000 Zagreb – **22)** Bjelovarska 62b, 10360 Zagreb – **23)** Jozefinska c. 8, 47250 Duga Resa – **24)** Varaždinska 49a, 42205 Vidovec – **25)** Rozag 23, 52470 Umag – **26)** Mile Budaka 1, 35000 Slavonski Brod – **27)** Toplička 5, 49240 Donja Stubica – **28)** Cehovska 8/1, 34000 Požega – **29)** Trg J. Broza Tita 2, 47000 Karlovac – **30)** Zrinsko Frankopanska 13, 23000 Zadar – **31)** Slatina Pokupska 80, 44400 Glina – **32)** F. Rusana 1/9, 33000 Virovitica – **33)** Trg žrtava fašizma 6, 10290 Zaprešić – **34)** Jurja Dalmatinca 29, 32100 Vinkovci – **35)** Hrvatske Republike 20, 31000 Osijek – **36)** Kvaternika 1, 32000 Vukovar – **37)** Đure Basaričeka 4, 10432 Bregana – **38)** Božidara Petranovića 3, 22000 Šibenik – **39)** Trg E. Kvaternika 7a, 43000 Bjelovar – **40)** Dr. Ante Starčevića 20, 20000 Dubrovnik – **41)** V. Nazora 19, 21480 Vis – **42)** Ambroza Vraniczanya 2, 47000 Karlovac – **43)** Gunduliceva 7, 35400 Nova Gradiška – **44)** Gajeva 10, 10000 Zagreb – **45)** Dr. Franje Tuđmana 13, 32000 Vukovar – **46)** Ivana Gorana Kovačića 25, 44320 Kutina – **47)** Trg republike 5, 40000 Čakovec – **48)** Trg Nikole Iločkog 13, 32236 Ilok – **49)** Zagrebačka bb, 48000 Koprivnica – **50)** Ante Starčevića 46, 44000 Sisak – **51)** Stjepana i Antuna Radica 2, 44000 Sisak – **52)** Zagrebačka 12a, 52210 Rovinj – **53)** Baruna Filipovića 23a, 10000 Zagreb – **54)** Haendelova 4 , 10000 Zagbreb – **55)** Budačka 12, 53000 Gospić – **56)** Don Mihovila Pavlinovića 1, 21300 Makarska – **57)** Šime Ljubica 30, 21000 Hvar – **58)** Trg Dr. Franje Tuđmana 14, 47240 Slunj – **59)** Put Mulina 2, 21220 Trogir – **60)** Stjepana Radića 24, 22000 Šibenik – **61)** Rudarska 3b, 52220 Labin – **62)** Trg Dr. Franje Tuđmana 10, 53220 Otočac.

DAB Transmitters (DAB+) (Trial)
Tx Operator: OIV **M:** Antena Zadar, Antena Zagreb, HR1, HR2, HR3, Laganini DAB+, Narodni R., Otvoreni R., R. Dalmacija, R. Trogir, Yammat FM.r

Bl	kW	Location	Bl	kW	Location
8C	-	SFN	10C	-	SFN
9C	-	SFN	11C	8	Učka
10A	5	Brač			

CUBA

L.T: UTC -5h (8 Mar-1 Nov: -4h) — **Pop:** 11.3 million — **Pr.L:** Spanish — **E.C:** 110V/60Hz — **ITU:** CUB

MINISTERIO DE COMUNICACIONES (MC)
Dirección General de Telecomunicaciones

✉ Plaza de la Revolución, Ciudad de la Habana **W:** www.mincom.gob.cu

IINSTITUTO CUBANO DE RADiO Y TELEVISIÓN (ICRT) - RADIO CUBANA (Gov)

✉ Edif. Radiocentro, Avda 23 N° 258, Vedado, Habana 4 ☎ +53 7 8324648 **E:** **W:** icrt.gob.cu; radiocubana.cu (includes links to national, provincial & municipal stns) **L.P:** Pres: Alfonso Noya Martínez

Hrs of tr. usually 24h – see address section for variations. Call CM–

MW	Call	kHz	kW	Primary network, location
N1)	BA	530	1	R. Rebelde, Guantánamo-R.Reloj, GU
N1)	BA	530		R. Rebelde, Caribe, IJ
N5)	BQ	530	10	R. Enciclopedia, Villa María, CH
N1)	BA	540	10	R. Rebelde, Santa Rita, Maisí, GU
N1)	BA	540	1	R. Rebelde, Sancti Spíritus-Progreso, SS
N1)	BA	550	12	R. Rebelde, Pinar del Río-San Juan, PR
N1)	BA	560	10	R. Rebelde, Ciego de Avila-Rebelde/Reloj, CA
N1)	BA	570	1	R. Rebelde, Pilón-Siguanea, GR
N2)	BD	570	25	R. Reloj, Santa Clara-Reloj, VC
N1)	BA	580	2.5	R. Rebelde, Mabujabo, GU
N1)	BA	590	10	R. Rebelde, Guantánamo-Burenes, GU
N3)	BF	590	25	R. Musical Nacional, La Julia, MB
N1)	BA	600	50	R. Rebelde, San Germán, HO
N1)	BA	610	1	R. Rebelde, Cienfuegos-Malecón, CI
N1)	BA	610	10	R. Rebelde, Bueycito, GR
N1)	BA	610	10	R. Rebelde, Guane, PR
N2)	BD	610	1	R. Reloj, Trinidad- R. Trinidad, SS
N1)	BA	620	25	R. Rebelde, Colón, MA
N4)	BC	630	5	R. Progreso, Camagüey-Isabel Hortensia, CM
N4)	BC	640	50	R. Progreso, Guanabacoa-Progreso, CH
N4)	BC	640	10	R. Progreso, Las Tunas-Progreso, LT
N4)	BC	650	10	R. Progreso, Ciego de Avila-Surco/Progreso, CA
N1)	BA	650	5	R. Rebelde, Santiago de Cuba-Eide, SC
N4)	BC	660	12	R. Progreso, Jovellanos, MA
N1)	BA	670	5	R. Rebelde, Bahía Honda, AR
N1)	BA	670	10	R. Rebelde, Central Brasil, Jaronú, CM
N1)	BA	670	10	R. Rebelde, Camagüey-Villa Rosita, CM
N1)	BA	670	50	R. Rebelde, Arroyo Arenas, CH
N1)	BA	670	5	R. Rebelde, Morón, CA
N1)	BA	670	10	R. Rebelde, El Coco, HO
N1)	BA	670		R. Rebelde, Mayarí, HO
N1)	BA	670		R. Rebelde, Caribe, IJ
N1)	BA	670	10	R. Rebelde, Las Tunas-Rebelde1180, LT
N5)	BQ	670	1	R. Enciclopedia, Cárdenas-2, MA
N1)	BA	670	5	R. Rebelde, Matanzas-Circunvalación, MA
N1)	BA	670	1	R. Rebelde, Los Palacios, PR
N1)	BA	670	1	R. Rebelde, Pinar del Río-Coloma, PR
N1)	BA	670	1	R. Rebelde, Santa Lucía, PR
N1)	BA	670	50	R. Rebelde, Santa Clara-Rebelde670, VC
N4)	BC	690	5	R. Progreso, Santiago de Cuba-Sta. María, SC
N4)	BC	690	10	R. Progreso, Santa Clara-Progreso, VC
N1)	BA	710	25	R. Rebelde, Camagüey-Tagarro, CM
N1)	BA	710	200	R. Rebelde, Chambas-Centro 6, CA
N1)	BA	710	50	R. Rebelde, Cacocúm, HO
N1)	BA	710	50	R. Rebelde, Martí-Centro 5, MA
N1)	BA	710	50	R. Rebelde, La Julia, MB
PR01)	AM	710	10	R. Guamá, La Palma, PR
N1)	BA	710	1	R. Rebelde, Yaguajay, SS
N1)	BA	710	50	R. Rebelde, Santa Clara-Reloj, VC
N1)	BC	720	2.5	R. Progreso, Mabujabo, GU
N4)	BC	730	10	R. Progreso, La Fe-Progreso, IJ
HO01)	KO	740	10	R. Angulo, Sagua de Tánamo, HO
N4)	BC	750	10	R. Progreso, Palmira, CI
N4)	BC	760	10	R. Progreso, Guane, PR
N4)	BC	760		R. Progreso, Mayarí Arriba-II Frente1, SC
N1)	BA	770	10	R. Rebelde, Las Tunas-Victoria, LT
AR01)	CW	770	10	R. Artemisa, La Salud, AR
N2)	BD	790	10	R. Reloj, Holguín, HO
N2)	BD	790	25	R. Reloj, Pinar del Río-Politécnico, PR
N4)	BC	810	10	R. Progreso, Guantánamo-Burenes, GU
N2)	BD	820	10	R. Reloj, Ciego de Ávila-Rebelde/Reloj, CA
CH02)	BU	820	10	R. Ciudad Habana, Arroyo Arenas, CH
N4)	BC	820	1	R. Progreso, Moa-Rolo Monterrey, HO
N2)	J	830		CMKC R. Revolucion, Mayarí Arriba-II Frente2, SC
SC01)	J	840	1	CMKC R. Revolución, Palma Soriano, SC
VC01)	E	840	10	R. CMHW, Santa Clara-CMHW, VC
N2)	BD	850	1	R. Reloj, Nueva Gerona, IJ
N4)	BC	850	1	R. Progreso, Trinidad-Tetraplexer, SS
N2)	BD	860		R. Reloj, Bolondrón, MA
N2)	BD	870	10	R. Reloj, Bueycito, GR
N2)	BD	870	10	R. Reloj, Baracoa-Van Van, GU
N2)	BD	870	1	R. Reloj, Sancti Spíritus-Reloj, SS
N4)	BC	880	12	R. Progreso, Pinar del Río-San Juan, PR
N4)	BC	890	200	R. Progreso, Chambas-Centro 6, CA
SC01)	J	890		CMKC R. Revolución, Santiago de Cuba, SC
N4)	BC	900	50	R. Progreso, San Germán, HO
CM01)	HA	910	25	R. Cadena Agramonte, Camagüey-Tagarro, CM
CH03)	BL	910	5	R. Metropolitana, Villa María, CH
N2)	BD	910	5	R. Reloj, Bolondrón, MA
N4)	BC	920	1	R. Progreso, Pilón-Siguanea, GR
N2)	BD	930	1	R. Reloj, Cienfuegos-Malecón, CI
N2)	BD	930	1	R. Reloj, La Jaiba, MA
N2)	BD	930	1	R. Reloj, Stgo de Cuba-Sta.María, SC
N4)	BC	940	1	R. Progreso, Sancti Spíritus-Progreso, SS
N2)	BD	950	10	R. Reloj, Camagüey-Isabel Hortensia, CM
N2)	BD	950	10	R. Reloj, Arroyo Arenas, HA
N2)	KC	950	1	R. R. Reloj, Mayarí Arriba-II Frente1, SC
N2)	BD	960	10	R. Reloj, Guantánamo-La Piña, GU
PR01)	AM	970	5	R. Guamá, Los Palacios, PR
N1)	BA	970	1	R. Rebelde, Trinidad-Tetraplexer, SS
CH04)	B	980	2.5	R. COCO, El Sapo, CH
N2)	BD	980	1	R. Reloj, Moa-Rolo Monterrey, HO
PR01)	AM	990	25	R. Guamá, Pinar del Río-Politécnico, PR
AR01)	CW	1000	10	R. Artemisa, Artemisa, AR
GR02)	NM	1000	5	R. Granma, Media Luna, GR
AR01)	CW	1020	5	R. Artemisa, Bahía Honda AR
GU01)	M	1020	10	CMKS R. Trinchera Antiimp., Baracoa-Van Van, GU
PR01)	AM	1020	1	R. Guamá, Santa Lucía, PR
MB01)	CL	1040	10	R. Mayabeque, Güines, MB
LT01)	LL	1050	10	R. Victoria, Las Tunas-Victoria, LT
MA01)	DL	1060	25	CMGW R. 26, Jovellanos, MA
GU01)	M	1070	10	CMKS R. Trinchera Antiimp., Guant.-Burenes, GU
PR01)	AM	1070	10	R. Guamá, Guane, PR
CA01)	IP	1080	10	R. Surco, Ciego de Ávila-Surco/Progreso, CA
CH01)	CH	1080	5	R. Cadena Habana, Villa María, CH
LT01)	LL	1090	1	R. Victoria, Amancio, LT
HO01)	KO	1100	1	R. Angulo, Mayarí, HO
HO01)	KO	1110	10	R. Angulo, Holguín, HO
N1)	BA	1130		R. Rebelde, Imías, GU
CA01)	IP	1140	25	R. Surco, Morón, CA
CI01)	FL	1140		R. Ciudad del Mar, Cienfuegos-Malecón, CI
CM02)	BQ	1140	1	R. Camagüey, Camagüey-Isabel Hortensia,CM
GR01)	NL	1140	1	R. Bayamo, Media Luna, GR
MA02)	DP	1140	1	R. Ciudad Bandera, Cárdenas-2, MA
MB01)	CL	1140	25	R. Mayabeque, La Salud, MB
N1)	BA	1140	10	R. Rebelde, Aguada, CI
N1)	BA	1140		R. Rebelde, Guantánamo-La Piña, GU
N1)	BA	1140		R. Rebelde, Caribe, IJ
N1)	BA	1140	5	R. Rebelde, Matanzas-Circunvalación, MA
N3)	BF	1140	10	R. Musical Nacional, Santa Clara-Progreso, VC
GR01)	NL	1150	10	R. Bayamo, Entronque Bueycito, GR
GR01)	NL	1160	1	R. Bayamo, Pilón-Siguanea, GR
GU01)	M	1170	10	CMKS R. Trinchera Antiimp., Sta. Rita, Maisí, GU
N1)	BA	1180	10	R. Rebelde, Artemisa, AR
N1)	BA	1180	5	R. Rebelde, Bahía Honda, AR
N1)	BA	1180	1	R. Rebelde, San Cristóbal, AR
N1)	BA	1180	10	R. Rebelde, Central Brasil, Jaronú CM
N1)	BA	1180	50	R. Rebelde, Camagüey-Villa Rosita, CM
N1)	BA	1180		R. Rebelde, Guáimaro, CM
N1)	BA	1180	10	R. Rebelde, Arroyo Arenas, CH
N1)	BA	1180	50	R. Rebelde, Guanabacoa, CH

MW	Call	kHz	kW	Primary network, location
N1)	BA	1180	10	R. Rebelde, Santa Catalina, CH
N1)	BA	1180	1	R. Rebelde, Ciego de Avila-Rebelde/Reloj, CA
N1)	BA	1180	50	R. Rebelde, Chambas-Centro 6, CA
N1)	BA	1180	5	R. Rebelde, Cienfuegos-1ra Tulipán, CI
N1)	BA	1180	1	R. Rebelde, Guantánamo-Radio Reloj, GU
GU02)	DX	1180	1	CMDX R. Baracoa "LV del Toa", Mabujabo, GU
N1)	BA	1180	1	R. Rebelde, Banes, HO
N1)	BA	1180	50	R. Rebelde, Cacocúm, HO
N1)	BA	1180	1	R. Rebelde, Moa-Rolo Monterrey, HO
N1)	BA	1180	5	R. Rebelde, Sagua de Tánamo, HO
N1)	BA	1180	5	R. Rebelde, Nueva Gerona, IJ
N1)	BA	1180	1	R. Rebelde, Puerto Padre, LT
N1)	BA	1180	10	R. Rebelde, Las Tunas-Rebelde1180, LT
N1)	BA	1180		R. Rebelde, Bolondrón, MA
N1)	BA	1180	5	R. Rebelde, Cárdenas-1, MA
N1)	BA	1180	25	R. Rebelde, Colón, MA
N1)	BA	1180	5	R. Rebelde, Matanzas-La Jaiba, MA
N1)	BA	1180	200	R. Rebelde, Martí-Centro 5, MA
N1)	BA	1180	10	R. Rebelde, Güines, MB
N1)	BA	1180		R. Rebelde, Hectométrico, MB
N1)	BA	1180	10	R. Rebelde, Sta Cruz del Norte-La Sierrita, MB
N1)	BA	1180		R. Rebelde, Pinar del Río-Coloma, PR
N1)	BA	1180	10	R. Rebelde, La Palma, PR
N1)	BA	1180	10	R. Rebelde, Los Palacios, PR
N1)	BA	1180	1	R. Rebelde, Santa Lucía, PR
N1)	BA	1180	1	R. Rebelde, Sancti Spíritus-Progreso, SS
N1)	BA	1180	1	R. Rebelde, Mayarí Arriba-II Frente1, SC
N1)	BQ	1180		R. Rebelde, Santiago de Cuba-Eide, SC
N1)	BA	1180		R. Rebelde, Corralillo, VC
N1)	BA	1180	10	R. Rebelde, Sagua la Grande, VC
N1)	BA	1180	10	R. Rebelde, Santa Clara-CMHW, VC
SC02)	JD	1190	10	R. Coral/R. Revolución, Chivirico, SC
SS01)	GL	1190	1	R. Sancti Spíritus, Trinidad-Tetraplexer, SS
SS01)	GL	1200	1	R. Sancti Spíritus, Yaguajay, SS
N2)	BA	1210		R. Rebelde, Las Tunas-Progreso, LT
SS01)	GL	1210	10	R. Sancti Spíritus, Sancti Spíritus-Reloj, SS
IJ01)	BY	1220	10	R. Caribe, La Fe-Progreso, IJ
N4)	BC	1230		R. Progreso, Bayamo, GR
GU01)	M	1250	1	CMKS R. Trinchera Antimperialista, Imías, GU
N4)	BC	1260	2.5	R. Progreso, Media Luna, GR
N5)	BQ	1280		R. Enciclopedia, Trinidad-RadioTrinidad, SC
SC03)	JN	1280	1	R. Mambí, Santiago de Cuba-Sta.María, SC
SC04)	JB	1300		R. Titán, Palma Soriano, SC
N5)	BQ	1310	1	R. Enciclopedia, Nueva Gerona, IJ
AR01)	CW	1320		R. Artemisa, San Cristóbal, AR
HO02)	KA	1320		Ecos de Sagua, Sagua de Tánamo, HO
MA01)	DL	1320	1	CMGW R. 26, Matanzas-La Jaiba, MA
CI01)	FL	1340	10	R. Ciudad del Mar, Palmira, CI
CI01)	FL	1350	10	R. Ciudad del Mar, Aguada, CI
LT03)	LM	1350	1	R. Libertad, Puerto Padre, LT
GU03)	MA	1370	1	R. Playita, Imías, GU
HO01)	KO	1380	1	R. Angulo, Banes, HO
VC02)	ES	1400	1	R. Sagua, Sagua La Grande, VC
LT02)	LN	1450	1	R. Maboas, Amancio Rodríguez, LT
MB01)	CL	1450	1	R. Mayabeque, Sta. Cruz del Norte-La Sierrita, MB
SC05)	JL	1460		R. 8SF, Mayarí Arriba-II Frente2, SC
LT04)	LB	1470	1	R. Chaparra, Puerto Padre, LT
HO03)	KN	1490	1	R. Mayarí, Mayarí, HO
SC06)	KZ	1520		R. Baraguá "LV del Cauto", Palma Soriano, SC
N1)	BA	1550		R. Rebelde, San Cristóbal, AR
N1)	BA	1550	5	R. Rebelde, Cienfuegos-1ra Tulipán, CI
CM		1550		R. Guaímaro, Guáimaro, CM
N1)	BA	1550		R. Rebelde, Jayamá, CM
N1)	BA	1550	10	R. Rebelde, Santa Catalina, CH
N1)	BA	1550	1	R. Rebelde, Guantánamo-La Piña, GU
N1)	BA	1550	5	R. Rebelde, Cárdenas-2, MA
N1)	BA	1550	5	R. Rebelde, Matanzas-Circunvalación, MA
N1)	BA	1550		R. Rebelde, Hectométrico, MB
N4)	BC	1550		R. Progreso, La Palma, PR
N1)	BA	1550	1	R. Rebelde, Yaguajay, SS
N1)	BA	1550		R. Rebelde, Corralillo, VC
N4)	BA	1550	1	R. Progreso, Sagua La Grande, VC
N1)	BA	1550	10	R. Rebelde, Santa Clara-Rebelde670, VC
N1)	BA	1620		R. Rebelde, El Sapo, CH
N1)	BA	1620	1	R. Rebelde, Guantánamo-R.Reloj, GU
N1)	BA	1620		R. Rebelde, El Coco, HO
N1)	BA	1620		R. Rebelde, Amancio Rodríguez, LT
GR01)	NL	1620		R. Bayamo, Bayamo GR

SW	Call	kHz	kW	Primary network, location
N4)		4765	50	R. Progreso, La Habana (Bejucal): 0130-0500
N1)	BA	5025	100	R. Rebelde, La Habana (Bauta)

Provinces: AR=Artemisa CA=Ciego de Avila CH=Ciudad Habana CI=Cienfuegos CM=Camagüey GR=Granma GU=Guantánamo HA=Habana HO=Holguín IJ=Isla de laJuventud LT=Las Tunas MA=Matanzas MB=Mayabeque PR=Pinar del Río SC=Santiago de Cuba SS=Sancti Spíritus VC=Villa Clara

NB: Esp. at night stns rel. an upper level station, i.e. municipal station rel. provincial station and provincial station rel. national station. Own prgr. for smallest stations is only few hrs per day. R. Rebelde carries sports events which are rel. by many other stns and other rel. may occur. Most txs operate 24h.

FM	MHz	Call	Station	Location
N6)	89.1	BV	R. Taíno	Loma de la Cruz, HO
N1)	90.3	BA	R. Rebelde	El Mamey, GR
N4)	90.3	BC	R. Progreso	Loma de la Cruz, CH
N5)	90.3	BQ	R. Enciclopedia	Cienfuegos, CI
N2)	90.5	BD	R. Reloj	TV Guanito, PR
N6)	90.5	BV	R. Taíno	Guardalavaca, HO
N1)	91.1	BA	R. Rebelde	Guamá, SC
N5)	91.1	BQ	R. Enciclopedia	Cumbre, MA
N5)	91.1	BQ	R. Enciclopedia	San Isidro, SS
N6)	91.5	BV	R. Taíno	TV Tunas, LT
N4)	91.7	BC	R. Progreso	La Vigía, SS
N2)	91.9	BD	R. Reloj	TV Miraflores, HO
N7)	91.9	BR	Habana R.	Plan Mangos, CI
N1)	92.1	BA	R. Rebelde	El Drinco, MA
N4)	92.3	BC	R. Progreso	El Mamey, GR
N5)	92.5	BQ	R. Enciclopedia	Cayo Santa María, VC
N7)	92.5	BR	Habana R.	San Isidro, SS
N1)	92.7	BA	R. Rebelde	Topes de Collantes, SS
N3)	92.7	BF	R. Musical Nacional	Bayamo, GR
N3)	92.7	BF	R. Musical Nacional	Cienfuegos, CI
N5)	92.7	BQ	R. Enciclopedia	Sierra Caballos, IJ
N6)	92.9	BV	R. Taíno	Cunagua, CA
N7)	92.9	BR	Habana R.	Loma dos Hermanas, VC
N4)	93.3	BC	R. Progreso	Los Guineos, GU
N6)	93.3	BV	R. Taíno	Loma de la Cruz, CH
N6)	93.3	BV	R. Taíno	TV FM Camagüey, CM
N6)	93.3	BV	R. Taíno	Viñales, PR
N1)	93.7	BA	R. Rebelde	La Vigía, SS
N3)	93.7	BF	R. Musical Nacional	Cumbre, MA
N5)	93.7	BQ	R. Enciclopedia	Bayamo, GR
N6)	93.7	BV	R. Taíno	Sierra Caballos, IJ
N3)	93.9	BF	R. Musical Nacional	San Isidro, SS
N4)	93.9	BC	R. Progreso	TV Miraflores, HO
N6)	93.9	BV	R. Taíno	Corralillo -CMHW, VC
N5)	94.1	BQ	R. Enciclopedia	Estudio Manzanillo, GR
N5)	94.1	BQ	R. Enciclopedia	Loma de la Cruz, CH
N2)	94.3	BD	R. Reloj	Los Guineos, GU
N2)	94.5	BD	R. Reloj	TV Tunas, LT
N4)	94.5	BC	R. Progreso	El Brinco, MA
N1)	94.7	BA	R. Rebelde	Corralillo -CMHW, VC
N1)	94.7	BA	R. Rebelde	TV Cajalbana, PR
N2)	94.7	BD	R. Reloj	Cienfuegos, CI
N6)	94.7	BV	R. Taíno	S.Miguel Baños Jacán, MA
N7)	94.7	BR	Habana R.	Sierra Caballos, IJ
N7)	94.9	BR	Habana R.	TV FM Camagüey, CM
N6)	95.1	BV	R. Taíno	Majayara, GU
N7)	95.1	BR	Habana R.	TV Guanito, PR
N1)	95.5	BA	R. Rebelde	Candelaria-TV Salón, AR
N1)	95.5	BA	R. Rebelde	TV la Capitana, PR
N4)	95.7	BC	R. Progreso	Corralillo, VC
N2)	95.9	BD	R. Reloj	San Isidro, SS
N7)	95.9	BR	Habana R.	TV Tunas, LT
N5)	96.3	BQ	R. Enciclopedia	Cueva Arriba, GU
N3)	96.5	BF	R. Musical Nacional	Sierra Caballos, IJ
N1)	96.7	BA	R. Rebelde	Bayamo, GR
N1)	96.7	BA	R. Rebelde	Loma de la Cruz, CH
N1)	96.7	BA	R. Rebelde	TV Miraflores, HO
N2)	96.7	BD	R. Reloj	Loma dos Hermanas, VC
N5)	97.1	BQ	R. Enciclopedia	Los Guineos, GU
N6)	97.1	BV	R. Taíno	Puerto Boniato, SC
N1)	97.5	BA	R. Rebelde	Bartolomé Masó, GR
N3)	97.5	BF	R. Musical Nacional	TV FM Camagüey, CM
N4)	97.5	BC	R. Progreso	Candelaria-TV Salón, AR
N4)	97.5	BC	R. Progreso	Cueva Arriba, GU
N6)	97.5	BV	R. Taíno	Loma dos Hermanas, VC

FM	MHz	Call	Station	Location
N1)	97.9	BA	R. Rebelde	Los Guineos, GU
N2)	98.1	BD	R. Reloj	TV Ciego de Ávila, CA
N3)	98.1	BF	R. Musical Nacional	Los Guineos, GU
N5)	98.1	BQ	R. Enciclopedia	Puerto Boniato, SC
N3)	98.3	BF	R. Musical Nacional	TV Tunas, LT
N3)	98.5	BF	R. Musical Nacional	Cueva Arriba, GU
N2)	98.7	BD	R. Reloj	Loma de la Cruz, HO
N3)	98.7	BF	R. Musical Nacional	TV Guanito, PR
N7)	98.7	BR	Habana R.	Cumbre, MA
N7)	98.7	BR	Playa Habana R.	Caibarién Playa, VC
N1)	99.1	BA	R. Rebelde	TV Tunas, LT
N3)	99.1	BF	R. Musical Nacional	Loma de la Cruz, CH
N1)	99.3	BA	R. Rebelde	TV Ciego de Ávila, CA
N4)	99.3	BC	R. Progreso	Puerto Boniato, SC
N1)	99.5	BA	R. Rebelde	TV Guanito, PR
N4)	99.9	BC	R. Progreso	Loma de la Cruz, HO
N6)	100.1	BV	R. Taíno	La Vigía, SS
N1)	100.3	BA	R. Rebelde	S.Miguel Baños Jacán, MA
N3)	100.3	BF	R. Musical Nacional	Puerto Boniato, SC
N4)	100.3	BC	R. Progreso	TV Las Llamadas, SS
N4)	100.5	BC	R. Progreso	Sierra Caballos, IJ
N5)	100.5	BQ	R. Enciclopedia	TV FM Camagüey, CM
N1)	100.7	BA	R. Rebelde	Cueva Arriba, GU
N3)	100.7	BF	R. Musical Nacional	Loma Dos Hermanas, VC
N5)	100.7	BQ	R. Enciclopedia	Candelaria-TV Salón, AR
N4)	100.9	BC	R. Progreso	TV Ciego De Ávila, CA
N5)	101.1	BQ	R. Enciclopedia	TV Tunas, LT
N1)	101.5	BA	R. Rebelde	TV FM Camagüey, CM
N2)	101.5	BD	R. Reloj	Televilla, CH
N6)	101.5	BV	R. Taíno	Guisa, GR
N7)	101.5	BR	Habana R.	Puerto Boniato, SC
N4)	101.9	BC	R. Progreso	S.Miguel Baños Jacán, MA
N4)	101.9	BC	R. Progreso	TV Guanito, PR
N4)	101.9	BC	R. Progreso	TV Tunas, LT
N7)	101.9	BR	Habana R.	Cueva Arriba, GU
N2)	102.1	BD	R. Reloj	TV Punta Alegre, CA
N1)	102.3	BA	R. Rebelde	Puerto Boniato, SC
N2)	102.3	BD	R. Reloj	TV FM Camagüey, CM
N5)	102.3	BQ	R. Enciclopedia	Loma dos Hermanas, VC
N5)	102.7	BQ	R. Enciclopedia	Loma de la Cruz, HO
N5)	102.7	BQ	R. Enciclopedia	TV Guanito, PR
N7)	102.9	BR	Habana R.	La Vigía, SS
N2)	103.1	BD	R. Reloj	Puerto Boniato, SC
N4)	103.1	BC	R. Progreso	Bartolomé Masó, GR
N4)	103.1	BC	R. Progreso	Loma dos Hermanas, VC
N4)	103.1	BC	R. Progreso	TV FM Camagüey, CM
N1)	103.5	BA	R. Rebelde	Loma de la Cruz, HO
N2)	103.5	BD	R. Reloj	S.Miguel Baños Jacán, MA
N7)	103.5	BR	Habana R.	TV Ciego de Ávila, CA
N1)	103.9	BA	R. Rebelde	Plan Mangos, CI
N1)	103.9	BA	R. Rebelde	San Antonio del Sur, GU
N2)	104.1	BD	R. Reloj	Sierra Caballos, IJ
N7)	104.1	BR	Habana R.	Bayamo, GR
N6)	104.5	BV	R. Taíno	Bartolomé Masó, GR
N1)	104.7	BA	R. Rebelde	Loma dos Hermanas, VC
N2)	105.1	BD	R. Reloj	Cueva Arriba, GU
N1)	105.7	BA	R. Rebelde	Sierra Caballos, IJ
N1)	105.7	BA	R. Rebelde	TV Tamarindo, CA
N3)	105.7	BF	R. Musical Nacional	Loma de la Cruz, HO
N6)	105.9	BV	R. Taíno	Cueva Arriba, GU
N6)	105.9	BV	R. Taíno	Cumbre, MA
N1)	106.3	BA	R. Rebelde	TV Ciego de Ávila, CA
N4)	106.3	BC	R. Progreso	Cumbre, MA
N4)	106.3	BC	R. Progreso	Focsa, CH
N4)	106.3	BC	R. Progreso	TV St. Cruz del Norte, MB
N5)	106.3	BQ	R. Enciclopedia	S.Miguel Baños Jacán, MA
N7)	106.9	BR	Habana R.	Loma de la Cruz, CH
N7)	106.9	BR	Habana R. (e)	Habana Radio, CH
N1)	107.9	BA	R. Rebelde	Cumbre, MA
N1)	107.9	BA	R. Rebelde	Sagua la Grande, VC
N1)	107.9	BA	R. Rebelde	TV St. Cruz del Norte, MB
N1)	107.9	BA	R. Rebelde	Alamar San Pedro, CH
N3)	107.9	BF	R. Musical Nacional	S.Miguel Baños Jacán, MA
N6)	107.9	BV	R. Taíno	Plan Mangos, CI
N6)	107.9	BV	R. Taíno	San Isidro , SS
N6)	107.9	BV	R. Taíno	TV Ciego de Ávila, CA

Provincial & Municipal FM Stations (MHz):

AR) R. Artemisa: 90.7 Candelaria, 90.9 Bahía Honda, 91.5 San Cristóbal, 92.1 Artemisa, 92.9 Alquízar, 93.7 Mariel, 94.5 Guanajay, 96.1 Bauta, 102.3 Candelaria-TV Salón, 104.1 Güira de Melena, 105.7 Caimito – **R. Ariguanabo:** 105.3 & 107.5 S.Antonio de los Baños

CA) R. Surco: 91.5 TV Ciego de Ávila, 93.7 Ciro Redondo, 94.1 Bolivia, 95.3 TV Ciego de Ávila, 96.1 Baraguá, 101.3 Tamarindo, 101.7 Majagua, 102.7 TV Ciego de Ávila, 107.9 TV Punta Alegre – **R. Morón**: 90.1 TV Tamarindo, 98.9 Morón – **R. Chambas:** 90.7 Estudios Chambas – **R. Amanecer:** 96.9 Primero de Enero

CH) R. Cadena Habana: 99.9 Televilla – **R. Ciudad Habana:** 94.7 Habana Libre, 94.7 Televilla – **R. Metropolitana:** 98.3 Habana Libre – R. Coco: 91.7 Habana Libre – **R. Habana Cuba:** 102.5 Focsa, 103.2 La Habana

CI) R. Ciudad del Mar: 91.1 Palmira, 95.9 Rodas, 98.5 Lajas, 98.9 Estudio Cienfuegos, 101.1 Abreus, 106.3 Plan Mangos – **R. Cumanayagua:** 95.1 Estud. Cumanayagua, 105.5 Crucecitas – **R. Cruces** "LV de los Molinos": 99.3 Cruces – **Aguada R.:** 105.1 Aguada

CM) R. Cadena Agramonte: 92.5 Jimaguayú, 96.7 Sibanicú, 99.7 Najasa, 105.3 TV FM Camagüey, 105.9 FM Sta. Cruz del Sur – R. Guáimaro: 90.3 Estudios Guáimaro – **R. Cubitas:** 95.7 Estudios Cubitas – **La Voz del Bayatabo**: 98.5 Minas – **R. Nuevitas:** 103.5 TV Nuevitas – **R. Santa Cruz:** 104.3 Sta. Cruz del Sur – R. Florida: 104.5 Florida Etecsa – **R. Esmeralda:** 105.9 Esmeralda – R. Vertientes: 104.1 Vertientes

GR) CMKX R. Bayamo: 90.1 Cauto Cristo, 90.7 Yara, 91.7 Campechuela, 96.3 Media Luna, 99.5 Bartolomé Masó, 100.3 Río Cauto, 102.1 Comunitaria Masó, 104.7 Comunitaria, 105.9 Buey Arriba – **R. Granma:** 96.5 Estudio Manzanillo – **CMND R. Jiguaní:** 91.9 Estudios Jiguaní – **R. Portada de la Libertad:** 95.1 El Mamey, 100.7 Niquero – **R. Ciudad Monumento:** 95.3 Bayamo

GU) CMKS R. Trinch.Antiimp: 92.1 Niceto Pérez, 93.1 Manuel Tames, 93.7 El Salvador, 94.7 Yateras, 95.5 Cueva Arriba, 99.9 Los Guineos, 100.3 Imías – **CMDX R. Baracoa**: 90.1 Los Guineos – **La Voz del Sol:** 91.1 Estudio Maisí – **R. Bahía:** 104.3 Estudios Caimanera – **R. Playita:** 100.3 Imías // 1370kHz

HO) R. Angulo: 91.7 Cueto, 92.9 Báguanos, 93.9 Rafael Freyre, 94.1 Cacocum, 95.1 Antillas, 97.7 Loma de la Cruz, 102.1 Frank País – **Ecos de Sagua:** 102.9 TV Miraflores – **La Voz del Níquel:** 92.7 TV Miraflores – **R. Juvenil:** 93.7 Calixto García, 93.7 Estudios C. García – **R. Gibara:** 94.9 Velasco, 107.9 Gibara – **R. Holguín:** 96.1 Loma de la Cruz – **R. SG** "LV del Azucar": 106.9 Estudios San Germán

IJ) R. Caribe: 93.5 Cocodrilo, 101.7 Sierra Caballos

LT) R. Victoria: 95.5 Puerto Padre, 103.9 Jobabo, 104.9 TV Tunas – **R. Libertad:** 93.3 Puerto Padre, 93.3 Puerto Padre – **R. Chaparra:** 90.9 Jesús Menéndez – **R. Manatí** "LV del Faro": 92.9 Estudios Manatí

MA) CMGW R. 37: 90.1 Jovellanos, 90.5 Los Arabos, 91.5 Perico, 92.1 Limonar, 92.7 Pedro Betancourt, 93.1 Martí, 96.3 Unión de Reyes, 97.3 Estudios Matanzas, 97.7 Calimete, 99.5 Ciénaga de Zapata, 99.9 El Brinco, 104.3 S.Miguel Baños Jacán – **R. Ciudad Bandera:** 99.7 Cárdenas – **R. Victoria de Girón:** 93.7 Ciénaga de Zapata, 95.3 Jagüey Grande – **R. Varadero:** 98.1 Varadero – **La Voz de la Victoria:** 99.5 Ciénaga de Zapata, 99.9 El Brinco – **R. Llanura de Colón:** 101.1 Colón

MB) R. Mayabeque: 90.7 Nueva Paz, 91.3 Madruga, 91.9 San Nicolás, 92.5 Batabanó, 95.9 Güines, 102.7 Bejucal, 104.7 Televilla, CH, 105.9 Melena del Sur – **R. Jaruco:** 92.3 Jaruco, 105.1 Loma Travieso – **CMCW R. Camoa:** 97.9 TV Loma la Candela, 103.9 S. José de Las Lajas – **La Voz del Litoral:** 102.5 TV St. Cruz del Norte

PR) R. Guamá: 90.1 La Palma, 91.3 San Juan y Martínez, 92.3 Los Palacios, 92.5 Viñales, 93.1 San Luis, 96.3 Cajalbana, 96.7 Consolación del Sur, 96.7 Mantua, 103.5 TV Guanito, 105.1 Guane – **R. Sandino:** 98.5 Estudios Sandino – **R. Minas:** 104.9 Estudios Minas de M

SC) CMKC R. Revolución: 95.1 Puerto Boniato – **CMKW R. Mambí:** 93.7 Puerto Boniato – **R. Titán:** 96.9 Estudios Mella – **R. 8SF:** 92.3 Estudios II Frente – **CMKZ R. Baraguá:** 91.3 Palma Soriano – **CMDV R. Siboney:** 90.5 Puerto Boniato – **R. Triple M/CMKC:** 92.5 Estudios III Frente – **R. Grito de Baire:** 103.9 Estudios Cotramestre – **R. Majaguabo:** 104.7 Estudios San Luis – **Sonido SM:** 105.5 Estud. Songo-La Maya

SS) R. Sancti Spíritus: 90.5 Fomento, 90.7 Topes de Collantes, 93.1 Taguasco, 96.5 La Vigía, 106.3 San Isidro, 106.3 TV las Llamadas, – **R. Trinidad:** 90.1 Trinidad – **R. Vitral/R.Sancti Spíritus:** 101.1 San Isidro – **R. Jatibonico:** 105.1 Jatibonico – **La Voz de Cabaiguán:** 105.5 Cabaiguán – **R. Yaguajay:** 91.3 Yaguajay, 94.5 TV las Llamadas

VC) CMHW: 92.3 Camajuani, 92.3 Corralillo, 94.3 Ranchuelo, 95.5 Santo Domingo, 99.1 Encrucijada, 99.7 Cifuentes, 101.5 Loma dos Hermanas, 105.7 Manicaragua – **R. Sagua:** 105.9 Quemado de Güines, 106.3 Sagua la Grande – **CMHS R. Caibarién:** 90.9 & 94.1 TV Caibarién, 95.7 Caibarién Playa, 107.1 Remedios – **Estereocentro:** 93.5 Loma dos Hermanas – **R. Placetas:** 94.9 Placetas

Addresses: & Other Information
National networks: N1) R. Rebelde, Ap. 6277, La Habana 10600 (or Edif. Del ICRT, Av. 23 N° 258, Vedado, La Habana 10400) **W:** radiorebelde.cu – **N2)** R. Reloj, Ap. 6277, Ciudad de La Habana (or Ed. Radiocentro, Calle 23 No. 258, (8avo piso), entre Ly M, Vedado, La Habana 10400 **W:** radioreloj.cu – **N3)** R. Musical Nacional, Edificio N, Calle N, entre 23 y 21, Vedado La Habana 10400 **W:** cmbfradio.cu – **N4)** R. Progreso, Ap. 4042, La Habana 10300 (or Infanta 105, Esq. A 25, Centro Habana) **W:** radioprogreso.cu – **N5)** R. Enciclopedia, Edificio N, Calle N. N° 266 (bajos), entre 21 y 23, Vedado, La Habana 10400 **W:** radioenciclopedia.cu – **N6)** R. Taíno, Ap. 6277, La Habana 10400 (or Av. 23 N° 258, Vedado, La Habana 10400) - FM only – **N7)** Lamparilla No. 2 Edificio Lonja del Comercio, 10100 La Habana **W:** habanaradio.cu - FM only
Provincial & Municipal Stations:
ARTEMISA: AR01) Calle 50 No. 2310, entre 23 y 25, Artemisa 33800 **W:** artemisaradioweb.icrt.cu
CIEGO DE ÁVILA: CA01) Ap. 183 (or Chicho Valdés 66), Ciego de Ávila 65100 **W:** radiosurco.icrt.cu
CIUDAD DE LA HABANA: CH01) Calle 15, esq. a J, No. 210, Vedado, Plaza de la Revolución, La Habana 10400 **W:** cadenahabana.cu – **CH02)** Ap. 6599, La Habana 10600 (or Calle N No. 266 (5to piso), entre 21 y 23, Vedadado, Plaza de la Revolución, La Habana 10400) **W:** radiociudadhabana.icrt.cu – **CH03)** Ed. Focsa, Calle N No. 301 (1er piso), esq. A 17, Vedado, Plaza de la Revolución, La Habana 10400 **W:** radiometropolitana.cu – **CH04)** Ed. Focsa, Calle N No. 301, esq. A 17, Vedado, Plaza de la Revolución, La Habana 10400 **W:** radiococo.icrt.cu
CIENFUEGOS: CI01) Calle 37 No. 3602, entre 36 y 38, Cienfuegos 55100 **W:** rcm.cu
CAMAGÜEY: CM01) Calle Cisneros # 310 entre Ignacio Agramonte y General Gómez, Camagüey 70100 **W:** cadenagramonte.cu – **CM02) W:** radiocamaguey.wordpress.com Camagüey 1200-1800, Cadena Agramonte 1800-1200
GRANMA: GR01) Ap. 74 (or Calle General Calixto García 156, entre Figueredo y Luz Vásquez 74) Bayamo 85100 **W:** radiobayamo.icrt.cu – **GR02)** Ap. 220 (or Calle Martí 341, entre Quintin Banderas y León), Manzanillo 87510 **W:** radiogranma.co.cu
GUANTÁNAMO: GU01) "Trinchera Antiimperialista", Ap. 96 (or Donato Mármol 409, entre José Martí y Pedro A. Pérez), Guantánamo 95100 **W:** radioguantanamo.icrt.cu – **GU02)** Calle Martí #122, % Frank País y Maraví, Baracoa 97310. H of tr: 1000-0200 **W:** radiobaracoa.icrt.cu – **GU03)** Calle B No. 2050, Imías 97500 **W:** facebook.com/Emisora-Radio-Playita-683062335045536
HOLGUÍN: HO01) Ap. 14 (or Calle Máximo Gómez 298 (3er piso) entre Frexes y Martí), Holguín 80100 **W:** radioangulo.cu – **HO02)** Sagua de Tánamo 83200 **W:** facebook.com/RadioEcosDeSagua – **HO03)** Calle Martí 46, Mayarí 83000
ISLA DE LA JUVENTUD: IJ01) Calle 26, entre 41 y 43, Nueva Gerona 25100 **W:** radiocaribe.icrt.cu
LAS TUNAS LT01) Ap. 211 (or Calle Colón 157, entre Julián Santana y Francisco Vega), Las Tunas 75100 **W:** tiempo21.cu – **LT02)** Avenida Sergio Reynó 19, Amancio Rodriguez 77700 **W:** radiomaboas.cu – **LT03)** Calle Donato Mármol # 65 Entre Avenida Máximo Gómez y Ángel Ameijeiras. Puerto Padre, Las Tunas 77210. **W:** radiolibertad.cu – **LT04)** Emisora Radio Chaparra. Municipio Jesús Menéndez. Las Tunas. **W:** twitter.com/cmlbradio
MATANZAS: MA01) Ap. 51 (or Milanés final, esq. a Guachinango), Matanzas 40100 **W:** radio26.icrt.cu – **MA02)** Calzada, esq. a Calvo, Cárdenas 42100 **W:** radiociudadbandera.wordpress.com
MAYABEQUE: MB01) Calle 76 No. 7707, entre 77 y 81, Güines 33900. 1100-0500 exc. 24h in July/August. **W:** radiomayabeque.icrt.cu
PINAR DEL RÍO: PR01) Calle Colón 14, entre Adela Azcuy y Juan Gualberto Gómez, Pinar del Río 20100 **W:** rguama.icrt.cu
SANTIAGO DE CUBA: SC01) Ap. 232 (or Aguilera 554, entre San Augustín y Barnada), Santiago de Cuba 90100 **W:** cmkc.cu – **SC02)** R. Coral, Calle C No. 64, Chivirico, Guamá 92800 – **SC03)** Calle 8 No. 56, entre A e Independencia, Reparto Sueño, Santiago de Cuba 90900 **W:** radiomambi.icrt.cu – **SC04)** Radio Titán, Calle Central - Esq. 3ra S/N, Mella, Santiago de Cuba **W:** radiotitan.icrt.cu – **SC05)** Mayarí Arriba, Stgo. de Cuba **W:** radio8sf.icrt.cu – **SC06)** Calle Massó # 59 esquina Agramonte, Palma Soriano, Stgo. de Cuba **W:** radiobaragua.cu
SANCTI SPÍRITUS: SS01) Circunvalación s/n, Los Olivos 1, Sancti Spíritus 60100. **W:** radiosanctispiritus.cu
VILLA CLARA: VC01) Ap. 376 (or Parque Leoncio Vidal 4, entre Martha Abreu y Pao Chao), Santa Clara 50100 **W:** cmhw.cu – **VC02)** Libertadores 100, esq. a Carmen Ribalta, Sagua la Grande, Villa Clara 52310 **W:** radiosagua.icrt.cu

Guantánamo Bay (leased to USA)

AFN GUANTÁNAMO BAY
🖂 Naval Media Center Broadcasting Detatchment, Guantánamo Bay, Cuba, PSC 1005, Box 22, FPO AE 09593, USA **W:** navy.mil/local/gtmo
MW: Talk Radio: Guantánamo Bay 1340kHz 0.25kW.
FM: The Mix: 102.1MHz 0.5kW, The Blitz: 103.1MHz 0.5kW

CURAÇAO (Netherlands)

L.T: UTC -4h — **Pop:** 162,000 — **Pr.L:** Papiamentu (official), Dutch (official), English (official), Spanish — **E.C:** 127/50Hz (most widespread), 220V/50Hz — **ITU:** CUW

Bureau Telecommunicatie en Post
🖂 Beatrixlaan 9, Emmastad; P.O. Box 2047, Curaçao ☎ +599 9 463 1700 📠 +599 9 736 5265 **W:** btnp.org **E:** gen.affairs@burtel.cw

MW	Call	kHz	kW	Station, location
1)	PJZ-86	860	10	Z-86 R. Curom, Willemstad

FM	MHz	kW	Station, location
1)	88.3		Rockorsou, Willemstad
23)	88.9		Blue Sky FM, Willemstad
12)	89.7		R. Krioyo, Willemstad
24)	90.9	0.83	How R., Willemstad
22)	91.5	0.75	HITradio 915, Willemstad
11)	92.1		R. Life 92.1 FM, Willemstad
9)	92.7		R. Edukativo, Deltha 92, Willemstad
20)	93.3	0.5	Tele Curaçao FM, Willemstad
3)	93.9	2.5	P.I08 R. Korsou FM, Willemstad
19)	94.5	0.5	R. 94.5 FM, Willemstad
8)	95.1	0.5	Clazz FM, Willemstad
1)	95.7	10	Mi-95FM, Willemstad
13)	96.5	0.5	New Song, Willemstad
10)	97.3	1	Dolfijn FM, Willemstad
8)	97.9	0.5	Easy 97.9 FM, Willemstad
4)	98.5	0.5	R. Semiya, Willemstad
21)	99.1	0.5	R. Lighthouse, Willemstad
15)	99.7		R. MAS, Santa Maria
7)	100.3		Hit 100.3, Willemstad
3)	101.1	2.5	PJ09 Laser 101, Willemstad
2)	101.9	2.5	R. Hoyer 1, Willemstad
5)	103.1	0.75	Paradise FM, Willemstad
8)	103.9	0.5	R. One FM, Willemstad
14)	104.5	1	R. Active FM, Willemstad
2)	105.1	2.5	R. Hoyer 2, Willemstad
16)	106.3		Fiesta FM, Willemstad
11)	107.1		R. Direct, Willemstad
6)	107.9	1	Rumbera Network, Willemstad

Addresses & other information:
1) Curom Broadcasting Curaçao, Roodeweg 62, Willemstad, Curaçao ☎ +599 9 462 2020 88Rockorsou: hip hop and R&B Mi-95FM: adult contemporary music Z86: news talk **W:** curom.cw– **2)** Plasa Horacio Hoyer 21, Willemstad, Curaçao ☎ +599 9 461 8679 **E:** sales@radiohoyer.com **W:** radiohoyer.com GM: Gwenny Visser R. Hoyer 1 in Papiamentu 0930-0400, R. Hoyer 2 in Dutch 1000-0400 – **3)** Bataljonweg 7, Willemstad, Dir.Dianthe Isa-Oosterhof ☎ +599 9 738 5670 📠 +599 9 737 2888. 24h in Dutch and Papiamentu **E:** studio@korsou.com **W:** korsou.com Separate prgrs on "Laser 101" on 101.1MHz, mainly music, announcements in English and Papiamentu ☎ +599 9 738 5670 **E:** studio@laser-101.com **W:** laser-101.com – **4)** Parmantierweg 2, Willemstad ☎ +599 9 462 4000/4002/4004/4005 Dir: Saïd R. Flores. Rlg 24h prgrs in English, Dutch, Spanish and Papiamentu **E:** radiosemiya@hotmail.com **W:** radiosemiya.org– **5)** Fokkerweg 26, Willemstad or PO Box 6103, Willemstad ☎ +599 9 462 8103 **W:** paradisefmcuracao.cw **E:** info@paradisefm.cw Dutch, with every hour Dutch news and every half hour local (Curaçao) news. Owner: C.L. Baas – **6)** Caracasbaaiweg 194, Willemstad ☎ +599 9 461 5027 **W:** rumberacuracao.com– **7)** Compleho Deportivo Casa Grandi Z/N Willemstad ☎ +599 9 747 3333 📠 +599 9 747 1003 Manager: Elmer Cijntje. 24h Prgrs in Papiamentu, Spanish, Creole and English – **8)** Arikokweg 19A, Willemstad ☎ +599 9 462 3162 📠 +599 9 462 8712. GM: Quintus Fliervoet ClazzFM **E:** info@clazzfm.com **W:** clazzfm.com 24h light music & jazz in E, Papiamentu & Dutch, R. One FM **E:** quintus@radioone.cw **W:** radioone.cw 24h dance & Top 40 music in E, & Dutch. Easy FM **W:** easyfm.com **E:** radio@easyfm.com 24h adult contemporary – **9)** Suffisantweg 18, Willemstad ☎ +599 9 868 8892📠 +599 9 888 5260 and + 599 9 869 3878 **E:** info@radiodeltha927.com – **10)** Sea Aquarium Beach Blvd

#21B, Willemstad ☎ +599 9 461 09734 🖹 599 9 461 9975 Station Manager: Egon Sybrandy **D.Prgr.** 24 hours in Dutch **E:** info@dolfijnfm.com **W:** dolfijnfm.com – **11)** Direct Media Curaçao, F.D Rooseveltweg 214, Tesoro Shopping Center, Willemstad Dir. Mrs. Jachmin Pinedo R. Direct: in Papiamentu and Spanish 1000-0400, other times music ☎ +599 9 888 5107 🖹 +599 9 888 8407 **W:** direct107.com Direct Life 92.1FM in Papiamentu and Dutch, interviews also in Dutch, English and Spanish 1030-1300 and 1800-2400 , other times music ☎+599 9 888 4107 🖹 +599 9 888 8407 **E:** 921local@gmail.com **W:** direct92.com – **12)** Gosieweg 133,Willemstad ☎ +599 9 736 4915 🖹 +599 9 736 4914 **E:** radiokrioyo@live.com – **13)** New Song Building, Muizenberg z/n ☎ +599 9 888 0965 🖹 +599 9 868 4343 **Dir.** Welton F.A. Esprit ; Christian prgrs 24 h in English, French, Papiamentu, Dutch, Spanish,– **14)** Kaya Simon Pieters Kwiers 67, Willemstad ☎+599 9 560 3302 Dir. Arthur Zimmerman 24h in Papiamentu **W:** active.fm **E:** info@active.fm – **15)** Fosfaatweg 8, Sta. Maria ☎+599 9 888 4997 🖹 +599 9 888 6997 **E:**info@mas99.com – **16)** Fatimaweg 2, Suffisant, Willemstad ☎+599 9 869 6606 🖹 +599 9 869 6613 Dir. Carlos S. de Abreu Ribeiro **W:** fiesta.fm– **19)** Arikokweg 30, Charo Dir: Feliciano da Silva Piloto ☎+599 717 5947 🖹 +599 717 8220 **W:** vozdibonaire.com **E:** vozdibonaire@gmail.com Music and information, 24 hrs in Papiamentu – **20)** Berg Arafat z/n, Willemstad , GMr: Hugo Lew Jen Tai ☎+599 9 777 1288 and +599 9 461 5933 Prgrs 24 hrs in Papiamentu **E:** hugo@telecuracao.com– **21)** Totonakenweg z/n, Groot Kwartier ☎+599 9 973 64805 Dir. Robert Braumuller **E:** radiolh01@gmail.com **D.Prgr.** 24h in Dutch, Papiamentu, English and Spanish – **22)** Fokkerweg 26, PO Box 6103, Willemstad ☎+599 9 462 8103, Dir. C.L. Baas **W:** hitradio915.com **E:** info@hitradio915.com **D.Prgr.** 24h in Dutch, non-stop latest hits News: every h; news highlights every half h. – **23)** ☎+599 9 463 6490 **E:**curacaoblueskyfm@gmail.com -**24)** Rondeklipweg 48, Willemstad, Dir.Beverley Mathilda ☎+599 9 738 4344 (office) and +599 9 747 8909 (live studio), Pgrs: International & local gospel music (this may include salsa, Latin, American music, local music); Languages: Papiamentu, Dutch, Spanish and English **W:**how-online.org **E:** howradiocuracao@gmail.com

CYPRUS

L.T: UTC +2h (28 Mar-31 Oct: +3h) — **Pop:** 1.2 million — **Pr.L:** Greek (official), Turkish (official), Armenian — **E.C:** 240V/50Hz — **ITU:** CYP

ARCHI RADIOTILEORASIS KYPROU
(Cyprus Radiotelevision Agency)

🖃 42 Athalassas Ave., 2012 Nicosia (P.O.Box 23377, 1682 Nicosia) ☎ +357 22512468 🖹 +357 22512472 **E:** crtauthority@crta.org.cy **W:** www.crta.org.cy **L.P:** Chair: Rona Petri Kassapi

CYPRUS BROADCASTING CORPORATION (CYBC) (Pub)

🖃 CyBC Street, Athalassa, P.O. Bxo 24824, CY-1397 Nicosia ☎+357 22 862000 🖹 +357 22 314050 **W:** cybc.com.cy **E:** info@cybc.com.cy

MW	kHz	kW	Ch.	MW	kHz	kW	Ch.
Nicosia	603	100	3	Nicosia	963	100	1

FM (MHz)	Ch. 1	Ch. 2	Ch. 3	Ch.4	kW
Armenochori	105.0	93.1	106.7	90.5	2
Mt. Olympos	97.2	91.1	94.8	88.2	30
Paphos	92.4	97.9	94.0	90.2	7
Paralimni	91.4	94.2	96.0	100.9	4

Ch. 1 (Proto) in Greek: 24h – **Ch. 2 (Deutero)** Turkish: 24h – **Ch. 3 (Trito)** in Greek: 24h – **Ch. 4 (Classic)** in Greek: 24h.
Ann: Greek: "Radiofonikon Idryma Kyprou". Turkish: "Burasi Kibris Radyo Yayin Korporasyonu". **IS:** "Avkoritssa" (guitar).

Other Stations (all MHz):
ANT1 FM: Larnaca 102.7, Paphos 103.7. **W:** ant1iwo.com/fm – **Dromos FM:** Larnaca 100.5, Limassol 100.3, Nicosia 106.7. **W:** facebook.com/dromosfmcy – **Kanali 6:** Limassol 98.6, Nicosia 106.0, Mount Phanos 107.0 **W:** kanali6.com.cy – **Kanali 7:** Nicosia 98.4, Limassol 102.1 **W:** kanali7.com – **Kiss FM:** Limassol 88.5, Nicosia 89.0. **W:** kissfm.com.cy – **Klik FM:** Limassol 89.6, Larnaca 98.2, Nicosia 105.5 **W:** klikfm.com.cy – **Logos R:** Mount Olympos 101.1, Larnaca 101.6 **W:** logosradio.com.cy – **Mix FM:** Limassol 90.8, Larnaca 102.2, Nicosia 102.3 **W:** mixfmradio.com – **R. Astra:** Mount Olympos 92.8, Larnaca 105.3 **W:** astra.com.cy – **R. Athina:** Limassol 88.7, Nicosia 100.7 **W:** radioathina.com – **R. Proto:** Agia Napa 87.9, Larnaca 89.4, Mount Olympos 99.3 **W:** radioproto.com.cy – **R. Sfera:** Paphos 96.8, Limassol 106.4 **W:** radiosfera.com.cy – **Rock FM:** Limassol 89.2, Paphos 98.5, Latchi 106.7 **W:** rockfmcyprus.com – **Russkoye Radio Cyprus:** Paphos 90.5, Larnaca 93.3, Nicosia 103.2, Limassol 105.7 **W:** russianwave.com.cy – **Super FM:** Larnaca 95.7, Paphos 103.4, Mount Olympos 104.8 **W:** superfmradio.com – **Super Sport FM:** Limassol 100.3, Larnaca 103.0, Nicosia 106.7 **W:** sport-fm.com.cy

Other Stations MW:
BBC World Sce: MW: Zakaki 639 & 720kHz: Arabic 0300-0700, 1800/1500-2100
Monte Carlo Doualiya & **Trans World R.** rel. on **MW:** 1233kHz 0200-2115.
For further details on these stns see International Radio section.

NORTHERN CYPRUS

YAYIN YÜKSEK KURULU (YYK)
(Supreme Broadcasting Council)

🖃 Server Somuncuoğlu Sk. No. 17, Köşklüçiftlik, Lefkoşa KKTC ☎ +90 392 2281368 **E:** info@kktcyyk.com **W:** www.kktcyyk.org
L.P: Chmn: Olgun Üstün

BAYRAK RADYO TELEVIZYON KURUMU (BRTK, Gov)

🖃 BRT Sitesi, Dr. Fasil Küçük Bulvari, Lefkoşa, Northern Cyprus, via Mersin 10, Turkey ☎+90 392 225 5555 🖹 +90 392 225 4991
W: brtk.net **E:** brt@brtk.net
L.P: DG: Mete Tümerkan. Head Tr. Dept: Mustafa Tosun.

FM	R.1	B.FM	B.Int.	R.Klasik	BTM	BRH	kW
Kantara	90.6	98.1	87.8	93.4			10/1
Selvilitepe	102.0	92.1/88.8	105.0	88.4/102.5	94.6	100.1	20/1
Lefkosa	89.6	94.2					0.3/10

R.1 (Bayrak Radyosu) in Turkish: 24h – **Bayrak FM** in Turkish: 24h – **Bayrak International** in English (also news in Turkish/Greek/German/Russian/French/Arabic): 24h – **Radyo Klasik:** 24h – **Bayrak Türk Müzigi**: 24h – **Bayrak Radyo Haber** (Turkish): 24h.

OTHER STATIONS FM (MHz):

	Station	W	E	kW	Location
1)	R. ODTÜ	103.1	-	1	Kalkanli
3)	As FM	97.7	95.2	1	Lefkoşa
4)	Sim FM	98.6	89.5	2.5/0.3	Lefkoşa
5)	Süper FM	98.9	-	1	Lefkoşa
6)	Metro FM	104.0	-	1	Lefkoşa
7)	Kral FM	106.9	-	1	Lefkoşa
8)	Kibris FM	103.4	100.2	5/2.5	Lefkoşa
9)	First FM	90.0	96.6	1/0.3	Lefkoşa
10)	Akdeniz FM	88.6	-	1	Lefkoşa
11)	R. Vatan Türkü	104.5	94.4	5/1	Lefkoşa
12)	R. Vatan Nihavent	100.4	89.8	5/3	Lefkoşa
13)	Dance FM	95.5	95.1	1	Lefkoşa
14)	Radyo T	96.6	-	1	Lefkoşa
15)	R. Güven	(89.2)90.4	90.8	5/2/5	Lefkoşa
16)	R. Plus	106.2	105.8	1	Magosa
17)	LAÜ FM	97.4	-	1	Lefke
18)	Mayis FM	96.0	101.3	1	Lefkoşa
21)	R. DAÜ	-	106.5	2	Magosa
22)	R. Enerji	93.1	100.0	1	Lefkoşa
23)	R. Havadis	107.8	-	2	Lefkoşa
24)	Ada FM	96.2	93.8	1	Lefkoşa
25)	Capital R.	93.8	99.4	1	Lefkoşa
26)	R. Vatan	87.5	104.3	5	Lefkoşa
27)	Ydü FM	88.0	-	1	Lefkoşa
28)	R. Juke	90.9	99.8	2.5/1	Lefkoşa
29)	Dream Live FM	104.2	102.8	2	Lefkoşa
30)	TRT FM	101.3	-	5	Lefkoşa
31)	R. Play FM	102.9	107.2	2/1	Lefkoşa

Tx sites: W (west) = Selvilitepe, E (east)= Kantara-Sinan Dagi.
All stns 24h.
1) radyoodtu.com.tr – **5)** superfm.gen.tr – **7)** kralfm.com.tr – **9)** kibrisfirstfm.net – **13)** dancefm.com.tr – **15)** radyoguven.com – **17)** radyo.eul.edu.tr – **18)** radyomayis.com – **21)** facebook.com/dautvradyodau – **22)** radyoenerji.com – **23)** radyohavadis.com – **24)** adafmkibris.com – **25)** capitalcyprus.com – **27)** neu.edu.tr – **28)** radyoujuke.com – **29)** dreamfmlivecyprus.com – **31)** playfm.com.tr

AKROTIRI & DHEKELIA (UK)

Pop: 15,700 (7,700 excl. UK military personnel and dependents) — **Pr.L:** English, Greek — **E.C:** 240V/50Hz — **ITU:** CYP

FORCES RADIO BFBS CYPRUS (Mil.)
✉ BFBS Akrotiri, BFPO 57, UK ☎ +357 2527 8518 🖷 +357 2527 8580
W: forces.net/radio/stations/bfbs-cyprus **E:** cyprus@bfbs.com

FM (MHz)	Forces R. CY	BFBS R.2	kW
Akrotiri	89.9	92.1	25
Ayios Nikolaos	107.3	89.7	
Dhekelia	99.6	95.3	25
Nicosia	91.7	89.7	1.5

D.Prgr: 24h. **Ann:** "Forces Radio BFBS"

CZECHIA

L.T: UTC +1h (28 Mar-31 Oct: +2h) — **Pop:** 10.1 million — **Pr.L:** Czech — **E.C:** 230V/50Hz — **ITU:** CZE

RADA PRO ROZHLASOVÉ A TELEVIZNÍ VYSÍLÁNÍ (RRTV) (Council for Radio and Television Broadcasting)
✉ Škrétova 44/6, 12000 Praha 2 ☎ +420 274813830 🖷 +420 274810885 **E:** podatelna@rrtv.cz **W:** www.rrtv.cz
L.P: Chmn: Ivan Krejci

CESKÉ RADIOKOMUNIKACE, a.s.
✉ U nákladového nádrazí 4, 130 00 Praha 3 ☎ +420 267 005 111 **E:** info@radiokomunikace.cz **W:** radiokomunikace.cz
Operates the TV and radio transmission facilities.

CESKY ROZHLAS (CZECH RADIO) (Pub)
✉ Vinohradská 12, 120 99 Praha 2 ☎ +420 221 551 111 🖷 +420 221 551 300 **E:** info@rozhlas.cz **W:** rozhlas.cz
L.P: DG: René Zavoral PD: Ondrej Novácek TD: Karel Zyka

LW & MW:	kHz	kW	Prgr.
Uherské Hradište	270	50	CRo 1
Praha (Liblice)	639	750	CRo 2
Ostrava-Svinov	639	30	CRo 2
Brno (Dobrochov)	954	200	CRo 2
Ceské Budejovice	954	30	CRo 2
Karlovy Vary	954	20	CRo 2
Ceské Budejovice	1071	5	CRo Plus
Ostrava-Svinov	1071	5	CRo Plus
Moravské Budejovice	1332	25	CRo 2

FM (MHz)	CRo 1	CRo 2	CRo 3	CRo 5	CRoPlus	kW
9) As	107.9	-	-	96.7	-	0.1/0.2
1) Benešov	-	-	-	99.0	104.0	1(5)/0.1
6) Brno	95.1	102.0	-	106.5	-	72/91/72
6) Brno (city)	-	-	90.4	93.1	92.6	6/6/2
2) C. Budejovice	91.1	103.7	96.1	106.4	-	80/1/40/80
C. Krumlov		-	-		98.2	0.2
9) Cheb	-	88.2	106.2	100.8	89.5	1
4) Chomutov	98.9	94.2	96.3	103.1	-	10
Decín	-	105.4	-		100.8	0.1
3) Domazlice	98.0	-		105.3	-	10
13) Frydlant	-	-	-	97.4	-	0.2
6) Hodonín	106.2	107.8	100.4	93.6	-	9/3/9
5) Hradec Králové	-	-	-	95.3	-	1
11) Hradec Králové	-	-	-	104.7	-	10
8) Hulín	-	-	-	101.6	-	1
13) Jablonné	-	-	-	105.4	-	0.1
9) Jáchymov	-	-	-	103.4	-	1
8) Jeseník	91.3	88.7	98.2	106.8	-	20/0.2/20/20
Jicín	-	106.9	-		-	1
10) Jihlava	90.7	107.1	88.4	87.9	95.4	20/10/20/10
Kaplice	-	-	105.9		-	0.2
9) Karlovy Vary	102.6	-	105.7	91.0	97.8	0.1/0.2/1
Kašperské Hory	-	-	107.2		-	0.5
1) Kladno		-	-	100.5	-	0.2
3) Klatovy	99.8	90.3	88.6	102.4	-	10
1) Kutná Hora	-	102.2	-	100.5	-	1/3
13) Liberec	95.9	89.9	103.9	102.3	-	20/20/20/1
Liberec	-	-	-		91.3	0.5
8) Lipník n.Becvou	-	-	-	88.7	-	0.1
Litomerice	-	100.0	-		92.8	0.1
9) Marián.Lázne	97.6	-	-	100.8	-	1
1) Mladá Boleslav	-	-	-	100.3	-	0.5
Nové Hrady	-	102.2	-		-	1
8) Olomouc	-	-	-	92.8	107.2	1
7) Opava	-	101.7	-	102.6	-	1/0.5
7) Ostrava	101.4	101.9	104.8	107.3	-	43/0.5/43/3
11) Pardubice	89.7	100.1	102.7	101.0	-	90/90/90/1
Písek	97.0	98.9	105.2		-	1
Plzen (North)	89.1	101.7	95.6		-	80
3) Plzen (East)	99.2	-	-	106.7	93.3	10
3) Plzen (city)	-	-	-	91.0	-	1
Prachatice	-	-	-		98.0	0.1
1) Praha	-	-	-	100.7	-	50
Praha (city)	94.6	91.2	105.0		92.6	5/3/5/7
1) Príbram	102.2	107.0	-	100.0	103.6	0.4/1/1
13) Prosec n.N.	-	-	-	102.3	-	1
1) Rakovník	-	-	-	100.4	-	1
5) Rychnov n.K.	-	-	-	96.5	-	1
2) Slavonice	-	103.3	-	88.2	-	1
3) Sokolov	94.3	-	-	98.2	-	0.4
Sušice	90.6	89.7	-	-	97.9	0.1
11) Svitavy	-	-	-	102.4	-	1
Sumperk					101.2	0.2
3) Tachov	-	-	-	106.3	-	0.4
Teplice	-	-	-	-	103.6	0.1
10) Trebíc	-	-	-	90.1	-	0.2
7) Trinec	92.1	-	-	105.3	-	1
5) Trutnov	88.5	93.4	-	90.5	101.9	10/10/20
13) Turnov	-	-	-	91.5	-	0.1
12) Uher. Hradište	-	-	-	99.1	-	0.2
12) Uhersky Brod	93.0	-	-	107.3	-	1
4) Ustí nad Labem	90.9	-	104.5	88.8	-	80
Ustí n.L.(city)	-	98.6	-	-	93.9	1
11) Ustí n. Orlicí	-	-	-	98.6	-	1
7) Val. Mezirící	92.5	89.9	96.8	99.0	-	7/1/7/7
4) Varnsdorf	-	-	88.4	98.5	-	0.2
11) Velké Opatovice	-	-	-	93.7	101.5	0.2
Vlašim					91.0	0.1
Votice	93.1	103.2	-	-	-	95
13 Vratislavice	-	-	-	91.3	-	0.5
7) Vrbno pod Prad.	-	103.6	-	95.5	-	1
12) Vsetín	92.1	102.9	98.3	89.5	-	0.1
11) Vysoké Myto	-	-	-	88.9	-	0.2
11) Zamberk	-	-	-	103.3	-	0.1
3) Zelezná Ruda	-	-	-	95.8	-	0.2
12) Zlín	99.5	107.7	94.8	97.5	-	6
6) Znojmo	101.2	89.6	99.2	97.3	-	1/3/3/1

CRo 1 (Radiozurnál): 24h (LW: Mon-Sat 0400-2300, Sun 0500-2300). **N:** on the h – **CRo 2 (Dvoyka):** 24h (MW: Mon-Fri 0300-2300, Sat+Sun 0400-2300) – **CRo 3 (Vltava):** 24h – **CRo 4 (Radio Wave):** 24h (on internet only **W:** rozhlas.cz/radiowave/portal) – **CRo 5 regional stations:** 24h own prgrs and relays of other regional stns (esp. in the night) – **CRo Plus:** 24h **N:** every 30 minutes

Addresses & other information:
CRo Radio DAB Praha, Hybešova 10, 186 72 Praha 8 **W:** rozhlas.cz/regina (On DAB+ only) – **1)** CRo Region - Strední Cechy, Hybešova 10, 186 72 Praha 8 **W:** rozhlas.cz/strednicechy – **2)** CRo Ceské Budejovice, U Trí lvu 1, 370 29 Ceské Budejovice **W:** rozhlas.cz/cb – **3)** CRo Plzen, Nám. Míru 10, 320 70 Plzen **W:** rozhlas.cz/plzen – **4)** CRo Sever (=North), Na schodech 10, 400 91 Ústí nad Labem **W:** rozhlas.cz/sever – **5)** CRo Hradec Králové, Havlíckova 292, 501 01 Hradec Králové **W:** rozhlas.cz/hradec – **6)** CRo Brno, Beethovenova 4, 657 42 Brno **W:** rozhlas.cz/brno – **7)** CRo Ostrava, Dr. Šmerala 2, 729 91 Ostrava (Polish: Mon-Fri 1804-1830) **W:** rozhlas.cz/ostrava – **8)** CRo Olomouc, Horní námestí 21, 771 06 Olomouc **W:** rozhlas.cz/ol – **9)** CRo Karlovy Vary, Zítkova 3, 360 00 Karlovy Vary: 0400-0800, 1300-1500, otherwise CRo Plzen **W:** vary.rozhlas.cz – **10)** CRo Vysocina, Masarykovo nám 42, 586 01 Jihlava **W:** vysocina.rozhlas.cz – **11)** CRo Pardubice, Sv. Anežky Ceské 29, 530 02 Pardubice **W:** rozhlas.cz/pardubice – **12)** CRo Zlín, Osvoboditelu 187, 760 01 Zlín **W:** zlin.rozhlas.cz – **13)** CRo Liberec, Modrá 1048, 460 06 Liberec **W:** rozhlas.cz/liberec/portal

EXTERNAL SERVICE: Radio Prague International
See International Broadcasting section.

MAJOR PRIVATE STATIONS/NETWORKS:
RADIO IMPULS (Comm.)
✉ Ortenovo nám. 15a, 170 00 Praha 7 ☎ +420 255 700 700 🖷 +420 255 700 727 **E:** impuls@radioimpuls.cz **W:** radioimpuls.cz
FM: see list below. **D.Prgr:** 24h
RADIO FREKVENCE 1 (Comm.)
✉ Wenzigova 4, 120 00 Praha 2 ☎ +420 257 001 111 🖷 +420 257 314 183 **E:** frekvence1@frekvence1.cz **W:** frekvence1.cz
FM: see list below. **D.Prgr:** 24h

EVROPA 2 (Comm.)
✉ Wenzigova 4, 120 00 Praha 2 ☎ +420 257 001 111 🖷 +420 257 001 807 **E:** info@evropa2.cz **W:** evropa2.cz
FM: see list below. **D.Prgr:** 24h
KISS (Comm.)
✉ Rícanská 3, 101 00 Praha 10-Vinohrady ☎ +420 601 111 601 **E:** studio@kiss.cz, program@kiss.cz **W:** kiss.cz **FM:** see list below. **D.Prgr:** 24h
RADIO PROGLAS (Relg)
✉ Barvicova 85, 602 00 Brno ☎ +420 543 217 241-3 🖷 +420 543 217 245 **E:** radio@proglas.cz **W:** proglas.cz **FM:** see list below. **D.Prgr:** 24h
COUNTRY RADIO (Comm.)
✉ Ricanská 3, 101 00 Praha 10-Vinohrady ☎ +420 251 024 111 🖷 +420 251 024 224 **E:** info@countryradio.cz **W:** countryradio.cz
MW: Praha 1062kHz 20kW (0500-1800), 1kW (1800-0500) **FM:** see list below. **D.Prgr:** 24h
RADIO DECHOVKA (Comm.)
✉ U Prutníku 232, 250 72 Predboj ☎ +420 311 280 281 **E:** program@radiodechovka.cz **W:** radiodechovka.cz

MW:	kHz	kW	MW:	kHz	kW
Hradec Králové	792	10	Ceské Budejovice	1233	2
Praha-Zbraslav	1233	10	Ostrava-Svinov	1233	2
Brno/Dobrochov	1233	5			

FM: see list below. **D.Prgr:** 24h
RADIO CESKY IMPULS (Comm.)
✉ Ortenovo nám. 15a, 170 00 Praha 7 ☎ (studio) +420 255 700 701 **E:** moderator@ceskyimpuls.cz **W:** ceskyimpuls.cz
MW: Praha (Líbeznice-Boranovice) 981kHz 10kW, Moravské Budejovice (Domamil) 981kHz 5kW, Litomysl 981kHz **(F.Pl.)**, Hradec Králové 981kHz **(F.Pl.)**. **D.Prgr:** 24h
RADIO ZET (Comm.)
✉ Wenzigova 4, 120 00 Praha 2 ☎ +420 257 001 240 **E:** info@zet.cz **W:** zet.cz **FM:** see list below. **D.Prgr:** 24h. Own prgr in Czech: Mon-Fri 0500-1700, Sat+Sun 0600-1700 (BBC WS relay in English: Sun-Thu 1700-0500, Fri+Sat 1700-0600).

Commercial FM Stations:

MHz	kW	Station	Location
87.6	70	R. Impuls	Brno
87.8	1	R. Blaník	Praha
87.8	1	Hitrádio Cerná hora	Králíky
88.1	1	R. Evropa 2	Liberec
88.1	10	Hitrádio Orion	Jeseník
88.2	5	R. Evropa 2	Praha
88.3	10	Kiss	Brno
88.4	1	R. Blaník	Ceské Budejovice
88.7	1	R. Proglas	Tábor
88.9	10	R. Jih	Breclav
89.0	1	R. Prácheň	Písek
89.0	45	R. Impuls	Ostrava
89.3	5	HEY R.	Benešov/Lbosín
89.5	1	R. Cas	Trinec
89.5	5	Country R.	Praha
89.6	1	R. Frekvence 1	Plzen
89.6	7	Rock Max	Zlín
89.8	1	R. Zet	Ceské Budejovice*
90.0	1	Hitradio Dragon	Cheb
90.0	1	R. Rubi	Sumperk
90.0	10	Kiss	Plzen
90.2	1	Kiss	Kutná Hora
90.3	5	Expres FM	Praha
90.3	3	Kiss	Zlín
90.5	1.6	R. Evropa 2	Ceské Budejovice
90.6	4	Hitrádio FM Most	Chomutov
90.6	1	R. Proglas	Bystrice pod Hostynem
91.0	70	R. Frekvence 1	Ostrava
91.0	1	R. Evropa 2	Mariánské Lázne
91.1	2	Kiss	Pardubice
91.4	66	R. Impuls	Plzen
91.6	1	R. Blanik	Decín
91.6	5	Fajn R.	Opatovice
91.7	4	R. Zlín	Zlín
91.9	1	R. 1	Praha
92.1	10	R. Impuls	Trutnov
92.3	1	R. Relax	Kladno
92.3	5	R. Haná	Pohorany
92.5	5	R. Egrensis	Mariánské Lázne
92.8	5	R. Cas	Ostrava
92.8	1	Hitradio Cerná Hora	Náchod
92.9	1	Kiss	Mladá Boleslav
92.9	1	R. Ceská Kanada	Dacice
93.2	1	R. Egrensis	Cheb
93.3	20	R. Proglas	Jeseník
93.4	20	R. Frekvence 1	Jihlava
93.5	50	R. Frekvence 1	Ustí nad Labem
93.6	1	Hitrádio Faktor	Písek
93.7	5	Hitrádio City	Praha
93.7	45	R. Hellax	Ostrava
93.8	1	R. Evropa 2	Karlovy Vary
93.9	80	R. Blaník	Pardubice
94.0	10	R. Impuls	Klatovy
94.1	10	R. Frekvence 1	Valašské Mezirící
94.1	50	R. Frekvence 1	Ceské Budejovice
94.3	10	Hitrádio Vysocina	Jihlava
94.5	0.1	R. Dechovka	Tábor
94.7	1	Country R.Mor.Sev.	Ostrava
95.0	95	R. Blaník	Votice
95.2	5	Fajn Radio	Ustí nad Labem
95.2	1	Rock R.	Klatovy
95.3	2.5	R. Beat	Praha
95.5	0.4	R. Dechovka	Cesnovice
95.7	2	Signál R. Praha	Praha
95.8	1	Hitrádio Vysocina	Trebíc
96.2	1	R. Spin	Praha
96.2	1	R. Zlín	Uherský Brod
96.4	4	Hitrádio Orion	Ostrava
96.5	1	Kiss	Sumperk
96.6	5	R. Impuls	Praha
96.7	5	R. Zet	Jihlava*
96.8	1	Country R.Mor.Jih	Brno
96.8	0.2	R. Dechovka	C.Budejovice
96.9	1	Country R.Vychod	Pardubice
97.1	5	R. Rubi	Pohorany
97.1	1	Country R.Sever	Liberec
97.2	5	Fajn R.	Praha
97.4	50	R. Frekvence 1	Pardubice
97.7	50	Kiss	Votice
97.7	1	Evropa 2	Ostrava
97.9	20	R. Proglas	Liberec
98.1	1	Fajn R.	Chomutov
98.1	2	Kiss	Praha
98.3	1	R. Cas	Trinec
98.4	20	R. Frekvence 1	Trutnov
98.4	5	R. Impuls	Kašperské Hory
98.6	1	R. Zet	Plzen*
98.7	1	Hitrádio Orion	Trinec
98.7	5	R. Classic FM	Praha
99.0	1	Hitradio Brno	Brno
99.1	1	R. Zet	Pardubice*
99.2	1	R. Zet	Liberec*
99.3	1	Kiss	Cesky Krumlov
99.3	10	R. Evropa 2	Jeseník
99.3	1	R. France Int./Fr. Mus.	Praha
99.4	0.1	R. Dechovka	Písek
99.5	1	R. Evropa 2	Pardubice-Opat.II
99.7	1	Hitradio Dragon	Karlovy Vary
99.7	1	Rock R.	Ceské Budejovice
99.7	5	R. Bonton	Praha
99.8	5	Hitradio Apollo	Valašské Mezirící
99.9	1	Hitrádio Crystal	Ceská Lípa
100.3	20	R. Impuls	Jihlava
100.5	7	R. Impuls	Valašské Mezirící
100.6	2	R. Blaník	Teplice
100.8	1	R. Beat	Slavonice
100.9	20	R. Impuls	Jeseník
101.1	1	Kiss	Frydek-Místek
101.1	0.2	R. Dechovka	Strakonice
101.1	3	R. Zet	Praha*
101.3	10	R. Evropa 2	Plzen
101.4	20	R. Contact (RCL)	Liberec
101.8	1	Country R.	Tábor
102.0	50	R. Impuls	Ustí nad Labem
102.5	5	R. Frekvence 1	Praha
102.8	5	Hitradio Dragon	Mariánské Lázne
102.8	1	Hitrádio FM Labe	Ustí nad Labem
102.9	50	R. Impuls	Ceské Budejovice
103.0	10	R. Krokodyl	Brno
103.4	1	R. Blaník	Hradec Králové
103.4	5	R. Blaník	Brno
103.6	1	Country R.Vychod	Chotebor

MHz	kW	Station	Location
103.6	1	R. Ceská Kanada	Jindrichuv Hradec
103.7	1	Oldies R.	Praha
103.8	10	R. Frekvence 1	Klatovy
103.9	7	Hitrádio Orion	Valašské Mezirící
104.1	50	R. Frekvence 1	Plzen
104.2	1	R. Blanik	Znojmo
104.3	20	R. Frekvence 1	Jeseník
104.3	32	Hitrádio Faktor	Ceské Budejovice
104.5	50	R. Frekvence 1	Brno
104.7	10	R. Blanik	Plzen
105.0	10	R. Frekvence 1	Zlín
105.3	3	Hitrádio Cerná hora	Trutnov
105.4	1	R. Rubi	Vrbno pod Pradedem
105.5	95	R. Evropa 2	Votice
105.5	1.5	R. Evropa 2	Brno
105.7	1	Signál R.	Mladá Boleslav
105.8	8	Hitrádio FM Plus	Klatovy
105.8	1	R. Zet	Ustí nad Labem*
105.9	1	R. Cas	Frenštát p. Radh.
106.0	50	R. Impuls	Pardubice
106.1	3	Hitrádio FM Plus	Plzen
106.3	1	R. Zet	Ostrava*
106.4	1	R. Evropa 2	Vrchlabí
106.5	10	R. Blaník	Chomutov
106.6	1	Fajn R.	Kutná Hora
106.7	1	R. Evropa 2	Znojmo
107.2	1	R. Evropa 2	Ustí nad Labem
107.4	1	Hitrádio FM Plus	Jáchymov
107.5	3	R. Proglas	Brno
107.5	2	R. Proglas	Nové Hrady

+ more than 70 txs below 1kW. *) rel. BBCWS at night

DIGITAL RADIO (DAB+)
CRo on Blocks: **12C** Praha (20kW), eské Budejovice (20kW), Pardubice (10kW), Plzen-Radec (10kW), Jáchymov-Klínovec (10kW), Ustí nad Labem (10kW), Trutnov (10kW), Votice (10kW), Klatovy (5kW), Plzen-Sylvan (1kW), Liberec (1kW), Sušice (1kW), Tachov (1kW); **12D** Ostrava (10kW), Jeseník (10kW), Zlín (10kW), Jihlava (10kW), Brno-Kojál 10kW), Brno-Hády (5kW), Olomouc (2kW), Trinec (1kW), Valašské Mezirící (1kW), Novy Jicín (1kW) + 10 low power repeaters (0.1 – 0.3kW) with various CRo sces.
Ceské Radiokomunikace on Blocks: **6D** Plzen-Košutka (1kW); **7A** Praha City (1kW), Praha-Strahov (1kW) + 2 low power repeaters (0.1 – 0.2kW) with various private stns.
TELEKO on Blocks: **5D** Trutnov (1kW); **6D** Ustí nad Labem (1kW); **8A** Jihlava (1kW), Benešov (1kW); **10B** Olomouc (1kW); **11A** Praha (0.2kW), Príbram (1kW); **11C** Zlín (0.5kW)+ 4 low power repeaters (0.1 – 0.2kW) with various CRo and private stns
RTI cz on Blocks: **5A** Praha (1kW), Beroun (1kW), Karlovy Vary (0,5kW); **5B** Plzen-Sylván (1kW), Klatovy (1kW), Trebounsky vrch (1kW); ; **7A** Ceské Budejovice (1kW), Kašperské Hory (1kW); **9C** Jáchymov-Klínovec (1kW) + 1 low power repeater (0.2kW) with various CRo and private stns.

DENMARK

L.T: UTC +1h (28 Mar-31 Oct: +2h) — **Pop:** 5.8 million — **Pr.L:** Danish — **E.C:** 230V/50Hz — **ITU:** DNK

RADIO- OG TV-NÆVNET (Radio and TV Board)

✉ H.C. Andersens Boulevard 2, 1553 Copenhagen V ☎ +45 33954200 **E:** post@slks.dk **W:** slks.dk/omraader/medier/radio

CIBICOM A/S

✉ Banestrøget 19-21, 2630 Taastrup ☎ +45 70118011 Cibicom is responsible for the operation of txs carrying prgrs of DR and TV 2.

DR RADIO (Pub.)

✉ DR Byen, Emil Holms Kanal 20, 0999 Copenhagen C ☎+45 35203040 **W:** dr.dk **L.P:** Chairman: Marianne Bedsted, DG: Maria Rørbye Rønn, News Dir.: Sandy French, Head of R.: Anette Kokholm.
LW: Kalundborg 243kHz 50kW

FM	P1/P2	P3	P4	kW
Bornholm	96.2	90.0	99.3	30
Copenhagen	90.8	93.9	96.5	60
Funen	89.0	92.6	96.8	60
Holstebro	90.2	92.9	98.5	60
Nakskov	89.4	94.1	92.2	30
Næstved	94.8	99.6	97.5	100
Skamlebæk	88.4	94.3	92.0	3
So. Jutland	95.1	97.2	99.9	60
Thisted	91.4	99.2	95.6	2
Tolne, N.Jutland	91.0	96.6	94.4	8
Varde	-	-	99.0	8
Vejle	95.5	90.7	94.0	10
Ølgod	88.7	92.3	97.7	10
Aalborg	93.3	89.7	98.1	60
Aarhus	88.1	91.7	95.9	60

+ 18 FM txs below 1kW. A full list is available at dr.dk/hjaelp/radio/sendemaster-og-frekvenser
DAB+: All prgrs from DR are also available on the internet and on DAB+: ch.11C on Sealand & Funen, ch. 8B in southern and western Jutland and ch.13B in northern and central Jutland
P1 on FM (MF 0500-1700, Sat 0700-1700, Sun 0854-1700) + DAB+ (24h). N: on the h (except Su 0900 & 1000). N in Danish from KNR, Greenland: MF 1755-1800 – **P2** on FM (MF 1700-0500, Sat 1700-0700, Sun 1700-0854) + DAB+ (24h): Classical music – **P3** on FM (24h) + DAB+ (24h): Popular music, news and sport. N: on the h + MF: 0530, 0630, 0730 – **P4** on FM + DAB+. News, entertainment and regional prgrs. **N:** nat. news on the h and regional news on the half h – **P5** on DAB+. Music etc. for +60, at times relays P4 – **P6 Beat** on DAB+. Indie/alternative music – **P8 Jazz** on DAB+. Jazz – **DR Langbølge** on LW 243kHz. 0445-0505, 0700-0805, 1045-1135, 1645-1710. Special prgrs.: Wrp: 0445-0500, 0745-0800, 1045-1100 & 1645-1700 & navigational warnings: 1703-1710. Also news from P4 or P1 at 0500-0505, 0700-0705, 0800-0805, 1100-1115 & 1700-1703.

Regional stations:
MF: 0505-0600, 0605-0700, 0705-0800, 0805-0900, 1130-1133, 1406-1500, 1510-1550 & 1610-1700. Sat 0603-0700, 0707-0800, 0807-0900 & 1130-1132. Sun: 0603-0700, 0703-0800, 0807-0900 & 1130-1132. P4 Trekanten and P4 Esbjerg are on the air at a reduced schedule. At other times national P4 prgrs are carried.
DR Nordjylland, Frederik Bajers Vej 9, 9220 Aalborg Ø: on 89.1/94.4/96.7/98.1MHz – **DR Midt- & Vest**, Vestergade 1, 7500 Holstebro: on 95.6/ 97.7/98.5/102.2MHz – **DR Østjylland**, Olof Palmes Alle 10-12, 8200 Aarhus N: on 88.9/95.9/96.4/102.0MHz – **DR Trekanten**, Den Hvide Facet 1, 4., 7100 Vejle: on 94.0MHz – **DR Syd**, H.P. Hanssensgade 9-11, 6200 Aabenraa: on 94.0/96.6/99.0/99.9/103.7MHz – **DR Esbjerg** (cf. DR Syd) on 99.0/103.7MHz – **DR Fyn**, Lille Tornbjerg Vej 9-10, 5220 Odense SØ: on 96.4/96.8MHz – **DR Sjælland**, Vadestedet 1, 4700 Næstved: on 92.0/92.2/97.5MHz – **DR København**, Emil Holms Kanal 20, 0999 Copenhagen: on 96.5MHz – **DR Bornholm**, Aakirkebyvej 52, 3700 Rønne: on 93.7/99.3MHz
Ann: FM: "Du lytter til P et/to/tre/fire" (1st, 2nd, 3rd & 4th prgr.) etc. LW: "Du lytter til DRs langbølgesender på 243 kHz"

RADIO4 (Pub.)

✉ Banegaardspladsen 11, 8000 Aarhus C ☎ +45 99199444 **E:** info@radio4.dk **W:** radio4.dk
L.P: MD: Anne-Marie Dohm
Radio 4: FM (all MHz): Nakskov 98.8 30kW, Holstebro 100.3 60kW, Funen 100.5 60kW, Tolne N. Jutland 100.7 10kW, Vejle 100.9 10kW, Skamlebæk 101.1 5kW, Thisted 101.3 3kW, Næstved 101.6 100kW, So.Jutland 102.1 60kW, Copenhagen 102.3 60kW, Varde 102.5 10kW, Aalborg 102.7 60kW, Aarhus 103.0 60kW, Bornholm 103.5 30kW + 4 FM tx below 1 kW. Also nationwide on DAB+ ch.12C
Format: News/talk

RADIO LOUD (Pub.)

✉ Wildersgade 10B,2., 1408 Copenhagen & Vestergade 165D,2., 5700 Svendborg ☎ +45 32421714 **W:** radioloud.dk
L.P: MD: Finn Høffner. Dir: Ann Lykke Davidsen
Radio Loud: DAB+ ch. 12C (nationwide). Also on the internet
Format: Talk and cultural radio for young people

BAUER MEDIA (Comm.)

✉ Mileparken 20A, 2740 Skovlunde ☎ +45 33119000 **E:** reception@bauermedia.dk **W:** bauermedia.dk
L.P: MD: Jim Receveur. CEN: Jan Andersen
Nova: AC. Varde 87.8MHz 10kW, So. Jutland 89.3MHz 3kW, Copenhagen 91.4MHz 12kW, Bornholm 92.2MHz 1kW, Funen 93.4MHz 1kW, Vejle 99.3MHz 1kW, Tolne N. Jutland 102.4MHz 1kW, Holstebro 103.4MHz 60kW, Næstved 103.9MHz 100kW, Aalborg 106.0MHz 6kW + 11 stns below 1kW (nominally). Also nationwide on DAB+ ch.12C –

The Voice: CHR. On 40 FM txs + nationwide on DAB+ ch.12C – **Pop FM**: Classic hits. On 26 FM txs + nationwide on DAB+ ch.12C – **Radio 100**: Hot AC: Copenhagen 100.0MHz 75kW, Randers 99.9MHz 0.5kW + nationwide on DAB+ ch.12C – **Radio Klassisk**: Classical Music on DAB+ Ch. 12C – **Radio Soft**: A/C Soft non-stop. On 22 FM txs – **MyRock**: Rock. On 24 FM txs + nationwide on DAB+ ch.12C.

HARTVIG MEDIA
PO Box 112, 8960 Randers SØ. **E:** wmr@wmr.dk & mail@radio208.dk **W:** wmr.dk & radio208.dk
L.P: Dir: Stig Hartvig Nielsen
World Music Radio (WMR): Hvidovre 927kHz (0.5kW), Bramming 5840kHz (0.5kW), Randers 15805kHz (0.2kW)(Sat/Sun only). Tropical world music.
Radio208: Ishøj 1440kHz (0.5kW), Hvidovre 5805kHz (0.15kW). Progressive classic rock (1964-84).
F.pl.: **NB24:** Copenhagen 846kHz (0.3kW) News.
All prgrs are also available on the internet

RADIO OZ-VIOLA (Priv.)
Engparken 35, 3400 Hillerød **E:** jansteendk@hotmail.com **W:** www.ozviola.dk **L.P:** Jan Sørensen
SW: Hillerød 5980kHz (0.15kW) 2100-2300 Wed, 1200-1400 Sat/Sun.

BBC WORLD SERVICE: DAB+ ch.12C (nationwide)

DK4DAB (Comm.)
Rådmandsgade 55, 2200 Copenhagen ☎ +45 70253535 **W:** dk4.dk
L.P: MD: Stig Hasner. Radio dir.: Steen Andersen
DAB+ ch.12C (nationwide)

PRIVATE STATIONS (all MHz):
Nominal power: 0.16-0.5kW at 40m. height. Major stns in the main cities are as follows (only main frequencies mentioned):
Aabenraa: Skala FM: 102.6/104.5 – Globus Guld: 90.6/106.7 – Classic FM: 92.0/104.0 – Radio Globus: 98.2
Aalborg: ANR, Langagervej 1, 9220 Aalborg Ø: 87.6/103.8 – Radio Nordjyske (same): 97.1/93.8 – The Voice: 100.2 – Radio Nord, Sigsgaardsvej 16, 9490 Pandrup: 95.1/98.9/102.2 – Radio 100: 101.4 – MyRock: 105.0 - Radio Soft: 97.4/104.4 – Folkets Radio/Lumi Radio: 92.2
Aarhus: Radio go!FM, Jens Baggesens Vej 90K, 8200 Aarhus N: 92.2/94.6/106.5 – The Voice: 93.1/93.7 – Radio 100: 100.1 – MyRock: 90.9 – Radio Soft: 96.9 – Pop FM: 98.3 – Øst FM, Storegade 7,1., 8382 Hinnerup: 95.0/105.1 – Radio ABC: 98.9/107.0 – Radio Alfa Aarhus: 104.2 – Radio Solo: 92.8 – Classic Rock: 103.8 – Classic FM: 105.6/107.6 – Grassroots/community stns: 89.5/98.7
Copenhagen: The Voice: 91.8/96.1/104.9 – Classic Rock: 88.2/107.1 – Radio Soft: 95.0/101.8 – MyRock: 92.7/103.6/104.4/105.6 – Pop FM: 97.2/101.2/106.9 – NRJ: 107.9 – Radio 902, Torvevej 27, 2740 Skovlunde: 90.2 - Grassroots/community stns: 87.6, 89.6, 90.4, 92.9, 94.5, 95.2, 95.5, 97.7, 98.9, 100.9, 102.9, 103.4, 105.9, 106.3
Esbjerg: Radio Victoria, Borgergade 66, 6700 Esbjerg: 106.3 – Skala FM: 101.7/106.8 – Globus Guld: 107.6 – VLR Esbjerg: 100.7 – Radio 100: 90.4 – Radio Soft: 93.5 – The Voice: 91.2 – Classic FM: 105.9 – Rlg. stations: 93.5
Fredericia: Radio Mælkebøtten, Prinsessegade 29B, 7000 Fredericia: 91.5 – Radio Viva: 98.0 - Skala FM: 94.4 - VLR Fredericia: 105.5 - Classic FM: 101.8 - Radio 100: 107.7 - Radio Soft: 98.8/101.3 - The Voice: 104.1 – Globus Guld: 89.5
Frederikshavn: Vendsyssel FM, Sønderjyllands Allé 35, 9900 Frederikshavn: 106.6 – ANR: 107.5 – Radio Nord: 96.1 – Radio 100: 90.1 – MyRock: 104.4 – The Voice: 99.6 – Radio Soft: 106.3
Haderslev: Skala FM: 88.4 – Classic FM: 107.4 – Radio Haderslev: 98.6 – Globus Guld: 88.0 – Radio Globus: 103.5/105.9
Helsingør/Hørsholm: The Voice: 89.1 – Guldkanalen, Klågerupsvägen 16, S-245 44 Steffanstorp, Sweden: 104.7 – grassroots stns: 92.8
Herning: Radio M, Østergade 21, 7400 Herning: 99.7/105.8 – Radio Alfa (same): 89.5 – Radio Solo (same): 91.2/105.3 – Radio Midtjylland Classic, Gl. Kirkevej 33, 7400 Herning: 96.2 – Radio 100: 104.3
Hillerød: Classic Rock: 88.6 – MTV Radio: 98.6 - The Voice: 107.3 - Pop FM: 89.4 - Radio Soft: 107.8 - MyRock: 106.2
Hjørring/Hirtshals: Skaga FM, Jørgen Fibigers Gade 20, 9850 Hirtshals: 105.6 – ANR: 104.7 – Radio Nordjyske: 88.6 – Nova 107.0 – Radio Nord: 88.0 – Radio Soft: 107.8
Holbæk: Holbæk Radio, Anders Larsens Vej 7, 1., 4300 Holbæk: 104.7 – SLR: 106.1 – The Voice: 104.3 – MyRock: 90.1 – Pop FM: 89.2/93.0 – Radio Odsherred: 107.0
Holstebro: Classic FM, Lægårdvej 86, 7500 Holstebro: 106.2 – VLR: 97.4 - Radio Solo: 107.1 – Radio Limfjord: 88.5 – Radio Alfa: 100.8 – Radio Skive: 107.6
Horsens: Radio VLR Horsens, Nørregade 42, 8700 Horsens: 91.1 – Classic FM: 105.3 – Skala FM: 104.6 - The Voice: 107.9 – MyRock: 107.0 – Nova 103.6 – Radio 100: 106.2 – Globus Guld: 89.5 – Radio Soft: 96.9/98.8 – Pop FM: 98.3
Kolding: Radio Viva, Skovvangen 42, 6000 Kolding: 106.3 – Skala FM, Dalbygade 40, 6000 Kolding: 105.2 – VLR/VLR Kolding: 103.2 – Radio Globus: 91.3 – Globus Guld: 100.3 – The Voice: 90.0 – Radio 100: 104.7 – Classic FM: 92.1
Køge: Radio Køge, Astersvej 23B, 4600 Køge: 98.2/106.8 – The Voice: 93.6 – Pop FM: 103.1 – MyRock: 95.6 – Radio Soft: 105.7 - Radio Midtsjælland: 89.9
Nykøbing F: Radio Sydhavsøerne, Tværgade 20, 4800 Nykøbing F: 87.8 – Pop FM: 93.0 – The Voice: 90.1/106.6 – Nova: 107.2 – Radio 100: 106.1 – Radio Soft: 104.6
Nykøbing M/Thisted: Radio Limfjord, Gasværksvej 10, 7900 Nykøbing Mors: 88.6/104.7/107.8 – Limfjord Mix (same): 94.7 – Limfjord Slager (same): 107.3 – ANR: 97.4 – Radio Nordjyske: 106.7 – Radio Nord: 92.1 – Nova 87.9 – Radio 100: 96.5 – The Voice 106.2
Næstved/Ringsted/Slagelse: Radio SLR, Dania 38, 4700 Næstved: 91.6/98.1/100.7/101.0/106.5 – The Voice: 104.9/107.5 – MyRock: 95.6 – Radio 100: 93.7/103.2 – Pop FM: 106.2 – Radio Soft: 104.5/107.1/107.7
Odense: Skala FM: 91.1/99.1 – The Voice: 98.0/107.6 – Classic FM: 98.7/103.5 – Radio 100: 101.2 – MyRock: 100.1 – Pop FM: 90.6 – VLR Fyn: 98.4 – Radio Soft: 104.2 – Grassroots stns: 107.1
Randers: Radio ABC, Brotoften 10, 8940 Randers SV: 95.3 – Radio Alfa (same): 89.4 – Radio Solo (same): 96.4 – Radio Randers, Garnisionsvej 17, 8930 Randers: 104.9 – The Voice: 101.8 – Radio 100: 99.9 – Nova: 92.5 – Pop FM: 99.1 – Radio Soft: 87.6
Roskilde: The Voice: 96.1/104.3./106.6 – Pop FM: 93.0/97.2 – MyRock: 90.1/92.7/103.6 – Radio Soft: 95.0/99.1/107.7 – Roskilde Dampradio, Vestergade 17,1., 4000 Roskilde: 97.8 – Umlando: 102.8 – SLR: 106.1 – Radio Køge: 106.8
Rødding: Radio Globus, Herredfogedvej 2, 6630 Rødding: 104.4 – Globus Guld (same): 91.9/93.0 – Radio Victoria: 95.7 – Skala FM: 100.6 – Grassroots stns: 107.8
Silkeborg: Radio Silkeborg, Papirfabrikken 18, 8600 Silkeborg: 101.2/107.7 – Radio Alfa: 94.5 – Radio Solo: 104.6/105.9 – Radio ABC: 97.4 – The Voice: 97.8 – Radio Soft: 107.1
Skive: Radio Skive, Nordbanevej 1A, 7800 Skive: 104.0 – Radio Alfa Skive (same): 101.8 – Radio Solo (same): 96.2 – Radio Viborg: 105.6 – Classic FM: 106.5
Svendborg: Radio Diablo, Vestergade 165D,1., 5700 Svendborg: 107.7 – Classic FM: 88.3 – Skala FM: 90.0/101.0 - Radio Aktiv/Svendborg Lokalradio: 106.5
Sønderborg: Classic FM Als, Peblingestien 1, 6430 Nordborg: 88.0 – Globus Guld: 95.4 – Skala FM: 104.4
Vejle: VLR, Bugattivej 8, 7100 Vejle: 88.5/101.7 – Classic FM: 98.2 – Skala FM: 87.6 - The Voice: 105.9 – MyRock: 89.9 – Radio 100: 106.9 – Radio Soft: 98.8 – Globus Guld: 89.5
Viborg: Radio Viborg, Vesterbrogade 8, 8800 Viborg: 105.0 – Classic FM: 93.8 – Radio Alfa Viborg: 87.6/95.2 – Radio ABC: 104.4 – Radio Solo: 107.9 – Grassrot stn: 90.9

DAB+: Some local/regional, commercial stns are also using these regional DAB+ muxes: 6D in W.Jutland (Herning, Brande & Ikast), 7A in S.Jutland (Sdr. Hygum)(LP) (F.pl. move to ch. 9B), 7C in Vejle (F.pl. move to ch. 8D), 8A in E.Jutland (Randers, Langaa, Grenaa, Rygårde, Aarhus & Silkeborg), 8C in Thisted, 9B in Copenhagen, 9D in Nivaa (local mux), 9D in Esbjerg, 11A in Nykøbing F., 11B in Aalborg, 11D in Viborg, Kjellerup, Skive & Durup, 12A in Svendborg and 12A on Bornholm. **F.pl.**:**DRM+**: Copenhagen 86.5MHz

DJIBOUTI

L.T: UTC +3h — **Pop:** 1 million — **Pr.L:** Arabic (official), French (official), Somali, Afar — **E.C:** 220V/50Hz — **ITU:** DJI

MINISTÈRE DE LA COMMUNICATION CHARGÉ DES POSTES ET DE TÉLÉCOMMUNICATIONS (MCPT)
B.P. 32, 1 Rue de Moscou, Djibouti ☎+253 21 353928 +253 21 353957
W: communication.gouv.dj **E:** contact@communication.gouv.dj

RADIODIFFUSION TÉLÉVISION DE DJIBOUTI (Gov.)
B.P. 97, 1 Rue St. Laurent du Var, Djibouti ☎+253 21 352294 🖷 +253 21 356502 **W:** rtd.dj **E:** rtd@intnet.dj

FM (MHz)	**1**	**2**	**Q**	**kW**
Ali Sabieh	90.3	94.2	103.0	0.5
Arta	93.5	89.5	104.0	3
Ballembaley	95.3	91.3	-	1
Dikhil	96.6	98.8	104.0	0.5/1
Djibouti	89.5/91.3/100.5	90.9/93.5/95.3	103.0	1

Channel 1 in Arabic/Somali: 24h on FM.
Channel 2 in Afar/French: 24h on FM.
Q=Quran prgr. **Ann:** "Radio Djibouti".

OTHER STATIONS:
BBC African Sce: Djibouti 99.2MHz 1kW.
China R. Int: Djibouti 98.2MHz.
Monte-Carlo Doualiya: Arta 97.2MHz 2kW.
VOA: FM: Arta 100.8MHz, Djibouti 102.0MHz 1kW **MW:** Djibouti (Pk 12) 1431kHz 600kW 1530-0330 (For schedule see Int. Radio section)

DOMINICA

L.T: UTC -4h — **Pop:** 72,000 — **Pr.L:** English (official), Dominican Creole, French — **E.C:** 230V/50Hz — **ITU:** DMA

MINISTRY OF INFORMATION, SCIENCE, TELECOMMUNICATIONS AND TECHNOLOGY
3rd Floor, Government Headquarters, Kennedy Ave, Roseau ☎ +1 767 2663294 🖷 +1 767 4480182 **E:** information@dominica.gov.dm **W:** information.gov.dm **L.P:** Minister: Kelver Darroux

DOMINICA BROADCASTING CORP. (Gov. Comm.)
Victoria Str, PO Box 148, Roseau ☎ +1 767 448 3282/3 🖷 +1 767 448 2918 **E:** dbsradio@cwdom.dm **W:** dbcradio.net **L.P:** Chairman: Bennette Thomas. GM: Cecil Joseph
DBS Radio: Eggleston Roseau 88.1MHz 1kW, Marigot 103.5MHz 0.3kW, Petite Soufriere 103.1MHz 0.1kW, Grand Bay 103.5MHz 0.1kW, Portsmouth 104.1MHz. Own prgrs: 0900-0300. Creole: 1800-2000MF. BBC relay: 1200-1205 & 0300-0900.
DBS Blaze FM: Roseau: 89.5MHz. Portsmouth: 104.7

OTHER STATIONS (FM in MHz):
DOMINICA CATHOLIC RADIO, Turkey Lane, Roseau ☎ +1 767 440 7985 **W:** dominicacatholicradio.org FM 96.1. Format: Rlg. – **KAIRI FM**, 42 Independence Str, PO Box 931, Roseau ☎ +1 767 448 7330 **E:** kairifm931@gmail.com **W:** kairifm.com L.P: CEO: Frankie Bellot. PD: Steve Vidal. FM: **Kairi FM:** 88.7/91.1/93.1/107.9 – **MY WORSHIP FM,** PO Box 905, Canefield Industrial Site, Roseau ☎ +1 767 245 9715 **W:** myworshipfm.com FM: Roseau 103.3 Format: Gospel – **POSSIE VIBRATIONS**, Bay Str, Portsmouth ☎ +1 767 616 1512 FM: 88.5. Format: Community – **Q95 FM**, 10 Hanover Str, PO Box 861, Roseau ☎ +1 767 448 5822 🖷 +1 767 448 5828 **W:** qfmda.com L.P: CEO: Sheridan G. Gregoire FM: 95.1/95.7/105.7 – **RADIO EN BA MANGO**, Grand Bay ☎ +1 767 446 3207 **W:** southcityagain.webs.com FM: 93.5/96.9/100.1. D.Prgr: Fr-Mo 2200-0300. Format: Community – **VIBES RADIO,** 36 Great George Str, 3rd floor, PO Box 1161, Roseau ☎ +1 767 440 8152 **W:** vibesradio.dm L.P: GM: Kimani St. Jean. FM 90.1(†) 93.9(†) 94.7(†) & 99.5 – **VOICE OF LIFE RADIO,** PO Box 205, Madrelle, Loubiere, Roseau ☎ +1 767 448 7017 **E:** volradio@cwdom.dm L.P: PD Gairy Didier FM: 24h Portsmouth 90.7 Roseau 102.1 Marigot 106.1. Format: Rlg

DOMINICAN REPUBLIC

L.T: UTC -4h — **Pop:** 11 million — **Pr.L:** Spanish — **E.C:** 110V/60Hz — **ITU:** DOM

INSTITUTO DOMINICANO DE LAS TELECOMUNICACIONES (INDOTEL)
Av. Abraham Lincoln No. 962, Santo Domingo 10148 ☎ +1 829 7325555 **E:** dau@indotel.gob.do **W:** www.indotel.gob.do
L.P: DG: Nelson de Jesús Arrollo.

ASOCIACIÓN DOMINICANA DE RADIODIFUSORAS (ADORA)
Calle Paul Harris No 3, Centro de Los Héroes, Santo Domingo ☎ +1 809 5354057 **W:** adora.com.do **E:** info@adora.com.do

Hrs of tr. 24h unless otherwise stated. Call HI—

MW	**Call**	**kHz**	**kW**	**Station, location and hr of tr.**
1)	B20	540	5	R. ABC, Santo Domingo: 0900-0400
2)	B22	570	10/5	R. Cristal/LV de la Liberación, Santo Domingo
3)	B24	590	10/5	R. Santa María, La Vega: 0900-0300
4)	B28	‡620	10	R. Santo Domingo, Santo Domingo: 1100-0400
5)	B31	650	15/5	R. Universal, Santo Domingo
6)	B32	660	3	R. Visión Cristiana, Santiago
7)	B33	670	5	R. Dial, San Pedro de Macorís
8)	B38	680	3	R. Zamba, S. Ignacio de Sabaneta: 0930-0300
9)	B39	690	10	R. Guarachita, Sto Domingo: 0900-0400
10)		710		Red Nacional Cristiana, Santo Domingo
11)	B41	‡710		Ondas del Caribe, San Cristóbal
12)	B42	720	1.5	R. Norte, Santiago: 0900-0500
13)	B48	‡720	5	R. Cayacoa, Higüey: 0900-0400
14)	B44	750	5	R. Jesús es el Señor, Santiago
15)	B47	‡780	0.5	R. Constanza, Constanza: 1100-0200
16)	B50	800	1	R. Bonao Bendición, Bonao: 1000-0400
17)	B52	810	5	R. Salvación Internacional, Baní: 1100-0300
18)	B54	830	10	Emisora HIJB, Santo Domingo: 1000-0300
19)	B59	870	4	R. La Vega, La Vega: 1000-0300
20)		890	3	Consentida, Mao: 1000-0400
21)	B68	950	10	R. Popular, Santo Domingo: 1000-0300
22)	B71	970	6	R. Olímpica, La Vega
23A)	B72	970	5/1	R. Barahona, Barahona
24)	C84	990	5/1	R. Eternidad, Sto Domingo: 1100-2400
25)	B80	1050	1.5	R. Hispaniola, Santiago
26)	B83	1070	5/1	HIBI Radio, S. Francisco de Macorís: 0900-0400
46)	B84	†1080	1	RPQ, Santo Domingo: 1200-0400
27)	B85	1090	2.5	R. Amistad, Santiago
28)	B86	1100	1	Aliento FM, San Pedro de Macorís
29)	B91	1110	1/0.5	R. Marién, Dajabón: 0930-0200
30)	B96	‡1150	5	Onda Musical, Sto Domingo: 1100-0500
31)	C23	1200	5	R. VEN/RTM RD, Sto Domingo
32)		1210	5	R. Merengue, San Francisco de Macorís
10)		‡1240	1	Red Nacional Cristiana, Puerto Plata
33)	C29	1250	5	R. Juventud, La Romana
34)	C32	1270	1	R. Ambiente, Baní: 1000-0400
35)	C36	1310	1	R. Real AM, La Vega: 1100-0400
7)	C38	1330	3	R. Visión Cristiana, Santo Domingo
36)	C41	1350	1	Ondas del Yuna, Bonao
37)	C47	1380	1	R. Nacional, Santiago: 1000-0300
38)		‡1380		Antena 13-80, Santo Domingo
39)	C54	1430	5	R. Emanuel, Santiago
40)	C55	1440	5	R. Impactante, Sto Domingo: 1100-0400
10)	C60	1470	1	Red Nacional. Cristiana, San Francisco de Macorís
23B)		1470		R. Barahona, Duvergé
41)	C67	1510	10/3	R. Pueblo, Sto Domingo: 1000-0400
47)		1560	1	R. Única, Santiago
23C)	C76	‡1580	1	R. Neyba, Neyba: 0900-0400
42)	C73	1590	1	R. Libertad, Santiago
48)	C78	†1600	5	R. Revelación en América, Santo Domingo
43)	C80	1640	1/0.5	R. Juventus Don Bosco, Santo Domingo
43)		1640	1/0.5	R. Juventus Don Bosco, Romana
43)		1640	1/0.5	R. Juventus Don Bosco, Boca
44)	C81	1670	3	LV del Yuna, Bonao
45)	C82	1680	1	R. Senda, San Pedro de Macorís

‡ = inactive, (r) = repeater, ± = varying fq.

Addresses & other information:
1) Av. Rómulo Betancourt N° 2078, (or Ap 517), Sto Domingo **W:** radioabc.org – **2)** Av. 27 de Febrero # 514, Edif. Manuel Arsenio Ureña, 6to Piso, Santo Domingo **W:** cristal570.com – **3)** Avenida Pedro A Rivera km 1.5 (or Ap 55), La Vega **W:** radiosantamaria.net – **4)** Ap. 869 (or Dr.Tejada Florentino N° 8), Sto Domingo **W:** radiosantodomingord.com – **5)** Av 27 de Febrero, Edificio Kira, Sto Domingo **W:** radiouniversalam.com – **6)** Calle Sabana Larga #64, Santiago / Calle César Dargán #26, El Vergel (Frente a la Plaza Criolla), Sto Domingo (or P.O. Box 2908, Paterson, NJ 07509-2908, USA) **W:** radiovision.net **Local prgr**: Mon-Fri 2000-2300 – **7)** Av. Independencia No. 169, San Pedro de Macorís **W:** facebook.com/RADIODIAL – **8)** Calle Restauración N° 60 (or: Ap 2), San Ignacio de Sabaneta **W:** radiozamba.com – **9)** Calle Palo Hincado 302, Sto Domingo – **10)** Avenida Lope de Vega, Santo Domingo **W:** rednacionalcristiana.org – **11)** San Cristóbal **W:** bocasondasdelcaribe.mex.tl – **12)** Urb. Las Hortensias (or Ap 454), Santiago **W:** norte720.com – **13)** Diócesis de la Alta Gracia, Calle General Santana 65, Higüey **W:** radiocayacoa.com – **14)** Calle Sánchez Esq Pedro F Bonó, Santiago **W:** radiojesus750am.com – **15)** Calle V. M de Robiou N° 18, Constanza **W:** radioconstanza.net – **16)**

Calle Libertad N° 15, Bonao **W:** linktr.ee/radiobonaobendicion - **FM:** 88.7MHz Latina 88 – **17)** Calle Mella esquina Calle 27 de Febrero, Baní **W:** facebook.com/radiosalvacion810 – **18)** Edif. Teleantillas, Carr Duarte km 7.5, Sto Domingo **W:** facebook.com/pages/Emisora-HIJB-830-AM/173438096006789 – **19)** Av. Pedro A. Rivera, km 0 (or Ap 203), La Vega **W:** radiolavega.com – **20)** Calle 27 de Febrero Esq. Agustin Cabral (or Ap 80), Valverde – **21)** Av. Charles Summer N° 33, Los Prados (or Ap 928), Sto Domingo **W:** radiopopularam.com – **22)** Av. Pedro A. Rivera, km 0, (or Ap 203), La Vega **W:** olimpica970.com – **23A-F)** Empresas Radiofónicas SA, Av. Tiradentes #35, Naco. Torre Marmer, Santo Domingo or C/ María Montés #24, Edificio Rodolfo Lama, Barahona **W:** empresasradiofonicas.com.do – **24)** Luís Amiama Tió # 105, Arroyo Hondo, Santo Domingo **W:** radioeternidad.com – **25)** Av. Rafael Vidal, Urb. Las Hortensias, Santiago **W:** radiohispaniola.com – **26)** Av 27 de Febrero N° 51 (orAp 201), San Francisco de Macorís **W:** hibiradio1070am.blogspot.com – **27)** C/Dr. Arturo Grullon, Edificio Cablenet, Jardines Metropolitanos, Santiago **W:** amistad1090.com - **FM:** 101.9MHz – **28) W:** facebook.com/aliento95.5fm – **29)** Pres Henriquez 53, Dajabón **W:** facebook.com/radiomarien - **FM:** 93.3MHz – **30)** Calle Palo Incado N° 161, Sto Domingo **W:** ondamusical1150.com – **31)** Ap. 2217 (Av. Leopoldo Navarro #34, Esq. Juan E. Dunant, Ensanche Miraflores), Sto Domingo **W:** radioven.com rtmdominicana.org – **32)** Calle 27 de Febrero N° (or Ap 57), San Francisco de Macorís **W:** circuitomerengue.wixsite.com/radiomerengue - **FM:** Digital 94.7MHz – **33)** Calle Santa Rosa N° 18 (orAp 151), La Romana **W:** esradiojuventud.com - **FM:** 107.5MHz – **34)** Sánchez esq Mella, Baní **W:** radioambiente.com.do - **FM:** 96.7MHz – **35)** Juan Rodríguez 76-A, La Vega **W:** radiorealam.net – **36)** Calle Duarte Esq Mella, Edif Fantino (2da planta), Bonao **W:** ondasdelyuna.com – **37)** Av Las Carreras, Esq Mella (4ta Planta), Santiago **W:** radionacional.net – **38)** Avenida Abraham Lincoln 1015, Paraíso, Santo Domingo **W:** antena1380.com – **39)** Calle Cuba No. 46, 3ra planta, Los Pepines, (or Ap. 897) Santiago **W:** radioemanuel.org – **40)** Ave Sarasota esquina Winston Churchill, Plaza Universitaria, Local 9B, Santo Domingo **W:** facebook.com/Radio-Impactante-1440-AM-339671216065657 – **41)** Av. Los Proceres #46, Suite 203, Arroyo Hondo, Santo Domingo **W:** radiopueblo.net – **42)** C/ Dr. Arturo Gullón, Esquina Transversal, Edificio CableNet, Los Jardines Metropolitanos, Santiago de los Caballeros **W:** radiolibertad1590.com – **43)** Calle Juan Evangelista Jiménez # 49, Barrio María Auxiliadora, (or Ap. 4848), Santo Domingo **W:** juventusdonbosco.com – **44)** 16 de Agosto esq. Luperón, Bonao **W:** lavozdelyuna.org - **FM:** 91.9MHz – **45)** Calle René del Risco Bermúdez No.17, Villa Progreso, San Pedro de Macorís **W:** radiosenda1680.org – **46)** Ave. Abraham Lincoln No. 476, Plaza Lincoln, Santo Domingo **W:** piodeportes.com – **47)** Santiago **W:** radiounica1560.com – **48)** Santo Domingo W: radiorevelacionam.net

FM in Sto Domingo (MHz):
88.1 Primera FM – 88.5 Studio 88 – 88.9 Escape – 89.3 Neón – 89.7 Renuevo FM – 90.1 Fuego 90 – 90.5 Estrella 90 – 90.9 R. France Int. - 91.3 La 91 FM – 91.7 La Roka FM – 92.1 Hits 92 – 92.5 CDN R. - 92.9 Pura Vida 92.9 – 93.3 Independencia FM – 93.7 Latidos FM – 94.1 Fidelity – 94.5 KQ94 – 94.9 Kiss 95 – 95.3 Ministerio de Educación – 95.7 La Nota Diferente – 96.1 Quisqueya FM – 96.5 Ritmo 96 – 96.9 Exa FM – 97.3 R. Disney – 97.7 Estación 97.7 – 98.1 R. Amanecer – 98.5 Rumba FM – 98.9 Dominicana FM – 99.3 Sonido Suave – 99.7 Listín – 100.1 "100.1" – 100.5 Cima – 100.9 Súper Q – 101.3 Z101 Digital – 101.7 Top Lantina – 102.1 La X 102 – 102.5 Escándalo FM – 102.9 Raíces FM - 103.3 Los 40 Principales – 103.7 Power FM - 104.1 R. Caliente – 104.5 Mixx - 105.3 ABC – 105.7 La Bakana FM – 106.1 Disco 106 – 106.5 Zol FM – 106.9 LV Cultural de las FF AA – 107.3 La Kalle – 107.7 La Súper 7

FM in Santiago (MHz):
88.1 Primera FM – 88.5 Comando FM – 88.9 Sistema 89 – 89.3 R. Disney – 89.7 CDN R. – 90.1 Primor FM – 90.5 Fuego 90 – 90.9 R. Amanecer – 91.3 La 91 FM (relay) – 91.7 Contacto FM – 92.1 ZOL FM (relay) – 92.7 Lider FM – 93.1 Concierto FM – 93.7 R. Luz – 94.1 Full FM – 94.7 KV 94 – 95.1 Raices – 95.5 Digital FM – 95.9 Clave FM – 96.3 La Kalle – 97.1 Caliente – 97.5 Tremenda – 98.3 Turbo 98 – 99.1 Mortal FM (relay) – 100.3 Monumental FM – 101.1 Premium – 101.5 Z-101 (relay) – 101.9 Amistad FM – 103.1 Super 103 – 103.5 La N – 103.9 Super Regional – 104.3 Sonido HD – 104.7 Matrix – 105.5 Ke Buena – 105.9 La Bakana FM – 106.1 Criolla 106 – 106.5 R. Luz FM – 106.9 La Nueva 107 – 107.3 Suave 107 – 107.9 Mix 107.9

FM in Puerto Plata (MHz):
88.7 Zona FM – 89.3 La 89.3 FM - 90.5 Fantasía FM – 91.7 Melody FM – 92.5 L'arena – 92.9 Orbita FM – 95.3 Arca de Salvación – 96.3 La Kalle – 97.3 La 97.3 FM – 99.7 La 99 FM – 101.7 Romance FM – 104.9 La 104.9 FM – 106.3 Perla FM – 106.9 Master FM

EASTER ISLAND (Chile)

L.T: UTC -6h (5 Sep 20-3 Apr 21, 4 Sep 21-2 Apr 22: -5h). **NB:** UTC times in schedules refer to DST period — **Pop:** 7,750 — **Pr.L:** Spanish, Rapanui — **E.C:** 220V/50Hz — **ITU:** PAQ

FM	MHz	kW	Station
1)	88.3		ADN R.
2)	88.9	1	R. Manukena
2)	99.1		R. Rapanui
5)	99.9		R. Maria
3)	104.3		Los 40 Principales
4)	107.3		R. Nuevo Tiempo

Addresses & other information
1) 24h satellite rel. ADN Santiago **W:** adnradio.cl – **2)** La Misma Municipalidad de Isla de Pascua, Calle Atamu Tekena, Hangaroa. Correo Isla de Pascua, Chile ☎+56 32 2255 1245 **W:** https://www.facebook.com/radiorapanui/ **LP:** Dir: Juan Herrera Torres. Local community radio stn. **D.Prgr:** 24h – **3)** 24h satellite relay from Santiago. **W:** los40.cl – **4)** 24h satellite relay from Santiago (Rlg.) **W:** nuevotiempo.org – **5)** 24h satellite relay from Santiago **W:** radiomaria.cl

ECUADOR

L.T: UTC -5h — **Pop:** 18 million — **Pr.L:** Spanish (official), Kichwa, Shuar — **E.C:** 120V/60Hz — **ITU:** EQA

AGENCIA DE REGULACIÓN Y CONTROL DE LAS TELECOMUNICACIONES (ARCOTEL)

✉ Av. Diego de Almagro entre Whymper y Alpallana, Quito - Ecuador ☎ +593-2 947 800 **E:** comunicacion@arcotel.gob.ec **W:** www.arcotel.gob.ec **L.P:** CEO: Xavier Aguirre

ASOCIACIÓN ECUATORIANA DE RADIODIFUSIÓN (AER)

✉ Cdla. Kennedy Norte, Edificio Mapfre Atlas Piso 8, Oficina 2, Guayaquil ☎ +593 4 2562448 **L.P:** Pres: Kléber Chica Zambrano

Hrs of tr. 24h unless otherwise stated. Call HC—

MW	Call	kHz	kW	Station, location, hr. of tr.
GU01)	FA2	540	25	R. Santiago, Guayaquil: 1100-0600
GU02)	AK2	560	10	CRE Satelital, Guayaquil
GU03)	FC2	580	10	Unión Radio, Guayaquil
PI04)	RF1	590	5	R. Super K800, Quito (r. 800kHz)
GU04)	XY2	600	40	R. Ciudadana, Guayaquil: 1100-0400
PI05)	MJ1	610	10	R. Caravana, Quito
LO01)	XY3	620	7	R. Ciudadana, Loja: 1100-0400
GU05)	BI2	640	10	R. Morena, Guayaquil
MA01)	FD4	650	5	R. Visión, Manta: 0900-0500
GU06)	VP2	680	10	R. Atalaya, Guayaquil
GU07)	RS2	700	50	R. Sucre, Guayaquil
EO01)	PR2	720	10	R. Única, Machala
PI09)	IC1	720	5	R. Municipal, Quito
GU09)	RC2	750	30	R. Caravana, Guayaquil
PI10)	QE1	760	10	R. Quito, Quito
GU10)	MF2	770	25/12	R. Revolución, Guayaquil
GU08)	ML2	800	10	R. Super K800, Guayaquil
CA01)	VI5	820	5	R. LV de Ingapirca, Cañar: 0900-0330
GU12)	RM2	830	10	R. Huancavilca, Guayaquil
PI16)	PN1	840	25	R. Vigía "LV de la Policía Nacional", Quito
GU13)	YS2	850	20	R. San Francisco, Guayaquil
PI17)	PC1	860	10	R. Positiva, Quito: 1015-0400
GU14)	LY2	870	16	R. Cristal, Guayaquil: 1000-0600
PI18)	FJ1	880	10	R. Católica Nacional, Quito: 1000-0200
GU15)	BO2	910	10	La Radio Redonda, Guayaquil
EO02)	RU3	920	10	CRO - Compañía Radiofónica Orense, Machala
PI40)	AB1	920	10	R. Democracia, Quito
TU03)	BA6	930	5	R. Ambato, Ambato
AZ21)	CP5	940	3	R. Caravana, Cuenca
PI21)	BZ1	940	10	R.CCE-Casa de la Cultura Ecuatoriana, Quito
CR05)	UE5	950	3	LV de AIIECH, Colta
IM02)	AV1	950	3	R. Chaskis del Norte, Ibarra
AZ02)	SA5	960	1.5	R. Sonoonda Int., Cuenca: 0900-0300
IM03)	MB1	970	1	R. Imperio, Ibarra: 1030-0300
CR06)	JI5	980	1	R. El Prado, Riobamba: 0900-0300
TU05)	NR6	1010	10	R. Líder TSB, Ambato: 0930-0300

MW	Call	kHz	kW	Station, location, hr. of tr.
EO03)	GO3	1020	5	R. Estelar, Santa Rosa
GU21)	RF2	1030	5	R. Ecuantena, Guayaquil: 1100-0500
TU06)	GB6	1040	1	R. Colosal, Ambato: 0930-0500
GU49)	RQ2	1050	5	R. Águila Sport, Guayaquil: 1000-0400
EO19)	CH2	1060	3	R. Fiesta, Machala: 1100-0500
AZ06)	CJ5	1070	5	LV del Tomebamba, Cuenca: 1000-0500
CP02)	BH6	1080	10	R. Latacunga AM, Latacunga: 0900-0230
GU22)	KD2	1080	10	Sistema 2, Guayaquil
MA11)	AB4	1080	1	R. Contacto, Manta: 0900-0300
PI30)	VC1	1090	3	R. Irfeyal "LV de Fe y Alegría", Quito
CP03)	GR6	1100	1	R. Novedades, Latacunga
NA02)	LE7	1100	1	R. Oriental, Tena: 0900-0400
EO20)	CC3	1130	1	R. Romántica, Machala
TU08)	PV6	1130	3	R. Centro, Ambato
AZ08)	AZ5	1140	1	R. Alpha Musical, Cuenca: 1100-0600
CA02)	CY5	1160	3	LV del Pueblo, Azogues
CP04)	UR6	1160	1	R. Runatacuyac, Latacunga
EO05)	VR3	1160	1	R. Vía, Machala
GU26)	RV2	1170	5	R. Filadelfia, Guayaquil
AZ09)	DP5	1180	2	R. Cuenca, Cuenca -2400v
CP05)	RF6	1190	1	R. El Sol Sol, Pujilí: 1100-0200
GU24)	DE2	1190	2	UCSG Radio, Guayaquil: 1100-0500
PI36)	CS1	1200	3	R. Super K 1200, Sangolquí: 1000-0100
TU09)	JM6	1210	1	R. SIRA, Ambato: 1000-0500
PI32)	PA1	1220	5	R. Marañón, Quito
GU48)	FV2	1230	5	R. Galáctica, Guayaquil: 1000-0400
PI37)	PA1	1240	1	R. Metropolitana, Yaruquí: 1200-0300
CC01)	EM1	1250	2	R. Ondas Carchenses, Tulcán: 1000-0400
AZ12)	CL3	1260	2	R. Contacto XG, Cuenca: 1100-0300
TU10)	RO6	1260	1	R. Calidad, Ambato: 0930-0600
GU23)	UM2	1270	10	R. Universal, Guayaquil
MA15)	LD4	1270	2	R. Junín, Junín: 1100-0500
AZ13)	JA5	1290	3	LV del Río Tarqui, Cuenca: 0900-0200
BO04)	AK6	1300	3.5	R. La Paz, Guaranda
SD04)	RU1	1300	2.5	R. Festival, Sto Domingo de los Colorados
CA03)	CI5	1310	3	R. Internacional TVO, Biblián
EO11)	CP3	1310	0.5	LV de El Oro, Pasaje
LR05)	FR2	1320	1	R. Guayaquil, Babahoyo: 1030-0300
TU11)	JD6	1320	3	R. Continental, Ambato: 0930-0400
ES03)	CO4	1340	5	LV de su Amigo, Esmeraldas
LO08)	RG3	‡1340	1	Ondas de Esperanza, Loja
AZ15)	SF5	1350	1	San Fernando Radio, San Fernando
GU47)	VR2	1350	3	Teleradio 1350 AM , Guayaquil
CA04)	AO5	1370	7	R. El Rocio, Biblián
GU32)	VO2	1370	5	LV de Milagro, Milagro
PI45)	CV1	1380	5	R. Cristal "RCQ", Quito: 0830-0300
TU13)	JR6	1380	1	R. Mera, Ambato
AZ16)	EA5	1390	1.5	R. Tropicana, Cuenca: 1200-0300
GU16)	FL2	1400	3	R. Z Uno, Guayaquil
AZ17)	KD5	1410	1	R. Centro Gualaceo, Gualaceo
PI59)	VE1	1410	1	R. El Tiempo "La Emisora del Amor", Quito
CP06)		1420		R. Integración, Salcedo
PI46)	GF1	1430	3.5	R. Futura, Quito
CA05)	OV5	1440	2	Ondas del Volante, Azogues: 1000-0400
IM11)	BA1	1440	1	R. Panorama, Ibarra: 1030-0400
CP12)	IC6	1460	3	R. Nuevos Horizontes, Latacunga: 1000-0200
GU37)	LD2	1470	1.5	R. Ecos de Naranjito, Naranjito
PI48)	ED1	1470	1	Rdif. Ecos de Cayambe, Cayambe
MA20)	HV4	1480	1	R. LV de Jipijapa, Jipijapa: 1100-0400
CA06)	AM5	1490	2	R. Santa María, Azogues
PI60)	MV1	1490	3	La Nueva R. Pasión, Quito
BO07)	RY6	1510	1	R. Runacunapac Yachana, Simiátug
GU39)	IO2	1510	0.5	R. Naval, Guayaquil 1030-0100
PI56)	BD1	1510	3	R. Monumental, Quito: 1300-0500
CR18)	RI5	1520	0.5	LV de Guamote, Guamote
CA08)	CC5	1530	5	Ondas Cañaris AM, Azogues
TU15)	MZ6	1530	3	R. Dorado Deportes, Pelileo: 1130-0230
LR10)	FM2	1540	3	R. Cristal de Ventanas, Babahoyo
GU42)	AD2	1550	1	LV de El Triunfo, El Triunfo: 1100-0400
IM15)	ZD1	1560	1.5	R. Ecos Culturales de Urcuquí, Urcuquí
MA23)	CC4	1570	0.5	R. La Voz, Manta
PI53)	RZ1	1590	1	R. Mensaje, Cayambe
TU17)	QT6	1590	1	R. Panamericana, Quero

Hrs of tr. 24h unless stated otherwise. Call HC—
° = also on SW, ‡ = inactive, (r) = repeater, ± = varying fq.

SW	Call	kHz	kW	Station, location, h of tr
PI08)		6050	1	R. HCJB, Quito: 0925-1400, 2100-0235

Province-abbreviations: AZ=Azuay BO=Bolívar CA=Cañar CC=Carchi CP=Cotopaxi CR=Chimborazo EO=El Oro ES=Esmeraldas GU=Guayas IM=Imbabura LO=Loja LR=Los Ríos MA=Manabí MS=Morona Santiago,NA=Napo PA=Pastaza PI=Pichincha SD=Santo Domingo de los Tsáchilas SE=Santa Elena SU=Sucumbios TU=Tungurahua ZC=Zamora Chinchipe **N.B.:** These abbreviations are not recognized by the Ecuadorian Post Office. Letters should carry the full name.

Addresses & other information:

AZ00) AZUAY

AZ02) Av.Remigio Crespo y Calle La Libertad, Cuenca **W:** sonoondainternacional.com – **AZ06)** Cas 01-01-0493, Cuenca **W:** www.lavozdeltomebamba.com – **AZ08)** Simon Bolívar 226, Cuenca **W:** facebook.com/RadioAlphaMusical1140Am – **AZ09)** Bomboiza 1-83, entre Loja-Pastaza, Cuenca **W:** https://twitter.com/radiocuenca1180 – **AZ12)** J. Dávila y C. Merchán, Cuenca **W:** 1260am.blogspot.com – **AZ13)** Manuel Vega 653 y Presidente Córdoba, Cuenca **W:** lavozdelriotarqui.com – **AZ15)** Av. José María Quito y Santiago de San Fernando, San Fernando **W:** sanfernandoradio.com – **AZ16)** Cas 830 (or Pumapungo 5-50), Cuenca **W:** tropicanalasuper.myl2mr.com – **AZ17)** Gran Colombia y 9 de Octubre 3102, Frente al Parque Central, Gualaceo **W:** radiocentrogualaceo.com – **AZ21)** J. Roldos 480, Edif El Consorcio, Cuenca **W:** radiocaravana.com

BO00) BOLÍVAR

BO03) 10 de Agosto 612, Guaranda - **FM:** 93.9MHz – **BO04)** G Moreno y 7 de Mayo, Guaranda **W:** radiolapaz1300am.com – **BO07)** Echeandia s/n y Barragán, 020108 Simiátug Guaranda **W:** radiorunacunapac.org

CA00) CAÑAR

CA01) Av Ingapirca, Cdla El Vergel, Cañar (or Cas 01-01-0447, Cuenca) **Quichua:** 0900-1300, 2100-0200 - **FM:** 94.5MHz mostly different programming **W:** radioingapirca.com.ec – **CA02)** General Vintimilla 1-10 y Oriente, Azogues **W:** radiolavozdelpueblo.com – **CA03)** Mariscal Sucre 722 y B Ochoa, Biblián (or Cas 729, Azogues) **W:** radiointernacionaltvo.com – **CA04)** Calle Mariscal Sucre 202 y Tarquí, Biblián **W:** radioelrocio1370.com – **CA05)** Bolivar y Azuay, Azogues **W:** facebook.com/ondasdelvolante – **CA06)** Cas 03-01-730, Azogues **W:** facebook.com/RadioSantaMariaAM – **CA08)** Universidad Católica de Cuenca - sede Azogues, Calle Rivera 613, Azogues **W:** ondascanaris.com.ec

CC00) CARCHI

CC01) Olmedo 52-025 y Ayacucho (or Cas. 30), Tulcán **W:** ondascarchenses.com

CP00) COTOPAXI

CP02) Cas 05-01-392 (or Calle Quito 14-56, Pasaje La Catedral), Latacunga **W:** radiolatacunga.com - **FM:** 97.1/102.1MHz – **CP03)** 2 de Mayo 438, entre Tarquí y General Maldonado, Latacunga **W:** facebook.com/SoloDeportesRadioNovedadesAm1100khz – **CP04)** Bel.Quevedo Caserio Illuchi, Latacunga **W:** radiorunatacuyac.org In Quichua/Spanish – **CP05)** B Quevedo 555, Pujilí **W:** radioelsolpujili.wixsite.com/radioelsol – **CP06)** Salcedo **W:** radiointegracion1420cotopaxi.jimdofree.com – **CP12)** Faustino Sarmiento 5046 y Vela, Latacunga **W:** rnh146.wix.com/rnh146

CR00) CHIMBORAZO

CR05) Cas.87A, Majipamba, Colta **W:** lavozdeaiiech.org.ec Prgrs in Quichua only - **FM:** 101.7MHz – **CR06)** Francia 1857 y Villaroel, Riobamba **W:** radioelprado.blogspot.com In Quichua&Spanish – **CR18)** Comunidad Sta Cruz, Guamote **W:** lavozdeguamote.org

EO00) EL ORO

EO01) Bolívar Madero 1313, via Pto Bolívar, Machala **W:** facebook.com/radiounica720 – **EO02)** Bolívar 601, Edif.Encasa, Machala **W:** radiocro920am.com – **EO03)** Av. General Eloy Alfaro, a una cuadra de la Terminal Terrestre Binacional, Santa Rosa **W:** radioestelaram.wixsite.com/1020-khz – **EO05)** Cas 07-01-0086, Machala (or 9 de Octubre y Paéz), Machala **W:** viaradio.globalmediahd.net – **EO11)** San Martín 720, Entre Municipalidad y Och, Pasaje **W:** facebook.com/lavozdeeloro – **EO19)** Av 9 de Octubre y 23 de Abril, Machala **W:** radiofiestamachala.com – **EO20)** Av 12va Norte y Buena Vista, Machala **W:** radioromanticamachala.blogspot.com

ES00) ESMERALDAS

ES03) Manuela Cañizares y Olmedo, Esmeraldas **W:** vozdesuamigo.com - **FM:** 96.3MHz

GU00) GUAYAS

GU01) Cdla. Bolivariana, Avda. del Libertador Mz K Villa 8, Guayaquil **W:** radiosantiago.com.ec – **GU02)** Boyacá 642 y Padre Solano, Edificio El Torreón, 8vo. piso, Guayaquil **W:** radiocre.com – **GU03)** Cas 2119, Guayaquil **W:** facebook.com/UnionRadio580AM – **GU04)** Quisquis 316 y Garaicoa, Edif Huancavelica, Guayaquil **W:** laciudadana.gob.

ec – **GU05)** Av. Quito 1200 y Aguirre, Guayaquil **W:** radiomorena640.com – **GU06)** Rumichaca 934 y Velez, Guayaquil **W:** radioatalaya.net – **GU07)** Cas 11714 (or Av.Francisco de Orellana y Juan Tanca Marengo), Guayaquil **W:** facebook.com/radiosucre700 – **GU08)** Av. Americas y Av. Constitución, dentro de TC Televisión, Guayaquil **W:** superk800.com – **GU09)** Cas 716, (or Av Juan Tanga Marengo km 3), Guayaquil **W:** radiocaravana.com/reproductores.php – **GU10)** Cas 09-01-4203 (or Colón 548 y Boyacá, P7), Guayaquil – **GU12)** Cas 856 (or Av. Guillermo Pareja Rolando, (Principal de la Alborada) y la novena (esquina), Cdla. IETEI, Mz 2, solar 7), Guayaquil **W:** radiohuancavilca.com.ec – **GU13)** Cas 09-01-5762, Guayaquil **W:** radiosanfrancisco850am.com – **GU14)** Cas 5062 (or Laque 1407 y Antepara), Guayaquil **W:** radiocristal.com.ec – **GU15)** Malecón 206 entre Juan Montalvo y Loja, Guayaquil - **W:** laradioredonda.ec/AM/ – **GU16)** radioz1.ec – **GU18)** 10 de Agosto 504 y Chimborazo, P3), Guayaquil **E:** servidor1000@hotmail.com – **GU21)** Los Ríos 609, Cond Orellana, P4, Ofc 2, Guayaquil **W:** radioecuantena.com.ec – **GU22)** Ciudadela Albatros Calle Fragata # 203, atrás de la Sociedad Italiana Garibaldi, Avenida de las Américas, Guayaquil **W:** radiosistema2.com Also r. R. Sucre 700kHz – **GU23)** Chimborazo 3407 Y El Oro, Guayaquil **W:** radiouniversalgye.com – **GU24)** Universidad Católica de Santiago de Guayaquil, Av. Carlos Julio Arosemena Km. 1 1/2 Vía Daule, Guayaquil **W:** ucsgrtv.com/radio – **GU26)** Veléz 905, Edif.Forum, P16 (or Cas 8729), Guayaquil. Also in Quchua **W:** radiofiladelfiamundial.com – **GU32)** Av. 17 de Septiembre y Azogues, esq. Edif. Radio, Milagro **W:** radiolavozdemilagro.com – **GU37)** Av 5 de Octubre 150, Naranjito **W:** radioecosdenaranjito.com – **GU39)** Cas 5940, Guayaquil **W:** inocar.mil.ec/web/index.php/radio-naval (Time signal overnight) – **GU42)** Jaime Roldos 700 y Av.8 de Abril, El Triunfo **W:** lavozdeltriunfo.com – **GU43)** Cdla.Belén Piedrahita y 1era, Daule – **GU47)** 9 de Octubre y Baquerizo Moreno, Edif.Plaza, P1, Guayaquil **W:** teleradio.com.ec – **GU48)** Edif El Forum, P5, Ofic 508, Guayaquil **W:** radiogalactica1230am.jimdo.com – **GU49)** Eloy Alfaro Duran en la Av. Samuel Cisneros, via al Secap, Guayaquil **W:** radioaguila1050am.com

IM00) IMBABURA

IM02) Celiano Aguinaga y Panamericana Sur, Atuntaqui, Ibarra – **IM03)** Cas 413 (or Olmedo 1178 y Av.Peréz Guerrero), Ibarra **W:** radioimperio970.com – **IM06)** Río Chinchipe 397 y Río Daule, Ibarra – **IM11)** Juan José Flores 11-26 y Jaime Rivadeneira, Ibarra **W:** radiopanorama1440.com – **IM15)** Antonio Ante s/n, Urcuquí **W:** ecosculturales.com – **IM16)** Jirón Roldos Aguilera y Panamericana Norte, Otavalo **E:** radiochaskis@hotmail.com

LO00) LOJA

LO01) Av.J.A Eguiguirren y Bolívar, Loja **W:** laciudadana.gob.ec – **LO03)** 24 de Mayo y Eloy Alfaro, Catamayo - **FM:** 93.7MHz – **LO08)** Olmedo 1146 entre Azuay y Mercadillo, Loja **W:** oeradio.org - **FM:** 94.1 MHz – **LO15)** Asociación Cristiana de Indigenas Saraguros, Saraguro - **FM:** 93.1MHz

LR00) LOS RÍOS

LR05) Cdla El Mamey, Babahoyo – **LR10)** 28 de Mayo 1412 y 6 de Octubre, Babahoyo **W:** radiocristal.com.ec

MA00) MANABÍ

MA01) Av.10ma y Calle 17, P2, Manta **W:** radiovisiondemanta.com – **MA11)** 9 y Malecón, Edif "Jacob Vera", P1 Ofc 7, Manta **W:** radiocontactoam.com.ec – **MA15)** 10 de Agosto 180 y Eloy Alfaro, Junín **W:** radiojunin1270.com – **MA20)** Noboa y Colón, Jipijapa – **MA23)** Edificio Jacob Vera 1, Primer Piso Alto Of. 1, Manta **W:** lavoz1570.com – **MA25)** Cas 13-02-0629 (or Montufar N° 1014 y Aguilera), Bahía de Caráquez - **FM:** 95.3

MS00) MORONA SANTIAGO

MS06) Federación de Centros Shuar, Domingo Comín 17-38, Sucúa (or Cas 17-01-4122, Quito).

NA00) NAPO

NA02) Cas 260 (or Av.Jumandy 536, Barrio 2 Rios), Tena **W:** radioorientaltena.com - **FM:** 89.7MHz

PI00) PICHINCHA

PI04) see GU08) – **PI05)** see GU09) – **PI08)** Cas 17-17-691(or Villalengua 884 y Av.10 de Agosto), Quito. **D.Prgr.** in Spanish, Quichua, Cofan, Waorani and Cha´palaa. For exact schedule see Internationa Radio section **W:** radiohcjb.org – **PI09)** García Moreno 751 entre Sucre y Bolívar, P3, Quito **W:** www.radiomunicipal.gob.ec – **PI10)** Cas 17-21-1971 (or La Coruña 2104 y Whimper, Edif.Aragones) Quito **W:** ecuadoradio.ec – **PI16)** Ramírez Dávalos 612 y 10 de Agosto, Quito **W:** radiovigiafm.com – **PI17)** Av.Amazonas y Colón, Edif.España, P4, Ofc.42, Quito **W:** radiopositiva.com.ec – **PI18)** Cas 17-03-540 (or Av.América 1830 y Mercadillo),Quito **W:** radiocatolica.org.ec – **PI21)** Cas 17-01-67, Quito **W:** radio.casadelacultura.gob.ec – **PI26)** Edif Sevilla, P9, J L Mera 565 y Carrión, Quito **W:** rtunoticias.com – **PI30)** Cas 17-03-31 (or Carrión 1288 y Av 10 de Agosto), Quito **W:** irfeyal.org – **PI32)** Cas. 17-11-2263 (or Bolivar 359 entre García Moreno y Venezuela), Quito **W:** facebook.com/RadioMaranon925Fm – **PI36)** Cas 17-23-47 (or Av General Enriquez N° 29-35 y Río Chinchipe), Sangolquí **W:** radiosuperk1200.com – **PI37)** 12 de Octubre 227, Quito **W:** facebook.com/Radio-Metropolitana-1240-AM-Yaruqui-Quito-Ecuador-274116546327076 – **PI40)** Edif Doral Mariscal, Of 86, Páez y Mercadillo, Quito **W:** democracia.ec – **PI45)** Av. de la Prensa N°60-22 y Av.de la Prensa, Quito **W:** rcq1380.wix.com/1380 – **PI46)** Av.Amazonas 3911 y Corea, Unicormio 2, P10, Ofc.1008, Quito **W:** radiofuturaecuador.com.ec – **PI48)** Cas.17-25-5 (or Terán 409 y Av 10 de Agosto, Cayambe **W:** facebook.com/RadiodifusoraEcos – **PI53)** Av.Natalia Jarrín 2-77 y Vivar, Cayambe **W:** facebook.com/radiomensajeam – **PI56)** Manuel Cajias E 14-09 y Toribio Hidalgo, Quito **W:** radiomonumental1510am.com – **PI59)** Gonzalo Díaz de Pineda 290 y Pedro del Alfaro, Quito **W:** radioeltiempo.com – **PI60)** Av Colón OE3-331 y Versalles, Edif. Villarre, Quito **W:** facebook.com/lanueva1490

SD00) SANTO DOMINGO DE LOS TSÁCHILAS

SD04) Quito e Ibarra, Santo Domingo de los Colorados **W:** radiofestivalfm.com

TU00) TUNGURAHUA

TU03) Cas 18-01-181 (or Sucre 09-42 y Quito), Ambato **W:** radioambato.com.ec - **FM:** 96.7MHz Amor – **TU05)** Cas 18-01-0674 (or Av.Cevallos 15-57 y Mera, P10, Ofc 1001), Ambato **W:** radioliderambato.com – **TU06)** Bolívar y Martinez, Ambato **W:** radiocolosal.com – **TU08)** Cas 18-01-0574 (or Castillo entre 12 de Noviembre y Olmedo, Edif.R.Centro), Ambato **W:** radiocentroambato.com - **FM:** 91.7MHz – **TU09)** Cas. 498, Imbabura 1652, Ciudadela Bellavista, Ambato **W:** radiosira.com – **TU10)** Cevallos 754 y Martinez (or Cas 18-01-0198), Ambato **W:** radiocalidadambato.com – **TU11)** Cotacachi 176 e Iliniza, Ambato **W:** gruporadialcontinental.com – **TU13)** Cas 618 (or Calle Ayllón 1753 y Darquea), Ambato **W:** radiomera.net – **TU15)** Av Padre Chancon s/n y Juan Velasco, Pelileo **W:** radiodoradodeportes.com – **TU17)** Montalvo 106, Quero **W:** radiopanamericana.com.ec

FM in Quito (MHz): 88.1 Latina FM – 88.5 Metro – PI08) 89.3 HCJB – 89.7 Majestad – 90.1 Tropicalida – 90.5 Disney – 90.9 Platinum – 91.3 Sabormix – PI17) 91.7 Visión – 92.1 Contacto Nuevo Tiempo – 92.5 Genial Exa FM – 92.9 Música y Sonido - PI33) 93.3 Eres 93.3 – 93.7 Galaxia – PI18) 94.1 Católica Nacional FM – 94.5 Rumba – 94.9 La Gitana – 95.3 Universal – 95.7 R. Legislativa – 96.1 Joya – 96.5 BBN - 96.9 Armónica FM – PI31) 97.3 La Otra FM – 97.7 Centro – 98.1 Proyección – 98.5 Alfa – 98.9 Colón – 99.3 La Luna – 99.7 Añoranza La Rumbera – 100.1 María – PI23) 100.5 Stereo Zaracay – 100.9 Nacional del Ecuador – 101.1 R. Pública – 101.3 Onda Azul – 101.7 Sucesos – 102.1 R.La Red – PI07) 102.5 Francisco Estéreo – 102.9 Distrito FM – 103.3 Onda Cero FM - 103.7 Sonorama – 104.1 Cobertura - 104.5 América – 104.9 Ecuashyri – 105.3 Kiss – 105.7 CRE – 106.1 Hot 106 R. Fuego – 106.5 Canela – 106.9 R. Genial – 107.3 JC – 107.7 Más Candela

FM in Guayaquil (MHz): 88.1 María – 88.5 Galaxia Stereo – 88.9 Di Blu – 89.3 R. City – 89.7 Punto Rojo FM – 90.1 Romance FM – 90.5 Canela – 90.9 Kiss – 91.3 Tropicalida Stereo – 91.7 Antena Tres – 92.1 Estrella – 92.5 Forever Music FM – 92.9 Colón FM – 93.3 Majestad – 93.7 Disney – 94.1 Onda Positiva – 94.5 Platinum FM – 94.9 La Otra FM – 95.3 Cupido – 95.7 Metro Stereo – 96.1 Onda Cero FM – 96.5 Pasión – 96.9 Más Candela – 97.3 Nuevo Tiempo – 98.1 Morena – 98.5 J C R. – 98.9 Impacto FM – 99.3 Sabormix FM – 99.7 Elite – 100.1 R. La Prensa – 100.5 RSN FM Stereo – 100.9 Mundial – 101.3 La Estación Musical – 101.7 Telequil R. Stereo – 102.1 WQ Dos – 102.5 HCJB – 102.9 Armonía Musical – 103.3 Joya Stereo – 103.7 Sonorama FM – 104.1 Alfa Stereo – 104.5 Corazón – 104.9 Once Q FM – 105.3 Nacional del Ecuador, R. Pública – 105.7 Fabustereo – 106.1 BBN – 106.5 Fuego – 106.9 Ciudadana – 107.3 Rumba – 107.7 Visión FM

EGYPT

L.T: UTC +2h — **Pop:** 101 million — **Pr.L:** Arabic — **E.C:** 220V/50Hz — **ITU:** EGY

SUPREME COUNCIL FOR MEDIA REGULATION (SCM)
Maspero, Nile Corniche, Cairo ☎ +20 2 25775595 +20 2 25748781 **E:** info@scm.gov.eg **W:** scm.gov.eg
L.P: Chmn: Makram Mohammed Ahmed

NATIONAL MEDIA AUTHORITY (Gov)
P.O. Box 1186, Cairo 11511 (Street: Radio & TV Building, Cornish El

Nil, Cairo) ☎+20 2 25757715, 25789145 🖹 +20 2 25789461
E: freqmeg@yahoo.com **W:** ertu.org (Arabic), egradio.eg (live audio)
L.P: Pres: Mr Husein Zein, Head Eng. Sector: Mrs Maissa Ali Kamel, Head Broadcasting Sector: Mr Mohamed Nawar

MW	kHz	kW	P	Times
Cairo	558	100	2j	1000-2200
Sohag	603	50	4	24h
Batra	621	300	6a	24h
Asswan	702	10	2e	0400-2000
Asswan	702	10	4	2000-2200
El Kharga	702	10	2h	0400-2000
El Kharga	702	10	4	2000-2200
Tanta	711	100	10	24h
Qena	756	10	2e	0400-2000
Qena	756	10	4	2000-2200
Abis	774	400	5	24h
Batra	819	300	1a	24h
Santah	864	400	4	24h
Matruh	882	10	1a	24h
Bawti	918	10	1a	24h
Cairo	936	50	11	1500-2000
Salum	936	10	1a	24h
Abu Simbel	981	1	1a	24h
Assiut	981	10	2d	0400-2000
Assiut	981	10	4	2000-2200
Baris	981	1	1a	0300-2400
El Arish	1008	50	6b	0600-1500
El Arish	1008	50	7	1500-2200
El Fayoum	1008	10	2d	0400-2000
Cairo	1071	100	1b	0300-1500
Cairo	1071	100	6c	1500-2100
El Minya	1080	10	1a	0300-2400
Luxor	1080	10	1a	0300-2400
Tanta	1161	100	2b	0400-2200
Qena	1179	10	1a	0300-2400
Asswan	1278	10	1a	0300-2400
Assiut	1305	10	1a	0300-2400
Abu Simbel	1314	1	2e	0400-2000
Abu Simbel	1314	1	4	2000-2200
Nag Hamadi	1314	1	1a	0300-2400
Cairo	1341	100	3c	1700-0100
Cairo	1341	100	8a	0500-1700
Bawiti	1341	10	2j	1300-2000
Bawiti	1341	10	4	2000-2200
Bawiti	1341	10	10	0500-1300
Idfu	1341	10	1a	0300-2400
Siwa	1341	10	1a	24h
Quseir	1350	10	1a	0300-2400
El Kharga	1368	10	1a	0300-2400
Luxor	1386	10	2e	0400-2000
Luxor	1386	10	4	2000-2200
Salum	1422	10	2i	0400-2000
Salum	1422	10	4	2000-2200
El Minya	1476	10	2d	0400-2000
El Minya	1476	10	4	2000-2200
El Arish	1503	25	4	2000-2200
Quseir	1575	10	2j	1300-2000
Quseir	1575	10	4	2000-2200
Quseir	1575	10	10	0500-1300
Baris	1584	1	2h	0400-2000
Baris	1584	1	4	2000-2200
Idfu	1584	10	2e	0400-2000
Idfu	1584	10	4	2000-2200
Matruh	1593	10	2i	0400-2000
Matruh	1593	10	4	2000-2200
Nag Hamadi	1602	10	2e	0400-2000
Nag Hamadi	1602	1	4	2000-2200
Siwa	1602	10	2i	0400-2000
Siwa	1602	10	4	2000-2200

MW Prgrs: 1a=General Prgr, 1b=Adults Prgr, 2=Local Prgrs (2b=Mid Delta, 2d=North Upper Egypt, 2e=South Upper Egypt, 2h=El Wady El Gadid, 2i=Matruh, 2j=Educational), 3c=Cultural Prgr, 4=Holy Koran Prgr, 5=Middle East Comm. Prgr, 6a=Voice of the Arabs, 6b=Palestine Prgr, 6c=Wadi el Nil, 7=Hebrew Prgr, 8a=Nile R. Netw. Songs Prgr, 10=Youth & Sports Prgr, 11=Om Kalthoum Prgr.

FM (MHz):

Site	D	E	G	K	M	N	R	S	Y
Abh	-	-	-	-	-	-	95.7	-	-
Abu	-	-	101.7	90.6	-	-	-	-	-
Ala	-	-	-	-	-	88.7	-	-	-
Alx	-	94.3	104.7	90.1	88.0	88.7	101.1	97.6	-
Al F	87.6	-	94.9	98.2	-	88.6	91.7	-	87.6
Asy	104.0	-	104.0	95.3	89.0	88.7	-	102.0	104.0
Asw	98.6		98.6	95.3	89.0	92.1	-	-	98.6
Baris	-	-	-	88.8	-	-	-	-	-
Bawiti	-	-	-	87.6	-	88.7	-	-	-
Ben	-	-	-	-	-	88.7	101.4	-	-
Cairo [a]	-	95.4	107.4	98.2	98.8	88.7	102.2	105.8	108.0
Dahab	-	-	98.5	92.0	-	-	-	-	-
Dum	-	-	-	93.8	-	88.7	-	-	-
El A [b]	-	-	94.1	87.8	-	90.9	97.4	97.4	87.8
El D	-	-	91.1	88.0	-	-	94.3	-	-
El Db	-	-	-	90.5	-	88.7	-	-	-
El F	-	-	-	89.8	-	-	-	-	-
El K	-	-	-	88.4	-	-	-	-	-
El M	91.0	-	91.0	97.5	101.0	87.9	94.2	104.6	91.0
El Tur	89.4	-	95.7	89.4	92.5	-	99.0	-	89.4
Hal	-	-	-	96.6	-	88.7	93.7	-	-
Ham	-	-	-	-	-	88.7	-	-	-
Hga	101.7	94.9	105.3	91.7	-	88.6	-	98.2	101.7
Idfu	-	-	-	101.7	-	-	-	-	98.2
Ism	-	-	-	-	93.5	90.4	96.7	-	-
Isna	-	-	-	90.3	-	-	-	-	-
Kat	-	-	90.0	87.6	-	-	-	-	-
Kom	-	-	-	92.8	-	-	-	-	-
Lux	93.1	-	93.1	103.1	90.0	96.3	-	-	93.1
Mah	-	-	-	99.6	93.1	89.8	-	89.2	-
Man	-	-	-	96.3	-	-	-	-	-
Mat	-	-	-	99.1	-	95.8	102.6	92.6	-
Nag	-	-	90.9	87.8	-	-	-	94.1	-
Nat	-	-	-	-	-	88.7	-	-	-
Nuw	99.1	-	92.6	99.1	89.5	-	95.8	-	99.1
Pt S	-	-	-	98.0	101.5	88.7	91.5	-	-
Qena	100.1	-	93.6	90.5	-	88.7	-	96.8	100.1
Qus	-	-	-	97.2	-	88.7	-	-	-
Ras	97.3	-	90.8	94.0	-	87.7	-	-	97.3
Saf	-	-	96.1	92.9	-	-	-	89.8	-
Salum	-	-	-	89.1	-	-	89.1	-	-
SeS [c]	97.6	-	91.1	97.6	88.0	-	94.3	-	97.6
Sha	-	-	103.5	93.5	-	-	-	-	-
Sid	-	-	-	101.2	-	-	-	-	-
Siwa	-	-	96.9	90.6	-	-	93.7	-	-
Soh	99.3	-	96.0	89.7	-	88.7	102.8	92.8	99.3
Suez	-	-	-	94.4	91.2	88.1	97.7	-	-

[a]=Site at Mokattam, also Cultural Prgr & Maspero FM on 91.5MHz 10kW, Middle East Prgr on 89.5MHz 10kW, Voice of the Arabs on 106.3MHz 10kW, [b]=Also Palestine Prgr on 94.1MHz 2kW [c]=Koran Prgr also on 101.1MHz 1kW

FM Prgrs: D=Educational Prgr, E=European Prgr, G=General Prgr, K=Koran Prgr, M=Musical Prgr, N=Radio Misr Prgr, R=Regional Prgr, S=Songs Prgr, T=Middle East Prgr, Y=Youth & Sport

Stations & powers: Abu=Abu Simbel 0.1kW, Abh=Abu Homus 0.5kW, Ala=Alamain 1kW, Alx=Alexandria 5kW/N 1kW, Al F=Al Farfra 2kW/Y,D 0.1kW, Asy=Assyout 2kW/M 1kW Asw=Aswan 2kW, Baris 0.1kW, Bawiti 0.1kW, Ben=Beni Suef 2kW/N 0.1kW, Cairo 10kW, Dahab 0.1kW, Dum=Dumyat 0.1kW, El A=El Arish 2kW, El D=El Dakhla 0.5kW/G 0.1kW, El Db=El Dabaa 1kHz, El F=El Fayoum 2kW, El K=El Kharga 1kW, El M=El Minyah 1kW/K 2kW/S 0.5kW, El Tur 1kW, Hal=Halayeb 1kW/R 0.1kW, Ham=Hammam 1kW, Hga=Hurghada 2kW/Y,D 0.5kW, Idfu 2.5kW, Ism=Ismailia 5kW/M 1kW, Isna 0.1kW, Kat=Katherina 0.1kW, Kom=Kom Ombo 0.5kW, Lux=Luxor 3kW, Mah=Mahalla 10kW/N 2kW, Man=Managem Bahariya 0.1kW, Mat=Matruh 1kW, Nag=Naga Hamadi 2kW, Nat=Natron 1kW, Nuw=Nuweiba 1kW, Pt S=Port Said 2kW, Qena 2kW/N 0.5kW, Qus=Quseir 2kW/K 0.5kW, Ras=Ras Gharb 2kW, Saf=Safaga 2kW, Salum 2kW, SeS=Sharm El Sheikh 1kW, Sha=Shalatin 2kW/K 0.1kW, Sid=Sidi Barani 2kW, Siwa 2kW/R 0.1kW, Soh=Sohag 2kW/R 0.5kW/N 0.1kW, Suez 2kW

Ann: General Prgr: "Idha'atu jumhuriya misr al'arabbiya min al-qahira". Voice of the Arabs: "Saut al-'arab, min al-qahira". Holy Koran prgr: "Idha'atu-l-Quran min al-qahira"

Other FM Stations (all MHz):
Radio Hits, 88.2 Cairo, Mahalla 10kW, Ismaila 5kW – **Radio Mix**, Cairo 87.8 10kW – **Nogoom FM**, 100.6 Cairo, Mahalla 10kW, Ismaila 5kW, Arabic music, 24h – **Nile FM**, 104.2 Cairo, Mahalla 10kW, Ismaila 5kW, mainly English pop & rock, 24h **W:** nilefmonline.com – **Mega FM**, 92.7: Cairo, Mahalla 10kW, Ismaila 5kW – **Nagham FM**, 105.3 Cairo, Mahalla 10kW, Ismaila 5kW – **Radio 9090**, Cairo 90.9 10kW – **Shaaby FM**, 95.0 Cairo, Mahalla 10kW, Ismaila 5kW – **NRJ Radio**, Cairo, Mahalla 92.1 10kW, Ismaila 5kW – **On Sport FM**, 93.7 Cairo, Mahalla 10kW, Ismaila 5kW – **R7**, Cairo, rel. R. Misr Prgr 88.7 1kW – **R8** Cairo, all 10kHz rel. Radio Hits 88.2, NRJ Radio 92.1, Mega FM 92.7, On Sport 93.7, Shaaby FM 95.0, Nogoom FM 100.6, Nile FM 104.2, Nagham FM 105.3

EXTERNAL SERVICES: Radio Cairo
see International Broadcasting Section.

Other Stations:
AFRTS Low-power broadcasts of NPR and AFN to US contingent of UN MFO in Sinai rep. on wide range of freqs from 92.7 to 106.1. Also 107.0 at Gebel Musa. **Energy FM** rep. active Cairo on 92.1MHz

EL SALVADOR

L.T: UTC -6h — **Pop:** 6.5 million — **Pr.L:** Spanish — **E.C:** 120V/60Hz — **ITU:** SLV

SUPERINTENDENCIA GENERAL DE ELECTRICIDAD Y TELECOMUNICACIONES (SIGET)

✉ Sexta Décima Calle Poniente y 3°Av.Sur N° 2001, Colonía Flor Blanca, San Salvador ☎ +503 2257-4438 **W:** siget.gob.sv **E:** info@siget.gob.sv

ASOCIACIÓN SALVADOREÑA DE RADIODIFUSORES (ASDER)

✉ Calle La Reforma, Centro Comercial Plaza San Benito, Primer Nivel, Local 1-2, San Salvador ☎ +503 22695334 **E:** asistente@asder.com.sv **W:** asder.com.sv

Call: YS—, ‡ = inactive, † = irregular, r. = relay, ± = varying frequency

MW	Call	kHz	kW	Station, location
1)	HV	540	5	La Estación de la Palabra, San Salvador
	KT	570	10	Nonstop music, San Salvador
3)	NK	600	3	Vox 94.5 FM, San Salvador
4)	LN	630	10	Voz Evangélica Santa Sion, San Salvador
7)	RA	720	1	Radio Qué Buena, San Salvador (r:88.9)
8)	KL	760	5	KL La Poderosa, San Miguel (r:770)
8)	KL	770	10	KL La Poderosa, San Salvador: 1030-0530
10)	AX	800	12	La Voz del Buen Pastor, San Salvador
13)	FB	840	10	R. Santa Biblia, San Salvador: 1030-0300
14)	AR	870	2	R. Renacer, San Salvador
22)	LA	890	3	R. Elohim, Santa Ana
2)	QJ	900	2	R. Tiempo, San Salvador
16)	TG	‡930	3	R. San José, San Salvador
17)	HG	950	1	R. Chaparrastique, San Miguel
18)	CA	1020	5	La Voz de la Liberación, San Salvador
19)	RM	1030	1	R. Frontera, Ahuachapán: 1200-0400
9)	U	1050	10	R. Evangélica Sinaí, San Miguel
20)	ME	1080	6	R. CRET, San Salvador
20)	IM	1080	1	R. CRET, San Miguel
21)	MG	1090	1	R. Cadena CRET, Atiquizaya (Santa Ana)
15)	RF	1100	6	R. Cristo Viene, San Salvador
22)	LR	1120	3	R. Elohim, San Salvador: 1045-0500
24)	GL	1130	1	R. Misionera Voz de Alerta, San Miguel
6)	TS	1140	10	LV del Rey de Gloria, San Salvador
26)	CG	1210	1	R. Salem, Zacatecoluca
28)	QN	1240	1	R. Norteña, San Miguel
29)	AA	‡1260	12	R. Abba, San Salvador
27)	QZ	1270	3.5	R. Visión, San Miguel
30)	MQ	1280	1	R. Emaús, San Vicente
31)	MA	1290	1	R. Chalatenango, Chalatenango: 1000-0300
33)	KG	1300		R. Unción y Presencia de Dios, San Miguel
45)	FG	‡1330		R. Cristo Te Llama, San Salvador
35)	KO	1370	1	R. Lluvias de Bendición, San Miguel: 1100-0300
36)	JU	1390	1	R. Getsemani, La Unión: 1100-0400
37)		‡1390		R. LV de la Palabra Que Cambia, Chalchuapa
38)	JS	1390	1	Sinaí R, LV del Rey de Gloria, Soyapango
39)	JI	1400	1	LV del Litoral, Usulután: 1100-0400
40)	KR	1450	1	R. Restauración, San Miguel: 1000-0400
41)	CS	1500	1	R. Pentecostal Bethel, Usulután
42)	DA	1500	1	R. Peniel, San Salvador
43)	CZ	‡1550	5	R. Sanidad Divina, San Salvador: 1000-0600
44)	MV	1600		R. Maya Visión, San Salvador
22)		1630		R. Elohim, San Salvador

Addresses & other information:
1) Misión Cristiana Elim, Ap. 2854 (or Calle al Matazano N° 1, A cien metros al occidente de bomba de ANDA), San Salvador **W:** elim.org.sv/540am – **2)** Colonia San Miguel, Cl Principal Pasaje Castillo, San Ramón Mejicanos, San Salvador. **W:** radiotiempoelsalvador.com – **3)** Edif. Alameda Manuel Enrique Araujo, San Salvador **W:** voxfm.com – **4)** 75 Av Norte, Prolongación Juan Pablo II, Col Jardines de Escalón, final Pasaje KL, San Salvador **W:** radiosantasion.com – **6)** San Salvador **W:** lavozdelreydegloria.com – **7)** Ap., 720, San Salvador **W:** quebuena.com.sv – **8)** 65 Av. Sur #192, , San Salvador **W:** radioyskl.com – **9)** Colonia Ciudad Real, Recidencial La Floresta, Pligono "E" N° 2, Calle Elizabeth, San Miguel **W:** ministerioradiosinai.com – **10)** 1a Calle Poniente N°3412, Col. Escalón, Frente al Seminario San José de la Montaña, San Salvador **W:** radioysax6.webnode.es – **13)** Iglesia San Pablo, Final 5a Calle Poniente, Colonia Escalón, San Salvador **W:** radiosantabibliasv.com – **14)** Jardines de la Cima, San Salvador **W:** facebook.com/RenacerAM – **15)** Centro de San Salvador, San Salvador **W:** radiocristoviene1100am.org – **16)** 1er Calle Josniente, San Salvador 503 **W:** radiosanjose.org – **17)** Bo El Calvario 4 Av Sur No 303 San Miguel **W:** radiochaparrastique.net – **18)** Avenida España Y 21 Calle Poniente Ex Cine Fausto #114, Esquina Opuesta Al Mercado San Miguelito, San Salvador **W:** ipda.com.sv/radio_en_vivo – **19)** Av.2 de Abril y 8a Calle Poniente, Ahuachapán – **20)** 10 Av. Norte, 3101 San Miguel **W:** radiocret.net/?page_id=65 – **21)** Santa Ana **W:** radiocadenacret.com/?page_id=391 – **22)** 8a Av. Norte #225, atrás de la Despensa Familiar, por el parque San José, San Salvador **W:** misioncristianaelohim.com/conectar-radio – **24)** 8va. Avenida Norte. Casa #108 Barrio La Cruz, San Miguel **W:** radiomisioneravda.com – **26)** 2a Calle Poniente 22, Zacatecoluca **FM:** 92.5 **W:** radiosalem.org – **27)** San Miguel **W:** radiovisionministeriosunidos.com – **28)** 14 Calle Poniente, San Miguel **W:** facebook.com/Radio-Norteña-El-Salvador-164392333624699 – **29)** Antigua Calle Ferrocarril, #2106, Colonia 3 de Mayo, San Salvador **W:** radioabba1260am.com – **30)** 2 Av N N° 10, San Vicente **W:** facebook.com/radioemaus1280am – **31)** Calle a San Francisco Lempa, Col. Veracruz, Chalatenango **W:** radiochalatenango.com.sv – **33) W:** radiouncionypresenciadedios.com – **34)** Bo El Centro, C.Bolivar y 4 Av.S, Stgo de María, Usulután – **35)** Carr.Panamericana, Crio El Alto, 300 mts al Norte, El Jalacatal, San Miguel. **W:** radiolluviasdebendicion.com.sv – **36)** Calle General Menéndez No. 2-3, La Unión **W:** radiogetsemani.net – **37)** Calle al trapiche, Chalchuapa, Santa Ana **W:** lavozdelapalabraquecambia.blogspot.com – **38)** Carretera al Plan del Pino. Una cuadra antes de la Ciudadela Don Bosco, Soyapango, San Salvador **W:** lavozdelreydegloria.com – **39)** 12 Av.Sur y final 5a Calle Oriente, Col. Santa Rosa, Usulután **W:** lavozdellitoral.com - **FM:** 90.1MHz – **40)** Iglesia Elim, 8a Calle Poniente, San Miguel **W:** elimsanmiguel.org – **41)** Kilómetro 112½, Carretera El Litoral, Frente a Desvío El Mora, Usulután **W:** radiopentecostalbethel.org – **42)** San Salvador **W:** radiopeniel1500am.com – **43)** Calle 25 de Abril Poniente, Barrio San José # 22B, San Marcos, San Salvador **W:** radiosanidaddivina.com – **44)** Calle a San Antonio Abad No. 2209, Col. Centroamérica, San Salvador **W:** radiomayavision.net – **45)** Carretera de Oro km. 8 1/2 Colonia Altavista Ilopango, San Salvador **W:** radiocristotellama.net

FM in San Salvador (MHz): 88.1 Legislativa – 88.5 Paz – (7) 88.9 Qué Buena – 89.3 Cool – 89.7 Bautista – 90.1 Láser (Spanish) – 90.5 Progreso – 90.9 UPA – 91.3 Exa – 91.7 YSUCA – 92.1 La Klave – 92.5 Club – 92.9 Láser (English) – 93.3 Globo – 93.7 El Mundo – 94.1 Super Estrella – 94.5 Vox FM – 94.9 La Urbana – 95.3 Órbita – 95.7 Verdad – 96.1 Scan – 96.5 Adventista – 96.9 R. El Salvador – 97.3 Corazón – 97.7 Luz – 98.1 Gospel FM – 98.5 Cadena Cuscatlán – 98.9 La Mejor – 99.3 Mesías – 99.7 Full FM – 100.1 ABC – 100.5 Restauración – 100.9 La Chévere – 101.3 Plus – 101.7 Mil80 –102.1 Vive –102.5 Femenina – 102.9 102 Nueve – 103.3 Clásica – 103.7 Cadena Central – (8) 104.1 KL La Poderosa – 104.5 Sonora – 104.9 Fiesta – 105.3 Punto 105 – 105.7 YXY – 106.1 El Camino – 106.5 Ranchera – 106.9 FM – 107.3 María – 107.7 Fuego.

FM in San Miguel (MHz): 90.1 Stereo Caliente - 90.5 Siglo 21– 90.9 Popular – 91.7 YSUCA – 92.5 Monseñor Romero – 94.1 Cadena Central – 96.5 Agape R. – 97.3 Carnaval – 98.1 La Pantera – 99.7 Mi

Consentida - 102.9 102 Nueve – 104.1 YSKL La Poderosa – 106.1 La Grande – 107.3 R. María.

FM in Santa Ana (MHz): 90.5 Supra Stereo - 91.7 YSUCA - 92.1 Fe y Alegría – (9) 92.5 R. Doremix – 93.3 Shabach – 95.3 Amor – 97.3 La Campirana – 97.9 Real FM – 99.7 Doble H - 102.9 102 Nueve – 104.1 YSKL La Poderosa – 105.3 Soda Stereo – 106.1 Bautista

EQUATORIAL GUINEA

L.T: UTC +1h — **Pop:** 1.4 million — **Pr.L:** Official languages: Spanish, French, Portuguese — **E.C:** 220V/50Hz — **ITU:** GNE

MINISTERIO DE INFORMACIÓN

✉ Barrio Nzalang (antiguo África 2000), Malabo ☎+240 333 078221 🖷 +240 333 072444

RADIO TELEVISIÓN DE GUINEA ECUATORIAL (RTVGE, Gov.)

✉ Ap. 749, Bata ☎+240 333 082592 🖷 +240 333 082093 ✉ Av. 3 de Agosto 90, Ap. 195, Malabo ☎+240 333 072260 🖷 +240 333 072097
W: (TV) tvgelive.gq **L.P:** Dir. Tech: Barila Sota.

SW	kHz	kW	Times
Bata	5005	50	0430-1730/2300v (irregular)
Malabo (Semu)	‡6250	20	0500-2300 (inactive)

FM: Bata 98.0MHz 1kW, Malabo 90.9MHz 12kW.
D.Prgr: in Spanish/ethnic.
Rural radio: La Voz de Kie-Ntem at Ebibeyín, Ecos de Wele Nzás at Mongomo and La Voz de Centro Sur at Evinayong.

Other Stations:
R. Asonga, Malabo 90.0/107.0MHz **W:** facebook.com/AsongaRadio
R. María, Malabo 94.0MHz **W:** radiomaria.gq
Africa Radio, Malabo 103.0MHz **W:** africaradio.com
BBC World Sce, Malabo 92.5MHz in English/French.
RFI Afrique, Bata 88.5, Malabo 88.0/97.5MHz in French/Spanish

ERITREA

L.T: UTC +3h — **Pop:** 3.6 million — **Pr.L:** Afar, Arabic, Tigrinya, Tigre — **E.C:** 230V/50Hz — **ITU:** ERI

MINISTRY OF INFORMATION

✉ P.O. Box 872, Asmara ☎+291 1 120478/201820 🖷 +291 1 126747
W: shabait.com **E:** nesredin@tse.com.er

VOICE OF THE BROAD MASSES OF ERITREA (Gov.)

✉ P.O. Box 242, Asmara ☎+291 1 117111/118711 🖷 +291 1 124847
L.P: DG: Ghirmay Berhe. TD: Mehreteab Tesfagiorgis. PD: Abdu Heji. Dir. Radio Eng.: Berhane Gerezgiher.
Station: Asmara (Selai Dairo).
MW: 837kHz 100kW (Prgr. 2), 945kHz 100kW (Prgr. 1). Alt. fq's used are 840 and 950 kHz.
SW: 7140kHz 100kW (Prgr. 1), 7180 kHz 100kW (Prgr. 2). Both irregular and frequency variable.
Prgr. 1 in Tigrinya/Tigre/Kunama: 0250-1900v – **Prgr. 2** in Arabic/Afar/Amharic/Oromo/Saho/Bilen: 0250-1900v.
Zara FM: 100MHz + others. **Numa FM:** 90MHz.
Ann: Amharic:"Yeh be Asmera ketema yemigegne yesifiw Yeritrea hezeb demts yeamarigna agelgilot new". Arabic: "Huna Asmara, Idha'at Sawt al-Jamahir al-Iritriyyah". Tigrigna: "Ezi kab Asmara Zemehalalef Medeber Radio Demtsi Hafash Eritrea Eyu"

ESTONIA

L.T: UTC +2h (28 Mar-31 Oct: +3h) — **Pop:** 1.3 million — **Pr.L:** Estonian (official), Russian — **E.C:** 230V/50Hz — **ITU:** EST

KULTUURIMINISTEERIUM (Ministry of Culture)

✉ Suur-Karja 23, 15076 Tallinn ☎ +372 6282222 **E:** min@kul.ee **W:** kul.ee **L.P:** Minister: Tõnis Lukas

EESTI RAHVUSRINGHÄÄLING (ERR) (Pub)

✉ F.R. Kreutzwaldi 14, 10124 Tallinn ☎ +372 6284100 **E:** err@err.ee
W: err.ee **L.P:** Chmn: Rein Veidemann

FM (MHz)	1	2	3	4	kW
Koeru	105.1	102.6	107.6	93.4	3x30/7.8
Kohtla-Nõmme	105.4	102.9	90.4	95.3	11.2
Kuressaare	105.6	103.1	107.0	-	1
Kõrgessaare	91.2	99.1	94.9	-	1
Mõksi	-	-	-	99.9	3
Orissaare	105.9	103.4	107.8	-	20/2x10
Pärnu	104.8	102.3	107.3	94.8	10
Tallinn	104.1	101.6	106.6	94.5	30
Valga	-	-	-	92.5	1.8
Valgjärve	106.1	103.6	105.7	-	2x40/12.5
Viiratsi	105.8	103.3	107.0	95.5	1

+ sites with only txs below 1kW.
D.Prgr: Prgr 1 (Vikerraadio): 24h – **Prgr 2 (Raadio 2)**: 24h – **Prgr 3 (Klassikaraadio):** 24h – **Prgr 4 (Raadio 4)** for ethnic minorities: 24h in Russian – **ERR Raadio Tallinn** 103.5MHz (1kW): 24h. Own prgrs 0500-2000; relays: 0300-0500 & 2000-2300 BBCWS (UK), 2300-0300 RFI (France).

OTHER STATIONS

MW	kHz	kW	Location	Station
13)	1035	100	Tartu (Kavastu)	R. Eli
FM	**MHz**	**kW**	**Location**	**Station**
2B)	87.7	1	Kehtna	Sky Plus
3A)	88.1	1	Koeru	Star FM
2C)	88.2	1	Kõmsi	Retro FM
8)	88.3	2	Tallinn	Relax FM
4)	88.6	3	Pärnu	Raadio 7
2F)	88.8	1	Tallinn	Rock FM
6)	89.0	1.3	Vanamõisa	Pereraadio
6)	89.0	2.3	Rõõmu	Pereraadio
6)	89.6	2.3	Tallinn	Pereraadio
1C)	89.8	1.2	Karitsa	MyHits
1A)	89.9	1	Pärnu	Raadio Kuku
9)	90.1	1	Käina	Raadio Kadi
9)	90.5	1	Aste	Raadio Kadi
1C)	91.0	3	Pärnu	MyHits
1B)	91.0	1	Kohtla-Nõmme	Raadio Elmar
1B)	91.2	6.5	Valgjärve	Raadio Elmar
5A)	91.3	1	Raikküla	Tre Raadio
1B)	91.5	1.5	Tallinn	Raadio Elmar
1B)	91.5	1	Kuressaare	Raadio Elmar
1B)	91.7	7.5	Koeru	Raadio Elmar
1B)	92.2	1	Haapsalu	Raadio Elmar
3A)	92.2	2.9	Karitsa	Star FM
1C)	92.3	1	Parksepa	MyHits
3B)	92.5	1	Karitsa	Power Hit R.
5A)	92.7	1.5	Pärnu	Tre Raadio
3A)	92.9	3	Haapsalu	Star FM
2E)	93.2	1.5	Tallinn	NRJ FM
3A)	93.3	2.2	Kuressaare	Star FM
2B)	93.8	3	Holsta	Sky Plus
2B)	95.2	1	Rõõmu	Sky Plus
2B)	95.4	2	Tallinn	Sky Plus
2C)	95.4	1	Aste	Retro FM
11)	96.0	1	Haapsalu	Äripäeva Raadio
4)	96.1	3	Tamsalu	Raadio 7
2B)	96.3	1.9	Vätta	Sky Plus
3A)	96.6	1.5	Tallinn	Star FM
7)	96.6	1	Sangaste	Ruut FM
2B)	96.8	1.6	Audru	Sky Plus
2B)	96.9	1.5	Sääre	Sky Plus
1C)	97.2	2	Tallinn	MyHits
1C)	97.2	1	Tartu	MyHits
1C)	97.4	3	Kuressaare	MyHits
1C)	97.4	2.5	Koeru	MyHits
2B)	97.6	1	Rohuküla	Sky Plus
12)	97.7	1.5	Kohtla-Nõmme	Jumor FM
2C)	97.8	4	Tallinn	Retro FM
2C)	97.9	1	Viiratsi	Retro FM
2C)	98.3	1.2	Audru	Retro FM
2A)	98.4	3	Tallinn	Sky R.
2C)	98.6	2.5	Rõõmu	Retro FM
9)	98.6	1	Liiva	Raadio Kadi
1B)	99.0	3	Pärnu	Raadio Elmar
3A)	99.4	2	Tartu	Star FM
1A)	99.6	3.2	Tüükri	Raadio Kuku
1A)	99.6	1	Karitsa	Raadio Kuku
2B)	99.7	1	Viiratsi	Sky Plus
1C)	99.8	2.5	Haapsalu	MyHits
1D)	100.0	1	Narva	Narodnoe R.
1A)	100.2	2	Tartu	Raadio Kuku
3A)	100.3	2	Pärnu	Star FM

FM	MHz	kW	Location	Station
1A)	100.4	1	Männamaa	Raadio Kuku
1A)	100.5	2	Koeru	Raadio Kuku
1A)	100.6	3	Kuressaare	Raadio Kuku
10)	100.7	3	Põlva	R. Marta
1A)	100.7	1.9	Tallinn	Raadio Kuku
1A)	100.8	1.5	Viiratsi	Raadio Kuku
1A)	100.9	2.5	Haapsalu	Raadio Kuku
5A)	101.0	3	Paide	Tre Raadio
2D)	101.2	1.3	Männamaa	Russkoe R.
2B)	101.3	1	Assamalla	Sky Plus
5B)	101.7	1	Mõksi	Ring FM
11)	101.7	3	Sauvere	Äripäeva Raadio
3B)	102.1	1.5	Tallinn	Power Hit R.
3A)	102.8	1	Valga	Star FM
3A)	103.2	3	Parksepa	Star FM
1C)	104.5	1	Orissaare	MyHits
5B)	104.7	1	Tartu	Ring FM
12)	104.9	1.5	Tallinn	Jumor FM
5B)	105.8	1	Tallinn	Ring FM
2B)	106.8	1	Kullamaa	Sky Plus
3C)	106.9	1	Kohtla-Nõmme	R. Volna

+ txs below 1kW.

Addresses & other information:

1A-D) Veerenni 58a, 11314 Tallinn, exc. 1B) Õpetaja 9a, 51003 Tartu. 1D in Russian – **2A-D)** Pärnu mnt. 139f, 11317 Tallinn. 2A,C,D in Russian – **3A-C)** Peterburi 81, 11415 Tallinn. 3C in Russian – **4)** Välja 18, 10616 Tallinn – **5A,B)** 5A) Asula 4c, 11315 Tallinn; 5B) Peterburi 49, 11415 Tallinn – **6)** Annemõisa 8, 50708 Tartu – **7)** Pikk 3a, 68206 Valga – **8)** Estonia puiestee 9, 10143 Tallinn – **9)** Kohtu 1, 93819 Kuressaare – **10)** Kesk 42, 63304 Põlva – **11)** Vana Lõuna 39/1, 19094 Tallinn – **12)** Osmussaare tee 8, 13619 Tallinn. In Russian – **13)** Kreenholmi 38a, 20205 Narva. In Russian. **E:** raadioeli@gmail.com

ESWATINI

L.T: UTC +2h — **Pop:** 1.2 million — **Pr.L:** Swati (official), English (official) — **E.C:** 230V/50Hz — **ITU:** SWZ

ESWATINI COMMUNICATIONS COMMISSION (ESCCOM)

✉ Mbabane Office Park, Fourth Floor North Wing, P.O. Box 7811, Mbabane **W:** www.sccom.org.sz **E:** info@sccom.org.sz

ESWATINI BROADCASTING AND INFORMATION SERVICES (EBIS, Gov.)

✉ P.O. Box 338, Corner Gwamile & Dzeliwe Streets, Mbabane H100 ☎+268 24061002 🖷 +268 24044678 **W:** gov.sz/index.php/ministries-departments/ministry-of-ict/swaziland-braodcating-a-information-services **E:** dlaminimart@gov.sz

FM: 88.5/91.6/93.6/105.2MHz 10kW + 4 low power relays.

English Sce: 0255-1800 on 91.6/93.6MHz.

Siswati Sce: 0255-2100 on FM 88.5/105.2MHz.

IS: at s/on, Cilongo (Swazi instrument). English Sce: cock crow, fanfare, spoken ID, instrumental theme.

TRANS WORLD RADIO - VOICE OF THE CHURCH

✉ P.O. Box 4544, Corner Martin & Tenbergen St, Manzini **W:** vocfm.org **W:** info@voc.org.sz ☎+268 25054845 🖷 +268 25054809 **L.P:** Nat. Dir: Nelson Vilakati, Adm: Tryphinah Dlamini, PM: Abel Vilakati.

FM: Mbabane 95.0, Siteki 96.0, Mankayane/Pigg's Peak 97.0, Manzini 97.1, Hlatikhulu 101.0MHz.

MW: TWR Africa, Mpangela Ranch 1170kHz 1800(Sun 1745)-2200 100kW & SW. For further details see Int. Radio section

ETHIOPIA

L.T: UTC +3h — **Pop:** 110 million — **Pr.L:** Amharic (official), Afar, Oromo, Sidamo, Somali, Tigrinya — **E.C:** 220V/50Hz — **ITU:** ETH

ETHIOPIAN BROADCASTING AUTHORITY (EBA)

✉ P.O. Box 43142, Hailalem Bldg. Kazanchis, Addis Ababa ☎+251 11 5538755 🖷 +251 11 5536767 **W:** www.eba.gov.et **E:** e.b.a1@ethionet.et

ETHIOPIA BROADCASTING CORPORATION RADIO ETHIOPIA (Gov.)

✉ P.O. Box 1020, Addis Ababa ☎+251 11 5516977 **W:** ebc.et **E:** ebc@ebc.et

MW	kHz	kW	MW	kHz	kW
Metu	684	100	Dese	891	100
Arba Minch	828	100	Robe (Bale)	972	100
Harar	855	100	Mekele	1044	200
Addis Ababa	873	100	Negele Borana	1485	10

Note: many transmitters are run on lower power.

FM(MHz): Addis Ababa 93.1 2.5kW, 96.3 3.5kW, 97.1, 104.7, Bahir Dar 94.5MHz, unknown sites: 88.7, 90.3, 91.9, 93.5, 98.7, 102.2.

National Sce in Amharic/Others: 24h (some MW's 0245-2100v). **Reg. prgrs** evenings until 1700. **FM Addis** in Amharic on 97.1MHz. **EBC R.** in English on 104.7MHz 0300-2100.

Ann: (National Sce) "Yeh Ethiopia Broadcasting Corporation".

FANA BROADCASTING CORPORATE

✉ P.O.Box 30702, near Black Lion Hospital, in front of Sweden Embassy, Addis Ababa. **W:** fanabc.com **E:** info@fanabc.com

L.P: GM: Woldu Yemessel. Tech. Dir: Mulugeta Mehari.

MW: Addis Ababa (Repi) 1080kHz 3kW.

SW: Addis Ababa (Geja) 6110kHz 100kW.

FM (MHz): Haromaya/Mekele 94.8, Dese 96.0, Nekemit 96.1, Addis Ababa/Gonder/Jimma 98.1, Wolayita 99.9, Shashemenie 103.4.

D.Prgr. "Fana National" in Afar/Amharic/Oromo/Somali/Tigrinya: 0255-2100 on MW & SW. **Fana FM:** on FM. **Ann:** Oromo: "Kun Radio Fana Broadcasting Corporate."

Regional Government Stations:

RADIO OROMIA (Oromia Broadcasting Network, OBN)

✉ P.O. Box 2919, Adama **W:** obnoromia.com **E:** obnoromiyaa@gmail.com

MW: Robe (Bale) 837kHz 100kW, Adama (Nazret) 1035kHz 10kW, Nekemte 1053kHz 100kW.

SW: Addis Ababa (Geja): 6030kHz 100kW.

FM (MHz): Addis Ababa (Intoto) 92.3, Degem 95.4, Ambo 96.4, Goba 96.5, Gimbi 99.2, Wadera 103.3, Adama 103.7, Wenchi 105.5, all 5kW.

D.Prgr. in Oromo (some Amharic&English): 0250-2000, irr. 24h. Also regional programming for west and southwest Oromia. **Ann:** Oromo: "Kun Radio Oromiya".

VOICE OF TIGRAY REVOLUTION (Gov)

✉ P.O.Box 450, Mekele, Tigray ☎+251 34 4410544/5 **W:** dimtsiwoyane.com

MW: Mekele 1359kHz 100kW.

SW: Addis Ababa 5950kHz 100kW.

FM: DWET FM: Axum 90.7, Shire 91.4, Humera 95.5, Mekele 102.2MHz 3kW.

D.Prgr in Tigrinya/Afar: MF 0300-2000, SS 0300-1730 (DWET FM 0300-2100). **Ann:** Tigrinya: **"**Dimtsi Woyane Tigray". **IS:** Melody played on washint (Ethiopian flute).

AMHARA RADIO (Pub.)

✉ Amhara Mass Media Agency, P.O. Box 955, Bahir Dar **W:** amharaweb.com **E:** amharamass@gmail.com

MW: Bahir Dar (Zege) 801kHz 100kW.

SW: Addis Ababa 6090kHz 100kW.

FM: Mt. Choke 95.1, Bahir Dar 96.9, Gondar 105.1MHz.

D. Prgr in Amharic/Awinya/Himtinya/Oromo: 0300-2100. **Ann:** Amharic: "Yeh ye Amhara Radio".

ETHIOPIAN SOMALI REGIONAL STATE RADIO (Gov.)

SW: Jigjiga (presumed loc.) 5940kHz 50kW. (inactive)

FM: Jigjiga (presumed loc.) 99.1MHz

D. Prgr in Somali: 0400-0600, 1300-1500, 1800-2100 (times variable). **Ann:** Somali: "Halkan wa Raadiyaha Dowlad Deegaanka Somalida Itoobia".

SIDAMA EDUCATIONAL RADIO

✉ c/o Furra Institute of Development Studies, P.O. Box 69, Yirga Alem: **MW:** 954kHz 2.5kW. **D.Prgr:** 0400-1800.

GIMBI EDUCATIONAL RADIO

MW: Gimbi 1215kHz 10kW 0400-2000 (irr., running on 2.5kW).

SOUTH FM (Gov)

✉ Southern Nations & Nationalities Mass Media Agency, P.O. Box 1080, Awassa.

FM: Awassa 96.9MHz, Arba Minch 90.9, Bensa 92.3, Bonga 97.4, Dire Dawa 106.1 2kW, Gedio 99.4, Jinka 87.8, Mizan 104.5, Waka

94.1, Wolkitie 89.2MHz.

Other Governmental Stations:
Addis Ababa R: 96.3MHz 4kW – **Bahir Dar FM:** 96.9MHz – **Debub FM,** Awassa: 100.6MHz – **Dire Dawa FM:** 106.1MHz 2kW – **Finfine FM:** Adama 92.3MHz – **Harari FM:** Harar: 101.4MHz – **Mekele FM:** 104.4MHz – **Somali FM,** Jigjiga 99.1MHz.

Other Stations:
Abay FM, Addis Ababa: 102.9MHz **W:** facebook.com/Abayfm102.9 – **Afro FM,** Addis Ababa: 105.3MHz 2.5kW. **W:** afro105fm.com – **Ahadu R,** Addis Ababa: 94.3MHz **W:** ahaduradio.com – **Bisrat R,** Addis Ababa: 101.1MHz **W:** bisratfm.com – **ECSU R,** Addis Ababa: 100.5MHz **W:** facebook.com/ECSU.FM.RADIO – **Ethio FM,** Addis Ababa: 107.8MHz **W:** ethiofmradio.com – **Ravos FM,** Awasa: 100.9MHz – **Sheger FM,** Addis Ababa: 102.1MHz. **W:** shegerfm.com – **Zami R,** Addis Ababa: 90.7MHz 2kW. **W:** zami.com.et

Community Radio:
Finote Selam Community R: 98.8MHz **W:** facebook.com/Finote-selam-community-Radio-FM-988-1928324040812967
HU FM, Haramaya 91.5MHz **W:** haramaya.edu.et/community/radio Korie 92.3MHz, Argoba 98.6MHz, Jimma 102.0MHz, Keffa 102.5, Kombolcha 104.8, Kembata 105.8MHz

FALKLAND ISLANDS (UK)

L.T: UTC -3h — **Pop:** 3,100 (excl. c. 300 military personnel) — **Pr.L:** English — **E.C:** 230V/50Hz — **ITU:** FLK

FALKLANDS RADIO (Pub)
✉ John Street, Stanley FIQQ 1ZZ (PO Box 786) ☎+500 27277. **W:** www.radio.co.fk **E:** stationmanager@radio.co.fk **L.P:** Stn Man.: Corina Goss, Content Lead: Liz Roberts, Engineer.: Jason Lewis
MW: 530kHz 15kW. **FM**(MHz): Stanley 96.5 2kW, North 88.2, West 88.4, South 88.6, East 88.8. **NB:** Rel. BBC World Service when Falklands R. off air

BRITISH FORCES BROADCASTING SERVICE
✉ Rockhopper Road, RAF Mount Pleasant. BFPO 655. ☎+500 73003. 🖷 +500 32193. **E:** fi@bfbs.com **W:** forces.net/radio
L.P: SM: Anthony Ballard. Eng. Mgr: Callum Pilkington.
BFBS Radio 2: W: forces.net/radio/stations/bfbs-radio-2
FM(MHz): Mt Sussex 88.2, Mt William 88.8, MPA West 93.8 2kW, 300W, Sapper Hill 94.5 300W, Port Howard 100.4, Byron Heights/Mt Alice/Mt Kent 104.2 10W
BFBS Falkland Islands: W: forces.net/radio/stations/bfbs-falkland-islands **FM**(MHz): Sapper Hill 91.1, MPA West 98.5, Port Howard 101.6, Byron Heights/Mt Alice/Mt Kent/ 102.4 10W, Mt Sussex 106.2, Mt William 106.8
BFBS Radio Gurkha: W: forces.net/radio/stations/bfbs-radio-gurkha **FM**(MHz): MPA West 96.0 2kW, Byron Heights/Mt Alice/Mt Kent 106.0 10W
D.Prgr: 24h **N:** Every hour from BFBS Radio UK News by satellite from London. **Ann:** "This is BFBS in the Falklands". **V.** by QSL-card. Rp.

FAROE ISLANDS (Denmark)

L.T: UTC (28 Mar-31 Oct: +1h) — **Pop:** 49,000 — **Pr.L:** Faroese (official), Danish (official) — **E.C:** 230V/50Hz — **ITU:** FRO

MENTAMÁLARÁÐIÐ (Ministry of Education, Research & Culture)
✉ Hoyvíksvegur 72, PO Box 3279, FO 110 Tórshavn ☎ +298 306500 **E:** mmr@mmr.fo **W:** www.mmr.fo **L.P:** Minister: Rigmor Dam

KRINGVARP FØROYA ÚTVARPIÐ (Pub.)
✉ Norðari Ringvegur 20, PO Box 1299, FO 100 Tórshavn ☎ +298 347500 🖷 +298 347501 **E:** netvarp@kvf.fo **W:** kvf.fo
L.P: SM: Ivan Hentze Niclasen. Head of news: Georg L. Petersen. TD: Hjallgrím P. Hentze.
MW: Akraberg 531kHz 10kW
FM (MHz): Tórshavn 89.9 31kW, Klaksvík 94.3 41kW, Hesturin Suðuroy 97.5 27kW, Støðlafjall 100.0 3kW, Knukur 92.1 1kW + 25 LP stns **D.Prgr:** 24h. All prgrs are in Faroese. **Ann:** 'Útvarpið"

MIÐLAR (Comm.)
✉ Grønlandsvegur 38, FO 100 Tórshavn ☎ +298 223910 **E:** midlar@midlar.fo **W:** midlar.fo L.P: Petur Zachariassen
FM1: Tórshavn 91.1/98.7, Klaksvík 88.7, Streymoy 95.9, Varmakelda 90.9, Høganesi 93.1. **D.Prgr:** 24h
VoxPop: Tórshavn 91.7/104.1, Klaksvík 90.7, Streymoy 104.8, Varmakelda 90.3, Høganesi 93.9. **D.Prgr:** 24h

R7 KRINGVARP (Comm.)
✉ PO Box 226, FO 600 Saltangará ☎ +298 207777 **E:** r7@r7.fo **W:** r7.fo **FM**(MHz): Tórshavn 102.0 1kW, Suðuroy 102.9 1kW, Streymoy 106.0 1kW, Klaksvík 107.0 1kW + 11 LP stns.

LINDIN KRISTILIGT KRINGVARP (Rlg.)
✉ Bøkjaragøta 9, PO Box 2063, FO 165 Argir (Tórshavn) ☎ +298 321377 🖷 +298 321379 **E:** lindin@lindin.fo **W:** lindin.fo
L.P: Chairman: Preben Hansen
FM(MHz): Tórshavn 101.0 3kW, Klaksvík 103.0 500W, Suðuroy 105.5 2.5kW, Norðurstreymoy 98.0 1kW + 10 LP stns. **D.Prgr:** 24h

LOCAL STATIONS (in MHz):
STAÐIÐ FM, Ungdómshúsið, FO 350 Vestmanna **Prgr:** Su&Th at 2100 LT. **FM:** 101.0 – **STREAM 98.7**, Skáltavegur 29, PO Box 242, FO 700 Klaksvík. **W:** stream.fo **L.P.:** Johnny Olsen **FM:** 98.7MHz

FIJI

L.T: UTC +12h (20 Dec 20-17 Jan 21, 14 Nov 21-16 Jan 22: +13h) **NB:** UTC times refer to DST period — **Pop:** 919,000 — **Pr.L:** Official languages: Fijian, English, Hindi — **E.C:** 240V/50Hz — **ITU:** FJI

DEPARTMENT OF COMMUNICATIONS
✉ 1st Floor, Credit Corporation Building, Suva ✉ PO Box 11689, Suva. ☎ +679 330 0766 🖷 +679 331 5167 **W:** communications.gov.fj
LP: Dep. Secretary: Josua Turaganivalu

TELECOMMUNICATIONS AUTHORITY OF FIJI
76 Gordon Street, GPO Box 13413, Suva ☎+679 3310101 🖷+679 3310110 **W:** taf.org.fj **E:** contact@taf.org.fj
Regulator of radio broadcasting in Fiji

FIJI BROADCASTING CORPORATION LTD (Pub/Comm)
✉ PO Box 334, Suva ☎+679 331 4333 🖷 +679 330 1643 **W:** fbc.com.fj **E:** infocenter@fbc.com.fj **LP:** CEO: Riyaz Saiyed Khaiyum C.E: Apisai Bakani
Netw.: RF1 (R.Fiji One Na Domoiviti) Fijian ☎ +679 322 0900 **W:** rf1.fbc.com.fj & facebook.com/radio-fiji-one-domoiviti E: rf1@fbc.com.fj– **RF2 (R.Fiji Two Desh ki Dhadkan)** Hindi ☎ +679 322 0902 **W:** rf2.fbc.com.fj & facebook.com/radio-fiji-two E: rf2@fbc.com.fj – **R.Mirchi** Hindi ☎ +679 322 0908 **W:** http://mirchifm.com.fj & facebook.com/mirchifm E: mirchifm1@fbc.com.fj – **RFGold (R.Fiji Gold)** English ☎ +679 322 0906 **W:** http://goldfm.com.fj & facebook.com/goldfmfiji E: goldfm@fbc.com.fj – **Bula FM** Fijian ☎ +679 322 0910 **W:** bulafm@fbc.com.fj & facebook.com/bula-fm E: bulafm@fbc.com.fj – **2dayFM** English ☎ +679 322 0904 **W:** www.2dayfm.com.fj & facebook.com/2dayfm-fiji E: 2dayfm@fbc.com.fj **Prgr:** All 24/7 audio streaming via individual station websites

MW	kHz	kW	Netw.
Suva	558	10	RF1
Suva	990	10	RFGold

FM	RF1	RF2	Bula FM	R.Mirchi	RFGOLD	2dayFM
1)	93.0	105.0	102.6	97.8	100.2	95.4
2)	92.8	104.8	102.4	97.6	100.0	95.2
3)	93.2	105.2	102.8	98.0	100.4	95.6
4)	93.4	105.4	103.0	98.2	100.6	95.8

1) Deuba, Navua, Lami, Suva, Nausori, Korovou, Nadi, Lautoka, Yasawas, Mamanuca, Savusavu, Tavenui – **2)** Coral Coast, Nabau, Serua, Ba – **3)** Tavua – **4)** Rakiraki

Private Commercial Network
COMMUNICATIONS FIJI LTD (Comm)
✉ 231 Waimanu Road [Private Mail Bag], Suva ☎ +679 331 4766 🖷 +679 330 3748 **W:** https://fijivillage.com **E:** info@fijivillage.com.fj **LP:** Man.Dir: William Parkinson, GM Fiji: Ian Jackson **E:** ian@fm96.com.fj CE: Philip Wilikibau **E:** philip@fm96.com.fj
Netw.: FM96 (English) **W:** http:/fm96.com.fj **E:** fm96@fm96.com.fj– **Legend FM** (English) **W:** htttps:/legendfm.com.fj **E:** legendfm@legendfm.com.fj – **Viti FM** (Fijian) W: https:/vitifm.com.fj **E:** vitifm.com.fj – **Navtarang** (Hindi) **W:** http:/navtarang.com.fj **E:** navtarang@navtrang.com.fj – **R. Sargam** (Hindi) **W:** https:/sargam.com.fj **E:** sargram@sargram.com.fj **Prgr:** All 24/7

FM	FM96	Navtarang	Viti FM	Legend FM	R.Sargam
1)	96.2	101.0	92.2	98.6	103.4
2)	96.0	100.8	92.0	98.4	103.2
3)	96.6	101.4	92.6	99.0	103.8

1) Suva, Nausori, Central Division, Nadi, Lautoka, Labassa – **2)** Sigatoka, Coral Coast, Ba, Tavua, Vatukoula – **3)** Rakiraki

OTHER STATIONS:

FM	MHz	Station	Location
1)	88.2	BBC	Nadi
1)	88.2	BBC	Suva
2)	89.0	fem'TALK 89 FM	Suva
2)	89.0	fem'TALK 89 FM	Labasa
3)	89.4	R. Pasifik	Suva
4)	89.8	Harvest R.	Suva/Navua/Nausori
5)	91.8	R. France Int.	Suva
6)	93.6	MIX 94FM	Sigatoka
6)	93.8	MIX 94FM	Suva/Lautoka/Nadi/ Mamanucas/Yasawas
6)	94.2	MIX 94FM	Ba/Tavua/RakiRaki
7)	94.6	R. Naya Jiwan	Suva/Navua/Nausori
7)	104.0	R. Light	Sigatoka/Nadi
7)	104.2	R. Light	Suva
8)	106.0	Hope FM	Vanualevu
9)	106.6	R. Australia	Suva
9)	106.6	R. Australia	Nadi
8)	107.0	Hope FM	Suva/Navua/Nausori
8)	107.4	Hope FM	Ba/Tavua/Vatukaola/Nadi/ Lautoka/Vanua Levu

Addresses and other information:

1) 24/7 Pacific stream via satellite from London – **2)** Community Media Center, 54 Ratu Sukuna Road, Suva ☎ +679 3318160/3310307 🖹 +679 323 1908 **W:** femlinkpacific.org.fj **L.P:** Exec.Dir: Sharon Bhagwan Rolls. Stations: Suva **Prgr:** 24/7, Labasa : **Prgr:** 2100-0500 (Monday-Friday) : Also operates a mobile community radio stn studio for women on Viti Levu **3)** School of Law, Arts & Media, University of the South Pacific, Private Mail Bag, Laucala, Suva ☎ 🖹+679 3231908 **L.P:** SM: Allan Stevens **W:** usp.ac.fj **D:Prgr:** 2000-1200 includes prgrs in English, Pidgin, Hindi and iTaukei languages. As all staff are volunteers, stn only on-air during academic year. Format local Pacific music— **4)** World Harvest Centre, 1 Corner of Kings and Khalsa Rd, Kinoya, Suva. PO Box 1499, Nabua, Suva ☎ +679 3398901 **W:** whbn.info **E**: whbn.info@gmail.com **L.P:** Mktg Mgr: Rajiv Puran **D.Prgr:** 24/7 rlg – **5)** RFI Satellite link from Paris. – **6)** 11 Nasoki St, Lautoka ☎ +679 666 8900 **W:** mix.com.fj **E:** info@mix,com.fj **ID:** "Fiji's Best Mix" 24h/7 – **7)** Pacific Islands Christian Network [PICN], Evangelical Bible Missions Trust Board. Studio: 15 Tower Street, Suva. PO Box 2525, Gov.Bldgs, Suva. Stns: R.Light (English) **W:** radiolight.org **E**: radiolight@connect.com.fj ☎ +679 331 9536, R. Naya Jiwan (Hindi) **W:** radiolight.org **E**: fm94.8@nayajiwan.org ☎ +679 331 9535 – **8)** Seventh Day Adventist Church Mission, 37 Queens Road, Suva ☎ +679 336 1022 **W:** facebook.com/hopefm107 **E**: hopechannelfiji@hopestudios.org **9)** 24/7 rel. ABC R. Australia in English via satellite.

FINLAND

L.T: UTC +2h (28 Mar-31 Oct: +3h) — **Pop:** 5.6 million — **Pr.L:** Finnish (official), Swedish (official) — **E.C:** 230V/50Hz — **ITU:** FIN

LIIKENNE- JA VIESTINTÄVIRASTO (TRAFICOM, Finnish Transport & Communications Agency)

✉ P.O. Box 320, FI-00059 Traficom ☎+358 29 5345000 **W:** traficom.fi **E:** info@traficom.fi **L.P:** DG: Mrs. Kirsi Karlamaa.

DIGITA OY (programme distributor)

✉ Jämsänk. 2, FI-00520 Helsinki ☎+358 20411711 🖹 +358 204117234 **W:** digita.fi **E:** info@digita.fi

YLEISRADIO (YLE, Pub.)

✉ FI-00024 Yleisradio ☎+358 9 14801 🖹 +358 9 14803216 **W:** yle.fi **L.P:** DG: Mrs. Merja Ylä-Anttila.

FM (MHz)	**1**	**2**	**3**	**4**	**5**	**6**	**7**	**kW**
Aavasaksa	87.9	89.8	94.7	-	-	-	-	3
Ahvenanmaa	-	-	100.3	-	104.9	93.1	-	10/3
Anjalankoski	88.5	92.8	96.9	91.4	-	99.5	-	30
Enontekiö	88.5	91.4	98.7	104.6	-	-	101.2	5
Espoo	87.9	91.9	94.0	103.7	98.9	101.1	-	60
Eurajoki	87.7	103.5	94.8	92.0	99.4	103.0	-	30
Fiskars	90.9	93.1	97.0	105.0	102.5	99.7	-	3
Haapavesi	89.0	96.1	98.4	101.9	-	-	-	30
Hämeenlinna	-	-	99.2	-	-	-	-	1
Iisalmi	87.7	92.8	96.5	107.9	-	-	-	2
Ilomantsi	-	-	-	106.1	-	-	-	1
Inari	88.4	92.8	98.8	105.3	-	-	101.9	50/30
Joensuu	-	-	106.9	101.2	-	-	-	1
Joutseno	88.0	90.9	98.5	100.7	-	-	-	30
Jyväskylä	89.9	87.6	99.3	92.5	103.5	-	-	3/30
Karigasniemi	89.5	93.4	96.8	103.7	-	-	100.8	2
Kerimäki	90.5	95.8	99.1	103.2	-	-	-	30
	-	-	97.7	-	-	-	-	6
Kiihtelysvaara	88.4	94.9	97.2	100.4	-	-	-	5
Koli	90.2	93.4	99.6	106.4	-	102.4	-	30/5
Kruunupyy	91.4	94.0	97.6	88.8	99.7	102.7	-	60/3
Kuopio	91.6	93.9	98.1	88.1	-	100.2	-	50
Kuttanen	94.1	97.2	99.6	105.6	-	-	102.2	3
Lahti	93.2	95.5	97.9	90.5	-	100.6	-	50/0.2
Lapua	88.2	90.1	93.1	97.5	95.2	101.5	-	60/2
Lohja	-	-	96.1	105.0	-	-	-	3
Mikkeli	88.9	92.1	94.6	101.8	-	-	-	30
Nuorgam	88.6	93.9	97.7	107.8	-	-	101.2	3
Oulu	90.4	93.2	97.3	107.7	-	100.3	-	50/5
Parikkala	-	-	95.1	-	-	-	-	1
Pello	90.2	97.0	99.7	103.4	-	-	-	3
Perho	-	-	95.9	92.2	-	-	-	3
Pernaja	89.5	92.3	95.0	96.4	102.2	98.3	-	3/1
Pieksämäki	89.4	95.3	97.4	104.9	-	-	-	2/0.5
Pihtipudas	88.6	91.1	97.0	94.7	-	100.8	-	50/2.5
Porvoo	-	-	90.8	-	-	95.9	-	1
Posio	87.6	91.5	98.6	104.0	-	-	-	30/3
Pyhätunturi	91.0	97.6	99.9	102.4	-	-	-	50
Pyhävuori	88.9	91.0	94.2/97.2	96.1	98.6	102.6	-	30/2
Rovaniemi	88.2	94.0	96.7	106.8	-	-	103.0	30/10
Ruka	90.7	92.8	95.1	104.3	-	-	-	3/2
Sievi	-	-	90.3	-	-	-	-	1
Sodankylä	87.8	90.1	94.3	106.5	-	-	101.3	3
Taivalkoski	89.2	91.9	99.2/103.6	106.5	-	-	-	60
Tammela	89.2	91.3	96.0	105.4	-	-	-	5
Tampere	90.7	93.7	99.9	88.3	-	102.1	-	60/6
Tenola(NOR)	89.0	94.1	95.8	-	-	-	100.5	0.02
Tervola	88.6	92.6	95.6	101.6	-	-	-	30
Turku	89.8	92.6	94.3	96.7	98.2	101.4	-	60/6
Utsjoki	90.7	93.1	99.4	107.1	-	-	102.6	2/5
Vaasa	87.8	89.6	94.8	105.2	97.3	101.0	-	1
Vuokatti	92.3	94.3	98.9	101.2	-	-	-	60
Ylläs	92.2	95.3	98.1	100.7	-	-	103.8	50
Ähtäri	91.9	94.6	96.6	102.9	-	-	-	3

+ approx. 30 transmitters under 1 kW.

D.Prgr: FM1 "YLE Radio 1" (classical music, culture, actualities): 24h (also on digital TV) – **FM2 "YleX"** (rock & pop culture for youth): 24h. (r. R. Suomi at night.) **N:** on the h – **FM3 "Radio Suomi"** (news, sports, popular music and regional prgrs): 24h. **N:** on the h – **FM4 "YLE Puhe"** (news & talk prgr.): 24h. Also on digital TV. – **FM5 "X3M"** (Swedish language prgr for young people). 24h (simultaneous night prgr. with R Vega) – **FM6 "YLE Vega"** (Swedish language prgr for grown-up people and regional prgrs). 24h – **FM7 "Yle Sámi Radio"** (Sámi language network). 24h. Carries YLE, SR & NRK Sámi Radio daytime weekdays, at other times relays FM3 – **"YLE Mondo"** (digital network carried also via Espoo 97.5MHz 5kW): 24h.

Regional prgrs:

In Finnish on FM3 Radio Suomi network): Mon-Fri 0430-0800, 1200-1600 excl. nationwide news on the h. Addit. reg. news at 0830, 0930 & 1130. Also Sat 0710-0950 divided to 10 regions. – **YLE Helsinki:** 88.4/90.3/94.0/95.0/96.1/97.0/99.1MHz – **YLE Tampere:** 99.9MHz – **YLE Lahti:** 97.9MHz – **YLE Hämeenlinna:** 96.0/99.2/107.1/107.8MHz – **YLE Turku:** 94.3/99.2/100.3/105.8/107.1MHz – **YLE Pori:** 94.8/97.2/106.9MHz – **YLE Jyväskylä:** 97.0/99.3MHz – **YLE Kotka:** 96.9MHz – **YLE Lappeenranta:** 89.1/95.1/97.2/98.5MHz – **YLE Joensuu:** 97.2/97.7/98.3/99.6/106.9MHz – **YLE Mikkeli** 94.6/97.4/99.1MHz – **YLE Kuopio:** 96.5/98.1MHz – **YLE Pohjanmaa:** 93.1/94.2/94.8/96.6MHz – **YLE Kokkola** 87.6/90.3/90.7/95.9/96.0/97.6MHz – **YLE Oulu:** 95.1/97.3/98.4/99.2/102.5MHz – **YLE Kajaani:** 98.9/103.6MHz – **YLE Kemi:** 94.7/95.6/103.7MHz – **YLE Rovaniemi:** 96.7MHz + 15 more freqs.

In Swedish on FM6: MF 0430-1000. **YLE Vega**

Huvudstadsregionen: Helsingfors: 100.2/101.1/102.1/103.5/104.4 MHz – **YLE Vega Östnyland,** Borgå: 95.9/98.3/99.5/100.6MHz – **YLE Vega Västnyland:** Ekenäs: 99.7/101.9MHz – **YLE Vega Åboland,** Åbo: 87.6/93.1/101.4/103.0MHz – **YLE Vega Österbotten,** Vasa: 98.5/100.3/100.8/101.0/101.5/102.6/102.7MHz.

OTHER STATIONS; main nationwide networks:

FM (MHz)	**1)**	**2)**	**3)**	**4)**	**5)**	**6)**	**7)**	**8)**	**9)**
Alajärvi	-	104.3	-	-	-	102.2	-	-	
Anjalankoski	105.7	-	102.7	90.0	89.3	-	104.9	96.2	
Espoo	106.2	-	-	-	-	-	92.5	-	
Eurajoki	90.4	105.1	104.5	96.5	106.0	-	101.7	95.7	
Forssa	-	98.5	103.6	107.5	103.3	-	90.1	-	
Haapavesi	104.1	100.1	96.8	-	105.6	93.4	106.1	-	
Hanko	-	107.5	96.2	-	104.5	95.7	95.3	-	
Harjavalta	-	-	-	-	-	93.9	-	-	
Heinola	-	87.6	-	-	-	-	-	-	
Helsinki	-	96.2	104.6	94.9	98.1	96.8	90.0	89.0	88.6
Huittinen	-	93.0	-	-	-	-	-	-	
Hyvinkää	-	-	-	95.7	-	104.0	-	-	89.4
Hämeenlinna	100.2	101.7	106.5	92.3	-	97.3	-	105.9	95.2
Iisalmi	-	89.5	103.1	104.7	89.1	-	95.6	-	102.5
Ikaalinen	-	99.0	-	-	-	-	-	-	
Imatra	-	105.3	-	-	101.5	102.5	-	-	
Inari	-	-	-	-	-	104.1	-	-	
Inkoo	-	-	-	-	-	-	105.5	-	
Joensuu	-	92.8	87.9	103.7	102.9	96.4	101.9	-	98.7
Joutseno	103.8	-	94.2	-	-	-	-	96.0	
Juuka	-	103.3	-	-	-	-	-	-	
Jyväskylä	105.8	107.1	101.6	97.7	95.1	97.3	101.0	94.1	107.8
Jämsä	-	100.0	94.4	-	-	88.8	89.6	-	
Järvenpää	-	-	-	-	-	-	101.8	-	
Kajaani	-	-	102.8	107.0	96.3	93.7	94.8	-	
Kalajoki	-	-	-	-	104.6	-	-	-	
Kemi	-	-	105.2	98.8	-	-	-	-	
Kemijärvi	104.7	-	-	-	-	-	-	-	
Kerimäki	107.7	-	104.2	-	-	-	-	91.3	
Kitee	-	102.2	-	-	-	-	-	-	
Kokkola	-	-	99.1	106.3	-	-	99.1	-	
Koli	104.3	-	95.7	-	94.7	-	-	107.4	
Kotka	-	87.7	-	-	-	101.5	-	-	
Kouvola	-	100.1	-	90.0	-	93.8	107.7	96.7	
Kristiinankaup.	-	105.1	93.4		-	-	-	-	
Kruunupyy	98.8	-	107.2	-	105.3	104.9	-	104.3	
Kuopio	106.7	96.7	93.0	100.9	107.3	101.6	89.1	106.1	92.0
Kurikka	-	92.3	-	-	100.1	-	-	-	
Köyliö	-	-	-	-	-	107.9	-	-	
Lahti	102.4	103.0	105.0	89.7	104.4	96.6	94.2	106.4	103.8
Lappeenranta	-	93.5	-	105.0	94.8	96.5	100.2	96.0	97.4
Lapua	106.5	96.9	105.4	100.4	-	-	-	89.4	
Lempäälä	-	-	-	-	-	102.8	-	-	
Lohja	-	96.5	-	104.8	-	88.8		107.2	
Loimaa	-	98.5	-	-	-	-	-	-	91.8
Loviisa	-	-	-	-	-	104.6	105.2	-	
Luumäki	-	-	-	-	-	-	-	96.0	
Mikkeli	106.9	89.7	100.5	93.0	104.8	106.3	100.9	87.8	
Mäntyharju	-	-	-	-	93.0	-	-	-	
Nilsiä	-	-	-	-	-	97.5	-	-	
Orivesi	-	103.8	101.2	89.3	-	-	-	-	
Oulu	104.8	89.4	101.4	95.8	96.4	99.1	106.2	106.9	101.0
Outokumpu	-	101.7	-	-	-	-	-	-	
Padasjoki	87.8	-	-	-	-	-	-	-	
Parkano	-	99.0	-	-	100.2	-	-	-	
Pieksämäki	-	102.2	101.3	-	103.0	96.5	-	-	
Pihtipudas	105.1	107.0	98.5	-	104.5	101.7	102.3	-	
Pohja	-	95.1	-	-	-	-	-	-	
Pori	91.6	100.4	104.5	96.5	90.4	98.7	-	95.7	101.0
Porvoo	-	99.8	107.9	-	-	93.5	-	-	
Pyhätunturi	105.8	-	-	-	-	106.2	-	-	
Pyhävuori	107.6	-	-	-	-	-	-	-	
Raahe	-	92.5	107.0	89.9	105.8	87.7	-	-	
Rauma	-	105.1	103.6	-	-	93.9	-	-	
Riihimäki	-	-	99.6	-	-	-	94.7	-	
Rovaniemi	105.5	89.3	102.0	106.3	103.3	101.1	-	93.4	
Ruka	100.8	-	-	-	-	96.3	-	-	
Ruovesi	-	103.8	-	-	-	-	-	-	
Salo	-	-	99.1	-	-	-	107.7	-	88.2
Savonlinna	-	96.7	104.2	-	101.4	105.2	-	91.3	93.6
Seinäjoki	-	96.9	-	100.4	103.3	91.2	-	89.4	101.8
Sievi	-	107.7	-	-	-	-	-	-	
Siilinjärvi	-	102.0	-	-	-	-	-	-	
Sonkajärvi	-	107.1	-	-	-	-	-	-	
Suomussalmi	-	-		-	88.8	104.5	-	-	
Sysmä	90.2	106.8	101.3	93.5	-	96.1	89.1	-	
Taivalkoski	106.5	-	-	-	-	94.6	-	-	
Tammisaari	-	95.1	100.2	91.4	103.2	-	107.0	-	
Tampere	104.7	100.9	89.6	104.2	91.6	90.0	105.6	98.8	94.1
Tervola	107.5	-	-	-	96.2	100.1	-	-	
Tornio	-	-	-	98.8	92.0	-	98.3	-	
Turku	103.9	100.1	98.7	97.6	103.4	104.6	102.4	107.3	89.0
Uusikaupunki	-	96.2	91.1	-	-	-	-	-	88.5
Vaasa	-	-	104.4	91.6	102.0	93.9	-	-	91.2
Valkeakoski	-	95.0	94.4	-	-	-	-	-	
Vammala	-	101.2	97.7	-	88.0	-	-	-	
Varkaus	-	92.7	-	-	91.0	105.5	102.8	-	
Vihti	-	105.6	-	-	-	-	-	-	
Vilppula	-	95.4	-	-	-	-	-	-	
Vuokatti	105.7	-	-	107.0	-	88.8	-	-	
Ylivieska	-	-	88.3	-	-	-	-	-	
Ylläs	107.9	-	-	-	-	91.6	-	-	
Ähtäri	-	97.8	102.9	-	104.9	98.4	105.5	-	

Addresses: & other information:

1) Nova, Tallberginkatu 1C, PL 123, 00180 Helsinki **W:** radionova.fi Powers 1-60kW – **2) Iskelmä,** Kehräsaari B5. 33200 Tampere. **W:** iskelma.fi Powers 0.1-3kW – **3) KISS,** Tallbergink 1C 7. krs, 00180 Helsinki **W:** kiss.fi Powers 0.1-60kW – **4) R. Rock,** Töölönlahdenkatu 2, PL 350, 00100 Helsinki **W:** radiorock.fi Powers 0.1-4kW – **5) R. Suomipop,** Lintulahdenk. 10, 00500 Helsinki **W:** radiosuomipop.fi Powers 0.1-3kW – **6) R. NRJ (Energy),** Kiviaidankatu 2 i, 00210 Helsinki **W:** nrj.fi Powers 0.1-30kW – **7) R. Aalto,** PL 350, Tehtaankatu 27-29 A, 00151 Helsinki. **W:** radioaalto.fi Powers 0.1-10kW – **8) R. Dei** (Rlg.), Ilmalankuja 2 i, 00240 Helsinki. **W:** radiodei.fi Powers 0.2-5kW – **9) Helmiradio,** PL 95, 00089 Sanoma **W:** helmiradio.fi Powers 0.2-2kW.

About 50 more stations are in operation.

ÅLAND (autonomous province)

SVERIGES RADIO cf. Sweden

FM (MHz)	**P1**	**P2**	**P3**	**P4**	**kW**
Mariehamn	95.0	97.1	88.6	102.3	10

Steel FM, Mariehamn: 95.9MHz 0.2kW. **W:** steelfm.net – **Rix FM** (cf. Sweden), Mariehamn: 101.8MHz 3kW – **R. Harmonica,** Mariehamn: 102.8MHz 1kW – **Soft FM,** Mariehamn: 107.2MHz 0.2kW. **W:** softfm.net – **Ålands R. (Gov.),** Mariehamn: 91.3MHz 10kW. **W:** alandsradio.ax

FRANCE

L.T: UTC +1h (28 Mar-31 Oct: +2h) — **Pop:** 65 million — **Pr.L:** French — **E.C:** 230V/50Hz — **ITU:** F

CONSEIL SUPÉRIEUR DE L'AUDIOVISUEL (CSA)

39/43 quai André Citroën, 75739 Paris cedex 15 ☎ +33 1 40583800 Fax +33 1 45790006 **W:** csa.fr **L.P:** Pres: Roch-Olivier Maistre

The CSA regulates TV and radio, and issues broadcast licences

TDF

155 bis avenue Pierre Brossolette, 92541 Montrouge cedex ☎ +33 1 55951000 **W:** tdf.fr **L.P:** Pres & DG: Olivier Huart

TDF operates the majority of radio and TV txs

TOWERCAST

46/50 avenue Théophile Gautier, 75016 Paris ☎ +33 1 40714071 **W:** towercast.fr **L.P:** Pres: Raphaël Eyraud

Towercast operates radio and TV txs

OUTRE-MER LA 1ère (Pub)

35/37 rue Danton, 92240 Malakoff ☎ +33 1 55227100 **W:** la1ere.francetvinfo.fr **L.P:** Dir.: Sylvie Gengoul

Outre-Mer 1ère is a part of France Télévisions and produces public service prgrs (radio & TV) in the French overseas territories

RADIO FRANCE (Pub)

116 Av. du Président Kennedy, 75220 Paris cedex 16 ☎ +33 1 56402222 **W:** radiofrance.fr **L.P:** Pres. & DG: Sybile Veil

HOME SERVICES:

FM: Station (MHz)	A	B	C	D	kW
Abbeville	93.1	97.4	89.8	-	2.5
Ajaccio	92.4	97.6	88.0	-	10
Ajaccio (La Punta)	88.6	103.9	-	105.6	4
Albi	-	-	-	105.5	1
Alençon	93.0	88.0	91.0	-	13
Ales	87.6	96.1	98.6	105.1	1
Amiens (St Just)	95.4	102.5	99.4	-	20
Amiens (Dury)	92.6	97.0	89.3	105.5	2
Angers	93.2	91.4	97.4	-	10
Angers (La Ballue)	-	-	-	105.5	1
Angoulême	92.4	87.8	95.1	105.5	2
Arcachon	88.3	97.0	91.0	105.5	1.2
Argenton sur Creuse	101.9	89.8	97.2	-	5
Arles	-	-	-	105.0	1
Arnay le Duc	94.6	90.3	100.3	105.5	3
Aurillac	94.5	98.0	91.9	-	7
Autun	88.1	97.3	94.1	-	10
Auxerre	99.5	89.5	92.8	-	5
Auxerre (Venoy)	-	-	-	105.5	1
Avallon	-	-	-	105.6	1
Avignon	97.4	90.7	93.2	-	4
Avignon (Sorgues)	-	-	-	105.2	2
Bar le Duc	90.9	88.4	92.7	104.5	10
Bastia	95.9	89.2	93.9	105.5	10
Bayonne	89.0	96.1	92.7	105.5	16
Beaucaire	-	-	-	105.2	1
Bergerac	92.3	94.0	97.1	-	26
Besançon (Montfaucon)	98.7	89.3	95.0	-	10
Besançon (Lomont)	90.0	97.7	92.9	-	18
Beziers	-	-	-	105.1	1
Bordeaux	89.7	97.7	93.5	105.5	6
Boulogne sur Mer	103.3	99.9	89.4	106.5	1
Bourges	94.9	88.5	91.8	-	74
Bourges (town)	-	-	-	105.5	1
Brest	95.4	97.8	89.4	-	200
Brest (town)	-	-	-	105.5	3
Briançon	91.5	97.8	89.5	105.4	1
Brignoles	106.7	104.0	105.5	-	1.5
Caen	99.6	91.5	95.6	-	100
Caen (town)	-	-	-	105.5	1
Calais	104.7	-	-	105.6	1
Cannes	-	-	-	105.9	1
Carcassone	88.3	96.5	90.9	-	80
Castres	-	-	-	105.5	2
Chambéry	93.5	90.5	98.6	-	8
Chambéry (town)	-	-	-	105.1	1
Champagnole	88.5	91.7	98.3	-	1
Charleville-Mézières	95.8	90.1	93.5	105.9	10
Chartres	94.6	98.1	89.7	-	32
Chartres (town)	-	-	-	105.7	4
Chateaubriant	-	-	-	105.5	1
Châteauroux	-	-	-	105.5	1
Chaumont	96.5	90.4	93.3	-	15
Chaumont (town)	-	-	-	105.5	1
Cherbourg en Cotentin	94.1	89.2	92.3	105.6	1
Cholet	-	-	-	105.9	1
Clermont-Fd	90.4	98.4	95.5	105.5	35
Compiègne	-	-	-	105.3	1
Corse (East)	96.8	92.3	99.8	-	17
Corte	98.2	91.0	94.8	105.5	1.3
Cosne Cours s.Loire	-	-	-	105.3	1
Creil	87.6	93.3	91.9	105.6	1
Dijon	95.9	93.7	99.2	-	25
Dunkerque	-	-	-	106.5	1
Epinal	98.6	92.4	89.4	106.5	10
Evreux	88.5	98.9	97.3	105.5	1
Falaise	-	-	-	105.3	1
Fontainebleau	-	-	-	105.5	2
Gap	98.3	88.5	95.3	105.5	5
Gex	94.4	96.7	89.6	101.1	25
Grenoble (Chamrousse)	99.4	88.2	91.8	-	1
Grenoble (T. s. Venin)	89.9	92.8	107.3	105.1	1
Guéret	100.7	98.8	90.8	105.5	12
Hirson	94.4	99.7	97.2	-	5
Hyères	91.6	97.5	94.5	107.1	1.5
Laon	-	-	-	105.3	1
Laval	95.1	88.3	92.1	105.5	5

FM: Station (MHz)	A	B	C	D	kW
La Rochelle	-	-	-	105.5	1
Le Havre	88.9	93.3	98.5	105.5	1
Le Mans	92.6	89.0	97.0	105.5	128
Le Puy	99.3	89.3	92.8	-	10
Lesparre	92.4	90.3	95.1	-	1.6
Lille (Bouvigny)	103.7	98.0	88.7	105.2	125
Limoges	93.0	89.5	97.5	-	150
Limoges (town)	-	-	-	105.5	2
Longwy	98.1	88.3	91.0	104.3	5
Lourdes	-	-	-	105.3	3.5
Lyon (Mont Pilat)	99.8	88.8	92.4	103.4	150
Lyon (Town)	101.1	94.1	98.0	105.4	1
Mantes la Jolie	95.0	92.4	97.1	-	5
Marseille	91.3	99.0	94.2	-	400
Marseille	-	-	-	105.3	13
Marseille (town)	91.7	98.6	94.7	-	1
Maubeuge	-	-	-	106.2	2
Melun	-	-	-	105.7	1
Mende	90.1	96.9	93.7	-	10
Menton	97.0	89.6	91.7	105.5	5
Metz	99.8	94.5	89.7	106.8	145
Millau	94.9	99.2	88.9	-	6
Mont de Marsan	-	-	-	105.5	6
Montargis	102.9	98.8	94.1	105.5	1
Montauban	-	-	-	105.7	1
Montereau	-	-	-	105.7	1
Montlieu la Garde	88.3	104.8	98.8	-	3.5
Montluçon	-	-	-	105.5	1
Montpellier	89.4	97.8	92.9	-	18
Montpellier (Town)	89.1	-	96.4	105.1	1
Morosaglia	97.1	88.8	93.4	-	1
Mulhouse	95.7	88.6	91.6	105.5	100
Nancy	96.9	88.7	91.7	105.9	5
Nantes	90.6	94.2	98.9	105.5	125
Neufchateau	96.3	100.3	91.5	-	1
Neufchatel-en-Bray	92.7	96.0	90.2	-	5
Nevers	-	-	-	105.5	1
Nice	100.2	101.9	92.2	105.7	100
Nimes	88.7	-	-	105.1	1/1.5
Niort	99.4	96.4	91.1	-	190
Niort (town)	-	-	-	105.5	1
Noyon	-	-	-	107.4	1
Orléans	99.2	95.8	90.7	-	4
Orléans (town)	-	-	-	105.5	1
Paris	87.8	93.5	91.7	105.5	10
Parthenay	93.8	87.9	98.5	105.5	12
Pau	-	-	-	105.5	1
Perpignan	92.1	99.8	97.2	105.1	10
Poitiers	97.7	92.3	95.5	105.5	1
Pto Vecchio (Col de Mela)	96.8	90.8	98.9	-	1.5
Pto Vecchio (Punto di a Varra)	92.6	87.9	94.6	100.4	1
Privas	89.8	96.5	94.7	105.2	1
Redon	-	-	-	95.8	1
Reims	96.8	98.8	89.2	105.5	135
Rennes	93.5	98.3	89.9	-	100
Rennes (town)	-	-	-	105.5	1
Roanne	-	-	-	105.5	1
Rochefort	-	-	-	95.7	1
Rouen	96.5	94.0	92.0	-	100
Rouen (town)	-	-	-	105.7	3
Ruffec	-	-	-	105.3	1
Saint Brieuc	-	-	-	105.5	1
Saint Etienne	99.5	89.1	92.7	105.6	2
Saint-Nazaire	95.2	92.2	102.6	105.5	1.5
Saint-Quentin	-	-	-	105.6	1
Saint-Raphaël	96.3	88.7	99.6	-	40
Saint-Raphaël (town)	-	-	-	106.0	1
Sainte Foy la Grande	-	-	-	105.5	1
Saintes	-	-	-	105.4	1
Sarrebourg	93.1	99.4	90.3	-	10
Sens	96.3	98.5	93.8	-	10
Sens (town)	-	-	-	105.7	1.3
Soissons	-	-	-	105.7	1
Strasbourg	97.3	87.7	95.0	104.4	48
Toulon	92.0	97.1	94.9	105.8	5
Toulouse (town)	88.1	96.3	91.1	105.5	2
Toulouse (Pic du Midi)	87.9	95.7	91.5	-	72
Tours	99.9	97.8	92.2	-	8

FM: Station (MHz)	A	B	C	D	kW
Tours (town)	-	-	-	105.5	1
Troyes	95.3	97.9	91.4	-	50
Troyes (town)	-	-	-	105.5	1
Ussel	96.0	88.2	99.7	-	10
Valence	-	-	-	105.4	3
Vannes	88.6	96.0	91.8	105.5	20
Verdun	92.1	99.3	97.4	106.3	6
Villebon sur Yvette	95.4	98.0	97.1	-	1
Villers-Cotterets	91.1	89.6	92.9	-	13
Vittel	98.2	89.0	94.0	-	8
Voiron	91.5	89.2	107.2	105.4	1

+ 1488 stns under 1kW. RDS on all txs.

France Inter (Network A) (stereo): **D.Prgrs**:24h **N:** Hourly, plus 0630 – **France Culture** (Network B) (stereo) **D.Prgrs**:24h **N:** 0500, 0530, 0600, 0700, 0800, 1130, 1700, 1800, 2100 – **France Musique** (Network C) (stereo): **D.Prgrs**:24h **N:** 0600, 0630, 07000, 1700 – **France Info** (Network D) (mono) News and informations **D.Prgrs**:24h

Mouv'

Station	MHz	kW	Station	MHz	kW
Ajaccio	92.0	4	Lyon	87.8	4
Amiens	91.0	1	Marseille	96.8	2.5
Angers	96.0	1	Marseille (town)	96.4	1
Annecy	99.4	1	Mende	107.2	0.2
Besançon	93.5	1	Montpellier	102.7	3
Bordeaux	87.7	1	Nantes	96.1	3
Brest	94.0	3	Nice	101.0	2.5
Caen	87.8	1	Paris	92.1	8
Cannes	101.0	0.2	Reims	101.1	0.5
Carcassonne	90.0	1	Rennes	107.3	2
Clermont-Fd	97.5	2	Rouen	95.8	1
Dijon	88.9	1	St Etienne	88.0	2
Grenoble	95.5	1	Toulouse	95.2	5
Lille	91.0	2	Tours	94.1	2
Limoges	107.6	2	Valence	100.7	0.5
Lorient	103.3	0.5			

D.Prgrs: 24h RDS on all txs (stereo)

Local Stations "FIP"
FIP Bordeaux, 12 allée Serr, 33100 Bordeaux ☎ +33 5 56241515 - Bordeaux 96.7MHz 2.5kW, Arcachon 96.5 0.5 kW
FIP Nantes, 2 bis quai François Mitterrand, 44100 Nantes ☎ +33 2 40717271 - Nantes 95.7MHz 2.5kW, St Nazaire 97.2MHz 1.5kW
FIP Paris, 116 avenue du Président Kennedy, 75220 Paris Cedex 16 – Paris 105.1MHz 10kW
FIP Strasbourg, 4 rue Joseph Massol, 67080 Strasbourg Cedex ☎ +33 3 88352400 - 92.3MHz 4kW
Sts without local news: Marseille 90.9MHz 4kW, Montpellier 99.7MHz 1kW, Rennes 101.2MHz 1kW, Toulouse 103.5MHz 2kW RDS on all txs **D.Prgrs:** 24h Prgrs consist of music and news

France Bleu
✉ 17/21 av du Général Mangin, 75016 Paris **D.Prgrs:** 24h uninterrupted music 0000-0358 (can vary on each France Bleu stn)
France Bleu Local Stations (F.B = France Bleu) - At certain times, local stns relay national France Bleu prgrs. 0400-0500, 0755-0800, 1100-1500, 1800-0400
F.B Alsace, 4 rue Joseph Massol, 67000 Strasbourg ☎ +33 3 88762000 **FM:** Strasbourg 101.4MHz 48kW, Mulhouse 102.6MHz 100kW
F.B Armorique, 14 av Jean Janvier, 35031 Rennes Cedex ☎ +33 2 99674321 **FM:** Vannes 101.3MHz 20kW, Rennes 103.1MHz 100kW
F.B Auxerre, 12 place Saint Amâtre, B.P 101, 89002 Auxerre Cedex ☎ +33 3 86723456 **FM:** Sens 100.5MHz 10kW, Auxerre 101.3MHz 5kW, Nevers 104.0MHz 1kW
F.B Azur, 2 place Grimaldi, 06000 Nice ☎ +33 4 97033636 **FM:** Nice 103.8MHz 100kW, Menton 94.8MHz 5kW, Saint Raphaël 100.7MHz 10kW
F.B Béarn, 5 place Clémenceau, 64000 Pau ☎ +33 5 59980909 **FM:** Oloron Sainte Marie 93.2MHz 1.5kW, Pau 102.5MHz 10kW
F.B Belfort Montbéliard, 10 rue des Capucins, 90000 Belfort ☎ +33 3 84579090 **FM:** Belfort 106.8MHz 2kW
F.B Berry, 10/12 rue de la République, 36000 Châteauroux ☎ +33 2 54273636 **FM:** Argenton 93.5MHz 5kW, Bourges 103.2MHz 19kW
F.B Besançon, 2 Place Granvelle, BP 591, 25027 Besançon Cedex ☎ +33 3 81212525 **FM:** Besançon 101.4MHz 18kW + 102.8MHz 10kW
F.B Bourgogne, 29 rue Guillaume Tell, BP 11888, 21018 Dijon Cedex ☎ +33 3 80592121 **FM:** Troyes 87.8 60kW, Arnay le Duc 103.4MHz 3kW, Dijon 103.7MHz 25kW
F.B Breizh Izel, 155 boulevard de Creac'h Gwenn, 29000 Quimper ☎ +33 2 98552929 **FM:** Brest 93.0MHz 200kW
F.B Champagne-Ardenne, 28 bd du Maréchal Joffre, BP 1094, 51054 Reims Cedex ☎ +33 3 26845151 **FM:** Charleville-Mézières 100.9MHz 10kW, Reims 95.1MHz 2kW, Châlons en Champagne 94.8MHz 1kW, Troyes 100.8MHz 1kW
F.B Cotentin, Hôtel Atlantique, impasse Piedagnel, 50100 Cherbourg en Cotentin ☎ +33 2 33885050 **FM:** Cherbourg en Cotentin 100.7MHz 4kW
F.B Creuse, 7 avenue de la République, BP 249, 23005 Guéret ☎ +33 5 55612323 **FM:** Guéret 94.3MHz 12kW
F.B Drôme Ardèche, 70 avenue de Romans, CS 10519, 26005 Valence Cedex ☎ +33 4 75401010 **FM:** Valence 87.9MHz 10kW, Privas 98.4MHz 1.5kW, Vals les Bains 103.8MHz 1kW
F.B Gard Lozère, 10 bd des Arènes, 30000 Nîmes ☎ +33 4 66363030 **FM:** Nîmes 90.2MHz 5kW, Alès 91.6MHz 2kW, Mende 104.9MHz 10kW
F.B Gascogne, 13 place Jean Jaurès, BP 289, 40005 Mont de Marsan Cedex ☎ +33 5 58465050 **FM:** Mont de Marsan 98.8MHz 20kW, Bayonne 100.5MHz 26kW, Mimizan 103.4MHz 20kW
F.B Gironde, 91 rue Nuyens, CS 91882, 33072 Bordeaux Cedex☎ +33 5 57812020 **FM:** Bordeaux 100.1MHz 6kW, Lesparre 101.6MHz 1.6kW
F.B Hérault, 474 allée Henri II de Montmorency, 34000 Montpellier ☎ +33 4 67066565 **FM:** Montpellier 101.1MHz 18kW + 100.6MHz 1kW
F.B Isère, 5 rue Eugène Faure, 38000 Grenoble ☎ +33 4 76503838 **FM:** Chambéry 99.1MHz 5kW, Lyon 101.8MHz 25kW, Grenoble 102.8MHz 1kW + 98.2MHz 1.2kW, Voiron 101MHz 1kW
F.B La Rochelle, 5 av Michel Crépeau, 17025 La Rochelle Cedex 01☎ +33 5 46351717 **FM:** Royan 103.6MHz 1kW, Saintes 103.9MHz 60kW, Angoulême 101.5MHz 2kW, La Rochelle 98,2MHz 1kW
F.B Limousin, 23 bd Gambetta, BP 3603, 87036 Limoges Cedex ☎ +33 5 55113811 **FM:** Chateauponsac 92.5MHz 1kW, Ussel 101.4MHz 10kW, Limoges 103.5MHz 150kW
F.B Loire Océan, 2 bis quai François Mitterrand, 44200 Nantes ☎ +33 2 40444546 **FM:** Saint Nazaire 88.1MHz 1.5kW, Nantes 101.8MHz 200kW, Angers 88.5MHz 1k W
F.B Lorraine Nord, 5 rue d'Austrasıe, B.P 50071, 57003 Metz cedex 03 ☎ +33 3 87682222 **FM:** Metz 98.5MHz 1kW, Sarreguemines 104 MHz 1kW
F.B Maine, 17 avenue Pierre Mendès France, 72000 Le Mans ☎ +33 2 43297272 **FM:** La Flèche 91.7MHz 1kW, Le Mans 96MHz 2.5 kW, Sablé sur Sarthe 105.7MHz 1kW
F.B Mayenne, 41 av Robert Buron, 53000 Laval ☎ +33 2 43495050 **FM:** Laval 96.6MHz 5kW
F.B Nord, 507 avenue du Président Hoover, 59000 Lille ☎ +33 3 20135962 **FM:** Lille (town) 87.8MHz 1kW, Lille (Bouvigny) 94.7MHz 125kW, Boulogne sur Mer 95.5MHz 1kW, Le Touquet 97.8MHz 2kW, Calais 106.2MHz 1kW
F.B Normandie (Calvados-Orne), 12 rue Rosa Parks, 14053 Caen Cedex 04 ☎ +33 2 31444844 **FM:** Le Havre 102.2MHz 2.5kW, Caen 102.6MHz 100kW
F.B Normandie (Seine Maritime-Eure), Hangar A, quai Boisguilbert, 76000 Rouen ☎ +33 2 35076666 **FM:** Le Havre 95.1MHz 1kW, Rouen 100.1MHz 100kW, Neufchâtel en Bray 101.6MHz 5kW, Evreux 89.5MHz 1kW
F.B. Occitanie, 78 allée Jean Jaurès, BP 50901, 31009 Toulouse ☎ +33 5 34417000 **FM:** Toulouse 91.8MHz 5 kW, Albi 103.7MHz 1 kW, Cahors 97.3MHz 1kW, Castres 91.8MHz 1kW, Mazamet 90.4MHz 1kW, Montauban 97.2 1kW, Rodez 106.2MHz 1kW, Saint Gaudens 96.4MHz 1kW
F.B Orléans, 5 place du Châtelet, 45000 Orléans ☎ +33 2 38714545 **FM:** Blois 93.9MHz 1kW, Orléans 100.9MHz 4kW, Montargis 106.8MHz 1kW
F.B Paris, 17/21 av du Général Mangin, 75016 Paris☎ +33 1 42301010 **FM:** Paris 107.1MHz 10kW, Chartres 97.3MHz 4kW.
F.B Pays Basque, 46 allées Marines, 64116 Bayonne Cedex ☎ +33 5 59466464 **FM:** Bayonne 101.3MHz 15kW
F.B Pays d'Auvergne, 80 bd François Mitterrand, 63000 Clermont-Ferrand ☎+33 4 73346363 **FM:** Clermont-Fd 102.5MHz 37kW, Aurillac 100.2MHz 1kW, Montluçon 96.7MHz 1kW
F.B Pays de Savoie, 256 rue de la République, 73000 Chambéry ☎ +33 4 79707374 **FM:** Annecy 95.2MHz 1kW, Chambéry 103.9MHz 8kW, Gex 106.1MHz 20kW
F.B Périgord, 1 cours Saint Georges, BP 3033, 24003 Périgueux

Cedex ☎ +33 5 53538282 **FM:** Limoges 91.7MHz 100kW, Bergerac 99.0MHz 26kW
F.B Picardie, 2 rue du Maréchal de Lattre de Tassigny, 80000 Amiens ☎ +33 3 22711515 **FM:** Amiens 100.2MHz 2kW, Abbeville 100.6MHz 5kW, Beauvais 106,8MHz 1kW, Hirson 101.3MHz 5kW, Noyon 94,4MHz 1kW, Sailly Saillisel 102.8MHz 15kW
F.B Poitou, 27, bd de Solférino, 86000 Poitiers ☎ +33 5 49605000 **FM:** Parthenay 106.4MHz 12kW, Niort 101.0MHz 1kW
F.B Provence, 560 av Mozart, 13100 Aix en Provence. ☎ +33 4 42991313 **FM:** Brignoles 102.1MHz 1.5kW, Hyères 102.5MHz 1.5kW, Toulon 102.9MHz 5kW, Marseille 103.6MHz 200kW
F.B RCFM, 1 Place du Donjon – 1 Piazza di a Corte, BP 130, 20292 Bastia Cedex ☎ +33 4 95329532 **FM:** Corse (east) 88.2MHz 17kW, Ajaccio 100.5MHz 10kW, + 97.0MHz 4kW + 1404kHz 20kW, Canavaggia 101.7MHz 1kW, Corte 100.0MHz 1.33kW, Bastia 101.7MHz 10kW, Porto Vecchio 101.8MHz 1.5kW + 105.4MHz 1kW, Morosaglia 104.6MHz 1kW
F.B Roussillon, 24 av du Maréchal Leclerc, 66000 Perpignan ☎ +33 4 68519000 **FM:** Perpignan 101.6MHz 10kW
F.B Saint-Étienne Loire, 5 rue Pablo Picasso, CS 10091, 42003 Saint-Étienne Cedex 1 ☎ +33 4 77520808 **FM:** Saint-Étienne 97.1MHz 2kW
F.B Sud Lorraine, 21 bd du Recteur Senn, 54042 Nancy Cedex ☎ +33 3 83362020 **FM:** Epinal 100.0MHz 1.5kW, Nancy 100.5MHz 5kW, Vittel 102.6MHz 1kW, Neufchateau 103.0MHz 1kW
F.B Touraine, 40 rue James Watt, 37206 Tours Cedex 3 ☎ +33 2 47363737 **FM:** Tours 105.0MHz 8kW +98.7MHz 1kW
F.B Vaucluse, 25 rue de la République, 84000 Avignon ☎ +33 4 90140404 **FM:** Avignon 100.4MHz 2kW
+ 335 txs less than 1kW not mentioned. Stereo and RDS on all txs

RADIO FRANCE INTERNATIONALE (Pub)

✉ 80 rue Camille Desmoulins, 92130 Issy les Moulineaux ☎ +33 1 84228484 **W:** rfi.fr **LP**: Marie-Christine Saragosse
RFI1 (French service): Paris **FM** 89.0MHz 10kW (stereo)
EXTERNAL SERVICE see International Broadcasting section

PRIVATE MW STATION

BRETAGNE 5 ✉ Le Pôle, Parc d'activités de l'Espérance Ouest, 10 rue de la Doucine, 22120 QUESSOY ☎ +33 2 96330504 **W:** bretagne5.fr **MW**: Saint Gouéno 1593kHz 5kW. **D.Prgrs**:24h

PRIVATE FM STATIONS:

FM Station	MHz	kW	FM Station	MHz	kW
25) Auxerre	87.6	1	7) Yvetot	87.9	1
23) Bayonne	87.6	3	10) Calais	88.0	1
20) Bernay	87.6	1	17) Châteauroux	88.0	1
17) Besançon	87.6	1	23) Colmar	88.0	1
23) Castres	87.6	1	6) Noyon	88.0	1
26) Laval	87.6	1	17) St Gilles Croix de Vie	88.0	1
20) Le Havre	87.6	1	17) Vesoul	88.0	1
26) Le Mans	87.6	1	3) Villefranche/Saône	88.0	1
22) Niort	87.6	1	9) Vitry le François	88.0	1
7) Orléans	87.6	2	17) Angers	88.1	1
22) Vannes	87.6	1	3) Avignon	88.1	1
8) Yssingeaux	87.6	1	6) Brive la Gaillarde	88.1	1
23) Bourges	87.7	1	18) Châtellerault	88.1	1
13) Clermont Ferrand	87.7	1	23) Dole	88.1	1
7) Corte	87.7	1	6) Nice	88.1	5
5) Figeac	87.7	1	17) Rouen	88.1	1
16) Marseille	87.7	1	6) Soissons	88.1	1
19) Nice	87.7	2	3) Fontenay le Comte	88.2	1
21) Saint Omer	87.7	1	17) Le Havre	88.2	1
9) Tours	87.7	2	10) Lille	88.2	1
20) Verneuil d'Avre	87.7	1	10) Metz	88.2	1
19) La Flèche	87.8	1	10) Nancy	88.2	1
7) Le Blanc	87.8	1	6) Saint Quentin	88.2	1
19) Mayenne	87.8	1	9) Strasbourg	88.2	4
23) Mazamet	87.8	1	22) Tours	88.2	2
7) Montluçon	87.8	1	13) Bonifacio	88.3	1
14) Nantes	87.8	1	17) Brioude	88.3	1
6) Verdun	87.8	1	17) Dijon	88.3	1
6) Dijon	87.9	1	9) L'Ile Rousse	88.3	1
21) Menton	87.9	1	8) Lorient	88.3	1
6) Montreuil	87.9	1	9) Moulins	88.3	1
17) Reims	87.9	2	17) Roanne	88.3	1
10) Saint Brieuc	87.9	1	17) Saint Flour	88.3	1
5) Saint Raphaël	87.9	1	14) Amiens	88.4	1
2) Toulon	87.9	1	12) Corte	88.4	1

FM Station	MHz	kW	FM Station	MHz	kW
5) Laon	88.4	1	18) Bayonne	89.4	2
9) Luxeuil les Bains	88.4	1	6) Chambéry	89.4	1
17) Lyon	88.4	4	23) Marmande	89.4	1
6) Mont de Marsan	88.4	1	6) Roanne	89.4	1
19) Nantes	88.4	2	8) Saint Dizier	89.4	1
21) Sarrebourg	88.4	1	15) Toulon	89.4	2
21) Sarreguemines	88.4	1	5) Saintes	89.4	1
6) Thouars	88.4	1	23) Chaumont	89.5	1
5) Tonnerre	88.4	1	6) Strasbourg	89.5	4
8) Bordeaux	88.5	4	18) Ajaccio	89.6	7
10) Compiègne	88.5	1	14) Angers	89.6	2
10) Gournay en Bray	88.5	1	4) Auch	89.6	1
6) Nogent le Rotrou	88.5	1	6) Clermont Ferrand	89.6	2
20) Quimper	88.5	1	10) La Rochelle	89.6	1
17) Annecy	88.6	1	23) Le Havre	89.6	1
17) Châlons en Champ.	88.6	1	17) Marseille	89.6	4
6) Châteaubriant	88.6	1	21) Mende	89.6	1
8) Chaumont	88.6	1	7) Vierzon	89.6	1
19) Confolens	88.6	1	5) Aubusson	89.7	1
22) Pamiers	88.6	1	23) Bastia	89.7	1
16) Paris	88.6	4	13) Nevers	89.7	1
23) Porto Vecchio	88.6	1	10) Nîmes	89.7	1
18) Vichy	88.6	1	23) Perpignan	89.7	3
10) Alençon	88.7	1	18) Saint Nazaire	89.7	1
7) Avallon	88.7	1	2) Tours	89.7	2
25) Bastia	88.7	1	6) Troyes	89.7	1
8) Caen	88.7	2	6) Agen	89.8	1
19) Chartres	88.7	1	6) Brioude	89.8	1
18) Châteauroux	88.7	1	23) Corte	89.8	1
19) Étampes	88.7	1	23) Gray	89.8	1
25) Ghisonaccia	88.7	2	14) Lyon	89.8	1
3) Gray	88.7	1	18) Quimper	89.8	1
22) Saint Gaudens	88.7	1	21) Roanne	89.8	1
13) Saintes	88.7	1	28) Rouen	89.8	1
22) Toulouse	88.7	5	6) Sablé sur Sarthe	89.8	1
6) Bonnières sur Seine	88.8	2	18) Toulon	89.8	4
12) Clermont Ferrand	88.8	1	19) Alès	89.9	1
4) Laval	88.8	1	17) Cognac	89.9	1
8) Nantes	88.8	3	18) Douai	89.9	1
6) Reims	88.8	2	20) Épinal	89.9	1
17) Saint Dizier	88.8	1	19) Montpellier	89.9	3
6) Verneuil d'Avre	88.8	1	20) Nancy	89.9	1
4) Bagnères de Bigorre	88.9	1	28) Paris	89.9	10
17) Bordeaux	88.9	1	3) Périgueux	89.9	1
13) Montluçon	88.9	1	6) Saint Dizier	89.9	1
23) Rennes	88.9	1	20) Saint Girons	89.9	1
6) Aurillac	89.0	1	18) Saint Raphaël	89.9	1
6) Avignon	89.0	1	20) Bagnères de Bigorre	90.0	1
6) Avranches	89.0	1	17) Bayeux	90.0	1
17) Brest	89.0	3	22) Brest	90.0	3
17) Clamecy	89.0	1	13) Cosne Cours/Loire	90.0	1
13) Moulins	89.0	1	23) Marseille	90.0	10
23) Bernay	89.1	1	21) Quimperlé	90.0	1
1) Bourges	89.1	1	9) Royan	90.0	1
5) Gien	89.1	1	3) Vichy	90.0	1
18) Perpignan	89.1	3	6) Béthune	90.1	1
8) Saint Nazaire	89.1	1	22) Évreux	90.1	1
22) Saint Quentin	89.1	1	18) Nantes	90.1	3
22) Valenciennes	89.1	1	9) Neufchâteau	90.1	1
9) Beauvais	89.2	1	19) Perpignan	90.1	3
19) Brive la Gaillarde	89.2	1	5) Poligny	90.1	1
23) Châteaubriant	89.2	1	9) Toul	90.1	1
9) Châtellerault	89.2	1	7) Angoulême	90.2	1
9) Decazeville	89.2	1	23) Bar le Duc	90.2	1
22) Lille	89.2	2	3) Bergerac	90.2	1
18) Marseille	89.2	10	9) La Ferté s/Jouarre	90.2	1
13) Montbard	89.2	1	13) Melun	90.2	1
17) Nevers	89.2	1	18) Mimizan	90.2	1
23) Ussel	89.2	1	28) Nevers	90.2	1
23) Verneuil d'Avre	89.2	1	14) Pau	90.2	1
17) Vichy	89.2	1	20) Porto Vecchio	90.2	1
17) Castres	89.3	1	9) Thionville	90.2	1
17) Cholet	89.3	1	17) Vannes	90.2	2
13) Longwy	89.3	1	5) Bastia	90.3	4
17) Niort	89.3	1	13) Compiègne	90.3	1
9) Nogaro	89.3	1	18) Decazeville	90.3	1
23) Rouen	89.3	2	17) Montargis	90.3	1
25) Arras	89.4	1	17) Montmorillon	90.3	1
17) Aurillac	89.4	1	24) Pamiers	90.3	1
18) Bayeux	89.4	1	3) Saumur	90.3	1

FM	Station	MHz	kW
19)	Valence	90.3	1
13)	Vivario	90.3	1
20)	Abbeville	90.4	1
18)	Auch	90.4	1
13)	Beauvais	90.4	1
5)	Bourg en Bresse	90.4	1
10)	Caen	90.4	2
5)	Calvi	90.4	1
13)	Châteaudun	90.4	1
22)	Dinan	90.4	1
21)	Longwy	90.4	1
13)	Paris	90.4	10
23)	Sablé sur Sarthe	90.4	1
3)	Alès	90.5	1
9)	Bourges	90.5	1
26)	Brest	90.5	1
13)	Chartres	90.5	1
23)	Le Mans	90.5	2
24)	Limoges	90.5	1
9)	Mont de Marsan	90.5	1
6)	Narbonne	90.5	1
13)	Rodez	90.5	1
23)	Tours	90.5	2
4)	Lourdes	90.6	3
7)	Maubeuge	90.6	1
20)	Melun	90.6	1
8)	Millau	90.6	1
4)	Noyon	90.6	1
26)	Creil	90.7	2
7)	Dijon	90.7	1
18)	Figeac	90.7	1
4)	Laon	90.7	1
9)	Laval	90.7	1
21)	Périgueux	90.7	1
6)	Soustons	90.7	1
13)	Troyes	90.7	1
6)	Avallon	90.8	1
1)	Bastia	90.8	1
9)	Château Thierry	90.8	1
9)	La Flèche	90.8	1
28)	Toulon	90.8	4
3)	Vannes	90.8	1
23)	Vesoul	90.8	1
17)	Annonay	90.9	1
19)	Brest	90.9	3
9)	Brive la Gaillarde	90.9	1
13)	Montreuil	90.9	1
14)	Poitiers	90.9	1
17)	Segré	90.9	1
7)	Villefranche/Saône	90.9	1
5)	Ajaccio	91.0	6.8
19)	Besançon	91.0	1
17)	Bourges	91.0	1
10)	Chambéry	91.0	1
9)	Colmar	91.0	1
13)	Fleurance	91.0	1
24)	Le Puy en Velay	91.0	1
17)	Sarrebourg	91.0	1
7)	Sens	91.0	1
10)	Vichy	91.0	1
25)	Boulogne sur Mer	91.1	1
23)	Dunkerque	91.1	1
19)	Malataverne	91.1	1
8)	Metz	91.1	1
19)	Montélimar	91.1	1
8)	Nancy	91.1	1
19)	Orange	91.1	1
23)	Pau	91.1	1
3)	Villeneuve sur Lot	91.1	1
7)	Aubusson	91.2	1
8)	Épinal	91.2	1
6)	Grenoble	91.2	1
6)	Laval	91.2	1
22)	Mulhouse	91.2	1
17)	Orléans	91.2	2
6)	Saint Tropez	91.2	1
19)	Agen	91.3	1
19)	Cahors	91.3	1
9)	Cambrai	91.3	1
3)	Clermont	91.3	1
5)	Dinan	91.3	1
3)	Paris	91.3	10
27)	Reims	91.3	1
6)	Valence	91.3	1
3)	Verneuil d'Avre	91.3	1
19)	Amiens	91.4	1
13)	Bastia	91.4	4
17)	Brive la Gaillarde	91.4	1
18)	Jonzac	91.4	1
21)	Morlaix	91.4	1
7)	Beaune	91.5	1
3)	Blois	91.5	1
6)	Boulogne sur Mer	91.5	1
8)	La Ferté s/Jouarre	91.5	1
22)	Le Puy en Velay	91.5	1
26)	Roanne	91.5	1
17)	Clermont Ferrand	91.6	1
9)	Corte	91.6	1
5)	Dunkerque	91.6	1
17)	Épernay	91.6	1
17)	La Châtre	91.6	1
5)	Lens	91.6	1
5)	Perpignan	91.6	3
13)	Royan	91.6	1
3)	Tours	91.6	2
10)	Agen	91.7	1
23)	Cholet	91.7	1
18)	La Tour du Pin	91.7	1
17)	Mortagne au Perche	91.7	1
14)	Saint Étienne	91.7	2
17)	Villefranche/Saône	91.7	1
7)	Amiens	91.8	1
7)	Bordeaux	91.8	5
8)	Brioude	91.8	1
18)	La Rochelle	91.8	1
21)	Montélimar	91.8	1
7)	Montpellier	91.8	3
7)	Saint Dizier	91.8	1
7)	Saint Malo	91.8	1
7)	Saint Quentin	91.8	1
2)	Vichy	91.8	1
7)	Bressuire	91.9	1
9)	Chalon sur Saône	91.9	1
19)	Chaumont	91.9	1
4)	Civray	91.9	1
9)	Épinal	91.9	1
7)	Le Puy en Velay	91.9	1
7)	Lessay	91.9	1
9)	Porto Vecchio	91.9	1
8)	Salon de Provence	91.9	1
5)	Vivario	91.9	1
8)	Aix en Provence	92.0	1
8)	Albi	92.0	1
7)	Arcachon	92.0	1
23)	Auxerre	92.0	1
6)	Lille	92.0	2
23)	Montargis	92.0	1
13)	Pamiers	92.0	1
8)	Saint Affrique	92.0	1
7)	Saint Brieuc	92.0	1
10)	Saintes	92.0	1
19)	Soissons	92.0	1
3)	Brive la Gaillarde	92.1	1
21)	Cambrai	92.1	1
6)	Menton	92.1	1
18)	Nontron	92.1	1
19)	Troyes	92.1	1
13)	Amiens	92.2	1
22)	Béthune	92.2	1
10)	Bordeaux	92.2	1
7)	Colmar	92.2	1
7)	Dunkerque	92.2	1
4)	Lannemezan	92.2	1
9)	Laon	92.2	1
7)	Limoges	92.2	2.2
22)	Metz	92.2	1
22)	Mont de Marsan	92.2	1
5)	Montélimar	92.2	1
7)	Mulhouse	92.2	1
9)	Noyon	92.2	1
18)	Carcassonne	92.3	1
30)	Melun	92.3	1
7)	Mimizan	92.3	1.1
10)	Rennes	92.3	1
13)	Vitry le François	92.3	1
23)	Albi	92.4	1
20)	Brest	92.4	1
14)	Montpellier	92.4	3
22)	Romilly sur Seine	92.4	1
5)	Saint Quentin	92.4	1
6)	Vannes	92.4	1
23)	Avignon	92.5	1
7)	Brive la Gaillarde	92.5	1
4)	Cahors	92.5	1
17)	Fontenay le Comte	92.5	1
17)	Issoudun	92.5	1
9)	Le Havre	92.5	1
5)	Lille	92.5	2
7)	Lourdes	92.5	3
19)	Rodez	92.5	1
1)	Aix en Provence	92.6	1
3)	Calvi	92.6	1
3)	Charolles	92.6	1
10)	Clermont Ferrand	92.6	1
3)	Corte	92.6	1
9)	Cosne Cours/Loire	92.6	1
23)	Nîmes	92.6	1
17)	Quimper	92.6	1
7)	Saint Raphaël	92.6	1
3)	Bastia	92.7	4
23)	Boulogne sur Mer	92.7	1
1)	Dreux	92.7	1
26)	Lorient	92.7	1
13)	Montélimar	92.7	1
22)	Rennes	92.7	1
9)	Béthune	92.8	1
10)	Blois	92.8	1
22)	Castres	92.8	1
8)	Châteauroux	92.8	1
25)	Marseille	92.8	4
22)	Nice	92.8	5
23)	Vannes	92.8	1
3)	Cambrai	92.9	1
20)	Château Gontier	92.9	1
26)	Colmar	92.9	1
13)	Lyon	92.9	10
22)	Menton	92.9	1
7)	Montauban	92.9	3
10)	Orléans	92.9	2
25)	Roanne	92.9	1
7)	Rochefort	92.9	1
5)	St Amand Montrond	92.9	1
13)	Ajaccio	93.0	8
22)	Bonifacio	93.0	1
5)	Cosne Cours/Loire	93.0	1
5)	Courtenay	93.0	1
18)	Hirson	93.0	1
21)	Lille	93.0	2
9)	Lourdes	93.0	3
22)	Saint Raphaël	93.0	1
17)	Verdun	93.0	1
13)	Annecy	93.1	1
13)	Arcachon	93.1	1
7)	Bayeux	93.1	1
13)	Bourg en Bresse	93.1	1
21)	Châlons en Champ.	93.1	1
6)	Châteaudun	93.1	1
7)	Coutances	93.1	1
13)	Dole	93.1	1
8)	Ernée	93.1	1
23)	Fontenay le Comte	93.1	1
13)	La Tour du Pin	93.1	1
20)	Mulhouse	93.1	1
23)	Royan	93.1	1
13)	Saint Étienne	93.1	2
7)	Toulon	93.1	4
19)	Avallon	93.2	1
6)	Bergerac	93.2	1
10)	Béziers	93.2	1
9)	Commercy	93.2	1
5)	Évreux	93.2	1
8)	Guéret	93.2	1
23)	Nevers	93.2	1
21)	Provins	93.2	1
21)	Romilly sur Seine	93.2	1
22)	Saint Tropez	93.2	1
5)	Ussel	93.2	1
13)	Arras	93.3	1
5)	Dreux	93.3	1
13)	Grenoble	93.3	1
7)	Lyon	93.3	1
6)	Marmande	93.3	1
23)	Meaux	93.3	3
4)	Montauban	93.3	3
8)	Montluçon	93.3	1
18)	Orléans	93.3	2
5)	Pamiers	93.3	1
3)	Poitiers	93.3	1
17)	Argentan	93.4	1
25)	Bourges	93.4	1
21)	Épernay	93.4	1
6)	Le Chambon s/Lignon	93.4	1
13)	Lille	93.4	1
8)	Marseille	93.4	4
7)	Moulins	93.4	1
10)	Narbonne	93.4	1
23)	Quimper	93.4	1
6)	Vic Fezensac	93.4	1
22)	Ajaccio	93.5	8
13)	Béthune	93.5	1
18)	Dax	93.5	1
14)	Metz	93.5	1
20)	Neufchâteau	93.5	1
6)	Amiens	93.6	1
10)	Angers	93.6	1
8)	Brest	93.6	1
4)	Calvi	93.6	1
18)	Évreux	93.6	1
23)	La Roche sur Yon	93.6	1
19)	Laon	93.6	1
17)	Mazamet	93.6	1
6)	Montbard	93.6	1
9)	Pau	93.6	1
18)	Verneuil d'Avre	93.6	1
22)	Grenoble	93.7	1
10)	Le Havre	93.7	1
8)	Lyon	93.7	1
17)	Nancy	93.7	1
13)	Orléans	93.7	2
25)	Reims	93.7	1
20)	Saint Nazaire	93.7	1
6)	Saintes	93.7	1
13)	Toulon	93.7	4
17)	Alençon	93.8	1
6)	Chaumont	93.8	1
27)	Marseille	93.8	4
18)	Montauban	93.8	3
7)	Orange	93.8	1
28)	Saint Raphaël	93.8	3
21)	Avallon	93.9	1
7)	Bar le Duc	93.9	1
17)	Bourg en Bresse	93.9	1
19)	Bourges	93.9	1
7)	Carcassonne	93.9	1
13)	Château Gontier	93.9	1
20)	Condom	93.9	1
9)	Épernay	93.9	1
18)	Guéret	93.9	1
20)	Jonzac	93.9	1
3)	Lille	93.9	1
25)	Nogent le Rotrou	93.9	1
13)	Saint Brieuc	93.9	1
20)	Vannes	93.9	1
7)	Verdun	93.9	1
7)	Avignon	94.0	1
6)	Pau	94.0	1
9)	Rochefort	94.0	1
22)	Saint Flour	94.0	1
17)	Thionville	94.0	1
1)	Troyes	94.0	1

FM	Station	MHz	kW
21)	Ussel	94.0	1
6)	Arcachon	94.1	1
25)	Chartres	94.1	1
13)	Creil	94.1	2
19)	Decazeville	94.1	1
12)	Dijon	94.1	1
18)	Grenoble	94.1	1
8)	Mayenne	94.1	1
24)	Mont de Marsan	94.1	1
13)	Montmorillon	94.1	1
5)	Narbonne	94.1	1
4)	Saint Gaudens	94.1	1
13)	Soissons	94.1	1
13)	Châlons en Champ.	94.2	1
3)	Chaumont	94.2	1
13)	Reims	94.2	1
5)	Saint Omer	94.2	1
23)	Tarbes	94.2	1
5)	Vierzon	94.2	1
6)	Bordeaux	94.3	5
21)	Cosne Cours/Loire	94.3	1
18)	La Côte Saint André	94.3	1
18)	Le Mans	94.3	2
23)	Lille	94.3	1
23)	Lorient	94.3	1
15)	Paris	94.3	4
23)	Saint Dizier	94.3	1
1)	Saint Étienne	94.3	2
10)	Saint Raphaël	94.3	1
21)	Sens	94.3	1
8)	Clermont Ferrand	94.4	1
8)	Le Puy en Velay	94.4	1
22)	Loches	94.4	1
19)	Orléans	94.4	1
17)	Parthenay	94.4	1
18)	Pau	94.4	1
6)	St Gilles Croix de Vie	94.4	1
9)	Saintes	94.4	1
19)	Toulouse	94.4	1
29)	Corte	94.5	1
5)	Creil	94.5	2
5)	Gournay en Bray	94.5	1
7)	La Rochelle	94.5	1
7)	Laval	94.5	1
9)	Mazamet	94.5	1
9)	Montmorillon	94.5	1
9)	Nevers	94.5	1
7)	Rennes	94.5	2
17)	Arcachon	94.6	1
13)	Chambéry	94.6	1
5)	Colmar	94.6	1
18)	Lannemezan	94.6	1
22)	Perpignan	94.6	3
13)	Pouzauges	94.6	1
12)	Reims	94.6	1
23)	Romilly sur Seine	94.6	1
7)	Saint Lô	94.6	1
5)	Béziers	94.7	1
18)	Fougères	94.7	1
18)	La Ferté Macé	94.7	1
13)	Le Havre	94.7	1
2)	Limoges	94.7	2
7)	Mende	94.7	1
6)	Nantes	94.7	3
17)	Poitiers	94.7	1
8)	Quimper	94.7	1
17)	Saint Étienne	94.7	2
22)	Sarrebourg	94.7	1
3)	Vesoul	94.7	1
6)	Angers	94.8	2
23)	Annecy	94.8	1
20)	Chalon sur Saône	94.8	1
9)	Chaumont	94.8	1
22)	Forbach	94.8	1
6)	Longwy	94.8	1
5)	Mulhouse	94.8	1
22)	Nancy	94.8	1
5)	Nîmes	94.8	1
20)	Riscle	94.8	1
5)	Avignon	94.9	1
12)	Bastia	94.9	1
14)	Bordeaux	94.9	1
17)	Caen	94.9	1
13)	Hirson	94.9	1
9)	La Roche sur Yon	94.9	1
13)	Le Puy en Velay	94.9	1
19)	Lyon	94.9	1
5)	Montpellier	94.9	3
8)	Rennes	94.9	1
24)	Alès	95.0	1
21)	Autun	95.0	1
7)	Chambéry	95.0	1
6)	Cholet	95.0	1
19)	Clermont Ferrand	95.0	1
8)	Dinan	95.0	1
19)	Grenoble	95.0	1
10)	Lorient	95.0	1
13)	Mimizan	95.0	1
9)	Montauban	95.0	3
7)	Nice	95.0	5
13)	Niort	95.0	1
13)	Porto Vecchio	95.0	1
3)	Aubusson	95.1	1
17)	Douai	95.1	1
23)	Épinal	95.1	1
17)	Mâcon	95.1	1
24)	Marseille	95.1	4
17)	Pithiviers	95.1	1
10)	Saint Étienne	95.1	2
9)	Saint Raphaël	95.1	1
3)	Ussel	95.1	1
3)	Béziers	95.2	1
21)	Dunkerque	95.2	1
21)	Fontenay le Comte	95.2	1
5)	Jussey	95.2	1
9)	Périgueux	95.2	1
24)	Tarascon	95.2	1
21)	Vivario	95.2	1
21)	Argentan	95.3	1
3)	Bordeaux	95.3	5
20)	Chartres	95.3	1
20)	Château Thierry	95.3	1
7)	Dax	95.3	1
21)	Évreux	95.3	1
10)	Le Puy en Velay	95.3	1
21)	Lisieux	95.3	1
2)	Lyon	95.3	10
3)	Mirande	95.3	1
3)	Montélimar	95.3	1
13)	Nancy	95.3	1
3)	Tarbes	95.3	1
3)	Toulon	95.3	4
18)	Cahors	95.4	1
18)	Chambéry	95.4	1
13)	Commercy	95.4	1
19)	Le Mans	95.4	2
23)	Orléans	95.4	2
17)	Pouzauges	95.4	1
17)	Ruffec	95.4	1
21)	Verneuil d'Avre	95.4	1
8)	Angers	95.5	1
3)	Annonay	95.5	1
24)	Bergerac	95.5	1
23)	Besançon	95.5	1
13)	Calvi	95.5	1
5)	Corte	95.5	1
17)	La Rochelle	95.5	1
6)	Mâcon	95.5	1
19)	Marseille	95.5	10
9)	Millau	95.5	1
19)	Nogent le Rotrou	95.5	1
6)	Niort	95.6	1
11)	Paris	95.6	4
9)	Saint Tropez	95.6	1
19)	Vannes	95.6	1
23)	Le Puy en Velay	95.7	1
19)	Lorient	95.7	1
22)	Lyon	95.7	4
23)	Metz	95.7	1
23)	Nancy	95.7	1
6)	Perpignan	95.7	3
17)	St Amand Montrond	95.7	1
13)	Angoulême	95.8	1
22)	Chambéry	95.8	1
6)	Montpellier	95.8	3
3)	Nice	95.8	5
21)	Saint Brieuc	95.8	1
23)	Thionville	95.8	1
6)	Toulon	95.8	4
23)	Beauvais	95.9	1
18)	Béthune	95.9	1
10)	Bourges	95.9	1
13)	Brioude	95.9	1
18)	Cavaillon	95.9	1
18)	Commercy	95.9	1
17)	La Tour du Pin	95.9	1
10)	Limoges	95.9	2
22)	Mazamet	95.9	1
23)	Montélimar	95.9	1
3)	Saint Étienne	95.9	2
3)	Annecy	96.0	1
9)	Brignoles	96.0	1
23)	Châteaudun	96.0	1
13)	Châtillon sur Seine	96.0	1
3)	Cognac	96.0	1
23)	Grenoble	96.0	1
18)	Lille	96.0	2
6)	Lisieux	96.0	1
13)	Marseille	96.0	4
23)	Paris	96.0	10
23)	Strasbourg	96.0	1.5
23)	Valence	96.0	2
22)	Auxerre	96.1	1
22)	Béziers	96.1	2
23)	Chartres	96.1	1
8)	Decazeville	96.1	1
6)	Le Puy en Velay	96.1	1
23)	Lyon	96.1	4
23)	Montauban	96.1	3
19)	Moulins	96.1	1
6)	Nancy	96.1	1
13)	Saint Dizier	96.1	1
6)	Tours	96.1	2
17)	Vire	96.1	1
25)	Aix en Provence	96.2	1
19)	Alençon	96.2	1
13)	Bagnères de Bigorre	96.2	1
13)	Bar le Duc	96.2	1
18)	Brive la Gaillarde	96.2	1
22)	Châteauroux	96.2	1
23)	Clermont Ferrand	96.2	1
23)	Compiègne	96.2	1
23)	Douai	96.2	1
6)	Dunkerque	96.2	1
23)	Montbard	96.2	1
6)	Saint Brieuc	96.2	1
13)	Sedan	96.2	1
12)	Amiens	96.3	1
6)	Bourg en Bresse	96.3	1
7)	Caen	96.3	2
7)	L'Aigle	96.3	1
23)	Le Péage/Roussillon	96.3	1
9)	Montluçon	96.3	1
6)	Morlaix	96.3	1
7)	Nogent le Rotrou	96.3	1
17)	Rennes	96.3	1
9)	Rodez	96.3	1
7)	Saint Étienne	96.3	2
2)	Annecy	96.4	1
22)	Bastia	96.4	4
17)	Blois	96.4	1
22)	Calvi	96.4	1
22)	Corte	96.4	1
20)	Cosne Cours/Loire	96.4	1
7)	Épernay	96.4	1
13)	Granville	96.4	1
2)	Lille	96.4	2
6)	Lorient	96.4	1
13)	Mont de Marsan	96.4	1
2)	Paris	96.4	4
9)	Saint Quentin	96.4	1
19)	Sarrebourg	96.4	1
20)	Bourges	96.5	1
6)	Brest	96.5	3
6)	Colmar	96.5	1
10)	Lyon	96.5	4
20)	Marmande	96.5	1
23)	Saint Flour	96.5	1
23)	Saint Nazaire	96.5	1
23)	Saint Omer	96.5	1
5)	Auxerre	96.6	1
6)	Châteauroux	96.6	1
7)	Clermont Ferrand	96.6	2
14)	Coulommiers	96.6	1
29)	Nice	96.6	1
3)	Nîmes	96.6	1
3)	Noyon	96.6	1
9)	Toulon	96.6	4
6)	Yssingeaux	96.6	1
23)	Abbeville	96.7	1
23)	Limoges	96.7	2
13)	Montargis	96.7	1
17)	Saint Lô	96.7	1
22)	Thionville	96.7	1
17)	Angoulême	96.8	1
23)	Brive la Gaillarde	96.8	1
6)	Caen	96.8	2
6)	Cahors	96.8	1
29)	Cannes	96.8	1
20)	Châtellerault	96.8	1
14)	Dreux	96.8	1
7)	Lille	96.8	1
18)	Mont de Marsan	96.8	1
13)	Nantes	96.8	3
13)	Redon	96.8	1
13)	Roanne	96.8	1
13)	Rochefort	96.8	1
13)	Valence	96.8	1
7)	Arras	96.9	1
13)	Guéret	96.9	1
7)	Montbard	96.9	1
3)	Montpellier	96.9	3
17)	Moulins	96.9	1
18)	Rennes	96.9	1
1)	Toulouse	96.9	1
25)	Calvi	97.0	1
21)	Chambéry	97.0	1
9)	Condom	97.0	1
3)	Mazamet	97.0	1
7)	Albi	97.1	1
9)	Bar le Duc	97.1	1
21)	La Ferté s/Jouarre	97.1	1
26)	Montélimar	97.1	1
6)	Montluçon	97.1	1
6)	Pouzauges	97.1	1
7)	Bagnères de Bigorre	97.2	1
10)	Bourg en Bresse	97.2	1
18)	Chaumont	97.2	1
19)	Épinal	97.2	1
23)	Propriano	97.2	1
18)	Saint Omer	97.2	1
20)	Alençon	97.3	1
21)	Auch	97.3	1
19)	Beauvais	97.3	1
13)	Bordeaux	97.3	5
22)	Le Havre	97.3	1
25)	Lyon	97.3	1
23)	Noyon	97.3	1
7)	Poitiers	97.3	1
8)	Rodez	97.3	1
6)	Vire	97.3	1
21)	Agen	97.4	1
22)	Bayeux	97.4	1
13)	Brest	97.4	3
21)	Grenoble	97.4	1
23)	Mont de Marsan	97.4	1
17)	Morhange	97.4	1
21)	Nice	97.4	5
19)	Paris	97.4	4
18)	Saint Malo	97.4	1

FM	Station	MHz	kW
3)	Toulouse	97.4	2
23)	Argentan	97.5	1
18)	Béziers	97.5	1
23)	Carmaux	97.5	1
13)	Corte	97.5	1
13)	Dijon	97.5	1
7)	Mayenne	97.5	1
21)	Neufchâteau	97.5	1
3)	Nogent le Rotrou	97.5	1
3)	Rouen	97.5	2
7)	Alès	97.6	1
18)	Avallon	97.6	1
23)	Caen	97.6	2
5)	Chambéry	97.6	1
22)	Fontenay le Comte	97.6	1
3)	Le Mans	97.6	2
7)	L'Île Rousse	97.6	1
18)	Menton	97.6	1
6)	Metz	97.6	1
13)	Montauban	97.6	3
7)	Pamiers	97.6	1
3)	Perpignan	97.6	1
13)	Rennes	97.6	3
6)	Bayonne	97.7	5
9)	Castres	97.7	1
7)	Compiègne	97.7	1
4)	Dreux	97.7	1
4)	Figeac	97.7	1
28)	Laval	97.7	1
5)	Maubeuge	97.7	1
9)	Montargis	97.7	1
22)	Nantes	97.7	3
8)	Ussel	97.7	1
15)	Vienne	97.7	1
24)	Brive la Gaillarde	97.8	1
6)	Chalon sur Saône	97.8	1
1)	Grenoble	97.8	1
17)	Porto Vecchio	97.8	1
2)	Reims	97.8	2
6)	Saint Étienne	97.8	2
4)	Bastia	97.9	1
9)	Cholet	97.9	1
13)	Parthenay	97.9	1
4)	Toulouse	97.9	5
9)	Angers	98.0	2
18)	Mirande	98.0	1
6)	Montélimar	98.0	1
23)	Montluçon	98.0	1
23)	Moulins	98.0	1
9)	Vannes	98.0	1
23)	Ajaccio	98.1	8
18)	Besançon	98.1	1
3)	Castres	98.1	1
6)	Dax	98.1	1
28)	Nice	98.1	5
5)	Périgueux	98.1	1
9)	Saint Flour	98.1	2
20)	Saintes	98.1	1
13)	Samatan	98.1	1
13)	Sens	98.1	1
12)	Strasbourg	98.1	1
5)	Annonay	98.2	1
13)	Auxerre	98.2	1
9)	Avignon	98.2	1
22)	Bernay	98.2	1
19)	Bordeaux	98.2	1
22)	Bourges	98.2	1
12)	Compiègne	98.2	1
12)	Gournay en Bray	98.2	1
19)	Limoges	98.2	2
6)	Lourdes	98.2	3
13)	Mâcon	98.2	1
17)	Narbonne	98.2	1
22)	Nevers	98.2	1
23)	Niort	98.2	1
12)	Paris	98.2	4
8)	Quimperlé	98.2	1
3)	Sablé sur Sarthe	98.2	1
1)	Toulon	98.2	1
14)	Tours	98.2	2

FM	Station	MHz	kW
13)	Aix en Provence	98.3	1
18)	Bar le Duc	98.3	1
9)	Gien	98.3	1
17)	Montpellier	98.3	3
22)	Rouen	98.3	2
21)	Saint Affrique	98.3	1
23)	Saint Quentin	98.3	1
20)	Sarrebourg	98.3	1
23)	Amiens	98.4	1
13)	Chaumont	98.4	1
21)	Falaise	98.4	1
3)	La Flèche	98.4	1
18)	Mazamet	98.4	1
12)	Meaux	98.4	1
5)	Mirande	98.4	1
8)	Royan	98.4	1
18)	Agen	98.5	1
3)	Alençon	98.5	1
18)	Bastia	98.5	1
17)	Béziers	98.5	1
28)	Bourg en Bresse	98.5	1
21)	Hirson	98.5	1
3)	Laval	98.5	1
5)	Albi	98.6	1
22)	Bergerac	98.6	1
9)	Cognac	98.6	1
20)	Dax	98.6	1
18)	La Roche sur Yon	98.6	1
18)	Vannes	98.6	1
7)	Auch	98.7	1
21)	Brioude	98.7	1
12)	Caen	98.7	1
10)	Chartres	98.7	1
13)	La Rochelle	98.7	1
9)	Le Puy en Velay	98.7	1
6)	Niederbronn l. Bains	98.7	1
5)	Argentan	98.8	1
20)	Cannes	98.8	1
21)	Castres	98.8	1
7)	Grenoble	98.8	1
20)	Lorient	98.8	1
20)	Nice	98.8	1
5)	Rodez	98.8	1
19)	Toulon	98.8	4
7)	Valence	98.8	1
3)	Arcachon	98.9	1
6)	Auxerre	98.9	1
7)	Brest	98.9	3
21)	Gournay en Bray	98.9	1
6)	Le Creusot	98.9	1
3)	Lyon	98.9	1
9)	Mende	98.9	1
3)	Montauban	98.9	3
21)	Nemours	98.9	1
6)	Sens	98.9	1
3)	Vierzon	98.9	1
9)	Amiens	99.0	1
22)	Bayonne	99.0	2
22)	Carcassonne	99.0	1
5)	La Ferté Macé	99.0	1
18)	Metz	99.0	1
29)	Paris	99.0	4
22)	Poitiers	99.0	1
7)	Royan	99.0	1
17)	Saint Raphaël	99.0	1
6)	Ussel	99.0	1
3)	Aurillac	99.1	1
9)	Cervione	99.1	2
7)	Châteauroux	99.1	1
5)	Châtillon sur Seine	99.1	1
9)	Limoges	99.1	2
20)	Provins	99.1	1
18)	Toulouse	99.1	5
3)	Abbeville	99.2	1
25)	Alençon	99.2	1
23)	Aubusson	99.2	1
7)	Bourges	99.2	1
13)	Brive la Gaillarde	99.2	1
22)	Calais	99.2	1
4)	Châtellerault	99.2	1

FM	Station	MHz	kW
7)	Condom	99.2	1
7)	Mont de Marsan	99.2	1
20)	Narbonne	99.2	1
9)	Nice	99.2	5
25)	Saint Lô	99.2	1
23)	Vichy	99.2	1
13)	Argentan	99.3	1
22)	Cambrai	99.3	1
13)	L'Aigle	99.3	1
14)	Laval	99.3	1
18)	Montpellier	99.3	3
6)	Saint Nazaire	99.3	1
10)	Avignon	99.4	1
7)	Bastia	99.4	4
5)	Calvi	99.4	1
5)	Charolles	99.4	1
25)	Clermont Ferrand	99.4	1
5)	Fontainebleau	99.4	2
3)	Mâcon	99.4	1
7)	Mazamet	99.4	1
27)	Metz	99.4	1
13)	Mulhouse	99.4	1
5)	Saint Malo	99.4	1
3)	Châteaudun	99.5	1
13)	Eauze	99.5	1
27)	Paris	99.5	4
13)	Toulouse	99.5	1
6)	Abbeville	99.6	1
25)	Aurillac	99.6	1
18)	Bordeaux	99.6	5
6)	Bourges	99.6	1
3)	Carcassonne	99.6	1
17)	Carmaux	99.6	1
22)	Cholet	99.6	1
24)	Corte	99.6	1
18)	Dijon	99.6	1
5)	Île de Ré	99.6	1
17)	Limoges	99.6	2
5)	Porto Vecchio	99.6	1
17)	Quimperlé	99.6	1
7)	Salon de Provence	99.6	1
9)	Vichy	99.6	1
6)	Bagnères de Bigorre	99.7	1
3)	Brest	99.7	3
13)	La Flèche	99.7	1
17)	Marseille	99.7	4
22)	Montauban	99.7	3
6)	Nevers	99.7	1
2)	Orléans	99.7	1
3)	Troyes	99.7	1
6)	Ajaccio	99.8	8
21)	Chartres	99.8	1
9)	Guéret	99.8	1
17)	Lavaur	99.8	1
9)	Menton	99.8	1
18)	Montargis	99.8	1
6)	Mulhouse	99.8	1
21)	Noyon	99.8	1
21)	Parthenay	99.8	1
19)	Argentan	99.9	1
9)	Mimizan	99.9	1
7)	Nîmes	99.9	1
24)	Paris	99.9	4
9)	Quimper	99.9	1
9)	Argentan	100.0	1
7)	Belfort	100.0	1
23)	Béziers	100.0	1
9)	Fontenay le Comte	100.0	1
2)	Laval	100.0	1
3)	L'Île Rousse	100.0	1
13)	Limoges	100.0	2
9)	Montélimar	100.0	1
9)	Pithiviers	100.0	1
9)	Poitiers	100.0	1
22)	Porto Vecchio	100.0	1
3)	Rodez	100.0	1
13)	Romilly sur Seine	100.0	1
23)	Toulouse	100.0	2
18)	Angers	100.1	1
9)	Bagnères de Bigorre	100.1	1

FM	Station	MHz	kW
3)	Bayonne	100.1	3
19)	Carcassonne	100.1	1
13)	Châteauroux	100.1	1
3)	Marseille	100.1	4
9)	Meaux	100.1	3
9)	Melun	100.1	1
22)	Reims	100.1	2
20)	Saint Brieuc	100.1	1
9)	Sens	100.1	1
23)	Alès	100.2	1
14)	Brest	100.2	1
7)	Chinon	100.2	1
5)	Coutances	100.2	1
13)	Gien	100.2	1
6)	Guéret	100.2	1
9)	La Rochelle	100.2	1
23)	Montpellier	100.2	3
3)	Orthez	100.2	1
9)	Troyes	100.2	1
9)	Valence	100.2	2
14)	Agen	100.3	1
6)	Angoulême	100.3	1
9)	Clermont	100.3	1
7)	Le Mans	100.3	2
6)	Lyon	100.3	4
13)	Mende	100.3	1
3)	Mont de Marsan	100.3	1
9)	Narbonne	100.3	1
9)	Paris	100.3	10
19)	St Gilles Croix de Vie	100.3	1
9)	Soissons	100.3	1
24)	Arcachon	100.4	1
6)	Besançon	100.4	1
21)	Bourges	100.4	1
9)	Chartres	100.4	1
22)	Chaumont	100.4	1
4)	Corte	100.4	1
13)	Lens	100.4	1
6)	Limoges	100.4	2
9)	Niort	100.4	1
9)	Orléans	100.4	2
22)	Royan	100.4	1
21)	Toulon	100.4	4
9)	Toulouse	100.4	5
17)	Tours	100.4	2
9)	Alençon	100.5	1
6)	Annecy	100.5	1
21)	Brive la Gaillarde	100.5	1
9)	Château Gontier	100.5	1
6)	Compiègne	100.5	1
3)	La Tour du Pin	100.5	1
12)	Marseille	100.5	2
23)	Mulhouse	100.5	1
9)	Nogent le Rotrou	100.5	1
18)	Rodez	100.5	1
9)	Rouen	100.5	2
18)	Ruffec	100.5	1
22)	Saint Étienne	100.5	2
9)	Saint Nazaire	100.5	1
9)	Albi	100.6	1
9)	Avallon	100.6	1
7)	Blois	100.6	1
3)	Bourg en Bresse	100.6	1
3)	Brioude	100.6	1
9)	Carcassonne	100.6	1
9)	Dijon	100.6	1
3)	Douarnenez	100.6	1
9)	Ghisonaccia	100.6	4
5)	Parthenay	100.6	1
9)	Reims	100.6	2
17)	Saint Brieuc	100.6	1
20)	Villeneuve sur Lot	100.6	1
13)	Béziers	100.7	1
6)	Decazeville	100.7	1
13)	Laon	100.7	1
13)	Laval	100.7	1
13)	Le Mans	100.7	2
3)	Le Puy en Velay	100.7	1
4)	Paris	100.7	10
9)	Aiti	100.8	1

FM	Station	MHz	kW
9)	Bastia	100.8	4
9)	Calvi	100.8	1
20)	Castres	100.8	1
23)	Chambéry	100.8	1
3)	Clermont Ferrand	100.8	1
2)	Grenoble	100.8	1
5)	Lisieux	100.8	1
4)	Nîmes	100.8	1
12)	Perpignan	100.8	1
7)	Saint Gaudens	100.8	1
8)	Thouars	100.8	1
9)	Verneuil d'Avre	100.8	1
20)	Vire	100.8	1
6)	Alençon	100.9	1
9)	Bayonne	100.9	5
9)	Besançon	100.9	1
13)	Coulommiers	100.9	1
10)	Marseille	100.9	10
3)	Nancy	100.9	1
22)	Rodez	100.9	1
3)	Amiens	101.0	1
24)	Aurillac	101.0	1
14)	Avignon	101.0	1
23)	Bergerac	101.0	1
13)	Château Thierry	101.0	1
9)	L'Aigle	101.0	1
5)	Lourdes	101.0	3
6)	Quimper	101.0	1
9)	Agen	101.1	1
9)	Aubusson	101.1	1
17)	Bar le Duc	101.1	1
10)	Beauvais	101.1	1
9)	Châteauroux	101.1	1
4)	Ghisonaccia	101.1	1
6)	La Roche sur Yon	101.1	1
10)	Laval	101.1	1
11)	Le Havre	101.1	1
13)	Metz	101.1	1
10)	Paris	101.1	10
23)	Poitiers	101.1	1
9)	Saint Malo	101.1	1
9)	Ajaccio	101.2	8
24)	Albi	101.2	1
9)	Arras	101.2	1
13)	Blois	101.2	1
21)	Chaumont	101.2	1
9)	Clermont Ferrand	101.2	1
7)	Épinal	101.2	1
3)	Chambéry	101.3	1
21)	Châtellerault	101.3	1
22)	Dreux	101.3	1
9)	Dunkerque	101.3	1
17)	Forbach	101.3	1
6)	Jonzac	101.3	1
22)	La Rochelle	101.3	1
7)	La Tour du Pin	101.3	1
21)	Le Blanc	101.3	1
9)	Lille	101.3	2
5)	Menton	101.3	1
20)	Orange	101.3	1
19)	Saint Étienne	101.3	2
9)	Sarlat la Canéda	101.3	1
10)	Amiens	101.4	1
9)	Caen	101.4	2
17)	Longwy	101.4	1
21)	Marseille	101.4	10
5)	Nice	101.4	5
10)	Noyon	101.4	1
21)	St Gilles Croix de Vie	101.4	1
12)	Toulouse	101.4	1
5)	Vic Fezensac	101.4	1
18)	Alès	101.5	1
9)	Cahors	101.5	1
14)	Évreux	101.5	1
5)	Montbard	101.5	1
18)	Nevers	101.5	1
14)	Paris	101.5	10
13)	Poitiers	101.5	1
21)	Redon	101.5	1
21)	Rodez	101.5	1

FM	Station	MHz	kW
17)	Valence	101.5	1
19)	Vendôme	101.5	1
18)	Cambrai	101.6	1
5)	Chaumont	101.6	1
18)	Issoudun	101.6	1
10)	Le Mans	101.6	2
5)	Mâcon	101.6	1
20)	Montargis	101.6	1
23)	Périgueux	101.6	1
10)	Quimper	101.6	1
21)	Saint Malo	101.6	1
13)	Valence	101.6	1
21)	Albi	101.7	1
6)	Bayeux	101.7	1
5)	Bayonne	101.7	5
18)	Compiègne	101.7	1
6)	Cosne Cours/Loire	101.7	1
17)	Le Puy en Velay	101.7	1
22)	Limoges	101.7	2
21)	Mazamet	101.7	1
18)	Montluçon	101.7	1
22)	Montpellier	101.7	1
23)	Morlaix	101.7	1
9)	Provins	101.7	1
7)	Reims	101.7	2
9)	Romilly sur Seine	101.7	1
22)	Tarascon	101.7	1
6)	Aubusson	101.8	1
9)	Auxerre	101.8	1
9)	Bergerac	101.8	1
23)	Brest	101.8	3
7)	Laon	101.8	1
6)	Le Havre	101.8	1
24)	Toulouse	101.8	1
17)	Aix en Provence	101.9	1
3)	Cahors	101.9	1
9)	Châtillon sur Seine	101.9	1
6)	Cognac	101.9	1
9)	Coutances	101.9	1
7)	Évreux	101.9	1
17)	Martigues	101.9	1
9)	Mayenne	101.9	1
18)	Moulins	101.9	1
7)	Paris	101.9	10
9)	Tonnerre	101.9	1
17)	Vendôme	101.9	1
7)	Abbeville	102.0	1
6)	Bar le Duc	102.0	1
17)	Beaune	102.0	1
5)	Épinal	102.0	1
6)	Falaise	102.0	1
23)	La Rochelle	102.0	1
17)	Metz	102.0	1
5)	Neufchâteau	102.0	1
22)	Quimper	102.0	1
6)	Rennes	102.0	3
21)	Saint Quentin	102.0	1
24)	Toulouse	102.0	60
7)	Annecy	102.1	1
20)	Avallon	102.1	1
20)	Calvi	102.1	1
9)	Charolles	102.1	1
26)	Coulommiers	102.1	1
18)	Limoges	102.1	2
26)	Melun	102.1	1
9)	Mulhouse	102.1	1
6)	Nîmes	102.1	1
7)	St Amand Montrond	102.1	1
18)	Strasbourg	102.1	4
9)	Arcachon	102.2	1
9)	Blois	102.2	1
21)	Dole	102.2	1
17)	La Ferté Macé	102.2	1
7)	Montargis	102.2	1
9)	Thouars	102.2	1
7)	Troyes	102.2	1
9)	Avranches	102.3	1
13)	Cahors	102.3	1
17)	Chambéry	102.3	1
6)	Forbach	102.3	1

FM	Station	MHz	kW
21)	Le Puy en Velay	102.3	1
6)	Marseille	102.3	10
9)	Montbard	102.3	1
18)	Nancy	102.3	1
21)	Nevers	102.3	1
26)	Paris	102.3	4
3)	Quimperlé	102.3	1
9)	Saint Brieuc	102.3	1
9)	Saint Omer	102.3	1
10)	Tours	102.3	2
7)	Auxerre	102.4	1
9)	Bordeaux	102.4	5
9)	Brest	102.4	1
6)	Castres	102.4	1
3)	Chalon sur Saône	102.4	1
20)	Chaumont	102.4	1
3)	Decazeville	102.4	1
10)	Grenoble	102.4	1
6)	Haguenau	102.4	1
5)	Montmorillon	102.4	1
9)	Nantes	102.4	3
7)	Perpignan	102.4	3
2)	Rennes	102.4	1
9)	Romorantin Lanthen.	102.4	1
5)	Thionville	102.4	1
6)	Toulouse	102.4	5
3)	Vienne	102.4	1
22)	Angers	102.5	1
18)	Calais	102.5	1
24)	Carmaux	102.5	1
5)	Chartres	102.5	1
6)	Commercy	102.5	1
3)	Dijon	102.5	1
18)	Gourdon	102.5	1
8)	Les Sables d'Olonne	102.5	1
7)	Melun	102.5	1
8)	Niort	102.5	1
6)	Sarrebourg	102.5	1
18)	Angoulême	102.6	1
13)	Bergerac	102.6	1
21)	Carcassonne	102.6	1
21)	Montauban	102.6	3
27)	Orléans	102.6	1
3)	Quimper	102.6	1
9)	Saint Gaudens	102.6	1
20)	Troyes	102.6	1
9)	Abbeville	102.7	1
22)	Avallon	102.7	1
3)	Limoges	102.7	2
5)	Morlaix	102.7	1
3)	Nérac	102.7	1
8)	Paris	102.7	10
20)	Rochefort	102.7	1
9)	Saint Dizier	102.7	1
5)	Saint Flour	102.7	1
18)	Valence	102.7	1
8)	Verneuil d'Avre	102.7	1
13)	Alès	102.8	1
9)	Annecy	102.8	1
18)	Annonay	102.8	1
13)	Avignon	102.8	1
23)	Bordeaux	102.8	5
9)	Bourg en Bresse	102.8	1
22)	Brive la Gaillarde	102.8	1
21)	Dax	102.8	1
17)	Lorient	102.8	1
20)	Parthenay	102.8	1
9)	Saint Étienne	102.8	2
2)	Saint Raphaël	102.8	3
7)	Tours	102.8	2
9)	Vitré	102.8	1
5)	Canavaggia	102.9	1
13)	Charolles	102.9	1
14)	Clermont Ferrand	102.9	1
21)	Confolens	102.9	1
5)	Guéret	102.9	1
1)	Le Mans	102.9	2
21)	Lourdes	102.9	3
9)	Lunéville	102.9	1
23)	Nantes	102.9	3

FM	Station	MHz	kW
9)	Saint Lô	102.9	1
24)	Villeneuve sur Lot	102.9	1
9)	Chambéry	103.0	1
9)	Châteaudun	103.0	1
13)	Colmar	103.0	1
6)	Condom	103.0	1
18)	Le Puy en Velay	103.0	1
9)	Lyon	103.0	10
3)	Metz	103.0	1
21)	Moulins	103.0	1
17)	Neufchâtel en Bray	103.0	1
12)	Poitiers	103.0	1
21)	Saint Gaudens	103.0	1
7)	Tonnerre	103.0	1
23)	Angoulême	103.1	1
21)	Arcachon	103.1	1
3)	Bar le Duc	103.1	1
20)	Bergerac	103.1	1
17)	Charensat	103.1	1
2)	Marseille	103.1	4
20)	Paris	103.1	10
5)	Roanne	103.1	1
24)	Saint Affrique	103.1	1
3)	Saint Dizier	103.1	1
13)	Saint Flour	103.1	1
10)	Toulouse	103.1	5
22)	Amiens	103.2	1
21)	Belfort	103.2	1
21)	Cervione	103.2	1
17)	Dole	103.2	1
6)	Douarnenez	103.2	1
9)	Grenoble	103.2	1
9)	Mirande	103.2	1
20)	Montmorillon	103.2	1
19)	Niort	103.2	1
20)	Nogent le Rotrou	103.2	1
24)	Perpignan	103.2	10
20)	Albi	103.3	1
21)	Annecy	103.3	1
18)	Aurillac	103.3	1
21)	Avesnes sur Helpe	103.3	1
6)	Carpentras	103.3	1
6)	Chartres	103.3	1
9)	Compiègne	103.3	1
5)	Guingamp	103.3	1
20)	La Rochelle	103.3	1
20)	Lille	103.3	2
7)	Nancy	103.3	1
7)	Nérac	103.3	1
20)	Orthez	103.3	1
19)	Rouen	103.3	2
20)	Sarlat la Canéda	103.3	1
5)	Strasbourg	103.3	4
10)	Toulon	103.3	1
7)	Vichy	103.3	1
2)	Bastia	103.4	1
25)	Cahors	103.4	1
13)	Carcassonne	103.4	1
7)	Metz	103.4	1
7)	Nantes	103.4	3
12)	Orléans	103.4	1
20)	Rodez	103.4	1
21)	Saint Lô	103.4	1
25)	Tours	103.4	2
6)	Beauvais	103.5	1
7)	Dinan	103.5	1
6)	Épinal	103.5	1
19)	Le Havre	103.5	1
6)	Le Mans	103.5	2
9)	Morlaix	103.5	1
6)	Paris	103.5	10
9)	Saint Affrique	103.5	1
23)	Angers	103.6	2
21)	Blois	103.6	1
25)	Corte	103.6	1
7)	Longwy	103.6	1
5)	Montluçon	103.6	1
20)	Saint Gaudens	103.6	1
7)	Saint Nazaire	103.6	1
23)	Alençon	103.7	1

FM	Station	MHz	kW
6)	Creil	103.7	2
6)	Fontainebleau	103.7	2
17)	Grenoble	103.7	1
23)	Laval	103.7	1
6)	Meaux	103.7	3
20)	Mirande	103.7	1
18)	Niort	103.7	1
21)	Bastia	103.8	4
21)	Bergerac	103.8	1
17)	Chinon	103.8	1
24)	Figeac	103.8	1
22)	Lorient	103.8	1
20)	Lourdes	103.8	3
4)	Nantes	103.8	2
5)	Saint Brieuc	103.8	2
18)	Troyes	103.8	1
9)	Ussel	103.8	1
24)	Bayonne	103.9	5
18)	Beauvais	103.9	1
21)	Calvi	103.9	1
18)	Épinal	103.9	1
18)	Le Havre	103.9	1
20)	Le Mans	103.9	2
13)	Montpellier	103.9	3
18)	Paris	103.9	10
9)	Rennes	103.9	3
21)	Saint Dizier	103.9	1
19)	Saint Flour	103.9	1
5)	Saint Lô	103.9	1
3)	Saint Quentin	103.9	1
21)	Toulouse	103.9	5
21)	Vierzon	103.9	1
20)	Arcachon	104.0	1
17)	Avignon	104.0	1
21)	Besançon	104.0	1
3)	Cervione	104.0	2
3)	Mauriac	104.0	1
2)	Metz	104.0	1
18)	Millau	104.0	1
21)	Pamiers	104.0	1
21)	Romorantin Lanthen.	104.0	1
18)	St Gilles Croix de Vie	104.0	1
21)	Tours	104.0	2
24)	Villefranche Rouerg	104.0	1
21)	Abbeville	104.1	1
21)	Alençon	104.1	1
9)	Bressuire	104.1	1
18)	Chartres	104.1	1
20)	Compiègne	104.1	1
17)	Confolens	104.1	1
21)	Coulommiers	104.1	1
21)	Laval	104.1	1
20)	Mâcon	104.1	1
24)	Mazamet	104.1	1
21)	Melun	104.1	1
8)	Menton	104.1	1
20)	Montauban	104.1	3
20)	Montélimar	104.1	1
21)	Montluçon	104.1	1
2)	Nancy	104.1	1
6)	Rouen	104.1	2
20)	Annecy	104.2	1
20)	Bordeaux	104.2	5
21)	Dijon	104.2	1
20)	Grenoble	104.2	1
20)	Lyon	104.2	4
20)	Mende	104.2	1
4)	Mirande	104.2	1
21)	Nogent le Rotrou	104.2	1
21)	Troyes	104.2	1
20)	Ajaccio	104.3	8
21)	Amiens	104.3	1
21)	Angers	104.3	1
20)	Bastia	104.3	4
20)	Bayonne	104.3	5
21)	Beauvais	104.3	1
20)	Béziers	104.3	1
20)	Bonifacio	104.3	1
21)	Brest	104.3	3
21)	Clermont Ferrand	104.3	2

FM	Station	MHz	kW
13)	Épinal	104.3	1
21)	La Ferté Macé	104.3	1
21)	La Rochelle	104.3	1
21)	Le Havre	104.3	1
21)	Le Mans	104.3	2
21)	Limoges	104.3	2
21)	Lorient	104.3	1
20)	Marseille	104.3	10
17)	Montbard	104.3	1
20)	Montpellier	104.3	3
21)	Nantes	104.3	3
13)	Neufchâteau	104.3	1
20)	Nîmes	104.3	1
21)	Orléans	104.3	2
21)	Paris	104.3	10
20)	Pau	104.3	1
21)	Péronne	104.3	1
20)	Perpignan	104.3	3
21)	Poitiers	104.3	1
21)	Quimper	104.3	1
21)	Rennes	104.3	3
20)	Saint Affrique	104.3	1
21)	St Amand Montrond	104.3	1
21)	Saint Nazaire	104.3	1
21)	Soissons	104.3	1
20)	Toulon	104.3	4
20)	Toulouse	104.3	5
20)	Valence	104.3	1
21)	Vannes	104.3	1
21)	Aubusson	104.4	1
21)	Auxerre	104.4	1
7)	Bourg en Bresse	104.4	1
21)	Jonzac	104.4	1
20)	Le Puy en Velay	104.4	1
19)	Montargis	104.4	1
2)	Nice	104.4	5
21)	Reims	104.4	2
24)	Rodez	104.4	1
18)	Romorantin Lanthen.	104.4	1
13)	Ruffec	104.4	1
20)	Saint Étienne	104.4	1
20)	Agen	104.5	1
5)	Alençon	104.5	1
20)	Arles	104.5	1
20)	Avignon	104.5	1
7)	Baccarat	104.5	1
20)	Chambéry	104.5	1
11)	Chartres	104.5	1
21)	Compiègne	104.5	1
5)	Coulommiers	104.5	1
19)	Forbach	104.5	1
19)	Gien	104.5	1
17)	La Roche sur Yon	104.5	1
5)	Laval	104.5	1
9)	Le Creusot	104.5	1
5)	Melun	104.5	1
17)	Redon	104.5	1
21)	Rouen	104.5	2
5)	Tours	104.5	2
1)	Alès	104.6	1
3)	Avallon	104.6	1
5)	Bayeux	104.6	1
5)	Bordeaux	104.6	5
5)	Grenoble	104.6	1
5)	L'Aigle	104.6	1
5)	Lyon	104.6	4
5)	Nevers	104.6	1
5)	Nogent le Rotrou	104.6	1
22)	Propriano	104.6	1
20)	Saint Flour	104.6	1
21)	Saint Raphaël	104.6	1
22)	Zonza	104.6	1
5)	Amiens	104.7	1
5)	Angers	104.7	1
5)	Beauvais	104.7	1
5)	Brest	104.7	3
24)	Carcassonne	104.7	80
5)	Cholet	104.7	1
5)	Clermont Ferrand	104.7	2
5)	Dijon	104.7	1

FM	Station	MHz	kW
22)	Ghisonaccia	104.7	2
5)	La Rochelle	104.7	1
5)	Le Havre	104.7	1
5)	Le Mans	104.7	2
5)	Limoges	104.7	2
5)	Lorient	104.7	1
24)	Montpellier	104.7	1
5)	Nantes	104.7	3
5)	Orléans	104.7	2
5)	Paris	104.7	10
5)	Poitiers	104.7	1
5)	Quimper	104.7	1
5)	Rennes	104.7	2
5)	Saint Nazaire	104.7	1
5)	Soissons	104.7	1
5)	Toulon	104.7	4
5)	Troyes	104.7	1
5)	Vannes	104.7	1
5)	Annecy	104.8	1
5)	Arcachon	104.8	1
3)	Argentan	104.8	1
20)	Aubusson	104.8	1
20)	Auxerre	104.8	1
5)	Bernay	104.8	1
5)	Cambrai	104.8	1
5)	Châlons en Champ.	104.8	1
4)	Gourdon	104.8	1
5)	La Tour du Pin	104.8	1
5)	Marseille	104.8	10
21)	Metz	104.8	1
18)	Neufchâteau	104.8	1
13)	St Amand Montrond	104.8	1
5)	Saint Étienne	104.8	2
18)	Saint Lô	104.8	1
5)	Valence	104.8	1
5)	Abbeville	104.9	1
5)	Agen	104.9	1
5)	Besançon	104.9	1
7)	Chartres	104.9	1
5)	Compiègne	104.9	1
7)	La Roche sur Yon	104.9	1
22)	Laval	104.9	1
5)	Mont de Marsan	104.9	1
7)	Montereau F/Yonne	104.9	1
5)	Moulins	104.9	1
7)	Parthenay	104.9	1
24)	Périgueux	104.9	1
5)	Rouen	104.9	2
21)	Royan	104.9	1
20)	Angoulême	105.0	1
20)	Auch	105.0	1
21)	Bar le Duc	105.0	1
21)	Caen	105.0	2
24)	Cahors	105.0	1
21)	L'Aigle	105.0	1
13)	Luxeuil les Bains	105.0	1
21)	Lyon	105.0	4
7)	Morlaix	105.0	1
23)	Reims	105.0	2
22)	Alençon	105.1	1
3)	Angers	105.1	2
21)	Bayonne	105.1	5
9)	Bonifacio	105.1	1
21)	Bordeaux	105.1	5
21)	Charolles	105.1	1
20)	Clermont Ferrand	105.1	2
6)	Corte	105.1	1
9)	Dinan	105.1	1
25)	Le Puy en Velay	105.1	1
20)	Limoges	105.1	2
21)	Nancy	105.1	1
20)	Niort	105.1	1
17)	Toulon	105.1	4
7)	Ajaccio	105.2	8
20)	Brive la Gaillarde	105.2	1
21)	Épinal	105.2	1
9)	Issoudun	105.2	1
3)	Lons le Saunier	105.2	1
5)	Montauban	105.2	3
21)	Saint Étienne	105.2	2

FM	Station	MHz	kW
13)	Saint Lô	105.2	1
21)	Vitré	105.2	1
3)	Chartres	105.3	1
19)	Cholet	105.3	1
5)	Metz	105.3	1
13)	Rouen	105.3	2
22)	Sens	105.3	1
13)	Strasbourg	105.3	4
18)	Dole	105.4	1
5)	Nancy	105.5	1
12)	Lens	105.6	1
9)	Béziers	105.7	1
23)	Bonifacio	105.7	1
7)	Lannemezan	105.7	1
21)	Le Creusot	105.7	1
20)	Lesparre Médoc	105.7	1
17)	Loches	105.7	1
14)	Marseille	105.7	1
7)	Neufchâteau	105.7	1
9)	Redon	105.7	1
3)	Saint Flour	105.7	2
19)	Sancerre	105.7	1
21)	Strasbourg	105.7	4
13)	Vesoul	105.7	1
17)	Argenton sur Creuse	105.8	1
5)	Carcassonne	105.8	1
10)	Dijon	105.8	1
3)	Grenoble	105.8	1
9)	Nîmes	105.8	1
23)	Segré	105.8	1
8)	Bourges	105.9	1
18)	Brest	105.9	3
5)	Caen	105.9	2
22)	Clermont Ferrand	105.9	1
21)	Corte	105.9	1
20)	Ghisonaccia	105.9	2
9)	Le Mans	105.9	2
18)	Mende	105.9	1
22)	Paris	105.9	10
7)	Pau	105.9	1
9)	Perpignan	105.9	3
18)	Poitiers	105.9	1
13)	Saint Nazaire	105.9	1
21)	Saintes	105.9	1
7)	Toulouse	105.9	5
23)	Troyes	105.9	1
21)	Valence	105.9	1
21)	Ajaccio	106.0	8
22)	Besançon	106.0	1
22)	Blois	106.0	1
24)	Bordeaux	106.0	5
7)	Cahors	106.0	1
5)	Forbach	106.0	1
17)	L'Aigle	106.0	1
8)	Limoges	106.0	2
9)	Lorient	106.0	1
3)	Martigues	106.0	1
20)	Mauriac	106.0	1
21)	Mayenne	106.0	1
21)	Montargis	106.0	1
21)	Niort	106.0	1
22)	Noyon	106.0	1
20)	Rennes	106.0	3
8)	Roanne	106.0	1
13)	St Gilles Croix de Vie	106.0	1
23)	Agen	106.1	1
3)	Albi	106.1	1
27)	Amiens	106.1	1
13)	Angers	106.1	2
8)	Aubusson	106.1	1
19)	Bastia	106.1	4
5)	Brive la Gaillarde	106.1	1
19)	Calvi	106.1	1
22)	Chartres	106.1	1
5)	Commercy	106.1	1
22)	Melun	106.1	1
9)	Montpellier	106.1	3
10)	Rouen	106.1	2
5)	Saint Dizier	106.1	1
5)	Sarrebourg	106.1	1

FM Station	MHz	kW
13) Tarbes	106.1	1
21) Angoulême	106.2	1
7) Argentan	106.2	1
19) Avignon	106.2	1
5) Bergerac	106.2	1
18) Étampes	106.2	1
20) Laval	106.2	1
13) Morlaix	106.2	1
3) Nantes	106.2	2
6) Neufchâteau	106.2	1
18) Tonnerre	106.2	1
22) Toulon	106.2	1
13) Vendôme	106.2	1
21) Arras	106.3	1
13) Bourges	106.3	1
5) Castres	106.3	1
25) Dijon	106.3	1
5) Ghisonaccia	106.3	1
6) Laon	106.3	1
20) Moulins	106.3	1
21) Pau	106.3	1
13) Quimper	106.3	1
22) Saint Brieuc	106.3	1
5) Sarlat la Canéda	106.3	1
5) Toulouse	106.3	5
13) Tours	106.3	2
8) Vannes	106.3	1
5) Avallon	106.4	1
15) Bordeaux	106.4	5
13) Caen	106.4	2
8) Chambéry	106.4	1
18) Clermont Ferrand	106.4	2
9) Marseille	106.4	10
5) Montargis	106.4	1
10) Troyes	106.4	1
10) Valence	106.4	1
7) Agen	106.5	1
5) Aurillac	106.5	1
5) Blois	106.5	1
5) Châteauroux	106.5	1
19) Corte	106.5	1
15) Évreux	106.5	1
9) Fougères	106.5	1
17) Lons le Saunier	106.5	1
22) Lourdes	106.5	1
13) Nogent le Rotrou	106.5	1
22) Périgueux	106.5	1
5) Reims	106.5	2
23) Saint Étienne	106.5	2
26) Strasbourg	106.5	1.5
17) Yvetot	106.5	1
22) Albi	106.6	1
10) Brest	106.6	3
20) Cahors	106.6	1
5) Châtellerault	106.6	1
17) Châtillon sur Seine	106.6	1
21) Commercy	106.6	1
15) Dreux	106.6	1
9) Gournay en Bray	106.6	1
18) La Flèche	106.6	1
6) La Rochelle	106.6	1
5) Le Puy en Velay	106.6	1
25) Montélimar	106.6	1
20) Montluçon	106.6	1
23) Quimperlé	106.6	1
13) Saint Malo	106.6	1
8) Toulon	106.6	1
9) Vire	106.6	1
18) Alençon	106.7	1
5) Angoulême	106.7	1
18) Bourges	106.7	1
6) Calvi	106.7	1
10) Carcassonne	106.7	1
5) Chalon sur Saône	106.7	1
5) Condom	106.7	1
18) Laval	106.7	1
25) Lisieux	106.7	1
15) Lyon	106.7	1
5) Mende	106.7	1
22) Moulins	106.7	1

FM Station	MHz	kW
10) Nantes	106.7	4
1) Paris	106.7	4
3) Roanne	106.7	1
5) Royan	106.7	1
5) Saint Gaudens	106.7	1
20) Ussel	106.7	1
6) Vitry le François	106.7	1
4) Alès	106.8	1
8) Avallon	106.8	1
22) Bordeaux	106.8	5
20) Brioude	106.8	1
4) Chartres	106.8	1
13) Château Renault	106.8	1
20) Grasse	106.8	1
17) La Côte Saint André	106.8	1
22) Marseille	106.8	4
5) Niort	106.8	1
5) Pau	106.8	1
13) Perpignan	106.8	1
3) Rennes	106.8	3
5) Rethel	106.8	1
18) Saint Affrique	106.8	1
23) Béthune	106.9	1
21) Bourg en Bresse	106.9	1
19) Châteauroux	106.9	1
8) Cholet	106.9	1
22) Compiègne	106.9	1
14) Corte	106.9	1
8) Grenoble	106.9	1
8) La Roche sur Yon	106.9	1
7) Le Havre	106.9	1
8) Le Mans	106.9	2
7) Lorient	106.9	1
9) Mantes la Jolie	106.9	2
5) Mazamet	106.9	1
23) Melun	106.9	1
3) Mers les Bains	106.9	1
21) Montpellier	106.9	3
8) Périgueux	106.9	1
18) Poligny	106.9	1
20) Propriano	106.9	1
5) Provins	106.9	1
5) Romilly sur Seine	106.9	1.2
28) Saint Brieuc	106.9	1
26) Saint Lô	106.9	1
2) Strasbourg	106.9	1
5) Bar le Duc	107.0	1
8) Bressuire	107.0	1
8) Cahors	107.0	1
7) Château Thierry	107.0	1
2) Clermont Ferrand	107.0	1
23) La Ferté Macé	107.0	1
6) L'Aigle	107.0	1
19) Le Puy en Velay	107.0	1
21) Mont de Marsan	107.0	1
8) Montauban	107.0	1
17) Montluçon	107.0	1
23) Nice	107.0	5
21) Nîmes	107.0	1
18) Porto Vecchio	107.0	1
7) Rouen	107.0	1
18) Saint Quentin	107.0	1
1) Valence	107.0	1
19) Abbeville	107.1	1
10) Arcachon	107.1	1
5) Bourges	107.1	1
2) Caen	107.1	2
21) Carmaux	107.1	1
23) Dijon	107.1	1
8) Laval	107.1	1
21) Mulhouse	107.1	1
9) Nancy	107.1	1
10) Poitiers	107.1	1
7) Quimper	107.1	1
18) Saint Étienne	107.1	2
21) Saint Flour	107.1	1
5) St Méen le Grand	107.1	1
21) Alès	107.2	1
2) Angers	107.2	1
21) Avignon	107.2	1

FM Station	MHz	kW
6) Bastia	107.2	1
20) Blois	107.2	1
21) Figeac	107.2	1
14) Limoges	107.2	2
19) Mâcon	107.2	1
2) Nantes	107.2	3
10) Pau	107.2	1
8) Rochefort	107.2	1
7) Soissons	107.2	1
2) Toulouse	107.2	1
20) Tours	107.2	2
24) Ussel	107.2	1
7) Arnay le Duc	107.3	1
3) Arras	107.3	1
10) Auxerre	107.3	1
2) Bordeaux	107.3	1
2) Brest	107.3	2.8
10) Brive la Gaillarde	107.3	1
1) Carcassonne	107.3	1
10) Chantilly	107.3	4
3) Châteauroux	107.3	1
21) Colmar	107.3	1
18) Corte	107.3	1
8) Dax	107.3	1
23) Évreux	107.3	1
3) Lens	107.3	1
18) Lorient	107.3	1

FM Station	MHz	kW
18) Lyon	107.3	4
6) Mazamet	107.3	1
2) Menton	107.3	1
9) Metz	107.3	1
5) Millau	107.3	1
10) Montpellier	107.3	3
20) Orléans	107.3	1
9) Parthenay	107.3	1
21) Perpignan	107.3	3
23) Saint Brieuc	107.3	1
23) Saint Raphaël	107.3	1
9) Verdun	107.3	1
23) Dreux	107.4	1
5) Granville	107.4	1
7) Lisieux	107.4	1
8) Nevers	107.4	1
18) Provins	107.4	1
28) Arcachon	107.5	1
4) Château Gontier	107.5	1
20) Châteaudun	107.5	1
21) Cherbourg/Cotentin	107.5	1
30) Paris	107.5	4
20) Saint Dizier	107.5	1
9) Canavaggia	107.7	1
25) Lorient	107.7	1
20) La Ferté Macé	107.9	1
20)L'Aigle	107.9	1

NB: Includes stns 1kW and over.
As of September 2020, 5403 licences (txs) were allocated to private commercial and non-commercial FM stns. Approx. 3700 stns are affiliated to one of the following private commercial national networks.

Addresses & other information:
1) Beur FM ✉ 2 rue du Nouveau Bercy, 94220 Charenton le Pont ☎ +33 1 53481057 **W:** beurfm.net + 4 txs less than 1kW – **2) BFM Business** ✉ 2 rue du Général Alain de Boissieu, 75015 Paris **W:** bfmbusiness.bfmtv.com + 7 txs less than 1kW – **3) Chérie FM** ✉ 22 rue Boileau, 75016 Paris ☎ +33 1 40714000 **W:** cheriefm.fr+ 68 txs less than 1kW – **4) COFRAC-Radio Notre Dame** ✉ 6 bd Edgar Quinet, 75014 Paris ☎+33 1 56564444 **W:** radionotredame.net + 18 txs less than 1kW – **5) Europe 1** ✉ 2 rue des Cévennes, 75015 Paris **W:** europe1.fr + 157 txs less than 1kW – **6) Virgin Radio** ✉ 2 rue des Cévennes, 75015 Paris **W:** virginradio.fr + 106 txs less than 1kW– **7) Fun Radio** ✉ 56 av Charles de Gaulle, 92200 Neuilly sur Seine ☎ +33 1 41924030. **W:** funradio.fr + 111 txs less than 1kW – **8) M Radio** ✉ 50 avenue Daumesnil, 75012 Paris **W:** mradio.fr + 39 txs less than 1kW – **9) NRJ** ✉ 22 rue Boileau, 75016 Paris ☎ +33 1 40714000 **W:** nrj.fr + 151 txs less than 1kW – **10) Radio Classique** ✉ 12 bis place Henri Bergson, 75382 Paris. Cedex 08 ☎ +33 1 40085000 🖷 +33 1 40085060 **W:** radioclassique.fr + 29 txs less than 1kW – **11) Radio Courtoisie** ✉ 61 bd Murat 75016 Paris ☎ +33 1 46510085 **W:** radiocourtoisie.fr + 3 txs less than 1kW – **12) Radio FG** ✉ 51 rue de Rivoli, 75001 Paris ☎ +33 1 40138800 **W:** radiofg.com + 11 txs less than 1kW – **13) Nostalgie** ✉ 22 rue Boileau, 75016 Paris ☎ +33 1 40714000. **W:** nostalgie.fr + 120 txs less than 1kW – **14) Radio Nova** ✉ 127 avenue Ledru Rollin, 75011 Paris ☎ +33 1 53333300 **W:** nova.fr + 6 txs less than 1kW – **15) Radio Orient** ✉ 98 bd Victor Hugo, 92110 Clichy ☎ +33 1 41061600 **W:** radioorient.com + 4 tx less than 1kW – **16) Radio Soleil** ✉ 57 rue d'Avron, 75020 Paris ☎ +33 1 43484343 **W:** radio-soleil.com + 2 txs less than 1kW – **17) RCF** ✉ 7 place Saint Irénée, 69321 Lyon Cedex 05 ☎ +33 4 72386210. **W:** rcf.fr + 118 txs less than 1kW – **18) RFM** ✉ 2 rue des Cévennes, 75015 Paris **W:** rfm.fr + 93 txs less than 1kW – **19) Rire et Chansons** ✉ 22 rue Boileau, 75016 Paris ☎ +33 1 40714000 **W:** rireetchansons.fr + 54 txs less than 1kW – **20) RMC** ✉ 2 rue du Général Alain de Boissieu, 75015 Paris **W:** rmc.bfmtv.com + 151 txs less than 1kW – **21) RTL** ✉ 56 av Charles de Gaulle, 92200 Neuilly sur Seine. ☎ +33 1 41924040 **W:** rtl.fr **LW:** 234kHz 750kW(d)/375kW(n) see Luxembourg. + 125 txs less than 1kW – **22) RTL 2** ✉ 56 av Charles de Gaulle, 92200 Neuilly sur Seine ☎ +33 1 41924020 **W:** 6play.fr/rtl2 + 74 txs less than 1kW – **23) Skyrock** ✉ 37 bis rue Greneta, 75002 Paris ☎ +33 1 44888200 **W:** skyrock.fm + 115 txs less than 1kW – **24) Sud Radio** ✉ 104 avenue du Pdt Kennedy, 75016 Paris ☎ +33 1 53920720 **W:** sudradio.fr + 32 txs less than 1kW – **25) Jazz Radio** ✉ 40 quai Rambaud, 69002 Lyon ☎ +33 4 72101535 **W:** jazzradio.fr + 27 txs less than 1 kW – **26) Ouï FM** ✉ 2 rue de la Roquette, 75011 Paris ☎ +33 1 55075801 **W:** ouifm.fr + 15 txs less than 1kW – **27) France Maghreb 2** ✉ 116 rue Haxo, 75019 Paris ☎ +33 1 47979721 **W:**

francemaghreb2.fr + 3 txs less than 1kW – **28) TSF Jazz** ✉ 127 avenue Ledru Rollin, 75011 Paris ☎ +33 1 53333300 **W:** tsfjazz.com + 9 txs less than 1kW – 29**) Latina** ✉ 167 rue du Chevaleret 75013 Paris ☎ +33 1 53600109 **W:** latina.fr + 3 txs less than 1kW – **30) Africa Radio** ✉ 33 rue du Faubourg Saint Antoine, 75011 Paris ☎ +33 1 55075801 **W:** africaradio.com+ 1 tx less than 1kW

DAB+:

Local Mux	1	2	3	4	5	6	kW
Bourgoin Jallieu	5C	-	-	-	-	-	5
Bourg en Bresse	6D	-	-	-	-	-	1.5
Calais	5B	-	-	-	-	-	3
Colmar	6D	11C	-	-	-	-	1.2/1
Dunkerque	8D	-	-	-	-	-	3
La Roche sur Yon	9A	-	-	-	-	-	6
Le Havre	10A	10D	-	-	-	-	10/4
Lens	8A	11D	-	-	-	-	10.5/4
Lille	7C	7D	8A	-	-	-	4x2/10
Lyon	5B	6A	11B	-	-	-	6/13/7
Marseille	7A	8A	8C	8D	-	-	10x2/4/10
Mulhouse	6D	11D	-	-	-	-	2.5/4
Nantes	5D	7B	12A	-	-	-	9/6/4
Nice	8D	9D	11A	11C	-	-	6/12x2/6
Paris	6A	6D	9A	9B	9D	11A	8x2/4x2/2/4
Pornic	8D	-	-	-	-	-	3
Rambouillet (tests)	5C	-	-	-	-	-	1.7
Roquevaire	8C	-	-	-	-	-	2
Rouen	9C	10A	10C	-	-	-	6/10/6
Saint Nazaire	5D	8D	-	-	-	-	2/3
Strasbourg	6C	6D	7C	-	-	-	4x2/5
Valenciennes	7A	-	-	-	-	-	8
Villefranche s/Saône	5B	6A	-	-	-	-	1.8/2.1

F.PI: .2 national mux and local mux in Amiens, Angers, Arcachon, Bayonne, Bordeaux, Brest, Caen, Clermont-Ferrand, La Rochelle, Le Mans, Limoges, Mâcon, Marmande, Metz, Montauban, Montpellier, Nancy, Nîmes, Orléans, Pau, Perpignan, Poitiers, Reims, Rennes, Tarare, Toulouse, Tours, Troyes.

FRENCH GUIANA

L.T: UTC -3h — **Pop:** 296,000 — **Pr.L:** French — **E.C:** 220V/50Hz — **ITU:** GUF — **Int. dialling code:** +594

COMITÉ TERRITORIAL DE L'AUDIOVISUEL DES ANTILLES ET DE LA GUYANE

see main entry under Martinique

GUYANE LA PREMIÈRE (Pub)

✉ Boulevard Docteur Lama Montjoly Cayenne ☎ 594 256700 **W:** la1ere.francetvinfo.fr/Guyana/ **E:** numerique-guyane@francetv.fr **L.P:** Dir: Anastasie Bourquin. Dir. Tec: Serge Sulpice-Timothe. PD: Jean-Pierre Karam

FM: Cacao, Ouanary 90.0MHz – Sinnamary Corossony, Saint Lauren, Grand Saint, Maripasoula 91.0MHz – Cayenne, Iracubo 92.0MHz – Mana, Kourou, Saint-Georges, Apatou, Kourou 94.0MHz – Papaichton, Camopi - 95.0MHz –Cayenne & Saint-Laurent 98.7MHz

D.Prgr: 24h **Ann:** "La Premiere"

Other stations in Cayenne: R. Mosaique 88.1MHz – Ouest FM 89.4MHz – R. Metis 90.6MHz – R. Jam 96.2MHz – R. 2000 96.9MHz – NRJ, 97.3MHz – RVLD 98.3MHz – Nostalgie Guyane 99.6MHz – Vinyl R. 102.9MHz – RTM 103.3MHz – Trace 104.3MHz – Chéri 104.7MHz – R. RMP 105.9MHz

FRENCH POLYNESIA

L.T: Tahiti: UTC-10h, Marquesas Is: -9½h Gambier Is: -9h — **Pop:** 290,000 — **Pr.L:** French (official), Tahitian — **E.C:** 220V/50Hz — **ITU:** OCE

COMITÉ TERRITORIAL DE L'AUDIOVISUEL DE LA POLYNÉSIE FRANÇAISE

✉ Immeuble Charles Lévy, Boulevard Pomaré, BP 20659, 98713 Papeete ☎ +689 689 40 54 38 88 **E:** cta.polynesie-francaise@csa.fr

FM MHz	Location	kW	Station
Iles du Vent			
15) 87.6	Papeete	1	R. Turiva
1) 87.6	Presqu'ile		R. Maria no Te Hau
2) 88.2	Mont Marau	3	R. Maohi
4) 88.2	Tumaraa		R. Polynésie la 1ère
3) 88.6	Moorea	4	R. NRJ Polynésie
4) 89.0	Moorea	10	R. Polynésie la 1ère
4) 89.5	Maupiti	0.2	R. Polynésie la 1ère
4) 89.5	Moorea/Maiao	0.2	R. Polynésie la 1ère
4) 89.6	Moorea/Papetoai	0.3	R. Polynésie la 1ère
4) 90.5	Tiarei	1	R. Polynésie la 1ère
4) 90.5	Moorea/Haapiti	0.2	R. Polynésie la 1ère
5) 90.9	Afaahiti	1	R. 1
6) 91.4	Mont Marau	1	R. Te Vevo o Te Tiaturiraa
4) 91.8	Mont Marau	1	R. Polynésie la 1ère
2) 92.3	Moorea	3.6	R. Maohi
9) 92.8	Mont Marau	3	R. Te Reo O Tefana
7) 93.2	Papara	1.3	R. Hiti FM
1) 93.8	Papeete		R. Maria no Te Hau
2) 94.8	Pueu	1	R. Maohi
4) 95.2	Mahaena	0.2	R. Polynésie la 1ère
4) 95.2	Papara	0.2	R. Polynésie la 1ère
4) 95.2	Pic Rouge	0.2	R. Polynésie la 1ère
8) 95.6	Mont Marau	2	R. La Voix de l'Espérance
16) 96.0	Mont Marau	3	R. Heipuni FM
1) 96.4	Mont Marau	3	R. Maria no Te Hau
9) 97.4	Moorea	4.2	R. Te Reo o Tefana
10) 97.8	Moorea	6	R. Taui FM
8) 98.2	Mahin		R. La Voix de l'Espérance
5) 98.3	Afaahiti	1	R. Tiare FM
4) 99.0	Pointe Vénus	0.3	R. Polynésie la 1ère
4) 99.0	Pueu	0.3	R. Polynésie la 1ère
4) 99.4	Taputapuatea	0.2	R. Polynésie la 1ère
8) 99.5	Maatea	3	R. La Voix de l'Espérance
5) 100.0	Maatea	3	R. 1
11) 101.1	Moorea	1.5	Rire et Chansons Tahiti
1) 101.5	Moorea	2	R. Maria no Te Hau
8) 102.2	Papeete	1	R. La Voix de l'Espérance
11) 102.6	Mont Marau	1	Rire et Chansons Tahiti
3) 103.0	Mont Marau	1.6	R. NRJ Polynésie
7) 103.4	Moorea	3	R. Hiti FM
5) 103.8	Mont Marau	3	R. 1
5) 104.2	Mont Marau	3	R. Tiare FM
12) 104.7	Moorea	2	R. Paofai ‡
5) 105.5	Moorea	3	R. Tiare FM
17) 106.4	Moorea	5	R. Manotahi
9) 107.0	Taiarapu		R. To Rco o Tefana
10) 107.3	Mont Marau	1	R. Faa'a Taui FM
+ 35 stns less than 1kW			
Iles Sous le Vent			
9) 90.0	Uturoa		R. Te Reo o Tefana
4) 94.0	Raiatea/ Uturoa	0.1	R. Polynésie la 1ère
10) 95.8			R. Taui FM
8) 96.2	Raiatea	0.2	R. La Voix de l'Espérance
4) 96.6	Bora Bora/Vaitape	0.1	R. Polynésie la 1ère
6) 97.2	Raiatea-Uturoa	0.5	R Te Vevo o Te Tiaturiraa
7) 100.3	Raromatai		R. Hiti FM
1) 105.4	Bora Bora		R. Maria no Te Hau
7) 106.2	Raiatea		R Hiti FM
+ 18 stns less than 1kW			
Archipel des Australes			
4) 89.6	Raivavae/Rurutu	0.1	R. Polynésie la 1ère
4) 99.4	Rapa/Rimatara/Tubuai	0.1	R. Polynésie la 1ère
+ 7 stns less than 1kW			
Les Isles Marquises			
4) 88.2	Hiva Oa	0.05	R. Polynésie la 1ère
4) 89.0	Nuku Hiva	0.5	R. Polynésie la 1ère
4) 89.5	Hiva Oa	0.1	R. Polynésie la 1ère
4) 91.0	Ua Huka	0.05	R. Polynésie la 1ère
4) 91.5	Ua Pou		R. Polynésie la 1ère
18) 92.5	Hiva	6	R. Te Oko Nui
6) 93.5	Taravo-Pueu	0.5	R. Te Vevo o Te Tiaturiraa ‡
18) 94.5	Nuku Hiva	6	R. Te Oko Nui
10) 100.0	Nuku Hiva	1	R. Taui FM
19) 101.3	Nuku Hiva	0.6	R. Marquises/ R. Henua Enana
19) 106.0	Hiva Oa/ Tapeata	1	R. Marquises/ R. Henua Enana
+ 9 stns less than 1kW			
Iles des Tuamotu Gambier			
4) 90.5	Arutua/Rautini	0.1	R. Polynésie la 1ère
4) 93.6	Kaukura/Raitahiti	0.1	R. Polynésie la 1ère
4) 93.6	Mataiva/ Pahua	0.1	R. Polynésie la 1ère

FM	MHz	Location	kW	Station
4)	93.6	Napuka/ Tepukamaruia	0.1	R. Polynésie la 1ère
4)	93.6	Takaroa/ Teavaroa	0.1	R. Polynésie la 1ère
4)	94.0	Rangiro (Airport)	0.1	R. Polynésie la 1ère
4)	94.0	Nukutavake/ Tavana	0.1	R. Polynésie la 1ère
4)	94.0	Pukapuka/ Teonemahina	0.1	R. Polynésie la 1ère
4)	94.0	Makemo/ Pouheva	0.1	R. Polynésie la 1ère
4)	94.0	Mangareva/ Rikitea	0.1	R. Polynésie la 1ère
4)	94.0	Faaite/ Hitianau	0.1	R. Polynésie la 1ère
4)	94.0	Niau/ Tapuna	0.1	R. Polynésie la 1ère
4)	94.4	Fakahina/Tarione	0.1	R. Polynésie la 1ère
4)	94.4	Fakarava/Rotava	0.1	R. Polynésie la 1ère
4)	94.4	Manihi/ Turipaoa	0.1	R. Polynésie la 1ère
4)	94.4	Hao/ Otepa	0.1	R. Polynésie la 1ère
4)	94.8	Anaa/ Tukuhora	0.1	R. Polynésie la 1ère
4)	94.8	Fangatau/ Teana	0.1	R. Polynésie la 1ère
4)	94.8	Takapoto/ Fakatopater	0.1	R. Polynésie la 1ère
4)	94.8	Tatakoto/ Tumukuru	0.1	R. Polynésie la 1ère
4)	94.8	Tikehau/ Tuherahera	0.1	R. Polynésie la 1ère
4)	94.8	Tureia/ Fakamaru	0.1	R. Polynésie la 1ère
4)	95.5	Apataki/Niutahi	0.1	R. Polynésie la 1ère
4)	95.5	Makatea/ Vaitepaua	0.1	R. Polynésie la 1ère
13)	96.0	Marutea Sud	1	R. Marutea Sud
1)	100.0	Gambier	0.2	R. Maria no Te Hau ‡
14)	101.0	Rangiroa	1	R. Te Reo Tuamotu

+ 9 stns less than 1kW ‡ = inactive

Addresses & other information:
1) BP 94, 98713 Papeete ☎689 40420011 2+689 40420635 **E:** radiomarianotehau@mail.pf **W:** radiomarianotehau.com & facebook.com/radiomarianotehau – **2)** BP 5038, 98716 Pirae ☎689 40501616 **E:** courrier@radiomaohi.pf **W:** radiomaohi.pf – **3)** BP 50, 98713 Papeete ☎689 40475283 🖷689 40464346 **E:** contact.nrj@pacfm.fr **W:** nrj.pf – **4)** POLYNÉSIE LA PREMIÈRE (Pub) + Centre Pamatai, BP 60-125, 98702 Faaa ☎689 40861600 🖷689 40861621 **W:** polynesie1ere.fr **E:** polynesie1ere@francetv.fr **Prgr:** 24h **LP:** Dir. Regional: Gérald Prufer – **5)** BP 3601, 98713 Papeete ☎689 40434100 🖷689 40422421 (R.1) ☎689 40423406 (R. Tiare FM) **E:** contact@radio1.pf **Brands:** Radio 1: **W:** radio1.pf & facebook.com/radio1tahiti/ Radio Tiare: **W:** tiarefm.pf & facebook.com/pages/tiarefm – **6)** BP 1817, 98713 Papeete, 51, rue Dumont D'Urville, Orovini, Papeete ☎689 40412341 🖷689 40412322 **E:** contacts@mail.pf **W:** facebook.com/Rtv-Tahiti-103877699955813 – **7)** Punaauia, ☎689 89932932 **W:** hitifm.pf, facebook.com/HITI-FM-Tahiti-802891306468692/ **E:** hitifmtahiti@gmail.com – **8)** 55 Cours de l'Union sacrée, Papeete (BP 140593, 98701 Arue) ☎689 40508259 🖷689 40451427 **E:** direction@lvdl.pf – **9)** BP 6295, 98703 Faaa ☎689 40819797 🖷689 40825493 **E:** tereo.com@mail.pf **W:** facebook.com/tereootefana – **10)** BP 62147, 98702 Faa'a-Centre ☎689 40854747 🖷689 40412555 **E:** tauifm@mail.pf **W:** tauifm.net – **11)** SARL Pac FM; BP 50 – 98713 Papeete ☎689 40421414 **E:** contact.rc@pacfm.fr **W:** rireetchansons.pf; facebook.com/rire.et.chansons – **12)** BP 113, 98713 Papeete ☎689 40460624 🖷689 40419357 [r. silent] – **13)** [atoll has no permanent population] – **14)** Cultural Association Iva Manu-Manu Arii, Avatoru, Rangiroa, Tuamotu-Gambier [r. silent] – **15)** No details available – **16)** No details available – **17)** No details available – **18)** BP 20, Nuku Hiva, Iles Marquises ☎689 40910155 🖷689 40910157 **W:** https://www.facebook.com/ArchipeldesMarquises **E:** teokonuiradio@Outlook.fr – **19)** ☎689 40920790 Facebook: https://www.facebook.com/Radio-Marquises-Radio-Henua-Enana-101246906591661

FRENCH SOUTHERN & ANTARCTIC LANDS

L.T: UTC+5h — **Pop:** (non-permanent) c.150 (wi), c. 300 (su) — **Pr.L:** French — **E.C:** 220V/50Hz — **ITU:** St. Paul & Amsterdam Islands: AMS, Terre Adélie: ATA, Crozet Islands: CRO, Kerguelen Islands: KER

FM	MHz	kW	Location	Station
1)	88.2		Dumont d'Urville, ATA	R. Skuarock †
2)	97.1	0.5	Port aux Français, KER	R. CNES
3)	97.9		Dumont d'Urville, ATA	Rires & Glaçons †
4)	98.0	0.5	Base Martin de Vivès, AMS	R. CNES
5)	100.0		Base Alfred Faure, CRO	R. CNES
6)	100.0	0.5	Port aux Français, KER	R. Ker

H of tr: 24h relay of France Inter (Mon-Fri) and RMC (Sat/Sun)
Addresses:
1) & 3) Terre Adélie, TAAF (Terres australes et antarctiques française) via Roissy HB BP 17615 Cargo 7 F- 95724 Roissy CDG Cedex France – **2) & 6)** Kerguelen, TAAF via F-97408 St Denis Messagerie France – **4)** Amsterdam, TAAF, F-97408 St Denis Messagerie France – **5)** Crozet, TAAF, F-97408 St Denis Messagerie France
NB: All stations (txs) are operated by staff of the geophysical laboratories of CNES (Centre National d'Etudes Spatiales) on the islands.

GABON

L.T: UTC +1h — **Pop:** 2.2 million — **Pr.L:** French (official), Fang, Myene, Nzebi, Punu — **E.C:** 220V/50Hz — **ITU:** GAB

HAUTE AUTORITÉ DE LA COMMUNICATION (HAC)
🖃 286, Av. de la Libération, BP 6437, Libreville ☎ +241 1 728259 🖷 +241 1 728271 **L.P:** Pres: Raphaël Ntoutoume Nkogue

RADIO-TÉLÉVISION GABONAISE - RADIO GABON (RTG, Gov.)
🖃 B.P. 10150, Boulevard Triomphal, Libreville ☎+241 01744051 🖷 +241 1739775 **W:** facebook.com/radiogabon.lareference

FM(MHz):	1	2
Franceville	87.9	89.9
Libreville	96.5	88.7
Koula-Moutou	88.2	91.8
Makokou	89.9	97.3
Oyem	103.2/98.8	89.2
Port-Gentil	90.4	93.5
Tchibanga	89.9	97.3

1 = **Chaîne 1** 24h in French. **2** = **Chaîne 2** (provincial netw.) 24h in French & ethnic languages.
Ann: 1: "Ici Libreville, vouz écoutez Radio Gabon, chaîne 1".

OTHER STATIONS:
Hit R, Libreville/Port-Gentil 98.5MHz **W:** facebook.com/HlitradioGabon
RBN-R. Bonne Nouvelle (Rlg.), Libreville: 95.5MHz **W:** twitter.com/radiorbngabon
R. Fréquence Protestante (Rlg.): Libreville 92.0MHz **W:** facebook.com/Top-Gospel-92-FM-354886124603116
R. Génération Nouvelle, Libreville: 97.4MHz **W:** facebook.com/generationnouvellefm
R. Nour (Rlg.), Libreville: 95.0MHz **W:** csaiag.ga
R. Sainte Marie (Rlg.):Port-Gentil 89.0MHz, Libreville 99.0MHz **W:** eglisecatholique.ga
RTN-Radio Télévision Nazareth (Rlg.), Libreville: 100.0MHz **W:** rtnagabon.org
R. Ubuntu, Libreville: 93.3MHz **W:** facebook.com/RadioUbuntu933Fm
Urban FM, Libreville: 104.5MHz **W:** urbanfm.fm
Africa Radio, Libreville: 91.1MHz **W:** africaradio.com
BBC African Sce, Libreville: 94.0MHz 4kW
Medi 1 Afrique Internationale, Libreville: 101.5MHz
RFI Afrique in Franceville/Libreville/Port-Gentil on 104.0MHz

GALAPAGOS ISLANDS (Ecuador)

L.T: UTC -6h — **Pop:** 25,000 — **Pr.L:** Spanish — **E.C:** 120V/60Hz — **ITU:** EQA (**WRTH**: GAL)

LA VOZ DE GALAPAGOS (Rlg.)
🖃 Prefectura Apostólica de Galápagos, Puerto Baquerizo Moreno ☎ +593 5 459435 **W:** lavozdegalapagos.net
FM: Galápagos Stereo 97.1MHz.
FM in Pto Baquerizo Moreno (MHz): 91.1 R. Pública/Nacional del Ecuador FM – 94.7 R. Mar – 97.1 LV de Galápagos FM – 100.7 R. María – 101.9 Encantada FM – 104.3 Telegalápagos FM
FM in Pto Ayora (MHz): 88.7 R. Santa Cruz – 89.9 Caravana AM – 93.5 Pacífica FM - 94.7 R. Mar – 95.9 Antena 9 FM – 98.3 Stereo Zaracay – 101.9 Encantada FM

GAMBIA

L.T: UTC — **Pop:** 2.4 million — **Pr.L:** English (official), Jola, Madinka, Pulaar, Soninke, Wolof — **E.C:** 230V/50Hz — **ITU:** GMB

PUBLIC UTILITIES REGULATORY AUTHORITY (PURA)
🖃 94 Kairaba Ave, Bakau, KSMD, Banjul ☎ +220 4399601 🖷 +220 4399905 **W:** pura.gm **E:** info@pura.gm

GAMBIA RADIO & TELEVISION SERVICE (GRTS) (Gov)
✉ Mile 7 Studios, P.O. Box 387, Banjul ☎+220 4495101/4497419 🖷 +220 4495102 **W:** grts.gm **L.P:** DG: Mr. Modou Sanyang. Deputy DG: Mr. Alhaji Modou Joof.
FM: Serrekunda 96.0MHz, Abuko 98.6MHz, Bonto 102.6MHz, Banjul 106.7MHz.
D.Prgr: in E/local langs: 0600-2400. N. in E: 0700, 1300, 1800, 2200. **Ann:** "GRTS Radio". **IS:** Cora (harp).

Other stations (all MHz**):**
Afriradio, Banjul: 107.6 **W:** africell.gm/FM.php – **Capital FM,** Banjul: 100.4 **W:** capitalfm.gm – **Choice FM,** Banjul: 106.4 **W:** choicefm.gm – **City Limits R,** Serrekunda: 93.6 0.25kW – **Hill Top R,** Serrekunda: 104.7 100W – **Hot FM,** Banjul: 104.3 **W:** hotfmgambia.gm – **Kora FM,** Banjul: 103.9 **W:** korafm.gm – **Paradise FM:** Farafenni105.5, Serrekunda 105.7, Basse 105.8 1kW. **W:** paradisefm.gm – **Star FM,** Banjul: 96.6 **W:** starfm.gm – **Unique FM,** Banjul/Basse: 100.7 **W:** uniquefm.gm Also r. VOA – **West Coast R,** Serrekunda: 92.1 & 95.3 (different prgr.) **W:** westcoast.gm – **Vibes FM,** Banjul: 106.1 **W:** vibesfm.gm
RFI Afrique: Banjul 89.0MHz

GEORGIA

L.T: UTC +4h; Abkhazia and South Ossetia (de facto): UTC +3h — **Pop:** 4 million — **Pr.L:** Georgian (official), Abkhaz (additional official regional language), Ossetic — **E.C:** 220V/50Hz — **ITU:** GEO

KOMUNIKATSIEBIS KOMISIA (Communications Commission)
✉ Ave. Ketevan Tsamebuli/Bochorma St. 50/18, 0144 Tbilisi ☎ +995 32 2921667 🖷 +995 32 2921625 **E:** post@comcom.ge **W:** comcom.ge
L.P: Chmn: Kakhi Bekauri

SAKARTVELOS SAZOGADOEBRIVI MAUTSQEBELI (Pub) (Georgian Public Broadcaster)
✉ M.Kostava St. 68, 0171 Tbilisi ☎ +995 32 2409477 **E:** info@gbp.ge **W:** gpb.ge **L.P:** DG: vacant

FM	1	2	kW	FM	1	2	kW
Akhaltsikhe	102.4	-	1	Kutaisi	100.3	-	2
Batumi*	102.4	-	1	Tbilisi	102.4	100.9	10/5
Telavi	100.6	-	1	Zugdidi	101.3	-	1

+ sites with only txs below 1kW. *) Located in Ajara (autonomous republic)
D.Prgr: Prgr 1 (Radio 1): 24h. – **Prgr 2 (Radio 2):** 0400-2200. – **Regional Branch** in Ajara: see below.

OTHER STATIONS

FM	MHz	kW	Location	Station
25)	92.3	1	Tbilisi	R. Tanamgzavri
22B)	93.1	1	Tbilisi	Qartuly Vinili
20)	93.5	1	Tbilisi	R. Tbilisi 93.5FM
14)	93.9	1	Tbilisi	Star FM
15)	94.3	1	Tbilisi	R. GIPA
1)	94.3	1	Dedoplistskaro	R. Iveria
22A)	94.7	1	Tbilisi	R. Maestro
5E)	95.1	1	Tbilisi	Avtoradio
3)	95.5	1	Tbilisi	R. Komersant
17)	96.3	1	Tbilisi	R. Jako
5C)	96.7	1	Tbilisi	R. Ar Daidardo
18)	97.1	1	Tbilisi	Dardimandi FM
34)	97.5	1	Akhaltsikhe	FM 97.5
31)	97.5	1	Kutaisi	42nd parallel
26)	97.5	1	Tbilisi	R. Kubrik
33)	97.8	1	Gori	R. Mosaic
10)	98.0	1	Tbilisi	R. Utsnobi
21)	98.5	1	Tbilisi	Shokoladi FM
7)	98.9	1	Kutaisi	Apkhazetis khma
7)	98.9	1	Tbilisi	Apkhazetis khma
23)	99.3	1	Tbilisi	R. Chveneburi
5D)	99.7	1	Tbilisi	R. Vinil
22A)	99.9	1	Kutaisi	R. Maestro
9)	100.0	1	Gori	R. Imedi
5E)	100.2	1	Dmasisi	Avtoradio
27)	100.3	1	Tbilisi	Beat FM 100.3
9)	100.9	1	Kutaisi	R. Imedi
12)	101.0	1	Dmanisi	R. Tavisupleba
9)	101.2	1	Akhalkalaki	R. Imedi
2)	101.4	1	Tbilisi	R. Monte-Karlo
12)	101.5	1	Gori	R. Tavisupleba
19)	101.9	1	Tbilisi	R. Kalaki
5E)	102.3	1	Kutaisi	Avtoradio
5C)	102.7	1	Kutaisi	R. Ar Daidardo
A)	102.9	1	Tbilisi	RFI relay
29)	102.9	1	Zugdidi	R. Odishi+
22A)	103.0	1	Tkibuli	R. Maestro
5B)	103.4	1	Tbilisi	R. Fortuna+
5B)	103.4	1	Gori	R. Fortuna+
5B)	103.4	1	Kutaisi	R. Fortuna+
12)	103.6	1	Zugdidi	R. Tavisupleba
22)	103.8	1	Dmansi	R. Maestro
6)	103.9	1	Tbilisi	R. Palitra
9)	104.1	5	Chiatura	R. Imedi
9)	104.2	1	Zugdidi	R. Imedi
4)	104.3	1	Tbilisi	R. Positive
9)	104.7	1	Dedoplistskaro	R. Imedi
28)	104.7	1	Tbilisi	NRJ
16)	104.8	1	Gori	R. Trialeti
18)	105.0	1	Kutaisi	Dardimandi FM
8)	105.1	1	Tbilisi	R. Obieqtivi
9)	105.1	5	Dmansi	R. Imedi
22A)	105.2	1	Ozurgeti	R. Maestro
30)	105.5	1	Kutaisi	R. Rioni
1)	105.5	1	Tbilisi	R. Iveria
9)	105.9	1	Tbilisi	R. Imedi
22A)	106.3	1	Gori	R. Maestro
11)	106.4	1	Tbilisi	Pirveli R.
11)	105.4	1	Kutaisi	Pirveli R.
5A)	106.9	1	Tbilisi	R. Fortuna
5A)	106.9	1	Gori	R. Fortuna
5A)	106.9	1	Kutaisi	R. Fortuna
7)	107.2	1	Zugdidi	Apkhazetis khma
12)	107.4	1	Tbilisi	R. Tavisupleba
12)	107.4	2	Kutaisi	R. Tavisupleba
13)	107.9	1	Tbilisi	Saqartvelos khma
24)	107.9	1	Kutaisi	R. Dzveli Kalaki

+ txs below 1kW.
Addresses & other information:
1) Erekle II square 1, 0105 Tbilisi – **2)** M.Kostava St. 14, 0169 Tbilisi. In Russian. – **3)** Nadiradze St. 8, 0102 Tbilisi – **4)** Dadiani 21, 0101 Tbilisi – **5A-D)** Beliashvili St. 9, 0159 Tbilisi – **6)** Iosebidze St. 49, 0160 Tbilisi – **7)** Kindzmarauli St. 15, 0121 Tbilisi – **8)** Agladze St. 31, 0119 Tbilisi – **9)** Lubliana St. 5, 0159 Tbilisi – **10)** M.Kostava St. 68, 0171 Tbilisi – **11)** Aleksidze St. 1, 0193 Tbilisi – **12)** Vazha-Pshavela Ave. 45, 0177 Tbilisi – **13)** Tashkenti St. 51, 0160 Tbilisi – **14)** Vazha-Pshavela Ave. 16, 0160 Tbilisi – **15)** Marie Brosset St. 2, 0108 Tbilisi – **16)** Chavchavadze St. 45, 1400 Gori – **17)** Tbilisi – **18)** Kindzmarauli St. 15, 0168 Tbilisi – **19)** Melikishvili St. 1, 0179 Tbilisi – **20)** Sanapiro St. 1, 0114 Tbilisi – **21)** M. Kostava St. 47/57, 0179 Tbilisi – **22A,B)** Akaki Beliashvili St. 8, 0159 Tbilisi – **23)** Gagarin St. 24, 0160 Tbilisi – **24)** Gaponov St. 30, 4600 Kutaisi – **25)** Tbilisi – **26)** Tbilisi – **27)** Tsinamdzgvrishvili St. 95, 0112 Tbilisi – **28)** Dolidze St. 2, 0171 Tbilisi – **29)** Zviad Gamsakhurdia 19, 2100 Zugdidi – **30)** Paliashvili St. 2, 4600 Kutaisi – **31)** Kutaisi – **32)** Tbilisi – **33)** Gori – **34)** Akhaltsikhe – **A)** Rel. RFI (France).

AJARA
(Autonomous republic)

AJARA RADIO & TV (Pub)
✉ Memed Abashidze Ave. 41, 6010 Batumi ☎ +995 422 274370 🖷 +995 422 274384 **E:** info@radioajara.ge **W:** radioajara.ge; ajaratv.ge
L.P: Dir: Natia Kapanadze
FM: Batumi 104.5MHz (0.5kW)
D.Prgr: R. Ajara 24h.
NB: Ajara Radio & TV is a branch of Georgian Public Broadcaster.

OTHER STATIONS

FM	MHz	kW	Location	Station
22A)	90.9	1	Batumi	R. Maestro
9)	100.1	1	Batumi	R. Imedi
5C)	101.9	1	Batumi	R. Ar Dadaido
5B)	103.4	1	Batumi	R. Fortuna+
1)	105.4	1	Batumi	R. Iveria
5A)	106.9	5	Batumi	R. Fortuna

+ txs below 1kW.
Addresses & other information: see main tx table.

ABKHAZIA
(Self-proclaimed "Republic of Abkhazia")

APSNYTWI AXWYNTKARRATW TELERADIO-EILAXWYRA (Gov*) (Abkhaz State Radio & TV Co.)
(* Run by the administration of the "Republic of Abkhazia")
✉ V.Ardzinba St. 16, Sokhumi, Abkhazia ☎ +7 840 2264867 **E:** apsua.radio@gmail.com **W:** apsua.tv **L.P:** DG: Ronald Bganba

MW	kHz	kW			
Sokhumi	1350	30			
FM	**MHz**	**kW**	**FM**	**MHz**	**kW**
Tkvarcheli	102.2	-	Ochamchire	104.0	-
Sokhumi	103.7	-	Gagra	107.1	-

D.Prgr: Apsua R. with own prgrs in Abkhaz, Russian. Outside of own prgrs, various other stns may be relayed (mainly Avtoradio). On MW: limited schedule, changing frequently.

OTHER STATIONS

FM	MHz	kW	Location	Station
1)	91.2		Ochamchire	R. Soma
A)	100.7		Ochamchire	R. Sputnik relay
3)	101.1		Sokhumi	R. Xara Xradio
A)	101.3		Gagra	R. Sputnik relay
3)	101.7		Gagra	R. Xara Xradio
4)	101.9		Sokhumi	R. Rio Rita
4)	102.2		Gagra	R. Rio Rita
A)	102.5		Gagra	R. Sputnik relay
A)	103.2		Sokhumi	R. Sputnik relay
2)	103.6		Gagra	Pervoye R.
A)	104.3		Sokhumi II	R. Sputnik relay
A)	105.2		Gagauta	R. Sputnik relay
5)	105.5		Sokhumi	Evropa plus
1)	106.1		Tkvarcheli	R. Soma
2)	106.5		Sokhumi	Pervoye R.
1)	107.9	0.3	Sokhumi	R. Soma

Addresses & other information:
1) Zvanba St. 9, Sokhumi **E:** info@radiosoma.com – **2)** Rel. Pervoye R. (Russia) – **3)** pr. Leona 17, Sokhumi **E:** reklama.sukhum@gmail.com – **4)** Sokhumi – **5)** Sokhumi – **A)** Rel. R. Sputnik (Russia).

SOUTH OSSETIA
(Self-proclaimed "Republic of South Ossetia")

GTRK "IR" (Gov*)
(* Run by the administration of the "Republic of South Ossetia")
✉ Geroev St. 37, Tskhinvali, South Ossetia ☎ +7 929 8066070 **E:** gtrk.ir@mail.ru **W:** gtrkir.ru **L.P:** Dir (Radio): Alan Yskhovrebov
FM: Tskhinvali 102.3MHz.
D.Prgr: R. Ir-FM in Russian, Ossetic: 24h.

OTHER STATIONS

FM	MHz	kW	Location	Station
3)	104.1		Tskhinvali	R. City
B)	104.5		Kaysa	Vesti FM relay
1)	105.9		Tskhinvali	Volna FM
A)	106.3		Tskhinvali	R. Sputnik relay
2)	107.3		Tskhinvali	R. Yuzhnyy gorod

Addresses & other information:
1) Tskhinvali – **2)** Geroev St. 1, Tskhinvali **E:** info@yugfm.ru – **2)** Tskhinvali. Incl. rel. R. Sputnik (Russia) – **A)** Rel. R. Sputnik (Russia) – **B)** Rel. Vesti FM (Russia)

GERMANY

L.T: UTC +1h (28 Mar-31 Oct: +2h) — **Pop:** 83 million — **Pr.L:** German — **E.C:** 50Hz, 230V — **ITU:** D

BUNDESNETZAGENTUR
✉ Postfach 8001, 53105 Bonn (office location: Tulpenfeld 4) ☎ +49 228 14 0 📠 + 49 228 14 8872 **W:** bnetza.de

NB: Broadcasting regulation, except aspects of spectrum use/ transmitter operations regulated by Bundesnetzagentur, is in Germany the sole responsibility of the federal states. Some of the public broadcasting institutions shown in section I are common operations by various states. Some states have also agreed a common regulation of the private sector as shown in section II.

I. PUBLIC STATIONS

ARBEITSGEMEINSCHAFT DER ÖFFENTLICH-RECHTLICHEN RUNDFUNKANSTALTEN DEUTSCHLANDS (ARD)
Formalised co-operation of institutions B)-J), Deutschlandradio and Deutsche Welle (see International Broadcasting section) are associated members.
Radio operations under ARD umbrella: Common overnight prgr. ARD-Hitnacht (2305-0500, oldies, produced by NDR), ARD-Popnacht (2305-0400, AC, produced by SWR), Die junge Nacht der ARD (2300-0400/0000-0500, produced by WDR), ARD-Nachtkonzert (2305-0500, classical, produced by BR), ARD-Infonacht (2200-0500, news, produced by MDR). Common summertime evening prgr. ARD-Radiofestival mid July to mid September daily 1900-2300.
Satellite radio: Most radio stations of member institutions B)-J) are carried on Astra 1M, 12.266 GHz

A) DEUTSCHLANDRADIO
Common operation of all federal states
Cologne seat: ✉ Raderberggürtel 40, 50968 Köln ☎ +49 221 345 0 📠 +49 221 345 4803
Berlin seat: ✉ Hans-Rosenthal-Platz, 10825 Berlin ☎ +49 30 8503 0 📠 +49 30 8503 6168 **W:** deutschlandradio.de

FM (MHz)	DLF	DK	kW
Baden-Württemberg			
Baden-Baden	-	107.9	0.1
Biberach	100.5	-	0.5
Blauen	105.1	-	10
Esslingen	96.7	-	0.1
Freiburg	-	90.6	0.2
Geislingen	-	87.7	0.2
Göppingen	99.8	-	0.1
Heidelberg	106.5	-	0.4
Heidenheim	94.0	100.8	0.1
Heilbronn	91.3	97.3	0.1
Hornisgrinde	106.3	-	80
Kirchheim	91.3	-	0.1
Konstanz	-	94.5	0.2
Lörrach	-	95.0	0.1
Ludwigsburg	94.1	97.3	0.5/0.1
Pforzheim	89.2	95.2	0.1/0.5
Rottweil	106.0	-	0.1
Schwäb. Hall	95.8	-	0.1
Schw. Gmünd	-	95.9	0.2
Stuttgart	96.0	87.9	0.5/1
Tübingen	93.9	99.4	0.5/1
Ulm	103.5	91.5	0.5/1
Witthoh	100.6	-	40
Bayern			
Ansbach	92.7	102.7	0.2
Aschaffenbg.	-	94.8	0.1
Augsburg	97.8	100.0	0.3/15
B. Reichenhall	-	92.6	0.1
Bad Tölz	87.8	93.2	0.1
Berchtesgd.	91.6	103.4	0.1
Brotjacklrieg.	100.1	-	100
Burgbernhm.	106.3	94.3	0.2/0.3
Burglengenf.	-	107.3	0.1
Cham	-	101.4	0.1
Freilassing	100.3	-	15
Hof Waldst.	-	89.3	20
Hohe Linie	-	101.3	0.2
Hohenpeißbg.	94.7		0.1
Ingolstadt	107.0	88.6	0.5
Kaufbeuren	-	107.3	0.1
Landsberg	90.3	107.9	0.1
München	101.7	96.8	0.3
Nürnberg	90.1	105.6	0.1
Oberstdorf	92.0	96.5	0.1
Ochsenkopf	100.3	-	100
Passau	-	97.7	0.5
Pfronten	96.5	-	0.02
Regensburg	95.5	101.3	0.2
Rhön	103.3	-	100
Rosenheim	97.2	96.2	0.1
Rosenh.-D'bg.	97.7	-	0.1
Starnberg	87.9	94.7	0.1
Straubing	-	88.7	0.4
Traunstein	-	88.3	0.1
Weiden	-	103.7	0.1
Würzburg	100.3	101.3	0.1
Berlin & Brandenburg			
Berlin A'platz	97.7	89.6	100
Calau	-	90.8	20
Casekow	105.2	-	6
Cottbus	88.6	-	3
Eisenhütt.st.	100.2	-	1
Frankfurt (Bo.)	97.3	92.7	0.5/5
Herzberg/Els.	94.5	-	0.3
Rhinow	-	103.7	0.2
Bremen			
Bremen	107.1	100.3	100/1
Bremerhaven	103.4	106.2	0.5/5
Hamburg			
Hamburg	88.7	89.1	3/0.1
Hessen			
Darmstadt	-	98.2	0.3
Eschwege	100.6	-	0.5
Feldberg	98.7	-	60
Frankfurt/M.	-	91.2	0.3
Fritzlar	-	96.0	0.1
Fulda	-	90.7	0.3
Gießen	-	107.5	0.3
Hanau	-	107.7	0.3
Heusenstamm	-	99.8	0.2
Hofgeismar	106.9	-	0.3
Kassel	92.7	-	0.1
Korbach	92.8	-	0.1
Limburg	-	105.1	0.3
Mainz-Kastel	-	107.2	0.4
Marburg	-	93.3	0.1
Michelstadt	100.5	107.2	0.2
Oberursel	-	101.8	0.1
Rimberg	91.3	-	50
Wetzlar	-	97.3	0.3
Mecklenburg-Vorpommern			
Anklam	107.4	-	1
Barth	100.3	-	0.1
Demmin	89.8	106.2	1/0.5
Greifswald	104.3	96.9	0.2
Güstrow	106.0	-	0.8
Helpterberg	96.5	97.1	10/30
Heringsdorf	98.4	107.1	0.5
Neukloster	90.6	-	0.3
Neustrelitz	97.9	-	1
Ribn.-Damg.	102.1	-	0.2
Röbel	102.4	90.0	3
Rostock	97.3	96.7	5/40
Sassnitz	104.0	101.4	8
Schwerin	106.3	95.3	2/100
Stralsund	89.3	92.1	0.4
Waren/Mü.	91.3	-	0.2

FM (MHz)	DLF	DK	kW
Niedersachsen			
Aurich	101.8	106.9	100/1
Cloppenbg.	-	95.5	0.1
Cuxhaven	101.6	107.7	2/20
Damme	95.4	97.5	0.3
Emden	-	93.4	1
Göttingen	101.0	-	0.1
Hannover	94.0	-	0.1
Hann. Münd.	98.5	-	0.5
Höhbeck	102.2	-	100
Jever	-	89.0	0.5
Leer	-	91.5	0.5
Lingen	102.0		25
		91.6*	0.4
		102.9*	0.3
Lüneburg	-	97.9	0.5
Meppen	-	100.7	0.3
Norden	-	105.3	0.3
Nordhorn	-	97.1	0.2
Oldenburg	-	102.8	1
Osnabrück	101.8	-	0.5
Seesen	88.0	-	0.1
Soltau	89.3	-	0.1
Stadthagen	106.1	-	1
Tecklenburg	-	101.1	0.5
Torfh./Harz	103.5	-	100
Uelzen	107.5	97.1	0.5/0.2
Visselhövede	-	88.8	1
Warendorf	107.2	-	1
Nordrhein-Westfalen			
Aachen	102.7	-	0.5
B. Oeynhsn.	93.9	-	0.1
Beckum	91.5	-	0.2
Bielefeld	95.5	106.2	0.1
Bonn	89.1	98.9	5/0.1
Eifel-Bärbelk.	-	106.1	20
Gronau	-	94.6	0.2
Kleve	-	90.1	1
Köln	91.3	-	0.1
Langenberg	-	96.5	35
Lemgo	92.2	88.9	0.3
Lennestadt	-	96.9	0.1
Lübbecke	-	97.7	0.2
Münster	104.5	97.5	0.3/0.1
Nordhelle	102.7	-	20
Olpe	-	96.3	0.1
Olsberg	-	106.1	10
Paderborn	94.5	-	0.2
Schwerte	104.4	-	0.2
Siegen	94.2	100.2	0.1
Stadthagen	106.1	-	1
Steinfurt	-	91.0	0.2
Tecklenburg	-	101.1	0.5
Warendorf	107.2	-	1
Warburg	106.6	-	0.2
Wesel	102.8	-	50
Wuppertal	91.0	-	0.3
Rheinland-Pfalz			
Bitburg	-	95.3	0.1
Idar-Oberst.	89.5	94.7	0.2
Kaiserslaut.	100.2	98.1	5/0.2
Koblenz	99.8	105.3	0.5
Linz	-	98.3	0.1
Ludwigshafen	-	97.3	0.1
Mayen	100.8	-	0.2
Pirmasens	106.1	94.4	0.4
Prüm	95.4	-	0.1
Saarburg	104.6	105.3	20/0.1
Traben-Trarb.	88.7	106.2	0.3

FM (MHz)	DLF	DK	kW
Trier	-	94.3	0.2
Wörth	-	96.6	0.2
Saarland			
Lebach	-	107.9	0.1
Neunkirchen	-	105.0	5
Oberperl	-	106.2	5
Saarbrücken	90.1	107.5	1/0.4
Saarlouis	-	96.3	0.1
Völklingen	-	88.6	0.1
Sachsen			
Bad Düben	-	99.4	0.2
Bärenstein	-	104.3	1
Belgern	-	101.1	1
Chemnitz	-	106.3	0.5
Collmberg	-	96.1	0.3
Döbeln	-	101.3	1
Dresden	97.3	93.2	100/1
Eilenburg	-	92.0	0.2
Freiberg	-	100.7	1
Geyer (Erzg.)	97.0	-	100
Grimma	-	91.6	0.1
Hoyerswerda	-	89.7	0.5
Leipzig-Holzh.	-	100.4	2
Löbau	99.5	103.0	5/2
Pulsnitz	-	106.7	0.5
Schöneck	94.5	-	3
Weißwasser	-	97.7	2
Wiederau	96.6	-	100
Zwickau	-	104.6	0.2
Sachsen-Anhalt			
Brocken/Harz	-	97.4	100
Dessau	107.1	-	0.3
Dequede	-	96.9	7
Eisleben	103.8	-	0.5
Schönebeck	102.0	-	20
Wittenberg	89.3	107.7	1/0.5
Zeitz	-	91.8	0.5
Schleswig-Holstein			
Bungsberg	101.9	103.1	95/0.2
Flensburg	103.3	92.1	20/0.2
Garding	102.3	101.7	0.5
Güby	-	105.0	0.2
Heide	104.4	92.2	1/0.1
Husum	-	101.0	0.1
Itzehoe	102.2	97.5	0.4/0.1
Kaltenkirchen	-	105.5	0.1
Kiel	-	104.7	0.3
Lauenburg	-	95.8	0.1
Neumünster	-	107.8	0.5
Niebüll	-	104.2	0.3
Rendsburg	-	95.2	0.3
Sylt	90.3	103.9	0.2
Thüringen			
Altenburg	-	97.3	0.4
Bleßberg	-	94.2	100
Eisenach	106.5	-	0.5
Erfurt	103.1	-	2
Gera	94.3	93.6	0.3
Gotha	94.0	-	0.1
Ilmenau	99.9	-	0.1
Inselsberg	-	97.2	100
Jena	104.5	98.2	0.3
Mühlhausen	107.0	-	1
Nordhausen	96.4	-	0.1
Pößneck	89.2	-	0.1
Saalfeld	98.7	-	0.1
Sondershaus.	101.9	-	0.1
Suhl	98.8	-	0.1
Weimar	89.7	-	0.5

*) directional with different beams. **N.B:** Txs with poor reach are being phased out.
DAB: See section II.
Satellite: Astra 1N, 11.954GHz h (operated by ZDF, see TV section).
D.Prgr: Deutschlandfunk from Köln studios, full sce. with strong emphasis on information – **Deutschlandfunk Kultur** from Berlin studios, culture, during daytime music format Alternative – **Deutschlandfunk Nova**, from Köln studios, for young audiences – **Dokumente & Debatten**, parliament coverage, audio of TV talkshows and other special prgrs.

B) BAYERISCHER RUNDFUNK (BR)

Public broadcasting institution of Bayern
✉ Bayerischer Rundfunk, 80300 München (location of radio operations: Rundfunkplatz 1) ☎ +49 89 5900 01 🖷 +49 89 5900 2375 **W:** br-online.de

FM (MHz)	B1	B2	B3	BR K	B5	kW
Augsburg	–	–	–	–	105.3	0.5
Bad Reichenhall	91.8	89.9	96.7	98.3	105.0	0.3
Bamberg	94.8N	98.6	99.8	102.9	97.4	25/5
Berchtesgaden	90.4	99.6	96.9	94.2	106.4	0.3/0.1
Brotjacklriegel	92.1R	96.5	94.4	100.9	106.9	100/50
Büttelberg	91.4N	88.2	99.3	95.5	104.0	25/10
Coburg	93.5N	88.3	99.2	97.7	92.8	5/0.3
Dillberg	88.9N	92.3	97.9	87.6	102.0	25
	104.5R					5
Eichstätt	101.6	90.5	97.6	89.0	106.1	25/10
Garmisch-Partenk.	89.2	93.5	97.7	95.9	104.9	0.1
Grünten (Allgäu)	90.7U	88.7	95.8	101.0	106.9	50/100
Herzogstand	88.1	97.0	91.0	–	106.7	0.1
Hochberg-Traunst.	98.0	91.5	95.9	97.0	107.1	5/0.5
Hohenpeißenberg	92.8	94.2	99.2	100.4	–	25
Hoher Bogen	96.8R	91.6	94.7	88.3	104.4	50/5
Hühnerberg	91.9U	96.1	99.5	93.1	107.6	25/11
Kreuzberg (Rhön)	98.3W	93.1	96.3	107.9	105.3	100/50
Landshut	90.2R	97.8	95.3	93.2	106.6	0.1
Lindau	88.1U	92.0	94.0	87.6	100.4	0.5/0.1
München-Ismaning	91.3	88.4	97.3	103.2	90.0	25
Ochsenkopf	90.7N	96.0	99.4	102.3	107.1	100/50
	91.2R					20
Passau	87.7R	93.2	90.4	95.6	105.9	0.5/0.3
Pfaffenberg	95.6W	88.4	93.4	98.0	106.4	25/1
Regensburg	95.0R	93.0	99.6	97.0	105.0	25/5
Untersb. Geiereck*)	87.8	92.9	96.1	100.7	–	0.1
Wallberg	94.0	87.7	99.7	97.9	101.8	0.1
Wendelstein	93.7	89.5	98.5	102.3	105.7	100
Würzburg	90.9W	90.0	97.6	89.0	105.7	5/0.2

*) site in Austria
DAB: See L).
D.Prgr: Bayern 1, oldies, 24h, Mon-Fri 1105-1200 regional prgr. from Nürnberg (N), Regensburg (R), Würzburg (W) and Ulm (U) – **Bayern 2**, various prgr., rel. ARD-Nachtkonzert – **Bayern 3**, AC, 24h – **BR Klassik**, classical music, 24h – **B5 aktuell**, news, on FM mono signal, rel. ARD-Infonacht – **Bayern Plus**, German "Schlager" music, 24h – **BR Heimat**, German/Bavarian folk music, 24h – **BR Puls**, for young listeners, 24h – **B5 Plus**, coverage of parliament, sports and other special prgr. – **BR Verkehr**, traffic announcements

C) HESSISCHER RUNDFUNK (HR)

Public broadcasting institution of Hessen
✉ 60222 Frankfurt am Main (office and studio location: Bertramstraße 8) ☎ +49 69 155 1 🖷 +49 69 155 2900 **W:** hr-online.de

FM (MHz)	hr1	hr2	hr3	hr4	kW
Alsfeld-Homberg	–	–	105.6	–	0.1
Bad Hersfeld	88.9	–	102.9	–	0.3
Bingen	–	–	91.1	–	0.3
Feldberg (Taunus)	94.4	96.7	89.3	102.5R	100
Frankfurt (HR headq.)	–	87.9	–	–	0.1
Fulda	–	106.6	88.5	103.9N	0.3
Habichtswald	–	–	101.2	103.2N	20
Hardberg (Odenw.)	90.6	–	92.7	101.6R	50
Heidelstein (Rhön)	104.8	–	106.2	107.3N	50
Hoher Meißner	99.0	95.5	89.5	101.7N	100
Kassel	94.3	93.7	–	–	0.5
Limburg	–	100.8	–	97.1M	0.3/0.2
Marburg	–	–	–	102.8M	1
Rimberg	–	–	–	91.9N	50/20
Rotenburg	–	–	105.7	–	0.3
Sackpfeife	91.0	–	87.6	104.3M	100
Schlüchtern	–	–	88.9	–	0.3
Weilburg	–	–	–	97.9M	0.1
Wetzlar	–	–	–	90.5M	0.3
Wiesbaden	98.3	93.1	–	–	0.1
Würzburg (Odenw.)	88.1	97.4	89.7	103.8R	5

FM (MHz)	You FM	hr-info	kW
Alsfeld	–	104.0	0.1
Bad Hersfeld	–	106.9	0.3
Bad Nauheim	–	88.9	0.3
Bad Orb	–	89.8	0.3

FM (MHz)	You FM	hr-info	kW
Bensheim	90.2	91.2	0.2/0.1
Bingen	92.3	–	0.3
Darmstadt	104.3	107.0	0.8/5
Eltville	96.2	–	0.5
Eschwege	106.6	–	0.1
Frankfurt/Main	90.4	103.9	0.5
Friedberg	94.0	92.1	0.3
Fritzlar	–	106.6	0.1
Fulda	93.6	89.7	0.3/0.2
Gelnhausen	99.4	–	0.3
Gießen	97.9	99.2	0.5/0.3
Hardberg	95.3	–	50
Herborn	103.4	–	0.5
Kassel-Wilhelmsh.	100.1	107.5	0.5/1
Korbach	91.6	102.6	0.5/1
Limburg	90.7	99.2	0.2/0.3
Marburg	93.9	98.5	1/0.3
Michelstadt	91.0	–	0.2
Reinhardshain	–	92.9	0.2
Rimberg	97.7	95.0	50
Rotenburg	–	96.8	0.3
Sackpfeife	102.3	99.6	10/100
Schlüchtern	88.2	91.5	0.3
Seeheim	–	88.2	0.1
Sontra	–	90.8	0.1
Wetzlar	105.5	93.2	0.3
Wiesbaden	99.7	97.2	0.2/0.1
Witzenhausen	91.1	–	0.3

DAB: 12 txs on ch. 7B.

D.Prgr: hr1, oldies, rel. ARD-Popnacht – **hr2**, culture and classical music, rel. ARD-Nachtkonzert, ARD-Radiofestival – **hr3**, AC, rel. ARD-Popnacht – **hr4**, produced at Kassel (Wilhelmshöher Allee 347, 34131 Kassel), light music format, rel. ARD-Hitnacht, regional news Nordhessen (N; Kassel/Fulda), Mittelhessen (M; Gießen) and Rhein-Main (R; Frankfurt/Darmstadt) – **You FM**, CHR, rel. Die junge Nacht – **hr-info**, news, rel. ARD-Infonacht with own insertions.

D) MITTELDEUTSCHER RUNDFUNK (MDR)

Public broadcasting institution of Sachsen, Sachsen-Anhalt and Thüringen. ✉ Kantstraße 71-73, 04360 Leipzig (TV, MDR Aktuell, administration) **W:** mdr.de
✉ Gerberstraße 2, 06110 Halle/Saale ☎ +49 345 300 0 🖷 +49 345 300 5544 (MDR Kultur, MDR Jump, MDR Sputnik)

FM (MHz)	MDR 1	Jump	Kult	Akt	Sputnik	kW
Txs in Sachsen:						
Altenburg	–	–	–	101.5	–	1
Annaberg-Buchholz	–	–	–	91.2	–	0.2
Aue	–	–	–	95.1	–	1
Auerbach	–	–	–	101.7	–	0.4
Bautzen	–	98.8	–	87.9	–	0.2/0.1
Chemnitz-Reichenh.	–	–	–	94.7	–	0.5
Collmberg	101.8L	103.7	98.9	105.9	–	2x5/0.5/30
Döbeln-Mockritz	–	–	–	99.6	–	0.1
Dresden-Wachwitz	92.2	90.1	95.4	106.1	–	3x100/0.5
Eilenburg	–	–	–	92.4	–	0.2
Freiberg	99.1C	–	–	93.7	–	1/0.2
Freital	–	–	–	95.9	–	0.2
Geyer (Erzgebirge)	92.8C	89.8	87.7	–	–	100
Grimma-Hohnstädt	–	–	–	100.6	–	0.2
Görlitz	–	–	–	106.9	–	1
Hoyerswerda	93.0B	89.0	94.7	94.2	–	1/0.5/1/1
	100.4					30
Kamenz	–	–	–	93.9	–	1
Klingenthal	93.7C	–	98.4	–	–	0.2
Leipzig city	–	–	–	95.6	–	0.5
Löbau	98.2B	91.8	96.2	–	–	5
Markneukirchen	104.8C	–	106.4	–	–	0.5
Meißen-Korbitz	–	–	–	94.9	–	1
Neustadt	–	–	–	89.6	–	0.2
Plauen	–	–	–	102.0	–	1
Raschau	–	–	–	91.6	–	0.2
Seifhennersdorf	94.5B	96.9	103.4	–	–	0.25/0.3
Schöneck	88.7C	101.2	98.7	–	–	3/30/3
Stollberg	–	–	–	89.3	–	0.1
Torgau	88.9L	–	93.0	–	–	0.5/0.2
Weißwasser	–	–	–	90.5	–	1
Wiederau (Leipzig)	93.9L	90.4	88.4	–	–	100
	106.5H					*30
Zittau	87.7B	107.1	95.4	106.4	–	0.2/0.5
Zschopau	–	–	–	99.5	–	0.2
Zwickau	–	–	–	91.4	–	1
Txs in Sachsen-Anhalt:						
Aschersleben	–	–	–	102.8	–	1
Brocken	94.6	91.5	107.8	–	–	60/100/10
Burg	–	–	–	89.6	–	1
Dequede	94.9St	98.9	89.4	–	–	10
Dessau-Mildensee	–	–	–	90.0	–	0.3
Fleetmark	–	–	–	90.1	105.0	2/1
Gernrode	–	–	–	91.0	–	0.1
Haidberg	–	–	–	–	100.7	5
Haldensleben	–	–	–	99.1	–	1
Halle Petersberg	100.8H	–	–	95.3	104.4	5/2/10
Halle city	–	89.6	107.3	–	–	0.1
Hergisdorf	92.9H	–	–	–	–	1
Jerichow	–	–	–	–	90.5	1
Jessen	–	–	–	87.6	–	1
Klötze	–	–	–	–	100.7	5
Köthen	–	–	–	106.4	–	0.3
Magdeburg	96.1	–	107.4	–	–	10/30
Naumburg	92.3H	–	–	–	93.1	1/0.5
Sangerhausen	101.1H	–	–	99.9	–	0.1/1
Schneidlingen	–	–	–	106.7	–	0.5
Schönebeck	–	–	–	91.1	105.2	2/1.5
Stendal-Borstel	–	–	–	87.8	104.8	1
Weißenfels	–	–	–	88.8	–	1
Wernigerode	–	–	–	98.6	–	1
Wittenberg	88.1D	101.6	104.0	–	–	30/2x55
Zeitz-Hainichen	–	–	–	–	89.4	0.5
Txs in Thüringen:						
Apolda	–	–	–	91.2	–	1
Arnstadt	–	–	–	106.1	–	0.5
Bad Salzungen	–	–	–	94.0	–	0.1
Bleßberg	91.7S	96.9	–	–	–	100/20
Eisenach	–	–	–	100.0	–	0.2
Erfurt	94.4	–	–	97.8	–	2/1
Gera	–	–	–	91.1	–	1
Gotha	–	–	–	88.8	–	0.1
Greiz	–	–	–	93.3	–	0.2
Heiligenstadt	93.6He	–	–	90.5	–	0.1
Ilmenau	–	–	–	93.0	–	0.1
Inselsberg	92.5	90.2	87.9	–	–	100/100/60
Jena-Oßmaritz	88.2G	101.9	96.4	89.5	–	1/0.2
Keula	98.5He	–	–	–	–	20
Lobenstein	95.5G	–	–	101.8	–	2/0.5
Magdala	92.9	–	–	99.2	–	0.01/0.05
Meiningen	–	–	–	94.7	–	0.2
Mühlhausen	–	–	–	105.8	–	0.1
Nordhausen	88.3He	–	–	93.7	–	0.1
Pößneck	–	–	–	101.6	–	0.2
Remda	103.6	105.6	100.7	–	–	60
Ronneburg	97.8G	100.9	103.9	–	–	10/30/30
Saalfeld	–	–	–	104.6	–	0.1
Schleiz	–	–	–	105.1	–	0.2
Schmalkalden	–	–	-	100.0	–	0.1
Schmölln	–	–	–	107.9	–	0.2
Sondershausen	100.1He	–	–	95.1	–	0.05/0.1
Sonneberg	–	–	–	105.8	–	0.1
Suhl Erleshügel	93.7S	91.1	89.8	97.5	–	1/0.1/0.2/5
Weimar Ettersberg	93.3	–	–	–	–	5
Weimar Belvedere	–	–	–	102.6	–	2

*) Directional, to north and west only

DAB: 8 txs in Sachsen-Anhalt on ch. 6B, 11 txs in Thüringen on ch. 8B, 10 txs in Sachsen on ch. 9A. Carry central prgr. plus respective MDR 1 stn. in all regional versions.

D.Prgr: MDR 1 Radio Sachsen, Königsbrücker Str. 88, 01099 Dresden, regional prgr. from studios Bautzen (freq. marked (B), Chemnitz (C) and Leipzig (L); **MDR Sachsen-Anhalt**, Stadtparkstr. 8, 39114 Magdeburg, regional prgr. Dessau (D), Halle (H) and Stendal (St); **MDR Thüringen**, Gothaer Str. 36, 99094 Erfurt; regional prgr. Gera (G), Heiligenstadt (He) and Suhl (S). 2200-0400 on all MDR 1 stns common prgr. – **MDR Jump**, AC – **MDR Kultur**, culture, rel. ARD-Nachtkonzert, ARD-Radiofestival – **MDR Aktuell**, news – **MDR Sputnik**, CHR, rel. Die junge Nacht – **MDR Klassik**, classical music, at times rel. MDR Kultur – **MDR Schlagerwelt**, German "Schlager" music – **Serbske Rozhlas**, Am Postplatz 3, 02607 Bautzen. Prgr. in Upper Sorbian on 100.4MHz Mon-Fri 0405-0700, Sat 0505-0800, Sun 1000-1130. Radio Satkula for young listeners Mon 1900-2100. Also rel. Bramborske Serbske Radio, see G).

E) NORDDEUTSCHER RUNDFUNK (NDR)

Public broadcasting institution of Hamburg, Mecklenburg-Vorpommern, Niedersachsen and Schleswig-Holstein
✉ Rothenbaumchaussee 132, 20149 Hamburg ☎ +49 40 4156 0 🖷 +49 40 447 602 **W:** ndr.de

FM (MHz)	NDR 1	NDR 2	NDR-K	Info	N-Joy	kW
Txs in Hamburg:						
Moorfleet	90.3	87.6	99.2	92.3	94.2	80/5/1
	89.5No					10
Txs in Mecklenburg-Vorpommern:						
Anklam	94.6Gr	–	–	–	103.0	6.3/1.25
Bad Doberan	94.3R	–	–	–	103.7	0.2/5
Barth	87.6Gr	–	–	–	95.0	0.4/0.3
Demmin	97.6N	92.5	91.8	101.5	95.1	0.1/1
Dömitz	88.3	–	–	–	–	1
Garz/Rügen	102.5Gr	99.8	91.5	88.6	95.5	50/10
Greifswald	101.0Gr	–	–	–	–	0.16
Grevesmühlen	100.7W	–	–	–	103.4	0.5/5
Güstrow-Strentz	92.5R	–	–	–	104.4	1.25/0.63
Helpterberg	90.5N	99.1	96.0	101.8	103.2	100/1.25
	94.2Gr					6.3
Heringsdorf	97.6Gr	94.0	102.7	100.5	92.3	1
Malchin	–	–	–	103.5	94.4	1
Neubrandenburg	–	–	–	–	89.5	1
Pasewalk	93.7Gr	–	–	–	94.8	2.5/1.25
Ribnitz-Damgarten	–	–	–	–	99.4	0.3
Röbel	88.5N	107.0	94.7	100.4	97.4	10/60/4
Rostock	91.0R	93.5	88.2	102.8	88.9	160/40/5
Schwerin	92.8	98.5	89.2	105.3	99.5	30/100/2
Stralsund	92.1Gr	–	–	–	–	0.4
Ueckermünde	90.1Gr	–	–	–	104.1	4/1.5
Wismar	96.2W	–	–	–	–	0.2
Wolgast-Moeckow	89.0Gr	–	–	–	93.2	0.4/0.3
Txs in and for Niedersachsen:						
Alfeld	87.8B	93.6	96.5	91.1	92.9	0.05
Aurich-Popens	95.8Ol	98.1	90.0	96.4	92.7	25/10/1
Bad Pyrmont	88.6	92.6	95.7	98.5		0.05
Bad Rothenfelde	–	–	–	97.9	91.2	0.2/0.1
Braunlage	–	–	–	–	96.1	0.02
Braunschweig	–	–	–	–	93.0	40
Bremen-Walle	–	–	–	95.0	–	1
Bremerhaven	–	–	–	98.9	92.8	0.5/0.05
Cloppenburg	–	–	–	103.7	93.5	1
Cuxhaven	105.4Ol	97.9	94.6	93.1	91.6	20/10/1/10
	98.4					1
Damme	–	–	–	106.5	105.0	0.5/1
Dannenberg	91.2L	96.4	93.3	90.7	94.0	25/10/3/1
Goslar	88.2B	93.7	95.1	96.0	96.5	0.1
Göttingen	88.5B	94.1	96.8	99.9	95.9	5/0.5/5/0.5
Hann. Münden	88.2B	96.1	90.8	92.9	94.8	0.05
Hannover-Hemm.	90.9	96.2	98.7	88.6	92.6	15/5/15/ 0.5/2.5
Hildesheim	–	–	–	–	95.7	0.5
Holzminden	92.7B	96.0	98.4	88.6	99.7	0.5/0.1
Jever	–	–	–	–	97.3	0.3
Königslutter-Elm	–	–	–	88.7	–	0.2
Lingen	92.8O	97.8	90.2	88.9	96.6	15/0.2/0.5
Meppen	–	–	–	–	93.3	0.05
Osnabrück	92.4O	89.2	98.8	87.6	96.4	8/2x0.2
Rinteln	–	–	–	95.3	105.2	0.1/0.04
Rosengarten	103.2L	–	–	–	91.4	20/0.3
Seesen	–	–	–	90.4	96.6	0.2/0.05
Stadthagen	100.8	102.6	104.4	98.2	91.3	25/1
Steinkimmen	91.1Ol	99.8	94.4	98.6	92.9	100/3/1
Torfhaus	98.0B	92.1	89.9	99.5	–	100/50
Visselhövede	91.8L	95.9	87.8	98.4	97.6	5/2/5/1/30
Wedel	–	–	–	–	95.6	0.2
Wolfsburg	–	–	–	88.2	–	0.1
Txs in Schleswig-Holstein:						
Bungsberg	97.8Lb	91.9	89.9	96.6	99.0	50/1/0.5
Flensburg	89.6F	93.2	96.1	87.7	91.0	25/10/0.5
Garding-Katingsiel	–	–	–	–	88.8	0.5
Heide-Welmbüttel	90.5H	96.3	99.4	87.9	94.9	15/0.5
Helgoland island	88.9H	93.4	97.0	92.5	91.5	0.01
Husum	–	–	–	–	93.7	0.05
Kiel-Kronshagen	91.3	98.3	95.7	99.7	94.5	15/1/0.4/15
Lauenburg	94.7Lb	–	–	96.8	99.8	0.3
Lübeck	93.1Lb	90.7	88.0	95.9	94.0	0.5/0.1/0.5
Mölln	104.5Lb	–	–	–	90.9	20/0.5
Neumünster	106.4No	–	–	90.8	98.7	20/1/0.5
Niebüll-Süderlügum	–	–	–	–	91.5	0.2
Sylt	90.9F	98.7	94.3	92.7	95.6	5
Wedel	–	–	–	–	95.6	0.2

DAB: Hamburg on ch. 7A; Mecklenburg-Vorpommern on ch. 8B (5 txs), 10C (Neubrandenburg/Röbel), 11B (Rostock/Güstrow), 12B (Schwerin/Wismar); Niedersachsen on ch. 6A (Visselhövede), 6D (Hannover), 7A (Hildesheim), 9B (Lüneburg/Stade), 10A (Osnabrück/Lingen/Damme), 11B (Braunschweig/Göttingen), 12A (Aurich/Steinkimmen/Bremerhaven); Schleswig-Holstein on ch. 9A (Lübeck), 9C (Kiel), 10C (Kaltenkirchen/Helgoland), 11B (Heide), 12B (4 txs).

D.Prgr: NDR 90,3 from Hamburg studios, on 90.3/98.4MHz – **NDR 1 Radio MV**, Schloßgartenallee 61, 19061 Schwerin; via txs in Mecklenburg-Vorpommern, regional prgr. Greifswald (Gr), Neubrandenburg (N), Rostock (R) and Wismar (W, from Schwerin studios) – **NDR 1 Niedersachsen**, Rudolf-von-Bennigsen-Ufer 22, 30169 Hannover; via txs in Niedersachsen, regional prgr. Braunschweig (B), Göttingen (G), Lüneburg area (L, from Hannover studios), Oldenburg (Ol) and Osnabrück (O) – **NDR 1 Welle Nord**, Postfach 34 80, 24033 Kiel (studio location: Eggerstr. 16); via txs in Schleswig-Holstein and 89.5MHz; regional prgr. Flensburg (F), Heide (H), Lübeck (Lb) and Norderstedt (No). 2110-0430 common prgr. on all NDR 1 stns – **NDR 2**, AC – **NDR Kultur**, classical music, rel. ARD-Nachtkonzert, ARD-Radiofestival – **NDR Info**, Mon-Fri 0500-1850 and Sat 0500-1700 news format, other times diverse prgr., at night music specials – **NDR Info Spezial**, special prgr., rel. ARD-Infonacht, Mon-Fri 1500-2000 Cosmo (see J), Sun 0500-0700 NDR 90,3 (for Hamburger Hafenkonzert prgr., broadcast since 1929). Sea weather forecasts at 2305 (also via NDR Info FM txs in Mecklenburg-Vorpommern), 0730 and 2105 – **N-Joy**, CHR, rel. Die junge Nacht – **NDR Blue**, alternative – **NDR Plus**, German "Schlager" music

F) RADIO BREMEN (RB)

Public broadcasting institution of Bremen
✉Diepenau 10, 28195 Bremen ☎ +49 421 246 0 🖷 +49 421 246 1010 **W:** radiobremen.de

FM (MHz)	Eins	Zwei	Vier	Next	Cosm	kW
Bremen-Walle	93.8	88.3	101.2	96.7	95.6	60/4/0.5
Bremerhaven	89.3	95.4	100.8	92.1	98.9	25/0.5

DAB: Bremen-Walle tx on ch. 7B, rel. also Kiraka, see J).

D.Prgr: Bremen Eins, oldies, rel. 2305-0400 (Sun to 0500) SWR1 – **Bremen Zwei**, culture, rel. ARD-Nachtkonzert – **Bremen Vier**, AC, rel. ARD-Popnacht – **Bremen Next**, for young audiences – **Cosmo** see J)

G) RUNDFUNK BERLIN-BRANDENBURG (RBB)

Public broadcasting institution of Berlin and Brandenburg, operating from two main seats:
Potsdam: ✉Marlene-Dietrich-Allee 20, 14482 Potsdam-Babelsberg ☎ +49 331 731 0 🖷 +49 331 731 3571
Berlin: ✉14046 Berlin (studio/office location: Masurenallee 8-14) ☎ +49 30 3031 0 🖷 +49 30)3015 062 **W:** rbb-online.de

Txs in Berlin:

MHz	kW	Site	Program
88.8	80	Scholzplatz	R. Berlin
92.4	80	Scholzplatz	Kulturradio
93.1	25	Scholzplatz	Inforadio
95.8	100	Alexanderplatz	radioeins
96.3	80	Scholzplatz	Cosmo
99.7	100	Alexanderplatz	Antenne Brandenburg
102.6	20	Alexanderplatz	Fritz

Txs in Brandenburg:

FM (MHz)	Ant.B.	Eins	Fritz	Kultur	Info	kW
Belzig-Lütte	106.2	99.3	91.9	100.2	–	100/10
Booßen	87.6F	89.1F	101.5	96.8	102.0	5/30/1.5
Calau	98.6C	95.1C	103.2	104.4	93.4+	100/30
Casekow	91.1Pr	106.1	100.1	104.4	–	60/10
Cottbus	–	–	–	–	99.9	1
Guben	100.9C	–	–	–	–	6
Lübben	–	–	–	–	92.4	0.4
Perleberg	–	–	–	–	92.3	1

FM (MHz)	Ant.B.	Eins	Fritz	Kultur	Info	kW
Prenzlau	99.4Pr	–	–	–	98.6	0.5
Pritzwalk	106.6Pe	99.9	103.1	91.7	–	100/10
Wittstock	–	–	–	–	97.7	1.3

+) Bramborske Serbske Radio

DAB: Berlin: Txs on ch. 7D, also rel. Bayern 2, BR Klassik (see B), MDR Jump (see D), SWR3 (see I), WDR 2 (see J). Branbenburg: 6 txs on ch. 10B.

D.Prgr from Berlin studios: Radio Berlin, AC, rel. ARD-Popnacht – **Inforadio**, news, rel. ARD-Infonacht with local insertions – **rbb kultur**, classical music, rel. ARD-Nachtkonzert, ARD-Radiofestival

D.Prgr from Potsdam studios: Antenne Brandenburg, light music, regional prgr. from studios Perleberg (Pe), Prenzlau (Pr), Frankfurt/Oder (F) and Cottbus (C), 2100-2305 common prgr. with Radio Berlin, rel. ARD-Nachtexpress – **radioeins**, progressive-style rock/pop and information, regional prgr. from Frankfurt/Oder and Cottbus – **Fritz**, youth, rel. Die junge Nacht

Cosmo: (see J)

Bramborske Serbske Radio: RBB, Studio Cottbus, Berliner Straße 155, 03046 Cottbus. Prgr. in Lower Sorbian Mon-Fri 1100-1200 and repeat at 1800-1900, Sundays and holidays 1130-1300. 93.4MHz otherwise rel. Inforadio and Serbske Rozhlas (see D)

H) SAARLÄNDISCHER RUNDFUNK (SR)

Public broadcasting institution of Saarland

✉ Funkhaus Halberg, 66100 Saarbrücken ☎ +49 681 602 0 🖷 +49 681 602 3874 **W:** sr-online.de

FM (MHz)	SR 1	SR 2	SR 3	UnserDing	kW
Bliestal-Webenheim	92.3	–	89.1	98.0	5
Göttelborner Höhe	88.0	91.3	95.5	103.7	100/20
Homburg	–	98.6	–	–	0.2
Merzig-Hilbringen	89.3	92.1	98.0	–	0.1
Neunkirchen	–	–	–	–	5
Oberperl	91.9	88.6	96.1	–	5
Sankt Wendel	–	–	–	90.3	0.1

DAB: 6 txs on ch. 9A, also rel. Kiraka (see J), R. Salü (see U)

D.Prgr: SR 1 Europawelle Saar, AC, rel. ARD-Popnacht – **SR 2 KulturRadio**, culture, rel. ARD-Nachtkonzert, ARD-Radiofestival – **SR 3 Saarlandwelle**, light music, news in French at 0805 – **Unser Ding**, CHR, at times rel. Das Ding (SWR) – **Antenne Saar**, rel. of SR 2, SWR Info and Radio France Internationale

I) SÜDWESTRUNDFUNK (SWR)

Public broadc.institution of Baden-Württemberg and Rheinland-Pfalz

✉ 76522 Baden-Baden (Location: Hans-Bredow-Straße) ☎ +49 7221 929 0 🖷 +49 7221 929 2010

Broadcasting house Mainz: ✉ Postfach 3740, 55122 Mainz (Location: Am Fort Gonsenheim 39) ☎ +49 6131 929 0

Broadcasting house Stuttgart: ✉ Postfach 106040, 70049 Stuttgart (Location: Neckarstraße 230) ☎ +49 711 929 0 **W:** swr.de

FM (MHz)	SWR1	SWR2	SWR3	SWR4	DasDing	kW
Txs in and for Baden-Württemberg:						
Aalen Braunenberg	95.1	91.1	98.1	96.9U	–	50/5
Albstadt-Mahlesfeld	–	–	–	99.5Tü	87.8	0.1/0.3
Bad Bellingen	–	–	–	96.6F	–	0.1
Bad Mergentheim	87.8	93.2	99.7	105.5H	100.5	10/0.1
Baden-Baden	90.9	98.9	99.6	88.5Ka	91.7	0.8/0.4
Baiersbronn	–	–	–	87.9O	–	0.1
Basel St. Crischona*	87.9	92.0	98.3	89.5L	–	5
Blauen-Hochblauen	89.2	92.6	97.0	–	–	8.4
Buchen	91.9	97.1	94.1	107.5M	100.6	0.1/25
Elzach Hörnleberg	–	–	–	101.8F	–	0.1
Feldberg	89.8	97.9	93.8	104.0F	–	5
Freiburg-Lehen	107.0	91.1	99.2	100.7F	–	0.1/1
Freudenberg	90.3	97.2	94.9	91.6H	–	0.01
Geislingen	93.0	88.5	95.5	107.9	–	0.5/0.1
Grünten*	98.7	–	103.0	–	–	30
Hausach Brandenkopf	95.4	–	99.7	97.6O	–	0.5/0.1
Heidelberg Königstuhl	97.8	88.8	99.9	104.1M	–	100
Heilbronn	–	–	–	99.5H	–	2
Hornisgrinde	93.5	96.2	98.4	94.0O	–	80/5
Karlsruhe-Ettlingen	–	–	–	97.0Ka	–	20
Klettgau	95.1	92.8	98.5	87.7Lö	–	2.6
Lichtenstein	99.1	–	–	89.0Tü	–	0.1
Mannheim	–	–	–	–	91.5	4
Mötzingen	–	–	97.2	87.6Tü	90.5	1
Mühlacker	–	–	–	95.7B	–	2
Pforzheim	92.9	88.1	99.3	87.6Ka	–	5/0.2/0.5
Raichberg	88.3	91.8	94.3	107.3Tü	–	40/25
Ravensburg	99.0	–	87.9	–	107.2	0.1
Reutlingen	–	–	–	–	97.7	2
Schiltach-Simonsberg	90.8	–	94.5	99.2O	–	0.1
Schwäbisch Gmünd	–	–	–	100.9U	–	0.1
Sigmaringen	–	–	–	101.2Fr	–	0.1
Strasbourg*	–	–	–	88.9O	–	1
Stuttgart-Degerloch	94.7	105.7	92.2	90.1	90.8	100/2
Stuttgart (town)	99.6	93.1	–	–	–	0.5/0.2
					†91.5	0.3
Tübingen	–	–	–	–	97.3	2
Ulm Kuhberg	92.6	89.2	97.4	94.5U	98.9	10/1
Vaihingen	–	98.6	–	–	–	0.1
Villingen-Schwenningen	–	–	–	91.1F	–	1
Waldenburg	98.8	93.8	96.5	106.6H	–	100/50
Waldburg	–	94.9	–	99.5H	–	60
				91.2Fr		25
Weinheim	97.1	–	99.5	100.7M	–	0.04/0.1
Wertheim	96.9	91.8	94.6	101.2H	–	0.1
Witthoh	92.4	90.4	97.1	89.0Fr	–	40/5
Zell Hohe Möhr	87.6	–	96.8	100.2F	–	0.1
Zwiefalten	93.7	–	92.8	87.6Fr	–	0.1

†) SWR Info. *Basel site in Switzerland, Strasbourg site in France, Grünten site in Bayern

FM (MHz)	SWR1	SWR2	SWR3	SWR4	DasDing	kW
Txs in and for Rheinland-Pfalz:						
Bad Kreuznach	–	–	–	–	90.9	0.1
Bleialf-Buchet	88.3	99.7	98.9	94.6T	–	0.1
Daun	91.1	–	98.5	93.6T	–	8
Diez-Geisenberg	88.4	93.4	98.2	87.9K	–	0.01/0.1
Donnersberg	99.1	92.0	101.1	105.6Kl	–	60
Haardtkopf	97.7	93.0	90.0	107.1T	–	50/25
Hohe Wurzel	–	–	–	107.9M	–	6.2
Idar-Oberstein	88.5	95.1	98.1	106.4T		0.01/1
Kaisersl. Bornberg	90.8	93.9	97.5	99.6Kl	92.5	25/0.3
Koblenz-Waldesch	96.1	94.0	91.6	107.4K	99.4	10/40/0.2
Kreuzweiler	–	–	–	97.3T	–	0.3
Linz	92.4	–	94.8	97.4K	–	50
Mainz-Kastel*	87.7	103.2	93.7	91.4M	105.2	1
Mainz-Wolfsheim	–	–	–	94.9M		5
Marienberger Höhe	89.8	95.4	92.8	106.3K	91.3	25/0.1
Nierstein-Oppenheim*	–	–	–	92.9M	98.4	0.1/0.3
Pirmasens Kettrichhof	100.8	–	107.2	104.2Kl	–	5
Rüdesheim*	–	99.4	93.3	88.6M		0.1/0.5
Saarburg	99.2	93.8	90.6	101.2T	–	5
Trier	94.9	89.4	98.2	98.8T	91.7	0.1/0.3
Tübingen Herrenberg	–	–	97.2	87.6Tü	90.5	1
Weinbiet	89.9	102.2	–	95.9L	–	25
Zweibrücken	–	–	–	90.5Kl	–	0.2

*) Site in Hessen. +20 stns below 0.1kW

DAB: Baden-Württemberg 4 txs on ch. 8A, 14 txs on ch. 8D, 12 txs on ch. 9D; Rheinland-Pfalz 13 txs on ch. 11A.

D.Prgr. from Stuttgart studios, via txs in Baden-Württemberg: **SWR1 Baden-Württemberg**, oldies, at night common SWR1 prgrs from Baden-Baden; **SWR4 Baden-Württemberg**, light music, with local prgr. from Freiburg (F), Friedrichshafen (F), Heilbronn (H), Karlsruhe (Ka), Lörrach (Lö), Mannheim (M), Offenburg (O), Tübingen (T) and Ulm (U), rel. ARD-Hitnacht

D.Prgr. from Mainz studios, via txs in Rheinland-Pfalz: **SWR1 Rheinland-Pfalz**, oldies, at night common SWR1 prgrs from Baden-Baden; **SWR4 Rheinland-Pfalz**, light music, with local prgrs from Kaiserslautern (Kl), Koblenz (K), Ludwigshafen (L) and Trier (T), rel. ARD-Hitnacht

D.Prgr. from Baden-Baden studios: SWR2, culture, 1740-1800 prgr. from Mainz/Stuttgart, at night rel. ARD-Nachtkonzert; **SWR3**, AC; **Das Ding**, youth, rel. Die junge Nacht; **SWR Info**, news, rel. ARD-Infonacht

J) WESTDEUTSCHER RUNDFUNK (WDR)

Public broadcasting institution of Nordrhein-Westfalen

✉ 50600 Köln (location: Appellhofplatz 1) ☎ +49 221 220 1 🖷 +49 221 220 4800 **W:** wdr.de

FM (MHz)	ELive	WDR 2	WDR 3	WDR4	WDR5	kW
Aachen-Stolberg	106.4	100.8A	95.9	93.9	101.9	20
Arnsberg	96.0	99.4S	97.5	91.7	88.5	0.1
Bad Oeynhausen	107.7	99.1B	92.7	90.1	87.7	0.1
Bergheim	–	88.4K	–	–	–	0.5
Bonn Venusberg	102.4	100.4K	93.1	90.7	88.0	50

FM (MHz)	ELive	WDR 2	WDR 3	WDR4	WDR5	kW
Dortmund	–	87.8D	–	–	–	2
Ederkopf	107.2	101.8S	–	100.7	95.8	15/20
Eifel-Bärbelkreuz	105.5	101.0	96.3	104.4	89.6	20/10/20/10
Gummersbach	–	91.8W	–	–	–	10
Hallenberg	105.7	–	–	96.1	88.3	0.1
Höxter Hasselberg	107.3	96.4B	95.2	87.8	93.9	0.5
Ibbenbüren	102.5	96.0M	97.3	99.5	88.5	0.5
Klever Berg	103.7	93.3Dü	97.3	101.7	99.7	2
Köln	87.6	98.6K	–	–	–	0.3/0.5
Langenberg	106.7	99.2Dü	95.1	101.3	88.8	100
					103.3+	100
Lübbecke	93.6	96.0B	91.7	99.6	88.6	0.1
Münster-Baumberge	107.9	94.1M	89.7	100.0	92.0	25
Nordhelle	104.7	93.5S	98.1	103.8	90.3	35
Olsberg	107.0	102.1S	–	104.1	98.6	10
Remscheid	–	95.7W	–	–	–	1
Schmallenberg	100.1	93.8S	97.8	101.1	90.0	0.1
Siegen	107.5	97.1S	98.4	101.2	97.6	0.5/1/0.5/1
Teutoburger Wald	105.5	93.2B	97.0	100.5	90.6	100
Warburg	98.2	91.8B	94.3	104.5	88.4	0.5
Wittgenstein	–	92.3S	88.7	–	–	15
Wuppertal	–	99.8W	–	–	–	1

*) Funkhaus Europa

DAB: 23 txs on ch. 11D, also rel. Domradio (see S)

D.Prgr: 1 Live, CHR – **WDR 2**, AC, incl. local news from Aachen (A), Bielefeld (B), Köln (K), Dortmund (D), Düsseldorf (Dü), Münster (M), Siegen (S), Wuppertal (W); at night rel. NDR 2 – **WDR 3**, culture, rel. ARD-Nachtkonzert, ARD-Radiofestival – **WDR 4**, light music, rel. ARD-Hitnacht – **WDR 5**, information, repeats overnight – **Cosmo**, for migrants, also via RBB and RB txs (see F/G) – **VERA**, continuous traffic jam information – **WDR Event**, live coverage of various events, otherwise silent – **1 Live Diggi**, continuous CHR music – **Kiraka**, for childrens

II. COMMERCIAL AND OTHER STATIONS

K) BADEN-WÜRTTEMBERG

Media institution: Landesanstalt für Kommunikation (LfK) ✉ Postfach 102927, 70025 Stuttgart (office location: Reinsburgstraße 27 ☎ +49 711 669910 🖷 +49 711 6699111 **W:** lfk.de

Commercial stations:

FM	MHz	kW	Site	Station
2)	87.8	1	Mannheim	big FM
6)	88.6	2	Langenburg	R. Ton
3)	89.1	0.5	Heilbronn	Hit-R. Antenne 1
3)	89.3	0.1	Bad Urach	Hit-R. Antenne 1
2)	89.5	10	Stuttgart Frauenkopf	big FM
3)	89.5	0.1	Wertheim	Hit-R. Antenne 1
2)	89.7	1	Tübingen	big FM
11)	90.4	2	Karlsruhe	Klassik R.
9)	90.5	2	Achern	Hitradio Ohr
2)	90.9	0.1	Heidelberg city	big FM
15)	91.4	3	Lützenhardt	R. TV R.
7)	91.4	0.5	Pforzheim	die neue welle
19)	92.4	1	Hockenheimring	Rennradio
2)	92.7	1	Horb	big FM
9)	93.0	0.1	Haslach	Schwarzwald R.
16)	93.1	1	Rottweil-Zimmern	R. Neckarburg
15)	94.7	0.5	Freiburg-Lehen	baden.fm
17)	95.4	0.1	Stuttgart SWR bldg.	Metropol FM
5)	95.6	1	Balingen	Neckaralb Live
6)	96.0	0.1	Künzelsau	R. Ton
10)	96.4	1	Überlingen	R. Seefunk
6)	96.8	0.3	Eppingen	R. Ton
4)	96.9	0.1	Schussental	R. 7
12)	97.2	1	Stuttgart-Münster	egoFM
2)	97.2	0.5	Sinsheim-Dühren	big FM
13)	97.5	0.5	Esslingen	Die Neue 107.7
8)	97.6	0.3	Rudersberg	Energy Stuttgart
2)	99.0	0.5	Rottweil	big FM
5)	99.0	0.1	Bad Urach	Neckaralb Live
15)	99.2	0.2	Herrenberg	R. TV R.
9)	99.2	0.1	Oberkirch	Hitradio Ohr
10)	99.3	5	Friedrichshafen	R. Seefunk
2)	99.7	1	Ulm	big FM
3)	100.1	50	Schwäbisch Hall	Hit-R. Antenne 1
6)	100.1	0.1	Hechingen	R. Ton
2)	100.3	5	Geislingen	big FM
1)	100.4	80	Hornisgrinde	R. Regenbogen
8)	100.7	20	Güglingen	Energy Stuttgart
5)	100.9	1	Tübingen	Neckaralb Live
7)	100.9	0.8	Baden-Baden	die neue welle
1)	101.1	8.4	Blauen-Müllheim	R. Regenbogen
4)	101.2	0.1	Villingen-Schwenningen	R. 7
3)	101.3	75	Stuttgart Frauenkopf	Hit-R. Antenne 1
9)	101.6	0.5	Brandenkopf	Hit-R. Ohr
7)	101.8	25	Karlsruhe	die neue welle
4)	101.8	10	Ulm-Ermingen	R. 7
10)	101.8	10	Konstanz	R. Seefunk
8)	101.8	1	Backnang	Energy Stuttgart
10)	101.9	0.1	Schopfheim	R. Seefunk
16)	102.0	3	Villingen-Schwenningen	R. Neckarburg
1)	102.1	25	Mudau	Regenbogen Zwei
10)	102.4	0.2	Laufenburg [Switzerl.]	R. Seefunk
4)	102.5	40	Witthoh-Tuttlingen	R. 7
6)	102.6	0.5	Schwäbisch Hall	R. Ton
10)	102.6	0.3	Ravensburg	R. Seefunk
8)	102.6	0.1	Bad Wildbad	die neue welle
8)	102.7	0.1	Nagold	die neue welle
1)	102.8	50	Heidelberg.Königstuhl	R. Regenbogen
2)	102.8	0.5	Freiburg	big FM
11)	103.0	1	Göppingen	Klassik R.
8)	103.0	0.3	Calw	die neue welle
10)	103.1	5	Rheinfelden	R. Seefunk
3)	103.1	0.1	Reutlingen	Hit-R. Antenne 1
6)	103.2	25	Heilbronn	R. Ton
3)	103.4	50	Raichberg	Hit-R. Antenne 1
6)	103.5	20	Bad Mergentheim	R. Ton
4)	103.7	50	Aalen	R. 7
16)	103.7	0.1	Schramberg	R. Neckarburg
2)	103.8	2	Baden-Baden	big FM
10)	103.9	10	Iberger Kugel	R. Seefunk
11)	103.9	2	Stuttgart-Münster	Klassik R.
10)	104.2	1	Sigmaringen	R. Seefunk
6)	104.2	0.1	Heidenheim	R. Ton
8)	104.3	2	Sindelfingen	Energy Stuttgart
10)	104.3	0.1	Lörrach	R. Seefunk
8)	104.5	2	Waiblingen	Energy Stuttgart
8)	104.5	0.1	Winnenden	Energy Stuttgart
16)	104.6	1	Oberndorf	R. Neckarburg
14)	104.6	0.3	Biberach	Donau 3 FM
1)	104.6	0.1	Buchen	R. Regenbogen
2)	104.7	0.2	Heilbronn	big FM
6)	104.7	0.1	Wertheim	R. Ton
13)	104.7	0.1	Geislingen	Die Neue 107.7
5)	104.8	1	Reutlingen	Neckaralb Live
9)	104.9	5	Offenburg-Ohlsbach	Hit-R. Ohr
18)	104.9	1	Stuttgart-Münster	sunshine live
4)	105.0	50	Grünenbach	R. 7
2)	105.1	0.2	Aalen	big FM
2)	105.2	20	Pforzheim	big FM
10)	105.3	0.5	Singen	R. Seefunk
3)	105.4	1	Geislingen	Hit-R. Antenne 1
3)	105.4	0.3	Balingen	Hit-R. Antenne 1
10)	105.4	0.1	Waldshut-Tiengen	R. Seefunk
9)	105.5	0.5	Bühl	Hit-R. Ohr
14)	105.9	5	Ulm-Ermingen	Donau 3 FM
15)	106.0	8.4	Blauen-Müllheim	baden.fm
3)	106.0	0.1	Bad Mergentheim	Hit-R. Antenne 1
1)	106.1	1	Heidelberg-Königstuhl	Regenbogen Zwei
13)	106.1	1	Göppingen	Die Neue 107.7
14)	106.2	0.5	Riedlingen	Donau 3 FM
13)	106.5	0.1	Kirchheim	Die Neue 107.7
15)	106.6	0.1	Titisee-Neustadt	baden.fm
13)	106.8	5	Nürtingen	Die Neue 107.7
3)	106.9	0.1	Leonberg	Hit-R. Antenne 1
10)	107.0	5	Wannenberg-Klettgau	R. Seefunk
3)	107.0	1	Pforzheim	Hit-R. Antenne 1
6)	107.1	20	Aalen	R. Ton
1)	107.1	0.1	Wiesloch	Regenbogen Zwei
7)	107.3	0.1	Bruchsal	die neue welle
9)	107.4	5	Lahr	Hit-R. Ohr
13)	107.4	0.1	Gosbach	Die Neue 107.7
13)	107.7	4	Stuttgart Frauenkopf	Die Neue 107.7

FM	MHz	kW	Site	Station
15)	107.7	0.5	Freiburg-Littenweiler	baden.fm
1)	107.7	0.1	Weinheim	Regenbogen Zwei
5)	107.9	1	Sickingen	Neckaralb Live
1)	107.9	0.1	Mosbach	Regenboen Zwei
7)	107.9	0.1	Bretten	die neue welle

Addresses & other information:
1) P.O.-Box 10 26 55, 68026 Mannheim (studio location: Dudenstr. 12-26); **W:** regenbogenweb.de AC, separate Regenbogen Zwei prgr. rock – **2)** Kronenstr. 24, 70173 Stuttgart; **W:** bigfm.de CHR, further txs see T), U) – **3)** Plieningerstr. 150, 70567 Stuttgart; **W:** antenne1.de AC – **4)** Gaisenbergstr. 29, 89073 Ulm; **W:** radio7.de AC – **5)** Obere Wässere 6-8, 72764 Reutlingen; **W:** neckaralblive.de AC – **6)** Allee 2, 74072 Heilbronn; **W:** radio-ton.de AC – **7)** Albert-Nestler-Str. 26, 76131 Karlsruhe; **W:** meine-neue-welle.de AC – **8)** Anton-Schmidt-Str. 36, 71332 Waiblingen; **W:** energy-stuttgart.de CHR – **9)** Postfach 20 80, 77610 Offenburg (studio location: Hauptstr. 83a); **W:** hitradio-ohr.de schwarzwaldradio.com AC – **10)** Konzilstr. 1, 78462 Konstanz; **W:** radio-seefunk.de AC – **11)** see O) – **12)** see L) – **13)** Königstr. 2, 70173 Stuttgart; **W:** dieneue1077.de Rock – **14)** Basteistr. 37, 89073 Ulm; **W:** donau3fm.de AC – **15)** Munzingerstr. 1, 79111 Freiburg; **W:** baden.fm AC – **16)** August-Schuhmacher-Str. 10, 78664 Eschbronn-Mariazell; **W:** radio-neckarburg.de – **17)** see M), stn. 15 – **18)** Grunewaldstr. 3, 12165 Berlin (studio); W: sunshine-live.de Techno, also via Astra 1N, 12.148GHz – **19)** during Hockenheimring races only

Non-commercial stations:

FM	MHz	kW	Site	Station
10)	88.4	0.3	Freiburg univ.	echo-fm
6)	88.6	1	Stuttgart-Münster	Hochschulr. Stuttg.
9)	89.2	0.1	Horb	Freies R. Freudens.
1)	89.6	0.1	Mannheim	bermuda.funk
4)	91.2	0.1	Bruchsal	LernR.
8)	96.6	1	Tübingen	Wüste Welle
2)	97.5	0.1	Schwäbisch Hall	R. StHörfunk
5)	99.2	0.3	Stuttgart-Münster	Freies R. f. Stuttg.
9)	100.0	0.5	Freudenstadt	Freies R. Freudens.
10)	102.3	1	Freiburg Vogtsberg	R. Dreyeckland
7)	102.6	1	Ulm-Ermingen	R. FreeFM
9)	104.1	0.1	Baiersbronn	Freies R. Freudens.
12)	104.5	0.5	Hohe Möhr	R. Kanal Ratte
3)	104.8	1	Karlsruhe	Querfunk
2)	104.8	0.1	Crailsheim	R. StHörfunk
1)	105.4	0.1	Heidelberg Königstuhl	bermuda.funk

Addresses & other information:
1) Brückenstr. 2-4, 68167 Mannheim; **W:** bermudafunk.org. Also rel. R. Aktiv (Universität Mannheim, Postfach 144, 68131 Mannheim); **W:** radioaktiv-online.de; Mon-Wed 0600-1000 and 1700-1900, Thu-Fri 2300-1000 and 1700-1900, Sun 1900-2100 – **2)** Haalstr. 9, 74523 Schwäbisch Hall; **W:** sthoerfunk.de – **3)** Steinstr. 23, 76133 Karlsruhe; **W:** querfunk.de, rel. Mon-Fri 0600-1100 and Mon-Thu 1600-2100 stn. 4) – **4)** Hochschule für Musik, Postfach 6040, 76040 Karlsruhe (studio location: Wolfartsweierer Str. 7a); **W:** lernradio.de – **5)** Freies R. für Stuttgart, Rieckestr. 24, 70190 Stuttgart; **W:** freies-radio.de – **6)** Hochschulradio Stuttgart, Nobelstr. 10, 70569 Stuttgart; **W:** horads.de – **7)** Söflinger Str. 206, 89077 Ulm; **W:** freefm.de – **8)** Hechinger Str. 203, 72072 Tübingen; **W:** wueste-welle.de Rel. Tue-Thu 0700-0800 Helle Welle (religious) – **9)** Freies R. Freudenstadt, Forststr. 23, 72250 Freudenstadt; **W:** radio-fds.de – **10)** Adlerstr. 12, 79098 Freiburg; **W:** rdl.de – **11)** Georges-Köhler-Allee Geb. 076, 79110 Freiburg; **W:** echo-fm.uni-freiburg.de – **12)** Bahnhofstr. 3, 79650 Schopfheim; **W:** kanalrattefm.de
DAB: 17 txs on ch. 5C Deutschlandfunk, Deutschlandfunk Kultur, Deutschlandfunk Nova, Dokumente & Debatten, Absolut Relax, Energy, ERF Plus, Klassik Radio, Radio Bob, Radio Horeb, Schlagerparadies, Sunshine Live, Schwarzwaldradio – 11 txs on ch. 11B Antenne 1, Baden FM, bigFM, Die neue 107.7, Die neue Welle, Donau 3 FM, egoFM, Hitradio Ohr, R. 7, R. B2 Schlager, R. Regenbogen, Regenbogen 2, R. Teddy, R. Ton, Rockantenne BW, Seefunk.

L) BAYERN

Media institution: Bayerische Landeszentrale für Neue Medien (BLM) ✉ Heinrich-Lübke-Straße 27, 81737 München ☎ +49 89 638 080 🖷 +49 89 63808140; **W:** blm.de
FM networks:

Location	Ant.B.	Rock.	Klass	egoFM	Galaxy	kW
Amberg	–	–	–	–	105.5	0.1
Ansbach	–	–	–	–	105.8	0.1
Aschaffenburg	103.0	–	–	–	91.6	25/0.1
Augsburg	104.2	87.9	92.2	94.8	–	0.1/0.3
Bad Reichenhall	103.7	–	–	–	–	0.3
Bamberg	101.1	–	–	–	104.7	25/0.5
Bayreuth	–	–	–	–	92.7	0.1
Bayrischzell	106.7	–	–	–	–	0.1
Berchtesgaden	107.9	–	–	–	–	0.3
Breithart	101.5	–	–	–	–	25
Brotjacklriegel	103.5	–	–	–	–	100
Coburg	103.8	–	–	–	90.4	5/0.2
Dillberg	100.6	–	–	–	–	25
Eichstätt	100.2	–	–	–	–	25
Enterbach	101.1	–	–	–	–	0.5
Erding	–	87.9	–	–	–	0.1
Erlangen	–	–	–	106.2	–	0.2
Freising	–	95,0	–	–	–	0.1
Fürth	–	–	–	91.0	–	0.2
Grünten	104.4	–	–	–	–	50
Heidelstein	101.9	–	–	–	–	100
Herzogstand	102.0	–	–	–	–	0.1
Hochries	107.7	–	–	–	–	50
Hof	–	–	–	–	94.0	0.2
Högl-Freilassing	105.3	–	–	–	–	1
Hohenpeißenb.	103.8	–	–	–	–	25
Hoher Bogen	101.9	–	–	–	–	50
Ingolstadt	–	–	–	–	107.9	0.1
Isen	–	88.8	–	–	–	0.5
Kirchseeon	–	93.0	–	–	–	0.6
Kempten	–	–	–	–	88.1	0.3
Konradsreuth	–	–	–	–	98.1	0.1
Landshut	99.3	–	–	–	99.8	0.2
Lindau	99.0	–	–	–	–	0.5
Moosinning	–	99.4	–	–	–	0.5
Münchberg	–	–	–	–	98.1	0.1
München	101.3	94.5	107.2	100.8	–	0.3
Naila	–	–	–	–	96.5	0.1
Nördlingen	103.3	–	–	–	–	25
Nürnberg	–	–	105.1	103.6	–	0.5/0.3
Oberaudorf	94.6	–	–	–	–	0.3
Ochsenkopf	103.2	–	–	–	–	100
Passau	102.1	–	–	–	91.7	1/0.2
Pfaffenhofen	92.6	–	–	–	–	0.5
Regensburg	103.0	–	91.1	107.5	–	25/0.3/0.3
Reit im Winkel	101.6	–	–	–	–	0.1
Rosenheim	–	–	–	–	106.6	0.1
Selb	–	–	–	–	93.4	0.1
Sonthofen	93.6	–	–	–	–	0.1
Traunstein	103.7	–	–	–	–	5
Ulm	104.8	–	–	–	–	0.1
Weiden	–	–	–	–	89.8	0.1
Weiler Simm.	106.0	–	–	–	–	0.1
Wunsiedel	–	–	–	–	97.3	0.2
Würzburg	104.4	–	92.1	95.8	–	5/0.3
Zugspitze	102.7	–	–	–	–	2

Addresses & other information:
Antenne Bayern (AC), **Rockantenne** (rock): Münchener Straße 101c, 85737 Ismaning; also via Astra 1N, 12.148GHz h; **W:** antenne.de rockantenne.de – **Klassik R.:** see O) – **egoFM:** Leopoldstraße 254, 80807 München; also via Astra 1M, 12.460GHz; **W:** egofm.de Alternative – **R. Galaxy:** Lilienthalstraße 3c, 93049 Regensburg, **W:** radiogalaxy.de CHR. Mon-Fri 1400-1800 local prgr, produced by stns 17), 26), 29), 30/31), 32), 33), 35) (R. Euroherz), 36), 41), 42), 43) and 48) listed below

Local stations:

FM	MHz	kW	Site	Station
39)	87.9	0.3	Straubing Bogenberg	R. AWN
35)	88.0	5	Großer Waldstein	extra~rad. / Euroherz
19)	88.1	0.1	Krumbach-Kirchberg	R. Prima 1
18)	88.2	0.2	Kaufbeuren	R. Ostallgäu
51)	88.2	0.1	Bad Reichenhall	R. Untersberg
32)	88.5	0.5	Bamberg Rothof	R. Bamberg
36)	88.5	0.1	Tirschenreuth	R. Ramasuri
27)	88.6	0.1	Karlstadt	R. Charivari
5)	89.0	0.3	München Olympiaturm	2DAY/Neues Europa
42)	89.0	0.1	Dingolfing	R. Trausnitz
51)	89.0	0.1	Högl-Freilassing	R. Untersberg

FM	MHz	kW	Site	Station
26)	89.1	0.1	Wassertrüdingen	R. 8
31)	89.2	0.5	Coburg Eckardtsberg	R. EINS
17)	89.3	0.1	Oberstdorf-Steinach	RSA R.
40)	89.3	0.2	Regen Geiskopf	Unser R. Deggendorf
26)	89.4	0.5	Ansbach Ludwigshöhe	R. 8
24)	89.7	0.1	Dillingen	RT.1 Nordschwaben
38)	89.7	0.3	Regensburg Ziegetsberg	gong fm
41)	89.7	0.3	Bad Griesbach	Unser R. Passau
26)	89.8	0.1	Dinkelsbühl	R. 8
45)	89.8	0.1	Landsberg-Stoffen	R. 106.4
31)	90.0	0.1	Kronach-Neuses	R. EINS
19)	90.2	0.32	Bad Grönenbach	R. Prima 1
26)	90.2	0.1	Gunzenhausen	R. 8
47)	90.2	0.1	Miesbach-Bergham	R. Alpenwelle
21)	90.3	0.1	Günzburg	Hitradio X
26)	90.4	0.2	Neuastadt / Aisch	R. 8
27)	90.4	0.1	Gemünden / Lohr	R. Charivari
49)	90.4	0.1	Mühldorf	Inn-Salzach-Welle
30)	90.5	0.1	Bad Kissingen	R. PrimaTon
29)	90.8	0.2	Alzenau	R. Primavera
47)	91.7	0.1	Holzkirchen Jasberg	R. Alpenwelle
42)	91.8	0.2	Pfeffenhausen-Stollnried	R. Trausnitz
47)	92.0	0.1	Wolfratshausen	R. Alpenwelle
6)	92.4	0.3	München Olympiaturm	(shared freq.)
16)	92.7	0.1	Weiler Simmerberg	Welle Bodensee
37)	92.7	0.4	Hoher Bogen	Charivari Regensbg.
49)	92.7	0.3	Reichertsheim	Inn-Salzach-Welle
13)	92.9	0.3	Nürnberg	Hi R. N1
17)	93.0	0.1	Immenstadt	RSA R.
49)	93.1	0.1	Burgkirchen-Gendorf	Inn-Salzach-Welle
2)	93.3	0.3	München Olympiaturm	Energy 93.3
33)	93.3	0.1	Pegnitz	R. Mainwelle
23)	93.4	0.3	Augsburg	R. Fantasy
9)	93.6	0.3	Erlangen	Energy Nürnberg
36)	93.6	0.1	Waidhaus Fischerberg	R. Ramasuri
19)	93.9	0.3	Mindelheim-Altensteig	R. Prima 1
41)	93.9	0.3	Vilshofen-Otterkirchen	Unser R. Passau
30)	94.0	0.1	Bad Brückenau	R. PrimaTon
37)	94.0	1	Seubersdorf Göschberg	Charivari Regensbg.
11)	94.5	0.3	Nürnberg	R. F / Jazztime
43)	94.6	0.1	Schrobenhausen	R. IN / R. ND1
47)	95.0	0.2	Bad Tölz	R. Alpenwelle
35)	95.1	0.1	Marktredwitz	extra~r. / Euroherz
36)	95.3	1	Hirschberg Rothbühl	R. Ramasuri
31)	95.4	0.3	Lichtenfels	R. EINS
43)	95.4	0.1	Ingolstadt	R. IN
3)	95.5	0.3	München Olympiaturm	Charivari 95.5
24)	95.6	1	Harburg Hühnerberg	RT.1 Nordschwaben
30)	95.7	0.1	Haßfurt/Main	R. PrimaTon
39)	95.7	0.1	Mallersdorf-Hofkirchen	R. AWN
14)	95.8	0.3	Nürnberg	R. Z
4)	96.3	0.3	München Olympiaturm	R. Gong 96,3
38)	96.3	0.32	Burglengenfeld	gong fm
25)	96.4	1	Fürth	star fm
32)	96.6	0.1	Forchheim Pinzberg	R. Bamberg
45)	96.6	0.1	Starnberg	R. 106.4
17)	96.7	0.1	Kempten town	RSA R.
22)	96.7	0.3	Augsburg	Kit R. RT.1
48)	96.7	0.3	Flintsbach Dandlberg	Charivari Rosenheim
12)	97.1	0.3	Nürnberg	Gong 97.1
24)	97.1	0.1	Donauwörth	RT.1 Nordschwaben
41)	97.2	0.1	Grafenau Liebersberg	Unser R. Passau
26)	97.3	0.3	Feuchtwangen	R. 8
38)	97.3	0.1	Schwandorf Weinberg	gong fm
46)	97.5	0.1	Weilheim	R. Oberland
17)	97.6	1	Kempten Blender	RSA R.
18)	98.0	0.1	Füssen	R. Ostallgäu
51)	98.1	0.1	Berchtesgaden	R. Untersberg
37)	98.2	0.3	Regensburg Ziegetsberg	Charivari Regensb.
41)	98.3	0.2	Passau-Haidenhof	Unser R. Passau
10)	98.6	0.3	Nürnberg	Charivari 98.6
40)	98.7	0.1	Deggendorf-Hochobernd.	Unser R. Deggendorf
37)	98.8	0.5	Burglengenfeld	Charivari Regensbg.
34)	98.9	0.1	Stadtsteinach	R. Plassenburg
25)	99.0	0.2	Lauf Moritzberg	star fm
27)	99.0	0.1	Marktheidenfeld	R. Charivari
43)	99.1	0.1	Eichstätt-Seuversholz	R. IN

FM	MHz	kW	Site	Station
50)	99.4	0.3	Haslach-Einham	R. Chiemgau
36)	99.9	0.2	Weiden Fischerberg	R. Ramasuri
47)	99.9	0.1	Herzogstand	R. Alpenwelle
29)	100.4	1	Aschaffenburg	R. Primavera
30)	100.5	0.5	Schweinfurth	R. PrimaTon
26)	100.8	0.1	Burgbernheim	R. 8
43)	101.2	0.2	Neuburg/Donau	R. IN / R. ND1
46)	101.2	0.1	Oberammergau	R. Oberland
46)	101.4	0.3	Sindelsdorf	R. Oberland
30)	101.5	1	Bad Neustadt-Unsleben	R. PrimaTon
41)	101.5	0.1	Freyung Geyersberg	Unser R. Passau
50)	101.5	0.3	Trostberg	R. Chiemgau
34)	101.6	5	Kulmbach Rehberg	R. Plassenburg
27)	102.4	0.3	Würzburg	R. Charivari
37)	102.6	0.32	Waldmünchen Perlhütte	Charivari Regensbg.
16)	103.6	0.5	Lindau Hoyerberg	Welle Bodensee
36)	103.9	0.1	Amberg Eisberg	R. Ramasuri
37)	103.9	0.5	Kelheim Leitenberg	Charivari Regensbg.
1)	104.0	0.1	München Blutenburgstr.	R. Arabella
42)	104.1	1	Landshut	R. Trausnitz
48)	104.2	0.3	Oberaudorf-Hölzelsau	Charivari Rosenheim
33)	104.3	10	Oschenberg	R. Mainwelle
47)	104.3	0.5	Enterbach-Ringberg	R. Alpenwelle
46)	104.6	0.1	Herzogstand	R. Oberland
43)	104.8	0.2	Pfaffenhofen Wolfsberg	R. IN
36)	105.1	0.5	Wiesau-Fuchsmühle	R. Ramasuri
1)	105.2	25	München-Isen	R. Arabella
18)	105.2	0.1	Obergünzburg	R. Ostallgäu
43)	105.4	0.1	Beilngries	R. IN
37)	105.5	0.3	Lam-Koppenhof	Charivari Regensbg.
42)	105.5	0.32	Landau	R. Trausnitz
20)	105.9	5	Ulm-Ermingen	R. Donau 1
37)	105.9	0.32	Nabburg Galgenberg	Charivari Regensbg.
32)	106.1	0.1	Burglesau Reisberg	R. Bamberg
46)	106.2	0.3	Garmisch-Partenkirchen	R. Oberland
47)	106.2	0.1	Schliersbergalm	R. Alpenwelle
18)	106.3	0.5	Eisenberg Schloßberg	R. Ostallgäu
36)	106.4	0.1	Königstein Gr. Ossinger	R. Ramasuri
45)	106.4	2	Fürstenfeldbruck	R. 106.4
49)	106.4	0.3	Lohkirchen	Inn-Salzach-Welle
8)	106.5	0.1	Nürnberg	afk max
28)	106.9	5	Würzburg	R. Gong 106,9
9)	106.9	0.3	Nürnberg	Energy Nürnberg
42)	107.4	1	Pfarrkirchen-Postm.	R. Trausnitz
25)	107.8	0.2	Schwabach Heidenberg	star fm
40)	107.9	0.2	Brotjacklriegel	Unser R. Deggendorf

+ 28 txs less than 0.1kW

Addresses & other information:

Dienstleistungsgesellschaft für Bayerische Lokal-Radioprogramme (BLR) Rosenheimer Straße 145c, 81671 München **W:** blr.de. Provides network prgr. and other content for many of the above listed stns

1) Paul-Heyse-Str. 2-4, 80336 München, **W:** radioarabella.de – **2)** Pestalozzistr. 15-19, 80469 München, **W:** energy.de/muenchen – **3)** Postfach 20 16 09, 80016 München (studio location as stn. 1), **W:** charivari.de – **4)** Franz-Joseph-Str. 14, 80801 München, **W:** radiogong.de – **5)** Schneemanstr. 25, 81369 München, **W:** radio2-day.de Rel. Sat 2300-Mon 0500 R. Neues Europa: Konviktstr. 1, 85049 Ingolstadt – **6)** Radio Horeb, Postfach 1165, 87501 Immenstadt; **W:** radiohoreb.de Religious. Also via Astra 1N, 12.604GHz h. On 92.4MHz Mon-Fri 0000-1300, Sat/Sun 2300-0500, Sun 0900-1200 and 1300-2300. Christliches Radio München, Postfach 310201, 80102 München; **W:** christlichesradio.de Religious, Mon-Fri 1300-1400, Sun 0800-0900 and 1200-1300. Lora München, Gravelottestr. 6, 81667 München, **W:** lora924.de Non-commercial. Mon-Thu 1500-2300, Fri 1500-2000. Feierwerk München, Hansastr. 39, 81373 München; **W:** feierwerk.de Non-commercial. Fr 2000-Sat 2300 and Sun 0500-0900 – **7)** M94.5 no longer on FM, freq. surrendered to Rockantenne – **8)** Fürther Str. 212, 90429 Nürnberg, **W:** afkmax.de Journalist training stn. – **9)** Ostendstr. 100, 90482 Nürnberg, **W:** energy.de/nuernberg – **10),11),12),13)** Funkhaus Nürnberg, Senefelder Str. 7, 90409 Nürnberg, **W:** funkhaus.de 92,0MHz also rel. Camillo 92.9 (Mon, Tue, Sun 2000-2200), R. AREF (Sun 0900-1100), Pray 92.9 (Sun 1100-1200), R. Meilensteine (Sun 0800-0900), 94.5MHz also rel. Jazztime Nürnberg (Mon 2100-2200, Thu 2000-2100). – **14)** Kopernikusplatz 12, 90459 Nürnberg, **W:** radio-z.net. 1300-0100 only, other times rel. stn. 25) – 15) left blank – **16) W:** welle-bodensee.de – **17)** Rottachstr. 17, 87439 Kempten, **W:** allgaeuseite.de/

rsa_radio – **18) W:** roal.de – **19)** Hirschgasse 1, 87700 Memmingen, **W:** prima1.de – **20)** Leipzigstr. 26, 88400 Biberach, **W:** radiodonau1.de – **21)** Augsburger Str. 112, 89312 Günzburg, **W:** hitradiox.de – **22)** Curt-Frenzel-Str. 4, 86167 Augsburg, **W:** radio-rt1.de – **23)** Ludwigstr. 1, 86150 Augsburg, **W:** fantasy.de Rel. Mon 2100-2400 Kanal C (university stn.): Eichleitnerstr. 30, 86159 Augsburg, **W:** kanal-c.de – **24)** Artur-Proeller-Str. 1, 86609 Donauwörth, **W:** rt1-nordschwaben.de – **25)** O´Brien Str. 2, 91126 Schwabach; **W:** rocksender.de/rocksender_nuernberg/ – **26)** Postfach 8, 91510 Ansbach (studio location: Schalkhäuser Landstr. 5), **W:** radio8.de – **27), 28)** Semmelstr. 15, 97070 Würzburg, **W:** charivari.fm and gong.fm Also rel. Radio Opera – **29)** Am Funkhaus 1, 63743 Aschaffenburg, **W:** radio-primavera.de – **30), 31)** Seifartshofstr. 21, 96450 Coburg, **W:** radioeins.com – **32)** Gutenbergstr. 5, 96050 Bamberg, **W:** radio-bamberg.de – **33)** Postfach 10 11 61, 95411 Bayreuth (studio location: Richard-Wagner-Str. 33), **W:** mainwelle.de – **34)** E.C.-Baumann-Str. 5, 95326 Kulmbach, **W:** radio-plassenburg.de – **35)** 0900-1000, 1200-1300 and 1800-2000 extra~radio, Postfach 1745, 95016 Hof (studio location: Kreuzsteinstr. 2-6), **W:** extra-radio.de; otherwise: R. Euroherz, Pfarr 1, 95028 Hof, **W:** euroherz.de – **36)** Unterer Markt 35, 92637 Weiden, **W:** ramasuri.de – **37), 38)** Lilienthalstr. 3c, 93049 Regensburg, **W:** radiocharivari.de and gongfm.de – **39), 40)** Bahnhofstr. 28, 94469 Deggendorf, **W:** unserradio.de – **41)** Medienstr. 5, 94036 Passau, **W:** as stn. 40) – **42)** Altstadt 361, 84028 Landshut, **W:** radio-trausnitz.de – **43)** Donaustr. 11, 85049 Ingolstadt, **W:** radio-in.de, rel. 0500-0900 on 94.6/101.2MHz R. ND1 – **44)** Hitwelle no longer in FM, freq. surrendered to Rockantenne – **45)** Schöngeisingerstr. 11, 82256 Fürstenfeldbruck, **W:** radio1064.de – **46)** Postfach 1752, 82467 Garmisch-Partenkirchen (studio location: Marienplatz 17), **W:** radio-oberland.de – **47) W:** radio-alpenwelle.de – **48)** Hafnerstr. 5-7, 83022 Rosenheim, **W:** radio-charivari.de – **49)** Mozartstr. 3a, 84508 Burgkirchen/Alz, **W:** inn-salzach-welle.de – **50)** Rupertistr. 40-42, 83278 Traunstein, **W:** radio-chiemgau.de – **51)** untersberg.de **N.B** stns 49), 50), 51) also rel. prgr. of independent producers

DAB: 21 txs on ch. 5C, use see K) – 58 txs on ch. 11D, Bayerischer Rundfunk prgr. and Antenne Bayern – Wendelstein tx on ch. 7A Alpenwelle, Arabella Kult, Charivari, Galaxy, R. Oberland – 9 txs on ch. 7D, Bayern 1, BR Verkehr, Absolut Hot, egoFM, R. AWN, R. Galaxy, R. Teddy, R. Trausnitz, Oldiewelle Niederbayern, Unser R. – 3 txs on ch. 8B Allgäu Hit, Allgäuer Melodie, Arabella Kult, Galaxy, Griaß di Allgäu, R. Schwaben, RSA, RT1 – 6 txs on ch. 8C Bayern 1, Bayern 2, BR Verkehr, Absolut Hot, egoFM, Galaxy, R. 8, R. Teddy, Rockantenne – Augsburg txs on ch. 9C Arabella Kult, Fantasy Classix, Fantasy Lounge, Galaxy, Mega 80s, Megaradio Bayern, R. Augsburg, R. Schwaben, RT1, RT1 in the mix, RT1 Relax, RT1 Nordschwaben, Smart R. – 26 txs (München/Ulm region) on ch. 10A, Bayern 1, Bayern 2, BR Verkehr, Absolut Hot, egoFM, R. Teddy, Rockantenne – 7 txs (Würzburg region) on ch. 10A Bayern 1, Bayern 2, BR Verkehr, Absolut Hot, Charivari, egoFM, Galaxy, Gong, Primaton, Primavera, R. Hashtag, R. Teddy, Rockantenne – 5 txs on ch. 10B Arabella Kult, Bayern 1, Bayern 2, BR Verkehr, Absolut Hot, R. Teddy, Rockantenne – Nürnberg txs on ch. 10C Charivari, Energy Nürnberg, Gong Nürnberg, Hitr. N1, Lieblingsradio, Max Neo, Megaradio Bayern, R. F, R. Z, Star FM – Ingolstadt txs on ch. 11A Arabella Kult, Galaxy Ingolstadt, Mega 80s, Megaradio Bayern, R. IN, RT1 – München txs on ch. 11C Arabella, Arabella Kult, Charivari, CRM, Digital Classix, Energy München, Feierwerk, Galaxy, Lora, M94.5, MKR-Kirchenradio, R. 2Day, R. Gong, Top FM – 12 txs on ch. 12D, Bayern 1, BR Verkehr, Absolut Hot, Bamberg, Charivari, egoFM, Eins, Euroherz, Extra-R. Hof, egoFM, Galaxy, Gong FM, Kulmbach, Mainwelle, R. Ramasuri, R. Teddy, Rockantenne

M) BERLIN & BRANDENBURG

Media institution: Medienanstalt Berlin-Brandenburg (MABB) Kleine Präsidentenstraße 1, 10178 Berlin ☎ +49 30 264 9670 🖹 +49 30 264 96730 **W:** mabb.de

Berlin txs:

FM	MHz	kW	Site	Station
14)	87.9	1	Alexanderplatz	Star FM
27)	88.4	2	Winterfeldtstraße	(shared)
24)	89.2	*0.5	Schäferberg	R Potsdam
19)	90.2	16	Alexanderplatz	R. Teddy
27)	90.7	0.1	Schäferberg	(shared)
16)	91.0	1	Winterfeldtstraße	ALEX
2)	91.4	100	Alexanderplatz	Berliner Rundfunk
10)	93.6	3	Alexanderplatz	JAM FM
3)	94.3	20	Alexanderplatz	rs2
12)	94.8	4	Schäferberg	BBC WS
17)	96.7	0.8	Winterfeldtstraße	RFI
13)	97.2	0.2	Winterfeldtstraße	R. Russkij
9)	98.2	8	Scholzplatz	R. Paradiso
11)	98.8	1	Alexanderplatz	KISS FM
4)	100.6	13	Alexanderplatz	Flux FM
8)	101.3	5	Alexanderplatz	Klassik R.
15)	101.9	0.5	Alexanderplatz	Metropol FM
5)	103.4	10	Alexanderplatz	Energy Berlin
18)	104.1	0.6	Winterfeldtstraße	KCRW Berlin
6)	104.6	10	Alexanderplatz	104.6 RTL
7)	105.5	5	Alexanderplatz	Spreeradio
21)	106.0	1	Alexanderplatz	R. B2
12)	106.8	2	Scholzplatz	Jazz R.
1)	107.5	40	Alexanderplatz	BB R.

*) directional towards Potsdam

Brandenburg txs:

FM	MHz	kW	Site	Station
24)	87.6	0.4	Brandenburg/Havel	R. Potsdam
5)	87.6	0.2	Prenzlau	Energy Berlin
6)	88.0	1	Crinitz	104.6 RTL
20)	88.3	0.5	Neuruppin	Power R.
6)	89.5	0.5	Elsterwerda-Hohenl.	104.6 RTL
23)	90.3	0.5	Spremberg	R. Cottbus
9)	90.4	0.2	Guben-Reichenbach	R. Paradiso
1)	90.9	0.8	Rhinow	BB R.
3)	91.3	1	Lauchhammer West	rs2
5)	91.6	1.3	Casekow	Energy Berlin
21)	91.6	0.5	Cottbus-Klein Oßnig	R. B2
5)	91.7	0.1	Herzberg/Elster	Energy Berlin
23)	92.1	1	Guben-Reichenbach	R. Cottbus
20)	93.3	0.5	Schwedt	Power R.
22)	93.9	3	Fürstenwalde	HitRadio SKW
20)	94.4	1.3	Perleberg	Power R.
23)	94.5	0.3	Cottbus-Madlow	R. Cottbus
3)	94.7	3	Booßen (Frankf./O.)	rs2
1)	95.0	0.8	Angermünde	BB R.
20)	95.2	0.4	Belzig-Lütte	Power R.
20)	95.3	0.1	Fürstenwalde	Power R.
25)	95.3	0.6	Potsdam	BHeins
1)	95.4	0.8	Eberswalde	BB R.
9)	95.5	0.2	Eisenhüttenstadt	R. Paradiso
3)	95.6	1.3	Cottbus-Klein Oßnig	rs2
5)	96.6	0.5	Wittstock	Energy Berlin
3)	96.7	1	Crinitz	rs2
6)	96.9	1	Luckenwalde	104.6 RTL
21)	97.0	0.6	Potsdam	R. B2
28)	98.0	0.7	Booßen (Frankf./O.)	Pure FM
20)	99.1	0.5	Erkner	Power R.
19)	99.3	0.8	Booßen (Frankf./O.)	R. Teddy
3)	100.1	3	Lübben	rs2
2)	100.9	5	Casekow	Berliner Rundfunk
21)	101.1	0.5	Fürstenwalde	R. B2
1)	102.1	20	Casekow	BB-R.
20)	102.1	0.6	Potsdam	Power R.
2)	102.2	3	Cottbus-Klein Oßnig	Berliner Rundfunk
23)	102.7	0.5	Forst	R. Cottbus
1)	103.7	0.6	Eisenhüttenstadt	BB R.
26)	103.8	1.5	Großräschen	Lausitzwelle
3)	103.9	6	Forst	rs2
2)	104.2	20	Booßen (Frankf./O.)	Berliner Rundfunk
1)	104.3	100	Pritzwalk-Buchholz	BB R.
21)	104.9	0.8	Eberswalde	R. B2
1)	105.0	3	Brandenburg-Krahne	BB R.
22)	105.1	0.8	Königs Wusterh.	HitRadio SKW
9)	105.9	1.6	Booßen (Frankf./O.)	R. Paradiso
3)	106.3	4	Spremberg	rs2
21)	106.9	0.2	Frankfurt/Oder	R. B2
1)	107.2	100	Calau	BB R.
3)	107.3	12	Casekow	rs2
1)	107.8	30	Booßen (Frankf./O.)	BB R.
1)	107.9	5	Gransee	BB R.

Addresses & other information:

1) Großbeerenstr. 185, 14482 Potsdam; **W:** bbradio.de. AC, with short local insertions – **2)** Grunewaldstr. 3, 12165 Berlin; **W:** berliner-rundfunk.de Oldies – **3)** as stn. 2); **W:** rs2.de. AC – **4)** Pfuelstr. 5, 10997 Berlin; **W:** fluxfm.de. Alternative – **5)** Hardenbergstr. 4-5, 10623 Berlin; **W:** energy.de/berlin. CHR – **6), 7)** Kurfürstendamm 207-208, 10719 Berlin; **W:** 104.6rtl.com (CHR), spreeradio.de (oldies) – **8)** see

O) – **9)** Am Kleinen Wannsee 5, 14109 Berlin; **W:** paradiso.de. Soft AC. Run by Protestant church – **10)** as stn. 9); **W:** jamfm.de. Black, also via Astra 1M, 12.460GHz – **11)** as stn. 2); **W:** kissfm.de. CHR – **12)** See International Broadcasting section under UK – **13)** Kochstr. 54, 10969 Berlin; **W:** radio-rb.de. In Russian – **14)** Dircksenstr. 48, 10178 Berlin; **W:** starfm.de. Rock – **15)** Markgrafenstr. 11, 10969 Berlin, **W:** metropolfm.de; prgr. in Turkish. Further txs see K) and T) – **16)** Voltastr. 5, 13355 Berlin; **W:** alex-berlin.de Citizen radio, run by MABB – **17)** See International Broadcasting section under France – **18)** Grunewaldstr. 3, 12165 Berlin; **W:** kcrwberlin.com – **19)** August-Bebel-Str. 26-53, 14482 Potsdam; **W:** radioteddy.de; childrens prgr., also via Astra 1N, 12.148GHz h. Further txs see P), Q), T) – **20)** Potsdamer Str. 131, 10783 Berlin; **W:** powerradio918.de. Oldies – **21)** Pfalzburger Str. 43-44, 10717 Berlin; **W:** radiob2.de German "Schlager" – **22)** Karl-Marx-Str. 116, 15745 Wildau; **W:** hitradio-skw.de. Oldies – **23)** Schloßkirchplatz 3, 03046 Cottbus; **W:** radiocottbus.de AC – **24)** Brandenburger Str. 48, 14467 Potsdam; **W:** radio-potsdam.de – **25)** August-Bebel-Str. 26-53, Fach 43, 14482 Potsdam; **W:** bheins.de – **26)** see V), stn. 8) – **27)** Shared use by various programmers, organized by stn. 16) **W:** 88vier.de – **28)** Wichertstr. 16, 10439 Berlin; **W:** pure-fm.de

DAB: 9 txs on ch. 5C see K) – Alexanderplatz tx on ch. 7B Berliner Rundfunk, Germany One, Jam FM, Kiss FM, Lulu FM, Maxx FM, Nice Mix, Pure FM, R. B2, R. Gold, R. Potsdam, R. Teddy, RS2, Starsat, Top 100 – Alexanderplatz/Booßen/Calau txs on ch. 12D 104.6 RTL, BB R., bigFM, Domradio, ERF Pop, Hit 104, Peli One, R. B2, R. Cottbus, R. Paloma, R. Paradiso, Rockantenne, Rockland, Spreeradio, Star FM.

N) BREMEN

Media institution: Bremische Landesmedienanstalt (Brema) ✉ Grünenweg 26, 28215 Bremen ☎ +49 421 334940 🖷 +49 421 323533 **W:** bremische-landesmedienanstalt.de

FM	MHz	kW	Site	Station
1)	89.8	1	Bremen-Walle	Energy Bremen
4)	90.7	0.2	Bremerhaven	R. Weser TV
4)	92.5	0.2	Bremen Neuenstr.	R. Weser TV
3)	97.2	0.5	Bremen-Walle	Metropol FM
1)	104.3	8	Bremerhaven	Energy Bremen
2)	104.8	0.1	Bremen-Walle	R. Teddy
5)	107.6	0.2	Bremen-Walle	R. 21
2)	107.9	0.3	Bremerhaven	R. Teddy

Addresses & other information:

1) Erste Schlachtpforte, 28195 Bremen; **W:** energy.de/bremen CHR – **2)** see M), stn. 19 – **3)** See M), stn. 15 – **4)** Richtweg 14, 28195 Bremen; **W:** radioweser.tv Citizen radio – **5)** see R)

DAB: Ch. 5C see K) – ch. 7D 90vier, Energy Bremen, ffn, Nordsee, R. B2, R. Roland.

O) HAMBURG & SCHLESWIG-HOLSTEIN

Media institution: Medienanstalt Hamburg / Schleswig-Holstein (MA HSH) ✉ Rathausallee 72-76, 22846 Norderstedt ☎ +49 40 3690050 🖷 +49 40 36900555 **W:** ma-hsh.de

FM	R.SH	delta	Bob	Klass.	kW
Ahrensburg	–	96.5	–	–	2
Bredstedt	–	–	98.1	–	0.1
Bungsberg (Eutin)	100.2	104.1	106.2	97.2	2x50/0.2
Flensburg-Freienwill	101.4	105.6	–	–	20
Flensburg-Harrislee	–	–	88.5	106.5	0.5
Garding	–	–	94.1	91.7	0.5
Hamburg-Bergedorf	102.0	107.7	93.7	–	0.1
Hamburg Hertz-T.	100.0	93.4	–	98.1	2x2/0.1
Heide-Welmbüttel	103.8	100.4	–	–	15
Heide (town)	–	–	96.9		0.3
Helgoland (island)	100.0	103.5	101.6	89.8	0.1
Husum	–	–	92.0	–	0.1
Itzehoe	–	–	104.9	92.7	1/0.5
Kaltenkirchen	102.9	107.4	101.1	–	20
Kiel	102.4	105.9	97.0	97.4	2x15/0.3
Lauenburg	102.5	105.6	97.4	–	1/1/0.3
Lübeck	–	–	91.5		0.3
Mölln-Berkenthin	101.5	107.9	91.5	93.6	2x20/0.3
Neumünster	–	–	88.9	–	0.5
Niebüll	–	–	107.2	94.7	0.2
Rendsburg	–	–	93.6	92.9	0.5
Schleswig (town)	–	–	92.4	100.8	1/0.5
Schleswig-Borgwedel	–	–	–	93.9	0.5
Westerland (Sylt)	102.8	104.8	89.1	89.8	5/5/1/0.5

Addresses & other information:

R.SH (AC), **delta radio** (CHR), **R. Bob** (rock): Wittland 3, 24109 Kiel; **W:** rsh.de deltaradio.de radiobob.de – **Klassik R.:** Planckstraße 15, 22765 Hamburg; **W:** klassikradio.de Light classical and lounge music. Further txs see K), L), M), R). Also via Astra 1M, 12.460GHz

Hamburg area only:

FM	MHz	kW	Site	Station
1)	88.1	0.1	Bergedorf	Hamburg Zwei
1)	88.5	2	Otterndorf*)	R. Hamburg
2)	91.7	0.1	H.-Hertz-Turm	917xfm
2)	93.6	2	Otterndorf*)	Alsterradio
1)	95.0	0.1	H.-Hertz-Turm	Hamburg Zwei
3)	97.1	0.1	H.-Hertz-Turm	Energy Hamburg
3)	100.9	0.1	Bergedorf	Energy Hamburg
3)	101.6	0.1	Wedel	Energy Hamburg
1)	103.6	80	Moorfleet	R. Hamburg
1)	104.0	0.2	H.-Hertz-Turm	R. Hamburg
1)	105.8	0.5	Ahrensburg	Hamburg Zwei
2)	106.8	40	Rahlstedt	106!8 rock'n pop

*) tx in Niedersachsen, serving Neuwerk and Scharhörn islands (belonging to Hamburg)

Addresses & other information:

1) Postfach 10 01 23, 20001 Hamburg (studio location: Spitalerstraße 10); **W:** radiohamburg.de (AC), hamburg-zwei.de (former Oldie 95, relaunched in 2014). On 104.0MHz at times prgr. from Flux FM, see M), stn. 4) – **2)** Messberg 4, 20095 Hamburg; **W:** 106acht.de (AC), 917xfm.de (alternative) – **3)** Winterhuder Marktplatz 6, 22299 Hamburg; **W:** energy.de/hamburg CHR. **F.Pl.:** Changes of freq. usage, subject of legal action at time of editing.

Non-commercial stations:

FM	MHz	kW	Site	Station
1)	93.0	0.1	Hamburg Hertz-Turm	Freies Sender Kombinat
2)	96.0	0.1	Hamburg Hertz-Turm	TIDE 96.0 / HLR
4)	97.6	0.5	Garding	OK Westküste
5)	98.8	0.5	Lübeck-Stockelsdorf	OK Lübeck
4)	98.8	0.1	Husum	OK Westküste
3)	101.2	0.1	Kiel	Kiel FM
5)	105.2	0.1	Heide	OK Westküste

Addresses & other information:

1) Schulterblatt 23c, 20357 Hamburg; **W:** fsk-hh.org – **2) TIDE 96.0**, Uferstraße 2, 22081 Hamburg; **W:** tidenet.de Run by Hamburg Media School. Mon 0500-2300 and thorough Tue 0500 til Sun 0500. **Hamburger Lokalradio,** Kulturzentrum LOLA, Lohbrügger Landstraße 8, 21031 Hamburg; **W:** hhlr.de On 96.0MHz Sun 0500 til Mon 0500 and night Mon/Tue 2300-0500 – **3)** Hamburger Chaussee 36, 24113 Kiel; **W:** kielfm.de – **4)** Landvogt-Johannsen-Str. 11, 25746 Heide; **W:** okwestkueste.de – **5)** Kanalstr. 42-48, 23554 Lübeck; **W:** ok-luebeck.de

DAB: 8 txs on ch. 5C see K) – Hamburg tx on ch. 11C 80s80s, 917XFM, Antenne Sylt, ERF Pop, ffn, Hamburg Zwei, HLRdigital, Lulu FM, Megaradio, Peli One, R. B2, R. Hamburg, R. Paradiso, Rockantenne, R.SH, Tide R.

P) HESSEN

Media institution: Hessische Landesanstalt für Privaten Rundfunk (LPR) ✉ Wilhelmshöher Allee 262, 34131 Kassel ☎ +49 561 935860 🖷 +49 561 9358630; **W:** lpr-hessen.de

FM	FFH	plan.	Bob	Ant	harm	kW
Alsfeld	88.1	–	101.5	–	94.1	4/0.1
Bad Camberg	–	99.8	–	–	105.4	0.2
Bad Hersfeld	95.9	–	99.8	–	88.4	0.1/0.3
Bad Nauheim	–	104.6	106.6	90.7	100.4	0.3/1
Bensheim	–	–	103.3	–	107.5	0.2
Bingen	106.9	103.4	–	–	101.8	0.2/0.3
Butzbach	–	–	–	–	–	0.1
Darmstadt	–	91.1	92.4	100.8	93.0	0.2/0.5
Delkenheim	–	–	–	88.0	–	0.3
Dieburg	–	90.1	99.5	–	104.7	1/0.2
Dillenburg	100.0	–	–	–	–	30
Driedorf	106.8	–	–	–	–	30
Eisenberg	–	100.3	–	–	–	50
Eltville	90.3	–	–	–	–	0.2
Eschwege	–	104.6	103.0	–	88.3	0.5/0.3
Feldberg	105.9	–	–	–	–	100
Frankfurt	–	100.2	101.4	95.1	97.6	1/0.1
Fritzlar	–	–	88.4	–	106.6	0.1
Fulda	–	99.9	105.7	–	95.7	0.2/0.3
Gelnhausen	–	93.9	–	–	–	0.2
Gießen	–	93.7	92.6	105.2	102.0	0.5/0.1
Glashütten	–	–	–	–	93.2	0.5

FM	FFH	plan.	Bob	Ant	harm	kW
Habichtsw.	103.7	–	–	–	–	20
Hanau	–	–	–	97.3	106.8	0.5
Heidelstein*	100.9	–	–	–	–	50
Hofgeismar	–	–	88.8	–	–	0.1
Hoherodskopf	–	–	94.7	–	–	0.1
Homberg	–	–	99.3	–	–	0.1
H. Meißner	105.1	–	–	–	–	100
Idstein	–	–	–	–	93.2	0.5
Kassel	–	104.6	99.4	–	96.6	0.5/0.2
Krehberg	105.0	–	–	–	–	20
Korbach	107.7	94.0	96.5	–	107.4	20/0.2
Limburg	–	97.6	90.2	–	92.1	0.5/0.2
Marburg	–	101.0	103.9	–	96.2	0.3/0.1
Michelstadt	96.1	–	98.5	–	104.6	0.1/1
Offenbach	–	–	–	–	99.3	0.3
Reinhardshain	–	92.9	–	–	–	0.2
Rimberg	–	–	90.5	–	–	0.1
Rotenburg	–	–	96.8	–	104.5	0.3/0.1
Schlüchtern	–	–	101.3	–	–	0.2
Schotten	–	–	94.7	–	–	0.1
Vogelsberg	–	–	94.7	–	–	0.1
Wetzlar	–	103.7	88.2	105.0	101.3	0.3/0.5
Wiesbaden	102.0	90.1	101.4	95.1	88.2	0.1/0.5

Addresses & other information:
Hit-R. FFH (AC)**, Planet R.** (black/CHR)**, harmony.fm** (oldies)**:** FFH-Platz 1, 61111 Bad Vilbel; **W:** ffh.de, planet-radio.de, harmonyfm.de; also via Astra 1L, 12.633GHz – **R. Bob**, Friedrich-Ebert-Str. 2, 34117 Kassel; **W:** radiobob.de. Rock – **Antenne Frankfurt**, Rüsselsheimer Str. 22, 60326 Frankfurt am Main; **W:** antenne-frankfurt.de

Other stations:

FM	MHz	kW	Site	Station
8)	90.0	0.1	Wetzlar	ERF Pop
5)	90.1	0.1	Marburg-Lahnberge	R. Unerhört
3)	90.9	0.3	Rüsselsheim	R. Rüsselsheim
9)	91.7	0.2	Kassel	R. Teddy
1)	91.8	0.1	Frankfurt-Ginnheim	R. X
9)	93.5	0.1	Rotenburg	R. Teddy
9)	93.8	0.3	Bad Hersfeld	R. Teddy
2)	92.5	0.1	Wiesbaden	R. RheinWelle 92,5
7)	96.5	0.3	Witzenhausen	RundFunk Meißner
10)	99.2	0.3	Fulda	Domradio
7)	99.4	0.1	Sontra	RundFunk Meißner
7)	99.7	0.5	Eschwege	RundFunk Meißner
7)	102.6	0.3	Hessisch Lichtenau	RundFunk Meißner
9)	102.8	0.3	Fulda	R. Teddy
4)	103.4	0.3	Darmstadt	R. Darmstadt
6)	105.8	0.5	Kassel Tannenwäldchen	Freies R. Kassel

Addresses & other information:
1) Schützenstr. 12, 60311 Frankfurt; **W:** radiox.de – **2)** Postfach 49 20, 65039 Wiesbaden; **W:** rheinwelle.de – **3)** Ludwigstr. 13-15, 65428 Rüsselsheim; **W:** radiok2r.de – **4)** Steubenplatz 12, 64293 Darmstadt; **W:** radiodarmstadt.de – **5)** Rudolf-Bultmann-Str. 2b, 35039 Marburg, **W:** radio-rum.de – **6), 7)** Niederhoner Str. 1, 37269 Eschwege, **W:** eschwege.de/rfm – **8)** Berliner Ring 62, 35576 Wetzlar, **W:** erf.de German affiliate of Trans World Radio (see International Broadcasting section under USA/Austria), now mostly using digital platforms – **9)** see M) – **10)** see S)
DAB: 10 txs on ch. 5C see K) – 4 txs on ch. 6A Absolut Hot, FFH, FFH Rock, FRK, harmony.fm, Planet Black Beats, Planet R., R. B2, RFM, Rockantenne – 4 txs on ch. 12C Absolut Hot, Antenne Mainz, Antenne Frankfurt, ERF Pop, FFH, harmony.fm, Lulu FM, Planet R., R. B2, R. Darmstadt, R. Rüsselsheim, R. X, Rheinwelle, Rockantenne.

Q) MECKLENBURG-VORPOMMERN

Media institution: Medienanstalt Mecklenburg-Vorpommern ✉Bleicheufer 1, 19053 Schwerin ☎ +49 385 5588 10 🖷 +49 385 5588 130 **W:** medienanstalt-mv.de

Location	A.MV	Osts	Parad	Tedd	B2	kW
Ahrenshoop	–	–	–	–	103.0	0.6
Demmin	–	107.9	–	–	–	0.2
Garz (Rügen)	105.1	107.6	–	–	–	50
Greifswald	–	–	–	–	87.8	0.8
Grevesmühlen	105.8	94.7	–	–	–	0.2/0.1
Güstrow	107.7	98.0	–	–	–	1/0.4
Helpterberg	103.8	105.8	–	–	–	100
Heringsdorf	105.4	103.3	–	–	–	10/2
Röbel	93.8	92.2	–	–	–	50/0.1
Rostock	100.8	104.8	89.7	95.8	106.5	130/0.3
Schwerin	101.3	107.3	103.9	102.9	90.1	100/0.2
Stralsund	–	–	103.6	93.0	98.9	0.1/0.4
Waren	98.3	93.0	–	–	–	0.2/0.1
Wismar	88.7	93.7	–	–	97.0	0.2/0.1
Wolgast	–	100.0	–	–	–	0.5

Addresses & other information:
Antenne MV, Rosa-Luxemburg-Straße 25/26, 18055 Rostock; **W:** antennemv.de. AC – **Ostseewelle**, Warnowufer 59a, 18057 Rostock; **W:** ostseewelle.de. CHR – **Radio Paradiso, Radio Teddy, Radio B2** see M)

Local stations:

FM	MHz	kW	Site	Station
1)	88.0	0.8	Neubrandenburg	NB-Radiotreff
3)	90.2	0.1	Rostock	LOHRO
4)	92.4	0.1	Rostock	sunshine live
2)	98.1	0.2	Greifswald	R. 98eins
1)	98.7	0.1	Malchin	NB-Radiotreff
4)	103.1	0.2	Stralsund	sunshine live
	105.6	(0.2)	Rostock	(to be allocated)

Addresses & other information:
1) Treptower Str. 9, 17033 Neubrandenburg; **W:** nb-radiotreff.de; run by Medienanstalt, also prgr. from Malchin studio – **2)** Domstr. 12, 17489 Greifswald; **W:** 98eins.de; run by university, Mon-Fri 1800-2200 only, otherwise rel. stn. 1) – **3)** Margaretenstr. 43, 18057 Rostock; **W:** lohro.de; non-commercial – **4)** see K), stn. 18
DAB: 6 txs on ch. 5C, see K).

R) NIEDERSACHSEN

Media institution: Niedersächsische Landesmedienanstalt für privaten Rundfunk (NLM), ✉Seelhorststraße 18, 30175 Hannover ☎ +49 511 28477 0 🖷 +49 511 28477 36 **W:** nlm.de

FM	ffn	Ant.	R. 21	Klass	kW
Aurich	103.1	104.9	100.6	–	2x25/1
Bad Rehburg	–	–	89.4	–	0.5
Barsinghausen	101.9	103.8	–	–	25
Braunschw.-Broitzem	103.1	106.9	104.1	–	15/13/1
Buxtehude	–	–	106.0	–	1
Celle	–	–	93.5	–	0.2
Cuxhaven	–	–	106.6	–	0.6
Cuxhaven-Otterndorf	102.6	104.6	–	–	20
Dannenberg-Zernien	102.7	106.1	–	–	25
Delmenhorst	–	–	107.6	–	0.1
Goslar	–	–	87.7	–	0.5
Göttingen	102.8	106.0	93.4	–	2x5/1
Hannoversch Münden	100.7	106.7	–	–	0.5
Hannover	–	–	104.9	107.4	0.5/0.2
Helmstedt	–	–	94.1	–	0.5
Hildesheim	–	–	105.8	–	1
Holzminden	102.2	105.7	–	–	0.5
Leer-Nüttermoor	–	–	104.5	–	0.3
Lingen-Damaschke	101.5	104.3	106.9	–	2x15/0.5
Lüneburg	–	–	91.9	–	0.1
Oldenburg	–	–	104.1	–	0.2
Osnabrück	103.4	105.9	95.3	–	2x10/0.1
Rosengarten	100.6	105.1	–	–	20
Seesen	–	100.9	–	–	0.1
Stade	–	–	97.3	–	0.2
Steinkimmen	102.3	105.7	–	–	100
Torfhaus (Harz)	102.4	106.3	–	–	100
Uelzen	–	–	99.7	–	0.5
Visselhövede	101.7	104.2	90.1	–	2x10/1
Wilhelmshaven	–	–	99.1	–	0.3
Wolfsburg	–	–	95.1	–	0.1

NB. Bremen txs on Hit-R. Antenne and R. 21 see N). R. Hamburg / 106!8 rock'n pop txs at Cuxhaven see O)

Addresses & other information:
R. ffn, Stiftstraße 8, 30159 Hannover; **W:** ffn.de AC – **Hit-R. Antenne**, Goseriede 9, 30159 Hannover; **W:** antenne.com. AC – **R. 21**, An der Feuerwache 3 5, 30823 Garbsen; **W:** radio21.de Rock, cooperates with Rockland Radio, see T) – **Klassik R.** see O)

Regional stations:

FM	MHz	kW	Site	Station
11)	87.6	0.1	Hannover Telemax	R. Hannover
4)	87.7	0.2	Emden	R. Ostfriesland
3)	87.8	1	Wilhelmshaven	R. Jade
1)	88.0	1	Uelzen	R. ZuSa

FM	MHz	kW	Site	Station
16)	88.2	0.3	Norden	R. Nordseewelle
1)	89.7	0.5	Dannenberg-Zernien	R. ZuSa
15)	90.4	1	Oldenburg	R. 90vier
16)	90.6	0.2	Borkum	R. Nordseewelle
14)	93.8	0.1	Wolfsburg	R. 38
4)	94.0	1	Aurich-Haxtum	R. Ostfriesland
7)	94.8	0.1	Bad Pyrmont	R. Aktiv
2)	95.2	0.2	Nordhorn	Ems-Vechte-Welle
1)	95.5	1	Lüneburg	R. ZuSa
5)	95.6	1	Lingen-Schepsdorf	Ems-Vechte-Welle
12)	98.2	0.3	Osnabrück	R. Osnabrück
5)	99.3	1	Molbergen-Cloppenburg	Ems-Vechte-Welle
16)	99.5	1	Aurich	R. Nordseewelle
7)	100.0	0.3	Hameln	R. Aktiv
16)	100.1	1	Neuharlingersiel	R. Nordseewelle
14)	100.3	15	Braunschweig Drachenb.	R. 38
13)	103.3	0.6	Nienburg	R. Mittelweser
4)	103.9	0.2	Leer	R. Ostfriesland
16)	104.0	0.1	Norderney	R. Nordseewelle
9)	104.6	0.5	Braunschweig-Broitzem	R. Okerwelle
6)	104.8	1	Osnabrück	OS R. 104,8
10)	105.3	1	Hildesheim	R. Tonkuhle
2)	106.5	1	Oldenburg-Wahnbek	Oldenburg Eins
	106.5	(0.3)	Hannover	(to be allocated)
8)	107.1	1	Göttingen	StadtR. Gött.

Addresses and other information:
1) Ilmenauufer 47, 29525 Uelzen and Scharnhorststr. 1, 21335 Lüneburg; **W:** zusa.de – **2)** Bahnhofstr. 11, 26122 Oldenburg; **W:** oeins.de **3)** Kieler Str. 31, 26382 Wilhelmshaven; **W:** radio-jade.de – **4)** VHS Emden, An der Berufsschule 3, 26721 Emden; **W:** radio-ostfriesland.com – **5)** Halle IV, Kaiserstr. 10a, 49809 Lingen; **W:** emsvechtewelle.de – **6)** Lohstr. 45a, 49074 Osnabrück; **W:** os-radio.de – **7)** Hefehof 23, 31785 Hameln; **W:** radio-aktiv.de – **8)** Groner Str. 2, 37073 Göttingen; **W:** stadtradio-goettingen.de – **9)** Rebenring 18, 38106 Braunschweig; **W:** okerwelle.de – **10)** Andreas-Passage 1, 31134 Hildesheim; **W:** tonkuhle.de – **11)** Münzstr. 3/4, 30159 Hannover; **W:** radio-hannover.de – **12)** Jürgensort 10, 49074 Osnabrück; **W:** radioosnabrueck.com – **13)** Wölper Str. 122, 31582 Nienburg; **W:** radionienburg.de – **14)** Hintern Brüdern 23, 38100 Braunschweig; **W:** radio38.de – **15)** Annenheider Str. 159, 27755 Delmenhorst; **W:** radio90vier.de – **16)** Am Markt 6, 26506 Norden; **W:** radio-nordseewelle.de
Permanent special stns: R. S.A.S. (**W:** radio-sas.de), Stadthagen 94.5MHz; **Lamberti-Kirchenfunk** (**W:** soerenkoenig.com/Radlam) Aurich 106.0MHz; **Kirchenfunk Esterwegen**, 106.6MHz; **Kirchenfunk Lorup**, 107.6MHz; **Kirchenfunk Herzlake**, 106.1MHz; **Pfarrfunk Breitenberg**, 98.4MHz.; **Kirchenfunk Meppen**, 95.0MHz; **Pfarrradio Warsingsfehn**, Moormerland 95.2MHz
DAB: 13 txs on ch. 5C (see K).

S) NORDRHEIN-WESTFALEN

Media institution: Landesanstalt für Medien Nordrhein-Westhalen (LFM) Postfach 10 34 43, 40025 Düsseldorf (office location: Zollhof 2) ☎ +49 211 77 007 0 🖷 +49 211 727 170 **W:** lfm-nrw.de
R. NRW, Essener Str. 55, 46047 Oberhausen; **W:** radionrw.de The following stns are affiliates with some hours of own prgrs per day, other times rel. R. NRW with local IDs inserted automatically.

FM	MHz	kW	Site	Station
5)	87.7	0.2	Krefeld-Oppum	Welle Niederrhein
26)	88.1	4	Eggegebirge	R. Hochstift
19)	88.2	0.5	Lüdinghausen	R. Kiepenkerl
37)	88.2	0.5	Siegen	R. Siegen
35)	88.3	0.1	Meinerzhagen	R. MK
16)	88.4	1	Bocholt	Westmünsterlandw.
36)	89.1	0.2	Schmallenberg	R. Sauerland
7)	89.4	1	Düsseldorf Rheinturm	NE-WS 89.4
6)	90.1	0.3	Mönchengladbach	R. 90,1
31)	90.8	0.1	Herne	Herne 90acht
30)	91.2	0.2	Dortmund	R. 91.2
39)	91.2	0.2	Siegburg	R. Bonn/Rhein-Sieg
42)	91.4	0.1	Bergheim	R. Erft
35)	91.5	0.1	Altena	R. MK
33)	91.5	0.1	Hattingen-Schierken	R. en
3)	91.7	0.1	Moers-Meerbeck	R. K.W.
23)	91.7	0.1	Vlotho	R. Herford
4)	92.2	0.1	Duisburg	R. Duisburg
35)	92.5	0.3	Iserlohn	R. MK
20)	92.6	1	Sendenhorst	R. WAF
43)	92.7	0.5	Düren-Hürtgenwald	R. Rur
13)	92.9	0.5	Mülheim-Saarn	R. Mülheim
29)	92.9	0.1	Selm	antenne unna
16)	93.0	0.5	Ahaus	Westmünsterlandw.
26)	93.7	0.1	Paderborn	R. Hochstift
39)	94.2	0.1	Much-Wersch	R.Bonn/Rhein-Sieg
9)	94.3	0.2	Solingen	R. RSG
15)	94.6	0.1	Recklinghausen	Hit R. Vest
20)	94.7	0.2	Warendorf	R. WAF
36)	94.8	0.1	Marsberg	R. Sauerland
23)	94.9	0.5	Herford	R. Herford
24)	95.1	0.1	Rahden	R. Westfalica
18)	95.4	0.2	Münster	Antenne Münster
15)	95.6	0.1	Berghaltern	Hit R. Vest
24)	95.7	0.5	Minden Jakobsberg	R. Westfalica
20)	95.7	0.3	Beckum	R. WAF
14)	96.1	0.1	Gelsenkirchen	REL
36)	96.2	0.4	Olsberg-Antfeld	R. Sauerland
20)	96.3	0.3	Oelde	R. WAF
38)	96.9	0.5	Leverkusen-Opladen	R. Berg
1)	97.2	0.1	Simmerath	Antenne AC
35)	97.2	0.1	Werdohl	R. MK
37)	97.3	0.1	Bad Laasphe	R. Siegen
29)	97.4	0.5	Lünen	Antenne Unna
11)	97.6	4	Langenberg	R. Neandertal
16)	97.6	1	Borken	Westmünsterlandw.
22)	97.6	0.4	Friedrichsdorf	R. Bielefeld
39)	97.8	0.5	Bonn Venusberg	R. Bonn/Rhein-Sieg
2)	98.0	1	Kleve	Antenne Niederrhein
22)	98.3	0.1	Bielefeld	R. Bielefeld
32)	98.5	0.5	Bochum	R. 98.5
14)	98.7	0.5	Bottrop	REL
37)	98.9	0.1	Neunkirchen	R. Siegen
35)	99.5	0.1	Plettenberg	R. MK
44)	99.7	0.1	Euskirchen	R. Euskirchen
38)	99.7	0.5	Gremberg	R. Berg
39)	99.9	0.5	Bonn-Königswinter	R. Bonn/Rhein-Sieg
1)	100.1	0.4	Aachen Karlshöhe	Antenne AC
35)	100.2	0.5	Lüdenscheid	R. MK
5)	100.6	1	Viersen	Welle Niederrhein
27)	100.9	1	Soest-Möhnesee	Hellweg R.
25)	101.0	0.5	Schieder-Schwalenbg.	R. Lippe
7)	102.1	0.3	Grevenbroich	NE-WS 89.4
12)	102.2	0.3	Essen-Werden	R. Essen
29)	102.3	1	Schwerte Sommerberg	Antenne Unna
5)	102.5	0.3	Viersen Süchtelner Höhe	Welle Niederrhein
16)	103.6	0.1	Gronau	Westmünsterlandw.
27)	103.6	0.1	Lippstadt	Hellweg R.
17)	104.0	1	Tecklenburg	R. RST
8)	104.2	1	Düsseldorf	Antenne Düsseldorf
33)	104.2	0.1	Witten-Stockum	R. en
26)	104.8	0.5	Neuhaus-Hasselberg	R. Hochstift
26)	104.8	0.1	Büren	R. Hochstift
36)	104.9	0.1	Meschede	R. Sauerland
1)	105.0	0.1	Monschau	Antenne AC
12)	105.0	0.1	Essen-Holsterhausen	R. Essen
28)	105.0	0.2	Hamm	R. Lippewelle
38)	105.2	4	Lindlar	R. Berg
17)	105.2	4	Schöppingen	R. RST
15)	105.2	0.1	Dorsten	Hit Radio Vest
37)	105.4	4	Aue-Kirchhundem	R. Siegen
38)	105.7	1	Waldbröl	R. Berg
2)	105.7	0.5	Geldern	Antenne Niederrhein
33)	105.7	0.1	Gevelsberg	R. en
42)	105.8	1	Köln-Ehrenfeld	R. Erft
13)	106.2	0.1	Oberhausen	R. Oberhausen
19)	106.3	0.2	Dülmen	R. Kiepenkerl
36)	106.5	0.5	Hallenberg	R. Sauerland
36)	106.5	0.3	Arnsberg	R. Sauerland
25)	106.6	1	Lemgo	R. Lippe
24)	106.6	0.1	Lübbecke	R. Westfalica
21)	106.8	0.4	Borgholzhausen	R. Gütersloh
45)	106.9	4	Schleiden (Eifel)	R. Euskirchen
41)	107.1	0.5	Köln Neumarkt	R. Köln
33)	107.2	0.1	Herdecke	R. en
27)	107.3	0.2	Wickede	Hellweg R.
19)	107.4	1	Coesfeld	R. Kiepenkerl

FM	MHz	kW	Site	Station
25)	107.4	1	Linderhofe-Dörenberg	R. Lippe
10)	107.4	0.5	Wuppertal	R. Wuppertal
44)	107.4	0.1	Bad Münstereifel	R. Euskirchen
21)	107.5	1	Oelde	R. Gütersloh
43)	107.5	0.1	Linnich	R. Rur
36)	107.6	0.5	Sundern	R. Sauerland
3)	107.6	0.2	Wesel-Büderich	R. K.W.
40)	107.6	0.1	Leverkusen-Wiesdorf	R. Leverkusen
27)	107.7	0.2	Belecke-Sennhöfe	Hellweg R.
34)	107.7	0.2	Hagen	R. Hagen
1)	107.8	0.4	Aachen Stolberg	Antenne AC
39)	107.9	0.1	Herchen-Rosbach	R. Bonn/Rhein-Sieg
9)	107.9	0.1	Remscheid	R. RSG

Addresses & other information:
1) Merzbrück 214, 52146 Würselen, **W:** antenne-ac.de – **2)** Stechbahn 2-8, 47533 Kleve, **W:** antenneniederrhein.de – **3)** Rheinstr. 24-26, 47495 Rheinberg, **W:** radiokw.de – **4)** Ruhrorter Str. 187, 47119 Duisburg, **W:** medien.freepage.de/guidojansen – **5)** Uerdinger Str. 543, 47800 Krefeld, **W:** welleniederrhein.de – **6)** Lüpertzender Str. 159, 41061 Mönchengladbach, **W:** radio901.de – **7)** Moselstr. 16, 41464 Neuss, **W:** news894.de – **8)** Kaistr. 7, 40221 Düsseldorf, **W:** antenneduesseldorf.de – **9)** Postfach, 42621 Solingen (studio location: Alleestr. 1) **W:** radiorsg.de – **10)** Friedrich-Engels-Allee 426, 42283 Wupperta, **W:** radiowuppertal.de – **11)** Elberfelder Str. 81, 40804 Mettmann **W:** radioneandertal.de – **12)** Sachsenstr. 36, 45128 Essen **W:** radio-essen.de – **13)** Essener Str. 99, 46047 Oberhausen **W:** 106.2.radiooberhausen.de and 92.9.radiomuelheim.de – **14)** Hochstr. 68, 45894 Gelsenkirchen, **W:** radio-emscher-lippe.de – **15)** Schaumburgstr. 14, 45657 Recklinghausen **W:** hitradiovest.de – **16)** Heinrich-Hertz-Str. 6, 46325 Borken **W:** radiowmw.de – **17)** Postnstr. 3, 48431 Rheine, **W:** radiorst.de – **18)** Nevinghoff 14/16, 48147 Münster, **W:** antennemuenster.de – **19)** Tiberstr. 21, 48249 Dülmen, **W:** radiokiepenkerl.de – **20)** Am Schweinemarkt 3, 48231 Warendorf, **W:** radiowaf.de – **21)** Feldstr. 14, 33330 Gütersloh **W:** radioguetersloh.de – **22)** Niedernstr. 21-27, 33602 Bielefeld **W:** radiobielefeld.de – **23)** Berliner Str. 30, 32052 Herford **W:** radioherford.de – **24)** Johanniskirchhof 2, 32423 Minden **W:** radiowestfalica.de – **25)** Lagesche Str. 17, 32756 Detmold **W:** radiolippe.de – **26)** Frankfurter Weg 22, 33106 Paderborn **W:** radiohochstift.de – **27)** Jakobistr. 46, 59494 Soest **W:** hellwegradio.de – **28)** Königstr. 39, 59065 Hamm **W:** lippewelle.de – **30)** Karl-Zahn-Str. 11, 44141 Dortmund **W:** radio912.de – **31)** Bahnhofstr. 45, 44623 Herne **W:** radio-herne.de – **32)** Westring 26, 44787 Bochum, **W:** ruhrwelle-bochum.de – **33)** Mühlenstr. 25, 58285 Gevelsberg **W:** radio-en.de – **34)** Rathausstr. 23, 58095 Hagen, **W:** radio-hagen.de – **35)** Vinckestr. 9-13, 58636 Iserlohn, **W:** radio-mk.de – **36)** Steinstr. 32, 59872 Meschede, **W:** radio-sauerland.de – **37)** Postfach 10 02 42, 57002 Siegen (studio location: Obergraben 33), **W:** radio-siegen.de – **38)** Friedrich-Ebert-Str., 51429 Bergisch Gladbach, **W:** radioberg.de – **39)** Kennedybrücke 4, 53225 Bonn, **W:** radio-bonn.de – **40)** Bismarckstr. 71, 51373 Leverkusen, **W:** radioleverkusen.de – **41)** Stolberger Str. 374, 50933 Köln, **W:** radiokoeln.de – **42)** Hürth Park, 50354 Hürth, **W:** radioerft.de – **44)** August-Klotz-Str. 21, 52349 Düren, **W:** radiorur.de – **45)** Rheinstr. 55, 53881 Euskirchen, **W:** radioeuskirchen.de

Stns not affiliated to Radio NRW:

FM	MHz	kW	Site	Station
12)	87.9	0.05	Bielefeld	Hertz 87.9
13)	89.4	0.03	Paderborn	L'Unico
9)	90.0	0.3	Bochum	CT das radio
11)	90.9	0.05	Münster university	R. Q
1)	92.0	0.05	Pulheim	Domradio
2)	92.1	0.03	Siegen university	Radius 92,1
8)	93.0	0.05	Dortmund university	Eldoradio
3)	94.3	0.05	Bielefeld-Bethel	Antenne Bethel
14)	94.7	0.05	Meschede	R. FH
7)	96.8	0.5	Bonn	(shared freq.)
6)	97.1	0.04	Düsseldorf-Bilk	Hochschulr. Düsseld.
15)	89.4	0.03	Paderborn university	L'Unico FM
4)	99.1	0.1	Aachen	Hochschulr. Aachen
5)	100.0	0.1	Köln Sternengasse	Kölncampus
1)	101.7	0.03	Köln Sternengasse	Domradio
11)	103.9	0.5	Steinfurt college	R. Q
10)	104.5	0.2	Essen university	Campus FM
10)	105.6	0.05	Essen university	Campus FM

Addresses & other information:
1) Domkloster 3, 50667 Köln; **W:** domradio.de; further txs see P) and T), also via Astra 1L, 12.460GHz h. Run by Catholic church – **2)** Hölderlinstr. 3, 57068 Siegen; **W:** radius921.de – **3)** Quellenhofweg 25, 33617 Bielefeld-Bethel; **W:** antenne-bethel.de Run by diacony – **4)** Wüllnerstr. 5, 52056 Aachen; **W:** hochschulradio-aachen.de – **5)** Albertus-Magnus-Platz, 50923 Köln; **W:** koelncampus.com – **6)** Universitätsstr. 1, 40225 Düsseldorf; **W:** hochschulradio.uni-duesseldorf.de – **7)** shared by six groups – **8)** Vogelpothsweg 74, 44227 Dortmund; **W:** eldoradio.de – **9)** 44780 Bochum (studio location: Ruhr university, room 04/452); **W:** radioct.de – **10)** Universitätsstr. 2, 45141 Essen; **W:** campusfm.info – **11)** Bismarckallee 3, 48151 Münster; **W:** radioq.de – **12)** Universitätsstr. 25, 33615 Bielefeld; **W:** radiohertz.de – **13)** Warburger Str. 100, 33098 Paderborn; **W:** l-unico.de – **14)** Jahnstr. 23, 59872 Meschede; **W:** radiofh.de – **15)** Warburger Str. 100, 33098 Paderborn; **W:** l-unico.de – **16)** Radio Triquency, Liebigstr. 87, 32657 Lemgo; **W:** triquency.de Via lp. txs on 95.9/96.1/99.4MHz **N.B** Stns 2) and 4)-16) university/college
F.Pl.: Allocation of FM chain Dülmen 92.5MHz, Wulfen 101.9MHz, Bielefeld 103.0MHz, Niederkrüchten 104.0MHz, Rheinberg 105.1MHz, Dortmund 106.0MHz.
DAB: 16 txs on ch. 5C see K). Domradio rel. by J).

T) RHEINLAND-PFALZ

Media institution: Landesanstalt für Medien und Kommunikation (LMK) Postfach 21 73 63, 67072 Ludwigshafen (office loc.: Turmstraße 8) ☎ +49 621 5252 0 +49 621 5252 152 **W:** lmk-online.de

FM	RPR 1	bigFM	Rockl.	Metrop	kW
Bad Bergzabern	103.3	–	–	–	0.3
Bad Dürkheim	98.1	96.4	–	–	0.1
Bad Kreuznach	89.7	104.8	–	–	0.1/0.2
Bad Marienberg	102.9	–	–	–	25
Bernkastel-Kues	–	100.5	–	–	0.1
Betzdorf	–	107.7	–	–	0.5
Bitburg	–	–	107.9	–	0.1
Bornberg-Eßweiler	103.1	107.6	–	–	25
Daun (Eifel)	102.1	106.6	–	–	20
Diezer Hain	101.2	100.4	–	–	0.1
Grünstadt/Mertesh.	103.3	–	–	–	0.1
Haardtkopf	100.1	–	–	–	50
Heckenbach	103.5	104.9	–	–	30
Hohe Wurzel	–	–	107.9	–	6
Idar-Oberstein	100.3	101.9	–	–	1
Kalmit	103.6	106.7	–	–	25
Kirchheimbolanden	–	–	97.1	–	0.2
Kleinkarlbach	91.1	–	–	–	0.1
Koblenz Kühkopf	101.5	104.0	–	–	40
Koblenz-Bendorf	–	–	88.3	107.8	0.3
Linz	–	–	96.9	–	0.2
Ludwigshafen	–	–	–	88.4	0.1
Mainz Ober-Olm	100.6	104.5	–	–	20
Mainz (city)	98.1	106.6	–	96.0	0.2/0.4
Mannheim	–	–	93.2	–	1
Pirmas. Kettrichhof	104.7	–	–	–	5
Pirmasens (town)	–	96.7	–	–	0.4
Rivenich	–	95.8	–	–	0.2
Saarburg	102.6	96.5	–	–	20
Trier Petrisberg	102.9	106.4	105.8	–	0.1/0.5
Zweibrücken	103.3	106.6	–	–	2/0.1

Addresses & other information:
RPR 1, Turmstr. 8, 67059 Ludwigshafen; **W:** rpr1.de – **bigFM:** see K), stn.2); rel. of adopted version in responsibility of RPR – **Rockland R.**, Wallstr. 1-5, 55122 Mainz; **W:** rockland.de; cooperates with R. 21, see R) – **Metropol FM** see M), stn. 15

Local stations:

FM	MHz	kW	Site	Station
3)	87.6	0.2	Idar-Oberstein	R. Idar-Oberstein
7)	87.8	0.1	Welschbillig	Cityradio Trier
10)	87.9	0.1	Bretzenheim (church)	Studio Nahe
2)	88.3	0.1	Bad Kreuznach	Antenne Bad Kreuznach
7)	88.4	0.5	Trier Petrisberg	Cityradio Trier
6)	88.4	0.3	Pirmasens	R. Pirmasens
8)	94.1	0.3	Mommenhein	Antenne Mainz
5)	94.2	1	Neustadt/Weinstr.	Antenne Pfalz
9)	94.7	0.2	Wittlich	R. Wittlich
7)	94.7	0.1	Trierweiler	Cityradio Trier
5)	94.8	0.1	Landau	Antenne Landau
4)	96.9	0.5	Kaiserslautern	Antenne Kaiserslautern
8)	97.1	0.1	Bodenheim	Antenne Mainz
11)	87.8	0.1	Koblenz	R. Teddy
1)	98.0	1	Koblenz Moselw. Str.	Antenne Koblenz

FM	MHz	kW	Site	Station
1)	98.0	1	Neuwied	Antenne Koblenz
1)	98.9	1	Koblenz-Bendorf	Antenne Koblenz
8)	106.6	0.1	Mainz	Antenne Mainz

Addresses & other information:
1) Friedrich-Ebert-Ring 54, 56068 Koblenz; **W:** akoblenz.de – **2)** Kreuzstr. 31-33, 55543 Bad Kreuznach; **W:** antenne-kh.de – **3)** Auf der Idar 2a, 55743 Idar-Oberstein; **W:** radio-io.de – **4)** Am Altenhof 11-13, 67655 Kaiserslautern; **W:** antenne-kl.de – **5)** Europastr. 3, 67433 Neustadt/Wstr.; **W:** antenne-landau.de antenne-pfalz.de – **6)** Schloßstr. 44, 66953 Pirmasens; **W:** radio-pirmasens.de – **7)** Paulinstr. 1, 54292 Trier; **W:** cityradio-trier.de – **8)** Hechtsheimer Str. 35, 55131 Mainz; **W:** antenne-mainz.de – **9)** Schloßstr. 7a, 54516 Wittlich; **W:** radio-wittlich.de – **10)** Obere Grabenstr. 29, 55450 Langenlonsheim; **W:** studio-nahe.de Run by Catholic church, mostly rel. Domradio, see S) – **11)** See M), stn. 19)
DAB: 7 txs on ch. 5C see K). BigFM and RPR1 via SWR txs, see I).

U) SAARLAND

Media institution: Landesmedienanstalt Saar (LMS) Postfach 11 01 64, 66070 Saarbrücken (office location: Nell-Breuning-Allee 6) ☎ +49 681 389880; Fax +49 681 3898820; **W:** lmsaar.de

LW	kHz	kW	Prgr.
Überherrn (Felsberg)	183	–	(closed down)

FM	Salü	C.Ro.	bigFM	Saar.	kW
Homburg	–	–	–	89.6	1
Lebach-Hoxberg	–	100.9	–	–	1
Merzig	103.0	–	92.6	105.1	0.1/0.5
Mettlach	104.2	–	–	106.1	0.1
Neunkirchen	–	99.3	–	94.6	1/0.6
Oberperl	100.3	–	–	–	5
Saarbr. Schoksbg.	101.7	–	–	–	100
Saarbr. Halberg	–	–	94.2	–	1
Saarbr. Winterberg	–	92.9	–	–	1
Saarbr. Schwarzenbg.	–	–	–	99.6	0.1
Saarlouis	–	102.8	99.5	–	1
St. Ingbert	–	100.6	–	–	0.1
Sulzbach	–	–	96.8	–	0.1
Webenheim	100.0	–	–	–	5

Addresses & other information:
R. Salü, Classic Rock R.: Postfach 10 08 44, 66008 Saarbrücken (studio location: Richard-Wagner-Str. 58-60); **W:** salue.de, classic-rock-radio.de – **bigFM Saarland**: Gutenbergstr. 11-23, 66103 Saarbrücken; **W:** bigfm-saarland.de; mostly rel. Stuttgart prgr. (see K), stn. 2) – **R. Saarbrücken, R. Merzig, R. Neunkirchen, R. Homburg**: Nell-Breuning-Allee 6, 66115 Saarbrücken; **W:** radio-sb.de, radiomerzig.de, antenneneunkirchen.de, radio-homburg.de
DAB: Schoksberg tx on ch. 5C see K). R. Salü via SR txs, see H).

V) SACHSEN

Media institution: Sächsische Landesanstalt für privaten Rundfunk und neue Medien (SLM) Postfach 10 16 62, 04016 Leipzig ☎ +49 341 22 59 0 Fax +49 341 22 59 199; **W:** slm-online.de; office location: Ferdinand-Lassalle-Straße 21

FM	PSR	R.SA	RTL	Radio	Energ.	kW
Annaberg-Buchholz	–	104.8	–	–	–	0.5
Auerbach	–	107.9	–	–	–	0.1
Bärenstein	–	–	–	107.2E	–	0.2
Beilrode	–	99.6	–	–	–	1
Borna	–	–	–	99.5L	–	0.1
Chemnitz-Reichenh.	–	91.0	–	102.1C	97.5	3
Collmberg	98.0	–	104.7	–	–	5/10
Döbeln	–	107.9	–	–	98.3	1/0.2
Dresden-Gompitz	–	–	–	91.1D	–	1
Dresden-Wachwitz	102.4	89.2	105.2	103.5D	100.2	100/2
Ebersbach	–	106.1	–	–	–	0.5
Elsterberg	–	99.7	–	–	–	0.2
Flöha	–	98.4	–	99.0C	–	0.1
Freiberg	–	90.6	–	104.2D	96.4	0.2/0.5
Freital	–	88.3	–	107.0D	–	0.2
Geyer (Erzgebirge)	100.0	–	105.4	–	–	100
Görlitz	–	105.1	–	–	–	1
Grimma	–	107.4	–	90.9L	93.3	2/0.3
Hoyerswerda-Zeißig	–	96.9	–	–	87.6	0.2/0.3
Kamenz	–	106.2	–	–	–	0.2
Leipzig-Holzhausen	–	–	–	91.3L	99.8	4
Leipzig-Reudnitz	–	98.2	–	–	–	1
Leisnig	–	100.5	–	–	–	0.2
Limbach-Oberfrohna	–	–	–	107.3C	–	0.1
Löbau Schafberg	101.0	–	105.6	107.6G	–	30
Löbau town	–	87.6	–	–	–	0.5
Markneukirchen	–	89.6	–	–	–	1
Meerane	–	–	–	89.2Z	–	0.1
Meißen-Korbitz	–	–	–	107.5D	–	0.2
Mittelherwigsdorf	–	100.0	–	94.3G	–	0.5/0.3
Mügeln	–	91.2	–	–	–	0.5
Neukirchen	–	–	–	95.8C	–	1
Niederschöna	–	94.4	–	–	–	0.5
Niesky	–	95.0	–	–	–	0.2
Nossen	–	91.4	–	–	–	0.2
Oelsnitz (Vogtland)	–	91.5	–	–	–	0.1
Olbernhau	–	101.0	–	–	–	0.5
Oschatz	–	89.1	–	–	–	0.3
Pirna	–	–	–	96.4D	–	0.1
Plauen	–	93.5	–	–	–	1
Reichenbach/Vogtl.	–	92.4	–	–	–	0.2
Riesa	–	106.4	–	–	91.7	2/1
Rothenburg	–	100.0	–	–	–	0.2
Schöneck	92.0	–	106.0	–	–	10/30
Sohland	–	107.0	–	–	–	0.2
Stollberg	–	93.4	–	–	–	1
Torgau	–	91.1	–	–	–	0.2
Weißwasser	–	101.9	–	–	–	0.5
Werdau	–	–	–	90.9Z	–	0.3
Wiederau (Leipzig)	102.9	–	106.9	–	–	100
Wilkau-Haßlau	–	92.3	–	103.4Z	–	0.5
Wilthen	–	106.5	–	–	104.9	1/0.5
Wurzen	–	95.0	–	–	–	0.4
Zittau	–	100.0	–	–	–	0.5
Zschopau	–	–	–	91.7C	–	0.3
Zwickau-Ebersbrunn	–	–	–	96.2Z	98.2	0.5/0.3
Zwickau-Planitz	–	95.5	–	–	–	0.5

Addresses & other information:
R. PSR (AC), **R.SA** (oldie-based), **Energy Sachsen** (CHR): Thomasgasse 2, 04102 Leipzig; **W:** radiopsr.de rsa-sachsen.de nrj.de – **Hitradio RTL** (AC), **R. Chemnitz / Dresden / Erzgebirge / Lausitz / Leipzig / Zwickau** (AC, on freq. marked C, D, E, G, L, Z, with some content from local studios): Ammonstr. 35, 01067 Dresden; **W:** bcs-sachsen.de
Other stations:

FM	MHz	kW	Site	Station
7)	88.2	0.4	Auerbach	Vogtland R.
9)	88.2	1	Weißig (Bernsdorf)	Lausitzwelle
1)	88.9	1	Chemnitz-Reichenhain	Apollo R.
10)	89.2	1	Weißwasser	R. WSW
2)	89.2	0.1	Leipzig-Reudnitz	R. Blau
2)	94.4	0.3	Leipzig-Stahmeln	R. Blau
10)	94.9	0.2	Wilthen	R. WSW
7)	95.4	2	Plauen	Vogtland R.
5)	97.6	4	Leipzig-Holzhausen	mephisto 97.6
3)	98.4	0.1	Dresden-Gompitz	coloRadio
2)	99.2	0.5	Leipzig-Connewitz	R. Blau
3)	99.3	0.1	Freital (Dresden)	coloRadio
6)	99.3	0.1	Mittweida	R. Mittweida
7)	100.5	1	Reichenbach/Vogtland	Vogtland R.
4)	102.7	1	Chemnitz-Reichenhain	R. T
9)	102.8	1	Hoyerswerda Neustadt	Lausitzwelle
7)	103.8	0.5	Markneukirchen	Vogtland R.
8)	107.7	2	Fichtelberg	R. Erzgebirge

Addresses & other information:
1) As Hitradio RTL; **W:** apolloradio.de; classical music and jazz, also Mon-Fri 2200-1700, Sat-Sun 2300-1100 via txs of stns 2), 3), 4) – **2)** Paul-Gruner-Str. 62, 04107 Leipzig; **W:** radioblau.de – **3)** Jordanstr. 5, 01099 Dresden; **W:** coloradio.org – **4)** Karl-Liebknecht-Str. 19, 09111 Chemnitz; **W:** radiot.de; rel. 1700-1800 Chemnitz university prgr. – **5)** Ritterstr. 9-13, 04109 Leipzig; **W:** mephisto976.uni-leipzig.de, run by Leipzig university; Mon-Fri 0900-1100 and 1700-1900, other times rel. R.SA – **6)** Leisniger Str. 9, 09648 Mittweida; **W:** radio-mittweida.de; run by Mittweida college – **7)** Haselbrunner Str. 114, 08225 Plauen; **W:** vogtlandradio.de. Further txs see X – **8)** Vierenstr. 11, 09484 Oberwiesenthal; **W:** radioerzgebirge-online.de – **9)** Schulstr. 15, 02977 Hoyerswerda; **W:** lausitzwelle.de, 103.8MHz tx see M) – **10)** Werner-Seelenbinder-Str. 54a, 02943 Weißwasser; **W:** radiowsw.de
DAB: 6 txs on ch. 5C see K). Local txs at Leipzig (ch. 6C) and Freiberg (ch. 10D). R.SA via MDR txs, see D).

W) SACHSEN-ANHALT

Media institution: Medienanstalt Sachsen-Anhalt (MSA) Reichardtstraße 9, 06114 Halle/Saale ☎ +49 345 52550 🖷 +49 345 5255 121 **W:** msa-online.de

FM	R Bro	RTL	SAW	Rock	kW
Bernburg	–	–	–	95.0	1
Blankenburg	99.9	–	95.7	–	0.3/0.1
Brocken	–	89.0	101.4	–	60/100
Dequede	101.0	–	95.6	–	60/1
Dessau-Mildensee	90.6	–	92.6	94.1	0.8/2/0.3
Eisleben	93.7	–	–	–	1
Fleetmark-Lüge	–	–	103.9	–	5
Halle Petersberg	93.5	–	103.3	–	5
Halle city	–	–	–	98.3	0.5
Hergisdorf-Wolferode	93.7	–	–	–	1
Köthen	–	–	–	97.1	1
Magdeburg-Buckau	–	–	–	98.7	0.2
Naumburg	98.8	–	95.1	99.6	10/0.5/1
Sangerhausen	107.1	–	99.4	–	0.1
Schneidlingen	–	–	–	107.2	2.5
Schönebeck	105.7	–	100.1	–	15/20
Stendal Tucholsky-Str.	–	–	100.5	–	0.5
Weißenfels	–	–	–	88.0	1
Wernigerode	105.4	–	90.8	–	0.5/1
Wiederau (Leipzig)	–	–	104.9	–	*90
Wittenberg-Gallun	102.3	–	98.4	–	4/5
Zeitz-Hainichen	99.1	–	–	–	0.5
Ziesar	–	–	102.8	–	2

*) tx in Sachsen, sharply directional towards Sachsen-Anhalt

Addresses & other information:

R. Brocken (oldie-based AC), **89.0 RTL** (CHR): Große Ulrichstr. 60D, 06108 Halle; **W:** brocken.de, 89.0rtl.de – **R. SAW** (AC), **Rockland Sachsen-Anhalt:** Hansapark 1, 39116 Magdeburg; **W:** radiosaw.de rockland-digital.de

Non-commercial stations:

FM	MHz	kW	Site	Station
2)	92.5	1	Aschersleben	R. hbw
1)	95.9	0.6	Halle Petersberg	R. Corax

Addresses and other information:

1) Unterberg 11, 06108 Halle; **W:** radiocorax.de – **2)** Herrenbreite 9, 06449 Aschersleben; **W:** radio-hbw.de

DAB: 6 txs on ch. 5C see K) – 5 txs on ch. 11C 1A Deutsche Hits, 89.0 RTL, R. Brocken, Rockland, SAW.

X) THÜRINGEN

Media institution: Thüringer Landesmedienanstalt (TLM) P.O.-Box 90 03 61 (office location: Steigerstraße 10), 99096 Erfurt ☎ +49 361 211770 🖷 +49 361 2117755 **W:** tlm.de

FM	Ant.T	LW	Top 40	Teddy	kW
Altenburg	–	–	98.4	–	0.5
Apolda	–	–	–	99.5	0.2
Arnstadt	–	–	–	96.5	0.1
Bleßberg	102.7	106.7	–	–	60
Dingelstädt	103.9	–	–	–	5
Eisenach	–	–	93.5	90.9	0.2
Erfurt-Windischh.	100.2	99.7	–	–	3/0.5
Erfurt-Hochheim	–	–	88.6	99.2	0.5
Gera	98.3	105.8	95.3	–	0.2/1
Gotha	–	–	90.8	99.3	0.1/0.2
Heiligenstadt	–	88.7	–	–	0.1
Ilmenau	–	–	94.8	–	0.1
Inselsberg	102.2	104.2	–	–	100
Jena-Oßmaritz	90.9	106.1	–	–	1
Jena Kernberge	–	–	94.8	–	0.2
Keula	–	104.5	–	–	10
Kulpenberg	104.7	96.8	–	–	3
Lobenstein	93.2	98.5	–	–	1/2
Meiningen	–	–	99.5	90.6	0.2/0.1
Mühlhausen	–	–	93.8	102.9	0.2/0.5
Nordhausen	106.8	105.8	103.0	107.4	0.1/0.2
Pößneck	–	–	98.9	–	0.2
Remda Kalmberg	107.6	95.7	–	–	60/10
Ronneburg	102.5	94.9	–	–	30/3
Saalfeld	–	–	97.6	–	0.1
Sömmerda	–	–	91.0	–	0.1
Sondershausen	–	–	90.7	–	0.2
Sonneberg	–	–	88.8	–	0.1
Suhl	101.3	88.6	92.1	–	2x1/0.1
Weimar Ettersberg	107.2	89.2	–	–	0.25
Weimar Belvedere	–	–	97.9	88.7	0.1

Addresses & other information:

Antenne Thüringen (AC), **Top 40** (rock): Schwanseestraße 143, 99427 Weimar; **W:** antennethueringen.de radiotop40.de – **LandesWelle Thüringen** (AC): Mehringstr. 5, 99086 Erfurt; **W:** landeswelle.de – **Radio Teddy** see M)

Local stations:

FM	MHz	kW	Site	Station
9)	92.4	0.2	Schleiz	Vogtland R.
1)	96.2	0.6	Erfurt-Hochheim	F.R.E.I.
4)	96.5	0.2	Eisenach	Wartburg-R.
3)	98.1	0.3	Ilmenau	hsf Studentenradio
6)	100.4	0.1	Nordhausen	R. Enno
8)	100.5	0.1	Artern	R. Artern
5)	103.4	0.3	Jena-Oßmaritz	R. OKJ
9)	104.5	0.1	Gera	Vogtland R.
7)	105.2	0.3	Saalfeld	SRB
2)	106.6	2	Weimar Belvedere	R. Lotte
9)	107.5	0.5	Altenburg	Vogtland R.

Addresses & other information:

1) Gotthardstr. 21, 99084 Erfurt; **W:** radio-frei.de – **2)** Herderplatz 14, 99423 Weimar; **W:** radiolotte.de. Rel. Bauhaus university prgr. Mon 1900-2300 – **3)** Postfach 100 565, 98684 Ilmenau; **W:** hsf.tu-ilmenau.de. Run by Ilmenau university – **4)** Georgenstr. 43, 99817 Eisenach; **W:** wartburgradio.com – **5)** Helmboldstr. 1, 07749 Jena; **W:** radio-okj.de – **6)** August-Bebel-Platz 6, 99734 Nordhausen; **W:** radio-enno.de – **7)** Tiefer Weg 7, 07318 Saalfeld; **W:** srb.fm – **8)** Solsteg 1, 06556 Artern; **W:** radio-artern.com – **9)** see V), stn. 7)

DAB: 8 txs on ch. 5C see K).

III. ARMED FORCES STATIONS

FM	MHz	kW	Site	Prgr.
Baden-Württemberg				
2)	102.3	100	Stuttgart	AFN Stuttgart
Bayern				
3)	89.9	0.2	Amberg	AFN Bavaria
3)	90.3	0.1	Garmisch-Partenk.	AFN Bavaria
3)	93.5	0.2	Hohenfels	AFN Bavaria
3)	98.5	0.1	Grafenwöhr	AFN Bavaria
3)	104.9	0.4	Illesheim	AFN Bavaria
3)	107.3		Ansbach	AFN Bavaria
3)	107.7	0.3	Vilseck	AFN Bavaria
Hessen				
4)	103.7	0.5	Wiesbaden	AFN Wiesbaden
Nordrhein-Westfalen				
7)	89.6	0.1	Minden	BFBS Radio 2
7)	91.2	0.1	Paderborn	BFSB Radio 2
7)	91.7	0.5	Friedrichsdorf	BFBS Germany
7)	96.9	0.1	Minden	BFBS Germany
7)	101.6	1.5	Herford	BFBS Germany
7)	103.0	(70)	Bielefeld	(closed down)
7)	105.0	0.3	Paderborn	BFBS Germany

NB: Geilenkirchen Air Base served by AFN and BFBS txs at Brunssum, see under Netherlands

FM	MHz	kW	Site	Prgr.
Rheinland-Pfalz				
5)	103.0	0.4	Pirmasens	AFN Kaiserslautern
5)	105.1	2	Kaiserslautern	AFN Kaiserslautern
6)	105.1	1	Spangdahlem	AFN Spangdahlem
5)	106.1	0.1	Baumholder	AFN Kaiserslautern

Addresses & other information:

1) Bundeswehr, Zentrum Operative Information, Kürrenberger Steig 34, 56727 Mayen; **W:** radio-andernach.de. Prgr. for Bundeswehr operations abroad presented as **Radio Andernach**, distributed via local FM txs – **2) AFN Stuttgart**, Robinson Barracks, 70376 Stuttgart; **W:** stuttgart.afneurope.net Own prgr. Mon-Fri 0400-0800 and 1400-1700 – **3) AFN Bavaria**, Rose Barracks, 92249 Vilseck; **W:** bavaria.afneurope.net Own prgr. Mon-Fri 0500-0800 and 1400-1700 – **4) AFN Wiesbaden**, Würgelstr. 1217, Flugplatz Erbenheim, 65205 Wiesbaden; **W:** wiesbaden.afneurope.net. Own prgr. Mon-Fri 0500-0900 and 1300-1700 – **5) AFN Kaiserslautern**, Vogelweh, Bldg. 2058, 67661 Kaiserslautern; **W:** kaiserslautern.afneurope.net Own prgr. Mon-Fri 0500-1700, Sat 0700-1100 – **6) AFN Spangdahlem**, Spangdahlem Air Base, 54529 Spangdahlem; **W:** spangdahlem.afneurope.net Own prgr. Mon-Fri 0500-0900 and 1300-1600, Sat 0800-1100 – **7) BFBS Germany**, Otto-Hahn-Straße 20, 33104 Paderborn, Sennelager; **W:** forces.net/radio. Also via Eutelsat 10A, 11.221GHz v. F.PI. for 103.0MHz see S) – **AFN Europe**, Sembach Kaserne, building 166, 67681 Sembach-Heuberg, **W:** afneurope.net. Produces network prgr., rel. by local AFN stns in Germany, Belgium and Italy.

GHANA

L.T: UTC — **Pop:** 31 million — **Pr.L:** English (official), Akan — **E.C:** 230V/50Hz — **ITU:** GHA

NATIONAL COMMUNICATIONS AUTHORITY (NCA)

✉ P.O. Box CT 1568, 1st Rangoon Close, Switchback Rd, Cantonments, Accra ☎+233 30 2776621 🖷 +233 30 2763449 **W:** nca.org.gh **E:** info@nca.org.gh **L.P:** Acting DG: Major J. R. K. Tandoh.

GHANA BROADCASTING CORPORATION (GBC, Pub.)

✉ P.O. Box 1633, Broadcasting House, Ring Road Central, Kanda, Accra ☎+233 30 2786567 🖷 +233 30 2773247
W: gbcghana.com **E:** info@gbcghana.com **L.P:** DG: Albert Don Chebe. Dir. Radio: Theo Agbam. Dir. Eng: Mrs. Sarah Boye.

GBC Regional & partnership stations:

FM	MHz	Name	Web/Addr./Area
Bolgatanga	89.5	URA R.	Upper East
Han	90.1	Upper West R.	Upper West
Tamale	91.2	R.Savannah	North
Ho	91.5	Volta Star R.	Volta
Kumasi	92.1	Garden City R.	Ashanti
Cape Coast	92.5	R.Central	Central
Accra	93.7	R. Ada	P.O. Box 9482, K.I.A
Wa	93.9	Upper West R.	Upper West
Sunyani	94.7	R. Bar	Brong Ahafo
Sekondi-Takoradi	94.7	Twin City R.	West
Dormaa-Ahenkro	94.9	R. Dormaa	Brong Ahafo
Accra	95.7	Uniiq FM	Greater Accra
Accra	96.5	Obonu FM	Greater Accra
Apam	96.5	Apam R.	Central
Swedru	98.6	Swedru R.	Central
Kumasi	99.5	Luv FM	P.O. Box 17207, Accra
Accra	99.7	Joy FM	myjoyonline.com
Koforidua	106.7	Sunrise FM	East

Other FM stations in Accra:
Asempa FM, P.O. Box 17013, Accra-North: 94.7MHz – **Atlantis R**, P.O. Box 14629, Accra: 87.9MHz 5kW – **Channel R**, P.O. Box AN 8135, Accra-North: 92.7MHz – **Choice FM**, Accra: 102.3MHz. **W:** choicefmghana.com – **Citi FM,** P.O. Box 30211, K.I.A, Accra: 97.3MHz – **Happy FM,** P.O. Box 1538, Dansoman, Accra: 98.9MHz – **Hot FM,** P.O. Box KD594, Kanda, Accra: 93.9MHz – **Peace FM,** Accra: 104.3MHz 5kW. **W:** peacefmonline.com – **R. Gold FM,** P.O. Box 17298, Accra: 90.5MHz – **R. Hit,** P.O. Box 17013, Accra-North: 103.7MHz – **R. Universe,** P.O. Box 25, Legon: 105.7MHz – **Sunny FM,** Box CT 3850, Cantonments, Accra: 88.7MHz – **Top R,** P.O. Box CT 4748, Cantonments, Accra: 103.1MHz – **Vibe FM,** Priv. Mailbag CT 183, Accra 91.9MHz.
+ 75 more stations elsewhere.
BBC World Sce: Accra 101.3MHz, Sekondi-Takoradi 104.7MHz.
RFI Afrique: Accra 89.5MHz, Kumasi 92.9MHz in French/English.
VOA African Sce: Accra 98.1MHz

GIBRALTAR (UK)

L.T: UTC +1h (28 Mar-31 Oct: +2h) — **Pop:** 34,900 — **Pr.L:** English (official), Spanish, Llanito — **E.C:** 230V/50Hz — **ITU:** GIB

GIBRALTAR REGULATORY AUTHORITY (GRA)

✉ 2nd Floor, Eurotowers 4, 1 Europort Road, Gibraltar GX11 1AA ☎ +350 20074636 🖷 +350 20072166 **E:** info@gra.gi **W:** www.gra.gi **L.P:** CEO: Paul Canessa

GIBRALTAR BROADCASTING CORPORATION (Pub) Radio Gibraltar

✉ Broadcasting House, 18 South Barrack Rd, Gibraltar GX11 1AA ☎ +350 200 79760 **W:** gbc.gi **E:** radiogibraltar@gbc.gi
L.P: CEO: Gerard Teuma, Head of R.: Ian Daniels, Head of Eng.: Michael Corcoran
MW: 1458kHz 4kW
FM: 91.3MHz 0.2kW, 92.6MHz 1.0kW, 100.5MHz 1.0kW
D. Prgr: 24h **Radio Gibraltar Plus** opt out in Spanish M-F 1300-1500, English M-F 1500-1700 on 100.5 MHz and 1458 kHz **Ann:** "Radio Gibraltar"

BRITISH FORCES BROADCASTING SCE. GIBRALTAR

✉ BFBS Gibraltar, BFPO 52, BF1 2AR; Oyster Cottage, Four Corners, Gibraltar ☎ +350 200 55389 **W:** forces.net/radio/stations/bfbs-gibraltar **E:** gib@bfbs.com
FM: BFBS Gibraltar: North Mole 93.5MHz 0.2kW; O'Hara's Battery 97.8MHz 1kW (Relays BFBS UK when not carrying local prgs.)
BFBS Radio 2: North Mole 89.4MHz 0.2 kW; O'Hara's Battery 99.5MHz 0.25kW. **D. Prgr:** 24h

‡ROCK RADIO (Comm) (inactive at time of publication)

✉ 61 Governors Str., Gibraltar GX11 1AA ☎ +350 225 0500 **W:** rockradio.gi **E:** hello@rockradio.gi
FM: 99.2 MHz **DAB:** DAB+ **D. Prgr:** 24h

DIGITAL RADIO (DAB+)

Block 12B (225.648MHz) & Block 12C (227.360)

GREECE

L.T: UTC +2h (28 Mar-31 Oct: +3h) — **Pop:** 10 million — **Pr.L:** Greek — **E.C:** 230V/50Hz — **ITU:** GRC

ETHNIKI EPITROPI TILEPIKOINONION KAI TAHIDROMION (EETT) (Hellenic Telecommunications & Post Commission)

✉ Leof. Kifisias 60, 15125 Maroussi ☎+30 210 6101500 🖷+30 210 6105049 **W:** eett.gr **E:** info@eett.gr **L.P:** President: Konstantinos Masselos.

ETHNIKO SIMVOULIO RADIOTILEORASIS (ESR) (National Council for Radio & Television)

✉ Panepistimiou & Amerikis 5, 10564 Athina ☎+30 213 1502300 🖷 +30 210 3319881 **W:** esr.gr **E:** ncrtv@otenet.gr
L.P: President: Athanasios Koutromanos.

ELLINIKI RADIOFONIA (ERA) (Greek Public Radio)

✉ Leof. Mesogeion 432, 153 42 Agia Paraskevi, Athina ☎+30 210 6066000 🖷+30 210 6002941 **W:** ert.gr **E:** info@ert.gr **L.P:** CEO: Christos Leontis. Tech. Dir: Petros Filos. Dir. Tech. Op. Radio: Kanavas Kreon

MW	kHz	kW	Prgr	MW	kHz	kW	Prgr
Athina	729	70	1	Tripoli	1305	1	1/R/K
Kerkira	1008	50	1/R/K	Komotini	1404	50	1/R/K

1=ERA1, R=Regional prgrs, K=ERA Kosmos (evenings) ‡) Inactive
NB: Most stations carry regional prgr. Mon-Fri 0400-1500 and Kosmos in the evening & overnight.

FM	ERA1	ERA2	ERA3	ERASp	Reg.	ERP
16) Aetos	-	-	-	-	104.4	1
5) Ahentrias	94.4	96.4	-	-	105.6	10
3) Ainos	96.9	98.9	104.2	106.8	93.2	20/10
2) Akarnanika	88.9	91.3	102.5	97.3	100.3	20/10
9) Assea	88.3	103.5	90.3	95.3	101.5	10/2
Borsa	90.5	102.6	95.6	106.6	-	2/1
1) Bournias	-	104.8	-	106.8	89.7	2
Delvinaki	-	102.4	-	-	-	1
Devas	93.5	-	-	-	-	6
Didima	101.2	99.4	97.4	103.2	-	2/1
9) Doliana	-	-	95.6	-	101.5	10
4) Dovroutsi	-	-	-	-	98.3	10
12) Erateini	-	96.5	94.5	-	89.9	10
Finiki	91.0	93.0	-	104.8	-	1
Geraneia	97.9	99.9	-	105.0	-	20/10
Hamezi	89.9	89.0	-	91.9	-	2
Hlomo	-	101.5	-	107.4	-	2
Hortiatis	88.0	90.0	92.0	93.9	-	20
1) Ikaria	102.5	-	-	-	89.1	3
Imittos	105.8	103.7	90.9	101.8	-	20/2
17) Kagias	-	91.2	105.8	87.6	89.6	2
12) Kalavrita	-	-	-	-	93.9	2
1) Karfas	-	-	-	102.1	100.1	2/1
19) Kastania	103.6	‡88.2	-	105.6	100.2	2/1
Katsikas	107.0	-	-	-	-	3
17) Kefalohori	96.4	-	105.8	-	101.5	3/1
Korylovos	92.4	99.5	-	104.2	-	
Lefkes	-	98.9	-	102.7	-	10
7) Lefkimi	89.8	91.8	-	107.7	87.8	10
1) Lepetimnos	-	-	-	-	99.4	1

FM	ERA1	ERA2	ERA3	ERASp	Reg.	ERP
Lidoriki	-	99.5	-	-	90.4	1
2) Ligiades	106.1	99.8	97.8	102.1	88.2	2/1
Lihada	88.7	104.2	-	-	-	10
Manoliassa	103.3	-	-	-	-	10
15) Malaxa	-	-	-	-	100.6	1
14) Monte Smith	-	-	-	-	93.1	1
18) Moustheni	102.4	104.4	100.5	107.3	106.0	2
1) Olympos	92.3	94.3	106.4	-	104.4	10
Orfanio	89.2	91.2	97.5	107.3	-	35
12) Panahaiko	-	104.3	102.3	87.9	92.5	10/2
6) Pantokratoras	91.8	93.8	89.8	101.1	99.3	20/10
Parnitha	91.6	102.9	95.6	100.9	-	20/10
16)Petalidi	92.2	94.2	89.3	100.4	107.2	10/3
13)Pilio	92.8	94.8	96.8	107.1	101.2	20/10
7) Pithio	98.9	93.8	88.1	89.4	101.0	10
11) Plaka	89.2	90.7	88.7	107.3	98.1	10/2
7) Plaka	-	-	-	-	103.5	2
1) Prof. Ilias (L)	-	-	97.2	-	103.0	2/1
14)Prof. Ilias (R)	88.4	90.4	103.4	101.4	92.7	10
5) Rogdia	104.8	99.2	91.3	93.9	97.5	2
15)Skloka	92.9	94.9	106.0	90.1	104.0‡	10
3) Skopos	-	-	-	-	95.2	2
10)Smerna	-	-	-	-	102.5	10
13) Soros	-	-	-	-	100.7	2
5) Stavros (Las.)	-	-	-	-	105.3‡	1
17) Strymoniko	96.4	-	105.8	87.6	101.5	2
14) Sympetro	-	96.1	100.3	107.9	98.4	1
1) Thanos	-	-	-	-	96.5	1
18)Thasos	95.1	106.7	100.8	104.7	96.3	10
1) Thosolopotami	-	-	-	-	95.2	2
Tsotili	89.1	-	-	-	-	1
1) Vathi	-	-	-	-	89.7	2
8) Vitsi	88.6	90.6	103.1	105.1	96.6	20/10
19) Vitsi	-	-	-	-	100.5	3

+about 75 stations under 1 kW. ‡) Inactive.
D.Prgr: All 24h. **ERA1 (Proto):** News, talk, current affairs. **ERA2 (Deftero):** Music and culture. **ERA3 (Trito):** Classical music, arts. **ERA Sport:** sports.
Other ERT Stations:
Kosmos Radio: Assea 93.6 1kW, Doliana 93.6 1kW, Parnitha 93.6 100kW, Borsa 94.0 1kW, Pithio 94.7 10kW, Moustheni 97.2 2kW, Kagias 97.5 1kW‡, Vasilaki 97.5 1kW, Skloka 104.4 10kW‡, Korilovos 104.2 1kW‡, Plaka 105.5 2kW, Imittos 107.0 6kW.

DAB: Mux featuring ERA1, ERA2, ERA3, ERA Sport, Kosmos, The Voice of Greece, and ERA7 (relaying audio from Vouli TV): Imittos & Parnitha 227.360MHz/12C 300w, Assea 213.360MHz/10C, Filippio (Thessaloniki) 174.928MHz/5C, Geraneia 206.352MHz/9C (90w), Panahaiko 188.928MHz/7A. **F.PI:** Network to be expanded nationwide.

Regional station addresses:
1) Northern Aegean: E. Bostani 69, 81100 Mitilini – **2) Ioannina:** N. Papadoupulou 2, 45444 Ioannina – **3) Zakynthos:** Ampelokipoi, 29100 Zakynthos – **4) Larissa** Iroon Politehniou 1, 1h Stratia, 41222 Larissa – **5) Heraklion:** Maxis Kritis 161, 71303 Iraklio – **6) Kerkiras:** Ethniki Lefkimis, 49100 Kerkira – **7) Orestiada:** Evripidou 15, 68200 Orestiada – **8) Florina:** Megarovou 20, 53100 Florina – **9) Tripolis:** Nafpliou & A. Soutsou 1, 22100 Tripoli – **10) Pirgos:** Olympion 70, Agia Paraskevi, 27100 Pirgos – **11) Komotinis:** P.O. Box 5, Kosmiou Terma, 69100 Komotini – **12) Patra:** Parodos Athinon 1, Ag. Georgios Riou, 26504 Patra – **13) Volou:** Pl. Agiou Konstantinou, 38222 Volos – **14) Southern Aegean:** 5o km. Rodou-Kallitheas, 851 00 Rhodes – **15) Chanion:** Ellis 40, 73200 Chania – **16) Kalamata:** Anataliko Kentro 10-11, 24100 Kalamata – **17) Serres:** P.O. Box 91, Stratopedo Kolokotroni, 62100 Serres – **18) Kavala:** Sof. Venizelou & Iokastis, Stratopedo Karakaosta, 65403 Kavala – **19) Kozani:** I. Tranta 19, 50100 Kozani **W:** webradio.ert.gr/periferia
IS: The opening notes of the Greek folk song "Tsopanakos imouna" (Once I Was A Shepherd Boy) played on flute and sheep bells.

EXTERNAL SERVICE: see International Radio section.

RADIOFONIKOS STATHMOS MAKEDONIAS (Pub)

✉ Aggelaki 14, 546 36 Thessaloniki ☎+30 2310 299600 🖷 +30 2310 299451 **W:** ert.gr **E:** makedonia@ert.gr
Makedonia 1: FM: Hortiatis 102.0MHz 20kW, 24h.
Makedonia 2: FM: Hortiatis 95.8MHz 20kW, 24h.
Ann: "Elliniki Radiophonia, Radiofonikos Stathmos Makedonias"

ERT OPEN - ELLINIKI RADIOFONIA & TILEORASIS (ERA, Greek Public Radio)

✉ Leof. Mesogeion 463, Agia Paraskevi, 153 43 Athina ☎+30 210 6002909-10 🖷 +30 210 6002941 **W:** ertopen.com E: ertopen@gmail.com
FM: Parnitha 106.7MHz 2kW.
NB: Operated by members of labour union of ERT administrative staff, using ERT transmission facilities and frequency assigned to ERT. Rebroadcast 24/7 on Stathmos ton Ergazomenon 96.5 MHz (Ktipas) and Radio Enosi 97.3 MHz (Xirovouni).

ILIDA RADIO (Comm.)

✉ Ag. Trifonos 5, 27200 Amaliada. **W:** ilida911.gr **E:** info@ilida911.gr **D.Prgr:** 24h.
MW: Kastro 1584kHz 1kW. **FM:** Frangapidima 91.1MHz 2kW.

1431 AM (Educ.)

✉ Aristotle University of Thessaloniki, 2os Orofos Ptergas Ilektrologon, Politehniki Sholi, 54124 Thessaloniki. **W:** 1431am.org **D.Prgr:** 24h. **MW:** Thessaloniki 1431kHz 350W **FM:** 97.3MHz.

UNOFFICIAL STATIONS (Athens area, Voreios Ihos & R. Makedonia in Thessaloniki): Diavlos 1 693kHz, Studio 1 801kHz, Studio 54 828kHz, R. Alfa Mike 846kHz, R. Ita-Vita 882kHz, Studio 7-40 918kHz, Black & White 927kHz, R. Galatsi 945kHz, R. Polytechnic 963kHz, R. Takis A5 972kHz, R. Vinylio 1035kHz, R. Daffy 1044kHz, R. Mesogeia 1071kHz, R. 322 1107kHz, Mini Watt 1125kHz, R. Asimatos 1134kHz, R. Nikolaos Elata 1188kHz, R. Sex Machine 1206kHz, R. 9 1206kHz, R. Apollon 1242kHz, R. FBI 1269kHz, LMG 1359kHz, Halastra R. 1368kHz, Supersonic 1377kHz, R. Macedonia 1386 kHz, R. Veteranos 1476kHz, Voreios Ihos 1539kHz and many others.

DAB: DigitalRadio473 197.648MHz/8B (Athens).

PRIVATE FM STATIONS in Athina, Thessaloniki and Patra
Athina

FM	MHz	Station	kW	FM	MHz	Station	kW
1)	87.5	Kriti FM	1	32)	97.8	Real FM	12
2)	87.7	En Lefko	10	33)	98.1	Free FM	1
3)	88.0	Menta 88	10	34)	98.3	Athina 9,84	10
4)	88.3	Meraki FM	2	35)	98.6	Mousikos 98,6	5
5)	88.6	Legend 88,6	8	36)	98.9	Alpha 989	10
6)	88.9	Hit 88,9	14	37)	99.2	Melodia 99,2	9
7)	89.2	Music 89,2	10	38)	99.5	Peiratikos FM	5
8)	89.5	Ekklesia Ell.	15	39)	99.8	Astro FM	3
9)	89.8	Dromos 89,8	10	40)	100.3	Skai 100,3	9
10)	90.1	Parapolitika FM	10	41)	100.6	Nostos 100,6	3
11)	90.4	Kanali 1	5	42)	101.3	Diesi 101,3	10
12)	90.6	ART FM	4	43)	101.6	Paradise R.	2
13)	91.2	Peiraiki Ekkl.	10	44)	102.2	Sfera 102,2	10
14)	91.4	Lyra FM	1	45)	102.5	Athens Voice	2
15)	92.0	Galaxy 92	10	46)	102.7	Palmos On Air	2
16)	92.3	Lampsi 92,3	7	47)	103.1	Firma FM	1
17)	92.6	Best 926	10	48)	‡103.3	Sport 24 Radio	10
18)	92.9	Kiss FM	12	49)	104.0	Party 104 FM	2
19)	93.2	Ellinikos 93,2	10	50)	104.3	Hristianismos FM	9
20)	93.8	93,8 FM	1	51)	104.6	Thema 104.6	9
21)	94.0	R. Epikoinonia	5	52)	104.9	Over FM	4
22)	94.3	Ellada FM	5	53)	105.2	Atlantis FM	5
23)	94.6	Spor FM	10	54)	105.5	Sto Kokkino	5
24)	94.9	Rythmos 949	10	55)	106.2	Mad Radio	10
25)	95.2	Athens Deejay	10	56)	106.4	R. Argosaronikos	5
26)	96.0	R. 96 FM	2	57)	106.5	106,5 FM	12
27)	96.3	Red 96,3	10	58)	107.2	Blue Space FM	3
28)	96.6	Pepper 96,6	10	59)	107.4	R. 107,4	2
29)	96.9	Rock 969	10	60)	107.6	Dias FM	1
30)	97.2	Easy 97,2	10	61)	107.8	Star FM	5
31)	97.5	Love Radio	10	62)	108.0	Ihorama FM	1

Thessaloniki

FM	MHz	Station	kW	FM	MHz	Station	kW
63)	87.6	Laikos FM	7	71)	91.4	Sto Kokkino	4
64)	88.5	88miso	1	72)	91.7	RSO 91,7	5
65)	89.0	89 Rainbow	6	73)	92.4	Karamela R.	5
66)	89.4	We Radio	6	74)	93.1	Ble FM	5
67)	89.7	Imagine 89.7	6	75)	93.4	Mythos FM	3
68)	90.4	904 Aristera	5	76)	93.7	R. Gnomi	1
69)	90.8	Zoo Radio	8	77)	94.2	R. Lydia	6
70)	91.1	VFM 91.1	1	78)	94.5	R. Thessaloniki	8

FM	MHz	Station	kW	FM	MHz	Station	kW
79)	94.8	Eroticos FM	5	96)	101.7	Yellow R.	5
80)	95.1	Cosmoradio	8	97)	102.3	R. Akrites	1
81)	95.5	Metropolis FM	8	98)	102.6	Plus R.	6
82)	96.1	Fresh 96.1	4	99)	103.6	Focus FM	5
83)	96.5	Alpha 96.5	4	100)	104.0	Fly FM	6
84)	96.8	Velvet 96.8	7	101)	104.4	Radiokymata	3
85)	97.5	Easy 97.5	7	102)	104.7	Rock R.	2
86)	98.0	R. North	6	103)	104.9	Praktoreio FM	1
87)	98.4	Panorama 98.4	5	104)	105.2	R. Apopsi	1
88)	98.7	R. Synora	5	105)	105.5	1055 Rock	5
89)	99.0	R. Ena	5	106)	105.8	Hroma FM	3
90)	99.4	Flash 99,4	2	107)	106.1	City International	2
91)	99.8	R. Ekrixi	2	108)	106.5	Love 106.5	5
92)	100.0	FM 100	5	109)	106.8	Iera Mt. Langada	2
93)	100.3	Tranzistor 100.3	5	110)	107.1	Real FM	4
94)	100.6	FM 100.6	1	111)	107.4	Libero 107.4	5
95)	101.3	Lelevose FM	5	112)	107.7	Status FM	5

Patra FM (MHz): Aroma 88.2 – Iera Mitropoli Patras 88.5 – Melody FM 88.8 – Skai Patras 89.4 – Skylos FM 90.0 – Laikos 90.4 – Yes R. 91.2 – Radio 91,5 91.5 – R. Enter 91.7‡ – Kiis Extra 92.2 – Top FM 93.0 – Max FM 93.4 – R. Gamma 94.0 – Alpha Patras 94.4 – Rythmos 94.9 – Oxygen 95.3 – Spor FM Patras 96.3 – Sfera Patras 96.6 – Wave R. 97.4 – R. Messatida 98.0 – Vima Patras 98.7 – R. Aigio 99.2 – Fasma FM 99.7 – You FM 100.1 – Melodia Patras 100.4 – Anoixi FM 100.7 – Free 101.1 – Hroma 102.1 – Loux FM 102.7 – Mousiki Lampsi 103.3 – Up FM 103.7 – Parea FM 104.1 – Mythos FM 104.8 – Antenna Patras 105.3 – Derti 105.7 – Galaxy FM 106.1 – R. Patra 106.5 – Sto Kokkino 107.7. Powers 1–5kW.
+ approx 1100 additional private stns nationwide. ‡=inactive
NB: No official information available about transmitter powers of most stations. Athina and Thessaloniki powers are mostly based on estimates.

DAB: Test broadcasts in Athens region by Digital Power (Gold, Pop, Jazz, Rock) on 216.928MHz/11A (Imittos).

Addresses & other information:
1) Peloponissou 42, 18121 Koridallos **W:** kritifm.com – **2)** Fraggoklisias 8, 15125 Maroussi, 15125 Maroussi **W:** enlefko.fm – **3)** Mesogeion 174, 15125 Maroussi **W:** menta88.gr – **4)** Athina **W:** penies.gr – **5)** Fraggoklisias 8, 15125 Maroussi **W:** facebook.com/legend886 – **6)** Fraggoklisias 8, 15125 Maroussi **W:** hit889.gr – **7)** Nikolaou Plastira 172, 13561 Agioi Anargiroi **W:** music892.gr – **8)** Iasiou 1 & Gennadiou, 11526 Athina **W:** ecclesia.gr/greek/ecclesiaradio/index.asp – **9)** Viltanioti 36, 14564 Kato Kifisia **W:** dromosfm.gr – **10)** Iasonos 2, 18537 Piraeus **W:** parapolitikaradio.gr – **11)** Evripidou 79, 18532 Piraeus **W:** kanaliena.gr – **12)** Kallirois 48, 11745 Kallithea **W:** artfm906.gr – **13)** Akti Themistokleous 190, 18539 Piraeus **W:** pe912fm.com – **14)** Athina **W:** lyrafm.gr – **15)** Pirronos 12, 16346 Ilioupoli **W:** galaxy92.gr – **16)** Viltanioti 36, 14564 Kato Kifisia **W:** lampsifm.gr – **17)** Viltanioti 36, 14564 Kato Kifisia **W:** best926.gr – **18)** Vas. Sofias 85, 15124 Maroussi **W:** kiss.gr – **19)** Dimitros 31, 17778 Tavros **W:** ellinikos932.fm – **20)** Iroon Polytechniou, Polytechnoupoli, 15773 Zografou **W:** radiozones.org – **21)** S. Karagiorgi 2 & M. Antypa, 14121 Iraklio **W:** 94fm.gr – **22)** Zitsis 54, 13123 Ilion **W:** elladafm.gr – **23)** Eth. Makariou/Delta Falireos 2, 18547 Neo Faliro **W:** sport-fm.gr – **24)** Theotokopoulou 4 & Astronafton, 15124 Maroussi **W:** rythmosfm.gr – **25)** Viltanioti 36, 14564 Kato Kifisia **W:** athensdeejay.gr – **26)** Athina – **27)** Amarousiou-Halandriou 89, 15125 Maroussi **W:** redfm.gr – **28)** Mesogeion 174, 15125 Maroussi **W:** pepper966.gr – **29)** Leof. Kifisias 40, 15125 Maroussi **W:** rockfm.gr – **30)** Leof. Kifisias 10-12, 15125 Maroussi **W:** easy972.gr – **31)** Dimitros 31, 17778 Tavros **W:** loveradio.gr – **32)** Leof. Kifisias 197, 15124 Maroussi **W:** realfm.gr – **33)** Athina – **34)** Peiraios 100, 11854 Athina **W:** athina984.gr – **35)** Nikolaou Plastira 172, 13561 Agioi Anargiroi **W:** mousikos986.gr – **36)** Thesi Petsa-Vakalopoulou, 15351 Pallini **W:** alpha989.com – **37)** Amarousiou-Halandriou 89, 15125 Maroussi **W:** melodia.gr – **38)** Athina **W:** peiratikos.gr – **39**) Leof. Salaminos 1, 18546 Keratsini **W:** astrofm.gr – **40)** Eth. Makariou/Delta Falireos 2, 18547 Neo Faliro **W:** skairadio.gr – **41)** Ag. Theklas 5, 153 43 Agia Paraskevi **W:** nostosradio.gr – **42)** Viltanioti 36, 14564 Kato Kifisia **W:** diesi.gr – **43)** Askeli Porou 18020 **W:** paradiseradio.gr – **44)** Nikolaou Plastira 172, 13561 Agioi Anargiroi **W:** sfera.gr – **45)** Harilaou Trikoupi 22, 10679 Athina **W:** athensvoice.gr/radio – **46)** 18020 Poros **W:** palmosradio.gr – **47)** Papanastasiou 25, 18755 Keratsini **W:** mariosblackman.gr – **48)** Leof. Syggrou 166, 17671 Kallithea **W:** sport24radio.gr – **49)** Papagou 2 & Leof. Dimokratias 1A, 15127 Melissia W: partyfm104.gr – **50)** Sofocleous 52 & Menandrou, 10552 Athina **W:** christianity.gr/radio-christianity – **51)** Agrafon 5 & Patmou, 15123 Maroussi **W:** themaradio.gr – **52)** Athina **W:** overfm.gr – **53)** Ag. Konstantinou 11, 18544 Piraeus **W:** atlantisfm.gr – **54)** Sarri 19, 10554 Athina **W:** stokokkino.gr – **55)** Eth. Antistaseos 253, 15351 Pallini **W:** madradio.gr – **56)** Dritseika Methanon, 18030 Methana **W:** radioargosaronikos.gr – **57)** Athina **W:** 1065radio.com – **58)** Athina **W:** bluespacefm.com – **59)** Athina – **60)** Athina – **61)** Athina **W:** starathens.blogspot.com – **62)** Athina – **63)** G. Kranidioti 2, 55535 Pylaia Thessaloniki **W:** laikos.gr – **64)** Armenopoulou 9, 54635 Thessaloniki **W:** radio88miso.gr – **65)** K. Karamanli 175, 54349 Thessaloniki **W:** 89rainbow.gr – **66)** Tsalouhidi 20, 54621 Thessaloniki **W:** we894.gr – **67)** Adrianoupoleos 20A, 55133 Kalamaria Thessaloniki **W:** imagine897.gr – **68)** Egnatias 69, 54631 Thessaloniki **W:** webradio.902.gr/904/stream.php – **69)** Kosti Palama 6G, 55535 Pylaia **W:** zooradio.gr – **70)** K. Karamanli 69, 4os Orofos, 54642 Thessaloniki **W:** 911.gr – **71)** 10 km. Filirou-Langada, 57010 Thessaloniki **W:** stokokkino.gr/liveThessaloniki.php – 72) G. Kranidioti 2, 55535 Pylaia Thessaloniki **W:** rso.gr – **73)** Fanariou 13 & Mouson, 56429 Stavroupoli Thessaloniki **W:** karamelaradio.gr – **74)** 4hs Avgoustou 6, 57003 Agios Athanasios Thessaloniki **W:** ble.fm – **75)** Karolou Diel 20, 54623 Thessaloniki **W:** mythosradio.gr – **76)** Ag. Sofias 43, 54623 Thessaloniki **W:** gnominet.gr – **77)** Eleftherias 15, 56123 Ambelokipi Thessaloniki **W:** radiolydia.com – **78)** 17o km Moudianon, Kombos Risiou, 57001 Thermi Thessaloniki **W:** rthess.gr – 79) 17o km Moudianion, Kombos Risiou, 57001 Thermi Thessaloniki **W:** eroticos.gr – **80)** Tsimiski 51, 6os Orofos, 54623 Thessaloniki **W:** cosmoradio.gr – **81)** K. Palama 6C, 54352 Pylaia Thessaloniki **W:** metropolisradio.gr – **82)** 17o km Moudianon, Kombos Risiou, 57001 Thermi Thessaloniki **W:** freshsalad.gr – **83)** K. Kristalli 4, 54630 Thessaloniki **W:** alpha965.gr – **84)** Kosti Palama 6G, 54630 Thessaloniki **W:** velvet968.gr – **85)** 26hs Oktovriou 90, 54627 Thessaloniki – **86)** Mitropoleos 34, 54623 Thessaloniki **W:** radionorth.gr – **87)** Andreou Georgiou 56, 54627 Thessaloniki **W:** panorama984.gr – **88)** Kentriki Plateia Polikastrou Kilkis & Ermou 4, 1os Orofos, P.O. Box 21, 61200 Polikastro Kilkis **W:** synorafm.gr – **89)** K. Karamanli 175, 54249 Thessaloniki **W:** 99fm.gr – **90)** 26hs Oktovriou 46, 54627 Thessaloniki **W:** flash994.gr – **91)** Melenikou 31A, 56224 Evosmos Thessaloniki **W:** ekrixifm.gr – **92)** N. Germanou 1, 54645 Thessaloniki **W:** fm100.gr – **93)** Kosti Palama 6G, 55535 Pylaia **W:** tranzistor1003.gr – **94)** N. Germanou 1, 54645 Thessaloniki **W:** fm100.gr – **95)** Antigonidon 19, 54630 Thessaloniki **W:** lelevose.gr/radio.html – **96)** K. Karamanli 171, Voulgari, 54249 Thessaloniki **W:** yellowradio.gr – **97)** Vas. Othonos 12, 54629 Stavroupoli Thessaloniki **W:** radioakrites.gr – **98)** Aristotelous 7, 54624 Thessaloniki **W:** plusradio.gr – **99)** Politehniou 21, 54623 Thessaloniki W: focusfm.gr – **100)** Andrianoupoleos 20A, 55133 Kalamaria Thessaloniki **W:** fly104.gr – **101)** A. Papandreou 27, 56334 Kordelio Thessaloniki **W:** radiokymata.gr – **102)** Kouskoura 5, 54625 Thessaloniki **W:** rockradio.gr – **103)** Egnatias 154, 54636 Thessaloniki **W:** praktoreiofm.gr – **104)** Promitheos 33 & Afroditis 12, 54630 Thessaloniki – **105)** Kosti Palama 6A, 54630 Thessaloniki **W:** 1055rock.gr – **106)** Kromnis 10, 54453 Toumpa Thessaloniki **W:** hroma.gr – **107)** Karatassou 31, 55132 Kalamaria Thessaloniki **W:** cityinternational.gr – **108)** 9o km. Thessalonikis-Moudanion, 57001 Thermi Thessaloniki **W:** love1065.gr – **109)** Meg. Alexandrou 25, 57200 Langadas **W:** imlagada.gr/default.aspx?catid=89 – **110)** Aristotelous 5, 54624 Thessaloniki **W:** real.gr/programma_thessalonikis – **111)** Leontos Sofou 18, 54625 Thessaloniki **W:** facebook.com/liberofm – **112)** Salaminos 5, 54626 Thessaloniki **W:** 1077statusfm.gr

AMERICAN FORCES NETWORK EUROPE (Mil.)

FM: "107.3 The Odyssey": Souda Bay 107.3MHz 0.5kW **W:** www.afneurope.net/Stations/Souda-Bay

GREENLAND (Denmark)

L.T: UTC -3h (DST*: -2h). Qaanaaq & Thule Air Base: UTC -4h (DST*: -3h; not Thule AB), Ittoqqortoormiit: UTC -1h (DST*: UTC), Danmarkshavn: UTC. *) 28 Mar-31 Oct — **Pop:** 57,000 — **Pr.L:** Greenlandic (official), Danish — **E.C:** 230V/50Hz — **ITU:** GRL

MINISTRY OF EDUCATION, CULTURE AND CHURCH

✉ Imaneq 4, Box 1029, DK-3900 Nuuk ☎ +299 345000 **E:** ikin@nanoq.gl **L.P:** Minister: Ane Lone Bagger

KALAALIT NUNAATA RADIOA – KNR (Pub. Comm.)

✉ Issortarfimmut 1A, Box 1007, DK-3900 Nuuk ☎ +299 361500 🖷 +299 361502 **W:** knr.gl **E:** info@knr.gl

L.P: Chrmn: Sofie Sandgreen. MD: Karl Henrik Simonsen. Hd of R.: Alice Sørensen

MW	kHz	kW	MW	kHz	kW
Nuuk	570	5	Qeqertarsuaq	650	5
Simiutaq	720	10			

FM	MHz	kW	FM	MHz	kW
Nuuk	90.5	0.5	Ilulissat	96.0	0.05
Sisimiut	95.0	0.1	Tasiilaq	96.0	0.05
Ummannaq	95.0	0.05	Sanderson Hope	96.0	0.1
Upernavik	95.0	0.05	Aasiaat	95.5	0.05
Qaqortoq	95.5	0.05	Maniitsoq	97.0	0.08
Kangerlussuaq	96.0	0.01	Dye Four	98.7	0.5

+ 62 additional stns 0.1kW or less. On 88.1-99MHz. Most txs use 94.0, 95.0, 95.4, 95.5, 96.0 or 97MHz **KNR:** 24h in Greenlandic (approx. 90%) and in Danish. N on the h in Greenlandic and Danish. Main N in Greenlandic: 1500, 2100. Danish: 1515, 2115
Ann: "Kallaallit-Nunaata Radioa", "Grønlands Radio" **IS:** "Sunnia Kalippoq" (The Whaleboat "Sonja" drags whale) played on celeste

DR P1, Denmark. Satellite relay 24h Nuuk 98.0MHz 0.1kW

INUUNERUP NIPAA (Rlg)
✉ Ilivinnguaq 1, Box 67, DK-3900 Nuuk ☎ +299 321382 🖷 +299 321226 **W:** inn.gl **E:** ino.nuuk@greennet.gl
L.P: Chrmn: John Østergaard Nielsen. Hd of Prgr.: Jan Berthelsen
FM: 88.5MHz (all txs are 0.05kW) in Aasiaat, Ilulissat, Kullorsuaq, Maniitsoq, Nanortalik, Nuuk, Qaanaaq, Qaqortoq, Sisimiut, Tasiilaq, Upernavik and Uummannaq
D.Prgr: 1030-1430, 1600-1930 & 2200-0230. Most prgrs in Greenlandic

PRIVATE STATIONS – local radio FM (MHz):
Ice FM, Industrivej 18, Box 1082, 3900 Nuuk ☎ +299 522840 **FM:** 93.5 0.1 kW – **Nanoq FM,** Box 1016, 3900 Nuuk ☎ +299 321911 **W:** nanoqmedia.gl/da/radio/ **FM:** 100.0 – **Nipi FM**, Box 279, 3921 Maniitsoq ☎ +299 547771/288362 **W:** nipifm.gl **FM:** 90.5/93.0 (Maniitsoq) & 99.0 (Kangaamiut) – **Qeqertarpaat Tusaataat 93 MHz**, Aqqusinersuaq 5, 3950 Aasiaat ☎ +299 +299 383290. L.P.: Arqalak Brandt Johansen. **FM:** 93.0 – **Radio Narsaq**, Josefip aqq. 543, 3961 Narsaq. L.P. Johan Henningsen. **FM:** 93.0 (0.025kW) – **Radio Upernavik**, Julius Olsvig-P Aqq, 3962 Upernavik. **FM:** 93.0 - **Seekon Radio**, Box 361, 3920 Qaqortoq ☎ +299 531994. **FM:** 103.0 – **Tusaataat**, Box 401, 3911 Sisimiut ☎ +299 864800 **W:** tusaataat.gl L.P. Jens Klaus Lennert. **FM:** 93.0 0.05kW

MILITARY STATION – local radio FM (MHz):
97.1 Thule Local Radio, Rec. Center Bldg. 362, Thule Air Base/ Pituffik. FM: 97.1. Format:: Multiple genres of American music

GRENADA

L.T: UTC -4h — **Pop:** 110,000 — **Pr.L:** English — **E.C:** 230V/50Hz — **ITU:** GRD

NATIONAL TELECOMMUNICATIONS REGULATORY COMMISSION (NTRC)
✉ P.O. Box 854, Maurice Bishop Highway, Grand Anse, St.George's ☎ +473 4356872 🖷 +473 4352132 **E:** gntrc@ectel.int **W:** ntrc.gd
L.P: Chmn: Spencer Thomas

GRENADA BROADCASTING NETWORK – G.B.N. Radio (Gov, Comm.)
✉ Observatory Rd, PO Box 535, St.George's ☎ +1 473 440 3033 🖷 +1 473 444 4180 **W:** gbn.gd **L.P:** GM: Odetta Best-Campbell
FM: HOTT FM: 98.5/98.7MHz 1000-0300 – **K105 FM:** 105.5/105.9MHz - **GBN Gospel**: 96.9/97.1MHz

HARBOUR LIGHT OF THE WINDWARDS (Rlg.)
✉ Harbour Light Way, Hillsborough PO, Tarleton Point, Carriacou ☎ +1 473 443 7628 🖷 +1 473 443 7628 **W:** harbourlightradio.org **E:** harbourlight@spiceisle.com **L.P:** SM: Randy Cornelius
MW: 1400kHz 5kW **FM:** 92.3MHz 0.25kW, 94.5MHz 0.25kW
D.Prgr: MW: 0900-0400. FM: 24h. **N:** rel. BBC
Ann: "This is the Harbour Light of the Windwards broadcasting from beautiful and friendly Carriacou"

PRIVATE STATIONS (FM in MHz):
Boss FM, Bruce Str Mall, St.George's ☎+1 473 442 1177 **W:** bossfmgrenada.net. FM 104.1/104.9 – **City Sound,** River Rd, St.George's **W:** citysoundfm.com. FM 97.5 – **CRFM Community Radio:** Morne Jaloux, St.George's ☎+1 473 440 4848 🖷 +1 473 440 4991. FM 89.5 – **GFN - Grenada Family Network,** Advent Ave, Grand Bras, PO Box 2747, St.George's ☎+1 473 435 4297 **W:** globalfamilynetwork.net. FM 91.3. Format: Rlg. (Adventist) – **GNCN - Good News Catholic Radio**, Church Str, PO Box 224, St.George's ☎+1 473 435 0143 **W:** catholicgnd.org FM 99.5/99.9. Format: Rlg – **GTC Radio,** Morne Rouge, Grand Anse, St.George's ☎+1 473 439 9700. FM 89.9/90.5 – **Kiss FM**, St.George's. FM 92.1 - **Live Wire HD,** Ross Point, PO Box 90, St.George's ☎/🖷+1 473 435 3563. FM 90.1 – **Magic FM**, Moving Target Co., Lagoon Rd, St.George's ☎+1 473 440 8171 **W:** magic103fm.com. FM 88.9/95.7/103.3 – **Power 95.1**, Melville Str, St.George's ☎+1 473 435 9500 **W:** power95fm.com. FM 95.1/95.3 – **Real FM Grenada,** Main Str, Sauters, St.Patrick ☎+1 473 442 0975 **W:** drealfmgrenada.com. FM 91.5/91.9 – **Secret Radio,** L'anse aux Epines, St.Geroge's. ☎+1 473 410 4512. FM 92.7 (inactive). F.pl.: Broadcasting again soon – **Sister Isle Radio,** Fort Hill, Hillsborough, Carriacou ☎+1 473 443 8141 **W:** sisterislandradio929.com. FM 92.9 – **Star FM 101.9,** Seaton James Str, Grenville, St.Andrew ☎+1 473 438 7827 **W:** starfmgrenada.com. FM 101.9 – **The Soul of Grenada (TSOG),** Grand Roy, St.John's. ☎+1 473 553 0400 **W:** thesoulofgrenada.com. FM 90.9 – **Topp FM,** Jubilee Str, Grenville ☎+1 473 440 8677 **W:** toppfm.com. FM 102.3/103.7 – **Vibes 101.3,** Church Str, Hillsborough, Carriacou ☎+1 473 439 0101. FM 101.3 – **Wee FM,** Grenada Wireless Comm Network, Cross Str, PO Box 555, St.George's ☎+1 473 440 4933 **W:** weefmgrenada.com. FM 93.3/93.9

GUADELOUPE (France)

L.T: UTC -4h — **Pop:** 396,000 — **Pr.L:** French (official), Guadeloupean Creole — **E.C:** 230V/50Hz — **ITU:** GLP

COMITÉ TERRITORIAL DE L'AUDIOVISUEL DES ANTILLES ET DE LA GUYANE see main entry under Martinique

GUADELOUPE LA PREMIÈRE (Pub)
✉ Morne Bernard-Destrellan, B.P. 180, F-97122 Baie-Mahault. ☎+590 590939696. 🖷+590 590939682 **W:** guadeloupe.la1ere.fr **L.P:** Dir: R.Surjus. Editor-in-Chief: Philippe Goudé. PD: L.Francil. Head Comms Dept: Sonia Gémieux
FM: Point-à-Pitre 88.9MHz 1kW, Haut du Morne des Pères 89.1MHz 1kW, Deshaies 96.8MHz 0.1kW, Basse-Terre 97.0MHz 3kW, Pointe-Noire 97.4MHz 16kW
D.Prgr: 24h. **N:** 1100, 1700, 2230, plus relays of France-Inter.
Ann: "Ici Point-à-Pitre, La Première Guadeloupe".
IS: "Biguin" (guitar) **V.** by QSL-card. Rp.

RADIO CARAÏBES INTERNATIONAL (Comm.)
✉ **RCI Guadeloupe**, B.P. 1309, 97187 Point-à-Pitre Cédex. ☎ +590 590839696 🖷 +590 590839697
FM: Basse-Terre 98.6MHz 1kW, Deshaies 98.6MHz 0.3kW, Morne-à-Louis 100.2MHz 2kW, Point-à-Pitre 106.6MHz 1kW, Haut du Morne 106.6MHz 0.05kW. **D.Prgr:** 24h.

RADIO BASSES INTERNATIONALE (Comm)
✉ Stations de radio, Lieu-dit les Basses, 97112 Grand Bourg ☎ +590 590977088 🖷 +590 590978062
FM: Haut du Morne des Pères 88.7MHz 1kW, Grand-Bourg 90.4MHz 1kW, Morne-à-Louis 98.2MHz 2kW, Basse-Terre 102.2MHz 1kW

RADIO MASSABIELLE (RCF) (Rlg)
✉ B.P. 607, 97168 Point-à-Pitre ☎+590 590832521 🖷 +590 590 834861. **L.P:** Pres: José Colat-Jolivière, Dir: Père Silvère Numa
W: radiomassabielle.fr **E:** contact@radiomassabielle.fr
FM: Point-à-Pitre 97.8MHz 0.6kW, Pointe-Noire 101.8MHz 1kW

RADIO SAPHIR FM
✉ rue Bel Air Bourg, 97170 Petit-Bourg ☎+590 590352274
E: saphirfm@live.fr **W:** radiosaphirfm.com
FM: Point-à-Pitre 89.4MHz 1kW
Other stations (all FM (MHz)**):**
France Inter, Pointe-à-Pitre 91.2 1kW, Haut du Morne des Pères 91.7 1kW, Morne-à-Louis 95.0 16kW, Basse-Terre 95.4 3kW – **NRJ Guadeloupe,** Pointe-à-Pitre, 100.6 1kW, Basse-Terre 102.6 1kW, Morne-à-Louis 107.2 2kW – **Antilles Infos**, 105.8 2kW, 106.5 1kW – **Bel'Radio**, 96.3 1kW, 106.9 1kW – **Fréquence Alizée**, 96.6 1kW,

103.4 2kW – **R. Éclair**, 96.0 1kW, 101.0 2kW – **R. Gaïac FM**, 99.8 1kW, 104.7 1kW – **R. Haute Tensi**, 89.8 1kW, 90.8 1kW – **R. Karata**, 90.6 1kW, 106.5 1kW – **Radio Madras FM**, 92.5 2kW, 92.9 1kW – **Radio Nostalgie**, 105.4 1kW, 107.6 2kW – **Trace FM**, 92.1 2kW, 94.1 1kW. **NB:** +11 other stations

GUAM (USA)

L.T: UTC +10h — **Pop:** 168,775 — **Pr.L:** English (official), Chamorro (official), Filipino — **E.C:** 120V/60Hz — **ITU:** GUM

FEDERAL COMMUNICATIONS COMMISSION (FCC)

see main entry under USA

	MW	kHz	kW		MW	kHz	kW
1)	KGUM	567	10	12)	KUSG	1350	0.09
3)	KTWG	801	10	13)	KVOG	1530	0.25
	FM	**MHz**	**kW**		**FM**	**MHz**	**kW**
4)	KHMG	88.1	8	16)	KZGU	99.5	17
5)	KPRG	89.3	9.2	9)	KOKU	100.3	50
15)	KKGU	90.1	0.25	11)	KNUT	101.1	8
6)	KOLG	90.9	5.7	10)	KTKB	101.9	46
7)	KSDA	91.9	3.8	8)	KISH	102.9	25
9)	KMOY	92.7	42	11)	KIJI	104.3	8.6
12)	KUSG	93.3	0.01	1)	KGUM	105.1	10.5
2)	KUAM	93.9	5.2	3)	KTWG*	105.9	0.2
8)	K3TO	95.5	2.5	14)	KGCA-LP	106.9	0.07
1)	KGUM*	96.5	0.25	14)	KGCA-LP	107.9	0.023
1)	KZGZ	97.5	37		*)= F.Pl.		

Addresses & other information:

1) Sorensen Pacific Broadcasting Inc 111 Chalan Santa Papa, Suite 800; Hagatna, GU 96910-5193 ☎+1 671 477-5700, +1 808 524-6495, 🖷+1 671 477-3982 **Brands:** KGUM-AM Talk, news **W:** k57.com; KZGZ Power98 CHR **W:** power98guam.com [KZGU 99.5 currently licenced to Garapan-Saipan, N Marianas but serves Guam as 'The Shark'] **W:** guamshark.com KGUM-FM 'The Kat' **W:** facebook.com/105thekat – **2) Pacific Telestations LLC** 600 Harmon Loop Road, Suite 102; Dededo, GU 96929-6536 ☎+1 671 637-KUAM (637-5826) 🖷+1 671 637-9865 **W**: kuam.com **Brands:** KUAM: Isla63 'Island Pride' contemporary island music; KUAM-FM: i94 Champion Radio CHR – **3) Edward H Poppe Jr & Frances W Poppe**, Cornerstone 800AM, 1868 Halsey Drive; Asan, GU 96910-1505 ☎+1 671 477-5894 🖷+1 671 477-6411 **W**: ktwg.com **E:** am800guam@gmail.com Format: Protestant Christian talk and instruction, gospel music **NB:** Korean Mon & Fri 0800-0830, Tagalog Wed 0800-0830, Chamorro Thu 0800-0815 & Sun 0700-0730, Japanese Thu 0815-0830 – **4) Harvest Christian Academy**, Harvest Family Radio, PO Box 23189 Barrigada, GU 96921 ☎ +1 671 477 6341🖷 +1 671 477 7136 **W:** hbcguam.net **E:** khmg@hbcguam.net **L.P:** GM: John Collier **Prgr:** 24h religious – **5) Guam Educational Radio Foundation** c/o University of Guam, 303 University Drive; UOG Station; Mangilao, GU 96923-1871 **NB:** BBCWS Daily 0700-0800, Sun 1900-2100, Mon 1900-2000, Tue 1400-2000, Wed & Thu 1400-1800 & 1900-2000, Fri 1400-1800, Sat 1700-2000 **W:** kprgfm.com STA 4.6kw because of typhoon damage and need to relocate tower – **6) Catholic Educational Radio**, Chalan Santo Papa; P.O. 23006, Guam Mail Facility, Barrigada, GU 96921-3006 **W:** kolg.com **L.P:** GM: Deacon Frank Tenorio, Dir. Prgr: Chuck White **Prgr:** 24h relig – **7) Good News Broadcasting Corp**, Joy FM, 290 Chalan Palasyo, Hagatna Heights, GU 96910-6405 ☎ +1 671 472 1111 🖷 +1 671 477 4678 **W:** joyfmguam.com **L.P:** GM: Matthew Dodd **Prgr:** 24h religious **Languages:** English, Chinese, Chuukese, Japanese, Korean, Tagalog – **8) Inter-Island Communications Inc**, Nimitz Hill, 1868 Halsey Drive, Piti, GU 96910-1505 – **9) Moy Communications**, Guam Hit Radio 100, 107 Julale Center, 424 West O'Brien Drive, Hagatna, GU 96910-5078 **W:** hitradio100.com **E:** marketing@hitradio100.com **KOKU:** "Guam's #1 Hit Music Station" CHR **KMOY** – **10) KM Broadcasting of Guam LLC**, 177-B Ilipog Drive, Suite 203; Tamuning, GU 96913-4107 **E:** rolly@ktkb.com **W:** ktkb.com **Brand:** Megamixx 101.9 Format: OPM Origil Pilipino Music **Prgr Language:** Tagalog – **11) Choice Broadcasting Company** 543A Top-Plaza Building, N Marine Dr, Tamuning, GU 96913-4217☎+1 671 478-0104 🖷+1 671 647-7480 **KNUT** Fun 101 FM "Guam's Hottest OPM & US Hit Station" **Prgr:** Filippino **W:** facebook.com/fun101Guam **KIJI** 3F La Casa de Colina Building, Tamuning GU 96913 "The Boss 104.3FM" **Prgr:** Classic Rock **L.P:** SM: Rich de Vera **W:** kijifm104.com **E:** rich@kijifm104.com **Other:** sister company to iConnect – **12) MCS LLC**, 125 Tun Jesus, Crisotomo Street #308, Tamuning GU 96913 ☎+1 671 648-4262 – **12)** Hagatna. ☎+1 671 648-4262 **W:** kusgthepulse.com – **13) Guam Power II Inc**, 1100 Alakea #1800, Honolulu HI 96813-2839 ☎+1 808 521-4711 – **14) KGCA Inc**, Melodies of Prayer Inc, 154 Calachucha Ave, Barrigada GU 96913 ☎+1 671 637 5975 **W:** melodiesofprayer.com **E:** mail@melodiesofprayer.com **L.P:** Chair: Edwin Supit **Prgr:** 24h religious – **15) Hurao Inc**, 264 Calle de los Marteres St, Agat GU 96935 ☎ +1 671 482-4630 – **16) Sorensen Pacific Broadcasting, Inc.** "The Shark" 962 Pale San Vitores Road, Suite 116, Tumon

ADVENTIST WORLD RADIO - ASIA (Rlg.) and TRANS WORLD RADIO - ASIA (Rlg.): See International Radio section

GUATEMALA

L.T: UTC -6h — **Pop:** 18 million — **Pr.L:** Spanish — **E.C:** 120V/60Hz — **ITU:** GTM

SUPERINTENDENCIA DE TELECOMUNICACIONES (SIT)

🖂 15 calle 1-95, zona 10, 01010 Ciudad de Guatemala ☎ +502 23211000 🖷 +502 23211004 **W:** sit.gob.gt

CÁMARA DE RADIODIFUSIÓN DE GUATEMALA

🖂 2 calle 1-25, zona 10, Edificio Géminis 10, 01010 Ciudad de Guatemala ☎ +502 23382974 **E:** camaraderadiodifusiongt@gmail.com

Call TG , ‡ = inactive, (r) = repeater, ± = varying fq.

MW Call	kHz	kW	Station, location, h. of tr.
GU01) RV	560		R. Poder y Unción/R. 5-60, Guatemala
M01)	560	1	R. Quetzal, Malacatán
ES01) PA	570	1	R. Palmeras, Escuintla
GU02) Y	580	5	R. Progreso, Guatemala: 1300-0100
QU01) RQ	590	5	R. Quiché, Sta Cruz del Quiché: 1100-0400
GU03) GA	610	5	R. Alianza, Guatemala: 1000-0500
TO01) PQ	620	5	R. 6-20, San Cristóbal: 1200-0400
QE01) Q	660	3	LV de Quetzaltenango: 1100-0400
JU01) VB	690	1	R. Tamazulapa, Jutiapa
ES03) AJ	700	1	R. Inspiración, Escuintla
GU05) HB	760	5	R. 760 AM, Guatemala
ZA01) CK	780	1	Sultana La Cristiana, Zacapa
PE02)	810		R. Moapán, Sta Elena
SA01)	810		R. Circuito San Juan, San Juan
TO02) END	‡810		R. Constelación, Totonicapán
GU06) TO	820	10	R. El Maestro en Casa, Guatemala
SU01) AV	830	5	R. Satélite, Mazatenango: 1100-0400
AV01)	840	2.5	R. Luz, San Pedro Carchá
JU04)	840	1	R. Idea Maranatha, Jutiapa: 1100-0400
SU02) L	870	0.5	R. Victoria, Mazatenango
ES04) HU	890	1	R. Escuintla, Escuintla
IZ02) MA	900	1	R. Amatique, Puerto Barrios
GU30) KL	‡910	10	R. Fe y Esperanza, Guatemala: 1130-0600
GU13)LV	940	10	Eventos Católicos R., San Pedro Sacatepéquez, Guatemala: 1200-0500
SU03) AF	950	1	R. Indiana, Mazatenango
GU14) AX	‡970	5	R. Continental, Guatemala: 1200-0430
CH01) AL	990	1	R. Perla de Oriente, Chiquimula
CM02)	1000		R. Cultural y Educativa, Patzún
GU32)	1000		R. Revelación y Verdad, Guatemala: 1055-0500
IZ06)	1010	1	R. Caribe, Izabal
QU03) XI	1010	1	R. Ixil, Nebaj: 1100-0200
SM05) CM	1020	5	R. Frontera, Pajapita: 1100-0400
HU01) SL	1050	5/1	LV de los Cuchumatanes, Huehuetenango: 1100-0600
QE04) D	1070	3/2	LV de Occidente, Quetzaltenango: 1200-0400
ZA02) LU	1080	1	R. Novedad, Zacapa
QE05) SR	1100	1	R. Superior, Coatepeque
GU17) C	1120	0.5	R. Dios es Amor, Guatemala
RE01) VR	1130	1	Em. Unidas LV de la Costa Sur, Retalhuleu
GU18) T	1150	10	R. Cadena Sonora, Guatemala: 1100-0600
QE06) RL	1170	5	R. Cadena Landívar, Quetzaltenango: 0900-0300
JU02) RJ	1200	12	R. Unción, Jutiapa
GU19) MX	1210	10/5	R. Miel Central, Guatemala 1100-0400
IZ04) AT	1230	1	R. Atlántida, Puerto Barrios: 1130-0500
SU04)	1230		R. América, Cuyotenango
CH02) PY	1250	1	R. Payakí, Esquipulas: 1100-0300
TO03)	1250	1	LV Cristiana, Totonicapán
GU21) CQ	1270	2.5	R. Exclusiva, Guatemala
ZA03)	1290		R. Miramundo "LV del Ejercito", Zacapa

MW	Call	kHz	kW	Station, location, h. of tr.
QE07)	AN	1310	1	R. LV de los Altos, Quetzaltenango: 1100-0700
JU03)	ME	1320	0.5	R. Quezada, Jutiapa
GU22)	MU	1330	5	Unión R, Guatemala
GU23)	LK	1360	10	R. Tic Tac "LV del Evangelio", Guatemala
QE08)	AC	1370	1	LV de Colomba, Colomba
TO04)	EB	1380	0.5	R. Momostenango Educativa, Momostenango:1100-0300
GU28	YC	1390	6	R. Fe y Esperanza, Guatemala
QE09)	GH	1410	5	Nueva R. Xelajú, Quetzaltenango: 1200-0600
GU29)	RP	1420	1	R. FGER, Guatemala
HU02)	AG	1430	1.2	LV de Huehuetenango: 1100-0400
SU05)	MS	1440	0.5	R. Nacional, Mazatenango: 0000-0400
GU24)	LG	1450	1	R. Hosanna, Guatemala: 1000-0400
PE04)	RN	1460	2.5	R. Petén, Flores: 1100-0500
RE02)	RE	1490	1	R. Modelo, Retalhuleu
GU26)	DX	1510		R. Centroamericana, Guatemala
PE05)		1520		R. Taysal, Sta Elena de la Cruz
QE10)		1560		R. Inspiración, Quetzaltenango
GU27)	VE	1570	10	R. VEA-Voz Evengélica de América, Guatemala: 1030-0600
CM01)	XC	1590	1	R. Triunfadora, Chimaltenango
SW	**Call**	**kHz**	**kW**	**Station, location & h. of tr**
CH04)	AV	‡4055	0.7	R. Verdad, Chiquimula: 0910-0600

Call TG—, ‡ = inactive, (r) = repeater, ± = varying fq.

State abbreviations: (Departamentos) AV = Alta Verapaz, BV = Baja Verapaz, CH = Chiquimula, CM = Chimaltenango, ES = Escuintla, GU = Guatemala, HU = Huehuetenango, IZ = Izabal, JA = Jalapa, JU = Jutiapa, PE = Petén, QE = Quetzaltenango, QU = Quiché, RE = Retalhuleu, SA = Sacatepéquez, SR = Santa Rosa, SM = San Marcos, SO = Sololá, SU = Suchitepéquez, TO = Totonicapán, ZA = Zacapa.
N.B: There is currently no postal service in Guatemala, courier service must be used.

Addresses & other information:

AV00) ALTA VERAPAZ
AV01) 11 Av Zona 1, Colonia Cuatro Caminos, San Pedro Carchá (or Apartado Postal 14, 16001 Cobán) - 1100-0400.

BV00) BAJA VERAPAZ
BV01) Inst de Educación Básica, Barrio Abajo San Jerónimo, 15001 Salamá. Prgrs. in Spanish, Achi and Q'eqchí

CH00) CHIQUIMULA
CH01) 7 Calle Av 4-00, Z-1, 20001 Chiquimula (or 6 Av 0-60, Z-4, Torre Prof II, Of 904, 01004 Guatemala) – **CH02)** 5 Av 6-37, Z-1, 20007 Esquipulas - **FM:** 91.5MHz – **CH04)** Estación Educativa Evangélica, Ap. 5, 20901 Chiquimula. **W:** radioverdad.org

CM00) CHIMALTENANGO
CM01) 2 Calle 3-33, Z-3, 04001 Chimaltenango – **CM02)** 6ta Calle 3-88, Zona 5, Patzún 050, Chimaltenango.

ES00) ESCUINTLA
ES01) 15 Calle 2-48, Z-3, 05001 Escuintla – **ES02)** Col 15 de Junio, Z-3, Tiquisate, 05001 Escuintla - **FM:** 92.3MHz – **ES03)** 4 Av 12-27, Z-1, 05001 Escuintla. **E:** radioinspiracion@gmail.com – **ES04)** 4 Av 11-38, Z-1, 05001 Escuintla

GU00) GUATEMALA
GU01) W: radiopoderyuncion.com – **GU02)** 9 Av 0-32, Z-2, 01002 Guatemala **W:** radioprogresoguatemala.com – **GU03)** 34 Av "A" 7-60 Tikal 2, Z-7, 01007 Guatemala **W:** radioalianza.gt – **GU05)** 3ª. Avenida 11-42, Zona 3 Mixco, Colonia El Rosario, Guatemala **W:** radio760online.com – **GU06)** Guatemala **W:** iger.edu.gt/content/grupo-radial – **GU08)** 30 Av 3-86, Z-11, Utatlán II, 01011 Guatemala – **GU09)** 11 Calle 2-43, Z-1, 01001 Guatemala – **GU11)** Calzada San Juan 7-90, Edif.Acuario, Z-7, 01007 Guatemala – **GU12)** 6a Av 0-60, Zona 4, Torre Profesional 1, Niv. 9, Of. 911, 01004 Guatemala – **GU13)** 10a Avenida "A" 2-43 Zona 1, 01001 Guatemala **W:** eventoscatolicos.com.gt – **GU14)** 15 Calle 3-45, Z-1, 01001 Guatemala – **GU16)** 10 Calle 5-20, Z-1, 01001 Guatemala – **GU17)** 11 ave. 15 -58 zona 1, 01001 Guatemala **W:** ipda.org.gt – **GU18)** 2 Calle 18-07, Zona 15, Vista Hermosa 1, 01015 Guatemala **W:** sonora.com.gt – **GU19)** 4 Av 1-14, Z-1, 01001 Guatemala. **W:** mielcentralguatemala.com/estudio-biblico-2-4-2 – **GU21)** Carretera Vieja a Antigua Guatemala, 2da Calle 23-70, Zona 1, Mixco, Guatemala **W:** radioexclusiva.org – **GU22)** Ap 51-C, 18 avenida 0-75 zona 15, Vista Hermosa II, 01015 Guatemala. **W:** unionradiogt.org – **GU23)** 1a Calle 35-48, Zona 7, Colonia Toledo, Guatemala **W:** facebook.com/radiotictacoficial – **GU24)** 8a Calle 10-54, Zona-11, Col. Roosevelt, Guatemala **W:** radiohosanna1450.blogspot.com – **GU26)** 17 Av.21, Cnt.Com Las Pergolas, Z-11, 01011 Guatemala **W:** facebook.com/1510am – **GU27)** Ap 1213, (or 30 Av "A" 7-33, Z-7, Col. Tikal, 01007 Guatemala), 01901 Guatemala **W:** radiovea.org – **GU28) W:** radiofeyesperanzadeguatemala.com – **GU29)** 2a. Calle 4-41 Zona 1, Guatemala City **W:** fger.org/radioenlinea – **GU30)** 10a Avenida 0-61, Z-19, Colonia La Florida, 01019 Guatemala – **GU32)** 17 Av. 5-47, Zona 11, Col. Miraflores, 01011 Guatemala **W:** radiorevelacionyverdad.com

HU00) HUEHUETENANGO
HU01) 2 Calle 4-42, Z-1, 13001 Huehuetenango – **HU02)** Ap 13, 13901 Huehuetenango **W:** lavozdehuehue.comlu.com – **HU04)** 13025 San Sebastián Coatán Programming in Spanish & Chuj Coatán **FM:** 92.5MHz –**HU05)** 13020 San Sebastián H, Huehuetenango **W:** tgmiradiobuenasnuevas.com

IZ00) IZABAL
IZ01) Calle Principal, Morales – **IZ02)** Ruta Atlántico km 291, 18001 Puerto Barrios – **IZ04)** Ap 425, 18901Puerto Barrios – **IZ05)** 8 Av 15 y 16 Calle, 18001 Puerto Barrios – **IZ06)** Izabal

JU00) JUTIAPA
JU01) 4 Avenida 4-79, Zona 1, Colonia El Latino, 22001 Jutiapa – **JU02)** Carr Interamericana km 117, 22001 Jutiapa. **W:** radiouncionjutiapa.com – **JU03)** Quezada – **JU04)** 6ta Calle 5-00, Zona 3, a un costado del puente del Incienso, 22001 Jutiapa **W:** radiomaranathajutiapa.com

PE00) PETÉN
PE02) Sta Elena de la Cruz – **PE04)** Isleta Sta Bárbara, 17001 Flores (or 1 Av 1-22, Z-1, Guatemala) **W:** radiopeten.com.gt - **FM:** 88.5MHz – **PE05)** Ministerio de la Defensa Nacional, Sta Elena de la Cruz

QE00) QUETZALTENANGO
QE01) Ap 113 (or 13 Av 8-19, Z-1), 09901 Quetzaltenango – **QE03)** 5 C 13-56, Zona 3, Xelajú (Ap 90), 09901 Quetzaltenango - **FM:** 99.1MHz– **QE04)** 7 Av 0-26, Z-2, 09002 Quetzaltenango **W:** radiotgd.com – **QE05)** 3 Calle 3-38, Z-1, Coatepeque – **QE06)** 14 Av "A" 0-78, Z-1, 09002 Quetzaltenango – **QE07)** Ap. 107, 09901 Quetzaltenango – **QE08)** Calle Principal, Z-2, Colomba - **FM:** 99.1MHz – **QE09)** 4 Calle 15A-62, Z-1, 09002 Quetzaltenango **W:** nuevaradioxelaju.com – **QE10)** Km 211, Aldea Duraznales, Concepción, Chiquirichapa, Quetzaltenango

QU00) QUICHÉ
QU01) 7 Calle 3-67, Z-5, 14001 Sta Cruz del Quiché **W:** radioscatolicasdequiche.com - **FM:** 90.7 MHz – **QU03)** 5 Av 1-32, Canton Batzbaca, 14013 Nebaj

RE00) RETALHULEU
RE01) Ap 84, 11901Retalhuleu – **RE02)** 7 Av 6-72, 11001 Retalhuleu (or Ap 183-A, Guatemala): 0900-0300

SA00) SACATEPÉQUEZ
SA01) San Juan Sacatepéquez **W:** radiocircuitosanjuan.com - **FM:** 105.3 MHz.

SR00) SANTA ROSA
SR01) Edif Municipal, Chiquimulilla

SM00) SAN MARCOS
SM01) 4 Avenida 4-32, Z-1, Malacatán – **SM04)** 5 Calle 8-21, Z-1, San Pedro – **SM05)** Pajapita, 12001 San Marcos

SU00) SUCHITEPEQUEZ
SU01) 10001 Mazatenango - 1100-0400 – **SU02)** La Libertad 9-91, Z-1, 10001 Mazatenango – **SU03)** 6 Av 10-54, Z-1, 10001 Mazatenango – **SU04)** 13 Av 23-60, Z-12, 10012 Coyotenango – **SU05)** Calle 30 de Junio 1a y 2a, Z-5, 10001 Mazatenango

TO00) TOTONICAPÁN
TO01) Barrio La Cienaga, 08002 San Cristóbal Totonicapán – **TO02)** Totonicapán www.radioconstelacion.com.gt – **TO03)** Totonicapán – **TO04)** Momostenango, 08001 Totonicapán

ZA00) ZACAPA
ZA01) 4 Calle 12-54, Z-1, 19001 Zacapa – **ZA02)** 4 Calle 10-34, Z-1, 19001 Zacapa – **ZA03)** Zona Militar N° 7, 19001 Zacapa

FM in Guatemala City (MHz): 88.1 Fabuestereo - 88.5 Galaxia La Picosa – 88.9 Fabulosa 88.9 – 89.3 Estrella – 89.7 Em.Unidas – 90.1 Yo Sí Sideral – 90.5 Punto – 90.9 Exitos – 91.3 Furia Musical – 91.7 Fiesta – 92.1 Universidad – 92.5 40 Principales – 92.9 Disney – 93.3 FM Joya – 93.7 Mía – 94.1 94 FM – 94.5 La Sabrosita – 94.9 Nueve Cuatro Nueve – 95.3 Kyrios – 95.7 Ranchero – 96.1 Nuevo Mundo – 96.5 Atmósfera - 96.9 Sonora – 97.3 Alfa – 97.7 Kiss FM - 98.1 Doble S – 98.5 Albavisión – 98.9 Globo – 99.3 La Grande - 99.7 Conga – 100.1 Infinita – 100.5 Cultural – 100.9 La Hit FM – 101.3 R. Extrema – 101.7 R. Activa – 102.1 Stereo 102 – 102.5 FM Fama – 102.9 Caliente – 103.3 R. María – 103.7 R. Fiesta – 104.1 Stereo Visión – 104.5 TGRF R. Faro Cultural – 104.9 Tropicálida – 105.3 Celebra FM – 105.7 Union – 106.1 Red Deportiva – 106.5 Clásica – 106.9 ¡UyUyUy! – GU04) 107.3 TGW LV de Guatemala – 107.7 Mega

FM in Quetzaltenango (MHz): 87.5 Estéreo Bendición – 88.1 Dinámica – 88.5 La Consentida – 89.5 Emisoras Unidas – 89.9 Prisima FM – 90.3 Tropicálida – 90.7 María – 91.1 La Nueva Mega – 91.7 La Rubia – 92.3 R. Cadena Sonora – 92.7 Cadena Caliente – 93.1 Nahual Estereo – 93.7 Fiesta – 94.3 Diamante – 94.7 Punto – 95.1 Ke Buena – 95.5 Evolución – 95.9 FM Globo – 96.3 FM Intima – 97.1 Exa FM – 97.5 Gaviota FM – 98.3 La Grande – 98.7 Yo Sí Sideral – 99.1 RTVA Arqueocesana – 99.5 Génesis – 99.9 Galaxia – La Picosa – 100.3 Stereo Cien – 100.7 R. Culturas – 101.1 R. Estéreo Tulán – 101.5 Estéreo Alegre – 102.3 Precencias R. – 102.9 Cristal – 103.3 La Voz de Dios – 104.3 Emisoras Unidas – 104.7 Razón – 105.3 La Voz del Evangelio – 105.9 FM Luna – 106.3 La Visión F – 106.7 Alfa – 107.1 R. Exitos – 107.9 R. Estéreo Vida

GUINEA

L.T: UTC — **Pop:** 13 million — **Pr.L:** French (official), Fulani, Mandinka, Susu — **E.C:** 220V/50Hz— **ITU:** GUI

HAUTE AUTORITÉ DE LA COMMUNICATION (HAC)

✉ Cité des Nations - Boulbinet, Kaloum, Conakry ☎ +224 657737376 **W:** hacguinee.org **L.P:** Pres: Martine Conde

RADIO TÉLÉVISION GUINÉENNE (RTG, Pub)

✉ B. P. 391, Conakry ☎+224 30 41 55 19 **W:** rtgkoloma.info **L.P:** DG: Alpha Kabinet Keita. Dir. Tech: Aladji Touré.
SW: Conakry (Sonfonia): 9650kHz 50kW (irregular): 0600-2400.
FM: Conakry 88.5/91.7MHz. **R. Kaloum Stereo:** 94.9MHz.
D.Prgr. in French/Ethnic: 24h.
Ann: F: "Radio Guineé". **IS:** Guitar.

RADIO RURALE (**RTG** rural stations):
Basse Guinée, Kindia: 98.7/99.2/99.3MHz – **Beyla:** 94.4/98.2MHz – **Bissikirima:** 91.0MHz – **Boké:** 95.3MHz – **Dinguiraye:** 98.6MHz – **Faranah:** 88.2MHz – **Gaoual:** 98.6MHz – **Guinée Forestiere,** Nzérékoré: 89.0MHz – **Haute Guinée**: Mandiana 88.2MHz, Kankan 92.1MHz, Dabadou 93.0MHz, Siguiri 97.0MHz, Douabou 99.0MHz – **Kérouané:** 92.2MHz – **Kindia:** 88.3MHz, Kakoulima 98.7MHz, Koliadi 99.9MHz – **Kissidougou:** 95.4/98.1MHz – **Koundara:** 98.6MHz – **Macenta:** 88.6/98.2MHz – **Mali:** 101.6MHz – **Mamou:** 91.1/101.1MHz – **Moyenne Guinée,** Pita: 87.6MHz – **Siguiri:** 94.4MHz – **Télimélé:** 97.7MHz – **Tougué:** 98.3MHz.

Private stations:
Atlantic FM: Conakry 96.5MHz – **Bambou FM:** Coyah/Faranah 89.3MHz– **Bolivar FM:** Mamou 99.4MHz **W:** bolivarmedia.webs.com – **Cherie FM:** Conakry 104.1MHz **W:** cheriefmguinee.com – **Djiguii FM,** Conakry: 105.7/107.7MHz. **W:** djiguii.com – **Djoliba FM:** Conakry/Siguiri 95.6MHz – **Espace FM:** Conakry 99.6MHz, Labé 99.7MHz **W:** espacefmguinee.info – **Gangan FM:** Conakry 101.1MHz – **Horizon FM:** Conakry/Kankan 103.4MHz – **R. Liberté FM:** Conakry/N'zérékoré 101.7MHz **W:** radiolibertefm.com – **R. Maria,** Conakry: 100.8MHz **W:** radiomaria.org – **R. Milo,** Kankan/Siguiri: 99.5MHz **W:** milo-fm.com – **R. Nostalgie Guinée:** Conakry 98.2MHz 1kW **W:** nostalgieguinee.net – **R. Renaissance:** Conakry 95.9MHz **W:** renaissancefmguinee.com – **Sabari FM,** Conakry: 97.3MHz 1kW. **W:** sabarifm.com – **Soleil FM:** Conakry 101.7MHz – **Swet FM:** Conakry 102.2MHz.
BBC World Sce: Conakry/Labé 93.9MHz.
R. France Int: Conakry 89.0, Kankan/Labé/Nzerékoré 89.9MHz

GUINEA-BISSAU

L.T: UTC — **Pop:** 2 million — **Pr.L:** Portuguese (official), Guinea-Bissau Creole — **E.C:** 220V/50Hz — **ITU:** GNB

AUTORIDADE REGULADORA NACIONAL (ARN)

✉ Enterramento/Traseiros do Hospital Militar, C.P. 1372, Bissau ☎+245 443204873 🖷 +245 443204876 **W:** arn.gw **E:** info@arn.gw

RADIODIFUSÃO NACIONAL (RDN, Gov.)

✉ C.P. 191, Av. Domingos Ramos, Bissau ☎+245 443212426 **W:** rdngbissau.com
FM: Nhacra 91.5, Catió 93.7, Gabú 94.5, Bissau 104.1MHz.
D.Prgr: 0600-2400.
Ann: "Escutam a Radiodifusão Nacional da República da Guiné-Bissau"

OTHER STATIONS:
R. Bombolom, Bissau: 106.2MHz. Also rel. BBC & DW **W:** facebook.com/Radio-bombolom-1375960895959569 – **R. Capital FM,** Bissau: 87.7MHz **W:** radiocapital.caster.fm – **R. Cidade FM,** Bissau: 105.6MHz **W:** radiocidadefmgbissau.blogspot.com – **R. Evangélica FM,** Gabú: 92.4MHz **W:** evangelicafmgabu.caster.fm – **R. Gandal,** Gabú: 105.7MHz **W:** radiocidadefmgbissau.blogspot.com – **R. Jovem,** Bissau: 102.8MHz **W:** radiojovem.info – **R. Luz,** Bissau: 97.7MHz **W:** radioluzafrica.com – **R. Mavegro,** Bissau: 100.0MHz. Also rel. BBC – **R. Nossa** (Rlg.), Bissau: 98.9MHz **W:** radionossabissau.com – **R. Pindjiguiti,** Bissau: 95.0MHz. Also rel. VOA **W:** facebook.com/Rádio-galáxia-de-pindjiguiti-1195284467171089 – **R. Sol Mansi** (Rlg.), Mansôa/Gabú 90.0MHz, Bissau/Bafatá/Canchungo 101.8MHz. 0630-2300. Also rel. Vatican R. and UN prgrs. **W:** facebook.com/Radio.Sol.Mansi – **R. Voz de Quelélé,** Bissau: 104.8MHz **W:** radio-voz-quelele.blogspot.com
RDP África: Nhacra 88.4MHz 25kW, Catió 96.9 & Gabú 100.0MHz 1kW.
RFI Afrique: Gabú 93.6, Bissau 94.0, Catió 101.5MHz.
+30 community radio stations

GUYANA

L.T: UTC -4h — **Pop:** 774 000 — **Pr.L:** English (official), Guyanese Creole — **E.C:** 110V/60Hz — **ITU:** GUY

GUYANA NATIONAL BROADCASTING AUTHORITY (GNBA)

✉ 8 Lamaha St, Queenstown, Georgetown ☎ +592 2317366 🖷 +592 2317367 **E:** info@gnba.gov.gy **W:** gnba.gov.gy **L.P:** Chmn: Leslie Sobers

NATIONAL COMMUNICATIONS NETWORK INC. (Gov)

✉ Broadcasting House, P.O. Box 10760, Georgetown ☎+592 223 6049, +592 223 1566/1577 🖷+592 226 2253 **W:** ncnguyana.com **E:** feedback@ncnguyana.com
L.P: SEO: Mohammed Sattaur GM: Mazrul Bacchus Prod. Mgr: Martin Goolsarran

VOICE OF GUYANA
MW: Georgetown 560kHz 10 kW
FM: Rupununi 97.1MHz – Georgetown 102.5MHz – Linden 106.5MHz
Hot FM: Georgetown 98.1 MHz – **Fresh FM** Georgetown 100.1MHz

Other FM stations (MHz): 88.5 Littlle Rock R., New Amsterdam – 89.1 NTN R., Georgetown – 89.7 R. Guyana, New Amsterdam – 89.5 R. Guyana, Georgetown – 90.1 Mix FM, Georgetown – 90.5 Freedom R., New Amsterdam – 91.1 Freedom R., Georgetown – 91.5 Mix FM, New Amsterdam – 93.1 Real FM, Georgetown – 94.1 – Boom FM, Georgetown

HAITI

L.T: UTC -5h (8 Mar-1 Nov: -4h) — **Pop:** 11 million — **Pr.L:** French (official), Haitian Creole (official) — **E.C:** 110V/60Hz — **ITU:** HTI

CONSEIL NATIONAL DES TÉLÉCOMMUNICATION (CONATEL)

✉ 4, Ave. Christophe, Port-au-Prince ☎ +509 22275454 **W:** www.conatel.gouv.ht

MW	kHz	kW	Station, location
1)	660	1	R. Lumière, Port-au-Prince
1)	760	5/1	R. Lumière, Les Cayes
11)	840	10	R. 4VEH, Cap Haitien
2)	1030		R. Ginen, Port-au-Prince
FM	**MHz**	**kW**	**Station, location**
3)	88.5		Caraibes FM, Cap-Haitien
6)	88.5		R. Kiskeya, Port-au-Prince
6)	88.9		R. Kiskeya, Camp-Perrin
34)	89.7		Voix de l'Espérance, Port-au-Prince
10)	89.9		R. Parole de Vie, Fort-Liberté
14)	88.9		R. Télé Express Continental, Jacmel
9)	90.3		R. Timoun, Jacmel
9)	90.5		R. Timoun, Cap-Haitien
40)	90.5		Signal FM, Port-au-Prince
9)	90.7		R. Timoun, Les Cayes
1)	90.9	1/0.3	R. Lumière, Les Cayes/Jérémie
5)	90.9		R. Vision 2000, Jacmel
9)	90.9		R. Timoun, Port-au-Prince
44)	91.3		Tropic FM, Port-au-Prince
9)	91.5		R. Timoun, Hinche/Port-de-Paix
10)	91.7		R. Ephphatha, Jacmel

FM	MHz	kW	Station, location
9)	91.9		R. Timoun, Jérémie
47)	92.1		Shekinah Radio, Port-au-Prince
2)	92.1		R. Ginen, Cap-Haitien
5)	92.5		R. Vision 2000, Port-de-Paix
21)	92.5		R. Commerciale d'Haiti, Port-au-Prince
2)	92.9		R. Télé Ginen, Port-au-Prince + 4 sites
11)	93.3		R. 4VEH, Pignon
19)	93.3		Canal du Christ, Port-au-Prince
41)	93.7		R. Vasco, Port-au-Prince
11)	94.1		R. 4VEH, Cap-Haitien
29)	94.1		R. Nouvelle Génération, Port-au-Prince
3)	94.5	3	Caraibes FM, Port-au-Prince
10)	94.7		R. Voix de la Paix, Port-de-Paix
4)	94.9		R. Metropole, Jacmel
9)	94.9		R. MBC, Port-au-Prince
27)	95.3		La Voix de l'Evangile, Port-au-Prince
10)	95.5		R. Men Kontre, Les Cayes
15)	95.7		R. Horizon 2000, Port-au-Prince
1)	95.9	1	R. Lumière, Les Irois
20)	95.9		R. Boukman, Port-au-Prince
36)	96.1		RCH 2000, Port-au-Prince
30)	96.5		Sky FM, Port-au-Prince
11)	96.7		R. 4VEH, Mirelabais
19)	96.9		R. Tele Antilles Int, Port-au-Prince
16)	97.3		R. Télémegastar, Port-au-Prince
1)	97.7	1/0.3	R. Lumière, Port-au-Prince/Hinche
5)	98.1		R. Vision 2000, Gonaives
28)	98.1		Maxima FM, Port-au-Prince
9)	98.5		R. Timoun, Gonaives
10)	98.5		R. Voix Ave Maria, Cap-Haitien
26)	98.5		R. Ibo, Port-au-Prince
10)	98.7		R. Christ Roi, Gonaives
13)	98.9		Alleluia FM, Port-au-Prince
5)	99.3		R. Vision 2000, Port-au-Prince
2)	99.5		R. Ginen, Miragoâne
32)	99.7		Sweet FM, Port-au-Prince
5)	99.9		R. Vision 2000, Saint-Marc
4)	100.1	2	R. Metropole, Port-au-Prince
11)	100.3		R. 4VEH, Ile de la Tortue
45)	100.3		R. Leve Kanpe, Hinche
23)	100.5		R. Eclair, Port-au-Prince
2)	100.7		R. Ginen, Miragoâne
1)	100.9	0.2	R. Lumière, Port-de-Paix/Jacmel
12)	100.9		Magik 9, Port-au-Prince
4)	101.3		R. Metropole, Saint-Marc
33)	101.3		Univers FM, Port-au-Prince
22)	101.3		R. Télé Digital, Port-au-Prince
5)	101.7		R. Vision 2000, Les Cayes
24)	101.7		Energie FM, Port-au-Prince
7)	102.1	5	R. Nationale d'Haiti, Port-au-Prince
3)	102.5		Caraibes FM, Port-de-Paix
4)	102.5		R. Metropole, Les Cayes
35)	102.5		R. Télé Zenith, Port-au-Prince
43)	102.7		Trace FM, Port-au-Prince
6)	102.9		R. Kiskeya, Saint-Marc
31)	102.9		R. Super Star, Port-au-Prince
4)	103.3		R. Metropole, Gonaives
17)	103.3		R. Melodie, Port-au-Prince
10)	103.5		R. de l'Immaculée Conception, Hinche
39)	103.7		R. Shalom, Port-au-Prince
25)	104.5		R. Galaxie, Port-au-Prince
37)	104.9		RFM, Port-au-Prince
7)	105.1	0.5	R. Nationale d'Haiti, Cap-Haitien
7)	105.3	2	R. Nationale d'Haiti, Port-au-Prince
5)	105.7		R. Vision 2000, Cap-Haitien
10)	105.7		R. Soleil, Port-au-Prince
10)	105.9		R. Tet Ansamn, Jérémie
7)	106.3	0.5	R. Nationale d'Haiti, Cap-Haitien
18)	106.5		Planet Kreyol, Port-au-Prince
6)	106.9		R. Kiskeya, Sans Souci
46)	107.1		R. Ideal, Port-de-Paix
42)	107.3		R. Solidarité, Port-au-Prince
38)	107.7		Scoop FM, Port-au-Prince

Addresses & other information:
1) Côte Plage 16, Carrefour, B.P .1050, Port-au-Prince **W:** radiolumiere.org – **2)** #28, Delmas 31, Port-au-Prince **W:** rtghaiti.com/radioginen – **3)** 45 Rue Chavannes, Port-au-Prince **W:** radiotelevisioncaraibes.com – **4)** 8, Delmas 52, B.P. 62, Port-au-Prince **W:** metropolehaiti.com – **5)** 184, Av. John Brown, Lalue, Port-au-Prince **W:** radiovision2000haiti.net – **6)** 42, Rue Villemenay, Bois Verna, Port-au-Prince **W:** radiokiskeya.com – **7)** Delmas 65, Impasse Orchidée, B.P. 1143, Port-au-Prince **W:** rnhhaiti.com – **8)** 11, Rue Rigaud, P.V, Port-au-Prince **W:** freewebs.com/radiombc – **9) W:** radiotimoun.com – **10)** 14, Rue Pinchinat, Pétionville, Port-au-Prince **W:** radiosoleil.org radiovoixavemaria.com – **11)** Route Nationale 1, Morne Rouge, B.P. 1, Cap-Haitien **W:** radio4veh.org – **12) W:** magik9haiti.com – **13) W:** alleluiafmhaiti.com – **14)** #35, Rue de l'Eglise, Jacmel **W:** radioteleexpress.com – **15)** Rue Butte # 2, Bourdon, Port-au-Prince 6111 **W:** radiohorizon2000endirect.com – **16) W:** radiotelemegastar.com – **17) W:** radiomelodiehaiti.com – **18)** Delmas 48 #34, Port-au-Prince **W:** planetkreyol.com – **19)** 77 Rue Metellus, Bas de la Montagne Noire, Pétionville, Port-au-Prince 6140 **W:** radioteleantilleshaiti.com – **20) W:** facebook.com/pages/Radio-Boukman/157901850906631 – **21)** 39 Blvd. 15 Octobre, Tabarre, Port-au-Prince **W:** radiocommercialedhaiti.com – **22) W:** radioteledigital.fr.ht – **23) W:** radioeclairhaiti.com – **24) W:** energiefm.com – **25) W:** radiogalaxiehaiti.com – **26) W:** radioibo.net – **27) W:** rvehaiti.org – **28)** facebook.com/maximafm.haiti – **29)** Delmas 64, No. 6, Port-au-Prince **W:** palimpalem.com/6/radionouvellegeneration – **30) W:** haitiskyfm.com – **31)** Delmas 68, Angle rues Safran et C. Henri, Pétionville, Haïti **W:** superstarhaiti.com – **32)** Rue Dr Coles #8, Résidences du soleil, Delmas 25, Port-au-Prince **W:** sweetfmhaiti.com – **33)** Rue Villate, Pétionville, Port-au-Prince **W:** universfm.ht – **34)** Diquini 63, Campus de l'Université Adventiste d'Haiti, B.P. 1339, Port-au-Prince **W:** 4vve.org – **35)** 33, Bon Repos, Route nationale #1,Port-Au-Prince **W:** radiotelezenith.net – **36) W:** rch2000.net – **37) W:** rfmhaiti.net – **38)** 93 Rue Vilatte, Pétionville, Port-au-Prince **W:** scoopfmhaiti.com – **39) W:** radioshalomhaiti.com **40)** #127 Rue Louverture, Pétionville, Port-au-Prince **W:** signalfmhaiti.com – **41) W:** radiovascohaiti.com – **42)** 6 Rue Fernand, Canape Vert, Port-au-Prince **W:** radiosolidaritehaiti.com – **43) W:** ht.trace.fm – **44) W:** tropicfmhaiti.com – **45) W:** radiolevekanpehaiti.com – **46)** 3 Rue Trois Grace, Port-de-Paix **W:** radioidealfm.com – **47) W:** facebook.com/ShekinahTel

RADIO FRANCE INTERNATIONALE
FM: Port-au-Prince 89.3, Gonaïves 90.5, Jeremie 92.7, Jacmel 96.9, Cap Haïtien 100.5, Les Cayes 106.9MHz

HAWAII (USA)

L.T: UTC -10h — **Pop:** 1.4 million — **Pr.L:** English (official), Hawaiian (official), Hawaiian Pidgin (official), Filipino, Japanese — **E.C:** 120V/60Hz — **ITU:** HWA

FEDERAL COMMUNICATIONS COMMISSION (FCC)
see main entry under USA

HAWAII ASSOCIATION OF BROADCASTERS, INC
✉ P.O. Box 61562, Honolulu, HI 96839 ☎ +1 808 5991455 **W:** jamie@hawaiibroadcasters.org **W:** www.hawaiibroadcasters.org
L.P: Pres: Chris Leonard; Exec. Dir: Jamie Hartnett

MW	kHz	kW	Island	City of License	Callsign
	530	0.01	OAH	Honolulu	WPIW528 (TIS)*
19)	550	5	MAU	Wailuku	KNUI
19)	570	1	KAU	Eleele	KUAI
6)	590	7.5	OAH	Honolulu	KSSK
26E)	650	10	OAH	Honolulu	KPRP
18)	670	5	HAW	Hilo	KPUA
25)	690	10	OAH	Honolulu	KHNR
22)	740	5	MAU	Kihei	KCIK
25)	760	10	OAH	Honolulu	KGU
6)	830	10	OAH	Honolulu	KHVH
8)	850	5	HAW	Hilo	KHLO
25)	880	2	OAH	Honolulu	KHCM (ch,jap,kor)
19)	900	5	MAU	Kahului	KMVI
26C)	940	10	OAH	Waipahu	KKNE
6)	990	5	OAH	Honolulu	KIKI
4)	1040	10	OAH	Honolulu	KLHT
23)	1060	5	HAW	Hilo	KIPA
21)	‡ 1080	5	OAH	Honolulu	KWAI
28)	1110	5	MAU	Kihei	KAOI
13A)	1130	1	OAH	Honolulu	KPHI
20)	1210	1	OAH	Honolulu	KZOO (jap)
28)	1240	5	MAU	Kahului	KEWE
10)	1270	5	OAH	Honolulu	KNDI (ethnic)
1)	‡ 1370	6.2	OAH	Pearl City	KUPA (ch)
3)	1420	5	OAH	Honolulu	KKEA

MW	kHz	kW	Island	City of License	Callsign
3)	1500	5	OAH	Honolulu	KHKA
14)	1540	5	OAH	Honolulu	KREA (kor)
8)	1570	15	MAU	Haiku	KUAU
FM	**MHz**	**kW**	**Island**	**City of License**	**Callsign**
11A)	88.1	39	OAH	Honolulu	KHPR
11A)	88.1	4	OAH	Makaha	KHPR-FM1
11A)	88.7	6.5	OAH	Kailua	KHPH
5)	88.9	2	KAU	Lihue	KHJC
11A)	89.1	18	HAW	Hilo	KANO
11B)	89.3	38.5	OAH	Honolulu	KIPO
11B)	89.3	4	OAH	Makaha	KIPO-FM1
11B)	89.7	14.5	MAU	Waikapu	KIPM
11A)	89.9	1	KAU	Lihue	KIPL
27)	90.1	7	OAH	Honolulu	KTUH
12) ‡	90.3	5	HAW	Hilo	KCIF
11A)	90.7	14.5	MAU	Wailuku	KKUA
11B)	91.3	18	HAW	Pahala	KAHU
4)	91.5	100	OAH	Honolulu	KLHT-FM
17)	91.7	1.2	MAU	Wailuku	KMNO
16)	91.9	6	KAU	Kilauea	KAQA
23)	92.1	4.5	HAW	Holualoa	KHWI
6) #	92.3	100	OAH	Waipahu	KSSK-FM
19)	92.5	1.7	MAU	Kahului	KLHI-FM
23)	92.7	7.5	HAW	Hilo	KHBC
19)	93.1	100	OAH	Honolulu	KQMQ-FM
18)	93.1	10	HAW	Captain Cook	KMWB
19)	93.5	69	MAU	Lahaina	KPOA
19)	93.5	51	KAU	Lihue	KQNG-FM
6) #	93.9	100	OAH	Honolulu	KUBT
19)	93.9	7.3	HAW	Kailua-Kona	KLUA
15)	94.3	2	KAU	Hanapepe	KHKU
28)	94.3	2	MAU	Makawao	KDLX
19)	94.7	100	OAH	Honolulu	KUMU-FM
18)	94.7	51	HAW	Hilo	KWXX-FM
28)	95.1	3.5	MAU	Wailuku	KAOI-FM
25)	95.5	100	OAH	Honolulu	KAIM-FM
19)	95.9	51	KAU	Poipu	KSRF
19)	95.9	39	HAW	Hilo	KPVS
7)	95.9	19	MAU	Kaunakakai	KKHI
26F)	96.3	75	OAH	Kailua	KRTR-FM
9)	96.9	100	KAU	Lihue	KFMN
18)	97.1	38	HAW	Hilo	KNWB
13C)	97.3	1.45	MAU	Wailea-Makena	KRKH
25)	97.5	80	OAH	Honolulu	KHCM-FM
19)	97.9	51	HAW	Hilo	KKBG
19)	98.3	9.4	MAU	Pukalani	KJMD
6) #	98.5	51	OAH	Honolulu	KDNN
19)	99.1	7.3	HAW	Waimea	KAGB
25)	99.5	100	OAH	Honolulu	KGU-FM
19)	99.9	69	MAU	Kahului	KJKS
26A) #	100.3	100	OAH	Honolulu	KCCN-FM
19)	100.3	35	HAW	Hilo	KAPA
19)	100.3	7.1	HAW	Puueo	KAPA-FM1
7)	100.7	3.5	MAU	Kihei	KMKV
13D) #	101.1	100	OAH	Waianae	KORL-FM
18)	101.5	6.5	HAW	Kealakekua	KAOY
6) #	101.9	100	OAH	Pearl City	KUCD
19)	102.7	61	OAH	Waipahu	KDDB
23)	102.7	15	HAW	Kurtistown	KTBH-FM
19)	103.1	51	KAU	Hanamaulu	KSHK
11A)	103.1	3.4	MAU	Kualapuu	KJHF
7)	103.5	100	OAH	Wahiawa	KLUU
28)	103.9	14.5	HAW	Paauilo	KNUQ
26D)	104.3	75	OAH	Kaneohe	KPHW
13C)	104.7	69	MAU	Lanai City	KONI
26B) #	105.1	100	OAH	Honolulu	KINE-FM
23)	105.3	25.5	HAW	Keaau	KBGX
23)	105.3	1	HAW	Naalehu	KBGX-FM5
24)	105.5	21	MAU	Haliimaile	KPMW
19)	105.9	100	OAH	Honolulu	KPOI-FM
19)	106.1	7.3	OAH	Kahaluu	KLEO
13B)	106.5	69	MAU	Haiku	KRYL
2)	106.7	1.85	OAH	Nanakuli	KNAN
23)	106.9	4.5	HAW	Kawaihae	KWYI
23)	107.7	25.5	HAW	Volcano	KKOA
23)	107.7	1	HAW	Hilo	KKOA-FM1
23)	107.7	1	HAW	Naalehu	KKOA-FM5
25)	107.9	100	OAH	Aiea	KKOL-FM

+ FM txs below 1kW.

Hawaiian Islands: HAW=Hawai'i, KAU=Kaua'i, MAU=Maui, OAH=O'ahu *) Travellers' Information Station (TIS) #) HD Radio (hybrid trs) ‡) Temporarily inactive at time of publication (FCC authorized "Silent STA" status). Languages (other than English): ch=Chinese, fil=Filipino, kor=Korean, jap=Japanese

Addresses & other information:
1) Beach Time Broadcast, LLC: 1773 W San Bernadino Rd, Bldg C31-C34, West Covina, CA 91791 – **2) Big D Consulting, Inc:** c/o Kemp Communications, Inc., 3800 Howard Hughes Parkway, 17th Floor, Las Vegas, NV 89169 – **3) Blow Up, LLC:** 126 Queen St, Ste 204, Honolulu, HI 96813 **W:** espnhonolulu.com (KKEA) (ESPN Radio); cbssportshawaii.com (KHKA) (CBS Sportsradio) – **4) Calvary Chapel of Honolulu, Inc:** 98-1016 Komo Mai Drive, Aiea, HI 96701 **W:** klight.org – **5) Calvary Chapel of Twin Falls, Inc:** P.O.Box 391, Twin Falls, ID 83303. KHJC: 2970 Kele St, Ste 117, Lihue, HI 96766 **W:** csnradio.com/stations/studiowaivered/KHJC.php – **6) Capstar TX, LLC:** 7136 S. Yale Ave, Ste 501, Tulsa, OK 74136. Studios: 650 Iwilei Rd, Ste 400, Honolulu, HI 96817 **W:** island985.iheart.com (KDNN); khvhradio.iheart.com (KHVH); foxsports990.iheart.com (KIKI) (Fox Sports Radio); ksskradio.iheart.com (KSSK/KSSK-FM); 939beat.iheart.com (KUBT); star1019.iheart.com (KUCD) – **7) Educational Media Foundation, Inc:** 5700 W Oaks Blvd, Rocklin, CA 95765 – **8) First Assembly King's Cathedral & Chapels:** 777 Mokulele Hwy, Kahului, HI 96732 **W:** kingscathedral.com – **9) FM 97 Associates:** 1860 Leleiona St, Lihue, HI 96766 **W:** kauaifm97.com – **10) Geronimo Broadcasting, LLC:** 94-1371 Hiaai Pl, Honolulu, HI 96797. KNDI: 1734 S. King St, Honolulu, HI 96826 **W:** kndi.com **Format:** multi-ethnic: Filipino (Ilocano, Tagalog, Visayan), Chinese (Cantonese & Mandarin), Okinawan, Vietnamese, Laotian, Spanish, Samoan, Tongan, Marshallese, Chuukese, Pohnpeian & English. – **11A,B) Hawaii Public Radio, Inc:** 738 Kaheka St, Ste 101, Honolulu, HI 96814 **W:** www.hawaiipublicradio.org. 11A) incl. rel. of BBC World Service at nighttime. – **12) Hilo Christian Broadcasting Corp:** 180 Kinoole St, Ste 310, Hilo HI 96720 **W:** kcifhawaii.org – **13A) Hochman-McCann Hawaii, Inc / 13B) Hochman Hawaii Five, Inc / 13C) Hochman Hawaii Publishing, Inc / 13D) Hochman Hawaii-Three, Inc:** 1164 Bishop St, Ste 1703, Honolulu, HI 96813 **W:** www.hhawaiimedia.com (H Hawaii Media); www.facebook.com/koni1047 (KONI); www.facebook.com/Krock1015 (KORL-FM); www.facebook.com/krock973 (KRKH); www.facebook.com/pg/mauicountry1065 (KRYL) – **14) JMK Communications, Inc:** 4525 Wilshire Blvd, Los Angeles, CA 90010. KREA: 1839 S. King St, Honolulu, HI 96826 – **15) Kauai Broadcast Partners, LLC:** 9408 Grand Gate Blvd, Las Vegas, NV 89143. KHKU: 4357 Rice St, Ste 201, Lihue, HI 96766 **W:** star943.com – **16) Kekahu Foundation, Inc:** 4520 D Hanalei Plantation Rd, Princeville, HI 96722. KAQA is a satellite of KKCR. – **17) Maui Media Initiative, Inc:** 72 Kono Pl, Kahului, HI 96732-1326 – **18) New West Broadcasting Corp:** 1145 Kilauea Ave, Hilo, HI 96720 **W:** www.facebook.com/newwestbroadcasting; b97hawaii.com (KMWB/KNWB); kwxx.com (KWXX-FM). KAOY is a satellite of KWXX-FM. – **19) Pacific Media Group, Inc**: **HAW:** 913 Kanoelehua Ave, Hilo, HI 96720-5116 **W:** pmghawaii.com (Pacific Media Group); kbigfm.com (KKBG), thebeathawaii.com (KLUA), nativefm.com (KPVS); 75-5852 Alii Drive, Ste B1 & B2, Lagoon Tower, Kailua-Kona, HI 96740 **W:** kaparadio.com (KAPA) **KAU:** 4271 Halenani St, Lihue, HI 96766 **W:** kongradio.com (KQNG-FM); shaka103.com (KSHK); hi95kauai.com (KSRF); kuaicountry.com (KUAI) **MAU:** 311 Ano St, Kahului, HI 96732-1304 **W:** kissfmmaui.com (KJKS), dajam983.com (KJMD), hi92maui.com (KLHI-FM), espnmaui.com (KMVI) (ESPN Radio), knuimaui.com (KNUI), kpoa.com (KPOA) **OAH:** 1000 Bishop St, Honolulu, HI 96813 **W:** 1027dabomb.net (KDDB-FM), alt1059.com (KPOI-FM), 931dapaina.com (KQMQ-FM), kumu.com (KUMU-FM) – **20) Polynesian Broadcasting, Inc:** 2454 S Beretainia St, Ste 203, Honolulu, HI 96826 **W:** kzoohawaii.com – **21) Radio Hawaii, Inc:** 2360 N E Coachman Rd, Clearwater, FL 33765 – **22) Relevant Radio, Inc:** 1496 Bellevue St, Ste 202, Green Bay, WI 54307 – **23) Resonate Hawaii, LLC:** 630 Kilauea Ave, Ste 202, Hilo, HI 96720 **W:** lava1053.com (KBGX); hawaiiswave.net (KHBC); hawaiiskoa.com (KKOA); hawaiisbeach.com (KTBH-FM) – **24) Rey-Cel Broadcasting, Inc:** 230 Hana Hwy, Kahului, HI 96732 **W:** www.facebook.com/mix1055FM – **25) Salem Media of Hawaii, Inc:** 4880 Santa Rosa Rd, Ste 300, Camarillo, CA 93012. Studios: 1160 N King St, Honolulu, HI 96817 **W:** thefishhawaii.com (KAIM-FM); honolulurealcountry.com (KGU); 995theword.com (KGU-FM); www.am880.net (KHCM) (rel. China R. International in Chinese, English, Japanese, Korean); 975country.com (KHCM-FM); theanswerhawaii.com (KHNR); 1079koolgold.com (KKOL-FM) – **26A) SM-KCCN-FM, LLC / 26B) SM-KINE, LLC / 26C) SM-KKNE-AM, LLC / 26D) SM-KPHW, LLC /**

26E) SM-KRTR-AM, LLC/ 26F) SM-KRTR-FM, LLC: 2700 Corporate Drive, Ste 115, Birmingham, AL 35242 **W:** summitmediacorp.com (Summit Media Corp). Studios: Pioneer Plaza, 900 Fort St, Ste 700, Honolulu, HI 96813 **W:** kccnfm100.com (KCNN-FM); hawaiian105.com (KINE-FM); power1043.com (KPHW); krater96.com (KRTR/KRTR-FM) – **27) The University of Hawaii:** 2444 Dole St, Bachman Hall, Ste 209, Honolulu, HI 96822. Studio: 2445 Campus Rd, Hemenway Hall, Ste 203, Honolulu, HI 96822 **W:** ktuh.org – **28) Visionary Related Entertainment, LLC**: 1900 Main St, Ste 6, Wailuku, HI 96793 **W:** www.kaoigroup.com (KAOI Radio Group); kaoi1110.com (KAOI); kaoifm.com (KAOI-FM); kdlx943.com (KDLX); kewe1240.com (KEWE); q103maui.com (KNUQ)

HONDURAS

L.T: UTC -6h — **Pop:** 10 million — **Pr.L:** Spanish — **E.C:** 110V/60Hz — **ITU:** HND

COMISIÓN NACIONAL DE TELECOMUNICACIONES (CONATEL)

Ap. 15012, Edificio CONATEL, Colonia Modelo, Sexta Avenida Suroeste Contigua a Hondutel, Tegucigalpa ☎ +504 2552 7484 +504 2236 8611 **W:** conatel.gob.hn **E:** transparencia@conatel.gob.hn

ASOCIACÍON NACIONAL DE RADIODIFUSORES DE HONDURAS (ANARH)

Edificio Power FM, Blvd. Del Norte, Costado Sur entrada al Liceo Militar del Norte, P.O.Box 868, San Pedro Sula ☎ + 504 25640500 **E:** presidencia@anarh.net **W:** anarh.net **L.P:** Pres: Francisco Xavier Sierra

Call HR—, ‡ = inactive, † =irregular
Hrs of tr 24h unless otherwise stated.

MW	Call	kHz	kW	Station, location
1)	XT	550	1	ABC Radio, Tegucigalpa
2)	XD	†550	0.5	R. Manantial, San Marcos: 1115-0300
4)	KL	560	1	R. Reloj, San Pedro Sula
6)	ZQ	580	3	R. Cadena Voces, Tegucigalpa
112)	EO	580	3	Super Estrella de Occidente, S. Rosa de Copán
5)	LP3	590	10	R. América, San Pedro Sula
5)		590	1	R. América, Tela
5)		610	1	R. América, Gracias
5)	LP4	610	3	R. América, Santa Rosa de Copán
5)		620	10	R. América, Siguatepeque
5)	LP	630	3.5	R. América, Choluteca
5)	LP7	630	5	R. América, La Ceiba
5)	LP	650	1	R. América, Danlí
5)		650	2.5	R. América, Olanchito
5)		650	1	R. América, Tocoa
7)	VS	650	2.5	R. Católica de Olancho, Juticalpa
8)	NN18	660	3	LV de Honduras, La Ceiba
8)	NN	670	10	LV de Honduras, Tegucigalpa
8)	NN20	670	1	LV de Honduras, Sta Rosa de Copán
8)	NN8	680	10	LV de Honduras, San Pedro Sula
8)	NN2	680	10	LV de Honduras, Siguatepeque
8)	NN7	680	1	LV de Honduras, Danlí
8)	NN3	690	1	LV de Honduras, Choluteca
11)	SG	710	2.5	R. LV de la Libertad, Catacamas
10)	NN4	730	1	R. Centro, Tegucigalpa
12)	QQ	740	1	R. Intibucá, La Esperanza: 1100-0100
13)	IH	740	5	La Super Grande, Juticalpa: 1230-0400
9)	TG2	740	1	R. Satélite, San Pedro Sula: 1100-0600
90)	VC	740	2.5	LV Evangélica, Olanchito (r. 1390)
16)	XW	760	2.5	R. Comayagüela, Tegucigalpa
14)	RD	770	1	R. Majestad, Juticalpa
9)	TG	790	3	R. Satélite, Tegucigalpa
21)	DL	‡800	1	R. Corporación, Comayagua: 1100-0400
17)	XS2	800	3	R. Moderna, San Pedro Sula (r. 820)
90)	VC	810	6	LV Evangélica, La Ceiba (r. 1390)
25)	LP24	810	3	R. Valle, Choluteca: 1000-0400
17)	LP16	820	5	R. Moderna, Tegucigalpa
84)	KW	820	7/3	R. Sultana, Sta Rosa de Copán: 1100-0400
24)	RU	830	1	R. Uno, San Pedro Sula
26)	JB	‡830	1	Cadena Radial Impacto, Comayagua
90)	QW	840	3	LV Evangélica, Tela (r. 1390)
19)		860	0.5	R. Río de Dios, Olanchito
20)	BV	860	1.5	R. Piedra Blanca, Catacamas
3)	H	880	10	R. Nacional de Honduras, Tegucigalpa
9)	UP6	‡900	1	R. Satélite, La Ceiba
29)	VS	910	10	La Voz de Suyapa, Tegucigalpa
21)	RM	‡920	1	R. Sistema, Comayagua
32)	SK	920	5	R. Catacamas, Catacamas: 1200-0400
91)	CQ	930	4	Cadena Radial Samaritano, La Ceiba
18)	CR	940	1	DCR (Dif. Cristiana de R.), Tegucigalpa
34)	QL	950	5	R. Centro de Honduras, Siguatepeque
38)	LY	970	2	R. Millenium, Tegucigalpa
41)	AO	†980	1	R. Tocoa, Tocoa
39)	ZC	980	2	R. Rhema, San Pedro Sula
90)	VC	980	5	LV Evangélica, Comayagua (r. 1390)
36)	PR	990	3.5	R. Paz, Choluteca: 1100-0200
30)	CY	†1000	3	R. Congolón, Gracias: 1100-0500
44)	XZ	1000	1	HCH Radio, Tegucigalpa
89)	CD	1010	1	R. Constelación. Juticalpa: 1200-0400
23)	LL	1010	1	R. Visión Cristiana, Tocoa
27)	PN	1020	3	R. Visión Cristiana Internacional, Marcovia
90)	VC	1040	5	LV Evangélica, Juticalpa
90)	VC	1040	1	LV Evangélica, Danlí
48)	KT	1060	1	R. La Catracha, Tegucigalpa
42)	BB	1070	3	R. Unidad Evangélica, Catacamas
53)	LE	1070	1	R. Unica, San Pedro Sula
43)	IE	1080	3	R. Senda de Vida, San Lorenzo: 1200-2300
91)	CQ	1090	10	Cadena Radial Samaritano, Tegucigalpa
57)	AJ	1100	1	Radio Gualaco, Gualaco
58)	ND	1100	1.5	R. La Esperanza, La Esperanza: 1100-0300
59)	VA	1100	1	R. Tiempo, San Pedro Sula
38)	TL	†1120	2	R. Fiesta, Tegucigalpa
63)	BT	1130	1	Ritmo 1130, Juticalpa
99)	HP	1130	2	Estéreo Pinares, Siguatepeque
65)	UL	‡1140	1	R. Pico Bonito, La Ceiba
90)	VC	1140	3	LV Evangélica, Choluteca
5)	LP12	1150	1	R. Universal, Tegucigalpa
35)	VZ	1160	1	R. Juan Pablo II, Siguatepeque
47)		1160		R. Nueva Palestina, Nueva Palestina
45)	AF	1170	2	La Campeonísima, Choluteca
19)		1180	1	R. Río de Dios, Belén
49)	AZ	1180	1	R. El Tigre, Tegucigalpa
6)	VW3	1190	5	R. Cadena Voces, El Progreso
72)	SI	‡1200	1	R. Impacto, Tela: 1200-0400
31)	ZB	1220	1	Una Voz Que Clama en el Desierto, S. P. S.
71)		1220	1	R. Destellos de Luz, Sabá
74)	OP	1220	1	R. Sintonía, Juticalpa
75)	YS	‡1220	1	R. Suari, Marcala
148)	SD	‡1220	3	R. Destellos de Luz, Sabá
91)	CQ	1230	3	Cad. R. Samaritano, San Marcos de Colón
133)	ZC	‡1240	1	R. Vanguardia, Tegucigalpa
37)	KF	1250	1	R. Garzel, Juticalpa
51)	YF	†1250	1	R. Renacimiento, Comayagua
77)	FP	1260	1	R. Amistad, San Marcos de Colón
107)	BN	1280	1	R. San Miguel, Marcala: 1000-0400
50)	OW	1280	1	LV de la Victoria, Juticalpa
82)	LR	‡1300	5	Estéreo Emaus, Santa Rosa de Copán
83)	IV	1300	5	CCI Radio, Tegucigalpa
90)	VC	1310	2.5	LV Evangélica, San Pedro Sula
52)	CM	1310	5	R. Universidad de Agricultura, Catacamas
153)	TQ	1340	10	R. Adventista Maranatha, San Pedro Sula
91)	CQ	1340	5	Cadena Radial Samaritano, Comayagua
28)	BS	1360	1	R. San Pedro, Tegucigalpa: 1100-0600
85)	UN	1370	5	LVC Radio, Catacamas
90)	VC	1390	10/5	LV Evangélica, Tegucigalpa
90)	VC	1390	1	LV Evangélica, Sata Rosa de Copán
86)	UV	†1400	1	R. Cristo Eterno, Catacamas
90)	FO	1430	1	LV Evangélica, Puerto Cortés
97)	VM	‡1430	1	R. Maranatha, La Paz
98)	RD	1440	5	R. Belén, La Ceiba
55)	MS2	1460	1	La Voz del Patuca, Campamento
56)	GC	‡1460	2.5	R. Reino, San Pedro Sula
102)	EZ	1480	1	R. Misiones Int. "R. MI", Comayagüela
60)	HY	1490	1	R. Boquerón, Juticalpa
106)	EM	1510	1	R. Emmanuel, Nueva Ocotepeque: 1100-2330
183)	DF	1520	1	R. Ríos de Agua Viva, Siguatepeque
192)	MQ	†1520	5	R. Manantial de Vida Eterna, Juticalpa
40)		1550	1	R. Miel, Sabá
181)	BX	1590	5	R. Perla, El Progreso

Addresses & other information:

1) Centro Sercano de Boulevard Suyapa, Tegucigalpa **W:** abcradiohn.com – **2)** San Marcos, Ocotepeque **W:** manantial550.radio12345.

com – **3)** Ap 403, Barrio La Guadalupe, Ave. República de Chile, Edificio Loyola segundo nivel, frente a CEDAC, Tegucigalpa **W:** rnh.gob.hn - **FM:** San Pedro Sula 94.1MHz – **4)** Ap. 24, San Pedro Sula – **5)** Edif Audio Video, Ap 259, Tegucigalpa **W:** radiouniversalhn.net – **6)** Blvd Morazán, Edificio Classic, 2ndo piso, Frente a Banco Ficohsa, Tegucigalpa **W:** radiocadenavoceshn.com – **7)** Juticalpa, Olancho **W:** rcolancho.org – **8)** Emisoras Unidas, Col Florencia, Blv Suyapa (or Ap 642), Tegucigalpa **W:** radiohrn.hn – **9)** Emisoras Unidas, Col Florencia, Blv Suyapa (or Ap. 642), Tegucigalpa **W:** radiosatelite.hn – **10) W:** radiocentro.hn – **11) W:** facebook.com/RadioEvangelicaLaVozDeLaLibertad – **12)** Barrio El Way, Calle Principal, La Esperanza, Intibucá **W:** radiointibuca.webs.com – **13)** Ap 9, Barrio de Jésus, 4ta y 5ta Ave, 6ta Calle, Juticalpa **W:** grupocnc.net/radio740.html – **14)** Ap 15, 16101 Juticalpa - **FM:** 106.3MHz Prgrs in Sp and E – **15)** Atras de Gasolinera Shell, La Entrada, Copán –**16) W:** facebook.com/radiocomayaguelahn – **17)** Colonia Alameda, Calle Las Flores, una cuadra al norte del Bloque Materno Infantil, Hospital Escuela, Ap 259, Tegucigalpa **W:** radiomoderna.net – **18)** Ap 3448 (or Iglesia Amor Viviente, Col Godoy frente a F.H.I.S.), Tegucigalpa **W:** dcr940.net – **19) W:** radioriodedios.org riodedios.net (separate feeds) – **20)** Barrio de Jésus, Catacamas, Olancho **W:** facebook.com/Radio-Piedra-Blanca-128514627243156 – **21)** Barrio San Francisco, Fte Parque, Comayagua - **FM:** 99.9MHz – **22)** Danlí, El Paraíso – **23)** Tocoa, Colón **W:** radiovisioncristianahn.com – **24)** 2 calle 7 y 8 avenida S.O, San Pedro Sula **W:** radiouno830.es.tl – **25)** Ap 29, Choluteca **W:** radiovalle.net - **FM:** 90.7MHz – **26)** Ap. 33, Avenida José Santos Guardiola, Comayagua **W:** facebook.com/CadenaRadialImpactoLaVozDeComayagua - **FM** 93.9MHz – **27)** Barrio El Tamarindo, contigo al Restaurante Kig Palace, Choluteca **W:** rvci.org - **FM:** 93.5MHz – **28)** Ap 364, Av.New Orleans, San Pedro Sula **W:** radiosanpedrohn.net - **FM:** San Pedro Sula 88.9MHz – **29)** Ap. 480, Suyapa Medios, Edificio Pablo VI atras del Santuario de Suyapa 1, Tegucigalpa 3404 **W:** suyapamedios.com/la-voz-de-suyapa – **30)** Frente al Parque "Lempira", Gracias, Lempira (or Ap.1579, Tegucigalpa) – **W:** facebook.com/radiocongolon – **31)** Ap 2918 (or 5 Calle, 10 y 11 Av S.O 91), San Pedro Sula **W:** facebook.com/Una-Voz-Que-Clama-En-El-Desierto-Honduras-603677789818059 - **FM:** 102.1MHz Radio Fabulosa – **32)** Ap 50, Catacamas **W:** radiocatacamas.net - **FM:** 104.5MHz – **33)** Ap 10, 12101 Comayagua 1100-2400 - **FM:** 89.1MHz R Vida – **34)** Barrio Abajo, 2 Ave, 2da. y 3era. Cll S. E, Siguatepeque **W:** lacentro.centroradialhn.net - **FM:** 96.3MHz – **35) W:** facebook.com/radiojuanpablo – **36)** Ap. 40, Barrio El Hospital, Calle Morazán CO 51101, Choluteca **W:** radiopazhn.org - **FM:** 95.5MHz – **37)** Juticalpa, Olancho **W:** facebook.com/Radio-Garzel-151178541726267 - **FM:** 97.9MHz – **38)** Ap 2821, Col. ave Guanacaste #1511, Tegucigalpa **W:** circuitopop.com – **39)** Ap 996 (or 9 Calle, S.O 44, Entre 8 y 9 Av), San Pedro Sula **W:** rhema.ebenezer.hn **FM:** 98.5MHz Estéreo Mass – **40)** Barrio el Chorro, 2da. Avenida, entre 7 y 8 calle, Sabá, Colón **W:** radiomielsaba.com – **41)** Bo la Esperanza, 2 cuadras y media del Mercado municipal, Tocoa, Colón **W:** radiotocoa.com – **42)** Barrio La Cruz, Contiguo a la Iglesia el Encuentro, Catacamas, Olancho **W:** facebook.com/Radio-Unidad-Evangelica-254226874988732 – **43)** Colonia Morazan, San Lorenzo, Valle **W:** radiosendadevida.net – **44)** Ap. 614, Lomas del Mayab, calle San Marcos esquina opuesta a Novel Center, Casa # 1647, Tegucigalpa **W:** hchradio.com – **45)** Ap 78, Choluteca **W:** emisorasaliadashn.com/html/la-campeonisima.html - **FM:** 105.1MHz – **47)** Nueva Palestina, Olanco **W:** facebook.com/Radio-Nueva-Palestina-Oficial-314955388985208 – **48)** Tegucigalpa – **49)** Tegucigalpa – **50)** Edif. Las Vegas 1/2 Cuadra al Norte de Banco Atlántidad, B° El Centro, Juticalpa, Olancho **W:** grupoecohn.com/vozvictoria.php – **51)** Barrio Cabañas 2 cuadras al Norte de la Planta de la ENEE, Comayagua **W:** facebook.com/Radio-Renacimiento-374089842665596 – **52)** Kilometro 9 en la Carretera que conduce al Municipio Dulce Nombre de Culmi, Catacamas, Olancho **W:** unag.edu.hn – **53)** 9 Av 4 Calle, Edif Las Fuentes, San Pedro Sula **W:** radiounicahn.com – **55)** - **FM:** 99.1MHz – **56)** Misión Cristiana Internacional El Shaddai, San Pedro Sula **W:** facebook.com/RadioReino – **57)** Gualaco, Olancho **W:** facebook.com/1100AMRADIO – **58)** Ap 25, La Esperanza, Intibucá **W:** facebook.com/Radio-La-Esperanza-1970762733210863 – **59)** Ap 906, Bo. Lempira, 10 Calle, 8-9 Ave., S.O, San Pedro Sula **W:** radiotiempohn.com - **FM:** Stero Fama 97.7MHz – **60)** Juticalpa, Olancho 16101 **W:** radioboqueron.net – **63)** Juticalpa **W:** ritmo1130.com – **65)** Barrio La Isla, La Ceiba **W:** facebook.com/radio-pico-bonito-1140-am-165026650238268 – **71)** Sabá, Colón - **W:** facebook.com/RadioDestellosDeLuz – **72)** Calle José Trinidad Cabañas, Edif Hotel Presidente, Tela - **FM:** 89.9 – **74) W:** zeno.fm/sintonia1220 – **75)** Calle Principal, Marcala, La Paz – **77)** Barrio Fátima, San Marcos de Colón, Choluteca **W:** radioamistad.biz – **81)** Barrio Campo Luna, Choluteca **W:** emisorasunidas.net - **FM:** 88.7MHz – **82)** Ap. 203, Diócesis de Santa Rosa de Copan, Iglesia Católica. Barrio El Carmen, Costado Este del Parque Infantil, Santa Rosa de Copan **W:** radiosantarosa.net - **FM:** 94.5MHz – **83)** Residencial El Trapiche, Boulevard Suyapa, 30694 Tegucigalpa **W:** cciradio.org – **84)** Ap 204, Sta Rosa de Copán **W:** facebook.com/RadioSultanaHN - **FM:** 90.3MHz – **85)** Barrio La Cruz, cuadra y media al Este de la Municipalidad de Catacamas, Olancho **W:** facebook.com/lavozdecatacamas - **FM** 97.9MHz – **86)** Catacamas, Olancho – **89)** Barrio Las Flores, Avenida La Trinidad, Casa 054, Juticalpa **W:** radioconstelacion.net - **FM:** 101.9MHz – **90)** Ap 3252, Tegucigalpa – (Owned and operated by Conservative Baptist Home Mission Society, Box 828, Wheaton, IL 60187, USA) **W:** hrvc.org – **91)** Colonia Payaqui, bulevar San Juan Bosco, frente a el segundo porton del instituto San Miguel, Casa 3658, 504, Tegucigalpa **W:** radiosamaritano.net - 1100-0500 – **95)** 12 Calle 2a Ave 206, Barrio La Curva, Puerto Cortés – **97)** Santiago de la Paz, La Paz (or Col.21 de Octubre, Sector 3, Bloque 2, Casa 5, Tegucigalpa) **W:** facebook.com/MaranathaHonduras – **98)** Ap. 614, Av San Isidro, Entre Calles 9 y 10, La Ceiba **W:** facebook.com/RadioBelenhn – **99)** Casa 269, Barrio Abajo, Siguatepeque 1155 **W:** pinares.centroradialhn.net - **FM:** 91.5MHz – **102)** Ap. 20583, Comayagüela (or IMF World Missions, 1115 S. Grove Ave. Ste. 104, Ontario, CA 91761) - 1100-0300 **W:** radiomi.com - **FM:** Talanga 99.3MHz – **106)** Barrio San Andrés, Ocotepeque **W:** facebook.com/Radio-Emmanuel-1510-AM-160416914020684 – **107)** Barrio Concepción, Marcala, La Paz (or Palacio Arzobispal, Av. Cervantes, Barrio El Centro, Tegucigalpa) **W:** radiosanmiguelhn.blogspot.com – **112)** Santa Rosa de Copán **W:** superestrella.org - **FM:** 93.1MHz – **128)** Radio Ensenanzas Evangelicas, Puerto Lempira – **133)** Ap 914, Tegucigalpa – **147)** Ap 888, (or Centro Comercial San José), La Ceiba **W:** applegatefellowship.org/missions/honduras.asp **E:** radiolitoral@psinet.hn – **148)** Barrio La Pava, Sabá, Colón **W:** radiodestellosdeluz.org – **153)** Ap 210 (or 5 Calle, 10 y 11 Av S.O., Barrio Beuque), San Pedro Sula **W:** 1340am.tk – **181)** 4 y 5 Ave, 3 Calle 442, Barrio Las Delicias, El Progreso, Yoro **W:** radioperla.com – **192)** Barrio de Jesús, Casa 7, Calle Principal, Juticalpa **W:** facebook.com/Radio-Manantial-de-Vida-Eterna-1520-AM/172815026105703

FM in Tegucigalpa (MHz): 88.1 Stereo Exitos – 88.7 Globo Grupera – 88.9 RDS R. – 89.3 Power – 89.9 R. Red de Radiodifusión Bíblica – 90.5 R. Corazón 90.5 – 91.1 R. Kairos FM – 91.7 R. Buenísima – 92.3 Rock n' Pop – 92.9 R. HRN – 93.3 Cadena Voces – 94.1 FM 94 – 94.7 América – 94.9 HCH Radio – 95.3 Digital – 95.9 R. Panamericana – 96.5 R. Estéreo Fiel – 97.1 EstéreoTic Tac – 97.7 Azul – 98.3 Estéreo Concierto – 98.9 Estéreo Fe – 99.5 Suprema – 100.1 Super 100 – 100.7 R. Exa FM – 101.3 Nacional de Honduras – 101.9 Vox – 102.5 Suave FM – 102.9 Tu Alternativa Siempre – 103.7 Luz – 104.5 Satélite – 104.9 Estéreo Amor – 105.5 Musiquera – 106.1 Romántica – 106.7 Stereo Rumba – 107.3 W107 Energía Estéreo – 107.9 Top Music con La Onda del Nuevo Mundo.

AFRTS (Air Force)
✉ JTF-B, APO AA 34042, USA **E:** PAO@jtfb-emh1.army.mil
FM: 106.3MHz Soto Cano Air Base, 0.25kW **D.Prgr:** 24h

HONG KONG (China, SAR)

L.T: UTC +8h — **Pop:** 7.5 million — **Pr.L:** Standard Chinese (official), English (official), Cantonese — **E.C:** 200V/50Hz, 220V/50Hz — **ITU:** HKG

COMMUNICATIONS AUTHORITY
✉ 20/F, Wu Chung House, 213 Queen's Road East, Wan Chai, Hong Kong ☎ +852 2961 6333 🖷 +852 25072219 **E:** webmaster@ofca.gov.hk **W:** www.coms-auth.hk **L.P:** Chair: Winnie Tam Wan-chi

RADIO TELEVISION HONG KONG (Gov.)
✉ Broadcasting House, 30 Broadcast Drive, Kowloon, Hong Kong ☎ +852 3691 2388 🖷 +852 2336 9314 **E:** ccu@rthk.org.hk **W:** rthk.hk **L.P:** Dir. of Broadc: Leung Ka-wing, Asst. Dir. (Radio & Corporate Programming): Chow Kwok-fung, Brian

MW	Netw.	Location	kW
567	R. 3	Golden Hill	20
621	P. Ch	Golden Hill	20
675	R. 6	Peng Chau	10
783	R. 5	Golden Hill	20
1584	R. 3	Chung Hom Kok	0.1

P. Ch = Putonghua Channel

FM	Netw.	kW	Tx Location	Target Div.
92.3	R. 5	0.025	Tin Shui Wai	
92.6	R. 1	3	Mt. Gough	Kowloon
92.9	R. 1	0.1	Golden Hill	Tsuen Wan
93.2	R. 1	0.5	Cloudy Hill	Fan Ling
93.4	R. 1	0.7	Castle Peak	Tuen Mun
93.5	R. 1	0.15	Beacon Hill	Sha Tin
93.6	R. 1	0.5	Lamma Isl.	HK Isl. south
93.6	R. 1	0.05	Hill 374	Yuen Long
94.4	R. 1	1	Kowloon Peak	HK Isl. north, Sai Kung
94.8	R. 2	3	Mt. Gough	Kowloon
95.2	R. 5	0.02	Mt. Nicholson	Jardine's Lookout
95.3	R. 2	0.5	Cloudy Hill	Fan Ling
95.6	R. 2	0.1	Golden Hill	Tsuen Wan
95.6	R. 2	0.05	Hill 374	Yuen Long
96.0	R. 2	0.5	Lamma Isl.	HK Isl. south
96.3	R. 2	0.15	Beacon Hill	Sha Tin
96.4	R. 2	0.7	Castle Peak	Tuen Mun,
96.9	R. 2	1	Kowloon Peak	HK Isl. north, Sai Kung
97.6	R. 4	3	Mt. Gough	Kowloon
97.8	R. 4	0.5	Cloudy Hill	Fan Ling
97.9	R. 3	0.02	Mt. Nicholson	Jardine's Lookout
98.1	R. 4	0.15	Beacon Hill	Sha Tin
98.2	R. 4	0.5	Lamma Isl.	HK Isl. south
98.2	R. 4	0.05	Hill 374	Yuen Long
98.4	R. 4	0.1	Golden Hill	Tsuen Wan
98.7	R. 4	0.7	Castle Peak	Tuen Mun,
98.9	R. 4	1	Kowloon Peak	HK Isl. north, Sai Kung
99.4	R. 5	0.015	Tseung Kwan O	Jank Bay
100.9	P. Ch	0.01	Mt. Nicholson	Jardine's Lookout
100.9	P. Ch	0.003	Castle Peak	Tuen Mun
103.3	P. Ch	0.015	Tseung Kwan O	Jank Bay
103.3	P. Ch	0.025	Tin Shui Wai	
106.8	R. 5	0.03	Castle Peak	Tuen Mun
106.8	R. 3	0.15	Chung Hom Kok	HK Isl. south
107.8	R. 3	0.015	Tseung Kwan O	Jank Bay
107.8	R. 3	0.025	Tin Shui Wai	

RTHK Radio 1 in Cantonese, partly relay BBCWS in Cantonese on Sat 2300-2400 : 24h – **RTHK Radio 2** in Cantonese: 24h, partly Indonesianon Sat 2300-2400 – **RTHK Radio 3** in English: 24h, partly Nepali on Sun 1105-1200, partly Urdu on Sun 1205-1300 – **RTHK Radio 4** in English/Cantonese, partly relay BBCWS English 1500-2300: 24h – **RTHK Radio 5** in Cantonese/Chinese: 24h – **RTHK Radio 6** Relay V.O. Hong Kong, 14th Prgr of China National Radio (CNR) in Beijing, in Chinese and Cantonese: 24h – **RTHK Putonghua Channel** in Chinese/Cantonese: 24h
Ann: Cantonese: "Heonggong dintoi dai (number) toi"

HONG KONG COMMERCIAL BROADC. CO. LTD

3 Broadcast Drive, Kowloon, Hong Kong ☎ +852 2336 5111 +852 2338 0021 **E:** cs@881903.com **W:** 881903.com

MW		kW	Location	Prgr.
864		10	Peng Chau	24h music
FM	**Netw.**	**kW**	**Tx Location**	**Target Div.**
88.1	CR1	3	Mt.Gough	Kowloon
88.3	CR1	0.5	Cloudy Hill	Fan Ling
88.6	CR1	0.7	Castle Peak	Tuen Mun
88.9	CR1	0.1	Golden Hill	Tsuen Wan
89.1	CR1	0.5	Lamma Isl.	HK Isl. south
89.2	CR1	0.15	Beacon Hill	Sha Tin
89.5	CR1	1	Kowloon Peak	HK Isl. north, Sai Kung
90.3	CR2	3	Mt.Gough	Kowloon
90.7	CR2	0.5	Cloudy Hill	Fan Ling
90.9	CR2	0.1	Golden Hill	Tsuen Wan
91.1	CR2	0.15	Beacon Hill	Sha Tin
91.2	CR2	0.7	Castle Peak	Tuen Mun
91.6	CR2	0.5	Lamma Isl.	HK Isl. south
92.1	CR2	1	Kowloon Peak	HK Isl. north, Sai Kung

HKCR CR1 (Supercharged 881) in Cantonese. 24h **N:** half-hourly
HKCR CR2 (Ultimate 903) in Cantonese 24h **N:** hourly **Ann:** "Chikja gaulingsaam"
HKCR AM864 in English, partly Filipino on Fri and Sat 1300-1500. 24h **N**: On the h from 2300-1500

METRO BROADCAST CORPORATION LTD.

Basement 2, Site 6, Whampoa Gardens Hunghom, Kowloon, Hong Kong ☎ +852 3698 8000 +852 2123 9889 **E:** prenquiry@mbc.com.hk **W:** metroradio.com.hk

MW	Network	kW	Location	
1044	Metro Plus	10	Peng Chau	
FM	**Network**	**kW**	**Tx Location**	**Target Div.**
99.7	Metro Info	3	Mt.Gough	Kowloon
100.0	Metro info	0.5	Cloudy Hill	Fan Ling
100.4	Metro info	0.7	Castle Peak	Tuen Mun
100.5	Metro Info	0.15	Beacon Hill	Sha Tin
101.0	Metro Info	0.01	Stanley	
101.6	Metro Info	0.1	Golden Hill	Tsuen Wan
101.8	Metro Info	1	Kowloon Peak	HK Isl. north
102.1	Metro Info	0.5	Lamma Isl.	HK Isl. south
102.4	Metro Finance	0.15	Beacon Hill	Sha Tin
102.5	Metro Finance	0.7	Castle Peak	Tuen Mun
102.6	Metro Finance	0.01	Stanley	
104.0	Metro Finance	3	Mt.Gough	Kowloon
104.5	Metro Finance	0.5	Lamma Isl.	HK Isl. south
104.7	Metro Finance	0.5	Cloudy Hill	Fan Ling
105.5	Metro Finance	0.1	Golden Hill	Tsuen Wan
106.3	Metro Finance	1	Kowloon Peak	HK Isl. north

Metro Plus in English (Partly Cantonese, Mandarin, Filipino, Hindi and Thai) 24h music, news and information **Metro Info** in Cantonese. 24h **Ann:** "Sansing jiseun toi" **Metro Finance** in Cantonese (Partly Mandarin) 24h

DIGITAL RADIO (DAB)
DAB has been discontinued since September 2017

HUNGARY

L.T: UTC +1h (28 Mar-31 Oct: +2h) — **Pop**: 9.68 million — **Pr.L**: Hungarian — **E.C**: 50Hz, 230V — **ITU**: HNG

MÉDIASZOLGÁLTATÁS-TÁMOGATÓ ÉS VAGYONKEZELŐ ALAP (MTVA) - Media Services and Support Trust Fund

MÉDIASZOLGÁLTATÁS-TÁMOGATÓ ÉS VAGYONKEZELŐ ALAP (MTVA) - Media Services and Support Trust Fund is Hungary's state-owned national public-service broadcasting organization and it is also a cooperation of the two public media services: **Duna Médiaszolgáltató Nonprofit Zrt.** (the former **Magyar Rádió**, **Magyar Televízió** and **Duna Televízió**) and **Magyar Távirati Iroda** (**Hungarian Telegraphic Office**).
1037 Budapest, Kunigunda útja 64 ☎ +36 1 7595050 +36 1 428 0222 **E:** info@mtva.hu **W:** www.mtva.hu **L.P:** CEO: Dániel Papp

NEMZETI MÉDIA- ÉS HÍRKÖZLÉSI HATÓSÁG (NMHH)

(National Media and Communications Authority)
1015 Budapest, Ostrom u. 23-25 ☎ +36 1 4577100 +36 1 3565520 **E:** info@nmhh.hu **W:** nmhh.hu **L.P:** Pres: Dr. Monika Karas

ANTENNA HUNGÁRIA ZRT.

1119 Budapest, Petzvál József u. 31-33 ☎ +36 1 4642464 +36 1 4642525 **E:** antennah@ahrt.hu **W:** ahrt.hu **L.P:** CEO: Zsolt Sárecz

HELYI RÁDIÓK ORSZÁGOS EGYESÜLETE (HEROE)

(National Association of Local Radios)
8000 Székesfehérvár, Donát u. 92 ☎ +36 22 505310 +36 22 505312 **E:** info@heroe.hu **W:** heroe.hu **L.P:** Pres: Zoltán Hauk

DUNA MÉDIASZOLGÁLTATÓ NONPROFIT ZRT. (former MAGYAR RÁDIÓ)

1038 Budapest, Bojtár utca 41-47 ☎ +36 1 7595050 **W:** www.dunamsz.hu **E:** kozonsegszolgalat@mtva.hu **L.P**: see: MTVA
Kossuth Rádió ☎ +36 1 3287945 **W:** mediaklikk.hu/kossuth **Petőfi Rádió** ☎ +36 1 3288555 **E:** petofilive@mtva.hu **W:** mediaklikk.hu/petofi **Bartók Rádió** ☎ +36 1 3288772 **W:** mediaklikk.hu/Bartok **E:** kozonsegszolgalat@mtva.hu

MW	kHz	kW	Pr	MW	kHz	kW	Pr
Solt	540	1000	1	Marcali	1188	300	4
Lakihegy	873	20	4	Szolnok	1188	100	4
Pécs	873	20	4	Szombathely	1251	25	D
Miskolc	1116	15	D	Nyíregyháza	1251	25	D
Mosonmagyaróvár	1116	5	D	Győr	1350	5	4

FM (MHz):	MR1	MR2	MR3	Dankó	kW(erp)
Aggtelek	94.6				2.3
Balassagyarmat	93.7				3
Barcs	89.5				2
Budapest	107.8	94.8	105.3	100.8	83/77/81/79
Cegléd	93.0				1.1
Csávoly	96.7	89.4			6.1/6.3
Debrecen	99.7	89.0	106.6	91.4	1.4/1/1/1.2

FM (MHz):	MR1	MR2	MR3	Dankó	kW(erp)
Dombóvár				100.2	1
Fehérgyarmat	105.9				5.6
Gerecse	105.6				10
Győr	87.6	93.1	106.8	106.4	7.6/7.5/7.5/0.8
Kab-hegy	107.2	93.9	105.0	102.3	87/65/69/5.4
Kaposvár	96.7				3.5
Karcag	97.9				10
Kecskemét	104.9				1.1
Kékestető	95.5	102.7	90.7	99.8	20/30/28/0.3
Keszthely				104.3	1
Kiskörös	88.4	95.1	105.9		2/1.7/3
Komádi	103.0	96.7	105.1	89.9	39/37/30/5
Miskolc	97.1		107.5	102.3	5.6/1.4/1.4
Mosonmagyaróvár	95.0				0.8
Nagykanizsa	90.2	94.3	104.7	106.7	8.3/12/20/5
Nyíregyháza				107.4	1
Pécs	95.9	103.7	107.6	104.6	25/50/10/5.6
Rábaszentandrás				105.2	4.9
Sátoraljaújhely	91.9				0.5
Siófok				93.6	3
Sopron	96.8	99.5	107.9	101.6	9.3/9/7/5.1
Szeged	90.3	104.6	105.7	93.1	0.6/5/2.2/1
Szekszárd	99.0				1.1
Szentes	100.4	98.8	107.3	91.6	34/32/34/2
Szolnok	94.3			101.2	6.3/2
Telkibánya	90.2				3.6
Tiszafüred				105.2	1
Tokaj	97.5	92.7	105.5	88.3	50/50/50/5
Úzd	101.5	90.3	106.9		3/3/3
Vasvár	91.6	98.2	106.9	103.6	6.8/7.5/3/3

+ 16 Kossuth txs & + 17 Dankó txs below 1kW

Programs: P1 = **Kossuth R.** (news-talk) P2 = **Petőfi R.** (pop) P3 = **Bartók R.** (classical) P4 = **Nemzetiségi adások** (Ethnic broadcasts), P5 = **Parlamenti adások** (Parliamentary broadcasts, internet/ satellite only), P6 = **Duna World Rádió** (internet/satellite only) D = **Dankó Rádió** (folk+operetta)
Daily pr: 24h exc. **P1** MW: Mo-Fr 0330-2130, Sa-Su: 0400-2130 & **P4** MW: 0700-1900
ANN: **P1**: "Kossuth Rádió, otthon a világban" **P2**: "Petőfi Rádió - a Te slágered" **P3**: "Bartók Rádió, több, mint klasszikus"
P4: Nemzetiségi (Ethnic pr): ☎ +36 (1) 328-8672 🖷 +36 (1) 328-8682. **W:** www.mediaklikk.hu/nemzetisegiradio/ **Daily:** Croatian 0700-0900, German 0900-1100, Bell at noon 1100-1103, Serbian 1300-1500, Romanian 1500-1700, Slovak 1700-1900 **Mon:** Hungarian 1103-1200, Slovenian 1200-1230, **Mon-Fri:** Music of nationalities 1230-1300 **Tue:** Rusyn 1200-1230 **Tue/Thu:** Roma (Lovari dialect) 1130-1200 **Tue-Fri:** Hungarian 1103-1130 **Wed:** Bulgarian 1200-1230 **Wed/Fri:** Roma (Boyash dialect) 1130-1200 **Thu:** Greek 1200-1230 **Fri:** Ukrainian 1200-1230, **Sat:** Armenian 1200-1230, Polish 1230-1300 **Sat/Sun:** Music of nationalities 1103-1200 **Sun:** Hungarian (In One Motherland) 1200-1300.
Dankó Rádió: 🖃 Kunigunda útja 64, 1037 Budapest ☎ +36 1 7596071 **W:** mediaklikk.hu/danko/ **E:** dankoradio@mtva.hu
Daily pr: 24h on FM; **Mo-Fr:** 0330-2005, **Sa-Su:** 0400-2005 on MW, **Ann:** "Dankó Rádió, csendül a nóta, száll a muzsika"
NB: DX data: radiosite.hu, frekvencia.hu

National network:
Retro Rádió (Comm.)
🖃 1016 Budapest, Hegyalja út 7-13 ☎ +36 20 2222122 **W:** www.retroradio.hu **E:** info@retroradio.hu

Location	MHz	kW	Location	MHz	kW
Kaposvár	89.0	0.05	Vasvár	101.2	1
Nagykanizsa	93.6	0.25	Győr	101.4	10
Szeged	94.9	1	Komádi	101.6	30
Szentes	95.7	0.2	Sopron	102.0	30
Miskolc	98.3	5.6	Fehérgyarmat	102.8	2.5
Szekszárd	98.4	1	Budapest	103.3	100
Gerecse	100.0	0.05	Tokaj	103.5	50
Kabhegy	100.5	100	Kékes	104.7	30
Debrecen	101.1	3	Pécs	105.5	50

Other Stations

FM	MHz	kW	Location	Station
27)	87.9	1	Szeged	Rádió 1
9)	88.1	1	Budapest	InfoRádió (news)
2)	88.3	1	Komárom	Mária R. (rlg)
2)	88.3	1	Cegléd	Mária R. (rlg)
2)	88.8	1.3	Budapest	Mária R. (rlg)
5)	90.3	0.4	Budapest	Tilos R. (community)
11)	90.5	0.8	Komárom	Forrás R.
7)	90.6	1	Sátoraljaújh.	Szent István R. (rlg)
27)	90.6	1.2	Veszprém	Rádió 1
26)	90.9	0.76	Budapest	Jazzy (smooth jazz)
13)	91.6	1	Cece	Karc FM (soon)
14)	91.7	1.2	Kiskörös	Magyar Katolikus R. (rlg)
7)	91.8	0.5	Eger	Szent István R. (rlg)
28)	92.1	1	Budapest	Klasszik R. (classical)
14)	92.5	0.63	Esztergom	Magyar Katolikus R. (rlg)
27)	92.6	1	Siófok	Rádió 1
24)	92.9	2.6	Budapest	Klubrádió (talk)
14)	92.9	1	Zalaegerszeg	Magyar Katolikus R. (rlg)
23)	93.4	1	Dabas	R. Dabas
25)	93.6	0.85	Nagykörös	Gong R.
18)	94.2	1	Budapest	Trend FM
20)	94.4	1	Debrecen	Európa R.
7)	95.1	1	Miskolc	Szent István R. (rlg)
8)	95.1	1	Zalaegerszeg	Egerszeg R.
7)	95.4	1	Encs	Szent István R. (rlg)
16)	95.4	0.9	Szeged	Rádió 88
29)	95.7	1	Balassagy.	Megafon R.
3)	95.8	2	Budapest	Sláger FM
14)	96.1	0.1	Székesfehérvár	Magyar Katolikus R. (rlg)
27)	96.3	5	Miskolc	Rádió 1
27)	96.4	2.5	Budapest	Rádió 1
25)	96.5	1	Kecskemét	Gong R.
13)	97.1	2	Szombathely	Karc FM
2)	97.3	1.3	Göd	Mária R. (rlg)
27)	97.7	1	Szombathely	Rádió 1
11)	97.8	0.8	Tatabánya	Forrás R.
1)	98.6	2	Budapest	Manna FM
13)	98.9	1	Szigetvár	Karc FM
4)	99.5	5	Budapest	99.5 Best FM
25)	99.6	0.76	Kecel	Gong R.
27)	99.9	2	Kaposvár	Rádió 1
10)	100.0	0.5	Kalocsa	Korona FM 100
33)	100.1	1	Győr	Győr+ R.
20)	100.5	1	Nyíregyháza	Európa R.
2)	100.6	3	Telkibánya	Mária R. (rlg)
6)	100.7	1	Eger	100.7 Best FM
14)	101.2	2	Pécs	Magyar Katolikus R. (rlg)
27)	101.3	1	Eger	Rádió 1
21)	101.6	1	Miskolc	Radio M
22)	101.6	0.1	Budapest	Sola R. (protestant rlg)
32)	101.7	2	Pécs	Pécs FM
39)	101.8	1	Székesfehérvár	101.8 Best FM
31)	101.9	1	Tamási	Tamási R.
14)	102.1	0.25	Budapest	Magyar Katolikus R. (rlg)
30)	102.4	0.8	Szolnok	Amadeus R.
14)	102.5	0.5	Szekszárd	Magyar Katolikus R. (rlg)
34)	102.7	0.95	Barcs	Dráva Hullám 102.7
37)	102.7	0.1	Pápa	AFN Europe, The Eagle
17)	103.0	1	Miskolc	Csillagpont R.
27)	103.1	0.1	Győr	Rádió 1
13)	103.8	3	Miskolc	Karc FM
12)	103.9	0.86	Nyíregyháza	103.9 Best FM
27)	104.0	1	Békéscsaba	Rádió 1
35)	104.6	0.8	Debrecen	104.6 Best FM
14)	104.6	1	Sopron	Magyar Katolikus R. (rlg)
2)	104.9	0.8	Dömös	Mária R. (rlg)
40)	104.9	1	Sátoraljaújh.	Zemplén FM (planned)
36)	105.1	0.74	Szekszárd	R. Antritt
13)	105.9	3.2	Budapest	Karc FM
13)	106.0	0.74	Debrecen	Karc FM (soon)
38)	106.6	5	Szentgotthárd	R. Monoster
15)	107.0	0.8	Kistelek	Rádió 7
19)	107.0	0.76	Szigetsz.mikl.	Lakihegy R.
14)	107.4	0.5	Szombathely	Magyar Katolikus R. (rlg)

+ approximately 170 additional FM txs from 50W to 1kW

Addresses & other information:1) 🖃 1147 Budapest, Gervay u. 4 ☎+36 1 9111986 **W:** mannafm.hu **E:** info@mannafm.hu – **2)** 🖃 1133 Budapest, Gogol u. 28 ☎+36 1 3730701 **W:** www.mariaradio.hu **E:** info@mariaradio.hu **NB:** total 22 txs. 4 hours local px from many regional studios – **3)** 🖃 1012 Budapest, Márvány u. 17

☎+36 1 2375300 **W:** slagerfm.hu **E:** online@slagerfm.hu – **4)** ✉ 1116 Budapest, Hegyalja út 7-13 ☎+36 20 5555155 **W:** www.bestfmbudapest.hu **E:** info@bestfmbudapest.hu **NB:** total 6 txs - **5)** ✉ 1085 Budapest, Mária u. 54. ☎+36 1 4768491 **W:** tilos.hu **E:** radio@tilos.hu **NB: English** every 2nd Sat 1400-1530 / **French** every 2nd Sat 1530-1630 / **German** every 2nd Sun 0600-0800 & every 2nd Sat 1530-1630 / **Spanish** every 2nd Sat 1400-1530 / **Russian+Hungarian** every 2nd Wed 1730-1830 / **Chinese** every 2nd Wed 1730-1830 / **Serbo-Croatian** every 2nd Tue 1900-2000 – **6)** ✉ 3300 Eger, Trinitárius u. 1 ☎ +36 36 410450 **W:** bestfmeger.hu **NB:** total 6 txs – **7)** ✉ 3300 Eger, Széchenyi utca 5. ☎+36 36 510-610 **W:** szentistvanradio.hu **E:** info@szentistvanradio.hu **NB:** total 8 txs – **8)** ✉ 8900 Zalaegerszeg, Kossuth u. 45-49 ☎+36 92 955955 **W:** egerszegradio.hu **E:** info@zegtv.hu – **9)** ✉ 1033 Budapest, Polgár u. 8-10 ☎ +36 1 4832950 **W:** inforadio.hu **E:** info@inforadio.hu – **NB:** BBC in **English** daily at 2300-0000 - **10)** ✉ 6300 Kalocsa, Szent István kir. út 34, ☎ +36 78 567662 **W:** www.koronafm100.hu **E:** info@koronaradio.hu – **11)** ✉ 2800 Tatabánya, Stúdium tér 1. ☎+36 34 310021 **W:** forrasradio.hu **E:** forras@forrasradio.hu **NB:** total 3 txs – **12)** ✉ 4400 Nyíregyháza, Eötvös u. 9/A ☎+36 42 444022 **W:** https://bestfmnyiregyhaza.hu/ **E:** info@bestfmnyiregyhaza.hu **NB:** total 6 txs – **13)** ✉ 1097 Budapest, Könyves Kálmán krt. 12-14 ☎+36 1 9111111 **W:** karcfm.hu **E:** info@karcfm.hu **NB:** total 14 txs – **14)** ✉ 1062 Budapest, Délibáb u. 15-17 ☎+36 1 255-3366 **W:** katolikusradio.hu **E:** info@katradio.hu **NB:** total 20 txs – **15)** ✉ 6800 Hódmezövásárhely, Szabadság tér 71. ☎+36 62 533777 **W:** www.radio7.hu **E:** radio7@radio7.hu **NB:** total 3 txs – **16)** ✉ 6725 Szeged, Kisfaludy u. 18 ☎+36 62 444088 **W:** www.radio88.hu **E:** program@radio88.hu – **17)** ✉ 3526 Miskolc, Szentpéteri Kapu 72-76 ☎/℻ +36 46 515276 **W:** csillagpontradio.hu **E:** info@cspr.hu – **18)** ✉ 1133 Budapest, Váci út 78/B ☎+36 1 8881500 **W:** trendfm.hu/ **E:** info@trendfm.hu – **19)** ✉ 2310 Szigetszentmiklós, Csepeli út 15. ☎+36 20 2754003 **W:** lakihegyradio.hu **E:** sales@lakihegyradio.hu – **20)** ✉ 3530 Miskolc, Toronyalja utca 13. (main HQ) ☎+36 46 509904 **W:** refradio.eu/radio/euradio **E:** euradio@euradio.hu, ✉ 4026 Debrecen, Péterfia u. 1-7. ☎+36 30 9027041 **E:** debrecen@euradio.hu, ✉ 4400 Nyíregyháza, Eötvös u. 9/A ☎+36 42 401035 **E:** nyiregyhaza@euradio.hu **NB:** total 6 txs – **21)** ✉ 3525 Miskolc, Széchenyi István út 46. I/5 ☎/℻+36 46 320075 **W:** fmradiom.hu/ **E:** reklam@fmradiom.hu – **22)** ✉ 1064 Budapest,Vörösmarty u. 65 ☎+36 1 3850835 **W:** www.solaradio.hu **E:** info@solaradio.hu – **23)** ✉ 2370 Dabas, Szent István tér 1/b ☎+36 29 562562 **W:** radiodabas.hu **E:** radiodabas@radiodabas.hu – **24)** ✉ 1037 Budapest, Bokor u 1-3-5 ☎+36 1 2406953 **W:** klubradio.hu **E:** info@klubradio.hu – **25)** ✉ 6000 Kecskemét, Petőfi Sándor u 1/b ☎+36 76 414030 **W:** gongradio.hu **E:** titkarsag@gongradio.hu **NB:** total 7 txs – **26)** ✉ 1022 Budapest Detrekö u. 12. ☎+36 1 7876992 **W:** jazzyradio.hu **E:** info@jazzy.hu – **27)** ✉ 1016 Budapest, Hegyalja út 7-13 ☎+36 20 3111111 **W:** radio1.hu **E:** radio1@radio1.hu **NB:** total 43 txs. 20 hrs. main px of Budapest on all 43 frequencies + 4 hrs. local px in other cities. – **28)** ✉ 1022 Budapest, Detrekö u 12 ☎+36 1 7866464 **W:** klasszikradio.hu **E:** info@klasszikradio.hu **NB: English** daily, BBC news several times – **29)** ✉ 2660 Balassagyarmat, Rákóczi Fejedelem út 50 ☎+36 35 957957 **W:** www.megafonfm.hu **E:** megafonfm@megafonfm.hu **30)** ✉ 5000 Szolnok, Baross út 3. ☎+36 56 221024 **W:** amadeusradio.hu **E:** amadeusradio@amadeusradio.hu – **31)** ✉ 7090 Tamási, Szabadság utca 41/B ☎+36 74 570260 **W:** tamasiradio.hu **E:** tamasiradio@tamasiradio.hu – **32)** ✉ 7623 Pécs, Rákóczi út 17 ☎+36 30 8891017 **W:** www.pecs.fm **E:** info@pecs.fm – **33)** ✉ 9023 Győr, Kodály Zoltán u. 32/A ☎+36 96 777777 **W:** www.gyorplusz.hu **E:** radio@gyorplusz.hu – **34)** ✉ 7570 Barcs, Köztársaság u. 2/1 ☎+36 82 462204 **W:** barcsihirek.hu/drava-hullam **E:** info@barcsmedia.hu – **35)** ✉ 4026 Debrecen, Darabos u. 35. ☎+36 52 450900 **W:** bestfmdebrecen.hu **E:** info@bestfm.hu **NB:** total 6 txs – **36)** ✉ 7100 Szekszárd, Wesselényi u. 16. ☎+36 74 444444 **W:** radioantritt.hu **E:** szerk@radioantritt.hu – **37)** ✉ 8500 Pápa, MH Airbase, Vaszari út **E:** dma.aviano.afn.mbx.afn-aviano@mail.mil **W:** www.afneurope.net/Stations/Aviano **38)** ✉ 9970 Szentgotthárd, Gárdonyi u. 1 ☎+36 94 554126 **W:** radiomonoster.hu **E:** info@radiomonoster.hu **NB:** On the air daily 1100-1500 UTC / Px in Slovenian & Hungarian // 97.7 - **39)** ✉ 8000 Székesfehérvár, Rákóczi út 1. ☎+36 30 3181000 **W:** www.bestfm.hu **E:** papp.klaudia@radio1.hu **NB:** total 6 txs – 40) ✉ 3980 Sátoraljaújhely

Kisközösségi rádió (lowpower community radio):
Non-profit low-power stns (0.1–10W) were granted licences in cities and country villages. In recent years the number of these stns has drastically decreased, mainly for financial reasons. Currently only 16 such stns are operating in the whole country.

See **W:** frekvencia.hu/fmlist-hng.htm
DAB+: Ceased on September 5, 2020
DRM: BME-HVT test transmissions on 26060 kHz (100W) from the Budapest University of Technology & Economics (**BME**), Department of Broadband Infocommunications and Electromagnetic Theory (**HVT**).

ICELAND

L.T: UTC — **Pop:** 340,000 — **Pr.L:** Icelandic — **E.C:** 230V/50Hz — **ITU:** ISL

FJÖLMIÐLANEFND (The Media Commission)

✉ Borgartúni 21, 105 Reykjavik ☎ +354 4150415 **E:** postur@fjolmidlanefnd.is **W:** fjolmidlanefnd.is **L.P:** Chmn: Einar Hugi Bjarnason

RÚV (Pub)

✉ Efstaleiti 1, 103 Reykjavík ☎ +354 5153000 **E:** frettir@ruv.is **W:** ruv.is **L.P:** DG: Stefán Eiríksson

LW	kHz	kW	Prgr	MW	kHz	kW	Prgr
Gufuskálar	189	100	1/2*	Eiðar	207	50	1/2*

*) Each tx has automatic fallback to Prgr 1 if time-shared feed is lost

FM (MHz)	1	2	3	kW
Almannaskarð	90.3	104.8	-	1
Auðsholt	91.3	95.3	-	2.5
Gagnheiði	99.8	87.7	-	12/9
Háfell	93.8	98.7	-	14/34
Hegranes	90.6	98.8	-	3/5
Hnjúkar	89.1	95.5	-	6/6.2
Skálafell	92.4	99.9	-	24
Snartastaðanúpur	101.3	88.7	-	1
Stykkishólmur	88.0	96.3	-	3/3.5
Úlfarsfell	93.5	90.1	87.7	2
Urðarhjalli	92.7	88.7	-	3
Vaðlaheiði	91.6	96.5	-	9.3
Vestmannaeyjar	97.1	88.1	-	17/24
Viðarfjall	88.1	96.1	-	3.3
Þjóðólfsholt	92.9	88.3	-	6

+ sites with only txs below 1kW.

D.Prgr: Prgr 1 (Rás 1): 24h – **Prgr 2 (Rás 2)**: 24h – **Prgr 3 (Rondó)**: 24h. **On LW:** 0000-0625 Rás 2, 0625-0900 (MF) Rás 1+2 (joint tr), 0625-0900 (SS) Rás 1, 0900-1000 Rás 2, 1000-1400 (Tue/Wed) Rás 1, 1000-1017 (exc. Tue/Wed) Rás 1, 1017-1220 (exc. Tue/Wed) Rás 2, 1220-1400 (Mon/Thu/Fri) Rás 1, 1220-1300 (Sat/Sun) Rás 1, 1400 (Sat/Sun 1300)-1800 Rás 2, 1800-1900 Rás 1, 1900-2200 Rás 2, 2200-2220 Rás 1, 2220-2400 Rás 2.

OTHER STATIONS

FM	MHz	kW	Location	Station
5)	88.5	1	Reykjavík	XA Radíó
2)	89.7	1	Háfell	K100
6)	89.9	1	Hrafnafell	Áttan FM
6)	89.9	1.6	Jórvík	Áttan FM
1E)	90.4	2	Vestmannaeyjar	X997
1C)	90.9	2	Úlfarsfell	GullBylgjan
6)	91.3	1	Hegranes	Áttan FM
1A)	92.7	2	Vaðlaheiði	Bylgjan
4)	93.3	1	Vestmannaeyjar	Suðurland FM
1A)	94.5	2	Háfell	Bylgjan
A)	94.5	2	Úlfarsfell	BBCWS relay
1B)	94.7	1	Egilsstaðir	FM957
1B)	95.1	1	Hegranes	FM957
1B)	95.7	2	Reykjavík	FM957
4)	96.3	1	Jórvík	Suðurland FM
1D)	96.5	2	Úlfarsfell	LéttBylgjan
4)	97.3	1	Reykjavík	Suðurland FM
1E)	97.7	2	Úlfarsfell	X997
1A)	97.9	1	Hegranes	Bylgjan
1A)	98.9	2	Reykjavík	Bylgjan
1A)	98.9	1	Hnjúkar	Bylgjan
2)	100.5	1	Bláfjöll	K100
1A)	100.9	2	Vestmannaeyjar	Bylgjan
1B)	101.7	2	Vestmannaeyjar	FM957
2)	101.7	1	Þrándur	K100
7)	102.1	1	Úlfarsfell	Útvarp Saga
1B)	102.5	1	Skáneyjarbunga	FM957
3)	102.9	2.5	Reykjavík	Lindin
1B)	103.2	1	Jórvík	FM957
1A)	103.3	1	Skáneyjarbunga	Bylgjan
1F)	103.9	1	Úlfarsfell	Íslenska Bylgjan

FM	MHz	kW	Location	Station
1A)	104.5	2	Grenjadalsfell	Bylgjan
2)	104.9	1	Strútur	K100

+ txs below 1kW.

Addresses & other information:
1A-1F) Suðurlandsbraut 8, 108 Reykjavík – **2)** Hádegismóum 2, 101 Reykjavík – **3)** Krókhálsi 4a, 110 Reykjavík – **4)** Hrísmýri 6, 800 Selfoss – **5)** Brávallagötu 18, 101 Reykjavík – **6)** Víkurhvarf 2, 203 Kópavogur – **7)** Þverholti 14, 105 Reykjavík – **A)** Rel. BBCWS (UK)

INDIA

L.T: UTC +5½h — **Pop**: 1.28 billion — **Pr.L**: Assamese, Bengali, Bodo, Dogri, English, Gujarati, Hindi, Kannada, Kashmiri, Maithili, Marathi, Malayalam, Nepali, Odia, Punjabi, Santhali, Sindhi, Tamil, Telugu & Urdu — **E.C**: 50Hz 230V — **ITU**: IND

MINISTRY OF INFORMATION & BROADCASTING

Main Secretariat: ✉ A-Wing, Shastri Bhawan, New Delhi-110001 **W**: mib.nic.in **L.P**: Union Minister of Info. & Broadcasting: Prakash Javadekar

PRASAR BHARATI (BROADCASTING CORPORATION OF INDIA) (Public Corporation)

✉ Prasar Bharati House, Copernicus Marg, New Delhi-110001 ☎ +91 11 23118400 **L.P:** Chairman: [position vacant] ☎+91 11 23118801/23118802 **E:** chairman@prasarbharati.gov.in **W:** prasarbharati.gov.in CEO: Shashi S. Vempati ☎ +91 11 23118803/23118804 **E:** ceo@prasarbharati.gov.in

AKASHVANI – ALL INDIA RADIO

Administration/Engineering: ✉ Directorate General, All India Radio, Akashvani Bhavan, Parliament Street, New Delhi-110001 ☎+91 11 23421006, 23715413 🖷 +91 11 23711956 **W:** prasarbharati.gov.in/AIR/
L.P: DG: Ms.Ira Joshi ☎+91 11 23421300 🖷 +91 11 23421956 **E:** dgair@prasarbharati.gov.in Eng. in Chief: C.B.S. Maurya ☎+91 11 23421058 🖷 +91 11 23421459 **E:** einc@prasarbharati.gov.in
Spectrum Management & Synergy: Room No.204, All India Radio, Akashvani Bhavan, Parliament Street, New Delhi 110001 ☎+91 11 23421062, 23421145 **E:** spectrum-manager@prasarbharati.gov.in
Programming: ✉ New Broadcasting House, 27 Mahadev Road, New Delhi-110 001 ☎ +91 (11) 23421218
✉ Akashvani Bhawan, Parliament Street, New Delhi-110001 ☎ +91 11 23715411
News Services Division: ✉ New Broadcasting House, 27 Mahadev Road, New Delhi-110 001 Newsroom ☎+91 11 23421100 🖷+91 11 23421219 **E:** nbhnews@prasarbharati.gov.in **W:** newsonair.nic.in www.newsonair.com **L.P.** Dir.Gen. (News): Jaideep Bhatnagar ☎+91 11 23421218 **E:** dgn.nsd@gmail.com
Entertainment Channel: (Vividh Bharati): All India Radio, ✉ Gorai Road, Borivli West, Mumbai-400 091, Maharashtra ☎ +91 22 28692698 **E:** vbsmumbai@gmail.com
Research & Development: ✉ Office of the Addl. Director General, R & D, All India Radio, 14-B, Indra Prashta Estate, Ring Road, New Delhi-110002 ☎+91 11 23379329, 23379255, **E:** cerdairdd@gmail.com
Monitoring: ✉ International Monitoring Stn., All India Radio, Dr. K.S. Krishnan Rd, Todapur, New Delhi-110012 ☎ +91 11 25842939 **E**.delhi.todapur@prasarbharati.gov.in ✉ Central Monitoring Stn, All India Radio, Ayanagar, New Delhi-110047 **E**: delhi.ayanagarcms@prasarbharati.gov.in
Audience Research: ✉ Audience Research Unit, AIR, Akashwani Bhavan, Parliament Street, New Delhi 110001 ☎ +91 11 23421022
Live streaming: W: prasarbharati.gov.in
Regional Headquarters: (Office of the Additional Director General)
North Zone: AIR & DD, Jamnagar House, Shahjahan Road, New Delhi-110011 ☎ +91 11 23382519
East Zone: AIR & DD, 4th Floor, Akashvani Bhawan, Eden Garden, Kolkata-700001 ☎ +91 33 22480158
North-East Zone: AIR & DD, Doordarshan Complex, KG Baruah Road, P.O. Zoo Road, Guwahati – 781024, Assam ☎ +91 361 2200326
West Zone: AIR & DD, 3rd Floor, AOA Building, Doordarshan Complex. Worli, Mumbai-400030, Maharashtra
South Zone: AIR & DD, Swami Sivanada Salai, Chepauk, Chennai-600005 ☎ +91 44 25383253

NB: Thiruvananthapuram is given in the schedules as 'Trivandrum.' and Rajamahendravaram as 'Rajamahen'.

MW: c) Vividh Bharati, e) ext.sce., r) relay stn
Some cities have more than 1 program channel on MW designated as A, B & C Channel. *=Tests #=to be decommissioned ‡=Inactive +=currently 1kW mobile tx

kHz	Station	kW	reg	kHz	Station	kW	reg
531	Jodhpur	300	N	1089	Naushera	20	N, r
540	Aizawl	20	NE	1107	Kalaburgi	20	S
549	Ranchi	100	E	1116	Srinagar A	300	N
558	Mumbai B	100	W	1125	Tezpur	20	NE
567	Dibrugarh	300	NE	1125	Udaipur	20	N
576	Alappuzha	200	S, r	1134	Chinsurah	*‡1000	E, e
585	Nagpur	300	W	1143	Ratnagiri	20	W
594	Chinsurah	1000	E, e	1143	Rohtak	20	N
603	Ajmer	200	N, r	1152	Kavaratti	10	S
612	Bengaluru	200	S	1161	Trivandrum	20	S
621	Patna	100	E	1179	Rewa	20	W
630	Thrissur	100	S	1188	Mumbai C	50	W, c
639	Kohima	100	NE	1197	Tirunelveli	20	S
648	Indore	200	W	1206	Bhawanipatna	200	E
657	Kolkata A	200	E	1215	Pudducherri	20	S
666	New Delhi B	100	N	1224	Srinagar C	10	N
675	Bhadravathi	20	S	1233	Tura	20	NE
675	Chhatarpur	20	W	1242	Varanasi	100	N
675	Itanagar	100	NE	1251	Sangli	20	W
684	Kozhikode	100	S	1260	Ambikapur	20	W
684	Port Blair	100	S	1269	Agartala	20	NE
684	Kargil A	200	N	1269	Madurai	20	S
702	Jalandhar B	‡200	N, e	1287	Panaji A	100	W
711	Siliguri	200	E	1296	Darbhanga	20	E
720	Chennai A	200	S	1305	Parbhani	20	W
729	Guwahati A	100	NE	1314	Bhuj	20	W
738	Hyderabad A	200	S	1323	Kolkata C	20	E, c
747	Lucknow	300	N	1332	Tezu	10	NE
756	Jagdalpur	100	W	1341	Kohima	1	NE
765	Dharwad	200	S	1350	Kupwara	20	N, r
774	Shimla	100	N	1377	Hyderabad B	20	S
792	Pune	100	W	1386	Gwalior	20	W
801	Jabalpur	200	W	1395	Bikaner	20	N
810	Rajkot A	300	W	1404	Gangtok	20	NE
819	New Delhi A	200	N	1413	Kota	20	N
828	Panaji B	20	W, c	1458	Barmer	20	N
828	Silchar	20	NE	1458	Bhagalpur	20	E
837	Vijayawada	100	S	1467	Jeypore	100	E
846	Ahmedabad	200	W	1485	Ahwa	1	W
864	Shillong	100	NE	1485	Chamoli	1	N
873	Jalandhar A	300	N	1485	Drass	1	N, cr
882	Imphal	300	NE	1485	Dunagrpur	1	N
891	Rampur	20	N	1485	Khaltsi	1	N, cr
900	Kadapa	100	S	1485	Nongstoin	1	NE
909	Gorakhpur	+100	N	1485	Nyoma	1	N, cr
918	Suratgarh	300	N	1485	Pithoragarh	1	N, r
927	Visakhapatnam	100	S	1512	Kokrajhar	20	E
936	Tiruchirappalli	100	S	1521	Tawang	20	NE
945	Sambalpur	100	E	1530	Agra	20	N
954	Najibabad	200	N	1584	Dharmanagar	1	NE
963	Jalgaon	20	W	1584	Diphu	1	NE
972	Cuttack	300	E	1584	Himmat Nagar	1	W
981	Raipur	100	W	1584	Kargil B	1	N
990	Jammu	300	N	1584	Mon	1	NE
999	Almora	1	N	1584	Padam	1	N,cr
999	Coimbatore	20	S	1584	Keonjhar	#1	E
1008	Kolkata B	100	E	1593	Bhopal	10	W
1017	Chennai B	20	S	1602	Diskit	1	N cr
1026	Prayagraj	20	N	1602	Pauri	1	N
1035	Guwahati B	20	NE	1602	Saiha	1	NE
1044	Mumbai A	100	W	1602	Tiesuru	1	N, cr
1053	Leh	20	N	1602	Tuensang	1	NE
1053	Tuticorin	‡200	S, e	1602	Uttarkashi	1	N, r
1062	Passighat	100	NE	1602	William Nagar	1	NE
1071	Rajkot	‡1000	W, e	1602	Ziro	1	NE
1089	Udipi	20	S, r				

DRM frequencies on MW (AM Frequency Minus 9 kHz):
Pure DRM at 1130-0930 UTC (22 hrs.).‡ Inactive * Proposed

kHz	Station	kW	reg	kHz	Station	kW	reg
540	Ranchi	100	E	603	Bengaluru	200	S
549	Mumbai B	100	W	612	Patna	100	E
558	Dibrugarh	300	NE	648	Kolkata A	200	E
585	Chinsurah	‡1000	E	666	Itanagar	200	NE
594	Ajmer	200	N	702	Siliguri	200	E

kHz	Station	kW	reg	kHz	Station	kW	reg
711	Chennai A	200	S	936	Sambalpur	*100	E
729	Hyderabad A	200	S	981	Jammu	300	N
747	Jagdalpur	*100	W	1008	Kolkata B	#100	E
738	Lucknow	300	N	1026	Guwahati B	20	NE
756	Dharwad	200	S	1044	Mumbai A	#100	W
783	Chennai	#20	S	1053	Pasighat	100	NE
783	Pune	100	W	1062	Rajkot	*‡1000	W
792	Jabalpur	200	W	1125	Chinsurah	‡1000	E
801	Rajkot	300	W	1197	Bhawanipatna	*200	E
810	New Delhi A	200	N	1233	Varanasi	100	N
828	Vijayawada	100	S	1278	Panaji	100	W
837	Ahmedabad	200	W	1368	New Delhi	#20	N
864	Jalandhar	300	N	1386	Bikaner	20	N
909	Suratgarh	300	N	1449	Barmer	20	N
918	Visakhapatnam	100	S	1458	Jeypore	*100	E
927	Tiruchirappalli	100	S	1512	Tawang	20	NE

NB: Full tx kW given but most txs use far fewer kW in DRM mode. DRM Schedule: Operates in Simulcast mode / Pure DRM at specific timings on their respective analogue frequency minus 9 kHz

D.Prgr: Most stations operate on MW from around 0000 to 1800 UTC. Varies from stn to stn. Some stns have 1 or 2 transmissions while others have 3. Extended coverage during sports or special events.

F.Pl: Replacement: 1kW MW to 1kW FM: Almora_

Addresses of MW stations (See also SW stn addresses):
1000kW MW stations:
1) AIR, Super Power Transmitter, Chinsurah-712102, West Bengal E: chinsurah@prasarbharati.gov.in – **2)** AIR, Super Power Transmitter, Radio Colony, Jamnagar Road, Rajkot-360006, Gujarat E: rajkot.spt@prasarbharati.gov.in

Other MW stations:
Agartala-799001, Tripura – Vivbhav Nagar, **Agra**-282001, Uttar Pradesh – Ashram Rd, Navarangpura, **Ahmedabad**-380009, Gujarat – **Ahwa**-394710, Dangs Dist., Gujarat – 21/10 Vaishali Nagar, **Ajmer**-305001, Rajasthan – Pathirapally, **Alappuzha**-688521, Kerala – **Almora**-263601, Kumaon Dist., Uttarakhand – Kumar Palace, **Ambikapur**-497001, Surguja Dist., Chhattisgarh –Raj Bhavan Rd, **Bengaluru**-560001, Karnataka – Laxmi Nagar, **Barmer**-344001, Rajasthan – J.P.S.Colony, Paper Tower, **Bhadravati**-577302, Karnataka – Port Campus, **Bhagalpur**-812001, Bihar – **Bhawanipatna**-766001, Nektiguda, Kalahandi Dist., Odisha – **Bhuj**-370001, Kutch Dist., Gujarat – **Bikaner**-334001, Rajasthan – **Chamoli**-246424, Gopeshwar, Uttarakhand – 7, Kamarajar Salai, Mylapore, **Chennai**-600004, Tamilnadu – **Chhatarpur**-471001, Madhya Pradesh – Trichy Rd, Ramanathapuram, **Coimbatore**-641045, Tamilnadu – Madhupur House, Bakshi Bazar, Cantonment Rd, **Cuttack**-753001, Odisha – **Darbhanga**-846004, Bihar – **Dharmanagar**-799250, Tripura – Saptapur, **Dharwad**-580008, Karnataka – Malakhubasa, **Dibrugarh**-786001, Assam – **Diphu**-782460, Kabri Anglong Dist., Assam – **Diskit**-194401, Leh Dist., Jammu & Kashmir – **Drass**-194102, Kargil, Jammu & Kashmir – Dungarpur-314001, Rajasthan –Town Hall, **Gorakhpur**-273001, Uttar Pradesh – Chandmari, **Guwahati**-781003 Assam – Gandhi Rd, **Gwalior**-474002, Madhya Pradesh – **Himmat Nagar** – 383001, Gujarat – Malwa House, Residency Area, **Indore**-452001, Madhya Pradesh – 373 Napier Town, **Jabalpur**-482001, Madhya Pradesh – Collectorate Rd, **Jagdalpur**-494 001, Bastar Dist., Chhattisgarh – **Jalandhar**-144001, Punjab – Jilhapet, **Jalgaon**-425001, Maharashtra – Palace Road,Panjtirthi, **Jammu**-180001, Jammu & Kashmir — Paoata 'C' Road, **Jodhpur**-342006, Rajasthan – Cooperative Colony, **Kadapa**-516001, YSR Dist., Andhra Pradesh – Aiwan-e-Shahi, Municipal Garden, **Kalaburagi** -585103, Karnataka – **Kargil**-194103, Jammu & Kashmir – **Kavaratti**-682555, Lakshadeep – **Khaltsi**–194106, Leh, Jammu & Kashmir – **Kokrajhar**-783370, Assam – Jawahar Rd, **Kota**-324001, Rajasthan – Beach Rd, **Kozhikode**-673001, Kerala – **Kupwara** – 193222, Jammu & Kashmir – Lady Doak College Rd, Chokkikulam, **Madurai**-625002, Tamilnadu – **Mon**-798621, Nagaland – Broadcasting House, Backbay Reclamation, Mumbai-400020, Maharashtra – Civil Lines, Palam Rd, **Nagpur**-440001, Maharashtra – Kotwali Rd, **Najibabad**-246763, Bijnor Dist., Uttar Pradesh – **Naushera**–193125, Jammu & Kashmir – **Nongstoin**-793119, West Khasi Hills, Meghalaya – **Nyoma**-194101, Leh Dist, Jammu & Kashmir – **Obra**-231219, Uttar Pradesh – **Padam**, Jammu & Kashmir - Altinho, **Panaji**-403001, Goa – Jamakar Colony, Nawa Mondha, **Parbhani**-431401, Maharashtra – **Pasighat**-791102, East Siang Dist., Arunachal Pradesh – Frazer Road, Chhaju Bagh, **Patna**-800001, Bihar – **Pauri**-246001, Uttarakhand – **Pithoragarh**-262501, Uttarakhand – Haddo Post, Dilanipur, Port Blair-744102, Andaman & Nicobar Islands – Z-9 Dayanand Marg, **Prayagraj** (Allahabad)-211001, Uttar Pradesh– Indira Nagar, Gorimedu, **Puducherry**-605006 – University Rd, Shivaji Nagar, **Pune**-411005, Maharashtra – Sitaram Pandit Marg, **Rajkot**-360001, Gujarat – **Rampur**-244901, Uttar Pradesh – 6 Ratu Rd, **Ranchi**-834001, Jharkhand – Thiba Palace Rd, **Ratnagiri**-415612, Maharashtra – 6 Civil Lines, **Rewa**-486001, Madhya Pradesh – Subhash Rd, **Rohtak**-124001, Haryana – **Saiha**-796901, Chhimtuipui Dist., Mizoram – 3, Kuchery Rd, **Sambalpur**-768001, Odisha – Market Yard, Kolhapur Rd, **Sangli**-416416, Maharashtra – Pomdngiem, Opposite GPO, **Shillong**-793001, Meghalaya - **Silchar**-788001, Cachar Dist., Assam – 2 Mile Sevoke Rd, **Siliguri**-734401, Darjeeling Dist., West Bengal –**Suratgarh**-335804, Sriganganagar Dist., Rajasthan – **Tawang**-790104, Arunachal Pradesh – **Tezpur**-784001, Sonitpur Dist., Assam – **Tezu**-792001, Lohit Dist., Arunachal Pradesh – Ramavarmapuram, **Thrissur**-680631, Kerala – **Tiesuru,** Jammu & Kashmir, 28-3 Promenade Rd, **Tiruchirappalli**-620001, Tamilnadu – Sarojini Park, Palayamkottai, **Tirunelveli**-627006, Tamilnadu – **Tuensang**-798612, Nagaland – Lower Chandmari, **Tura**-794001, Meghalaya – Millerpuram, Playamkottai Road, **Tuticorin**-628008, Tamilnadu – Chetak Circle, **Udhagamandalam**-643001, Nilgris, Tamilnadu – **Udaipur**-313001, Rajasthan – Brahmavar, **Udipi**-576213, Dakshina Kanara Dist., Karnataka – **Uttar Kashi**-249193, Uttarakhand –Mahmoorganj, **Varanasi**-221010, Uttar Pradesh – Bandar Rd, Punnammathota, **Vijayawada**-520010, Andhra Pradesh – Siripuram, **Visakhapatnam**-530003, Andhra Pradesh – **William Nagar**, Meghalaya – **Ziro**-791120, Lower Subansiri Dist., Arunachal Pradesh.

Email: Id of AIR stns is normally location followed by @prasarbharati.gov.in e.g.: hyderabad@prasarbharati.gov.in

Regional Domestic SW stations:

kHz	kW	Station	H. of tr.
4760	2.5	Leh	s0130/w0210-0430, 1130-1700
4835	10	Gangtok	0100-0500, 1030-1700
4870#‡	100	Delhi (Kingsway)	0230-0330, 1430-1530
4950	50	Srinagar	0120-0215, 1120-1744 (2145v-2245v in Ramadan)
5040	30	Jeypore	0025-0436, 0700-0915, 1130-1742
5050†	10	Aizawl	0025-0400, 1130-1700
6000	10	Leh	0630-0930
6030†	25	Delhi (Khampur)	0230-0230, 1430-1530
6085	10	Gangtok	0630-0930
6100	25	Delhi (Khampur)	0730-0830
6110	50	Srinagar	0225-0505(Sun s -1115), 0600-1115
7250#†	10	Delhi (Kingsway)	1130-1140
7270#†	10	Chennai	0130-0430 (FM Gold)
7295†	10	Aizawl	0700-0930
7505	10	Delhi	0230-0300
7555†	10	Delhi (Kingsway)	1430-1600
9620	25	Aligarh	1130-1140
9865‡	500	Benguluru	0025-0435, 0900-1200, 1245-1740 (Vividh Bharati)
9950	10	Delhi (Kingsway)	1130-1140

s=summer, w=winter, v=timing/frequency varies. †=irregular ‡= inactive, #= frequency also used by External Services at other times

F.Pl: New 50 kW SW DRM transmitter at Kurseong_

NB: Extended broadc. for special events, important Parliament sessions, sports and on January 26 (Republic Day) and August 15 (Independence Day).

V. by QSL-card. Reception Reports to: ✉ Dy. Director General (Spectrum Management & Synergy), All India Radio, Room No.204, Akashvani Bhavan, New Delhi-110001 ☎ 91-11-23421062, 23421145: **E:** spectrum-manager@prasarbharati.gov.in .Local stns also verify directly in many cases by letter or email. No return postage necessary.

Addresses of SW stations (R. rpts may be sent to the Stn Engineer): **1) Aizawl**: R. Tila, Tuikhuahtlang, Box 13, Aizawl-796001 ☎+91 389 2322415 **E:** aizawl@prasarbharati.gov.in – **2) Aligarh**: Anoopshahar Road, Aligarh-202001, Uttar Pradesh ☎+91 571 2700972 **E:** aligarh@prasarbharati.gov.in – **3) Bengaluru**: Super Power Transmitters, Yelahanka New Town, Bengaluru-560064, Karnataka ☎+91 80 27601149 **E:**bangalore.spt@prasarbharati.gov.in – **4) Bhopal**: Shyamla Hills, Bhopal-462002, Madhya Pradesh ☎+91 755 4950128 **E:** bhopal@prasarbharati.gov.in – **5) Chennai**: S.M.Nagar PO, Avadi,

Chennai-600062, Tamilnadu. Tel. 91 44 26383204. **E:** chennai.avadi@prasarbharati.gov.in **6) Gangtok**: Old MLA Hostel, Gangtok-737101, Sikkim ☎+91 3592 202636 **E:** gangtok@prasarbharati.gov.in – **7) Hyderabad**: Rocklands, Saifabad, Hyderabad-500004, Telangana ☎+91 40 23234904. **E:** hyderabad@prasarbharati.gov.in – **8) Jaipur**: 5 Park House, Mirza Ismail Road, Jaipur-302001, Rajasthan ☎ +91 141 2366263 **E:** jaipur@prasarbharati.gov.in – **9) Jeypore**:764005, Odisha ☎+91 6854 232524 **E:**jeypore@@prasarbharati.gov.in –**10) Leh**:Leh-194101, Ladakh ☎+91 1982 252063 **E:** leh@prasarbharati.gov.in – **11A) New Delhi**: High Power Transmitters, Khampur, New Delhi -110036 ☎+91 11 27831474 **E:** hptkhampur@prasarbharati.gov.in **11B)** High Power Transmitters, Kingsway, New Delhi-110009 ☎+91 11 27606661 **E:** delhi.kingsway@prasarbharati.gov.in – **12) Panaji**: Goa University PO, Panaji-403206 ☎+91 832 2459096 **E:** panaji.spt@prasarbharati.gov.in –**13) Srinagar:** Sherwani Rd, Srinagar-190001, Jammu & Kashmir ☎+91 194 2452100 **E:**srinagar@prasarbharati.gov.in – **14) Thiruvanathapuram:** Bhakti Vilas, Vazuthacaud, Thiruvanathapuram-695014, Kerala ☎+91 471 2325009 **E:** thiruvanathapuram @prasarbharati.gov.in

FM Stations: b) FM Rainbow c) Vividh Bharati g) FM Gold r) relay stn

MHz	location	kW	reg	MHz	location	kW	reg
93.9	Vadodara	10	W,C	100.9	Port Blair	10	S,C
96.7	Ahmedabad	10	W,C	101.0	Balurghat	10	E, r
100.1	Ahmednagar	10	W	101.0	Bhaderwah	5	N
100.1	Bengaluru	1	S	101.0	Daporijo	1	NE
100.1	Chennai	20	S, g	101.0	Nagercoil	10	S
100.1	Gorakhpur	10	N,C	101.0	Pune	10	W,C
100.1	Kanpur	10	N, b	101.0	Sambalpur	5	E
100.1	Keonjhar	10	E	101.0	Suryapet	10	S, r
100.1	Kolkata	20	E, g	101.1	Bathinda	6	N
100.1	Kothagudem	6	S	101.1	Jowai	5	NE
100.1	Ludhiana	5	N, g	101.1	Nanded	10	W
100.1	Mumbai	20	W, g	101.1	Panaji	10	W, C
100.1	New Delhi	20	N,g	101.1	Surat	10	W,C
100.2	Adilabad	10	S	101.1	Thrissur	1	S
100.2	Ambikapur	5	W	101.1	Tuticorin	1	S
100.2	Darjeeling	10	E	101.2	Banda	10	N, r
100.2	Haflong	10	NE	101.2	Jaipur	10	W
100.2	Patiala	6	N	101.2	Khandwa	10	W
100.2	Shivpuri	10	W	101.2	Mahabubnagar	10	S, r
100.3	Prayagraj	10	N,C	101.2	New Tehri	1	N,c
100.3	Asansol	10	E, r	101.2	Nutan Bazar	1	NE r
100.3	Bhawanipatna	5	E	101.2	Udaipur	1	NE
100.3	Bomdila	1	NE	101.3	Aligarh	10	N,B,r
100.3	Jaipur B	10	N,C	101.3	Balaghat	10	W
100.3	Jammu A	3	N	101.3	Banswara	10	N
100.3	Karaikal	10	S	101.3	Bengaluru	10	S,B
100.3	Mangaluru	10	S	101.3	Cuttack	6	E,B
100.3	Tuipang	1	NE	101.3	Dibrugarh	1	NE
100.4	Bareilly	6	N	101.3	Osmanabad	10	W
100.4	Cuttack	10	E,C	101.3	Vijayawada10		S,c
100.4	Karimganj	1	NE	101.4	Chennai	20	S,B
100.4	Mandla	1	W	101.4	Churachandpur	5	NE
100.5	Chhatarpur	5	W	101.4	Devikulam	5	S
100.5	Dehradun	10	N	101.4	Kurukshetra	10	N
100.5	Dhule	10	W	101.4	Nashik	10	W
100.5	Hospete	10	S	101.4	Siliguri	10	E,C
100.5	Kodaikanal	10	S,B	101.5	Amravati	10	W,C,r
100.5	New Delhi		F.Pl.	101.5	Bageshwar	5	N
100.5	Ranchi	10	E	101.5	Bardhaman	10	E,r
100.5	Ukhrul	1	NE r	101.5	Kannur	10	S
100.6	Berhampur	10	E	101.5	Lumding	1	NE r
100.6	Jalandhar	10	N,C	101.5	Markapur	10	S
100.6	Mysuru	10	S	101.5	Ratnagiri	1	W
100.6	Nagpur	10	W,C	101.5	Sawai Madhopur10		N
100.6	Sangli	10	W, C	101.6	Agartala	10	NE
100.6	Varanasi	10	N, C	101.6	Guwahati	10	NE
100.7	Aizawl	6	NE	101.6	Indore	10	W,C
100.7	Churu	6	N	101.6	Lucknow	10	N,C
100.7	Lucknow	10	N,B	101.6	Patna	10	E,b
100.7	Poonch	6	N	101.6	Raipur	10	W, C
100.7	Raigarh	6	W	101.7	Anantapur	10	S
100.7	Rajgarh	3	W	101.7	Aurangabad	10	W,C
100.8	Fazilka	20	N, r	101.7	Chaibasa	10	E
100.8	Guwahati	10	NE,C	101.7	Junagadh	10	W
100.8	Jamshedpur	10	E,C	101.7	Meerut	10	N
100.9	Kasauli	10	N, r	101.7	Tura	5	NE
100.9	Mokokchung	5	NE	101.7	Udaipur	10	N,C

MHz	location	kW	reg	MHz	location	kW	reg
101.8	Gwalior	5	W	102.3	Karwar	5	S
101.8	Hamirpur	5	N	102.3	Kochi A	10	S
101.8	Jaisalmer	10	N	102.3	Kurseong	5	E,B
101.8	Kolkata	10	E,C	102.3	Lakhimpur Kheri	10	N, r
101.8	Udagamandalam	10	S	102.4	Akola	10	W
101.8	Vijayapura	10	S	102.4	Gairsain	1	N
101.8	Wokha	1	NE	102.4	Jamshedpur	10	E
101.9	Bolangir	10	E	102.4	Kurnool	10	S
101.9	Faizabad	6	N	102.4	Pithoragarh	1	N
101.9	Hyderabad	10	S,B	102.4	Rajkot	10	W,C
101.9	Kotpuli	10	N	102.4	Rewa	5	N
101.9	Lungleh	5	NE	102.4	Tezpur	1	NE
101.9	Rajouri	10	N, r	102.5	Dharmapuri	10	S
101.9	Trivandrum	10	S,C	102.5	Kullu	5	N, r
102.0	Kota	1	N	102.5	Longtherai	5	NE
102.0	Rairangpur	1	E	102.5	Patna	10	E,C
102.0	Parbhani	1	W	102.5	Ujjain	5	W,r
102.0	Shahdol	6	W	102.6	Chitradurga	6	S
102.0	Soro	1	E	102.6	Goalpara	1	NE r
102.0	Visakhapatnam	10	S,B	102.6	Naushera	10	N
102.1	Hazaribagh	6	E	102.6	New Delhi	20	N,B
102.1	Jalgaon	5	W	102.6	Rourkela	6	E
102.1	Jodhpur	10	N,C	102.6	Sagar	10	W
102.1	Mussoorie	10	N,Br	102.6	Srinagar	10	N,C
102.1	Phek	1	NE r	102.6	Tirunelveli	10	S, B
102.1	Raichur	10	S	102.7	Jalandhar	10	N,B
102.1	Tiruchirappalli	10	S,B,c	102.7	Kolhapur	10	W
102.2	Chindwara	10	W	102.7	Manjeri	3	S,B
102.2	Godhra	10	W	102.7	Nagaon	6	NE
102.2	Hassan	10	S	102.7	Nellore	10	S, r
102.2	Joranda	1	E	102.7	Obra	6	N
102.2	Kathua	10	N	102.7	Srikakulam	1	S, r
102.2	Mathura	10	N	102.7	Yavatmal	10	W
102.2	Maunath Bhanjan10		Nr	102.8	Hyderabad	10	S,C
102.2	Murshidabad	6	E	102.8	Mumbai	20	W,C
102.2	Vijayawada	10	S,B	102.8	Puducherry	10	S,B
102.3	Chautan Hill	20	N r	102.8	Raebareilly	20	N
102.3	Chennai	20	S, C	102.8	Saraipali	1	W
102.3	Daman	5	W	102.9	Baripada	5	E
102.3	Guna	10	W	102.9	Beed	6	W
102.3	Hissar	10	N	102.9	Bengaluru	10	S,C
102.3	Karimnagar	5	S, r	102.9	Chittorgarh	10	N

MHz	location	kW	reg	MHz	location	kW	reg
102.9	Jabalpur	10	W,C	103.5	Bhadravathi	1	S
102.9	Rampur	1	N	103.5	Bhopal	10	W,C
103.0	Chandrapur	6	W	103.5	Dhanbad	10	E
103.0	Coimbatore	10	S,B	103.5	Imphal	10	NE
103.0	Daltonganj	10	E	103.5	Kurseong	10	E
103.0	Dharwad	10	S,C	103.5	Mount Abu	6	N
103.0	Gangtok	10	NE	103.5	Rohtak	10	N,C
103.0	Jhansi	10	N	103.5	Silchar	5	NE
103.0	Kohima	10	NE	103.5	Srinagar	10	N
103.1	Alwar	10	N	103.5	Warangal	10	S
103.1	Amethi	5	N	103.6	Amritsar	20	N
103.1	Betul	6	W	103.6	Bundi	10	N, r
103.1	Chandigarh	10	N,C	103.6	Jeypore	1	E
103.1	Itanagar	10	NE	103.6	Kozhikode	10	S,C
103.1	Macherla	3	S	103.6	Kadapa	1	S
103.1	Madikeri	10	S	103.6	Oros	5	W
103.1	Patni Top	10	N	103.6	Shillong	10	NE,B
103.1	Satara	6	W	103.7	Belonia	10	NE
103.1	Shanthinikethan	3	E	103.7	Bhuj	5	W
103.2	Bilaspur	6	W	103.7	Kalaburagi	10	S,C
103.2	Jhalawar	10	N	103.7	Kalpa	1	N, r
103.2	Kailashahar	6	NE	103.7	Kanpur	10	N,C
103.2	Nizamabad	10	S	103.7	Krishnanagar	10	E r
103.2	Tirupati-I	10	S	103.7	Nagaur	6	N
103.3	Ajmer	5	N	103.7	Purnea	10	E
103.3	Bellary	10	S	103.7	Shimla	10	N
103.3	Dhubri	10	NE, r	103.7	Udhampur	10	N
103.3	Madurai	10	S	104.5	Jammu B	10	N,C
103.3	Ranchi	10	E,C	105.4	Panaji	6	W,B
103.4	Agra	5	N	106.4	New Delhi	20	N, C
103.4	Dharamsala	10	N	106.6	Bikaner	10	N
103.4	Jorhat	10	NE	107.0	Kolkata	20	E,B
103.4	Puri	5	E	107.1	Mumbai	20	W,B
103.4	Sasaram	6	E	107.2	Kasauli	10	N,C,R
103.4	Solapur	10	W	107.5	Tirupati II	3	S
103.5	Alappuzha	5	S				

+ about 233 relay stns of 100W operating mostly on 100.1MHz
NB: AWR, FEBA, TWR etc. also broadcasting via AIR stns on MW/FM.
F.PI: 100W FM transmitters at 111 locations,**1kW:** Anini,Champai, Champawat, Changlang, Khonsa, Kolasib, **Namsai,** Tamenglong, Zunheboto. 5 nos. of 5kW Mobile Transmitters in Jammu & Kashmir **5kW:** Almora**10kW:** Amethi, Bathanaha, Coochbehar, **Green Ridge,** Dahod, Etawah, Gadania, Gurej, Haldwani, Himbotingla, Jaspur, **Kokrajhar,** Kupwara, Ludhiana, **Maharajganj,** Muzzafarpur, Narkatiaganj, Nanpara, Rajahmundry, Rampur(UP), Sitamarhi, Sultanpur 20kW: Rameswaram

Addresses of FM stations (see also SW & MW stn addresses): **Adilabad**-504002, Telangana – **Ahmednagar**-414001, Maharashtra – **Akola**-444001, Maharashtra – Scheme No 6, Mangal Vihar, **Alwar**-301001, Rajasthan – **Amritsar**-143001, Punjab – **Amethi**, Uttar Pradesh – Tapovan Gate, Camp, **Amravati**-444602, Maharashtra – Near Collectorate, **Anantapur**-515001, Andhra Pradesh – **Asansol**-713301, Burdwan Dist., West Bengal – Jalna Rd, **Aurangabad**-431005, Maharashtra – **Aurangabad**-842101, Bihar– **Bageshwar,** 263642, Uttarakhand – **Balaghat**-481001, Madhya Pradesh–**Balurghat**-733101, West Bengal – **Banda**-210001, Uttar Pradesh – Bardhaman-713101, West Bengal - **Banswara**-327001, Rajasthan – No 15, Lal Phatak, Badaun Road, **Bareilly**-243004, Uttar Pradesh – **Baripada**-757001, Mayurbhanj Dist., Odisha – Khandeshwari Road, **Beed**-431122, Maharashtra – **Bellary**-583101, Karnataka – **Belonia**-799155, Tripura – **Berhampur**-760001, Ganjam Dist., Odisha – **Betul**-460001, Madhya Pradesh – **Bathinda**-151005, Punjab – **Bhaderwah**-182222, Doda Dist., Jammu & Kashmir– Nutan Colony, **Bilaspur**-495001, Chhattisgarh – **Bolangir**-767001, Odisha – Bomdila-790001, West Kameng Dist. Arunachal Pradesh - **Bundi**-323001, Rajasthan - Tungri Maidan, **Chaibasa**-833201, Singhbhum Dist., Jharkhand – **Chandrapur**-442401, Maharashtra – Sector-19B, **Chandigarh**-160019 – **Cherrapunji**-793108, East Khasi Hills, Meghalaya – **Chindwara**-480001, Madhya Pradesh – **Chitradurga**-577501, Karnataka – Sector 4, Gandhi Nagar, **Chittorgarh**-312001, Rajasthan – **Churu**-331001, Rajasthan – **Churachandpur**-795128, Manipur – **Daltonganj**-822101, Jharkhand – Opp. Mota Fliya, Varkunt, **Daman**-396210, Daman & Diu – Daporijo-791122, Upper Subabsiri, Arunachal Pradesh - **Darjeeling**-734101, West Bengal – **Dehradun** 248001, Uttarakhand – **Devikulam**-685613, Idukki Dist., Kerala – **Dharmapuri**-636701, Tamilnadu – **Dharmasala**-176215, Kangra Dist., Himachal Pradesh – **Dhubri**-783301, Assam – **Dhule**-424001, Maharashtra – Begumganj Garahiya, **Faizabad**-224001, Uttar Pradesh – **Fazilka**-152123, Firozpur Dist, Punjab – **Gairsain**-246248, Chamoli Dist, Utarakhand – **Goalpara**-783101, Assam – **Godhra**-389001, Gujarat – **Guna**-473001, Madhya Pradesh – **Haflong**-788819, Assam – **Hamirpur**-177001, Himachal Pradesh – Salagame Road, **Hassan**-573201, Karnataka – Jail Road, **Hazaribagh**-825301, Jharkhand – **Hissar**-125001, Haryana – **Hospete**-583201, Karnataka – Vyas Colony, **Jaisalmer**-345001, Rajasthan – Adityapur, Gamharia Rd, **Jamshedpur**-831013, Jharkhand –Jungle Road, **Jhalawar**-326001, Rajasthan – Kanpur Road, **Jhansi**-284128, Uttar Pradesh – **Joranda**-759014, Dhenkanal Dist., Odisha – **Jorhat**-785001, Assam – **Jowai**-793150, Jaintia Hills, Meghalaya – **Junagadh,** Gujarat – **Kailashahar**-799277, Tripura – **Kalpa**-172108, Kinnaur Dist., Himachal Pradesh –**Kannur**-670001, Kerala – Radio Avenue, Nehru Ngr., **Karaikal**-609606, Puducherry – **Kanpur**-208001, Uttar Pradesh – **Karimganj**-787710, Assam – **Karimnagar**-505001, Telangana – **Karwar**-581301, Karnataka – **Kasauli**-173204, Solan Dist., Himachal Pradesh – **Kathua**-184104, Jammu & Kashmir – **Keonjhar**-758001, Odisha – **Khandwa**-450001, Nimar Dist., Madhya Pradesh – BMC PO, **Kochi**-682021, Ernakulam Dist., Kerala – Anandagiri, **Kodaikanal**-624101, Tamilnadu – Sardar Cly, Taravai Park, **Kolhapur**-416003, Maharashtra – Ramavaram, **Kothagudam**-507118, Telangana – Krishnanagar,Nadia Dist.741101, West Bengal – **Kulu**-175101, Himachal Pradesh – Bellary Road, **Kurnool**-518003, Andhra Pradesh – **Kurseong**: Mehta Club Bldg, Kurseong-734203, Darjeeling Dist., West Bengal– **Kurushetra**-132118, Haryana – **Lakhimpur Kheri**-262701, Uttar Pradesh – **Longtherai**-799275, Dhalai Dist, Tripura – **Ludhiana**-141001**,** Punjab – **Lumding**-782447, Nagaon Dist, Assam – **Lungleh**-796701, Mizoram – **Macherla**-522426, Guntur Dist, Andhra Pradesh – **Madikeri**-571201, Kodagu Dist., Karnataka – **Mahabubnagar**-509001, Telangana – Kadri Hills, **Mangaluru**-575004, Dakshin Kanara Dist., Karnataka – **Manjeri**-676121, Kerala – **Mandla**-481661, Madhya Pradesh – **Markapur**-523316, Prakasam Dist., Andhra Pradesh – Vrindavan Rd, Gayatri Tapobhumi, **Mathura**-281003, Uttar Pradesh – **Maunath Bhanjan**-275101, Mau Dist. Uttar Pradesh – **Mokokchung**-798601, Nagaland – **Mount Abu**-307501, Sirohi Dist., Rajasthan – **Murshidabad**-742101, West Bengal – **Mussoorie**-248179, Dehradun Dist., Uttarakhand – Yadavagiri, **Mysuru**-570020, Karnataka – **Nagaon**-782002, Assam – Basni Rd, **Nagaur**-341001, Rajasthan – Konam, **Nagercoil**-629004, Kanya Kumari Dist., Tamilnadu – Vasrania, **Nanded**-431601, Maharashtra – **Nashik**-422001, Maharashtra – **New Tehri**-249001**,** Tehri Garhwal Dist, Utarakhand – **Nizamabad**-503012, Telangana – **Nutan Bazar**-788115, Cachar Dist, Assam – Tambri Vibhag, **Oros**-416812, Sindhudurg Dist, Maharashtra – **Osmanabad**-413501, Maharashtra – Phase-I, Urban Estate, Rajpura Rd, **Patiala**-147002, Punjab – Patnitop-182142, Jammu & Kashmir – **Phek**-797108, Nagaland – **Poonch**-185101, Jammu & Kashmir – **Puri**-751001, Odisha – **Purnea**-854302, Bihar – **Raebareily**-229001, Uttar Pradesh – **Raichur**-584101, Karnataka – Chote Atarmude, **Raigarh**-496001, Chhattisgarh – Kamla Nehru Marg, Civil Lines, **Raipur**-492001, Chhattisgarh – **Rairangpur**-757043, Mayurbhanj Dist., Odisha – **Rajgarh**-465661, Madhya Pradesh – **Rajouri**-185131, Jammu & Kashmir – **Rourkela**-769001, Odisha – **Sagar**-470001, Madhya Pradesh – **Saraipali**-493558, Raipur, Chhatisgarh – **Sasaram**-821115, Rohtas Dist., Bihar – **Satara**-415001, Maharashtra – Pali Road, **Shahdol**-484001, Madhya Pradesh – **Shanthinikethan**, West Bengal – Physical College, **Shivpuri**-473551, Madhya Pradesh – **Solapur**-413006, Maharashtra – **Soro**-756045 , Balasore Dist, Odisha –_**Srikakulam**-532001, Andhra Pradesh – **Surat**-395001, Gujarat – **Suryapet**-508213, Telangana – **Swai Madhopur**-322001, Rajasthan – **Tirupati**-517501, Andhra Pradesh – **Tuipang**-796901,Saiha Dist, Mizoram - **Ujjain**-456001, Madhya Pradesh – Udagamandalam-643006, Tamilnadu - **Udaipur**-799120, Tripura – **Ukhrul**-795142, Manipur – Makarpura Rd, **Vadadora**-390009, Gujarat –**Vijapura**-586101, Karnataka–**Warangal**-506002, Telangana – **Yavatmal**-445001, Maharashtra.

EXTERNAL SERVICES: All India Radio
see International Broadcasting section

Private FM Stations:

Location	MHz	Station	Location	MHz	Station
Agartala	92.7	Big FM	Agra	94.5	FM Tadka
Agartala	95.0	Red FM	Ahmedabad	91.1	R. City
Agra	91.9	R. City	Ahmedabad	93.5	Red FM
Agra	92.7	Big FM	Ahmedabad	94.3	My FM
Agra	93.7	Fever FM	Ahmedabad	98.3	R.Mirchi

Location	MHz	Station
Ahmedabad	95.0	R. One
Ahmedabad	104.0	Mirchi Love
Ahmednagar	91.1	R. City
Ahmednagar	92.7	Big FM
Ahmednagar	104.0	My FM
Ahmednagar	106.4	R.Dhamaal
Aizawl	92.7	Big FM
Aizawl	93.5	Red FM
Aizawl	94.3	R. Gup Shup
Ajmer	92.7	Big FM
Ajmer	94.3	My FM
Ajmer	104.8	R. City
Ajmer	106.4	FM Tadka
Akola	91.1	R. City
Akola	91.9	R. Orange
Akola	94.3	My FM
Akola	95.0	R. Mirchi
Alappuzha	92.7	R.Mango
Alappuzha	104.8	Club FM
Aligarh	94.1	Current FM
Aligarh	92.7	Big FM
Aligarh	94.9	Fever FM
Aligarh	104.6	FM Tadka
Amravati	92.1	R. Mirchi
Amritsar	92.7	Big FM
Amritsar	93.5	Red FM
Amritsar	94.3	My FM
Amritsar	104.8	R. Mirchi
Asansol	92.7	Big FM
Asansol	93.5	Red FM
Asansol	95.0	R. Mirchi
Aurangabad	92.7	Big FM
Aurangabad	93.5	Red FM
Aurangabad	94.3	My FM
Aurangabad	98.3	R. Mirchi
Bareilly	91.1	FM Tadka
Bareilly	91.9	R. City
Bareilly	92.7	Big FM
Bareilly	94.3	Fever FM
Bengaluru	91.1	R. City
Bengaluru	91.9	R. Indigo
Bengaluru	92.7	Big FM
Bengaluru	93.5	Red FM
Bengaluru	94.3	R. One
Bengaluru	95.0	R. Mirchi
Bengaluru	98.3	R. Mirchi
Bengaluru	104.0	Fever FM
Bhaderwah	94.3	Top FM
Bharuch	92.3	R. Mirchi
Bharuch	105.2	Top FM
Bhavnagar	91.5	R. Mirchi
Bhavnagar	93.1	Top FM
Bhilai	91.9	R.Mirchi
Bhopal	92.7	Big FM
Bhopal	93.5	Red FM
Bhopal	94.3	My FM
Bhopal	98.3	R. Mirchi
Bikaner	91.1	R. City
Bikaner	92.7	Big FM
Bikaner	94.3	My FM
Bikaner	95.0	FM Tadka
Bilaspur	91.1	FM Tadka
Bilaspur	91.9	R. Orange
Bilaspur	92.7	R. Rangila
Bilaspur	94.3	My FM
Chandigarh	92.7	Big FM
Chandigarh	93.5	Red FM
Chandigarh	94.3	My FM
Chandigarh	98.3	R. Mirchi
Chennai	91.1	R. City
Chennai	91.9	Fever FM
Chennai	92.7	Big FM
Chennai	93.5	Suryan FM
Chennai	94.3	R. One
Chennai	95.0	Suryan FM
Chennai	98.3	R. Mirchi
Chennai	104.8	Chennai Live
Chennai	106.4	Hello FM
Coimbatore	91.1	R. City
Coimbatore	93.5	Suryan FM

Location	MHz	Station
Coimbatore	98.3	R. Mirchi
Coimbatore	106.4	Hello FM
Cuttack	91.9	Sarthak FM
Cuttack	92.7	Big FM
Cuttack	93.5	Red FM
Cuttack	104.0	R. Choklate
Dehradun	93.5	Red FM
Dhubri	94.3	R. Gup Shup
Dhule	93.5	Red FM
Dhule	95.0	My FM
Dhule	106.4	R. Dhamaal
Durg	91.9	R. Mirchi
Erode	91.9	Suryan FM
Erode	92.7	Hello FM
Gangtok	93.5	Red FM
Gangtok	95.0	R. Misty
Godhra	93.1	Top FM
Gorakhpur	91.1	FM Tadka
Gorakhpur	91.9	R. City
Gorakhpur	92.7	Big FM
Gorakhpur	94.3	Fever FM
Guwahati	92.7	Big FM
Guwahati	93.5	Red FM
Guwahati	94.3	R. Gup Shup
Guwahati	95.0	R. Mirchi
Gwalior	91.9	Suno Lemon
Gwalior	92.7	Big FM
Gwalior	94.3	My FM
Gwalior	95.0	FM Tadka
Haflong	94.3	R. Gup Shup
Hissar	91.9	R. City
Hissar	92.7	Big FM
Hissar	94.5	My FM
Hissar	106.4	R. Dhamaal
Hubli	93.5	Red FM
Hubli	98.3	R.Mirchi
Hyderabad	91.1	R. City
Hyderabad	92.7	Big FM
Hyderabad	93.5	Red FM
Hyderabad	94.3	Fever FM
Hyderabad	95.0	Mirchi 95
Hyderabad	98.3	R. Mirchi
Hyderabad	104.0	Kool FM
Hyderabad	106.4	Magic FM
Indore	92.7	Big FM
Indore	93.5	Red FM
Indore	94.3	My FM
Indore	98.3	R. Mirchi
Itanagar	92.7	Big FM
Itanagar	94.3	R. Gup Shup
Jabalpur	93.5	Red FM
Jabalpur	94.3	My FM
Jabalpur	98.3	R. Mirchi
Jabalpur	106.4	R. Dhamaal
Jaipur	91.1	R. City
Jaipur	93.5	Red FM
Jaipur	94.3	My FM
Jaipur	95.0	FM Tadka
Jaipur	98.3	R. Mirchi
Jaipur	104.0	Mirchi Love
Jalandhar	91.9	R. City
Jalandhar	92.7	Big FM
Jalandhar	94.3	My FM
Jalandhar	98.3	R. Mirchi
Jalgaon	91.1	R. City
Jalgaon	94.3	My FM
Jalgaon	98.3	FM Tadka
Jalgaon	106.4	R. Dhamaal
Jammu	91.9	Red FM
Jammu	92.7	Big FM
Jammu	95.0	FM Tadka
Jammu	98.3	R. Mirchi
Jamnagar	91.9	Top FM
Jamnagar	95.0	R. Mirchi
Jamshedpur	91.1	R. City
Jamshedpur	92.7	Big FM
Jamshedpur	93.5	Red FM
Jamshedpur	104.8	R. Dhoom
Jhansi	91.1	FM Tadka
Jhansi	92.7	Big FM

Location	MHz	Station
Jhansi	104.8	R. Mirchi
Jhansi	106.4	Red FM
Jodhpur	92.7	Big FM
Jodhpur	93.5	Red FM
Jodhpur	94.3	My FM
Jodhpur	98.3	R. Mirchi
Junagadh	91.9	Top FM
Junagadh	95.0	R.Mirchi
Kalaburagi	93.5	Red FM
Kannur	91.9	R. Mango
Kannur	93.5	Red FM
Kannur	94.3	Club FM
Kanpur	91.9	Mirchi Love
Kanpur	92.7	Big FM
Kanpur	93.5	Red FM
Kanpur	95.0	Fever FM
Kanpur	98.3	R. Mirchi
Kanpur	104.8	R. City
Kargil	91.1	Top FM
Kargil*	98.3	
Karnal	91.9	R. City
Karnal	94.5	My FM
Karnal	106.4	R. Dhamaal
Kathua	91.1	Top FM
Kathua	106.4	
Kochi	91.9	R. Mango
Kochi	93.5	Red FM
Kochi	94.3	Club FM
Kochi	104.0	R. Mirchi
Kolhapur	92.7	Big FM
Kolhapur	94.3	Tomato FM
Kolhapur	95.0	R. City
Kolhapur	98.3	R. Mirchi
Kolkata	91.9	Radio City
Kolkata	92.7	Big FM
Kolkata	93.5	Red FM
Kolkata	94.3	R. One
Kolkata	98.3	R. Mirchi
Kolkata	104.0	Fever FM
Kolkata	104.8	Ishq FM
Kota	91.1	R. City
Kota	92.7	Big FM
Kota	94.3	My FM
Kota	95.0	FM Tadka
Kozhikode	91.9	R. Mango
Kozhikode	92.7	R. Mirchi
Kozhikode	93.5	Red FM
Kozhikode	104.8	Club FM
Leh	91.1	Top FM
Leh	93.5	Red FM
Leh*	98.3	
Lucknow	91.1	R. City
Lucknow	93.5	Red FM
Lucknow	94.3	Big FM
Lucknow	98.3	R. Mirchi
Lucknow	104.0	Fever FM
Lucknow	107.2	Mirchi Love
Madurai	91.9	R. City
Madurai	93.5	Suryan FM
Madurai	98.3	R. Mirchi
Madurai	106.4	Hello FM
Mangaluru	92.7	Big FM
Mangaluru	93.5	Red FM
Mangaluru	98.3	R. Mirchi
Mehsana	91.9	R.Mirchi
Mehsana	92.7	Top FM
Mokokchung*	93.5	
Mumbai	91.1	R. City
Mumbai	91.9	R. Nasha
Mumbai	92.7	Big FM
Mumbai	93.5	Red FM
Mumbai	94.3	R. One
Mumbai	98.3	R. Mirchi
Mumbai	104.0	Fever FM
Mumbai	104.8	Ishq FM
Mumbai	106.4	Magic FM
Muzaffarpur	91.9	FM Tadka
Muzaffarpur	92.7	Big FM
Muzaffarpur	94.3	Red FM
Muzaffarpur	106.4	R.Dhamaal

Location	MHz	Station
Mysuru	92.7	Big FM
Mysuru	93.5	Red FM
Mysuru	104.8	R. Mirchi
Nagpur	91.1	R. City
Nagpur	93.5	Red FM
Nagpur	91.9	Mirchi Love
Nagpur	92.7	Big FM
Nagpur	94.3	My FM
Nagpur	98.3	R. Mirchi
Nanded	91.1	R. City
Nanded	93.5	Red FM
Nanded	94.3	My FM
Nashik	93.5	Red FM
Nashik	95.0	R. City
Nashik	98.3	R. Mirchi
Nashik	104.2	My FM
Nellore	93.5	Red FM
New Delhi	91.1	R. City
New Delhi	92.7	Big FM
New Delhi	93.5	Red FM
New Delhi	94.3	R. One
New Delhi	95.0	Hit FM
New Delhi	98.3	R. Mirchi
New Delhi	104.0	Fever FM
New Delhi	104.8	Ishq FM
New Delhi	107.2	R. Nasha
Palanpur	93.7	R.Mirchi
Panaji	91.9	R. Indigo
Panaji	92.7	Big FM
Patiala	91.1	R. City
Patiala	92.7	Big FM
Patiala	104.8	R. Mirchi
Patiala	106.4	R.Dhamaal
Patna	91.1	R. City
Patna	93.5	Red FM
Patna	95.0	Big FM
Patna	98.3	R. Mirchi
Poonch	94.3	Top FM
Poonch	106.4	
Porbandar	93.5	Top FM
Prayagraj	92.7	Big FM
Prayagraj	93.5	Red FM
Prayagraj	94.3	Fever FM
Prayagraj	106.4	FM Tadka
Puducherry	92.7	Big FM
Puducherry	93.5	Suryan FM
Puducherry	104.0	R.Mirchi
Puducherry	106.4	Hello FM
Pune	91.1	R. City
Pune	93.5	Red FM
Pune	94.3	R. One
Pune	95.0	Big FM
Pune	98.3	R. Mirchi
Pune	104.2	Mirchi Love
Raigarh	91.1	R.Mirchi
Raipur	94.3	My FM
Raipur	95.0	FM Tadka
Raipur	98.3	R. Mirchi
Raipur	104.8	Rangila FM
Rajamahen.	91.1	R.Mirchi
Rajamahen.	92.7	E FM
Rajamahen.	93.5	Red FM
Rajkot	92.7	Big FM
Rajkot	93.5	Red FM
Rajkot	94.3	My FM
Rajkot	98.3	R. Mirchi
Ranchi	91.9	R. City
Ranchi	92.7	Big FM
Ranchi	104.8	R. Dhoom
Ranchi	106.4	R. Dhamaal
Rourkela	91.9	Sarthak FM
Rourkela	92.7	Big FM
Rourkela	98.3	Radiodisha
Rourkela	104.0	R. Choklate
Salem	91.5	Hello FM
Salem	93.9	Suryan FM
Sangli	91.1	R. City
Sangli	91.9	Aapla FM
Sangli	93.5	Radio Orange
Sangli	104.0	My FM

Location	MHz	Station
Shillong	91.1	R. Mirchi
Shillong	93.5	Red FM
Shillong	98.3	Big FM
Shimla	95.0	Big FM
Shimla	98.3	R. Mirchi
Shimla	106.4	R. Dhamaal
Siliguri	92.7	High FM
Siliguri	93.5	Red FM
Siliguri	94.3	R. Misty
Siliguri	98.3	R. Mirchi
Solapur	91.1	R. City
Solapur	92.7	Big FM
Solapur	95.0	My FM
Solapur	104.8	FM Tadka
Srinagar	92.7	Big FM
Srinagar	93.5	Red FM
Srinagar	95.0	FM Tadka
Srinagar	98.3	R. Mirchi
Surat	91.1	R. City
Surat	91.9	Mirchi Love
Surat	92.7	Big FM
Surat	94.3	My FM
Surat	95.0	Red FM
Surat	98.3	R. Mirchi
Trivandrum	92.7	Big FM
Trivandrum	93.5	Red FM
Trivandrum	94.3	Club FM
Trivandrum	98.3	R. Mirchi
Thrissur	91.9	R. Mango
Thrissur	95.0	Red FM
Thrissur	104.8	Club FM
Tiruchirappalli	93.5	Suryan FM
Tiruchirappalli	95.0	R. Mirchi
Tiruchirappalli	106.4	Hello FM
Tirunelveli	93.5	Suryan FM
Tirunelveli	95.0	R. Mirchi
Tirunelveli	106.4	Hello FM
Tirupati	92.7	Big FM
Tirupati	93.5	Red FM
Tirupati	104.0	E FM
Tuticorin	93.5	Suryan FM
Tuticorin	106.4	Hello FM
Udaipur	91.9	R. City
Udaipur	92.7	Big FM
Udaipur	94.3	My FM
Udaipur	95.0	FM Tadka
Ujjain	91.9	R.Mirchi
Vadodara	91.1	R. City
Vadodara	92.7	Big FM
Vadodara	93.5	Red FM
Vadodara	98.3	R. Mirchi
Varanasi	91.9	R. City
Varanasi	93.5	Red FMF
Varanasi	95.0	Big FM
Varanasi	98.3	R. Mirchi
Vellore	91.5	Hello FM
Vellore	93.9	Suryan FM
Veraval	93.5	Top FM
Vijayawada	91.9	E FM
Vijayawada	93.5	Red FM
Vijayawada	98.3	R. Mirchi
Visakhapatnam	91.1	R. City
Visakhapatnam	93.5	Red FM
Visakhapatnam	98.3	R. Mirchi
Warangal	91.9	R. Mirchi
Warangal	93.5	Red FM
Warangal	104.8	E FM

*= F.Pl. **NB:** Big FM rel. R. Japan in Hindi 1835-1900 UTC via Bengaluru, Hyderabad, Kolkata, Mumbai, New Delhi on 92.7 MHz.

Web addresses: Best FM: bestfm95.in **Chennai Live:** chennailive.fm **Club FM:** clubfm.in **E FM:** eenadufm.net **Fever FM:** fever.fm **Hit FM:** hit95fm.in**Ishq FM:** ishq.com **My FM:** myfmindia.com **R. Chaska:** radiochaska.com **R. Choklate:** radiochoklateonline.com **R. City:** radiocity.in/radiocity **R. Dhamaal:** dhamaal24.com**R. Gup Shup:** radiogupshup.com **R. High:** radiohigh927fm.com **R. Mango:** radiomango.fm **R. Mirchi:** radiomirchi.com **R. Misty:** radiomisty.co.in **R. Nasha:** radionasha.com **R. One:** radioone.in **R. High:** radiohigh927fm.com **Red FM:** redfmindia.in **Suryan FM:** suryanfm.in **Top FM:** topfm.in

Gyan Vani (Educational FM Channel)
✉ Electronic Media Production Centre, Sanchar Kendra, Indira Gandhi National Open University (IGNOU), Maidan Garhi, New Delhi-110068 ☎+91 11 2953 3103, 2953 6131 🖷 91-11-2953 4299 E: gyandarshan@ignou.ac.in
W: http://ignou.ac.in/ignou/aboutignou/icc/empc/gyanvani

Location	MHz	kW	H. of Tr.
Agra ‡	105.6	10	
Ahmedabad ‡	105.6	6	
Aurangabad	105.6	10	0030-0430, 1230-1630
Bengaluru	106.4	10	0030-0430, 1130-1630
Bhopal ‡	105.0	10	
Chandigarh	105.6	10	0230-1430
Chennai ‡	105.6	10	
Coimbatore ‡	91.9	10	
Cuttack ‡	105.6	10	
Guwahati ‡	107.8	10	
Hyderabad ‡	105.6	10	
Indore	105.6	10	0230-1430
Jabalpur ‡	105.6	10	
Jaipur	105.6	10	0025-0430, 1225-1630
Jalandhar	105.6	10	0230-1430
Kanpur ‡	106.4	10	
Kochi	105.6	10	0230-1430
Kolkata ‡	105.4	10	
Lucknow	105.6	10	0030-0430, 1230-1630
Madurai	105.6	10	0230-1430
Mumbai ‡	105.6	10	
Mysuru ‡	105.6	10	
Nagpur	105.6	10	0030-0430, 1230-1630
New Delhi	105.6	10	0230-1430
Panaji ‡	107.8	10	
Patna ‡	105.6	10	
Prayagraj ‡	107.4	10	
Pune	105.6	10	0230-1430
Raipur	105.6	10	0230-1430
Rajkot ‡	105.6	10	
Shillong ‡	103.6	10	
Srinagar ‡	107.8	10	
Trivandrum ‡	105.6	10	
Tiruchirappalli ‡	104.8	10	
Tirunelveli	105.6	10	0230-1430
Varanasi	105.6	10	0230-1430
Visakhapatnam ‡	106.4	10	

NB: Txs located at and maintained by AIR. ‡ = off air.

Community FM Radio Stations: About 300 stations run by educational institutions, NGOs and others with 50W on **FM (MHz)**: 89.6, 90.0, 90.4, 90.7, 90.8, 91.2, 96.9, 106.8, 107.2, 107.4 and 107.8. **F.Pl.** More community stns to be started.

INDONESIA

L.T: We. Indonesia (Java, Sumatra, We. & Ce. Kalimantan): UTC +7; Ce. Indonesia (Bali, Ea. N. & S. Kalimantan, Nusa Tenggara, Sulawesi): +8h; Ea. Indonesia (Maluku Is, Papua): +9h — **Pop:** 274 million — **Pr.L:** Bahasa Indonesia (Indonesian) (official), Acehnese, Balinese, Banjarese, Buginese, Javanese, Madurese, Malay, Minangkabau, Palembang Malay, Sundanese — **E.C:** 220V/50Hz — **ITU:** INS

DIRECTORATE GENERAL OF POSTS & TELECOMMUNICATIONS (Direktorat Jenderal Pos dan Telekomunikasi)
✉ Gedung Sapta Pesona, Medan Merdeka Barat 17, Jakarta 10110 ☎ +62 21 3835955 🖷 +62 21 3860754 **W:** postel.go.id **E:** admin@postel.go.id

INDONESIAN BROADCASTING COMMISSION (Komisi Penyiaran Indonesia, KPI)
✉ Gedung Sekretariat Negara Lt VI, Jl. Gajah Mada 8, Jakarta 10120 ☎ +62 21 6340713 🖷 +62 21 6340667 **W:** kpi.go.id
LP: Head: Mr Agung Suprio. Dep. Head: Mr Mulyo Hadi Purnomo

RADIO REPUBLIK INDONESIA (RRI) (Pub)
National Station: RRI, Jakarta ✉ Jl. Medan Merdeka Barat 4-5, Jakarta 10110, or Tromolpos 1157 (or Kotak Pos 356), Jakarta 10001 ☎ +62 21 3842083 🖷 +62 21 3457132 **W:** rri.co.id **E:** info@rri.co.id
LP: Man. Dir.: Mr Muhammad Rohanudin, Dir. of Tech. & New Media: Mr Rahadian Gingging MK
Pro 1 (Prosatu): Information and entertainment on 91.2MHz **Pro 2 (Produa):** Prgrs for young people on 105.0MHz **Pro 3 (Protiga):** National news network on 999kHz, 88.8MHz 24h, also relayed in full on FM by most regional stns. N: on the h. Sports N. (Berita Olahraga): 0400, 0800 **Pro 4 (Proempat):** Educational and cultural prgrs on 1332kHz, 92.8MHz 24h. Relays Pro 3 1700-2200
Local Stations: Pro 1 (music and information), Pro 2 (for young people), Pro 3 (relay of Pro 3 Jakarta), Pro 4 (education and culture). MW and SW freqs below carry the local Pro 1 sce except where marked '3' or '4'. **H of tr:** Pro 3 24h, others usually 0430/0500-2400 local time

MW	kHz	kW	Station
JB01)	540	10	Bandung 4
JT01)	585	50	Surabaya 4
SL01)	630	50	Makassar
PB01)	702	10	Manokwari
MA01)	720	10	Ambon
PA06)	729	10	Nabire
BE01)	747	10	Bengkulu
JH03)	756	10	Purwokerto
MA02)	765	1	Tual
PB02)	774		Fak-Fak
NT02)	783	10	Ende
JH01)	801	10	Semarang
PA02)	810	7.5	Merauke
NB01)	‡855	10	Mataram
JB03)	864	10	Cirebon
JT02)	891	10	Malang 4
MU01)	891	10	Ternate
PB03)	909	10	Sorong
RI01)	927	25	Pekanbaru 4
SG01)	954	10	Kendari
JT03)	‡963	10	Jember
JH02)	972	50	Surakarta
JB01)	999		Bandung 3
JB03)	999		Cirebon 3
JK01)	‡999	150	Jakarta 3
GO01)	1008	10	Gorontalo
JT04)	1008	10	Madiun
PA03)	1026	5	Serui
LA01)	1035	5	Bandar Lampung
SH01)	1035		Palu
PA04)	1044	2	Biak
ST02)	‡1044	10	Tahuna
SU02)	1044	10	Sibolga
BA02)	‡1080	10	Singaraja
JA01)	1098	10	Jambi
JT05)	1098	10	Sumenep

MW	kHz	kW	Station	MW	kHz	kW	Station
NT01)	1107	5	Kupang	AC01)	1251	10	Banda Aceh 4
YG01)	1107	10	Yogyakarta 4	SS01)	1287	25	Palembang
SB01)	1179	10	Padang	JK01)	‡1332	10	Jakarta 4
ST01)	1188	10	Manado 4	KU01)	‡1350	10	Tarakan
KH01)	1197	10	Palangkaraya	SH02)	‡1377	10	Tolitoli
BA01)	1206	10	Denpasar	PA05)	1395	1	Wamena
KT01)	1215	10	Samarinda	BB01)	1413	5	Sungai Liat
KB01)	1233	5	Pontianak	KR02)	1467	10	Ranai
JB02)	1242	10	Bogor	SB02)	1512	10	Bukittinggi

SW	kHz	kW	Station, h. of tr.
KH01)	$3325	10	Palangkaraya.
JK01)	$4750	10	Cimanggis
PA06)	‡6125		Nabire
PA06)	±7290		Nabire: 2200-2300, 0500-0830v

NB: ‡=r. inactive at editorial deadline, ±=variable frq, v.=variable times. $ = carries VO Indonesia (Ext. Sce). During Ramadan several stns begin morning transmissions as early as 1800. A synchronised network across Java is planned on 999kHz for Pro-3.

Addresses (Jl = Jalan). All **FM:** in MHz. FM freqs are listed in order of prgr (Pro 1, Pro 2, Pro 3, Pro4) exc. where noted. Local FM relays are marked after + and generally carry Pro-1.

AC01) Jl Sultan Iskandar Muda 13, P.O Box 112, Banda Aceh 23423, Nanggroe Aceh Darussalam - **FM:** 97.7/92.6/87.8/88.6 + 90.5 Tapaktuan, 91.9 Langsa, 92.0 Sinabang, 92.3 Kutacane, 93.0 Subulussalam, 95.1 Lamno, 97.3 Jantho, 97.5 Calang, 99.7 Beuneuruen – **AC02)** Jl Peutua Ibrahim 75, Teumpok Teungoh, Lhokseumawe 24352, Nanggroe Aceh Darussalam - **FM:** 89.3/100.9/95.2 – **AC03)** RRI Sabang, Jl Yos Sudarso 65, Cot Bak U, Kecamatan Sukajaya, Sabang, Nanggroe Aceh Darussalam - **FM:** 94.0 – **AC04)** RRI Takengon, Jl Lembaga Kemili, Takengon, Aceh Tengah, Nanggroe Aceh Darussalam - **FM:** 93.0 – **AC05)** RRI Meulaboh, Meulaboh, Nanggroe Aceh Darussalam - **FM:** 97.0 (Pro 1)/88.7 (Pro 3) – **AC06)** RRI Singkil, Singkil, Nanggroe Aceh Darussalam – **FM:** 92.2

BA01) Jl Hayam Wuruk 70, Keladis, Denpasar 80233 (Kotak Pos 31, Denpasar 80001), Bali - **FM:** 88.6/95.3/93.0/106.6 + 99.5 Tamblingan, 100.9 Karangasem – **BA02)** Jl Gajah Mada 144, Tromolpos 153, Singaraja 81113, Bali - **FM:** 97.9/103.7/102.0

BB01) Jl Jend Ahmad Yani, Sungai Liat 33211, Bangka, Bangka Belitung - **FM:** 96.4/101.4/97.2 + 90.4 Toboali, 95.4 Mentok, 95.5 Tanjung Pandan, 99.8 Pangkalpinang

BE01) Jl Let Jend S Parman 25, Kotak Pos 13, Bengkulu 38227, Bengkulu - **FM:** 92.5/105.1/90.9 + 95.4 Muko-Muko, 97.0 Bintuhan, 98.0 Curup, 101.3 Ipuh

BN01) RRI Banten, Kompleks Pendopo Gubernur Banten, Serang, Banten - **FM:** 94.9

GO01) Jl Jenderal Sudirman 30, Gorontalo 96128, Gorontalo - **FM:** 101.8/92.4/96.7 + 92.5 Baroko, 94.9 Paguyaman, 97.0 Marisa

JA01) Jl Jendral A Yani 5, Telanaipura, Jambi 36122, Jambi - **FM:** 88.5/90.9/94.4 + 95.8 Bangko, 99.0 Kualatungkal, 99.0 Sarolangun, 99.8 Sungai Penuh, 99.8 Tungkal Ilir, 101.0 Muara Bungo - **JA02)** RRI Sungai Penuh, Sungai Penuh, Jambi - **FM:** 97.1/101.0

JB01) Jl Diponegoro 61, Bandung 40122 (Kotak Pos 1055, Bandung 40001), Jawa Barat - **FM:** 97.6/96.0 + 95.0 Gunung Malang, 97.0 Purwakarta/Subang, 97.8 Tasikmalaya, 98.0 Bayah, 98.2 Puncak Surangga, 98.9 Saketi, 102.5 Cikuray, 103.3 Garut – **JB02)** Jl Pangrango 30, P.O Box 232, Bogor 16161, Jawa Barat - **FM:** 93.7/106.8 – **JB03)** Jl Brigjen Dharsono/By Pass, Cirebon 45132, Jawa Barat - **FM:** 94.8/97.5/99.6

JH01) Jl Ahmad Yani 144-146, Kotak Pos 1307, Semarang 50241, Jawa Tengah - **FM:** 89.0/95.3/88.2/91.4 + 94.2 Colo, 96.7 Batang, 97.7 Gunung Gantungan, 99.5 Gunung Periksa – **JH02)** Jl Abdul Rahman Saleh 51, Kotak Pos 40, Surakarta 57133, Jawa Tengah - **FM:** 101.0/105.5/105.9 + 96.3 Tawangmangu – **JH03)** Jl Jendral Sudirman 427, Kotak Pos 5, Purwokerto 53116, Jawa Tengah - **FM:** 93.1/99.0/97.1

JK01) Jl Medan Merdeka Barat 4-5, Jakarta 10110 (Tromolpos 1157, Jakarta 10001).

JT01) Jl Pemuda 82-90, Kotak Pos 239, Surabaya 60271, Jawa Timur - **FM:** 99.2/95.2/106.3/96.8 + 91.1 Cemoro Lawang, 97.9 Pacitan, 99.2 Alas Malang, 102.3 Pulau Bawean; Studio 5 (additional music sce for Surabaya area): 91.7MHz – **JT02)** Jl Candi Panggung 58, Kotak Pos 78, Mojolangu, Malang 65142, Jawa Timur - **FM:** 91.5/87.9/94.6/105.3 – **JT03)** Jl D.I Panjaitan 61, Jember 68110 (Kotak Pos 166, Jember 68101), Jawa Timur - **FM:** 95.4/89.5/87.9 + 91.6 Banyuwangi/Bondowoso, 95.8 Lumajang – **JT04)** Jl Mayjen Panjaitan 10-12, Madiun 63133, Jawa Timur - **FM:** 99.7/95.2/104.0 + 96.3 Kemiri – **JT05)** Jl Urip Sumoharjo 26, Sumenep 69411, Madura, Jawa Timur - **FM:** 101.3/94.6/93.0 – **JT06)** RRI Sampang, Jl Peliang Km 2, Torjun, Sampang, Madura, Jawa Timur - **FM:** 100.8 – **JT06)** RRI Kediri, Pare Kediri, Jawa Timur - **FM:** 100.2

KB01) Jl Jendral Sudirman 7, Kotak Pos 6, Pontianak 78111, Kalimantan Barat - **FM:** 104.2/101.8/90.3 + 95.0 Nangamerakai, 96.8 Ketapang, 97.0 Sanggau) 97.7 Sambas, 97.7 Singkawang, 98.0 Kendawangan, 98.2 Semitau, 99.3 Sanggau Ledo, 100.2 Balaikarangan – **KB02)** RRI Sintang, Jl Oevang Oeraya, Baning, Sintang, Kalimantan Barat - **FM:** 96.6/90.7/102.5 – **KB03)** RRI Entikong, Jl Lintas Negara Indonesia-Malaysia, Entikong Sanggau, Kalimantan Barat - **FM:** 100.2

KH01) Jl M Husni Thamrin 1, Palangkaraya 73112, Kalimantan Tengah - **FM:** 89.2/92.4/95.9 + 93.6 Kuala Kapuas, 93.6 Sampit, 96.0 Muara Teweh, 97.1 Pulang Pisau, 97.3 Buntok, 99.2 Pangkalan Bun

KR01) Jl Ahmad Yani Km 4, Kotak Pos 8, Tanjung Pinang 29133, Bintan, Kepulauan Riau - **FM:** 98.3/92.1/88.6/101.3 + 96.6 Karimun, 99.6 Tarempa – **KR02)** RRI Ranai, Jl Sepempang, Ranai, Pulau Natuna Besar 29183, Kepulauan Riau - **FM:** 105.9/99.2/90.2 – **KR03)** RRI Batam, Komplek Politeknik Batam, Batam Centre, Batam, Kepulauan Riau - **FM:** 105.1/105.5

KS01) Jl Jenderal A. Yani Km 3.5 No 234, Kotak Pos 117, Banjarmasin 70234, Kalimantan Selatan - **FM:** 97.6/95.2/92.5/87.7 + 89.4 Batu Licin, 90.2 Kotabaru, 90.7 Amuntai, 99.6 Banjarbaru,105.7 Kandangan

KT01) Jl Moh Yamin 8, P.O Box 45, Samarinda 75110, Kalimantan Timur - **FM:** 97.6/88.5/98.4 + 96.0 Penajam, 96.7 Berau, 96.8 Tanah Grogot, 97.0 Balikpapan, 97.4 Melak, 97.4 Bontang/Sangata, 99.0 Tenggarong – **KT02)** RRI Sendawar, Jl D.I. Panjaitan 61, Dusun Busur, Kampung Barong Tongkok, Sendawar, Kutai Barat, Kalimantan Timur - **FM:** 103.3 – **KT03)** RRI Long Bagun, Mahakam Hulu, Kalimantan Timur **FM:** freq. not yet conf.

KU01) Jl Sungai Mahakam 10, Kampung Empat, Tarakan Timur 77125, Kalimantan Utara - **FM:** 97.9/101.9/88.8 – **KU02)** Jl Pelajar Perumda II, Malinau, Kalimantan Utara - **FM:** 95.5 – **KU03)** Jl TVRI 77, Nunukan, Kalimantan Utara - **FM:** 97.1/89.6 + 95.5 Pulau Sebatik (Pro 3)

LA01) Jl Gatot Subroto 26, Kotak Pos 24, Pahoman, Bandar Lampung 35213, Lampung - **FM:** 90.9/92.5/87.7 + 94.7 Rajabasa (Pro 3), 95.8 Kotabumi, 97.0 Kota Agung, 99.0 Simpang Pematang, 99.4 Liwa, 99.7 Padang Cermin, 100.2 Tulungbawang – **LA02)** Way Kanan, Lampung- FM: 103.6

MA01) Jl Jendral Akhmad Yani 1, Ambon 97124, Maluku - **FM:** 95.4/98.4/102.0 + 92.0 Amahai/Masohi, 94.3 Saumlaki – **MA02)** Jl Sukarno-Hatta, Kec Wat Deh, Tual 97661, Pulau Kai, Maluku - **FM:** 93.2/97.6/103.6 – **MA03)** RRI Bula, Seram Bagian Timur, Maluku **FM:** 90.0.

MU01) Jl Sultan Khairun 2, Kedaton, Ternate 97720, Maluku Utara - **FM:** 101.8/96.7/104.1 + 92.8 Pulau Morotai, 93.7 Soasiu

NB01) Komplek Perumahan RRI Mataram, Jl Majapahit, P.O Box 2, Mataram, Lombok, Nusa Tenggara Barat - **FM:** 89.2/104.2/94.3 + 89.1 Dompu, 89.3 Sumbawa Besar, 92.7 Kuripan, 96.3 Aik Bukak, 97.9 Lombok Timur **NB02)** Jl Lintas Tente Godo, Desa Kalampa, Bima, Sumbawa - **FM:** 91.4

NT01) Jl Tompello 8, Kupang 85225, Timor, Nusa Tenggara Timur - **FM:** 94.4/90.0/101.9 + 88.8 Soe, 90.7 Kefamenanu – **NT02)** Jl Durian, Ende 86317, Flores, Nusa Tenggara Timur - **FM:** 100.5/92.2 + 89.0 Bajawa (Pro 3), 89.2 Labuhan Baju (Pro 3) – **NT03)** RRI Rote Ndao, Baa, Rote 85371, Nusa Tenggara Timur - **FM:** 93.3 – **NT04)** RRI Atambua, Komplek Kantor Bupati Belu, Jl Eltari 1, Atambua, Timor, Nusa Tenggara Timur - **FM:** 91.5

PA01) Jl Tasangkapura 23, Kotak Pos 1077, Jayapura 99200, Papua - **FM:** 96.0/90.1/105.9/89.3 + 93.5 Sentani, 94.5 Timika, 96.5 Sarmi, 96.7 Sorendiweri, 97.6 South Jayapura, 100.0 Genyem – **PA02)** Jl Jendral Ahmad Yani 11, Mopa Baru, Merauke 99611 (Kotak Pos 111, Merauke 99601), Papua - **FM:** 90.0&95.4 (Pro-1)/98.1/105.0 – **PA03)** Jl Pattimura, Serui 98213, Papua - **FM:** 96.4/101.5/94.5 – **PA04)** Jl Majapahit, Kotak Pos 505, Biak 98117, Papua - **FM:** 96.9/95.3/95.8 + 96.3/97.6 Numfor – **PA05)** Jl Jendral A Yani 64, Wamena 99511 (Kotak Pos 10, Wamena 99501), Papua - **FM:** 97.1/96.3/94.7 – **PA06)** Jl Merdeka 74, Nabire 98811 (Kotak Pos 110, Nabire 98801), Papua - **FM:** 97.6/90.1/94.4 – **PA07)** RRI Boven Digul, Jl Trans Papua 17, Tanah Merah, Papua – **FM:** 93.6 – **PA08)** RRI Oksibil, Jl. Perbukitan Okpol, Oksibil, Papua - **FM:** 90.0 – **PA09)** RRI Skow, Jl RRI Stasiun Perbatasan, Skow, Papua - **FM:** 98.3

PB01) Jl Merdeka 68, Manokwari 98311, Papua Barat - **FM:** 94.3/97.8/95.1 – **PB02)** Jl Kapt P Tendean, Kotak Pos 154, Fak-Fak 98612, Papua Barat - **FM:** 97.2/99.0/93.15 + 98.1 Kokas – **PB03)** Jl Sam Ratulangi 4, Kotak Pos 146, Sorong 98414, Papua Barat - **FM:** 102.6/95.9/95.1 + 95.9 Bintuni, 96.3 Teminabuan – **PB04)** Jl Air

Merah, Kaimana, Papua Barat - **FM:** 96.3
RI01) Jl Jend Sudirman 440, Kotak Pos 51, Pekanbaru 28115, Riau - **FM:** 99.1/88.4/89.2/95.9 + 92.6 Pasir Pangaraian, 93.0 Dumai, 94.7 Selat Panjang, 96.5 Sei Pakning, 98.5 Baserah, 99.3 Tembilahan, 99.9 Siak – **RI02)** Bengkalis, Riau - **FM:** 90.6 (Pro-1)/89.8 (Pro-3)
SB01) Jl Jendral Sudirman 12, Kotak Pos 77, Padang 25124, Sumatera Barat - **FM:** 97.5/90.8/88.4 + 88.4 Pandai Sikek Padang Pariaman, 89.5 Bukit Gompong Solok, 92.0 Bungkit Palakat, 96.0 Lubuk Sikaping, 96.8 Pasaman Barat, 97.9 Bukit Langkisau Painan, 97.9 Dharma Seraya, 98.5 Mentawai – **SB02)** Jl.Prof Muhammad Yamin 199, Kotak Pos 3, Aurkuning, Bukittinggi 26131, Sumatera Barat - **FM:** 94.8/97.2/90.5 – **SB03)** Jl Diponegoro 48, Pariaman, Sumatera Barat - **FM:** 97.1
SG01) Jl Laute Mandonga 44, Kotak Pos 7, Kendari 93111, Sulawesi Tenggara - **FM:** 96.7/90.8/91.6 + 93.5 Boepinang, 97.0 Raha, 99.5 Lasolo
SG02) Bau-Bau, Sulawesi Tenggara - **FM:** 99.4
SH01) Jl R.A Kartini 39, Palu 94112, Sulawesi Tengah - **FM:** 90.8/105.0/92.4 + 95.4 Ampana, 95.5 Tanjung Santigi, 96.0 Banggai, 96.2 Poso, 97.1 Toboli, 99.2 Luwuk – **SH02)** Jl Jenderal Sudirman, Tolitoli 94514, Sulawesi Tengah - **FM:** 102.0/90.2/94.5 – **SH03)** RRI Ampana, Jl Tanjungulu Tojo Una-Una, Ampana, Sulawesi Tengah - **FM:** 93.0
SL01) Jl Riburane 3, Kotak Pos 103, Makassar 90111, Sulawesi Selatan - **FM:** 94.4/96.8/106.3/92.9 + 90.6 Bontu Tabang, 94.0 Baraka, 99.0 Parepare, 99.0 Bantaeng – **SL02)** RRI Bone, Jl Ahmad Yani, Watampone, Sulawesi Selatan - **FM:** 97.7
SR01) Jl H. Abdul Malik Pattana Endeng, Mamuju, Sulawesi Barat - **FM:** 96.0
SS01) Jl Radio 2 Km 4, Palembang 30128, Sumatera Selatan - **FM:** 92.4/91.6/97.1/88.4 + 90.3 Sekayu, 90.5 Baturaja, 90.5 Pagar Alam, 95.1 Lubuklinggau, 97.7 Prabumulih, 99.9 Muara Enim
ST01) Jl Radio 1, Kotak Pos 1110, Tikala Ares, Manado 95124, Sulawesi Utara - **FM:** 94.5/97.7/104.4/88.6 + 88.2 Pineleng, 92.0 Lirung, 92.5 Buroko, 98.1 Tondano, 99.5 Melonguane (Pro-3) – **ST02)** Jl Tona, Tahuna, Sangihe, Sulawesi Utara - **FM:** 98.7/92.0/105.4 – **ST03)** RRI Talaud - **FM:** 101.2
SU01) Jl Jend Gatot Subroto Km 5.6, Medan 20123, Sumatera Utara - **FM:** 94.3/92.4/88.8/88.4 + 90.0 Natal, 90.6 Rantau Prapat, 91.9 Kotanopan, 92.0 Prapat, 92.0 Sidikalang, 94.5 Simar Jarunjung, 96.1 Pematang Siantar, 96.3 Tarutung, 99.1 Sibuhan, 99.3 Pulau Raja – **SU02)** Jl Ade Irma Suryani Nasution 11, Sibolga 22513, Sumatera Utara - **FM:** 97.2/94.8/103.1 + 99.9 Padangsidempuan – **SU03)** RRI Gunungsitoli, Desa Iraonogeba, Gunungsitoli, Nias, Sumatera Utara - **FM:** 96.2/101.3/90.3– **SU04)** RRI Nias Selatan, Teluk Dalam, Nias Selatan, Sumatera Utara - **FM:** 93.1
YG01) Jl Ahmad Jazuli 4, Tromolpos 18, Kotabaru, Yogyakarta 55224, Daerah Istimewa Yogyakarta - **FM:** 91.1/102.5/102.9/106.6

EXTERNAL SERVICES: The Voice of Indonesia
see International Broadcasting section.

FEDERATION OF INDONESIAN NATIONAL COMMERCIAL BROADCASTERS (Persatuan Radio Siaran Swasta Nasional Indonesia)

✉ Jl Raya Mabes Hankam 19-A, Setu, Cipayung, Jakarta Timur 13880 ☎ +62 21 84591855 🖷 +62 21 29066878 **E:** ppjkt@indosat.net.id **LP:** Chmn: Rohmad Hadiwojoyo.

LOCAL PUBLIC BROADCASTING STATIONS (Lembaga Penyiaran Publik Lokal)

Local government stns have made the transition to local government-owned but autonomous public broadcasters. As a result, the names of most former local government radio stns (Radio Siaran Pemerintah Daerah, RSPD) have been changed.

INDONESIAN COMMUNITY RADIO NETWORK (Jaringan Radio Komunitas Indonesia)

✉ Sekretariat, Jaringan Radio Komunitas Indonesia, Jl Dwi Sri 10, Bandung, Jawa Barat ☎ +62 22 5224205 **W:** jrki.wordpress.com **E:** suara.jrki@gmail.com or jrk_kongres04@yahoo.com
LP: Chrmn: Bowo Usodo
The FM frequencies 107.7, 107.8 & 107.9MHz are reserved for community stns. Maximum permitted power is 50W

MW	kHz	kW	Station, location
JB04)	549		Inyong R., Depok
BN02)	576		R. Hutama Buana Swara (Neo HBS), S. Tangerang
JK02)	594		R. Prima Nusantara, Jakarta
JH18)	612		Radio Silaturahim Semarang (Rasil), Demak
JK03)	630	1	R. Samhan, Jakarta
JK12)	‡648		R. Rahmat Emmanuel Ministries (REM), Jakarta
JB05)	675		R. Syair Tauhid, Depok
JK04)	693		R. Musik Asik Nusantara (R. Muara), Jakarta
YG02)	711		R. Suara Konco Tani, Sidokarto
JB06)	720		R. Silaturahim, Cibubur
JH05)	720	0.25	R. Lusiana Namberwan (R. Silaturahim), Semarang
BN03)	738		R. Bharata Bhakti Nusa (Jakarta Music & News R.), Tangerang
JB07)	756		R. Rodja, Cileungsi – Bogor
JB08)	774		R. Ismail Mubarak, Bekasi
KS02)	±783		R. Dakwah Masjid Raya Sabilal Muhtadin Banjarmasin
YG03)	783		R. Swara Kenanga, Yogyakarta
JK05)	792	1	R. As Syafi'iyah, Jakarta
JB09)	‡810		RSPD Kabupaten Bandung (R. Kandaga)
JK15)	810		R. Politik, Jakarta (irreg.)
JK06)	828		R. Berita Klasik (RBK), Jakarta
SL03)	828		R. Swara Christy Ria, Makassar
JK07)	‡837		R. Muslim Jakarta
JH08)	‡846		R. Immanuel, Surakarta
JT08)	846		R. Suara Al Iman, Surabaya
JB10)	855		R. Kabar Empat, Bekasi
YG04)	±855		R. Gemma Satunama, Gunung Kidul
JH09)	873	0.5	R. Buana Asri (R. Publik Kabupaten Sragen), Sragen
JK08)	882		R. Pelangi Nusantara, Jakarta (irreg.)
JK09)	‡900		R. Sindajaya, Jakarta
SU05)	±900		R. Aksi Bethany, Medan
BN04)	909		R. Suara Guntur Laras, Tangerang
JB11)	‡918		R. Mustaqbal (Al Binaa), Bekasi
YG05)	‡927		R. Suara Parangtritis, Parangtritis
JK10)	936	0.25	R. Puspa Dwi Swara Cipta (P2SC), Jakarta
JH11)	945		R. Swara Buana Asri, Wonosobo
JB12)	954		R. Bekasi Banget (BaBe), Bekasi
JT10)	954	0.25	R. El Bayu, Gresik
SS02)	954	0.15	R. Garuda Kenten Jaya (Bazz R., Islamic R. Palembang), Palembang
SL04)	954		R. Wadhatama Nusantara (Makkah AM), Makassar
JK17)	981		R. Pesona Jakarta, Jakarta
KS03)	990		R. Bahana Al-Mursyidul Amin, Martapura
SL05)	1008		R. Suara Adyafiri, Watansoppeng
BN05)	±1017		R. Swara Angkasa Semesta (RASS), Teluknada, Tangerang
JK11)	‡1026		R. Suara Khatulistiwa (SK), Jakarta
JB13)	1044		R. Purna Yudha (i-Dream R.), Depok
JH12)	1062		R. P.T.D.I. Unisa 205, Semarang
JT11)	1062	1	R. Sangkakala, Surabaya
SU06)	1062		R. Tembang Perbaungan Indah, Perbaungan
YG09)	1062		R. Bin Baz, Yogyakarta
BN06)	1080		R. Gema Pesona Muda (GPM), S. Tangerang
SL06)	1080		R. Suara Viktori, Makassar
JB14)	1089		R. Daarul Qur'an (RadioQu), Bogor
JB15)	1116	1	R. Barani, Bandung
JT12)	±1117	0.25	R. Carolina Arjuno, Surabaya
BN07)	1125		R. Pendidikan Al-Fitroh (Rapa R.), Tangerang
JH13)	1125		R. Suara Diponegoro, Semarang
JK13)	1134	2	R. Swara Mega Asri (R. Safari), Jakarta
JH14)	±1143		R. Swara Delanggu (Swadesi), Delanggu-Klaten
JK14)	±1152		R. Ikadi, Jakarta
JT13)	1152		R. Yasmara, Surabaya
PA10)	1170		R. Suara Nusa Bahagia, Jayapura
BN08)	1179		GES Radio, Tangerang
YG06)	1179		R. Unisia Media Umat, Sleman
JH15)	±1180	0.5	RSPD Wonogiri
JT14)	1188		R. Swara Perak Jaya P.T.D.I., Surabaya
BN08)	1197		R. Swara Mitra, Tangerang
SB04)	1206		R. Suara Dikara Bawana (Dirgan Bravo), Padang
JH16)	1224		R. Angkasa Bahana Citra (A.B.C.), Surakarta
YG07)	‡1251		R. Edukasi, Yogyakarta
JB16)	1278		R. Sonata Bandung
YG08)	1323		R. Kartini Indah Swara, Yogyakarta
JB17)	1368		R. Attaqwa, Bekasi
YG10)	1395		R. Muhammadiyah (Radiomu), Yogyakarta
BN09)	‡1440		R. Edukasi, Tangerang
JH19)	1440		R. Muria, Jepara

MW	kHz	kW	Station, location
JT15)	±1449	0.7	R. Pertanian Wonocolo, Surabaya
JB18)	1458		R. Fajri, Bandung
SH05)	1458	1	R. Kareme Nuvula (RPK Parigi Moutong), Parigi
YG11)	1467		R. Muslim AM, Yogyakarta
JB19)	1476		R. Rodja Bandung, Bandung
ST04)	‡1494		R. Swara Kasih, Tahuna
KT04)	1512	0.25	R. Swara Mitra Dirgantara (Rasmira), Balikpapan
JK16)	1530		R. Mesjid Sunda Kelapa, Jakarta
BN10)	±1566		R. Bhalqist, Tangerang

NB: ‡ = r. inactive ± = variable. A number of unlicensed stns operating in the Tangerang area, Banten province, are not included in the list above.

Addresses (Jl = Jalan)
BN00) BANTEN
BN02) Jl Musyawarah, Sawa Lama, Ciputat, Tangerang – **BN03)** Jl Radeh Fatah, Perum Lembang Baru I/3, Ciledug, Tangerang 15151 (carries China Radio International prgr) – **BN04)** Jl Kayu Gede 2, Paku Jaya, Serpong Utara, Tangerang – **BN05)** Jl Kampung Melayu Barat, Teluknaga, Tangerang – **BN06)** Jurang Mangu Barat, Pondok Aren, S. Tangerang – **BN07)** Yayasan Pendidikan Al-Fitroh, Jl Panglima Polim, N. Poris Plawad, Cipondoh, Tangerang – **BN08)** Jl Komplek Peruri, Ciledug, Tangerang **BN09)** Pusat Teknologi Informasi dan Komunikasi (PUSTEKKOM), Departemen Pendidikan Nasional (DEPDIKNAS), Ciputat, Tangerang – **BN10)** Pondok Serut, Serpong Utara, Tangerang Selatan.
JB00) JAWA BARAT (West Java)
JB04) Jl Perintis I, Kalimulya, Depok – **JB05)** Jl Rawakalong 122, Grogol, Limo, Depok – **JB06)** Jl Masjid Silaturahim 36, Kalimanggis, Cibubur, Bekasi – **JB07)** Masjid Al Barkah, Jl Pahlawan kp Tengah, Cileungsi - Bogor – **JB08)** Jl Kemang Sari IV no 2, Jatimakmur, Pondok Gede, Bekasi – **JB09)** Jl Adikusumah, Bale Endah, Dayeuh Kolot, Bandung – **JB10)** Jl Kain Raya 3, Rawa Lumbu, Bekasi – **JB11)** Kompleks Pondok Pesantren Al Binaa IBS, Jalan Raya Pebayuran, Kertasari, Pebayuran, Bekasi 17110 – **JB12)** Jl PLTU. Babelan, Bekasi – **JB13)** Jl Rawa Pule I, Kukusan, Beji, Depok 16425 – **JB14)** Gang H. Mantik, Karadenan, Cibinong, Bogor 16425 – **JB15)** Jl Raya Cinunuk 84, Cileunyi, Bandung 40393 – **JB16)** Jl Soekarno-Hatta 260, Bandung – **JB17)** Jl KH. Noer Alie, Ujung Harapan, Babelan, Bekasi 17612 – **JB18)** Jl Nagrak Cangkuang RT 02/10, Soreang, Bandung – **JB19)** Masjid Umar Ibnul Khatab, Desa Selacau RT 02/05, Lembur Tengah, Batujajar, Bandung Barat 40561.
JH00) JAWA TENGAH (Central Java)
JH05) Jl Raung 7, Candi Baru, Semarang – **JH06)** Jl Kendeng (Pesayangan) 55, Kroya, Cilacap – **JH07)** Jl Letjend S Parman 28, Banjarnegara – **JH08)** Jl DI Panjaitan 3, Surakarta – **JH09)** Jl Veteran 21, Sragen 57211 – **JH11)** Jl Raya Kertek-Kalikajar 33, Wonosobo 56311 – **JH12)** Yayasan Badan Wakaf Sultan Agung (YBWSA), Universitas Islam Sultan Agung, Jl Raya Kaligawe Km 4, Semarang 50012 – **JH13)** Jl Perentis Kemerdekaan, Watugong, Semarang – **JH14)** Jl Raya Delanggu Utara 53, Delanggu, Klaten 57471 – **JH15)** Komplek Perluasan Kota, Jl Plongkowati, Wonogiri – **JH16)** Jl Kapt Mulyadi 117, Surakarta 57113 – **JH18)** Kalitengah, Mranggen, Demak. – **JH19)** Jl. Yos Sudarso 28, Jepara 59416.
JK00) JAKARTA
JK02) Jl Matraman 39, Jakarta – **JK03)** Jl Swadaya Raya 26/143, Raden Inten, Jakarta – **JK04)** Jl Cipinang Timur 15, Rawamangun, Jakarta 13240 – **JK05)** Jl Masjid Al Barkah 17, Tebet, Jakarta Selatan – **JK06)** Jl Danau Agung II/5-7, Sunter Agung, Podomoro, Jakarta Utara 14350 – **JK07)** J Swadaya 1, Pondok Ranggon, Cipayung, Jakarta Timur – **JK08)** Gedung Sasana Kriya TMII Lantai 2, Jl Pondok Gede Arena Taman Mini Indonesia Indah, Jakarta Timur – **JK09)** Kampung Beting, Jakarta Utara – **JK10)** Jl Dakota V/1, Kemayoran, Jakarta 10630 – **JK11)** Jl Tipar Cakung 9, Cilincing, Jakarta Utara – **JK12)** Apartemen Robinson Lantai 6, Jl Jembatan Dua Raya 2, Jakarta Utara 14450 – **JK13)** Gedung AKA, Jl Bangka Raya 2, Kebayoran Baru, Jakarta Selatan 12720 – **JK14)** Ikatan Da'i Indonesia, Jl Bambu Apus Raya 62, Jakarta Timur 13890 – **JK16)** Menteng, Jakarta.
JT00) JAWA TIMUR (East Java)
JT08) Komplek STAI Ali Bin Abi Thalib, Jl Sitopo Kidul 51, Surabaya – **JT09)** Jl Simolawang I/96, Surabaya 60144 – **JT10)** Jl Aipda Karel Sasuit Tubun 15, Gresik 61114 – **JT11)** Kompleks Manyar Indah Plaza, Jl Ngagel Jaya Selatan, Surabaya – **JT12)** Jl Ngagel Jaya Utara IV/21, Surabaya 60283 – **JT13)** Jl Amir Hamzah 18, Surabaya 60241 – **JT14)** Jl Teluk Aru 68, Surabaya 60165 – **JT15)** Jl Ahmad Yani 112, Wonokromo, Surabaya.
KB00) KALIMANTAN BARAT (West Kalimantan)
KB04) Jl Raya Sambas Bukitluwing 1, Sambas.
KS00) KALIMANTAN SELATAN (South Kalimantan)
KS02) Jl Jend. Sudirman 1, Banjarmasin 70114 – **KS03)** Jl Barintik 35, P.O Box 48, Martapura 70613
KT00) KALIMANTAN TIMUR (East Kalimantan)
KT04) Jl A Yani 50, Balikpapan 76123.
PA00) PAPUA (formerly Irian Jaya)
PA10) Jl Skyline, Jayapura
SB00) SUMATERA BARAT (West Sumatra)
SB04) Jl W.R Mongonsidi 4B, Lantai 2, Padang.
SH00) SULAWESI TENGAH (Central Celebes)
SH05) Jl Toraraga 234, Parigi 94371
SL00) SULAWESI SELATAN (South Celebes)
SL03) Jl Manggis 16, Makassar 90112 – **SL04)** Masjid Wihdatul Ummah, Jl Abdullah Daeng Sirua 52J, Makassar – **SL05)** Jl Poros Cabenge 1, Watansoppeng – **SL06)** Kompleks Ruko Somba Opu Blok B/19, Tanjung Bunga - Makassar
SS00) SUMATERA SELATAN (South Sumatra)
SS02) Jl Dr M Isa 38, 8 Ilir, Palembang 30114.
ST00) SULAWESI UTARA (North Celebes)
ST04) Manente, Tahuna, Kepulauan Sangihe.
SU00) SUMATERA UTARA (North Sumatra)
SU05) Jl Pabrik Tenun 102, Medan – **SU06)** Jl Deli Gg Kereta Api 6, Perbaungan, Deli Serdang 20586.
YG00) DAERAH ISTIMEWA YOGYAKARTA (Yogyakarta Special Reg.)
YG02) Jl Godean Km 9, Dukuh Sidokarto Godean, Sleman – **YG03)** Jl Panti Wreda 5, Giwangan, Umbulharjo, Yogyakarta 55163 – **YG04)** USC Satunama, Wiladeg, Gunung Kidul – **YG05)** Jl Parangtritis 22, Tegalsari RT46, Donotirto Kretek, Parangtritis 55772, Bantul – **YG06)** Universitas Islam Indonesia, Jl Demanangbaru 24, Sleman – **YG07)** Balai Pengembangan Media Radio, Pusat Teknologi Informasi dan Komunikasi Pendidikan, Departemen Pendidikan Nasional, Jl Sorowajan Baru 367, Banguntapan, Yogyakarta 55198 – **YG08)** Bantul, Yogyakarta – **YG09)** Islamic Centre Bin Baz (ICBB), Jl Wonosari km 10, Karanggayam Sitimulyo, Piyungan, Bantul, Yogyakarta Yogyakarta – **YG10)** Komplek Gedoeng Muhammadiyah, Jl. KH. Ahmad Dahlan no. 103, Notoprajan, Ngampilan, Yogyakarta – **YG11)**, Jl. C. Simanjuntak no. 72, Terban, Gondokusuman, Yogyakarta.

FM Stations: A large number of FM stns operate throughout the country. See RRI address list for RRI FM freqs.
Jakarta area FM (MHz): 87.6 Antarnusa Jaya (Hard Rock) – 87.8 Bogor Swaratama (Sheba), Bogor – 88.0 Mustang Utama – 88.2 M2, Bekasi – 88.4 Arief Rahman Hakim (ARH/Global R.) – 89.2 Power R.– 89.4 Sipatahunan (RSPK Bogor), Bogor – 89.6 Mustika Abadi (I R.) – 90.0 Elshinta – 90.2 Harmoni FM, Bekasi – 90.4 Muara Abdi Nusa (Cosmopolitan) – 90.6 RH56, Bekasi – 90.8 Suara Gema Pembangunan Utama (Oz R. Jakarta) – 91.0 Cherry Black R., Bogor – 91.6 Indika Millenia – 92.0 Sonora – 92.2 Radiotemen Nagaswara, Bogor – 92.4 Primaswara Adi Spirit Semesta (PAS/R. Bisnis Jakarta) – 93.0 Teman, Bogor – 93.2 Merpati Dharmawangsa (Hot FM) – 93.4 Kancah Irama Suara Indonesia (KISI), Bogor – 93.6 Gema Wargakarya Satnawa (Gaya), Bekasi – 93.9 Swara Mersidiona (Mersi), Tangerang – 94.3 Gardia Asia Bumi (XChannel) – 94.5 Ganadas, Bogor – 94.7 Agustina Yunior (U) – 95.1 Kirana Indah Suara (KIS) – 95.3 Pertanian Ciawi, Bogor – 95.5 Siaran Alaikassalam Sejahtera (RAS) – 95.7 Win FM, Bogor – 95.9 Smart Media Utama – 96.3 Pelita Kasih (RPK) – 96.7 Swara Rhadana Dunia (Hitz FM) – 97.1 Suara Monalisa (RDI) – 97.5 Safari Bina Budaya (Motion) – 97.9 Bahana Sanada Dunia (Female), Tangerang – 98.1 One Center, Bekasi – 98.3 Cakrawala Gita Swara (Mandarin Station) – 98.5 Islamic Centre Dakwah Al-Awwabin (Rida), Depok – 98.7 Attahiriyah (Gen) – 99.1 Delta Insani – 99.3 Fajri, Bogor – 99.5 Kayumanis (Smooth) – 99.7 Bahana Suara Alam (WADI), Bogor – 99.9 Draba (Virgin Radio Jakarta)– 100.1 Lesmana, Bogor – 100.3 Elgangga, Bekasi – 100.6 Jati Yaski Mandiri (Heartline), Tangerang – 100.8 Megaswara, Bogor – 101.0 Suara Irama Indah (Jak) – 101.4 Suara Kejayaan (Trax on Sky) – 101.8 Terik Matahari Bahana Pembangunan – 102.2 Prambors – 102.4 Media Akbar Zhapin (ZFM), Depok – 102.6 Camajaya Surya Nada – 102.8 Gema Annisa Persada, Cikarang-Bekasi – 103.0 Irnusa Ria, Depok – 103.2 Duta Swara Parahyangan, Bekasi – 103.4 Taman Mini (DFM) – 103.6 Swara Irama Kusuma Sena (Elpas), Bogor – 103.8 Pesona Gita Anindita (Brava) – 104.0 Forum 77 (8EH), Bekasi – 104.2 Media Suara Trisakti (MS-Tri) – 104.4 Swara Widya Sari (Puncak), Bogor – 104.6 Trijaya Sakti (Sindo Trijaya R.) – 105.4 Niaga Chakti Bhudi Bhakti (CBB) – 105.6 Suara Pendikikan Al-Ihya dan Insan Kamil, Bogor – 105.6 Gema Annisa,

Cikarang-Bekasi – 105.8 Ramako Jaya Raya (Most R.) – 106.0 Siaran Gema Nury (Elnury), Bogor – 106.2 Bergaya Nyanyian Irama Sejati, Tangerang (Bens) – 106.4 R. Attaqwa FM, Bekasi – 106.6 Sabda Sosok Sohor (V Radio) – 107.0 Nada Komunikasi Utama (Dakta), Bekasi – 107.2 Cemerlang, Depok – 107.3 Suara Tunggal Angkasa Raya (Star), Tangerang – 107.5 Mitra Carita Enambelas (Music City / MC), Depok – 107.7 Prestasi – 107.7 Islamic R. – 107.7 Sahabat Pramuka (Scout R.), Cibubur – 107.7 UG, Depok – 107.7 Komunitas Institut Pertanian Bogor (Agri), Bogor – 107.7 Jalesviva Jayamahe (Suara Samudera) – 107.9 Suara Sorak Kemenangan – 107.9 R. Airmen (Air Force R.) – 107.9 Telekomunikasi Cipta (UI FM), Depok.

Bandung FM (MHz): 87.7 Ekacita Swara Buana (Hard Rock FM) – 88.1 Swara Emas (SE) – 88.5 Mora Purna Karsa – 88.9 Hasil Era Reformasi (Auto Radio) – 89.3 Cipta Swara Global (Elshinta) – 89.7 Media Wisata Sariasih (Global R.) – 90.1 Karang Tumaritis (Zora) – 90.5 Cakra – 90.9 Lita Sari – 91.3 Manca Suara (Sindo R.) – 91.7 Citra Bahana Limbangan (INB) – 92.1 Bandung Suara Indah (Mei Sheng) – 92.5 Madah Ekaristi Swaratronika (Maestro) – 92.9 Arus Rizki (ARFM), Cimahi– 93.3 Ganesha Nada (Walagri) – 93.7 Paramuda – 94.1 Sanndy Qyu, Soreang – 94.4 Bandung Cipta Perdana (Delta FM) – 94.8 Galang Wahana Raya (Fit Radio) – 95.2 Swara Pandawa Lima Shakti (Bandung R.) – 95.6 Suara Burinyay (B Radio) – 96.4 Swaratama Cicalengka (Bobotoh) – 96.8 Nada Kencana Agung – 97.2 Shinta Buana – 98.0 Maya Nada – 98.4 Suara Sembilan Delapan Lima (Prambors) – 98.8 Candrika Widya Swara (Sonora) – 99.2 Manggala Gemini Bandung (Kids FM) – 99.6 Thomson – 100.0 Swara Milliard Artha (Ninety-Niners) – 100.4 Ilnafir Karanglayung Citra Budaya Suara (KLCBS) – 100.7 RSPD Kabupaten Bandung (R. Kandaga), Bale Endah – 101.1 Swakarsa Megantara (MGT) – 101.5 Dahlia Flora – 101.9 Putramas Mulia Rahayu (Cosmo) – 102.3 Tiara Rase Perdana – 102.7 Madinatussalam Bandung (MQ) – 103.1 Mitragamma Swara (Oz FM) – 103.5 Citrahutama Eltravidya (Chevy) – 103.9 Antassalam Bagja (Hits) – 104.3 Generasi Muda (U FM) – 104.7 Salam Rama Dwihasta – 105.1 Gema Dwipa (I R.) – 105.5 Garuda Tunggal Angkasa – 105.9 Ardan Swaratama – 106.3 Bhakti Musik Wastukencana (Urban R) – 106.7 Mara Ghita – 107.1 Lintas Kontinental (K-Lite) – 107.5 Mustika Parahyangan (PR FM) – 107.9 Jabar One

Batam FM (MHz): 87.6 Discovery Minang – 91.7 Aljabar Serumpun – 100.7 Ramako Batam (Batam FM) – 101.6 Matra Komersial Batam (Zoo FM) – 102.3 Kencana Ria Indah Suara (Kei FM) – 103.2 Artha Media Juanesha (Juan FM) – 104.3 Lintas Sei Ladi (Silaturahim) – 104.7 Batam Indah Gelora Suara (BiGSFM) – 106.0 Media Hang Batam (Hang FM) – 106.5 Suara Marga Semesta (Sing FM) – 107.0 Be FM – 107.7 R. Alfa Omega– 107.8 Rabbani Generation (RG FM) – 107.9 R. Komunitas Hang Tuah

Denpasar (Bali) FM (MHz): 87.8 Baturiti Menara Swara (Hard Rock) – 89.4 Gema Sunari Indah – 89.8 Organik Lestari Sejahtera (Pak Oles), Tabanan – 90.2 Suara Yudha (Urban R. Bali) – 90.6 Gema Megantara Pratama (Megantara Bali), Tabanan – 91.0 Gita Bakti Persada (Phoenix) – 91.4 Beat – 91.8 Flamboyant Bali Indah (FBI) – 92.2 Gema Megantara Pesona (Heartline) – 92.6 RPKD Denpasar – 93.3 Berita Bagus Sejati (Thomson News R.), Kuta – 94.1 Swara Swarga (Thomson Dangdut) – 94.9 Click Gita Saraswati, Bangli – 96.1 Genta Suara Bali – 96.5 Swara Kinijani (Global), Tabanan – 96.9 Elang Kosa Gagana (Elkoga) – 97.3 Sonata Indah (Thomson Bali) – 97.7 Gema Merdeka – 98.1 Gia, Gianyar – 98.5 Plus – 98.9 Bali Perkasa (Bali FM), Gianyar – 99.3 Duta Dewata (Duta Female) – 99.7 Srinadi FM, Klungkung – 100.5 Dunia Bokashi Raya, Klungkung – 101.2 Bali Swara Mitragama (D'Oz R. Bali), Kuta – 102.0 Suara Denpasar Chakti (Cassanova) – 102.4 R. Publik Kabupaten Bangli (RPKB) – 102.8 Menara – 103.2 Mega Nada, Tabanan – 103.6 Pinguin – 104.4 Aneka Rama (AR) – 104.8 R. Gelora Gianyar – 105.6 Bali Mandala Perkasa, Gianyar – 106.0 Swara Kreasi Utama (Kuta R.), Kuta – 106.9 Swara Bukit Bali Indah (Bali United FM), Kuta – 107.2 Swara Smarapura Shakti, Klungkung – 107.7 Komunitas Dwijendra

Medan FM (MHz): 87.6 DASS FM, Lubuk Pakam – 88.0 Cikal Anugrah Fiesta (La Femme) – 88.9 RPDK Deli Serdang, Lubuk Pakam – 89.2 Pasopati Perkasa (P FM) – 89.6 Visi Orang Medan Sumatera – 90.0 Gebyar Nada Satuwarna (Hot 90 FM), Deli Serdang – 90.4 Swara Teladan Anugrah (Sonora) – 90.8 Garuda Pentasindo Hutama (Mix FM) – 91.2 Swara Belmera (Istana MBC) – 91.6 Surya Damusu (Umsu FM) – 92.0 Mom's 99, Binjai – 92.8 Suara Dirgantara (Lite FM), Namorambe – 93.2 Berita Jaringan Global (Elshinta) – 94.7 Bonita Jaya (Suara Medan) – 95.1 Prapanca Buana Suara (Sindo Trijaya R.) – 95.5 Citra Buana Indah (CB) – 95.9 Mutiara Mandiri Buana Swara (City R.) – 96.3 Rhodesa (Medan FM) – 96.7 Citra Ayu Senada (R. Dangdut Indonesia, RDI) – 97.1 Sikamoni – 97.5 Swara Kencana Yuda (Prambors) – 97.9 Tuah Singalorlau (Narwastu FM), Deli Serdang – 98.3 Komersil Siaran Nusantara (I Radio) – 99.1 Khamasutra (Moze FM) – 99.5/106.2 Kardopa – 99.9 Istana Merpati Jaya (Istana MBC) – 100.5 Pelangi Lintas Nusa (Mutiara FM) – 101.0 Suara Binuang (Joy FM) – 101.4 Roris Shinta Rama – 101.8 Radio Media Indah Suara Handalan (Smart FM) – 102.2 Bonsita – 102.6 Alnora (Star News FM) – 103.4 Simponi – 103.8 Gitasukma Bahana (A R.) – 104.2 Mitramedia Dirgantara (R. Maria Indonesia) – 104.6 Anugrah Pradana Muda (Star FM), Deli Serdang – 105.0 Kindung Indah Seleras Suara (KISS FM) – 105.4 Pesona Ciptaswara (RPC), Binjai – 105.8 Medan Cipta Perdana (Delta FM) – 106.6 Sonya Portibi – 107.3 Lips FM– 107.8 Raja FM

Surabaya FM (MHz): 87.7 R. Zodiac (Colors) – 88.1 Kota Buaya Mandiri – 88.5 Metro Gema Mega – 88.9 JT-FM (Smart FM)– 89.3 Surabaya Pesona Femina (Prambors) – 89.7 Hafini Jaya Mandiri (Hard Rock FM.) – 90.1 Media Caraka Angkasa – 90.4 Ampel Denta– 90.6 Swara Laras Varia Citra Torasih (Rosco R.)– 90.9 Global Nada Prima – 91.3 Suzana Suara Bhakti – 92.5 Kreasi Indah Dunia Swara (Kosmonita) – 92.9 BFM – 93.3 Eka Laras Vicaksana Torya (El Victor) – 93.8 Shamsindo Indonusa (Suara Muslim Surabaya) – 94.4 Suara Digital Indonesia (My Radio) – 94.8 Devina Jelita (DJ FM) – 95.6 TOC FM (R. Spirit) – 96.0 Mercury Masa Depan Sukses – 96.4 Bahtera Yudha – 97.1 Suara Masa Depan Cerah (Life R.) – 97.6 Shinta Warga Gemilang (Elshinta) – 98.0 Salvatore Surabaya (Sonora) – 98.4 Giri Swara Indah Sakti (Swara Giri FM), Gresik – 98.8 Kartika Bahari Dirgantara (M R.) – 99.6 Gitaya Gegana (She R.) – 100.0 Fiskaria Jaya Suara Surabaya – 100.5 Delta FM – 101.1 Laras Pancar Istana Suara (Istara) – 101.5 Cakrawala Bhakti – 101.9 Stratosfir (Strato) – 102.3 X Channel –102.7 Suara Mahasiswa Turun Bekerja (MTB) – 103.1 Camar (Gen FM) – 103.5 Wijaya – 103.8 Rajawali Megah (Primaradio) – 104.3 Bisnis Surabaya (PAS FM) – 104.7 Cakra Awigra (Sindo Trijaya R.) – 105.1 Wahana Informasi Gemilang (JJ R.) – 105.5 Star Wibawa Anugrah, Pandaan – 105.9 Era Bimasakti Selaras (EBS) – 106.7 Merdeka Lokatama – 107.5 Media Assalam Surabaya (SAS FM) – 107.9 Suara An-Nida

IRAN

L.T: UTC +3½h (22 Mar-22 Sep: +4½h) — **Pop:** 84 million — **Pr.L:** Farsi (Persian) — **E.C:** 220V/50Hz — **ITU:** IRN

ISLAMIC REPUBLIC OF IRAN BROADCASTING (Gov.)
P O. Box 19395-333, Tehran ☎+98 21 2204 1093 🖷 +98 21 2222 1508 **W:** radio.ir **E:** radio@irib.ir **L.P:** President: Abdolali Ali Asgari.

MW	Region, location	kHz	kW	N	Language*, H of trs
3)	Azarshahr	558	500	I	
4)	Bushehr	558	200	I	
5)	Shahr-e-Kord	558	50	I	
6)	Habibabad	558	200	I	
7)	Shiraz (Dehnow)	558	400	I	
8)	Kiashahr	558	100	I	
9)	Gonbad-e Kavus	558	300	I	
10)	Hamadan	558	100	I	
13)	Sirjan	558	400	I	
15)	Shushtar	558	400	I	
21)	Tehran (Goldasteh)	558	600	I	
23)	Shahroud	558	50	I	
24)	Iranshahr	558	600	I	
24)	Zahedan	558	50	I	
26)	Yazd	558	50	I	
26)	Ardakan	558	200	I	
27)	Zanjan	558	50	I	
29)	Mashhad	558	200	I	
30)	Birjand	558	150	I	
15)	Mahshahr	576	600	E	Arabic 0330-1630
2)	Maku	576	50	I	Azeri
21)	Tehran (Gheslagh)	585	1000	F	
29)	Bajgiran	603	10	R	
14)	Qasr-e-Shirin	612	600	E	Arabic 0430-1630
11)	Bandar Abbas	621	50	R	
3)	Bonab	639	400	E	Kurd/Turk 0420-1920
8)	Kiashahr	657	100	R	
7)	Abadeh	666	50	R	
7)	Darab	666	60	R	
7)	Kazerun	666	10	R	
7)	Lamerd	666	50	R	
7)	Lar	666	50	R	
7)	Qir	666	50	R	
7)	Shiraz (Dehnow)	666	400	R	
29)	Kashmar	684	50	R	

MW	Region, location	kHz	kW	N	Language*, H of trs
29)	Mashhad	684	100	R	
11)	Bandar Lengeh	693	100	R	
8)	Kiashahr	702	500	E	VOIRI various 2330v-1930
15)	Ahvaz	711	600	R	Arabic/Farsi
29)	Taybad	720	400	R/E	VOIRI 0050-1720
12)	Ilam	729	100	A	
4)	Dayyer	738	50	R	
26)	Yazd	747	100	R	
5)	Shahr-e-Kord	756	200/50	R	
24)	Chabahar	765	600	R/E	
19)	Arak	774	100	R	
24)	Iranshahr	783	150	R	Baluchi
27)	Zanjan	792	50	R	Azeri
24)	Zahedan	801	100	R	Baluchi
18)	Khorramabad	810	100	R	
20)	Chalus (Darya)	819	60	R	
20)	Sari	819	30	R	
30)	Tabas	828	50	R	
6)	Habibabad	837	300	R	
3)	Miyaneh	846	50	R	Azeri
14)	Qasr-e-Shirin	864	50	R	
28)	Bojnurd	873	50	R	
32)	Mahabad	882	60	R	Kurdish
16)	Dehdasht	891	50	R	Luri
16)	Yasouj	891	50	R	Luri
25)	Tehran (Goldasteh)	900	600	Q	Arabic
13)	Sirjan	909	150	R	
13)	Jiroft	918	50	R	
18)	Dorud	927	50	R	
2)	Miandoab	936	300	R	Azeri/Kurdish
2)	Urmia	936	50	R	Azeri/Kurdish
17)	Dehgolan	945	100	R	
30)	Birjand	963	150	R	
12)	Ilam	972	100	R	
10)	Hamadan	981	100	R	
17)	Baneh	999	50	R	Kurdish
23)	Semnan	1008	100	R	
11)	Bandar Abbas	1017	50	I	
3)	Azarshahr	1026	200	R	Azeri
12)	Dehloran	1044	50	R	
18)	Khorramabad	1053	100	I	
24)	Saravan	1053	30	R	Baluchi
13)	Kerman	1062	200	R	
22)	Qom (Alborz)	1071	100	M	
15)	Mahshahr	1080	600	E	Arabic 1630-0030
23)	Shahrud	1089	50	R	
24)	Zabol	1098	200	E	Afghan langs. 0130-1720
29)	Sabzevar	1107	50	R	
21)	Qazvin	1125	50	R	
3)	Kaleybar	1134	10	R	Azeri
16)	Yasuj	1143	50	I	
14)	Qasr-e-Shirin	1161	600	E	Arab. 0130-0420,1630-2130
24)	Chabahar	1179	50	I	
25)	Tehran	1188	300	P	
1)	Parsabad-Moghan	1197	50	R	Azeri
30)	Nehbandan	1206	10	R	
11)	Kish Island	1224	300	E	Arabic
13)	Kerman	1224	50	I	
6)	Khur	1260	10	R	
1)	Khalkhal	1269	50	R	Azeri
14)	Kermanshah	1278	300	R	
24)	Zabol	1296	50	R	Baluchi
4)	Bushehr	1305	50	R	
1)	Ardabil	1314	50	I	
3)	Jolfa	1323	50	E/R	Azeri 0030-2030
25)	Tehran (Goldasteh)	1332	300	R	
13)	Bam	1341	20	R	
9)	Gonbad-e Kavus	1368	150	R	
24)	Chabahar	1377	50	R	Baluchi
14)	Paveh	1377	50	R	
11)	Hajiabad	1395	50	R	
9)	Gorgan	1395	50	E	Turkmen 1420-1820
7)	Qir	1404	10	I	
7)	Estahban	1413	10	R	
9)	Bandar-e-Torkamen	1449	400	E	Turkmen 1220-1820
30)	Ghayen	1458	10	R	
22)	Alborz	±1467	50	R	
17)	Marivan	±1476	20	R	Kurdish
2)	Khoy	1485	10	R	Azeri
7)	Jahrom	1485	10	R	
23)	Damghan	1485	1	I	
29)	Taybad	1494	10	R	
33)	Jamshidabad	1485	400	R	Arabic
1)	Ardabil	1512	50	R	Azeri
9)	Gorgan	1539	50	R	
23)	Garmsar	1539	10	I	
16)	Gachsaran	1548	10	R	
20)	Larijan	1548	10	I	
30)	Ferdows	1548	10	R	
24)	Zabol	1557	50	I	
13)	Bam	1566	50	I	
23)	Biyarjomand	1584	50	R	
23)	[unk. location]	1584	10	R	
15)	Dezful	1602	10	R	
23)	Damghan	1602	10	R	
23)	Garmsar	1602	10	R	
26)	Bahabad	1602	10	R	

± variable frequency. *Languages excluding Farsi. Times given if known, by monitoring, not to be 24h.

FM	Location	J	I	V	A	R	M
1	Ardabil	88.3	90.3	92.3	102.3	94.1	96.1
2	Urmia	88.5	90.5	92.5	98.5	94.5	96.5
3	Tabriz 1	88.0	90.0	92.0	102.0	94.0	96.0
3	Tabriz 2	-	91.0	93.0	99.0	-	97.0
4	Bushehr					92.2	
5	Shahr-e-Kord	88.0	90.0	92.0	102.0	94.0	96.0
6	Isfahan 1	89.0	91.0	93.0	93.5	95.0	97.0
6	Isfahan 2	88.5	90.5	92.5	107.5	94.5	96.5
7	Shiraz	88.0	90.0	92.0	93.5	94.0	96.0
8	Rasht	89.0	91.0	93.0	93.5	95.0	97.0
9	Gorgan	88.3	90.3	92.3	99.0	94.3	96.3
10	Hamadan	88.0	90.0	92.0	93.5	94.0	96.0
11	Bandar Abbas	87.9	90.1	91.8	93.4	94.2	96.0
11	Kish Island	87.6	89.9	93.0	93.5	99.2	96.8
12	Ilam	88.0	90.0	92.0	-	94.0	96.0
13	Kerman	88.0	90.0	92.0	93.5	94.0	96.0
14	Kermanshah	88.0	90.0	92.0	-	94.0	96.0
15	Abadan	87.6	89.7	92.7	-	93.8	95.6
15	Ahwaz	88.0	90.0	92.0	93.5	94.0	96.0
16	Yasuj	88.0	90.0	92.0	-	94.0	96.0
17	Sanandaj	88.0	90.0	92.0	-	94.0	96.0
18	Khorramabad	88.0	90.0	92.0	-	94.0	96.0
19	Arak	88.3	90.3	92.3	93.3	94.3	96.3
20	Sari	88.0	90.0	92.0	93.5	94.0	96.0
21	Qazvin	88.2	90.2	92.2	-	94.2	96.2
22	Qom	88.5	90.5	92.5	-	94.5	96.5
23	Semnan	88.0	90.0	92.0	-	94.0	96.0
24	Zahedan	88.0	90.0	92.0	-	94.0	96.0
25	Tehran	88.0	90.0	92.0	93.5	94.0	96.0
26	Yazd	88.0	90.0	92.0	93.5	94.0	96.0
27	Zanjan	88.5	90.5	92.5	93.5	94.5	96.5
28	Bojnurd	88.0	90.0	92.0	-	94.0	96.0
29	Mashhad	88.0	90.0	92.0	93.5	94.0	96.0
30	Birjand	88.0	90.0	92.0	-	94.0	96.0
31	Karaj	88.9	90.9	92.9	-	94.9	96.9
32	Mahabad	87.8	89.8	91.8	-	95.8	

FM	Location	Eg	Q	S	P	F
1	Ardabil	98.3	100.3		104.3	106.3
2	Urmia	98.8	100.5	102.5	104.5	106.5
3	Tabriz 1	98.0	100.0	-	104.0	106.0
3	Tabriz 2	-	-	103.0	-	107.0
4	Bushehr					
5	Shahr-e-Kord	98.0	100.0	-	104.0	106.0
6	Isfahan 1	99.0	101.0	103.0	105.0	107.0
6	Isfahan 2	98.5	100.5	102.5	104.5	106.5
7	Shiraz	98.0	100.0	102.0	104.0	106.0
8	Rasht	99.0	101.0	103.0	105.0	107.0
9	Gorgan	98.3	100.3	102.3	104.3	106.3
10	Hamadan	98.0	100.0	102.0	104.0	106.0
11	Bandar Abbas	98.6	100.2	101.8	104.3	106.6
11	Kish Island	97.7	99.7	102.8	104.6	105.8
12	Ilam	98.0	100.0	102.0	104.0	106.0
13	Kerman	98.0	100.0	102.0	104.0	106.0
14	Kermanshah	98.0	100.0	102.0	104.0	106.0
15	Abadan	97.6	99.6	101.6	104.9	106.7
15	Ahwaz	98.0	100.0	102.0	104.0	106.0
16	Yasuj	98.0	100.0	102.0	104.0	106.0

FM	Location	Eg	Q	S	P	F
17	Sanandaj	98.0	100.0	102.0	104.0	106.0
18	Khorramabad	98.0	100.0	102.0	104.0	106.0
19	Arak	98.3	100.3	102.3	104.3	106.3
20	Sari	98.0	100.0	102.0	104.0	106.0
21	Qazvin	98.2	100.2	102.2	104.2	106.2
22	Qom	98.5	100.5	102.5	104.5	106.5
23	Semnan	98.0	100.0	102.0	104.0	106.0
24	Zahedan	98.0	100.0	102.0	104.0	106.0
25	Tehran	98.0	100.0	102.0	104.0	106.0
26	Yazd	98.0	100.0	102.0	104.0	106.0
27	Zanjan	98.5	100.5	102.5	104.5	106.5
28	Bojnurd	98.0	100.0	102.0	104.0	106.0
29	Mashhad	98.0	100.0	102.0	104.0	106.0
30	Birjand	98.0	100.0	102.0	104.0	106.0
31	Karaj	98.9	100.9	102.9	104.9	106.9
32	Mahabad	-	99.8	-	103.8	105.8

NB: Only main FM transmitter sites for each production studio listed. Iran authorities have not provided comprehensive update information regarding their transmitter network in recent years and all information is based on various web sources and monitoring observations.

Stations of provincial or regional centres: 1) Ardabil (Parsabad own programming 3 hours a day) – **2)** West Azerbaijan: Radio Chichest – **3)** East Azerbaijan – **4)** Bushehr – **5)** Chaharmahal & Bakhtiari: R. Jahanbin – **6)** Isfahan – **7)** R. Fars – **8)** Gilan – **9)** Golestan – **10)** Hamadan – **11)** Hormozgan: R. Khalij e Fars & R. Kish 99.2 MHz – **12)** Ilam – **13)** Kerman – **14)** Kermanshah – **15)** R. Khuzestan, Ahvaz (also Arabic, Dezful 1602 kHz & 94.2 MHz own prgr. 5h between 0340-1630) – **16)** Kohgiluyeh & Boyerahmad: R. Dena – **17)** Kurdistan – **18)** Lorestan – **19)** Markazi (R. Aftab) – **20)** Mazandaran – **21)** Qazvin – **22)** Qom – **23)** Semnan – **24)** Zahedan, Sistan & Baluchestan (R. Hamoon, Zabol own prgr. 5h between 0340-1630) – **25)** Tehran – **26)** Yazd – **27)** Zanjan – **28)** Bojnurd, North Khorasan (R. Atrak) – **29)** Razavi Khorasan: R. Mashhad – **30)** Birjand, South Khorasan (R. Khorasan-e Jonubi, R. Kharavan) – **31)** Alborz (regional prgr. on 94.9 MHz only) – **32)** Mahabad – **33)** Abadan

NB: Access to regional web pages via **W:** dpp.irib.ir/radio

Networks:

I=Radio Iran: 24h, but hrs. of operation vary by station. Frequencies for R. Iran and provincial prgrs at the same transmitter site may be swapped. Gradually all R. Iran MW transmitters will be concentrated to 558 kHz synchronous frequency. **N:** on the half hour – **R=Regional (Provincial) network.** Studios in 33 centres producing prgrs in Farsi and local langs, including some locally produced Ext. Sce prgrs. Regional prgrs are in usually 24h. Most provincial stations also carry "Shabhaye Iran" (Iran Nights) between 2030-2230, produced in turn by each studio. **E=External Service** – **J=R. Javan** (Youth): 24h on FM – **V=R. Varzesh** (Sports) on FM – **A=R Ava** (Music Radio): 24h on FM – **M=R. Ma'aref** ("Religious Knowledge", rlg.): 24h on MW 1071kHz & FM. – **Eg=R. Eghtesad** (Economy) on FM – **Q=R. Quran**(rlg.): 24h on MW 900kHz and FM – **S=R. Salamat** (Health R): 24h on FM – **P=R. Payam** ("Message", music, traffic, news): 24h on MW 1188kHz + FM – **F=R. Farhang** (cultural): 24h on MW 585kHz & FM – **Ar=R. Arbayeen** 24h on 729kHz, only 4 weeks in Sept./ Oct. – **R. Tartil** (Quran): Tehran 101.5MHz - **R. Goftogoo** (Dialogue), Tehran: 24h on 103.5MHz – **R. Saba** (Humour): Tehran 105.5MHz – **R. Namayesh** (Theatre): Tehran 107.5MHz - **R. Monasebati** (seasonal event channel): Tehran/others on 95.5MHz (for example carrying R. Arbaeen in autumn).

Foreign Language prgrs in Tehran: English 91.5MHz, Arabic 97.5MHz, various languages 99.5MHz.

Ann: J: "Inja Tehran ast, Sedaye Jomhuriye Islamiye Iran, Shabakeye Radyoe-ye Javan". **I:** "Inja Tehran ast, Sedaye Jomhuriye Islamiye Iran, Shabakeye Radyoe-ye Iran". **V:** "Inja Tehran ast, Sedaye Jomhuriye Islamiye Iran, Shabakeye Radyoe-ye Varzesh". **A:** "Inja Tehran ast, Sedaye Jomhuriye Islamiye Iran, Radyoe Ava". **R:** "Inja (capital) ast, Sedaye Jomhuriye Islamiye Iran, shabakeye ostaniye (province)." **M:** "Inja Qom ast, Sedaye Jomhuriye Islamiye Iran, Shabakeye Radyoe-ye Ma'aref". **Eq:** "Inja Tehran ast, Sedaye Jomhuriye Islamiye Iran, Shabakeye Radyoe-ye Eghtesad". **Q:** "Inja Tehran ast, Sedaye Jomhuriye Islamiye Iran, Shabakeye Radyoe-ye Qur'an". **S:** "Inja Tehran ast, Sedaye Jomhuriye Islamiye Iran, Shabakeye Radyoe-ye Salamat". **P:** "Inja Tehran ast, Sedaye Jomhuriye Islamiye Iran, Shabakeye Radyoe-ye Payam". **F:** "Inja Tehran ast, Sedaye Jomhuriye Islamiye Iran, Shabakeye Radyoe-ye Farhang".

EXTERNAL SERVICE: Pars Today: see International Radio section

IRAQ

L.T: UTC +3h — **Pop:** 40 million — **Pr.L:** Arabic (official), Kurdish (official), Assyrian, Turkoman — **E.C:** 230V/50Hz — **ITU:** IRQ

COMMUNICATIONS AND MEDIA COMMISSION (CMC)

P.O. Box 2044, District 929, Street 32, Building 18 , Jadreiah, Baghdad ☎+964 1 7180009 +964 1 719 5839 **W:** cmc.iq **E:** enquiries@cmc.iq

IRAQI MEDIA NETWORK (Pub)

near Al-Mansoor Melia Hotel, Salihiya, Baghdad **W:** imn.iq **E:** info@imn.iq

MW	kHz	kW	Prgr.
Baghdad	792	20	Main

FM	MHz	kW	Prgr.	FM	MHz	kW	Prgr.
Diwaniya	88.1		Provincial	Salah al-Din	98.0		Al-Iraqiya
Mosul	88.7		Main/Prov.	Baghdad	98.3	1	Main
Ninewa	88.7		Main	Kut	98.5	1	Al-Iraqiya
Sinjar	90.5		Main	Qaim	98.5		Main
Ramadi	90.8		Main	Rutba	99.0		Main
Kirkuk	91.5		Main	Nasiriya	99.0		Quran
Hit	92.0		Main	Babylon	99.0		Provincial
Karbala	92.2	1	Main	Haditha	99.0		Al-Iraqiya
Muthanna	92.7		Main	Falluja	99.9	1	Main
Karbala	93.3		Provincial	Basra	100.5	5	Main
Shomali	94.2	10	Main	Najaf	101.0	5	Provincial
Baquba	94.8	10	Provincial	Baghdad	103.3		Al-Iraqiya
Ali Al-Garbi	95.0		Main	Mosul	103.3		Main/Prov.
Diyala	96.0		Al-Iraqiya	Amara	104.1		Quran
Maysan	96.1		Al-Iraqiya	Baghdad	105.0		Al Jel
Tikrit	96.1		Main	Amara	106.0		Main
Najaf	96.5	5	Quran				

Main Prgr (Republic of Iraq R.): 24h in Arabic on on MW and FM except for Provincial programmes on some transmitters during the day. **R. Al-Iraqiya:** 24h. **Quran prgr (R. Furqan):** 24h. **R. Al Jel** (for youth). **R. Nineva:** daytime on Mosul trs. **Ann:** Main prgr: "Idha'at Jumhuriyah al-Iraq min Baghdad".

Other stations:

MW	kHz	kW	Location	Station	H of tr
5)	999	20	Baghdad	R. Al-Bilad/Al-Amal	0240-1810
10)	1116	20	Baghdad	R. Dar as-Salam	0230-2100

FM	MHz	kW	Location	Station
14)	87.5		Penjwin	R. Garmyan (Yekgirtu R.)
21)	87.7	1	Baghdad	Monte-Carlo Doualiya
10)	88.0		Kirkuk	R. Dar as-Salam
20)	88.0		Sulaimaniya	R. Sawa
21)	88.1	1	Mosul	Monte-Carlo Doualiya
1)	88.3		Karbala	Imam Hussein FM
43)	88.3		Baghdad	R. Dijla
22)	88.3	1	Sulaimaniya	R. Nawxo
22)	88.4		Erbil	R. Nawxo
22)	88.4		Halabja	R. Nawxo
46)	88.5		Mosul	R. Nawa (Arabic)
18)	88.5		Sulaimaniya	Traffic FM
23)	88.6	1	Baghdad	Panorama FM
38)	88.6	1	Halabja	R. Dênge Nwe
20)	88.8		Sulaimaniya	VOA
47)	88.9		Erbil	R. Duhok
19)	89.0	2	Baghdad +2 stns	BBC Arabic
39)	89.0		Kirkuk	R. Ashur
47)	89.0		Amediye	R. Duhok
46)	89.1		Penjwin	R. Nawa (Kurdish)
14)	89.1		Kalar	R. Garmiyan (Yekgirtu R.)
3)	89.1		Basra	R. Al-Amal
8)	89.1		Sulaimaniya	R. Al-Hayat Al-Jadida
46)	89.3		Saidsadeq	R. Nawa (Kurdish)
46)	89.3		Halabja	R. Nawa (Kurdish)
10)	89.4		Mosul	R. Dar as-Salam
45)	89.4	10	Amara	Al-Mirbad R.
46)	89.5	4	Kirkuk	R. Nawa (Kurdish)
47)	89.5		Duhok	R. Duhok

FM	MHz	kW	Location	Station
20)	89.6		Amara	VOA
31)	89.7		Karbala	Al-Huda Islamic R.
4)	89.9		Mosul	R. Al-Ghad
46)	89.9	5	Baghdad	R. Nawa (Kurdish)
46)	89.9	1	Kalar	R. Nawa (Kurdish)
19)	90.0	1	Basra	BBC Arabic
24)	90.0		Kirkuk	Turkoman FM
1)	90.2		Muthanna	Imam Hussein FM
36)	90.3		Sulaimaniya	Ur FM
20)	90.4	1	Hilla	R. Sawa
42)	90.4		Basra	R. Al-Ahad
26)	90.5		Baghdad	Al-Yaum FM
1)	90.6		Maysan	Imam Hussein FM
46)	90.7	1	Sulaimaniya	R. Nawa (Arabic)
46)	90.7	2	Duhok/Zakho	R. Nawa (Arabic)
39)	90.9		Erbil	R. Ashur
27)	91.0		Najaf	Ministry of Interior Radio
7)	91.1		Samawa	R. Al-Kafeel
10)	91.1	1	Baghdad/Tikrit	R. Dar as-Salam
46)	91.1	2	Zakho	R. Nawa (Kurdish)
3)	91.3		Najaf	R. Al-Amal
28)	91.5	5	Baghdad	Al-Rasheed R.
47)	91.5		Zakho	R. Duhok
20)	91.6		Amara	R. Sawa
28)	91.6	5	Basra	Al-Rasheed R.
19)	91.7		Nasiriya	BBC Arabic
20)	91.7		Mosul	VOA
46)	90.7	8	Ramadi	R. Nawa (Arabic)
40)	91.8		Basra	Sumer FM
46)	91.9	3	Duhok/Halabja	R. Nawa (Kurdish)
46)	91.9	9	Sara-Dokan	R. Nawa (Kurdish)
21)	92.0	1	Basra	Monte-Carlo Doualiya
46)	92.0	9	4 locations	R. Nawa (Kurdish)
28)	92.1		Kirkuk	Al-Rasheed R.
20)	92.2		Hilla	VOA
34)	92.3		Erbil/Duhok	Zed R.
46)	92.3	1	Sulaiminiya	R. Nawa (Music)
19)	92.5	2	Sulaimaniya	BBC Arabic
34)	92.5		Kirkuk	Zed R.
42)	92.5		Al-Amara	R. Al-Ahad
46)	92.5		Basra/Koya	R. Nawa (Arabic)
46)	92.7		Erbil	R. Nawa (Arabic)
40)	92.8		Sulaimaniya	Sumer FM
19)	92.9	2	Kirkuk	BBC Arabic
7)	93.0		Maysan	R. Al-Kafeel
11)	93.0		Baghdad	Voice of Iraq
43)	93.1		Sulaimaniya	R. Dijla
1)	93.3		Al-Diwaniya	Imam Hussein FM
43)	93.3		Nineve	R. Dijla
45)	93.3	5	Basra	Al-Mirbad R.
1)	93.5		Baghdad	Imam Hussein FM
20)	93.6		Samawa	VOA
5)	93.7		Baghdad	R. Al-Bilad
52)	93.7		Sulaimaniya	R. Taxi
46)	93.9	17	Kalak/Khanaqin	R. Nawa (Arabic)
20)	94.0		Baquba	VOA
27)	94.0		Baghdad	Ministry of Interior Radio
6)	94.3		Sulaimaniya	Gorran Radio
61)	94.3	2	Erbil	R. Al-Salam
46)	94.6		Kirkuk	R. Nawa (Arabic)
4)	94.7		Mosul	R. Al-Ghad
2)	95.0		Baghdad	Sawt al-Khaleej
1)	95.3		Al-Kut	Imam Hussein FM
7)	95.3		Dhi-Qar/Karbala/ Najaf	R. Al-Kafeel
28)	95.5		Mosul	Al-Rasheed R
4)	95.5			R. Al-Ghad
20)	95.6	10	Samawa	R. Sawa
43)	95.7		Erbil	R. Dijla
53)	95.7		Sulaimaniya	Voice of Kurdsat (English)
19)	96.0	2	Mosul	BBC Arabic
53)	96.3		Sulaimaniya	Dengê Kurdsat (Kurdish)
43)	96.5		Basra	R. Dijla
60)	96.5	5	Baghdad	R. Al-Nas
46)	96.5		Koya/Qaladezi	R. Nawa (Kurdish)
20)	96.8		Kirkuk	VOA
19)	96.9	2	Baghdad	BBC English
8)	97.1		Sulaimaniya	R. Al-Hayat Al-Jadida
20)	97.1	2	Tikrit	R. Sawa
27)	97.1		Dhi Qar/Muthanna	Ministry of Interior Radio
46)	97.1		Ranya/Sara	R. Nawa (Kurdish)
7)	97.3		Diwaniya	R. Al-Kafeel
20)	97.5		Baquba	R. Sawa
28)	97.5		Mosul	Al-Rasheed R.
46)	97.5		Penjwin/Zmnako	R. Nawa (Kurdish)
20)	97.6		Ramadi	VOA
12)	97.7		Baghdad	Al-Hurriyah R.
27)	97.7		Basra	Ministry of Interior Radio
45)	97.7	10	Samawa	Al-Mirbad R.
36)	97.9		Basra	Ur FM
7)	98.0		Baghdad	R. Al-Kafeel
24)	98.0	0.1	Erbil	Turkoman FM
40)	98.2		Erbil	Sumer FM
46)	98.5		Mosul	R. Nawa (Arabic)
2)	98.7		Basra	Sawt al-Khaleej
27)	98.7		Babylon	Ministry of Interior Radio
20)	98.8	1	Kirkuk	R. Sawa
36)	98.9	5	Baghdad	Ur FM
45)	99.3	0.3	Kut	Al-Mirbad R.
54)	99.3	1	Sulaimaniya	Babylon FM
39)	99.4		Baghdad	R. Ashur
27)	99.5		Diyala	Ministry of Interior Radio
20)	99.6		Ramadi	R. Sawa
22)	99.9		Kirkuk	R. Nawxo
40)	99.9	5	Baghdad	Sumer FM
40)	99.9		Dohuk	Sumer FM
14)	100.2		Tawella	R. Garmiyan (Yekgirtu R.)
42)	101.0		Baghdad	R. Al-Ahad
20)	101.1		Tikrit	VOA
27)	101.1		Diwaniya	Ministry of Interior Radio
7)	101.3		Kut	R. Al-Kafeel
45)	101.4	10	Nasiriya	Al-Mirbad R.
7)	101.9		Babylon/Basra	R. Al-Kafeel
55)	102.1		Sulaimaniya	Nalia FM
20)	102.4	10	Baghdad	R. Sawa (alt. fq 100.5)
30)	102.5		Basra	R. Times Square
21)	103.0		Erbil	Monte-Carlo Doualiya
14)	103.4		Kifri	R. Garmiyan (Yekgirtu R.)
1)	103.7		Dhi Qar	Imam Hussein FM
1)	103.9		Basra	Imam Hussein FM
12)	104.0		Kirkuk	R. Kirkuk
42)	104.9		Nasiriya	R. Al-Ahad
58)	104.9		Erbil	R. Mariam
20)	105.0	10	Basra	VOA
42)	105.0		Hilla	R. Al-Ahad
19)	105.2		Nasiriya	BBC English
14)	105.4		Darbandikhan	R. Garmiyan (Yekgirtu R.)
57)	105.7		Sulaimaniya	X FM Radio
20)	105.8	1	Najaf	R. Sawa
40)	105.8		Diwaniya	Sumer FM
1)	106.3		Najaf	Imam Hussein FM
7)	106.3		Salah al-Din	R. Al-Kafeel
21)	106.3		Tikrit	Monte-Carlo Doualiya
20)	106.6	5	Erbil/Mosul	R. Sawa
59)	106.8		Baghdad	Sound of Joy
20)	107.0	10	Basra	R. Sawa
20)	107.8		Najaf	VOA
43)	107.9		Kirkuk	R. Dijla
20)	108.0		Erbil	VOA

Addresses & other information:
1) W: imamhussain-fm.com – **2)** See main entry under Qatar – **3) W:** radioalamalfm.com – **4) W:** alghad.fm – **5)** own programming until 0900, after that r. Radio Al-Amal **W:** albilad.org – **6) W:** gorran.net – **7) W:** alkafeel.net/radio – **8) W:** laii.org – **10) E:** darusalam.radio@gmail.com – **11) W:** voiraq.com – **12) W:** facebook.com/alhurriafm – **14) W:** facebook.com/garmyan.fm – **16) W:** facebook.com/RadioAlSalam – **18) W:** facebook.com/traffic.FM.Sulaimaniyah – **19)** BBC Arabic Service **W:** bbc.com/arabic – **20)** Also on MW via Kuwait 1593kHz 150kW 24h. For more details see International Radio section (USA) – **21)** R. France Internationale & Monte-Carlo Doualiya. Prgrs in Arabic/French. For details see International radio section (France) – **22) W:** facebook.com/nawxonewsagency – **23)** See MBC entry under UAE – **24) W:** kerkuk.net Prgrs in Turkoman/Arabic – **26) W:** alyaumfm.net – **27) W:** moi.gov.iq/index.php?name=Pages&op=page&pid=104 – **28) W:** alrasheedmedia.com Different prgr. to each region – **30)** facebook.com/btsfmradio – **31) W:** al-hodaonline.com – **36) W:** urradio.fm – **38) W:** facebook.com/Radio-Dangi-NWE-813632082138820 – **39) W:** facebook.com/radioashur In Assyrian/Arabic – **40) W:** sumerfm.

com – **42) W:** facebook.com/Radio.AlAhad – **43) W:** radiodijla.net – **45) W:** almirbad.com – **46) W:** radionawa.com – **47) W:** facebook.com/Radio-Duhok-130660366987960 – **52) W:** radiotaxi.fm – **53) W:** facebook.com/DengiKurdsat – **54) W:** babylonfm.net – **55) W:** facebook.com/NaliaFM – **57) W:** facebook.com/xfm105.7 – **58) W:** radiomariam.org – **59) W:** sojfm.com – **60) W:** facebook.com/radio.alnas – **61) W:** radioalsalam.com

IRELAND

L.T: UTC (28 Mar-31 Oct: +1h) — **Pop:** 4.7 million — **Pr.L:** Irish Gaelic (official), English (official) — **E.C:** 230V/50Hz — **ITU:** IRL

BROADCASTING AUTHORITY OF IRELAND (BAI)

2-5 Warrington Place, Dublin D02 XP29 ☎ +353 1 644 1200 🖷 +353 1 644 1299 **E:** info@bai.ie **W:** bai.ie **L.P:** Chief Exec: Michael O'Keeffe.
Responsible for regulation of commercial broadcasting in the Irish Republic. Full list of licensed stns can be found on BAI website.

RAIDIÓ TEILIFÍS EIREANN (Statutory Corporation)

Donnybrook, Dublin 4 ☎ +353 1 208 3111 🖷 +353 1 208 3080 **E:** info@rte.ie **W:** rte.ie
L.P: DG: Dee Forbes; Ch. Fin. Offr.: Richard Collins; Dir. Content: Jim Jennings; Ch Technology Officer.: Richard Waghorn, MD News: Jon Williams
Raidió Na Gaeltachta: Casla, Conamara, Co Galway ☎ +353 91 506677 **E:** rnag@rte.ie **W:** rte.ie/rnag
Lyric FM: Cornmarket Square, Limerick ☎ +353 61 207300 🖷 +353 61 207390 **E:** lyric@rte.ie **W:** rte.ie/lyricfm **Pub.:** RTE Guide

LW	**kHz**		**kW**	**Prg.**	
Summerhill	252		150/300	1	
FM (MHz)	**1**	**2**	**3**	**4**	**kW**
Achill	89.9	92.1	94.3	99.5	3
Aranmore	89.6	91.8	94.0	99.2	3
Ballybofey	89.7	91.9	94.1	99.3	0.5
Bantry	88.7	90.9	93.1	98.3	1
Cahirciveen	89.5	91.7	93.9	99.1	3
Cairn Hl (Longford)	89.8	-	-	-	20
Casla	88.4	90.6	92.8	98.0	2
Castlebar	89.3	91.5	93.7	98.9	3
Castletownbere	88.3	90.5	92.7	97.9	3
Clermont Carn	87.8	97.0	102.7	95.2	40
Clifden	89.5	91.7	93.9	99.1	3
Clonmel	88.3	90.5	92.7	97.9	1
Cnoc an Oir	89.2	91.4	93.6	98.7	1
Cork (Spur Hill)	89.2	91.4	93.6	98.8	5
Crosshaven	88.2	90.4	92.6	97.8	3
Dungarvan	88.5	90.7	92.9	98.1	3
Fanad	89.8	92.0	94.2	99.4	4
Greystones	89.5	91.7	93.9	99.1	1
Holywell Hill	89.2	91.4	93.6	98.8	6
Kilduff	90.2	92.4	99.8	-	3
Kippure	89.1	91.3	93.5	98.7	50
Knockmoyle	88.4	90.6	92.8	98.0	1
Limerick City	89.4	91.6	93.8	99.0	2.5
Maghera	88.8	91.0	93.2	98.4	160
Malin	89.9	91.1	93.3	98.5	2
Monaghan	88.9	91.1	93.3	98.5	2.5
Moville	88.3	90.5	92.7	97.9	1
Mt. Leinster	89.6	91.8	94.0	99.2	200
Mullaghanish	90.0	92.2	94.4	99.6	160
Suir Valley	89.0	91.2	93.4	98.6	3
Three Rock	88.5	90.7	92.9	96.7	10
Truskmore	88.2	90.4	92.6	97.8	120

+ 10 relays below 0.5kW

1) RTE R. 1: 24h mainly in English. **N. in English:** on the h **N. in Irish Gaelic:** 2150 – **2) 2FM:** 24h in English. – **3) Raidió Na Gaeltachta:** 24h in Irish Gaelic – **4) Lyric FM:** 24h classical music.

DIGITAL RADIO (DAB): DAB/DAB+ **RTE national multiplex** (Block 12C) trs. in Dublin, NE Ireland, Cork, Limerick carrying RTE services: R1, R1+, R1 Extra, 2FM, 2FM+, 2XM, Chill, Gold, Junior, Lyric FM, Pulse, R Na Gaeltachta. Local multiplex **RTE Dublin 1** (Block 5A) **RTE Dublin 2** (Block 5B) carry RTE and a variety of commercial sces. **FreeDAB** (unofficial) reported in Cork (Block 5A) and Dublin (Block 5D)

2RN (formerly RTE Network)

Block B, Cookstown Court, Old Belgard Road, Dublin 24 ☎ +353 1 208 2259 **E:** 2rntech@2rn.ie **W:** 2rn.ie
Distributes RTE radio and TV, Today FM and some local and regional broadcasters

TODAY FM (Comm.)

Marconi House, Digges Lane, Dublin D02 TD60 ☎ +353 1 804 9000 **E:** info@todayfm.com **W:** todayfm.com

FM	**MHz**	**kW**	**FM**	**MHz**	**kW**
Crosshaven	100.0	6	Knockanore	101.0	2
Truskmore	100.0	250	Castlebar	101.1	6
Moville	100.1	2	Woodcock Hill	101.2	5
Clonmel	100.1	2	Greystones	101.3	1
Knockmoyle	100.2	2	Clifden	101.3	6
Dungarvan	100.3	6	Kilkeaveragh	101.3	6
Maghera	100.6	320	Mt. Leinster	101.4	400
Monaghan	100.7	5	Fanad	101.6	8
Suir Valley	100.8	6	Achil	101.7	6
Kippure	100.9	100	Mullaghanish	101.8	320
Holywell Hill	101.0	12	Three Rock	101.8	2
Spur Hill, Cork	101.0	10	Clermont Carn	105.5	80

+ 5 trs.under 1kW
D.Prgr: 24h **N:** on the h, also on the half h at peak times

NEWSTALK (Comm.)

Marconi House, Digges Lane, Dublin D02 TD60 ☎ + 353 1 644 5100 🖷 + 353 1 644 5101 **W:** newstalk.com **E:** info@newstalk.com

FM	**MHz**	**kW**	**FM**	**MHz**	**kW**
Monaghan	103.3	2.5	Mohercrom	107.4	10.0
Capard	105.8	4	Waterford	107.4	2.0
Three Rock	106.0	10	Mullaghanish	107.4	80.0
Clonmel	106.0	1	Truskmore	107.4	80.0
Nagles	106.4	4	Fanad	107.6	4
Achill	106.8	1.3	Maghera	107.6	32.0
Holywell Hill	106.9	12	Saggart	107.6	2.0
Longford	106.9	5	Dungarvan	107.6	5.0
Limerick City	107.0	2	Cork City	107.8	5
Ballyguile	107.0	2	Cahirciveen	107.8	4.0
Clifden	107.0	4	Kilduff	107.8	2.0
Castlebar	107.2	6	Gorey	107.8	1.0
Mt Leinster	107.2	2	Wexford	107.8	0.4
Knockmoyle	107.2	4	Clermont Carn	107.9	4

+4 trs. under 0.4 kW **D.Prgr:** 24h

SPIRIT RADIO (Rlg.)

Radio Centre, Killarney Rd., Bray, Co Wicklow A98 R6F6 ☎ + 353 1 272 4760 **W:** spiritradio.ie **E:** info@spiritradio.ie

MW	**kHz**	**kW**			
Carrickroe	549	25			
FM	**MHz**	**kW**	**FM**	**MHz**	**kW**
Letterkenny	87.7	0.4	Cork	90.9	0.5
Tralee	88.0	0.4	Galway	91.7	0.4
Limerick	89.8	0.4	Drogheda	92.1	0.2
Dublin	89.9	0.4	Saggart	92.2	0.5
Waterford	90.1	0.4	Navan	92.4	0.2
Bray	90.1	0.2	Kilkenny	93.1	0.2
Ennis	90.3	0.5	Sligo	93.4	0.2
Dundalk	90.4	0.1	Wexford	94.5	0.2
Carlow	90.5	0.5			

D.Prgr: 24h

Local Stations:

FM	**MHz**	**kW**	**Station, tx location**
31)	87.8	1	Connemara Community R., Clifden
30)	94.6	1	Classic Hits, Saggart
32)	94.7	5	Spin South West, Clifden
18)	94.8	4	Northern Sound, Slieve Glah
30)	94.8	3	Classic Hits, Churchfield (Mallow)
1)	94.9	9	East Coast FM, Avoca
30)	94.9	3	Classic Hits, Three Rock
2)	95.0	10	Limerick's Live 95 FM, Woodcock Hill
16)	95.1	10	WLR FM, Faha, Dungarvan
10)	95.2	2	Highland R, Aran Mor
30)	95.4	9	Classic Hits, Nowen Hill
7)	95.5	2	Clare FM, Kilrush
17)	95.6	1	Cork's 96 FM, Kilworth,NE Cork
3)	95.6	4	South East R, Mt.Leinster

FM	MHz	kW	Station, tx location
4)	95.8	10	LM FM, Mt. Oriel
17)	95.8	10	Cork's 96 FM, Nowen Hill
7)	95.9	2	Clare FM, Woodcock Hill
8)	96.0	1	KCLR, Corbally Wood
5)	96.1	10	MWR FM, Kiltimagh
17)	96.1	2	Cork's 96 FM, Mount Hillary
20)	96.2	6	R. Kerry, Cahirciveen
1)	96.2	10	East Coast FM, Bray
18)	96.3	10	Northern Sound, Monaghan
7)	96.4	10	Clare FM, Maghera
17)	96.4	10	Cork's 96 FM, Holly Hill
8)	96.6	10	KCLR, Johns Well
9)	96.8	10	Galway Bay FM, Knockroe
8)	96.9	4	KCLR, Rossmore
34)	96.9	9	iRadio, Scalp Mountain
20)	97.0	40	R. Kerry, Mullaghanish
11)	97.1	10	Tipp FM, Scrouthea
5)	97.1	3	MWR FM, Achill
12)	97.3	5	KFM, Rossmore
30)	97.4	4	Classic Hits, Bweeng Mountain
9)	97.4	2	Galway Bay FM, Redmount Hl
9)	97.4	1	Galway Bay FM, Seanafaistin
16)	97.5	10	WLR FM, East Waterford
20)	97.6	2	R. Kerry, Knockanore
12)	97.6	4	KFM, Slieve Thuile
13)	98.1	5	98 FM, Three Rock
1)	99.9	5	East Coast FM, Saggart Hill
33)	100.3	12	R. Nova, Three Rock
24)	102.0	13	Beat 102-103 FM, Mount Leinster
34)	102.1	9	iRadio, South Galway
10)	102.1	1.3	Highland R., Feirn Hill
24)	102.2	6	Beat 102-103 FM, West Waterford
26)	102.2	5	Q 102, Three Rock
32)	102.3	1	Spin South West, Ennistymon
24)	102.4	10	Beat 102-103 FM, Clonmel
21)	102.5	4	Ocean FM, Truskmore
32	102.5	5	Spin South West, Knockmoyle
17a)	102.6	10	C103, Cork City
32)	102.7	9	Spin South West, Maghera
24)	102.8	10	Beat 102-103 FM, East Waterford
1)	102.9	16	East Coast FM, Ballyguille
1)	102.9	2	East Coast FM, Baltinglass
17)	102.9	1	C103, NE Cork
32)	102.9	9	Spin South West, Cahirciveen
32)	103.0	2.5	Spin South West, Woodcock Hill
34)	103.1	9	iRadio, Longford
34)	103.1	3	i102-104, Achill
34)	103.1	1	iRadio, Senafaistin
22)	103.2	0.5	Dublin City FM, Three Rock
10)	103.3	10	Highland R, Scalp Mountain
17a)	103.3	10	C103, Nowen Hill
34)	103.3	4	iRadio, Clifden
6)	103.5	2.5	Midlands 103, Sliabh Bloom
32)	103.5	1	Spin South West, Knockanore
17a)	103.7	5	C103, Mt. Hillary
34)	103.7	9	iRadio, Castlebar
25)	103.8	5	Spin 103.8, Three Rock
11)	103.9	3.2	Tipp FM, Kilduff
34)	104.0	2	iRadio, Aranmore
14)	104.1	2.5	Shannonside 104FM, Sliabh Bawn
30)	104.2	9	Classic Hits, Limerick
15)	104.4	5	FM 104, Three Rock
34)	104.4	9	iRadio, Sligo (Truskmore)
28)	104.5	10	Red FM, W. Cork (Nowen Hill)
10)	104.5	2	Highland R., Back Mountain
30)	104.6	9	Classic Hits, Maghera,Co Clare
34)	104.7	1	iRadio, Saggart
19)	104.8	10	Tipperary Mid-West R, Dangandargan
34)	104.8	2.5	iRadio, Cavan (Sliabh Giah)
30)	104.9	9	Classic Hits, Galway City
21)	105.0	10	Ocean FM, Mt.Charles
34)	105.0	5	iRadio, Mt Oriel (Louth)
28)	105.7	5	Red FM, North Cork (Nagles)
28)	106.1	10	Red FM, Churchfield, Cork
34)	106.2	5	iRadio, Capard
23)	106.4	2	Raidió Na Life, Three Rock
34)	106.7	10	iRadio, Monaghan
27)	106.8	4	Sunshine 106.8, Three Rock

+ approx 110 additional txs of less than 1kW

Addresses & other information:
1) Radio Centre, Killarney Rd, Bray, Co Wicklow A98 R6F6 **E:** reception@eastcoast.fm **W:** eastcoast.fm – **2)** Radio House, Richmond Court, Dock Rd, Limerick V94 HF91 **E:** info@live95fm.ie **W:** live95fm.ie – **3)** Custom House Quay, Wexford Town **E:** info@southeastradio.ie **W:** southeastradio.ie – **4)** Broadcasting House, Rathmullen Rd, Drogheda, Co Louth A92 T274 **E:** info@lmfm.ie **W:** lmfm.ie – **5)** Clare Str, Ballyhaunis, Co Mayo **W:** midwestradio.ie – **6)** Tindle House, Axis Business Park, Tullamore, Co Offaly R35 R588 **E:** info@midlandsradio.fm **W:** midlandsradio.fm – **7)** Abbeyfield Centre, Francis Str, Ennis, Co Clare V95 FN40 **W:** clare.fm – **8)** Leggettsrath Business Park, Carlow Rd, Kilkenny R95 YTD5 **E:** info@kclr96fm.com **W:** kclr96fm.com – **9)** Unit 13, Sandy Rd, Galway H91 CC97 **E:** info@galwaybayfm.ie **W:** galwaybayfm.ie – **10)** Pine Hill, Letterkenny, Co Donegal **E:** enquries@highlandradio.com **W:** highlandradio.com – **11)** Broadcast Centre, 4A Gurtnafleur Business Park, Clonmel, Co Tipperary E91 TW77 **E:** reception@tippfm.com **W:** tippfm.com – **12)** KFM Broadcast Centre, M7 Business Park, Newhall, Naas, Co Kildare W91 HX03 **E:** info@kfmradio.com **W:** kfmradio.com – **13)** Marconi House, Digges Lane, Dublin D02 TD60 **E:** website@98fm.com **W:** 98fm.com – **14)** Unit 1E Master Tech Business Park, Athlone Rd, Longford N39 RR67 **W:** shannonside.ie – **15)** Macken House, Mayor Str Upper, North Wall, Dublin 1 **E:** sales@fm104.ie **W:** fm104.ie – **16)** Broadcast Centre, Ardkeen, Dunmore Rd, Waterford X91 C4VN **E:** reception@wlrfm.com **W:** wlrfm.com – **17)** Broadcasting House, St Patrick's Place, Cork T23 E183 **E:** info@96fm.ie **W:** 96fm.ie – **17a)** Majestic Business Park, Goulds Hill, Mallow, Co. Cork **E:** info@c103.ie **W:** c103.ie - **18)** Unit 3 Milltown Business Park, Monaghan **E:** reception@norththernsound.ie **W:** northernsound.ie – **19)** St Michael Str, Tipperary E34 K156 **W:** tippmidwestradio.com – **20)** Maine Str., Tralee, Co Kerry **E:** info@radiokerry.ie **W:** radiokerry.ie – **21)** Ocean FM, North West Business Park, Collooney, Co Sligo F91 NX02 **E:** reception@oceanfm.ie **W:** oceanfm.ie – **22)** Docklands Innovation Park, Unit 6, 128-130 East Wall Rd, Dublin 3 **E:** admin@dublincityfm.ie **W:** dublincityfm.ie – **23)** 63-66 Amiens Str., Dublin 1 **E:** eolas@raidionalife.ie **W:** raidionalife.ie (Irish language stn) – **24)** Broadcast Centre, Ardkeen, Dunmore Rd, Waterford **E:** sales@beat102103.com **W:** beat102103.com – **25)** Marconi House, Digges lane, Dublin D02 TD60 **E:** info@spin1038.com **W:** spin1038.com – **26)** Macken House, 39-40 Upper Mayor Str, Dublin 1, D01 C9W8 **E:** info@q102.ie **W:** q102.ie – **27)** Castleforbes House, Castleforbes Rd., Dublin D01 A8NO **E:** mail@sunshineradio.ie **W:** sunshine1068.com – **28)** 1 University Technology Centre, Curraheen Rd., Bishopstown, Cork **E:** info@redfm.ie **W:** redfm.ie – **30)** Ground Floor, Castleforbes House, Castleforbes Rd., Dublin D01 A8NO. **E:** info@classichits.ie **W:** classichits.ie – **31)** Connemara West Centre, Letterfrack, Co Galway **E:** info@connemarafm.com **W:** connemarafm.com – **32)** 2nd Floor, City Gate House, Raheen, Limerick **E:** info@spinsouthewst.com **W:** spinsouthwest.com – **33)** 1st Floor, Castleforbes House, Castleforbes Rd, Dublin D01 A8NO **E:** info@nova.ie **W:** nova.ie – **34)** iRadio, Level 3, Unit C, Monksland Business Park, Athlone. **E:** reception@iradio.ie **W:** iradio.ie

Unofficial MW stations:

kHz	kW	Station, tx location
846	3	R. North, Redcastle, Co Donegal
981	1	R. Star Country, Emyvale, Co Monaghan
1395	0.3	Energy Power AM, Dublin (SS & public holidays)

Community/special interest stns: Approx 20 stns in operation at October 2020. **Hospital/Institutions:** 5 stns. **Temporary/Special Event services:** see BAI **W:** bai.ie **Wireless Public Address System (WPAS):** religious and other sces broadc. to the housebound via CB radio 27.600-27.995 MHz - licensed by Comreg - www.comreg.ie. **Parish radio** Some church services are relayed on FM frequencies with low power.

ISRAEL

L.T: UTC +2h (26 Mar-31 Oct: +3h) — **Pop:** 8.7 million — **Pr.L:** Hebrew (official), Arabic — **E.C:** 230V/50Hz — **ITU:** ISR

KAN – Israeli Public Broadcasting Corporation (IPBC)

Kanfei Nesharim 35, Jerusalem ☎+972 76 809 8000 **W:** kan.org.il **E:** info@kan.org.il kanenglish@kan.org.il

FM (MHz)	A	H	B	C	D	M	X	R	kW
Akko	104.9	-	95.0	-	99.3	-	-	101.3	40
Arad	-	-	95.0	89.7	-	-	-	101.3	
Ariel	105.3	90.5	95.2	97.5	-	-	88.2	-	4

FM (MHz)	A	H	B	C	D	M	X	R	kW
Atara	105.3	-	95.2	97.5	93.7	103.7	88.2	100.5	16/40
Bar Yehuda	-	-	94.5	-	-	-	-	-	
Beersheba	104.7	100.7	94.5	105.5	92.3	98.5	88.5	101.8	4/80
Bnei Yehuda	-	-	94.5	105.5	92.3	-	-	-	
Efrat	105.3	90.5	95.2	97.5	93.7	-	88.2	100.5	8
Eilat	-	-	94.5	105.5	92.3	98.5	88.5	-	4
Ein Yahav	-	-	95.2	97.5	-	-	88.2	-	4
Eitanim	105.1	92.5	95.5	97.8	88.8	91.3	87.6	100.3	160/100
Gidron	-	-	94.5	105.5	92.3	-	-	-	
Grofit	-	-	95.5	97.8	-	91.3	87.6	-	16
Haifa	104.7	100.7	94.5	105.5	92.3	98.5	88.5	-	80
Heletz	-	90.8	95.0	-	99.3	-	-	101.3	20
Jerusalem	104.9	90.8	95.0	89.7	99.3	103.7	88.0	101.3	8/2
Kalya	-	-	95.5	97.8	88.8	91.3	-	-	8/0.5
Katzir	-	-	95.2	-	93.7	-	-	-	40
Kohav Hayarden	104.9	90.8	95.0	89.7	-	97.2	-	101.3	40
Manara	104.9	-	95.0	89.7	-	97.2	-	101.3	2
Mitzpe Ramon	-	-	95.0	89.7	-	97.2	-	88.0	20
Nazareth	-	-	95.2	97.5	93.7	-	-	100.5	
Netanya	-	90.5	-	-	-	-	-	100.5	8
Safed	105.1	92.5	95.5	97.8	88.8	91.3	87.6	100.3	40
Tefen	-	90.5	95.2	97.5	-	-	88.2	-	
Tel Aviv	104.9	90.8	95.0	89.7	-	97.2	88.0	101.3	10/4/2

(Part of the sites are located in West Bank & Gaza)

Prgrs (in Hebrew if not mentioned otherwise):
A: "Kan Tarbut" (Culture Network): Talk & cultural programming 24h. **N.** in Hebrew: rel. Prgr. B. – **H: "Kan Moreshet"** (Heritage Network): Sun-Fri 24h – **B: "Kan Bet"**: 24h. News, current affairs & sports. **Ann** (for news): "Kan Kol Yisrael". **N:** on the h. – **C: "Kan Gimel"**: 24h Israeli popular music. **N:** rel. Prgr. B. – **D: "Kan Dalet, Makan Radio"** (Arabic). 24h. – **X: "Kan 88 FM"**: 24h. **N:** rel. Prgr. B. Light music, traffic reports – **R: Kan REQA** (Reshet Qlitat Aliya): immigrants network, 24h mostly in Russian but also in Amharic, French, Yiddish, Ladino, Romanian, Spanish, Moghrabi, Bukharian, Georgian and Hungarian, and in English 1800-1900. – **M: "Kol Ha Musica"** (VO Music): 24h, classical music and drama. – **Educational radio** "Kol HaCampus" is operating on 106.0MHz with 1kW in Holon, Tiberias, Beersheba, Haifa, Bet El and other trs in colleges around Israel. **W:** 106fm.co.il

GALEI TZAHAL (Israel Defence Forces R, Mil.)

✉ 1 Dror St, corner of Yehuda Hayamit St, Tel Aviv. Military ✉ MPO Box 01005 Jaffa ☎+972 3 5126666 **W:** glz.co.il **E:** glz@galatz.co.il
L.P: Commander: Yaron Dekel.

FM (MHz)	Main	kW	GalGalatz	kW
Beersheba	102.3	10	99.8	10
Beit She'an	104.0	5	91.8	5
Efrat	102.3		91.8	
Eilat	104.0	1	107.0	1
Grofit	96.6	10	93.5	10
Haifa	102.3	10	107.0	10
Jerusalem	104.0	1	107.1	1
Kalya	104.0	2	99.8	2
Kiryat Shmona	104.0	1	107.0	1
Ma'ale Adumim	104.0	0.3	-	
Ma'ale Efraim	96.6	1	107.0	1
Mitzpe Ramon	104.0	5	107.0	5
Ramla	96.6	20	91.8	10
Safed	96.6	5	93.5	5
Sapir	102.3	2	91.8	2
Tel Aviv	104.0	2	93.5	2
Wadi Ara	104.0	5	99.8	5

Main Prgr: 24h. (news, talk show, music). **N:** on the h.
GalGalatz (traffic reports and music): 24h.
Ann: Main Prgr: "Galei Tzahal, Shidure Tsva Hagana Le'Yisrael".

SECOND AUTHORITY FOR TELEVISION & RADIO

✉ 20 Beit Hadfus St, P.O.Box 3445, Jerusalem ☎+972 2 6556222 **W:** rashut2.org.il **E:** rashut@rashut2.org.il

Regional commercial FM radio (all in Hebrew except as noted): **Eco99fm**, Hertzliyah: 99.0MHz **W:** eco99fm.maariv.co.il – **Galey Israel:** Benjamin area 89.3MHz, Central Israel 94.0MHz, South 102.5MHz, Dan area 106.5 MHz. **W:** srugim.co.il/galeyisrael – **Pervoye R,** Rishon Le'Zion. In Russian: Ashdod 89.1MHz. **W:** 891fm.co.il – **R. A'shams** (The Sun) in Arabic at Nazareth-Ein Hahoresh area. 98.1 & 101.1MHz. **W:** ashams.com – **R. Cham Esh,** Haifa: 99.5MHz. **W:** 995.co.il – **R. Darom** (Southern R.): Beersheba 97.0MHz, Kiryat Gat, Ashkelon. Arava & Dead Sea settlements: 95.8MHz. **W:** radiodarom.co.il **R. Darom** (Southern R.) :101.5MHz. **W:** radiodarom.co.il/?page_id=2880 – **R. Haifa,** Haifa: 107.5MHz. **W:** 1075.fm – **R. Jerusalem:** Jerusalem 101.0MHz, Bet Shemesh 89.5MHz. **W:** tapuz.co.il/minisites/radiojerusalem – **R. Kol Barama,** Tel Aviv 92.1MHz, Beersheva 104.3MHz, Jerusalem 105.7MHz. **W:** kol-barama.co.il – **R. Kol Chai**: Bene Brak 92.8, Jerusalem 93.0/102.5MHz **W:** 93fm.co.il – **R. Kol Rega**: Galilee 96.0MHz, Tiberias 91.5MHz. **W:** 96fm.co.il – **R. Lev Ha Medina**: Shfela 91.0MHz, Beersheba 93.3MHz. **W:** 91fm.co.il – **Kol Ha Yam Ha Adom** (VO the Red Sea): 101.1, 102.0MHz 1kW. **W:** fm102.co.il – **R. L'Lo Hafsaka** (Nonstop): Upper Galilee 101.5MHz, Ramat Gan 103.0MHz, Lower Galilee 104.5MHz. **W:** 103.fm – **R. Tel Aviv**: 102.0MHz. **W:** 102fm.co.il – **R. Tishim,** (90), Tel Aviv: 90.0, 94.7MHz. **W:** 90fm.co.il – **Radius 100 FM**, Tel Aviv: 100.0MHz. **W:** 100fm.co.il

WEST BANK & GAZA STRIP (Palestinian Authority)

L.T: UTC +2h (26 Mar-30 Oct: +3h; suspended during month of Ramadan; dates subject to confirmation) — **Pop:** 5.2 million — **Pr.L:** Arabic — **E.C:** 230V/50Hz— **ITU:** XWB (West Bank), XGZ (Gaza)

MINISTRY OF TELECOMMUNICATIONS & INFORMATION TECHNOLOGY

✉ Ramallah ☎ +970 2 2943333 **E:** info@mtit.gov.ps **W:** www.mtit.pna.ps **L.P:** Minister: Allam Mousa

PALESTINIAN BROADCASTING CORPORATION (Gov)

✉ P.O. Box 984, Al-Bireh, Ramallah, West Bank ☎+970 2 2988888 **W:** vop.ps **E:** info@pbc.ps
FM: Ramallah 90.7MHz, Hebron 99.4MHz, Gaza 108.0MHz. Regional service: Jenin 89.5MHz.
D.Prgr. in Arabic: 0400-2300 **Ann:** "Sawt Filastin".

OTHER STATIONS, main networks (MHz):
Ajyal Radio: Jenin 92.8, Qalqiliya 93.8, Tubas 95.0, Salfit 95.7, Jericho 100.3, Nablus 100.4, Ramallah 103.4MHz, Bethlehem 105.6, Hebron 105.8, Tulkarem 106.6, Bethlehem 106.9MHz, Gaza 107.2MHz **W:** arn.ps
Al-Balad FM, Jenin: 95.6/105.2 **W:** albaladfm.ps
Amwaj Radio: Nablus 89.8, Ramallah 91.5, Jerusalem 104.8 **W:** amwajfm.ps
Angham Radio: Ramallah 92.3, Hebron 93.3, Jericho/Tulkarem 98.6, Nablus/Salfit 101.7, Qalqiliya 106.2, Jenin 106.8, Bethlehem 106.9, Tubas 107.4 **W:** arn.ps
Holy Quran Radio: Hebron 88.2, Jerusalem 88.4, Nablus 96.9 **W:** quran-radio.com
Najah FM: Nablus 91.4/104.4, Tulkarem 91.6, Ramallah 91.7, Jenin 102.8 **W:** najah.edu/en/about/nnu-offices/media-center/najah-fm
R. Bethlehem 2000: Bethlehem: Gaza 102.9, Bethlehem 106.3, Hebron 107.6, all 5kW **W:** rb2000.ps
Raya FM: Nablus 96.4, Jericho/Hebron/Gaza 96.8, Ramallah 98.3, Nablus 103.9 **W:** raya.fm

Monte-Carlo Doualiya: Ramallah 94.6, Nablus 97.3, Hebron 99.7
R. Japan: Ramallah 87.8, Nablus 107.8, Jericho 107.9
R. Sawa: Jenin 93.5, Ramallah 94.2, Nablus 94.5, Hebron 100.2

ITALY

L.T: UTC +1h (28 Mar-30 Oct: +2h) — **Pop:** 60.2 million — **Pr.L:** Italian — **E.C:** 230V/50Hz — **ITU:** I

AUTORITÀ PER LE GARANZIE NELLE COMUNICAZIONI (AGCOM)

(Italian Communications Authority)
✉ Centro Direzionale, Isola B5, 80143 Napoli (NA) ☎ +39 081 7507111 🖷 +39 081 7507616 **E:** info@agcom.it **W:** www.agcom.it
L.P: Pres. Giacomo Lasorella, Dir. Infrastrutture: Antonio Provenzano **E:** rpd@agcom.it

RAI-RADIOTELEVISIONE ITALIANA (Pub.)

✉ **Listeners:** Viale G. Mazzini 14, 00195 Roma (RM) ☎ +39 06 38781 🖷 +39 06 3227061 **E:** ufficiostampa@rai.it **W:** rai.it
✉ **RAI Teche:** Via G. Verdi 31, 10124 Torino (TO), ☎ +39 011 8104666 🖷 +39 011 8104549 **Dir.** Maria Pia Ammirati **W:** teche.rai.it **E:** teche@rai.it

RAI Way: Via Teulada 66, 00195 Roma (RM) ☎ +39 06 94809596 🖷 +39 06 36869771 **L.P:** Pres.: Giuseppe Pasciucco **W:** raiway.it **E:** raiway@rai.it **V:** QSL-card. No Rp. **W:** contactcenter.rai.it/app/scriverai
Sedi Regionali: W: sediregionali.rai.it **E:** sedi.regionali@rai.it **L.P:** Dir. Sedi Reg. ed Estere: Luigi Meloni, Dir. RAI Italia: Marco Giudici.
Regional Centres: **1)** Abruzzo: Viale Edmondo de Amicis 27, 65123 Pescara (PE) – **2)** Alto Adige: Piazza Mazzini 23, 39100 Bolzano/Bozen (BZ) – **3)** Basilicata: Via dell'Edilizia 2, 85100 Potenza (PZ) – **4)** Calabria: Viale Guglielmo Marconi 1, 87100 Cosenza (CS) – **5)** Campania: Via Guglielmo Marconi 9, 80125 Napoli (NA) – **6)** Emilia-Romagna: Viale della Fiera 13, 40127 Bologna (BO) – **7)** Friuli-Venezia-Giulia: Via Fabio Severo 7, 34133 Trieste (TS) – **8)** Lazio: Largo Willy de Luca 4, 00188 Roma (RM) – **9)** Liguria: Corso Europa 125, 16132 Genova (GE) – **10)** Lombardia: Corso Sempione 27, 20145 Milano (MI) – **11)** Marche: Scalo Vittorio Emanuele 1, 60121 Ancona (AN) – **12)** Molise: Viale Principe di Piemonte 59/65, 86100 Campobasso (CB) – **13)** Piemonte: Via Giuseppe Verdi 16, 10121 Torino (TO) Museo Radio TV RAI Torino **W:** www.museoradiotv.rai.it ☎ +39 011 8104360 – **14)** Puglia: Via Dalmazia 104, 70121 Bari (BA) – **15)** Sardegna: Via Barone Rossi 27, 09125 Cagliari (CA) – **16)** Sicilia: Viale Strasburgo 19, 90146 Palermo (PA) – **17)** Toscana: Via Ettore Bernabei 1, 50136 Firenze (FI) – **18)** Trentino: Via Fratelli Perini 141, 38122 Trento (TN) – **19)** Umbria: Via Luigi Masi 2, 06121 Perugia (PG) – **20** Valle d'Aosta: Loc.Grande Charriere 70, 11020 Saint Cristophe (AO) – **21)** Veneto: Palazzo Labia, Campo S. Geremia, Sestiere Cannaregio 275, 30121 Venezia (VE).

MW	Station	kHz	kW	Prg
17)	Pisa (Coltano)	657	100	R1
10)	Milano (Siziano)	900	100/50	R1
21)	Venezia(Campalto)	936	10/5	R1 (+a)
7)	Trieste(Monte R.)	981	20/10	S
13)	Torino (Volpiano)	999	50/10	R1
11)	Ancona(Montagnolo)	1062	10/6	R1
15)	Cagliari(Decimoputzu)	1062	60/10	Rp (d)
16)	Catania(Barriera del B.)	1062	20/2	R1 (c)
8)	Roma(Monte Ciocci)	1107	10	R1
16)	Palermo(Mte Pellegrino)	1116	10	R1 (c)
14)	Foggia	1431	5/2	R1
21)	Belluno (Cortina)	1449	2	R1 (+a)
9)	Genova(Portofino)	1575	50/30	R1

FM	TX	R1	R2	R3	R4/R5	GRP	kW
6)	Bertinoro 90.8	93.4	99.6	-	89.7		30
6)	Bologna	89.5	91.7	93.9	-	93.6	60
2)	Bolzano	91.5	93.7	97.1	99.6	95.1	14
6)	Ca'delVento	92.1	96.5	98.5	-	90.6	40
8)	Canepina-P. Nibbio	93.7	99.4	-	-	-	12
4)	Capo Spartivento	95.6	97.6	99.7	-	104.2	10
21)	Col Visentin	91.1	93.1	95.5	-	-	30
4)	Crotone	94.9	97.9	99.9	-	97.4	10
17)	Firenze	87.8	91.1	98.4	-	88.0	10
7)	Friscano	88.4	90.5	94.1	-	-	10
4)	Gambarie	95.3	97.3	99.3	-	-	40
	Sicilia Regional	103.9	-	-	-	-	40
9)	Genova	89.5	91.9	95.1	-	104.5	80
5)	Golfo Policastro	88.5	90.5	92.5	-	-	10
5)	Golfo Salerno	95.1	97.1	99.1	-	-	20
7)	Gorizia	89.5	92.3	94.6	98.3	106.8	10
14)	Martina Franca	89.1	91.1	93.1		90.3	100
10)	Milano	90.6	93.7	99.4	102.2	88.3	60
17)	Mte Argentario	90.1	92.1	94.3	-	99.6	70
	Lazio Regional	89.0	-	-	-	-	16
9)	Mte Beigua	91.5	94.6	98.9	-	100.5	40
14)	Mte Caccia	94.6	96.7	99.2	-	98.2	100
16)	Mte Cammarata	91.1	95.9	99.9	-	98.3	100
6)	Mte Canate	95.9	-	- -	-		24
8)	Mte Cavo	87.6	91.2	98.4	-	99.4	80
11)	Mte Conero88.3	90.3	92.3	-		105.2	100
5)	Mte Faito	94.1	96.1	98.1	-	91.0	100
16)	Mte Lauro	94.7	96.7	98.7	-	89.0	100
15)	Mte Limbara	88.9	95.3	99.3	-	-	60
17)	Mte Luco	88.1	92.5	96.2	-	103.2	30
11)	Mte Nerone	94.7	96.6	98.7	-	88.1	100
19)	Mte Miranda	95.7	97.7	99.7	-	102.1	60
	Lazio Regionale	88.3	-	-	-	-	30
10)	Mte Penice	94.2	97.4	99.9	-	88.2	120
	Piemonte Regionale	103.0	-	-	-	-	120
3)	Mte Pierfaone	88.1	90.1	92.1	-	91.2	45
19)	Mte Sambuco	88.6	90.7	93.5	-	-	100
	Campania Regionale	100.7	-	-	-	-	100
4)	Mte Scuro	88.5	90.5	92.5	-	98.4	30
15)	Mte Serpeddi	90.7	92.7	96.3	-	106.5	70
17)	Mte Serra	88.5	90.5	92.9	-	88.2	70
16)	Mte Soro	89.9	91.9	93.9	-	104.2	30
19)	Mte Subasio	89.3	91.4	93.5	-	104.6	30
21)	Mte Venda	88.1	89.0	89.9	-	-	160
5)	Mte Vergine	87.9	90.3	92.3	-	93.0	20
5)	Napoli Camaldoli	89.3	91.3	93.3	1103	101.1	2
3)	Nova Siri	-	-	89.5	-	-	10
16)	Palermo Mte Pell.	94.9	96.9	98.9	-	90.3	40
1)	Pescara S. Silves.	89.2		94.3	96.4	-102.0	70
3)	Pomarico	88.7	92.7	95.7	-	-	10
15)	Pta Badde Urbara	91.3	93.3	97.3	-	-	70
8)	Roma MteMario	89.7	91.7	93.7	100.3	-	100
4)	Roseto CpoSpulico	94.7	96.5	98.5	-	-	10
14)	SalentoTurrisi	90.7	95.5	97.5	-	91.0	60
17)	SanCerbone	95.3	97.3	99.3	-	-	12
21)	S. Zenodi Montagna	93.2	96.5	98.5	-	89.5	10
10)	SelvaPiana	88.4	90.3	92.4	-	-	20
13)	Torino Eremo	92.1	95.6	98.2	101.8	88.2	100
16)	TrapaniEricc	88.4	90.5	92.5	-	90.8	60
7)	Trieste Mte Belvedere	91.5	93.6	95.8	103.9	106.7	30
7)	Udine	94.9	97.2	99.8	-	-	60
8)	Velletri	88.7	90.7	92.7	-	-	15

+ over 8000 stns below 1kW
D.Prgr: All MW stns transmit from 0500 to 2300, except Pisa 657kHz, Milano 900kHz, Roma 1107kHz 24h
All FM stns transmit 24h **R1**=Radiouno, **R2FM**=Radiodue, **R3FM**=Radiotre, **S**=Special Prgrs.

Regional Prgrs: 0620-0628 Mon/Sat RAI1; 1110-1127 RAI1 Mon/Sat; 1730-1735 RAI1 Mon/Fri; 1115-1126 RAI1 Sun.
(a) Friuli: 0618-0657 Mon-Sat RAI1; 1003-1157 Mon-Sat RAI1; 1130-1157 Sun RAI 1; 1300-1415 Mon-Fri RAI1; 1330-1400 Sat RAI1; 1730-1756 Mon/Fri RAI1; 1715-1756 Sat RAI1; 0740-0910, 1108-1157, 1730-1756 Sun sport RAI1; (+a): "L'ora della Venezia Giulia" 1345-1445 Mon/Sat RAI1; 1330-1400 Sun RAI1 – (b) Sicilia: 1230-1245, Mon/Sat RAI1; Arabic sce only on FM stns – (c) Sicilia: 0630-0657,1110-1127,1315-1400,1730-1756 Mon/Sat; RAI1; 1140-1157,1730-1756 Sun sport RAI1 – (d) Sardegna: 0630-0657,1130-1145,1315-1400,1730-1756 Mon/Sat RAI1; 1730-1756 Sun sport RAI1 – (f) Valle D'Aosta: 1315-1400 Mo/Sat, 1730-1756 Sun sport RAI1 (Bilingual) – (e) Alto Adige 0630-0657, 1110-1127, 1130-1145, 1315-1400, 1730-1756 Mon/Sat; 1730-1756 Sun sport RAI1.
NB: All 1h earlier in summertime

SPECIAL PRGRS:
RAI Isoradio : 24h sce for motorway users on 103.3MHz FM (250 txs of 5kW or less);103.2MHz Milano,Como,Lecco area; 103.5MHz, Roma area **E:** isoradio@rai.it **W:** isoradio.rai.it **Dir.:** Danilo Scarrone.
RAI GR Parlamento: 24h sce Italian Parliament channel. FM (150 txs of 5kW or less) **W:** grparlamento.rai.it **Dir.;** Riccardo Berti. **RAI Südtirol**: **Prgr** in German on FM (46 txs of 1kW or less) **DPrgr**: 0500 (Sun 0600)-2300. N. 0615 (W), 0800 (Sun), 1000 (W), 1100, 1200, 1300, 1700 (W), 1930 **W:** raisudtirol.rai.it **E:** kontakt@rai.it **E PgrMgr:** dieter.scoz@rai.it

Regional Prgr. in Slovene: Trieste 981kHz 20/10 kW + 103.9MHz 20kW (and 22 additional FM-txs). **W:** sedezfjk.rai.it
D. Prgr: 0500 (Sun 0600)-1900. **N:** W 0500, 0700, 0900, 1200, 1300, 1600, 1800; Sun 0700, 1200, 1300, 1800. Dir. : Guido Corso. **N.** in German: 0900 (W). Night :**Relay** RAI 1 FM 1900-0500. **Ann:** Home Sce: "RAI Radiouno", "RAI Radiodue", "RAI Radiotre" as appropriate.

R.A.S.
✉ Europaallee 164/A, 39100 Bozen ☎ +39 0471 546666 🖷 +39 0471 200378 **E:** info@ras.bz.it **W:** ras.bz.it **L.P:** Pres: Rudi Gamper MD: Georg Plattner, Dir. Tec: Dr. Johann Silbernagl
NB: R.A.S. is a public body of the autonomous Region of Southern Tyrol whose purpose is to relay TV and radio from Germany, Austria and Switzerland to the German-speaking population.

FM TX(MHz)	**RAS 1**	**RAS 2**	**RAS 3**	**kW**
Kronplatz	100.7	103.0	104.7	2
Meransen	101.3	103.9	107.3	1
Obervinschgau	100.5	103.0	106.1	0.6
Penegal	103.3	100.3	104.7	2
Perdonig	101.8	104.0	106.0	1
Plose	99.8	102.0	105.6	1
Vinschgau	101.1	102.9	105.0	2

+ 880 low power stns
RAS 1: rel. OE-3 (Austria) - **RAS-2**: rel. OE-R (Austria) - **RAS-3**: rel. OE-1 (Austria)
DAB+: RAI & RAS on Blocks 12A-12DA, 223.936MHz - 229.072MHz Consorzio DAB Italia on block 9D. 208.064MHz **W:** dab.it **W Freq.List:** diretta.frequence-radio.com/dab.php

PRIVATE STATIONS
Only stns with MW broadcasts and FM networks are listed. A number of other stns are heard irr. There are approx. 600 FM stns

MW	**kHz**	**kW**	**Station, location and h of tr.**
1)	594	5	Challenger R., Villa Estense (PD) (0300-1600)
2)	693	2	R. Zai.net, Siziano (PV)
3)	711	0.5	Media R. Castellana, Castel San Pietro Terme (BO) (0300-1600)
4)	720	0.1	Baby Radio AM, Trieste (TS) irr. (0300-1600)
4)	819	2,5	R. Diffusione Europea, Trieste (TS)
5)	990	1	R. Z100 Milano, Zinasco Nuovo, (PV) irr.
6)	1017	1	Amica R. Veneta, Peraga di Vigonza (PD)
3)	1098	0.5	Media R. Castellana, Castel San Pietro Terme (BO)
5)	1350	1	R. Z100 Milano, Zinasco Nuovo, (PV) irr.
7)	1404	0.15	R. 106, Chiozza di Scandiano (RE) 0500-1700 irr.
5)	1440	1	R. Z100 Milano, Zinasco Nuovo, (PV) irr.
8)	1485	1.5	Regional R., Terni (TR)
9)	1485	1	R. Studio X, Livorno (LI)
10)	1566	0.5	R. Kolbe Sat, Schio (VI) irr. (ex legge 223/90)
4)	1584	1	R. Diffusione Europea, Trieste (TS)
8)	1584	2	Regional R., Guadamello / Narni (TR)
11)	1602	0.02	Dot R., Spello (PG) (morning rel. R. Spoleto Int.)
12)	1602	0.15	R. 3 Network, Poggibonsi (SI) irr.
13)	1602	0.2	R. a Colori, Bologna (BO)
14)	1602	1	R. Milano 1602 (MI)
15)	1602	0.2	R. Treviso, Treviso (TV) irr.

F.Pl.: Expected to be activated/reactivated soon:

MW	**kHz**	**kW**	**Station, location**
16)	603	1	Nuova Radio AM, Spoltore (PE)
17)	711	0.05	Radio King Italia, Cerveteri (RM)
18)	774	1	Viva la R. Network, Firenze (FI)

Addresses & other information:
1) Via Legnaro 6, 35040 Villa Estense (PD) 🖷 +39 0429 662280 **W:** challenger.it **E:** challenger@challenger.it **V.** by email letter Rp. **SM:** Maurizio Anselmo – **2)** Via Nota 7, 10122 Torino 🖷 +39 011 4143052 **W**: radiozai.net **F.PL.** 774 Milano/Napoli, 801 Genova, 1305 Pisa – **3) W:** www.mediaradiocastellana.it **E:** info@mediaradiocastellana.it **SM**: Andrea Lannutti – **4)** Via Franca 10, 34123 Trieste (TS) 🖷 +39 040 314772 / +39 345 9945637 **W**: radiodiffusioneeuropea.net **E:** redazione@radiodiffusioneeuropea.net **SM**: Maurizio Castelli **V.**by E-QSL qsl@radiodiffusioneeuropea.net **VS:** Roberto Scaglione **F.PL.** 1485/1584 Belluno, 1602 Palermo/Catania – **5) E:** z100milano@ondemedie.am **VS:** Alessandra Grumetti – **6)** Via Paradisi, 35010 Vigonza (PD) ☎ +39 049 7387987 **W:** amicaradioveneta.it **V.**by E-QSL **SM:** Roberto Saccardo – **7)** Via Brolo Sotto 52, 42019 Chiozza di Scandiano (RE) ☎+39 0522 856598 🖷+39 0522 5263255 **W:** radio106.it **E:** info@radioluna.com - **FM:** 104.4,105.9MHz 5kW **SM:** Battista Francia – **8)** Via Palombara 7, 05030 Otricoli (TR) ☎ +39 06 81153603 **W:** www.regionalradio.it **E:** info@regionalradio.it **SM:** Naldino Forti V.by E-QSL – **9)** Via Mammianese 687, Marliana (PT) **W:** www.radiostudiox. it **E**: qsl@radiostudiox.it **V.**by E-QSL **SM:** Pier Luca Betti **F.PL.** 1188 Sanremo, 1584 Arezzo – **10)** R. Kolbe Sat, Via Ischia 9, 36015 Schio (VI) ☎ +39 0445 505035 **W:** radiolkolbe.it **E**: segreteria@radiokolbe.net **SM:** Alberto De Pretto **V.**by E-QSL – **11)** Via G. di Vittorio 11, 06038 Spello (PG) ☎ +39 0742 436030 **W:** www.dotradio.eu **E:** info@dotradio.eu **SM:** Marco Cocco – **12)** Via S. Pertini 20, 53036 Poggibonsi (SI) ☎ +39 0577 980900 **W:** radio3.net **E:** posta@radio3.net **V.**by E-QSL SM: Mirco Roppolo – **13)** Via Saliceto 5 , 40128 Bologna (BO) ☎ +39 051 4151311 🖷 +39 051 4151300 **E:** urpnavile@comune.bologna.it **W:** www.icoloridelnavile.org – **14) W**: www.radiomilano1602.it **E:** qsl@radiomilano1602.it **V.** by E-QSL **F.PL.** 720 Sanremo, 1584 Alessandria, 1602 Biella, 1602 Brescia – **15)** ☎ +39 333 7066699 **E:** rtv1602@libero.it – **16) W**: nuovaradio1485.altervista.org **E:** nuovaradio.am@gmail.com **SM:** Franco Probi – **17) W:** www.rki711.it **E:** radiokingrrr@gmail.com **SM:** Fabrizio Di Giammarino – **18) W:** www.vivalaradio.fm SM: Emanuele Scatarzi **F.PI:** 702 Roma, 774 North Italy, 873 Napoli, 1296 Firenze **V.** by E-QSL.

FM NETWORKS IN MAJOR CITIES (MHz):

	Network	**TO**	**MI**	**VE**	**BO**	**GE**
1)	Circuito Margherita	91.8	-	-	-	90.1
2)	Kiss Kiss	92.4	97.6	89.7	92.5	104.9
3)	InBlu R.	92.4	95.3	94.6	-	88.8
4)	LatteMiele	88.5	92.6	106.2	91.2	-
5)	m2o	93.0	91.0	87.8	94.5	88.6
6)	Popolare Network		-	107.6	96.5	96.3-
7)	R. Capital	90.3	90.1	98.5	99.4	93.9
8)	R. 105	99.6	99.1	104.4	96.0	99.5
9)	R. 101	101.0	100.9	107.3	103.5	105.1
10)	R. Cuore	92.7	101.7	-	-	-
11)	R. Deejay	106.9	99.7	94.8	99.7	96.9
12)	R. RDS	96.4	107.3	103.4	97.9	95.7
13)	R. Italia Anni 60	103.7	106.3	99.5	102.1	91.3
14)	R. Italia	106.6	98.4	98.1	100.6	106.3
15)	R. Maria	107.7	107.9	106.5	90.8	106.6
16)	R. Mater	105.75	95.3	100.1	-	-
17)	R. Freccia	90.9	91.4	99.0	107.6	96.0
18)	R. Radicale	102.8	96.8	104.7	92.0	95.4
19)	R. RMC	105.5	105.3	100.4	101.3	104.2
20)	R. Sportiva	101.5	92.8	-	87.9	90.7
21)	R. 24	105.0	104.8	106.9	107.0	97.2
22)	RTL 102.5	102.5	102.5	102.5	101.6	102.4
23)	Virgin R.	90.9	104.5	93.1	106.5	105.5
	Network	**FI**	**RM**	**NA**	**BA**	**PA**
1)	Circuito Margherita	96.7	-	100.7	95.2	95.2
2)	Kiss Kiss	92.8	97.2	88.8	94.1	-
3)	InBlu R.	88.8	96.3	99.45	88.3	88.0
4)	LatteMiele	-	-	-	97.5	94.6
5)	m2o	105.8	97.0	98.3	88.5	107.8
6)	Popolare Network	93.6	-	-	-	-
7)	R. Capital	97.4	95.5	104.6	87.5	92.9
8)	R. 105	105.0	107.4	99.7	87.9	105.1
9)	R. 101	104.5	100.0	93.0	107.3	97.2
10)	R. Cuore 90.4	-	-	-	89.1	
11)	R. Deejay	100.6	101.0	92.3	93.2	107.5
12)	R. RDS	92.3	103.0	107.5	95.65	106.6
13)	R. Italia Anni 60	-	93.0	104.1	107.0	-
14)	R. Italia	107.6	105.6	96.8	103.5	104.8
15)	R. Maria	88.8	95.1	105.6	102.0	89.4
16)	R. Mater	93.9	93.5	-	95.45	-
17)	R. Freccia	91.4	102.1	95.2	105.2	97.8
18)	R. Radicale	97.0	88.6	101.6	89.3	92.0
19)	R. RMC	106.6	106.3	91.6	92.0	90.0
20)	R. Sportiva	94.2	-	90.8	100.2	100.5
21)	R. 24	103.8	107.9	103.5	88.2	104.5
22)	RTL 102.5	100.9	92.4	102.6	102.7	102.3
23)	Virgin R.	107.2	98.7	93.7	106.6	93.2

TO=Torino MI=Milano VE=Venezia BO=Bologna GE=Genova FI=Firenze RM=Roma NA=Napoli BA=Bari PA=Palermo

Addresses & other information:
1) Via Marchese di Villabianca 82, 90143 Palermo (PA) ☎+39 800 303464 🖷+39 091 8724835 **W:** radiomargherita.com **E:** info@radiomargherita.com SM: Giuseppe Orobello **V.** by letter. Rp. – **2)** Via Sgambati 61, 80131 Napoli (NA) ☎+39 081 5461212 🖷+39 081

5467789 **W:** kisskiss.it **E:** info@kisskiss.it PRES: Lucia Niespolo TM: Ugo Lombardi **V.** by letter. Rp. – **3)** Via Aurelia 796, 00165 Roma (RM) ☎+39 06 6650851 🖷+39 06 66508516 **W:** radioinblu.it **E:** info@radioinblu.it SM: Vincenzo Morgante. **V.** by eQSL. Rp – **4)** Via Andrea Costa 10, 40013 Castel Maggiore (BO) ☎+39 051 70928 🖷+39 051 6325710 **W:** lattemiele.com **E:** info@lattemiele.com SM: Franco Mignani – **5)** Via Andrea Massena 2, 20154 Milano (MI) ☎+39 02 342522 🖷+39 02 342888 **W:** m2o.it **E:** contatti@m2o.it PM: Albertino **V.** by QSL-card. Rp. – **6)** Via Ulderico Ollearo 5, 20155 Milano (MI) ☎+39 02 392411 🖷+39 02 39273125 **W:** radiopopolare.it **E:** Radiopop@radiopopolare.it SM: Michele Migone **V.** by eQSL-letter. – **7)** Via Cristoforo Colombo 90, 00147 Roma (RM) ☎+39 06 494321 🖷+39 06 44702290 **W:** capital.it **E:** infoline@capital.it SM: Massimo Giannini. **V.** by eQSL-card. – **8)** Largo Guido Donegani 1, 20121 Milano (MI) ☎+39 02 6596116 🖷 39 02 6592272 **W:** 105.net **E:** diretta@105.net SM: Barbara Rossetti **V.** by eQSL-Card. – **9)** Largo Guido Donegani 1, 20121 Milano (MI) ☎+39 02 6596116 🖷 39 02 6592272 **W:** r101.it **E:** infor101@r101.it SM: Daniele Tognacca **V.** by eQSL-card – **10)** Via Giovanni da Verrazzano 16, Localita Le Melorie, 56038 Ponsacco (PI) ☎ +39 0587 2861 🖷+39 0587 286284 **W:** mediahit.it **E:** info@mediahit.it SM: Loriano Bessi **V.** by letter. Rp – **11)** Via Andrea Massena 2, 20154 Milano (MI) ☎+39 02 342522 🖷+39 02 342888 **W:** deejay.it **E:** segnalazioni@deejay.it SM: Linus **V.** by eQSL-card – **12)** Via Pier Ruggero Piccio 55, 00136 Roma (RM) ☎+39 06 37704242 🖷+39 06 37704250 **W:** rds.it **E:** ufficiotecnico@rds.it SM: Stefano Montefusco **V.** by email letter **W**: rds.it/frequenze/ – **13)** Via Zambra 11, 38121 Trento (TN) ☎ +39 0461 828990 🖷+39 0461 428960 **W:** radioitaliaanni60.it **E:** info@radioitaliaanni60.it SM: Franco Nisi **V.** by letter. Rp. – **14)** Viale Europa 49, 20093 Cologno Monzese (MI) ☎+39 02 25441 🖷+39 02 25444220 **W:** radioitalia.it **E:** info@radioitalia.it SM: Mario Volanti **V.** by letter. Rp. – **15)** Via Milano 12 , 22036 Erba (CO) ☎+39 031 610600 🖷+39 031 611288 **W:** radiomaria.it **E:** info.ita@radiomaria.org SM: Don Livio Fanzaga **V.** by QSL-card. Rp. Rpt requested to **E:** QSL@radiomaria.org QSL Mgr. Giampiero Bernardini, St Eng, Claudio Re – **16)** Via XXV Aprile 1, 22031 Albavilla (CO) ☎+39 031 645214 🖷+39 031 6490527 **W:** radiomater.com **E:** info@radiomater.com SM: Don Mario Galbiati **V.** by letter. Rp. – **17)** Viale Piemonte 61/63, 20093 Cologno Monzese (MI) ☎+39 366 663446 🖷+39 02 25096489 **W:** radiofreccia.it **V.** by email letter SM: Pier Luigi Tornari – **18)** Centro di Produzione, Via Principe Amedeo 2, 00185 Roma (RM) ☎+39 06 488781 🖷+39 06 4880196 **W:** radioradicale.it **E:** ioascolto@radioradicale.it SM: Alessio Falconio **V.** by letter. Rp. – **19)** Via Principe Amedeo 2, 20121 Milano (MI) ☎+39 02 29001636 🖷 +39 02 6551451 **W:** radiomontecarlo.net **E:** rmc@radiomontecarlo.net SM: Stefano Bragatto **V.**by email QSL-card – **20)** Via Giovanni da Verrazzano 16, Localita Le Melorie,56038 Ponsacco (PI) ☎+39 334 7330020 🖷+39 0587 733861 **W:** radiosportiva.com **E:** redazione@radiosportiva.it SM: Loriano Bessi **V.** by letter. Rp – **21)** Via Monte Rosa 91, 20149 Milano (MI) ☎+39 800 240024 🖷+039 02 30224462 **W:** www.radio24.ilsole24ore.com **E:** info@radio24.ilsole24ore.com SM: Fabio Tamburini V. TM: Dario Arbulla **E:** darioarbulla@radio24.ilsole24ore.com by email letter – **22)** Viale Piemonte 61/63, 20093 Cologno Monzese (MI) ☎+39 02 251515 🖷+39 02 25096201 **W:** rtl.it **E:** qualita@rtl.it **V.** QSL Man.: Armando Finocchi (Chief Eng.) SM:Pier Luigi Tornari **V.** by eQSL-card – **23)** Largo Guido Donegani 1, 20121 Milano (MI) ☎+39 02 6575661 🖷 +39 02 62537460 **W:** virginradio.it **E:** guastivirgin@virginradio.it SM: Francesco Migliozzi. **V.** by eQSL-card

EXTERNAL SERVICES:
NEXUS - INTERNATIONAL BROADCASTING ASSOCIATION
See International Broadcasting section
BCLNEWS – STUDIO DX

AMERICAN FORCES NETWORK EUROPE (U.S. Mil.)
W: afneurope.net/AFN-360/ **E:** harringtonj@afns.vicenza.army.mil
FM (MHz): **1)** 107.0 Castaldia, Aviano. c/o Base NATO, Via Pordenone 52, Aviano (PN) ☎ +39 0434 308236 **W:** aviano.afneurope.net **E:** dma.aviano.afn.mbx.afn-aviano@mail.mil **V.** by email or letter - **2)** 106.0 - 107.0 10kW Camaldoli, Napoli (NA). PSC 817, Box 31,FPO AE 09622, USA ☎ +62 969 05629 **W:** naples.afneurope.net **E:** dma.afnnaples@mail.mil **V.** by email or letter – **3)** 105.9 2kW Sigonella, Motta Sant'Anastasia (CT). Strada Provinciale 69II snc, Località Sigonella, 96016 Lentini (SR) ☎ +39 095 563971 **W:** sigonella.afneurope.net **E:** brett.p.cote.mil@mail.mil **V.** by email or letter – **4)** 106.0 Verona / 106.0 – 107.0 Monte Caina, Bassano del Grappa (VI). c/o Caserma Ederle, Via della Pace 100, 36100 Vicenza (VI) ☎ +39 0444 715243 **W:** vicenza.afneurope.net **E:** dma.usag-italy.afn.mbx.afn-vicenza@mail.mil - **V.** by email or letter

IVORY COAST

See CÔTE D'IVOIRE

JAMAICA

L.T: UTC -5h — **Pop:** 2.96 million — **Pr.L:** English — **E.C:** 110V/60Hz — **ITU:** JMC

BROADCASTING COMMISSION OF JAMAICA
✉ 5th Floor, Victoria Mutual Building, 53 Knutsford Boulevard, Kingston 5 ☎ 1 876 9209537 🖷 +1 876 9291997 **E:** info@broadcom.org **W:** www.broadcastingcommission.org **L.P:** Chmn: Anthony Clayton

RJR GLEANER COMMUNICATIONS GROUP
RADIO JAMAICA LTD (Comm.)
✉ 32 Lyndhurst Rd, Kingston 5 ☎ +1 876 926 1100 🖷 +1 876 929 7467 **W:** rjrgleanergroup.com **L.P:** Chmn. Joseph M. Matalon. MD: Gary Allen. GM (Radio & TV): Claire Grant
FM(MHz): **Radio Jamaica 94 (RJR94):** 94.1/94.3/94.5/94.7/94.9 – **Fame95**: 95.1/95.3/95.5/95.7/95.9 – **Hitz92**: 92.1/92.3/92.5/92.7/92.9 – **Music99**: 99.1/99.3/99.5/99.7/99.9 – **Power106FM**: 106.1/106.3/106.5/106.7/106.9. **Note:** Music99 and Power106FM are still being run from 7 North Str, Kingston.

CORNWALL BROADCASTING COMPANY LTD
✉ 63 Barnett Str, Montego Bay ☎ +1 876 971 4163/9124 **W:** mellofmjamaica.com **L.P:** CEO Al Robinson
FM(MHz): **Mello FM**: 88.1/88.3/88.5/88.7 – **Riddim 96 FM**: 96.5/96.7/96.9 – **Energy FM**: 102.1/102.3/102.5/102.7/102.9
Note: The company also operates from 3 Cargill Av, Kingston 10

S&B COMMUNICATIONS LTD
✉ 40-41 Beechwood Ave, Kingston 5 ☎ +1 876 754 4182 **W:** edge105.com & fyah105.com **L.P:** GM: Ronald Sutherland
FM(MHz): **The Edge**: 105.1 (mid-island) & 105.3 (Kingson & Western Jamaica) - **Fyah FM**: 105.7 (Kingston & Western Jamaica) & 105.9 (mid-island)
NB: The company is an affiliate of The Jamaican Observer

OTHER STATIONS (FM in MHz):
BBC FM: 104.1/104.3/104.5/104.7/104.9. 24h relay of the BBC World Service – **Bes' FM**, 4 East Bloomsbury Rd, Kingston 10 ☎ +1 876 678 2326 **W:** bessfm.com L.P: Antonio Shaw. FM: 100.1/100.3/100.5/100.7/100.9 – **Earth FM**, 6 Queen Str, Morant Bay PO, St Thomas ☎ +1 876 734 5385. L.P.: CEO Michael McDowell FM: 96.9 – **Gospel JA**, Unit 5, Tri 7 Business Green Crescent, Kingston 10 ☎ +1 876 906 3423 **W:** gospelja.com FM: 91.7/91.9 – **Irie FM,** P.O Box 282, Coconut Grove, Ocho Rios ☎ +1 876 974 5051 **E:** info@iriefm.net **W:** iriefm.net L.P: MD Debbian Dewar. FM: 107.1/107.3/107.5/107.7/107.9. Format: Reggae – **Klas FM,** 17 Haining Rd, Kingston 5 ☎ +1 876 929 1344 **W:** klassportsradio.com FM: 89.1/89.3/89.5/89.9. Format: Sport – **Kool 97 FM,** 1 Braemar Ave, Kingston 10 ☎ +1 876 978 9161 **W:** kool97fm.com L.P: GM Howard Armstrong. FM: 97.1/97.3/97.5/97.7/97.9 – **Love FM,** 81 Hagley Pk Rd, Kingston 11 ☎ +1 876 968 9596 **W:** love101.org FM: 101.1/101.3/101.5/101.7/101.9. Format: Rlg. – **Mega Jamz**, 40A Mannings Hill Rd, Kingston 8 ☎ +1 876 579 6342 **W:** megajamz98fm.com L.P.: MD Katherine Chong. FM: 98.1/98.3/98.5/98.7/98.9. Format: Oldies – **Nationwide 90FM,** Natiowide News Network, Bradley Ave, Kingston ☎ +1 876 630 1210 **W:** nationwideradiojm.com L.P: Cliff Hughes. FM: 90.3/90.5/90.7 – **NCU FM,** Northern Caribbean University, East Campus, Manchester Rd, Mandeville ☎ +1 876 963 7716 **W:** ncumediagroup.com FM: 91.1/91.3/91.5. Format: Rlg. (Adventist) – **Newstalk 93FM,** Universal Media Company, 18 Ring Rd, Mona, Kingston 7 ☎ +1 876 927 1660 **W:** newstalk93fm.com FM: 93.1/93.3/93.5/93.7/93.9 – **Roots FM,** 1 Mahoe Drive, Kingston 11 ☎ +1 876 923 6488 FM: Kingston 96.1 – **Stylz FM,** 4 Boundbrooke Ave, Port Antonio P.O., Portland ☎ +1 876 518 2399 **W:** stylzfm.com L.P: Huel Jackson. FM: 96.3/96.7 – **SunCity Radio**, Shop #30-32, Portmore Pines Plaza, Portmore, St. Catherine ☎ +1 876 572 6416 **W:** suncityradio.fm L.P: CEO Doreen Billings FM: 104.9 – **TBC FM (The Breath of Change)**, 51 Molynes Rd, Kingston 10 ☎ +1 876 754 5120 **W:** tbcradio.org FM: Kingston 88.5. Format: Rlg (Baptist) – **Zip 103,** 1B Courtney Walsh Drive, Kingston 10 ☎ +1 876 618

0351 🖷 +1 876 960 0523 **W:** zipfm.net L.P: MD Debbian Dewar FM: 103.1/103.3/103.5/103.7/103.9. Format: Techno/dance/alternative. + 10 low-power stns

JAPAN

L.T: UTC +9h — **Pop:** 126 million — **Pr.L:** Japanese — **EC:** 100V/50Hz (Ea. Japan), 100V/60Hz (We. Japan) — **ITU:** J

INFORMATION AND COMMUNICATIONS BUREAU, MINISTRY OF INTERNAL AFFAIRS AND COMMUNICATIONS (SOUMU SHO)

✉ 1-2, Kasumigaseki 2-chome, Chiyoda-ku, Tokyo 100-8926 ☎ +81 3 5253 5111 **W:** soumu.go.jp **L.P:** Minister: R.Takeda

NIPPON HOSO KYOKAI (NHK) (Pub)
(The Japan Broadcasting Corporation)

✉ 2-1, Jinnan 2-chome, Shibuya-ku, Tokyo 150-8001 ☎ +81 3 3465 1111 **W:** nhk.or.jp

L.P: Chmn. (Board of Governors): S.Morishita. Pres:T.Maeda. Exec. Vice-Pres: S.Masagaki. Exec. Dirs: C.Matsuzaka, Y.Itano. Exec. Dir & Chief of Eng: A.Chigono. Sen. Dirs: H.Nakata, H.Kado, H.Wakaizumi, K.Matsuzaki, H.Koike, H.Tanaka, R.Hayashi

Pub: NHK Nenkan (Japanese), NHK Update (English)

MW Loc. & Prgr	Call	kHz	kW	MW Loc. & Prgr	Call	kHz	kW
E2) Nago 1		531	1	E7) Fukue 1		945	1
F2) Morioka 1	QG	531	10	G7) Muroran 1	IQ	945	3
A2) Matsumoto 1		540	1	H2) Tokushima 1	XK	945	5
C2) Nanao 1		540	1	D3) Hagi 1		963	1
E2) Ishigaki 1		540	1	D4) Yonago 1		963	1
E3) Miyazaki 1	MG	540	5	E9) Saga 1	SP	963	1
E4) Kitakyushu 1	SK	540	1	F6) Aomori 1	TG	963	5
F3) Yamagata 1	JG	540	5	H1) Matsuyama 1	ZK	963	5
E2) Okinawa 1	AP	549	10	A2) Kisofukushima 1		981	1
G1) Sapporo 1	IK	567	100	E7) Sasebo 1		981	1
C3) Hamamatsu 1	DG	576	1	H3) Kochi 1	RK	990	10
E5) Kagoshima 1	HG	576	10	D1) Fukuyama 1		999	1
G2) Kushiro 1	PG	585	10	F6) Hachinohe 1		999	1
A1) Tokyo 1	AK	594	300	H3) Nakamura 1		999	1
D2) Okayama 1	KK	603	5	E1) Fukuoka 2	LB	1017	50
G3) Obihiro 1	OG	603	5	C4) Toyama 2	IC	1035	1
E1) Fukuoka 1	LK	612	100	F3) Tsuruoka 2		1035	1
A2) Iida 1		621	1	H4) Takamatsu 2	HD	1035	1
E3) Nobeoka 1		621	1	D1) Hiroshima 1	FK	1071	20
G4) Asahikawa 1	CG	621	3	F1) Sendai 2	HB	1089	10
C3) Shizuoka 2	PB	639	10	C5) Takayama 2		1125	1
E6) Oita 1	IP	639	5	D3) Hagi 2		1125	1
C4) Toyama 1	IG	648	5	D4) Tottori 2	LC	1125	1
B1) Osaka 1	BK	666	100	E2) Okinawa 2	AD	1125	10
D3) Yamaguchi 1	UG	675	5	G3) Obihiro 2	OC	1125	1
G5) Hakodate 1	VK	675	5	G4) Nayoro 2		1125	1
E7) Nagasaki 1	AG	684	5	G7) Muroran 2	IZ	1125	1
A1) Tokyo 2	AB	693	500	G2) Kushiro 2	PC	1152	10
D1) Hiroshima 2	FB	702	10	H3) Kochi 2	RB	1152	10
G6) Kitami 2	KD	702	10	G6) Kitami 1	KP	1188	10
C1) Nagoya 1	CK	729	50	C2) Kanazawa 1	JK	1224	10
G1) Sapporo 2	IB	747	500	D5) Matsue 1	TK	1296	10
E8) Kumamoto 1	GK	756	10	F2) Yamada 1		1323	1
F4) Akita 2	UB	774	500	F5) Fukushima 1	FP	1323	1
A3) Takada 1		792	1	E8) Minamata 1		1341	1
C5) Takayama 1		792	1	F5) Iwaki 1		1341	1
E5) Naze 1		792	1	D4) Tottori 1	LG	1368	1
G4) Enbetsu 1		792	1	F3) Tsuruoka 1		1368	1
A2) Nagano 1	NK	819	5	H4) Takamatsu 1	HP	1368	5
B1) Osaka 2	BB	828	300	D3) Yamaguchi 2	UC	1377	5
A3) Niigata 1	QK	837	10	E7) Nagasaki 2	AC	1377	1
G4) Nayoro 1		837	1	F6) Hachinohe 2		1377	1
E8) Hitoyoshi 1		846	1	C2) Kanazawa 2	JB	1386	10
F5) Koriyama 1		846	5	D2) Okayama 2	KB	1386	5
H1) Uwajima 1		846	1	E5) Kagoshima 2	HC	1386	10
E8) Kumamoto 2	GB	873	500	F2) Morioka 2	QC	1386	10
C3) Shizuoka 1	PK	882	10	A2) Nagano 2	NB	1467	1
F1) Sendai 1	HK	891	20	E3) Miyazaki 2	MC	1467	1
C1) Nagoya 2	CB	909	10	E6) Oita 2	ID	1467	1
A4) Kofu 1	KG	927	5	G4) Wakkanai 2		1467	1
C6) Fukui 1	FG	927	5	G5) Hakodate 2	VB	1467	1
D2) Tsuyama 1		927	1	A2) Iida 2		1476	1
G4) Wakkanai 1		927	1	E8) Aso 1		1503	1
B3) Hikone 1	QP*	945	1	F4) Akita 1	UK	1503	10
A2) Matsumoto 2		1512	1	D5) Matsue 2	TB	1593	10
F5) Koriyama 2		1512	1	A4) Kofu 2	KC	1602	1
H1) Matsuyama 2	ZB	1512	5	D1) Fukuyama 2		1602	1
C3) Hamamatsu 2	DC	1521	1	E3) Nobeoka 2		1602	1
C6) Fukui 2	FC	1521	1	E4) Kitakyushu 2	SB	1602	1
D4) Yonago 2		1521	1	E5) Naze 2		1602	1
E2) Ishigaki 2		1521	1	E8) Hitoyoshi 2		1602	1
F3) Yamagata 2	JC	1521	1	F5) Fukushima 2	FD	1602	1
F6) Aomori 2	TC	1521	1	G4) Asahikawa 2	CC	1602	1
H3) Nakamura 2		1521	1	G4) Enbetsu 2		1602	1
A3) Niigata 2	QB	1593	10	H1) Uwajima 2		1602	1

+ approx 240 stns below 1kW. There are multiple stns on 1026, 1161 and 1584kHz broadc. R. One, and on 1359 & 1539kHz, broadc. R. Two. **1:** NHK R. One, **2:** NHK R. Two. **Call: JO(call)**. *stn announces its callsign as "JOBK"

FM Location	Call	MHz	kW	FM Location	Call	MHz	kW
A5) Utsunomiya	BP	80.3	1	F5) Fukushima	FP	85.3	1
A6) Chiba	MP	80.7	5	D3) Yamaguchi	UG	85.3	0.5
C4) Toyama	IG	81.5	1	E8) Kumamoto	GK	85.4	1
A7) Maebashi	TP	81.6	1	A4) Kofu	KG	85.6	1
E9) Saga	SP	81.6	0.5	E5) Kagoshima	HG	85.6	1
C7) Tsu	NP	81.8	3	E4) Kitakyushu	SK	85.7	0.25
A8) Yokohama	GP	81.9	5	G4) Asahikawa	CG	85.8	0.5
F3) Yamagata	JG	82.1	1	D5) Hamada		85.8	1
C2) Kanazawa	JK	82.2	1	G6) Kitami	KP	86.0	0.25
A3) Niigata	QK	82.3	1	F6) Aomori	TG	86.0	3
A1) Tokyo	AK	82.5	10	H4) Takamatsu	HP	86.0	1
C1) Nagoya	CK	82.5	10	E3) Miyazaki	MG	86.2	0.5
F1) Sendai	HK	82.5	5	B4) Kobe	PP	86.5	0.5
B2) Kyoto	OK	82.8	1	F4) Akita	UK	86.7	3
F2) Morioka	QG	83.1	1	G5) Hakodate	VK	87.0	0.25
A9) Mito	EP	83.2	1	B6) Nara	UP	87.4	0.5
C6) Fukui	FG	83.4	1	G3) Obihiro	OG	87.5	0.25
H2) Tokushima	XK	83.4	1	H3) Kochi	RK	87.5	0.5
A3) Yamato		83.5	1	H1) Matsuyama	ZK	87.7	1
C5) Gifu	OP	83.6	1	G7) Muroran	IQ	88.0	0.25
A2) Nagano	NK	84.0	0.5	B1) Osaka	BK	88.1	10
B3) Otsu	QP	84.0	1	E2) Okinawa	AP	88.1	1
B4) Himeji		84.2	1	G4) Nayoro		88.2	1
E5) Tanegashima		84.4	1	D1) Hiroshima	FK	88.3	1
D5) Matsue	TK	84.5	0.5	G2) Kushiro	PG	88.5	0.25
E7) Nagasaki	AG	84.5	0.5	D2) Okayama	KK	88.7	1
B5) Wakayama	RP	84.7	0.5	C3) Shizuoka	PK	88.8	1
E1) Fukuoka	LK	84.8	3	E6) Oita	IP	88.9	1
E2) Miyakojima		85.0	1	G4) Chikoma		89.1	1
A10) Saitama	LP	85.1	5	G2) Nakashibetsu		89.9	1
G1) Sapporo	IK	85.2	5				

+ approx 481 relay stns below 1kW. **Call: JO (call)-FM**

Addresses of regional HQs and stns:

A) Kanto-Koshinetsu area = Tokyo **A1**): same as NHK general HQ address – **A2**) Nagano: 210-2, Inaba, Nagano 380-8502 – **A3**) Niigata: 1-49, Kawagishi-cho, Chuo-ku, Niigata 951-8508 – **A4**) Kofu: 1-1-20, Marunouchi, Kofu 400-8552 – **A5**) Utsunomiya: 3-1-2, Chuo, Utsunomiya 320-8502 – **A6**) Chiba: 5-1, Chibaminato, Chuo-ku, Chiba 260-8610 – **A7**) Maebashi: 189, Motosojyamachi, Maebashi 371-8555 – **A8**) Yokohama: 281, Yamashita-cho, Naka-ku, Yokohama 231-8324 – **A9**) Mito: 3-4-4, Omachi, Mito 310-8567 – **A10**) Saitama: 6-1-21, Tokiwa, Urawa-ku, Saitama 330-9310 – **B)** Kinki area = Osaka – **B1**): 1-20, Otemae 4-chome, Chuo-ku, Osaka 540-8501 – **B2**) Kyoto: 576,Toraya-cho, Nakakyo-ku, Kyoto 604-8515 – **B3**) Otsu: 3-30, Uchidehama, Otsu 520-0806 – **B4**) Kobe: 24-7, Nakayamate-dori 2-chome, Chuo-ku, Kobe 650-8515 – **B5**) Wakayama: 2-3-47, Fukiage, Wakayama 640-8556 – **B6**) Nara: 1-20, Sanjyo-oji 1-chome, Nara 630-8540 – **C)** Tokai-Hokuriku area = Nagoya **C1**): 13-3, Higashisakura 1-chome, Higashi-ku, Nagoya 461-8725 – **C2**) Kanazawa: 2-10, Hirooka 3-chome, Kanazawa 920-8644 – **C3**) Shizuoka: 6-1, Yahata 1-chome, Suruga-ku, Shizuoka 422-8787 – **C4**) Toyama: 3-1, Shinsogawa, Toyama 930-8502 – **C5**) Gifu: 2-3, Kyomachi, Gifu 500-8554 – **C6**) Fukui: 3-3-5, Hoei, Fukui 910-8680 – **C7**) Tsu: 4-8, Marunouchi Yousei-cho, Tsu 514-8531. **D)** Chugoku area = Hiroshima **D1**): 11-10, Otemachi 2-chome, Naka-ku, Hiroshima 730-8672 – **D2**) Okayama: 15-1, Ekimotomachi, Kita-ku, Okayama 700-8621 – **D3**) Yamaguchi: 2-1, Nakazono-cho, Yamaguchi 753-8660 – **D4**) Tottori: 100, Teramachi, Tottori 680-8701 – **D5**) Matsue: 1-21, Nadamachi, Matsue 690-8601. **E)** Kyushu area = Fukuoka – **E1**): 1-10, Ropponmatsu 1-chome, Chuo-ku, Fukuoka

810-8577 – **E2**) Okinawa: 2-6-21, Omoromachi, Naha 900-8535 – **E3**) Miyazaki: 2-2-15, Ehiranishi, Miyazaki 880-8633 – **E4**) Kitakyushu: 1-1-20, Muromachi 1-chome, Kokurakita-ku, Kitakyushu 803-8555 – **E5**) Kagoshima: 4-6, Honko Shinmachi, Kagoshima 892-8603 – **E6**) Oita: 2-36, Takasagomachi, Oita 870-8660 – **E7**) Nagasaki: 1-1, Nshizakamachi, Nagasaki 850-8603 – **E8**) Kumamoto: 5-1, Hanabatacho, Chuo-ku, Kumamoto 860-8602 – **E9**) Saga: 2-15-8, Jyonai, Saga 840-8601. **F**) Tohoku area = Sendai – **F1**): 20-1, Honmachi 2-chome, Aoba-ku, Sendai 980-8435 – **F2**) Morioka: 1-3, Ueda 4-chome, Morioka 020-8555 – **F3**) Yamagata: 2-50, Sakura+-cho, Yamagata 990-8575 – **F4**) Akita: 4-2, Higashidori Nakamachi, Akita 010-8501 – **F5**) Fukushima: 1-2, Wase-cho, Fukushima 960-8588 – **F6**) Aomori: 2-1-1, Matsubara, Aomori 030-8633. **G**) Hokkaido area = Sapporo – **G1**): 1, Odori Nishi 1-chome, Chuo-ku, Sapporo 060-8703 – **G2**) Kushiro: 3-8, Nusamai-cho, Kushiro 085-8660 – **G3**) Obihiro: 2-2, Nishi 5-jyo Minami 7-chome, Obihiro 080-0015 – **G4**) Asahikawa: 27, 6-jyo Dori 6-chome, Asahikawa 070-8680 – **G5**) Hakodate: 13-1, Chitose-cho, Hakodate 040-8680 – **G6**) Kitami: 3-24, Hokutocho 2-chome, Kitami 090-0035 – **G7**) Muroran: 3-50, Yamatecho 1-chome, Muroran 051-0012. **H**) Shikoku area = Matsuyama – **H1**): 5, Horinouchi, Matsuyama 790-8501 – **H2**) Tokushima: 1-28, Terashimahoncho Higashi, Tokushima 770-8544 – **H3**) Kochi: 3-12, Honmachi 3-chome, Kochi, 780-8512 – **H4**) Takamatsu: 1-12-7, Nishikimachi, Takamatsu, 760-8686.

NHK R. One (General prgr): 24h **N:** every h (exc Sun 0000, Mon-Fri 1300). **Regional and local prgrs** (the amount of local prgrs varies between stns) 2055wrp, 2125N/wrp/inf, 2155wrp/inf, 2220(Fri&Sat 2215)N/wrp, 2250(Sat 2255)N/wrp/inf, 0055(exc Sun)N/wrp/inf, 0250wrp/inf, 0315(SS 0310)N/wrp, 0455N/wrp/inf, 0555(exc Sat)N/wrp/inf, 0755(exc Sat)N/wrp/inf, 0805(Mon-Fri)N, 0855N/wrp/inf, 0950N/wrp/inf, 1015(SS)N, 1055N/wrp/inf, 1255N/wrp/inf, 1355N/wrp. **IS:** Original music played by Celesta. **Ann:** "JO (call), NHK (location) Daiichi Hoso desu". Local ID's with call letters, network & location given by studio stns just before: 2000, 0300, 1000
NHK R. Two (Educational prgr): 2100-1540. No regular regional and local prgrs. **Foreign language N** (rel. NHK World - R. Japan): **Chinese:** 0400. **Korean:** 0415 (SS 0440). Vietnamese: Mon-Fri 1330. Indonesian: Mon-Fri 1340. Thai: Mon-Fri 1350. **English:** 0430(SS 0500). **Portuguese:** 0900(SS 1440). **Spanish:** 0500(SS 0450). **Russian:** Mon-Fri 0510. Weather map: 0700. **IS:** Original music played by Celesta. Nat. Anthem at s/on on national holidays & s/off. **Ann:** "JO (call), NHK (location) Daini Hoso desu". Local IDs on certain stns (as 1st Netw) just before 2100, 0415 (Mon-Fri), 0410 (SS), 0720 and s/off.
NHK FM Netw: 24h. 1600-2000 relays R. One, **N:** 2200, 0300, 0950(local), 1000. **Ann:** "JO (call)-FM, NHK (location) FM Hoso desu". Local IDs just before 2000, 0300, 1000
V: NHK officially has no organised QSL sce. However, many local stns verify by QSL card or letter for DX reports.

EXTERNAL SERVICES:
RADIO JAPAN, NHK WORLD NETWORK
See International Broadcasting section

THE JAPAN COMMERCIAL BROADCASTERS ASSOCIATION (NIPPON MINKAN HOSO RENMEI)
✉ 3-23, Kioi-cho, Chiyoda-ku, Tokyo 102-8577 ☎ +81 3 5213 7711 🖷 +81 3 5213 7703 **W:** j-ba.or.jp
L.P: Pres: Y.Okubo. Vice-Presidents: T.Sasaki, H.Kamiguchi, Y.Kosugi, K.Kameyama, R.Endo, S.Komago, K.Maruyama, S.Yamamoto, S.Hamu, R.Inoue. Exec. Dir: S.Nagahara. **Pub:** Nippon Minkan Hoso Nenkan, Gekkan Minpo, Minkan Hoso (all Japanese) and NAB Handbook (English) etc.

MW	Call	kHz	kW	ID	Station, location & h of tr
1)	CR	558	20	CRK	R. Kansai, Kobe
2)	WN	639	5	STV	STV R., Hakodate
3)	DF	684	5	IBC	Iwate Hoso, Morioka
3)	LO	684	1	IBC	Iwate Hoso, Ofunato
4)	IL	720	1	KBC	Kyushu Asahi Hoso, Kitakyushu
5)	LR	738	5	KNB	Kita Nihon Hoso, Toyama
5)		738	1	KNB	Kita Nihon Hoso, Takaoka
6)	RR	738	10	RBC	Ryukyu Hoso, Naha
7)	JF	765	5	YBS	Yamanashi Hoso, Kofu
8)	PF	765	5	KRY	Yamaguchi Hoso, Shunan
9)	XR	864	10	ROK	R. Okinawa, Naha: 2000-1800(Sun1530)
10)	SO	864	1	SBC	Shin'etsu Hoso, Matsumoto
11)	HE	864	3	HBC	Hokkaido Hoso, Asahikawa
11)	QF	864	3	HBC	Hokkaido Hoso, Muroran
11)		864	1	HBC	Hokkaido Hoso, Enbetsu
12)	PR	864	5	FBC	Fukui Hoso, Fukui
13)	XN	864	1	CRT	Tochigi Hoso, Nasu
2)	WS	882	3	STV	STV R., Kushiro
2)		882	1	STV	STV R., Esashi
11)	HO	900	5	HBC	Hokkaido Hoso, Hakodate
14)	HF	900	5	BSS	San'in Hoso, Yonago: (off air Sat1800-1955, Sun1505-1955)
15)	ZR	900	5	RKC	Kochi Hoso, Kochi
2)	VX	909	5	STV	STV R., Abashiri
16)	EF	918	5	YBC	Yamagata Hoso, Yamagata
16)		918	1	YBC	Yamagata Hoso, Tsuruoka
16)		918	1	YBC	Yamagata Hoso, Yonezawa
16)		918	1	YBC	Yamagata Hoso, Shinjo
8)	PM	918	1	KRY	Yamaguchi Hoso, Shimonoseki
8)	PN	918	1	KRY	Yamaguchi Hoso, Iwakuni
17)	TR	936	5	ABS	Akita Hoso, Akita
18)	NF	936	5	MRT	Miyazaki Hoso, Miyazaki
18)		936	1	MRT	Miyazaki Hoso, Nobeoka
18)		936	1	MRT	Miyazaki Hoso, Nichinan
18)		936	1	MRT	Miyazaki Hoso, Kobayashi
18)		936	1	MRT	Miyazaki Hoso, Takachiho
19)	KR	954	100	TBS	TBS R., Tokyo
20)	NR	1008	50	ABC	Asahi Hoso, Osaka
21)	AR	1053	50	CBC	Chubu Nippon Hoso, Nagoya: (S)
2)	WM	1071	5	STV	STV R., Obihiro
10)	SR	1098	5	SBC	Shin'etsu Hoso, Nagano
10)	SW	1098	1	SBC	Shin'etsu Hoso, Iida
22)	MF	1098	1	NBC	Nagasaki Hoso, Sasebo
23)	GF	1098	5	OBS	Oita Hoso, Oita
24)	WO	1098	5	RFC	R. Fukushima, Koriyama
25)	CF	1107	20	MBC	Minami Nihon Hoso, Kagoshima
25)		1107	1	MBC	Minami Nihon Hoso, Akune
25)		1107	1	MBC	Minami Nihon Hoso, Oguchi
25)		1107	1	MBC	Minami Nihon Hoso, Sendai
26)	MR	1107	5	MRO	Hokuriku Hoso, Kanazawa
26)		1107	1	MRO	Hokuriku Hoso, Nanao
27)	AF	1116	5	RNB	Nankai Hoso, Matsuyama
27)	AL	1116	1	RNB	Nankai Hoso, Niihama
27)	AM	1116	1	RNB	Nankai Hoso, Uwajima
28)	DR	1116	5	BSN	Niigata Hoso, Niigata
29)	QR	1134	100	NCB	Bunka Hoso, Tokyo
30)	BR	1143	20	KBS	KBS Kyoto, Kyoto
31)	OR	1179	50	MBS	Mainichi Hoso, Osaka
15)		1197	1	RKC	Kochi Hoso, Nakamura
32)	FO	1197	1	RKB	RKB Mainichi Hoso, Kitakyushu
33)	BF	1197	10	RKK	Kumamoto Hoso, Kumamoto
33)		1197	1	RKK	Kumamoto Hoso, Hitoyoshi
33)		1197	1	RKK	Kumamoto Hoso, Aso
33)		1197	1	RKK	Kumamoto Hoso, Goshoura
34)	YF	1197	5	IBS	Ibaraki Hoso, Mito: (off air 2000-2100, Fri -2050, Sat-2045, Sun1500-2100)
2)	WL	1197	3	STV	STV R., Asahikawa
2)		1197	1	STV	STV R., Wakkanai
2)		1197	1	STV	STV R., Nayoro
2)		1197	1	STV	STV R., Enbetsu
30)	BO	1215	2	KBS	KBS Kyoto, Maizuru
30a)	BW	1215	1	KBS	KBS Shiga, Hikone
22)	UR	1233	5	NBC	Nagasaki Hoso, Nagasaki
35)	GR	1233	5	RAB	Aomori Hoso, Aomori
36)	LF	1242	100	NBS	Nippon Hoso, Tokyo: (S)
37)	IR	1260	20	TBC	Tohoku Hoso, Sendai
11)	HW	1269	5	HBC	Hokkaido Hoso, Obihiro
11)	FM	1269	1	HBC	Hokkaido Hoso, Esashi
38)	JR	1269	5	JRT	Shikoku Hoso, Tokushima
38)		1269	1	JRT	Shikoku Hoso, Ikeda
32)	FR	1278	50	RKB	RKB Mainichi Hoso, Fukuoka
11)	HR	1287	50	HBC	Hokkaido Hoso, Sapporo
39)	UF	1314	50	OBC	R. Osaka, Osaka: (S)
40)	SF	1332	50	Tokai	R. Hoso, Nagoya
41)	ER	1350	20	RCC	Chugoku Hoso, Hiroshima
11)	TS	1368	1	HBC	Hokkaido Hoso, Wakkanai
1)	CE	1395	1	CRK	R. Kansai, Toyooka
24)	WE	1395	1	RFC	R. Fukushima, Wakamatsu
11)	QL	1404	5	HBC	Hokkaido Hoso, Kushiro
42)	VR	1404	10	SBS	Shizuoka Hoso, Shizuoka
42)	VO	1404	1	SBS	Shizuoka Hoso, Hamamatsu

MW	Call	kHz	kW	ID	Station, location & h of tr
4)	IF	1413	50	KBC	Kyushu Asahi Hoso, Fukuoka
43)	RF	1422	50	RF	RF R. Nippon, Yokohama
14)	HL	1431	1	BSS	San'in Hoso, Tottori: (as 900kHz)
14)		1431	1	BSS	San'in Hoso, Izumo: (as 900kHz)
22)		1431	1	NBC	Nagasaki Hoso, Fukue
24)	WW	1431	1	RFC	R. Fukushima, Iwaki
44)	VF	1431	5	WBS	Wakayama Hoso, Wakayama: (S)
45)	ZF	1431	5	GBS	Gifu Hoso, Gifu: 2100-1500
2)	WF	1440	50	STV	STV R., Sapporo
2)		1440	3	STV	STV R., Muroran
2)		1440	1	STV	STV R., Tomakomai
11)	QM	1449	5	HBC	Hokkaido Hoso, Abashiri
46)	KF	1449	5	RNC	Nishi Nippon Hoso, Takamatsu
46)		1449	1	RNC	Nishi Nippon Hoso, Marugame
22a)	UO	1458	1	NBC	Nagasaki Hoso, Saga
24)	WR	1458	1	RFC	R. Fukushima, Fukushima
34)	YL	1458	1	IBS	Ibaraki Hoso, Tsuchiura
34)		1458	1	IBS	Ibaraki Hoso, Sekijo
41)		1458	1	RCC	Chugoku Hoso, Shobara
8)	PL	1485	1	KRY	Yamaguchi Hoso, Hagi
35)	GO	1485	1	RAB	Aomori Hoso, Hachinohe
11)	TL	1494	1	HBC	Hokkaido Hoso, Nayoro
47)	YR	1494	10	RSK	Sanyo Hoso, Okayama
47)		1494	1	RSK	Sanyo Hoso, Takahashi
47)		1494	1	RSK	Sanyo Hoso, Tsuyama
47)		1494	1	RSK	Sanyo Hoso, Niimi
47)		1494	1	RSK	Sanyo Hoso, Bizen
47)		1494	1	RSK	Sanyo Hoso, Ochiai
28)	DO	1530	1	BSN	Niigata Hoso, Joetsu
13)	XF	1530	5	CRT	Tochigi Hoso, Utsunomiya
41)	EO	1530	1	RCC	Chugoku Hoso, Fukuyama
41)		1530	1	RCC	Chugoku Hoso, Mihara

+ approx 125 relay stns below 1kW. Of these some exist multiply on 801, 1026, 1062 and 1557kHz.

Simultaneous FM broadcasts of MW stns

FM	MHz	kW	Stn, loc	FM	MHz	kW	Stn, loc
17)	90.1	1	ABS, Akita	14)	92.2	0.5	BSS, Matsue
5)	90.2	1	KNB, Toyama	8)	92.3	1	KRY, Shunan
4)	90.2	1	KBC, Fukuoka	16)	92.4	1	YBC, Yamagata
46)	90.3	1	RNC, Takamatsu	43)	92.4	5	RF, Yokohama
18)	90.4	1	MRT, Miyazaki	22)	92.6	1	NBC, Nagasaki
45)	90.4	1	GBS, Gifu	28)	92.7	1	BSN, Niigata
2)	90.4	5	STV, Sapporo	25)	92.8	1	MBC, Kagoshima
19)	90.5	7	TBS, Tokyo	40)	92.9	7	Tokai R., Nagoya
3)	90.6	1	IBC, Morioka	36)	93.0	7	NBS, Tokyo
31)	90.6	7	MBS, Osaka	38)	93.0	1	JRT, Tokushima
15)	90.8	0.5	RKC, Kochi	9)	93.1	1	ROK, Naha
24)	90.8	0.5	RFC, Fukushima	20)	93.3	7	ABC, Osaka
7)	90.9	1	YBS, Kofu	23)	93.3	1	OBS, Oita
32)	91.0	1	RKB, Fukuoka	37)	93.5	5	TBC, Sendai
1)	91.1	1	CRK, Kobe	21)	93.7	7	CBC, Nagoya
33)	91.4	0.8	RKK, Kumamoto	42)	93.9	1	SBS, Shizuoka
47)	91.4	0.7	RSK, Okayama	26)	94.0	1	MRO, Kanazawa
11)	91.5	5	HBC, Sapporo	13)	94.1	1	CRT, Utsunomiya
29)	91.6	7	NCR, Tokyo	44)	94.2	0.5	WBS, Wakayama
27)	91.7	1	RNB, Matsuyama	12)	94.6	1	FBC, Fukui
35)	91.7	1	RAB, Aomori	34)	94.6	1	IBS, Mito
39)	91.9	7	OBC, Osaka	41)	94.6	1	RCC, Hiroshima
6)	92.1	1	RBC, Naha	30)	94.9	3	KBS, Kyoto
10)	92.2	1	SBC, Nagano				

+ Relay stns below 1kW.

Call: JO(call). **(S):** AM Stereo (C-QUAM System). **Schedule:** 24h unless otherwise indicated above. Most 24h stns are off the air for 1 to 5 hours until 1900 or 2000 on Sun unless mentioned. All other days a network prgr is aired 1600 or 1800 to 2000 on most stns. Network prgrs may also be broadcast at other times of day. **ID:** Company initials are usually used as stn identification

Addresses & other information:

1) R. Kansai Co., Ltd., 5-7, Higashi Kawasaki-cho 1-chome, Chuo-ku, Kobe 650-8580 **W:** jocr.jp – **2)** The STVradio Broadcasting Co., Ltd, 1-1, Nishi 8-chome, Kita 1-jo, Chuo-ku, Sapporo 060-8705 **W:** stv.jp – **3)** Iwate Broadc Co., Ltd., 6-1, Shike-cho, Morioka 020-8566 **W:** ibc.co.jp/ – **4)** Kyushu Asahi Broadc Co., Ltd, 1-1, Nagahama 1-chome, Chuo-ku, Fukuoka 810-8571 **W:** kbc.co.jp – **5)** Kita-nihon Broadc Co., Ltd.,10-18, Ushijima-machi, Toyama 930-8585 **W:** knb.ne.jp – **6)** Ryukyu Broadc Corp., 3-1, Kumoji 2-chome, Naha 900-8711 **W:** rbc.co.jp – **7)** Yamanashi Broadc System, Inc., 6-10, Kitaguchi 2-chome, Kofu 400-8525 **W:** ybs.jp – **8)** Yamaguchi Broadc Co., Ltd., Koen-ku, Shunan 745-8686 **W:** kry.co.jp – **9)** R Okinawa Corp., 4-8, Nishi 1-chome, Naha 900-8604 **W:** rokinawa.co.jp – **10)** Shin-etsu Broadc Co., Ltd., 1200, Toigoshomachi, Nagano 380-8521 **W:** sbc21.co.jp – **11)** Hokkaido Broadc Co., Ltd., Nishi 5-chome, kita 1-jo, Chuo-ku, Sapporo 060-8501 **W:** hbc.co.jp – **12)** Fukui Broadc Corp., 510, Owada 2-chome, Fukui 910-8588 **W:** fbc.jp –**13)** Tochigi Broadc Co., Ltd., 2-2-5, Showa, Utsunomiya 320-8601 **W:** crt-radio.co.jp – **14)** Broadc System of San-in, 1-71, Nishi-Fukubara 1-chome, Yonago 683-8670 **W:** bss.jp – **15)** Kochi Broadc Co., Ltd., 2-15, Hon-machi 3-chome, Kochi 780-8550 **W:** rkc-kochi.co.jp – **16)** Yamagata Broadc Co., Ltd., 5-12, Hatago-machi 2-chome, Yamagata 990-8555 **W:** ybc.co.jp – **17)** Akita Broadc System,Inc., 1-2, Nakadori-7 chome, Akita 010-8611 **W:** akita-abs.co.jp – **18)** Miyazaki Broadc Co., Ltd., 6-7, Tachibanadori-nishi 4-chome, Miyazaki 880-8639 **W:** mrt.jp – **19)** TBS Radio, Inc., 3-6, Akasaka 5-chome, Minato-ku, Tokyo 107-8006 **W:** tbsradio.jp – **20)** Asahi Radio Broadc Corp., 1-30, Fukushima 1-chome, Fukushima-ku, Osaka 553-8503 **W:** abc1008.com – **21)** CBCradio Co., Ltd., 2-8, Shinsakae 1-chome, Naka-ku, Nagoya 460-8405 **W:** hicbc.com – **22)** Nagasaki Broadc Co., Ltd., 1-35, Uwa-machi, Nagasaki 850-8650 **W:** nbc-nagasaki.co.jp – **22a)** Nagasaki Broadc Co., Ltd Saga station, 4-17, Ekimaechuo 1-chome, Saga 840-0801 **W:** nbc-saga.jp – **23)** Oita Broadc System, 1-1, Imazuru 3-chome, Oita 870-8620 **W:** e-obs.com – **24)** R Fukushima Broadc Co., Ltd., 8, Shimoarako, Fukushima 960-8655 **W:** rfc.jp – **25)** Minaminihon Broadc Co., Ltd., 5-25, Korai-cho, Kagoshima 890-8570 **W:** mbc.co.jp – **26)** Hokuriku Broadc Co., Ltd., 2-1, Honda-machi 3-chome, Kanazawa 920-8560 **W:** mro.co.jp – **27)** Nankai Broadc Co., Ltd., 1-1, Honmachi 1-chome, Matsuyama 790-8510 **W:** rnb.co.jp – **28)** Broadc System of Niigata, Inc., 18, Kawagishi-cho 3-chome, Chuo-ku, Niigata 951-8655 **W:** ohbsn.com – **29)** Nippon Cultural Broadc., Inc.,31, Hamamatsu-cho 1-chome, Minato-ku, Tokyo 105-8002 **W:** joqr.co.jp – **30)** Kyoto Broadc System Co., Ltd., Kamichojamachi, Karasumadori, Kamigyo-ku, Kyoto 602-8588 **W:** kbs-kyoto.co.jp – **30a)** KBS Shiga Station, 6-19, Tachibana-cho, Hikone 522-0062 – **31)** Mainichi Broadc System, Inc., 17-1, Chayamachi, Kita-ku, Osaka 530-8304 **W:** mbs.jp – **32)** RKB Mainichi Broadc Corp., 3-8, Momochihama 2-chome, Sawara-ku, Fukuoka 814-8585 **W:** rkb.jp – **33)** Kumamoto Broadc Co., Ltd., 30, Yamasaki-machi, Kumamoto 860-8611 **W:** rkk.jp – **34)** Ibaraki Broadc System, 2084-2, Senba-cho, Mito 310-8505 **W:** ibs-radio.com – **35)** Aomori Broadc Corp., 8-1, Matsumori 1-chome, Aomori 030-8655 **W:** rab.co.jp – **36)** Nippon Broadc System, Inc., 9-3, Yurakucho 1-chome, Chiyoda-ku, Tokyo 100-8439 **W:** jolf.co.jp – **37)** Tohoku Broadc Co., Ltd., 26-1, Kasumi-cho, Yagiyama, Taihaku-ku, Sendai 980-8668 **W:** tbc-sendai.co.jp – **38)** Shikoku Broadc Co., Ltd., 5-2, Nakatokushima-cho 2-chome, Tokushima 770-8573 **W:** jrt.co.jp – **39)** Osaka Broadc Corp., 2-4, Benten 1-chome, Minato-ku, Osaka 552-8501 **W:** obc1314.co.jp – **40)** Tokai Radio Broadc Co., Ltd., 14-27, Higashisakura 1-chome, Higashi-ku, Nagoya 461-8503 **W:** tokairadio.co.jp – **41)** RCC Broadc Co., Ltd., 21-3, Moto-machi, Naka-ku, Hiroshima 730-8504 **W:** rcc.jp – **42)** Shizuoka Broadc System, 1-1, Toro 3-chome, Suruga-ku, Shizuoka 422-8680 **W:** at-s.com – **43)** RF Radio Nippon Co., Ltd., 85, Choja-machi 5-chome, Naka-ku, Yokohama 231-8611 **W:** jorf.co.jp – **44)** Wakayama Broadc System, 3, Minato-honmachi 3-chome, Wakayama 640-8577 **W:** wbs.co.jp – **45)** Gifu Broadc System, 52, Hashimotocho 2-chome, Gifu 500-8588 **W:** zf-web.com – **46)** Nishi-nippon Broadc Co., Ltd., 8-15, Marunouchi, Takamatsu 760-8575 **W:** rnc.co.jp – **47)** Sanyo Broadc Co., Ltd., 1-3, Marunouchi 2-chome, Okayama 700-8580 **W:** rsk.co.jp.

V: Most stns verify by QSL-card. Rec acc. Rp

NIKKEI RADIO BROADCASTING CORPORATION (RADIO NIKKEI)

✉ 2-8, Toranomon 1-chome, Minato-ku, Tokyo 105-8565 ☎ +81 3 6205 7810 🖷 +81 3 6205 7809 **W:** radionikkei.jp

SW	kHz	kW	Prgr	SW	kHz	kW	Prgr
JOZ	‡3925	50	1	JOZ6	6115	50	2
JOZ4	*3925	10	1	JOZ3	‡9595	50	1
JOZ5	‡3945	10	2	JOZ7	‡9760	50	2
JOZ2	6055	50	1				

*) Nemuro; others Nagara (Chiba), ‡ inactive

1st Prgr: Sun-Thu 2215-1500(Fri -1530) on 6055kHz, 2215-2300 & 0750-1500(Fri -1530) on 3925kHz (Nemuro). Fri-Sat 2340-1000 on 6055KHz, 0750-1000 on 3925kHz (Nenuro).

2nd Prgr: Sun-Thu 2329-1000 on 6115kHz, Fri-Sat 2359- 0800 on 6115kHz.

IS: Slow tempo chime with Japanese instrument "Koto" at sign on and sign off - **V.** by QSL card. Rp.

COMMERCIAL FM STATIONS:

FM	Call	MHz	kW	Station, location & h of tr
1)	QU	76.1	1	FM Iwate, Morioka
2)	LU	76.1	1	FM Fukui, Fukui
3)	FW	76.1	1	Love FM, Fukuoka
4)	SV	76.4	1	R. Berry, Utsunomiya
5)	AW	76.5	10	FM COCOLO, Osaka
6)	VV	76.8	1	FM Okayama, Okayama
7)	UV	77.0	1	E-R. LAKESIDE, Otsu
8)	JU	77.1	5	Date FM, Sendai
9)	SU	77.4	1	FM Kumamoto, Kumamoto
10)	VU	77.4	0.5	V-air, Matsue
11)	XU	77.5	1	FM Niigata, Niigata
12)		77.6	1	Kiss-FM Kobe, Himeji
13)	QV	77.8	10	ZIP FM, Nagoya
14)	NV	77.9	0.5	FM Saga, Saga
15)	GV	78.0	5	bayfm, Chiba
16)	GU	78.2	1	Hiroshima FM, Hiroshima
17)	YU	78.6	1	FM Kagawa, Takamatsu
18)	RV	78.7	3	CROSS FM, Kitakyushu (Fukuoka)
19)	NU	78.9	3	R. Cube, Tsu
20)	KU	79.2	1	K-MIX, Hamamatsu (Shizuoka)
21)	UU	79.2	1	FM Yamaguchi, Yamaguchi
22)	HU	79.5	1	FM Nagasaki, Nagasaki
23)	DV	79.5	5	NACK 5, Saitama
24)	EU	79.7	1	FM Ehime, Matsuyama: 2057-1803 (v.)
25)	ZU	79.7	1	FM Nagano, Matsumoto (Nagano)
26)	OV	79.8	1	μ FM, Kagoshima
27)	WU	80.0	1	FM Aomori, Aomori
28)	AU	80.0	10	Tokyo FM, Tokyo
29)	XV	80.0	1	FM Gifu, Ogaki (Gifu)
30)	FV	80.2	10	FM 802, Osaka
31)	FU	80.4	5	AIR-G', Sapporo
32)	EV	80.4	1	Rhythm Station, Yamagata
33)	HV	80.5	1	Hello Five, Kanazawa
34)	CU	80.7	10	FM Aichi, Nagoya
35)	MV	80.7	1	FM Tokushima, Tokushima
36)	DU	80.7	3	FM Fukuoka, Fukuoka
37)	AV	81.3	7	J-WAVE, Tokyo
38)	LV	81.6	0.5	Hi-six, Kochi
39)	TV	81.8	1	Fukushima FM, Koriyama(Fukushima)
40)	PV	82.5	5	FM North Wave, Sapporo
41)	OU	82.7	1	FM Toyama, Toyama
42)	PU	82.8	3	FM Akita, Akita
43)	CV	83.0	1	FM Fuji, Kofu: 1950-1700 (v.)
44)	MU	83.2	1	Joy FM, Miyazaki
45)	TU	84.7	5	FM Yokohama, Yokohama
46)	BU	85.1	10	FM Osaka, Osaka
47)	RU	86.3	1	FM Gunma, Maebashi
11)		86.5	1	FM Niigata, Yamato
10)		86.6	1	V-air, Hamada
48)	IU	87.3	1	FM Okinawa, Naha
49)	JV	88.0	1	Air R., Oita
50)	KV	89.4	3	Alpha-Station, Kyoto
51)	DW	89.7	10	Inter FM, Tokyo
12)	IV	89.9	1	Kiss-FM Kobe, Kobe

NB: Relay stns below 1kW and community stns are not included.
Call: JO (call)-FM. Schedule: 24h unless otherwise indicated above. Most 24h stns are off the air for 2 to 5 hours until 1900, 2000 or 2100 on Sun.

Addresses & other information:
1) FM Iwate Broadc Co., 2-10, Uchimaru, Morioka 020-8512 **W:** fmii.co.jp – **2)** Fukui FM Broadc Co., Ltd., 1-1, Miyuki 1-chome, Fukui 910-8553 **W:** fmfukui.jp – **3)** LOVE FM International Broadc Co., Ltd., 12-23, Imaizumi 1-chome, Chuo-ku, Fukuoka 810-8516 Prgr in English, Chinese and Korean etc **W:** lovefm.co.jp – **4)** FM Tochigi Brordc co.,ltd., 2-1, Chuo 1-chome, Utsunomiya 320-8550 **W:** berry.co.jp – **5)** FM 802 Co., Ltd., See 30). Foreign language prgr in English, Chinese, Korean, etc. Since April 2012, the business has been transfered from Kansai Intermedia Corp. to FM 802 Co. Ltd. **W:** cocolo.jp – **6)** Okayama FM Broadc Co., Ltd., 1-8-45, Nakasange, Okayama 700-0821 **W:** fm-okayama.co.jp – **7)** FM Shiga Co., Ltd., 19-10, Nishinosho, Otsu 520-0818 **W:** e-radio.co.jp – **8)** Sendai FM Broadc., Inc., 10-28, Honcho 2-chome, Aoba-ku, Sendai 980-8420 **W:** datefm.co.jp – **9)** FM Kumamoto Broadc Co., Ltd., 5-50, Chibajomachi, Kumamoto 860-0001 **W:** fmk.fm – **10)** FM San-in Co., Ltd., 2-1, Gakuenminami 1-chome, Matsue 690-8508 **W:** fm-sanin.co.jp – **11)** FM Radio Niigata Co., Ltd., 3-5, Saiwainishi 4-chome, Chuo-ku, Niigata 950-8581 **W:** fmniigata.com – **12)** Kiss-FM KOBE Inc., 5-4 Hatoba-cho, Chuo-ku, Kobe 650-8589 **W:** kiss-fm.co.jp – **13)** ZIP-FM Inc., 20-17, Marunouchi 3-chome, Naka-ku, Nagoya 460-8578 **W:** zip-fm.co.jp – **14)** FM Saga Co., Ltd., 286-5, Fukuro, Honjo-machi, Saga 840-0023 **W:** fmsaga.co.jp – **15)** bayfm78 Co., Ltd., 6-1, Nakase 2-chome, Mihama-ku, Chiba 261-7127 **W:** bayfm.co.jp – **16)** Hiroshima FM Broadc Co., Ltd., 8-2, Minamimachi 1-chome, Minami-ku, Hiroshima 734-8511 **W:** hfmweb.jp – **17)** FM Kagawa Broadc Co., Ltd., 4-23, Saiho-cho 1-chome, Takamatsu 760-8584 **W:** fmkagawa.co.jp – **18)** Cross FM Co., Ltd, 1-1, Kyomachi 3-chome, Kokurakita-ku, Kitakyushu 802-8570 **W:** crossfm.co.jp – **19)** Mie FM Broadc co., Ltd., 1043-1, Kannonji-cho, Tsu 514-8505 **W:** fmmie.jp –20) Shizuoka FM Broadc Co., Ltd, 133-24, Tokiwa-cho, Naka-ku, Hamamatsu 430-8575 **W:** k-mix.co.jp – 21) FM Yamaguchi Co., Ltd., 3-31, Midori-cho, Yamaguchi 753-8521 **W:** fmy.co.jp – 22) FM Nagasaki Co., Ltd., 5-5, Sakae-machi, Nagasaki 850-8550 **W:** fmnagasaki.co.jp – 23) FM Nack 5 Co Ltd., 682-2, Nishiki-cho, Omiya-ku, Saitama 330-8579 **W:** nack5.co.jp – 24) FM Ehime Broadc Co., 10-7, Takewara-machi 1-chome, Matsuyama 790-8565 **W:** joeufm.co.jp – 25) Nagano FM Broadc Co., Ltd, 13-5, Honjo 1-chome, Matsumoto 390-8520 **W:** fmnagano.co.jp – 26) FM Kagoshima Co., Ltd., 1-38, Higashisengoku-cho, Kagoshima 892-8579 **W:** myufm.jp – 27) Aomori FM Broadc Co., Ltd., 7-19, Tsutsumi-machi 1-chome, Aomori 030-0812 **W:** afb.co.jp – 28) Tokyo FM Broadc Co., Ltd., 7, Kojimachi 1-chome, Chiyoda-ku, Tokyo 102-8080 **W:** tfm.co.jp – 29 FM Gifu Broadc. Inc 35-10, Kono 4-chome, Ogaki 503-8580 **W:** fmgifu.com – 30) FM 802 Co., Ltd., Kita 2-6, Tenjinbashi 2-chome, Kita-ku, Osaka 530-8580 **W:** funky802.com – 31) FM Hokkaido Broadc Co., Ltd., 1, Nishi 2-chome, kita 1-jo, Chuo-ku, Sapporo 060-8532 **W:** air-g.co.jp – 32) FM Yamagata Co., Ltd., 14-69, Matsuyama 3-chome, Yamagata 990-9543 **W:** rfm.co.jp – 33) FM Ishikawa Broadc Co., Ltd., 1-45, Hikoso-machi 2-chome, Kanazawa 920-8605 **W:** hellofive.jp – 34) FM Aichi Broadc Co., Ltd., 15-18, Chiyoda 2-chome, Naka-ku, Nagoya 460-8388 **W:** fma.co.jp – 35) FM Tokushima Broadc Co., 61, Terashimahonchonishi 1-chome, Tokushima 770-8567 **W:** fm807.jp – 36) Fukuoka FM Broadc Co., Ltd., 9-19, Kiyokawa 1-chome, Chuo-ku, Fukuoka 810-8575 **W:** fmfukuoka.co.jp – 37) J-WAVE Inc., Roppongi Hills Mori Tower 33F, 10-1, Roppongi 6-chome,, Minato-ku, Tokyo 106-6188 **W:** j-wave.co.jp – 38) FM Kochi Broadc Co., Ltd., 1-5, Takashocho 2-chome, Kochi 780-8532 **W:** fmkochi.com –39) FM Fukushima Inc., 4-4, Shinmei-cho, Koriyama 960-8013 **W:** fmf.co.jp –40) FM North Wave Co., Ltd., 3-1, Nishi 4-chome, Kita 7-jo, Kita-ku, Sapporo 060-8557 **W:** fmnorth.co.jp – 41) Toyama FM Broadc Co., Ltd., 2-11, Okuda-machi, Toyama 930-8567 **W:** fmtoyama.co.jp – 42) FM Akita Broadc Co.,Ltd., 7-10, Yabase-Honcho 3-chome, Akita 010-0973 **W:** fm-akita.co.jp – 43) FM Fuji Co Ltd., Aria 105, Kawadamachi, Kofu 400-8550 **W:** fmfuji.jp – 44) Miyazaki FM Broadc Co., Ltd., 78, Gion 2-chome, Miyazaki 880-8583 **W:** joyfm.co.jp – 45) Yokohama FM Broadc Co., Ltd., 2-1, Minato-Mirai 2-chome, Nishi-ku, Yokohama 220-8110 **W:** fmyokohama.co.jp –46) FM Osaka Co., Ltd., 3-1, Minatomachi 1-chome, Naniwa-ku, Osaka 556-8510 **W:** fmosaka.net – 47) FM Gunma Broadc Co., Ltd., 4-8, Wakamiyacho 1-chome, Maebashi 371-8533 **W:** fmgunma.com – 48) FM Okinawa Broadc Corp., 40, Kowan, Urasoe, Okinawa 901-2525 **W:** fmokinawa.co.jp – 49) FM Oita Broadc., Co., Ltd., 3-8-8, funai-machi, Oita 870-8558 **W:** fmoita.co.jp –501) FM Kyoto, Inc., CoCon Karasuma 8F, 620, Suiginya-cho, Karasuma-dori Shijo-sagaru, Shimogyo-ku, Kyoto 600-8566 **W:** fm-kyoto.jp – 51) Inter FM 897 Co., Ltd., 3-3, Higashi-shinagawa 1-chome, Shinagawa-ku, Tokyo 140-0002 - Prgr in English & foreign languages **W:** interfm.co.jp
V. Most stns verify by QSL card. Rec acc. Rp.

AMERICAN FORCES NETWORK (AFN) (U.S. Mil.)
The network serves the members of the US forces. The stns in Japan broadcast by authority of Commander, US Forces, Japan, in cooperation with the Information and Communications Policy Bureau in Japan. Stns are linked by land line and microwave.
AFN Tokyo, Det 10, Unit 5091 Bldg 3266, Yokota Air Base, Fussa, Tokyo 197-0001 or Det 10, Unit 5091 Bldg 3266, APO/AP 96328-5091 ☎+81 42 552 2511 ext 52374 📠+81 42 552 2511 ext 52386 **E:** dma.Yokota.afn.list.publicity@mail.mil **W:** afnpacific.net/Local-Stations/Tokyo
Other stns: **AFN Okinawa:** Okinawa **E:** DMA.Kadena.AFN.list.publicity@mail.mil **W:** afnpacific.net/Local-Stations/Okinawa – **AFN Misawa:** Misawa, Aomori **E:** afn@misawa.af.mil **W:** afnpacific.net/Local-Stations/Misawa **AFN Iwakuni:** Iwakuni, Yamaguchi **W:** afnpacific.net/Local-Stations/Iwakuni – **AFN Sasebo:** Sasebo, Nagasaki **W:** afnpacific.net/Local-Stations/Sasebo

MW	kHz	kW	MW	kHz	kW
Okinawa	648	10	Misawa	1575	1
Tokyo	810	50	Sasebo	1575	0.30
Iwakuni	1575	1			

FM: Okinawa 89.1MHz 20kW
D. Prgr: 24h **N:** on the h. **Ann:** "This is the American Forces Network" **V.** by QSL card or letter

JORDAN

L.T: UTC +2h (26 Mar-29 Oct: +3h) — **Pop:** 10 million — **Pr.L:** Arabic — **E.C:** 230V/50Hz — **ITU:** JOR

MEDIA COMMISSION (MC)

Amman ☎ +962 6 5650231 **W:** www.mc.gov.jo; www.facebook.com/mediacommissionjo

JORDAN RADIO & TELEVISION CORP. (JRTV, Pub)

Al-Shara Al-Musharrafah St, P.O.Box 909, JO-11118 Amman ☎+962 6 4773111 🖷 +962 6 4778 578 **W:** jrtv.gov.jo **E:** rj@jrtv.gov.jo

MW	kHz	kW	Prgr.	Times
Shobak	612	100	Main	24h
Amman	*855	20	Main	24h

*inactive, but expected to return

FM	Main	Amman FM	R. Jordan	Quran	Hadaf	kW
Ajlun	95.8	95.8	90.9	-		10/5
Amman	90.0	99.0	96.3	93.1	88.0	5/10
Aqaba	101.5	98.1/105.6	99.7	91.5	-	5/1
Irbid	103.8	95.4		98.7		1
Karak	103.6	-	-	98.7	-	1
Salt	-	105.0	-	-		1
Tafeleh	90.8					1

Main Arabic sce: 24h. Jordan Armed Forces R: 1400-1600. **Amman FM** in Arabic: 24h (Irbid with some local prgr). **R. Jordan 96.3:** 24h in English exc. **French** 1100-1300. **Quran Prgr:** 24h. **Hadaf** (sports prgr.): 24h. **Ann:** Arabic: "Huna Amman, Idha'atu-l-Mamlaka al-Urdoniya al-Hashemiya". Armed forces R: "Idha'at Al-Quwaat Al-Musala al-Urdoniya, al-Gayish al-Arabi". E: "This is R. Jordan broadcasting from Amman".

OTHER STATIONS (**FM** MHz):
Amen FM: Amman/Aqaba 89.5, Irbid 89.7 **W:** amenfm.jo – **Ayyam FM:** Amman 91.5, Irbid 91.9, Petra 92.1 **W:**ayaamfm.jo – **Beat FM,** Amman: 102.5 English. **W:** mybeat.fm – **Bliss FM,** Amman: 104.3 English. **W:** bliss.jo – **Energy FM,** Amman: 97.7 English. **W:** energyradio.jo – **Global FM:** Amman 94.5 2kW. **W:** globaljo.fm Also r. CRI – **Hala FM:** Aqaba 91.1, Irbid/Ruweished 91.3, Al-Karak 94.3, Al-Salt/Tafilaq 94.7, Ajlun 94.3, Amman 102.1, Petra 105.4 **W:** hala.jo – **Hawa FM,** Amman: 105.9MHz **W:** ammancity.gov.jo – **Hayat FM:** Irbid 94.7, Amman 104.7, Azraq 105.4 **W:** hayat.fm – **Mazaj FM:** Amman 95.3, Irbid 101.7 **W:** mazajfm.com – **Melody FM:** Amman 91.1, Zarqa 105.5 – **Mood FM,** Amman: 92.0 English. **W:** mood.fm – **Play FM:** Amman 99.5, Irbid 105.3. English **W:** play.jo – **R. Al-Balad,** Amman: 92.4 **W:** balad.fm – **R. Fann:** Aqaba 91.1, Irbid/Ruweished 91.3, Ajlun/Karak 94.3, Salt/Tafileh 94.7, Amman 102.1/104.2, Petra/Azraq 105.4 **W:** radiofann.com – **R. Farah Al-Nas,** Amman: 98.5 **W:** farahalnas.jo – **R. Yaqeen,** Amman: 103.7, Irbid 97.7 **W:** yaqeen.jo1jo.org – **Rotana R:** Irbid 90.5, Amman 99.9 **W:** rotana.net – **Sawt Al-Janoub,** Ma'an: 90.5 – **Sawt al-Madina:** Amman: 88.7.**W:** sawtalmadenah.net – **Sawt el-Ghad:** Amman 101.5 **W:** sawtelghad.com (see main entry under Lebanon) – **Spin Jordan:** Irbid 88.3, Ma'an 88.5, Amman 94.1, Aqaba 103.5 English. **W:** spin.jo – **Sunny,** Amman: 105.1 English. **W:** sunny.jo – **Watar FM:** Amman 88.3, Irbid 91.5, Aqaba 102.5 **W:** watar.fm – **Virgin R. Jordan,** Amman: 93.7 **W:** virginradiojordan.com – **Yarmouk FM,** Irbid: 105.7 **W:** yu.edu.jo
BBC Arabic Sce: Amman 103.1 5kW, Ajlun 89.1 10kW.
Monte-Carlo Doualiya: Amman 97.4, Ajlun 106.2MHz.
R. Sawa: Amman 98.1 10kW, Ajlun 107.4MHz

KAZAKHSTAN

L.T: UTC +6h (Western Kazakhstan: +5h) — **Pop:** 18.5 million — **Pr.L:** Kazakh (official), Russian (official) — **E.C:** 220V/50Hz — **ITU:** KAZ

MÁDENIET JÁNE SPORT MINISTRLIGI (Ministry of Culture and Sport)

Máńgilik el k. 8, 010000 Nur-Sultan ☎ +7 7172 740251 **E:** p.pressa@mcs.gov.kz **W:** mks.gov.kz **L.P:** Minister: Aqtoty Raıymqulova

QAZAQ RADIOLARY JSS (Gov)

Qonaev k. 4, 010000 Nur-Sultan ☎ +7 7172 757302 **E:** qazaqradiolary@gmail.com **W:** qazradio.fm **L.P:** DG: Nurjan Muhamedjanova
Almaty studios: Jeltoqsan k. 177, 050013 Almaty

MW	kHz	kW	Prgr	MW	kHz	kW	Prgr
Jetisaı	1098	-	1	Sapaq	1548	-	1
Shardara	1098	-	1	Lepsi	1557	-	1
Aqtaý	1341	25	1				

FM (MHz)	1*	2	kW		1*	2	kW
Aıagóz	101.0m	103.2	1	Oktıabrskoe	104.8i	-	1
Almaty	101.0a	106.5	1	Oral	101.2e	103.2	1
Amangeldi	103.2e	-	1	Óskemen	104.0m	105.6	1
Aqadyr	101.0j	-	1	Pavlodar	101.0i	106.7	1
Aqjal	101.3j	-	1	Petropavl	106.8n	104.7	1
Aqqý	106.4i	-	1	Prıozersk	100.7j	-	1
Aqsaı	101.4e	-	1	Qandyaǵash	101.8c	-	1
Aqtaý	100.5g	102.1	1	Qarabalyq	103.2k	-	1
Aqtóbe	102.2c	105.7	1	Qarabutaq	104.3c	-	1
Aral	101.3l	-	1	Qaraǵaıly	103.0j	-	1
Arqalyq	105.7k	101.4	1	Qaraǵandy	103.4j	102.3	1
Atasý	101.8j	-	1	Qarajal	102.1j	-	1
Atbasar	104.5b	-	1	Qarataý	103.0f	-	1
Atyraý	101.0d	102.8	1	Qaratóbe	102.4e	-	1
Baıanaýyl	103.5i	-	1	Qaraýylkeldi	101.6c	-	1
Balqash	101.0j	-	1	Qazyǵurt	106.1h	-	1
Baqanas	104.4a	100.6	1	Qorǵaljyn	101.6b	-	1
Barshatas	101.6o	-	1	Qostanaı	105.4k	107.4	1
Chapaev	101.9e	-	1	Qulsary	102.2d	106.0	1
Derjavınsk	100.3b	-	1	Qushmuryn	104.9k	-	1
Dostyq	106.2h	-	1	Qyzylorda	102.0l	101.0	1
Ekibatuz	106.9i	-	1	Rýzaevka	101.2n	-	1
Esil	102.5b	-	1	Sarqan	102.2a	105.2	1
Hromtaý	102.0c	-	1	Saryaǵash	102.3h	-	1
Inderbor	101.5d	103.2	1	Semeı	100.1m	104.4	1
Jangyztóbe	104.5m	106.9	1	Soldatovo	101.3m	-	1
Jalpaqtal	103.1e	-	1	Stepnıak	101.0b	-	1
Jarkent	101.0a	104.2	1	Stepnogor	102.2b	103.5	1
Jaryq	103.1j	-	1	Taraz	100.8f	102.6	1
Jetisaı	107.9h	-	1	Tasqala	105.6e	-	1
Jezqazǵan	103.1j	-	1	Tolqyn	-	105.0	1
Jitiqara	100.9h	-	1	Torǵaı	100.9k	-	1
Jolymbet	104.5b	-	1	Túrkistan	101.0h	102.2	1
Jympıty	102.4e	-	1	Uzynkól	104.7k	-	1
Kárim Myńbaev	105.2j	-	1	Shaǵan	101.0a	102.8	1
Kishkenekól	102.9n	-	1	Shalqar	101.4c	-	1
Kókpekti	102.2m	-	1	Shıeli	101.8l	-	1
Kókshetaý	101.0b	103.7	1	Shý	107.6f	-	1
Lısakovsk	107.2k	-	1	Shymkent	106.4h	102.7	1
Maqanshy	101.0m	103.6	1	Vozvyshenka	101.0n	-	1
Maqkat	101.2d	102.5	1	Yrgyz	101.9c	-	1
Nıkolaevka	103.8n	-	1	Zaısan	103.2m	-	1
Nur-Sultan	106.8	100.4	1	Zapadnaıa	104.7f	-	1

+ sites with txs below 1kW *) incl. reg. prgrs a-o (see below)
D.Prgrs: Prgr 1 (Qazaq radiosy): 24h in Kazakh, Russian – **Prgr 2 (Shalqar radiosy)** 0000-1800 in Kazakh – **Prgr 3 (Classic radiosy)** 24h on (MHz) Nur-Sultan 102.7, Almaty 102.8, Atasý 103.0 – **Local station: Astana radiosy** on Nur-Sultan 101.4MHz (1kW) in Kazakh, Russian: 24h.

Qazaqstan RTRK Regional Services
The regional branches (filialy) of Qazaqstan RTRK (the holding enterprise of Qazaq Radiolary JSS) broadcast at various times via txs of Prgr 1 (see FM chart). In addition, some branches are also broadcasting on own FM frequencies in Kazakh and languages of ethnic minorities.
a) Almaty qalaliq filialy: Jeltoqsan k. 177, 050013 Almaty. **E:** almatytrk@kaztrk.kz – **b) Aqmola oblystyq filialy:** Kýıbyshev k. 19, 020000 Kókshetaý. **E:** akmola@kaztrk.kz – **c) Aqtóbe oblystyq filialy:** Ahtanov k. 54, 030002 Aqtóbe. **E:** tvaktobe@gmail.com – **d) Atyraý oblystyq filialy:** Moldaǵalıev k. 29, 060005 Atyraý **E:** qazaqstan.atyrau@mail.ru. Own prgrs on 102.0MHz (Atyraý 0.25kW) – **e) Batys Qazaqstan oblystyq filialy:** Sydyqov k. 1, 090000 Oral. **E:** oral.tv@mail.ru – **f) Jambil oblystyq filialy:** Súleimenov k. 6, 080000 Taraz. **E:** taraztv@kaztrk.kz – **g) Mangistaý oblystyq filialy:** 24 shaǵyn aýdan, 130000 Aqtaý. **E:** aktautrk@gmail.com – **h) Ontýstik Qazaqstan oblystyq filialy:** Qazybek bı k. 20, 160000 Shymkent. **E:** shymkenttv@

kaztrk.kz – **i) Pavlodar oblystyq filialy:** Suraǵanov k. 21, 140006 Pavlodar. **E:** kaz.pavlodar@mail.ru. "R. Jalyk" on 100.5MHz (Pavlodar 0.5kW) + translators – **j) Qaragandy oblystyq filialy:** Jaýyngerler-internasıonalıst k. 14, 100000 Qaraǵandy. **E:** kartv@kaztrk.kz – **k) Qostanai oblystyq filialy:** Ál-Farabi dańǵyly 126, 110003 Qostanaı. **E:** office_kst@kaztrk.kz – **l) Qyzylorda oblystyq filialy:** Jeltoqsan k. 11, 120014 Qyzylorda – **m) Shygys Qazaqstan oblystyq filialy:** Stahanovskaıa k. 70, 070010 Óskemen. **E:** oskementv@kaztrk.kz. **Local station (Semei qalalyq filialy):** Shýǵaev k. 157, 071403 Semeı. "R.7" on 106.9MHz (Semeı 0.25kW) – **n) Soltýstik Qazaqstan oblystyq filialy:** Brýsılovskıı k. 1, 150000 Petropavl. **E:** petropavltv@gmail.com.

OTHER STATIONS

FM	MHz	kW	Location	Station
10)	87.7	2	Almaty	Lux FM
3)	89.6	1	Shymkent	Gakku FM
9)	89.6	2	Almaty	Business FM
13)	91.3	2	Almaty	R. Dacha
8)	91.7	1	Aqtóbe	Dala FM
2)	100.1	1	Taraz	Avtoradio
8)	100.2	2	Almaty	Dala FM
13)	100.3	1	Shymkent	R. Dacha
4B)	100.4	1	Taldyqorǵan	Juldyz FM
4A)	100.5	1	Qaraǵandy	Vostok FM
4B)	100.8	1	Nur-Sultan	Juldyz FM
14)	101.1	1	Jezagazgan	Energy FM
11)	101.2	1	Qaraǵandy	Jańa FM
5)	101.2	1	Shymkent	Love R.
13)	101.4	1	Qyzylorda	R. Dacha
2)	101.4	1	Shaǵan	Avtoradio
4A)	101.4	1	Aqtaý	Vostok FM
4A)	101.4	1	Semeı	Vostok FM
4B)	101.4	1	Almaty	Juldyz FM
14)	101.5	1	Balqash	Energy FM
13)	101.6	1	Atyraý	R. Dacha
3)	101.8	1	Almaty	Gakku FM
8)	101.8	1	Nur-Sultan	Dala FM
5)	101.9	1	Qostanaı	Love R.
14)	102.2	1	Almaty	Energy FM
13)	102.3	1	Óskemen	R. Dacha
10)	102.4	1	Taldyqorǵan	Lux FM
4B)	102.4	1	Qyzylorda	Juldyz FM
4A)	102.7	1	Aqtóbe	Vostok FM
1A)	102.8	1	Qyzylorda	Russkoye R.
13)	102.9	1	Pavlodar	R. Dacha
4B)	102.9	1	Óskemen	Juldyz FM
10)	103.1	1	Shymkent	Lux FM
14)	103.2	1	Ekibatuz	Energy FM
6)	103.2	1	Nur-Sultan	Orda FM
13)	103.3	1	Oral	R. Dacha
4A)	103.5	1	Óskemen	Vostok FM
5)	103.5	2	Almaty	Love R.
1A)	103.6	1	Taldyqorǵan	Russkoye R.
2)	103.8	1	Qostanaı	Avtoradio
5)	103.8	1	Pavlodar	Love R.
14)	104.0	1	Qyzylorda	Energy FM
1B)	104.0	1	Qaraǵandy	Europa Plus
8)	104.1	1	Petropavl	Dala FM
13)	104.3	1	Aqtóbe	R. Dacha
4A)	104.5	1	Nur-Sultan	Vostok FM
13)	104.6	1	Taraz	R. Dacha
2)	104.6	1	Qyzylorda	Avtoradio
2)	104.7	1	Óskemen	Avtoradio
4A)	104.7	1	Shymkent	Vostok FM
10)	104.8	1	Atyraý	Lux FM
1B)	105.0	1	Nur-Sultan	Europa Plus
2)	105.0	1	Pavlodar	Avtoradio
2)	105.2	1	Aqtóbe	Avtoradio
2)	105.2	1	Shymkent	Avtoradio
5)	105.2	1	Qyzylorda	Love R.
1A)	105.4	1	Aqtaý	Russkoye R.
9)	105.4	2	Nur-Sultan	Business FM
12)	105.6	1	Qaraǵandy	R. NS
2)	105.6	1	Pavlodar	Avtoradio
2)	105.8	1	Ekibatuz	Avtoradio
4A)	105.8	1	Oral	Vostok FM
12)	105.9	1	Shymkent	R. NS
11)	106.0	1	Aqsaı	Jańa FM
3)	106.0	1	Óskemen	Gakku FM
4B)	106.1	1	Kókshetaý	Juldyz FM
2)	106.2	1	Jezqazǵan	Avtoradio
8)	106.2	1	Atyraý	Dala FM
2)	106.3	1	Qaraǵandy	Avtoradio
4B)	106.3	1	Petropavl	Juldyz FM
8)	106.3	1	Shaǵan	Dala FM
10)	106.4	1	Qyzylorda	Lux FM
2)	106.4	1	Nur-Sultan	Avtoradio
13)	106.5	1	Kókshetaý	R. Dacha
4B)	106.5	1	Semeı	Juldyz FM
11)	106.6	1	Jezqazǵan	Jańa FM
4A)	106.7	1	Shaǵan	Vostok FM
4B)	106.7	1	Taraz	Juldyz FM
4B)	106.8	1	Taraz	Juldyz FM
1B)	107.0	1	Almaty	Europa Plus
4B)	107.2	1	Atyraý	Juldyz FM
8)	107.2	1	Qyzylorda	Dala FM
13)	107.3	2	Nur-Sultan	R. Dacha
8)	107.3	1	Taraz	Dala FM
10)	107.4	1	Óskemen	Lux FM
4A)	107.5	1	Almaty	Vostok FM
4A)	107.6	1	Kókshetaý	Vostok FM
14)	107.7	1	Shaǵan	Energy FM
2)	107.7	1	Atyraý	Avtoradio
4A)	107.7	1	Taraz	Vostok FM
8)	107.7	1	Qaraǵandy	Dala FM
9)	107.7	1	Shymkent	Business FM
5)	107.8	1	Aqkól	Love R.
7)	107.9	1	Óskemen	R. Miks

+ txs below 1kW.

Addresses & other information:
1A,B) Respýblıka alańy 13, 050013 Almaty – **2)** Satpaev k. 30a, 050057 Almaty – **3)** Klochkov k. 116, 050000 Almaty – **4A,B)** Qarasaı batyr k. 88, 050000 Almaty – **5)** Mynbaev k. 53, 050057 Almaty – **6)** Jeltoqsan k. 49, 010000 Nur-Sultan – **7)** Gagarın dańǵyly 11, 070000 Óskemen – **8)** Jetysu-2 39a, 050063 Almaty – **9)** Ulyqbek k. 40b, 050000 Almaty – **10)** Dostyq dańǵyly 132, 050020 Almaty – **11)** Lenın k. 10a, 100000 Qaraǵandy – **12)** Samal-1 36, 050059 Almaty – **13)** Seıfýllın dańǵyly 498, 050004 Almaty – **14)** Bógenbaı batyr k. 156/1, 050000 Almaty

KENYA

L.T: UTC +3h — **Pop:** 54 million — **Pr.L:** Swahili (official), English (official), Kikuyu, Luhya, Luo, Kalenjin, Somali — **E.C:** 240V/50Hz — **ITU:** KEN

COMMUNICATIONS AUTHORITY OF KENYA

✉ P.O. Box 14448, Nairobi 00800 ☎+254 20 4242000 **W:** ca.go.ke **E:** info@ca.go.ke

KENYA BROADCASTING CORPORATION (KBC, Pub.)

✉ P.O. Box 30456, Nairobi 00100 ☎+254 20 2766000 🖷 +254 20 2220675 **W:** kbc.co.ke **E:** md@kbc.co.ke

MW	kHz	kW	Netw.	MW	kHz	kW	Netw.
Garissa	567	50	S	Marsabit	1233	50	N
Garissa	639	50	S	Maralal	1386	50	E/N
Marsabit	675	50	S				

FM	S	E	Co	Pw	Mi	Ki	Ma	Mw	I
Limuru*	92.9	95.6	99.5	-	-	98.0	-	-	101.9
Malindi	96.5	93.3	-	93.7	-	-	-	-	-
Meru**	90.4	103.5	-	-	-	-	-	100.3	-
Nyeri	87.6	100.7	102.3	-	-	-	-	-	-
Mombasa	100.7	103.1	-	104.7	-	-	-	-	-
Timboroa	88.6	91.5	-	-	-	-	-	-	-
Nakuru	104.1	96.5	-	-	-	-	-	-	-
Eldoret						92.9			
Kisumu	88.6	91.5	-	-	-	-	93.5		
Kisii	103.3	-	-	-	101.7	-	-	-	-
Nyadundo	-	-	99.7	-	-	-	-	-	-

*Limuru txs serve Greater Nairobi. **) also called Nyambene.

Networks (from Nairobi studios unless stated):
S=Swahili Sce "Radio Taifa": 0200-2100 on MW, 24h on FM. – **E=English Sce**: 0200-2105 (on FM, non-stop music 2105-0200). Includes relays of CRI 1700-1800 & BBC. Also on 1386 kHz mornings and irregularly overnight – **N= Northeastern Sce**: 0230-2105: Turkana on 1386kHz in the evening, Borana, Burji & Rendille on 1233kHz – **I= Iftiin FM** in Somali on 101.9MHz – **Co=Coro FM**

in Kikuyu – **Pw=Pwani FM** from Mombasa studios – **Mi=Minto FM** (from Keroka studios in Kisii) – **Ki=Kitwek FM** in Kalenjin – **Ma=Mayienga FM** (from Kisumu studios in Luo) – **Mw=Mwago FM** in Meru – **Ingo FM**: western Kenya on 100.5MHz in Luhya – **Mwatu FM**: Kibwezi 93.1MHz in Kamba – **Nosim FM:** Narok 90.5MHz in Masai.
Ann: E: "This is KBC English Service". **IS:** Flute & drum melody in some services.

ROYAL MEDIA SERVICES LTD. (RMS)
P.O. Box 7468, Nairobi 00300 ☎+254 20 2721415/6 +254 20 2724211 **W:** royalmediaservices.co.ke **E:** info@royalmedia.co.ke

FM(MHz): **R. Citizen** in Swahili/Eng: Eldoret 90.4, Voi 91.8, Chuka 93.1, Machakos 94.2, Meru 94.3, Kibwezi 95.4, Narok 95.5, Garissa 95.7, Maralal 95.9, Kapenguria 96.1, Kanyenyeini 96.5, Wajir 97.0, Mombasa 97.3, Malindi 97.4, Kisumu 97.6, Marsabit 98.0, Kitui 98.6, Nakuru 100.5, Nyadundo 103.6, Nyeri 104.3, Homa Bay 105.2, Nairobi/Namanga 106.7 – **Hot 96 FM** in Eng/Sheng/Swahili: Nairobi 96.0, Eldoret 87.6, Kisumu 103.1, Mombasa 90.4, Nakuru 102.5, Nyeri 88.6

RMS also operates the following stns for specific lang. communities:

FM(MHz)**: Bahari FM** (in Swahili & coastal langs): Mombasa&Nairobi 94.2 – **Chamgei FM** (in Kalenjin): Kericho 90.2, Nairobi 90.4, Nakuru 95.0, Eldoret 97.5 – **Egesa FM** (in Kisii): Kisii 94.6, Nairobi 103.2 – **Inooro FM** (in Kikuyu): Nyadundo 88.9, Nakuru 89.8, Meru 95.1, Muranga 96.9, Nyeri 97.8, Nairobi 98.9, Mombasa 99.2, Chuka 102.0, Eldoret 107.0 – **Mulembe FM** (in Luhya): Webuye 89.6, Rift Valley 94.0, Eldoret 95.8, Nairobi 97.9 – **Musyi FM** (in Kamba): Nairobi 102.2, Kitui 103.6 – **Muuga FM** (in Meru): Nairobi/Meru 88.9 – **R. Maa** (in Maasai): 103.5 – **Ramogi FM** (in Luo): Nakuru 95.4, Mombasa 96.0, Homa Bay 97.0, Siaya 98.4, Nairobi 107.1, Kisumu 107.6 – **Sulwe FM** (in Bukusu): Nairobi 89.6 – **Wimwaro FM** (in Embu): Embu 93.0 – **Vuuka FM** (in Maragoli): Nairobi 95.4, Kisumu 100.4.

RADIO AFRICA LTD.
P.O. Box 74497, Nairobi ☎+254 20 4244000 +254 20 4447410 **W:** the-star.co.ke **E:** info@kissfm.co.ke

FM(MHz): **Kiss 100** in Eng/Swahili: Nairobi 100.3, Eldoret 89.1, Kisumu 92.5, Meru 93.5, Mombasa 88.7, Nakuru 98.1, Nyeri 100.1, Webuye 104.7 – **Classic 105 FM** in Eng/Swahili: Nakuru 95.7, Nairobi 105.2, Mombasa 107.5 – **East FM** (Asian): Nairobi 106.3, Mombasa 89.5 – **Jambo Turkana**: Lokakuma 90.1, Lokori 90.5, Lokichogio 92.1, Lokapedo 92.4, Lodwar 92.7, Lokitaung 94.5, Lokalokol 96.7, Lotodonyang 96.1 – **R. Jambo** (sports): Kisii 89.3, Mombasa 92.3, Meru 92.7, Webuye 95.3, Nakuru 96.9, Maralal/Narok/Nyahururu 97.3, Nairobi 97.5, Malindi 98.1, Nyeri 99.3, Eldoret 99.5, Kapenguria 99.7, Kisumu 100.1, Garissa 104.3, Kibwezi/Lamu 104.7, Kitui 104.9, Voi 105.7 – **Smooth FM** (old pop favourites): Nairobi 105.5 – **Relax FM** (R&B music): Nairobi 103.0.

MEDIAMAX NETWORK LTD
P. O. Box 103618, 3rd Floor, DSM Place, Kijabe St., Nairobi 00101 ☎+254 20 4944 100 **W:** mediamaxnetwork.co.ke
E: info@mediamax.co.ke

FM(MHz): **Emoo FM** (in Kalenjin): Kericho 90.8, Eldoret 91.8, Narok 92.6, Nakuru 100.2, Nairobi 104.2, Bomet 105.3 – **Kameme FM** (mainly in Kikuyu): Meru 88.3, Nyeri 92.3, Nakuru 99.3, Nairobi 101.1, Eldoret 101.9. Also rel. BBC – **Mayian FM** (in Maasai): Maralal 100.5, Kajiado, Narok 100.7 – **Meru FM**: Meru 88.3, Mombasa&Garissa 100.3, Nakuru&Nyeri 101.3, Machakos 107.8 – **Milele FM** (in Swahili): Kapenguria 88.3, Voi 89.7, Nakuru/Nyahururu 90.2, Kitui/Lamu 91.3, Nyeri 91.7, Webuye 92.7, Kisii 95.1, Migori 95.7, Mombasa 96.7, Maralal 98.7, Kisumu 99.7, Garissa 99.9, Malindi 101.3, Meru 101.5, Eldoret 103.1, Kibwezi 104.3, Nairobi 104.8 – **Msenangu FM** (in Mijikenda): Malindi 92.5, Lamu 94.7, Mombasa 99.5, Kilifi 101.0, Kwale&Voi 102.1

OTHER FM STNS IN NAIROBI (including relays elsewhere; freqs are in Nairobi unless stated, & in MHz): **ATG Radio**: 91.1, Voi 88.5, Kibwezi 95.1 – **Biblia Husema Broadcasting** (Christian): 96.7, Eldoret 96.3, Lokichokio 102.5, Nakuru 102.9, Machakos 96.7, Timboroa 101.5 – **Capital FM** (in Eng): 98.4, Garissa 102.7, Kitui 106.5, Malindi 104.5, Meru 103.9, Mombasa 98.4, Nakuru 98.5, Nyeri 98.5, Timboroa 93.0, Voi 104.9 – **Choice R.** (in Eng): 87.7 **W:** facebook.com/ChoiceRadioKE – **East Africa R.** (in Eng/Swahili - relay of Tanzanian stn): 94.7 – **Family R. 316** (Christian): 103.9, Kisumu 96.5, Mombasa 97.9, Nakuru 102.1 – **FunX Cool:** 91.3 **W:** facebook.com/FunXCoolKe – **Gukena FM:** 92.2, Mt. Kenya/Nakuru 92.8 – **Homeboyz R.:** 103.5, Eldoret 91.2 **W:** hbr.co.ke – **Hope FM** (Pentecostal Church): 93.3, Mombasa 101.9, Timboroa 93.9 – **Iqra FM** (Islamic): 95.0 – **Kass FM** (in Kalenjin): 89.1, Eldoret 90.0, Kisumu 91.0, Nakuru 92.5, Kisii 99.3, Mombasa 102.7 – **Kubamba R.**: 91.6 – **Mbaitu FM**: 92.5, Kitui 100.4, Makueni 100.5 – **Qwetu R:** 95.3, Kisumu 99.1, Mombasa 92.0, Webuye 98.0 – **R. Maisha** 102.7, Nakuru 104.5, Mombasa/Meru 105.1, Kisumu 105.3, Nyeri 105.7 – **R. Nam Lolwe:** 101.5, Kisumu 97.3, Mombasa 94.7, Nakuru 87.7 – **R. Waumini:** 88.3. **W:** catholicchurch.or.ke – **Sound Asia:** 88.0, Mombasa 89.9 – **Star FM** (in Somali/Swahili/Eng): 105.9, Dadaab/Garissa 97.1, Wajir 97.3, Mandera 97.5. Also rel. BBC **W:** starfm.co.ke – **Truth FM:** 90.7 – **Uptown Radio:** 91.1– **Virgin R:** 97.1 **W:** virginradio.com
NB: 99.9MHz is assigned for use in Nairobi by several very low-powered community stns. There are many private FM stns outside Nairobi.

Relays of international stations:
BBC WS (E/Swahili): Kisumu 88.1, Nairobi/Mombasa 93.9MHz
China R. Int: Nairobi 91.9MHz
RFI Afrique (F/E/Swahili): Nairobi 89.9, Mombasa 105.5MHz
VOA (E/Swahili): Nairobi 107.5MHz

KIRIBATI

L.T: Gilbert Islands: UTC +12h, Phoenix Islands: +13h, Line Islands: +14h — **Pop:** 120,000 — **Pr.L:** Kiribati (official), English (official) — **E.C:** 240V/50Hz — **ITU:** KIR

COMMUNICATIONS COMMISSION OF KIRIBATI
PO Box 529, Betio, Tarawa ☎ +686 75125431/75125488 **W:** cck.ki
E: enquiry@cck.ki
Regulator of broadcasting in Kiribati [including Kiritimati Island]

RADIO KIRIMATI
Ronton, Kiritimati Island, Kiribati, Central Pacific

MW	kHz	kW	Station
1) London Settlement	846	10	R. Kiribati
1) Bairiki	1440	10	R. Kiribati
FM	**MHz**	**kW**	**Station**
1) Ronton	93.5	0.5	R. Kiribati Kiritimati FM

Other Stations:

FM	MHz	kW	Station
1) Bairiki	88.0	0.1	Mauri FM 88
2) Betio	89.0		Newair FM
3) Bairiki	90.0		R. Australia
4) Bairiki	95.0		BBC
4) Tarawa	100.0		BBC
2) Bairiki	101.0		Newair FM

Addresses & other information
1) BROADCASTING & PUBLICATIONS AUTHORITY – Radio Kiribati PO Box 78, Bairiki, Tarawa **LP:** CEO Teannaki Tongaua **E:** ceo@bpa.org.ki Mgr Program & Publications Mrs Reita Andrew **E:** program-publications@bpa.org.ki Engineering Netw. Mgr Babera Marewenimakin **E:** engineering-network@bpa.org.ki ☎ +686 75121457 +686 75121096. **E:** radio.kiribati@gmail.com **W:** bpa.org.ki Audio streaming at Icecast 202.6.120.13:8000 **MW:** Bairiki 1440kHz 10kW **FM:** 88.0MHz 0.1kW [relays MW] **D.Prgr:** I-Kiribati (90%) English (10%): 1855-2030, 0000-0130, 0500-1000 **N. in English:** 2000, 0100, 1800 (RNZI) followed by local news bulletin [r.relaying other RNZI programs irregularly]. Incl. sponsored programs from government agencies, international agencies on AM, with spot advertising only on FM. **Ann:** "This is Radio Kiribati, the national broadcasting service of Kiribati in the Central Pacific" "Aio bwanaan Kiribati te botaki ni kanako bwanaa I bukin Kiribati I nukan te Betebeke".
Radio Kiribati Kiritimati FM Prgr: Satellite feed from R. Kiribati 88.0 FM and local originated prgrs for Kiritimati (Christmas) Island in the Line Islands [Responsibility of Kiritimati Branch Broadcasting Services via Engineering Netw Mgr]. – **2)** PO Box 204, Bairiki, Tarawa. **LP:** Sir Ieremia Tabai. **D.Prgr:** Local commercial prgrs in English & I-Kiribati ☎ +686 75121671 **E:** newairfm89kiribati@gmail.com – **3)** 24/7 Pacific stream in English via satellite from Melbourne – **4)** 24/7 Pacific stream in English via satellite from London.

KOREA, North

L.T: UTC +9h — **Pop:** 26 million — **Pr.L:** Korean — **E.C:** 220V/50Hz — **ITU:** KRE

THE RADIO AND TELEVISION BROADCASTING COMMITTEE OF THE DEMOCRATIC PEOPLE'S REPUBLIC OF KOREA

✉ Jonsung-dong, Moranbong District, Pyongyang ☎ +850 2 816035

KOREAN CENTRAL BROADCASTING STATION (Joson Jung-ang Pangsong)

✉ Jonsung-dong, Moranbong District, Pyongyang ☎ +850 2 812301

MW	kHz	kW	Prgr	MW	kHz	kW	Prgr
Chongjin	‡702	50	C	Sinuiju	873	250	C#
Wiwon	*720	500	C	Wonsan	‡882	250	C
Hyesan	‡765	50	C	Hwangju	+‡927	50	C
Kaesong	810	50	C	Hamhung	‡999	250	C
Pyongyang	819	500	C	Pyongyang	1368	2	E

SW	kHz	Prgr	SW	kHz	Prgr
Sariwon	‡2350	C	Kanggye	3959	C
Pyongyang	‡2850	C	Wonsan	‡3968	C
Pyongyang	3205	C	Chongjin	‡3980	C
Hamhung	3220	C	Kanggye	6100	C
Pyongyang	3250	C	Pyongyang	9665	C
Pyongsong	‡3350	C	Kanggye	11680	C
Hyesan	3920	C			

*= Kanggye, += Sariwon, ‡=inactive, C = Central Broadcast from Pyongyang, # = carries Pyongyang Broadcasting Station between 0300-0500 (local time) E = rel. Ext. Sce

NB: all freqs variable **FM:** Kaesong 102.3MHz

D.Prgr. in Korean: 2000-1800 on all freqs exc. 6100 (2000-0850 & 1300-1800). **N:** 2100, 2200, 0100, 0300, 0600, 0800, 1100, 1200, 1300. Regional Prgrs: W0500-0600. Rel. Pyongyang Broadc. St: 1500-1800 on 702/720/864kHz 1500-2000 on 102.3MHz 1800-2000 on 3220kHz **Ann:** "Joson Jung-ang Pangsong-imnida". Reg. Prgrs: "(location) Pangsong-imnida". **IS:** Song of General Kim Il Sung. Opening & closing music: Nat. Anthem. **V:** not verified

EXTERNAL SERVICES: Voice of Korea, Pyongyang Broadcasting Station, Echo of Unification– See International Radio section

PYONGYANG FM BROADCASTING STATION (Pyongyang FM Pangsong)

FM	MHz	kW	FM	MHz	kW
Pyongsong	90.1	2	Sariwon	103.0	2
Kaesong	92.5	2	Haeju	103.7	10
Kanggye	93.3	5	Pyongyang	105.2	20
Hyesan	93.8	2	Chongjin	105.5	10
Wonsan	95.1	5	Hamhung	106.1	20
Sinuiju	‡101.3	5	Nampo	107.2	2
Komdok	102.1	1			

‡=inactive

D.Prgr: 0700-2000, 2100-0000 (National holidays: 2100-2030) (music and drama) **Ann:** "Pyongyang FM Pangsong-imnida". **IS:** Song of General Kim Jong Il. Opening music: Pyongyang Is My Heart

KOREAN PEOPLE'S ARMY FM BROADCASTING STATION (Joson Inmingun FM Pangsong)

FM: 95.5MHz **Ann:** "Joson Inmingun FM Pangsong-imnida"

KOREA, South

L.T: UTC +9h — **Pop:** 51 million — **Pr.L:** Korean — **E.C:** 220V/60Hz — **ITU:** KOR

KOREA COMMUNICATIONS COMMISSION

✉ 47 Gwanmun-ro, Gwacheon-si, Gyeonggi-do, Republic of Korea ☎ +82 2 5009000 **W:** kcc.go.kr **L.P:** Chair: Han Sang-Hyuk

KOREAN BROADCASTING SYSTEM (KBS) (Hanguk Bangsong Gongsa) (Public Corporation)

✉13, Yeouigongwon-ro, Yeongdeungpo-gu, Seoul 07235 ☎ +82 2 781 1000 🖷 +82 2 761 2499 **W:** kbs.co.kr

L.P: Pres & CEO: Yang Sung-dong. Auditor Gen.: Kim Young-Heon. Exec.Vice Pres: Lim Byung-Kul, Exec. Man. Dirs:Han Chang-Rok (Programming), Kook Eun-Ju (Strategy & Planning), Kim Jong-Myong (N & Sports), Rhee Sang-Woon (Content Production 1), Lee Hun-Hee (Content Production 2), Lee Chang-Hyung (Tech), Cho Hyun-Guk (Man.).

MW	Location	Call	kHz	kW	MW	Location	Call	kHz	kW
13)	Daegu+2	QH	558	250	16)	Changwon 3	-	936	10
9)	Jeonju+	KF	567	100	19)	Jeju+	KS	963	10
12)	Suncheon 3		576	1	14)	Andong+	CR	963	10
N2)	Namyang*	SA	603	500	K1)	Dangjin*	CA	972	1500
12)	Yeosu	-	630	10	15)	Pohang+	CP	1035	10
3)	Chuncheon+	KM	657	50	6)	Cheongju+	KQ	1062	50
9)	Jeonju 3	-	675	10	18)	Jinju+	CJ	1098	20
N1)	Sorae*	KA	711	500	N3)	Hwaseong*	KC	1134	500
13)	Daegu+	KG	738	100	5)	Wonju+	CW	1152	10
10)	Gwangju+	KH	747	100	K2E)	Gimje*	SR	1170	500
4)	Gangneung+	KR	864	100	17)	Ulsan+	QB	1449	10
8)	Daejeon+	KI	882	20	11)	Mokpo+	KN	1467	50
2)	Busan+	KB	891	250					

MW: N1 = KBS R. One, N2 = KBS R. Two, N3 = KBS R. Three, K1 = Global Korean Network 1, K2 = Global Korean Network 2, E = also used for Ext. sce., KBS WORLD R, N = Netw. or local stn. area

*) = Key stn, +) = Regional key St, 2 = rel N2 exc. for local prgrs, 3 = rel N3 (other local stns take N1), **Call**: HL (call)

NB: Global Korean Network stns and FM-stns do not use call letters (even if assigned). Other stns without call letters use the calls from their regional key stns.

FM	Location	I	II	III	kW
1)	Gwanaksan	97.3*	93.1	89.1a	10/10/10
1)	Gwanaksan	-	-	106.1b	10
1)	Gwanaksan	-	-	104.9c	2
1)	Yongmunsan	90.3*	-	-	1
2)	Hwangnyeongsan	103.7	92.7	97.1b	3/5/3
3)	Hwaaksan	99.5*	91.1	98.7b	5/5/3
4)	Gwaebangsan	98.9*	89.1	102.1b	3/5/5
5)	Baegunsan	97.1	89.5	-	1/3
5)	Taegisan	95.5*	-	-	1
4)	Hambaeksan	93.7*	97.3	-	1/3
4)	Chorokbong	88.5	-	-	1
6)	Sikchangsan	-	102.1	-	3
8)	Sikchangsan	-	-	100.9b	3
8)	Heukseongsan	89.9*	-	-	1
6)	Uamsan	89.3	94.1	90.9b	1/1/1
7)	Gayeopsan	92.1*	100.3	-	1/3
8)	Gyeryongsan	94.7*	98.5	-	3/5
9)	Moaksan	96.9*	100.7	92.9b	5/5/3
9)	Nogodan	88.3*	104.5	-	1/3
10)	Mudeungsan	90.5*	92.3	95.5b	5/5/3
11)	Yangulsan	-	98.3	-	1
11)	Daedunsan	105.9	-	-	2
12)	Namsan	-	-	102.7b	1
12)	Mangunsan	95.7*	94.5	-	1/3
13)	Palgongsan	101.3*	89.7	102.3b	5/5/3
14)	Ilwolsan	90.5*	-	-	1
14)	Hakkasan	-	88.1	-	3
15)	Johangsan	95.9*	93.5	-	1/3
15)	Hyeonjongsan	93.9	-	-	1
16)	Bulmosan	91.7*	93.9	106.1b	5/1/3
17)	Muryongsan	90.7*	101.9	-	1/3
18)	Gamaksan	-	92.1	-	3
18)	Mangjinsan	90.3	89.3	-	1/1
19)	Gyeonwolak	99.1*	96.3	91.9b	3/3/3
19)	Sammaebong	95.3	99.9	89.7b	3/3/3

+ low power relay stns

Reg = region in MW section. I-Standard FM (R. One); II-KBS FM One; III a = KBS FM Two, b = R. Two, c=R. Three. *) also SCA (R. Three)

KBS R. One (KBS Je-il Radio, HLKA): 24h Non-commercial nationwide news sce. Key freqs 711kHz, 90.3/97.3MHz. Also rel. by Standard FM stns and most reg. stns. Reg. stns may broadcast local prgrs at designated times. **N:** hourly 2000-1500 except 1100(W), 2000(Sat & Sun). Local N: 2205(Sun), 2210(W), 0000(Sun), 0005(w), 0310(Sun), 0315(W), 0605, 0805(Mon-Fri), 0900(Sun), 0905(W)

KBS R. Two (KBS Je-i Radio, Happy FM, HLSA): 2000-1800 (558kHz to 1500). Commercial. Key freq's 603kHz/106.1MHz. Reg. stns may broadcast local prgrs at designated times. **N:** 2200(w), 1100(w). Global Korean Network prgr 1700-1800

KBS R. Three (KBS Je-sam Radio, Sarang-ui Sori Bangsong, HLKC): 2100-1800. Non-comm. sce. **N:** 0100(W), 0300(W), 0500(w), 1200.

Global Korean Network prgr 2100-2200
KBS FM One (KBS Je-il FM Bangsong, Classic FM, HLKA-FM): 24h. Mainly Korean traditional and western classical music
KBS FM Two (KBS Je-i FM Bangsong. Cool FM, HLKC-FM): 24h. Mainly Korean and western popular and light classical music
Ann: N1: "AM Chilbaek-sib-il (711)kHz, FM Gusib-chil-jeom-sam(97.3)MHz, KBS II Radiomnida. HLKA". **N2:** "KBS Happy FM, Je-i Radiomnida". **N3:** "KBS Sam Radio, Sarang-ui Sori Bangsong-imnida. HLKC".

Addresses of key regional stations:
2) 429, Suyeong-ro, Suyeong-gu, Busan 48316 – **3)** 109, Bangsong-gil, Chuncheon-si, Gangwon-do 24363 – **4)** 13, Imyeong-ro 131beon-gil, Gangneung-si, Gangwon-do 25534 – **5)** 37, Wonil-ro, Wonju-si, Gangwon-do 26432 – **6)** 1428, Seobu-ro, Heungdeok-gu, Cheongju-si, Chungcheongbuk-do 28637 – **7)** 3448, Jungwon-daero, Chungju-si, Chungcheongbuk-do 27428 – **8)** 128, Dunsan-daero 117beon-gil, Seo-gu, Daejeon 35203 – **9)** 30, Majeonjungang-ro, Wansan-gu, Jeonju-si, Jeollabuk-do 54962 –**10)** 287, Uncheon-ro, Seo-gu, Gwangju 61946 – **11)** 221, Yangeul-ro, Mokpo-si, Jeollanam-do 58613 – **12)** 250, Jungang-ro, Suncheon-si, Jeollanam-do 57938 – **13)** 30, Dalgubeol-daero 496-gil, Suseong-gu, Daegu 42095 – **14)** 27, Gamnamu 3-gil, Andong-si, Gyeongsangbuk-do 36647 – **15)** 72, Jungseom-ro, Nam-gu, Pohang-si, Gyeongsangbuk-do 37771 – **16)** 178, Jungang-daero, Changwon-si, Gyeongsangnam-do 51444 – **17)** 212, Beonyeong-ro, Nam-gu, Ulsan 44702 – **18)** 85, Sinan-ro, Jinju-si, Gyeongsangnam-do 52695 – **19)** 8, Bokji-ro 1-gil, Jeju-si, Jeju 63220.
Local identifications: Within local prgrs. **N1**: just before the h. 2000, 2100(Sat & Sun), 2200, 2300, 0000(W), 0100-0900, 1000(W), 1100(Sat & Sun), 1300-1600, 1700(Sat & Sun), 1800, 1900. **N2**: just before the h. 2000-1700. **N3**: just before the h. 2100-1800. **FM One**: just before the h. at 2000-2200, 0000, 0200, 0300, 0500, 0700-0900, 1100, 1300, 1500, 1600, 1800. **FM Two**: just before the h

Digital service (UKBS Music): 177.008MHz (Daegu/Pohang/Suncheon), 183.008MHz (Gwangju/Mokpo/Seogwipo), 189.008MHz(Jinju/Andong), 201.008MHz (Daejeon/Cheongju/Chungju), 207.008MHz (Seoul/Busan/Ulsan/Changwon/Jeonju), 213.008MHz (Chuncheon/Gangneung/Wonju/Jeju-si): 24h

EXTERNAL SERVICES: KBS WORLD RADIO, KBS Global Korean Network (Hanminjok Bangsong) See International Radio section

KOREA EDUCATIONAL BROADCASTING SYSTEM (EBS) (Gyoyuk Bangsong) (Pub.)

✉ 281, Hallyu world-ro, Ilsandong-gu, Goyang-si, Gyeonggi-do 10393 ☎ +82 2 526 2000 🖷 +82 2 526 2419 **W:** ebs.co.kr
Call letters HLQL used for all the stns.

FM	Tx location	MHz	kW
Chungju	Gayeopsan	104.1	3
Changwon	Bulmosan	104.3	3
Seoul	Gwanaksan	104.5	10
Jinju	Gamaksan	104.7	3
Gangneung	Gwaebangsan	104.9	3
Wonju	Baegunsan	104.9	3
Seogwipo	Sammaebang	104.9	3
Daegu	Palgongsan	105.1	5
Gwangju	Mudeungsan	105.3	5
Daejeon	Gyeryongsan	105.7	5
Ulsan	Muryongsan	105.9	3
Yeosu	Mangunsan	106.3	3
Chuncheon	Hwaaksan	106.5	3
Pohang	Johangsan	106.7	3
Jeonju	Moaksan	106.9	5
Taebaek	Hambaeksan	107.1	3
Jeju	Gyeonwolak	107.3	3
Namwom	Nogodan	107.5	3
Daegu	Ilwolsan	107.7	3
Busan	Hwangnyeongsan	107.7	3
Cheongju	Sikjangsan	107.9	3

+ low power relay stns
D.Prgr: 2000-1700 **Ann:** "EBS, Gyoyuk Bangsong-imnida"

GUGAK FM BROADCASTING SYSTEM (Gugak Bangsong) (Pub.)

✉ DMS Bldg., 12, World Cup Buk-ro 54-gil, Mapo-gu, Seoul 03925 ☎ +82 2 300 9990 🖷 +82 2 300 9959
W: gugakfm.co.kr

Stations: Seoul HLQA-FM 99.1MHz 5kW: 24h, Daejeon HLEK-FM 90.5MHz 1kW: 24h, Namwon 95.9MHz 1kW: 24h, Namdo 94.7MHz 0.5kW: 24h, Gyeongju/Pohang 107.9MHz 1kW: 24h, Jeonju 95.3MHz 1kW: 24h, Busan 98.5MHz 1kW: 24h, Gangneung 103.3MHz 1kW: 24h, Daegu 107.5MHz 1kW: 24h, Gwangju HLEG-FM 99.3MHz 1kw: 24h, Jeju(Hallasan) 91.3MHz 1kW: 24h, Jeju(Sammaebong) 106.9MHz 1kW: 24h. + low power relay stns **Ann:** "Gugak Bangsong-imnida"

MUNHWA BROADCASTING CORP. (MBC) (Munhwa Bangsong) Nationwide comm. netw.

✉267, Seongam-ro, Mapo-gu, Seoul 03925 ☎ +82 2 789 0011 **W:** imbc.com

MW	Call	kHz	kW	Station	MW	Call	kHz	kW	Station
1)	CQ	765	10	Daejeon MBC	11)	AT	1080	10	Yeosu MBC
2)	AJ	774	10	Jeju MBC	12)	AV	1107	10	Pohang MBC
3)	AN	774	10	Chuncheon MBC	13)	KU	1161	20	Busan MBC
4)	CT	‡810	20	Daegu MBC	14)	AK	1215	10	Jinju MBC
5)	CN	819	20	Gwangju MBC	15)	SB	1242	10	Wonju MBC
6)	AU	846	10	Ulsan MBC	16)	AF	1287	10	Gangneung MBC
7)	CX	855	10	Jeonju MBC	17)	AX	1287	10	Cheongju MBC
8)	KV	900	50	Seoul MBC	18)	AO	‡1332	10	Chungju MBC
9)	AP	‡990	10	Changwon MBC	19)	AQ	1350	10	Samcheok MBC
10)	AW	1017	10	Andong MBC	20)	AM	1386	10	Mokpo MBC

‡=inactive
D.Prgr: All 24h

FM	Location	Music FM MHz	Music FM kW	Standard FM MHz	Standard FM kW
8)	Seoul	91.9	10	95.9	10
13)	Busan	88.9	5	95.9	3
4)	Daegu	95.3	5	96.5	5
5)	Gwangju	91.5	5	93.9	5
	Gwangju	95.1	3	-	
1)	Daejeon	97.5	5	92.5	3
7)	Jeonju	99.1	5	94.3	2
	Jeonju (Namwon)	-		101.7	3
9)	Changwon	100.5	1	98.9	3
3)	Chuncheon	94.5	3	92.3	3
17)	Cheongju	99.7	1	107.1	1
2)	Jeju	90.1	3	97.9	1
	Jeju (Seogwipo)	102.9	3	97.1	1
6)	Ulsan	98.7	3	97.5	1
16)	Gangneung	94.3	5	96.3	3
14)	Jinju	97.7	1	91.1	3
	Jinju	96.1	3	93.5	1
20)	Mokpo	102.3	1	89.1	2
11)	Yeosu	98.3	2	100.3	1
10)	Andong	91.3	3	100.1	3
15)	Wonju	98.9	3	92.7	1
	Wonju	-		102.5	1
18)	Chungju	88.7	3	96.1	1
19)	Samcheok	98.1	3	101.5	1
	Samcheok	99.9	1	93.1	3
12)	Pohang	97.9	3	100.7	3
	Pohang (Uljin)	94.9	1	102.7	1

+low power relay stations
NB: Standard FM stns simulcast with the MW stn in the same city. A separate sce. is provided to the Music FM stns. All regional stns broadcast a combination of a feed from Seoul and their own local prgrs. Standard FM stns follow the same schedule as their corresponding MW outlet. Music FM of Seoul MBC sched: 24h
Ann: "(freq. and location) Munhwa Bangsong-imnida. (Call)" or "Munhwa Bangsong-imnida" or "MBC". Seoul: "Jungpa Gubaek (900)kHz, Pyojun FM Gushib-o-jeom-gu 95.9MHz Munhwa Bangsong-imnida"

Addresses & other information:
NB: Add "(location) Munhwa Broadc. Corp." to addr.
1) 161, EXPO-ro, Yuseong-gu, Daejeon 34125 **W:** tjmbc.co.kr – **2)** 35, Munyeon-ro, Jeju-si, Jeju Special Self-do 63120 **W:** jejumbc.co.kr – **3)** 54, Subyengongwon-gil, Chuncheon-si, Gangwon-do 24239 **W:** chmbc.co.kr – **4)** 400, Dongdaegu-ro, Suseong-gu, Daegu 42020 **W:**dgmbc.co.kr – **5)** 17, Wolsan-ro 116byeon-gil, Nam-gu, Gwangju 61629 **W:** kjmbc.co.kr – **6)** 65, Seowon 3-gil, Jung-gu, Ulsan 44512 **W:**usmbc.co.kr – **7)** 50, Sanneomeo 1-gil, Wansan-gu, Jeonju-si, Jeollabuk-do 54986 **W:** jmbc.co.kr – **8)** National addr. – **9)** 11-11, Yangdeokseo 9-gil, Masan Hoewon-gu, Changwon-si, Gyeongsangnam-do 51322 **W:** mbcgn.co.kr – **10)** 20, Dangwon-ro, Andong-si, Gyeongsangbuk-do 36645 **W:** andongmbc.co.kr – **11)**

135, Munsu-ro, Yeosu-si, Jeollanam-do 59700 **W:** ysmbc.co.kr – **12)** 421, Saecheingnyeng-ro, Pohang-si, Gyeongsangbuk-do 37685 **W:** phmbc.co.kr – **13)** 69, Gamporo 8beon-gil, Suyeong-gu. Busan 48276 **W:** busanmbc.co.kr – **14)** 13, Gaho-ro, Jinju-si, Gyeongsangnam-do 52817 **W:** mbcgn.co.kr – **15)** 67, Hakseong-gil, Wonju-si, Gangwon-do 26412 **W:** wjmbc.co.kr – **16)** 267, Gajak-ro, Gangneung-si, Gangwon-do 25477 **W:** mbceg.co.kr – **17)** 1322, 2 Sunhwan-ro, Heungdeok-gu, Cheongju-si, Chungcheongbuk-do 28382 **W:**mbccb.co.kr – **18)** 3250, Jungwon-daero, Chungju-si, Chungcheongbuk-do 27480 **W:**mbccb.co.kr – **19)** 629-59, Saecheongnyeon-doro, Samcheok-si, Gangwon-do 25909 **W:** mbceg.co.kr – **20)** 334, Yeongsan-ro, Mokpo-si, Jeollanam-do 58700 **W:**mpmbc.co.kr

CHRISTIAN BROADCASTING SYSTEM (CBS) (Gidokkyo Bangsong)

MW	Call	kHz	kW	Station and h.of tr.
1)	KY	837	50	CBS Seoul: 24h
2)	CL	999	10	CBS Gwangju: 2000-1600
4)	KT	1251	10	CBS Daegu: 2000-1600
5)	CM	1314	10	CBS Jeonbuk: 2000-1600
6)	KP	1404	10	CBS Busan: 2000-1600

CBS FM	Call	MHz	kW	h. of tr.
1) CBS-FM Seoul	HLKY-FM	93.9	7	24h (Music FM)
1) CBS Seoul	HLKY-SFM	98.1	10	24h
2) CBS Gwangju	HLCL-SFM	103.1	5	2000-1600
2) CBS-FM Gwangju	HLEM-FM	98.1	1	24h (Music FM)
3) CBS Jeonnam	HLCL-FM	102.1	2	2000-1600
4) CBS Daegu	HLKT-SFM	103.1	5	2000-1600
4) CBS-FM Daegu	HLKT-FM	97.1	1	24h (Music FM)
5) CBS Jeonbuk	HLCM-SFM	103.7	5	2000-1600
6) CBS Busan	HLKP-SFM	102.9	5	2000-1600
6) CBS-FM Busan	HLKP-FM	102.1	1	24h (Music FM)
7) CBS Cheongju	HLAC-FM	91.5	3	2000-1600
8) CBS Gangwon	HLDC-FM	93.7	3	2000-1600
8) CBS Gangwon	(W)	94.9	1	2000-1600
9) CBS Daejeon	HLDX-FM	91.7	5	2000-1600
10) CBS Pohang	HLCB-FM	91.5	3	2000-1600
11) CBS Gyeongnam	HLCC-FM	106.9	5	2000-1600
12) CBS Jeju	HLKO-FM	93.3	3	2000-1600
12) CBS Jeju	(S)	90.9	1	2000-1600
13) CBS Yeongdong	HLCO-FM	91.5	3	2000-1600
14) CBS Ulsan	HLKP-FM	100.3	3	2000-1600

+low power relay stns. (W)=Wonju relay st. (S)= Seogwipo relay st

Addresses & other information:

1) 159-1, Mokdongseo-ro, Yangcheon-gu, Seoul 07997 ☎ +82 2 2650 7000 **W:** cbs.co.kr **Ann:** "Jeongjikhan Sesang eul Gakkuneun AM Palbaek-samsip-chil(837)kHz, Pyojun FM Gusip-pal-jeom-il(98.1)MHz, CBS-mnida. HLKY." – **2)** 89, Uncheon-ro, Seo-gu, Gwangju 62002 ☎ +82 62 376 8500 – **3)** 166, Jungang-ro, Suncheon-si, Jeollanam-do 57939 ☎ +82 61 902 1000 – **4)** 612, Jungang-daero, Buk-ku, Daegu 41561 ☎ +82 53 426 8001 – **5)** 453, Beonyeong-ro, Deokjin-gu, Jeonju-si, Jeollabuk-do 54806 ☎ +82 63 256 1000 – **6)** 141, Sinam-ro, Busanjin-gu, Busan 47344 ☎ +82 51 636 0050 – **7)** 17, Sugok-ro 5beon-gil, Seowon-gu, Cheongju-si, Chungcheongbuk-do 28697 ☎ +82 43 292 4100 – **8)** 892, Baksa-ro, Seo-myeon, Chuncheon-si, Gangwon-do 24461 ☎ +82 33 255 0937 – **9)** 1712, Gyebaek-ro, Jung-gu, Daejeon 34956 ☎ +82 42 259 8888 – **10)** 10, Sanggong-ro, Nam-gu, Pohang-si, Gyeongsangbuk-do 37831 ☎ +82 54 277 5500 – **11)** Room 404, 510, Changi-daero, Uichang-gu, Changwon-si, Gyeongsangnam-do 51430 ☎ +82 55 224 5600 – **12)** 15, Singgwang-ro, Jeju-si, Jeju Teukbyeol Jachido 63125 ☎ +82 64 744 0933 – **13)** 32, Won-daero 26-gil, Gangneung-si, Gangwon-do 25506 ☎ +82 33 642 9131 – **14)** 216, Jungang-ro, Nam-gu, Ulsan44690 ☎ +82 52 256 3333

Ann: stns 2)-8): "Jeongjikhan Sesang-eul Kakkuneun (freq.), CBS (location) Bangsong-imnida (call)" or "Maeumgwa Maeumi Mannaneun Bangsong (freq.), CBS (location) Bangsong-imnida (call)"

F.PI: Relay stns in Chungju, Wonju, Jinju, Gongju, Seosan. Music FM in Daejeon, Jeju, Ulsan, Jeonbuk (Jeonju), Gyeongnam (Changwon)

SEOUL BROADCASTING SYSTEM (SBS)

✉ 161, Mok-dong Seo-ro, Yangcheon-gu, Seoul 07996 ☎ +82 2 2061 0006 🖷 +82 2 2113 3169 **W:** sbs.co.kr

MW: HLSQ Goyang (near Seoul) 792kHz 50kW **D.Prgr:** 24h

Standard FM (Love FM): 103.5MHz HLSQ-SFM 10kW: 24h

Music FM (Power FM): 107.7MHz HLSQ-FM 10kW: 24h + lp rel. stn.

Ann: "AM Chilbaek-gusib-I 792kHz, FM Baek-sam-jeom-o 103.5MHz, SBS Love FM-imnida. HLSQ", "FM Baek-chil-jeom-chil 107.7MHz, Yeoreobune SBS Power FM-imnida. HLSQ"

FAR EAST BROADCASTING CO., KOREA (Rlg.)

MW	kHz	kW	Station, location
1)	1188	100	HLKX, Seoul
2)	1566	250	HLAZ, Jeju
FM	**MHz**	**kW**	**Station, location**
1)	106.9	5	HLKX-SFM, Seoul
2)	104.7	1	HLAZ-SFM, Jeju
3)	93.3	5	HLAD-FM, Daejeon
4)	98.1	5	HLDD-FM, Changwon
5)	90.1	3	HLDY-FM, Yeongdong
6)	100.5	1	HLKW-FM, Mokpo
7)	90.3	3	HLDZ-FM, Pohang
8)	107.3	3	HLQR-FM, Ulsan
9)	93.3	1	HLQQ-FM, Busan
10)	91.9	1	HLKK-FM, Daegu
11)	93.1	1	HLED-FM, Gwangju
12)	97.5	1	HLEI-FM, Jeonnam Dongbu
13)	91.1	1	HLEN-FM, Jeonbuk

+ low power relay stns

Addresses & other information:

1) Far East Broadc. Co.(Geukdong Bangsong), 56, Wausan-ro, Mapo-gu, Seoul 04067 ☎ +82 2 320 0114 🖷 +82 2 320 0229 **W:** febc.net **D.Prgr:** 24h. Korean: 1900-1000, 1600-1700 (Stangdard FM: 24h) **English:** 1000-1100(1188kHz) **Chinese:** 1900-2000(1188kHz). **VOA Relay in Korean:** 1100-1500(1188kHz). **RFA Relay in Korean:** 1500-1900(1188kHz). **Ann:** Korean "Jungpa Cheonbaek-palsip-pal(1188)kHz, Pyojun FM Paeng-nyuk-jeom-gu(106.9)MHz, Areumdaun Chanyanggwa Gibbeun Sosigeul Jeonhaneun Geukdong Bangsong-imnida.". English: "This is HLKX Radio broadcasting with 100,000 watts of power on 1188kHz" **FI:** by contributions & free will offerings – **2)** Jeju Geukdong Bangsong, 67, Gamundongsan 4-gil, Aewol-up, Jeju-si, Jeju Teukbyeol Jachido 63050 ☎ +82 64 799 8100 **D.Prgr:** 24h. **Korean:** 1600-1700, 1900-1100 (Stangdard FM: 24h). **Chinese:** 1100-1230(1566kHz), 1345-1600(1566kHz). **Japanese:** 1230-1345(1566kHz). **Russian:** 1830-1900. **RFA Relay in Korean:** 1000-1100(1566kHz). **VOA Relay in Korean:** 1700-1800(1566kHz). **Voice of Wilderness**, see COTB North Korea, 1900-2000 on Sat. – **3)** Daejeon Geukdong Bangsong, 38-8, Jijok-ro 364-gil, Yuseong-gu, Daejeon 34076 ☎ +82 42 828 9330. **D.Prgr:** 24h – **4)** Changwon Geukdong Bangsong, 147, Du-daero, Seongsan-gu, Changwon-si, Gyeongsang-nam-do 51519 ☎ +82 55 269 9810 **D.Prgr:** 24h – **5)** Yeongdong Geukdong Bangsong, 465 Jungang-ro, Sokcho-si, Sokcho-si, Gangwon do 24803 ☎ +82 33 638 9000 **D.Prgr:** 1900-1700 – **6)** Mokpo Geukdong Bangsong, 61, Bipa-ro, Mokpo-si, Jeollanam-do 58690 ☎ +82 61 284 9000 **D.Prgr:** 1900-1700 – **7)** Pohang Geukdong Bangson, 164, Yongdang-ro, Buk-gu, Pohang-si, Gyeongsangnam-do 58690 ☎ +82 54 256 3000 **D.Prgr:** 24h – **8)** Ulsan Geukdong Bangsong, 145, Beonyeong-ro, Nam-gu, Ulsan-si 44695 ☎ +82 52 256 2000 **D.Prgr:** 24h – **9)** Busan Geukdong Bangsong, 105, Senteom Jungang-ro, Haeundae-gu, Busan 48058 ☎ +82 51 759 6000 **D.Prgr:** 24h – **10)** Daegu Geukdong Bangsong, 90, Hwarang-ro, Suseong-gu, Daegu 42037 ☎ +82 53 770 3000 **D.Prgr:** 24h – **11)** Gwangju Geukdong Bangsong, 73, Sangmubeonyeong-ro, Seo-gu, Gwangju 61946 ☎ +82 62 373 1000 **D.Prgr:** 24h – **12)** Jeonnam Dongbu Geukdong Bangsong, 14, Munsu-ro, Yeosu-si, Jeolla-nam-do 59706 ☎ +82 61 650 3800 **D.Prgr:** 24h – **13)** Jeonbuk Geukdong Bangsong, 145, Mahan-ro, Iksan-si, Jeolla-buk-do 54540 ☎ +82 63 854 0911 **D.Prgr:** 24h

F.PI: Power up for HLKX, Seoul

CATHOLIC PEACE BROADCASTING CORP. (CPBC) (Gatollik Pyeonghwa Bangsong) Endowment by the Catholic Church.

Stations:

1) Seoul HLQP-FM 105.3MHz 5kW: 1957-1702 – **2)** Gwangju HLDL-FM 99.9MHz 5kW, 99.5MHz 1kW(rel. stn in Yeosu): 1957-1702 – **3)** Deagu HLDK-FM 93.1MHz 3kW, 96.9MHz 0.5kW(rel. st. in Pohang), 100.7MHz 0.5kW(rel. stn in Andong): 1957-1702 – **4)** Busan HLDW-FM 101.1MHz 3kW, 94.3MHz 0.5kW(rel. st in Ulsan), 105.5MHz(rel. st. in Changwon): 1957-1702 – **5)** Daejeon HLQO-FM 106.3MHz 3kW: 1957-1702 + low power rel. stn.

Addresses:

1) 330, Samil-daero, Jung-gu, Seoul 04552 ☎ +82 2 2270 2114 🖷

+82 2 2270 2210 **W:** pbc.co.kr **Ann:** " Gatollik Pyeonghwa FM Baeg-o-jeom-sam(105.3)MHz, Gibbeun Sosik, Balgeun Sesang, CPBC Gatollik Pyeonghwa Bangsong-imnida. HLQP." – **2)** 75, Sangmusimin-ro, Seo-gu, Gwangju 61951 – **3)** 20, Seoseong-ro, Jung-gu, Daegu 41933 – **4)** 71, Junggu-ro, Jung-gu, Busan 48968 – **5)** 471, Daejong-ro, Jung-gu, Daejeon 34915 ☎ +82 42 250 3200

BUDDHIST BROADCASTING SYSTEM (BBS)
(Bulgyo Bangsong) Owned and operated by the Buddhists
Stations:
1) Seoul HLSG-FM 101.9MHz 5kW: 2000-1700 – **2)** Gwangju HLDB-FM 89.7MHz 3kW, 105.7MHz 0.5kW(rel. stn in Gwnagyang): 2000-1700 – **3)** Busan HLDA-FM 89.9MHz 5kW, 89.5MHz 0.5kW (rel. stn in Changwon), 88.1MHz 0.5kW(rel. stn in Jinju): 2000-1700 – **4)** Daegu HLDI-FM 94.5MHz 3kW, 105.5MHz 0.5kW (rel. stn in Pohang), 97.7MHz 1kW (rel. stn in Andong): 2000-1700 – **5)** Cheongju HLDJ-FM 96.7MHz 3kW: 2000-1700 – **6)** Chuncheon HLQM-FM 100.1MHz 3kW, 104.3MHz 1kW(rel. stn in Gangneung): 2000-1700 – **7)** Ulsan HLQU-FM 88.3MHz 1kW: 2000-1700 – **8)** Jeju HLEL-FM 94.9MHz 1kW, 100.5MHz 1kW(rel. stn in Seogwipo) + low power rel. stns

Addresses:
1) Dabo Building;20, Mapo-daero, Mapo-gu, Seoul 04175 ☎ +82 2 705 5114 🖷 +82 2 705 5229 **W:** bbsi.co.kr – **2)** Dongyang Bldg, 9, Sangmu Jungang-ro, Seo-gu, Gwangju 61962 ☎ +82 62 520 1114 – **3)** Boseong Bldg, 102, Beomil-ro, Dong-gu, Busan 48738 ☎ +82 51 520 5114 – **4)** Jingak Bldg, 261, Myeongdeok-ro, Jung-gu, Daegu 41956 ☎ +82 53 427 5114 – **5)** 101, Wolpyeong-ro 184beon-gil, Sangdang-gu, Cheongju-si, Chungcheongbuk-do 28776 ☎ +82 43 294 5114 – **6)** 10, Jungang-ro, Chuncheon-si, Gangwon-do 24270 ☎ +82 33 250 2114 – **7)** 201, Samsan-ro, Nam-gu, Ulsan 44703 ☎ +82 52 279 8114 – **8)** 14, Imhang-ro, Jeju-si, Jeju Teukbyeol Jachido 63277 ☎ +82 1811 0818
Ann: 1) "FM Baeg-il-jeom-gu (101.9)MHz, BBS Bulgyo Bangsong-imnida. HLSG."
F.Pl: Local sts in Jeonbuk, Daejeon

SEOUL TRAFFIC BROADCASTING (TBS)
(Gyotong Bangsong)(Pub.)
✉ S-PLEX Center, 31, Maebongsan-ro, Mapo-gu, Seoul 03909 ☎ +82 2 311 5114 🖷 +82 2 311 5219 **W:** tbs.seoul.kr
Station: HLST-FM (Live FM) 95.1MHz 5kW: 24h in Korean. HLSW-FM (Soul FM) 101.3MHz 1kW: 24h in English.
Ann: "FM Gusib-o-jeom-il(95.1)MHz, TBS Gyotong Bangsong-imnida","You're listening to 101.3 tbs-eFM"

TRAFFIC BROADCASTING NETWORK (TBN)
(Hanguk Gyotong Bangsong)
✉ 2, Hyeoksin-ro, Wonju-si, Gangwon-do 26466 ☎ +82 33 749 5000 🖷 +82 33 749 5908 **W:** tbn.or.kr
Stations:
1) Busan 94.9MHz HLDN-FM 3kW: 24h – **2)** Gwangju 97.3MHz HLDM-FM 3kW, 103.5MHz 3kW (rel. st. in Gwangyang): 24h – **3)** Daejeon 102.9MHz HLDT-FM 3kW: 24h – **4)** Daegu 103.9MHz HLDU-FM 3kW: 24h – **5)** Incheon 100.5MHz HLSU-FM 1kW: 24h – **6)** Gangwon(Wonju) 105.9MHz HLSV-FM 3kW: 24h, Gangwon(Chuncheon) 103.7MHz 3kW: 24h , Gangwon(Gangneung) 105.5MHz 3kW: 24h, Gangwon(Donghae) 95.3MHz 1kW: 24h – **7)** Jeonju 102.5MHz HLCM-FM 3kW: 24h – **8)** Ulsan 104.1MHz HLCV-FM 1kW: 24h+ low power relay stns– **9)** Changwon 95.5MHz HLEE-FM 1kW: 24h, Changwon(Jinju) 100.1MHz 1kW: 24h – **10)** Gyeongbuk(Gyeongju) 103.5MHz HLEF-FM 1kW: 24h, Gyeongbuk(Uljin) 103.7MHz 1kW: 24h – **11)** Jeju 105.5MHz HLEH-FM 1kW, 105.9MHz 1kW(rel. st. in Seogwipo): 24h + low power rel. stns.
F.Pl: Local st in Chungbuk

Addresses & other information:
1) 68, Yongso-ro, Nam-gu, Busan 48501 ☎ +82 51 6105 114 **Ann:** "FM Gusib-sa-jeom-gu(94.9)MHz, Busan Gyotong Bangsong-imnida. HLDN-FM" – **2)** 40, Cheomdanjungang-ro 182-gil, Gwangsan-gu, Gwangju 62274 ☎ +82 62 9701 114 **Ann:** "FM Gusib-chil-jeom-sam(97.3)MHz, Gwangju Gyotong Bangsong-imnida. HLDM" – **3)** 17, Singalma-ro, Seo-gu, Daejeon 35280 ☎ +82 42 6001 114 **Ann:** "FM Baeg-i-jeom-gu(102.9)MHz, Dallineun Radio Daejeon Gyotong Bangsong-imnida." – **4)** 120, Hyeonchug-ro, Nam-gu, Daegu 42420 ☎ +82 53 6060 114 **Ann:** "FM Baek-sam-jeom-gu(103.9)MHz, Daegu Gyotong Bangsong-imnida. HLDU-FM" – **5)** 251, Maesohol-ro, Nam-gu, Incheon 22201 ☎ +82 32 4531 114 **Ann:** "FM Baek-jeom-o(100.5) MHz, TBN Incheon Gyotong Bangsong-imnida. HLSU" – **6)** 183, Dongbusunhwan-ro, Wonju-si, Gangwon-do 26457 ☎ +82 33 7490 114 **Ann:** "Haengbogui Giljabi, Ggumi Inneun Bangsong, FM Baeg-o-jeom-gu(105.9)MHz, Gangwon Gyotong Bangsong-imnida." – **7)** 1097-10, Jeogyeorip-ro, Deokjin-gu, Jeonju 54859 ☎ +82 63 2593 114 **Ann:** "FM Baeg-i-jeom-chil(102.7)MHz, TBN Jeonju Gyotong Bangsong-imnida. HLCM" – **8)** 11, Hamwol 7-gil, Jung-gu, Ulsan 44426. ☎ +82 52 290 8514 **Ann:** "FM Baeg-sa-jeom-il(104.1) MHz, TBN Ulsan Gyotong Bangsong-imnida. HLCV" – **9)** 82-4, Changwoncheon-ro 94-gil, Uichang-gu, Changwon-si 51409. ☎ +82 55 272 6114 **Ann:** "FM Gusib-o-jeom-o(95.5)MHz, Changwon Gyotong Bangsong-imnida. HLEE" – **10)** 95, Samheung-ro, Buk-gu, Pohang-si 37613. ☎ +82 54 240 6214 **Ann:** "FM Baek-sam-jeom-o(103.5) MHz, TBN Gyeongbuk Gyotong Bangsong-imnida. HLEF" – **11)** 101, Gija-gil, Jeju-si, Jeju 63246 ☎ +82 64 717 8114 **Ann:** "FM Baeg-o-jeom-o(105.5)MHz, TBN Jeju Gyotong Bangsong-imnida. HLEH"

KOREA NEW NETWORK CORP. (KNN)
✉ 30, Senteomseo-ro, Haeundae-gu, Busan 48058 ☎ +82 51 850 9000 **W:** knn.co.kr **Station:** HLDG-FM(Power FM) 99.9MHz 5kW, 102.5MHz 1kw(rel. stn in Changwon), 105.5MHz 1kW(rel. stn in Jinju): 24h, HLDG-SFM(Love FM) 105.7MHz 1kW, 90.9MHz 1kw(rel. stn in Changwon), 98.7MHz 1kW(rel. stn in Jinju): 24h.
+low Power rel. stns
Ann: "Busan Gusip-gu-jeom-gu(99.9), Gijang, Yangsan Gusim-nyuk-jeom-sam(96.3), Changwon Baeg-i-jeom-o(102.5), Jinju Baeg-o-jeom-o(105.5)MHz, jeulgeoumeul cheongchwijawa hamgge mandeuneun KNN Power FM-imnida.", "Busan Baeg-o-jeom-chil(105.7), Yangsan Palsip-pal-jeom-o(88.5), Changwon, Gimhae, Geoje Gusip-jeom-gu(90.9), Jinju Gusip-pal-jeom-chil(98.7)MHz, KNN Love FM-imnida."

TAEGU BROADCASTING CORPORATION (TBC)
(Daegu Bangsong)
✉ 23, Dongdaegu-ro, Susong-gu, Daegu 42175 ☎ +82 53 760 1900 **W:** tbc.co.kr **Station:** HLDE-FM(Dream FM) 99.3MHz 5kW: 24h. Relay stn: Pohang 99.7MHz 1kW, Andong 106.5MHz 0.5kW. **Ann:** "HLDE-FM TBC Dream FM-imnida"

KWANGJU BROADCASTING CO., LTD. (KBC) (Gwangju Bangsong)
✉ 919, Mujin-daero, Seo-gu, Gwangju, 61915 ☎ +82 62 650 3114 **W:** ikbc.co.kr **Station:** HLDH-FM (MY FM) 101.1MHz 5kW: 24h. Relay stn: Yeosu 96.7MHz 1kW. **Ann:** "HLDH, FM 101.1MHz, 96.7MHz, Yeollin Sesang, Joheun Chingu, KBC MY FM"

TAEJON BROADCASTING CO., LTD. (TJB)
(Daejeon Bangsong)
✉ 131, EXPO-ro, Yuseong-gu, Daejeon 34125 ☎ +82 42 281 1101 **W:** tjb.co.kr **Station:** HLDF-FM (Power FM) 95.7MHz 5kW: 24h Relay stn: Seosan 96.5MHz 0.5kW. **Ann:** "Gusib-o-jeom-chil(95.7), Gusim-nyuk-jeom-o(96.5)MHz, TJB Power FM-imnida. HLDF"

JEONJU TELEVISION CORPORATION (JTV)
(Jeonju Bangsong)
✉ 1083, Jeongyeorip-ro, Deokjin-gu, Jeonju-si, Jeollabuk-do 54859 ☎ +82 63 250 5200 **W:** jtv.co.kr **Station:** HLDQ-FM(Magic FM) 90.1MHz 5kW: 24h **Ann:** "FM Gusib-jeom-il(90.1)MHz, JTV Magic FM-imnida. HLDQ"

CHEONGJU BROADCASTING CORPORATION (CJB)
(Cheongju Bangsong)
✉ 59-1, Saun-ro, Seowon-gu, Cheongju-si, Chungcheongbuk-do 28654 ☎ +82 43 265 7000 **W:** cjb.co.kr **Station:** HLDI-FM (Joy FM) 101.5MHz 5kW, 97.9MHz 2kW (rel. stn in Eumseong): 24h
Ann: "FM Baeg-il-jeom-o (101.5)MHz, CJB Joy FM-imnida. HLDI"

ULSAN BROADCASTING CORPORATION (UBC)
(Ulsan Bangsong)
✉ 41, Gugyo-ro, Jung-gu, Ulsan 44520 ☎ +82 52 228 6000 **W:** ubc.co.kr **Station:** HLDP-FM(Green FM) 92.3MHz 3kW: 24h **Ann:** "Gusib-i-jeom-sam(92.3)MHz, UBC Green FM Bangsong-imnida. HLDP"

JEJU FREE INTERNATIONAL CITY BROADCASTING SYSTEM (JIBS) (Jeju Gukje Jayu Dosi Bangsong)
✉ 95, Yeonsam-ro, Jeju-si, Jeju Teukbyeol Jachido 63148 ☎ +82 64 740 7800 **W:** jibstv.com **Station:** HLQC-FM (Power FM) 101.5MHz 3kW: 24h. Relay stn: Seogwipo 98.5MHz 1kW
Ann: "JIBS New Power FM Bangsong-imnida"

GANGWON NO.1 BROADCASTING CO., LTD (G1) (Gangwon Minbang)
✉ 274, Soyanggang-ro, Dong-myeon, Chuncheon-si, Gangwon-do 24210 ☎ +82 33 248 5000 **W:** g1tv.co.kr **Station:** HLCG-FM(Fresh FM) 105.1MHz 3kW: 24h. Relay stn: Gangneung 106.1MHz 1kW, Wongju 103.1MHz 0.5kW +low Power rel. stns
Ann: "Wonju Baeg-sam-jeom-il (103.1), Chuncheon Baeg-o-jeom-il (105.1), Gangneung Baeng-ryuk-jeom-il(106.1), Taebaek Gusib-gu-jeom-sam(99.3)MHz, G1 Fresh FM, HLCG"

KYONGGI BROADCASTING CO. (KFM) (Gyeonggi Bangsong)
✉ 111, Maeyeong-ro 345-gil, Yeongtong-gu, Suwon-si, Gyeonggi-do 16703 ☎ +82 31 210 0999 **W:** kfm.co.kr
Station: HLDS-FM 99.9MHz 5kW: 24h **Ann:** "FM Gusib-gu-jeom-gu(99.9)MHz, Gyeonggi Bangsong-imnida. HLDS"

Kyung-In Broadcasting (Gyeong-in Bangsong)
✉ 7, Aam-daero 287beon-gil, Nam-gu, Incheon 22196 ☎ +82 32 830 1000 **W:** ifm.kr **Station:** HLDO-FM 90.7MHz 5kW: 24h **Ann:** "FM Gusib-jeom-chil (90.7)MHz, Gyeong-In Bangsong"

YTN RADIO(YTN FM)
✉ 76, Sangamsan-ro, Mapo-gu, Seoul 03926 ☎ +82 2 398 8000 **W:** radio.ytn.co.kr **Station:** HLQV-FM 94.5MHz 3kW: 24h **Ann:** "FM Gusib-sa-jeom-o (94.5)MHz, YTN FM-imnida. HLQV"

WON-BUDDHISM BROADCASTING SYSTEM (WBS) (Woneum Bangsong)
✉ **1)** 233, Mok-dong Dong-ro, Yangcheon-gu, Seoul 07995 ☎ +82 2 2102 7700 **W:** wbsi.kr – **2)** 10, Gwangbokjungang-ro 33beon-gil, Jung-gu, Busan 48947 ☎ +82 51 247 3844 – **3)** 501, Iksan-daero, Iksan-si, Jeollabuk-do 54536 ☎ +82 63 837 0979 – **4)** 31, Sangmuowol-ro Seo-gu, Gwanju 61966 – **5)** 42, Jungang-daero 66-gil, Jung-gu, Daegu 41961 ☎ +82 53 425 0983.
Stations: 1) Seoul HLQK-FM 89.7MHz 3kW: 24h – **2)** Busan HLQJ-FM 104.9MHz 3kW: 24h – **3)** Jeonbuk(Iksan) HLDV-FM 97.9MHz 3kW: 24h – **4)** Gwangju HLQN-FM 107.9MHz 1kW: 24h – **5)** Daegu HLCS-FM 98.3MHz 1kW: 24h.
Ann: 1) FM Palsip-gu-jeom-chil(89.7)MHz, WBS Woneum Bangsong-imnida. HLQK" – **2)** "FM Baek-sa-jeom-gu(104.9)MHz, WBS Busan Woneum Bangsong-imnida. HLQJ" – **3)** "FM Gusip-chil-jeom-gu(97.9) MHz, WBS Jeonbuk Woneum Bangsong-imnida. HLDV" – **4)** "FM Baek-chil-jeom-gu(107.9)MHz, WBS Gwangju Woneum Bangsong-imnida. HLQN" – **5)** "FM Gusip-pal-jeom-sam(98.3)MHz, WBS Daegu Woneum Bangsong-imnida. HLCS"

KOREA INTERNATIONAL BROADCASTING FOUNDATION (Arirang Radio)
✉ Arirang Tower, 2351, Nambusunhwan-ro, Seocho-gu, Seoul 06713 ☎ +82 2 3475 5000 **W:** arirang.co.kr **Station:** Jeju HLSE-FM 88.7MHz 3kW: 24h in English. Relay stn: Seogwipo 88.1MHz 1kW. **Ann:** "You're listening to Arirang Radio"

GFN FOUNDATION
✉ 17, Sajik-ro, Nam-gu, Gwangju 61640 ☎ +82 62 460 0987 **W:** gfn.or.kr **Station:** HLSY-FM 98.7MHz 1kW, 93.7MHz 1kW(rel. stn in Yeosu): 2000-1700 in English. **Ann:** "Listen more Feel more! GFN 98.7 FM"

BUSAN e-FM
✉ Centum venture town 4F, 41, Centum dong-ro, Haeundae-gu, Busan 48059 ☎ +82 51 861 8601 **W:** befm.or.kr **Station:** HLSX-FM 90.5MHz 1kW: 2000-1700 in English. **Ann:** "Now you're listening to Busan e-FM 90.5"

KOREAN FORCES NETWORK (Friends FM) (Gukpang FM)
✉ 54-99, Duteopbawi-ro, Yongsan-gu, Seoul 04353 **W:** radio.dema.mil.kr/web/fm/main.do **Stations: FM** (operated by KBS): Namsan HLSF-FM 96.7MHz 2kW, Hwaaksan 96.7MHz 5kW, Yongmunsan 101.1MHz 3kW, Gwaebangsan 92.5MHz 3kW , Jeju 94.1MHz 3kW + 8 lp stns
D.Prgr: 24h. Own prgrs 2100-1500, other times relay KBS R. One (HLKA). prgrs for soldiers. **Ann:** "Yuneunghan anbo teunteunhan gukpang, yeoreobun-ui gukpang FM-imnida"

AMERICAN FORCES NETWORK KOREA (AFN)
✉ As below ☎ +82 2 7914 6495/6 **W:** afnkorea.com

	MW & FM Stations	kHz	kW	MHz	kW
1)	Pyeongtaek/Camp Humphreys	+1440	*5	88.3	3
2)	Daegu/Camp Walker	-	-	88.5	1
3)	Busan/Camp Hialeah	-	-	88.1	0.25
	Chuncheon/Camp Page	1044	1	88.5	0.1
	Uijeongbu/Camp Red Cloud	1161	0.25	88.5	0.25
4)	Dongducheon/Camp Casey	+1197	1	88.3	0.3
5)	Songtan/Osan Air Base	-	-	88.5	0.05
6)	Seoul/Yongsan	-	-	102.7	5
7)	Gunsan/Gunsan Air Base	1440	1	88.5	0.25
	Waegwan/Camp Carrol	1440	5	-	-
	Pohang/Camp Libby	1512	0.25	-	-
	Jinhae/Naval St.	1512	0.25	88.5	0.05
	Gwanju/Gwangju Air Base			88.5	0.05

+= local prgrs 2005-0000 Mon-Fri; otherwise rel.1). *= **F.Pl:** 10kW
D.Prgr: 24h (MW/FM sep. prgrs). **N.** on the h. Formal sign on at 1505
Ann: AM: "American Forces Network Korea", FM (Seoul): "This is Eagle FM"
Addresses: 1) Headquarters, American Forces Network Korea, Unit #15877. APO AP 96271-0543, USA ☎ +82 2 7914 6495. Commanding Officer: LTC Eric Badger – **2)** Unit #15029, APO AP 96218-0186, USA – **3)** Unit #15184. APO AP 96259-0274, USA – **4)** Unit #15116, APO AP 96224-0380, USA – **5)** Unit #2034. APO AP 96278-5000, USA – **6)** Unit #15324, APO AP 96205-0097, USA – **7)** Unit #2011, APO AP 96264-5000, USA

KOSOVO

L.T: UTC +1h (28 Mar-31 Oct: +2h) — **Pop:** 1.7 million — **Pr.L:** Albanian (official), Serbian (official) — **E.C:** 230V/50Hz — **ITU:** pending (**WRTH**: RKS)

KOMISIONI I PAVARUR PËR MEDIA (KPM) (Independent Media Commission)
✉ Rr. Perandori Justinian nr. 14, Qyteza Pejton, 10000 Prishtinë ☎🖷 +383 38 245031 **E:** info@kpm-ks.org **W:** kpm-ks.org
L.P: Chmn: Muja Ferati

RADIOTELEVIZIONI I KOSOVËS (RTK) (Pub)
✉ Rr. Xhemail Prishtina nr. 12, 10000 Prishtinë ☎+383 38 230102 **E:** post@rtklive.com **W:** rtklive.com **L.P:** DG/CEO: Ngadhnjim Kastrati

MW	kHz	kW	Prgr
Prishtinë	549	1	1

FM (MHz)	1	2	kW	FM	1	2	kW
Cërnusha	87.6	91.5	0.4	Prishtinë	91.9	93.3	0.5
Maja e Gjelbërt	88.5	90.5	0.4	Prishtinë II	-	99.2	0.5
Golesh	95.7	97.7	3.5	Zatriq	88.9	92.4	0.5
Leposaviq*		97.3	0.3	*) KFOR Camp Nothing Hill			

D.Prgr: Prgr 1 (R. Kosova 1): 24h in Albanian – **Prgr 2 (R. Kosova 2):** 0600-1300 Albanian, 1300-2000 prgrs for ethnic minorities (1300-1500 Serbian, 1500-1700 Turkish, 1700-1900 Bosnian, 1900-2000 Romany), 2000-2400 in Albanian.

OTHER STATIONS

FM	MHz	kW	Location	Station
23)	88.1	1	Podujevë	R. Vizioni
24)	88.6	1	Prishtinë	Glam R.
12)	89.1	1	Zubin Potok	R. Kolašin
4)	89.4	1	Ljubinjë e Epërme	R. Astra
25A)	90.2	2	Golesh	R. K4
11)	92.2	1	Mitrovicë	R. Kiss
6)	92.6	1	Ferizaj	R. Ferizaj
2)	92.7	1	Maja e Gjelbërt	R. Dukagjini
15)	92.9	1	Leposaviq	R. Mir
3)	94.0	1	Kamenicë	R. 24
2)	94.5	2.5	Zariq	R. Dukagjini
1)	94.8	1	Maja e Gjelbërt	Virgin R.
19)	94.9	1	Mitrovicë	R. Ylberi
9)	95.4	1	Kaçanik	R. Kaçaniku
A)	96.2	1	Prishtinë	VOA relay
18)	96.4	1	Dragash	R. Sharri
20)	96.4	1	Gjilan	R. Star
25B)	96.6	2	Golesh	R. K4
22)	97.9	1	Gjilan	R. Victoria
17)	98.4	1	Gjilan	R. Rinia
B)	98.6	1	Golesh	BBCWS relay
10)	98.8	1	Kamenicë	R. Kamenica
16)	99.0	1	Mitrovicë	R. Mitrovica

FM	MHz	kW	Location	Station
2)	99.7	30	Golesh	R. Dukagjini
8)	100.3	1	Leposaviq	R. Impuls
5A)	100.9	1	Gjilan	R. Shqip FM
C)	101.0	1	Prishtinë	RFI relay
13)	101.9	1	Mitrovicë	R. Kontakt Plus
14)	102.4	1	Shillovë	R. Max
1)	102.8	30	Golesh	Virgin R.
5B)	103.3	1	Gjilan	R. Energji
1)	103.9	2.5	Zatriq	Virgin R.
7)	104.1	1	Viti	R. Iliria
21)	105.7	1	Vushtrri	R. Vicianum

+ txs below 1kW.

Addresses & other information:

1) Pallati i mediave, aneks II, 10000 Prishtinë – **2)** Rr. Ismail Qemajli nr. 7, 30000 Pejë – **3)** 70000 Lagjja Liria – **4)** 20000 Ljubinjë e Epërme. In Bosnian – **5A,B)** Rr. "Abdullah Presheva" nr. 63, 60000 Gjilan – **6)** Rr. Dëshmoret e Kombit, 70000 Ferizaj – **7)** Rr. Hoxhë Jonuzi p.n., 61000 Viti – **8)** Rr. 24 Novembar p.n., 40000 Leposaviq. In Serbian. – **9)** Rr. Vellezerit Çaka p.n., 71000 Kaçanik – **10)** Shtëpia e Kultures, 62000 Kamenicë – **11)** Rr. Kralj Petar I p.n., 40000 Mitrovicë – **12)** Rr. Arsenija Carnojevica nr. 48, 40650 Zubin Potok. In Serbian – **13)** Rr. Lole Ribara nr. 58, 40000 Mitrovicë – **14)** 60000 Shillovë. In Serbian – **15)** Rr. Vojske Jugoslavije nr. 26, 40000 Leposaviq. In Serbian – **16)** Sheshi Jasharaj, 40000 Mitrovicë – **17)** Rr. Skenderbeu nr. 13, 60000 Gjilan – **18)** Rr. "Rruga e Dëshmorve", 22000 Dragash – **19)** Sheshi Agim Hajrizi p.n., 40000 Mitrovicë – **20)** Rr. Lagja Dardania nr. 1, 60000 Gjilan – **21)** Rr. Faruk Beqiri p.n., 42000 Vushtrri – **22)** Rr. Dardania I nr. 12/9, 60000 Gjilan – **23)** Rr. Zahir Pajaziti p.n., 11000 Podujevë – **24)** Rr. Enver Zymberi nr. 5, 10000 Prishtinë – **25A,B)** KFOR HQ, Camp Film City, 10000 Prishtinë. 25A) in Albanian, 25B) in Serbian. – **A)** Rel. VOA (USA) – **B)** Rel. BBCWS (UK) – **C)** Rel. RFI (France)

KUWAIT

L.T: UTC +3h — **Pop:** 4.3 million — **Pr.L:** Arabic — **E.C:** 240V/50Hz — **ITU:** KWT

COMMUNICATION & INFORMATION TECHNOLOGY REGULATORY AUTHORITY (CITRA)

P.O. Box 898, 13009 Kuwait City **W:** citra.gov.kw **E:** info@citra.gov.kw

RADIO OF THE STATE OF KUWAIT (Gov)

P.O. Box 967, 13010 Safat ☎+965 22436193 🖷+965 22417830 **W:** media.gov.kw **E:** kwtfreq@media.gov.kw
L.P: Mr. Hani Al-Naqi, Dir. Freq. Mgmt.
Stations: MW: Magwa 630/963/1341kHz, Kabd 540/1134/1269kHz. **FM:** Madinat-al-Kuwait

MW(kHz)	kW	Prgr.	Times
540	600	Main Arabic	24h
630	10	Quran prgr.	24h
963	20	Main Arabic	1200-1600, 2100-0500
		Multilingual	0500-1200, 1600-2100
1134	100	Main Arabic	24h
1269	100	Classical Arab Music	24h
1341	100	Quran prgr.	2200-0400
		2nd Arabic	0400-2200

FM(MHz)	kW	Prgr.	Times
87.9/101.0	20	Arab Music	24h
89.5/95.3	20	Main Arabic	24h
88.4/93.9	20/10	OFM	24h
92.5/96.3	10/5	Easy FM	24h
93.3	5	Multilingual	0500-1800
94.9	5	Folklore prgr.	24h
98.9/105.1	20	Quran	24h
97.5	20	Quran	2200-0400
		2nd Arabic	0400-2200
94.5	20	2nd Arabic	0400-2200
99.7	20	Super Station	24h
100.5	10	TV sound (Prgr. 1)	24h
103.2/103.7	20	R. Kuwait Al-Arabi	24h

Main Arabic prgr: 24h. **N:** 0300, 0500, 1000, 1700, 2100 – **2nd Arabic prgr:** 0400-2200 – **Classical Arab Music prgr:** 24h – **Kuwait 103.7** (Modern Arab Music prgr): 24h – **Multilingual prgr:** English 0500-0800, 1800-2100, Persian 0800-1000, Filipino 1000-1200, Urdu 1600-1800 – **OFM** (youth prgr.): 24h – **Quran prgr:** 24h – **"Easy FM" in English**: 24h – **"FM Super Station"** in English: 24h. **N:** on the hour.
Ann: "Idha'at al-Dawlat Al Kuwait".
Programmes also transmitted on DAB channel 11B.

Other stations:
Arabian Gulf R, 91.5MHz (See main entry under Bahrain)
Marina FM, 90.4MHz 5kW. **W:** marinafm.com
Q8 Pulse, 88.8MHz. **W:** fm888.info
U FM, 98.4MHz. **W:** ufm4u.com
Sowt al-Khaleej, 102.4MHz 5kW. See Qatar for main entry.
Sowt al-Rayan, 102.0MHz. See Qatar for main entry.
AFN: Al-Jabber/Camp Doha 101.5/104.3/107.9MHz 50 W/5kW.
BBC World Sce: Arabic 90.1MHz, English 100.1MHz, both 5kW.
Monte Carlo Doualiya: 107.4MHz 2kW. **RFI:** 106.3MHz 2kW.
R. Sawa: 1548kHz 600kW, 1593kHz 150kW.
Voice of America "VOA 1": 95.7&96.9MHz 5kW

KYRGYZSTAN

L.T: UTC +6h — **Pop:** 6.4 million — **Pr.L:** Kyrgyz (official), Russian (official), Uzbek — **E.C:** 220V/50Hz — **ITU:** KGZ

MADANIYAT, MAALYMAT JANA TURIZM MINISTRILIGI (Ministry of Culture, Information and Tourism)

Pushkin St. 78, 720040 Bishkek ☎ +996 312 620482 🖷 +996 312 623589 **E:** minculture.kg@gmail.com **W:** www.minculture.gov.kg
L.P: Minister: Azamat Jumagulov

KOOMDUK TELERADIOBERÜÜ KORPORATSIYASY (KTRK) (Pub) (Public Broadcasting Corp.)

Jash Gvardiya blvd. 59, 720010 Bishkek ☎ +996 312 392059
E: public@ktrk.kg **W:** ktrk.kg **L.P:** DG: Usen Jaynak

MW	kHz	kW	Prgr
Bishkek (a)	*612	100	1

*) Tx is timeshared with TWR relays (see International Radio section).

SW	kHz	kW	Prgr	SW	kHz	kW	Prgr
Bishkek (a)	4010	100	1	Bishkek (a)	4820	15	2

FM (MHz)	1	2	3	FM	1	2	3
Balykchy	105.3	-	-	Karakol	102.4	106.0	100.6
Batken	104.2	-	102.2	Naryn	100.5	103.2	107.7
Bishkek	104.1	106.9	103.7	Osh	100.7	-	-
Jalalabat	104.7	105.9	106.3	Talas	102.0	107.6	105.7

+ translators (a) Krasnaya Rechka

D.Prgr: Prgr 1 (Birinchi radio): 0000-1800 in Kyrgyz, Russian; Rel. Dostuk radiosu: 0400-1200 (Sat), 1100-1500 (Sun) – **Prgr 2 (Kyrgyz radiosu):** 24h in Kyrgyz on FM; limited schedule on SW – **Prgr 3 (Ming kyyal FM):** 24h in Kyrgyz – **Prgr 4 (Dostuk radiosu):** 0000-1800 via DTT & webcasting (+ via Birinchi R. on weekends). For ethnic minorities in Kyrgyz, Dungan, Polish, Russian, Tatar, Turkish, Uighur, Ukrainian, Uzbek.

OTHER STATIONS

FM	MHz	kW	Location	Station
A)	66.26	17	Karakol	R. Rossii relay
A)	67.94	17	Bishkek	R. Rossii relay
A)	68.66	17	Karaköl	R. Rossii relay
A)	69.92	17	Osh	R. Rossii relay
A)	69.95	17	Kazarman	R. Rossii relay
A)	70.07	17	Arstanbap	R. Rossii relay
A)	70.40	17	Sülüktü	R. Rossii relay
A)	70.82	17	Naryn	R. Rossii relay
A)	72.20	17	Jalalabat	R. Rossii relay
A)	72.44	17	Sülüktü	R. Rossii relay
5)	87.5	6.3	Kumaryk	Kyrgyzstan Obondoru
13)	87.5	3	Bishkek	R. Mir
2A)	87.6	3.2	Chon-Döbö	Evropa Plus
22)	87.6	6.3	Mayly-Suu	R. Kaskad
9)	87.7	1	Isfana	R. Almaz
5)	87.9	16	Balykchy	Kyrgyzstan Obondoru
B)	88.0	3	Bishkek	Vesti FM relay
6A)	88.1	1.6	Talas	Manas FM
14)	88.3	6.3	Karaköl	R. OK
7)	88.5	3	Bishkek	Maral FM
14)	88.8	4	Cholponata	R. OK
15)	89.0	4	Bishkek	R. Rekord
C)	89.3	2	Karabalta	R. Sputnik relay
2B)	89.3	6.3	Kumaryk	Retro FM
2B)	89.4	3.2	Chon-Döbö	Retro FM
12)	89.6	3	Bishkek	El FM

FM	MHz	kW	Location	Station
2B)	89.7	10	Balykchy	Retro FM
14)	89.8	1.6	Talas	R. OK
8)	90.2	1	Bishkek	Parlament R.
8)	90.3	6.3	Kumaryk	Parlament R.
20)	90.6	2	Kara-Balta	Next FM
13)	90.8	1.6	Talas	R. Mir
6B)	90.9	2	Bishkek	Manas Zhanyrygy
13)	91.1	4	Karakol	R. Mir
2A)	91.3	6.3	Kumaryk	Evropa Plus
8)	91.5	1.6	Balykchy	Parlament R.
1)	92.6	1	Talas	TNT Music R.
8)	92.6	1.6	Karakol	Parlament R.
5)	93.3	1	Naryn	Kyrgyzstan Obondoru
6A)	93.7	1	Naryn	Manas FM
C)	95.1	3.2	Naryn	R. Sputnik relay
7)	95.3	1	Osh	Maral FM
B)	96.2	1.6	Karakol	Vesti FM relay
11)	96.9	4	Naryn	Sanjyra R.
11)	98.0	4	Karakol	Sanjyra R.
8)	98.7	1	Naryn	Parlament R.
11)	99.7	1	Jalalabat	Sanjyra R.
8)	100.0	1.6	Chon-Döbö	Parlament R.
14)	100.5	3	Bishkek	R. OK
25)	100.5	1.6	Talas	Radiomost
1)	100.9	3	Bishkek	TNT Music R.
15)	101.1	1	Cholponata	R. Rekord
C)	101.1	1.6	Talas	R. Sputnik relay
16)	101.3	3	Bishkek	Tumar FM
3)	101.4	1	Karakol	Hit FM
3)	101.4	3	Balykchy	Hit FM
8)	101.4	1.6	Sülüktü	Parlament R.
C)	101.4	1	Bishkek	R. Sputnik relay
2B)	101.4	1.6	Osh	Retro FM
8)	101.5	2	Batken	Parlament R.
2B)	101.5	8	Naryn	Retro FM
2A)	101.7	1	Bishkek	Evropa Plus
17)	101.8	1.6	Karakol	Radio LW
9)	102.0	1	Jalalabat	R. Almaz
9)	102.0	1	Kochkor	R. Almaz
9)	102.1	3	Bishkek	R. Almaz
10)	102.5	3	Bishkek	Pyramida FM
20)	102.6	2	Talas	Next FM
3)	102.7	1.6	Cholponata	Hit FM
6A)	102.9	1	Bishkek	Manas FM
12)	102.9	1.6	Nookat	El FM
16)	103.2	1.6	Cholponata	Tumar FM
16)	103.2	2	Osh	Tumar FM
11)	103.3	3	Bishkek	Sanjyra R.
5)	104.3	1.6	Batken	Kyrgyzstan Obondoru
11)	104.4	1.6	Talas	Sanjyra R.
2B)	104.5	4	Bishkek	Retro FM
4)	104.6	20	Sülüktü	Jash FM
7)	105.0	1.6	Batken	Maral FM
8)	105.0	3	Osh	Parlament R.
C)	105.0	1	Bishkek	R. Sputnik relay
11)	105.3	1	Kara-Balta	Sanjyra R.
11)	105.3	2	Batken	Sanjyra R.
7)	105.5	1.6	Karakol	Maral FM
9)	105.5	3	Naryn	R. Almaz
3)	105.6	1	Bishkek	Hit FM
11)	105.6	1.6	Osh	Sanjyra R.
4)	105.8	1.6	Özgen	Jash FM
4)	105.8	2.5	Gülchö	Jash FM
8)	105.9	1	Kochkor	Parlament R.
18)	106.0	4	Bishkek	Atom FM
7)	106.1	1.6	Talas	Maral FM
21)	106.1	3	Osh	Yntymak R.
7)	106.3	1.6	Naryn	Maral FM
24)	106.4	2	Batken	R. Salam
5)	106.5	1	Bishkek	Kyrgyzstan Obondoru
5)	106.5	4	Osh	Kyrgyzstan Obondoru
2A)	106.7	8	Naryn	Evropa Plus
9)	106.8	1.6	Cholponata	R. Almaz
2A)	107.1	1	Balykchy	Evropa Plus
19)	107.4	2	Bishkek	Ekho Moskvy
26)	107.5	1.6	Cholponata	Volna Issykkulya
8)	107.7	1	Kara-Kulja	Parlament R.
12)	107.7	2	Osh	El FM
11)	107.7	3	Jalalabat	Sanjyra R.
23)	107.8	1	Bishkek	R. Romantika
11)	107.9	1.6	Cholponata	Sanjyra R.

+ txs below 1kW.

Addresses & other information:
1) Akhunbaev k. 119a, 720000 Bishkek – **2A,B)** Shabdan Baatyra k. 4b, 720000 Bishkek **E:** 2A) office@europa.kg, 2B) info@retrofm.ru – **3)** pr. Chuy 36, 720000 Bishkek **E:** advert@hitfm.kg – **4)** Akhunbaev k. 129, 720000 Bishkek **E:** office.jashfm@gmail.com – **5)** Shabdan Baatyra k. 4b, 720000 Bishkek **E:** radio@obondoru.kg – **6A,B)** 720000 Bishkek **E:** info@mediamanas.kg – **7)** Frunze k. 387, 720000 Bishkek **E:** info.maralfm@gmail.com – **8)** 720000 Bishkek – **9)** Chuykov k. 133a, 720000 Bishkek **E:** almazradio@gmail.com – **10)** Jantosheva k. 70, 720000 Bishkek – **11)** Tokumbaev k. 46a, 720000 Bishkek – **12)** Lenin k. 330, 723500 Osh **E:** elfm@gmail.com – **13)** Abdrakhmanov k. 170, 720000 Bishkek – **14)** Shabdan Baatyra k. 6, 720000 Bishkek **E:** okradio@elcat.kg – **15)** 720000 Bishkek **E:** office@mixmedia.kg – **16)** Jantoshev k. 70, 720000 Bishkek **E:** info@tumar.fm – **17)** 1 may k. 61, 722360 Karakol – **18)** Abdrakhmanov k. 192, 720000 Bishkek **E:** atom-fm@gmail.com – **19)** 720000 Bishkek – **20)** Sataev k. 52/67, 722720 Talas – **21)** Nurmatov k. 3, 4-kabat, 723500 Osh **E:** yntymakunalgysy@gmail.com – **22)** 721600 Toktogul – **23)** Akhunbaev k. 119a, 720000 Bishkek **E:** romantika.bishkek@gmail.com – **24)** 8 Mart k, 25, 715100 Batken – **25)** 59-kvartal, 8-uy, 1-batir, 722720 Talas – **26)** 18 mkr Voskhod 66, 722200 Karakol – **A)** Rel. R. Rossii (Russia) – **B)** Rel. Vesti FM (Russia) – **C)** Rel. R. Sputnik (Russia).

Radio via DTT: see National TV section

LAOS

L.T: UTC +7h — **Pop:** 7.3 million — **Pr.L:** Lao (official), French, Hmong, Khmu — **E.C:** 230V/50Hz — **ITU:** LAO

MINISTRY OF INFORMATION, CULTURE AND TOURISM (MICT)

✉ Lane Xang Avenue (P.O.Box 3556), Vientiane ☎ +856 21 212251 🖷 +856 21 212769

LAO NATIONAL RADIO – LNR (Gov.)

✉ PO Box 310, Vientiane; Phaynam Rd, Ban Sisakhet, Chantabouly District, Vientiane **L.P:** DG: Mr Phosy Keomanivong ☎ +856 21 243250 🖷 +856 21 212430 **W:** lnr.org.la

City and Provincial sces: These are operated by the local governments + Sisavangvong Rd, Ban Pakhame, Luang Prabang – Km 2 Route 13 South, Oudomsavane Village, Pakse, Champassak Province - Manthatulat Road, Vientiane – Houamouangtai Village, Savannakhet, Khantabouly – Nongbouakham Village, Tha Khek, Khammouane

MW	kHz	kW	S	H of tr
Vientiane*	567	200	N	2200-0800, 0900-1630
Khantabouly, Sa	585	20	P	2230-1300
Luang Prabang	705	10	P	2200-0800, 1025-1500
SW	**kHz**	**kW**	**S**	**H of tr**
Vientiane	6130	50	N	2200-0800, 0900-1630

S=Sce, N=National, P=Provincial, Sa=Savannakhet prov.
*) Tx loc.: Kilometre 49 (GC: 18N20 102E27)
Reg. stns generally rel. national news at 0000, 0500, 1200

National Sce in Lao: 2300-0600, 0900-1330; **Hmong:** 2200-2230, 0600-0700; **Khmu:** 2230-2300, 0700-0800; **Foreign Language Sce in Chinese:** 1400-1430; **English:** 1430-1500; **French:** 1500-1530; **Khmer:** 1330-1400; **Thai:** 1530-1600; **Vietnamese:** 1600-1630; **N:** 2300, 0000, 0500, 0800, 1200
Ann: LNR: 'Thini Sathani Vitthayou Krachaisiang Hengsat'
IS: Music on Khéne (mouth organ) & Solo (bamboo instrument)

LNR FM (MHz): Vientiane FM 103.7 20kW: 2300-1700 – **Happy Radio** 97.3 20kW: 2300-1700 – **Climax Radio** 95.0: 2300-1700 – **Butterfly Radio** 94.3: 2200-1700
Vientiane City FM (MHz): **Love Lao FM** 105.5 1kW: 2330-1700 – **VV Radio** 98.8 10kW
Provincial FM (MHz): Attapeu: 95.0 10kW – Paksan, Bolikhamsay Prov: 101.5 5kW – Houai Xay, Bokeo Prov: 102.75 1kW – Khantabouly, S: 100.75 1kW Luang – Namtha Prov: 98.0 1kW Luang Prabang: 103.5MHz 0.3kW. Muang Hay, Oudomxay Prov: 100MHz 0.1kW – Pakse, Champassak Prov: 103.7 1kW – Phonsavan, Xieng Khuang Prov: 97.5 5kW – Phongsali Prov: 102 0.1kW – Sam Neua, Houa Phan Prov: 102.0 10kW – Saravane: 101.2 0.3kW – Saiyabouly: 96.5

5kW – Saysomboun Special Reg.: 100 5kW – Sekong: 102.7 1kW – Siphandon, Champassak Prov: 97.3 0.33kW – Tha Khek, Khammouane Prov: 95.5 0.1kW

LAO YOUTH RADIO STATION
Lao People's Revolutionary Youth Union
✉ Phonthan Village, Xaysetha District, Vientiane **W:** laoyouth-radio.com
FM: Vientiane 90.0MHz 2.5kW. D.Prgr: 2300-1600

LAO PEOPLE'S ARMY BROADCASTING (Mil.)
✉ Phonkheng Village, Vientiane
FM: Vientiane 99.7MHz 10kW. Rel. on 99.7MHz: Attapeu, Bolikhamsay, Houai Xay, Houai Xe, Luang Prabang, Nam Bak, Pak Lay, Paksan, Pakse, Paksong, Phonsavan, Saiyabouly, Saravane, Savannakhet, Sekong, Siphandon. Tha Khek, Viengxay.

PUBLIC SECURITY RADIO STATION (Gov.)
✉ Ministry of Public Security, Sengsavang Village, Saysettha District, Vientiane
FM: PS Radio Vientiane 101.5MHz 10kW

OTHER STATIONS:
China R. International: Vientiane 93.0MHz 10kW D.Prgr: 0300-1530 rel. CRI from Beijing in Chinese, English & Lao
R. France Internationale: Vientiane 100.5 MHz 5kW D.Prgr: 24h rel. RFI from Paris in French

LATVIA

L.T: UTC +2h (28 Mar-31 Oct: +3h) — **Pop:** 1.9 million — **Pr.L:** Latvian (official), Russian — **E.C:** 230V/50Hz — **ITU:** LVA

NACIONALA ELEKTRONISKO PLAŠSAZINAS LIDZEKLU PADOME (NEPLP)
(National Council for Electronic Media)
✉ Doma laukums 8A, LV-1939 Rīga ☎ +371 67221848 🖷 +371 67220448 **E:** neplpadome@neplpadome.lv **W:** neplpadome.lv
L.P: Chmn: Ivars Āboliņš

LATVIJAS RADIO (Pub)
✉ Doma laukums 8, LV-1505 Rīga ☎ +371 67206722 **E:** radio@latvijasradio.lv **W:** latvijasradio.lsm.lv **L.P:** Chair: Una Klapkalne

FM (MHz)	**1**	**2**	**3**	**4**	**5**	**6**	**kW**
Aizpurve	106.0	-	-	100.0	-	-	10/2
Alūksne	106.8	104.3	-	100.5	-	-	3.5
Cesvaine	102.5	105.0	103.5	-	-	-	2x20/4.5
Dagda	102.6*	98.6	-	99.1	-	-	1.7/1/0.9
Daugavpils	90.6*	100.7	88.1	88.7	104.0	-	4/7.9/1.3/6.3/3.2
Dundaga	91.1	106.7	104.2	-	-	-	4
Evarži	-	-	-	-	102.4	-	-
Kuldīga	95.9	101.3	92.0	-	-	-	10/16.6/3.3
Lielauce	99.6	-	-	-	-	-	1
Liepāja	107.1	101.0	104.6	97.9	102.1	-	2x12.6/3.2/6.3/0.2
Limbaži	105.5	-	-	-	100.5	-	5.6/4.7
Māle	100.3	-	-	-	-	-	1
Rēzekne	107.5*	101.0	101.8	104.2	103.8	-	2x20/5/20/0.4
Rīga	90.7	91.5	103.7	107.7	93.1	95.8	2x35/9.5/6.6/8.9/0.7
Skaista	92.7*	102.6	-	94.5	-	-	2x2.5/2
Valmiera	104.0	101.5	87.6	-	89.5	-	2x20/2x2.4
Ventspils	99.2	103.0	89.8	95.3	96.5	-	3x0.3/1/0.2
Viesīte	107.6	104.7	102.2	91.1	-	-	3x5/1.6

*) Incl. reg prgrs (see below)

D.Prgr: Prgr 1 (Latvijas R.1): 24h – **Prgr 2 (Latvijas R.2):** 24h – **Prgr 3 (Latvijas R.3 - Klasika):** 24h – **Prgr 4 (Latvijas R.4 - Doma laukums)** for ethnic minorities: 24h in Russian (exc. Mon-Wed 1810-1900 for other ethnic communities (e.g. Georgian, German, Polish, Tatar, Ukrainian communities), rotating. These prgrs may be in Latvian, Russian and/or the respective ethnic minority language) – **Prgr 5 (Latvijas R.5 - Pieci.lv):** 24h – **Prgr 6 (Latvijas R.6 - NABA):** 24h. This outlet provides a relay of the Latvijas Universitāte student webradio station R. NABA (✉Aspazijas blvd. 5, LV-1050 Rīga), and live broadcasts from parliament (Saeima). – **Regional Studio:** LR Latgales studija, Atbrīvošanas aleja 90, LV-4601 Rēzekne. On FM (see main tx table) in Latgalian: MF 1305-1400 ("Latgolys stuņde").

OTHER STATIONS

MW	**kHz**	**kW**	**Location**	**Station**
20A)	1485	0.3¹	Rīga	R. Merkurs
20B)	1602	1¹	Rīga	R. Centrs

¹) permitted (licensed) power for each freq is 1kW
The site for both freqs is located in the northwest of Rīga (Dzintara iela 20), in the Daugavgrīva neighbourhood at the Baltic Sea shore (on third-party owned antenna terrain shared with an amateur radio club, formerly used for military maritime navigation and since privatized; G.C: 57N02'11" / 024E00'27").

FM	**MHz**	**kW**	**Location**	**Station**
3C)	87.7	1.6	Liepāja	EHR Russkie Hity
1B)	87.9	1	Ventspils	R. SWH+
2)	87.9	2.5	Madona	Star FM
3A)	88.4	1	Gulbene	EHR
9)	88.4	1.3	Liepāja	Kurzemes R.
4C)	88.6	1	Rīga	R. 88.6 FM
2)	89.1	2.5	Sēlpils	Star FM
1C)	89.2	4	Rīga	R. SWH Rock
1A)	89.3	1	Dundaga	R. SWH
18)	89.5	1.1	Aizpute	R. Tev
19)	90.1	3.2	Daugavpils	Divu Krastu R.
3B)	90.3	1	Matīši	EHR Superhits
18)	90.4	2.2	Kuldīga	R. Tev
5)	90.8	1	Ventspils	Kristīgais R.
3B)	90.9	3	Madona	EHR Superhits
2)	91.0	1.9	Liepāja	Star FM
2)	91.9	1.5	Rēzekne	Star FM
8)	91.9	2	Iecava	Top R.
2)	92.0	1	Viļķene	Star FM
12A)	92.3	1	Liepāja	Retro FM
8)	92.4	1	Daugavpils	Top R.
9)	92.4	1.3	Tukums	Kurzemes R.
3A)	92.9	2	Daugavpils	EHR
16)	93.5	2.2	Liepāja	XOFM
4D)	93.9	2.8	Rīga	Baltkom R.
18)	94.0	1	Valka	R. Tev
1C)	94.1	1.1	Jēkabpils	R. SWH Rock
3B)	94.3	1.6	Talsi	EHR Superhits
6B)	94.6	1	Valka	R. Skonto Vidzeme
1A)	94.7	1	Broceni	R. SWH
7)	94.9	1.3	Rīga	Relax FM
18)	95.0	2.5	Dundaga	R. Tev
17)	95.2	6.3	Daugavpils	Latgales R.
3B)	95.2	1.6	Liepāja	EHR Superhits
8)	95.4	1	Rīteri	Top R.
17)	95.8	1	Jēkabpils	Latgales R.
7)	95.9	1	Valmiera	Relax FM
12B)	96.1	2.1	Kraslava	RU FM
3A)	96.1	1.6	Liepāja	EHR
3C)	96.2	2	Rīga	EHR Russkie Hity
3B)	96.8	1	Rīga	EHR Superhits
6B)	97.0	1	Valmiera	R. Skonto Vidzeme
10)	97.3	2.6	Rīga	R. Marija Latvija
6A)	97.5	3.2	Liepāja	R. Skonto Kurzeme
2)	97.7	1.1	Pūre	Star FM
8)	97.7	1	Līvāni	Top R.
18)	98.1	1	Valmiera	R. Tev
8)	98.3	2.3	Rīga	Top R.
5)	98.5	3.3	Kuldīga	Kristīgais R.
1C)	98.6	2	Gulbene	R. SWH Rock
1C)	98.8	7.2	Valmiera	R. SWH Rock
13)	99.0	1	Jūrmala	R. Jūrmala
12A)	99.4	1.6	Daugavpils	Retro FM
17)	99.5	2	Balvi	Latgales R.
4B)	99.5	2.8	Rīga	Lounge FM
6B)	99.8	2	Cesvaine	R. Skonto Vidzeme
5)	99.9	2	Daugavpils	Kristīgais R.
15)	100.0	2.5	Rīga	R. PIK
1A)	100.1	1.9	Kuldīga	R. SWH
6A)	100.5	1	Ventspils	R. Skonto Kurzeme
A)	100.5	1.3	Rīga	BBCWS relay
5)	100.6	1.6	Liepāja	Kristīgais R.
3A)	100.8	1	Talsi	EHR
8)	100.9	1	Cēsis	Top R.
16)	101.0	2.6	Rīga	XOFM
1A)	101.2	4.5	Jēkabpils	R. SWH
5)	101.3	1.1	Kraslava	Kristīgais R.
14)	101.6	3.2	Daugavpils	Alise Plus
5)	101.8	5.6	Rīga	Kristīgais R.
3A)	101.9	1	Ventspils	EHR
2)	102.0	2.3	Broceni	Star FM

FM	MHz	kW	Location	Station
1A)	102.2	4	Talsi	R. SWH
4A)	102.7	2.8	Rīga	Mix FM
5)	102.8	1	Jēkabpils	Kristīgais R.
17)	103.0	1.8	Rēzekne	Latgales R.
2)	103.2	5	Svente	Star FM
3B)	103.2	1	Kuldīga	EHR Superhits
2)	103.8	1.3	Kuldīga	Star FM
3A)	104.3	4.8	Rīga	EHR
16)	104.7	1.1	Cēsis	XOFM
2)	105.0	1.6	Pope	Star FM
1A)	105.1	5	Liepāja	R. SWH
11)	105.1	1.3	Rēzekne	R. Rēzekne
1A)	105.2	3.6	Daugavpils	R. SWH
1A)	105.2	13.2	Rīga	R. SWH
1A)	105.4	1.3	Ventspils	R. SWH
12A)	105.5	2	Rēzekne	Retro FM
1B)	105.7	4.1	Rīga	R. SWH+
5)	105.9	3.5	Cesvaine	Kristīgais R.
6B)	106.1	3.5	Daugavpils	R. Skonto Vidzeme
2)	106.2	6.3	Rīga	Star FM
9)	106.4	11.5	Kuldīga	Kurzemes R.
1A)	106.5	4	Rēzekne	R. SWH
1A)	106.5	5	Valmiera	R. SWH
2)	106.6	1	Bauska	Star FM
1B)	107.2	6.3	Daugavpils	R. SWH+
6)	107.2	4	Rīga	R. Skonto
2)	107.4	2	Valmiera	Star FM
3A)	107.4	1.3	Kuldīga	EHR
8)	107.6	1.6	Liepāja	Top R.
1A)	107.9	5	Cesvaine	R. SWH
9)	107.9	1	Ventspils	Kurzemes R.

+ txs below 1kW.

Addresses & other information:

1A-C) Ganību dambis 24D, LV-1013 Rīga. 1B) in Russian – **2)** Dzelzavas iela 120G, LV-1021 Rīga – **3A-C)** Elijas iela 17, LV-1050 Rīga. 3C) In Russian – **4A-D)** Kr.Valdemāra iela 8, LV-1010 Rīga. In Russian – **5)** Lāčplēša iela 37, LV-1011 Rīga – **6)** Kr.Valdemāra iela 100, LV-1013 Rīga. Reg. stns: 6A) Graudu iela 27/29, LV-3401 Liepāja; 6B) Rīgas iela 13, LV-4201 Valmiera – **7)** L.Nometņu iela 62, LV-1002 Rīga – **8)** Tērbatas iela 83B, LV-1001 Rīga. In Russian – **9)** Pilsētas laukums 4A, LV-3301 Kuldīga – **10)** Ojāra Vācieša iela 6, LV-1004 Rīga – **11)** Atbrīvošanas aleja 108-1, LV-4601 Rēzekne. In Russian – **12A,B)** Kr.Valdemāra iela 76, LV-1013 Rīga. In Russian – **13)** Brīvības bulv. 30-6, LV-1050 Rīga. In Russian – **14)** Raiņa iela 28, LV-5401 Daugavpils. In Russian – **15)** Brīvības bulv. 30, LV-1050 Rīga. In Russian – **16)** Kr.Valdemāra iela 76-1A, LV-1013 Rīga – **17)** Latgales iela 82, LV-4601 Rēzekne. Partly in Latgalian – **18)** Kr.Valdemāra iela 100, LV-1013 Rīga – **19)** Atbrīvošanas aleja 98, LV-4601 Rēzekne – **20A,B)** Recording studio: L.Nometņu iela 62, LV-1002 Rīga (programming on both stn's generally consists of pre-recorded broadcasts). 20A) licensed by the regulator NEPLP to SIA "RNI Radio" (**L.P:** Chair: Inese Kreicberga) **E:** rni@apollo.lv; 20B) in Russian (Ann: "R. Tsentr"), licensed by NEPLP under the Latvian language brand "R. Centrs" to the Latvian association "Radio Centrs 1602" (**L.P:** Chmn: Raimonds Kreicbergs) as interdenominal, local religious station for listeners in Rīga & vicinity (coverage defined in license: Rīga & 20km radius around the tx site), **E:** radiocenter@inbox.lv. Both SIA "RNI Radio" and Biedrība "Radio Centrs 1602" are registered at Kadiķu iela 5-1, LV-2008 Jūrmala. Postbox address for R. Centrs: P.O.Box 166, LV-1050 Rīga. 12B prgrs are produced in cooperation with/supplied by the U.S. based non-profit corporation Russian Christian Radio Center, Inc (**L.P:** Pres/CEO: Andrey Nekrasov), **E:** rcrc@radiocenter.net – **A)** Rel. BBCWS (UK)

LEBANON

L.T: UTC +2h (28 Mar-31 Oct: +3h) — **Pop:** 6.8 million — **Pr.L:** Arabic (official), French, Armenian — **E.C:** 230V/50Hz — **ITU:** LBN

CONSEIL NATIONAL DE L'AUDIOVISUEL (CNA)

Beirut ☎ +96 1 1744310 🖷 +96 1 1744314 **E:** cnaliban@gmail.com **W:** www.cna-liban.com

RADIO LIBAN (Pub.)

Rue Lyon, Sanayeh, P.O. Box 4848, Beirut ☎+961 1 743531 **W:** radioliban.gov.lb **E:** radiolibanonline@hotmail.com

1st Prgr. in Arabic: Tyros 98.1MHz, Beit Mery/Jabal Safi 98.5 MHz. **2nd Prgr. in French/English:** 4 sites on 96.2MHz. **Rel. R. France Int:** 12h per day.

OTHER STATIONS:

FM	MHz	Station	FM	MHz	Station
41)	87.5	Irtiqaa Way	11)	96.9	Sawt el-Ghad
43)	87.9	Vo Youth	38)	97.9	Vo Grace
20)	88.1	R. Nostalgie	41)	98.5	Irtiqaa Way
4)	88.5	R. Orient	36)	98.9	R. Aghani Aghani
44)	88.5	R. Liban Culture	5)	99.1	NRJ
7)	89.1	Risala R.	15)	99.7	Fame FM
32)	89.5	Virgin R.	1)	100.3	Voice of Lebanon
42)	89.7	Flash FM	37)	100.7	R. Al-Fajir
35)	89.7	Ciel FM	25)	101.0	R. Jaras Scoop
16)	90.1	Sawt al Hurriya	24)	101.3	Power FM
12)	90.3	Sawt al-Jadeed	31)	101.5	R. Sevan
17)	90.5	R. Light FM	22)	101.9	R. Delta
31)	90.8	R. Sevan	9)	102.5	R. Free Lebanon
33)	91.0	Sawt al-Injil	21)	103.0	Pax R.
8)	91.3	Nidaa al-Maarifa	2)	103.8	Sawt al-Shaab
3)	91.9	R. Al-Nour	39)	104.1	Play FM
44)	92.3	R. Liban Culture	19)	104.5	Mix FM
28)	92.7	Sawt el-Mada	37)	104.9	R. Al-Fajir
23)	93.3	Voice of Lebanon	45)	105.7	Star FM
13)	94.0	Holy Quran R	14)	106.1	Voice of Charity
33)	94.5	Sawt al-Injil	27)	106.7	Al-Balad R. Station
10)	94.9	Voice of Van	18)	107.3	R. MBS
34)	95.5	Al-Bachaer Radio	30)	107.7	Sawt el-Noujoum
30)	95.9	Sawt el-Noujoum	37)	107.7	R. Al-Fajir
41)	96.5	Irtiqaa Way Radio	46)	107.9	Jabal Loubnan

NB: most stns have been allocated 400kHz frequency range, of which mostly the centre freq. is listed above. In many cases the trs from various sites are placed on both upper and lower limits of the range.

Addresses & other information:

1) P.O. Box 165271, Ashrafieh, Bachir el Gemayel Ave, Beirut **W:** sawtlebnan.com – **2)** Jabal el Arab St, Wata el Mousaitbeh, P.O.Box 14/5425, Beirut **W:** sawtachaab.com – **3)** Al-Nour Bldg, Abdel Nour St, Haret Hreïk, P.O.Box 25-197, Ghbeiry, Beirut **W:** alnour.com.lb/radio Also relayed via in Syria via Tartus on 1071kHz and Aleppo 98.7MHz – **4)** Annajah Centre, Mar Elias St, Karakol Druz, P.O. Box 11-6362, Beirut **W:** radioorientlb.com – **5)** Studiovision Bldg, Naccache, Metn, Beirut **W:** nrjlebanon.com 24h in English. – **7)** Fraiha Bld. 3rd Floor, Barbour Beirut **W:** risalaradio.com – **8)** Shaykh Ahmad Iskandarani Centre, Bourj Abi Haidar, Beirut.**W:** nidaa.fm – **9)** Kebbe Bldg, Adonis, Zouk Mosbeh, P.O.Box 110, Zouk Mekhael, Jounieh **W:** rll.com.lb – **10)** 2nd floor, Shaghzoyan Centre, Borj Hammoud, P.O. Box 80-860, Beirut **W:** voiceofvan.net 24h in Armenian & Arabic – **11)** Jal el Dib, Beirut 60073 **W:** facebook.com/sawtelghadlb – **12)** Watta al-Museitbeh, Ghbeiri, Beirut **W:** aljadeed.tv hawacom.tv/radio – **13)** Dar al Fatwa, P.O. Box 14-5380, Al Mazraa-Beirut **W:** quranradio.com.lb – **14)** Couvent St. Jean, Fouad Chehab St, P.O. Box 850, Jounieh **W:** voiceofcharity.org 24h in Arabic/French/others – **15)** 3rd floor, La Perla Centre, Sabra Highway, Jounieh **W:** famefm.com – **16)** Achrafieh, Kobayate St, Tutunji Center 7th floor, Beirut 1100 **W:** facebook.com/SawtelhouriaRadio – **17)** cityrama, dekwaneh, sin el fil the private club, 3rd floor, Beirut **W:** radiolightfm.com in English/French – **18)** 1st floor, Pères Paulistes building, Off Highway, Haret Sakhre, Kesrouane **W:** facebook.com/radiombsfm – **19)** Alfred Naccache Ave, P.O. Box 166-815, Achrafieh, Beirut **W:** mixfm.com.lb 24h in English – **20)** Mont Liban Bldg, Ave. Fouad Chehab, Fassouh, P.O.Box 16-6000, Achrafieh, Beirut **W:** nostalgie.com.lb 24h in French – **21)** P.O. Box 116-5104, Beirut 24h in English **W:** paxradio.net – **22)** Kahalé Bldg, Old St, P.O.Box 1306, Beit Meri el Metn **W:** radiodelta.fm – **23)** c/o Modern Media Company, Dbayeh, Beirut **W:** vdl.com.lb – **24)** powerfmlebanon.com – **25)** 4th Floor, Hawa Chicken Building, Damascus Highway, Hazmiyé **W:** jarasfm.com – **27)** Centre Nasrallah, Rue Al-Anwar, Jdeideh, P.O. Box 90-1119, Beirut **W:** albaladonline.com – **28)** Mirna el Chalouhi Centre 2nd floor, Sin el-Fil, Beirut **W:** sawtelmada.com – **30)** Kreshet Bldg. 7th floor, Suyoufi St, Algazlep, Achrafieh, Beirut **W:** sawtelnoujoum.com – **31)** Khatchadurian Street, Khederlarian Building, Ground Floor, Beirut **W:** radiosevan.com – **32)** Jal al-Dib highway, Beirut **W:** virginradiolebanon.com – **33)** Sawt al-Injil, Maronite Archdiocese of Beirut **W:** facebook.com/voiceofgospel – **34)** Sawt al-Bachaer, Beirut **W:** albachaer.com – **35) W:** facebook.com/CielFMLebanon – **36)** Beirut Media Zone, Studiovision Bldg #1, Naccache, Beirut **W:** aghaniaghani.com – **37)** Beirut **W:** fajrradio.com – **38) W:** antiochpatriarchate.org/radio.php – **39) W:** facebook.com/PlayFmLebanon In Arabic & English – **41) W:** irtiqaaway.com – **42)** unlicensed **W:** facebook.com/RadioFlashLebanon – **43)** unlicensed **W:** yeridasartoutiantsayne.com – **44) W:** radiolibanculture.com

– **45) W:** starfmlebanon.com – **46) W:** jaballebnan.fm– **47)** Beirut

R. Sawa: Beirut/Bekaa/Jabal Safi/Tripoli 87.7MHz, Al-Qubayat/Deir el-Acher 98.7MHz

LESOTHO

L.T: UTC +2h — **Pop:** 2.2 million — **Pr.L:** Sesotho (official), English (official) — **E.C:** 220V/50Hz — **ITU:** LSO

LESOTHO COMMUNICATIONS AUTHORITY (LCA)

P.O. Box 15896, 6th Floor, Moposo House, Kingsway Road, Maseru ☎+266 22224300 🖹 +266 22310984 **W:** lca.org.ls **E:** lca@lca.org.ls

LESOTHO NATIONAL BROADCASTING SERVICES (LNBS) (Pub.)

P. O. Box 552, Lerotholi St, Opposite Royal Palace, Maseru 100 ☎+266 22321460 🖹 +266 22313980 **W:** communications.gov.ls/pages/lnbs.php

MW: Maseru (Lancer's Gap): 639kHz 100kW, 891kHz 50kW.

FM	MHz	kW(TRP)	FM	MHz	kW(TRP)
Leribe	88.6		Likhoele	97.2	1
Katse	90.8	0.3	Maseru (Berea)	99.8	5
Ha-Sottho	92.6	0.25	Thaba-Putsoa	100.2	1
Lebelonyane	93.2	1	Sheep Stud Hill	102.4	1
Maseru (Berea)	93.3	5	Popa	103.6	1
Leribe	96.0	1	Souru	105.4	1
Matshoana	96.8	1	Sehonghong	106.1	0.25

R. Lesotho in Sesotho/English: 24h on 639kHz & FM excl. two Ultimate FM freq's.
Ultimate FM in English: 891kHz and 88.6 & 99.8MHz 24h.

OTHER STATIONS:
357 Sublime Radio, Maseru: 94.3MHz **W:** 357fm.com
Bokamoso FM, Maseru: 97.4 700W **W:** facebook.com/bokamoso974
Harvest FM (Rlg.) Maseru: 98.9MHz 500W **W:** harvestfm.co.ls
LM Radio: Maseru 104.0MHz **W:** facebook.com/www.lmradio.net
Mafeteng Community Radio: Maseru 107.7MHz **W:** facebook.com/Mafeteng-Community-Radio-1729087884010915
MoAfrika FM: Berea 89.7MHz 500W, Mafeteng 90.7MHz **W:** moafrika.co.ls
Motjoli FM, Thaba-Tseka: 87.9MHz **W:** motjolifm879.wordpress.com
MXXL, Maseru 91.0MHz. **W:** facebook.com/mxxl910
PCFM: Leribe 92.8MHz, Maseru: 95.6MHz **W:** pcfm.co.ls
Radio Maria Lesotho, Maseru: 103.3MHz **W:** radiomaria.co.ls
T'senolo FM, Maseru: 104.6MHz 1kW **W:** tsenolofm.co.ls
VOG-Voice of God (Rlg.), Maseru: 106.0MHz 1kW **W:** facebook.com/Voice-of-God-fm-VOG-FM-1060-MHZ-765979953530829
BBC African Sce, Maseru (Berea): 90.2MHz.
RFI Afrique, Maseru (Berea): 96.5MHz in French/English

LIBERIA

L.T: UTC — **Pop:** 5.1 million — **Pr.L:** English (official), indigenious languages — **E.C:** 120V/60Hz — **ITU:** LBR

LIBERIA TELECOMMUNICATIONS AUTHORITY (LTA)

National Investment Commission Annex, 12th Street, Sinkor, Tubman Boulevard, Monrovia ☎+231 27302012 **W:** lta.gov.lr **E:** info@lta.gov.lr

LIBERIA BROADCASTING SYSTEM (LBS, Pub.)

P.O. Box 594, Paynesville **W:** elbcradio.com **E:** lbs@yahoo.com
L.P: DG: Darryl Ambrose Nmah, Sr. Deputy DG: Ledgerhood Rennie.
FM: ELBC Radio 99.9MHz 10kW **D.Prgr:** 0530-2400.

RADIO ELWA (Rlg.)

P.O. Box 192, Monrovia **W:** elwaministries.org **E:** elwaradio54@gmail.com **L.P:** GM: Moses T. Nyantee.
SW: Monrovia 6050kHz 1kW.
FM: Monrovia 94.5MHz 2kW.
D.Prgr in English/local lang's: 0530-1000, 1700-2400 (SS -2230).

ECOWAS RADIO (Economic Community of West African States)

Monrovia **W:** ecowas.int **W:** info@ecowas.int
FM: Gbarnga 90.5MHz, Harper/Monrovia/Zwedru 91.5MHz, Sanniquellie 95.1MHz. Greenville/Voinjama 97.1MHz (Harper/Sanniquelle 1kW, others 5kW). **D.Prgr**: 24h in English/French/Portuguese

OTHER STATIONS:
ABCU R, Yekepa: 95.7MHz 0.6kW **W:** africanbiblecolleges.org/abcu_liberia.php – **City FM,** Monrovia: 90.2MHz – **Crystal FM,** Monrovia: 95.5MHz – **DC 101.1 FM,** Monrovia: 101.1MHz. Also rel. BBC African Sce – **King's FM,** Monrovia: 88.5MHz. Also rel. VOA. – **Liberian Christian Broadcasting Network,** Monrovia: 102.3MHz – **Love FM,** Monrovia: 105.5MHz – **Power FM,** Monrovia: 93.3MHz – **Magic FM,** Monrovia: 99.2MHz – **R. Monrovia**: 92.1MHz **W:** radiomonrovia247.com – **Sky FM,** Monrovia: 107.0MHz. **E:** skyliberia@yahoo.com – **Truth FM,** Monrovia 96.1MHz. **W:** truthfm.com.lr – **United Metodist Church R,** Monrovia: 98.7MHz 0.3kW.

BBC African Sce, Monrovia: 103.1MHz
RFI Afrique: Monrovia 106.0MHz in French/English/Mandinka.
About 35 community radio stations are in operation

LIBYA

L.T: UTC +2h — **Pop:** 6.9 million — **Pr.L:** Arabic — **E.C:** 230V/50Hz — **ITU:** LBY

GENERAL AUTHORITY FOR COMMUNICATIONS AND INFORMATICS (GACI)

Zawia St., Tripoli ☎ +218 21 3619811 🖹 +218 21 3622452 **E:** info@cim.gov.ly **W:** www.cim.gov.ly **L.P:** Chmn: Sami Al-Fintazi

LIBYAN RADIO & TELEVISION NETWORK (Gov)

El Fath Rd, P.O. Box 80237, Tripoli ☎+218 21 4442252 🖹 +218 21 3403458. **W:** facebook.com/radio.alwatania.ly facebook.com/903-Radio-Libya-FM-1530899760490235

MW	kHz	kW	Prgr.
Benghazi	‡675	100	Vo Homeland
Tripoli	‡1053	100	Vo Homeland

FM (MHz): El Beida 87.9, Tripoli 88.8 (youth channel), Benghazi 89.3, Riqdalin 89.7, Ajdabiya 89.9, Misrata 90.3 (regional), Tripoli 90.3, Gharyan 91.9, Al-Marj/Bani Walid 92.3, Sebha 92.9, Sabha 93.4, Sirte 95.3, Misrata 95.5 (Koran), Sabha 96.1, Tripoli 96.6, El Beida 98.0, Benghazi 98.9, Sirte 101.1, Al-Zawiya 101.3, Tobruk 102.6, Sultan 103.0, Tripoli 103.4/105.3 (city council).
Ann: "Radio Libya al-Wataniya".

Other Stations:

FM	MHz	Station & other info
Tripoli	87.7	Al Saba FM
Janzur	87.9	Al-Badia FM
Tarhuna	87.9	R. Holy Koran
Benghazi	88.1	Voice of America
Surman	88.1	R. Aloula **W:** facebook.com/radioloulasurman
Msallata	88.3	R. Misallata **W:** facebook.com/msallata.radio
Benghazi	88.5	Libya FM **W:** facebook.com/LFM88.5
Tripoli	88.5	Ajwa FM
Waddan	88.5	Waddan FM **W:**facebook.com/885-253268675138765
Tripoli	88.8	Al-Shababiya **W:** alshbabya.net
Hun	88.9	Hun FM **W:** facebook.com/hun.fm
Misrata	89.1	Tanasuh FM (see 102.1)
Tripoli	89.1	Assheya FM
Derna	89.3	R. Assaraya (see 99.3)
Misallata	89.3	Tanasuh FM (see 102.1)
Tripoli	89.5	Al-Qitab wa al-Sunna **W:** kwsfm.ly
Qaser al Khiar	90.1	R. Al-Shorooq **W:** facebook.com/ksfm90.1
Misrata	90.5	Al-Furqan R. **W:** furqan.ly
Tripoli	90.5	Qimam al-Andalus R. **W:** facebook.com/qimam.fm
Tripoli	90.7	R.Alsaa **W:** facebook.com/Radio-Alsaa-907-fm-1511278569136196
Benghazi	90.9	Minhaj al-Sunna **W:** facebook.com/MinhajAlssuna
Jadu	90.9	R. Sawt al-Haq **W:** facebook.com/radiosawt
Tripoli	91.1	Libo FM **W:**facebook.com/LIBO-FM-422922221078165
3 sites	91.5	BBC Arabic Sce **W:** bbc.com/Arabic
Tripoli	92.1	Al-Amal FM **W:** facebook.com/alamalfm
Tripoli east	92.3	Tanasuh FM (see 102.1)
Misrata	92.5	Flash FM **W:** facebook.com/-925-Flash-fm-442113809190890
Tripoli	92.5	Echo FM **W:** echo.net.ly

FM	MHz	Station & other info
Benghazi	92.9	R. Sanabil **W:** facebook.com/sanabillibya92.9
Tripoli	92.9	Ranwa FM **W:** facebook.com/RanwaFM
Benghazi	93.1	R. Assaraya (see 99.3)
Tripoli	93.4	Al-Rasmiya FM **W:**facebook.com/alrasmiyafm934
Nalut	93.7	Al-Seean FM **W:**facebook.com/Radio.AlseeanFM
Tripoli	93.8	Lebda FM **W:** rtvlebda.com
Tripoli	94.1	Karawan FM **W:**facebook.com/Radio.karawan.fm
Castelverde	94.3	R. Garabulli **W:** facebook.com/-Fm943-1234822709880714
Sirte	94.3	R. Al-Tawhid **W:**facebook.com/AttawheedChannel
Tripoli	94.5	Raqmia FM
Alrujban	94.8	Alrujban FM **W:** facebook.com/alrujban.fm
Ain Zara	95.1	R. Ain Zara **W:** facebook.com/951-444412692975552
Tripoli	95.1	Zain FM **W:** facebook.com/Radio-zain-fm-951-174552360128811
Benghazi	95.5	Jawak FM **W:** facebook.com/jawakfm
Tripoli	95.5	Al-Madena FM **W:** facebook.com/AlmadenaFM
Misrata	95.9	Libya Cultural R. **W:**facebook.com/499370350240827
Tripoli	96.3	Al-Kalema Al-Taiba Islamic R.
Misrata	96.5	Wadah FM
Tripoli	96.9	LY Radio **W:** lyradio.webs.com
Tripoli	97.1	Monte Carlo Doualiya **W:** mc-doualiya.com
Tripoli	97.5	Al-Turath FM **W:**facebook.com/FM-230187014471338
Al-Khums	97.9	R. Biladi FM **W:** facebook.com/FM-979-1211700278916218
Tripoli	97.9	R. Ittihad **W:** facebook.com/RadioIttihad
Zuwara	98.1	R. Assaraya (see 99.3)
Nalut	98.3	Nalut R. **W:** facebook.com/NalutFM
Tripoli&4 sites	98.7	Al-Wasat R. **W:** alwasat.ly
Al Zawiya	98.9	R. Sada **W:** facebook.com/radio.sada.fm98.9
Tripoli	99.0	R.Tajoura **W:** facebook.com/RTaj99FM
Misrata	99.1	Voice of America
Tarhouna	99.1	R. Al-Shoroq **W:** facebook.com/ShoroukTarhona
Tripoli	99.3	R. Assaraya **W:** facebook.com/radioassaraya
Benghazi	99.5	R. Madinaty **W:** facebook.com/radiomycity
Az-Zawiya	99.7	As-Shorouk FM
Tripoli	99.7	Al-Sooq FM **W:** facebook.com/radioalsooqFM
Ajdabiya	99.9	Future FM **W:** facebook.com/fut.fm
Misrata	99.9	Misrata FM **W:** facebook.com/misratafm99.9
Tripoli	99.9	Al-Iman R. **W:** facebook.com/999.ly
Benghazi	100.1	Libyana Hits **W:** libyanahits.fm, English
El Beida	100.1	R. Sowt Libya **W:**facebook.com/radio.sout.libya.fm100.1
Tripoli	100.3	Salaf Way FM **W:** facebook.com/salafwayfm
Sebha	101.1	R. Ramadan FM **W:**ramadan1011fm26.wixsite.com/radioramadan101
Tripoli	101.1	Waad FM **W:** waadfm.com
Al-Zawia	101.3	Al-Zawia FM **W:** facebook.com/AlzawiaFM
Benghazi	101.5	R. Shabab **W:** facebook.com/Radioshababbenghzi
Tripoli	101.5	R. Burkan Algadb
Wazin	101.6	Wazin FM **W:** wazenfm.blogspot.com
Tripoli	101.7	University R. **W:** facebook.com/uot.radio
Tripoli	101.9	West Tripoli R. **W:** facebook.com/WT.RadioO
Tripoli	102.1	Tanasuh FM **W:** fm.tanasuh.tv
Jalu	102.3	R. Jalu **W:** facebook.com/Radio.Jalu.Free
Nalut	102.3	R. Nalut **W:**facebook.com/fm-1023-1661201574139356
Tobruk	102.5	R. Nidaa al-Iman **W:** facebook.com/RadioneydaaalaemaanTbrq
Tripoli	102.5	Tripoli FM **W:** facebook.com/TripoliFM
Tripoli	102.9	Libya Sport FM **W:** facebook.com/LibyaSportFM
Tripoli	103.4	Vo Tripoli **W:**facebook.com/1034-136638183158287
Zliten	103.5	Zliten FM **W:** facebook.com/ZlitenFM
Zuwara	103.7	R. Quran **W:** facebook.com/323272227711369
Tripoli	104.5	Nass FM **W:** nass.fm
Sabrata	104.8	Sabrata FM **W:** facebook.com/Sabratah-FM-1048-375630675784277
Tripoli/9 sites	105.3	Al-Aan FM (**W:** alaan.fm)
Bani Walid	105.5	R. Ades **W:** facebook.com/RadioAdes
Benghazi	105.5	Monte-Carlo Doualiya **W:** mc-doualiya.com
Al-Aziziya	105.7	R.Zawiya **W:**facebook.com/-1057fm-597897223748407
Zliten	105.7	R.Nour Al-Iman **W:**facebook.com/RadioNourAleman
Benghazi	105.9	R. Power FM **W:**facebook.com/radiopower105.9fm
Misrata	106.0	University R. **W:** facebook.com/RRRR2017
Tripoli	106.1	Al-Watan FM **W:** facebook.com/-Fm-1061-1034191363300506
Yefren	106.3	Awal FM **W:** facebook.com/Awal.fm
Benghazi	106.5	Zain FM **W:** facebook.com/Zain106.5FM
Tripoli	106.6	Voice of America 2kW
Misrata	106.9	Libya Al-Watan Sound **W:** facebook.com/-Libya-alwatan-sound-1861839720772012
Tripoli	107.0	Quran R. **W:** facebook.com/142635977581107
Tripoli	107.3	Tadamon FM **W:** tadamon.gov.ly/site/?page_id=219
Bani Walid	107.7	Zaytona FM **W:** facebook.com/ZaytonaFM
Tripoli	107.7	Jawhara FM **W:** facebook.com/JawFM2012
Al-Qalaa	107.9	Al-Qalaa FM **W:** facebook.com/AlqalaaFM

LIECHTENSTEIN

L.T: UTC +1h (28 Mar-31 Oct: +2h) — **Pop:** 38,000 — **Pr.L:** German — **E.C:** 230V/50Hz — **ITU:** LIE

LIECHTENSTEINISCHER RUNDFUNK (LRF) (Pub)

✉ Dorfstr. 24, 9495 Triesen ☎+423 3991313 **E:** office@radio.li **W:** radio.li **L.P:** CEO:Thomas Mathis

FM (MHz): Balzers 88.8 (0.05kW), Buchs* 89.2 (0.5kW), Steg 96.6 (0.25kW), Vaduz 96.9 (0.1kW), Nendeln 100.2 (0.05kW), Vilters* 103.4 (0.1kW), Thal* 105.9 (0.2kW), Rüthi* 106.1 (1kW). *) Located in Switzerland. Also on DAB Block 9D via txs in Eastern Switzerland (see Switzerland entry).

D.Prgr: Radio L 24h

LITHUANIA

L.T: UTC +2h (28 Mar-31 Oct: +3h) — **Pop:** 2.8 million — **Pr.L:** Lithuanian (official), Polish, Russian — **E.C:** 230V/50Hz — **ITU:** LTU

LIETUVOS RADIJO IR TELEVIZIJOS KOMISIJA (LRTK)

(Radio and TV Commission of Lithuania)

✉ Šeimyniškių g. 3a, 09312 Vilnius ☎ +370 5 2330660 🖷 +370 5 2647125 **E:** lrtk@rtk.lt **W:** rtk.lt **L.P:** Chmn: Mantas Martišius

LIETUVOS NACIONALINIS RADIJAS IR TELEVIZIJA (LRT) (Pub)

✉ S.Konarskio g. 49, 03123 Vilnius ☎ +370 5 2363000 **E:** lrt@lrt.lt **W:** lrt.lt **L.P:** DG: Monika Garbačiauskaitė-Budrienė

FM (MHz)	1	2	3	kW
Biržai	100.8	87.5	-	5/1.3
Bubiai	100.9	103.4	90.5	2x20/0.8
Druskininkai	102.3	103.7	91.7	8.2/5/0.6
Giruliai	102.8	105.3	91.9	27.5/29/0.5
Joniškis	89.4	94.4	-	2/0.5
Juragiai	102.1	96.2	98.0	2x10/1.9
Kalvarija	104.8	-	-	1
Mažeikiai	93.3	101.8	89.9	2x2/0.7
Pažagieniai	107.5	105.3	93.7	2x1.5/1.7
Plungė	88.0	105.0	-	1/0.7
Skuodas	99.3	103.5	-	0.7/2
Tauragė	98.8	107.4	104.2	13/2/1
Viešintos	101.9	104.4	106.5	17.4/18/0.9
Vilnius	89.0	105.1	98.3	20/6.5/3.5
Visaginas	102.9	100.4	-	10

+ sites with only txs below 1kW.

D.Prgr: Prgr 1 (LRT Radijas): 24h. For ethnic minorities: 1405-1430 Russian – **Prgr 2 (LRT Klasika):** 24h. For ethnic minorities: 1200-1230 Belarusian (Tue), Russian (Mon/Wed/Fri/Sat); Russian for the Jewish community (Thu/Sun), 1230-1300 Polish – **Prgr 3 (LRT Opus):** 24h.

OTHER STATIONS

FM	MHz	kW	Location	Station
2D)	87.8	5.3	Vilnius	Rock FM
2B)	88.2	3.2	Bubiai	ZIP FM
16)	88.3	1	Utena	Relax FM
19)	88.5	5	Vilnius	Extra FM
22)	88.8	4	Bubiai	XXL FM
19)	89.1	1	Marijampolė	Extra FM
2A)	89.6	3	Vilnius	Radiocentras
9)	89.7	3.5	Bubiai	Power Hit R.
3B)	90.1	2	Perkūnai	Pūkas 2
2D)	90.3	20	Juragiai	Rock FM
2C)	90.6	2.3	Giruliai	Rusradio LT
2A)	91.2	4	Tryškiai	Radiocentras
14)	91.4	3.2	Klaipėda	XFM

FM	MHz	kW	Location	Station
7)	91.4	2.1	Marijampolė	Marijos radijas
19)	91.5	1	Ukmergė	Extra FM
2B)	91.6	2	Skuodas	ZIP FM
7)	91.8	2	Bubiai	Marijos radijas
2A)	92.2	3.5	Bubiai	Radiocentras
4A)	92.3	1.5	Utena	Žinių radijas
3B)	92.4	3.2	Kaunas	Pūkas 2
2B)	92.5	4.5	Giruliai	ZIP FM
2B)	92.7	2.1	Mažeikiai	ZIP FM
1A)	92.8	11.7	Krakės	M-1
7)	93.1	1.3	Vilnius	Marijos radijas
4A)	93.4	1	Marijampolė	Žinių radijas
5)	93.5	1	Utena	Gold FM
3A)	94.0	2.5	Lelionys	Pūkas
3A)	94.2	4.8	Liktėnai	Pūkas
3A)	94.6	2	Ukmergė	Pūkas
3A)	94.8	2.5	Daukšiai	Pukas
15A)	94.9	3.2	Giruliai	Laluna
7)	95.0	4	Viešintos	Marijos radijas
3B)	95.4	4	Liepkalnis	Pukas 2
A)	95.5	3.2	Vilnius	BBCWS relay
3A)	95.7	2	Šiauliai	Pūkas
4)	96.0	1.8	Biržai	Žinių radijas
4)	96.4	1.8	Mažeikiai	Žinių radijas
10)	96.6	1	Panevėžys	Pulsas
9)	96.7	2.3	Giruliai	Power Hit R.
1B)	97.6	4	Juragiai	M-1 Plius
21)	97.8	1.6	Šiauliai	RS2
7)	98.2	1.9	Biržai	Marijos radijas
1B)	98.3	3.4	Giruliai	M-1 Plius
1B)	98.7	1.6	Utena	M-1 Plius
12)	99.0	3.2	Alytus	FM 99
13)	99.7	1	Vilnius	European Hit R.
6)	99.8	2	Giruliai	Kelyje
2A)	99.9	2	Raseiniai	Radiocentras
2B)	100.1	4	Vilnius	ZIP FM
1B)	100.2	5	Pažagieniai	M-1 Plius
19)	100.2	1	Klaipėda	Extra FM
8)	100.4	4	Mažeikiai	Mažeikiu aidas
2C)	100.4	2.4	Kaunas	Rusradio LT
1B)	100.5	3	Bubiai	M-1 Plius
15B)	100.8	1.3	Klaipėda	Raduga
3B)	100.9	1.1	Vilnius	Pūkas 2
2A)	101.1	1.4	Alytus	Radiocentras
2A)	101.4	3.8	Pažagieniai	Radiocentras
2A)	101.5	2	Giruliai	Radiocentras
4B)	101.5	2.3	Vilnius	Easy FM
3A)	101.6	1.7	Tauragė	Pūkas
2A)	101.6	1.9	Druskininkai	Radiocentras
16)	101.7	1.6	Bubiai	Relax FM
2A)	101.8	2	Marijampolė	Radiocentras
3A)	102.0	1	Karlai	Pūkas
4A)	102.2	1.6	Giruliai	Žinių radijas
17)	102.5	3.4	Bubiai	Saules radijas
3A)	102.6	1	Skuodas	Pūkas
5)	102.6	5.8	Vilnius	Gold FM
2A)	102.7	1.5	Tauragė	Radiocentras
18)	102.9	4	Kaunas	Tau
1C)	103.0	2.2	Pažagieniai	Lietus
1C)	103.0	1.1	Tryškiai	Lietus
1C)	103.1	2.5	Vilnius	Lietus
1C)	103.1	1.7	Tauragė	Lietus
1C)	103.3	1	Biržai	Lietus
1C)	103.4	1.1	Utena	Lietus
1C)	103.5	4.2	Juragiai	Lietus
1C)	103.7	1.6	Giruliai	Lietus
4A)	103.7	1.1	Visaginas	Žinių radijas
20)	103.8	1.8	Vilnius	Znad Wilii
1C)	103.9	3.7	Bubiai	Lietus
5)	104.1	4	Klaipėda	Gold FM
2B)	104.1	20	Juragiai	ZIP FM
1B)	104.3	2	Marijampolė	M-1 Plius
5)	104.3	1.2	Šiauliai	Gold FM
5)	104.5	4	Kaunas	Gold FM
5)	104.8	1.2	Panevėžys	Gold FM
4A)	104.8	2.2	Tauragė	Žinių radijas
4A)	104.9	1	Juragiai	Žinių radijas
2B)	105.0	1	Utena	ZIP FM
2B)	105.2	1.3	Raseiniai	ZIP FM
19)	105.4	3.9	Kaunas	Extra FM
2B)	105.4	10	Visaginas	ZIP FM
2A)	105.5	1.7	Biržai	Radiocentras
11)	105.6	3.2	Mažeikiai	Mažeikiai.FM
2C)	105.6	2.2	Vilnius	Rusradio LT
2B)	105.7	2	Tauragė	ZIP FM
2C)	105.8	4.2	Bubiai	Rusradio LT
1A)	105.9	3.2	Ignalina	M-1
1A)	106.0	2.2	Pažagieniai	M-1
1A)	106.0	2	Tryškiai	M-1
1A)	106.2	1.5	Tauragė	M-1
1B)	106.2	4	Vilnius	M-1 Plius
1A)	106.3	3.9	Marijampolė	M-1
1A)	106.3	2.5	Bubiai	M-1
1A)	106.3	2	Utena	M-1
1A)	106.4	2	Raseiniai	M-1
1A)	106.5	3	Giruliai	M-1
1A)	106.6	4	Juragiai	M-1
2B)	106.7	2	Laukuva	ZIP FM
1A)	106.8	1	Vilnius	M-1
2A)	107.1	3.9	Juragiai	Radiocentras
3A)	107.3	2	Vilnius	Pūkas
10)	107.3	3.2	Biržai	Pulsas
3A)	107.6	3.7	Kaunas	Pūkas
3A)	107.8	4.5	Perkūnai	Pūkas
4A)	107.9	1	Pažagieniai	Žinių radijas

+ txs below 1kW.

Addresses & other information:
1A-C) Laisvės pr. 60, 05120 Vilnius – **2A-D)** Laisvės pr. 60, 05120 Vilnius. 2C) in Russian – **3A,B)** Šaldytuvų g. 25, 45123 Kaunas – **4A,B)** A.Smetonos g. 6, 01115 Vilnius – **5)** Gedimino pr. 50/2, 01110 Vilnius – **6)** Savanorių pr. 151, 50174 Kaunas – **7)** M.Daukšos g. 21, 44282 Kaunas – **8)** Sodų g. 13-93, 89116 Mažeikiai – **9)** P. Lukšio g. 23, 09132 Vilnius – **10)** Respublikos g. 28, 35174 Panevėžys – **11)** Ventos g. 8a, 89111 Mažeikiai – **12)** Rotušės a. 2a, 62141 Alytus – **13)** Odminių g. 8, 01112 Vilnius – **14)** Pylimo g. 20-10, 01118 Vilnius – **15A,B)** Taikos pr. 81, 94114 Klaipėda. 15B) in Russian – **16)** Laisvės pr. 60, 05120 Vilnius – **17)** Aušros al. 64, 76240 Šiauliai – **18)** Draugystės g. 19, 51230 Kaunas – **19)** Konstitucijos pr. 7, 09308 Vilnius – **20)** Laisvės pr. 60, 05120 Vilnius. In Polish – **21)** Varpo g. 22, 76297 Šiauliai – **22)** Saulėtekio g. 17-44, 87101 Telšiai – **A)** Rel. BBCWS (UK).

Int. relays on MW: (Upon demand; provided by R. Baltic Waves International; tx operated by LRTC) Viešintos 1386kHz 200kW (run at 75kW). See International Radio section

LORD HOWE ISLAND (Australia)

L.T: UTC +10½h (4 Oct 20-4 Apr 21, 3 Oct 21-3 Apr 22: +11½h). **NB:** UTC times in schedules refer to DST period — **Pop:** 382 — **Pr.L:** English — **E.C:** 230V/50Hz — **ITU:** AUS (**WRTH:** LHW)

AUSTRALIAN BROADCASTING CORP. [ABC]
ABC Classic FM 2ABCFM: FM: 104.1MHz 0.02kW

LORD HOWE ISLAND RADIO
✉ The Shack, New Jetty Complex, Lagoon Road [PO Box 52], Lord Howe Island NSW 2898 ☎+61 2 6563 2123 🖷 +61 2 6563 2127
FM: 100.1MHz, 40W **Prgr:** Irr. Local prgr. Wed midday, and Thurs night 2130-0230. Local community stn

LUXEMBOURG

L.T: UTC +1h (28 Mar-31 Oct: +2h) — **Pop:** 597,000 — **Pr.L:** Official languages: Luxembourgish, French, German — **E.C:** 230V/50Hz — **ITU:** LUX

AUTORITÉ LUXEMBOURGOISE INDEPENDENTE DE L'AUDIOVISUEL (ALIA)
✉ 19, rue du Fossé, L-1536 Luxembourg ☎ +352 24782089 🖷 +352 27858464 **E:** info@alia.etat.lu **W:** www.alia.lu
L.P: Chmn: Thierry Hoscheit

RADIO 100.7 (Pub)
✉ 21a, Avenue J.F. Kennedy, L-1855 Luxemburg ☎ +352 4400441 🖷 +352 440044980 **E:** info@100komma7.lu **W:** www.100komma7.lu
L.P: Pres: Laurent Loschetter
FM: Neidhausen 95.9 MHz 3 kW, Dudelange 100.7 MHz 100 kW
D.Prgr: 24h in Luxembourgish

RTL (Comm.)
45 blvd. Pierre Frieden, L-1543 Luxembourg ☎ +352 4214 22175 🖷 +352 4214 22756 **W:** radio.rtl.lu **L.P:** Pres: Jacques Santer.
Luxembourg Sce: RTL Radio Lëtzebuerg: ☎ +352 4214 23 🖷 +352 4214 22737 **W:** rtl.lu
German Sce: RTL Radio: Kurfürstendamm 207-208, D-10719 Berlin ☎ +49 30 88484120 🖷 +49 30 88484121 **W:** rtlradio.de **L.P:** Station Manager: Frank Jaeger
LW: 234kHz 750kW(d)/375kW(n) (227° towards Paris) via Beidweiler, 24h Fr. sce

FM	Station	Location	kW
88.9	R. Lëtzebuerg	Dudelange	100
92.5	R. Lëtzebuerg	Hosingen	50
93.3	RTL R.	Dudelange	100
97.0	RTL R.	Hosingen	100

Also FM relays in France & Germany.
RTL Radio Lëtzebuerg 24h in Luxembourgish: 24h on 92.5MHz
DAB: Block 7D have started via Dudelange (10kW) and a support transmitter in Hosingen (0.5kW).

OTHER STATIONS (all MHz and 1 kW or more)
R. Ara, 2 rue de la Boucherie, 1247 Luxembourg **W:** ara.lu - **FM:** 87.8/102.9 – **R. Latina**, 2 rue Astrid, 1143 Luxembourg **W:** radiolatina.lu - **FM:** 91.7/101.2 – **Antenne Luxemburg** - **FM:** 94.3/103.4 – **R. Eldoradio**, B.P. 1344, 1013 Luxembourg **W:** eldoradio.lu - **FM:** 95.0 – **L'Essentiel R.** - **FM:** 97.5/107.7 **W:** lessentielradio.lu
+ several other stns of less than 1kW

MACAU (China, SAR)

L.T: UTC +8h — **Pop:** 650,000 — **Pr.L:** Standard Chinese (official), Portuguese (official), Cantonese — **E.C:** 220V/50Hz — **ITU:** MAC

TELEDIFUSÃO DE MACAU, SARL (Priv. Comm.)
Avenida Dr. Rodrigo Rodrigues, No. 223-225, Edificio Nam Kwong 7°Andar, Macau ☎ +853 28517758 🖷 +853 28716579 **E:** enquiry@tdm.com.mo **W:** tdm.com.mo
FM: 98.0MHz 2.5kW **D.Prgr:** Portuguese 24h except Indonesian on Sun 1200-1400 and Tagalog on Sat 1200-1300, including relay RDP Antena 1 on Sun 1400-2300, Mon-Thu 1600-2300, Fri 1600-2400 and Sat 1300-2400. **FM:** 100.7MHz 2.5kW **D.Prgr:** Cantonese and Chinese 24h

RÁDIO VILA VERDE LDA (Priv. Comm.)
Hipódromo da Taipa, Macau ☎ +853 28820338 🖷 +853 28820337 **E:** helpdesk@am738.com **W:** am738.com
FM: 99.5MHz **D.Prgr:** Cantonese 24h

MACEDONIA

See North Macedonia

MADAGASCAR

L.T: UTC +3h — **Pop:** 28 million — **Pr.L:** Malagasy (official), French (official) — **E.C:** 220V/50Hz — **ITU:** MDG

AUTORITÉ DE RÉGULATION DES TECHNOLOGIES DE COMMUNICATION (ARTEC)
Rue Ravoninahitriniarivo, Alarobia, 101 Antananarivo ☎ +261 20 2242119 **E:** artec@artec.mg **W:** www.artec.mg
L.P: Chmn: Jean Rakotomalala

RADIO MADAGASIKARA - RADIO NATIONALE MALAGASY (RNM) (Pub.)
BP 4422, Anosy, 101 Antananarivo **W:** facebook.com/radio.madagasikara (stream on anio-info.com) **E:** r.radiomadagaskara@yahoo.fr ☎ +261 20 2221745 🖷 +261 20 2232715
L.P: Dir: Johary Ravoajanarahy.

MW	kHz	kW	H of tr
Fenoarivo	630	50	0300-1900
SW	**kHz**	**kW**	**H of tr**
Ambohidrano	v5010	10	0300-0500, 1500-1900
Ambohidrano	6135	30	0500-1500

NB: All transmitters operate irregularly.
FM: Antananarivo 99.3MHz (0.5kW) & relay txs.
D.Prgr: 0300-1900 (SS 2200) in Malagasy & French.
Ann: Malagasy: "R. Madagasikara"; F: "R. Madagascar".

OTHER STATIONS

FM	MHz	kW	Location	Station
2)	88.6		Antananarivo	R. Fahazavana
	89.2		Antananarivo	BBCWS relay
	89.8		Fianarantsoa/Toamasina	BBCWS relay
3)	92.0		Antananarivo	Alliance FM (also r. RFI)
	92.0		Antsirabé/others	R. France Int.
4)	93.4		Antananarivo	R. Don Bosco
5A)	94.4		Antananarivo	R. Tana
	96.0		Antananarivo/others	Radio France Int.
6)	96.6		Antananarivo	R. Des Jeunes
7)	97.6		Antananarivo	R. Antsiva
	98.0		Antsiranana	R. France Int.
8)	98.2		Toamasina	R. Voanio
5B)	102.0		Antananarivo	R. 102
1)	105.0	0.75	Ambositra	R. Maria
9)	105.2		Antananarivo	Ma FM
10)	106.0		Antananarivo	R. Lazan Iarivo
11)	107.4		Antananarivo	R. FMFOI

NB: Unlicensed stns are operating in many parts of the country.

Addresses & other information:
1) W: radiomaria.org – **2)** BP 623, Lot II J 11, Faravohitra, Rue Joël Rakotomalala, 101 Antananarivo. **W:** radiofahazavana.agilityhoster.com – **3)** Enceinte Maison Laborde, Andohalo, 101 Antananarivo. **W:** alliancefr.mg – **4)** BP 60, Maison Don Bosco, Ivato Airport, 105 Antananarivo. **W:** radiodonbosco.mg – **5A-B)** Enceinte Sitram, Ankorondrano, 101 Antananarivo. **W:** rta.mg . A) in Malagasy, B) in French –**6)** BP 4370, Immeuble Vitasoa, Analakely, 101 Antananarivo. **W:** rdeejay.net – **7)** BP 12170, Zone Zital Ankorondrano, Enceinte RTA, 101 Antananarivo. **W:** radio-antsiva.com –**8)** BP 489, 11 Rue Grandidier, 501 Toamasina. **W:** voanio.com – **9)** BP 1414, Ankorondrano, 101 Antananarivo. **W:** matv.mg – **10)** BP 6319, V.A 49 Andafiavaratra, 101 Antananarivo. **W:** rli106fm.com – **11)** Rue Docteur Ralarosy V W01, Ambohipotsy, 101 Antananarivo **W:** fmfoi.ifrance.com

MADEIRA (Portugal)

L.T: UTC (28 Mar-31 Oct: +1h) — **Pop:** 290,000 — **Pr.L:** Portuguese — **E.C:** 230V/50Hz — **ITU:** MDR

ANACOM-Autoridade Nacional de Comunicações, Delegação da Madeira
Rua do Vale das Neves, 19, São Gonçalo, 9050-332 Funchal ☎ +351 291 79 02 00 🖷 +351 291 79 02 01

RÁDIO E TELEVISÃO DE PORTUGAL, S.A. (RTP) (Pub) Centro Regional da RTP-Madeira (radio & TV)
Caminho de Santo António, n.º 145 , 9020-002 Funchal ☎ +351 291 20 20 00 🖷 +351 291 23 07 53 **W:** rtp.pt **E:** rdpmadeira@rtp.pt
L.P: Dir: Martim Santos

FM(MHz)	Ant. 1	Ant.2	Ant. 3	kW
Achada da Cruz	104.3		105.0	0.8
Cabo Girão	96.7	99.4	94.8	1/3/1
Calheta	105.4		107.5	0.1
Caniço	101.6	99.0	89.3	0.5
Encumeada	93.1		90.8	0.06
Gaula	98.5	106.3	91.3	1/0.7/1
Maçapez	92.0		95.7	0.1
Monte	104.6	102.4	89.8	1/1/0.7
Paúl da Serra	101.9		93.3	1
Pico do Areeiro	95.5	88.4	94.1	13/15
Pico do Facho	93.1		90.8	0.03
Ponta do Pargo	90.2		94.6	1
Porto Santo	100.5	103.3	96.5	10
Ribeira Brava	105.6		103.1	1
Santa Clara *	104.6	102.4	89.8	

* Tunnel tx at Funchal
D.Prgr: all networks 24h. Antena 1 of RDP Madeira provides regional prgrs M-F 0700-2000, Sat & Sun 0900-1900 LT; Antena 2 relays Lisboa 24h; Antena 3 Madeira carries own prgrs. M-T 0700-2300, F 0700-0000 LT, Sat & Sun 24h. Technical info may be obtained from **E:** gabinete.tecnologias@rtp.pt
V. by QSL-card via RTP Lisboa

RÁDIO RENASCENÇA – Em. Católica Portuguesa (Rlg., Comm) (see Portugal) - **FM:** Pico do Silva 88.0MHz 44kW (RR), 93.6MHz 44kW (RFM)

PEF – Posto Emissor de Radiodifusão do Funchal (Priv., Comm.) Rua Ponte de São Lázaro 3, 9000-027 Funchal ☎ +351 291 23 03 93 & +351 291 208 950 🖷 +351 291 22 17 97 **E:** radiopef@gmail.com, noticiaspef@gmail.com **W:** pef.pt
Channel 1 MW: Funchal 1530kHz 3kW (nominal power: 10kW)
Channel 2 FM: Funchal 92.0MHz 2kW **D.Prgr:** 24h Both channels relay R. Renascença, Lisboa, at certain times **Ann:** "PEF - a sua rádio regional"
NB: The two channels have different programmes most of the day.

Local FM stations:

FM	Island	Station & location	MHz	kW
4)	Madeira	R. Jornal da Madeira, Funchal	88.8	1
13)	Madeira	R. São Vicente, São Vicente	89.2	0.5
6)	Madeira	R. Zarco, Machico	89.6	1
9)	Pto Santo	R. Praia, Pto Santo	91.6	0.5
12)	Madeira	Santana FM, Santana	92.5	0.5
11)	Madeira	R. Palmeira, Santa Cruz	96.1	0.5
10)	Madeira	R. Festival da Madeira, Ribeira Brava	98.4	0.5
1)	Madeira	R. Calheta, Calheta	98.8	0.5
5)	Madeira	TSF Madeira, Funchal	100.0	2
2)	Madeira	R. Popular da Madeira, Câm. de Lobos	101.0	2
8)	Madeira	R. Porto Moniz, Porto Moniz	102.9	0.5
7)	Madeira	R. Sol, Ponta do Sol	103.7	0.5
3)	Madeira	R. Clube da Madeira, Funchal	106.8	0.4

+ five 50W repeaters used by three stns
NB: Some programmes are simulcast on R. Popular da Madeira, R. Zarco, R. Sol, R. Festival da Madeira & R. Palmeira.
Addresses & other information (add +351 to tel/fax nos):
1) & 12) Edifício Ondaparque, Av.ª D. Manuel I, 9370-133 Calheta ☎ 291 820132/6 & 961 220 552 🖷 291 820138 **E:** radiocalheta@gmail.com, santanafm@gmail.com **W:** radiocalheta.pt, santanafm.com.pt – **2), 3) & 10)** Avenida Estados Unidos da América n º 146-150, 9000-090 Funchal ☎291 766101/291 761 068 & 291 762 984 **W:** popular.radiosmadeira.pt, clube.radiosmadeira.pt & festival.radiosmadeira.pt **E:** ssfranco75@gmail.com, radiofestival98.4@gmail.com – **4)** Rua 31 de Janeiro, n.º 73 e 74, 9050-013 Funchal ☎ 291 210 408/9 🖷291 210 401 **E:** rjm@jm-madeira.pt, gerencia@jm-madeira.pt **W:** jm-madeira.pt/radio88 – **5)** (relays TSF Lisboa) Rua Fernão de Ornelas, 56-3º, 9050-021 Funchal ☎ 291 202300 🖷 291 20 23 87 **E:** info@tsfmadeira.pt **W:** tsfmadeira.pt – **6) & 11)** Conjunto Habitacional da Bemposta, Ap-A1/A2, Água de Pena, 9200-012 Machico ☎ 291 526896 & 291 526961 **E:** radiozarcomachico@gmail.com & radiopalmeira96.1@gmail.com **W:** zarco.radiosmadeira.pt **W:** palmeira.radiosmadeira.pt –**7)** Estrada Murteiras-Canhas, 9360-303 Canhas☎ 291 972 282 **E:** radiopontadosol@gmail.com **W:** sol.radiosmadeira.net – **8)** Bombeiros Voluntários de S. Vicente e Porto Moniz, Vila de S. Vicente, 9240 São Vicente ☎ 291 842135 🖷 291 842666 – **9)** Rua Estevão Alencastre, 9400-161 Porto ☎ 291 980130 🖷 291 980137 **E:** radiopraia91.6fm@gmail.com **W:** radiopraia.com/estatico.asp – **13)** Bombeiros Voluntários de São Vicente e Porto Moniz, Sítio do Pé do Passo, 9240-225 São Vicente ☎ 291 842 694 🖷 291 842393 **E:** radiosaovicente@gmail.com **W:** radiosaovicentemadeira.pt

MALAWI

L.T: UTC +2h — **Pop:** 19 million — **Pr.L:** English (official), Chichewa (official), Lomwe, Tumbuka, Yao — **E.C:** 230V/50Hz — **ITU:** MWI

MALAWI COMMUNICATIONS REGULATORY AUTHORITY (MACRA)

9 Salmin Amour Road, (Private Bag 261), Blantyre ☎ +265 1 810497 🖷 +265 1 812890 **E:** info@macra.org.mw **W:** www.macra.org.mw **L.P:** DG: Godfrey Itaye; Dir of Broadcasting: Fegus Lipenga

MALAWI BROADCASTING CORPORATION (MBC, Pub.)

P.O. Box 30133, Chichiri, Blantyre 3 ☎+ 265 1 871461 **W:** mbc.mw **E:** dgmbc@mbc.mw **L.P:** DG: Dr. Benson Tembo. Ag. Dir. Prgr. & News: Hamilton Chimala. Dir. of Signal Distr. &Projects: Joseph Chikagwa.

MW	kHz	kW	MW	kHz	kW
Mangochi	540	10	Blantyre	756	10
Karonga	558	10	Chitipa	1404	10
Lilongwe	‡594	30	Matiya	1422	10

FM	R1	R2FM	kW	FM	R1	R2FM	kW
Bangula	104.5	88.1	1	Mangochi	98.3	91.8	1
Chikangawa	105.9	103.0	1	Mchinji	88.0	95.4	1
Chitipa	90.7	100.5	1	Mpingwe	95.4	92.2	1/5
Dedza	90.1	104.5	1	Nkhotakota	95.6	-	1
Dwangwa	103.6	93.6	1	Nsanje	95.5	94.4	0.05
Ekwendeni	92.2	100.5	1	Ntchisi	100.5	92.4	2
Kanengo	94.7	91.5	5/1	Salima	105.9	100.0	1
Karonga	95.5	98.7	2	Zomba	94.1	96.8	2/5
Kasungu	94.5	96.2	1				

Radio 1 in English/Chichewa/Others on MW/FM: 24h exc. 540/1422kHz 0200-2200.
Radio 2FM in English/Chichewa on FM: 24h.
Ann: E: R1: "Radio 1", R2: "Radio 2FM". Chichewa: "Kuno ndi ku Radio ya MBC".

Other stations (FM MHz):
R. Alinafe, Lilongwe: 97.1 **E:** radioalinafe@sdnp.org.mw – **Calvary Family Church R,** Blantyre 3: 105.8 0.25kW **E:** calvaryministries@hotmail.com – **Capital R**: Blantyre/Mzuzu 102.5, Dedza 105.2, Lilongwe 102.8, Zomba 96.1, all 1kW **W:** capitalradiomalawi.com – **Channel For All Nations,** Lilongwe: 101.5 – **Galaxy FM:** (all 1kW): Lilongwe 90.8, Blantyre 94.6, Mzuzu 100.9 **W:** facebook.com/Galaxy-Radio-Malawi-595098733871458 – **FM 101 Power:** (all txs 0.5/1kW): Ntcheu 88.1, Livingstonia 93.2, Chintheche 98.6, Mzuzu 99.0, Nkhoma 100.3, Blantyre/Lilongwe/Nkhota-kota 101.0, Dedza 103.9, Ntchisi 104.0, Dwangwa 107.2 **W:** fm101.malawi.net – **Joy R,** Blantyre: 89.6 – **MIJ FM**: Blantyre/Lilongwe/Mzuzu: 90.3 **W:** mijmw.net – **R. Islam:** Blantyre 97.6, Dedza 105.7, Dowa 89.7, Karonga 97.7, Lilongwe 97.6, Mtengo Wa Ung'ono 99.7, Mangochi 101.8, Mzuzu 97.0, Namwera 97.4, Zomba 102.9, all 1kW **W:** radioislam.org.mw – **R. Maria Malawi:** Mangochi 88.5 1kW, Dowa 94.0 1kW, Blantyre 99.2 1kW, Zomba 99.4 2kW, Dedza 99.7 2kW. **W:** radiomaria.mw – **Star FM,** Blantyre: 89.0 – **Trans World Radio Malawi:** Blantyre 89.1, Ntchis 90.7, Mvera 91.1, Dedza 96.4, Yawo 106.2, Chikangawa/Zomba 106.4, Lilongwe 106.5, Thyolo 107.1, all 2kW **W:** twrmalawi.wordpress.com – **Ufulu FM:** Blantyre 92.5MHz **W:** ufulufm.com – **YONECO FM:** Lilongwe 90.0, Blantyre 101.9, Zomba 101.9, Mzuzu 104.0 **W:** yoneco.org – **Zodiak BS:** Chitipa 89.5, Dedza 89.0, Dowa 92.9, Karonga 93.7, Lilongwe 95.1, Livingstonia 95.0, Mpingwe 97.0, Mzuzu 95.1, Namwera 103.3, Zomba 89.3 **W:** zbsmw.com
BBC African Sce: Mzuzu 87.9, Lilongwe 98.0, Blantyre 98.7MHz

MALAYSIA

L.T: UTC +8h — **Pop:** 32.5 million — **Pr.L:** Malay (official), English, Chinese, Tamil — **E.C:** 240V/50Hz — **ITU:** MLA

MALAYSIAN COMMUNICATIONS AND MULTIMEDIA COMMISSION (MCMC) (Suruhan Komunikasi dan Multimedia Malaysia, SKMM)

Regulatory body for the communications & multimedia industries
MCMC Tower 1, Jalan Impact, Cyber 6, 63000 Cyberjaya, Selangor ☎ +60 3 8688 8000 🖷 +60 3 8688 1000 **W:** skmm.gov.my **L.P:** Chairman: YBrs. Dr. Fadhlullah Suhaimi Abdul Malek

JABATAN PENYIARAN MALAYSIA (Dept of Broadcasting of Malaysia) (Gov.)

Parent body of RTM Angkasapuri, 50614 Kuala Lumpur ☎ +60 3 2282 5333 🖷 +60 3 2282 5103

RADIO TELEVISION MALAYSIA - RTM (Gov.)

Dept. of Broadcasting, Angkasapuri, Bukit Putra, 50614 Kuala Lumpur ☎ +60 3 2282 5333 🖷 +60 3 2282 7146 **W:** rtm.gov.my **E:** aduan@rtm.net.my **L.P:** DG: Nor Yahati Awang. Prgr Dir (Radio): Puan Malinaziah Datu Mohd Julaspi

FM (MHz)	Site	1	2	4	5	6	kW
Alor Setar	a	94.9	100.5	98.7	101.3	96.7	5
Balik Pulau	b	101.7	93.9	88.5	92.1	98.9	0.1
Baling	c	88.7	89.7	91.7	92.5	93.3	1
Besut	d	94.3	98.8	97.0	97.8	95.3	0.1
Bukit Gantang	88.3	-	-	-	-	-	0.1
Cameron	e	89.1	93.1	101.1	103.5	104.3	0.1
Dabong		-	104.1	-	-	-	-
Damak	f	-	89.4	-	-	-	
Dungun	g	95.9	96.9	98.9	99.7	100.7	1
FELDA Tenang		91.0	89.4	90.2	87.8	-	

FM (MHz)	Site	1	2	4	5	6	kW
Gambang		89.2	88.3	-	-	-	0.5
Gerik	h	97.8	95.4	98.4	100.8	100.0	0.1
Gua Musang	i	89.7	91.1	94.1	94.9	93.2	
Ipoh	j	88.3	90.9	90.1	92.1	98.9	0.5
Jeli	k	88.4	89.2	90.8	91.6	92.4	0.1
Jerantut	l	88.1	93.5	89.9	90.7	91.9	0.1
Johor Bahru	m	106.7	105.7	102.9	104.9	101.1	0.5
Kg Keruak		89.7	91.7	92.5	103.3	-	
Kota Bharu	n	101.1	101.9	104.7	105.7	106.7	1
Kuala Lumpur	o	87.7	88.5	90.3	89.3	92.3	1
KL2	p	-	95.3	-	-	-	5
KL2	p	98.3	-	100.1	106.7	96.3	2
KT	q	92.5	91.7	89.7	90.5	87.9	1
Kuantan	r	107.9	107.1	105.3	106.1	103.3	1
Lawin	-		102.9	-	-	-	0.25
Lenggong	s	-	92.3	-	-	-	
Machang	t	95.5	96.5	98.5	99.3	100.9	2
Maran	u	87.9	91.2	94.7	89.6	90.4	0.25
Melaka	v	93.6	96.6	97.4	100.4	103.3	0.5
Mersing	w	90.1	90.9	92.9	89.1	88.3	1
Paloh		-	90.7	-	-	-	0.1
Penang	x	101.7	93.9	88.5	92.1	98.9	
Raub	y	-	106.2	-	-	-	0.5
Rompin		93.7	-	90.7	88.9	-	
Sedeli		100.5	96.5	-	-	-	
Seremban	z	87.9	91.7	88.7	89.7	90.5	0.1
Sik	aa	99.5	102.7	105.9	106.7	107.5	1
Sintok (UUM)		99.5	102.7	105.9	106.7	107.5	
Taiping	bb	103.3	107.1	105.3	106.1	107.9	0.5
Tapah	cc	88.7	-	-	-	-	0.5
Terolak		90.3	88.5				
U. Tembeling	dd	90.1	89.3	88.5	87.7	-	0.1

National networks 1-6: see below. KL2=KL/Selangor/Pahang (West). KT=Kuala Terengganu.
Sites: a) Gunung Jerai, b) Bukit Genting (Penang) c) Bukit Palong, d) Bukit Bintang, e) Gunung Berinchang, f) Bukit Botak, g) Bukit Bauk, h) RTM Gerik (Mempelam Sari), i) Bukit Chupak, j) Bukit Keledang, k) Bukit Tangki Air, l) Bukit Istana, m) Gunung Pulai, n) Telipot, o) Menara KL (Bukit Nanas), p) Gunung Ulu Kali, q) Bukit Besar, r) Bukit Pelindung, s) Bukit Ladang Teh, t) Bukit Bakar, u) Bukit Senggora, v) Gunung Ledang (Mt Ophir), w) Bukit Tinggi, x) Bukit Penara, y) Bukit Fraser, z) Bukit Telapa Burok, aa) Bukit Dedap, bb) Bukit Larut (Maxwell Hill) cc) Changkat Rembian,dd) Kampung Bantal, Ulu Tembeling.

Asyik FM/Salam FM: Cameron Highlands (G. Berinchang) 105.1MHz 0.1kW, Damak (Bukit Botak) 99.9MHz, Gunung Ledang 95.6MHz 0.25kW, Gunung Ulu Kali 102.5MHz 5kW, Kuala Lumpur 91.1MHz 1kW, Lenggong 97.3MHz, RTM Gerik (Mempelam Sari) 96.7MHz 0.1kW
NB: All **FM** powers throughout are TRP

RTM national services
1) Klasik FM (R. Klasik): 24h news, information & Malay oldies in Malay. **2) Nasional FM:** 24h General sce in Malay. **4) Traxx FM:** 24h News, music and travel sce in English. **5) Ai FM:** 24h General Sce in Chinese (Mandarin exc. news at 0200 in Hakka, 0500 Cantonese, 0700 Hakka & 1300 Chaozhou). **6) Minnal FM:** 24h General sce in Tamil. **Asyik FM:** 0000-1500 for Orang Asli in Jakun, Malay, Semai, Temiar & Temuan. **Salam FM:** Rlg. prgrs in Malay from Jabatan Kemajuan Islam Malaysia 1500-2400 **V.** occasionally by letter or email. **Ann:** names of networks and regional sces are sometimes preceded by the words 'Radio Malaysia'

RTM regional services in West Malaysia:
Most sces. operate 24h in Malay. Exceptions include Langkawi, which carries local & tourist information in English and Malay. Some sces relay RTM Klasik Nasional overnight. Refer to above lists for tx sites and powers for frequencies marked a-dd.
Johor: Johor FM (JFM), Karung Berkunci 716, 80990 Johor Bahru, Johor. On 92.1MHz w, 101.9MHz m, 105.3MHz v – **Kedah:** Kedah FM, Kompleks Penerangan dan Penyiaran Sultan Abdul Halim, KM 3, Jalan Kuala Kedah, 05400 Alor Setar, Kedah. On 88.5MHz Selama-Bandar Baru (site Bukit Sungai Kecil Hilir) 0.25kW, 90.5MHz c, 97.5MHz a, 105.1MHz aa, 105.1MHz Sintok (UUM), 105.7MHz Gunung Raya 1kW – **Kelantan:** Kelantan FM, Peti Surat 143, 15720 Kota Bharu, Kelantan. On 88.1MHz FELDA Paloh 1kW, 97.3MHz t 102.9MHz n, 92.0MHz i 0.1kW, 90.0MHz i, 107.1MHz d, 107.2MHz Dabong – **Kuala Lumpur:** KL.fm On 97.2MHz o – **Langkawi (Kedah):** Langkawi FM, Tingkat 2, Bangunan Tabung Haji, Jalan Padang Mat Sirat, 07000 Kuah, Langkawi. On 87.5MHz Kuah 0.1kW, 104.8MHz Gunung Raya 1kW **English:** 0100-0400, 0700-1000 Malay/English 1300-1600 – **Melaka:** Melaka FM (MFM), Jalan Taming Sari, 75614 Melaka. On 102.3MHz v – **Negeri Sembilan:** Negeri FM, Jalan Raja Ali, 71000 Seremban, Negeri Sembilan. On 92.5MHz z, 95.7MHz Gunung Tampin 0.1kW, 107.7MHz v – **Pahang:** Pahang FM, Peti Surat 152, 25710 Kuantan, Pahang. On 88.0MHz Bandar Muadzam Shah (Bukit Sembilan), 91.9MHz Rompin 0.25kW, 92.0MHz Maran 0.25kW, 92.7MHz l, 95.5 Gambang (Bukit Sulai), 100.3MHz e, 102.2 y, 104.1MHz r, 107.2 f, 107.5MHz p – **Perak:** Perak FM, Jalan Dairy, 31400 Ipoh, Perak. On 89.6MHz Tanjung Malim (Bukit Asa) 0.25kW, 94.2MHz Lenggong (Bukit Ladang Teh) 0.025kW, 94.7MHz e, 95.6MHz j, 96.2MHz h, 96.7MHz Gerik, 97.3MHz Changkat Rembian 0.5kW, 102.9MHz Lawin 0.25kW, 104.1MHz bb – **Perlis:** Perlis FM, Tingkat 6, Bangunan WSP, Jalan Bukit Lagi, 01000 Kangar, Perlis. On 102.9MHz Pauh 2kW – **Pulau Pinang (Penang):** Mutiara FM, Jalan Burmah, Peti Surat 433, 10350 Pulau Pinang. On 90.9MHz b, 93.9MHz a, 95.7MHz Bukit Penara 1kW – **Selangor:** Selangor FM Bangunan Sultan Salehudin Abdul Aziz Shah, 40000 Shah Alam, Selangor. On 99.8MHz Hulu Langat, 100.9MHz p – **Terengganu:** Terengganu FM, Peti Surat 63, 20914 Kuala Terengganu, Terengganu. On 88.7MHz q, 88.9MHz FELDA Tenang, 90.0MHz FELDA Cerul, 96.2MHz d, 97.7MHz g,

RADIO TELEVISION MALAYSIA SABAH (Gov)

✉ Kompleks Bersepadu Kementerian Komunikasi dan Multimedia, Off Jalan Lintas Kepayan, 88200 Kota Kinabalu ☎ +60 88 712344
Addresses of local stns: ✉ Tingkat 6, Wisma Persekutuan, W.D.T. 52, 90500 Sandakan – Jalan Chong Thien Vun, Peti Surat 606, 91008 Tawau - Aras Bawah Rumah Persekutuan Keningau, Peti Surat 424, 89008 Keningau
L.P: Dir. Broadcasting: .Puan Nor'ain Binti Haji Bakir

RADIO TELEVISION MALAYSIA LABUAN (Gov)

✉ Jalan Tanjung Taras, Peti Surat 81311, 87023 WP Labuan ☎ +60 87 415677 🖷 +60 87 416658

FM (MHz)	Tx	SF	SV	1	2	4	5	kW
FELDA S	a	104.1	106.7	99.9	102.9	104.9	105.7	0.1
Gadong	b	89.3	92.6	88.0	88.9	90.7	91.6	0.1
Kg Lanas		91.9	-	-	87.7	-	-	
Kota Belud	c	101.5	104.1	99.9	100.7	102.5	103.3	0.1
K. Kinabalu	d	89.9	92.7	88.1	88.9	90.7	91.9	1
Kudat	e	95.9	98.9	94.1	94.9	96.7	98.1	1
Labuan	f	-	93.3	87.6	88.5	90.3	92.3	0.1
Lahad Datu	g	89.7	92.6	87.9	88.7	90.5	91.7	1
Langkon		97.1	91.1	101.6	90.1	89.0	87.7	0.1
Layang-L.	h	104.5	107.1	99.5	100.3	105.3	106.3	1
Luasong		-	-	87.7	88.5	89.3	90.1	0.1
Nabawan		-	-	88.3	89.1	89.9	90.6	
Sandakan	j	92.9	96.1	91.1	92.1	94.3	95.1	1
Sapulut		88.9	-	-	88.0	-	-	
Sipitang	k	97.9	102.9	95.5	96.5	99.1	99.9	1
Tawau	l	95.7	99.3	93.9	94.7	97.1	98.1	1
Tenom	m	90.3	93.1	88.5	89.3	91.7	92.3	1

Sites: , a) FELDA Sahabat, b) Bukit Gadong, c) Bukit Pompoda d) Kota Kinabalu (Bukit Lawa Mandau) e) Bukit Kelapa, f) Bukit Timbalai, g) Gunung Silam, h) Layang-Layang (Mount Kinabalu) j) Bukit Trig, k) Bukit Tampulagus, l) Gunung Andrassy, m) Bukit Sigapon
National networks: 1-5: see RTM national sces above
State networks: SF= Sabah FM in Malay 24h. **Reg. N:** 2200, 2330, 0400, 0530, 0830, 1400. **SV= Sabah V FM** in **English** 0400-0700 & 1700-1900, Mandarin 0100-0400 inc. news in Hakka at 0100, Bajau 0700-1100; Dusun 1300-1700, Kadazan 2030-0100 & 0600-0830, Murut 1100-1300. **N.** (English): 0500
Local Sces: Labuan FM on 89.4MHz 0.1kW (Bukit Timbalai) & 103.7MHz i 0.1kW (RTM Labuan): 2145-1200 incl. English 0100-0300 – Tawau FM on 93.6MHz 1 kW (Guning Silam), 99.1MHz 0.1kW (FELDA Sahabat), 100.1MHz 1kW (Gunung Andrassy): 2245-1100 in Malay – Sandakan FM on 90.1MHz 1kW (Bukit Trig): 2150-1100 – Keningau FM on 94.7MHz (Tenom), 98.4MHz (Keningau): 2300-0900 in Malay, Dusun and Murut

RADIO TELEVISION MALAYSIA SARAWAK (Gov.)

✉ Broadcasting House, Jalan P. Ramlee, 93614 Kuching ☎ +60 82 248422 🖷 +60 82 246523
L.P: Dir. Broadcasting: Encik Abdull Hadi bin Mohd Yusoff

Addresses of local stns: Bangunan Penyiaran, 98700 Limbang – Bangunan Penyiaran, Jalan Brighton, 98000 Miri – Bangunan Penyiaran, 96009 Sibu – Bangunan Penyiaran, 95000 Sri Aman – Bangunan Penyiaran, Jalan Sommerville, Bintulu

Stations: Kajang (near Kuala Lumpur)

SW	kHz	kW	Netw.	SW	kHz	kW	Netw.
Kajang	9835	100	SF	Kajang	11665	100	W

FM (MHz)	Tx	SF	Red	1	2	4	5	kW
Belaga		105.4	107.8	103.8	104.6	106.2	107.0	0.1
Betong	a	94.4	97.8	92.8	93.6	95.2	96.0	0.1
Bintulu	b	93.7	100.5	87.9	90.3	98.5	99.3	1
Dalat		-	96.9	-	-	-	-	0.1
Kanowit		107.1	-	-	104.5	-	-	
Kapit	d	92.7	89.9	90.7	91.9	88.1	88.9	0.1
Kuching	e	88.9	91.9	92.9	88.1	89.9	90.7	10
Lambir Hills	f	88.1	90.7	91.9	92.7	88.9	89.9	1
Lawas	g	97.5	100.5	94.7	96.7	98.5	99.3	0.1
Limbang	h	101.5	104.1	97.1	98.1	102.3	103.3	1
Limbang	j	100.0	107.7	95.3	99.2	106.0	106.8	0.1
Long Lama		98.1	-	-	95.5	-	-	
Lubok Antu		98.4	-	-	97.0	-	-	
Marudi	k	-	-	102.9	-	-	-	0.1
Miri	l	100.3	106.3	107.1	99.3	104.5	105.3	0.1
Mukah		89.9	92.3	88.3	89.1	90.7	91.5	0.5
Sarikei	m	91.5	89.2	87.9	90.3	92.3	93.6	10
Serian	n	94.8	97.2	98.0	94.0	95.6	96.4	0.5
Sibu	o	101.5	104.1	95.5	98.5	102.5	103.3	0.1
Song	p	95.7	99.0	91.1	92.2	96.7	97.5	1
Sri Aman	q	100.3	106.3	107.3	98.9	92.3	105.3	1
Stapong	r	95.1	101.1	93.3	94.1	95.9	97.1	1
Suai	s	97.1	-	95.1	-	-	-	

SF=Sarawak FM, W=Wai FM, Red=Red FM L=Limbang FM S=Sibu

National networks: 1, 2, 4, 5: see RTM national sces

SW: 9835kHz: 2200-1600 (rel. Sarawak FM). 11665kHz: 2200-1600 (rel. Wai FM). SW freqs operating irregularly at editorial deadline.

FM: Additional local sce. freqs: Gunung Serapi (Kuching) 101.3MHz 10kW (Wai FM Iban) & 106.1MHz (Wai FM Bidayuh / Kayan-Kenyah), Bukit Ampangan 101.7MHz 0.5kW (Wai FM Bidayuh / Kayan-Kenyah) & 106.9MHz 0.5kW (Wai FM Iban).

Sites: a) Off. Spaoh b) Bukit Setiam c) Bukit Nyabau d) Bukit Kapit e) Gunung Serapi f) Bukit Lambir g) Bukit Tiong h) Bukit Mas j) Bukit Sagan Rudang, k) BukitDabei, l) RTM Miri, m) Bukit Dabei, n) Bukit Ampangan o) Bukit Lima p) Bukit Song q) Bukit Temunduk r) Bukit Singgalang s) Bukit TT 844

State networks: Sarawak FM in Malay 24h. **N.** (Kuching): 2200, 0400, 1000, 1400. **Red FM** 2200-1600, in Chinese: 2200-0200, 0700-1300; English: 0200-0700, 1300-1600. Educational prgs during school terms: MF 0100-0300. **N.** (Kuching): English 0400, 0700, 1300; Chinese 0000, 0801, 1000, 1245; Hakka 1030; Hokkien 1045. **Wai FM:** 2200-1600 in Iban. Relays Limbang FM Mon/Thurs 1300-1400. **Wai FM:** 2200-1600, in Bidayuh: 2200-0400 & 1000-1600; Kayan/Kenyah: 0400-1000. FM txs of all state networks relay Sarawak FM 1600-2200

Local sces: Bintulu FM: 0100-1100 in Malay and Iban. RTM Bintulu 95.3MHz 1kW, Bukit Setiam 97.5MHz 1kW. **Limbang FM:** in Malay 0100-0400, 1000-1300; Lun Bawang (Murut) 0400-0700, also relayed via Kuching 7270kHz; Bisaya 0700-1000; Iban 1300-1400 also relayed by Wai FM Iban Mon/Thurs. Bukit Mas 104.9MHz 1kW, Bukit Tiong 101.1MHz 0.1kW, Bukit Sagan Rudang 94.5MHz 0.1kW. **Miri FM**: in Malay 0000-0300, 1000-1300, Chinese 0700-1000, Iban 0400-0700, Kenyah 0300-0400. Lambir Hills 95.7MHz 1kW, Miri (RTM Miri) 98.0MHz 0.1kW **Sibu FM:** in Malay 0100-0400, 1000-1300, Chinese 0700-1000, Iban 0400-0700. Bukit Lima 87.6MHz 0.1kW, Bukit Kayu Malam 94.6MHz 1kW, Bukit Song 99.8MHz 1kW, Bukit Kapit 94.3MHz 0.1kW, Belaga 103.0MHz 0.1kW, Bukit Singgalang 102.1MHz 1kW, Mukah 98.7MHz 0.5kW. **Sri Aman (RaSa FM):** in Malay, Iban, Chinese. Bukit Temunduk 89.5MHz 1kW. **NB** Local sces relay Wai FM Iban 2200-0100 and from close of local prgrs until 1600, and relay Sarawak FM 1600-2200

IS: A musical phrase (played on a native instrument, the Sape), alternating between A and F.

ASTRO RADIO SDN. BHD. (Comm.)

All Asia Broadcast Centre, Technology Park Malaysia, Bukit Jalil, 57000 Kuala Lumpur **W:** astroradio.com.my

L.P: CEO: Mr Jake Abdullah

FM(MHz)	Tx	MY	ERA	Lite	Mix	Hitz	Sin	Mel	THR	Zay
Alor Setar	a	99.7	103.6	104.4	91.0	92.8	97.1	106.5	102.4	98.1
Ipoh	b	100.6	103.7	101.5	94.3	92.7	96.9	98.5	102.7	106.4
Johor Bahru	c	95.4	104.5	94.6	99.1	97.6	87.8	98.4	103.7	92.8
Johor Bahru	d	-	-	-	-	-	-	103.3	-	-
Kota Bharu	e	102.3	103.3	104.3	94.6	92.8	93.8	99.8	88.1+	-
KK	f	104.0	102.4	103.2	101.6	100.8	104.9	98.6	-	-
KT	g	101.2	102.8	105.9	98.3	94.8	97.5	104.0	100.2+	-
KL/Selangor	h	101.8	103.3	105.7	94.5	92.9	96.7	103.0	99.3	104.9
Kuantan	i	101.1	98.0	104.7	94.1	93.2	97.2	100.0	88.8+	91.6
Kuching	j	96.9	96.1	100.1	97.7	95.3	102.1	103.7	-	-
Langkawi	k	100.1	90.7	-	-	92.4	100.9	-	101.9	-
Melaka	l	106.4	90.3	92.2	91.1	93.0	96.0	107.3	99.7	98.9
Miri	m	103.2	101.3	-	-	105.8	87.7	102.4	-	-
Penang	n	-	-	-	-	-	-	-	99.3	-
Sandakan	o	100.6	103.0	-	-	99.8	106.9	102.2	-	-
Seremban	p	100.6	103.6	104.6	94.2	95.0	96.9	97.9	101.5	-
Sibu	q	105.9	96.3	-	-	105.1	-	-	-	-
Taiping	r	100.2	95.2	89.3	91.3	93.6	96.4	104.9	102.1	-
Tapah	s	-	102.0	-	-	-	-	-	-	-

Prgrs: MY FM: Music channel in Mandarin & Cantonese. **ERA:** Contemporary Malaysian music channel in Malay. **Lite FM:** Easy listening music in English. **Mix FM:** Music and variety in English. **Hitz.fm:** Top 40 presented in English. **Sinar FM:** Malay oldies. **Melody FM:** Programming in Chinese. **THR Raaga**:Music and traffic information presented in Tamil: 24h. **THR Gegar**: Separate prgrs in Malay for East Coast on freqs marked +. **Zayan FM:** Islamic music presented in Malay.

GoXuan FM: 24h in Chinese on Kuala Lumpur/Klang Valley (Gunung Ulu Kali) 88.9MHz 2kW, Penang (Bukit Penara & Batu Ferranghi) 107.6MHz.

Sites: a) Gunung Jerai b) Bukit Keledang c) Gunung Pulai d) Metropolis Tower, JB e) Bukit Panau f) Kota Kinabalu (Bukit Kokol) g) Kuala Terangganu (Bukit Jerung) h) Gunung Ulu Kali i) Bukit Pelindong j) Bukit Djin k) Gunung Raya l) Gunung Ledang m) Tanjong Lobang n) Bukit Penara o) Bukit Trig p) Telapa Barok q) Bukit Lima r) Bukit Larut s) Changkat Rembian. **TRP:** generally 2kW, exc. Sinar FM at sites e, f, j, k and l: 0.25kW, THR 1kW exc 0.5kW at sites b, n and q.

BFM MEDIA (Comm.)

5.01 Wisma BU8, 11 Lebuh Bandar Utama, 47800 Petaling Jaya ☎ +60 3 7629 7112 **W:** bfm.my **L.P:** Exec. Dir: Malek Ali

BFM: Kuala Lumpur/Klang Valley (Gunung Ulu Kali) 89.9MHz, 24h business prgrs and music in E and Malay.

CENSE MEDIA SDN. BHD. (Community Radio)

L-72-3 Block L, KK Times Square, Off Coastal Highway, 88100 Kota Kinabalu, Sabah **W:** kupikupifm.my

City Plus: Seremban 106.0MHz (Gunung Telapa Burok), 24h in Chinese.

Kupi-Kupi FM: Kota Kinabalu (Bukit Keratong) 96.3 MHz, 24h in Malay & English.

DIGITAL MEDIA BROADCASTING SDN. BHD. (Bernama News Agency) (Gov.)

15th Fl, Wisma Bernama, 28 Jalan 1/65A, off Jalan Tun Razak, 53300 Kuala Lumpur ☎+60 3 2692 7939 🖷 +60 3 2692 8939 **W:** radio24.com.my

Bernama Radio: Kuala Lumpur/Klang Valley (Bukit Nanas), 93.9MHz 1kW, Johor Bahru (Gunung Pulai) 107.5MHz 1kW, Kota Kinabalu (Bukit Keratong) 107.9 MHz, Kuching (Bukit Antu) 100.9 MHz, 24h in E and Malay.

EPHRATA SERVICES SDN. BHD.

Lot 2, 2nd floor, Mile 7 1/2 Golden Hill Industrial Park Jln Tuaran, Inanam, Kota Kinabalu, Sabah **W:** vokfmsabah.my

Voice of Kinabalu (VOKfm): Keningau 106.6MHz (Bukit Sigapon), in Malay.

HUSA NETWORK SDN. BHD. (Comm.)

Tingkat 2&3, Bangunan Epic Pavilion, Jalan Pejabat, 20200 Kuala Terangganu ☎ +60 9 6262255 🖷 +60 9 6262266 **W:** manis.fm

Manis FM: Kota Bharu (Tunjung) 90.6MHz, Kuantan (Bukit Pelindong) 95.1MHz, Kuala Terengganu (Bukit Jerung) 102.0MHz, Maran (Bukit Senggora) 103.8MHz. Prgrs in Malay.

INSTITUT KEFAHAMAN ISLAM MALAYSIA (Institute of Islamic Understanding) (Gov., Rlg.)
✉ No 2, Langgak Tunku, Off Jalan Duta, 50480 Kuala Lumpur ☎+60 3 62046273 🖷 +60 3 620462779 **W:** ikimfm.my
L.P: Dir. of R.: Nik Roskiman bin Abdul Samad

FM	Tx	MHz	FM	Tx	MHz
Alor Setar	a	89.0	Kuching	h	93.6
Ipoh	b	102.7	Lahad Datu	n	107.3
Johor Bahru	c	106.2	Melaka	j	89.5
Kota Bharu	d	89.9	Miri	o	104.0
Kota Kinabalu	e	93.9	Negeri Sembilan	k	102.7
Kuala Lumpur	i	91.5	Penang (Balik Pulau)	l	102.7
Kuala Terengganu	f	100.2	Tawau	m	100.7
Kuantan	g	89.5			

Radio Ikim (IKIM.FM): 24h in Malay with limited Arabic and English. **Sites:** a) Gunung Jerai, b) Bukit Keledang, c) Gunung Pulai, d) Bukit Panau, e) Bukit Kokol, f) Bukit Besar, g) Bukit Pelindong 2, h) Pending, i) Bukit Cincin, j) Gunung Ledang, k) Gunung Telapa Burok l) Bukit Genting m) Gunung Andrassy. n)Gunung Silam o)Tanjung Lobang **TRP:** sites a-k: 2kW

KRISTAL HARTA SDN. BHD. (CATS RADIO) (Comm.)
✉ Lot 287, Jalan Bako, Petra Jaya, 93050 Kuching, Sarawak ☎ +60 82 311799 🖷 +60 82 254993 **W:** catsfm.my **L.P:** Chmn: Tan Sri Datuk Amar Haji Bujang Mohd Nor. GM: Haji Mohd Iskandar Hajni Mohd Nawawi

FM	Tx location	MHz	FM	Tx location	MHz
Bintulu	Bukit Setiam	88.3	Sarikei	Bt. K. Malam	96.7
Kuching	Gunung Serapi	99.3	Sibu	Bukit Lima	88.4
Limbang	Bukit Mas	88.7	Sibu	Bt. Singgalang	99.9
Miri	Lambir Hills	93.3	Sri Aman	Bt. Temudok	88.7
Mukah	Mukah	97.9			

Prgr.: 24h in Malay, E and Iban. **TRP:** all sites 1kW

MEDIA PRIMA BHD. (Comm.)
✉ Tingkat 2, South Wing, Sri Pentas, Persiaran Bandar Utama, 47800 Petaling Jaya, Selangor Darul Ehsan ☎ +60 3 77105022 🖷 +60 3 77107098 **W:** hotfm.com.my or flyfm.com.my or onefm.com.my
L.P: Head of Radio Ntwks: Ahmad Izham Omar

FM(MHz)	Tx	Hot	Fly	One	FM(MHz)	Tx	Hot	Fly	One
Alor Setar	a	88.2	99.1	87.8	Kuantan	h	92.4	87.6	100.4
Ipoh	b	104.5	07.9	87.6	Kuching	i	94.3	-	98.3
Johor Bahru	c	90.1	102.5	105.3	Melaka	j	104.3	94.0	88.1
Kota Bharu	d	105.1	107.4	-	Penang	k	-	89.9	-
Kota Kinabalu	e	87.7	-	95.7	Seremban	l	99.5	98.6	88.3
KL/Selangor	f	97.6	95.8	88.1	Taiping	m	90.5	-	-
KT	g	105.0	107.5	-					

Hot FM: 24h in Malay. Hot FM freqs are licensed to Synchrosound Studios Sdn Bhd. **Fly FM**: 24h in English/Malay. FlyFM freqs are licensed to Malaysian Airports (Sepang) Sdn. Bhd. **One FM**: 24h in Mandarin and Cantonese **Kool FM**: 24h in Malay on 101.3MHz in KL area (Bukit Sungai Besi) 1kW, 90.2MHz Penang area (Bukit Penara) 2kW, 88.6MHz Kota Bharu (Peringat), 93.6MHz Kuala Terengganu (g), 107.3MHz Alor Setar (Menara Alor Setar)
Sites: a) Gunung Jerai exc. 99.1MHz: Menara Alor Setar b) Bukit Keledang c) Gunung Pulai exc. 105.3MHz: Taman Sentosa, JB d) Peringat e) Hot FM: Bukit Kokol, One FM: Bukit Karatong f) Gunung Ulu Kali g) Kuala Terengganu (Bukit Besar) h) Bukit Pelindung i) Hot FM: Gunung Serapi, One FM: Bukit Djin j) Gunung Ledang k) Bukit Penara l) Bukit Telapa Burok exc. One FM: Bukit Gan m) Bukit Larut. **TRP:** Fly FM 0.25kW exc. Bukit Cincin: 2kW

RIMAKMUR SDN. BHD. (Comm.)
✉ Tropicana City Office Towers, Level 2.01, No. 3, Jalan SS 20/27, 47400 Petaling Jaya, Selangor Darul Ehsan ☎ +60 3 78851188 🖷 +60 3 78851099 **W:** suriafm.com.my
L.P: COO: Engku Emran Engku Zainal Abidin

FM	Tx	MHz	FM	Tx	MHz
Alor Setar	a	106.9	Kuala Terengganu	g	102.4
Ipoh	b	96.0	Kuantan	h	96.1
Johor Bahru	c	101.4	Melaka	i	88.5
Klang Valley (KL)	d	105.3	Seremban	j	107.0
Kota Bharu	e	106.1	Taiping	k	91.7
Kota Kinabalu	f	105.9			

Suria FM: 24h in Malay. **Sites:** a) Gunung Jerai b) Bukit Keledang c) Gunung Pulai d) Gunung Ulu Kali e) Bukit Panau f) Bukit Kokol g) Bukit Besar h) Bukit Pelindong 2 i) Gunung Ledang j) Gunung Telapa Burok k) Bukit Larut. Kota Kinabalu 105.9MHz carries local prgrs at times.

SENANDUNG SONIK SDN. BHD. (Comm.)
Tea FM: Kota Kinabalu (Bukit Keratong) 102.8MHz, Kuching (Bukit Antu) 102.7MHz, Sibu (Bukit Lima) 100.7MHz. 24h in Chinese

STAR RFM SDN. BHD. (Comm.)
✉ Tropicana City Office Towers Level 2.01 No 3, Jalan SS20/27, 47400 Petaling Jaya, Selangor Darul Ehsan ☎ +60 3 78851188 🖷 +60 3 78851099 **W:** 988.com.my **E:** rfm988@silicon.net.my

FM	Tx	MHz	FM	Tx	MHz
Alor Setar	a	96.1	Kuantan	e	90.4
Ipoh	b	99.8	Melaka	f	98.2
Johor Bahru	c	99.9	Penang	g	94.5
KL/Selangor	d	98.8	Seremban	h	93.3

988 (jiu ba ba): 24h in Mandarin & Chinese dialects. **Sites:** a) Gunung Jerai b) Gunung Keledang c) Gunung Pulai d) Gunung Ulu Kali e) Bukit Pelindong f) Gunung Ledang g) Bukit Penara h) Bkt Telapa Burok

SUARA JOHOR (Comm.)
✉ Bukit Pelangi, Jalan Pasir Pelangi, 80050 Johor Bahru, Johor ☎ +60 7 3314104 🖷 +60 7 3351104 **L.P:** CEO: Haji Bakhtiar Haji Arshad
BEST 104: Melaka & Segamat (Gunung Ledang) 94.8MHz, Johor Bahru (Gunung Pulai) 104.1MHz 10kW TRP, Kuala Lumpur/Selangor (Gunung Ulu Kali) 104.1MHz, Mersing (Bukit Tinggi) 102.5MHz
D.Prgr: 24h (Malay & E music)

University stations:
Putra FM, ✉ Tingkat 2 Jabatan Komunikasi, Fakulti Bahasa Moden dan Komunikasi, Universiti Putra Malaysia, 43400 UPM Serdang, Selangor **W:** putrafm.upm.edu.my **Station:** 90.7MHz 1kW: Mon-Fri 0200-1600 in Malay & E
Radio UiTM (UFM), ✉ Level 13, Menara Ilmu Universiti Teknologi MARA, 40450 Bandaraya Shah Alam, Selangor **W:** uitm.edu.my/ufm **Station:** 93.6MHz 1kW
KK FM, ✉ University Malaysia Sabah (UMS), Jalan UMS, 88400 Kota Kinabalu, Sabah **W:** kkfm.my **Station:** 91.1MHz

MALDIVES

L.T: UTC +5h — **Pop:** 540,000 — **Pr.L:** Dhivehi (Maldivian) (official), English (official) — **E.C:** 230V/50Hz — **ITU:** MLD

MALDIVES BROADCASTING COMMISSION
✉ G. Billoorijehige (3rd Floor), Majeedhee Magu, Malé ☎+960 3334333 🖷 +960 3334334 **W:** broadcom.org.mv **E:** info@broadcom.org.mv

PUBLIC SERVICE MEDIA (Pub.)
✉ Radio Building, Ameenee Magu, 20331 Malé ☎+960 300 0300 🖷 +960 331 7273 **W:** psm.mv **E:** info@psm.mv
Dhivehi Raajjeyge Adu (Radio of Dhivehi People):
MW: Thilafushi 1449kHz 25kW **FM:** Malé 89.0MHz 1kW, Foahmula 89.0MHz 0.5kW. **D.Prgr.** in Dhivehi: 24h (MW occ. only 0058-1930). English: 1300-1310.

Dhivehi FM (Youth prgr.): Malé 91.0MHz 1kW 24h. **Dheenuge Adu:** Malé 90.0MHz.
Ann: "Dhivehi Raajjeyege Adu - Raayithung Radio" (Radio of Dhivehi People - Citizens' Radio).

Other stations:
R. Atoll, Malé: 96.0MHz **W:** facebook.com/radioatoll
Saathanai Minivan, Malé: 97.0MHz **W:** facebook.com/97Minivan
Sun FM, Malé: 94.6MHz **W:** en.sun.mv
V FM, Malé: 99.0MHz **W:** vnews.mv/vfm

MALI

L.T: UTC — **Pop:** 20 million — **Pr.L:** French (official), Bambara — **E.C:** 220V/50Hz — **ITU:** MLI

HAUTE AUTORITÉ DE LA COMMUNICATION (HAC)
✉ B.P. 116, Bamako ☎+223 20232101
OFFICE DE RADIODIFFUSION TÉLÉVISION DU MALI (ORTM, Pub)
✉ B.P. 171, Rue del Marne 287, Bamako ☎+223 20212019 🖷 +223 20214205 **W:** ortm.ml **E:** info@ortm.ml

SW: Bamako (Kati) 50/100kW

kHz	Times	kHz	Times
†5995	0555-0800, 1800-2400	†9635	0800-1800

FM Stations:
National R. Bamako: 92.0MHz 1 kW + 47 txs of 0.5/0.25kW
Regional R. (Channel 2)

Location	MHz	kW	Location	MHz	kW
Mopti	94.4	10	Ségou	96.8	1
Bamako	95.2	1	Sikasso	98.3	1
Kayes	95.4	10			

National R. (Radio Mali) in French/Arabic/English/Bambara/others: **D.Prgr:** SW & FM 0555-2400. **N. in English:** Sat 1855-1910.
Regional R. (Channel 2) on FM only: **D.Prgr:** 0800-1945.
Ann: "Vous écoutez l'Office de Radiodiffusion-Télévision de Mali émettant de Bamako". **E:** "This is Bamako, Mali Radio Telecommunications". **IS:** Guitar.

MIKADO FM (United Nations' Minusma operation)
☎+223 44927070 **W:** minusma.unmissions.org/mikado-fm-la-radio-de-la-paix **E:** radio.mikado@gmail.com
FM(MHz): Bamako 106.6, Gao 94.0, Mopti 91.8, Timbuktu 92.6.

Other stations in Bamako:
R. Patriote FM: 88.1MHz – **R. Canal 2000:** 90.7MHz. **W:** membres.lycos.fr/canal2000 – **R. Mirador** 91.1MHz – **La Voix de la Verité** 91.5MHz – **Fréquence 3** 93.8MHz – **R. Tabalé** 94.3MHz – **R. Guintan** 94.7MHz – **R. Benkan** 97.1MHz – **R.Liberté** 97.7MHz **W:** comfm.com/live/radio/radioliberte **E:** liberte@mtelecom-mali.net – **R. Bamakan** 100.3MHz – **R. Klédu** FM 101.2MHz – **R Jekafo** 100.7MHz – **R. Kayira FM** 104.4MHz – **R. Voix de l'Islam** 107.4MHz.

R. Rurale: Kolondieba 93.7MHz, Koutiala, Macina and others.
RFI Afrique: Gao 92.1, Segou 93.6, Sikasso 95.0, Mopti 97.7, Bamako 98.5, Kayes 102.2MHz in French/Mandinka.
BBC African Service: Bamako 88.9MHz.
VOA African Sce: Timbuktu 90.3, Gao 92.9, Bamako 102.0MHz

MALTA

L.T: UTC +1h (28 Mar-31 Oct: +2h) — **Pop:** 430,000 — **Pr.L:** Maltese (official), English (official) — **E.C:** 230V/50Hz — **ITU:** MLT

MALTA BROADCASTING AUTHORITY (Regulatory Authority)

✉ 7 Mile-end Rd, Hamrun HMR1719 ☎ +356 21221281 / 22016000 🖷 +356 21240855 **E:** info.ba@ba.org.mt **W:** ba-malta.org **L.P:** Chief Exec.: Dr Joanna Spiteri

PUBLIC BROADCASTING SERVICES LTD

✉ 75, St. Luke's Road, Gwardamangia MSD 09 ☎ +356 22913395-6 🖷 +356 21244601 **E:** info@tvm.com.mt **W:** tvm.com.mt/mt/radju
L.P: Chief Exec.: Charles Dalli. Head of News: Norma Saliba. Consultant Manager: Costantino Abela. Technical Officer: David Mizzi

RADIO MALTA

MW: Bizbizja 999kHz 5kW **FM:** Bizbizja 93.7MHz 8kW, 107.5MHz 0.025kW **D.Prgr:** 24h **N:** D.Prgr: 24h. N: 0700 - 0800 - 1000 - 1200 - 1600 - 1800 - 2000. BBC News 0900 - 1100.
RADJU MALTA 2: FM: 105.9MHz 8kW **N:** D.Prgr: 24h.
MAGIC MALTA: FM: 91.7MHz 8kW, 24h **N:** D.Prgr: 24h. N: BBC News 0800 - 0900 - 1200 - 1700 - 1800.
DIGI B NETWORK LTD: ✉ 136, Alwetta Street, Mosta MST4508 ☎ +356 27420570 **E:** info@digibnetwork.com **W:** dab.com.mt **LP:** Man. Dir: Sergio D'Amico.
DAB+: 6A, 6C, 12A. Includes local, gov. and international stns.

COMMERCIAL STATIONS:
103, Archdiocese of Malta and Diocese of Ghawdex, Triq Nazzjonali, Blata-Badja HMR02 ☎+356 2569 9400/2124 6714-5 🖷+356 2569 9151/9160 **E:** live@103.mt **W:** 103.mt **LP**: Chmn: Gege Gatt, Editor in chief: Sylvana Debono, Technical Manager: George Pollacco - **FM:** 103.0MHz 8kW, Ghawdex 97.8MHz 400W, Malta 97.6MHz 250W – **89.7 BAY**, Eden Place, St. Augustine Street, St. George's Bay, St. Julian's STJ3310 ☎+356 23710800 🖷+356 23710845 **E:** info@bay.com.mt **W:** bay.com.mt **LP**: Stn Mngr: Kevin De Cesare Jnr - **FM:** 89.7MHz 8kW – **CALYPSO R.**, 28 New Street in Valletta Road, Luqa ☎+356 21801403 / 52102055 **E:** 101.8@calypsomalta.com **W:** calypsomalta.com **LP**: S.M.: Gordon Pace, Sales executive: Victor Debattista - **FM:** 101.8MHz 8kW – **CAMPUS FM**, University Broadcasting Services, Old Humanities Building, University of Malta, Tal-Qroqq Msida MSD 2080 ☎+356 21333313 🖷+356 21314485 **E:** campusfm@um.edu.mt **W:** campusfm.um.edu.mt **LP**: Stn Mngr: Celaine Buhagiar. - **FM:** 103.7MHz 8kW. Also rel. BBC WS – **NET FM**, 2 Triq Herbert Ganado, Pieta' PTA1450 ☎+356 21230101 🖷+356 21240261 **W:** netfm.com.mt - **FM:** 101.0MHz 8kW, 95.5MHz 300W. (Operated by Maltese Nationalist Partys) – **ONE R.**, A28B, Industrial Estate, Marsa, LQA 06 ☎+35625682568 🖷+35621248249 **E:** onenews@one.com.mt **W:** one.com.mt/oneradio **LP**: Chmn: Jason Micallef, Radio Head: Clint Bajada, Broadc Exec. Head.: Ms. Ruth Vella, Man. R.: Pierre Borg, Head of News: Owen Galea - **FM:** 92.7MHz 8kW, 88.2MHz 200W, 88.0MHz 25W.(Operated by Maltese Labour Party) – **R. MARIJA**, 40 Triq San Vinċenz Ferreri, Rabat RBT 2521 ☎+356 21453105 / 21452474 🖷+356 21453103 **E:** info.mal@radiomaria.org **W:** radjumarija.org **LP**: Coordinator: Michael Amato - **FM:** 102.3MHz 8kW, 107.8MHz 200W – **SMASH R.**, 4 Thistle Lane, Paola PLA 19 ☎+356 21667777 🖷+356 21697830 - **FM:** 104.6MHz 8kW – **VIBE FM**, Triq Tas-Sliema, Kappara, San Gwann, SGN4411 ☎+356 21385887 🖷+356 21383826 **E:** info@vibefm.com.mt **W:** vibefm.com.mt **LP**: Head: Justin Chircop - **FM:** 88.7MHz 8kW – **XFM 100.2**, 111, Triq Lunzjata, St Venera, SVR1021 ☎+356 21378871 **E:** info@xfm.com.mt **W:** xfm.com.mt - **FM:** 100.2MHz 8kW

Established Community Stations (all MHz):
Bastjanizi FM 95,0 Qormi, BKR Radio 94,5 Birkirkara, Deejays Radio 95,6 San Gwann, Lehen il-Belt Gorgjana 105,6 Qormi, Le en il-Belt Victoria 104,0 Victoria, Mics FM 93,3 Rabat, Radio 105 105,0 Hamrun, Radio City 107,6 Valletta, Radju Bambina 98,3 Xaghra, Radju Hompesch 90,0 zabbar, Radju Katidral 90,9 Victoria, Radju Kazin Banda San Filep 106,3, Radju Leħen il-Qala 106,3 Qala, Radju Luminaria 106,9 Nadur, Radju Prekursur 99,3 Xewkija, Radju Sacro Cuor 105,2 Fontana, Radju Santa Katarina 90,6 Zurrieq, Radju Sokkors 95,1 Kercem, Radju Vizitazzjoni 92,4 Gharb, Radju Xeb-er-ras 90,8 Valletta, Radju Ghazziela 101,4 Zebbug

Temporary Community Stations (all MHz):
Temporary licences up to 1 month, usually during the period preceding the festa of the town or village, and powers of 0.25-1W: 12th May Radio 96.5 Ħaz-Zebbuġ, Lehen il-Karmelitani 101.4 Zurrieq, Radju 15 t'Awwissu 98.3 Qrendi, Radju Lauretana 89.3 Ghajnsielem, Radju Lehen il-Ġuzeppini 89.1 Ghaxaq, Radju Leonardo 105.2 Kirkop, Radju Margerita 96.1 Sannat, Radju Sant'Andrija 88.4 Luqa, Tal-Gilju FM 95.4 Mqabba

MARSHALL IS (USA associated)

L.T: UTC +12h — **Pop:** 59,190 — **Pr.L:** English (official), Kajin Majol (official) — **E.C:** 120V/60Hz — **ITU:** MHL

RADIO MARSHALL ISLANDS (Gov/Comm)

✉ PO Box 18, Majuro 96960 ☎+692 625 8413 Studio ☎ + 692 625 8411 **E** v7ab1098@gmail.com: **W:** www.facebook.com/groups/166418142050l222/ Audio Streaming: v7ab.radiostreaming321.com
L.P: GM: Antari Elbon, majuro.letao@gmail.com PD: Arden Sorimle, CE: Stanny Wottokna
MW: V7AB 1098kHz 25kW **FM:** 89.9MHz **D.Prgr:** 1830(Sun 1900)-1130 **News:** Local bulletins, also RNZI & BBC.

OTHER STATIONS:

FM	MHz	kW	Station	FM	MHz	kW	Station
5) Majuro	90.7	0.3	Joy-FM	4) Majuro	101.1		Power FM
3) Majuro	96.5	0.03	WSO-FM	4) Majuro	103.5		Power 103.5
6) Majuro	‡98.5		BBC	2) Majuro	‡104.1		V7AA

‡ Reported inactive

Addresses & other information:
2) Majuro Independent Baptist Church, PO Drawer H, Majuro 96960-1008 ☎+692 625 3141 🖷+692 625 3141 **E:** v7aafm@ntamar.net **ID:** "The Change 104.1FM" – **3) National Weather R.**, Long Island Road, Rairok P.O. Box 78, Majuro 96960-0078. Live and recorded local weather and emergency information for the Majuro atoll area, 24h – **4)** Rairikku, Majuro Atoll, 96960 ☎+692 247 1035 **W:** www.facebook.com/majuropower103.5fm/ – **5)** C/o Delap Seventh-day Adventist School, PO Box I, Majuro, MH 96960 – **6)** Broadcasting House, Portland Place, London W1A 1AA **E:** worldservice.letters@bbc.co.uk

MARTINIQUE (France)

L.T: UTC -4h — **Pop:** 375,000 — **Pr.L:** French (official), Martiniquan Creole — **E.C:** 220V/50Hz — **ITU:** MRT

COMITÉ TERRITORIAL DE L'AUDIOVISUEL DES ANTILLES ET DE LA GUYANE

Centre d'affaires Beterbat, Angle de la rue Victor Lamon et de la route du Stade, Place d'armes, 97232 Le Lamentin ☎ +596 596300963 **E:** cta.antillesguyane@csa.fr

MARTINIQUE LA 1ÈRE (Pub)

1 Rue Loulou Boislaville, Pointe-Simon Tour Lumina, 97200 Fort-de-France ☎+596 596595200 +596 596595226
W: la1ere.francetvinfo.fr/martinique/radio
L.P: Dir. Régional: Augustin Hoareau
FM: 92.0/93.0/93.2/94.3/100.9MHz
D.Prgr: 24h. **Main N:** 1000, 1100, 1200, 1700, 2000. Rel. France-Inter & France Info

RADIO CARAÏBES INTERNATIONAL MARTINIQUE (Comm)

2 Boulevard de la Marne, 97200 Fort-de-France ☎+596 596639870
W: rci.fm **L.P:** Dir: José Anelka
FM: 91.2/92.6/98.6/98.7/98.9/100.2/103.0/104.6/106.6MHz
D.Prgr: 24h **N:** on the h (rel. Europe 1). **Ann.:** RCI

Other FM stations in Fort-de-France (in MHz):
88.9 FM Plus – 89.3 Radio Sud-Est – 90.1 Radio Intertropicale – 91.6 Radio Esperance – 92.4 Radio Transat – 92.8 Radio Actif – 93.6 RFA Radio Frequence Atlantique – 94.0 Bel Radio – 94.9 Radio APAL – 95.3 Radio Fusion – 95.8 France Inter – 96.2 Radio Imagine – 96.7 Nostalgie – 97.1 Trace FM – 97.5 RLDM Radio Lévé Doubout Matinik – 98.1 Super Radio – 99.1 REM Radio Evangile Martinique – 99.5 Radio Saint Louis – 100.6 Radio Canal Antilles & Radio France Internationale – 101.6 Chérie FM – 102.0 Ekla FM – 103.4 RBR – 103.9 Fun Radio – 104.4 NRJ – 104.8 Mouv' FM – 105.4 Campus FM – 106.2 Radio AS & Radio France Internationale – 107.3 Maxxi RMC

MAURITANIA

L.T: UTC — **Pop:** 4.7 million — **Pr.L:** Arabic (official), French, Hassaniya Arabic, Malinke, Pulaar, Soninke, Wolof — **E.C:** 220V/50Hz — **ITU:** MTN

HAUTE AUTORITÉ DE LA PRESSE ET DE L'AUDIOVISUEL (HAPA)

BP 3192, Ilot C Lot 406, Tevragh Zeina, Nouakchott ☎+222 45241088 +222 45241051 **W:** hapa.mr **L.P:** Dir: M. Imam Cheikh Ould Ely.

RADIO MAURITANIE (RM, Gov.)

Av. Gamal Abdel Nasser 387, BP 200, Nost Ksar, Nouakchott ☎+222 45253 266 +222 4525 4069 **W:** radiomauritanie.mr radiocoran.mr radiochabab.mr radioculturelle.com **E:** rm@radiomauritanie.mr **L.P:** DG: Yeslem Ben Abdem.

MW: Nouakchott 783kHz 50kW (inactive).
FM (MHz, 2nd frequency for Quran prgr.): Aïoun 94.7/88.1, Akjoujt 90.4/98.7, Aleg 94.0/87.7 1kW + 90.8 1kW (local stn), Amourj 99.1/95.8, Aoujeft 92.4, Atar 98.0/90.2, Bababé 96.2/89.9, Barkéol 100.0, Bir-Moghrein 90.0, Boghe 88.1/90.2, Boutilimit 92.2/95.4, Boulenouar 97.5, Chami 88.2, Chinguitti 102.0, Djigueni 92.5/89.4, Guerou 99.3/103.8, Kaedi 97.2/89.0, Keur Macene 102.5/94.4, Kiffa 91.4/96.7, Maghama 97.2/90.7, Magta Lahjar 89.0/94.0, MBagne 90.8/103.8, M'Bout 98.4/93.2, Medredra 94.2/91.0, Moudjeria 96.9/93.7, Mounghel 94.8/88.5, N'Beiket Lahouach 97.0/93.4, Néma 98.5/90.1, Nouadhibou 94.7/91.5, Nouakchott 93.3 6kW/98.0 2kW, Ouadane 98.6, Oualata 98.0, R'Kis 104.3/96.1, Rosso 98.0/94.0, Sélibabi 97.7/92.4, Tembedra 96.9/107.3, Tichit 98.0, Tidjikja 98.5/90.2, Tintane 94.8/98.2, Zouérate 97.5/93.3.
Regional Prgrs(FM MHz): R. Aleg 90.8, R. Atar 98.0 , R. Aioun 94.0, R. Kaedi 97.2, R. Kiffa 91.4/96.7 , R. Nema 98.0 , R. Nouadhibou 93.0/98.0, R. Nouakchott 96.1, R. Zouérate 98.0.
NB: Where no power is shown, stns are 0.1kW.
Youth R: Nouakchott 98.0MHz 1kW.
D.Prgr. in Arabic/French/others: 24h. N: Arabic: 0700, 1100(not Fri), 1200, 1300, 1500(not Fri), 1600(Fri), 2200, 2400. French: 1330(Fri), 1430, 1800v. **Quran prgr:** 24h. **Ann:** A: "Huna Nouakchott, Idha'at al-Gumhuriyati al-Islamiyya al-Mauritaniya". F: "Ici Nouackchott, R. Mauritanie". **IS:** Mauritanian guitar.

Other Stations:
R. Koubeni: Nouakchott 94.2MHz **W:** facebook.com/R.koubeni
Mauritanid FM: Nouakchott 100.5MHz, Nouadhibou 101.5MHz **W:** facebook.com/mauritanidFM
R. Nouakchott: Nouadhibou 92.0, Nouakchott 99.5MHz
R. Sahara Media: Nouakchott 92.8MHz, Nouadhibou 95.6MHz **W:** saharamedias.net
R. Tenwire: Nouakchott 97.1MHz **W:** facebook.com/radiotenwire

BBC Arabic Sce: Nouadhibou 102.4MHz, Nouakchott 106.9MHz
China R. Int, Nouakchott 95.7MHz
Medi 1 Maghreb: Nouakchott 102.4MHz
Monte-Carlo Doualiya, Nouakchott: 90.2MHz 2kW
RFI Afrique: Nouadhibou 88.0, Nouakchott 103.3MHz
VOA: Nouakchott 93.8MHz

MAURITIUS

L.T: UTC +4h — **Pop:** 1.3 million — **Pr.L:** Mauritian Creole, English, French, Bhojpuri, Tamil, Hindi, Marathi, Urdu, Telugu, Odia, Chinese — **E.C:** 230V/50Hz — **ITU:** MAU (Rodrigues: ROD)

INDEPENDENT BROADCASTING AUTHORITY (IBA)

Level 2, The Celi Court 6, Sir Celicourt Antelme Str, Port Louis ☎+230 213 3890 +230 213 3894 **W:** iba.mu **E:** iba@intnet.mu

MAURITIUS BROADCASTING CORPORATION (MBC, Pub)

1 Louis Pasteur Str, Forest Side ☎+230 6021200 +230 6757332
W: mbcradio.tv **E:** mbceng@mbc.intnet.mu
MBC R. Maurice, Malherbes: 684kHz 10kW **D.Prgr:** 24h in Creole, French, English & Chinese.
MBC R. Mauritius, Malherbes: 819kHz 10kW. **D.Prgr:** 24h in Indian languages.
Rodrigues FM, Citronelle: 1206kHz 1kW, 97.3Mhz 0.5kW.
Best FM in English & Hindi: Jurançon 96.4Mhz 0.5kW, Plaine Wilhelms 99.4MHz 1kW, Signal Mt. 103.5MHz 1kW.
Kool FM in Creole, English, French: Jurançon 89.3Mhz 1kW, Signal Mt. 91.7MHz 1kW, Plaine Wilhelms 97.3MHz 10kW.
Taal FM in Bhojpuri, Chinese and Hindi: Plaine Wilhelms 94.0MHz 1kW, Jurançon 95.6MHz 0.5kW, Signal Mt. 98.2MHz 1kW.

Other stations:
NRJ Maurice: Curepipe 90.8, Jurançon 92.4, Signal Mt. 94.9 **W:** nrj.mu – **R. Plus**: Malherbes 87.7, Port Louis 88.6, Jurançon 98.9 **W:** radioplus.mu – **R. One**: Malherbes 100.8, Port Louis 101.7, Jurançon 102.4 **W:** r1.mu – **Top FM**: Malherbes 104.4, Port Louis 105.7, Jurançon 106.0 **W:** topfmradio.com
BBC World Sce: Bigara 1575kHz 2kW. 24h.
RFI Afrique: Curepipe/Jurançon/Port Louis/Rodrigues 93.2MHz

MAYOTTE (France)

L.T: UTC +3h — **Pop:** 273,000 — **Pr.L:** French (official), Bushi, Shimaore — **E.C:** 220V/50Hz — **ITU:** MYT

COMITÉ TERRITORIAL DE L'AUDIOVISUEL DE LA RÉUNION ET DE MAYOTTE see main entry under Réunion

MAYOTTE LA PREMIÈRE (Pub)

B.P. 103, Rue de Jardins, 97610 Dzaoudzi ☎+262 269601017 +262 269601852 **W:** la1ere.francetvinfo.fr/mayotte
FM: Dzaoudzi 91.0MHz 0.1kW, M'lima Combani 92.0MHz 0.5kW, Kanikeli-Choungui 101.3MHz 0.5kW, Mtsanboro-Madjabalini 103.2MHz 0.5kW.
D.Prgr in French/Mahorian: Local prgr. Mon-Sat 0000-1900, Sun 0145-1830. Relays RFI overnight.
IS: Melody on guitar.

Europe 2: Boueni 90.2MHz, Mamoudzou 99.1MHz, Pamandzi 97.7MHz
France-Inter: Dzaoudzi 101.0MHz 24h

MEXICO

L.T: UTC -6h (DST*: -5h). QR: UTC -5h. BS, CH, NA, SN: UTC -7h (DST*: -6h). SO: UTC -7h. BC: UTC -8h (DST**: -7h) *) 4 Apr-31 Oct **) as (*) except 14 Mar-7 Nov in certain locations along the border with USA — **Pop:** 129 million — **Pr.L:** Spanish — **E.C:** 60Hz, 127V — **ITU:** MEX

INSTITUTO FEDERAL DE TELECOMUNICACIONES (IFT)
Unidad de Sistemas de Radio y Televisión
✉ Insurgentes Sur #1143, Col. Noche Buena, Delegación Benito Juárez, CP 03720, México D.F. **W:** ift.org.mx **E:** quejas@ift.org.mx ☎ +52 55 50154000.

DIRECCION DE RADIO
Departamento de Asignación de Frecuencias
✉ Eugenia 197, Col.Narvarte, 03020 Delg. Benito Juárez México, D.F ☎ +52 55 5015 4785.

Call XE–,° = also on SW, ‡= inactive, # = HD Radio (IBOC), d = daytime operation. The letters preceding the stn number indicate the state. Addresses are listed by state in alphabetical order. Hrs of tr usually 24h – see address section for variations.
NB: most stations carry "La Hora Nacional" (official prgr.) Mon. 0400-0500 (Sun. local time), first half hour nationwide prgr, second regional programming.

MW	Call	kHz	kW	Station, location
BC01)	SURF	540	25/3.5	R. Zion, Tijuana
CH15)	TX	540	4/1	La Ranchera de Paquimé, Nuevo Casas Grandes (r. XHTX 90.5)
CS01)	MIT	540	5/1	R. IMER, LV de Balún Canán, Comitán (r. XHEMIT 107.9 HD1)
ME01)	WF	540	20/2.5	Heraldo R. Estado de México, Tlalmanalco
NL01)	WA	540	1.5/1	Los 40, Monterrey (r. XHWAG 88.5 HD)
SL01)	WA	540	150	Los 40, San Luis Potosí (r. XHEWA 103.9)
SN01)	HS	540	5/2.5	La Mejor, Los Mochis (r. XHHS 90.9)
CH01)	PL	550	5/0.15	La Super Estación, Cd. Cuauhtémoc (r. XHEPL 91.3)
NA01)	GNAY	550	2.5/0.15	R. Aztlán, "Nuestra Radio", Tepic
CO01)	GIK	560	1.4/0.25	La Acerera, Monclova (r. XHGIK 88.1)
DF01)	OC	560	1.5/0.5	R. Chapultepec, México
DG01)	SRD	560	10/1	La Tremenda, Santiago Papasquiaro (r. XHSRD 89.3)
CL01)	MZA	560	10/1	Sol FM, Manzanillo (Cihuatlán JL) (r. XHMZA 89.7)
MI01)	LQ	570	2/1.7	Candela, Morelia (r. XHLQ 90.1)
NL02)	BJB	570	5/2	BJB Regional Mexicana, Monterrey (r. XHGBO 92.1)
OX02)	OA	570	5/2.5	La Mexicana, Oaxaca (r. XHEOA 94.9)
CH08)	FI	580	5/0.7	Fiesta Mexicana, Chihuahua (r. XHFI 96.5)
CO02)	LRDA	580	5/2.5	La Rancherita del Aire, Piedras Negras (r. XHEMU 103.7)
JL02)	AV	580	10/1	Canal 58, Guadalajara
QR02)	YI	580	1/0.25	Mix FM, Cancún (r. XHYI 93.1)
DF02)	PH	590	25/10	Sabrosita 590, México
DG03)	E	590	1	R. Fórmula Durango, Durango(r. XHE 105.3)
GJ01)	GTO	590	10/0.25	Éxtasis Digital, León (r. XHGTO 95.9)
TM02)	FD	590	5/0.5	La Mejor, Reynosa
CS05)	OCH	600	10/0.5	K'in Radio, Ocosingo
GR02)	BB	600	5/1	La Comadre, Puros Éxitos, Acapulco (r. XHBB 101.5)
NL03)	MN	600	1/0.5	Acustik R., Monterrey
SN02)	HW	600	5/1	La Mejor, Chametla (r. XHHW 102.7)
CO34)	SORN	610	1	Viva Saltillo, Saltillo
MI03)	UF	610	5/1	La Z, Uruapan (r. XHUF 100.5)
SN03)	GS	610	6/1	Chavez R. GS, Guasave (r. XHGS 106.1)
YU04)	UM	610	10/0.2	La Nueva Candela, Valladolid (r. XHUM 92.7)
BC02)	SS	620	5	Unánimo Deportes, Ensenada
DF03)	NK	620	50/5	R. 6.20, México (Ecatepec ME)
SL02)	PBSD	620		Origen R., Soledad Diez Gutiérrez (F.Pl.)
TB15)	GMSR	620	2.5	620 AM, La R. Que Se Ve, Villahermosa
TM03)	GH	620	1/0.25	La Lupe, Río Bravo (r. XHCAO 89.1)
JL05)	PBGJ	630	10/0.5	Jalisco Radio AM, Guadalajara (// 1080)
NL03)	FB	630	10	La FB 6-30, Monterrey
QR03)	CCQ	630	0.5	La Z, Cancún (r. XHCCQ 91.5)
SO05)	FX	630	1/0.25	Amor 101, Guaymas (r. XHFX 101.3)
TM04)	ERO	630	1/0.15	R. Tamaulipas, Esteros
VE03)	FU	630	10/0.75	F-U, LV Amiga de la Cuenca, Cosamaloapan (r. XHFU 103.3)
CH27)	JUA	640	5	La Lupe Chihuahua, Cd.Juárez(r. XHCHA 104.5)
HG01)	NQ	640	50/25	NQ Radio, Tulancingo (r. XHNQ 90.1)
TM05)	TAM	640	5/1	Romántica, Cd.Victoria (r. XHTAM 96.1)
JL06)	CSBK	650	10/2.5	Puerto Vallarta (F.Pl.)
OX05)	PX	650	5/0.2	LV del Ángel, Puerto Ángel (r. XHEPX 99.9)
SN05)	TNT	650	5/1	Chavez R. 65, Los Mochis (r. XHTNT 100.5)
SO40)	HEEP	650	1/0.1	Acustik Radio, Hermosillo (F.Pl.)
YU03)	VG	650	2.5/0.02	R. Fórmula Yucatán, Mérida (r. XHVG 94.5)
AG01)	EY	660	50/10	La Kaliente, Aguascalientes(r. XHEY 102.9)
BS06)	SJC	660	2.5/0.25	KVOZ, San José del Cabo (r. XHESJC 93.1)
DF04)	DTL	660	50/1	Ciudadana 6-60, México
DG10)	DGEP	660	1	Acustik R., Durango (F.Pl.)
NL02)	FZ	660	10/1	ABC R., Monterrey
QR04)	CPR	660	30d	R. Chan Santa Cruz, Felipe Carrillo Puerto
GR06)	CHG	680	5/2.5	Súper 102.7, Chilpancingo (r. XHCHG 102.7)
BC03)	WW	690	78/50	U Radio, Tijuana
DF05)	N	690	100/5	R. Centro y El Fonógrafo, México (Tlalnepantla ME)
NL04)	RG	690	10/1	RG La Deportiva, Monterrey (r. XHFMTU HD2 103.7)
CA09)	XPUJ	700	5	LV del Corazón de la Selva, X'pujil
JL08)	DKR	700	10/0.15	La Octava y Universal, Guadalajara
MI02)	LX	700	5	La Grande de Michoacán, Zitácuaro(r. XHLX 95.1)
SO07)	ETCH	700	5d	LV de los Tres Ríos, Etchojoa
DF04)	MP	710	10/1	R. 710, México
GR02)	MAR	710	1	98.5 FM, Acapulco (r. XHMAR 98.5)
OX24)	OAEP	710	5/0.5	Acustik Radio, Oaxaca (F.Pl.)
SL03)	SLEP	710	1/0.25	Acustik Radio, San Luis Potosì (F.Pl.)
CH30)	JCC	720	1	La Zeta, Cd. Juárez (r. XHEM 103.5)
CO07)	DE	720	8/0.25	La Kaliente, Saltillo (irr, r. XHDE 105.7)
MI06)	KN	720	5d	La Ke Buena, Huetamo (r. XHKN 95.5)
ZC09)	JAGC	720	2	La Bonita del Norte, Juan Aldama
CH03)	HB	730	50/1	La Mexicana, Hidalgo del Parral (r. XHEHB 107.1)
DF06)	X	730	60	W Deportes, México
JL10)	GDL	730	5/1	Arroba FM, Guadalajara (r. XHGDL 88.7)
YU07)	PET	730	10d	LV de los Mayas, Peto (r. XHPET 105.5)
CO09)	QN	740	10/1	R. Fórmula, Torreón (r. XHQN 105.9)
JL11)	VAY	740	1	Amor FM, Puerto Vallarta (r. XHVAY 92.7)
OX08)	POR	740	5/1	TPrende, Putla de Guerrero(r. XHPOR 98.7)
QR06)	CAQ	740	20/10	R. Fórmula QR, Cancún (r. XHCAQ 92.3)
TBYY)	KV	740	10/1	Exa FM, Villahermosa (r. XHKV 88.5)
GR23)	ACEP	750	5	Acustik R., Acapulco (F.Pl.)
MI31)	UORN	750	10	Media Group R. Michoacán, Uruapan
NA02)	JMN	‡750	10d	LV de los Cuatro Pueblos, Jesús María
SN08)	CSI	750	5/0.25	Romántica, Culiacán (r. XHCSI 89.5)
CS11)	RA	760	5/0.5	R. Uno, San Cristóbal de las Casas
DF07)	ABC	760	70/10	ABC Radio, México (La Paz ME)
JL12)	ZZ	760	5/1	R. Gallito, Guadalajara
SO11)	NY	760	5/0.1	R. Xeny, Nogales
MI08)	ML	770	5/1.5	La Ranchera, Apatzingán (r. XHEML 98.3)
NL05)	ACH	770	25/1	R. Fórmula Monterrey 770, Monterrey
SL04)	ANT	770	10	LV de las Huastecas, Tancanhuitz de Santos
ZC08)	FRTM	770	25/1	XEFRTM, Fresnillo (F.Pl.)
GR08)	XY	780	2.5/1	La Poderosa Voz del Balsas, Cd.Altamirano
JL13)	LD	780	5/0.5	R. Costa, Autlán (r. XHLD 103.9)
OX10)	GLO	780	10d	LV de la Sierra Juárez, Guelatao de Juárez
TM09)	SFT	780	5/1	La Poderosa, San Fernando(r.XHSFT 103.7)
TM34)	TMEP	780	1/0.25	Acustik Radio, Tampico (F.Pl.)
BC05)	SU	790	1/0.25	La Dinámica, Mexicali (r. XHSU 105.9)
BS01)	NT	790	5/0.75	R. Fórmula, La Paz (r. XHNT 97.5)
JL14)	GAJ	790	0.25	Fórmula Jalisco 7-90 AM, Guadalajara
BC06)	SPN	800	0.5/0.25	Cadena 800, Tijuana
CH12)	ROK	800	50	R. Cañón, Cd.Juárez
GR09)	ZV	800	5d	LV de la Montaña, Tlapa de Comonfort
NL06)	ERG	800	10/2.5	RG La Deportiva 92.9 FM, Montemorelos (r. XHERG 92.9)
VE09)	QT	800	1	La Poderosa, Veracruz (r. XHQT 106.9)
GJ05)	EMM	810	1/0.5	Salmantina, Salamanca
GR10)	AGR	810	7/0.6	R. Fórmula, Acapulco (r. XHAGR 105.5)
QR07)	RB	810	2.5/0.25	Sol Estéreo, Cozumel (r. XHRB 89.9)
SO12)	RSV	810	5d	Tribuna Radio, Cd. Obregón
TM11)	RI	810	5/0.1	R. Rey, Reynosa
TX01)	HT	810	5/1	R. Huamantla, Huamantla (r. XHHT 106.9)
BC07)	ABCA	820	3.5/0.5	ABC R. Canal 820, Mexicali (r.XHABCA 101.3)
GR11)	GRC	820	1d	RTG Más Radio, Coyuca de Catalán
JL36)	BA	820	10/1	R. Cañón, Guadalajara
SL05)	BM	820	10/1	Ke Buena, San Luis Potosí (r. XHBM 105.7)

MW	Call	kHz	kW	Station, location
DF08)	ITE	830	25/5	Radio Capital, México
MI09)	PUR	830	8d	LV de los P'urhépechas, Cheran
NL07)	LN	830	5/0.25	La Caliente, Linares (r. XHR 105.7)
OX11)	TLX	830	1/0.5	La Poderosa, Tlaxiaco (r. XHTLX 100.5)
JL16)	XXX	840	5/1	Fiesta Mexicana, Tamazula(r. XHXXX 97.5)
NA03)	TEY	840	1/0.25	Fiesta La Más Picuda, Tepic(r. XHTEY 93.7)
BC10)	ZF	850	1	Buenísima, Mexicali
BC08)	MO	860	5	La Poderosa/Uniradio, Tijuana
CH33)	ZOL	860	1/0.5	R. Noticias 860, Cd. Juárez
DF09)	UN	860	45/10	R. UNAM AM, México
NL04)	NL	860	5/1.5	R. Recuerdo, Monterrey (r. XHFMTU-HD2 103.7)
QR08)	CTL	860	10/1	R. Chetumal, Chetumal (r. XHCHE 100.9)
CH18)	TAR	870	10d	LV de la Sierra Tarahumara, Guachochi
GR12)	GRO	870	1	RTG Más Radio, Chilpancingo
OX12)	ACC	870	10/0.25	LV del Puerto, Pto. Escondido (r. XHACC 93.3)
CH38)	CHEP	880	5/0.25	XECHEP, Chihuahua (F. Pl.)
JL18)	AAA	880	20/1	R. Mujer, Guadalajara (r. XHEAAA 92.7)
GJ06)	AK	890	5/0.5	La Mejor, Acámbaro (r. XHAK 89.7)
DF06)	W	900	100	W Radio, México (r. XEW-FM 96.9)
NL08)	OK	900	10/2.5	Amor FM, Monterrey (r. XHOK 90.9)
BC10)	AO	910	0.25	R. Mexicana, Mexicali
GJ24)	LNEP	910	5/0.1	Acustik Radio, León (F.Pl.)
CA10)	STRC	920	1.5/0.5	Voces, Campeche
GJ08)	RE	920	5/1	La Comadre, Celaya (r. XHRE 88.1)
JL21)	LT	920	10/1	R. María México, Tlaquepaque
MI11)	LCM	920	5/2.5	La Poderosa, Lázaro Cárdenas (r. XHLCM 95.7)
PU07)	ZAR	920	1	Arroba FM, Puebla (r. XHEZAR 96.1)
CO33)	SAME	930	1	SJ 103.3 FM, Saltillo (r XHSJ 103.3)
OX14)	TLA	930	5d	LV de la Mixteca, Tlaxiaco (r. XHPBSD 95.9)
BC07)	MMM	940	1/0.1	940 AM Oldies, Mexicali
BS08)	RLA	940	10/1	R. Surcalifornia, Santa Rosalía
DF06)	Q	940	30	Ke Buena, México (r. XEQ 92.9)
TM15)	RKS	940	1d	Romántica, Reynosa (r. XHRKS 103.3)
BC09)	KAM	#950	20/5	R. Fórmula BC Tijuana, Tijuana
CA02)	MAB	950	3/0.9	Heraldo R, Cd. del Carmen(r. XHMAB 101.3)
CH02)	FA	950	1/0.5	La Poderosa, Chihuahua (r. XHFA 89.3)
JL23)	MEX	950	5/0.5	La Mexicana, Cd.Guzmán (r. XHMEX 104.9)
OX15)	OJN	950	10d	LV de la Chinantla, San Lucas Ojitlán
DG09)	TPH	‡960	5d	Las Tres Voces de Durango, Santa María de Ocotán
JL24)	HK	960	10/2.5	HK 9-60, LV de Guadalajara, Guadalajara
VE08)	OZ	†960	1/0.25	Amor FM, Xalapa (r. XHOZ 91.7)
CH22)	SW	970	1/0.5	R. Madera, Cd. Madera (r. XHESW 96.1)
CH30)	J	970	5	La Jota Mexicana, Cd.Juárez
DF10)	RFR	970	50/4	Fórmula 970, México
GJ10)	UG	970	1	R. Universidad de Guanajuato, Guanajuato
MI08)	CJ	970	1/0.25	Los 40, Apatzingán (r. XHCJ 94.3)
TM17)	O	970	1	NotiGAPE, Matamoros
MI15)	LC	980	5/0.2	Radio Pía, La Piedad (r. XHLC 92.7)
PU01)	LFFS	980	5	XELFFS Mi Gente, Izúcar de Matamoros
BC05)	CL	†990	1.4/3	La Rocola 9-90, Mexicali
NL04)	T	990	50	La T Grande, Monterrey
OX16)	IU	990	2.5/1	Stereo Cristal, Oaxaca (r. XHIU 105.7)
CH33)	FV	1000	1	La Rancherita, Cd.Juárez
DF02)	OY	1000	50/20	Mil AM, México
YU01)	MYL	1000	5/0.35	So Good, Mérida (r. XHMYL 92.1)
HG03)	HGO	1010	1d	Hidalgo Radio, Huejutla
JL36)	HL	1010	50/5	R. Cañón, Guadalajara
MI18)	TUX	1010	5d	LV de la Sierra Oriente, Tuxpan(r. XHTUMI 107.9)
PU02)	PA	1010	20/2	Ke Buena, Puebla (r. XHEPA 89.7 HD)
SO19)	XN	1010	0.5/0.2	Toño, Ures (r. XHHER 105.9 MHz)
CL11)	COEP	1020	1	Acustik Radio, Colima (F.Pl.)
QR11)	WO	1020	1/0.25	Sol Stereo, Chetumal (r. XHWO 97.7)
VE11)	PR	1020	5/0.5	Éxtasis Digital, Poza Rica (r. XHPR 102.7)
BC02)	SDD	1030	5	La Tremenda/PSN Radio, Puerto Nuevo
CS18)	VFS	1030	10/0.25	LV de la Frontera Sur, Las Margaritas
DF05)	QR	1030	50/5	R. Centro y El Fonógrafo, México (r. 690kHz)
JL34)	ROPJ	1030	10/1	W Radio Bajío, Lagos de Moreno
QR14)	FEL	1030	5d	LV del Gran Pueblo, Felipe Carrillo Puerto (r. XHNKA 104.5)
SL06)	IE	1030	5/1	Oye Digital, Matehuala (r. XHIE 105.5)
CS19)	PLE	1040	5/0.5	R. Palenque, Palenque
GJ09)	SAG	1040	5/0.25	R. Lobo Bajío, Irapuato
JL18)	BBB	1040	10/1	ESNE R, Guadalajara
BC05)	D	1050	10d	La Poderosa, Mexicali (r. XHMUG 96.9)
BS05)	BCS	1050	10/1	La Radio de Sudcalifornia, La Paz (r. 99.1)
MI07)	IP	1050	1	La Poderosa, Uruapán (r. XHIP 89.7)
NL10)	G	1050	100	La Ranchera 1050, Monterrey

MW	Call	kHz	kW	Station, location
DF11)	EP	°1060	100/20	R. Educación "Señal 1060 AM", México (r. XHEP-HD 96.5)
TM30)	RDO	1060	7/2.5	La Raza 1060, Reynosa
CA05)	IT	1070	1/0.25	Exa FM, Cd. del Carmen (r. XHIT 99.7)
GR02)	AGS	1070	1/0.2	Estéreo Pop, Acapulco (r. XHAGS 103.1)
JL05)	PBPV	1080	5d	Jalisco Radio AM, Puerto Vallarta (// 630)
ME03)	TUL	1080	5/0.25	R. Mexiquense Valle de México, Tultitlán
BC12)	PRS	1090	50	KJAV Ultra 104.9, Rosarito
NL04)	AU	1090	5/0.5	Milenio R, Monterrey (r. XHFMTU-HD3 103.7)
PU03)	HR	1090	1	La HR, Puebla
TM20)	WL	1090	1d	Xtrema, Nuevo Laredo (r. XHWL 103.7)
GJ11)	BV	1100	5	R. Alegría, Moroleón (r. XHBV 95.7)
GR17)	GRM	1100	1d	RTG Radio Guerrero, Ometepec
ZC07)	TGO	1100	5/0.5	R. Cañón, Tlaltenango (r. XHTGO 90.1)
CH33)	WR	1110	1/0.5	Cristo Rey Radio, Ciudad Juarez
CO20)	PU	1110	0.25	La P-U, Monclova
JL20)	PVJ	‡1110	1/0.2	Fiesta Mexicana, Pto Vallarta(r. XHPVJ 94.3)
SO23)	VS	1110	1/0.25	Maxima 96-3, Hermosillo (r. XHVS 96.3)
TM21)	OQ	1110	1	NotiGAPE, Reynosa
BC13)	MX	1120	0.4/0.1	Noticias 1120, Mexicali
JL29)	UNO	1120	0.5	Acustik Radio, Guadalajara
PU10)	POP	1120	5	Fórmula 11-20 AM, Puebla
TB14)	TQE	1120	5/0.5	La R. de Tabasco, Tenosique(r. XETVH 1230kHz)
YU09)	RUY	1120	1d	R. Universidad, Mérida (r. XHRUY 103.9)
ME10)	CHAP	1130	5	R. Chapingo, Chapingo
MI19)	FN	1130	1/0.1	Candela, Uruapan (r. XHFN 91.1)
NA11)	LUP	1130	1d	R. Lupita, Las Varas (r. XHLUP 89.1)
SO24)	HN	1130	1	Los 40, Nogales (r. XHHN 89.9)
CS20)	TEC	1140	1/0.5	R. Tecpatán, Tecpatán
HG03)	PEC	1140	1	R. San Bartolo, San Bartolo Tutotepec (r. XHPEC 103.9)
NL02)	MR	1140	50	R. Esperanza, Monterrey
BC14)	RM	#1150	1	R. Fórmula BC Mexicali, Mexicali
DF25)	JP	1150	50/10	Acustik Radio, México
JL10)	AD	1150	50/1	R. Metrópoli, Guadalajara
OX20)	XP	1150	10/1	La Mejor, Tuxtepec (r. XHESO 104.9)
SN17)	UAS	1150	10/0.15	R. UAS, Culiacán (r. XHUAS 96.1)
VE24)	TVR	1150	1.5/0.5	Vida Azul, Tuxpan (r. XHTVR 106.9)
BC15)	QIN	1160	10	LV del Valle, San Quintín
SO26)	FEM	1170	5/0.1	R. Disney, Hermosillo (r. XHFEM 99.5)
TM15)	RT	1170	5d	Ke Buena, Reynosa
BS05)	UBS	1180	10	R. Universidad Autonoma de Baja California Sur, La Paz
CH35)	DCH	1180	5/1.5	Ke Buena, Cd. Delicias
DF12)	FR	1180	35/25	R. Felicidad, México
BC16)	MBC	1190	0.25/0.1	Cadena 1190 AM, Mexicali
CH30)	PZ	1190	1/0.1	R. Centro 11-90, Cd.Juárez
JL12)	WK	1190	50/10	W Radio, Guadalajara
MO02)	JOEP	1190	5	Acustik Radio, Jojutla (F.Pl.)
NL10)	CT	1190	10/0.1	Contacto 11-90, Monterrey
SL07)	XQ	1190	25/1	R. Universidad, San Luís Potosí
BS11)	PAS	1200	1	R. Punta Abreojos, Punta Abreojos
ME06)	QY	1200	2.5	La Bestia Grupera, Toluca (r. XHQY 103.7)
QE01)	CPAC	1200	5	RTQ "Consumo Libre", Jalpan
CS21)	COPA	1210	5d	LV de los Vientos, Copainalá
PU10)	PUE	1210	5/1	92.1 FM, Puebla (r. XHPUE 92.1)
CO22)	SAL	1220	4.5d	R. Universidad Agraria, Saltillo
DF04)	B	1220	100	La B Grande, México
JL14)	DKN	1230	0.5	Fórmula Jalisco 12-30 AM, Guadalajara
NL05)	IZ	1230	10/1	R. Fórmula Monterrey 1230, Monterrey
TB14)	TVH	1230	20/1	La Radio de Tabasco, Villahermosa
SN23)	CSEP	1230	10	Acustik Radio, Culiacán (F.Pl.)
CH12)	WG	1240	1	Bengala 1240/R. Guadalupana, Cd.Juárez
HG05)	RD	1240	1	La Comadre, Pachuca (r. XHRD 104.5)
MI31)	MEFM	1240	‡25	MG Radio Michoacán, Morelia
SO24)	CG	1240	1	Ke Buena, Nogales (r. XHCG 89.5)
JL24)	DK	1250	10/1	DK 12-50, Guadalajara
ME07)	TEJ	1250	1/0.25	R. Mexiquense, Tejupilco (r. XEGEM 1600)
PU04)	ZT	1250	5/0.5	La Magnífica 1250 AM, Puebla
VE55)	VREP	1250	1	Acustik Radio, Veracruz (F.Pl.)
CH20)	OG	1260	5/0.25	XEOG La Primera, Ojinaga (r. XHOG 101.7)
DF12)	L	1260	50/35	La Comadre, México
GJ14)	ZH	1260	1/0.25	La Estación que se Escucha, Salamanca
JL31)	JY	1260	5/1	La Mejor, Autlán (r. XHJY 101.5)
OX22)	JAM	1260	10d	LV de la Costa Chica, Santiago Jamiltepec
SO30)	MW	1260	1/0.25	Río Digital 93.9, San Luis Río Colorado
VE22)	MTV	1260	1	El Lobo de Mina, Minatitlán (r. XHMTV 100.9)
BC17)	AZ	1270	0.5	La Z, Tijuana

MW	Call	kHz	kW	Station, location
CO33)	TGME	1270	10	XETGME, Torreón (F.Pl.)
GJ16)	RPL	1270	10/0.15	La Poderosa RPL, León (r. XHRPL 93.9)
SO31)	GL	1270	1/0.5	La Verdad Radio, Navojoa
VE11)	RRR	1270	1/0.25	La Huasteca, Papantla
GJ17)	SQ	1280	2.5/1	R. San Miguel, S. M. de Allende (r. XHSQ 103.3)
NL04)	AW	1280	10/1	La Gran AW, Monterrey (r. XHAW 101.3)
PU05)	EG	1280	1/0.5	ABC Radio, Puebla
TM24)	TUT	1280	1d	R. Tamaulipas, Tula
MI24)	IX	1290	1/0.5	La Pantera, Sahuayo
SO16)	AP	1290	1/0.25	Romántica, Cd.Obregón (r. XHAP 96.9)
CH30)	P	1300	38/1	R. Mexicana Nuestras Noticias, Cd.Juárez
GJ19)	XV	1300	10/0.75	La Z, León (r. XHXV 88.9)
HG07)	AWL	1300	1/0.25	El Corazón de la Sierra,Jacala
SO24)	XW	1300	1/0.1	La Bestia Grupera, Nogales
VE36)	CPAD	1300	-	Radio UV, Xalapa (F.Pl.)
BC18)	C	1310	1	R. Enciso/PSN Radio, Tijuana
CS25)	RAM	1310	1	R. Amanecer, LV Indígena, Betania
GR18)	GRT	1310	1d	RTG Más Radio Taxco, Taxco de Alarcón
JL10)	TIA	1310	10/1	R. Vital, Guadalajara
NL02)	VB	1310	5/0.25	R. 13 Más Vallenata, Monterrey
TM25)	AM	1310	1/0.25	La Radio de Matamoros, Matamoros
CO33)	PNME	1320	10	XEPNME, Piedras Negras (F.Pl.)
BC19)	AA	‡1340	1	R. Variedades, Mexicali
HG08)	QB	1340	1	Super Stereo Miled, Tulancingo(r. XHQB 97.1)
JL24)	DKT	1340	5/1	Radiorama 13-40, Frecuencia Deportiva, Guadalajara
MI08)	APM	1340	1	Candela, Apatzingán (r. XHAPM 95.1)
MI26)	CR	1340	1	La Zeta, Morelia (r. XHCR 96.3)
NL02)	NV	1340	1	Romántica 1340, Monterrey
TM25)	MT	1340	0.6	R. Diamante, Matamoros
TM26)	BK	1340	1	La BK, Nuevo Laredo (r. XHBK 95.7)
CO06)	TB	1350	5/0.5	R. Laguna, Torreón
CS23)	CAH	1350	5/1	La Popular, LV de Soconusco, Cacahoatán (r. XHCAH 89.1)
DF04)	QK	1350	5/1	Tropicalísima 13-50, México
PU06)	CTZ	1350	10d	LV de la Sierra Norte, Cuetzalán
SO30)	LBL	1350	8d	R. Centro, San Luis Río Colorado (r. XHLBL 93.9)
TM27)	ZD	1350	0.25	La Mandona, Camargo
CH02)	DI	1360	1/0.4	@FM, Chihuahua (r. XHDI 88.5)
GR23)	IGEP	1360	-	Acustik Radio, Iguala (F.Pl.)
VE42)	ZON	1360	10d	LV de la Sierra de Zongolica, Zongolica
BC10)	HG	1370	0.5	Vida 13-70, Mexicali
DG08)	RPU	1370	1/0.25	La Lupe, Durango (r. XHRPU 102.9)
JL24)	PJ	1370	10/1	R. Ranchito, Guadalajara
TM20)	GNK	1370	5/0.5	La La Ranchera Norteña, Nuevo Laredo
DF14)	CO	1380	50/5	Romántica 13-80, México
VE27)	TP	1380	10/1	Sensación FM, Xalapa (r. XHTP 95.5)
CL10)	TY	‡1390	10/2.5	@FM, Tecomán (r. XHTY 91.3)
HG06)	ZG	1390	10/2.5	R. Mezquital, Ixmiquilpan (r. XHD 96.5)
MO01)	CTAM	1390	1	IMRyT Señal de Identidad, Cuautla (r. XHVACM 102.9)
TM13)	XO	1390	5/1	La Super Buena, Cd.Mante (r. XHXO 95.7)
TM21)	OR	1390	1	NotiGAPE, Reynosa
ME08)	XI	1400	2.5/1	Lokura FM, Ixtapan de la Sal (r. XHXI 99.5)
NL11)	SH	1400	51	R. Sabinas, Cd.Sabinas
OX23)	UBJ	1400	1	R. Universidad, Oaxaca
CA13)	CUA	1410	1/0.25	R. Universidad, Campeche
DF02)	BS	1410	25/1	Bandolera 14-10, México
JL32)	KB	1410	25/10	Alfa FM, Guadalajara (r. XHKB 99.9)
TM20)	AS	1410	1/0.25	Fiesta Mexicana, Nuevo Laredo (r. XHAS 101.5)
BC20)	XX	1420	10/2	TUDN Radio, Tijuana
CH33)	F	1420	5/0.5	Activa 14-20, Cd.Juárez
NL03)	H	1420	5/0.4	Antología Vallenata, Monterrey
TM21)	EW	1420	1	W1420/LV del Bajo Bravo, Matamoros
TM29)	WD	1430	5/0.15	R. X, Cd. Miguel Alemán (r. XHWD 95.9)
TX02)	TT	1430	5/1	R. Tlaxcala, La Doble T, Tlaxcala
DF15)	EST	1440	25/5	Ondas de Paz, México
GR21)	RY	1450	2/1	La Poderosa Voz del Sur, Arcelia
MI24)	RNB	1450	1	R. Impacto, Sahuayo y Jiquilpan
VE55)	PREP	1450	1	Acustik Radio, Poza Rica (F.Pl.)
CH32)	YC	1460	1	R. Fórmula Juárez, Cd.Juárez
GR12)	GRA	1460	1	RTG Radio, Acapulco (r. XHGRC 97.7)
OX07)	KC	1460	5/0.5	Planeta, Oaxaca (r. XHKC 100.9)
SO30)	CB	1460	10/0.25	R. Ranchito, San Luis Río Colorado (r. XHDY 107.1)
BC08)	RCN	1470	10/5	RCN/Uniradio 14-70, Tijuana (r. CRI 12h)
CA11)	BAL	1470	2.5/0.5	R. Voz Maya de México, Bécal
DF10)	AI	1470	50/5	Fórmula 1470, México
HG10)	IND	1470	1/0.5	Hidalgo R., Tlanchinol
SN22)	ACE	1470	1/0.1	R. Fórmula, Mazatlán (r. XHACE 91.3)
TM31)	HI	1470	10/0.25	La Consentida, Ciudad Miguel Alemán
HG11)	CARH	1480	5	LV del Pueblo Hña-hñu, Cárdonal (r. XHCARH 89.1)
JL24)	ZJ	1480	20/1	14-80 Simplemente Supérate, Guadalajara
NL04)	TKR	1480	10/1	La TKR, Rancherita y Regional, Monterrey
SO18)	NS	1480	1/0.25	Z107.1, Navojoa (r. XHENS 107.1)
TM32)	VIC	1480	5/0.15	R. Tamaulipas, Cd.Victoria
CH37)	CJC	1490	1	R. Net, Cd.Juárez
TM33)	MS	1490	1	R. Mexicana, Matamoros
VE28)	YTM	1490	1	R. Teocelo, Teocelo
DF10)	DF	1500	50/5	Fórmula 1500, México
GJ23)	FL	1500	1/0.5	La FL, Guanajuato (r. XHFL 90.7)
HG12)	HUI	1510	0.25	R. Huichapan, Huichapan
JL35)	PBGR	1510	10	Radio Miled, Guadalajara
NL12)	QI	1510	10d	Opus 1510, Monterrey
CO31)	VUC	1520	1d	La Norteñita, Allende (r. XHVUC 95.9)
ME07)	ATL	1520	1/0.25	R. Mexiquense, Atlacomulco
SO38)	EH	1520	1d	La Primera, San Luis Río Colorado
DF14)	UR	1530	50/1	Éxtasis Digital, México
GJ01)	SD	1530	10/0.1	Arroba FM León, Silao (r. XHSD 99.3)
NL13)	STN	1540	5/0.5	La Octava y Universal, Monterrey
SO39)	HOS	1540	5	La Invasora, Hermosillo
BC06)	BG	1550	1	Cadena 1550 AM, Tijuana
MI29)	REL	1550	1	La 15-50, Morelia
TM20)	NU	1550	5/0.25	La Rancherita, Nuevo Laredo
CH33)	JPV	1560	1d	R. Deportiva 15-60, Cd. Juárez
GJ15)	MAS	1560	1/0.25	La Estación Familiar, Salamanca
CO32)	RF	1570	100	La Poderosa, Cd.Acuña (r. XHRF 103.9 HD)
GR06)	LI	1580	1/0.25	Máxima, Chilpancingo (r. XHLI 94.7)
SO26)	DM	1580	10	Mix, Hermosillo (r. XHDN 102.7)
DF14)	VOZ	1590	20/1	Arroba FM CDMX, México (La Paz ME)
ME07)	GEM	1600	5	R. Mexiquense, Metepec
CH..)	CSCGU	1620	1	Creo Radio, Guachochi
BC21)	UT	1630	10/1	UABC Radio, Tijuana (r.XHBA 104.1 Mexicali)
DF16)	ARZ	1650	5	ZER R. 16-50, México
ME11)	ANAH	1670	1	R. Anáhuac, Huixquilucan
TE36)	FCR	1670	10/1	Reynosa (F.Pl.)
BC12)	PE	1700	10	Heraldo Radio Tijuana, Tecate

SW	Call	kHz	kW	Station, location & h of tr
DF11)	PPM	6185	5	Señal Cultura México, México: 2200-1000

State abbreviations: AG = Aguascalientes; BC = Baja California; BS = Baja California Sur; CA = Campeche; CH = Chihuahua; CL = Colima; CO = Coahuila; CS = Chiapas; DF = Distrito Federal; DG = Durango; GJ = Guanajuato; GR = Guerrero; HG = Hidalgo; ME = Estado de México; MI = Michoacán; MO = Morelos; NA = Nayarit; NL = Nuevo León; OX = Oaxaca; PU = Puebla; QE = Querétaro; QR = Quintana Roo; SL = San Luis Potosí; SN = Sinaloa; SO = Sonora; TB = Tabasco; TM = Tamaulipas; TX = Tlaxcala; VE = Veracruz: YU = Yucatán; ZC = Zacatecas.

N.B: These abbreviations are not officially recognized by the Mexican Post Office. Letters should therefore carry the abbreviations in brackets or full state name.

Addresses & other information:

AG00) AGUASCALIENTES (Ags.)

AG01) Grupo Radiofónico Zer, San Miguel 117-A, Col. Salud, 20240 Aguascalientes **W:** facebook.com/LaKaliente102.9

BC00) BAJA CALIFORNIA (B.C.)

BC01) Calle lluvia 2554, Fracc. Playas de Tijuana 22500, Tijuana (or: P.O. Box 40231 Downey, CA. 90239 USA) **W:** radiozion.net – **BC02)** Av. General Ferreira 3250, Col. Madero Sur, Tijuana **W:** unanimosports.com latremenda1030.com – **BC03)** Carr. Libre Tijuana- Ensenada No. 3100, 22710 Playas de Rosarito (or: 3500 W. Olive Ave. Suite 250 Burbank, CA 91505 USA) **W:** uradio.ifengus.com – **BC05)** Radiorama Mexicali, Pasaje Vallarta 1128, Centro Cívico, 21000 Mexicali **W:** facebook.com/LaDinamicaMexicali facebook.com/RocolaMexicali radioramamexicali.com/poderosa – **BC06)** Grupo Cadena, Av.de los Olivos 3401, Fracc. Cubillas, 22410 Tijuana **W:** cadenanoticias.com – **BC07)** Grupo ABC Radio, Ave. Francisco I. Madero 1345, Col. Nueva, 21100 Mexicali **W:** abcradio.com.mx facebook.com/ABCRadio820AMMexicali 940oldies.com – **BC08)** Uniradio, Gral. Manuel Márquez de León 950, Zona Urbana Río, 22010 Tijuana (or: 5030 Camino de la Siesta, Suite 403, San Diego, CA 92108, USA) **W:** uniradio.com – **BC09)** Radio Fórmula Tijuana, Blvd. Agua Caliente 8710. local 17 y 18. Plaza Pio Pico, Centro, 22000 Tijuana **W:** radioformulabc.com – **BC10)** Audiorama Mexicali, Av. Calafia 519, Centro Cívico, 21000 Mexicali **W:** audioramabc.

com – **BC12)** Blvd. Agua Caliente 10535-506, Fracc. Chapultepec, 22420 Tijuana **W:** heraldodemexico.com.mx/seccion/heraldo-radio-tijuana-xepe-am-1700-am – **BC13)** Francisco L. Montejano 2200, Fracc. Fovisste, 21030 Mexicali (or: P.O.Box 872125, Calexico, CA 92232) **W:** noticias1120am.com – **BC14)** Pasaje Cozumel 1140, Centro Cívico, 21000 Mexicali **W:** radioformulabc.com – **BC15)** Calle Octava n° 139, Fracc. Cd. San Quintín, 22930 San Quintín **W:** inpi.gob.mx/ecosgobmx/xeqin.php - 1200-0200 (Sun –2200) Prgrs in Sp., Mixteco, Triqui and Zapateco – **BC16)** Grupo Cadena, Prolongación Alfareros No. 253 Centro Cívico, 21000 Mexicali **W:** cadenanoticias.com/radio/cadena.1190-am – **BC17)** Baja California 1310, Zona Norte, 22100 Tijuana (or: Box 430233, San Ysidro, CA 92073, USA) - 1400-0800 – **BC18)** Blvd. Agua Caliente esq. Blvd. Cuauhtémoc 2513-6, 22400 Tijuana (or P.O.Box 430521, San Ysidro, CA. 92143 USA) **W:** radioenciso1310am.com psn.si – **BC19)** Boulevard Benito Juárez No 1990, Local 12, Plaza Fimbres, Col Jardines del Valle, 21270 Mexicali – **BC20)** Audiorama Tijuana, Carlos Robirosa 3110-B, Fracc. Aviación, 22420 Tijuana **W:** tudn.com/TUDN-radio – **BC21)** Edif. Rectoría, Av. Álvaro Obregón y Calle Julián Carrillo s/n, Col. Nueva, 21100 Mexicali (or: UABC Radio, 233 Paulin Avenue, P O Box MSC 5163, Calexico, CA 92231-2646, USA) **W:** radio.uabc.mx - 1400-0800

BS00) BAJA CALIFORNIA SUR (B.C.S.)

BS01) Plaza Cuatro Molinos, Ignacio Manuel Altamirano 2790, Zona Central, 23000 La Paz **W:** radioformulapaz.com - 1300-0700 – **BS05)** Ap.19-B, 23010 La Paz **W:** iert.bcs.gob.mx centroderadioytelevision.weebly.com – **BS06) W:** kvoz.com – **BS08)** Av de Las Flores 1, 23920 Santa Rosalía – **BS11)** 23970 Punta Abreojos

CA00) CAMPECHE (Camp.)

CA02) Calle 22 N° 131, 24100 Cd.del Carmen **W:** heraldodemexico.com.mx/seccion/heraldo-radio-ciudad-del-carmen-xhmab-101-3-fm – **CA05)** Calle 32 N° 23-2 P.B., Centro, 24100 Cd.del Carmen W: exafm.com/ciudaddelcarmen - 1200-0500 – **CA09)** Domicilio Conocido, 24640 X'pujil **W:** inpi.gob.mx/ecosgobmx/xexpuj.php - 1100-1600, 2000-0000 - Prgrs in Sp., Maya and Chol – **CA10)** Prol. Calle 53, Esq. Av.16 de Septiembre s/n, 24000 Campeche **W:** vocescampeche.gob.mx - 1200-0600 – **CA11)** Calle 30 No. 269, Barrio Pablo García, 24930 Becal **E:** cadenacultural@prodigy.net

CH00) CHIHUAHUA (Chih.)

CH01) Calle Agustín Melgar 473, 31500 Cd.Cuauhtémoc **W:** xepl.com.mx – **CH02)** Julián Carrillo No 701, 31000 Chihuahua **W:** radiorama.mx – **CH03)** Boulevard Ortíz Mena 54, 3er. piso, Col. Centro, 33800 Hidalgo del Parral – **CH08)** Julián Carrillo 705-A, 31000 Chihuahua **W:** radiorama.mx/aradios.php?id=126 – **CH12)** Av.Insurgentes 2127, Col.Ex-Hipódromo, 32330 Cd Juárez **W:** gruposiete.com.mx/radio radiobengala.mx radioguadalupana.com (1200-2400) – **CH15)** Jesús Urueta 504, 31700 Nuevo Casas Grandes **W:** gbmradio.com - 1200-0400 – **CH18)** CDI, Francisco M. Plancarte y Felipe Ángeles, Col. El Salto, 33180 Guachochi **W:** inpi.gob.mx/ecosgobmx/xetar.php – **CH20)** Calle de la Paz 602, 32880 Ojinaga **W:** gbmradio.com/ojinaga – **CH22)** Calle 3a N° 1204, 31940 Cd.Madero **W:** radiomadera.com – **CH27)** Avenida Tecnológico 1770, Colonia Fuentes del Valle, Galería C, Local D-07, 32000 Cd.Juárez **W:** multimedios.com/radio/programas/la-lupe-1045-fm-chihuahua – **CH30)** Av Vicente Guerrero 2329, Col. Partido Romero, 32280 Cd.Juárez **W:** radiorama.mx lazradio.com.mx/juarez radiomexiconoticias.com - 1300-0700 – **CH32)** Av. de la Raza 3585, Int. 503, Plaza Grande, Col. Mascareñas, 32340 Cd. Juárez **W:** radioformulajuarez.com – **CH33)** Mega Radio, Av. Chapultepec 316, Col. Cuauhtémoc, Edificio Megaradio, 32010 Cd.Juárez **W:** megaradio.mx 860noticias.com.mx larancherita1000.com.mx cristoreyradio.com activa1420.mx radiodeportiva1560.com – **CH37)** Grupo NET, José Borunda 1178, 32000 Cd.Juárez **W:** radionet1490.com.mx – **CH38)** Escápate al Paraíso S.A. de C.V., N/A **W:** grupoacustik.com.mx/radio – **CH39)** Grupo Radio México, Elisa Dosamantes 400, Fracc. Los Colorines, 32380 Cd.Juárez **W:** radiorama.mx – **CH40)** Grupo Radio México, Elisa Dosamantes 400, Fracc. Los Colorines, 32380 Cd.Juárez **W:** olivoministerio200.wixsite.com/creoradio

CL00 COLIMA (Col.)

CL01) Grupo Radiofónico ZER, Blvd. Costero Miguel de la Madrid 505, Col. Playa Azul, 28218 Manzanillo **E:** xemza@hotmail.com **W:** grupozer.net – **CL10)** Radiorama Tecomán, Av. Antonio Leaño del Castillo 663, Col. Ponciano Arriaga, 28160 Tecomán - 1100-0300 – **CL11)** Escápate al Paraíso S.A. de C.V., N/A **W:** grupoacustik.com.mx/radio

CO00) COAHUILA (Coah.)

CO01) De la Fuente 223 Pte., Col. Los Telefonistas, 25700 Monclova **W:** laacerera.mx – **CO02)** San Juan 819, Fracc. San José, 26014 Piedras Negras **W:** rancherita.com.mx – **CO06)** Grupo Radio México, Priv. Eulogio Ortiz y Jesús Pamanes, Col. Ampl. Los Ángeles, 27140 Torreón **W:** grmtorreon.webs.com/radioranchito.htm – **CO07)** Av. Universidad 1035, Col Universidad, 25260 Saltillo – **CO09)** Grupo Radio Fórmula, Independencia 706, Mza 29, Col. Los Ángeles, 27140 Torreón **W:** radioformulatorreon.com – **CO20)** GRM Radio, Venustiano Carranza 612-2 Ote., 25700 Monclova - **W:** grmradio.com – **CO22)** Universidad Autónoma Agraria, "Antonio Narro", Periférico Luis Echeverría S/N, Lourdes, 25070 Saltillo **W:** radionarro.com – **CO32)** Madero 600, Centro, 26200 Cd. Acuña **W:** imer.mx/lapoderosa – **CO33)** 25000 Saltillo **W:** rcg.com.mx/xhsj-103-3-fm – **CO34)** Grupo M, Hidalgo 2757 Norte, Col. República Norte, 25280 Saltillo **W:** grupomradio.mx/vivasaltillo

CS00 CHIAPAS (Chis.)

CS01) Instituto Mexicano de la Radio, Av. Chichimá 405, (or A. P. 16) 30000 Comitán - 1100-0700 **W:** imer.mx/radioimer – **CS05)** Radio Chiapas, Segunda Sur Oriente 132, 29950 Ocosingo **W:** radiotvycine.chiapas.gob.mx **E:** xeoch@radiotvycine.chiapas.gob.mx – **CS11)** Radio Chiapas, Avenida Benito Juárez 48, Interior Altos, 29200 San Cristóbal de las Casas **E:** xera@radiotvycine.chiapas.gob.mx – **CS18)** 14a Sur-Poniente s/n, Barrio San Sebastián, 30180 Las Margaritas **W:** inpi.gob.mx/ecosgobmx/xevfs.php - 1200-0030 (SS – 2400) Prgrs in Sp., Tojobal, Mame, Tzeltal and Tzotzil – **CS19)** Radio Chiapas, Av. 5 de Mayo entre Aldama y Allende s/n, Centro, 29960 Palenque 1000-0400 **W:** radiotvycine.chiapas.gob.mx – **CS20)** Radio Chiapas, 2ª Sur y 1ª s/n, 29610 Tecpatan **W:** radiotvycine.chiapas.gob.mx – **CS21)** Primera Oriente s/n, Barrio Siete Huesos, 29620 Copainalá 1230-2230 Prg in Sp., Zoque and Tzotzil – **CS23)** Instituto Mexicano de la Radio, Km. 1.5 Carr. Cacahoatán-Unión Juárez, Ejido Rosario Ixtal, 30890 Cacahoatán **W:** imer.mx/lapopular – **CS25)** CS25) La Fuente de Poder Educativa Indígena de Chiapas, A.C., Sinaí 3, 29416 Betania, Prg in Sp. and Tzotzil

DF00) CIUDAD DE MÉXICO (D.F.)

DF01) Grupo Radio Digital, Paseo de las Palmas 751, Col. Lomas de Chapultepec, 11000 México **W:** radiochapultepec.mx - 1100-0700 – **DF02)** NRM Comunicaciones, Prolongación Paseo de la Reforma 115, Col. Paseo de las Lomas, 01330 México **W:** nrm.com.mx – R. Mil: Ap.21-1000, 04021 México – **DF03)** Radiodifusoras Asociadas, Durango 341, Planta Baja, Col. Roma, 06700 México **W:** radio620.com – **DF04)** Instituto Mexicano de la Radio, Real de Mayorazgo 83, Barrio Xoco, 03330 México **W:** imer.mx – **DF05)** Grupo R. Centro, Av. Constituyentes 1154, Col. Lomas Altas, 11950 México **W:** radiocentro.com – **DF06)** Televisa Radio, Calzada de Tlalpan 3000, Col. Espartaco, 04870 México **W:** televisa.com wradio.com.mx wdeportes.com los40.com.mx kebuena940.com.mx – **DF07)** Grupo ABC Radio, Basilio Vadillo 29, Col Tabacalera, 06030 México **W:** abcradio.com.mx – **DF08)** Grupo Radiodifusoras Capital, Montes Urales 425, Col. Lomas de Chapultepec, 11000 México **W:** gruporadiocapital.com.mx – **DF09)** Universidad Nacional Autónoma de México, Adolfo Prieto 133, Col. del Valle, 03100 México **W:** radio.unam.mx – **DF10)** Grupo R. Fórmula, Av. Universidad 1273, Col. del Valle, 03100 México **W:** radioformula.com.mx – **DF11)** Radio Educación, Ángel Urraza 622, Col. del Valle 03100 México **W:** radioeducacion.edu.mx emisorasre.gob.mx – **DF12)** Grupo ACIR, S.A., Pirineos 770, Lomas de Chapultepec, 11000; **W:** grupoacir.com.mx – **DF14)** Radiorama Valle de México, Paseo de la Reforma 56, P1, Col. Juárez, 06000 México **W:** radioramavm.mx/romantica extasisdigital.mx arroba.fm – **DF15)** Grupo 7 División Radio, Montecito 59, Col. Nápoles, 03810 México **W:** gruposiete.com.mx radiocapital.mx ondasdepaz1440.mx – **DF16) W:** facebook.com/GrupoRadiofonicoZer – **DF17)** Grupo Imagen Multimedia, Av. Universidad 2014, Col. Copilco Universidad, 04350 México **W:** imagen.com.mx imagenradio.com.mx rmx.com.mx – **DF18)** Universidad Iberoamericana, Av. Prol. Paseo de la Reforma 880, Lomas de Santa Fe, 01219 México. **W:** ibero909.fm – **DF19)** Universidad Autónoma Metropolitana, Av. Constituyentes 1054, Col. Lomas Altas, 11950 México **W:** uamradio.uam.mx – **DF20)** Instituto Politécnico Nacional, Av. Santa Ana 1000, San Fco. Culhuacán, 04430, México **W:** radio.ipn.mx – **DF21)** MVS Radio, Mariano Escobedo 532, Col. Anzures, 11300 México **W:** mvsradio.com – **DF22)** Av. de la República 157, Col. Tabacalera, 06030 México **W:** airelibre.fm – **DF23)** Alianza por el Derecho Humano de las Mujeres a Comunicar **W:** violetaradio.org – **DF24)** Heraldo Media Group, Torre Carracci, Av. Insurgentes Sur 1271, Col. Extremadura Insurgentes, 03740 México **W:** heraldodemexico.com.mx/seccion/heraldo-de-mexico-radio – **DF25)** Paseo de la Reforma 250, Piso 15, Col. Juárez, 06000 México **W:** grupoacustik.com.mx/radio arre.acustik.mx

DG00) DURANGO (Dgo.)

DG01) Fco. I. Madero y Heroico Colegio Militar s/n, Col. Altamira, 34600 Santiago Papasquiaro **W:** santiago.latremenda.com.mx – **DG03)** Jesús Contreras 111, Col. Guillermina, 34279 Durango **W:** radioformuladurango.com – **DG08)** Grupo Radio México, Capitán de Ibarra 1203 Ote., Fracc. del Lago, 34080 Durango

W: multimedios.com/radio/programas/la-lupe-1029-fm-durango – **DG09)** DCI, Domicilio conocido, 34985 Santa María de Ocotán **W:** inpi.gob.mx/ecosgobmx/xetph.php – **DG10)** Escápate al Paraíso S.A. de C.V., N/A **W:** grupoacustik.com.mx/radio

GJ00) GUANAJUATO (Gto.)

GJ01) Boulevard Algeciras 1504, Col. Lomas de Arbide, 37368, León **W:** radiorama.mx/emisoras.php arroba.fm – **GJ05)** Morelos 110, 36500 Irapuato **W:** radioirapuato.com - 1200-0600 – **GJ06)** Allende 17, 38600 Acámbaro. **W:** radioconsentida.com.mx - 1200-0400 – **GJ08)** Corporación ACIR Celaya, Guanajuato 106, Col Alameda, 38090 Celaya **W:** lacomadre.mx/la-comadre-88-1-celaya – **GJ09)** Corporación Bajío Comunicaciones, Av.Guerrero y Francisco Sarabia, Centro Plaza Magna, Locales 1,2 y 3 C, 36500 Irapuato **W:** elyella.mx radiolobobajio.mx – **GJ10)** Palacio Federal, Casa de Moneda, Sopeña 1, P2, 36000 Guanajuato **W:** radiouniversidad.ugto.mx - 1300-0500 – **GJ11)** Elodia Ledezma 658, Fracc. Las Flores, 38890 Moroleón **W:** radiomoroleon.mx - 1200-0600 – **GJ14)** Aldama 301(or Ap.24) , 36700 Salamanca - 1300-0500 – **GJ15)** Morelos 110, Centro, 36500 Salamanca **W:** estacionfamiliar.com - 1300-0500 – **GJ16)** Cañada 310, Esq.Roca, Col Jardines de Moral, 37160 León **W:** lapoderosa.com.mx – **GJ19)** 10 de Mayo No. 126, Centro, 37000 León **W:** lazradio.com.mx/leon – **GJ23)** Municipio Libre 8, 36080 Guanajuato **W:** 907santafe.com - 1300-0300 – **GJ24)** Escápate al Paraíso S.A. de C.V., N/A **W:** grupoacustik.com.mx/radio

GR00) GUERRERO (Gro.)

GR02) Grupo ACIR, Av. La Suiza 19, Fracc. Las Playas, 39390 Acapulco **W:** 101.5acapulco.comadre.mx iheart.com/live/estereo-pop-1031-8074 (geoblocked) – **GR06)** Audiorama Guerrero, Av. Del Sur 14, Col. Margarita Vigurí, 39060 Chilpancingo **W:** radioramaguerrero.com.mx maxima.com.mx – **GR08)** Fray Bautista Moya 410, Centro, 40660 Cd. Altamirano **W:** radioxexy780.mx - 1200-0430 – **GR09)** Av. Heroico Colegio Militar No 234, Col Aviación, 41304 Tlapa de Comonfort **W:** inpi.gob.mx/ecosgobmx/xezv.php - 1200-0100 (SS -2000) Prgrs in Sp., Náhuatl, Mixteco and Tlapaneco – **GR10)** Carretera Escénica 109, Col. Villas Guitarrón, Acapulco **W:** radioformulaguerrero.com – **GR11)** Av. Revolución 6, 40700 Coyuca de Catalán **W:** rtvgro.net/radio – **GR12)** Monteblanco 37, Fracc. Hornos Insurgentes, 39350 Acapulco **W:** rtvgro.net - 1200-0700 – **GR17)** Benito Juárez 19-A, Barrio del Carmen, 41700 Ometepec **W:** rtvgro.net/radio – **GR18)** Hacienda del Cernillo, Casa Gallos s/n, 40200 Taxco **W:** rtvgro.net/radio - 1200-0400 – **GR21)** Avenida Lázaro Cárdenas 54, Col Héroes Surianos, 40500 Arcelia **W:** radioarcelia.com - 1200-0400 – **GR23)** Escápate al Paraíso S.A. de C.V., N/A **W:** grupoacustik.com.mx/radio

HG00 HIDALGO (Hgo.)

HG01) Plaza de la Constitución y Manuel F Soto (or Ap.96), 43600 Tulancingo **W:** nqradio.com - 1200-0600 – **HG03)** R. y Televisión de Hidalgo, Blvd. Adolfo López Mateos s/n, Col. Aviación Civil, 43000 Huejutla **W:** radioytelevision.hidalgo.gob.mx - 1100-0300 – **HG05)** Plaza Juárez 103 (or Ap.123), 42000 Pachuca **W:** 104.5pachuca.comadre.mx - 1200-0600 – **HG08)** Hidalgo Ote.209, Col. Centro, 43600 Tulancingo **W:** facebook.com/miledtulancingo - 1200-0600 – **HG11)** Domicilio Conocido, Col Buenos Aires, 42370 Cárdonal **W:** inpi.gob.mx/ecosgobmx/xecarh.php - 1300-0100. Prgrs in Sp., Otomí and Náhuatl – **HG12)** Chávez Macotela 8, 42400 Huichapan **W:** radioytelevision.hidalgo.gob.mx

JL00) JALISCO (Jal.)

JL02) México Radio, Calzada Independencia Sur 324, Col. Centro, 44100 Guadalajara **W:** canal58gdl.com – **JL03)** Blvd. Francisco Medina Asencio km. 7.5, Plaza Marina Local 101, Col. Marina Vallarta, 48300 Puerto Vallarta **W:** kebuenapv.com – **JL05)** C7 Jalisco, Francisco Rojas González 155, Col. Ladrón de Guevara, 44600 Guadalajara **W:** jaliscoradio.com – **JL06)** – **JL08)** Lorenzana 884, Col. Chapalita, 45040 Guadalajara **W:** laoctava.com – **JL10)** Notisistema, Av. México 3150 Fracc. Moraz, 44670 Guadalajara **W:** notisistema.com – **JL11)** Grupo ACIR, Paseo de Las Gaviotas 198, Col. Las Gaviotas, 48351 Puerto Vallarta – **JL12)** Rubén Darío 158, Circunvalación Vallarta, 44680 Guadalajara **W:** radiogallito.com.mx wradio.com.mx/emisora/guadalajara – **JL13)** Av. Hidalgo 111, Centro, 48900 Autlán. **W:** radiocosta.com.mx – **JL14)** Av. México 3370, Plaza Bonita, Local Subanda P, 45120 Guadalajara **W:** radioformulaguadalajara.com - 1300-0700 – **JL16)** Promomedios, Portal Hidalgo 13, Int.10, Centro, 49650 Tamazula **W:** promomediosjalisco.com - 1200-0600 – **JL17)** Grupo ACIR, Av. Lázaro Cárdenas 2820, Jardines del Bosque, 44520 Guadalajara - 1200-0600 **W:** matchmx.fm – **JL18)** Av. Mariano Otero 3405, Fracc. Verde Valle, 45060 Guadalajara **W:** radiomujer.com.mx elsembradorministries.com/radio/jalisco-guadalajara – **JL20)** Radiorama Puerto Vallarta, Honduras 309, Int. 161, Col.5 de Diciembre, 48350 Puerto Vallarta – **JL21)** Calle San Juan Bosco 3623, Fracc. Jardines de San Ignacio, 45050 Zapopan **W:** radiomariamexico.com – **JL23)** Primero de Mayo 126-8, 49000 Cd. Guzmán - 1200-0600 **W:** radiolamexicana.negocio.site – **JL24)** Radiorama de Occidente, Av. Niños Héroes 1555, 6to. Piso, Col. Moderna, 44190 Guadalajara **W:** radioramadeoccidente.com – **JL29)** Hidalgo 2055 Esq. Tomas de Gómez, Col Arcos Sur, 44500 Guadalajara **W:** arre.acustik.mx – **JL32)** Av. Francia 1783, Col. Moderna, Sector Juárez, 44190 Guadalajara **W:** alfaenlinea.com – **JL34)** Radio Operadora Pegasso, S.A. de C.V., N/A **W:** wradio.com.mx/tag/el_bajio/a/ – **JL35)** Radio de Ayuda A.C. **W:** miled.com – **JL36)** NTR Guadalajara, Morelos 2027, Col. Arcos Vallarta, 44130 Guadalajara **W:** ntrguadalajara.com

ME00) ESTADO DE MÉXICO (Edo.Méx.)

ME01) Radiorama del Valle de México, Paseo de la Reforma 56, P1, Col.Juárez, 06000 México - 1100-0600 **W:** heraldodemexico.com.mx/radio – **ME03)** Sistema de R. y Televisión Mexiquense, Av. Quintana Roo 44, Col. Prado Sur, Tultitlan **W:** radioytvmexiquense.mx – **ME06)** Radiorama Toluca, Av. José María Morelos 903, esq. con Quintana Roo, Col. La Merced (Alameda), 50080 Toluca **W:** radiorama.com.mx – **ME07)** Sistema de R. y TV Mexiquense, Av. Estado de México km 1, Col. La Virgen, 52140 Metepec **W:** radioytvmexiquense.mx - 1200-0600 – **ME08)** José María Morelos 948, Esq. Carretera a Tonatico, 51900 Ixtapan de la Sal **W:** facebook.com/LokuraFM.MX – **ME10)** Universidad Autónoma de Chapingo, Carr. México-Texcoco km 38.5, 56235 Chapingo **W:** radio.chapingo.mx - 1300-0100 – **ME11)** Cabina 5, Edificio CAD, Escuela de Comunicación, Av. Universidad Anáhuac 46, Col. Lomas Anáhuac, Huixquilucan **W:** anahuac.mx/mexico/radio

MI00) MICHOACÁN (Mich.)

MI01) Aqua 78, Col.Prados del Campestre, 58297 Morelia **W:** rasacandela.com - 1200-0300 – **MI02)** Av. Revolución Sur 66, Col. Mariano Matamoros, 61506 Zitácuaro **W:** radiozitacuaro.com - 1200-0600 (SS -0400) – **MI03)** Privada de Diligencias 53, Int. 1, Fraccionamiento El Mirador (or Ap.61), 60100 Uruapan **W:** lazeta.mx/Uruapan – **MI07)** Macarena 32, Inguambo, 60130 Uruapan **W:** radioramamichoacan.com/lapoderosa – **MI08)** Av.Constitución de 1814 Norte 2 Altos, 60600 Apatzingan **W:** rasa-apatzingan.com - 1200-0500 – **MI09)** CDI, Av. Lázaro Cárdenas 30, Col. San Marcos, 60270 Cherán **W:** inpi.gob.mx/ecosgobmx/xepur.php - 1300-0020 Prgrs in Sp and Purépecha – **MI11)** Carr. Lázaro Cárdenas-La Mira, 5 de Mayo, 60990 Lázaro Cárdenas – **MI15)** Madero 116, Col. Centro, 59300 La Piedad **W:** radiopia.mx – **MI18)** Carretera Federal N° 15 Morelia-Zitácuaro km 125.6, 61420 Tuxpan **W:** inpi.gob.mx/ecosgobmx/xhtumi.php - 1200-2330 Prgrs in Sp., Mazahua, Otomí & Matlatzinca – **MI19)** Juan Ayala 10, Int 102, Centro, 60000 Uruapan **W:** candelauruapan.com – **MI24)** Av. Díaz Ordaz 225A (Ap.60), 59000 Sahuayo **W:** promoradio.com.mx - 1300-0400 – **MI26)** Aquiles Serdán 548 , 58020 Morelia **W:** facebook.com/LaZMoreliaOficial – **MI29)** José Rosas Moreno 200, Col. Vista Bella, 58090 Morelia **W:** sistemamichoacano.tv/radio-am-vivo – **MI31)** Media Group, Torre Victoria, Av. Acueducto 2800, Piso 6, Col. Lomas de Hidalgo, 58241Morelia **W:** mediagroup.mx/senal-en-vivo/acustik-michoacan/

MO00) MORELOS (MoR)

MO01) 62746 Cuautla (alt.address: Hidalgo 109, Col. Cuauhtémoc, 62220 Ocotepec, Cuernavaca) **W:** imryt.org/radio – **MO02)** Escápate al Paraíso S.A. de C.V., N/A **W:** grupoacustik.com.mx/radio

NA00) NAYARIT (Nay.)

NA01) Radio Aztlán, Av. Victoria 213 A Pte, 63940 Tepic **W:** radioaztlan.com – **NA02)** Domicilio Conocido, 63530 Jesús María **W:** www.inpi.gob.mx/ecosgobmx/xejmn.php - 1200-2400 Prgrs in Sp., Cora, Huichol, Tepehuáno and Náhuatl – **NA03)** Radiorama Nayarit, Puebla 64 Sur, Centro, 63060 Tepic **W:** radioramanayarit.mx

NL00) NUEVO LEÓN (N.L.)

NL01) Parque Industrial Regiomontano, 64540 Monterrey **W:** escucha.los40.com.mx/emisora/40_monterrey – **NL02)** Grupo Radio Alegría, Av. Madero Oriente 1110, 64000 Monterrey **W:** gruporadioalegria.com abcnoticias.mx/radio radioesperanza.mx facebook.com/Radio13MasVallenata – **NL03)** Grupo Radio Centro, Juan Ignacio Ramón 506 Oriente, P20, Edif. Latino, 64000 Monterrey **W: W:** arre.acustik.mx fb630.com facebook.com/xeh1420am – **NL04)** Paricutín Sur 316, Col. Roma, (or: Ap.203) 64700 Monterrey **W:** mmradio.com - 1200-0700 – **NL05)** Edificio Santos, Francisco I. Madero 1955, Int. 210, 64000 Monterrey **W:** radioformulamonterrey.com – **NL06)** Capitán Alonso de León s/n o Antigua Carretera Nacional km 904, Barrio Zaragoza, 67500 Montemorelos. **W:** multimedios.com/radio/programas/rg-la-deportiva-929-fm-monterrey – **NL07)** Carr. Nacional Km. 856, Col. La Amistad, 67700 Linares (or. Ap.81), 67700 Linares - 1200-0600 – **NL08)** Radio ACIR, Monterrey 698, Esq. Cerralvo, Col. Libertad, 64130 Guadalupe **W:** amorfm.mx/amor-90-9-monterrey

– **NL10)** NRM Comunicaciones, Av. Cuauhtémoc 725 Nte., Centro (or Ap.118), 64000 Monterrey **W:** larancherademonterrey.com.mx contacto1190.com.mx – **NL11)** Grupo Radio Alegría, Reforma s/n, Col. Enrique Lozano, 65290 Cd. Sabinas Hidalgo - 1200-0600 – **NL12)** Av. San Francisco y Loma Grande, Col. Loma Grande, 64000 Monterrey **W:** nl.gob.mx/escucha-radio-nuevo-leon – **NL13)** Grupo Radio Centro, Padre Mier Poniente 439, Centro, 64000 Monterrey

OX00) OAXACA (Oax.)

OX05) Cerro El Panteón, Ap.35, 70900 Puerto Ángel **W:** lavozdelangel.com.mx - 1200-0200 – **OX06)** Aquiles Serdán y Mina 502, Col. Benito Juárez Norte, 70301 Matías Romero **W:** encuentroradiotv.com - 1200-0100 – **OX07)** Grupo Radio México, Netzahualcóyotl 216, Col Reforma, 68050 Oaxaca - 1200-0600 – **OX08)** Morelos 6-2, 71000 Putla de Guerrero **W:** facebook.com/TPrendeRadio - 1200-0130 – **OX10)** Lázaro Cárdenas s/n, 68770 Guelatao de Juárez **W:** inpi.gob.mx/ecosgobmx/xeglo.php - 1200-2400. Prgrs in Sp., Zapoteco, Mixe and Chinanteco – **OX11)** 5 de Mayo 21-A, Centro, 69800 Tlaxiaco - 1200-0500 **W:** lapoderosatlaxiaco100-5.com – **OX12)** Carr. Puerto Escondido-Pochutla Km. 143, 71980 Puerto Escondido **W:** lavozdelpuerto.mx - 1300-0600 – **OX14)** CDI, Blvd. Rafael Reyes Spíndola 1, 69800 Tlaxiaco **W:** cdi.gob.mx/ecosgobmx/xetla.php - 1200-2400. Prgrs in Sp., Mixteco and Triqui – **OX15)** Independencia s/n, Sección Segunda, 68470 San Lucas Ojitlán **W:** inpi.gob.mx/ecosgobmx/xeojn.php - 1400-2200 Prgrs in Sp., Mazateco, Cuicateco and Chinanteco – **OX16)** Amapolas 808, Col. Reforma, 68050 Oaxaca - 1200-0600 – **OX22)** Plaza de la Constitución y Negrete s/n, 71700 Santiago Jamiltepec. Prgrs in Sp., Mixteco, Amuzgo and Chatino **W:** inpi.gob.mx/ecosgobmx/xejam.php - 1200-2400 – **OX24)** Escápate al Paraíso S.A. de C.V., N/A **W:** grupoacustik.com.mx/radio

PU00) PUEBLA (Pue.)

PU01) Morelos No. 10, Centro, Izúcar de Matamoros, 74400 Puebla **W:** migente980am.net – **PU02)** Blvd. Atlixco 37, Local 218, Plaza JV, Col. San José, 72170 Puebla **W:** kebuena1010.com.mx – **PU03)** Av. 15 de Mayo 2939, Col. Las Hadas, 72070 Puebla **W:** cincoradio.com.mx – **PU04)** Calle Matamoros 77, esq. San Martin Texmelucan, Col. La Paz, 72160 Puebla. **W:** lamagnificafm.com – **PU05)** 3 Oriente no, 201, col. Centro Histórico, 72000 Puebla **W:** abcradiopuebla.com.mx – **PU06)** Priv. Miguel Alvarado s/n, 73560 Cuetzalán **W:** inpi.gob.mx/ecosgobmx/xejam.php - 1200-0100 prgrs in Sp, Náhuatl and Totonaco – **PU07)** Radiorama Puebla, Tonanzintla 13, Col. La Paz, 72160 Puebla **W:** arrobapueplafm.com

QE00) QUERÉTARO (Qro.)

QE01) Camino de Piedras Anchas 100, Cabecera Municipal de Jalpan de Serra, 76000 Jalpan **W:** rtq.mx/copia-de-100-3-fm-qro - 1100-0200

QR00) QUINTANA ROO (Q.Roo.)

QR02) Calle 63, Supermanzana 61, Mzna 7, Lote 1, 77500 Cancún **W:** mixfm.mx/mix-93-1-cancun - 1100-0600 – **QR03)** Grupo Radio México, Av. López Portillo, Supermanzana 59, Manzana 8 Lote 2, Local 1433-A, Col. Benito Juárez, 77515 Cancún **W:** lazradio.com.mx/cancun - 1200-0300 – **QR04)** Sistema Quintanarroense de Comunicación Social, Carretera a Tulum, Km. 1.5, 77200 Félipe Carillo Puerto. **W:** sqcs.com.mx – **QR06)** Plaza Hollywood local 86, Supermanzana 35, 77508 Cancún **W:** radioformulaqr.com – **QR07)** 20 Av. Sur 965, Entre 13 y 15, Sur. Col. Andrés Quintana Roo. (or:Ap.299) 77600 Cozumel **W:** sol899.com – **QR08)** Av. Miguel Hidalgo 201, 77000 Chetumal **W:** sqcs.com.mx - 1100-0700 – **QR09)** Av. Uxmal 30, Supermanzana 62, 77513 Cancún **W:** sqcs.com.mx - 1100-0500 – **QR11)** Prol. Av.Héroes 680, 77000 Chetumal **W:** sol899.com - 1200-0400 – **QR14)** CDI, Av. Altamirano 83, Col. Emiliano Zapata, 77200 Felipe Carrillo Puerto - 1200-0000 Prgrs in Sp. and Maya **W:** cdi.gob.mx/ecosgobmx/xenka.php

SL00) SAN LUIS POTOSÍ (S.L.P.)

SL01) Radiorama San Luis Potosí, Eucaliptos 565, Col. Jardín, 78270 San Luis Potosí **W:** globalmedia.mx/los40 – **SL02)** Radio de Ayuda A.C. **W:** origen.tv/?page_id=1579 – **SL03)** Escápate al Paraíso S.A. de C.V., N/A **W:** acustik.mx/radiodifusoras-afiliadas – **SL04)** CDI, Josefa Ortíz de Domínguez 5, 79800 Tancanhuitz de Santos **W:** inpi.gob.mx/ecosgobmx/xeant.php - 1200-0100. Prgrs in Sp., Náhuatl, Pame and Huasteco – **SL05)** Globalmedia, Av. Dr. Salvador Nava Martínez No 278, Col El Paseo, 78320 San Luis Potosí **W:** globalmedia.mx/KeBuena – **SL06)** Betancourt No 401, Col. Centro, 78700 Matehuala **W:** oye105fmdigital.com – **SL07)** General Mariano Arista 245, Centro Histórico, 78000 San Luis Potosí **W:** uaslp.mx/RadioYTelevision/Paginas/Radio Universidad/1190AM.aspx

SN00) SINALOA (Sin.)

SN01) Aquiles Serdán 860 Pte, Col. Scally, 81200 Los Mochis - 1300-0700 **W:** lamejor.com.mx/losmochis/home – **SN02)** RSN, Av. Rafael Buelna 202, Fracc. Hacienda Las Cruces, 82126 Mazatlán **W:** lamejor.com.mx/#!/mazatlan/home – **SN03)** Grupo Chávez R., Ignacio Zaragoza 200, 2do.piso, Centro, 81000 Guasave **W:** grupochavezradio.com - 1230-0800 – **SN04)** Av. Benemérito de las Américas 400, Lomas del Mar, 82010 Mazatlán **W:** exafm.com/#!/mazatlan/home – **SN05)** Cjon. Sinaloa 442 Pte., Centro, 81200 Los Mochis **W:** grupochavezradio.com – **SN08)** Radiorama Culiacán, Av. Álvaro Obregón 24 Sur, Local 53 2do. piso, Plaza Paladio, Centro, 80000, Culiacán **W:** radiorama.mx/aradios.php?id=193 – **SN17)** Radio Universidad Autónoma de Sinaloa, Agustina Ramírez 1249, Col. Gabriel Leyva, 80030 Culiacán **W:** radiouas.org - 1300-0200 – **SN22)** Insurgentes 313, Col. Flamingos, 82149 Mazatlán **W:** radioformulamazatlan.com – **SN23)** Escápate al Paraíso S.A. de C.V., N/A **W:** grupoacustik.com.mx/radio

SO00) SONORA (Son.)

SO05) Av. Serdán, y Calle 29 N° 415, Centro, (or: Ap.630) 85480 Guaymas **W:** amor101.mx – **SO07)** Carr. a Novojoa km 27, 85280 Etchojoa **W:** inpi.gob.mx/ecosgobmx/xeetch.php - 1300-0100. Prgrs in Sp., Mayo, Yaqui and Guarijío – **SO11)** Obregón 38, 1 Altos, Centro, 84000 Nogales (or: Box 1472, Nogales, AZ 85628, USA) **W:** xenygenial.com/radio-xeny-760-am – **SO12)** Durango 901 Sur Altos, Col. Campestre, 85160 Cd. Obregón **W:** tribunaradio.com.mx - 1300-0200 – **SO19)** Pino Suarez 99, 84900 Ures **W:** larsavision.tv/estaciones/ures/toño_1010AM - 1300-0500 – **SO23)** Heriberto Aja 96 y Nayarit, 83000 Hermosillo **W:** maxima.com.mx – **SO24)** Vázquez 127, Col. Fundo Legal, 84000 Nogales **W:** isamultimedia.com/los-40 isamultimedia.com/kebuena – **SO30)** Ave. Francisco Eusebio Kino y Calle 5 No 470, Barrio Comercial (Ap.44), 83449 San Luis Río Colorado **W:** radiogrupooir.com/zeta radiogrupooir.com/centro radiogrupooir.com/ranchito – **SO31)** Av. Morelos y Ramón Corona s/n, Col. Constitución, 85830 Navojoa - 1200-0700 – **SO38)** Carr. del Valle y Prol. Ave. Madero, 83449 San Luis Río Colorado – **SO39)** Uniradio, Blvd Navarrete 38, Local 2, Col. Valle Hermoso, 83209 Hermosillo **W:** uniradionoticias.com/invasora1019 – **SO40)** Escápate al Paraíso S.A. de C.V., N/A

TB00) TABASCO (Tab.)

TB14) Comisión de Radio y Televisión de Tabasco, Prolongación 27 de Febrero No.1001, 86035 Villahermosa **W:** corat.mx – **TB15)** Grupo Multimedios Sin Reservas, Prol. Av. 27 de Febrero 3117, Fracc. Galaxias 86035 Villahermosa **W:** sinreservas.mx

TM00) TAMAULIPAS (Tamps.)

TM02) Blvd. Miguel Hidalgo 200 A, Col. Polanco, 88710 Reynosa **W:** notigapc.com/estaciones.html - 1300-0100 – **TM03)** BMP Radio, Lázaro Cárdenas 210, Local 19,20 y 21, Col. Centro, 88500 Reynosa **W:** es-la.facebook.com/lalupe891 – **TM04)** Altamira Calle Principal de Esteros, Carr. Tampico-González, 89600 Altamira **W:** radio.tamaulipas.gob.mx - 1200-0400 – **TM05)** Grupo AS, Carretera Victoria-Mante Km 2 s/n, Col Las Brisas, 87180 Cd. Victoria **W:** grupoasradio.com/victoria – **TM09)** Zaragoza 85, 87600 San Fernando **W:** facebook.com/LaPoderosaSanFer - 1200-0600 – **TM11)** Tiburcio Garza Zamora 335, Rodríguez, 88630 Reynosa **W:** radio.notireytamaulipas.mx/web - 1200-0600 – **TM15)** Radiorama Reynosa, Tiburcio Garza Zamora No 1245, Col Beatty, 88630 Reynosa **W:** grupoasradio.com/reynosa/xerks.html - 1200-0400 – **TM17)** Calle 14 y Abasolo, No 76, 87300 Matamoros **W:** notigape.com/estaciones.html - 1200-0600 – **TM20)** Guanajuato #3332 Col. Jardin C.P 88260 Nuevo Laredo **W:** grupoasradio.com/laredo/xewl.html – **TM21)** Blvd. Hidalgo 22 A, Fracc. Polanco, 88710 Reynosa **W:** notigape.com/estaciones.html – **TM24)** Diego Acuña, 87900 Cd. Tula **W:** radio.tamaulipas.gob.mx - 1200-0400 – **TM25)** Sexta 75, Centro, (or Ap.540), 87300 Matamoros **W:** corporativoradiofonicodemexico.com - 1200-0700 – **TM26)** Morelos 2513, Col. Juárez, (or. Ap.232), 88000 Nuevo Laredo **W:** laraza957.com - 1155-0600 (Sat –0800, Sun -0200) – **TM27)** Carretera Ribereña KM 62, 88440 Cd. Camargo - 1200-0400 **W:** grupomiradio.mx/portal/estaciones/reynosa – **TM29)** Quinta 226, Centro, (or Ap.13), 83000 Cd. Miguel Alemán **W:** notigape.com/estaciones.html – **TM30)** Grupo R. Avanzado, Ignacio Zaragoza 660, Local 4, 88500 Reynosa **W:** radioavanzado.com/laraza1060 - 1200-0600 – **TM31)** Séptima 233 Altos, Centro, 88300 Ciudad Miguel Alemán **W:** grupomiradio.mx/portal/estaciones/miguelaleman - 1155-0200 – **TM32)** Calle 8 y Cuauhtémoc 125, Col. Pedro Sosa, 87120 Cd Victoria **W:** radio.tamaulipas.gob.mx - 1200-0800 – **TM33)** Sexta y Fuerza Aérea, Edif. María Rebeca, 87300 Matamoros – **TM34)** Escápate al Paraíso S.A. de C.V., N/A **W:** grupoacustik.com.mx/radio – **TM36)** Fomento Cultural Reynosa, A.C., N/A

TX00) TLAXCALA (Tlax.)

TX01) Av.Juárez Norte 203, 90500 Huamantla **W:** radiohuamantla.net - 1200-0600 – **TX02)** Calle Uno 420, Col. Xicohtencatl, 90070 Tlaxcala **W:** radiotlaxcala1430.mx - 1200-0600

VE00) VERACRUZ (Ver.)

VE03) Ruíz Cortines 303, Col. Centro, 95400 Cosamaloapan **W:** xefuradio.com.mx – **VE08)** Moctezuma 77, Bis Col. Centro, 91000 Xalapa **W:** amorfm.mx/amor-91-7-xalapa – **VE09)** Benjamín Franklin

4, Col. Centro, 91700 Veracruz **W:** lapoderosaveracruz.fm/site – **VE22)** Eulalio Vela 15, Col. Obrera, 96700 Minatitlán **W:** gruporadiomina.com – **VE24)** Morelos No. 37 Altos 3er. Piso Frente al Parque Reforma, Col. Centro, 92800 Tuxpan **W:** facebook.com/Azul106.9fm – **VE27)** Plaza Crystal, Local 20, 91150 Xalapa **W:** 955sensacionfm.com - 1200-0600 – **VE28)** Bernarda Soto Mercado No. 2, Barrio de San Pedro, 91615 Teocelo **W:** radioteocelo.org.mx - 1100-0200 – **VE36)** Universidad Veracruzana, Francisco de Clavijero 24, 91000 Xalapa. W: uv.mx/radio - 1300-0700 – **VE42)** CDI, Callejón de las ánimas s/n, Col. Centro, 95000 Zongolica **W:** inpi.gob.mx/ecosgobmx/xezon.php – **VE55)** Escápate al Paraíso S.A. de C.V., N/A **W:** grupoacustik.com.mx/radio

YU00) YUCATÁN (Yuc.)

YU01) Grupo Rivas, Calle 62 N° 465, Entre 53 y 55, Centro, 97000 Mérida **W:** gruporivas.com.mx - 1130-0100 – **YU03)** Calle 33-B No. 513, Col. García Gineres, 97070 Mérida **W:** radioformulayucatan.com – **YU04)** Cadena RASA, Km 1 Carr. Valladolid-Carillo Puerto, 97780 Valladolid **W:** cadenarasa.com/candela_valladolid - 1100-0500 – **YU07)** Carretera Peto-Tzucacab Km 2, 97930, Peto **W:** inpi.gob.mx/ecosgobmx/xepet.php - 1100-0100 (Sun - 1300-2200) Prgrs in Sp And Maya – **YU09)** Universidad Autónoma de Yucatán, Calle 60 No. 491-A, Esquina con 57, Centro, 97000 Mérida **W:** radio.uady.mx - 1200-0600

ZC00) ZACATECAS (Zac.)

ZC07) Josefa Ortiz de Dominguez 51, P3, 99700 Tlaltenango **W:** 1100am.tv - 1200-0600 – **ZC08)** Transmisiones MIK, S.A. de C.V., N/A – **ZC09)** Domicilio conocido, 98300 Juan Aldama **W:** comunicacionesjfj.com

FM in México City (MHz): (HD Radio): **DF05)** 88.1 (HD1: La Octava y Universal) – **DF12)** 88.9 Noticias – **DF02)** 89.7 Oye 89.7 – **DF17)** 90.5 Imagen R. – **DF18)** 90.9 (HD1: Ibero 90.9, HD2: Ibero 2) – **DF05)** 91.3 Alfa 91.3 – **DF15)** 92.1 Radio Disney – **DF06)** 92.9 La Ke Buena – **DF05)** 93.7 (HD1: Joya) – **DF19)** 94.1 UAM R. – **DF04)** 94.5 Opus 94 – **DF12)** 95.3 Amor – **DF20)** 95.7 R. IPN – **DF09)** 96.1 R. UNAM – **DF11)** 96.5 (HD1: R.Educación, Señal 96.5) – **DF06)** 96.9 W Radio – **DF05)** 97.7 La Mejor – **DF24)** 98.5 Heraldo Radio – **DF12)** 99.3 Match – **DF02)** 100.1 Stereo Cien – **DF02)** 100.9 Beat – **DF06)** 101.7 Los 40 – **DF21)** 102.5 MVS – **DF10)** 103.3 (HD1: Grupo Fórmula Digital HD 103.3, HD2: Grupo Fórmula Digital HD 103.3 – 1hr., HD3: Grupo Fórmula Digital HD 1470, HD4: Grupo Fórmula Trión) – **DF10)** 104.1 (HD1: Grupo Fórmula Digital HD 104.1, HD2: Grupo Fórmula Digital HD 104.1 – 1hr., HD3: Jazz FM, HD4: Fórmula Acústica) – **DF21)** 104.9 Exa FM – **DF22)** 105.3 (HD1: Aire Libre, HD2: Origen Radio) – **DF04)** 105.7 Reactor – **DF23)** 106.1 R. Violeta – DF12) 106.5 Mix 106 – **DF05)** 107.3 La Z – **DF04)** 107.9 Horizonte 108

MICRONESIA (USA associated)

L.T: Chuuk, Yap: UTC +10h; Kosrae, Pohnpei: +11h — **Pop:** 115,023 — **Pr.L:** English (official), Chuukese, Kosraean, Pohnpeian, Yapese — **E.C:** 120V/60Hz — **ITU:** FSM

FEDERATED STATES OF MICRONESIA BROADCASTING SERVICE (FSMBS) (Gov)

✉ Public Information Office, P.O. Box 34, Palikir Station, Pohnpei State FSM 96941 **L.P:** Chairman: Shelten G Neth **E:** chairman@mail.fm ☎ +691 320 2548 🖷 +691 320 4356

Stations: see FSMBS entries below

CHUUK STATE

MW	Call	kHz	kW
2)	V6AK	1593	5

FM	Call	MHz	kW	FM	Call	MHz	kW
1)	BBC*	88.5		1)	BBC*	89.9	
4)	V6CWS	89.5		*=R. Chuuk			

Addresses & other information

1) Baptist Mid-Missions P.O. Box 819, Weno, Chuuk State FSM 96942 **L.P:** Pastor Jody J Colson ☎ +691 330 3453 **E:** jtcolson@mail.fm – **2)** Baptist Radio stations in Chuuk Micronesia, R. Chuuk, PO Box 189, Weno, Chuuk State FSM 96942 **L.P:** Mgr Ennis Timothy ☎+691 3302374 🖷 +691 3302593 **W:** fm/chuuk/radio **ID:** "Ach nenien appio V6AK ion Chuuk' **D.Prgr:** 1900-0700 daily – **3)** Baptist Church, Weno, Chuuk State FSM 96942 **L.P:** Rev.Tom Phillips **Prgr:** conservative religious music and supplied paid prgrs – **4)** National Weather R. [WSO FM], PO Box A, Weno, Chuuk State, FSM 96942. Live and recorded local weather and emergency information for Chuuk Lagoon area 24h

KOSRAE STATE

FM	Call	MHz
1)	V6AJ	89.7

Addresses & other information

1) FSMBS R. Kosrae, PO Box 147, Tofol, Kosrae State FSM 96944 **L.P:** Mgr Keitson Jonas ☎ +691 370 3040 🖷 +691 370 3880 **W:** fm/kosrae/radio **E:** v6aj@mail.fm **ID:** "Painge station V6AJ, fwin an Kosrae" **D.Prgr:** 2000-1400, 24h during adverse weather.

POHNPEI STATE

SW	Station	kHz	kW	
4)	V6MP	‡4755	1	(currently inactive, awaiting parts)

MW	Station	kHz	kW	MW	Station	kHz	kW
1)	V6AF	999	1	2)	V6AH	1449	10

FM	Station	MHz	kW	FM	Station	MHz	kW
4)	V6MA	88.5	0.3	7)	Magic FM	100.3	
7)		88.9		1)	V6AF	104.1	
6)	V6WI	89.5					

Addresses & other information

1) Baptist R. Pohnpei, PO Box H, Kolonia, Pohnpei State FSM 96941. ☎+691 3202475 **E:** v6afpohnpei@gmail.com **LP:** Gabe Eiben **D.Prgr:** 24h – **2)** FSMBS R. Pohnpei, PO Box 1086, Kolonia, Pohnpei State FSM 96941 **L.P:** Commissioner Shelten G Neth ☎+691 320 2296 🖷+691 320 5212 **W:** fm/pohnpei/radio **E:** pohnpeiradio@outlook.com**ID:** "Met Station V6AH nan Pohnpei" **D.Prgr:** 1900-1105, 24h during adverse weather – **3)** Bernard's Enterprises, Kolonia, Pohnpei State FSM 96941 ☎+691 320 2441 🖷+691 320 2444 – **4)** The Cross, Pacific Missionary Aviation, Radio Station, PO Box 517, Kolonia, Pohnpei State FSM 96941 ☎ +691 320 1122/2496 **W:** pmapacific.org **E:** radio@pmapacific.org **SW:** Ninseitamw, Kolonia, simulcast of 88.5MHz – **6)** R. Paradise, Paradise Media, PO Box 1748, Kolonia, Pohnpei State FSM 96941 **W:** paradisemediapni.com **E:** paradiseradiopni@gmail.com **L.P:** GM: William Hoffman **Format:** hiphop & reggae music, community news – **7)** Kolonia, Pohnpei State FSM 96941, joint ownership with KWAW Saipan CNM

YAP STATE

MW	Station	kHz	kW	MW	Station	kHz	kW
2)	V6AG	1260	1	1)	V6AI	1494	5

FM	Station	MHz	kW	FM	Station	MHz	kW
1)	KUTE FM	88.1		2)	V6JY	88.9	0.25

Addresses & other information

1) FSMBS R. Yap, PO Box 117, Colonia, Yap State FSM 96943 **L.P:** Mgr Sebastian Tamagken ☎ +691 350 2174 🖷 +691 350 2160 **W:** fm/yap/radio **E:** s_tamagken@yahoo.com **ID:** "Pary e radio station V6AI nu Waab" **D.Prgr:** 2000-1400, 24h during adverse weather. KUTE-FM is repeater – **2)** Joy Family R., PO Box 1219, Yap State FSM 96943 ☎ +691 350 8483 **D.Prgr:** 24h religious

MOLDOVA

L.T: UTC +2h (28 Mar-31 Oct: +3h) — **Pop:** 4 million — **Pr.L:** Romanian (official), Gagauz, Russian — **E.C:** 230V/50Hz — **ITU:** MDA

CONSILIUL COORDONATOR AL AUDIOVIZUALULUI (CCA) (Coordinating Audio-Visual Council)

✉ str. Vlaicu Parcalab 46, 2012 Chişinău ☎ +373 22277551 🖷 +373 22277471 **E:** office@cca.md **W:** cca.md **L.P:** Pres: Dragoş Vicol

TELERADIO MOLDOVA (Pub)

✉ str. Mioriţa 1, 2028 Chişinău ☎ +373 22721388 **E:** trm@trm.md **W:** trm.md **L.P:** Pres: Olga Bordeianu

MW	kHz	kW	Prgr	MW	kHz	kW	Prgr
Chişinău (Codru)	873	50	1	Edineţ	1494	20	1
Cahul	1494	20	1				

FM (MHz)	1	2	kW	FM	1	2	kW
Bălţi	-	99.4	1	Mîndreştii Noi	104.9	-	2
Cahul	100.7	-	4	Straşeni	100.5	-	5
Căuşeni	106.8	-	4	Trifeşti	103.3	-	4
Cimişlia	103.5	-	2	Ungheni	102.0	-	4
Edineţ	101.3	-	4	+ sites with only txs below 1kW.			

D.Prgr: Prgr 1 (R. Moldova Actualitati) 24h. For ethnic minorities: 0700-0710 Russian, 0900-0910 (SS 0905) Russian, 1200-1210 (SS 1205) Russian, 1600-1610 Russian; 1815-1835 Romany (Tue); 1815-1855 Gagauz (Mon), Ukrainian (Thu), Bulgarian (Fri); 1835-1855 Russian (Tue), 1900-1915 Russian (MF) – **Prgr 2 (R. Moldova Tineret):** 24h. – **Prgr 3 (R. Moldova Muzical):** 24h via webcasting.

OTHER STATIONS

FM	MHz	kW	Location	Station
B)	68.48	17	Straşeni	RFE-RL relay
B)	69.53	17	Ungheni	RFE-RL relay
B)	70.31	17	Edineţ	RFE-RL relay
3)	71.57	2.5	Chişinău	Vocea Basarabiei
6)	87.9	1.2	Edineţ	R. Noroc
2)	88.0	1	Chişinău	Muz FM
19)	88.7	4	Edineţ	Publika FM
14)	89.1	2	Chişinău	Retro FM
9)	89.4	1	Leova	R. Plai
17)	89.6	1	Chişinău	R. Chişinău
15)	90.4	1.8	Cahul	Radio.md
21)	90.7	3.2	Chişinău	Aquarelle FM
8)	91.0	3.2	Bălţi	Jurnal FM
8)	91.2	7.9	Rezina	Jurnal FM
3)	91.9	2	Căuşeni	Vocea Basarabiei
20)	95.9	1	Proteagailovca	Diaspora FM
16)	96.7	2	Chişinău	Comedy R.
9)	97.2	3.1	Chişinău	R. Plai
19)	98.0	2.5	Comrat*	Publika FM
9)	98.8	2.5	Cimişlia	R. Plai
7)	98.5	2	Ştefan Vodă	Eco FM
6)	99.7	1.4	Chişinău	R. Noroc
6)	99.9	3.2	Căuşeni	R. Noroc
22)	99.9	3.2	Glodeni	R. Prim
8)	100.1	3.2	Chişinau	Jurnal FM
3)	100.3	1	Glodeni	Vocea Basarabiei
9)	100.5	1	Briceni	R. Plai
9)	100.6	1	Ştefan Vodă	R. Plai
5)	100.7	1.3	Mîndreştii Noi	Micul Samaritean
12)	100.9	2	Chişinău	Kiss FM
6)	100.9	1.6	Iargara	R. Noroc
1)	101.1	1.3	Proteagailovca	Hit FM
18)	101.3	2	Chişinău	Russkii Hit
20)	101.4	1	Cahul	Diaspora FM
9)	101.5	16	Căuşeni	R. Plai
1)	101.7	1	Chişinău	Hit FM
7)	101.9	(37)	Taraclia	Vocea Basarabiei
5)	102.0	1	Căuşeni	Micul Samaritean
7)	102.3	10	Straşeni	Vocea Basarabiei
13)	102.7	1	Chişinău	Virgin R.
9)	102.9	16	Mîndreştii Noi	R. Plai
10)	102.9	1.1	Nisporeni	Cultura Divină
4)	103.0	3.2	Căuşeni	Novoye R.
5)	103.2	1	Ciadîr-Lunga	Micul Samaritean
6)	103.4	2.2	Călărasi	R. Noroc
3)	103.5	1.6	Bălţi	Vocea Basarabiei
4)	103.7	1.6	Chişinău	Novoye R.
5)	103.8	10	Edineţ	Micul Samaritean
5)	104.2	1	Chişinău	Micul Samaritean
6)	104.3	5	Floreşti	R. Noroc
1)	104.5	20	Ungheni	Hit FM
1)	105.2	20	Cahul	Hit FM
5)	105.4	10	Trifeşti	Micul Samaritean
11)	105.6	1.6	Bălţi	Megapolis FM
3)	105.7	5	Nisporeni	Vocea Basarabiei
17)	106.1	2.5	Proteagailovca	R. Chişinău
1)	106.6	5	Comrat*	Hit FM
9)	106.8	1.6	Floreşti	R. Plai
5)	107.0	20	Ungheni	Micul Samaritean
A)	107.3	10	Straşeni	RFI relay
1)	107.6	20	Mîndreştii Noi	Hit FM
5)	107.7	20	Cahul	Micul Samaritean
8)	107.9	10	Edineţ	Jurnal FM

+ txs below 1kW. *) situated in Gagauzia (autonomous territorial unit)

Addresses & other information:
1) str. Bucovinei 9, 2075 Chişinău – **2)** str. Ghioceilor 1, 2008 Chişinău – **3)** 4829 Măgdăceşti – **4)** şos. Hînceşti 59/1, 2028 Chişinău. Rel. Novoye R. (Russia) – **5)** str. Bucureşti 68, 2012 Chişinău – **6)** bd. Negruzzi 6, 2001 Chişinău – **7)** şos. Balcani 7/7, 2069 Chişinău – **8)** str. M.Sadoveanu 21, 2044 Chişinău – **9)** str. Ion Inculeţ 105, 2025 Chişinău – **10)** 6421 Cioreşti – **11)** str. Alba Iulia 75, 2028 Chişinău – **12)** str. Ismail 33, 2011 Chişinău. Rel. Kiss FM (Romania) – **13)** str. Alecu Russo 1, 2068 Chişinău. Rel. Virgin R. (Romania) – **14)** str. Frumusica 1, 2002 Chişinău. Rel. Retro FM (Russia) – **15)** str. Independenţei 50, 2072 Chişinău – **16)** str. Bucureşti 68, 2012 Chişinău. Rel. R. Sputnik (Russia) – **17)** str. Bucureşti 42A-3, 2012 Chişinău. Own prgrs & rel. R.România Actualităţi (Romania) – **18)** str. Alexei Mateevici 46/1, 2009 Chişinău – **19)** str. Ghioceilor 1, 2071 Chişinău – **20)** str. Primar Carol Smidt 7, 2021 Chisinau – **21)** str. Puşkin 47/1C, 2012 Chişinău – **22)** str. Suveranităţii 5, 2002 Glodeni – **A)** Rel. RFI (France) – **B)** Rel. RFE-RL (USA).

DAB Transmitter (DAB+) (Trial)
Tx Operator: Radiocom **M:** various tests **Txs:** Block 12C (Chişinău)

GAGAUZIA
(Autonomous territorial unit)

GAGAUZIYA RADIO TELEVISIONU (GRT) (Pub)

str. Lenin 164, 3805 Comrat ☎ +373 29823086 **E:** radio@grt.md **W:** grt.md **L.P:** Chair: Tatyana Donçeva

FM	MHz	kW	FM	MHz	kW
Comrat	102.1	5	Baurci	104.6	1.25
Vulcăneşti	103.6	0.2			

D.Prgr: GRT FM in Gagauz, Russian: 0500-2200.

OTHER STATIONS

FM	MHz	kW	Location	Station
22)	100.3	1	Comrat	PRO 100 R.

+ txs below 1kW.

Addresses & other information:
22) str. Lenin nr. 204a, 3800 Comrat.

TRANSNISTRIA
(Self-proclaimed "Pridnestrovian Moldavian Republic")

PRIDNESTROVSKAYA GTRK (PGTRK) (Gov*)

(* Run by the administration of the "Pridnestrovian Moldavian Republic")
per. Khristoforova 5, 3300 Tiraspol, Transnistria ☎ +373 53373074 **E:** radio1@pgtrk.ru **W:** radio.pgtrk.ru **L.P:** Dir: Igor Nikitenko

MW	kHz	kW	Prgr
Maiac	621	150	2

FM (MHz)	1	2	kW	FM	1	2	kW
Camenca	105.0	106.4	-	Tiraspol	104.0	105.0	0.2
Caterinovca	104.0	-	-	Valea Adîncă	100.1	-	-
Dnestrovsc	100.3	-	-	Voroncovo	106.0	-	1
Maiac	-	106.0	1.5				

D.Prgr: Prgr 1 (R. 1): 24h – **Prgr 2 (R. 1 plyus):** 24h on FM, limited schedule on MW.

OTHER STATIONS

FM	MHz	kW	Location	Station
3)	88.8	3	Tiraspol[1]	R. Shanson
6)	89.3	-	Varniţa	R. Novaya volna
2)	89.6	-	Tiraspol	Hit FM
7)	90.1	-	Slobozia	Retro FM
12)	90.5	-	Tiraspol	R. Rekord
8)	91.2	-	Tiraspol	Russkoye R.
9)	91.5	-	Slobozia	R. Maksimum
14)	91.7	-	Dubăsari	Dubossary FM
A)	92.1	-	Pervomaisc	R. Sputnik relay
15)	93.7	-	Chitcani	R. Dacha
11)	96.2	-	Rîbniţa	Beat FM
A)	100.1	-	Tiraspol[1]	R. Sputnik relay
10)	100.3	0.03	Dubăsari	Dubossarskoye R.
B)	100.7	-	Tiraspol	R. Rossii relay
5)	100.9	-	Voroncovo	Dorozhnoye R.
4)	102.5	-	Tiraspol	Nik FM
A)	104.6	-	Rîbniţa	R. Sputnik relay
C)	104.6	0.1	Slobozia	Mayak relay
5)	105.4	2	Bender	Dorozhnoye R.
A)	106.5	-	Maiac	R. Sputnik relay
A)	105.8	-	Slobozia	R. Sputnik relay
13)	107.1	-	Tiraspol	Avtoradio
1)	107.7	1	Tiraspol[1]	R. Inter FM

[1]) Synchro-network with txs in several towns

Addresses & other information:
1) ul. K.Libnikhta 1/2, 3300 Tiraspol – **2)** Rel. Hit FM* – **3)** ul. K.Libnikhta 1/2, 3300 Tiraspol. Rel. R. Shanson* – **4)** 3300 Tiraspol – **5)** 3300 Tiraspol. Rel. Dorozhnoye R.* – **6)** ul. Internatsionalistov 13, Bender. Rel. Love R.* – **7)** Rel. Retro FM* – **8)** ul. Yunosti 1, 3300 Tiraspol. Rel. Russkoye R.* – **9)** Rel. R. Maksimum* – **10)** ul. Dzerzhinskogo 4, 4501 Dubăsari. Rel. Dorozhnoye R.* – **11)** ul. Kirova 130, 5500 Rîbniţa – **12)** Rel. R. Rekord* – **13)** Rel. Avtoradio* – **14)** 4501 Dubăsari – **15)** Rel. R. Dacha* – **A)** Rel. R. Sputnik* – **B)** Rel. R. Rossii* – **C)** Rel. Mayak* (*= Relays from Russia)

MONACO

L.T: UTC +1h (28 Mar-30 Oct: +2h) — **Pop:** 33,000 — **Pr.L:** French — **E.C**: 50Hz, 220V — **ITU:** MCO

MONACO MEDIA DIFFUSION (Comm.)

10-12 Quai Antoine 1er, MC-98000 Monaco ☎ +377 97974700 🖷 +377 97974707 **W:** mmd.mc **E:** contact@mmd.mc
L.P: Jean Pastorelli

MW	kHz	kW	Prgr.
Col de la Madone (France)	702	200	‡
Roumoules (France)	1467	1000	TWR relay (2045-2245, excl. Sat. 2115-2245)*
Col de la Madone (France)	1467	40	‡
Roumoules (France)	216	900	‡

*) mainly Polish & Arab Prgs

RMC (Comm.)

HQ: 15 rue Général Alain de Boissieu 75015 Paris, France ☎ +33 1 71191191 🖷 +33 1 71191190 **W:** http://rmc.bfmtv.com
L.P: Pres: Alain Weill, GD: Franck Lanoux
FM: Col de la Madone 98.5MHz 50kW; Monaco Herculis 98.8MHz 0.1kW 24h.

RADIO MONACO (Comm.)

HQ: 7 Rue du Gabian, Gildo Pastor Centre, MC-98000 Monaco ☎ +377 97700700 🖷 +377 97700701 **W**: radio-monaco.com
FM: Monaco Mont Agel Site 1 98.2MHz 0.5 kW; Mont Agel Site 1 95.4MHz 1kW, Grasse (France) 103.2MHz 0.5kW **E:** info@radio-monaco.com

RADIO MONTE CARLO ITALIE (Comm.)

8 Quai Antoine 1er, MC-98000 Monaco ☎ +377 97976666 🖷 +377 97708661 **W:** radiomontecarlo.net **E:** rmc@radiomontercarlo.net
FM: RMC1 Monaco Mont Agel Site 1 106.8MHz 1kW

RIVIERA RADIO (Comm)

10 Quai Antoine 1er, MC-98000 Monaco ☎ +377 97979494 🖷 +377 97979495 **W:** rivieraradio.mc **E:** info@rivieraradio.mc
L.P: MD: Paul Kavanagh. Tech. Manager: Peter Miller
FM: Monaco Musée Océanographique 106.3MHz 1kW; Col de la Madone 106.5MHz 50kW **D.Prgr.** in English: 24h Rel. BBCWS N every h

Other FM stations (all sces. 24h):

FM	MHz	kW	Station, location
1)	88.2	0.01	R. Maria Italia, Escorial
2)	90.3	50	M R., Col de la Madone
3)	90.6	0.2	Médi 1, Mont Agel Site 2
)	91.4	0.16	Mont Agel Site 2
)	92.7	0.1	Herculis
4)	93.2	0.2	Jazz R., Mont Agel Site 2
5)	93.5	50	R. Nostalgie,Col de la Madone
5)	93.8	1	R. Nostalgie, Mont Agel Site 1
)	94.5	0.1	Escorial
)	95.1	0.1	Musée Océanographique
4)	95.7	0.16	Jazz R., Mont Agel Site 2
7)	96.1	0.7	R. FG Mont Agel Site 2
8)	96.4	0.3	Chérie FM, Mont Agel Site 1
9)	96.7	0.05	R. Ethic , Escorial
10)	97.9	0.2	Sud R., Mont Agel Site 2
11)	99.1	0.03	R. 105 Italia, Escorial
12)	101.1	0.16	Fun R., Mont Agel Site 1
6)	102.1	0.1	R. Pitchoun, Mont Agel Site 2
13)	102.4	0.3	R. Rire & Chansons, Mont Agel Site 1
14)	102.7	50	R. Classique, Col de la Madone
15)	103.0	1	RFM, Mont Agel Site 1
16)	103.3	0.4	RDS Italia, Musée Océanographique
8)	104.5	0.1	Cherie FM, Musée Océanographique

Addresses and other information:
1) W: radiomaria.it **2) W:** mradio.fr **3) W:** medi1.com **4) W:** jazzradio.fr **5) W:** nostalgie.fr **6) W:**tvradio-pitchoun.fr **7) W:** radiofg.com **8)W:** cheriefm.fr **9) W:** radioethic.com **10) W:** sudradio.fr **11) W:** radio105.net **12) W:** funradio.fr **13) W:** rireetchansons.fr **14) W:** radioclassique.fr **15) W:** rfm.fr **16) W:** rds.it

DAB+ from Mont Agel.
8A (195.936 MHz) 10kW Radio. 105 – RMC Italie – Riviera Radio. – R. Maria (France) – Médi 1 – RMC 2 – R. Latina – R. Ethic – Crooner Radio – Swigg FM – MC Doualiya – R. Monaco
12B (225.648 MHz) 10kW Fréquence Mistral – R. Pitchoun – R. Orient – AMI radio – Melody – RCF Côte d'Azur – Radio Yacht – KISS FM Nice- Sud Radio

MONGOLIA

L.T: UTC +8h (Western Mongolia: +7h) — **Pop:** 3.2 million — **Pr.L:** Mongolian — **E.C:** 230V/50Hz — **ITU:** MNG

KHARILTSAA KHOLBOONY ZOKHITSÜÜLAKH KHOROO (Communications Regulatory Commission)

Sükhbaatar district, Metro Business Center, Sükhbaatar St. 13, 5th floor, Ulaanbaatar 14201 ☎ +976 1 1304257 🖷 +976 1 1327720 **E:** info@crc.gov.mn **W:** crc.gov.mn
L.P: Chmn/CEO: Gonchig Chinzorig

MONGOLYN ÜNDESNII OLON NIITIIN RADIO TELEVIZ (MÜONRT) (Pub)
(Mongolian National Broadcaster)

Bayangol district, 11th subdistrict, Khuvisgalyn Rd. 3, Ulaanbaatar 16061 ☎ +976 91 915575 **E:** contact@mnb.mn **W:** mnb.mn
L.P: DG: Ninjjamts Luvsandash

LW	kHz	*kW	Prgr	LW/MW	kHz	kW	Prgr
Ulaanbaatar (a)	164	250	MR	Ölgii	209	40	MR+R
Choibalsan	209	40	MR	Altai	227	40	MR+²
Dalanzadgad	209	40	MR+¹	Mörön	882	40	MR

*) All txs are officially run on reduced power: 250kW instead of 500kW, 40kW instead of 75kW (a) Khonkhor; R=incl. MÜONRT regional prgr (see below); ¹ ² =Txs also carry prgrs of non-affiliated regional public broadcasting stations (see under "Regional Public Service Stations"): ¹ Goviin Dolgion Büsiin Olon Niitiin R. ² Govi-Altain Olon Niitiin R.

SW	kHz	kW	Prgr	SW	kHz	kW	Prgr
Altai	4830	10	R3°	Ulaanbaatar (a)	7260	50	R3
Mörön	4895	10	R3°	(a) Khonkhor (°) alternatively MR			

NB: All SW txs are officially scheduled to be on the air on a regular basis 2300-0500 & 0700-1500. Speculations that the txs on 4830/4895 may have been on the air irregularly or are off the air, have not been independently confirmed by local monitoring or official information.

FM (MHz)	MR	R3	kW	FM	MR	R3	kW
Altai	107.0	-	0.05	Ölgii	107.0	-	0.05
Choibalsan	101.5	106.7	0.05	Sainshand	100.9	-	1
Dalanzadgad	107.5	-	1	Ulaanbaatar	106.0	100.9	1
Mörön	103.0	103.6	0.05	Zamyn-Üüd	105.2	-	0.1

+ translators

D.Prgr: Mongolyn R. (MR): 2200-1500 – **R3:** 2300-1500. **MÜONRT Regional Branch: Bayan-Ölgii R.** on Ölgii 209kHz. Incl. prgrs in Kazakh.
International Service (Voice of Mongolia): See Int. Radio section.

REGIONAL PUBLIC SERVICE STATIONS

Govi-Altain Olon Niitiin R.: Yesönbulag district (Altai), Badsuuriin Rd. On Altai 227kHz*. – **Goviin Dolgion Büsiin Olon Niitiin R.:** Dalanzadgad. On Dalanzadgad 209kHz* + 103.6MHz. – **Züün Büsiin Olon Niitiin R.:** Choibalsan. On Choibalsan 106.4MHz.
*Timeshared with the prgr Mongolyn R. of Mongolian National Broadcaster (MÜONRT). **NB:** These stns are not part of, or affiliated with MÜONRT.

OTHER STATIONS

FM	MHz	kW	Location	Station
22)	88.8	1	Ulaanbaatar	Medee medeelliin R.
20B)	89.3	1	Ulaanbaatar	UBM R.
23)	89.7	1	Ulaanbaatar	Zokhist ayalguu R.
24)	90.5	1	Ulaanbaatar	VIP R.
25)	91.1	1	Ulaanbaatar	Tsag üe zaluus R.
2)	91.7	1	Ulaanbaatar	Metro Lounge R.
1)	92.1	1	Ulaanbaatar	Toim R. 92.1
3)	92.5	1	Ulaanbaatar	Star FM
4)	95.1	1	Ulaanbaatar	Khamag Mongol R.
5)	95.7	1	Ulaanbaatar	Arga bilig R.
26)	96.3	1	Ulaanbaatar	Avto R.
6)	96.9	1	Ulaanbaatar	Elgen nutag R.
7)	97.5	1	Ulaanbaatar	Lavain egshig R.
8)	98.1	1	Ulaanbaatar	Formula FM

FM	MHz	kW	Location	Station
9)	98.5	1	Ulaanbaatar	Best R.
10)	98.9	1	Ulaanbaatar	Business R.
11)	99.3	1	Ulaanbaatar	Ineemseglel R.
12)	99.7	1	Ulaanbaatar	Ikh Mongol
13)	100.1	1	Ulaanbaatar	Kiss FM
14)	100.5	1	Ulaanbaatar	Giingoo R.
15)	101.7	1	Ulaanbaatar	Shine Mongol R.
27)	102.1	1	Ulaanbaatar	MGL R.
16)	102.5	1	Ulaanbaatar	R. UB
21)	102.5	1	Darkhan	Shine dolgion R.
A)	103.1	1	Ulaanbaatar	BBCWS relay
17)	103.6	1	Ulaanbaatar	Tani R.
18)	104.0	1	Ulaanbaatar	Mongolyn duu kholoi
19)	104.0	1	Khovd	Ger büüliin R.
19)	104.0	1	Erdenet	Ger büüliin R.
19)	104.5	1	Ulaanbaatar	Ger büüliin R.
19)	104.5	1	Darkhan	Ger büüliin R.
19)	104.5	1	Mörön	Ger büüliin R.
28)	105.0	1	Ulaanbaatar	Övör Mongolyn R.
20)	105.5	1	Ulaanbaatar	Vibe 105.5
19)	106.5	1	Bayankhongor	Ger büüliin R.
19)	106.5	1	Bulgan	Ger büüliin R.
19)	106.5	1	Sainshand	Ger büüliin R.
B)	106.6	1	Ulaanbaatar	VOA relay
29)	107.0	1	Ulaanbaatar	Smart FM
21)	107.5	1	Ulaanbaatar	Shine dolgion R.

+ txs below 1kW.

Addresses & other information:
1) Chingeltei district, 2nd subdistrict, Sansar Cable LLC Building, Ulaanbaatar – **2)** Bayangol district, 11th subdistrict, Khuvisgalyn Rd. 3, Ulaanbaatar **E:** info@evsegmongol.mn – **3)** Ulaanbaatar – **4)** Sükhbaatar district, 5th subdistrict, N&N center, 3rd floor, Room 302, Ulaanbaatar 14192 **E:** hamagmongol@yahoo.com – **5)** Sükhbaatar district, 8th subdistrict, Independence Palace, Amar St., 1st floor, Ulaanbaatar 14200 **E:** argabilig_fm@yahoo.com – **6)** Khan-Uul district, 15th subdistrict, Narkhan khotkhon 61-r Building, Room 32, Ulaanbaatar 13380 **E:** dnaba_d@yahoo.com – **7)** Chingeltei district, 2nd subdistrict, Khudaldaa St., Javzandamba Center, 3rd floor, Ulaanbaatar **E:** info@lavain-egshig.mn – **8)** Chingeltei district, 5th subdistrict, Narny Titem Building, 2nd floor, Ulaanbaatar **E:** ubradio@mail.mn – **9)** Chingeltei district, 4th subdistrict, Business Development Centre, Ulaanbaatar Bank building, 2nd floor, Ulaanbaatar 15160 **E:** best_985@yahoo.com – **10)** Ulaanbaatar **E:** info@business-radio.mn – **11)** Sükhbaatar district, 8th subdistrict, Amar St., CT House, 5th floor, Room 433, Ulaanbaatar 14200 – **12)** Bayangol district, Enkhtaivan Ave., Grand Plaza, 14th floor, Room 1404, Ulaanbaatar 16050 **E:** fm_997@yahoo.com – **13)** Chingeltei district, 1st subdistrict, Ulaanbaator Bank bair, 13th floor, Room 1302, Ulaanbaatar **E:** gerlees2002@yahoo.com – **14)** Ulaanbaatar – **15)** Ulaanbaatar **E:** shine_mongolradio@yahoo.com – **16)** Bayangol district, Enkhtaivan Ave., Grand Plaza, 14th floor, Room 1108, Ulaanbaatar 16050 **E:** fmub1025@yahoo.com – **17)** Ulaanbaatar – **18)** Ulaanbaatar – **19)** Bayanzürkh district, 2nd subdistrict, 15th microdistrict, 10A-r Building, Ulaanbaatar **E:** windfm1045@yahoo.com – **20)** Ulaanbaatar **E:** hulan@bproduction.mn – **21)** Bayanzürkh district, 6th subdistrict, 13th microdistrict, Namiianjugiin St., Ereliin 40-r Building, Ulaanbaatar – **22)** Ulaanbaatar – **23)** Ulaanbaatar – **24)** Ulaanbaatar – **25)** Ulaanbaatar – **26)** Chingeltei district, 4th subdistrict, 4th District City Administration, Ulaanbaatar **E:** mongol_media@yahoo.com – **27)** Sükhbaatar district, 14th subdistrict, Altai St., New World Tower, 5th floor, Room 501, Ulaanbaatar **E:** info@mglradionews.com – **28)** Ulaanbaatar. Incl. rel. CRI (P.R. China) – **29)** Sükhbaatar district, 8th subdistrict, STÖ Building, 4th floor, Ulaanbaatar 13381 – **A)** Rel. BBCWS (UK) – **B)** Rel. VOA (USA)

MONTENEGRO

L.T: UTC +1h (28 Mar-31 Oct: +2h) — **Pop:** 630,000 — **Pr.L:** Montenegrin, Serbian — **E.C:** 230V/50Hz — **ITU:** MNE

RADIO TELEVIZIJA CRNE GORE

✉ Bul. Revolucije 19, 81000 Podgorica ☎ +382 20 245595 **W:** rtcg.me **E:** marketing@rtcg.org **L.P:** DG: S. Sestic

FM (MHz)	**RCG 1**	**R. 98**	**kW**	**FM** (MHz)	**RCG 1**	**R. 98**	**kW**
Bjelasica	92.1	99.3	54	Podgorica	96.5	89.3	10
Durmitor	96.1	91.3	10	Tovic	88.0	98.9	10
Lovcen	94.9	98.0	54	Velji Grad	99.8	89.6	10
Mozura	97.3	93.4	10				

+ 11 txs.less than 1kW

Local/private stations
R. Antena M, Podgorica 87.6MHz + 5 relays – **R. Cetinje** 94.5MHz + 1 relay – **R. Elmag**, Podgorica 96.0MHz + 7 relays – **R. Bar** 91.8MHz + 1 relay – **R. Berane** 88.2MHz + 1 relay – **R Bijelo**, Polje 101.1MHz + 1 relay – **R. Budva** 98.7MHz + 1 relay – **R. Corona**, Bar 88.9MHz +1 relay – **R. D**, Podgorica 88.6MHz + 2 relays – **R. Danilovgrad** 92.9MHz – **R. Fokus**, Bijelo Polje 93.9MHz – **R. Free Montenegro**, Podgorica 103.0.MHz – **R. Glas** Plava, Plav 102.9.MHz – **R. Gorica**, Podgorica 93.3MHz – **R. Herceg** Novi 90.0MHz +1 relay – **R. Jupok**, Rozaje 98.7MHz + 1 relay – **R. Kotor** 95.3MHz + 1 relay – **R. Max**, Danilovgrad 107.5MHz + 1 relay – **R. Mir**, Tuzi 106.1MHz + 1 relay – **R. Mojkovac** 92.8MHz – **R. Montena**, Podgorica 105.7MHz + 5 relays – **R. Niksic** 89.8MHz + 2 relays – **R. Ozon**, Kolasin 97.6MHz – **R. Panorama**, Pljevlja 89.2MHz – **R. Pljevlja** 94.8MHz – **R. Rozaje** 104.4MHz – **R. Svetigora**, Cetinje 101.0.MHz – **R. Tivat** 88.5.MHz – **R. Ulcinj** 91.3MHz + 1 relay – **R. Zeta**, Podgorica 93.8.MHz – **R. City**, Podgorica 107.3MHz

MONTSERRAT (UK)

L.T: UTC -4h — **Pop:** 5,000 — **Pr.L:** English — **E.C:** 230V/50Hz — **ITU:** MSR

ZJB RADIO MONTSERRAT (Gov. Comm.)

✉ PO Box 51, Sweeneys ☎ +1 664 491 2885 **E:** zjb@gov.ms **W:** zjbradio.com **L.P:** SM: Herman Sargeant. Techn: Ivor Greenaway
FM: 88.3MHz, 0.1kW (Isles Bay Hill), 95.5MHz, 5kW (Silver Hills)
D.Prgr: 24h BBC relay at night
Ann: "ZJB Radio Montserrat, the Voice of Montserrat"

MOROCCO

L.T: UTC +1h (during month of Ramadan 11 Apr - 16 May: UTC) — **Pop:** 37 million — **Pr.L:** Arabic (official), Tamazight (official), Hassaniya Arabic, French — **E.C:** 220V/50Hz — **ITU:** MRC

HAUTE AUTORITÉ DE LA COMMUNICATION AUDIOVISUELLE (HACA)

✉ Espace les Palmiers, Lot 26,Angle Avenues Anakhil et Mehdi Ben Barka, B.P. 20590, Rabat Ryad ☎+212 53 7579600 🖷 +212 53 7714274 **W:** haca.ma **E:** info@haca.ma **L.P:** DG: Ahmed Akhchichine.

SOCIÉTÉ NATIONALE DE RADIODIFFUSION ET DE TÉLÉVISION (SNRT) - RADIO MAROCAINE (Pub.)

✉ 1, Rue El Brihi, B.P. 1042, MA-10000 Rabat ☎+212 53 7700 319 🖷 +212 53 772 2047 **W:** snrt.ma **E:** lemediateur@snrt.ma **Reg.** ✉ B.P. 459, Laayoune. **L.P:** DG: Mohamed Ayad. Dir. Tech: Allal Kacimi.

MW	**kHz**	**kW**	**N**	**MW**	**kHz**	**kW**	**N**
Sidi Bennour	540	600	A/R	Laâyoune	711	300	R
Oujda	*596	50	A/R	Agadir	936	200	A/R
Sebaa-Aioun	612	300	A	*nominal fq. 594kHz			

FM (MHz)	**A**	**B**	**C**	**Q**	**R**	**kW**
Agadir	91.0	94.2	97.5	87.9	105.3	20
Al Hoceima	105.7	92.1	95.3	89.0	104.4	5
Beni Mellal	92.9	89.8	96.1	-	-	10
Bouarfa	88.0	91.1	94.3	-	-	20
Casablanca	96.0	90.0	95.3	98.6	103.1	10
Dakhla	93.5	91.8	-	98.3	-	
El Houceima	105.7	92.1	95.3	89.0	-	8
El Jadida	90.4	-	-	-	-	
Erfoud	91.8	-	98.3	-	-	12
Errachidia	91.3	97.8	94.5	-	-	20
Essaouira	97.9	91.4	-	-	-	
Fès	88.8	95.1	101.9	98.4	-	10
Figuig	91.9	95.1	98.4	-	-	5
Ifrane	90.5	93.6	96.8	-	-	
Kenitra	91.6	-	87.7	-	-	12
Khenifra	91.6	87.9	104.6	94.2	-	10
Khourigba	87.6	-	-	-	-	
Lâayoune	93.9	97.9	91.1	91.0	-	10
Marrakech	94.9	98.8	89.7	91.7	-	30
Meknès	88.8	95.1	101.9	92.5	-	10
Nador	87.6	93.9	97.2	-	-	12
Ouarzazate	90.3	93.4	96.6	-	-	6
Oujda	89.9	99.4	91.3	96.1	104.0	12
Rabat	91.0	87.9	104.6	94.2	-	20
Safi	90.9	-	94.1	-	-	5

FM (MHz)	A	B	C	Q	R	kW
Settat	92.1	89.0	107.3	-	-	5
Tanger	88.7	91.8	95.0	88.7	-	20
Tantan	90.3	-	-	-	-	
Taounate	96.1	-	-	-	-	
Taourirt	96.6	93.4	90.3	-	107.0	10
Tarfaya	90.2	91.8	95.5	98.4	100.0	5
Taroudant	92.2	-	-	-	-	
Taza	94.9	98.2	-	-	-	12
Tétouan	90.6	100.2	96.9	93.7	-	12
Zougara	94.3	97.6	91.1	-	-	5

A: Al-Idaa al-Watania in Arabic: 24h. **N:** on the h. – **B: Chaîne Inter:** 24h. **Spanish:** 1330-1345, **English:** 1345-1300. Other times in French. – **C: Al-Idaa al-Amazighia in Berber/Arabic dialects:** 0800-2400. **Q: Quran R. "R. Mohammed VI":** 24h. – **R: Regional Prgrs. MW: Agadir:** 936kHz&105.3MHz. **Casablanca:** 103.1MHz. **Laâyoune/Dakhla:** 711kHz/100.0MHz. **Oujda,** 595kHz&104.0&107.0MHz. **Tanger:** 540kHz&104.1MHz. **Marrakech:** 540kHz.

Ann: Arabic: "Huna Ribat, Idha'atu-l-Mamlaka al Maghribiyya" or "Idha'at al-Wataniya". French: "Ici Rabat, Radiodiffusion Télévision Marocaine". Berber: "Dahab Rbad al-idaa al-Amazighia Li Mamlaka L'Maghrib".

MEDI 1 RADIO (Comm, Semi-Gov.)

✉ B.P. 2055, 3/5 rue Emsallah, 90000 Tanger ☎&🖷 +212 539936363 **W:** medi1.com **E:** technique@medi1.com **L.P:** Dir: Hassan Kiyar.
Two separate streams acc. to target area: Antenne Maghreb in Arabic/French and Antenne Afrique Internationale in French.
LW: Nador 171kHz 1600kW
FM (MHz):Agadir 104.6 20kW, Al Hoceima 88.5 16kW, Beni Mellal/Oujda 102.9 12kW, Bouarfa 97.2 1kW, Casablanca 99.6 9kW, Dakhla 96.4, El Jadida 96.7, Enjil/Erfoud/Figuig 97.0, Errachadia 96.0 16kW, Essaouira 94.6 12kW, Fès 101.4 2kW, Goulmima 96.8 16kW, Ifrane 97.9 3kW, Khenifra 97.6 16kW, Kenitra 97.7, Khouribga 104.4, Laâyoune 101.0 10kW, Larache 91.3, Marrakech 105.3 1kW, Meknès 105.5 10kW, Merchiche 87.6, Nador 89.6 10kW, Ouarzazate/Zaio 99.9, Rabat 97.5 20kW, Safi 97.0, Slokia 95.3, Semara 96.8, Taliouine 92.2, Tanger 101.0 1kW, Tantan 93.4, Taounate 103.1, Taourirt 97.5 16kW, Tarfaya 97.9, Taroudante 95.4, Taza 96.2 16kW, Tetouan 103.7 12kW, Tiznit 96.9, Zagora 97.0.
D.Prgr. in Arabic/French: 24h. **Ann:** "Médi 1".

Other stations, main networks:

FM	1)	2)	3)	4)	5)	6)	7)	8)	9)	10)
Agadir	100.4	93.1	96.5	-	95.6	-	89.3	103.7	-	-
Al Hoceima	97.7	93.3	98.6	102.1	90.8	-	-	103.3	94.4	-
Béni Mellal	94.0	93.5	89.2	-	98.1	-	-	94.7	91.6	105.1
Bouarfa	89.1	93.1	106.5	-	89.9	-	95.9	105.6	90.6	-
Boujdour	-	93.1	88.0	106.0	102.0	-	88.9	105.6	-	-
Casablanca	104.3	93.1	88.7	-	100.3	92.5	88.2	100.8	91.2	102.1
Dakhla	89.7	93.1	93.9	106.0	99.7	-	88.7	88.0	-	-
El Jadida	95.1	93.1	102.5	92.7	100.5	97.3	89.3	96.2	91.5	101.3
Erfoud	-	-	-	-	88.7	-	105.4	104.5	-	-
Errachadia	102.5	93.5	102.9	-	104.1	-	100.5	105.6	-	-
Essaouira	92.8	93.3	99.9	104.1	96.1	-	89.8	98.5	-	-
Fès	103.9	93.7	106.9	-	94.1	98.8	88.3	91.4	89.4	100.4
Figuig	101.9	93.1	88.1	105.5	97.8	-	106.4	91.3	88.8	-
Guelmin	91.9	93.1	100.3	-	98.5	96.8	88.7	94.3	-	-
Goulmima	96.4	93.2	105.0	97.5	-	-	91.0	103.2	-	-
Ifrane	103.6	-	106.7	-	94.6	-	-	89.9	-	103.2
Kenitra	-	93.3	101.6	-	107.6	106.9	-	98.1	-	99.5
Khenifra	102.4	-	-	-	101.2	-	-	104.7	95.6	-
Khouribga	106.6	-	97.2	-	101.4	-	-	92.3	93.9	-
Laâyoune	104.6	93.1	107.1	106.3	91.6	-	89.4	98.6	94.8	-
Larache	99.3	93.1	100.8	104.4	96.7	-	92.8	-	-	-
Marrakech	100.6	93.8	97.7	106.5	94.4	90.5	88.6	97.1	98.2	-
Meknès	99.9	93.7	102.5	106.1	96.6	97.2	104.2	90.3	90.7	92.9
Nador	104.3	91.9	105.3	90.7	92.6	-	-	95.7	100.7	101.4
Oujda	102.0	93.5	101.0	92.9	98.5	-	92.2	106.5	97.7	103.4
Ouarzazate	91.2	93.1	105.6	-	92.0	-	88.9	103.4	-	-
Rabat	95.7	93.5	100.5	-	99.8	106.9	90.2	103.7	96.5	97.0
Safi	103.6	93.5	105.4	-	99.5	92.3	90.3	104.5	-	-
Settat	103.8	92.9	102.9	105.7	98.9	106.4	93.4	97.9	94.7	96.4
Skhour	102.2	-	102.6	-	95.8	92.2	88.0	103.7	-	-
Smara	93.5	93.1	95.0	106.0	95.4		91.8	105.4	-	-
Tafraoute	88.5	-	-	99.2	89.6	95-.9	102.7	93.3	-	-
Tantan	103.5	93.1	99.9	-	97.0	95.2	91.8	101.3	-	-
Tanger	102.3	93.3	104.7	105.4	96.4	103.3	89.6	94.3	92.3	91.1
Taounate	91.5	93.9	105.8	93.1	103.6	95.6	-	90.0	-	99.6
Taourirt	91.5	-	106.0	-	98.8	-	105.1	94.8	94.2	-
Tarfaya	95.9	-	95.0	102.7	97.2	-	89.6	-	-	-
Targuist	-	-	104.5	95.8	106.2	90.8	103.7	92.7	-	-
Taroudante	101.3	93.9	87.7	99.9	104.9	97.8	-	88.1	-	-
Taza	95.8	93.5	105.3	88.0	99.5	103.0	88.6	89.9	100.1	101.7
Tétouan	105.9	93.9	-	104.5	97.8	87.8	101.1	107.3	-	93.0
Tiznit	90.6	-	104.2	-	91.5	103.1	88.4	105.1	-	-
Zagora	104.7	93.1	95.8	-	91.8	-	88.0	105.9	-	-

1) Aswat FM, Casablanca **W:** radioaswat.ma – **2) Radio 2M** (Semi-Gov.), Casablanca **W:** radio2m.ma – **3) MFM Atlas/Oriental/Sahara/Saïss/Souss & Casa FM**, Casablanca **W:** mfmradio.ma radiocasafm.ma – **4) Cap Radio**, Tanger **W:** capradio.ma – **5) Hit Radio**, Rabat **W:** hitradio.ma Also transmitters in many West & Central African French speaking countries – **6) R. Atlantic**, Casablanca **W:** atlanticradio.ma – **7) Med Radio**, Casablanca **W:** medradio.ma – **8) R. Chada FM**, Casablanca **W:** chadafm.net – **9) R. Mars**, Casablanca **W:** radiomars.ma – **10) Medina FM,** Rabat **W:** radiomedinafm.ma
Voice of America: Meknès 91.9MHz, Fès 97.9MHz 2kW, Rabat/Agadir 101.0MHz 20kW, Casablanca 101.5MHz 10kW, Marrakech 101.7MHz 12kW, Tanger 101.8MHz 20kW.

CEUTA (Spain)

L.T: see Spain — **Pop:** 85,000 — **Pr.L:** Spanish — **E.C:** 230V/50Hz — **ITU:** E (**WRTH:** CEU)

R. Nacional de España, Real 90, E-51001 Ceuta. **FM:** RNE-1 97.2MHz, R. Clásica 100.8MHz, RNE5TN 101.9MHz, RNE-3 106.8MHz, all 1kW.
SER Radiolé - R. Ceuta, Poblado Marinero, Local 32, E-51001 Ceuta. **MW:** 1584kHz 5kW 24h rel. of Radiolé netw. **FM:** 96.2MHz R. Ceuta
COPE, Sargento Mena 5-8,1°izq, E-51001 Ceuta. **FM:** 89.8MHz.
Onda Cero R, Calle Delgado Serrano 1, 1°, E-51001 Ceuta. **FM:** 101.4MHz 3kW.
RTV Ceuta, Paseo Alcalde Sánchez Prado, 5 entreplanta, 51001 Ceuta. **FM:** 99.0MHz. **W:** rtvce.es
R. Solidaria:107.1MHz **W:** radiosolidaria.com
Radio Adventista: 107.8 MHz **W:** adventistaes.radio.es

MELILLA (Spain)

L.T: see Spain— **Pop:** 85,000 — **Pr.L:** Spanish — **E.C:** 230V/50Hz — **ITU:** E (**WRTH:** MEL)

R. Nacional de España, Altos de la Vía 3, E-52004 Melilla **MW: RNE1** 972kHz 5kW. **FM:** (0.3kW): 97.7MHz (R1), 100.1MHz (RNE5TN), 105.3MHz (R3), 107.6MHz (R. Clásica).
SER R. Melilla, Calle Cardenal Cisneros 8 bajo, E-52001 Melilla **W:** cadenaser.com/tag/melilla/a/ . **MW:** 1485kHz 1kW 24h. **FM:** (MHz): 92.2MHz, 96.3 Los 40 Melilla, 101.1 Dial Melilla.
COPE, C/ Pablo Vallescá 6 "Edificio Ánfora"2º - 1, E-52001 Melilla **W:** copemelilla.com **FM:** 102.2MHz Cadena 100, 98.4MHz COPE Melilla.
Onda Cero R, Calle de Musico Granados 2, E-52004 Melilla **FM:** 89.6MHz
RTV Melilla, C/ General Macías, 11, 1º izquierda – 52001 Melilla **W:**inmusa.es **FM:** 104.0 MHz .
R. Maria: 92.9 MHz. **W:** radiomaria.es
R. Adventista W: adventistaes.radio.es **FM:** 103.2/106.2MHz

MOZAMBIQUE

L.T: UTC +2h — **Pop:** 31 million — **Pr.L:** Portuguese (official), Bantu languages — **E.C:** 220V/50Hz — **ITU:** MOZ

INSTITUTO NACIONAL DAS COMUNICAÇÕES (INCM)

✉ Av. Eduardo Mondlane, 123/127, PO Box 848, Maputo ☎+258 21 490131 🖷 +258 21 494435. **W:** incm.gov.mz **E:** info@incm.gov.mz

RÁDIO MOÇAMBIQUE (Pub.)

✉ Rua da Rádio n.º 2, C.P. 2000, Maputo ☎+258 21 431687 🖷 +258 21 321816 **W:** www.rm.co.mz **E:** caprimoe@zebra.uem.mz
L.P: Chmn/CEO: Ricardo Malate, TD: Hermenegildo Basílio Mula, Int. Rel. Dir: Maria Cremilda Massingue, Fin. Dir: Arlindo Piedade de Sousa

MW	kHz	kW	N	MW	kHz	kW	N
1) Maputo	738	50	AN	4) Chimoio	1026	50	EP
3) Nampula	765	50	EP	7) Quelimane	1179	50	EP
10) Xai-Xai	810	50	EP	5) Inhambane	1206	50	EP
2) Beira(Dondo)	†873	50	EP	8) Pemba	1224	50	EP
9) Tete	963	50	EP	6) Lichinga	1260	50	EP
1) Maputo	1008	50	EP				

FM	MHz	kW	N	FM	MHz	kW	N
10) Chicumbane	87.8	1	AN	10) Chokwe	96.7	1	AN
4) Chimoio	88.5	1	D	8) Palma	97.4	1	EP
6) Metangula	88.5	1	AN	2) Beira	97.6	1	AN
9) Tete	88.5	0.3	D	2) Quelimane	97.8	1	EP
5) Vilaculos	88.9	1	AN	1) Maputo	97.9	1	C
6) Lichinga	89.1	0.25	EP	10) Massangena	97.9	1	EP
4) Mossorize	89.2	1	AN	5) Inhambane	98.1	0.25	D
7) Milange	89.2	1	AN	6) Matchedje	98.2	1	AN
2) Gorongosa	89.9	1	EP	2) Caia	98.6	1	AN
5) Masinga	89.9	1	AN	7) Beira	99.2	1	D
8) Pemba	89.9	0.25	D	2) Quelimane	99.5	1	AN
6) Cuamba	90.4	1	AN	8) Metoro	100.7	5	AN
8) Macomia	90.4	1	EP	9) Tete	100.7	1	EP
8) M. da Praia	90.6	1	EP	8) Montepuez	100.9	1	AN
10) Xai-Xai	90.9	1	EP	5) Maxixe	101.6	1	AN
5) Mabote	91.2	1	AN	6) Lichinga	101.7	1	AN
6) Mecanhelas	91.3	1	AN	10) Massingir	101.7	1	AN
2) Dondo	91.6	5	AN	5) Homoíne	102.1	2	AN
7) Mocuba	91.7	1	EP	1) Maputo	102.3	1	EP
7) Namacata	92.1	1	AN	9) Ulóngue	103.7	1	AN
1) Maputo	92.3	5	AN	4) Catandica	104.8	1	AN
1) Maputo	93.1	1	D	5) Inhambane	105.1	0.3	EP
3) Nampula	93.6	0.25	D	2) Beira	105.2	1	C
3) Nampula	95.1	1	AN	3) Nampula	105.5	0.25	EP
2) Beira	96.5	1	EP	6) Marrupa	105.6	1	AN
4) Chimoio	96.6	0.25	EP	1) Maputo	105.9	1	E

+22 more tx's under 1kW.

(AN) Antena Nacional in Portuguese: 24h.
(C) Cidade FM in Portuguese: 24h. Also rel. BBC.
(D) RM Desporto in Portuguese: 0300-2200.
(E) Maputo Corridor R. in English: 1000-2200. Also rel. BBC.
(EP Emissor Provincial) in Portuguese/ethnic: Provincial prgrs Mon-Fri 0250-2200, SS 24h on FM & other MW except 765, 810, 873kHz. FM relays Antena Nacional overnight weekdays.

Addresses:
1) EP de Maputo – **2)** EP de Sofala, C.P. 1942, Beira – **3)** EP de Nampula, C.P. 93, Nampula – **4)** EP de Manica, C.P. 390, Chimoio – **5)** EP de Inhambane, C.P. 196, Imhambane – **6)** EP do Niassa, C.P. 171, Lichinga – **7)** EP de Zambézia, C.P. 333, Quelimane – **8)** EP de Cabo Delgado, C.P. 45, Pemba – **9)** EP de Tete, C.P. 384, Tete – **10)** EP de Gaza, C.P. 130, Xai-Xai.
Ann: "Rádio Moçambique, Antena Nacional", EP: "Rádio Moçambique, (province)". **IS:** Mbira (indigenous xylophone). Opens and closes with National Anthem.

Other Stations (FM MHz):
A Voz do Islão, Maputo: 96.3 – **KFM**, Maputo: 88.3 – **Lifetime Music R,** Maputo: 87.8 1kW **W:** lmradio.net – **R. Capital,** Maputo: 90.7 (also rel. TWR) – **R. Haq,** Nampula: 104.4 – **R. Índico**: Maputo 89.5, Inhambane 89.7, Quelimane 88.2, Beira/Chimoio/Lichinga/Nampula/Pemba/Tete/Xai-Xai 90.0 **W:** teste.radioindico.fm – **R. Maria Moçambique**: Maputo 103.1, Villankulo/Xai Xai 102, Chokwe 101.4, Govure 102.5, Quissico 106.4, Maxixe 104.2, Nova Mambone 104.0 **W:** radiomaria.org.mz – **R. Miramar**, Maputo: 101.4, Beira 98.1, Nampula 98.4 **W:** radiomiramarfm.blogspot.com – **R. N'tyana,** Maputo: 93.5 – **R. Savana,** Maputo: 100.2 **W:** savana.co.mz – **R. SFM,** Maputo: 94.6 – **R. Terra Verde,** Maputo: 98.6 – **99FM**: Maputo 99.3, Beira 89.3, Tete/Xai-Xai 95.0, Inhambane 96.0, Nampula 97.3, Pemba 99.5 **W:**99fm.co.mz – **R. Viva:** Maputo 99.6 1kW, Nampula 90.8. **W:** radioviva.fm – **Top R,** Maputo: 104.2 **W:** topradiomoz.blogspot.com

BBC African Service: Tete 87.8, Nampula 88.3, Beira 88.5, Quelimane 95.3, Maputo 95.5, Chimoio 99.0, Xai-Xai 100.9MHz
RDP África: Beira 94.8, Maputo 89.2, Nampula 91.9, Quelimane 89.0 (all 50kW)
RFI Afrique: Maputo 105.0 2kW in French/Portuguese.
In addition about 100 community radio stations are in operation

MYANMAR

L.T: UTC + 6½h — Pop: 55 million — **Pr.L:** Burmese (Bamar) (official), English, Kachin, Kayah, Karen, Chin, Mon, Rakhine, Shan — **E.C:** 230V/50Hz — **ITU:** BRM

MINISTRY OF INFORMATION
Yaza Thingaha Rd, Zeya Theiddhi Ward, Naypyidaw ☎+95 67 412323 **W:** www.moi.gov.mm

MYANMA RADIO AND TELEVISION DEPT, MRTV (Gov.) MYANMA RADIO
Tatkon Township, Naypyidaw ☎ +95 67 79483 ⎙ +95 67 79403 **Yangon centre:** Pyay Rd, Kamayut-11041, Yangon ☎+95 1 527119 ⎙+95 1 534211 **W:** mrtv.gov.mm **E:** mrtv@mptmail.net.mm **L.P:** DG: U Ye Naing. Dir. R.: U Zay Yar CE: U Myo Win

MW	kHz	kW	Prgr	Times
Yangon	576	200+	N	2300-1700
Naypyidaw	594	400+	N	2300-1700
Yangon	729	100	Y	2330 (SS 2300)-1630

+) operates on half power during early morning and evening

SW	kHz	kW	Prgr	Times
Naypyidaw	5915	50	Mi	2300-1700
Yangon	5985	50	N	2300-0130, 1130-1700
Yangon	9730	50	N	0130-1130

FM	MHz	kW	Region/State
Yangon	87.6	2	Yangon Region
Hsipaw	88.0	0.3	Shan State
Kawthaung	88.0	1	Tanintharyi Region
Nyaunglaybin	88.3	2	Bago Region
Pyin U Lwin	88.3	1	Mandalay Region
Taungdwingyi	88.3	2	Magwe Region
Theinni	88.3	0.15	Shan State
Ye-U	88.3	2	Sagaing Region
Maungdaw (Buthidaung)	88.9	2	Rakhine State
Taunggyi	88.9	2	Shan State
Myawaddy	89.0	0.3	Kayin State
Tachilek	89.0	0.3	Shan State
Naypyidaw (Tatkon)	89.2	2	Union Territory
Yanbye	89.2	2	Rakhine State
Kanbalu	89.5	0.3	Sagaing Region
Sittwe	89.8	2	Rakhine State
Kennedy Peak	90.4	2	Chin State
Loikaw	90.7	2	Kayah State
Lashio	91.3	2	Shan State
Mawlamyine	91.3	2	Mon State
Bago	92.5	2	Bago Region
Minbu	92.5	2	Magwe Region
Pathein	92.5	2	Pathein District
Magwe (Popa)	94.3	2	Magwe Region
Sagaing	94.6	2	Sagaing Region
Pyinmana	94.9	2	Union Territory

NB: Approx. 50 additional FM relays are in operation, details not available. FM network carries N prgr, but some FM freqs opt out to carry Mi or Y prgrs in minority languages at times.
Prgr: N=National prgr in Burmese, English. Also language lessons in English and Japanese from Voice of America, Australian Broadcasting Corporation and NHK World. Mi=Upper Myanmar minorities prgr from Naypyidaw in Kachin, Shan, Phalan Chin, Mindat Chin, Rakhine, Wa and Kokang. Y=Lower Myanmar minorities prgr from Yangon in Sakaw Kayin, Po Kayin, Mon, Kayah, Gekho and Gebo. **English** (in N Prgr): 0230-0330, 0700-0730, 1530-1630. **N:** Generally 30 mins past the UTC h on N prgr; in English on N prgr at 0230, 0700, 1530. **Mayu FM:** 2330-0330, 0930-1330 in Burmese, Rakhine and Rohingya on Maungdaw (Buthidaung) 90.1MHz
Ann: E: 'This is Myanma Radio' IS: Myanma Orchestral Music

THAZIN RADIO (Mil.)
Tatmadaw Broadcasting, Thin Village, Pyin U Lwin ☎ +95 33 60165 **W:** thazinfm.com.mm
Operated by the Directorate of Public Relations and Psychological Warfare, Ministry of Defence
Station (MW/SW): Thin Village, Pyin U Lwin

MW	kW	Pr	H. of tr.
639	400	M	2330-0200, 0430-0700, 0930-1500

SW	kW	Pr	H. of tr.
6165	100	Mi	2330-0130

SW	kW	Pr	H. of tr.
7345	100	Mi	0930-1330
9590	100	Mi	0130-0330, 0430-0830

Thazin FM: 2230-1630 in Burmese. Bago/Magwe/Naypyidaw/Taunggyi 87.6MHz, Hakha/Lashio/Meikhtila/Myeik/Sagaing/Sittwe/Yangon 88.6MHz, Myitkyina 89.2MHz, Monywa/Pathein/Pyin U Lwin/Tachilek 89.5MHz, Dawei/Muse 91.0MHz

Pr=Prgr: M=Main prgr in Burmese, exc.English 0130-0200, 0630-0700, 1430-1500. Mi=minorities prgr in Chin, Kachin, La, Po, Geba, Kokang, Karen, Shan, Kayah, Gekho and Mon.

Other Stations:
Cherry FM (Comm.) Operated by Zay Kaba Co. ✉ Pyay Garden Residence & Office Tower, 346 Pyay Rd, Yangon. **FM:** Hpa-an/Kawkareik 88.3MHz, Yangon 89.3MHz, Loikaw/Muse 89.5MHz, Hsipaw/Kunlong/Kyaingtong/Lashio/Laukkaing/Pyin U Lwin/Tachilek/Taunggyi 89.8MHz, Pathein 91.3MHz, Sagaing 92.2MHz, Naypyidaw/Pyay 92.5MHz, Popa 93.1MHz – **City FM (FM-89) (Gov.)** ✉ 573 Pyay Rd, Kamayut Township, Yangon ☎ +95 1 536042 **FM:** Yangon 89.0MHz – **FM Bagan (Comm.)** Operated by Htoo Co. ✉ A-2, Min Dhama Road, Mayangone Township, Yangon ☎ +95 1 655301-3 **W:** fmbagan.com **FM:** Popa 88.3MHz, Ganga/Kennedy Peak 89.2MHz, Hakha/Minbu 89.8MHz, Yangon 89.9MHz, Sagaing 93.4MHz, Mawlamyine/Pyinmana/Taunggyi 93.7MHz, Myeik 94.6MHz, Pathein/Pyay 94.9MHz – **Khayae FM (Community R.) FM:** Htantabin 104.8MHz – **Mandalay FM (Gov.)** Joint venture of Forever Group and Mandalay City Development Committee (MCDC). ✉ Mandalay. Yangon office: Rm 1402-3, Olympic Twr, Bo Aung Kyaw St, Yangon.**FM:** Mandalay (Sagaing Hill)/Taungoo/Yangon 87.9MHz, Naypyidaw 88.3MHz, Hpa-an 90.4MHz, Minhla 90.7MHz, Bago 96.1MHz – **Myanmar International Radio (MIRadio) (Comm.)** Operated by Monnect Group Co. Ltd. ✉ Room 05-05, 53 Strand Rd, Yangon **W:** miradio.com.mm **FM:** Yangon 96.1MHz, Mandalay 96.5MHz, Naypyidaw 96.7MHz in English – **Padamyar FM (Comm.) (Ruby FM)** Operated by Thein Kyaw Kyaw Co. ✉ 301-305 Crystal Office Tower, Kyun Taw Street, Kamayut Township, Yangon ☎ +95 1 9339293 **W:** padamyarfm.com **FM:** Yangon 88.2, Kanbalu/Monywa 88.6MHz, Bhamo/Katha/Myitkyina/Nam Mar/Sagaing 88.9MHz, Naypyidaw 89.5MHz, Bilin/Minbu/Popa 90.7MHz, Bago/Pyay 91.3MHz, Taunggyi 92.2MHz, Mawlamyine 92.5MHz, Pathein 93.7MHz – **Pyinsawaddy FM (Teen Radio) (Comm.)** Operated by Forever Group. ✉ Rm 1402-3, Olympic Twr, Bo Aung Kyaw St, Yangon ✉ Sittwe, Rakhine State. **FM:** Labutta 87.9MHz, Sitwe 88.3MHz, Pathein/Thandwe 88.9MHz, Bogale 90.4MHz, Yangon 91.0MHz, Kyaungon 100.6MHz – **Shwe FM (Comm.) (Gold FM)** Operated by Shwe Thanlwin Co. ✉ 131/133 Botahtaung Pagoda Road, Yangon ☎ +95 1 9010082 **W:** shwefmradio.com **FM:** Bilin/Nyaunglaybin/Pyay 89.5MHz, Yangon 89.6MHz, Bago/Dawei/Hpa-an/Kawthaung/Kyaikto/Mawlamyine/Myawaddy/Myeik/Taungoo 89.8MHz, Sagaing/Taunggyi 91.0MHz, Naypyidaw 91.3MHz, Popa 91.9MHz

NAMIBIA

L.T: UTC +2h — **Pop:** 2.6 million — **Pr.L:** English (official), Afrikaans, German, Oshiwambo — **E.C:** 220V/50Hz — **ITU:** NMB

COMMUNICATIONS REGULATORY AUTHORITY OF NAMIBIA (CRAN)

✉ Private Bag 13309, Communication House, 56 Robert Mugabe Ave, Windhoek ☎+264 61 222666 🖷 + 264 61 238646 **W:** www.cran.na **E:** info@cran.na **L.P:** CEO: Stanley Shanapinda. Head Eng.: Ronel le Grange.

NAMIBIAN BROADCASTING CORPORATION (Pub.)

✉ P.O. Box 321, Pettenkofer Str, Windhoek West 9000 ☎+264 61 2919111 🖷 + 264 61 2913325 **W:** nbc.na **E:** pr@nbc.na

FM (MHz)	**Hart**	**Nat**	**Funk**	**Kati**	**Omu**	**Kai**	**Nwa**	**TYS**	**Wat**
Aminuis	88.9	92.0	-	-	95.2	-	-	98.5	-
Andara	-	92.5	-	95.7	-	-	102.5	-	-
Aroab	87.9	94.2	-	-	-	104.6	-	-	-
Aus	92.5	-	95.8	102.6	-	106.2	-	-	-
Aussenkehr	92.5	95.7	-	98.7	-	102.5	-	-	-
Bethanien	88.1	91.2	94.4	97.7	101.2	104.8	-	-	-
Brukkaros	90.2	96.5	-	-	-	106.9	-	-	-
Buitepos	-	95.0	-	98.3	101.8	-	-	105.4	-
Ekuli	-	91.5	-	88.4	-	-	98.0	-	-
Epukiro	91.6	98.1	-	-	101.6	-	-	105.2	-
Erongo	90.6	93.7	96.9	100.2	103.7	107.3	-	-	-
Gam	-	92.6	-	102.6	99.1	-	-	-	95.8
Gibeon	-	-	-	-	-	100.7	-	-	-
Gobabis	87.6	90.7	93.9	102.9	100.7	104.3	92.9	97.2	-
Grossherzog Fr.	88.6	91.7	94.9	98.2	101.7	105.3		-	-
Kamanjab	89.7	-	-	-	-	106.4	-	-	-
Katima Mulilo	89.5	92.6	90.9	99.1	94.1	106.2	95.8	87.8	-
Keetmanshoop	87.6	90.7	93.9	97.2	89.3	104.3	-	-	-
Kl. Waterberg	89.6	92.7	95.9	99.2	102.7	106.3	-	-	-
Koës	88.8	95.1	-	-	-	105.5	-	-	-
Kongola	-	88.3	-	91.4	-	-	97.9	-	-
Lüderitz	89.7	92.8	96.0	99.3	100.2	103.7	-	-	-
Maltahöhe	88.5	-	94.8	-	-	105.2	-	-	-
Mariental	87.7	90.8	94.0	101.8	105.4	104.4	-	-	-
Nakop	90.6	93.7	-	100.2	-	103.7	-	-	-
Nkurenkuru	-	90.7	-	87.6	97.2	-	93.9	-	-
Noordoewer	87.7	90.8	-	97.3	-	100.8	-	-	-
Okongo	-	89.0	-	92.1	-	95.3	-	-	-
Omega	-	89.4	-	92.5	-	-	99.0	-	-
Omuthiya	-	89.2	-	98.8	102.3	105.9	-	-	-
Opuwo	-	91.1	-	97.6	101.1	-	-	-	-
Oranjemund	90.0	93.1	-	99.6	-	106.7	-	-	-
Oshakati	89.2	87.8	96.4	97.4	98.8	105.9	90.9	99.7	-
Otjimbingwe	-	-	-	-	102.3	105.9	-	-	-
Otjinene	90.2	93.5	-	-	96.7	-	-	103.5	-
Paresis	88.7	91.8	95.0	98.3	101.8	105.4	-	-	-
Renosterkop	87.9	91.0	-	-	101.0	104.6	-	-	-
Rietfontein	-	92.2	-	89.1	95.4	-	-	98.7	-
Rosh Pinah	90.3	93.4	-	96.6	-	99.9	-	-	-
Rundu	88.7	90.1	91.8	96.4	99.7	106.8	95.0	98.3	103.2
Rössing	89.7	92.8	96.0	99.3	101.1	106.4	-	-	-
Rundu	-	89.6	-	-	-	-	-	-	-
Sesfontein	-	91.6	-	98.1	101.6	105.2	-	-	-
Shamvura	-	91.3	-	97.8	-	-	104.9	-	-
Signalberg	87.7	90.8	94.0	97.3	100.8	104.4	-	-	-
Stampriet	89.7	92.8	96.0	-	-	106.4	-	-	-
Terrace Bay	-	104.3	-	-	-	-	-	-	-
Tsumeb	88.6	91.7	94.9	98.2	-	105.3	-	-	-
Tsumkwe	-	90.4	-	100.0	93.5	-	-	-	103.5
Ur	89.8	92.9	96.1	99.4	102.9	106.5	-	-	-
Windhoek	89.5	92.6	95.8	-	-	-	93.5	90.4	-

Hartklop FM (Hart) in Afrikaans: 24h – **National FM (Nat)** in English: 24hrs – **Funkhaus Namibia (Funk)** in German: 24h – **Kati FM (Kati)** in Oshivambo: 0350-2200 – **Omurari FM (Ormu)** in Otjihero: 0300-2200 – **Kaisames FM (Kai)** in Damara/Nama: 0500-2000 – **Nwanyi FM (Nwa)** in Lozi: 0400-2200 (SS 1900) – **Tirelo ya Setswana (TYS)** in Tswana: 0500-2000 – **Wato FM (Wat)** in Kwangali, Rumanyo, Rugciriku, Thimbukushu: 0400-2200 (SS 1900).
Also **R. Opuwo:** Rundu, 103.2MHz 5kW.

OTHER STATIONS, main networks (FM MHz):
Energy 100 FM: Walvis Bay 88.8 0.5kW, Tsumeb 99.1 0.5kW, Klein Windhoek 100.0 0.5kW, Rundu 100.7 5kW, Oshakati 100.9 2kW **W:** energy100fm.com . In English
Fresh FM: Otjiwarongo 87.8 1kW, Swakpomund 89.3, Oshakati 90.1, Grootfontein 91.3 1kW, Tsumeb 91.4 0.5kW, Rundu 102.7 0.5kW, Windhoek 102.9 1kW **W:** freshfm.com.na . In Enlissh
Hitradio Namibia: Otjiwarongo 90.0 5kW, Tsumeb 90.4 5kW, Swakopmund 97.5 1kW, Windhoek 99.5 5kW, Oshakati 101.1 5kW **W:** hitradio.com.na . In German
JACC FM: Lüderitz 93.7, Swapakopmund 94.3, Omaruru 94.6, Henties Bay 95.1, Grootfontein 95.2, Oshakati 95.5, Oranjemund 97.3, Usakos 98.7, Okahandja/Windhoek 103.5. All 0.5/1kW + a dozen more tx's of 0.1kW **W:** jacc.com.na . In English
Kanaal 7: Buitebos/Gamsberg 88.1 1kW, Oshakati 90.9 0.5kW, Gobabis 92.4 1kW, Outapi 94.3 1kW, Klein Vaterberg 97.7 2kW, Swakopmund 98.4 1kW, Soutblok 101.6 0.5kW, Rundu 101.8 0.5kW, Koës 101.9 0.5kW, Duineweld/Klein Windhoek 102.3 1kW, Lüderitz/Rössing/Stampriet 102.8 0.5/5kW, Tsumeb 103.0 1kW, Noordoever 104.4 1kW, Windhoek 104.5 1kW, Tsumeb 107.0 1kW + 10 more tx's of 0.1kW. **W:** k7.com.na . Rlg. in Afrikaans.
Kosmos: Klein Windhoek 94.1, Rundu 95.9, Mariental 98.3, Erongoberg 101.4, Otjiwarongo 104.5, Gobabis 105.4, Grootfontein 105.6, Tsumeb 106.2, Keetmanshoop 107.7. All 0.5/1kW **W:** www.kosmos.com.na In Afrikaans
Omulunga R: Otjiwarongo 87.8 0.1kW, Grootfontein 92 0.1kW, Mariental 95.0 0.1kW, Rundu 99.2 0.1kW, Rehoboth/Windhoek

100.9 1kW, Ongwediva/Oshakati 102.3 1kW, Swakopmund/Walvis Bay 105.5 0.1kW, Keetmanshoop 106 0.1kW, Lüderitz 106,4 0.1kW, Gobabis 107.5 0.1kW **W:** omulunga.com.na . In Oshiwambo

Radiowave: Windhoek 87.8 5kW, Mareintal 91.8 0.5kW, Usakos 92.2 1kW, Tsumeb 95.8 1kW, Klein Windhoek 96.7 1.5kW, Katima Mulilo 104.5 0.35kW, Rundu 105.4 0.35kW, Gobabis 106.0 1kW, Oshakati 106.8 0.35kW + 8 more tr's 0.1kW **W:** radiowave.com.na In English

99 FM: Walvis Bay & Swakopmund 96.5, Windhoek 99.0, Otjiwarango 99.9, Tsumeb 101.7, Oshakati & Ondangwa 104.5 **W:** 99fm.com.na. In English

West Coast FM: Walvis Bay 106.9 0.5kW, Swakopmund 107.7 0.5kW **W:** westcoastfmnamibia.com . In English

R. France Int, Windhoek: 107.9MHz 1kW in English/French

NAURU

L.T: UTC +12h — **Pop:** 11,843 — **Pr.L:** English, Nauruan — **E.C:** 50Hz, 110/240V — **ITU:** NRU

NAURU BROADCASTING SERVICE (Gov)
Nauru Media Bureau, Home Affairs Department

P O Box 429, Rep. of Nauru, Ce. Pacific ☎ +674 4443190 🖷 +674 4443153 **E: (none listed)**

FM: ‡105.1MHz (Government of the Republic of Nauru website states "On behalf of Radio Nauru. The public is advised that due to hardware failure, Radio Nauru is off the air via radio transmission until further notice. However Radio Nauru can still be accessed via the app radionauru.nr:8000/live" This live stream is not working either at present.

NEPAL

L.T: UTC +5¾h — **Pop:** 25.3 million — **Pr.L:** Nepali (official), Bhojpuri (official), Maithili (official), English — **E.C:** 230V/50Hz — **ITU:** NPL

MINISTRY OF COMMUNICATIONS & INFORMATION TECHNOLOGY (MOCIT)

Kathmandu 44600 ☎ +977 1 4211556 🖷 +977 1 4211729 **E:** info@mocit.gov.np **W:** mocit.gov.np **L.P:** Minister: Gokul Prasad Baskota

RADIO NEPAL (Pub, Comm.)

Radio Broadcasting Service, G.P.O. Box 634, Singha Durbar, Kathmandu ☎+977 1 4231804 🖷+977 1 4221952 **W:** radionepal.gov.np **E:** program@radionepal.gov.np **E:** engg@wlink.com.np (Eng. div: ☎+977 1 4211842)

L.P: Exec. Dir: Er. R.S. Karki. Dep. Exec. Dirs: Mr Rajendra Prasad Sharma & Mr Sushil Koirala. Chief Eng.: Er. Ramesh Jung Karkee

MW	kHz	kW	MW	kHz	kW
Surkhet	576	100	Kathmandu	792	100
Dhankuta	648	100	Dipayal	810	10
Pokhara	684	100	Bardibas	1143	10

SW: Khumaltar 5005kHz 100kW/5kW (‡, but irr.15-20kW test with open carrier or dummy load 0815-1115) **F.Pl.:** New 100kW DRM-capable tx.

D.Prgr on MW/SW: 2315-1720. **N.** in **Nepali** at 0015, 0115, 0315, 0415, 0515, 0615, 0715, 0915, 1015, 1115, 1315, 1515, 1715**; Other language N.** in **English:** 0215, 0815, 1415; in **Sanskrit** 0010; in **Sherpa** 1020; in **Tamang** 1120; in **Bhojpuri** 1205; in **Urdu** 1210; in **Maithili** 1215; in **Hindi**: 1615; **Variation at Regional Centres:** 0400-0415 & 1215-1300. **Sponsored Prog Madhurima** on Thu and Sat at 1625

Ann: Nepali: 'Yo Radio Nepal Ho'; English: 'This is Radio Nepal'

IS: Instruments used are conch shell, violin, piano and jal tarang

V. by QSL-card

FM STATIONS:

FM	MHz	Station
Achhaam	88.2	R. Vaijnath FM
Achhaam	92.0	R. Ramaroshan
Arghakhanchi	101.0	R. Deurali
Arghakhanchi	105.8	R. Argakhanchi
Baglung	91.6	Saypatri FM
Baglung	96.4	Baglung FM
Baglung	98.6	Dhaulagiri FM
Baglung	104.1	R. Dhorpatan
Baglung	107.4	Sarathi FM#
Baitadi	103.6	Saugat FM
Baitadi	106.6	R. Sansher
Bajhang	93.6	Seti FM
Bajhang	98.0	R. Nepal
Bajhang	100.6	Saipal R
Bajura	104.0	R. Bajura
Banke	88.4	R. Xpress FM
Banke	94.0	R. Krishnasar
Banke	94.6	R Bageshori
Banke	95.6	R Bheri Aawaj
Banke	96.8	Youth FM#
Banke	97.3	R Jana Aawaj
Banke	97.9	Image FM
Banke	101.2	R. Kohalpu
Banke	101.8	Kantipur FM
Banke	102.4	R. Pratibodh
Banke	104.2	Naya Nepal Sanchar
Banke	104.5	R. Rubaru
Banke	104.8	Nepalgunj FM
Banke	105.4	Bheri FM
Bara	88.8	Sanskar FM#
Bara	106.0	R. Simara
Bardiya	100.6	Fulbari FM
Bardiya	106.0	R. Babai
Bardiya	106.4	R. Gurubaba
Besisahar	95.0	R. Marsyangdi#
Bhairahawa	98.8	Siddhartha FM
Bhairahawa	102.0	Rupandehi FM
Bhaktapur	88.8	NepaliKo R.
Bhaktapur	105.4	Bhaktapur FM#
Bharatpur	91.0	Kalika FM#
Bharatpur	91.6	Synergy FM#
Bharatpur	94.0	Hamro FM#
Bharatpur	94.6	Chitawan FM
Bharatpur	95.2	Kalika FM#
Bharatpur	96.1	Kantipur FM
Bharatpur	96.8	V. of Youth FM#
Bharatpur	97.9	Image FM
Bhedetar	90.0	Saptakoshi FM#
Bhedetar	96.8	V. of Youth FM#
Bhedetar	97.9	Image FM
Bhojpur	98.6	R. Chomolungma
Bhojpur	103.6	R. Bhojpur
Biratnagar	88.2	Kankai Sangeet
Biratnagar	91.2	Birat FM
Biratnagar	94.3	Koshi FM
Biratnagar	105.6	SaptaKoshi FM#
Biratnagar	106.7	Sky FM
Birgunj	91.4	Gadimai FM
Birgunj	92.2	Kalika FM#
Birgunj	96.1	Kantipur FM
Birgunj	96.8	V. of Youth FM#
Birgunj	97.0	Image FM
Birgunj	97.6	Indreni FM#
Birgunj	99.0	Birgunj FM
Birgunj	100.0	R. Nepal
Birgunj	103.8	Narayani FM#
Birgunj	105.4	Star FM
Birtamod	92.6	Kanchanjunga FM
Birtamod	105.0	Kankai Samaaj
Buditola	100.0	R. Nepal
Butwal	92.2	Kalika FM#
Butwal	92.8	R. Namaste
Butwal	93.6	Jagaran R.
Butwal	94.4	Butwal FM#
Butwal	96.1	Kantipur FM
Butwal	97.9	Image FM
Butwal	98.2	Tinau FM#
Butwal	99.4	R. Jagran
Byash	105.8	Madi Seti FM
Chainpur	100.6	Saipal R.
Chainpur	105.2	R. Kailash
Chainpur	106.6	Saipal R.
Charpane	103.6	R. Kechana
Chitawan	89.8	R. Dhruvatara
Chitawan	91.0	Kalika FM#
Chitawan	91.6	Synergy FM#
Chitawan	94.0	Hamro FM#
Chitawan	94.6	R Chitawan
Chitawan	95.2	Kalika FM#
Chitawan	96.1	Kantipur FM
Chitawan	96.8	Youth FM#
Chitawan	97.9	Image FM
Chitawan	100.6	R. Triveni#
Chitawan	103.0	R. Nepal
Chitawan	104.5	R. Arpan
Chitawan	105.2	R. Narayani
Chitawan	107.6	R. Madi
Dadeldhura	95.0	R. Sudur Aawaj
Dadeldhura	96.0	Paschim Nepal Media
Dadeldhura	97.4	Vikash Nyaya Manch
Dadeldhura	104.8	Aafno FM
Dailekh	89.8	R. Dhurbatara FM
Dailekh	104.0	R. Panchakoshi FM#
Damak	91.8	Star FM
Damak	93.6	Pathibhara FM#
Damak	101.6	Saptarangi FM#
Daman	97.0	Prathidhwani FM
Damauli	94.2	Damauli FM
Dang	88.0	R. Jharana
Dang	89.0	R. Hamro Pahuch
Dang	91.4	R Madhya.
Dang	92.4	Indreni FM#
Dang	93.4	R. Prakriti
Dang	95.1	R. Ganatantra Rapti
Dang	98.0	R. Nepal
Dang	100.2	R Tulsipur
Dang	102.8	R Swargadwari
Dang	103.5	R. Highway
Dang	104.0	R. Saryu Ganga
Dang	106.4	Super FM
Dang	107.0	Dang FM
Dang	107.3	R. Naya Yug
Darchula	98.0	R. Nepal
Darchula	102.2	Kalapani FM
Darchula	104.5	R. Naya Nepal
Daunne	100.0	R. Nepal
Dhading	89.4	R. Loktranta FM
Dhading	92.1	Rajmarga Sanchar Kendra
Dhading	97.6	Shree Sahid Smriti Sanchar
Dhading	105.0	Krishi R.
Dhading	105.6	R. Trishuli
Dhading	106.0	R. Dhading#
Dhangadi	89.4	R. Jana Aawaj
Dhangadi	91.4	Khaptad FM
Dhangadi	93.8	Dinesh FM#
Dhangadi	101.8	Kantipur FM
Dhankuta	87.6	Heart FM
Dhankuta	92.2	R. Makalu
Dhankuta	96.1	R Kantipur
Dhankuta	96.8	Youth FM#
Dhankuta	97.9	Image FM
Dhankuta	105.2	R. Laliguransh
Dhankuta	106.2	R. Dhankuta
Dhanusha	91.0	R Today
Dhanusha	93.8	City Sahakari R.
Dhanusha	95.0	Kamalamai FM
Dhanusha	97.0	R Janakpur
Dhanusha	99.4	Mithilanchal FM
Dhanusha	106.0	Janaki FM
Dhanusha	106.6	Mithila Sanchar Samuha
Dharan	95.1	R. Ganatantra
Dharan	95.6	Star FM
Dharan	106.6	Budasubba FM
Dhulikhel	104.0	Madhya. FM
Dolakha	103.4	Hamro R.
Dolakha	104.0	R. Sailung
Dolakha	106.0	Gaurishankar FM
Dolakha	106.4	R. Kalinchowk
Dolakha	108.8	Chyomongmo Media Pvt. Ltd.
Dolpa	100.0	R. Nepal
Dolpa	106.3	Se Foksundo Sanchar
Doti	94.4	Triveni FM
Doti	105.9	R. Shaileshwari FM
Gaidakot	101.6	Vijay FM
Ghorahi	91.4	R. Madhya.
Ghorahi	102.8	R. Swargadwari FM
Godawari	104.2	ECR FM
Gorkha	102.4	R. Manakamana
Gorkha	103.6	Gorakhkali FM
Gorkha	103.9	R. Manaslu
Gorkha	104.6	R. Lamjung
Gorkha	105.4	R. Harmi
Gorkha	106.4	Deurali FM
Gorkha	107.2	Mero Saathi

FM	MHz	Station
Gulariya	100.6	Phoolbari FM
Gulmi	88.4	R. Sky FM
Gulmi	91.2	R. Gulmi
Gulmi	94.8	Ruru FM
Gulmi	100.0	R. Nepal
Gulmi	106.2	R Resunga
Hetauda	90.4	National FM
Hetauda	92.9	Manakamana FM
Hetauda	96.6	Hetauda FM#
Hetauda	103.4	Shakti FM
Humla	94.2	Ekikrit Vikash Kendra
Humla	96.8	V. of Youth FM#
Humla	100.0	R. Nepal
Humla	101.4	Sarkegad FM
Humla	103.4	R. Kailash
Illam	90.6	R. Fikkal FM
Illam	93.0	Illam FM
Illam	94.9	R. Nepalbani
Illam	100.0	R. Nepal
Illam	104.0	Sandakpur FM
Itahari	107.2	Namaste FM
Jajarkot	97.9	Asal Sashan Jilla Samiti
Jajarkot	105.0	R. Paila
Jajarkot	107.6	Khalanga FM
Jalweshwor	106.7	R. Appan Mithila
Janakpur	91.0	R. Today#
Janakpur	97.0	R. Janakpur
Janakpur	100.8	R. Mithila#
Janakpur	101.8	Janakpur FM#
Janakpur	105.0	Mithilanchal FM
Janakpur	106.0	Janaki FM
Jhapa	88.8	R. Saragam
Jhapa	89.1	Hamro Sanchar Samuha
Jhapa	92.6	Kanchanjungha FM
Jhapa	96.8	FM Mechi Tunes
Jhapa	101.6	Saptarangi FM#
Jhapa	103.9	R. Sandesh
Jhapa	105.0	Birta FM
Jhapa	105.9	R. Sunrise
Jhapa	106.9	Seemana FM
Jhapa	107.5	Nagarik FM#
Jomsom	100.0	R. Nepal
Jumla	100.0	R. Nepal
Jumla	100.6	Hamro Aawaj Hamro Sarokar
Jumla	105.2	R. Karnali FM#
Kailali	87.9	Godavari FM#
Kailali	88.8	Paschim Today FM
Kailali	91.4	Ghodaghodi FM
Kailali	93.2	Fulbari FM
Kailali	93.8	Dinesh FM#
Kailali	98.2	Khaptad FM
Kailali	101.0	Tikapur FM
Kailali	101.8	Kantipur FM
Kailali	103.0	R. Nepal
Kailali	103.7	R. Kailali FM#
Kailali	105.3	Sita Sanchar Samuha
Kailali	105.6	Ujyalo Sudur Paschhim
Kailali	107.0	Hamra Malika FM
Kailali	107.3	Hamro Fulbari FM
Kalikot	100.0	R. Nepal
Kalikot	101.2	R. Bhek Aawaj
Kalikot	101.8	R. Chulimalika
Kalikot	102.8	R. Malika
Kalyanpur	106.8	Nuwakot FM
Kamalamai	103.6	R. Sindhuligadi
Kanchanpur	104.3	Angel FM
Kapilvastu	89.6	R. Buddha Aawaj
Kapilvastu	104.2	R. Kapilvastu#
Kapilvastu	105.4	R. Samanata
Kapilvastu	106.1	Janakpur Sanchar Samuha
Kapilvastu	107.6	Tilarakot R. FM
Kaski	87.9	R. Chhunumunu
Kaski	90.6	R. Gandaki
Kaski	91.0	Machhapucchre FM
Kaski	92.2	Himchuli FM#
Kaski	93.4	R Annapurna
Kaski	95.8	Pokhara FM
Kaski	96.8	Youth FM#
Kaski	97.9	Image FM
Kaski	99.6	Annapurna Music FM
Kaski	101.2	Big FM
Kaski	101.8	Kantipur FM
Kaski	102.2	Sunaulo FM
Kaski	102.6	R. Apostle
Kaski	103.4	R. Safalta
Kaski	106.0	Gorkhali R.
Kaski	106.6	R. Lekhnath
Kaski	107.6	Tarang Pvt. Ltd
Kathmandu	87.6	R. Upatyaka
Kathmandu	88.2	Jana Sandesh
Kathmandu	88.8	Nepaliko R.
Kathmandu	89.4	R. Mirmire
Kathmandu	90.6	Times FM
Kathmandu	91.2	Hits FM
Kathmandu	91.8	Nepal FM
Kathmandu	92.4	Capital FM
Kathmandu	93.0	Gorkha FM
Kathmandu	93.5	R. Jana Sandesh
Kathmandu	94.0	HBC FM
Kathmandu	94.6	Metro FM
Kathmandu	95.2	Star FM
Kathmandu	96.8	V. of Youth FM#
Kathmandu	97.9	Image FM
Kathmandu	98.3	Keeps Media
Kathmandu	98.8	R. City FM
Kathmandu	99.4	Maittri FM
Kathmandu	100.0	R. Nepal
Kathmandu	100.6	RBC FM
Kathmandu	101.8	GopiKrishna FM
Kathmandu	103.0	BBC WS#
Kathmandu	103.6	R. Bagmati
Kathmandu	104.8	FM Adhyatma Jyoti
Kathmandu	105.1	Good News FM
Kathmandu	106.0	CJMC FM#
Kathmandu	106.3	R. Audio
Kathmandu	107.0	TU FM
Kavre	87.9	R. Masti#
Kavre	88.4	R. Shepherd
Kavre	89.8	R ABC
Kavre	104.0	Madhyapurva FM
Kavre	104.5	R. Naya Sandesh
Kavre	106.7	R. Namobuddha
Kavre	107.3	R. Janasanchar
Kavre	107.6	Grace FM
Khalanga	92.0	R. Pyuthan
Khalanga	101.0	R. Salyan
Khanigau	103.6	R. Parbat
Khotang	102.4	R. Haleshi
Khotang	105.0	Rupakot R.
Kirtipur	106.7	Newa FM
Kohalpur	101.2	R. Kohalpur
Lahan	102.6	Samad FM
Lahan	105.4	Fulbari R.
Lalitpur	90.0	Ujyaalo FM
Lalitpur	96.1	Kantipur FM
Lalitpur	97.2	Headlines & Music FM
Lalitpur	100.0	R. Nepal
Lalitpur	100.9	R. Lalipur
Lalitpur	101.2	Classic FM
Lalitpur	102.4	R. Sagarmatha#
Lalitpur	104.2	Paryawaran Chakra R.
Lalitpur	105.7	BFBS or R. Nepal
Lamahi	105.8	R. Deukhuri
Lamjung	88.4	R. Lamjung
Lamjung	95.0	R. Marsyangdi#
Liwang	93.8	R. Rolpa
Mahend.	90.2	Kanchanpur FM
Mahend.	96.2	R. Mahakali
Mahend.	99.4	Suklafanta FM
Mahottari	88.4	R. Darpan
Mahottari	90.4	Jaleshwarnath FM
Mahottari	94.4	R. Appan Mithila
Mahottari	103.4	R. Rudraksha#
Mahottari	103.7	R. Gunjan
Mahottari	107.0	R. Sungava FM
Makwanpur	88.0	Hetauda Media
Makwanpur	88.5	R. Aakash Ganga#
Makwanpur	96.6	Hetauda FM#
Makwanpur	97.0	R. Pratidhwani
Makwanpur	98.0	R. Nepal
Makwanpur	99.6	R. Thaha Sansar
Makwanpur	101.3	R. Makwanpur
Makwanpur	103.4	R. Sakti
Makwanpur	106.6	R. Asmita
Makwanpur	107.2	R. Palung
Mechinagar	96.8	FM Mechi Tunes
Morang	87.9	Jagriti FM
Morang	91.2	B FM
Morang	94.3	Koshi FM
Morang	95.1	Janasanchar Kendra
Morang	101.0	R. Chamatkar
Morang	102.1	R. Makalu
Morang	102.6	R. Sunakhari
Morang	104.4	R. Purwanchal
Morang	104.8	Sajha R.
Morang	105.6	Saptakoshi FM#
Morang	106.3	R. Suseli FM
Morang	106.6	Sky FM
Mugu	100.0	R. Nepal
Mugu	102.2	R. Suryadaya FM
Mugu	104.6	R. Rara
Mugu	106.6	Mugali Chalchitra Vikash Sang
Mugu	107.4	R. Mugu
Musikot	92.8	R. Sisne FM
Mustang	89.0	Gramin Suchana Vikash Kendra
Mustang	96.8	V. of Youth FM#
Mustang	103.0	R. Nepal
Myagdi	88.2	Myagdakali FM
Myagdi	104.4	R. Myagd
Myanglung	104.2	R. Samhaltung
Nawalparasi	90.2	R. Parasi
Nawalparasi	100.0	R. Nepal
Nawalparasi	101.0	R. Madhyavindu FM
Nawalparasi	101.6	Vijaya FM#
Nawalparasi	103.4	Daunne FM
Nepalgunj	94.6	R. Bageshwori
Nepalgunj	95.6	R. Bheri Aawaj#
Nepalgunj	96.8	V. of Youth FM#
Nepalgunj	97.3	R. Jana Aawaj
Nepalgunj	97.9	Image FM
Nepalgunj	101.8	Kantipur FM
Nepalgunj	104.8	R. Nepalgunj
Nilkantha	106.0	Dhading FM
Nuwakot	104.5	R. Jalapa
Nuwakot	107.4	R. Abhiyan
Okhaldhunga	100.6	Ramailo Com. R.
Okhaldhunga	104.8	Afno FM
Okhaldhunga	107.6	R. Okhaldhunga
Palpa	90.8	Muktinath FM
Palpa	93.2	Shrinagar FM
Palpa	99.4	R Paschimanchal
Palpa	103.6	R. Rampur
Palpa	103.9	R. Palpa
Palpa	106.9	R. Madanpokhara#
Palung	107.2	R. Palung FM
Panchthar	97.3	Simhalila FM
Panchthar	99.2	Eagle FM
Panchthar	104.2	Sumhatlung FM
Parbat	95.2	R. Didi Bahini
Parbat	100.6	R. Shaligram
Parsa	91.4	Gadimai FM
Parsa	92.8	Bhojpuriya FM
Parsa	96.1	R. Kantipur
Parsa	96.8	Youth FM#
Parsa	97.6	Indreni FM#
Parsa	97.9	Image FM
Parsa	99.0	R Birganj
Parsa	100.0	R. Nepal
Parsa	101.9	Aakas FM
Parsa	103.8	Narayani FM#
Parsa	105.8	Birgunj Musical FM
Parsa	107.0	R. Tarang
Pokhara	91.0	Machhapuchhre FM
Pokhara	92.2	Himchuli FM#
Pokhara	93.4	R. Annapurna#
Pokhara	95.8	Pokhara FM
Pokhara	96.8	V. of Youth FM#
Pokhara	97.9	Image FM
Pokhara	99.2	R. Barahi FM#
Pokhara	104.6	R. Sarangkot
Prithivinarayan	92.8	R. Gorkha#
Putalibazar	90.2	Syangja FM
Pyuthan	90.0	R. Mahila Aawaj
Pyuthan	92.0	R Pyuthan
Pyuthan	97.0	R. Mandhawi
Pyuthan	103.6	R. Lishne Aawaj
Rajbiraj	105.8	R. Rajbiraj
Ramechhap	88.6	R. Tinlal
Ramechhap	102.1	Hajurko R.
Rasuwa	100.9	Durgam FM
Rasuwa	102.1	Rasuwa FM
Rautahat	89.6	R. Madhes
Rautahat	90.4	R. Jivan Jyoti
Rautahat	90.8	Rautahat FM#
Rautahat	93.2	Rajdevi FM
Rautahat	98.2	R. Sanskriti
Rautahat	98.6	Madhesh Jana Aawaj
Rautahat	102.2	Gaur FM
Rautahat	102.6	R. Nunthar FM
Rolpa	93.8	R. Rolpa
Rolpa	104.5	R. Jaljala
Rukum	89.2	R. Sani Bheri
Rukum	92.8	R. Sisne
Rukum	100.8	R. SanoBheri
Rukum	102.0	Uttarjganga Sanchar Kendra
Rupandehi	88.2	R. Republic
Rupandehi	88.6	R. Malmala
Rupandehi	92.8	Star FM
Rupandehi	93.6	R. Jagaran
Rupamdehi	94.4	Butwal FM#
Rupandehi	95.5	R. Mukti
Rupandehi	96.1	R. Kantipur
Rupandehi	96.8	R. Lumbini#
Rupandehi	97.6	Image FM
Rupandehi	98.2	Tinau FM#
Rupandehi	98.8	Siddhartha FM
Rupandehi	102.0	Rupandehi FM
Rupandehi	105.0	R. Samabesi
Rupandehi	106.6	R. Devdaha
Rupandehi	107.2	Aasha ko Sandesh
Salleri	94.6	R. Dudhkoshi
Salleri	102.2	Solu FM#
Salyan	101.0	R. Salyan
Salyan	102.2	R. Sharada FM
Salyan	103.8	R. Sahara
Salyan	104.8	R. Rapti FM
Salyan	106.1	R. Kapurkot
Sankhuwa.	100.8	R. Arun Sandesh
Sankhuwa.	107.5	Gurans FM
Sankhuwa.	105.8	Khadbari FM
Saptari	91.8	Today FM
Saptari	92.8	Bhorukawa
Saptari	101.4	R. Chhinnamasta
Saptari	102.1	Janak Sanchar Samuha
Saptari	104.6	Appan FM
Sarlahi	89.3	R. Madhes
Sarlahi	94.6	R. Ekata
Sarlahi	104.8	Malangwa FM
Sarlahi	105.6	R. Sarlahi

FM	MHz	Station
Sarlahi	107.4	Mai FM
Siligadi	96.8	V. of Youth FM#
Simikot	100.0	R. Nepal
Sindhuli	92.0	R. Sindhuligadi
Sindhuli	104.2	R. Sahara
Sindhup.	89.1	R. Avarv
Sindhup.	96.8	Youth FM#
Sindhup.	102.8	Sindhu FM
Sindhup.	105.0	R. Sindhu
Siraha	88.1	R. Saugat
Siraha	88.8	Bhaluwahi Samudaik R.
Siraha	107.8	R. Samagra
Solukhumbu	94.6	R. Dudhkoshi
Solukhumbu	101.2	Solu FM#
Solukhumbu	105.3	R. Everest
Sunsari	88.5	Dantakali FM
Sunsari	89.4	R. Jaya Nepal
Sunsari	90.0	Saptakoshi FM#
Sunsari	95.1	Ganatantra FM
Sunsari	95.6	Star FM
Sunsari	96.1	R. Kantipur
Sunsari	98.8	Vijaypur FM
Sunsari	99.5	Popular FM#
Sunsari	103.6	Jana Sanchar Kendra Nepal
Sunsari	107.2	Namaste FM
Surkhet	90.2	R. Surkhet
Surkhet	90.8	Jagaran FM
Surkhet	92.6	R. Himal
Surkhet	98.6	R. Bheri#
Surkhet	101.2	R. Bheka Aawaj
Surkhet	103.4	Bulbule FM
Surkhet	106.7	Himal FM
Syangja	89.2	R. Waling
Syangja	89.6	R. Syangja
Tamghas	106.2	R. Resunga#
Tanahu	88.2	Dhorbarahi FM
Tanahu	88.8	R. Bandipur
Tanahu	94.2	Damauli FM
Tanahu	97.2	R. Tanahun
Tanahu	102.6	R. Devghat
Tanahu	104.2	R. Bhanubhakta
Tansen	90.8	Muktinath FM
Tansen	93.2	Shreenagar FM
Tansen	99.4	R. Paschimanchal
Taplejung	94.0	R. Taplejung
Taplejung	102.0	R. Tamor
Tawlihawa	104.2	R. Kapilbastu
Tehrathum	102.6	R.Menchhyayam
Thulasen	92.0	R. Ramaroshan
Tikapur	101.0	Tikapur FM
Tribhuwan.	92.4	Indreni FM#
Tulsipur	100.2	R. Tulsipur FM#
Udaypur	91.6	Amurta FM
Udaypur	102.4	R. Udayapur
Udaypur	104.0	R. Triyuga
Udaypur	106.8	UK FM#
Walling	105.4	R. Aandhikhola

NB: Madhya. = Madhyapashchim Mahend. = Mahendranagar, Sankhuwa. = Sankhuwasabha, Sindhup. = Sindhupalchok, Tribhuwan. = Tribhuwannagar. #=BBC Nepali rel. daily 0130-0145,1500-1530

Other Stations:
Guru-Baba FM: Bansgadi, 106.4MHz 0.1kW. Prgrs in Tharu
BFBS Radio: Kathmandu 105.7MHz (Nepali & English) ; **Dharan** 107.5MHz

NETHERLANDS

L.T: UTC +1h (28 Mar-31 Oct: +2h) — **Pop:** 17.2 million — **Pr.L:** Dutch — **E.C:** 230V/50Hz — **ITU:** HOL

COMMISSARIAAT VOOR DE MEDIA

✉ Hoge Naarderweg 78, 1217 AH Hilversum ☎ +31 35 7737700 **E:** cvdm@cvdm.nl **W:** www.cvdm.nl

NEDERLANDSE OMROEP STICHTING (NOS)

✉ Mediapark, Journaalplein 1, 1217 ZK Hilversum; Postbus 26600, 1202 JT Hilversum ☎ +31 35 6779222
W: nos.nl **E:** publieksvoorlichting@nos.nl

NTR (PUBLIEKE TAAKOMROEP)

✉ Mediapark, Wim T. Schippersplein 5-7, 1217WD Hilversum or P.O. Box 29000, 1202 MA Hilversum ☎ +31 88 7799 999 **W:** ntr.nl **E:** info@ntr.nl

NEDERLANDSE PUBLIEKE OMROEP (NPO)

✉ Bart de Graaffweg 2, 1217ZL Hilversum or P.O. Box 26444, 1202 JJ Hilversum ☎ +31 35 677 8899 **W:** npo.nl
Representing the following broadcasting organisations: AVROTROS, BNNVARA, EO, Human, KRO-NCRV, MAX, NOS, NTR, VPRO, WNL, PowNed
Dutch national public prgrs are provided by the **NOS**, **NTR** and the broadcasting organisations of the **NPO**.

FM	NPO1	NPO2	NPO3	NPO 4	kW
Alphen ad Rijn-	-		96.5		0.06
Amsterdam	98.6	92.3	96.5	94.5	0.03/0.03/0.03/0.03
Arnhem	98.6	92.9	96.5	92.1	0.06/0.06/0.06/0.06
Den Haag	105.5	92.9	96.5	94.1	0.013/0.04/0.003/0.008
Emmaberg	105.3	93.4	103.9	98.7	10/10/10/10
Eys	-	97.2	-	-	10
Goes	104.4	94.4	99.8	95.0	40/0.1/11/11
Hoogersmilde	91.8	88.0	88.6	94.8	93/93/40/93
Hoorn	98.6	105.1	96.5	-	0.4/0.01/0.4
Hulst	-	107.1	-	-	0.04
IJsselstein	98.9	92.6	96.8	94.3	70/70/70/50
Jirnsum	104.3	-	-	-	0.07
Loon op Zand	-	-	-	98.2	55
Markelo	98.4	104.6	96.2	91.4	80/80/80/80
Mierlo	104.6	92.3	97.1	-	0.03/0.07/0.07
Roermond	104.8	88.2	90.9	94.5	100/100/100/100
Roosendaal	92.1	95.9	96.5	87.6	0.06/0.02/0.03/0.02
Rotterdam	98.6	92.9	97.1	94.7	0.08/0.08/0.04/13
Wageningen	-	-	-	94.7	0.05
West Terschelling	-	89.9	-	-	0.05
Westdorpe	-	97.8	-	-	100
Wieringerwerf	95.0	92.9	97.1	101.6	14/16/16/35

Ann: "Dit is de KRO-NCRV", "Dit is de VPRO" etc. **NPO R. 1:** news, sport; **NPO R. 2** and **NPO 3 FM:** music; **R. 4:** classical music

Regional stations:

FM	Mhz	kW	Location	Station
2)	87.6	8	Mierlo	Omroep Brabant
4)	87.9	15	Goes	Omroep Zeeland
9)	88.7	1	Alkmaar	NH R.
9)	88.9	10	Amsterdam	NH R.
6)	89.1	5	Megen	R. Gelderland
13)	89.3	20	Rotterdam	R West
10)	89.4	10	Hengelo	R. Oost
12)	89.8	25	Lelystad	Omroep Flevoland
6)	90.4	10	Ruurlo	R. Gelderland
5)	90.8	3	Hoogersmilde	R. Drenthe
2)	91.0	15	Roosendaal	Omroep Brabant
2)	91.9	2	Loon op Zand	Omroep Brabant
3)	92.2	25	Jirnsum	Omrop Fryslân
3)	92.5	1	Hoogersmilde	Omrop Fryslân
7)	93.1	4	IJsselstein	R. M Utrecht
11)	93.4	10	Rotterdam	R. Rijnmond
9)	93.9	11	Wieringerwerf	NH R.
1)	95.3	10	Emmaberg	L1 R.
10)	95.6	5	Markelo	R. Oost
2)	95.8	5	Megen	Omroep Brabant
8)	97.5	20	Groningen	R. Noord
7)	97.9	1	Rhenen	R. M Utrecht
10)	99.4	25	Zwolle	R. Oost
6)	99.6	4	Zaltbommel	R. Gelderland
1)	100.3	100	Roermond	L1 R.
6)	103.5	20	Ugchelen	R. Gelderland

+4 low-power relays

Addresses: & other information:
1) Postbus 31, 6200 AA Maastricht ☎ +31 43 850 60 00 🖷 +31 43 850 61 01 **E:** redactie@L1.nl **W:** l1.nl – **2)** Postbus 108, 5600 AC Eindhoven ☎ +31 40 2949494 **E:** info@omroepbrabant.nl **W:** omroepbrabant.nl – **3)** Postbus 7600, 8903 JP Leeuwarden ☎ +31 58 299 7799 **E:** ynfo@omropfryslan.nl **W:** omropfryslan.nl – **4** Kanaalstraat 64,4388BP Oost-Souburg ☎ +31 118 499900 **E:** nieuws@omroepzeeland.nl **W:** omroepzeeland.nl – **5)** Postbus 999, 9400 AZ Assen ☎ +31 592 338080 **E:** redactie@rtvdrenthe.nl **W:** rtvdrenthe.nl – **6)** Postbus 747, 6800 AS Arnhem ☎ +31 26 3713713 **E:** omroep@gelderland.nl **W:** omroepgelderland.nl – **7)** Postbus 1012, 3500 BA Utrecht ☎ +31 30 8500600 🖷 +31 30 8500601 **E:** vraag@rtvutrecht.nl **W:** rtvutrecht.nl – **8)** Postbus 30101, 9700 RP Groningen ☎ +31 50 3199999 **E:** info@rtvnoord.nl and redactie@rtnoord.nl **W:** rtvnoord.nl– **9)** Postbus 9823, 1006AM Amsterdam ☎ +31 88 850 5050 **E:** radio@nhradio.nl **W:** nhradio.nl – **10)** Postbus 1000, 7550BA Hengelo (Ov) ☎ +31 74 2456456 **E:** info@rtvoost.nl **W:** rtvoost.nl – **11)** Postbus 1515, 3000 BM Rotterdam ☎ +31 10 7075 707 **E:** info@rijnmond.nl **W:** rijnmond.nl – **12)** Postbus 567, 8200 AN Lelystad ☎ +31 320 285085 **E:** rtv@omroepflevoland.nl **W:** omroepflevoland.nl – **13)** Postbus 24025, 2490 AA Den Haag ☎ +31 70 3078888 **E:** online@omroepwest.nl **W:** omroepwest.nl

Public local stations in major cities: FM(MHz):
Amsterdam 96.1 FUN X, 99.4 Radio SALTO, 105.2 Radio Zuid Oost (RAZO), 106.8 Radio SALTO, 107.9 Caribbean FM – **Den Haag** 92.0 Den Haag FM 98.4 FUN X – **Rotterdam** 91.8 FUN X– **Utrecht** 96.1 FUN X, 105.7 Bingo FM, 107.7 Bingo FM
Addresses & other information:
FUN X Rotterdam, Lloydstraat 21,3024EA Rotterdam ☎ +31 10

22 14 900 🖷 +31 10 22 14 918 – **FUN X Amsterdam**, Piet Heinkade 181K, 1019HC Amsterdam ☎ +31 20 530 4960 – **FUN X Utrecht**, Hengeveldstraat 29, 3572KH Utrecht ☎ +31 30 303 1250 **Fun X Den Haag**: Laan van 's-Gravenmade 4, 2495AJ, Den Haag ☎ +31 70 317 4900 **W:** funx.nl – **Radio Zuid Oost,(RAZO), RadioSALTO,Caribbean FM** Piet Heinkade 181E, 1019HC Amsterdam ☎ +31 20 638 6386 **W:**salto.nl –**Den Haag FM**: Laan van 's-Gravenmade 4, 2495AJ, Den Haag ☎ +31 70 317 8899 **W:** denhaagfm.nl **E:** info@denhaagfm.nl – **Bingo FM**, postbus 1012, 3500BA Utrecht ☎ +31 30 850 0600 🖷 +31 30 850 0601 **W:** bingofm.nl **E:** info@bingofm.nl

Digital services DAB+:
National Public Radio (NPO): 12C – National Commercial Radio: 11C Regional and commercial Radio North West: 9D – Regional and commercial Radio East: 6B and 6C – Regional and commercial Radio West: 8A – Regional Radio South West: 9D – Regional and commercial Radio South: 7A
MTVNL Regional: 5A, 5B, 7C, 8C, 9C, 11A and 12B
Local (incl. future plans) : 5A, 5C, 6A, 7B, 8B, 8C, 9B, 10B, 10C, 11B and 12D

OTHER STATIONS

MW	kHz	kW	Location	Station
60)	1566	1	Den Haag	Vahon Hindustani R.

LPAM stations on: **675kHz**: Radio Nostalgie,Kollumerzwaag 0.1kW, Radio Calypso,Oostwold 0.1kW, Unique AM 675,Wijchen 0.1kW – **747kHz**: MCB Radio,Alphen aan den Rijn 0.1kW, Radio 4 Brainport,Eindhoven 0.1kW, Cupra Radio,Emmer-Compascuum 0.1kW, Different Radio 747 AM,Nijkerkerveen 0.05kW, Radio0511 (06-18h),Pietersbierum 0.1kW, Radio Seagull (18-06h),Pietersbierum 0.1kW, Radio Vrij Zwolle,Zwolle 0.1kW – **801kHz**: Radio (Jong) Europa (1),Alphen a.d.Rijn 0.1kW, Stem van Drenthe,Hoogeveen 0.1kW – **819kHz**: Studio Denakker,Klazienaveen 0.1kW, Keukenduin,Wassenaar 0.1kW – **828kHz**: Radio President,Hoogvliet 0.05kW, Radio 4 Brainport (daytime),Nuenen 0.1kW Radio Nederwetten,Nuenen 0.1kW – **846kHz**: Haaglanden Radio Internationaal,Honselersdijk 0.1kW, Veluws Genot,Oldebroek 0.1kW, Fryskeheide,Twijzelerheide 0.1kW, Album AM (1),Uden 0.1kW – **891kHz**: HOTRADIO Hits,Huissen 0.1kW – **900kHz**: Theonex AM,Hoogeveen 0.1kW – **918kHz**: Citrus AM,Emst 0.1kW, Radio T-Pot,Gasselternijveen 0.1kW, Radio Monique 963,Velsen-Noord 0.1kW, Radio Sitara FM,Vianen 0.1kW – **1008kHz**: Radio Transparant,Creil 0.1kW, Radio Babylona,Musselkanaal 0.1kW, United AM,Neede 0.1kW, Radio Experience,Wageningen 0.1kW, Impact AM,Wassenaar 0.1kW – **1035kHz**: Neverland AM,Venlo 0.1kW – **1098kHz**: Radio Popcorn,Schiedam 0.1kW, Radio Gasselte,Gasselte 0.05kW,MasterFM,Nuland 0.1kW, Milano Team,Punthorst 0.1kW – **1134kHz**: Eye AM Radio,Alkmaar 0.1kW, Freya AM,Bergen op Zoom,. Japie de portier,Buitenpost 0.1kW, Like FM,Den Bosch 0.05kW,60-AM-Radio,Rotterdam (Noord) 0.1kW, Groove Radio,Wierden 0.1kW – **1179kHz**: Radio Heideruiter,Zwagerbosch 0.1kW, Antenne Domstad,Utrecht 0.1kW – **1224kHz**: Amplivier Radio,Damwald 0.1kW, Radio Emmeloord,Emmeloord 0.1kW, Piratensound,Lemele 0.05kW,Radio 1224,Lunteren 0.1kW, De Rode Adelaar,Waalwijk 0.05kW – **1251kHz**: Album AM (2),Uden 0.1kW – **1287kHz**: Radio Seagull (18-06h),Ternaard 0.1kW, Kilrock,'s-Gravendeel 0.1kW, HOTRADIO Hits ,Bornerbroek 0.1kW – **1332kHz**: Extra AM,Amsterdam 0.1kW, Radio Beilen AM,Beilen 0.1kW, De Parel van Twente,Goor 0.1kW – **1395kHz**: Columbia AM,Aalst 0.1kW, Radio Seabreeze,Grou 0.1kW, Loostad Radio,Apeldoorn 0.1kW, Sterrekijker AM,Elim 0.1kW, Happy AM,Nieuw- en Sint Joosland 0.1kW, Nostalgie AM,Siddeburen 0.1kW, Haaglanden Radio Internationaal,Voorburg 0.1kW – **1467kHz**: Radio Eldorado ,Damwâld 0.1kW, Zuidwest Brabant AM,Heerle 0.1kW, Radio Paradijs,Utrecht 0.1kW, Hit AM,Zwartemeer 0.1kW – **1485kHz**: Radio (Jong) Europa (2),Alphen a.d.Rijn 0.001kW, Radio Impuls,Amersfoort 0.001kW, AMsterdam 1485,Amsterdam 0.001kW, Flashback 1485 AM,Baarn 0.001kW, Radio0511 (06-18u),Bellingwolde 0.001kW, Radio Seagull (18-06u),Bellingwolde 0.001kW, Radio Armada,Blerick 0.001kW, Radio 220,Buitenpost 0.001kW, Radio de Zwarte Hond,Drachten 0.001kW, Radio Jupiter A.M.,Groningen 0.001kW, TalentCast (sundays 07-19h),Groningen 0.001kW, Radio Elvira,Heerhugowaard 0.001kW, Wijkradio,Helvoirt 0.001kW, Midden Groningen AM,Hoogezand 0.001kW, Radio Las Vegas,Hoogezand 0.001kW, Olde Iesel Radio,Lochem 0.001kW, Radio de Vliegende Hollander,Meppel 0.001kW, Radio Koekoek,Rijswijk 0.001kW, Good Country,Rotterdam (Lombardijen) 0.001kW, Radio Colinda,Rozenburg 0.001kW, Monti Radio,'s-Heerenberg 0.001kW, Vintage Music Radio,Vlissingen 0.001kW, Haaglanden Radio Internationaal,Voorburg 0.001kW, Radio Mebo 2,Westerlee 0.001kW, Backyard AM,Zaandijk 0.001kW, Hollands Palet,Zoetermeer 0.001kW, Radio Nomen Nescio,Goes 0.001kW – **1584kHz**: Fidelio Radio,Driebergen-Rijsenburg 0.1kW – **1602kHz**: Radio Flandria,Hemelum 0.1kW, Radio0511 (06-18h),Ternaard 0.1kW. **F.Pl.: 828kHz**: Stichting Middengolf,Utrecht – **918kHz**: Radio Sitara,Vianen – **1134kHz**: Klaassen, Bergen op Zoom – **1179kHz**:Luth, Nieuw Amsterdam 1287kHz: Stichting Audiovisuele Faciliteiten, Malden – **1332kHz**: Telecom Bennekom B.V., Bennekom – **1485kHz**: Akse, Beilen; Broek, Bladel; Engels, Elim; Tiqs B.V., Leiden; Prenter,Schiedam; Stichting Middengolf, Utrecht; Stichting Radio 182 Midden Holland,Waddinxveen.

FM	MHz	kW	Location	Station
20)	87.6	1	Enschede	Joy R.
61)	87.6	45	Hoogersmilde	R. 10
61)	87.7	115	Lelystad	R. 10
61)	87.9	10	Den Bosch	R. 10
61)	88.1	4	Hilversum	R. 10
23)	88.2	1	Ugchelen	100%NL
23)	88.3	2	Wieringerwerf	100%NL
9)	88.4	43	Roosendaal	Slam!
3)	88.6	26	Mierlo	BNR Nieuws R.
57)	88.8	1	Vlissingen	Sublime
61)	88.9	1	Vught	R. 10
23)	89.0	3	Lochem	100%NL
26)	89.1	4	Groningen	R NL Grunn FM
19)	89.1	2	Wieringerwerf	R. Veronica
9)	89.2	1	Venlo	Slam!
20)	89.2	2	Zwolle	R. NL
62)	89.2	1	Amersfoort	EVA R.
61)	89,2	1	Breda	R. 10
61)	89.3	3	Eindhoven	R. 10
23)	89.5	10	Alkmaar	100%NL
23)	89.5	5	Utrecht	100%NL
3)	89.6	5	Hoogersmilde	BNR NieuwsR.
30)	89.6	1	Nieuwbergen	Maasland R.
57)	89.7	2.5	Mierlo	Sublime
57)	89.7	2	Breda	Sublime
11)	89.9	1	Emmen	R. NL
23)	90.0	3	Vlissingen	100%NL
23)	90.0	17	Loon op Zand	100%NL
80)	90.1	1	247Spice	Diemen
23)	90.2	50	Roosendaal	100%NL
11)	90.3	4	Eindhoven	R.NL
57)	90.3	5	Hoogezand	Sublime
57)	90.4	25	Hoorn	Sublime
57)	90.5	8	Rotterdam	Sublime
57)	90.5	15	Hoogersmilde	Sublime
11)	90.5	4	Helmond	R.NL
57)	90.7	50	Ijsselstein	Sublime
57)	90.7	6	Enschede	Sublime
57)	90.8	2	Terneuzen	Sublime
9)	91.0	10	Tjerkgaast	Slam!
9)	91.0	1	Markelo	Slam!
61)	91.1	2	Maastricht	R. 10
9)	91.1	40	Hilversum	Slam!
48)	91.1	1	Gemert	Omroep Centraal
9)	91.2	4	Jirnsum	Slam!
18)	91.3	2	Hoogezand	Simone FM
18)	91.3	1	Stadskanaal	Simone FM
3)	91.3	70	Rotterdam	BNR Nieuws R.
3)	91.3	1	Tilburg	BNR Nieuws R.
3)	91.5	3	Biervliet	BNR Nieuws R.
3)	91.5	10	Eys	BNR Nieuws R.
19)	91.6	4	Amsterdam	R. Veronica
23)	91.9	1	Venlo	100%NL
23)	92.1	10	Emmaberg	100%NL
78)	92.3	1	Rijssen	R. 350
11)	92.4	8	Westdorpe	R. NL
58)	92.4	4	Hoogezand	R. Continu
58)	92.4	2	Ommen	R. Continu
47)	92.9	1	Wellerooi	Maasland R.
44)	93.0	1	Meppel	R. TV Meppel
18)	93.0	2	Assen	Simone FM
61)	93.0	12	Westdorpe	R. 10
9)	93.1	1	Emmen	Slam!
11)	93.1	1	Ommen	R. NL
26)	93.2	8	Jirnsum	Waterstad FM

FM	MHz	kW	Location	Station
71)	93.2	1	Eindhoven	R. JND
11)	93.3	1	Enschede	R. NL
11)	93.3	1	Loon op Zand	R. NL
61)	93.3	1	Vlissingen	R. 10
69)	93.3	1	Amsterdam	Ujala R.
11)	93.5	3	Markelo	R. NL
75)	93.5	1	Beers	Omroep Land van Cuijk
29)	93.6	3	Amsterdam	Wild FM Hit R.
71)	93.6	1	Eindhoven	Radio JND
9)	93.6	6	Zwolle	Slam!
9)	93.7	2	Hoogezand	Slam!
9)	93.7	2	Hengelo	Slam!
40)	93.7	2	Leiden	R. NL
9)	93.8	17	Megen	Slam!
23)	93.8	1	Haarlem	100%NL
61)	93.9	4	Roosendaal	R. 10
19)	94.0	1	Emmen	R. Veronica
72)	94.0	1	Favoriet FM	Zevenaar
11)	94.1	1	Vught	R. NL
11)	94.1	2	Tjerkgaast	R. NL
23)	94.2	1	Hoogersmilde	100%NL
11)	94.5	1	Den Helder	R. NL
23)	94.9	12	Mierlo	100%NL
23)	95.0	2	Amersfoort	100%NL
23)	95.0	4	Nijmegen	100%NL
9)	95.2	25	Alphen aan den Rijn	Slam!
61)	95.2	2.5	Weert	R. 10
3)	95.3	20	Zwolle	BNR Nieuws R.
43)	95.3	2	Scharmer	Regio FM
3)	95.4	1	Emmen	BNR Nieuws R.
3)	95.4	15	Gilze	BNR Nieuws R
3)	95.5	30	Tjerkgaast	BNR Nieuws R.
61)	95.5	1	Mierlo	R. 10
79)	95.6	2	Vianen	SRC FM
13)	95.7	5	Amsterdam	QMusic
11)	95.7	1	Meppel	R. NL
13)	95.9	3	Alphen a.d.Rijn	QMusic
58)	96.0	2	Wieringerwerf	R. Continu
66)	96.2	1	Zoetermeer	ZFM
19)	96.3	20	Loon op Zand	R. Veronica
29)	96.3	1	Alkmaar	Wild FM Hitradio
76)	96.5	2	Oostburg	Scheldemond FM
19)	96.6	1	Goes	R. Veronica
11)	96.6	1	Leeuwarden	R. NL
11)	97.0	2	Hoogeveen	R. NL
11)	97.1	1	Assen	R. NL
19)	97,1	1	Vlissingen	R. Veronica
29)	97.3	2	Haarlem	Wild FM Hitradio
29)	97.4	1	Almere	Wild FM Hitradio
63)	97.6	2	Maastricht	Q-Music Limburg
36)	97.6	36	Rotterdam	R. Decibel
19)	97.7	8	Arnhem	R. Veronica
19)	97.7	6	Mierlo	R. Veronica
63)	97.7	15	Landgraaf	Q-Music Limburg
19)	97.8	2	Ijsselstein	R. Veronica
58)	97.9	3	Tjerkgaast	R Continu
36)	98.0	12	Amsterdam	R. Decibel
58)	98.2	3	Jirnsum	Radio Continu
36)	98.3	15	Alkmaar	R. Decibel
20)	98.5	2	Groningen	Joy R.
20)	98.5	1	Tjerkgaast	Joy R.
63)	98.5	1	Weert	Q-Music Limburg
20)	98.7	20	Hoogersmilde	Joy R.
23)	99.1	15	Enschede	100%NL
23)	99.1	3	Hoogezand	100%NL
23)	99.1	5	Tjerkgaast	100%NL
32)	99.1	1	Geleen	Bie Os
9)	99.2	9	Vlissingen	Slam!
9)	99.4	30	Mierlo	Slam!
9)	99.4	1	Breda	Slam!
36)	99.4	2	Den Haag	R. NL
68)	99.5	2	Hengelo	R. Ideaal
9)	99.6	25	Hoorn	Slam!
11)	99.6	3	Rotterdam	R. NL
9)	99.6	6	Hoogersmilde	Slam!
3)	99.9	1	Dedemsvaart	BNR Nieuws R.
3)	99.9	3	Ugchelen	BNR Nieuws R.
3)	99.9	27	Wormer	BNR Nieuws R.
3)	100.1	60	IJsselstein	BNR Nieuws R.
3)	100.1	4	Nijmegen	BNR Nieuws R.
3)	100.2	20	Lochem	BNR Nieuws R.
13)	100.4	25	Westdorpe	QMusic
13)	100.4	7	Roosendaal	QMusic
13)	100.4	20	Rotterdam	QMusic
13)	100.4	95	Hoogersmilde	Qmusic
13)	100.4	25	Doetinchem	QMusic
13)	100.5	5	Wieringerwerf	QMusic
13)	100.5	2	Nijmegen	QMUsic
13)	100.7	10	Vlissingen	QMusic
13)	100.7	6	Hengelo	QMusic
13)	100.7	68	IJsselstein	QMusic
13)	100.7	10	Lichtenvoorde	Qmusic
24)	101.0	93	Hoogersmilde	Sky R.
24)	101.1	5	Nijmegen	Sky R.
24)	101.2	200	Hilversum	Sky R.
24)	101.2	1	Biervliet	Sky R.
24)	101.2	32	Enschede	Sky R.
24)	101.3	5	Roosendaal	Sky R.
24)	101.4	10	Deventer	Sky R.
24)	101.5	4	Arnhem	Sky R.
24)	101.5	8	Rotterdam	Sky R.
24)	101.5	7	Vught	Sky R.
24)	101.6	5	Mierlo	Sky R.
24)	101.6	2	Roermond	Sky R.
24)	101.7	2	Gilze	Sky R.
18)	101.7	2	Emmen	Simone FM
24)	101.8	5	Boxtel	Sky R.
24)	101.9	8	Tilburg	Sky R.
24)	101.9	36	Goes	Sky R.
11)	101.9	1	Zieuwent	R. NL
14)	101.9	3	Megen	R. 538
14)	102.1	100	Hilversum	R. 538
14)	102.2	10	Hoogersmilde	R. 538
14)	102.3	13	Alkmaar	R. 538
14)	102.3	40	De Mortel	R. 538
14)	102.3	15	Lochem	R. 538
14)	102.3	2	Roermond	R. 538
14)	102.4	1	Arnhem	R. 538
14)	102.4	1	Amsterdam	R. 538
14)	102.4	20	Westdorpe	R. 538
14)	102.4	1	Dedemsvaart	R. 538
14)	102.5	8	Tilburg	R. 538
14)	102.5	100	Tjerkgaast	R. 538
14)	102.5	1	Utrecht	R. 538
14)	102.6	2	Nijmegen	R. 538
14)	102.6	13	Hengelo	R. 538
14)	102.7	10	Emmen	R. 538
14)	102.7	100	Rotterdam	R. 538
14)	102.9	3	Stadskanaal	R. 538
19)	103.0	40	Hilversum	R. Veronica
19)	103.1	20	De Lutte	R. Veronica
190	103.1	11	Markelo	R. Veronica
19)	103.1	8	Megen	R. Veronica
19)	103.2	40	Rotterdam	R. Veronica
19)	103.2	3	Hoorn	R. Veronica
19)	103.2	32	Hoogersmilde	R. Veronica
19)	103.3	2	Emmeloord	R. Veronica
19)	103.3	6	Terneuzen	R. Veronica
19)	103.4	3	Hoogezand	R. Veronica
19)	103.5	7	Roosendaal	R. Veronica
61)	103.6	15	Amsterdam	R. 10
61)	103.6	10	Tilburg	R. 10
61)	103.8	5	Emmen	R. 10
61)	103.8	1	Goes	R. 10
61)	103.8	20	Rotterdam	R. 10
61)	103.8	10	Tjerkgaast	R. 10
61)	103.9	1	Enschede	R. 10
61)	104.0	1	Haarlem	R. 10
61)	104.1	100	Arnhem	R. 10
11)	104.2	3	Alkmaar	R. NL
11)	104.3	1	Breda	R. NL
23)	104.4	50	Hilversum	100%NL
11)	104.4	2	Groningen	R. NL
23)	104.6	87	Rotterdam	100%NL
45)	104.8	1	Zuidwolde	DNO.
81)	105.4	1	Coevorden	ZO!34

FM	MHz	kW	Location	Station
74)	106.6	1	Hippolytushoef	Noordkop R.
34)	106.7	1	Lochem	Uniekk FM

+ 449 stns below 1kW

Addresses and other information:
3) Prins Bernhardplein 173 1097BL Amsterdam or Postbus 651, 1000 AR Amsterdam ☎ +31 20 592 8500 **E:** operations@bnr.nl **W:** bnr.nl –**9)** Postbus 34 1400AA Bussum ☎ +31 88 101 00 10 **E:** info@slam.nl **W:** slam.nl – **11)** Postbus 248, 8600AE Sneek ☎ +31 515 432360 **W:** radionl.fm **E:** info@radionl.fm and techniek@radionl.fm –**13)** De Kauwgomballenfabriek, Paul van Vlissingenstraat 10D, 1096BK Amsterdam ☎ +31 20 7970 500 **E:** info@qmusic.nl **W:** qmusic.nl – **14)** Postbus 2538, 1200 CM Hilversum ☎ +31 35 5385538 **W:** 538.nl **E:** info@538.nl –**18)** Nijbracht 138, 7821CE Emmen ☎ +31 591 652 025 **E:** info@simonefm.nl **W:** simone.nl – **19)** Postbus 2538, 1200CM Hilversum ☎ +31 35 625 2727 **E:** info@radioveronica.nl **W:** radioveronica.nl – **20)** Postbus 248, 8600AE Sneek ☎ +31 515 432360 **W:** joyradio.nl **E:** techniek@joyradio.nl – **23)** Postbus 34, 1400AA Bussum ☎ +31 88 101 00 10 **E:**info@100p.nl **W:** 100p.nl – **24)** Postbus 2538, 1200CM Hilversum ☎ +31 35 750 5905 **E** :info@skyradio.nl **W:** skyradio.nl **26)** Postbus 248, 8600AE Sneek ☎ +31 515 432 360 **E:** techniek@waterstadfm.nl **W:** waterstadfm.nl– **29)** Prof. W.H. Keesomlaan12 1183DJ Amstelveen ☎ +31 20 447 0030 **W:** wildfm.nl **E:** info@wildfm.nl – **30)** Raadhuisstraat 5, 5854AX Nieuwbergen ☎ +31 485 34 1939 **W:** maaslandradio.nl **E:** kantoor@maaslandradio.nl – **32) Raadhuisstraat 64, 6129CE Urmond** ☎ +31 46 4747555 **W:** bioes-omroep.nl **E:**bestuur@bieos-omroep.nl– **34)**Markt 3, 7240AA Lochem ☎ +31 575 556 560 **W:** uniekfm.nl – **36)** Postbus 94443, 1090GK Amsterdam ☎ +31 62 064 2229 **W:** radiodecibel.nl **E:** info@radiodecibel.nl –**40)** Middelstegracht 87A 2312TT Leiden ☎ +31 71 523 5907 **W:** sleutelstad.nl **E:** info@sleutelstad.nl – **43)** Hoofdweg 118 9628CS Siddeburen **W:** regiofm.info **E:** info@regiomediagroningen.nl and studio@gegiofm.nl ☎ +31 598 42 32 00– **44)** Postbus 510, 7940AM Meppel ☎ +31 522 241404 **W:** rtvmeppel.nl **E:** secretariaat@rtvmeppel.nl – **45)** Postbus 8, 7920AA Zuidwolde ☎ +31 528 373444 **W:** wijzijndno.nl **E:** info@dnomedia.nl and techniek@dnomedia.nl –**48)** St. Annastraat 60, 5421KC Gemert ☎ +31 492 366833 **W:** omroepcentraal.nl **E:** redactie@omroepcentraal.nl -**57)** Tractieweg 41, Studio E, , 3534AP Utrecht ☎ +31 303 5443 **W:** sublime.nl **E:** info@sublime.nl – **58)** Exloërkijl Zuid 38, 9571AC Tweede Exloërmond ☎ +31 909 9223 **W:** radiocontinu.nl **E:** studio@radiocontinu.– **60)** Newtonstraat 25, 2562KC Den Haag ☎ +31 70 365 2247 and +31 70 362 2077 24 hr in Sarnami Hindustani and Dutch **W:** vahonfm.nl **E:** info@vahonfm.nl– **61)** Postbus 2538, 1200CM Hilversum ☎ +31 35 750 5900 **W:** radio10.nl **E:** info@radio10.nl– **62)** Van Persijnstraat 19a, 3811LS Amersfoort ☎ +31 33 8893 492 **W:** mediagroep-eva.nl/radio/ **E:** redactie@mediagroep-eva.nl –**66)** Postbus 841, 2700AV Zoetermeer ☎ +31 79 331 7287 **E:** studio@zfmzoetermeer.nl **W:** insidezoetermeer.nl/zoetermeer-fm/ – **68)** Postbus 50, 7020AB Zelhem .☎ +31 314 62 40 02 🖷 +31 314 624 242 **W:** radioideaal.nl **E:** redactie@ideaal.nl and info@ideaal.nl – **69)** Hoogoord 51B 1102CC Amsterdam ☎ +31 20 4 09 08 07 **E:** info@ujala.nl **W:** ujala.nl –**71)** IBCweg 3n, 5683PK Best ☎ +31 85 760 99 32 **W:** radiojnd.nl – **72)** Ringbaan Zuid 8b, , 6905DB Zevenaar ☎ +31 316 342 242 **W:** rtv-favoriet.nl **E:** redactie@rtv-favoriet.nl –**74)**Torplaan 4, 1785BA Den Helder ☎ +31 223 684 609 **W:** regionoordkop.nl **E:** nieuws@regionoordkop.nl – **75)** Breestraat 1D, 5845AX Sint Anthonis, ☎ +31 485 381 777 **W:** omroeplvc.nl **E:** info@omroeplvc.nl - **76)** Schorpioen 21, 4501HA Oostburg ☎ +31 117 383 897 **W:** rtvscheldemond.nl **E:** info@rtvscheldemond.nl - **78)** Oosterhofweg 49, 7461BT Rijssen ☎ +31 548 681 010 **W:** radio350.nl **E:** info@radio350.nl – **79)** Postbus 178, 4100AD Culemborg ☎ +31 345 520 405 **W:** src.fm **E:** info@src.fm **80)** Johan Huizingalaan 763A, 1066VH Amsterdam **W:** 247spice.com **E:** sales@247spice.nl **81)** Postbus 34, 7800AA Emmen ☎ +31 591 392 220 W: zo34.nl **E:** info@zo34.nl and techniek@zo34.nl

Military stations

FM	MHz	kW	Location	Station
2)	90.2	0.05	Brunssum	BFBS
1)	99.7	0.3	Brunssum	AFN The Eagle
1)	107.9	0.1	Zeeland	AFN The Eagle

Addresses & other information:
1) W: afneurope.net **E:** dma.afnbenelux@mail.nl **D.Prgr:** 24h – **2)** ☎ +44 203 750 4567 🖷 +44 2037 550 **E:** info@bfbs.com and media@bfbs.com**W:** forces.net **D.Prgr:** Relays BFBS prgrs Germany

NEW CALEDONIA (France)

L.T: UTC +11h — **Pop:** 280,000 — **Pr.L:** French (official), New Caledonian languages — **E.C:** 220V/50Hz — **ITU:** NCL

COMITÉ TERRITORIAL DE L'AUDIOVISUEL DE NOUVELLE-CALÉDONIE ET DES ÎLES WALLIS-ET-FUTUNA 🖂 Nouville - commune de Nouméa, BP 739, F-98845 Nouméa Cedex ☎ +687 25 40 51 **E:** cta.nouvelle-caledonie@csa.fr
Regulator of broadcasting for New Caledonia & Wallis and Futuna

FM	MHz	kW	Station
1) Port Boisé-Oungoné	88.0	1	Nouvelle Calédonie la 1ère
1) Mont Do-Boulouparis	88.0	2.2	Nouvelle Calédonie la 1ère
1) Ouaco/Tsiba	88.0	1.2	Nouvelle Calédonie la 1ère
1) Touho:Popomé	88.0		Nouvelle Calédonie la 1ère
1) Kouaoua: Mé-Firo	88.5		Nouvelle Calédonie la 1ère
1) Maré:Tadine	88.5		Nouvelle Calédonie la 1ère
1) Aoupinie/Ponerihouen	89.0	3	Nouvelle Calédonie la 1ère
1) Île des Pins: Pte-Ita	89.0		Nouvelle Calédonie la 1ère
1) Nouméa-Mt Coffyn	89.0	2.3	Nouvelle Calédonie la 1ère
1) Pouébo:Mandjélia	89.0		Nouvelle Calédonie la 1ère
1) Île des Pins: Déété-Kari	89.5		Nouvelle Calédonie la 1ère
1) Ouvéa-Pte Gervaise	89.5	1.3	Nouvelle Calédonie la 1ère
1) Canala:Prokoméo	90.0		Nouvelle Calédonie la 1ère
1) Koné-Kaféaté	90.0	3	Nouvelle Calédonie la 1ère
1) Nouméa -Mont Koghi	90.0	5	Nouvelle Calédonie la 1ère
1) Kone/Mont Kaféaté	90.0	3.5	Nouvelle Calédonie la 1ère
1) Poum:Pt-Géodisique	90.0		Nouvelle Calédonie la 1ère
1) Yaté: Gouemba	90.0		Nouvelle Calédonie la 1ère
1) Lifou/Nawagued	90.5	11	Nouvelle Calédonie la 1ère
1) Poya-Château-Eau	90.5		Nouvelle Calédonie la 1ère
1) Koumac/Dôme de Tiébaghi	91.0	4	Nouvelle Calédonie la 1ère
1) Houaïlou/Pic Bâ	91.0	2	Nouvelle Calédonie la 1ère
1) Mont Dore: Plum	91.0		Nouvelle Calédonie la 1ère
1) Thio:St-Philippe	91.0		Nouvelle Calédonie la 1ère
1) Yaté Mamié	91.9		Nouvelle Calédonie la 1ère
1) Lifou-Waé	91.5	2	Nouvelle Calédonie la 1ère
1) Houailou-Pic Ba	91.0	2.1	Nouvelle Calédonie la 1ère
1) Koumac-Tiébaghi	91.0	4.3	Nouvelle Calédonie la 1ère
1) Bourail-Château d'Eau	91.0	1.3	Nouvelle Calédonie la 1ère
2) Nouméa -Mont Coffyn	93.0	2.2	France Inter Nlle Calédonie
3) Nouméa -Mont Coffyn	93.5	2	NRJ
4) Dumbéa (Nouméa)	95.0	1	R. Océane
5) Mont Do/ Boulupari	96.0	2.2	R. Djiido
5) Aoupinie/Ponerihouen	97.0	1.5	R. Djiido
5) Nouméa/Tour de Montravel	97.4	1.5	R. Djiido
6) Dumbéa	98.0		R. Rythme Bleu
6) Koné	98.0	1	R. Rythme Bleu
6) Nouméa -Mont Koghis	98.0	1.5	R. Rythme Bleu
5) Lifou	98.5	1.5	R. Djiido
6) Koumac	99.0	1.5	R. Rythme Bleu
6) Bouloupari	100.0	1	R. Rythme Bleu
6) Goro	100.0	1	R. Rythme Bleu
6) Nouméa	100.4	1.5	R. Rythme Bleu
6) Poya	101.0	1	R. Rythme Bleu
5) Dumbéa (Nouméa)	102.0	1.5	R. Djiido
6) Lifou	102.5	1.5	R. Rythme Bleu
5) Koumac	103.0	1.5	R. Djiido
6) Ouvéa	103.5		R. Rythme Bleu

+ 55 stns less than 1kw

Addresses & other information:
1) Nouvelle Calédonie La Première (Pub) 1 rue Maréchal Leclerc, Mt Coffyn, B.P. G3, 98848 Nouméa Cedex ☎ +687 239907 🖷 +687 239975 **W:** la1ere.francetvinfo.fr/nouvellecaledonie/rado (live streaming) **E:** info.NC@francetv.fr **L.P:** Reg. Dir: Jean Phillipe Pascal **D.Prgr:** 24h in French and local languages (local and Réseau Outre-Mer Première common prgr satellite feed) – **2) Radio France Inter (Pub):** satellite relay from Paris 24h in French – **3) NRJ,** 41 rue de Sébastopol, B.P G5, 98848 Nouméa Cedex ☎ +687 279592 🖷 +687 279447 **W:** nrj.nc; facebook.com/NRJ.Nouvelle.Caledonie 24h **E:** nrj@nrj.nc – **4) R. Océane**, 282 rue Jacques Lékawé, 7KM, 98800 Nouméa ☎ +687 410095 🖷+687 410099 **L.P:** President, Dumbéa Communications – Robert Lucas, Dir: Lucia Alikifaitunu **E:** contact@oceanefm.nc **W:** oceanefm.nc 24h – **5) R. Djiido**, 31 rue Édouard Unger, 98800 Nouméa ☎ + 687 253515 🖷 +687 272187 **W:** radiodjiido.nc; facebook.com/RDK.kanalk/ **E:** radiodjiido@radiodjiido.

nc **L.P:** Thierry Kameremoin 24h – **6) R. Rythme Bleu**, 4 Avenue de Sebastopol, 98800 Nouméa, B.P 578, 98845 Nouméa Cedex ☎ +687 254646 🖷 +687 284928 **W:** rrb.nc **E:** rrb@lagoon.nc **L.P:** Dir: Elizabeth Nouar **Prgr:** local + prgrs from Europe 1. 24h

NEW ZEALAND

L.T: UTC +12h (27 Sep 20-4 Apr 21, 26 Sep 21-3 Apr 22: +13h) **NB:** UTC times in schedules refer to DST period — **Pop:** 4.82 million — **Pr.L:** English (official), Maori (official), Samoan — **E.C:** 230V/50Hz — **ITU:** NZL

RADIO SPECTRUM MANAGEMENT GROUP
Ministry of Business, Innovation & Employment

✉ P.O. Box 2847, Wellington 6140 ☎ +64 4 962 2603 NZ Freephone 0508 776 463 🖷 +64 4 978 3162 **W:** rsm.govt.nz **E:** info@rsm.govt.nz **L.P:** Mgr Policy Planning: Len Starling Mgr Licensing: Siegmund Wieser. **RSMG** is the statutory authority responsible for radio spectrum licensing & administration.

BROADCASTING STANDARDS AUTHORITY

✉ P.O. Box 9213, Wellington 6141 ☎ +64 4 382 9508 🖷+64 4 382 9543 NZ Freephone 0800 366 996 **W:** bsa.govt.nz **E:** info@bsa.govt.nz **L.P:** CE: Glen Scanlan. The BSA statutory authority has codes of broadc. practice and a complaints procedure.

NEW ZEALAND ON AIR

✉ P.O. Box 9744, Wellington 6141 ☎ +64 4 382 9524 **W:** nzonair.govt.nz **E:** info@nzonair.govt.nz **L.P:** CE: Cameron Harland. **NZOA** is an independent government funding agency delivering quality and diverse NZ public media found on TV, online and on radio.

RADIO NEW ZEALAND (Non-commercial, Pub)

✉ P.O. Box 123, Wellington 6140 ☎ +64 4 474 1999 🖷 +64 4 474 1730 **W:** radionz.co.nz **L.P:** CE: Paul Thompson; Chief Tech & Ops Officer (CTOO). Mark Bullen; Trs. Ops Mgr: Gary Fowles
Network Stations: RNZ National (**N**), RNZ Concert (**C**), RNZ AM Network (**AM**). For full FM listings see website. **Prgr:** 24h from Wellington studios except for RNZ AM Network which only broadc. when Parliament in session [rel. commercial stn Star at other times]. **N:** RNZ News bulletins.

Network Stations:

MW	kHz	kW	Net	MW	kHz	kW	Net
Wellington	567	50	N	Napier	909	5	AM
Napier	630	10	N	Timaru	918	2.5	N
Tauranga	657	10	AM	Christchurch	963	10	AM
Wellington	657	50	AM	Kaikohe	981	2	N
Christchurch	675	10	N	Masterton	1071	2.5	N
Invercargill	720	10	N	Nelson	1116	2.5	N
Tokoroa	729	2.5	N	Hamilton	1143	2.5	N
Auckland	756	10	N	Rotorua	1188	0.4	N
Dunedin	810	10	N	Gisborne	1314	2	N
Tauranga	819	10	N	Palmerston Nth	1449	2	N
Kaitaia	837	2	N	Westport	1458	2.5	N
Whangarei	837	2.5	N	Gisborne	1314	2	N
Auckland	882	10	AM	Westport	1458	2.5	N
Dunedin	900	6	AM	Hamilton	1494	3	AM

FM (MHz)	N	C	FM (MHz)	N	C
Far North	[a]101.1	[b]98.3	Kapiti Coast	101.5	98.3
Whangarei	[c]101.2	[d]100.4	Wairarapa	101.5	99.1
Auckland	101.4	92.6	Wellington	[g]101.3	[h]92.5
Hamilton	101.0	91.4	Blenheim	101.7	99.3
Tauranga	[e]101.0	91.4	Nelson	101.6	91.2
Whakatane	101.7	95.3	Christchurch	101.7	[i]89.7
Rotorua	101.5	90.3	Greymouth	101.1	95.5
Gisborne	101.3	97.3	Westport	-	98.9
Taupo	[f]101.6	98.4	Ashburton	101.3	-
New Plymouth	101.2	91.6	Timaru	101.1	99.5
Hawkes Bay	101.5	91.1	Dunedin	101.4	[j]92.6
Whanganui	101.6	99.2	Queenstown	101.6	98.4
Palmerston N.	101.0	89.0	Invercargill	101.2	90.0

Also on: [a]101.5, [b]100.3, [c]104.4, [d]105.2, [e]101.4, [f]104.8, [g]101.7, [h]96.1, [i]99.7& 95.1, [j]99.0 & 99.4
Low powered network stations at Russell (C) 97.3, Tokoroa (N) 729, Te Kuiti (N) 94.0, Takaka (N) 98.2, Tekapo (N) 93.4,
Twizel (N) 92.6 Omarama (N) 97.3, Otematata (N) 106.7, Wanaka (N) 101.0, Alexandra (N) 101.5 & (C) 97.5, Te Anau (N) 101.6 & Milford Sound (N) 92.0. Some of these are community-funded relays rather than RNZ operations.

EXTERNAL SERVICE: Radio New Zealand Pacific
See International broadcasting section

COMMUNITY ACCESS RADIO

12 independent stns affiliated to the **Community Access Media Alliance (CAMA) W:** cama.nz **E:** info@cama.nz. Each stn serves local urban communities with a variety of ethnic language, cultural and comm. group prgrs. BBC WS is carried overnight on several stns.
H. of tr: 24h

MW	KHz	kW	Station
2) Palmerston Nth	999	1.5	Manawatu Peoples R.
4) Hawkes Bay	1431	3	R. Kidnappers
5) Dunedin	1575	2.5	OAR FM
FM	**MHz**	**kW**	**Station**
6) Blenheim	88.9	0.1	Fresh FM
3) Hamilton	89.0	5	Free FM89
7) Masterton	92.7	0.8	Arrow FM
6) Takaka	95.0	0.1	Fresh FM
9) Invercargill	96.4	3.2	R. Southland
8) Christchurch	96.9	5	Plains FM
12) New Plymouth	104.4	5	Access R. Taranaki
10) Auckland	104.6	15.8	Planet FM
4) Hawkes Bay	104.7	4	R. Kidnappers
11) Kapiti Coast	104.7	0.63	Coast Access R.
6) Nelson	104.8	1.6	Fresh FM // 107.2
5) Dunedin	105.4	7.9	OAR FM
1) Wellington	106.1	2.5	Wellington Access R.

Addresses & other information

1) P.O. Box 9073, Wellington 6141 ☎ +64 4 385 7210 **W:** accessradio.org.nz **E:** info@accessradio.org.nz – **2)** P.O. Box 4666, Palmerston North 4442 ☎+64 6 357 9340 **W:** mpr.nz **E:** info@MPR.nz **Prgr:** BBC WS overnight 1200-2000 overnight daily – **3)** P.O. Box 110, Hamilton 3204 ☎ +64 7 834 2170 **W:** freefm.org.nz **E: info@freefm.org.nz** – **4)** Taikura House, 304 Fitzroy Avenue, Hastings 4122 ☎+64 6 878 8710 **W:** radiokidnappers.org.nz **E:** info@radiokidnappers.org.nz – **5)** 301 Moray Place, Dunedin 9016 ☎ +64 3 471 6161 **W:** oar.org.nz **E:** manager@oar.org.nz **Prgr:** BBC WS overnight 1100-1900 daily – **6)** 87 Atawhai Drive, Nelson 7010 ☎ +64 3 546 9891 **W:** freshfm.net **E:** helen@freshfm.net – **7)** 5 Church Street, Masterton ☎ +64 6 378 0255 **W:** arrowfm.co.nz **E:** quiver@arrowfm.co.nz – **8)** 154 Madras Street, Christchurch 8011 ☎ +64 3 365 7997 **W:** plainsfm.org.nz **E:** info@plainsfm.org.nz **Prgr:** BBC WS overnight Su-Th 1200-1900 Fr-Sa 1200-1800 – **9)** P.O. Box 1, Invercargill ☎ +64 3 218 9891 **W:** radiosouthland.org.nz **E:** admin@radiosouthland.org.nz **Prgr:** BBC WS overnight Su-Th 1200-1900 Fri 1200-1900, Sat 1600-2000 – **10)** P.O. Box 44215, Pt Chevalier, Auckland 1246 ☎ +64 9 815 8600 **W:** planetaudio.org.nz **E:** info@planetaudio.org.nz – **11)** P.O. Box 213, Waikanae 5250 ☎/🖷 +64 4 293 4838 **W:** coastaccessradio.org.nz **E:** admin@ coastaccessradio.org.nz – **12)** PO Box 445, New Plymouth 4340 ☎ 06 751 3720 **W:** accessradiotaranaki.com **E:** anne@accessradiotaranaki.com

COMMUNITY RADIO

Independent unaffiliated community stns.

FM	MHz	kW	Station
1) Raglan	98.1	0.06	Raglan Community R.
4) Dargaville	98.6	1	Big River FM
2) Hamner	103.7	0.3	Compass FM
2) Rangiora	104.9	2	Compass FM
3) Eketahuna	106.5	0.5	R. Eketahuna

Addresses & other information

1) 41 Bow St, Raglan ☎ +64 7 825 2981 **W:** raglanradio.com **E:** manager@raglanradio.com – **2)** 79 High Street, Rangiora 7400 ☎ +64 3 311 7101 **W:** compassfm.org.nz **E:** managercompassfm@gmail.com – **3)** Main St, Eketahuna ☎ 06 375 8080 **W:** radioeketahuna.co.nz **E:** admin@radioeketahuna.co.nz **Netw:** 88.3 – **4)** P O Box 199, Dargaville 0310 ☎ +64 9 439 3003 **W:** bigriverfm.co.nz **E:** office@bigriverfm.co.nz **Netw:** 88.2 at Ruawai & Aranga.

TE MANGAI PAHO

✉ P.O. Box 10004, Wellington 6143 ☎ +64 4 915 0700 🖷 +64 4 915 0701 **W:** tmp.govt.nz **E:** thomas@tmp.govt.nz **L.P:** Mgr Radio Portfolio: Carl Goldsmith, Corporate Services Mgr: Thomas Hood
Te Māngai Pāho is the broadc. funding agency providing operational

funding to 21 independent community Mâori radio stns connected to the iwi radio distribution system, Punga.net: an internet distribution system for sharing radio prgrs, audio and data between the netw. of Mâori radio stns, Mâori TV Service and other system users.

MAORI RADIO STATIONS (Comm.)

MW	KHz	kW	Station
1) Ruatoria	585	2	R. Ngâti Porou
2) Auckland	603	5	R. Waatea
3) Hawkes Bay	765	2.5	R. Kahungunu
4) Wellington	1161	5	Te Ūpoko o te Ika
5) Tauranga	1440	2.5	Moana R.
FM	**MHz**	**kW**	**Station**
6) Rotorua	88.7	0.8	Te Arawa FM
6) Matata	88.9	0.04	Te Arawa FM
8) Timaru	89.1	5	Tahu FM
1) Tikitiki	89.3	0.6	R. Ngâti Porou
7) Palmerston Nth	89.8	1	Kia Ora FM
1) Tolaga Bay	90.5	0.6	R. Ngâti Porou
8) Christchurch	90.5	15.8	Tahu FM
9) Hamilton	90.6	4	Raukawa FM
8) Kaikoura	90.7	0.15	Tahu FM
21) Ruapehu	91.0	0.1	Awa FM
11) Gisborne	91.7	0.8	Turanga FM
17) Taupo	92.0	6	Tuwharetoa FM
20) Coromandel	92.2	0.2	Nga Iwi FM
20) Thames	92.4	4	Nga Iwi FM
20) Waihi	92.8	0.2	Nga Iwi FM
9) Mangakino	93.2	0.08	Raukawa FM
1) Gisborne	93.3	1.6	R. Ngâti Porou
21) Taumarunui	93.5	0.3	Awa FM
6) Rotoiti	93.9	0.4	Te Arawa FM
3) Hawkes Bay	94.3	4	R. Kahungunu
14) New Plymouth	94.8	5	Te Korimako o Taranaki
16) Wellington	94.9	1	Atiawa Toa FM
8) Dunedin	95.0	3.2	Tahu FM
17) Taumarunui	95.1	2	Tūwharetoa FM
15) Ngaruwahia	95.4	7.9	R. Tainui
11) Gisborne	95.7	0.8	Turanga FM
9) Tokoroa	95.7	1	Raukawa FM
15) Kawhia	96.5	0.05	Tainui FM
18) Whakatane	96.9	4	Tūmeke FM
13) Kaitaia	97.1	4	Te Hiku 97.1 FM
10) Mangamuka	97.5	6.3	Tautoko FM
17) Turangi	97.6	4	Tūwharetoa FM
11) Gisborne	98.1	0.15	Turanga FM
5) Tauranga	98.2	0.8	Moana R.
14) Opunake	98.4	2	Te Korimako o Taranaki
1) Ruatoria	98.5	0.8	R. Ngâti Porou
13) Kaitaia	98.7	10	Tai FM
19) Kaikohe	99.1	10	Ngâti Hine FM
22) Tolaga Bay	99.3	-	Uawa FM
10) Mangamuka	99.5	6	Tautoko FM
19) Whangarei	99.6	0.1	Ngâti Hine FM
20) Paeroa	99.6	0.1	Nga Iwi FM
12) Te Kuiti	99.6	0.8	Maniapoto FM
8) Invercargill	99.6	8	Tahu FM
21) Whanganui	100.0	0.8	Awa FM
16) Hutt Valley	100.9	1.6	Atiawa Toa FM
6) Reporoa	103.6	0.1	Te Arawa FM
13) Kaitaia	104.3	4	Sunshine FM
1) Te Araroa	105.3	0.8	R. Ngâti Porou
15) Huntly	106.4	-	Radio Tainui
1) Tokomaru Bay	106.5	0.1	R. Ngâti Porou
18) Whakatane	106.5	1.6	Sun FM

Addresses & other information (all MHz):
1) P.O. Box 55, Ruatoria 4043 ☎ +64 6 864 8020 **W:** radiongatiporou.com **E:** info@radiongatiporou.co.nz – **2)** P.O. Box 43157, Mangere, Manukau 2153 ☎ +64 9 275 9070 **W:** waateanews.com **E:** admin@waatea603am.co.nz – **3)** P.O. Box 2615, Hastings 4153 ☎ +64 6 872 8943 **W:** radiokahungunu.nz **E:** pat@radiokahungunu.nz – **4)** P.O. Box 11812, Wellington 6011 ☎ +64 4 801 5002 **W:** teupoko.co.nz **E:** info@teupoko.co.nz **Netw:** 87.6 FM – **5)** 104 Spring Street, Tauranga 3112 ☎ +64 7 571 0009 **W:** moanaradio.co.nz **E:** admin@moanaradio.co.nz – **6)** 2C Ranolf St, Rotorua ☎ +64 7 349 2959 **W:** facebook.com/TeArawaFM/ – **7)** P.O. Box 1341, Palmerston North 4440 ☎ +64 6 353 1881 **W:** kiaorafm898.maori.nz **E:** kfmstudio@rangitaane.iwi.nz – **8)** P.O. Box 13469, Christchurch 8141 ☎+64 3 366 4344 **W:** tahufm.com **E:** dee.henry@ngaitahu.iwi.nz – **9)** P.O. Box 842, Tokoroa 3444 ☎+64 7 886 0127 **W:** raukawafm.co.nz **E:** tammi@raukawafm.com – **10)** 4317 SH1, Mangamuka, Okaihau 0476 ☎+64 9 401 8991 **W:** tautokofm.com **E:** radiotautoko@tautokofm.com **FM Netw.:** 97.5/99.5 – **11)** P.O. Box 1224, Gisborne 4040 ☎ +64 6 868 6821 **W:** turangafmmedia.com **E:** turangafm@turangafm.maori.nz **FM Netw.:** 91.7/95.7/98.1 – **12)** P.O. Box 416, Te Kuiti 3941 ☎ +64 7 878 1160 **W:** mfmradio.co.nz **E:** jaqui@mfmradio.co.nz **FM Netw.:** 91.8/92.7/99.6 – **13)** P.O. Box 458, Kaitaia 0441 ☎ +64 9 408 3944 **W:** tehiku.nz/te-hiku-radio/ **E:** peterlucas@tehiku.co.nz **FM:** 97.1FM, 98.7, 104.3FM – **14)** P.O. Box 4232, New Plymouth 4340 ☎+ 64 6 757 9055 **W:** tekorimako.co.nz **E:** office@tekorimako.co.nz – **15)** P.O. Box 208, Ngaruawahia 3742 ☎ +64 7 824 5650 **W:** radiotainui.co.nz **E:** info@radiotainui.co.nz – **16)** P.O. Box 36111, Wellington Mail Centre, Lower Hutt 5043 ☎+64 4 569 7993 **W:** atiawatoafm.co.nz **E:** info@atiawa.co.nz – **17)** PO Box 198, Turangi 3334 ☎+64 7 386 0935 **W:** tuwharetoafm.net/ **E:** charmaine@tuwharetoafm.net **FM Netw:** 89.4 Waiouru & Taihape 100.6 (inactive) – **18)** P.O. Box 2090, Kopeopeo, Whakatane 3159 ☎+64 7 308 0403 **W:** tumekefm.co.nz **E:** jarrod@tumekefm.co.nz – **19)** P.O. Box 1127, Whangarei 0110 ☎ +64 9 438 6115 **W:** ngatihinefm.co.nz **E:** manager@ngatihinefm.co.nz – **20)** P.O. Box 135, Paeroa 3640 ☎+ 64 7 862 6247 **W:** ngaiwifm.co.nz **E:** nifm@ngaiwifm.co.nz – **21)** 70 Campbell St, Whanganui 4500 ☎+ 64 6 347 1402 **W:** awafm.co.nz – **22)** Tolaga Bay 4077 ☎+ 64 6 862 6826 **W:** facebook.com/pg/UAWALIVE/ **FM Netw:** 88.3, 99.3.

NATIONAL PACIFIC R. TRUST (PACIFIC MEDIA NETW., Comm)
✉ PO Box 97601, Manukau, Auckland 2241 ☎+64 9 361 6656 **W:** pacificmedianetwork.com **E:** info@pmn.co.nz **LP:** CE Don Mann **Stns: 531PI E:** info@radio531pi.com Market: older Pacific people – this is now relayed on all FM frequencies nationwide exc Auckland 103.8 FM which carries the Niu FM prgr. **NiuFM Auckland 103.8** Market: Pacific youth in Auckland **Prgr: 531PI** 24/7 English/individual Pacific languages **NiuFM** 24/7pan-Pacific English 1800-0600 daily 10 Pacific languages 0600-1800 daily. **Other:** Pacific R. News Independent charitable trust funded by NZ On Air and Ministry for Culture & Heritage.
MW: 531PI, Auckland 531Khz 5kW

FM	MHz	kW	FM	MHz	kW
Whangarei	103.6	0.4	Manawatu	103.4	10
Hamilton	103.4	79.4	Wellington	103.7	7.9
Rotorua	103.9	0.8	Christchurch	104.1	15.8
Taupo	104.0	1.6	Wellington	104.1	0.8
Taranaki	103.6	5	Dunedin	103.8	4
Hawkes Bay	103.9	6.3	Invercargill	103.6	4
FM: NiuFM Network:			Auckland	103.8	15.8

RADIO BROADCASTERS ASSOCIATION
✉ PO Box 8049, Auckland 1150 ☎ +64 9 378 0788 **W:** rba.co.nz **E:** jana@rba.co.nz **L.P:** CE: Jana Rangooni. **RBA** represents NZ commercial radio industry and sponsors NZ Radio Awards.

MAJOR COMMERCIAL NETWORKS
Full FM listings at individual netw. or local brand websites.

MEDIAWORKS, Level 2, 239 Ponsonby Road, Ponsonby, Auckland 1011. ✉ P.O. Box 8880, Symonds Street, Auckland 1150 ☎ 64 9 928 9300 🖷 +64 9 373 4000 **W:** mediaworks.co.nz **L.P:** Group CEO Michael Anderson, Dir Radio Content: Leon Wratt.
Prgrs: 24h **Owner: MediaWorks Holdings Ltd**
Netw. Brands ✉ P.O. Box 47560, Ponsonby, Auckland 1144 ☎ +64 9 928 9000 🖷 +64 9 361 1677 **Magic Talk:** ✉ 3 Flower St, Eden Terrace, Auckland☎+64 9 928 9270 **W:** magic.co.nz **E:** talk@magic.co.nz **Magic Music:** ✉ 239 Ponsonby Road, Auckland ☎+64 9 928 9270 **W:** magic.co.nz **E:** studio@magic.co.nz **George FM:** ✉ P.O. Box 47664, Ponsonby, Auckland 1144 ☎ +64 9 928 9150 🖷 +64 9 360 0044 **W:** georgefm.co.nz **The Edge W:** theedge.co.nz – **The Rock W:** therock.co.nz – **The Sound W:** thesound.co.nz – **Mai FM W:** maifm.co.nz

MW	Khz	kW	Station	MW	Khz	kW	Station
Alexandra	531	2	MORE FM	Tauranga	1107	5	Magic Talk
Auckland	702	10	Magic Talk	Wellington	1233	2	Magic Talk
Christchurch	738	5	Magic Talk	Dunedin	1305	2.5	R. Dunedin
Wellington	891	5	Magic Music	Queenstown	1359	1	MORE FM
Rotorua	1107	3	Magic Talk	Hawkes Bay	1368	1	Magic Talk

FM	1	2	3	4	5	6	7
Far North	94.0	-	-	90.0	-	-	-
Kerikeri	-	-	-	-	92.0	-	-

FM	1	2	3	4	5	6	7
Whangarei	94.0	90.8/100.7	-	90.0	98.0	-	107.3
Rodney	-	-	104.9	100.1	92.9	-	-
Auckland	94.2	-	100.6	90.2	93.8	96.6	88.6
Coromandel	93.1	-	104.4	105.5	-	-	-
Hamilton	97.8	100.2	-	93.0	93.8	107.3	105.8
Tauranga	99.8	100.6	88.6	94.2	92.6	107.4	96.6
Whakatane	104.1	92.1	-	-	105.7	-	-
Rotorua	99.9	95.1	100.7	92.7	91.1	-	105.5
Reporoa	-	98.0	-	-	92.4	-	-
Taupo	88.8	-	99.2	94.4	100.0	-	-
Gisborne	99.7	94.9	-	94.1	96.5	-	89.3
Hawkes Bay	98.3	106.3	92.7	95.1	91.9	-	105.5
New Plymouth	94.0	89.2	-	95.6	98.0	-	-
Whanganui	88.8	96.0	90.4	95.2	94.4	-	-
Palmerston Nth	93.0	93.8	104.2	95.4	94.6	107.1	97.0
Masterton	95.9	98.3	105.5	95.1	93.5	-	-
Kapiti Coast	97.5	99.1	95.1	91.9	94.3	-	-
Wellington	91.7	98.9	104.5	96.5	97.3	106.7	100.5
Marlborough	104.9	95.3/92.3	105.7	91.3	96.1	-	-
Nelson	88.8	96.0	99.2	94.4	98.4	95.2	-
Christchurch	88.9	-	99.3	93.7	92.9	106.9	95.3
West Coast	-	90.1	87.9	-	-	-	-
Ashburton	93.3	-	103.7	97.3	95.7	-	-
Timaru	95.5	105.9	103.5	91.5	**90.7	-	-
Wanaka	98.6	-	-	89.8	93.8	-	-
Oamaru	96.0	100.8	94.4	104.8	99.2	-	-
Dunedin	91.8	96.6	99.8	93.4	90.2	107.1	-
Queenstown	95.2	91.2	104.0	100.0	97.6	96.8	-
Central Otago	88.7/98.6	95.9	-	98.3	93.5	-	-
Invercargill	97.2	94.0	106.0	90.8	98.0	-	-

1=The Edge, **2**=Magic Talk, **3**=Magic Music, **4**=The Rock, **5**=The Sound **6**=George **7** =Mai FM
** also on 97.1, 104.6, 105.6

Local Brands: The Breeze W: thebreeze.co.nz – **MORE FM W:** morefm.co.nz – **R. Dunedin W:** radiodunedin.co.nz **NB:** Overnight and weekends often networked from Auckland except for R. Dunedin. **Prgr:** 24h.

FM Location	1	2	FM Location	1	2
4) Northland	-	[o]91.6	18) Kapiti	100.7	90.3
4) Bay of Isl.	-	95.2/107.3	2) Wellington	94.1/98.5	[a]99.7
24) Orewa	-	88.9/97.8	19) Nelson	97.6	[k]92.8
5) Auckland	93.4	91.8	20) Marlborough	[b]89.7	92.9
6) Waikato	99.4	92.2	21) Kaikoura	97.1	89.9
7) Tauranga	95.8	93.4	21) Christchurch	94.5	[c]92.1
8) Coromandel	[h]96.7	[d]90.3	25) Ashburton	106.1	[p]98.9
9) Rotorua	91.9	95.9	25) Timaru	89.9/92.3	[e]93.1
9) Reporoa	-	89.1	25) Twizel	-	[j]89.4
10) Taupo	100.8	[v]93.6	25) Oamaru	97.6	100.0
11) Gisborne	-	98.9/90.1	3) Dunedin[f]	98.2	[s]97.4
12) Hawkes Bay	97.5	88.7	1) Cent..Otago	[g]96.7	90.3
13) Taranaki	92.4	[n]93.2	13) South Otago	-	[u]92.9
14) Whanganui	97.6	92.8	22) Queenstown	[m]99.2	92.0
15) Manawatu	98.6	92.2	22) Te Anau	-	96.0
16) Masterton	99.9	[r]89.5	23) Southland	91.6	89.2

1= The Breeze, **2**= MORE FM
Also on: [a]95.3, [b]94.7/98.7, [c]94.9/99.1, [d]89.1/89.9/90.6/93.2/93.8/93.9/94.0/97.2/104.2/106.7, [e]95.0/96.8/97.9, [f]R. Dunedin on 95.4 & 106.7, [g]97.8/99.4. [h]90.7/90.8/99.5, [i]105.9, [j]90.9/94.2/98.1, [k]92.0/94.1, [m]92.8/96.8/97.2, [n]92.8/96.8/100.0, [o]94.4, [p]94.9, [q]92.9/97.8, [r]92.9, [s]100.6/106.9, [t]94.3/99.4, [u]93.7, [v]107.2

Addresses & other information
1) P.O. Box 143, Alexandra 9340 ☎ +64 3 901 6200 📠 +64 3 448 6502 – **2)** P.O. Box 11441, Manners Street, Wellington 6142 ☎+64 4 915 1000 📠 +64 4 915 1009 – **3)** P.O. Box 1957, Dunedin 9054 **R. Dunedin:** ☎ +64 3 477 6934 **FM:** 106.7MHz **The Breeze/MORE FM:** ☎ +64 3 951 3600 📠 +64 3 477 6874 – **4)** P.O. Box 100, Whangarei 0140 ☎ +64 9 986 9990 📠 +64 9 438 2348 – **5) The Breeze/MORE FM:** P.O. Box 8880, Symonds Street, Auckland 1150 ☎+64 9 928 9300 📠 +64 9 373 4000 **Mai FM:** P.O. Box 68886, Newton, Auckland ☎ +64 9 977 7800 📠 +64 9 977 7801 – **6)** P.O. Box 19293, Hamilton 3244 ☎ +64 7 958 7050 📠 +64 7 838 2893 – **7)** P.O. Box 13344, Tauranga 3141 ☎ +64 7 928 7300 📠 +64 7 577 0294 – **8)** P.O. Box 16, Whitianga +64 7 866 5696 📠 +64 7 866 2553 – **9)** P.O. Box 92, Rotorua 3040 ☎ +64 7 921 7630 📠 +64 7 348 3830 – **10)** P.O. Box 393, Taupo 3351 ☎+64 7 906 7500 📠 +64 7 378 2701 – **11)** P.O. Box 468, Gisborne 4040 ☎+64 6 986 3700 📠 +64 6 869 0037 – **12)** P.O. Box 193, Hastings 4156 ☎ +64 6 974 6150 📠 +64 6 876 5626 – **13)** P.O. Box 869, Taranaki Mail Centre, New Plymouth ☎ +64 6 968 6200 📠 +64 6 757 5020 – **14)** P.O. Box 928, Whanganui 4540 ☎ +64 6 965 6300 📠 +64 6 345 5592 – **15)** P.O. Box 446, Palmerston North Central, Palmerston North 4440 ☎ +64 6 952 6420 📠 +64 6 356 1317 – **16)** P.O. Box 881, Masterton ☎+64 6 370 2548 📠 +64 6 378 8877 – **17)** P.O. Box 603, Levin ☎+64 6 368 2827 📠 +64 6 368 0415 – **18)** P.O. Box 132, Paraparaumu 5254 ☎ +64 4 903 0400 📠 +64 4 297 2999 – **19)** P.O. Box 907, Nelson 7040 ☎+64 3 546 9670 📠 +64 3 546 9427 – **20)** P.O. Box 930, Blenheim ☎+64 3 579 0393 – **21) The Breeze:** Private Bag 4750, Christchurch 8140 ☎ +64 3 961 3102 📠 +64 3 366 5301 **MORE FM:** P.O. Box 25209, Victoria Street, Christchurch 8144 ☎+64 3 961 3322 📠 +64 3 377 1993 – **22)** P.O. Box 224, Queenstown ☎+64 3 901 0810 📠 +64 3 442 7799 – **23)** P.O. Box 1740, Invercargill ☎ +64 3 948 3900 📠 +64 3 218 8015 – **24)** The Village, 292 Hibiscus Coast Highway, Orewa 0931 ☎ +64 9 928 9940 📠 +64 9 427 0251 – **25)** 56 Woollcombe Street, Timaru ☎ +64 3 6889886.

NZ MEDIA & ENTERTAINMENT [NZME]
✉ **NZME:** 2 Graham Street, Auckland 1010, New Zealand. ✉ **Postal:** Private Bag 92198, Victoria St West, Auckland 1142 ☎ +64 9 379 5050 **W:** nzme.co.nz **L.P:** CEO: Michael Boggs
Netw. Brands: Prgr: 24h from Auckland studios **N:** Newstalk ZB bulletins.
Brands: Coast **W:** thecoast.net.nz - Flava **W:** flava.co.nz – Gold **W:** gold.co.nz - Radio Hauraki **W:** hauraki.co.nz –Newstalk ZB **W:** newstalkzb.co.nz - ZM **W:** zmonline.com – The Hits **W:** thehits.co.nz – Mix **W:** mixonline.co.nz (online only)

Gold AM

MW	kHz	kW	MW	KHz	kW
Nelson	549	1	Palmerston N	1089	2.5
Invercargill	558	5	Hawkes Bay	1125	1
Dunedin	693	5	Auckland	1332	10
Ashburton	702	1	Rotorua	1350	1
Whangarei	729	3	Timaru	1494	2.5
New Plymouth	774	5	Christchurch	1503	2.5
Hamilton	792	5	Wellington	1503	5
Whanganui	1062	1	Tauranga	1521	1

NewstalkZB

MW	kHz	kW	MW	KHz	kW
Rotorua	747	0.4	Auckland	1080	10
Masterton	846	2	Christchurch	1098	5
Invercargill	864	10	Timaru	1152	2
Ashburton	873	1	Whanganui	1197	2
Palmerston N.	927	2	Kaikohe	1215	2
Gisborne	945	2	Napier-Hastings	1278	2
Tauranga	1008	10	Westport	1287	2
Christchurch	1017	10	Hamilton	1296	2.5
Kaitaia	1026	2	Nelson	1341	2
Whangarei	1026	2	Oamaru	1395	2
Wellington	1035	20	Tokoroa	1413	2
Dunedin	1044	10			

Coast

MW	kHz	kW	MW	KHz	kW
Whangarei	900	2.5	Palmerston North	1548	1
Dunedin	954	1	Christchurch	1593	2.5
Hawera	1323	3			

Radio Hauraki

MW	kHz	kW	MW	KHz	kW
Dunedin	1125	-	Hawkes Bay	1584	1

FM	1	2	3	4	5	6
Far North	-	-	93.2/105.1	-	89.2	94.8
Russell	89.6	-	93.6	-	-	-
Whangarei	106.0	-	93.2	-	89.2	94.8
Auckland	98.2	95.8	99.0	89.4	105.4	91.0
Coromandel	97.9	-	-	-	-	-
Hamilton	105.0	-	96.2	97.0	-	89.8
Tauranga	97.4	-	91.0	90.2	99.0	89.4
Rotorua	96.7	89.5	94.3	-	-	98.3
Taupo	-	-	92.8	96.0	107.7	90.4
Gisborne	88.3	-	105.3	-	106.1	107.4
Hawkes Bay	99.9	-	96.7	90.3	-	95.9
New Plymouth	106.0	-	90.8	96.4	-	98.8
Whanganui	98.4	-	-	-	-	96.8
Palmerston Nth	105.8	-	87.6-	100.2	-	90.6
Masterton	91.9	-	-	-	87.6	94.3
Kapiti Coast	95.9	-	-	89.5	-	91.1

FM	1	2	3	4	5	6
Wellington	95.7	-	93.3	89.3	93.7	90.9
Nelson	100.8		90.4		104.0	96.8
Ashburton	-	-	-	98.1	-	-
Blenheim	94.5	-	98.5	92.1	-	90.5
Christchurch	105.7	-	106.5	100.1	91.7	91.3
	90.1	-	89.3	-	-	90.9
Reefton	-		-	-	99.9	-
Greymouth	-	-	105.1	103.5	91.5/97.1	89.9
Westport	-	-	89.3	95.7	92.5	91.7
Hokitika	-	-		105.9	91.5	-
Timaru	-	-	-	-	-	96.3
Wanaka	94.6	-	-	90.6	-	100.2
Dunedin	104.6	106.2	95.8	-	-	88.6
Queenstown	-	-	-	89.6	-	88.8
Alexandra	-	-	-	95.1	-	-
Invercargill	92.4	-	93.2	-	-	95.6

1=Coast, **2**=Flava, **3**=R.Hauraki, **4**=NewstalkZB, **5**=Gold, **6**=ZM

Local Brand: The Hits W: thehits.co.nz **MW:** 1) Takaka 1269kHz 1.25kW

FM	MHz	FM	MHz	FM	MHz
27) Picton	89.1	12) S Taranaki	91.2	4) Auckland	97.4
20) Ashburton	89.3	19) Kaikoura	91.5	7) Rotorua	97.5
23) Dunedin	89.4	18) Westport	92.5	18) Reefton	97.5
11) Hawkes Bay	89.5	16) Kapiti	92.7	19) Christchurch	97.7
1) Nelson	89.6	18) Hokitika	93.1	14) Manawatu	97.8
13) Whanganui	89.6	21) Timaru	94.7	22) Oamaru	98.4
12) Taranaki	90.0	6) Tauranga	95.0	5) Waikato	98.6
17) Wellington	90.1	3) Northland	95.6	21) Timaru	98.7
15) Masterton	90.3	24) Wanaka	96.2	25) Southland	98.8
24) Queenstown	90.4	23) Dunedin	96.2	10) Wairoa	99.7
25) Te Anau	90.4	3) Far North	96.4	18) Reefton	99.9
18) Westland	*90.5	19) Sumner	96.5	24) Alexandra	99.9
18) Greymouth	90.7	9) Taupo	96.8	6) Coromandel	+100.3
7) Reporoa	90.8	2) Blenheim	96.9	3) Doubtless Bay	105.9
10) Gisborne	90.9	8) Tokoroa	97.3	3) Russell	106.1
18) Westport	90.9				

* Also on 97.1, 97.5 FM + Also on 106.0, 106.9

Addresses & other information

1) P.O. Box 43, Nelson 7043 ☎ +64 3 546 2557 – **2)** P.O. Box 225, Blenheim ☎+64 3 578 0129 – **3)** P. O. Box 845, Whangarei ☎ +64 9 430 4950 – **4)** Private Bag 92198, Auckland ☎ +64 9 379 5050 – **5)** P.O. Box 489, Hamilton ☎+64 7 858 0700 – **6)** P.O. Box 642, Tauranga ☎ +64 7 578 9139 – **7)** P.O. Box 1147, Rotorua ☎ +64 7 348 9089 – **8)** P.O. Box 272, Tokoroa ☎ +64 7 886 8399 – **9)** P.O. Box 967, Taupo ☎ +64 7 376 0550 – **10)** P.O. Box 1040, Gisborne ☎+64 6 867 2139 – **11)** P.O. Box 241, Napier ☎ +64 6 833 8400 – **12)** P.O. Box 141, New Plymouth ☎ +64 6 759 2460 – **13)** P.O. Box 632, Wanganui ☎ +64 6 345 8564 – **14)** P.O. Box 1045, Palmerston North ☎ +64 6 350 3550 – **15)** P.O. Box 220, Masterton ☎+64 6 370 5014 – **16)** P.O. Box 462, Paraparaumu ☎+64 4 296 1201 – **17)** P.O. Box 300, Wellington ☎+64 4 802 4710 #NewstalkZB 1035MW/90.1FM carries local breakfast show – **18)** P.O. Box 378, Greymouth ☎+64 3 768 7068 – **19)** P.O. Box 1484, Christchurch ☎ +64 3 379 9600 #NewstalkZB 1098MW/89.3FM carries local breakfast show – **20)** P.O. Box 465, Ashburton ☎+64 3 307 8927 – **21)** P.O. Box 275, Timaru ☎ +64 3 684 8152 – **22)** P.O. Box 426, Oamaru ☎ +64 3 433 1090 – **23)** P.O. Box 888, Dunedin ☎+64 3 474 8400 – **24)** PO Box 1769, Queenstown ☎ +64 3 447 3175 – **25)** P.O. Box 802, Invercargill ☎+64 3 211 1500 – **26)** P.O. Box 292, Gore ☎ +64 3 208 9325 – **27)** P.O. Box 43, Nelson ☎ +64 3 546 2557

Associated local NZME stations:

Hokonui R.

MW: Hawera 1557KHz 2kW

FM: Ashburton 92.5 FM & 96.5 FM, Southland 94.8 FM, Gore/Tapanui 95.2 FM, Balclutha 91.3 FM (and in town on 88.3 FM), Taranaki 2 LPFM outlets.

✉ PO Box 292, Gore 9700 ☎+64 3 208 9325 **W:** hokonui.co.nz **Prgr:** 24/7 breakfast live from local studios in Gore, Ashburton & Taranaki then networked from Dunedin/Gore **N:** NewstalkZB NB: Hokonui is privately owned but under long-term lease to NZME

Humm 106.2 FM

FM: 106.2 FM 16kw

✉ 16 Taylors Road, Morningside, St.Lukes, Auckland 1025 **W:** hummfm.com **E:** connect@hummfm.com **Prgr:** 24/7 Hindi

RHEMA MEDIA

✉ **Corporate:** 53 Upper Queen Street, Eden Tce, Auckland.1010 ✉ **Postal:** Private Bag 92636, Symonds Street, Auckland 1150. ☎ +64 9 307 1251 🖷 +64 9 309 6888 **W:** rhemamedia.co.nz **L.P:** Chief Exec: Andrew Fraser **Dir.Prgr-Radio:** Luke Weston **Other Media:** Shine TV, NZ charitable organization.

Netw. Stns: Prgr: 24h from Auckland studios. Star also broadc. on RNZ AM Netw. txs when Parliament not in session. A duplicate network in several markets carries Star 24/7 so that listeners can hear it without interruption when Parliament is in session. **N:** NZME bulletins. **Netw. Brands:** Life **W:** lifefm.co.nz – Rhema **W:** rhema.co.nz – Star **W:** star.net.nz – Full FM listings at individual netw. brand websites.

Rhema

MW	kHz	kW	MW	KHz	kW
Tauranga	540	5	Nelson	801	1.5
New Plymouth	540	2	Hamilton	855	2
Christchurch	540	1	Wellington	972	5
Kaitaia	549	2	Auckland	1251	5
Whangarei	621	2	Invercargill	1404	5
Dunedin	621	2			

Star

MW	kHz	kW	MW	KHz	kW
Hamilton	576	2.5	Wellington	657	*50
Whanganui	594	2	Auckland	882	*10
Timaru	594	5	Hawkes Bay	909	*5
Nelson	612	2	Hawkes Bay	909	*5
Christchurch	612	2	Invercargill	1026	2.5
New Plymouth	612	5	Dunedin	1377	2
Tauranga	657	*10			

*shares freq with RNZ AM Netw. Duplicate freqs in same market carry Star 24/7 when alternate * freq carrying RNZ AM Netw.

FM	1	2	3	FM	1	2	3
Kaitaia	-	-	103.5	Picton	103.5	-	91.5
Kaikohe	99.9	-	-	Blenheim	104.1	-	93.7
Whangarei	-	-	98.8	Nelson	-	-	93.6
Whangarei	-	-	98.8	Murchison	97.3	88.3	-
Auckland	-	-	99.8	Kaikoura	105.1	-	-
Hamilton	-	-	94.6	Christchurch	-	-	87.6
Tauranga	104.6	-	94.6	Westport	94.9	103.7	104.5
Whakatane	-	-	104.9	Reefton	95.9	-	-
Tokoroa	99.7	-	-	Greymouth	92.3	104.3	94.7
Rotorua	93.5	-	106.3	Ashburton	-	-	91.7
Tokoroa	99.7	-	-	Twizel	91.8	-	-
Taupo	95.2	88.3	105.6	Timaru	104.3	-	105.1
Taumarunui	97.5	95.9	96.7	Oamaru	106.4	-	95.2
Raetihi	95.0	92.6	98.2	Dunedin	-	-	94.2
Gisborne	103.7	92.5	100.5	Wanaka	89.0	87.7	105.0
Wairoa	92.5	-	-	Cromwell	89.5	87.6	91.1
Hawkes Bay	99.1	-	93.5	Alexandra	92.7	100.7	103.9
Taranaki	-	-	99.6	Queenstown	94.4	107.0	-
Opunake	93.6	-	-	Tapanui	99.2	-	-
Whanganui	104.8	-	100.8	Gore	99.2	-	105.6
Palmerston Nth	91.4	-	96.2	Balclutha	96.1	88.9	92.1
Masterton	97.5	100.7	88.7	Te Anau	94.4.4	91.2	89.6
Kapiti Coast	103.9	-	96.7	Invercargill	-	-	100.0
Wellington	-	-	98.1				

1 = Rhema, **2** = Star, **3** = Life FM

STUDENT RADIO (bNet affiliated stations)

FM	MHz	kW	Station
1) Wellington	88.6	1	R. Active
2) Dunedin	91.0	2.5	R. One
3) Auckland	95.0	12.6	95bFM
4) Christchurch	98.5	1.6	RDU 98.5FM
5) Palmerston North	99.4	0.15	R. Control

1) PO Box 11971 Wellington **W:** radioactive.fm **E:** info@radioactive.fm – **2)** PO Box 1436, Dunedin 9016 **W:** r1.co.nz **E:** r1@r1.co.nz – **3)** c/o AUSA, Private Bag 92019, Auckland 1142 **W:** 95bfm.com **E:** gm@95bfm.com – **4)** PO Box 699, Christchurch Central **W:** rdu.org.nz **E:** james@rdu.org.nz – **5)** c/o MUSA, Students Centre Bldg, Massey University, Private Bag 11-222, Palmerston North **W:** radiocontrol.org.nz **E:** manager@radiocontrol.org.nz

INDEPENDENT STATION - BRIAN FM

✉ 18 Algarve Close, Blenheim 7201. Studios in Blenheim &

Springvale [Whanganui] **Brands:** Brian FM & Reelworld FM **W:** brianfm.com & facebook.com/brianfm Reelworld FM **E:** brian@brianfm.com

Brian FM	MHz	kW	FM	MHz	kW
Ruapehu	90.2	1.6	Ward	105.9	0.3
Whanganui	91.2	0.8	Kaikoura	100.3	0.5
Taihape	93.2	1	Timaru	93.9	1
Takaka	91.0	0.8	Twizel	99.0	0.08
Havelock	100.1	0.8	Ashburton	99.7	8
Blenheim	100.9	0.8	Mt Hutt	105.3	0.3
Seddon	104.3	0.3	Oamaru	88.8	0.6
Murchison	105.3	0.8	Wanaka	91.4	0.5
Nelson	105.6	5	Cromwell	105.5	0.1
Okiwi Bay	105.9	0.1	Alexandra	105.5	1.6
Picton	105.9	0.15			
Reelworld R.:			Whanganui	92.0	0.8

OTHER INDEPENDENT STATIONS

MW	kHz	kW	Station
2) Palmerston	756	1	Puketapu R.
4) Auckland	810	2	BBC World Service NZ
5) Auckland	936	1	AM936 Chinese R.
6) Auckland	990	1	Apna 990
7) Auckland	1179	5	Ake 1179
8) Whakatane	1242	2	One Double X
9) Tauranga	1368	0.8/0.1	Village R.
10) Auckland	1386	10	R. Tarana
11) Christchurch	1413	1	R. Ferrymead
17) Hawkes Bay	1530	1	The Wireless Station
5) Wellington	1566	-	AM936 Chinese R. (FPI)
13) Auckland	1593	5	R. Samoa

FM	MHz	kW	Station
Northland			
12) Mangawhai	90.4	0.1	The Wireless
15) Waipu	105.6	0.2	Smooth FM
12) Mangawhai	106.4	0.1	Heads FM
Auckland			
18) Auckland	90.6	1.6	Chinese R 90.6FM
19) Station Rock GBI	94.6	1	Aotea FM
5) Auckland	99.4	1.6	Chinese R. FM99.4
19) Port Fitzroy GBI	104.0	0.1	Aotea FM
5) Auckland	104.2	3	Chinese R. FM104.2
Waikato			
24) Pio Pio	88.7	0.8	Cruise FM
24) Te Kuiti	104.4	0.8	Cruise FM
240 Mangakino	104.4	0.1	Cruise FM
24) Tokoroa	105.3	0.3	Cruise FM
Coromandel, Bay of Plenty & Lakes			
27) Waihi Beach	89.0	0.008	The Rhythm
8) Whakatane	89.7	3w	1XX
8) Whakatane	90.5	16	1XX
26) Opotiki	91.7	0.1	Bridge 91.7FM
8) Whakatane	92.9	0.15	One Double X
8) E. BOP	93.7	1.6	Bayrock
3) Thames	94.0	2.5	Coromandel's CFM
3) Whitianga*	95.1	0.1	Coromandel's CFM
21) Waihi	96.4	0.1	Gold FM
21) Coromandel Town	96.4	0.1	Gold FM
-) Whitianga	97.5	0.1	Yesterday FM
8) E. BOP	97.7	2	Q97
21) Whitianga	99.1	0.1	Gold FM
14) Rotorua	99.1	0.25	The Heat
8) Whakatane	99.3	0.16	Q97
21) Waihi Beach	99.4	0.06	Gold FM
8) Ohope Beach	100.1	0.1	Bayrock
22) Tauranga	105.4	8	The Station

* also licenced for synch tx on 95.1 at Coromandel Township, Pauanui & Whangamata

FM	MHz	kW	Station
Central North			
24) Pio Pio	88.7	0.8	Cruise FM
1) Taupo	89.6	6	Lake FM
32) Taihape	90.0	0.6	Ski FM
32) Taumarunui	91.1	1	Ski FM
32) Turoa	91.8	1.6	Ski FM
24) Taumarunui	92.7	1.6	Peak FM
32) Whanganui	93.6	0.16	Ski FM
24) Taumarunui	94.3	1	Cruise FM
34) Ruapehu	95.8	1.6	Peak FM
24) Raetihi	99.0	1.6	Cruise FM
34) Taihape	99.6	0.8	Peak FM
34) Taumarunui	99.9	0.16	Peak FM
36) New Plymouth	100.4	1.6	The Most
33) Ruapehu	104.6	1.6	Reelworld R.
39) Foxton	105.4	0.16	R. Foxton
32) National Park	105.4	0.8	Ski FM
40) Whanganui	105.6	0.8	The Avenue
32) Ohakune	106.2	0.1	Ski FM
25) Taupo	106.4	6.3	Timeless Taupo
HB-East Coast			
31) Dannevirke	99.4	0.03	Central FM
35) Woodville	99.6	0.05	R. Woodville
30) Hawkes Bay	100.7	4	R. Bay FM
31) Takapau	105.2	2	Central FM
31) Waipukurau	106.0	2	Central FM
Wellington			
37) Wellington	105.3	2	Wellington 105.3FM
16) Kapiti Coast	106.3	0.63	Beach FM
Nelson/Marlborough			
29) Takaka	95.8	0.1	XS80s
33) Blenheim	106.5	0.8	Reelworld FM
Canterbury			
42) Akaroa	90.3	0.1	Akaroa R.
42) Akaroa	91.1	0.3	Akaroa R.
49) Sumner	93.3	0.1	Pulzar FM
44) Mt Hutt Skifield	94.1	0.15	Mt Hutt R.
45) Twizel	95.8	0.08	R. Twizel
29) Akaroa	95.9	0.3	XS80s
46) Christchurch	96.1	16	The 96 One
48) Timaru	100.3	2.5	100.3 FM
49) Christchurch	100.9	5	Pulzar FM
West Coast			
43) Reefton	90.3	0.5	Coast FM
43) Franz Josef	94.5	0.08	Coast FM
43) Westport	96.5	1.6	Coast FM
43) Greymouth	97.9	0.5	Coast FM
43) Karamea	99.3	1.6	Coast FM
43) Greymouth	99.5	1.6	Coast FM
43) Hokitika	100.3	2.5	Coast FM
Otago & Southland			
51) Glenorchy	89.2	0.3	Glenorchy Country R.
52) Cromwell	91.9	0.1	R. Central
52) Alexandra	91.9	0.8	R. Central
53) Wanaka	92.2	0.5	R. Wanaka
52) Roxburgh	94.3	0.02	R. Central
52) Queenstown	96.0	0.8	R. Central
53) Wanaka	97.0	0.5	R. Wanaka
29) Wanaka	103.4	0.1	XS80s
41) Oamaru	104.0	0.6	Real R.
53) Wanaka	104.2	0.5	Roy FM
52) Ranfurly	104.3	0.6	R. Central
47) Invercargill	105.2	4	Country R.
54) Gore	106.4	0.8	Cave FM

Addresses & other information

1) W: facebook.com/pages/category/Radio-Station/Lake-FM-Taupo **E:** lakefmtaupo@gmail.com – **2)** 114 Ronaldsay St, Palmerston 9430 **W:** http://puketapuradiopalmerston.yolasite.com/ **E:** puketapuradio@xtra.co.nz – 3) Radio Coromandel Ltd, 71a Cook Drive, Whitianga 3510 **W:** cfm.co.nz/ **E:** hello@cfm.co.nz **Netw:** 88.2 Coromandel Town, 94.0, 95.1 sync tx in Pauanui/Tairua, Whangamata & Whitianga – **4)** Auckland Radio Trust, PO Box 28622, Remuera, Auckland **W:** worldservice.co.nz **E:** vince@worldservice.co.nz **Prgr:** BBC World Service satellite relay from London 24/7, RNZI Dateline Pacific. Local advertising on hr & half-hr achieved by trimming seconds per minute off the satellite feed and 'saving' about 3 minutes per hour – **5)** PO Box 12743, Penrose, Auckland 1642 **W:** chinesevoice.co.nz **E:** info@wtv.co.nz **Prgr:** 936AM Mandarin [incl satellite services from China & Taiwan], 99.4 FM Cantonese [incl satellite services from Hong Kong], **104.2 FM** Mandarin [12h daily], China R. International English [12h daily] – **6)** Level 3, 362 Great North Rd, Henderson, Waitakere 0612 **W:** apna990.com **E:** info@apna990.com **Prgr:** Hindi – **7)** Te Reo o Ngati Whenua, Te Runanga o Ngati Whatua, PO Box 1784, Whangarei. **W:** ngatiwhatua.iwi.nz/manaakitanga/ake-1179am **E:** ake1179@ngatiwhatua.iwi.nz **Prgr:** Maori reggae favorites, soul, R&B music – **8)** Radio Bay of Plenty Ltd, 267 The Strand, Whakatane 3121 **Brands:** 1XX **W:** 1xx.co.nz – Bayrock **W:** bayrock.co.nz – Q97 **W:** q97.co.nz **E:** reception@1xx.co.nz – **9)** PO Box 841 Seventh Avenue,

Tauranga 3140 **W:** villageradio.co.nz **E:** info@villageradio.co.nz **Prgr:** Nostalgia Mon-Fri 2000-0400 Sat-Sun 2100-0500 – **10)** PO Box 5956, Wellesley Street, Auckland 1141 **W:** facebook.com/RadioTaranaNZ/ **E:** info@tarana.co.nz **Prgr:** Hindi – **11)** PO Box 19090, Woolston, Christchurch 8241 **W:** radioferrymead.co.nz **Prgr:** Thu 2000-Mon 1200 non-stop including automated prgrs, Statutory Holidays & Christmas New Year period – **12)** Perryscope Productions Ltd, PO Box 180, Mangawhai 0540 **Brands:** Heads FM **W:** headsfm.co.nz The Wireless **W:** wirelessfm.co.nz **E:** mark@perryscope.co.nz – **13)** 3/36 Hobill Ave, Wiri, Auckland 2104 **W:** radiosamoa.co.nz **E:** sales@samoatimes.co.nz **Prgr:** Samoan **Other:** Samoa Times newspaper – **14)** theheat.co.nz/– **15)** Waipu, Bream Bay 0510 **W:** smoothfm.co.nz **E:** info@smoothfm.co.nz – **16)** PO Box 157, Paraparaumu **W:** beachfm.co.nz & facebook.com/beachfm106.3 **E:** beachfm@kapiti.co.nz – **17)** PO Box 8947, Havelock North **Prgr:** mostly automated standards, rock & roll music, obs. with some live anncrs in primetime. – **18)** 194 Marua Road, Mt Wellington, Auckland 1051 **W:** fm906.co.nz **E:** info@fm906.co.nz **Prgr:** 24/7 Mandarin – **19)** Hector Sanderson Road, Claris, Great Barrier Island **W:** aoteafm.org & facebook.com/aoteafm **E:** aoteafm@xtra.co.nz **Prgr:** 1930-0600 daily – **21)** PO Box 341, Waihi 3641 **W:** goldfm.co.nz **E:** info@goldfm.co.nz **Other:** 88.0/88.3 – **22)** 52 Devonport Road, Tauranga **W:** vinyldestination.co.nz – **24)** Level 1, 203 Leith Place, Tokoroa 3420 **W:** cruisefm.co.nz **E:** johnnydryden@xtra.co.nz – **25)** Great Lake Taupo R Ltd, 23 Scannell Street, Taupo **W:** timelesstaupo.co.nz **E:** radio@timelesstaupo.co.nz – **26)** PO Box 593, Opotiki **W:** wwt.org.nz **E:** wwt@xtra.co.nz – **27)** 7 The Crescent Waihi Beach **W:** http://therhythm.co.nz/ **E:** info@therhythm.co.nz – **29) W:** xs80s.com **E:** studio@xs80s.com - **30)** PO Box 220, Hastings **W:** facebook.com/radiobayfm **E:** radiobayfm@xtra.co.nz – **31)** PO Box 195, Waipukurau **W:** centralfm.co.nz **E:** centralfm@xtra.co.nz – **32)** PO Box 661, Taupo **W:** skifmnetwork.co.nz **E:** info@skifmnetwork.com **Other:** FPL 1251 MW Taupo – **34)** PO Box 37, Raetihi. **W:** peakfm.nz & facebook.com/peak-fm **E:** geoff@peakfmruapehu.co.nz – **35)** 59c McLean St, Woodville **W:** radiowoodville.co.nz **E:** station@radiowoodville.co.nz + 88.3 – **36)** 27 Liardet St, New Plymouth 4310 **W:** mostfm.co.nz **E:** mostfm@mostfm.com – **37)** 18 Ashwood Street, Woodridge, Newlands, Wellington **W:** facebook.com/wellington105.3fm/ **E:** info@wellington105.3fm.co.nz **Prgr:** 24/7 Hindi – **39)** MAVTECH The National Museum of Audio Visual Technology, Avenue Road, Foxton **W:** mavtech.co.nz & facebook.com/mavtechnz **E:** mavtech@xtra.co.nz – **40)** 180 Upper Roberts Avenue, RD14, Whanganui **W:** theavenue.co.nz – **41)** PO Box 504, Oamaru **W:** real104.com – **42)** 4 Vangioni Lane, Akaroa, Banks Peninsula 7520 **W:** akaroaradio.co.nz **E:** dave@akaroaradio.co.nz – **43)** 165 Palmerston Street, Westport **W:** coastfm.net.nz **E:** studio@coastfm.net.nz **Other:** Westport News newspaper – **44)** seasonal only station based at Mt Hutt Skifield, associated with Mediaworks – **45)** 36 Mount Cook St, Twizel **W:** facebook.com/RadioTwizel95.8FM/ **E:** twizelcommunityradio@xtra.co.nz – **46)** NZ Broadcasting School, PO Box 540, Christchurch 8140 **W:** nzbs.com/ **NB:** each year the NZBS rebrands its station on 96.1 to give students broadcasting experience. – **47)** 145 Islington Street, Invercargill **W:** countryradio.co.nz **E:** countryradio@xtra.co.nz + 88.2 also 88.1 Gore/87.7 Dunedin – **48)** James Valentine, 8 Lisava Street, Timaru. **W:** 100point3fm.co.nz – **49)** PO Box 13-209, Christchurch 8141 **W:** pulzarfm.co.nz **E:** info@pulzarfm.co.nz – **51) W:** glenorchycommunity.nz/community-services/glenorchy-country-radio **E:** glenorchycountry@gmail.com – **52)** 2/22 Centennial Ave, Alexandra 9320 **W:** radiocentral.nz **E:** studio@radiocentral.nz – **53)** PO Box 825, Wanaka **W:** radiowanaka.co.nz & facebook.com/radiowanaka & facebook.com/royfmwanaka **E:** info@radiowanaka.co.nz – **54)** PO Box 117, Gore 9710 **W:** cavefm.co.nz & facebook.com/cavefmgore **E:** studio@cavefm.co.nz

NB: Comprehensive list of authorised NZ FM stns at **W:** radiodx.com is regularly updated by members of the NZ Radio DX League.
NZ Radio Guide from the Radio Heritage Foundation **W:** radioheritage.net additionally includes LPFM [1w or less] stns broadc. on 87.6-88.3 and 106.7-107.7MHz throughout the country.

NICARAGUA

L.T: UTC -6h — **Pop:** 6.6 million — **Pr.L:** Spanish — **E.C:** 120V/50Hz — **ITU:** NCG

INSTITUTO NICARAGÜENSE DE TELECOMUNICACIONES Y CORREOS (TELCOR)

✉ Av. Bolívar, Managua 12001 ☎ +505 22227350 **W:** www.telcor.gob.ni **L.P:** DG: Orlando José Castillo Castillo

Call YN—. ‡ = inactive, ± = varying fq

MW	Call	kHz	kW	Station, location & h. of tr.
MA01)	A3OW	540	25	R. Corporación, Managua: 0950-0505
MA02)	A3LP	580	10	R. 580, Managua: 1030-0000
MA03)	A3MD	600	10	La Nueva R. Ya, Managua: 1000-0600(SS 24h)
MA04)	N	620	50	R. Nicaragua, Managua: 1000-0400
MA05)		†660	5	R. Máxima, Managua
MA06)	AM	680	10/2	R. La Primerísima, Managua: 1045-0500
MT01)	RH	†690	10/5	R. Hermanos, Matagalpa: 1000-0400
MA07)	A3RC	720	25	R. Católica, Managua: 1000-0430
CT01)		‡720		R. Asunción, Juigalpa: 24h
MA08)	A3LS	740	50	La Sandino "La S Grande", Managua
MA09)	A3RO	800	50	R. Cadena 800, Managua: 0800-0500
MA10)	A3NT	840	5	R. Fe 840, Managua: 24h
CT02)	CD	870	10	R. Centro, Juigalpa: 1000-0200
MA11)	A3EP	880	10	R. El Pensamiento, Managua: 1100-0300
JI01)		910	5	R. Jinotega, Jinotega: 24h
MA13)	W	920	10	R. Mundial, Managua: 1100-0400
RS01)	ACTH	960	2.5	R. Trópico Húmedo, San Carlos: 1000-0300
MA15)	FF	1000	10	R. Hosanna, Managua: 1200-0400
NS01)	FAVP	‡1010	5	R. LV del Pinar, Ocotal: 1100-0400
MA17)	A3CP	1120	5	R. CEPAD "El Arco Iris del Amor", Managua
MA20)	A3RR	1240	5	R. Vida, Managua: 24h
MA21)	A2CC	‡1300	1	Canal 130 AM, Managua: 1200-2330
MA24)	A3MR	1440	25	R. Maranatha, Managua: 1000-0500
CA02)	A4TS	†1530	0.5	R. LV de Teresa, Santa Teresa: 1400-2200

Addresses & other information:

CA00) CARAZO

CA02) Entrada II Calle, ½ c abajo, Sta Teresa **W:** lavozdeteresa.es.tl

CT00) CHONTALES

CT01) de Catedral 1/2c al Sur, Juigalpa **W:** facebook.com/estereo.juigalpanicaragua **FM:** 93.7 – **CT02)** Caracoles negros, Juigalpa **W:** radiocentro870am.com

JI00) JINOTEGA

JI01) Escuela Gabriela Mistral, ½ al Norte, Avenida Ernesto Rosales, Jinotega. **W:** radiojinotega.com **FM:** 102.1

MA00) MANAGUA

MA01 Cd. Jardín Q-20, Av. Ponciano Lombillo (Apartado Postal 2442), Managua **W:** radio-corporacion.com – **MA02)** Reparto El Carmen, Costado Oeste del Parque, Managua **W:** radiola580.com – **MA03)** Frente a la Universidad Centroamericana, Managua **W:** nuevaya.com.ni – **MA04)** Villa Fontana, Contiguo a TELCOR, Managua **W:** radionicaragua.com.ni – **MA05)** Managua **W:** canal31.com.ni – **MA06)** Apartado Postal 4003 (or Barrio Bolonia, de Tica bus, 100 metros al sur, 100 metros al este), Managua **W:** radiolaprimerisima.com – **MA07)** Altamira D'Este 621, Managua **W:** radiocatolica.org – **MA08)** Av. Colón, Managua 11121 **W:** lasandino.com.ni – **MA09)** Semaforos de Lozelsa 1c al lago, ½ abajo, Managua **W:** radio800ni.com – **MA10)** Mansión Teodolinda 6C. al sur, ½ C. al oeste M/I, Managua **W:** fe840.com – **MA11)** Distribuidora Vicky, 4C Al lago, Casa 73, Managua **W:** radioelpensamientoonline.com – **MA13)** Reparto Miraflores, Rest. Munich 4c Al lago 1 c al Oe, Managua **W:** radiomundialdenicaragua.com – **MA15)** Rotonda Jean Paul Genie 300 mts al oeste sobre la pista, Comunidad Hosanna 2821, Managua **W:** facebook.com/RadioHosanna – **MA17)** Apartado 3091, Managua **W:** radiocepad.org – **MA20)** Carret. Vieja a León, km 10 ¾, 500 m al N 200 al Oe, Managua **W:** facebook.com/RadioVida1240Am – **MA21)** Carretera a Masaya, Km 12 ¾, 450 Metros al este, Managua – **MA22)** Bo La Cruz, Cine Blanca, 5c al N, ½ c al E, Casa 1112, Managua – **MA24)** Rotonda Metrocentro 1 c al sur, ½ C Abajo, Casa 41, Managua **W:** facebook.com/radiomaranatha

MS00) MASAYA

MS01) Carr. a Managua km 24½, Masaya

MT00) MATAGALPA

MT01) Bo. Liberación Igl. Catedral. 1c al N 25 vs al Oe, Matagalpa **FM:** 92.3 **W:** radiohermanos.net

NS00) NUEVA SEGOVIA

NS01) En el Centro Histórico de la ciudad, del Templo Nuestra Señora de la Asunción una cuadra al norte, Ocotal **W:** radiolavozdelpinar.com **FM:** 100.9MHz Stereo Mogotón

RS00) RIO SAN JUAN

RS01) Costado Norte de la Iglesia Católica, San Carlos **W:** facebook.com/tropicohumedo.tk **FM:** 89.3

FM in Managua (MHz): 87.7 Canal 6 – 88.9 Israel – 89.5 Enlace – 89.9 Tropicálida – 90.5 R. Nicaragua – 90.9 La Marka – 91.3 Futura – 91.7 R. La Primerísima – 92.1 Estación X – 92.7 Advent Estéreo –

93.1 La Buenísima – 93.5 Alfa Radio – 93.7 La Gran Cadena – 93.9 La Tigre – 94.3 Ondas de Luz – 94.7 Mujer – 95.1 La Pachanguera – 95.5 Amor – 95.9 Estéreo Ritmo – 96.3 La Gran Cadena – 96.7 Furia Magic – 96.9 La Nueva R. Ya – 97.1 Estéreo Mía – 97.5 Corporación – 97.9 Salsa 98 – 98.3 R. Viva – 98.7 Romántica – 99.1 La Nueva R. Ya – 99.5 Universidad – 99.9 María – 100.3 R. Tuani – 100.7 Disney – 101.1 Güegüense – 101.5 Juvenil – 101.9 R. Clásica – 102.3 Universidad – 102.7 Magic – 103.1 Bautista – 103.5 Maranatha – 103.9 Joya FM – 104.3 Estrella del Mar – 104.7 Hit – 105.1 Mi Preferida – 105.5 Rock FM – 105.9 Rica – 106.3 Galaxia, La Picosa – 106.7 Eco Romántico – 107.1 Sol – 107.5 La Sandino – 107.9 Restauración

NIGER

LT: UTC +1h — **Pop:** 24 million — **Pr.L:** French (official), Arabic, Buduma, Fulfulde, Gourmanchéma, Hausa, Kanuri, Tamashek, Tassawaq, Tebu, Zarma — **E.C:** 220V/50Hz — **ITU:** NGR

CONSEIL SUPÉRIEUR DE LA COMMUNICATION (CSC)

Plateau I, Niamey ☎+227 20 722356 🖷+227 20 722667 **W:** www.csc-niger.ne **L.P:** Chmn: Daouda Diallo. Vice Chmn: Hamidou Kô.

LA VOIX DU SAHEL – OFFICE DE RADIODIFFUSION-TÉLÉVISION DU NIGER (ORTN, Gov.)

Maison de la Radio, B.P. 309, Niamey ☎+227 20 722272 🖷+227 20 722548 **W:** ortn.ne **E:** ortny@ortn-niger.com **L.P:** DG: Amadou Harouna Yayé. Dir. Voix du Sahel: Mahaman Chamsou Maïgary. Gen. Secr: Mrs. Diaffra Fadimou Moumouni. Tech. Dir: Maraka Laouali.

FM (MHz): Maradi 88.4, Doutchi 89.7, Niamey 91.3, Zinder 91.3 2.5kW, Diffa 92.0, B. Konni 96.2, Madaoua 97.2, Tillaberi 99.0 10kW, Dosso 99.8, Tahoua 100.0, Agadez 106.8. All 1kW if not given otherwise. In addition 16 txs under 1kW.

D.Prgr in French/ethnic: 0500-2300 (Sun -2200). Local prgrs: 0700-1130 & 1500-1700. **N. in French:** 0545, 1200, 1900. **IS:** Local flute. **Ann:** F:"Ici la Voix du Sahel", A: "Idha'at al-Jumhuriya al-Niger, Sawt as-Sahel min Niamey".

Other Stations:
Alternative FM: Niamey/Agadez/Zinder: 99.4MHz. **W:** alternativeniger.org – **Anfani FM:** Niamey/Birni Nkonni/Diffa/Maradi/Zinder 100.0MHz 1.5kW. **W:** anfani-info.com – **Dounia FM,** Niamey: 89.0MHz 3kW. **E:** radioteledounianiger@yahoo.fr – **Espoir FM,** Niamey: 101.0MHz **E:** espoirfm@iniger.ne – **Hit R,** Niamey: 88.7MHz **W:** hitradio.co – **La Voix de l'Hemicycle,** Niamey: 95.1MHz – **Radio & Musique (R&M)**, Niamey: 104.5MHz 1kW **E:** retm@intnet.ne – **R. Bonferey,** Niamey: 105.0MHz 1kW **W:** sites.google.com/a/bonferey.com/www – **R. Dounia**, Niamey: 99.0MHz 1kW **E:** nodiabaoba@yahoo.fr – **R. Saraounia**, Niamey/Birnin Konni/Madoua/Maradi/Tahoua: 102.1MHz – **Sahara FM**, Agadez: 97.0MHz **W:** radiosahara.blog.fr – **Tambara FM**, Niamey: 107.0MHz 0.5kW **E:** tambarafm@yahoo.fr – **Ténére FM**, Niamey/Agadez/Diffa/Dosso/Maradio/Tahoua/Tillaberi/Zinder: 98.0MHz 1kW.
R. Rurale stations on FM in Agadez, Bankilaré, Diffa, Dosso, Gaya, Maradi, Niamey, Tahoua, Tillabéri, Zinder.

BBC African Sce, Niamey: 100.4MHz.
China R. Int: Agadez/Maradi/Niamey/Zinder 106.0MHz
RFI Afrique: Agadez 94.5, Diffa/Maradi/Niamey/Tahoua/Zinder 96.2MHz in French/Hausa.
VOA African Sce: Niamey 102.5MHz

NIGERIA

LT: UTC +1h — **Pop**: 207 million — **Pr.L:** English (official), Hausa, Igbo, Yoruba — **E.C:** 240V/50Hz — **ITU**: NIG

NATIONAL BROADCASTING COMMISSION (NBC)

Road 14, Badagry Rd, Gwarinpa, Abuja ☎+234 1 2647867 **W:** nbc.gov.ng

FEDERAL RADIO CORPORATION OF NIGERIA (FRCN) - RADIO NIGERIA (Pub)

Radio House, Herbert Macauley Way, Area 10, PMB 452, Garki, Abuja, Federal Capital Territory +234 9 2341103 🖷 +234 9 2346486 **W:** radionigeria.gov.ng **E:** info@radionigeria.gov.ng

1) R. Nigeria Lagos, Broadcasting House, P.M.B. 12504, Ikoyi Road, Ikoyi, Lagos, Lagos State. ☎+234 1 2690301-5. L.P: Exec. Dir: Prince Atilade Atoyebi. R. One in English. NB: Nigerian N. from Lagos or Abuja at 0600, 1500 & 2100 is relayed by all FRCN stations and most state stations. Ann: "This is R. Nigeria, Lagos". Metro FM, Ikeja in English: 0500-2300 on 97.7MHz 20kW. Bond FM, Ikeja in Pidgin/English/Yoruba/Hausa/Igbo on 92.9MHz 20kW: 0430-2300. R. One, Ikoyi: 103.5Mhz. – **2) R. Nigeria Abuja**, 12th Floor, Radio House, Garki, P.M.B. 7, Abuja, Federal Capital Territory ☎+234 9 88210410 L.P: Exec. Dir: Shuaibu Ibrahim. D.Prgr: 0530-2305 in English/Hausa/Igbo/Yoruba and others. Kapital FM, Abuja: 92.9MHz. Ann: "This is R. Nigeria, Abuja". – **3) R. Nigeria Enugu**, Broadcasting House, Onitsha Rd, P.M.B. 1051, Enugu, Enugu State **W:** radionigeriaenugu.com 0500-2315 in English/Igbo/Tiv/Efik/Izon. Coal City FM, Enugu: 92.8MHz – **4) R. Nigeria Ibadan**, Broadcasting House, Oba Adebimpe Rd, P.M.B. 5003, Dugbe, Ibadan, Oyo State **W:** radionigeriaibadan.org.ng **E:** radionigeriaibadan@gmail.com L.P: Exec. Dir: Princess Banke Ademola. D.Prgr: 0430-2305 in English/Yoruba/Edo/Igala/Urhobo. Premier FM, Ibadan: 93.5MHz. Amuludun FM, Ibadan: 96.3MHz. Ann: "R. Nigeria Ibadan, Station with distinction". – **5) R. Nigeria Kaduna**, Broadcasting House, No. 7 Yakubu Gowon Way, P.O.Box 250, Kaduna, Kaduna State ☎+234 62 235390 🖷 + 234 62 245392 **L.P:** Ag. Zonal Dir: Alhaji Muhammad Sani Suleiman. Chief Tech. Officer: Shehu A. Muhammad. Ch. 1 in Hausa: 0430-2300 on 594/6090kHz. Ch. 2 in English/Hausa/Fulfulde/Kanuri/Nupe: 0430-2300 on 1107kHz. Supreme FM in English: 0500-2400 on 96.1MHz. Karama FM in Hausa: 92.1MHz. Ann: "This is R. Nigeria, Kaduna".

MW	kHz	kW	MW	kHz	kW
5) Jaji	594	200	5) Jaji	1107	25
3) Enugu	828	100			

FM (MHz): **1)** 92.9/97.7 **2)** 92.9 **3)** 92.8 **4)** 93.5/96.3 **5)** 92.1/96.1

Further federal FM stations (MHz): Abakaliki 101.5, Abeokuta 94.5, Ado-Ekiti 100.5, Akure 102.5, Asaba 104.4, Awka 102.5, Bauchi 98.5, Benin 101.5, Bida (Minna) 100.5, Birnin-Kebbi 103.5, Calabar 99.5, Damaturu 104.5, Dutse 100.5, Gombe 103.5, Gusau 102.5, Ilesha 95.5, Idofian (Ilorin) 103.5, Jalingo 104.5, Jos 101.5, Kano 103.5, Katsina 104.5, Kwara 103.5, Lafia 102.5, Lokoja 98.1, Maiduguri (Borno) 102.5, Makurdi (Benue) 91.1, Osogbo 93.5, Owerri 100.5, Port-Harcourt 98.5, Sokoto 101.5, Umuahia 103.5, Uyo 104.5, Yenagoa 106.5, Yola 101.5.

Aso FM: Abuja: 93.5MHz. **W:** asoradioonline.com

STATES RADIO STATIONS:

MW	Location	kHz	kW	MW	Location	kHz	kW
17)	Sokoto	540	50	43)	Yola	917	50
44)	Kano	549	50	10)	Makurdi	918	30
18)	Abeokuta	603	25	27)	Birnin Kebbi	945	10
16)	Ilorin	612	50	25)	Dutsin-Ma	972	25
8)	Katabu	639	50	21)	Bauchi	990	50
30)	Damaturu	684	50	33)	Dutse	1026	25
14)	Jogana	729	50	31)	Jalingo	1269	10
42)	Kaduna	747	60	39)	Gombe	1404	10
15)	Ibadan	756	100	11)	Yola	1440	10

FM (MHz): **6)** 96.1 **7)** 95.8 **8)** 89.9/90.9 **9)** 94.5/95.3 **10)** 95.0 **11)** 95.8 **12)** 91.3 **13)** 94.4 **14)** 89.3 **15)** 98.5 **16)** 99.0 **17)** 96.4 **18)** 90.5 **19)** 96.5 **20)** 107.5 **21)** 94.6 **22)** 99.1 **23)** 92.7 **24)** 90.5 **26)** 90.5 **28)** 88.5 **29)** 88.6/97.9 **30)** 89.5 **31)** 90.6 **32)** 88.1 **34)** 89.5/104.5 **35)** 90.5/93.5/94.1/97.1 **36)** 97.1 **37)** 91.5 **38)** 97.3 **39)** 96.8 **41)** 98.1

States Radio information:
6) Enugu State Broadc. Sce (ESBS), Broadcasting House, Independence Layout, P.M.B. 01600, Enugu, Enugu State. Prgr 1 on MW: 0430-2300 in English/others. Prgr. 2 on FM ("Sunrise 96"): 0500-2100 – **7)** Edo State Broadc. Sce, P.M.B. 1012, Aduwawa, Benin City, Edo State. 0400-2305 in English + 12 local languages – **8)** Kaduna State Media Corp. (KSMC), Wurno/Rabah Road, PMB 2013, Kaduna North, Kaduna State **W:** facebook.com/ksmckaduna Kada 1 AM: 0430-2315 in English/Hausa on 639kHz. Kada 2 on 89.9MHz. Capital Sound on 90.9MHz – **9)** Borno Radio & TV Corp., P.M.B. 1020, Broadcasting House, Along Shehu Laminu Way, Maiduguri, Borno State **E:** brtvnews@yahoo.com 0400-2305 in English/Hausa/Kanuri/Marghi/Suwa/Babur-Bura – **10)** R. Benue, P.M.B. 102202, Makurdi, Benue State **W:** radiobenue.com Prgr. 1: 0430-2305 in English/others. Prgr. 2 on FM: 0500-2105. Ann: "This is R. Benue, Makurdi" – **11)** Adamawa Broadc. Corp. (ABC), P.M.B. 2123, Yola, Adamawa State **W:** facebook.com/ABC-YOLA-HAUSA-478623719171601 0500-2300 in English/Hausa + 6 Nigerian languages. On MW: 0500-2100. Ann: "This is ABC Yola, your No. 1 radio station" – **12)** Niger State Media Corp., Radio House, Ibrahim Babangida St, P.M.B. 88, Minna, Niger State **E:** info@nigermedia.com 0430-2130 in English/others – **13)** Imo Broadc. Corp, Ebu Rd, P.O. Box

329, Owerri, Imo State. Prgr. 1: 0425-2305 on MW. Prgr. 2: 0440-2305 on FM. English: 0430-0630, 1100-1830, 2100-2300 (Sat/Sun 0100), other times Igbo – **14)** Kano State BC, 1 Ibrahim Taiwo Rd, Gidan Bello Dandago, P.M.B. 3014, Kano, Kano State. **W:** radiokano.com Prgr. 1 on MW: 0430-2320. Prgr. 2: on FM: 0550-2320 in English/Hausa. Ann: "Radio Kano" – **15)** Broadc. Corp. of Oyo State, P.M.B. 1, Akodi Post Office, Ibadan, Oyo State. R. O-y-o on 756kHz: 0400-2200 in English/Yoruba. R. Oluyole on FM: 0700-2100 – **16)** Kwara State Broadc. Corp, Akpata Yakuba, P.M.B. 1345, Ilorin, Kwara State **W:** radiokwara.com 0400-2305 in English/others – **17)** Sokoto State BC, Moliba Adamawa Rd, Tudua Wada, P.M.B. 2156, Sokoto, Sokoto State. 0430-2305 in English/Hausa. Ann: "Rima Radio" – **18)** Ogun State BC, Ibara Housing Estate, P.M.B. 2084, Abeokuta, Ogun State **W:** ogunradio.ng OGBC1 on MW, Ogun Radio on 90.5 FM: 0400-2400 in English/Yoruba – **19)** Ondo State Radio Corp, Broadcasting House, Oba-Ile, P.M.B. 709, Akure, Ondo State. 0400-2300 in English/others – **20)** Lagos State Broadc. Corp, Obafemi Awolowo Way, P.M.B. 21035, Ikeja, Lagos State **W:** radiolagos.net 0430-0005 in English/Yoruba – **21)** Bauchi Radio Corp, 18 Ahmadu Bello Way, P.M.B. 0133, Bauchi, Bauchi State. **W:** facebook.com/brcbauchi.info Prgr 1: 0430-2300 on MW, Prgr. 2: 24h on 94.6MHz and 10 other txs – **22)** Rivers State Broadc. Corp, 4 Degema St, P.M.B. 5170, Port Harcourt, Rivers State. Prgr. 1: 0450-2310 on MW, Prgr. 2: 0450-2310 on FM in English/others – **23)** Cross River Broadc. Corp. (CRBC), No. 8 IBB Way, P.M.B. 1035, Calabar, Cross River State. 0430-2315 in English/others – **24)** Plateau Radio TV Corp. (PRTVC), 5 Joseph Gomwalk Rd, P.M.B. 2043, Jos, Plateau State **W:** prtvc.tv R. Plateau on MW: 0500-2300. Peace FM on 90.5MHz: 0500-2300 in English/others – **25)** Katsina State Radio & TV Sce (KSRTV), Former SDP State Headquarters, Batsari Rd, P.M.B. 2163, Katsina, Katsina State. **W:** ktrs.com.ng 0430-2300 in English/others. Ann: "This is Katsina State R." – **26)** Akwa Ibom Broadc. Corp, 205 Aka Rd, P.M.B. 1122, Uyo, Akwa Ibom State. 0500-2300 in English/others – **27)** Kebbi Radio, km 9 Kalgo Rd, Birnin Kebbi, Kebbi State. **W:** facebook.com/kebbiradio 0500-2300 in English/others – **28)** Anambra Broadc. Sce (ABS), off Arroma Junction, P.M.B. 5070, Awka, Anambra State. 0500-2300 in English/Igbo – **29)** Delta State Broadc. Sce, Broadc. House P.M.B. 5032, Asaba, Delta State. 0500-2300 in English/others – **30)** Yobe Broadc. Corp, km 6 Gujba Rd, P.M.B. 1044, Damaturu, Yobe State. Sahel Radio 0500-2300 in English/others on MW&FM – **31)** Taraba State Broadc. Sces(TSBS), "Voice of Unity", Broadc. House, adjacent Gen. Sani Abacha State Secretariat, P.M.B. 1038, Jalingo, Taraba State **W:** tsbs.com.ng 0500-2305 in English/others, 25 kW tx on MW, operated at 10 kW: 0500-1100, 1430-2300 – **32)** Broadc. Corp. of Abia State (BCA), Broadc. House, Government Station Layout, B.M.P. 7276, Umuahia, Abia State. **W:** bcanigeria.com 0500-2300 in English/Igbo – **33)** Jigawa Broadc. Corp, Broadc. House, Kiyawa Rd, P.M.B. 7032, Dutse, Jigawa State. 0500-2205 **W:** radiojigawa.com – **34)** Osun State Broadc. Corp, Studio 1, Ita-Akogun St, P.M.B. 4425, Osogbo, Osun State **W:** osbcng.org 0500-2300 in English/others – **35)** Kogi State Broadc. Corp, 1 Danladi Zakari Rd, P.M.B. 1095 GRA, Lokoja, Kogi State. 0500-2300 in English/others. Ann: "R. Kogi" – **36)** Nasawara Broadc. Sce (NBS), Tudun K. Nasarawa auri, Makurdi Rd, P.M.B. 97, Lafia, Nasarawa State. 24h in English/others – **37)** Vo Ekiti, Broadc. Sce of Ekiti State, Old Ado Ekiti Local Government Secretariat, Okeyinmi, P.M.B. 5343, Ado, Ekiti State – **38)** Bayelsa State Broadc. Corp, P.M.B. 56, Ekeki, Yenagoa, Bayelsa State. "Glory FM" in English/others – **39)** Gombe State Broadc. Sce, Buhari Estate Rd, GRA, Gombe, Gombe State. 0500-2300 English/others – **40)** Zamfara State R, Mall. Yahaya Secretariat, Off Zaria Road, P.M.B. 01007, Gusau, Zamfara State – **41)** Ebonyi Broadcasting Service (EBBS), Ministry of Information Building, Government House Annex, Abakaliki, Ebonyi State – **42)** Nagarta R, Nagarta Communications Complex, Katabu, Mararraban, Jos, P.O. Box 574, Kaduna **W:** facebook.com/Nagarta-radio-kaduna-1374512406167747 D.Prgr: 0430-2305 – **43) R. Gotel,** P.O. Box 5759, Modire (After Yola Bridge), Off Yola-Mubi Expressway, Jimeta-Yola, Adamawa State. D.Prgr: 24h in English/French **W:** gotelonline.net – **44) Manoma R,** Kano. F.Pl.

EXTERNAL SCE: Voice of Nigeria: see International Radio section.

Private FM stations:
Alheri R: Kaduna 97.7MHz **W:** ditvalheriradiokaduna.9f.com – **Brila FM:** Abuja/Lagos/Kaduna/Onitsha 88.9MHz **W:** brilafm.net – **Choice FM**: 103.5MHz – **Cool FM**, 267A, AIM Plaza, Etim Inyang Crescent Victoria Island Annex.P.M.B. 10096, Victoria Island, Lagos: Port Harcourt 95.9, Abuja/Lagos 96.9MHz. **W:** coolfm.us – **Cosmo FM,** Plot 18, Pocket Estate, Independence Layout, Enugu: 105.5MHz – **Crown FM,** Warri: 89.9MHz 5kW **W:** crownfmng.com – **Defence FM** (Mil), Abuja: 107.7MHz – **Eko-FM**, Lagos: 89.75MHz – **Freedom R**: Kaduna 92.9MHz, Dutse/Kano 99.5MHz **W:** freedomradionig.com – **Independent R**, Benin City: 92.3MHz **W:** itvradionigeria.com – **Lafiya Dole R,** Maiduguri: 108.0MHz **W:** facebook.com/lafiyadoleradio – **Liberty R,** Kaduna: 91.7MHz – **Naija FM,** Ibadan/Lagos: 102.7MHz **W:** naija102.com – **Ray Power 1:** Lagos/Abuja 100.5MHz. **Ray Power 2:** Lagos/Kano 106.5MHz + rel. in other towns (Incl. rel. of BBC African Sce in English/Hausa) – **Rhythm FM,** 17A Commercial Ave, Yaba, Lagos: 93.7MHz – **Rhythm 94.7,** Hilltop, Karu, Abuja: 94.7MHz – **Rockcity FM,** Abeokuta: 101.9MHz **W:** srockcityfmradio.com –**Space FM,** Ibadan: 90.1MHz **W:** spacefm901.org.ng – **Splash FM,** Ibadan: 105.5MHz **W:** splashfm1055.com – **Sweet FM,** Abeokuta: 107.1MHz **W:** facebook.com/sweetfm1071 – **The Beat:** Ibadan: 97.9MHz. Lagos 99.9MHz **W:** thebeat97.com thebeat99.com – **Wazobia FM:** for addr. see Cool FM above. Port Harcourt 94.1MHz, Lagos 95.1MHz, Abuja 99.5MHz. **W:** wazobiafm.com – **We FM:** Abuja 106.3MHz. **W:** facebook.com/wefmng – **Vo Women:** Lagos 91.7MHz **W:** wfm917.com **F.Pl:** transmitters in other states. **NB:** about 20 community radio stations also in operation

NIUE

L.T: UTC -11h — **Pop:** 1,600 — **Pr.L:** Niuean (official), English (official) — **E.C:** 230V/50Hz — **ITU:** NIU

BROADCASTING CORPORATION OF NIUE (BCN)

P.O. Box 68, Alofi, Niue, South Pacific. Studio: Fonuakula, Alofi ☎ +683 4226 **E:** sunshine@mail.gov.nu
L.P: CEO: Trevor Tiakia
FM: 88.6MHz 0.1kW, 91.0MHz 0.5kW
D.Prgr: Mon-Sat. N: international news bulletins from R. Australia/RNZI 1800, 1900, 0200 **Ann:** "This is Radio Sunshine"

NORFOLK ISLAND (Australia)

L.T: UTC +11h (4 Oct 20-4 Apr 21, 3 Oct 21-3 Apr 22: +12h). **NB:** UTC times in schedules refer to DST period — **Pop:** 1,748 — **Pr.L:** English (official), Pitcairn Norfolk (official) — **E.C:** 230V/50Hz — **ITU:** NFK

NB: Since 2016, Norfolk Island has been transitioning to greater integration with Australia. The Broadcasting Section of the Norfolk Island Regional Council manages all broadc. sces on the island including R. Norfolk and the ABC radio retransmissions.

AM	kHz	Call	kW	Programme
1)	1566	VL2NI	0.1	R. Norfolk
FM	**MHz**	**Call**	**kW**	**Programme**
1)	89.9	VL2NI	0.25	R. Norfolk [stereo]
1)	*91.9	2ABCRN	0.15	ABC R. National [mono]
1)	95.9	2ABCRR	0.15	ABC Local R.**
1)	98.2	2JJJ	0.25	ABC Triple J [stereo]
2)	99.9		-	Pines FM***

*Broadc. local council meetings live with repeats at 0930 the following day. **Western Plains, Dubbo, NSW. ***Local community prgrs

Addresses & other information:
1) R Norfolk, New Cascade Road (PO Box 95), Norfolk Island 2899, Australia ☎ +6723 22137 🖷 +6723 23298 **E:** manager@radio.gov.nf & news@radio.gov.nf **L.P:** Louci Reynolds ASM Gary Summerscales Contract Tech. **D.Prgr:** 2000-0530 M-F, 2000-0100 Sat-Sun **MW**: relay R. New Zealand National rnz.co.nz from Wellington via satellite overnight daily 0530-2000 **FM**: rel. MW during the day, pre-programmed music nightly M-F from 0530 but volunteer announcers with individual prgrs daily evenings (except Wed) at various times. **V:** responds promptly to email reports – **2)** Norfolk Island Community Radio 866 Taylors Road, Norfolk Island NSW 2899 ☎+6723 22899 **E:** Pinesfm999@outlook.com, **FB:** facebook.com/NIcommunityradio

NORTH MACEDONIA

L.T: UTC +1h (28 Mar-31 Oct: +2h) — **Pop:** 2.1 million — **Pr.L:** Macedonian (official), Albanian (official); additional official regional languages: Aromanian, Bosnian, Romany, Serbian, Turkish — **E.C:** 230V/50Hz — **ITU:** MKD

AGENCIJA ZA AUDIO I AUDIOVIZUELNI MEDIUMSKI USLUGI (AVMU) (Agency for Audio & Audiovisual Media Services)

bul. Makedonija 38, 1000 Skopje ☎ +389 2 3103400 🖷 +389 2

3103401 **E:** contact@avmu.mk **W:** avmu.mk
L.P: Dir: Zoran Trajcevski

NACIONALNA RADIO TELEVIZIJA (NRT) (Pub)
bul. Goce Delčev 18, 1000 Skopje ☎ +389 2 519899 **E:** direkci-jamrt@mrt.com.mk **W:** mrt.com.mk **L.P:** DG: Marjan Cvetkovski
NB: In 2019, Makedonska Radio Televizija (MRT) was re-branded Nacionalna Radio Televizija (NRT). The former brand may still be found in use in many instances during a transition period.

MW	kHz	kW	Prgr
Sveti Nikole	810	100	1, International Service

FM (MHz)	1	2	3	kW
Belasica	91.5	97.8	106.8	10
Boskija	95.3	98.1	105.4	10
Buković	89.2	95.9	104.3	1
Cocon	88.8	93.8	98.1	1
Crn Vrv	97.3	94.1	101.3	100
Gevgelija	99.2	102.4	96.5	10
Golak	94.5	97.0	107.7	10
Mali Vlaj	93.3	97.7	91.0	10
Pelister	92.3	96.1	102.6	20
Popova Šapka	88.8	96.3	98.3	5
Stogovo	95.3	101.0	91.3	3
Tepavci	94.9	103.4	91.5	1
Turtel	93.3	90.5	99.7	50
Vodno	98.9	92.4	87.8	10

+ txs below 1kW.
D.Prgr: Prgr 1 (R. Skopje): 24h on FM; also on MW except W 1830-0400 (see below) – **Prgr 2 (R. 2):** 24h – **Prgr 3 (R. Shkupi):** 24h in Albanian & other ethnic minority languages (Bosnian, Romany, Serbian, Turkish, Vlakh) – **International Service (R. Makedonija):** W 1830-0400 on MW (see Int. Radio section).

OTHER STATIONS

FM	MHz	kW	Location	Station
2)	89.7	1	Vodno	Kanal 77
A)	91.3	1	Skopje	RFI relay
1)	92.9	1	Pelister	Antena 5
1)	95.5	1	Vodno	Antena 5
1)	104.8	1	Turtel	Antena 5
1)	106.3	1	Boskija	Antena 5

+ txs below 1kW.
Addresses & other information:
1) ul. Tetovska 35, 1000 Skopje – **2)** ul. 5-ta Partiska Konferencija bb, 2000 Štip – **A)** Rel. RFI (France)

NORTHERN MARIANA ISLANDS (USA Commonwealth)

L.T: UTC +10h — **Pop:** 57,559 — **Pr.L:** English (official), Chamorro (official), Carolinian (official), Filipino — **E.C:** 120V/60Hz — **ITU:** MRA

FEDERAL COMMUNICATIONS COMMISSION (FCC)
see USA for details

MW	kHz	kW	Station
2)	1440	1.1	KKMP

FM	MHz	kW	Station	FM	MHz	kW	Station
3)	88.1	1.8	KRNM	2)	92.3		CP
3)	89.1	0.25	KRNM	4)	97.9	6.5	KPXP
6)	89.9	1.8	KORU	4)	99.5	17	KZGU
3)	90.7	0.6	KCKD	5)	100.3	1.1	KWAW
3)	91.5	0.6	KMOP	1)	103.9	3.2	KZMI
2)	92.1	0.01	KKMP				

Addresses & other information:
1) Choice Broadcasting Company LLC, PO Box 500914, Saipan 96950-0914 ☎+1 671 2347239 +1 671 2340447 **KCNM**: News/ Talk **KZMI**: Adult Contemporary **L.P:** GM Bob Webb **Prgr:** 24h – **2) Blue Continent Communications Inc.** PO Box 500815, Saipan 96950-0815 ☎+1 670 233 1440 **W:** cnmiradio.com **E:** kkmp670@gmail.com **L.P:** CEO: Rosemond Santos, VP: Gary Sword **Format:** 'Strickly Island' Islands Music – **3) Marianas Educational Media Services Inc** Sunny Plaza, 125 Tun Jesus Crisostomo St #301, Tamuning GU 96913 **E:** darryl@guamtech.com **L.P:** CEO: Robert F Kelly, Community Radio Mgr: Darryl Taggerty **KRNM 88.1:** Chalan Kanoa simulcast 24h KPRG Guam, **KRNM 89.1:** Capital Hill simulcast 24h KPRG Guam **Format:** NPR, Public Radio International and BBC World Service, **KCKD**: **Format:** relay WCPE Wake Forest NC **W:** theclassicalstation.org 24h classical music, **KMOP**: **Format:** Melodies of Prayer **W:** melodiesofprayer.com 24h religious – **4) Sorensen Pacific Broadcasting Inc.** PPP415 Box 10000, Saipan 96950 ☎+1 670 2357996 +1 670 2357998 **W:** sorensenmediagroup.com **L.P:** SM: Tina Palacios **KZGU** and **KPXP:** 'Power99' Top 40/Islands Music [STA 1.5kw because of typhoon damage] **D.Prgr:** 24h – **5) Magic 100FM** 1st Fl, Naru Building, Susupe, Saipan 96950 ☎+1 670 2345929 +1 670 2342262 **W:** magic100radio.com **E:** kwaw100.3@magic100radio.com **D.Prgr:** 24h – **6) Good News Broadcasting Corp.** 290 Chalan Palasyo, Agana Heights, GU 96910 ☎+1 671 472 1111 +1 671 4774678 **W:** joyfmguam.com **L.P:** GM: Matthew Dodd **Format:** simulcast 24h KSDA-FM Guam religious Joy FM Family Friendly Radio

NORWAY

L.T: UTC +1h (28 Mar-31 Oct: +2h) — **Pop:** 5.4 million — **Pr. L:** Norwegian — **E.C:** 230V/50Hz — **ITU:** NOR

MEDIETILSYNET (Norwegian Media Authority)
Nygata 4, N-1607 Fredrikstad ☎ +47 69301200 +47 69301201
E: post@medietilsynet.no **W:** www.medietilsynet.no
L.P: DG: Mari Velsand

NORWEGIAN COMMUNICATIONS AUTHORITY
PB 93, NO-4791 Lillesand ☎ +47 22824600 +47 22824640
W: nkom.no

NORKRING (Transmission provider)
PB 1, NO-1331 Fornebu ☎ +47 67892000 +47 67893611
W: norkring.no

NRK - NORSK RIKSKRINGKASTING AS (Pub.)
NO-0340 Oslo ☎ +47 23047000 +47 23047575 **Inf.Dpt:** ☎ +47 81565900 **E:** info@nrk.no **W:** nrk.no
L.P: DG: Thor Gjermund Eriksen

DAB: Oslo, Akershus, Østfold 12C. Hedmark, Oppland 13E, Buskerud, Telemark, Vestfold 13A. Trøndelag, Møre og Romsdal 12C. Agder, Rogaland 13F. Nordland, Sør-Troms 13E, Hordaland, Sogn og Fjordane 12B, Nord-Troms, Finnmark12B
Programmes:
P1 NO-7005 Trondheim ☎ +47 73881400 +47 73881809
24h. **N:** MF on the h also 0530, 0630, 0730, 1130, 1530, 1630. Sat on the h also 0630, 1130. Sun on the h also 0430. Reg. prgrs: see below
P2: NO-0340 Oslo ☎ +47 23047297 +47 23047480
24h cultural prgr. **N:** MF on the h 0500-0000 except 1800, 1900 2000 and 2200. Also 0530, 0630, 0730, 1130, 1630. Sat: on the h. 0500-0000 except 0900, 1200, 1800, 1900, 2000. Also 0630, 1130, 1530. Sun: on the h 0500-2300 except 1200, 1300, 1600, 1800, 1900. Also 1530.
P3: NO-7005 Trondheim ☎ +47 73881600 +47 73881609
24h youth prgr. Rly P1 2300-0500. **N:** MF on the h 0500-2300 except 1600, 1800, 2000, 2200, also 0530, 0630, 0730, 0830. Sat: on the h except 1600, 1800, 2000, 2100, 2200. Sun: on the h except 2200
Sàpmi: PB 183, NO-9730 Karasjok ☎ +47 78469200 +47 78469223; 24h in Sami language. Also on P2 MF 1230-1300. Additional prgrs on P2 in northern Norway and Oslo: MF 0600-0800, 1300-1630, (Fri also 1200-1230, 1630-1700), Sat/Sun 1700-1800
Klassisk: NO-0340 Oslo ☎ 47 23047882 +47 23048575. 24h classical music. Some rly P2
Alltid Nyheter: NO-0340 Oslo ☎ +47 23047000 +47 23045141 24h rolling news. Rly BBC World Service most of the day Sat/Sun and 2100-0500 weekdays
MP3: NRK MPETRE: NO-7005 Trondheim ☎ +47 73881600 +47 73881609. 24h teenage ch. with techno/dance music. Some rly of P3

NRK REGIONAL SERVICES:
On **P1**. **D.Prgr:** MF 0503-0530, 0533-0600, 0603-0630, 0640-0700, 0703-0730, 0733-0800, 0903-0905, 1003-1005, 1103-1105, 1230-1232, 1303-1400, 1405-1500, 1503-1600. Sat: 0703-0705, 0803-0805, 0903-0905
NRK Innlandet, Storhove, NO-2624 Lillehammer – **NRK Møre og Romsdal**, PB 1516, NO-6025 Ålesund – **NRK Nordland**, PB 1446, NO-8038 Bodø. – **NRK Oslo og Viken**, PB 4555 Nydalen, NO-0421 Oslo or PB 733 Strømsø, NO-3003 Drammen or PB 33, NO-1629 Gamle Fredrikstad - **NRK Rogaland**, PB 614, NO-4090 Hafrsfjord – **NRK Sørlandet**, PB 413, NO-4664 Kristiansand – **NRK Troms og**

Finnmark, PB 6138 Langnes, NO-9291 Tromsø or PB 1333, NO-9506 Alta – **NRK Trøndelag**, PB 2450 Torgarden, NO-7005 Trondheim – **NRK Vestfold og Telemark,** Øvre Langgate 50, NO-3110 Tønsberg or PB 284, NO-3901 Porsgrunn – **NRK Vestland,** PB 7777, NO-5020 Bergen or PB 100, NO-6801 Førde.
Ann: 1st Prgr: "P1". 2nd Prgr: "P2". 3rd Prgr: "Petre". Sami: "Datlae Sáméradio, Kárássjagás"

OTHER STATIONS:
RADIO NORGE (Comm.)
✉ Jernbanetorget 4, NO-0154 Oslo ☎ +47 07270 **W:** bauermedia.no / radionorge.com **L.P:** MD: Lasse Kokvik
D.Prgr: 24h on **DAB**. **N:** M-F: on the h. 0500-2300, also 0630, 0730, 1430, 1530. Sat: on the h. 0800-2300. Sun: on the h.0800-2300
P4 – RADIO HELE NORGE (Comm.)
✉ PB 817, NO-2626 Lillehammer ☎ +47 61248444 🖷 +47 61248445 **W:** p4.no **L.P:** MD: Trygve Rønningen
D.Prgr: 24h on **DAB**. **N:** M-F: on the h 0500-2300, also 0530, 0630, 0730, 1430, 1530, 1630. Sat-Sun: on the h 0700-2300
RADIO 1 HITS (Comm.)
✉ PB 1102 Sentrum, NO-0104 Oslo ☎ +47 22023300 🖷 +47 22952202 **W:** radio1.no **FM**(MHz): Oslo: 103.4, Bergen: 90.4, 97.1, 106.4, 107.1, Stavanger: 107.2, Trondheim: 96.3. All txs below 1 kW
RADIO METRO (Comm.)
✉ Akersgata 45, NO-0158 Oslo ☎ +47 21555910 **W:** radiometro.no
FM: Main freqs (MHz): Oslo: 106.8, Askim: 105.4, Lillestrøm: 107.9, Drammen: 101.8, Hønefoss: 103.5, Gjøvik: 105.8, Lillehammer: 105.0, Elverum/Hamar: 102,9, Trondheim: 104.2/107.0, Stjørdal: 97.5, Levanger: 99.8, Steinkjer: 95.2. All txs below 1 kW
NRJ NORGE (Comm.)
✉ Akersgata 73, NO-0180 Oslo ☎ +47 22797500 🖷 +47 22797501 **W:** nrj.no **FM:** Main freqs (MHz): Oslo: 90.5, Drammen: 95.3, Kristiansand: 93.2/106.9, Stavanger: 99.3, Bergen: 98.2, Trondheim: 95,5/105.1/106.7 All txs below 1 kW

Internet: Most stns provide webstreams and/or on-demand audio sces. **Satellite:** Most NRK-channels, radio and TV (incl NRK regional TV), Radio Norge and P4 are available through satellite.

LOCAL FM STATIONS
Around 300 low power FM commercial stns are in operation, some sharing freqs. Many of them organised through Lokalradioforbundet.

DAB: Almost all local FM stns have been granted an extension until 2022 for using FM. **W:** lokalradioforbundet.no

AFRTS (U.S. Mil.)
FM: Lifjell 101.5MHz (Stavanger). D.Prgr: 24h rly AFN Europe

SVALBARD (SPITSBERGEN)
(Norwegian Territory)

L.T: UTC +1h (28 Mar-31 Oct: UTC +2h) — **Pr.L:** Norwegian — **E.C:** 50Hz, 230V

NRK - NORSK RIKSKRINGKASTING AS (Pub.)
MW: Longyearbyen: 1485kHz 1kW (F.pl. 3 kW)
D.Prgr: 24h relay NRK P1 on DAB and FM (incl. reg. prgr NRK Troms)

FM	P1	P2	P3	kW
Isfjord R.	89.7	93.6	97.3	0.05
Ny-Ålesund	91.3	94.8		0.12
Svea	89.1	92.0		0.025

DAB: Svalbard (Platåfjellet and Longyearbyen) 12B

OMAN

L.T: UTC +4h — **Pop:** 5.1 million — **Pr.L:** Arabic — **E.C:** 240V/50Hz — **ITU:** OMA

MINISTRY OF INFORMATION
✉ Off Al Ilam Street, Madinat Al Ilam, Mina Al Fahal, 116 Muscat ☎ +968 24603222 **E:** info@omaninfo.om **W:** omaninfo.om
L.P: Minister: Abdulmunim bin Mansour bin Said al-Hasani

PUBLIC AUTHORITY FOR RADIO AND TV - RADIO SULTANATE OF OMAN (RSO)
✉ P.O. Box 1130, Madinat Al Ilam, 133 Masqat ☎+968 24 601538 🖷+968 24 602831 **W:** part.gov.om/omanradio
L.P: DG Radio: Nasser Al-Sybani. DG Eng.: Mohd Salim Al Marhouby. Dir. Freq: Salim Al-Nomani. Dir. Trs: Saif Al-Rashedi

MW	kHz	kW	MW	kHz	kW
Haima	576	100	Salalah	738	100
Bidiya	603	500	Barka (Seeb)	1242	500
Buraimi	639	100	Bahla	1278	100

FM	G	Q	Y	E	kW(TRP)
Bahla	107.3	96.5	-	-	1
Barka	101.8	107.3	-	-	5
Batina	-	-	91.7	-	
Buraimi	96.1	93.0	-	-	5
Dhalkut	-	-	94.5	-	
Dhank	-	-	91.2	-	
Haima	-	106.5	98.8	-	
Hasikiya	96.5	-	-	-	1
Dakhiliya	-	-	98.8	-	
Ibra	93.2	-	98.8	-	2
Ibri	99.1	106.9	-	-	5
Jalan Bani Buali	88.1	97.7	-	-	5
Khasab	100.6	-	-	-	1
Madha	97.4	-	-	-	0.1
Masqat	94.4	93.2	100.0	90.4	5
Mazyunah	88.2	88.5	-	-	1
Murbat	-	-	100.0	-	
Nizwa	88.5	100.5	-	-	1
Quriyat	100.4	-	-	-	2.5
Sadah	88.2	-	100.0	-	1
Saham	91.1	93.6	-	-	5
Salalah	-	-	100.0	90.4	
Sayq	89.3	94.0	-	-	5
Sur	97.2	87.6	-	-	2
Taqah	-	-	100.0	-	
Thumrait	-	93.0	100.0	91.3	

G=General Arabic prgr: 24h on MW & FM. **N:** 0300, 0700 (Fri 0830), 1300, 1600, 1700, 1900, 2000. **Q=Quran prgr:** 24h. **Al-Shabab (Youth) channel**: 24h. **R. Oman FM in English:** 24h.
Ann: A: "Idha'atul Saltanat al-Oman min Masqat." E: "This is the English Service of Radio Sultanate of Oman from Masqat".

EXTERNAL SERVICE: See International Broadcasting section.

Other Stations:
Al Wisal FM, Masqat: 96.5MHz. **W:** wisal.fm – **Hala FM,** Masqat: 102.7MHz. **W:** halafm.com – **Hi FM,** Masqat: 95.9MHz. **W:** hifmradio.com – **Merge FM,** Masqat: 104.8MHz. **W:** radiomerge.fm – **Sowt al-Khaleej**, Masqat: 107.7MHz. See Qatar for main entry.
BBC relay: Masqat 89.8 (Arabic), 103.2MHz (English).
R. France Int: Masqat 92.2MHz in Arabic.
BBC relay station: MW (702kHz 1500-2100 & 1413kHz 0030-0400, 1300-2100) & **SW:** for details see International Broadcasting section

PAKISTAN

L.T: UTC +5h — **Pop:** 221 million — **Pr.L:** Urdu (official), English (official), Balochi, Punjabi, Saraiki, Sindhi, Pashto — **E.C:** 230V/50Hz — **ITU:** PAK

PAKISTAN ELECTRONIC MEDIA REGULATORY AUTHORITY (PEMRA)
✉ Green Trust Tower, 6th Floor F-6, Jinnah Ave, Blue Area, Islamabad **W:** pemra.gov.pk **E:** info@pemra.gov.pk

PAKISTAN BROADCASTING CORPORATION (PBC, Gov.) RADIO PAKISTAN
✉ Broadcasting House, Constitution Avenue, Islamabad 44000 ☎+92 51 9214278 🖷 +92 51 9223827 **W:** radio.gov.pk **E:** info@radio.gov.pk

MW	kHz	kW	MW	kHz	kW
Khuzdar	567	*300	Multan	1035	100
Islamabad	585	500	Larkana	1053	100
Lahore-I	630	100	Quetta (city)	1134	100
Karachi (Landhi)	639	10	Rawalpindi	1152	100
Dera Ismail Khan	711	100	Peshawar-III	1170	100
Quetta (Yaru)	756	*100	Loralai	1251	10
Turbat	981	*100	Peshawar-II	1260	400
Hyderabad (city)	1008	100	Lahore (city)	1332	100

MW	kHz	kW	MW	kHz	kW
Bhawalpur	1341	10	Sibi	1584	0.25
Gilgit	1512	10	Abbotabad	1602	0.3
Skardu	1557	10	*running on low power		

NCAC: News & Current Affairs Channel on MW: 0200-1810/1900 in Urdu & English. Also regional programmes in other languages. Times vary by frequency. **N. in English**: 0300, 0800, 1100, 1300, 1600, 1700. 585/630/756kHz carry Voice of Quran 0200-0700.
FM93 (community radio stations): on 93.0MHz in Abbottabad, Bannu, Chitral, Dera Ismail Khan, Faisalabad, Gilgit, Gwadar, Hyderabad, Islamabad, Karachi, Kohat, Lahore, Muzaffarabad, Mianwali, Mithi, Multan, Larkana, Quetta, Skardu and Sargodha. Powers 2-5 kW. (Also r. CRI in Urdu & English).
Voice of Quran: 93.4MHz in Islamabad, Karachi, Lahore, Narowal, Peshawar, Quetta, Multan, Bannu, Gwadar, Sibb, Gilgit and Skardu.
Dhanak FM 94 (music): Islamabad, Karachi and Lahore on 94.0MHz.
FM101: information and entertainment channel on 101.0MHz in Abbottabad, Faisalabad, Hyderabad, Islamabad, Kalarkahar, Karachi, Lahore, Larkana, Multan, Muree, Peshawar, Quetta and Sialkot. Powers 2kW except Karachi 5kW.
Regional prgr: Khairpur 93.3MHz, Bhit Shah & Rawalpindi 93.5MHz. In tribal areas: R. Paktunhkhwa 92.2MHz. R. Swat 96.0MHz.
D.Prgr: as above in Urdu, English and regional languages. Local IDs are usually heard at sign on/off.
Ann: "This is Radio Pakistan".

AZAD KASHMIR RADIO (AKR, Gov.)

Broadcasting House, Muzaffarabad (AJK) 13100. **W:** fm93mirpur.com
MW: Mirpur 936kHz 100kW.
SW: Islamabad (Rewat) 7265kHz 100kW.
FM: Mirpur 101.4MHz, Muzaffarabad 93.0MHz.
D.Prgr: Muzaffarabad channel: 0045-0445 & 1000-1810 on FM. Mirpur: MW: 0045-0515 & 1100-1810, FM: 0045-1900. Rawalpindi-III ("Trarkhel") channel (from Islamabad 100kW): 7265kHz: 0700-0800, 1110-1300 & 1500-1810 (irr.). Prgrs on all channels also include R. Pakistan NCAC relays.
Ann: "Yeh Azad Kashmir Radio Muzaffarabad hay". 936kHz: "Mediumwave na-sau-chattis (936) kHz par. Yeh Azad Kashmir Radio hay".
IS: "Azad Kashmir" anthem at open and close.

Other, non-PBC stations (**FM** in MHz). Powers normally in Islamabad/Karachi/Lahore 2kW, other cities 1kW and university/public radio 200-500W):
Apna Karachi 107: Karachi 107.0. **W:** apnakarachi107.fm – **City FM 89:** Karachi/Lahore/Islamabad/Faisalabad 89.0 **W:** cityfm89.com – **FM98 Dosti Channel:** Karachi/Lahore/Islamabad 98.0 **W:** dostiradio.com – **FM 99 Baltistan:** Gilgit/Skardu 99.0 **W:** fm99gb.com – **FM 100 Pakistan:** Abbottabad/Gujrat/Hyderabad/Islamabad/Jhelum/Karachi/Lahore/Multan/Rahim Yar Khan 100.0 **W:** fm100pakistan.com – **FM Sunrise:** Jhelum 95.0, Sardogha/Sahiwal 96.0, Hassan Abdal/Islamabad 97.0 **W:** facebook.com/SunriseFm96 – **Hamara FM Network:** Kharian 97.0, Mandi Bahuddin 98.0 **W:** hamarafm.com.pk – **Hot FM 105,** Karachi & 13 other cities on 105.0MHz **W:** hotfm.com.pk – **Hum FM,** Islamabad & 5 other cities: 106.2 **W:** hum.fm – **Humara FM,** Faisalabad: 90.0 **W:** humara.fm – **Josh FM,** Hyderabad/Karachi/Lahore: 99.0 – **Mast FM 103,** Faisalabad/Karachi/Lahore/Multan: 103.0 **W:** mast103.com – **Power FM,** Abbottabad/Islamabad/Vehari: 99.0 **W:** power99.live – **R. Awaz:** Karachi 99.0, Hyderabad/Lahore 99.4, Bhalwal/Rajanpur 104.0, Bahawalpur/Gujrat/Jhang/Okara/Sadiqabad/Sahiwal/Sheikhpura 105.0, Gujranwala/Khanpur 106.0, Attock/Pakpattan 107.0 **W:** radioawaz.com.pk – **R. One,** Gwadar/Islamabad/Karachi/Lahore: 91.0 **W:** fm91.com.pk – **Suno FM,** 50 transmitters on 89.4MHz **W:** sunofm.pk – **VO Kashmir**: Muzaffarabad 105.4, Bagh 105.6, Rawalakot 105.8 **W:** vokfm.com.pk – **Zab FM,** Islamabad/Karachi/Larkana: 106.6 0 **W:** zabfm.org

China R. Int. (Urdu/English): Karachi/Islamabad 98.0, Kohat/Lahore/Multan 93.0.
VOA Radio Aap ki Dunyaa: via Orzu TJK 972kHz 800kW 1400-0200

PALAU (USA associated)

L.T: UTC +9h — **Pop:** 18,094 — **Pr.L:** Official languages: English, Palauan, Japanese, Sonsorolese, Tobian — **E.C:** 120V/60Hz — **ITU:** PLW

DEPARTMENT OF TRANSPORTATION, COMMUNICATION & INFRASTRUCTURE

(Communications Division) P.O.Box PS-2, Palikir, Pohnpei, FM 96941 ☎ +691 3202865 🖷 +691 3205853 **E:** transcom@mail.fm **W:** www.ict.fm/communications.html

T8AA BROADCASTING STATION (Gov)

Bureau of Domestic Affairs PO Box 279, Koror State, Republic of Palau 96940 ☎ +680 4882417 🖷 +680 4881932 **L.P:** SM: Ms Eunice Akiwo **E:** ecoparadise@palaugov.net
FM: Eco-paradise FM 87.9MHz and 89.1MHz 1900-1300 **N:** includes R. Australia via satellite. **Format:** local news, music and talkback

Other Stations:

FM	MHz	kW	Station	FM	MHz	kW	Station
2)	88.5	0.45	WWFM	4)	89.9	0.6	PWFM
1)	88.9	-	WPKR	3)‡	102.5	0.2	T8WH-FM
2)	89.5	0.45	WWFM		‡ Reported inactive		

Addresses & other information:
1) Rudimich Enterprises, Sure Save Store, PO Box 2000, Koror 96940 ☎+680 4880889 **E:** rudimch@palaunet.com **ID:** "Island Rhythm" **Format:** Contemporary Top 40 **D.Prgr:** 24h in English/Palauan – **2)** Diaz Broadcasting Co, PO Box 1327, Koror 96940 ☎**+**680 4884848 🖷 +680 4884420 **L.P:** GM Alfonzo Diaz, WWFM English & Palaun, KDFM Filipino, classical, jazz, easy listeningformat**W:**https://www.facebook.com/pages/category/Radio-Station/Diaz-Broadcasting-Company-150219442210740/ **E:** wwfm@palaunet.com **D.Prgr:** 24h – **3)** World Harvest Radio, 61300 Ironwood Rd,South Bend, IN 46614, USA ☎+1 574 2918200 🖷+1 574 2918200 **W:** whr.org **Prgr:** Music and Family Broadcasting Corporation programs in English, also available via Intelsat 19 – **4)** 1A Building [above Dollar 99 store], Room S, Floor 3, Medalai hamlet, Koror ☎ +680 4885350, 🖷 +680 488 5250 **E:** pwfm89.9@gmail.com **TXT:** +680 778 5490 US based message line +1 503 928 7718 **W:** palauwaveradio.com **ID:** "Palau Wave Radio" **L.P:** Sha Merirei Ongelungel, GM **Format:** social, cultural & political news, information and music. **D.Prgr:** 24h
NB: Calls beginning K and W are unofficial as Palau regulates its own broadc. spectrum. American-style calls are more familiar to locals.

EXTERNAL SERVICES: T8WH (Rlg.) See Int. Broadcasting section

PANAMA

L.T: UTC -5h — **Pop:** 4.3 million — **Pr.L:** Spanish — **E.C:** 120V/60Hz — **ITU:** PNR

AUTORIDAD NACIONAL DE LOS SERVICIOS PÚBLICOS (ASEP)

Vía España, Edificio Office Park, Ciudad de Panamá (Apartado Postal 0816-01235, Zona 5, Ciudad de Panamá) ☎ +507 5084500 🖷 +507 5084600 **E:** atencionalusuario@asep.gob.pa **W:** www.asep.gob.pa **L.P:** Dir: Carmela Castillo Correa

ASOCIACÍON PANAMEÑA DE RADIODIFUSIÓN (APR)

Via Brasil y Calle 50, Edificio Plaza 50, Oficina# 4, Piso 3, Ciudad de Panamá ☎ +507 3977695
L.P: Pres: José Antonio Miro Quesada Ferreyros

Call HO—, ‡ = inactive, (r) = repeater, ± = varying fq.
H of tr 24h unless otherwise stated.

MW	Call	kHz	kW	Station, location, hr. of tr.
HE01)	J35	630	2	R. Provincias, Chitré
PA01)	S22	650	5	R. Mía, Panamá
PA02)	LY	670	1	R. Hogar, Panamá
PA03)		690	5	R. Evangelio Vivo, Panamá
VE01)	R43	690	10	R. Veraguas AM, Santiago
PA04)	Q51	710	10	KW Continente, Panamá
HE02)	B50	720	10	R. República, Chitré: 1200-0300
CH01)	N26	740	5	R. Cristal, David
HE03)		750	5	R. Amistad, Los Pozos: 1000-2300
PA05)	XO	‡760	5	LV del Istmo, Panamá
PA06)		780	5	MQV Radio, Panamá
LS01)	R56	830	5	R. Península, Macaracas: 1000-0200
PA07)	L80	840	10	Nacional FM, Panamá
HE04)	L55	860	10	R. Reforma, Chitré: 1030-0400
HE05)	Q62	890	5	R. Ritmo Stereo, Chitré
PA07)	L81	910	10	Nacional FM, David
LS02)	S56	920	5	R. Mía, Los Santos

MW	Call	kHz	kW	Station, location, hr. of tr.
CH02)	K85	930	2	R. Mi Preferida,Pto. Armuelles:1000-0400
VE02)	S97	970	3	Ondas Centrales, Santiago: 1000-0200
PA08)		990	5	COC Radio (W Radio aff.), Panamá
PA09)		†1020	5	R. Ancón, Panamá
LS03)	J2	1040	2.5	Canajagua AM Stereo, Las Tablas
CE01)		1070	3	R. Mi Favorita, Penonomé
PA10)	M92	1100	5	LV de la Liberación, Panamá
PA11)	M21	1120	5	R. Sonora, Panamá: 1030-0300
PA12)	B49	1140	5	R. Panamericana, Panamá: 1100-0500
PA13)		1180	10	R. Chinavisión, Panamá (Chinese)
VE03)	U	1180	10	AM Original, Santiago: 1100-0200
LS04)		1290	5	La Nueva 1290 AM, Las Tablas
CH04)	I417	1300	1	R. Baha'í, Boca del Monte: 1200-2400
PA14)	Z38	1350	5	BBN R., Panamá
PA15)		1380	10	Bendición Radio, Panamá
LS04)	H779	1410	5	R. Mensabé, Las Tablas: 1000-0300
PA15)		1470	5	La Primerísima, Panamá
PA16)		1530	10	R. Avivamiento, Panamá
VE04)		1540	4	Festival 1540 AM, Santiago
PA17)		1560	10	R. Adventista "LV de Panamá", Panamá

Province abbreviations: (Provincias) BT = Bocas del Toro, CE = Coclé, CH = Chiriquí, CN = Colón, DA = Darién, HE = Herrera, LS = Los Santos, PA = Panamá, VE = Veraguas. **N.B:** These abbreviations are not recognized by the Post Office. Letters should carry the full name.

Addresses & other information:
BT00) BOCAS DEL TORO
BT01) Finca 13, Empalme, Changuinola - **FM:** 90.1MHz **W:** bocasondasdelcaribe.com
CE00) COCLÉ
CE01) Calle Damian Carles, Penonomé **W:** mifavorita.com.pa - **FM:** 91.9MHz
CH00) CHIRIQUÍ
CH01) Ap. 540 (or Av. 8 y Calle A Norte, Barrio Bolívar), David **W:** cristal740am.com – **CH02)** Ap. 44 (or Barriada San José), Puerto Armuelles **W:** mipreferidapanamafm.com - **FM:** 105.3MHz – **CH04)** Ap. 1187, David **W:** facebook.com/panamabahai
HE00) HERRERA
HE01) Ap. 423 (or Urb.Las Mercedes), Chitré – **HE02)** Ap. 191, Chitré **W:** facebook.com/radiorepublicalacampeona - **FM:** 93.9MHz – **HE03)** Calle Central, Los Pozos **W:** radioamistadlospozos.com – **HE04)** Ap. 194, Chitré **W:** radioreformaseoye.com - **FM:** 102.7MHz – **HE05)** Av. Pérez, Chitré **W:** facebook.com/ritmostereotellega
LS00) LOS SANTOS
LS01) Calle Central, Macaracas - **FM:** 93.7MHz – **LS02)** La Villa de Los Santos, Calle Sergio González Ruiz **W:** radiomia920.com – **LS03)** Av. Belisario Porras Final, Las Tablas **W:** canajaguaamstereo.com – **LS04)** Zahita SA, Calle 45, Bella Vista, Ed. El Conquistador, Panamá – **LS05)** Ap. 20 (or Av. Agustín Cano Castillero), Las Tablas **W:** radiomensabe.com
PA00) PANAMÁ
PA01) Ap. 5117, Panamá 5 **W:** radiomiapanama.com – **PA02)** Ap. 102 (or San Francisco de la Caleta, via Cincuentario y Av. José Matilde Pérez), Panamá 9-A **W:** radiohogar.org – **PA03)** Condomino Dorado N° 2, Ofc. 10A, Vía Ricardo J. Alfaro, Panamá **W:** radioevangeliovivo.net - **FM:** Los Santos 101.3MHz — **PA04)** Ap. 87-1324, Panamá 7 (or Vía Argentina, Edif. Carillón, Panamá) **W:** kwcontinente.com – **PA5)** Ap. 6-1192, (or 66 Oeste N° 641) El Dorado, Panamá **W:** lavozdelistmo.org – **PA06)** Alcalde Díaz, Calle Principal, Panamá **W:** imqv.com/i/radio - **FM:** Darién 95.9MHz – **PA07)** Ap. 0843-0256, Sistema Estatal de Radio y Televisión, Av. Dulcidio González, Panamá **W:** sertv.gob.pa – **PA08)** Edificio Casa de Oración Cristiana, Santa Elena, Parque Lefevre, Panamá **W:** cocradio.com – **PA09)** Calle Cuba y Calle 37, Panamá **W:** radioancon.com – **PA10)** Rua Estudiante, Antigui Cine Central, 1861, Santa Ana, Panamá **W:** facebook.com/IPDAPANAMAOFICIAL – **PA11)** Ap. 87-1165 (or Calle 63 Oeste N° E-21, Urb. Los Angeles), Panamá 7 **W:** sonora1120.com – **PA12)** Ap. 6956 (or Vía José Agustín Arango), Panamá 5 **W:** radiopanamericanapanama.com – **PA13)** Sun Tower Mall, Av. Ricardo J.Alfaro, Panamá **W:** chinavision1180am.com – **PA14)** Ap. 0860-00356, (or Vía Cincuentenario final, a 300 metros del McDonald's de Río Abajo, después del Edificio La Reina) Panamá **W:** bbnradio.org – **PA15)** Entrada de Nuevo Chorillo, frente a la Barriada Fundavico, Distrito Arraijan, Panamá **W:** bendicion-radio.com – **PA15)** Edif.La Marqueta, Vía Porras, Panamá **W:** primerisimaradioam.com – **PA16)** Av. Ernesto T. Lefevre, Panamá **W:** sopladios.org.pa/radio-avivamiento – **PA17)** Ap. 3244, Panamá 3 (or Carrasquilla, Calle 2da N° 39, Panamá) **W:** lavozdepanama.org
VE00) VERAGUAS
VE01) Ap. 48 (or Calle 9 y vía Panamericana), Santiago **W:** radioveraguas.org - Veraguas FM 101.9MHz – **VE02)** Ap. 131, Santiago **W:** ondascentrales.com - **FM:** Superstereo 99.5MHz – **VE03)** Ap. 286 (or Calle 10), Santiago **W:** amoriginal.net - **FM:** 90.7MHz – **VE04)** Calle Calidonia, Ave B Norte, Mercado Público, Santiago **W:** festival1540am.com

FM in Panamá City (MHz): 88.1 R. 10 – 88.5 88.5 FM Stereo – 88.9 Sol 88.9 – 89.3 Cool FM – 90.1 Estéreo 89 – 90.5 Super Q – 90.9 RPC Radio – 91.3 Besame – 91.7 Máxima – 92.1 Ancón – 92.5 La KY – 92.9 YXY – 93.3 Metrópolis – 93.7 María – 94.5 W Radio Panamá – 94.9 Hosanna Capital – 95.3 La Exitosa – 95.7 KW Continente – 96.1 Stereo Fe – 96.5 TVN R. – 96.9 Caliente Panamá –97.3 WAO 97½ – 97.7 Mix – 98.1 La Mega – 98.9 Ultra Estéreo – 99.3 La 99 – 99.7 Tropic Q – 100.1 Antena 8 – 100.5 Fabulosa Estereo – 100.9 Estéreo Azul – 101.3 R. Disney – 101.7 Nacional FM – 102.1 Lo Nuestro – 102.5 FM Corazón – 102.9 Blast – 103.3 Quiubo Estéreo – 103.7 Play FM – 104.1 Telemetro Radio – 104.5 K-Latin – 104.9 Estéreo Vida – 105.7 40 Principales – 106.1 Boom! – 106.5 Rock & Pop – 107.3 Omega Stereo – R. Estéreo Universidad 107.7

PAPUA NEW GUINEA

L.T: UTC +10h; Bougainville: +11h — **Pop:** 8.9million (estimated) — **Pr.L:** English, Tok Pisin, Motu + 860 ethnic langs — **E.C:** 50Hz, 240V — **ITU:** PNG

NATIONAL INFORMATION & COMMUNICATIONS TECHNOLOGY AUTHORITY (Gov)

P.O Box 8444, Boroko, NCD ☎ +675 3033200 🖷 +675 3256868, 3004829 **W:** nicta.gov.pg **E:** licensing@nicta.gov.pg **L.P:** CEO: Charles Punaha. Regulator of broadcasting. and communications (re-appointed in 2015 for a 5 year term)

NATIONAL BROADCASTING CORPORATION (Gov)

P.O. Box 1359, Boroko NCD ☎ +675 3255233 🖷 +675 3256296 **W:** www.facebook.com/NBCNewsPNG **L.P:** MD: Memafu Kapera, Dir. Engineering: Robin Vuvut
Netw.: NBC National (English/Tok Pisin), **NBC Kundu** (Prov.: English/Tok Pisin & local vernaculars), **Tribe FM** (Nat. English/Tok Pisin)
NBC National (Voice of Papua New Guinea):

MW	kHz	kW	
Port Moresby	585	10	(Some prgrs now streamed via Facebook or You Tube)

FM	MHz	kW	FM	MHz	kW
Port Moresby	90.7	1	Rabaul	100.8	0.3

D.Prgr: 1900-1400 daily **N:** on the h 1900-1400 **Format:** National public service prgr. **V:** card or letter **F.PL:** FM coverage of NBC National is being expanded nationwide at existing NBC Kundu transmitter sites.
NBC Kundu Network (local provincial stns often funded in partnership with provincial govs): 90.7MHz from Port Moresby carries some prgrs for the Voice of Blessed Peter Tarot which used to be heard on FM from several locations. It was reported in the PNG Post Courier in August 2020 that a new 10kW Medium Wave transmitter is to be installed in the Eastern Province at the Goroko site. The transmitter is being shipped from Canada when ready. Further to this announcement the NBC hopes to renovate about 5 stns per year over the next ten years, which would see major renovation work being done to most of its provincial stns. (Reported by EMTV March 15, 2020)

MW	kHz	kW	Station, slogan, location
1)	585	2	NBC Karai, "Maus Bilong Sandaun", Vanimo *
5)	810	10	NBC Morobe, "Maus Bilong Kund", Lae
9)	810	2	NBC Rabaul, "Maus Bilong Tavuvu", Rabaul
2)	900	10	NBC Kimbe, "Singaut Bilong Tavur", Kimbe *
6)	900	2	NBC Eastern Highlands, Goroka
7)	1107	10	NBC Alotau, "Maus Bilong Caauka, V. of Kula**
SW	**kHz**	**kW**	**Station, slogan, location**
10)	3260	10	NBC Madang, "Maus Bilong Garamut", Madang
11)	3325	10	NBC Bougainville, "Maus Bilong Sankamap", Buka ARB
FM	**MHz**	**kW**	**Station, slogan, location**
7)	90.4	-	NBC Milne Bay, "V. of Kula", Alotau
3)	91.5	-	NBC Western Highlands, "Eagle FM", Mt Hagen
8)	95.5	-	NBC Central "V of the Conch Shelll", Port Moresby

FM	MHz	kW	Station, slogan, location
4)	98.3	-	NBC East New Britain, "Maus Blong Tavuvur", Kenabot
6)	100.3	-	NBC Manus, "Maus Bilong Chauka", Lorengau
5)	105.0	-	NBC Morobe, "Maus Bilong Kundu", Lae

*active briefly 2017 **active briefly 2018

D.Prgr: 2000-2200, 0800-1200v. **Format:** Non-commercial local music and health, education, public safety and sports prgrs. **N:** NBC National Network. **V:** card or letter, email; send reports direct to stn.

FM: An increasing number of Kundu stns now also broadcast locally on FM from existing transmitter sites. **NB:** A full list of current Kundu FM stns is currently still unavailable.

NBC Tribe FM: c/o NBC, 1359 Boroko NCD, Port Moresby. 92.3 FM Nationwide. New youth netw. delivered via satellite. **W:** facebook.com/tribefm **F.PL:** FM coverage being expanded nationwide with local relays broadc. from Kundu tx sites but locations currently unavailable.

NB: A recent review of provincial stns may result in consolidation of NBC stns; some SW stns are not being repaired or replaced when equipment fails. Satellite delivery of NBC National and Tribe FM to be expanded via local FM txs as funding allows. Local NBC Kundu studio prgrs continue on FM (and SW only as necessary) giving 3 NBC prgr streams (2 national 1 local) at all proposed remaining locations as FM equipment also installed in association with national expansion of Kundu2 TV svce. Funding for provincial Kundu stns allocated at provincial level. National NBC services are centrally funded but need provincially funded infrastructure to be available.

Addresses & other information:

Regions: ARB=Autonomous Region of Bougainville, Cen=Central, Chi=Chimbu, EHP=Eastern Highlands, ENB=East New Britain, Eng=Enga, ESP=East Sepik, Gul=Gulf, Mad=Madang, Man=Manus, MBP=Milne Bay, Mor=Morobe, NCD=National Capital District, NIP=New Ireland, Or=Oro, SHP=Southern Highlands, WHP=Western Highlands, WNB=West New Britain, WP=Western, WSP=West Sepik

1) P.O.Box 37, Vanimo, WSP ☎ +675 8571144/1149 🖷 +675 8571305 -**2)** P.O Box 412, Kimbe, WNB ☎ +675 9835600/5185/5010 🖷 +675 9835600 **3)** P.O.Box 311, Mount Hagen WHP ☎ +675 5421000 🖷 +675 5421001 – **4)** P.O.Box 393, Rabaul, ENB ☎ +675 982 8966/67/68/69/70 🖷 +675 9828971 – **5)** P.O.Box 1262, Lae, Mor ☎ +675 472 1311/7520/4209 🖷 +675 4726423 – **6)** P.O Box 505, Lorengau, Man ☎ +675 4709079 🖷 +675 4709079 – **7)** P.O. Box 111, Alotau MBP ☎ +675 6411028/1334 🖷 +675 6411028 - **8)**1359, Boroko NCD ☎ +675 3217155 🖷 +675 3217110 **FM:** 90.7 carries Karai Network including Tribe FM [youth prgr] Sa 2100-0000 local – **9)** P.O. Box 393, Rabaul, ENB ☎ +675 9828966/67/68/69/70 🖷 +675 9828971 -**10)**P.O. Box 2036, Jomba, Mad. ☎ +675 8522415/2301/2360 🖷 +675 8522360 – **11)**P.O. Box 35 Buka, ARB ☎ +675 9739911 🖷 +675 9739912

MAJOR COMMERCIAL NETWORKS:

FM 100 Kalang Advertising Ltd (Telikom PNG subsidiary)

🖃 P.O. Box 1534, Boroko, NCD ☎ +675 3004300 🖷 +675 3004316 **L.P:** CEO: John Mong, Ops Mgr: Bonner Tito **D.Prgr:** 24h via satellite **F.PL:** Continued FM expansion nationwide

FM(MHz): Brands FM100: W Facebook FM100 PNGs Information And Music Leader) E Facebook Messaging Format: Contemporary music "PNG's Information & Music Leader" **Sports** relay 2GB Sydney NRL Live Fri/Sat/Sun - 100.1 Kandrian, 100.2 Kavieng/Goroka/Tabubil, 100.3 1kW Pt Moresby/Lorengau/Kimbe/Tabubil/Finschafen/Mendi, 100.4 Mt Hagen, 100.5 Popondetta/Lae/Namatanai/Daru/Tari, 100.6 Pomio/Buka, 100.8 1kW Rabaul/Madang/Wewak, 101.1 Kundiawa, 102.0 Paga Hill, 107.1 Mt Horeatoa/Mt Kainguma, 107.3 Mt Boregoro/Mt Waterholes, 107.7 Mt Dimodimo **Hot FM: W:** facebook.com/hot97fm **E:** sashahot97fm@gmail.com **Format:** youth oriented contemporary music - Port Moresby 97.0 and other locations

PNGFM

🖃 P.O Box 774, Port Moresby NCD ☎ +675 3234288 🖷 +675 3231628 **L.P:** MD: Rosemarie Botong, CE: Clezy Rakole **W:** cfl.com.fj/radiopng **E:** aau@naufm.com.pg **D.Prgr:** 24h via satellite

Netw.: Nau FM PD: Turner Arifeae **Format:** E, urban westernized youth market **Yumi FM** PD: **Format:** Tok Pisin, local and adult contemporary music **Legend FM Bikpla 101:** E, Hits of 1970s-2000s. **F.PL:** Continued FM expansion nationwide.

FM(MHz): Nau FM: 96.1 1kW Goroka, 96.3 1kW Lae/Madang, 96.5 1kW Kimbe/Port Moresby/Lihir/Rabaul/Lorengau, 96.7 Alotau, 96.9 1kW Mt Hagen. **Yumi FM: W:** facebook.com/pages/93yumifm 1kW Pt Moresby/Lihir, 93.3 Tinputz, 93.5 Mt Hagen, 93.7 1kW Lae/Madang, 93.9 Rabaul/Goroka, 95.0 Kundiawa, 96.3 Balimo **Legend FM Bikpla: W:** facebook.com/pages/legend-fm-png 101.1 Port Moresby/Lae/Madang/Goroka/Mt Hagen/Rabaul/Kokopo

MAJOR NON-COMMERCIAL NETWORKS

Wantok Radio Light – PNG Bible Church

🖃 Papua New Guinea Christian Broadcasting Network, Gerehu Stage 2, Sivari Rd, Port Moresby NCD ☎ +675 326 0946 +675 3262933 🖷 +675 326 1104 **L.P:** GM: Pawa Warena **W:** wantokradio.org **E:** admin@wantokradio.org **D.Prgr:** 24h via satellite **N:** NBC National bulletins 0700, 1900 **Format:** religious **F.PL:** Continued FM expansion nationwide via satellite **Affiliation:** HCJB/Evangelical Bible Missions through Life Radio Ministries, Griffin GA, USA.

SW: †7325kHz1kW Pt Moresby NCD **QSL:** r. to **E:** qsl@wantokradio.org (broadcasts periodically)

FM(MHz): 93.9 1kW Port Moresby, 105.9 Wewak/Kimbe/Buka/Popondetta/Lae/Kokopo/Kiunga/Goroka/Mt Hagen/Ialibu/Wabag/Alotau/Mendi/Kainantu/Madang

CRN (Catholic Radio Network) – Radio Maria

🖃 Radio Maria PNG Inc, PO Box 8719, Boroko, NCD ☎ +675 3259178 **L.P:** Father Martin We-en **W:** radiomariapng.net **E:** studios.pg@radiomaria.org **Format:** religious **D.Prgr:** 24h via satellite **F.PL:** continued FM expansion nationwide via satellite

FM(MHz): 98.1 Mt Hagen 101.0 Kimbe/Mendi 103.5 Port Moresby/Wewak 103.7 Lae

OTHER STATIONS:

FM	MHz	kW	Location	Station
1)	95.3		Buka ARB	New Dawn FM
2)	97.9	1	Port Moresby NCD	2G 97.9 FM

Addresses & other information:

1) Buka ARB ☎+675 9739319 🖷+675 9739285 **L.P:** Stn Mgr Aloysius Laukai **W:** bougainville.typepad.com/newdawn **E:** tambolema@daltron.com.pg – **2)** Pacific Adventist University (PAU), PMB, Boroko NCD ☎+675 3280400 **W:** pau.ac.pg facebook.com/2g.97.9fm **E:** 2g@pau.ac.pg **ID:** "Exalting God above all the earth. Psalms 97.9" NBPOL

PARAGUAY

L.T: UTC -4h (4 Oct 20-28 Mar 21, 3 Oct 21-27 Mar 22: -3h). **NB:** UTC times in schedules refer to DST period — **Pop:** 7 million — **Pr.L:** Spanish (official), Guarani (official) — **E.C:** 220V/50Hz — **ITU:** PRG — **Int. dialling code:** +595

COMISIÓN NACIONAL DE TELECOMUNICACIONES (CONATEL)

🖃 Presidente. Franco N° 780 y Ayolas, Edif. Ayfra, Asunción ☎ 21 438 2000 **W:** conatel.gov.py **E:** ccenter@contel.gov.py **L.P:** Pres: Juan Carlos Duarte Duré

UNIÓN DE RADIODIFUSORES DEL PARAGUAY (URP)

🖃 Cptan. Grauchover 2909, esq. Inglaterra, Asunción ☎ 21 290773 **E:** info@urp.com.py **W:** urp.com.py **L.P:** Pres: Javier Correa

MW	Call	kHz	kW	Station, location, h. of tr
AP01)	ZP16	550	20/12	R. Parque, Ciudad del Este
AM01)	ZP15	570	1	R. LV del Amambay, Pedro Juan Caballero
MI03)	ZP39	570	12	R. San Roque Gonzáles, Ayolas
SP01)	ZP32	590	5	R. Ycuámandyjú, San Pedro
BO01)	ZP30	610	50	R. ZP30 - LV del Chaco, Filadelfia
SP02)	ZP40	±620	5	R. Ñasaindý, San Estanislao:
CG01)	ZP19	±640	15	R. Caaguazú, Coronel Oviedo
CA01)	ZP4	650	50	R. Uno, Chaco (Asunción)
CO05)	ZP74	660	10	R. Regional, Concepción
AP02)	ZP26	660	5	R. Itapirú, Ciudad del Este
CA02)	ZP11	680	50	R. Caritas, Ñemby (Asunción)
NE01)	ZP12	700	12	R. Nacional, Pilar: (rel. R. Nal 920)
PH01)	ZP17	720	50	R. Pai Puku, Teniente M.I. Fernández:
CA03)	ZP7	730	50	R. ABC Cardinal, Nueva Italia
CZ01)	ZP38	740	1/0.5	R. Hechizo, Caazapá
CA04)	ZP42	750	5	R. LV de la Policía Nacional,San Lorenzo (Asunción)
IP01)	ZP80	760	25/10	R. Encarnación, Encarnación
CA05)	ZP70	780	30	R. Primero de Marzo, Asunción
CN01)	ZP27	800	5/3	R. Mbaracayú, Salto del Guairá
CA13)	ZP73	800	5	La Union R.800, Asunción:
GU01)	ZP6	840	5	R. Guairá, Villarrica
CR01)	ZP28	±860	1	LV de la Cordillera, Caacupé
CE01)	ZP33	±890	5/0.5	R. Tres de Febrero, Itá (895 at night)
CA06)	ZP1	920	20/100	R. Nal. del Paraguay, Chaco-i (Asuncion)
PH02	ZP9	970	80	Universo 970 AM , Villa Hayes

MW	Call	kHz	kW	Station, location, h. of tr
AM02)	ZP31	980	5	R. Mburucuyá, Pedro Juan Caballero: 0900-0100
CE02)	ZP36	1000	5	R. Mil, Chaco-i (Asuncion)
CA08)	ZP14	±1020	25	R. Ñandutí,San Lorenzo (Asunción)
MI01)	ZP43	1040	5	R. Arapysandú, San Ignacio
CE03)	ZP25	1080	10	R. Monumental, Chaco-i
AM03)	ZP71	1100	5	R. Ñú Verá, Capitán Bado
CE04)	ZP24	1120	10	La Deportiva, San Lorenzo
CR02)	CP22	1140	5/2	R. Central de Notícias, Atyrá
CA09)	ZP72	1160	10	R. Antena Dos, Asunción
CG02)	ZP52	1180	5/1	R. Coronel Oviedo – RCO-AM, Coronel Oviedo
AP03)	ZP45	1190	5	LV de la Libertad, Henendarias
CE05)	ZP44	1200	10	R. Libre, Luque
CG03)	ZP21	1230	3	Fénix AM, Caaguazú
CA10)	ZP3	1250	5	R. Asunción, Asunción
GU03)	ZP34	1260	5	R. Panambi Vera, Villarrica
CA11)	ZP53	1300	5	R. Fe y Alegria, Villa Hayes (Asuncion)
CG04)	ZP53	1310	10/0.5	LV del Este, J.E. Estgarribia
CA12)	ZP13	1330	10	R. Chaco Boreal, Asunción
CO01)	ZP37	1360	1	R. Yby Yaú, Yby Yaú
CO02)	ZP8	1380	1	R. Concepción, Concepción
CO03)	ZP42	1420	5	R. Güyrá Campana, Horqueta
MI02)	ZP35	1430	2	R. Mangoré, San Juan Bautista:
CO04)	ZP29	1450	5	Mercedita AM, Vallemi
AM04)	ZP23	1480	1	R. Dos Fronteras, Bella Vista Norte
CE06)	ZP20	1480	5	R. América, Villeta

SW	Call	kHz	kW	Station, location
BO1)	ZP30	6884	0.1	LV del Chaco Paraguayo, Filadelfia: (USB – Audio Feeds)
PH1)	ZP17	6890	0.1	R. Pa´i Puku, Tte. Irala Fernández: (USB – Audio Feeds)

NB: ± = varying freq.

Addresses & other information:

AM00 (AMAMBAY)

AM01) 14 de Mayo 485 esq Cerro León, Pedro Juan Caballero ☎336 272537 **W:** amambay570.com.py **E:** amambay570@gmail.com - **FM:** 100.5MHz – **AM02)** Villa María Victoria, Fracción San Jorge, Pedro Juan Caballero ☎336 272598 **W:** mburucuya.com.py– **AM03)** Estrella c/4 de Enero, Capitán Bado, Amambay ☎337 230 262 **W:** facebook.com/radio1100/**E:** radiozp71@gmail.com – **AM04)** Calle Iturbe 146, Bella Vista Norte **E:** fronterafm92@gmail.com - **FM:** 92.5MHz

AP00 (ALTO PARANA)

AP01) Av. Amado Benitez Gamarra, 7000 Ciudad del Este ☎ 61 572 190 **W:** radioparquecde.com **E:** radioparquecde_102.550@hotmail.com – **FM:** 102.5 MHz – **AP02)** San Blas esquina Coronel Sánchez, Ciudad del Este ☎ 61 572 208 **W:** radioitapiru.com **E:** radioitapiru@hotmail.com - **FM:** 96.1MHz – **AP03)** Juan E.O´Leary 152, 1a piso, Oficina 5, Hernandarias **W:** radiolavozdelalibertad1190.jimdo.com

BO00 (BOQUERÓN)

BO01) 29 Filadelfia, 9300 Fernheim ☎491 432 330 🖷491 432 501 **W:** zp30.com.py **E:** avisos@zp30.com.py

CA00 (CAPITAL)

CA01) Av Mariscal López 2948 c/MacArthur, Asunción ☎ 21 555-111 **W:** radiouno.com.py **E:** contacto@radiouno.com.py – **CA02)** Kubischek 661 y Azara, (Cas 1313), Asunción ☎21 213-570 **W:** caritas.com.py **E:** caritas@caritas.com.py – **CA03)** Yegros 745, Asunción ☎21 415 1730 **W:** abc.com.py/730am/ **E:** 730am@abc.com.py – **CA04)** Comandancia de la Policia Nacional, El Paraguayo Independiente c/Chile, Asunción ☎ 21 202 585 **W:** fmenvivo.com/la_voz_de_la_policia **E:** rrpnacional@gmail.com – **CA05)** Av Perón y Concepción Prieto, Asunción ☎21 300-380 **W:** facebook.com/780am **E:** administracion@780am.com.py – **CA06)** Av Blas Garay entre Iturbe y Yegros, Asunción ☎21 390 375 **W:** radionacional.gov.py **E:** radionacionaldelparaguay@gmail.com – **CA08)** Choferes del Chaco 1194 esq Carmen Soler, Asunción ☎21 218-6000 **W:** nanduti.com.py **E:** publicidad@holdingderadio.com.py – **CA09)** Estados Unidos 2019, Asunción – **E:** pastorcarlosrodriguez@hotmail.com – **CA10)** Capitán Lombardo 174 y Av Artigas, Asunción ☎992 730-600 **W:** radioasunciontv.com.py **E:** miguelfermin_fernandez@yahoo.es – **CA11)** O´Leary 1847 e66ta. y 7ma., Asunción ☎21 374-746 **W:** radiofeyalegriapy.org **E:** prensa@feyalegriapy.org – **CA12)** Alejo Garcia 2589 con Rio de la Plata, Asuncion ☎ 21 425 589 **W:** chacoboreal.com.py – **CA13)** Av Republica Argentina y Sousa, Villa Morra, Asunción ☎21 611-370 **W:** launion.com.py **E:** info@launion.com.py

CE00 (CENTRAL)

CE01) Av Enrique Doldán Ibieta y Presidente Franco, Itá ☎24 32543 **Guaraní:** 0900-1000, 1330-1430, 1800-1845 – **CE02)**Av. Luis Maria Argaña c/Felicidad, Lambaré, Asuncion ☎21 302-600 **W:** radio1000.com.py **E:** info@radio1000.com.py – **CE03)** Andrade y O´Higgins, Morra, Luque ☎21 644-330 **W:** monumental.com.py **E:** 1080monumental@gmail.com - **FM:** 91.9 MHz Estación 40 – **CE04)** Av Médicos del Chaco 6229, Lambaré, Asuncion ☎21 307 1012 **W:** ladeportiva.com.py – **CE05)** Av Zavalaa Cué 1615, Zona Su, 2300 Fernando de la Mora☎21 509 087 **W:** facebook.com/radiolibrepy**E:** jfernandez@radiolibre.com.py – **CE06)** Cas 2220, Asunción ☎21 964-100 **W:** radioiglesia.com **E:** iglesiaradio@gmail.com –

CG00 (CAAGUAZÚ)

CG01) Jóvenes por la Democracia c/Padre Molas, 3300 Coronel Oviedo ☎521 202 251 **W:** https://www.facebook.com/RadioCaaguazu/ **E:** info@radiocaaguazudigital.com - **FM:** 102.3MHz R.Más – **CG02)** Tuyuti y Antonio Vera Centurion, 3300 Coronel Oviedo ☎ 595 993 118000 **W:** rco1180.com **E:** rco1180@hotmail.com - **FM:** 91.9MHz FM del Sol – **CG03)**Caaguazú – **CG04)** Avenida San Blás No 353, Ciudad del Este ☎61 512-583 **W:** lavoz.com.py **E:** lavoz@lavoz.com.py

CN00 (CANINDEYÚ)

CN01) 1er. Intendenta c/R Méndez, Salto del Guairá ☎462 42 350

CO00 (CONCEPCIÓN)

CO01) Av San Juan y alas Paraguayo, Ybu Ya'u ☎39 210 263 **W:** Facebook: Radio Yby Yby ZP37 **E:** carlosescobar777@hotmail.es – **CO02)** Ypané. Av Boquerón, Concepción ☎971 816-303 **W:** facebook.com/radio-concepcion-1380-am **E:** mcvelaztiqui@yahoo.com **CO03)** José Luís Arbues c/Ruta 5, Horqueta ☎32 222-364 **W.:** facebook.com/radioguyracampana **E:** radioguyracampana@hotmail.es – **CO04)** Zona Urbana, Vallemi ☎351 230329 – **CO05)** Av Pinedo y Mayor Lorenzo Medina, Concepción ☎331 243-589 **W:** regional660.com**E:** contacto@regional660.com

CZ00 (CAAZAPA)

CZ01) Mariscal Estigarribia esquina Boulevard Villarica, Caazapá ☎542 232607 **E:** causacomunpy@hotmail.com

CR00 (CORDILLERA)

CR01) Dr Venancio Pino y 2nda Proyectada, Caacupé ☎511 243326 **W:** radiozp28.com **E:** cordillera860am@hotmail.com – **CR02)** Atyrá

GU00 (GUAIRA)

GU01) Pte Franco 788 y Alejo Garcia, 5000 Villarrica ☎ 541 42385 **W:** radioguaira.com.py **E:** info@radioguaira.com.py - **FM:** 103.5MHz – **GU03)** Gral Caballero 748, Villarrica ☎541 42229 **W:** panambidigital.com **E:** radiopanambivera@gmail.com

IP00 (ITAÚA)

IP01) Mcal Estigarribia-casi 14 de Mayo – Centro, Encarnación ☎71 205195 **W:** facebook.com/Encarnacion **E:** gerencia@radioencarnacion.com - **FM:** 95.7 MHz

MI00 (MISIONES)

MI01) Av Mariscal López y Capitan del Puerto, San Ignacio ☎82 232374 **W:**facebook.com/people/arapysandu-amplitud-modulada/100009510759966**E:** arapysanduam@gmail.com – **MI02)** Coronel Alfredo A Ramos esq San Juan, San Juan Bautista☎21 7212 306 **W:**radiomangore.wixsite.com/1430am **E:** mangoream@hotmail.es – **MI03)** 7° y 2° Projectadas, Villa Permanente,Ayolas ☎595 072 222 **W:** radiosanroque.com **E:** radiosanroque570@gmail.com

NE00 (ÑEEMBUCÚ)

NE01) Alberdi y Av Iralda, Pilar ☎786 232219 **W:** radionacional.gov.py **E:** zp12pilar@gmail.com

PH00 (PRESIDENTE HAYES)

PH01) Ruta Transchaco km. 389, Tte. Irala Fernández, Chaco ☎21 3386140(In Asuncion J. Eulogio Estigarribia c/ M. Molas ☎21 605754) **W:** radiopaipuku.org.py **E:** rppuku@tigo.com.py – **PH02)** Av Mariscal López 2948 casi McArthur, Asunción ☎21 450 283 **W:** radio970am.com.py **E:** info@radio970am.com.py – produccion.970am@gmail.com

SP00 (SAN PEDRO)

SP01) Ruta 11 Juana M de Lara, Villa de San Pedro ☎34 2222300 **E:** radioycuamandyyu@gmail.com – **SP02)** Av Cnl. Zoilo González casi. Pedro Juan Caballero, San Pedro ☎343 420957 **W:** radionasaindy.com.py **E:** rnasaindy@click.com.py

FM in Metro Asunción and Central (MHz): 88.3 R.Ñemby – 89.1 R. Conquistador – 90.1 Mix 90.1 FM – 90.7 Ysapy – **CE03)** 91.1 Estacion 40 – 91.5 R.Top Milenium – 91.9 HEi – 92.3 Los 4o Principales – 92.7 R.Vibras – 93.9 R.Universal – 94.3 RQP – 94.7 R. Azul y Oro – **CA06)** 95.1 R.Nacional – 95.9 R. Amor – 96.5 R. Disney – **CA05)** 97.1 FM Latina – 97.9 R.Nuevo Tiempo – 98.5 ABC FM – 99.1 R.Corazón – 99.5 CFA Radio – 100.1 Canal Cien – 100.5 La Klasikera – 100.9 Monte Carlo – 101.3 R. Farra – 102.1 R. Obedira – 103.1 FM Popular – 103.7 R.Exclusiva – 105.1 R.Venus – 106.1 Emisoras Paraguay – 106.5 Global Mix – 106.9 R.Urbana – 107.3 R. Maria – 25) 107.7 FM Concert

PERU

L.T: UTC -5h — **Pop:** 32.9 million — **Pr.L:** Official languages: Spanish, Aymara, Quechua — **E.C:** 220V/60Hz — **ITU:** PRU — **Int. dialling code:** +51

MINISTERIO DE TRANSPORTES Y COMUNICACIONES (MTC)

✉ Jr. Zorritos 1203, Cercado de Lima, Lima 1 ☎ 1 6157800 **E:** atencionalciudadano@mtc.gob.pe **W:** www.mtc.gob.pe
L.P: Minister: Edmer Trujillo Mori

SOCIEDAD NACIONAL DE RADIO Y TELEVISIÓN (SNRTV)

✉ Edificio Capital Golf, Av. Circunvalación del Club Golf Los Incas 154, Oficina N° 202, Santiago de Surco, Lima ☎ 1 3992100 **E:** contacto@snrtv.org.pe **W:** snrtv.org.pe **LP:** Pres: José Antonio Miro Quesada Ferreyros

MW	Call	kHz	kW	Station, location, h of tr.
LM01)	OBX4E	540	10	R. Inca del Perú, Lima: 24h
LL01)	OCX2D	540	1	R. San Antonio, El Porvenir
TC20)	OBU6W	550	1	R. Bacan Sat // 750, Pocollay
JN49)	OBU4M	560	1	R. Bacan Sat, Sicaya
LM02)	OBZ4L	±560	5	R. Oriente, Lima
LB01)	OBX1H	560	5	Radiomar, Chiclayo
IC33)	OAM5I	570	1	R. OAM5I, Salas
LB02)	OAU1M	570	3	R. Univ. Nal. Pedro Ruiz Gallo, Lambayeque
LL51)	OAM2M	570	3	R. Antena 9, Huamachuco
CJ01)	OAX2E	580	10	R. Marañón, Jaén: 24h
LL02)	OCY2L	580	1	R. El Sol, La Esperanza
LM03)	OAX4M	580	12	R. Maria, Lima: 24h
PU58)	OAM7N	580	1	R&TV Aswanqhari, Azángaro: 0900-0200
AQ02)	OCX6V	590	1	NSE Radio, Arequipa
IC28)	OAM5E	590	1	R. Sembrador, Chincha
TC28)	OCU6P	590	1	R. OCU6P, Candarave
LL03)	OBX2B	600	1	R. Onda de Paz (IPDA), Trujillo: 24h
LM04)	OBZ4W	‡600	10	R. Cora, Lima: 24h
MQ19)	OCU6S	600	1	R. OCU6S, Marsical Nieto
PI55)	OCU1K	600	1	R. Frias, Frias
CJ32)	OCY2I	610	6	R. Santa Monica, Chota: 1100-0100, Sun 1145-1700
PU61)	OAM7M	610	1	R. Continental, Ayaviri
TC19)	OBU6V	610	1	R. OBU6V, Pocollay
AQ53)	OCX6K	620	1	R. Maria, Uchumayo, Aqp
LL04)	OAX2M	620	0.4	R. Chepen, Chepen
LM05)	OBU4B	620	10	R. Ovación, San Isidro
CU72)	OBU7I	630	1	Chaski R., Urubamba: 1000-1500, 1700-0100
PI04)	OBX1U	630	18	R. Cutivalú "LV del Desierto", Castilla: 1000-0100 Sat/Sun 1100
LB03)	OAU1Y	640	3	R. La Luz, José Leonardo Ortiz
LM06)	OAZ4K	640	10	R. Del Pacifico, Lima: 1030-0430
PU01)	OBX7B	640	10	R. Onda Azul, Puno. 0800-0400, S/S -0300
AM11)	OAU9D	‡650		R. Kampagkis, Nieva
CJ67)	OBU2P	650	1.5	R. Bendición Cristiana, Huambos: 1000-0400
IC25)	OCU5Q	650	1	R. OCU5Q, Pueblo Nuevo
LL05)	OAX2N	650	1	R. Regional del Norte, Trujillo
PU57)	OBM7C	650	1	R. OBM7C, Sandia
TC24)	OCU6L	650	1	R. OCU6L, Alto de la Alianza
CU35)	OAZ7J	660	3	R. Santa Monica, Wanshaq
LB04)	OCX1U	660	3	R. J.H.C., Chiclayo
LM07)	OCX4R	660	10	R. La Inolvidable, Lima: 1100-0700
PU02)	OAX7H	670	10	R. Nal. del Perú, Puno
CJ03)	OCY2Y	680	5	R. San Luis, Jaén
CU73)	OBU7G	680	1	R. Vida, Cusco
IC01)	OAX5E	680	5	Emisora del Pacifico, Ica: 1100-0600
LL06)	OBX2L	680	0.5	R. Amauta, Chócope
LM08)	OBX4A	680	20	R. RBC, San Isidro
MQ20)	OCU6Q	680		R. Americana, Moquegua
PA13)	OAM4B	680	5	R. OAM4B, Chaupimarca
CU74)	OAM7C	690	1	R. Altiva, Yanaoca
CU04)	OBU7K	700	1	R. La Salle, Maras
JN01)	OBU4J	700	3	R. La Luz, El Tambo
LL07)	OBU2T	700	1	R. Sausal Superior, Ascope
LM09)	OBZ4H	700	25	R. R. Integridad, San Miguel
SM15)	OAU9A	700	10	R. Maria, Moyobamba
AQ04)	OAU6L	710	1	R. Amor, Socabaya, Aqp
CJ63)	OCU2X	710	5	R. TurboMix, Cajamarcal
C02)	OBX5Q	710	5	R. Programas del Perú, Ica
MD01)	OCX7I	‡710	10	R. Nacional del Peru, Puerto Maldonado
CU05)	OBU7D	720	3	NSE R., Santiago
JN04)	OAU4E	720	10	R. Sideral, La Oroya: 24h
LL08)	OAX2J	‡720	25	R. Nal.. del Perú, Trujillo
LB06)	OAU1O	720	0.5	R. Frecuencia Oceánica, San José
PU45)	OCU7J	720	2	R. Noticias, Puno
CJ05)	OBU2Q	730	2.5	R. Maria, Cajamarca
LM10)	OAX4G	730	50	R. Programas del Perú - RPP, San Isidro:24h
PI05)	OAX1D	730	10	R. del Pacifico, Piura: 1100-0500
PU52)	OAM7X	730	1	R. Altura, Macusani: 0900-0100
TC20)	OCU6G	730	1	R. OCU6G, Tacna
AQ05)	OAX6C	740	10	R. Continental, Paucarpat Aqp
CJ38)	OBX2U	740	5	R. Ilucan, Cutervo: 1000-0400
CU06)	OBU7C	740	1	R. Rede, Cusco
JN46)	OCU4X	740	3	R. Vision, Huancayo
LL09)	OCX2X	740	1	R. El Puerto, Pascamayo
PU50)	OAM7R	740	1	R. Publica, Juliaca
CU75)	OCU7Q	750	1	R. Tupac Anaru/FM, Yanaoca Canas: 0900-0200
PA01)	OCX4X	750	10	R. Los Andes, Cerro de Pasco: 1000-0400
IC27)	OAM5D	750	1	R. OAM5D, Chincha
TC14)	OBU6I	750	1	R. Bacan Sat, Pocollay
SM19)	OAU9G	750	5	R. OAU9G, Bellavista
AP11)	OBU5B	760	1	R. Municipal, Chincheros
CU91)	OCX7V	760		R. Cadena Los Andes, Chaski
LL10)	OBX2K	760	0.5	R. Andino, Otuzco
LM11)	OCU4G	760	10	R. Bienstar, Chorillos //1360 24h
MD10)	OBM7K	760	1	R. OBM7K, Mazuku
PU59)	OAM7Q	760	1	R. Azángaro, Azángaro
AQ06)	OBX6H	770	2.5	R. La Inolvidable, Caiama, Aqp
CU76)	OCU7K	770	1	R. LV Evangelica, Urcos
LB31)	OCX1T	770	3	R. Vision, José Leonardo Ortiz: 24h
PU03)	OAU7D	770	2.5	R. LV de Allincapac, Macusani
AY31)	OCU5L	780	2	R. OCU5L, Ayacucho
CJ07)	OBU2N	780	1	R. Coremarca, Bambamarca: 1000-0200
LM12)	OAX4X	780	3	R. Victoria,Lima: 24h
PU04)	OAZ7S	780	10	R. Nuevo Tiempo, Juliaca: 24h
TB01)	OAX1K	780	10	R. Nal. del Perú, Tumbes
CU07)	OAZ7H	790	3	R. La Luz, Cusco
LL11)	OAX2I	790	10	R. Programas del Perú - RPP, Trujillo
TC16)	OBU6D	790	2.5	R. Uno, Tacna
AQ07)	OBX6A	800	0.3	Contacto Sur, Cerro Colorado, Aqp
CJ71)	OCU2Y	800	3	R. Vision, Cajamarca: 24h
IC03)	OBX5B	‡800	0.5	R. Sur, Ica
JN05)	OBU4D	800	1	R. Vida, Huancayo
LM13)	OAU4H	800	0.5	R. La Luz, Huaral
PI06)	OCX1P	800	1	Telecom del Norte, Piura
AY19)	OBU5F	810	1.5	ABC R. TV, Huamanga
AP19)	OCU5Z	810	3	R. Asociación Cultural Tintaya, Cotabambas
CJ80)	OCU2V	810	1	R. Onda Popular, Jaen
CU70)	OAM7E	‡810	5	R. Jerusalen, Cusco
LL12)	OAU2G	810	1	R. Apocali, Trujillo
MQ14)	OCU6Q	810	2	R. R.Santa Cruz, Moquegua
MQ16)	OCU6R	810	1	R. OCU6R, General Sanchec
PU05)	OAX7T	810	10	R. Programas del Perú - RPP, Juliaca: 24h
CJ43)	OBX2J	820	0.5	R. Nuevo Continente, Cajamarca
PI54)	OBU1X	820		R. Vision, Piura
LM14)	OAX4O	820	20	R. Libertad, Lima: 1000-0900
CU08)	OAZ7U	830	1	R. Inti Raymi, Santiago: 0900-0100
CJ62)	OCU2M	830	1	R. Universo, Bambamarca
JN06)	OAU4C	830	10	R. Capital, El Tambo
LL52)	OAM2A	830	5	R. Educacion, Trujillo
PU53)	OAM7W	830	1	R. OAM7W, Macusani
TC02)	OAX6D	830	10	R. Nacional del Perú, Tacna
AN01)	OAU3Q	840	1	R. Vision, Casma: 24h
AN25)		840		R. Campesina, Huari: 24h
AP15)	OCU5N	840	1	R. OCU5N, Abancay
AQ01)	OBX6Y	840	1	R. Azul, Cayama Aqp: 24h
CJ08)	OAU2E	840	1	R. Nuevo Continente, San Ignacio
CU58)	OCU7I	840	1	R. Santa Cruz, Kunturkanki
PI50)	OCU1C	840	1	R. Campesina de Ayabaca), Ayabaca
AM12)	OBX9W	850	1	R. OBX9W, Chachapoyas
CU77)	OAM7I	850	5	R. Lorena, San Sebastian
HN19)	OBU3B	850	1	R. OBU3B. Cerro Jactay
HV08)	OAM5L	850	1	R. OAM5L, Acori
LB49)	OCU1Y	850	1	R. OCU1Y, Chiclayo
LM15)	OAX4A	850	40	R. Nal. del Perú, Lima: 24h
PI56)	OBU1M	850	1	R. Nal. del Peru, Ayabaca
TC11)	OAU6S	‡850		R. Nal. del Peru, Tarata
PU35)	OBU7Z	850		R. Pachamama, Puno: 0830-0300
PI08)	OCX1M	860	3	R. Nuevo Norte, Sullana
PU609	OBM7B	860		R. OBM7B, Sandia

MW	Call	kHz	kW	Station, location, h of tr.
AQ52)	OCX6F	870	2.5	R. Impacto Universal, Uchumayo Aqp
CU10)	OCX7R	870	1	R. Mundo, Wanchaq: 24h
JN34)	OCX4D	870	2.5	R. Huancayo, El Tambo: 24h
LB08)	OBX1F	870	10	R. Programas del Perú - RPP, Chiclayo: 24h
PU06)	OAU7O	870	5	R. Libertad, Puno
AY22)	OBU5W	880	1	R. OBU5W
LL15)	OAX2P	880	2	R. Sintonia, Trujillo
LM16)	OBZ4N	880	50	R. Union, Lima: (IPDA) 24h
PU09)	OCU4S	880	5	R. Cumbre, Chaupimarca
AP16)	OCU5J	890	1	R. Cielo, San Pedro de Cachora
CU56)	OCU7C	890	1	R. Laramani, Espinar
IC29)	OCU5W	890	1	R. OCU5W, Ica
PU07)	OBX7S	890	3	R. Bahá'í del Lago Titicaca, Chiucuito: 0900-0200
CJ10)	OAU2N	890	1	R. Nor Andina, Celendin
AQ11)	OBX6K	900	3	R. Nevada, Uchumayo, Aqp: 24h
HN02)	OAX3E	900		R. Ribereña, Aucaycu
LM17)	OBX4X	‡900	10	R. Felicidad, Lima: 24h
MD11)	OBM7M	900	1	R. OBM7M, Inambari (F.PI)
PI52)	OCU1P	900	1	R. Huarmaca, Huarmaca
AY02)	OAU5M	910	1	R. Estacion Wari, Ayacucho
CU40)	OAU7M	910	1	R. Regional – R.Quechua, Sicuani
PU08)	OAU7G	910	1	R. Frontera, Juliaca
CJ66)	OAM2G	920	3	R. Vision, Samangay: 24h
CU66)	OAM7H	920	1	CVC La Voz, Cusco
IC04)	OCX5C	920	1	R. Stelar, Chinca Alta
MD07)	OCU7W	920	1	R. R.Red Andina, Tambopata
LL16)	OBX2S	920	1	R. Ollantay, Virú
PI10)	OBX1J	920	10	R. Programas del Peru - RPP, Piura: 24h
PU42)		920		R. Campesina, Juli: 0900-0300
SM01)	OAX9V	920	1	R. Marginal, Tocache
TC16)	OBU6M	920	2.5	R. Uno, Tacna: 24h
AM13)	OBX9V	930	5	R. OBX9V, Huambo
AQ12)	OBX6T	930	5	R. Yaravi, Cerro Colorado, Aqp.
AY23)	OBU5S	930	1	R. OBU5S, Pucar del Sara Sara
CU67)	OAM7J	930	1	R. Cadena Sur, Espinar
LB40)	OCU1O	930	3	R. Nor Andina, Olmos: 0900-0300
LL17)	OCX2V	930	1	R. Inti, Chepén
LM18)	OAX4E	930	5	Moderna - R.Papa, Lima: 24h
PU09)	OBU7T	930	3	R. Cadena Colca, Juliaca
AQ55)	OBU6G	940	1	R. OBU6G, Cotahuasi
CJ58)	OBX2G	940		R. Cutervo, Cutervo - 0500
CU13)	OBX7P	940	1.5	R. Las Vegas – W Radio, Wanchaq: 24h
JN08)	OBU4E	940	1	R. Luz, Jauja
PI47)	OBU1Y	940	1	R. Studio Satelite, Tambo Grande
AN02)	OBX3S	950	1	R. Programas del Perú - RPP, Chimbote
AP12)	OBU5R	950	1	Radio y TV Mallmanya, Callhuahuacho
AY24)	OBU5N	950	1	R. OBU5N, Paucar del Sara Sara
CJ72)	OAM2H	950	1.5	Onda Popular, Bambamarca
PU46)	OAM7S	950	1	R. OAM7S, Juliaca
SM20)	OAU9K	950	1.5	R. OAU9K, Shucshuyacu
TC13)		950		R. Campesina, Tarata
AQ13)	OBX6S	960	18	R. El Pueblo 960, Mariano Melgar, Aqp
CU14)	OBU7P	960	1	R. Concierto Santa Monica, Espinar
JN09)	OCY4V	960	1	R. Manantial, Chilca
LB11)	OBX1Y	±960	3	R. WSP, Chiclayo: (r. on 958): 0900-0400
LM19)	OAX4D	960	10	R. Panamericana, Lima: 24h
CJ13)	OAU2K	970	1	R. Lider del Norte, Cajamarca
CU15)	OAU7A	970	5	R. Tropicana, Wanchaq
IC05)	OBX5A	970	1	R. Comericial Sonora, Ica
PI11)	OBX1V	‡970	1.5	R. La Capullana, Sullana
PU11)	OBU7B	970	1	R. Union Qollasuyo, Juliaca
AQ14)	OAU6F	980	1.5	R. Universidad, Arequipa: 1000-0100
AM14)		980		R. Comercial Cosmos, La Peca
AY14)	OBU5K	980	1	R. LV de Huamanga, Huamanga
CJ42)	OCX2R	980	1	Andina R., Chota
CU78)	OCU7X	980	1	R. Caden Sur, Sicuani
JN10)	OBU4H	980	1	R. OBU4H, Huancayo
LB12)	OAU1N	980	1	R. Primavera, Lambayeque
PI51)	OBU1N	980	1	R. Campesina, Huancabamba
AN04)	OBX3L	990		R. Peruana, Chimbote
CJ14)	OBX2M	990	0.5	R. Contumaza, Contumaza
LM20)	OBX4J	990	12	R. Latina, Miraflores: 24h
PA07)	OCU4A	990		R. Oro, Huayllay
PI57)	OCU1H	990	3	R. Bendicion Cristiana, Piura
PU47)	OCU7T	990	2.5	R. Milagros, Juliaca
TC04)	OAX6K	‡990	10	R. Continental, Tacna
AQ15)	OBX6R	1000	2.5	R. Edesa, Cerro Colorado, Aqp
CU16)	OAZ7P	‡1000	2	R. Prensa al Dia, Cusco

MW	Call	kHz	kW	Station, location, h of tr.
HV01)	OBX5W	1000	1	R. Lircay, Lircay
HN03)	OBX3V	1000	1	R. Huanuco
JN50)	OBU4Z	1000	1	R. OBU4Z, Pariahuanaca
LB44)	OCU1N	1000	7	R. OCU1N, San José
LM75)	OAM4N	1000	1	R. OAM4N, Barranca
AM10)	OBX9T	1010	1	R. Fé, Bagua Grande
AQ56)	OBU6L	1010	1	R. Orcopampa, Orcopampa
AP13)	OBU5T	1010	1	R. OBU5T, Cotabambas
CJ15)	OBX2P	‡1010	1.5	R. San Francisco, Cajamarca
CJ86)		1010		R. Cajamarca, Cajamarca
LM54)	OAX4U	1010	10	R. Cielo, Lima: 24h
PI13)	OBU1L	1010	1	LV de las Huaringas, Huancabamba
PU48)	OCU7P	1010	1	R. Nac. del Peru, Juli
TB02)	OBZ1C	1010	1	R. Sonora, Tumbes
AY25)	OBU5M	1020	0.5	R. AM Vida, Huamanga
CJ41)	OAU2P	1020	2	R. Bambamarca, Bambamarca
LB45)	OCU1M	1020	1	R. OCU1M, José Leonardo Ortiz
CU17)	OBU7O	1020	1	R. Informes, Sicuani
CU85)	OAM7Y	1020	5	R. Kinsachata Tintaya, Espinar
JN11)	OBU4F	1020	1	R. Cristo Vive, Huancayo
PI14)	OBU1D	1020	1	R. La Luz, Piura
TC05)	OAU6J	‡1020	1	R. Internacional, Tacna
AQ16)	OCX6L	1030	1	R. Cumbia, Arequipa
CJ73)	OAM2E	1030	5	R. La Beta Cajamarca
CU18)	OCX7O	1030	1	R. HG-AM, Cusco
LL19)	OAU2U	1030	5	R. Los Andes, Huamachuco
PU12)	OAX7N	1030	1	R. LV del Altiplano, Puno
SM16)	OBX9Z	1030	1	R. OBX9Z, San Ramon
AN29)	OAU3P	1040	1	R. Nueva Vida, Chimbote
CJ74)	OAM2L	1040	1	R. OAM2L, Pomahuaca
CU19)	OAU7H	1040	1	R. Los Andes, Espinar
IC06)	OBX5U	1040	1	R. La Luz, Ica
LM21)	OBX4O	1040	10	R. Metropolitiana, Miraflores
PI15)	OAZ1D	1040	1	R. Vecinal, Piura
AQ17)	OBX6B	1050	3	Bethel R., Uchumayo, Aqp
CJ89)		1050		R. Tigre, Rejopampa, Sorochuco
JN12)	OBZ4J	1050	1	Bethel R., Huancayo
LB42)	OCU1E	1050	3	R. Bendición Cristiana, Chiclayo
LL20)	OCX2B	1050	1	R. San Sebastian (R. Maria), Chepen
PI58)	OAZ1C	1050	1	R. Superior, Chulucanas
PU13)	OAZ7Q	1050	1	R. Noticias, Juliaca: 24h
AN27)	OAU3S	1060	3	R. R.Cielo, Chimbote
AP14)	OBU5Q	1060	2	R. Restauracion, Andahuaylas
AY26)	OAU5P	1060	1	Estacion Wari, Huamanga
CJ17)	OCY2O	±1060	5	R. Sudamerica, Cutervo
CU20)	OAU7U	1060	1	R. Estudio 1060, Cusco
LM22)	OCY4D	1060	1	R. Exito, Lima
MD04)	OCU7V	1060	1	Tambopata
MQ10)	OBU6O	1060	1	R. Municipilidad, Omate
PI41)	OBU1F	1060		R. Studio 1060. Piura
TU10)	OCU1V	1060	2	R. OCU1V, Tumbes
AQ18)	OAU6K	1070	1	R. Trinidad, Paucarpata, Aqp.: 1000-0200
HN13)	OAU3N	1070	1	R. OAU3N, Huánuco
HV09)	OAM5K	1070	1	R. OAM5K, Huancavelica
IC07)	OAX5A	1070	0.2	R. San Juan, San Juan de Marcona
JN13)	OBX4G	1070	1	R. Visión, San Ramón
LB14)	OAU1J	1070	1	R. Vida, José Leonardo Ortiz
SM03)	OBX9J	1070	3	R. Andes, Tarapoto
CJ18)	OAU2L	1080	1	R. Nueva Vida, Cajamarca
CU21)	OAX7S	1080	2.2	R. Salkantay, Cusco
JN51)	OBU4W	1080	1	R. Cielo, Huancayo
LM23)	OAU4I	1080	10	R. La Luz, Lima: 24h
MQ11)	OBU6H	1080	1	R. LV del Sur, Moquegua
PA10)	OCU4O	1080	5	R. Mineria, Chaupimarca
PI16)	OBX1D	±1080	1.5	R. La Luz, Piura
PU14)	OCU7O	1080	1	R. Nacional, Ayaviri
AQ61)	OBX6X	1090	1	R. Amistad (IPDA), Arequipa
AY05)	OAU5F	1090	1	R. Inti Andina, Aucara
TU11)	OCU1Z	1090	2	R. Vision, Tumbes (F.PI)
JN14)	OCY4G	1100	1	Sonorama R., Huancayo
LB15)	OBX1L	1100	1	R. Ondas de Paz (IPDA), Chiclayo
LM64)	OAZ4W	1100	1	R. Programas del Peru - RPP, Barranca
LM71)	OCU4N	1100	1	R. OCU4N, Cañete
LL46)	OCU2E	1100		R. 1000, Julcan
PU15)	OBX7Z	1100	1	R. LTC, Juliaca
CJ20)	OCX2U	1110	1	R. Jaén, Jaén: 1030-0600
CU22)	OCX7T	1110	5	R. Machupicchu, Cusco
HN17)	OAU3R	1110	3	R. Cielo, Huánuco
LM24)	OAU4J	1110	1	R. Feliz, Lima: 24h

MW	Call	kHz	kW	Station, location, h of tr.
MQ04)	OBU6F	1110	1	R. Austral, Ilo
PI17)	OCX1R	1110	0.5	R. Centro Popular, La Union
AQ20)	OCX6U	1120	1	R. Municipal, Cerro Colorado, Aqp
AY06)	OAU5H	1120	1	R. Quispillaccta, Ayacucho: 0900-1400. 2100-0100
CJ61)	OAM2F	1120	3	R. Paz, Chota: 1000-0100
HV03)	OAU5W	1120	0.5	R. Huayllahuara
JN58)		1120		R. San Bartolome, Junin
LL21)	OBX2I	1120	1.5	R. Dinamica, Trujillo
LM67)	OCU4E	1120	1	R. Bendición, Barranca
LT05)	OAX8A	1120	5	R. Nacional, Iquitos
UC09)	OBX8R	±1125	1	R. Nuevo Tiempo, Campoverde (nf 1120)
AQ63)	OCU6I	1130	1	R. OCU6I, Camaná
CJ21)	OAX2V	1130	1.2	R. Onda Popular, Cajamarca
CU65)	OAM7F	1130	5	R. Ondas de Paz, Cuzco (IPDA)
JN60)	OAM4K	1130		R. OAM4K, Junin
LM27)	OAX4N	1130	2.6	R. Bacán Sat., Lima: 24h
MQ09)	OBU6Q	1130	3	R. Cielo, Moquegua
PI53)	OCU1R	1130	1	R. OCU1 R. Huarmaca)
PU16)	OAU7B	1130	1	R. Onda Popular, Juliaca
AN07)	OAU3C	1140	1	R. Bahia, Chimbote: 1000-0200(Sun -2200)
AQ21)	OAX6L	1140	1	R. Capital, Cerro Colorado, Aqp: (rel. Lima)
CJ83)	OAM2O	1140	5	R. Maria, Chota
IC08)	OAX5W	1140	0.5	R. Chinchaysuyo, Chinca Alta
JN16)	OCY4C	1140	1	R. Programas del Perú - RPP, Pilcomayo
LB16)	OAU1T	1140	5	R. Fraternal, Ferreñafe
LL48)	OCU2D	1140		Chami R., Otuzco
PI18)	OBX1W	1140	1.5	R. Piura, Piura
CJ22)	OCY2E	1150	0.5	R. Chasquillacta, Pedro Galvez: 1030-2200
CU23)	OCX7Q	1150	2.5	R. Universal, Wanchaq: Mon-Sat 0900-1200
PA02)	OBU4K	1150	5	R. Mineria, Cerro de Pasco
PA16)	OAM4R	1150	1	R. OAM4R, Huayllay (F.PI)
PU17)	OAU7X	1150	2.5	R. La Sureña, Juliaca:
AY07)	OBX5O	1160	1	R. Huanta 2000, Huanta : 1030-0130
JN52)	OCU4V	1160	1	R. Maranatha, Huancayo
LL22)	OAX2C	1160	0.3	R. Libertad Mundo, Trujillo: 24h
LB17)	OCX1S	1160	1	Radiales Nor Oriental del Marañon, Chiclayo
LM56)	OAX4C	1160	5	R. 1160/R.Onda Cero Lima: 24h
MD02)	OCX7Z	1160	1	R. del Sur, Tambopata
MQ05)	OBX6G	‡1160	1	R. Nac. del Perú, Moquegua
PI59)	OCU1Q	1160	1	R. LV Campesino, Huarmaca
AN08)	OAZ3K	‡1170	1	R. Nor Peruana Chimbote
AQ22)	OBX6L	1170	10	R. Programas del Perú, Uchumayo, Aqp
CJ24)	OAU2M	1170	1	R. Jerusalen, Cajamarca (IPDA 24/7)
CU24)	OBU7F	1170	1	Bethel R., Cusco
HV06)	OAM5B	1170	2	R. OAM5B, Acobamba
IC19)	OAU4N	1170	1	R. Horizonte La Voz del Agro, Pueblo Nuevo
JN58)	OAM4I	1170	1	R. COSAT, Satipo
LM72)	OAM7A	1170	1	R. OAM4E, Paramonga
PU18)	OCX7Y	1170	0.5	R. Constelación, Puno
CJ25)	OAM2K	1180	1	Municipalidad Provincial de Jaen, Jaen
CJ23)	OAU2T	1180	1	R. Siglo 21, Chota
JN18)	OCY4Z	1180	1	R. Libertad Junin
LM62)	OCU4K	1180	10	NSE R., Lima
PI60)	OAZ1H	1180	2.5	R. Vencinal, Piura
TC14)	OCU6N	1180	1	R. Bacan Sat 2, Pocollay
AN09)	OBX3D	1190	5	R. Ancash, Huaraz
AQ23)	OCX6G	1190	1	R. Central de Noticias, Miraflores Aqp
AY27)	OBU5U	1190	2	R. OBU5U, Huamanga
LB18)	OAX1E	1190	10	Bravasa R., Chiclayo
CU25)	OAX7B	1190	2	R. Tawantinsuyo, Cusco
MD08)	OAM7V	1190	3	R. Cielo, Tambopata
SM21)	OAU9J	1190	3	R. Vision, Nueva Cajamarca (F.PI)
TB08)	OCU1S	1190	3	R. Cielo. Tumbes
AP03)	OBX5X	1200	1	R. Comercial, Abancay
CJ26)	OAU2A	1200	1	LV de Cumbe, Cajamarca: 1000-0200
JN19)	OAU4G	1200	3	R. Andes, Huancayo
LM60)	OAX4B	1200	3	Cadena R. 1200, Lima
PI61)	OCU1A	1200	1	R. Fe, Piura
PU19)	OCX7S	1200		R. Continental, Juliaca
PU55)	OAM7O	1200	1	R. Universidad, Puno
TC06)	OAU6P	1200	3	R. La Luz, Tacna
HV05)		1200		R. Master Mix, Huancavelica
AN34)	OBU3D	1210	1	R. OBU3D, Chimbote
CJ75)	OCU2W	1210	1	R. OCU2W, Querocoto
CU26)	OAX7M	1210	1	R. Quillabamba, Quillabamba: 1000-0300
CU55)	OCU7B	1210	1	R. Qorilazo, Chumbivilcas
HN12)	OBX3X	1210	1	R. Ondas de Paz, Huanuco (IPDA)
JN20)	OCY4T	1210	1	R. Galaxia, Satipo
LL24)	OAX2Q	1210	1	R. Universo, Trujillo: 24h
AQ24)	OAX6X	1220	10	R. Melodia, Hunter, Aqp: 24h
CU02)	OAU7N	1220	1	R. Universidad de San Antonio Abad , Cusco: 24h
IC20)	OBU5I	1220		R. Bethel, San Clemente
JN53)	OCU4W	1220	1.5	R. Cora, Huancayo
LB19)	OCX1X	1220	3	R. Libertad, Chiclayo: 0900-0400
LM63)	OCU4H	1220		R. Fe, Lima: 24h
CJ76)	OAM2B	1230	1	R. Fé, Cajamarca
JN21)	OBZ4Y	1230	1	R. Selecciones,Tarma: 1100-0200(Sun -1800)
LM65)	OCU4C	1230		R. La Luz, Huacho
MD06)	OAM7T	1230	2.5	R. Tambopata, Tambopata
MQ12)	OBU6T	1230	1	R. OBU6T, Moquequa
PA03)	OBX4Z	‡1230	1	R. LV de Oxapampa, Oxapampa
PU20)	OAU7V	1230	1	R. Surupana, Caminca
PU62)		1230		R. Frecuencia Amistad, Juliaca
AM01)	OAU9B	1240	1	R. Bagua Grande, Chachapoyas
AN10)	OAU3L	1240	1	R. La Luz, Chimbote
AQ25)	OAU6D	1240	15	R. Lider, Socabaya, Aqp
CU27)	OCU7Z	1240	5	R. Pachatusán, Sicuani
IC10)	OAU5U	1240	1	R. Eco, Ica
JN22)	OAU4V	1240	12	R. Cumbre, Huancayo -0000
LB21)	OAZ1A	1240	1	R. Ferreñafe, Ferrañafe
LL26)	OAU2Y	1240	1	R. Nor Andino, Santiago de Chuco
PI69)	OCX1C	1240	1	R. Sechura, Sechura
PU44)	OCX1C	1240		R. Campesina, Ayaviri
CJ27)	OAU2V	1250	1	R. HGV, Santa Cruz
CU28)	OBX7A	1250	3	R. Solar, Cusco: 1000-0500
LM30)	OAX4L	1250	5	R. Cora, Lima
MQ08)	OAU6I	1250	1	R. Campesina, Omate
PI23)	OBZ1B	1250	1.5	R. Dif. BNS, Talara Alta
SM07)	OAX9C	1250	1	R. Americana, Nueva Cajamarca
UC10)	OBX8S	1250	3	R. Cielo, Calleria
AN11)	OAU3G	1260	3	R. El Pregonero, Chimbote
AQ26)	OBX6D	1260	1	R. Manahaim, Uchumayo Aqp
HN04)	OAU3F	1260	1	R. La Luz, Huanuco
JN54)	OCU4F	1260	1	R. Corazón Andino, El Tambo
LB20)	OCX1O	1260	1	R. Nova, Chiclayo
LL49)	OBX2C	1260		R. Otuzco, Otuzco
LL56)		1260		R. Cielo, Trujullo – relay of R.Cielo, Lima (r)
LM68)	OCU4B	1260	3	R. La Luz, San Vicente de Cañete
AY08)	OBX5S	1260	0.3	R. Nal. del Perú, Ayacucho
AQ46)	OBU6P	1270	1	R. San Antonio, Callalli
CU30)	OAU7S	1270	2	R. Horizonte – LV de Agro, Cusco
HV07)	OAM5A	1270	2	R. OAM5A, Huancavelica
JN23)	OBZ4I	1270	0.4	R. La Merced, Chanchamayo
LL28)	OCX2Z	1270	1	R. Estacion Latina, Cepén
LM31)	OAZ4H	1270	0.4	R. Huacho, Huacho
PI24)	OAU1S	1270	1	R. Nor Peru, Paita
TC21)	OBU6N	1270	3	R. Cielo, Tacna
AN12)	OBX3C	‡1280		R. El Puerto, Chimbote
AQ27)	OBX6P	1280	0.5	R. Fénix, Camaná
CJ28)	OBX2F	1280	1	R. Modema, Cajamarca: 1000-0400(Sun -0300)
CU61)	OCU7R	1280	1	R. Fé, Sicuani
HN01)	OAX3Y	1280	1	R. La Selva, Rupa-Rupa
IC21)	OBU5J	1280	3	Yeshua R., Chinca Alta
LB22)	OAU1R	1280	1	R. Bethel, San Jose
PA11)		1280		R. Bethel, Chaquimarca
PU49)	OCU7S	1280	2.5	R. Continental, Macusani
AQ28)	OCX6B	1290	5	R. Cielo, Cerro Colorado Aqp
AY20)	OBU5V	1290	1	R. OBU5V, Ayacucho
CJ69)	OAM2C	1290	1	R. Estelar, Chota: 1000-0200
JN24)	OBU4S	1290	1	R. Exito, La Oroya
LM32)	OBU4Q	1290	1	S & RD, Hualmay
LM69)	OCU4P	1290	1	San Vicente de Cañete
LL53)	OBU2D	1290	1	R. Sonorama, Trujillo
TB04)	OCX1Q	1290	1	R. Programas del Perú - RPP, Tumbes: 24h
AN13)	OAX3O	1300	0.5	R. Cielo, Independencia
AQ64)	OCU6W	1300	1	R. OCU6W, Mariscal Cáceres (F.PI)
CJ29)	OAU2I	1300	1	R. Paraiso, Cajabamba
CU31)	OAX7P	‡1300	5	R. Onda Imperial, Cusco: 1200-2130
CU89)		1300		R. Chumpiwilkas, Santo Tomas Chumbivilcas
JN55)	OCU4R	1300	2.5	R. OCU4R, Ahuac
LB23)	OAU1U	1300	1	R. Frecuencia Lider, Morro
LM33)	OAX4S	1300	5	R. Comas, Comas: 24h
PU21)	OAX7X	1300	0.35	R. La Decana – R. Juliaca, Juliaca
SM08)	OBX9P	‡1300	1	R. La Luz, Tarapoto
TC18)	OBU6X	1300	3	R. Candarave, Ilabaya
UC03)	OAZ8B	1300	1	R. Nuevo Mundo, Pucallapa

MW	Call	kHz	kW	Station, location, h of tr.
AQ50)	OAU6N	1310	6	R. Libertad, Alto Selva Alegre Aqp
AY21)	OBU5X	1310	3	Ayacucho
CJ30)	OBX2D	1310	1	R. Chota, Chota: 1100-0300
LM34)	OBX4L	1310	1	R. Irvisa, Huacho
HN15)	OAU3T	1310	5	R. OAU3T, Rupa Rupa
LT09)	OBX8L	1310	12	R. Vision Amazonia (R. MIVIA), Iquitos
PI62)	OCU1D	1310	3	Bethel R., Piura
AN31)	OAU3W	1320	5	R. OAU3W, La Caleta
AP19)	OCU5V	1320	5	R. Cultural Tintaya, Cotabambas
AQ60)	OBU6B	1320	0.5	R. Majes
IC22)	OBU5L	1320	1	La Luz del Mundo, Pueblo Nuevo
JN26)	OCU4T	1320	2.5	R. Bacan Sat., Huancayo
LB24)	OBU1S	1320	1	R. Frecuencia Popular, Olmos
LM55)	OAX4I	1320		R. La Cronica, Lima
PU22)	OAU7W	1320	3	R. TV Peru, Juliaca: 1000-0300
TC17)	OBU6A	1320	1	R. OBU6A, Tacna
AQ30)	OVX6E	1330	1	Frequencia 1330, Arequipa
AY09)	OBU5P	1330	0.5	R. Bethel, Huamanga
CU32)	OCX7K	1330	1	R. San Miguel, Wanchaq
JU61)	OAM4L	1330	2	R. OAM4L, Tarma
LB25)	OAU1A	1330	1	R. Amistad, Chiclayo
LL54)	OAM2D	1330	1	R. Fé, La Esperanza
PI63)	OCU1J	1330	1	R. Frecuencia Ideal, Frias
SM17)	OBX9Y	1330	1	R. Fé, Tarapoto
AN33)	OBU3C	1340	1	R. OBU3C, Casma
AQ65)	OCU6U	1340	1	R. OCU6U, Mejia Sur
CJ31)	OAU2S	1340	1	R. Shalom, Cajamarca
CU87)		1340		R. Choque, Chumbivilcas
IC11)	OAX5D	1340	0.5	R. Chincha, Chincha Alta
JN27)	OAU4N	1340	1	R. Jauja, Jauja
LM35)	OAU4Q	1340	10	R. Alegria, Pucasana
PI64)	OBX1K	1340	1	R. San Francisco, Piura
PU23)	OBU7V	1340	1	R. Sudamericana, Juliaca
AY18)	OBU5O	1350	1	R. Atlantis, Huamanga
HN16)	OAU3X	1350	1	R. OAU3X, Pillco Marca
LB31)	OAU1H	1350	1	R. Vision, Chiclayo: 24h
LM73)	OAM4H	1350	1	R. Paraiso, Huacho
MQ1)	OCU6D	1350	3	R. Municipal, Ichuña
TB09)	OCU1I	1350	1	R. Fé, Tumbes
UC04)	OBX8D	1350		R. Super, Pucallpa
AN16)	OAU3A	1360	1	R. Intercontinental, Yungay
AQ32)	OCX6T	1360	7.5	R. Popular, Mariano Melgar
CJ77)	OCU2Z	1360	2	R. Las Palmas, Querocotillo: 1100-0200
CU34)	OAX7R	±1360	2.5	R. Sicuani, Sicuani
IC12)	OBZ5Z	1360	1	R. Cruz del Sur, Palpa
JN28)	OAU4O	1360	1	R. Sudamericana, Tarma
LM58)	OCU4I	1360	10	R. Bienestar, Lima: 24h
PI25)	OBZ1A	1360	1	R. Cielo, Piura
AP05)	OCX5A	1370	1	Inti R., Abanacy
AP17)	OCU5Y	1370	3	R. Chalhuahuacho, Chalhuahuacho
AQ62)	OBU6Y	1370	1	R. OBU6Y, Viraco
CU79)	OAM7G	1370	3	R. Qosqo Wayra, Cusco
MQ07)	OAX6T	‡1370		R. Moquegua, Moquegua
SM18)	OAU9E	1370	5	R. OAU9E, Moyobamba
PA01)	OCU4U	1370	10	R. Los Andes, Cerro de Pasco
AN32)	OAU3U	1380	1	R. R.dif San Juan, Chimbote
AQ33)	OAX6O	1380	3	R. San Martin, Arequipa: 1055-0500
CJ33)	OAX2W	‡1380	1	R. Atahualpa, Cajamarca
CJ34)	OAU2H	1380	1	R. Campesina, Cajamarca
JN29)	OBU4L	1380		R. Rescate,Huancayo
HN06)	OBX3I	±1380	1	R. Pilco Mozo, Huanuco
IC31)	OAM5E	1380	1	R. OAM5E, Salas
LM38)	OCY4U	1380	1	R. Nuevo Tiempo, Lima: 24h
MD05)	OCU7U	1380	1	R. OCU7U, Tambopata
PI26)	OBZ1D	1380	1	RB - R. Bellavista, Bellavista
PU24)	OUA7L	1380	2.5	R. Andina, Juliaca
AY28)	OCU5C	1390	2.5	R. Cielo, Ayacucho
CJ70)	OBU2U	1390	0.5	Frequencia del Norte, Santa Cruz
CU36)	OAU7T	1390	1	R. Enlace, Kunturkanki
CU69)	OAM7A	1390	3	R. Exitosa, Sicuani: 24h
LL32)	OAU2Z	1390	3	R. La Luz, Trujillo
LB41)	OCU1G	1390		R. Fe, Pimentel
PU63)		1390		Corp. R. TV Continental Ayaviri, Umachiri
AN35)	OBU3E	1400	1	R. OBU3E, Chimbote
CJ88)	OAU2H	1400	1	R. Agricultura, Cajamarca
CU37)	OAX7I	1400	1	R. La Hora, Cuzco
HV10)	OCU5S	1400	1	R. OCU5S, Preov
IC30)	OAM5G	1400	1	R. OAM5G, Ica
JN30)	OBX4H	1400	1	R. Luz, Tarma
LM39)	OBX4W	1400	2.5	R. Ecco, Lima: 24h
TC22)	OCU6F	1400	1	R. Candaravena, Candaravna
AY33)	OCU5G	1410	3	R. Genesis, Huanta
CJ64)	OCU2Q	1410	1	R. Huracana, Pedro Galvez
HN18)	OAU3Y	1410	1	R. Ke Buena, Paucarbambilia
LB29)	OBU1G	1410	1	R. Olmos, Olomos
LM40)	OBZ4V	1410	1	R. Bethel, Huacho
PU26)	OBU7A	1410	1	R. Corporacion Wayra, Juliaca
TB05)	OBU1H	1410	3	R. La Luz, Tumbes
UC05)	OBX8I	1410	1	Dif. Comercial, Pucallapa
AQ57)	OBU6C	1420	1	R. Fe, Arequipa
IC23)	OBU5H	1420	0.5	R. la Luz, Salas
CJ85)	OAM2P	1420	5	R. La Positiva, Bambamarca
CU88)	OAM7K	1420	1.5	R. San Luis, Pallpata
LM41)	OBZ4G	1420	1	R. San Isidro, Lima
PI65)	OCU1F	1420	2	R. OCU1F, Tambo Grande
AM03)	OBX9H	1430	1	R. Utcubamba, Bagua Grande
AN18)	OAZ3H	‡1430	1	R. Chavin, Chimbote
CJ78)	OCU2U	1430	1	R. LV de Salvación, Jaén
CU39)	OAZ7M	1430	1	R. Programas Peru - RPP, Cusco
JN31)	OAZ4V	1430	0.5	R. Universal, El Tambo: 1100-0500
LM42)	OCU4L	1430	1	Chilca, Cañete
PU27)	OBU7U	1430	3	R. Red Andina, Juliaca
TC08)	OAU6M	‡1430	1	R. Lider, Tacna
AQ19)	OAX6R	1440	2.5	R. Santa Monica, Hunter, Aqp:
AY32)	OCU5K	1440	2.5	R. OCU5K, Ayacucho
CU71)	OAM7L	1440	3	R. Solar, Espinar
CJ35)	OAU2O	1440	2	R. Frecuencia VH, Celendin
IC26)	OCU5P	1440	3	R. Cielo, Ica
LB30)	OBX1T	1440	2	R. Tumán, Tumán
LM43)	OAX4K	1440	1	R. Imperial 2, Lima
PI66)	OBU1Z	1440	1	R. OBU1Z, Vice
AQ58)	OBU6K	1450	1	R. OBU6K, Chivay
CJ81)	OAU2W	1450		R. Manantial de Vida, Cajamarca:1100-0100 (Sun -1300)
CJ82)		1450		R. Libertad, Bambamarca
JN45)	OBU4Y	1450	1	R. Andina (IPDA) Huancayo
LL35)	OCX2J	1450	1	R. San Juan, Trujillo
LM44)	OBX4K	1450	1	R. Fortaleza, Barranca
MO15)	OCU6E	1450		R. Santa Cruz, Ichuña
PA08)	OAM4A	1450	1	R. Vida, Tinyahuarco
AN30)	OAU3V	1460	2.5	R. Municipal, Cabana
AQ37)	OBU6R	1460	1	R. Bahia, Mollendo
CU42)	OBU7M	1460		R. OBU7M, Marcapata
IC32)	OAM5C	1460	1	Rdif. Disaga, Pueblo Nuevo
JN32)	OCY4I	1460	0.5	R. Imperial, Junin
JN33)	OAZ4F	1460	1	R. La Oroya, La Oroya: 1000-0500
JN48)	OCU4Y	1460	1	R. Voz Cristiana, Chongo Bajo: 24h (n.f. 1470)
PI29)	OAX1V	1460	1	R. Sullana "LV de Chira", Sullana
PU28)	OAX7W	1460	10	R. Sol de los Andes, Juliaca: 0900-0300
AQ38)	OAU6E	1470	2.5	R. Victoria, Alto Selva Alegre Aqp
CU43)	OAX7G	1470	1	R. Cusco, Cusco
JN48)	OCU4Y	1470	1	R. Voz Cristiana, Chongo Bajo: 24h (r. 1460)
LB46)	OAU1P	1470	1	R. California, Lambayeque
LL37)	OCY2G	1470	1	R. Amistad, Quiruvilca
LM45)	OAU4B	1470	20	R. Felicidad, Lima
TC09)	OAX6M	1470	0.8	R. Tacna, Tacna: 1100-1300
CU44)	OAZ7G	1480	1	R. Espinar, Yauri
CJ44)	OBU2H	1480	0.2	R. Santa Ana, Cutervo: 1000-0100
JN35)	OAU4A	1480	1	R. Mineria, Santa Rosa de Sacco: 1100-2300
LL38)	OCX2C	1480	0.6	R. Comercial San Pedro, Virú
LM70)	OAM4F	1480	1	R. OAM4F, Barranca
MD09)	OBM7F	1480		R. OBM7F, Tambopata
AQ39)	OAX6Q	1490	1.3	R. Fidelidad, Cerro Colorado, Aqp
AP10)	OBU5C	1490	2.5	Rdif. los Chankas, Andahuaylas
AP18)		1490		R. Patron Santiago, Challhuacho
CU80)	OCU7Y	1490	2.5	Cadena Sur del Peru, Cusco (IPDA)
IC15)	OAX5N	1490	1	R. Nazca, Nazca
LB47)	OAX1L	±1490	1	R. Imperio, Chiclayo
LT14)	OAX8F	1490	1	R. Atlántiada, Iquitos
PA15)	OCX4P	1490	0.5	R. La Luz, Cerro de Pasco
PU51)	OAM7P	1490	1	R. OAM7P, Capachica
CJ39)	OBU2J	1500	2	R. San Pablo, San Pablo
CU81)	OAM7B	1500	1	R. TV Cristiana, Sicuani
HN07)	OBX3J	1500	1	R. Luz y Sonido, Huanuco: 0900-0300
JN56)	OCU4Q	1500	1	LV Liberacion, Huancayo
LL39)	OBX2X	1500	0.5	R. Comercial, Trujillo
LM47)	OBX4I	±1500	18	R. Santa Rosa, Lima: 24h
TC10)	OAU6B	‡1500	1	R. Bulevar, Tacna

MW	Call	kHz	kW	Station, location, h of tr.
AQ40)	OCX6Q	±1510	3	R. Alegria, Mariano Melgar, Aqp
CU82)	OBX7P	1510	1	R. Las Vegas, Wanchaq
JN37)	OCX4J	1510	1	R. Tarma, Tarma: 1000-0200, Sun 1100-2300
LB50)	OAM1C	1510	1	R. TV Motupe, Motupe
LB32)	OBU1B	1510	1	R. Super Real, Olmos
LM66)	OCU4M	1510	1	R. OCU4M, San Vicente de Cañete
LM78)	OAM4Q	1510	1	R. OAM4Q, Supe Puerto
TB06)	OCX1V	1510	1	R. Tumbes, Tumbes
UC06)	OBX8K	1510	1	R. Centro de los Medios, Sepahua
CJ84)	OAM2Q	1516	1	R. Charles, Bambamarca (nf 1530)
AY29)	OCU5F	1520	2	R. OCU5F, Huanta
CU48)	OBU7X	1520	1	R. Avance - Voz Evangelica, Espinar
LB26)	OAX1C	1520	1	R. Cristal, Chiclayo
HV04)	OBU5Z	1520	3	R. Municipal, Castrovirreyna
MQ13)	OBU6Z	1520	6	R. OBU6Z, Mascal Nieto
PA12)	OAM4C	1520		R. OAM4C, San Juan
PI68)	OCU1T	1520	1	R. LV del Campesino, Ayabacha
PU56)		1520		R. Andina, Lampa
CJ06)	OBX2R	1530	3	R. Oriental, Jaén
CJ84)	OAM2Q	1530	1	R. Charles, Bambamarca
CU49)	OAZ7F	1530	0.5	Rdif. Espinar, Yauri
CU50)	OBU7N	1530	1	R. Ondas del Sur Oriente, Quillabamba
IC17)	OAU5R	1530	1	R. Universidad San Juan Bautista, Subtanjalla
JN38)	OBZ4S	1530	1	R. 15-50, Huancayo: 24h
LM49)	OBU4C	1530	10	R. Milenia, Lima
PI70)	OCX1Y	1530		R. La Jefa, Sullana
AQ41)	OAU6A	1540	1	R. Milenio Universal, Alto Selva Alegre
CU51)	OCX7V	‡1540	1	R. Los Andes, Cusco
LL42)	OBU2A	1540	2	R. Mundial, Trujillo
LM74)	OAM4G	1540	1	R. Angie@Net, Barranca
PA05)	OBX4N	1540	0.3	R. Corporacion, Cerro de Pasco: 0900-0500
TB07)	OBX1B	1540	1	R. LV de la Frontera, Tumbes
TC23)	OCU6H	1540	1	R. OCU6H, Pocollay
AN22)	OAU3D	‡1550	1	R. Cruz, Chimbote
AY10)	OBX5J	1550	1	R. Maria, Huamanaga
CJ88)		1550		R. Integracion, Cutervo
CU83)	OAM7D	±1550	1	R. San Sebastian, Livitaca
IC24)	OAU5Z	1550	3	R. La Luz del Mundo, Subtanjalla
LB48)	OCU1W	1550	1	R. OCU1W, Monsefú
LM51)	OBX4P	1550	5	R. Independencia, Independencia
PI67)	OCU1B	1550	1	R. La Clave, Castilla
AQ42)	OCX6N	1560	1	R. Sabor, Arequipa
CJ79)	OAM2I	1560	1	R. R. Antena Norte, Cajabamba
CU52)	OAZ7N	1560	1	R. Maria, Wanchaq
JN57)	OCU4Z	1560	2.5	R. Rumba, Hualhuas
LB51)	OAM1B	1560	1	R. Moderna, Olmos
TC25)	OCU6K	1560	1	R. OCU6K, Alto de la Alianza
AY34)	OCU5O	1570	2.5	R. Musuq Chaski Radio, Huamanga
CJ54)	OBU2L	1570		R. Jesus es la Vida, Granja Porcón
CU62)	OCU7L	1570	1	R. Vilcanota, Sicuani
HN20)	OBU3A	1570	1	R. OBU3A. Cerro Jactay
IC31)	OAM5H	1570	1	R. OAM5H, Chinca Alta
LM59)	OCU4J	1570	25	R. Bethel, Lima
LL47)	OCU2C	1570	1	Rdif. Julcan, Otuzco
PI32)	OCX1Z	1570	1	R. La Nueva Esperanza, Tambo Grande
PU32)	OAU7Z	1570	1	R. Carraviz, Juliaca (IPDA)
AQ59)	OBU6S	1580	1	R. OBU6S, Orcopampa
CJ87)	OAM2R	1580		R. OAM2R, Jaen
HV02)	OAU5J	1580	1	R. Virgen del Carmen, Huancavelica: 24h
JN40)	OAU4P	1580	1	R. San Juan, Tarma
LB36)	OBX1M	1580	1	R. Naylamp, Lambayeque
LM76)	OAM4O	1580	2.5	R. Andina, Huacho
TC27)	OCU6M	1580		R. Bacan Sat., Tacna
AQ44)	OCX6S	1590	1	R. Mundo, Arequipa
AY30)	OBU5F	1590	1	R. OBU5F, Lucanas
CJ68)	OAM2S	1590		R. Municipal, San Marcos
IC34)	OAM5J	1590	3	R. OAM5J, Ica
LL43)	OBU2C	1590	1	R. Bendicion, Trujillo
LM52)	OAZ4Z	‡1590	1.5	R. Vida, Lima
PU33)	OAU7C	1590	1	R. Asillo, Azangaro
CU86)	OBM7A	1600	3	R. Antena 5, Wanchaq
JN44)	OBU4R	1600	2.5	R. Nuevo Tiempo, Huancayo: 24h
MO18)	OCU6C	1600	3	R. OCU6C Moquequa
AQ45)	OAU6O	1610	0.5	R. El Sol, Arequipa
PU54)		1610		R. Inka, Acora
CU90)		1620		R. Choquechamaca, Chamaca
LL57)		1650		R. Santa Roas, San Ignacio, Otuzco (r)

SW	Call	kHz	kW	Station, location, h of tr.
CU93)	OAW7N	3270	1	R. OAW7N, Pitumarca (F.Pl)
AP20)	OAW5F	3295	1	R. OAW5F, Tambobamba (F.Pl)
AY07)	OAZ5B	4747	0.5	R. Huanta 2000, Huanta: (n.f.: 4755): 1100-0100
JN37)	OCX4E	4775	0.5	R. Tarma, Tarma: 1000-1400 2200-0000, Sun: 1100-1400 2000-2300
CU94	OAW7O	4800	1	R. OAW7O, Sicuani (F.Pl)
SM14)	OAW9A	4810	1	R. Logos, Chazuta
LL55)	OAW2H	4920	1	R. LV Del Pueblo, Santiago de Chuco
CU92)	OAW7M	4930		R. Sur Andina, Pitumarca
LM77)	OAW4Z	4935	1	R. OAW4Z, San Antonio (F.Pl)
UC07)	OAW8A	†4940	1	R. San Antonio, Villa Atalaya
AY13)	OAX5S	4955	5	R. Cultural Amauta, Huanta: 1000-1400, 2100-0100
CU26)	OAX7Q	5025	5	R. Quillabamba, Quillabamba: 1000-0200
CU72)	OBX4M	5980	5	Chaski R., Urubamba: 1000-1500, 2200-0100
AN36)	OAD3A	6090	1	R. OAD3A, Independencia (F.Pl)
CU25)	OAX7C	6174	1	R. Tawantinsuyo, Cusco

NB: ‡ = inactive, ± = varying freq., † = irregular
° = on-air stn name not confirmed, Aqp = Provincia de Arequipa

Addresses & other information:
NB: Names of *departamentos* should be added to addresses.
AM00 (AMAZONAS):
AM01) Jr.Grau N° 617, 01001 Chachapoyas – **AM03)** Jr F Villareal N° 400, 01671 Bagua Grande - **FM:** 96.9MHz – **AM04)** Jr Amazonas N° 1717 (Ap 69), 01001 Chachapoyas ☎41 777793 **W:** horizonteperu.com **E:** rhorizonte@hotmail.com - **FM:** 99.9MHz –**AM10)** Calle Higos Urcos 651, 01671 Bagua Grande, Utcubamba – **AM11)** Av.Gonzalo Puerta s/n, 01131 Nieva, Condorcanqui - **FM.** 91.7 MHz – **AM12)** Jr Salamanca N° 1183, 01001 Chachapoyas - **AM13)** Jr Amazonas s/n, Urb. Tupac Amaru, 01321 Huambo – **AM14)** Av La Circunvalacion N° 1249, 01651 La Peca
AN00 (ANCASH):
AN01) Tabon Alta, Fundo El Milagro, 02661 Casma ☎43 711266 **W:** visionradioperu.com - **FM:** 93.7 MHz – **AN02)** Av Francisco Pizzarro, 02741 Chimbote - **FM:** 95.5MHz – **AN04)** Urb. el Trapecio 2da etapa, MZ G, Lote 18, 02741 Chimbote - **FM:** 97.5MHz – **AN07)** Jr Elias Aguirre N° 755 cerca a Panamericana Television, 02741 Chimbote ☎44 272639 – **AN08)** Pasaje Los Jardines N° 129, 02741 Chimbote - **FM:** 104.3MHz – **AN09)** Jr Francisco Araoz 146, Independencia 02001 Huaraz ☎43 421359 **W:** invierteenhuaraz.com.pe/radioa/ **E:**radioancashhuaraz@gmail.com - **FM:** 101.3MHz – **AN10)** Av Enrique Meiggs N° 2013, 02741 Chimbote ☎43 805591 **W:** radiolaluz.com **E:** programacion@radiolaluz.com - **FM:** 89.9MHz – **AN11)** Jr Elias Aguirre N° 549, 2do Piso Oficina 205, 02741 Chimbote – **AN12)** Jr Alfonso Ugarte N° 554, 02741 Chimbote - **FM:** 89.9MHz – **AN13)** Jr San Martin N° 655, 02001 Huaraz **W:** radiocielo.pu - **FM:** 104.5MHz – **AN16)** Casero el Rayan, 02816 Yungay – **AN18)** Urb. San Juan ZN 5, 02741 Chimbote - **FM:** 92.3MHz – **AN22)** Jr Alfonso Ugarte N° 627 4° piso, 02741 Chimbote – **AN25)** Huari **W:** agrorural.gob.pe/pagina/huari-ancash – **AN27)** Av Jorge Chávez N° 364, 02741 Chimbote **W:** radiocielo.pe – **AN29)** Jr John F.Kennedy MZ. 36, Lote 1, Miraflores Alto, 02741 Chimbote – **AN30)** Plaza de Armas N° 106, Cabana– **AN31)** Av Malecón s/n, La Caleta – **AN32)** Av Santa Cruz 397, Chimbote – **AN33)** Av Peru 1263, Casma – **AN34)** Av Jorge Chavez 364, Chimbote – **AN35)** Jr Francisco Pizarro 610, Chimbote – **AN36)** Jr Los Jardines 670, Independencia
AP00 (APURIMAC): AP03) Av Nuñez 401, 03001 Abancay – **AP05)** Av Seoane 375, Region Inca, 03001 Abancay ☎8 332 4087 **W:** corporacionsolar.com **E:** intiradio@corporacionsolar.com - **FM:** 103.3 Solar FM – **AP10)** Jr. Juan Antonio Trellers N° 278, 03281 Andahuaylas ☎83 721511 - **FM:** 94.9 MHz – **AP11)** Tres Cruces, 03141 Ocobamba – **AP12)** Av Cristo de Los Andes S/N, Barrio El Salvador, 03301 Challhuahuacho ☎ 961 220 820 **W:** facebook.com/Radiotvmallmany950Am/ **E:** radiomallmanya950@gmail.com – **AP13)** Barrio Pampaña Calle Apurimac s/n, 03341 Cotabambas – **AP14)** Jr Los Sauces N° 283, U.V. Pochccota, 03281 Andahuaylas **W:** restauracionandahuaylas.com – **AP15)** Jr Manuel Seone 320, Abancay – **AP16)** Comunidad Campesina de Totoray, San Pedro de Cachora **W:** radiocielo.pe – **AP17)** Comunidad de Fuerobamba, Challhuahuacho ☎953 283062 **W..** facebook.com/rchallhuahuachooficial **E.:** radiochallhuahuacho@gmail.com – **AP18)** Ca 8 de Agosto, 03301 Challhuahuacho – **AP19)** Comunidad de Fuerabamba, Dist. Callhuahuach, Cotabambas – **AP20)** Calle Martinelly S/N, Dist. de Tambobamba, Prov. de Cotabambas
AQ00 (AREQUIPA):
AQ01) Ca Colon 121 Cercado, 04001 Arequipa ☎54 200982 **W:** radioazularequipaperu.com **E:** radioazulamfm@hotmail.com - **FM:**

89.5MHz – **AQ02)** Ca San Juan de Dios 210, 04001 Arequipa **W:** nseradio.com **E:** nsearequipa@nseradio.com – **AQ04)** Av. Salaverry 103, Socabaya, 04051 Arequipa ☎54 507362 – **AQ05)** Centro Comercial, Av Independencia 600, Of 401-A, Cercado, 04001 Arequipa ☎54 406175 - **FM:** 93.5MHz – **AQ06)** Jr.Palacio Viejo 216, Cayma, 04016 Arequipa - **FM:** 89.5 MHz – **AQ07)** Av Emmel 216, Yanahuara, 04020 Arequipa **W:** radiohuanta2000fm.com **E:** radioportena@hotmail.com – **AQ11)** Av Victor A Belaúnde C-8, Umacollo, 04001 Arequipa ☎54 255888 🖷54 251822 - **FM:** 97.1MHz – **AQ12)** Ca Los Robles 139, Urb. Orrantia, 04001 Arequipa ☎54 289952 - Quechua: Sat.2h **W:** radioyaravi.org.pe **E:** yaraviaqp@gmail.com - **FM:** 106.3MHz – **AQ13)** Calle Palacio Viejo 401, 04001 Arequipa ☎54 223080 **W:** radioelpueblo960.pe - **FM:** 98.5MHz in Majes, 102.1 in Tacna – **AQ14)** Av Independencia s/n 2° piso, Pabellón de la Cultura, Ciudad Universitaria (Cas 23), 04001 Arequipa. ☎54 287771 **W:** unsa.edu.pe and radiouniversidadaqp.blogspot.no **E:** radiouniversidad@unsa.edu.pe – **AQ15)** At 200 Millas La Pino, 04039 Paucarpata – **AQ16)** Av Independencia 905 - 2do piso, 04001 Arequipa ☎54 204904 - **FM**: 107.7MHz – **AQ17)** Av Union 225, Miraflores, 04009 Arequipa (Also in Lima: LI59) **W:** bethelradio.fm **E:** betheltradio@bethelradio.fm – **AQ18)** Av. La Paz 504, 04001 Arequipa ☎54 204847 **Quechua:** 1000-1200 – **AQ19)**Av Independencia 905 2° piso, Ur. Municipal 04001 Arequipa ☎54 204904 **W:** radiosantamonicaarequipa.com **E:** gerencia@radiosantamonicaarequipa.com – **AQ20)** Calle 28 de Julio N° 129 – La Libertad, Cerro Colorado, 04023 Arequipa – **AQ21)** Av.La Paz 512, Costado Grifo Repsol, 04001 Arequipa ☎54 446053 - **FM:** 95.8MHz – **AQ22)** Av La Paz 511 "A", Of 312 – 3er piso, 04001 Arequipa ☎54 287821 **W:** rpp.com.pe – **AQ23)** Av La Salle 124, Urb. Daniel Alcides Carrión G-14, 04044 José Luis Bustamente y Rivero 04001 Arequipa ☎54 431051 – **AQ24)** Calle San Camilo 501-A Cercado, 04001 Arequipa ☎54 204420 **W:** radiomelodia.com.pe - **FM:** 104.3MHz – **AQ25)** Av Independencia 1819 Pl:3 Cercado, 04001 Arequipa ☎54 330033 **W:** radiotelevisionlider.com **E:** lideraqp@gmail.com - **FM:** 98.7MHz – **AQ26)** Ca Pierola 209, Of 205, 04001 Arequipa ☎54 284411 – **AQ27)** Esq Av Lima y Calle Bolognesi, 04446 Camaná – **AQ28)** Av. Independencia 600, Edifico C.C. Independencia N° 321D, 04001 Arequipa **W:** radiocielo.pe – rel. of R.Cielo, Lima 24h – **AQ30)** Parque Azángarao 105 2° Pisa, Miraflores, 04009 Arequipa ☎54 659893 **W:** frecuencia1330arequipa.blogspot.com – **AQ32)** Av.Independencia N° 600, Oficina 302-A, 04001 Arequipa **W:** Facebook: Radio Popular Arequipa – **AQ33)** Calle Deán Valdivia 221, Cercado, 04001 Arequipa **W:** radiosanmartin.pe **E:** director@radiosanmartin.pe ☎54 215190 - **FM:** 97.7MHz – **AQ37)** C.Baca Flor 410, (Cas 128), 04466 Mollendo ☎54 532521 **W:** radiobahiaperu.es.tl **E:** radiobahiadelvalle@hotmail.com - **FM:** 101.5MHz – **AQ38)** Dean Valdivia 418, Piso 3, Cercado, 04001 Arequipa ☎54 505479 **W:** radiovictoriaaqp.com **E:** aqpvictoria@gmail.com – **FM:** 92.9 MHz – **AQ39)** Santo Domingo 113 , Galerias Gamesa Of 700, 04001 Arequipa, (Ap 2330) ☎54 214997 **E:** radiominuto@terra.com.pe - **FM:** 99.9MHz – **AQ40)** Centro Comercial Independencia, Av Independencia N° 403-A, Ofic 433, 4° piso, 04001 Arequipa ☎54 287211 - **FM:** 95.1 MHz – **AQ41)** Ca Puente Grau 122, 04001 Arequipa ☎54 507643 **W:** radiomileniouniversal.blogspot.no **E:** radiomileniouniversal@hotmail.com – **AQ42)** Sebastian Luna 105a, Parque Azángarao 2° Pisa, Miraflores, 04009 Arequipa , Arequipa – **AQ44)** Ca Castilla 39, Urb. Municipal, 04001 Arequipa – **AQ45)** C.C Héroes Anónimos 3er piso, Oficina 301-a,. Paucarpata con Independencia, 04000 Arequipa ☎54 299887 **W:** radioelsolaqp.blogspot.com E: radioelsol1610@gmail.com – **AQ46)** Parroquia San Antonio de Padua, Plaza Principal s/n, 04201 Callalli, Prov de Caylloma **E:** rsan_antonio14@hotmail.com - **FM:** 94.5MHz – **AQ50)** Ca Trabada 105, VI Centenario, 04001 Arequipa ☎54 202022 **W:** radiolibertadaqp.com **E:** radiolibertadaqp@hotmail.com – **AQ52)** Calle Puente Arnao 705, 3 Cdras de la Av. Progreso, 04001 Arequipa – **AQ53)** 04001 Arequipa **W:** radiomariaperu.org – **AQ55)** Casinino Peralta 102, 04101 Cotahuasi, La Union – **AQ56)** Ca 22 de Octubre s/n, Urb. Los Miradores, 04231 Orcopampa – **AQ57)** Calle Ugarte N° 504, Arequipa ☎54 384463 **W:** facebook.com/radiofe1420amarequipa/ – **AQ58)** Sector Escalera, 04341 Chivay – **AQ59)** Av Buena Ventura s/n, 04231 Orcopampa – **AQ60)** Mz. 3E Lte. 18 Pedregal, 04426 Majes – **AQ61)** Av Independecia 905, 04001 Arequipa ☎54 288787 **W:** ipda.com.pe/radioarequipa.htm – **AQ62)** Plaza de Armas s/n, 04556 Viraco – **AQ63)** Jr. Pizarro N° 121, Camaná – **AQ64)**Sector Santa Luzmila, Mariscal Cáceres – **AQ65)** La Hacienda Pampa Meija Sur S/N, Mejia

AY00 (AYACUCHO):

AY02) Ca Nazareno 108H, 05001 Ayacucho **E:** macebu90@hotmail.com - **FM:** 95.3MHz – **AY05)** Plaza Mayor Felipe Guzman Poma, 05411 Aucara, Lucanas **E:** radioia1090@hotmail.com – **AY06)** Jr Chorro 274 - Int "A", 05001 Ayacucho, ☎66 326042 **W:** radioquispillaccta.com Prgr mainly in **Quechua** – **AY07)** Jr Gervasio Santillana 455, 05111 Huanta ☎66 322105 **W:** radiohuanta2000fm.com **E:** webmaster@radiohuanta2000fm.com - **FM**: 92.9MHz – **AY08)** Jr Piura s/n, 05001 Ayacucho – **FM:** 97.9MHz – **AY09)** Jr. Los Girasoles 194, Canan Bajo, 05001 Ayacucho – **FM:** 93.9 MHz – **AY10)** Local de Obispado, 05021 Carmen Alto, **W:** radiomariaperu.org - **FM:**106.7MHz – **AY13)** Jr Cahuide 278, 05111 Huanta (Cas 24) ☎66 322153 **W:** radioamautafm.net/ **E:** radioamauta@hotmail.com - **FM:** 99.9MHz – **AY14)** Ca El Nazareno, 2do Pasaje 159, Cercado, 05001 Ayacucho ☎66 528523 **W:** diariolavozdehuamanga.com **E:** diariolavozdehuamanga@yahoo.com.ar - **FM:** 91.1MHz. – **AY18)** Ca Manco Capac 157, 05001 Ayacucho **W:** Facebook: R.Atlantis - **FM:** 99.3 MHz – **AY19)** Jr Angel del Señor MZ C Lote 01A, Asociacion Los Mecanicos ☎528594, Huamanga – **AY20)** Av Mariscal Cáceres 641, 05001 Ayacucho – **AY21)** Jr Arequipa N° 231, 05001 Ayacucho – **AY22)** Av Mariscal Cáceres 641, 05001 Ayacucho – **AY23)** Jr Bolognes 147-149, Barrio Huánuco, 05571 Pausa, Paúcar del Sara Sara – **AY24)** Av 28 de Julio s/n, 05571 Pausa – **AY25)** Jr Dos de Mayo 610, 05001 Ayacucho **W:** radioamvida1020khz.blogspot.no **E:** radioamvida1020@yahoo.com.pe – **AY26)** Urb. Mariscal Cáceres, Mz. K Lote 12, 05001 Ayacucho ☎966 905992 **W:** Facebook: Estacion Wari 1060 khz A.M.– **AY27)** Jr Primavera 175, Santa Ana, 05001 Ayacucho – **AY28)** Av.Miguel Grau 256, 05001 Ayacucho **W:** radiocielo.pe – **AY29)** Jr Miller 177, 05111 Huanta – **AY30)** Jr Tacna N° 617, 05601 Pucuio – **AY31)** Jr Cesar Vallejo 325 – San Juan Bautista, 05001 Ayacucho – **AY32)** Av. Los Andes 624, 05001 Ayacucho – **AY33)** Jr. Libertad 153, 05111 Huanta – **AY34)** Av. Javier Pérez de Cuellar 546, Urb. José Ortiz Vergara Mx. "S", Ayacucho ☎97 8465290 **W:** FB: Musuq Chaski Radio 1570 AM

CJ00 (CAJAMARCA)

CJ01) Jr Francisco de Orellana 343 (Apt 50), 06101 Jaén **W:** radiomaranon.org.pe **E:** correo@radiomaranon.org.pe ☎76 431147 - **FM:** 96.1 & 97.5 MHz – **CJ03)** Km 5 Carretera Jaen-San Ignacio, 06101 Jaen - **FM:** 90.9MHz – **CJ05)** Predio Coliga, 06001 Cajamarca **W:** radiomariaperu.org – **CJ06)** Av Mesones Muro 157, 06101 Jaén – **CJ07)** Jr 28 de Julio 712, 06115 Bambamarca ☎76 353462 **W:** radiocoremarca.com **E:** coremarca@radiocoremarca.com - **FM:** 100,5 – **CJ08)** Jr Villanueva Pinillos N°N330, 06151 San Ignacio – **CJ10)** Celendin ☎76 639577 **W:** radionorandina.com **E:** norandina101.9@hotmail.com - **FM.** 101.9 MHzz – **CJ13)** Jr Huánuco 2363, 06001 Cajamarca ☎76 341347 **W:** radiolider.com.pe **E:** radiolidersac@yahoo.com - **FM:** 90.3MHz – **CJ14)** Jr David León N° 601, 06001 Contumazá – **CJ15)** Jr Dos de Mayo 271, 06001 Cajamarca ☎76 369915 **W:** radiosanfranciscoperu.com **E:** radiosanfrancisco@gmail.com - **FM:** 91.9MHz – **CJ17)** Jr Orozco 320, 06858 Cutervo ☎76 737090 **W:** radiosudamerica.net – **CJ18)** Av Via de Evitamiento Norte 280, 06001 Cajamarca ☎76 343725 **W:** radionuevavidacomunicaciones.com **E:** radiotvnc@radionuevavidacomunicaciones.com or radiotvnvc@hotmail.com – **CJ20)** Jr Mariscal Castilla 439, 06101 Jaén – **CJ21)** Av Miguel Carducci 101 Br Saman Cruz, 06002 Cajamarca ☎931 027 136 **W.**radioondapopular.com **E:** servicios@radioondapopular.com – **CJ22)** Jr LeSoncio Prado 330, 06501 San Marcos ☎76 858083 – **CJ23)** Av Inca Garcilazo de la Vega 473, 05301 Chota – **CJ24)** Jr Mariano Melgar 138 , Cajamarca ☎76 368975 **W:** layzonradio.com **E:** radiolayzon@yahoo.com - **FM:** 90.5MHz – **CJ25)** Ca. San Martin 1371, Jaèn ☎76 433414 – **CJ26)** Jr. Huanuco 100, Barrio San Pedro, 06001 Cajamarca ☎76 368952 **W:** facebook.com/rtvlavozdelcumbe/ **E:** cia.radioytvlavozdelcumbe@hotmail.com – **CJ27)** Jr Simon Bolivar 280, 06813 Santa Cruz – **CJ28)** Jr. Revilla Peréz 540, Barrio Pueblo Nuevo, 06001 Cajamarca ☎76 344465 **W:** radiomoderna.pe **E:** radio_moderna@yahoo.es - **FM:** 98.1 & 106.5 MHz – **CJ29)** Jr Silva 673, 06001 Cajabamba ☎76 551421 **E:** radioparaiso1300@hotmail.com – **CJ30)** Jr Santa Rosa 674-680, 06301 Chota ☎76 351240 **W:** radiochota.com **E:** radiochota@hotmail.com – **CJ31)** Av La Paz N° Cd Int 11, 06001 Cajamarca ☎76 885580 – **CJ32)** Jr. 27 de Noviembre 557, 06301 Chota **W:** radiosantamonica.org **E:** radiosantamonica@hotmail.com ☎76 351477 🖷76 351132 - **FM:** 95.7MHz – **CJ33)** Juan XXIII s/n (Plaza Bolognesi), 06001 Cajamarca - **FM:** 89.9MHz – **CJ34)** Av. Independencia 102 – 3er piso, 06001 Cajamarca ☎999491668 **W:** radiocampesina.pe **E:** campesinaradio@hotmail.com – **CJ35)** Jr. Arica cuadra. 5 s/n, Celendin ☎76 555115 **E:** frecuenciavh_1440@hotmail.com – **CJ36)** Jr. Alfonso Ugarte N° 668, 06001 Cajamarca ☎7655 7075 **W:** facebook.com Radio San Miguel Cajamarca **E:** sanmiguelradioradio@hotmail.com - **FM:** 101.1MHz – **CJ38)** Jr. Lima 290, 06858 Cutervo ☎76 437010 **W:** radioilucan.com **E:** radioilucan@hotmail.com - **FM:** 96.5MHz – **CJ39)** Av Bolognesi 501, 06652 San Pablo - **FM:** 95.3 MHz – **CJ41)** Jr Jorge Chávez 416, 06115 Bambamarca ☎76 501297 **W:** radiobambamarca.

com - **FM:** 101.3 MHz "Stereo Líder" – **CJ42)** Anaximandro Vega 481, Plaza de Armas, 06031 Chota ☎76 351442 🖷76 352027 **W:** andinaradio.net **E:** webmaster@andinaradio.net – **CJ43)** Jr Manuel Seoane 385, Cajamarca ☎76 3575525 **W:** radiocontinente.pe **E:** radiocontinenete820@gmail.com – **CJ44)** Av San Juan 835, 06858 Cutervo. ☎76 437272 **W:** www,radiosantaana.com **E:** info@radiosantaana.com – **CJ54)** Granja Porcón ☎ 930 122 280 **W:** facebook.com/Radio-Jesus-es-la-1570am-Vida-102072254848780 **E:** radiojesuseslavida1570am@gmail.com – **CJ58)** Cutervo ☎65 4654 5454 **W:** radiocutervo.com **E:** radiocutervo@hotmail.com - **FM:** 101.1 MHz – **CJ61)** Cajamarca 1119, Oficina del distrito Perú Andino Iglesia del Nazareno, 06121 Chota ☎937 580 962 **W:** radiopaz1120 - **FM:** 98.5 MHz – **CJ62)** Jr Los Libertadores 250, 06115 Bambamarca **W:** universobambamarca,com – **FM:** 98.5 MHz – **CJ63)** Jr Miguel Iglesia 483-489, 06001 Cajamarca ☎76 366985 **W:** turbomix.com.pe - **FM:** 92.5MHz – **CJ64)** Jr Leonico Prado 550, 06501 Pedro Galvez, San Marcos **W:** Facebook.com/Radio-Huracan-San-Marcos-600351456767398 – **CJ66)** 06115 Samangay **W:** visionradioperu.com – **CJ67)** José Osores 331, 06301 Chota ☎97 6163606 **W:** corporacionrbc.org **E:** carranzamori@hotmail.com – **CJ68)** Jr Leoncios Prado 360, 06501 San Marcos ☎76 558338 **W:** munisanmarcos.gob.pe/portal/index.php/radio **E:** radiomunicipalsanmarcos@hotmail.com - **FM:** 106.1 MHz – **CJ69)** Jr Anaximando Vega 688, 06301 Chota ☎97 68011212 **E:** digitelssac@hotmail.com - **FM:** 105.9 MHz – **CJ70)** Jr Cutervo 543, 06813 Santa Cruz ☎76 844068 **W:** frecuenciadelnorte.globered.com – **CJ71)** Carretera Agocucho s/n, Parimarca Baja, Zona Rural Marcopampa, 06001 Cajamarca **W:** visionradioperu.com – **CJ72)** Jr. San Martin 950 & Av Miguel Carducci 101, 06115 Bambamarca ☎97 6407575**W:** ondapopular.pe/bambamarca **E:** ondapopular.radio@hotmail.com – **FM:** 96.5 MHz – **CJ73)** Jr Eten 152, 06001 Cajamarca ☎976 372920 **W:** radiolabeta.com **E:** envivo@radiolabeta.com - **FM:** 101.3 MHz – **CJ74)** Cerro Chamusco, 06873 Pomahuaca – **CJ75)** Vista Alegre, Querocoto ista Alegre, 06846 Querocoto – **CJ76)** Las Dalias 147, 06001 Cajamarca – **CJ77)** Prolongacion Arequipa s/s, Barrios Altos,06861 Querocotillo ☎995 583160 **W:** radiolaspalmasdequerocotillo.com **E:** radiolaspalmas1360@hotmail.com – **CJ78)** Iglesia Pentecostal La Cosecha, Caserio San Lorenzo de Shumba km 46 Carretera San Ignacio, Jaen – **CJ79)** Jr Marañon 345, Tacshana, 06536 Cajabamba ☎76 774441 **W:** Facebook – **CJ80)** Ca Lambayeque 156, 06101 Jaen ☎949 917090 **W:** facebook.com/pg/OndaPopular – **CJ81)** Jr. Teresa de Journet 131, Urb. Alameda, 06001 Cajamarca ☎94 2021465 **W:** manantialdevida1450.com **E:** manantialdevidaradio@hotmail.com – **CJ82)** Bambamarca **W:** facebook.com/radiolibertadbambamarca – **FM:** 104.1 MHz – **CJ83)** Jr.Juan XXIII 287, 06031 Chota – **CJ84)** Jr Alfonso Ugarte 212, Bambamarca ☎76 353642 **W:**.radiocharles.com **E:** radiocharles91.1@hotmail.com - **FM:** 91.1 MHz – **CJ85)** Jr Fray Juose Arana 738, Chota ☎97 5801485 **W:** facebook.com/lapositiva.chota.bambamarca/ **E:** loloperiiodista@hotmail.com - **FM:** 90.1 MHz – **CJ86)** Jr Huancavelica No 387, Urb. Las Margaritas - Barrio San José, Cajamarca ☎76 601795 **W:** radiotvcajamarca.com – **CJ87)** Pasaje Shililique s/n, Jaen – **CJ88)** Cutervo **W:** FB - **FM.:** 91.1 MHz – **CJ88) W:** radioagriculturacajamarca.com **E:** Francisco.cortez@radioagricultura.com – **CJ89)** Rejopampa, Sorochuco

CU00 (CUSCO):

CU02) Universidad Nacional de San Antonio Abad del Cusco, Av. de la Cultura 733, 08001 Cusco ☎84 786874 **W:** abel-ww.wix.com/radiouniversidad-unsaac-cusco **E:** radio_universidad@hotmail.com – **CU04)** Av Charcahuaylla s/n, 08028 Maras, Prov Urubamba ☎84 201410 **W:** radiolasalle.com.pe **E:** webmaster@radiolasalle.com.pe - **FM:** 91.7MHz – **CU05)** Prolongacion Av. Grau 30, Huancaro, 08001 Cusco ☎🖷84 221045 **W:** nseradio.com **E:** nsecusco@nseradio.com – **CU06)** Ca Tres Cruces de Oro 430, 3er piso, 08001 Cusco ☎84 232717 **W.:** facebook.com/radioredecusco **E.:** redecusco@yahoo.com – **CU07)** Ca Puputi K-3B, Cercado de Cusco, 08001 Cusco ☎84 505364 **W:** radioluzcusco.org – **CU08)** Ca Inca 650, Santiago, 08001 Cusco ☎84 228649 **W:**radiointiraymi.com **E:** intiraymiradio@hotmail.com - **Quechua:** 2 hrs: - 1100, 1500 – **CU10)** Ca Daniel A Carrioón 602, Urb. Fideranda, 08006 Wanchaq ☎84 255491 – **CU13)** Av Tupac Amaru, Urb. Progreso D3, 08006 Wanchaq ☎84 504961 **W:** radiolasvegas.pe **E:** administracion@grupovegas.com.pe - **FM:** 100.1 MHz – **CU14)** Jr Cusco 805 - Yauri, 08451 Espinar ☎84 773692 **W:** http//radioconciertocusco.galeon.com - **FM:** 103.9MHz – **CU15)** Asoc. Pro-Vivendi el Periodista Lt B-13, 08006 Wanchaq ☎84 261556 **W:** radiotropicanacusco.blogspot.no **E:** RadioTropicanaCusco@gmail.com – **CU16)** Urb. Villa el Periodista Lote E-1, 08001 Cusco ☎84 239514 **W:** cuscoctv47.com **E:** prensaaldiaperu@gmail.com – **CU17)** Ca Sucre 107, 08351 Sicuaní – **CU18)** Jr Ricardo Palma M 2, Wanchaq, 08001 Cusco ☎84 246201 - **FM:** 100.7MHz – **CU19)** Ca Anta s/n, Antanampa, 08541 Espinar **W:** radiolosandesdelperu.es.tl - **FM :** 98.9MHz – **CU20)** Jr Juan Espinoza Medrano P-13, Urb Rosas Pata, 08001 Cusco **E:** sernaquem@hotmail.com – **CU21)** Ca Retiro 296-A, 08001 Cusco ☎84 224567 - **FM:** 92.7MHz – **CU22)** Lote E-11, Urb Bancopata, 08001 Cusco **W:** machupicchuradio.com **E:** machupicchuradio@hotmail.com - **FM:** 100.1MHz – **CU23)** Jr José Santos Chocano, Bloque G-11, Urb. Santa Monica, 08001 Cusco ☎84 226765 🖷84 234494 **W:** radiouniversalcusco.com.pe **E:** radiouniversal@speedy.com.pe - **FM:** 103.3MHz – **CU24)** Ca Meloc 417, 08001 Cusco **W:** bethelradio.fm – **CU25)** Av El Sol N° 830, 08001 Cusco ☎84 228411 **W:** facebook.com/www.radiotawantinsuyo- **FM:** 91.3MHz – **CU26)** Av Martin Pio Concha 339, 08141 Santa Ana **Quechua:** 1300-1430, 2100-0100 ☎84 281002 **W:** radioquillabamba.com - **FM:** 91.1MHz – **CU27)** Jr Bolivar 217, 08351 Sicuani **W:** radiopachatusan.com**E:** pachatusanradio1240@hotmail.com – **CU28)** Pasaje Constancia 102, Of 410, 08006 Wanchaq **W:** solimperiotvradio.blogspot.com – **CU30)** Jr José Olaya Mz H-9, Urb Bancopata, 08009 Santiago ☎84 252591 – **CU31)** Ca Sacsaywaman K-10, Urb. Manuel Prado, 08001 Cusco - **FM:** 104.1MHz – **CU32)** Av. Garcilazo de la Vega 604, 08006 Wanchaq ☎84 226912 **E:** campesinaprensa@gmail.com – **CU34)** Jr 2 de Mayo 206, 08351 Sicuani ☎🖷84 351136 **W:** radiosicuani.org.pe **E:** radiosicuani@gmail.com - **Quechua:** 0930-1100, 2300-0300 0900-0300 - **FM:** 91.1MHz – **CU35)** Urb. Marcavalle, P-20, 08002 Wanchaq ☎84 226555 **W:** rtvsantamonica.com **E:** radiosantamonica@gmail.com - **FM:** 93.9MHz – **CU36)** Plaza de Armas s/n, El Descanso, 08371 Kunturkanki Canas, Prov. de Canas **E:** cpmaldonado@caritas.org.pe – **CU37)** Conjunto Habitacional Pachacútec A-105, 08001 Cusco ☎84 211371 **W:** radiovidacusco.org – **CU39)** Jr Matara 526, 08001 Cusco - **FM:** 106.5MHz – **CU40)** Av Manuel Callo Zevallos 161, 08351 Sicuani ☎84 351700 **W:** radioquechua.pe **E:** radioquechus@gmail.com - **FM:** 97.7MHz – **CU42)** Plaza de Armas s/n, 08281 Marcapata, Provincia de Quispicanchi – **CU43)** Ca Saphi 601, Cusco ☎84 225851 - **FM:** 90.1MHz – **CU44)** Av El Sol 230, Yauri, 08451 Espinar - **FM:** 103.1MHz – **CU48)** Av Panamericana 105, Yauri, 08451 Espinar – **CU49)** Av Cusco s/n, Yauri, 08451 Espinar – **CU50)** Jr Ricardo Palma 516, 08141 Quillabamba - **FM:** 96.5MHz – **CU51)** Ca Choquechaca 152, 08001 Cusco ☎84 802444 – **CU52)** Ca Heladeros 220, 08006 Wanchaq **W:** radiomariaperu.org - **FM:** 102.1MHz – **CU55)** Comunidad de Usañaje, Ca 28 de Junio 507, 08551 Santo Tomas, Chumbivilcas **W:** radioqorilazo.zragteam.com – **CU56)** Av San Martin 305, Yauri, 08451 Espinar ☎84 301099 **W:** radiolaramani.com **E:** radiolaramani@latinmail.com – **CU58)** Plaza de Armas s/n, El Descanso, 08371 Kunturkanki, Prov de Canas ☎84 812761 **E:** radiosantacruz@peru.com - **FM:** 97.7MHz – **CU61)** Ca Arequipa 590, 08351 Sicuani – **CU62)** Av Arequipa s/n, 08351 Sicuani ☎84 352373 **W:** Facebook.com/radiovilcanotasicuani/ **E:**. rperzquispe@hotmail.com – **CU65)** Sede Nacional Cusco, Av Huayarurupata 1707, Wanchaq, Cusco – **CU66)** Puputi 208, Int. N° 01, 08001 Cusco – **CU67)** Av Sol s/n Plazoleta Terminal Antiguo, 08451 Espinar ☎84 634240 **W:** facebook.com/RadioCadenaSurEspinar **E:** waldervalero@hotmail.com - **FM:** 103.1 MHz – **CU69)** Malecón Sicuani s/n, 08351 Sicuani,**W:** radioexitosa.pe – **CU70)** Av Infancia 551, 08001 Cusco ☎84 784397 **W:** facebook.com R. Jerusalen – **CU71)** Cl San Pedro esquina con calle Tres de Mayo, Espinar ☎84 301125 **W:** radiosolarespinar.com – **CU72)** Ca Belen 600, 08031 Urubamba ☎99 6783273 **W:** radiochaski.com **E:** chaskiradio@hotmail.com - **FM:** 94.9 MHz – **CU73)** Av Ejercito 200, 08001 Cusco ☎84 775511 **W:** radiovidacusco.org – **CU74)** Av Tupac Amaru 535, 08386 Yanaoca **W:** Facebook Radio Altiva Canas – **CU75)** Av Tupac Amaru 321 08386 Yanaoca Canas ☎968666649 **W:** radiotupacamaru.blogspot.no – **CU76)** Urb. Tambillo L-5, 08086 Urcos – **CU77)** Av de la Cultura 3035 A-1, 08058 San Sebastian – **CU78)** Av Carrion 313, 08351 Sicuani **W:** redinformativadelsur.blogspot.se – **CU79)** Ca Mojospata 745, Cusco ☎98 665 5540 **W:** radiowayraperu.com – **CU80)** Av Huayruropata 1707, Cusco **W:** ipda.com.pe – **CU81)** Esquina Calle Alegria 205 con Av.Arequipa No 119, 08351 Sicuani – **CU82)** Av Tupac Amaru D-3, Urb. Progreso, 08006 Wanchaq ☎84 246832 **W:** radiolasvegas.pe – **CU83)** Ca Concepcion MZ J-4, Lote 4, 08531 Livitica – **CU85)** Calle Nueva Baja 206, Espinar ☎973 583596 **W:** kinsachata.pe **E:** radiokinsachata@hotmail.com – **CU86)** Av. Diagonal Ramon Zabaleta 117 5° piso, Wanchaq, 08000 Cusco **W:** antena5cusco.com **E:** rantena5@hotmail.com – **CU87)** Chumbbivilcas – **CU88)** Pallpata, Espinar – **CU89)** Bolivar esq. Bolognesi, Santo Tomás, Chumbbivilcas ☎84 612178 **W:** radiochumpiwillkas.com – **CU90)** Chamaca, Chumbivilcas – **CU91)** Av Cultura No 2405, Oficina 203, Cusco **W:** radio760cuscoam.com **E:** radiolosandes760cusco@gmail.com – **CU92)**Sicuani ☎91 0361334 **W:** radiosurandina.com **E:**contacto@radiosurandina.com – **CU93)**Barrio Bañupata, Distr. Pitumarca, Prov. de

Canchis – **CU94)** Cerro Lechemoco, Distr. de Sicuani
HN00 (HUANUCO):
HN01) Av Raymondi N° 432, 10221 Rupa-Rupa ☎6256 2024 – **HN02)** Malecón Huallaga 1038, 10261 Aucayacu – **HN03)** Jr Tacna 693, 10001 Huanuco ☎62 517996 **W:** radiohuanuco.com – **HN04)** Jr Hermilio Valdiz 272,10001 Huanuco ☎62 516360 **W:** radiolaluz.com – **HN06)** Ruben Dario 128, 10051 Amarilis, 10001 Huánuco ☎62 512428 – **HN07)** Jr Dos de Mayo 1286, Of 208, 10001 Huánuco **E:** luzysonido@hotmail.com ☎62 518500 🖷62 511985 **Quechua:** 1000-1200, 2300-0200 - **FM:** 105.7MHz – **HN12)** Jr. Aguilar N° 560, 2do Piso, 10001 Huanuco – **HN13)** Sector San Cristóbal de Huayllabamba, 10066 San Francisco de Cayran – **HN15)** Pasaje Uchiza 170, Int 7, 10221 Rupa-Rupa – **HN16)** Sector Mesepata, 10061 Pilco Marca – **HN17)** Jr Leonicio con Libertad, 10001 Huanuco **W:** radiocielo.pe – **HN18)** Jr. Ambo 112, Amarilis **W:** kebuenaradioytv.com – **FM:** 99.7 – **HN19)** Jr Colonial 312, 10021 Amarilis – **HN20)** Jr Colonial N° 312, 10021 Amarilis
HV00 (HUANCAVELICA):
HV01) Puno 110, 09481 Lircay, Prov de Angaraes – **HV02)** Plaza Bolognesi 142, Cercado,09001 Huancavelica ☎67 451257 **E:** jlopez_alvarado@hotmail.com - **FM**: 99.1MHz – **HV03)** Ca Arequipa S/N, 09841 Huayllahuara – **HV04)** Av Los Libertadores s/n, Castrovirreina – **HV05)** Cl Mercurio 101, Urb. Santa Bárbara, Huancavelica ☎67 451376 **W:** radiomastermixfm.com **E:** mastermixfm@hotmail.com – **HV06)** Jr Armado Revorredo 588, Acobamba – **HV07)** Jr Sebastián 353, Huancavelica – **HV08)** Plaza San Lorenzo S/N,Acoria – **HV09)** Av Andrés Avelino Cáceres No 381, Huancavelica – **HV10)** Ca. Lima s/n, Preov
IC00 (ICA):
IC01) Conde de Nieva 125, 11001 Ica – **IC02)** Av Ayacucho Esq Grau s/n, 11001 Ica ☎56 231956 - **FM:** 105.3MHz – **IC03)** Av Conde de Nieva, Urb Luren, 11001 Ica - **FM:** 90.7MHz – **IC04)** Av San Martín 305, 2º piso, 11101 Chincha Alta – **IC05)** Ca Cajamarca 195, 11001 Ica - **FM:** 103.3MHz – **IC06)** Av Leon de Bivero 100 2do Piso, 11001 Ica ☎56 237326 **W:** radiolaluz.com – **IC07)** Zona M-6, San Juan de Marcona, 111521 Marcona ☎56 525268 – **IC10)** Ca Bolivar 473, 11001 Ica. ☎56 219300 – **IC11)** Calle Grocio Prado 122, 11101 Chincha Alta – **IC12)** Los Portales de Escribanos 167, Plaza de Armas, Palpa **E:** radiocruzdelsur@hotmail.com - **FM:** 99.7 MHz – **IC15)** San Martín 120, Urb Pencal, 11521 Nazca – **IC17)** Km 300, Panamericana Sur, 11011 Subtanjalla **E:** epcc@upsjb.edu.pe – **IC19)** Jr Los Ángeles 296 3er Piso, Publo Nuvo, 11141 Chincha ☎56 263278 – **IC20)** Ca San Francisco 301, 11241 San Clemente☎56 312416 **W:** facebook.com/carlosalberto.bautistagutierrez – **IC21)** Jr Lima 529,11141 Chincha Alta **W:** yeshuaradiofm.blogspot.se - **FM:** 107.5 MHz – **IC22)** Urb. Fernando de Leon de Vivero R` 1-7, 11146 Pueblo Nuevo **W:** bethelradio.fm **E:** bethelradio@bethelradio.fm – **IC23)** Ca Camino Real s/n, Sector Guadeloupe, 11021 Salas **W:**radiolaluz.com – **IC24)** Programa de Vivienda Vallea Hermoso, 11011 Subtanjalla – **IC25)** Jirón Miraflores 342, 4588 Pueblo Nuevo – **IC26)** Av Arenales 697, Ica – **IC27)** Ca San Francisco s/n – Sector Coloradio, Chincha – **IC28)** Av. Las Gaviotas Cdra. 17 A27, Urb. Sagitario, Santiago de Surco, Lima ☎1 2577315 **W.:** elsembrador.com **E.:** elsembradortv@gmail.com – **IC29)** Av Arenales 685, Ica – **IC30)** Av Arenales 685, Ica – **IC31)** Av Progreso 168, Chinca Alta – **IC31)** Prolongación Cañete Mz. D- 1, LT21-A, Salas – **IC32)** Jr. Ica 357, Pueblo Nuevo – **IC33)** Prolongación Cañete s/n, Salas – **IC34)** Ica
JN00 (JUNIN):
JN01) Jr Los Manzanos 695, 12009 El Tambo ☎64 789459 **W:** radiolaluz.com - **FM:** 101.7MHz – **JN04)** Av Tayacaja 324, Of 202, 12851 La Oroya – **JN05)** Av Jorge Chavez 851, Anexo Zaños Grande, 12009 El Tambo **E:** radiovida@hotmail.com – **JN06)** Ca Ancash 543, Of 208, 12001 Huancayo - **FM:** 103.1MHz – **JN08)** Jr Bolognesi 484 2de Piso, 12741 Jauja **W:** radioluzdetarma.com – **JN09)** Av Calmell del Solar 469-481, Sn Carlos Hye, 12001 Huancayo ☎64 211312 **W:** rmanantial.webcindario.com **E:** manantialradio960@hotmail.com - **FM:** 94.9 MHz – **JN10)** Jr. Huancas 251, a San Carlos, 12001 Huancayo – **JN11)** Esquina Prolongación Pachitea 136 y Pasaje Andaluz 106 4° piso, 12001 Huancayo – **JN12)** Paraje Aliguata, Anexo A Azapampa, 12014 Chilca **W:** bethelradio.fm – **JN13)** Ca Mercado 194, 12321 San Ramón – **JN14)** Ca Real 270, El Tambo, 12001 Huancayo ☎64 245396 🖷64 253921 - **FM:** 96.7MHz "R Futura" – **JN16)** Paseo La Breña 174 2 piso Of 202, 12001 Huancayo ☎64 219990 – **JN18)** Jr Cerro de Pasco 582, (Ap 2), 12101 Junín ☎64 344029 **W:** rlibertadjunin.com **E:** radiolibertadjunin@yahoo.es - **FM:** 98.9MHz – **JN19)** Av Ayacucho 7300, 12001 Huancayo - **FM:** 105.7MHz – **JN20)** Av Manuel Prado 239,12411 Satipo – **JN21)** Jr Moquegua 648 Int. 28, 12221 Tarma **W:** facebook.com/radioselecciones – **FM:** 104.1 MHz – **JN22)** Jr Puno 430, Huancayo ☎64 218080 **W:** radiocumbre.org.pe **E:** radiocumbre985fmcom@gmail.com - **FM:** 98.5MHz – **JN23)** Jr Junín 163, 12331 La Merced Chanchamayo – **JN24)** Jr Dario Leon 198, 4° piso, 12851 La Oroya **W:** Facebook - **FM:** 91.7 MHz – **JN26)** Ca Real 1453, 12001 Huancayo **W:** radiobacan.com **E:** corplus@radiobacan.com – **JN27)** Jr Junin 843 , 2° piso, 12741 Jauja ☎64 362428 🖷64 361850 – **JN28)** Jr Jauja 494, 12221 Tarma – **JN29)** Jr Manuel Fuentes N° 490, El Tambo, Huancayo ☎964 614 403 **W:** facebook.com/MisionCristianaRescate/ **E:** edemiperu@hotmail.com – **JN30)** Jr Moquegua 642, 12221 Tarma ☎64 321864 **W:** radioluzdetarma.com – **JN31)** Av Jose Carlos Mariátegui 699, Urb Tambo, 12001 Huancayo ☎64 241941 🖷64 252840 - **FM:** 102.5MHz – **JN32)** Ca Bolivar 481, 12101 Junin – **JN33)** Marcavelle Block "F" 191,Santa Rosa de Sacco, 12851 La Oroya **W:** Facebook – Radio La Oroya **E:** radio_la_oroya@hotmail.com ☎64 391401 🖷64 391748 - **FM:** 100.1MHz – **JN34)** Ca Real 517, Of 403, 12001 Huancayo ☎64 231831 **W:** radiohuancayo.com.pe - **FM:** 104.3MHz – **JN35)** Av Arevaldo 484, Anexo Chuccus, 12841 Santa Rosa de Sacco, Prov de Yauli **W:** mineriaradiotv.com – **JN37)** Jr Molino del Amo 167 (Cas.167), 12221 Tarma ☎64 321510 🖷6432 1167 **W:** radiotarma.com **E:** informacion@grupomonteverde.com - **FM:** 99.3 & 101.7MHz "R Tropicana" in La Merced – **JN38)** Av Huancavelica 430, 2° piso (Ap 230), 12001 Huancayo ☎64 233851 **W:** radio1550.com **E:** radio@radio1550.com - **FM:** 88.9MHz – **JN40)** Jr Pasco y Amazonas 420 2 piso Edifico San Juan, 12221 Tarma ☎64 321820 - **FM:** 106.5 MHz – **JN44)** Ca Principal de Lama, Pariahuanca, 12001 Huancayo **W:** nuevotiempo.org.pe – **JN45)** Av.Huancavlica 439 4to pisi, 12001 Huancyo – **JN46)** Prolongacion ICA y la Ca. Real s/n, 12001 Huancayo **W:** visionradioperu.com – **JN48)** Jr Santa Cecilia 107 12014 Chilca ☎64 201011 **W:** radiovozcristianaperu.com **E:** radiovozcristiana1470am@hotmail.com – **JN49)** Pasaje Omacoto, 12072 Sicaya – **JN50)** Ca Principal de Lampa s/n, 12006 Pariahuanca – **JN51)** Jr Ayacucho 297, 12001 Huancayo **W:**radiocielo.pu – **JN52)** Av los Incas 421, Huancán ☎64 248362 **W:** ministerioevangelicoapocalipsis.com – **JN53)** Conjunto Habitacional Villa Mercedes, Block 03, Tiends 1, 12001 Huancayo **W:** radiocora.net – **JN54)** Av Deusta 548,12009 El Tambo – **JN55)** Jr La Victoria 322, Costado Colegio Casillo, 12009 El Tambo ☎64 249121 – **JN56)** Jr Cajamarca 178, Huancayo ☎64 215038 **W:** facebook.com/ipda.huancayo **E:** escalaradio@hotmail.com - **FM:** 107.1 MHz – **JN57)** Jr Ayacucho 297,12001 Huancayo **W:** FB- **E:** rumbaradioactiva@hotmail.com - **FM:** 91.1 MHz – **JN58)** Centro Poblado de Tzancuvatziari, Satipo – **JN59)** Junin – **JN60)** Altura de Puente Chacachimpa, Carretera Junin Ondores, Junin – **JN61)** Pasaje Las Orquidias s/n, Tarma
LB00 (LAMBAYQUE):
LB01) Km 4 de la Carretera Pimentel, 14001 Chiclayo - **FM:** 105.1MHz – **LB02)** Ca Juan XXXIII 391 (Ciudad Universitaria), 14601 Lambayeque **W:** unprg.edu.pe **E:** universitariaradio@hotmail.com – **LB03)** Psje.Woyke 179,Oficina Radio, Edifico Angelica, 14011 San José ☎74 237850 **W:** radiolaluz.com – **LB04)** Juan Cuglievan 984, 14001 Chiclayo – Quechua: **Sun:** 0600-1100 – **LB06)** Alfonso Ugarte 505, 14011 San José ☎74 608991 – **LB08)** Ca San José 462, Of 207, 14001 Chiclayo ☎74 204786 - **FM:** 96.7MHz – **LB11)** Av Pedro Ruiz 1123, 3° piso, 14001 Chiclayo – **LB12)** Calle 28 de Julio 440, 14041 San Jose ☎74 650332 **W:** radioprimaverachiclayo.com – **LB14)** Colombia 1637, Urb. V.R.Haya de la Torre, 14001 Chiclayo ☎74 208523 – **LB15)** Av Saenz Peña 1046, 14001 Chiclayo ☎74 208872 - **FM:** 98.3MHz – **LB16)** Av Tupac Amaru 532, 14301 Ferreñafe ☎73 286044 **E:** aflff@hotmail.com – **LB17)** Ca San José 1084, 14001 Chiclayo – **LB18)** Av. Lora y Lora 1505, Urb. San Isidro, 14001 Chiclayo ☎74 320616 - **FM:** 94.1MHz – **LB19)** Ca Manuel Seano 918, 14001 Chiclayo ☎74 236363 – **LB20)** Ca Las Violetas s/n, 14001 Chiclayo **W:** radionova.com.pe/nova_chiclayo.html - **FM:** 94.9MHz – **LB21)** Ca Francisco Gonzales Burgán 717, 14301 Ferreñafe ☎74 286351 **E:** radioferrenafe@hotmail.com – **LB22)** Ca 1 de Mayo 278, Urrunaga, 14001 Chiclayo – **LB23)** Caserio Tranca Falupe, 14101 Morrope – **LB24)** Ca San Francisco 1499 - P.J.Cruz de Chalpo, 14161 Olmos – **LB25)** Jr. Juan Cuglievan 984, 14001 Chiclayo ☎98 1877701 **W:** radioamistadperu.net – **LB26)** Empresa Capimag S.R.L., Calle Justicia 102, Urb. Túpac Amaru, 14001 Chiclayo – **LB29)** Ca San José 148, 14161 Olmos **E:** clori1009@yahoo.es – **LB30)** Av el Tren s/n, 14001 Chiclayo **W:** facebook.com/radiotuman.net – **LB31)** Ca Juan Fanning N° 457, Urb San Juan, 14001 Chiclayo ☎74 239889 **W:** visionradioperu.com **E:** informes@visionradioperu.com – **LB32)** Ca Tarata 931, 14161 Olmos **W:** Facebook – Radio Super Real 1510 – **LB36)** Av Huamaucho 1080, 14601 Lambayeque ☎74 284085 **W:** radionaylamp.com **E:** naylamp@llampallec.rep.net.pe - **FM:** 96.1MHz – **LB40)** Ca Amadeo Ruiz 320, 14161 Olmos **W:** radionorandinaolmos.

com - **FM:** 102.7 MHz – **LB41)** Ca Nazca 300, 14021 La Victoria ☎74 232559 **W:** radiofechiclayo.tk **E** jesusmiguela1077@hotmail.com att.: Pastor José Huamán – **LB42)** Ca Vicente de la Vega 873, 14001 Chiclayo ☎74 224287 **W:** corporacionrbc.org **E:** carranzamori@hotmail.com – **LB44)** Av Lora y Lora 399, Urb. Patazca, 14001 Chiclayo – **LB45)** Av Los Andes No 950, 14021 La Victoria – **LB46)** Prolongacion 8 de Octubre No 263, 14601 Lambayeque – **LB47)** Av Pedro Ruiz 1250, 14001 Chiclayo ☎74 229494 – **LB48)** Ca Diego Ferre 637, Monsefú – **LB49)** Av Pacifico 483, Chiclayo – **LB50)** M "A" S/N serur Letica, Motupe ☎942 376 603 **W:** radiotvmotupe **E:** radiotvmotupe@gmail.com – **LB51)** Calle Bolognesi S/N, Olmos - **FM:** 101.7 MHz

LL00 (LA LIBERTAD):

LL01) Av.Gonzales Prada 695-12, 13001 Trujillo ☎44 436007 – **LL02)** Jr Benito Juarez 1753, 13009 La Esperanza – **LL03)** Daniel Alcides Carrión 306,13001 Trujillo ☎44 291058 - **FM:** 98.3MHz – **LL04)** Ca Lima 599, 13171 Chepén – **LL05)** San Martín 472, 13001 Trujillo ☎44 251792 – **LL06)** Av Los Incas s/n, Anexo Facala, Ascope – **LL07)** Ca Junín 23, Sausal, 13261 Ascope – **LL08)** Francisco Pizarro 532, Of 205, 13001 Trujillo – **LL09)** Jr Ayacucho 65, 13111 Pacasmayo ☎44 583042 – **LL10)** Jr San Antonio 880 Piso 2, 13301 Otuzco ☎44 436007 – **LL11)** Jr Marcelo Corne 224, Urb San Andrés, 13001 Trujillo ☎44 294050 - **FM:** 90.9MHz – **LL12)** Av V Belaunde MZ.L lote 15, Urb Santo Dominguito, 13001 Trujillo – **LL15)** Av Gran Chimu 1791 – Esperanza Alta, 13009 La Esperanza – **LL16)** Jr Apurimac Caja, 13052 Virú ☎44 371046 **W:** radioollantay.com.pe **E:** publicidad@radioollantay.com.pe - **FM:** 102.3MHz – **LL17)** Ca Trujillo 699-A, 13171 Chepén – **LL19)** Psje. Damián Niculau 108, 13501 Huamachuco. ☎44 441502 **W:** radiolosandesdehuamachuco.com **E:** radiolosandesdireccion@yahoo.es – **LL20)** Psje. Rosa Elvira Farro Solis 3, Urb. Ignacioa Reaño, 13171 Chepen ☎44 561430 **W:** sansebastianradio.com **E:** info@sansebastianradio.com - **FM:** 103.3 MHz – **LL21)** Miguel Grau 439, Of. 213, 13001 Trujillo ☎44 217885 – **LL22)** Zepita 452, 13001 Trujillo ☎44 249326 ℻44 252970 **W:** radiolibertadmundo.com **E:** contactanos@radiolibertadmundo.com – **LL24)** Bolívar 780 (Cas 1029), 13001 Trujillo ☎44 233981 – **LL26)** Ca Cáceres 1338, 13761 Santiago de Chuco ☎44 230277 – **LL28)** Jr Progreso 987, 13171 Chepén - **FM:** 98.7MHz – **LL32)** Av. Geronimo La Torro 175, Urb. Las Quintanas, 13001 Trujillo ☎44 803207 **W.:** Facebook - Radio La Luz 1390 – **LL35)** Pasaje San Martin 300, Urb Alto Mochica, (Ap 352) 13001 Trujillo ☎44 201606 **W:** sanjuansuperradio.com **E:** radiosanjuan@hotmail.com – **LL37)** Jr. Trujillo 350, 13701 Quiruvilca ☎949 611963 **W:** facebook.com/Radio-Amistad-1470-am-101046394619384 – **LL38)** Av. Virú N° 1205, 13052 Virú – **LL39)** Av. España 1238 – oficina 305, 13001 Trujillo ☎44 210494 – **LL42)** Av. Cesar Vallejo 390, 13001 Trujillo **W:** radiomundialam.com - **FM:** 96.9MHz – **LL43)** Av España 1210, 13001 Trujillo ☎44 295214 **W:** facebook **E:** pastormamerto@hotmail.com – **LL46)** Ca Victor Julio Rossel 324, 13831 Julcan – **LL47)** Ca Progreso 551, 13301 Otuzco ☎44 220221 – **LL48)** Ca La Libertad 120, 13301 Otuzco ☎44 436565 **W:** chamiradio.org.pe **E:** direccion@chamiradio.org.pe – **LL49)** Ca Progreso 551, 13301 Otuzco **W:** radiootuzco.blogspot.no – **LL51)** Jr Lara 591, 13501 Huamachuco **W:** radioantena9.com – **LL52)** Av America Sur 3145, Urb. Monserrat (Apt. 1075), 13001 Trujillo ☎44 604444 **W:** upao.edu.pe/radio **E:** cceli@upao.edu.pe – **LL53)** Jr Francisco Pizarro 970, 13001 Trujillo – **LL54)** Panamericana Norte Km 570 – El Milagro, 13009 La Esperanza – **LL55)** Ca Simón Bolivar 675, Santiago de Chuco **FB:** Radio-La-Voz-Del-Pueblo-Santiago-De-Chuco-137302053483702 – **LL56)** Trujillo – **LL57)** San Ignacio, Otuzco

LM00 (LIMA):

LM01) Juan Vargas 147, Chorrillos, Lima 09 ☎1 617 6606 **W:** radioinca.com.pe – **LM02)** Jr Camana 615 of 605, Lima 01 ☎1 4272639 **W:** radiooriente.com **E:** radiooriente@hotmail.es – **LM03)** Av Garzón 2031, Jesús Maria, Lima 11 ☎1 7001600 ℻1 4333276 **W:** radiomariaperu.org **E:** info.per@radiomaria.org – **LM04)** Jr, Contunaz No 933 Ofic 601, Lima 15001 ☎1 4280938 **W:** radiocora.net **E:** soporteradiocora@gmail.com – **LM05)** Ca Miguel Dasso 144, Of 2A, San Isidro, Lima 27 ☎1 5922291 **W:** ovacion.com.pe/radio/ **E:** radioovacion@ovacion.com.pe – **LM06)** Av Guzman Blanco 465, oficina 203-701, (Ap 4236) Lima 01 ☎1 4333275 **W:** pacificocomunicaciones.com/radio640.html **E:** informes@pacificocomunicaciones.com – **LM07)** Justo Pastor Davila 197, Chorillos, Lima 09 ☎1 6176600 **W:** radiolainolvidable.com.pe **E:**crpradio@crpradio.com.pe – **LM08)** Los Robles 297, San Isidro, Lima **W**: rbcradio.pe/ **E:** contacto@rbcradio.pe – **LM09)** Jr. Alejandro Tirado 508, Urb. Santa Beatriz, Lima 01 (✉ C.P. 138, La Molina, Lima 12) ☎1 2653291 **W:** redradiointegridad.com **E:** info@redradiointegridad.org – **LM10)** Av Paseo de la República 3866, 2° piso, San Isidro, Lima 27 ☎1 2150200 **W:** rpp.com.pe **E:** info@gruporpp.com.pe – **LM11)** Justo Pastor Dávila 197, Chorillos, Lima 09 ☎1 6176600 ℻1 2513324 **W:** radiomar.com.pe – **LM12)** Alfonso Ugarte 1428 of 904, Lima ☎1 4241805 – **LM13)** Prolongación los Angeles 676, Huaral, Lima 18 ☎1 2465296 **W:** Facebook Radio la Luz Huaral **E:** radiolaluzhuaral@hotmail.com - **FM:** 94.7 MHz – **LM14)** Jr Mayta Cápac 1385, Jesús Maria Central, Lima 11 **W:** radiolibertad.com.pe **E:** info@radiolibertad.com.pe ☎1 2660777 – **LM15)** Av Petit Thouars 447, Santa Beatriz, Lima 01 **W:** radionacional.com.pe **E:** webmaster@irtp.com.pe ☎1 4338956 – **LM16)** Av José Pardo 138, Of. 1501, Miraflores, Lima 18 ☎1 7120145 **W:** radiounion.pe **E:** informes@unionlaradio.com – **LM17)** Av Paseo de la Republica 3866, San Isidro, 15046 Lima 27 ☎1 2150266 **W:** felicidad.com.pe – **LM18)** Av Republica de Chile 295, Of. 1104, Santa Beatriz, Lima 01 ☎1 3327779 **W:** modernaradiopapa.com.pe **E:** info@modernaradiopapa.com.pe – **LM19)** Paseo Parodi 340, San Isidro, Lima 27 **W:** radiopanamericana.com **E:** radio@panamericana.com ☎1 4388585 ℻1 4221223 – **LM20)** Jr Ignacio Merino 230, Santa Cruz, Miraflores, Lima 18 ☎1 4428810 **W:** radiolatina.com.pe **E:** contacto@radiolatina.com.pe – **LM21)** Julio C.Tello 152, Lince, Lima 14 ☎1 4714291 **W:** metropolitanaradioperuana.com **E:** metropolitanaradioperuana@gmail.com – **LM22)** Julio C.Tello 152, Lince, Lima 14 ☎1 4714291 **W:** radioexitoperu.com **E:** radioexitoperu@gmail.com – **LM23)** Av Alfonso Ugarte 1465, 01 Lima ☎1 3320080 **W:** radiolaluz.com **E:**dr.davidlozano@hotmail.com – **LM24)** Gerardo Unger 6347, San Martin de Porres, Lima 31 ☎1 5373204 **W:** radiofelizperu.com – **LM27)** Jr Bernardo Alcedo 375, Lince, Lima 14 ☎1 2652333 **W:** radiobacan.com **E:** corplus@radiobacan.com – **LM30)** Jr. Contunaz No 933 Ofic 601, Lima 15001 ☎1 4280938 **W:** radiocora.net **E:** soporteradiocora@gmail.com – **LM31)** Jr Echenique 140, 15140 Huacho – **LM32)** Mz L, Lt 7, Urb La Esperanza, 15146 Hualmay – **LM33)** Av Estados Unidos 327, Urb Huaquillay, Comas, Lima 07 **W:** radiocomas.com **E:** comas@radiocomas.com ☎1 5250094 ℻1 5250859 – **LM34)** Ca MCDO Sur 105, 15140 Huacho – **LM35)** Cl Felipe Arancibia 861, San Juan de Miraflores Lima☎1 368 6829 **W:** radioalegria1340am.com – **LM38)** Av Comandante Espinar N° 680, Miraflores, Lima 18 ☎1 6107760 ℻1 6107761 **W:** nuevotiempo.org.pe **E:** radio@nuevotiempo.org.pe – **LM39)** Av. Paseo de la Republica 3832 – Oficina 602, 01 San Isidro, Lima ☎1 4405790 **W:** eccoradio.pe **E:** eccoradiopropusa@gmail.com – **LM40)** Av 28 de Julio 1781, La Victoria. Lima 13 ☎1 6131701 **W:** bethelradio.fm **E:** betheltradio@bethelradio.fm – **LM41)** Av Petit Thouars 1806, Lince, Lima 14 ☎1 4711278 **W:** radiosanisidroam.com – **LM42)** Mz C, Lte. 5, Asoc. Virgen de la Familia, 15857 Chilca – **LM43)** Av Separadora Industrial s/n, Lote 4, MZ5, M25, Parcela 1, Villa El Salvador, Lima 42 ☎1 2913012**W:** radioimperial2peruam.com – **LM44)** Alfonso Ugarte 149, 15170 Barranca ☎1 2354238 – **FM:** 101.5 MHz – **LM45)** A.Paseo de la República 3866, San Isidro **W:** capital.com.pe – **LM47)** Jr Camaná 170, (Apt 4451 San Miguel), El Cercado, Lima 01 **W:** radiosantarosa.com.pe **E:** contacto@radiosantarosa.com.pe ☎1 4277488 – **LM49)** Calle Las Lucumas 4168 4to.Piso Urb. Naranjal – Independencia(, Antes San Martin de Porres, Lima ☎1 7153268 **W:** radiomileniaperu.com – **LM51)** Jr. Napo 3916, Independencia, Lima 28 ☎1 5234319 **W:** radioindependenciaperu.com.pe **E:** wbaldeon@radioindependecniaperu.com.pe – **LM52)** Av Colombia 325, Pueblo Libre, Lima ☎1 4236201 **W:** radiovida1590.com/public_html/ – **LM54)** Jr. Almirante Guisse N° 1885, Lince, Lima 14 ☎1 4723110 **W:** radiocielo.com.pe – **LM55)** Av Petit Thouars 447, Santa Beatriz, Lima 01 **W:** radionacional.com.pe ☎1 4331404 – **LM56)** Av. Paseo Parodi 340, San Isidro, Lima 43 ☎1 4413050 **W:** radio1160.com.pe – **LM58)** CRP – Justo Pastor Davila 197, Chorrillos, Lima 09 ☎1 617 6606 **W:** radiobienestar.pe – **LM59)** Av 28 de Julio 1781, La Victoria. Lima 13 ☎1 6131701 **W:** bethelradio.fm **E:** bethelradio@bethelradio.fm – **LM60)** Jr. Morales Bermúdez 140, Pueblo Libre, Lima 21 ☎1 4248122 **W:** cadena1200.org **E:** contacto@cadena1200.org – **LM62)** Av.Salaverry 862, Jesus Maria, Lima 11 **W:** nseradio.com **E:** nselima@nseradio.com ☎1 4714172 – **LM63)** Av.Gerardo Unger 6995, Independencia, Lima 28 ☎1 5331848 **W:** radiofeperu.org **E:** gerencia@radiofeperu.org – **LM64)** KM 193 Panamericana Norte, Barranca, Lima 04 – **LM65)** Urb. Lever Pacocha "D" 13 Av. San Martin 1 Piso, 15140 Huacho ☎1 3045427 **W:** radiolaluz.com – **LM66)** Luis Alberto Lizarraga Alva, Cerro Laguna, 15703 San Vicente de Cañete, Provinca de Cañete – **LM67)** Jr Mariano Melgar 235, 15173 Barranca **W:** radiobendicionbarranca.blogspot.no – **LM68)** Mz. E Lt. 1 AAHH Cocharcas Asuncion 8, 15708 Imperial – **LM69)** Ca Tupac Amaru 140, Urb. Casuarina, 15703 San Vicente de Cañete – **LM70)** Jr. Lima 1398, 15173 Barranca – **LM71)** Jr.Cusco s/n, Cuadra 1, Quilmana, 15875 Cañete – **LM72)** Av Miguel Grau s/n, Paramonga – **LM73)** Av Grau 592, Oficina 502, Huacho ☎1 3970739 **W:** radioparaisofm.com - **FM:** 103.5 MHz – **LM74)** Pampa de Lara s/n, Barranca ☎992 619756 **W:** angienetradio.com **E:** alzejara@

hotmail.com – **LM75)** Av Arics S/n, Barranca – **LM76)** Sector Pampa Colorado, Huacho, Huara – **LM77)**Sector Sicicaya, San Antonio – **LM78)** Sector La Minka S/N, Supe Puerto

LT00 (LORETO):

LT05) Av Antonio Raymondi 331, 16001 Iquitos - **FM:** 101.3MHz – **LT09)** Jr Arica 737, 16001 Iquitos – **LT10)** Ca Progreso 112-114, 16421 Yurimaguas, Alto Amazonas **W:** roriente.org **E:** oriente995@yahoo.com ☎65 351611 - **FM:** 99.5MHz – **LT14)** Arica 441, 16001 Iquitos

MD00 (MADRE DE DIOS):

MD01) Jr Guillermo Billingurst 406 PTO, 17001 Puerto Maldonado - **FM:** 101.3MHz – **MD02)** Nueva Plaza de Armas 200, 17001 Puerto Maldonado – **MD04)** Av Fitzcarrald 130, 17001 Madre de Dios – **MD05)** Av Andres Avelino Caceres km 4.5, Carreter de Tambopata a Cusco – Zona La Pastora, 17001 Madre de Dios – **MD06)** Jr Apurimac Psj. Tacna Lt.10 Mz.B5, 17001 Tambopata – **MD07)** Sector Triunfo s/n, Tambopata ☎51 324846 **W.:** radioredandina.com **E.:** radioredandina@gmail.com – **MD08)** Jr Lerón 368, Tambopata **W:** radiocielo.pe – **MD09)** Jr Apurimac s/n, Tambopata – **MD10)** Pasaje Túpac Amaru S/N, Mazuko – **MD11)** Centro Poblado Dos de Mayo S/N, Inambari

MQ00 (MOQUEGUA):

MQ04) PP.JJ. John F. Kennedy, Mz. E Lte. 48, 18311 Ilo – **MQ05)** Jr Tarapaca 260, 18001 Moquegua - **FM:** 101.0 – **MQ07)** Jr Ayacucho N° 639 (Ap 22), 18001 Moquegua ☎53 461542 - **FM:** 105.3MHz – **MQ08)** Mollejo s/n, 18401 Omate **W:** agrorural.gob.pe/escuchar-radios-campesinas – **MQ09)** Marsical Andrés A.Cáceres 193, 18001 Moquegua **W:** radiocielo.pu – **MQ10)** Ca Grau 101 - Frenta a la Plazade Armas, 18401 Omate – **MQ11)** Ca Libertad 1015, 18001 Cercado Moquegua ☎53 463276 **W:** radiolavozdelsurmoquegua.com **E:** radiolavozdelsur@yahoo.com – **MQ12)** Sector Charsawa-Centro Poblado Menor Los Angeles, 18001 Moquegua – **MQ13)** Pse San Antonio s/n, Mascal Nieto – **MQ14)** Jr Ancash 555-2, Moquegua **W:** radiosantacruzmoqquegua - **FM:** 94.7 MHz – **MO15)** Calle Moquegua S/N, Ichuña, ☎53 338433 **W.:** facebook.com/radioo.cruzichuna – **MO16)** Ca 2 de Enero S/N, Ichuña ☎9990 25026 **W:** mdi.gob.pe **E:** munichuna@gmail.com – **MO17)** Anexo Santa Cruz Oyo Oyo, Prov. General Sanchez – **MO18)** Plaza de Armas s/n, Moquequa – **MQ19)** Sector Chojasirca Alta, Distr. de San Cristobal, Prov de Mariscal Nieto – **MQ20)** Calle Ãncash No 556, Cercado, Moquegua ☎953 601958 **W.:** radioamericana.com.pe **E.:** americanafm@hotmal.com - **FM.:** 95.7, 101.7MHz

PA00 (PASCO):

PA01) Plazuela Gamaniel Blanco, 127- 2°Nivel - Ninguno, 19001 Chaupimarca ☎63 422398 **W:** radioalturatv.com **E:** radiotalturatv@hotmail.com - **FM:** 90.9MHz R.Alrura;: 97.7 MHz R.Los Andes – **PA02)** Jr Puno s/n, 19001 Chaupimarca - **FM:** 102.5MHz – **PA03)** Jr Mullembruck 468, Urb Cercado, 192110Oxapampa ☎63 762689 - **FM:** 101.5MHz – **PA05)** Jr Huamachuco 214, Cerro de Pasco ☎63 330109 **W:** radiocorporacion.com.pe – **PA07)** Jr Daniel Alcids Carrion 250, 19026 Huayllay – **PA08)** Av Tupac Amaru 1066, Colquijirca, 19016 Tinyahuarco – **PA09)** Jr.Pedro Caballero y Lira s/n, Galeria Mina de Oro, 19001 Chaupimarca **W:** radiocumbre.com.pe - **FM:** 103.1 MHz – **PA10)** Jr.Bolognesi 225, 19001 Chaupimarca **W:** radiomineria.com.pe/radiomineria - **FM:**102.5 MHz – **PA11)** Jr Lima 365, 19001 Chaquimarca – **PA12)** Av Simon Bolivar 410, San Juan, 19151 Yanacancha – **PA13)** Pasajae Jauja 106, Chaupimarca – **PA14)** Oxapampa – **PA15)** Cerro de Pasco – **PA16)** Jr San Juan, Mz E. Lot7, Huayllay

PI00 (PIURA):

PI04) Jr San Ignacio de Loyola 300, 20011 Castilla ☎73 342802 **W:** radiocutivalu.org **E:** cutivalu@radiocutivalu.org - **FM:** 100.5MHz – **PI05)** Ica 419, Of 206, 20001Piura - **FM:** 92.1MHz – **PI06)** Santa Maria C., 20001 Piura - **FM:** 94.5MHz.– **PI08)** Ugarteche 490, 20201 Sullana - **FM:** 99.3MHz – **PI10)** Ca Tacna 260 4 piso, (frente al banco de la nación), 20001 Piura ☎73 303369 – **PI11)**Ca San Martin 1041, 20201 Sullana ☎73 503071 **W:** Facebook Radio Capullana **E:** capullanaradio@latinmail.com.pe - **FM:** 95.7MHz – **PI13)** Calle el Altillo 282, 20541 Huancabamba ☎73 473259 **W:** lavozdelashuaringas.com **E:** radio@lavozdehuarinjas.com - **FM:** 103.7 MHz – **PI14)** Av Sánches Cerro 582 2do Piso, 20001 Piura ☎73 304221 **W:** radiolaluz.com - **FM:** 107.9MHz – **PI15)** Carretera Piura-Chulucanas km 4, 20011 Castilla ☎73 324180 – **PI16)** Av. Sanches Cerro 582 - 2° piso, 20001 Piura ☎73 304221 **W:** radiolaluz.com - **FM:** 107.9 MHz – **PI17)** Ca Unión 515 – B, Barrio Punta Arena, 20001 Piura ☎73 374106 – **PI18)** Zona Industrial Mz D Km 5, Carretera Piura, 20201 Sullana **E:** piuraradio@terra.com.pe - **FM:** 101.9MHz – **PI23)** Ca 8 s/n, 20131 Talara Alta, ☎383 750 **W:** radiobns.com **E:** radiobns1992@hotmail.com – **PI24)** Mz "E" Lote 8, Urb. Isabel Barreto I Etapa, 20801 Paita ☎73 211885 **W:** radionorperu.blogspot.no - **FM:** 102.9MHz – **PI25)** Jr Leoncio Prado 425, 20201 Sullana **W:** radiocielo.pu – **PI26)** Madre de Dios 258, 20201 Sullana ☎73 505026 **W:** facebook.com/www.radiobellavista.sullana.com.pe – **PI32)** Av Grau Cuadra N° 5, Cruceta San Lorenzo, 20701 Tambo Grande – **PI41)** Km 993.8, Carretera Panamericana, Predio Don Bosco, Sector Coscomba, 20001 Piura – **PI47)** Av Principal, Caserio La Peñita, 20701 Tambo Grande – **PI50)** Av.Miguel F. Cerro s/n, AA HH, San Jose, 20046 Vice **W:** agrorural.gob.pe/radio-ayabaca-de-piura.html – **PI51)** Jr 9 de Octubre 110, 20571 Huarmaca **W:** agrorural.gob.pe/radio-huancabamba-de-piura.html – **PI52)** Jr 9 de Octubre 110, 20571 Huarmaca **W:** radiohuarmaca.com **E:** radiohuarmaca@hotmail.com - **FM:** 98.1 MHz – **PI53)** Bolivar 114, 20441 Ayabaca – **PI54)** Km. 248 Panamericana Carretera a Chulucanas, 20011 Castilla **W:** visionradioperu.com – **PI55)** Ca Piura 508, 20611 Frias ☎73 631459 **W:** Facebook: R.Frias - **FM:** 96.5 MHz– **PI56)** Barrio Santa Rosa s/n, 20441 Ayabaca – **PI57)** Jr Morro Solar, Block F, 20001 Piura **W:** corporacionrbc.org – **PI58)** Jr Pisagua 812, 20601 Chulucanas ☎73 378627 **E:** radiosup263@hotmail.com – **PI59)** Esq. Calle Jorge Chavez y 9 de Octubre, 20571 Huarmaca **W:** rvclagrande1160am.es.tl – **PI60)** MZ. H. LT 14 – Urb. San Eduardo, 20001 Piura – **PI61)** Av Circunvalacion Lopez Albujar MZ. B.LT. 8, 20001 Piura – **PI62)** Predio de Mercedec Vite Quezada s/n, San Miguel – Valle Medio, 20001 Piura **W:** bethelradio.fm – **PI63)** Cl. Piura 311, 20611 Frias 944360440 **W:** radiofrecuenciaideal.com **E:** contacto@radiofrecuenciaideal.com – **PI64)** Calle Tacna No 235 – Edif. El Sol – 3er Piso, 20001 Piura – **PI65)** Parcela T15.8 – 42 Sector 7, 20701 Tamboa Grande – **PI66)** Calle Alfonso Ugarte 118, 20046 Vice – **PI67)** Av Progreso 101, Castilla ☎73 340301 **W:** laclave.com.pe **E:** laclave100mail.com - **FM:** 104.5 MHz – **PI68)** Ca Bolognesi s/n, 20441 Ayabacha – **PI69)** Tambopata – **PI70)** Calle Leonicio Prado 515-B, Sullana ☎73 507979 **W:** radiolajefa1530.com

PU00 (PUNO):

PU01) Jr Conde Lemos 212, 21001 Puno ☎51 351562 **W:** radioondaazul.com **E:** ondazul@radioondaazul.com - Quechua & Aymara: 6h daily - **FM:** 95.7MHz "Stereo Azul" – **PU02)** Jr Arequipa 385, 21001 Puno – **PU03)** Jr Miraflores MZ E-1, Lt-4 – Barrio Jorge Chavez, 21111 Macusani ☎51 51837009 **E:** rvamacusani@terra.com.pe - **FM:** 90.5MHz – **PU04)** Jr Jauregui 966, 21621 Juliaca ☎51 800601 **W:** nuevotiempo.org **E:** nuevotiempojuliaca@hotmail.com – **PU05)** Ca San Román 116, 21621 Juliaca ☎51 325357 – **PU06)** Simon Bolivar 442, 21001 Puno – **PU07)** "Lugar Denominado ""Barco Chuco"",21061 Chucuito **Aymara & Quechua** 0900-1400, 1900-0100 – **PU08)** Jr.Huanynacapac T4,Centro Comerical No2, 21621 Juliaca ☎51 322313 **W:** radiofronterajuliaca.blogspot.no - **FM:** 107.9MHz – **PU09)** Jr. San Isidro MZ. S, Lote 14-.B, Urb. Señor de Huanca, 21621 Juliaca ☎51 502319 – **PU11)** Jr 2 de Mayo 418 – 4to nivel, 21621 Juliaca **W.** 24horasradionoticias.com **E:** radionoticias24horasamotmail.com – **PU12)** Jr. Moquegua 180, 21001 Puno ☎51 351502 **W:** Facebook – Radio La Voz Del Altiplano – **PU13)** Ca Mariano Pandía 166, 2° piso, 21621 Juliaca **W:**radiocielo.pu – **PU14)** Jr.Leonicio Prado, 21001 Puno – **PU15)** Jr Unión 242, 21621 Juliaca **E:** radioltcj@latinmail.com ☎51 322452 📠51 369450 – **PU16)** Jr Apurimac 640, 21621 Juliaca ☎51 207007 **W:** radioondapopular.pe - **FM:** 88.9Mhz – **PU17)** Jr Antonio (Sierra) 178, prolongación Ramón Castilla, a dos cuadras del Cuartel Bolognesi, 21621 Juliaca ☎+51 793059 – **PU18)** Jr Piura 167, 21001 Puno ☎51 9731663 - **Aymara & Quechua:** 0900-1100 – **PU19)** Jr. Carabaya 998, Juliaca **W:** andino.pe **E:** info@radiotvcontinental.com – **PU20)** Jr Lima s/n, 21666 Caminaca **E:** trebol34@mixmail.com – **PU21)** Ramon Castilla 949, 21621 Juliaca ☎51 321372 **W:** ladecana.pe **E:** guadalupee8@hotmail.com - **FM:** 90.9MHz – **PU22)** Jr Apurimac 644 Cercado, 21621 Juliaca ☎51 641342 **W:** radiotvperu.pe **E:** radiotvperu@hotmail.com - **FM:** 106.7 MHz – **PU23)** Jr 2 de Mayo 790, 21621 Juliaca – **PU24)** Jr 2 de Mayo No 795 – Plaza de Armas, 21621 Juliaca ☎51 470000 **W:** radioandinajuliaca.com **E:** gerencia@radioandinajuliaca.com – **PU26)** Jr Raúl Porras 210, 21621 Juliaca ☎51 502005 **W:** radiocorporacionwayrajuliaca.com – **PU27)** Jr Chachani 220, , 21621 Juliaca ☎51 324846 **W:** radioredandina.com **E:** radioredandina@gmail.com – **PU28)** Jr 2 de Mayo 209, Oficina 406, 21621 Juliaca ☎51 321115 **W:** radiosoldelosandes.com - **FM:** 104.5MHz "El Sol de los Andes FM" – **PU32)** Jr 2 de Mayo , 21621 Juliaca **E:** carraviz@gmail.com or carraviz@hotmail.com - Listeners correspondence to: Iván Tito Vizcarra – **PU33)** Azangaro **W:** radioasillo.com – **PU35)** Jr Acora 222, 21001 Puno ☎51 366222 **W:** pachamamaradio.org **E:** info@pachamamaradio.org – **PU42)** Túpac Amaru Altura Coliseo Juli s/n, 21401 Juli ☎51 554173 **W:** agrorural.gob.pe/radio-juli-de-puno **E:** radiocampesinajuli@hotmail.com – **PU44)** 21701 Ayaviri **W:** agrorural.gob.pe/radio-ayaviri-de-puno.html– **PU45)** Jr

Jose Galvez 542, Urb Bellavista, 21001 Puno ☎51 323546 **W.** 24horasradionoticias.com **E:** radionoticias24horasamotmail.com – **PU46)** Jatun Pampa Chejollani Cupi-Esquen, 21621 Juliaca – **PU47)** Ca s/n – Sector Taparachi Zona Industrial, Urb. La Rinconada 3ra E-17, 21621 Juliaca **W:** radiomilagros.com – **PU48)** Zona Fortaleza Pucara, Sector Chuñawi, 21401 Juli – **PU49)** Jr Ayacucho 679, 21601 Caracoto **E: W.:** coorporativocontinental.com **E..** informes@coorporativocontinental.com – **PU50)** Jr Tumbes 220 3ere nivel, Juliaca ☎51 1327311 **W:** radiopublica.pe **E:** webmaster@radiopublica.pe – **PU51)** Jr Arequipa 403, 21051 Capachica – **PU52)** Jr. Alfonso Ugarte Nº 608 Macusani, Carabaya, 21 111 Macusani ☎950 300420 **W:** coorporativocontinental.com **E:** informes@coorporativocontinental.com - **FM:** 100.9MHz – **PU53)** Pasaje Echenique 110, Cercado, 21 111 Macusani – **PU54)** Acora **W:** Facebook: R. Inca-Acora – **PU55)** Jr Lima 317, Puno **W:** Facebook: R.Universidad Puno - **FM:** 92.9 MHz – **PU56)** Jr 2 de Mayo s/n, Lampa ☎950 984 787 **W:** actiweb.es/radioandinalampa – **PU57)** Jr Pedro de Candida s/n, Sandia – **PU58)** Jr Sandia 280, 21157 Azángaro ☎999 011 494 **W:** facebook.com/radioaswanghari580am **E:** radiotvaswanqhari@gmail.com – **PU59)** Azángaro – **PU60)** Cl Sandia s/n, Cuyocuyo, Sandia – **PU61)** Jr. Carabaya No 998 - 5to piso (esquina con Benigno Ballón), Juliaca ☎51 323030 **W:** facebook.com/radiotvcontinental– **PU62)** Jr Azangaro 575, Juliaca **W:** radiofrecuenciaamistad.blogspot.no – **PU63)** Rua Carabaya N° 998, Juliaca ☎51 323030 **W:** Facebook.com/RadioTvContinental

SM00 (SAN MARTIN):

SM01) Jr San Martín 257, 22411 Tocache ☎42 551031 - **FM:** 100.1 MHz – **SM03)** Av Compagñón 410, 22221 Tarapoto – **SM07)** Jr Imperio 764, 22056 Nueva Cajamarca– **FM:** 100.3 MHz – **SM08)** Jr Bolognesi 180 Altos, 22221 Tarapoto **W:** radiolaluz.com – **SM14)** Jr Loreto 300, 22251 Chazuta **W:** ethnicradio.org **E:** agiazo@hotmail.com – **SM15)** Jr Callao 650 (Apt. 133), 22001 Moyobamba ☎42 562353 – **SM16)** Av Celedin s/n, 22066 San Fernando – **SM17)** Av Alfonso Ugarte Cdra 18, Los Olivos, 22221 Tarapoto – **SM18)** Jr Libertad 157, Moyobamba – **SM19)** Jr Las Dalias s/n Mz 17, Lt E, Bellavista – **SM20)**Fundo Via Television, Shucshuyacu – **SM21)** Jr Piura 309,Nueva Cajamarca

TC00 (TACNA)

TC02) Prolong Unanue 1041 (Cas 113), 23001 Tacna - **FM:** 99.9MHz – **TC04)** Jr Sir Jones s/n (Cas 281), 23001 Tacna – **TC05)** Arias y Araguez 584, 23001 Tacna – **TC06)** Cl Tarata 665, Urb San José - Bacigalup, 23001 Tacna **W:** radiolaluz.com – **TC08)** Av Internacional 484, Alto de la Alianza, 23001 Tacna ☎52 804100 - **FM:** 106.7 MHz – **TC09)** Av.Dos de Mayo 2-A 23001 Tacna ☎52 414871 **W:** radiotacna.com.pe **E:** gerencia@radiotacna.com.pe - **FM:** 104.3 & 104.7MHz – **TC10)** Av San Martín de Porras 209, Natividad, 23001 Tacna **E:** radiobulevar@hotmail.com ☎5284 8537 – **TC11)** Jose Olaya s/n 2° piso, 23341 Tarata – **TC13)** 23341 Tarata **W:** agrorural.gob.pe/escuchar-radios-campesinas.html – **TC14)** Villa Universitaria Capannique A 20, 23031 Pocoally **W:** radiobacan.com – **TC16)** Ca 2 de Mayo 263, 23001 Tacna ☎52 428184 **W:** radiouno.pe **E:** prensa@radiouno.pe - **FM:** 93.7 MHz – **TC17)** Ca Progreso 43, Vigila, 23001 Tacna – **TC18)** Barrio Azul S-27, Ilabaya **W:** Facebook. Radio Candarave – **TC19)** Sector Buganvillas - A 200m. Cruze de Tarapaca con Buganvillas, Distr. de Pocollay, Dept. de Tacna – **TC19)** Villa Universitaria Capanique A-20, Pocollay – **TC20)** Calle Gil de Herrera 186, Tacna – **TC21)** Av El Sol 427, Tacna **W:** radiocielo.pu – **TC22)** Candarave **W:** FB radiocandaravena.com – **TC23)** Calle Gil de Herrera 186, Pocoally – **TC24)** Pampa de Layagache – Alt. Km 25 Carretera a Tarata, Alto de la Alianza – **TC26)** Prolongación Hermanos Reynosa s/n, Pocollay – **TC27)** Carretera Calana, Sector Santa Rita,Tacna **W:**radiobacan.com – **TC28)** Av Alamded N° 241, Candarave

TB00 (TUMBES):

TB01) Pza Alipio Rosales s/n, 24001 Tumbes - **FM:** 99.7MHz – **TB02)** Ca Tarapaca 163, 24001 Tumbes – **TB04)** Panamericana Norte Km 1321, 24001 Tumbes **W:** rpp.com.pe - **FM:** 100.5MHz – **TB05)** Av.Mayor Novoa 814 2° piso, 24001 Tumbes ☎72 527002 – **TB06)** Jr Bolívar 117, 24001 Tumbes ☎72 523003 – **TB07)** Jr Piura 1010, 24001 Tumbes – **TB08)** Av.Mariscal Castilla 432, 24001 Tumbes **W:** radiocielo.pe – **TB09)** Paseo Concordia y Bolognesi 2° piso, 24001 Tumbes – **TU10)** Zona Rural de Pampa Grande, Tumbes – **TU11)** El Bebedro S/N, Tumbes

UC00 (UCAYALI):

UC03) Av 9 de Diciembre 646, Pucallpa – **UC04)** Jr Coronel Portillo 448-A, Pucallpa ☎61 573876 **W:** radiousa.com **E:** radiosuper103.3@gmail.com - **FM :** 103.3MHz – **UC05)** Zona San Fernando, Callería – **UC06)** Ca Padre Francisco Alvares s/n, Sephua - **FM:** 100.5MHz – **UC07)** Ca Iquitos 499, Villa Atalaya, Distrito de Raymondi, Prov de Atalaya ☎64 461240 - **FM:** 95.5MHz – **UC09)** Carretera Federico Basadre Km 37, Los Pinos, Campoverde **W:** nuevotiempo.org.pe **E:** radio@nuevotiempo.org.pe – **UC10)** Av Tupac Amaru 957, Calleria **W:** radiocielo.pe

FM in Lima (MHz): 88.3 R.Magica,San Isidro – **LM17)** 88.9 R.Felicidad – 89.7 Emisoras Perúanos (RPP), San Isidro – 90.1 Cieneguilla – 90.1 R:Bethel, Ate-Amauta – 90.1 R.Silde, Lurigancho – 90.5 R.La Zona, Lurigancho – 91.1 R.San Borja – 91.5 R.Planicie – 91.5 R.del Sur, Lurin – 91.5 R.Chalaca, Cieneguilla – 91.5 R.Andina, Ate-Huayacan - 91.9 Okey Radio, San Isidro – 92.5 R.Studio 92, San Isidro – 93.1 R.Ritmo Romantico, Chorrillos – **LM07)** 93.7 La Inolvidable – 94.3 R.Bravaza, San Isidro – 94.9 R.La Karibeña, Chorillos – 94.9 R.A, Corillos – 95.5 R.La Exitosa, Chorillos – 96.1 Z Rock & Pop, Chorillos – **LM45)** 96.7 R.Capital – 97.3 R.Moda, Chorillos – 97.7 R.Kandela, Ate – 97.7 R.Canto Grande, San Juan de Lurigancho – LM03) 97.7 R.Maria - 97.7 R.Sencación, Chaclayo – 97.7 R.Vitarte, Cieneguilla – **LM56)** 98.1 R.1160 – 98.7 R.Magica, Punta Hermosa – 98.7 R.Karibeña, San Luis – 99.1 R.Doble Nueve, Jesus Maria – 99.5 Ate-Huaycan – 99.5 Comas – 99.5 Cieneguilla – 99.5 Chaclacayo – **LM43)** 99.5 R.Imperial 2 – **LM22)** 100.1 R.Exito – 100.1 R.Oasis, San Isidro – 100.5 R.Enmanuel, Ate – 100.7 R.Satelite, Ventanilla – 100.7 R.La Familia, Carabayllo – **LM19)**101.1 R.Panamericana – **LM54)** 101.7 R.Cielo – **LM33)** 101.7 R.Comas – **LM54)** 101.7 R.Cielo – 101.7 R.Stereo Villa, Villa El Salvador – 101.7 Chaclavayo – 101.7 San Juan – **LM33)** 102.1 R.Oxigeno, San Isidro **LM51)** R.Nacional, Barranco – 103.3 R.Unión, Miraflores – **LM15)**103.9 R.Nacional, Lima –104.7 Viva FM, San isidro – **LM47)**105.1 R.Santa Rosa, Carabayllo – 105.5 R.Fiesta, Lince – **LM11)**106.3 R. Mar Plus, Chorillios – **LM58)** 107.1 R.Nueva Q, Chorillos – 107.7 R. Planeta, Chorillos

PHILIPPINES

L.T: UTC +8h — **Pop:** 110 million — **Pr.L:** Filipino (Tagalog) (official), English (official) — **E.C:** 230V/60Hz — **ITU:** PHL

NATIONAL TELECOMMUNICATIONS COMMISSION (NTC) (Dept. of Transportation and Communications)

✉ NTC Bldg., BIR Road, East Triangle, Diliman, Quezon City 1104 ☎ +63 2 9254651 or 9267722 **W:** ntc.gov.ph

L.P: Commissioner: Gamaliel A. Cordoba. Dep. Commissioners: Delilah F. Deles, Edgardo V. Cabarios. Chief Broadcast Sces Div: Alvin Bernard N. Blanco

KAPISANAN NG MGA BRODKASTER NG PILIPINAS (KBP) (Assoc. of Broadcasters of the Philippines)

✉ 6th Flr, LTA Bldg, 118 Perea Str, Legaspi Village, Makati C, 1226 NCR ☎ +63 2 815 1992 🖷 +63 2 8815 1989 **W:** kbp.org.ph

L.P: Pres: Ruperto S. Nicdao, Chmn: Herman Z. Basbaño. Most stns are KBP members

CATHOLIC MEDIA NETWORK (CMN)

✉ Unit 201 Sunrise Condominium, 226 Ortigas Ave, North Greenhills, San Juan, Manila 1503 NCR ☎ +63 2 7249850 🖷 +63 2 7249962

L.P: Pres: Fr. Francis B. Lucas. Chmn: Bishop Bernardino Cortez (28 affiliated stns on MW, 20 on FM)

PHILIPPINE BROADCASTING SERVICE (PBS, 'Radyo Pilipinas') (Gov.)

✉ 4/F Government Media Center Bldg., Vasra, Quezon C, 1128 NCR ☎ +63 2 9242607 **W:** pbs.gov.ph **L.P:** Dir. Gen: Rizal Giovanni "Bong" Aportadera, Jr.

Manila stns: DZRB "RP1" (news sce) 738 kHz, DZSR "RP3" Sports Radio 918 kHz, DZRM "RP2" Radyo Magasin 1278 kHz, DWFO-FM "FM-1" 87.5MHz, DWBR-FM "FM2" 104.3MHz

Regional MW stns on MW: DWBT, San Antonio, Basco, 3900 Batanes. **DWFB**, Mariano Marcos State University Campus, Laoag C, 2900 Ilocos Norte. **DWFR**, Multipurpose Bldg, Provincial Capitol Compound, Bontoc, 2616 Mountain Province. **DWJS**, Legazpi C., 4500 Albay. **DWLC**, Perez Park, Lucena C, 4301 Quezon Province. **DWPE**, CSU Campus, Caritan Highway, Tuguegarao, 3500 Cagayan. **DWRB**, City Civic Center, Taal Ave, Naga C, 4400 Camarines Sur. **DWRM**, City Hall Compound, Puerto Princesa C, 5300 Palawan. **DWRS**, Poblacion, Tayug, 2445 Pangasinan. **DXBN**, City Hall Compound, Brgy. Doongan, Butuan C, 8600 Agusan del Norte. **DXIM**, A. Velez Str, Cagayan de Oro C, 9000 Misamis Oriental. DXJS, Capitol Hills, Tandag, 8300 Surigao del Sur. DXJT, Brgy Maloro,Tangub C, 7214 Misamis Occidental. **DXMR**, Baliwasan Chico, Zamboanga C, 7000

Zamboanga del Sur. **DXPT**, Tubig Boh, Bongao, 7500 Tawi-Tawi. **DXRG**, Dugenio Str, Gingoog C, 9014 Misamis Oriental. **DXRP**, Door 5, PTA Complex, Magsaysay Park, 2nd District, Agdao, 8000 Davao C. **DXSM**, Camp Asturias, Jolo, 7400 Sulu. **DXSO**, Satellite Office, MSU Campus, Marawi C, 9700 Lanao del Sur. **DYES**, Capitol Compd, Borongan, 6800 Eastern Samar. **DYLL**, PNRC Youth Center Bldg, Bonifacio Drive, Iloilo C, 5000 Iloilo. **DYMP**, Govt Center, Candahug, Palo, Leyte. **DYMR**, CSCST Compound, Vicente Sotto, 6000 Cebu C. **DYOG**, Butel Building, Calbayog C, 6710 W. Samar. **DYSL**, Southern Leyte State University Compound, Sogod, 6606 Southern Leyte. **DZAG**, Don Mariano Marcos Memorial State University, Agoo, 2504 La Union. **DZEQ**, Polo Field, Pacdal Circle, Baguio C, 2600 Benguet. **DZER**, Boac, 4900 Marinduque. **DZMQ**, Tondaligan Beach, Dagupan C, 2400 Pangasinan. **DZRK**, Capitol Compound, Tabuk, 3800 Kalinga. **DZVC** Virac, State College Campus, 4800 Catanduanes
See **PB)** entries in the MW frequency list below for frequencies and powers. Regional stns usually relay news from Manila on the h., and also carry networked prgrs at times.
NB: A number of stns are operating irr or are inactive

Callsigns: ____-AM

MW	Call	kHz	kW	Net
118)	DYDW	‡531	10	cm
4)	DZBR	531	10	
67)	DXGH	540	5	dz
83)	DYRB	540	1	
54)	DZWT	540	10	cm
PB)	DWRB	549	10	
16)	DXHM	549	5	cm
84)	DZXL	558	40	
67)	DXCH	567	5	dz
73)	DXMF	576	10	bo
PB)	DYMR	576	10	
PB)	DZMQ	576	10	
17)	DZHR	576	5	dz
16)	DXCP	585	5	cm
PB)	DYLL	585	1	su
16)	DXDB	594	5	cm
60)	DYWR	‡594	10	bo
36)	DZBB	594	20	su
10)	DZLL	603	10	cm
84)	DXPR	±603	5	
22)	DZVV	603	5	bo
75)	DWSP	612	5	dz
84)	DYHP	612	10	
PB)	DWJS	621	1	
84)	DXDC	621	10	
PB)	DZVC	621	1	
85)	DZTG	621	5	
2)	DZMM	‡630	50	
22)	DYWB	630	10/5	bo
84)	DXKR	639	5	
85)	DZRL	639	1	
67)	DWRH	648	10	dz
PB)	DWRM	648	10	
84)	DXMB	648	3	
50)	DYRC	648	5	ak
77)	DWRN	657	5	
130)	DXDD	657	5	cm
PB)	DYES	657	1	
84)	DYVR	657	5	
98)	DZLU	657	1	
PB)	DXRP	‡666	10	
50)	DZRH	666	35	
103)	DXGD	675	1	cm
85)	DYKC	675	5	
43)	DWJJ	684	5	
50)	DYEZ	684	10	ak
33)	DZCV	684	5	
84)	DXBC	693	10	ag
85)	DXDX	693	1	
50)	DYKX	693	1	dz
50)	DYPH	693	10	dz
106)	DZTP	693	10/5	
31)	DZAS	702	50	
84)	DXIC	711	5	ag
58)	DXRD	711	5	ss
29)	DYBR	‡711	5	
60)	DZVR	711	5	bo

MW	Call	kHz	kW	Net
58)	DZYI	711	5	ss
50)	DYOK	720	1	ak
7)	DZJO	720	5	
60)	DZSO	720	5	bo
PB)	DWPE	729	10	
60)	DXIF	729	10	bo
84)	DXMY	729	5	
70)	DXOR	729	5	
72)	DZGB	729	5	
PB)	DZRB	738	60	
62)	DXND	747	5	cm
84)	DYHB	747	10	
50)	DZJC	747	10	ak
PB)	DWRS	756	10	
9)	DWHL	756	1	
121)	DXBZ	756	10	
82)	DXJM	756	2	
83)	DXGS	765	5	
68)	DYAP	‡765	10	
58)	DYAR	765	5	ss
58)	DZYT	765	5	ss
41)	DWWW	774	25	
PB)	DXSM	774	10	
PB)	DXSO	774	10	
84)	DYRI	774	10	ag
94)	DXRA	783	10	
51)	DYME	783	5	
75)	DZNL	783	5	ak
95)	DWES	792	5	
38)	DWGV	792	5	
PB)	DXBN	792	10	
73)	DXPD	792	5	bo
66)	DYRR	792	5	
58)	DXBL	801	1	ss
22)	DXES	801	5	bo
16)	DYKA	801	5	cm
35)	DYWC	801	5	cm
60)	DZNC	801	10	bo
PB)	DXRG	810	1	
90)	DZRJ	810	10	
58)	DWAR	819	5	ss
114)	DWMG	819	1	
101)	DXSC	‡819	1	
53)	DXUM	819	10	
50)	DYVL	819	10	ak
39)	DWZR	828	5	
84)	DXCC	828	10	ag
135)	DZTC	828	1	
PB)	DXJS	837	10	
58)	DXRE	837	5	ss
22)	DYFM	837	10	bo
30)	DZXE	‡837	5	
87)	DZRV	846	50	cm
67)	DXGO	855	5	ak
42)	DXWG	‡855	1	
17)	DXZH	855	5	dz
33)	DZGE	855	10	

MW	Call	kHz	kW	Net
58)	DWSI	864	5	ss
97)	DYHH	864	10	
140)	DZIP	864	10	
134)	DZWM	864	5	cm
58)	DXRB	873	5	ss
58)	DXRT	‡873	5	
127)	DYUP	873	5	
1)	DZPA	873	5	cm
33)	DZRC	873	5	
3)	DWIZ	882	50	
62)	DXMS	882	10	cm
PB)	DYOG	882	10	
73)	DZGR	891	5	
63)	DWNE	900	5	
84)	DXRZ	900	5	ag
22)	DYOW	900	5	bo
115)	DYLA	909	5	
91)	DYSP	909	5	su
16)	DZEA	909	5	cm
84)	DXRS	918	5	ag
PB)	DZSR	918	50	
122)	DWRS	927	5	
64)	DXDA	927	5	
84)	DXMD	927	5	ag
103)	DXMM	927	5	cm
73)	DZLG	927	5	bo
40)	DWIM	936	5	
111)	DXDN	936	5	uk
PB)	DXIM	936	10	
84)	DYCC	936	1	
85)	DYKW	936	1	
82)	DZXT	936	1	
116)	DXDV	945	10	
58)	DXRO	945	5	ss
4)	DYRO	‡945	5	
PB)	DWFB	954	10	
PB)	DXJT	954	1	
110)	DYMM	‡954	5	
20)	DZEM	954	40	
62)	DXOM	963	10	
58)	DXYZ	963	5	ss
73)	DYMF	963	10	bo
136)	DZNS	963	5	cm
PB)	DWFR	972	5	
45)	DWTI	972	5	
17)	DXKH	972	5	dz
17)	DYSM	972	1	ak
75)	DWMT	981	5	dz
22)	DXBR	981	10	bo
84)	DXDR	981	5	ag
88)	DXOW	981	10	
42)	DYBQ	981	10	
58)	DZRD	981	5	ss
107)	DZIQ	990	10	
91)	DXBM	990	5	su
67)	DYTH	990	5	dz
67)	DZMT	990	5	dz
45)	DWMI	999	5	D
84)	DXHP	999	1	
PB)	DXPT	999	1	
91)	DYSS	999	5	su
PB)	DZEQ	999	5	
16)	DWBS	1008	5	cm
102)	DWGO	1008	5	
85)	DXXX	±1008	10	
42)	DWDC	1017	10	
PB)	DWLC	1017	10	
44)	DXRR	1017	10	
138)	DXSN	1017	5	cm
73)	DXMC	1026	5	bo
58)	DZAR	1026	10	ss
139)	DXUZ	±1035	5/1	
88)	DYRL	1035	10	
22)	DZWX	1035	5	bo
88)	DXCO	1044	5	
81)	DXLL	1044	5	uk
17)	DYMS	±1044	5	ak
60)	DZNG	±1044	10	bo
85)	DXKD	1053	10	

MW	Call	kHz	kW	Net
112)	DYSA	1053	5	cm
31)	DXKI	1062	5	
46)	DYEC	1062	10/5	
28)	DZEC	1062	40	
85)	DXKT	1071	5	
110)	DYXT	1071	1	
123)	DZSL	1071	1	
28)	DWIN	1080	5	
83)	DWRL	1080	5	
85)	DXKS	1080	1	
67)	DYBH	1080	5	dz
111)	DXCM	1089	10	uk
39)	DYHR	‡1089	1	
23)	DWAD	1098	10	
58)	DXCL	1098	5	ss
61)	DWDY	1107	10	
141)	DXBB	1107	5	
129)	DYIN	1107	5	bo
8)	DZOM	1107	1	
13)	DYAG	1116	5	
31)	DXAS	1116	5	
104)	DYTR	1116	10	
113)	DZLB	1116	5	
69)	DXGL	1125	10	
91)	DXGM	1125	5	su
22)	DZWN	1125	10	bo
26)	DWDD	1134	10	
95)	DWJS	1134	5	
111)	DXMV	1134	5	uk
79)	DXOS	1134	10	
77)	DYRM	±1134	1	
PB)	DWBT	1134	1	
137)	DYAF	1143	10	cm
31)	DZMR	1143	10	
51)	DYCM	1152	5	
75)	DWCM	1161	10	
111)	DXDS	1161	1	uk
84)	DYKR	1161	5	ag
11)	DYRD	1161	5	cm
72)	DZMD	1161	5	
PB)	DXMR	1170	10	
PB)	DYSL	1170	10	
65)	DZCA	‡1170	10	
142)	DWET	1179	10	
91)	DXYK	1179	5	su
60)	DYCX	1179	5	
36)	DYSB	1179	5	su
86)	DZRS	1179	1	
22)	DXLX	1188	5	bo
2)	DYRV	‡1188	1	
82)	DZLT	1188	5	
114)	DZXO	1188	5	
98)	DWBA	1197	5	
31)	DXFE	1197	5	
4)	DYRH	‡1197	5	
118)	DYRF	1215	10	cm
50)	DWSR	1224	5	dz
28)	DXED	1224	10	
PB)	DZAG	1224	10	
87)	DWRV	1233	5	cm
31)	DYVS	1233	5	
32)	DWBL	1242	20	
105)	DXSY	1242	5	
27)	DXZB	1242	5	
42)	DYRG	1251	1	
72)	DZMS	1251	2.5	
49)	DWMC	1260	5	
50)	DXRF	1260	5	dz
97)	DYDD	1260	10	
28)	DZEL	1260	5	
91)	DWRC	1269	10	
PB)	DZRM	1278	10	
50)	DZZH	1287	5	dz
133)	DWPR	1296	5	
2)	DXAB	‡1296	10	
42)	DYJJ	1296	5	
25)	DWXI	1314	10	
57)	DXAD	±1322	5	
19)	DXHR	±1323	10	

MW	Call	kHz	kW	Net
36)	DYSI	1323	10	su
PB)	DZRK	1323	10	
58)	DWAY	1332	5	ss
85)	DZKI	1332	1	
91)	DXRL	‡1341	10	su
48)	DWUN	1350	50	
PB)	DZER	‡1350	5	
129)	DYSJ	1359	1	
77)	DZYR	1359	5	
58)	DWTT	‡1368	5	
85)	DXKO	1368	10	
85)	DZBS	1368	2.5	
15)	DZRA	1368	1	
85)	DXKP	1377	10	
55)	DXCR	1386	10	
16)	DYVW	1386	5	cm
17)	DYCH	1395	10	dz
132)	DZVT	1395	5	cm
58)	DXAQ	‡1404	-	ss
85)	DYKB	1404	1	
91)	DWRA	1413	5	su
33)	DYXW	1413	5	
11)	DYZD	‡1422	5	
89)	DYRS	‡1431	5	
50)	DWDH	1440	10	dz
100)	DXSI	1440	0.01	
52)	DXSA	1449	5	

MW	Call	kHz	kW	Net
97)	DYZZ	1458	10	
120)	DZJV	1458	10	
87)	DWVR	1467	1	cm
131)	DXVP	1467	5	cm
92)	DWRB	1476	1	
90)	DXRJ	1476	10	
88)	DZYA	1476	1	
67)	DYDH	1485	5	dz
108)	DWSS	1494	10	
83)	DXOC	1494	5	
2)	DYAB	‡1512	10	
125)	DZAT	1512	10	
14)	DZME	1530	25	
77)	DZYM	1539	5	
36)	DZSD	1548	10	su
16)	DYDM	1548	5	cm
5)	DXID	1566	10	
PB)	DYMP	‡1566	7.8	
18)	DXJR	1575	10	
24)	DWBR	1584	1	
124)	DXSK	1593	10	
113)	DZUP	1602	1	
84)	DWNX	1611	10	
37)	DWGI	1638	0.6	
56)	DZBF	1674	1	

NB: ‡ = r. inactive, ± = variable

GENERAL NOTES:

Station identifications: Generally, stn IDs are given on the h and half h. The English alphabet is used for the call letters, while the freq. is usually expressed in Spanish- or English-language numerals. Extensive stn details are included in sign on and sign off Anns.

Callsign assignments: DU = Shortwave only; DW = Luzon; DX = Mindanao and Sulu; DY = Visayas and Palawan; DZ = Luzon

Administrative divisions: Level 1: regions, 2: provinces, cities (C.), 3: municipalities, 4: barangays (brgy.). The National Capital Region (NCR) is also known as Metropolitan Manila or Metro-Manila.

NB: Cities may be referred to with or without 'City', e.g. Baguio City or Baguio. Quezon City is always referred to by its full name.

Prgr. networks: ag=R. Agong, ak=Aksyon R. bo=Bombo R., cm=Catholic Media Network (CMN, see above and entry **16)** below), dz=DZRH (key: 666kHz), ss=Sonshine R. (key: 1026kHz), su=Super R., uk=Radyo Ukay

Web addresses for broadcast networks: FEBC: **W:** febc.org – Bombo R. **W:** bomboradyo.com – R. Mindanao Netw **W:** rmn.ph – Manila Broadc. Co **W:** manlilabroadcasting.com – Sonshine R. **W:** sonshineradio.com – DZRH: dzrh.com.ph

FM: A large number of FM stns are operating throughout the country.

Callsigns: _____-FM

Manila FM(MHz): – **PB)** 87.5 DWFO 'FM1' – 88.3 DWCT 'Jam 88.3' (Raven Broadc. Corp.) – 89.1 DWAV 'Wave 89.1' (Blockbuster Broadc. System) – 89.9 DWTM 'Magic 89.9' (Quest Broadc. Inc.) – **50)** 90.7 DZMB 'Love R.' – 91.5 DWKY 'Win R.' (Mabuhay Broadc. System Inc.) – 92.3 DWFM 'Radyo5 92.3 News FM' (Nation Broadc. Corp.) – 93.1 DWRX 'Monster RX' (Audiovisual Communicators Inc.) – **84)** 93.9 DWKC 'iFM' – **32)** 94.7 DWLL 'Mellow 947' – **28)** 95.5 DWDM 'Pinas FM' – **17)** 96.3 DWRK 'Easy Rock' – **36)** 97.1 DWLS 'Barangay LS' – **3)** 97.9 DWQZ '97dot9 Home R.' – **31)** 98.7 DZFE 'The Master's Touch' – 99.5 DWRT 'Play FM' (Real R. Network Inc.) – **90)** 100.3 DZRJ 'RJ 100' – **67)** 101.1 DWYS 'Yes the Best' – **2)** 101.9 DWRR 'MOR 101.9 For Life!' (inactive) – **73)** 102.7 DWSM 'Star FM' – 103.5 DWKX 'K-Lite' (Advanced Media Broadc. Syst.) – **PB)** 104.3 DWBR 'FM2.' – 105.1 DWBM 'Crossover' (Mareco Broadc. Network) – 105.9 DWLA 'Lite FM' (Bright Star Broadc Network) – 106.7 DWET 'Energy FM' (Ultrasonic Broadc. Syst. Inc.) – **141)** 107.5 DWNU 'Wish FM.'

Cebu City FM(MHz): – 88.3 DYAP 'Mom's R.' (Southern Broadc. Network) –**16)** 89.1 DYDW 'Power 89'– 89.9 DYKI 'MemoRies FM' (Primaxx Broadc. Network) – 90.7 DYAC 'Crossover' (Mareco Broadc. Network) –**17)** 91.5 DYHR 'Yes the Best' – 92.3 DYBN 'Magic 92.3' (Quest Broadc., Inc.) – **115)** 93.1 DYWF 'Brigada News FM'– **84)** 93.9 DYXL 'iFM'– 94.7 DYLL 'Energy FM' (Ultrasonic Broadc. System) – **22)** 95.5 DYMX 'Star FM' – 96.3 DYRK 'W- Rock' (Exodus Broadc. Co.) – **2)** 97.1 DYLS 'MOR for Life!'(inactive) – **50)** 97.9 DYBU 'Love R.' – **31)** 98.7 DYFR 'UP 987' – **91)** 99.5 DYRT 'Barangay RT' – **90)** 100.3 DYRJ 'RJ 100' – 101.1 DYIO 'Y 101' (GVM Radio/TV Corp.) – 101.9 DYNC 'Radyo5 News FM' (Nation Broadc. Corp.) – **17)** 102.7 DYTC 'Easy Rock' – 103.5 DYCD 'Retro Cebu' (Ditan Communications/ Univ. of Mindanao Broadc. Network) – 105.1 DYUR 'Halo-Halo 105.1' (Ultimate Entertainment) – 105.9 DYBT 'Monster R.' (Capricorn Production & Management Corp.) – **3)** 106.7 DYQC 'Home R.' – 107.5 DYNU 'Win R.' (Progressive Broadc. Corp.)

Davao City FM (MHz): – **PB)** 87.5 DXRP R. Pilipinas – 88.3 DXDR 'Energy FM' (Ultrasonic Broadc. System) – 89.1 DXBE 'Magic 89.1' (Quest Broadc. Inc) – **16)** 89.9 DXGN 'Spirit FM' – **50)** 90.7 DXBM 'Love R.' – **82)** 91.5 DXKX 'Brigada News FM' – **111)** 92.3 DXWT 'Wild 92.3' – 93.1 DXAC 'Crossover' (Mareco Broadc. Network) – **84)** 93.9 DXXL 'iFM' – **32)** 94.7 DXLL 'One Radio Davao' – **107)** 95.5 DXKR 'Retro 95.5' – **22)** 96.3 DXFX 'Star FM' – 97.1 DXUR 'Halo-Halo R. 97.1' (Ultimate Entertainment Inc.) – 97.9 DXSS 'Mom's R.' (Southern Broadc. Network) – **3)** 98.7 DXQM 'Home R.' – 99.5 DXBT 'Monster R.' (Ausiovisual Communicators Inc. – **90)** 100.3 DXDJ 'RJ 100' – **2)** 101.1 DXRR 'MOR for Life!'(inactive) – 101.9 DXFM 'Radyo5 News FM' (Nation Broadc. Corp.) – 102.7 DXDM 'Mango Radyo' (Multipoint Broadc. Network) – **91)** 103.5 DXRV 'Barangay 103.5' – 104.3 DXMA 'Hope Radio' (United Christian Broadcasters) – **17)** 105.1 DXYS 'Easy Rock' – 105.9 DXMX 'Balita FM' (Omarco Broadc. Corp.) – 106.7 DXET 'Dream FM' (ABC Development Corp.) – 107.5 DXNU 'Win R.' (Progressive Broadc. Corp.)

Addresses:

For each entry the organisation or company name is followed by the call letters (in alphabetical order) and addresses of the stns licensed to the organisation. When contacting a stn, use Radio Station + the call letters as stn name. In some cases the stn may be operated by a different organisation than the licensee mentioned below.

PB) See separate listing for Philippine Broadc. Sce Above. – **1)** Abra Community Btcg. Corp. DZPA R. Totoo, Blessed Arnold Janssen Communication Center, Zamora Str corner Rizal Str, Bangued, 2800 Abra – **2)** ABS-CBN Broadc. Corp (R. Patrol). DXAB, KM-4, Shrine Hills, Matina, 8000 Davao C. DYAB, ABS-CBN Broadc. Center, Jagobiao, Mandaue C, 6014 Cebu. DYRV, Catbalogan, 6700 Samar. DZMM, ABS-CBN Broadcast Center, Sergeant Esquerra Avenue corner of Mother Ignacia Street, Barangay South Triangle, Quezon C, 1103 NCR **NB**: all freqs went off air from 5 May 2020 following government legal action – **3)** Aliw Broadc. Corp. DWIZ, 5th Floor, Citystate Center, 809 Shaw Boulevard, Barangay Oranbo, Pasig C, 1600 NCR – **4)** Allied Broadc. Center, Inc. DYRH, JTL Bldg, North Drive, Bacolod C, 6100 Negros Occidental. DYRO. Roxas C., Capiz – DZBR Bible R., President Jose P. Laurel Highway, Batangas C, 4200 Batangas – **5)** Association of Islamic Dev't. Cooperative. DXID, Banale Dist, Pagadian C, 7016 Zamboanga del Sur – **7)** Bayanihan Broadc. Corp. DZJO, Infanta, 4336 Quezon Province – **8)** Ben Viduya (OMARCO). DZOM, Calapan C, 5200 Mindoro Oriental – **9)** Beta Broadc. Syst. DWHL R. Apo, 8 Kessing Str, Olongapo C, 2200 Zambales – **10)** Bicol Broadc. Syst. DZLL, BBS Bldg, Balagtas Road, Magsaysay Ave, Naga C, 4400 Camarines Sur – **11)** Bohol Chronicle Radio Corp. DYRD, Dejaresco Bldg, 56 Bernardino Inting Str, Tagbilaran C, 6300 Bohol. DYZD, Brgy Tapon, Ubay, 6315 Bohol – **13)** Cadiz Radio & TV Netw. DYAG, Cadiz C, 6121 Negros Occidental – **14)** Capitol Broadc. Center. DZME Kinze Trenta, OMM-Citra Bldg, Ortigas Center, Padig C, 1309 NCR – **15)** Catanduanes State College. DZRA, Virac, 4800 Catanduanes – **16)** Catholic Media Network (CMN). Most MW sts ID as R. Totoo. DWBS Radio Veritas, 2/F Landco Business Park, Legaspi C, 4500 Albay. DXCP, Lagao, Gen. Santos C, 9500 South Cotabato. DXDB Radyo Bandilyo, Communications Media Center, San Isidro Cathedral Compound, Malaybalay C, 8700 Bukidnon. DXHM, Clergy House Compound, Madang, Mati C., Davao Oriental. DYDM, SJC Extension Campus, Mambajao, Maasin C, 6600 Southern Leyte. DYKA, St Joseph Bldg, San Jose de Buenavista, 5700 Antique. DYVW, Clergy House, Baybay Blvd, Borongan, 6800 Eastern Samar. DZEA, Brgy. Nalbo, Laoag C, 2900 Ilocos Norte – **17)** Cebu Broadc. Co. DXKH, Bayabas, Cagayan de Oro C, 9000 Misamis Oriental. DXZH, Zamboanga C, 7000 Zamboanga del Sur. DYCH, Tanke, Talisay C, 6045 Cebu. DYMS, San Bartolome Str, Catbalogan, 6700 Samar. DYSM, Brgy. Cawayan, Catarman, 6400 Northern Samar. DZHR, Carig, Tuguegarao, 3500 Cagayan. – **18)** Cagayan de Oro Media Corp. DXJR R. Higala, Manolo Fortich, Bukidnon – **19)** Gateway UHF Broadcasting (Seventh Day Adventist). DXHR Hope R., km 43 Baan Hwy, Butuan C., 8600 Agusan del Norte – **20)** Christian Era Broadc. Sce DZEM, Barn Studio Bldg, New Era Studio Campus, 9 Central Avenue, Quezon C, 1107 NCR – **22)** Consolidated Broadc. Syst, Inc. DXBR, Bombo R. Broadc. Center, Arujville Subd, Brgy. Libertad, Butuan C, 8600 Agusan del Norte.

DXES Bombo R. Broadc. Center, Amao Rd, Brgy. Bula, Gen. Santos C, 9500 South Cotabato. DXLX, Tambo, Brgy. Hinaplon, Iligan C, 9200 Lanao del Norte. DYFM, Sky City Tower, Mapa Str, Jaro, Iloilo C, 5000 Iloilo. DYOW, Bombo R. Broadc. Center, Arnaldo Blvd, Roxas C, 5800 Capiz. DYWB, Bombo R. Broadcast Center, Lacson Str, Mandalagan, Bacolod C, 6100 Negros Occidental. DZVV, Bombo R. Broadc. Center, Brgy. Tamag, Vigan, 2700 Ilocos Sur. DZWN, Bombo R. Broadc. Center, Maramba Bankers' Village, Bonuan Catacdang, 2400 Dagupan C, Pangasinan. DZWX, Bombo R. Broadc. Center, 87 Lourdes Subdivision Rd, Baguio C, 2600 Benguet – **23)** Crusaders Broadc. Syst, Now Radio. DWAD, 209 E. de la Paz Str, Mandaluyong C, 1550 NCR – **24)** Dawnbreaker's Foundation. DWBR R. Baha'i, Bulac, Talavera, 3114 Nueva Ecija or P. O.Box 27, San José City 3121 – **25)** Delta Broadc. Syst., Himpilang Pinagpala. DWXI, Mathew Str, Multinational Village, Parañaque C, 1708 NCR – **26)** Dept. of National Defense, Armed Forces R. (Ka-Tropa Radio). DWDD, PVAO Building, Camp Aguinaldo, EDSA, Quezon C, 1110 NCR – **27)** DXZB/TV13 Cooperative, Inc. DXZB, Zamboanga C, 7000 Zamboanga del Sur – **28)** Eagle Broadc. Corp. DWIN, Bo. Lucao, Dagupan C, 2400 Pangasinan. DXED, Cabiguio Ave, Agdao, 8000 Davao C. DZEC, EBC Building, 25 Central Avenue, Quezon C, 1107 NCR. DZEL, Bo. Mayao, Lucena C, 4301 Quezon Province – **29)** East Visayan Broadc. DYBR, Sagcahan Rd, P.O. Box 80, Tacloban C, 6500 Leyte – **30)** Fairwaves Broadc. Netw. DZXE R. Tirador, Mira Hills, Vigan, 2700 Ilocos Sur – **31)** Far East Broadc. Co. . DXAS, P.O. Box 349, Tugbungan, Zamboanga C, 7000 Zamboanga del Sur. DXFE, Circumferential Rd, Dona Vicente Village, 8000 Davao C. DXKI, P.O. Box 8004, Brgy Morales, Koronadal C, 9506 South Cotabato. DYVS, P.O. Box 393, Km. 7, Pahanocoy, Bacolod C, 6100 Negros Occidental. DZAS, 46th Floor, One Corporate Center, Meralco Avenue corner Dona Julia Vargas Avenue, Ortigas Center, Pasig C, 1600 NCR. DZMR Missions Radio, Maharlika Highway, Sefton Village, Santiago City, 3311 Isabela – **32)** FBS Radio Netw., Unit 908, Paragon Plaza, EDSA corner Reliance Str, Mandaluyong C, 1554 NCR – **33)** Filipinas Broadc. Netw. DYXW, Baruyan, San Jose, Tacloban C, 6500 Leyte. DZCV, Ugac Norte, Tuguegarao, 3500 Cagayan. DZGE R. Numero Uno, Nordia Resort, Baras, Canaman, Naga C, 4400 Camarines Sur. DZRC R. Champion, Capt. Aquendes Drive, Legaspi C, 4500 Albay – **35)** Franciscan Broadc. Corp. DYWC R. Bandilyo, Parish Compound, St Anthony of Padua Parish, Sibulan, Dumaguete C, 6201 Negros Oriental – **36)** GMA Netw, Inc. DZSD, Arellano St., Dagupan C, 2400 Pangasinan. DYSB, Bacolod C, 6100 Negros Occidental. DYSI, GMA Compound, MacArthur Drive, Jaro, Iloilo C, 5000 Iloilo. DZBB, GMA Netw. Center, EDSA corner Timog Ave, Diliman, 1103 Quezon C – **37)** Guzman Institute of Tech. DWGI, 509 Z.P. de Guzman, Quiapo, Manila, NCR – **38)** GV Broadc. Syst. DWGV R. Centro, Rizal Extension, Cut-Cut, Angeles C, 2009 Pampanga – **39)** Hypersonic Broadc. Center. DWZR Zoom Radio, Penaranda Str, Legaspi C, 4500 Albay. DYHR, Calbayog C, 6710 W. Samar – **40)** Insular Broadc. Syst. DWIM R. Mindoro, Brgy. Bayanihan, Calapan, 5200 Mindoro Oriental – **41)** Interactive Broadcast Media, Inc. DWWW, Units 807-808 Atlanta Center, Annapolis Street, Greenhills, San Juan C, 1502 NCR – **42)** Intercontinental Broadc. Corp, R. Budyong. DWDC, A.B. Fernandez Ave, Dagupan C, 2400 Pangasinan. DXWG, Iligan C, 9200 Lanao del Norte. DYBQ, Datu Puti Subdivision, ,Cubay, Jaro, Iloilo C, 5000 Iloilo. DYJJ, Roxas Ave, Roxas C, 5800 Capiz. DYRG, Roxas Ave Extension, Andagao, Kalibo, 5600 Aklan – **43)** Kaissar Broadc. Netw. DWJJ R.bisyon (Double J Ad Ventures), Celcor Compound, Bitas, Cabanatuan C, 3100 Nueva Ecija – **44)** Kalayaan Broadc. Syst. DXRR R. Rapido, Bug-ac, Matina, 8000 Davao C – **45)** Katigbak Enterprises (ConAmor Broadcasting Systems). DWMI, Calapan, 5200 Mindoro Oriental. DWTI, Broadcast Village, Ibabang Dupay, Lucena C, 4301 Quezon Province – **46)** Puerto Princesa Broadc. Co. DYEC Environment Radio, Puerto Princesa C, 5300 Palawan – **48)** Progressive Broadcasting Corporation. DWUN UNTV Radio La Verdad, UNTV Bldg, 907 EDSA, Brgy Philam, Quezon C, 1104 NCR – **49)** Magiliw Community Broadc. Co. DWMC, Tomana, Rosales, 2441 Pangasinan – **50)** Manila Broadc. Co. DWDH, Lucao District, Dagupan C, 2400 Pangasinan. DWSR, Talipan, Pagbilao, Lucena C, 4301 Quezon Province. DXRF, Matina, 8000 Davao C. DYEZ, Wilrose Building, Burgos Str, Bacolod C, 6100 Negros Occidental. DYKX, Kalibo, 5600 Aklan. DYOK, Suite 301Carlos Uy Bldg, Diversion Rd, Manurriao, Iloilo C, 5000 Iloilo. DYPH, Gabinete Rd, Bancao-Bancao, Puerto Princesa C, 5300 Palawan. DYVL, J. Romualdez corner Real Streets, Tacloban C, 6500 Leyte. DYRC Radyo Cebu, 3rd Floor, Cinco Centrum Building, Fuente Osmeña Blvd, 6000 Cebu C. DZJC, Brgy. 29, Rizal Street, St. Joseph District, Laoag C, 2900 Ilocos Norte. DZRH, MBC Bldg, Vicente Sotto Str, CCP Complex, Pasay C, 1300 NCR. DZZH, Cabit-an, Sorsogon C, 4700 Sorsogon – **51)** Masbate Community Broadc. Co. DYCM, 201 Dona Luisa Bldg, Fuente Osmena Ave, Cebu City, 6000 Cebu. DYME, Tugbo Str, Masbate C, 5400 Masbate – **52)** Mindanao Broadc. Co, Inc. DXSA, Marawi C, 9700 Lanao del Sur – **53)** Univ. of Mindanao Broadcasting Netwk. DXUM R. Ukay, UMBN Broadcast Center, Multi-test Bldg, Ponciano Reyes St, 8000 Davao C – **54)** Mt. Province Broadc. Corp. DZWT, P.O. Box 156, Mount Beckel, La Trinidad, Baguio C, 2600 Benguet – **55)** Mt. View College. DXCR Hope R., MVC, Valencia, 8709 Bukidnon – **56)** Municipality of Marikina. DZBF, R. Marikina, Second Floor, City Hall, Shoe Avenue, Marikina C, 1800 NCR – **57)** Mindanao Dev. Multi-Purpose Coop. DXAD Radio Ranao, Marcos Blvd, Saduc, Marawi C, 9700 Lanao del Sur – **58)** Swara Sug Media Corporation. DWAR, Laoag C, 2900 Ilocos Norte. DWAY, Cabanatuan C, 3100 Nueva Ecija. DWSI, North Eastern Foundation College, Santiago, 3311 Isabela. DWTT, Tarlac C, 2300 Tarlac. DXBL, Mangagoy, Bislig C, 8311 Surigao del Sur. DXAQ, Philippine-Japan Friendship Hwy, Catitipan, Davao C. DXCL, Cagayan de Oro C, 9000 Misamis Oriental. DXRB, Brgy Libertad, Butuan C, 8600 Agusan del Norte. DXRD, J.P Laurel Ave, Bajada, 8000 Davao C. DXRE, Lagao, Gen. Santos C, 9500 South Cotabato. DXRO, Don Roman Vilo Str, Cotabato C, 9600 Maguindanao. DXRT, Jolo, 7400 Sulu. DXYZ, San Jose Rd, Baliwasan, 7000 Zamboanga C. DYAR, 3rd Fl. Astron Gestus Bldg, Gorordo Ave, 6000 Cebu C. DZAR, 3rd Floor, ACQ Tower, Santa Rita Street, Barangay Guadelupe Nuevo, Makati C, 1212 NCR. DZRD, Banuan Guesset, Dagupan C, 2400 Pangasinan. DZYI, Calamagui 2nd, Ilagan, 3300 Isabela. DZYT, Cagayan Teachers College, Tuguegarao, 3500 Cagayan – **60)** Newsounds Broadc. Netw. DXIF, Bombo R. Broadc. Center, Corrales Ave, Cagayan de Oro C, 9000 Misamis Oriental. DYCX, San Jose de Buenavista, Antique. DYWR, Bombo R. Broadc. Center, Sto. Nino cor. Imelda Ave, Tacloban C, 6500 Leyte. DZNC, Bombo R. Broadc. Center, Barrio Menante II, Cauayan, 3305 Isabela. DZNG, Bombo R. Broadc. Center, Diversion Road, Brgy. Tabuko, Naga C, 4400 Camarines Sur. DZSO, Bombo R. Broadcast Center, Pennsylvania Ave, Parian, San Fernando C, 2500 La Union. DZVR, Bombo R. Broadcast Center, 48 A, Cabungaan Airport Ave, Laoag C, 2900 Ilocos Norte – **61)** Northeastern Broadc. Sce DWDY, Ground Floor, Isabela Hotel, Mirante Uno, Cauayan, 3305 Isabela – **62)** Notre Dame Broadc. Corp. DXMS, Sinsuat Ave cor. Rizal Ave, Cotabato C, 9600 Maguindanao. DXND, Daang Maharlika, Kidapawan C, 9400 North Cotabato. DXOM R. Bida, General Santos Drive, Morales, Koronadal C., S, Cotabato – **63)** Nueva Ecija Provincial Gov. DWNE, Brgy Singalat, Palayan C, 3132 Nueva Ecija – **64)** Office of the Governor, Prov. of Agusan del Sur. DXDA R. Agusan, Patin-ay, Prosperidad, 8500 Agusan del Sur – **65)** Office of the Civil Defense. DZCA, Agham Rd. Science Garden, Pag-asa Planetarium, NCR – **66)** Ormoc Broadc. Co. DYRR, Bantigue, Ormoc C, 6541 Leyte – **67)** Pacific Broadc. Syst (subsidiary of Manila Broadc. Co.). DWRH, Rizal, Santiago C, 3311 Isabela.. DXCH, Krislamville, Kakar, Cotabato C, 9600 Maguindanao. DXGH, Purok Malakas, Lagao, Gen. Santos C, 9500 South Cotabato. DXGO, MBC Compound, Brgy. Duterte, R. Castillo Str, Agdao, 8000 Davao C. DYBH, Bacolod C, 6100 Negros Occidental. DYDH, Iloilo Cadastre, Iloilo C, 5000 Iloilo. DYTH, Real Str, Tacloban C, 6500 Leyte. DZMT, Santo Tomas, Laoag C, 2900 Ilocos Norte – **68)** Palawan Broadc. Corp. DYAP, Rey Olivar Bldg., 61 Mabini St. Puerto Princesa C, 5300 Palawan. – **69)** PEC Broadc. Corp. DXGL, Butuan C, 8600 Agusan del Norte – **70)** Pedro N. Roa Broadc. DXOR, Don A. Velez Str, Cagayan de Oro C, 9000 Misamis Oriental – **72)** People's Broadc. Netw. DZGB, Mayona Building, Imperial Court Subdivision, Legaspi C, 4500 Albay. DZMD, Vinzons Ave, Daet, 4600 Camarines Norte. DZMS, Balobo Str, Sorsogon C, 4700 Sorsogon – **73)** People's Broadc. Sce DXMC, Bombo R. Broadc. Center, Km 4 General Santos Drive, Koronadal C, 9506 South Cotabato. DXMF, Bombo R. Broadc. Center, San Pedro Str, 8000 Davao C. DXPD, Bombo R. Broadc. Center, North Diversion Road, Brgy. Banale, Pagadian C, 7016 Zamboanga del Sur. DYMF, 87-A. Borromeo Str, 6000 Cebu C. DZGR, Bombo R. Broadc. Center, Taft Str Extension, Brgy 5, Tuguegarao, 3500 Cagayan. DZLG, Bombo R. Broadc. Center, Tahao Road, Legaspi C, 4500 Albay. – **75)** Philippine Broadc. Corp. DWCM, Caranglaan District, Dagupan C, 2400 Pangasinan. DWMT, San Isidro, Magarao, Naga C, 4400 Camarines Sur. DWSP, Tuding, Itogon, nr Baguio City, Benguet. DZNL, Brgy. Pagdalagan, San Fernando C, 2500 La Union. – **77)** Philippine Radio Corp. DWRN R. Asenso, Manipit Rd, Queborac Bagumbayan, Naga C, 4400 Camarines Sur. DYRM, Bo. Calindangan, Dumaguete C, 6200 Negros Oriental. DZYM R. Asenso, Puerto Gallenero, Pag-asa, San Jose, 5100 Mindoro Occidental. DZYR, Catbangen, San Fernando C, 2500 La Union – **79)** Public Affairs Sce, Armed Forces of the Philippines. DXOS, Basilan Island, Basilan – **81)** R.T. Broadc.

Specialistns Philippines. DXLL, Campaner Str, Zamboanga C, 7000 Zamboanga del Sur – **82)** Radio Corp. of the Philippines. DXJM, J & M Bldg, Villakananga, Butuan C, 8600 Agusan del Norte. DZLT, Bo. Ibabang Dupay, Lucena C, 4301 Quezon Province. DZXT, MacArthur H-way, Tarlac C, 2300 Tarlac – **83)** DWRL Radio, Inc (subsidary of 82 above). DWRL, Purok 5, Rawis, Legaspi C, 4500 Albay. DXGS R. Asenso, NLSA Rd, Lagao, Gen. Santos C, 9500 South Cotabato. DXOC R. Asenso, Manabay, Catadman, Ozamis C, 7200 Misamis Occidental. DYRB, C. Padilla St., 6000 Cebu C – **84)** Radio Mindanao Netw. DWNX, 2/F Ramaida Centrum, East Angeles Str, Naga City, 4400 Camarines Sur. DXBC, Montilla Blvd, Butuan C, 8600 Agusan del Norte. DXCC, Canoy Bldg., Don Apolinar Velez Str, Cagayan de Oro C, 9000 Misamis Oriental. DXDC, San Vincente Bldg, cor. Anda & Bonifacio Stns, 8000 Davao C. DXDR, Bo. Mario Turno, Dipolog C, 7100 Zamboanga del Norte. DXHP, Flomencia Bldg. P. Castillo Mangagoy, Bislig C, 8311 Surigao del Sur. DXIC, Pafs Mejia Bldg, Roxas Str. cor Aguinaldo Str, Iligan C, 9200 Lanao del Norte. DXKR, Gen. Santos Drive, Koronadal C, 9506 South Cotabato. DXMB, Fortich Str, Malaybalay C, 8700 Bukidnon. DXMD, Bo. Obrero National Highway, Gen. Santos C, 9500 South Cotabato. DXMY, Esteros, RH 10, Cotabato C, 9600 Maguindanao. DXPR, Mercedes Str, San Jose Dist, Pagadian C, 7016 Zamboanga del Sur. DXRS, Km. 1 Rizal Str, Surigao C, 8400 Surigao del Norte. DXRZ, Zamaveco Bldg, Pilar Str, Zamboanga C, 7000 Zamboanga del Sur. DYCC, Brgy. Obrero, Calbayog C, 6710 W. Samar. DYHB, 4th Flt, SSS Bldg. Lacson Str, Bacolod C, 6100 Negros Occidental. DYHP, 2nd Flr, Gold Palace Bldg, 168 Osmeña Blvd, 6000 Cebu C. DYKR, C. Laserna Str, Kalibo, 5600 Aklan. DYRI, St Anne Bldg, Luna Str, La Paz, Iloilo C, 5000 Iloilo. DYVR, Punta, Tabuc, Roxas C, 5800 Capiz. DZXL, 4/F, Guadelupe Commerical Complex, Guadelupe Nuevo, Makati C, 1200 NCR – **85)** Radio Philippines Netw. DXDX R. Ronda, Acharon Blvd, Gen. Santos C, 9500 South Cotabato. DXKD, Gonzales corner Lopez Jaena Str, Biasong, Dipolog C, 7100 Zamboanga del Norte. DXKO R. Ronda, Gusa, National Hwy, Cagayan de Oro C, 9000 Misamis Oriental. DXKP R. Ronda, Araulio Str, Brgy Datoc, Pagadian C, 7016 Zamboanga del Sur. DXKS, Capitol Rd, Surigao C, 8400 Surigao del Norte. DXKT R. Ronda, Marfori Heights, 8000 Davao C. DXXX R. Ronda, Brgy Tugbungan, 7000 Zamboanga C. DYKB R. Ronda, Bo. Sumag, Bacolod C, 6100 Negros Occidental. DYKC, Barangay Maguikay, Mandaue C, 6014 Cebu. DYKW R. Ronda, Cagamayan, Binalbagan, 6107 Negros Occidental. DZBS R. Ronda, Agrix Supermarket cor. Magsaysay Ave. & Bakawkan, Baguio C, 2600 Benguet. DZKI R. Ronda, San Agustin, Iriga C, 4431 Camarines Sur. DZRL R. Ronda, Bo. Kawayan, Batac, 2906 Ilocos Norte. DZTG, 46 Rizal Str, Tuguegarao, 3500 Cagayan – **86)** Radio Sorsogon Netw, Inc. DZRS, Don Luis Lee Bldg, Plaza Bonifacio, Sorsogon C, 4700 Sorsogon – **87)** Radio Veritas Global Broadc. Syst. DWRV, Maharlika Highway, Bayombong, 3700 Nueva Vizcaya. DWVR, San Jose C, 3121 Nueva Ecija. DZRV, R. Veritas, 20/F The Centerpoint Bldg 1, 162 West Ave corner EDSA, Ortigas Center, Pasig C, 1600 NCR – **88)** R. Pilipino Corp (R. Asenso). DXCO, Atco Bldg, Capistrano & Gomez Str, Cagayan de Oro C, 9000 Misamis Oriental. DXOW, Mapa, 8000 Davao C. DYRL, Camaroli Av, Lupit Subd, Bacolod C, 6100 Negros Occidental. DZYA 2/F Tanglao Bldg, Balibago, Angeles C, 2009 Pampanga. – **89)** Ragde, Vicente & Sons. DYRS, Ragde Comp, Corner M. Endrinda Str and Broce Str, San Carlos C, 6127 Negros Occidental – **90)** Rajah Broadc. Netw (R. Bandido). DXRJ, RJ Clubhouse, Sta. Filomena, Iligan C, 9200 Lanao del Norte. DZRJ (The Voice of the Philippines), Ventures Bldg 1, Gen. Luna Str, Makati C, NCR – **91)** Republic Broadc. Syst. (owned by GMA Network Inc.) DWRA, Baguio C, 2600 Benguet. DWRC, San Nicolas, 2901 Ilocos Norte. DXBM, Cotabato C, 9600 Maguindanao. DXGM, Shrine Hills, Matina, 8000 Davao C. DXRL, 3/F Carisma Bldg., General Santos Drive, Koronadal C, 9506 South Cotabato. DXYK, Butuan C, 8600 Agusan del Norte. DYSP, Solid Rd, Brgy San Manuel, Puerto Princesa C, 5300 Palawan. DYSS, GMA Network Center, Nivel Hills, Apas, 6000 Cebu C – **92)** Ribbon Broadc. Netw. DWRB, 5/F, LCC Bldg, Lipa C, 4217 Batangas – **94)** RMC Broadc. Co, Inc (Rizal Memorial Colleges). DXRA R. Arangkada, A. Pichon St., 8000 Davao C – **95)** Rolin Broadc. Enterprises (sts relay RMN DWAR 103.9MHz, Puerto Princesa). DWES, Narra, 5303 Palawan. DWJS, Roxas, 5308 Palawan – **97)** Sarraga Integration and Management Corp. (SIAM), El Nuevo Bantay R. DYHH Bantay R.DYDD, Martinez, Cebu C, 6000 Cebu. DYZZ, Bogo, 6010 Cebu. DYZZ, Guihulngan, 6214 Negros Oriental – **98)** Satellite Broadc. Corp. DWBA, Bangued, 2800 Abra. DZLU, National College of Technology Campus, Barangay 1, San Fernando C, 2500 La Union –**100)** Southern Institute of Tech. DXSI, Cagayan de Oro C, 9000 Misamis Oriental – **101)** Southern Philippines Mass Comm. DXSC, Camp Navarro, Calarian, 7000 Zamboanga C – **102)** Subic Broadc. Corp. DWGO Gabay ng Olangapo, 1 Kasarinlan Rd, Olongapo, 2200 Zambales – **103)** Sulu Tawi-Tawi Broadc. Foundation. DXGD Radio for Peace, Bongao, 7500 Tawi-Tawi. DXMM R. Totoo, Gandasuli Str, Jolo, 7400 Sulu – **104)** Tagbilaran Broadc. Corp. DYTR, CAP Bldg, CPG Ave crnr Borja Str, Dampas, Tagbilaran C, 6300 Bohol – **105)** Times Broadc. Corp. DXSY, Mariano Marcos, Ozamis C, 7200 Misamis Occidental – **106)** Tirad Pass R/TV Broadc. Netw. DZTP R. Tirad Pass, San Nicolas, Candon, 2710 Ilocos Sur – **107)** Trans-Radio Broadc. Corp. (operated by Philippine Daily Inquirer). R. Inquirer, 2/F Media Resources Plaza, Pasong Tirad cor. Mola Str, Brgy La Paz, Makati C, 1204 NCR – **108)** Supreme Broadc. Systems. DWSS, Paragon Plaza, EDSA, Mandaluyong C, 1554 NCR – **110)** Universal Broadc. Syst (owned by Radio Mindanao Network). DYMM, Sunshine Village, Esperos Str, Tacloban C, 6500 Leyte. DYXT, Luna Str, Tagbilaran C, 6300 Bohol – **111)** University of Mindanao Broadc. Netwk (UMBN). DXCM, UM School Compound, Cotabato C, 9600 Maguindanao. DXDN, UM Tagum School Compound, Tagum C, 8100 Davao del Norte. DXDS, Digos C, 8002 Davao del Sur. DXMV, Mt. Kitangcad Cor. Kanlaon Street, Valencia, 8709 Bukidnon. – **112)** University of San Agustin. DYSA R. San Agustin, 2/F Univ. of S. Agustin, Gen. Luna Str, Iloilo C, 5901 Iloilo – **113)** University of the Philippines. DZLB, UP Los Banos College, 4031 Laguna. DZUP, Media Center, College of Mass Comunications, UP Campus Diliman, R, Magasay Ave corner Apacible Str, Quezon C, 1104 NCR – **114)** Vanguard Radio Netw (Radio Vanguard). DWMG, Solano, 3709 Nueva Vizcaya. DZXO, Ground Floor Diego Building, Maharlika Highway, Cabanatuan C, 3100 Nueva Ecija – **115)** Visayas Mindanao Confederation of Trade Unions. DYLA, Alu-Vimcontu Welfare Center, Pier Area, 6000 Cebu C – **116)** Vismin Radio & TV Broadc. Net. DXDV, Baan, Butuan C, 8600 Agusan del Norte – **118)** Word Broadc. Corp. DYDW Radio Diwa, Burayan, San José, Tacloban C, 6500 Leyte. DYRF R. Fuerza, Univ. of San Carlos, Pelaez Str, 6000 Cebu C – **120)** ZOE Broadc. Netw., Radyo Calabarzo. DZJV, 140 Brgy Parian, Calamba, 4027 Laguna – **121)** Baganian Broadc. Corp. DXBZ R. Bagting, Bana Str, Sta Maria District, Pagadian C., 7015 Zamboanga del Sur – **122)** Solidnorth Broadcasting System. DWRS Commando Radio, Tamag, Vigan, 2700 Ilocos Sur – **123)** S.O.L. Telebroadcasting Station. DZSL, Purok 2, Talisay, Camarines Norte – **124)** Ranao Radio & TV Broadcast System Corp. DXSK R. Ranaw, Pangarungan Village, Marawi C, 9700 Lanao del Sur – **125)** End Time Mission (Pentecostal Missionary Church of Christ 4th Watch). DZAT, Purok Rosal, Bo. Silangan Mayao, Lucena C., 4301 Quezon Province – **127)** University of the Philippines in the Visayas. DYUP UPV Radio, Miagao, Iliolo – **129)** Inter-Island Broadc. Corp. (IBC), owned by 73) above. DYIN, Bombo R. Broadcast Center, Oyo Torong Str, cor. J. Magno. Str, Kalibo, 5600 Aklan. DYSJ, San Jose de Buenavista, Antique – **130)** Dan-ag sa Dakbayan Broadc. Corp. DXDD R. Kampana, New DXDD Bldg, Rizal. Str, Ozamis C, 7200 Misamis Occidental – **131)** Roman Catholic Archdiocese of Zamboanga Broadc. Network (RCA-ZBN). DXVP R. Verdadero, Sacred Heart Center, R.T. Lim Bvd, Zamboanga C, 7000 Zamboanga del Sur – **132)** Apostolic Vicariate of San Jose de Mindoro. DZVT R. Totoo, Labangan Poblacion, San Jose, 5100 Mindoro Occidental – **133)** Multipoint Broadc. Netwk. DWPR Power Radio, A.B. Fernandez Ave, Bolosan District, Dagupan C, 2400 Pangasinan – **134)** Alaminos City Broadc. Corporation. DZWM R. Totoo, St Joseph Cathedral Compound, Alaminos, 2404 Pangasinan – **135)** Government of Tarlac Province. DZTC, MacArthur Hwy, Tarlac C, 2300 Tarlac – **136)** Archdiocese of Nueva Segovia. DZNS R. Totoo, Brgy Pantay Fatima, Vigan, 2700 Ilocos Sur – **137)** Diocese of Bacolod. DYAF R. Veritas Bacolod, Rizal Str corner San Juan Str, Brgy. 11, Bacolod C, 6100 Negros Occidental – **138)** Silangan Broadcasting Corporation. DXSN R. Magbalantay or R. Totoo, 55 Jules Chevalier Str, Surigao C, 8400 Surigao del Norte – **139)** Universitad de Zamboanga. DXUZ R. Lipay, Ipil, 7001 Zamboanga Sibugay – **140)** Itransmission, Inc. DZIP R. Palaweño, Dimalanta Bldg, Rizal Ave, Puerto Princesa, Palawan – **141)** Sarangani Broadcasting Netwk. DXBB R. Alerto, Yumang Str, Brgy San Isidro, Gen. Santos C, 9500 South Cotabato – **142)** End-Time Mission Broadcasting Service. DWET Life R, Batal, Santiago C, 3311 Isabela.

PITCAIRN ISLANDS (UK)

L.T: UTC -8h — **Pop:** 50 — **Pr.L:** Pitcairn English — **E.C:** 240V/50Hz — **ITU:** PTC

PITCAIRN ISLAND RADIO
✉ Adamstown, Pitcairn Island
NB: All broadcasting ceased.

POLAND

L.T: UTC +1h (28 Mar-31 Oct: +2h) — **Pop:** 37.9 million — **Pr.L:** Polish — **E.C:** 230V/50Hz — **ITU:** POL

KRAJOWA RADA RADIOFONII I TELEWIZJI (KRRiT)

(National Broadcasting Council)
Skwer kard. S.Wyszyńskiego 9, 01-015 Warszawa ☎ +48 225973000 🖷 +48 225973180 **E:** krrit@krrit.gov.pl **W:** krrit.gov.pl
L.P: Pres: Witold Kołodziejski

RADA MEDIÓW NARODOWYCH (RMN)

(National Media Council)
Kancelaria Sejmu, ul. Wiejska 4/6/8, 00-902 Warszawa ☎ +48 226942500 **E:** krzysztof.czabanski@rmn.sejm.pl **W:** rmn.sejm.pl
L.P: Chmn: Krzysztof Czabański

POLSKIE RADIO S.A. (PR) (Pub)

al. Niepodległości 77/85, 00-977 Warszawa ☎ +48 226459212 **E:** public.relations@polskieradio.pl **W:** www.polskieradio.pl
L.P: Chair: Agnieszka Kamińska

LW	kHz	kW	Prgr	
Solec Kujawski	225	1200*	1	*) 700kW at night

FM (MHz)	1	2	3	5	kW
Białogard (Sławoborze)	106.0	98.2	101.5	-	10/2x15
Białystok	-	106.4	-	-	1
Białystok (Krynice)	92.3	-	96.0	-	30
Bielawa	-	-	-	103.5	1
Bogatynia (G.Wysoka)	92.8	-	-	-	1
Bydgoszcz	-	-	-	96.2	1
Bydgoszcz (Trzeciewiec)	106.6	97.6	102.1	-	60/2x120
Częstochowa	-	-	-	98.9	2
Częstochowa (Wręczyca)	87.5	90.6	91.7	-	10/2x60
Elbląg (Jagodnik)	-	102.3	-	101.2	5/0.25
Gdańsk (Chwaszczyno)	95.7	-	99.9	-	120
Gdynia	-	97.2	-	-	2
Giżycko (Miłki)	97.1	92.6	94.4	-	6/2x10
Gołańcz	101.3	-	-	-	3
Gorlice	105.4	-	91.6	-	10/0.2
Gorzów Wlkp.	-	-	-	105.4	1
Iława (Kisielice)	94.8	102.7	-	104.8	2x10/5
Jelenia Góra (Śnieżne Kotły)	92.5	-	94.0	-	10
Kalisz (Mikstat)	100.0	95.6	102.5	94.2	10
Katowice (Kosztowy)	97.9	105.6	99.7	-	60
Kielce (Święty Krzyż)	92.3	-	96.2	-	60
Kielce	-	102.7	-	87.6	1/0.1
Kłodzko	-	92.4	-	-	2
Kłodzko (Czarna Góra)	97.6	-	89.2	-	10
Konin (Żółwieniec)	87.7	-	103.3	-	30
Koszalin (Gologóra)	107.9	93.8	97.4	-	60
Kraków (Chorągwica)	89.4	-	99.4	-	60
Kraków (Krzemionki)	-	102.0	-	97.2	1/0.4
Krosno (Sucha Góra)	88.0	-	92.0	-	120
Krynica (G.Jaworzyna)	106.4	89.6	-	98.4	1/0.1/1
Kutno	101.8	96.9	-	-	8.9/0.8
Lębork (Skórowo Nowe)	100.5	88.2	106.3	107.5	2x10/5/10
Legnica	-	105.3	-	103.3	2/0.3
Leszno	-	88.7	-	107.9	0.25/1
Leżajsk (Giedlarowa)	96.8	-	98.9	-	10
Łobez (Toporzyk)	-	-	-	100.6	3
Łódź	107.8	91.4	103.8	107.3	30/2x10/1.5
Lowicz	101.6	-	-	-	10
Lubaczów (Boble)	100.0	88.4	96.0	-	10
Lubań (Nowa Karczma)	99.0	-	91.5	-	10/60
Lublin (Piaski)	90.8	-	104.2	-	30/90
Nowy Tomyśl (Bolewice)	-	107.7	-	-	10
Olsztyn (Pieczewo)	93.0	93.7	99.1	97.9	30/2/120/0.1
Opole (Chrzelice)	88.3	94.5	90.3	-	60/10/60
Ostrołęka (Ławy)	106.7	96.3	98.5	93.4	10/5/10/0.2
Piła (Staszyce)	-	102.5	-	-	10
Płock (Rachocin)	92.2	98.1	96.1	-	60/2.5/60
Poznań (Śrem)	92.3	-	96.4	-	120
Przasnysz	105.9	107.1	-	-	10
Przemyśl (Tatarska Góra)	87.8	94.1	99.6	91.0	5/1/5/1
Przysucha (Kozłowiec)	92.0	104.8	-	-	10
Rabka (G.Luboń Wielki)	93.4	90.4	-	-	5
Radom (Wacyn)	-	100.3	-	97.5	1/0.1
Ryki	105.1	88.7	-	-	10
Rzeszów	-	105.8	-	91.5	1
Siedlce (Łosice)	88.3	-	90.5	-	30
Słupsk	104.3	-	-	106.8	2.8/5
Solina (G.Jawor)	90.7	-	96.3	-	30
Stargard	-	107.6	-	-	1
Suwałki (G.Krzemianucha)	105.5	92.0	96.6	88.7	20/2x30/0.2
Świeradów-Zdrój	-	93.2	-	90.5	10/1
Świnoujście (Chrobrego)	107.7	-	-	-	10
Szczawnica (G.Prehyba)	88.0	-	94.7	-	10/5
Szczecin (Kołowo)	100.3	-	102.3	-	60
Szczecin (Warszewo)	-	96.3	-	88.4	1
Tarnów (G.Św. Marcina)	-	-	-	99.9	2.5
Tarnów (Lichwin)	91.1	88.6	-	-	10
Toruń	-	-	-	89.7	1
Wałbrzych (G.Chełmiec)	-	87.9	99.8	94.3	2x5/0.5
Wałcz (Rusinowo)	101.9	-	90.9	-	30
Warszawa	92.4	104.9	99.1	92.0	0.3/2.5/0.1/0.2
Warszawa (Raszyn)	102.4	-	98.8	-	120
Wisła (G.Skrzyczne)	91.5	-	100.8	-	10
Włocławek (Szpetal Górny)	-	93.9	-	-	1
Włodawa (Żołnierzy)	-	102.5	-	-	9.1
Włoszczowa (Dobromierz)	88.9	-	-	-	3.2
Wrocław (G.Ślęża)	98.8	-	100.2	-	120
Wrocław (Żórawina)	-	87.7	-	107.5	10/5
Żagań (Wichów)	91.2	104.7	87.8	-	30
Zakopane (G.Gubałówka)	92.8	90.9	98.2	-	10/0.3/10
Zamość (Feliksówka)	105.7	-	-	95.3	10/1
Zamość (Tarnawatka)	-	87.6	91.3	-	30
Zielona Góra (Jemiołów)	105.0	89.9	94.1	-	60
Zielona Góra (Wilkanowo)	-	-	-	104.0	2

+ sites with only txs below 1kW.

D.Prgr: Prgr 1 (Jedynka): 24h – **Prgr 2 (Dwójka):** 24h – **Prgr 3 (Trójka):** 24h – **Prgr 4 (Czwórka):** 24h via DAB – **Prgr 5 (PR24):** 24h – **Prgr 6 (R. Chopin):** 24h via DAB – **Prgr 7 (R. Dzieciom):** 24h via DAB – **International Service (R. Poland):** 24h via DAB.

PR Regional Stations

D.Prgr: All stations broadcast 24h. **PR R.Bialystok:** ul. Świerkowa 1, 15-328 Białystok **E:** radiobia@radio.bialystok.pl. On (MHz) 87.9 (Łomża 0.2kW), 89.4 (Białowieża 0.1kW), 98.6 (G.Krzemianucha 30kW), 99.4 (Krynice 30kW), 104.1 (Makarki 10kW), DAB 5C (Krynice 2kW) – **PR R.Dla Ciebe (RDC):** ul. Myśliwiecka 3/5/7, 00-977 Warszawa **E:** radio@rdc.pl. On (MHz) 87.6 (Ostrów Mazowiecka 1kW), 89.1 (Wacyn 5kW), 100.8 (Ostrołęka 0.25kW), 101.0 (Warszawa 12.9kW), 101.9 (Rachocin 60kW), 103.4 (Łosice 120kW), DAB 6B (Warszawa PKiN 6kW) – **PR R.Gdansk:** ul. Grunwaldzka 18, 80-006 Gdańsk **E:** poczta@radio.gdansk.pl. On (MHz) 91.1 (Skórowo Nowe 10kW), 102.0 (Słupsk 1kW)*, 103.7 (Chwaszczyno 120kW), 106.0 (Kwidzyn 1kW), 107.0 (Bytów 10kW), DAB 5B (Chwaszczyno 24kW). *) incl. prgrs from Słupsk studio – **PR R.Katowice:** ul. Ligonia 29, 40-953 Katowice **E:** sekretariat@radio.katowice.pl. On (MHz) 89.3 (Zabrze 0.5kW), 97.0 (Racibórz 1kW), 98.4 (Wręczyca 60kW), 101.2 (Bytków 1kW), 102.2 (Kosztowy 60kW), 103.0 (G.Skrzyczne 10kW), DAB 11A (Kosztowy 19kW) – **PR R.Kielce:** ul. Radiowa 4, 25-317 Kielce. **E:** radio@radio.kielce.com.pl. On (MHz) 90.4 (Kielce 0.25kW), 100.0 (Włoszczowa 1kW), 101.4 (Święty Krzyż 120kW), DAB 10D (SFN) – **PR R.Koszalin:** ul. Piłsudskiego 43-49, 75-502 Koszalin **E:** radio@radio.koszalin.pl. On (MHz) 88.1 (Rusinowo 3kW), 91.0 (Kołobrzeg 0.1kW), 92.5 (Sławoborze 15kW), 95.3 (Słupsk 2kW)*, 97.8 (G.Chełmska 0.1kW), 103.1 (Gołogóra 60kW), DAB 11B (SFN)*. *) incl. prgrs from Słupsk studio (ul. Filmowa 2 76-200 Słupsk **E:** radioslupsk@radio.koszalin.p) – **PR R.Kraków:** al. Słowackiego 22, 30-007 Kraków. **E:** redakcja@radiokrakow.pl. On (MHz) 87.6 (G.Luboń Wielki 5kW), 90.0 (G.Prehyba 10kW), 97.4 (Gorlice 10kW), 98.8 (Andrychów 1kW), 100.0 (G.Gubalówka 10kW), 101.0 (G.Św. Marcina 10kW), 101.6 (Chorągwica 60kW), 102.1 (G.Jaworzyna 1kW), DAB 11B (Chorągwica 10kW) – **PR R.Lódz:** ul. Narutowicza 130, 90-146 Łódz **E:** studio@radiolodz.pl. On (MHz) 96.7 (Sieradz 0.5kW), 99.2 (Łódź 30kW), 104.0 (Wieruszów 1kW), DAB 5C (Łódź 9.3kW) – **PR R.Lublin:** ul. Obronców Pokoju 2, 20-030 Lublin **E:** poczta@radio.lublin.pl. Prgr 1 (R. Lublin): on (MHz) 93.1 (Biała Podlaska 5kW), 102.2 (Piaski 90kW), 103.1 (Ryki 10kW), 103.2 (Feliksówka 30kW), DAB 11B (Piaski 5kW). Prgr 2 (R. Freee): on 89.9MHz (Lublin 1kW) – **PR R.Olsztyn:** ul. Radiowa 24, 10-206 Olsztyn **E:** radio@ro.com.pl. On (MHz) 99.6 (Miłki 10kW), 103.2 (Pieczewo 120kW), 103.4 (Jagodnik 0.5kW), DAB 11B (Pieczewo 7.6kW) – **PR R.Opole:** ul. Strzelców Bytomskich 8, 45-084 Opole **E:** info@radio.opole.pl. On (MHz) 88.0 (Brzeg 1kW), 89.1 (Olesno 1kW),

92.6 (Paczków 1kW), 94.8 (Głubczyce 1kW), 96.3 (Kłuczbork 30kW), 101.2 (Opole 1kW), 103.2 (Chrzelice 60kW), 105.1 (Strzelce Opolskie 1kW), 107.7 (Namysłów 1kW), DAB 11C (SFN). Prgr 2 (R. Opole Kultura): on 96.5MHz (Opole 0.05kW) + DAB. – **PR R.PiK:** ul. Gdańska 48-50, 85-006 Bydgoszcz **E:** radio@radiopik.pl. On (MHz) 100.1 (Trzeciewiec 120kW), 100.3 (Włocławek 1kW), 106.9 (Brodnica 10kW), DAB 11A (SFN) – **PR R.Poznan:** ul. Berwińskiego 5, 60-765 Poznań **E:** office@radiopoznan.fm. Prgr 1 (R. Poznań): On (MHz) 91.1 (Mikstat 10kW), 91.9 (Żółwieniec 30kW), 100.9 (Śrem 120kW), 102.4 (Bolewice 3kW), 103.6 (Rusinowo 60kW), DAB 12A (SFN). Prgr 2 (MC R.): on 102.7MHz (Piątkowo 2kW) – **PR R.Rzeszów:** ul. Zamkowa 3, 35-032 Rzeszów **E:** sekretariat@radio.rzeszow.pll. On (MHz) 90.3 (Machów 1kW), 90.5 (Sucha Góra 120kW), 96.4 (Mielec 1kW), 99.2 (G.Jawor 5kW), 102.0 (Tatarska Góra 10kW), 102.9 (Giedlarowa 30kW), 103.7 (Boble 10kW), 106.7 (Magdalenka 2kW), DAB 11A (SFN) – **PR R.Szczecin:** al. Wojska Polskiego 73, 70-481 Szczecin. **E:** sekretariat@radio.szczecin.pl. Prgr 1 (R. Szczecin): on (MHz) 92.0 (Kołowo 60kW), 98.7 (Sławoborze 10kW), 106.3 (Chrobrego 10kW), DAB 11A (SFN). Prgr 2 (R. Szczecin Extra): on 94.4MHz (Warszewo 0.5kW) + DAB – **PR R.Wroclaw:** ul. Karkonoska 8-10, 53-015 Wrocław **E:** sekretariatzarzadu@radiowroclaw.pl. Prgr 1 (R. Wrocław): on (MHz) 89.0 (G.Wysoka 1kW), 95.5 (G.Chełmiec 5kW), 96.0 (Czarna Góra 10kW), 96.7 (Śnieżne Kotły 10kW), 98.0 (G.Parkowa 0.1kW), 102.3 (G.Ślęża 120kW), 103.6 (Nowa Karczma 60kW), DAB 5B (Żórawina 5kW). Prgr 2 (R. RAM): on 89.8MHz (Żórawina 6kW). Prgr 3 (R. Wrocław Kultura): on DAB. – **PR R.Zachód:** ul. Kukułcza 1, 65-472 Zielona Góra **E:** radio@zachod.pl. Prgr 1 (R. Zachód): on (MHz) 103.0 (Jemiołów 120kW), 106.0 (Wichów 30kW), DAB 11C (SFN). Prgr 2 (R. Zielona Góra): on 97.1MHz (Zielona Góra 1kW).

OTHER STATIONS

MW	MHz	kW	Location	Station
69A)	963	0.1	Lipsko	Twoje R. Lipsko/R. AM
69B)	1584	0.8	Andrychów	R. Andrychów/R. AM
69)	1602	0.8	Kraków	R. AM

FM	MHz	kW	Location	Station
27)	87.7	1.2	Białystok	R. Akadera
3)	87.7	3	Międzyzdroje	R. Maryja
1B)	87.8	1	Kraków	R. RMF Classic
3)	87.8	1	Biała Podlaska	R. Maryja
3)	87.9	10	Łódź	R. Maryja
4C)	87.9	25	Lublin	R. Plus
2A)	88.0	3	Gołańcz	R. ZET
1C)	88.1	1	Zabrze	R. RMF MAXXX
36)	88.1	1	Wieluń	R. Fiat
67)	88.1	1	Płock	R. Płock FM
1A)	88.2	1	Polkowice	R. RMF FM
1A)	88.2	120	Kielce	R. RMF FM
3)	88.2	1	Ostrów Wlkp.	R. Maryja
5A)	88.2	1	Toruń	R. TOK FM
2A)	88.3	60	Zielona Góra	R. ZET
3)	88.3	1	Kutno	R. Maryja
3)	88.4	10	Bielsko-Biała	R. Maryja
5B)	88.4	5	Poznań	R. Złote Przeboje
3)	88.5	1	Bydgoszcz	R. Maryja
3)	88.5	10	Słupsk	R. Maryja
61)	88.6	1	Skierniewice	R. RSC
2A)	88.7	1	Koszalin	R. ZET
3)	88.7	1.6	Gołańcz	R. Maryja
3)	88.7	1.6	Wągrowiec	R. Maryja
4D)	88.8	1	Kraków	R. WAWA
3)	88.9	2	Gdańsk	R. Maryja
3)	88.9	120	Wrocław	R. Maryja
4C)	88.9	12	Szczecin	R. Plus
3)	89.0	5	Warszawa	R. Maryja
39)	89.2	5	Białystok	R. Jard
5A)	89.2	1	Elbląg	R. TOK FM
1A)	89.3	30	Lublin	R. RMF FM
1A)	89.3	60	Koszalin	R. RMF FM
2A)	89.4	60	Lubań	R. ZET
3)	89.4	2	Stargard	R. Maryja
3)	89.5	1	Wegrów	R. Maryja
4A)	89.5	1	Sanok	R. Eska
4C)	89.5	10	Gniezno	R. Plus
2D)	89.6	1	Łódź	Antyradio
33)	89.6	1	Opole	R. DOXA
3)	89.8	1	Mielec	R. Maryja
30)	89.8	1	Poznań	R. Emaus
5B)	89.8	1	Szczecin	R. Złote Przeboje
4D)	89.8	1	Warszawa	R. WAWA
19)	90.0	2	Rybnik	R. 90
5B)	90.0	4	Legnica	R. Złote Przeboje
13)	90.1	10	Zamość	Katolickie R. Zamość
4A)	90.1	2	Łódź	R. Eska
7)	90.1	1	Kościerzyna	R. Kaszëbë
3)	90.2	10	Kamieńsk	R. Maryja
4B)	90.1	1	Pobiedziska	R. VOX FM
43)	90.2	1	Kolobrzeg	R. Kołobrzeg
63)	90.2	1	Bielsko-Biała	R. Aniol Beskidów
3)	90.3	1	Zielona Góra	R. Maryja
66)	90.3	2	Stargard	Twoje R.
5B)	90.4	3	Wrocław	R. Złote Przeboje
3)	90.6	5	Kraków	R. Maryja
32)	90.6	1	Słupsk	R. FAMA
4A)	90.7	2	Gdynia	R. Eska
4C)	90.7	2	Gryfice	R. Plus
4C)	90.7	5	Radom	R. Plus
16)	90.8	1	Mława	R. 7
1C)	90.8	1	Inowrocław	R. RMF MAXXX
14)	90.9	1	Jelenia Góra	Muzyczne R.
14)	90.9	4.7	Wałbrzych	Muzyczne R.
1A)	91.0	120	Warszawa	R. RMF FM
5B)	91.2	2	Katowice	R. Złote Przeboje
1A)	91.3	10	Łobez	R. RMF FM
38)	91.4	1	Pelplin	R. Głos
1A)	91.5	15	Ostrołęka	R. RMF FM
2A)	91.6	10	Ryki	R. ZET
1A)	91.7	2	Gołańcz	R. RMF FM
4C)	91.7	1	Zielona Góra	R. Plus
2A)	91.8	10	Świnoujście	R. ZET
3)	91.8	1	Ciechanów	R. Maryja
1A)	91.9	30	Siedlce	R. RMF FM
2D)	92.0	1	Gdańsk	Antyradio
59)	92.0	2.5	Wrocław	R. Rodzina
15)	92.1	4	Zduńska Wola	Nasze R.
2A)	92.1	1	Włodawa	R. ZET
5B)	92.1	1	Bydgoszcz	R. Złote Przeboje
2A)	92.2	10	Opole	R. ZET
55)	92.3	1	Łaziska Górne	R. Express FM
7)	92.3	2	Gdańsk	R. Kaszëbë
4D)	92.4	1	Nowy Sacz	R. WAWA
5B)	92.5	1	Kraków	R. Złote Przeboje
2A)	92.6	120	Łódź	R. ZET
42)	92.6	1	Sępólno Kraj.	R. Weekend
4D)	92.6	1	Krosno	R. WAWA
3)	92.7	7	Lębork	R. Maryja
2C)	92.8	1	Toruń	Meloradio
5B)	92.8	1	Opole	R. Złote Przeboje
5B)	92.8	2	Tarnów	R. Złote Przeboje
1A)	92.9	10	Wrocław	R. RMF FM
2A)	92.9	10	Gryfice	R. ZET
32)	92.9	1	Tomaszów Maz.	R. FAMA
1A)	93.0	60	Katowice	R. RMF FM
4A)	93.0	10	Poznań	R. Eska
3)	93.1	1	Krynica	R. Maryja
4D)	93.2	2	Szczecin	R. WAWA
5B)	93.2	5	Jędrzejów	R. Złote Przeboje
1A)	93.3	120	Bydgoszcz	R. RMF FM
4E)	93.3	1	Warszawa	R. Eska Rock
25)	93.4	2	Gliwice	R. CCM
1A)	93.5	10	Łódź	R. RMF FM
2A)	93.6	120	Wrocław	R. ZET
2B)	93.7	1	Kraków	R. Chillizet
1A)	93.8	60	Lubań	R. RMF FM
4A)	93.8	10	Gorzów Wlkp.	R. Eska
52)	93.8	1	Kutno	R. Victoria
65)	93.8	1	Częstochowa	R. Jura
54)	93.9	1	Kędzierzyn-Koźle	R. Park FM
4C)	94.0	1	Końskie	R. Plus
5B)	94.0	1	Tokarnia	R. Złote Przeboje
2C)	94.0	1	Warszawa	Meloradio
12)	94.1	1	Jasło	VIA - Kat. R. Rzeszów
4A)	94.1	1	Elbląg	R. Eska
38)	94.2	1	Kartuzy	R. Głos
1A)	94.3	60	Płock	R. RMF FM
3)	94.3	2	Racibórz	R. Maryja
3)	94.4	1	Tarnobrzeg	R. Maryja
4A)	94.4	5	Bydgoszcz	R. Eska
5B)	94.4	1	Żary	R. Złote Przeboje
23)	94.5	1	Grodzisk Maz.	R. Bogoria
3)	94.5	1	Ustrzyki Dolne	R. Maryja

FM	MHz	kW	Location	Station
1A)	94.6	120	Poznań	R. RMF FM
4A)	94.6	1	Gdańsk	R. Eska
36)	94.7	10	Częstochowa	R. Fiat
52)	94.7	1	Rawa Maz.	R. Victoria
1A)	94.8	30	Żagań	R. RMF FM
59)	94.8	2	Strzelin	R. Rodzina
25)	94.9	1	Oświęcim	R. CCM
31)	94.9	1	Sochaczew	R. Sochaczew
4C)	94.9	1	Jelenia Góra	R. Plus
5A)	94.9	1	Kielce	R. TOK FM
2A)	95.0	20	Leżajsk	R. ZET
3)	95.0	3	Szczecinek	R. Maryja
1A)	95.1	1.6	Suwałki	R. RMF FM
2C)	95.1	1	Zabrze	Meloradio
3)	95.1	1	Nowy Sącz	R. Maryja
1B)	95.1	1	Bydgoszcz	R. RMF Classic
2A)	95.2	60	Szczecin	R. ZET
3)	95.2	1	Sieradz	R. Maryja
3)	95.2	1	Świeradów-Zdrój	R. Maryja
5A)	95.2	1	Gdynia	R. TOK FM
49)	95.2	1	Sanok	Trendy R.
1A)	95.3	60	Olsztyn	R. RMF FM
1A)	95.3	60	Opole	R. RMF FM
1A)	95.4	10	Tarnów	R. RMF FM
3)	95.4	1	Gniezno	R. Maryja
3)	95.4	5	Skierniewice	R. Maryja
39)	95.5	4	Bielsk Podl.	R. Jard
2A)	95.6	120	Bydgoszcz	R. ZET
5B)	95.6	1	Lublin	R. Złote Przeboje
2A)	95.7	10	Wisła	R. ZET
4B)	95.7	1	Szczecin	R. VOX FM
5B)	95.7	1	Rzeszów	R. Złote Przeboje
1C)	95.8	1	Warszawa	R. RMF MAXXX
1C)	95.8	2	Konin	R. RMF MAXXX
3)	95.8	1	Hrubieszów	R. Maryja
48)	95.8	1	Krapkowice	R. Vanessa
4A)	95.9	1	Koszalin	R. Eska
57)	95.9	1	Olsztyn	R. UWM FM
1A)	96.0	60	Kraków	R. RMF FM
1C)	96.0	1	Olesnica	R. RMF MAXXX
53)	96.0	6	Łódź	R. Parada
1A)	96.1	1	Gorzów Wlkp.	R. RMF FM
1A)	96.1	1	Legnica	R. RMF FM
10)	96.2	2	Zabrze	R. Silesia
1A)	96.4	15	Białogard	R. RMF FM
1C)	96.4	1	Gdańsk	R. RMF MAXXX
3)	96.5	10	Zamość	R. Maryja
4C)	96.5	10	Warszawa	R. Plus
1A)	96.6	30	Wałcz	R. RMF FM
2A)	96.6	10	Lębork	R. ZET
5B)	96.6	1	Częstochowa	R. Złote Przeboje
5B)	96.6	1	Zabrze	R. Złote Przeboje
1C)	96.7	2	Kraków	R. RMF MAXXX
4D)	96.7	3	Toruń	R. WAWA
52)	96.7	1	Skierniewice	R. Victoria
3)	96.9	7.5	Iława	R. Maryja
4A)	96.9	1	Szczecin	R. Eska
2A)	97.0	30	Poznań	R. ZET
3)	97.0	2	Ciechanowiec	R. Maryja
3)	97.0	1	Lublin	R. Maryja
1A)	97.1	12	Włoszczowa	R. RMF FM
54)	97.1	1	Brzeg	R. Park FM
24)	97.2	2.5	Puławy	R. Impuls
2A)	97.2	1	Wałbrzych	R. ZET
9)	97.2	1	Wągrowiec	Wasze R. FM
2A)	97.3	60	Płock	R. ZET
4A)	97.3	1	Zamość	R. Eska
5A)	97.4	1	Katowice	R. TOK FM
1C)	97.5	1	Łomża	R. RMF MAXXX
2A)	97.5	30	Żagań	R. ZET
4A)	97.7	1	Kraków	R. Eska
2A)	97.8	2.5	Szczawnica	R. ZET
2C)	97.8	1.35	Wrocław	Meloradio
2A)	97.9	60	Wałcz	R. ZET
1A)	98.0	10	Kalisz	R. RMF FM
22)	98.1	120	Białystok	R. Racja
2C)	98.1	1	Inowrocław	Meloradio
4A)	98.1	2	Tarnów	R. Eska
52)	98.1	1	Mszczonów	R. Victoria
34)	98.2	1	Przemyśl	R. Fara
28)	98.3	1	Polkowice	R. Elka
1A)	98.4	120	Gdańsk	R. RMF FM
28)	98.5	1	Leszno	R. Elka
5A)	98.5	1	Bydgoszcz	R. TOK FM
2A)	98.6	1	Nysa	R. ZET
51)	98.6	2	Łódź	R. Niepokalanów
2A)	98.7	10	Iława	R. ZET
3)	98.8	10	Gorzów Wlkp.	R. Maryja
1A)	98.9	30	Konin	R. RMF FM
7)	98.9	2	Reda	R. Kaszëbë
1B)	99.0	1	Kielce	R. RMF Classic
4A)	99.0	1	Szczecinek	R. Eska
22)	99.2	10	Biała Podlaska	R. Racja
42)	99.3	2	Chojnice	R. Weekend
2C)	99.4	10.7	Poznań	Meloradio
8)	99.4	1	Włocławek	R. Kujawy
1A)	99.5	1	Kluczbork	R. RMF FM
3)	99.5	1	Lipiany	R. Maryja
4C)	99.5	1	Słupsk	R. Plus
5B)	99.5	1	Żmudź	R. Złote Przeboje
2C)	99.6	1	Konin	Meloradio
1C)	99.7	1	Koszalin	R. RMF MAXXX
9)	99.7	1	Mogilno	Wasze R. FM
3)	100.0	5	Zielona Góra	R. Maryja
1A)	100.1	120	Krosno	R. RMF FM
5B)	100.1	4	Warszawa	R. Złote Przeboje
1A)	100.2	120	Białystok	R. RMF FM
64)	100.2	5	Zabrze	R. Fest
)	100.2	1	Giżycko	R. Maryja
3)	100.3	1	Bogatynia	R. Maryja
48)	100.3	3	Racibórz	R. Vanessa
3)	100.4	1	Nysa	R. Maryja
3)	100.4	5.5	Ostrów Maz.	R. Maryja
4C)	100.4	5	Łódź	R. Plus
3)	100.4	5	Ostróda	R. Maryja
3)	100.6	5	Parczew	R. Maryja
3)	100.6	10	Glogów	R. Maryja
3)	100.6	10	Krosno	R. Maryja
3)	100.6	10	Toruń	R. Maryja
40)	100.6	60	Częstochowa	R. Jasna Góra
2A)	100.7	2	Zamość	R. ZET
3)	100.7	5	Rabka	R. Maryja
4C)	100.7	10	Gorzów Wlkp.	R. Plus
1A)	100.8	10	Jelenia Góra	R. RMF FM
32)	100.8	5	Kielce	R. FAMA
1A)	100.9	10	Słupsk	R. RMF FM
3)	100.9	1	Włocławek	R. Maryja
2D)	101.0	1	Kraków	Antyradio
1A)	101.1	30	Solina	R. RMF FM
1C)	101.1	5	Wałbrzych	R. RMF MAXXX
3)	101.1	10	Złotów	R. Maryja
4A)	101.1	2	Kalisz	R. Eska
13)	101.2	1	Lubaczów	Katolickie R. Zamość
1A)	101.2	10	Świnoujście	R. RMF FM
1C)	101.2	1	Bytów	R. RMF MAXXX
3)	101.2	10	Żagań	R. Maryja
58)	101.2	2.5	Szczawnica	R. RDN
5A)	101.2	1	Płock	R. TOK FM
2C)	101.3	1	Kraków	Meloradio
3)	101.3	3	Łomża	R. Maryja
5B)	101.3	10	Pabianice	R. Złote Przeboje
2A)	101.4	30	Suwałki	R. ZET
3)	101.4	10	Czersk	R. Maryja
4B)	101.5	1	Wrocław	R. VOX FM
1A)	101.6	10	Kłodzko	R. RMF FM
2D)	101.6	1	Poznań	Antyradio
3)	101.6	1	Szczecin	R. Maryja
3)	101.6	10	Pisz	R. Maryja
28)	101.7	1	Jarocin	R. Elka
46)	101.7	35	Siedlce	Katolickie R. Podlasie
4C)	101.7	120	Gdańsk	R. Plus
62)	101.7	1	Kępno	R. Sud
1A)	101.8	10	Zakopane	R. RMF FM
1A)	101.8	60	Leżajsk	R. RMF FM
28)	101.8	1	Jarocin	R. Elka
49)	101.9	1	Jasło	Trendy R.
1A)	102.0	10	Giżycko	R. RMF FM
3)	102.0	10	Bielsk Podl.	R. Maryja

FM	MHz	kW	Location	Station
4A)	102.0	1	Leszno	R. Eska
3)	102.3	10	Lubaczów	R. Maryja
3)	102.4	1	Kartuzy	R. Maryja
5D)	102.4	1	Kraków	R. Pogoda
6)	102.4	1	Mielec	R. Leliwa
18)	102.6	1	Ełk	R. 5 Elk
1C)	102.6	1	Częstochowa	R. RMF MAXXX
3)	102.6	10	Tarnów	R. Maryja
4C)	102.6	1	Bydgoszcz	R. Plus
4C)	102.6	1	Koszalin	R. Plus
4C)	102.6	20	Polkowice	R. Plus
37)	102.7	1	Białystok	R. Orthodoxia
4C)	102.7	5	Rabka	R. Plus
51)	102.7	1	Skierniewice	R. Niepokalanów
2A)	102.8	5	Katowice	R. ZET
2A)	102.8	10	Ostrołęka	R. ZET
3)	102.8	2	Chełm	R. Maryja
3)	102.8	10	Kluczbork	R. Maryja
4C)	102.8	1	Świeradów-Zdrój	R. Plus
1A)	102.9	8	Wałbrzych	R. RMF FM
1C)	102.9	1	Lębork	R. RMF MAXXX
2A)	102.9	12	Przysucha	R. ZET
2C)	102.9	1	Słupca	Meloradio
3)	102.9	10	Gryfice	R. Maryja
5A)	102.9	1	Kraków	R. TOK FM
44)	103.0	3	Warszawa	R. Kolor 103 FM
5B)	103.0	2	Gdańsk	R. Złote Przeboje
2A)	103.1	30	Solina	R. ZET
60)	103.1	1	Kalisz	R. Rodzina Kalisz
1A)	103.2	10	Szczawnica	R. RMF FM
41)	103.3	1	Białystok	R. i
4A)	103.3	1	Kielce	R. Eska
1A)	103.4	7	Lębork	R. RMF FM
1A)	103.4	10	Przemyśl	R. RMF FM
2A)	103.4	60	Częstochowa	R. ZET
3)	103.5	3	Trzcińsko-Zdrój	R. Maryja
52)	103.5	5	Lowicz	R. Victoria
5D)	103.5	1	Bydgoszcz	R. Pogoda
21)	103.6	2	Nysa	R. Nysa FM
50)	103.6	10	Łomża	R. Nadzieja
58)	103.6	30	Tarnów	R. RDN
4A)	103.6	1	Lublin	R. Eska
3)	103.7	3	Katowice	R. Maryja
56)	103.7	1	Wrocław	R. MUZO.FM
12)	103.8	10	Rzeszów	VIA - Kat. R. Rzeszów
2A)	103.8	10	Klodzko	R. ZET
5C)	103.8	1	Kraków	Rock R.
2C)	103.9	2	Kielce	Meloradio
45)	103.9	1.5	Ciechanów	KRDP FM
2A)	104.0	10	Giżycko	R. ZET
3)	104.0	10	Swiecie	R. Maryja
1C)	104.1	5	Piła	R. RMF MAXXX
2A)	104.1	60	Kraków	R. ZET
32)	104.1	1	Żyrardów	R. FAMA
2A)	104.2	10	Białogard	R. ZET
2A)	104.2	9.1	Jelenia Góra	R. ZET
3)	104.2	10	Elbląg	R. Maryja
45)	104.3	1	Płock	KRDP FM
4C)	104.3	1	Myślibórz	R. Plus
2A)	104.4	10	Kalisz	R. ZET
3)	104.4	1	Stalowa Wola	R. Maryja
4B)	104.4	1	Gdańsk	R. VOX FM
2C)	104.5	1	Łódź	Meloradio
3)	104.5	5	Wieleń	R. Maryja
3)	104.5	10	Włodawa	R. Maryja
34)	104.5	1	Krosno	R. Fara
3)	104.6	2	Opole	R. Maryja
4A)	104.6	1	Toruń	R. Eska
15)	104.7	2	Sieradz	Nasze R.
1A)	104.7	3	Rabka	R. RMF FM
3)	104.7	10	Łobez	R. Maryja
3)	104.7	120	Białystok	R. Maryja
11)	104.9	1	Chełm	Bon Ton R.
1A)	104.9	1	Koszalin	R. RMF FM
2C)	104.9	1.5	Mrągowo	Meloradio
4A)	104.9	10	Krosno	R. Eska
4A)	104.9	60	Wrocław	R. Eska
56)	104.9	1	Kraków	R. MUZO.FM
2A)	105.0	120	Gdańsk	R. ZET
2D)	105.0	1	Bielsko-Biała	Antyradio
3)	105.1	1	Przemyśl	R. Maryja
3)	105.1	10	Ełk	R. Maryja
3)	105.1	30	Konin	R. Maryja
20)	105.2	1	Zakopane	R. Alex
3)	105.2	5	Wieluń	R. Maryja
2A)	105.3	30	Koszalin	R. ZET
2A)	105.3	60	Kielce	R. ZET
3)	105.3	1	Płońsk	R. Maryja
2A)	105.4	30	Siedlce	R. ZET
5A)	105.4	2	Zduńska Wola	R. TOK FM
5C)	105.4	1	Poznań	Rock R.
4D)	105.5	3	Wrocław	R. WAWA
3)	105.6	1	Kalisz	R. Maryja
4A)	105.6	1	Piła	R. Eska
4A)	105.6	5	Warszawa	R. Eska
4B)	105.6	1	Gdynia	R. VOX FM
5B)	105.6	1	Międzyzdroje	R. Złote Przeboje
2A)	105.7	20	Olsztyn	R. ZET
4D)	105.7	1	Opole	R. WAWA
14)	105.8	10	Jelenia Góra	Muzyczne R.
9)	105.8	2	Gołańcz	Wasze R. FM
1A)	105.9	60	Częstochowa	R. RMF FM
46)	106.0	1	Garwolin	Katolickie R. Podlasie
1C)	106.1	5	Bydgoszcz	R. RMF MAXXX
4C)	106.1	10	Kraków	R. Plus
5D)	106.1	10	Wrocław	R. Pogoda
7)	106.1	1	Hel	R. Kaszëbë
4B)	106.1	2	Lublin	R. VOX FM
17)	106.2	1	Radom	R. Rekord FM
2C)	106.2	1	Opole	Meloradio
3)	106.2	11	Lidzbark Warm.	R. Maryja
30)	106.2	1.5	Poznań	R. Emaus
35)	106.2	1	Warszawa	R. Warszawa
5B)	106.2	1	Jelenia Góra	R. Złote Przeboje
2A)	106.3	8	Zakopane	R. ZET
3)	106.3	5	Kłodzko	R. Maryja
3)	106.3	20	Leżajsk	R. Maryja
3)	106.3	60	Płock	R. Maryja
1A)	106.4	60	Zielona Góra	R. RMF FM
26)	106.4	10	Kalisz	R. Centrum
2D)	106.4	1	Zabrze	Antyradio
1A)	106.5	10	Ełk	R. RMF FM
1C)	106.5	20	Kielce	R. RMF MAXXX
4A)	106.5	1	Łobez	R. Eska
4A)	106.6	5	Żary	R. Eska
5C)	106.6	4	Opole	Rock R.
14)	106.7	5	Świeradów-Zdrój	Muzyczne R.
1A)	106.7	60	Szczecin	R. RMF FM
1C)	106.7	3	Gdynia	R. RMF MAXXX
47)	106.7	1	Bielsko-Biała	R. Bielsko
3)	106.8	110	Poznań	R. Maryja
4A)	106.8	1	Bochnia	R. Eska
2D)	106.9	2	Wrocław	Antyradio
4A)	106.9	10	Radom	R. Eska
2A)	107.0	40	Lublin	R. ZET
2C)	107.0	2	Giżycko	Meloradio
3)	107.0	10	Częstochowa	R. Maryja
4B)	107.0	1.6	Kraków	R. VOX FM
1B)	107.1	1	Gdynia	R. RMF Classic
2A)	107.1	30	Konin	R. ZET
3)	107.2	120	Kielce	R. Maryja
59)	107.2	2	Bystrzyca Klodzka	R. Rodzina
2A)	107.3	120	Białystok	R. ZET
1A)	107.4	10	Iława	R. RMF FM
2A)	107.4	1	Kluczbork	R. ZET
2A)	107.4	30	Krosno	R. ZET
3)	107.4	1	Koszalin	R. Maryja
3)	107.4	2.5	Wałbrzych	R. Maryja
4B)	107.4	1	Poznań	R. VOX FM
2A)	107.5	30	Warszawa	R. ZET
68)	107.5	1	Nakło	R. Nakło
29)	107.6	60	Katowice	R. eM
1A)	107.7	15	Zamość	R. RMF FM
3)	107.7	10	Siedlce	R. Maryja
3)	107.7	20	Olsztyn	R. Maryja
2A)	107.8	10	Tarnów	R. ZET
29)	107.9	1	Kielce	R. eM
2A)	107.9	10	Przemyśl	R. ZET

FM	MHz	kW	Location	Station
3)	107.9	10	Ryki	R. Maryja
3)	107.9	20	Suwałki	R. Maryja
33)	107.9	10	Opole	R. DOXA

+ txs below 1kW.

Addresses & other information:
1A-C) al. Waszyngtona 1, 30-204 Kraków – **2A-D)** ul. Żurawia 8, 00-503 Warszawa – **3)** ul. Żwirki i Wigury 80, 87-100 Toruń – **4A-E)** ul. Jubilerska 10, 04-190 Warszawa – **5A-D)** ul. Czerska 14, 00-732 Warszawa – **6)** ul. Wyspiańskiego 12/5, 39-400 Tarnobrzeg – **7)** ul. Mireckiego 12, 81-229 Gdynia – **8)** ul. Piaski 9, 87-800 Włocławek – **9)** ul. Przemysłowa 7A, 62-100 Wągrowiec – **10)** Park Hutniczy 3-5, 41-800 Zabrze – **11)** ul. Lubelska 31, 22-100 Chełm – **12)** ul. Zamkowa 4, 35-032 Rzeszów – **13)** ul. Hetmana J. Zamoyskiego 1, 22-400 Zamość – **14)** pl. Kat. S. Wyszyńskiego 45/1, 58-500 Jelenia Góra – **15)** ul. Rynek 14, 98-200 Sieradz – **16)** ul. Żwirki 21B, 06-500 Mława – **17)** ul. Okulickiego 39, 26-600 Radom – **18)** ul. Małeckich 2, 19-300 Ełk – **19)** ul. Rudzka 13E, 44-200 Rybnik – **20)** ul. Smrekowa 26A, 34-500 Zakopane – **21)** ul. Podolska 22, 48-300 Nysa – **22)** ul. Ciepła 1/7, 15-472 Białystok – **23)** Spółdzielcza 9, 05-825 Grodzisk Mazowiecki – **24)** Gen. Fieldorfa-Nila 8, 24-100 Puławy – **25)** ul. Pszczyńska 44A, 44-100 Gliwice – **26)** ul. Częstochowska 12, 62-800 Kalisz – **27)** ul. Zwierzyniecka 4, 15-333 Białystok – **28)** ul. Sienkiewicza 30A, 64-100 Leszno – **29)** ul. Wita Stwosza 11, 40-042 Katowice – **30)** ul. Chartowo 5, 61-245 Poznań – **31)** ul. Narutowicza 1, 96-500 Sochaczew – **32)** ul. Kozia 2, 25-514 Kielce – **33)** ul. Koraszewskiego 7-9, 45-011 Opole – **34)** ul. Grodzka 11, 37-700 Przemyśl – **35)** ul. Floriańska 3, 03-707 Warszawa – **36)** ul. Ogrodowa 24/44, 42-200 Częstochowa – **37)** ul. Antoniuk Fabryczny 13, 15-762 Białystok – **38)** ul. Biskupa Dominika 11, 83-130 Pelplin – **39)** al. Jana Pawła II 54, 15-703 Białystok – **40)** ul. O. Augustyna Kordeckiego 2, 42-225 Częstochowa – **41)** ul. Św. M.M. Kolbego 8, 15-174 Białystok – **42)** ul. Jana Pawła II 1B, 89-804 Chojnice – **43)** ul. Czarnieckiego 7, 78-100 Kołobrzeg – **44)** ul. Narbutta 41/43, 02-536 Warszawa – **45)** ul. ks. Piotra Ściegiennego 18, 06-400 Ciechanów – **46)** ul. Biskupa Świrskiego 56, 08-110 Siedlce – **47)** ul. Olszówka 62, 43-309 Bielsko-Biała – **48)** ul. Batorego 5, 47-400 Racibórz – **49)** ul. Rynek 25, 38-400 Krosno – **50)** ul. Sadowa 3, 18-400 Łomża – **51)** ul. O.Maksymiliana Kolbego 5, 96-515 Teresin – **52)** ul. Seminaryjna 6A, 99-400 Łowicz – **53)** ul. Piłsudskiego 141, 92-318 Łódź – **54)** ul. Piastowska 1, 47-200 Kędzierzyn-Koźle – **55)** ul. Olszówka 62, 43-309 Bielsko-Biała – **56)** ul. Ostrobramska 77, 04-175 Warszawa – **57)** ul. Kanafojskiego 1/14, 10-724 Olsztyn – **58)** ul. Gen. Józefa Bema 14, 33-100 Tarnów – **59)** ul. Katedralna 13, 50-328 Wrocław – **60)** ul. Złota 144, 62-810 Kalisz – **61)** ul. Sobieskiego 81, 96-100 Skierniewice – **62)** al. Marcinkowskiego 12k, 63-600 Kępno – **63)** ul. Św. Jana Chrzciciela 14, 43-346 Bielsko-Biała – **64)** ul. Pszczyńska 44A. 44-100 Gliwice – **65)** ul. Wilsona 6, 42-200 Częstochowa – **66)** ul. Piłsudskiego 105, 73-110 Stargard – **67)** Stary Rynek 5, 09-402 Płock – **68)** ul. Mickiewicza 3, 89-100 Nakło – **69)** ul. Fatimska 13A, 31-831 Kraków. Affiliates with own prgrs at times: 69A) ul. Iłżecka 6A, 27-300 Lipsko **E:** radio@lipsko.eu; 69B) ul. Krakowska 74, 34-120 Andrychów **E:** radio@andrychow.eu.

DAB Transmitters (DAB+)
Licensee Mux PR: Polskie R. **M:** PR1-4, PR24, PR R. Chopin, PR R. Dzieciom, PR Regional stns, PR R. Poland – **Licensee Mux Dabcast:** BCAST Sp. z o.o. **M:** R. Kolor 103 FM, R. MUZO.FM, R. Maryja, R. RAM, R. Bezpieczna Podróż, Mega R., R. Profeto, Akademickie R. Kampus, R. 7, R. Rekord FM (Mux is subject to local variations) – **Local/Experimental Muxes:** not shown.

Block	kW	Location	Mux
5B	24	Gdańsk (Chwaszczyno)	PR
5B	5.9	Wrocław (Żórawina)	PR
5C	2	Białystok (Krynice)	PR
5C	9.3	Łódź	PR
5D	1	Gdańsk	Dabcast
6B	11	Warszawa (PKiN)	PR
10A	1	Warszawa	Dabcast
10A	0.5	Wrocław	Dabcast
10D	-	SFN (Kielce)	PR
11A	10	Bydgoszcz (Solec Kujawski)	PR
11A	19	Katowice (Kosztowy)	PR
11A	15	Rzeszów (Sucha Góra)	PR
11A	15	Szczecin (Kołowo)	PR
11B	-	SFN (Kołobrzeg, Koszalin)	PR
11B	10	Kraków (Chorągwica)	PR
11B	5	Lublin (Piaski)	PR
11B	7.6	Olsztyn (Pieczewo)	PR
11C	-	SFN (Opole)	PR
11C	-	SFN (Zielona Góra)	PR
12A	-	SFN (Poznań)	PR

PORTUGAL

L.T: UTC (28 Mar-31 Oct: +1h) — **Pop:** 10.3 million — **Pr.L:** Portuguese — **E.C:** 230V/50Hz — **ITU:** POR

ANACOM – Autoridade Nacional de Comunicações
🖃 HQ: Avenida José Malhoa, 12, 1099-017 Lisboa ☎ +351 21 721 10 00 🖷 +351 21 721 10 01 **W:** anacom.pt **E:** info@anacom.pt
Gov. body responsible for licensing & monitoring radio & TV txs

APR – Associação Portuguesa de Radiodifusão (Assoc. of Portuguese Broadcasters)
🖃 Avenida Defensores de Chaves, nº 65 - 3º, 1000-113 Lisboa ☎ +351 213 015 453/+351 213 015 459/ +351 213 016 999 🖷 +351 21 301 65 36 **W:** apradiodifusao.pt **E:** apr@apradiofusao.pt

RTP-Rádio e Televisão de Portugal, SGPS (Pub)
🖃 Av. Marechal Gomes da Costa, 37, 1849-030 Lisboa ☎ +351 21 794 70 00 🖷 +351 21 794 75 70 **W:** rtp.pt **E:** info@rtp.pt **LP:** Chmn: Gonçalo Reis
Antena 1/Antena 2/Antena 3/RDP Africa/RDP Açores/RDP Madeira/RDP Internacional: ☎ +351 21 382 00 00. Antena 1 🖷 +351-21-382 00 70 🖷 +351-21-382 00 05, Antena 2 ☎ +351-21-382 02 82 🖷 +351-21-382 01 99, Antena 3 +351-21-382 02 02 ☎ +351-21-382 00 17, RDP África ☎ +351-21-382 02 12 🖷 +351-21 382 00 81.
News Dept: ☎ +351-21 382 00 02 🖷 +351-21 382 01 83
L.P: Chmn. bd of Dirs: Gonçalo Reis, Dir. of Antena 1, RDPi & RDP África: Rui Fernandes Pêgo, Dir. of Antena 2: João Almeida, Dir. of Antena 3: Nuno Reis, Dir. of RDP África: Jorge Oliveira Gonçalves , Reg. Dir. Açores & Madeira: see respective country entries, Technical info. & support may be obtained from **E:** gabinete.tecnologias@rtp.pt
Ann: "Antena 1, a rádio que liga Portugal", "Antena 2, a rádio clássica", "Antena 3, a alternativa pop"

MW Antena 1	kHz	kW	MW Antena 1	kHz	kW
Miranda do Douro	630	2	Viseu	666	10
Montemor-o Velho	630	10	Elvas	720	10
Bragança	666	2	Guarda	720	10
Castª Ribatejo* #	666	2	Castelo Branco	720	10
Covilhã	666	10	Mirandela	720	10
Valença #	666	2.5	Lamego ‡	756	2
Vila Real #	666	8	Portalegre	1287	2

*) Castanheira do Ribatejo, North of Lisbon; also known as "CEN" (Centro Emissor Nacional)
‡ inactive due to technical breakdown # 10kW nominal

FM (MHz)	Ant. 1	Ant. 2	Ant. 3	kW
Alcoutim	88.9	91.5	101.9	0.2
Arestal (Aveiro)	106.7	95.2	-	0.5
Bornes %	92.8	91.1	102.1	10
Braga (Sameiro)	91.3	88.0	103.0	10/2/10
Bragança	96.4	98.2	104.2	9
Castelo Branco	89.9	94.9	104.3	0.5
Coimbra (a)	94.9	-	-	4
Elvas (Vª Boim)	103.8	93.2	101.6	5.4
Faro (S.Miguel) (b)	97.6	93.4	100.7	10
Gardunha	96.4	93.9	101.3	10
Grândola	99.2	90.6	103.6	10
Gravia $	104.5	106.8	107.9	0.1
Guarda	94.7	88.4	100.6	6.4
Janas (Sintra)	96.9	96.0	103.8	0.2
Leiria	98.7	104.2	106.4	1
Lisboa (Banática)	99.4	88.9	100.0	1/0.3/0.3
Lisboa (Monsanto) (c)	95.7	94.4	100.3	10
Lousã	87.9	89.3	102.2	34/34/39
Manteigas	104.8	91.6	100.3	0.5
Marão (Vila Real)	95.2	99.8	101.5	9
Marofa §	97.2	93.4	104.6	20/20/10
Mendro	87.7	91.1	102.4	20/20/44
Mértola	90.9	92.2	100.1	0.4
Minhéu (V. P. Aguiar)*	94.9	88.0	104.7	10
Miranda do Douro	90.3	95.7	98.9	0.05
Moledo	102.9	88.0	92.3	0.5
Monchique (Fóia)	88.9	91.5	101.9	25
Montargil	93.6	99.6	105.0	3

FM (MHz)	Ant. 1	Ant. 2	Ant. 3	kW
Montejunto	98.3	88.7	105.2	10
Muro	88.3	94.6	102.0	10
Paredes de Coura	102.9		92.3	0.1
Pte. de Lima (Rendufe)	89.2	92.2	104.9	0.3
Portalegre	97.9	92.9	102.8	10
Porto (Mte. da Virgem)	96.7	92.5	100.4	44/44/50
Santarém	98.8	-	-	0.4
S. Domingos	87.9	89.3	103.7	0.2
Serra de Ossa	88.4	95.0	102.1	2/0.5/0.5
Tróia (Setúbal)	106.7	99.7	107.9	0.07
Túnel do Marão #	95.2	-	101.5	
Valença	98.2	89.6	104.0	10
Viseu	88.2	97.5	101.8	0.5/0.5/0.7

* District of Vila Real; § District of Guarda
# Tunnel tx in motorway A4 between Amarante and Vila Real
% District of Bragança; $ São Pedro do Sul, near Viseu

RDP África: a) 103.4MHz 1kW, **b)** 99.1MHz 1kW, **c)** 101.5MHz 4kW
D.Prgrs: 24h **Ant. 1**=Antena 1 (general pt rgrs, sport), **Ant. 2**=Antena 2 (classical music, culture), **Ant. 3**=Antena 3 (pop/rock music), **RDP África** (general prgrs for the Portuguese-speaking African community.
RDP abroad: txs in Cape Verde, Guinea-Bissau, São Tomé e Príncipe, Mozambique, all relaying RDP África, txs in Timor (Díli), relaying RDPi and Antena 1 and one tx for RDPi in Bosnia for the Portuguese peace-keeping force, operated by the military (see respective country entries). **RDP África:** ✉ Av. Marechal Gomes da Costa, 37, 1849-030 Lisboa ☎ +351 21 382 00 00 🖷 +351 21 382 00 81 **LP:** Dir: Jorge Oliveira Gonçalves **E:** rdpafrica@rtp.pt

Web Radio: Audio feeds at **W:** rtp.pt/play Antenas 1, 2 & 3, RDP-África, RDP-Internacional, RDP-Madeira (Antena 1 Madeira and Antena 3 Madeira) and RDP-Açores, plus 7 web-only radios.
Satellite: Europe, N. Africa & Mid. East: Hot Bird 13C (13° E), Transponder 7 (11.33433 GHz), Ku Band, H. Pol., FEC: ¾, SyR: 27.5 Ms/s, RDPi: PID 2502 (stereo), RDP Ant. 1: PID 2602 (mono), 24h. **Africa:** Intelsat 901 (27.5° W), DVB-S2 standard, Transponder 22, C Band, Right Circ. Pol., Symbol Rate 8.843 MSps. Freq. 3830.320 MHz; prgrs: RDP África: audio PID d 412 (mono), RDPi: audio PID d 413 (stereo), Ant. 1: audio PID d 411 (mono). **Asia & Oceania:** Asiasat 5 (digital) (100.5°E), DVB-S2 standard, "European Bouquet", Transponder C06V (3860 MHz), C Band, Ver. Pol. on 30.000 Ms/s, FEC ¾. RDP Int. stereo on the audio ch. 29, RDP Ant. 1 aired on the audio ch. 30. **N.America & Hawaii:** Galaxy 19 (digital) (97° W), Transponder K26, Frequency 12125.5 MHz, Ku Band, H. Pol., SyR 20.4667 Ms/s, FEC ¾. RDP Int. audio PID: 4001 (stereo). **The Americas**: Intelsat 34 (55.5° W), DVB-S2 standard, Transponder AE17C/AE17C (4100.6 MHz), C Band, V. Pol., SyR 2.2222 Ms/s, FEC 8/9. RDP Int.: PID 413. **S.America:** Telstar 14 / Estrela do Sul 2 (63°W), transponder 13, 11710MHz, ku Band, Vert. Pol., Sy.Rate 3200, FEC 2/3. RDP Int.: PID 268 (stereo).
DAB: RDP halted T-DAB broadcasts in June 2011. The network may be restored but there are no current plans to reactivate this service.

RÁDIO COMERCIAL, S.A. (Priv., comm.)
Owned by Media Capital Rádio – Radiofonia e Publicidade, S.A. **W:** mcr.iol.pt **E:** contacto@mcr.iol.pt
✉ Rua Sampaio e Pina, 24-26, 1099-044 Lisboa ☎ +351 21 382 15 00 🖷 +351 21 382 15 89 **E:** programas@radiocomercial.iol.pt, Northern office: Rua Tenente Valadim, 181, 4100 Porto ☎ +351 22 605 75 00 **W:** radiocomercial.iol.pt **LP:** Dir. Gen. MCR Rádios: Salvador Bourbon Ribeiro

FM	MHz	kW	FM	MHz	kW
Fóia (Monchique)	88.1	10	Guarda	96.1	10
Moledo	88.5	0.2	São Miguel (Faro)	96.1	10
Lamego	88.7	5	Grândola	96.8	10
Minhéu (Vila Real)	88.9	10	Monsanto (Lisboa)	97.4	44
Leiria	89.0	1	Monte da Virgem (Porto)	97.7	44
Viana do Castelo	89.3	0.4	Gardunha	98.2	10
Lousã	90.8	44	Valongo	98.2	0.1
Bornes	91.9	10	Sintra	98.5	0.3
Mendro	92.0	50	Portalegre	98.9	10
Aveiro	92.2	0.2	Valença	99.0	10
Bragança	93.9	10	Braga	99.2	10
Soajo*	94.2	0.4	Montejunto	99.8	10
Viseu	94.3	0.5	Pico da Pena (Vouzela)	103.1	0.2
Mértola	95.8	0.4	Vila Boim (Elvas)	105.9	1

* Arcos de Valdevez, district of Viana do Castelo

D.Prgr: 24h **Ann:** Rádio Comercial. **Format**: music stn
Web Radio: R. Comercial plus 5 web-only radios selectable at **W:** radiocomercial.iol.pt/player

Local FM stns in the same group:
M80: (see Southern network) – **Cidade FM** (**W:** cidadefm.iol.pt): txs in Lisboa 91.6MHz 5 kW, Montijo (Lisboa region) 106.2MHz 1kW , Vila Nova de Gaia (Monte da Virgem, near Porto) 107.2MHz 0.5kW, Alcanena (Santarém) 99.3MHz 2kW, Penacova (Coimbra) & Loulé (Algarve province), 99.7MHz 1/2kW , Redondo (Alentejo province) 97.2MHz 0.5kW, Vale de Cambra (near Aveiro) 101.0 MHz 0.5kW, Viseu 102.8 MHz 2kW, Amares (Braga) 104.4MHz 1 kW, – **Smooth FM** (**W:** smoothfm.iol.pt) : txs in Lisboa 96.6 MHz 5kW, Barreiro (Lisboa region) 103.0MHz 2kW, Matosinhos (near Porto) 89.5MHz 1.5kW, Figueiró dos Vinhos (near Coimbra) 92.8MHz 1kW & Santarém 97.7MHz 2kW – **Vodafone FM** (**W:** vodafone.fm): txs in Amadora (Lisboa reg.) 107.2MHz 1.5kW, Moita (near Lisboa) 101.1MHz 1.5kW, Maia (near Porto) 94.3MHz 1.5kW & Cantanhede (near Coimbra) 103.0MHz 2 kW

RÁDIO RENASCENÇA – Em. Católica Portuguesa (Rlg/Comm)
✉ Quinta do Bom Pastor, Estrada da Buraca 8-12, 1549-025 Lisboa ☎ +351 21 323 92 00 🖷 +351 21 323 92 99 **E:** mail@rr.pt (**PR: E:** rp@rr.pt) **W:** rr.sapo.pt & rfm.sapo.pt & radiosim.sapo.pt & megahits.sapo.pt
L.P: News Dir.: Drª Graça Franco, PD (R. Renascença): Drª Dina Isabel, PD (RFM): Dr. António Mendes, PD (Mega Hits): Nelson Cunha

NB: Rádio Sim was discontinued by RR and it is expected to close soon. MW & FM frequencies belonging to RR national network broadcast now Rádio Renascença (main channel). As of September 2020, local FM stations at Palmela, Maia & Portel (see below) still broadcast R. Sim (automated station playing music continuously).

MW: RR	kHz	kW	MW: RR	kHz	kW
Castelo Branco	1251	1	Seixal*	963	1
Chaves	1251	1	Vilamoura#	891	2.5
Coimbra#	981	3			

* 1x10 kW main tx; 1x1kW standby unit. RR has been broadcasting using the latter. ‡ inactive # 10kW nominal

FM (MHz)	RR	RFM	kW
Aveiro	102.5	97.4	0.2
Arrábida	105.8	89.9	10/12
Bornes	89.6	101.1	10
Braga	101.1	89.7	10/1
Bragança	105.7	99.5	10
Elvas	102.3	-	0.1
Elvas/V.ª Boim	99.8	107.1	1
Fóia (Monchique)	98.6	104.9	12
Gardunha	103.4	99.5	10
Guarda	90.2	104.0	10
Lamego	98.6	106.2	12
Leiria	95.1	107.7	2/3
Lisboa	103.4	93.2	50
Lousã	106.0	91.7	50/56
Marofa	94.2	103.0	16/10
Mendro	96.5	100.9	50
Minhéu	89.8	102.6	10
Monte da Virgem	93.7	104.1	50
Montejunto	90.2	106.8	10
Muro	103.4	90.4	10/20
Pena (Vouzela)	93.8	95.0	0.4
Penafiel	90.2	102.3	1
S. Mamede	95.3	101.1	10
São Miguel	103.8	89.6	10
Serra de Ossa	98.5	89.7	2
Sintra	105.0	106.6	0.3
Túnel do Marão	94.2	-	
Valença	100.0	95.4	10
Valongo	104.5	106.2	0.4/1
Viseu	103.6	99.4	1

D.Prgr.: 24h. **Ann:** "Renascença - música e informação dia-a-dia.", "RFM - só grandes músicas"
Some prgs are simulcast on RR Canal 1 & R. Sim
Web Radio: RR, RFM, Mega Hits & R. Sim have audio feeds available at the respective websites. RFM has 4 webradios selectable at **W:** rfm.sapo.pt

Local FM stns of the R. Renascença group: Mega Hits (**W:** megahits.sapo.pt): txs in Lisboa 92.4MHz 5kW, Sintra (west of Lisboa) 88.0MHz 1 kW, Rio Maior (near Santarém) 92.6MHz 1kW & 99.5MHz 0.05kW; Coimbra 90.0MHz 5kW, Aveiro 96.5MHz 2kW, Gondomar (Porto region) 90.6MHz 2kW, Braga 92.9MHz 2kW and Viseu 106.4 MHz 2kW
Local FM stns airing R. Sim: R. Sim Pal Palmela (near Lisboa): 102.2MHz 2kW; **R. Sim Porto** Maia (near Porto): tx in Valongo 100.8MHz 1.5kW; **R. Sim Alentejo** Portel (near Évora): 97.5 MHz 0.5kW.

Regional FM networks:
Northern network
RÁDIO NOTÍCIAS, PRODUÇÕES E PUBLICIDADE, S.A.
✉ Rua Tomás da Fonseca, Torres de Lisboa, Torre E - 4º Piso, 1600-209 Lisboa ☎ +351 21 861 25 00 🖷 +351 21 861 25 07/8/10 **LP:** Chmn.: José Pedro Soeiro, TD: Pedro Pinheiro, Dir tx network: José de Sousa
TSF Northern office & Radiopress HQ: ✉ Rua Gonçalo Cristóvão, 195, 4017-001 Porto ☎ +351 222 096 350🖷 +351 222 096 163
E: tsf@tsf.pt **W:** tsf.pt
Station: TSF (priv., comm.)

FM	MHz	kW	FM	MHz	kW
Pena (Vouzela)	102.5	0.1	Guarda	106.6	10
Bornes	103.2	10	Minhéu	106.7	10
Gardunha	105.1	10	Braga	106.9	10
Valongo (Porto)	105.3	50	Bragança	107.0	10
Marofa	105.4	10	Lousã	107.4	50
Valença	105.7	10	Marão	107.6	10
Muro	106.5	10	Túnel do Marão	107.6	

NB: the whole netw. relays key stn TSF 89.5MHz 5kW Lisboa . TSF broadcasts 24 hours/day via **R. Jovem** 105.4MHz 2kW Évora , **R. Santa Maria** 101.6MHz 2kW Faro (Algarve) and **R. Caldas** 103.1 MHz 1kW Caldas da Rainha; in the Açores via **R. Comercial dos Açores-TSF** 99.4MHz 3kW Ponta Delgada (São Miguel isl.) and in Madeira via **R. Notícias-TSF** 100.0MHz 2kW Funchal.
SATELLITE: Europe, N. Africa & Mid. East: Hispasat 30W-5 (30º W), DVB-S2 standard, Transponder 117 (12437 GHz), Ku Band, H. Pol., FEC: ¾, SyR: 27.5 Ms/s, audio PID: 2048
Format: mainly news. **D.Prgr.:** 24h

Southern network
LICENSEE: RÁDIO REGIONAL DE LISBOA, S.A.
(Owned by Média Capital Rádio) ✉ see R. Comercial **W:** m80.iol.pt
Station: M80 Rádio (priv., comm.)

FM	MHz	kW	FM	MHz	kW
Bragança# (Nogueira)	89.2	1	Coimbra #	98.4	5
Porto #	90.0	5	Fafe #	103.8	1
Bragança#	90.0	0.05	Monsanto (Lisboa)	104.3	50
Leiria#	93.0	2	Manteigas#	104.4	0.5
Mogadouro#	93.1	1	Valongo#	105.8	1.5
Aveiro#	94.4	2	São Miguel (Faro)	106.1	10
Penalva do Castelo#	95.6	0.5	Mendro	106.4	50
Montejunto	96.4	10	Portalegre	106.7	10
Sabugal#	96.8	0.5	Fóia (Monchique)	107.1	10
Vila Real #	97.4	1	Grândola	107.5	10

#) txs of associated local stns. **Format:** music oldies from 1970s-2000s. **N:** every h on the h. **D.Prgr:** 24h **Ann:** "M80 Rádio"
Web Radio: M80 plus 10 web-only radios available at W: m80.iol.pt

Other Networks:
Golo FM (Priv., comm.)
✉ Avenida Ramos Pinto, Cais de Gaia, Loja 350, 4400-266 Vila Nova de Gaia ☎+351 221 450 010 **E:** correio@golo.fm **W:** golo.fm **FM:** 89.2MHz 2kW Amarante (near Porto), Bombarral 94.8MHz 1kW (often inactive) & Ponte de Sor (near Portalegre) 96.0MHz 2kW + 105.6MHz 0.050kW (both inactive). **D.Prgr:** 24h **Format:** sports
Rádio Amália (Priv., comm.)
✉ Rua Viriato nº 25, 3º Esqº- 1050-234 Lisboa ☎+351 210 105 740 🖷+351 210 105 769 **W:** amalia.fm **E:** geral@amalia.fm
FM: Loures (near Lisboa) 92.0MHz 2kW & Setúbal 100.6MHz 2kW **D.Prgr:** 24h **Format:** Portuguese music (Fado)
Rádio Dom Bosco (Priv., comm.)
✉ Vilarinho do Tanha, 5000-011 Abaças - Vila Real ☎+351 254 905 108/+351 967 453 017 (☎+351 259 010 069 - studios in Abaças & +351 254 090 144 - studios in Régua) 🖷+351 223 759 675 **E:** radiodombosco@sapo.pt
FM: Lamego 94.1MHz 2kW & Trancoso 92.1MHz 1kW (near Guarda) **D.Prgr:** 24h **Format:** general
Rádio Meo Sudoeste (Priv., comm.)
✉ Rua Viriato, 25 - 4º/6º, 1050-234 Lisboa ☎+351 210 105 765 🖷+351 210 105 769 **W:** radiomeosudoeste.pt **E:** geral@radiomeomusic.pt & info@radiomeomusic.pt
FM: Almada (near Lisboa) 100.8MHz 2kW & Monte da Virgem (V. N. Gaia) 102.7MHz 2kW **D.Prgr:** 24h **Format:** pop/dance music
Rádio SBSR (Priv., comm.)
✉ Rua Viriato, 25 - 3º, 1050-234 Lisboa ☎+351 210 105 730 **W:** sbsr.fm **E:** mail@sbsr.fm
FM: Lisboa 90.4MHz 5kW & Porto 91.0MHz 1.5kW **D.Prgr:** 24h **Format:** indie rock/ independent music
Rádio Estádio (Priv., comm.
✉ Avenida Visconde de Barreiros, 89, 5440-151 Maia ☎+351 937 517 190 **W:** radioestadio.pt **E:** geral@radioestadio.pt
FM: Barreiro (near Lisboa) 96.2MHz 2kW & Póvoa de Varzim (Porto reg.) 89.0MHz 2kW **D.Prgr:** 24h **Format:** sports and music (automated station)
NB: Rádio Estádio ceased activity. As of September 2020, the station has been playing music and recorded sport programmes continuously. The future of the frequencies is not known yet.
Rádio Nova Era (Priv., comm.)
✉ Rua das Camélias, 134 B, 4430-038 Vila Nova de Gaia ☎+351 223 770 180🖷+351 223 759 675 **W:** radionovaera.pt **E:** geral@radionovaera.pt **FM:** Monte da Virgem (V. N. Gaia) 101.3MHz 2kW & Paredes 100.1MHz 2kW (both near Porto) **D.Prgr:** 24h **Format:** dance music
Rádio Observador (Priv., comm.)
✉ Rua João Saraiva, 7, 1700-248 Lisboa ☎ +351 211 937 400 **W:** observador.pt/radio **E:** leitor@observador.pt
FM: Seixal (near Lisboa) 98.7 MHz 1.5 kW & Vila do Conde (near Porto) 98.4 MHz 2 kW **D. Prgr:** 24h **Format:** news
Record FM (Priv., Rlg/Comm)
✉ Rua Dr. Coutinho Pais 25-A, 2770-180 Paço de Arcos ☎+351 214 406 380 **E:** geral@recordfm.pt **W:** recordfm.pt
FM: Sintra (near Lisboa) 107.7MHz 1kW, Monte da Virgem (V. N. Gaia) 95.5MHz 2kW, Silves (Algarve region) 91.8MHz 2kW, Leiria 101.3MHz 2kW, Santarém 101.7MHz 2kW & 105.5MHz 0.05kW. All frequencies carry also local prgs. **D.Prgr:** 24h **Format:** general, religious prgrs. **NB:** Associated local VHF-FM stns relaying prgs from Record FM: **Antena Sul** (**W:** antenasul.pt): Viana do Alentejo (near Évora) 95.5MHz 0.5kW & Almodôvar 90.4MHz 0.5kW

Local Stations (all priv. & comm.)
Rádio Altitude
✉ Rua Batalha Reis - Parque da Saúde, 6300-668 Guarda +351 271 22 19 95 🖷 +351 271 227 193 **E:** altitude@altitude.fm **W:** altitude.fm **LP:** Dir: Rui Isidro
FM: 90.9MHz 2kW 24h **Ann:** "Altitude FM"
NB: R. Altitude owns a MW licence (1584kHz 1kW), but broadcasts only on VHF-FM. As the MW tower had to be dismantled, there are no current plans to reactivate the service soon.
Rádio Elvas
✉ Rua dos Chilões,1 - R/C, 7350-078 Elvas ☎+351 268 62 20 44 🖷 +351 268 62 20 46 **E:** radioelvas@gmail.com
FM: 91.5MHz 0.5kW Vila Boim (Elvas), 103.0MHz 0.05kW São Vicente (Elvas), 104.3MHz 0.05kW Elvas **D.Prgr:** 24h
NB: Associated local VHF-FM stns relaying Rádio Elvas: **Rádio Nova Antena (Montemor-o-Novo)**: 101.3MHz 2kW **W:** radionovaantena.com; **Rádio Campo Maior**: 95.9MHz 0.5kW Campo Maior (near Elvas) **W:** radiocampomaior.com

Other FM stations:

FM	MHz	kW	Station, location
43)	88.2	2	Ultra FM, Vila Franca de Xira
36)	88.6	2	R. Jornal de Setúbal, Setúbal: (effective 0.03kW)
42)	88.6	2	R. Linear, Vila do Conde
44)	89.1	2	R. Lezíria, Vila Franca de Xira
1)	89.7	2	R. Antena Livre, Abrantes
40)	90.5	2	R. Cidade de Tomar, Tomar
41)	90.8	2	R. Geice, Viana do Castelo
9)	91.4	2	R. Íris FM, Benavente
29)	91.8	2	R. Clube de Penafiel, Penafiel
6)	91.9	2	R. Barcelos, Barcelos
12)	92.0	2	R. Castelo Branco, Castelo Branco
19)	92.1	2	R. Maiorca, Figueira da Foz (often open carrier)
5)	92.7	2	ERA FM-Emissora Reg. de Amarante, Amarante
27)	92.8	2	Horizonte FM, Bobadela (Loures)

FM	MHz	kW	Station, location
3)	93.9	2	R. Telefonia do Sul, Alcácer do Sal
46)	94.0	2	R. Cidade Hoje, Vila Nova de Famalicão
24)	94.0	2	R. 94 FM, Leiria
16)	94.1	2	Diana FM, Évora
15)	94.5	2	R. Despertar, Estremoz
14)	94.7	2	R. Voz do Sorraia, Coruche
31)	94.8	5	R. Festival, Porto
38)	94.8	2	R. Gilão, Tavira
21)	95.8	2	R. Fundação, Guimarães
33)	96.1	2	R. Onda Viva, Póvoa de Varzim
37)	96.9	2	R. Horizonte Algarve, Tavira
23)	97.0	2	R. Clube de Lamego, Lamego
4)	97.8	2	Radar, Almada
22)	98.0	2	R. Santiago, Guimarães
39)	98.0	2	R. Hertz, Tomar
11)	98.1	3	R. Marginal, Cascais
32)	98.9	5	R. Nova, Porto
35)	98.9	2	R. Azul, Setúbal: (effective power 0.3 kW)
18)	99.1	2	Foz do Mondego Rádio, Figueira da Foz
2)	99.3	2	R. Soberania, Águeda
30)	100.5	2	R. Portalegre, Portalegre
7)	101.4	2	R. Pax, Beja
26)	101.9	2	Orbital, Sacavém (Loures)
34)	102.7	2	R. M24, Santiago do Cacém
25)	103.1	2	Total FM, Loulé
17)	103.2	2	R. Telefonia do Alentejo, Évora
28)	103.7	2	R. Canção Nova, Ourém
8)	104.5	2	R. Voz da Planície, Beja
45)	105.0	2	Fama Rádio, Vila Nova de Famalicão
47)	105.5	2	RCI-R. Clube do Interior, Viseu
20)	105.8	2	R. "F", Guarda
10)	106.0	2	R. Antena Minho, Braga
13)	107.9	2	R. Universidade de Coimbra, Coimbra

Some stns use 0.05kW repeaters + over 200 stns of less than 2kW

Addresses & other information:

Many stns have websites and may also have webcasting; most, if not all, have an email address. Add country code to tel. & fax nos

1) Rua General Humberto Delgado, Edifício Mira Rio cv / Apartado 65, 2204-909 Abrantes ☎ 241 360170/1 🖷 241 360179 **E:** geral@mediaon.com.pt & luisabludias@mediaon.com.pt **W:** antenalivre.pt – **2)** Rua dos Marnotos, 1 - 1.° D, 3800-220 Aveiro & Rua José Sucena, 120, 3° E, 3750-157 Águeda ☎ 234 331 234 & 234 602 133 🖷 241-624 334 **E:** radiosoberania99.3aveiro@gmail.com **W:** radiosoberania.pt– **3)** Travessa João Rosa, 5A, 7005-665 Évora ☎ 266 703 812 & 917 278 022 **E:** dialogohabil@gmail.com **W:** televisaodosul.pt – **4)** Rua Pêro da Covilhã 34, Restelo, 1400-296 Lisboa ☎ 213 011 901 & 933 035 321 **E:** geral@radarlisboa.fm **W:** radarlisboa.fm – **5)** Rua João Pinto Ribeiro, 186, Edifício de Sta. Luzia, Apartado 64, 4600-035 São Gonçalo, Amarante, ☎ 255 136 045 **E:** geral.erafm@gmail.com **W:** erafm.pt – **6)** Centro Comercial Bolívar, lojas 45-49 / Apartado 129, 4750-180 Arcozelo, Barcelos ☎ 253 823530 /1 🖷 253 823 531 **E:** geral@radiobarcelos.com **W:** radiobarcelos.pt – **7)** Rua de Angola, Torre C-11°, 7800-468 Beja ☎ 284 325 011 🖷 284 326312 **E:** radio@radiopax.com **W:** radiopax.com – **8)** Rua da Misericórdia, 4 / Apartado 368, 7800-285 Beja ☎ 284 311 330 🖷 284 321446 **E:** radio@vozdaplanicie.pt **W:** vozdaplanicie.pt – **9)** Rua dos Operários Agrícolas, 5B, 2135-322 Samora Correia ☎ 263 650 730 🖷 263 650 739 **E:** director@irisfm.pt, informacao@irisfm.pt **W:** irisfm.pt – **10)** Praceta Escola do Magistério, 36 / Apartado 2186, 4700-222 Braga ☎ 253 309560 🖷 253 309569 **E:** info@antenaminho.pt **W:** antenaminho.pt– **11)** Rua Viriato, 25, 4°E , 105-234 Lisboa ☎210 105 742/63 🖷21 0105769 **E:** geral@marginal.fm **W:** marginal.fm – **12)** Avª 1° de Maio, 89, 1° Esquerdo, 6000-086 Castelo Branco ☎ 272 347 346 & 272 321 050 **E:** racabgeral@gmail.com , racabcomercial@gmail.com **W:** radiocastelobranco.pt – **13)** Apartado 1178, 3001-501 Coimbra ☎ 239 851 058/80 🖷239 835 446 **E:** info@ruc.pt, tecnica@ruc.pt & prog@ruc.pt **W:** ruc.pt – **14)** Rua do Couço, 29-r/c frt, 2100-169 Coruche ☎ 243 617436/100 & 927 600 421 🖷 243 617100 **E:** radiovozsorraia@sapo.pt,rvsinformacao@gmail.com **W:** radiovozsorraia.blogspot.com – **15)** Rua Bento de Jesus Caraça, Bloco C 1° Andar, Apartado 76 , 7100-104 Estremoz ☎ 268 339 454 🖷 268 339 456 **E:** geral@radiodespertar.net **W:** radiodespertar.net – **16)** MARÉ, EE08, 7005-873 Évora ☎ 266 700333 🖷 266 700555 **E:** geral@dianafm.com **W:** dianafm.com – **17)** Estrada de Arraiolos, km 2, Arcos da Cartuxa. 7001-951 Évora ☎ 266 730 415 🖷 266 730411 **E:** rtalentejo@gmail.com **W:** radiotelefoniadoalentejo.com.pt– **18)** Rua Detrás da Alfândega n.° 1-A, 3080-063 Figueira da Foz ☎ 233 040 620 🖷 233 428134 **E:** comercialfozdomondego@gmail.com – **19)** Rua Poeta João de Lemos, 6, 3080-476 Maiorca ☎233930500 🖷233 930 499 – **20)** Rua Soeiro Viegas, 2-B, 6300-758 Guarda ☎ 271 221468 🖷 271 221482 **E:** radiof@gmpress.pt **W:** radiof.gmpress.pt – **21)** Rua Arqueólogo Mário Cardozo, Ed. Guimarães Palace 411, Apartado 358, 4800-116 Guimarães ☎ 253 420520/2/5/6 🖷 253 420529 **E:** geral@radiofundacao.net **W:** radiofundacao.net – **22)** Edifício Santiago, Rua Dr. José Sampaio, 264, Apartado 485, 4810-275 Guimarães ☎ 253 421700 🖷 253 421709 **E:** santiago@guimaraesdigital.com, geral@guimaraesdigital.com **W:** guimaraesdigital.com – **23)** Urbanização da Urtigosa, Bloco 6 - R/C, 5100-183 Lamego ☎ 254 609300/1 🖷 254 609309 **E:** geral@rclamego.pt & rclamego97@gmail.com **W:** rclamego.pt – **24)** Av. dos Combatentes da Grande Guerra, Edifício Liz – 10° , 2400-122 Leiria ☎ 244 860090/4 🖷 244 860098 **E:** geral@radio94fm.pt **W:** radio94fm.pt – **25)** Rua da Rádio, Sítio do Troto, 8135-030 Almancil ☎ 289 391 031& 962 437 023 **E:** totalfm@totalfm.pt **W:** totalfm.pt – **26)** Travessa do Olival, 6, 2685-086 Sacavém ☎ 21 9401019 & 21 9427750 🖷 21 9427757 **E:** orbital@orbital.pt **W:** orbital.pt – **I** Rua da Boa Vista, N.° 2-B, 2685-027 Bobadela, Loures ☎ 21 9559215 & 21 9553113 /219 🖷 21 9558465 **E:** geral@horizontefm.pt **W:** horizontefm.pt – **28)** Estrada da Batalha, 68, Edifício Canção Nova/ Apartado 199, 2495-405 Fátima ☎249 530600/3 🖷249 530609 **E:** direcaoradio@cancaonova.pt **W:** radio.cancaonova.pt – **29)** Rua Alfredo Pereira, 14-2°, 4564-909 Penafiel ☎ 255 710040 🖷 255 710049 **E:** info.mail@radioclube-penafiel.pt,jose.ferreira@radioclube-penafiel.pt **W:** radioclube-penafiel.pt – **30)** Av. de Santo António, 22 , Edifício Régio 1, Atelier "A" e "B" /Apartado 154, 7300 -074 Portalegre ☎ 245 300550/7 🖷 245 331630 **E:** geral@radioportalegre.pt **W:** radioportalegre.pt – **31)** Rua da Alegria, 582 - 9 esq°, 4000-037 Porto ☎ 225 101 008 **E:** geral@radiofestival.pt **W:** radiofestival.pt – **32)** Rua Júlio Dinis, 270 Bloco A, 3° piso, 4050-318 Porto ☎ 226 151 000🖷 22 6151001 **E:** nova@radionova.fm **W:** radionova.fm – **33)** Praça dos Combatentes, 15, 4990-439 Póvoa de Varzim ☎ 252 299 570 🖷252 613898 **E:** radioondaviva@sapo.pt **W:** radioondaviva.com – **34)** Rua Condes de Avillez, 19-21, 7540-152 Santiago do Cacém ☎ 269 750600 **E:** mail@radiom24.pt **W:** radiom24.pt – **35)** & **36)** Av. Dr. António Rodrigues Manito, 58 - r/c "B", 2900-061 Setúbal ☎ 265 112023 & 265 119 947 🖷 265 089053, 265 573639 & 969 584 349 **E:** radioazul98.9@gmail.com, radiojornalsetubal@gmail.com **W:** radioazul.pt– **37)** Rua dos Pelames, Terminal Rodoviário, 1°, 8800-411 Tavira ☎ 281 380 240 🖷 281 380 249 **E:** horizontesecretaria@gmail.com **W:** radiohorizonte.com – **38)** Largo de Santa Ana, 1, 8800-701 Tavira ☎ 281 320240 🖷281 325523 **E:** radiogilao@net.vodafone.pt & radiogilao@gmail.com **W:** radiogilao.com – **39)** Rua Centro Republicano, 135, 2300-909 Tomar ☎ 249 323100/20 🖷 249 316995 **E:** radiohertz@radiohertz.pt **W:** radiohertz.pt – **40)** Travessa da Cascalheira, n.° 27, 2300 Tomar ☎ 249 310010 🖷 249 310016 **E:** radio@cidadetomar.pt & redaccao@cidadetomar.pt **W:** radio.cidadetomar.pt – **41)** Rua José Espregueira N°23 R/C, 4900-459 Viana do Castelo ☎ 258 800400 🖷 258 800409 **E:** geral@radiogeice.com **W:** radiogeice.com – **42)** Rua das Donas, 3, 4480-910 Vila do Conde ☎ 252 642426/7/8/9 🖷 252 642303 **E:** radiolinear@gmail.com & radio.linear@outlook.pt **W:** radiolinear.pt – **43)** R. Dr. Sousa Martins, Lote 2, 2725-461 Algueirão-Mem Martins☎ 218 007 558 **E:** geral@ultrafm.pt **W:** ultrafm.pt – **44)** Praça Marquês de Pombal, 2-7°,2600-222 Vila Franca de Xira ☎ 263 3286000 & 917 920 452 🖷 263 3286007 **E:** radioleziria@gmail.com **W:** radioleziria.com– **45)** Rua 8 de Dezembro, 214, Antas S. Tiago, 4760-016 Vila Nova de Famalicão☎ 252 308145 & 963 964 191 🖷 252 308 149 **E:** info@famaradio.pt **W:** famaradio.pt – **46)** R. 5 de Outubro, Edifício Vilarminda, loja 204, 4760-289 Vila Nova de Famalicão ☎ 252 301 780/3 & 917 221 645 🖷 252 301789 **E:** radio@cidadehoje.pt & geral@cidadehoje.pt **W:** cidadehoje.pt – **47)** R. Dom Duarte, 13, 3500-135 Viseu ☎ 232 431 249 & 963 926 687 **E:** info@rci.pt **W:** rci.pt

PUERTO RICO (USA Commonwealth)

L.T: UTC -4h — **Pop**: 2.8 million — **Pr.L:** English (official), Spanish (official) — **E.C:** 120V/60Hz — **ITU:** PTR

FEDERAL COMMUNICATIONS COMMISSION (FCC)
See main entry under USA.

ASOCIACIÓN DE RADIODIFUSORES DE PUERTO RICO
✉ Urb. Caribe, Calle Bori #1554, San Juan, PR 00927 ☎ +1 787 7838810 **E:** radiodifusorespr@gmail.com **W:** www.radiodifusorespr.com

MW	Call	kHz	kW	Station, location, h. of tr.
1)	WPAB	550	5	WPAB 550 "La Radio del Sur", Ponce
2)	WKAQ	580	4.5	R. KAQ "La Numero Uno", San Juan
3)	WYEL	600	5	Mayagüez (r. WKAQ 580)
4)	WEXS	610	1/0.25	X-61, Patillas
5)	WUNO	630	5	NotiUno 6-30, San Juan
6)	WAPA	680	10	Cadena WAPA R. "La Poderosa", San Juan
7)	WKJB	710	10/0.75	KJB "Radio Isla", Mayagüez: 0915-0400
8)	WIAC	740	10	WIAC 740, San Juan: 0700-0300
9)	WORA	760	5	NotiUno, Mayagüez (r. 630)
10)	WKVM	810	25	R. Paz 810, San Juan: 0900-0500
11)	WXEW	840	5/1	R. Victoria "La Reina del Caribe", Yabucoa
12)	WABA	850	5/1	WABA "La Grande", Aguadilla
13)	WQBS	870	1.25	WQBS Radio, San Juan: 0900-0400
14)	WYKO	880	1/0.5	La Poderosa 880, Sabana Grande
15)	WFAB	890	0.25	R. Unidad Cristiana "La Nave 890", Ceiba
16)	WPRP	910	4.4	NotiUno, Ponce (r. 630)
17)	WYAC	930	2.5	WIAC 740, Cabo Rojo (r. WIAC 740)
18)	WIPR	940	10/2.5	Máxima 940 AM, San Juan
19)	WDNO	960	1/1.7	Cima Norte, Quebradillas (r. 1600)
20)	WPRA	990	0.91	La Primera, Mayagüez: 0900-0400
21)	WOQI	1020	1/0.3	R. Casa Pueblo, Adjuntas: 1000-0200
23)	WNVI	1040	9/0.25	R. Nueva Vida, Moca
24)	WCGB	1060	5/0.5	Rock R. Network, Juana Díaz (r. 1190)°
6)	WMIA	1070	0.5/2.5	Cadena WAPA R. "La Poderosa", Arecibo
26)	WLEY	1080	0.25	R. Ley, Cayey
27)	WSOL	1090	0.2/0.7	R. Sol, San Germán: 0930-0400
28)	WVJP	1110	2.5/0.5	Z101 Digital, Caguas
29)	WMSW	1120	2.6/5	R. Once, Hatillo: 1000-0200
30)	WOIZ	1130	0.2/0.7	R. Antillas, Guayanilla: 0900-0200
31)	WQII	‡1140	10	Once Q Cadena Nac., San Juan:1000-0400
32)	WBQN	1160	5/2.5	R. Borinquén, Barceloneta-Manatí: 1100-0200
33)	WLEO	1170	0.2	R. Leo, Ponce
34)	WBMJ	1190	10/5	Rock R. Netw./"La Roca", San Juan°
35)	WGDL	1200	0.25/1	La Mejor AM, Lares
36)	WHOY	1210	5	R. Hoy "La Señal Activa", Salinas
37)	WNIK	1230	1	Única Radio, Arecibo
38)	WALO	1240	1/5	Walo Radio, Humacao
39)	WJIT	1250	0.25/1	R. Hit, Sabana
6)	WISO	1260	2.5/2	Cadena WAPA R, Ponce (r. 680)
41)	WCMN	1280	5/1	NotiUno, Arecibo (r. 630)
42)	WTIL	1300	5/1	Cadena WAPA Radio, Mayagüez (r. 680)
43)	WSKN	1320	5/2.3	R. Isla 1320, San Juan
44)	WENA	1330	1.5	La Buena 1330, Yauco
45)	WWNA	1340	0.95	R. Una, Aguadilla: 0900-0300
46)	WEGA	1350	2.5	Candelita 7, Vega Baja
48)	WIVV	1370	5/1.2	Rock R. Network,Vieques Island (r. 1190)°
49)	WOLA	1380	1	R. Prócer "Voz de la Montaña", Barranquitas
50)	WISA	1390	1	La Voz del Noroeste, Isabela (also r. WIAC 740)
51)	WIDA	1400	1	R. Vida, Carolina (r. 90.5 MHz)
52)	WRSS	1410	1	R. Progreso, San Sebastián
2)	WUKQ	1420	1	Ponce (r. WKAQ 580)
54)	WNEL	1430	5	NotiUno, Caguas (r. 630)
55)	WCPR	1450	1	Coamomall Radio, Coamo
56)	WRRE	1460	0.5/0.3	Maranatha Radio Ministries, Juncos
57)	WLRP	1460	0.5	R. Raíces, San Sebastián: 0900-0400
58)	WKUM	1470	2/4	Cumbre, Orocovis: 0900-0200
59)	WMDD	1480	5	El 14-80, Fajardo
60)	WDEP	1490	5/1	R. Isla, Ponce (r. 1320)
61)	WMNT	1500	1/0.25	R. Atenas, Manatí: 1030-0200
62)	WBSG	1510	1	Super 15-10, Lajas
63)	WRSJ	1520	25	Activa 15-20/IBC News Network, San Juan
64)	WUPR	1530	1/0.25	Exitos 1530, Utuado: 1000-0400
65)	WIBS	1540	1d	Caribe 1540 AM, Guayama
66)	WKFE	1550	0.25	R. Café Dinámica, Yauco
67)	WBYM	1560	5/0.75	La Mas Z Radio, Bayamón
68)	WPPC	1570	1/0.1	R. Felicidad, Peñuelas
6)	WVOZ	1580	5/2	Cadena WAPA R, Morovis (r. 680)
6)	WXRF	1590	1	Cadena WAPA R, Guayama (r. 680)
69)	WCMA	1600	5	Cima 103.7, Bayamón: 1100-0500
70)	WGIT	1660	10/1	Faro de Santidad, Canóvanas

Addresses & other information:

1) Box 7243, Ponce 00732-7243 **W:** pab550.com - **FM:** WOQI 93.3MHz, WIOC 105.1MHz, WOYE 94.1MHz, Mayagüez – **2)** Box 364668, San Juan 00936-4668 **W:** wkaq580.univision.com - **FM:** KQ-105 La Primera 104.7MHz – **3)** Box 1370, Mayagüez 00681-1370 - **FM:** WAEL-FM 96.1MHz, Maricao – **4)** Box 640, Patillas 00723-0640 **W:** x61radio.com – **5)** Box 363222, San Juan 00936-3222 **W:** notiuno.com – **6)** Urb Baldrich, 134 Domenech Ave, Hato Rey 00918-3502 **W:** waparadiopr.com – **7)** Box 1293, Mayagüez 00709-1293 **W:** radioisla1320.com – **8)** Box 9023916, San Juan 00902-3916 **W:** wiac740.com – **9)** Box 43, Mayagüez 00681-0043 (or P.O.Box 363222, San Juan, PR 00936) **W:** notiuno.com – **10)** Urb. Roosevelt, 415 Calle Carbonell, Hato Rey 00918-2866 **W:** radiopaz810.com – **11)** Box 100, Yabucoa 00767 **W:** victoria840.com – **12)** 6 Calle Munoz Rivera St., Aguadilla 00603-5154 (or P.O.Box 188, Aguadilla, PR 00605) **W:** waba850.com – **13)** Calle Bori 1508, Urb Autonsanti, San Juan 00927 **W:** wqbsradio.com – **14)** Calle Dr. Felix Tio 34, Sabana Grande, PR 00637 **W:** wyko880am.com – **15)** P.O.Box 318, Río Blanco, PR 00744. **W:** radiounidadcristiana.com – **16)** Box 7771, Ponce 00732-7771 **W:** notiuno.com – **17)** Box 681, Cabo Rojo 00623-0681 **W:** wiac740.com – **18)** Box 190909, Hato Rey 00918-0909 **W:** wipr.pr – **19)** P.O.Box 846, Aguada, PR 00602. **W:** cima103.com - **FM:** 103.7MHz – **20)** Box 1293, Mayagüez 00681-1293 **W:** wpra990.com – **21)** Box 704, Adjuntas 00601-0704 **W:** casapueblo.org – **23)** Box 846, Aguada, PR 00602-0846 **W:** nuevavida.fm - **FM:** 104.5MHz – **24)** Box 1414, Juana Díaz 00795-1414 (or P.O.Box 367000, San Juan, PR 00936) - Mon-Fri 1300-1700 local prgrs in Spanish – **W:** rockradionetwork.org – **26)** Box 1186, Cayey 00737-1186 (or 100 Gran Bulevar Paseo #403A, San Juan, PR 00926) **W:** radioisla1320.com/radio-ley-1080-am – **27)** Box 5000, Suite 442, San Germán 00683-0442 **W:** radiowsol.com – **28)** Box 207, Caguas 00726-0207. Relays Z101 Digital 101.3MHz from Santo Domingo, Dom. Rep. **W:** z101digital.com – **29)** 550 Calle Truncado, Hatillo 00659-2712 (or P.O.Box 140961, Arecibo, PR 00614) **W:** radioonce.com – **30)** Box 561130, Guayanilla 00656-1130 **W:** radioantillas.4t.com – **31)** Cobian's Plaza, Santurce 00909-1820 (or Box 193779, San Juan, PR 00919) **W:** 11qradio.com – **32)** Box 1625 (or Calle 16 H-6 Urb. Flamboyán), Manatí 00674-1625 – **33)** Box 7213, Ponce 00732-7213 **W:** unoradio.com – **34)** Box 367000, San Juan 00936-7000 (or Av Ponce de León N° 1409, P4, Santurce 00907) – Mon-Fri 2300-0540 Spanish, 0540-2300 English, Sun English 24h **W:** rockradionetwork.org – **35)** Box 872, Lares, PR 00669 – **W:** wgdl1200am.com – **36)** Box 1148, Salinas 00751-1148 **W:** radiowhoy.com – **37)** Box 141526, Arecibo 00614 **W:** unicaradio1230.com - **FM:** 106.5MHz – **38)** Box 1240 (or P.O.Box 9230), Humacao 00792 **W:** waloradio.com – **39)** Box 316, Coamo 00769-0316 (or P.O.Box 878, Vega Alta, PR 00692) **W:** radiohit1250.com – **41)** Box 436, Arecibo 00613-0436 **W:** notiuno.com – **42)** Box 1360, Mayagüez 00681-1360 **W:** waparadiopr.com - **FM:** 106.9MHz – **43)** Box 363222, San Juan 00936-3222 **W:** radioisla1320.com – **44)** Box 1330, Yauco 00698-1330 **W:** labuena1330.com – **45)** Box 7, Moca 00676-0007 **W:** radiouna1340.com **FM:** 98.3MHz– **46)** BHC 03 Box 12110, Carolina, P.R. 00987 **W:** candelita7.com – **48)** HC02 Box 13903, Vieques Island, PR 00765 – Sat 1000-1300 local programming in English **W:** rockradionetwork.org 34) – **49)** Box 669-A, Barranquitas, PR 00794 – **50)** Box 750, Isabela 00662-0750 **W:** wisa1390am.com - **FM:** WKSA 101.5MHz – **51)** Box 188, Carolina 00986-0188 **W:** cadenaradiovida.net - **FM:** 90.5MHz – **52)** Box 1410, San Sebastián 00685-1410 **W:** radioprogreso1410.com – **54)** Box 487, Caguas 00726-0487 **W:** radiotiempo.net – **55)** Box 1863, Coamo 00769-1863 **W:** coamomall.com/coamomallradio – **56)** Box 1460, Las Piedras, PR 00771-1460 **W:** maranatharadioministries.com – **57)** Box 1670, San Sebastián 00685-1670 **W:** wlrpam.net – **58)** 10 Calle Pedro Arroyo, Orocovis 00720-2202 (or P.O.Box 1210, Orocovis, PR 00720) **W:** cumbre1470.com – **59)** Box 948, Fajardo 00738-0948 **W:** wmdd.radio.net – **60)** Box 7213, Ponce 00732-7213 **W:** radioisla1320.com – **61)** Box 6, Manatí 00674-0006 **W:** radioatenas1500.net – **62)** Box 593, Lajas 00667-0593 **W:** super1510.com – **63)** Calle Bori 1554, San Juan, PR 00927 – **64)** Box 868, Utuado 00641-0868 **W:** exitos1530radio.com – **65)** Box 1540, Guayama 00785-1540 **W:** caribe1540am.com – **66)** Box 324, Yauco 00698-0324 (or 100 Gran Bulevar Paseo #403A, San Juan, PR 00926) **W:** facebook.com/radiocafe1550 – **67)** Box 4036, Carolina 00984-4036 (or Calle Bori 1554, San Juan, PR 00927) **W:** metroradio1560.com – **68)** Box 9064, Ponce 00732-9064 **W:** radiofelicidadpr.com – **69)** Box 9394, Santurce 00908-9394 **W:**cima103.com - **FM:** 103.7MHz – **70)** Calle Bori 1554, San Juan, PR 00927 **W:** farodesantidad.com

FM in San Juan (MHz): 89.7 WRTU Universidad – 90.5 WIDA – 91.3 WIPR Allegro – 92.5 WORO Oro – 93.7 WZNT La Zeta – 94.7 La Nueva – 95.7 WFID Didelity – 97.3 WOYE Magic – 97.7 WNVM Nueva Vida – 99.1 WPRM Salsoul – 99.5 Rock Radio Network – 99.9 WIOA Fresh – 100.7 WXYX La X – 102.5 WTOK Hot 102 – 103.3 WVJP Dimensión 103 – 104.7 WKAQ KQ105 – 105.7 WCAD Alfa Rock – 107.7 WVOZ Mix

QATAR

L.T: UTC +3h — **Pop:** 2.9 million — **Pr.L:** Arabic — **E.C:** 240V/50Hz — **ITU:** QAT

COMMUNICATIONS REGULATORY AUTHORITY (CRA)

✉ Al Nasr Tower B, Corniche, Doha ☎ +974 44995535 🖷 +974 44995515 **E:** info@cra.gov.qa **W:** cra.gov.qa

QATAR MEDIA CORPORATION (QMC, Gov.)

✉ P.O. Box 1414, Doha ☎+974 44 894444 🖷 +974 44 882888 **W:** qmc.qa **E:** info@qmc.qa
Main Arabic Prgr: 24h. **MW:** Al-Arish 675kHz 600kW. **FM:** Al-Jumailiya 90.8MHz 40kW, Umm Said 93.4MHz, Al-Markhiyah 96.0MHz 10kW, Al Kohr 97.6MHz 10kW, Al-Khaisah 103.4MHz, Al Ruwais 106.0MHz. **W:** qatarradio.qa
English prgr (QBS Radio): Doha 97.5MHz 10kW **W:** qbsradio.qa
Qabayan Radio: Doha 94.3MHz
QFM Bangla: Doha 95.3MHz 10kW **W:** fb.com/qfm953bangla
Quran prgr: Khawr al-Udayd 103.4MHz 0.5kW, Doha 105.7Mhz.
Malayalam Radio: Doha 98.6MHz
Urdu prgr: Doha 107.0MHz 5kW **W:** urduradio.qa
Oryx FM, Doha, 94.0MHz (joint QMC and RFI project in French.) **W:** oryxradio.qa
Sowt al-Khaleej (Vo the Gulf): Doha 93.4/99.0/100.8MHz. **W:** skr.fm
Al-Jazeera TV audio in Doha: English 101.7, Arabic 102.6MHz.
Al-Kass TV audio: Doha 100.3MHz 20kW. **W:** alkass.net
Qatar TV Arabic audio: Al-Khaisah 104.6MHz 20kW.
Ann: Main Arabic prgr: "Idha'at Qatar min al-Doha".

OTHER STATIONS:
Emarat FM, Doha: 104.0MHz. See UAE – **Malayalam FM,** Doha 98.6MHz **W:** radio986.com – **Middle East BC,** Markhiya 92.0MHz – **One FM,** Doha 89.6MHz. In Hindi **W:** facebook.com/oneFMQatar – **R. Olive,** Doha 106.3MHz. In Hindi **W:** olive.qa – **R. Suno,** Doha 98.6MHz. In Malayalam **W:** suno.qa – **QF Radio,** Doha: 91.7MHz English, 93.7MHz Arabic. **W:** qfradio.org.qa – **Sowt Al-Rayyan-Souq Waqif:** Doha 97.0Mhz 20kW, Markhiyah 102.0MHz 10kW. **W:** soutalrayyan.com
AFN, Al Udeid Airbase: 98.9/101.3MHz – **BBC World Sce,** Doha: 107.4MHz 8kW – **Monte Carlo Doualiya,** Doha: 99.6MHz 5kW – **R. Sawa,** Al-Jumailiya: 92.6MHz 20kW

RÉUNION (France)

L.T: UTC +4h — **Pop:** 900,000 — **Pr.L:** French (official), Réunion Creole — **E.C:** 220V/50Hz — **ITU:** REU

COMITÉ TERRITORIAL DE L'AUDIOVISUEL DE LA RÉUNION ET DE MAYOTTE

✉ Immeuble Darwin, 4 rue Emile-Hugot, CS 60584, 97495 Sainte-Clotilde Cédex ☎ +262 262298710 **E:** cta.reunion-mayotte@csa.fr

RÉUNION LA PREMIÈRE (Pub)

✉ 12 rue René Demarne, BP 47716, 97804 Saint-Denis Cedex 9 ☎+262 262406767 🖷 +262 262216484 **W:** la1ere.francetvinfo.fr/reunion/radio

FM	MHz	kW	FM	MHz	kW
Saint-Joseph	87.8	2	Saint-Leu	90.7	1
Saint-Denis	89.2	2	Le Port	91.0	2
Piton Textor	89.6	3	Saint-Benoît	106.7	2
Piton Hyacinthe	90.7	2			

+about 10 trs under 1kW.
D.Prgr: 24h. During nighttime 2000-0100 relay of RFI.
Ann: "Réunion la première".

Other stations, main networks:

FM (MHz)	1	2	3	4	5	6	7	8	kW
Cilaos	103.5	98.8	107.4	-	-	-	88.5	100.7	0.2
Etang-Salé		89.3	-	-	-	-	-	94.7	1
La Possession		93.4	-	-	-	-	103.0	-	1
Le Port	91.6	93.4	94.2	105.2	93.8		103.3	-	1-2
Le Tampon	99.2	97.4	-	98.6	104.0	105.7	-	-	1-3
Petite-Ile	91.1	-	-	105.5			-	-	1-2
Plaine des-Chafres	91.3	-	-	105.1	96.5	93.0	-	-	1-2
Plaine des-Palm.	99.2	88.2	100.1	-	-	-	93.6	-	1-3
Saint-André	-	-	94.2	-	-	-	-	-	2
Saint-Benoit	97.5	101.3	-	-	88.5	-	-	105.2	0.2-1
Saint-Denis	98.8	97.8	101.5	95.1	107.7	103.4	95.5	91.3	0.2-2
Sainte-Rose	99.8	-	87.6	107.5	89.0	93.6	102.1	-	0.2-1
Sainte-Suzanne	99.6	106.2	-	-	101.1	-	95.7	-	0.1-1
Saint-Joseph	107.8	-	98.8	98.0	107.0	90.5	103.5	88.3	0.1-1
Saint-Leu	91.5	95.0		105.3	96.7	92.8	103.1	106.8	1
Saint-Paul	-	107.1	103.7	105.7	96.6	89.6	90.0	87.6	1-2
Saint-Philippe	101.1	91.6	-	-	-	-	102.6	96.3	0.2-1
Salazie	93.2	101.7	89.0	104.4	-	103.2	-	105.7	0.2
Saline-les-Hauts	-	95.2	-	105.5	106.6	89.4	103.3	-	1
Trois Bassins	91.3	-	107.9	-	-	-	-	95.6	1
Vincendo	-	-	-	-	101.6	105.8	-	-	1

1) France Inter W: franceinter.fr – **2) R. Freedom W:** freedom.fr – **3) Kréol FM W:** kreol.tv – **4) RER** (Radio Est Réunion) **W:** rer.re – **5) RTL Réunion W:** rtl.re – **6) Antenne Réunion Radio W:** antennereunion.fr – **7) Fun R. W:** funradio.re – **8) R. Arc en Ciel W:** radioarcenciel.re

ROMANIA

L.T: UTC +2h (28 Mar-31 Oct: +3h) — **Pop:** 19.4 million — **Pr.L:** Romanian (official), Hungarian, German — **E.C:** 230V/50Hz — **ITU:** ROU

CONSILIUL NATIONAL AL AUDIOVIZUALULUI (CNA)

(National Audiovisual Council)
✉ Bd. Libertății nr. 14, sector 5, 050706 Bucureşti ☎ +40 213055350 🖷 +40 213055354 **E:** cna@cna.ro **W:** www.cna.ro
L.P: Pres: Maria Monica Gubernat

SOCIETATEA ROMÂNA DE RADIODIFUZIUNE (SRR) (Pub)

✉ Str. Berthelot nr. 60-64, sector 1, 010171 Bucureşti ☎ +40 213031777 **E:** relatii.public@radioromania.ro **W:** radioromania.ro
L.P: DG: Georgică Severin

LW/MW	kHz	kW	Prgr	MW	kHz	kW	Prgr
Braşov (Bod)	153	200	AS	Miercurea Ciuc	945	15	1
Petroşani	531	15	1	Iaşi (Uricani)	1053	400	R5
Urziceni	531	15	AS	Cluj-Napoca (b)	1152	400	1
Târgu Jiu	558	400	1	Bacău (Galbeni)	1179	400	1
Braşov (Bod)	567	50	1	Reşiţa (Vaşcău)	1179	10	1
Satu Mare	567	50	1	Braşov (Bod)	1197	15	R2+M
Botoşani	603	50	1	Constanța (d)	1314	50	AS
Bucureşti	603	30	AS+M	Craiova	1314	15	R6
Oradea	603	50	1	Timişoara (e)	1314	25	AS+M
Drobeta-T. Severin	603	15	R6	Târgu Mureş	1323	15	R8+M
Timişoara (a)	630	400	R9	Galați	1332	50	1
Voineşti	630	50	AS	Sighetu M.	1404	50	R3/L+M
Sighetu M.	711	50	1	Sibiu	1404	15	1
Baia Mare	720	10	1	Băile Olăneşti	1422	10	1
Nufăru	720	15	1	Constanța (d)	1458	100	1
Sinaia	720	15	1	Nufăru	1530	15	R4
Lugoj (Boldur)	756	400	1	Rădăuți	1530	15	1
Bucureşti (c)	855	400	1	Miercurea Ciuc	1593	15	R8+M
Cluj-Napoca (b)	909	200	R3+M	Ion Corvin	1593	15	1
Timişoara (e)	909	50	1	Oradea	1593	15	R3+M
Constanța (d)	909	25	R4	Sibiu	1593	10	R2+M

(a) Orțişoara (b) Jucu (c) Tâncăbeşti (d) Valu lui Traian (e) Săcălaz
R=Regional stns (2-9 see under SRR Regional Stations), L=Local prgr (R. Sighet), M=Ethnic Minority Service in Hungarian/German

FM (MHz)	1	2	4	AS	kW
Alexandria	91.8	89.7	-	-	10
Arad (Şiria)	103.8	106.8	-	-	60
Bacău	98.8	101.8	-	-	10
Baia Mare (Mogoşa)	102.5	100.1	-	-	60
Băneasa	106.6	89.1	-	-	30
Bârlad (Popeni)	103.9	102.8	-	-	10
Bihor (Curcubăta Mare)	91.0	105.8	-	-	60
Bistrița (Heniu)	103.9	101.3	-	-	40
Botoşani (Săveni)	100.8	106.0	-	-	10
Bucureşti	105.3	101.3	104.8	-	2x100/2
Buzău	107.0	103.7	-	-	14
Calafat (Plenița)	90.2	101.1	-	-	10
Câmpulung M. (Rarău)	96.0	98.7	-	-	30
Cluj-Napoca (Feleac)	88.8	101.0	-	-	30
Comăneşti	104.7	101.4	-	89.0	2x30/1
Constanța	102.7	-	-	-	2
Constanța (Techirghiol)	105.5	-	-	-	60
Craiova	88.7	-	-	-	30
Deva (Măgura Boiului)	103.4	105.0	-	-	30

FM (MHz)	1	2	4	AS	kW
Drobeta - T.Severin (Balota)	91.4	105.8	-	-	30
Faget	89.8	-	-	-	5
Focşani (Măgura Odobeşti)	102.5	101.0	-	-	60
Galaţi (Văcăreni)	106.4	101.6	-	-	60
Gheorgheni (Harghita-Băi)	103.4	106.8	-	-	60
Iaşi (Pietrăria)	101.1	103.1	-	-	100
Mahmudia	100.5	102.0	-	-	10
Novaci (Cerbu)	92.9	89.5	-	-	100
Oradea	104.1	96.1	-	-	10/60
Petroşani (Parâng)	88.1	90.6	-	-	10
Piatra Neamţ (Pietricica)	103.6	100.3	-	-	30/10
Ploeşti (Coştila)	102.2	104.1	97.6	-	100
Râmnicu Vâlcea (Cozia)	103.4	102.5	-	-	30
Reşiţa (Semenic)	102.5	-	-	-	100
Sibiu (Paltiniş)	101.8	103.7	-	-	60
Suceava (Mihoveni)	99.6	101.6	-	-	30
Sulina	-	-	-	103.2	1
Târgu Mureş	93.6	104.9	-	-	10
Timişoara (Urseni)	106.4	100.7	-	-	10
Tulcea	99.4	105.4	-	-	10
Tulcea (Topolog)	105.0	103.0	-	-	30
Turnu Măgurele	105.1	101.1	-	-	30
Vărătec	91.2	100.8	-	-	10
Zalău (Meseş)	88.1	105.0	-	-	10

+ sites with only txs below 1kW.

D.Prgr: Prgr 1 (R. „România Actualitati"): 24h – **Prgr 2 (R. „România Cultural"):** 24h – **Prgr 3 (R. 3 Net „Florian Pittis"):** 24h via DAB – **Prgr 4 (R. „România Muzical"):** 24h – **Antena Satelor (AS):** 24h – **Service for Hungarian & German ethnic minorities („Programul maghiar-german"):** W 1200-1300 German & 1300-1400 Hungarian; Sun 0800-0820 Hungarian & 0820-0830 German.

SRR Regional Stations

✉ **R. România Regional**, Str. Berthelot nr. 60-64, sector 1, 010171 Bucureşti ☎ +40 21 3031469 **E:** radio.regional@radioromania.ro **W:** romaniaregional.ro

NB: All reg. stns relay news from national networks at times, and some stns may relay R. "România Actualităţi" outside of own prgrs (esp. at nighttime). – Ethnic minority prgrs may be in the language of the minority and/or in Romanian (monolingual or bilingual).

1) R. Bucuresti FM: Str. Berthelot nr. 60-64, sector 1, 010171 Bucureşti. **E:** radiobucuresti@srr.ro. On 98.3MHz (Bucureşti 100kW): 24h – **2) R. România Brasov FM:** Bd. Eroilor nr. 29, 500036 Braşov. **E:** secretariat@radiobrasovfm.ro On (kHz) 1197 (Bod), 1593 (Sibiu) + (MHz) 93.3 (Braşov): 24h – **3) R. România Cluj:** Str. Donath nr. 160, 400293 Cluj-Napoca. **E:** office@radiocluj.ro. On (kHz) 909 (Cluj), 1404 (Sighetu)*, 1593 (Oradea): 0400-2000 + (MHz) 87.6 (Satu Mare 2kW), 93.3 (Negreşti-Oaş 2kW), 95.4 (Paltiniş 0.1kW)*, 95.6 (Feleac 20kW), 101.7 (Sighetu 2kW): 24h (*= except for prgrs from substudio R. Sighet, see below). For ethnic minorities: Hungarian ("Kolozsvári Rádió"): 0000-0200 (W)*, 0600-0800 (W), 1300-1400 (W)*, 1400-1600 (W), 1200-1600 (Sun) (*= FM only). Local station **"Kolozsvári Rádió"** on 98.8MHz (Feleac 0.5kW): 24h in Hungarian, exc. Sun 0500-0520 Ukrainian. Local substudio with own prgrs (otherwise rel. R. Cluj): **"R. Sighet"** Str. Plevnei nr. 8, 435500 Sighetu M. **E:** radiosighet@yahoo.com. On 1404kHz: 0400-0600 (MF), 0800 (Sun 0830)-1200, 1600-1900; incl. prgrs for ethnic minorities: Hungarian ("Máramarosszigeti Rádió"): 0440-0450 (Mon), 0520-0525 (W), 1620-1630 (Tue), 1730-1755 (Thu); Ukrainian 1700-1755 (Fri) – **4) R. România Constanta:** Vila nr. 1, 900001 Mamaia. **E:** secretariat@radioconstanta.ro. On (kHz) 909 (Valu lui Traian), 1530 (Nufăru): 0400-2200 + (MHz) 90.8 (Techirghiol 30kW)*, 93.0 (Tulcea 0.5kW)*, 100.1 (Techirghiol 5kW, Mangalia 5kW)*, 106.2 (Sulina 2kW)*: 24h. (*= 1 July to first week in September (ca) FM txs are carrying prgr "R. Vacanţa" for tourists 0800-1700; incl. N. produced by SRR's "R. Romania International" service in English, French, German, Italian, Russian). MW+FM txs may separate for different programming at times. For ethnic minorities: MF 1905-2000 Greek (Mon), Armenian (Tue), Russian (for the Russio-Lipovanian ethnic minority) (Wed), Tatar (Thu), Turkish (Fri); Aromanian: 1610-1700 (Sun) – **5) R. România Iasi:** Str. Lascăr Catargi nr. 44, 700107 Iaşi. **E:** secretariat@radioiasi.ro. On 1053kHz: 0400-2000 + (MHz) 90.8 (Rarău 30kW), 94.5 (Huşi 1kW), 96.3MHz (Pietrăria 100kW): 24h (MW+FM txs carry separate prgrs Sun 0603-0700 & 0710-0900). For ethnic minorities: Mon-Thu 1830-1900 Romany (Mon), Yiddish (Tue), Russian (for the Russio-Lipovanian ethnic minority) (Wed), Ukrainian (Thu). – **6) R. România Oltenia - Craiova:** Bd. Ştirbei Vodă nr. 3, 200352 Craiova. **E:** office@radiocraiova.ro. On (kHz) 603 (Drobeta-Turnu Severin), 1314 (Craiova) + (MHz) 99.8 (Râmnicu Vâlcea 0.2kW), 102.9 (Craiova 10kW), 105.0 (Cerbu 100kW): 24h – **7) R. România Resita:** Str. Petru Maior nr. 71, 320111 Reşiţa. **E:** contact@radioresita.ro. On (MHz) 91.9 (Moldoviţa 0.05kW), 93.8 (Berzeasca 0.5kW), 105.6 (Semenic 100kW): 24h. For ethnic minorities: 1710-1740 Ukrainian (Mon), Serbian (Tue), Hungarian (Wed), German (Thu), Croatian (Fri), Slovak (Sat), Czech (Sun) – **8) R. România Târgu Mures:** Bd. 1 Decembrie 1918 nr. 109, 540445 Târgu Mureş. **E:** office@radiomures.ro. Prgr 1 on (MHz) 94.9 (Borsec), 98.9 (Harghita-Băi 60kW), 102.9 (Târgu Mureş 10kW): 0400-2000; Prgr 2 on (kHz) 1323 (Târgu Mureş), 1593 (Miercurea Ciuc) + (MHz) 92.3 (Gheorgheni 0.05kW), 96.0 (Târgu Mureş 0.2kW), 106.8MHz (Harghita-Băi 60kW): 0400-2200. For ethnic minorities on Prgr 2: Hungarian ("Marosvásárhelyi Rádió"): W 0400 (Sat 0500)-1900, Sun 0500-2000; German ("R. Neumarkt"): W 1900-2000 – **9) R. România Timisoara:** Str. Pestalozzi nr. 14A, 300115 Timişoara. **E:** secretariat@radiotimisoara.ro. On 630kHz + (MHz) 101.5 (Parâng 10kW), 102.9 (Arad 2kW)*, 103.8 (Faget 5kW)*, 105.9 (Timişoara 0.3kW): 24h (*= exc. for prgrs from substudio Arad, see below). MW+FM txs carry separate programming at times. For ethnic minorities: German ("R. Temeswar"): 1100-1200 on MW & 1700-1800° on 105.9MHz (°= Italian on 1st Mon); Hungarian ("Temesvári Rádió"): 1200-1300 on MW & 1800-1900 on 105.9MHz; Serbian: 1300-1400 on MW & 1900-2000 on 105.9MHz; Sun, only on MW: 1400-1500 Czech, 1500-1600 Slovak, 1600-1700 Ukrainian, 1700-1800 Bulgarian, 1800-1900 Romany. Local substudio with own prgrs **"Arad FM"**: Bd. Revoluţiei nr. 77, 310130 Arad. On (MHz) 102.9 (Arad 2kW), 103.8 (Faget 5kW): MF 1600-2000 (otherwise rel. R. Timişoara).

OTHER STATIONS

MW	kHz	kW	Location	Station
3)	1485	1	Botoşani	R. Vocea Speranţei
3)	1485	1	Mediaş	R. Vocea Speranţei
3)	1485	1	Oradea	R. Vocea Speranţei
3)	1584	1	Iaşi	R. Vocea Speranţei
3)	1584	1	Sighetu M.	R. Vocea Speranţei
3)	1584	1	Tecuci	R. Vocea Speranţei
3)	1584	1	Vatra Dornei	R. Vocea Speranţei
37)	1584	1	Timişoara	ALT FM
37)	1602	1	Arad	ALT FM
3)	1602	1	Piatra Neamţ	R. Vocea Speranţei
FM	**MHz**	**kW**	**Location**	**Station**
16)	88.0	2	Bucureşti	R. Impuls
4A)	88.0	30	Bârlad	Kiss FM
1A)	88.2	5	Botoşani	Europa FM
20)	88.2	1.5	Olteniţa	Stil FM
6)	88.3	3	Tulcea	Itsy Bitsy
2A)	88.4	10	Vărătec	Digi FM
1B)	88.5	1	Comăneşti	Virgin R.
2A)	88.5	100	Reşiţa	Digi FM
4A)	88.5	2	Vaslui	Kiss FM
22)	88.6	1	Câmpina	Best FM
4A)	88.7	3	Focşani	Kiss FM
6)	88.7	2	Satu Mare	Itsy Bitsy
5)	88.9	2	Mahmudia	R. ZU
5)	89.0	3	Bucureşti	R. ZU
2A)	89.1	10	Târgu Mureş	Digi FM
1A)	89.2	2	Braşov	Europa FM
9)	89.2	1	Sulina	R. Trinitas
1A)	89.3	4.5	Arad	Europa FM
23)	89.3	2	Sighetu M.	Sighet FM
5)	89.3	1	Piatra Neamţ	R. ZU
1A)	89.4	2	Giurgiu	Europa FM
2D)	89.5	2	Bucureşti	Dance FM
6)	89.5	3	Tulcea	Itsy Bitsy
14)	89.7	22	Gheorghieni	Mária R. Erdély
4B)	89.8	2	Slobozia	Magic FM
2B)	89.9	1	Braşov	Pro FM
2B)	89.9	2	Medgidia	Pro FM
1A)	90.0	4.5	Bistriţa	Europa FM
2A)	90.0	60	Focşani	Digi FM
9)	90.1	2	Topliţa	R. Trinitas
5)	90.3	5	Comăneşti	R. ZU
1A)	90.4	2	Râmnicu Vâlcea	Europa FM
1A)	90.5	4.5	Baia Mare	Europa FM
5)	90.6	5	Tulcea	R. ZU
1A)	90.7	4	Târgu Mureş	Europa FM
7)	90.7	30	Turnu Măgurele	Naţional FM
4A)	90.8	2	Târgu Bujor	Kiss FM
4B)	90.8	2	Bucureşti	Magic FM
1A)	90.9	1	Satu Mare	Europa FM

FM	MHz	kW	Location	Station
5)	90.9	2	Slobozia	R. ZU
7)	90.9	5	Mahmudia	Naţional FM
4A)	91.1	1	Constanţa	Kiss FM
4C)	91.2	1	Vaslui	Rock FM
2A)	91.3	10	Timişoara	Digi FM
4A)	91.3	30	Buzău	Kiss FM
2A)	91.4	60	Gheorghieni	Digi FM
16)	91.4	2	Tulcea	R. Impuls
1B)	91.5	5	Râmnicu Vâlcea	Virgin R.
7)	91.7	1	Bucureşti	Naţional FM
A)	91.7	30	Cluj-Napoca	RFI Relay
2A)	91.8	10	Bacău	Digi FM
2A)	92.0	60	Galaţi	Digi FM
16)	92.0	6	Craiova	R. Impuls
4A)	92.0	10	Bistriţa	Kiss FM
1A)	92.1	4.5	Petroşani	Europa FM
1C)	92.1	2	Bucureşti	Vibe FM
25)	92.2	1	Oneşti	Dream FM
2A)	92.4	60	Sibiu	Digi FM
10)	92.5	10	Zalău	R. Maria
5)	92.5	5	Buzău	R. ZU
9)	92.5	2	Giurgiu	R. Trinitas
9)	92.7	1	Iaşi	R. Trinitas
4A)	92.8	1	Galaţi	Kiss FM
9)	93.0	60	Gheorghieni	R. Trinitas
19)	93.2	2	Negreşti-Oaş	Smile FM
1A)	93.2	5	Oradea	Europa FM
4A)	93.3	1	Slobozia	Kiss FM
9)	93.3	3	Ceahlău	R. Trinitas
1A)	93.4	2	Alexandria	Europa FM
7)	93.4	30	Bistriţa	Naţional FM
9)	93.5	2	Comăneşti	R. Trinitas
A)	93.5	1	Bucureşti	RFI Relay
3)	93.6	1	Tulcea	R. Vocea Speranţei
9)	93.6	30	Râmnicu Vâlcea	R. Trinitas
4A)	93.8	1	Drăgăneşti-Olt	Kiss FM
2A)	93.9	30	Băneasa	Digi FM
4B)	93.9	1	Ploieşti	Magic FM
7)	94.0	2	Zimnicea	Naţional FM
21A)	94.2	2	Bucureşti	R. Vocea Evangheliei
2A)	94.3	30	Râmnicu Vâlcea	Digi FM
9)	94.3	1	Baia Mare	R. Trinitas
14)	94.4	2	Topliţa	Mária R. Erdély
12)	94.6	10	Zalău	R. Transilvania
33)	94.7	1	Piatra Neamţ	Viva FM
26)	94.8	1.5	Bucureşti	R. Guerrilla
2B)	94.9	60	Sibiu	Pro FM
4B)	94.9	2	Satu Mare	Magic FM
6)	95.0	10	Botoşani	Itsy Bitsy
4A)	95.1	1	Bacău	Kiss FM
5)	95.1	2	Medgidia	R. ZU
9)	95.3	100	Munţii Bucegi	R. Trinitas
8)	95.5	1	Craiova	R. Galaxy
2A)	95.7	10	Bârlad	Digi FM
31)	95.8	1	Tulcea	R. Delta
2A)	95.9	30	Deva	Digi FM
1B)	96.0	1	Negreşti-Oaş	Virgin R.
4B)	96.0	1	Bacău	Magic FM
1C)	96.1	2	Zimnicea	Vibe FM
4A)	96.1	2.5	Bucureşti	Kiss FM
7)	96.1	2	Timişoara	Naţional FM
2A)	96.2	60	Comăneşti	Digi FM
8)	96.4	5	Râmnicu Vâlcea	R. Galaxy
9)	96.4	1	Nucet	R. Trinitas
2B)	96.5	2	Satu Mare	Pro FM
9)	96.5	60	Galaţi	R. Trinitas
5)	96.6	6	Sibiu	R. ZU
2A)	96.7	10	Botoşani	Digi FM
27)	96.8	2	Bechet	Favorit FM
4A)	96.8	2	Mahmudia	Kiss FM
28)	96.9	3.5	Bucureşti	Gold FM
32)	96.9	29	Baia Mare	Social FM
15)	97.0	5	Focşani	Focus FM
1B)	97.1	30	Suceava	Virgin R.
5)	97.2	2	Braşov	R. ZU
8)	97.2	30	Turnu Măgurele	R. Galaxy
5)	97.3	10	Bârlad	R. ZU
24)	97.4	2	Sighetu M.	City Rádió
29)	97.5	2	Medgidia	R. Terra
1B)	97.7	10	Zalău	Virgin R.
6)	97.8	6	Constanţa	Itsy Bitsy
1B)	97.9	2	Voineasa	Virgin R.
2A)	97.9	3	Bucureşti	Digi FM
13)	98.0	2	Bacău	Romantic FM
4B)	98.1	2	Botoşani	Magic FM
7)	98.1	10	Văratec	Naţional FM
9)	98.1	1	Hârşova	R. Trinitas
9)	98.2	1	Băileşti	R. Trinitas
2A)	98.5	30	Comăneşti	Digi FM
2A)	98.5	10	Petroşani	Digi FM
4A)	98.5	30	Canlia	Kiss FM
5)	98.5	5	Baia Mare	R. ZU
9)	98.5	1	Drobeta-T.Severin	R. Trinitas
1B)	98.7	6	Buzău	Virgin R.
1A)	98.8	1	Slatina	Europa FM
4B)	99.1	3	Galaţi	Magic FM
2A)	99.2	100	Iaşi	Digi FM
35)	99.2	1	Ploieşti	R. Prahova
4A)	99.2	30	Râmnicu Vâlcea	Kiss FM
4B)	99.3	30	Bistriţa	Magic FM
6)	99.3	1.5	Bucureşti	Itsy Bitsy
1A)	99.5	5	Călăraşi	Europa FM
2A)	99.6	60	Munţii Bucegi	Digi FM
17)	99.7	1	Comăneşti	R. Dobrogea
1A)	100.0	5	Bârlad	Europa FM
1A)	100.0	2	Drobeta-T.Severin	Europa FM
1A)	100.2	5	Gheorghieni	Europa FM
1B)	100.2	5	Bucureşti	Virgin R.
1A)	100.3	2	Buzău	Europa FM
1A)	100.3	1	Vaslui	Europa FM
4C)	100.6	6	Bucureşti	Rock FM
6)	100.6	2	Bacău	Itsy Bitsy
7)	100.6	2	Târgu Mureş	Naţional FM
2A)	100.7	2	Braşov	Digi FM
2A)	100.7	100	Novaci	Digi FM
1A)	100.9	2	Slobozia	Europa FM
7)	100.9	5	Făget	Naţional FM
2A)	101.6	10	Zalău	Digi FM
34)	101.7	2	Ploieşti	R. S.O.S.
13)	101.9	3	Bucureşti	Romantic FM
1A)	102.0	2	Nucet	Europa FM
2A)	102.3	2	Topliţa	Digi FM
1A)	102.7	1	Câmpulung M.	Europa FM
1A)	102.7	5	Zalău	Europa FM
2B)	102.8	2	Bucureşti	Pro FM
9)	103.1	2	Bechet	R. Trinitas
18)	103.4	3	Bucureşti	R. Seven
1A)	103.4	10	Galaţi	Europa FM
2A)	103.4	10	Suceava	Digi FM
3)	103.5	2	Cobadin	R. Vocea Speranţei
2C)	103.8	1	Bucureşti	Chill FM
2A)	104.0	2	Satu Mare	Digi FM
1B)	104.1	1	Mangalia	Virgin R.
4A)	104.1	10	Petroşani	Kiss FM
1A)	104.2	4	Bacău	Europa FM
2A)	104.2	2	Voineasa	Digi FM
36)	104.3	2	Topliţa	R. Son
1A)	104.4	5	Timişoara	Europa FM
1A)	104.5	2	Craiova	Europa FM
2A)	104.5	30	Cluj-Napoca	Digi FM
3)	104.5	1	Zimnicea	R. Vocea Speranţei
1A)	104.8	2	Negreşti-Oaş	Europa FM
2A)	104.8	30	Câmpulung M.	Digi FM
1A)	105.1	4.5	Piatra Neamţ	Europa FM
1B)	105.2	30	Băneasa	Virgin R.
2A)	105.3	60	Arad	Digi FM
2A)	105.3	60	Baia Mare	Digi FM
5)	105.3	2	Hârlău	R. ZU
1B)	105.4	1	Bacău	Virgin R.
1A)	105.5	5	Suceava	Europa FM
2A)	105.5	30	Craiova	Digi FM
5)	105.5	2	Negreşti-Oaş	R. ZU
1A)	105.8	7.5	Odobeşti	Europa FM
7)	105.9	10	Petroşani	Naţional FM
1A)	106.1	5	Comăneşti	Europa FM
1A)	106.2	6	Sibiu	Europa FM
1A)	106.3	5	Comăneşti	Europa FM
33)	106.3	1	Botoşani	Viva FM

FM	MHz	kW	Location	Station
24)	106.4	2	Satu Mare	City Rádió
1A)	106.5	5	Iaşi	Europa FM
1A)	106.6	12	Cluj-Napoca	Europa FM
1B)	106.6	2	Drăgăneşti-Olt	Virgin R.
21B)	106.6	2	Moldova Nouă	9FM
1A)	106.7	30	Bucureşti	Europa FM
1A)	107.1	10	Novaci	Europa FM
1A)	107.1	2.5	Vărătec	Europa FM
2B)	107.1	2	Mangalia	Pro FM
11)	107.2	10	Câmpulung M.	Impact FM
4B)	107.2	2	Adjud	Magic FM
1B)	107.3	2	Zimnicea	Virgin R.
1D)	107.3	5	Bucureşti	Smart R.
1A)	107.4	5	Tulcea	Europa FM
2A)	107.4	2	Negreşti-Oaş	Digi FM
1A)	107.5	100	Munţii Bucegi	Europa FM
1A)	107.5	5	Reşiţa	Europa FM
5)	107.5	2	Comăneşti	R. ZU
2A)	107.6	60	Oradea	Digi FM
9)	107.6	2	Voineasa	R. Trinitas
1A)	107.7	5	Deva	Europa FM
2A)	107.8	30	Bistriţa	Digi FM
2B)	107.8	10	Bacău	Pro FM
30)	107.8	2	Moldova Nouă	Popular FM
1B)	107.9	1	Tulcea	Virgin R.
2A)	107.9	60	Bihor	Digi FM
2A)	107.9	30	Drobeta-T.Severin	Digi FM
4A)	107.9	2	Satu Mare	Kiss FM

+ txs below 1kW

Addresses & other information:
1A-D) Str. Admiral Horia Macelăriu nr. 36-38, sector 1, 013932 Bucureşti – **2A-D)** Şos. Panduri nr. 71, sector 5, 061344 Bucureşti – **3)** Str. Erou Iancu Nicolae nr. 38-38A, 077190 Voluntari **E:** rvs@rvs.ro – **4A-C)** Splaiul Independenţei nr. 202A, sector 6, 060022 Bucureşti – **5)** Str. Maior Gheorghe Şonţu nr. 8, sector 1, 011448 Bucureşti – **6)** Str. Leonida nr. 19, sector 2, 030167 Bucureşti – **7)** Str. Fabricii nr. 46B, sector 6, 060823 Bucureşti – **8)** str. 9 Mai 6B, sector 6, 060353 Bucureşti – **9)** Al. Dealul Mitropoliei nr. 25, sector 4, 040163 Bucureşti – **10)** Str. Spartacus nr. 33, 410466 Oradea – **11)** Bd. George Enescu 24, 720232 Suceava – **12)** Str. Borşului 45, 410605 Oradea – **13)** Şos. Bucureşti-Ploieşti nr. 81, sector 1, 077190 Bucureşti – **14)** Str. Bârsei nr. 18, 410423 Oradea. In Hungarian – **15)** Str. Ion Băieşu, bl. D3-D4, et. 1, 120252 Buzău – **16)** Bd. Mărăşti nr. 65-67, sector 1, 011465 Bucureşti – **17)** Str. Arhiepiscopiei 23, 900178 Constanţa – **18)** Str. Doamnei 15, sector 3, 030056 Bucureşti – **19)** Str. Traian 329, 730142 Vaslui – **20)** Bd. Nicolae Titulescu nr. 36-37, 910011 Călăraşi – **21A,B)** Str. Orzari nr. 84, sector 2, 021554 Bucureşti – **22)** Str. Teilor nr. 11, 105600 Câmpina – **23)** Str. Bucureşti nr. 149-151, 910011 Călăraşi – **24)** Str. Ion C. Brătianu nr. 1, 440010 Satu Mare. In Hungarian – **25)** Str. Drumul Muntele Găina nr. 107-109, sector 1, 013913 Bucureşti – **26)** Str. G-ral Dimitrie Salmen nr. 20, ap.7, sector 2, 021371 Bucureşti – **27)** Str. Ianus Pannonius nr. 25A, 410150 Oradea – **28)** Bd. Iuliu Maniu nr. 51, sector 6, 061077 Bucureşti – **29)** Str. 24 Ianuarie nr. 9E, 905200 Cernavoda – **30)** Str. Grisellini nr. 43, 325550 Moldova Nouă – **31)** Str. Podgoriilor nr. 32, 820185 Tulcea – **32)** Bd. Traian nr. 14, 430212 Baia Mare – **33)** Str. Mărăşti nr. 18, 720188 Suceava – **34)** Str. DN1 Ploieşti-Câmpina km 5, 107070 Blejoi – **35)** Str. Democraţiei nr 28A, 100559 Ploieşti – **36)** Str. Baraţilor nr. 18, 545400 Sighişoara – **37)** Str. Sinaia nr. 17, 310084 Arad **E:** contact@altfm.ro. In Romanian & Hungarian – **A)** Rel. RFI (France).

DAB Transmitter (DAB+) (Trial)
Tx Operator: Radiocom **M:** România Actualităţi, România Cultural, România Muzical, R. 3Net, Antena Satelor, Bucureşti FM **Tx:** Block 12A (Bucureşti 0.5kW)

RUSSIA

L.T: KA: UTC +2h; AD, AR, BE, BR, CC, CV, DA, IN, IV, KB, KC, KD, KL, KO, KS, KT, KU, KV, KX, LI, MD, ME, MO, MU, NE, NN, NO, OL, PS, PZ, RO, RY, SM, SO, SP, ST, TA, TL, TS, TV, VL, VN, VO, YA: +3h; AS, SA, SR, UD, UL, VG: +4h; BA, CB, KG, KY, OB, PR, SV, TY, YN: +5h; OM: +6h; AK, KE, KN, NS, RA, RK, RT, TO: +7h; BU, IR: +8h; RS (Western), YV, ZB: +9h; AM, KH, PM, RS (Central): +10h; MA, RS (Eastern), SL: +11h; CK, KM: +12h. Resp. Krym & Sevastopol: +3h. — **Pop:** 146 million — **Pr.L:** Russian (official); additional official languages in the republics: Abaza, Adyghe, Altay, Avar, Azeri, Bashkir, Buryat, Chechen, Chuvash, Erzya, Ingush, Kabardian, Kalmyk, Karachay-Balkar, Khakas, Komi-Zyrian, Lezgi, Mansi, Mari, Moksha, Nogai, Ossetic, Tatar, Tuvan, Udmurt, Yakut. Resp. Krym & Sevastopol: Ukrainian, Crimean Tatar. — **E.C:** 230V/50Hz — **ITU:** RUS

FEDERALNAYA SLUZHBA PO NADZORU V SFERE SVYAZI, INFORMATSIONNYKH TEKHNOLOGIY I MASSOVYKH KOMMUNIKATSII (ROSKOMNADZOR)

(Federal Service for the Supervision of Communications, Information Technology, and Mass Media)
✉ 109074 Moskva, Kitaygorodskiy proyezd 7 ☎ +7 495 9876800 🖷 +7 495 9876801 **E:** rsoc_in@rsoc.ru **W:** rkn.gov.ru
L.P: Head: Aleksandr A.Zharov

VSEROSSIYSKAYA GOSUDARSTVENNAYA TELEVIZIONNAYA I RADIOVESHCHATELNAYA KOMPANIYA (VGTRK) (Gov)

✉ 125040 Moskva, Yamskogo polya 5-ya ul. 19/21 ☎ +7 495 2514050 **E:** vgtrk@vgtrk.com **W:** vgtrk.com **L.P:** GD: Oleg B.Dobrodeyev
FM (MHz)
R. Rossii (RR): tx list see VGTRK Regional Services.

Rg	Location	RM*	VFM*	kW
AD	Maykop	104.0	-	4
AK	Barnaul	101.0	101.5	2/1
AK	Biysk	107.2	-	1
AK	Rybtsov	102.7	107.9	1
AM	Blagoveshchensk	90.2	-	1
AR	Arkhangelsk	106.0	90.8	1
AR	Severodvinsk	90.4	106.2	1/0.1
AS	Astrakhan	101.2	107.4	1
BA	Ufa	100.6	102.1	1
BA	Steplitamak	106.7	-	2
BE	Belgorod	88.7	105.9	1
BE	St. Oskol	105.0	p106.5	1
BR	Bryansk	90.6	104.0	1
BU	Ulan-Ude	103.2	88.4	1
CB	Chelyabinsk	93.6	92.6	1
CB	Magnitogorsk	101.8	p95.4	1
CC	Goragorskiy	104.1	103.3	1
CC	Groznyy	90.1	99.4	1
CC	Gudermes	104.9	102.6	1/0.1
DA	Makhachkala	98.6	100.3	1
IR	Angarsk	103.5	-	1
IR	Bratsk	99.9	100.3	1
IR	Irkutsk	88.1	101.7	1/2
IV	Ivanovo	104.2	100.7	1
KA	Kaliningrad	102.5	95.1	4/1
KB	Nalchik	101.1	96.6	1
KC	Cherkessk	p99.6	p97.4	1
KD	Krasnodar	91.4	100.6	1
KE	Kemerovo	102.3	90.6	1/0.5
KE	Novokuznetsk	103.0	95.2	1
KG	Kurgan	102.0	87.9	1
KH	Khabarovsk	90.6	104.8	1
KL	Kaluga	98.7	107.1	1/0.5
KM	Petropavlovsk-Kam.	103.5	107.0	1/0.1
KN	Krasnoyarsk	106.6	94.0	1
KO	Syktyvkar	90.8	88.3	1
KO	Ukhta	p91.0	103.9	0.5/1
KT	Petrozavodsk	107.9	p98.0	0.5/1
KS	Kostroma	100.9	-	1
KU	Kursk	95.3	102.9	1
KV	Kirov	101.4	105.3	0.5/1
KX	Elista	102.2	p105.6	1
KY	Nizhnevartovsk	89.5	p106.9	1
KY	Surgut	107.0	100.7	1/0.5
LI	Lipetsk	106.6	90.3	1
MA	Magadan	105.0	-	1
MD	Saransk	102.6	90.6	1
ME	Yoshkar-Ola	102.7	90.9	1
MO	Moskva	103.4	97.6	5
MO	Shatura	-	91.4	1
MU	Murmansk	103.5	107.8	1
NN	Arzamas	p91.6	p101.7	1
NN	N.Novgorod	92.4	98.6	4/1
NO	V.Novgorod	101.2	-	5
NS	Novosibirsk	93.2	104.6	1/2
OB	Orenburg	106.3	90.5	1
OB	Orsk	101.1	p95.4	1
OM	Omsk	88.6	107.8	1
OR	Oryol	99.2	p92.0	1
PE	Penza	95.2	96.0	1

Rg	Location	RM*	VFM*	kW
PM	Ussuriysk	p92.5	p98.8	1
PM	Vladivostok	88.8	89.8	1
PR	Berezniki	101.9	107.0	1
PR	Perm	96.2	88.5	1
PS	Pskov	104.1	p87.7	1
RA	Gorno-Altaysk	104.2	-	1
RO	Dyoktevo	-	104.5	1
RO	Morozovsk	-	106.5	1
RO	Rostov-na-Donu	91.8	90.2	0.1/1
RO	Salsk	-	102.8	1
RO	Shakhty	100.5	106.8	1/0.1
RO	Volgodonsk	105.8	91.4	0.5/1
RO	Vyoshenskaya	105.5	-	1
RS	Yakutsk	89.7	p87.5	1
RT	Kyzyl	103.4	p107.5	1
RY	Ryazan	99.1	97.7	1
SA	Samara	92.1	93.5	1
SA	Syzran	94.6	104.2	0.1/1
SA	Zhigulyovsk	90.8	87.5	1
SL	Yuzhno-Sakhalinsk	103.5	107.2	5/1
SO	Vladikavkaz	89.6	106.3	1
SM	Vyazma	104.2	-	1
SP	St.Peterburg	107.0	89.3	5
SR	Balakovo	101.3	-	1
ST	Pyatigorsk	102.5	-	1
ST	Stavropol	104.3	96.3	1
SV	Nizhniy Tagil	99.6	97.5	1
TA	Tambov	89.8	91.8	2
TL	Tula	103.9	100.9	1
TO	Tomsk	106.6	91.1	1
TS	Kazan	93.9	94.3	1
TS	Nab.Chelny	99.4	91.1	1
TS	Nizhnekamsk	88.2	p97.9	1
TV	Tver	93.1	92.7	1
TY	Tyumen	100.0	103.6	1
UD	Izhevsk	94.4	104.9	1
UL	Ulyanovsk	100.6	102.5	1
VG	Kamyshin	92.0	99.1	1
VG	Volgograd	95.3	106.8	1
VL	Kovrov	p101.0	102.2	0.25/1
VL	Vladimir	103.9	96.5	1
VN	Rossosh	106.5	101.9	1
VN	Voronezh	105.7	96.3	1
VO	Cherepovets	102.5	100.7	1
VO	Vologda	102.3	100.6	1
YA	Yaroslavl	107.9	99.9	1
ZB	Chita	104.5	101.5	1

+ sites with only txs below 1kW. Rg=Region (see VGTRK Regional Services chapter) *) Txs may carry local/regional opt-outs (produced by the regional VGTRK branches) p=Planned

Remaining txs of Mayak in the OIRT-FM band (to be replaced by CCIR FM txs): Salekhard 66.80 (0.03kW), Smogiri 67.13 (4kW), Naryan-Mar 67.76 (0.1kW), Khanty-Mansiysk 68.60 (2kW). Abakan 68.63 (4kW), Sochi 70.07 (2kW), Cherkessk 72.11 (4kW), Saratov 72.65 (4kW).

D.Prgr: R. Rossii (RR): 24h (time-shifted editions for all timezones) – **Mayak (RM):** 24h – **Vesti FM (VFM):** 24h – **R. Kultura:** 24h on Moskva 91.6MHz 5kW.

VGTRK Regional Services

D.Prgr: Reg. prgrs produced by the regional VGTRK branches are generally broadcast at local prime time hours (morning/noon/early evening) on freqs shared with R. Rossii on FM (txs see below) & via the national DVB-T2 multiplex 1 (txs see National TV section). In addition, some branches broadcast short news bulletins and/or local advertsing via the freqs of Mayak or Vesti FM. A few branches also have separate local or reg. outputs on exclusive freqs (txs see below).

NB: GTRK=gosudarstvennaya teleradiokompaniya, state broadcasting company. Synchronized networks: due to limited space, for each freq only one tx is listed; the number of other sites on the same freq is indicated by "(+2)" etc.

AD) Respublika Adygeya (Adygeya): GTRK "Adygeya", 385000 Maykop, ul. Zhukovskogo 24. **E:** trkra@radnet.ru **Reg:** On (MHz) Guzeripl 68.00, Krasnogvardeyskoye 69.38, Khamyshki 70.70, Koshekhabl 71.93, Takhtamukay 73.76, Maykop 98.8, Sevastopolskaya 100.2, Ust-Sakhrayskiy 100.3, Dakhovskaya 100.8, Kamennomostskiy 101.1, Novoprokhladnoye (+1) 103.9 in Russian, Adyghe. Also on Krasnodar (KD) 107.2MHz. **SW prgr for the Circassian ethnic minority in the Near East:** see International Radio section.

AK) Altayskiy kray: GTRK "Altay", 656045 Barnaul, Zmeinogorskiy trakt 27. **E:** altai@gtrk22.ru **Reg:** On (MHz) Yeltsovka 100.1, Kytmanovo 100.2, Ovsyannikovo (+1) 100.3, Tyumenskoye 100.7, Shipunovo 100.9, Ust-Kalmanka 101.2, Reprikha 101.3, Mayak 101.4, Burla (+1) 101.5, Alekseyevka (+2) 102.0, Kurya 102.4, Pospelikha 102.5, Ust-Charyshskaya Pristan 102.6, Verkh-Suyetka 102.7, Kulunda (+3) 102.8, Mikhaylovskoye 102.9, Gornyak (+1) 103.0, Klyuchi (+1) 103.2, Zalesovo (+1) 103.3, Barnaul (+3) 103.4, Maralikha (+3) 103.5, Berezovka 103.6, Novichikha 103.7, Galbshtadt 103.9, Pavlovsk (+1) 104.2, Krasnoshchekovo 104.3, Aleysk 104.6, Biysk 104.7, Bayevo 104.8, Blagoveshchenka (+1) 105.1, Topchikha 105.2, Shelabolikha 105.7, Rubtsovsk 106.0, Krasnogorskoye 106.8, Tabuny 106.9, Talkmenka 107.1, Zmeinogorsk 107.2, Belokurikha 107.4, Bystryy Istok (+1) 107.5, Local channel "Heart FM" on (MHz) Barnaul 69.80/105.9, Kamen-na-Obi 100.6, Zarinsk 101.2.

AM) Amurskaya oblast: GTRK "Amur", 675000 Blagoveshchensk, per. Svyatitelya Innokentiya 15. **E:** info@gtrkamur.ru **Reg:** On (MHz) Belogorsk 67.82, Progress 68.36, Shimanovsk 68.72, Svobodnyy 69.92, Poyarkovo 88.4, Blagoveshchensk 91.0, Arkhara (+1) 100.0, Yekaterinoslavka 101.9, Zavitinsk 102.4, Zen 103.4, Tynda 106.2, Konstantinovka 106.7, Skovorodino 107.1.

AR) Arkhangelskaya oblast: GTRK "Pomorye", 163069 Arkhangelsk, ul. Troitskiy 73. **E:** agtrk@pomorie.ru **Reg:** "R. Pomorye" on (MHz) Urdoma 66.38, Nizhneye Ustye 66.98, Nyandoma 67.31, Karpogory 67.76, Konosha 67.91, Rogachevo 68.00, Pinega 68.30, Glubokiy 68.45, Mezen 68.48, Plesetsk 69.23, Lekushonskoye 69.50, Vazhskiy 69.56, Sorga 69.71, Kizema 69.80, Pogost 69.92, Pogor 70.19, Alferovskaya 70.34, Okulovskaya 70.55, Pervomayskiy 72.14, Stroyevskoye 72.38, Vershinino 72.50, Shangaly 73.19, Morshchikhinskaya 73.52, Severodvinsk 88.7, Voznesenskoye 100.3, Obozerskiy 100.6, Arkhangelsk 102.0, Svetlyy 102.1, Ilinsko-Podomskoye (+2) 102.5, Kargopol 102.6, Avnyugskiy 102.9, Yemetsk (+1) 103.0 (also relayed via txs in region NE).

AS) Astrakhanskaya oblast: GTRK "Lotos", 414040 Astrakhan, ul. Lyakhova 4. **E:** lotos@lotos.rfn.ru **Reg:** "R. Lotos" on (MHz) Tambovka 103.4, Astrakhan 104.5, Chernyy Yar 105.3.

BA) Respublika Bashkortostan: GTRK "Bashkortostan", 450076 Ufa, ul. Gafuri 9/1. **E:** gtrk@gtrk.tv **Reg:** "R. Bashkortostana" on (MHz) Zilay 66.80, Dyurtyuli 66.86, Akyar 67.37, Rayevka 68.42, Chishmy 72.89, Tuymazy (+1) 87.9, Ufa 89.5, Oktyabrskiy 90.6, Belebey 98.2, Blzhbulyak 100.8, Abzanovo 101.1, Idelbakovo 101.3, Birsk 101.4, Karaidel 101.7, Isyangulovo 102.0, Starosubkhangulovo 102.1, Sharan 102.2, Mesyangutovo 102.3, Beloretsk (+1) 102.4, Verkhneyarkeyevo 102.6, Fyodorovka 102.7, Steplitamak 102.9, Baymak (+1) 103.4, Bakaly 103.7, Komsomolsk 104.1, Kugarchi 104.6, Verkhniy Avzyan 105.4, Krasnousolskiy 105.6, Davlekanovo 106.3, Tolbazy 107.3 in Bashkir, Russian.

BE) Belgorodskaya oblast: GTRK "Belgorod", 308009 Belgorod, pr. Slavy 60. **E:** trcblg@gtrktv.ru **Reg:** On (MHz) Valuyki 66.80, Staryy Oskol 107.0, Belgorod 107.2.

BR) Bryanskaya oblast: GTRK "Bryansk", 241033 Bryansk, ul. Stanke Dimitrova 77. **E:** radio@br-tvr.ru **Reg:** On (MHz) Navlya 67.37, Shvedchiki 70.04, Unecha 70.55, Pocheb 71.54, Belaya Beryozka 73.19, Novozybkov 89.5, Bryansk 91.6.

BU) Respublika Buryatiya: GTRK "Buryatiya", 670000 Ulan-Ude, ul. Yerbanova 7. **E:** bgtrk@bgtrk.ru **Reg:** On (MHz) Armak (+1) 66.68, Mikhaylovka (+1) 68.24, Altsak (+1) 68.48, Babushkin (+6) 68.60, Ashanga (+1) 69.08, Sosnovo-Ozerskoye (+5) 69.56, Kyakhta 70.16, Balakta 71.12, Botsiy 72.44, Zaigrayevo 87.5, Ulan-Ude 90.0, Bayangol (+5) 100.0, Sorok 100.4, B.Rechka (+6) 101.0, Ust-Barguzin 101.1, Mikhaylovka 101.4, Barykino 101.5, Gusinoozersk (+3) 101.6, Petropavlovka 101.7, Zakamensk 101.8, Bardarin (+2) 102.0, Kurumkan (+1) 102.2, Bichura 102.3, Ilinka 102.4, Mukhorshibir (+2) 102.5, Taksimo (+1) 102.7, Tataurovo (+2) 103.0, Kyren (+4) 103.3, Severobaykalsk (+1) 103.7, Nizhniy Torey (+1) 103.8, Kabansk (+2) 104.0, Kika (+1) 104.5, Zhemchuk 105.0, Tashir 105.7, Yelan 106.0, Kyakhta 106.3, Naushki 106.8, Ust-Muya 107.0, Novoilinsk 107.1, Tarbagatay 107.2, Bilyutay (+6) 107.5 in Russian, Buryat.

CB) Chelyabinskaya oblast: GTRK "Yuzhnyy Ural", 454000 Chelyabinsk, ul. Ordzhonikidze 54b. **E:** radio@cheltv.ru **Reg:** "R. Yuzhnyy Ural" on (MHz) Kyshtym 67.13, Yuryuzan 67.25, Stepnoye 68.36, Mezhozernyy 88.8, Miass 95.0, Chelyabinsk 97.8, Magnitogorsk 99.3*, Novoburino 100.2, Satka 100.4, Kartaly 101.2, Asha 102.8, Verkhniy Ufaley 103.6, Oktyabrskoye 103.7, Yuzhnouralsk 107.1, Zlatoust 107.2, Troitsk 107.9. *) Tx also carries prgrs by reg. substudio (Territorialnoye otdeleniye GTRK "Yuzhnyy Ural"): 455025 Magnitogorsk, ul. Lesoparkovaya 97. **E:** info@mgtrk.ru.

CC) Chechenskaya respublika: GTRK "Vaynakh", 364000 Groznyy, ul. A. Aydamirova 147. **E:** gtrkvainah@mail.ru **Reg:** "R. Vaynakh" on

(MHz) Gvardeyskoye 68.84, Goragorskiy 72.44, Gukhoy 88.1, Tevzana 90.4, Bulgat-Irzu 92.0, Dargo 95.2, Guni 98.7, Ersenoy 99.6, Day (+4) 100.0, Dyshne-Vedeno 100.2, Bolshiye Varandy (+1) 100.5, Benoy 100.6, Naurskaya 101.2, Zandak 101.6, Nikhaloy (+1) 101.7, Oyskhara 102.2, Tazbichi 102.5, Shelkovskaya (+2) 103.1, Assinovskaya 103.2, Groznyy 103.6, Khal-Kiloy (+1) 104.3, Kharachoy 105.0, Borzoy (+1) 105.1, Kargalinskaya 106.0, Terskoye 106.4, Gilyany 106.6, Dabrankhi (+1) 106.8, Benoy 106.9, Gudermes (+1) 107.3 in Russian, Chechen.

CK) Chukotskiy avtonomnyy okrug: GTRK "Chukotka", 686710 Anadyr, ul. Lenina 18. **E:** gtrk@anadyr.ru **Reg:** On (MHz) Ust-Belaya 100.1, Lorino (+7) 100.5, Alkatvaam (+5) 101.6, Beringovskiy (+3) 102.8, Anadyr (+22) 104.7 in Russian, Chukchi.

CV) Chuvashskaya respublika - Chuvashiya: GTRK "Chuvashiya", 428003 Cheboksary, ul. Nikolayeva 4. **E:** chradio@tvr.chtts.ru **Reg:** "R. Chuvashii" on (MHz) Ibresi 70.85, Yadrin 71.12, Tsivilsk 99.9 in Russian, Chuvash.

DA) Respublika Dagestan: GTRK "Dagestan", 367032 Makhachkala, ul. M.Gadzhiyeva 182. **E:** gtrk_dagestan@mail.ru **Reg:** On (MHz) Kochubey 67.04, Gergebil 69.95, Dubki 100.1, Derbent 104.9, Makhachkala 105.6 in Russian, Avar, Chechen, Kumyk, Lak, Nogai, Rutul, Tsakhur; Aghul, Azeri, Dargwa, Lezgi, Tabassaran, Tat.

IN) Respublika Ingushetiya: GTRK "Ingushetiya", 386100 Nazran, per. Naberezhnyy 8 **E:** pressari@mail.ru **Reg:** On (MHz) Nazran 101.3, Karabulak 104.0 in Russian, Ingush.

IR) Irkutskaya oblast: GTRK "Irkutsk", 664025 Irkutsk, ul. Gorkogo 15. **E:** news@vesti.irk.ru **Reg:** On (MHz) Ust-Ilimsk 91.3, Bratsk 99.1, Mama (+2) 100.0, Kachug 100.8, Rudnogorsk 101.0, Ust-Ordynskiy 101.1, Tubinskiy (+1) 101.5, Yerbogachen (+1) 102.0, Kuytun (+1) 102.2, Bayanday 102.4, Novaya Igirma 102.6, Chunskiy 102.8, Zhigalovo 103.4, Kirensk 103.5, Yelantsy (+1) 103.6, Ust-Uda 103.7, Magistralnyy 103.8, Bodaybo 104.3, Baykalsk 104.4, Irkutsk 105.0, Tulun 106.3, Zheleznogorsk-Ilimskiy 106.4, Bokhan 106.6, Tayshet 106.8, Zima 107.0, Osa 107.6, Angarsk 107.9. NB: Tx also carries prgrs by reg. substudio (Territorialnoye otdeleniye GTRK "Irkutsk"): 666110 Ust-Ordynskiy, ul. Kalinina 10. **E:** info@mgtrk.ru.

IV) Ivanovskaya oblast: GTRK "Ivteleradio", 153000 Ivanovo, ul. Teatralnaya 31. **E:** admin@ivtele.ru **Reg:** On (MHz) Rodniki 70.13, Furmanov 73.64, Ivanovo 89.1.

KA) Kaliningradskaya oblast: GTRK "Kaliningrad", 236016 Kaliningrad, ul. Klinicheskaya 19. **E:** redaktor@gtrk39.ru **Reg:** On (MHz) Veselovka 65.90, Bolshakovo 70.19, Kuybyshevskoye 102.1, Kaliningrad 103.9.

KB) Kabardino-Balkarskaya respublika: GTRK "Kabardino-Balkariya", 360030 Nalchik, pr. Lenina 1a. **E:** vestikbr@mail.ru **Reg:** On (MHz) Samarkovo (+3) 66.62, Verkhnyaya Balkariya 71.51, Zayukovo 88.2, Nalchik 101.8, Anzorey 102.6, Nizhniy Cherem 103.9, Bulungu 104.0, Elbrus (+1) 106.5, Karasu 106.8 in Russian, Kabardian, Karachay-Balkar.

KC) Karachayevo-Cherkesskaya respublika: GTRK "Karachayevo-Cherkesiya", 369000 Cherkessk, ul. Krasnoarmeyskaya 51. **E:** gtrk_kchr@rambler.ru **Reg:** On (MHz) Krasnogorskaya 66.98, Karachayevsk (+1) 67.34, Kavkazkiy 68.21, Adyge-Khabl 68.66, Zelenchuskaya 68.81, Pregradnaya 69.80, Ispravnaya 69.83, Ust-Dzheguta 69.89, Teberda 69.98, Arkhyz 70.07, Dombay 70.25, Cherkessk 70.31, V.Mara 71.06, Storozhevaya 71.72, Kurdzhinovo 71.81, Khabez 71.84, Urup 72.44, Cherkessk 91.2, Uchkeken 98.8, Teberda 102.8, Dombay 104.0 in Russian, Abaza, Karachay-Balkar, Nogai.

KD) Krasnodarskiy kray: GTRK "Kuban", 350038 Krasnodar, ul. Radio 5. **E:** owl@kubantv.ru **Reg:** On (MHz) Tbilisskaya 66.20, Goryachiy Klyuch 66.41, Abrau-Dyurso 66.62, Novorossiysk (+1) 67.97, Gelendzhik 68.30, Kanevskaya 68.36, Armavir 68.57, Vyshestebliyevskaya 68.72, Primorsko-Ahktarsk 69.08, Kropotkin (+1) 69.23, Pavlovskaya 69.59, Temryuk 70.22, Tuapse 70.46, Gubskaya 71.21, Sochi 71.93*, Apsheronsk 72.20, Imretinskaya 72.71, Otradnaya 72.98, Krasnodar 90.2, Primorsko-Akhtarsk 91.8, Armavir 100.4, Tuapse 101.4, Belaya Glina 102.0, Adler 102.8, Kushchevskaya 103.5, Krasnodar 107.2, Yeysk 107.4, Arkhipo-Osipovka 107.6. NB: *) Tx also carries prgrs by reg. substudio (Territorialnoye otdeleniye GTRK "Kuban"): 354000 Sochi, ul. Teatralnaya 11a. **E:** tv@sochi.com.

KE) Kemerovskaya oblast: GTRK "Kuzbass", 650000 Kemerovo, ul. Teletsentr 3. **E:** post@gtrk.kuzbass.net **Reg:** "R. Kuzbassa" on (MHz) Yurga 66.11, Klyuchevaya 67.04, Tashtagol 69.80, Anzhevo-Sudzhensk 70.40, Novokuznetsk 97.9, Kiselyovsk 100.0, Mezhdurechensk 100.8, Kemerovo 103.7, Leninsk-Kuznetskiy 103.8. Reg. channel "Kuzbass FM" on (MHz) Kemerovo 91.0, Klyuchevaya 101.2, Leninsk-Kuznetskiy 101.3, Anzhevo-Sudzhensk 101.6, Mezhdurechensk 101.8, Novokuznetsk 102.0, Guryevsk 102.5, Yurga 103.6, Belovo 104.5, Sheregesh 105.7, Prokopyevsk 107.4.

KG) Kurganskaya oblast: GTRK "Kurgan", 640018 Kurgan, ul. Sovetskaya 105. **E:** report@gtrk-kurgan.ru **Reg:** On (MHz) Shumikha 66.89, Makushino 68.48, Shadrinsk 69.23, Shatrovo 71.18, Kurgan 105.0.

KH) Khabarovskiy kray: GTRK "Dalnevostochnaya", 680632 Khabarovsk, ul. Lenina 4. **E:** vesti@dvtrk.com **Reg:** On (MHz) Khabarovsk 91.4, Aim (+2) 100.0, Amgun (+5) 100.1, Glebovo 100.3, Chegdomyn 100.5, Tyrma 100.9, im. P.Osipenko 101.3, Nikolayevsk-na-Amure (+1) 101.6, Okhotsk (+1) 101.9, Berezovyy (+3) 102.0, Bichevaya 102.2, Ayan (+1) 102.4, Tugur 102.5, Sovetskaya Gavan 102.6, Duki 103.3, Arka 104.0, Poletnoye 104.5, Komsomolsk-na-Amure 105.2*, Dolmi 105.3, Bikin 106.4, Mukhen 107.0, Pereyaslavka 107.3, Amursk 107.5, Vyazemskiy 107.6 (also via txs in region YV). Local channel "R. 101.8" on Khabarovsk 101.8MHz. NB: *) Tx also carries reg. prgrs by reg. substudio (Territorialnoye otdeleniye GTRK "Dalnevostochnaya"): 681000 Komsomolsk-na-Amure, ul. Molodogvardeyskaya 7 **E:** studio@kmscom.ru.

KL) Kaluzhskaya oblast: GTRK "Kaluga", 248021 Kaluga, Pole Svobody 40a. **E:** mail@gtrk-kaluga.ru **Reg:** On (MHz) Lyudinovo 67.91, Medyn 68.03, Baryatino 70.79, Mosalsk 71.39, Spassk-Demensk 72.05, Zhizdra 72.92, Khvastovichi 73.07, Sukhinichi 101.3, Kaluga 104.3, Yukhnov 104.9, Obninsk 106.4.

KM) Kamchatskiy kray: GTRK "Kamchatka", 683000 Petropavlovsk-Kamchatskiy, ul. Sovetskaya 62. **Reg:** On (MHz) Palana (+4) 69.68, Ust-Kamchatsk 71.12, Klyuchi 71.90, Sobolevo 72.86, Ust-Bolsheretsk 100.5, Petropavlovsk-Kamchatskiy 102.0, Apacha 102.3, Milkovo 102.6, Nachiki 102.7. Incl. prgrs in Koryak, Itelmen, Evenki produced by sub-studio (Territorialnoye otdeleniye GTRK "Kamchatka"): 684620 Palana, ul. Obukhova 4.

KN) Krasnoyarskiy kray: GTRK "Krasnoyarsk", 660028 Krasnoyarsk, ul. Mechnikova 44a. **E:** referent@kgtrk.ru **Reg:** On (MHz) Balakhta 66.32, Motygino 66.44, Karatuzskoye 67.37, Zelenogorsk 68.21, Solyanka 68.84, Uzhur 69.56, Pirovskoye 70.76 Tyukhtet 71.42, Krasnoturansk 71.48, Kodinsk 71.66, Igarka 72.00, Yeniseysk 72.74, Norilsk 87.9, Krasnoyarsk 94.5, Pervomansk 100.6, Dikson (+1) 101.0, Norilsk 101.4, Tura (+1) 101.5*, Borodino (+1) 101.8, Aginskoye (+2) 102.0, Novobirilyussy 102.3, Motorskoye 102.4, Mina 102.5, Bolshaya Irba 102.6, Anash (+1) 102.7, Lesosibirsk (+2) 102.8, B.Salba 103.1, Bogotol (+1) 103.2, Dudinka 103.7, Achinsk (+1) 104.0, Nazarovo 104.8, Sukhobuzimskoye 104.9, Kozulka 106.3, Divnogorsk (+1) 107.9. NB: *) Tx also carries prgrs by reg. substudio (Territorialnoye otdeleniye GTRK "Krasnoyarsk") in Russian, Evenki: 663370 Tura, ul. 50 let Oktyabrya 28. **E:** heglen@tura.evenkya.ru.

KO) Respublika Komi: GTRK "Komi Gor", 167005 Syktyvkar, Oktyabrskiy pr. 164. **E:** komigor@komi.rfn.ru **Reg:** On (MHz) Yarashyu 65.90, Storozhevsk 66.32, Priuralsk 66.35, Vorkuta 66.60, Sludka 67.16, Pomozdino 67.85, Yaksha 68.36, Troitsko-Pechorsk 68.60, Shoshka 68.72, Kartayol (+2) 68.93, Inta 69.08, Krasnobor 69.11, Okunevo 69.20, Usogorsk 69.56, Myyeldino (+1) 69.83, Petrun 70.28, Vetyu 70.40, Voyvozh 70.64, Spasporub 70.73, Vuktyl 71.06, Kuratovo 71.09, B.Pyssa 71.15, Chukhlom 73.19, Vekshor 73.31, Ukhta 87.9, Syktyvkar 91.6 in Russian, Komi-Zyrian.

KS) Kostromskaya oblast: GTRK "Kostroma", 156961 Kostroma, pl. Konstitutsii 1. **E:** gtrk@gtrk.kmtn.ru **Reg:** On (MHz) Galich 66.74, Sharya 67.10, Kologriv 68.66, Soligalich 69.02, Makaryev 71.60, Nerekhta 89.3, Kostroma 91.6, Pyshchuk 103.5, Vokhma 103.7, Chukhloma 103.8, Pavino 103.9, Parfenevo 104.0, Ostrovskoye 107.3.

KT) Respublika Kareliya: GTRK "Kareliya", 185002 Petrozavodsk, ul. Pirogova 2. **E:** gtrk@petrozavodsk.rfn.ru **Reg:** "R. Karelii" on (MHz) Kostomuksha 101.5, Petrozavodsk 102.2, Muyezerskiy 102.7, Loukhi 103.0, Medvezhyegorsk 103.7, Naiystenyarvi 105.0, Sortavala 105.6, Segezha 106.0, Belomorsk 106.4 in Russian, Finnish, Karelian, Vepsian.

KU) Kurskaya oblast: GTRK "Kursk", 305016 Kursk, ul. Sovetskaya 32. **E:** gtrk@kursk.rfn.ru **Reg:** On (MHz) Lgov 66.83, Kshenskiy 72.41, Kursk 101.7.

KV) Kirovskaya oblast: GTRK "Vyatka", 610002 Kirov, ul. Uritskogo 34. **E:** tv@gtrk-vyatka.ru **Reg:** On (MHz) Vyatskiye Polyarny 66.35, Kirs 66.86, Sovetsk 67.07, Klyuchi 67.91, Falyonki 68.33, Pinyug (+1) 70.55, Shmelevo 70.73, Sanchursk 73.28, Omutninsk (+1) 103.1, Podosinovets 104.0, Pinyug 106.2, Kirov 106.3, Urzhum 107.7.

KX) Respublika Kalmykiya: GTRK "Kalmykiya", 358000 Elista, ul. M.Gorkogo 34. **E:** kalmradio@mail.ru **Reg:** "R. Kalmykiya" on (MHz) Sadovoye 66.95, Utta 68.24, Ulan-Kholl 69.59, Elista 102.7 in Russian, Kalmyk.

KY) Khanty-Mansiyskiy avtonomnyy okrug - Yugra (NB: KY is subordinated to region TY): GTRK "Yugoriya", 628012 Khanty-Mansiysk, ul. Gagarina 4. **E:** gtrk@ugoria.tv **Reg:** "R. Yugry" on (MHz) Agirish 65.96, Kondinskoye 66.20, Kommunisticheskiy 66.32, Beloyarskiy 66.44, Oktyabrskoye 66.68, Bobrovskaya 66.77, Uray 67.22, Langepas 67.28, Kuminskiy 67.52, Igrim (+1) 68.33, Batovo 69.47, Mezhdurechenskiy

70.28, Vakhovsk 70.67, Nyagan 70.82, Gornopravdinsk 71.00, Kogalym 71.30, Beryozovo 71.42, Yugorsk 71.78, Raduzhnyy 72.08, Pyt-Yakh 72.86, Khanty-Mansiysk 88.3, Surgut 89.9, Nizhnevartovsk 107.8 in Russian, Khanti, Mansi. Txs also relay reg. prgrs by GTRK "Region-Tyumen", TY.

LI) Lipetskaya oblast: GTRK "Lipetsk", 398050 Lipetsk, pl. Plekhanova 1. **E:** teleradio@lipetsk.rfn.ru **Reg:** On (MHz) Chernava 69.26, Izmalkovo 73.79, Lipetsk 89.1, Yelets 101.7, Terbuny 101.9, Dankov 102.4, Ploty 102.6, Dobrinka 102.7, Dolgorukovo 102.9, Chaplygin 103.3, Lev Tolstoy 103.8, Usman 104.0, Volovo 104.4.

MA) Magadanskaya oblast: GTRK "Magadan", 685024 Magadan, ul. Kommuny 8/12. **E:** vesti.gtrk.magadan@gmail.com **Reg:** On (MHz) Ola 101.3, Stekolnyy 103.3, Magadan 103.5, Sokol 104.0.

MD) Respublika Mordoviya: GTRK "Mordoviya", 430030 Saransk, ul. Dokuchayeva 29. **E:** gtrkmordoviya@yandex.ru **Reg:** On (MHz) Tengushevo 66.35, Vechkusy 66.95, Dubenki 67.28, Krasnoslobodsk 67.31, Yavas 67.67, Umet 68.33, B.Berezniki 68.42, Atyashevo 68.51, Yelniki 68.78, Lyambir 68.96, Temnikov 68.99, Kadoshkino 69.41, Ardatov 69.53, St.Shaygovo 69.65, Insar 71.03, Saransk 91.2, Atyuryevo 106.0 in Russian, Erzya, Moksha.

ME) Respublika Mariy El: GTRK "Mariy-El", 424031 Yoshkar-Ola, ul. Mashinostroiteley 7a. **E:** gtrkradio@yandex.ru **Reg:** On (MHz) Volzhsk 69.29, Sovetskiy 71.21, Kozmodemyansk 72.20, Zvenigovo 73.16, Yoshkar-Ola 106.0 in Russian, Mari.

MO) Moskva (Federal City) & Moskovskaya oblast: no regional branch of VGTRK.

MU) Murmanskaya oblast: GTRK "Murman", 183032 Murmansk, ul. Varnichnaya Sopka 1. **E:** radio@tvmurman.com **Reg:** On (MHz) Krasnoshchelye 72.38, Zelenoborskiy 100.5, Revda 101.6, Olenegorsk 101.8, Kirovsk 102.0, Lovozero 102.1, Kandalaksha 102.2, Umba 102.3, Tumannyy 102.7, Alakurtti 103.1, Teriberka 103.8, Prirechnyy 105.6, Ostrovnoy 106.1, Murmansk 107.4, Polyarnyye Zori 107.7, Zapolyarnyy 107.9.

NE) Nenetskiy avtonomnyy okrug (NB: NE is subordinated to region AR): Territorialnoye otdeleniye GTRK "Pomorye", 164700 Naryan-Mar, ul. Smidovicha 19. **E:** zapolyarie@mail.ru **Reg:** On (MHz) Naryan-Mar 66.20 in Russian, Nenets. Tx also relays reg. prgrs by GTRK "Pomorye", Arkhangelsk, AR.

NN) Nizhegorodskaya oblast: GTRK "Nizhniy Novgorod", 603950 Nizhniy Novgorod, ul. Belinskogo 9a. **E:** radio@nnov.rfn.ru **Reg:** On (MHz) Vacha 66.65, Sokolskoye 66.92, Sergach 67.16, Semyonov 67.43, Uren 68.84, Shakhunya 69.59, Diveyevo 69.80, Lyskovo 70.43, Krasnyye Baki 70.64, Vyksa 71.09, Kstovo 73.97, N.Novgorod 93.9, Kovernino 101.1, Belogorka 102.2, Lukoyanov 103.3, Sarov 103.5, Arzamas 106.6.

NO) Novgorodskaya oblast: GTRK "Slaviya", 173620 Velikiy Novgorod, ul. B.Moskovskaya 106. **E:** vestira@mail.ru **Reg:** "R. Slaviya" on (MHz) Pestovo 100.0, Zaluchye 101.1, Valday 101.6, Novgorod 102.2, Kresttsy 106.3, Chudovo 107.3.

NS) Novosibirskaya oblast: GTRK "Novosibirsk", 630048 Novosibirsk, ul. Rimskogo-Korsakova 9. **E:** radio@nsk.rfn.ru **Reg:** On (MHz) Aleksandro-Nevskoye 68.24, Zdvinsk 68.96, Sharchino 69.62, Kuybyshev 69.68, Kayly (+1) 69.83, Kochki (+1) 69.95, Listvyanka 69.98, Bolotnoye 71.66, Zyryanka 72.23, Raduga 72.95, Novosibirsk 97.8, Listvyanskiy 100.3, Kochenevo 100.4, Ubinskoye 100.6, Bystrovka 101.0, Severnoye (+1) 101.2, Kyshtovka 101.5, Druzhinino 101.8, Novoyarkovo 101.9, Tatarsk 102.0, Lyanino (+2) 102.2, Pryamskoye 102.3, Proletarskiy 102.4, Novosilish 102.5, Pautovskiy 102.8, Kargat 102.9, Ordynskoye (+1) 103.0, Vengerovo 103.2, Boltovo (+2) 103.3, Degostayevo 103.4, Gornyy (+1) 103.5, Chistoozernoye 104.1, Chany 104.2, Osinovskiy 104.3, Novoselovo 104.4, Karasevo 104.5, Uspenskiy 104.7, Maslyanino 105.0, Beloye (+1) 105.1, Berezovka 105.4, Zavyalovo 105.5, Bagan 105.7, Zhuravka 106.1, Shipunovo 106.3, Kochenevo (+1) 106.9, Karasuk (+2) 107.1.

OB) Orenburgskaya oblast: GTRK "Orenburg", 460024 Orenburg, per. Televizionnyy 3. **E:** gtrc@orenburg.rfn.ru **Reg:** On (MHz) Buzuluk 66.62, Yasnyy 69.71, Kuvandyk 70.04, Orenburg 91.0, Uralskoye 101.9, Sorochinsk 102.0, Bikkulovo (+1) 102.1, Tashla 102.6, Svetlyy 102.9, Pervomayskiy 103.0, Kvarkeno 103.1, Saraktash 103.3, Donetskoye 103.4, Izobilnoye 103.5, Ilek 103.6, Novosergiyevka 103.9, Sol-Iletsk 104.6, Abdulino 105.1, Pleshanovo 105.2, Akbulak 105.5, Sharlyk 106.4, Alekseyevo 106.5, Tyulgan 106.6, Ponomarevka 106.9, Severnoye 107.0, Buguruslan (+1) 107.5, Aleksandrovka 107.8 in Russian, Chuvash, Tatar.

OL) Orlovskaya oblast: GTRK "Oryol", 302028 Oryol, ul. 7 Noyabrya 43. **E:** info@ogtrk.ru **Reg:** On (MHz) Livny 67.19, Oryol 102.3.

OM) Omskaya oblast: GTRK "Irtysh", 644050 Omsk, pr. Mira 2. **E:** reklama@omsk.rfn.ru **Reg:** On (MHz) Khutora 70.43, Omsk 87.7, Nazyvayevsk 101.3, Tara 101.4, Ust-Ishim 102.6, Sherbakul 102.8, Isilkul 103.8, Odesskoye 104.2, Cherlak 107.1.

PM) Primorskiy kray: GTRK "Vladivostok", 690090 Vladivostok, ul. Uborevicha 20a. **E:** gtrk@vestiprim.ru **Reg:** "R. Primorskogo kraya" on (MHz) Olga 67.58, Arsenyev 68.60, Kraskino 68.84, Kavalerovo 69.20, Dalnerechensk 69.32, Dalnegorsk 70.04, Novozhatkovo 70.64, Plastun (+1) 71.00, Chkalovka 72.08, Nakhodka 101.4, Kamenka (+4) 101.5, Moryak-Rybolov (+2) 102.0, Vladivostok (+2) 102.1, Kavalerevo 102.6, Ust-Sobolevka 102.9, Plastun 103.1, Agzu (+3) 103.5, Maksimovka 103.9, Olga 104.4, Lesozavodsk 105.5, Ussuriysk 106.0.

PR) Permskiy kray: GTRK "Perm", 614990 Perm, ul. Tekhnicheskaya 7. **E:** main@perm.t7.ru **Reg**: "R. Permskogo kraya" on (MHz) Kungur 66.65, Barda 67.10, Kudymkar 67.19*, Kizel 67.67, Chastye 68.63, Oktyabrskiy 68.72, Vaya 68.78, Ust-Chernoye 68.84*, Ilyinskiy 68.93, Serebryanka 69.14, Karagay 69.53, Osa 70.55, Chusovoy 70.67, Chernushka 70.70, Krasnovishersk 71.33, Chaykovskiy 71.42, Berezniki 71.87, Ochyor 72.02, Perm 90.2, Kochevo 101.1*, Uinskoye 101.5, Nyrob 102.7, Kosa 103.0*, Gayny 103.5*, Siva 103.8, Berezniki 104.2. NB: *) Txs also carry prgrs by reg. substudio (Territorialnoye otdeleniye GTRK "Perm") in Russian, Komi-Permyak: 617240 Kudymkar, ul. Volodarskogo 18. **E:** kudtv@mail.ru.

PS) Pskovskaya oblast: GTRK "Pskov", 180024 Pskov, Rizhskiy pr. 71. **E:** tv@pvi.ru **Reg:** On (MHz) Trutnevo 67.34, Novosokolniki 67.94, Dedovichi 69.86, Glubokoye 70.01, Pskov 91.1, Pytalovo 101.8, Sebezh 103.3, V.Luki 103.8, Strugi Krasnyye 104.4, Bezhanitsy 104.8.

PZ) Penzenskaya oblast: GTRK "Penza", ul. Lermontova 39, 440602 Penza. **E:** gtrk@penza-trv.ru **Reg:** On (MHz) Meshcherskoye 68.84, Penza 94.2, Gorodishche 100.9, Pachelma 103.6, Belinskiy 105.0, Neverkino 105.1, Malaya Serdoba 105.4, Kuznetsk 107.0, Nikolsk 107.3, Issa 107.7.

RA) Respublika Altay: GTRK "Gornyy Altay", 659000 Gorno-Altaysk, pr. Kommunisticheskiy 37. **E:** info@elaltay.ru **Reg:** On (MHz) Tashanta 67.10, Tiyakhty 71.66, Iohach 101.5, Aktash 102.0, Shebalino 102.3, Onguday 102.5, Ust-Kan 102.8, Ulagan 103.3, Kosh-Agach 103.5, Turochak 103.8, Ust-Koksa 104.8, Gorno-Altaysk 105.0 in Russian, Altai.

RK) Respublika Khakasiya: GTRK "Khakasiya", 655017 Abakan, ul. Vyatkina 12. **E:** vgtrk2003@mail.ru **Reg:** "R. Khakasiya" on (MHz) Kopyevo 68.00, Priiskovyy 68.51, Shira 70.16, Tashtyp (+1) 71.00, Bogdan 72.50, Askiz 72.59, Sorsk 73.19, Sonskiy 73.52, Saragash 73.61, Kommunar 73.85, Abakan 91.0, Sayanogorsk 102.7, Abaza 103.3 in Russian, Khakas.

RO) Rostovskaya oblast: GTRK "Don-TR", 344101 Rostov-na-Donu, ul. 1-ya Barrikadnaya 18. **E:** info@dontr.ru **Reg:** On (MHz) Rostov-na-Donu 89.0, Kamensk-Shakhtinskiy 90.0, Volgodonsk 99.0, Veshenskaya 101.4, Shakhty 102.9, Morozovsk 104.0, Taganrog 104.8, Novocherkassk 105.4, Salsk 105.9.

RS) Respublika Sakha (Yakutiya): GTRK "Sakha", 677892 Yakutsk, ul. Ordzhonikidze 48. **E:** gtrksakha@yandex.ru **Reg:** "R. Yakutii" on (MHz) Neryungri 66.68, Aldan 69.38, Berdigestyakh 100.0, Batagay (+1) 100.5, Lensk 100.9, Namtsy 101.2, Olyokminsk 101.4, Pokrovsk 101.7, Belaya Gora (+3) 102.0, Khandyga 103.1, Yakutsk 104.9 in Russian, Yakut.

RT) Respublika Tyva: GTRK "Tyva", 667010 Kyzyl, ul. Gornaya 31. **E:** gtrk-tuva@gtrktuva.ru **Reg:** On (MHz) Shagonar 70.64, Kyzyl 105.5 in Russian, Tuvinian.

RY) Ryazanskaya oblast: GTRK "Oka", 390006 Ryazan, ul. Skomoroshinskaya 20. **E:** zavtv@ryazan.rfn.ru **Reg:** "R. Ryazani" on (MHz) Ryazan 99.7, Yermish 100.9, Sasovo 101.2, Pronsk 101.7, Miloslavskoye 101.8, Mosolovo 103.5, Kasimov 103.7, Spas-Klepiki 103.8, Mikhaylov (+1) 104.7, Ryazhsk 105.2, Lesnoye Konobeyevo 106.3, Kadom 106.5, Skopin 106.9.

SA) Samarskaya oblast: GTRK "Samara", 443011 Samara, ul. Sovetskoy Armii 205. **E:** info@tvsamara.ru **Reg:** On (MHz) Tolyatti 88.9, B. Glushitsa 91.7, Podlesnyy 94.8, Kurumoch 95.0, Samara 95.3, Borskoye 96.1, Novyy Kutuluk 98.5, Petrovka 99.0, Kinel 99.5, Bereznyaki (+1) 100.0, Beregovoy 100.3, Oktyabrsk 100.4, Chapayev 100.7, Chetyrla 101.2, Kamyshla 102.6, Mordovo-Adelyakovo 103.0, Syzran (+1) 103.4, Chelno-Vershiny 103.5, Androsovka (+1) 103.9, Alekseyevka (+1) 104.0, Pokhvistnevo 104.1, Yelkhovka 104.2, Klyavlino (+1) 104.4, Koshki 105.1, Neftegorsk 105.2, Isakly 105.3, Staraya Racheyka 105.4, Novokurovka 105.5, Krasnoarmeyskoye 105.8, Sergiyevsk 105.9, Khvorostyanka 107.1, Kinel-Cherkassy 107.7.

SL) Sakhalinskaya oblast: GTRK "Sakhalin", ul. Komsomolskaya 209, 693000 Yuzhno-Sakhalinsk. **E:** gtrksakhalin@gmail.com **Reg:** On (MHz) Khoe 66.80, Nogliki 88.0, Val 100.3, Vostochnoye 100.6, Tymovskoye 100.9, Reydovo 101.0, Smirnykh (+1) 101.4, Shebunino (+2) 101.5, Pravda 101.8, Tomari 101.9, Dolinsk (+1) 102.0, Nevelsk 102.1, Aleksandrovsk-Sakhalinskiy (+1) 102.2, Novikovo 102.4, Kurilsk 102.5, Krabozavodskoye 102.6, Yablochnoye (+2) 102.7, Golovnino

102.8, Okha 102.9, Malokurilskoye 103.1, Poronaysk 103.2, Chaplanovo (+1) 103.9, Chekhov 104.0, Kholmsk 104.8, Yuzhno-Sakhalinsk 106.0, Gornozavodsk 106.1, Okhotskoye 106.2, Yasnomorskoye 106.9, Ozerskoye 107.2, Uglegorsk 107.5, Korsakov 107.6, Pyatirechye 107.7, Yuzhno-Kurilsk 107.8. Incl. prgr in Korean.

SM) Smolenskaya oblast: GTRK "Smolensk", 214000 Smolensk, ul. Dzerzhinskogo 17. **E:** rukovodstvo@smolgtrk.rfn.ru **Reg:** On (MHz) Smolensk 68.54, Smogiri 68.96, Vyazma 69.20, Roslavl 70.91.

SO) Respublika Severnaya Osetiya - Alaniya: GTRK "Alaniya", 362007 Vladikavkaz, Osetinskaya gorka 2. **E:** mail@alaniatv.ru **Reg:** On (MHz) Verkhniy Fiagdon 69.47, Mozdok 71.78, Vladikavkaz 90.0 in Russian, Ossetic. Local channel "Alaniya FM" on Vladikavkaz 104.5MHz.

SP) Sankt Peterburg (Federal City) & Leningradskaya oblast: GTRK "Sankt-Peterburg", 197022 St.Peterburg, nab. reki Karpovki 43. **E:** info@rtr.spb.ru **Reg:** On (MHz) Tikhvin 66.14, St.Peterburg 66.30/99.0, Kingisepp 67.67, Podporozhye 69.95, Luga 70.88.

SR) Saratovskaya oblast: GTRK "Saratov", 410004 Saratov, 2-ya Sadovaya ul. 7. **E:** top@gtrk.renet.ru **Reg:** On (MHz) Perelyub 66.44, Yershov 68.48, Aleksandrov Gay 69.68, Balashov 70.16, Saratov 71.09, Balakovo 100.4.

ST) Stavropolskiy kray: GTRK "Stavropolye", 355000 Stavropol, ul. Dzerzhinskogo 149-151. **E:** referent@stavropolye.tv **Reg:** On (MHz) Ipatovo 66.77, Neftekumsk 70.01, Stavropol 95.6, Budyonnovsk 106.9, Pyatigorsk 107.8. NB: Txs also carry prgrs by reg. substudio (Territorialnoye otdeleniye GTRK "Stavropolye"): 357500 Pyatigorsk, ul. Mira 1. **E:** office@ptv.ru.

SV) Sverdlovskaya oblast: GTRK "Ural", 620026 Yekaterinburg, ul. Lunacharskogo 212. **E:** radio@sgtrk.ru **Reg:** "R. Urala" on (MHz) Talitsa 65.93, Novaya Lyalya 66.08, Petrokamenskoye 66.32, Talitsa 66.71, Zaykovo 66.83, Nizhniye Sergi 67.01, Ivdel 67.76, Sankino 68.66, Basyanovskiy 68.69, Sredniy Bugalysh 68.93, Rezh 69.17, Bisert 69.20, Baranchinskiy 69.29, Serov 69.65, Klevakinskoye 69.74, Andronovo 70.16, Andryushino 70.34, Afanasyevskoye (+1) 70.43, Arti 70.73, Pyshma 71.24, Verkhnyaya Salda 72.92, Yuzhakovo 73.10, Severouralsk 73.25, Verkhoturye 73.34, Turinsk 73.85, Vostochnyy 73.91, Yekaterinburg 95.5, Sukhoy Log 98.7, Alapayevsk 101.1, Artyomovskiy 103.8, Kamyshlov 106.4.

TA) Tambovskaya oblast: GTRK "Tambov", 392000 Tambov, ul. Michurinskaya 8a. **E:** radio@intmb.ru **Reg:** On (MHz) Tambov 100.9.

TL) Tulskaya oblast: GTRK "Tula", 300600 Tula, Staronikitskaya ul. 1. **E:** info@tula.rfn.ru **Reg:** On (MHz) Yevremov 66.92, Novomoskovsk 72.35, Tula 90.2, Suvorov 102.4, Arsenyevo 103.7.

TO) Tomskaya oblast: GTRK "Tomsk", 634045 Tomsk, ul. Yakovleva 5. **E:** adm@tvtomsk.ru **Reg:** "R. Tomsk" on (MHz) Kozhevnikovo 67.01, Krivosheino 67.31, Beregayevo (+2) 67.40, Staraya Yuvala (+1) 68.15, Voznesenka 68.33, Vysokiy Yar 68.54, Teguldet 68.60, Kyonga 69.29, Parbig 69.80, Bakchar 70.01, Malinovka 70.55, Sayka 71.33, Krasnyy Yar 72.17, Chilino 72.20, Podgornoye 72.44, Zyryanskoye 73.01, Plotinkovo 73.22, Komsomolsk 101.1, Vertikos 101.5, Kolpashevo 101.6, Volodino 101.9, Baturino (+4) 102.0, Aleksandrovskoye (+2) 102.3, Sredniy Vasyugan 102.4, Tomsk 102.9, Molchanovo 103.2, Parabel 103.3, Narym 103.7, Almyakovo 103.9, Belyy Yar 104.2, Kedrovyy (+1) 104.6, Mikhaylovka 105.0, Strezhevoy 105.7, Melnikovo 107.9.

TS) Respublika Tatarstan (Tatarstan): GTRK "Tatarstan", 420095 Kazan, ul. Sh. Usmanova 10. **E:** vesti@trttv.ru **Reg:** "R.Tatarstana"/ "Tatarstan radiosi" on (MHz) Abdakhmanovo 72.59, Nurlat 87.6, Bilyarsk (+1) 92.1, Muslyumovo 92.4, Aznakayevo 95.3, Sarmanovo 96.4, Sovkhoz im. Kirova 98.2, Novosheshminsk 98.8, B.Atnya 98.9, Kazan (+1) 99.2, Leninogorsk 99.9, Bavly 100.3, Nizhnekamsk 101.1, Kushmany 101.6, Cheremshan 102.9, Kutlu-Bukash 103.5, Buinsk 103.8, Almetyevsk 103.9, Tetyushi 104.8, Shemordan 107.5, Bazarnyye Mataki 107.8, Aktanysh (+1) 107.9 in Russian, Tatar.

TV) Tverskaya oblast: GTRK "Tver", 170000 Tver, ul. Vagzhanova 9. **E:** secretar@vesti-tver.ru **Reg:** On (MHz) V.Volochyok 87.5, Kimry 88.1, Selizharovo 88.2, Novozavidovskiy 88.9, Tver 93.5, Bologoye 99.2, Maksatikha (+1) 99.5, Krasnyy Kholm 100.5, Olenino 101.5, Spirovo 101.7, Nelidovo 102.5, Staritsa 103.1, Rameshki 103.5, Toropetsk 104.0, Zharkovskiy 104.1, Torzhok 104.6, Konakovo (+1) 105.1, Belyy (+1) 107.1, Kashin 107.7, Vesyegonsk 107.9.

TY) Tyumenskaya oblast: GTRK "Region-Tyumen", 625013 Tyumen, ul. Permyakova 6. **E:** gtrk@region-tyumen.ru **Reg:** On (MHz) Berdyuzhye 66.41, Aromashevo 66.68, Gagarino 66.89, Yarkovo 66.95, Vagay 68.60, Armizonskoye 68.84, Masali 68.96, Yurginskoye 69.11, Demyanskoye 69.32, B.Sorokino 69.95, Nizhnyaya Tavda 70.34, Shabanovo 70.55, Uvat 71.42, Uporovo 73.19, Tyumen 90.8, Isetskoye 100.8, Tobolsk 102.0 (also relayed via txs in region KY).

UD) Udmurtskaya respublika: GTRK "Udmurtiya", 426069 Izhevsk, ul. Pesochnaya 9. **E:** adm@udmtv.ru **Reg:** On (MHz) Kizner 71.81, Balezino 96.3, Izhevsk 96.6, Sarapul 96.8, Alnashi 98.3, Karakulino 98.4, Debyosy 101.0, Vavozh 102.7, Kambarka (+1) 103.6, Mozhga 104.0, Krasnogorodskoye 104.7, Valamaz 105.0, Yar 106.5, Syumsi 107.2, Votkinsk 107.9 in Russian, Udmurt, Tatar, Mari.

UL) Ulyanovskaya oblast: GTRK "Volga", 432030 Ulyanovsk, ul. Narimanova 62. **E:** volgaulsk@gmail.ru **Reg:** On (MHz) Novospasskoye 67.07, Veshkayma 70.40, Gladchikha 73.49, Ulyanovsk 89.6, Kuzovatovo 102.8, Barysh 103.3, Dimitrovgrad 107.2

VG) Volgogradskaya oblast: GTRK "Volgograd-TRV", 400005 Volgograd, ul. Marshala Rokossovskogo 100. **E:** radioinfo@volgograd-trv.ru **Reg:** On (MHz) Volgograd 98.3, Chilekovo 100.4, Yelan 102,7, Uryupinsk 103.4, Zhirnovsk 103.6, Uspenka 103.9, Kamyshin 105.2, Surovikino 105.4, Novoanninskiy 106.1, Mikhaylovka 106.5, Kletskiy 107.0. Local channel "Volgograd 24" on Volgograd 93.5MHz.

VL) Vladimirskaya oblast: GTRK "Vladimir", 600000 Vladimir, ul. Bol. Moskovskaya 62. **E:** adm@vladtv.ru **Reg:** On (MHz) Petushki 66.71, Gorokhovets 69.08, Yuryev-Polskiy 69.17, Sobinka 70.61, Kolchugino 73.55, Murom 88.7, Aleksandrov 88.9, Vyazniki 90.1, Melenki 92.7, Kirzhach 96.2, Kovrov 98.3, Gus-Khrustalnyy 103.1, Vladimir 106.3, Kolchugino 106.7.

VN) Voronezhskaya oblast: GTRK "Voronezh", 394625 Voronezh, ul. Karl Marksa 114. **E:** tv@vgtv.vrn.ru **Reg:** On (MHz) Bobrov 67.04, Kalach 67.37, Boguchar 71.90, Voronezh 95.9, Ertil 101.5, Borisoglebsk 104.1.

VO) Vologodskaya oblast: GTRK "Vologda", 160000 Vologda, ul. Predtechenskaya 32. **E:** secretar@gtrk35.ru **Reg:** On (MHz) Kurilovo 70.07, Vologda 98.0, Andomskiy Pogost 100.8, Tarnogorskiy Gorodok 101.5, Syamzha 101.8, Nyuksenitsa 102.0, Vytegra 102.1, Kharovsk 102.2, Vozhega 102.5, Novaya Derevnya (+1) 102.7, Shuyskoye 102.9, Verkhovazhye 103.2, Cherepovets 103.4, Totma 104.6, V.Ustyug 105.2, Babayevo 106.0, Litin Bor 107.7.

YA) Yaroslavskaya oblast: GTRK "Yaroslaviya", 150014 Yaroslavl, ul. Bogdanovicha 20. **E:** gtrk@yaroslavl.rfn.ru **Reg:** On (MHz) Yaroslavl 99.1, Rybinsk 102.8, Lyubim 103.6, Danilov 104.3.

YN) Yamalo-Nenetskiy avtonomnyy okrug - Yugra (NB: YN is subordinated to region TY): GTRK "Yamal", 629007 Salekhard, ul. Lambinykh 3. **E:** gtrk@gtrk-yamal.ru **Reg:** On (MHz) Gubkinskiy 66.74, Pangody 67.55, Yar-Sale 69.32, Kharp 70.76, Nadym 71.78, Salekhard (+1) 100.6, Muzhi 102.2, Muravlenko 104.7. Txs also relay reg. prgrs by GTRK "Region-Tyumen", Tyumen, TY.

YV) Yevreyskaya avtonomnaya oblast: GTRK "Bira", 679016 Birobidzhan, ul. Oktyabrskaya 15. **E:** gtrkbira@biratv.rfn.ru **Reg:** On (MHz) Bidzhan (+1) 70.07, Kuldur 73.64, Amurzet 101.3, Birakan 101.9, Pashkovo 104.3, Birobidzhan 104.6, Obluchye 106.1, Bidzhan 107.5, Khingansk 107.6.

ZB) Zabaykalskiy kray: GTRK "Chita", 672027 Chita, ul. Kostyushko-Grigorovicha 27. **E:** gtrk-chita@mail.ru **Reg:** On (MHz) Kokuy (+1) 66.14, Nerchinskiy Zavod 66.44, Krasnyy Chikoy 66.53, Kyra 68.00, Khilok 68.09, Karymskoye 68.81, Novopavlovka 69.05, Baley 69.17, Ulety 69.41, Khada-Bulak 69.56, Kholbon 69.80, Verkh-Usugli 69.98, Orlovskiy 70.07*, Krasnokamensk 70.67, Priargunsk 73.85, Chita 91.6, Narasun 101.9, Kurulga (+1) 102.4, Aleksandrovskiy Zavod (+6) 102.5, Kokuy 102.6, Tokhtor 102.8, Chara 103.0, Duldurga 103.3, Gazimurskiy Zavod (+2) 103.6, Maleta (+1) 103.7, Darasun (+1) 104.1, Batakan (+6) 104.2, Novokurgatay (+1) 104.4, Kalga 106.9 in Russian, Buryat. NB: *) Tx also carries prgrs by reg. substudio (Territorialnoye otdeleniye GTRK "Chita"): ul. Bazara Rinchino 7, 687000 Aginskoye. **E:** abgtrk_agi@aginsk.chita.ru.

RADIO ORFEY (Gov)

✉ 115326 Moskva, ul. Pyatnitskaya 25 ☎ +7 495 9514340 **E:** rgmc@muzcentrum.ru **W:** muzcentrum.ru **L.P:** DG: Irina Gerasimova

Rg	Location	MHz	kW	Rg	Location	MHz	kW
PR	Perm	66.80	4	TL	Tula	71.93	4
SV	Yekaterinburg	69.92	1	MO	Moskva	99.2	5
LI	Lipetsk	70.07	4	SM	Smolensk	104.3	0.5
VG	Volgograd	71.33	2	KG	Kurgan	106.0	1
SP	St.Peterburg	71.66	5				

D.Prgr: 24h.

OTHER STATIONS (¦=time-shared tx)

MW	kHz	kW	Rg	Location	Station
172)	684	10	SP	Olgino, E	R. Radonezh
117)	765	20	KH	Khabarovsk, FE	R. Vostok Rossii
117)	765	20	KH	Komsomolsk-na-A., FE	R. Vostok Rossii
117)	765	5	KH	Berezovyy, FE	R. Vostok Rossii
117)	765	5	KH	Bikin, FE	R. Vostok Rossii

MW	kHz	kW	Rg	Location	Station
117)	765	5	KH	Bogorodskoye, FE	R. Vostok Rossii
117)	765	5	KH	Chegdomyn, FE	R. Vostok Rossii
117)	765	5	KH	De-Kastri, FE	R. Vostok Rossii
117)	765	5	KH	Nikolayevsk-na-A., FE	R. Vostok Rossii
117)	765	5	KH	Troitskoye, FE	R. Vostok Rossii
117)	765	5	KH	Tsimmermanovka, FE	R. Vostok Rossii
117)	765	5	KH	Vyazemskiy, FE	R. Vostok Rossii
117)	765	5	KH	Yagodnyy, FE	R. Vostok Rossii
121)	¦828	10	SP	Olgino, E	Radiogazeta Slovo
123)	¦828	10	SP	Olgino, E	Pravoslavnoye R.
128)	1053	10	SP	Olgino, E	R. Mariya
223)	1584	0.3	KD	Belorechensk, E	Chistaya volna

SW	kHz	kW	Rg	Location	Station
222)	5935+	20	KH	Komsomolsk-na-A., FE	R. Purga (2000-1000)
222)	6025+	20	KH	Komsomolsk-na-A., FE	R. Purga (0600-1000)
222)	6025+	20	KH	Komsomolsk-na-A., FE	R. Purga (2000-2200)
222)	11860+	20	KH	Komsomolsk-na-A., FE	R. Purga (2200-0100)
222)	15325+	20	KH	Komsomolsk-na-A., FE	R. Purga (0100-0600)

+) DRM (registered times for B20 season shown, actual schedule may vary)

NB: R. Purga (Anadyr) live streaming is available on the stn's website (radiopurga.org). During local nighttime (UTC+12h timezone: i.e. 0000 LT = 1200 UTC), the stn is playing mainly nonstop music.

FM	MHz	kW	Rg	Location	Station
12)	66.23	1	TS	Nab. Chelny	Brezhnev FM
124C)	66.68	4	BA	Ufa	R. Ashkadar
148)	67.79	1	TS	Nab. Chelny	R. Kunel
1)	68.00	5	MO	Moskva	Avtoradio
4)	68.09	1	PZ	Penza	Europa plus
60)	68.51	4	SV	Irbit	Kanal Voskreseniye
60)	68.87	4	SV	Nizhniye Sergi	Kanal Voskreseniye
9C)	68.90	1	KN	Krasnoyarsk	R. dlya dvoikh
7)	69.74	1	UL	Ulyanovsk	Militseyskaya volna
60)	71.21	4	SV	Nizhniye Tagil	Kanal Voskreseniye
60)	71.69	4	SV	Serov	Kanal Voskreseniye
60)	72.11	4	SV	Afanasyevskoye	Kanal Voskreseniye
60)	72.11	4	SV	Tavda	Kanal Voskreseniye
99)	72.29	1	ZB	Chita	Populyarnoye R.
60)	72.83	4	SV	Yekasterinburg	Kanal Voskreseniye
172)	72.92	10	MO	Moskva	R. Radonezh
56)	73.10	10	SP	Sankt-Peterburg	Grad Petrov
130B)	73.55	1	VN	Voronezh	R. Blagovestiye
43)	73.94	1	YA	Yaroslavl	Marusya FM
134A)	87.5	1	BR	Bryansk	Studio 21
15)	87.5	1	VO	Cherepovets	DFM
157)	87.5	1	SR	Saratov	R. Monte-Karlo
178)	87.5	1	TS	Nab. Chelny	Tatarskoye R.
19)	87.5	1	RO	Salsk	Dorozhnoye R.
19)	87.5	5	SP	Sankt-Peterburg	Dorozhnoye R.
27)	87.5	1	ST	Pyatigorsk	R. Dacha
28)	87.5	5	MO	Moskva	Biznes FM
6)	87.5	1	KY	Surgut	Love R.
134A)	87.6	1	BE	Belgorod	Studio 21
19)	87.6	1	IV	Kineshma	Dorozhnoye R.
21)	87.6	1	SV	Yekaterinburg	R. Zvezda
23)	87.6	1	PR	Perm	Detskoye R.
25)	87.6	1	KE	Kemerovo	R. Mir
1)	87.7	1	AM	Blagoveshchensk	Avtoradio
134A)	87.7	1	SM	Smolensk	Studio 21
134A)	87.8	1	BA	Ufa	Studio 21
45A)	87.8	1	PM	Vladivostok	Novoye R.
65)	87.8	2	KY	Nizhnevartovsk	PIFM
1)	87.9	1	SL	Yu-Sakhalinsk	Avtoradio
134A)	87.9	1	TY	Tyumen	Studio 21
16)	87.9	1	KH	Khabarovsk	Retro FM
216)	87.9	1	AK	Barnaul	R. Kniga
220)	87.9	1	OB	Orenburg	Planeta FM
24)	87.9	1	SR	Saratov	NRJ
27)	87.9	1	VO	Cherepovets	R. Dacha
31)	87.9	10	MO	Moskva	Like FM
6)	87.9	1	IV	Ivanovo	Love R.
72)	87.9	1	BR	Bryansk	32 R.
8)	87.9	1	AS	Astrakhan	Nashe R.
14)	88.0	1	MA	Magadan	R. Shanson
16)	88.0	5	SP	Sankt-Peterburg	Retro FM
2)	88.0	1	SA	Tolyatti	Russkoye R.
21)	88.0	1	MU	Murmansk	R. Zvezda
4)	88.0	1	KE	Kemerovo	Europa plus
86)	88.0	1	PR	Perm	Bolid FM
19)	88.1	1	SM	Velizh	Dorozhnoye R.

FM	MHz	kW	Rg	Location	Station
9A)	88.1	1	OM	Omsk	R. Vanya
23)	88.2	1	RO	Rostov-na-Donu	Detskoye R.
24)	88.2	1	BA	Ufa	NRJ
5)	88.2	1	KY	Surgut	Hit FM
97)	88.2	1	KE	Leninsk-Kuznetskiy	Pioner FM
1)	88.3	2	PM	Vladivostok	Avtoradio
16)	88.3	5	MO	Moskva	Retro FM
16)	88.3	1	SL	Yu-Sakhalinsk	Retro FM
17)	88.3	1	TS	Kazan	Serebryanyy dozhd
171)	88.3	2	BE	Belgorod	R. Radio
18)	88.3	1	TY	Tyumen	Yumor FM
19)	88.3	1	AK	Barnaul	Dorozhnoye R.
22)	88.3	1	KH	Khabarovsk	R. KP
23)	88.3	1	SR	Saratov	Detskoye R.
27)	88.3	1	AS	Astrakhan	R. Dacha
27)	88.3	1	KD	Krasnodar	R. Dacha
35)	88.3	1	OB	Orenburg	R. Vera
5)	88.3	1	SV	Yekaterinburg	Hit FM
24)	88.4	1	MD	Saransk	NRJ
24)	88.4	1	SA	Tolyatti	NRJ
36)	88.4	5	SP	Sankt-Peterburg	Avtoradio S-Peterburg
6)	88.4	1	KE	Kemerovo	Love R.
1)	88.5	1	MO	Yegoryevsk	Avtoradio
1)	88.5	1	KH	Komsomolsk-na-A.	Avtoradio
21)	88.5	1	TO	Tomsk	R. Zvezda
35)	88.5	1	IR	Irkutsk	R. Vera
17)	88.6	1	IV	Ivanovo	Serebryanyy dozhd
5)	88.6	1	UL	Dimitrovgrad	Hit FM
1)	88.7	2	KH	Khabarovsk	Avtoradio
134A)	88.7	1	MU	Murmansk	Studio 21
14)	88.7	1	AM	Blagoveshchensk	R. Shanson
174)	88.7	1	AS	Astrakhan	R. Astrakhan
18)	88.7	10	MO	Moskva	Yumor FM
23)	88.7	1	KD	Krasnodar	Detskoye R.
25)	88.7	1	SA	Samara	R. Mir
26)	88.7	1	SR	Saratov	R. Rekord
7)	88.7	1	AK	Barnaul	Militseyskaya volna
9A)	88.7	1	SM	Safonovo	R. Vanya
134A)	88.8	1	UL	Ulyanovsk	Studio 21
17)	88.8	1	SV	Yekaterinburg	Serebryanyy dozhd
185)	88.8	1	IN	Nazran	R. Ingushetiya
22)	88.8	1	ST	Pyatigorsk	R. KP
26)	88.8	1	TY	Tyumen	R. Rekord
88)	88.8	1	BU	Ulan-Ude	R. MSM
18)	88.9	1	PR	Perm	Yumor FM
18)	88.9	1	KM	Petropavlovsk-K.	Yumor FM
18)	88.9	5	SP	Sankt-Peterburg	Yumor FM
19)	88.9	1	TS	Kazan	Dorozhnoye R.
26)	88.9	1	SL	Yu-Sakhalinsk	R. Rekord
8)	88.9	1	IR	Irkutsk	Nashe R.
14)	89.0	1	UL	Dimitrovgrad	R. Shanson
18)	89.0	1	BA	Ufa	Yumor FM
139)	89.1	5	MO	Moskva	R. Jazz
22)	89.1	1	AS	Astrakhan	R. KP
24)	89.1	1	OM	Omsk	NRJ
9A)	89.1	1	MU	Murmansk	R. Vanya
176)	89.2	1	SR	Saratov	Taksi FM
23)	89.2	1	SV	Yekaterinburg	Detskoye R.
27)	89.2	1	KE	Kemerovo	R. Dacha
27)	89.2	1	UL	Ulyanovsk	R. Dacha
53)	89.2	1	SA	Samara	R. Russkiy khit
6)	89.2	1	BU	Ulan-Ude	Love R.
183)	89.3	1	OB	Orenburg	R. Sibir
25)	89.3	1	IR	Irkutsk	R. Mir
45A)	89.3	1	KD	Krasnodar	Novoye R.
19)	89.4	1	PM	Vladivostok	Dorozhnoye R.
27)	89.4	1	RK	Abakan	R. Dacha
4)	89.4	1	PR	Perm	Europa plus
134A)	89.5	1	OM	Omsk	Studio 21
25)	89.5	1	AS	Astrakhan	R. Mir
25)	89.5	1	MU	Murmansk	R. Mir
53)	89.5	1	KY	Surgut	R. Russkiy khit
76)	89.5	10	MO	Moskva	Megapolis FM
2)	89.6	1	KH	Khabarovsk	Russkoye R.
24)	89.6	1	SV	Yekaterinburg	NRJ
27)	89.6	1	TY	Tyumen	R. Dacha
45A)	89.6	1	SA	Samara	Novoye R.
176)	89.7	1	TS	Kazan	Taksi FM
202)	89.7	4	SP	Sankt-Peterburg	R. Zenit
18)	89.8	1	RK	Abakan	Yumor FM

FM	MHz	kW	Rg	Location	Station
21)	89.8	1	IR	Irkutsk	R. Zvezda
22)	89.8	1	KE	Kemerovo	R. KP
46)	89.8	1	PR	Perm	Comedy Radio
2)	89.9	1	SL	Yu-Sakhalinsk	Russkoye R.
26)	89.9	1	SV	Serov	R. Rekord
49)	89.9	5	MO	Moskva	Strana FM
134A)	90.0	1	AR	Arkhangelsk	Studio 21
23)	90.0	1	UL	Ulyanovsk	Detskoye R.
25)	90.0	1	TY	Tyumen	R. Mir
157)	90.1	1	OB	Orenburg	R. Monte-Karlo
159)	90.1	5	SP	Sankt-Peterburg	R. Ermitazh
23)	90.1	1	AS	Astrakhan	Detskoye R.
134A)	90.2	1	KE	Kemerovo	Studio 21
27)	90.2	1	BR	Bryansk	R. Dacha
27)	90.2	1	TS	Kazan	R. Dacha
46)	90.2	1	SR	Saratov	Comedy Radio
9A)	90.2	1	TA	Tambov	R. Vanya
1)	90.3	20	MO	Moskva	Avtoradio
19)	90.3	2	KY	Surgut	Dorozhnoye R.
157)	90.4	1	TY	Tyumen	R. Monte-Karlo
16)	90.4	1	SA	Tolyatti	Retro FM
19)	90.4	1	KE	Leninsk-Kuznetskiy	Dorozhnoye R.
22)	90.4	2	PM	Vladivostok	R. KP
22)	90.4	1	BU	Ulan-Ude	R. KP
216)	90.5	1	SM	Smolensk	R. Kniga
35)	90.5	1	OM	Omsk	R. Vera
219)	90.6	1	KS	Kostroma	Kostroma FM
22)	90.6	1	SR	Saratov	R. KP
23)	90.6	1	BA	Ufa	Detskoye R.
24)	90.6	1	KD	Krasnodar	NRJ
43)	90.6	1	SA	Samara	Marusya FM
9A)	90.6	1	KG	Kurgan	R. Vanya
9A)	90.6	5	SP	Sankt-Peterburg	R. Vanya
1)	90.7	1	PR	Perm	Avtoradio
124A)	90.7	1	BA	Verkhneyarkeyevo	R. Yuldash
19)	90.7	1	TL	Tula	Dorozhnoye R.
2)	90.7	1	TS	Kazan	Russkoye R.
208)	90.7	1	NN	Arzamas	Rock FM
23)	90.7	2	IR	Irkutsk	Detskoye R.
70)	90.7	1	LI	Lipetsk	Lipetsk FM
8)	90.7	1	KY	Surgut	Nashe R.
8)	90.7	1	TO	Tomsk	Nashe R.
207)	90.8	5	MO	Moskva	Relaks FM
27)	90.8	1	MU	Murmansk	R. Dacha
35)	90.8	1	KV	Kirov	R. Vera
45A)	90.8	1	SV	Yekaterinburg	Novoye R.
54)	90.8	1	BU	Ulan-Ude	Burgyaad FM
61)	90.8	1	SO	Vladikavkaz	Kavkaz R.
25)	90.9	1	PM	Vladivostok	R. Mir
25)	90.9	1	OM	Omsk	R. Mir
27)	90.9	1	TA	Tambov	R. Dacha
6)	90.9	1	RS	Yakutsk	Love R.
9A)	90.9	1	BR	Unecha	R. Vanya
131)	91.0	1	TS	Alyoshkin Saplyk	R. Bolgar
156)	91.0	1	CC	Groznyy	Put islama
157)	91.0	1	SA	Samara	R. Monte-Karlo
21)	91.0	1	KG	Kurgan	R. Zvezda
22)	91.0	1	KD	Krasnodar	R. KP
24)	91.0	1	KH	Khabarovsk	NRJ
27)	91.0	1	SR	Saratov	R. Dacha
9A)	91.0	1	KS	Kostroma	R. Vanya
10)	91.1	1	BR	Bryansk	R. 7
18)	91.1	1	TS	Kazan	Yumor FM
18)	91.1	1	KY	Surgut	Yumor FM
19)	91.1	1	IR	Irkutsk	Dorozhnoye R.
27)	91.1	1	LI	Lipetsk	R. Dacha
3)	91.1	1	BA	Ufa	Ekho Moskvy
45A)	91.1	1	AK	Barnaul	Novoye R.
45A)	91.1	10	SP	Sankt-Peterburg	Novoye R.
8)	91.1	1	KN	Norilsk	Nashe R.
14)	91.2	1	KV	Kirov	R. Shanson
14)	91.2	1	BU	Ulan-Ude	R. Shanson
17)	91.2	1	TY	Tyumen	Serebryanyy dozhd
18)	91.2	1	RO	Rostov-na-Donu	Yumor FM
19)	91.2	1	SO	Vladikavkaz	Dorozhnoye R.
3)	91.2	5	MO	Moskva	Ekho Moskvy
3)	91.2	1	PR	Perm	Ekho Moskvy
98)	91.2	1	AR	Arkhangelsk	Uyezdnoye R.
14)	91.3	1	KE	Belovo	R. Shanson
19)	91.3	1	VL	Murom	Dorozhnoye R.
4)	91.3	1	SA	Tolyatti	Europa plus
16)	91.4	1	AS	Astrakhan	Retro FM
23)	91.4	1	UD	Izhevsk	Detskoye R.
23)	91.4	1	OM	Omsk	Detskoye R.
24)	91.4	1	UL	Ulyanovsk	NRJ
3)	91.4	1	SV	Yekaterinburg	Ekho Moskvy
4)	91.4	1	TS	Almetyevsk	Europa plus
43)	91.4	1	BE	Belgorod	Marusya FM
6)	91.4	1	AM	Blagoveshchensk	Love R.
131)	91.5	1	TS	Kazan	R. Bolgar
14)	91.5	1	SA	Samara	R. Shanson
15)	91.5	1	BA	Ufa	DFM
17)	91.5	1	KE	Kemerovo	Serebryanyy dozhd
25)	91.5	1	TO	Tomsk	R. Mir
3)	91.5	5	SP	Sankt-Peterburg	Ekho Moskvy
45A)	91.5	1	KN	Norilsk	Novoye R.
8)	91.5	1	SR	Saratov	Nashe R.
93)	91.5	1	SL	Yu-Sakhalinsk	R. Iskatel
18)	91.6	1	UL	Dimitrovgrad	Yumor FM
25)	91.6	1	SO	Vladikavkaz	R. Mir
25)	91.6	1	TS	Nab. Chelny	R. Mir
27)	91.6	1	KV	Kirov	R. Dacha
27)	91.6	1	KY	Surgut	R. Dacha
27)	91.6	1	BU	Ulan-Ude	R. Dacha
6)	91.6	1	MD	Saransk	Love R.
1)	91.7	1	CC	Groznyy	Avtoradio
97)	91.8	1	PR	Perm	Pioner FM
134A)	91.9	1	TS	Kazan	Studio 21
191)	91.9	1	SA	Tolyatti	Samarskoye gub. R.
26)	91.9	1	SV	Yekaterinburg	R. Rekord
22)	92.0	5	SP	Sankt-Peterburg	R. KP
25)	92.0	1	UD	Izhevsk	R. Mir
35)	92.0	1	KS	Kostroma	R. Vera
80A)	92.0	5	MO	Moskva	Moskva FM
22)	92.3	1	SV	Yekaterinburg	R. KP
24)	92.3	2	TS	Kazan	NRJ
27)	92.4	5	MO	Moskva	R. Dacha
35)	92.4	1	TY	Tyumen	R. Vera
5)	92.4	5	SP	Sankt-Peterburg	Hit FM
191)	92.5	1	SA	Samara	Samarskoye gub. R.
1)	92.6	1	MO	Orekhovo-Zuyevo	Avtoradio
1)	92.6	1	MO	Taldom	Avtoradio
35)	92.6	1	VG	Volgograd	R. Vera
35)	92.6	1	TO	Tomsk	R. Vera
134A)	92.7	1	SV	Yekaterinburg	Studio 21
216)	92.7	1	VO	Vologda	R. Kniga
46)	92.7	2	KN	Krasnoyarsk	Comedy Radio
10)	92.8	3	NS	Novosibirsk	R. 7
141)	92.8	5	MO	Moskva	R. Karnaval
18)	92.8	1	KE	Novokuznetsk	Yumor FM
183)	92.8	1	TY	Tyumen	R. Sibir
216)	92.8	1	UD	Izhevsk	R. Kniga
22)	92.8	1	NN	N.Novgorod	R. KP
39)	92.9	2	SP	Sankt-Peterburg	IZ.RU
8)	92.9	1	SA	Samara	Nashe R.
168)	93.1	1	TS	Kazan	R. Tartip
102)	93.2	1	RY	Ryazan	TKR FM
134A)	93.2	5	MO	Moskva	Studio 21
134A)	93.2	1	KE	Novokuznetsk	Studio 21
216)	93.2	1	NS	Novosibirsk	R. Kniga
11)	93.5	1	UD	Izhevsk	R. Maksimum
28)	93.5	1	TS	Kazan	Biznes FM
45A)	93.5	1	KN	Krasnoyarsk	Novoye R.
8)	93.5	1	NN	N.Novgorod	Nashe R.
10)	93.6	1	KA	Kaliningrad	R. 7
64)	93.6	5	MO	Moskva	Kommersant FM
35)	93.7	1	SV	Yekaterinburg	R. Vera
15)	93.8	1	KE	Novokuznetsk	DFM
25)	93.8	1	VG	Volgograd	R. Mir
88)	93.9	1	IR	Bratsk	R. MSM
9A)	93.9	1	UD	Izhevsk	R. Vanya
154)	94.0	5	MO	Moskva	Vostok FM
25)	94.0	1	CB	Chelyabinsk	R. Mir
21)	94.1	5	SP	Sankt-Peterburg	R. Zvezda
6)	94.2	1	NS	Novosibirsk	Love R.
152)	94.4	5	MO	Moskva	Vesna FM
35)	94.6	1	NS	Novosibirsk	R. Vera
6)	94.6	1	CB	Chelyabinsk	Love R.
15)	94.7	1	NN	N.Novgorod	DFM
35)	94.7	1	PZ	Penza	R. Vera

FM	MHz	kW	Rg	Location	Station
212)	94.8	5	MO	Moskva	Govorit Moskva
8)	94.8	1	SV	Yekaterinburg	Nashe R.
10)	94.9	1	VG	Volgograd	R. 7
209)	95.0	1	KN	Krasnoyarsk	Russkiye pesni
24)	95.0	4	SP	Sankt-Peterburg	NRJ
25)	95.0	2	NS	Novosibirsk	R. Mir
35)	95.0	1	PR	Perm	R. Vera
208)	95.2	5	MO	Moskva	Rock FM
22)	95.3	1	CB	Chelyabinsk	R. KP
134A)	95.4	1	UD	Izhevsk	Studio 21
19)	95.4	1	SP	Svetogorsk	Dorozhnoye R.
25)	95.4	1	PR	Perm	R. Mir
35)	95.4	1	KN	Krasnoyarsk	R. Vera
8)	95.4	1	NS	Novosibirsk	Nashe R.
134A)	95.5	5	SP	Sankt-Peterburg	Studio 21
134A)	95.5	1	SA	Tolyatti	Studio 21
157)	95.5	1	TV	Tver	R. Monte-Karlo
16)	95.5	1	KA	Kaliningrad	Retro FM
45A)	95.5	1	VO	Vologda	Novoye R.
14)	95.6	1	VL	Vladimir	R. Shanson
14)	95.6	1	KS	Kostroma	R. Shanson
16)	95.6	1	PZ	Penza	Retro FM
21)	95.6	10	MO	Moskva	R. Zvezda
23)	95.6	1	KE	Novokuznetsk	Detskoye R.
64)	95.6	1	NN	N.Novgorod	Kommersant FM
171)	95.7	1	BE	Rakitnoye	R. Radio
18)	95.7	1	SA	Samara	Yumor FM
21)	95.7	1	RY	Ryazan	R. Zvezda
23)	95.7	1	VG	Volgograd	Detskoye R.
6)	95.7	1	TO	Tomsk	Love R.
158)	95.8	1	KA	Gusev	R. na Vostoke
183)	95.8	1	KN	Krasnoyarsk	R. Sibir
19)	95.8	1	DA	Makhachkala	Dorozhnoye R.
21)	95.8	1	TY	Tyumen	R. Zvezda
23)	95.8	1	NS	Novosibirsk	Detskoye R.
35)	95.8	1	OB	Orsk	R. Vera
45A)	95.8	1	PR	Perm	Novoye R.
46)	95.8	1	UD	Izhevsk	Comedy Radio
93)	95.8	1	YA	Yaroslavl	R. Iskatel
18)	95.9	1	TA	Tambov	Yumor FM
46)	95.9	1	SV	Yekaterinburg	Comedy Radio
46)	95.9	4	SP	Sankt-Peterburg	Comedy Radio
1)	96.0	1	SA	Tolyatti	Avtoradio
19)	96.0	4	MO	Moskva	Dorozhnoye R.
24)	96.0	1	CB	Chelyabinsk	NRJ
25)	96.0	1	KE	Novokuznetsk	R. Mir
35)	96.0	1	VO	Vologda	R. Vera
47)	96.0	1	NN	N.Novgorod	Dinamit N.Novgorod
23)	96.1	1	RY	Ryazan	Detskoye R.
5)	96.1	1	TV	Tver	Hit FM
6)	96.1	1	VG	Volgograd	Love R.
193)	96.2	1	KN	Krasnoyarsk	Krasnoyarsk FM
2)	96.2	2	NS	Novosibirsk	Russkoye R.
207)	96.2	1	OL	Oryol	Relaks FM
22)	96.2	1	YA	Yaroslavl	R. KP
24)	96.2	1	UD	Izhevsk	NRJ
27)	96.2	1	CB	Magnitogorsk	R. Dacha
45A)	96.2	1	SV	Nizhniy Tagil	Novoye R.
2)	96.3	1	KA	Kaliningrad	Russkoye R.
204)	96.3	1	SA	Samara	Radiola
4)	96.3	1	KE	Belovo	Europa plus
16)	96.4	1	CB	Chelyabinsk	Retro FM
176)	96.4	5	MO	Moskva	Taksi FM
6)	96.4	1	VO	Vologda	Love R.
6)	96.4	1	PZ	Penza	Love R.
22)	96.5	1	VG	Volgograd	R. KP
25)	96.5	1	CV	Cheboksary	R. Mir
27)	96.5	1	RY	Ryazan	R. Dacha
45A)	96.5	1	TV	Tver	Novoye R.
17)	96.6	1	NS	Novosibirsk	Serebryanyy dozhd
21)	96.6	1	KN	Krasnoyarsk	R. Zvezda
22)	96.6	1	SV	Nizhniy Tagil	R. KP
22)	96.6	1	PR	Perm	R. KP
24)	96.6	1	TY	Tyumen	NRJ
38)	96.6	1	PR	Berezniki	Beloye R.
8)	96.6	1	SA	Tolyatti	Nashe R.
27)	96.7	1	KE	Belovo	R. Dacha
9A)	96.7	1	SP	Lyuban	R. Vanya
23)	96.8	5	MO	Moskva	Detskoye R.
23)	96.8	1	CB	Chelyabinsk	Detskoye R.
24)	96.8	1	NN	N.Novgorod	NRJ
35)	96.8	1	SA	Samara	R. Vera
8)	96.8	1	TS	Kazan	Nashe R.
17)	96.9	1	KE	Novokuznetsk	Serebryanyy dozhd
16)	97.0	2	NS	Novosibirsk	Retro FM
23)	97.0	1	KN	Krasnoyarsk	Detskoye R.
27)	97.0	4	SP	Sankt-Peterburg	R. Dacha
35)	97.1	1	SV	Nizhniy Tagil	R. Vera
22)	97.2	10	MO	Moskva	R. KP
8)	97.2	1	VG	Volgograd	Nashe R.
134A)	97.3	1	RY	Ryazan	Studio 21
19)	97.3	1	SA	Samara	Dorozhnoye R.
25)	97.4	1	KN	Krasnoyarsk	R. Mir
46)	97.4	2	NS	Novosibirsk	Comedy Radio
138)	97.5	1	PZ	Penza	R. Stantsiya
8)	97.5	1	TV	Tver	Nashe R.
24)	97.6	1	PR	Perm	NRJ
27)	97.6	1	VG	Volgograd	R. Dacha
17)	97.7	1	KA	Kaliningrad	Serebryanyy dozhd
22)	97.7	1	VN	Voronezh	R. KP
10)	97.8	1	KN	Krasnoyarsk	R. 7
139)	97.8	1	SA	Samara	R. Jazz
6)	97.8	1	UD	Izhevsk	Love R.
67)	97.8	1	VG	Leninsk	Belyy lebed
27)	97.9	1	VL	Vladimir	R. Dacha
4)	97.9	1	SA	Syzran	Europa plus
161)	98.0	1	NN	N.Novgorod	R. Obraz
18)	98.0	1	SV	Nizhniy Tagil	Yumor FM
181)	98.0	5	MO	Moskva	R. Shokolad
22)	98.0	1	TS	Kazan	R. KP
65)	98.1	1	RY	Ryazan	PIFM
22)	98.2	1	SA	Samara	R. KP
216)	98.3	1	KE	Novokuznetsk	R. Kniga
22)	98.3	1	NS	Novosibirsk	R. KP
15)	98.4	1	TY	Tyumen	DFM
19)	98.4	1	TO	Tomsk	Dorozhnoye R.
27)	98.4	1	PR	Perm	R. Dacha
45A)	98.4	10	MO	Moskva	Novoye R.
134A)	98.5	1	OL	Oryol	Studio 21
21)	98.5	1	TV	Tver	R. Zvezda
45A)	98.5	1	VN	Voronezh	Novoye R.
53)	98.5	1	RY	Mosolovo	R. Russkiy khit
6)	98.5	2	SV	Yekaterinburg	Love R.
79)	98.5	1	BE	Borisovka	Mir Belogorya
1)	98.6	1	MO	Zaraysk	Avtoradio
111)	98.6	2	SP	Sankt-Peterburg	Royal R.
154)	98.6	1	KB	Nalchik	Vostok FM
16)	98.6	1	SA	Samara	Retro FM
4)	98.6	1	KE	Yurga	Europa plus
1)	98.7	2	NS	Novosibirsk	Avtoradio
16)	98.7	2	KN	Krasnoyarsk	Retro FM
18)	98.7	1	BA	Steplitamak	Yumor FM
25)	98.7	1	ST	Stavropol	R. Mir
27)	98.7	1	TS	Nab. Chelny	R. Dacha
27)	98.7	1	CB	Chelyabinsk	R. Dacha
65)	98.7	1	KE	Novokuznetsk	PIFM
97)	98.7	1	PR	Berezniki	Pioner FM
11)	98.8	1	TO	Tomsk	R. Maksimum
20)	98.8	10	MO	Moskva	R. Romantika
24)	98.8	1	VG	Volgograd	NRJ
36)	98.8	1	SP	Lyuban	Avtoradio S-Peterburg
43)	98.8	1	LI	Lipetsk	Marusya FM
8)	98.8	1	VO	Vologda	Nashe R.
17)	98.9	1	PR	Perm	Serebryanyy dozhd
19)	98.9	1	SV	Yekaterinburg	Dorozhnoye R.
24)	98.9	1	KS	Kostroma	NRJ
25)	98.9	1	SA	Tolyatti	R. Mir
4)	98.9	1	PM	Arsenyev	Europa plus
9A)	98.9	1	SM	Gagarin	R. Vanya
18)	99.0	1	MO	Taldom	Yumor FM
25)	99.0	2	KB	Nalchik	R. Mir
4)	99.0	1	TS	Chistopol	Europa plus
1)	99.1	2	CB	Chelyabinsk	Avtoradio
113)	99.1	1	KN	Krasnoyarsk	R. 99.1 FM
18)	99.1	1	VN	Voronezh	Yumor FM
23)	99.1	1	NN	N.Novgorod	Detskoye R.
23)	99.1	1	PZ	Penza	Detskoye R.
24)	99.1	2	NS	Novosibirsk	NRJ
3)	99.1	1	SA	Samara	Ekho Moskvy
11)	99.2	1	VG	Volgograd	R. Maksimum

FM	MHz	kW	Rg	Location	Station
19)	99.2	1	SR	Balakovo	Dorozhnoye R.
22)	99.2	1	VO	Vologda	R. KP
27)	99.2	1	KT	Petrozavodsk	R. Dacha
45A)	99.2	1	TO	Tomsk	Novoye R.
53)	99.2	1	MD	Saransk	R. Russkiy khit
6)	99.2	1	TS	Almetyevsk	Love R.
6)	99.2	1	SV	Nizhniy Tagil	Love R.
8)	99.2	1	TY	Tyumen	Nashe R.
18)	99.3	1	KS	Kostroma	Yumor FM
21)	99.3	1	KO	Syktyvkar	R. Zvezda
22)	99.3	1	TV	Tver	R. KP
27)	99.3	2	BA	Steplitamak	R. Dacha
4)	99.3	1	SP	Kingisepp	Europa plus
5)	99.3	1	KE	Leninsk-Kuznetskiy	Hit FM
6)	99.3	1	VL	Vladimir	Love R.
6)	99.3	1	SM	Vyazma	Love R.
6)	99.3	1	KU	Kursk	Love R.
16)	99.4	5	PR	Perm	Retro FM
18)	99.4	1	LI	Lipetsk	Yumor FM
19)	99.4	1	SA	Tolyatti	Dorozhnoye R.
28)	99.4	2	SV	Yekaterinburg	Biznes FM
4)	99.4	1	MO	Kolomna	Europa plus
45A)	99.4	1	TS	Chistopol	Novoye R.
140)	99.5	2	KB	Nalchik	R. Kabardino-Balkariya
18)	99.5	1	NS	Novosibirsk	Yumor FM
203)	99.5	2	RS	Aldan	Radiogora
21)	99.5	1	KA	Kaliningrad	R. Zvezda
216)	99.5	1	KN	Krasnoyarsk	R. Kniga
218)	99.5	1	TA	Tambov	Global FM
22)	99.5	1	IR	Bratsk	R. KP
23)	99.5	1	VN	Voronezh	Detskoye R.
3)	99.5	1	CB	Chelyabinsk	Ekho Moskvy
4)	99.5	1	KE	Novokuznetsk	Europa plus
45A)	99.5	1	YA	Yaroslavl	Novoye R.
46)	99.5	1	NN	N.Novgorod	Comedy Radio
139)	99.6	1	TO	Tomsk	R. Jazz
16)	99.6	1	VO	Vologda	Retro FM
169)	99.6	1	SR	Balakovo	R. Aktivnoye
19)	99.6	1	SP	Lyuban	Dorozhnoye R.
19)	99.6	1	OL	Oryol	Dorozhnoye R.
22)	99.6	1	TY	Tyumen	R. KP
24)	99.6	1	PZ	Penza	NRJ
35)	99.6	1	TS	Almetyevsk	R. Vera
53)	99.6	10	MO	Moskva	R. Russkiy khit
24)	99.8	1	TV	Tver	NRJ
27)	99.8	1	CB	Asha	R. Dacha
27)	99.8	1	KE	Mezhdurechensk	R. Dacha
6)	99.8	1	SP	Vyborg	Love R.
1)	99.9	5	MO	Kurovskoye	Avtoradio
2)	99.9	1	KD	Vyshestebliyevskaya	Russkoye R.
25)	99.9	1	VN	Voronezh	R. Mir
4)	99.9	1	SA	Samara	Europa plus
10)	100.0	1	NN	N.Novgorod	R. 7
104)	100.0	1	CB	Chelyabinsk	R. 100
14)	100.0	1	VG	Volgograd	R. Shanson
16)	100.0	1	SV	Yekaterinburg	Retro FM
16)	100.0	1	RY	Mosolovo	Retro FM
2)	100.0	1	OL	Oryol	Russkoye R.
217)	100.0	1	KA	Sovetsk	Mediakit FM
45A)	100.0	1	NS	Novosibirsk	Novoye R.
7)	100.0	1	OB	Akbulak	Militseyskaya volna
8)	100.0	1	PR	Perm	Nashe R.
1)	100.1	1	PR	Berezniki	Avtoradio
1)	100.1	1	KA	Kaliningrad	Avtoradio
10)	100.1	1	PZ	Penza	R. 7
17)	100.1	5	MO	Moskva	Serebryanyy dozhd
18)	100.1	1	CB	Magnitogorsk	Yumor FM
45A)	100.1	1	VL	Vladimir	Novoye R.
5)	100.1	1	RO	Rostov-na-Donu	Hit FM
6)	100.1	1	SA	Tolyatti	Love R.
83)	100.1	1	UD	Izhevsk	Moya Udmurtiya
18)	100.2	1	TS	Almetyevsk	Yumor FM
2)	100.2	1	SM	Vyazma	Russkoye R.
4)	100.2	1	VO	Vologda	Europa plus
4)	100.2	1	KU	Zheleznogorsk	Europa plus
9A)	100.2	1	LI	Khlebnoye	R. Vanya
10)	100.3	1	TA	Tambov	R. 7
18)	100.3	2	KN	Krasnoyarsk	Yumor FM
2)	100.3	1	SA	Samara	Russkoye R.
24)	100.3	1	KE	Mariinsk	NRJ

FM	MHz	kW	Rg	Location	Station
25)	100.3	1	IR	Irkutsk	R. Mir
36)	100.3	1	SP	Kingisepp	Avtoradio S-Peterburg
4)	100.3	1	BR	Bryansk	Europa plus
4)	100.3	1	VN	Voronezh	Europa plus
4)	100.3	1	KS	Kostroma	Europa plus
4)	100.3	1	KO	Syktyvkar	Europa plus
7)	100.3	1	OB	Sol-Iletsk	Militseyskaya volna
146)	100.4	2	CB	Chelyabinsk	R. Kontinental
166)	100.4	5	SV	Yekaterinburg	R. Pilot
17)	100.4	4	NN	N.Novgorod	Serebryanyy dozhd
2)	100.4	1	UL	Dimitrovgrad	Russkoye R.
24)	100.4	1	KT	Petrozavodsk	NRJ
27)	100.4	1	SM	Gagarin	R. Dacha
51)	100.4	1	OL	Oryol	Ekspress R.
1)	100.5	1	TY	Tobolsk	Avtoradio
16)	100.5	1	TL	Tula	Retro FM
177)	100.5	1	RS	Aldan	R. Sakha
178)	100.5	1	TS	Kazan	Tatarskoye R.
182)	100.5	1	SV	Nizhniy Tagil	R. Si
19)	100.5	1	VN	Bobrov	Dorozhnoye R.
2)	100.5	1	KS	Buy	Russkoye R.
2)	100.5	1	UD	Izhevsk	Russkoye R.
215)	100.5	1	PR	Solikamsk	SK FM
34)	100.5	1	KE	Novokuznetsk	Apeks-R.
4)	100.5	5	SP	Sankt-Peterburg	Europa plus
69)	100.5	10	MO	Moskva	Zhara FM
7)	100.5	1	VL	Kovrov	Militseyskaya volna
87)	100.5	1	CV	Yardin	Nats. R. Chuvashii
16)	100.6	1	VL	Murom	Retro FM
18)	100.6	1	SR	Saratov	Yumor FM
184)	100.6	2	TY	Tyumen	R. Siti
2)	100.6	1	BA	Kumertau	Russkoye R.
2)	100.6	1	TV	Tver	Russkoye R.
23)	100.6	1	AK	Barnaul	Detskoye R.
24)	100.6	1	KE	Kemerovo	NRJ
26)	100.6	1	MD	Saransk	R. Rekord
4)	100.6	1	VG	Volgograd	Europa plus
6)	100.6	1	KL	Kaluga	Love R.
8)	100.6	1	OM	Omsk	Nashe R.
93)	100.6	1	RA	Gorno-Altaysk	R. Iskatel
10)	100.7	1	ST	Stavropol	R. 7
115)	100.7	1	RO	Rostov-na-Donu	FM-na Donu
120)	100.7	1	SA	Otradnyy	R. Aprel
124B)	100.7	1	BA	Davlekanovo	Sputnik FM
170)	100.7	1	DA	Makhachkala	R. Priboy
19)	100.7	1	MU	Apatity	Dorozhnoye R.
19)	100.7	1	KT	Peldozha	Dorozhnoye R.
200)	100.7	3	NS	Novosibirsk	R. Yuniton
24)	100.7	1	KB	Nalchik	NRJ
27)	100.7	1	KU	Kursk	R. Dacha
4)	100.7	1	BR	Unecha	Europa plus
4)	100.7	1	PM	Ussuriysk	Europa plus
5)	100.7	1	PR	Perm	Hit FM
6)	100.7	1	RY	Ryazan	Love R.
8)	100.7	1	VN	Voronezh	Nashe R.
9A)	100.7	1	SM	Vyazma	R. Vanya
9A)	100.7	1	OB	Orsk	R. Vanya
124A)	100.8	1	BA	Burayevo	R. Yuldash
16)	100.8	1	BR	Bryansk	Retro FM
18)	100.8	1	VL	Vladimir	Yumor FM
19)	100.8	1	KN	Krasnoyarsk	Dorozhnoye R.
24)	100.8	1	OB	Orenburg	NRJ
28)	100.8	1	CB	Chelyabinsk	Biznes FM
51)	100.8	1	OL	Livny	Ekspress R.
6)	100.8	1	AR	Arkhangelsk	Love R.
6)	100.8	1	KM	Petropavlovsk-K.	Love R.
1)	100.9	1	KD	Kushchyovskaya	Avtoradio
10)	100.9	1	IR	Irkutsk	R. 7
157)	100.9	1	KA	Kaliningrad	R. Monte-Karlo
16)	100.9	1	KD	Novorossiysk	Retro FM
183)	100.9	1	ZB	Aginskoye	R. Sibir
19)	100.9	1	LI	Lipetsk	Dorozhnoye R.
22)	100.9	1	AK	Biysk	R. KP
25)	100.9	1	TS	Kazan	R. Mir
25)	100.9	1	YA	Rybinsk	R. Mir
26)	100.9	4	NN	N.Novgorod	R. Rekord
35)	100.9	5	MO	Moskva	R. Vera
4)	100.9	1	OL	Oryol	Europa plus
45A)	100.9	1	UD	Izhevsk	Novoye R.
46)	100.9	1	RK	Abakan	Comedy Radio

FM	MHz	kW	Rg	Location	Station
79)	100.9	1	BE	Belgorod	Mir Belogorya
94)	100.9	1	PR	Kudymkar	Okrug FM
9B)	100.9	10	SP	Sankt-Peterburg	Piter FM
126)	101.0	1	PM	Artyom	R. AVN
14)	101.0	1	TY	Ishim	R. Shanson
14)	101.0	1	SV	Nizhniy Tagil	R. Shanson
14)	101.0	1	TY	Tyumen	R. Shanson
176)	101.0	1	SA	Samara	Taksi FM
19)	101.0	1	VO	Vologda	Dorozhnoye R.
19)	101.0	1	VO	Lipin Bor	Dorozhnoye R.
19)	101.0	1	CB	Magnitogorsk	Dorozhnoye R.
2)	101.0	2	TS	Bugulma	Russkoye R.
21)	101.0	1	PR	Berezniki	R. Zvezda
27)	101.0	1	OM	Omsk	R. Dacha
29)	101.0	1	KD	Otradnaya	Pervoye R.
3)	101.0	1	KV	Kirov	Ekho Moskvy
34)	101.0	2	KE	Kemerovo	Apeks-R.
35)	101.0	5	RY	Mosolovo	R. Vera
35)	101.0	1	KT	Petrozavodsk	R. Vera
4)	101.0	1	MU	Murmansk	Europa plus
9A)	101.0	1	KO	Ukhta	R. Vanya
1)	101.1	1	KD	Sochi	Avtoradio
1)	101.1	1	RS	Yakutsk	Avtoradio
10)	101.1	1	PR	Perm	R. 7
124A)	101.1	1	BA	Neftekamsk	R. Yuldash
16)	101.1	1	ZB	Chita	Retro FM
187)	101.1	1	NS	Kuybyshev	R. 54
19)	101.1	1	ME	Yoshkar-Ola	Dorozhnoye R.
20)	101.1	1	DA	Makhachkala	R. Romantika
207)	101.1	1	SR	Saratov	Relaks FM
217)	101.1	1	KA	Chernyakhovsk	Mediakit FM
24)	101.1	1	VN	Voronezh	NRJ
3)	101.1	1	VG	Volgograd	Ekho Moskvy
35)	101.1	1	KD	Yeysk	R. Vera
7)	101.1	1	KE	Novokuznetsk	Militseyskaya volna
15)	101.2	10	MO	Moskva	DFM
16)	101.2	1	KD	Krasnodar	Retro FM
18)	101.2	1	CB	Chelyabinsk	Yumor FM
19)	101.2	1	MU	Monchegorsk	Dorozhnoye R.
24)	101.2	1	IV	Ivanovo	NRJ
24)	101.2	1	KM	Petropavlovsk-K.	NRJ
27)	101.2	1	AR	Arkhangelsk	R. Dacha
4)	101.2	5	SV	Yekaterinburg	Europa plus
43)	101.2	1	SA	Tolyatti	Marusya FM
5)	101.2	1	KO	Pechora	Hit FM
87)	101.2	1	CV	Ibresi	Nats. R. Chuvashii
16)	101.3	1	VL	Vladimir	Retro FM
16)	101.3	1	BA	Tuymazy	Retro FM
18)	101.3	1	UD	Izhevsk	Yumor FM
19)	101.3	1	RK	Abakan	Dorozhnoye R.
2)	101.3	1	AK	Biysk	Russkoye R.
2)	101.3	1	MD	Saransk	Russkoye R.
25)	101.3	1	AK	Rubtsovsk	R. Mir
3)	101.3	1	OB	Orenburg	Ekho Moskvy
4)	101.3	1	LI	Lipetsk	Europa plus
45A)	101.3	1	TS	Kazan	Novoye R.
6)	101.3	2	KN	Krasnoyarsk	Love R.
6)	101.3	1	ST	Pyatigorsk	Love R.
65)	101.3	1	TO	Tomsk	PIFM
8)	101.3	1	KA	Kaliningrad	Nashe R.
1)	101.4	1	VN	Rossosh	Avtoradio
1)	101.4	1	BA	Steplitamak	Avtoradio
1)	101.4	1	TV	Tver	Avtoradio
11)	101.4	1	PR	Berezniki	R. Maksimum
131)	101.4	2	TS	Bilyarsk	R. Bolgar
14)	101.4	1	KH	Khabarovsk	R. Shanson
16)	101.4	1	KS	Kostroma	Retro FM
17)	101.4	1	PZ	Penza	Serebryanyy dozhd
18)	101.4	1	KT	Petrozavodsk	Yumor FM
19)	101.4	1	ST	Stavropol	Dorozhnoye R.
24)	101.4	1	OL	Oryol	NRJ
24)	101.4	1	TL	Tula	NRJ
27)	101.4	1	VO	Vologda	R. Dacha
5)	101.4	5	IR	Irkutsk	Hit FM
5)	101.4	1	NN	N.Novgorod	Hit FM
52)	101.4	10	SP	Sankt-Peterburg	Eldoradio
55)	101.4	2	NS	Novosibirsk	Gorodskaya volna
81)	101.4	1	KO	Ukhta	R. Kabriolet
1)	101.5	1	BR	Bryansk	Avtoradio
1)	101.5	1	TS	Nab. Chelny	Avtoradio
1)	101.5	1	KY	Nyagan	Avtoradio
1)	101.5	1	CV	Cheboksary	Avtoradio
110B)	101.5	3	VG	Volgograd	Volgograd FM
14)	101.5	1	SR	Saratov	R. Shanson
18)	101.5	1	OM	Omsk	Yumor FM
18)	101.5	1	IR	Tayshet	Yumor FM
19)	101.5	1	RY	Ryazan	Dorozhnoye R.
2)	101.5	1	KE	Yurga	Russkoye R.
206)	101.5	1	PR	Perm	R. Nostalzhi
24)	101.5	1	KE	Novokuznetsk	NRJ
26)	101.5	2	SA	Samara	R. Rekord
27)	101.5	1	DA	Makhachkala	R. Dacha
4)	101.5	1	SV	Nizhniy Tagil	Europa plus
46)	101.5	1	MO	Shatura	Comedy Radio
62)	101.5	2	AD	Maykop	Kazak FM
85)	101.5	1	NO	Malaya Vishera	MV Diapazon
1)	101.6	1	AR	Arkhangelsk	Avtoradio
10)	101.6	1	VN	Voronezh	R. 7
108)	101.6	1	BA	Ufa	R. 1-y Kanal
14)	101.6	1	SV	Krasnoturinsk	R. Shanson
16)	101.6	1	IV	Ivanovo	Retro FM
19)	101.6	1	PZ	Kuznetsk	Dorozhnoye R.
2)	101.6	1	MU	Apatity	Russkoye R.
24)	101.6	1	VG	Mikhaylovka	NRJ
4)	101.6	1	CB	Chelyabinsk	Europa plus
6)	101.6	1	RO	Rostov-na-Donu	Love R.
7)	101.6	1	OB	Pleshanovo	Militseyskaya volna
7)	101.6	1	OB	Saraktash	Militseyskaya volna
1)	101.7	1	AS	Astrakhan	Avtoradio
1)	101.7	1	VN	Borisloglebsk	Avtoradio
10)	101.7	1	YA	Yaroslavl	R. 7
131)	101.7	1	TS	Bugulma	R. Bolgar
14)	101.7	2	KN	Krasnoyarsk	R. Shanson
14)	101.7	1	SL	Yu-Sakhalinsk	R. Shanson
15)	101.7	1	RK	Abakan	DFM
15)	101.7	1	BA	Neftekamsk	DFM
19)	101.7	1	VO	Babayevo	Dorozhnoye R.
195)	101.7	4	PM	Vladivostok	R. VBC
2)	101.7	1	YV	Birobodzhan	Russkoye R.
204)	101.7	1	SR	Balakovo	Radiola
4)	101.7	1	UL	Ulyanovsk	Europa plus
45A)	101.7	1	BE	Belgorod	Novoye R.
7)	101.7	1	AK	Kamen-na-Obi	Militseyskaya volna
8)	101.7	10	MO	Moskva	Nashe R.
1)	101.8	1	VN	Bobrov	Avtoradio
1)	101.8	1	KO	Syktyvkar	Avtoradio
1)	101.8	1	PR	Chusovoy	Avtoradio
10)	101.8	1	OL	Oryol	R. 7
105)	101.8	1	PZ	Penza	R. 101.8
134A)	101.8	1	KV	Kirov	Studio 21
134A)	101.8	1	KT	Petrozavodsk	Studio 21
15)	101.8	1	KE	Kemerovo	DFM
16)	101.8	1	UD	Izhevsk	Retro FM
16)	101.8	1	NO	V. Novgorod	Retro FM
16)	101.8	1	OB	Orenburg	Retro FM
19)	101.8	2	VL	Vladimir	Dorozhnoye R.
2)	101.8	1	KD	Krasnodar	Russkoye R.
2)	101.8	1	ST	Stavropol	Russkoye R.
25)	101.8	1	SA	Syzran	R. Mir
28)	101.8	1	KA	Kaliningrad	Biznes FM
4)	101.8	1	TV	Tver	Europa plus
4)	101.8	1	KD	Tuapse	Europa plus
4)	101.8	1	TY	Tyumen	Europa plus
7)	101.8	1	OB	Buzuluk	Militseyskaya volna
1)	101.9	1	AK	Biysk	Avtoradio
1)	101.9	4	NN	N.Novgorod	Avtoradio
10)	101.9	1	KY	Surgut	R. 7
124B)	101.9	2	BA	Steplitamak	Sputnik FM
14)	101.9	1	AK	Barnaul	R. Shanson
17)	101.9	5	KD	Sochi	Serebryanyy dozhd
19)	101.9	1	KO	Ukhta	Dorozhnoye R.
2)	101.9	1	DA	Makhachkala	Russkoye R.
23)	101.9	1	VO	Vologda	Detskoye R.
23)	101.9	1	BU	Ulan-Ude	Detskoye R.
26)	101.9	1	TS	Kazan	R. Rekord
4)	101.9	1	TS	Nab. Chelny	Europa plus
4)	101.9	1	KD	Novorossiysk	Europa plus
4)	101.9	1	OM	Omsk	Europa plus
5)	101.9	1	IR	Tulun	Hit FM
8)	101.9	1	TL	Tula	Nashe R.

FM	MHz	kW	Rg	Location	Station
1)	102.0	1	VN	Boguchar	Avtoradio
1)	102.0	1	TV	Zapadnaya Dvina	Avtoradio
1)	102.0	1	SR	Pugachyov	Avtoradio
1)	102.0	1	RY	Ryazan	Avtoradio
10)	102.0	1	ST	Ipatovo	R. 7
101)	102.0	1	CV	Cheboksary	R. Rodnykh dorog
14)	102.0	1	OB	Orsk	R. Shanson
17)	102.0	1	KY	Khanty-Mansiysk	Serebryanyy dozhd
177)	102.0	1	RS	Sangar	R. Sakha
18)	102.0	1	SV	Yekaterinburg	Yumor FM
183)	102.0	1	ZB	Krasnokamensk	R. Sibir
183)	102.0	1	ZB	Kholbon	R. Sibir
19)	102.0	1	BR	Bryansk	Dorozhnoye R.
19)	102.0	1	AR	Velsk	Dorozhnoye R.
19)	102.0	1	NS	Novosibirsk	Dorozhnoye R.
19)	102.0	1	PR	Perm	Dorozhnoye R.
26)	102.0	1	MU	Murmansk	R. Rekord
4)	102.0	1	SO	Vladikavkaz	Europa plus
4)	102.0	1	MD	Saransk	Europa plus
4)	102.0	1	SM	Smolensk	Europa plus
4)	102.0	1	ZB	Chita	Europa plus
45A)	102.0	1	CB	Chelyabinsk	Novoye R.
49)	102.0	10	SP	Sankt-Peterburg	Strana FM
92)	102.0	2	VG	Volgograd	Novaya volna
1)	102.1	1	LI	Lipetsk	Avtoradio
1)	102.1	1	SR	Saratov	Avtoradio
11)	102.1	1	SV	Nizhniy Tagil	R. Maksimum
131)	102.1	2	TS	Leninogorsk	R. Bolgar
14)	102.1	1	IR	Bratsk	R. Shanson
14)	102.1	1	KY	Nizhnevartovsk	R. Shanson
157)	102.1	5	MO	Moskva	R. Monte-Karlo
2)	102.1	1	TO	Tomsk	Russkoye R.
27)	102.1	1	SA	Samara	R. Dacha
33)	102.1	1	UL	Ulyanovsk	2x2 R.
4)	102.1	1	PS	Pskov	Europa plus
45A)	102.1	1	PM	Arsenyev	Novoye R.
88)	102.1	1	IR	Irkutsk	R. MSM
9A)	102.1	1	KE	Belovo	R. Vanya
9A)	102.1	1	KE	Mariinsk	R. Vanya
1)	102.2	1	SM	Vyazma	Avtoradio
1)	102.2	1	MO	Serebryanyye Prudy	Avtoradio
16)	102.2	1	RY	Sasovo	Retro FM
16)	102.2	1	TV	Tver	Retro FM
16)	102.2	1	YA	Yaroslavl	Retro FM
17)	102.2	3	KN	Krasnoyarsk	Serebryanyy dozhd
182)	102.2	1	SV	Kamensk-Uralskiy	R. Si
19)	102.2	1	AR	Vazhskiy	Dorozhnoye R.
19)	102.2	1	NO	Valday	Dorozhnoye R.
19)	102.2	1	SP	Volkhov	Dorozhnoye R.
19)	102.2	1	RO	Rostov-na-Donu	Dorozhnoye R.
2)	102.2	1	RK	Abakan	Russkoye R.
2)	102.2	1	BE	Belgorod	Russkoye R.
4)	102.2	1	KD	Krasnodar	Europa plus
4)	102.2	1	KB	Nalchik	Europa plus
6)	102.2	2	AS	Astrakhan	Love R.
1)	102.3	1	KD	Armavir	Avtoradio
1)	102.3	1	AM	Belogorsk	Avtoradio
1)	102.3	2	OB	Orenburg	Avtoradio
1)	102.3	1	PZ	Penza	Avtoradio
112)	102.3	1	TY	Uvat	R. 7 Tyumen
125)	102.3	1	SA	Tolyatti	R. Avgust
129)	102.3	1	MO	Kolomna	R. Blago
131)	102.3	2	TS	Shemordan	R. Bolgar
19)	102.3	1	VN	Voronezh	Dorozhnoye R.
2)	102.3	1	BA	Neftekamsk	Russkoye R.
25)	102.3	1	KH	Khabarovsk	R. Mir
27)	102.3	1	IR	Usolye-Sibirskoye	R. Dacha
4)	102.3	1	BU	Ulan-Ude	Europa plus
45A)	102.3	1	BA	Steplitamak	Novoye R.
6)	102.3	1	KO	Syktyvkar	Love R.
9A)	102.3	1	TL	Bogoroditsk	R. Vanya
1)	102.4	1	PM	Dalnegorsk	Avtoradio
112)	102.4	1	TY	Vikulovo	R. 7 Tyumen
127)	102.4	10	SP	Sankt-Peterburg	R. Metro
134A)	102.4	1	CB	Chelyabinsk	Studio 21
15)	102.4	1	AK	Barnaul	DFM
15)	102.4	1	VL	Vladimir	DFM
15)	102.4	1	TS	Nurlat	DFM
157)	102.4	1	NN	N.Novgorod	R. Monte-Karlo
16)	102.4	1	TS	Kazan	Retro FM
164)	102.4	5	IN	Nazran	R. Republic
179)	102.4	1	PM	Lukhovitsy	Vladivostok FM
19)	102.4	1	KS	Galich	Dorozhnoye R.
19)	102.4	1	PS	Sebezh	Dorozhnoye R.
2)	102.4	1	KO	Ukhta	Russkoye R.
27)	102.4	1	UD	Izhevsk	R. Dacha
29)	102.4	1	KD	Yeysk	Pervoye R.
35)	102.4	1	TV	Rzhev	R. Vera
4)	102.4	1	DA	Makhachkala	Europa plus
4)	102.4	1	PM	Nakhodka	Europa plus
54)	102.4	1	BU	Sulkhara	Burgyaad FM
6)	102.4	1	TA	Tambov	Love R.
62)	102.4	5	KD	Novorossiysk	Kazak FM
1)	102.5	1	MU	Murmansk	Avtoradio
1)	102.5	4	IV	Rodniki	Avtoradio
122)	102.5	1	BA	Kumertau	R. Aris
14)	102.5	1	KD	Sochi	R. Shanson
146)	102.5	1	CB	Magnitogorsk	R. Kontinental
16)	102.5	1	SV	Serov	Retro FM
16)	102.5	1	TO	Tomsk	Retro FM
19)	102.5	1	KT	Kotkozero	Dorozhnoye R.
19)	102.5	1	SM	Safonovo	Dorozhnoye R.
2)	102.5	1	OM	Omsk	Russkoye R.
2)	102.5	1	TY	Tyumen	Russkoye R.
24)	102.5	2	SA	Samara	NRJ
27)	102.5	1	KM	Petropavlovsk-K.	R. Dacha
35)	102.5	1	RY	Ryazan	R. Vera
4)	102.5	1	AK	Biysk	Europa plus
4)	102.5	1	CV	Cheboksary	Europa plus
4)	102.5	1	SL	Yu-Sakhalinsk	Europa plus
4)	102.5	1	RS	Yakutsk	Europa plus
46)	102.5	10	MO	Moskva	Comedy Radio
5)	102.5	1	MU	Kirovsk	Hit FM
50)	102.5	5	SV	Yekaterinburg	Dzhem FM
62)	102.5	1	KD	Psebay	Kazak FM
8)	102.5	1	BA	Ufa	Nashe R.
1)	102.6	1	IR	Sayansk	Avtoradio
10)	102.6	1	SR	Saratov	R. 7
131)	102.6	2	TS	Nizhnekamsk	R. Bolgar
16)	102.6	1	VG	Volgograd	Retro FM
18)	102.6	1	VN	Ostrorozhsk	Yumor FM
183)	102.6	1	ZB	Chita	R. Sibir
19)	102.6	1	KT	Leppyasilta	Dorozhnoye R.
19)	102.6	1	KS	Makaryev	Dorozhnoye R.
19)	102.6	4	SP	Tikhvin	Dorozhnoye R.
2)	102.6	1	BR	Bryansk	Russkoye R.
2)	102.6	1	YA	Yaroslavl	Russkoye R.
26)	102.6	1	NS	Novosibirsk	R. Rekord
27)	102.6	1	KE	Novokuznetsk	R. Dacha
3)	102.6	1	PS	Pskov	Ekho Moskvy
4)	102.6	1	KL	Kaluga	Europa plus
45A)	102.6	1	IR	Irkutsk	Novoye R.
45B)	102.6	5	ST	Stavropol	Kalina krasnaya
9A)	102.6	1	TA	Morshansk	R. Vanya
1)	102.7	1	KU	Zheleznogorsk	Avtoradio
10)	102.7	1	BE	Belgorod	R. 7
124A)	102.7	1	BA	Baymak	R. Yuldash
124A)	102.7	1	BA	Oktyabrskiy	R. Yuldash
14)	102.7	1	VO	Vologda	R. Shanson
14)	102.7	1	MU	Kandalaksha	R. Shanson
15)	102.7	5	PR	Perm	DFM
150)	102.7	4	PM	Vladivostok	R. Lemma
196)	102.7	1	KH	Khabarovsk	Mix FM
214)	102.7	1	IR	Nizhneudinsk	Udachnoye R.
29)	102.7	5	KD	Krasnodar	Pervoye R.
4)	102.7	1	AS	Astrakhan	Europa plus
5)	102.7	1	KO	Syktyvkar	Hit FM
96)	102.7	1	TV	Tver	Pilot R.
9A)	102.7	2	SA	Tolyatti	R. Vanya
1)	102.8	1	PM	Arsenyev	Avtoradio
1)	102.8	1	RA	Gorno-Altaysk	Avtoradio
1)	102.8	1	NS	Kuybyshev	Avtoradio
11)	102.8	10	SP	Sankt-Peterburg	R. Maksimum
124B)	102.8	1	BA	Uchaly	Sputnik FM
14)	102.8	1	VN	Voronezh	R. Shanson
14)	102.8	1	IR	Cheremkhovo	R. Shanson
19)	102.8	1	KS	Ostrovskoye	Dorozhnoye R.
2)	102.8	1	AM	Belogorsk	Russkoye R.
21)	102.8	1	SO	Vladikavkaz	R. Zvezda
3)	102.8	1	BU	Ulan-Ude	Ekho Moskvy

FM	MHz	kW	Rg	Location	Station
4)	102.8	1	PR	Berezniki	Europa plus
4)	102.8	1	OB	Orsk	Europa plus
4)	102.8	1	OM	Takmyk	Europa plus
40)	102.8	1	TS	Kazan	BIM-R.
63)	102.8	5	KN	Krasnoyarsk	Krasnoyarsk glavnyy
79)	102.8	1	BE	Valuyki	Mir Belogorya
82)	102.8	1	PZ	Penza	Most R.
9A)	102.8	1	KE	Kemerovo	R. Vanya
1)	102.9	1	IR	Bratsk	Avtoradio
1)	102.9	1	PM	Nakhodka	Avtoradio
1)	102.9	1	RS	Neryungri	Avtoradio
1)	102.9	1	TA	Tambov	Avtoradio
15)	102.9	1	SA	Samara	DFM
19)	102.9	1	SP	Podporozhye	Dorozhnoye R.
2)	102.9	5	NN	N.Novgorod	Russkoye R.
208)	102.9	1	SL	Yu-Sakhalinsk	Rock FM
24)	102.9	1	KO	Ukhta	NRJ
4)	102.9	1	VL	Vladimir	Europa plus
46)	102.9	1	AK	Barnaul	Comedy Radio
58)	102.9	1	CB	Chelyabinsk	Intervolna
6)	102.9	1	KA	Kaliningrad	Love R.
62)	102.9	4	KD	Armavir	Kazak FM
75)	102.9	1	KV	Kirov	Mariya FM
92)	102.9	1	VG	Mikhaylovka	Novaya volna
1)	103.0	1	MA	Magadan	Avtoradio
14)	103.0	1	TS	Bugulma	R. Shanson
14)	103.0	10	MO	Moskva	R. Shanson
15)	103.0	1	CB	Magnitogorsk	DFM
160)	103.0	1	YN	Noyabrsk	R. Noyabrsk
175)	103.0	1	BA	Ufa	R. Roksana
19)	103.0	1	VN	Borisloglebsk	Dorozhnoye R.
19)	103.0	1	IV	Ivanovo	Dorozhnoye R.
19)	103.0	1	SP	Kirishi	Dorozhnoye R.
2)	103.0	1	UL	Ulyanovsk	Russkoye R.
204)	103.0	1	SR	Saratov	Radiola
23)	103.0	1	CV	Cheboksary	Detskoye R.
4)	103.0	1	UD	Izhevsk	Europa plus
5)	103.0	2	OB	Orenburg	Hit FM
8)	103.0	1	YV	Birobodzhan	Nashe R.
8)	103.0	1	MU	Murmansk	Nashe R.
0)	103.0	1	KM	Petropavlovsk-K.	Nashe R.
8)	103.0	1	PS	Pskov	Nashe R.
1)	103.1	1	VG	Volgograd	Avtoradio
1)	103.1	1	CB	Ozyorsk	Avtoradio
1)	103.1	1	KT	Petrozavodsk	Avtoradio
1)	103.1	3	PM	Spassk-Dalniy	Avtoradio
112)	103.1	1	TY	Tyumen	R. 7 Tyumen
16)	103.1	1	SV	Krasnoturinsk	Retro FM
16)	103.1	1	ST	Stavropol	Retro FM
197B)	103.1	1	RS	Yakutsk	R. Viktoriya
2)	103.1	1	KD	Sochi	Russkoye R.
4)	103.1	1	BE	Staryy Oskol	Europa plus
6)	103.1	1	KS	Kostroma	Love R.
62)	103.1	1	KD	Primorsko-Akhtarsk	Kazak FM
7)	103.1	1	OB	Abdulino	Militseyskaya volna
7)	103.1	1	MU	Apatity	Militseyskaya volna
7)	103.1	1	OB	Kuvandyk	Militseyskaya volna
7)	103.1	1	AK	Slavgorod	Militseyskaya volna
89)	103.1	1	KL	Kaluga	Nika FM
1)	103.2	1	KD	Krasnodar	Avtoradio
11)	103.2	1	PR	Perm	R. Maksimum
112)	103.2	1	TY	Bol. Sorokino	R. 7 Tyumen
124A)	103.2	1	BA	Davlekanovo	R. Yuldash
14)	103.2	4	PM	Vladivostok	R. Shanson
14)	103.2	1	SV	Yekaterinburg	R. Shanson
14)	103.2	1	IR	Tayshet	R. Shanson
15)	103.2	1	SA	Tolyatti	DFM
18)	103.2	1	TS	Nab. Chelny	Yumor FM
19)	103.2	1	SM	Vyazma	Dorozhnoye R.
19)	103.2	1	MD	Saransk	Dorozhnoyc R.
2)	103.2	1	AS	Astrakhan	Russkoye R.
2)	103.2	1	ST	Pyatigorsk	Russkoye R.
21)	103.2	1	ME	Yoshkar-Ola	R. Zvezda
21)	103.2	1	AR	Plesetsk	R. Zvezda
38)	103.2	1	PR	Krasnovishersk	Beloye R.
4)	103.2	1	VL	Kovrov	Europa plus
4)	103.2	3	NS	Novosibirsk	Europa plus
4)	103.2	1	NO	Pestovo	Europa plus
4)	103.2	1	RY	Ryazan	Europa plus
43)	103.2	1	MO	Kashira	Marusya FM

FM	MHz	kW	Rg	Location	Station
5)	103.2	1	KG	Kurgan	Hit FM
1)	103.3	2	TS	Kazan	Avtoradio
1)	103.3	2	KY	Surgut	Avtoradio
124A)	103.3	1	BA	Bakaly	R. Yuldash
14)	103.3	1	KE	Kemerovo	R. Shanson
15)	103.3	1	PR	Berezniki	DFM
15)	103.3	1	VL	Murom	DFM
179)	103.3	1	PM	Dalnerechensk	Vladivostok FM
2)	103.3	1	AM	Blagoveshchensk	Russkoye R.
2)	103.3	1	MU	Kandalaksha	Russkoye R.
2)	103.3	1	IR	Sayansk	Russkoye R.
24)	103.3	1	OB	Buzuluk	NRJ
24)	103.3	2	KN	Krasnoyarsk	NRJ
26)	103.3	1	OL	Livny	R. Rekord
27)	103.3	1	SR	Balakovo	R. Dacha
27)	103.3	1	UD	Balezino	R. Dacha
27)	103.3	1	OB	Orsk	R. Dacha
27)	103.3	1	RO	Rostov-na-Donu	R. Dacha
27)	103.3	1	YA	Yaroslavl	R. Dacha
29)	103.3	4	KD	Tbilisskaya	Pervoye R.
37)	103.3	1	KA	Dobrovolsk	Baltik plyus
46)	103.3	2	KH	Khabarovsk	Comedy Radio
7)	103.3	1	TL	Tula	Militseyskaya volna
99)	103.3	1	ZB	Chita	Populyarnoye R.
1)	103.4	1	NO	Valday	Avtoradio
1)	103.4	1	VN	Voronezh	Avtoradio
1)	103.4	1	KV	Vyatstkiye Polyarny	Avtoradio
1)	103.4	1	KV	Kirov	Avtoradio
1)	103.4	1	KL	Obinsk	Avtoradio
134A)	103.4	1	KA	Kaliningrad	Studio 21
15)	103.4	5	SP	Sankt-Peterburg	DFM
173)	103.4	4	NN	N.Novgorod	R. Randevu
19)	103.4	1	AR	Arkhangelsk	Dorozhnoye R.
19)	103.4	1	RA	Gorno-Altaysk	Dorozhnoye R.
2)	103.4	1	VL	Vladimir	Russkoye R.
42)	103.4	1	TL	Yefremov	Pervoye setevoye
1)	103.5	1	SO	Vladikavkaz	Avtoradio
1)	103.5	1	KD	Labinsk	Avtoradio
1)	103.5	1	KA	Chernyakhovsk	Avtoradio
109)	103.5	5	OM	Omsk	R. 3
133)	103.5	1	AR	Velsk	R. 29
15)	103.5	1	BR	Bryansk	DFM
16)	103.5	1	MU	Kirovsk	Retro FM
16)	103.5	1	KT	Petrozavodsk	Retro FM
16)	103.5	1	CV	Cheboksary	Retro FM
179)	103.5	1	PM	Dalnegorsk	Vladivostok FM
179)	103.5	5	PM	Novozhatkovo	Vladivostok FM
19)	103.5	1	UL	Ulyanovsk	Dorozhnoye R.
2)	103.5	1	SM	Smolensk	Russkoye R.
24)	103.5	1	MO	Shatura	NRJ
4)	103.5	1	VO	Lipin Bor	Europa plus
4)	103.5	1	SR	Saratov	Europa plus
4)	103.5	1	KO	Ukhta	Europa plus
46)	103.5	1	BA	Ufa	Comedy Radio
7)	103.5	1	AK	Aleysk	Militseyskaya volna
7)	103.5	1	OB	Tyulgan	Militseyskaya volna
76)	103.5	1	KN	Norilsk	Megapolis FM
8)	103.5	1	CB	Chelyabinsk	Nashe R.
9A)	103.5	1	OL	Oryol	R. Vanya
101)	103.6	1	VL	Kolchugino	R. Rodnykh dorog
132)	103.6	2	PR	Perm	Nashi pesni
134A)	103.6	1	SV	Nizhniy Tagil	Studio 21
155)	103.6	2	SA	Samara	R. Megapolis
18)	103.6	1	RS	Yakutsk	Yumor FM
19)	103.6	1	VG	Volgograd	Dorozhnoye R.
19)	103.6	1	TV	Vyshniy Volochyok	Dorozhnoye R.
2)	103.6	1	TS	Nab. Chelny	Russkoye R.
24)	103.6	1	CB	Magnitogorsk	NRJ
4)	103.6	1	BE	Belgorod	Europa plus
4)	103.6	1	VL	Gus-Khrustalnyy	Europa plus
4)	103.6	1	ST	Stavropol	Europa plus
88)	103.6	1	IR	Cheremkhovo	R. MSM
1)	103.7	1	NO	V. Novgorod	Avtoradio
1)	103.7	1	MD	Saransk	Avtoradio
11)	103.7	10	MO	Moskva	R. Maksimum
117)	103.7	2	KH	Khabarovsk	R. Vostok Rossii
134A)	103.7	1	VO	Vologda	Studio 21
14)	103.7	1	AS	Astrakhan	R. Shanson
143)	103.7	1	OB	Orsk	R. Khit
149)	103.7	1	KU	Kursk	R. Kurs

FM	MHz	kW	Rg	Location	Station
157)	103.7	1	RO	Rostov-na-Donu	R. Monte-Karlo
16)	103.7	1	PM	Vladivostok	Retro FM
16)	103.7	1	KX	Elista	Retro FM
182)	103.7	5	SV	Yekaterinburg	R. Si
183)	103.7	1	RK	Abakan	R. Sibir
19)	103.7	1	NN	Vorotynets	Dorozhnoye R.
19)	103.7	1	KD	Krasnodar	Dorozhnoye R.
19)	103.7	1	KG	Kurgan	Dorozhnoye R.
19)	103.7	1	BU	Ulan-Ude	Dorozhnoye R.
191)	103.7	1	SA	Isakly	Samarskoye gub. R.
2)	103.7	1	KE	Mezhdurechensk	Russkoye R.
24)	103.7	1	SR	Balakovo	NRJ
27)	103.7	1	KD	Sochi	R. Dacha
4)	103.7	1	OB	Orenburg	Europa plus
103)	103.8	1	ME	Yoshkar-Ola	Puls R.
124A)	103.8	1	BA	Steplitamak	R. Yuldash
14)	103.8	1	PR	Berezniki	R. Shanson
15)	103.8	1	TO	Tomsk	DFM
16)	103.8	1	KO	Syktyvkar	Retro FM
17)	103.8	1	TV	Tver	Serebryanyy dozhd
177)	103.8	1	RS	Neryungri	R. Sakha
19)	103.8	1	NO	Borovichi	Dorozhnoye R.
19)	103.8	1	YA	Yaroslavl	Dorozhnoye R.
2)	103.8	4	AR	Arkhangelsk	Russkoye R.
2)	103.8	1	RT	Kyzyl	Russkoye R.
25)	103.8	1	KN	Yeniseysk	R. Mir
4)	103.8	1	IR	Irkutsk	Europa plus
4)	103.8	2	KN	Krasnoyarsk	Europa plus
4)	103.8	1	PZ	Penza	Europa plus
4)	103.8	1	ST	Pyatigorsk	Europa plus
6)	103.8	1	VN	Voronezh	Love R.
8)	103.8	1	UD	Izhevsk	Nashe R.
89)	103.8	1	KL	Sukhinichi	Nika FM
1)	103.9	1	AK	Barnaul	Avtoradio
1)	103.9	1	PM	Dalnerechensk	Avtoradio
134A)	103.9	1	TA	Tambov	Studio 21
15)	103.9	1	MO	Lukhovitsy	DFM
15)	103.9	2	NS	Novosibirsk	DFM
16)	103.9	1	VG	Mikhaylovka	Retro FM
18)	103.9	1	OL	Oryol	Yumor FM
183)	103.9	1	OM	Omsk	R. Sibir
19)	103.9	1	BA	Birsk	Dorozhnoye R.
2)	103.9	3	PM	Dalnegorsk	Russkoye R.
2)	103.9	1	KV	Kirov	Russkoye R.
2)	103.9	1	KM	Petropavlovsk-K.	Russkoye R.
4)	103.9	1	SV	Irbit	Europa plus
4)	103.9	5	NN	N.Novgorod	Europa plus
45A)	103.9	1	PM	Partizansk	Novoye R.
45A)	103.9	1	SR	Saratov	Novoye R.
7)	103.9	5	UL	Veshkayma	Militseyskaya volna
1)	104.0	1	SV	Kamensk-Uralskiy	Avtoradio
112)	104.0	1	TY	Ishim	R. 7 Tyumen
124B)	104.0	1	BA	Kugarchi	Sputnik FM
14)	104.0	1	TS	Kazan	R. Shanson
14)	104.0	1	KE	Novokuznetsk	R. Shanson
151)	104.0	1	ST	Svetlograd	Svoye R.
16)	104.0	1	MU	Murmansk	Retro FM
16)	104.0	1	BA	Ufa	Retro FM
19)	104.0	1	TV	Rzhev	Dorozhnoye R.
19)	104.0	1	RS	Yakutsk	Dorozhnoye R.
26)	104.0	1	SA	Tolyatti	R. Rekord
4)	104.0	1	KY	Nizhnevartovsk	Europa plus
45A)	104.0	1	VG	Volgograd	Novoye R.
8)	104.0	10	SP	Sankt-Peterburg	Nashe R.
91)	104.0	1	KD	Novorossiysk	Novaya Rossiya
9A)	104.0	1	PZ	Pachelma	R. Vanya
1)	104.1	1	RO	Dyogtevo	Avtoradio
1)	104.1	1	AR	Plesetsk	Avtoradio
1)	104.1	1	RO	Rostov-na-Donu	Avtoradio
118)	104.1	5	PR	Perm	R. Alfa
15)	104.1	1	OB	Orsk	DFM
15)	104.1	1	CB	Tryokhgornyy	DFM
188)	104.1	1	AS	Astrakhan	Yuzhnaya volna
19)	104.1	1	AM	Shimanovsk	Dorozhnoye R.
2)	104.1	1	PM	Arsenyev	Russkoye R.
2)	104.1	1	IR	Bratsk	Russkoye R.
2)	104.1	1	CB	Chelyabinsk	Russkoye R.
24)	104.1	1	RY	Ryazan	NRJ
27)	104.1	1	SV	Yekaterinburg	R. Dacha
6)	104.1	1	SV	Krasnoturinsk	Love R.
8)	104.1	1	NO	V. Novgorod	Nashe R.
9A)	104.1	1	SM	Roslavl	R. Vanya
9A)	104.1	1	MD	Saransk	R. Vanya
14)	104.2	1	KY	Surgut	R. Shanson
161)	104.2	4	NN	Arzamas	R. Obraz
18)	104.2	2	TO	Tomsk	Yumor FM
19)	104.2	1	SP	Kingisepp	Dorozhnoye R.
192)	104.2	2	VO	Babayevo	R. Transmit
192)	104.2	1	VO	Totma	R. Transmit
2)	104.2	1	CB	Magnitogorsk	Russkoye R.
221)	104.2	1	SP	Kirishi	VFM-Rock
23)	104.2	1	TY	Tyumen	Detskoye R.
24)	104.2	1	BE	Belgorod	NRJ
24)	104.2	15	MO	Moskva	NRJ
28)	104.2	1	KN	Krasnoyarsk	Biznes FM
4)	104.2	1	RK	Abakan	Europa plus
4)	104.2	1	MU	Apatity	Europa plus
4)	104.2	3	PM	Vladivostok	Europa plus
5)	104.2	1	KD	Krasnodar	Hit FM
6)	104.2	1	IR	Irkutsk	Love R.
6)	104.2	1	CV	Cheboksary	Love R.
69)	104.2	1	AR	Arkhangelsk	Zhara FM
7)	104.2	1	OB	Tashla	Militseyskaya volna
1)	104.3	1	OL	Oryol	Avtoradio
11)	104.3	1	KT	Petrozavodsk	R. Maksimum
15)	104.3	1	VN	Voronezh	DFM
15)	104.3	2	OB	Orenburg	DFM
16)	104.3	1	SR	Saratov	Retro FM
19)	104.3	1	PZ	Penza	Dorozhnoye R.
19)	104.3	1	KH	Khabarovsk	Dorozhnoye R.
2)	104.3	1	BA	Steplitamak	Russkoye R.
2)	104.3	1	KD	Tikhoretsk	Russkoye R.
213)	104.3	2	SA	Samara	Samara-Maksimum
216)	104.3	1	TV	Tver	R. Kniga
22)	104.3	1	VL	Vladimir	R. KP
46)	104.3	1	KE	Kemerovo	Comedy Radio
9A)	104.3	1	KV	Kirov	R. Vanya
1)	104.4	5	TL	Tula	Avtoradio
10)	104.4	1	BE	Ivnya	R. 7
14)	104.4	5	SP	Sankt-Peterburg	R. Shanson
16)	104.4	1	AK	Barnaul	Retro FM
16)	104.4	1	TA	Tambov	Retro FM
19)	104.4	1	AM	Blagoveshchensk	Dorozhnoye R.
19)	104.4	1	PS	Pushkinskiye Gory	Dorozhnoye R.
19)	104.4	1	NO	Khvoynaya	Dorozhnoye R.
192)	104.4	1	VO	Vologda	R. Transmit
192)	104.4	1	VO	Nikolsk	R. Transmit
2)	104.4	1	PR	Chusovoy	Russkoye R.
24)	104.4	1	KE	Yurga	NRJ
26)	104.4	1	OM	Omsk	R. Rekord
27)	104.4	1	BA	Tuymazy	R. Dacha
4)	104.4	1	YN	Noyabrsk	Europa plus
4)	104.4	5	KD	Sochi	Europa plus
6)	104.4	1	KA	Sovetsk	Love R.
6)	104.4	1	SL	Yu-Sakhalinsk	Love R.
7)	104.4	1	VL	Murom	Militseyskaya volna
75)	104.4	2	TS	Shemordan	Mariya FM
9A)	104.4	1	KE	Novokuznetsk	R. Vanya
1)	104.5	1	KM	Petropavlovsk-K.	Avtoradio
1)	104.5	1	SM	Safonovo	Avtoradio
1)	104.5	1	BE	Staryy Oskol	Avtoradio
1)	104.5	1	YA	Yaroslavl	Avtoradio
100)	104.5	1	MU	Murmansk	Power Hit R.
114)	104.5	1	UD	Izhevsk	R. Adam
16)	104.5	1	MU	Kandalaksha	Retro FM
163)	104.5	1	CB	Chelyabinsk	R. Olimp
167)	104.5	1	MD	Saransk	Start FM
170)	104.5	1	DA	Kizilyurt	R. Priboy
18)	104.5	1	VG	Volgograd	Yumor FM
19)	104.5	1	KT	Lakhdenpokhya	Dorozhnoye R.
197A)	104.5	1	RS	Yakutsk	R. Viktoriya-Sakha
199)	104.5	1	KY	Nyagan	R. Yugra
2)	104.5	1	BA	Ufa	Russkoye R.
210)	104.5	5	SV	Yekaterinburg	Rok-Arsenal
25)	104.5	1	NO	V. Novgorod	R. Mir
27)	104.5	2	NN	N.Novgorod	R. Dacha
29)	104.5	5	KD	Kanevskaya	Pervoye R.
33)	104.5	1	UL	Dimitrovgrad	2x2 R.
35)	104.5	1	TV	Vyshniy Volochyok	R. Vera
4)	104.5	1	ME	Yoshkar-Ola	Europa plus

FM	MHz	kW	Rg	Location	Station
4)	104.5	1	KA	Kaliningrad	Europa plus
45A)	104.5	1	RY	Ryazan	Novoye R.
5)	104.5	1	KO	Ukhta	Hit FM
7)	104.5	1	OB	Sharlyk	Militseyskaya volna
1)	104.6	1	KV	Kilmez	Avtoradio
1)	104.6	1	KD	Tuapse	Avtoradio
124A)	104.6	1	BA	Akyar	R. Yuldash
15)	104.6	1	RO	Rostov-na-Donu	DFM
16)	104.6	5	IR	Irkutsk	Retro FM
179)	104.6	1	PM	Arsenyev	Vladivostok FM
183)	104.6	1	TO	Tomsk	R. Sibir
192)	104.6	1	VO	Cherepovets	R. Transmit
24)	104.6	1	SA	Syzran	NRJ
27)	104.6	2	KN	Krasnoyarsk	R. Dacha
40)	104.6	1	TS	Almetyevsk	BIM-R.
41)	104.6	1	BU	Ulan-Ude	Barguzin FM
6)	104.6	1	PR	Berezniki	Love R.
6)	104.6	1	LI	Lipetsk	Love R.
65)	104.6	1	IR	Bratsk	PIFM
66)	104.6	1	TY	Tyumen	Krasnaya Armiya
7)	104.6	1	AK	Zarinsk	Militseyskaya volna
9A)	104.6	1	VN	Liski	R. Vanya
1)	104.7	1	RK	Abakan	Avtoradio
1)	104.7	1	CB	Magnitogorsk	Avtoradio
1)	104.7	1	KY	Nizhnevartovsk	Avtoradio
10)	104.7	10	MO	Moskva	R. 7
124A)	104.7	1	BA	Belebey	R. Yuldash
124B)	104.7	1	BA	Neftekamsk	Sputnik FM
131)	104.7	1	TS	Nurlat	R. Bolgar
15)	104.7	1	TS	Kazan	DFM
16)	104.7	1	KH	Komsomolsk-na-A.	Retro FM
2)	104.7	1	KT	Petrozavodsk	Russkoye R.
24)	104.7	1	KE	Mezhdurechensk	NRJ
26)	104.7	1	PR	Perm	R. Rekord
27)	104.7	5	PM	Vladivostok	R. Dacha
46)	104.7	1	BE	Belgorod	Comedy Radio
8)	104.7	1	AR	Arkhangelsk	Nashe R.
8)	104.7	1	KD	Krasnodar	Nashe R.
97)	104.7	1	KS	Sharya	Pioner FM
9B)	104.7	1	SP	Luga	Piter FM
1)	104.8	1	VL	Vladimir	Avtoradio
1)	104.8	1	SA	Samara	Avtoradio
134A)	104.8	1	KD	Sochi	Studio 21
14)	104.8	1	TV	Tver	R. Shanson
157)	104.8	1	OL	Oryol	R. Monte-Karlo
16)	104.8	1	SM	Smolensk	Retro FM
16)	104.8	1	BA	Steplitamak	Retro FM
17)	104.8	1	SR	Saratov	Serebryanyy dozhd
18)	104.8	1	MO	Kolomna	Yumor FM
19)	104.8	1	KB	Nalchik	Dorozhnoye R.
19)	104.8	1	OB	Orenburg	Dorozhnoye R.
19)	104.8	1	KO	Syktyvkar	Dorozhnoye R.
194)	104.8	1	DA	Makhachkala	R. Assa
2)	104.8	1	VN	Voronezh	Russkoye R.
2)	104.8	1	TY	Zavodoukovsk	Russkoye R.
2)	104.8	1	KE	Kemerovo	Russkoye R.
2)	104.8	1	KS	Kostroma	Russkoye R.
2)	104.8	1	PZ	Penza	Russkoye R.
24)	104.8	1	TS	Nab. Chelny	NRJ
35)	104.8	1	RT	Kyzyl	R. Vera
6)	104.8	1	MU	Monchegorsk	Love R.
7)	104.8	1	UL	Sengiley	Militseyskaya volna
77)	104.8	4	SP	Sankt-Peterburg	R. Baltika
1)	104.9	1	YN	Noyabrsk	Avtoradio
124A)	104.9	1	BA	Beloretsk	R. Yuldash
131)	104.9	1	TS	Kutlu-Bukash	R. Bolgar
137)	104.9	1	MO	Noginsk	R. Noginska
16)	104.9	1	KV	Kirov	Retro FM
18)	104.9	1	MD	Saransk	Yumor FM
2)	104.9	1	VO	Vologda	Russkoye R.
23)	104.9	1	TA	Tambov	Detskoye R.
29)	104.9	5	KD	Novorossiysk	Pervoye R.
4)	104.9	1	AK	Barnaul	Europa plus
4)	104.9	1	TL	Tula	Europa plus
6)	104.9	1	TS	Bavly	Love R.
6)	104.9	1	NN	N.Novgorod	Love R.
62)	104.9	1	KD	Yeysk	Kazak FM
7)	104.9	1	UL	Novospasskoye	Militseyskaya volna
71)	104.9	1	CB	Chelyabinsk	L-Radio
95)	104.9	1	SO	Vladikavkaz	R. MSS
1)	105.0	2	SV	Yekaterinburg	Avtoradio
1)	105.0	1	KE	Novokuznetsk	Avtoradio
1)	105.0	1	KA	Sovetsk	Avtoradio
10)	105.0	1	RY	Ryazan	R. 7
131)	105.0	1	PR	Barda	R. Bolgar
14)	105.0	1	VO	Cherepovets	R. Shanson
16)	105.0	1	BU	Ulan-Ude	Retro FM
18)	105.0	1	AS	Astrakhan	Yumor FM
198)	105.0	1	RS	Neryungri	R. Voyazh
199)	105.0	5	KY	Surgut	R. Yugra
216)	105.0	5	MO	Moskva	R. Kniga
24)	105.0	1	KD	Tuapse	NRJ
26)	105.0	1	KO	Ukhta	R. Rekord
27)	105.0	1	BA	Ufa	R. Dacha
29)	105.0	1	KD	Belaya Glina	Pervoye R.
29)	105.0	1	KD	Psebay	Pervoye R.
3)	105.0	1	TO	Tomsk	Ekho Moskvy
6)	105.0	1	OB	Buguruslan	Love R.
6)	105.0	1	OM	Omsk	Love R.
7)	105.0	1	KU	Kursk	Militseyskaya volna
8)	105.0	1	ST	Kislovodsk	Nashe R.
87)	105.0	2	CV	Tsivilsk	Nats. R. Chuvashii
1)	105.1	1	ME	Yoshkar-Ola	Avtoradio
1)	105.1	1	ST	Stavropol	Avtoradio
110A)	105.1	1	VG	Volgograd	R. Sputnik
124A)	105.1	1	BA	Kumertau	R. Yuldash
134A)	105.1	1	LI	Lipetsk	Studio 21
14)	105.1	1	PR	Perm	R. Shanson
14)	105.1	1	RO	Rostov-na-Donu	R. Shanson
156)	105.1	1	MO	Shatura	R. 1
16)	105.1	1	TY	Tyumen	Retro FM
16)	105.1	1	IR	Ust-Ilimsk	Retro FM
2)	105.1	1	PR	Berezniki	Russkoye R.
27)	105.1	1	SL	Yu-Sakhalinsk	R. Dacha
4)	105.1	1	YA	Yaroslavl	Europa plus
9A)	105.1	1	TV	Vyshniy Volochyok	R. Vanya
1)	105.2	2	KN	Krasnoyarsk	Avtoradio
1)	105.2	1	ZB	Chita	Avtoradio
10)	105.2	1	CB	Magnitogorsk	R. 7
135)	105.2	1	PZ	Penza	R. Ekspress
149)	105.2	1	KU	Zheleznogorsk	R. Kurs
2)	105.2	1	KO	Syktyvkar	Russkoye R.
23)	105.2	1	KT	Petrozavodsk	Detskoye R.
27)	105.2	1	SA	Tolyatti	R. Dacha
27)	105.2	1	OB	Yasnyy	R. Dacha
3)	105.2	1	DA	Makhachkala	Ekho Moskvy
37)	105.2	1	KA	Kaliningrad	Baltik plyus
4)	105.2	1	SM	Vyazma	Europa plus
46)	105.2	2	KY	Megion	Comedy Radio
5)	105.2	2	NS	Novosibirsk	Hit FM
62)	105.2	5	KD	Krasnodar	Kazak FM
8)	105.2	1	KD	Sochi	Nashe R.
1)	105.3	1	KE	Kemerovo	Avtoradio
131)	105.3	1	TS	Abasalyamovo	R. Bolgar
15)	105.3	1	PM	Vladivostok	DFM
16)	105.3	1	VN	Voronezh	Retro FM
17)	105.3	1	VO	Vologda	Serebryanyy dozhd
171)	105.3	1	IR	Usolye-Sibirskoye	R. Radio
18)	105.3	1	VN	Rossosh	Yumor FM
19)	105.3	1	UD	Izhevsk	Dorozhnoye R.
2)	105.3	1	SR	Saratov	Russkoye R.
2)	105.3	1	TL	Tula	Russkoye R.
207)	105.3	1	TS	Kazan	Relaks FM
27)	105.3	1	KS	Kostroma	R. Dacha
27)	105.3	1	OB	Orenburg	R. Dacha
6)	105.3	1	SO	Vladikavkaz	Love R.
6)	105.3	5	SP	Sankt-Peterburg	Love R.
8)	105.3	1	RS	Yakutsk	Nashe R.
80B)	105.3	5	MO	Moskva	Capital FM
1)	105.4	1	NO	Borovichi	Avtoradio
1)	105.4	1	TO	Tomsk	Avtoradio
10)	105.4	1	CB	Chelyabinsk	R. 7
124A)	105.4	1	BA	Uchaly	R. Yuldash
124A)	105.4	1	BA	Fyodorovka	R. Yuldash
134A)	105.4	1	IV	Ivanovo	Studio 21
16)	105.4	1	AR	Arkhangelsk	Retro FM
16)	105.4	1	RY	Ryazan	Retro FM
177)	105.4	1	RS	Mirnyy	R. Sakha
18)	105.4	1	VN	Kalach	Yumor FM
19)	105.4	1	NN	N.Novgorod	Dorozhnoye R.

FM	MHz	kW	Rg	Location	Station
19)	105.4	1	KG	Shardinsk	Dorozhnoye R.
2)	105.4	1	AK	Barnaul	Russkoye R.
29)	105.4	4	KD	Armavir	Pervoye R.
46)	105.4	1	SA	Samara	Comedy Radio
57)	105.4	1	CC	Groznyy	R. Groznyy
7)	105.4	1	OB	Pervomayskiy	Militseyskaya volna
1)	105.5	1	YA	Rybinsk	Avtoradio
1)	105.5	1	MO	Uvarovka	Avtoradio
106)	105.5	1	SL	Yu-Sakhalinsk	R. ASTV
124A)	105.5	1	BA	Ufa	R. Yuldash
131)	105.5	2	TS	Nab. Chelny	R. Bolgar
144)	105.5	1	SP	Kirishi	R. Kirishi
15)	105.5	1	OL	Oryol	DFM
16)	105.5	1	UL	Ulyanovsk	Retro FM
19)	105.5	1	MA	Magadan	Dorozhnoye R.
192)	105.5	4	VO	Lipin Bor	R. Transmit
2)	105.5	1	MU	Murmansk	Russkoye R.
2)	105.5	1	KB	Nalchik	Russkoye R.
2)	105.5	1	KE	Novokuznetsk	Russkoye R.
2)	105.5	1	BE	Staryy Oskol	Russkoye R.
211)	105.5	1	IR	Ust-Kut	Lena FM
23)	105.5	1	AM	Blagoveshchensk	Detskoye R.
25)	105.5	1	BU	Ulan-Ude	R. Mir
46)	105.5	2	SV	Nizhniy Tagil	Comedy Radio
59)	105.5	1	VN	Elista	Kanal Melodiya
6)	105.5	1	TV	Tver	Love R.
6)	105.5	1	KD	Tuapse	Love R.
65)	105.5	1	RA	Gorno-Altaysk	PIFM
7)	105.5	1	OB	Kvarkeno	Militseyskaya volna
77)	105.5	1	SP	Vyborg	R. Baltika
84)	105.5	1	ME	Yoshkar-Ola	R. Mariy El
14)	105.6	5	IR	Irkutsk	R. Shanson
14)	105.6	1	LI	Lipetsk	R. Shanson
16)	105.6	1	TY	Ishim	Retro FM
191)	105.6	2	SA	Kinel-Cherkassy	Samarskoye gub. R.
2)	105.6	2	VG	Volgograd	Russkoye R.
25)	105.6	1	KO	Syktyvkar	R. Mir
26)	105.6	1	TS	Almetyevsk	R. Rekord
29)	105.6	1	KD	Primorsko-Akhtarsk	Pervoye R.
30)	105.6	1	TS	Shemordan	Dulkyn radiosy
4)	105.6	2	KH	Khabarovsk	Europa plus
48)	105.6	1	TY	Tyumen	Dipol FM
6)	105.6	1	CB	Magnitogorsk	Love R.
7)	105.6	1	OB	Novosergiyevka	Militseyskaya volna
7)	105.6	1	MD	Saransk	Militseyskaya volna
1)	105.7	1	MU	Apatity	Avtoradio
1)	105.7	1	BR	Unecha	Avtoradio
124B)	105.7	1	BA	Oktyabrskiy	Sputnik FM
14)	105.7	1	RK	Abakan	R. Shanson
14)	105.7	1	UD	Izhevsk	R. Shanson
147)	105.7	1	RS	Yakutsk	STV-R.
157)	105.7	1	PM	Vladivostok	R. Monte-Karlo
16)	105.7	1	OM	Omsk	Retro FM
18)	105.7	1	SA	Tolyatti	Yumor FM
19)	105.7	1	PR	Berezniki	Dorozhnoye R.
19)	105.7	4	NO	V. Novgorod	Dorozhnoye R.
2)	105.7	1	SV	Yekaterinburg	Russkoye R.
2)	105.7	10	MO	Moskva	Russkoye R.
22)	105.7	1	ST	Stavropol	R. KP
28)	105.7	2	NS	Novosibirsk	Biznes FM
29)	105.7	1	KD	Sochi	Pervoye R.
4)	105.7	1	RO	Rostov-na-Donu	Europa plus
4)	105.7	1	SV	Serov	Europa plus
78)	105.7	1	KD	Krymsk	R. Elektron
10)	105.8	1	VL	Vladimir	R. 7
124A)	105.8	1	BA	Mesyagutovo	R. Yuldash
14)	105.8	1	ST	Pyatigorsk	R. Shanson
19)	105.8	1	SM	Roslavl	Dorozhnoye R.
2)	105.8	1	KN	Krasnoyarsk	Russkoye R.
201)	105.8	1	KG	Shardinsk	R. Za oblakami
205)	105.8	1	KS	Kostroma	RDV-FM
24)	105.8	1	BA	Neftekamsk	NRJ
27)	105.8	1	KO	Ukhta	R. Dacha
3)	105.8	1	TS	Kazan	Ekho Moskvy
5)	105.8	1	OB	Orsk	Hit FM
59)	105.8	1	VN	Borisloglebsk	Kanal Melodiya
6)	105.8	4	TL	Tula	Love R.
62)	105.8	4	KD	Tbilisskaya	Kazak FM
7)	105.8	1	OB	Buguruslan	Militseyskaya volna
7)	105.8	1	OB	Orenburg	Militseyskaya volna
8)	105.8	1	IR	Usolye-Sibirskoye	Nashe R.
1)	105.9	1	TS	Bugulma	Avtoradio
14)	105.9	1	RY	Ryazan	R. Shanson
14)	105.9	2	CB	Chelyabinsk	R. Shanson
142)	105.9	1	KC	Karachayevsk	R. Kavkaz Khit
157)	105.9	5	SP	Sankt-Peterburg	R. Monte-Karlo
16)	105.9	1	SO	Vladikavkaz	Retro FM
16)	105.9	1	RT	Kyzyl	Retro FM
187)	105.9	2	NS	Raduga	R. 54
19)	105.9	1	VN	Kalach	Dorozhnoye R.
19)	105.9	1	KA	Kaliningrad	Dorozhnoye R.
199)	105.9	1	KY	Nizhnevartovsk	R. Yugra
2)	105.9	1	TA	Tambov	Russkoye R.
4)	105.9	2	KY	Surgut	Europa plus
4)	105.9	1	TV	Tver	Europa plus
7)	105.9	1	NN	N.Novgorod	Militseyskaya volna
73)	105.9	1	RO	Zverevo	Ataman FM
79)	105.9	1	BE	Svistovka	Mir Belogorya
1)	106.0	1	MO	Kolomna	Avtoradio
10)	106.0	1	KB	Nalchik	R. 7
134A)	106.0	1	VG	Volgograd	Studio 21
15)	106.0	1	KD	Krasnodar	DFM
16)	106.0	1	SV	Nizhniy Tagil	Retro FM
171)	106.0	1	IR	Nizhneudinsk	R. Radio
18)	106.0	1	IR	Irkutsk	Yumor FM
19)	106.0	1	AS	Astrakhan	Dorozhnoye R.
19)	106.0	1	MU	Murmansk	Dorozhnoye R.
2)	106.0	1	SR	Balakovo	Russkoye R.
4)	106.0	1	SP	Vyborg	Europa plus
4)	106.0	1	IV	Ivanovo	Europa plus
4)	106.0	1	CB	Magnitogorsk	Europa plus
4)	106.0	1	KM	Petropavlovsk-K.	Europa plus
4)	106.0	1	BA	Ufa	Europa plus
5)	106.0	1	TS	Nab. Chelny	Hit FM
1)	106.1	1	VO	Vologda	Avtoradio
1)	106.1	1	UD	Izhevsk	Avtoradio
1)	106.1	1	TY	Tyumen	Avtoradio
124A)	106.1	1	BA	Bikkulovo	R. Yuldash
124A)	106.1	1	BA	Verkhniye Tatyshly	R. Yuldash
124A)	106.1	1	BA	Kugarchi	R. Yuldash
17)	106.1	1	KL	Kaluga	Serebryanyy dozhd
19)	106.1	1	AM	Belogorsk	Dorozhnoye R.
2)	106.1	1	RS	Yakutsk	Russkoye R.
21)	106.1	1	KX	Elista	R. Zvezda
24)	106.1	1	KE	Belovo	NRJ
24)	106.1	1	KD	Sochi	NRJ
24)	106.1	1	TO	Tomsk	NRJ
25)	106.1	1	ZB	Chita	R. Mir
9A)	106.1	2	SA	Samara	R. Vanya
9B)	106.1	1	SP	Kirishi	Piter FM
10)	106.2	1	LI	Lipetsk	R. 7
157)	106.2	5	SV	Yekaterinburg	R. Monte-Karlo
157)	106.2	1	OM	Omsk	R. Monte-Karlo
16)	106.2	1	OB	Orsk	Retro FM
16)	106.2	1	ST	Pyatigorsk	Retro FM
179)	106.2	5	PM	Spassk-Dalniy	Vladivostok FM
18)	106.2	1	KG	Shardinsk	Yumor FM
187)	106.2	2	NS	Novosibirsk	R. 54
19)	106.2	1	AK	Biysk	Dorozhnoye R.
19)	106.2	1	KS	Kostroma	Dorozhnoye R.
19)	106.2	1	KU	Kursk	Dorozhnoye R.
19)	106.2	1	KE	Novokuznetsk	Dorozhnoye R.
19)	106.2	1	PZ	Pachelma	Dorozhnoye R.
2)	106.2	5	PR	Perm	Russkoye R.
21)	106.2	1	NO	V. Novgorod	R. Zvezda
216)	106.2	1	CV	Cheboksary	R. Kniga
27)	106.2	1	KH	Khabarovsk	R. Dacha
29)	106.2	1	KD	Pavlovskaya	Pervoye R.
4)	106.2	10	MO	Moskva	Europa plus
45A)	106.2	1	RK	Abakan	Novoye R.
6)	106.2	1	VL	Murom	Love R.
6)	106.2	1	UL	Ulyanovsk	Love R.
10)	106.3	1	TV	Tver	R. 7
124B)	106.3	1	BA	Baymak	Sputnik FM
13)	106.3	2	RO	Taganrog	Donskoye R.
15)	106.3	1	KY	Nizhnevartovsk	DFM
15)	106.3	1	MD	Saransk	DFM
16)	106.3	1	BE	Belgorod	Retro FM
19)	106.3	1	IR	Bratsk	Dorozhnoye R.
19)	106.3	1	SR	Saratov	Dorozhnoye R.

FM	MHz	kW	Rg	Location	Station
19)	106.3	1	CB	Chelyabinsk	Dorozhnoye R.
191)	106.3	1	SA	Khvorostyanka	Samarskoye gub. R.
2)	106.3	1	KD	Goryachiy Klyuch	Russkoye R.
2)	106.3	1	SM	Roslavl	Russkoye R.
25)	106.3	1	AM	Blagoveshchensk	R. Mir
25)	106.3	1	RY	Ryazan	R. Mir
26)	106.3	5	SP	Sankt-Peterburg	R. Rekord
5)	106.3	1	DA	Khasavyurt	Hit FM
7)	106.3	1	TS	Kazan	Militseyskaya volna
1)	106.4	1	YV	Birobodzhan	Avtoradio
11)	106.4	1	AS	Astrakhan	R. Maksimum
11)	106.4	1	KA	Kaliningrad	R. Maksimum
11)	106.4	1	TL	Tula	R. Maksimum
16)	106.4	1	TS	Nab. Chelny	Retro FM
16)	106.4	1	NN	N.Novgorod	Retro FM
179)	106.4	5	PM	Vladivostok	Vladivostok FM
19)	106.4	1	TA	Tambov	Dorozhnoye R.
216)	106.4	1	VG	Volgograd	R. Kniga
24)	106.4	10	IR	Irkutsk	NRJ
26)	106.4	1	KY	Surgut	R. Rekord
4)	106.4	1	RA	Gorno-Altaysk	Europa plus
45A)	106.4	1	SA	Tolyatti	Novoye R.
59)	106.4	4	VN	Bobrov	Kanal Melodiya
8)	106.4	1	AK	Barnaul	Nashe R.
9A)	106.4	1	PZ	Kuznetsk	R. Vanya
9A)	106.4	1	KE	Mezhdurechensk	R. Vanya
9A)	106.4	1	SV	Nizhniy Tagil	R. Vanya
1)	106.5	1	BA	Ufa	Avtoradio
15)	106.5	1	SR	Balakovo	DFM
156)	106.5	1	MO	Zaraysk	R. 1
16)	106.5	1	ME	Yoshkar-Ola	Retro FM
16)	106.5	1	KG	Kurgan	Retro FM
16)	106.5	1	KM	Petropavlovsk-K.	Retro FM
16)	106.5	1	TS	Chistopol	Retro FM
171)	106.5	1	IR	Zima	R. Radio
18)	106.5	1	BR	Bryansk	Yumor FM
18)	106.5	1	VO	Vologda	Yumor FM
183)	106.5	1	BU	Ulan-Ude	R. Sibir
19)	106.5	1	SP	Luga	Dorozhnoye R.
19)	106.5	1	SL	Yu-Sakhalinsk	Dorozhnoye R.
23)	106.5	1	SM	Smolensk	Detskoye R.
27)	106.5	1	OB	Kuvandyk	R. Dacha
35)	106.5	1	KD	Tuapse	R. Vera
4)	106.5	1	BA	Neftekamsk	Europa plus
43)	106.5	1	YA	Yaroslavl	Marusya FM
45A)	106.5	1	MU	Murmansk	Novoye R.
46)	106.5	1	KN	Achinsk	Comedy Radio
6)	106.5	1	TY	Tyumen	Love R.
68)	106.5	1	RS	Yakutsk	Lena R.
8)	106.5	1	MA	Magadan	Nashe R.
15)	106.6	1	AK	Biysk	DFM
153)	106.6	1	SP	Kirishi	Volkhov FM
19)	106.6	1	KS	Sharya	Dorozhnoye R.
199)	106.6	2	KY	Khanty-Mansiysk	R. Yugra
2)	106.6	1	ZB	Chita	Russkoye R.
24)	106.6	1	RO	Rostov-na-Donu	NRJ
25)	106.6	1	UL	Ulyanovsk	R. Mir
27)	106.6	1	PR	Berezniki	R. Dacha
6)	106.6	10	MO	Moskva	Love R.
6)	106.6	3	SA	Samara	Love R.
1)	106.7	1	KD	Yeysk	Avtoradio
1)	106.7	1	KD	Kropotkin	Avtoradio
119)	106.7	4	IV	Rodniki	Ivanovo FM
157)	106.7	1	PM	Nakhodka	R. Monte-Karlo
16)	106.7	1	RK	Abakan	Retro FM
18)	106.7	2	PZ	Penza	Yumor FM
183)	106.7	1	OB	Orsk	R. Sibir
19)	106.7	1	SP	Vyborg	Dorozhnoye R.
19)	106.7	1	KV	Kirov	Dorozhnoye R.
19)	106.7	1	TV	Tver	Dorozhnoye R.
26)	106.7	1	MU	Apatity	R. Rekord
27)	106.7	1	NS	Novosibirsk	R. Dacha
29)	106.7	1	KD	Temryuk	Pervoye R.
35)	106.7	1	VO	Cherepovets	R. Vera
4)	106.7	1	KV	Vyatstkiye Polyarny	Europa plus
45B)	106.7	1	RY	Ryazan	Kalina krasnaya
5)	106.7	1	TS	Bugulma	Hit FM
6)	106.7	1	KO	Ukhta	Love R.
8)	106.7	1	KE	Kemerovo	Nashe R.
88)	106.7	1	IR	Listvyanka	R. MSM
9A)	106.7	1	VN	Borisloglebsk	R. Vanya
1)	106.8	1	SV	Nizhniy Tagil	Avtoradio
1)	106.8	1	OM	Omsk	Avtoradio
101)	106.8	1	PS	Velikiye Luki	R. Rodnykh dorog
124B)	106.8	1	BA	Bakaly	Sputnik FM
14)	106.8	1	KD	Krasnodar	R. Shanson
156)	106.8	1	MO	Volokalamsk	R. 1
156)	106.8	1	MO	Taldom	R. 1
19)	106.8	5	BE	Belgorod	Dorozhnoye R.
19)	106.8	1	VN	Boguchar	Dorozhnoye R.
2)	106.8	1	SV	Serov	Russkoye R.
22)	106.8	1	AK	Barnaul	R. KP
24)	106.8	1	AS	Astrakhan	NRJ
25)	106.8	1	MD	Saransk	R. Mir
4)	106.8	2	TS	Kazan	Europa plus
4)	106.8	1	VL	Murom	Europa plus
45A)	106.8	2	KH	Khabarovsk	Novoye R.
59)	106.8	1	VN	Voronezh	Kanal Melodiya
6)	106.8	1	SR	Saratov	Love R.
8)	106.8	1	KE	Novokuznetsk	Nashe R.
90)	106.8	1	KY	Yugorsk	Nord FM
93)	106.8	1	CB	Chelyabinsk	R. Iskatel
134A)	106.9	1	VL	Vladimir	Studio 21
14)	106.9	1	NN	N.Novgorod	R. Shanson
19)	106.9	1	KD	Sochi	Dorozhnoye R.
24)	106.9	1	VO	Vologda	NRJ
27)	106.9	1	TL	Tula	R. Dacha
32)	106.9	1	SA	Tolyatti	106.9 FM
44)	106.9	1	MU	Murmansk	Bolshoye R.
45A)	106.9	1	TS	Nab. Chelny	Novoye R.
8)	106.9	1	BU	Ulan-Ude	Nashe R.
9A)	106.9	1	KE	Yurga	R. Vanya
1)	107.0	1	KE	Belovo	Avtoradio
124B)	107.0	1	BA	Ufa	Sputnik FM
131)	107.0	1	TS	Novosheshminsk	R. Bolgar
14)	107.0	1	SR	Balakovo	R. Shanson
14)	107.0	1	KN	Norilsk	R. Shanson
15)	107.0	1	UD	Izhevsk	DFM
165)	107.0	2	SV	Yekaterinburg	Sputnik 107 FM
19)	107.0	1	TY	Tyumon	Dorozhnoye R.
2)	107.0	1	PM	Vladivostok	Russkoye R.
2)	107.0	1	CV	Cheboksary	Russkoye R.
21)	107.0	1	CB	Magnitogorsk	R. Zvezda
23)	107.0	1	YA	Yaroslavl	Detskoye R.
39)	107.0	5	MO	Moskva	IZ.RU
62)	107.0	5	KD	Kanevskaya	Kazak FM
9A)	107.0	1	BR	Bryansk	R. Vanya
1)	107.1	1	IR	Irkutsk	Avtoradio
124B)	107.1	1	BA	Kumertau	Sputnik FM
131)	107.1	1	TS	Aznakayevo	R. Bolgar
131)	107.1	2	TS	Bazarnyye Mataki	R. Bolgar
136)	107.1	1	PS	Pskov	Semoye nebo
14)	107.1	1	KG	Kurgan	R. Shanson
177)	107.1	2	RS	Yakutsk	R. Sakha
189)	107.1	1	DA	Makhachkala	R. Stolitsa
2)	107.1	1	MA	Magadan	Russkoye R.
22)	107.1	1	KN	Krasnoyarsk	R. KP
27)	107.1	1	IV	Ivanovo	R. Dacha
27)	107.1	1	TO	Tomsk	R. Dacha
35)	107.1	1	KY	Khanty-Mansiysk	R. Vera
7)	107.1	1	AK	Rubtsovsk	Militseyskaya volna
124B)	107.2	1	BA	Belebey	Sputnik FM
124B)	107.2	1	BA	Beloretsk	Sputnik FM
130A)	107.2	1	VN	Voronezh	R. Borneo
16)	107.2	1	KO	Ukhta	Retro FM
162)	107.2	1	RY	Ryazan	R. OK
19)	107.2	1	KT	Petrozavodsk	Dorozhnoye R.
19)	107.2	1	SM	Smolensk	Dorozhnoye R.
2)	107.2	1	OB	Orenburg	Russkoye R.
22)	107.2	1	KA	Kaliningrad	R. KP
23)	107.2	1	SA	Samara	Detskoye R.
35)	107.2	1	IR	Bratsk	R. Vera
45A)	107.2	1	LI	Lipetsk	Novoye R.
8)	107.2	1	CB	Snezhinsk	Nashe R.
1)	107.3	1	PM	Lukhovitsy	Avtoradio
131)	107.3	1	TS	Menzelinsk	R. Bolgar
134)	107.3	1	TS	Kazan	R. Millenium
15)	107.3	1	CB	Chelyabinsk	DFM
19)	107.3	1	PS	Novosokolniki	Dorozhnoye R.
191)	107.3	1	SA	Sergiyevsk	Samarskoye gub. R.

FM	MHz	kW	Rg	Location	Station
2)	107.3	1	VL	Murom	Russkoye R.
26)	107.3	1	SP	Luga	R. Rekord
45A)	107.3	1	OM	Omsk	Novoye R.
5)	107.3	1	KE	Kemerovo	Hit FM
1)	107.4	1	KS	Kostroma	Avtoradio
133)	107.4	1	AR	Arkhangelsk	R. 29
14)	107.4	2	TA	Tambov	R. Shanson
18)	107.4	5	NN	N.Novgorod	Yumor FM
2)	107.4	1	VN	Rossosh	Russkoye R.
21)	107.4	1	ZB	Chita	R. Zvezda
27)	107.4	1	AK	Barnaul	R. Dacha
28)	107.4	10	SP	Sankt-Peterburg	Biznes FM
35)	107.4	1	KN	Norilsk	R. Vera
4)	107.4	1	MU	Kandalaksha	Europa plus
45A)	107.4	1	SR	Balakovo	Novoye R.
45B)	107.4	1	SA	Tolyatti	Kalina krasnaya
5)	107.4	1	KN	Achinsk	Hit FM
5)	107.4	5	MO	Moskva	Hit FM
7)	107.4	1	OB	Ilek	Militseyskaya volna
74)	107.4	1	KD	Sochi	Maks FM
79)	107.4	1	BE	Staryy Oskol	Mir Belogorya
1)	107.5	1	SM	Roslavl	Avtoradio
10)	107.5	1	RK	Abakan	R. 7
131)	107.5	1	TS	Bavly	R. Bolgar
134A)	107.5	1	KC	Karachayevsk	Studio 21
134A)	107.5	1	KH	Khabarovsk	Studio 21
14)	107.5	1	TL	Tula	R. Shanson
15)	107.5	1	TS	Nizhnekamsk	DFM
186)	107.5	1	SV	Irbit	R. Skit
19)	107.5	1	SM	Gagarin	Dorozhnoye R.
190)	107.5	1	CV	Ibresi	Tavan R.
2)	107.5	1	VL	Kovrov	Russkoye R.
2)	107.5	1	BU	Ulan-Ude	Russkoye R.
27)	107.5	1	IR	Irkutsk	R. Dacha
28)	107.5	1	BA	Ufa	Biznes FM
3)	107.5	1	PZ	Penza	Ekho Moskvy
45A)	107.5	1	RO	Rostov-na-Donu	Novoye R.
5)	107.5	1	AK	Rubtsovsk	Hit FM
8)	107.5	1	KG	Kurgan	Nashe R.
1)	107.6	1	KD	Kanevskaya	Avtoradio
11)	107.6	1	KE	Leninsk-Kuznetskiy	R. Maksimum
16)	107.6	1	RS	Yakutsk	Retro FM
17)	107.6	1	KU	Kursk	Serebryanyy dozhd
18)	107.6	1	PZ	Pachelma	Yumor FM
180)	107.6	1	SV	Yekaterinburg	Gorod FM
19)	107.6	1	SP	Priozersk	Dorozhnoye R.
22)	107.6	1	UD	Izhevsk	R. KP
4)	107.6	1	TO	Tomsk	Europa plus
6)	107.6	1	BR	Bryansk	Love R.
1)	107.7	1	BE	Belgorod	Avtoradio
1)	107.7	1	KE	Mezhdurechensk	Avtoradio
107)	107.7	1	KD	Krasnodar	R. 107
124B)	107.7	1	BA	Burayevo	Sputnik FM
124B)	107.7	1	BA	Mesyagutovo	Sputnik FM
134A)	107.7	1	PM	Vladivostok	Studio 21
134A)	107.7	1	OB	Orenburg	Studio 21
14)	107.7	2	NS	Novosibirsk	R. Shanson
18)	107.7	1	IR	Bratsk	Yumor FM
18)	107.7	1	SM	Smolensk	Yumor FM
2)	107.7	1	IV	Ivanovo	Russkoye R.
26)	107.7	1	VL	Murom	R. Rekord
27)	107.7	1	SV	Nizhniy Tagil	R. Dacha
4)	107.7	1	BA	Tuymazy	Europa plus
7)	107.7	1	CC	Groznyy	Militseyskaya volna
7)	107.7	1	OB	Yasnyy	Militseyskaya volna
8)	107.7	1	KO	Ukhta	Nashe R.
1)	107.8	1	SV	Krasnoturinsk	Avtoradio
10)	107.8	1	KD	Novorossiysk	R. 7
16)	107.8	1	PR	Berezniki	Retro FM
16)	107.8	1	KN	Norilsk	Retro FM
19)	107.8	1	VN	Rossosh	Dorozhnoye R.
2)	107.8	10	SP	Sankt-Peterburg	Russkoye R.
26)	107.8	1	SR	Volsk	R. Rekord
27)	107.8	1	AK	Biysk	R. Dacha
28)	107.8	1	NN	N.Novgorod	Biznes FM
29)	107.8	1	KD	Kushchyovskaya	Pervoye R.
6)	107.8	1	TS	Kazan	Love R.
7)	107.8	5	MO	Moskva	Militseyskaya volna
1)	107.9	1	MU	Monchegorsk	Avtoradio
1)	107.9	5	PM	Novozhatkovo	Avtoradio
10)	107.9	1	BE	Staryy Oskol	R. 7
14)	107.9	1	KD	Tikhoretsk	R. Shanson
145)	107.9	1	VL	Vladimir	Vladimir - Novaya volna
16)	107.9	1	KE	Kemerovo	Retro FM
16)	107.9	1	KD	Sochi	Retro FM
19)	107.9	1	KM	Petropavlovsk-K.	Dorozhnoye R.
19)	107.9	1	BA	Ufa	Dorozhnoye R.
2)	107.9	1	SO	Vladikavkaz	Russkoye R.
2)	107.9	1	RY	Ryazan	Russkoye R.
21)	107.9	1	AK	Barnaul	R. Zvezda
23)	107.9	1	KV	Kirov	Detskoye R.
24)	107.9	2	KY	Surgut	NRJ
35)	107.9	1	TV	Mednoye	R. Vera
35)	107.9	1	KH	Khabarovsk	R. Vera
36)	107.9	1	SP	Vyborg	Avtoradio S-Peterburg
4)	107.9	1	OB	Buguruslan	Europa plus
7)	107.9	1	SA	Tolyatti	Militseyskaya volna

+ txs below 1kW. MW txs: E = European part of Russia, FE = Far Eastern part of Russia.

Addresses and other information:

1) 127083 Moskva, ul. 8-go Marta 8 – **2)** 123298 Moskva, 3-ya Khoroshevskaya ul. 12 – **3)** 119992 Moskva, ul. Novyy Arbat 11 – **4)** 109004 Moskva, ul. Stanislavskogo 21 – **5)** 123298 Moskva, 3-ya Khoroshevskaya ul. 12 – **6)** 127299 Moskva, ul. Bolshaya Akademicheskaya 5a – **7)** 109180 Moskva, 3-y Golutinskiy per. 8/10 – **8)** 123060 Moskva, ul. Narodnogo Opolcheniya 39 – **9A-C)** 199406 St.Peterburg, ul. Shevchenko 27 – **10)** 109004 Moskva, ul. Stanislavskogo 21 – **11)** 123298 Moskva, 3-ya Khoroshevskaya ul. 12 – **12)** 423822 Nab.Chelny, Naberezhnochelinskiy pr. 21 – **13)** 347936 Taganrog, Noviy 17-y per. 108 – **14)** 119049 Moskva, ul. Shabolovka 10 – **15)** 123298 Moskva, 3-ya Khoroshevskaya ul. 12 – **16)** 109004 Moskva, ul. Stanislavskogo 21 – **17)** 109004 Moskva, ul. Stanislavskogo 21 – **18)** 127083 Moskva, ul. 8-go Marta 8 – **19)** 199406 St.Peterburg, ul. Shevchenko 28 – **20)** 127083 Moskva, ul. 8-go Marta 8 – **21)** 129164 Moskva, pr. Mira 126 – **22)** 127993 Moskva, Staryy Petrovsko-Razumovskiy proyezd 1/23 – **23)** 129226 Moskva, ul. Vilgelma Pika 3 – **24)** 127083 Moskva, ul. 8-go Marta 8 – **25)** 107076 Moskva, ul. Krasnobogatyrskaya 44 – **26)** 198303 St.Peterburg, pr. Stachek 105 – **27)** 127299 Moskva, ul. B. Akademicheskaya 5a – **28)** 127287 Moskva, 2-ya Khutorskaya ul. 38a – **29)** 350038 Krasnodar, ul. Korolenko 2/1 – **30)** 420066 Kazan, ul. Dekrabristov 2 – **31)** 129226 Moskva, ul. Vilgelma Pika 3 – **32)** 445051 Tolyatti, Primorskiy bul. 2b – **33)** 432030 Ulyanovsk, ul. Narimanova 75 – **34)** 650007 Novokuznetsk, ul.Ordzhonikidze 35 – **35)** 107553 Moskva, B.Cherkizovskaya ul. 17 – **36)** 197376 St.Peterburg, ul. Ak.Pavlova 5 – **37)** 236000 Kaliningrad, ul. Narvskaya 58 – **38)** 618400 Berezniki, Klyuchevaya ul. 17 – **39)** 115093 Moskva, Partiynyy per. 1 – **40)** 420021 Kazan, ul. Gabdully Tukaya 91 – **41)** 670000 Ulan-Ude, Smolina, 54b – **42)** 398059 Lipetsk, ul. Sovetskaya 64c – **43)** 308023 Belgorod, Studencheskaya ul. 28 – **44)** 183038 Murmansk, ul. Lenina 68 – **45A,B)** 123308 Moskva, ul. D.Bednogo 24 – **46)** 129272 Moskva, ul. Trifonovskaya 57 – **47)** 603022 N.Novgorod, Okskiy syezd 8 – **48)** 625000 Tyumen, ul. Geologorazvedchikov 28 – **49)** 123290 Moskva, 1-y Magistralnyy proyezd 11 – **50)** 620075 Yekaterinburg, pr. Lenina 41 – **51)** 302028 Oryol, ul. 7-ye Noyabrya 43 – **52)** 197376 St.Peterburg, ul. Prof.Popova 47 – **53)** 129164 Moskva, Zubarev per. 15 – **54)** 670000 Ulan-Ude, ul. Borsoyeva 105 – **55)** 630087 Novosibirsk, ul. Nemirovicha-Danchenko 122 – **56)** 199034 St. Peterburg, nab. L. Shmidta 39.– **57)** 364014 Groznyy, ul. Mayakovskogo 92 – **58)** 454091 Chelyabinsk, ul. Ordzhonikidze 81 – **59)** 394000 Voronezh, ul. Lenina 73 – **60)** 620086 Yekaterinburg, ul. Repina 6a – **61)** 362047 Vladikavkaz, ul. Vesennaya 5 – **62)** 350038 Krasnodar, ul. Korolenko 2/1 – **63)** 660075 Krasnoyarsk, ul. Severo-Yeniseyskaya 33 – **64)** 125080 Moskva, ul. Vrubelya 4 – **65)** 650001 Kemerovo, ul. Sevastopolskaya 6 – **66)** 625019 Tyumen, ul. Respubliki 211a – **67)** 400081 Volgograd, ul. Angarskaya 71 – **68)** 677000 Yakutsk, ul. Bestuzheva-Marlinskogo 9/3 – **69)** 143402 Krasnogorsk, ul. Mezhdurarodnaya 12 – **70)** 398050 Lipetsk, ul. Plekhanova 1 – **71)** 454091 Chelyabinsk, ul. Ordzhonikidze 41 – **72)** 241007 Bryansk, ul. Duki 80 – **73)** 346512 Shakhty, ul. Smidovicha 121 – **74)** 354000 Sochi, ul. Severnaya 12 – **75)** 610000 Kirov, Oktyabrskiy pr. 120 – **76)** 127015 Moskva, Bolshaya Novodmitrovskaya ul. 36 – **77)** 97046 Sankt-Peterburg, Petrogradskaya nab. 18a – **78)** 353380 Krymsk, ul. K.Libknekhta 21 – **79)** 308000 Belgorod, pr. Slavy 60 – **80A,B)** 127137 Moskva, ul. Pravdy 24/2. 80B) in English – **81)** 746903 Ukhta, Oktyabrskkaya ul. 21 – **82)** 440026 Penza, ul. Lermontova 39 – **83)** 426069 Izhevsk, ul. Pesochnaya 9 – **84)** 424038 Yoshar-Ola, pr. Tsargradskiy 37 – **85)** 174260 Malaya Vishera, ul. Moskovskaya 21 – **86)** 614015 Perm, ul. Kuybysheva 37 – **87)** 428003 Cheboksary, pr. Lenina 15 – **88)** 664047 Irkutsk, ul. Baykalskaya 105 – **89)** 248021 Kaluga, ul. Moskovskaya 189 – **90)** 628260 Yugorsk, ul. Lenina 18 – **91)** 353915 Novorossiysk, ul. Revolutsii 1905 goda 19 – **92)** 400131

Volgograd, ul. Komsomolskaya 8 – **93)** 649002 Gorno-Altaysk, pr. Kommunisticheskiy 1 – **94)** 619001 Kudymkar, ul. Polevaya 3 – **95)** 362013 Vladikavkaz, ul. Nikolayeva 84 – **96)** 170000 Tver, ul. Mednikovskaya 55/25 – **97)** 115035 Moskva, Sofiyskaya nab. 30 – **98)** 164570 Bereznik, Dvinskaya ul. 20 – **99)** 672010 Chita, ul. Amurskaya 36 – **100)** 183038 Murmansk, ul. Yegorova 14 – **101)** 428018 Cheboksary, ul. Nizhegorodskaya 6 – **102)** 390000 Ryazan, ul. Pravolybedskaya 35 – **103)** 424038 Yoshkar-Ola, ul. Voinov-Internatsionalistov 37 – **104)** 454084 Chelyabinsk, ul. Kalinina 21 – **105)** 440046 Penza, ul. Mira 1a – **106)** 693023 Yuzhno-Sakhalinsk, ul. Komsomolskaya 213a – **107)** 350000 Krasnodar, ul. Gimnazicheskaya 51 – **108)** 450075 Ufa, ul. Blyukhera 15 – **109)** 644010 Omsk, ul. Dekabristov 130 – **110A,B)** 400131 Volgograd, ul. Krasnoznamenskaya 25 – **111)** 191186 Sankt-Peterburg, ul. Italyanskaya 15 – **112)** 625013 Tyumen, ul. Tekstilnaya 1 – **113)** 620151 Krasnoyarsk, ul. Baumana 22 – **114)** 426035 Izhevsk, ul. Avangardnaya 4b – **115)** 344006 Rostov-na-Donu, ul. Suvorova 26 – **116)** 236022 Kaliningrad, pr. Sovetskiy 12 – **117)** 680000 Khabarovsk ul. Lenina 4 – **118)** 514017 Perm, ul. Turgeneva 33a – **119)** 153003 Ivanovo, ul. Parizhskoy Kommuny 16 – **120)** 403348 Mikhaylovka, ul. Mira 81 – **121)** 197022 St.Peterburg, P.O.Box 122. **E:** radioslovo@mail.ru – **122)** 453300 Kumertau, PKiO im. Gagarina – **123)** 196084 St.Peterburg, ul. Tsvetochnaya 16b **E:** radio_rusk@mail.ru – **124A-C)** 450076 Ufa, ul. Gafuri 9 124A,B) in Bashkir. – **125)** 445010 Tolyatti, ul. Sovetskaya 74a – **126)** 692760 Artyom, ul. Kirova 68 – **127)** 192007 St. Peterburg, Ligovskiy pr. 174 – **128)** 190068 St.Peterburg, P.O.Box 732. **E:** d.kravchenko@radiomaria.ru – **129)** 140400 Kolomna, ul. Shilova 9 – **130A,B)** 394071 Voronezh, ul. 20-letnaya Oktyabrya 66 – **131)** 420015 Kazan, ul. Gorkogo 15 – **132)** 614060 Perm, ul. Uralskaya 119 – **133)** 63002 Arkhangelsk, Novgorodskiy pr. 32 – **134A,B)** 109004 Moskva, ul. Stanislavskogo 21 – **135)** 440434 Penza, ul. Markina 1 – **136)** Paromenskaya ul. 21/32, 180007 Pskov – **137)** 142400 Noginsk, ul. Sovetskaya 42 – **138)** 440046 Penza, ul. Mira 1b – **139)** 125190 Moskva, Leningradskiy pr. 80 – **140)** 360000 Nalchik, pr. Lenina 5 – **141)** 115054 Moskva, ul. Valovaya 32/75 – **142)** 369200 Karachayevsk – **143)** 462411 Orsk, ul. Leninskogo Komsomola 4b – **144)** 187110 Kirishi, ul. Sovetskaya 20 – **145)** 600000 Vladimir, Vorontsovskiy per. 4 – **146)** 454080 Chelyabinsk, ul. Ordzhonikidze 58a – **147)** 677007 Yakutsk, ul. Kirova 17/3 – **148)** 423827 Nab.Chelny, bul. Yunykh Lenintsev 9 – **149)** 305004 Kursk, ul. Dimitrova 76 – **150)** 690091 Vladivostok, ul. Pologaya 53 – **151)** 355008 Stavropol, ul. Grazhdanskaya 9 – **152)** 129626 Moskva, Zubarev per. 15 – **153)** 187401 Volkhov, ul. Kommunarov 18 – **154)** 129164 Moskva, Zubarev per. 15 – **155)** 443070 Samara, ul. Partizanskaya 19 – **156)** 364014 Groznyy – **157)** 123298 Moskva, 3-ya Khoroshevskaya ul. 12 – **158)** 238050 Gusev, ul. Shkolnaya 11 – **159)** 194044 St. Peterburg, Krapivnyy per. 5 – **160)** 629807 Noyabrsk, ul. Lenina 47 – **161)** 603068 N.Novgorod, Yarmarochnyy proyezd 10 – **162)** 390023 Ryazan, ul. Tsiolkovskogo 20 – **163)** 454090 Chelyabinsk, ul. Tsvillinga 46a – **164)** 386140 Nazran, ul. Moskovskaya 29 – **165)** 620026 Yekaterinburg, ul. Vazhova 162 – **166)** 620075 Yekaterinburg, ul. Lenina 41 – **167)** 430000 Saransk, ul. Kommunisticheskaya 89 – **168)** 420066 Kazan, ul. Dekabristov 2 – **169)** 413851 Balakovo, ul. Volzhskaya 74a – **170)** 368120 Kyzylyurt, pr. Imama Shamilya 43/13 – **171)** 123001 Moskva, Vspolnyy per. 18 – **172)** 113326 Moskva, ul. Pyatnitskaya 25. **E:** radonezh@radonezh.ru – **173)** 603006 N.Novgorod, ul. Semashko 37 – **174)** 414040 Astrakhan, ul. Lyakhova 4 – **175)** 450075 Ufa, ul. Blyukhera 15 – **176)** 127299 Moskva, ul. B.Akademicheskaya 5a – **177)** 677027 Yakutsk, ul. Ordzhonikidze 48 – **178)** 420094 Kazan, ul. Golubyatnikova 20a – **179)** 690091 Vladivostok, ul. Pologaya 66 – **180)** 620014 Yekaterinburg, pr. Lenina 24a – **181)** 127287 Moskva, 2-ya Khutorskaya ul. 38a – **182)** 620014 Yekaterinburg, ul. Lenina 41 – **183)** 634003 Tomsk, per. Mariniskiy 8 – **184)** 625013 Tyumen, ul. Permyakova 7 – **185)** 386245 Stanitsa Troitskaya, ul. Krestyanskaya 4 – **186)** 623850 Irbit, ul. Zhukova 6a – **187)** 630011 Novosibirsk, ul. Kirova 3 – **188)** 414000 Astrakhan, ul. Nab. 1-ya Maya 75 – **189)** 367000 Makhachkala, ul. Gamidova 18 – **190)** 428003 Cheboksary, pr. Lenina 15 – **191)** 443068 Samara, ul. Novo-Sadovaya 106 – **192)** 162610 Cherepovets, ul. Lenina 151 – **193)** 660028 Krasnoyarsk, ul. Baumana 22 – **194)** 367020 Makhachkala, ul. Nuradilova 2 – **195)** 690091 Vladivostok, ul. Uborevicha 20a – **196)** 680000 Krasnoyarsk, ul. Frunze 58 – **197A,B)** 677027 Yakutsk, ul. Oktyabrskaya 16/2 – **198)** 678960 Neryungi, teletsentr – **199)** 628011 Khanty-Mansiysk, ul. Gagarina 4 – **200)** 630087 Novosibirsk, ul. Nemirovicha-Danchenko 122 – **201)** 640021 Kurgan, ul. Tobolnaya 54 – **202)** 197101 St.Peterburg, ul. Kronverskaya 23 – **203)** 678901 Aldan, Sportivnyy per. 2 – **204)** 620144 Yekaterinburg, ul. Khokhryakova 104 – **205)** 156005 Kostroma, ul. Lagernaya 15 – **206)** 614990 Perm, ul. Lenina 50-141 – **207)** 117105 Moskva, Varshavskoye shosse 9 – **208)** 123060 Moskva, ul. Narodnogo Opolcheniya 39 – **209)** 660000 Krasnoyarsk – **210)** 620075 Yekaterinburg, ul. Lenina 41 – **211)** 666784 Ust-Kut, ul. Kirova 88 – **212)** 123298 Moskva, 3-ya Khoroshevskaya ul. 12 – **213)** 443110 Samara, ul. Novo-Sadovaya 44 – **214)** 680000 Khabarovsk, ul. Frunze 58 – **215)** 618551 Solikamsk, ul. Vseobucha 80 – **216)** 127238 Moskva, Lokomotivnyy proyezd 21 – **217)** 236010 Kaliningrad, pr. Mira 136 – **218)** 392016 Tambov, ul. Pushkarskaya 45 – **219)** 156000 Kostroma, ul. Sverdlova 34a – **220)** 460024 Orenburg, ul. Turkestanskaya 15 – **221)** 187401 Volkhov, ul. 8-go Marta 7 – **222)** 689000 Anadyr, ul. Lenina 18a. **E:** purgainfo@yandex.ru **W:** radiopurga.org. **NB:** R. Purga (launched in 2001) is a music/infotainment stn (format: Hot AC), produced by the administration of the Chukotka autonomous okrug and available on FM throughout the region – **223)** 352630 Belorechensk, ul. Lenina 50 **E:** stl1ferap@gmail.com.

Radio via DTT: see National TV section.

CRIMEA
NB: The station listing can be found at the end of the Ukraine entry

RWANDA

L.T: UTC +2h — **Pop:** 13 million — **Pr.L:** Official languages: Kinyarwanda, Swahili, French, English — **E.C:** 230V/50Hz — **ITU:** RRW

RWANDA UTILITIES REGULATORY AGENCY (RURA)
✉ B.P. 6929, Kigali ☎+250 252584562 🖷 +250 252584563 **W:** rura.rw **E:** info@rura.rw

RWANDA BROADCASTING AGENCY (RBA) (Pub)
✉ B.P. 83, Kigali ☎+250 252572276 **W:** rba.co.rw **E:** radiorwanda@yahoo.com **L.P:** Dir. Broadc: Mweusi Karake. Dir. Prgrs: Paul Ndamage. Ag. Ch.Editor: Willy Rukundo. Tech. Dir: Charles Nahayo.
FM: Channel I (MHz): 89.8 Kinanira 0.5kW, 93.5 Nyarupfubire 0.5kW, 95.1 Mugogo/Rushaki 0.5kW, 97.6 Karongi 1kW, 100.7 Mt. Jali 5kW, 103.2 Byumba 0.5kW, 103.9 Butare 0.5kW + 8 trs under 0.5kW.
Channel II (Magic FM): Kigali 90.7MHz 5kW.
D.Prgr in Kinyarwanda/Swahili/French/English: 24h. N. in English: 0515, 1830. **Ann:** F: "Vous écoutez Radio Rwanda émettant de Kigali".

OTHER STATIONS FM(MHz)
City R, Kigali: 88.3 1kW – **Contact FM:** Kigali 89.7 0.5kW **W:** facebook.com/897-Contact-FM-365864343554684 – **Flash FM,** Kigali: 89.2 0.5kW – **Kiss FM,** Kigali: 102.3 **W:** kissfm.rw – **KT R,** Kigali: 96.7 **W:** ktradio.rw – **R. Izuba,** Kibungo: 100.0 0.25kW –**R. Isango Star,** Kigali: 91.5 **W:** isangostar.rw – **R. Maria Rwanda:** Gitarama 88.6 1kW, Kigali 97.3 2kW, Karongi 99.8 **E:** radiomariar@yahoo.fr – **R. 10 FM:** Kigali (Mont Jari) 87.6 0.5kW **W:** danslevent.com/rwanda **E:** contact@danslevent.com – **R. Salus** (University R.), Butare: 97.0 1kW, Kigali 101.9 1kW. **W:** salus.nur.ac.rw – **R. Sana uRwanda** (Rlg.): Kigali 98.0 – **R. Umucyo,** Kigali: 102.8 0.1kW **Rwanda Community Radio Network:** Rubavu, 94.6, Nyagatare 95.5, Musanze 98.4, Huye 100.4, Rusizi 103.2MHz **W:** rwandaradioscommunautaires.org

AWR: 106.4 0.3kW – **BBC African Sce:** Kibuye 93.3, Kigali (Mont Jari) 93.9 3kW, Butare 106.1 3kW – **RFI Afrique**: Kigali 92.1 in French/Swahili – **Voice of America:** Kigali 104.3 2kW – **Deutsche Welle:** Kigali 96.0MHz 2kW

SABA (Netherlands)

L.T: UTC -4h — **Pop:** 1,900 — **Pr.L:** Dutch (official), English — **E.C:** 110V/60Hz — **ITU:** BES

AGENTSCHAP TELECOM (Bonaire, Saba, Sint Eustatius)
✉ Kaya Grandi 69, P.O. Box 791, Bonaire ☎ + 599 717 3140 🖷 +599 717 3554 **W:** agentschaptelecom.nl **E:** bes@agentschaptelecom.nl

SABA RADIO
✉ PO Box 27,The Bottom, Saba ☎ +599 4 16 3213 🖷 +599 416 3525 **LP:** Dir. Michael Nicholson **E:** sabaradiopjf2@yahoo.com **W:** q939.fm
FM: PJF2 93.9MHz 0.6 kW 24h in English; Dutch Saturdays 2200-2300 and Sundays 1615-1715; Spanish Thursdays 1800-2200; Papiamentu Mondays to Thursdays 1600-1800, Fridays and Saturdays 1600-2200

SAMOA

L.T: UTC +13h (27 Sep 20-4 Apr 21, 26 Sep 21-3 Apr 22: +14h). **NB:** UTC times in schedules refer to DST period — **Pop:** 199,000 — **Pr.L:** Samoan (official), English (official) — **E.C:** 230V/50Hz — **ITU:** SMO

OFFICE OF THE REGULATOR
✉ Private Bag, Apia, Samoa; OOTR Building, Mulinuu, Apia, Samoa

☎ +685 30282 🖷 +685 30281 **E:** admin regulator.gov.was **W:** regulator.gov.ws **L.P:** Regulator: Lefaoali'i Unutoa Auelua-Fonoti

MW	kHz	kW	MW	kHz	kW
1) 2AP Apia	#540	5	1) 2AP Apia	#747	5

FM	MHz	kW
2) Showers of Blessings FM	88.1	
3) Talofa FM	88.5	0.25
4) Mai FM	89.1	1
3) Magik FM	89.5	
2) Showers of Blessings FM	89.9	
5) Aiga Fesilafa'i	90.5	1
6) EFKS FM*	90.9	
3) Talofa FM*	91.5	0.25
7) Samoa FM	93.7	
8) Laufou o le Talaleilei	95.1	
3) Star FM	96.1	0.25
9) Power FM	96.9	
2) Showers of Blessings FM	97.5	0.5
3) Magik FM	98.1	0.3
6) EFKS FM	98.9	
3) Talofa FM	99.9	0.25
10) China R. Int.	100.4	
3) K-Lite FM	101.1	0.25
11) R. Australia	102.0	
8) Laufou o le Talaleilei	103.1	
7) Samoa FM*	104.1	
12) NUS Campus R.	105.0	
9) Power FM	106.7	
6) EFKS FM	106.9	

NB: Location Apia & Upoulu except *) Savai'i. #) 2AP Apia is replacing its transmission mast and may be off air.

Addresses & other information:

1) **NATIONAL RADIO 2AP (Gov)** 🖃 Ministry of Communications and Information Technology, Government of Samoa, Level 1, CA & CT Plaza, Savalolo, Apia, Samoa ☎ +685 26177 🖷 +685 24671 **W:** mcit.gov.ws **E:** mcit@mcit.gov.ws ☎ 2AP Studio, Mulinu'u, Apia: +685 21422 **E:** a.ahsam@mcit.gov.ws **L.P:** CEO: Tua'imalo Asamu Ah Sam, Senior Programmer: Vaasiliega Lupati Lagaia Samoan/English: 1700 (Sun 2200)-1000 on 540kHz Edu: broadcs on some weekdays for Samoa and Tokelau 1930-2030 on 747kHz World N: 1800W, 1900W, 1930W. Local N: 1630W, 1730W, 1830W, 0730W Ann: "National Radio 2AP" or "Voice of the Nation" – **2)** Samoa Worship Centre Church, PO Box 3026, Apia. ☎ +685 21447/23887/29153 🖷 +685 20657 **W:** samoa.worshipcentre-worldwide.org & facebook.com/uagaofaamanuiago/info incl live streaming audio. Prgr: Samoan/English religious – **3)** R. Polynesia Ltd, P.O.Box 762, Svalalo, Apia ☎+685 25148/49/50 🖷 +685 25147 Brands: Magik FM - "Samoa's #1 Hit Music Station' (English) ☎ Studio +685 33981, Talofa FM "100% Local" (Samoan) Studio ☎+685 33999, K-Lite FM "Memories are Good' (English) ☎+685 33101 **N:** RNZI throughout the day, Star FM "Absolute Music Variety" (English) ☎ +685 33961 **W:** fmradio.ws **E:** corey@fmradio.ws **L.P:** CEO Corey Keil D.Prgr: 24h – **4)**Samoa Quality Broadcasters, Mulinu'u, Apia ☎+685 24790/91, 21735 🖷 +685 24789 CEO: Galuemalemana Ms Faresea Matafeo **E:** ceo@sbcl.ws **D.Prgr:** 24h (Samoan/English) Other: technical services for R. Australia 102.0FM – **5)** Catholic Archdiocese of Samoa, PO Box 532, Muli'vai, Apia. ☎ +685 21156/21051/7521051 **E:** daman-auisavelio@yahoo.com Prgr: Samoan religious – **6)** Ekalesia Faapotopototoga Kerisiano Samoa [EFKS] - Congregational Christian Church in Samoa, 5th Floor, John Williams Building, Tamalagi, Apia. ☎ +685 24414 **F:** +685 20429 **W:** cccs.org.ws Prgr: Samoan religious Other: EFKS-TV – **7)** Talamua Media & Publications Ltd, Level 2, Nia Mall, Fugalei, Apia. PO Box 1321, Apia. ☎ +685 7777937, 7513937 **W:** talamua.com **E:** samoafm93.7@gmail.com L.P: MD: Angela Kronfeld-Polu. **ID:** "The People's Station" D.Prgr: 24h in Samoan/English – **8)** Youth for Christ Samoa, PO Box 3706, Apia. ☎ +685 22663 **W:** yfcsamoa.org **LP:** Manasa Aloalii Prgr: Samoan religious – **9)** Silver & Gold Radio Imaging Ltd, Vaea Street, Apia. ☎ 685 28894 **W:** facebook.com/power-969-1067-fm-samoa **ID:** 'The Station that Rocks the Nation' Prgr: Samoan/English – **10)** 24/7 English language via satellite from Beijing – **11)** 24/7 Pacific English stream via satellite from Melbourne – **12)** Faculty of Arts, Media & Journalism program, National University of Samoa, Le Papaigalagala Campus, To'omatgi ☎+685 20072 🖷 +685 25489 **E:** info@nus.edu.ws **W:** nus.edu.ws **LP:** Nora Tumua **E:** n.tumua@nus.edu.ws Vicky Lepou **E:** v.lepou@nus.edu.ws Prgr: student campus radio in Samoan/English.

SAMOA, AMERICAN (USA)

L.T: UTC -11h — **Pop:** 56,000 — **Pr.L:** Samoan (official), English (official) — **E.C:** 120V/60Hz — **ITU:** SMA

FEDERAL COMMUNICATIONS COMMISSION (FCC)

see main entry under USA

FM	MHz	Call	kW	FM	MHz	Call	kW
6) Tafuna	88.1	KGIF	1.5	2) Pago Pago	93.1	KKHJ-FM	1.1
7) PagoPago	88.9	KKBT	0.3	2) Pavaiai	93.7	KKHJ-FM	0.01
8) Nu'uuli	89.7	KMOA	1.5	10) Tafuna	94.5	KKAS-LP	0.1
9) Mapusaga	90.5	KPPO	0.75	4) Ili'Ili	95.1	KULA-LP	0.1
6) Utulei	91.3	KIOE	1.5	4) W. District	97.1	KULA-LP	0.011
3) Pago Pago	92.1	KSBS-FM	15.5	4) C. District	99.1	KULA-LP	0.011
4) E. District	102.5	KULA-LP	0.023	5) Pago Pago	104.1	KNWJ	‡0.01
2) Fagaitua	103.1	WVUV-FM	1.3	5) Leone	104.7	KNWJ	0.28

‡ reported silent

Addresses & other information:

2) South Seas Broadcasting Inc, PO Box 6758, Pago Pago, American Samoa 96799. L.P: Joey Cummings, GM ☎+1 684 633 4493 **W:** KKHJ-FM: khjradio.com **ID:** '93KHJ' **W:** WVUV-FM: wvuv.com **ID:** "WVUV-FM is V103 The People's Station' in Samoan/English, D.Prgr: both 24h **Other Media:** KKHJ-TV Island TV Cable 10 – **3)** Samoa Technologies Inc, PO Box 793, Pago Pago, American Samoa 96799-0793 ☎+1 684 633 7000 🖷+1 684 633 5727 **W:** ksbsfm92.com **E:** info@ksbsfm92.com L.P: Esther Prescott, GM **ID:** 'Island 92 - The Station That Belongs to You' **News:** hourly bulletins from RNZI, R. Australia, BBC, NPR, VOA. D.Prgr: 24h – **4)** Pacific Islands Bible School, PO Box 1268, Pago Pago, American Samoa 96799 – **5)** Showers of Blessings R., PO Box 997777, Pago Pago, American Samoa 96799 ☎+1 684 699 8123. 🖷+1 684 699 8126 **W:** fm104.org **E:** info@fm104.org – **6)** Leone Church of Christ, PO Box 5093, Pago Pago, American Samoa 96799 –**7)** Rev Shannon Cummings dba Pure Truth Ministries, PO Box 6008, Pago Pago, American Samoa 96799 – **8)**Teen Challenge American Samoa P.O.Box 277, Pago Pago, American Samoa 96789. **L.P:** Otto and Vickie Haleck ☎ +1 684 699 2635 **W:** globaltc.org – **9)** Second Samoan Congregational Church of Long Beach, 655 Cedar Ave, Long Beach CA 90802-1222 – **10)** Life Inc Ministry, PO Box 1744, Pago Pago, American Samoa 96799.

SAN MARINO

L.T. UTC +1h (28 Mar-31 Oct: +2h) — **Pop:** 33,700 — **Pr.L:** Italian — **E.C:** 230V/50Hz — **ITU:** SMR

SAN MARINO RTV (Pub)

🖃 Viale J.F. Kennedy 13, 47890 San Marino Città, Repubblica di San Marino ☎ +378 0549 882000 🖷 +378 0549 882840 **E:** radio@sanmarinortv.sm **W:** sanmarinortv.sm/radio **L.P:** Dir. Carlo Romeo, Prgr.Dir.: Giuseppe Cesetti, T.Dir.: Fabio Pelliccioni
FM: 102.7MHz 10kW **D.Prgr:** 24h

San Marino Classic, **E:** radiosanmarinoclassic@sanmarinortv.sm **LP:** Prgr. Dir. Stefano Coveri FM: 103.2MHz 2kW **D.Prgr:** 24h Also carries govt meetings, live service.
F.Pl. no plans to start on MW assigned freq. 711kHz
V: by QSL-letter. Rpts to **E:** ufficiotecnico@sanmarinortv.sm

SÃO TOMÉ E PRÍNCIPE

L.T: UTC — **Pop:** 220,000 — **Pr.L:** Portuguese (official), Angolar Creole, Foro Creole, Principense Creole — **E.C:** 220V/50Hz — **ITU:** STP

RÁDIO NACIONAL DE SÃO TOMÉ E PRÍNCIPE (RNSTP (Pub)

🖃 Avenida Marginal 12 de Julho, C.P. 44, São Tomé ☎/🖷 +239 222 13 42 **W:** facebook.com/radionacional.stp **E:** atendimento@rnstp.st
MW: Pinheira: 945kHz 20kW **FM:** 89.7/95.4/99.3MHz.
D.Prgr: 24h in Portuguese. **N:** 0700, 1300, 1630, 1930.

Other stations:
R. Jubilar: São Tomé 91.9MHz **W:** facebook.com/radiojubilar91.9
RDP África: São Tomé 92.8MHz 3kW, Príncipe 101.9MHz 70W.
RFI Afrique: 102.8MHz in French/Portuguese.
VOA Africa: São José 105.5MHz 0.2kW in English/Portuguese.
VOA relay station: MW 1530kHz 600kW 0300-0630, 1600-2200 & SW. For further details see International Radio section under USA

SAUDI ARABIA

L.T: UTC +3h — **Pop:** 35 million — **Pr.L:** Arabic — **E.C:** 230V/50Hz (being phased out: 127V/60Hz & 220V/60Hz) — **ITU:** ARS

MINISTRY OF CULTURE & INFORMATION (MOCI)

Nasseriya Str, Riyadh 11161 ☎+966 1 4014440 +966 1 402 3570. **W:** moci.gov.sa

GENERAL COMMISSION FOR AUDIOVISUAL MEDIA (GCAM)

Riyadh ☎ +966 11 425352 **E:** info@gcam.gov.sa **W:** www.gcam.gov.sa

SAUDI BROADCASTING AUTHORITY (SBA, Gov.)

P.O. Box 61718, Riyadh 11575 or P.O. Box 8525, Riyadh 11492 ☎+966 1 4425170 +966 1 4041692 **W:** sba.sa **E:** saudi-radio@moci.gov.sa

MW	kHz	kW	H of tr & Prgr.
Bisha	531	10	24h (Q)
Ar-Rass	549	10	0300-2300 (R)
Jizan	549	1	24h (A)
Qurayyat	549	2000	0300-1500 (R)
Rafha	549	20	24h (R)
Abha	558	5	24h (Q)
Jeddah (Bahrah)	567	200	24h (Q)
Afif	567	15	24h (Q)
Jizan	576	20	24h (Q)
Riyadh	585	1200	24h (R)
Hofuf	594	10	0300-2300 (R)
Duba	594	2000	0300-1500 (R)
Makkah	594	50	24h (I)
Aflaj	612	15	24h (R)
Hail	612	5	24h (J)
Jizan	630	20	0300-2200 (J)
Najran	630	10	24h (Q)
Jeddah (Khumra)	648	2000	0300-2300 (R)
Rafha	657	20	24h (Q)
Abha	675	5	0300-2300 (R)
Afif	675	20	0300-2300 (R)
Jeddah (Bahrah)	684	200	24h (J)
Riyadh	684	10	24h (J)
Bisha	702	10	24h (J)
Duba	702	40	24h (J)
Najran	747	10	24h (A)
Buraidah	747	10	0300-2300 (J)
Aflaj	765	20	24h (Q)
Hofuf	765	10	24h (Q)
Qurayyat	765	20	24h (Q)
Ras al-Khair	783	100	24h (I)
Jeddah (An-Nuziah)	792	50	24h (Q)
Abha	810	5	24h (Q)
Hafar al-Batin	810	20	24h (Q)
Buraida	846	20	24h (Q)
Ras al-Khair	855	100	24h (Q)
Ar-Rass	873	10	24h (Q)
Dammam	882	100	24h (Q)
Qurayyat	900	1000	1500-0300 (R)
Hofuf	927	20	24h (J)
Makkah	936	50	24h (Q)
Riyadh	936	50	24h (Q)
Hail	945	50	24h (R)
Madinah	981	20	24h (Q)
Duba	999	20	24h (Q)
Rafha	1035	20	24h (J)
Afif	1044	20	0300-2300 (J)
Bisha	1071	50	24h (R)
Najran	1080	10	0300-2200 (J)
Qurayyat	1089	20	24h (J)
Dammam	1098	100	24h (J)
Madinah	1116	20	24h (J)
Aflaj	1206	20	24h (J)
Hafar al-Batin	1215	20	24h (J)
Madinah	1215	20	24h (R)
Dammam	1260	500	24h (R)
Riyadh	1422	20	24h (I)
Ras al-Khair	1440	1600	24h (R)
Jeddah (Bahrah)	1449	200	24h (R)
Hafar al-Batin	1467	50	24h (R)
Jeddah (Khumra)	1512	1000	1500-0300 (Q)
Duba	1521	2000	1500-2230 (R)

Some transmitters running on lower power.

FM(MHz)	R	J	Q	I/M	E
Abha	-	-	-	-	89.0
Aflaj	93.3	96.5	99.8	-	-
Almandaq	-	-	-	-	99.1
Al-Artawiya	-	-	-	-	102.9
Al-Bad'	-	-	-	-	107.3
Al-Bahah	98.0	88.4	91.5	-	104.1
Al-Duwadimi	-	-	-	-	98.1
Al-Henakiya	-	-	-		98.4
Al-Huwayd	-	-	-	-	102.0
Al-Kharj	-	-	-	-	94.2
Al-Madha	-	-	-	-	97.7
Al-Musayjid	-	-	-	-	97.7
Al-Nuhaitiya	-	-	-	-	98.0
Al-Ula	-	-	-	-	103.6
Al-Uwayqilah	-	-	-	-	99.2
Al-Wajh	-	-	-	-	105.5
Ar-Rass	96.1	102.9	99.4	-	-
Arafat	92.2	94.0	90.8	92.2	95.4
Arar	94.1	97.4	88.4	-	-
Buraydah	89.3	95.6	93.2	-	98.9
Dammam	92.8/93.8	94.7	90.0	-	103.6
Darma	-	-	-	-	102.3
Duba	89.5	95.8	92.6	-	-
Ethnen	-	-	-	-	107.3
Farasan Island	-	-	-		99.3
Halat Ammar	-	-	-	-	97.5
Haradh	-	-	-	-	101.3
Hubuna	-	-	-	-	98.6
Huraymila	-	-	-	-	95.5
Jeddah	92.0/99.5	93.0	89.9	-	96.2
Jizan	95.1	88.8	91.9	-	-
Jubail	107.8	105.6	95.3	-	-
Khamis Mushait	-	-	-	-	107.3
Kharj	94.0	96.0	90.0	95.2	-
Makkah	94.7	98.0	91.5	-	87.7
Medina	90.5	93.0	96.8	-	100.1
Rabigh	-	-	-	-	96.8
Rafha	-	-	-	-	100.2
Riyadh	91.2	94.4	100.0	-	97.0
Sabt Alalayah	-	-	-	-	98.3
Sajir	-	-	-	-	102.7
Taif	96.5	93.3	99.8	-	106.9
Turaif	-	-		-	101.5
Turbah	-	-	-	-	98.2
Uqlat as-Suqur	-	-	-	-	101.7
Wadi Al-Fora'a	-	-	-	-	98.8
Yanbu	97.4	93.6	90.9	-	-

+ numerous low power stations under 10kW for local coverage.

R=R. Riyadh in Arabic: 24h. – **J=R. Jeddah in Arabic**: 24h, on most MW fqs 0300-2200. – **Q=Quran prgr:** 24h incl. Call of Islam 0100-0300 – **I=Call of Islam prgr:** 24h – **E=English prgr. "Saudia Radio"** (from either Riyadh or Jeddah studios): 24h. – **M=Music prgr:** 24h. **A:** "R. Al-Azm", a programme for Yemen (also on FM Dhahran al-Janub 94.9, Fayfa 99.0, Jizan/Najran 107.0MHz. For more details see International section.

Ann: R. Riyadh: "Idha'at ar-Riyadh", "Idha'atu'l-mamlakah al-arabiyah t'il-saudiayh min al-Riyadh". R. Jeddah: "Idha'at al-Jiddah", "Idha'atu'l-mamlakah al-arabiyah t'il-saudiayh min Jiddah". 'Quran prgr: "Idha-atu'l-Koran al-Kareem min al-mamlakah al-arabiyah t'il-saydiah". Call of Islam: "Idha'at Nidaa Al-Islam min Makka al-Mukaram". E: "This is Saudia Radio".

IS: 'Ud' (oriental lute). Opens and closes with National Anthem.

F.PI: separate FM network for Call of Islam prgr.

EXTERNAL SERVICE: Saudi Radio International: see International Radio section.

SAUDI ARAMCO RADIO (Serving the staff of Saudi Aramco)

P.O.Box 5000, Dhahran 31311 **W:** saudiaramco.com **E:** webmaster@aramco.com.sa

Studio 1 (pop, rock and country music): Udhailiyah 88.8MHz, Dhahran 91.4MHz, Safaniya/Tanajib/Haradh 103.8MHz – **Studio 2** (easy listening, jazz and classical music): Udhailiyah 91.9MHz, Dhahran 101.4MHz, Safaniya/Tanajib/Haradh 107.9MHz. **D.Prgr:** 24h in English.

Other Stations (FM MHz):
Alif Alif FM: Najran/Riyadh 94.0, Al-Bahah 94.7, Jeddah 101.0, Hafar al-Batin 101.7, Arar/Madinah/Rafha 104.0, Hail 105.0, Dammam 107.5 + more LP txs **W:** alifaliffm.com
Arabian Gulf R, 107.5MHz (See main entry under Bahrain)
MBC FM: Yanbu 100.9, Az-Zulfi 101.0, Dhahran 101.9, Riyadh 102.0, Najran 102.9, Jeddah/Medina 103.0 + more LP txs **W:** mbc.net/mbcfm . See main entry under UAE
Mix FM: Tabuk 93.0MHz, Riyadh/Hail 98.0, Hafar al-Batin 98.2, Jubayl/Gizan 98.4, Nazran 101.0, Taif 101.4, Kharj/Sakaha 103.0, Burayda/Jeddah 105.5, Makkah/Yanbu 106.0, Majmaa 106.2, Baha 106.4 + more LP txs **W:** mixfm-sa.com
Panorama FM: Dammam 91.9, Riyadh 96, Tabuk 101.7, Jeddah 102.0, Madinah 102.3, Buraidah (Al Qassim) 103.3, Abha/Taif 104.0. See main entry under UAE
R. Rotana: Al-Qurayat/Jeddah 88.0, Hafar al-Batin 88.6, Dammam 100.0, Gizan 105.5 + more LP txs. **W:** rotana.net
U FM Radio: Riyadh 90.0, Al-Qurayat/Taif 90.3, Madina 91.0, Al-Kharj/Arar/Al-Dawadimi 91.5, Hafar al-Batin 91.7, Jeddah 97.0, Rabigh 101.7, Gizan 101.9, Yanbu 102.5, Al-Bahah 105.1 + more LP txs **W:** ufmradio.com
American Forces Network: Jeddah 93.7/100.7/103.9, Riyadh 100.7/103.1/105.1/103.9/105.9/107.9

SENEGAL

L.T: UTC — **Pop:** 17 million — **Pr.L:** French (official), Mandinka, Pulaar, Soninke, Wolof — **E.C:** 230V/50Hz — **ITU:** SEN

CONSEIL NATIONAL DE REGULATION DE L'AUDIOVISUEL (CNRA)

🖃 15ème étage, Immeuble Fahd, Blvd Djily Mbaye, B.P. 50059, Dakar RP ☎+221 33 8499120 🖹 +221 33 8234785 **W:** cnra.sn
L.P: Chairperson: Nancy Ngom Ndiaye.

RADIODIFFUSION TÉLÉVISION SÉNÉGALAISE (Pub)

🖃 Triangle Sud x Avenue El-Hadj Malick SY, B.P. 1765, Dakar ☎+221 33 8491212 🖹 +221 33 8223490 **W:** rts.sn **E:** rts@rts.sn
L.P: DG: Babacar Diagne. Dir. Radio: Oumar Seck. Dir. New Tech. & Development: Papa Abdou Diallo.

FM	N	I	R	M	kW
Bakel	95.9	107.3	-	-	5
Dakar	95.7	92.5	94.5	95.2	10
Diourbel	97.6	96.6	101.1	-	2
Fatick	95.7	-	92.8	-	0.5/2
Goudiry	106.0	-	91.1	-	0.5
Kaolack	103.0	107.0	97.9	-	5
Kédougou	94.6	97.7	100.0	-	2
Kolda	100.0	102.2	92.2	-	2
Koungheul	89.7	-	107.0	-	1
Linguère	92.1	89.0		-	5
Louga	95.0	101.8	88.7	-	5/2
Matam	95.6	89.1	100.6	-	2
Ndioum	-	98.4	92.7	-	5
Ourossogui	96.5	89.1	105.3	-	5/2
Podor	-	-	100.6	-	0.25
Richard Toll	-	-	89.6	-	0.1
Saint-Louis	91.9	90.1	96.3	-	10/5
Tambacounda	102.0	88.1	92.0	-	5
Thiès	96.9	94.9	100.6	-	5
Touba	-	-	99.2	-	0.25
Vélingara	99.0	89.1	92.2	-	2
Ziguinchor	95.2	100.2	98.9	-	5

N=Chaîne Nationale: 24h in French, Wolof and other national languages – **I=R. Sénégal Internationale:** 24h in French, Arabic, Portuguese and other languages – **M=RTS Mag FM**: 24h in French – **R=Chaîne Régionale:** 0600-2400, regional programming for 9 to 18 hours a day depending on station.
Ann: N: "Radiodiffusion Télévision Sénégalaise émettant de Dakar". Int: "Radio Sénégal Internationale". **IS:** Melody on "Cora" (local harp).

Other Stations (main networks):

FM	1)	2)	3)	4)	5)	6)	7)
Bakel	-	-	93.7	100.8	-	-	-
Banlieue	91.7	-	-	-	-	-	-
Bignona	-	91.4	-	88.3	-	-	-
Dagana	-	-	-	91.7	-	-	-
Dakar	98.5	94.0	88.9	101.0	103.9	98.7	97.8
Diourbel	91.1	92.4	90.9	-	-	106.0	105.5
Fatick	-	99.3	102.5	-	99.3	-	102.8
Joal	-	-	92.4	-	-	-	-
Kaffrine	-	95.0	102.4	-	-	-	-
Kaolack	94.6	93.9	105.0	92.7	99.7	93.1	91.9
Kébémer	-	-	91.5	101.3	-	-	-
Kédogou	-	99.7	98.6	106.4	-	-	-
Kidira	-	-	105.0	-	-	-	-
Kolda	95.4	93.2	98.7	91.9	102.2	99.7	88.1
Linguere	-	-	102.8	-	-	-	-
Louga	-	88.3	91.8	-	98.3	107.0	103.4
Matam	98.4	95.0	-	89.3	96.9	91.8	88.7
Mboro	-	-	98.6	-	-	-	-
Mbour	106.9	95.8	102.8	-	-	104.1	-
Ndioum	93.9	-	-	-	-	-	-
Nioro	-	98.4	-	-	-	-	-
Ourossogui	-	-	99.5	-	-	-	-
Podor	-	100.0	98.7	-	95.4	-	-
Richard Toll	-	99.0	106.0	-	-	-	-
Saint-Louis	93.2	99.3	106.3	88.3	94.6	88.9	88.1
Sédhiou	88.0	-	95.3	-	-	-	-
Tambacounda	98.5	93.2	91.0	94.0	105.6	100.5	90.3
Thiès	102.2	102.5	93.7	106.9	92.3	107.1	105.1
Toubambacké	92.8	92.4	-	89.1	106.2	-	-
Velingara	-	96.4	102.4	-	-	-	-
Ziguinchor	95.6	92.0	92.4	-	-	106.0	103.4

Addresses: 1) Sud FM Sen R, Immeuble Fahd, Bld. Djily Mbaye x rue Macodou Ndiaye (5ème étage), Dakar ☎+221 33 8650888 🖹 +221 33 8220250 **W:** sudfm.net – **2) R. Futurs Medias (RFM)**, Rue 15x Corniche, Immeuble Elimane Ndour , B.P. 17795, Dakar ☎+221 33 8491640 **W:** futursmedias.net – **3) R. Dunyaa**: HLM 1, Rue 14 prolongée, Dakar ☎+221 33 8242424 **E:** dunyaa@sentoo.sn – **4) Express An-Nour FM** – **5) Convergence FM,** Immeuble Lambert, Avenue Bourguiba, Dakar ☎+221 33 8253989 **W:** convergencefm.wordpress.com – **6) Océan FM** – **7) Sénégal Info**

Community radio FM (MHz):
Afia FM, Dakar: 93.0 5kW – Biyen FM, Thiès 89.5 2kW – Ferlo FM, Dahra: 94.0 2kW – Gaynaako FM, Podor 99.4 0.5kW. **W:** gaynaakofm.org – Jéeri FM, Keur Momar Sarr 97.0 0.3kW – Manoore FM, Dakar: 89.4 5kW – R. Penc Mi, Fissel: 90.6 1kW. **E:** pencmi_fm@yahoo.fr – R. Tim-Timol, Matam: 91.8 1kW.

Other stations (MHz):
BBC African Sce: Dakar 105.6 10kW in French.
China R. Int, Dakar/St.Louis 102.9, Kaolack/Ziguinchor 106.6MHz
Medi 1 Afrique Internationale: Dakar 93.8
RFI Afrique: Ziguinchor 87.6, Tambacounda 88.9, Kaolack 91.4, Dakar 92.0, Richard Toll 94.3, Mbacké 94.4, Bakel 98.2, St.-Louis 99.7, Thiès 100.2MHz.
VOA Africa: Dakar 102.0MHz in French & Wolof

SERBIA

L.T: UTC +1h (28 Mar-31 Oct: +2h) — **Pop:** 8.7 million — **Pr.L:** Serbian — **E.C:** 230V/50Hz — **ITU:** SRB

REGULATORNO TELO ZA ELEKTRONSKE MEDIJE (REM) (Regulatory Authority of Electronic Media)

🖃 Trg Nikole Pasica 5, 11003 Beograd ☎ +381 11 2028700 🖹 +381 11 2028745 **E:** office@rem.rs **W:** www.rem.rs
L.P: Vice Pres: Goran Petrovic

JP. EMISIONA TEHNIKA I VEZE/ETV (PUBLIC ENTERPRISE BROADCASTING AND COMMUNICATION)

🖃 Kneza Viseslava 88, 11030 Beograd ☎ +381 11 3693251 🖹 +381 11 3693260, Tech.: ☎ +381 11 3212650 **W:** etv.rs **E:** etv@etv.rs, tehnika@etv.rs, etv@etv.rs **L.P:** Branko Gogic

RADIO-TELEVIZIJA SRBIJE (Pub)

🖃 Takovska 10, 11000 Beograd ☎ +381 11 3212000
E: kontaktcentar@rts.rs **W:** rts.rs **L.P:** DG: Dragan Bujosevic
R. Beograd: Hilendarska 2, 11000 Beograd ☎ +381 11 3248888
L.P: Dir: Milivoje Mihajlovic **W:** radiobeograd.co.rs

MW	kHz	kW	Prgr	
Sjenica	1602	0.5	Radio Beograd 1 (rel.)	
FM (MHz)	**I**	**II/III**	**202**	**kW**
Avala	95.3	97.6	104.0	75/75/130
Bajina Basta	91.9	93.0	94.0	2
Beograd	88.3	-	-	2
Besna Kobila	91.7	95.3	100.1	25/25/40
Bitovik	91.7	92.9	104.3	25
Crni Vrh	89.7	99.3	101.0	25
Crveni Cot	94.5	96.5	101.8	75/75.130
Deli Jovan	87.7	94.9	98.9	25/25/40
Jastrebac	96.9	89.3	103.5	100
Kopaonik	90.9	93.7	102.1	50/50/100
Ljubovija	104.0	94.0	105.6	25
Maljen	104.5	107.9	93.4	25
Ovcar	88.1	90.1	101.6	25
Pirot	98.5	102.5	101.0	15
Subotica	88.9	101.1	98.5	50/50/0.3
Tornik	90.6	97.5	100.2	15
Trgoviste	90.1	92.3	96.9	15
Tupiznica	92.5	96.1	100.4	25
Vrsac	95.7	98.1	103.0	30

Additional low power local stns not mentioned.

R. Beograd 1: 24h **N:** W 0303, 0330, 0400, 0430, 0500, 0540, 0700, 0800, 0900, 1000, 1100, 1200, 1300, 1400, 1600, 1700, 1830, 2100, 2200, 2300; Sun 0430, 0500, 0530, 0600, 0700, 0800, 0900, 1000, 1100, 1200, 1400, 1600, 1830, 2000, 2200, 2300 – **R. Beograd 2:** W 0400-1900 (Sun 0600-1900). **N:** W 1130, 1230, 1330, 1500, 1600, 1850. Sun 0630, 0730, 0930, 1055, 1130, 1330, 1730, 1850 – **R. Beograd 3:** 1900-2300 (Serious prgr.) – **R. Beograd 202: 24h** on 104.0MHz + FM 202 – **Stereorama:** 0700-1900SS on FM 202. Other times rel. Beograd 202

Local stations:

FM	MHz	FM	MHz	FM	MHz
Arandjelovac	98.9	Leskovac	99.0	Smed. Palanka	88.3
Bor	91.7	Loznica	107.4	Smederevo	96.1
Cacak	92.8	Majdanpek	96.7	Soko Banja	90.5
Jagodina	97.3	Mladenovac	97.0	Uzice	92.0
Kladovo	89.0	Novi Pazar	90.0	Valjevo	88.6
Kragujevac	88.9	Pirot	95.8	Vranje	96.5
Kraljevo	87.6	Pozarevac	90.1	Vrnjacka Banja	96.5
Krusevac	92.2	Priboj	88.7	Zajecar	98.1
Lazarevac	89.3	Prijepolje	98.9		

E: R. Bella Amie: belami.rs **R. Vranje:** rtv-vranje.rs **R. Leskovac:** radioleskovac.rs **R. Kragujevac:** rtk.co.rs **R. Valjevo:** patak.co.rs

FM stations with national coverage:

FM	MHz	FM	MHz
R. S2	88.9	R. S1	94.9
Play	92.5	FM Hit R.	98.5

All stns have relays.

E: Index: indexradio.rs **Play:** b92.net **R.S:** radios.rs **Hit Music:** hitmusicfm.rs

Local FM stations in Beograd:

FM	MHz	FM	MHz	FM	MHz
R. S2	88.9	R. S1	94.9	R. S4	102.2
Bum Bum	89.4	TRI	95.8	Novosti	104.7
R. JAT	90.2	Rock R.	96.2	Nostalgie	105.2
R. S3	90.9	Naxi	96.9	Karolina	106.3
Pink	91.3	FM Hit R.	98.5	Top FM	106.8
TDI	91.8	Studio B	99.1	S. Ljubve	107.3
Play	92.5	Sport FM	100.4	AS FM R.	107.9
Laguna	93.7				

NB: There are numerous local FM stns.

VOJVODINA (Autonomous Province)

RADIO TELEVIZIJA NOVI SAD

✉ Ignjata Pavlasa 3, 21000 Novi Sad ☎ +381 21 210-1420 🖷 +381 21 423348 **E:** office@rtv.rs **W:** rtv.rs

FM (MHz)	I	II	III	kW
Novi Sad	87.7	90.5	100.0	50
Subotica	99.3	92.5		50
Vrsac	99.6	91.7	107.1	30

I) in Serbian, II) in Hungarian, III) prgrs for national minorities

R. Novi Sad 1: 24h in Serbian **R. Novi Sad 2:** 24h in Hungarian **R.Novi sad** 3: 24h for national minorities

Local stations

FM	MHz	FM	MHz	FM	MHz
Apatin	98.7	Kovin	89.5	St. Pazova	91.5
B. Palanka	95.1	Odzaci	89.7	Subotica	91.5
B. Topola	97.8	Pancevo	92.1	Temerin	93.5
B. Petrovac	91.4	Ruma	102.7	Vrbas	95.5
Beocin	97.8	Sid	89.1	Vrsac	94.0
Indjija	96.0	Sombor	97.5	Zrenjanin	103.6
Kovacica	93.2	Srbobran	102.6		

There are numerous low-power local FM stns.

E: R. Pancevo: rtvpancevo.rs **R. Panon:** pannonrtv.com **R. Zrenjanin:** radiozrenjanin.rs

DAB+

Location	Ch	ERP	Location	Ch	ERP
Avala	11A	15kW	Subotica	11B	10kW
Crveni Cot	11B	10kW	Tupiznica	11B	10kW
Jastrebac	11D	15kW	Ovcar	11B	15kW

MUX: Belgrade1, Belgrade2/3, Belgrade 202, R. Play, R. FM Hit, R.S1, R.S2

SEYCHELLES

L.T: UTC +4h — **Pop:** 99,000 — **Pr.L:** English (official), French (official), Seychellois Creole (official) — **E.C:** 240V/50Hz— **ITU:** SEY

DEPARTMENT OF INFORMATION COMMUNICATIONS TECHNOLOGY (DICT)

✉ P.O. Box 737, Third Floor, Caravelle House, Manglier St, Victoria, Mahé ☎+248 4286609 🖷 +248 4324643 **W:** www.ict.gov.sc **E:** psoffice@ict.gov.sc **L.P:** Principal Secretary: Benjamin Choppy

SEYCHELLES BROADCASTING CORPORATION (SBC, Pub.)

✉ P.O. Box 321, Hermitage, Mahé ☎+248 4289600 🖷 +248 4225641 **W:** sbc.sc **E:** ceo.secretary@sbc.sc

L.P: DCEO: Mr. Jude Louange. Head of Marketing & Corporate Affairs: Ms. Cindy Wirtz Head of Eng. & Tech : Mr. Jean-Paul Gamatis. Head of Radio Prgr: Mrs. Jeannette Julienne

MW: Victoria 1368kHz 10kW.

FM: St. Louis 93.6MHz 1kW, Praslin 100.8MHz 0.03kW.

D.Prgr: **MW: Radyo Sesel** (spoken word): 0200-1800. **N: English**: 0300, 0600, 0900, 1500. **French**: 0330, 0700, 1300, 1700. **Creole**: 0230, 0500, 0800, 1600.

FM: **Paradise FM** (musical prgr.): 24h.

Ann: E: "This is SBC Radio". F: "Ici la Radio SBC". C: "Isi Radyo Sesel"

IS: Instrumental music.

Other Stations:

K-Radio: 96.8/97.0/97.2/99.0MHz. **W:** k-ent.sc

Pure FM: Anse Soleil 90.0MHz, St. Louis 90.7MHz, Praslin 95.7MHz. **W:** purefm.sc

RFI Afrique: Anse Soleil 102.8MHz 0.25kW, Pointe au Sel 103.2MHz, Victoria 103.8MHz 1kW.

BBC World Sce: Anse Soleil 105.2MHz, Pointe au Sel 105.6MHz, St. Louis/Victoria 106.2MHz

SIERRA LEONE

L.T: UTC — **Pop:** 8 million — **Pr.L:** English (official), Krio — **E.C:** 230V/50Hz — **ITU:** SRL

INDEPENDENT MEDIA COMMISSION (IMC)

✉ Kissy House, 54 Siaka Stevens Street, Freetown ☎+232 22 221835 **W:** www.facebook.com/IndependentMediaCommissionImc

L.P: Commissioner: Augustine Garmoh.

SIERRA LEONE BROADCASTING CORPORATION (SLBC, Pub.)

✉ New England, Freetown ☎+232 22 241919 🖷 +232 22 240922 **W:** slbc.sl

L.P: DG: Elvis Gbanabom Hallowell. Dir. Eng.: Alhajie Bangura.

FM: Freetown 100.0MHz 8kW. Regional stations (mostly own programming): Bo 96.5MHz 2kW, Kenema 93.5MHz 2kW, Kono 90.2MHz 1kW, Makeni 88.0MHz 1kW. In addition 4 trs under 1kW.

D.Prgr: 0600-2400.

Other Stations FM (MHz):
Africa Young Voices (AYV), Freetown: 101.6. **W:** ayvnews.com – **Believers Broadcasting Network (BBN)** (Rlg.), Freetown: 93.0 2kW. **W:** bbn-sl.org – **Capital R**: Freetown 104.9 8kW, Bo 102.3 50W, Kenema 104.9 30W, Makeni 103.3 30W. **W:** capitalradio.sl – **Eastern R**: Kenema 101.9, Kono 96.5 – **Joy FM,** Segbwema 88.5 – **Kids Radio Network,** Freetown 103.0 **W:** facebook.com/kidsradionetwork – **Kiss FM**, Bo: 104.0 (Also rel. VOA) – **R. Bintumani**, Kabala: 93.7 – **R. Bontico**, Bonthe: 96.9 – **R. Democracy,** Freetown: 98.1 **W:** radiodemocracy.sl – **R. Galaxy**, Mahera: 106.1 – **R. Gbafth**, Mile 91: 91.0 – **R. Kolenten**, Kambia: 92.4 – **R. Mankneh,** Makeni: 95.1 – **R. Moa,** Kailahun: 105.5 – **R. Modcar,** Moyamba: 94.8 – **R. Maria**, Makeni 101.1 0.5kW – **R. Mount Aureol**, Fourah Bay College, Freetown: 107.3MHz – **Njala University R**, Njala 92.5 – **R. Numbura**, Bumbuna: 102.5 – **R. Wanjei**, Pujehun: 101.1 – **R. Viascity**, Waterloo: 100.6 – **Star R**, Freetown 103.5 – **Skyy R**, Freetown: 106.6 – **Unity R,** Freetown: 98.4 – **Voice of Islam,** Freetown: 102.0 – **VO the Handicapped,** Freetown: 96.2 (mostly rel. BBC) – **VO the Peninsula,** Tombo: 96.0 – **VO Women**, Mattru Jong: 88.5.

BBC African Sce: Freetown 94.3 8kW, Makeni 91.7 60W, Bo 94.35120W, Kenema 95.3MHz 60W – **RFI Afrique**, Freetown: 89.9 in French/English/Mandinka – **VOA Africa:** Freetown 102.5MHz

SINGAPORE

L.T: UTC +8h — **Pop:** 5.9 million — **Pr.L:** English, Chinese, Tamil, Malay — **E.C:** 230V/50Hz — **ITU:** SNG

INFO-COMMUNICATIONS MEDIA DEVELOPMENT AUTHORITY OF SINGAPORE (IMDA)
(Government statutory board)
✉ #10 Pasir Panjang Road, Mapletree Business City, Singapore 117438 ☎ +65 6377 3800 🖷 +65 6577 3888 **W:** imda.gov.sg
LP: Chmn: Mr Chan Yeng Kit, CEO: Mr Lew Chuen Hong.

MEDIACORP RADIO SINGAPORE PTE LTD (Comm.)
✉ Mediacorp Campus, 1 Stars Avenue, Ayer Rajah, Singapore 138507 ☎ +65 6333 3888 🖷 +65 6251 5828 **W:** mediacorp.sg (corporate), toggle.sg/en (programming)
L.P: Chmn: Chiang Meng Niam. CEO: Ms Tham Loke Kheng
Stations: FM tx centre at Bukit Batok

FM	MHz	kW	Network	Format	Lang.
1)	89.7	6	Ria 89.7FM	CHR	Malay
2)	90.5	6	Gold 90FM	Gold	English
3)	92.4	10	Symphony 92FM	Classical	English
4)	93.3	6	YES 93.3FM	AC	Chinese
5)	93.8	6	CNA938	N./Info	English
6)	94.2	10	Warna 94.2FM	N./Info	Malay
7)	95.0	6	Class 95FM	AC	English
8)	95.8	10	Capital 95.8FM *	N./Info	Chinese
9)	96.8	10	Oli 96.8FM	Full sce	Tamil
10)	97.2	6	Love 97.2FM **	Easy	Chinese
11)	98.7	6	987FM	CHR	English

*) in Chinese: 'Chengshi Pindao' **) in Chinese: 'Zui'ai Pindao'
D.Prgr: all networks 24h Tr. powers shown are TRP
Ownership: MediaCorp is wholly owned by Temasek Holdings, an investment company of the Government of Singapore.

SO DRAMA! ENTERTAINMENT (Comm.)
Operated by the Singapore Armed Forces Reservists' Assoc.
✉ Tower B #12-04, Defence Technology Towers, 5 Depot Rd, Singapore 109681 ☎ +65 6373 1920 🖷 +65 6278 3039 **W**: sodrama.sg
883JiaFM: 88.3MHz 5kW, 24h in Chinese
Power98FM: 98.0MHz 12kW, 24h in English

SPH RADIO PTE LTD (Singapore Press Holdings, Comm.)
✉ 1000 Toa Payoh North, News Centre Podium Block Level 3, Singapore 318994 ☎ +65 6319 1900 🖷 +65 6319 1099 **W:** sphradio.sg **L.P:** Chairman: Mr Anthony Tan. Gen. Mgr: Mr Sim Hong Huat
Money FM: 24h in English on 89.3 MHz **One FM:** 24h in English on 91.3MHz **Kiss92 FM:** 24h in English on 92.0MHz **96.3 Hao FM:** 24h in Chinese on 96.3MHz **UFM 1003:** 24h in Chinese on 100.3MHz

BBC SINGAPORE 88.9 FM
24h rel. of BBCWS in English. The 5kW FM tx at Bukit Batok is operated by MediaCorp.

FAR EASTERN RELAY STATION
Encompass Digital Media Services Ltd, ✉ 51 Turut Track, Singapore 718930 ☎ +65 6793 7511 See International Radio section

SLOVAKIA

L.T: UTC +1h (28 Mar-31 Oct: +2h) — **Pop:** 5.5 million — **Pr.L:** Slovak — **E.C:** 230V/50Hz — **ITU:** SVK

RADA PRE VYSIELANIE A RETRANSMISIU (RVR) Council for Broadcasting and Retransmission
✉ Palisády 36, 81106 Bratislava ☎ +421 22090650 🖷 +421 220906535 **E:** office@rvr.sk **W:** www.rvr.sk
L.P: Chair: Marta Danielová

ROZHLAS A TELEVÍZIA SLOVENSKA (Radio and Television of Slovakia) - RTVS (Pub) SLOVENSKY ROZHLAS (SLOVAK RADIO)
✉ Mytna 1 (P.O.Box 55), 817 55 Bratislava 15 ☎ + 421 2 57273111 🖷 + 421 2 57273559 **W:** rozhlas.sk **E:** info@rozhlas.sk **Radio FM: W:** radiofm.sk **E:** info@radiofm.sk **L.P:** DG: Jaroslav Rezník. PD: Michal Dzurjanin. TD: Roman Skrivánek

MW	kW	kHz	Prgr
Kosice	702	5	S5 (daytime) + S3 (nighttime)
Nitra (Jarok)	1098	25	S5 (daytime) + S3 (nighttime)
Rimavská Sobota	1521	10	S5 (daytime) + S3 (nighttime)

FM (MHz)	S1	S2	S3	S4	S5	kW
Banská Bystrica	90.1	101.5	102.0	105.4	-	100/100/0.1/2
Banská Stiavnica	99.0	-	102.6	-	-	20/20
Bardejov	93.5	89.3	88.8	101.7	-	10/1/10/10
Borsky Mikulás	-	-	95.6	102.8	-	1
Bratislava	96.6	99.3	104.4	89.3	-	100/10/10/10
Cadca	-	-	-	91.8	-	0.5
Dolny Kubin	-	-	-	91.7	-	1
Dubnica n.V.	92.2	-	-	-	-	0.5
Gemer					89.6	0.5
Kosice	96.6	100.3	-	-	-	100/35
Kosice (city)	-	-	96.2	101.2	-	0.5/1
Lucenec	103.6	88.2	-	98.0	-	10/2/10
Modry Kamen	90.9	88.5	103.1	98.3	-	10
Námestovo	102.4	100.4	88.7	-	-	10
Nitra	91.2	102.2	-	-	-	10/10
N. Mesto n.V.	103.2	100.7	90.8	-	-	10
Nové Zámky	-	-	94.6	102.8	98.7	1
Poprad	92.2	96.9	94.2	104.3	-	30
Presov	-	-	106.7	101.5	-	0.5
Rim. Sobota	-	95.0	-	-	-	1
Roznava	97.3	88.6	90.0	105.9	-	1/1/1/1
Ruzomberok	103.8	100.6	104.6	102.1	-	5
Snina	91.2	-	102.2	107.6	-	10
Stará Lubovna	89.1	102.3	96.1	-	-	10
Šamorín					91.4	0.1
Sturovo	96.3	91.7	106.2	103.7	-	10
Trebisov	-	89.2	106.7	101.3	-	10
Trencín	-	95.9	97.8	101.2	-	10
Trnava (F.PI.)	90.8	-	-	-	-	10
Trstená	-	-	-	91.9	-	10
Zilina	103.5	100.1	97.2	94.5	-	20/20/30/20
Zvolen	-	-	99.8	89.0	-	0.5/1

Addresses & other information:
S1 = Radio Slovensko: 24h (national prgr news) **S2** = Radio Regina: 24h (regional prgrs + prgrs for national minorities in Hungarian, Ukrainian, Ruthenian, German, Czech, Polish and Gypsy/Roma + relays of Radio Slovensko – S1) **S2 BA** = Radio Regina Bratislava, ✉ Mytna 1, 817 55 Bratislava 15 **S2 BB** = Radio Regina Banská Bystrica ✉ L. Sáru 1, 975 68 Banská Bystrica **S2 KE** = Radio Regina Kosice ✉ Masarykova 7, 041 61 Kosice **S3** = Radio Devín: 24h (cultural prgr) on FM and 1700-0500 on 702, 1098 and 1521kHz **S4** = Radio FM: 24h (rock, pop and alternative music). N: on the h **S5** = Radio Patria – production of prgrs for national minorities in Hungarian, Ukrainian, Ruthenian, German, Czech, Polish, Gypsy/Roma relayed on S2 and S5 txs ✉ Slovensky Rozhlas, HRNEV, Moyzesova 7, 040 01 Kosice **E:** nev@slovakradio.sk Prgrs for minorities (S5): Hungarian 0500-1700 on 702, 1098 and 1521kHz). Prgrs for national minorities (S5) on Radio Regina (S2): Mon+Wed+Fri+Sat+Sun 1700-1800, Tue+Thu 1700-1800, 1900-2000

EXTERNAL SERVICE: Radio Slovakia International
See International Broadcasting section

MAJOR PRIVATE STATIONS/NETWORKS:

ASOCIÁCIA NEZÁVISLYCH ROZHLASOVYCH A TELEVÍZNYCH STANÍC (Association of Independent Radio Stations)
Gröslingova 63, 811 09 Bratislava ☎ +421 2 5296 2370 **W:** anrts.sk **E:** anrts@anrts.sk
FUN RADIO (Comm.) Leskova 5, 815 25 Bratislava ☎ +421 2 52494601 🖷 +421 2 52495535 **W:** funradio.sk – **RADIO JEMNÉ (Comm.)** Dr. Vladimíra Clementisa 10, 815 25 Bratislava ☎ +421 2 48484811 🖷 +421 2 52492701 **W:** jemne.sk **FM:** see list below **D.Prgr:** 24h – **RADIO EXPRES (Comm.)** Lamacská cesta 1, 841 04 Bratislava ☎ +421 2 59308900 🖷 +421 2 59308991 **W:** expres.sk **FM:** see list below **D.Prgr:** 24h – **EUROPA 2 (Comm.)** Seberíniho 1, 821 03 Bratislava ☎ +421 2 48224201 **W:** europa2.sk **FM:** see list below **D.Prgr:** 24h – **RADIO LUMEN (Relig.)** Kapitulská 2, 974 01 Banská Bystrica ☎ +421 48 4710800 🖷 +421 48 4710840 **W:** lumen.sk **FM:** see list below **D.Prgr:** 24h – **RADIO ANTÉNA ROCK (Comm.)** Siberíniho 1, 821 03 Bratislava ☎ +421 2 48484811 **W:** antenarock.sk **FM:** see list below **D.Prgr:** 24h – **RADIO VLNA (Comm.)** Siberíniho 1, 821 03 Bratislava ☎ +421 2 48484855 **W:** radiovlna.sk **FM:** see list below **D.Prgr:** 24h

Private Commercial FM Stations:

FM	MHz	kW	Station
Kosice	87.7	80	Fun R.
Banská Bystrica	87.7	10	R. Jemné
Nové Mesto n.V.	88.0	8.5	R. Jemné
Hlohovec	88.4	2	R. Expres
Ruzomberok	88.4	1	R. Expres
Snina	88.5	10	R. Vlna
Banská Bystrica	88.6	1	F.Pl.
Nitra	88.8	10	R. Anténa Rock
Trencín	89.1	10	Fun R.
Rimavská Sobota	89.3	1	R. Expres
Ruzomberok	89.7	1	R. Lumen
Nitra	89.7	1	R. Expres
Banská Bystrica	90.5	2	R. Beta
Prievidza	90.5	1	R. WOW
Presov	90.8	2	R. Kosice
Zilina	90.8	1	R. Goldies
Moldava nad Bodvou	91.0	1	R. Expres
Ruzomberok	91.1	1	R. Vlna
Lucenec	91.6	10	Fun R.
Banská Bystrica	92.0	2	R. Goldies
Stropkov	92.4	1	R. Vlna
Zvolen	92.6	1	R. Expres
Zámky	92.7	1	R. Expres
Zilina	92.7	1	R. Vlna
Ruzomberok	92.8	1	R. Vlna
Trencín	93.3	10	R. Lumen
Banská Stiavnica	93.3	2	R. Lumen
Bratislava	93.8	6	R. Lumen
Košice	93.8	2	R. Best FM
Prievidza	93.9	1	R. Beta
Bratislava	94.3	100	Fun R.
Nové Zámky	94.6	1	R. Maria
Banská Bystrica	94.7	1	BB FM R.
Košice	94.8	1	R. Anténa Rock
Liptovsky Mikuláš	95.0	1	Fun R.
Nitra	95.2	10	Europa 2
Kosice	95.2	2	R. Expres
Levoca	95.3	1	R. Expres
Bardejov	95.6	1	R. Vlna
Roznava	95.7	1	R. Expres
Snina	95.9	10	R. Anténa Rock
Lucenec	96.0	5	R. Vlna
Cadca	96.1	1	R. Frontinus
Martin	96.2	1	R. Frontinus
Partizánske	96.4	1	R. Expres
Trstená	96.5	2	R. Expres
Zilina	96.5	1	R. Expres
Michalovce	97.0	5	F.Pl.
Banská Bystrica	97.6	100	R. Anténa Rock
Stropkov	97.8	1	R. Lumen
Handlová	98.1	1	R. Lumen
Bardejov	98.2	1	R. Expres
Nové Mesto n.V.	98.5	8.8	Europa 2
Kosice	98.6	50	R. Jemné
Ruzomberok	98.8	5	R. Anténa Rock
Michalovce	99.0	2	R. Vlna
Bardejov	99.1	1	R. Lumen
Zilina	99.2	20	Fun R.
Sturovo	99.4	10	R. Expres
Vychodna	99.5	1	R. Expres
Cadca	99.6	1	R. Vlna
Bratislava	100.3	1	R. Anténa Rock
Poprad	100.9	30	Europa 2
Lucenec	101.1	5	R. Expres
Roznava	101.4	1	R. Vlna
Bratislava	101.8	100	R. Vlna
Trencín	102.5	1	R. Expres
Poprad	102.5	1	Fun R.
Roznava	102.8	1	Fun R.
Strbské Pleso	102.9	2	R. Lumen
Kosice	102.9	1	Fun R.
Michalovce	103.3	2	R. Lumen
Presov	103.7	8	Europa 2
Banská Bystrica	104.0	100	Fun R.
Presov	104.1	1	R. Kiss
Zilina	104.6	1	R. Frontinus
Bratislava	104.8	50	Europa 2
Poprad	104.8	1	R. Vlna
Martin	104.9	1	R. Vlna
Banská Stiavnica	105.1	20	R. Vlna
Povazská Bystrica	105.2	1	R. Expres
Prešov	105.2	1	R. Anténa Rock
Trencín	105.5	10	R. Vlna
Stará Lubovna	105.7	10	R. Expres
Námestovo	105.8	10	R. Lumen
Presov	105.8	2	R. Vlna
Banská Bystrica	106.0	50	Europa 2
Kosice	106.2	20	R. Expres
Lucenec	106.3	3	R. Lumen
Roznava	106.3	1	R. Lumen
Prievidza	106.4	1	F.Pl.
Modry Kamen	106.5	1	R. Expres
Bratislava	106.6	10	R. Jemné
Banská Bystrica	106.6	1	R. Vlna
Partizánske	106.7	1	R. WOW
Zilina	106.9	3	R. Jemné
Dobsiná	107.0	1	R. Vlna
Bardejov	107.1	10	Europa 2
Levice	107.1	4	Fun R.
Poprad	107.3	2	R. Anténa Rock
Prievidza	107.5	1	R. Expres
Bratislava	107.6	10	R. Expres
Stará Lubovna	107.7	1	R. Jemné

+ over 60 relays of less than 1kW

DIGITAL RADIO (DAB+)
Towercom on Blocks: **12A** Zilina (2kW), Banská Bystrica (2kW); **12B** Košice (2kW); **12C** Bratislava (4kW), Dunajská Streda (1kW) with various Slovensky Rozhlas and private stns.
AVIS on Blocks: **10B** Banská Bystrica (3kW); **10C** Nitra (20kW) with various Slovensky Rozhlas and private stns.

SLOVENIA

L.T: UTC +1h (28 Mar-31 Oct: +2h) — **Pop:** 2.1 million — **Pr.L:** Slovenian — **E.C:** 230V/50Hz — **ITU:** SVN

AGENCIJA ZA KOMUNIKACIJSKA OMREZJA IN STORITVE (AKOS)
Stegne 7, 1000 Ljubljana ☎+386 1 5836300 🖷+386 1 5111101 **W:** srdf.si akos-rs.si **E:** info.box@akos-rs.si

RADIOTELEVIZIJA SLOVENIJA (Pub.)
Kolodvorska ulica 2, SI-1550 Ljubljana / Tavcarjeva ul. 17, SI-1550 Ljubljana ☎+386 1 4752151 ☎ +386 1 4752111 **W:** rtvslo.si **E:** pr@rtvslo.si **L.P:** DG: Igor Kadunc.

MW	kHz	kW	Prgr.	MW	kHz	kW	Prgr.
Beli Kriz	549	15	1/K	B. Kriz	1170	15	C
Nemcavci	558	15	1/MMR				

C=R. Capodistria in Italian, **K**=R. Koper in Slovenian, **MMR**=Muravideki Magyar R. in Hungarian.

FM (MHz)	Slo 1	Slo 2	Slo 3	Reg.	kW
Beli Kriz	92.0	94.1	96.1	104.3k/97.7c	5
	-	-	-	102.0si	1
Blejska Dobrava	-	-	-	100.4si	1
Boc	-	-	-	90.4m	2
Golnik	-	-	-	89.0si	1
Koper	92.2	-	-	104.1k	1
Krim	88.0	93.5	96.5	-	5
Krvavec	91.8	98.9	102.0	-	100
Kuk	90.8	87.8	96.4	100.6k	5
Kum	94.1	99.9	103.9	-	30
Ljubljana-Šance	-	-	-	100.8si	1
Nanos	92.9	95.3	105.7	88.6k	50/50/50/25
	-	-	-	103.1c	100
Pec	100.1	104.0	106.0	-	5
Pecarovci	-	-	-	87.6h	5
Plešivec	90.0	92.4	101.4	-	10
Pohorje	88.5	96.9	105.3	93.1m102.8si	30/20/50/20/50
Skalnica	-	-	-	100.3k	2
Tinjan	89.3	98.9	98.1	107.6k/103.6c	6/6/6/6/5
	-	-	-	94.6si	6
Trdinov Vrh	90.9	97.6	100.6	-	7.5/10/11
Trstelj	92.6	94.3	102.2	96.7si	5

Reg. stns: c=R. Capodistria in Italian, h=MMR in Hungarian, k=R. Koper, m=R. Maribor, si=R. Slovenija Int.

R. Slovenija 1 "Prvi program": 24h – **R. Slovenija 2 "Val 202":** 24h. Other times relay R. Slovenija Int. Pop + entertainment – **R. Slovenija 3 "Program ARS":** 24h. Serious music, educational – **R. SI, R. Slovenija International**, Ilichova ulica 33, SI-2106 Maribor **W:** radiosi.eu . Music and information channel 24h in English, German and Slovenian on **FM** ("si").

RADIO KOPER – CAPODISTRIA (Pub.)

✉ ulica OF 15, SI-6000 Koper-Capodistria ☎+386 5 6685050 (Slovenian Dept.) ☎+386 (5)6685440 🖷 +386 (5) 6684500 (Italian Dept.) **W:** rtvslo.si/radiokoper rtvslo.si/radiocapodistria **E:** radio.koper@rtvslo.si radio.capodistria@rtvslo.si **R. Koper in Slovenian:** 0430-2300 on 549kHz + FM ("k"). Other times rel. Slovenija 1 – **R. Capodistria in Italian:** 24h on 1170kHz + FM ("c").

RADIO MARIBOR (Pub.)

✉ Ilichova ulica 33, SI-2000 Maribor ☎+386 2 4299111 **W:** rtvslo.si/radiomaribor **E:** radio.maribor@rtvslo.si **FM:** ("m"). **D.Prgr:** Mon-Sat 0440-2100, Sun 0600-2100. At other times rel. Slovenia 1.

MURAVIDEKI MAGYAR RADIO (Pub.)

✉ Kranjceva ulica 10, SI-9220 Lendava +386 2 4299700 🖷+386 2 4299712 **W:** rtvslo.si/mmr **E:** mmr@rtvslo.si
MW 558kHz + **FM:** ("h"). **D.Prgr:** 24h.

OTHER STATIONS:

MW	kHz	kW	Station	Location
A)	648	10	R. Murski Val	Nemcavci

A) Ul. Arhitekta Novaka 13, SI-9000 Murska Sobota **W:** murskival.si **D.Prgr:** 24h. A joint night prgr. of Koroski R., Murski val, R. Celje, R. Kranj, R. Ptuj, R. Slovenske Gorice, R. Sora, R. Triglav, R. Univox and R. Velenje is broadcast.

FM	MHz	kW	Station	Location
1)	87.6	1	R. Bob	Ljubljana-Šance
2)	87.8	1	R. Salomon	Blejska Dobrava
3)	88.3	1	R. 1 Portoroz	Malija
3)	88.4	2	R. 1 Kranj	Krvavec
5)	89.3	1	R. Študent	Ljubljana-Šance
18)	89.8	1	R. Ptuj	Majšperg
6)	90.0	5	R. Maxi	Ljutomer
3)	90.1	1	R. 1 Primorska	Nova Gorica
7)	90.2	1	R. Hit	Vrhnika
3)	90.6	1	R. 1 Krim	Krim
30)	91.0	5	R. Ognjišce	Tinjan
8)	91.7	1	R. Capris	Markovec
9)	92.6	1	R. 2	Ljubljana-Šance
25)	93.1	1	R. Zeleni Val	Polzevo
10)	93.7	2	Štajerski Val	Boc
4)	93.8	3	R. Gorenc	Golnik
26)	93.8	1	Hitradio Center	Markovec
40)	94.6	5	Murski Val	Pecarovci
43)	94.6	1	R. Sraka	Trdinov Vrh
11)	94.9	1	R. Veseljak	Ljubljana-Šance
41)	95.1	2	R. Celje	Boc
7)	95.6	3	R. Hit	Dobeno
6)	95.7	1	R. Maxi	Pecarovci
12)	95.9	1	R. MARŠ	Maribor
13)	96.0	1	R. Triglav	Ravni Valvazor
14)	97.2	1	Koroški R.	Plešivec
3)	97.3	1	R. 1 Primorska	Hrvatini
15)	97.3	1	R. Kranj	Smarjetna Gora
3)	97.4	1	R. 1 Štajerska	Ljubicna
21)	98.1	1	R. Aktual Kum	Kum
17)	98.2	1	R. 94	Postojna
18)	98.2	1	R. Ptuj	Ptuj
3)	99.1	5	R. 1 Primorska	Trstelj
3)	99.3	1	R. 1 Celjski val	Celje
20)	99.5	1	R. Robin	Nova Gorica
21)	99.5	1	R. City	Ljubljana-Šance
30)	99.7	1	R. Ognjišce	Beli Kriz
20)	100.0	1	R. Robin	Trstelj
21)	100.2	5	R. Aktual	Krim
22)	100.2	1	Net FM	Maribor
23)	100.6	1	R. City	Maribor
23)	100.8	1	R. City	Topolšica
21)	101.2	1	R. Aktual	Ljubljana-Šance
19)	101.3	1	R. Pohorje	Maribor
2)	101.6	1	R. Salomon	Ljubljana-Šance
24)	101.8	1	R. Rogla	Konjiška Gora
3)	102.1	4	R. 1 Pomurje	M.Sobota/Bogojina
26)	102.4	1	Hitradio Center	Ljubljana-Šance
21)	102.4	5	R. Aktual Obala	Hrvatini
21)	102.8	1	R. Aktual Obala	Portoroz/Šentanje
21)	103.0	5	R. Aktual Studio D	Trdinov Vrh
26)	103.2	1	Hitradio Center	Rahtelov Vrh
26)	103.7	1	Hitradio Center	Maribor
42)	103.7	1	Primorski Val/R. Odmev	Javornik
17)	104.1	1	R. 94	Ilirska Bistrica
30)	104.5	100	R. Ognjišce	Krvavec
30)	104.5	5	R. Ognjišce	Trstelj
21)	104.8	2	R. Aktual	Boc
26)	104.9	1	Hitradio Center	Nova Gorica
3)	105.0	1	R. 1 Dolenjska	Krško
8)	105.1	5	R. Capris	Slavnik
32)	105.1	1	Primorski Val/Alpski Val	Kobariški Stol
34)	105.2	1	R. Antena	Ljubljana-Šance
40)	105.7	2	Murski Val	Zlatolicje
30)	105.9	5	R. Ognjišce	Kum
26)	106.4	5	Hitradio Center	Hrvatini
35)	106.4	4	R. Ekspres	Krim
36)	106.6	15	R. Krka	Trdinov Vrh
27)	106.8	1	R. Brezje	Maribor
37)	107.0	1	Moj R.	Topolšica
7)	107.0	1	R. Hit	Markovec
17)	107.1	1	R. 94 Notrajnska	Rovte
30)	107.3	2	R. Ognjišce	Boc
8)	107.9	1	R. Capris	Portoroz
3)	107.9	1	R. 1 Štajerska	Maribor
3)	107.9	1	R. 1 Ljubljana	Ljubljana-Šance

NB: Txs 1kW or higher are listed.

Addresses: 1) Stegne 11B, 1000 Ljubljana **W:** radiobob.si – **2)** Papirniški trg 17, 1260 Ljubljana-Polje **W:** radiosalomon.si – **3)** Stegne 11B, 1000 Ljubljana **W:** radio1.si Loc.Prgr. 0100-0400 – 4) Balos 4, 4290 Trzic **W:** radiogorenc.si – **5)** Svetceva ul. 9, 1000 Ljubljana **W:** radiostudent.si – **6)** Prešernova ul. 3, 9240 Ljutomer **W:** radiomaxi.si – **7)** Ljubljanska Cesta 36, 1230 Domzale **W:** radiohit.si – **8)** ul. 15.maja 10B, 6000 Koper **W:** radiocapris.si – **9)** Stegne 11b, 1000 Ljubljana **W:** radio2.si – **10)** Drofenikova 1, 3230 Šentjur **W:** stajerskival.si – **11)** Papirniški trg 17, 1260 Ljubljana-Polje **W:** veseljak.si – **12)** Tkalski prehod 4, 2000 Maribor **W:** radiomars.si – **13)** Trg Toneta Cufarja 4, 4270 Jesenice **W:** radiotriglav.si – **14)** Meškova 21, 2380 Slovenj Gradec **W:** koroski-radio.si – **15)** Stritarjeva 6, 4000 Kranj. **W:** radio-kranj.si – **17)** Kazarje 10, 6230 Postojna **W:** radio94.si – **18)** Osojnikova cesta 3, 2250 Ptuj **W:** radio-ptuj.si – **19)** Partizanska cesta 24, 2000 Maribor **W:** radiopohorje.si – **20)** Kromberk, Industrijska cesta 5, 5000 Nova Gorica **W:** robin.si – **21)** Papirniški trg 17, 1260 Ljubljana-Polje **W:** radioaktual.si – **22)** Loska ul. 13, 2000 Maribor **W:** radionet.si – **23)** Slovenska ul. 35, 2000 Maribor **W:** radiocity.si – **24)** Škalska 7, 3210 Slovenske Konjice **W:** radiorogla.si – **25)** Taborska cesta 38d, 1290 Grosuplje **W:** zelenival.com – **26)** Zelezna cesta 14, 1000 Ljubljana **W:** radiocenter.si – **27)** Partizanska cesta 24, 2000 Maribor **W:** radiobrezje.si – **30)** Trg Brolo Št 11, 6000 Koper **W:** radio.ognjisce.si – **32)** Prešernova 4, 5220 Tolmin **W:** primorskival.si D.Prgr:

1500-1900 Alpski Val. 1900-1500 Primorski Val (a joint programme of Alpski Val and R. Odmev) – **34)** Stegne 11B, 1000 Ljubljana **W:** hitradioantena.si – **35)** Stegne 21C, 1000 Ljubljana **W:** radioekspres.si – **36)** Ljubljanska Cesta 26, 8000 Novo Mesto **W:** radiokrka.com – **37)** Kidriceva 2B, 3320 Velenje **W:** mojradio.com – **40)** see A) – **41)** Prešernova 19, 3000 Celje **W:** radiocelje.si – **42)** Licarjeva 7, 5282 Cerkno **W:** primorskival.si D.Prgr: 1500-1900 R. Odmev & 1900-1500 Primorski Val (a joint programme of Alpski Val and R. Odmev) – **43)** Valanticevo 17, 8000 Novo Mesto **W:** radiosraka.com

DAB: Mux SLO DAB+ R1: Beli Kriz, Kranjska Gora, Krim, Krvavec, Kuk, Malic Laško, Ljubljana-Šance, Nanos, Plešivec, Pohorje, Skalnica, Tinjan, Tolmin, Trdinov vrh on 215.072 MHz (channel 10D): Slo1, Slo2, Slo3, R. SI, R. Ognjišce, R. Antena, R. Center, Rock R. Slovenija, R. 1 DAB, R. 2, Odprti R., R. Bob, R. Ekspres, R. Veseljak, R. Študent, R.Maxi, R. Net FM, R. Aktual – **Mux SLO DAB+ R2:** Boc, Plešivec, Pohorje, Trdinov vrh on 225.648 MHz (channel 12B) and Beli Kriz, Kuk, Nanos, Skalnica, Tinjan on 227.360 MHz (channel 12C) – **Mux SLO DAB+ R3:** Ljubljana-Šance on 194.064 MHz (channel 7D)
NB: Due to CoV-19 licensing process for programmes on R2 and R3 is delayed. At editorial deadline R3 is on the air with RTVSLO test programmes only, start of R2 is postponed

SOLOMON ISLANDS

L.T: UTC +11h — **Pop:** 695,000 — **Pr.L:** English (official), Pijin — **E.C:** 240V/50Hz — **ITU:** SLM

TELECOMMUNICATIONS COMMISSION OF THE SOLOMON ISLANDS (TCSI)

✉ 2nd Floor, Alvaro Building, Honiara ☎+677 23850 **W:** tcsi.org.sb
E: ictpolicy@tcsi.org.sb
Regulator of broadcasting in the Solomon Islands

SOLOMON ISLANDS BROADCASTING CORP. (Statutory Authority, Comm.)

✉ **Honiara**: P.O. Box 654, Honiara ☎ +677 20051 🖷 +677 23159. **W:** sibconline.com.sb **E:** sibcnews@solomon.com.sb **L.P:** GM: R. Buaoka. Wantok FM ☎ +677 29600 🖷 +677 29600 ✉ **Gizo**: P. O. Box 78, Gizo, Western Province ☎ +677 60160 ✉ **Lata**: P. O. Box 46, Lata, Santa Cruz ☎ +677 53047
SW relays SIBC MW. **Schedule:** 5020kHz 0500v-1200, 1900-2200, 9545kHz 2200-0500v. **FM format:** Common urban breakout 0600 for Wantok FM network otherwise relay SIBC 1035 AM//5020 SW.
D.Prgr: local 1900-0000, BBC 1300-1900 **N. in English:** 2000, 2200 (R. Australia), 0130W, 0200 (R. Australia), 0500, 0600 (BBC), 0730, 1000 (R. Australia), 1100 **Ann:** "This is the SIBC" **IS:** Drum and Bamboo Pipes **V.** by QSL-card

MW	**kHz**	**kW**	**Station**
Honiara, Guadalcanal	1035	6	SIBC
SW	**kHz**	**kW**	**Station**
Honiara, Guadalcanal	5020	10	SIBC
Honiara, Guadalcanal	9545	10	SIBC
FM	**MHz**	**kW**	**Station**
Gizo, Gizo Isl	96.3	*1	Gizo FM, SIBC
Honiara, Guadalcanal	96.3		Wantok FM, SIBC
Kirakira, Makiri Isl	96.3	*0.5	Kirakira FM, SIBC
Lata, Nendo Isl	96.3	*0.5	Lata FM, SIBC

NB: F.pl. power increase (*), and other provincial FM stns.

Other Stations:

FM	**MHz**	**kW**	**Station**
2) Honiara, Guadalcanal	88.1		Hope FM
3) Honiara, Guadalcanal	93.5		Laef FM
3) Munda, New Georgia	93.5	0.5	Laef FM
4) Gizo, Gizo Isl	95.3	0.5	One Life FM
4) Atoifi, Malaita	95.3	0.025	One Life FM
4) Takwa, Malaita	95.3	0.025	One Life FM
4) Kijabelo, Marovo	95.3	0.025	One Life FM
5) Honiara, Guadalcanal	97.7		Paoa FM
6) Honiara, Guadalcanal	99.5		ZFM
5) Auki, Malaita	101.7		Paoa FM
3) Auki, Malaita	103.9		Laef FM
7) Honiara, Guadalcanal	104.1	1	Barava FM
8) Honiara, Guadalcanal	105.9		BBC
9) Honiara, Guadalcanal	107.0		R. Australia

Addresses & other information
2) Kukum SDA church, Honiara. Solomon Islands Mission Office, PO Box R145, Honiara ☎ +677 39267/39269/39281 🖷 +677 38862 **W:** facebook.com/hopefm88.1 **E:** hopefm88.1@sim.adventist.org.sb – **3)** Ebenezer House, Vura, Honiara. **F.Pl:** Low power outlet on 107.5 at Gizo. Additional stn at Kirakira, Makira/Ulawa Province – **4)** P.O. Box 26, Gizo, Western Province. **L.P.** Station Manager, Derald Michael. E: klezyderaldmichael@gmail.com **F.Pl.:** All day broadcasting and new station at Lata, Temotu – **5)** PO Box R331, Panatina Plaza, Prince Philip Hwy, Honiara ☎+677 38984 🖷+677 38980 **W:** solomonstarnews.com & facebook.com/paoafm **E:** paoafm@solomon.com.sb or paoafm.news@gmail.com **L.P:** GM Joel Lamani, News Editor: Uriel Matangani **Other:** Pacific Star newspaper – **6)** P.O. Box 100, Honiara ☎+677 21100 🖷 +677 21100 **L.P:** Sammy 'Sharzy' Saeni **E:** zfm@solomon.com.sb – **7)** Big Maos Communications Ltd, PO Box 2025, Honiara. ☎+677 27104 **E:** barava104.1@gmail.com **L.P:** Station Manager: John Adifaka, Jnr. – **8)** 24/7 Pacific stream via satellite from London – **9)** 24/7 Pacific stream via satellite from Melbourne

SOMALIA

L.T: UTC +3h — **Pop:** 16 million — **Pr.L:** Somali (official), Arabic (official), English, Italian — **E.C:** 220V/50Hz — **ITU:** SOM

MINISTRY OF INFORMATION, CULTURE & TOURISM

✉ Mogadishu ☎ +252 612777736
W: moi.gov.so **E:** media@moi.gov.so

RADIO MOGADISHU (Gov.)

✉ Mogadishu ☎ +252 851013
W: radiomuqdisho.net **E:** radiomogadishu@gmail.com
FM: Dhusomareb 87.7, Adado/Guricel 88.5, Baledweyn/Galkacyo 88.8, Abudwaq/Mogadishu 90.0, Baidoa 99.9MHz.
D.Prgr: 24h in Somali, incl. limited English segments. Also rel. VOA Somali.
Ann: "Raadiyo Muqdisho, Codka Jamhuuriyadda Soomaaliya"

WARSAN RADIO

✉ Baidoa **W:** warsanradio.com **E:** warsanradiobaidoa@gmail.com
L.P: Dir: Mr. Hilal Sheikh Shueb.
SW: 7120kHz AM/U 0.1kW. **FM:** 88.2MHz. **D.Prgr:** 0300-1930.

Other stations:
Ciyaaraha FM, Mogadishu: 103.0MHz
Dalsan R: Baydhabo 87.7, Jowhar 88.2, Mogadishu 91.5MHz. **W:** radiodalsan.com
Gool FM, Mogadishu: 99.0MHz **W:** goolfm.net
Hubal FM: Mogadishu 99.5MHz **W:** hubalnews.net
Mustaqbal R: Mogadishu 89.7MHz. **W:** mustaqbalradio.net
R. Al Furqaan: Mogadishu 106.5MHz **W:** radioalfurqaan.com
R. Banadir: Mogadishu 103.4MHz **W:** radiobanadir.com
R. Bar-Kulan: Mogadishu 92.0/98.0MHz, Puntland: Bosaso 89.5MHz **W:** bar-kulan.com
R. Danan: Mogadishu 94.0MHz **W:** danannews.com
R. Kulmiye: Mogadishu 88.0MHz **W:** radiokulmiye.net
R. Hiddo, Mogadishu: 98.5MHz **W:** facebook.com/radiohiddo
R. Maanta: Mogadishu 95.5MHz **W:** radiomaanta.com
R. Risaala: Mogadishu 102.2MHz. Also rel. BBC **W:** radiorisaala.com
R. Simba: Mogadishu 95.0MHz 1kW **W:** simbanews.net
Star FM: Dhusamareb 88.5MHz, Mogadishu 97.0MHz **W:** starfmsomalia.com See main entry under Kenya
Vo Democracy (R. Xamar): Mogadishu: 93.5MHz **W:** xamarradio.com
BBC African Sce: Beledweyne 88.4, Kismayo 90.5, Baydhabo 90.8, Mogadishu 91.0, Marka 95.1, Jawhar 96.1, Galkacyo 96.6. Somaliland: Burco 88.8, Baki 89.0, Hargeisa 98.0MHz.
VOA Africa: Mogadishu 99.9MHz, Somaliland: Hargeisa 88.0 1kW.

SOMALILAND

(self-declared autonomous state in northwest Somalia)

RADIO HARGEISA

✉ Nala soo xidhiidh, Head Quarter, Near SLNTV, Hargeisa. **W:** radiohargaysa.net **E:** radiohargeisa@yahoo.com
SW: 7120kHz 100kW (inactive) **FM:** 89.7/98.0MHz 1kW.
D.Prgr in Somali/Amharic/English: 0330-2100, SW 0330-0500, 0900-1400, 1500-1900. **N.** in E: 1300, 1930.
Ann: "Halkani wa Radio Hargeysa, codka jamhuriyada Somaliland".

Other stations:
Koran R: Hargeisa 88.6MHz 0.3kW.

PUNTLAND

(self-declared autonomous state in northeast Somalia)

Horseed R: Bosaso 89.2MHz 1kW **W:** horseedmedia.net
R. Daljir: Burtinle/Garowe 88.0MHz, Bosaso/Buuhoodle/Cabudwaq/Qardho 88.8MHz, Galkacyo 89.1MHz **W:** daljir.com
R. Gaalkacyo: Gaalkacyo 88.2MHz, Garowe 89.0MHz **W:** facebook.com/radiogaalkacyo
R. Garowe: Eyl 88.8MHz, Garowe 89.5MHz. **W:** garoweonline.com
R. Midnimo: Bosaso 97.5MHz **W:** midnimo.com
SBC R.: Qardho 88.7, Bosaso 89.0, Garowe 89.2MHz **W:** allsbc.com
R. Vo Peace: Gaalkacyo 88.8MHz **W:** facebook.com/codkanabadda

SOUTH AFRICA

L.T: UTC +2h — **Pop**: 58 million — **Pr.L**: Official languages: Afrikaans, English, Ndebele, Northern Sotho, Sotho, SiSwati, Tsonga, Tswana, Venda, Xhosa, Zulu — **E.C**: 230V/50Hz — **ITU**: AFS

INDEPENDENT COMMUNICATIONS AUTHORITY OF SOUTH AFRICA (ICASA)

✉ Private Bag X10, Highveld Park, 0168 ☎ +27 12 568 3000 **E:** info@icasa.org.za **W:** icasa.org.za
The ICASA is the regulator of telecommunications and the broadcasting sectors. It issues licences for commercial and community stns.

SOUTH AFRICAN BROADCASTING CORPORATION (SABC) (Pub)

✉ Private Bag X1, Auckland Park 2006 ☎ +27 11 714 9111 🖷 +27 11 714 9744 **W:** sabc.co.za **E**: contactcentre@sabc.co.za **Regional offices:** PO Box 2551, Cape Town 8000 – PO Box 1588, Durban 4000 – PO Box 563, Bloemfontein 9300 – PO Box 1040, Port Elizabeth 6000 – PO Box 395, Polokwane 0700 – Private Bag X11301, Nelspruit 1200 – PO Box 1008, Kimberley 8300 – Private Bag X2158, Mafikeng 2735 – PO Box 1198, Hatfield (Pretoria) 0001. **L.P.**: Chmn: Bongumusa Makhatini Group CEO: Madoda Mxakwe COO: Ian Plaatjies GE Media Technology Infrastructure: Alan Visser
NB: All txs belong to SENTECH (the common carrier for broadcasting in South Africa), ✉ Private Bag X06, Honeydew 2040, **W**: www.sentech.co.za

MW HOME SERVICES (Comm.)

Location	Station	kHz	kW
Komga	Umhlobo Wenene FM	†846	50 (irr.)

COUNTRYWIDE FM (Comm.)

Limpopo FM (MHz)	R. Sonder Grense	SAfm	R. 2000	5 FM	R. Metro
Blouberg	102.3	105.9	-	-	-
Hoedspruit	102.0	105.6	98.5	-	-
Louis Trichardt	100.7	104.3	97.2	-	-
Modimolle	102.9	106.5	-	-	-
Mokopane	101.4	105.0	97.9	91.4	106.7
Thabazimbi	101.9	105.5	98.4	-	-
Tzaneen	102.6	106.2	107.7	-	-

NW Province FM (MHz)	R. Sonder Grense	SAfm	R. 2000	5 FM	R. Metro
Christiana	103.6	107.2	-	-	-
Groot Marico	102.3	105.9	-	-	-
Klerksdorp	101.2	104.8	97.7	-	-
Piet Plessis	102.8	106.4	-	-	-
Pomfret	101.1	104.7	-	-	-
Rustenburg	100.7	104.3	97.2	-	-
Schweizer-Reneke	103.1	106.7	99.6	-	-
Zeerust	102.6	106.2	99.1	-	-

Gauteng FM (MHz)	R. Sonder Grense	SAfm	R. 2000	5 FM	R. Metro
Heidelberg	100.8	104.4	97.3	-	-
Helderkruin	-	-	-	104.0	-
Johannesburg	101.5	105.1	99.7	98.0	96.4
Menlo Park	102.1	105.7	98.6	-	-
Pretoria	101.0	104.6	97.5	89.9	92.4
Sunnyside	-	-	-	103.6	-
Welverdiend	102.0	105.6	104.1	107.3	-

Mpumalanga FM (MHz)	R. Sonder Grense	SAfm	R. 2000	5 FM	R. Metro
Carolina	103.0	106.6	-	-	-
Davel	103.5	107.1	100.0	90.4	-
Dullstroom	100.8	104.4	-	-	-
Mashishing	102.8	106.4	-	-	-
eMalahleni	101.8	105.4	98.3	97.0	100.3
Nelspruit	102.5	106.1	99.0	91.1	-
Piet Retief	102.1	105.7	-	-	-
Sabie	104.2	107.9	-	-	-
Volksrust	102.6	106.2	-	-	-

Northern Cape FM (MHz)	R. Sonder Grense	SAfm	R. 2000	5 FM	R. Metro
Alexander Bay	102.2#	105.8#	98.7	92.2	
Calvinia	101.5	105.1	-	-	-
Carnavon	102.5	106.1	-	-	-
Colesberg	103.8	107.5	-	-	-
De Aar	102.0	105.6	-	-	-
Douglas	102.9	106.5	-	-	-
Faans Grove	103.0	106.6	-	-	-
Garies	100.7#	104.3#	-	-	-
Kimberley	101.0	104.6	97.5	91.0	-
Kuruman Hills	102.4	106.0	-	-	-
Pofadder	102.8	106.4	-	-	-
Prieska	100.8	104.4	-	-	-
Springbok	101.6	105.2	-	-	-
Upington	101.7	105.3	-	-	-
Victoria West	101.1	104.7	-	-	-
Williston	103.2	-	-	-	-

Free State FM (MHz)	R. Sonder Grense	SAfm	R. 2000	5 FM	R. Metro
Bethlehem	101.9	105.5	98.4	-	-
Bloemfontein	103.0	106.6	99.5	91.6	98.1
Boesmanskop	101.2	104.8	-	-	-
Ficksburg	103.7	107.3	-	-	-
Kroonstad	103.4	107.0	99.9	93.4	-
Ladybrand	102.1	105.7	-	-	-
Petrus Steyn	102.3	105.9	98.8	-	-
Senekal	101.1	104.7	97.6	-	-
Springfontein	102.6	106.2	99.1	-	-
Theunissen	102.5	106.1	99.0	92.5	-
Witsieshoek	101.3	104.9	-	-	-

Kwazulu Natal FM (MHz)	R. Sonder Grense	SAfm	R. 2000	5 FM	R. Metro
Donnybrook	102.7	106.3	99.2	-	-
Durban	100.8	104.4	97.3	89.9	93.0
Durban North	102.5	106.1	99.0	103.8	107.9
Eshowe	103.4	107.0	99.9	-	90.3
Glencoe	103.1	106.7	99.6	-	-
Greytown	101.7	105.3	98.2	-	-
Kokstad	101.0	104.6	-	-	-
Ladysmith	101.0	104.6	97.5	-	-
Matatiele	101.5	105.1	-	-	-
Mooi River	102.2	105.8	98.7	-	-
Nongoma	102.9	106.5	99.4	-	89.8
Pietermaritzburg	101.4	105.0	97.9	100.3	-
Port Shepstone	101.3	104.9	97.8	-	-
The Bluff	102.0	105.6	98.5	107.4	-
Ubombo	102.4	106.0	98.9	-	-
Vryheid	101.2	104.8	97.7	-	-

Western Cape FM (MHz)	R. Sonder Grense	SAfm	R. 2000	5 FM	R. Metro
Beaufort West	100.7@	104.3@	-	-	-
Constantiaberg	102.1	105.7	98.6	89.0	-
Ceres	103.7	107.3	-	-	-
Franschhoek	100.7	104.3	97.2	-	-
George	101.7	105.3	98.2	91.7	-
Grabouw	101.7	105.3	-	-	-
Hermanus	100.8	104.4	-	-	-
Hex River	102.0	105.6	-	-	-
Hout Bay	100.9	104.5	97.4	87.8	-
Kleinmond	104.2	107.9	-	-	-
Knysna	102.2	105.8	98.7	92.2	-
Ladysmith	101.4	105.0	-	-	-
Matjiesfontein	102.8	106.4	-	-	-
Montagu	104.2	107.9	-	-	-
Napier	102.4	106.0	-	-	-
Oudtshoorn	102.6	106.2	99.1	92.6	-
Paarl	101.6	105.2	98.1	88.5	-
Piketberg	101.1	104.7	97.6	-	-
Plettenberg	100.8	104.4	-	-	-
Riversdale	100.9	104.5	-	-	-
Sea Point	103.5	107.1	100.0	90.4	91.7
Simonstown	100.7	104.3	97.2	87.6	-

FM (MHz)	R. Sonder Grense	SAfm	R. 2000	5 FM	R. Metro
Stellenbosch	100.9	104.5	97.4	87.8	-
Table Mountain	102.6	106.2	99.1	89.9	88.6
Tygerberg	103.0	106.6	99.5	88.2	93.0
Uniondale	103.4	107.0	-	-	-
Vanrhynsdorp	103.4	107.0	-	-	-
Villiersdorp	103.3	106.9	99.8	-	-
Eastern Cape FM (MHz)	**R. Sonder Grense**	**SAfm**	**R. 2000**	**5 FM**	**R. Metro**
Aliwal North	101.7	105.3	-	-	-
Andrieskraal	103.2	106.8	-	-	-
Barkly East	100.9	104.5	-	-	-
Bedford	100.8	104.4	-	-	-
Burgersdorp	103.9	107.6	-	-	-
Butterworth	101.1	104.7	97.6	-	-
Cala	103.4	107.0	-	-	-
Cradock	102.7	106.3	-	-	-
East London	101.6	105.2	98.1	88.5	107.7
Elliot	101.4	105.0	-	-	-
Graaff-Reinet	103.3	106.9	-	-	-
Grahamstown	103.5	107.1	100.0	90.4	-
Hankey	101.0	104.6	-	-	-
Kareedouw	102.9	106.5	-	-	-
King Williams Tn	103.0	106.6	-	-	-
Mount Ayliff	103.2	106.8	99.7	-	-
Noupoort	101.4	105.0	-	-	-
Patensie	101.5	105.0	-	-	-
Parsons Hill (PE)	101.0	104.6	97.5	-	87.9
Paul Sauer Dam	103.6	107.2	-	-	-
Port Elizabeth	102.3	105.9	98.8	89.2	100.5
Port St.Johns	103.7	107.3	100.2	-	-
Queenstown	102.2	105.8	98.7	-	-
Suurberg	101.8	105.4	-	-	-
Ugie	102.6	106.2	-	-	-
Umtata	102.0	105.6	98.5	-	-
Willowmore	101.2	104.8	-	-	-

= mono – no RDS @ = mono RDS

SABC PUBLIC BROADCASTING SERVICES (PBS) (Comm.)
Ikwekwezi FM (isiNdebele): ✉ P.O.Box 11620, Hatfield 0028 **W:** ikwekwezifm.co.za ☎+27 12 431 5477 🖷+27 12 431 5312 - **FM**(MHz): Middelburg 91.8/Pretoria 96.8/Dullstroom 107.7/Johannesburg 106.3/Davel 94.5 + 4 rel. – **Lesedi FM** (Sesotho): ✉ PO Box 20707, Bloemfontein 9300 **W:** lesedifm.co.za ☎+27 51 503 3090 🖷+27 51 503 3269 - **FM**(MHz): Bloemfontein 89.9/Durban 106.6/ Johannesburg 88.4/Kroonstad 90.3 + 13 rel. – **Ligwalagwala FM** (siSwati): ✉ Private Bag X11301, Nelspruit 1200 **W:** ligwalagwalafm.co.za ☎+27 13 759 6611 🖷+27 13 755 3065 - **FM**(MHz): Nelspruit 92.5/Pretoria 89.3/Middelburg 103.9 + 8 FM rel. – **Lotus FM** ✉ PO Box 1588, Durban 4000 **W:** lotusfm co.za ☎ +27 31 362 5444 - **FM**(MHz): Durban 87.7/Johannesburg 106.8/Pretoria 100.3/Port Elizabeth 98.3 + 8 rel. – **Motsweding FM** (Setswana): ✉ Private Bag X2150, Mmabatho 2735 **W:** motswedingfm.co.za ☎+27 18 389 7111 🖷+27 18 389 7326 - **FM**(MHz): Mmabatho 88.7/Johannesburg 89.6/Bloemfontein 93.0/Pretoria 91.0/Rustenburg 87.6/Blouberg 92.3 + 22 rel. – **Munghana Lonene FM** (xiTsonga): ✉ PO Box 395, Polokwane 0700 **W:** munghanalonenefm.co.za ☎+27 15 290 0262 🖷+27 15 290 0171 - **FM**(MHz): Johannesburg 103.2/Pretoria 95.6/ Tzaneen 92.6/Nelspruit 89.4 + 4 rel. – **Phalaphala FM** (TshiVenda): ✉ PO Box 985, Polokwane 0700 **W:** phalaphalafm.co.za ☎+27 15 290 0260 🖷+27 15 290 0170 - **FM**(MHz): Johannesburg 107.8/ Louis Trichard 90.7/Tzaneen 99.1 + 11 rel. – **Radio Sonder Grense** (National service in Afrikaans): ✉ Private Bag X1, Auckland Park 2006 **W:** rsg.co.za ☎+27 11 714 2244 - on FM (as above) – **Radio X-K FM** (in !Xu and Khwe languages for Khoi San communities in N.Cape): ✉ PO Box 1008, Kimberley 8300 ☎+27 53 831 8131 🖷+27 53 831 8127 - **FM**(MHz): Kimberley 107.9 – **R.2000** ✉ Private Bag X1, Auckland Park 2006 **W:** radio2000.co.za ☎+27 11 714 4085 - **FM:** (as above) – **SAfm** (Nat. sce in English): ✉ PO Box 91162, Auckland Park 2006 **W:** safm.co.za ☎ +27 11 714 4442 🖷+27 11 714 5829 - **FM:** (as above) – **Thobela FM** (Sepedi): ✉ PO Box 395, Polokwane 0700 **W:** thobelafm.co.za ☎+27 15 290 0264 🖷+27 15 290 0172 - **FM**(MHz): Johannesburg 90.1/Pretoria 87.9/Tzaneen 89.5+ 9 rel. – **TruFM** (isiXhosa & English): ✉ Private Bag X0037, Bhisho 5605 **W:** trufm.co.za ☎+27 40 609 1800 🖷+27 40 636 4112 - **FM**(MHz): East London 104.1/Bhisho 100.0 + 2 rel. – **Ukhozi FM** (isiZulu): ✉ PO Box 1588, Durban 4000 **W:** ukhozifm.co.za ☎+27 31 362 5111 🖷+27 31 362 5203 - **FM**(MHz): Durban 90.8, 92.0, 92.5/Johannesburg 91.5/Pretoria 102.4 + 21 rel. – **Umhlobo Wenene FM** (isiXhosa): ✉ PO Box 1040, Port Elizabeth 6000 **W:** umhlobowenenefm.co.za ☎+27 41 391 1911 - **FM**(MHz): Port Elizabeth 92.3/King Williams Town 93.0/Durban 96.2/ Johannesburg 93.2/Cape Town 92.1/Bloemfontein 94.8 + 46 FM rel.

SABC COMMERCIAL BROADCASTING SERVICES (CBS) (Comm.)
Good Hope FM ✉ PO Box 2551, Cape Town 8000 ☎ +27 21 430 8276 🖷 +27 21 434 3392 **W:** goodhopefm.co.za - **FM:** Cape Town 95.3MHz + 7 rel – **R. Metro FM** ✉ PO Box 91136, Auckland Park 2006 **W:** metrofm.co.za ☎ +27 89 110 3377 🖷+27 11 714 4166 - **FM:** (as above) – **5 FM** ✉ PO Box 91555, Auckland Park 2006 ☎ +27 11 714 2905 🖷 +27 11 714 5714 **W:** 5fm.co.za - **FM:** (as above)

PRIVATE STATIONS (Comm.) – (Excl. v. low power repeaters)

MW	kHz	kW	Station	Location
1)	567	25	Cape Talk	Klipheuwel (Cape Town)
20)	702	50	LM R.	Springs
21)	828	25	Magic 828 AM	Klipheuwel (Cape Town)
FM	**MHz**	**kW**	**Station**	**Location**
12)	88.6	10	Gagasi FM	Greytown
15)	88.8	0.1	Heart FM	Hermanus
2)	89.0	8.9	Rise FM	Piet Retief
12)	89.1	10	Gagasi FM	Mooi River
2)	89.7	0.01	Rise FM	Mashishing
3)	89.8	4	You FM	Rustenburg
4)	89.9	-	Capricorn FM	Thohoyandou
18)	90.4	10	Smile FM	Cape Town
7)	91.5		KFM	Camps Bay
4)	91.7	10	Capricorn FM	Pankop
3)	91.8	10	You FM	Mmbabatho
3)	91.9	5	You FM	Taung
5)	92.7	3.5	Talk R. 702	Johannesburg
3)	93.5	11	You FM	Zeerust
6)	93.7	0.5	OFM	Sasolburg
7)	93.9	10	KFM	Beaufort West
7)	93.9	3	KFM	Garies
8)	93.9	4	R. Jacaranda	Rustenburg
8)	93.9	15	R. Jacaranda	Louis Trichardt
9)	94.0	0.04	Algoa FM	Plettenberg Bay
9)	94.0	5	Algoa FM	Bedford
8)	94.0	10	R. Jacaranda	Dullstroom
6)	94.0	9	OFM	Prieska
6)	94.0	0.65	OFM	Potchefstroom
10)	94.0	25	East Coast R.	Durban
11)	94.0	0.1	Highveld Stereo	Heidelberg
7)	94.0	0.1	KFM	Hermanus
7)	94.1	13	KFM	Riversdale
8)	94.2	110	R. Jacaranda	Pretoria
9)	94.2	0.1	Algoa FM	Parson's Hill
10)	94.2	0.05	Kokstad	East Coast R.
10)	94.2	0.1	East Coast R.	Ladysmith
6)	94.2	10	OFM	Kimberley
6)	94.3	10	OFM	Senekal
7)	94.3	10	KFM	Piketberg
2)	94.3	12	Rise FM	Nelspruit
9)	94.3	0.2	Algoa FM	Knysna
10)	94.4	10	East Coast R.	Vryheid
6)	94.4	22	OFM	Bosmanskop
6)	94.4	10	OFM	Klerksdorp
10)	94.5	10	East Coast R.	Port Shepstone
7)	94.5	1.3	KFM	Tygerberg
7)	94.6	2.5	KFM	Ladismith
8)	94.6	10	R. Jacaranda	Mokopane
10)	94.6	0.3	East Coast R.	Pietermaritzburg
9)	94.6	10	Algoa FM	Noupoort
12)	94.7	30	Gagasi FM	Ulundi
12)	94.7	-	Gagasi FM	Richards Bay
10)	94.7	12	East Coast R.	Matatiele
11)	94.7	38	R. 947	Johannesburg
7)	94.7	10	KFM	Calvinia
7)	94.8	10	KFM	Springbok
2)	94.8	8.9	Rise FM	Carolina
8)	94.8	0.3	R. Jacaranda	Enzelberg
9)	94.8	10	Algoa FM	East London
9)	94.8	0.01	Algoa FM	Patensie
7)	94.9	0.01	KFM	Grabow
7)	94.9	10	KFM	George
6)	94.9	8	OFM	Upington
10)	94.9	10	East Coast R.	Greytown
9)	94.9	10	Algoa FM	Aliwal North
9)	95.0	11	Algoa FM	Port Elizabeth

FM	MHz	kW	Station	Location
8)	95.0	11	R. Jacaranda	Middelburg
6)	95.1	10	OFM	Bethlehem
8)	95.1	11	R. Jacaranda	Thabazimbi
8)	95.2	18	R. Jacaranda	Hoedspruit
7)	95.2	0.2	KFM	Hex River
11)	95.2	20	Highveld Stereo	Welverdiend
10)	95.2	0.1	East Coast R.	The Bluff
8)	95.3	0.04	R. Jacaranda	Menlo Park
8)	95.3	9	R. Jacaranda	Piet Retief
6)	95.3	10	OFM	Ladybrand
9)	95.4	12	Algoa FM	Queenstown
10)	95.4	10	East Coast R.	Mooi River
7)	95.4	0.05	KFM	Alexander Bay
7)	95.4	0.2	KFM	Knysna
8)	95.5	0.13	R. Jacaranda	Groot Marico
8)	95.5	0.2	R. Jacaranda	Blouberg
6)	95.5	11	OFM	Petrus Steyn
9)	95.5	-	Algoa FM	Jeffreys Bay
9)	95.5	16	Algoa FM	Port Elizabeth
10)	95.6	15	East Coast R.	Ubombo
6)	95.6	11	OFM	Kuruman Hills
7)	95.6	3	KFM	Napier
7)	95.6	2.5	KFM	Ladismith
10)	95.7	6	East Coast R.	Durban North
8)	95.7	12	R. Jacaranda	Nelspruit
6)	95.7	10	OFM	Theunissen
7)	95.7	10	KFM	Carnavon
7)	95.8	9	KFM	Oudtshoorn
8)	95.8	10	R. Jacaranda	Volksrust
8)	95.8	11	R. Jacaranda	Zeerust
8)	95.8	12	R. Jacaranda	Tzaneen
6)	95.8	-	OFM	Colesberg
10)	95.9	10	East Coast R.	Donnybrook
9)	95.9	12	Algoa FM	Cradock
13)	95.9	35	Kaya FM	Johannesburg
8)	96.0	0.01	R. Jacaranda	Mashishing
9)	96.0	10	Algoa FM	George
4)	96.0	10	Capricorn FM	Mokopane
7)	96.0	10	KFM	Matjiesfontein
7)	96.0	5	KFM	Pofadder
6)	96.1	9	OFM	Douglas
8)	96.1	0.2	R. Jacaranda	Modimole
10)	96.1	10	East Coast R.	Nongoma
9)	96.1	6	Algoa FM	Kareedouw
9)	96.2	10	Algoa FM	King Williams Town
6)	96.2	10	OFM	Bloemfontein
8)	96.2	9	R. Jacaranda	Carolina
10)	96.3	10	East Coast R.	Glencoe
6)	96.3	10	OFM	Schweitzer-Reineke
9)	96.4	0.01	Algoa FM	Andrieskraal
9)	96.5	10	Algoa FM	Graaf-Reinet
7)	96.5	10	KFM	Villiersdorp
7)	96.6	17	KFM	Vanrhynsdorp
10)	96.6	10	East Coast R.	Eshowe
6)	96.6	10	OFM	Kroonstad
9)	96.7	-	Algoa FM	Port Alfred
9)	96.7	10	Algoa FM	Grahamstown
8)	96.7	10	R. Jacaranda	Davel
6)	96.8	11	OFM	Christiana
10)	96.9	1	East Coast R.	Newcastle
7)	96.9	20	KFM	Ceres
6)	96.9	0.01	OFM	Ficksburg
3)	97.0	10	You FM	Klerksdorp
8)	97.1	0.02	R. Jacaranda	Sabie
7)	97.1	0.08	KFM	Kleinmond
7)	97.1	0.02	KFM	Montagu
3)	97.3	10-	You FM	Schweitzer Reneke
4)	97.6	12	Capricorn FM	Tzaneen
4)	98.0	18	Capricorn FM	Hoedspruit
12)	98.5	0.1	Gagasi FM	Pietermaritzburg
17)	98.7	11	Power FM	Johannesburg
14)	99.2	35	Y-FM	Johannesburg
3)	99.4	-	You FM	Potchefstroom
12)	99.5	25	Gagasi FM	Durban
15)	100.0	0.02	Heart FM	Fishhoek
12)	100.1	6	Gagasi FM	Durban North
7)	100.1	-	KFM	Hout Bay
2)	101.6	10	Rise FM	Dullstroom
15)	102.7	0.1	Heart FM	Paarl
16)	102.7	35	Classic FM	Johannesburg
19)	103.0	5	Vuma FM	Umhlanga
12)	103.5	10	Gagasi FM	Port Shepstone
17)	103.6	-	Power FM	Soweto
3)	103.9	8	You FM	Garankuwa
17)	104.4	-	Power FM	Vaal
15)	104.9	0.25	Heart FM	Tygerberg
4)	105.4	15	Capricorn FM	Makhado
2)	105.8	10	Rise FM	Davel
5)	106.0	33	Talk R. 702	Pretoria
15)	106.3	-	Heart FM	West Coast
2)	106.4	11	Rise FM	eMalahleni
15)	107.0	0.02	Heart FM	Hout Bay
7)	107.2	-	KFM	Stellenbosch
17)	107.2	-	Power FM	Erkuhukeni
15)	107.8	0.01	Heart FM	Grabow
12)	107.9	-	Gagasi FM	Newcastle

Addresses & other information:

1) Private Bag 567, Vlaeberg 8018 ☎ +27 21 446 4700 **W:** capetalk.co.za **E:** comments@capetalk.co.za – **2)** Shop 38, The Grove Shopping Centre, Cnr. R40 & George St., Riverside Park, Nelspruit, 1201 ☎ +27 13 757 0263 **LP**: Mark Schormann **W:** risefm.co.za **E:** info@risefm.co.za – **3)** 214 Beyers Naude Dr., Rustenburg 2999 ☎ +27 861 444 898 **LP:** Lawrence Tlhabane **W:** youfm.co.za **E:** info@youfm.co.za – **4)** Postnet Suite 93, Private Bag X9676, Polokwane, 0700 ☎ +27 15 590 0900 **LP**: Simphiwe Mdlalose **W:** capricornfm.co.za **E:** info@capricornfm.co.za – **5)** PO Box 5572, Rivonia 2128. ☎ +27 (11) 506 3200 **W:** 702.co.za **E:** comment@702.co.za – **6)** PO Box 7117, Bloemfontein 9300 ☎ +27 51 505 0900 🖹 +27 51 505 0905 **LP**: Nick Efstathiou **W:** ofm.co.za **E:** info@ofm.co.za – **7)** Private Bag X945, Cape Town, 8000 ☎ +27 21 446 4700 **W:** kfm.co.za **E:** kfm@kfm.co.za – **8)** PO Box 11961, Centurion 0046 ☎ +27 11 063 5700 **LP**: Alan Khan **W:** jacarandafm.com **E:** enquiries@jacarandafm.com – **9)** PO Box 5973, Walmer, 6065 ☎ +27 41 505 9497 **LP**: Dave Tiltmann **W:** algoafm.co.za **E:** info@algoafm.co.za – **10)** P.O. Box 25095, Gateway, Umhlanga Rocks 4321 ☎ +27 31 570 9495 🖹 +27 86 679 4951. **LP:** Trish Taylor **W:** ecr.co.za **E:** hazelp@ecr.co.za – **11)** PO Box 3438, Rivonia 2128 ☎ +27 11 506 3947 🖹 +27 86 501 2014 **LP**: Tery Volkwyn **W:** 947.co.za **E:** webmaster947@947.co.za – **12)** U128 Cornubia Mall, Fkanders & Tacoma Dr., Blackburn Estate, Mount Edgecombe, 4319 ☎ +27 31 580 5300 **LP:** Pearl Sokhulu **W:** gagasiworld.co.za **E:** info@gagasiworld.co.za – **13)** PO Box 395, Parklands, 2112 **W:** kayafm.co.za ☎ +27 11 634 9500 **LP**: Charlene Deacon **E:** pr@kayafm.co.za – **14)** 2 Abury Rd., Dunkeld Cresc., Dunkeld West Ext.8, Sandton, 2196 ☎ +27 11 772 0800 **LP**: Kanthan Pillay **W:** yfm.co.za **E:** info@yfm.co.za – **15)** Second Floor, Media Centre, Greenpoint 8051 ☎ +27 21 406 8900 **LP**: Gavin Meiring **W:** heartfm.co.za **E:** info@heartfm.co.za – **16)** PO Box 782, Auckland Park 2006 ☎ +27 10 590 4554 **LP**: Mike Ford **W:** classic1027.co.za **E:** info@classic1027.co.za – **17)** 79 Central St., Houghton Estate, 2198 **W:** power987.co.za **E:** info@power987.co.za **LP**: Dawn Klatzko ☎ +27 11 014 9200 – **18)** PO Box 50194, Waterfront, 8002 ☎+27 21 818 8904 🖹+27 21 818 8810 **LP**: Lois O'Brien **W:** smile904.fm **E:** lois@smile904.fm – **19)** 6th Floor, Centenary Building, Cnr. Equinox & Zenith Dr., Umhlanga New Town Centre, Unhlanga Rocks, 4319 ☎+27 31 833 3000 **LP**: Patrick Bogatsu **W:** vumafm.co.za **E**: zamak@vumafm.co.za – **20)** Genesis House, 18 Wessel Road, Rivonia 2128 ☎+27 11 234 2691 **W:** lmradio.co.za **E:** studio@lmradio.net - **21)** DBN Gardens, Golf Park, 45 Raapenberg Rd., Mowbray, 7700 ☎+27 21 001 4828 **LP**: Frank Creese **W**: magic828@co.za **E**: info@magic828@co.za

COMMUNITY AND RELIGIOUS STATIONS

Numerous licences issued by ICASA with about 200 stns currently on the air, mainly on FM, most of them low power.

MW	kHz	kW	Station	Location
1)	576	50	R. Veritas	Meyerton
2)	657	50	R. Pulpit/R.Kansel	Meyerton
7)	729	25	Cape Pulpit	Klipheuwel (Cape Town)
3)	1269	2	Arrowline Chinese R.	Edenvale
9)	1368	0.4	Eden R.	Edenvale (irr)
4)	1422	1	Hellenic R.	Bedfordview
5)	1485	1	R. Today	Honeydew
6)	1548	10	R. Islam	Lenasia
8)	1584	0.25	R. 1584	Laudium (Pretoria)

Addresses & other information:

1) PO Box 4599, Edenvale 1610 **W:** radioveritas.co.za ☎ +27 11 663 4700 🖹 +27 11 452 7625 **LP:** Fr. Emil Blaser OP – **2)** 42 Jakobus Street, Kilner Park, 0186 **W:** radiokansel.co.za or radiopulpit.co.za **E:** gospel@

radiopulpit.co.za ☎ +27 12 334 1200 🖷 +27 86 663 0766 Relig. prgrs in English, Afrikaans and other African languages, 24h – **3)** PO Box 2241, Edenvale 1610 **W:** arrowline.co.za **E:** info@arrowline.co.za ☎ +27 11 454 5808 🖷 +27 86 685 2447 prgrs in Chinese, 24 h – **4)** PO Box 4077, Edenvale 1610 ☎ +27 11 453 3786 🖷 +27 86 591 5621 **W:** hellenicradio.org.za **E:** info@hellenicradio.org.za **LP:** Tulla Critsotakis, Prgrs in Greek and English 24h – **5)** PO Box 2820, Parklands 2121 **W:** 1485.org.za ☎ +27 11 880 0329 🖷 +27 86 601 2950 **E:** info@1485.org.za **LP**: Daryl Peel, Prgrs in English for over 50s, rel. BBCWS 2300-0400, 24h – **6)** PO Box 2580, Lenasia, 1820 **W:** radioislam.org.za **E:** support@radioislam.co.za ☎ +27 11 854 7022 Prgrs in English, 24h – **7)** 2nd floor, Santyger Building, Willie van Schoor Drive, Bellville, 7535 ☎+27 21 917 7000 **W:** capepulpit.co.za **E:** gospel@capepulpit.co.za relig. prgrs in English, Afrikaans, Zulu and Xhoza, 24h – **8)** PO Box 46001, Belle Ombre 0142☎+27 12 374 1584 🖷+27 12 374 2488 **W:** radio1584.co.za **E:** islamic1584@gmail.com prgrs of Institute for Islamic Services, 24h – **9)** Park Meadows Shopping Centre, Cor. Cumberland & Allum Rds., Bedfordview, 2416 ☎+27 84 585 2001 **W**: edenradio.co.za **E**: studio@edenradio.co.za **LP:** Nick Megens, Stn. Manager, 24h **F.PI**: relaunch early 2021 with 5kW

SOUTH SUDAN

L.T: UTC +3h — **Pop:** 11 million — **Pr.L:** Arabic (official), English (official), Dinka, Juba Arabic, Nuer — **E.C:** 230V/50Hz — **ITU:** SSD

SOUTH SUDAN MEDIA AUTHORITY (SSMA)

🖃 Juba ☎+211 95 5010147 **L.P:** MD: Elijah Alier Kuai.

SOUTH SUDAN BROADCASTING CORPORATION (SSBC, Gov.)

🖃 P.O. Box 126, Juba ☎+211 91 2452275 **L.P:** DG: Mr. Arop Bagat. Dir. of Eng: Kamil Ramadan.
MW: Juba 693kHz (inactive). **FM:** Bentiu 99.0MHz, Juba 105.0MHz, Kwajok 99.0MHz, Rumbek 98.0MHz, Torit/Kapoeta 97.5MHz, Yambio 90.0MHz 1kW.
F.PI: on 693 kHz a new 50 kW transmitter being installed.

RADIO MIRAYA (operated by UN Mission in South Sudan)
N.B: operation suspended in early 2018 by South Sudan Media Authority.
🖃 c/o UNMISS, Tongping, Juba, Central Equatoria State ☎+211 91 2062616 **W:** radio-miraya.org facebook.com/radiomiraya **E:** mirayafm@un.org **L.P:** Chief of Op: Ratomir Petrovic. Head of Tech. Op: Sonam Tobgyal.
FM: Bor/Juba/Malakal/Rumbek/Wau 5kW, Aweil/Bentiu/Bunj/Ezo/Melut/Naseer/Pibor/Turalei 1kW, all on 101.0MHz, Kuajok/Torit/Yambio/Yei 101.5 1kW, Ar-Rank/Raja/Gok-Machar 101.0 250W, Kapoeta/Maridi/Mundri 101.5 250W. 24h in Arabic and English.

EYE RADIO (joint project of Internews and Eye Media)
🖃 P.O. Box 425, Plot 48, Block 1 Korok, Juba ☎ +211 92 4486980 **W:** eyeradio.org **L.P:** CEO: Stephen Omiri.
FM: Juba 98.6 2kW, Aweil/Bor/Rumbek/Wau 88.6,Kuajok 88.8, Torit 98.8, Yambio 89.0, all 500W.

CATHOLIC RADIO NETWORK (Rlg.)

🖃 P.O. Box 258, Hai Jerusalem, Juba ☎ +211 92 4217188 **W:** catholicradionetwork.org **E:** crn.director@gmail.com **L.P:** Dir: Enrica Valentini.
Stations: Bakhita R, Juba: 91.0 – **Easter R,** Yei: 94.0 1kW – **Good News R,** Rumbek: 89.0 2.5kW – **R. Anisa,** Yambio: 92.0 – **R. Don Bosco,** Tonj: 91.0 2kW – **R. Emmanuel,** Torit: 89.0 – **Vo Hope,** Wau: 98.65 – **Vo Love,** Malakal: 93.6 2kW – **Vo Peace,** Gidel: 107.9.

INTERNEWS stations: **Akol Yam,** Aweil 91.0 – **JamJang FM,** Ajuong Thok 89.4 600W – **Kondial FM,** Bentiu 97.2 600W – **Mayardit FM,** Turalei 90.7 1kW – **Mingkaman 100 FM,** Mingkaman: 100.0 MHz – **Nile FM,** Malakal: 98.0 600W – **Nhomlaau FM,** Malualkon 88.0 1kW – **Singaita FM,** Kapoeta 88.0 1.5kW **W:** internews.org – **Vo Freedom,** Magwi: 93.0 **W:** facebook.com/93fm-Voice-of-Freedom-Magwi-741739775952307

Other Stations (FM MHz):
Amadi FM, Mundri: 93.8 **W:** facebook.com/Amadi-FM-938-101638888392187 – **Capital FM,** Juba: 89.0 **W:** capitalfmjuba.com – **City FM,** Juba: 88.4 **W:** facebook.com/88.4CityFmJuba – **Classic FM,** Juba: 92.4 **W:** facebook.com/Classicfm924 – **Equatoria R,** Juba: 89.4 **W:** facebook.com/EquatorBroadcastingCorporation – **Jesus' Voice,** Juba: 90.3 **W:** facebook.com/JICS-FM-RADIO-1827281477489409 – **Malakal FM,** Malakal: 105.0 – **Nehemiah Trumpet Call R,** Nimule: 97.3 350W **W:** operationsnehemiah.org/#!nehemiah-gospel-radio-973-fm/cis7 – **Malakal FM,** Malakal: 105.0 – **R. Jonglei,** Bor: 95.9 **W:** facebook.com/RadioJonglei959Fm – **R. Magwi,** Magwi: 92.5 – **R. One,** Juba: 87.9 **W:** facebook.com/RadioOneSouthSudan – **Raja FM,** Raja: 95.0 – **Sama FM,** Juba: 99.3 **W:** facebook.com/SAMA-FM-993-157712584921735 – **Spirit FM,** Yei: 99.9 – **Top FM,** Juba: 90.7 **W:** facebook.com/Topfmjuba – **Wau FM,** Wau: 88.6
BBC World Sce: Juba 88.2 (English), Juba/Malakal/Wau 90.0 (Arabic).
R.France Int.: Juba 91.4MHz.
VOA Africa: Juba 93.6MHz

SPAIN

L.T: UTC +1h (28 Mar-31 Oct: +2h) — **Pop:** 46 million — **Pr.L:** Spanish (Castilian) (official), Basque, Catalan, Galician — **E.C:** 230V/50Hz — **ITU:** E

MINISTERIO DE FOMENTO

Secretaría General de Comunicaciones
🖃 Paseo de la Castellana, 67, Palacio de Comunicaciones, 28071 Madrid **W:** fomento.gob.es **E:** fomento@fomento.es

COMISIÓN NACIONAL DE LOS MERCADOS Y LA COMPETENCIA

🖃 Directorate for Telecommunications and Audiovisual, Carrer de Bolívia 56, 08018 Barcelona ☎ +34 93 6036126 **E:** internacional-dtysa@cnmc.es **W:** www.cnmc.es **L.P:** Dir (Directorate for Telecommunications and Audiovisual): Alejandra de Iturriaga

RADIO NACIONAL DE ESPAÑA (RNE) (Pub)

🖃 Casa de la Radio, Avenida de la Radio y la Televisión, 4, Prado del Rey, 28223 Pozuelo de Alarcón
☎ +34 91 581 70 00 🖷 +34 91 346 1769 **W:** rne.es **E:** rtve.dircom@rtve.es
RNE1 (R. Nacional) and **RNE5** (R. 5 Todo Noticias)

MW	kHz	kW	Net	Rg	Location
AS01)	531	20	RNE5	AS	Oviedo °
AN02)	531	10	RNE5	AN	Córdoba
GA02)	531	10	RNE5	GA	Pontevedra
NA01)	531	10	RNE5	NA	Pamplona °
VA01)	558	50	RNE5	VA	València °
GA01)	558	20	RNE5	GA	A Coruña °
EU02)	558	20	RNE5	EU	Donosti-San Sebastián
MU01)	567	50	RNE5	MU	Murcia °
CA01)	576	100	RNE5	CA	Barcelona °
MA01)	585	600	RNE1	MA	Madrid °
AN01)	603	50	RNE5	AN	Sevilla °
CL02)	603	10	RNE5	CL	Palencia
CA02)	612	10	RNE1	CA	Lleida (relay)
EU01)	612	10	RNE1	EU	Vitoria-Gasteiz °
AN04)	621	10	RNE1	AN	Jaén (relay)
BA01)	621	10	RNE1	BA	Palma de Mallorca °
CL03)	621	10	RNE1	CL	Avila (relay)
GA01)	639	300	RNE1	GA	A Coruña °
AR01)	639	50	RNE1	AR	Zaragoza °
EU03)	639	50	RNE1	EU	Bilbo-Bilbao (relay)
AN05)	639	20	RNE1	AN	Almería (relay)
CM03)	639	10	RNE1	CM	Albacete (relay)
EX02)	648	10	RNE1	EX	Badajoz (relay)
MA01)	657	50	RNE5	MA	Madrid °
AN01)	684	600	RNE1	AN	Sevilla °
AS01)	693	5	RNE1	AS	Boal (rel. of Oviedo)
CM01)	693	20	RNE1	CM	Toledo °
CA03)	693	10	RNE1	CA	Tortosa (rel.of Catalunya)
AS01)	729	100	RNE1	AS	Oviedo °
AN06)	729	20	RNE1	AN	Málaga
RI01)	729	20	RNE1	RI	Logroño °
CL01)	729	10	RNE1	CL	Valladolid °
CM04)	729	10	RNE1	CM	Cuenca
VA02)	729	10	RNE1	VA	Alacant-Alicante (relay)
CA01)	738	600	RNE1	CA	Barcelona °
AN07)	747	10	RNE5	AN	Cádiz
VA01)	774	100	RNE1	VA	València °
EX01)	774	60	RNE1	EX	Cáceres °
EU02)	774	50	RNE1	EU	Donosti-San Sebastián
GA03)	774	20	RNE1	GA	Ourense (relay)

MW	kHz	kW	Net	Rg	Location
AN08)	774	10	RNE1	AN	Granada (relay)
AN09)	774	10	RNE1	AN	La Línea (relay)
CL04)	774	10	RNE1	CL	León (relay)
CL05)	774	10	RNE1	CL	Soria (relay)
CM05)	801	25	RNE1	CM	Ciudad Real (relay)
GA04)	801	20	RNE1	GA	Lugo (relay)
CA04)	801	10	RNE1	CA	Girona (relay)
CL06)	801	10	RNE1	CL	Burgos
CL07)	801	10	RNE1	CL	Zamora
VA03)	801	10	RNE1	VA	Castelló (relay)
MU01)	855	300	RNE1	MU	Murcia °
CT01)	855	50	RNE1	CT	Santander °
CA03)	855	20	RNE1	CA	Tarragona (relay)
GA02)	855	20	RNE1	GA	Pontevedra (relay)
AN10)	855	10	RNE1	AN	Huelva (relay)
AR02)	855	10	RNE1	AR	Teruel (relay)
CL08)	855	10	RNE1	CL	Ponferrada (relay)
CL09)	855	10	RNE1	CL	Salamanca (relay)
NA01)	855	10	RNE1	NA	Pamplona-Iruñea °
AN03)	855	5	RNE1	AN	Marbella (relay)
CM02)	864	10	RNE1	CM	Socuellamos (rel.of Toledo)
BA01)	909	5	RNE5	BA	Palma de Mallorca °
AR01)	936	20	RNE5	AR	Zaragoza °
CL01)	936	20	RNE5	CL	Valladolid °
VA02)	936	10	RNE5	VA	Alacant-Alicante
AN11)	972	5	RNE1	AN	Cabra (rel.of Sevilla)
GA05)	972	2	RNE1	GA	Monforte de Lemos (relay)
AN08)	1017	10	RNE5	AN	Granada
CL06)	1017	10	RNE5	CL	Burgos°
AN05)	1098	25	RNE5	AN	Almería
GA04)	1098	20	RNE5	GA	Lugo
CL03)	1098	10	RNE5	CL	Avila
AN10)	1098	5	RNE5	AN	Huelva
RI01)	1107	25	RNE5	RI	Logroño °
CT01)	1107	20	RNE5	CT	Santander °
EX01)	1107	20	RNE5	EX	Cáceres °
AR02)	1107	10	RNE5	AR	Teruel (rel.of zaragoza)
CL08)	1107	10	RNE5	CL	Ponferrada (rel.of León)
CL05)	1125	10	RNE5	CL	Soria
CM01)	1125	10	RNE5	CM	Toledo °
EU01)	1125	10	RNE5	EU	Vitoria-Gasteiz °
VA03)	1125	10	RNE5	VA	Castelló
EX02)	1125	5	RNE5	EX	Badajoz
AN06)	1152	20	RNE5	AN	Málaga
CA02)	1152	10	RNE5	CA	Lleida
CL07)	1152	10	RNE5	CL	Zamora
CM03)	1152	10	RNE5	CM	Albacete
MU02)	1152	10	RNE5	MU	Cartagena
GA03)	1305	25	RNE5	GA	Ourense
CM05)	1305	20	RNE5	CM	Ciudad Real
EU03)	1305	20	RNE5	EU	Bilbo-Bilbao
CL04)	1305	10	RNE5	CL	León
CM04)	1314	20	RNE5	CM	Cuenca
CA03)	1314	10	RNE5	CA	Tarragona
CL09)	1314	10	RNE5	CL	Salamanca
GA06)	1413	20	RNE5	GA	Vigo
AN04)	1413	10	RNE5	AN	Jaén
CA04)	1413	5	RNE5	CA	Girona
AN09)	1503	5	RNE5	AN	La Linea (rel.of Cádiz)
GA05)	1503	2	RNE5	GA	Monforte de Lemos (rel.of. Lugo)

°= regional key stn

FM	Location	RNE1	RNE2	RNE3	RNE4	RNE5	kW
Andalucía							
AN08)	Baza	92.6	97.3	-	-	-	5
AN02)	Cabra	95.1	89.5	103.8	-	88.0	1
AN02)	Córdoba	-	-	-	-	99.8	2
AN08)	Granada	104.2	96.4	94.4	-	98.5	1
AN01)	Guadalcanal	-	90.6	-	-	-	5
AN07)	Jerez	103.5	94.5	96.7	-	106.3	80
AN02)	Lagar de la Cruz	92.2	97.5	98.6	-		10
AN06)	Málaga	-	99.2	104.0	-	92.5	1
AN03)	Marbella	-		-	-	87.6	1
AN06)	Mijas	106.6	98.1	99.8	-	88.0	10
AN08)	Parapanda	103.0	91.1	93.9	-		5
AN05)	Pechina	100.9	92.4	94.9	-	106.7	70
AN10)	Punta Umbria	95.2	92.6	99.0	-	88.8	5
AN06)	Ronda	106.1	99.3	91.6	-	102.3	1
AN04)	Sierra Almadén	105.4	90.0	96.0	-	-	10
AN08)	Sierra Lújar	96.7	90.4	94.2	-	-	5
AN07)	Tajo	105.0	94.0	103.1	-	-	5
AN01)	Valencina	91.2	93.7	98.8	-	90.0	5
Aragon							
AR02)	Alcañiz	89.5	-	-	-	99.3	1
AR03)	Arguis	100.9	94.4	103.7	-	92.8	5
AR03)	Barbastro	89.6	97.4	105.1	-	100.2	1
AR01)	Caspe	90.2	99.0	-	-	103.7	1
AR01)	Ejea de los C.	94.8	98.9	106.4	-	91.2	
AR03)	Fraga	95.0	96.3	102.2	-	98.8	1
AR01)	Inogés	89.4	92.4	99.7	-	105.0	5
AR03)	Jaca	103.7	94.4	100.3	-	98.7	1
AR02)	Javalambre	-	90.0	93.9	-	-	1
AR01)	La Muela	94.5	90.9	96.3	-	103.6	10
AR02)	Montalban	90.5	92.7	96.4	-	105.1	
AR02)	Peracense	88.3	98.1	100.6	-	106.1	
AR02)	Teruel	104.7	89.2	94.5	-	95.6	1
Asturias							
AS01)	Avilés	100.0	87.9	95.6	-	102.9	1
AS01)	Boal	93.2	97.8	88.2	-	90.5	1
AS01)	Cangas Narcea	97.2	99.0	87.7	-	90.9	1
AS01)	Cangas Onis	88.8	92.5	104.0	-	100.3	1
AS01)	Gamoniteiro	102.5	92.2	94.4	-	104.4	10
AS02)	Gijón	99.2	98.5	102.0	-	89.9	5
AS01)	Ibias	95.8	98.7	102.9	-	105.1	1
AS01)	Llanes	106.1	-	-	-	97.3	1
AS01)	Los Oscos	89.7	104.0	105.7	-	96.1	1
AS01)	Luarca	96.8	93.8	100.3	-	-	1
AS01)	Mieres	-	-	-	-	101.8	1
AS01)	Oviedo	89.4	96.0	90.3	-	99.6	1
AS01)	Peñamelleras	93.9	96.4	100.7	-	104.6	
AS01)	San Martín	88.3	96.7	100.2	-	93.3	1
Baleares							
BA01)	Alfabia	90.1	87.9	92.3	-	104.5	10
BA01)	Ibiza	101.6	104.0	105.7	-	94.9	1
BA01)	Menorca	94.6	97.1	105.8	-	100.4	1
BA01)	Pollensa	93.2	95.4	97.4	-	99.7	1
Cantabria							
CT03)	Embalse Ebro	89.0	94.0	98.2	-	101.9	1
CT01)	Liérganes	96.9	93.0	102.9	-	105.0	10
CT02)	Torrelavega	99.5	97.9	103.4	-	89.4	1
Catalunya							
CA02)	Alpicat	94.6	89.2	97.8	87.9	-	10
CA02)	Baquéira	92.2	87.7	89.0	93.3	-	1
CA02)	Bossost	94.4	100.5	105.2	102.3	-	1
CA01)	Collserola	88.3	93.0	98.6	100.8	99.0	20
CA01)	Collsuspina	99.2	97.9	103.1	104.7	-	1
CA01)	Igualada	89.4	90.9	105.1	106.9	-	1
CA03)	Monte Caro	104.3	96.6	99.6	90.7	-	5
CA01)	Montserrat	94.3	99.0	-	103.8	98.8	2
CA03)	Musara	106.5	91.5	94.5	88.8	94.0	5
CA01)	Sant Pere Ribes	89.4	95.2	97.5	106.3	101.3	1
CA04)	Rocacorba	93.3	91.1	95.9	106.2	94.0	5
CA02)	Soriguera	99.9	103.6	106.4	90.6	97.2	1
CA03)	Ulldecona	95.0	-	-	-	-	5
CA02)	Viella	90.0	96.2	104.4	102.6	-	1
CA04)	Olot	93.8	106.6	-	-	-	
CA02)	Pont de Suert	88.2	94.9	96.8	104.9	-	
Castilla-León							
CL06)	Aranda Duero	90.0	92.7	101.6	-	106.2	1
CL03)	Arenas Pedro	102.4	90.3	-	-	-	1
CL03)	Avila	87.6	92.0	97.8	-	102.4	1
CL09)	Béjar	99.9	101.6	104.7	-		1
CL07)	Benavente	87.8	91.3	97.9	-	100.2	1
CL05)	Burgo Osma	96.1	98.4	88.7	-	102.8	1
CL06)	Burgos	93.6	90.3	91.2	-	106.6	1
CL04)	Castropodame	103.3	93.0	99.9	-	105.9	5
CL02)	Cervera	88.6	94.8	97.3	-	100.4	1
CL09)	El Cabaco	102.9	92.4	95.4	-	-	5
CL02)	Guardo	89.8	105.6	-	-	104.0	1
CL04)	León	97.1	91.1	89.3	-	102.2	1
CL02)	Palencia	91.8	101.0	97.6	-	88.0	1
CL06)	Pancorbo	89.7	92.0	101.7	-	104.5	1
CL07)	Pbla Samabria	93.6	103.5	100.3	-	91.9	1
CL09)	Salamanca	94.5	88.1	91.4	-	102.2	1
CL10)	Segovia	97.0	-	-	-	91.5	1
CL05)	Soria	89.7	91.5	94.3	-	104.7	2
CL01)	Valladolid	97.3	93.1	92.2	-	95.1	5
CL04)	Villablino	98.1	89.0	91.4	-	99.4	1
CL06)	Villadiego	-	102.3	103.3	-	-	1
CL04)	Villafranca	90.9	89.7	97.5	-	104.1	1

FM	Location	RNE1	RNE2	RNE3	RNE4	RNE5	kW
CL07)	Zamora	101.8	96.7	98.5	-	88.8	5
Castilla La Mancha							
CM03)	Almansa	91.2	98.6	95.6	-	94.4	1
CM03)	Chincilla	91.8	93.6	99.0	-	106.3	5
CM05)	Ciudad Real	95.7	92.8	94.1	-	88.8	1
CM04)	Cuenca	105.6	93.0	92.0	-	96.1	1
CM06)	Guadalajara	103.7	93.5	96.9	-	102.1	1
CM05)	La Mancha	101.0	89.8	94.5	-	106.8	10
CM05)	Puertollano	93.1	99.1	91.8	-	101.8	5
CM05)	Socuéllamos	94.0	-	-	-		1
CM01)	Talavera	97.8	105.5	94.7	-	89.4	5
CM01)	Toledo	102.0	103.9	106.4	-	99.9	1
CM05)	Valdepeñas	92.6	95.5	97.3	-	102.1	
Euskadi							
EU03)	Archanda	100.7	90.6	99.2	-	96.3	5
EU02)	Azcoitia	88.7	104.9	106.9	-	-	1
EU02)	Beasain	100.2	98.4	94.9	-	-	1
EU02)	Eibar	92.9	98.7	95.9	-	-	1
EU02)	Jaizquibel	104.7	90.0	92.1	-	-	10
EU02)	Monte Igueldo	87.6	99.5	98.9	-	93.3	1
EU03)	Oiz	106.4	105.3	102.1	-	-	5
EU01)	San León	-	-	-	-	93.3	1
EU03)	Sollube	105.9	93.9	95.4	-	-	5
EU02)	Tolosa	101.9	98.8	96.0	-	-	1
EU01)	Vitoria-Gasteiz	92.5	96.9	99.5	-	89.4	1
Extremadura							
EX02)	Badajoz	94.9	90.1	92.2	-	106.0	1
EX01)	Cáceres	95.1	101.7	93.7	-	88.2	1
EX02)	Mérida	-	-	-	-	101.3	1
EX01)	Montánchez	105.3	97.7	99.3	-	-	5
EX01)	Plasencia	88.6	-	99.3	-	104.4	1
Galicia							
GA03)	Barco	94.7	96.4	100.3	-	104.6	
GA02)	Domayo	90.1	92.1	97.4	-	-	5
GA04)	Monforte	-	-	-	-	88.8	1
GA03)	Monte Meda	102.8	91.2	94.3	-	106.8	5
GA01)	Monte Xalo	100.4	91.6	94.5	-	95.8	10
GA03)	Ourense	100.6	97.2	99.4	-	95.1	5
GA04)	Páramo	101.7	88.2	99.6	-	92.8	5
GA04)	Piedrafita	89.4	92.6	105.3	-	95.2	
GA02)	Pontevedra	-	88.3	-	-	-	1
GA07)	Santiago	103.1	98.1	99.0	-	93.7	5
GA03)	Verin	90.7	98.4	106.4	-	94.1	1
GA06)	Vigo	-	-	-	-	96.0	5
GA04)	Xistral	89.5	96.3	104.2	-	106.6	1
Madrid							
MA01)	Navacerrada	104.9	98.8	95.8	-	-	30
MA01)	Torrespaña	88.2	96.5	93.2	-	90.3	10
Murcia							
MU01)	Carrascoy	101.7	98.2	96.0	-	92.1	5
MU02)	Cartagena	102.9	94.5	97.5	-	103.5	1
MU01)	Cieza	91.0	93.7	99.0	-	96.9	
MU01)	Jumilla	89.1	93.1	100.1	-	-	1
MU01)	Yecla	88.8	93.4	103.7	-	-	1
Navarra							
NA01)	Estella	89.0	101.2	100.5	-	90.9	1
NA01)	Gorramendi	88.3	99.0	100.6	-	95.3	1
NA01)	Ibañeta	89.6	93.8	103.4	-	101.9	1
NA01)	Isaba	90.3	95.1	103.0	-	91.8	1
NA01)	Leire	88.9	101.0	99.6	-	90.5	1
NA01)	Lesaka	90.6	94.8	97.0	-	102.2	1
NA01)	Monreal	106.1	97.5	93.0	-	95.7	5
NA01)	Pamplona	104.8	97.1	102.3	-	103.7	
NA01)	San Miguel	96.7	100.0	90.3	-	102.7	1
NA01)	Tudela	100.9	102.2	91.3	-	88.3	1
La Rioja							
RI01)	Logroño	95.4	88.1	89.9	-	97.2	1
RI01)	Moncalvillo	102.0	88.5	94.6	-	103.3	40
RI01)	Monte Yerga	87.6	106.8	96.5	-	105.4	1
Comunitat Valenciana							
VA02)	Aitana	104.8	88.6	99.7	-	-	10
VA02)	Alcoi	95.8	92.3	91.1	-	105.9	1
VA02)	Alicante	105.2	99.4	97.1	-	103.6	
VA03)	Benicasim	89.3	90.3	92.8	-	95.5	5
VA02)	Benidorm	87.6	97.8	102.1	-	-	
VA02)	Elda	93.9	88.1	97.6	-	-	1
VA01)	Monduber	97.4	99.3	100.1	-	-	5
VA01)	Monte Picayo	89.8	106.6	95.1	-	88.2	10
VA01)	Ontinyent	100.7	96.7	102.4	-	-	1
VA02)	Santa Pola	92.5	100.1	94.3	-	104.2	5
VA02)	Santa Pola	-	-	-	-	105.8	5
VA01)	Utiel	98.1	96.6	89.1	-	87.9	1
VA02)	Villena	90.7	97.1	101.1	-	-	1

RNE1 R. Nacional: (MW and FM): 24h. **N:** On the h. Regional prgrs from key stn of each region: Mon-Fri UTC Local 0625-0630 RNE5; - Reg 0645-0700 RNE1 and RNE5 (*); - Local 0745-0800 RNE5; - Reg. 0904-0906 RNE1 and RNE5; - Reg. 1004-1006 RNE and RNE5; - Reg. 1104-1106 RNE1 and RNE5; -Reg 1210-1300 RNE1 and RNE5; -Reg. 1504-1506 RNE1 and RNE5; -Reg. 1604-1606 RNE1 and RNE5; -Reg. 1704-1706 RNE1 and RNE5; Reg. 1804-1806 RNE1 and RNE5; Reg. 1850-1900 RNE5; - Sa-Su: Reg. 0805-0815 RNE5 ;- Reg. 1230-1300 RNE1 and RNE5. – **RNE2:** R.Clasica: (FM): Classical music & cultural prgrs: 24h. – **RNE3:** (FM): Young people's music prgr: 24h. – **RNE4:** (FM): Regional network in Catalunya: 24h. in Catalán. – **RNE5-RADIO 5 TODO NOTICIAS (R5TN):** (MW and FM): Informacion. 24h. RNE1/RNE5 simulcasting times): 2300-0800 (except 0625-0630 and 0745-0800 for local news on RNE5), 1200-1300, and 2000-2200.

Addresses for RNE regional key stns:
AN Andalucia: Edif.RTVE, Parque del Alamillo, Isla de la Cartuja,41092 Sevilla – **AR Aragón**: José Luís Albareda 1-3, 50004 Zaragoza – **AS Asturias**: Calle San Esteban de las Cruces 92, 33195 Oviedo – **BA Balears**: Aragó 26, 07006 Palma de Mallorca – **CA Catalunya**: C. Roc Boronat 127, 08018 Barcelona – **CL Castilla y León**: García Morato 27-29, 47007 Valladolid – **CM Castilla La Mancha**: Plaza de San Cristóbal s/n, 45002 Toledo – **CT Cantabria**: Polígono de Raos s/n, 39609 Camargo (Santander) – **EU Euskadi**: Plaza de Simón Bolívar 13, 01003 Vitoria-Gasteiz – **EX Extremadura**: Av. Ruta de la Plata 10, 10001 Cáceres – **GA Galicia**: Paseo Méndez Nuñez 12, 15006 A Coruña – **MA Madrid**: Casa de la Radio, Prado del Rey, 28223 Pozuelo de Alarcón – **MU Murcia**: La Olma 27-29, 30005 Murcia – **NA Navarra**: Calle Aoiz,17, 31004 Pamplona-Iruñea – **RI La Rioja**: Vara de Rey 42, 26002 Logroño – **VA Comunitat Valenciana**: Av.Colóm 13, 46004 València

OTHER STATIONS

Only stns with MW broadcasts and FM networks are listed. A number of other stns are heard irr. There are approx. 2,400 FM stns.

NATIONAL NETWORKS:
(COPE) CADENA DE ONDAS POPULARES ESPANOLAS (Comm)
✉ Alfonso XI N° 4, 28014 Madrid ☎ +34 91-3090000 🖷 +34 91-5317517 **W:** cope.es stns list: www.cope.es/emisoras **E:** programas.madrid@cadenacope.net
Local and regional prgr on AM and FM stns: Mon-Fri 0555, 0624, 0650, 0724, 1809-1859, generally at xx27 and xx57 0757-1700, 1930, 2030, 2130, 2230, 2255, 2357. Sat xx27 and xx57 0757-1400, 1557, 1657, 1810, 1840, 1910, 1940, 2040, 2257, 2330. Sun xx27 and xx57 0957-1300, xx10 and xx40 1510-1840, 2157, 2330 **(C100) Cadena 100** (music on FM only) **W**: cadena100.es stns list: cadena100.es/emisoras.php **E:** jplane@cadena100.es
COPE MAS, 30 stns, local prgr on FM only) **(MEGA) MegaStar FM** (music on FM only) **W:** megastar.fm
ROCK FM, st.music rock, see: ROCK.
(D) CADENA DIAL (Comm) Part of Grupo Prisa-SER
✉ Gran Vía 32, 28013 Madrid ☎ +34 91-3470880 🖷 +34 91-5211753 **W:** cadenadial.com stns list: cadenadial.com/nosotros/emisoras **E:** ccampillo@cadenadial.com
(EFM) EUROPA FM (Comm) Part of Grupo Antena 3- Atresmedia
✉ Fuerteventura 12, 28703 San Sebastian de los Reyes ☎+34 91-4366400 🖷+34 91-4366116 **W:** europafm.com stns list: europafm.com/frecuencias
MELODIA FM (Comm) Part of Grupo Antena 3- Atresmedia
(ES) esRADIO (Comm)
✉ C/ Juan Esplandiú 13, 28007 Madrid ☎+34 91-4094766 🖷+34 91- 4094899 **W:** esradio.fm stns list: esradio.fm/escuchenos.html
(LOCA) LOCA RADIO ESPAÑA (Comm) Part of RTL Group France
✉ C/ Enrique Larreta 12 bajo izq., 28036 Madrid ☎+34 90-2302024 **W:** locafm.com **E:** contacto@locaradio.es
(HFM) Hit FM (Comm) Part of Grupo KISS Media
✉ José Isbert 6, Ciudad de la Imagen, 28223 Pozuelo de Alarcón **W**: hitfm.es
(IE) INTERECONOMÍA (Comm)
✉ Velázquez 105, 28003 Madrid.☎+34 90-2996556 🖷+34 91-5771314 **W:** intereconomia.com **E:** redaccion@intereconomia.com
(KFM) KISS FM (Comm)
✉ José Isbert 6, Ciudad de la Imagen - 28223 Pozuelo de Alarcón

☎+34 91-4440490 🖷+34 91-8379189 **W:** kissfm.es stns list: kissfm.es/contacta-kiss **E:** kissfm@kissfm.es
(L40) LOS 40 (Comm) Part of Grupo Prisa
✉ Gran Vía 32, 7ª planta, 28013 Madrid. ☎ +34 91-3477700 🖷 +34 91-5228693 **W:** los40.com **E:** los40@los40.com
(40D) LOS 40 DANCE (Comm) Part of Grupo Prisa
✉ C/ Gran Vía 32, 7ª planta, 28013 Madrid ☎+34 91-3477624 🖷+34 91-5325808 **W:** los40.com/seccion/los40dance **E:** ADSanchez@prisaradio.com. **LP:** Dir.: Toni Sánchez
(40C) LOS 40 CLASSIC (Comm) Part of Grupo Prisa
✉ Gran Vía 32, 7ª planta, 28013 Madrid ☎ +34 91-3477700 🖷 +34 91-5228693 **W:** los40.com/seccion/los40classic stns list: los40.com/los40/emisoras/
(40UR) LOS 40 URBAN (Comm) Part of Grupo Prisa-SER. New Channel from April 2020. Only this stations in FM: 103.9 MHz Madrid; 104.9 MHz Pontevedra; 92.4 MHz La Roda, Albacete; and 97.1 MHz Las Pedroñeras, Cuenca.
(OCR) ONDA CERO RADIO (Comm) Part of Grupo Antena 3-Atresmedia
✉ C/ Fuerteventura 12, 28703 San Sebastián de los Reyes, Madrid ☎ +34 91-4366400 🖷 +34 91-5386332 **W:** ondacero.es stns list: ondacero.es/frecuencias **E:** ondacero@ondacero.es **Prgrs:**.Melodia FM and Europa FM. Local and regional programming on AM stations: Mon-Fri 0527, 0555, 0620, 0655, 0720, 0827, 0855, 0927, 0955, 1025, 1130, 1400, 1527, 1557, 1627, 1657, 1727, 1757, 1800, 2030, 2130, 2230, 2257, 2340, 0030. Sat-Sun 0527, 0727, 0757, 0827, 0857, 0927, 0957, 1027, 1227, 1457, 1850, 2255, 2320, 2340. Times vary.
(RA) RADIO TELEVISION AMISTAD (Rlg)
✉ Apartado 269, 08211 Castellar del Vallés (Barcelona) 🖷+34 93-7242380 **W:** rtvamistad.net **E:** info@rtvamistad.tv
(RI) RADIO INTERNACIONAL (Comm)
✉ Orense 68, Planta 12, 28020 Madrid. **W:** radiointernacional.es **E:** info@radiointernacional.es – Stations: Radio Inter (918 MW, FM 93.5 ; R. Internacional FM 97.5 ; China FM 92.9, Madrid
(RKM) RKM RADIO (Rlg)
✉ Carretera de Ajalvir a Daganzo km 1.7, Ajalvir, 28864 Madrid ☎ +34 91- 8844180 **W:** rkmradio.com **E:** madrid@rkmradio.com
(RM) RADIO MARÌA (Rlg)
✉ Paseo de Lanceros 2 (Centro Comercial), Planta 1ª, 28024 Madrid ☎+34 90-2500518 🖷 +34 91-7057727 **W:** radiomaria.es **E:** radiomaria@radiomaria.es Total 225 Stations in Spain
(RMA) RADIO MARCA (Comm)
✉AvenidadeSanLuís25,28033Madrid☎+34 90 2996111 **W:** marca.com **E:** radiomarca@radiomarca.com **LP:** Dir.: Francisco Garcia Caridad
(RO) Radiolé (Comm) Part of Grupo Prisa
✉ Gran Vía 32, 7ª planta, 28013 Madrid ☎ +34 91-3477740 🖷 +34 91-5324769 **W:** radiole.com stns list: radiole.com/emisoras **E:** direccion@radiole.com **LP:** Dir.: Miguel Ángel Corral Salas
(ROCK) ROCK FM (Comm) Part of Grupo **COPE**
✉ Alfonso XI N° 4, 28014 Madrid ☎ +34 91-5951210 🖷 +34 91 3090721 **W:** rockfm.fm stns list: www.rockfm.fm/emisoras
(SER) SOCIEDAD ESPANOLA DE RADIODIFUSION (Comm)
Part of Grupo Prisa
✉ Gran Vía 32, 7ª planta, 28013 Madrid ☎ +34 91-3477700 🖷 +34 91-3470779 **W:** cadenaser.com stns list: cadenaser.com/emisoras **E:** redaccion@cadenaser.com **FM stns:** Local and regional prgr **AM stns:** Mon-Fri 0550, 0620, 0650, 0720, 0827, 0855, 0930, 0957, 1003, 1030, 1057, 1120, 1410, 1530, 1630, 1720, 1810-1855, 1925, 2157, 2255, 2330, 0000, 0030, 0159, 0259. Sat-Sun 0750, 0855, 0955, 1055, 1105 and xx23 or xx53 in the evening. Times vary
SER+, local stations in FM.

REGIONAL NETWORKS:
(AR) ARAGÓN RADIO
✉ María Zambrano 2, 50018 Zaragoza. ☎ +34 876-256500 🖷 +34 876-256519 **W:** aragonradio.es **E:** jmartinez@cartv.es **LP:** Dir. Mktg: Javier Martinez López
(CR) CORPORACIO CATALANA DE MITJANS AUDIOVISUALS
✉ Av. Diagonal 614-616, 08021 Barcelona ☎ +34 93-3069200 🖷 +34 93-3069201 **W:** catradio.cat **E:** correu@catradio.com **Prgrs:** Catalunya Ràdio; Catalunya Informació; Catalunya Música; Icat FM
(CER) CANAL EXTREMADURA RADIO
✉ Av. de las Américas 1, 1°, 06800 Mérida (Badajoz) ☎ +34 924-382000 **W:** radio.canalextremadura.es **E:** cexma@canalextremadura.es
(CLR) CASTILLA LEON RADIO
✉ Calle Manuel Canesi Acevedo 1, ES-47016 Valladolid ☎ +34 98 3131313 🖷 +34 98 3131314 **W:** puntoradiocyl.com **E:** puntoradiocyl@edigrup.es
(CSR) CANAL SUR RADIO
✉ Carretera Edificio Canal Sur. Avda. José Gálvez 1, 41092 Isla de la Cartuja, Sevilla ☎ +34 95-5054600 🖷 +34 95- 5054740 **W:** canalsur.es **E:** comunicacion@rtva.es **Prgrs:** Canal Fiesta: (Int. music and Spanish pop and rock music); Canal Sur Radio: (Andalucian and Spanish music, news and sports); Radio Andalucía Información.
(DH) DIGITAL HITS,Catalunya
Freq.: 89.5 MHZ Barcelona; 93.5 MHZ Girona; 106.0 MHZ Tarragona; 95.8 MHZ Lleida; 95.7 MHZ Osona; 100.9 MHZ Penedés. W: www.digitalhits.cat
(EI) EUSKA IRRATI TELEBISTA – RADIO TELEVISIÓN VASCA
✉ EiTB Donostia: Paseo Miramon 172, 20014 Donostia-San Sebastián ☎ +34 94-30116 00 🖷 +34 94-301 1995 – ✉ EiTB Bilbao: Capuchinos de Basurto 2, 48013 Bilbo-Bilbao ☎ +34 94-6563000 🖷 +34 94-6563095 – ✉ EiTB Vitoria: Domingo Martinez de Aragón, 5-7 bajo, 01006 Vitoria-Gasteiz ☎ +34 94-5012500 🖷 +34 94-5012695 – ✉ EiTB Iruña: Calle Tomás Caballero 2, 31005 Pamplona-Iruña ☎ +34 94-8012200 🖷 +34 94-8153485. **Prgrs:** Euskadi Irratia (AM + FM), R. Euskadi (AM + FM), R. Vitoria (AM + FM), EiTB Músika (FM), Gaztea Irratia (FM) **W:** eitb.com **E :** info@eitb.com
(GR) GRUP FLAIX (Comm)
✉ Passeig de Gràcia 55, novena planta, 08007 Barcelona ☎ +34 93-5055555 🖷 +34 93-4880776 **W:** flaixfm.cat and radioflaixbac.com **E:** flaixfm@grupflaix.cat & flaixbac@grupflaix.cat **Prgs:** Flaix FM and Flaixbac
(IB3) IB3 RADIO ✉ C/ Manuel Azaña 7-A, 07006 Palma de Mallorca ☎ +34 971-139931 🖷 +34 971-139930 **W:** ib3tv.com **E :** info@eprtvib.com
(OC) ONA CATALANA (Comm) Part of Grupo Prisa. NOW is **SER CAT, SER Catalunya**.
✉ C/ Casp 6, 08010 Barcelona ☎ +34 93-3441400 **W:** ona-fm.cat **E:** info@onafm.cat
(OM) ONDA MADRID
✉ Paseo del Príncipe 3, 28223 Pozuelo de Alarcón (Madrid) ☎ +34 91-5128200 🖷 +34 91-5128300
W: ondamadrid.es **E :** ondamadrid@ondamadrid.es
(ORM) ONDA REGIONAL MURCIA
✉ Avda. Libertad 6, 30009 Murcia ☎+34 968-200000 🖷+34 968-272665 **W:** orm.es **E :** info@orm.es
(RAC) RAC (Comm) Belongs to Grupo Godò
Av. Diagonal 477, Planta 15, 08036 Barcelona ☎+34 93-2704400 🖷+34 93-2704464 **W:** rac1.cat and rac105.cat **E :** rac1@rac1.net and rac105@rac105.net. **Prgrs:** RAC1 and RAC 105
(RCM) RADIO CASTILLA-LA MANCHA
✉ Edificio RTVCM, C/ Río Alberche s/n, Polígono Santa María de Benquerencia, 45007 Toledo. ☎ +34 925-288600 🖷 +34 925-288607 **W:** rtvsm.es **E:** comercial@rtvcm.es
(RCL) RADIO CASTILLA Y LEÓN
✉ Edificio Promecal Burgos, Avenida Castilla y León 62-64, 09006 Burgos ☎ +34 947-266868 🖷 +34 947-202752 **W:** rtvcyl.es **E:** burgos@rtvcyl.es
(RE) RÀDIO ESTEL (Rlg)
✉ Comtes de Bell-lloc 67-69, 08014 Barcelona ☎ +34 93-4092770 🖷 +34 93-4092775 **W:** radioestel.com **E:** estudis@radioestel.com Dir.: Jaume Aymar
(RG) RADIO GALEGA – COMPAÑÍA DE RADIO TELEVISION DE GALICIA
✉ Casa da Radio, Edificio de Usos Múltiples San Marcos, 15820 Santiago de Compostela ☎ +34 981-540640 🖷 +34 981-540949 **W:** crtvg.es/rg **E:** info@crtvg.es
(RP) RADIO POPULAR - HERRI IRRATIA
✉Alameda Mazarredo 47, 48009 Bilbo-Bilbao ☎+34 94-4239200 🖷+34 94-4234703 **W:** radiopopular.com **E:** direccion@radiopopular.com
(RPA) RADIO DEL PRINCIPADO DE ASTURIAS
✉ Camino de las Clarisas 263, 33203 Gijón ☎+34 985-185900 🖷 +34 985-185939 **W:** rtpa.es/radio **E:** comunicacion@rtpa.es
(RTT) RADIO TELE TAXI (Comm)
✉ C/ Sant Carles 40, 08922 Sta Coloma de Gramenet (Barcelona) ☎+34 93-4665656 🖷 +34 93-4661534 **W:** radioteletaxi.com **E:** radioteletaxi@radioteletaxi.com
(RV) RADIO VOZ
✉ Av. De la Prensa 84-85, Arteixo, 15142 A Coruña ☎ +34 981-180600 🖷 +34 981-180477 **W:** radiovoz.com **E:** director@radiovoz.com
(XAR) La XARXA (Comm)
✉ Travessera de les Corts 131-159, 08028 Barcelona ☎ +34

93-5080600 **W:** xarxaradio.cat **E:** laxarxa@laxarxa.com
SER CAT, SER Catalunya, c/Casp 6, 08010 Barcelona –Part of Grupo PRISA. Stations only in Catalonia, in **FM:**
89.6 MHZ Pallars; 89.8 Cerdanya; 92.3 Osona; 95.5 Garrotxa; 95.7 Terres de L'Ebre; 97.2 Val D'Aran; 97.4 Girona; 97.7 Tarragona; 99.2 Segarra; 101.9 Baix Emporda; 103.5 Barcelona; 103.6 Lleida; 104.0 Penedés; 104.0 Alt Emporda; 104.4 Alt Emporda; 104.4 Catalunya Central.
Radio France Internationale (RFI) Relay in Barcelona, **FM:** 105.3 MHZ.In French.

MW	kHz	kW	Net	Rg	Station, location	FM (MHz)
CA07)	540	50	OCR	CA	Onda Cero Catal., Barcelona	93.5
CA08)	666	50	SER	CA	R. Barcelona, Barcelona	93.9
MU05)	711	5	COPE	MU	COPE, Murcia	89.7
CA09)	783	50	COPE	CA	COPE Catalunya i Andorra, Barcelona	
AN15)	792	50	SER	AN	R. Sevilla, Sevilla	97.1
MA05)	810	20	SER	MA	R. Madrid, Madrid	93.9
CA13)	828	5	HFM	CA	HIT FM Catalunya, Terrassa	‡A
AN16)	837	10	COPE	AN	COPE, Sevilla	99.6
CL15)	837	10	COPE	CL	COPE, Burgos	95.5
GA09)	837	5	COPE	GA	COPE, El Ferrol	101.3
AR05)	873	25	SER	AR	R. Zaragoza, Zaragoza	95.3
GA10)	873	10	SER	GA	R. Galicia, Stgo de Comp.	90.0
VA07)	882	5	COPE	VA	COPE, Alacant-Alicante	95.6
AN17)	882	5	COPE	AN	COPE, Málaga	89.8
AS05)	882	5	COPE	AS	COPE, Gijón	94.8
CL16)	882	5	COPE	CL	COPE, Valladolid	88.5
EU10)	900	10	RP	EU	R. Popular, Bilbo-Bilbao	97.8
AN18)	900	5	COPE	AN	COPE, Granada	87.6
GA11)	900	5	COPE	GA	COPE, Vigo	87.8
MA06)	918	20	RI	MA	R. Inter, Madrid	93.5
MA13)	954	50	OCR	MA	Onda Cero R., Madrid	98.0
EU11)	990	10	SER	EU	R. Bilbao, Bilbo-Bilbao	89.5
AN19)	990	5	SER	AN	R. Cádiz, Cádiz	89.4
MA08)	999	50	COPE	MA	COPE, Madrid	106.3
CA11)	1008	10	SER	CA	R. Girona, Girona	98.5
EX06)	1008	5	SER	EX	R. Extremadura, Badajoz	96.9
VA08)	1008	5	SER	VA	R. Alacant, Alacant-Alicante	91.7
CA12)	1026	10	SER	CA	R. Reus, Reus	97.7
AS06)	1026	5	SER	AS	R. Asturias, Oviedo	97.5
GA12)	1026	5	SER	GA	R. Vigo, Vigo	99.4
AN20)	1026	5	SER	AN	R. Jaén, Jaén	96.9
AN21)	1026	5	SER	AN	R. Jerez, J. de la Frontera	97.8
CL17)	1026	5	SER	CL	R. Salamanca, Salamanca	96.9
EU12)	1044	10	SER	EU	R. San Sebastián, Donosti-S Se	97.2
CL18)	1044	5	SER	CL	R. Valladolid, Valladolid	90.9
AR06)	1053	25	COPE	AR	COPE, Zaragoza	97.5
VA09)	1053	5	COPE	VA	COPE, Vila-Real	90.6
AN22)	1080	10	SER	AN	R. Granada, Granada	93.2
AR07)	1080	10	SER	AR	R. Huesca, Huesca	96.9
BA06)	1080	5	SER	BA	R. Mallorca, P. de Mallorca	94.1
CM11)	1080	5	OCR	CM	Onda Cero R., Toledo	100.8
GA13)	1080	5	SER	GA	R. Coruña, A Coruña	91.0
CM12)	1116	5	SER	CM	R. Albacete, Albacete	100.3
GA14)	1116	5	SER	GA	R. Pontevedra, Pontevedra	89.1
CL19)	1134	10	COPE	CL	COPE, Salamanca	90.0
AN23)	1134	5	COPE	AN	COPE, Jerez de la Frontera	92.4
NA05)	1134	5	COPE	NA	COPE, Pamplona-Iruñea	87.9
AN24)	1143	5	COPE	AN	COPE, Jaén	94.2
GA15)	1143	5	COPE	GA	COPE MAS, Ourense	102.4
VA10)	1179	50	SER	VA	R. València, València	94.2
RI05)	1179	2	SER	RI	R. Rioja, Logroño	91.7
AN25)	1215	5	COPE	AN	COPE, Córdoba	87.6
CL21)	1215	5	COPE	CL	COPE, León	97.7
CT05)	1215	5	COPE	CT	COPE Cantabria, Santander	88.4
MU06)	1215	5	COPE	MU	COPE, Lorca	89.2
AN26)	1224	5	COPE	AN	COPE, Huelva	91.9
AN27)	1224	5	COPE	AN	COPE, Almería	97.1
BA08)	1224	5	COPE	BA	COPE, Palma de Mallorca	97.6
CA15)	1224	5	COPE	CA	COPE, Lleida	97.4
GA16)	1224	2	COPE	GA	COPE MAS, Lugo	88.9
AN28)	1260	5	SER	AN	R. Algeciras, Algeciras	95.7
MU07)	1260	5	SER	MU	R. Murcia, Murcia	100.3
CL22)	1269	5	COPE	CL	COPE, Zamora	94.9
EX07)	1269	5	COPE	EX	COPE, Badajoz	87.6
CA17)	1287	10	SER	CA	R. Lleida, Lleida	93.4
CL23)	1287	5	SER	CL	R. Castilla, Burgos	89.1
GA17)	1287	5	SER	GA	R. Lugo, Lugo	91.8
VA11)	1296	50	COPE	VA	COPE, València	99.0
AN29)	1341	10	OCR	AN	Onda Cero R., Almería	93.8
CL24)	1341	5	SER	CL	R. León, León	88.2
CM16)	1341	5	OCR	CM	Onda Cero R., Ciudad Real	92.1
CL25)	1485	10	SER	CL	R. Zamora, Zamora	89.8
CT06)	1485	10	SER	CT	R. Santander, Santander	90.9
VA12)	1485	5	SER	VA	R. Alcoi, Alcoi	96.3
VA13)	1521	5	SER	VA	R. Castelló, Castelló	94.8
VA14)	1539	6	SER	VA	R. Elche - R. Elx, Elx	99.1
CA19)	1539	5	SER	CA	R. Manresa, Manresa	95.8
AN31)	1575	5	SER	AN	R. Córdoba, Córdoba	96.6
GA18)	1584	5	SER	GA	R. Ourense, Ourense	87.6
VA15)	1584	5	SER	VA	R. Gandia, Gandia	96.5
AN32)	1602	5	SER	AN	R. Linares, Linares	94.9
CL26)	1602	5	SER	CL	R. Segovia, Segovia	93.6
MU08)	1602	5	SER	MU	R. Cartagena, Cartagena	91.8
VA16)	1602	5	SER	VA	R. Ontinyent, Ontinyent	95.3

NB: ‡A inactive on AM

FM	MHz	kW	Net	Rg	Station, location
AN41)	87.6	5	CSR	AN	Canal Sur R., Santo Pitar,Málaga
CL20)	87.6		CL		COPE Astorga
CA25)	87.6		CR	CA	Icat FM, L'Estartit, Girona
CA25)	87.6		CR	CA	Icat FM, Camprodón, Girona
CA25)	87.6		CR	CA	Catalunya Informació, Soriguera, Lleida
CA25)	87.6		CR	CA	Catalunya Música, Portbou, Girona
AN35)	87.7	6	HIT	AN	HIT FM, Jerez de Frontera
CA34)	87.7	20	RAC	CA	RAC1, Barcelona Collserola
CA25)	87.7		CR	CA	Icat FM, El Vendrell, Tarragona
CA25)	87.7		CR	CA	Catalunya Música, El Vendrell, Tarragona
CA25)	87.8		CR	CA	Catalunya Música, Calonge, Girona
CA09)	87.8		ROCK	CA	ROCK FM, Figueres, Girona
AN36)	87.9	5	SER	AN	R. Morón, Morón de la Frontera ,Sevilla
CA25)	87.9		CR	CA	IcatFM, Igualada, Barcelona
CA25)	87.9		CR	CA	IcatFM, Collsuspina, Barcelona
CA37)	88.0	25	CR	CA	Icat FM, La Mussara, Tarragona
CA25)	88.0		CR	CA	Catalunya R., Arenys de Munt, Barcelona
EU25)	88.0	5		EU	R. Nervión, Bilbao
CA25)	88.1	10	L40	CA	LOS 40, Rocacorba, Girona
CA25)	88.2		CR	CA	IcatFM, Puigdevall, Lleida
AN37)	88.3	5	CSR	AN	Canal Fiesta R., Algeciras
CA25)	88.3		CR	CA	Catalunya R., Ponts, Lleida
CA25)	88.4	5	CR	CA	Catalunya R., Montcaro, Tortosa
CA25)	88.4		CR	CA	Catalunya R., Cabra del Camp, Tarragona
CA25)	88.4		CR	CA	Catalunya Música, La Molina, Girona
CA25)	88.5		CR	CA	Catalunya R., Olot, Girona
CA25)	88.5		CR	CA	Catalunya R., Arbucies, Girona
CA25)	88.6		CR	CA	Catalunya Informació, Boí, Lleida
CA25)	88.6	20	CR	CA	Catalunya Música, Soriguera, Lleida
CA25)	88.6		CR	CA	Icat FM, Guardiola Berguedá, Barcelona
CA35)	88.7	10	OCR	CA	Melodia FM, Barcelona Collserola
CA25)	88.7		CR	CA	Catalunya R., Cubells, Lleida
AN70)	88.8	40		AN	Stereo Vision, Sevilla
CA25)	88.8		CR	CA	Catalunya Informació, Ripoll, Girona
CA25)	88.8		CR	BA	Catalunya Música, Alfábia, Mallorca
CA38)	88.9	25	CR	CA	Icat FM, Rocacorba, Girona
CA25)	88.9		CR	CA	Catalunya R., Almacelles, Lleida
EU07)	88.9	20	EI	EU	Euskadi Irratia, Bilbo-Bilbao
MU17)	88.9	5	RMA	MU	R. Marca, Murcia
MA05)	89.0	20	40C	MA	Los 40 Classic, Madrid
CA25)	89.0		CR	CA	Icat FM, Vilaller, Lleida
CA25)	89.0		CR	CA	Icat FM, Portilló, Val D'Aran
CA07)	89.1	8	RMA	CA	R,Marca,, Barcelona Collserola
EU10)	89.2	5	ROCK	EU	ROCKFM. Bilbo-Bilbao
EU26)	89.2	5		EU	Segura Irratia, Segura, Vitoria
GA29)	89.2	8	RMA	GA	R. Marca, A Coruña
VA21)	89.2	8	KFM	VA	Kiss FM, Alacant-Alicante
NA11)	89.3	6	KFM	NA	Kiss FM, Pamplona
CA25)	89.3		CR	CA	Icat FM, Bellmunt
GA28)	89.4	6	RA	GA	Ondas de Vida, R. Amistad, Vigo
MU14)	89.4	6	COPE	MU	COPE, Cartagena
CA25)	89.4		CR	CA	Catalunya Informació, Falset, Tarragona
CA09)	89.4	10	COPE	CA	Cadena 100, Rocacorba, Girona
AN42)	89.5	20	CSR	AN	Canal Fiesta R., Huelva
BA11)	89.5	8	KFM	BA	Kiss FM, Palma de Mallorca
EX11)	89.5	6	KFM	EX	Kiss FM, Cáceres
CA25)	89.5		CR	CA	Catalunya R., La Figuerassa, Barcelona
CA25)	89.5		CR	CA	Catalunya R., Artesa de Segre, Lleida
CA25)	89.5		CR	CA	Catalunya R., Vielha, Val D'Arán

FM	MHz	kW	Net	Rg	Station, location
CA25)	89.5		CR	CA	Catalunya Informació, Arenys de Munt, Barcelona
BA07)	89.6		COPE	BA	COPE Menorca
AR13)	89.7	40	ROCK	AR	ROCKFM.Zaragoza
CA25)	89.7		CR	CA	Icat FM, Sant Carles, Tarragona
CA25)	89.7		CR	CA	Catalunya R., Almenar, Lleida
CA25)	89.7		CR	CA	Catalunya Música, Solsona, Lleida
AN43)	89.8	8	CSR	AN	RAI R.Andalucía Informacion, Granada
CA09)	89.8	10	ROCK	CA	ROCKFM., Barcelona Collserola
AS03)	89.8	8	RPA	AS	RPA, R.Principado Asturias, Gijón
CA36)	89.9	10	ROCK	CA	ROCKFM., Rocacorba, Girona
CA09)	89.9	10	COPE	CA	COPE Catalunya, Rocacorba, Girona
VA08)	90.0	8	SER	VA	SER+ , Alicante
CA25)	90.0		CR	CA	Catalunya R., Pont de Suert, Lleida
CA25)	90.0		CR	CA	Catalunya R., Ulldemolins, Tarragona
CA25)	90.0		CR	CA	Catalunya Informació, Flix, Tarragona
AN38)	90.1	8	KFM	AN	Kiss FM, Málaga
VA30)	90.1	5		VA	Peque R., Valencia
CA25)	90.1		CR	CA	Catalunya R., Guardiola, Barcelona
CA25)	90.1		CR	CA	Catalunya Informació, Ribes de Freser
CA25)	90.2	10	CR	CA	Icat FM, Sant Celoni, Barcelona
CA25)	90.2		CR	CA	IcatFM, Oliana, Lleida
AN35)	90.3	6	OCR	AN	Onda Cero R., Jerez de la Frontera
EX12)	90.4	5	OCR	EX	Onda Cero Melodía, Mérida
AN57)	90.5	70	CSR	AN	RAI R.Andalucía Informacion, Almería
CA08)	90.5	8	40C	CA	Los 40 Classic, Barcelona Collserola
AR05)	90.5	40	40C	AR	Los 40 Classic, Zaragoza
CL31)	90.5	5	SER	CL	SER R. Miranda, Miranda de Ebro Burgos
CA25)	90.5		CR	CA	IlcatFM, Montblanc, Tarragona
CA25)	90.7		CR	CA	Catalunya R., Calella, Barcelona
CA25)	90.7		CR	CA	Catalunya R., Sant Hilari, Girona
AN39)	90.8	5	SER	AN	SER R. Puerto, El Puerto de S.M., Cadiz
AN38)	90.8	10	OCR	AN	Onda Cero R., Málaga
AN59)	90.8	64	CSR	AN	RAI R.Andalucía Informacion, Sevilla
GA29)	90.8	5	RG	GA	R. Galega Música, Vigo
CA25)	90.8		CR	CA	Catalunya Música, Maçanet, Girona
EU09)	90.9	20	EI	EU	R. Euskadi, Vitoria
CA25)	90.9		CR	CA	Catalunya Informació, Ponts, Lleida
MA11)	91.0	100	EFM	MA	Europa FM, Madrid
AS06)	91.1	6	D	AS	Cadena Dial Asturias, Oviedo
RI02)	91.1	6	COPE	RI	COPE Rioja, Logroño
CA25)	91.1		CR	CA	Catalunya R., Puigdevall, Lleida
EU07)	91.2	20	EI	EU	Euskadi Gaztea, Bilbo-Bilbao
CM08)	91.3	5	RCM	CM	R. Castilla-La Mancha, Guadalajara
CA25)	91.3		CR	CA	Catalunya Música, La Figuerassa, Barcelona
AR04	91.4	40	HIT	AR	HIT FM, Zaragoza
EX13)	91.4	10	L40	EX	Los 40, Plasencia
AN40)	91.4	8	EFM	AN	Europa FM, Córdoba
CA25)	91.4		CR	CA	IcatFM, Ripoll, Girona
CA25)	91.4		CR	CA	Catalunya Informació, Cogulló, Lleida
CL27)	91.5	8	KFM	CL	Kiss FM, Astorga
EU21)	91.5	8	KFM	EU	Kiss FM, Donosti-San Sebastián
CA25)	91.5		CR	CA	Catalunya R., Montagut, Girona
CA25)	91.5		CR	CA	Catalunya Música, Pont de Suert, Lleida
EX05)	91.6	6	COPE	EX	COPE, Cáceres
VA17)	91.6	10	EFM	VA	Europa FM, La RIbera València
CA25)	91.6		CR	CA	Catalunya Informació., Cadaqués, Girona
EU07)	91.7	20	EI	EU	R. Euskadi, Bilbo-Bilbao
MA05)	91.7	100	D	MA	Cadena Dial, Madrid
CL40)	91.7	5	KFM	CL	Kiss FM, Salamanca
VA08)	91.7	8	SER	VA	SER R. Alicante, Alicante
CA25)	91.7		CR	CA	Catalunya R., Cabrils, Barcelona
CA25)	91.9	15	CR	CA	Catalunya Música, Alpicat, Lleida
CA25)	91.9		CR	C	Catalunya Música, Sant Pere de Ribes, Barcelona
CA34)	91.9	10	RAC	CA	RAC105, Rocacorba, Girona
CM08)	91.9	5	RCM	CM	R. Castilla-La Mancha, Toledo
CT11)	91.9	6	OCR	CT	Onda Cero R., Santander
AR05)	92.0	40	40D	AR	Los 40 Dance, Zaragoza
CA25)	92.0	100	CR	CA	Catalunya Informació, Barcelona Collserola
CA25)	92.0		CR	CA	Catalunya Informació, Sant Carles, Tarragona
CA25)	92.0		CR	CA	Catalunya R., Senterada, Lleida
VA29)	92.0	10	MEGA	VA	MegaStar FM, València
EU10)	92.2	24	RP	EU	Popular Irratia Bilbo-Bilbao
CA25)	92.2		CR	C	Catalunya Música, Falset, Tarragona
VA34)	92.2		VA		R. Vila-Real, Castellón
CA25)	92.3		CR	CA	Catalunya Informació, L'Estartit, Girona
MA05)	92.4	14	SER	MA	Radiolé, Madrid
CA25)	92.5	100	CR	CA	Icat FM. Barcelona Collserola
CA25)	92.5		CR	CA	Catalunya R., Calonge, Girona
EX08)	92.6	6	L40	EX	Los 40, Cáceres
GA21)	92.6	8	RV	GA	R. Voz, A Coruña
CA25)	92.6		CR	C	Catalunya R., Camprodón, Girona
CM21)	92.7	6	KFM	CM	Kiss FM, Albacete
CA25)	92.7		CR	CA	Catalunya R., Portbou, Girona
AN22)	92.8	8	D	AN	Cadena Dial, Granada
VA18)	92.8	6	EFM	VA	Europa FM, Elx-Elche
CA25)	92.8		CR	CA	Catalunya Música, Baqueira, Val D'Arán
CL34)	92.9	6	CLR	CL	Castilla Leon R ., Burgos
CA25)	92.9		CR	CA	Catalunya R., Palafrugell, Girona
MA06)	92.9		RI	MA	China FM, Madrid
CA25)	93.0		CR	CA	IcatFM, Boí, Lleida
CA25)	93.0		CR	CA	IcatFM, Ponts, Lleida
CA25)	93.0		CR	CA	Catalunya R., Sant Feliu de Guixols, Girona
AN43)	93.1	5	CSR	AN	Canal Fiesta R. Baza, Granada
AN72)	93.1	8	D	AN	Cadena Dial, Málaga
EU18)	93.1	8		EU	R.Gorbea, Vitoria-Gasteiz
GA22)	93.1	5	RV	GA	R. Voz,. Pontevedra
CA25)	93.1		CR	CA	IcatFM, Pujalt, Tarragona
CA25)	93.1		CR	CA	IcatFM, Solsona, Lleida
VA11)	93.1	5	ROCK	VA	ROCK FM, València
AN73)	93.2	5	ROCK	AN	ROCKFM , Sevilla
VA08)	93.2	8	D	VA	Cadena Dial, Alicante
CA25)	93.2		CR	CA	IcatFM, Mur, Lleida
CA25)	93.3	5	CR	BA	Catalunya R., Alfabia, Palma M.
CA25)	93.3		CR	CA	IcatFM, Sant Pere de Ribes, Barcelona
CA25)	93.3		CR	CA	Catalunya Música, Guardiola, Barcelona
GA13)	93.4	8	SER	GA	SER R. Coruña, A Coruña
CA30)	93.4	5	SER	CA	SER, R. LLeida
AR05)	93.5	8	SER	AR	R. Zaragoza 2, Zaragoza
CA25)	93.5	20	OCR	CA	Onda Cero R., Collserola Barcelona
CA14)	93.5		COPE	CA	COPE Reus
CM15)	93.6		COPE	CM	COPE Ciudad Real
CA25)	93.6		CR	CA	Catalunya Informació, Senterada, Lleida
CA25)	93.7		CR	CA	IcatFM, Sant Hilari, Girona
CA25)	93.7		CR	CA	Catalunya Música, Cadaqués, Girona
CA25)	93.7		CR	CA	Catalunya Música, Sant Carles, Tarragona
CA25)	93.7		CR	CA	Catalunya Música, Almacelles, Lleida
AN47)	93.8	5	EFM	AN	Europa FM, Almería
AN72)	93.8	5	RO	AN	Radiolé, Málaga
CA25)	93.8		CR	CA	Catalunya R., Falset, Tarragona
CA25)	93.8		CR	CA	Catalunya Informació, Pujalt
CA25)	93.8		CR	CA	Catalunya Música, Artesa de Segre, Lleida
CA25)	93.9		CR	CA	Catalunya Informació, Montblanc, Tarragona
MA05)	93.9	100	L40	MA	Los 40, Madrid
CA08)	93.9	8	L40	CA	Los 40, Collserola Barcelona
AN42)	94.0	10	CSR	AN	Canal Sur R., Huelva
GA23)	94.0	6	OCR	GA	Kiss FM, Vigo
GA07)	94.1	20	RG	GA	R. Galega, Santiago de Compostela
CA25)	94.1		CR	CA	Catalunya Informació, Calonge, Girona
AN12)	94.2	5	ROCK	AN	ROCKFM, Jaén
CT03)	94.2	6	RMA	CT	R. Marca, Santander
CA25)	94.2		CR	CA	Catalunya Informació, Sant Celoni, Barcelona
AN59)	94.3	20	CSR	AN	RAI R.Andalucía Informacion., Sevilla
AN55)	94.3	10	CSR	AN	Canal Sur R., Córdoba
CL23)	94.3	6	D	CL	Cadena Dial, Burgos
CA25)	94.3		CR	CA	Catalunya R., Flix, Tarragona
CA11)	94.4	10	40C	CA	Los 40 Classic, Girona, Rocacorba
CL39)	94.4	8	EFM	CL	Europa FM, Valladolid
EU08)	94.4	20	EI	EU	Euskadi Irratia,Donosti-S Sebastián
EX08)	94.4	6	SER	EX	SER, Cáceres
CA25)	94.5	5	CR	CA	Catalunya Informació, Collsuspina Barcelona
AN43)	94.6	5	CSR	AN	Canal Fiesta R., Loja,Granada
CA25)	94.6		CR	CA	Catalunya Informació, Guardiola, Barcelona
EU07)	94.7	20	EI	EU	Euskadi Gaztea, Bilbo-Bilbao
CA25)	94.7		CR	CA	IcatFM, Arbucies, Girona
CA25)	94.7		CR	CA	Catalunya R., Tossa de Mar, Girona
CA25)	94.7		CR	CA	Catalunya Informació, Sant Pere de

FM	MHz	kW	Net	Rg	Station, location
					Ribes, Barcelona
CA25)	94.7		CR	CA	Catalunya Información, Sant Pere de Ribes
AN15)	94.8	40	40C	AN	Los 40 Classic, Sevilla
CA25)	94.8		CR	CA	Catalunya Informació, La Molina, Girona
AN41)	94.9	60	CSR	AN	RAI R.Andalucía Informacion. Málaga
CA07)	94.9	20	EFM	CA	Europa FM, Collserola Barcelona
CM10)	95.0	6		CM	R. Surco, Albacete
EU09)	95.0	20	EI	EU	Euskadi Irratia, Vitoria-Gasteiz
CA25)	95.0		CR	CA	Catalunya Informació, Vielha, Val D'Arán
CA25)	95.0		CR	CA	Catalunya Música, Cabra del Camp, Tarragona
AN43)	95.1	5	CSR	AN	Canal Sur R., Granada
CA11)	95.1	10	D	MA	Cadena Dial Girona, Rocacorba
MA17)	95.1	100	IE	MA	R.Intereconomia, Madrid
CA25)	95.1		CR	CA	Catalunya Música, Ponts, Lleida
CA08)	95.1	10	SER	CA	Cadena Dial, Rocacorba, Girona
AS08)	95.2	6	OCR	AS	Onda Cero R., Oviedo
CA25)	95.2		CR	BA	Catalunya R., Monte Toro, Menorca
AR05)	95.3	13	L40	AR	Los 40, Zaragoza
CA31)	95.3	5	OCR	CA	Onda Cero R., Tarragona
CA25)	95.3		CR	CA	Catalunya R., Ripoll, Girona
AS03)	95.4	10	RPA	AS	RPA,R.Principado Asturias, Boal
AN44)	95.4	8	KFM	AN	Kiss FM, Cádiz
CM14)	95.4		COPE	CM	COPE Albacete
CA25)	95.4		CR	CA	Catalunya R., Soriguera, Lleida
CA25)	95.4		CR	CA	Catalunya R., Boí, Lleida
CA25)	95.5		CR	BA	Catalunya R., S. Llorenç, Eivissa i Formentera
CA25)	95.5		CR	CA	Catalunya Inform. Ulldemolins, Tarragona
CA28)	95.5	20	KFM	CA	Kiss FM, Barcelona
AN52)	95.6	8	KFM	AN	Kiss FM, Córdoba
CA25)	95.6		CR	CA	Catalunya R., Sant Pere de Ribes, Barcelona
CA25)	95.6		CR	CA	Catalunya Informació, Puigdevall, Lleida
CA25)	95.7		CR	CA	Catalunya Informació, Artesa de Segre, Lleida
BA02)	95.8	5		BA	Insel R., Mallorca
AN22)	95.8		RO	AN	Radiolé, Granada
AN45)	95.9	40	OCR	AN	Onda Cero R., Sevilla
CA32)	95.9	5	RTT	VA	R. Tele Taxi, Benicassim, Valencia
CA08)	96.0	20	RO	CA	Radiolé, Collserola Barcelona
MA02)	96.0	20	FUN	MA	FUN R. Madrid
RI03)	96.0	6	KFM	RI	Kiss FM, Logroño
EU04)	96.1	20	EI	EU	Euskadi Gaztea, Zaldiaran
VA10)	96.1	10	40C	VA	Los 40 Classic, València
CA25)	96.1		CR	CA	Catalunya R., Solsona, Lleida
CL32)	96.2	6	OCR	CL	Europa FM, Salamanca
AN67)	96.2	6	D	AN	Cadena Dial Almería, Almería
CA25)	96.2		CR	CA	Catalunya R., Bellmunt, Lleida
AN33)	96.3	8	OCR	AN	Melodia FM, Malaga
MU03)	96.3	5	AMC	MU	R. 5, Cartagena
CM12)	96.4	6	RO	CM	Radiolé, Albacete
CA25)	96.4		CR	BA	Catalunya R., Alcúdia, Balears
CA25)	96.4		CR	CA	Catalunya Música, Cabrils, Barcelona
EU08)	96.5	20	EI	EU	R. Euskadi, Donosti-San Sebastián
AS09)	96.5	8	SER	AS	R. Gijón, Gijón
VA22)	96.5	8	R9	VA	R. Nou, Alacant-Alicante
CL35)	96.5		KFM	CL	Kiss FM, León
CA25)	96.5	10	CR	CA	IcatFM, Montserrat, Barcelona
AN43)	96.6	5	CSR	AN	Canal Sur R., Loja, Granada
GA08)	96.6	6	RG	GA	R. Galega Música, Friol
CA25)	96.7	25	CR	CA	Catalunya Música, Girona, Rocacorba
CA25)	96.7		CR	CA	IcatFM, Ribes de Fresser, Girona
MU11)	96.7	6	KFM	MU	Kiss FM, Cartagena
AN22)	96.8	3	40D	AN	Los 40 Dance, Granada
VA25)	96.9	20	KFM	VA	Kiss FM, València
CA08)	96.9	8	SER	CA	R. Barcelona, SER Catalunya, Collserola Barcelona
MA16)	96.9	20	RM	MA	R. María España, Madrid
CA25)	96.9		CR	CA	Catalunya R., Oliana, Lleida
EX08)	97.0	6	D	EX	Cadena Dial, Cáceres
CA25)	97.0		CR	CA	IcatFM, Palafrugell, Girona
CA25)	97.0		CR	CA	Catalunya Informació, Alpicat, Lleida
AN15)	97.1	40	L40	AN	Los 40, . Sevilla
AN43)	97.1	30	CSR	AN	Canal Fiesta R., Granada
AR05)	97.1	40	D	AR	CadenaDial Zaragoza, Zaragoza
CL23)	97.1	6	SER	CL	R. Castilla, Burgos
MU04)	97.1	5		MU	Onda Mediterranea R., Cartagena

FM	MHz	kW	Net	Rg	Station, location
CA25)	97.1		CR	CA	Catalunya Música, Sant Feliu de Guixols, Girona
CA25)	97.1		CR	CA	Catalunya Música, Olot, Girona
CA25)	97.1		CR	CA	Catalunya Música, Sant Hilari, Girona
MA07)	97.2	100		MA	Top R. Latina , Madrid
CA25)	97.2		CR	CA	Catalunya R., Sant Celoni, Barcelona
CA25)	97.2		CR	CA	Catalunya Informació, Calella, Barcelona
CA25)	97.3	10	CR	CA	Catalunya R., Montserrat Barcelona
CA25)	97.3		CR	CA	Catalunya Música, Flix, Tarragona
EU05	97.3	8	C100	EU	Cadena 100, Vitoria-Gasteiz
EU06)	97.3	5		EU	Fórmula Hit, Portugalete, Gipuzcoa
VA 05)	97.3	8	OCR	VA	Melodía FM, Altea.Alicante
CA11)	97.4	10	SER	CA	SER CAT, Rocacorba, Girona
CA25)	97.4		CR	CA	Catalunya R., Sant Carles, Tarragona
CA25)	97.4		CR	CA	Catalunya Música, Mur, Lleida
AR06)	97.5	40	COPE	AR	COPE, Zaragoza
CM13)	97.5		COPE	CM	COPE Puertollano
CA25)	97.5		CR	CA	IcatFM, Artesa de Segre, Lleida
CA25)	97.5		CR	CA	IcatFM, Senterada, Lleida
CA25)	97.5		CR	CA	Catalunya R., Montblanc, Tarragona
MA06)	97.5		RI	MA	R. Internacional, Madrid
GA13)	97.6	8	40C	GA	Los 40 Classic, A Coruña
MA18)	97.6	4	OCR	MA	Onda Cero R., Alcalá de Henares, Madrid
CL32)	97.6	6	OCR	CL	Onda Cero R., Salamanca
CA25)	97.6		CR	CA	IcatFM, Portbou, Girona
CA25)	97.6		CR	CA	Catalunya R., Baqueira, Val D'Arán
CA32)	97.7	20	RTT	CA	R. Tele Taxi, Collserola Barcelona
VA27)	97.7	20	VA	LA	97 Punto 7, València
AN48)	97.9	30	CSR	AN	Canal Fiesta R., Jaén
AR06)	97.9	40	C100	AR	Cadena 100, Zaragoza
CA25)	97.9		CR	CA	Catalunya R., Pujalt, Tarragona
CA25)	97.9		CR	CA	Catalunya Informació, Ponts, Lleida
CA25)	97.9		CR	CA	Catalunya Informació, Tossa de Mar, Girona
AN13)	98.0	30	COPE	AN	COPE, Alanis, Sevilla
EU13)	98.0	8	COPE	EU	Cope Más, Donosti-San Sebastián
EU15)	98.0	8		EU	R. Álava,Onda Vasca, Vitoria-Gasteiz
MA13)	98.0	100	OCR	MA	Onda Cero R., Madrid
CA14)	90.0		COPE	CA	COPE Tortosa
CA25)	98.0		CR	CA	Catalunya Informació, Vilaller, Lleida
CA25)	98.0		CR	CA	Catalunya Informació, Portilló, Val D'Arán
AN49)	98.1	5	SER	AN	R. Huelva, Huelva
CL18)	98.1	8	40CL	CL	Los 40 Classic, Valladolid
EX03)	98.1	5	CER	EX	Canal Extremadura R., Zafra, Badajoz
VA07)	98.1	10	ROCK	VA	ROCK FM, Alicante
CA25)	98.1		CR	CA	Catalunya Informació, Cabra del Camp
RI04)	98.2	6	MEGA	RI	MegaStar FM, Logroño
CA25)	98.2		CR	CA	Catalunya R., El Vendrell, Tarragona
CA25)	98.2		CR	CA	Catalunya Informació, Lloret, Girona
CA25)	98.3	10	CR	CA	Catalunya Informació, Montserrat, Barcelona
CM25)	98.3	5	KFM	CM	Kiss FM, Toledo
BA06)	98.4	5	D	BA	Cadena Dial, Alfábia, Palma M.
VA10)	98.4	20	D	VA	Cadena Dial Mediterraneo, València
CA25)	98.4		CR	CA	Catalunya Informació, Baqueira, Val D'Arán
CA25)	98.4		CR	CA	Catalunya Informació, Arenys de Munt, Barcelona
CA25)	98.5	5	CR	CA	Catalunya Informació, Montcaro, Tortosa
CA40)	98.5	10	SER	CA	SER, Girona
CT11)	98.5	5	KFM	CT	Kiss FM, Santander
CM22)	98.5	5	OCR	CM	Onda Cero R., Talavera de la Reina, Toledo
CL36)	98.6	8		CL	R. Arlanzón, Burgos
CM08)	98.6	5	RCM	CM	R. Castilla-La Mancha, Valdepeñas, Ciudad Real
EU11)	98.8	5	40C	EU	Los 40 Classic, Llodio, Alava
MU17)	98.8	6	RMA	MU	Solo R. R, Marca , Cartagena
BA16)	98.8	5	ROCK	BA	ROCK FM, Ultima Hora., Palma de Mallorca
CA25)	98.8		CR	CA	Catalunya Música, Camprodón, Girona
CA22)	98.9	10	OCR	CA	Onda Cero R., Rocacorba Girona
VA26)	98.9	5	COPE	VA	COPE, R.Sirena, Benidorm
CA25)	98.9		CR	CA	Catalunya Música, Oliana, Lleida
CA25)	98.9		CR	CA	Catalunya Música, Cubells-Balaguer, Lleida
VA11)	99.0	40	C100	VA	Cadena 100, València
CA25)	99.0		CR	CA	Catalunya Música, Almenar, Lleida
CA25)	99.0		CR	CA	Catalunya Música, Arbúcies, Girona
CL42)	99.1	5	KFM	CL	Kiss FM, Zamora

FM	MHz	kW	Net	Rg	Station, location
EU04)	99.1	5		EU	Euskadi Gaztea Vitoria-Gasteiz
MA03)	99.1	10	ES	MA	esRadio, Madrid
CA25)	99.1		CR	CA	Catalunya Música, Calella, Barcelona
CA25)	99.2		CR	CA	IcatFM, Calonge, Girona
CA25)	99.2		CR	CA	IcatFM, Montagut, Girona
CA25)	99.2		CR	CA	Catalunya R., Igualada, Barcelona
CL17)	99.3	6	D	CL	Cadena Dial, Salamanca
MU09)	99.3	8	KFM	MU	Kiss FM, Murcia
AN74)	99.4	30	CSR	AN	RAI R. Andalucía Informacion., Cádiz
AN55)	99.4	60	CSR	AN	RAI R. Andalucía Informacion., Córdoba
AR12)	99.4	40	OCR	AR	Onda Cero R., Zaragoza
CA08)	99.4	10	D	CA	Cadena Dial Barcelona, Barcelona
CL33)	99.4	8	KFM	CL	Kiss FM, Valladolid
CA25)	99.4		CR	CA	Catalunya Informació, Maçanet, Girona
AN51)	99.5	8	EFM	AN	Europa FM, Granada
MA08)	99.5	100	C100	MA	Cadena 100, Madrid
CA05)	99.6	10	GR	CA	Flaix FM, Girona, Rocacorba
CA25)	99.7	5	CR	CA	Catalunya R., Collsuspina, Barcelona
CA25)	99.7		CR	CA	IcatFM, Arenys de Munt, Barcelona
CA25)	99.7		CR	CA	Catalunya Informació, El Vendrell, Tarragona
MA04)	99.8	10		MA	R. Sol XXI, Madrid
CA25)	99.8		CR	CA	IcatFM, Ulldemolins, Tarragona
CA25)	99.8		CR	CA	IcatFM, Tossa de Mar, Girona
AN19)	99.9	8	D	AN	Cadena Dial Bahía, Cádiz
BA18)	99.9	8	RM	BA	R. Maria, Palma de Mallorca
AS03)	100.0	8	RPA	AS	R.Principado Asturias, Los Oscos
CA09)	100.0	20	C100	CA	Cadena 100, Collserola Barcelona
CA25)	100.0		CR	CA	Icat FM, Vielha, Val D'Aran
CA25)	100.1	10	CR	CA	Catalunya R., Girona, Rocacorba
CA34)	100.1	10	RAC	CA	RAC 1, Rocacorba, Girona
EU07)	100.1	20	EI	EU	EITB IrratiaMusika, Bilbo-Bilbao
CA25)	100.2	35	CR	CA	Catalunya R., La Mussara,Tarragona
GA08)	100.2	5	RG	GA	R. Galega Música, Xistral
AN58)	100.3	40	KFM	AN	Kiss FM, Sevilla
CM12)	100.3	5	SER	CM	SER Albacete
AN72)	100.4	6	SER	AN	SER, Málaga
CL18)	100.4	8	D	CL	Cadena Dial, Valladolid
EU22)	100.4	5	L40	EU	Los 40, Vitoria-Gasteiz
MA09)	100.4	5		MA	R. Círculo, Madrid
VA10)	100.4	20	SER	VA	R. Valencia 2, Valencia
CA25)	100.4		CR	CA	Icat FM, La Molina, Girona
CA25)	100.4		CR	CA	Catalunya Música, Palafrugell, Girona
NA06)	100.4		SER	NA	Radio Pamplona, also in 89.0 MHz
AR12)	100.5	10	EFM	AR	Europa FM, Zaragoza
AS03)	100.5	20	RPA	AS	R.Principado Asturias, Gijón
CA25)	100.5	5	CR	CA	Catalunya Música, Collsuspina, Barcelona
CA25)	100.5		CR	CA	Catalunya Informació, Mur, Lleida
CM08)	100.5	5	RCM	CM	R. Castilla-La Mancha, Guadalajara
CM23)	100.5	5		CM	R. Santa María, Toledo
GA12)	100.6	8	SER	GA	SER. Vigo 2, Vigo
AN48)	100.6	30	CSR	AN	Canal Sur R., Jaén
BA16)	100.6	5	GR	BA	Flaix FM, Mallorca
GA08)	100.6	5	RG	GA	R. Galega Música, Monte Páramo
CA25)	100.7	80	CR	CA	Catalunya R., Alpicat, Lleida
CA05)	100.7	10	GR	CA	Flaixbac FM, Girona, Rocacorba
MA08)	100.7	20	MEGA	MA	MegaStar FM, Madrid
AN55)	100.8	5	CSR	AN	Canal Sur R., Córdoba
EX03)	100.8	5	CER	EX	Canal Extremadura R., Badajoz
VA19)	100.8	6	COPE	VA	COPE,Elche
GA24)	100.9	30	RG	GA	R. Galega, Xesteiras, Pontevedra
BA11)	101.0	5	OCR	BA	Melodía FM Mallorca
CA34)	101.0	5	RAC	CA	Catalunya R., Mont Caro, Tortosa
CA25)	101.0		CR	CA	Icat FM, Cogulló, Lleida
EU05)	101.0	8	COPE	EU	COPE, Vitoria
AN72)	101.1	10	40D	AN	Los 40 Dance, Málaga
CT06)	101.1	6	40C	CT	Los 40 Classic, Santander
CA25)	101.1		CR	CA	Icat FM, La Figuerassa, Barcelona
VA23)	101.2	20	OCR	VA	Onda Cero R., València
AN56)	101.2	5	OCR	AN	Onda Cero R., Huelva
GA12)	101.2	6	40C	GA	Los 40 Classic, Vigo
CA25)	101.2		CR	CA	Icat FM, Lloret, Girona
CA25)	101.2		CR	CA	Catalunya Música, Vilaller, Lleida
CA25)	101.2		CR	CA	Catalunya Música, Portilló, Val D'Arán
MA14)	101.3	100		MA	Onda Madrid, Madrid
AN55)	101.3	30	CSR	AN	Canal Fiesta R., Córdoba
AN43)	101.3	5	CSR	AN	RAI R. Andalucía Informacion Loja, Granada
CA25)	101.3		CR	CA	Catalunya Informació, Solsona, Lleida
AS03)	101.4	10	RPA	AS	R. Principado Asturias, Avilés
RI02)	101.4	6	COPE	RI	Cadena 100, Logroño
CA25)	101.4		CR	CA	Catalunya R., Ribes de Freser, Girona
CA25)	101.4		CR	CA	Catalunya Informació, Sant Feliu de Guixols, Girona
AN15)	101.5	40	SER	AN	Radiolé, Sevilla
CA25)	101.5	8	CR	CA	Catalunya Música, Collserola Barcelona
EU07)	101.5	24	OCR	EU	Onda Cero R., Bilbo-Bilbao
AN53)	101.6	5	EFM	AN	Europa FM Costa del Sol, Mijas, Malaga
CM08)	101.6	5	CLR	CM	Castilla Leon R, Cuenca
CA38)	101.7	25	CR	CA	Catalunya Informació, Girona, Rocacorba
CA25)	101.7		CR	CA	Catalunya Informació, Almacelles, Lleida
AN67)	101.8	6	L40	AN	Los 40, Almería
CA06)	101.8	5	GR	CA	Flaix FM, Tarragona
AN59)	101.9	60	CSR	AN	Canal Fiesta R., Sevilla
EU04)	101.9	8	EI	EU	Euskadi Irratia, Amurrio,Alava
GA30)	101.9	6	RMA	GA	R. Marca, Vigo
CA25)	101.9		CR	CA	Catalunya Informació, Cubells-Balaguer, Lleida
AN14)	102.0	8	COPE	AN	COPE, Cádiz
CA09)	102.0	20	COPE	CA	COPE, Barcelona
CA25)	102.0		CR	CA	Catalunya R., Cogulló, Lleida
CA25)	102.0		CR	CA	Catalunya Música, Bellmunt
CA25)	102.0		CR	CA	Catalunya Música, Senterada, Lleida
CA25)	102.0		CR	CA	Catalunya Música, Ulldemolins, Tarragona
CA25)	102.2	25	CR	CA	Catalunya R, Girona, Rocacorba
AN42)	102.2	30	CSR	AN	Canal Fiesta R., Huelva
CA25)	102.2		CR	CA	Catalunya Música, Igualada, Barcelona
BA06)	102.3	4	40C	BA	Los 40 Classic Mallorca, Palma de Mallorca
CA42)	102.3	10	FUN	CA	FUN R., Barcelona
GA25)	102.3	40	RG	GA	R. Galega, Domaio
AN68)	102.4	40	D	AN	Cadena Dial Sevilla, Sevilla
CA25)	102.4	10	CR	CA	Catalunya Música, Montserrat, Barcelona
CT06)	102.4	6	SER	CT	SER, Liérganes, Santander
EU28)	102.4	6	OCR	EU	Onda Cero R., Vitoria
AN57)	102.5	70	CSR	AN	Canal Fiesta R., Almería, Pechina
CA25)	102.5	10	CR	CA	Catalunya Música, Mont Caro, Tortosa
CM08)	102.5	12	RCM	CM	R. Castilla-La Mancha, Ciudad Real
EU29)	102.5	8	OCR	EU	Onda Cero R., Donosti-San Sebastián
AN22)	102.5	8	D	AN	Cadena Dial, Granada
EX03)	102.6	60	CER	EX	Canal Extremadura R., Montánchez
EU23)	102.6	15	COPE	EU	Bizkaia Irratia, Bilbo-Bilbao
CA25)	102.6		CR	CA	Icat FM, Olot, Girona
CA25)	102.6		CR	CA	Catalunya Música, L'Estartit, Girona
MA13)	102.7	100	KFM	MA	Kiss FM, Madrid
GA26)	102.7	8	ES	GA	esRADIO.,A Coruña
AN72)	102.8	8	L40	AN	Los 40,, Mijas, Málaga
CA25)	102.8	100	CR	CA	Catalunya R. Collserola Barcelona
CA25)	102.8		CR	CA	IcatFM, Maçanet, Girona
CL43)	102.8	8	CLR	CL	Castilla Leon R,, Valladolid
BA15)	102.8	5	SER	BA	SER Ibiza, Ibiza
VA32)	102.8	90	R9	VA	Sí R., Benicassim
CA25)	102.9		CR	CA	Catalunya Informació, Pont de Suert, Lleida
CA25)	103.0		CR	CA	Icat FM, Almenar, Lleida
CA25)	103.0		CR	CA	Catalunya R., Mur, Lleida
CA25)	103.0		CR	CA	Catalunya Música, Cogulló, Lleida
AN71)	103.1	5		AN	R. Pinomar, Málaga
CA25)	103.1		CR	CA	Catalunya Informació, Cabrils, Barcelona
AN15)	103.2	28	SER	AN	SER Sevilla 2, Sevilla
EU07)	103.2	20	EI	EU	R. Euskadi, Bilbo-Bilbao
MA22)	103.2	5		MA	RTC - Radio TV Cristiana, Madrid
VA23)	103.2	10	EFM	VA	Europa FM, València
CA25)	103.2		CR	CA	IcatFM, Almacelles, Lleida
CA25)	103.2		CR	CA	Catalunya Informació, Montagut, Lleida
CA25)	103.3		CR	CA	Icat FM, Cubells-Balaguer, Lleida
CA29)	103.4	10	RE	CA	R. Estel, Girona, Rocacorba
CL37)	103.4	6	CLR	CL	Castilla Leon R, Salamanca
CM08)	103.4	5	RCM	CM	R. Castilla-La Mancha, Puertollano, Ciudad Real
EU09)	103.4	20	EI	EU	EITB Musika, Vitoria-Gasteiz
BA19)	103.4		COPE	BA	COPE Ibiza – Eivissa
CA25)	103.4		CR	CA	Icat FM, Baqueira, Val D'Aran
AN43)	103.5	60	CSR	AN	Canal Sur R., Sierra de Lújar, Córdoba
CA08)	103.5	20	SER	CA	SER CAT, Collserola Barcelona
EU08)	103.5	20	EI	EU	Euskadi Gaztea,Donosti-S. Sebastián

FM	MHz	kW	Net	Rg	Station, location
CA25)	103.5		CR	CA	Catalunya Informació, Camprodón, Girona
AN55)	103	6	30	CSR	AN Canal Sur R., Córdoba
EU30)	103.7	24	ROCK	EU	ROCK FM , Bilbo-Bilbao
GA08)	103.7	70	RG	GA	R.Galega, Monte Páramo
GA30)	103.8	6	RV	GA	R. Voz, Vigo
CA25)	103.8		CR	CA	Catalunya Informació, Bellmunt
AN59)	103.9	30	CSR	AN	Canal Fiesta R., Sevilla, Valencina
GA25)	103.9	40	RG	GA	R. Galega, Monte Faro
MA05)	103.9	30	40UR	MA	Los 40 Urban, Madrid
MU07)	103.9	8	D	MU	Cadena Dial, Murcia, Murcia
CA25)	103.9		CR	CA	Icat FM, Calella, Barcelona
CA25)	103.9		CR	CA	Catalunya Música, Sant Celoni, Barcelona
CM08)	104.0	10	RCM	CM	R. Castilla-La Mancha, Chinchilla, Albacete
EX03)	104.0	5	CER	EX	Canal Extremadura R., Cáceres
CA25)	104.0		CR	VA	Catalunya R., Ontinyent, Valencia
CA25)	104.0		CR	CA	Catalunya Informació, Oliana, Lleida
CA25)	104.0		CR	CA	Catalunya Informació, Igualada, Barcelona
AN24)	104.1	5	ROCK	AN	ROCK FM, Córdoba
AN63)	104.1	6	KFM	AN	Kiss FM, Almería
CA25)	104.1		CR	CA	Icat FM, Sant Feliu de Guixols, Girona
CA25)	104.1		CR	CA	Catalunya R., Cadaqués, Girona
EU09)	104.1	20	EI	EU	R. Vitoria/Gasteiz Irratia, Vitoria-Gasteiz
AN43)	104.2	8	CSR	AN	Canal Sur R., Granada
AS11)	104.2	5		AS	R. Amistad, Hevia-Siero, Gijón
CA08)	104.2	20	40D	CA	Los 40 Dance, Collserola Barcelona
GA31)	104.2	5	RG	GA	R. Galega Música, Santiago de Compostela
MA05)	104.3	37	SER	MA	SER+, Madrid
CA25)	104.3		CR	CA	Catalunya Música, Ribes de Freser, Girona
AN42)	104.4	30	CSR	AN	Canal Sur R., Huelva
EU07)	104.4	20	EI	EU	Euskadi Irratia, Bilbo-Bilbao
CA25)	104.4		CR	CA	Catalunya Informació, Arbúcies, Girona
CA25)	104.5	2	CR	CA	Catalunya Informació, La Mussara, Tarragona
AN41)	104.6	30	CSR	AN	Canal Sur R., Málaga
AN59)	104.6	60	CSR	AN	RAI R.Andalucía Informacion, Sevilla
MU16)	104.6	6	ORM	MU	Onda Regional Murcia, Cartagena
CA25)	104.6		CR	CA	Catalunya R., Lloret, Girona
VA20)	104.7	5	LOCA	VA	LOCA R., Elx
GA12)	104.7	6	40D	GA	Los 40 Dance, Vigo
CA25)	104.7		CR	CA	Catalunya R., Vilaller, Lleida
CA25)	104.7		CR	CA	Catalunya R., Portilló, Val D'Arán
AN37)	104.8	30	CSR	AN	Canal Sur R., Jerez de la Frontera
AN57)	104.8	20	CSR	AN	Canal Sur R., Almería
AR14)	104.8	10	RKM	AR	RKM, Zaragoza
EU31)	104.8	5	RKM	EU	RKM, Vitoria-Gasteiz
GA25)	104.8	40	RG	GA	R. Galega, Monte Meda
CA25)	104.8		CR	CA	Catalunya Informació, Palafrugell, Girona
CA25)	104.8		CR	CA	Catalunya Música, Montagut, Girona
AN43)	104.9	30	CSR	AN	Canal Sur R., Granada
EU23)	104.9	8	EI	EU	Euskadi Gaztea, Amurrio
CA25)	104.9		CR	CA	Icat FM, Cabra del Camp, Tarragona
CA25)	104.9		CR	CA	Icat FM, Montcaro, Tarragona
CA25)	104.9		CR	CA	Icat FM, Falset, Tarragona
CA34)	105.0	20	RAC	CA	RAC105, Collserola Barcelona
CA25)	105.0		CR	CA	Catalunya Informació, Almenar, Lleida
AN59)	105.1	30	CSR	AN	Canal Sur R., Sevilla
CA32)	105.1	10	RTT	CA	R. Tele Taxi, Girona, Rocacorba
MA10)	105.1	5		MA	Super Q FM , Madrid
CA25)	105.1		CR	CA	Catalunya Música, Pujalt, Tarragona
CA25)	105.2		CR	CA	Catalunya Música, Lloret, Girona
BA18)	105.2	30	RM	BA	R. Maria, Alfabia, Palma M.
CL39)	105.2	8	OCR	CL	Onda Cero R., Valladolid
MU16)	105.3	60	ORM	MU	Onda Regional, Murcia
CA25)	105.3		CR	CA	Catalunya R., La Molina, Girona
AS03)	105.4	8	RPA	AS	R.Principado Asturias, Oviedo
CA25)	105.4	20	CR	CA	Catalunya Música, La Mussara, Tarragona
CA25)	105.4		CR	CA	Icat FM, Cabrils, Barcelona
CA25)	105.4		CR	CA	Catalunya Informació, Olot, Girona
MA05)	105.4	100	SER	MA	SER Madrid 2, Madrid
AN55)	105.5	6	CSR	AN	Canal Fiesta R. Cabra, Cordoba
CL38)	105.5	6	KFM	CL	Kiss FM, Burgos
CA25)	105.5		CR	CA	Icat FM, Soriguera, Lleida
CA25)	105.5		CR	CA	Catalunya R., Maçanet, Girona
CA25)	105.5		CR	CA	Catalunya Informació, Sant Hilari, Girona
CA25)	105.5		CR	CA	Catalunya Música, Boí, Lleida
CA25)	105.5		CR	CA	Catalunya Música, Vielha, Val D'Arán
AN60)	105.6	16	CSR	AN	Canal Sur R., Algeciras
EU32)	105.6	8	C100	EU	Cadena 100,, Vitoria-Gasteiz
CA25)	105.6		CR	CA	Catalunya Música, Puigdevall, Lleida
CA41)	105.7	20	GR	CA	Flaix FM, Collserola Barcelona
CA25)	105.7		CR	CA	Icat FM, Cadaques, Girona
AR12)	105.8	40	KFM	AR	Kiss FM, Zaragoza
AN41)	105.8	30	CSR	AN	Canal Fiesta R., Málaga
CA25)	105.8		CR	CA	Catalunya R., L'Estartit, Girona
CA25)	105.8		CR	CA	Catalunya Informació, Portbou, Girona
CA25)	105.8		CR	CA	Catalunya Música, Ripoll, Girona
CA25)	105.9		CR	CA	Icat FM, Pont de Suert, Leida
MA14)	106.0	30		MA	Onda Madrid R., Madrid
AN55)	106.1	6	CSR	AN	RAI R. Andalucía Información, Cabra, Cordoba
BA06)	106.1	8	D	BA	Cadena Dial, Palma de Mallorca
CA41)	106.1	20	GR	CA	Flaixbac FM, Collserola Barcelona
GA27)	106.1	8	RV	GA	R. Voz, Santiago de Compostela
CA25)	106.1		CR	CA	Icat FM, Alpicat, Lleida
EU33)	106.2	8	C100	EU	CADENA100,, Donosti-San Sebastián
MA08)	106.3	10	COPE	MA	COPE , Madrid
CA25)	106.3		CR	CA	Icat FM, Flix, Tarragona
CA25)	106.3		CR	VA	Catalunya R., Perentxissa, Valencia
AS03)	106.4	60	RPA	AS	R.Principado Asturias, Gamoniteiro
CA25)	106.4		CR	CA	Catalunya Informació, La Figuerassa, Barcelona
CA25)	106.4		CR	CA	Catalunya Música, Montblanc, Tarragona
CA25)	106.4		CR	CA	Catalunya Música, Tossa de Mar, Girona
VA28)	106.5	5	OCR	VA	Onda Cero Alicante, Alicante
AN76)	106.9	20	RMA	AN	R. Marca, Sevilla
CA29)	106.6	20	RE	CA	R. Estel, Collserola Barcelona
EU34)	106.7	8	KFM	EU	Kiss FM, Vitoria-Gasteiz
CA25)	106.7		CR	VA	Catalunya R., Bartolo, Castellón
BA09)	106.8	100	IB3	BA	IB3, Alfábia, Palma M.
CA04)	106.8	10	EFM	CA	Europa FM, Girona, Rocacorba
CA25)	106.8		CR	VA	Catalunya R., Carrasqueta, Alicante
CA43)	106.9	5		CA	RKB, R. Kanal Barcelona
MU18)	106.9	8	ROCK	MU	ROCK FM , Murcia
MA27)	107.0	2		MA	Libertad FM., Madrid
AN65)	107.1	5		AN	R. Guadalate, Bornos, Jerez de la F.
MA20)	107.2	15		MA	Fiesta FM, Madrid
CA20)	107.9	15	RA	CA	R. Amistad,Barcelona.Turó d'en Fotjà

NB: stns less than 2kW omitted

DAB: 18 DAB stns and 1 DAB+ stn, only in Barcelona and Madrid (20% population). **Ch. 8A:** SER Digital, Onda Cero, Kiss FM, R.María, Cadena 100, Melodía FM, and R. María DAB+ – **Ch. 9D:** Madrid and **10A** Barcelona: RNE1, RNE5, COPE Digital, Intereconomía DAB, R.Marca, esRadio (off)-rep.R.Marca) – **Ch. 11B:** RNE1, R.Clásica RNE, RNE3, REE Europa, Megastar FM, Los 40 Classic.

DAB+ TEST in Costa del Sol, Málaga, Ch.7B: JAMM Radio; RRN Marbella; The One; JAZZ; Spectrum FM; ZZ.

Addresses & other information:

AN00) ANDALUCIA

AN01) Edif.RTVE, Parque del Alamillo, 41092 Sevilla. – **AN02)** Góngora 3, 14002 Córdoba. – **AN03)** Av.Ricardo Soriano 11, 29600 Marbella. – **AN04)** Av.de Granada 57, P1, 23001 Jaén. – **AN05)** Hermanos Machado 23, 04004 Almería. – **AN06)** Av.de la Aurora 40, 29006 Málaga. – **AN07)** Av.de Andalucía 67, 11007 Cádiz. – **AN08)** Plaza Carretas 5, 18009 Granada. – **AN09)** Plaza de Europa s/n, 11300 La Línea de la Concepción. – **AN10)** La Fuente 4, 21004 Huelva. – **AN11)** Cervantes 11, 14940 Cabra. – **AN12)** C/ Bartolomé 32 bajo, 23001 Jaén. – **AN13)** C/ Triana 8, 41380 Alanis. – **AN14)** C/ Algeciras 1, 2º módulo 8 "Edificio Fenicia", 11011 Cádiz. – **AN15)** Rafael González Abreu 6, 41001 Sevilla **E:** radiosevilla@cadenaser.com – **AN16)** Rioja 4, 41001 Sevilla. **E:** sevilla@cadenacope.net – **AN17)** Linaje 2, 29001 Málaga **E:** malaga@cadenacope.net – **AN18)** Gran Vía de Colón 28, 18001 Granada **E:** granada@cadenacope.net – **AN19)** Paseo Marítimo 1, Edif.Reina Victoria, 11010 Cádiz **E:** sercadiz@cadenaser.com – **AN20)** Obispo Aguilar 1, 23001 Jaén. **W:** radiojaen.es – **AN21)** Guadalete 12, 11403 Jerez de la Frontera. **W:** radiojerez.com – **AN22)** Santa Paula 2 (or: Ap.158), 18001 Granada **W:** radiogranada.es **E:** radiogranada@radiogranada.es – **AN23)** San Agustín 11 (or: Ap.364), 11403 Jerez de la Frontera **E:** jerez@cadenacope.net – **AN24)** Federico Mendizábal 10, 23001 Jaén **E:** jaen@cadenacope.net – **AN25)** Plaza Cardenal Toledo 4, 14001 Córdoba **E:** cordoba@cadenacope.net – **AN26)** José María Amoz 2, 21001 Huelva **E:** huelva@cadenacope.net – **AN27)** Padre Luque 11, 04001 Almería. **E:** almeria@cadenacope.net – **AN28)** General

Castaños 2, 11201 Algeciras. **E:** radioalgeciras@unionradio.es – **AN29)** Av.Federico García Lorca 105, 04005 Almería. – **AN30)** San Agustín 4, 29200 Antequera. – **AN31)** García Lovera 3, 14002 Córdoba. **W:** radiocordoba.com –**AN32)** Plaza Ramón y Cajal 8, 23700 Linares **E:** radiolinares@unionradio.es – **AN33)** C/ Peregrinos 3 "Edif. Galaxia 2º" Puerta 7, 29002 Málaga **AN35)** Gaitan 10, 11402 Jerez de la Frontera. – **AN36)** Pozo Nuevo 40 bajo, 41530 Morón de la Frontera. – **AN37)** C/ Carpinteros de Ribera 2, 11007-Cádiz. – **AN38)** C/ Peregrino 3 "Edif. Galaxia 2º" Puerta 7, 29002 Málaga. – **AN39)** Misericordia 10, 11500 Puerto de Santa María. – **AN40)** C/ Doctor Manuel Ruiz Maya 8,5º, 14004 Córdoba – **AN41)** Avenida Velazquez 307, 29004 Malaga – **AN42)** Carretera Huelva-San Juan del Puerto, km. 6,36. 21007 Huelva. – **AN43)** Urb. Bola de Oro, C/ Laguna de Aguas Verdes 11, 18008 Granada. – **AN44)** C/ Dr. Manuel Ruíz Maya 8, 11004 Cádiz. – **AN45)** Pabellón Once, Isla de Cartuja, 41092 Sevilla. – **AN46)** Plaza de España 15, 11006 Cádiz. – **AN47)** Avenida Federico García Lorca 105, 04005 Almería. – **AN48)** Prolongación Av. De Granada s/n, Recinto Institución ferial, 23009 Jaén. – **AN49)** Mendez Nuñez 15-5-6, 21001 Huelva. – **AN50)** Corredera 53, 11402 Jerez de la Frontera. – **AN51)** Recogidas 37, 18005 Granada. – **AN52)** Barroso 4-2, 14003 Córdoba. – **AN53)** C/ Ramón Gómez de la Serna 22 "Edificio King Edward II", 29600 Marbella. –**AN55)** Glorieta de Guadalhorce s/n, "Antigua Estación de RENFE", 14008 Córdoba. – **AN56)** Arquitecto Pérez Carasa 14-16, 21001 Huelva. – **AN57)** Centro Residencial Oliveros, C/ Maestro Serrano 9, 2º-B, 04004 Almería. — **AN58)** Sevilla. – **AN59)** Edificio Canal Sur, Av. José Gálvez 1, 41092 Isla de la Cartuja (Sevilla). – **AN60)** C/ Patriaca Pérez Rodríguez 36, 11201 Algeciras. – **AN61)** Placentines 2, 41004 Sevilla. – **AN62)** Av.de la Borbolla 47, 41013 Sevilla. – **AN63)** Almería. – **AN65)** San Jerónimo 7, 11640 Bornos. –**AN67)** Av. Mediterráneo 159, 2º "Edificio Laura", 04007 Almería– **AN68)** Rafael Gonzáles Abreu 6, 41001 Sevilla. – **AN69)** C/ San Agustín 4, 29200 Antequera. –**AN70)** Pasaje Comercial, Gran Plaza Letra F, 41005 Sevilla **W:** ministerioselshaddaisevilla.net – **AN71)** CL. Coín Parcela 1273, 29130 Alhaurín de la Torre (Málaga). – **AN72)** C/ Dr. Manuel Domínguez "Ed. Bulevar 2", 29001 Málaga. – **AN73)** Edificio de Oficinas del Estadio Olímpico, Isla de la Cartuja, 41092 Sevilla. – **AN74)** C/ Capinteros de Ribera 2, 11002 Cádiz.– **AN76)** Av. República Argentina 25-9º-B, 41011 Sevilla.

AR00) ARAGON

AR01) José Luís Albareda 1-3, 50004 Zaragoza. – **AR02)** Nueva 1, 44001 Teruel. – **AR03)** José Gil Caves 1, 22005 Huesca. **AR04)** Zaragoza. **W:** hitfm.es – **AR05)** Paseo de la Constitución 21, 50001 Zaragoza **E:** radiozaragoza@unionradio.es – **AR06)** Paseo de Sagasta 50 (or: Ap.42), 50006 Zaragoza. **E:** programas.zaragoza@cadenacope.net – **AR07)** Calle Alcalde Carderera 1, 22080 Huesca. **W:** radiohuesca.com – **AR11)** Coso 46, 50004 Zaragoza. – **AR12)** Zaragoza. – **AR13)** Calle Bilbao, 2, 1ª planta, 50004 Zaragoza. – **AR14)** REMAR, Av. Cataluña 225, 50003 Zaragoza.

AS00) ASTURIAS

AS01) C/ San Esteban de las Cruces 92, 33195 Oviedo. – **AS02)** Plaza del Instituto 3, 33201 Gijón. – **AS03)** Camino de las Clarisas 263, 33203 Gijón. –**AS05)** Carr.de la Costa 87 (or: Ap.235), 33205 Gijón. – **AS06)** Asturias 19, Bajo, 33004 Oviedo. **W:** radioasturias.com – **AS07)** Prado Picón 16, 33008 Oviedo. **W:** copeasturias.com **E:** c-oviedo@arrakis.es – **AS08)** C/ Cervantes 27, 5°,33003 Oviedo. – **AS09)** Jovellanos 1, 33202 Gijón. – **AS11)** C/ Lugar Orial 16, 33187 Hevia-Siero

BA00) BALEARES

BA01) Aragó 26, 07006 Palma de Mallorca. – **BA02)** Paseo Marítimo 26, 07014 Palma de Mallorca. – **BA03)** C/ Font i Monteros 21, 07003 Palma de Mallorca. – **BA05)** Felip II N° 28, 07800 Eivissa **E:** ibiza@cadenacope.net – **BA06)** Rector Bertomeu Martorell 35, Son Xigala, 07013 Palma de Mallorca **E:** informativos.mallorca@cadenaser.com – **BA07)** Av.Capitá Negrete 2-3N,07760 Ciutadella Menorca **E:** menorca@cope.es – **BA08)** Av.Jaume III N° 18, 07012 Palma de Mallorca **E:** mallorca@cadenacope.net – **BA09)** C/ Manuel Azaña 7-A, 07006 Palma de Mallorca. – **BA11)** Forners 7, Edif.Once, 07002 Palma de Mallorca.– **BA13)** Menacor 171, 07007 Palma de Mallorca. – **BA15)** Avenida Sant Jordi s/n, 07800 Figueretes (Ibiza). – **BA16)** C/ Gremi Selleters i Basters 14, "Polígon Son Castelló", 07009 Palma de Mallorca. – **BA18)** Mallorca. – **BA19)** Felipe II, 18 - 2ª, 07800 Ibiza-Eivissa **E:** informativos.ibiza@cadenacope.net

CA00) CATALUNYA

CA01) C. Roc Boronat 127, 08018 Barcelona. – **CA02)** Carrer Lluis Companys 1, 25003 Lleida. – **CA03)** Rambla Nova 23, 43003 Tarragona. – **CA04)** Gran Vía Jaume I N° 60, 17001 Girona. E-mail: emisora.girne@rtve.es – **CA05)** Av. Jaume I 76, 17002 Girona. – **CA06)** Plaça del Pati 2, entlo, 43800 Valls – **CA07)** Av. Diagonal 460, 3º, 08006-Barcelona **W:** radiomarcabarcelona.com **E:** info@radiomarcabarcelona.com – **CA08)** Casp 6, 08010 Barcelona. **E:** radiobarcelona@unionradio.es **W:** radiobarcelona.cat – **CA09)** Diputació 238, 08013 Barcelona **W:** fm/copebarcelona **E:** barcelona@cadenacope.net – **CA10)** Travessera de les Corts 131-159, Recinte Martenitat, Pavello Cambo, 08028 Barcelona **W:** comradio.com – **CA11)** Placa Josep Pla 2, 17001 Girona. **E:** radiogirona@unionradio.es – **CA12)** Tomàs Bergadà 3, 43204 Reus **E:** radioreus@unionradio.es – **CA13)** Carrer de Aragón 390-394, 2a planta, 08013 Barcelona – **CA14)** Llovera 54-56, 43201 Reus **E:** tarragona@cope.es – **CA15)** Acadèmia 14, 25002 Lleida. **W:** copelleida.com **E:** lerida@cadenacope.net – **CA16)** Sèquia 3, 17001 Girona **E:** girona@cadenacope.net – **CA17)** Vila Antònia 5, 25007 Lleida **E:** lleida@cadenaser.com – **CA18)** Relay Onda Rambla Barcelona (Local adress: Rambla Nova 69, 43003 Tarragona) – **CA19)** Calle Nou 47, 08240 Manresa **E:** informatius@els40.com – **CA20)** Apartado 269, 08211 Castellar del Vallès – **CA21)** Avda. Diagonal 441, 1º, 08006-Barcelona – **CA22)**Avda. Jaume I, 37, 7é 2a, 17001 Girona – **CA25)** El Palau Nou, Ramblas 88-94, 4ª, 08002-Barcelona **CA25)** Av Diagonal 614-616, 08021 Barcelona. **E:** info@catradio.cat – **W:** catradio.cat – **CA27)** Bulidor s/n, Polígnon Industrial 1, 08960 St Just D (Barcelona) – **CA28)** Aragó 390-394, P2, 08013 Barcelona. **E:** onamusica@onacataluna.com – **CA29)** C/ Comtes de Bell-lloc 67-69, 08014 Barcelona **E:** radioestel@radioestel.com – **CA30)** Del Riu 6, 25007 Lleida. – **CA31)** Rambla Nova 38, 43004 Tarragona – **CA32)** C/ Sant Carles 40, 08922 Sta Coloma de Gramenet (Barcelona). – **CA34)** Av. Diagonal 477, 15ª, 08006 Barcelona. – **CA35)** Camí Real 551, 1º, 08302 Mataró. – **CA36)** Rambla de la Llibertat 6, 17004 Girona. – **CA37)** C/ Ramón y Cajal 36, 3º, 43001 Tarragona. – **CA38)** Carretera de Barcelona 33, 4º, 17001 Girona. – **CA39)** Rambla d'Arago 43, 1º, 25003 Lleida.- **CA40)** Gran via de Jaume I 29-2º, 17001 Girona. – **CA41)** Paseo de Gràcia 55-57, 9º, 08007 Barcelona. – **CA42)** Barcelona. **W:** facebook.com/Locafuncatalunya – **CA43)** Gran vía de les Corts Catalanes 645, 2º-1, 08007 Barcelona.

CL00) CASTILLA Y LEÓN

CL01) García Morato 27-29, 47007 Valladolid. – **CL02)** Becerro de Bengoa 9, 34002 Palencia. – **CL03)** Santa Clara 2, 05001 Avila. – **CL04)** Ordoño II N° 28, 24001 León. – **CL05)** Campo 5, 42001 Soria. – **CL06)** Calle Barrio Gimeno 11, 09004 Burgos. – **CL07)** Av.de Requejo 21, 49012 Zamora. – **CL08)** Ave María 11, (or Apartado de Correos 105, 24480 Ponferrada) 24400 Ponferrada. – **CL09)** Plaza de Colón 4, 37001 Salamanca. – **CL10)** Paseo Ezequiel Gonzales 24, 40002 Segovia. – **CL15)** Av.del Cid 8, 09005 Burgos **E:** informativos.burgos@cadenacope.net – **CL16)** Duque de la Victoria 23, 47001 Valladolid **E:** direccion.valladolid@cadenacope.net – **CL17)** C/ Veracruz 2 bajo, 37008 Salamanca **W:** radiosalamanca.com – **CL18)** C/ La Estación 3, 47004 Valladolid **E:** radiovalladolid@cadenaser.com – **CL19)** Sol Oriente 11-15, 37002 Salamanca **E:** salamanca@cadenacope.net – **CL20)** Hermanos La Salle 2, 24700 Astorga **E:** astorga@cadenacope.net – **CL21)** Lope de Vega 1, 24002 León **W:** copeleon.com **E:** leon@cadenacope.net – **CL22)** Plaza Fernández Duró 3 (or: Ap.42), 49001 Zamora **E:** zamora@cadenacope.net – **CL23)** Plaza de España 3, 09005 Burgos **E:** radiocastilla.redaccion@unionradio.es – **CL24)** Villafranca 6, 24001 León **W:** radioleon.com **E:** radioleon@radioleon.com – **CL25)** Calle Santa Ana 6, 49006 Zamora **E:** radioz@teleline.es – **CL26)** Plaza Cirilo Rodríguez 2, 40001 Segovia **W:** radiosegovia.com – **CL27)** Astorga. – **CL31)** Vitoria 24, 09200 Miranda de Ebro. – **CL32)** Bermejeros 14, 37001 Salamanca. – **CL33)** Rastrojo 5, 47014 Valladolid. – **CL34)** Plaza de Aragón 5, 09001 Burgos. – **CL35)** Julio del Campo 4-6, 24002 León. – **CL36)** Plaza de los Vadillos 5, 09005 Burgos. **W:** radioarlanzon.com – **CL37)** Aliso 2 bajo, 37004 Salamanca. – **CL38)** Burgos. – **CL39)** Edif.Promecal, c/los Astros s/n, 47009 Valladolid. **CL40)** Salamanca. – **CL41)** Valladolid. – **CL42)** Zamora. – **CL43)** C/ Manuel Canesi Acevedo 1, 4706 Valladolid.

CM00) CASTILLA-LA MANCHA

CM01) Paseo de San Cristóbal s/n, 45002 Toledo. – **CM02)** Ramiro Ledesma 8, 13630 Socuéllamos. – **CM03)** Nuestra. Sra. De Araceli 1, Edif.Las Torres, 02002 Albacete. – **CM04)** Radio Nacional de España 2 (or: Ap.18), 16003 Cuenca. – **CM05)** Ronda del Carmen s/n (or: Ap.150), 13002 Ciudad Real **E:** emisora.cr.rne@rtve.es – **CM06)** Plaza de Consejo, Centro Civico, 19001 Guadalajara. – **CM07)** Ronda del Canillo 35, 45600 Talavera de la Reina. – **CM08)** Polígono Santa María de Benquerencia, C/ Río Alberche s/n, 45007 Toledo. – **CM10)** C/ Gaona 8 , 4º-B, 02001 Albacete. **W:** radiosurco.es – **CM12)** Avenida de la Estación 5, 02001 Albacete. **E:** radioalbacete@unionradio.es – **CM13)** Alejandro Prieto 2, 13500 Puertollano **E:** puertollano@cadenacope.net – **CM14)** Tesifonte Gallego 9, 02002 Albacete **E:** albacete@cadenacope.net – **CM15)** Pasaje San Isidro 3, 13001 Ciudad Real **E:** ciudadreal@cadenacope.net – **CM21)** Av.de la

Estación 5, 02001 Albacete. – **CM22)** C/ Joaquina Santander 13, 1º, 45600 Talavera de la Reina. – **CM23)** Calle Trinidad 12, 45002 Toledo. **W:** rtvd.org/radio.htm **E:** rtvdiocesana@planalfa.es – **CM24)** 02001 Albacete. – **CM25)** Toledo.

CT00) CANTABRIA

CT01) Polígono de Raos s/n, 39609 Camargo (Santander) – **CT02)** Av.del Besaya 1 (or: Ap.46), 39300 Torrelavega – **CT03)** C/ José María Pereda 23, 39100 Santa Cruz de Bezana. – **CT05)** Rualasal 5, 39001 Santander **E:** santander@cadenacope.net – **CT06)** Pasaje de la Peña 2, int 7, Edif.Simeon 39008 Santander **W:** radiosantander.com **E:** informativos@radiosantander.com – **CT11)** Fernandez de Isla 14,2º, 39008 Santander.

EU00) EUSKADI

EU01) Plaza de Simón Bolívar 13, 01003 Vitoria-Gasteiz – **EU02)** Paseo de los Fueros 2, 20006 Donosti-San Sebastián **E:** emisora.ss.rne@the.es – **EU03)** Licenciado Poza 55, 48013 Bilbo-Bilbao. – C/ Polorínviejo 4, 01003 Vitroria-Gasteiz. – **EU04)** C/ Domingo Martínez de Aragón 5-9, 01006 Vitoria-Gasteiz. **W:** eitb.com/eu/gaztea – **EU05)** C/ San Antonio 2 bajo, 01005 Vitoria-Gasteiz. – **EU06)** C/ Alonso Allende 21, Lonja izquierda, 48920 Portugalete. – **EU07)** Capuchinos de Basurto 2, Edificio Bami, 48013 Bilbo-Bilbao **E:** radio_euskadi@eitb.com – **EU08)** Miramón 172, 20004 Donostia-San Sebastián **W:** www eitb.com/euskara/ – **EU09)** C/ Domingo Martínez de Aragón 5-9, 01006 Vitoria-Gasteiz **W:** eitb.com/radiovitoria – **EU10)** Calle Alameda Mazarredo 47,7°, 48009 Bilbo-Bilbao **W:** radiopopular.com – **EU11)** C/ Industrialdea s/n, 01400 Llodio-Alava **E:** vitoria@los40.com – **EU12)** Paseo Portuetxe 51, Edificio ACB, 20018 Donostia-San Sebastián **E:** radiosansebastian@cadenaser.com – **EU13)** Miracruz 9, 20001 Donostia-San Sebastián –**EU15)** C/Portal de Gamarra, 23. Pabellón A, 01002 Vitoria-Gasteiz . **W:** ondavasca.com – **EU17)** Vitoria-Gasteiz. – **EU20)** Bulevar de Beurko 4, local 2, 48902-Barakaldo. **EU18)** C/ La Habana s/n, 01012 Vitoria **W:** radiogorbea.com **EU21)** Av.de la Libertad 17, 20004 -Donosti-San Sebastián – **EU22)** General Alava 10-6 Depto 9, 01005 Vitoria-Gasteiz – **EU23)** Fontecha y Salazar 9-5, 48007 Bilbo-Bilbao – **EU24)** Eziago Poligonoa 10B, 20120 Hernani. – **EU25)** C. Hurtado de Amezaga 27,17piso, 48008 Bilbo-Bilbao. – **EU26)** C/ Esteban Zurbano 20, 20214 Segura (Guipúzcoa). – **EU27)** Gordóniz 44, 12º, 48002 Bilbao. – **EU28)** C/ San Prudencio 8-A,, 5º, 01005 Vitoria-Gasteiz. – **EU29)** Paseo Federico García Lorca 10, 4º, Puerta 1-2, 20014 Donosti-San Sebastián. – **EU30)** Ribera de Elorrieta 7, 48015 Bilbo-Bilbao. – **EU31)** C/ José Lejarreta 11, 01003 Vitoria-Gasteiz. – **EU32)** C/ Portal de Legutiano 6, 01002 Vitoria-Gasteiz . – **EU33)** Parque Empresarial Zuazu, Ed. Ulía 8, 20018 Donosti-San Sebastián. – **EU34)** Vitoria-Gasteiz.

EX00) EXTREMADURA

EX01) Av.Ruta de la Plata 10, 10001 Cáceres – **EX02)** Plaza de España 5, 06002 Badajoz. – **EX03)** Avenida de las Américas 1, 1º, 06800 Mérida. – **EX05)** C/ Comandante Sánchez Herrero 2, 1º, 10004 Cáceres **E:** caceres@cadenacope.net – **EX06)** Ramón Albarrán 2, 06002 Badajoz **E:** radioextremadura@unionradio.es – **EX07)** Menacho 12, 06001 Badajoz **E:** badajoz@cadenacope.net – **EX08)** C/ Profesor Rodríguez Moñino 1, 8º-A, 10003 Cáceres. – **EX11)** Av.de España 9-6, 10004 Cáceres – **EX12)** Av.de Portugal s/n, Ctro Comercial El Foro, 06800 Mérida – **EX13)** Santa Isabel 4, 10600 Plasencia – **EX16)** Luis Alvarez Lancero 8, 10001 Cáceres.

GA00) GALICIA

GA01) Paseo Méndes Nuñez 12, (or: Ap.199), 15006 A Coruña – **GA02)** Lepanto 7, 36001 Pontevedra – **GA03)** Rua de Progreso 115 (or: Ap.268), 32003 Ourense – **GA04)** Ourense 59-63 (or: Ap.73), 27004 Lugo – **GA05)** Plaza de España 4, 27400 Monforte de Lemos – **GA06)** Av.García Barbón 36, 36201 Vigo – **GA07)** San Marcos s/n, Edif.TVE, 15780 Santiago de Compostela. – **GA08)** Rúa Pascual Veiga 12-14 baixo dereita, 27002 Lugo. – **GA09)** Plaza de España 5-6, 15403 El Ferrol **E:** ferrol@cadenacope.net – **GA10)** San Pedro de Mezonzo 3 (or: Ap 469), 15701 Santiago de Compostela **E:** radiogalicia@unionradio.es – **GA11)** Principe 57, 36202 Vigo **E:** vigo@cadenacope.net – **GA12)** Areal 6-8, 36201 Vigo **W:** radiovigo.es – **GA13)** Plaza de Ourense 3, 15004 A Coruña **W:** radiocoruna.com – **GA14)** Castelao 3 B, 36001 Pontevedra **E:** ser@radiopontevedra.com – **GA15)** Rua de Progreso 89, 32003 Ourense **E:** orense@cadenacope.net – **GA16)** Rua de Valiño s/n, 27002 Lugo **E:** lugo@cadenacope.net – **GA17)** Plaza de Santo Domingo 3, 27001 Lugo **W:** radiolugo.com – **GA18)** Rua do Paseo 30 (or: Ap.1017), 32003 Ourense **W:** radioourense.com **E:** cadenaser@radioourense.com – **GA21)** Ronda de Outeiro, Nº1 y 3 Bajo, 15006 A Coruña– **GA22)** Salvador Moreno 30, 36001 Pontevedra – **GA23)** Av.García Barbón 104, 36201 Vigo – **GA24)** Rúa Benito Corbal 14, 2º, 36001 Pontevedra – **GA25)** Casa de la Radio, San Marcos, 15820 Santiago de Compostela – **GA26)** . **W:** esradio.fm – **GA27)** Salguiriños de Arriba 44, bajo, 15890 Santiago de Compostela. – **GA28)** Apartado de Correos 3114, 36208 Vigo. **W** : ondasdevida.org - **GA29)** C/ Torreiro 13-15, 3º-E, 15005 A Coruña. – **GA30)** Av. García Barbón 28, 36201 Vigo. – **GA31)** Rúa Costa Rica 6, 7º, 15005 A Coruña.

MA00) MADRID

MA01) Casa de la Radio, Prado del Rey, 28223 Pozuelo de Alarcón – **MA02)** C/ Enrique Larreta 12, 28036 Madrid. – **MA03)** C/ Juan Esplandiú 15, 2ª, 28007 Madrid. – **MA04)** C/ San Bernardo 20, 3º, Centro, 28015 Madrid – **MA05)** Gran Vía 32, 28013 Madrid **E:** redaccion@cadenaser.com – **MA06)c/Orense 68, 28020 Madrid** Web: radiointer.es – **MA07)** C/ Juan Esplandiú 15, 2ª, 28007 Madrid – **MA08)** Alfonso XI N° 4, 28014 Madrid **W:** cope.es **E:** programas.madrid@cadenacope.net – **MA09)** Círculo de Bellas Artes, C/ Alcalá 42, 5 planta, 28014 Madrid.- **MA10) W:** superqfm.es . – **MA11)** Bueso Pineda 7, 28043 Madrid – **MA13)** José Isbert 6, Ciudad de la Imagen - 28223 Pozuelo de Alarcón **W:** kissfm.es **E:** kissfm@kissfm.es – **MA14)** Pso del Principe 3, Cd.de la Imagem, 28223 Pozuelo de Alarcón **W:** telemadrid.com – **MA16)** Av.de los Arqueros s/n, 28024 Madrid **E:** radiomaria@arsenet.com – **MA17)** c/Velázquez, 105 , 28006 Madrid **W:** intereconomia.com – **MA18)** Sta Clara 7, 28801 Alcalá de Henares – **MA20)** C/ Juan Español 47, local bajo, 28026 Madrid. **W:** fiestafm.net. – **MA21)** C. Francisco Silvela 122 bajo, 28002 Madrid. – **MA22)** Calle de Secoya 29, Planta 3 Puerta 1, 28054 Madrid – **MA24)** C/ Orense 18, piso 8, of. 9, 28020 Madrid. **W:** rtcespana.es – **MA26)** Juan Ignacio Luca de Tena 7, 28027 Madrid. – **MA27)** Paseo de la Castellana 129, 1º-C, 28046-Madrid

MU00) MURCIA

MU01) La Olma 27-29, 30005 Murcia **E:** emisora.mu.rne@rtve.es – **MU02)** Paseo Alfonso XIII N° 51, 30203 Cartagena. – **MU03)** C/ Bucarest 29, 30391 Cartagena. – **MU04)** C/ Carmen Conde 46, 1º, 30203 Cartagena. – **MU05)** Arco de Santo Domingo 2-3, Edif. Fontanar, 30001 Murcia **E:** murcia@cadenacope.net – **MU06)** Av.Juan Carlos I N° 63, 30800 Lorca **E:** lorca@cadenacope.net – **MU07)** Calle Radio Murcia 4, 30001 Murcia **E:** radiomurcia@unionradio.es – **MU08)** Real 70, 30201 Cartagena **E:** informativos.cartagena@cadenaser.com – **MU09)** Murcia – **MU11)** Edif.Mediterráneo, Puerta Murcia 11, 30201 Cartagena – **MU12)** C/ Carmen 51, 1° A, 30201 Cartagena – **MU13)** Madre de Dios 15, 30004 Murcia – **MU14)** Mayor 31, 30200 Cartagena – **MU16)** Av.Libertad 6, bajo, 30009 Murcia. – **MU17)** Pza de los Apóstoles 7, 30001 Murcia. – **MU18)** Ed.del Periódico La Verdad, Camino Viejo de Monteagudo s/n, 30160 Murcia.

NA00) NAVARRA

NA01) Emilio Arrieta 8, P8, 31002 Pamplona-Iruñea – **NA02)** Aoiz 17, 31004 Pamplona-Iruñea. – **NA03)** Ed. Ciencias Sociales, Universidad de Navarra, Campus Universitario s/n, 31080 Pamplona.-Iruñea **W:** unav.es/98.3 – **NA05)** Amaya 2-B, 31002 Pamplona-Iruñea **E:** pamplona@cadenacope.net – **NA06)** Polígono Plazaola, Manzana F, 2° A, 31195 Aizoain (or Apartado de Correos 71, 31080 Pamplona) **E:** informativosnavarra@cadenaser.com – **NA11)** Plaza del Castillo 43, 31001 Pamplona-Iruñea – **NA12)** Cortes de Navarra 1, 31002 Pamplona-Iruñea.

RI00) LA RIOJA

RI01) Vara de Rey 42, (or: Ap.247), 26002 Logroño – **RI02)** Residencia Universitaria Francisco Jordán, Av. Madre de Dios 17, 26001 Logroño – **RI03)** C/ Estambrera 36, 1º, 26006 Logroño. – **RI04)** C/ General Vara del Rey 74, 26002 Logroño. – **RI05)** Av.de Portugal 12 (or: Ap.149), 26001 Logroño **W:** radiorioja.com – **RI11)** Logroño – **RI12)** Miguel Villanueva 2, Ofc.5, 26001 Logroño.

VA00) CUMUNITAT VALENCIANA

VA01) Av Colóm 13, 46004 València – **VA02)** Angel Lozano 18, 03001 Alacant-Alicante – **VA03)** Passeig de la Ribalta 5, 12001 Castelló – **VA04)** Juan Carlos I 37, 03202 Elx. – **VA05)** Plaça dels Sports 7-8, Ed. Sabater, 03590 Altea – **VA07)** Rambla de Méndez Nuñez 45, 03002 Alacant-Alicante **E:** alicante@cadenacope.net – **VA08)** Calderón de la Barca 26, 03004 Alacant-Alicante **E:** alicante@cadenaser.com – **VA09)** Av.Francisco Tàrrega 69, 12540 Vila-Real **E:** castellon@cadenacope.net – **VA10)** Don Juan de Austria 3, 46002 València **E:** valencia@cadenaser.com – **VA11)** Passatge Dr.Sierra 2, 46004 València **W:** cope.es/valencia – **VA12)** Doctor Sempere 16B y C, Bajos, 03803 Alcoi **E:** radioalcoy@radioalcoy.com – **VA13)** Moyano 5, 12002 Castelló **W:** radiocastellon.comdc – **VA14)** Dr.Caro 43, 03201 Elx **W:** radioelche.com – **VA15)** Calle Loreto 32, 46700 Gandia **E:** ser@radiogandia.net **W:** radiogandia.net – **VA16)** Ereta 2A (or: Ap.84), 46870 Ontinyent **W:** radioontinyent.com – **VA 17)** C/ Hort dels Frares 12, 46600 Alzira. – **VA18)** C/ Doctor Caro 18 entresuelo derecha, 03201 Elx. – **VA19)** C/ La Fira 10, 03202 Elx. – **VA20)** C/ Almorida 2, 4º derecha, 03201 Elx. – **VA21)** Alacant-Alicante. **E** : alicante@kissfm.es

– **VA23)** C/ San Vicente 16, entreplanta 1°, 46001 València – **VA24)** Av.Blasco Ibañez 136, 46022 València – **VA25)** València – **VA26)** Vía Emilia Ortuño 5, 3°, 03500 Benidorm – **VA27)** Edificio Levante. Polígono Vara de Quart. Calle Traginers, 7 46014 València **W:** la977.com – **VA28)** Paseo Explanada de España 26, 03001 Alicante – **VA29)** C/ Els Gremis 1, Polígono Vara de Quart, 46014 Valencia **W:** abc.es/radio/valencia – **VA30)** C.C. Alfafar, Pl. Alquería de la Culla 4, Planta14, of.01, 46910 Alfafar,Valencia. **W:** pequeradio.es – **VA32)** Av. Blasco Ibáñez 134, 46022 València. – **VA33)** Av. Aragón 30, 46031 Valéncia.- VA34) c/Ausias March 1 bajos, 12540 Vila-Real, Castellón E: direccio@radiovila-real.info
For more information see W: lalistadelafm.com Also in: guiadelaradio.com

AMERICAN FORCES RADIO & TV SERVICE (Mil.)
AFN Rota 102.5 MHZ(4 Kw), AFN Morón 92.1 MHZ (0,1 Kw). US Naval Station, PSC 816, Box 27, FPO AE 09645, USA. **W:** www.facebook.com/AFNRota **E:** afn1025rota@gmail.com D.Prgr: 24h

SRI LANKA

L.T: UTC +5½h — **Pop:** 21 million — **Pr.L:** Sinhala (official), Tamil (official), English — **E.C:** 230V/50Hz — **ITU:** CLN

TELECOMMUNICATIONS REGULATORY COMMISSION OF SRI LANKA
276, Elvitigala Mawatha, Colombo 08 ☎ +94 11 2689345 +94 11 2689341 **E:** dgtsl@trc.gov.lk **W:** www.trc.gov.lk
L.P: Chmn: Austin Fernando

SRI LANKA BROADCASTING CORPORATION (Pub)
P.O. Box 574, Independence Square, Colombo 7 ☎+94 11 2697491 +94 11 2691568 **E:** ddge@slbc.lk **W:** slbc.lk
L.P: Chairman: Mr Malaka Talwatte, DG: Mr Erananda Hettiarachchi, Dir Eng.: Mr M.G.W. Priyadarshana

FM (MHz)	A	B	C	D	E	F
Colombo	91.7	94.3	102.1	104.7	97.4	89.6
Deniyaya	91.7	94.3	102.1	104.7	97.4	89.6
Haputale	91.9	94.5	102.3	104.9	90.1	89.8
Hunasgiriya	91.7	94.3	102.1	104.7	97.4	89.6
Jaffna	-	-	-	104.7	-	-
Karagahatenna	91.7	94.3	102.1	104.7	97.4	89.6
Kovavil	-	-	107.5	104.9	-	89.8
Radella	91.7	94.3	102.1	104.7	97.4	89.6
Yatiyantota	91.9	94.5	102.3	104.9	97.6	89.8

A = Sinhala National Sce (Swadeshiya Sevaya) 2300-1600., **B** = Sinhala Commercial Sce (Velenda Sevaya) 24h, **C** = Tamil National Sce 2300-1715, **D** = Tamil Commercial Sce 2300-1700, **E** = English Sce 0000-1700 (includes rel. of BBC World Sce), **F** = City FM 24h.
Sports Sce: operates irr. on FM freqs of Vidula Sce and YAL FM.
Vidula (Children's channel): Colombo 107.3MHz, Yatiyantota 107.5MHz: 0000-1630 in Sinhala, Tamil and English.

Regional services:
FM(MHz): **Akkaraipattu:** Haputale 102.1 (Thirayi Sevaya) – **Anuradhapura:** Anuradhapura 90.1, Karaghatenna 107.3 (Rajarata Sevaya) – **Batticaloa:** Karaghatenna 102.3 (Pirai FM in Tamil) – **Jaffna:** Jaffna 90.1, Palali 102.1 (Palali Sevaya/YAL FM in Tamil & Sinhala) – **Kandy:** Hanthana 90.1, Hunasgiriya 107.5, Radella/Nuwara Eliya 107.3 (Kandurata Sevaya) – **Kurunegala:** Karaghatenna 90.1 (Wayamba Handa) – **Matara:** Haputale 107.5, Deniyaya 107.3 5kW (Ruhunu Sevaya).
Regional Sce operates 2300-0230 & 1000-1530.
Community Stations: Badulla 97.6 (Uva Com, R.), Girandurukotte 97.6 (Dambana R.), Mawathura 97.6 0.3kW (Kothmale FM)
Ann: A: "Me Sri Lanka Guwan Viduli Sansthave Welanda Sevaya". **B:** "Me Sri Lanka Guwan Viduli Sansthava Swadeshiya Sevaya". **C:** "Illangar Oliparappu Kootuthapanam Tamil Sevai". **E:** "This is the Sri Lanka Broadcasting Corporation"

EXTERNAL SERVICE: SLBC see International Broadcasting section

MAJOR COMMERCIAL NETWORKS (FM MHz):

ASIA BROADCASTING CORPORATION (Pvt) Ltd
35th Floor, East Tower, World Trade Center, Colombo 1 ☎+94 11 2337555 **E:** md@abcradio.lk **W:** abcradio.lk **Stns: Gold FM** in English: Colombo/Kandy/Matale/Matara 93.0, Badulla/Jaffna/Nuwara Eliya/Ratnapura 93.2 – **Hiru FM** in Sinhala: Colombo/Kandy/Matale/Matara 96.1, Badulla/Jaffna/Nuwara Eliya 96.3 – **Shaa FM** in Sinhala: Colombo/Kandy/Matale/Matara 90.9, Badulla/Jaffna/Nuwara Eliya/Ratnapura 91.1 – **Sooriyan FM** in Tamil: Badulla/Jaffna/Mannar/Nuwara Eliya/ Trincomalee/Vauniya 103.4, Colombo/Kandy/Matale/Matara 103.6 – **Sun FM** in English: Badulla/Kilinochchi/Nuwara Eliya/Ratnapura 98.7, Colombo/Jaffna/Kandy/Matale/Matara 98.9

ASSET RADIO BROADCASTING (Pvt) Ltd
09C Ocean Tower Building, Station Road, Bambalapitya, Colombo 4 ☎+94 11 2507080 +94 11 5342434 **E:** eng@nethfm.com **W:** nethfm.com **Stn: Neth FM** (Sinhala): Bandarawela/Kandy/Kegalla/ 94.8, Colombo/Kandy/Matale/Matara/Ratnapura 95.0. **Fox Fm** (English): Kandy & Colombo 91.4.

COLOMBO COMMUNICATIONS (Pvt) Ltd
686 Galle Road, Colombo 3 ☎+94 11 5577777 +94 11 2505796 **E:** info@efm.lk **W:** efm.lk **Stns: E! FM** (English): Colombo/Kandy/Matara 88.3 – **RANONE FM** (Sinhala): Kegalle/Matale/Matara 88.1, Bandarawela/Colombo//Ratnapura 100.5 – **Shree FM** (Sinhala): Bandarawela/Colombo/Kandy/Ratnapura 100.0, Kegalle/Matale/Matara 100.2

INDEPENDENT TELEVISION NETWORK
Wickramasinghepura, Battaramulla 10120 ☎+94 11 2774424 +94 11 2774591 **E:** itn@slt.lk **W:** itn.lk **L.P:** Chmn.: Rosmand Senarathna, Gen Mgr: W Wijesinghe. **Stns: ITN FM** (Sinhala): Bandarawela/Kandy/Kegalla/Kokavil 93.5, Colombo/Matale/Matara 93.7 – **Vasantham** (Tamil): Bandarawela/Kegalla/Kokavil 102.6, Colombo/Jaffna/Matale/Uda 102.8

MBC NETWORKS (Pvt) Ltd
PO Box 25, 36 Araliya Uyana, Depanama, Pannipitiya ☎+94 11 2851371 +94 11 2851373 **W:** www.mbc.lk **Stns: Shakthi FM** (Tamil): 7 Braybrooke Place, Colombo. Bandarawela/Kalutara/Kandy/Kilinochchi/ Nuwara Eliya/Trincomalee/Vavuniya 103.9, Colombo/Jaffna/Kandy/Mannar/Matale/Matara 104.1 – **Sirasa FM** (Sinhala) PO Box 25, Araliya Uyana: **E:** radio@sirasafm.maharaja.lk Colombo/Jaffna/Kandy/Kurunegala/Magalkanda/Matale/Matara 106.5, Bandarawela/Kalutara/Kandy/Nuwara Eliya/Ratnapura 106.7 – **Y FM** (Sinhala) 7 Braybrooke Place, Colombo: Bandarawela/Colombo/Jaffna/Kalutara/Kandy/Kurunegela/Matale/Matara/Ratnapura 92.7– **Yes FM** (English) as MBC Networks: Nuwara Eliya 100.8, Colombo/Jaffna/Kandy/Kurunegala/Matara101.0

TNL RADIO NETWORK Pvt Ltd
No.52, 5th Lane, Colombo 3 ☎+94 11 7669966 **W:** www.tnlradio.com **Stns: Lite 87** (English): Nuwara Eliya 87.6, Colombo/Kandy/Matara 87.8 – **Rhythm World** (Sinhala): Colombo/Kandy/Matale/Matara 95.6, Nuwara Eliya 95.8 – **TNL Radio** (English): Colombo/Kandy 99.2, Colombo 101.8.

Other Stations:
Trans World Radio India MW: Puttalam 882kHz 200/400kW Broadcasts for Sri Lanka and southern India.
SLBC tx stn Puttalam 1125kHz 50kW Available for hire by Int. broadc.
SLBC tx stn Trincomalee 1548kHz 300kW and 250kW SW facility available for hire by Int. broadc.

ST BARTHÉLEMY (France)

LT: UTC -4h — **Pop:** 7,200 — **Pr. L:** French (official), Saint-Barthélemy French, Antillean Creole — **E.C:** 230V/50Hz — **ITU:** BLM

COMITÉ TERRITORIAL DE L'AUDIOVISUEL DES ANTILLES ET DE LA GUYANE
see main entry under Martinique

GUADELOUPE LA PREMIÈRE (Pub)
c/o Morne Bernard-Destrellan, B.P. 180, 97122 Baie-Mahault, Guadeloupe. ☎+590 590 939696 +590 590939682.
FM: 88.6MHz 0.3kW

RADIO SAINT-BARTH
BP 1113, 97014 St Barthélemy. ☎+590 590 27 74 74 & +590 690 242874 (Admin). **W:** radiostbarth.com **E:** radio@radiostbarth.com
L.P: Président: Bruno Magras
FM: 98.7MHz 0.3kW, 103.7MHz 0.3kW.

R. France Internationale: via R. Saint-Barth 98.7 & 103.7MHz outside local programming

ST EUSTATIUS (Netherlands)

L.T: UTC -4h — **Pop:** 3,100 — **Pr.L:** Dutch (official), English — **E.C:** 110V/60Hz — **ITU:** BES

AGENTSCHAP TELECOM (Bonaire, Saba, Sint Eustatius)
Kaya Grandi 69, P.O. Box 791, Bonaire ☎ + 599 717 3140 🖷 +599 717 3554 **W:** agentschaptelecom.nl **E:** bes@agentschaptelecom.nl

PJB-50 RADIO STATIA
Sint Eustatius Broadcasting Foundation
Statia Mall, Chaple Piece ☎ +599 318 2722 🖷 +599 318 2168
L.P: Dir.: Ivan Rivers; English prgrs **E:** radio_statia@yahoo.com
FM: PJB50 92.3MHz 0.5kW 24h

CTCreativity / CTC-Radio /Empire Radio
Statia Mall, Chaple Piece **FM**: 101.9MHz

PJE-3 FAB Radio
Golden Rock, Oranjestad ☎ +599 318 3300
W: fabradio903.com **E:** fabradio903@gmail.com **FM:** 90.3Mhz

ST HELENA (UK)

L.T: UTC — **Pop:** 4,500 — **Pr. L:** English — **E.C:** 230V/50Hz — **ITU:** SHN

SOUTH ATLANTIC MEDIA SERVICES LTD (SAMS) (Gov)
The Media Centre, Castle Gardens, Jamestown, St Helena STHL 1ZZ ☎+290 22727 **L.P:** CEO: Richard Wallis, SM: [vacant]
E: news@sams.sh **W:** sams.sh (live audio stream)
FM(MHz): **SAMS Radio 1**: High Knoll Fort 90.5, Jamestown 102.7, Levelwood 105.1, Blue Hill 105.3 **SAMS Radio 2** (rel. BBC World Service): High Knoll Fort 88.1, Jamestown 100.7. **D.Prgr.:** 24h.

Saint FM Community Radio
Association Hall, Main St, Jamestown, St Helena STHL 1ZZ. ☎+290 22660 **E:** admin.fm@helanta.co.sh **W:** saint.fm (live audio stream) **L.P:** Chair: [vacant], Dir: Liz Johnson, SM: Tammy Williams
FM(MHz): Half Tree Hollow 93.1 0.25kW, Deadwood Plain 95.1 0.05kW, Jamestown 106.7 0.05kW
F.Pl: Sandy Bay or Blue Hill 91.1MHz 0.05kW.

ST KITTS & NEVIS

L.T: UTC -4h — **Pop:** 53,000 — **Pr.L:** English — **E.C:** 230V/60Hz — **ITU:** SCN

NATIONAL BROADCASTING CORPORATION OF ST. KITTS & NEVIS (Gov. Comm.)
PO Box 331, Springfield, Basseterre, St. Kitts ☎ +1 869 465 2621 🖷 +1 869 466 2159 **L.P:** GM: Clement O'Garro **E:** info@zizonline.com **W:** zizonline.com
FM: Radio ZIZ 95.9/96.1/96.9MHz – **Big Wave 96.7 FM** 96.7MHz

SON POWER RADIO (Rlg.)
Flowing Streams, PO Box 690069, Vero Beach FL 32969-0069, USA ☎ +1 772 569 8880 **L.P:** Doc Burkhart
F.pl.: MW: Conaree, St. Kitts ‡820kHz 10kW (inactive)

VOICE OF NEVIS (Comm.)
Bath Plains, PO Box 195, Charlestown, Nevis ☎ +1 869 469 1616/1700 🖷 +1 869 469 5329 **E:** vonradio@sisterisles.kn **W:** vonradio.com
L.P: GM: Evered Herbert
MW: 860kHz 10kW **D.Prgr:** 24h **Ann:** "This is VON Radio on 860 AM"

OTHER STATIONS (in MHz):
Dominion Radio, Fort Thomas Rd, PO Box 513, Basseterre ☎ +1 869 465 1597 **W:** dominionradioskn.com FM 91.5. Format: Rlg. – **Freedom FM**, The Cable Bldg., Suite 2, Cayon St., Basseterre. ☎ +1 869 465 6474 **W:** freedomskn.com L.P: CEO Clement Juni Liburd. FM 106.5 – **Kyss FM**, Suite A6, The Sands Complex, Bay Rd, Basseterra ☎ +1 869 466 5978 **E:** info@kyssonline.com FM 102.5 – **Praise FM,** Hamilton Estate, 00265 Charlestown, Nevis ☎ +1 869 663 6491 **W:** praisefmnevis.com L.P: Steve Huggins. FM 99.3. Format: Gospel – **Radio St. Kitts Nevis**, Victoria Rd, Basseterre and Reef Broadcasting, 6079A Castle Coakley, Christiansted, VI 99820, USA ☎ +1 869 465 7528 **W:** reefbroadcasting.com FM 90.7 (relays WAXJ 103.5, US Virgin Isl.) – **Screen IT**, Ponds Extension, Basseterre. FM 88.5 (50W) (Community station) - **Sugar City FM**, 8 Greenlands Park, Basseterre ☎ +1 869 466 1113 **W:** sugarcityfmstkitts.com FM 90.3 – **Winn FM,** Unit C24, The Sands Complex, Bay Rd, Basseterre, St. Kitts ☎ +1 869 466 9586 **E:** info@winnfm.com **W:** winnmediaskn.com FM 98.9

ST LUCIA

L.T: UTC -4h — **Pop:** 180,000 — **Pr.L:** English (official), Saint Lucian Creole — **E.C:** 240V/50Hz — **ITU:** LCA

MINISTRY OF TOURISM INFORMATION AND BROADCASTING
3rd Floor, Sir Stanislaus James Building, Waterfront, Castries ☎ +1 758 4684629 🖷 +1 758 4517414 **W:** tourism.govt.lc **L.P:** Minister: Dominic Fedee

HOT FM/KISS FM, Old Victoria Rd, Morne Fortune, PO Box MF 7096, Castries ☎ +1 758 452 6040 🖷 +1 758 458 1462 **W:** caribbeanhotfm.com & caribbeankissfm.com **L.P:** CEO: Patrick Smith. Mgr.: Sandra Recai. Stns: **Hot FM:** 96.1(South)/105.3(North), **Kiss FM:** 105.5 (South)/105.9(North) – **IBAS RADIO,** Rodney Bay, Castries ☎ +1 758 384 1045. **FM:** 104.5/106.7 – **JOY FM,** PO Box MF 7149, Castries ☎ +1 758 453 6962 **FM:** 90.1 (North)/96.9 (South). Format: Rlg – **KAIRI FM,** Morne Du Don, PO Box 1730 Castries ☎ +1 758 451 1079 **W:** kairifm.com **FM:** 93.1/107.9 – **PRAYZ FM RADIO,** Sir John Compton Highway, Sans Soucis, PO Box CP6141, Castries ☎ +1 758 452 1022 **W:** prayzfm.org **FM:** 92.5/98.5 Format: Rlg., Adventist – **RADIO CARIBBEAN INTERNATIONAL,** Sans Souci, PO Box 121, Castries ☎ +1 758 452 2636 **W:** rcistlucia.com **FM:** 99.1(South) /101.1(North) – **RADIO 100 HELEN FM,** Morne Fortune, PO Box 621, Castries ☎ +1 758 452 4982 🖷 +1 758 453 1737. **FM:** 100.1(Castries)/100.3(North)/103.5(South) – **REAL FM,** Barnard Hill, PO Box CP 6279, Castries ☎ +1 758 453 7458 **W:** realfm.mbcslu.com. **FM:** 91.3/91.5 – **RFI 102.1 (RADIO FREE IYANOLA),** 22 Delieu Str, Soufriere ☎ +1 758 489 1021 **W:** rfi1021fm.com **FM:** 102.1. Format: Reggae – **RHYTHM FM/BLAZIN FM INC.,** Julian Charles Rd, PO Box 584, Castries ☎ +1 758 450 9494 Stns: **Rhythm FM:** 95.5 & **Blazin FM:** 99.3 – **RIZZEN 102FM,** McVane Rd, Sans Souci, Castries ☎ +1 758 451 3001 **W:** rizzen102.com **FM:** 99.7/102.5/102.9. Format: Rlg. – **SOUFRIERE FM,** Sir Arthur Lewis Str LC09 101, PO Box 272, Soufriere ☎ +1 758 459 7885/7888 🖷 +1 758 457 1071 **W:** 885soufrierefm.com **FM:** 88.5 (local community stn) – **THE WAVE,** Karlione Court, Rodney Bay, Castries ☎+1 758 451 6400 **W:** thewavestlucia.com L.P: PD Michael Rogers. **FM:** 93.7 (South)/94.5 (North)

ST MAARTEN (Netherlands)

L.T: UTC -4h — **Pop:** 41,500 — **Pr.L:** Dutch (official), English (official), Papiamentu, Simaatn Creole — **E.C:** 110/60Hz — **ITU:** SXM

BUREAU TELECOMMUNICATIONS AND POST
Kannegieter Street 15 – Unit 5.1, P.O. Box 5054, Philipsburg, St. Maarten ☎ +1 721 542 4699 🖷 +1 721 542 5517 **W:** sxmregulator.com **E:** info@sxmregulator.com

	MW Call	kHz	kW	Station, location
1)	PJD-2	1300	1	The Voice of St. Maarten, Philipsburg

FM	MHz	kW	Station, location
4)	91.9	1	Island 92, Simpson Bay
6)	94.7	1	Mix 94.7, Philipsburg
6)	96.3	1	Oasis 96.3, Philipsburg
8)	98.1	1	Pearl FM, Philipsburg
6)	101.1	1	Laser 101 FM
1)	102.7	3.5	PJD3, The VO St. Maarten/Power 102.7, Philipsburg
7)	104.3	1.5	PJM1, X 104.3, Philipsburg
4)	105.1	1	Z105.1 FM, Simpson Bay
6)	105.5	1	Tropixx 105.5, Philipsburg
2)	107.9	1	Gov. R., Philipsburg

Addresses & other information:
1) Back Street, Plaza 21, Philipsburg ☎ +1 721 542 2580 🖷 +1 721 542 2356 **E**: info@pjd2radiosxm.com **W:** pjd2radiosxm.com – **2**) Government Administration Building, Soualuiga Road #1, Pond Island, Great Bay ☎721-542-0349,721-542-0640,721-542-0651 and 721-542-2026 official weather and government related information **W:** sintmaartengov.org/government/AZ/dcomm/Pages/Products-and-

Services.aspx – **4)** Caribe Broadcasting Network, Welfare Road # 64, Federal Express Building, Simpson Bay ☎ +1 721 544 3377; Island 92: 24 hours in Eng : Classic Rock, Blues and Good Time Music; Z105.1: 24 hr in Eng: Classic Hits; Managing Director: Jeffrey W. Sochrin, **E:** info@island92.com **W:** island92.com **W:** z1051.net –**6)** A.Th. Illidge Road 106 Philipsburg ☎ +1 721 543 2200 🖷 +1 721 543 2200; Oasis, Laser and Mix: 24h in English; Tropixx: 24h in English, Papiamentu and Spanish; Laser,Tropixx, Oasis and Mix: Dir: Gary Euton Mix 94.7: **E:** marketing@philbroad.com **W:** oasis963.fm **E:** request@oasis963.fm **W:** laser101.fm **E:** request@laser101.fm **W:** tropixx.fm **E:** request@tropixx.fm – **7)** Media One Corporation, #9, Walter Nisbeth Road, Suite B, Philipsburg ☎+1 721 543 8104 Studio Line: + 1 721 543 9104 24h in English, Dir. Mr E. Brown, **E:** info@x1043.com and info@mediaoneco.com – **8)** Fort Belair Road 3, Philipsburg ☎+1 721 5430 462 and ☎+1 721 5202 981 prgrs : 24 hours, **E:** 981pearlfm@gmail.com **W:** pearlfmradio.sx

ST MARTIN (France)

L.T: UTC -4h — **Pop:** 36,000 — **Pr. L:** French (official), English, Simaatn Creole — **E.C:** 220V/60Hz — **ITU:** MAF

COMITÉ TERRITORIAL DE L'AUDIOVISUEL DES ANTILLES ET DE LA GUYANE see main entry under Martinique

GUADELOUPE LA PREMIÈRE (Pub)

🖃 Quartier Bellevue-Marigot, 97100 Saint Martin ☎+590 590291716
FM: St. Martin 88.9MHz 0.3kW

RADIO SAINT MARTIN (Comm.)

🖃 Port de Marigot, 97150 Saint Martin **L.P.:** Mgr: H. Cocks.
FM: 101.5MHz 0.3kW **D.Prgr:** 1000-0500(Sun -0400) in French & English exc. Spanish: 2000-2100W.

RADIO CALYPSO

🖃 10, rue du Général de Gaule, 97150 Saint Martin
☎+590 590 522222 🖷 +590 590 52 22 23 **W:** radiocalypso.net **E:** calypsopub@powerantilles.com **FM:** 102.1MHz 1kW

Other Stations FM:
R. Laser Îles du Nord 89.9MHz 1kW – **France Inter** 91.1MHz – **Youth R.** 92.5MHz 1kW – **R.** 94.3MHz 1kW – **R. Music FM** 95.1MHz 1kW – **R. SOS** 95.9MHz 1kW – **R. Maranatha** 100.3MHz 1kW – **R. Saint-Barth/RFI** 100.7MHz 0.3kW – **R. Tropik FM** 104.7MHz 1kW – **Sun FM Music** 107.1MHz 1kW

ST PIERRE ET MIQUELON (France)

L.T: UTC -3h (14 Mar-7 Nov: -2h) — **Pop:** 6,400 — **Pr.L:** French — **E.C:** 230V/50Hz — **ITU:** SPM

COMITÉ TERRITORIAL DE L'AUDIOVISUEL DE PARIS

🖃 39/43 quai André-Citroën, 75739 Paris Cedex 15 ☎ +33 140583475 **E:** cta.paris@csa.fr **NB:** The CTA Paris branch is regulating broadcasting stations on St Pierre et Miquelon.

RADIO ST PIERRE ET MIQUELON LA PREMIÈRE (Pub)

🖃 B.P. 4227-97500 St. Pierre et Miquelon ☎+508 411111 **W:** la1ere.francetvinfo.fr/saintpierremiquelon/radio
LP: Tech. Dir: Etienne Grisel, Head of N.: Frederic Lahiton
FM: Miquelon 98.9 500W, St. Pierre 99.9 100W
D.Prgr: 0930-0230. **Rel. France-Inter:** 0230-0930. **N (local):** 1000, 1530, 2200. **Rel. France-Inter N:** 1100, 1200, 1300, 1400, 1800, 1900
Ann: "Ici Radio Saint-Pierre et Miquelon la Première"

R. Atlantique 🖃 B.P. 1282-97500 ☎+508 412493 **W:** radioatlantique.com **FM:** 94.5 1kW, 102.1 1kW (also rel. R. France Int.)

ST VINCENT & THE GRENADINES

L.T: UTC -4h — **Pop:** 110,000 — **Pr.L:** English — **E.C:** 230V/50Hz— **ITU:** VCT

NATIONAL BROADCASTING CORPORATION RADIO ST VINCENT AND THE GRENADINES – NBCSVG (Gov. Comm.)

🖃 Richmond Hill, PO Box 705, Kingstown ☎ +1 784 457 1111 🖷 +1 784 456 2749 **W:** nbcsvg.com **E:** nbcadmin@nbcsvg.com **L.P:** GM: Dionne John. PM: Colvin Harry
FM: 90.7MHz 1kW, 107.5MHz 1kW
D.Prgr: 24h. Relays BBC W 0400-0900, Fri-Sat 0500-0930, Sun 0400-0930. **N:** 1130, 1630, 2230 – Su 1230 only. **Ann:** "NBC Radio"

OTHER STATIONS (FM in MHz):
Adoration FM, North Union, Charlotte ☎ +1 784 529 5480 **E:** adoration88@gmail.com **W:** adoration88.com FM 88.9 Format: Rlg – **Boom SVG,** Paul's Ave, Prospect, PO Box 592, Kingstown ☎ +1 784 455 1069 FM 92.5/106.9 – **Christlike Radio,** PO Box 701, Kingstown ☎ +1 784 526 4057 **E:** christlikeradiosvg@gmail.com FM 99.1 Format: Rlg – **Hot 97.1FM,** 1 Melville Str, PO Box 1716, Kingstown ☎ +1 784 485 9797 **W:** hot97svg.com FM 93.1/97.1. Format: Urban Caribbean – **Jem Radio,** Hopewell Rd, PO Box 1419, Kingstown ☎ +1 784 451 3827 **W:** jemradio.com FM 89.1. Format: Rlg. – **Magic 103.7,** St Vincent Broadc. Corp., Dorsetshire Hill, P.O. Box 617, Kingstown ☎ +1 784 451 1037 **W:** magic1037.com FM 91.5/103.7. Format: Urban Caribbean – **Nice Radio,** BDS Company Ltd., Dorsetshire Hill, PO Box 324, Kingstown ☎ +1 784 458 1013 🖷 +1 784 456 5556 **W:** niceradio.info L.P: Mgr: Douglas Defreitas. FM 90.3/96.7/101.3 – **Praise FM,** Sion Hill, PO Box 443, Kingstown ☎ +1 784 456 1057 **W:** praisefmsvg.com. FM 95.7/105.7 Format: Rlg – **Star FM,** Murray's Rd, McKies Hill, PO Box 1651, Kingstown ☎ +1 784 451 7827 🖷 +1 784 485 7827 **W:** star983fm.com FM 98.3/104.7 – **WEFM,** Windy Pt., Lower Questelles, PO Box 1346, Kingstown ☎ +1 784 457 9994 **E:** wefm@vincysurf.com **W:** 999wefm.com FM 99.9 – **Xtreme 104.3,** Vigie Highway, Kingstown ☎ +1 784 457 1043 **W:** x104fm.com FM 88.5/104.3 Format: Urban

SUDAN

L.T: UTC +2h — **Pop:** 44 million — **Pr.L:** Arabic (official), English (official), Beja, Nubian languages — **E.C:** 230V/50Hz — **ITU:** SDN

TELECOMMUNICATIONS AND POST REGULATORY AUTHORITY (TPRA)

🖃 P.O.Box 2869, 11111 Khartoum ☎ +249 187 171144 🖷 +249 183 562355 **E:** itisalat@tpra.gov.sd **W:** tpra.gov.sd

SUDAN RADIO & TV CORPORATION - SUDAN RADIO (Gov.)

🖃 P.O. Box 1094, Mulazmin, Omdurman ☎+249 1 87572956 🖷 +249 1 87556006. **W:** sudanradio.gov.sd **E:** web form
L.P: Dir: Ibrahim Mohammed Ibrahim al-Bazi'i.

MW	kHz	kW	Prgr.	MW	kHz	kW	Prgr.
Nyala	540	50	R	Dongola	819	10	R
Unknown site	621		G	Wad Madani	873	10	R
Unknown site	621		G	Wadi Halfa	873	5	R
Al-Ubayyid	639	10	R	Singa	891	5	R
Kassala	666	10	R	Al-Foula	945	5	R
Khartoum	747	10	R	Khartoum Soba	963	100	S/G
Port Sudan	747	5	R	Al-Damazin	1026	5	R
Khartoum Soba	765	50	G	Al Qadarif	1485	12	R
Atbara	783	5	R	Kosti	1584	5	R
Al-Fashir	801	5	R	Kadugli	1602	5	R

SW: Omdurman (Al-Fatihab) 100kW: General prgr: 7205kHz 0330-2200 (irreg.)
FM: Khartoum: 88.6MHz (W), 90.0MHz (S/Q), 93.0MHz (Y), 95.0MHz (G), 98.0MHz (E/U), 100.0MHz (N), 105.0MHz (Q).
Prgr. S: Khartoum 90.0MHz & Darfur: Al-Fashir/Al-Junayna 95.0MHz, Nyala 98.0MHz.

Regional stations: Al-Gadarif/Dongola/El Obeid/Kassala/Nyala/Sinja 98.0MHz, Port Sudan 105.0MHz, Khartoum 107.0MHz.
Prgrs: G=General Prgr (incl. **National Unity R.** 1100-1300) in Arabic: 24h. 963kHz 2100-020. **H=Quran R:** 0300-1100. **K=Khartoum State R:** 0400-0800, 1400-2000. **N="Sudan Home Radio":** 24h. **S=R. As-Salam** (Peace): 020-2100 on 90.0MHz & 963kHz. **U="Nation's Memory Radio":** 1200-1600, 2000-2400. **E=European prgr.** in English/French: 1600-2000. **W: Wadi al-Nil** (Nile Valley R.). **Y=Youth & Sports R.**
R=Regional stations. D.Prgr: mostly 0300-2100. Also relay **G** prgr.
VO the Armed Forces, Khartoum: 97.0MHz. **W:** mod.gov.sd
VO the Police, Khartoum: 99.6MHz **W:** facebook.com/sahiroon.fm
Ann: "Huna Omdurman, Idha'atu-l-Gumhuriya as-Sudan"
IS: Sudanese music.

EXTERNAL SERVICE: See International Radio section.

Other Stations (FM MHz**):**
Al-Basira FM, Khartoum: 96.3 **W:** facebook.com/albasiraa1
Al-Hia R, Khartoum: 98.3 **W:** alhiaradio.net
Al-Kawthar R.(rlg.), Khartoum: 92.0 **W:** alkawtherfmsd.com
Al-Rabaa FM, Khartoum: 94.0. By Channel 4, UAE **W:** alrabaafm.com
Beladi FM, Khartoum: 96.6 **W:** beladifm.com
BN FM, Khartoum: 91.0 **W:** facebook.com/BN-FM-1493950377551282
Bokra FM, Khartoum: 104.6 **W:** facebook.com/BokraFm1046
Capital R, Khartoum: 91.6. **W:** facebook.com/91.6fm
Darfur FM, Khartoum: 90.3 **W:** facebook.com/190201404415447
Furqan FM (rlg.): Khartoum 99.0, unk. loc. 102.0/105.0 **W:** facebook.com/furganradio99
Future R, Khartoum: 92.6 **W:** facebook.com/Future92.6fm
Hala FM: Khartoum/Port/Sudan/Wad Madani 96.0 **W:** hala96.fm
Khartoum FM: 89.0 **W:** facebook.com/89-915352691893353
Life and Health R, Khartoum: 106.0 **W:** fm106.net
Masa FM, Khartoum: 101.0 **W:** windwhispergroup.wixsite.com/almasaaradio
Noor TV audio, Khartoum: 105.3 **W:** facebook.com/noorchannel.tv
OUS R, Khartoum: 89.5 **W:** media.ous.edu.sd/RadioBroadcast.html
Profession FM, Khartoum: 106.6 **W:** acst.edu.sd/ar/radio
R. Al-Tibbiya, Khartoum: 99.3 **W:** facebook.com/ALTbia99.3
R. Hawana, Khartoum: 88.3 **W:** facebook.com/Fm-1193031280727839
R. Hawas, Khartoum: 92.3 **W:** facebook.com/RadioHawasOfficial
SIU R, Khartoum: 102.6 **W:** facebook.com/102.6fm
Sports FM, Khartoum: 104.0 **W:** facebook.com/Fm-104-413817798673775
Tayba FM (rlg.), Khartoum: 103.0. **W:** facebook.com/tayba.fm
Vision FM, Khartoum: 101.3 **W:** visionfmradio.com

BBC Arabic Sce: El Obeid/Port Sudan 91.0MHz.
Voice of America, Khartoum: 97.5MHz.
UNAMID R, Darfur region **W:** unamid.unmissions.org/audio . Broadcasting some programmes via Khartoum 98.0MHz, Al-Fatihab 7205kHz and Al-Fashir 801kHz & 95.0Mhz

SURINAME

L.T: UTC -3h — **Pop:** 552,000 — **Pr.L:** Dutch (official), Sranan Tongo, Sarnami Hindi, Javanese — **E.C:** 127V/60Hz — **ITU:** SUR — **Int. dialling code:** 597

TELECOMMUNICATIE AUTORITEIT SURINAME (TAS)

Lalla Rookhweg perc. 228, Paramaribo ☎ 532523 🖷 462985 **E:** dsecretariaat@tas.sr **W:** www.tas.sr **L.P:** Dir: Wendy Jap A Joe

STICHTING RADIO-OMROEP SURINAME (SRS) (Pub)

P.O. Box 271, Paramaribo ☎ 498115 🖷 498116 **W:** radiosrs.com **E:** adm@radiosrs.com
FM: Paramaribo 96.3MHz 1kW, Coronie, Nickerie, Moengo, Brokopando all 94.7MHz 0.1kW, Wageningen 95.6 MHz, Albina 105.7MHz 0.1kW **D.Prgr:** 0900-0700

PRIVATE COMMERCIAL STATIONS:
SW: 8) R. Apintie, Paramaribo 4990kHz 1kW (irregular)
FM (MHz): **1) R. 10** 88.1, 88.7 & 103.7 – **2) Radika** 98.3 – **3) R. Garuda** 97.5, 103.4 & 105.7 – **4) Sky** R. 94.1 & 102.7 – **5) R. Katoilica** 93.1 – **6) R. Trishul** 90.5 – **7) R. Zon** 107.5 – **8) R. Apintie** 97.1 – **9) R. Ishara** 100.7 – **10) R. Noer** 92.1 – **11) R. Paramaribo Rapar "The Hot-One"** 89.7 – **12) RP Acme** 91.3 – **13) RTV Mustika** 106.5 – **14) Sangeetmala R.** 99.3 & 100.1 – **15) R. Shalom** 94.5 – **16) R. Pertjajah** 95.3 – **17) R. Koyeba** 104.9 – **18) Rasonic R.** 102.3 & 105.3 – **19) Kara´s Broadcasting Corp.** 101.1 & 103.1 – **20) R. ABC** 101.7

Addresses & other information:
1) Stadionlaan 3 (P.O.Box 110), Paramaribo ☎ 410881 🖷 422294 **W:** radio10.sr **E:** info@radio10.sr – **2)** Indira Gandhiweg 165, Paramariba ☎ 482800 – **3)** Goudstraat 20 Maretrait 4, Paramaribo 454 926 **W:** rtvgaruda.com **E:** info@rtv-garuda.com – **4)** Ormosiastraat 2 (P.O.Box 1597), Paramaribo ☎ 530015 **W:** skyradioasuriname.com **E:** info@skyradio.sr – **5)** Paramaribo – **6)** Flocislaan 4, Boyen ☎ 439500 **W:** trishul.sr **E:**info@trishul.sr – **7)** Burenstraat No 60, Paramaribo ☎475261 🖷 420233 **W:** radiozon.com **E:**admin@radiozon.com – **8)** verl. Gemenelandsweg 37, Paramaribo ☎ 400455 🖷 400684 **W:** apintie.sr **E:** apintie@sr.net – **9)** 109 Fredericiweg, Nickerie ☎231244 **W:** isharafm.com **E:** info@isharafm.com – **10)** Zwartenhovenbrugstraat 154, Paramaribo **W:** dbsuriname.com/radionoer.php **E:** radionoer@gmail.com – **11) 18)** Coppenamstraat 34 (P.O. Box 975), Paramaribo ☎ 497774 Paramaribo **W:** dbsuriname.com/radiorpthehotone.php **E:** rpthehot1@gmail.com – **12)** Zwartenhovenbrugstraat 154, Paramaribo **W:** dbsuriname.com/radiorpthehotone.php – **13)** Paramaribo **W:** rtvmustika.net **E:** rtvmustikacontact@gmail.com – **14)** Indira Gandhiweg No 40, Wanicxa ☎ 482392 **W:** sgmsuriname.com **E:** info@sgmsuriname.com – **15)** Malebatrumstraat 10-12 BV, Paramaribo ☎ 422630 🖷 422737 **W:** shalomsuriname.com **E:** shalom@sr.net – **16)** Gemenlandsweg/Daneil Coutinhostraat 31, Paramaribo ☎ 401919 **W:** twitter.com/#!/PertjajahLuhur – **17)** van`t Hogerhuystraat 88 ☎ 403115 **W:**radiokoyebasuriname.com **E:** odjahh@yahoo.com – **18)** Bataviastraat 25, NW. Nickerie ☎ 231447 **W:** rasonictv.com – **19)** Verlengde Gemenelandsweg 177, Paramaribo ☎ 4300666 – **20)** Maystraat 57, Paramaribo ☎ 465092 **W:** abcsuriname.com **E:** info@abcsuriname.com

SWAZILAND

See ESWATINI

SWEDEN

L.T: UTC +2h (28 Mar-31 Oct: +3h) — **Pop:** 10 million — **Pr.L:** Swedish (official); official minority languages: Finnish, Meänkieli, Sami, Romany, Yiddish — **E.C:** 230V/50Hz — **ITU:** S

MYNDIGHETEN FÖR PRESS, RADIO OCH TV (MPRT) (Swedish Press and Broadcasting Authority)

P.O.Box 33, 12125 Stockholm ☎ +46 8 58007000 🖷 +46 8 7410870 **E:** registrator@mprt.se **W:** www.mprt.se
L.P: DG: Charlotte Ingvar-Nilsson

POST- OCH TELESTYRELSEN (PTS)

P.O.Box 5398, 10249 Stockholm ☎ +46 8 6785500 🖷 +46 8 6785505 **E:** pts@pts.se **W:** pts.se **L.P:** DG: Dan Sjöblom

SVERIGES RADIO AB (SR) (Pub)

Radiohuset, Oxenstiernsgatan 20, 10510 Stockholm ☎ +46 8 7845000 **E:** lyssnarservice@sverigesradio.se **W:** sverigesradio.se
L.P: CEO: Cilla Benkö
FM (MHz)

Location	1	2#	3	4°	L°	kW
Arvidsjaur	89.4	94.2	97.1	100.6m	-	60
Bollnäs	88.4	91.7	96.0	103.8d	-	60
Borlänge	89.4	93.0	97.7	101.3b	-	60
Borås	88.5	94.6	97.9	102.9n	-	10
Bäckefors	92.7	96.8	99.1	102.2t	-	60
Emmaboda	93.0	96.7	99.7	101.8k	-	60
Emmaboda	-	-	-	95.6i	-	60
Enköping	-	-	-	95.2r	-	5
Eskilstuna	-	-	-	100.1q	-	6
Filipstad	88.5	90.1	98.8	103.2s	-	3
Finnveden*	90.1	94.2	99.9	103.4h	-	30
Färjestaden	-	-	-	107.8i	-	1
Gällivare	88.3	94.9	98.5	100.9m	-	60
Gävle	88.1	97.4	99.8	102.0d	-	60
Göteborg	89.3	96.3	99.4	101.9e	-	60
Halmstad	87.7	91.2	95.4	97.3f	-	60
Halmstad	-	-	-	102.6j	-	3
Helsingborg	89.8	95.7	98.4	103.2l	-	30
Hudiksvall	87.6	90.2	93.8	100.7d	-	60
Härnösand	88.8	91.1	95.1	100.5v	-	1.5
Hörby	88.8	92.4	97.0	89.5l	-	3x60/5
Hörby	-	-	-	101.4j	-	60
Jönköping	91.6	93.7	97.1	100.8h	-	5
Kalix	91.3	93.6	97.9	102.2m	-	60
Karlshamn	90.3	93.4	98.3	100.4a	-	15
Karlskrona	89.1	95.0	97.7	100.7a	-	10
Karlstad	90.5	94.2	96.5	103.5s	-	15
Kiruna	89.1	92.7	96.4	102.7m	-	60
Kisa	90.5	92.5	96.9	103.6y	-	30
Kramfors	88.3	92.4	97.2	102.4v	-	1.2
Kungsbacka	-	-	-	101.3f	-	1
Lycksele	92.9	95.4	98.7	103.3u	-	60

Location	1	2#	3	4°	L°	kW
Malmö	87.9	93.3	98.0	102.0l	100.6l[1]	6
Markaryd	101.9	95.0	102.2	99.5k	-	3
Mora	92.2	96.7	99.0	101.0b	-	60
Motala	91.1	94.0	98.2	101.2y	-	20
Norrköping	90.0	93.5	98.7	94.8y	-	60
Norrköping	-	-	-	103.2q	-	60
Nässjö	89.6	92.1	99.0	102.1h	-	60
Pajala	90.8	93.0	95.9	100.2m	.	60
Skellefteå	93.8	96.3	100.0	103.9u	-	60
Skövde	88.9	95.1	97.5	100.3o	-	60
Sollefteå	89.3	93.5	98.1	101.2v	-	60
Stockholm	92.4	96.2&	99.3	103.3p	-	60
Stockholm	-	-	-	93.8p	89.6p[2]	1.5/0.9
Storuman	87.6	91.2	99.0	102.5u	-	60
Strängnäs	-	-	-	96.9q	-	4
Sundsvall	92.7	96.9	99.2	102.8v	-	60
Sunne	90.9	94.5	98.5	101.8o	-	60
Sveg	90.6	94.9	97.9	102.2g	-	60
Södertälje	-	-	-	97.6p	102.7p[2]	3/0.1
Trollhättan	91.9	95.7	99.8	103.7t	-	3
Tåsjö**	89.9	94.7	97.5	100.8g	-	60
Tåsjö**	-	-	-	88.2u	-	60
Törntorp	-	-	-	89.8x	-	3
Uddevalla	89.9	93.1	97.2	103.3t	-	8
Uppsala	90.3	93.3	96.6	102.5r	-	20
Varberg	90.4	93.6	98.8	103.8f	-	10
Visby	87.6	94.1	97.2	100.2c	-	60
Vislanda	88.0	90.6	94.7	101.0k	-	30
Väddö	-	-	-	94.7p	-	3
Vännäs	88.5	92.1	95.8	103.6u	-	60
Västervik	88.3	91.8	96.0	102.7i	-	60
Västerås	90.7	95.8	98.0	100.5w	-	60
Ånge	93.2	95.6	99.6	103.1v	-	60
Ånge	-	-	-	94.5g	-	60
Älvsbyn	90.6	94.5	99.4	102.9m	-	60
Ängelholm	-	-	-	103.6j	-	1
Örebro	87.9	91.5	99.6	102.8s	-	60
Örnsköldsvik	90.8	94.4	97.8	100.1v	-	60
Östersund	87.9	91.5	94.0	100.4g	-	60
Östhammar	89.1	92.8	95.5	101.6r	-	60
Överkalix	88.9	91.7	99.0	103.2m	-	15

+ sites with txs below 1kW *) Bredaryd **) Hoting #) P2 Språk & musik &) P2 (see below) °) Regional studios a-y: see below L = Local outlets (see below) [1]) P3 Din Gata [2]) P6

D.Prgrs: Prgr 1 (P1): 24h – **Prgr 2 (P2):** 24h on Stockholm 96.2MHz. **P2 Språk & musik:** 24h (as P2, plus prgrs for ethnic minorities and immigrants in Swedish, Arabic, English, Finnish, Romany, Sami) via P2 FM txs exc. Stockholm 96.2MHz – **Prgr 3 (P3):** 24h – **Prgr 4 (P4):** 24h. Reg. prgrs MF 0459-1635; SS 0730-0733, 0830-0833, 0930-0933, 1130-1133 & 1230-1233 (studios see below); national prgr at other times– **Local outlets: P3 Din Gata:** 24h. **P6:** 24h in Swedish, Arabic, English, Finnish, Romany, Sami. Rel. BBC World Service (English) MF 1730-0500 (Sat -0600), SS 1800-0600 (Mon -0500) – **SR Sameradion:** (✉Österleden 21, 98138 Kiruna) (for Sami ethnic minority) 24h in Sami, Swedish via webcast; selected prgrs are relayed via P2 Språk & musik, P4, P6 – **SR Sisuradio:** (for Finnish ethnic minority) 24h in Finnish, Meänkieli dialects, Swedish via DAB & webcast; selected prgrs are relayed via P2 Språk & musik, P4, P6.

SR Regional Studios

a) SR Blekinge, P.O.Box 305, 37125 Karlskrona – **b)** SR Dalarna, P.O. Box 123, 79123 Falun – **c)** SR Gotland, P.O.Box 1324, 62124 Visby – **d)** SR Gävleborg, P.O.Box 311, 80104 Gävle – **e)** SR Göteborg, Pumpgatan 2, 40513 Göteborg – **f)** SR Halland, P.O.Box 133, 30104 Halmstad – **g)** SR Jämtland, P.O.Box 476, 83126 Östersund – **h)** SR Jönköping, Barnarpsgatan 35D, 55192 Jönköping – **i)** SR Kalmar, Norra vägen 22, 39183 Kalmar – **j)** SR Kristianstad, P.O.Box 505, 29125 Kristianstad – **k)** SR Kronoberg, P.O.Box 62, 35103 Växjö – **l)** SR Malmöhus, Baltzarsgatan 16, 21101 Malmö – **m)** SR Norrbotten, Nygatan 3, 97171 Luleå – **n)** SR Sjuhärad, P.O.Box 27, 50330 Borås – **o)** SR Skaraborg, Norra Bergvägen 4, 54124 Skövde – **p)** SR Stockholm, Oxenstiernsgatan 20, 10510 Stockholm – **q)** SR Sörmland, P.O.Box 641, 63108 Eskilstuna – **r)** SR Uppland, P.O.Box 1552, 75145 Uppsala – **s)** SR Värmland, P.O.Box 98, 65103 Karlstad – **t)** SR Väst, P.O.Box 654, 45124 Uddevalla – **u)** SR Västerbotten, Mariehemsvägen 4, 90615 Umeå – **v)** SR Västernorrland, Krönvägen 18, 85179 Sundsvall – **w)** SR Västmanland, P.O.Box 850, 72122 Västerås – **x)** SR Örebro, Västra Bangatan 15, 70180 Örebro – **y)** SR Östergötland, P.O.Box 500, 60107 Norrköping.

NÄRRADIONS RIKSORGANISATION (NRO)

✉ c/o Ragnar Smittberg, Skogsängsgatan 8C, 63357 Eskilstuna ☎ +46 70 8869160 **E:** ordforande@nro.se **W:** www.nro.se
L.P: Chmn: Ragnar Smittberg

OTHER STATIONS

FM	MHz	kW	Location	Station
1A)	87.6	7	Karlstad	RIX FM
2B)	88.1	2	Skövde	NRJ
4)	88.1	1	Ängelholm	Retro FM
2B)	88.3	1	Landskrona	NRJ
2A)	88.6	1	Emmaboda	Mix Megapol
1A)	88.6	2	Ånge	RIX FM
2B)	88.7	3	Västerås	NRJ
1B)	89.0	1	Bollnäs	Star FM
2B)	89.1	3	Vindeln	NRJ
16)	89.2	1.5	Malmö	Malmökanalen 89,2
1A)	89.3	2	Arvika	RIX FM
2A)	89.4	2	Oskarshamn	Mix Megapol
2A)	89.5	1	Norrköping	Mix Megapol
7)	89.7	1	Skellefteå	R. Skellefteå
5)	89.9	1	Sandviken	R. Sandviken
1B)	90.1	2.5	Luleå	Star FM
2C)	90.2	3	Motala	Rockklassiker
1A)	90.3	1	Normaling	RIX FM
1A)	90.4	1	Lindesberg	RIX FM
2B)	90.8	1	Aneby	NRJ
2B)	90.8	1	Bollnäs	NRJ
1B)	90.9	1	Karlskrona	Star FM
1B)	90.9	2	Skellefteå	Star FM
1A)	91.0	3	Trollhättan	RIX FM
2B)	91.0	1.2	Hässleholm	NRJ
2B)	91.2	2	Trelleborg	NRJ
1B)	91.3	2.5	Örnsköldsvik	Star FM
2C)	91.5	1	Visby	Rockklassiker
15)	91.6	1	Kristianstad	Kristianstad närradio
1A)	91.7	1	Älmhult	RIX FM
2C)	91.7	1	Vellinge	Rockklassiker
1B)	91.9	1	Piteå	Star FM
1A)	92.1	4	Uppsala	RIX FM
13)	92.2	1	Karlstad	KN R.
2B)	92.2	1.5	Färjestaden	NRJ
2B)	92.4	1	Filipstad	NRJ
2B)	92.4	3	Skellefteå	NRJ
24)	92.5	1	Borås	Borås närradio
2A)	92.6	1	Hagfors	Mix Megalpol
2B)	92.6	5	Karlskrona	NRJ
2B)	92.7	1	Mora	NRJ
1A)	92.8	1	Habo	RIX FM
1A)	92.9	1	Törntorp	RIX FM
1A)	93.2	1	Traryd	RIX FM
1A)	93.2	1	Ödeshög	RIX FM
2B)	93.4	5	Alingsås	NRJ
23)	93.7	2	Kiruna	R. Kiruna
2B)	93.8	1	Älmhult	NRJ
1B)	93.9	2	Borås	Star FM
1A)	94.0	1	Bromölla	RIX FM
6)	94.1	1	Mora	R. Siljan
1A)	94.4	1	Linköping	RIX FM
2C)	94.5	2	Landskrona	Rockklassiker
2C)	94.7	2	Uddevala	Rockklassiker
2A)	94.9	1	Filipstad	Mix Megapol
2A)	94.9	5	Lund	Mix Megapol
2A)	95.2	1	Olofström	Mix Megapol
10)	95.3	4	Svedala	Fun Radio 95.3
2C)	95.3	1	Hudiksvall	Rockklassiker
18)	95.4	1	Kungälv	Pirate Rock
2B)	95.4	1	Borlänge	NRJ
2C)	95.5	2	Karlstad	Rockklassiker
2C)	95.9	1	Kävlinge	Rockklassiker
1A)	96.0	2	Karlskrona	RIX FM
1B)	96.3	1	Gävle	Star FM
2C)	96.3	6	Sundsvall	Rockklassiker
11)	96.4	1	Alvesta	Gold FM
3)	96.7	1	Bjuv	Guldkanalen
1A)	97.4	5	Nyköping	RIX FM
2A)	97.6	1	Älmhult	Mix Megapol
2B)	97.6	1	Hudiksvall	NRJ
1A)	98.3	1	Vännäs	RIX FM

FM	MHz	kW	Location	Station
2A)	98.3	1	Trelleborg	Mix Megapol
17)	98.7	1	Revsund	Mittradion
1A)	98.8	1	Karlshamn	RIX FM
1A)	99.1	1	Eskilstuna	RIX FM
2A)	99.2	4	Motala	Mix Megapol
12)	99.2	3	Helsingborg	Helsingborgs närradio
2A)	99.3	1	Avesta	Mix Megapol
2A)	99.4	2	Vimmerby	Mix Megapol
1A)	99.5	5	Jönköping	RIX FM
3)	99.7	1	Skurup	Guldkanalen
1A)	99.8	1	Älvsbyn	RIX FM
25)	99.8	2	Torekov	R. Båstad
2A)	99.9	1	Ludvika	Mix Megapol
1A)	100.0	3.6	Kisa	RIX FM
2B)	100.1	1	Uddevalla	NRJ
4)	100.3	1	Helsingborg	Retro FM
14)	100.6	1.5	Sunne	R. Fryksdalen
1A)	100.6	1.7	Valdemarsvik	RIX FM
2A)	100.8	3	Södertälje	Mix Megapol
2C)	100.9	5	Norrköping	Rockklassiker
2C)	101.1	1	Borås	Rockklassiker
19A)	101.1	1.6	Lycksele	Pop och Rock
1B)	101.3	2	Färjestaden	Star FM
1B)	101.5	1	Hudiksvall	Star FM
2A)	101.6	2	Västervik	Mix Megapol
2A)	101.7	1	Ullånger	Mix Megapol
1B)	101.7	1	Linköping	Star FM
2B)	101.8	1	Gällivare	NRJ
1C)	101.9	3	Stockholm	Bandit Rock
2B)	101.9	3	Sundsvall	NRJ
2C)	102.1	2	Örnsköldsvik	Rockklassiker
19B)	102.3	2	Umeå	Rockstar
1A)	102.3	2	Borås	RIX FM
2B)	102.4	1	Ystad	NRJ
1A)	102.5	5	Habo	RIX FM
1A)	102.6	1	Borlänge	RIX FM
22)	102.7	1	Gävle	R. Gävle
19A)	103.0	2	Vännäs	Pop och Rock
2B)	103.0	1	Arvika	NRJ
1A)	103.1	7	Växjö	RIX FM
2B)	103.1	1	Visby	NRJ
2C)	103.2	5	Linköping	Rockklassiker
8)	103.8	1.5	Degerfors	Cityradion
2B)	103.9	4	Södertälje	NRJ
1A)	104.0	3	Färjestaden	RIX FM
1A)	104.0	3	Östersund	RIX FM
2D)	104.0	1	Ludvika	NRJ
2A)	104.2	10	Halmstad	Mix Megapol
2A)	104.2	4	Uddevalla	Mix Megapol
2A)	104.2	5	Umeå	Mix Megapol
2B)	104.2	1	Lund	NRJ
2B)	104.2	1	Charlottenberg	NRJ
2A)	104.3	16	Kalix	Mix Megapol
2A)	104.3	3	Stockholm	Mix Megapol
2B)	104.3	6	Linköping	NRJ
2B)	104.3	5	Växjö	NRJ
1A)	104.4	23	Visby	RIX FM
1A)	104.4	1	Perstorp	RIX FM
2B)	104.4	13	Karlstad	NRJ
2B)	104.4	1	Kiruna	NRJ
1A)	104.5	5	Vindeln	RIX FM
2B)	104.5	5	Eskilstuna	NRJ
2A)	104.5	1	Landskrona	Mix Megapol
4)	104.5	1	Kristianstad	Retro FM
1A)	104.6	5	Mora	RIX FM
2A)	104.6	3	Gnosjö	Mix Megapol
2B)	104.6	1	Älvsbyn	NRJ
2A)	104.7	6	Örebro	Mix Megapol
2F)	104.7	1	Stockholm	Lugna Klassiker
3)	104.7	2	Karlebo*	Guldkanalen
2A)	104.8	10	Örnsköldsvik	Mix Megapol
2A)	104.8	1	Vetlanda	Mix Megapol
2C)	104.8	5	Göteborg	Rockklassiker
1A)	104.9	3	Norrköping	RIX FM
1B)	104.9	1	Skövde	Star FM
2A)	104.9	5	Gävle	Mix Megapol
1A)	105.0	3	Överkalix	RIX FM
1A)	105.0	1	Piteå	RIX FM
1A)	105.0	5	Robertsfors	RIX FM
2B)	105.0	14	Trollhättan	NRJ

FM	MHz	kW	Location	Station
2A)	105.0	1	Timrå	Mix Megapol
2A)	105.1	3	Hudiksvall	Mix Megapol
2A)	105.1	5	Jönköping	Mix Megapol
2E)	105.1	3	Stockholm	Svensk Pop
2A)	105.2	10	Gällivare	Mix Megapol
2B)	105.2	1	Mjällom	NRJ
2B)	105.2	5	Malmö	NRJ
2B)	105.2	6	Örebro	NRJ
1A)	105.3	3.5	Göteborg	RIX FM
1B)	105.3	3	Östersund	Star FM
2A)	105.3	4	Uppsala	Mix Megapol
1A)	105.4	1	Hässleholm	RIX FM
2A)	105.4	3	Färjestaden	Mix Megapol
2A)	105.4	12	Karlstad	Mix Megapol
2A)	105.4	2	Skellefteå	Mix Megapol
1A)	105.5	5	Helsingborg	RIX FM
2A)	105.5	1.9	Borås	Mix Megapol
2A)	105.5	5	Borlänge	Mix Megapol
2A)	105.5	5	Sundsvall	Mix Megapol
2B)	105.5	1	Stockholm	NRJ
1A)	105.6	1	Västervik	RIX FM
1B)	105.6	1.5	Eskilstuna	Star FM
2B)	105.6	5	Luleå	NRJ
1A)	105.7	10	Uddevalla	RIX FM
2A)	105.7	4	Nyköping	Mix Megapol
1A)	105.8	1	Kiruna	RIX FM
2A)	105.8	7	Växjö	Mix Megapol
2B)	105.8	2	Sunne	NRJ
1A)	105.9	3	Kristianstad	RIX FM
2B)	105.9	1	Åsele	NRJ
2B)	105.9	10	Göteborg	NRJ
2D)	105.9	1	Stockholm	Vinyl FM
1A)	106.0	1	Kristinehamn	RIX FM
2A)	106.0	1.9	Helsingborg	Mix Megapol
2B)	106.0	10	Jönköping	NRJ
2B)	106.0	1	Örnsköldsvik	NRJ
1A)	106.1	5	Malmö	RIX FM
1A)	106.1	1	Storuman	RIX FM
1B)	106.1	1	Falkenberg	Star FM
2A)	106.1	3	Västerås	Mix Megapol
2A)	106.1	25	Visby	Mix Megapol
2A)	106.1	3	Älvsbyn	Mix Megapol
1B)	106.2	1	Trollhättan	Star FM
2B)	106.2	5	Umeå	NRJ
2B)	106.2	1	Gävle	NRJ
1B)	106.3	1	Mora	Star FM
2A)	106.3	5	Luleå	Mix Megapol
2B)	106.3	6	Örebro	NRJ
2B)	106.3	1.2	Värnamo	NRJ
2C)	106.3	1	Stockholm	Rockklassiker
1A)	106.4	1	Torsby	RIX FM
2A)	106.4	3	Skövde	Mix Megapol
2B)	106.4	5	Karlshamn	NRJ
1A)	106.5	1	Gällivare	RIX FM
2A)	106.5	1	Varberg	Mix Megapol
2B)	106.5	3	Norrköping	NRJ
2B)	106.5	4	Uppsala	NRJ
3)	106.5	1	Höör	Guldkanalen
1B)	106.6	5	Sundsvall	Star FM
2B)	106.6	1	Kristinehamn	NRJ
2B)	106.6	5	Kalix	NRJ
1A)	106.7	1	Charlottenberg	RIX FM
1A)	106.7	3	Stockholm	RIX FM
1A)	106.7	5	Gävle	RIX FM
2A)	106.7	2.5	Malmö	Mix Megapol
2B)	106.7	10	Skellefteå	NRJ
1A)	106.8	3.2	Finnveden	RIX FM
2A)	106.8	7.4	Mora	Mix Megapol
1A)	106.9	2.5	Luleå	RIX FM
1A)	106.9	5	Västerås	RIX FM
2A)	106.9	7	Linköping	Mix Megapol
2A)	106.9	10	Trollhättan	Mix Megapol
1A)	107.0	10	Hudiksvall	RIX FM
1A)	107.0	3	Umeå	RIX FM
1B)	107.0	2.1	Jönköping	Star FM
2A)	107.0	2	Kiruna	Mix Megapol
4)	107.0	1	Lund	Retro FM
1A)	107.1	10	Örnsköldsvik	RIX FM
1B)	107.1	1	Borlänge	Star FM
1B)	107.1	1	Stockholm	Star FM

FM	MHz	kW	Location	Station
2B)	107.1	6.3	Borås	NRJ
1A)	107.2	1	Halmstad	RIX FM
2B)	107.2	3	Östersund	NRJ
1A)	107.3	1	Kristianstad	RIX FM
2A)	107.3	3	Eskilstuna	Mix Megapol
2A)	107.3	2	Göteborg	Mix Megapol
2B)	107.3	1	Söderhamn	NRJ
1A)	107.4	5	Sundsvall	RIX FM
1B)	107.4	2.5	Norrköping	Star FM
2A)	107.4	2	Kristinehamn	Mix Megapol
2A)	107.4	1	Nässjö	Mix Megapol
1D)	107.5	3	Stockholm	Power Hit R.
21)	107.5	1	Lysekil	R. Bohuslän
2A)	107.5	2	Växjö	Mix Megapol
1A)	107.6	5	Skövde	RIX FM
2B)	107.6	4.4	Helsingborg	NRJ
20)	107.7	1	Svenstavik	R. Berg
2B)	107.7	10	Nyköping	NRJ
1B)	107.8	3	Göteborg	Star FM
1B)	107.8	1	Orebro	Star FM
2A)	107.8	1	Arvika	Mix Megapol
9)	107.8	1.2	Norrtälje	R. Roslagen

+ txs below 1kW *) Located in Denmark

Addresses & other information:
1A-D) Nordic Entertainment Group (NENT), Ringvägen 52, 11867 Stockholm – **2A-F)** Bauer Media, Gjörwellsg. 30, 11260 Stockholm – **3)** Klågerupsvägen 16, 24 544 Staffanstorp – **4)** Hyllie stationsväg 2, 21532 Malmö – **5)** Solbergsvägen 2, 81134 Sandviken – **6)** P.O.Box 131, 79222 Mora – **7)** Åsgatan 24A, 93141 Skellefteå – **8)** P.O.Box 147, 69123 Karlskoga – **9)** Stora Brogatan 6, 76130 Norrtälje – **10)** Tornavägen 13, 22363 Lund – **11)** Klostergatan 2, 35230 Växjö – **12)** Ärlevägen 4, 25284 Helsingborg – **13)** Kungsgatan 16, 65224 Karlstad – **14)** Svetsarevägen 2, 68633 Sunne – **15)** P.O.Box 81, 29121 Kristianstad – **16)** P.O.Box 30079, 20061 Limhamn – **17)** Riksvägen 1, 840 60 Bräcke – **18)** Olvonvägen 9, 44277 Romelanda – **19A,B)** Bölevägen 38, 90431 Umeå – **20)** Industrivägen 27, 84531 Svenstavik – **21)** P.O.Box 535, 45121 Uddevalla – **22)** Södra Centralgatan 10, 80250 Gävle – **23)** Gruvvägen 1, 98131 Kiruna – **24)** Kungsgatan 58, 50335 Borås – **25)** P.O.Box 1087, 26921 Båstad.

Community Radio (Närradio) & Special Event Radio
Närradio: there are about 150 community radio stations on FM, most of them with a power below 1kW. Each tx is licensed by MPRT & PTS to a local community radio association (närradioförening); the airtime is usually shared by a variety of different non-profit associations and religious organisations (ca 800) that are individually licensed by MPRT and are transmitting their prgrs under their own names. **Special Event Radio:** MPRT & PTS are issuing short-term licenses for non-professional (hobby) broadcasting with very low power txs on FM, MW or SW for the duration of up to 2 weeks each.

DAB Transmitters (DAB+)
Tx Operator: Teracom **M:** SR P1, P2, P3 Din Gata, SR P4 (regional studios), SR Knattekanalen, SR P7 Sisuradio – **Tx Operator:** NENT **M:** Bandit Rock, Bandit Classic, Gamla Favoriter, Lugna Favoriter, Rockklassiker, Star FM, Mix Megapol, Power Millenium, R. Rainbow, Svenska Favoriter, Dansbandsfavoriter, Guldkanalen, Power Hit R., Skärgårdsradion – **Tx Operator:** Bauer Media **M:** Mix Megapol, NRJ, Hårdrock, Rockklassiker, Svensk Pop, Vinyl FM.

Block	kW	Location	Mux
6C	20	Göteborg	NENT
7C	20	Malmö	NENT
10B	20	Gävle	NENT
10D	20	Uppsala	NENT
12A	4	Stockholm	Bauer Media
12B	2	Göteborg	Teracom
12B	-	SFN (Malmö)	Teracom
12B	2	Uppsala	Teracom
12B	6	Älvsbyn	Teracom
12C	-	SFN (Stockholm)	Teracom
12D	-	SFN (Stockholm)	NENT

SWITZERLAND

L.T: UTC +1h (28 Mar-31 Oct: +2h) — **Pop:** 8.6 million — **Pr.L:** Official languages: German, French, Italian, Rumantsch — **E.C:** 230V/50Hz — **ITU:** SUI

BUNDESAMT FÜR KOMMUNIKATION (BAKOM)
(Federal Office of Communications)
Zukunftstrasse 44, 2501 Biel ☎+41 32 3275511 Fax +41 32 3275555
E: info@bakom.admin.ch **W:** www.bakom.admin.ch
L.P: Dir: Bernard Maissen

SRG SSR (Pub)
Giacomettistrasse 1, 3000 Bern 31 ☎+41 31 3509111 **E:** info@srgssr.ch **W:** www.srgssr.ch
L.P: Pres: Jean-Michel Cina; DG: Gilles Marchand
NB: SRG SSR is the administrative holding for the regional branches Schweizer Radio und Fernsehen (SRF), Radiotelevisiun Svizra Rumantscha (RTR), Radio Télévision Suisse (RTS) and Radiotelevisione svizzera (RSI).

Schweizer Radio und Fernsehen (SRF)
Fernsehstrasse 1-4, 8052 Zürich ☎+41 44 3056611 **E:** srf@srf.ch **W:** srf.ch **L.P:** Dir: Nathalie Wappler
Radio studios: Brunnenhofstrasse 22, 8057 Zürich (exc. R. SRF 2 Kultur); Novarastrasse 2, 4002 Basel (R. SRF 2 Kultur), subreg. studios.

FM (MHz)	1	2	3	kW
Arth (Rigi-Kulm)	90.9	96.6	103.8	20
Beatenberg (Niederhorn)	93.6	97.2	105.8	4
Bettingen (St. Chrischona)	90.6	99.0	103.6	32
Bolligen (Bantiger)	88.2	93.2	99.3	5
Bregenz (Pfänder)**	96.3	97.7	107.5	2
Carona (Monte San Salvatore)	96.3	-	-	20
Castel San Pietro (Caviano)	93.0	-	-	10
Celerina (Laret)	91.9	100.3	106.3	2
Evilard (Hohmatt)	96.0	99.7	91.7	0.1/1/0.1
Feschel (Wilerzälg)	88.2	90.3	101.5	1.6
Gerra (Lutri)	95.4	-	-	1.3
Haute-Nendaz (La Crête)	92.0	-	-	2
Ins (Schaltenrain)	90.7	-	-	1
Lostorf (Froburg)	96.0	98.7	91.3	1.3
Martigny (Ravoire)	107.7	-	-	2
Mt. Salève*	87.8	-	-	2
Nods (Chasseral)	103.0	-	105.3	20
Oberdorf (Nesselboden)	89.7	-	-	1.6
Pianezzo (Monti di Paudo)	96.9	-	-	2.5
Port Valais (Chalavornaire)	93.6	-	-	1
Schattenhalb (Geissholzli)	95.4	98.4	105.6	2
Tarasp (Sparsels)	101.3	103.9	95.1	1.3
Thollon (Leucel)*	88.1	-	-	6.3
Valzeina (Mittagplatte)	93.8	102.5	104.3	1.6
Visperterminen (Gebidem)	89.4	93.9	103.9	2.5
Widen (Gugelholz)	98.3	-	-	1
Wildhaus (Säntis)	101.5	95.4	105.6	63
Zürich (Uetliberg)	94.6	99.6	105.8	2/0.6/2

+ sites with only txs below 1kW. *) Located in France **) Located in Austria
D.Prgr (in Swiss German, exc. news/traffic info and *= in German): **Prgr 1 (R. SRF 1):** 24h. **Subregional prgrs:** 0532-0537 (MF), 0632-0637 (MF), 0732-0737 (MF), 1103-1110 (MF), 1630-1640 (Sat), 1630-1700 (Sun-Fri), 1655-1700 (Sat; Graubünden only) – **Prgr 2 (R. SRF 2 Kultur)*:** 24h – **Prgr 3 (R. SRF 3):** 24h – **Prgr 4 (R. SRF 4 News)*:** 24h – **Prgr 5 (R. SRF Musikwelle):** 24h – **Prgr 6 (SRF Virus):** 24h.

Radiotelevisiun Svizra Rumantscha (RTR)
Via da Masans 2, 7002 Cuira ☎+41 81 2557575 **E:** esther.bigliel@rtr.ch **W:** rtr.ch **L.P:** Dir: Pius Paulin

FM	MHz	kW	FM	MHz	kW
Celerina (Laret)	89.1	2	Tarasp (Sparsels)	98.7	1.3
Valzeina (Mittagplatte)	90.3	1.6	+ txs below 1kW.		

D.Prgr (in Rumantsch): **R. RTR:** 24h. Incl. relay of selected R.SRF prgrs in Swiss German/German.

Radio Télévision Suisse (RTS)
Administration/studios: Quai Ernest-Ansermet 20, 1211 Genève 8 ☎+41 58 2367444 **W:** rts.ch **L.P:** Dir: Pascal Crittin
Radio studios: Avenue du Temple 40, 1010 Lausanne.

FM (MHz)	1	2	3	4	kW
Abbaye (Pont-Agouillons)	99.5	87.6	101.4	-	1
Bolligen (Bantiger)	95.1	-	-	-	5
Bourrignon (Ordons)	94.2	99.6	104.8	-	10
Carona (Monte San Salvatore)	104.0	-	-	-	20
Castel San Pietro (Caviano)	87.8	-	-	-	10
Chardonne (Mt. Pèlerin)	91.6	101.5	90.6	-	1.6

FM (MHz)	1	2	3	4	kW
Chaux-de-Fonds (Cornu)	92.3	96.3	103.4	-	1.3
Cudrefin (Tremblex)	91.3	92.0	89.1	-	4
Feschel (Wilerzälg)	91.4	96.1	107.4	-	1.6
Gerra (Lutri)	93.2	-	-	-	1.6
Gingins (Barillette)	91.2	100.1	105.6	-	20
Haute-Nendaz (La Crête)	94.4	96.5	106.0	-	2
Ins (Schaltenrain)	96.9	-	-	-	1
Martigny (Ravoire)	93.2	106.9	100.5	-	2
Mt. Salève*	94.9	100.7	104.4	90.8	1
Nods (Chasseral)	102.3	100.3	104.2	-	20
Ollon (Chamossaire)	98.1	95.0	88.6	-	1
Ollon (Chamossaire)	105.1	-	-	-	0.3
Pianezzo (Monti di Paudo)	105.3	-	-	-	2.5
Premier (Buclards)	94.7	100.8	104.7	-	10
Saint-Sulpice (Haut de la Vy)	102.0	95.3	104.5	-	1
Sorens (Gibloux)	91.0	92.5	88.6	-	1
Thollon (Leucel)*	102.6	96.2	98.5	-	6.3
Visperterminen (Gebidem)	90.8	-	-	-	2.5
Wildhaus (Säntis)	99.9	-	-	-	63

+ sites with only txs below 1kW. *) Located in France
D.Prgr (in French): **Prgr 1 (La 1ère):** 24h – **Prgr 2 (Espace 2):** 24h **Prgr 3 (Couleur 3):** 24h – **Prgr 4 (Option Musique):** 24h.

Radiotelevisione svizzera (RSI)
Via Canevascini 5, 6900 Lugano ☎+41 91 8035111 **E:** info@rsi.ch **W:** rsi.ch **L.P:** Dir: Maurizio Canetta

FM (MHz)	1	2	3	kW
Arth (Rigi-Kulm)	106.2	-	-	20
Carona (Monte San Salvatore)	88.1	91.5	106.0	20
Castel San Pietro (Caviano)	88.8	98.8	104.5	10
Celerina (Laret)	104.3	-	-	2
Gerra (Lutri)	99.2	94.1	92.5	1.3
Mt. Salève*	97.1	-	-	2
Nods (Chasseral)	107.3	-	-	20
Pianezzo (Monti di Paudo)	89.4	93.5	107.4	2.5
Thollon (Leucel)*	97.8	-	-	6.3
Valzeina (Mittagplatte)	95.8	-	-	1.6
Visperterminen (Gebidem)	96.7	-	-	2.5
Wildhaus (Säntis)	107.8	-	-	63

+ sites with only txs below 1kW. *) Located in France
D.Prgr (in Italian): **Prgr 1 (Rete Uno):** 24h – **Prgr 2 (Rete Due):** 24h **Prgr 3 (Rete Tre):** 24h.

OTHER STATIONS

FM	MHz	kW	Location	Station
16B)	87.6	2	Stockeren	R. Freiburg
24)	88.0	2.8	Rooterberg	R. Sunshine
7)	88.4	2	Mt. Salève*	LFM
24)	88.8	1	Schüepenloch	R. Sunshine
24)	88.8	2	Gugelholz	R. Sunshine
3)	88.9	4	Dornegg	R. 32
10)	89.2	1	Utzenstorf	R. Bern1
15)	89.3	1	Rorschacherberg	R. FM1
16A)	89.4	1.75	Gibloux	R. Fribourg
19)	89.8	1	Lenzerheide	R. Südostschweiz
25)	90.0	1	St. Gallen	R. Top
11)	90.5	1	Rigi-Kulm	R. Central
14)	90.6	1	Monti di Paudo	R. Ticino
8)	91.6	2	Gugelholz	R. Argovia
18)	91.8	2	Mt. Salève*	R. Lac
2)	92.1	1	Honegg	R. 24
13)	92.2	1	Mt. Salève*	R. Cité Genève
18)	92.3	4	Champs Maître	R. Lac
12)	92.6	1	Giettes	R. Chablais
15)	92.7	3	Mittagplatte	R. FM1
27A)	92.8	1	Elemoos	Canal 3
14)	93.0	1	Monte Laura	R. Ticino
24)	93.2	1	Rigi-Kulm	R. Sunshine
27B)	93.9	1	Elemoos	Canal 3
18)	94.0	1	Champs Lequet	R. Lac
18)	95.6	6	Leucel*	R. Lac
21)	95.7	1	Rigi-Kulm	R. Pilatus
29)	96.3	1	Ins	RJB
4)	96.5	4	Alpe del Tiglio	R. 3i
1)	97.0	1	Champs Lequet	One FM
12)	97.1	1	Chamossaire	R. Chablais
7)	97.4	4	Champs Maître	LFM
26)	97.5	1	Uetliberg	R. LoRa
23)	97.5	1	Ins	R. RTN
20)	97.6	2	Mt. Salève*	Rouge FM
10)	97.7	1	Bantiger	R. Bern1
11)	99.2	1.5	Rooterberg	R. Central
1)	99.3	2	Grand Devin	One FM
24)	99.6	1.5	Alpnach	R. Sunshine
19)	99.7	1.2	Davos	R. Südostschweiz
14)	100.0	4	Monte San Salvatore	R. Ticino
11)	100.1	1	Sonnenberg	R. Central
17)	100.6	1	Loge	RFJ
6)	100.6	1	Schaltenrain	GRRIF
17)	100.8	4.6	Ordons	RFJ
5C)	100.9	1	Uetliberg	Energy Zürich
5B)	101.0	1	Utzenstorf	Energy Bern
23)	101.7	1	Loge	R. RTN
5A)	101.7	4	St.Chrischona	Energy Basel
5B)	101.7	1	Bantiger	Energy Bern
28)	101.9	4	Tresillet	Rouge FM
21)	102.1	1.5	Rooterberg	R. Pilatus
22)	102.2	1.5	Gebidem	R. Rottu Oberwallis
11)	102.6	2	Urmiberg	R. Central
2)	102.8	1	Uetliberg	R. 24
11)	103.0	1.5	Alpnach	R. Central
7)	103.3	6	Leucel*	LFM
28)	104.3	1.2	Martigny	Rhône FM
21)	104.9	1	Sonnenberg	R. Pilatus
20)	106.5	6	Leucel*	Rouge FM
4)	106.5	10	Caviano	R. 3i
1)	107.2	3	Publier*	One FM
23)	107.6	1	Montela	R. RTN
9)	107.6	4	St. Chrischona	R. Basilisk
1)	107.9	4	Champs Maître	One FM

+ sites with onlt txs below 1kW. *) Located in France

Addresses & other information:
NB. Stns broadcast in Swiss German/German exc. where indicated otherwise. **1)** Rue des Bains 33, 1205 Genève. In French – **2)** Limmatstrasse 264, 8005 Zürich – **3)** Zuchwilerstrasse 21, 4501 Solothurn – **4)** Via Carona 15, 6815 Melide. In Italian – **5A)** Münchensteinerstrasse 43, 4052 Basel, **5B)** Optingenstrasse 56, 3001 Bern **5C)** Dufourstrasse 23, 8008 Zürich – **6)** Rue du Marché 3, 2800 Delémont. In French – **7)** Chemin de Mornex 1 Bis, 1003 Lausanne. In French – **8)** Bahnhofstrasse 41, 5001 Aarau – **9)** Marktgasse 8, 4001 Basel – **10)** Dammweg 9, 3001 Bern – **11)** Postfach 464, 6440 Brunnen – **12)** Rue des Fours 11A, 1870 Monthey 1. In French – **13)** Rue du Pré-de-la-Fontaine 2, 1217 Meyrin 2. In French – **14)** Via Varenna 18, 6600 Locarno. In Italian – **15)** Bionstrasse 4, 9001 St.Gallen – **16A,B)** Rue de Romont 35, 1701 Fribourg. 16A) in French – **17)** Rue du 23-Juin 20, 2800 Delémont. In French – **18)** Rue des Bains 35, 1205 Genève. In French – **19)** Sommeraustrasse 32, 7007 Chur – **20)** En Budron A6, 1052 Le-Mont-sur-Lausanne. In French – **21)** Zürichstr. 5, 6004 Luzern – **22)** Treichweg 1, 3930 Visp – **23)** Champs-Montants 16a, 2074 Marin. In French – **24)** Erlenstrasse 2, 6343 Rotkreuz – **25)** Bürglistrasse 31a, 8401 Winterthur – **26)** Militärstrasse 85a, 8004 Zürich – **27A,B)** Robert-Walser-Platz 7, 2501 Biel. 27B) in French – **28)** Chemin Saint-Hubert 5, 1950 Sion. In French – **29)** L'Orgerie 9, 2710 Tavannes. In French.

Special Event Radio
BAKOM is issuing short-term licenses for non-professional broadcasting with low power txs on FM, related to public events.

DAB Transmitters (DAB+)
Licensee: SRG SSR **M1:** R. SRF 1 (incl. subreg), R. SRF 2 Kultur, R. SRF 3, R. SRF 4 News, R. SRF Musikwelle, SRF Virus, Swiss Pop, RTS La 1ère, RTS Couleur 3, RSI Rete Uno, RSI Rete Tre, R. RTR **M2:** RTS La 1ère, RTS Espace 2, RTS Couleur 3, RTS Option Musique, Swiss Pop, Swiss Classic, Swiss Jazz, R. SRF 1 (incl. subreg), R. SRF 3, R. SRF Musikwelle, R. SRF 4 News, SRF Virus, RSI Rete Uno, RSI Rete Tre, RTR R. Rumantsch **M3:** RSI Rete Uno, RSI Rete Due, RSI Rete Tre, Swiss Pop, Swiss Classic, Swiss Jazz, R. SRF 1, R. SRF 3, R. SRF 4 News, R. SRF Musikwelle, RTS La 1ère, RTS Couleur 3, RTS Option Musique, R. RTR, R. Fiume Ticino, R. 3i **M4:** R. SRF 1 (incl. subreg), R. SRF 2 Kultur, R. SRF 3, R. SRF 4 News, R. SRF Musikwelle, SRF Virus, Swiss Pop, Swiss Classic, Swiss Jazz, RTS La 1ère, RTS Couleur 3, RSI Rete Uno, RSI Rete Tre, R. RTR – **Licensee:** SwissMediaCast AG **M5:** R. Central, Energy Basel, Energy Bern, Energy Zürich, ERF Plus, Eviva, R. FM1, Life Channel, R. Pilatus, R. Argovia, R. 24, R. Maria, R. Melody, R. Top, R. Zürisee, R. Top Two, Schlager R., RSI Rete Tre **M6a-d: Regional muxes** (on all muxes: Swiss Classic, Swiss Jazz); 6c includes R. L (Liechtenstein) – **Licensee:** Romandie Médias SA **M7:** BNJ-RJB,

BNJ-RTN, BNJ-RFJ, GRIFF, LFM, One FM, R. Chablais, R. Fribourg, R. Fribourg Music, R. Lac, R. Maria, Rhône FM, Rouge FM, Vertical, SRF Virus, RSI Rete Tre – **Licensee:** Digris AG **M: Local muxes** in key agglomerations (not shown).

Bl	Location	Mux	Bl	Location	Mux
7A	SFN (Nordschweiz)	6a	11C	SFN (Oberwallis)	6d
7D	SFN (Deutschschweiz)	5	12A	SFN (Romandie)	2
8B	SFN (Mittelland)	6b	12A	SFN (Ticino)	3
9B	SFN (Ostschweiz)	6c	12C	SFN (Deutschschweiz[1])	1
10B	SFN (Romandie)	7	12D	SFN (Graubünden)	4

Bl=Block [1]) exc. Graubünden

SYRIA

L.T: UTC +2h (26 Mar-29 Oct: +3h) — **Pop:** 18 million — **Pr.L:** Arabic — **E.C:** 220V/50Hz — **ITU:** SYR

MINISTRY OF INFORMATION

Mezzeh Autostrad, Dar al Ba'th Building, Damascus ☎+963 11 6664681 +963 11 6664681 **W:** moi.gov.sy **E:** info@moi.gov.sy **L.P:** Talib Qadi Amin, Asst. Minister.

SYRIAN RADIO AND TV (Gov)

Radio & TV Directorate, Ommayad Square, Damascus ☎+963 11 2720700 +963 11 2234930 **W:** en.ortas.gov.sy **E:** editor@rtv.gov.sy **L.P:** DG: Fayez Al Sayegh. Dir. Eng: Adnan Salhah. Dir. Radio: Mahmoud Al Joma'at.

MW	kHz	kW	Prgr	MW	kHz	kW	Prgr
Damascus	567	300	1	Homs	936	100	1
Damascus	666	100	Y	Tartus	1071	100	*
Tartus	783	300	1/E	*relays R. Al-Nour, LBN			

FM (MHz)	1	Y	kW	FM	1	Y	kW
Abu Kamal	-	92.6		Homs	-	99.3	
Afrin	93.0	96.6		Maliqiyah	89.4	99.0	
Al-Hassake	89.9	99.5		Nabi Saleh	89.0	98.8	
Aleppo	96.1	89.9	10	Raqqah	103.7	93.7	
Ayn al-Arab	89.4	105.1		Slenfe	94.9	88.6	150
Bloudan	93.5	96.7		Suwayda	92.6	100.9	150
Damascus	95.5	88.7		Tartus	-	95.5	
Deir ez-Zor	90.0	87.8	150/1	Yabrud	-	93.0	

General Prgr "Radio Dimashk" (1): 24h. **Voice of Youth (Y)** 24h.
Other stations (**W:** ortas.gov.sy/index.php?d=100461):
Amwaj FM, Latakia 98.2, Tartus 105.3MHz. **W:** facebook.com/Amwaj.Latakia – **Al-Karma FM,** Suwayda: 88.5/104.5MHz. **W:** facebook.com/al-karma.fm – **Syriana FM** (news prgr.), Damascus 88.3MHz, Tartus 90MHz – **Zenobia FM,** Homs: 98.0MHz
Ann: 1: "Idha'at Dimashq". 2: "Huna Idha'at Sowt as-Sha'ab min Dimashq". Y: "Huna Sowt as-Shabab".

EXTERNAL SERVICE: see International Radio section.

Other Stations (FM MHz):
Al Aan FM: Al Bab 104.4, Aleppo 96.6, Atme 99.7, Damascus 96.9, Daraa 98.2/99.4, Homs 97.6, Latakia 96.3 **W:** alaan.fm – **Al Madina FM:** Slenfe 100.5, Aleppo/Damascus 101.5.**W:** almadinafm.com – **Alwan FM:** Idlib 93.3 **W:** alwan.fm – **Arabesque FM:** Aleppo/Damascus 102.3, Slenfe 106.9 **W:** arabesque.fm – **ARTA FM:** Deir ez-Zor 97.0, Aamouda 99.5 **W:** artafm.com – **Fann FM:** Aleppo/Damascus 89.0, Slenfe 106.1 **W:** fann-fm.com – **Farah FM:** Aleppo/Damascus 97.3 **W:** farah.fm – **Hala FM:** 99.9/103.8 **W:** 7la.fm – **R. Al-Kul** (opposition) Aleppo: 95.5 **W:** radioalkul.com – **R. Gecko (UN)**, Camp Faouar, Golan: 103.8 **W:** radio-gecko.com – **Melody FM:** Aleppo/Damascus 97.9 **W:** melodysyria.com – **Mix FM,** Damascus: 105.7 **W:** mixfmsyria.com – **Ninar FM:** Aleppo 88.3, Damascus 89.6, Damascus 93.5, Tartus 101.1 **W:** ninar.net – **R. Amal FM:** Raqqa 99.0 **W:** radioamalfm.com – **R. Nasaem Syria:** Aleppo 98.5 **W:** nasaem-syria.fm – **Rotana Style FM:** Slenfe 103.3, Aleppo/Damascus 105.0 **W:** rotanastyle.com – **Sawt el-Ghad,** Damascus: 99.9 **W:** sawtelghad.com (see main entry under Lebanon) – **Shahba FM,** Aleppo 94.0 **W:** shahbafm.com – **Sham FM:** Damascus 92.3, Aleppo 95.3, Slenfe 101.8 **W:** shamfm.fm – **Syria Al-Ghad FM:** Damascus 104.2, Aleppo 104.4, Slenfe 107.4 **W:** syriaalghad.com – **Watan FM:** Aleppo 90.2, Idlib 90.3, Damascus 102.8 **W:** watan.fm – **Version FM:** Damascus 94.4 **W:** versionfm.com
R. Al-Nour: Aleppo 98.7, Damascus 91.3/91.5, Homs/Tartus 92.3 **W:** alnour.com.lb/radio (See main entry under Lebanon) **Orient Radio** (studios in Turkey): Homs/Idlib 94.6, Deraa 99.2, Antakya (TUR) 94.4, Reyhanli (TUR) 95.8. **W:** orient-radio.net

NB: Many stns and txs rep. off the air or operating irregularly. Many stns operate without licence.

TAIWAN (Rep. of China)

L.T: UTC +8h — **Pop:** 23.8 million — **Pr.L:** Chinese (Amoy, Mandarin, Hakka) — **E.C:** 110V/60Hz — **ITU:** CHN (**WRTH:** TWN)

NATIONAL COMMUNICATIONS COMMISSION (NCC)

RenAi Rd. Office: No. 50, Sec. 1, RenAi Rd., Taipei 10052 ☎ + 886 800 177177 + 886 2 2343 3994 **W:** ncc.gov.tw **E:** po2@ncc.gov.tw
L.P: Chairperson: Yaw-Shyang Chen

CHUNGKUO KUANGPO KUNGSSU (Broadcasting Corporation of China - BCC) (Priv. Comm.)

375 Sungchiang Rd, Chungshan Ward, Taipei 104 ☎ + 886 2 2501 9688 + 886 2 2501 8834 **W:** bcc.com.tw **E:** pr@bcc.com.tw
L.P: Chairman: Chao Shao Kang
Call: BE followed by the callsign below

MW	Call	Location	kHz	kW	Netw.
1)	D57	Taipei (Tucheng)	531	10	L
9)	D65	Ilan*	630	10	N
1)	D34	Taipei (Tucheng)	648	20	N
6)	D92	Tainan	711	10	C
4)	D58	Taichung	720	10	N
10)	D28	Taitung*	819	10	N
8)	D27	Hualien	855	4.6	N
7)	D25	Kaohsiung	864	10	N
2)	G77	Hsinchu	882	10	N
6)	D24	Tainan	891	10	L
4)	D43	Taichung	927	10	C
1)	D55	Taipei (Tucheng)	963	20	C
10)	D88	Taitung*	1008	10	C
2)	D53	Hsinchu	1017	10	C
5)	D26	Chia-i	1035	10	C
4)	D77	Taichung	1062	10	L
11)	D72	Yuli*	1116	3.5	N
12)	D68	Puli*	1152	1	C
9)	D86	Ilan*	1161	10	C
3)	D89	Miaoli	1161	10	C
8)	D32	Hualien	1188	5	C
7)	D79	Kaohsiung	1224	10	C
6)	D47	Tainan	1296	10	N
5)	D63	Chia-i	1350	10	N
11)	D74	Yuli*	1386	3.5	C
3)	D54	Miaoli	1413	10	N
12)	D67	Puli*	1413	1	N

N=News Netw, C=Country Netw, L=local *) relay stn

FM	Call	Location	MHz	kW	FM	Call	Location	MHz	kW
13)	G30	Kinmen*	96.3	10	5)	G86	Chentoushan	103.1	10
4)	D4	Taichung	102.1	35	1)	D3	Taipei	103.3	35
8)	D6	Hualien	102.1	5	7)	D5	Kaohsing	103.3	35
9)	D80	Ilan*	102.1	2.5	11)	D51	Yuli*	103.3	1
10)	D52	Taitung*	102.1	5	12)	G96	Puli*	107.3	1
3)	G85	Huoyenshan	102.9	10					

Pop Netw, *) relay stn
D.Prgr: News Network: 24h in Mandarin – **Country Network:** 24h in Taiwanese – **Taipei Local R. (i go 531):** 24h mainly in Taiwanese – **Pop Network (i like radio):** 24h in Mandarin

Addresses of local stations:
2) 125-1, Chingpu Rd, Chiingpu, Hsinfeng Village, Hsinchu 304 – **3)** 78, Lane 1008, Chungshan Rd, Kaomiao Li, Miaoli 360 – **4)** 35th Flr, 758 Chungming So. Rd, Taichung 402 – **5)** 121 Wufeng So. Rd, Chia-i 600 – **6)** 5, 19th Flr, 248, Sec. 2, Yunghua Rd, Anping, Tainan 708 – **7)** 4, 16th Flr, 91 Chungshan 2nd Rd, Chienchen, Kaohsiung 806 – **8)** 2nd Flr. 108, Fu'an Rd, Hualien 970 – **9)** Ilan (relay st.) – **10)** Taitung (relay st.) – **11)** Yuli (relay st.) – **12)** Puli (relay st.) – **13)** Kinmen (relay st.), relays also News Netw at certain times
Ann: Mandarin: "Chungkuo Kuangpo Kungssu" or "Chungkuo Kuangpo Kungssu, (location) Kuangpo Tientai", Amoy: "Tiyon Gok Kon Po Kon Sih, (location) Kon Po Den Tai"
Notes: Two networks, Formosa Network and Music Network, both ceased FM broadcasting on 14 April,2017. Of these Former Music Network only continues to broadcast via internet as "I Radio"

EXTERNAL SERVICES: Chungyang Kuangpo Tiantai (Radio Taiwan International) see International Broadcasting section

HAN SHENG KUANGPO TIENTAI (Voice of Han Broadcasting Network) (Gov)

(operated by General Political Warfare Bureau, Ministry of National Defense)
✉ B, 5th Flr, 3, Sec. 1, Hsin-i Rd, Chungcheng Ward, Taipei 10048 ☎ + 886 2 2321 5191 🖷 + 886 2 2396 2657 **W:** voh.com.tw

MW	Call	Location	kHz	kW
1)	C22	Taipei	684	10
1b)	C25	Taoyuan	693	10
2b)	C32	Tainan	693	8
4)	C33	Hualien	792	10
2c)	C38	Penghu	846	10
1b)		Taoyuan	936	5
1)	C23	Taipei	1116	10
4b)	C30	Ilan	1116	10
2)	C29	Kaohsiung	1251	10
2c)	C44	Penghu	1269	10
3)	C27	Taichung	1287	10
2)	C36	Kaohsiung	1332	10
4)	C40	Hualien	1359	5
3b)	C31	Yunlin	1377	10

FM	Call	Location	MHz	kW
2b)	C28	Tainan (Chentoushan)	101.3	35
1)	C26	Miaoli (Huoyenshan)	104.5	35
4)	C35	Hualien	104.5	3
4c)	C39	Taitung	105.3	3
4d)		Kuanshan	105.3	3
1)	C24	Taipei	106.5	35
4b)		Ilan	106.5	
2)	C34	Kaohsiung	107.3	35
1c)		Kinmen	107.3	0.1

D.Prgr: 24h on MW & FM. Same prgr broadcasts at certain times. – **1b)** Taoyuan **1c)** Kinmen (relay Taipei) – **2)** 40 Mingte New Village, Tsoying, Kaohsiung 813 – 2b) Tainan 2c) 1 Makong, Penghu (relay Kaohsiung) – **3)** 178 Chenhsing Rd, East Ward, Taichung 401 – 3b) Yunlin (relay Taichung) – 4) 643 Chungcheng Rd, Hualien 970 – 4b) Ilan 4c) Taitng 4d) Kuanshan (relay Hualien)

BROADCASTS TO MAINLAND: KUANGHUA CHIH SHENG (Voice of Kuanghua)

✉ P.O.Box 1700, Taipei ☎+ 886 2 2603 0429 🖷+ 886 2 2603 0433 **W:** khmusic. tw

MW location	kHz	kW	Location	kHz	kW
Hsinfeng	711	250	Kuanyin	‡846	250
Kuanyin	‡801	250	Hsinfeng	981	250

D.Prgr. 0755-0005

SW Location	kHz	kW
Kuanyin	‡9745	250 ‡ inactive

D.Prgr. 0755-0005 **Ann:** "Kuanghua chih Sheng"

FU HSING KUANGPO TIENTAI (Fu Hsing Broadcasting Station) (Gov)

(operated by Ministry of National Defence)
✉ 5, Lane 280, Sec. 5, Chungshan No. Rd, Shihlin Ward, Taipei 111 ☎ + 886 2 2882 3450 🖷 + 886 2 2881 8218 **W:** fhbs.com.tw

MW	Call	Location	kHz	kW
1)	H2	Taipei 1	594	10
2)	H38	Taichung 1	594	5
3)	H44	Kaohsiung 1	594	10

SW	Call	Location	kHz	kW
1)		Unknown	9410	10
1)		Unknown	9774	10
1)		Unknown	15375	10

FM	Call	Location	MHz	kW
2)	I44	Taichung 1	107.8	10

D.Prgr: 1st Netw. 24h on MW, **2nd Netw.** 0500-0900 on SW for China Mainland.
Local (relay) Stations: 2) 81 Chungtai Rd, Chunshe Li, Nantun, Taichung 408. – **3)** 819 Chengching Rd, Niaosung Village, Kaohsiung 833. **Ann:** "Fu Hsing Kuangpo Tientai."
Editorial note: The 'unknown' SW location is not Kuanyin. We visited Kuanyin area including Voice of Kuanghua tx site twice last year, however the signal is not strong and it was not enough to judge Fu Hsing SW as transmitting from Kuanyin area.

OTHER PUBLIC STATIONS (Call: BE_)

MW	Call	Station	Location	kHz	kW
3)	L2	Yuyeh	Penghu	738	100
5)	G28	Kaohsiung	Kaohsiung	1089	10
4)	G26	Taipei	Taipei	1134	10
3)	L3	Yuyeh	Penghu	1143	100
1c)	P33	Ching Cha	Tainan	1314	1
2)	E32	Chiao Yu	Taipei	1494	10
2a)	E34	Chiao Yu	Changhua	1494	5
1a)	P26	Ching Cha	Hsinchu	1512	10
3a)		Yuyeh	Ilan	1593	1

FM	Call	MHz	kW	FM	Call	MHz	kW	FM	Call	MHz	kW
2f)		88.9	1	2i)		98.1	3	3d)		104.3	10
2l)		88.9	1	2k)		99.1	4	1)	P29	104.9	35
2n)		91.5		2m)		99.3	3	1)		104.9	2
1d)	P42	93.1	25	2e)		100.1		1)		104.9	2
1h)		93.1	1	2f)	E39	100.3	1	1e)		104.9	2
1j)		93.1	2	2d)		100.5	3	1c)	P31	104.9	5
4)	G25	93.1	10	2d)		100.5	1	1d)	P32	104.9	12
1)	P41	94.3	10	1e)	P39	101.3	1	1j)		104.9	2
1f)	P44	94.3	5	1f)	P35	101.3	1.5	1b)	P30	105.1	35
1g)	P45	94.3		1g)	P37	101.3	1.6	2k)		105.3	3
1i)		94.3	1	7b)		101.5	30	7e)		105.7	5
5)	G29	94.3	16	2)	E33	101.7	30	7f)		105.7	3
1b)	P43	94.5	30	2b)	E36	101.7	30	7)		105.9	30
6z)		96.1		7c)		102.9	5	7a)		105.9	30
6)		96.3	15	2d)	E38	102.9	5	1f)	P36	106.5	1.5
6a)		96.3	30	2a)	E35	103.5	30	7g)		106.9	5
6b)		96.3	5	2g)	E40	103.5	10	7f)		106.9	5
6c)		96.3	5	2c)	E37	103.7	5	7b)		106.9	3
2c)	E47	97.3	3	2h)	E41	103.9	3	2j)		107.7	3

Addresses & other information:
1) Chingcha Kuangpo Tientai (Police Broadcasting Service), 17 Kuangchou Str, Chungcheng, Taipei 10066. Two networks in 24h: Nat. Traffic Netw. of Public Security (NTN) on FM, and Reg. Traffic Netw. of Public Security (RTN) on AM and FM. NTN on 104.9MHz (2 relay stns on same freq) RTN on 94.3MHz – **1a)** 389 Sec.2, Hsinglung Rd, Chupei City, Hsinchu 30274. RTN on 1512kHz – **1b)** 99 Po-ai Str, Nantun, Taichung 40844. NTN on 105.1MHz, RTN on 94.5MHz – **1c)** 85-21, Nanshih, Nanshih Li, Matou, Tainan 72153. RTN on 1314kHz, NTN on 104.9MHz – **1d)** 455 Po-ai 4th Rd, Tsoying Ward, Kaohsiung 81369. NTN on 104.9MHz, RTN on 93.1MHz – **1e)** 89 Sec. 2, Minchuan Rd. Ilan 26049. RTN on 101.3MHz, NTN 2 relay stations on 104.9MHz – **1f)** 21-2 Fuchien Rd, Hualien 97058, NTN on 101.3, 106.5MHz, RTN on 94.3MHz – **1g)** 289, Chungshan Rd. Taitung 95043. NTN on 101.3MHz, RTN on 94.3MHz – **1h)** Peililungshan (relay Kaohsing RTN) – **1i)** Senyung (relay Taitung RTN) – **1j)** Hengchun (relay Kaohsing NTN on 104.9MHz, RTN on 93.1MHz) **W:** pbs.gov.tw – **2)** Chiao Yu Broadc. System (National Education R.), 45 Nanhai Rd, Taipei 10066. On MW, FM both 24h **Ann:** "Chiao Yu chih Sheng, Chiao Yu Kuangpo Tientai" – **2a)** 5-1 Hukang Rd, Changhua 50080 – **2b)** 380 Kuangtung 3rd Rd, Chienchen Ward, Kaohsiung 80656 – **2c)** 457 Tunghsing Rd, Hualien 97063. 1st prgr on 103.7MHz, 2nd prgr on 97.3MHz – **2d)** 135, Ma Hengheng Rd, Taitung 95047. 1st prgr on 102.9MHz, 2nd prgr on 100.5MHz –**2e)** Keelung relay Taipei – **2f)** Yuli (1st prgr on 100.3MHz, 2nd prgr on 88.9MHz) relay Hualien – **2g)** Ilan relay Taipei – **2h)** Miaoli relay Changhua – **2i)** Nantou relay Changhua – **2j)** Chia-I relay Kaohsiung – **2k)** Penghu (1st prgr on 99.1MHz relay Taipei FM, 2nd prgr on 105.3MHz relay Taipei AM) – **2l)** Kinmen relay Taipei – **2m)** Hengchun relay Kaohsiung – **2n)** Matzu relay Taipei **W:** ner.gov.tw – **3)** Yuyeh Broadc. St (Fishery R. Station), 5 Yukang No. 2nd Rd, Chienchen Ward, Kaohsiung 80672. 24h Weather rpt. at every h. 1520-1600 in English & Indonesian. Sun-Thu 1920-2000 in Indonesian, 2120-2200 in Vietnamese.Sat & Sun 0620-0700 in Indonesian, 0720-0800 in Tagalog. **Ann:** "Hi-giap Kong-po'-tian-tai"– **3a)** Ilan (relay stn) **W:** frs. gov.tw – **4)** Taipei Broadc. St, 4th Flr, 62-2, Sec. 3, Chungshan No. Rd, Chungshan Ward, Taipei 10452 (operated by Taipei City Council). AM "Ho Hi Yan" Ch. on 1134kHz, 2300-1600. FM "City Info" Ch. on 93.1MHz, 24h. Rel: BBC-WS: MF1400-1500, Sun-Thu2200-2300 on FM. **W:** radio.gov. taipei . – **5)** Kaohsiung Broadc. St, 90 Hsinchiang Rd, Kushan, Kaohsiung 80472 (operated by Kaohsiung City Council). Two prgr. on 1089kHz, 94.3MHz, both 2200-1800 **W:** kbs.gov.tw – **6)** Alian Radio, 5th Flr, 120, Chungyang Rd, Nankang Ward, Taipei 11573. 24h **W:** alian963.ipcf.org.tw – 6**a)** Kaohsiung – **6b)** Hualien – **6c)** Taitung **–6z)** Hsingchu(10kW), Miaoli(15kW), Nantou(1kW, 3stn), Kaohsiung(1kW, 3stn), Pintung(1kW) Hengchun(3kW), Ilan(5kW),Taitung(10kW,1kW)– **7)** Hakka Radio, 10th Flr, 49, Sec. 1, Chingfeng Rd, Chungli Ward, Taoyuan 320. 24h **W:** hakkaradio.org.tw

– **7a)** Kaohsiung – **7b)** Miaoli – **7c)** Ilan – **7d)** Tainan – **7e)** Hsinchu – **7f)** Hualien – **7g)** Taitung

OTHER PRIVATE & COMMERCIAL STATIONS (Call: BE_)

MW	Call	Station	Location	kHz	kW
1a)		Taiwan	Tahsi	621	1
1c)		Taiwan	Sungling	630	10
2b)	V59	Cheng Sheng	Taichung 2	657	20
2c)		Cheng Sheng	Peikang	675	5
3)	E43	Shih Hsin	Taipei	729	0.5
4)		Sheng Li	Makung	756	1
2b)	V94	Taiwan	Taichung	774	20
5)	V88	Hsien Sheng	Taoyuan	774	20
4)	V56	Sheng Li	Tainan 1	774	1
61)	V79	Keelung	Keelung	792	1
7)		Chien kuo	Hsinhua	801	1
8)	V54	Kuo Sheng	Changhua	810	10
2)	V35	Cheng Sheng	Taipei	819	5
2a)	V72	Cheng Sheng	Chia-i	855	1
9)	V24	Min Pen	Taipei 2	855	1
10)		Feng Ming	Penghu	882	1
11)	V98	Cheng Kung	Kaohsiung	936	1
7)	V85	Chien Kuo	Hsinying	954	10
1c)	V84	Taiwan	Chunghsing	963	10
10)	V68	Feng Ming	Kaohsiung 2	981	2.2
2b)	V58	Cheng Sheng	Taichung 1	990	20
12)	V92	Tien Nan	Taipei	999	1
2f)	V60	Cheng Sheng	Kaohsiung	1008	1
13)		Tien Sheng	Yuanli	1026	1
14)	V51	Chung Hua	Sanchung 2	1026	1
15)	V64	Yen Sheng	Hualien 1	1044	5
2d)	V82	Cheng Sheng	Ilan	1062	1
16)	V74	Min Li	Pingtung	1062	5
1a)		Taiwan	Tahsi	1062	1
17)	V96	Tien Sheng	Tainan	1071	1
2c)	V36	Cheng Sheng	Yunlin	1125	5
18)	V70	Hua Sheng	Taipei 1	1152	5
10)	V67	Feng Ming	Kaohsiung 1	1161	1.2
8)		Kuo Sheng	Erhlin	1179	2.5
1)	V46	Taiwan	Taipei 2	1188	1
4)	V57	Sheng Li	Tainan 2	1188	1
1a)	V62	Taiwan	Hsinchu	1206	10
13)		Tien Sheng	Pengshan	1215	1
18)	V71	Hua Sheng	Taipei 2	1224	1
14)		Chung Hua	Juifang	1233	1
15)		Yen Sheng	Hualien 2	1242	1
2a)		Cheng Sheng	Taipao	1260	1
2e)	V37	Cheng Sheng	Taitung	1269	1
19)		Fuhsingkang	Peitou	1278	1
9)	V23	Min Pen	Taipei 1	1296	1
13)	V76	Tien Sheng	Chunan	1314	10
1)	V45	Taiwan	Taipei 1	1323	1
1c)		Taiwan	Puli	1332	1
14)	V50	Chung Hua	Sanchung 1	1350	2.5
16)		Min Li	Fangliao	1368	1
2f)		Cheng Sheng	Tafa	1395	1
20)	V78	Yi Shih	Keelung	1404	10
7)		Chien Kuo	Kuanyin	1422	1
21)		Fuhsing B.C.	Kaohsing	1458	1

FM	Call	MHz	kW	FM	Call	MHz	kW	FM	Call	MHz	kW
3)		88.1		48)		96.9	3	65)		98.5	
32)		92.1	3	49)	N61	97.1	3	66)		98.7	3
33)	N82	92.1	3	50)	N99	97.1	3	67)	N72	98.7	3
34)	N42	92.3	3	51)	M84	97.1	3	68)		98.7	3
35)		92.7	3	52)		97.3	3	69)	M31	98.9	3
36)	N58	92.9	3	53)		97.3	3	70)		98.9	3
37)		92.9	3	54)	N74	97.5	1	71)		99.1	3
38)	N24	93.3	3.0	55)	M40	97.5	3	72)	N79	99.1	3
39)		93.5	3.0	56)		97.7	3	73)		99.3	3
40)	N84	93.5	3.0	57)		97.7	3	74)	M24	99.5	3
41)	N50	93.7	3	58)	N32	97.9		75)	N77	99.5	3
42)		93.7	3	59)		97.9	3	76)		99.5	3
43)		93.7	3	60)	M23	98.1	3	77)		99.7	3
44)		93.9	3	61)	N93	98.3	3	78)	N33	99.7	3
45)		96.7	3	62)		98.3	3	79)	M30	99.9	3
46)	N40	96.7		63)	N51	98.3	3	31b)		100.1	13
47)		96.9	3	64)		98.5	3	80)	M33	100.3	

FM	Call	MHz	kW	FM	Call	MHz	kW	FM	Call	MHz	kW
81)	M26	100.7	3	86)	M27	102.5	3	93)	N65	106.5	3
31)	M3	100.7	30	87)		103.9	3	94)		106.7	3
31a)		100.7	27	2)	M22	104.1	3	95)	M28	106.9	3
31c)		100.8		88)		105.5	3	96)		107.1	3
82)		101.1	1	89)	N54	105.5	3	97)		107.3	3
83)		101.1		90)		105.7	3	98)	M32	107.7	3
84)		102.3	3	91)	M29	106.1	3	99)	M25	107.7	3
85)		102.5	1	92)		106.3	1				

NB: + more than 80 low-powered community FM stns

Addresses & other information: Following 1) to 21) for MW or MW/FM stns, **31) to 99)** for FM-only stns

1) Taiwan Broadc. Co, 9th Flr, 2, Sec 2, Jen-ai Rd, Chungcheng, Taipei 100. 1st prgr on 1323kHz, 24h 2nd prgr on 1188kHz, 24h **W:** taiwanradio.com.tw –**1a)** 2, Lane 506, Kaofeng Rd, Hsinchu 300. 24h – **1b)** 25th Flr, 787, Chungming So. Rd, So. Ward, Taichung 402. 24h – **1c)** 258-1 Fentsao Rd, Tsaotun Town, Nantou 542. 24h – **2)** Chengsheng Broadc. Corp., 7th Flr, 1, Lane 66, Sec. 1, Chungching So. Rd, Taipei 10045. 819kHz, 104.1MHz both 24h – **2a)** 17, Chuiyang Rd. Chia-i 60043. 24h – **2b)** 760, Sec. 2, Chunghsing Rd, Tali Ward, Taichung 41244. 1st prgr on 990kHz, 2nd prgr on 657kHz, both 24h. – **2c)** 10 Shuiyuan Rd, Huwei Town, Yunlin 63244. Yunlin St on 1125kHz, Peikang St on 675kHz, both 24h. – **2d)** 45 Chienchun Rd, Ilan 26051. 24h – **2e)** 21, Lane 380, Hsinsheng Rd, Taitung 95052. 24h – **2f)** 838 Chengching Rd, Niaosung Ward, Kaohsiung 83347. Kaohsiung St. on 1008kHz, Tafa St. on 1395kHz, both 24h **W:** csbc.com.tw – **3)** Shih Hsin Radio St, 1, Lane 17, Sec. 1, Mushan Rd, Wenshan Ward, Taipei 11604. AM: and FM both 0155-1405 **W:** shrs.shu.edu.tw – **4)** Shengli chih Sheng (Voice of Victory) Broadc. Co, 22, Sec. 1, Chienkang Rd, Chunghsi Ward, Tainan 700. 1st Prgr. on 774kHz, 24h 2nd Prgr. on 1188kHz, 24h Makung St. on 756kHz, 24h **Ann:** "Tainan Sheng Li chih Sheng Kuangpo Tientai" **W:** victory-radio.com.tw – **5)** Hsien Sheng Broadc. Co, 1, 16th Flr, Lane 505, Chungshan Rd, Taoyuan Ward, Taoyuan 330. 24h – **6)** Keelung Broadc. Co, 12th Flr, 13 Chungsu Rd, Keelung 200. 24h **W:** am792.com.tw – **7)** Chien Kuo Broadc. Co, 78 Chienkuo Rd, Hsinying , Tainan 730. 24h **W:** ckbam954. byethost10. com – **8)** Kuo Sheng Broadc. Co, 35 Wenchuan Rd, Pakuashan, Changhua 500. 24h **W:** ksbc. Com tw – **8a)** 2 Taiping Rd, Erhlin Town, Changhua 526 – **9)** Ming Pen Broadc. Co, 6th Flr, 325, Sec. 3, Huanho So. Rd, Wanhua Ward, Taipei 108. 1st Prgr on 1296kHz, 2nd Prgr on 855kHz, both 24h **W:** mingpen.com.tw – **10)** Feng Ming Broadc. Co, 492 Chiuju 2nd Rd, Sanmin Ward, Kaohsiung 807. 1st Prgr on 1161kHz, 2nd Prgr on 981kHz, both 24h **W:** fengmin.com.tw – **10a)** Chentieh Hsien, Li 38, Makung, Penghu 880 – **11)** Chengkung Broadc. Co, 63 Chunghua 3rd Rd, Chienchin Ward, Kaohsiung 801. 24h (exc. Sun 1600-2100). **W:** ckb. tw – **12)** Tien Nan Broadc. Co, 7th Flr. 235, Sec. 4, Chengte Rd, Shihlin Ward, Taipei 111. 24h **W:** tnbcam999.business. site – **13)** T'ien Sheng Broadc. Co, 285 Kungyi Rd, Chunan Town, Miaoli 350. 24h – **13a)** 8, Chuchung Rd, Yuanli Town, Miaoli 358. Yuanli St. on 1026kHz, Pengshan St. on 1215kHz, both 24h – **14)** Chung Hwa (China) Broadc. Co, 5th Flr, 130, Sec 4 Chungyang Rd, Sanchung, New Taipei 241. 1st Prgr on 1350kHz, 2nd prgr on 1026kHz, both 24h **Ann:** "Chung Hua Kuangpo Tientai Ti I/Erh Tai". Juifang St,. mostly relays 1st prgr on 1233kHz, 24h **W:** chbc. wunme.com – **15)** Yen Sheng Broadc. Co, 31, Sec. 1, Nanpin Rd, Tungchang, Chi-an Village, Hualien 973. On 1044, 1242kHz, both 24h **W:** am10441242.tw – **16)** Min Li Broadc. Co, 57-20 Minsheng Rd, Pingtung 900. 24h – **17)** Densen Broadc. Company, 11, 15th Flr, 149, Sec. 1, Linsen Rd, Ea. Ward Tainan 701. 24h (exc. Sun 1600-2100 **W:** am1071.com.tw – **18)** Hua Sheng Broadc. Co, 18 Huasheng Str, Shihlin Ward, Taipei 111. 1st Prgr on 1152kHz, 2nd Prgr on 1224kHz, both 24h **W:** hsradio.com.tw – **19)** Fuhsingkang Broadac. Stn. 70, Sec .2, Chungyang No. Rd, Peitou, Taipei 112 – **20)** Yi Shih Broadc. St, 75 Paisan Str, Chitu Ward, Keelung 206. 24h **Ann:** "Keelung Yi Shih Kuangpo Tientai" **21)** Fuhsing Broadc. Co, 6th Flr, 118-1, Ssuwei 2nd Rd, Lingya Ward, Kaohsiang 80247. **E:** A3309077@gmail.com **NB** It differs from Fu Hsing Broadc. Stn operated by Ministry of National Defense **31)** International Community R. Taipei (ICRT), 19-5F, No.5 Sec 3, New Taipei Blvd, Hsinchuang Ward, New Taipei 24250. 24h in English Rel. BBC News Sun, Mon, Wed & Thu 2200-2230 – **31a)** Kaohsiung – **31b)** Taichung – **31c)** Chia-i **W:** icrt.com.tw – **32)** Fei Tieh (UFO) Broadc. Co (UFO Netw), 25th Flr, 102, Sec. 2, Lossufou Rd, Chungcheng Ward, Taipei 100. 24h **W:** uforadio.com.tw– Other UFO Netw stns: Miaoli 91.3MHz, Taichung 89.9MHz, Yunlin & Chia-i district 90.5MHz, Kaohusing 103.9MHz, Ilan 89.9MHz, Hualien 91.3MHz, Taitung 91.3MHz, Penghu 89.7MHz – **33)** Chin Sheng Broadc. Co, 25th Flr, 206 Kuanghua 1st Rd, Lingya, Kaohsiung 802. 24h – **34)** Chia Le Broadc Co, 1, 16th Flr, 193, Hsiaoya

Rd, East Ward, Chia-i 600. 24h – **35)** Yachou (Asia) Broadc. Co (Asia FM Netw), 2, 22nd Flr, 102 Chungping Rd, Taoyuan Ward, Taoyuan 33060. 24h **W:** asiafm.com.tw – Other Asia FM Netw stns: Hsinchu 92.3MHz, Taoyuan (Feiyang) 89.5MHz. – **36)** Cheng Shih Broadc. Co, 28th Flr, 758 Chungming So. Rd, So. Ward, Taichung 402. 24h **W:** cityfm.com.tw – Other City FM Netw st: Taipei 90.1MHz, Miaoli 98.3MHz, Nantou 99.7MHz, Tainan 97.1MHz – **37)** Taiwu chih Chun Broadc.(Yes R.) Co. 9, Lane 240, Sec. 1, Poyu Rd. Panglin, Chinning, Kinmen 89248. 24h – **38)** Yun Chia Broadc. Co, 7th Flr, 52, Minchuan Rd, East Ward, Chia-i 600. 24h **W:** fm933.com.tw – **39)** Hsin Kechia Broadc. Co (New Hakka R.), 3, 13th Flr, 411 Huannan Rd, Pingchen Ward, Taoyuan 324. 24h **W:** fm935newhakka.com.tw – **40)** Lien Hua Broadc. Co. (Best 935) 3, 8th Flr. 65, Kuolienssu Rd. Hualien 970 24h – **41)** Pao Tao Kechia Broadc. St, (Formosa Hakka R. Stn.) 2, 17th Flr, 91, Sec. 2, Lossufu Rd, Ta'an Ward, Taipei 10646. 24h **W:** formosahakka.org.tw – **42)** Sheng Tu Broadc. Co, 850, Sec 2, Fentsao Rd, Tsaotun Town, Nantou 542. 24h **W:** fm937.com.tw – **43)** Ling Hsiu Broadc. Co, – 1, Lane 181, Tachiaoi Str, Yungkang, Tainan 710. 24h – **44)** Ta Ti chih Sheng Broadc. Co. 10, Chengpei Village, Huhsi, Makung, Penghu 880. 24h – **45)** Huan Yu Broadc. Co (Uni R.), 3, 6th Flr, 675, Sec. 1, Chingkuo Rd, Hsinchu 300. 24h **W:** uni967.com – **46)** Penghu Broadc. Co. 2nd Flr. 1-204, I-lin Shihchuan-li, Makung, Penghu 880. 24h – **47)** Tien Tien (Sky) Broadc. Co, 42nd Flr, 760 Chungming So. Rd, So. Ward, Taichung 402. 24h **W:** sky969.groups.com.tw – **48)** Chu Jen (Boss Radio) Broadc. Co. 17th Flr, 155, Fujen Rd, Linyang Ward, Kaohsiung 80288. 24h **W:** boss969.com – **49)** Ta Han chih Yin (Voice of Hakka) Broadc. Co, 1-1 Hsintung Rd, Toufen Town, Miaoli 351. 24h **W:** fm971.com.tw – **50)** Tainan chih Yin Broadc. Co, 1-134 Chunghua Rd, Yongkang, Tainan 710 – **51)** Chung Shan Broadc. Co, 2nd Flr, 151, Sec 2, Chungshan Rd, Ilan 260. 24h – **52)** Green Peace Broadc. Co, 1, 14th Flr, 97, Sec. 4, Chunghsing Rd, Sanchung New Taipei 241. 24h **W:** greenpeace.com.tw – **53)** Ai Yu chih Sheng Broadc. Co, 12th Flr, 173, Linsen Rd, Changhua 500. 24h – **54)** IC chih Yin, IC Broadc. Co. Ltd., 2, 11th Flr, 287, Sec. 2, Kuangfu Rd, Hsinchu 30071. 24h **W:** ic975.com – **55)** Kuai Le (Happy) Broadc. Co, 1st Flr, 70, Ling-an Rd, Lingya Ward, Kaohsiung 80249. 24h. **W:** happyradio.com.tw – Other Happy R. Netw stns: Taipei 89.3MHz, Taichung 89.5MHz, Chia-I 92.3MHz, Hualien 98.3MHz, Penghu 91.3MHz & 96.7MHz – **56)** Taiwan Sheng Yin Broadc. Co. 9th Flr. 76, Sec. 1, Minchuan East Rd. Chungshan Ward, Taipei, 10491. 24h – **57)** Hao Chia Ting Broadc. Co (Family 977 Broadc. Network), 37th Flr, 789 Chungming So. Rd, So. Ward, Taichung 402. 24h **W:** family977.com.tw – Other Family 977 Netw stn: Taipei 91.3MHz – **58)** Tainan Kaihsuan Broadc. Co, 2, 21th Flr, 425 Chunghua Rd, Yungkang, Tainan 710 – Other Smile Netw stns: Ilan 97.9 MHz, Taoyuan 101.1 MHz, Hsinchu 90.3 MHz, Nantou 105.5 MHz, Chia-I 107.1 MHz, Kaohsiung 90.5 MHz, Pingtung 90.9/91.3/92.5MHz, Kimmen 106.3MHz. 24h – **59)** Ka Ma Lan Broadc. Co, 46, Lane 455, Kungyuan Rd, Ilan 260. 24h **W:** kamalan979.com.tw– **60)** Taiwan National Broadc. Com. (News 98), 26th Flr, 102, Sec. 2, Lossufu Rd, Chungcheng Ward, Taipei 100. 24h **W:** news98.com.tw– **61)** Ta Miaoli FM Broadc. Co, 3, 16th Flr, 1 Chanchien, Shangmiao Li, Miaoli 360. 24h – **62)** Kang Tu Broadc. Co (Best R.), 1, 34th Flr, 80 Mintsu 1st Rd, Sanmin Ward, Kaohsiung 807. 24h **W:** bestradio.com.tw - Other Best Netw stns: Taipei 98.9MHz, Taichung 90.3MHz, Hualien 93.5MHz –**63)** Hualien (Huan Le) Broadc Co, 3rd Flr, 196, Linsen Rd, Hualien 970. 24h – **64)** Pao Tao Hsin Sheng (Super FM 98.5) Broadc. Co, 7th Flr. 56, Sec 1, Hsinsheng So. Rd, Chungcheng Ward, Taipei 100. 24h **W:** superfm98-5.com.tw – Other Superfm Netw stns: Taichung 99.1 MHz, Chia-I 91.3 MHz, Hualien 90.5MHz – **65)** Feifanyin Broadc. Co (Libra R.), 6, Chingshui Village, Nankan, Lienchiang 209. 24h **W:** libraradio.com.tw – **66)** Mei Jih Broadc. Co (Sakura R.), 1, 7th Flr, 1-67 Wuchuan Rd, We. Ward, Taichung 403. 24h **W:** fm987.com.tw – **67)** Ching Chun Broadc. Co, 15-2, 53, Sec. 2, Lin'an Rd, No. Ward, Tainan 704. 24h – Other A-Line stn: Chia-I 98.9MHz – **68)** Tung Min Broadc. Co. 156, Fuyu Rd. Chihpen, Taitung 950. 24h – **69)** Jen Jen Broadc. Co (Best 989), 2nd Flr, 142, Sec. 3, Minchuan East Rd, Chungshan Ward, Taipei 104. 24h – **70)** Cheng Kang Broadc. Co. 2, 4th Flr. 73, Teming Rd. Chia-i, 600. 24h – **71)** Ta Chien Broadc. Co (Super 99.1), 2, 22nd Flr, 309, Sec. 2, Taiwan Tatao, We. Ward, Taichung 403.24h **W:** superfm99-1.com.tw – **72)** Yang Kuang Broadc. Co, 7, 21st Flr, 3, Tzuchiang 3rd Rd, Lingya, Kaohsiung 802. 24h – Other Ching Chun Online Stns: Tainan 106.5MHz, Penghu 93.9MHz – **73)** Hsin Sheng FM Broadc. Co, 1, 19th Flr, 37 Chienchung 1st Rd, Hsinchu 300. 24h – **74)** Sen Nong (Farmer R.) Broadc. Co., 10th Flr, 234 Peiping Rd, Huwei Town, Yunlin 632.24h **W:** fm995.com.tw – **75)** Tung Fang Broadc. Co, 13rd Flr, 168, Sec. 3, Chunching Rd, Lotung Town, Ilan 265. 24h – **76)** Lan Yu Broadc. St, 147, Yujen, Hongtou, Lanyu Village, Taitung 95241. 24h **W:** lanan.org.tw/radio – **77)** Taipei Ai Yue Broadc. Co, 7th Flr, 47 Tunghsing Rd, Hsin-i Ward, Taipei 110. 24h **W:** e-classical.com.tw – **78)** Nantou Broadc. Co, 28th Flr, 758 Chungming So. Rd, So. Ward, Taichung 402. 24h – **79)** Ta Chung Broadc. Co (Kiss R.), 2, 34th Flr, 6 Minchuan 2nd Rd, Chienchen Ward, Kaohsiung 806. 24h **W:** kiss.com.tw – **80)** Pao Tao Broadc. Co. 1, 12th Flr. 287, Wenya St. Chia-i 600. 24h **W:** fm1003.com.tw – 81) Taichung Broadc.Co, 21st Flr, 489, Sec. 2, Taiwan Tatao, We. Ward, Taichung 40309. 24h **W:** fm1007lucky.com – **82)** Kuo Chi Broadc. Co, 14th Flr, 1, Lane 72, Shujen 3rd St, Taoyuan Ward, Taoyuan 330. 24h – **83)** Ching Shan Broadc. Co. 12th Flr, 20, Talung Rd. We. Ward, Taichung 403. 24h – **84)** Ai Miao Broadc. Co, 78, Huatung Str, Chunan Town, Miaoli 350. 24h – **85)** Hsing Fu Broadc. Co (Transformation R.), 3rd Flr. 333, Hsinfu 2nd Rd, Neihu Ward, Taipei 114. 24h – **86)** Ku Tu Broadc. Co, 1, 15th Flr, 77, Sec. 2, Chunghua East Rd, Tainan 70155. 24h **W:** fm1025.com.tw – **87)** Nan Taiwan chih Sheng Broadc.Co (Voice of South Taiwan), 38th Flr, 38, Hsinkuang Rd, Lingya Ward, Kaohsiung 80247 24h – **88)** Huanhsi chih Sheng Broadc. Co (Happy R.), 37th Flr, 760 Chungming So. Rd, So. Ward, Taichung 402. 24h – **89)** Tung Shan He Broadc. Co, 13th Flr, 162-5, Sec. 3, Chunching Rd, Lotung Town, Ilan 265. 24h – **90)** Tzumei Broadc. Co (Sister R.), 4th Flr, 32, Lane 416, Sec. 1, Linsen Rd, Huwei Town, Yunlin 632. 24h **W:** sister-radio.com.tw – **91)** Chuan Kuo Broadc. Co (M Radio), 1, 8th Flr, 659, Sec.2, Taiwan Tatao, Hsitun Ward, Taichung 40759. 24h – **92)** Ta Chin Broadc. Co, 3rd Flr. 331, Hsinfu 2nd Rd, Neihu Ward, Taipei 114. 24h – **93)** Chih Nan Broadc. Co, 15th Flr, 53, Sec.2, Lin-an Rd, No. Ward, Tainan 704. 24h – **94)** Kao Ping Hsi Broadc. Co, 17th Flr, 161 Chiuta Rd, Chiuchu, TashuWard, Kaohsiung 840. 24h – **95)** Taoyuan Broadc. Co (TBC R.), 9th Flr, 859, Sec. 1, Chunghua Rd, Chungli, Taoyuan 320. 24h – **96)** Chia-i Huanchiu Broadc. Co, 1, 19th Flr, 25 Pingtien, Chianghsi Village, Fanlu, Chia-i 602. 24h – **97)** Lan Yang FM Broadc. Co, 12th Flr, 186, Sec. 3, Chungcheng Rd, Wuchie Village, Ilan 268. 24h – **98)** Taipei chih Yin Broadc. Co, (Hito R.) 15-1, Sec. 1, Hanchou So. Rd, Chungcheng Ward, Taipei 10050. 24h **W:** hitoradio.com – Other Hit FM Netw stns: Taichung 91.5MHz, Kaohsiung 90.1MHz, Ilan 97.1MHz, Hualien 107.7 MHz – **99)** Tung Taiwan Broadc. Co, 31, Sec. 1, Nanpin Rd, Tungchang, Chi-an Village, Hualien 973. 24h

TAJIKISTAN

L.T: UTC +5h — **Pop:** 9.3 million — **Pr.L:** Tajik (official), Uzbek — **E.C:** 220V/50Hz — **ITU:** TJK

KUMITAI TELEVIZION VA RADIOI
(State Committee for TV & Radio)

k. Sheroz 31, 734025 Dushanbe ☎ +992 37 2277497
E: info@ktr.tj; radiotojikiston@gmail.com **W:** ktr.tj; radiotoj.tj; sadoi-dushanbe.tj **L.P:** Chmn: Asadulloi Rahmon
NB: In addition to being a state broadcaster, the committee is also responsible for issuing licenses to private radio stations in Tajikistan.

MW	kHz	kW	Prgr	MW	kHz	kW	Prgr
Dushanbe	549	40	2	Dushanbe (a)	1143	150	F
Orzu	702	150	1	Orzu	1161	40	2
Khujand	819	15	1	Dushanbe	1323	7	1

(a) Yangiyul F=International Service

SW	kHz	kW	Prgr
Dushanbe (Yangiyul)	4765	100	1

FM (MHz)	1	2	3	kW
Ayvanj	103.1	107.8	-	-
Dushanbe	104.7	102.2	106.5	2x4/-
Khorugh*	104.5	104.0	103.0	-
Khujand	102.7	100.2	106.1	4
Panj	-	100.3	-	-
Qurghonteppa	101.7	-	-	4

+ low power txs. *) Located in Kuhistan-Badakhshan (autonomous province)

D.Prgr: Prgr 1 (Radioi Tojikiston): 24h on FM; limited schedule on MW/SW. – **Prgr 2 (Sadoi Dushanbe):** 24h. For ethnic minorities: 0600-0800 (Russian). – **Prgr 3 (Radioi Farhang):** 24h. – **Regional Stations: R. Badakhshon (Khorugh)** planned. **R. Khatlon (Qurghonteppa)** on Qurghonteppa 101.3MHz, **R. Sughd (Khujand)** on Khujand 101.1MHz – **International Service (Ovozi Tojik):** see International Radio section. On FM: Dushanbe 105.5MHz.

OTHER STATIONS

FM	MHz	kW	Location	Station
16)	88.8	1	Khujand	Love R.
1)	92.2	1	Istaravshan	Dunyo FM

FM	MHz	kW	Location	Station
15)	93.3	1	Buston	R. Salom
19)	95.5	1	Dushanbe	Novoye R.
12)	95.5	1	Isfara	R. Diyor
17)	97.7	1	Khujand	R. Shahri Man
A)	100.3	1	Dushanbe	R. Sputnik relay
14)	100.6	1	Khujand	R. Payvand
9)	101.5	1	Dushanbe	FM Khovar
10)	101.5	1	Panjakent	Sadoi Panjakent
2)	102.4	1	Qurghonteppa	R. Vatan
7A)	103.0	1	Dushanbe	R. Rusii Oriyono
7B)	103.0	1	Khujand	R. Imruz
2)	103.3	1	Khujand	R. Vatan
5)	104.0	1	Dushanbe	AFM
3B)	104.4	1	Khujand	R. Aziya Plus
3A)	104.5	1	Dushanbe	R. Aziya FM
2)	105.0	1	Khorugh*	R. Vatan
11)	105.2	1	Isfara	R. Isfara
12)	105.5	1	Asht	R. Diyor
13)	105.7	1	Khujand	Sadoi Khujand
4)	105.9	1	Isfara	R. Mavji ozod
2)	106.0	1	Dushanbe	R. Vatan
6)	106.1	1	Istaravshan	R. AVIS-Plus
18)	106.8	1	Tursunzade	Sadoi Osiyo
3B)	107.0	1	Dushanbe	R. Aziya Plus
3B)	107.0	1	Qurghonteppa	R. Aziya Plus
B)	107.1	1	Khujand	R. Sputnik relay
7B)	107.4	1	Dushanbe	R. Imruz
7B)	107.4	1	Kulob	R. Imruz
7B)	107.4	1	Qurghonteppa	R. Imruz
8)	107.5	1	Ghafurov	R. Jahonoro

+ txs below 1kW *) Located in Kuhistan-Badakhshan (autonomous province)

Addresses & other information:
1) 1. Mikrorayon 6-65, 735000 Tursunzade – **2)** pr. S.Sherozi 16, 734018 Dushanbe **E:** info@vatan.tj – **3A,B)** pr. S.Sherozi 16, 734018 Dushanbe **E:** radio@asiaplus.tj – **4)** k. Umari Hazom 18, 735330 Vose – **5)** pr. S.Ayni 27/17, 734000 Dushanbe **E:** info@afm.tj – **6)** k. A.Mirrajabov 10, 735610 Istaravshan **E:** avis@avis.tj – **7A,B)** pr. Rudaki 100, 734001 Dushanbe **E:** info@orionomedia.tj. 7A) rel. Russkoye R. (Russia) – **8)** k. Lenin 22, 735690 Ghafurov – **9)** Dushanbe. **E:** sadrshamsi67@mail.ru – **10)** k. Bobodajarov 7a, 735500 Panjakent **E:** simo-tv@mail.ru – **11)** k. Markazi 40, 735920 Isfara **E:** sahbon@mail.ru – **12)** k. I.Somoni 91a, Shaydon **E:** mail@diyorfm.com – **13)** 735700 Khujand – **14)** k. Lenin 303a, 735700 Khujand **E:** akram_urunov@mail.ru – **15)** 735730 Chkalov **E:** radiosalom@mail.ru – **16)** 735700 Khujand – **17)** k. Tanburi 9, 735700 Khujand **E:** shahriman.97.70@gmail.com – **18)** k. Lenin 134, 735000 Tursunzade – **19)** k. Kutbi Kirom 1, 734000 Dushanbe. **E:** info@newradio.tj. Rel. Novoye R. (Russia) – **A)** Rel. R. Sputnik (Russia)

TANZANIA

L.T: UTC +3h — **Pop:** 60 million — **Pr.L:** Swahili (official), English (official) — **E.C:** 230V/50Hz — **ITU:** TZA

TANZANIA COMMUNICATIONS REGULATORY AUTHORITY (TCRA)

Mawasiliano House, Plot 304, Ali Hassan Mwinyi/Nkomo Rd, P.O Box 474, Dar es Salaam ☎+255 22 2118947 🖷 +255 22 2116664 **W:** tcra.go.tz **E:** dg@tcra.go.tz

TANZANIA BROADCASTING CORPORATION (TBC) (Gov)

P. O. Box 9191, Nyerere Rd, Dar es Salaam ☎+255 22 2860760 🖷 +255 22 2866383 **W:** tbc.go.tz **E:** info@tbc.go.tz

MW	kHz	kW	MW	kHz	kW
Mbeya	†621	50/10	Kigoma	711	100/10

FM (MHz): Arusha 91.6, Dar es Salaam 89.9/92.35, Dodoma 87.7, Kigoma 88.4, Lindi 93.5, Mbeya/Masasi/Nachingwea 92.3, Mwanza 89.2, Songea 98.7, Dar es Salaam 94.6/95.3MHz.
TBC Taifa in Swahili on MW: 0200-2100. **TBC FM in Swahili:** 24h. **TBC International in English:** Dar es-Salaam 95.3MHz. Also relays RFI.

Other Stations, main networks:
R. Free Africa, P.O. Box 1732, Post Road, Mwanza **W:** radiofreeafrica.co.tz **E:** info@radiofreeafricatz.com Swahili Sce: **MW:** Mwanza 1377kHz 50kW (irr.). **FM:** Katavi 87.9, Himo/Shinyanga 88.2MHz, Singida 88.3, Geita 88.4, Mbeya 88.8, Iringa/Simiu 88.9, Arusha/Bukoba/Dodoma/Kigoma/Mtwara 89.0, Sumbawanga 89.1, Manyara/Songea 89.6, Mwanza 89.8, Njoluma 89.9, Kagera/Tabora 90.0, Musoma 93.5, Morogoro 93.8, Lindi 96.7, Dar es-Salaam/Pwanii/Zanzibar 98.6, Pemba/Tanga 99.3. English sce: **Kiss FM**: Mbeya 88.2, Mwanza 88.7, Iringa 89.2, Dodoma/Sindiga 89.4, Arusha/Manyara/Kilimanjaro 89.9, Morogoro 90.2, Tanga 92.7, Bugoba/Kagera 94.1, Dar es Salaam/Pwani/Zanzibar 98.9MHz.
R. One, P.O. Box 4374, Dar es Salaam **W:** radio1.co.tz **MW:** Moshi 1323kHz 10kW, 1500-1800 only with CRI English relay. **FM** (MHz, all 5kW): Dar es Salaam 89.7, Bukoba 92.1, Arusha 95.3, Moshi 97.2, Tabora 98.1, Dodoma 100.8, Mwanza 102.9, Morogoro 103.2, Tanga 106.3. In Swahili.
Capital Radio, W: capitalradio.co.tz **FM** (MHz): Morogoro 88.9, Bukoba 95.3, Mbeya 96.4, Dodoma 97.3, Dar es Salaam 101.3, Mwanza 101.2, Arusha 102.1, Moshi 103.3
Clouds FM, W: facebook.com/CloudsFmRadio **FM** MHz: Mwanza 88.1, Kibaha 88.4 2kW, Dar es Salaam 88.5, Arusha 98.6MHz
East Africa R, W: eastafricaradio.com **FM** MHz: Dar es Salaam 88,1, Bukoba 90.1, Iringa 90.9, Mwanza 92.1, Moshi 93.5, Arusha 93.7, Musoma 96.8, Tanga 97.7, Mtwara 98.6, Dodoma 99.6, Mbeya 100.1, Singida 101.4, Morogoro 103.1, Tabora 105.2 (also relayed on FM in Kampala, Uganda, & Nairobi, Kenya)
Ebony FM, W: facebook.com/ebonyfmradiostation **FM** MHz: Iringa 87.8, Njombe 88.2, Mbeya 94.7, Songea 102.2, Dar es Salaam 106.9
Imaan FM (Rlg.) **W:** islamicftz.org **FM** MHz: Mbeya 90.3, Arusha 90.8, Mtwara 90.9, Kigoma 92.5, Songeo 94.2, Morogoro 96.0, Tabora 101.6, Dodoma 102.0, Pemba 104.4, Masingin/Dar es Salaam 104.5, Mwanza 106.5
Kiss FM, W: facebook.com/kissfmtz **FM** MHz: Mbeya 88.2, Dodoma 88.4, Mwanza 88.7, Iringa 89.2, Arusha 89.9, Tanga 92.7, Bukoba 94.1, hinyanga 96.4, Dar es Salaam 98.9
Morning Star R, W: morningstaradio.or.tz **FM** MHz: Morogoro 89.9, Mwanza 102.1, Arusha 102.5, Tabora 102.9, Kigoma 103.3, Tanga 104.1, Iringa 104.9, Dar es Salaam 105.3, Mbeya 106.9
R. Maria Tanzania (Rlg.), **W:** www.radiomariatanzania.co.tz **FM** MHz: Songea 89.1, Iringa 90.4, Mpanda 90.9, Singida 91.4, Mbeya 91.9, Mtwara 95.3, Morogoro 102.0, Pemba 103.5, Dar es Salaam// Unguja 103.7, Mwanza 106.0, Arusha 106,7, Mwanga 107.6
R. Sauti ya Injili (Rlg.), **W:** sautiyainjili.org **FM** MHz: Moshi 92.3, Ngorongoro 94.0, Arusha 96.1, Rombo 96.3, Tanga 96.5, Morogoro 99.9, Same 100.3, Usambara 102.6, Kibaya 102.9
Sibuka FM, W: sibukamedia.com **FM** MHz: Dodoma 92.0, Bukoba 92.6, Dar es Salaam 94.0, Mwanza 95.5, Mtwara 96.2, Maswa 97.0, Kigoma/Mbeya 97.6, Arusha 104.6, Shinyanga 104.9
Uhuru FM, W: facebook.com/uhurufmradio **FM** MHz: Dodoma 88.2, Mwanza 92.9, Dar es Salaam 95.7, Arusha 99.7, Mbeya 103.0

ZANZIBAR
(semi-autonomous archipelago)

ZANZIBAR BROADCASTING CORPORATION (Pub.)

P.O. Box 314, Zanzibar, Tanzania ☎+255 24 2330000 🖷 +255 24 233000 **W:** zbc.co.tz **E:** zanzibarbroadcasting@zbc.co.tz
MW: Chumbuni 585kHz 50kW.
SW: Dole: 6015 & 11735kHz 50kW.
FM: Zanzibar 97.7MHz, Pemba 90.5MHz.
D.Prgr in Swahili: 0300-2100 on 585kHz. **FM** ("Spice FM"): 0300-2100. **N:** Local bulletins at 0400, 1200, 1600, 1800, 1900. Rel. R.Tanzania from Dar es Salaam at 1700, 1900. **In English:** irr. 1800.
Relays on shortwave: see International Radio section.

Other Stations:
Al-Noor FM (Rlg.), Zanzibar: 93.3MHz 2kW. **W:** alnoorcharity.org
Assalam FM (Rlg.), Zanzibar: 92.1MHz.
Bomba FM, Zanzibar: 87.5MHz **W:** facebook.com/bombafmzanzibar
Chuchu FM, Zanzibar: 90.9MHz. **W:** chuchufm.com
Coconut FM, Zanzibar: 88.9MHz **W:** facebook.com/CoconutFm88.9
Hits FM, Zanzibar: 92.5MHz
Mwenze FM, Zanzibar: 95.4MHz
R. Adhana (Rlg.). Zanzibar: 104.9MHz. **W:** facebook.com/Adhana-fm-1487495931462046
Swahiba FM, Zanzibar: 102.9MHz **W:** facebook.com/swahibafm
Zenji FM, Zanzibar: 96.9MHz **W:** facebook.com/ZenjiFMRadio
BBC African Sce: Zanzibar 94.1MHz, Pemba 93.5MHz, both 4kW.
RFI Afrique: Dar es Salaam 94.6MHz in F/E/Swahili

THAILAND

L.T: UTC +7h — **Pop:** 70 million — **Pr. L:** Thai — **E.C:** 220V/50Hz — **ITU:** THA

NATIONAL BROADCASTING AND TELECOMMUNICATIONS COMMISSION (NBTC)

87 Phahonyotin Rd. Soi 8 (Soi Silom), Samsen Nai, Phayathai Bangkok 10400 ☎ +66 2670 8888 🖷 +66 2290-5240 **W:** nbtc.go.th
L.P: Chmn: Gen. Sukit Khamasunthorn. Sec. Gen.: Takorn Tantasith
The NBTC controls administrative, legal, technical and programming aspects of broadcasting in Thailand.

GOVERNMENT PUBLIC RELATIONS DEPT. (Gov.)

9 Rama VI Road, Bangkok 10400
☎ +66 2618-2323 🖷 +66 2618-2358 **W:** thailand.prd.go.th (general info in English). This body operates the NBT radio & TV services (R. Thailand & Television Thailand).
L.P: DG: Lt. Gen Sansern Kaewkamnerd

THE NATIONAL BROADCASTING SERVICES OF THAILAND (NBT) – RADIO THAILAND (Sathani Witthayu Krachaisiang Haeng Prathet Thai, Sor. Wor. Thor.) (Gov.)

236 Vibhavadi Rangsit Rd, Din Daeng, Huay Khwang, Bangkok 10320 ☎ +66 2277-1966 🖷 +66 2277-2809
W: nbt.prd.go.th **L.P:** Exec. Dir. R. Thailand: Thongthot Mahamontri

MW STATIONS:

kHz	kW	Location +)	kHz	kW	Location +)
531	25	Maha Sarakham	981	25	Yala
549	10	Mukdahan	1026	25	Phitsanulok
558	10	Kanchanaburi	1026	10	Betong (Yala)
639	10	Chiang Mai$	1062	10	Phuket
639	20	N. Si Thammarat	1098	10	Mae Sot
648	25	Khon Kaen	1116‡	10	Takua Pa (Phang Nga)
720	5/10	Krabi	1125	25	Chanthaburi
729	25	N. Ratchasima	1134	10	Lampang
783	10	Ranong	1215	25	Surat Thani
810	20	Nong Khai	1260	25	Chiang Rai
810	10	Sangkhlaburi%	1296	10	Pattani
810	10	Trang	1341	20	Loei
819	10	Pathum Thani#	1341	25	U. Ratchathani
837	10	Pathum Thani#	1341	10	Phangnga
846	10	Phetchabun	1368	25	Nan
864	10	Tak	1368	10	Buri Ram
864	10	Si Sa Ket	1377	10	Chumphon
891	400	Sara Buri#	1404	25	Songkhla
909	10	Dansai (Loei)	1422	10	Amnat Charoen
909	25	Surin	1476	50	Chiang Mai*
918	10	Pathum Thani#	1557	10	Trat
981	25	Mae Hong Son	1593	10	Ratchaburi
981	20	N. Phanom			

‡) r. inactive at editorial deadline +) N.=Nakhon, U.=Ubon. %) Kanchanaburi Prov. #) Bangkok area *) tr. loc. in Lamphun Prov.
D.Prgr: Main sces: 2200-1700 on 891kHz (tx site: Nong Khae, Sara Buri), 819kHz (tx site: Rangsit, Pathum Thani) & 92.5MHz (Bangkok 10kW) and in full or in part on many RT regional AM stns. N: On the h – AM 837: 2300-1700 on 837kHz (tx site: Bang Phun, Pathum Thani).– AM 918 (tx site: Rangsit, Pathum Thani): 2200-1700 ASEAN languages sce. in English & Thai exc. Malay: 0600-0730, Chinese: 0730-0900, Lao: 0910-1000, Burmese: 1010-1100, Khmer: 1110-1200, on 918kHz, also in part on some RT regional FM stns inc. Chiang Mai 98MHz, Phuket 90.5MHz, Samui 96.75MHz, Songkhla 102.25MHz – Bangkok FM prgrs: 88.0MHz Foreign Lang Prgr in English (10kW), 93.5MHz 'Digital FM HD One' (10kW), 95.5MHz 'Virgin Hitz'in English (10 kW), 97.0MHz (10kW) 'Quality News Station', 105.0MHz (10kW) 'Smile Thailand' prgr for young people and families.

Selected Reg. Stations: 49 Prachasamphan Rd., Tambon Chang Khlan, Mueang Dist., Chiang Mai 50100 **FM:** 93.25 & 98.0MHz; 1476 kHz: Prgr in Thai and minority langs for hill tribes 2200-1600 Kasikon Thungsang Rd, Mueang Dist., Khon Kaen 40000 **FM:** 98.5 & 99.5MHz. Soi Sathaban Ratchaphat Phuket, Thepkasatri Rd, Tambon Ratsada, Mueang Dist., Phuket 83000 **FM:** 90.5MHz 'Blue Wave' & 96.75MHz 'Sunshine R.' 439 Mu 2, Songkhla - Ko Yo Road, Tambon Phawong, Mueang Dist., Songkhla 90100 **FM:** 89.5, 90.5 & 102.25MHz
Addresses of other regional stations: Most stns can be reached by quoting 'Sathani Witthayu Sor. Wor. Thor.' or 'Radio Thailand' and the location given in the freq. list. **D.Prgr** of reg. sts: generally 2200-1700

EXTERNAL SERVICE: Radio Thailand
see International Broadcasting section

NATIONAL EDUCATION RADIO (Sathani Witthayu Krachaisiang Haeng Prathet Thai Phuea Kan Sueksa, Sor. Wor. Sor.)

Soi Aree Samphan, Rama VI Rd, Samsen, Phaya Thai, Bangkok 10400 ☎ +66 2271-3448 🖷 +66 2245-7083 **W:** edu.prd.go.th
D.Prgr: 2200-1700 on 1467kHz in the Bangkok area. Regional stns carry own prgrs and relay Bangkok.

MW:

kHz	kW	Location	kHz	kW	Location
549	100	Lampang	‡936	50	Nakhon Sawan
‡558	50	Songkhla	963	25	Krabi
621	100	Khon Kaen	‡1242	50	Surat Thani
711	20	Ubon Ratchathani	1467	100	Pathum Thani
‡927	20	Chanthaburi			

‡) inactive at editorial deadline

OTHER STATIONS:

MW	kHz	kW	Location +)	MW	kHz	kW	Location +)
39)	540	5	Bangkok	12)	1017	10	Prachuap KK
24)	567	5	Chaiyaphum	31)	1035	10	Bangkok
17)	576	5	Bangkok	35)	1044	10	Khon Kaen
7)	585	5	Phrae	1)	1053	10	Bangkok
32)	585	5	Chumphon	12)	1062	10	Udon Thani
9)	594	5	Bangkok	4)	1071	10	Bangkok
32)	603	5	Khon Kaen	32)	1080	10	Chiang Rai
10)	612	5	Lop Buri	32)	1080	10	N. Sawan
25)	612	5	Chiang Mai	32)	1080	10	Yala
1)	630	5	Bangkok	30)	1098	10	Songkhla
24)	657	5	Bangkok	25)	1107	10	Samut Sakhon#
6)	666	5	Surin	6)	1107	10	Khon Kaen
29)	675	5	Bangkok	7)	1116	10	Phitsanulok
8)	684	5	N. Si Thammarat	6)	1134	10	N. Ratchasima
39)	684	5	Udon Thani	27)	1143	10	Bangkok
11)	693	5	Saraburi	37)	1152	10	Chiang Mai
19)	711	5	Chiang Mai	37)	1152	10	Khon Kaen
10)	711	5	Lop Buri	20)	1161	20	Bangkok
29)	720	5	Chon Buri	29)	1161	10	U. Ratchathani
32)	738	5	Chiang Mai	29)	1170	10	Chanthaburi
32)	738	5	Songkhla	29)	1170	10	Phitsanulok
37)	747	5	Bangkok	36)	1179	10	Bangkok
6)	747	5	Udon Thani	34)	1179	10	Chiang Rai
34)	756	5	Narathiwat	35)	1188	10	Sakon Nakhon
35)	756	5	Surin	7)	1188	10	Phitsanulok
31)	765	5	Lampang	5)	1188	10	Sa Kaeo
12)	765	5	Lop Buri	26)	1197	10	Lop Buri
18)	774	5	Rayong	5)	1206	10	Prachuap KK
36)	774	5	Udon Thani	35)	1215	10	Phrae
7)	783	5	Kamphaeng Phet	6)	1215	10	U. Ratchathani
19)	792	5	Bangkok	12)	1224	10	Chiang Rai
3)	801	5	N. Sawan	12)	1224	10	N. Sawan
12)	801	5	Chiang Rai	12)	1233	10	Bangkok
12)	801	5	U. Ratchathani	32)	1233	10	Udon Thani
32)	828	5	N. Si Thammarat	24)	1251	10	Roi Et
7)	828	5	Sukhothai	12)	1251	5	Bangkok
34)	837	5	Sakon Nakhon	25)	1269	10	Songkhla
2)	855	5	Prachin Buri	15)	1269	10	Bangkok
16)	873	5	Bangkok	28)	1287	10	Samut Prakan#
30)	918	10	Chiang Mai	32)	1287	10	U. Ratchathani
8)	936	10	Pattani	7)	1287	10	Uttaradit
12)	945	10	Bangkok	39)	1305	10	Sara Buri
6)	945	10	Kalasin	25)	1314	10	Khon Kaen
12)	954	10	Phitsanulok	12)	1323	10	Chiang Mai
12)	954	10	Chanthaburi	12)	1323	10	Surat Thani
18)	963	10	Bangkok	14)	1332	10	Bangkok
34)	972	10	Phetchabun	12)	1332	10	Maha Sarakham
38)	981	10	Pathum Thani#	32)	1350	10	Trang
30)	990	10	N. Ratchasima	33)	1350	10	Bangkok
7)	999	10	Chiang Rai	6)	1359	10	Sakhon Nakhon
33)	999	10	Bangkok	12)	1368	10	N. Pathom
32)	1008	10	N. Ratchasima	22)	1377	10	Phitsanulok

MW	kHz	kW	Location +)
34)	1395	10	Chiang Rai
24)	1404	10	Yasothon
5)	1404	10	Suphan Buri
33)	1422	10	Bangkok
30)	1422	10	Phitsanulok
12)	1431	10	N. Ratchasima
29)	1431	5	Songkhla
6)	1440	10	N. Phanom
32)	1440	10	Samut Sakhon
7)	1449	10	Phichit
10)	1449	10	Chumphon
24)	1458	10	Si Sa Ket
29)	1458	10	Phuket
27)	1494	10	Bangkok
24)	1503	10	Surat Thani
35)	1512	10	Phayao
12)	1512	10	Songkhla
34)	1521	10	Bangkok
32)	1530	10	Uttaradit
5)	1530	10	Chanthaburi
23)	1539	10	Kanchanaburi
11)	1557	10	Phetchabun
-)	1575	1000	Ayutthaya

‡) r. inactive. +) N.=Nakhon, U.=Ubon, KK=Khiri Khan. #) Bangkok area

GENERAL NOTES: News: Stns are generally required to relay N. from R. Thailand at 0000 & 1200 daily, each 30 mins, and to relay time signal and national anthem at 0000 and 1100. Many stns operated by army departments relay Jor. Sor. Like FM, Bangkok 103.0MHz overnight and/or at other times. **Station IDs:** Both short names, e.g. Wor. Por. Tho, and long names may serve as stn identifications, usually preceded by 'Thini' ('This is'), 'Thini Sathani Witthayu (Krachaisiang)' ('This is R. St.') or 'Khun kamlang rap fang' ('You are listening to'). Changwat=province. Amphoe=district (dt.). Prgrs are often supplied by separate production companies. The Thai name for Bangkok is 'Krung Thep' or 'Krung Thep Mahanakhon'. **Thai numerals:** 0 = sun, 1 = nueng (et), 2 = song, 3 = sam, 4 = si, 5 = ha, 6 = hok, 7 = chet, 8 = paet, 9 = kao, 10 = sip, 20 = yi sip, 100 = roi, 1000 = phan; thi = number, chut = decimal point

1) Mor. Thor. Bor. Sip Et (Monthon Thahan Bok Thi Sip Et, 11th Military Circle) ✉ 145 Rama V Rd, Dusit Region, Bangkok 10300 Ann: 'Suan Mitsakawan' – **2) Mor. Thor. Bor. Sip Song** (Monthon Thahan Bok Thi Sip Song, 'Siang Khai Chakkrapong', 12th Military Circle, 'Voice of Chakkrapong Camp') Chakkrapong Camp, Dong Phra Ram, Prachin Buri 25000 – **3) Mor. Thor. Bor. Thi Sam Sip Et** (Monthon Thahan Bok Thi Sam Sip Et, 31st Military Circle). ✉ Jiraprawat Camp, Nakhon Sawan 60000 – **4) Sathani Witthayu Rattasapha** (Parliament R. Station). ✉ Parliament House, Uthong Nai Rd, Dusit Region, Bangkok 10300. **N in English:** Mon-Fri 1230 – **5) Thor. Phor. Nueng** (Kongthap Phak Thi Nueng, 1st Army Area). HQ: ✉ Headquarters of the 1st Army Area, Suan Mitsakawan, Rajchadamnern Nok Ave, Dusit Region, Bangkok 10300. **Regional stns:** 9 Mu 4, Bang Kacha, Chanthaburi 22000 – Phairirayodet Camp, Suwansri Rd, Tha Kasem, Sa Kaeo 27000 – Kao Kuat, Kraw Plub Pla, Ratchaburi 70000 – Ban Sam Liam, Mu 4, Don Pho Thong, Suphan Buri 72000 – **6) Thor. Phor. Song** (Kongthap Phak Thi Song, 2nd Army Area). HQ: ✉ Suranari Camp, Ratchadamnoen Rd, Nong Phailom, Nakhon Ratchasima 30000. **Regional stns:** Aphai Rd, Nai Mueang, Kalasin 46000 – Si Phatcharin Camp, Sila, Khon Kaen 40000 – Phra Yot Mueang Khwang Camp, Nakhon Phanom-Sakon Nakhon Rd, Khurukhu, Nakhon Phanom 48000 – Krit Siwara Camp, That Naveng, Sakon Nakhon 47000 – Wirawatyothin Camp, Phakdichumphon Rd, Nok Mueang, Surin 32000 – Sapphasiti Prasong Camp, Warin Chamrap District, Ubon Ratchathani 34190 – Yutthasin Prasit Camp, Non Sung Rd, Udon Thani 41330 – **7) Thor. Phor. Sam** (Kongthap Phak Thi Sam, 3rd Army Area). ✉ Headquarters of the 3rd Army Area, Somdet Phra Ekathosarot Camp, Aranyik, Phitsanulok 65000. **Regional stns:** Mengrai Maharat Camp, Chiang Rai 57000 – 236/5 Mu 3, Nakhon Sawan - Kamphaeng Phet Rd, Nakhon Chum, Kamphaeng Phet 62000 – 104/1 Mu 5, Ban Krot Ngam, Ban Na, Wachirabarami District, Phichit 66140 – Ban Mai, Ratsadon Uthit Rd, Nai Wiang, Phrae 54000 – Bypass Road, Pak Khwae, Sukhothai 64000 – 109 Mu 8, Tha Sao, Uttaradit 53000 – **8) Thor. Phor. Si** (Kongthap Phak Thi Si, 4th Army Area). HQ: ✉ Wachirahwud Camp, Ratchadamnoen-Pak Nun Rd, Nakhon Si Thammarat 80000. **Regional stns:** Senanarong Camp, Kho Hong, Hat Yai District, Songkhla 90110 – Ban Na San District, Surat Thani 84120 – Charoen Pradit Rd, Rusamilae, Pattani 94000 – **9) Phon Por. Thor. Or.** (Kong Phon Thahan Puen Yai Tosue Akart Yan, Anti-Aircraft Artillery Division), ✉ Kiak Kay Junction, Thahan Road, Bangsue, Dusit Region, Bangkok 10300 – **10) Wor. Sor. Por.** (Witthayu Sun Kan Thahan Puen Yai, Artillery Centre R. St.). ✉ 301 Phahonyothin Camp, Artillery Centre, Khao Phra Ngam, Lop Buri 15160. Regional st: Khet Udomsak Camp, Wang Mai, Chumphon 86000 – **11) Siang Adison** (Sun Kan Thahan Ma, Cavalry Centre, 'Voice of Adison'). ✉ Saraburi Cavalry Centre, Adison Camp, Mitraphap Rd, Pak Phrieo, Saraburi 18000. Regional st: Saraburi-Lom Sak Rd, Nong Khwai, Lom Sak District, Phetchabun 67110 – **12) Thor. Or.** (Thahan Akart, Royal Thai Airforce). ✉ Tor. Or. 01, 1233kHz, Don Mueang: 171 Mu 2, Phahonyothin Rd, Khlong Thanon, Sai Mai, Bangkok 10220. Tor. Or. 01, 945kHz, Min Buri: 74 Mu 2, Nimit Mai, Sai Kong Tin, Min Buri, Bangkok 10510. Tor. Or. 06, 1251kHz: The Empress Hotel, 1091/343 Phetchaburi Tat Mai Road, Charurat, Makassan, Ratcha Thewi, Bangkok 10400. **Regional stns:** Thor. Or. 02: 301 Wing 2, 1st Air Division, Khao Phra Ngam Rd, Lop Buri 15160 – Thor. Or. 03: Wing 1, Mu 3, Nong Phai Lom, Nakhon Ratchasima 30000 – Thor. Or. 04: 305 Mu 4, Wing 4, 3rd Air Division, Takhli District, Nakhon Sawan 60140 – Thor. Or. 05: Wing 53, 4th Air Division, Ko Lak, Prachuap Khiri Khan 77000 – Thor. Or. 7: Surat Thani Airport Entrance, Huatoey, Phunphin District, Surat Thani 84130 – Thor. Or. 08: 38 Mu 14, Ban Nongphai, Chayangkun Rd, Khamyai, Ubon Ratchathani 34000 – Thor. Or. 09: 549 Mu 9, Wing 23, Thahan Rd, Makkhaeng, Udon Thani 41000 – Thor. Or. 10: Wing 46, 3rd Air Division, Yaek Khok Matum, Phitsanulok - Wangthong Rd, – **14) Or. Sor.** (Sathani Witthayu Amphon Sathan, Phraratchawang Dusit, Amphon Sathan Throne Radio Station). ✉ Dusit Palace, Ratchawithi Rd, Chitralada, Dusit Region, Bangkok 10303 – **15) Kho. Sor. Thor. Bor.** (Kromkan Khon Song Thahan Bok, Army Transportation Dept.). ✉ Army Transportation Broadcasting Station, Transport School Compound, Thahan Road, Dusit Region, Bangkok 10300 – **16) Wor. Kor. Thor. Mor.** (Sathani Witthayu Krung Thep Mahanakhon, Bangkok Radio Station), ✉ 192 Sarasin Rd, Lumphini Park, Pathum Wan Region, Bangkok 10330 – **17) Tor. Chor. Dor.** (Tamruat Trawen Chaidaen, Border Patrol Police). ✉ Bang Khen Police Dept. Club, Vibhavadi-Rangsit Rd, Bang Khen Bangkok 10210 – **18) Phon Mor. Song** (Sathani Witthayu Kong Phan Thahan Ma Thi Song, 2nd Cavalry Division). ✉ Samsen Rd, Bang Krabue, Dusit Region, Bangkok 10300 Bangkok. Regional st: Rayong-Ban Khai Rd, Nam Khok, Rayong 21000 – **19) Wor. Phor. Thor.** (Witthayu Kromkan Phalang Ngan Thahan, Defence Energy Dept. R. St.). ✉ New Building, Sukhumvit 24, Phra Khanong, Bangkok 10250. Regional st: 141/3 Mu 4, Don Kaeo Rd, Chotana, Mae Rim District, Chiang Mai 50180 – **20) Wor. Sor. Sor.** (Witthayu Sueksa, Educational Radio). ✉ Educational Technology Centre, Si Ayutthaya Rd, Ratcha Thewi, Bangkok 10400 – **22) Wor. Phon Si** (Witthayu Kong Phon Thi Si, 4th Infantry Division). ✉ Headquarters of the 4th Infantry Division, Somdet Phra Naresuan Maharat Camp, Phitsanulok 65000 – **23) Phon Ror. Kao** (Kong Phon Thahan Rap Thi Kao, 9th Infantry Division). ✉ Surasi Camp, Kanchanaburi 71190 – **24) Jor. Sor.** (Krom Chaye Thahan Suesarn, Army Signals Department). ✉ Jor. Sor. 1, Rama V Rd, Saphan Daeng, Bangsue, Dusit Region, Bangkok 10300. **Regional stns:** Jor. Sor. 2, Tharathibodi Rd, Thakham, Phunphin District, Surat Thani 84130 – Jor. Sor. 3, Prasert Songkhram Camp, Kongphon Si Rd, Nuea, Roi Et 45000 – Jor. Sor. 4, 104 Thetsaban 1 Rd, Nai Mueang, Yasothon 35000 – Jor. Sor. 5, 5 Mu 2 Ban Lao, Ban Lao, Chaiyaphum 36000 – Jor. Sor. 6, 1543/23 Srisumang Rd, Mueang Tai, Si Sa Ket 33000 – **25) Mor. Kor.** (Mahawitthayalai Kasetsat, Kasetsart University). HQ: ✉ 50 Phahonyothin Rd, Bang Khen, Chatuchak, Bangkok 10900. Bangkok. Tr. located at Nongkhaem in Samut Sakhon province. **Regional stns:** 301/1 Mu 5, Paphai, Sansai District, Chiang Mai 50210 – 86/8 Maliwan Rd, Mueang Kao, Sitan, Khon Kaen 40000 – 424 Mu 3, Kanchanawanit Rd, Phawong, Songkhla 90100 – **26) Jor. Tor. Lor.** (Changwat Thahan Bok Lop Buri, Lop Buri Army Province). ✉ 13th Military Circle, Narai Maharat Rd, Lop Buri 15000 – **27) Or. Sor. Mor. Thor.** (Ongkan Suesan Muanchon Haeng Prathet Thai, Mass Communications Org. of Thailand, MCOT Radio Network). ✉ 63/1 Rama IX Rd, Huay Khwang, Bangkok 10320 – **28) Sor. Or. Thor.** (Sathani Witthayu Krom Utiniyom Witthaya, Meteorological Department R. St.). ✉ 4353 Sukhumvit Rd, Bangna, Bangkok 10260 – **29) Sor. Thor. Ror.** (Siang Chak Thahan Ruea, Voice of the Navy). ✉ Sor. Thor. Ror. 2: Phutianan Stadium, Phra Khanong, Bangna District, Bangkok 10260. **Regional stns:** Sor. Thor. Ror. 3: 99/1 Mu 1, Phuket 83000 – Sor. Thor. Ror. 4: 9/9 Thetsaban-Phatthana Rd, Wat Mai, Chanthaburi 22000 – Sor. Thor. Ror. 5: 652 Mu 2, Sattahip District, Chon Buri 20180 – Sor. Thor. Ror. 6: Songkhla Naval Station, Thale Luang Rd, Bo Yang, Songkhla 90000 – Sor. Thor. Ror. 7: Mae Klang River Operation Unit, Nakhon Phanom 48000 – Sor. Thor. Ror. 8: Ban Khlong Mek, Tha Chang, Phrom Phiram District, Phitsanulok 65150 – Sor. Thor. Ror. 9: Ban Thung Sawang, Ubon-Takan Rd, Rai Noi, Ubon Ratchathani 34000 – **30) Sor. Wor. Phor.** (Sathani Witthayu Phitaksantirat, Police R. St.). ✉ Radio Broadcasting Section, 2nd Communication Division, Directorate of Police Communications, Police Department, Bang Khen Region, Bangkok 10900. **Regional stns:** 40 Mu 1, Chotana Rd, Maesa, Mae Rim District, Chiang Mai 50180 – Sor. Wor. Phor. 2, Suranarai Rd, Cho Ho, Nakhon Ratchasima 30310 – Sor. Wor. Phor. 3, Banphru, Hat Yai District, Songkhla 90250 – Sor. Wor. Phor. 4, Pracha Uthit Rd, Nai Mueang, Phitsanulok – **31)**

Nueng. Por. Nor. (Krom Praisani Thoralek, Post & Telegraph Dept.). ✉ Chaengwattana-Thungsonghong Rd, Don Mueang, Bangkok 10210. **Regional stns:** 219 Mu 4, Lampang-Hang Chat Rd, Pong Yang Khok, Hang Chat District, Lampang 52190 – Ban Nong Bu, Rop Mueang Rd, Samphrao, Udon Thani 41000 – **32) Wor. Por. Tho.** (Witthayu Pracham Thin, Local R, Communications Division, Signals Dept, Royal Thai Army) ✉ Wor. Por. Tho. 8: Kamphaeng Phet Akkharayothin Camp, Suan Luang, Krathum Baen District, Samut Sakhon 74110. **Regional stns:** Wor. Por. Tho. 2: Kawila Camp, Kongsai, Wat Ket, Chiang Mai 50000 – Wor. Por. Tho. 3: 001 Na Khai Suranari, Phanibut Rd, Pho Klang, Nakhon Ratchasima 30000 – Wor. Por. Tho. 4: Thep Sattri Si Sunthon Camp, Kabang, Thung Song District, Nakhon Si Thammarat 80310 – Wor. Por. Tho. 5: 5 Kanchanawanit Rd, Hat Yai District, Songkhla 90110 – Wor. Por. Tho. 6: Sapphasiti Prasong Camp, Warin Chamrap District, Ubon Ratchathani 34190 – Wor. Por. Tho. 7: Khai Prachak Sinlaprakhom, Thahan Rd, Mak Khaeng, Udon Thani 41000 – Wor. Por. Tho. 9: Chiraprawat Camp, Na Khai Chiraprawat Rd, Nakhon Sawan 60000 – Wor. Por. Tho. 10: Mengrai Maharat Barracks, Chiang Rai 57000 – Wor. Por. Tho. 12: 140 Kasikonthungsang Rd, Sila, Khon Kaen 40000 – Wor. Por. Tho. 14: Phichai Dap Hak Camp, 13/7 Prachanimit Rd, Tha It, Uttaradit 5 – **33) Phon Nueng Ror. Or.** (Kong Phon Thi Nueng Raksa Phra Ong, 1st Infantry Division, Royal Guard). ✉ Phitsanulok Rd, Dusit Region, Bangkok 10300 – **34) Nor. Thor. Phor.** (Nuai Bannachakan Thahan Phatthana, Armed Forces Development Command AFDC, Royal Thai Armed Forces HQ). ✉ Sathani Witthayu 919, Phitsanulok Rd, Dusit Region, Bangkok 10300. **Regional Stns:** Sathani Witthayu 914, Suan Sak Kieo Tap Yong, Ban Pong O, Mae Chan, Mae Chan District, Chiang Rai 57110. 1395kHz in Thai, 1179kHz prgr in Thai and minority langs for hilltribes – Sathani Witthayu 912, 13 Chan Uthit Rd, Bang Nak, Narathiwat 96000 in Thai and Malay – Sathani Witthayu 921, 114 Mu 1, Na Saeng, Lom Kao District, Phetchabun 67120 – Sathani Witthayu 909, Ban Rung Phatthana, Sakon Nakhon-Nakhon Phanom Rd, That Naweng, Sakon Nakhon 47000 – **35) Kor. Wor. Sor.** (Kitkan Witthayu Krachaisiang, Radio & TV Division, Army Signals Dept). HQ: ✉ Radio Broadcasting & Television Division, Signals Department, Royal Thai Army, Rama V Rd, Saphan Daeng, Bangsue, Dusit Region, Bangkok 10300. **Regional stns:** Kor. Wor. Sor. 1, Surin-Prasat Rd, Nok Mueang, Surin 32000 – Kor. Wor. Sor. 2, Yantarakit Sokon Rd, Sung Men District, Phrae 54130 – Kor. Wor. Sor. 3, 1879 Mu 14, That Choeng Chum, Sakon Nakhon 47000 – Kor. Wor. Sor. 4, 383 Super Highway, Ban Dom, Phayao 56000 – Kor. Wor. Sor. 5, 252 Mitraphap Rd, Ban Phai District, Khon Kaen 40110 – **36) Sor. Sor. Sor.** (Siang Sam Yot, Crime Suppression Division, Royal Thai Police). ✉ Section 1, Superintendency 2, Command Division, Crime Suppression Division, Phahonyothin Rd, Bangkok 10900. Regional st: 195 Mu 8, Udon-Nong Samrong Rd, Mumon, Udon Thani 41000 – **37) Ror. Dor.** (Kromkan Raksa Dindaen, Territorial Defence Dept.). HQ: ✉ 2 Charoen Krung Rd, Suan Chaochet, Phra Nakhon Region, Bangkok 10200. **Regional stns:** Nong Ho, Chotana Rd, Chang Phueak, Chiang Mai 50000 – Sri Phatcharin Camp, Rat Khanueng Rd, Nai Mueang, Khon Kaen 40000 – **38) Mahawitthayalai Thammasat** (Thammasat University). ✉ Faculty of Journalism and Mass Communications, Thammasat University, Prachan Rd, Phra Nakhon Region, Bangkok 10200 D.Prgr: Mon-Fri 0300-1400 – **39) Yan Kraw** (4th Cavalry Battalion, Armoured Unit, Royal Guard). HQ: ✉ Military Armoured Car School, 1156 Samsen Road, Bangkabrue, Dusit Region, Bangkok 10300. **Regional stns:** Saraburi Cavalry Centre, Adison Camp, Mitraphap Rd, Pak Phrieo, Saraburi 18000 Mitraphap Rd, Nong Bua Udon Thani 41000.

FM STATIONS IN SELECTED CITIES (MHz) (exc. R. Thailand, commercial, institutional and community radio stns):
Bangkok: 87.5 Sathani Witthayu Ratthasapha (Parliament R. St.) – 88.5 Sor. Thor. Ror. 1, 'Lukthung Family' – 89.0 Yan Kraw, 'Gift FM' – 89.5 Rajamangala University of Technology 'Sweet FM' – 90.0 Phon Nueng Ror. Or. 'Lukthung Rak Thai' – 90.5 Wor. Phor. Thor. – 91.0 Sor. Wor. Phor. 'Traffic Pro' – 91.5 Yan Kraw, 'FresZ' – 92.0 Wor. Sor. Sor. – 93.0 Sor. Thor. Ror. 1, 'Cool Fahrenheit' – 94.0 Thor. Thor. Bor. (Sathani Witthayu Thorathat Kongthap Bok, Army TV Station), 'EFM' – 94.5 Jor. Sor, 'Lukthung Network' – 95.0 Or. Sor. Mor. Thor 'LTM FM Lukthung Mahanakhon' – 96.0 Ror. Dor, 'Sport R.' – 96.5 Or. Sor. Mor. Thor, 'Khluen Khwam Khit, Thinking Radio' – 97.5 Or. Sor. Mor. Thor, 'Mellow 97.5' – 98.0 Phon Nueng Ror. Or. 'EDS Everyday Station' – 98.5 Nueng Por. Nor, 'Goodtime R.' – 99.0 Or. Sor. Mor. Thor, 'Active R.' – 99.5 Sathani Witthayu 9-1-9, 'Happy Life Radio' – 100.0 Jor. Sor. Roi – 100.5 Or. Sor. Mor. Thor. 'Modern R. News Network' – 101.0 Sathani Witthayu Kong Banchakan Thahan Sungsut (Royal Thai Armed Forces Command HQ) 'Radio Report One' – 101.5 Sathani Witthayu Chula (CU FM, Chulalongkorn Univ.) – 102.0 Khor. Sor. Thor. Bor. 'Khluen Khon Tham Ngan' – 102.5 Thor. Or, 'Flex 102.5' – 103.0 Jor. Sor 'Like FM' – 103.5 Thor. Thor. Bor, 'FM One' – 104.0 Or. Sor. – 104.5 Phon Por. Thor. Or. (Kong Phon Thahan Puen Yai Tosue Akat Yan, Anti-Aircraft Artillery Division), 'Travel R.' – 105.5 Or. Sor. Mor. Thor 'Eazy FM' – 106.0 Sor. Thor. Ror. 1, 'Family News Station' – 106.5 Nueng Por. Nor, 'Green Wave' – 107.0 Or. Sor. Mor. Thor, 'Met 107'.
Chiang Mai: 88.0 Sor. Thor. Ror. – 100.0 Mor. Chor. (Chiang Mai Univ.) – 100.75 Or. Sor. Mor. Thor. – 101.5 Thor.Phor. Sam – 102.5 Thor. Or 013– 105.75 Sor. Sor. Sor. – 106.75 Sathani Witthayu Ratthasapha (Parliament R. St.)
Khon Kaen: 88.25 Thor. Phor. Song 'KCS Radio' – 90.75 Or. Sor. Mor. Thor. – 103.0 Mor. Khor. (Khon Kaen Univ.) – 104.5 Sor. Wor. Phor. – 107.0 Thor Or. 020
Phuket: 88.0 Sor. Thor. Ror. 'Nice Peak FM' – 89.0 Nueng Por. Nor 'Power Zone FM'– 95.0 Sor. Sor. Sor, 'Kiss FM' – 99.25 Sathani Witthayu Ratthasapha (Parliament R. St.) – 101.5 Or. Sor. Mor. Thor. – 102.5 Ror. Dor. – 107.25 Sor. Or. Thor. 'Smart R.'
Songkhla/Hat Yai: 88.0 Mor. Or. (Prince of Songkhla Univ.), Hat Yai – 94.5 Sor. Thor. Ror. 6 'Sweet FM' – 96.5 Or. Sor. Mor. Thor., Hat Yai – 103.25 Sathani Witthayu Ratthasapha (Parliament R. Stn). – 104.0 Tor. Chor. Dor., Hat Yai 'Smart R.'– 107.0 Thor. Or. 011, Khlong Hoi Khong – 107.75 Thor. Phor. Si, Hat Yai 'Power FM.'

OTHER FM STATIONS: FM stns belonging to R. Thailand and other operators are on air throughout Thailand. A large number of local commercial, institutional and community radio stns are also operating, with transmitter powers up to 500 watts.

International Relays: See International radio section

TIMOR-LESTE

L.T: UTC +9h — **Pop:** 1.3 million — **Pr. L:** Tetun (official), Portuguese (official), Indonesian — **E.C:** 220V/50Hz — **ITU:** TLS

AUTORIDADE NACIONAL DE COMUNICAÇÕES (ANC)

✉ Ground Floor, Telecom Building, Av. Xavier do Amaral 8, Caicoli, Díli ☎ +670 3311415 **E:** info@anc.tl **W:** anc.tl **L.P:** Exec. Pres: João Olívio Freitas

RÁDIO TELEVISAUN TIMOR-LESTE (RTTL) (Pub.)

✉ Edifício da Rádio e Televisão, Estrada Mercado Municipal, Caixa Postal 114, Díli ☎ +670 73960050 **W:** rttlep.tl **E:** info@rttlep.tl **L.P:** Dir: Milena Soares Abrantes. RTTL administers R. Timor-Leste (RTL) and TV Timor-Leste (TVTL)

RÁDIO TIMOR-LESTE (RTL) (Pub.)

✉ Estrada Mercado Municipal, Caixa Postal 114, Díli ☎ +670 73960050 **W:** rttlep.tl **E:** info@rttlep.tl; radiotimorleste@gmail.com **L.P:** Dir: Rosário Maia Martins. PD: Martinho Tavares

FM(	MHz	kW	FM	MHz	kW
Maliana	88.9	0.5	Manatuto	95.0	0.3
Aileu	90.3	0.3	Kutulau	96.7	
Ermera	90.6		Lospalos	96.8	0.5
Ainaro	90.9		Same	97.0	1
Díli	91.7	4	Viqueque	98.9	0.3
Oecussi	92.1	0.3	Liquisa	99.1	
Suai	93.3	0.3	Baucau	105.4	1

D.Prgr in Tetun, Portuguese and Indonesian: 2100-1500. **N.** in **Tetun/ Portuguese/Indonesian:** 2200-2300, 0330-0430, 1100-1200

RÁDIO MAUBERE (Operated by Fretilin Party)

✉ Avenida dos Mártires da Pátria, Lurumata, Díli ☎ +670 3322599 **W:** facebook.com/radiomaubere **E:** radio-maubere@live.com **FM (MHz):** Manatuto 93.8, Viqueque 94.8, Baucau 96.0, Oecusse 96.2, Ermera 96.4, Suai 96.5, Aileu & Ainaro 97.9, Liquisa 97.9, Lospalos 98.0, Same 98.2, Maliana 99.5, Díli 99.9

TIMOR-LESTE ASSOCIATION OF COMMUNITY RADIO STNS (Asosiasaun Radio Komunidade Timor-Leste) (ARKTL)

✉ National Press Centre, Rua Martires da Patria, Fatuhada, Dili ☎ +670 77066650 **W:** facebook.com/ARKTL **E:** arktl.info@gmail.com **L.P:** Pres: Prezado Ximenes. ARKTL's main role is as advocate for all community and independent stns. Member stns: 5, 9, 11, 12, 14, 16, 18, 20, 22, 23, 24, 28, 29, 30, 31 and 34.

COMMUNITY RADIO CENTRE (Centru Radio Comunidade) (CRC) ✉ CNE Building, Rua Bispo de Medeiros, Kintal Ki'ik, PO Box 160, Santa Cruz, Díli ☎ +670 77237890 **W:** facebook.com/dcrctl **L.P:** Dir:Abel da Conceição. CRC supports stns 5, 9, 11, 12, 14, 16, 17, 18, 20, 22, 23, 24, 27, 29, 30 and 34.

COMMUNITY AND INDEPENDENT STATIONS

FM	MHz	kW	Station
1)	88.2		R. Gardamor, Díli
2)	88.5		R. Na'i Feto, Laleia
3)	88.8	0.15	M3 R., Díli
4)	89.5	1	Voz FM, Díli
5)	89.7		R. Comunidade Maubisse Mau-Loko, Maubisse
6)	90.0		R. Akademika, Díli
7)	90.6		R. Lian Dame, Díli
8)	91.2		R. Lalenok Ba Ema Hotu (Labeh), Díli
9)	91.7	0.2	R. Comunidade Maliana, Maliana
10)	92.3		R. Advent Suara Pengharapan, Díli
11)	92.3	0.1	R. Comunidade Café Ermera, Gleno
12)	92.3	0.1	R. Comunidade Tokodede, Liquisa
13)	92.9		R. Parlamento Nacional, Díli
14)	93.3	0.1	R. Comunidade Atoni Lifau, Oecussi
15)	94.1		R. Comunidade Comoro, Díli
16)	94.1	0.1	R. Comunidade Cova Taroman, Suai
17)	94.7	0.3	R. Metro, Díli
18)	95.1	0.1	R. Comunidade 1912 Dom Boaventura, Same
19)	95.8		R. Liberdade, Díli
20)	96.1	0.1	R. Comunidade Ili Uai, Manatuto
21)	97.0		R. Suara Timor Lorosae (STL), Díli
22)	97.1	0.1	R. Comunidade Rai Husar, Aileu
23)	97.9	0.8	R. Povo Viqueque, Viqueque
24)	98.1	0.1	R. Comunidade Lian Tatamailau, Ainaro
25)	98.5	1	R. Timor Kmanek, Díli
26)	98.9		R. Kolejiu Fatumaka, Fatumaka
27)	99.0		R. Comunidade Lian Manu-Koko, Vila
28)	99.4	0.16	R. Rakambia, Díli
29)	99.9	0.1	R. Comunidade Lian Matebian, Baucau
30)	100.1	0.3	R. Comunidade Lospalos (Vox Populi), Lospalos
31)	100.5	0.1	R. Lorico Lian, Díli
32)	101.1		R. Nacional, Díli
33)	102.0		R. Klibur, Díli
34)	102.5	0.15	R. Comunidade Coulelemai Sahe, Bukoli
35)	107.9		R. Fini Lorosae, Baucau

Addresses & other information:

1) 2nd Floor, Gardamor Building, Fatuhada, Díli **W:** facebook.com/gardamor **E:** rtvgardamor@gmail.com – **2)** Paróquia de Laleia, Laleia, Munisipiu Manatuto **W:** facebook.com/paroquiadelaleia **E:** paroquiadelaleia@gmail.com – **3)** Rua da Guiné, Palapaso, Díli **W:** facebook.com/M3Radio **E:** m3radiodili@gmail.com – **4)** Rua Mundo Perdido II 28 (Caixa Postal 153), Delta, Díli **W:** radiovoz895.com **E:** radiovozfm@hotmail.com (Repeater stns at Aileu, Ainaro, Baucau, Lospalos, Maliana, Manatuto, Oecussi, Suai, Viqueque all on 89.5MHz 0.015 kW and at Same on 100.5MHz 0.015 kW)– **5)** Rua Mau-Corro, Maubisse Villa, Munisipiu Ainaro **W:**radiomauloko.org **E:** Radio. Komunidade.Maubisse@gmail.com – **6)** Universidade Nacional de Timor-Leste, Díli – **7)** Universidade da Paz, Rua Osindo 1, Manleuana, Díli **W:** facebook.com/Radio-Lian-Dame-RLDUNPAZ-203306513016774 **E:** radioliandame@yahoo.com – **8)** Rua 30 de Agosto depan SDN 05, Malinamoc, Comoro, Díli **W:** labeh.org **E:** info@labeh.org – **9)** Estrada Antigo Hospital, Maliana, Munisipiu Bobonaro **W:** radiomaliana.org **E:** maliana26radio@yahoo.com – **10)** Adventist World Radio, Díli – **11)** Traseiras do Campo de Futebol, Gleno, Munisipiu Ermera **W:** radio-café.org **E:** info@radio-cafe.org – **12)** Avenida Venancio Mau Sera, Suco Dato, Liquisa, Munisipiu Liquisa **W:** radiotokodede.org **E:** info@radiotokodede.org – **13)** Rua Formosa, Díli **W:** ww1.parlamento.tl **E:** relacoes.publicas@parlamento.tl - **14)** Rua de Santa Rosa, Oecussi, Munisipiu Oecussi-Ambeno **W:** radioatonilifau.org **E:** info@radioatonilifau.org – **15)** Avenida Presidente Nicolau Lobato, Comoro, Díli **W:** radiocomoro.org – **16)** Rua de Santa Rosa, Orun, Antigo Rezidensia Administrador Munisipiu, Suai, Munisipiu Covalima **W:** facebook.com/rcctinfo **E:** info@radiocovataroman.org – **17)** Díli **W:** facebook.com/dilimetrofm – **18)** Rua Pousada, Same, Munisipiu Manufahi **W:** radio1912.org **E:** info@radio1912.org – **19)** Avenida Hudi Laran, Usindo, Díli **W:** radioliberdadedili.com **E:** info@radioliberdadedili.com – **20)** Manatuto, Munisipiu Manatuto **W:** radioiliwai.org **E:** info@radioiliwai.org – **21)** STL Park, Surik Mas, Díli **W:** suara-timor-lorosae.com **E:** stl@redaksi.yahoo.com – **22) Rua** de Aileu Vila, Aileu, Munisipiu Aileu **W:** radioraihusar.org **E:**info@radioraihusar.org – **23)** Rua Central, Viqueque, Munisipiu Viqueque **W:** radiopovoviqueque.org **E:** info@radiopovoviqueque.org – **24)** Ainaro, Munisipiu Ainaro – **25)** Rua Foho Nain Feto, Ailok Laran (Caixa Postal 354), Maloa, Díli **W:** rtk.tl **E:** radio.rtk@gmail.com – **26)** Kolejiu Don Bosco Fatumaka, Fatumaka, Munisipiu Baucau – **27)** Rua Vila Mau-Meta, Vila, Atauro **W:** facebook.com/lianmanukoko **E:** lianmanukoko@gmail.com – **28)** Rua Kampung Alor, Díli **W:** facebook.com/Radio-Rakambia-TL-1215021985372938 **E:** radiorakambia@gmail.com – **29)** Campus Universitário, Rua Watulete-Tirilolo, Kota Baru, Baucau, Munisipiu Baucau **W:** radiolianmatebean **E:** info@radiolianmatebean.org – **30)** Rua Central, Lospalos, Munisipiu Lautém **W:** radiolospalosvoxpopuly.org **E:** info@radiolospalosvoxpopuly.org – **31)** Rua Governador Serpa Rosa, Farol, Díli **W:** facebook.com/radiolorico **E:** radiolorico@gmail.com – **32)** Rua D. Boaventura 8, Díli **W:** gmntv.tl **E:** comercial@gmntv.tl – **33)** Rua Pertamina, Praia dos Coqueiros, Pantai Kelapa, Díli **E:** radiokliburfm@yahoo.com – **34)** Bukoli, Munisipiu Baucau **W:** radiosahebucoli.org **E:** info@radiosahebucoli.org – **35)** Diocese de Baucau, Baucau, Munisipiu Baucau.

Relays of International Stations: RTP Antena 1, Díli 103.1MHz - **RDP Internacional**, Díli 105.3MHz 1KW - **BBC World Service**, Díli 95.1MHz - **Radio Australia**, Díli 106.4MHz

TOGO

L.T: UTC — **Pop:** 8.3 million — **Pr.L:** French (official), Éwé, Kabiyè — **E.C:** 230V/50Hz — **ITU:** TGO

HAUTE AUTORITÉ DE L'AUDIOVISUEL ET DE LA COMMUNICATION (HAAC)

✉ Lomé.

RADIO LOMÉ (Gov.) ✉ B.P. 434, Lomé ☎+228 2221 2493 🖷 +228 2221 3673 **W:** radiolome.tg **E:** radiolome@radiolome.tg
FM: Agou 88.3MHz, Alédjo 92.7MHz, Dapaong 88.3MHz, Badou 99.3MHz, Lomé 99.5MHz.
D.Prgr: French/Ethnic: 24h. **English:** 1940. **IS:** Soft tempo chime.

RADIO KARA (Gov.) ✉ B.P. 21, Kara **W:** radiokara.tg **E:** radiokara14@yahoo.fr
FM: Dapaong/Kara 91.5MHz, Agou 94.7MHz, Pya Kadjika 96.7MHz, Alédjo 99.2MHz, Lomé 101.5MHz.
D.Prgr: 24h.

Other Stations (FM MHz):
Hit R, Lomé: 104.7 **W:** hitradio.ma – **R. Avenir**, 76 Blvd. de la Kara, Quartier Doumassessé, B.P. 20183, Lomé: 104.3 – **R. de L'Evangile**, Lomé: 100.3. – **R. Delta Santé,** Aneho: 106.1. (Also rel. RFI) – **R. Evangile Jésus Vous Aime**, Bretelle de Klimamé, B.P. 2313, Lomé. **FM:** Lomé 100.2, Agou 104.1 – **R. Maria Togo**, n°155 de la rue 158, Hédzranawoé, B.P. 30162, Lomé **W:** radiomaria.org **E:** rmariatg@ids.tg **FM:** Dapaong 88.5 0.25kW, Lomé 98.8, Kara 101.5, Kpalimé/Sokodé 104.5 – **R. Missionnaire,** Quartier Tomdé Kara, B.P. 170, Kara: 106.3. **E:** emc_kara@yahoo.com – **R. Nana FM**, Angle Rues Tanou et Djossi, B.P. 6035, Lomé: 95.5. **E:** petdog2@yahoo.fr – **Océan FM,** Aneho: 93.1 – **R. Rurale:** Pagouda 88.9, Notsè 100.1, Dapaong 102.5 – **Sport FM,** Tokoin Habitat, B.P. 8675, Lomé: 91.9 **W:** radiosportfm.com – **R. Tropik FM**, Quartier Wuiti, B.P. 2276, Lomé: 93.1. **E:** tropikfm@nomade.fr – **Zephyr FM,** B.P. 20017, Lomé. **W:** zephyr.tg **E:** zephyr@zephyr.tg **FM:** Lomé 92.3, Kara 95.5, Atakpamé 102.9 – **R. Zion**, Adidogomé, B.P. 13853, Lomé. **FM:** Lomé 94.3, Kpalimé 102.5.
BBC African Sce in English/French: Lomé 97.5MHz.
RFI Afrique: Lomé 91.5, Kara/Kpalimé 98.3MHz
VOA: Lomé 102.3MHz

TOKELAU (New Zealand)

L.T: UTC +11h — **Pop:** 1,600 — **Pr.L:** Tokelauan (official), English (official) — **E.C:** 240V/50Hz — **ITU:** TOK

TOKELAU COMMUNITY RADIO

✉ National Public Service - Tokelau Office, PO Box 3298 Apia, Samoa **LP**: Acting GM: Seiuli Aleta ☎ +685 20822 **W:** tokelau.org.nz
Prgr: local community news and information, educational talks, weather reports and music. Each stn operates independently, with studios on each atoll.

FM	MHz	kW	Station
Atafu Atoll	‡107.5	0.005	R. Atafu FM
Fakaofo Atoll	‡107.5	0.005	R. Fakaofo FM

FM	MHz	kW	Station
Nukunonu Atoll	‡107.5	0.005	R. Nukunonu FM

NB: ‡ Tokelau Community Radio and transmitters currently inactive. Discussions ongoing about reactivation.

TONGA

L.T: UTC +13h — **Pop:** 106,000 — **Pr.L:** Tongan (official), English (official) — **E.C:** 240V/50Hz — **ITU:** TON

COMMUNICATION DEPARTMENT, Ministry of Information & Communications (MIC)

MIC (Communication Department) is the government ministry responsible for broadcasting policy and spectrum administration.
✉ P.O. Box 1380, Nuku'alofa ☎ +676 20100 **W:** mic.gov.to **E:** enquiries1@mic.gov.to **LP:** CEO: Mr Paula P. Ma'u Dir. Communication: Mr 'Alifeleti Tu'ihalamaka

TONGA BROADCASTING COMMISSION (Independent Statutory Board, part-Comm.)

✉ P.O. Box 36, Nuku'alofa, Tongatapu ☎+676 23555 ✉ Fangatongo, Neiafu, Vava'u ☎+676 70827, 70843 **W:** tonga-broadcasting.net **E:** info@tonga-broadcasting.net **LP:** CEO: Viola Ulakai

MW	Location	KHz	kW	Station
	Nuku'alofa	1017	10	A3Z R. Tonga 1
FM	**Location**	**MHz**	**kW**	**Station**
	Neiafu, Vava'u	90.0		Kool FM R. Tonga 2
	Nuku'alofa	90.0	0.5	Kool FM R. Tonga 2
	Neiafu, Vava'u	97.2		A3Z R. Tonga1
	Nuku'alofa	101.7		A3Z R. Tonga 1

R. Tonga "The Call of the Friendly Isles" 1017kHz **D.Prgr:** 1900-1110(SS-1200). **N. in English:** 1800 (BBC), 1900 (ABC), 0000 (ABC or RNZI), 0700 (local), 0715 (ABC), 1100. **Kool FM** "Kool 90FM" & "Vava'u Kool 90FM" **N:** local and RNZI **D.Prgr:** 24h

OTHER STATIONS:

FM	Location	MHz	kW	Station
6)	Nuku'alofa	87.5		FM87.5 Tonga Daily News
6)	Neiafu, Vava'u	87.9		89.5FM
2)	Vaipoa	00.0		A3NTT R. Niuatoputapu
3)	Nuku'alofa	88.1		FM88.1 Letio Le'o 'o Tonga
4)	Nuku'alofa	88.6	1	R. Nuku'alofa
5)	Neiafu, Vava'u	88.6		R. Waves of Vava'u
8)	Neiafu. Vava'u	89.0		Letio Faka-Kalistiane 89FM
9)	Nuku'alofa	89.1		A3V Tonga R. Magic 89.1
10)	Neiafu, Vava'u	89.3		PIG FM
6)	Nuku'alofa	89.5		R. Tonga Vake-Tali-Folau
7)	Unknown	91.5		R. FM 91.5
13)	Nuku'alofa	92.1		China R. International
8)	Nuku'alofa	93.1	0.2	A3R Letio Faka-Kalistane 93FM
11)	Nuku'alofa	98.0	0.1	Letio le'o 'o e kakai
12)	Nuku'alofa	103.0		R. Australia

Addresses and other information

2) Old Catholic Priests residence, Vaipoa, Niuatoputapu, Northern Tonga – **3)** Vaiola Motu'a, Nuku'alofa ☎ +676 27477 **W:** taimi-online.com **E:** info@tonga881fm.com **Prgr:** news/talk/talkback – **4)** Teufaiva, Nuku'alofa ☎ +676 872 6282 **W:** facebook.com/radionukualofa/ **E**: radionukualofa886@gmail.com **Prgr:** 24/7 – **5)** ☎ +676 71128 – **6)** Broadcom Ltd, Vikilani House, Nuku'alofa. ☎ +676 22296 **W:** facebook.com/875fm E: 87.5fmbroadcom@gmail.com **LP**: MD Katalina Tohi, C.Ops Mgr Siaosi Lavaka Prgr: 24/7 in Tongan/English – 7) Unknown broadcaster – details required – **8)** Tonga Christian Radio, PO Box 478**,** Nuku'alofa ☎+676 27328 **W:** tcrfm.org **E:** info@pacificpartners.org **L.P:** Stn M: Willy Florian **Prgr:** 24/7 Tongan religious – **9)** Kaipongipongi,13 Vaha'akolo Road, Nuku'alofa ☎ +676 25891 **W:** tongaradio.com **E:** a3v@tongaradio.com or magic@tongaradio.com **LP:** Mgr Phillip Vea – **10) T:** +676 71479 **W:** facebook.com/pigfm-893 **LP:** Greg Carlson **Prgr:** eclectic 'Radio that Rocks the South Pacific' – **11)** Voice of the People, Ma'a Fafine moe Famili Inc, Community Media Centre, Fasi, Nuku'alofa. **E:** 98fm.mff@gmail.com **LP:** Bale Huni **Prgr:** community radio – **12)** 24/7 relay of ABC R. in English via satellite from Melbourne – **13)** 24/7 in English & Chinese via satellite from Beijing

TRINIDAD & TOBAGO

L.T: UTC -4h — **Pop:** 1.4 million — **Pr.L:** English — **E.C:** 115V/60Hz — **ITU:** TRD

TELECOMMUNICATIONS AUTHORITY OF TRINIDAD & TOBAGO (TATT)

✉ #5, Eighth Ave Extension, off Twelfth Str, Barataria ☎ +1 868 6758288 **E:** info@tatt.org.tt **W:** tatt.org.tt **L.P:** Chmn: Gilbert Peterson

TTT LTD. (Gov. Comm.)

✉ 11A Maraval Rd, Port of Spain ☎ +1 868 622 4141 **W:** talkcity91fm.com & next99fm.com & sweet100fm.com **L.P:** CEO: David Roberts
FM: Talk City 91.1MHz – **Next** 99.1MHz – **Sweet** 100.1MHz

TBC RADIO NETWORK – GUARDIAN MEDIA LTD. (Comm.)

✉ Second Floor, Guardian Building, 22-24 St. Vincent St, P.O. Box 716, Port of Spain ☎ +1 868 623 3802-5 **W:** tbcradionetwork.co.tt
FM: 951 Remix: 95.1MHz (Rock) – **Sky**: 99.5MHz (Rlg.) – **Slam**: 100.5MHz (Caribbean) – **The Vibe CT 105:** 105.1MHz (Local music + sport) – **Sangeet:** 106.1MHz (East Indian) – **Aakash Vani:** 106.5MHz (Easy Listening). Note: TBC also runs Mix90.1FM in Guyana

ONE CARIBBEAN MEDIA LTD (Comm.)

✉ 7-9 Shine Str, Port of Spain ☎ +1 868 625 8426 🖷 +1 868 624 3234 **W:** onecaribbeanmedia.net **L.P:** CEO: Dawn Thomas PD: Keichel Walter-Ramroop (Taj 92.3FM), Warren Pereira (Hott 93), Tamara Williams (Red 96.7FM)& Jamie Thomas (W107). Contact person for i95.5: Rhonda Fullerton
FM: Taj 92.3 FM: 92.3MHz (East Indian) – **Hott 93:** 93.1MHz (Top40/mainstream), 93.5MHz (Port of Spain) – **i95.5 FM**: 95.5MHz (News, talk, current affairs) – **Red 96.7FM**: 96.7MHz (Urban) – **W107 The Word**: 107.1MHz (Gospel) Note: Also runs The Wave in St.Lucia, Starcom in Barbados and The Grenada Broadcasting Network

CARIBBEAN LIFESTYLE COMMUNICATIONS (Comm.)

✉ #4 Herbert Str, St. Clair, Port of Spain ☎ +1 868 622 4124 🖷 +1 868 622 6693 **E:** sales@clcommunications.com **W:** caribbeanlifestylecommunications.com **L.P:** MD Kiran Maharaj
FM: Radio 90.5: 90.5MHz (East Indian/Bollywood) – **Music Radio 97.1:** 97.1MHz (AC/Easy Listening) – **Heartbeat 104.1:** 104.1MHz (Women/Adult Pop)

OJO WORLD (Comm)

✉ 153 Tragarete Rd, Newtown, Port of Spain ☎ +1 868 628 9696 **W:** ojoworldtt.com **L.P:** MD: Tony Chow Lin On GM: Robert Dash PD: Paul Richards **FM: Star 947:** 94.7MHz (Rock) – **WEFM**: 96.1MHz (Urban Caribbean) – **Music for Life**: 107.7 (Soul)

RADIO VISION LIMITED (Comm.)

✉ 88-90 Abercromby St., Port of Spain ☎ +1 868 627 6937 **W:** boomchampionstt.com & power102fm.com **L.P:** CEP: O'Brian Haynes MD Brian Knight **FM: Boom Champions** 94.1MHz (Urban) – **Power 102:** 102.1/102.5 (all talk)

OTHER STATIONS (FM in MHz):

BBC relay: Port-of-Spain & Scarborough **FM:** 98.7 – **Isaac 98.1**, Family Focus Broadcasting Network, 105 Woodford Str, Newtown, Port of Spain ☎+1 868 622 8981 **W:** isaac981.com **L.P:** CEO Margaret Elcock **FM:** 98.1 (Gospel) – **Lime Radio,** Heritage Communications Ltd, 104 Woodford Str, New Town, Port of Spain ☎+1 868 221 8585 **W:** lime101.com **FM:** 101.7 – **More FM,** PBCT Ltd, 177 Tragarete Rd, Woodbrook, Port of Spain ☎ +1 868 628 9595 **FM:** 104.7 (Top 40) – **103FM,** Level 4, Long Circular Mall, St. James, Post of Spain ☎ +1 868 628 9222 **W:** 103fm.net **FM**: 103.1 (East Indian) – **Parliament of the Republic of Trinidad & Tobago,** Abercromby St, Port of Spain **FM:** 105.5 – **Platinum Hits**, #7-9 Shine Str, Port of Spain **W:** platinumhitstt.com **FM:** 103.5 – **Pulse 89.5,** Trico Industries Ltd., 65-67 Lambeau Signal Hill Rd, Signal Hill, Tobago ☎+1 868 635 1005 **W:** pulse895fm.com **FM:** 89.5 – **Radio Jaagriti,** Corner Pasea Main Rd Ext and Churchill Roosevelt Highway, Tunapuna ☎+1 868 663 2250 **FM:** 102.7 (Rlg., hindu) – **Radio Tambrin,** 3 Picton Str, Scarborough, Tobago ☎+1 868 639 3437 🖷+1 868 660 7351 **E:** contact@ttambrintobago.com **W:** tambrintobago.com **L.P:** GM: George Leacock **FM:** 92.7 – **Radio Toco,** Victoria Pritchard Resource Centre, Galera Road, Toco ☎+1 868 670 0068 **W:** www.ilannet/com/radiotoco/index.html **FM:** 106.7 1.2kW, Community Radio for NE Trinidad – **The Street 91.9FM**, Trini Bashment Ltd., 8 Pro de Verteuil, Arima ☎ +1 868 628 4531 **W**: www.facebook.com/theStreet919fm **FM:** 91.9 – **U97.5 Hot Like Pepper**, Lot 41 Unit 2, Exchange Lots, Couva ☎+1 868 720 5858 **W**: www.facebook.com/U97.5FM/ **FM:**

97.5 (Asian Multicultural) – **Wack FM,** KMP Music Group Ltd, 129C Coffee Str, San Fernando ☎ +1 868 652 9774 **E:** wack901fm@gmail.com **W:** wackradio901fm.com **L.P:** CEO: Kenny Phillips **FM:** 90.1

TRISTAN DA CUNHA (UK)

L.T: UTC — **Pop:** 250 — **Pr.L:** English — **E.C:** 230V/50Hz — **ITU:** TRC

TRISTAN BROADCASTING SERVICE (Gov.)

✉ The Administrator, Tristan da Cunha, So. Atlantic via Cape Town, South Africa. **E:** tristan.radio@yahoo.co.uk **L.P:** Head of Telecommunications: Andy Repetto.

FM: Atlantic FM, 93.5MHz 25W **D.Prgr:** Sun 1000-1200. Satellite relay of **Forces Radio BFBS** rebroadcast on 93.5MHz outside own programming.

TUNISIA

L.T: UTC +1h — **Pop:** 12 million — **Pr.L:** Arabic (official), French — **E.C:** 230V/50Hz — **ITU:** TUN

HAUTE AUTORITÉ INDÉPENDANTE DE LA COMMUNICATION AUDIOVISUELLE (HAICA)

✉ 50 Ave de l'Indépendance, Le Bardo 2000 ☎+216 7166 0177 **W:** haica.tn **E:** contact@haica.tn

RADIO TUNISIENNE (Pub)

✉ 71 Avenue de la Liberté, 2002 Tunis ☎+216 71 847300 **W:** radionationale.tn telediffusion.net.tn/?page_id=135&lang=fr **E:** contact@radionationale.tn Ont@telediffusion.net.tn

MW	kHz	kW	Prgr.	Times
Gafsa	585	200	N	0400-2400
Tunis	630	300	N	24h
Medenine	684	50	N	0400-2400
Tunis	963	100	I	24h

FM (MHz)	N	C	I	Y	kW
Ain Draham	90.3	103.4	93.4	96.6	6
Beni Khiar	93.9	101.1	98.5	102.0	0.5
Gabes	95.5	93.3	-	90.2	1
Gafsa (Biadha)	104.6	105.4	101.8	95.0	50
Gorrâa	89.1	98.7	95.4	89.1	4
Harkoussia	-	-	-	92.5	
Kasserine	94.6	102.7	99.2	89.6	49
Kchabta	102.6	89.5	93.8	97.0	
Kef Errand	89.8	96.1	88.2	99.4	
Ksour-Essaf	102.0	103.7	-	92.5	1
Remada	88.9	99.9	93.4	90.3	80
Sfax (Ghraba)	93.0	103.0	99.5	93.0	60
Souk Jomaa	104.9	101.3	88.2	91.3	1
Tataouine	106.4	101.2	-	97.7	1
Tozeur	94.6	105.9	-	97.3	1
Trozza	105.9	87.7	-	90.8	
Tunis	105.3	101.1	98.2	88.6	1
Zaghouan	94.3	101.1	92.0	96.5	20
Zarzis	106.1	90.7	97.2	93.9	72

National Channel (N) in Arabic on MW & FM: 24h. **N.** on the h **W:** radionationale.tn – **Cultural channel (C)** in Arabic: 1100-2400 on FM **W:** radionationale.tn – **R. Tunis Chaîne Internationale (RTCI) (I):** on 963kHz & FM: **French** 24h except English 1403-1430, Italian 1430-1500, Spanish 1903-1930, German 1930-2000 **W:** rtci.tn – **R. Jeunes** (Youth R.) **(Y):** 24h on FM **W:** radiojeunes.tn

Regional stations (FM MHz): R. Gafsa, Av. Habib Bourguiba, 2100 Gafsa **W:** radiogafsa.tn **FM:** Tozeur 89.2, Gafsa 91.8 40kW, Chambi 92.7 50kW, Sidi Bouzid 102.7 – **R. El Kef,** Rue Mongi Slim, 7100 El Kef **W:** radiokef.tn **FM:** Souk-Jomaa 90.0, 92.2 50kW, Ain Draham 90.3, Ghardimaou 94.1, Sidi Youssef 95.8, Sidi Salem 96.2, Le Kef 96.8, Nefta 99.6, Nebeur 100.1, Goraa 102.2, Siliana 103.1, Tabarka 106.7 – **R. Monastir,** Rue Farhat Hached, 5019 Monastir **W:**radiomonastir.tn **FM:** Harkoussia 95.7 2kW, Trozza 97.3 2kW, Beni Khiar 98.5 0.5kW, Sousse 99.0 1kW, Zaghouan 104.7 2kW, Monastir 106.1 1kW – **R. Panorama:** Tunis 92.5MHz **W:** facebook.com/RadioPanoramaTunisie – **R. Sfax,** Route de Menzel Chaker Road, 3058 Sfax **W:** radiosfax.tn **FM:** Djerba/Skhira 89.0, Ksour-Essaf 100.2, Trozza 100.8, Sfax 105.2 3kW, El Ghraba 106.6 – **R. Tataouine**, Cité 7 Novembre, 3263 Tataouine **W:** radiotataouine.tn **FM:** Zarzis 87.6 70kW, Tataouine 88.1 70kW, Techout 89.5, Medenine 95.8, Remda 96.6 80kW, Ghomrassen 102.6, Gabes 103.3, Djerba 105.7.

Ann: National Channel: "Huna Tunis, Idha'atu-l-Wataniya at-Tunisiya". Cultural Channel: "Huna idha'at-Tunis at-thakafiya". F: "Ici Radio Tunisie Internationale".

Other stations, main networks (FM MHz):
Cap FM: Kef-Errand 91.5, Sidi Abdessalem 95.2, Hammamet 105.6 **W:** capradio.tn – **iFM:** Kef-Errand 87.6, Nefta 89.7, Tataouine 89.9, Remada 91.6, Sousse 93.4, Zarzis 94.7, Gafsa 96.8, Kef 97.6, Tozeur 97.8, Tunis 100.6, Gabès 102.8, Bizerte 107.3 **W:** ifm.tn – **Knooz FM:** Sousse/Hammamat/Zaghouan 105.1, Mahdia/Monastir 98.0 **W:** knoozfm.net – **Nejma FM:** Zeramdine 88.4, Mahdia 88.9, Sousse 95.9 **W:** nejmafm.com – **Oasis FM:** Gabès 96.5, Medenine 94.4 **W:** oasisfm.tn – **Ulysse FM:** Djerba 92.1, Zarzis 104.3 **W:** ulysse-fm.com – **R. Express FM:**Sousse 91.1, Bizerte 100.2, Tunis 103.6, Sfax 104.0, Monastir 104.5, Cap Bon 106.0. **W:** radioexpressfm.com – **R. Jawhara FM:** Kairouan 89.4, Tunis 90.7, Mahdia 91.6, Cap Bon 103.2, Chambi 104.4, Sousse 107.3 1kW.**W:** jawharafm.net – **R. Med:** Tunis 93.5, Zaghouan 100.0, Cap Bon 104.1 **W:** radiomed.tn – **R. MFM:** Sousse 94.7/105.5 **W:**facebook.com/RadioMfmTunisie – **R. Mosaïque FM:** Gafsa 88.2,Hammamet 88.9, Médenine 89.2, Sousse 90.1, Sidi Bou Said 90.3 0.1kW, Kasserine 91.1, Tozeur 92.3, Nabul 92.9, Tunis 94.9 5kW, Sfax 95.3, Nefta 101.4, Béja 105.8, Bizerte 106.8, Ain Deraham/ Tataouine 107.0, Mehdia 107.5 **W:** mosaiquefm.net – **R. Oxygene FM:** Bizerte 90.0/104.5 **W:** oxygene.fm – **R. Sabra FM:** Kairouan 89.0, Monastir 98.8 **W:** radiosabrafm.net – **Shems FM:** Gafsa 88.7, Monastir 90.6, Sousse 93.7, Bizerta 95.7, Sfax 96.2, Tunis 101.7, Cap Bon 106.5, Kairouan 107.0 **W:** shemsfm.net – **Zitouna FM**: Zaghouan 88.0 80kW, El Ghraba/Sfax 89.9 60kW, Nefta 91.4 1kW, Gorraa 92.2 3kW, Trozza 94.0 5kW, Tataouine 94.4 1kW, Ksour-Essaf 96.9, Zaghouan 97.6 80kW, Souk-Jomaa 97.8, Biadha 98.3 35 kW, Bizerte 99.1 5kW, Medenine 99.3, Gabes 99.8 1kW, Ain Draham 100.4 5kW, Zarziz 100.7 63kW, Kef Errand 100.9, Tozeur 102.3 1kW, Nabeul 102.9 7kW, Remada 103.4 80kW, Chambi 106.3, Sidi Bou Said 106.9 **W:** zitounafm.net

DAB: Al Ghraba 10D, Djebel Zaghouan 12C/12D 215.072MHz

TURKEY

L.T: UTC +1h (28 Mar-31 Oct: +2h) — **Pop:** 85 million — **Pr.L:** Turkish — **E.C:** 220V/50Hz — **ITU:** TUR

SUPREME BOARD OF RADIO & TELEVISION (RTÜK)

✉ Bilkent Plaza B2 Blok, 06530 Bilkent/Ankara ☎+90 312 2975000 **W:** rtuk.gov.tr **E:** rtuk@rtuk.gov.tr **L.P:** Pres: Ilhan Yerlikaya.

TÜRKIYE RADYO-TELEVIZYON KURUMU (TRT) (Pub) (Turkish Radio-Television Corporation)

✉ TRT Genel Müdürlügü, Turan Günes Bulvari, 06109 OR-AN, Ankara ☎+90 312 4634343 🖷 +90 312 4632335
W: radyo.trt.net.tr **E:** rdb@trt.net.tr
L.P: DG: Ibrahim Eren. Dep. DG (Eng.): Murat Akgüç. Dep. DG (Admin): Erkan Durdu. Dep. DG (Broadc.): Mustafa Alcan. Dept. DG (Admin.) Osman Urgun. Dept. DG (TRT International (World Arabic) Admin.) Serdar Karagoz. Head of Radio Dept: Ahmet Akçakaya. Head of Transmitters Dept: Yusuf Tashdemir.

MW	kHz	kW	N	MW	kHz	kW	N
Mersin	630	300	1/R	Trabzon	954	300	1/R
Antalya	891	300	1/R	Diyarbakir	1062	300	1/R
Izmir	927	100	1				

1=TRT1, R=regional prgr.

FM main txs	1	2	3	4	5	6	kW
Adana	96.7	92.5	89.2			102.4	30
Adiyaman	88.8	94.4		103.3	90.8		30
Afyon	89.5	93.2	94.7	94.0	92.0	92.7	5
Aksehir	89.2	95.8			92.4		30
Alanya	90.3	92.7	96.4	105.3	99.0	91.2	5
Amasya	97.3	93.9	99.6	98.9	101.9	107.6	30
Ankara	93.3	88.0	91.2	102.8	98.6	95.0	30
Antalya	88.4	95.6	91.6	92.1	88.4	107.0	10
Ardahan	90.4	94.8	99.8	101.7	104.7	99.3	5
Artvin	94.4	98.4	88.4		101.3	90.0	5
Avanos	99.6	95.0	93.7				5
Aydin	98.5	91.7	97.6	106.3	95.0	92.9	5
Ayvalik	88.4	90.4	95.4		99.1		5
Bingöl	89.3	92.5		97.6	99.6	96.0	5
Bitlis	98.0	94.2			102.6	102.0	5
Bodrum	94.6	99.3	89.4	97.4		92.8	5
Bolu	89.6	92.6	94.8	87.7	98.9	88.6	5
Bozkir	93.1	103.6			106.7		5

FM main txs	1	2	3	4	5	6	kW
Bozkurt	101.5	97.5			103.5		30
Bucak	101.5	107.8			105.8		5
Giresun (Bulancak)	91.7	88.0				88.4	5
Burdur	101.5	107.8	100.5	99.2	102.4		5
Burhaniye	107.5	93.1			99.1		5
Bursa	99.5	95.0	96.3	96.7	99.5		30
Çanakkale	96.5	98.9		104.2	97.0	96.4	30
Çankiri	98.1	100.5		100.8	98.8	107.7	30
Caykuma	106.9	104.9			100.5		5
Cizre	101.9	97.7					30
Çorum	105.7	103.7		101.2	98.2	100.2	5
Datça	95.8	107.1	102.9				30
Denizli	95.2	93.2	90.0	88.6	101.5	107.9	30
Diyarbakir	89.6	93.6		100.8	105.0	106.8	30
Edirne	97.4	99.4		100.9	105.8	91.7	30
Elazig	100.7	105.7		102.7	107.5	98.0	30
Elbistan	91.4	96.4			94.0	103.5	30
Eleskirt	88.2	92.2			95.2		30
Ermenek	103.8	90.3			95.8		5
Erzincan	88.0	93.2	104.5	94.7	91.2	107.9	30
Erzurum	90.8	98.8	96.8	92.7	102.6	94.8	30
Eskisehir	89.0	96.8	94.4	107.8	101.3	107.2	30
Fethiye	97.7	94.5	89.3	93.7			5
Gaziantep	92.0	97.6	95.2	102.2	101.9	100.7	30
Gebze	105.5	100.9	103.3		97.8		5
Gökceada	99.0	95.4	93.4		101.6		5
Gümüshane	98.0	96.0	90.0	90.0	100.2		5
Gürpinar	96.4	93.8	100.0				5
Hadim	94.0	92.8			90.1		5
Hinis	91.8	93.9			88.9		5
Ilgaz	93.2	98.4			90.0		30
Iskenderun	93.6	91.2	100.0	100.0	88.8	93.0	10
Isparta	95.1	97.3	92.7	99.2	102.4	95.7	5
Istanbul	95.6	91.4	88.2	101.6	103.4	99.6	100
Izmir	94.7	91.2	88.0	88.7	101.6	99.1	100
Izmit	90.5	96.0	93.6				30
Kahramanmaras	99.8	105.8		107.9	87.8	107.6	5
Kangal	97.6	94.4			88.0		5
Karabük	100.0	94.0		97.8		96.0	5
Karaburun	90.8	93.8	99.1	88.7	101.6	100.2	5
Karaman	96.4	98.6		106.5	90.8	102.3	30
Kars	100.8	89.5		91.3	103.3	92.7	30
Kas	88.1	90.5	92.5	95.2	103.0		5
Kastamonu	104.0	91.5		101.9	97.9	88.2	5
Kayseri	89.4	97.2	99.2	103.2	107.0	101.3	30
Kilis	94.4	90.8		88.8		89.7	5
Kirikkale	105.9	89.0			88.8	93.4	5
Kirklareli	94.5	90.0	103.6	98.5	91.0	101.9	30
Kirsehir	97.6	92.0		102.5	88.8	100.8	30
Konya	103.2	90.5		92.9	107.6	88.8	5
Kurtalan	99.6	105.6					30
Kusadasi	98.7	90.2	93.5		103.8	88.6	30
Kütahya	90.2	95.4	92.1	101.5	88.1	92.4	30
Gumushane Köse	90.2	92.5	94.7				5
Köycegiz	105.1	99.8	95.4				30
Malatya	101.3	103.7		105.8	97.6	95.6	30
Manisa	92.1	93.1	98.9	103.7	93.9	95.2	30
Mardin	91.4	96.1			92.8	101.5	5
Marmaris	98.2	90.9	95.0				5
Mersin	92.0	90.0	95.8	102.1	92.0	104.3	5
Mudanya	87.9	98.9	91.1	99.5	95.5		5
Mugla	105.3	92.9	106.5	94.9	100.6		30
Mus	90.9	98.7		105.9	102.7	95.5	5
Nigde	90.0	95.6		105.7	93.2	89.5	30
Nusaybin	96.8	93.4	89.0			100.0	30
Oltu	95.6	93.6			89.1		5
Ordu-Persembe	99.9	95.6	91.5	102.8	96.0	105.5	30
Pinarbasi-Kayseri	107.1	105.1		103.2	102.8		5
Posof	107.4	102.0			104.0		5
Rize-Dagsu	103.0	107.1	104.9	104.9	101.1	98.7	5
Salihli-Gölmarmara	100.1	96.2		88.6	103.0		5
Samsun	94.8	92.8	90.8	97.5	96.8	103.8	30
Sanliurfa	98.1	102.5		107.5	90.8	95.7	5
Sariz-Yesilkent	107.3	90.9	93.3		100.1		5
Sarkisla	106.9	101.6			103.8		5
Savsat	107.9	105.4			101.3		5
Silifke	97.0	88.8	94.4	97.0	102.2		30
Sindirgi	92.6	98.4	102.0				30
Sinop	96.4	92.4			89.2		5
Sivas	93.6	98.3	90.4	95.8	100.9	91.7	30
Sivrihisar	90.2	98.4	96.2				30
Soma	94.0	96.3			87.6		5
Suruc	97.1	100.3	90.0				30
Tekirdag	99.6	92.2		94.2	97.0		2
Trabzon	88.8	95.0	92.0	92.0	97.0	99.0	30
Trabzon-Boztepe	90.0	107.7		105.7	103.7		5
Tunceli	91.5	93.1		101.1	106.3		30
Ulukisla	88.4	102.2			104.2		5
Usak	105.5	101.9		95.7	98.4		30
Van	94.8	89.3	92.8	93.8	100.3	95.8	30
Yozgat	98.0	96.0			104.0	107.8	5
Zonguldak	88.8	97.2	99.2	87.8	93.4		30
Ödemis	92.9	97.9			87.8		5
Özalp	93.2	91.2			97.6		5

1=Radyo Bir (Educational, Culture and News channel): 24h on FM. **MW:** 0250-1015 on 891/927/954kHz, 0300-2200 on 630kHz, 0250-1900 on 1062kHz, opt-out for reg. prgr as below:
R=Regional prgr: Mon-Fri 0700-1000, SS 0700-0930: Çukurova Radio 630kHz, Antalya Radio 891kHz, Trabzon Radio 954kHz, Diyarbakir Radio 1062kHz.
2=TRT FM (popular music): 24h
3=Radyo Üc (classical music): 24h in Turkish exc. N. in English/French/German (3 min's each) at certain hours. Tourist Prgrs (3 min's each on Saturdays): English: 1615, French: 1415, German: 1915
4=TRT Nagme (Turkish art music): 24h on FM
5=TRT Türkü (Turkish folk music): 24h on FM
6=TRT Radyo Haber: news channel 24h in Ankara on 95.0MHz
TRT Radyo Kurdî in Kurdish: 24h on **FM** (MHz): Diyarbakir 88.4, Besiri 89.5, Bagisli 90.0, Solhan 90.2, Bitlis 90.6, Shanlıurfa 91.0, Hakkari 92.3, Cizre/Gercüs 94.5, Nusaybin 98.4, Mardin 102.1, Van 102.3, Siirt 103.6, Mus 105.0
TRT World Radio (carrying TRT World TV audio): Izmir 99.1MHz, Ankara 105.6MHz & Istanbul 106.8MHz. 24h.
TRT Arabic TV audio: Istanbul 91.6MHz, Ankara 107.8MHz.
Ann: TRT-1: "Burasi TRT Radyo Bir". Reg.: e.g. Antalya: "Burasi TRT Antalya Radyosu."

TRT DAB+: Block 12B: 225.648MHz Ankara & Istambul

EXTERNAL SERVICE: Voice of Turkey
See International Radio section.

Other stations; main networks:

FM (MHz)	1)	2)	3)	4)	5)	6)	7)	8)	9)	10)
Adana	105.4	89.6	102.9	103.8	96.0	88.6	106.3	101.9	92.0	98.7
Adiyaman						92.0		100.5		91.2
Afyon		101.2	95.1	90.4		95.2		96.2		102.4
Agri						100.4		96.2		104.7
Aksaray		96.0				90.5	97.2	105.0		107.3
Aksehir							104.5	105.0		
Alanya			100.0	89.3	98.0		89.9	93.5	104.8	
Amasya		92.8				102.7	106.5	101.6		89.1
Ankara	102.4	88.8	100.0	105.3	97.2	95.5	89.8	107.4	90.8	94.6
Antalya	90.2	89.7	100.0	89.3	102.6	90.9	101.2	95.3	94.2	95.8
Ardahan						95.5		99.0		103.7
Artvin								100.4		106.8
Aydin				92.3		95.8		91.1		93.2
Ayvalik				98.3		93.6		105.2		
Balikesir	98.7	88.8	100.0	90.7	93.6	94.3	97.2	88.5	100.8	99.6
Bandirma			89.8			107.7	106.2	107.0		87.8
Bartin						95.5	98.4	100.0		105.7
Batman							99.5	95.0		102.8
Bayburt						91.5		95.0		107.0
Bilecik					89.9			102.5		96.0
Bingöl								103.3		102.5
Bitlis								101.0		106.3
Bodrum	104.8	103.5	100.0	94.2	96.8		89.0			
Bolu		88.9	100.0	94.3		97.1	89.2	107.6	104.8	93.4
Boyabat								100.0		
Bucak								100.0		
Burdur		93.5					88.0	104.5		93.8
Bursa	92.0	89.8	100.0	89.2	97.2	101.6	104.6	107.6	90.8	97.9
Ceyhan							107.7	88.9		

FM (MHz)	1)	2)	3)	4)	5)	6)	7)	8)	9)	10)
Çanakkale		88.0		89.3		99.5	105.3	101.0		106.7
Çankiri						90.1		92.8		97.0
Çesme		89.6	95.0	89.3	97.2	98.6		93.3		
Çorlu			100.0					91.3		107.5
Çorum							91.3	89.5		90.7
Demirci							104.6			
Denizli		88.0	100.0	89.3	96.0		107.7	96.8	90.8	90.5
Develi							102.0	99.0		
Diyarbakir	92.0	89.8	100.3	92.3	91.2	90.4	98.0	101.0	97.5	88.0
Düzce								107.6	96.3	93.4
Edirne				101.3	102.6	90.5	103.0	91.3	98.4	93.4
Edremit		89.7				90.7		96.0		
Elazig	91.2	97.5				104.0	92.4	94.1		101.2
Erzincan						89.5		93.8		107.2
Erzurum	91.8	90.4	100.7	89.3	103.5	94.6	91.5	94.0		89.6
Eskisehir	88.6	100.0	100.5	89.3	97.2	92.6	106.3	106.6	97.8	89.6
Fethiye	102.0	89.0	100.3	96.7	94.6		98.9	98.5	93.2	
Gaziantep	107.5	92.4	104.6	102.5	103.7	96.6	107.0	103.0	99.3	88.0
Gerede		89.1				94.5	102.7	107.4	104.8	90.5
Giresun						91.1		93.0		106.3
Gümüshane						92.0		102.5		101.8
Hakkari						98.0		90.0		91.8
Hatay		105.5				88.5	106.7	101.0		99.5
Igdir						95.5		99.5		89.8
Iskenderun			101.3				94.6	95.6		107.6
Isparta		93.5		91.8		96.0		100.0		87.7
Istanbul	92.0	89.8	100.0	89.2	97.2	94.1	104.6	107.6	90.8	102.6
Izmir	96.2	89.6	100.0	89.3	97.2	96.7	101.3	96.9	90.8	98.8
K.Maras		91.2		89.0		89,7	98.2	94.0		102.3
Karaman							107.2	103.9		96.1
Kars		102.0				90.6	104.6	102.7		100.4
Kastamonu				89.6				101.0		104.3
Kayseri	93.9	105.0	100.0	88.7	98.9	104.7	100.2	88.5	96.2	106.7
Kirikkale						105.5		105.0		94.0
Kirklareli						87.5	89.8	107.6		100.3
Kirsehir								94.4		91.3
Kocaeli	92.0	89.8	100.0	89.3	100.7	94.6	104.6	107.6	90.8	99.5
Konya	95.1	89.9	97.0	89.3	101.7	98.0	92.1	102.0	93.4	96.1
Kusadasi	104.5		100.0		92.7					103.0
Kütahya				91.3	97.2		107.0	93.8	90.8	100.8
Malatya		89.9	103.3	97.8	101.7	91.7	104.6	105.5	94.5	91.3
Manisa				89.1		87.8	101.3	103.3	105.4	94.3
Mardin		89.0				102.5	104.0			87.7
Marmaris	103.6	105.5	100.0	89.3	96.1		97.3		93.0	
Mersin		93.5	105.0	90.3	94.0	94.5	103.0	105.3	97.4	103.5
Mugla			100.3	89.3			104.6	102.6	90.1	106.8
Mus					93.3			102.0		104.2
Nevsehir					96.3			102.0		91.3
Nigde	91.7				97.0	94.5		103.0		97.3
Ordu								92.5		96.5
Osmaniye		89.6				98.4	99.9	101.7	100.5	89.4
Rize					95.2			102.5		105.3
Sakarya	101.3	88.0	100.7	101.8	91.2		104.6	107.8	97.8	91.5
Samsun	99.7	106.2	100.0	88.0	98.8	88.3	94.0	103.0	96.3	105.8
Sanliurfa		106.2					92.0	93.5	105.4	103.6
Siirt						89.4		91.0		102.8
Sinop						94.2		99.0		107.4
Sivas	96.2						91.0	100.1		92.3
Sivrihisar						97.5		94.9		89.3
Tekirdag	96.2	90.1		90.3	96.0		104.6	105.4	91.8	95.2
Tokat						87.5		96.0		97.7
Trabzon				89.3		94.6	93.0	102.8	90.3	92.5
Tunceli						94.5		94.0		106.2
Usak						106.0		99.0		107.5
Van				97.5		94.5	104.6	96.0		103.3
Yalova						94.1				102.6
Yozgat						105.4		100.4		106.6
Zile								96.4		
Zonguldak				90.0			104.6	107.0	91.0	94.1

Addresses & other information:
1) Kral FM ✉ Ahi Evran Cad. No: 4, 34398 Maslak-Istanbul **W:** kralmuzik.com.tr – **2) Show R.** ✉ Levent Mah. Yeni Sülün Cad. Hardal Sk. No: 6, 34330 Besiktas/Istanbul Ust Zeren Sokak No 40, Levent-Besiktas-Istanbul **W:** showradyo.com.tr – **3) Power FM** ✉ Altunizade Mah., Kusbakisi Sk. No 43, 34665 Üsküdar/Istanbul **W:** powerfm.com.tr – **4) Alem FM** ✉ Bahariye Cad. No: 31, Ikitelli, Basın Ekspres Yolu, 34307 Küçükçekmece/Istanbul **W:** alemfm.com – **5) Metro FM** ✉ Maslak Mah. A.O.S. 55, Sok. No: 2, Aksoy Plaza Kat: 2, 34398 Sarıyer/Istanbul **W:** metrofm.com.tr – **6) Polis Radyosu** ✉ Ayrancı Mahallesi, Selimiye Caddesi No: 17, 06540 Çankaya/Ankara **W:** polisradyosu.pol.tr – **7) Radyo 7** ✉ Otakçılar Cad. No. 78, Eyüp/Istanbul **W:** radyo7.com – **8) Akra FM** ✉ Barbaros Mah., Mütevelli Çesme cd. No: 21/1, 34662 Üsküdar/Istanbul **W:** akradyo.net – **9) Süper FM** ✉ Maslak Mah. A.O.S. 55, Sok. No: 2, Aksoy Plaza Kat: 2, 34398 Sarıyer/Istanbul **W:** superfm.com.tr
10) Diyanet Radyo (operated by the State Directorate of Religious Affairs) ✉ Üniversiteler Mah. Dumlupýnar Bulv. No: 147/A 06800 Çankaya/Ankara **W:** diyanetradyo.com - **Diyanet Kuran R.: W:** diyanetkuranradyo.com **FM:** Ankara 88.2, Istanbul 106.4, Izmir 90.3, Adana 106.6, Gaziantep 99.7, Konya 88.2 + 76 more transmitters - **Diyanet Risalet R.: W:** risaletradyo.com **FM:** Ankara 94.0, Istanbul 95.1, Izmir 104.5, Konya 94.6, Sivas 102.8, Manisa 107.8, Gaziantep 107.8, Tekirdag 106.7, Trabzon 96.7, Canlýurfa 95.9, Samsun 101.3, Eskisehir 102.9, Malatya 100.2, Diyarbakýr 101.9, Adana 107.0, Balýkesir 104.7, Antalya 107.8, Aydin 104.8, Bolu 101.8, Bursa 97.4, Canakkale 105.0, Denizli 101.2, Edirne 98.8, Elazig 103.2, Erzurum 106.5, Hatay 103.7, K.Maras 98.7, Kayseri 107.7, Kocaeli 107.9, Mardin 94.3, Mersin 105.9, Mugla 88.5, Ordu 104.8, Sakarya 87.8, Van 99.4.
CRI Türk FM: W: criturk.com

AMERICAN FORCES NETWORK (Mil.)

W: www.afneurope.net/Stations/Incirlik **MW:** 1593kHz 5W. **FM:** 107.1MHz on cable

TURKMENISTAN

L.T: UTC +5h — **Pop:** 6 million — **Pr.L:** Turkmen — **E.C:** 220V/50Hz — **ITU:** TKM

TELEWIDENIÝE, RADIOGEPLESIKLER WE KINEMATOGRAFIÝA BARADAKY DÖWLET KOMITETI

(State Committee for TV, Radio and Cinematography)
✉ Magtymguly köçesi 89, 744000 Aşgabat ☎ +993 12 351515
L.P: Chmn: Arslan Aşirow

LW	kHz	kW	Prgr
Aşgabat	279	150	1

FM (MHz)	1	2/3	4	kW
Arçabyl	102.3	-	100.3	4
Aşgabat	103.2	104.4	101.3	4
Atamyrat	102.8	-	100.3	4
Baharly	101.6	104.1	-	4
Balkanabat	100.4	101.9	103.9	1
Boldumsaz	105.6	106.9	104.0	4
Daşoguz	100.7	103.0	100.1	1
Magdanly	104.2	106.7	102.2	4
Mary	103.2	104.4	102.3	4
Türkmenabat	104.4	106.0	100.8	4
Türkmenbaşy	100.2	101.7	100.7	10
Uly Balkan Gerşi	-	-	103.0	4

+ translators
D.Prgr: Prgr 1 (Watan): 24h – **Prgr 2 (Çar tarapdan):** 0200-0400, 0700-0900, 1400-1700 – **Prgr 3 (Miras):** 0400-0700, 0900-1400, 1700-2300 – **Prgr 4 (Owaz):** 24h. N. in English 0000, Turkmen 0100, Russian 0200; continues in 3h cycles.

DAB Transmitters (DAB+)
Tx Operator: Ministry of Communications **M:** Watan, Çar tarapdan, Miras, Owaz **Txs:** Block 7B & 13B (Aşgabat 3.1kW)

TURKS & CAICOS ISLANDS (UK)

L.T: UTC -5h (14 Mar-7 Nov: -4h) — **Pop:** 39,000 — **Pr.L:** English — **E.C:** 120V/60Hz — **ITU:** TCA

RADIO TURKS & CAICOS (Gov. Comm.)

✉ Unit 8, Pond Breeze Plaza, Good Str., Grand Turk ☎ +1 649 946 2455 🖷 +1 649 946 1600 **W:** rtc89fm.com **L.P.:** Dir. Christopher Jarret
FM: 89.1MHz
D.Prgr: 24h Local prgr: 1100-0300; at other times relays country satellite stn.
Ann: "This is Radio Turks & Caicos on Grand Turk, Turks & Caicos Islands"

RADIO VICIÓN CRISTIANA (Rlg.)
✉ PO Box 2908, Paterson NJ 07509, USA ☎ +1 973 881 8700 **W:** radiovision.com **L.P.**: Mgr. Bob Rodríguez
MW: So. Caicos ‡530kHz 80kW **D.Prgr** in Spanish: relays WWRV 1330, NY **F.Pl.:** Currently inactive, back on air in 2021

WIV FM RADIO LTD (Comm.)
✉ WIV Building, Leeward Highway, Box 324, Providenciales ☎ +1 649 333 4487 **FM: Kiss FM** 102.5MHz 0.25kW (Light rock) – **Power 92** 92.5MHz 0.25kW (Hit music)

OTHER STATIONS (FM in MHz):
Abundant Life Ministries, Leeward Highway, PO Box 696, Cooper Jack Bay **W**: almi.tc **FM:** 98.3 0.5kW – **88 Jamz**, Princess Drive, Grace Bay, PO Box 865, Providenciales ☎ +1 649 946 8028 **W**: 88jamz.com **FM:** 88.7 0.1kW Freq leased from D&D Ewing – **Faith FM,** Rock of Jesus Ministry, Five Cays, Providenciales. **FM:** 98.9 0.25kW Freq leased from D&D Ewing. Format: Gospel – **Hope Radio**, A18 Millennium Highway, Blue Hills, Providenciales ☎ +1 649 331 2323 **W**: hoperadiotci.com FM 89.7 (0.5kW). Format: Gospel – **Island FM**, Pinnacle Broadc. Enterprises, 10 Woodland Str., Blue Hills, Providenciales ☎ +1 649 247 4487 **W**: islandfmtci.com **FM:** 93.9 0.35kW Format: Hits – **Life Radio-ZIBF,** Providenciales. **FM:** 103.5 0.5kW West Caicos-North Caicos & 105.5 0.5kW Middle Caicos-Grand Turk – **91Sun FM,** Sun Media, Airport Hotel Plaza, Airport Rd, PO Box 435, Providenciales. **FM:** 91.1 0.75kW Format: Urban AC – **Platinum Sounds Radio**, Blue Hills, Providenciales. **FM:** 88.5 0.5kW Format: R&B – **Radio Example of Christ**, PO Box 1095, Providenciales. **FM:** 95.1 0.5kW – **Radio VHTC**, PO Box 500, Melletus Plaza, Blue Hills, Providenciales. **FM:** 91.5 0.5kW – **Smooth FM**, Connolly Productions Co. Ltd., Tropicana Plaza, Leeward Highway, Providenciales. **FM:** 88.1 0.1kW – **Tropical Vibes**, Leeward Highway, Stubbs Rd, Providenciales. **FM:** 103.5 0.5kW Middle Caicos-Grand Turk & 105.5 0.05kW West Caicos-North Caicos – **Victory in Christ Radio - VIC 96.7FM**, Butterfield Square, PO Box 32, Providenciales. **FM:** 96.7 1kW.
Inactive: ‡88.3 (CGA), ‡90.5 (WIV), ‡96.9 (House of Rock)

TUVALU

L.T: UTC +12h — **Pop:** 11,000 — **Pr.L:** Tuvaluan (official), English (official) — **E.C:** 240V/50Hz — **ITU:** TUV

TUVALU MEDIA DEPARTMENT (Gov.)
✉ Private Mail Bag, Vaiaku, Funafuti ☎ +688 20139 🖷 + 688 20732 **L.P:** GM Melali Taape **Prgr Prod:** Ms Afasene Pese, Head of Tech. Sces: John Sammons
E: meltaape@govt.tv, apese@govt.tv
MW: Radio Tuvalu AM: 621kHz 5kW Funafuti (24h nationwide)
FM: Funafuti (local coverage) 100.1MHz 0.02kW
D.Prgr: 1830-2000, 2325-0100, 0625-1000 daily. **N. in English:** 1910, 0710 **Ann:** "This is Radio Tuvalu" **V.** by letter
BBC Pacific stream via satellite from London at other times: 2000-2325, 0100-0625, 1000-1830

UGANDA

L.T: UTC +3h — **Pop:** 46 million — **Pr.L:** Swahili (official), English (official), Luganda — **E.C:** 240V/50Hz — **ITU:** UGA

UGANDA COMMUNICATIONS COMMISSION (UCC)
✉ 12th Floor, Communications House, Plot 1, Colville Street, P. O. Box 7376, Kampala ☎+256 41 4339000 🖷 +256 41 4348832
W: ucc.co.ug **E:** ucc@ucc.co.ug

UGANDA BROADCASTING CORPORATION (UBC, Pub.)
✉ P.O. Box 2038, Plot 17-19, Nile Ave, Kampala ☎+256 41 4257034 🖷 + 256 41 4257252 **W:** ubc.ug **E:** customerservice@ubc.ug

FM (MHz)	UBC R.	West	Butebo	Star FM	Magic
Fort Portal	-	98.8	-	-	-
Hoima	-	99.1	-	-	-
Jinja	-	-	-	95.7	-
Kabale	-	93.7	-	-	-
Kampala	98.0	107.5	107.3	87.5	100.0
Kisoro	-	97.7	-	-	-
Lira	100.0	-	-	-	-
Masaka	-	99.5	-	96.9	-
Mbale	-	-	96.9	-	-
Mbarara	-	97.4	-	-	-
Masindi	-	105.0	-	-	-
Soroti	-	-	96.7	-	-

UBC R. in English, Swahili, Luo and Nubian: 24h – **UBC West** in 5 ethnic languages: 0300-2105 – **Butebo Channel** in 11 ethnic languages – **Star FM** in Luganda. **Magic FM** in English.
Buruli FM in 5 ethnic languages: Nakasongola 107.0MHz.
Mega FM in Luo/others: Gulu 102.1, Moro 103.1MHz 2kW.
Ngeya FM in 5 languages: Kasese 101.5MHz.
Vo Bundibugyo: Bundibugyo 93.3MHz.
West Nile FM: Arua 94.1MHz.

Other stations (FM MHz):
African R, Kampala: 104.5 – **All Karamoja FM,** Moroto: 94.7 – **Arua One FM,** Arua: 88.7 2kW – **Bamboo FM,** Jinja: 107.6 – **Basoga Bainho,** Jinja: 87.7 – **Beat FM,** Kampala: 96.3 – **Bob FM,** Kampala: 92.7 **W:** facebook.com/927BobFM – **Buddu BS,** Masaka: 98.8 – **Bukedde FM:** Kampala 100.5, Masaka 106.8 **W:** bukedde.co.ug – **Bunuyoro BS,** Masindi: 98.2 – **Busiro FM,** Kakiri: 107.5 – **Busoga FM,** Jinja: 96.0 – **Campus FM,** Kampala: 106.6 – **Capital FM:** Kampala 91.3, Mbale 90.9, Mbarara 88.7 – **City FM,** Kampala: 98.1 – **Continental FM,** Kumi: 94.7 – **Dembe FM,** Kampala: 90.4 **W:** dembefm.ug – **Dunamis FM,** Kampala: 103.0 – **East Africa R,** Kampala: 99 (cf. Tanzania) – **Eastern Voice,** Bugiri: 102.3 – **Elgon FM,** Kapchorwa 89.2 – **Etop R,** Soroti: 99.4 – **Eye FM,** Iganga: 98.8 – **Impact & Alpha FM**: Mbale 98.5, Masaka 101.5 1kW, Kampala 102.1 4kW. **W:** victoryuganda.org – **Juice FM,** Kampala: 103.4 **W:** facebook.com/1034-JUICE-FM-Sports-542359682519594 – **K FM,** Kampala: 93.3 **W:** kfm.co.ug – **Kaboozi R. Two,** Kampala: 87.9 **W:** akaboozi.fm – **Kibaale Community R:** 91.7 – **Kiira FM,** Jinja: 88.6 – **Kings R,** Masindi 88.2 – **Liberty FM,** Hoima 89.0 – **Maranatha FM,** Jinja: 104.7 – **Mbale FM**: 90.1 – **Nile BS,** Jinja: 89.4 – **Open Gate FM,** Mbale: 103.2 – **Power FM,** Kampala: 104.1 – **Prime R,** Kampala: 91.9 – **R FM,** Iganga: 91.1 **W:** rfm.co.ug – **R. Apac,** Apac 92.9 0.4kW, Odokomit 106.5 0.1kW **W:** radioapac.tripod.com – **R. Kitara,** Masindi: 101.8 – **Kyoga Veritas R,** Soroti: 91.5 1kW. **W:** facebook.com – **R. Lira,** Lira: 95.3 – **R. Mama,** Kampala: 101.7 **W:** interconnection.org/umwa/community_radio.html – **R. Maria Uganda,** Masaka 94 40W, Mbale 101.8, Kampala 103.7 40W, Fort Portal 104.6, Mbarara 105.4. **W:** radiomaria.org – **R. Onc,** Kampala: 90.0 – **R. Pacis,** Arua: 90.9/94.5 1kW. **W:** radiopacis.org – **R. Paidha,** Nebbi: 87.8 – **R. Rukungiri:** 96.9 – **R. Rupiny:** Kampala 95.7, Lira 98.1 **W:** visiongroup.co.ug – **R. Sapientia,** Kampala: 94.4 5kW. **W:** radiosapientia.com – **R. Simba,** Kampala: 97.3 **W:** simba.fm – **R. Skynet,** Mityana: 96.9 – **R. Unity,** Lira: 97.7 – **R. Wa,** Lira: 89.8 – **R. West FM:** Mbarara 102.2, Tooro 91.0, Kabale & Masak – **Rhino FM,** Lira: 96.1 – **Rock Mamba FM,** Tororo 106.8 – **Safari FM,** Mayuge 103.9 – **Sanyu FM,** Kampala 88.2 – **Speak FM,** Gulu 89.5 **W:** fowode.org – **Spirit FM,** Mukono: 96.6 – **Ssuubi FM,** Kampala 104.9, Masaka 88.1. **W:** ssuubifmradio.com – **Star FM,** Kampala: 100.0 – **Step FM,** Mbale: 99.8 – **Super FM,** Kampala: 88.5 – **Truth FM,** Mbale: 105.3 – **VO Africa:** Kampala 92.3 – **VO Kigezi,** Kabale 89.5 – **VO Life,** Arua: 100.9 **W:** vol-radio.net – **VO Teso,** Soroti: 88.4 – **Top R,** Kampala: 89.6 – **VO Toro,** Kampala 100.5, Fort Portal 101.0, Mbarara 95.0, Mubende 97.5 – **Touch FM,** Kampala: 95.9 1kW. **W:** touch.fm – **X FM:** Kampala: 94.8, Mbarara 96.6 **W:** xfm.co.ug

BBC African Sce: Arua 99.4, Kampala 101.3, Mbale/Mbarara 107.3MHz in English/Swahili/Kinyarwanda.
RFI Afrique: Kampala 93.7MHz in French/English/Swahili

UKRAINE

LL.T: UTC +2h (28 Mar-31 Oct: +3h); Crimea and Donets Basin (de facto): UTC +3h — **Pop:** 44 million — **Pr.L:** Ukrainian (official), Russian — **E.C:** 230V/50Hz — **ITU:** UKR

NATSIONALNA RADA UKRAINY Z PYTAN TELEBACHENNIA I RADIOMOVLENNIA
(National Council of Television and Radio Broadcasting in Ukraine)
✉ vul. Prorizna 2, 01001 Kyiv ☎ +380 44 2787575 🖷 +380 44 2787575 **E:** nrada@nrada.gov.ua **W:** nrada.gov.ua
L.P: Deputy Chair: Olha Herasymiuk

DERZHAVNYI KOMITET TELEBACHENNIA I RADIOMOVLENNIA UKRAINY (DERZHTELERADIO)
✉ vul. Prorizna 2, 01001 Kyiv ☎ +380 44 2785349 **E:** pr@comin.gov.ua **W:** comin.kmu.gov.ua **L.P:** Chmn: Oleh Nalyvaiko

NATSIONALNA SUSPILNA TELERADIOKOMPANIIA UKRAINY (NSTU) (Pub)

vul. Khreshchatyk 26, 01001 Kyiv ☎ +380 44 2396224 **E:** nrcu-zw@nrcu.gov.ua **W:** ukr.radio **L.P:** Chmn: Zurab Alasania

MW	kHz	kW	Prgr
Chasiv Yar	873	25	1

FM (MHz)	1*	2	3	kW
Andriivka	103.4w	101.2	105.7	5/2x0.1
Antopil	87.8r	103.0	66.52	1
Bakhmutivka	92.4	-	-	1
Balanivka	105.1u	-	71.93	1
Buky	106.9b	-	-	1
Cherkasy	91.4b	-	-	1
Chernivtsi	91.8c	105.0	67.97	0.25/2x1
Chonhar	100.7	102.6	-	5/1
Dnipro	87.5d	104.8	66.74	0.5/2x1
Hirnyk	90.7	95.3	102.6	1/2x0.5
Horokhiv	106.5v	105.2	-	1/0.1
Ivano-Frankivsk	100.4g	72.80	91.0	1/0.1
Izium	102.5g	106.5	-	0.25/0.1
Kamianets-Pod.	101.5k	-	102.8	0.1/1
Kamin-Kashyrskyi	105.8v	-	1	
Kharkiv	106.1h	100.5	91.6	2x1/0.1
Kherson	100.6i	88.1	71.90	1
Khmelnytskyi	104.6k	-	-	1
Kholmy	106.1a	68.27	101.2	0.5/1/0.2
Korosten	104.2w	94.1	-	2/0.25
Kostianynivka	98.6d	103.1	-	0.5/1
Krasnohorivka	106.3q	68.60	-	3/4
Kropyvnytskyi	91.2j	88.7	91.8	0.25/1/0.5
Kryvyi Rih	90.4d+e	98.7	69.56	0.1/0.5/1
Kulchiivtsi	70.76k	72.89	-	1
Kyiv	105.0l	97.2	97.6	5/1/0.5
Lozova	87.7t	71.75	-	0.25/1
Lviv	103.3n	102.5	67.04	1
Liubeshiv	107.8v	-	105.2	0.1/1
Lutsk	88.3v	107.3	101.9	1
Lysychansk	88.2	92.1	-	0.3/1
Mariupol	107.3g	103.2	69.44	0.25/0.5/1
Melitopol	107.7y	-	66.14	0.25/1
Mykolaiv	92.0o	88.8	100.1	0.5/2x1
Novohrad-Vol.	89.3	-	103.2	1/0.5
Odesa	91.4p	-	72.14	2/1
Olevsk	100.2w	69.80	101.9	2x1/0.1
Pervomaisk	105.9o	-	68.03	0.1/1
Pidhorivka	71.66	107.6	69.65	1/0.2/1
Podilsk	103.6p	-	69.35	0.5/1
Poltava	101.8q	100.0	89.5	2x1/0.5
Shostka	107.8s	67.49	-	1
Shyrokyi	100.4	106.5	106.9	5/2x1
Tokmak	90.2y	103.9	71.84	0.5/1/0.1
Trostianets	104.1s	69.92	-	0.5/1
Uzhhorod	107.2x	103.0	-	1/0.5
Vasylivka	105.8i	-	-	5
Vinnytsia	88.6u	100.3	100.9	0.5/2x1
Volnovakha	88.7d	96.5	-	1
Volochysk	68.72k	-	-	3
Zaporizhia	103.7y	106.2	87.8	2x1/0.5
Zarichne	103.8v	104.9	-	1
Zhashkiv	-	105.4	-	1

+ sites with only txs below 1kW. * Incl. reg prgrs (a-y, see below)
NB: The remaining OIRT FM freqs are being replaced by txs in the CCIR FM band.
D.Prgr: Prgr 1 (Ukrainske radio): 24h – **Prgr 2 (R. Promin):** 24h.– **Prgr 3 (R. Kultura):** 24h.

NSTU Regional Services

D.Prgr: 1010-1100, 1510-1600, 1810-1850 on FM freqs of Prgr 1 (exc. f+m - see below). **a) Chernihivska obl.:** pr. Peremohy 62, 14000 Chernihiv **E:** tvodtrk@ukr.net – **b) Cherkaska obl.:** vul. B.Vishnevetskoho 35/1, 18002 Cherkasy **E:** rosradio@ua.fm – **c) Chernivetska obl.:** vul. Holovna 91, 58001 Chernivtsi **E:** bukdtrk-net@ukr.net – **d+e) Dnipropetrovska obl.: d)** vul. Televiziina 3, 49010 Dnipro **E:** dodtrk@email.ua **e)** vul. Annenka 2, 50099 Kryvyi Rih **E:** kdt@kdtro.com.ua – **f) Donetska obl.:** vul. Shkadinova 48, 84313 Kramatorsk. **E:** dogtrk3@gmail.com. Reg: "Holos Donbasu" 24h on (MHz) 87.9 (Bakhmut 0.3kW), 88.0 (Bakhmutivka 0.3kW & Mariupol 0.2kW), 90.4 (Kramatorsk 0.2kW), 95.7 (Hirnyk 0.5kW), 100.3 (Volnovakha 0.1kW) – **g) Ivano-Frankivska obl.:** vul. Sichovykh striltsiv 30a, 76000 Ivano-Frankivsk **E:** ifodtrk@gmail.com – **h) Kharkivska obl.:** pl. Svobody 5, 61506 Kharkiv. **E:** oblradio_kharkiv@ukr.net – **i) Khersonska obl.:** vul. Perekopska 10, 73000 Kherson **E:** khersonodtrk@skifiya.ks.ua – **j) Kirovohradska obl.:** pl. Heroiv Maidanu 1, 25022 Kropyvnytskyi **E:** tvkirovograd@gmail.com – **k) Khmelnytska obl.:** vul. Volodymyrska 92, 29000 Khmelnytskyi **E:** office@odtrk.km.ua – **l) Kyivska obl.:** vul. Melnykova 42, 04119 Kyiv – **m) Luhanska obl.:** vul. Vilesova 1v, 93400 Severodonetsk. **E:** lgtrk@ukrpost.ua. Reg: "Puls FM" 0400-2000 on (MHz) 89.3 (Stantsia Luhanska 0.2kW), 96.2 (Bakhmutivka 1kW), 99.5 (Shyrokyi 1kW), 100.1 (Zorynivka 0.1kW), 100.6 (Pidhorivka 1kW), 101.9 (Bilolutsk 0.1kW), 102.1 (Troitske 0.25kW & Bilovodsk 0.25kW), 102.9 (Markivka 0.25kW), 103.5 (Sosnovyi 0.25kW), 105.9 (Lysychansk 1kW) – **n) Lvivska obl.:** vul. Vysokyi Zamok 4, 79008 Lviv **E:** lodtrk12@gmail.com – **o) Mykolaivska obl.:** pr. Tsentralyi 24-b, 54029 Mykolaiv **E:** mksuspilne@gmail.com – **p) Odeska obl.:** Fontanska doroha 3, 65963 Odesa **E:** odt@ukr.net – **q) Poltavska obl.:** vul. R.Kyrychenko 1, 36014 Poltava **E:** info@ltava.poltava.ua – **r) Rivnenska obl.:** vul. Kotliarevskoho 20-a, 33028 Rivne **E:** rodtrk@ukr.net – **s) Sumska obl.:** vul. Petropavlivska 125, 40030 Sumy **E:** trksumy@ukr.net – **t) Ternopilska obl.:** bul. T.Shevchenka 17, 46021 Ternopil **E:** todtrk@poshta.te.ua – **u) Vinnytska obl.:** vul. Teatralna 15, 21100 Vinnytsia **E:** trk_vintera@ukr.net – **v) Volynska obl.:** vul. Slovatskoho 9, 43025 Lutsk **E:** voltv.lutsk@gmail.com – **w) Zhytomyrska obl.:** vul. Liubarska 1a, 10014 Zhytomyr **E:** 103fm@ukr.net – **x) Zakarpatska obl.:** Kyivska nab. 18, 88018 Uzhhorod **E:** tisafm@gmail.com – **y) Zaporizka obl.:** vul. Matrosova 24, 69057 Zaporizhia **E:** zdtrk@zp.ukrtel.net.

ARMIA FM (Mil)

vul. Hrushevskoho 30/1, 01021 Kyiv ☎ +380 50 3049407 **E:** army-fm@ukr.net **W:** www.armyfm.com.ua

FM	MHz	kW	FM	MHz	kW
Bakhmutivka	90.8	1	Chonhar	103.0	1
Kyiv	94.6	1	Hirnyk	106.4	5
Vinnytsia	99.3	1	+ txs below 1kW.		

D.Prgr: 24h.

OTHER STATIONS

MW	kHz	kW	Location	Station
51)	648	25	Chonhar	Krym.Realii
FM	**MHz**	**kW**	**Location**	**Station**
30)	66.14	1	Khmelnytskyi	R. Emmanuil
12)	66.26	1	Lviv	R. Maria
30)	67.82	1	Lviv	R. Emmanuil
11)	68.36	2	Odesa	R. M
18)	69.02	1	Kyiv	Yaskave R.
30)	69.20	1	Kharkiv	R. Emmanuil
30)	69.26	1	Chernivtsi	R. Emmanuil
12)	69.68	1	Kyiv	R. Maria
30)	69.92	1	Zaporizhia	R. Emmanuil
12)	70.04	2	Andriivka	R. Maria
30)	70.79	1	Chernihiv	R. Emmanuil
12)	70.91	2	Vinnytsia	R. Maria
20)	70.97	4	Olevsk	Holos Nadii
18)	72.47	4	Vinnytsia	Yaskave R.
11)	87.5	1	Kramatorsk	R. M
41)	87.5	1	Odesa	Pershe R. FM1
6)	87.9	1	Odesa	R. NV
2E)	88.0	1	Kharkiv	Russkoye R. Ukraina
48)	88.4	1	Kyiv	Priamyi FM
1B)	88.5	1	Odesa	Retro FM
2C)	88.5	1	Dnipro	Relax FM
6)	88.6	1	Lviv	R. NV
2A)	89.0	1	Ternopil	Kiss FM
2F)	89.1	1	Lviv	R. Roks Ukraina
32)	89.6	1	Shatsk	Lvivska khvylia
4B)	89.7	1	Odesa	Europa Plus
2F)	90.2	1	Odesa	R. Roks Ukraina
2G)	90.3	1	Sumy	Nashe R.
32)	90.3	1	Liuboml	Lvivska khvylia
1A)	90.9	1	Dnipro	Avtoradio-Ukraina
27)	90.9	1	Kramatorsk	Hromadske R.
6)	90.9	1	Sumy	R. NV
2C)	91.0	1	Cherkasy	Relax FM
5)	91.0	1	Odesa	Kraina FM
1A)	91.1	1	Kryvyi Rih	Avtoradio-Ukraina
34)	91.2	2	Kharkiv	M-FM
1B)	91.3	1	Sumy	Retro FM
3A)	91.3	1	Vinnytsia	Power FM
1B)	91.5	1	Berdiansk	Retro FM
2B)	91.5	1	Lviv	Melodia FM
4A)	91.6	1	Kryvyi Rih	Lux FM

FM	MHz	kW	Location	Station
1B)	92.4	1	Kyiv	Retro FM
1C)	92.8	2	Kyiv	NRJ
3C)	93.8	1	Kyiv	Biznes-R.
4B)	94.2	1	Kyiv	Maximum FM
2B)	95.2	1.5	Kyiv	Melodia FM
1F)	95.6	2	Kyiv	Dzhem FM
6)	96.0	2	Kyiv	R. NV
2D)	96.4	2	Kyiv	Hit FM Ukraina
3D)	96.8	2	Kyiv	DJ FM
7)	97.0	1	Hirnyk	Stilnoye R. "Perets FM"
45)	98.0	1	Kyiv	Kyiv FM
8)	98.0	1	Karlivka	Tryzub FM
2E)	98.5	2	Kyiv	Russkoye R. Ukraina
6)	98.9	1	Nikopol	R. NV
38)	99.0	2	Kyiv	R. Nostalgie
1B)	99.1	1	Melitopol	Retro FM
1B)	99.1	1	Poltava	Retro FM
27)	99.4	1.5	Kyiv	Hromadske R.
4A)	99.4	1	Kherson	Lux FM
5)	100.0	4	Kyiv	Kraina FM
41)	100.2	2	Kamianske	Pershe R. FM1
5)	100.2	1	Kryvyi Rih	Kraina FM
5)	100.3	1	Zaporizhia	Kraina FM
29)	100.4	1	Odesa	Avtoradio-Odesa
4A)	100.5	1	Dnipro	Lux FM
4C)	100.5	2	Kyiv	R. Miami
1A)	100.6	1	Chernihiv	Avtoradio-Ukraina
33)	100.6	2	Korosten	Rekord FM
2G)	100.7	1	Antopil	Nashe R.
2D)	100.8	1	Mariupol	Hit FM Ukraina
2F)	100.8	1	Mykolaiv	R. Roks Ukraina
2F)	100.8	1	Zaporizhia	R. Roks Ukraina
32)	100.8	1	Lviv	Lvivska khvylia
1B)	100.9	1	Kremenchuk	Retro FM
46)	100.9	1	Lutsk	Avers FM
4A)	100.9	1	Vasylivka	Lux FM
16)	101.0	1	Horbkiv	R. Sokal
2D)	101.0	1	Odesa	Hit FM Ukraina
3B)	101.0	1	Kryvyi Rih	R. Shanson
4B)	101.0	1	Cherkasy	Maximum FM
1C)	101.1	1	Kharkiv	NRJ
1D)	101.1	3	Kyiv	R. Piatnytsia
2E)	101.1	1	Dnipro	Russkoye R. Ukraina
49)	101.1	1	Bakhmutivka	R. 49 paralel
2A)	101.2	1	Kherson	Kiss FM
4A)	101.2	1	Khmelnytskyi	Lux FM
6)	101.2	1	Melitopol	R. NV
2C)	101.3	1	Zhytomyr	Relax FM
7)	101.3	1	Poltava	Stilnoye R. "Perets FM"
10)	101.4	5	Chonhar	R. Meidan
1D)	101.4	1	Odesa	R. Piatnytsia
2B)	101.4	1	Sumy	Melodia FM
2C)	101.4	1	Antopil	Relax FM
7)	101.4	1	Kryvyi Rih	Stilnoye R. "Perets FM"
1B)	101.5	1	Kropyvnytskyi	Retro FM
1D)	101.5	1	Dnipro	R. Piatnytsia
2C)	101.5	4	Kyiv	Relax FM
2E)	101.5	1	Krasnohorivka	Russkoye R. Ukraina
7)	101.5	1	Kharkiv	Stilnoye R. "Perets FM"
13)	101.6	1	Kholmtsi	R. Versia
1C)	101.6	1	Cherkasy	NRJ
2A)	101.7	1	Mariupol	Kiss FM
2D)	101.7	1	Lviv	Hit FM Ukraina
2E)	101.7	1	Khmelnytskyi	Russkoye R. Ukraina
2E)	101.7	1	Zhytomyr	Russkoye R. Ukraina
2F)	101.7	1	Kramatorsk	R. Roks Ukraina
2A)	101.8	3	Odesa	Kiss FM
3B)	101.9	4	Kyiv	R. Shanson
7)	101.9	1	Kherson	Stilnoye R. "Perets FM"
28)	102.0	1	Pryluky	Halaktyka plius
2D)	102.0	2	Dnipro	Hit FM Ukraina
2A)	102.1	1	Mykolaiv	Kiss FM
4B)	102.1	1	Lviv	Maximum FM
43)	102.2	2	Odesa	R. Fil
2D)	102.3	1	Poltava	Hit FM Ukraina
2A)	102.4	1	Kharkiv	Kiss FM
2F)	102.4	1	Cherkasy	R. Roks Ukraina
4A)	102.4	1	Chernivtsi	Lux FM
5)	102.4	1	Kholmtsi	Kraina FM
2B)	102.5	1	Tokmak	Melodia FM
2C)	102.5	1	Khmelnytskyi	Relax FM
2D)	102.5	1	Kherson	Hit FM Ukraina
4A)	102.5	2	Kyiv	Prosto R.
1B)	102.6	1	Lubny	Retro FM
2D)	102.6	1	Vinnytsia	Hit FM Ukraina
36)	102.6	1	Kamianske	Hrad FM
2C)	102.7	1	Kovel	Relax FM
2G)	102.7	4	Kryvyi Rih	Nashe R.
2G)	102.7	1	Zhytomyr	Nashe R.
19)	102.8	1	Pryluky	R. Planeta
23)	102.8	1	Mariupol	Best FM
2G)	102.8	1	Mykolaiv	Nashe R.
2G)	102.9	1	Cherkasy	Nashe R.
2G)	102.9	3	Dnipro	Nashe R.
1D)	103.0	1	Kharkiv	R. Piatnytsia
2A)	103.1	1	Zaporizhia	Kiss FM
2G)	103.1	1	Khmelnytskyi	Nashe R.
3D)	103.1	1	Kherson	DJ FM
4A)	103.1	5	Kyiv	Lux FM
1C)	103.2	1	Kryvyi Rih	NRJ
1D)	103.2	1	Melitopol	R. Piatnytsia
4D)	103.2	2	Odesa	Narodnoye R.
3D)	103.3	1.2	Dnipro	DJ FM
6)	103.3	1	Cherkasy	R. NV
2D)	103.4	1	Sumy	Hit FM Ukraina
36)	103.4	2	Petrovirivka	Hrad FM
4B)	103.4	1	Dniprorudne	Maximum FM
2B)	103.5	1	Kremenchuk	Melodia FM
2F)	103.5	1	Ternopil	R. Roks Ukraina
2F)	103.6	1	Kyiv	R. Roks Ukraina
3A)	103.6	2	Kryvyi Rih	Power FM
15)	103.7	1	Vinnytsia	R. TAKT
2D)	103.7	1	Antopil	Hit FM Ukraina
2E)	103.7	1	Cherkasy	Russkoye R. Ukraina
6)	103.7	1	Kherson	R. NV
2E)	103.8	1	Kropyvnytskyi	Russkoye R. Ukraina
2G)	103.8	1	Poltava	Nashe R.
36)	103.8	3	Odesa	Hrad FM
4A)	103.8	1	Ivano-Frankivsk	Lux FM
21)	103.9	1	Kramatorsk	Klasne R.
2E)	103.9	1	Kremenchuk	Russkoye R. Ukraina
6)	103.9	1	Zhytomyr	R. NV
1A)	104.0	1	Mariupol	Avtoradio-Ukraina
3A)	104.0	1	Dnipro	Power FM
3A)	104.0	4	Kyiv	Power FM
4B)	104.0	2	Kharkiv	Maximum FM
2E)	104.1	1	Vinnytsia	Russkoye R. Ukraina
6)	104.1	1	Chonhar	R. NV
2B)	104.3	1	Polohy	Melodia FM
2G)	104.3	1	Chernihiv	Nashe R.
4A)	104.3	2	Odesa	Lux FM
9)	104.3	1	Lviv	Duzhe R.
1D)	104.4	1	Kherson	R. Piatnytsia
24)	104.4	1	Novovolynsk	R. Nova
35)	104.4	1	Kamianske	TopRadio
2B)	104.5	1	Cherkasy	Melodia FM
2G)	104.5	1	Kharkiv	Nashe R.
3B)	104.5	1	Zaporizhia	R. Shanson
4A)	104.5	1	Ternopil	Lux FM
2H)	104.6	2	Kyiv	R. Jazz
6)	104.6	1	Kropyvnytskyi	R. NV
2C)	104.7	1	Kryvyi Rih	Relax FM
2D)	104.7	1	Chernihiv	Hit FM Ukraina
3B)	104.7	1	Melitopol	R. Shanson
4A)	104.7	1	Lviv	Lux FM
6)	104.7	5	Hirnyk	R. NV
2E)	104.8	1	Kherson	Russkoye R. Ukraina
2E)	104.8	5	Shyrokyi	Russkoye R. Ukraine
2G)	104.8	1	Lutsk	Nashe R.
4A)	104.9	1	Zhytomyr	Prosto R.
3B)	105.0	1	Poltava	R. Shanson
1D)	105.1	1	Mykolaiv	R. Piatnytsia
2C)	105.1	1	Sumy	Relax FM
3A)	105.1	1	Zaporizhia	Power FM
50)	105.1	1	Balanivka	R. Lada
1B)	105.2	1	Krasnohorivka	Retro FM
4A)	105.2	1	Kharkiv	Lux FM
4A)	105.2	1	Uzhhorod	Lux FM
1B)	105.3	1	Shostka	Retro FM
2B)	105.3	1	Kamianets-Pod.	Melodia FM

FM	MHz	kW	Location	Station
2D)	105.3	1	Kropyvnytskyi	Hit FM Ukraina
2E)	105.3	1	Mariupol	Russkoye R. Ukraina
31)	105.3	1	Severodonetsk	STV
3B)	105.3	2	Dnipro	R. Shanson
4A)	105.3	4	Odesa	Prosto R.
2H)	105.4	1	Lviv	R. Jazz
40)	105.4	1	Khmelnytskyi	OK FM
4A)	105.4	1	Chernihiv	Lux FM
2C)	105.5	1	Lutsk	Relax FM
7)	105.5	2	Kyiv	Stilnoye R. "Perets FM"
2D)	105.6	1	Krasnohorivka	Hit FM Ukraina
2D)	105.6	1	Ternopil	Hit FM Ukraina
2E)	105.6	1	Sumy	Russkoye R. Ukraina
2G)	105.6	1	Zaporizhia	Nashe R.
3A)	105.7	1	Kharkiv	Power FM
2C)	105.8	1	Kropyvnytskyi	Relax FM
4A)	105.8	1	Dnipro	Prosto R.
4C)	105.8	1	Petrovirivka	R. Miami
7)	105.8	1	Mariupol	Stilnoye R. "Perets FM"
2E)	105.9	1	Kryvyi Rih	Russkoye R. Ukraina
51)	105.9	5	Chonhar	Krym.Realii
1G)	106.0	1	Kyiv	Lounge FM
22)	106.0	1	Berdiansk	Azovska khvylia
2E)	106.0	1	Hirnyk	Russkoye R. Ukraina
39)	106.0	1	Odesa	R. 106 FM
2B)	106.1	1	Ternopil	Melodia FM
4A)	106.1	1	Cherkasy	Lux FM
1B)	106.2	1	Bila Tserkva	Retro FM
2G)	106.2	1	Kherson	Nashe R.
7)	106.2	1	Kropyvnytskyi	Stilnoye R. "Perets FM"
2B)	106.3	1	Melitopol	Melodia FM
14)	106.4	2	Antopil	R. Trek
1A)	106.4	1	Ivano-Frankivsk	Avtoradio-Ukraina
2G)	106.4	1	Vinnytsia	Nashe R.
2A)	106.5	2	Kyiv	Kiss FM
2G)	106.5	1	Mariupol	Nashe R.
25)	106.6	1	Chernivtsi	Blysk FM
2D)	106.6	1	Zaporizhia	Hit FM Ukraina
44)	106.6	2	Odesa	R. Hlas
1B)	106.7	1	Kherson	Retro FM
3B)	106.7	1	Kropyvnytskyi	R. Shanson
17)	106.8	2	Debeslavtsi	R. Siaivo
2A)	106.8	3	Dnipro	Kiss FM
3B)	106.8	1	Chernihiv	R. Shanson
47)	106.8	1	Ternopil	Faine misto
2D)	106.9	1	Kryvyi Rih	Hit FM Ukraina
4A)	106.9	1	Lutsk	Lux FM
1B)	107.0	1	Zaporizhia	Retro FM
26)	107.0	1	Sumy	Diva-R.
2A)	107.0	1	Kramatorsk	Kiss FM
4B)	107.0	1	Kyiv	Europa Plus
4C)	107.0	1	Odesa	R. Miami
6)	107.0	1	Kharkiv	R. NV
32)	107.1	1	Zarichne	Lvivska khvylia
3A)	107.1	1	Cherkasy	Power FM
4A)	107.1	1	Mykolaiv	Lux FM
4C)	107.1	1	Izmail	R. Miami
2E)	107.2	1	Chernihiv	Russkoye R. Ukraina
42)	107.2	1	Lviv	R. Vrolos
37)	107.3	1	Dnipro	Informator FM
4B)	107.4	1	Odesa	Maximum FM
5)	107.4	1	Kharkiv	Kraina FM
6)	107.4	1	Kryvyi Rih	R. NV
2B)	107.5	1	Zaporizhia	Melodia FM
7)	107.5	1	Dubrovytsia	Stilnoye R. "Perets FM"
2F)	107.6	2	Kherson	R. Roks Ukraina
48)	107.6	1	Hirnyk	Priamyi FM
2F)	107.7	1	Chernihiv	R. Roks Ukraina
4B)	107.7	1	Dnipro	Maximum FM
6)	107.8	1.2	Mykolaiv	R. NV
1A)	107.9	1	Sumy	Avtoradio-Ukraina
2C)	107.9	1	Zaporizhia	Relax FM
2G)	107.9	1	Kropyvnytskyi	Nashe R.
2G)	107.9	5	Kyiv	Nashe R.
2G)	107.9	1	Odesa	Nashe R.

+ txs below 1kW.

Addresses & other information:
1A-G) vul. Kyrylivska 108a, 04080 Kyiv – **2A-H)** vul. V.Khvoiky 15/15, 04655 Kyiv – **3A-D)** b-r T.Shevchenka 54/1, 01032 Kyiv – **4A-D)** vul. O.Shmidta 6, 04107 Kyiv– **5)** vul. Saksahanskoho 91, 01032 Kyiv – **6)** pr-t Povitrianoflotskyi 54, 03151 Kyiv – **7)** vul. Dovzhenka 14, 03057 Kyiv – **8)** vul. Evenyhorodska 5-40, 69093 Zaporizhia – **9)** vul. Horbachevskoho 16, 79000 Lviv – **10)** vul. Syretska 33b, 04073 Kyiv – **11)** vul. Marshala Vasylevskoho 14-5, 84116 Sloviansk – **12)** vul. Sribnokilska 8, 02095 Kyiv – **13)** vul. Erdeli 1, 88018 Uzhhorod – **14)** vul. Kavkazka 2, 33013 Rivne – **15)** vul. Soborna 59, 21050 Vinnytsia – **16)** vul. Sichovykh striltsiv 18, 80000 Sokal – **17)** vul. Sichovykh striltsiv 23, 78200 Kolomyia – **18)** b-r L. Ukrayinky 3, 01133 Kyiv – **19)** vul. Piriatynska 129, 17500 Pryluky – **20)** vul. Lukianivska 9/10a, 041074 Kyiv – **21)** vul. Soborna 56a, 64309 Izium – **22)** Melitopolske shose 20, 77108 Berdiansk – **23)** vul. Chernyshevskoho 15, 61057 Kharkiv – **24)** pr-t Druzhby 27, 45400 Novovolynsk – **25)** vul. Eminesku 2, 58000 Chernivtsi – **26)** vul. Kharkivska 5, 40024 Sumy – **27)** vul. Holosiivska 7, 03039 Kyiv – **28)** vul. Piriatynska 129, 17500 Pryluky – **29)** vul. Kanatna 83, 65107 Odesa – **30)** vul. Velyka Vasylivska 131a, 03150 Kyiv – **31)** vul. Haharina 93, 93400 Severodonetsk – **32)** vul. Hutsulska 9a, 79008 Lviv – **33)** vul. Rylskoho 9, 10014 Zhytomyr – **34)** vul. Petrovskoho 3, 61002 Kharkiv – **35)** vul. Vasylia Stusa 15b, 51900 Kamianske – **36)** vul. Balkivska 120/1, 65005 Odesa – **37)** vul. Koltsova 8, 49000 Dnipro – **38)** vul. Y.Konovaltsiia 32a, 01133 Kyiv – **39)** vul. Zaslavskoho 10/12, 65004 Odesa – **40)** pr-t Miru 69, 29000 Khmelnytskyi – **41)** vul. Balkivska 120/1, 65005 Odesa – **42)** vul. Pidvalna 3, 79008 Lviv – **43)** vul. Troitska 50, 65045 Odesa – **44)** vul. Kanatna 83, 65107 Odesa – **45)** vul. Khreshchatyk 44, 01044 Kyiv – **46)** vul. Elektroaparatna 3, 43026 Lutsk – **47)** vul. Sichovykh striltsiv 1, 46001 Ternopil – **48)** vul. Mechynkova 2a, 01601 Kyiv – **49)** Obolonskyi pr. 16e-214, 04205 Kyiv – **50)** vul. Protsyshyna 45-91, 24321 Ladyshkyn – **51)** vul. Khreshchatyk 19a, 01001 Kyiv **E:** krym_redaktor@rferl.org.

DAB Transmitters (DAB+) (Trial)
Tx Operator: Concern RRT **M:** Ukrainske radio, R. Promin, R. Kultura, R. Meidan, R. Maria, Armia FM, Bisnes-R., Priamyi FM **Txs:** Block 1D (Kyiv 2kW).

DONETS BASIN

(Self-proclaimed "Donetsk People's Rep." and "Luhansk People's Rep.")

Territory controlled by "Donetsk People's Republic" (DPR)

RADIO RESPUBLIKA (Gov*) (* Run by the "DPR" administration)
✉ vul. Kuibysheva 61, 83016 Donetsk (de facto: ul. Kuybysheva 61, 283016 Donetsk, DNR ☎ +380 62 3028245 **E:** dnr.tv@yandex.ru **W:** vk.com/radio_respublica
FM: Donetsk 99.0MHz (0.5kW).
D.Prgr: R. Respublika 24h in Russian, incl. rel. Vesti FM (Russia).

OTHER STATIONS

FM	MHz	kW	Location	Station
	100.0	1	Donetsk	R. Stolitsa
	104.7	1	Donetsk	Russkoye R.*
	105.1	2	Donetsk	DFM*
	106.8	3	Donetsk	R. Novorossiya - Roks

+ txs below 1kW. *) Relays from Russia

Territory controlled by "Luhansk People's Republic" (LPR)

GTRK LNR (Gov*) (* Run by the "LPR" administration)
✉ vul. Demokhina 25, 91016 Luhansk (de facto: ul. Demekhina 25, 291016 Lugansk, LNR ☎ +380 642 585552 **E:** gtrk.lnr@mail.gtrklnr.com **W:** gtrklnr.com

FM (MHz)	**1**	**2**	**3**	**4**	**kW**
Luhansk	106.9	103.6	104.8	107.9	1

+ sites with txs below 1kW.
D.Prgr: Prgr 1 (R. Pobyeda) 24h in Russian – **Prgr 2 (Svoye R.)** 24h in Russian – **Prgr 3 (R. Respublika):** 24h in Russian – **Prgr 4 (Vesti Plyus):** 24h in Russian, incl. rel. Vesti FM (Russia)

OTHER STATIONS

FM	MHz	kW	Location	Station
	106.5	1	Luhansk	R. Sputnik relay*

+ txs below 1kW. *) Relay from Russia

CRIMEA

(under Russian administration)

L.T: UTC +3h — **Pop:** 2.4 million — **Pr.L:** Russian, Ukrainian, Crimean Tatar

UPRAVLENIYE ROSKOMNADZORA PO RESPUBLIKE KRYM I G. SEVASTOPOL
✉ 295034 Simferopol, ul. Moskovskaya 12 ☎ +7 3652 669293 **E:**

rsockanc82@rkn.gov.ru **W:** 82.rkn.gov.ru **L.P:** Head: Viktoriya Dunayeva

VSEROSSIYSKAYA GOSUDARSTVENNAYA TELEVIZIONNAYA I RADIOVESHCHATELNAYA KOMPANIYA (VGTRK) (Gov)
Contact details see under "Russia"

FM	MHz	kW	Prgr	FM	MHz	kW	Prgr
Simferopol	87.5	1	VFM	Krasnoperekopsk	102.6	1	VFM
Sevastopol	*90.8	1	VFM	Belogorsk	105.9	1	VFM
Kerch	91.6	1	VFM	+ txs below 1kW *) Incl reg prgrs			

D.Prgr: Vesti FM (VFM): see under "Russia".

VGTRK Regional Services
GTRK "Sevastopol": 299011 Sevastopol, ul. Lenina 3. **E:** radio@vesti92.ru **Reg:** On Sevastopol 90.8MHz.
GTRK "Vesti-Krym": 295001 Simferopol, ul. Studencheskaya 14. **E:** vesticrimea@vesti-k.ru.

TELERADIOKOMPANIYA "KRYM" (Gov)
295001 Simferopol, ul. Studencheskaya 14 ☎ +7 3652 788444 **E:** tv@tv.crimea.ru **W:** 1tvcrimea.ru **L.P:** DG: Yekaterina Kozyr

FM (MHz)	1	2	kW	FM	1	2	kW
Dzhankoy	107.9	105.9	1	Sevastopol	91.3	90.4	1/0.5
Chapayevka	101.5	104.9	1	Simferopol	100.1	100.6	1
Kerch	88.5	100.3	1/0.1	Sol. Ozero	90.8	107.8	1
Krasnoperekopsk	101.4	105.0	1	+ sites with only txs below 1kW.			

D.Prgr: Prgr 1 (R. Krym): 24h – **Prgr 2 (R. Morye):** 24h.

OBSHCHESTVENNAYA KRYMSKOTATARSKAYA TELERADIOKOMPANIYA (OKTT) (Pub)
295011 Simferopol, ul. Kozlova 45a ☎ +7 978 9809009 **E:** ok_trk@mail.ru **W:** trkmillet.ru **L.P:** DG: Ervin Musayev

FM	MHz	kW	FM	MHz	kW
Simferopol	99.5	1	Sol. Ozero	105.9	1
Chapayevka	102.5	1	Krasnoperekopsk	107.0	1

+ txs below 1kW.
D.Prgr: Vatan Sedasi 24h in Crimean Tatar, Russian.

OTHER STATIONS

FM	MHz	kW	Location	Station
224)	87.7	1	Dzhankoy	R. Sputnik v Krymu
21)	88.3	1	Sevastopol	R. Zvedzda
27)	89.1	1	Sevastopol	R. Dacha
21)	89.2	1	Kerch	R. Zvezda
15)	92.3	1	Simferopol	DFM
5)	96.2	1	Simferopol	Hit FM
21)	98.3	1	Simferopol	R. Zvezda
224)	100.7	1	Belogorsk	R. Sputnik v Krymu
224)	100.7	1	Sol. Ozero	R. Sputnik v Krymu
4)	101.4	1	Kerch	Europa plus
225)	102.0	1	Sevastopol	Sevastopol FM
16)	102.2	1	Kerch	Retro FM
224)	102.3	1	Simferopol	R. Sputnik v Krymu
16)	103.9	1	Yevpatoriya	Retro FM
62)	104.3	1	Simferopol	Kazak FM
224)	105.6	1	Sevastopol	R. Sputnik v Krymu
10)	107.0	1	Sevastopol	R. 7

+ txs below 1kW.
Addresses & other information:
Contact details see "Other Stations" chart under "Russia" (stn numbers refer to that chart) **224)** 299011 Sevastopol, 4-ya Bastionnaya ul. – **225)** 295005 Simferopol, ul. Sevastopolskaya 8.

Radio via DTT: see National TV section

UNITED ARAB EMIRATES

L.T: UTC +4h — **Pop:** 10 million — **Pr.L:** Arabic — **E.C:** 220V/50Hz — **ITU:** UAE

NATIONAL MEDIA COUNCIL (NMC)
P.O.Box 3790, Abu Dhabi ☎ +971 2 4044333 🖷 +971 2 4450408 **E:** info@nmcuae.ae **W:** nmc.gov.ae
L.P: Chmn: Sultan bin Ahmad Sultan Al Jaber

ABU DHABI MEDIA (Gov)
4th St, Sector 18, Zone 1, Abu Dhabi ☎+971 2 4144000 🖷 +971 2 4144001 **W:** adradio.ae **L.P:** CEO: Ahmed Ali Mohamed Al Bloushi. Dir. Radio: Jaber Obaid. Head R&TV Eng: Mahmood Al-Redha.
FM (MHz):
Abu Dhabi R.: Ras al-Khaimah 89.7, Abu Dhabi 90.0, Jabal Al-Dhanna 97.3, Dubai 98.4, Habshan 100.1, Liwa 103.7, Fujairah 106.0.
Classic FM (in English): Dubai 87.9. Abu Dhabi 91.6, Al-Ain 105.2
Emarat FM: 24h on FM (MHz): Ras al-Khaimah 88.5, Jabal al-Dhanna 92.4, Al-Ain 94.9, Abu Dhabi 95.8, Liwa 95.6, Dubai 97.1, Habshan 98.4, Fujairah 103.9
Quran R: 24h on FM (MHz) Jabel Dhana 87.7, Dubai 88.2, Al-Ain 88.6, Habshan 88.8, Liwa 89.3, Abu Dhabi 98.1, Ras al-Khaimah 105.2
R. Mirchi (in Hindi/English): Dubai/Sharjah 88.8, Al-Ain 95.6, Abu Dhabi 97.3
Star FM: Abu Dhabi 92.4, Dubai 99.9. Al-Ain 100.1
Radio 1 (in English): Abu Dhabi 100.5, Dubai 104.1
Radio 2 (in English): Abu Dhabi 106.1, Dubai 99.3

PRAVASI BHARATHI (Comm)
P.O. Box 77914, Two Four 54, Media Zone Authority, Abu Dhabi ☎+971 2 3043 818 **W:** pravasibharathi.com **L.P:** GM: K. Chandrasenan.
MW: Al-Dhabbaya 810kHz. **D.Prgr** in Malayalam: 0100-2010 200 kW AM & 2010-0100 50 kW DRM.

RAS AL-KHAIMAH BROADCASTING STATION (Gov)
RAK Media, P.O. Box 141, Ras al Khaimah **W:** facebook.com/rak1035fm **RAK FM** (Arabic): 103.5MHz 20kW. **Quran R:** 87.6MHz.

SHARJAH MEDIA CORPORATION (Gov)
P.O. Box 111, Sharjah ☎+971 6 566 1111 🖷 +971 6 566 9999 **W:** smc.ae **E:** info@smc.ae
R. Sharjah in Arabic: Sharjah 94.4, Abu Dhabi 96.3, Al-Ain 107.6, Kalba 107.7MHz. **Quran R:** Sharjah 102.7MHz.

UMM AL-QUWAIN BROADCASTING NETWORK (Gov)
P.O. Box 1106, King Faisal St, Umm al Quwain **W:** ubn.ae **E:** admin@ubn.ae
MW: Holy Quran R: 846kHz 20kW 24h.
FM: R. Hala: 95.6MHz in Arabic **W:** radiohala.com – **Dance FM**: 97.8MHz in English **W:** dancefm.com – **Jio FM,** Umm al Quwain: 100.3MHz **W:** facebook.com/JioFMUAE **Big FM**: 106.2MHz in Hindi/Urdu. **W:** bigfm.ae – **R. Gilli**: 106.5MHz **W:** radiogilli.com – **Heart FM**: 107.1MHz in English **W:** iheartuae.com

ARABIAN RADIO NETWORK (ARN) (Comm)
P.O. Box 502255, CNN Bldg, Media City 103, Dubai ☎+971 4 3912000 🖷 +971 4 3912007 **W:** arn.ae **E:** amghrteam@arabmediagroup.ae
FM: Tag 91.1: 91.1MHz in Filipino – **Dubai 92:** 92.0MHz 5kW in Arabic&English – **Fujairah FM:** 92.6MHz 2kW – **R. Shoma:** 93.4MHz in Farsi – **Hit FM:** 96.7MHz 5kW in English – **Zayed Quran R.:** Fujairah 97.6MHz 2kW – **Al-Arabiya:** 99.0MHz 10kW – **Al-Khaleejiya:** 100.9MHz 5kW – **City FM:** 101.6MHz 5kW in Hindi – **Dubai Eye:** 103.8MHz 5kW in English – **Virgin R:** Dubai 104.4MHz 30kW – **R. Spice:** Fujairah 105.4MHz 1kW

DUBAI MEDIA INCORPORATED (DMI) (Gov)
W: dmi.ae **Dubai FM:** 93.0MHz. **Noor Dubai:** 93.9MHz 5kW.

CHANNEL 4 RADIO NETWORK (Comm)
P.O Box 442, Ajman ☎+971 6 746 1444 **W:** ch4.ae
FM: all in Ajman. **R. 4 FM:** 89.1MHz 1kW in Hindi – **Channel 4 FM:** 104.8MHz 1kW in English – **Gold FM:** 101.3MHz in Malayalam – **Al Rabia FM**: 107.8MHz 1kW in Arabic – **Avtoradio FM:** 90.8MHz in Russian **W:** autoradio.ae

MBC FM & PANORAMA FM (Comm)
P.O. Box 75335, MBC Building, Media City, Dubai ☎+971 4 3919713 🖷 +971 4 3916683 **W:** mbc.net/ar/panorama-fm **E:** contactus@mbc.ae
L.P: Dir: Hassan Muawad. **FM:** Txs in Bahrain, Iraq, Jordan, Kuwait, Qatar, Saudi Arabia, Sudan and Palestine West Bank.

Other Sations:
A-Oula FM, Dubai: 107.4MHz **W:** aloularadio.ae – **Club FM,** Dubai: 99.6MHz in Malayalam **W:** clubfm.ae – **Dubai Holy Quran,** Dubai: 91.4MHz **W:** dubaiholyquran.ae – **Pearl FM,** Dubai: 102.0MHz **W:** pearlfm.ae – **Pulse FM**, Sharjah: 95.0MHz in English **W:** pulse95radio.com – **R. Asia**, Ras al-Khaimah: 94.7 in Malayalam **W:**

radioasiauae.com – **Sky News Arabia:** Abu Dhabi 90.3, Dubai 90.5 **W:** skynewsarabia.com – **Sowt al-Khaleej**, Abu Dhabi: 105.2MHz. See Qatar for main entry – **Suno FM**, Dubai: 102.4MHz in Hindi/Urdu **W:** suno1024.com – **Tamil FM**, Dubai: 89.4MHz **W:** tamil894fm.com

Monte Carlo Doualiya: Ras al-Khaimah 95.3MHz

UNITED KINGDOM

L.T: UTC (28 Mar-31 Oct: +1h) — **Pop:** 67 million — **Pr.L:** English (official), Welsh — **E.C:** 230V/50Hz — **ITU:** G — **Int.Dialing Code:** +44

CROWN DEPENDENCIES: The **Channel Islands** and the **Isle of Man** are dependencies of the British Crown and are not part of the United Kingdom. They are included here for editorial convenience.

OFFICE OF COMMUNICATIONS (Ofcom) (Regulatory Authority)

Riverside House, 2A Southwark Bridge Rd, London SE1 9HA ☎20 7981 3040 20 7981 3333 **W:** ofcom.org.uk

BRITISH BROADCASTING CORPORATION (Pub)

The BBC is an independent body created by Royal Charter and operates under licence.
Broadcasting House, Portland Place, London W1A 1AA ☎ 20 7580 4468 **W:** bbc.co.uk **LP:** DG: Tim Davie; CEO BBC Studios: Tom Fussell; Chief Content Off: Charlotte Moore; Dir Nations & Regions: Ken MacQuarrie; Dir Radio & Education: James Purnell; Dir News & Current Affairs: Fran Unsworth.

LW/MW:

Radio 4	kHz	kW	Radio 4	kHz	kW
Burghead	198	50	Crystal Palace	720	0.8
Westerglen	198	50	Redruth	756	2
Droitwich	198	500	Enniskillen	774	1
Newcastle	603	2	Plymouth	774	1
Londonderry	720	0.3	Redmoss	1449	2
Lisnagarvey	720	10	Carlisle	1485	1

Radio 5 Live	kHz	kW	Radio 5 Live	kHz	kW
Barrow	693	1	Brookmans Park	909	150
Brighton	693	1	Clevedon	909	50
Burghead	693	25	Exeter	909	1
Droitwich	693	150	Fareham	909	1
Enniskillen	693	1	Lisnagarvey	909	10
Folkestone	693	1	Londonderry	909	1
Postwick	693	10	Moorside Edge	909	200
Redmoss	693	1	Redruth	909	2
Stagshaw	693	50	Westerglen	909	50
Start Point	693	50	Whitehaven	909	1
Bexhill	693	1	Tywyn	990	1
Bournemouth	909	0.3			

England, Isle of Man, Channel Is FM (all stereo)

FM	R1	R2	R3	R4	kW
Barnstaple	98.1	88.5	90.7	92.9	1
Beacon Hill	98.4	88.7	90.9	93.1	1
Belmont	98.3	88.8	90.9	93.1	16
Bilsdale	98.6	89.0	91.2	93.4	5
Bow Brickhill	98.2	88.6	90.8	93.0	10
Bristol	98.9	89.3	91.5	93.7	1.3
Chatton	99.7	90.1	92.3	94.5	5.6
Crystal Palace	98.5	88.8	91.0	93.2	4
Douglas (I.O.M.)	98.0	88.4	90.6	92.8	11
Guildford	97.7	88.1	90.3	92.5	3
Caversham	99.4	89.8	92.0	94.2	1
Holme Moss	98.9	89.3	91.5	93.7	250
Keighley	98.5	88.9	91.1	93.3	1
Les Platons (C.I.)	97.1	89.6	91.1	94.8	16
Manningtree	97.7	88.1	90.3	92.5	5
Morecambe Bay	99.6	90.0	92.2	94.4	10
North Hessary Tor	97.7	88.1	90.3	92.5	160
Oxford	99.1	89.5	91.7	93.9	46
Pendle Forest	97.8	90.2	92.6	94.6	1
Peterborough	99.7	90.1	92.3	94.5	40
Pontop Pike	98.1	88.5	90.7	92.9	134
Redruth	99.3	89.7	91.9	94.1	25
Ridge Hill	98.2	88.6	90.8	93.0	10
Rowridge	98.2	88.5	90.7	92.9	250
Sandale	97.7	88.1	90.3	92.5	250
Stanton Moor	99.4	89.8	92.0	94.2	1.2
Sutton Coldfield	97.9	88.3	90.5	92.7	250
Swingate (Dover)	99.5	90.0	92.4	94.4	11
Tacolneston	99.3	89.7	91.9	94.1	250
Winter Hill	98.2	88.6	90.8	93.0	4
Woolmoor	99.6	90.2	92.2	94.4	5
Wrotham	*98.8	89.1	91.3	93.5*	125/250

+ 74 low power txs less than 1kW

STATIONS: Radio 1: New music for youth audience 24h **N:** Newsbeat M-F 1245, 1745 – **Radio 1Xtra** (digital only) – **Radio 2:** Adult contemporary and specialist music: 24h **N:** on the h – **Radio 3:** Classical music, jazz, world music, arts: 24h **N:** 0700, 0800, 0900(SS), 1300, 1700(MF), 1800(MF) – **Radio 4:** News, documentaries, drama, entertainment; cricket on LW/MW in season: 0520-0100; relays BBCWS 0100-0520 **N:** 0530, then on the h (not 1000 Sun, 1100 Sun, 1500 Sat) – **Radio 4Extra** (digital only) – **Radio 5 Live:** News & sport: 24h **N:** on the h and half h – **Radio 6 Music:** New and archive music: 24h (digital only)

BBC LOCAL RADIO

MW	Station	Location	kHz	kW
11)	Essex	Manningtree	729	0.2
15)	Hereford & Worcs	Worcester	738	0.4
8)	R. Cumbria	Carlisle	756	1
11)	Essex	Chelmsford	765	0.5
20)	R. Leeds	Farnley	774	0.5
10)	R. Devon	Barnstaple	801	2
8)	R. Cumbria	Barrow	837	1
19)	R. Lancashire	Preston	855	1
26)	R. Norfolk	West Lynn	873	0.3
10)	R. Devon	Exeter	990	1
4)	R. Cambridgeshire	Chesterton Fen	1026	0.5
17)	R. Jersey	Trinity	1026	1
31)	R. Sheffield	Sheffield	1035	1
9)	R. Derby	Burnaston Lane	1116	1
14)	R. Guernsey	Rohais	1116	0.5
12)	R. Gloucestershire	Berkeley Heath	1413	0.5
12)	R. Gloucestershire	Bourton-on-the-Water	1413	0.5
34)	R. Stoke	Sideway	1503	1
3a)	R. Somerset	Taunton	1566	1
15)	Hereford & Worcs.	Woofferton	1584	0.3

FM	Station	Location	MHz	kW
31)	R. Sheffield	Sheffield	88.6	0.3
17)	R. Jersey	Les Platons	88.8	3.8
1)	Three Counties R.	Epping Green	90.4	0.1
20)	R. Leeds	Holme Moss	92.4	5.6
14)	R. Guernsey	Les Touillets	93.2	1
34)	R. Stoke	Alsagers Bank	94.6	6.1
2)	R. Berkshire	Henley	94.6	0.25
15)	Hereford & Worcs.	Ridge Hill	94.7	2
1)	Three Counties R.	Aylesbury	94.7	0.2
31)	R. Sheffield	Chesterfield	94.7	0.4
7)	CWR (Coventry & Warks)	Meriden	94.8	2.2
10)	R. Devon	Huntshaw Cross	94.8	0.675
24)	R. London	Crystal Palace	94.9	4
3)	R. Bristol	Dundry Lane	94.9	0.5
22)	R. Lincolnshire	Belmont	94.9	6
30)	R. Sussex	Newhaven	95.0	0.1
5)	R. Tees	Bilsdale	95.0	10
12)	R. Gloucestershire	Stroud	95.0	0.1
13)	R. Manchester	Holme Moss	95.1	5.6
28)	R. Nottingham	Newark	95.1	0.2
26)	R. Norfolk	Stoke Holy Cross	95.1	4
6)	R. Cornwall	Caradon Hill	95.2	4.3
8)	R. Cumbria	Kendal	95.2	0.1
29)	R. Oxford	Beckley	95.2	5.8
11)	Essex	South Benfleet	95.3	1.2
30)	R. Sussex	Brighton	95.3	1.2
9)	R. Derby	Stanton Moor	95.3	1.2
20)	R. Leeds	Luddenden	95.3	0.083
2)	R. Berkshire	Windsor	95.4	0.5

FM	Station	Location	MHz	kW
25)	R. Newcastle	Pontop Pike	95.4	10
1)	Three Counties R.	Sandy Heath	95.5	1
3a)	R. Somerset	Mendip	95.5	9
19)	R. Lancashire	Hameldon Hill	95.5	1.6
28)	R. Nottingham	Mansfield	95.5	2
35)	R. Suffolk	Lowestoft	95.5	2
37)	R. York	Olivers Mount	95.5	0.25
26)	R. Norfolk	West Runton	95.6	2
8)	R. Cumbria	Sandale	95.6	15
38)	R. WM (West Midlands)	Sutton Coldfield	95.6	11
4)	R. Cambridgeshire	Peterborough	95.7	5.1
10)	R. Devon	Plymouth	95.7	1
23)	R. Merseyside	Allerton Park	95.8	8
5)	R. Tees	Whitby	95.8	0.1
10)	R. Devon	Exeter	95.8	0.4
35)	R. Suffolk	Aldeburgh	95.9	2
16)	R. Humberside	High Hunsley	95.9	9.6
4)	R. Cambridgeshire	Cambridge	96.0	1
9)	R. Derby	Buxton	96.0	1.5
32)	R. Shropshire	The Wrekin	96.0	4.8
25)	R. Newcastle	Chatton	96.0	5.6
8)	R. Cumbria	Morecambe Bay	96.1	3.2
33)	R. Solent	Rowridge	96.1	10
18)	R. Kent	Wrotham	96.7	8.7
18)	R. Kent	Folkestone	97.6	0.1
1)	Three Counties R.	High Wycombe	98.0	0.2
20)	R. Leeds	Keighley	102.7	0.5
10)	R. Devon	North Hessary Tor	103.4	15
11)	Essex	Great Braxted	103.5	12
36)	R. Wiltshire	Salisbury	103.5	1
3)	R. Bristol	Weston-S-Mare	103.6	0.1
36)	R. Wiltshire	Swindon	103.6	0.5
27)	R. Northampton	Geddington	103.6	0.8
7)	CWR (Coventry & Warks)	Lark Stoke	103.7	1.4
37)	R. York	Acklam Wold	103.7	2
25)	R. Newcastle	Hexham	103.7	0.1
1)	Three Counties R.	Zouches Farm	103.8	0.5
28)	R. Nottingham	Mapperley Ridge	103.8	1
33)	R. Solent (Dorset)	Bincombe Hill	103.8	0.5
6)	R. Cornwall	Redruth	103.9	18
19)	R. Lancashire	Winter Hill	103.9	2
20)	R. Leeds	Beecroft Hill	103.9	0.1
35)	R. Suffolk	Manningtree	103.9	5
15)	Hereford & Worcester	Great Malvern	104.0	2
30a)	R. Surrey	Reigate	104.0	3.8
8)	R. Cumbria	Whitehaven	104.1	1
31)	R. Sheffield	Holme Moss	104.1	4.4
34)	R. Stoke	Stafford	104.1	0.075
2)	R. Berkshire	Hannington	104.1	3
18)	R. Kent	Swingate	104.2	10
27)	R. Northampton	Northampton	104.2	4
36)	R. Wiltshire	Naish Hill	104.3	0.6
10)	R. Devon	Beacon Hill	104.3	1
37)	R. York	Woolmoor	104.3	0.5
2)	R. Berkshire	Reading	104.4	1
26)	R. Norfolk	Great Massingham	104.4	4.2
15)	Hereford & Worcester	Redditch	104.4	0.1
30)	R. Sussex	Heathfield	104.5	10
1)	Three Counties R.	Bow Brickhill	104.5	2.2
9)	R. Derby	Drum Hill	104.5	5.4
19)	R. Lancashire	Lancaster	104.5	2
13)	R. Manchester	Saddleworth	104.6	0.1
15)	Hereford & Worcester	Kidderminster	104.6	0.5
30a)	R. Surrey	Guildford	104.6	3
3)	R. Bristol	Bath	104.6	0.082
35)	R. Suffolk	Great Barton	104.6	2
12)	R. Gloucestershire	Churchdown Hill	104.7	2
30)	R. Sussex	Burton Down	104.8	2
21)	R. Leicester	Copt Oak	104.9	8
36)	R. Wiltshire	Marlborough	104.9	0.1

+ 15 low power txs less than 0.1kW

Addresses and other information:
1) Unit 4 Grove Park, Court Drive, Dunstable LU5 4GP ☎1582 636900 **E:** threecounties@bbc.co.uk – **2)** 550 Thames Valley Park Drive, Reading RG6 1PT ☎118 9464200 **E:** radio.berkshire.news@bbc.co.uk – **3)** Whiteladies Rd, Bristol BS8 2LR ☎117 9741111 **E:** radio.bristol@bbc.co.uk **3a)** Broadcasting House, Park Street, Taunton TA1 4DA ☎1823 323956 **E:** somerset@bbc.co.uk – **4)** Cambridge Business Park, Cowley Rd, Cambridge CB4 0WZ ☎1223 259696 **E:** cambs@bbc.co.uk– **5)** Broadcasting House, Newport Rd, Middlesbrough TSI 5JA ☎1642 225211 **E:** tees.studios@bbc.co.uk– **6)** Phoenix Wharf, Truro TR1 1UA ☎1872 275421 **E:** radio.cornwall@bbc.co.uk – **7)** Priory Place, Coventry CV1 5SQ ☎24 76551000 **E:** coventry.warwickshire@bbc.co.uk– **8)** Annetwell Street, Carlisle CA3 8BB ☎1228 592444 **E:** radio.cumbria@bbc.co.uk – **9)** 56 St Helen's Street, Derby DE1 3HY ☎1332 361111 **E:** radio.derby@bbc.co.uk – **10)** Seymour Rd., Plymouth PL3 5BD ☎1752 260323 **E:** radio.devon@bbc.co.uk – **11)** PO Box 765, Chelmsford CM2 9XB ☎1245 616000 **E:** essex@bbc.co.uk– **12)** London Rd, Gloucester GL1 1SW ☎1452 308585 **E:** radio.gloucestershire@bbc.co.uk – **13)** Quay House, BBC Media City UK, Salford M50 2QH ☎161 335 6000 **E:** radio.manchester@bbc.co.uk – **14)** Bulwer Ave, St Sampson, Guernsey GY2 4LA ☎ 1481 200600 **E:** bbcguernsey@bbc.co.uk – **15)** Hylton Rd, Worcester WR2 5WW ☎1905 748485 **E:** bbchw@bbc.co.uk and 43 Broad Street, Hereford HR4 9HH ☎1432 355255 – **16)** Queens Court, Queens Gardens, Hull HU1 3RH ☎1482 323232 **E:** radio.humberside@bbc.co.uk – **17)** 18-21 Parade Rd, St. Helier, Jersey JE2 3PL ☎1534 870000 **E:** radiojersey@bbc.co.uk – **18)** The Great Hall, Mount Pleasant Rd, Tunbridge Wells TN1 1QQ ☎1892 670000 **E:** radio.kent@bbc.co.uk – **19)** 20-26 Darwen Street, Blackburn BB2 2EA ☎1254 262411 **E:** radio.lancashire@bbc.co.uk – **20)** 2 St Peters Square, Leeds LS9 8AH ☎113 244 2131 **E:** radioleeds@bbc.co.uk – **21)** 9 St Nicholas Place, Leicester LE1 5LB ☎116 251 6688 **E:** radioleicester@bbc.co.uk – **22)** Radion Buildings, Newport, Lincoln LN1 3XY ☎1522 511411 **E:** radio.lincolnshire@bbc.co.uk – **23)** 31 College Lane, Liverpool L1 3DS ☎151 708 6161 **E:** radio.merseyside@bbc.co.uk – **24)** Egton Wing, Broadcasting House, Portland Place, London W1A 1AA ☎20 8743 8000 **E:** yourlondon@bbc.co.uk – **25)** Broadcasting Centre, Barrack Rd, Newcastle-Upon-Tyne NE99 1RN ☎191 222 4141 **E:** bbcnewcastle@bbc.co.uk – **26)** The Forum, Millennium Plain, Norwich NR2 1BH ☎1603 619331 **E:** norfolk@bbc.co.uk – **27)** Broadcasting House, Abington Street, Northampton NN1 2BH ☎1604 239100 **E:** northamptonshire@bbc.co.uk – **28)** London Rd, Nottingham NG2 4UU ☎115 955 0500 **E:** radio.nottingham@bbc.co.uk – **29)** 269 Banbury Rd, Oxford OX2 7DW ☎8459 311444 **E:** oxford@bbc.co.uk – **30)** Broadcasting House, 40 42 Queen's Rd, Brighton BN1 3XB **E:** sussex@bbc.co.uk – **30a)** Broadcasting Centre, Guildford GU2 7AP ☎1483 306306 **E:** surrey@bbc.co.uk – **31)** 54 Shoreham Street, Sheffield S1 4RS ☎114 2731177 **E:** radio.sheffield@bbc.co.uk – **32)** 2-4 Boscobel Drive, Shrewsbury SY1 3TT ☎1743 248484 **E:** shropshire@bbc.co.uk – **33)** Broadcasting House, 10 Havelock Rd, Southampton SO14 7PW ☎23 8063 1311 **E:** radio.solent@bbc.co.uk – **34)** Cheapside, Hanley, Stoke-on-Trent ST1 1JJ ☎01782 08080 **E:** radio.stoke@bbc.co.uk– **35)** Broadcasting House, St. Matthew's Street, Ipswich IP1 3EP ☎1473 250000 **E:** radiosuffolk@bbc.co.uk– **36)** 56-58 Prospect Place, Swindon SN1 3RW ☎ 1793 513626 **E:** wiltshire@bbc.co.uk – **37)** 20 Bootham Row, York Y030 7BR ☎1904 641 351 **E:** northyorkshire.news@bbc.co.uk – **38)** The Mailbox, Wharfside Street, Birmingham B1 1AY ☎121 567 6767 **E:** radio.wm@bbc.co.uk

D.Prgr: Stns generally carry local or regional prgrs from 0600-0100, then BBC Radio 5 Live overnight

BBC SCOTLAND

40 Pacific Quay, Glasgow G51 1DA ☎ 141 422 6000
W: bbc.co.uk/radioscotland

MW: R. Scotland:

Location	kHz	kW	Location	kHz	kW
Burghead	810	100	Westerglen	810	100

D.Prgr: R.Scotland 0600-0100. Rel. BBC R. 5 overnight

FM stereo	R1	R2	R3	R4	RS/L	kW
Ashkirk	98.7	89.1	91.3	103.9	93.5f	50
Ben Gullipen	98.3	88.7	90.9	104.9	93.1	1
Black Hill	99.5	89.9	92.1	95.8	94.3	250/200
Bressay	97.9	88.3	90.5	94.9	92.7ac	43
Clettraval	97.7	88.1	90.3	95.1	92.5d	2
Daliburgh	98.9	89.3	91.5	95.9	93.7d	1
Darvel	99.1	89.5	91.7	104.3	93.9	10
Durris	99.0	89.4	91.6	95.9	93.8a	2.1
Eitshal	99.4	89.8	92.0	95.1	94.2d	2
Forfar	97.9	88.3	90.5	94.9	92.7	17
Fort William	98.9	89.3	91.5	95.9	93.7d	3
Glengorm	99.1	89.5	91.7	96.1	93.9d	5

FM stereo	R1	R2	R3	R4	RS/L	kW
Keelylang Hill	98.9	89.3	91.5	96.0	93.7ab	41
Kirkton Mailer	98.6	89.0	91.2	94.6	93.4	1
Meldrum	98.3	88.7	90.9	95.3	93.1a	150
Melvaig	98.7	89.1	91.3	95.7	93.5d	50
Oban	98.5	88.9	91.1	95.3	93.3d	3.6
Rosemarkie	99.2	89.6	91.8	103.6	94.0d	20
Rumster Forest	99.7	90.1	92.3	95.6	94.5d	10
Sandale	97.7	88.1	90.3	92.5	94.7e	250
Skriaig	98.1	88.5	90.7	94.8	92.9d	30
So. Knapdale	98.9	89.3	91.5	95.6	93.7	2.2

+ 32 low power txs less than 1kW
RS/L=R. Scotland + local news – a) RS: Aberdeen – b) RS: Orkney – c) RS: Shetland – d) RS: Inverness – e) RS: Dumfries – f) RS: Selkirk.

Local Services (FM only). Freqs as above.
a) Beechgrove Terrace, Aberdeen AB15 5ZT. M-F: 0630, 0730, 0830, 1230, 1630, 1730. **W:** bbc.co.uk/northeastscotland – **b)** Castle Str, Kirkwall, Orkney KW15 1DF: M-F 0730-0800, Fri 1810-1900 – **c)** Pitt Lane, Lerwick, Shetland ZE1 0DW: M-F 1730-1800, Fri 1810-1900 – **d)** 7 Culduthel Rd, Inverness IV2 4AD M-F: 0630, 0730, 0830, 1230, 1630, 1730 – **e)** Elmbank, Lovers Walk, Dumfries DG1 1NZ: M-F: 0630, 0730, 0830, 1230, 1630, 1730. **W:** bbc.co.uk/southscotland – **f)** Ettrick Riverside, Dunsdale Rd, Selkirk TD7 5EB M-F 0630, 0730, 0830, 1230, 1630, 1730

BBC RADIO NAN GAIDHEAL

✉ 54 Seaforth Rd., Stornoway HS1 2SD ☎ 1851 705000 **E:** stornoway@bbc.co.uk **W:** bbc.co.uk/radionangaidheal

FM	MHz	kW	FM	MHz	kW
Glengorm	103.5	5	Meldrum	104.2	150
Clettraval	103.7	2	Eitshal	104.3	2
So. Knapdale	103.7	2.2	Kirkton Mailer	104.5	1
Forfar	103.7	17	Rumster Forest	104.5	10
Melvaig	103.9	50	Oban	104.6	3.6
Craigkelly	104.1	5	Black Hill	104.7	10
Daliburgh	104.2	1	Skriaig	104.7	30
Fort William	104.2	3	Rosemarkie	104.9	20

+ 16 low power txs less than 1kW
D.Prgr: Own prgrs in Gaelic and relays of BBC R. Scotland

BBC CYMRU WALES

✉ Central Square, Cardiff CF10 1FS
☎ 29 2032 2000 🖷 29 2055 5960
E: radiowales@bbc.co.uk **W:** bbc.co.uk/radiowales

MW: R. Wales:

Location	kHz	kW	Location	kHz	kW
Wrexham	657	2	Washford	882	100
Penmon	882	10			

FM stereo	R1	R2	R3	R4	kW
Blaenplwyf	98.3	88.7	90.9	104.0	250
Carmel	98.0	88.4	90.6	92.8	2.5
Haverfordwest	98.9	89.3	91.5	104.9	20
Kilvey Hill	99.1	89.5	91.7	94.6	1
Llanddona	99.4	89.8	92.0	103.6	21
Llandrindod Wells	98.7	89.1	-	103.8	2.8
Llangollen	98.5	88.9	-	93.3	15.6
Wenvoe	99.5	89.9	92.1	94.3	250

FM stereo	R. Wales	R. Cymru	kW
Blaenplwyf	95.3	93.1	250/120
Carmel	95.1	104.6	3/3.2
Haverfordwest	95.9	93.7	20
Kilvey Hill	93.9	104.2	1
Llanddona	94.8	94.2	21/10
Llandrindod Wells	91.3	93.5	2.8
Llangollen	91.9	104.3	15.6
Wenvoe	103.9	-	40
Wenvoe	-	96.8	250

+ 42 low power txs less than 1kW
D.Prgr: R. Wales: 0600-0100. Rel. BBC R5 overnight. **R. Cymru:** 0530-0000. Rel. BBC World Service overnight

BBC NORTHERN IRELAND

✉ Broadcasting House, 25-27 Ormeau Avenue, Belfast BT2 8HQ ☎ 28 9033 8000 🖷 28 9032 6453 **W:** bbc.co.uk/radioulster

MW: R. Ulster:

Location	kHz	kW	Location	kHz	kW
Enniskillen	873	1	Lisnagarvey	1341	100

FM stereo	R1	R2	R3	R4	R. Ulster	kW
Brougher Mntn	99.0	89.4	91.6	95.6	93.8	9.8
Camlough	98.3	88.7	90.9	104.6	93.1	4
Divis	99.7	90.1	92.3	96.0	94.5	250/125
Limavady	99.2	89.6	91.8	94.0	95.4	3.4
Londonderry	98.3	88.7	90.9	94.9	93.1h	31/10

+ 5 low power txs of less than 1kW – h) **R. Foyle** (see below)
D.Prgr: MF 0630(SaSu0700)-0000. Other times rel. BBC R5

BBC RADIO FOYLE

✉ 8 Northland Rd, Londonderry BT48 7GD ☎ 28 7137 8600 **W:** bbc.co.uk/radiofoyle **E:** radio.foyle@bbc.co.uk
MW: Londonderry 792kHz 1kW **FM:** 93.1MHz 31kW
D.Prgr: 24h. Own prgs. and relay BBC R. Ulster. Local N. M-F hourly 0700-1700

BBC ASIAN NETWORK

✉ The Mailbox, Birmingham B1 1RF **E:** asiannetwork.enquiries@bbc.co.uk **W:** bbc.co.uk/asiannetwork

MW	kHz	kW	MW	kHz	kW
Sedgley	828	0.2	Gunthorpe	1449	0.15
Freemen's Common	837	0.5	Langley Mill	1458	5

D.Prgr: 24h mainly in English.
BBC Asian Network relays

MW	kHz	kW
R. Leeds[a]	774	0.7

NB: [a]) Mon-Fri 1900-2200. Local Asian prog. also carried on some BBC local radio stns at various times.

EXTERNAL SERVICE: BBC World Service

See International Broadcasting section

ARQIVA

✉ Crawley Court, Winchester SO21 2QA ☎1962 823434
W: arqiva.com Operates most BBC domestic and many commercial radio tx sites.

DIGITAL RADIO (DAB/DAB+): DAB trs are on Band 3. **National Multiplexes: BBC (DAB)** On Block 12B, 225.648MHz: BBC Radios 1, 1Xtra, 2, 3, 4, 4 Extra, 5 Live, 5 Live Sports Extra, 6 Music, Asian Network and World Service. **Digital One (DAB/DAB+) W:** arqiva.com - In England, Wales & Northern Ireland on Block 11D, 222.064MHz; in Scotland on Block 12A, 223.936MHz.: Absolute, Capital, Capital Xtra, Capital Xtra Reloaded, Classic FM, Gold, Heart Dance, Heart UK, Heart 70s, Heart 80s, Heart 90s, Kiss, Kisstory, LBC, LBC News, Magic, Radio X, Smooth, Smooth Chill, TalkSport, UCB 1. **Sound Digital (Digital Two) (DAB/DAB+): W:** sounddigital.co.uk On Block 11A, 216.928MHz: Absolute 80s, Absolute 90s, BFBS UK, Fun Kids, Jack, Jazz, Love Sport, Mellow Magic, Planet Rock, Premier Christian, Premier Praise, Scala, Sunrise, TalkRadio, TalkSport 2, Times, UCB 2, Union Jack, Virgin, Virgin Anthems, Virgin Chilled. **Local Multiplexes:** Aberdeen (11C), Ayr (11B), Birmingham (11C), Bournemouth (11B), Bradford & Huddersfield (11B), Bristol & Bath (11B), Cambridge (11C), Cardiff & Newport (12C), Central Lancashire (12A), Central Scotland (11D), Cornwall (11B), Coventry (12D), Derbyshire (10B), Dundee & Perth (11B), Edinburgh (12D), Exeter & Torbay (11C), Glasgow (11C), Gloucestershire (10C), Greater London I (12C), Greater London II (12A), Greater London III (12B), Hereford & Worcester (12A), Herts, Beds & Bucks (10D), Humberside (10D), Inverness (11B), Kent (11C), Leeds (12D), Leicester (11B), Lincolnshire (12A), Liverpool (10C), Manchester (12C), Mid & W Wales (12D), NE Wales & W Cheshire (10D), Northampton (10C), North Devon (12C), North Yorkshire (10C), Northern Ireland (12D), Norwich (10B), Nottingham (12C), Oxford (10B), Peterborough (12D), Plymouth (12D), Reading & Basingstoke (12D), Somerset (10B), Southend & Chelmsford (12D), South Hampshire (11C), South Yorkshire (11C), Stoke-on-Trent (12D), Suffolk (10C), Surrey (10C), Sussex (10C), Swansea (12A), Swindon (11C), Teesside (11B), Tyne & Wear (11C), West Wiltshire (10D), Wolverhampton/Shrewsbury & Telford (11B), **Small scale test multiplexes (mostly DAB+)**: Aldershot (8A), Birmingham (9A), Brighton (9A), Bristol (9A), Cambridge (7D), Glasgow (10B), London (9A), Manchester (10B), Norwich (9A), Portsmouth (7D).

RADIOCENTRE

✉ 6th Floor, 55 New Oxford St. London W1A 1BS ☎20 7010 0600

W: radiocentre.org - Radiocentre represents commercial radio to Government, Ofcom, Copyright Societies and other organisations concerned with radio.

NATIONAL COMMERCIAL STATIONS:

ABSOLUTE RADIO

✉ 1 Golden Square, London W1F 9DJ ☎20 7434 1215 📠20 7434 1197 **W:** absoluteradio.co.uk

MW	kHz	kW	MW	kHz	kW
Bournemouth	1197	0.25	Norwich	1215	1.2
Brighton	1197	1.1	Washford	1215	50
Trowell	1197	0.5	Westerglen	1215	50
Gloucester	1197	0.3	Wrekenton	1215	2.2
Oxford	1197	0.25	Kings Heath	1233	0.5
Brookmans Pk.	1215	62.5	Manningtree	1233	0.5
Dartford Tunnel	1215	0.004	Boston	1242	2
Droitwich	1215	52.5	Sideway	1242	0.5
Fareham	1215	1	Stockton	1242	1
Lisnagarvey	1215	16	Lydd	1260	1
Moorside Edge	1215	50			

D.Prgr: 24h (rock & contemporary music). **N:** on the h
FM: London (Crystal Palace) 105.8MHz 4kW

CAPITAL FM

✉ 30 Leicester Square, London WC2H 7LA ☎ 20 7054 8000 **W:** capitalfm.com

FM	MHz	kW	Location	FM	MHz	kW	Location
33)	95.8	4	London	49)	105.1	3.1	Emley Moor
69)	96.2	1	Nottingham	36)	105.3	8.4	Burnhope
116)	96.2	0.1	Coventry	69)	105.4	5	Leicester
100)	96.3	1.25	Llandudno	49)	105.6	0.5	Bradford
45)	96.3	0.1	Chorley	49)	105.6	0.25	Sheffield
100)	97.1	1	Wirral	122)	105.7	10	Edinburgh
42)	97.4	0.5	Newport	36)	105.8	0.2	Hexham
45)	99.8	0.75	Burnley	49)	105.8	9.6	Hull
116)	102.0	2.6	Stratford	122)	106.1	20	Glasgow
45)	102.0	0.5	Manchester	36)	106.4	10	Bilsdale
9)	102.2	1	Birmingham	45)	106.5	0.1	Preston
116)	102.4	0.1	Burton	45)	107.0	0.5	Blackburn
69)	102.8	0.9	Derby	116)	107.1	0.1	Rugby
100)	103.0	5	Caernarfon	43)	107.2	0.2	Brighton
42)	103.2	2	Cardiff	116)	107.3	0.2	Warwick
43)	103.2	2	Southampton	17)	107.6	0.4	Liverpool
100)	103.4	1.4	Wrexham	116)	107.6	0.2	Banbury

NB: Numbers refer to regional studio addresses - see list below

CLASSIC FM

✉ 30 Leicester Square, London WC2H 7LA ☎ 20 7343 9000 **W:** classicfm.com

FM	MHz	kW	FM	MHz	kW
Cumbria	99.9	250	Blaen Plwyf	101.1	10
No.Hessary Tor	100.0	160	Holme Moss	101.1	250
Angus	100.1	10	Darvel	101.3	8
Sutton Coldfield	100.1	250	Oxford	101.3	46
Bath	100.2	0.2	Swansea	101.3	1
Douglas I.O.M.	100.2	1	Bristol	101.4	0.2
Rowridge	100.3	250	Inverness	101.4	11
Bradford	100.3	0.5	Tacolneston	101.5	250
Pontop Pike	100.3	130	Redruth	101.5	10
Milton Keynes	100.4	10	Gt. Ormes Hd	101.6	2.5
Ridge Hill	100.4	5	Bilsdale	101.6	2
Belmont	100.5	6	Leeds	101.6	0.5
Londonderry	100.5	31	Black Hill	101.7	250
Meldrum	100.5	150	Sheffield	101.7	0.5
Preseli	100.5	7	Wenvoe	101.7	250
Crystal Pal.	100.6	2	Dover	101.8	5
Arfon	100.7	19	Morecambe Bay	101.8	6
Swindon	100.8	0.7	Reading	101.8	0.5
Selkirk	100.9	10	Brighton	101.9	0.4
Wrotham	100.9	250	Divis	101.9	250
Fenham	101.0	0.1	Peterborough	101.9	35

D.Prgr: 24h **N:** on the h

GREATEST HITS RADIO

✉ Castle Quay, Castlefield, Manchester M15 4PR ☎161 288 5000 **W:** planetradio.co.uk/greatest-hits

MW	kHz	kW	Location	MW	kHz	kW	Location
56)	828	0.12	Leeds	51)	1170	0.32	Stockton
56)	990	0.25	Doncaster	51)	1170	0.2	Stoke-on-Trent
51)	999	0.28	Preston	56)	1278	0.43	Bradford
127)	1170	0.58	Swansea	56)	1530	0.74	Huddersfield
51)	1152	1.5	Manchester	53)	1305	0.15	Barnsley
61)	1152	1.8	Newcastle	53)	1548	0.74	Sheffield

FM	MHz	kW	Location	FM	MHz	kW	Location
107)	96.0	0.125	Bridport	50)	103.4	2	Lowestoft
56)	96.1	0.2	Rotherham	56)	103.5	0.2	Northallerton
56)	96.3	2.5	Leeds	56)	104.7	2.5	York
107)	96.2	1	Aylesbury	34)	105.2	11	Sutton Coldfield
50)	96.2	2.6	N. Norfolk	84)	105.5	1.6	Torbay
56)	96.2	0.625	Scarborough	84)	105.6	0.4	Yeovil
56)	96.3	2.5	Leeds	107)	105.6	0.1	Newbury
107)	96.4	3	Guildford	52)	105.9	7.5	Liverpool
56)	96.4	0.1	Grimsby	107)	106.0	4	Solent
51)	96.5	0.4	Blackpool	107)	106.4	0.1	Andover
107)	96.6	0.1	Blandford	34)	106.5	0.5	Shrewsbury
107)	96.6	0.4	Chichester	107)	106.6	0.3	Poole
50)	96.7	3	King's Lynn	84)	106.6	0.25	Chard
107)	97.1	0.275	Haslemere	107)	106.6	0.4	Midhurst
107)	97.2	0.7	Weymouth	56)	106.8	0.5	Wakefield
56)	97.2	1	Harrogate	107)	107.0	0.2	Reading
107)	97.4	0.125	Shaftesbury	56)	107.1	0.5	Doncaster
50)	97.4	0.24	Southwold	56)	107.1	0.1	Ilkley&Pateley
54)	99.8	0.75	Hull	34)	107.1	0.1	Oswestry
50)	99.9	0.5	Norwich	52)	107.2	0.18	Warrington
50)	100.2	2	Clacton-on-Sea	34)	107.2	0.2	Oakham
84)	100.8	0.13	Porlock	84)	107.2	0.66	Bristol
107)	101.6	0.1	Alton	34)	107.2	0.2	Kidderminster
107)	101.8	0.11	Petersfield	84)	107.3	0.1	Bridgwater
56)	102.0	0.45	Barnsley	56)	107.4	0.2	Chesterfield
56)	102.0	0.1	Matlock	34)	107.4	0.1	Telford
107)	102.0	1.25	Salisbury	51)	107.3	0.18	Bolton
107)	102.0	0.1	Alton	84)	107.5	0.1	Cheltenham
107)	102.3	0.5	Littlehampton	84)	107.5	0.1	Warminster
56)	102.3	0.1	Thirsk	107)	107.6	0.1	Basingstoke
84)	102.4	4	Minehead	84)	107.7	0.2	Swindon
56)	102.4	0.1	Bridlington	84)	107.7	0.1	Weston-S-Mare
52)	102.4	0.1	Wigan	34)	107.7	0.17	Wolverhampton
56)	102.8	1	Skipton	56)	107.8	1	Skipton
56)	103.1	0.12	Whitby	56)	107.9	0.1	Worksop
50)	103.2	0.25	N.Norfolk	84)	107.9	0.2	Bath

Note: Local prgs Mon-Fri 1600-1900
Numbers refer to regional studio address - see list below.

HEART

✉ 30 Leicester Square, London WC2H 7LA ☎20 7766 6000 **W:** heart.co.uk

FM	MHz	kW	Location	FM	MHz	kW	Location
100)	88.0	1.4	Wrexham	72)	97.5	0.1	Southend
43)	95.9	0.3	Thanet	72)	97.6	1	Luton
43)	96.1	0.2	Ashford	122)	100.3	20	Black Hill
72)	96.1	0.5	Colchester	86)	100.5	0.3	Totnes
86)	96.2	2.5	N. Devon	34)	100.7	11	Birmingham
86)	96.3	2	Bristol	36)	100.7	10	Bilsdale
72)	96.3	1	Southend	86)	100.8	0.1	Dartmouth
86)	96.4	1.6	Torbay	122)	101.1	10	Edinburgh
72)	96.4	2	Bury St.Eds	122)	101.1	0.2	Rosneath
86)	96.5	0.1	Taunton	36)	101.2	0.2	Hexham
72)	96.6	4	Northampton	86)	101.2	1.25	Kingsbridge
23)	96.6	0.5	Watford	72)	101.7	0.1	Harlow
43)	96.7	0.5	Winchester	36)	101.8	8.5	Burnhope
72)	96.9	0.8	Bedford	86)	101.9	0.5	Ivybridge
43)	96.9	0.1	Newhaven	43)	102.0	0.2	Hastings
45)	96.9	3.2	Morecambe	86)	102.2	0.5	W. Wiltshire
43)	97.0	0.5	Dover	42)	102.3	0.5	Pontypridd
86)	97.0	1	Exeter	43)	102.3	2	Bournemouth
43)	97.0	1	Reading	43)	102.4	8.2	Eastbourne
86)	97.0	2	Plymouth	86)	102.4	2	Gloucester
86)	97.1	0.2	W. Somerset	72)	102.4	3.3	Norwich
72)	97.1	3.4	Ipswich	72)	102.6	2	Chelmsford
86)	97.2	0.7	Swindon	43)	102.6	9	Oxford
86)	97.3	0.1	Ilfracombe	86)	102.6	4	Mendip
43)	97.4	0.3	Banbury	43)	102.7	3.6	Reigate
43)	97.5	0.85	Portsmouth	72)	102.7	4	Peterborough

FM	MHz	kW	Location	FM	MHz	kW	Location
43)	102.8	1	Dunkirk	42)	105.7	9.4	Preseli
100)	102.8	0.2	Long Mountain	100)	105.7	1.3	Llandudno
43)	102.9	3.4	Hannington	42)	105.9	1	Newport
72)	103.0	1	Cambridge	42)	106.0	1	Swansea
86)	103.0	1	Stockland Hl	49)	106.2	3.1	Emley Moor
86)	103.0	0.1	Stroud	42)	106.2	0.5	Fishguard
86)	103.0	0.1	W-S-Mare	33)	106.2	4	London
43)	103.1	4	Maidstone	23)	106.7	0.1	Stevenage
45)	103.2	0.1	Kendal	100)	106.9	0.4	Meol-y-Parc
122)	103.3	0.5	Penicuik	23)	106.9	0.1	Hertford
72)	103.3	2	Milton Keynes	86)	107.0	11	W. Cornwall
43)	103.4	0.1	Henley-on-Th	100)	107.2	3.1	Arfon
43)	103.5	1	Brighton	100)	107.3	0.15	Bargoed
86)	105.1	2.5	E.Cornwall	49)	107.6	0.2	Bradford
42)	105.2	3	Carmel	100)	107.7	10.3	Blaenplwyf
45)	105.4	5	Winter Hill	49)	107.7	0.2	Sheffield
42)	105.4	5	Cardiff				

D.Prgr: 24h **N:** on the h (Numbers refer to regional address - see list below)

SMOOTH RADIO

30 Leicester Square, London WC2H 7LA ☎20 7766 6000 **W:** smoothradio.com

MW	kHz	kW	Location	MW	kHz	kW	Location
43)	603	0.4	Littlebourne	72)	1170	0.28	Ipswich
86)	774	0.14	Gloucester	43)	1170	0.12	Portsmouth
72)	792	0.28	Bedford	43)	1242	0.32	Maidstone
43)	828	0.27	Bournemouth	72)	1251	0.76	Bury St.Eds.
72)	828	0.2	Luton	100)	1260	0.64	Wrexham
86)	936	0.18	Naish Hill	43)	1323	0.5	Brighton
43)	945	0.7	Bexhill	72)	1359	0.28	Chelmsford
72)	1152	0.83	Norwich	72)	1431	0.35	S'thend-on-Sea
86)	1152	0.32	Plymouth	43)	1557	0.5	Southampton
86)	1161	0.16	Swindon				

FM		MHz	kW	FM		MHz	kW
36)	Newton	96.4	0.2	33)	Croydon	102.2	4
69)	Wellingboro'	97.2	0.12	122)	Glasgow	105.2	30
36)	Burnhope	97.5	9	9)	Sutton Cldfld	105.7	11
45)	Kendal	100.1	0.2	69)	Waltham	106.6	10.8
45)	Winter Hill	100.4	5	69)	Peterborough	106.8	0.2
45)	Windermere	100.8	0.12	69)	Kettering	107.4	0.2
45)	Keswick	101.4	0.1	36)	Eston Nab	107.7	5
69)	Derby	101.4	0.2				

D.Prgr: 24h (Numbers refer to regional studio address - see list below)

TALKSPORT

18 Hatfields, London SE1 8DJ ☎20 7959 7800 20 7959 7808 **W:** talksport.com

MW	kHz	kW	MW	kHz	kW
Bournemouth	1053	1	Brookmans Pk	1089	400
Brighton	1053	2	Dartford Tunnel	1089	0.004
Droitwich	1053	500	Lisnagarvey	1089	13
Dumfries	1053	10	Moorside Edge	1089	100
Dundee	1053	1	Washford	1089	80
Hull	1053	1	Westerglen	1089	125
Postwick	1053	18	Boston	1107	1
Stockton	1053	1	Fareham	1107	1
Tonbridge	1053	4	Lydd	1107	2
Clipstone	1071	1	Reigate/Crawley	1107	1
Newcastle	1071	1	Wallasey	1107	1

D.Prgr: 24h

OTHER LOCAL RADIO STATIONS:

MW	kHz	kW	Station or Slogan	Location
11)	558	1	Panjab R.	London
12)	648	1	R. Caroline*	Orford Ness
128)	855	0.15	Sunshine R.	Ludlow
7)	936	0.15	Dales R*	Hawes
69)	945	0.2	Gold	Derby
1)	963	0.95	Sunrise R.	E. London
93)	963	0.2	Asian Sound R.	Haslingden
1)	972	1	Sunrise R.	Southall
69)	999	0.25	Nottingham	Gold
3)	1026	1.7	Downtown R.	Belfast
160)	1035	0.32	West Sound	Ayr
31)	1035	1.6	Lyca Dilse	Southall
20)	1107	1.5	MFR 2	Inverness
-)	1134	0.001	LPAMs	
33)	1152	23.5	LBC News	London
97)	1152	3.6	Clyde 2	Glasgow
58)	1161	0.35	Magic	Hull
29)	1161	1.4	Tay 2	Dundee
-)	1251	0.001	LPAMs	
89)	1260	0.29	Sabras R.	Leicester
-)	1278	0.001	LPAMs/RSLs	
-)	1287	0.001	LPAMs	
104)	1296	10	R. XL	Birmingham
98)	1305	0.5	Premier Christian R.	Epsom
98)	1305	0.5	Premier Christian R.	Chingford
78)	1323	0.003	Akash R*	Leeds
72)	1332	0.6	Gold	Peterborough
98)	1332	1	Premier Christian R.‡	London (Bow)
87)	1332	0.1	R. Warrington*	Warrington
-)	1350	0.001	LPAMs	
93)	1377	0.08	Asian Sound R.	Ashton Moss
-)	1386	0.001	LPAMs	
98)	1413	0.5	Premier Christian R.	Heathrow
98)	1413	0.5	Premier Christian R.	Dartford Marshes
44)	1413	0.04	Bradford Asian R.*	Bradford
-)	1431	0.001	LPAMs	
-)	1449	0.001	LPAMs	
31)	1458	125	Lyca R.	London
45)	1458	5	Gold	Manchester
57)	1476	0.25	Carillon Wellbeing R*	Coalville
137)	1521	0.07	Flame CCR*	Wirral
117)	1521	0.04	R. Panj*	Coventry
15)	1530	0.04	R Ramadhan 365*	Glasgow
33)	1548	97.5	Gold	London
85)	1548	2.2	Forth 2	Edinburgh
98)	1566	0.8	Premier Christian R.	Guildford
72)	1557	0.76	Gold	Northampton
147)	1566	0.06	Salaam BCR*	Bury
131)	1575	0.003	R Seerah*	Leicester
29)	1584	0.21	Tay 2	Perth
11)	1584	0.2	Asian FX R.	N. London
83)	1602	0.07	Desi R.*	Southall

*community radio stns.

FM	MHz	kW	Name or Slogan	Location
-)	87.7	-	RSLs/LPFMs	
-)	87.9	-	RSLs	
41)	93.6	0.1	R. Tyneside*	Newcastle
12)	94.7	0.1	Caroline C.R.*	Maldon
91)	95.2	0.2	Kingdom FM	Dunfermline
91)	96.1	0.5	Kingdom FM	Glenrothes
124)	96.2	4	SIBC	Shetland
63)	96.2	0.2	KMFM	Tonbridge
138)	96.2	0.1	Revolution	Oldham
67)	96.3	4	Nation R.	Glasgow
47)	96.3	0.2	Seahaven FM*	Newhaven
3)	96.4	2	Downtown R.	Limavady
34)	96.4	10	Free R,	Birmingham
127)	96.4	1.5	The Wave	Swansea
29)	96.4	0.8	Tay FM	Perth
35)	96.4	0.25	Signal 1	Congleton
16)	96.4	3	CFM	Carlisle
63)	96.4	0.2	KMFM	Folkestone
136)	96.5	0.12	West Sound	Stranraer
3)	96.6	8.2	Downtown R.	Brougher Mountain
26)	96.6	0.2	R North Angus	Arbroath
59)	96.6	10	TFM R.	Bilsdale
8)	96.6	0.4	Nation R. Ceredigion	Lampeter
142)	96.6	0.3	Nevis R.*	Fort William
20)	96.6	0.45	MFR	Cairngorm
160)	96.7	2.2	West FM	Ayr
52)	96.7	8	R. City	Liverpool
135)	96.7	0.55	Q R.	Belfast
96)	96.7	0.2	Imagine R.	Ashbourne
70)	96.7	0.1	Free R.	Kidderminster
20)	96.7	0.1	MFR	Fraserburgh
4)	96.8	5	R. Borders	Selkirk
125)	96.8	0.5	Lochbroom FM	Polbain

FM	MHz	kW	Name or Slogan	Location
54)	96.9	9.4	Viking FM	Hull
146)	96.9	10.4	Northsound 1	Aberdeen
35)	96.9	0.2	Signal 1	Stafford
136)	97.0	1	West Sound	Dumfries
34)	97.0	1.8	Free R.	Coventry
61)	97.1	10	Metro R.	Newcastle
3)	97.1	0.08	Downtown R.	Larne
66)	97.1	3	R. Carmarthenshire	Carmel
34)	97.2	2	Free R.	Wolverhampton
58)	97.2	0.3	Kiss	Bristol
135)	97.2	0.31	Q R.	Coleraine
33)	97.3	4	LBC	London
85)	97.3	9.8	Forth 1	Edinburgh
20)	97.4	6.25	MFR	Inverness
51)	97.4	2	Rock FM	Preston/Blackpool
3)	97.4	3.2	Cool FM	Belfast
53)	97.4	0.4	Hallam FM	Sheffield
8)	97.4	0.4	Nation R. Ceredigion	Penwaun
106)	97.5	0.5	Pulse 1	Bradford
28)	97.5	0.4	Heartland FM	Pitlochry
71)	97.5	0.15	West FM	Girvan
66)	97.5	0.2	R. Carmarthenshire	Llanelli
70)	97.6	0.8	Free R.	Hereford
85)	97.6	0.1	Forth 1	Edinburgh
33)	97.7	1	R. X	Manchester
108)	97.8	0.15	Gateway*	Basildon
111)	97.8	0.1	LDC R.*	Leeds
60)	99.9	0.2	Witney R.*	Witney
58)	100.0	4	Kiss	London
63)	100.4	0.3	KMFM	Hoo St.Werburgh
135)	100.5	1	Q R.	Newry
48)	100.7	0.8	Star R.	Cambridge
58)	101.0	40	Kiss	Mendip
135)	101.1	0.4	Q R.	Kilkeel
135)	101.1	0.125	Q R.	Newcastle
68)	101.1	0.15	Unity 101*	Southampton
64)	101.2	1.37	Waves R.	Peterhead
135)	101.2	6.26	Q R.	Brougher Mountain
88)	101.4	0.1	Flex FM*	SW London
63)	101.6	0.4	KMFM	Wrotham
2)	102.0	1	Ipswich 102	Ipswich
73)	102.0	0.2	Pure R.	Dundee
8)	102.1	1.2	Swansea Bay R.	Swansea
89)	102.1	0.2	Sabras R.	Loughborough
85)	102.2	0.5	Forth 1	Penicuik
112)	102.2	6.4	Lincs FM	Belmont
37)	102.2	2.5	Pirate FM	Caradon Hill
16)	102.2	0.815	CFM	Workington
125)	102.2	0.7	Lochbroom FM	Ullapool
97)	102.3	0.6	Clyde 1	Rothesay
3)	102.3	0.5	Downtown R.	Ballymena
142)	102.3	0.8	Nevis R.*	Fort William
3)	102.4	10	Downtown R.	Londonderry
97)	102.4	0.6	Clyde 1	Rosneath
142)	102.4	0.5	Nevis R.*	Glenachulish
97)	102.5	24.5	Clyde 1	Glasgow
106)	102.5	2	Pulse 1	Halifax
20)	102.5	1.2	MFR	Thurso
102)	102.5	20	R. Pembrokeshire	Haverfordwest
16)	102.5	0.1	CFM	Penrith
144)	102.5	0.2	Mon FM*	Anglesey
35)	102.6	4	Signal 1	Stoke-on-Trent
61)	102.6	0.125	Metro R.	Alnwick
39)	102.6	0.1	Sun FM	Richmond
62)	102.7	9	R. Skye	Isle of Skye
39)	102.8	0.33	Sun FM	Sacriston
70)	102.8	1	Free R.	Worcester
29)	102.8	5	Tay FM	Dundee
37)	102.8	10	Pirate FM	Redruth
20)	102.8	1	MFR	Keith
74)	102.8	0.2	YO1 R.*	York
115)	102.8	0.1	Canalside*	Macclesfield
8)	102.9	3.2	Nation R	Carmel
53)	102.9	0.45	Hallam FM	Barnsley
135)	102.9	3.14	Q R.	Londonderry
51)	103.0	4	Hits R.	Manchester
143)	103.0	3.6	Isles FM	Stornoway

FM	MHz	kW	Name or Slogan	Location
146)	103.0	0.174	Northsound 1	Peterhead
67)	103.0	0.1	Your R.	Dumbarton
136)	103.0	0.7	West Sound	Kirkcudbright
7)	103.0	0.1	Dales R.*	Ingleton
34)	103.1	2.7	Free R.	Shrewsbury
14)	103.1	0.5	Central FM	Stirling
3)	103.1	1.8	Downtown R.	Newry
32)	103.2	0.1	Mansfield 103.2	Mansfield
123)	103.2	0.5	Sunrise FM	Bradford
39)	103.2	0.365	Sun FM	Darlington
61)	103.2	0.12	Metro R.	Hexham
96)	103.3	0.2	Imagine R.	Buxworth
114)	103.3	0.2	London Greek R.	N. London
8)	103.3	5.8	Nation R. Ceredigion	Blaenplwyf
97)	103.3	0.1	Clyde 1	Rosneath
6)	103.3	0.4	Oban FM	Oban
53)	103.4	1.6	Hallam FM	Doncaster
3)	103.4	0.2	Downtown R.	Newcastle
4)	103.4	0.5	R. Borders	Eyemouth
39)	103.4	0.3	Sun FM	Sunderland
16)	103.4	0.4	CFM	Whitehaven
21)	103.7	4	Channel 103 FM	Jersey
105)	104.5	0.1	R. Ninesprings*	Yeovil
5)	104.7	1.25	Island FM	Guernsey
140)	104.9	0.64	Imagine R.	Stockport
33)	104.9	2.9	R. X	London
79)	105.0	0.5	Uckfield FM*	Uckfield
95)	105.1	0.5	R. Essex	Southend-on-Sea
25)	105.1	0.3	First FM*	Oxford
101)	105.2	10	Wave 105	Solent
81)	105.3	0.2	Seaside FM*	Withernsea
91)	105.4	0.1	Kingdom FM	Fife
58)	105.4	4	Magic	Croydon
58)	105.6	1	Kiss	Cambridge
63)	105.6	0.15	KMFM	Maidstone
99)	105.6	0.15	Mearns FM*	Stonehaven
10)	105.8	1.9	U105	Belfast
101)	105.8	0.625	Wave 105	Poole
128)	105.9	1	Sunshine R.	Woofferton
38)	106.0	8	Gem 106	Copt Oak
135)	106.0	0.5	Q R.	Cookstown
63)	106.0	0.1	KMFM	Canterbury
75)	106.0	0.6	Two Lochs R.	Gairloch
58)	106.1	4	Kiss	Stoke Holy Cross
45)	106.1	1	XS	Manchester
121)	106.1	0.2	R Newquay*	Newquay
103)	106.2	1.5	Sunshine R.	Hereford
91)	106.3	0.15	Kingdom FM	Fife
30)	106.3	0.9	Bridge FM	Bridgend
19)	106.3	0.175	Original 106	Peterhead
27)	106.3	0.2	Dee	Chester
58)	106.4	20	Kiss	Mendelsham
55)	106.4	0.4	More R.	Haywards Heath
96)	106.4	0.25	Imagine R.(2 txs)	Buxton/Glossop
13)	106.5	0.5	Argyll FM	Campbeltown
40)	106.5	1.2	Caithness FM*	Ben Dorrey
84)	106.5	1	Sam FM	Bristol
75)	106.6	2	Two Lochs R.	Loch Ewe
73)	106.6	0.25	Pure R.	Perth
109)	106.6	0.2	BCB*	Bradford
80)	106.6	0.3	Koast *	Ashington
106.6	0.1		N. Manchester*	Manchester
71)	106.7	0.6	West FM	Rothesay
18)	106.7	0.62	R. Plymouth	Ft Staddon
130)	106.7	0.2	LCR*	Liverpool
8)	106.8	4	Nation R.	Cardiff
55)	106.8	0.1	More R.	Lewes
63)	106.8	0.1	KMFM	Dover
65)	106.8	0.3	Jack FM	Oxford
19)	106.8	19	Original FM	Aberdeen
134)	106.8	0.05	Rinse FM*	C London
22)	106.9	0.3	Silk FM	Macclesfield
24)	107.0	0.1	Fosse 107	Loughborough
113)	107.0	0.1	Isle of Wight R.	Chillerton Down
135)	107.0	0.62	Q R.	Ballymena
103)	107.0	1	Sunshine R.	Monmouth
33)	107.1	0.13	Capital Xtra	N. London

FM	MHz	kW	Name or Slogan	Location
8)	107.1	2.5	Nation R.	Preseli
48)	107.1	0.14	Speysound R.*	Aviemore
46)	107.1	0.12	Star R.	Ely
13)	107.1	0.625	Argyll FM	Ballygroggan
135)	107.2	0.25	Q R.	Dungannon
107)	107.2	0.2	Hits R.	Winchester
63)	107.2	0.1	KMFM	Thanet
119)	107.3	2	R. Exe	Exeter
8)	107.3	1.25	Nation R.	Swansea
77)	107.3	0.18	Reprezent*	S. London
141)	107.3	0.16	Alive*	Dumfries
99)	107.3	0.1	Mearns FM*	Laurencekirk
107)	107.4	0.2	Hits R.	Portsmouth
102)	107.5	0.1	R. Pembrokeshire	Fishguard
126)	107.5	0.4	Time	Romford
55)	107.5	0.15	More R.	Eastbourne
-	107.5	0.1	Paisley FM*	Paisley
90)	107.6	0.2	Vibe*	Watford
107)	107.6	1	Fire R.	Bournemouth
63)	107.6	0.5	KMFM	Ashford, Kent
136)	107.6	0.15	Q R.	Larne
129)	107.7	0.85	KCR*	Keith
95)	107.7	0.1	R. Essex	Chelmsford
58)	107.7	0.2	Kiss	Peterborough
55)	107.7	0.1	More R.	Worthing
13)	107.7	0.5	Argyll FM	South Knapdale
55)	107.8	0.1	More R.	Hastings
139)	107.8	0.8	R. Jackie	SW London
107)	107.8	0.5	Hits R.	Southampton
82)	107.8	0.2	The Voice*	Bideford
24)	107.9	0.2	Fosse 107	Hinckley
65)	107.9	0.2	Jack 3	Oxford
63)	107.9	0.5	KMFM	Rochester
92)	107.9	0.1	Islands FM*	St Mary's
94)	107.9	0.1	GTFM*	Pontypridd
76)	107.9	0.1	The Cat*	Crewe
118)	107.9	0.1	Riviera*	Torquay

+approx 260 stns of less than 0.1kW *community radio stns

H. of tr: Most stns operate 24h Some stns carry automated prgrs outside peak hours

MAJOR COMMERCIAL RADIO GROUPS:

BAUER MEDIA 1 Golden Square, London W1W 9DJ ☎ 20 7434 1215 **W:** bauermedia.co.uk

COMMUNICORP UK Level 7, XYZ Building, Hardman Blvd., Manchester M3 3AQ ☎ 161 886 8800 **W:** communicorpuk.com/radio

GLOBAL 30 Leicester Square, London WC2H 7LA ☎ 20 7766 6000 🖷 20 7766 6111 **W:** global.com/radio

Addresses & other information:

1) Unit 2, 694-712 London Rd., Hounslow TW3 1PG ☎ 20 8574 6666 **W:** sunriseradio.com – **2)** Unit 5 Alton Business Centre, Valley Lane, Ipswich IP9 2AX ☎ 1473 550714 **W:** ipswich102radio.com – **3)** Kiltonga Ind. Estate, Newtownards, Co Down BT23 4ES ☎ 28 9181 5555 **W:** planteradio.co.uk/downtown, planetradio.co.uk/cool-fm – **4)** Tweedside Park, Galashiels TD1 3TD ☎ 1896 759444 **W:** planetradio.co.uk/borders – **5)** 12 Westerbrook, St Sampsons, Guernsey GY2 4QQ ☎ 1481 242000 **W:** islandfm.com – **6)** 132 George Street, Oban PA34 5NT ☎ 1631 570057 **W:** obanfm.com – **7)** Colvend, Hebden Rd., Grassington, BD23 5LB **W:** dalesradio.co – **8)** St Hilary Transmitter, St Hilary, Cowbridge, CF71 1DP ☎ 1792 716200 **W:** nationradio.wales swanseabayradio.wales – **9)** Eleven Brindley Place, 2 Brunswick Square, Birmingham B1 2LP ☎ 121 695 0000 – **10)** Level 7, City Quays 2, Clarendon Rd., Belfast BT1 3FG ☎ 28 9033 3105 **W:** u105.com – **11)** Panjab Radio House, Springfield Rd, Hayes UB4 0TH ☎ 20 848 8877 **W:** panjabradio.co.uk, asianfx.co.uk – **12)** PO Box 12524, Maldon, Essex CM9 9EX ☎ 208 340 3831 **W:** radiocaroline.co.uk – **13)** 27-29 Longrow, Campbeltown PA28 6ER ☎ 1586 551800 **W:** argyllfm.com – **14)** 9 Munroe Rd., Stirling FK7 7UU ☎ 1324 611164 **W:** centralfm.co.uk – **15)** 70 Coplow Str., Glasgow G42 7JG ☎ 141 3753434 **W:** radioramadhan.scot – **16)** Atlantic House, Fletcher Way, Parkhouse, Carlisle CA3 0LJ ☎ 1228 818964 **W:** planetradio.co.uk/cfm – **17)** 33-39 Strand Str., Liverpool L1 8LT ☎ 151 550 5800 **W:** capitalfm.com/liverpool – **18)** 3 Crescent Ave. Mews, Plymouth PL1 3AP ☎ 1752 389532 **W:** radioplymouth.com – **19)** 1 Marischal Square, Broad Str., Aberdeen AB10 1BL ☎ 1224 294860 **W:** originalfm.com – **20)** Scorguie Place, Inverness IV3 8UJ ☎ 1463 224433 **W:** planetradio.co.uk/mfr – **21)** 6 Tunnell Street, St Helier, Jersey JE2 4LU ☎ 1534 888103 **W:** channel103.com –**22)** Adelaide House, Aldelaide Str., Macclesfield SK10 2QS ☎ 1625 268000 **W:** silk1069.com – **23)** Unit 5 The Metro Centre, Dwight Rd., Watford WD18 9UD ☎ 1923 801955 **W:** heart.co.uk/hertfordshire – **24)** Graphic House, Druid Str., Hinckley LE10 1QH ☎ 1455 442772 **W:** fosse107.co.uk – **25)** 70A Hollow Way, Oxford OX4 2NH **W:** first105.com **26)** Arbroath Infirmary, Rosemount Rd, Arbroath DD11 2AT ☎ 1241 871446 **W:** radionorthangus.co.uk – **27)** 2 Chantry Court, Chester CH1 4QN ☎ 1244 391000 **W:** dee1063.com – **28)** 23 Atholl Rd., Pitlochry PH16 5BX ☎ 1796 474040 **W:** heartlandfm.org – **29)** 6 North Isla Street, Dundee DD3 7JQ ☎ 1382 200800 **W:** planetradio.co.uk/tay – **30)** Tondu Road, Bridgend CF31 4LH ☎ 1656 838620 **W:** bridgefmradio.wales – **31)** Wallbrook Bldg., 195 Marsh Wall, London E14 9SG ☎ 20 7132 1458 **W:** lycadilse.com, lycaradio.com – **32)** Unit 4, Brunts Business Centre, Samuel Brunts Way, Mansfield NG18 2AH ☎ 1623 646666 **W:** mansfield103.co.uk – **33)** 30 Leicester Square, London WC2H 7LA ☎ 20 7766 6000 **W:** capitalfm.com Capital Xtra: capitalxtra.com Gold: mygoldmusic.co.uk LBC: lbc.co.uk R.X: radiox.co.uk – **34)** Nine Brindleyplace, 4 Oozells Square, Birmingham B1 2DJ ☎ 121 566 5200 **W:** planetradio.co.uk/free, planetradio.co.uk/greatest-hits – **35)** 67-73 Stoke Rd, Stoke-on-Trent ST4 2SR ☎ 1782 441 300 **W:** signal1.co.uk – **36)** Wellbar Central, 36 Gallowgate, Newcastle upon Tyne NE1 4TD☎ 191 444 2500 – **37)** Barncoose Ind. Estate, Wilson Way, Redruth TR15 3XX ☎ 1209 314400 **W:** piratefm.co.uk – **38)** City Link, Nottingham NG2 4NG ☎ 115 910 6100 **W:** planetradio.co.uk/gem-106 – **39)** Unit 63-36T, Business & Innovation Centre, Sunderland Enterprise Park, Sunderland SR5 2TA ☎ 191 548 1034 **W:** sun-fm.com – **40)** Neil Gunn Drive, Thurso KW14 7QU ☎ 1847 890000 **W:** caithnessfm.co.uk – **41)** 3 North Terrace, Newcastle-upon-Tyne NE2 4AD ☎191 222 0789 **W:** radiotyneside.co.uk – **42)** Red Dragon Centre, Hemingway Rd., Cardiff CF10 4JY ☎ 29 2031 5100– **43)** Radio House, Apple Ind. Estate, Whittle Ave, Fareham PO15 5SX ☎ 345 481 1111 – **44)** 8th Floor, West Riding Business Centre, 41 Cheapside, Bradford BD1 4HR ☎ 1274 306677 **W:** bradfordasianradio.co.uk – **45)** XYZ Building, 2 Hardman Blvd, Manchester M3 3AQ ☎ 161 662 4700 **W:** capitalfm.com, mygoldmusic.co.uk smoothradio.com xsmanchester.co.uk – **46)** PO Box 1387, Cambridge CB1 0JZ ☎ 1223 735100 **W:** star.radio – **47)** Unit 3 The Courtyard, Saxon Lane, Seaford BN21 1QL **W:** www.seahavenfm.com – **48)** Suite 5, Aviemore Shopping Centre, Grampian Rd., Aviemore PH22 1RH ☎ 1479 811888 **W:** speysound.com – **49)** 2a Joseph's Well, Hanover Walk, Leeds LS3 1AB ☎ 113 308 5100 – **50)** Stanton House, 29 Yarmouth Rd, Norwich NR7 0EE ☎ 845 345 1035 **W:** planetradio.co.uk/greatest-hits – **51)** Castle Quay, Castlefield, Manchester M15 4PR ☎ 161 288 5000 **W:** planetradio.co.uk/hits-radio planetradio.co.uk/greatest-hits planetradio.co.uk/rock-fm – **52)** St Johns Beacon, 1 Houghton Street, Liverpool L1 1RL ☎ 151 472 6800 **W:** planetradio.co.uk/city planetradio.co.uk/greatest-hits – **53)** 900 Herries Rd, Sheffield S6 1RH ☎ 114 2091000 **W:** planetradio.co.uk/hallam – **54)** The Block, Springfield Way, Anlaby, Hull HU10 6RG ☎ 1482 325141 **W:** planetradio.co.uk/Viking – **55)** Guildbourne Centre, Worthing BN11 1LZ ☎1903 233271 **W:** moreradio.online – **56)** 51 Burley Rd, Leeds LS3 1LR ☎ 113 283 5500 **W:** planetradio.co.uk/greatest-hits – **57)** Loughborough Hospital, Epinal Way, Loughborough LE11 5JY ☎1509 276575 **W:** carillonradio.com – **58)** 1 Golden Square, London W1F 9DJ ☎ 20 7434 1215 **W:** planetradio.co.uk/greatest-hits planetradio.co.uk/magic planetradio.co.uk/kiss – **59)** Addr as 61 **W:** planetradio.co.uk/tfm – **60)** Blanket House, Witney OX29 7DX **W:** witneyradio.co.uk – **61)** 55 Degrees North, Pilgrim St., Newcastle upon Tyne NE1 6BF ☎ 191 230 6100 **W:** planetradio.co.uk/metro – **62)** Stormyhill Rd, Portree IV51 9DT ☎ 1478 611796– **W:** radioskye.com – **63)** Medway House, Sir Thomas Longley Rd, Medway City Estate, Strood, Rochester ME2 4DU ☎ 1634 711079 **W:** kmfm.co.uk – **64)** 7 Blackhouse Circle, Blackhouse Industrial Estate, Peterhead AB42 1BN ☎ 1779 491012 **W:** wavesfm.com – **65)** 1 Oasis Park, Stanton Harcourt Rd, Eynsham OX29 4TP ☎ 1865 315980 **W:** jackfm.co.uk; jack3.co.uk – **66)** Parc y Scarlets, Llanelli SA14 9UZ ☎ 1267 679250 **W:** radiocarmarthenshire.wales– **67)** 272 Bath Str., Glasgow, G2 4JR ☎ 141 811 0470 **W:** nationradio.scot yourradio.scot – **68)** 107 St Mary's Rd, Southampton SO14 0AN **W:** unity101.org – **69)** 2 Chapel Quarter, Mount Str., Nottingham NG1 6HQ ☎ 115 986 1066 **W:** capitalfm.com; mygoldmusic.co.uk – **70)** Kirkham House, John Comyn Drive, Worcester WR3 7NS ☎ 1905 545510 **W:** planetradio.co.uk/free – **71)** Ladykirk House, Skye Rd, Prestwick KA9 2TA ☎ 1292 270500 **W:** planetradio.co.uk/west – **72)** 4th Floor, CBX II, Midsummer Blvd, Milton Keynes MK9 2EA ☎ 345 481 0077– **73)** 50 High Craighall Rd., Glasgow, G4 9UD **W:** pureradioscotland.com–

74) 8 Marsden Park, York YO30 4WX **W:** yo1radio.co.uk – **75)** Mansegate, Gairloch IV21 2LR ☎ 870 712106 **W:** 2lr.co.uk – **76)** C206 South Cheshire College, Danebank Ave., Crewe CW2 8AB ☎ 1270 654686 **W:** thisisthecat.com – **77)** Pop Brixton, 49 Brixton Station Rd., London SW9 8PQ ☎20 7639 8512 **W:** reprezent.org.uk – **78)** 122 Potternewton Lane, Leeds, LS7 2EG **W:** akashradioleeds.co.uk – **79)** Upper Barn, Bird in Eye Farm, Uckfield TN22 5HA **W:** uckfieldfm.co.uk – **80)** 30 Woodhorn Villas, Ashington NE63 9JD **W:** koastradio.co.uk - **81)** 29-31 Seaside Road, Withernsea HU19 2DL **W:** seasideradio.co.uk - **82)** Belle Meadow Court, Albert Lane, Barnstaple EX32 8RJ ☎1271 323010 **W:** thevoicefm.co.uk – **83)** Panjabi Centre, 30 Sussex Rd, Southall UB2 5EG ☎ 20 8574 9591 **W:** desiradio.org.uk – **84)** County Gates, Ashton Rd, Bristol BS3 2JH ☎ 117 966 6107 **W:** samfm.co.uk/bristol planetradio.co.uk/greatest-hits – **85)** Forth House, Forth Street, Edinburgh EH1 3LE ☎ 131 556 9255 **W:** planetradio.co.uk/forth – **86)** One Passage Str., Bristol BS2 0JF ☎ 345 481 0888 – **87)** Unit 54, Warrington Temporary Market, Academy Str., Warrington WA1 2LH ☎ 1925 555110 **W:** radiowarrington.co.uk – **88)** First Floor, Unit 13, 193 Garth Rd., Morden SM4 4LZ ☎208 330 4455 **W:** flexfm.co.uk – **89)** 63 Melton Rd, Leicester LE4 6PN ☎ 116 261 0666 **W:** sabrasradio.com – **90)** 59 Clarendon Rd, Watford WD17 1LA ☎1923 888650 **W:** vibe1076.co.uk – **91)** Elizabeth House, Barclay Court, Mitchelston Ind. Est., Kirkcaldy KY1 3WE ☎ 1592 753753 **W:** kingdomfm.co.uk – **92)** Porthmellon, St Mary's, Isles of Scilly TR21 0JY ☎1720 423417 **W:** islandsfm.org – **93)** 42 Southall Str, Manchester M3 1LQ ☎ 161 288 1000 **W:** asiansoundradio.co.uk – **94)** Pinewood Studios, Pinewood Ave, Rhydyfelin, Pontypridd CF37 5EA ☎1443 406111 **W:** gtfm.co.uk – **95)** Icon Bldg., Western Esplanade, Southend-on-Sea SS1 1EE ☎ 1702 455070 **W:** radioessex.com – **96)** St Monicas House, Windmill Lane, Ashbourne DE6 1EY ☎ 1335 346967 **W:** imagine.radio – **97)** Clydebank Business Park, Clydebank, Glasgow G81 2RX ☎ 141 565 2200 **W:** planetradio.co.uk/clyde – **98)** 22 Chapter Street, London SW1P 4NP ☎ 20 7316 1300 **W:** premierchristianradio.com – **99)** 64 Allerdice Str, Stonehaven AB39 2AA **W:** www.mearnsfm.co.uk – **100)** The Studios, Mold Rd, Wrexham LL11 4AF ☎ 1978 722200 – **101)** 5 Manor Court, Barnes Wallis Rd, Segensworth East, Fareham PO15 5TH ☎ 1489 481050 **W:** planetradio.co.uk/wave-105 – **102)** Unit 14, Old School Estate, Station Rd, Narberth SA67 7DU ☎1834 887160 **W:** radiopembrokeshire.wales – **103)** Suite 5, Penn House, Broad Street, Hereford HR4 9AP ☎ 1432 360246 **W:** sunshineradio.co.uk/hfm – **104)** KMS House, Bradford Street, Birmingham B12 0JD ☎ 121 753 5353 **W:** radioxl.net – **105)** Waterloo House, Waterloo Lane, Yeovil BA20 1TF **W:** radioninsprings.co.uk – **106)** 1 St James Business Park, New Augustus Str., Bradford BD1 5LL ☎ 1274 203040 **W:** pulse1.co.uk – **107)** 4th Floor, Roman Landing, Kingsway, Southampton SO14 1BN ☎ 845 466 1107 **W:** planetradio.co.uk/greatest-hits; planetradio.co.uk/hits-radio; fireradio.co.uk – **108)** The Galleries, Eastgate Centre, Basildon SS14 1AN **W:** gateway978.com – **109)** 11 Rawson Rd, Bradford BD1 3SH ☎ 1274 771677 **W:** bcbradio.co.uk – **110)** 40 Melton Rd, Oakham LE15 6AY ☎ 1572 757868 **W:** rutlandradio.co.uk – **111)** James Graham Bldg, Headingley Campus, Leeds LS6 3QS **W:** ldcradio.co.uk– **112)** Witham Park, Waterside South, Lincoln LN5 7JN ☎ 1472 362964 **W:** lincsfm.co.uk – **113)** Dodnor Park, Newport, Isle of Wight PO30 5XE ☎ 1983 822557 **W:** iwradio.co.uk – **114)** LGR house, 437 High Rd, London N12 0AP ☎ 20 8349 6950 **W:** lgr.co.uk – **115)** Canal 2B Clarence Mill, Bollington SK10 5JZ **W:** canalsideradio.net– **116)** Unit G3-G4, Holly Farm Business Park, Honily, Kenilworth CV8 1NP ☎ 1788 220140 **W:** capitalfm.com – **117)** 6 Longford Rd, Coventry CV6 6DX ☎ 24 7668 1521 **W:** radiopanj.com –**118)** 34 Castle Circus House, Union Str., Torquay TQ2 5QG**W:** riviera.fm– **119)** 1 Oak Tree Place, Manaton Close, Matford Business Park, Exeter EX2 8WA ☎ 1392 823557 **W:** radioexe.co.uk – **120)** 115 Southwark St., London SE1 0JF **W:** lovesportradio.com – **121)** Prow Park, Newquay TR7 2SX ☎ 16377 806111 **W:** radionewquay.com – **122)** 8th Floor, 1 West Regent Street, Glasgow G2 1RW ☎ 141 781 1011 – **123)** 55 Leeds Rd, Bradford BD1 5AF ☎ 1274 735043 **W:** sunriseradio.fm – **124)** Market Street, Lerwick, Shetland ZE1 0JN ☎ 1595 695299 **W:** sibc.co.uk – **125)** Mill Street Industrial Estate, Ullapool IV26 2UN ☎ 1854 613131 **W:** lochbroomfm.com – **126)** Laurie Walk, The Liberty Centre, Romford RM1 3RT ☎ 1708 710075 **W:** time1075.net – **127)** Victoria Rd, Gowerton, Swansea SA4 3AB ☎ 1792 511964 **W:** thewave.co.uk – **128)** Unit 11, Burway Trading Estate, Ludlow SY8 1EN ☎ 1584 873795 **W:** sunshineradio.co.uk – **129)** 59a Land Street, Keith AB55 5AN ☎ 1542 866080 **W:** kcr.fm – **130) W:** l-c-r.co.uk – **131)** Melbourne Centre, Melbourne Rd, Leicester LE2 0GU ☎116 3848786 **W:** radioseerah.com – **133) W:** northmanchester.fm– **134)** 93 Kingsland Rd, London E2 8AG ☎ 20 7247 7252 **W:** rinse.fm – **135)** 1st Floor, Fountain Centre, College Str., Belfast, BT1 6ET ☎ 28 9023 4967 **W:** goqradio.com – **136)** Unit 40, Loreburn Centre, High Street, Dumfries DG1 2BD ☎ 1387 250999 **W:** planetradio.co.uk/westsound-fm – **137)** St Pauls Road Mission Church, Birkenhead CH42 3UZ ☎ 151 643 1696 **W:** flameradio.org – **138)** Sarah Moor Studios, Henshaw St., Oldham OL1 3EN ☎ 161 621 6500 **W:** revolutionon962.com – **139)** 110 Tolworth Broadway, Surbiton KT6 7JD ☎ 20 8288 1300 **W:** radiojackie.com – **140)** 116 Wellington Place, Stockport SK1 1YH ☎ 161 399 0148 **W:** imagine.radio – **141)** 32 Annan Rd, Dumfries DG1 3AD **W:** aliveradio.net– **142)** Unit 4A, Ben Nevis Industrial Estate, Fort William PH33 6PR ☎ 1397 700007 **W:** nevisradio.co.uk – **143)** 50 Seaforth Rd, Stornoway, Isle of Lewis HS1 2SH ☎ 1851 703333 **W:** islesfm.com – **144)** 12 Ffordd yr Efail, Llangefni, Anglesey LL77 7ER ☎ 1248 722224 **W:** monfm.net – **145)** Paisley Grammar School, Glasgow Rd, Paisley PA1 3PR **W:** paisleyfm.co.uk– **146)** Abbottswell Rd, West Tullos, Aberdeen AB12 3AJ ☎ 1224 337000 **W:** planetradio.co.uk/northsound – **147)** Project 29, 52 Moorgate, Bury BL9 7AF **E:** salaambcr@gmail.com

MANX RADIO (Comm.)

✉ Broadcasting House, Douglas Head, Douglas, Isle of Man IM1 5BW ☎ 1624 682600 **W:** manxradio.com **E:** reception@manxradio.com **L.P:** MD: Chris Sully, PC Alex Brindley
MW: 1368kHz Foxdale 20kW **FM:** 89.0MHz Snaefell 4kW / 89.5MHz Ramsey 0.1kW / 97.2MHz Carnane 11kW / 103.7MHz Jurby 4kW
D.Prgr: 24h Separate prgrs on MW at various times & during Manx TT motorcycle events

ENERGY FM (Comm.)

✉ PO Box 986, Douglas, Isle of Man IM99 2TB ☎ 1624 611936 **W:** energyfm.net **FM:** 91.2MHz Snaefell 1.2kW, 93.4MHz Jurby 1kW, 98.6MHz Carnane 2kW, 102.4 Beary Park 0.33kW (+ relays on 98.4/105.2) **D.Prgr:** 24h

3FM (Comm.)

✉ Skanco Court, Cooil Rd., Douglas, Isle of Man IM2 2SR ☎ 1624 616333 🖷 1624 616333 **W:** three.fm
FM: 104.2MHz (Ramsey & Mull Hill), 105MHz (Carnane 2kW), 106.6MHz (Snaefell), 106.2MHz (Peel) **D.Prgr:** 24h

BRITISH FORCES BROADCASTING SERVICE

(a division of Services Sound & Vision Corp.)
✉ SSVC, Narcot Lane, Gerrards Cross SL9 8TN ☎ 1494 878354 🖷 1494 878552 **E:** admin.officer@bfbs.com **W:** forces.net/radio/
L.P: Dir. Forces Broadcasting: Nicky Ness
FORCES RADIO BFBS in English **FM**: 89.3MHz Blandford, 94 MHz Glencorse, 98.5MHz Edinburgh, 100.6MHz Lisburn, 101MHz Belfast, 102.5MHz Aldershot, 106.1 Brize Norton, 106.5MHz Antrim, 106.8MHz Salisbury, 106.9MHz Catterick, 107MHz Colchester. **MW:** Low power relay on 1287kHz (Bovington). **DAB:** Digital One (National).
BFBS GURKHA RADIO in Nepali, news hourly in English. **MW:** Low power sce on 1134kHz (Abingdon, Bramcote, Bulford, Catterick, Sandhurst), 1251kHz (York), 1278kHz (Folkestone-main studio, Tidworth, Stafford), 1287kHz (Aldershot, Blandford, Brecon, Gloucester, Hullavington, Maidstone, Warminster)
See Afghanistan, Bosnia, Ascension Island, Belgium, British Indian Ocean Territory, Brunei, Canada, Cyprus, Falkland Islands, Germany, Gibraltar, Nepal, Netherlands for other BFBS sces.

RSL (Restricted Service Licences) Licences are granted for low power special event stns operating for up to 28 days (occ. longer) usually on FM
LPAM (Low Power AM stations) There are currently about 40 stns on the air (including BFBS relays - see above) with txs of 0.001kW e.r.p. Freqs used: 1134, 1251, 1278, 1287, 1350, 1386, 1431, 1449kHz
LPFM (Low Power VHF/FM stations) There are currently about 25 stns on the air, most on 87.7MHz, with txs of typically 50mW

COMMUNITY RADIO Small-scale, low-power, non-profit community radio sces to serve a particular neighbourhood. Most on FM with 25 - 300W. approx 300 stns on air as of October 2020. MW community radio sces and FM sces above 100W are included in the main frequency lists above. For updated listing of short-term RSLs, long-term RSLs (LPAMs) and Community Radio see Radio Broadcast Licensing at **W:** ofcom.org.uk

Community Audio Distribution Systems (CADS) licence-exempt service for religious and community events using 27MHz Citizens Band.

UNITED STATES OF AMERICA

L.T: See World Time Table (DST where applicable: 14 Mar-7 Nov) — **Pop:** 329 million — **Pr.L:** English — **E.C:** 120V/60Hz — **ITU:** USA

FEDERAL COMMUNICATIONS COMMISSION (FCC) (Independent U.S. Govt. agency)
45 L St NE, Washington, DC 20554 ☎ +1 888 2255322 +1 866 4180232 **E:** pra@fcc.gov **W:** fcc.gov
L.P: Chmn: Ajit Pai; Commissioners: Brandan Carr, Michael O'Rielly, Jessica Rosenworcel, Geoffrey Starks

CORPORATION FOR PUBLIC BROADCASTING
401 9th St NW, Washington, DC 20004-2129 ☎ +1 202 8799600 **W:** www.cpb.org **L.P:** Chmn: Bruce Ramer

NATIONAL ASSOCIATION OF BROADCASTERS (NAB)
1 M St SE, Washington, DC 20003 ☎ +1 202 4295300 **E:** nab@nab.org **W:** www.nab.org **L.P:** Pres/CEO: Gordon H. Smith

NATIONAL ASSOCIATION OF SHORTWAVE BROADCASTERS, Inc (NSAB)
10400 NW 240th St, Okeechobee, FL 34972 ☎ +1 305 5599764 **E:** nasbshortwave@gmail.com **W:** shortwave.org **L.P:** Pres: John D. Tayloe, Vice Pres: Jerry Plummer

NATIONAL FEDERATION OF COMMUNITY BROADCASTERS (NFCB)
P.O. Box 806, Paonia, CO 81428 ☎ +1 970 2793411 **E:** membership@nfcb.org **W:** nfcb.org **L.P:** Pres: Sonya Green

NATIONAL RELIGIOUS BROADCASTERS (NRB)
660 North Capitol St NW, Suite 210, Washington, DC 20001 ☎ +1 202 5430073 **E:** info@nrb.org **W:** nrb.org
L.P: Pres/CEO: Troy Miller

MAJOR PRODUCERS/DISTRIBUTORS OF NETWORK PROGRAMMING FOR LOCAL STATIONS

ABC RADIO (ABC, Inc - a division of The Walt Disney Co)
47 West 66th St, New York, NY 10023 ☎ +1 212 4565101 **W:** abcradio.com **L.P:** Vice Pres/GM: Stacia Deshishku

AMERICAN PUBLIC MEDIA GROUP (Non-Comm)
480 Cedar St, St. Paul, MN 55101 ☎ +1 651 2901373 **W:** americanpublicmedia.org **L.P:** Pres/CEO: Jon McTaggart

AMERICAN URBAN RADIO NETWORKS (AURN) (ACCESS.1 COMMUNICATIONS CORP)
960 Penn Ave, 4th Floor, Pittsburgh, PA 15222-3811 ☎ +1 412 4564000 **W:** aurn.com
L.P: CEO (Access.1 Communications Corp): Chesley Maddox-Dorsey

BIBLE BROADCASTING NETWORK, Inc (Rlg)
11530 Carmel Commons Blvd, Charlotte, NC 28226 ☎ +1 704 5235555 **W:** bbnradio.org

BOTT RADIO NETWORK (BOTT COMMUNICATIONS, Inc) (Rlg)
10550 Barkley St, Suite 100, Overland Park, KS 66212 ☎ +1 913 6427770 **E:** comments@bottradionetwork.com **W:** bottradionetwork.com **L.P:** Chmn: Dick Bott

COMPASS MEDIA NETWORKS, LLC
150 Purchase St, Suite 11, Rye, NY 10580 ☎ +1 914 6005099 **E:** info@compassmedianetworks.com **W:** compassmedianetworks.com
L.P: CEO: Peter Kosann

CUMULUS MEDIA, Inc
3280 Peachtree Rd NW, Suite 2300, Atlanta, GA 30305 ☎ +1 404 9490700 **W:** cumulus.com
L.P: Pres/CEO: Mary G. Berner

ENTERCOM COMMUNICATIONS CORP.
2400 Market St, Philadelphia, PA 19103 ☎ +1 212 3149200 **W:** entercom.com **L.P:** CEO: David J. Field

ESPN RADIO (ESPN, Inc)
ESPN Plaza, 935 Middle St., Bristol, CT 06010 ☎ +1 860 7662000 **W:** www.espn.com/espnradio; espnpressroom.com
L.P: Pres (ESPN): Jimmy Pitaro

FAMILY LIFE NETWORK (FAMILY LIFE MINISTRIES, Inc) (Rlg)
7634 Campbell Creek Rd, Bath, NY 14810 ☎ +1 607 7764151 **W:** fln.org **L.P:** Chairman (Family Life Ministries): Norb Fuest

FAMILY LIFE RADIO (FAMILY LIFE COMMUNICATIONS, Inc) (Rlg)
7355 N. Oracle Rd, Tucson, AZ 85704 ☎ +1 520 7426976 **E:** correspondence@flc.org **W:** myflr.org
L.P: Pres (Family Life Communications): Evan Carlson

FOX NEWS RADIO (FOX NEWS NETWORK, LLC - a subsidiary of 21st Century Fox, Inc)
1211 Avenue of the Americas, 18th floor, New York, NY 10036 ☎ +1 212 3015439 **E:** foxnewsradio@foxnews.com **W:** radio.foxnews.com **L.P:** CEO (Fox News Network): Suzanne Scott

GENESIS COMMUNICATIONS NETWORK, Inc (GCN)
190 Cobblestone Lane, Burnsville, MN 55337 ☎ +1 877 9964327 **W:** gcnlive.com **L.P:** Pres/CEO: Ted Anderson

IHEARTMEDIA, Inc
20880 Stone Oak Pkwy, San Antonio, TX 78258 ☎ +1 210 8222828 **W:** iheartmedia.com **L.P:** Chmn/CEO: Bob Pittman

NATIONAL PUBLIC RADIO, Inc (Non-Comm)
635 Massachusetts Avenue NW, Washington, DC 20001 ☎ +1 202 5133232 **W:** npr.org **L.P:** Pres/CEO: John Lansing

PREMIERE NETWORKS, Inc (Subsidiary of iHeartMedia, Inc)
15260 Ventura Blvd, Suite 400, Sherman Oaks, CA 91403 ☎ +1 818 3775300 **E:** feedback@premierenetworks.com **W:** www.premierenetworks.com **L.P:** Pres: Richard J. Bressler

RADIO 74 (RADIO 74 INTERNATIONALE) (Rlg)
1209 West Robert Avenue, Ridgecrest, CA 93556-0716 ☎ +1 760 3752355 **E:** contact@radio74.net **W:** radio74.net
L.P: Pres: Everet W. Witzel

RELEVANT RADIO (IMMACULATE HEART MEDIA, Inc) (Rlg)
1496 Bellevue St, Suite 202, Green Bay, WI 54311 ☎ +1 920 8841460 **E:** info@relevantradio.com
W: relevantradio.com **L.P:** CEO: Francis J. Hoffman

SALEM RADIO NETWORK (SALEM MEDIA GROUP, Inc)
4880 Santa Rosa Rd, Camarillo, CA 93012 ☎ +1 805 9870400 **W:** salemmedia.com **L.P:** CEO (Salem Media Group): Edward G. Atsinger

UNIVISION RADIO (UNIVISION COMMUNICATIONS, Inc)
605 Third Avenue, 33rd Floor, New York, NY 10158 ☎ +1 212 4555200 **W:** univision.com
L.P: CEO (Univision Communications): Vincent L. Sadusky
Univision Radio is a Spanish language network.

USA RADIO NETWORKS (NEVADA RADIO, LLC)
1111 W Mockingbird Ln, Dallas, TX 75247 ☎ +1 214 6283111 **E:** contact@usaradio.com **W:** usaradio.com **L.P:** CEO: Fred Weinberg

WESTWOOD ONE, LLC (Subsidiary of Cumulus Media, Inc)
220 West 42nd St, Candler Tower, New York, NY 10036 ☎ +1 212 9672888 **W:** www.westwoodone.com **L.P:** Pres: Suzanne M. Grimes

LOCAL STATIONS
There are more than 17,000 local stns operating on AM and FM. As of September 30, 2020: AM stns: 4,560 - FM (Full Power) Commercial stns: 6,704 - FM (Full power) Educational stns: 4,196 - FM Low power stns (LPFM): 2,143. There are also 8,339 FM translators and boosters.

Call Letter Assigments: For broadcasting stns in the U.S., callsigns consist of four letters, beginning with K or W, to which "-FM" or "-LP" may be added for FM stns. Calls with leading K are assigned to stns west of the Mississippi River (incl. Guam and No. Mariana Is), while a leading W is assigned to broadcast stns east of the Mississippi (incl. Puerto Rico). Exceptions: a few stns east of the Mississippi using a "K" callsign and stns west of the Mississippi using a "W" callsign will be noted. These are old callsigns that were assigned for various reasons (e.g. reflecting the initial geographic division in the early days of U.S. radio, or were requested by the stn owner) and are retained by special permission. Similarly some very old callsigns using only three letters may be retained by the stns that were once assigned these callsigns.

Program Formats: Especially in multi-station markets, **commercial radio stns** concentrate their prgrs to appeal to a given segment of the population or a given listening taste. Many stns devote their entire broadcast day to news and/or talk prgrs, or sports coverage. Others specialize in various types of music: Hit music (e.g. Contemporary Hit Radio), Country music, Classic Hits or Oldies, African American music (e.g. Urban Contemporary), Latin music (e.g. Mexican Regional), Classical music, etc. The number of Spanish language stns targeting the Hispanic audience has increased considerably in recent years. Some stns address other ethnic communities (e.g. African, Asian, European), incl. relays of foreign radio prgrs. Many stns change to a new format from time to time. **Non-commercial Educational radio stns** include public radio, religious radio, community radio, college radio, high school radio, etc.
Local radio stns make extensive use of programming produced and/or distributed by network providers (typically fed by satellite), and many may have only one local identification per hour, usually on top of the hour.

AM Stations: In the U.S. the AM band 540-1600kHz & expanded band 1610-1700kHz is divided into "clear", "regional" and "local" channels, and the AM stns are divided into domestic classes A, B, C, D. "Clear channel" stns in the highest class A today have a protected area extending to 750 miles (c. 1200 km). Outside this area, the frequencies are also used by other stns. In order to combat interference from neighbouring countries, a few stns have been granted temporary licenses for increased powers, and many daytime stns may now operate after local sunset, using low or very low powers. 530kHz is reserved for very low power Travelers' Information Stations (TIS). Also 1610kHz was initially reserved for TIS, but is now available for regular stns (Class C&D), although so far no stn (exc. TIS) has been licensed on this frequency.

Travelers' Information Stations (TIS): State and local governments or institutions may create local stns or networks to provide non-commercial travel- or emergency-related public safety information using LPFM stations, or AM stns of up to 10 Watts primarily on 530kHz, or on any other available AM freq up to 1700kHz.

Low Power FM Stations (LPFM): This type of FM license is open to non-commercial educational entities and public safety/travelers' information entities, but not individuals or commercial operations.

Digital Broadcasting ("HD Radio"): An increasing number of stns is transmitting additional digital audio in the FM band, using the IBOC system, while the number of hybrid AM stns still remains relatively small. With the hybrid IBOC system digital signals are emitted on both sides of a transmitter's analogue signal, so that both analogue and digital receivers can recover the audio. Analogue listeners may experience the IBOC signal as an increased noise level on freqs adjacent to the nominal channel of the emitting transmitter. While in the AM band the IBOC signal is limited to one digital audio channel, IBOC in the FM band offers the option for multicasting on several digital subchannels. Most stns are using this possibility to transmit various additional programme feeds. A directory of FM stns carrying IBOC transmissions and the content of their subchannels can be found on **W:** hdradio.com/stations, a list of AM stns with IBOC trs on **W:** topazdesigns.com/iboc/station-list.html.

MEDIUMWAVE (AM)
Call: Station call letters. All stns are required to announce their actual call letters and city of licence once per hour as close as possible to the top of the hour.
Ant: Use of antenna (CH=Critical Hours; ND=Non-directional). **U** = Unlimited time operation (typically 24h): **U1** ND at all hours, **U2** with directional antenna at night only, **U3** with directional antenna at all hours (same pattern day & night), **U4** as U3, but with different patterns day and night, **U5** with directional antenna daytime, ND at night, **U6** with directional antenna at night & during CH, **U7** as U3, but with three different patterns day, CH and night, **U8** as U7 but ND daytime, **U9** with directional antenna day & night (different patterns), but non-directional during CH (usually on reduced power), **U10** with directional antenna during CH, **U11** with directional antenna with separate patterns for daytime & CH, ND at night, **U12** ND daytime & CH, directional antenna at night, **U13** with directional antenna (same pattern day & CH, different pattern at night), **U14** with directional antenna day and night (different patterns), ND during CH. **D** = Daytime operation (between local sunrise and local sunset): **D1** with non-directional antenna, **D2** with directional antenna during CH only, **D3** with directional antenna, **D4** with directional antenna (different patterns during critical and non-critical hours), **D5** with directional antenna except CH. **L** = Limited time operation (usually based upon sunrise or sunset at the dominant station's location on a Clear Channel): **L1** with ND antenna, **L3** with directional antenna. **N** = Nighttime operation (between local sunset and local sunrise): **N1** with ND antenna, **N3** with directional antenna.
D: Daytime power in kW. **N:** Nighttime power in kW.
City of License and Sta: City (or Community) and State that the license has been issued to. **NB:** Hawaii (HI) and Alaska (AK) are listed under separate country headings.
Scope: Due to the large number of stns in operation, the listing has been limited to stns operating at 2.5kW or more during day- or nighttime. Stations on 530 (TIS), and on the "local channels" 1230, 1240, 1340, 1400, 1450, 1490 kHz have been omitted due to their low power.

STATES: AL Alabama, AR Arkansas, AZ Arizona, CA California, CO Colorado, CT Connecticut, DE Delaware, FL Florida, GA Georgia, IA Iowa, ID Idaho, IL Illinois, IN Indiana, KS Kansas, KY Kentucky, LA Louisiana, MA Massachusetts, MD Maryland, ME Maine, MI Michigan, MN Minnesota, MO Missouri, MS Mississippi, MT Montana, NC North Carolina, ND North Dakota, NE Nebraska, NH New Hampshire, NJ New Jersey, NM New Mexico, NV Nevada, NY New York, OH Ohio, OK Oklahoma, OR Oregon, PA Pennsylvania, RI Rhode Island, SC South Carolina, SD South Dakota, TN Tennessee, TX Texas, UT Utah, VA Virginia, VT Vermont, WA Washington, WI Wisconsin, WV West Virginia, WY Wyoming. **Federal District:** DC (District of Columbia).

NB: **#**=Stn's reported transmitting IBOC signals (regularly or intermittently) at day- and/or nighttime. **+**= all-digital stn (HD Radio). **‡**=inactive at editorial deadline. *****=WNZK uses diff. frqs for daytime (690kHz) and nighttime (680kHz)

MW	Call	kHz	Ant.	D	N	Sta	City of License
		530	Various stns of 0.01kW or less (TIS only)				
1	WASG	**540**	U1	2.5	0.01	AL	Daphne
2	KRXA	540	U4	10	0.5	CA	Carmel Valley
3	KVIP	540	U1	2.5	0.01	CA	Redding
4	WFLF	540	U4	50	46	FL	Pine Hills
5	WDAK	540	U1	4	0.03	GA	Columbus
6	KWMT	540	U4	5	0.17	IA	Fort Dodge
7	KMLB	540	U1	4	0.02	LA	Monroe
8	WRGC	540	U1	5	0.14	NC	Sylva
9	WETC	540	U4	10	0.5	NC	Wendell-Zebulon
10	KNMX	540	U4	5	0.02	NM	Las Vegas
11	WBWD	540	U4	10	0.22	NY	Islip
12	WWCS	540	U4	5	0.5	PA	Canonsburg
13	WKFN	540	U1	4	0.05	TN	Clarksville
14	KFYI	**#550**	U1	5	1	AZ	Phoenix
15	KUZZ	550	U4	5	5	CA	Bakersfield
16	KRAI	550	U2	5	0.5	CO	Craig
17	WAYR	550	U4	5	0.5	FL	Fleming Island
18	WDUN	550	U2	10	2.5	GA	Gainesville
19	KFRM	550	U4	5	0.11	KS	Salina
20	KTRS	550	U2	5	5	MO	Saint Louis
21	KBOW	550	U2	5	1	MT	Butte
22	KFYR	550	U2	5	5	ND	Bismarck
23	WGR	550	U2	5	5	NY	Buffalo
24	WKRC	550	U4	5	1	OH	Cincinnati
25	KOAC	550	U4	5	5	OR	Corvallis
26	KCRS	550	U4	5	1	TX	Midland
27	KTSA	550	U2	5	5	TX	San Antonio
28	WSVA	550	U2	5	1	VA	Harrisonburg
29	WDEV	550	U4	5	1	VT	Waterbury
30	KARI	550	U4	5	2.5	WA	Blaine
31	WSAU	550	U4	15	20	WI	Wausau
32	WOOF	**560**	U1	5	0.11	AL	Dothan

MW	Call	kHz	Ant.	D	N	Sta	City of License
33	KSFO	560	U2	5	5	CA	San Francisco
34	KLZ	#560	U3	5	5	CO	Denver
35	WQAM	560	U1	4.1	1	FL	Miami
36	WIND	560	U4	5	5	IL	Chicago
37	WMIK	560	U1	2.5	0.08	KY	Middlesboro
38	WHYN	560	U4	5	1	MA	Springfield
39	WFRB	560	U1	5	0.05	MD	Frostburg
40	WGAN	560	U4	5	5	ME	Portland
41	WEBC	560	U4	5	5	MN	Duluth
42	KWTO	560	U4	5	4	MO	Springfield
43	KMON	560	U2	5	5	MT	Great Falls
44	WFIL	560	U4	5	5	PA	Philadelphia
45	WVOC	560	U2	5	5	SC	Columbia
46	WNSR	560	U4	4.5	0.07	TN	Brentwood
47	WHBQ	560	U4	5	1	TN	Memphis
48	KLVI	560	U2	5	5	TX	Beaumont
49	KPQ	560	U2	5	5	WA	Wenatchee
50	WJLS	560	U2	4.5	0.47	WV	Beckley
51	WAAX	**570**	U2	5	0.5	AL	Gadsden
52	KCFJ	570	U1	5	0.04	CA	Alturas
53	KLAC	570	U2	5	5	CA	Los Angeles
54	WTBN	570	U4	5	5	FL	Pinellas Park
55	WWRC	570	U4	5	1	MD	Bethesda
56	WWNC	570	U2	5	5	NC	Asheville
57	KWML	570	U1	5	0.15	NM	Las Cruces
58	WMCA	570	U3	5	5	NY	New York
59	WSYR	570	U4	5	5	NY	Syracuse
60	WKBN	570	U2	5	5	OH	Youngstown
61	WNAX	570	U2	5	5	SD	Yankton
62	KLIF	570	U4	5	2.4	TX	Dallas
63	KNRS	570	U3	5	5	UT	Salt Lake City
64	KVI	570	U1	5	5	WA	Seattle
65	KSAZ	**580**	U2	5	0.39	AZ	Marana
66	KMJ	580	U3	50	50	CA	Fresno
67	KUBC	580	U2	5	1	CO	Montrose
68	WDBO	580	U2	5	5	FL	Orlando
69	WGAC	#580	U2	5	0.84	GA	Augusta
70	KIDO	580	U2	5	5	ID	Nampa
71	WILL	580	U4	5	0.1	IL	Urbana
72	WIBW	580	U2	5	5	KS	Topeka
73	KJMJ	580	U2	5	1	LA	Alexandria
74	WTAG	580	U4	5	5	MA	Worcester
75	WTCM	580	U4	50	1.1	MI	Traverse City
76	WKSK	580	U1	5	0.03	NC	West Jefferson
77	WHP	580	U2	5	5	PA	Harrisburg
78	WXRH	580	U1	5	0.04	TN	Rockwood
79	WKTY	580	U4	5	0.74	WI	La Crosse
80	WCHS	580	U2	5	5	WV	Charleston
81	KTIE	**590**	U4	2.5	0.96	CA	San Bernardino
82	KTHO	590	U2	2.5	0.5	CA	South Lake Tahoe
83	WDIZ	590	U2	1.7	2.5	FL	Panama City
84	WDWD	590	U4	12	4.5	GA	Atlanta
85	KID	590	U2	5	1	ID	Idaho Falls
86	WVLK	590	U4	5	1	KY	Lexington
87	WEZE	590	U3	5	5	MA	Boston
88	WJMS	590	U1	5	0.11	MI	Ironwood
89	WKZO	590	U2	5	5	MI	Kalamazoo
90	KXSP	590	U1	5	5	NE	Omaha
91	WROW	590	U4	5	1	NY	Albany
92	KUGN	590	U2	5	5	OR	Eugene
93	KLBJ	590	U2	5	1	TX	Austin
94	KSUB	590	U2	5	1	UT	Cedar City
95	KQNT	590	U1	5	5	WA	Spokane
96	KOGO	**#600**	U4	5	5	CA	San Diego
97	KCOL	600	U4	5	0.5	CO	Wellington
98	WBOB	600	U2	50	9.7	FL	Jacksonville
99	WMT	600	U2	5	5	IA	Cedar Rapids
100	WKYH	600	U1	5	0.04	KY	Paintsville
101	WCAO	#600	U3	5	5	MD	Baltimore
102	WFST	600	U1	5	0.12	ME	Caribou
103	KGEZ	600	U4	5	1	MT	Kalispell
104	WSJS	600	U4	5	5	NC	Winston-Salem
105	KSJB	600	U3	5	5	ND	Jamestown
106	WREC	600	U4	5	5	TN	Memphis
107	KROD	600	U2	5	5	TX	El Paso
108	KTBB	600	U4	5	2.5	TX	Tyler
109	WAGG	**610**	U1	5	0.61	AL	Birmingham
110	KAVL	610	U4	4.9	4	CA	Lancaster
111	KEAR	610	U1	5	5	CA	San Francisco
112	WIOD	610	U4	5	5	FL	Miami
113	KDAL	610	U2	5	5	MN	Duluth
114	KCSP	610	U1	5	5	MO	Kansas City
115	WFNZ	#610	U4	5	1	NC	Charlotte
116	WGIR	610	U4	5	1	NH	Manchester
117	KNML	610	U2	5	5	NM	Albuquerque
118	WTVN	610	U2	5	5	OH	Columbus
119	KRTA	610	U4	2.5	5	OR	Medford
120	WTEL	610	U3	5	5	PA	Philadelphia
121	KILT	610	U4	5	5	TX	Houston
122	KVNU	610	U2	10	1	UT	Logan
123	WPLY	610	U4	5	1	VA	Roanoke
124	KONA	610	U4	5	5	WA	Kennewick-Richland-Pasco
125	KTAR	**#620**	U2	5	5	AZ	Phoenix
126	KJOL	620	U1	5	0.07	CO	Grand Junction
127	WDAE	620	U2	5.6	5.5	FL	Saint Petersburg
128	WTRP	620	U1	2.5	0.12	GA	La Grange
129	WZON	620	U2	5	5	ME	Bangor
130	WJDX	620	U2	5	1	MS	Jackson
131	WSNR	620	U4	3	7.6	NJ	Jersey City
132	WHEN	620	U2	5	1	NY	Syracuse
133	KPOJ	620	U2	25	10	OR	Portland
134	WKHB	620	U1	5.5	0.05	PA	Irwin
135	WFMV	620	U1	2.5	0.12	SC	Cayce
136	WRJZ	620	U2	5	5	TN	Knoxville
137	KTNO	620	U4	5	4.5	TX	Plano
138	WVMT	620	U4	5	5	VT	Burlington
139	WTMJ	620	U4	50	10	WI	Milwaukee
140	WWNR	620	U1	5	0.02	WV	Beckley
141	KHOW	**630**	U4	5	5	CO	Denver
142	WSBN	630	U4	10	2.7	DC	Washington
143	WBMQ	‡630	U1	4.8	0.04	GA	Savannah
144	WNEG	630	U1	5	0.04	GA	Toccoa
145	KFXD	630	U4	5	5	ID	Boise
146	WLAP	630	U4	5	1	KY	Lexington
147	WREY	630	U4	3	2.4	MN	Saint Paul
148	KYFI	630	U4	5	5	MO	Saint Louis
149	KPLY	630	U2	5	1	NV	Reno
150	KWRO	630	U1	5	0.04	OR	Coquille
151	WPRO	630	U2	5	5	RI	Providence
152	KSLR	630	U4	5	4.3	TX	San Antonio
153	KCIS	630	U2	5	2.5	WA	Edmonds
154	KFI	**640**	U1	50	50	CA	Los Angeles
155	WMEN	640	U4	7.5	0.46	FL	Royal Palm Beach
156	WGST	640	U4	50	1	GA	Atlanta
157	WOI	640	U2	5	1	IA	Ames
158	WMFN	640	U4	4.4	1.6	IL	Peotone
159	KTIB	640	U4	5	1	LA	Thibodaux
160	WNNZ	640	U4	50	1	MA	Westfield
161	WFNC	640	U1	10	1	NC	Fayetteville
162	WWJZ	640	U4	50	0.95	NJ	Mount Holly
163	WHLO	640	U4	5	0.5	OH	Akron
164	KWPN	#640	U4	5	1	OK	Moore
165	WXSM	640	U2	10	0.81	TN	Blountville
166	WCRV	640	U2	50	0.48	TN	Collierville
167	KSTE	**650**	U4	21.4	0.92	CA	Rancho Cordova
168	WNMT	650	U2	10	1	MN	Nashwauk
169	WSM	650	U1	50	50	TN	Nashville
170	KMTI	650	U4	10	0.9	UT	Manti
171	KGAB	650	U2	8.5	0.5	WY	Orchard Valley
172	WXQW	**660**	U1	10	0.01	AL	Fairhope
173	KTNN	660	U2	50	50	AZ	Window Rock
174	KGSV	660	U4	8	6	CA	Oildale
175	WDYZ	660	U4	3.5	1	FL	Altamonte Springs
176	WBHR	660	U4	10	0.5	MN	Sauk Rapids
177	KEYZ	660	U4	5	5	ND	Williston
178	WFAN	660	U1	50	50	NY	New York
179	KXOR	660	U1	10	0.07	OR	Junction City
180	WESC	‡660	D1	50		SC	Greenville
181	KSKY	660	U4	20	0.7	TX	Balch Springs
182	KAPS	660	U4	10	1	WA	Mount Vernon
183	WYLS	**670**	D1	4.8		AL	York
184	KHGZ	670	D1	5		AR	Glenwood
185	KIRN	670	U4	5	3	CA	Simi Valley
186	KLTT	#670	U4	50	1.4	CO	Commerce City
187	WWFE	670	U4	50	1	FL	Miami
188	KBOI	670	U2	50	50	ID	Boise

MW	Call	kHz	Ant.	D	N	Sta	City of License
189	WSCR	670	U1	50	50	IL	Chicago
190	KMZQ	670	U4	25	0.6	NV	Las Vegas
191	WLUI	670	D1	5.4		PA	Lewistown
192	WRJR	670	U4	20	0.003	VA	Claremont
193	KNBR	**680**	U1	50	50	CA	San Francisco
194	WCNN	680	U4	50	10	GA	North Atlanta
195	WRKO	680	U4	50	50	MA	Boston
196	WCBM	680	U4	50	20	MD	Baltimore
197	WNZK*	680	N2		2.5	MI	Dearborn Heights
198	WDBC	680	U4	6	1	MI	Escanaba
199	KFEQ	680	U4	5	5	MO	Saint Joseph
200	KKGR	680	D1	5		MT	East Helena
201	WPTF	680	U2	50	50	NC	Raleigh
202	WINR	680	U4	5	0.5	NY	Binghamton
203	WMFS	680	U2	8	5	TN	Memphis
204	KKYX	680	U2	50	10	TX	San Antonio
205	KOMW	680	D1	5		WA	Omak
206	WOGO	680	U4	2.5	0.5	WI	Hallie
207	WKAZ	680	U2	10	0.22	WV	Charleston
208	WJOX	**690**	U2	50	0.5	AL	Birmingham
209	WADS	690	D3	3.2		CT	Ansonia
210	WOKV	690	U2	50	25	FL	Jacksonville
211	KGGF	690	U4	10	5	KS	Coffeyville
212	WQNO	690	U2	9.1	2.1	LA	New Orleans
213	WNZK*	690	D3	2.5		MI	Dearborn Heights
214	KTSM	690	U4	10	10	TX	El Paso
215	WZAP	690	U1	10	0.01	VA	Bristol
216	WELD	690	U1	3	0.01	WV	Fisher
217	KMBX	**700**	U1	2.5	0.7	CA	Soledad
218	WPVQ	700	D1	2.5		MA	Orange-Athol
219	WDMV	700	D3	5		MD	Walkersville
220	WLW	700	U1	50	50	OH	Cincinnati
221	KGRV	700	U1	23	0.47	OR	Winston
222	KSEV	700	U4	15	1	TX	Tomball
223	KALL	700	U4	50	10	UT	North Salt Lake City
224	KXLX	700	U2	10	0.6	WA	Airway Heights
225	KBMB	**710**	U4	22	3.9	AZ	Black Canyon City
226	KFIA	710	U4	25	1	CA	Carmichael
227	KSPN	710	U2	50	10	CA	Los Angeles
228	KNUS	710	U3	5	5	CO	Denver
229	WAQI	710	U4	50	50	FL	Miami
230	WUFF	710	D1	2.5		GA	Eastman
231	WEKC	710	L1	4.2		KY	Williamsburg
232	KEEL	710	U4	50	5	LA	Shreveport
233	KCMO	710	U4	10	5	MO	Kansas City
234	WEGG	710	D1	2.5		NC	Rose Hill
235	KXMR	710	U4	4	4	ND	Bismarck
236	WOR	710	U4	50	50	NY	New York
237	KGNC	710	U4	10	10	TX	Amarillo
238	WFNR	710	D3	10		VA	Blacksburg
239	KIRO	710	U2	50	50	WA	Seattle
240	WDSM	710	U2	10	5	WI	Superior
241	WRZN	**720**	U2	10	0.25	FL	Hernando
242	WVCC	720	D1	7.97		GA	Hogansville
243	WGN	720	U1	50	50	IL	Chicago
244	WGCR	720	D1	50		NC	Pisgah Forest
245	KDWN	#720	U2	50	50	NV	Las Vegas
246	KFIR	720	U1	10	0.14	OR	Sweet Home
247	KSAH	720	U4	10	0.89	TX	Universal City
248	WSTT	**730**	U1	5	0.02	GA	Thomasville
249	KDBI	730	U4	15	0.5	ID	Boise
250	WACE	730	U1	5	0.008	MA	Chicopee
251	KYYA	730	U1	5	0.23	MT	Billings
252	WZGV	730	U1	10	0.16	NC	Cramerton
253	WPIT	730	U1	5	0.02	PA	Pittsburgh
254	WLTQ	730	U1	5	0.1	SC	Charleston
255	WTNT	730	U1	8	0.02	VA	Alexandria
256	WMSP	**740**	U4	10	0.23	AL	Montgomery
257	KBRT	#740	U4	50	0.19	CA	Costa Mesa
258	KCBS	740	U4	50	50	CA	San Francisco
259	KVOR	#740	U4	3.3	1.5	CO	Colorado Springs
260	WSBR	‡740	U4	2.5	0.94	FL	Boca Raton
261	WYGM	740	U4	50	50	FL	Orlando
262	WNOP	740	U4	2.5	0.03	KY	Newport
263	WPAQ	740	U1	10	0.007	NC	Mount Airy
264	KNFL	740	U7	50	0.94	ND	Fargo
265	WNYH	740	U4	25	0.04	NY	Huntington
266	KRMG	740	U4	50	25	OK	Tulsa
267	KTRH	740	U4	50	50	TX	Houston
268	WDGY	740	D3	5		WI	Hudson
269	WSB	**750**	U1	50	50	GA	Atlanta
270	WNDZ	750	D3	15		IN	Portage
271	KBNN	750	D1	5		MO	Lebanon
272	KERR	750	U2	50	1	MT	Polson
273	KMMJ	750	L3	10.5		NE	Grand Island
274	KXTG	750	U4	50	20	OR	Portland
275	KAMA	750	U4	10	1	TX	El Paso
276	KOAL	#750	U2	10	6.8	UT	Price
277	KMTL	**760**	D1	10		AR	Sherwood
278	KFMB	760	U2	5	50	CA	San Diego
279	KDFD	760	U4	50	1	CO	Thornton
280	WLCC	760	U4	10	1	FL	Brandon
281	WEFL	760	U4	3	1.5	FL	Tequesta
282	KCCV	760	U4	6	0.2	KS	Overland Park
283	WVNE	760	D1	25		MA	Leicester
284	WJR	760	U1	50	50	MI	Detroit
285	WCIS	760	D1	3.5		NC	Morganton
286	WCHP	760	U4	35	0.01	NY	Champlain
287	KTKR	760	U4	50	1	TX	San Antonio
288	WVNN	**770**	U2	7	0.25	AL	Athens
289	KCBC	#770	U4	50	4.1	CA	Manteca
290	WJBX	770	U4	10	0.63	FL	North Fort Myers
291	KUOM	770	D1	5		MN	Minneapolis
292	KATL	770	U2	10	1	MT	Miles City
293	WLWL	770	D1	5		NC	Rockingham
294	KKOB	770	U2	50	50	NM	Albuquerque
295	WABC	770	U1	50	50	NY	New York
296	WTOR	770	D3	13		NY	Youngstown
297	KAAM	770	U4	10	1	TX	Garland
298	WYRV	770	D1	5		VA	Cedar Bluff
299	KTTH	770	U4	50	5	WA	Seattle
300	KAZM	**780**	U2	5	0.25	AZ	Sedona
301	WBBM	780	U1	35	42	IL	Chicago
302	WXME	780	U1	5	0.06	ME	Monticello
303	WIIN	780	D1	4.4		MS	Ridgeland
304	WCKB	780	U1	7	0.001	NC	Dunn
305	WWOL	780	D1	10		NC	Forest City
306	KKOH	780	U2	50	50	NV	Reno

MW	Call	kHz	Ant.	D	N	Sta	City of License
307	WAVA	780	D1	12		VA	Arlington
308	WTSK	**790**	U1	5	0.03	AL	Tuscaloosa
309	KURM	790	U2	5	0.5	AR	Rogers
310	KNST	790	U4	5	0.5	AZ	Tucson
311	KFPT	790	U4	5	2.5	CA	Clovis
312	KEJY	790	U1	5	0.11	CA	Eureka
313	KABC	#790	U2	6.6	7.9	CA	Los Angeles
314	WLBE	‡790	U2	5	1	FL	Leesburg-Eustis
315	WAXY	790	U4	5	5	FL	South Miami
316	WQXI	790	U2	28	1	GA	Atlanta
317	KXXX	790	U1	5	0.02	KS	Colby
318	WKRD	790	U4	5	1	KY	Louisville
319	WSGW	790	U4	5	1	MI	Saginaw
320	KGHL	790	U1	5	1.8	MT	Billings
321	WBLO	790	U1	10	0.02	NC	Thomasville
322	KFGO	790	U2	5	5	ND	Fargo
323	WAEB	790	U4	3.6	1.5	PA	Allentown
324	WPRV	790	U2	5	5	RI	Providence
325	WETB	790	U1	5	0.07	TN	Johnson City
326	WMC	790	U2	5	5	TN	Memphis
327	KBME	790	U4	5	5	TX	Houston
328	KFYO	790	U4	5	1	TX	Lubbock
329	WNIS	790	U3	5	5	VA	Norfolk
330	KGMI	790	U2	5	1	WA	Bellingham
331	KJRB	790	U4	5	3.8	WA	Spokane
332	WAYY	790	U1	5	0.12	WI	Eau Claire
333	KBRV	**800**	U1	10	0.15	ID	Soda Springs
334	WNNW	800	U1	3	0.24	MA	Lawrence
335	WVAL	800	U4	2.6	0.85	MN	Sauk Rapids
336	WTMR	800	U4	5	0.5	NJ	Camden
337	KQCV	800	U4	2.5	1	OK	Oklahoma City
338	WSVS	800	U1	10	0.27	VA	Crewe
339	WPCA	800	U4	5	0.5	WI	Waupaca
340	WVHU	800	U1	5	0.18	WV	Huntington
341	WCKA	**810**	U4	50	0.5	AL	Jacksonville
342	KGO	810	U3	50	50	CA	San Francisco
343	WRSO	810	U4	20	0.4	FL	Orlovista
344	WZYN	810	D1	2.5		GA	Hahira
345	WEKG	810	D1	5		KY	Jackson
346	WMJH	810	D1	3.6		MI	Rockford
347	WHB	810	U2	50	5	MO	Kansas City
348	WSJC	810	U2	50	0.5	MS	Magee
349	KSWV	810	U1	5	0.01	NM	Santa Fe
350	WGY	#810	U1	50	50	NY	Schenectady
351	WWOS	810	D1	5		SC	Walterboro
352	KBHB	810	U1	25	0.06	SD	Sturgis
353	WMGC	810	U1	5	0.006	TN	Murfreesboro
354	WPIN	810	D1	4.2		VA	Dublin
355	KTBI	810	D1	50		WA	Ephrata
356	WWBA	**820**	U4	50	1	FL	Largo
357	WCPT	820	U2	5.8	1.5	IL	Willow Springs
358	WWFD	820	U2	4.3	0.43	MD	Frederick
359	WBKK	820	U4	10	0.75	MN	Wilton
360	WWLZ	820	U2	4.1	0.85	NY	Horseheads
361	WNYC	820	U4	10	1	NY	New York
362	WVSG	#820	U2	6.5	0.79	OH	Columbus
363	WBAP	820	U1	50	50	TX	Fort Worth
364	KUTR	#820	U8	50	2.5	UT	Taylorsville
365	WNTW	820	U4	10	1	VA	Chester
366	KGNW	820	U4	50	5	WA	Burien-Seattle
367	KDRI	**830**	U2	50	1	AZ	Tucson
368	KNCO	830	U2	5	5	CA	Grass Valley
369	KLAA	830	U2	50	20	CA	Orange
370	KGLA	830	U4	5	0.75	LA	Norco
371	WCRN	830	U4	50	50	MA	Worcester
372	WCCO	830	U1	50	50	MN	Minneapolis
373	WTRU	830	U4	50	10	NC	Kernersville
374	WEEU	830	U4	20	6	PA	Reading
375	WUMY	830	D1	3		TN	Memphis
376	KUYO	830	D1	25		WY	Evansville
377	WBHY	**840**	D1	10		AL	Mobile
378	KMPH	840	U4	5	5	CA	Modesto
379	WHGH	840	D1	10		GA	Thomasville
380	WHAS	840	U1	50	50	KY	Louisville
381	KWDF	840	D1	8		LA	Ball
382	KTIC	840	D1	5		NE	West Point
383	KXNT	#840	U4	50	25	NV	North Las Vegas
384	WCEO	840	D3	50		SC	Columbia
385	KVJY	840	U4	5	1	TX	Pharr
386	WKTR	840	D3	8.2		VA	Earlysville
387	KMAX	840	U1	10	0.28	WA	Colfax
388	WXJC	**850**	U4	50	1	AL	Birmingham
389	KOA	850	U1	50	50	CO	Denver
390	WAXB	850	D1	2.5		CT	Ridgefield
391	WRUF	850	U2	5	5	FL	Gainesville
392	WFTL	850	U4	50	20	FL	West Palm Beach
393	WAIT	850	D3	2.5		IL	Crystal Lake
394	WEEI	850	U4	50	50	MA	Boston
395	WQRM	850	D1	50		MN	Duluth
396	KFUO	#850	L1	5		MO	Clayton
397	WPTK	850	U2	10	5	NC	Raleigh
398	WKNR	850	U4	50	4.7	OH	Cleveland
399	WKGE	850	U3	10	10	PA	Johnstown
400	KJON	850	D3	5		TX	Carrollton
401	KEYH	850	U4	10	0.18	TX	Houston
402	WTAR	850	U4	50	25	VA	Norfolk
403	KHHO	850	U4	10	1	WA	Tacoma
404	KTRB	**860**	U2	50	50	CA	San Francisco
405	WGUL	860	U4	5	1.5	FL	Dunedin
406	WAEC	860	U12	5	0.5	GA	Atlanta
407	WDMG	860	U2	5	5	GA	Douglas
408	KKOW	860	U2	10	5	KS	Pittsburg
409	WSBS	860	U1	2.7	0.004	MA	Great Barrington
410	WFSI	860	U4	2.5	0.06	MD	Baltimore
411	KPAM	860	U2	50	15	OR	Troutdale
412	WWDB	860	D3	10		PA	Philadelphia
413	KONO	860	U2	5	0.9	TX	San Antonio
414	KKAT	860	U1	10	0.19	UT	Salt Lake City
415	WOAY	860	U1	10	0.01	WV	Oak Hill
416	WQRX	**870**	D1	10		AL	Valley Head
417	KRLA	870	U4	50	3	CA	Glendale
418	WWL	870	U3	50	50	LA	New Orleans
419	WLVP	870	U4	10	1	ME	Gorham
420	WKAR	870	D3	10		MI	East Lansing
421	KPRM	870	U2	50	2.5	MN	Park Rapids
422	WTCG	870	D1	5		NC	Mount Holly
423	KLSQ	‡870	U2	5	0.43	NV	Whitney
424	WHCU	870	U2	5	1	NY	Ithaca
425	WPWT	870	D1	10		TN	Colonial Heights
426	KFLD	870	U1	10	0.25	WA	Pasco
427	KLRG	**880**	U2	50	0.22	AR	Sheridan
428	KKMC	880	U4	10	10	CA	Gonzales
429	WZAB	880	U4	4	5	FL	Sweetwater
430	KJJR	880	U1	10	0.5	MT	Whitefish
431	WPEK	880	D1	5		NC	Fairview
432	KRVN	880	U2	50	50	NE	Lexington
433	KHAC	880	U1	10	0.43	NM	Tse Bonito
434	WCBS	#880	U1	50	50	NY	New York
435	WRFD	880	D1	23		OH	Columbus-Worthington
436	KWIP	880	U1	5	1	OR	Dallas
437	WMDB	880	U1	2.5	0.002	TN	Nashville
438	KJOZ	880	U4	10	1	TX	Conroe
439	KIXI	880	U4	50	10	WA	Mercer Island-Seattle
440	WMEQ	880	U2	10	0.21	WI	Menomonie
441	WYAM	**890**	D1	2.5		AL	Hartselle
442	KIHC	890	U4	5	5	CA	Arroyo Grande
443	KVMX	890	U2	10	0.27	CA	Olivehurst
444	KJME	890	U4	5	0.58	CO	Fountain
445	WJTP	890	D1	5		GA	Lithia Springs
446	KYWN	890	U2	50	0.25	ID	Meridian
447	WLS	890	U1	50	50	IL	Chicago
448	WAMG	890	U4	25	6	MA	Dedham
449	WHJA	890	D1	10		MS	Laurel
450	WBAJ	890	D1	50		SC	Blythewood
451	KVOZ	890	U2	10	1	TX	Del Mar Hills
452	KTXV	890	U4	20	0.25	TX	Mabank
453	KDXU	890	U2	10	10	UT	Saint George
454	WKNV	890	D3	10		VA	Fairlawn
455	KALI	**900**	U4	5	0.15	CA	West Covina
456	WMOP	900	U1	2.7	0.02	FL	Ocala
457	WJLG	900	U1	4.35	0.15	GA	Savannah
458	WLSI	900	U1	3.5	0.12	KY	Pikeville
459	KTIS	900	U4	50	0.5	MN	Minneapolis
460	WYCV	900	U1	2.5	0.25	NC	Granite Falls
461	WCPA	900	U4	2.5	0.5	PA	Clearfield
462	WKDA	900	U1	5	0.13	TN	Lebanon

MW	Call	kHz	Ant.	D	N	Sta	City of License
463	KREH	900	U4	5	0.01	TX	Pecan Grove
464	WKDW	900	U1	2.5	0.12	VA	Staunton
465	KGME	**#910**	U2	5	5	AZ	Phoenix
466	KECR	910	U4	5	5	CA	El Cajon
467	KKSF	910	U2	20	5	CA	Oakland
468	KOXR	910	U4	5	1	CA	Oxnard
469	KPOF	#910	U1	5	1	CO	Denver
470	WLAT	910	U2	5	2.8	CT	New Britain
471	WTWD	910	U3	5	5	FL	Plant City
472	WSUI	910	U2	5	4	IA	Iowa City
473	WTOS	910	U2	5	5	ME	Bangor
474	WFDF	#910	U4	50	25	MI	Farmington Hills
475	WMOG	910	U1	5	1	MS	Meridian
476	WSRP	910	U2	5	5	NC	Jacksonville
477	KCJB	910	U4	5	5	ND	Minot
478	KKBE	910	U1	5	0.03	NM	Roswell
479	WLTP	910	U5	5	0.01	OH	Marietta
480	WXJX	910	U4	5	0.06	PA	Apollo
481	WSBA	910	U4	5	1	PA	York
482	WOLI	910	U4	3.6	0.89	SC	Spartanburg
483	WJCW	910	U2	5	1	TN	Johnson City
484	WEPG	910	U1	5	0.09	TN	South Pittsburg
485	KRIO	910	U4	5	5	TX	McAllen
486	WRNL	910	U2	5	1.5	VA	Richmond
487	KMTT	910	U4	3.3	4.3	WA	Vancouver
488	WCBN	910	U1	5	0.07	WI	Hayward
489	KARN	**920**	U2	5	5	AR	Little Rock
490	KVIN	920	U4	0.5	2.5	CA	Ceres
491	KKGX	920	U4	5	1	CA	Palm Springs
492	KLMR	920	U2	5	0.5	CO	Lamar
493	WDMC	920	U4	8	4	FL	Melbourne
494	WGKA	920	U1	14	0.49	GA	Atlanta
495	KYFR	920	U4	5	2.5	IA	Shenandoah
496	WBAA	#920	U2	5	1	IN	West Lafayette
497	WTCW	920	U1	4.2	0.04	KY	Whitesburg
498	KDHL	920	U4	5	5	MN	Faribault
499	WPCM	920	U1	5	0.05	NC	Burlington - Graham
500	KRLV	920	U2	5	0.5	NV	Las Vegas
501	KIHM	920	U2	4.8	0.85	NV	Reno
502	WHJJ	920	U2	5	5	RI	Providence
503	KKLS	920	U4	5	0.11	SD	Rapid City
504	KYST	920	U4	5	1	TX	Texas City
505	KVEL	920	U2	5	1	UT	Vernal
506	WURA	920	U4	7	0.97	VA	Quantico
507	KGTK	920	U1	3	0.007	WA	Olympia
508	KXLY	920	U1	20	5	WA	Spokane
509	WOKY	920	U4	5	1	WI	Milwaukee
510	WMMN	920	U1	5	0.2	WV	Fairmont
511	WGAD	**930**	U2	5	0.5	AL	Rainbow City
512	KAPR	930	U1	2.5	0.07	AZ	Douglas
513	KAFF	930	U1	5	0.03	AZ	Flagstaff
514	KHJ	930	U2	5	5	CA	Los Angeles
515	KIUP	930	U1	5	0.1	CO	Durango
516	KRKY	930	U1	4.5	0.12	CO	Granby
517	WFXJ	#930	U2	5	5	FL	Jacksonville
518	WLSS	930	U4	5	3	FL	Sarasota
519	WMGR	930	U2	5	0.5	GA	Bainbridge
520	KSEI	930	U2	5	5	ID	Pocatello
521	WTAD	930	U2	5	1	IL	Quincy
522	WKBM	930	U4	2.5	4.2	IL	Sandwich
523	WKCT	930	U1	5	0.05	KY	Bowling Green
524	WFMD	930	U4	5	2.5	MD	Frederick
525	WFAT	930	U4	5	1	MI	Battle Creek
526	KKIN	930	U1	2.5	0.36	MN	Aitkin
527	KWOC	930	U2	5	0.5	MO	Poplar Bluff
528	WSFZ	930	U1	3.7	0.06	MS	Jackson
529	KMPT	930	U2	5	1	MT	East Missoula
530	WYFQ	930	U2	5	1	NC	Charlotte
531	WDLX	930	U2	5	1	NC	Washington
532	WPKX	930	U2	5	5	NH	Rochester
533	WPAT	930	U4	5	5	NJ	Paterson
534	WBEN	930	U2	5	5	NY	Buffalo
535	WKY	930	U1	5	0.51	OK	Oklahoma City
536	KAGI	930	U1	5	0.12	OR	Grants Pass
537	KSDN	930	U4	5	1	SD	Aberdeen
538	WSEV	930	U1	5	0.14	TN	Sevierville
539	KLUP	930	U2	5	1	TX	Terrell Hills
540	WLLL	930	U1	9	0.04	VA	Lynchburg
541	KYAK	930	U1	10	0.12	WA	Yakima
542	WLBL	#930	U1	5	0.07	WI	Auburndale
543	WRVC	930	U2	5	1	WV	Huntington
544	KROE	930	U1	5	0.11	WY	Sheridan
545	KFIG	**940**	U4	50	50	CA	Fresno
546	WINZ	940	U2	50	10	FL	Miami
547	WMAC	940	U2	50	10	GA	Macon
548	KPSZ	940	U4	10	5	IA	Des Moines
549	WMIX	940	U4	5	1.5	IL	Mount Vernon
550	WYLD	940	U4	10	0.5	LA	New Orleans
551	WIDG	940	U1	5	0.004	MI	Saint Ignace
552	WCPC	940	U4	31	0.007	MS	Houston
553	WKYK	940	U2	4.6	0.25	NC	Burnsville
554	KVSH	940	U1	5	0.01	NE	Valentine
555	WECO	940	U1	5	0.01	TN	Wartburg
556	KIXZ	940	U4	5	1	TX	Amarillo
557	KTFS	940	U1	2.5	0.01	TX	Texarkana
558	WNRG	940	U1	5	0.01	VA	Grundy
559	WKGM	940	U2	10	3.1	VA	Smithfield
560	KXJK	**950**	U1	5	0.08	AR	Forrest City
561	KAHI	950	U4	5	5	CA	Auburn
562	KKSE	950	U3	5	5	CO	Parker
563	WORL	950	U2	12	5	FL	Orlando
564	WGUN	950	U1	3.5	0.06	GA	Valdosta
565	KOEL	950	U4	5	0.5	IA	Oelwein
566	KMHR	950	U1	3.5	0.03	ID	Boise
567	KOZE	950	U4	5	1	ID	Lewiston
568	WNTD	950	U2	1	5	IL	Chicago
569	WROL	950	U1	5	0.09	MA	Boston
570	WCTN	950	U4	2.5	0.35	MD	Potomac - Cabin John
571	WWJ	950	U4	50	50	MI	Detroit
572	KWOS	950	U2	5	0.5	MO	Jefferson City
573	WHSY	950	U1	5	0.06	MS	Hattiesburg
574	KCAP	#950	U2	5	5	MT	Helena
575	KNFT	950	U1	5	0.22	NM	Bayard
576	KDCE	950	U1	4.2	0.08	NM	Española
577	WIBX	950	U3	5	5	NY	Utica
578	KTBR	950	U1	3.4	0.02	OR	Roseburg
579	WKDN	950	U4	43	21	PA	Philadelphia
580	WCDC	950	U4	10	6	SC	Moncks Corner
581	WORD	950	U2	5	5	SC	Spartanburg
582	WAKM	950	U1	5	0.07	TN	Franklin
583	KPRC	950	U2	5	5	TX	Houston
584	KJTV	950	U4	5	0.5	TX	Lubbock
585	WXGI	950	U1	3.9	0.04	VA	Richmond
586	KJR	950	U4	50	50	WA	Seattle
587	WBES	950	U2	5	1	WV	Charleston
588	WERC	**960**	U2	5	5	AL	Birmingham
589	WLPR	960	U1	6	0.03	AL	Prichard
590	KCGS	960	U1	5	0.04	AR	Marshall
591	KKNT	960	U2	5	5	AZ	Phoenix
592	KIXW	960	U1	5	0.02	CA	Apple Valley
593	KNEW	960	U3	5	5	CA	Oakland
594	WELI	#960	U2	5	5	CT	New Haven
595	WJYZ	960	U4	5	0.39	GA	Albany
596	WRFC	960	U2	5	2.5	GA	Athens
597	KMA	960	U2	5	5	IA	Shenandoah
598	WSBT	960	U4	5	5	IN	South Bend
599	WPRT	960	U1	3.8	0.01	KY	Prestonsburg
600	WFGL	960	U4	2.5	1	MA	Fitchburg
601	WTGM	960	U4	5	5	MD	Salisbury
602	WHAK	960	U1	5	0.13	MI	Rogers City
603	KLTF	960	U1	5	0.03	MN	Little Falls
604	KZIM	960	U2	5	0.5	MO	Cape Girardeau
605	KFLN	960	U1	5	0.09	MT	Baker
606	WCRU	960	U4	10	0.5	NC	Dallas
607	WRNS	960	U2	5	1	NC	Kinston
608	KNEB	960	U4	5	0.35	NE	Scottsbluff
609	KNDN	960	U1	5	0.16	NM	Farmington
610	WEAV	960	U4	5	5	NY	Plattsburgh
611	KLAD	960	U2	5	5	OR	Klamath Falls
612	WHYL	960	U4	5	0.02	PA	Carlisle
613	WATS	960	U1	5	0.05	PA	Sayre
614	KGKL	960	U2	5	1	TX	San Angelo
615	KOVO	960	U1	5	0.14	UT	Provo
616	WFIR	960	U2	10	5	VA	Roanoke
617	KALE	960	U2	5	1	WA	Richland
618	WTBF	**970**	U1	5	0.04	AL	Troy

MW	Call	kHz	Ant.	D	N	Sta	City of License
619	KVWM	970	U1	5	0.19	AZ	Show Low
620	KHTY	970	U4	1	5	CA	Bakersfield
621	KNWZ	970	U4	5	0.36	CA	Coachella
622	KFEL	970	U1	3.2	0.18	CO	Pueblo
623	WFLA	970	U4	25	11	FL	Tampa
624	WNIV	970	U1	5	0.03	GA	Atlanta
625	WVOP	970	U1	4	0.06	GA	Vidalia
626	KXTA	970	U2	2.5	0.9	ID	Rupert
627	WFSR	970	U1	5	0.02	KY	Harlan
628	WGTK	970	U4	5	5	KY	Louisville
629	WZAN	970	U2	5	5	ME	Portland
630	WZAM	970	U1	5	0.06	MI	Ishpeming
631	KQAQ	970	U4	5	0.5	MN	Austin
632	KBUL	970	U2	5	5	MT	Billings
633	WYSE	970	U1	5	0.03	NC	Canton
634	WDAY	970	U4	10	10	ND	Fargo
635	KJLT	970	U1	5	0.05	NE	North Platte
636	WNYM	970	U4	50	5	NJ	Hackensack
637	KNIH	970	U4	5	0.5	NV	Paradise
638	WDCZ	970	U3	5	5	NY	Buffalo
639	WFUN	970	U4	5	1	OH	Ashtabula
640	KCFO	970	U4	2.5	1	OK	Tulsa
641	KUFO	970	U2	5	5	OR	Portland
642	WBGG	970	U4	5	5	PA	Pittsburgh
643	WWRK	970	U1	10	0.03	SC	Florence
644	WKCI	970	U4	5	1	VA	Waynesboro
645	KTTO	970	U2	5.3	0.75	WA	Spokane
646	WHA	#970	U1	5	0.05	WI	Madison
647	KCAB	**980**	U1	5	0.03	AR	Dardanelle
648	KWSW	980	U2	5	0.5	CA	Eureka
649	KFWB	#980	U1	5	5	CA	Los Angeles
650	KDBV	980	U4	10	10	CA	Salinas
651	WTEM	980	U4	50	5	DC	Washington
652	WDVH	980	U1	5	0.16	FL	Gainesville
653	WRNE	980	U2	4	1	FL	Gulf Breeze
654	WHSR	‡980	U4	5	2.2	FL	Pompano Beach
655	WDDO	980	U1	2.6	0.08	GA	Perry
656	KSPZ	980	U4	5	1	ID	Ammon
657	KOKA	980	U1	5	0.07	LA	Shreveport
658	WCAP	980	U4	5	5	MA	Lowell
659	KKMS	980	U3	5	5	MN	Richfield
660	KMBZ	980	U2	9	5	MO	Kansas City
661	WAAV	980	U2	5	5	NC	Leland
662	KMIN	980	U1	5	0.23	NM	Grants
663	KVLV	980	D1	5		NV	Fallon
664	WOFX	#980	U2	5	5	NY	Troy
665	WONE	#980	U2	5	5	OH	Dayton
666	WILK	980	U2	5	1	PA	Wilkes-Barre
667	WULR	980	U4	3	0.16	SC	York
668	KDSJ	980	U2	5	1	SD	Deadwood
669	WYFN	980	U2	5	5	TN	Nashville
670	KQUE	980	U4	5	4	TX	Rosenberg-Richmond
671	KSVC	980	U2	10	1	UT	Richfield
672	WWTB	980	U2	5	1	VA	Bristol
673	KTCR	980	U4	5	0.5	WA	Selah
674	WCUB	980	U4	5	5	WI	Two Rivers
675	WHAW	980	U1	2.5	0.04	WV	Lost Creek
676	KTKT	**990**	U4	10	0.49	AZ	Tucson
677	KATD	990	U4	10	5	CA	Pittsburg
678	KTMS	990	U4	5	0.5	CA	Santa Barbara
679	KRKS	990	U2	6.5	0.39	CO	Denver
680	WNTY	990	U4	2.5	0.08	CT	Southington
681	WMYM	990	U4	7.5	5	FL	Kendall
682	WTLN	990	U4	50	14	FL	Orlando
683	WISK	990	D1	2.5		GA	Lawrenceville
684	WDEO	990	U4	9.2	0.25	MI	Ypsilanti
685	KRMO	990	U1	2.5	0.04	MO	Cassville
686	WEEB	990	U1	10	0.03	NC	Southern Pines
687	WDCX	#990	U4	5	2.5	NY	Rochester
688	WNTP	990	U4	50	10	PA	Philadelphia
689	WNTI	990	U4	10	0.1	PA	Somerset
690	WNML	990	U2	10	10	TN	Knoxville
691	KWAM	990	U4	10	0.45	TN	Memphis
692	KFCD	990	U4	7	0.92	TX	Farmersville
693	WNRV	990	U1	5	0.01	VA	Narrows-Pearisburg
694	KCEO	**#1000**	U4	10.53	0.97	CA	Vista
695	WYBT	1000	D1	5		FL	Blountstown
696	WMVP	1000	U4	50	50	IL	Chicago
697	WXTN	1000	D1	5		MS	Benton
698	KKIM	1000	U1	10	0.05	NM	Albuquerque
699	WLNL	1000	D1	5		NY	Horseheads
700	KTOK	1000	U4	5.8	5.8	OK	Oklahoma City
701	WIOO	1000	D1	15		PA	Carlisle
702	KSOO	1000	U4	10	0.1	SD	Sioux Falls
703	WHNY	1000	D4	5		TN	Paris
704	KOMO	1000	U2	50	50	WA	Seattle
705	KXXT	**1010**	U5	15	0.25	AZ	Tolleson
706	KCHJ	1010	U4	5	1	CA	Delano
707	KIQI	1010	U4	10	10	CA	San Francisco
708	KXPS	1010	U4	3.6	0.4	CA	Thousand Palms
709	KSIR	1010	U4	25	0.28	CO	Brush
710	WJXL	1010	U4	50	30	FL	Jacksonville Beach
711	WHFS	1010	U4	50	5	FL	Seffner
712	WTZA	‡1010	U1	50	0.07	GA	Atlanta
713	KXEN	1010	U4	50	0.5	MO	Saint Louis
714	WKJW	1010	U10	47	0.09	NC	Black Mountain
715	WCNL	1010	U1	10	0.03	NH	Newport
716	WINS	#1010	U3	50	50	NY	New York
717	KOOR	1010	D1	4.5		OR	Milwaukie
718	WHIN	1010	U1	5	0.04	TN	Gallatin
719	KTNZ	1010	U4	5	0.5	TX	Amarillo
720	KLAT	1010	U4	5	3.6	TX	Houston
721	KBBW	1010	U4	10	2.5	TX	Waco
722	KIHU	1010	U13	50	0.19	UT	Tooele
723	WPMH	1010	U4	5	0.44	VA	Portsmouth
724	KTNQ	**1020**	U4	50	50	CA	Los Angeles
725	WHDD	1020	D1	2.5		CT	Sharon
726	WLVJ	1020	U4	4.7	1.5	FL	Boynton Beach
727	KMMQ	1020	U4	50	1.4	NE	Plattsmouth
728	KCKN	1020	U4	50	50	NM	Roswell
729	KDKA	1020	U1	50	50	PA	Pittsburgh
730	WRIX	1020	D1	10		SC	Homeland Park
731	KDYK	1020	U5	4	0.4	WA	Union Gap
732	KFAY	**1030**	U4	6	1	AR	Farmington
733	KVOI	1030	U4	10	1	AZ	Cortaro
734	KJDJ	1030	U1	2.5	0.7	CA	San Luis Obispo
735	WONQ	1030	U2	45	1.7	FL	Oviedo
736	WEBS	1030	U1	5	0.003	GA	Calhoun
737	WNVR	1030	U7	10	0.12	IL	Vernon Hills
738	KBUF	1030	U2	2.5	1.2	KS	Holcomb
739	WBZ	#1030	U3	50	50	MA	Boston
740	WWGB	1030	D3	50		MD	Indian Head
741	WUFL	1030	D3	5		MI	Sterling Heights
742	WCTS	1030	U4	50	4	MN	Maplewood
743	KCWJ	1030	U4	5	0.5	MO	Blue Springs
744	WDRU	1030	D3	50		NC	Creedmoor
745	WNOW	1030	D3	9.4		NC	Mint Hill
746	KDUN	1030	U1	50	0.63	OR	Reedsport
747	WGSF	1030	U12	50	1	TN	Memphis
748	KCTA	1030	L1	50		TX	Corpus Christi
749	KMAS	1030	U1	10	1	WA	Shelton
750	WTHQ	1030	D5	10		WV	Point Pleasant
751	KTWO	1030	U2	50	50	WY	Casper
752	KCBR	**#1040**	D1	15		CO	Monument
753	WURN	1040	U4	50	5	FL	Miami
754	WHBO	1040	U2	3.6	0.42	FL	Pinellas Park
755	WPBS	1040	D1	50		GA	Conyers
756	WHO	1040	U1	50	50	IA	Des Moines
757	WSGH	1040	U4	9.1	0.18	NC	Lewisville
758	WCHR	1040	U7	15	1.5	NJ	Flemington
759	WYSL	1040	U7	20	0.5	NY	Avon
760	WZSK	1040	D1	2.5		PA	Everett
761	WJBE	1040	D1	10		TN	Powell
762	KGGR	1040	D1	3.3		TX	Dallas
763	KJPG	**1050**	D3	10		CA	Frazier Park
764	KTCT	1050	U4	50	10	CA	San Mateo
765	WJSB	1050	D1	3.1		FL	Crestview
766	WROS	1050	U4	5	0.01	FL	Jacksonville
767	WFAM	1050	U1	5	0.08	GA	Augusta
768	WBQH	1050	U1	10	0.04	MD	Silver Spring
769	WTKA	1050	U4	10	0.5	MI	Ann Arbor
770	KLOH	1050	U4	9.38	0.43	MN	Pipestone
771	KMTA	1050	U1	10	0.13	MT	Miles City
772	WFSC	1050	U1	5	0.15	NC	Franklin
773	WBVG	1050	U4	2.5	0.01	NY	Baldwinsville
774	WEPN	1050	U4	50	50	NY	New York

MW	Call	kHz	Ant.	D	N	Sta	City of License
775	KORE	1050	U1	5	0.1	OR	Springfield-Eugene
776	WAYS	1050	U4	5	0.47	SC	Conway
777	WBRG	1050	U1	3.8	0.09	VA	Lynchburg
778	WVXX	1050	U4	5	0.35	VA	Norfolk
779	KFIO	1050	U1	25	0.26	WA	Dishman
780	KBLE	1050	U1	5	0.44	WA	Seattle
781	WLYQ	1050	U1	5	0.14	WV	Parkersburg
782	KDUS	**1060**	U2	5	0.5	AZ	Tempe
783	KTNS	1060	U1	5	0.02	CA	Oakhurst
784	KRCN	1060	U1	50	0.11	CO	Longmont
785	WIXC	1060	U7	50	5	FL	Titusville
786	WKNG	1060	D1	15		GA	Tallapoosa
787	KBGN	1060	D1	10		ID	Caldwell
788	WMCL	1060	U5	2.5	0.002	IL	McLeansboro
789	WLNO	1060	U4	50	5	LA	New Orleans
790	WQOM	1060	U4	50	2.5	MA	Natick
791	WHFB	1060	U1	5	0.001	MI	Benton Harbor-St Joseph
792	WXNC	1060	D1	4		NC	Monroe
793	KKVV	1060	U1	5	0.04	NV	Las Vegas
794	KFOY	1060	U2	5	0.5	NV	Sparks
795	WILB	1060	D4	15		OH	Canton
796	KYW	#1060	U3	50	50	PA	Philadelphia
797	KGFX	1060	U4	10	1	SD	Pierre
798	KXPL	‡1060	D1	10		TX	El Paso
799	KIJN	1060	D3	10		TX	Farwell
800	KDYL	1060	U1	10	0.14	UT	South Salt Lake
801	WAPI	**1070**	U2	50	5	AL	Birmingham
802	KNX	#1070	U1	50	50	CA	Los Angeles
803	WNVY	1070	U1	15	0.02	FL	Cantonment
804	WFRF	1070	D1	10		FL	Tallahassee
805	WFNI	#1070	U4	50	10	IN	Indianapolis
806	KFTI	1070	U2	10	1	KS	Wichita
807	KSKK	1070	U2	10	5	MN	Verndale
808	KHMO	1070	U4	5	1	MO	Hannibal
809	KATQ	1070	U1	5	0.05	MT	Plentywood
810	WNCT	1070	U4	50	10	NC	Greenville
811	WPLB	1070	D1	5		NY	Plattsburgh
812	WZUN	1070	D1	2.5		NY	Sandy Creek-Pulaski
813	WKOK	1070	U2	10	1	PA	Sunbury
814	WCSZ	1070	U4	50	1.5	SC	Sans Souci
815	WFLI	1070	U4	50	2.5	TN	Lookout Mountain
816	WDIA	1070	U4	50	5	TN	Memphis
817	KNTH	1070	U4	10	5	TX	Houston
818	KWEL	1070	D1	2.5		TX	Midland
819	WINA	1070	U2	5	5	VA	Charlottesville
820	WTSO	1070	U4	10	5	WI	Madison
821	WBKW	1070	D1	10		WV	Beckley
822	WKAC	**1080**	D1	5		AL	Athens
823	KSCO	1080	U2	10	5	CA	Santa Cruz
824	WTIC	#1080	U2	50	50	CT	Hartford
825	WQOS	1080	U4	50	10	FL	Coral Gables
826	WHOO	1080	U4	6	0.05	FL	Winter Park
827	WFTD	1080	D4	50		GA	Marietta
828	KVNI	1080	U2	10	1	ID	Coeur d' Alene
829	WNWI	1080	U2	5	2.6	IL	Oak Lawn
830	WKJK	1080	U4	10	1	KY	Louisville
831	WKGX	1080	D1	5		NC	Lenoir
832	KFXX	1080	U4	50	9	OR	Portland
833	WWNL	1080	D4	50		PA	Pittsburgh
834	WALD	1080	D1	9		SC	Johnsonville
835	KRLD	#1080	U2	50	50	TX	Dallas
836	KSLL	1080	D1	10		UT	Price
837	KAAY	**1090**	U2	50	50	AR	Little Rock
838	KNCR	1090	D1	10		CA	Fortuna
839	KMXA	#1090	U4	50	0.5	CO	Aurora
840	WFCV	1090	D4	2.5		IN	Fort Wayne
841	WILD	‡1090	D1	4.8		MA	Boston
842	WBAL	1090	U2	50	50	MD	Baltimore
843	KEXS	1090	D4	10		MO	Excelsior Springs
844	KBOZ	‡1090	U2	5	5	MT	Bozeman
845	WTSB	1090	D1	9		NC	Selma
846	WCZZ	1090	D1	5		SC	Greenwood
847	WHGG	1090	D1	10		TN	Kingsport
848	KVOP	1090	U4	5	0.5	TX	Plainview
849	KFNQ	1090	U4	50	50	WA	Seattle
850	WAQE	1090	D1	5		WI	Rice Lake
851	KFNX	**1100**	U4	50	1	AZ	Cave Creek
852	KAFY	1100	U2	4.2	0.8	CA	Bakersfield
853	KFAX	1100	U3	50	50	CA	San Francisco
854	KNZZ	1100	U12	50	10	CO	Grand Junction
855	WWWE	1100	D1	5		GA	Hapeville
856	WCGA	‡1100	D1	10		GA	Woodbine
857	WZFG	1100	U2	50	0.44	MN	Dilworth
858	KKLL	1100	D1	5		MO	Webb City
859	KWWN	1100	U4	22	2	NV	Las Vegas
860	WHLI	1100	D3	10		NY	Hempstead
861	WTAM	1100	U1	50	50	OH	Cleveland
862	KDRY	1100	U2	11	1	TX	Alamo Heights
863	WTWN	1100	D1	5		VT	Wells River
864	WISS	1100	D1	2.5		WI	Berlin
865	WTOF	**1110**	D1	10		AL	Bay Minette
866	KGFL	1110	D1	5		AR	Clinton
867	KRDC	1110	U4	50	20	CA	Pasadena
868	KLIB	1110	U4	5	0.5	CA	Roseville
869	WTIS	1110	D1	10		FL	Tampa
870	WMBI	1110	D1	4.2		IL	Chicago
871	WUPE	1110	D3	5		MA	Pittsfield
872	WJML	1110	U4	10	0.01	MI	Petoskey
873	WBT	1110	U2	50	50	NC	Charlotte
874	KFAB	1110	U2	50	50	NE	Omaha
875	WMVX	1110	D3	5		NH	Salem
876	KEJL	1110	D1	5		NM	Humble City
877	WGNZ	1110	U7	5	0.002	OH	Fairborn
878	KBND	1110	U2	10	5	OR	Bend
879	WNAP	1110	D5	4.8		PA	Norristown
880	WPMZ	1110	D3	5		RI	East Providence
881	WSLV	1110	D1	2.5		TN	Ardmore
882	KTEK	1110	D3	2.5		TX	Alvin
883	KVTT	1110	D4	50		TX	Mineral Wells
884	WKQA	1110	D3	50		VA	Norfolk
885	KZSJ	**1120**	U1	5	0.15	CA	San Martin
886	KCRN	1120	D3	50		CO	Limon
887	WUST	1120	D5	50		DC	Washington
888	WBNW	1120	U4	5	1	MA	Concord
889	KMOX	#1120	U1	50	50	MO	Saint Louis
890	WTWZ	1120	D1	10		MS	Clinton
891	WSME	1120	D1	6		NC	Camp Lejeune
892	WKAJ	1120	U4	10	0.4	NY	Saint Johnsville
893	KETU	1120	D4	10		OK	Catoosa
894	KPNW	1120	U3	50	50	OR	Eugene
895	KTXW	1120	U4	5.6	0.15	TX	Manor
896	KANN	1120	U4	10	1.1	UT	Roy
897	WALQ	**1130**	D1	25		AL	Carrville
898	KRDU	1130	U4	5	6.2	CA	Dinuba
899	KSDO	1130	U4	10	10	CA	San Diego
900	WWBF	1130	U2	2.5	0.5	FL	Bartow
901	WLBA	1130	D1	10		GA	Gainesville
902	KWKH	1130	U2	50	50	LA	Shreveport
903	WDFN	1130	U4	50	10	MI	Detroit
904	KTLK	1130	U4	50	25	MN	Minneapolis
905	WPYB	1130	D1	6.5		NC	Benson
906	KBMR	1130	U1	10	0.02	ND	Bismarck
907	WBBR	1130	U2	50	50	NY	New York
908	KXET	‡1130	U4	25	0.49	OR	Mount Angel
909	WEAF	1130	U1	5	0.007	SC	Camden
910	KTMR	1130	D3	25		TX	Converse
911	WISN	1130	U4	50	10	WI	Milwaukee
912	WBXR	**1140**	D4	15		AL	Hazel Green
913	KLTK	1140	D1	5		AR	Centerton
914	KNWQ	1140	U4	10	2.5	CA	Palm Springs
915	KHTK	#1140	U4	50	50	CA	Sacramento
916	WPNS	‡1140	U1	3	0.01	FL	Destin
917	WQBA	1140	U4	50	10	FL	Miami
918	WURB	1140	U2	5	0.008	FL	Orlando
919	KGEM	1140	U2	10	10	ID	Boise
920	WVEL	1140	L1	5		IL	Pekin
921	WVHF	1140	D3	5		MI	Kentwood
922	KCXL	1140	U1	4	0.006	MO	Liberty
923	KXST	1140	U2	10	2.5	NV	North Las Vegas
924	WCJW	1140	D4	8		NY	Warsaw
925	KXRB	1140	U2	10	5	SD	Sioux Falls
926	KHFX	1140	U4	5	0.71	TX	Cleburne
927	KYOK	1140	D3	5		TX	Conroe
928	WRVA	1140	U3	50	50	VA	Richmond
929	WXLZ	1140	D1	2.5		VA	Saint Paul
930	KZMQ	1140	D1	10		WY	Greybull

MW	Call	kHz	Ant.	D	N	Sta	City of License
931	WJRD	**1150**	U2	20	1	AL	Tuscaloosa
932	KCKY	1150	U4	5	1	AZ	Coolidge
933	KEIB	1150	U4	50	44	CA	Los Angeles
934	KNRV	1150	U4	10	1	CO	Englewood
935	WMRD	1150	U1	2.5	0.04	CT	Middletown
936	WDEL	1150	U4	5	5	DE	Wilmington
937	WTMP	1150	U4	10	0.5	FL	Egypt Lake
938	WJEM	1150	U4	5	0.1	GA	Valdosta
939	KWKY	1150	U4	2.5	1	IA	Des Moines
940	WGGH	1150	U4	5	0.04	IL	Marion
941	KSAL	1150	U2	5	5	KS	Salina
942	WMST	1150	U1	2.5	0.05	KY	Mount Sterling
943	WJBO	1150	U4	15	5	LA	Baton Rouge
944	WWDJ	1150	U4	5	5	MA	Boston
945	KSEN	1150	U4	10	5	MT	Shelby
946	WGBR	1150	U4	5	0.8	NC	Goldsboro
947	WCUE	1150	U4	5	0.5	OH	Cuyahoga Falls
948	KAGO	1150	U2	5	1	OR	Klamath Falls
949	KGDD	1150	U1	5	0.01	OR	Portland
950	WAVO	1150	U1	5	0.05	SC	Rock Hill
951	KIMM	1150	U1	5	0.03	SD	Rapid City
952	WGOW	1150	U2	5	1	TN	Chattanooga
953	WCRK	1150	U2	5	0.5	TN	Morristown
954	KHRO	1150	U1	5	0.38	TX	El Paso
955	WNLR	1150	U1	2.5	0.03	VA	Churchville
956	KQQQ	1150	U1	11	0.02	WA	Pullman
957	KKNW	1150	U2	10	6	WA	Seattle
958	WEAQ	1150	U1	5	0.04	WI	Chippewa Falls
959	WHBY	1150	U4	20	25	WI	Kimberly
960	WELC	1150	D1	5		WV	Welch
961	WEWC	**1160**	U5	5	0.25	FL	Callahan
962	WRLZ	1160	U4	2.5	0.5	FL	Saint Cloud
963	WCFO	1160	U4	50	0.16	GA	East Point
964	WYLL	1160	U4	50	50	IL	Chicago
965	WCVX	1160	U4	5	0.99	KY	Florence
966	WKCM	1160	U1	2.5	0.05	KY	Hawesville
967	WMET	1160	U4	50	1.5	MD	Gaithersburg
968	WSKW	1160	U1	10	0.73	ME	Skowhegan
969	WCXI	1160	U4	15	0.4	MI	Fenton
970	KCTO	1160	U4	5	0.23	MO	Cleveland
971	WYDU	1160	U1	5	0.25	NC	Red Springs
972	WWQT	1160	U2	25	0.5	NC	Tryon
973	WOBM	1160	U4	5	8.9	NJ	Lakewood Township
974	WVNJ	1160	U4	20	2.5	NJ	Oakland
975	WSSV	1160	U1	5	0.57	NY	Mechanicville
976	WPIE	1160	U4	5	0.31	NY	Trumansburg
977	WCCS	1160	U4	10	1	PA	Homer City
978	WBYN	1160	U4	4	1	PA	Lehighton
979	WCRT	1160	U2	50	1	TN	Donelson
980	KBDT	1160	U4	35	1	TX	Highland Park
981	KRDY	1160	U4	10	1	TX	San Antonio
982	KSL	#1160	U1	50	50	UT	Salt Lake City
983	WODY	1160	U2	5	0.25	VA	Fieldale
984	KYET	**1170**	U1	6	0.001	AZ	Golden Valley
985	KCBQ	1170	U4	50	2.9	CA	San Diego
986	KLOK	#1170	U4	50	9	CA	San Jose
987	WAVS	1170	U2	5	0.25	FL	Davie
988	KFOW	1170	U1	2.5	0.005	MN	Waseca
989	WCXN	1170	D1	7.7		NC	Claremont
990	WCLN	1170	D1	5		NC	Clinton
991	KFAQ	#1170	U2	50	50	OK	Tulsa
992	WDEK	1170	D1	10		SC	Lexington
993	KPUG	1170	U2	10	5	WA	Bellingham
994	WWVA	1170	U2	50	50	WV	Wheeling
995	WGUE	**1180**	U7	5	0.02	AR	Turrell
996	KERN	1180	U4	50	10	CA	Wasco - Greenacres
997	-	1180	U3	100	100	FL	Marathon (R. Marti)
998	WZQZ	1180	D1	5		GA	Trion
999	WXLA	1180	D4	10		MI	Dimondale
1000	KYES	1180	U7	50	5	MN	Rockville
1001	WJNT	1180	U12	50	0.5	MS	Pearl
1002	KOFI	1180	U2	50	10	MT	Kalispell
1003	WLTT	1180	D3	10		NC	Carolina Beach
1004	KZOT	1180	U4	25	1	NE	Bellevue
1005	KCKQ	1180	U2	4	0.19	NV	Sparks
1006	WHAM	1180	U1	50	50	NY	Rochester
1007	WFGN	1180	D1	2.5		SC	Gaffney
1008	WKCE	1180	D1	10		TN	Knoxville

MW	Call	kHz	Ant.	D	N	Sta	City of License
1009	KGOL	1180	U4	50	3	TX	Humble
1010	KLPF	1180	U1	25	0.21	TX	Midland
1011	KLAY	1180	U2	5	1	WA	Lakewood
1012	WEUV	**1190**	D1	2.5		AL	Moulton
1013	KREB	1190	D1	5		AR	Bentonville-Bella Vista
1014	KJJI	1190	U2	25	0.35	AR	White Hall
1015	KNUV	1190	U4	5	0.25	AZ	Tolleson
1016	KGBN	1190	U4	20	1.3	CA	Anaheim
1017	KDYA	1190	D3	3		CA	Vallejo
1018	KVCU	1190	U1	6.8	0.11	CO	Boulder
1019	WAMT	1190	U2	4.7	0.23	FL	Pine Castle - Sky Lake
1020	WAFS	1190	D1	25		GA	Atlanta
1021	KQQZ	1190	U4	10	0.65	IL	Fairview Heights
1022	WOWO	#1190	U2	50	9.8	IN	Fort Wayne
1023	KKOJ	1190	D3	5		MN	Jackson
1024	KDMR	1190	U2	5	0.5	MO	Kansas City
1025	WMEJ	1190	D1	5		MS	Bay Saint Louis
1026	WIXE	1190	U1	5	0.07	NC	Monroe
1027	KXKS	1190	U1	10	0.02	NM	Albuquerque
1028	WLIB	1190	U4	10	30	NY	New York
1029	KEX	1190	U2	50	50	OR	Portland
1030	WSDQ	1190	D1	5		TN	Dunlap
1031	KFXR	1190	U4	50	5	TX	Dallas
1032	WCRW	1190	U4	50	1.2	VA	Leesburg
1033	WNWC	1190	U4	4.8	0.02	WI	Sun Prairie
1034	WVUS	1190	U1	4.5	0.02	WV	Grafton
1035	KPSF	**1200**	U4	5	1.3	CA	Cathedral City
1036	KYAA	1200	U2	25	10	CA	Soquel
1037	WRTO	1200	U4	20	4.5	IL	Chicago
1038	WXKS	1200	U4	50	50	MA	Newton
1039	WMUZ	1200	U4	50	15	MI	Taylor
1040	WXIT	1200	D1	4.2		NC	Blowing Rock
1041	WSML	1200	U2	10	1	NC	Graham
1042	KFNW	1200	U4	50	13	ND	West Fargo
1043	WRKK	1200	U4	10	0.25	PA	Hughesville
1044	WKST	1200	U2	5	1	PA	New Castle
1045	WJXY	1200	U1	6.5	0.01	SC	Atlantic Beach
1046	WFCN	1200	D1	10		TN	Nashville
1047	WOAI	#1200	U1	50	50	TX	San Antonio
1048	WYSN	1200	U1	5	0.009	WV	Huntington
1049	WTXK	**1210**	U1	10	0.003	AL	Pike Road
1050	KEVT	‡1210	U2	10	1	AZ	Sahuarita
1051	KQEQ	1210	U5	5	0.37	CA	Fowler
1052	KRPU	1210	U5	5	0.5	CA	Rocklin
1053	KPRZ	1210	U4	20	10	CA	San Marcos
1054	WNMA	1210	U4	47	2.5	FL	Miami Springs
1055	WILY	1210	U11	10	0.003	IL	Centralia
1056	WJNL	1210	D1	50		MI	Kingsley
1057	KGYN	1210	U2	10	10	OK	Guymon
1058	WPHT	1210	U1	50	50	PA	Philadelphia
1059	WANB	1210	D1	5		PA	Waynesburg
1060	KOKK	1210	U4	5	0.87	SD	Huron
1061	WMPS	1210	U4	10	0.25	TN	Bartlett
1062	WSBI	1210	D1	10		TN	Static
1063	KUBR	1210	U4	10	5	TX	San Juan
1064	KHKR	1210	U1	10	0.23	UT	Washington
1065	KMIA	‡1210	U4	27.5	0.22	WA	Auburn-Federal Way
1066	KRSV	1210	U1	5	0.25	WY	Afton
1067	KHAT	1210	U2	10	1	WY	Laramie
1068	KDOW	**1220**	U1	5	0.14	CA	Palo Alto
1069	WSLM	1220	U4	5	0.08	IN	Salem
1070	KLBB	1220	U1	5	0.25	MN	Stillwater
1071	WDYT	1220	U5	25	0.1	NC	Kings Mountain
1072	WENC	1220	U1	5	0.15	NC	Whiteville
1073	WGNY	1220	U4	10	0.18	NY	Newburgh
1074	WHKW	1220	U3	50	50	OH	Cleveland
1075	WFAX	1220	U1	5	0.04	VA	Falls Church
		1230	Various stns of 1kW or less				
		1240	Various stns of 1kW or less				
1076	WZOB	**1250**	U1	5	0.12	AL	Fort Payne
1077	WRBZ	1250	U1	5	0.08	AL	Wetumpka
1078	KHIL	1250	U1	5	0.19	AZ	Willcox
1079	KZER	1250	U4	2.5	1	CA	Santa Barbara
1080	KLLK	1250	U4	5	2.5	CA	Willits
1081	WHNZ	#1250	U4	25	5.9	FL	Tampa
1082	KYYS	1250	U4	25	3.7	KS	Kansas City
1083	WARE	1250	U4	5	2.5	MA	Ware
1084	WJMK	1250	U4	5	1.1	MI	Bridgeport

MW	Call	kHz	Ant.	D	N	Sta	City of License
1085	KBRF	1250	U2	5	2.2	MN	Fergus Falls
1086	KIKC	1250	U1	5	0.13	MT	Forsyth
1087	WGHB	1250	U4	5	2.5	NC	Farmville
1088	WBRM	1250	U1	5	0.05	NC	Marion
1089	WGAM	1250	U4	5	5	NH	Manchester
1090	WMTR	1250	U4	5	7	NJ	Morristown
1091	WLEM	1250	U1	2.5	0.03	PA	Emporium
1092	WPGP	1250	U2	5	5	PA	Pittsburgh
1093	WTMA	1250	U2	5	1	SC	Charleston
1094	KDEI	1250	U2	5	1	TX	Port Arthur
1095	KZDC	1250	U4	25	0.92	TX	San Antonio
1096	KNEU	1250	U1	5	0.12	UT	Roosevelt
1097	WDVA	1250	U2	5	5	VA	Danville
1098	WRCW	1250	U4	3	0.12	VA	Warrenton
1099	KWSU	#1250	U1	5	2.5	WA	Pullman
1100	KKDZ	#1250	U2	5	5	WA	Seattle
1101	WSSP	1250	U4	5	5	WI	Milwaukee
1102	WYKM	1250	D1	5		WV	Rupert
1103	WYDE	**1260**	U1	5	0.04	AL	Birmingham
1104	KBSZ	1260	U1	4.5	0.05	AZ	Apache Junction
1105	KSUR	1260	U4	20	7.5	CA	Beverly Hills
1106	KSFB	1260	U1	5	1	CA	San Francisco
1107	WQOF	1260	U4	35	5	DC	Washington
1108	WFTW	1260	U1	2.5	0.13	FL	Fort Walton Beach
1109	WSUA	1260	U4	50	20	FL	Miami
1110	WUFE	1260	D1	5		GA	Baxley
1111	WMDG	‡1260	U1	5.1	0.05	GA	East Point
1112	KDLF	1260	U5	5	0.03	IA	Boone
1113	KNBL	1260	U1	5	0.06	ID	Idaho Falls
1114	KKOO	1260	U1	8.4	0.03	ID	Weiser
1115	WSDZ	1260	U4	20	5	IL	Belleville
1116	WNDE	#1260	U2	5	5	IN	Indianapolis
1117	KBRH	1260	U1	5	0.12	LA	Baton Rouge
1118	WBIX	1260	U2	5	5	MA	Boston
1119	WPNW	1260	U4	10	1	MI	Zeeland
1120	KSGF	1260	U2	5	5	MO	Springfield
1121	WKXR	1260	U4	5	0.5	NC	Asheboro
1122	WFJS	1260	U4	5.9	2.5	NJ	Trenton
1123	KTRC	1260	U1	5	1	NM	Santa Fe
1124	WSKO	1260	U2	5	5	NY	Syracuse
1125	WCCR	#1260	U4	10	5	OH	Cleveland
1126	WNXT	1260	U4	5	1	OH	Portsmouth
1127	WRIE	1260	U4	5	5	PA	Erie
1128	WPHB	1260	U1	5	0.03	PA	Philipsburg
1129	WPJF	1260	U1	5	0.01	SC	Greenville
1130	WHYM	1260	U1	5	0.05	SC	Lake City
1131	KWYR	1260	U1	5	0.14	SD	Winner
1132	WNOO	1260	U1	5	0.02	TN	Chattanooga
1133	WDKN	1260	U1	5	0.01	TN	Dickson
1134	KSML	1260	U1	4.5	0.07	TX	Diboll
1135	WCHV	1260	U4	5	2.5	VA	Charlottesville
1136	WWVT	#1260	U1	5	0.02	VA	Christiansburg
1137	WXCE	1260	U4	5	5	WI	Amery
1138	KPOW	1260	U2	5	1	WY	Powell
1139	WIJD	**1270**	U1	5	0.1	AL	Prichard
1140	KDJI	1270	U1	5	0.13	AZ	Holbrook
1141	KGAY	1270	U4	5	0.75	CA	Thousand Palms
1142	KVMI	1270	U2	5	1	CA	Tulare
1143	WIWA	1270	U4	25	5	FL	Eatonville
1144	WNOG	1270	U4	5	5	FL	Naples
1145	WTLY	1270	U1	5	0.11	FL	Tallahassee
1146	WBOJ	1270	U1	5	0.23	GA	Columbus
1147	WJJC	1270	U1	5	0.17	GA	Commerce
1148	KTFI	1270	U1	5	0.86	ID	Twin Falls
1149	WKBF	1270	U2	5	5	IL	Rock Island
1150	WCMR	1270	U4	5	1	IN	Elkhart
1151	KSCB	1270	U1	5	0.02	KS	Liberal
1152	WACM	1270	U4	5	1	MA	Springfield
1153	WCBC	1270	U4	5	1	MD	Cumberland
1154	WMKT	1270	U2	27	5	MI	Charlevoix
1155	WXYT	#1270	U4	50	50	MI	Detroit
1156	WWWI	1270	U2	5	5	MN	Baxter
1157	KFAN	1270	U4	5	1	MN	Rochester
1158	WCGC	1270	U4	10	0.5	NC	Belmont
1159	WMPM	1270	U1	5	0.14	NC	Smithfield
1160	WTSN	1270	U4	5	5	NH	Dover
1161	KBZZ	1270	U2	13	5	NV	Sparks
1162	WHLD	1270	U4	5	1	NY	Niagara Falls
1163	WDLA	1270	U1	5	0.08	NY	Walton
1164	KRXO	1270	U4	5	1	OK	Claremore
1165	KAJO	1270	U1	10	0.04	OR	Grants Pass
1166	WLBR	1270	U4	5	1	PA	Lebanon
1167	WHGS	1270	U1	10	0.21	SC	Hampton
1168	KNWC	1270	U4	5	2.3	SD	Sioux Falls
1169	WLIK	1270	U2	5	0.5	TN	Newport
1170	KFLC	#1270	U4	50	5	TX	Benbrook
1171	WHEO	1270	D1	5		VA	Stuart
1172	KBAM	1270	U1	5	0.08	WA	Longview
1173	KIML	1270	U2	5	1	WY	Gillette
1174	WMXB	**1280**	U2	5	0.5	AL	Tuscaloosa
1175	KXEG	‡1280	U1	2.5	0.04	AZ	Phoenix
1176	KXTK	1280	U4	10	2.5	CA	Arroyo Grande
1177	KBNO	1280	U4	5	5	CO	Denver
1178	WDSP	‡1280	U1	5	0.04	FL	De Funiak Springs
1179	WIHB	1280	U1	5	0.09	GA	Macon
1180	WGBF	1280	U2	5	1	IN	Evansville
1181	WODT	1280	U3	5	5	LA	New Orleans
1182	WPKZ	1280	U4	5	1	MA	Fitchburg
1183	WHTP	1280	U1	5	0.04	ME	Gardiner
1184	WWTC	1280	U4	10	15	MN	Minneapolis
1185	KVXR	1280	U4	5	1	MN	Moorhead
1186	WYAL	1280	D1	5		NC	Scotland Neck
1187	KRZE	1280	U1	5	0.1	NM	Farmington
1188	KQLL	1280	U1	5	0.02	NV	Henderson
1189	WADO	1280	U4	50	7.2	NY	New York
1190	WHTK	1280	U2	5	5	NY	Rochester
1191	KRVM	1280	U4	5	1.5	OR	Eugene
1192	WHVR	1280	U4	5	0.5	PA	Hanover
1193	WUZZ	1280	U2	4.9	1	PA	New Castle
1194	WANS	1280	U2	5	1	SC	Anderson
1195	WJAY	1280	U1	4.2	0.27	SC	Mullins
1196	WMCP	1280	U4	5	0.5	TN	Columbia
1197	KZNS	1280	U4	50	0.67	UT	Salt Lake City
1198	WYVE	1280	U1	2.5	0.16	VA	Wytheville
1199	KZFS	1280	U4	5	0.12	WA	Spokane
1200	KIT	1280	U1	5	1	WA	Yakima
1201	WNAM	1280	U4	5	5	WI	Neenah-Menasha
1202	WOPP	**1290**	U4	2.5	0.5	AL	Opp
1203	KUOA	1290	U1	5	0.03	AR	Siloam Springs
1204	KPAY	1290	U2	5	5	CA	Chico
1205	KAZA	1290	U4	5	0.08	CA	Gilroy
1206	KKDD	1290	U4	5	5	CA	San Bernardino
1207	WWTX	#1290	U1	2.5	0.03	DE	Wilmington
1208	WJNO	1290	U4	10	4.9	FL	West Palm Beach
1209	WCHK	1290	U2	10	0.5	GA	Canton
1210	WTKS	1290	U2	5.3	5	GA	Savannah
1211	KOUU	1290	U5	50	0.02	ID	Pocatello
1212	WIRL	1290	U4	5	5	IL	Peoria
1213	KMMM	1290	U4	5	0.5	KS	Pratt
1214	WCBL	1290	U1	5	0.05	KY	Benton
1215	WKLB	1290	U1	5	0.03	KY	Manchester
1216	KGVO	1290	U2	5	5	MT	Missoula
1217	WHKY	1290	U4	50	1	NC	Hickory
1218	WJCV	1290	U1	5	0.04	NC	Jacksonville
1219	KOIL	1290	U2	5	5	NE	Omaha
1220	WKBK	1290	U3	5	5	NH	Keene
1221	WNBF	1290	U2	9.3	5	NY	Binghamton
1222	WHIO	1290	U2	5	5	OH	Dayton
1223	KUMA	1290	U2	5	5	OR	Pendleton
1224	WFBG	1290	U2	5	1	PA	Altoona
1225	WRPA	1290	U4	10	10	RI	Providence
1226	KIVY	1290	U1	2.5	0.17	TX	Crockett
1227	KRGE	1290	U2	5	5	TX	Weslaco
1228	KWFS	1290	U1	5	0.07	TX	Wichita Falls
1229	WDZY	1290	U1	25	0.04	VA	Colonial Heights
1230	WZTI	1290	U4	5	5	WI	Greenfield
1231	WKLJ	1290	U1	5	0.05	WI	Sparta
1232	WVOW	1290	U2	5	1	WV	Logan
1233	KOWB	1290	U4	5	1	WY	Laramie
1234	KSMD	**1300**	D1	5		AR	Searcy
1235	KWRU	1300	U2	5	1	CA	Fresno
1236	KPMO	#1300	U1	5	0.07	CA	Mendocino
1237	KAZN	1300	U4	23	4.2	CA	Pasadena
1238	KCSF	#1300	U1	5	1	CO	Colorado Springs
1239	WKQK	1300	U4	5	1	FL	Cocoa Beach
1240	WFFG	‡1300	U3	2.5	2.5	FL	Marathon

MW	Call	kHz	Ant.	D	N	Sta	City of License
1241	WQBN	1300	U5	5	0.16	FL	Temple Terrace
1242	WMTM	1300	U1	5	0.06	GA	Moultrie
1243	KGLO	1300	U4	5	5	IA	Mason City
1244	KLER	1300	U2	5	1	ID	Orofino
1245	WRDZ	1300	U4	4.5	4	IL	La Grange
1246	WLXG	1300	U2	2.5	1	KY	Lexington
1247	KSYB	1300	U1	5	0.03	LA	Shreveport
1248	WJZ	1300	U4	5	5	MD	Baltimore
1249	WOOD	1300	U3	20	20	MI	Grand Rapids
1250	KPMI	1300	U2	2.5	0.6	MN	Bemidji
1251	WOAD	1300	U1	3.6	0.73	MS	Jackson
1252	WSYD	1300	U2	5	1	NC	Mount Airy
1253	KBRL	1300	U4	5	0.13	NE	McCook
1254	WPNH	1300	U1	5	0.08	NH	Plymouth
1255	WIMG	1300	U4	3.2	1.3	NJ	Ewing
1256	KCMY	1300	U1	5	0.12	NV	Carson City
1257	WXRL	1300	U4	5	2.5	NY	Lancaster
1258	WGDJ	1300	U4	10	8	NY	Rensselaer
1259	WJMO	1300	U3	5	5	OH	Cleveland
1260	KAKC	1300	U4	5	1	OK	Tulsa
1261	KAPL	1300	U2	20	5	OR	Phoenix
1262	WODS	1300	U4	5	0.5	PA	West Hazleton
1263	KOLY	1300	U1	5	0.11	SD	Mobridge
1264	WMTN	1300	U1	5	0.09	TN	Morristown
1265	WNQM	1300	U2	50	5	TN	Nashville
1266	KVET	1300	U4	5	1	TX	Austin
1267	WKCY	1300	U1	6.4	0.005	VA	Harrisonburg
1268	KKOL	1300	U4	50	3.2	WA	Seattle
1269	WFGM	1300	U1	2.5	0.04	WV	Morgantown
1270	WHEP	**1310**	U1	2.5	0.04	AL	Foley
1271	WJUS	1310	U1	5	0.03	AL	Marion
1272	KIHP	1310	U1	3.4	0.26	AZ	Mesa
1273	KIQQ	1310	U4	5	0.11	CA	Barstow
1274	KMKY	1310	U3	5	5	CA	Oakland
1275	KFKA	1310	U2	5	1	CO	Greeley
1276	WICH	1310	U4	5	5	CT	Norwich
1277	WYND	1310	U1	10.4	0.11	FL	DeLand
1278	WAUC	1310	U4	5	0.5	FL	Wauchula
1279	WJZA	1310	U1	2.5	0.03	GA	Decatur
1280	KLIX	1310	U2	5	2.5	ID	Twin Falls
1281	WTLC	1310	U2	5	1	IN	Indianapolis
1282	WDOC	1310	U1	5	0.02	KY	Prestonsburg
1283	KMBS	1310	U1	5	0.04	LA	West Monroe
1284	WORC	1310	U4	5	1	MA	Worcester
1285	WLOB	1310	U4	5	5	ME	Portland
1286	WDTW	1310	U4	5	5	MI	Dearborn
1287	WCCW	1310	U4	15	7.5	MI	Traverse City
1288	KGLB	1310	U4	2.5	0.27	MN	Glencoe
1289	KZRG	1310	U4	5	1	MO	Joplin
1290	KEIN	1310	U1	5	1	MT	Great Falls
1291	WISE	1310	U2	5	1	NC	Asheville
1292	WGSP	1310	U2	5	0.24	NC	Charlotte
1293	WTIK	1310	U4	5	1	NC	Durham
1294	KNOX	1310	U2	5	5	ND	Grand Forks
1295	WADB	1310	U4	2.5	1	NJ	Asbury Park
1296	KKNS	1310	U2	5	0.5	NM	Corrales
1297	WRVP	1310	U4	5	0.03	NY	Mount Kisco
1298	WTLB	1310	U4	5	0.5	NY	Utica
1299	KNPT	1310	U2	5	1	OR	Newport
1300	WBFD	1310	U1	2.5	0.08	PA	Bedford
1301	WICU	1310	U1	5	0.09	PA	Warren
1302	WDKD	1310	U1	5	0.06	SC	Kingstree
1303	WDXI	1310	U2	5	1	TN	Jackson
1304	KTCK	1310	U4	25	5	TX	Dallas
1305	KAHL	1310	U4	5	0.23	TX	San Antonio
1306	WDCT	1310	U4	5	0.5	VA	Fairfax
1307	WGH	1310	U4	20	5	VA	Newport News
1308	KZXR	‡1310	U1	5	0.06	WA	Prosser
1309	WIBA	1310	U2	5	5	WI	Madison
1310	WSLW	1310	D1	5		WV	White Sulphur Springs
1311	WENN	**1320**	U1	5	0.11	AL	Birmingham
1312	KWHN	1320	U2	5	5	AR	Fort Smith
1313	KIFM	1320	U4	5	5	CA	West Sacramento
1314	WATR	1320	U4	5	1	CT	Waterbury
1315	WLQY	1320	U4	5	5	FL	Hollywood
1316	WJNJ	1320	U2	50	5	FL	Jacksonville
1317	WDDV	1320	U4	5	1	FL	Venice
1318	WHIE	1320	U1	5	0.08	GA	Griffin
1319	KNCB	1320	U1	5	0.05	LA	Vivian
1320	WARA	1320	U4	5	5	MA	Attleboro
1321	WILS	1320	U4	25	1.9	MI	Lansing
1322	WDMJ	1320	U1	5	0.13	MI	Marquette
1323	KOZY	1320	U2	5	5	MN	Grand Rapids
1324	KSIV	1320	U2	4.6	0.27	MO	Clayton
1325	WRJW	1320	U1	5	0.07	MS	Picayune
1326	WCOG	1320	U4	5	5	NC	Greensboro
1327	WKRK	1320	U1	5	0.06	NC	Murphy
1328	KHRT	1320	U1	2.5	0.31	ND	Minot
1329	WDER	1320	U4	10	1	NH	Derry
1330	WJAS	1320	U4	7	3.3	PA	Pittsburgh
1331	WISW	1320	U2	5	2.5	SC	Columbia
1332	KELO	1320	U2	5	5	SD	Sioux Falls
1333	WGOC	1320	U2	5	0.5	TN	Kingsport
1334	WMSR	1320	U1	5	0.07	TN	Manchester
1335	KXYZ	1320	U4	10	5	TX	Houston
1336	WVNZ	1320	U4	5	0.008	VA	Richmond
1337	KXRO	1320	U2	5	1	WA	Aberdeen
1338	WFHR	1320	U2	5	0.5	WI	Wisconsin Rapids
1339	WZCT	**1330**	U1	5	0.03	AL	Scottsboro
1340	KWFM	1330	U2	2	5	AZ	South Tucson
1341	KWKW	1330	U2	5	5	CA	Los Angeles
1342	KLBS	1330	U2	0.42	5	CA	Los Banos
1343	WJNX	1330	U4	5	1	FL	Fort Pierce
1344	WEBY	1330	U5	25	0.07	FL	Milton
1345	WCVC	1330	I1	3.2	0.02	FL	Tallahassee
1346	KPTY	1330	U4	5	5	IA	Waterloo
1347	WKTA	1330	U4	5	0.11	IL	Evanston
1348	WBGW	1330	U2	5	1	IN	Evansville
1349	KNSS	1330	U2	5	5	KS	Wichita
1350	WKDP	1330	U4	5	0.01	KY	Corbin
1351	KVOL	1330	U2	5	1	LA	Lafayette
1352	WRCA	1330	U4	25	17	MA	Watertown
1353	WHGM	1330	U2	5	0.5	MD	Havre de Grace
1354	WTRX	1330	U4	5	1	MI	Flint
1355	WLOL	1330	U4	9.7	5.1	MN	Minneapolis
1356	WNIX	1330	U1	3.8	0.05	MS	Greenville
1357	KGAK	1330	U2	5	1	NM	Gallup
1358	WWRV	1330	U4	10	3.8	NY	New York
1359	WEBO	1330	U1	5	0.03	NY	Owego
1360	KKPZ	#1330	U3	5	5	OR	Portland
1361	WFNN	1330	U4	5	5	PA	Erie
1362	WPJS	1330	U1	3.2	0.02	SC	Conway
1363	WYRD	1330	U2	5	5	SC	Greenville
1364	KCKM	1330	U2	12	1	TX	Monahans
1365	WBTM	1330	U2	5	1	VA	Danville
1366	WESR	1330	U1	5	0.05	VA	Onley-Onancock
1367	KYOZ	1330	U1	5	0.02	WA	Spokane
1368	WHBL	1330	U4	5	1	WI	Sheboygan
1369	KOVE	1330	U1	5	0.25	WY	Lander
		1340	Various stns of 1kW or less				
1370	WTDR	**1350**	U2	5	1	AL	Gadsden
1371	KZTD	1350	U1	2.5	0.07	AR	Cabot
1372	KPWK	1350	U4	5	0.6	CA	San Bernardino
1373	KSRO	1350	U2	5	5	CA	Santa Rosa
1374	WINY	1350	U1	5	0.07	CT	Putnam
1375	WFNS	1350	U1	2.5	0.11	GA	Blackshear
1376	WBML	1350	U2	15	0.5	GA	Warner Robins
1377	KRNT	1350	U2	5	5	IA	Des Moines
1378	KRLC	1350	U1	5	0.15	ID	Lewiston
1379	KTIK	1350	U2	5	0.6	ID	Nampa
1380	WIOU	1350	U4	5	1	IN	Kokomo
1381	WWWL	1350	U2	5	5	LA	New Orleans
1382	WZGM	1350	U1	10	0.05	NC	Black Mountain
1383	WEZS	1350	U1	5	0.11	NH	Laconia
1384	WHWH	1350	U4	5	5	NJ	Princeton
1385	KABQ	1350	U2	5	0.5	NM	Albuquerque
1386	WARF	#1350	U3	5	5	OH	Akron
1387	WOYK	1350	U2	5	1	PA	York
1388	KCOX	1350	U1	5	0.03	TX	Jasper
1389	KXTN	1350	U2	5	5	TX	San Antonio
1390	WBLT	1350	U1	5	0.04	VA	Bedford
1391	WNVA	1350	U1	5	0.03	VA	Norton
1392	WGPL	1350	U4	5	5	VA	Portsmouth
1393	WIXI	**1360**	U1	12	0.04	AL	Jasper
1394	WMOB	1360	U4	9	0.2	AL	Mobile
1395	KPXQ	1360	U2	50	1	AZ	Glendale

MW	Call	kHz	Ant.	D	N	Sta	City of License
1396	KFIV	1360	U4	4	0.95	CA	Modesto
1397	KLSD	1360	U1	5	1	CA	San Diego
1398	KHNC	1360	U2	10	1	CO	Johnstown
1399	WDRC	1360	U2	5	5	CT	Hartford
1400	WHNR	1360	U4	5	2.5	FL	Cypress Gardens
1401	WCGL	1360	U1	5	0.08	FL	Jacksonville
1402	WQVN	1360	U1	9.3	0.4	FL	North Miami
1403	KSCJ	1360	U2	5	5	IA	Sioux City
1404	WKMI	1360	U2	5	1	MI	Kalamazoo
1405	KKBJ	1360	U2	5	2.5	MN	Bemidji
1406	WCHL	1360	U2	5	1	NC	Chapel Hill
1407	WNJC	1360	U4	5	0.8	NJ	Washington Twnshp
1408	KBUY	1360	U1	5	0.2	NM	Ruidoso
1409	WYOS	1360	U4	5	0.5	NY	Binghamton
1410	WSAI	1360	U2	5	5	OH	Cincinnati
1411	WWOW	1360	U1	5	0.03	OH	Conneaut
1412	KOHU	1360	U2	4.3	0.5	OR	Hermiston
1413	KUIK	1360	U2	5	5	OR	Hillsboro
1414	WPPA	1360	U4	5	0.5	PA	Pottsville
1415	WELP	1360	U1	5	0.03	SC	Easley
1416	KDJW	1360	U4	6	0.32	TX	Amarillo
1417	KWWJ	1360	U4	5	1	TX	Baytown
1418	KMNY	1360	U4	50	0.89	TX	Hurst
1419	WCGX	1360	U1	5	0.03	VA	Galax
1420	WHBG	1360	U1	5	0.009	VA	Harrisonburg
1421	KKMO	1360	U1	5	5	WA	Tacoma
1422	WTAQ	1360	U4	10	5	WI	Green Bay
1423	WMOV	1360	D1	5		WV	Ravenswood
1424	KRKK	1360	U2	5	1	WY	Rock Springs
1425	KWRM‡	**1370**	U4	5	2.5	CA	Corona
1426	KRAC	1370	U4	4	0.2	CA	Red Bluff
1427	KZSF	1370	U3	5	5	CA	San Jose
1428	WOCA	1370	U1	5	0.03	FL	Ocala
1429	WCOA	1370	U2	5	5	FL	Pensacola
1430	WLOP	1370	U1	5	0.03	GA	Jesup
1431	KDTH	1370	U2	5	5	IA	Dubuque
1432	WGCL	1370	U4	5	0.5	IN	Bloomington
1433	KGNO	1370	U1	5	0.23	KS	Dodge City
1434	WGOH	1370	U1	5	0.02	KY	Grayson
1435	WQLL	1370	U4	50	24	MD	Pikesville
1436	WDEA	1370	U4	5	5	ME	Ellsworth
1437	WLJW	1370	U4	5	1	MI	Cadillac
1438	KXTL	1370	U1	5	5	MT	Butte
1439	WLLN	1370	U4	5	0.04	NC	Lillington
1440	WGIV	1370	U1	16	0.04	NC	Pineville
1441	WTAB	1370	U1	5	0.1	NC	Tabor City
1442	KWTL	1370	U1	12	0.27	ND	Grand Forks
1443	WFEA	1370	U4	5	5	NH	Manchester
1444	WJIP	1370	D1	5		NY	Ellenville
1445	WXXI	1370	U2	5	5	NY	Rochester
1446	WSPD	1370	U2	5	5	OH	Toledo
1447	WKMC	1370	U4	5	0.03	PA	Roaring Spring
1448	WXCT	1370	U2	5	5	TN	Chattanooga
1449	KJCE	1370	U4	5	0.5	TX	Rollingwood
1450	KSOP	1370	U2	5	0.5	UT	South Salt Lake
1451	WHEE	1370	D1	5		VA	Martinsville
1452	WSHV	1370	U1	4.2	0.41	VA	South Hill
1453	WCCN	1370	U1	5	0.04	WI	Neillsville
1454	WVMR	1370	D1	5		WV	Frost
1455	WVLY	1370	U1	5	0.02	WV	Moundsville
1456	WVSA	**1380**	U1	5	0.03	AL	Vernon
1457	KZTS	1380	U4	5	2.5	AR	North Little Rock
1458	KLPZ	1380	U1	2.5	0.05	AZ	Parker
1459	KTKZ	1380	U4	5	5	CA	Sacramento
1460	WFNW	1380	U4	3.5	0.35	CT	Naugatuck
1461	WELE	1380	U4	5	2.5	FL	Ormond Beach
1462	WWMI	1380	U2	9.8	6.5	FL	Saint Petersburg
1463	WAOK	1380	U2	25	4.2	GA	Atlanta
1464	WBEL	1380	U2	5	5	IL	South Beloit
1465	WKJG	1380	U4	5	5	IN	Fort Wayne
1466	KCNW	1380	U1	2.5	0.02	KS	Fairway
1467	WMJR	1380	U1	5	0.03	KY	Nicholasville
1468	WPYR	1380	U4	5	0.06	LA	Baton Rouge
1469	WPHM	1380	U4	5	5	MI	Port Huron
1470	KLIZ	1380	U2	5	5	MN	Brainerd
1471	KXFN	1380	U4	5	1	MO	Saint Louis
1472	WKJV	1380	U2	25	1	NC	Asheville
1473	WWNT	1380	U4	5	2.5	NC	Winston-Salem
1474	WABH	1380	U4	10	0.45	NY	Bath
1475	WKDM	1380	U4	5	13	NY	New York
1476	KMUS	1380	U4	7	0.25	OK	Sperry
1477	WNRI	1380	U1	2.5	0.01	RI	Woonsocket
1478	WNRR	1380	U1	4	0.07	SC	North Augusta
1479	KOTA	1380	U2	5	5	SD	Rapid City
1480	WHEW	1380	D1	2.8		TN	Franklin
1481	WLRM	1380	U4	2.5	1	TN	Millington
1482	KHEY	1380	U1	5	0.5	TX	El Paso
1483	KWMF	1380	U5	4	0.16	TX	Pleasanton
1484	KRCM	1380	U4	22	0.05	TX	Shenandoah
1485	WBTK	1380	U4	5	5	VA	Richmond
1486	WSYB	1380	U1	5	0.02	VT	Rutland
1487	KRKO	1380	U2	50	50	WA	Everett
1488	WOTE	1380	U4	3.9	1.8	WI	Clintonville
1489	WHMA	**1390**	U2	5	1	AL	Anniston
1490	KFFK	1390	U1	5	0.03	AR	Rogers
1491	KLTX	1390	U4	5	3.6	CA	Long Beach
1492	KLOC	1390	U4	5	5	CA	Turlock
1493	KGNU	1390	U1	5	0.13	CO	Denver
1494	WAJD	1390	U1	5	0.05	FL	Gainesville
1495	WGRB	#1390	U4	5	5	IL	Chicago
1496	WKIC	1390	D1	5		KY	Hazard
1497	WPLM	1390	U4	5	5	MA	Plymouth
1498	WZHF	1390	U4	9	1	MD	Capitol Heights
1499	WEGP	1390	U4	25	10	ME	Presque Isle
1500	WLCM	1390	U4	5	4.5	MI	Holt
1501	KXSS	1390	U4	2.5	1	MN	Waite Park
1502	KJPW	1390	U1	5	0.11	MO	Waynesville
1503	WROA	1390	U4	5	5	MS	Gulfport
1504	WMER	1390	U1	5	0.1	MS	Meridian
1505	WEED	1390	U1	5	0.03	NC	Rocky Mount
1506	KRRZ	1390	U1	5	1	ND	Minot
1507	KENN	1390	U2	5	1.3	NM	Farmington
1508	KHOB	1390	U2	5	0.5	NM	Hobbs
1509	WEOK	1390	U4	5	0.1	NY	Poughkeepsie
1510	WFBL	1390	U4	5	5	NY	Syracuse
1511	WMPO	1390	U1	5	0.12	OH	Middleport-Pomeroy
1512	WNIO	#1390	U2	9.5	4.8	OH	Youngstown
1513	KZGD	‡1390	U1	5	0.69	OR	Salem
1514	WSPO	1390	U2	5	5	SC	Charleston
1515	WYXI	1390	U1	2.5	0.06	TN	Athens
1516	WLLI	1390	U2	5	1	TN	Jackson
1517	KLGN	1390	U2	5	0.5	UT	Logan
1518	WPLI	1390	U1	4.7	0.03	VA	Lynchburg
1519	WCAT	‡1390	U2	5	5	VT	Burlington
1520	KBBO	1390	U4	5	0.39	WA	Yakima
1521	WRIG	1390	U4	10	7.2	WI	Schofield
		1400	Various stns of 1kW or less				
1522	WNGL	**1410**	U2	5	4.6	AL	Mobile
1523	KMYC	‡1410	U4	5	1	CA	Marysville
1524	KCAL	1410	U2	5	4	CA	Redlands
1525	WPOP	1410	U4	5	5	CT	Hartford
1526	WDOV	1410	U4	5	5	DE	Dover
1527	WMYR	1410	U2	5	5	FL	Fort Myers
1528	WQBQ	1410	U1	5	0.08	FL	Leesburg
1529	WHBT	‡1410	U1	5	0.01	FL	Tallahassee
1530	WKKP	1410	U1	2.5	0.05	GA	McDonough
1531	KKLO	1410	U4	5	0.5	KS	Leavenworth
1532	KGSO	1410	U4	5	1	KS	Wichita
1533	WHLN	1410	U1	5	0.04	KY	Harlan
1534	WRJD	1410	U4	5	0.29	NC	Durham
1535	KOOQ	1410	U2	5	0.5	NE	North Platte
1536	WELM	1410	U2	5	1	NY	Elmira
1537	WNER	1410	U1	3.5	0.05	NY	Watertown
1538	WING	1410	U2	5	5	OH	Dayton
1539	KBNP	1410	U1	5	0.009	OR	Portland
1540	WLSH	1410	D3	5		PA	Lansford
1541	KQV	1410	U1	5	0.07	PA	Pittsburgh
1542	WRTZ	1410	U1	5	0.07	VA	Roanoke
1543	WIZM	1410	U2	5	5	WI	La Crosse
1544	WSCW	1410	D1	5		WV	South Charleston
1545	KWYO	1410	U1	5	0.35	WY	Sheridan
1546	WACT	**1420**	U1	5	0.1	AL	Tuscaloosa
1547	KBHS	1420	U1	5	0.08	AR	Hot Springs
1548	KMOG	1420	U2	2.5	0.5	AZ	Payson
1549	KSTN	1420	U4	5	3.5	CA	Stockton
1550	WLIS	1420	U2	5	0.5	CT	Old Saybrook

MW	Call	kHz	Ant.	D	N	Sta	City of License
1551	WDJA	1420	U4	5	0.5	FL	Delray Beach
1552	WBRD	1420	U4	2.5	1	FL	Palmetto
1553	WRCG	1420	U1	5	0.08	GA	Columbus
1554	WKWN	1420	U1	2.5	0.11	GA	Trenton
1555	WOC	1420	U4	5	5	IA	Davenport
1556	KIGO	1420	U1	32	0.01	ID	Saint Anthony
1557	WIMS	1420	U4	5	5	IN	Michigan City
1558	WBSM	1420	U4	5	1	MA	New Bedford
1559	KTOE	1420	U2	5	5	MN	Mankato
1560	WASR	1420	U1	5	0.13	NH	Wolfeboro
1561	WACK	1420	U4	5	0.5	NY	Newark
1562	WLNA	1420	U4	5	1	NY	Peekskill
1563	WHK	1420	U2	5	5	OH	Cleveland
1564	WCOJ	1420	U2	5	5	PA	Coatesville
1565	WCED	1420	U1	4.2	0.005	PA	Du Bois
1566	WEMB	1420	U1	5	0.02	TN	Erwin
1567	WKCW	1420	U4	22	0.06	VA	Warrenton
1568	KITI	1420	U4	5	5	WA	Centralia - Chehalis
1569	KUJ	1420	U1	5	0.9	WA	Walla Walla
1570	WZWB	1420	U2	5	0.5	WV	Kenova
1571	WFHK	**1430**	D1	5		AL	Pell City
1572	KYNO	1430	U3	5	5	CA	Fresno
1573	KMRB	1430	U4	50	9.8	CA	San Gabriel
1574	KVVN	1430	U4	1	2.5	CA	Santa Clara
1575	KEZW	1430	U2	10	5	CO	Aurora
1576	WTMN	1430	U1	10	0.04	FL	Gainesville
1577	WOIR	1430	U2	5	0.5	FL	Homestead
1578	WLKF	1430	U1	5	1	FL	Lakeland
1579	WLTG	1430	U4	5	5	FL	Panama City
1580	WYKG	1430	U1	3.9	0.21	GA	Covington
1581	WDAL	1430	U1	2.5	0.07	GA	Dalton
1582	WXNT	1430	U2	5	5	IN	Indianapolis
1583	WCWC	1430	U1	4.6	0.03	KY	Williamsburg
1584	WKOX	1430	U2	5	1	MA	Everett
1585	WNAV	1430	U2	5	1	MD	Annapolis
1586	WION	1430	U2	4.7	0.33	MI	Ionia
1587	KZQZ	1430	U4	50	5	MO	Saint Louis
1588	WDEX	1430	U4	2.5	2.5	NC	Monroe
1589	WMNC	1430	U1	2.7	0.04	NC	Morganton
1590	WDJS	1430	U4	10	5	NC	Mount Olive
1591	KRGI	1430	U2	5	1	NE	Grand Island
1592	WNSW	1430	U4	10	7	NJ	Newark
1593	WENE	1430	U2	5	5	NY	Endicott
1594	KTBZ	1430	U4	25	5	OK	Tulsa
1595	KYKN	1430	U2	5	5	OR	Keizer
1596	WTNA	1430	U2	5	1	PA	Altoona
1597	WBLR	1430	U1	5	0.16	SC	Batesburg
1598	WOWW	1430	U2	2.5	2.5	TN	Germantown
1599	WPLN	1430	U2	15	1	TN	Madison
1600	KEES	1430	U2	5	1	TX	Gladewater
1601	KSHJ	1430	U4	5	1	TX	Houston
1602	KLO	1430	U4	25	5	UT	Ogden
1603	WDIC	‡1430	U1	5	0.05	VA	Clinchco
1604	KCLK	1430	U4	5	1	WA	Asotin
1605	KBRC	1430	U2	5	1	WA	Mount Vernon
1606	WLWI	**1440**	U2	5	1	AL	Montgomery
1607	KTUV	1440	U2	5	0.24	AR	Little Rock
1608	KAZG	1440	U1	5	0.05	AZ	Scottsdale
1609	KVON	1440	U4	5	1	CA	Napa
1610	KUHL	1440	U2	5	1	CA	Santa Maria
1611	KRDZ	1440	U1	5	0.21	CO	Wray
1612	WWCL	1440	U4	5	1	FL	Lehigh Acres
1613	WPRD	1440	U2	5	1	FL	Winter Park
1614	WGMI	1440	U1	2.5	0.06	GA	Bremen
1615	WGIG	1440	U2	5	1	GA	Brunswick
1616	WGEM	1440	U4	5	1	IL	Quincy
1617	WROK	1440	U5	5	0.27	IL	Rockford
1618	KMAJ	1440	U4	5	1	KS	Topeka
1619	WVEI	1440	U2	5	5	MA	Worcester
1620	WRED	1440	U2	5	5	ME	Westbrook
1621	WMAX	1440	U4	5	2.5	MI	Bay City
1622	WKPR	1440	U1	4	0.02	MI	Kalamazoo
1623	KYCR	1440	U2	5	0.5	MN	Golden Valley
1624	WVGG	1440	D1	5		MS	Lucedale
1625	WBLA	1440	U1	5	0.19	NC	Elizabethtown
1626	WLXN	1440	U2	5.3	1	NC	Lexington
1627	WFNY	1440	U2	5	0.5	NY	Gloversville
1628	WHKZ	1440	U4	5	5	OH	Warren
1629	KMED	1440	U1	5	1	OR	Medford
1630	WCDL	1440	U1	5	0.03	PA	Carbondale
1631	WNPV	1440	U4	2.5	0.5	PA	Lansdale
1632	WGVL	1440	U2	5	5	SC	Greenville
1633	WZYX	1440	U1	5	0.06	TN	Cowan
1634	KPUR	1440	U2	5	1	TX	Amarillo
1635	KETX	1440	U1	5	0.09	TX	Livingston
1636	KEXB	1440	U4	50	0.35	TX	University Park
1637	WKLV	1440	U1	5	0.07	VA	Blackstone
1638	WNFL	1440	U4	5	0.5	WI	Green Bay
1639	WHIS	1440	U1	5	0.5	WV	Bluefield
1640	WAJR	1440	U4	5	0.5	WV	Morgantown
		1450	Various stns of 1kW or less				
1641	WMCJ	**1460**	U2	5	0.5	AL	Cullman
1642	WGSY	1460	U1	4	0.14	AL	Phenix City
1643	KTYM	1460	U4	5	0.5	CA	Inglewood
1644	KION	1460	U3	10	10	CA	Salinas
1645	KZNT	1460	U2	5	0.54	CO	Colorado Springs
1646	WQXM	1460	U5	10	0.15	FL	Bartow
1647	WZEP	1460	U1	10	0.18	FL	Defuniak Springs
1648	WNPL	1460	U4	7	2	FL	Golden Gate
1649	WQOP	1460	U2	15	5	FL	Jacksonville
1650	WXEM	1460	U1	5	0.19	GA	Buford
1651	KXNO	#1460	U2	5	5	IA	Des Moines
1652	WKAM	1460	U2	2.5	0.5	IN	Goshen
1653	WEKB	1460	U1	5	0.11	KY	Elkhorn City
1654	WXOK	1460	U1	4.7	0.29	LA	Port Allen
1655	WBMS	1460	U1	5	0.03	MA	Brockton
1656	WBRN	1460	U2	5	2.5	MI	Big Rapids
1657	KKAQ	1460	U1	2.5	0.15	MN	Thief River Falls
1658	KHOJ	1460	U4	12	0.21	MO	Saint Charles
1659	WEWO	1460	U4	5	5	NC	Laurinburg
1660	WHBK	1460	U1	5	0.13	NC	Marshall
1661	KLTC	1460	U1	5	0.77	ND	Dickinson
1662	KXPN	1460	U1	5	0.05	NE	Kearney
1663	WIFI	1460	U4	5	0.5	NJ	Florence
1664	KENO	1460	U4	10	0.62	NV	Las Vegas
1665	WOPG	1460	U2	5	5	NY	Albany
1666	WHIC	1460	U2	3.7	5	NY	Rochester
1667	WBNS	1460	U2	5	1	OH	Columbus
1668	WTKT	1460	U2	5	4.2	PA	Harrisburg
1669	WZMF	1460	U4	5	1	PA	Tunkhannock
1670	KCLE	1460	U4	11	0.7	TX	Burleson
1671	KBRZ	1460	U1	5	0.12	TX	Missouri City
1672	WKDV	1460	U4	5	5	VA	Manassas
1673	WRAD	1460	U1	5	0.03	VA	Radford
1674	KARR	1460	U4	5	2.5	WA	Kirkland
1675	KUTI	1460	U2	5	3.7	WA	Yakima
1676	WBUC	1460	U1	5.5	0.02	WV	Buckhannon
1677	KXSL	**1470**	U1	5	0.08	AZ	Show Low
1678	KNXN	1470	U1	2.5	0.04	AZ	Sierra Vista
1679	KUTY	1470	U4	5	5	CA	Palmdale
1680	KIID	1470	U4	5	1	CA	Sacramento
1681	WBOM	1470	U4	2.5	2.5	CT	Meriden
1682	WMGG	1470	U4	2.8	0.8	FL	Egypt Lake
1683	WWNN	1470	U4	50	2.5	FL	Pompano Beach
1684	WRGA	1470	U2	5	5	GA	Rome
1685	WMBD	1470	U4	5	5	IL	Peoria
1686	WBFC	1470	U1	2.5	0.02	KY	Stanton
1687	KLCL	1470	U1	5	0.5	LA	Lake Charles
1688	WAZN	1470	U4	1.4	3.4	MA	Watertown
1689	WJDY	1470	U4	5	0.04	MD	Salisbury
1690	WLAM	1470	U3	5	5	ME	Lewiston
1691	WFNT	1470	U4	5	1	MI	Flint
1692	KMNQ	‡1470	U4	5	5	MN	Brooklyn Park
1693	WNAU	1470	U2	2.5	0.5	MS	New Albany
1694	WWBG	1470	U4	10	5	NC	Greensboro
1695	WTOE	1470	U1	5	0.1	NC	Spruce Pine
1696	WNYY	1470	U2	5	1	NY	Ithaca
1697	WSAN	#1470	U2	5	5	PA	Allentown
1698	WQXL	1470	U1	11	0.1	SC	Columbia
1699	WVOL	1470	U4	5	1	TN	Berry Hill
1700	KYYW	1470	U1	5	0.11	TX	Abilene
1701	KWRD	1470	U1	5	0.08	TX	Henderson
1702	WBTX	1470	U1	5	0.03	VA	Broadway-Timberville
1703	WTZE	1470	D1	5		VA	Tazewell
1704	KELA	1470	U1	5	1	WA	Centralia-Chehalis
1705	KBSN	1470	U4	5	1	WA	Moses Lake

MW	Call	kHz	Ant.	D	N	Sta	City of License
1706	WIBD	1470	U4	2.5	2.5	WI	West Bend
1707	WMMA	**1480**	U1	5	0.02	AL	Irondale
1708	WABF	1480	U2	5	4.4	AL	Mobile
1709	KTHS	1480	U1	5	0.06	AR	Green Forest
1710	KPHX	1480	U2	5	0.5	AZ	Phoenix
1711	KGOE	1480	U1	5	1	CA	Eureka
1712	KYOS	1480	U1	4.3	0.07	CA	Merced
1713	KVNR	1480	U4	5	5	CA	Santa Ana
1714	WKGC	‡1480	U1	5	0.03	FL	Southport
1715	WYZE	1480	U1	10	0.04	GA	Atlanta
1716	KRXR	1480	U1	5	0.09	ID	Gooding
1717	WPFR	‡1480	U4	5	1	IN	Terre Haute
1718	KQAM	1480	U4	5	1	KS	Wichita
1719	WNKW	1480	D1	5		KY	Neon
1720	WSAR	1480	U3	5	5	MA	Fall River
1721	WGVU	#1480	U2	2	5	MI	Kentwood
1722	WSDS	1480	U4	0.75	3.8	MI	Salem Township
1723	KKCQ	1480	U1	5	0.09	MN	Fosston
1724	WGFY	1480	U4	12	5	NC	Charlotte
1725	WQTM	1480	U1	10	0.04	NC	Fair Bluff
1726	WPFJ	1480	U1	5	0.01	NC	Franklin
1727	WLEA	1480	U1	2.5	0.01	NY	Hornell
1728	WZRC	1480	U4	5	5	NY	New York
1729	WRCK	1480	D1	5		NY	Remsen
1730	WHBC	1480	U4	15	5	OH	Canton
1731	WDJO	1480	U4	4.5	0.3	OH	Cincinnati
1732	WDAS	1480	U4	5	1	PA	Philadelphia
1733	WBBP	1480	U1	5	0.04	TN	Memphis
1734	KNGO	1480	U4	50	1.9	TX	Dallas
1735	KLVL	1480	U4	5	0.5	TX	Pasadena
1736	KCHL	1480	U4	2.5	0.09	TX	San Antonio
1737	WPWC	1480	U4	5	0.5	VA	Dumfries-Triangle
1738	WTOX	1480	U4	6.3	1.5	VA	Glen Allen
1739	WTOY	1480	U1	5	0.02	VA	Salem
1740	WCFR	1480	U1	5	0.02	VT	Springfield
1741	KBMS	1480	U2	1	2.5	WA	Vancouver
1742	WLMV	1480	U4	5	5	WI	Madison
		1490	Various stns of 1kW or less				
1743	KSJX	**1500**	U4	10	5	CA	San Jose
1744	WFIF	1500	D3	5		CT	Milford
1745	WFED	1500	U4	50	50	DC	Washington
1746	WDPC	1500	D4	5		GA	Dallas
1747	WBRI	1500	D3	5		IN	Indianapolis
1748	WLQV	1500	U4	50	10	MI	Detroit
1749	KSTP	1500	U2	50	50	MN	Saint Paul
1750	KFNN	**1510**	U4	22	0.1	AZ	Mesa
1751	KIRV	1510	D3	10		CA	Fresno
1752	KSPA	‡1510	U4	10	1	CA	Ontario
1753	KSFN	1510	U4	8	2.4	CA	Piedmont
1754	KPLS	1510	U4	10	25	CO	Littleton
1755	WWBC	1510	D4	50		FL	Cocoa
1756	WMEX	1510	U1	10	0.1	MA	Quincy
1757	KCTE	1510	D3	10		MO	Independence
1758	KMRF	1510	D4	5		MO	Marshfield
1759	WVJJ	1510	D3	2.5		NJ	Salem
1760	KOAZ	1510	U1	5	0.02	NM	Isleta
1761	WWSM	1510	D3	5		PA	Annville-Cleona
1762	WPGR	1510	U11	5	0.001	PA	Monroeville
1763	KMSD	1510	U1	5	0.01	SD	Milbank
1764	WLAC	1510	U2	50	50	TN	Nashville
1765	KBED	1510	D3	5		TX	Nederland
1766	KGA	1510	U4	50	15	WA	Spokane
1767	WRRD	1510	D4	23		WI	Waukesha
1768	KMPG	**1520**	D4	5		CA	Hollister
1769	KKZZ	1520	U4	10	1	CA	Port Hueneme
1770	WNDO	1520	U4	5	0.35	FL	Apopka
1771	WEXY	1520	U2	5	0.8	FL	Wilton Manors
1772	WDCY	1520	D1	2.5		GA	Douglasville
1773	WHOW	1520	D1	5		IL	Clinton
1774	KFXZ	1520	U6	10	0.5	LA	Lafayette
1775	WIZZ	1520	D3	10		MA	Greenfield
1776	WTRI	1520	D3	17		MD	Brunswick
1777	KOLM	1520	U8	10	0.8	MN	Rochester
1778	KRHW	1520	U7	5	1.6	MO	Sikeston
1779	WDSL	1520	D1	5		NC	Mocksville
1780	WARR	1520	D1	5		NC	Warrenton
1781	WWKB	1520	U3	50	50	NY	Buffalo
1782	KOKC	1520	U2	50	50	OK	Oklahoma City
1783	KQRR	1520	U4	50	15	OR	Oregon City
1784	KYND	1520	D4	25		TX	Cypress
1785	KQQB	1520	D3	2.5		TX	Stockdale
1786	KKXA	1520	U2	50	50	WA	Snohomish
1787	KVDW	**1530**	D1	2.5		AR	England
1788	KFBK	1530	U4	50	50	CA	Sacramento
1789	KQSC	1530	U1	15	0.01	CO	Colorado Springs
1790	WYMM	1530	D3	50		FL	Jacksonville
1791	WTTI	1530	D4	10		GA	Dalton
1792	WVBF	1530	U14	5	0.004	MA	Middleborough Center
1793	WLCO	1530	D3	5		MI	Lapeer
1794	KQSP	1530	U4	8.6	0.01	MN	Shakopee
1795	WLLQ	1530	D3	10		NC	Chapel Hill
1796	WCKY	#1530	U2	50	50	OH	Cincinnati
1797	KXTD	1530	D3	5		OK	Wagoner
1798	WZTE	1530	D1	4.8		PA	Union City
1799	KZNX	1530	U7	10	0.22	TX	Creedmoor
1800	KGBT	1530	U8	50	10	TX	Harlingen
1801	KLBW	1530	D1	2.5		TX	New Boston
1802	KASA	**1540**	U4	10	0.01	AZ	Phoenix
1803	KMPC	1540	U4	50	37	CA	Los Angeles
1804	WKVQ	1540	D1	10		GA	Eatonton
1805	KXEL	1540	U2	50	50	IA	Waterloo
1806	WACA	1540	D1	5		MD	Wheaton
1807	WYNC	1540	D1	2.5		NC	Yanceyville
1808	WXEX	1540	U1	5	0.003	NH	Exeter
1809	KENT	1540	U7	10	0.27	NV	Enterprise
1810	WNWR	‡1540	U4	50	0.25	PA	Philadelphia
1811	WECZ	1540	D1	5		PA	Punxsutawney
1812	WTBI	1540	D1	10		SC	Pickens
1813	KGBC	1540	U4	2.5	0.25	TX	Galveston
1814	KEDA	1540	U4	5	1	TX	San Antonio
1815	KZMP	1540	U4	32	0.75	TX	University Park
1816	KXPA	1540	U2	5	5	WA	Bellevue
1817	WLOR	**1550**	U4	50	0.04	AL	Huntsville
1818	KUAZ	1550	D1	50		AZ	Tucson
1819	KWRN	1550	U2	5	0.5	CA	Apple Valley
1820	KXEX	1550	U4	5	2.5	CA	Fresno
1821	KGMZ	1550	U4	10	10	CA	San Francisco
1822	WSDK	1550	U4	5	2.4	CT	Bloomfield
1823	WNZF	1550	U1	5.5	0.05	FL	Bunnell
1824	WRHC	1550	U4	10	0.5	FL	Coral Gables
1825	WAMA	1550	U1	10	0.13	FL	Tampa
1826	WTHB	1550	U1	5	0.01	GA	Augusta
1827	WAZX	1550	U4	50	0.01	GA	Smyrna
1828	WKTF	1550	U1	10	0.02	GA	Vienna
1829	WPFC	1550	U1	5	0.04	LA	Baton Rouge
1830	WNTN	1550	U1	6.7	0.003	MA	Cambridge
1831	KAPE	1550	U4	5	0.04	MO	Cape Girardeau
1832	KESJ	1550	U2	2.5	0.5	MO	Saint Joseph
1833	KRZD	1550	U1	5	0.02	MO	Springfield
1834	KQNM	1550	U1	10	0.02	NM	Albuquerque
1835	KXTO	1550	U1	2.5	0.09	NV	Reno
1836	KYAL	1550	U4	2.5	0.04	OK	Sapulpa
1837	WITK	1550	U4	10	0.5	PA	Pittston
1838	WIGN	1550	U1	35	0.006	TN	Bristol
1839	KMRI	‡1550	U1	10	0.34	UT	West Valley City
1840	WKBA	1550	D3	10		VA	Vinton
1841	KRPI	1550	U4	50	10	WA	Ferndale
1842	KKOV	1550	U2	50	12	WA	Vancouver
1843	WHIT	1550	D3	5		WI	Madison
1844	WMRE	1550	U1	5	0.006	WV	Charles Town
1845	KNZR	**1560**	U2	25	10	CA	Bakersfield
1846	WLZR	1560	D1	5		FL	Melbourne
1847	KLNG	1560	D1	10		IA	Council Bluffs
1848	WTOU	1560	D3	4.1		MI	Portage
1849	WYZD	1560	D1	4.2		NC	Dobson
1850	WFME	1560	U4	50	50	NY	New York
1851	WCNW	1560	D4	5		OH	Fairfield
1852	WAHT	1560	D1	15		SC	Cowpens
1853	KKAA	1560	U4	10	10	SD	Aberdeen
1854	KGOW	1560	U4	46	15	TX	Bellaire
1855	KTXZ	1560	U4	2.5	2.5	TX	West Lake Hills
1856	WSBV	1560	D1	2.5		VA	South Boston
1857	KVAN	1560	U4	10	0.7	WA	Burbank
1858	KZIZ	1560	U12	5	0.9	WA	Pacific
1859	WGLB	1560	U7	2.5	0.25	WI	Elm Grove
1860	WCRL	**1570**	U1	2.5	0.06	AL	Oneonta

MW	Call	kHz	Ant.	D	N	Sta	City of License
1861	KCVR	#1570	U4	5	0.5	CA	Lodi
1862	KTGE	1570	U4	5	0.5	CA	Salinas
1863	WTWB	1570	U1	5	0.01	FL	Auburndale
1864	WVOJ	1570	U1	10	0.03	FL	Fernandina Beach
1865	WIGO	1570	U1	5	0.05	GA	Morrow
1866	WFRL	1570	U4	5	0.5	IL	Freeport
1867	WUBG	1570	U1	44	0.14	MA	Methuen
1868	WNST	1570	U1	5	0.23	MD	Towson
1869	KDIZ	1570	U1	4	0.22	MN	Golden Valley
1870	KAKK	1570	U1	9.5	0.25	MN	Walker
1871	KBCV	1570	U4	5	3	MO	Hollister
1872	WIZK	1570	D1	3.2		MS	Bay Springs
1873	WNCA	1570	U1	5	0.28	NC	Siler City
1874	WECU	1570	U1	8	0.2	NC	Winterville
1875	WFLR	1570	U1	5	0.44	NY	Dundee
1876	WPGM	1570	U1	2.5	0.22	PA	Danville
1877	WISP	1570	U4	5	0.9	PA	Doylestown
1878	WCLE	1570	U1	5	0.08	TN	Cleveland
1879	WYTI	1570	U1	2.5	0.22	VA	Rocky Mount
1880	WLKD	1570	U1	5	0.5	WI	Minocqua
1881	WVOK	**1580**	U1	2.5	0.02	AL	Oxford
1882	KQFN	1580	U1	50	0.09	AZ	Tempe
1883	KBLA	1580	U4	50	50	CA	Santa Monica
1884	KFCS	1580	U1	10	0.14	CO	Colorado Springs
1885	WNTF	1580	D3	10		FL	Bithlo
1886	WTCL	1580	D1	10		FL	Chattahoochee
1887	WSRF	1580	U4	10	1.5	FL	Fort Lauderdale
1888	WWTF	1580	U4	10	0.04	KY	Georgetown
1889	WJFK	1580	U4	50	0.27	MD	Morningside
1890	WPMO	1580	U4	5	0.05	MS	Pascagoula-Moss Point
1891	WNYG	1580	U2	10	0.5	NY	Patchogue
1892	WVKO	1580	U4	3.2	0.29	OH	Columbus
1893	KGAL	1580	U2	5	1	OR	Lebanon
1894	WNPZ	1580	D1	5		TN	Knoxville
1895	WLIJ	1580	U1	5	0.01	TN	Shelbyville
1896	WTTN	1580	U15	5	0.004	WI	Columbus
1897	WVNA	**1590**	U2	5	1	AL	Tuscumbia
1898	KBJT	1590	U1	4.7	0.03	AR	Fordyce
1899	KYNG	1590	U1	2.5	0.05	AR	Springdale
1900	KLIV	‡1590	U2	5	5	CA	San Jose
1901	KVTA	1590	U4	5	5	CA	Ventura
1902	WPSL	1590	U1	5	0.06	FL	Port Saint Lucie
1903	WTPA	1590	U4	5	1	FL	Saint Pete Beach
1904	WALG	1590	U1	3.3	0.04	GA	Albany
1905	WQCH	1590	D1	5		GA	LaFayette
1906	WXRS	1590	U1	2.5	0.02	GA	Swainsboro
1907	WCGO	1590	U2	10	2.5	IL	Evanston
1908	WNTS	1590	U4	5	0.5	IN	Beech Grove
1909	KVGB	1590	U2	5	5	KS	Great Bend
1910	WHGT	1590	U4	15	0.05	MD	Maugansville
1911	WTVB	1590	U2	5	1	MI	Coldwater
1912	KGFK	1590	U4	5	1	MN	East Grand Forks
1913	WCSL	1590	U1	10	0.03	NC	Cherryville
1914	WHPY	1590	U4	5	0.02	NC	Clayton
1915	KCTY	1590	U4	2.5	0.04	NE	Wayne
1916	WGGO	1590	U1	5	0.01	NY	Salamanca
1917	WAKR	1590	U2	5	5	OH	Akron
1918	KTIL	1590	U2	5	1	OR	Netarts
1919	WPWA	1590	U2	2.5	1	PA	Chester
1920	WPSN	1590	U1	2.5	0.01	PA	Honesdale
1921	WARV	1590	U4	8	5	RI	Warwick
1922	WKTP	1590	U3	5	5	TN	Jonesborough
1923	KGAS	1590	U1	2.5	0.12	TX	Carthage
1924	KELP	1590	U4	5	0.8	TX	El Paso
1925	KMIC	1590	U2	5	5	TX	Houston
1926	KEKR	1590	U4	2.5	0.06	TX	Mexia
1927	WFTH	1590	U1	5	0.01	VA	Richmond
1928	KLFE	1590	U4	20	5	WA	Seattle
1929	WGBW	1590	U4	10	0.5	WI	Denmark
1930	WIXK	1590	U1	5	0.09	WI	New Richmond
1931	WHIY	**1600**	U2	5	0.5	AL	Huntsville
1932	WXVI	1600	U4	5	1	AL	Montgomery
1933	KGST	1600	U2	5	5	CA	Fresno
1934	KAHZ	1600	U2	5	5	CA	Pomona
1935	KUBA	1600	U2	5	2.5	CA	Yuba City
1936	KEPN	1600	U2	5	5	CO	Lakewood
1937	WZNZ	1600	U1	5	0.08	FL	Atlantic Beach
1938	WPOM	1600	U4	5	4.7	FL	Riviera Beach
1939	WAOS	1600	U1	20	0.06	GA	Austell
1940	KGYM	1600	U2	5	5	IA	Cedar Rapids
1941	KLEB	1600	U4	5	0.25	LA	Golden Meadow
1942	WUNR	1600	U3	20	20	MA	Brookline
1943	WLZX	1600	D1	2.5		MA	East Longmeadow
1944	WAAM	1600	U4	5	5	MI	Ann Arbor
1945	KPNP	1600	U3	5	5	MN	Watertown
1946	KATZ	1600	U2	6	3.5	MO	Saint Louis
1947	WIDU	1600	U4	5	0.14	NC	Fayetteville
1948	WTZQ	1600	U1	5	0.03	NC	Hendersonville
1949	KIVA	1600	U1	10	0.17	NM	Albuquerque
1950	WEHH	1600	U4	5	0.17	NY	Elmira Hts-Horseheads
1951	WWRL	1600	U4	25	5	NY	New York
1952	KUSH	1600	U1	5	0.07	OK	Cushing
1953	KOPB	1600	U2	5	1	OR	Eugene
1954	WAYC	1600	U1	2.7	0.01	PA	Bedford
1955	WKZK	1600	U1	4	0.02	SC	North Augusta
1956	WUCT	1600	U1	2.5	0.02	TN	Algood
1957	WMQM	1600	U1	50	0.03	TN	Lakeland
1958	KRVA	1600	U4	25	0.93	TX	Cockrell Hill
1959	KOKE	1600	U4	5	0.7	TX	Pflugerville
1960	KTUB	1600	U2	5	1	UT	Centerville
1961	WCPK	1600	U1	4.2	0.02	VA	Chesapeake
1962	KVRI	1600	U4	50	10	WA	Blaine
1963	WRPN	1600	U4	5	5	WI	Ripon
1964	WZZW	1600	U1	5	0.02	WV	Milton
1965	WKKX	1600	U1	5	0.03	WV	Wheeling
		1610	Various stns of 0.01kW or less (TIS)				
1966	KSMH	**1620**	U1	10	1	CA	West Sacramento
1967	WNRP	1620	U1	10	1	FL	Gulf Breeze
1968	KOZN	1620	U1	10	1	NE	Bellevue
1969	WTAW	#1620	U1	10	1	TX	College Station
1970	KYIZ	1620	U1	10	1	WA	Renton
1971	KCJJ	**1630**	U1	10	1	IA	Iowa City
1972	KKGM	1630	U1	10	1	TX	Fort Worth
1973	KRND	1630	U1	10	1	WY	Fox Farm
1974	KDIA	**1640**	U2	10	10	CA	Vallejo
1975	WTNI	1640	U1	10	1	MS	Biloxi
1976	KZLS	1640	U4	10	1	OK	Enid
1977	KDZR	#1640	U1	10	1	OR	Lake Oswego
1978	KBJA	1640	U1	10	1	UT	Sandy
1979	WSJP	1640	U1	10	1	WI	Sussex
1980	KFSW	**1650**	U1	10	1	AR	Fort Smith
1981	KFOX	1650	U1	10	0.49	CA	Torrance
1982	KBJD	1650	U1	10	1	CO	Denver
1983	KCNZ	1650	U1	10	1	IA	Cedar Falls
1984	KSVE	1650	U1	8.5	0.85	TX	El Paso
1985	WHKT	1650	U1	10	1	VA	Portsmouth
1986	KBRE	**1660**	U1	10	1	CA	Merced
1987	WCNZ	1660	U1	10	1	FL	Marco Island
1988	KWOD	1660	U1	10	1	KS	Kansas City
1989	WQLR	1660	U1	10	1	MI	Kalamazoo
1990	WBCN	#1660	U1	10	1	NC	Charlotte
1991	KQWB	1660	U1	10	1	ND	West Fargo
1992	WWRU	1660	U4	10	10	NJ	Jersey City
1993	KRZI	1660	U1	10	1	TX	Waco
1994	KHPY	**1670**	U4	10	9	CA	Moreno Valley
1995	KQMS	1670	U1	10	1	CA	Redding
1996	WMGE	1670	U1	10	1	GA	Dry Branch
1997	WOZN	1670	U1	10	1	WI	Madison
1998	KGED	**1680**	U1	10	1	CA	Fresno
1999	WOKB	1680	U1	10	1	FL	Winter Garden
2000	KRJO	1680	U1	10	1	LA	Monroe
2001	WPRR	1680	U1	10	0.68	MI	Ada
2002	WTTM	1680	U1	10	1	NJ	Lindenwold
2003	KNTS	1680	U1	10	1	WA	Seattle
2004	KFSG	**1690**	U1	10	1	CA	Roseville
2005	KDMT	#1690	U1	10	1	CO	Arvada
2006	WMLB	1690	U1	10	1	GA	Avondale Estates
2007	WVON	1690	U1	10	1	IL	Berwyn
2008	WPTX	1690	U1	10	1	MD	Lexington Park
2009	WEUP	**1700**	U1	10	1	AL	Huntsville
2010	WJCC	1700	U1	10	1	FL	Miami Springs
2011	KBGG	1700	U1	10	1	IA	Des Moines
2012	WRCR	1700	U1	10	1	NY	Ramapo
2013	KVNS	1700	U1	8.8	0.88	TX	Brownsville
2014	KKLF	1700	U1	5	1	TX	Richardson

Addresses:
– **1)** 3929 Airport Blvd #2-403, Mobile, AL 36609 – **2)** 20720 Marilla St, Chatsworth, CA 91311-4407 – **3)** 1139 Hartnell Ave, Redding, CA 96002-2113 – **4)** 2500 Maitland Center Pkwy #401, Maitland, FL 32751-4122 – **5)** 1501 13th Ave, Columbus, GA 31901-1908 – **6)** 200 N 10th St, Fort Dodge, IA 50501-3925 – **7)** 1109 Hudson Lane, Monroe, LA 71201-6003 – **8)** 1846 Skyland Dr, Sylva, NC 28779-8008 – **9)** 2411 E. Millbrook Rd, #114, Raleigh, NC 27604 – **10)** 304 S Grand Ave, Las Vegas, NM 87701-3873 – **11)** 2395 Ocean Ave #3, Ronkonkoma, NY 11779-5670 – **12)** 32500 Parklane St, Garden City, MI 48135-1572 – **13)** 1640 Old Russellville Pike, Clarksville, TN 37043-1709 – **14)** 4686 E Van Buren St #300, Phoenix, AZ 85008-6967 – **15)** 3223 Sillect Ave, Bakersfield, CA 93308-6329 – **16)** 1111 W Victory Way, Craig, CO 81625-2950 – **17)** 2500 Russell Rd, Green Cove Springs, FL 32043-9492 – **18)** 1102 Thompson Bridge Rd, Gainesville, GA 30501-1706 – **19)** 1815 Meadowlark Rd, Clay Center, KS 67432-8201 – **20)** 638 West Port Plaza, Saint Louis, MO 63146-3106 – **21)** 660 Dewey Blvd, Butte, MT 59701-2318 – **22)** 3500 E Rosser Ave, Bismarck, ND 58501-3398 – **23)** 500 Corporate Parkway #200, Buffalo, NY 14226-1263 – **24)** 8044 Montgomery Rd #650, Cincinnati, OH 45236-2959 – **25)** 7140 SW Macadam Ave, Portland, OR 97219-3013 – **26)** 1330 E 8th St #207, Odessa, TX 79761-4731 – **27)** 4050 Eisenhauer Rd, San Antonio, TX 78218-3409 – **28)** 1820 Heritage Center Way, Harrisonburg, VA 22801-8451 – **29)** 9 Stowe St, Waterbury, VT 05670-1820 – **30)** 4840 Lincoln Rd, Blaine, WA 98230-9602 or PO Box 75150 RPO White Rock, White Rock, BC V4B 5L3 – **31)** 557 Scott St, Wausau, WI 54403-4829 – **32)** 2518 Columbia Hwy, Dothan, AL 36303-5402 – **33)** 55 Hawthorne St #1000, San Francisco, CA 94105-3966 – **34)** 2821 S Parker Rd #1205, Aurora, CO 80014-2708 – **35)** 194 NW 187th St, Miami, FL 33169-4050 – **36)** 25 NW Point Blvd #400, Elk Grove, IL 60007-1030 – **37)** PO Box 608, Middlesboro, KY 40965-0608 – **38)** 1331 Main St, Springfield, MA 01103-1669 – **39)** 350 Byrd Ave, Cumberland, MD 21502-3219 – **40)** 420 Western Ave, South Portland, ME 04106-1704 – **41)** 207 W. Superior St #130, Duluth, MN 55802 – **42)** 3000 Chestnut Expressway, Springfield, MO 65802-2528 – **43)** 20 3rd St N #231, Great Falls, MT 59401-3188 – **44)** 117 Ridge Pike, Lafayette Hill, PA 19444-1900 – **45)** 316 Greystone Blvd, Columbia, SC 29210-8007 – **46)** 1815 Division St #110, Nashville, TN 37203-2753 or PO Box 90972, Nashville, TN 37209-0972 – **47)** 6080 Mount Moriah Rd Ext, Memphis, TN 38115-2698 – **48)** 2885 Interstate 10 E, Beaumont, TX 77702-1001 – **49)** 231 N Wenatchee Ave, Wenatchee, WA 98801-2009 – **50)** 102 N Kanawha St, Beckley, WV 25801-4715 – **51)** 6510 Whorton Bend Rd, Gadsden, AL 35901-8873 – **52)** PO Box 580, Alturas, CA 96101-0580 – **53)** 3400 Olive Ave #550, Burbank, CA 91505-5544 – **54)** 5211 W Laurel St #101, Tampa, FL 33607-1725 – **55)** 1801 Rockville Pike #405, Rockville, MD 20852-5604 – **56)** 13 Summerlin Rd, Asheville, NC 28806-2800 – **57)** 1355 California Ave, Las Cruces, NM 88001-4130 – **58)** 111 Broadway #302, New York, NY 10006-1901 – **59)** 500 Plum St #100, Syracuse, NY 13204-1427 – **60)** 7461 South Ave, Youngstown, OH 44512-5789 – **61)** WNAX Bldg - 1609 E Hwy 50, Yankton, SD 57078-6406 – **62)** 3090 Olive St #400, Dallas, TX 75219-7640 – **63)** 2801 Decker Lake Dr, West Valley City, UT 84119-2330 – **64)** 140 4th Ave N #340, Seattle, WA 98109-4932 – **65)** 1110 S Park Ave, Tucson, AZ 85719-6745 – **66)** 1071 W Shaw St, Fresno, CA 93771-3702 – **67)** 106 Rose Lane, Montrose, CO 81401-3823 – **68)** 4192 N John Young Pkwy, Orlando, FL 32804-2696 – **69)** 4051 Jimmie Dyess Pkwy, Augusta, GA 30909-9469 – **70)** 827 Park Blvd #1001, Boise, ID 83712-7781 – **71)** Campbell Hall - 300 N Goodwin Ave, Urbana, IL 61801-2316 – **72)** 1200 SW Executive Dr, Topeka, KS 66615-3850 – **73)** 601 Washington St, Alexandria, LA 71301-8028 – **74)** 96 Stereo Lane, Paxton, MA 01612-1376 – **75)** 314 E Front St, Traverse City, MI 49684-2528 – **76)** 240 Radio Road, West Jefferson, NC 28694-ND – **77)** 600 Corporate Cir #100, Harrisburg, PA 17110-9787 – **78)** 319 W Rockwood St, Rockwood, TN 37854-2245 – **79)** 201 State St, La Crosse, WI 54601-3246 – **80)** 1111 Virginia St E, Charleston, WV 25301-2406 – **81)** 701 N Brand Blvd #550, Glendale, CA 91203-1235 – **82)** 1001 Heavenly Village Way #36A, South Lake Tahoe, CA 96150-6985 – **83)** 1834 Lisenby Ave, Panama City, FL 32405-3713 – **84)** 900 Circle 75 Pkwy SE #1320, Atlanta, GA 30339-3095 – **85)** 1406 Commerce Way, Idaho Falls, ID 83401-1233 – **86)** 300 W Vine St 3rd Flr, Lexington, KY 40507-1807 – **87)** 500 Victory Rd #2, Quincy, MA 02171-3132 – **88)** 222 S Lawrence St, Ironwood, MI 49938-2524 – **89)** 4200 W Main St, Kalamazoo, MI 49006-2766 – **90)** 10714 Mockingbird Dr, Omaha, NE 68127-1942 – **91)** 6 Johnson Rd, Latham, NY 12110-5638 – **92)** 1200 Executive Pkwy #440, Eugene, OR 97401-2169 – **93)** 8309 N Interstate 35, Austin, TX 78753-5771 – **94)** 750 Ridgeview Dr #204, St. George, UT 84770-2697 – **95)** 808 E Sprague Ave, Spokane, WA 99202-2126 – **96)** 9660 Granite Ridge Dr, San Diego, CA 92123-2657 – **97)** 4270 Byrd Dr, Loveland, CO 80538-7074 – **98)** 4190 Belfort Rd #450, Jacksonville, FL 32216-1405 – **99)** 600 Old Marion Rd NE, Cedar Rapids, IA 52402-2152 – **100)** 330 2nd Ave, Paintsville, KY 41240-1034 – **101)** 711 W 40th St #350, Baltimore, MD 21211-2190 – **102)** 670 Sweden St, Caribou, ME 04736-3419 – **103)** 2995 US Highway 93 S, Kalispell, MT 59901-8640 – **104)** 875 W 5th St, Winston-Salem, NC 27101-2505 – **105)** 2400 8th Ave SW #D1, Jamestown, ND 58401-6623 – **106)** 2650 Thousand Oaks Blvd #4100, Memphis, TN 38118-2451 – **107)** 4180 N Mesa St, El Paso, TX 79902-1420 – **108)** 1001 E Southeast Loop 323 #455, Tyler, TX 75701-9600 – **109)** 2700 Corporate Dr #115, Birmingham, AL 35242-2735 – **110)** 352 "E" Ave #K4, Lancaster, CA 93535-4505 – **111)** 260 Hegenberger Rd, Oakland, CA 94621-1491 – **112)** 7601 Riviera Blvd, Miramar, FL 33023-6574 – **113)** 11 E Superior St #380, Duluth, MN 55802-3016 – **114)** 7000 Squibb Rd, Mission, KS 66202-3233 – **115)** 1520 South Blvd #300, Charlotte, NC 28203-3701 – **116)** 195 McGregor St #810, Manchester, NH 03102-3755 – **117)** 500 4th St NW, Albuquerque, NM 87102-5324 – **118)** 2323 W 5th Ave #200, Columbus, OH 43204-4988 – **119)** 511 Rossanley Dr, Medford, OR 97501-1771 – **120)** 555 E City Ave #330, Bala Cynwyd, PA 19004-1137 – **121)** 24 E Greenway Plaza #1900, Houston, TX 77046-2428 – **122)** 810 W 200 N, Logan, UT 84321-3726 – **123)** 3934 Electric Rd, Roanoke, VA 24018-4513 – **124)** 2823 W Lewis St, Pasco, WA 99301-6700 – **125)** 7740 N 16th St #200, Phoenix, AZ 85020-4482 – **126)** 1354 E Sherwood Dr, Grand Junction, CO 81501-7546 – **127)** 4002 W Gandy Blvd, Tampa, FL 33611-3410 – **128)** 806 New Franklin Rd, La Grange, GA 30240-1859 – **129)** 861 Broadway, Bangor, ME 04401-2916 – **130)** 1375 Beasley Rd, Jackson, MS 39206-2018 – **131)** 2508 Coney Island Ave 2nd Flr, Brooklyn, NY 11223-5026 – **132)** 500 Plum St #100, Syracuse, NY 13204-1427 – **133)** 13333 SW 68th Pkwy, Tigard, OR 97223-8304 – **134)** 1918 Lincoln Hwy, North Versailles, PA 15137-2706 or PO Box 990, Greensburg, PA 15601-0990 – **135)** 2440 Millwood Ave, Columbia, SC 29205-1128 or PO Box 2355, West Columbia, SC 29171-2355 – **136)** 1621 E Magnolia Ave, Knoxville, TN 37917-7825 – **137)** 6400 N Belt Line Rd #110, Irving, TX 75063-6065 – **138)** 118 Malletts Bay Ave, Colchester, VT 05446-2009 – **139)** 720 E Capitol Dr, Milwaukee, WI 53212-1308 – **140)** 306 S Kanawha St, Beckley, WV 25801-5619 – **141)** 4695 S Monaco St, Denver, CO 80237-3403 – **142)** 4400 Jenifer St NW #400, Washington, DC 20015-2183 – **143)** 214 Television Circle, Savannah, GA 31406-4519 – **144)** 145 N Alexander St, Toccoa, GA 30577-2371 – **145)** 827 Park Blvd #100, Boise, ID 83712-7782 – **146)** 2601 Nicholasville Rd, Lexington, KY 40503-3307 – **147)** 205 Cesar Chavez St, Saint Paul, MN 55107-2309 – **148)** 10845 Olive Blvd #160, Saint Louis, MO 63141-7792 or PO Box 7300, Charlotte, NC 28241-7300 – **149)** 2900 Sutro St, Reno, NV 89512-1616 – **150)** 320 Central Ave #519, Coos Bay, OR 97420-2272 – **151)** 1502 Wampanoag Trail, Riverside, RI 02915-1075 – **152)** 9601 McAllister Freeway #1200, San Antonio, TX 78216-4686 – **153)** 19319 Fremont Ave N, Shoreline, WA 98133-3800 – **154)** 3400 Olive Ave #500, Burbank, CA 91505-5544 – **155)** 2100 Park Central Blvd #100, Pompano Beach, FL 33064-2219 – **156)** 1819 Peachtree Rd NE #700, Atlanta, GA 30309-1849 – **157)** 1013 WOI Rd, Ames, IA 50011-1067 – **158)** 21700 Northwestern Hwy. Tower 14 #1190, Southfield, MI 48075 – **159)** 108 Green St, Thibodaux, LA 70301-3144 – **160)** 131 County Circle, Amherst, MA 01003-9257 – **161)** 1009 Drayton Rd, Fayetteville, NC 28303-3887 – **162)** 501 Office Center Dr #190, Fort Washington, PA 19034-3268 – **163)** 7755 Freedom Ave NW, North Canton, OH 44720-6905 – **164)** 4045 NW 64th St #600, Oklahoma City, OK 73116-2615 – **165)** 162 Free Hill Rd, Gray, TN 37615-3144 – **166)** 6401 Poplar Ave #640, Memphis, TN 38119-4808 – **167)** 1545 River Park Dr #500, Sacramento, CA 95815-4693 – **168)** 807 W 37th St, Hibbing, MN 55746-2856 – **169)** 2644 McGavock Pike, Nashville, TN 37214-1202 – **170)** 1600 W 500 N, Manti, UT 84642-5503 – **171)** 1912 Capitol Ave #300, Cheyenne, WY 82001-3659 – **172)** 2800 Dauphin St #104, Mobile, AL 36606-2400 – **173)** PO Box 2569, Window Rock, AZ 86515-2569 – **174)** 3000 W MacArthur Blvd #500, Santa Ana, CA 92704-7947 – **175)** 1188 Lake View Dr, Altamonte Springs, FL 32714-2713 – **176)** 1010 2nd St N, Sauk Rapids, MN 56379-2527 – **177)** 410 E 6th St, Williston, ND 58801-5552 – **178)** 345 Hudson St Fl10, New York, NY 10014-4502 – **179)** 2911 Tennyson Ave, #400, Eugene, OR 7408-4811 or PO Box 40231, Downey, CA 90239-1231 – **180)** 2420 Wade Hampton Blvd, Greenville, SC 29615-1107 – **181)** 6400 N Belt Line Rd #110, Irving, TX 75063-6065 – **182)** 2029 Freeway Dr, Mount Vernon, WA 98273-5470 – **183)** 11474 US Hwy 11, York, AL 36925-9764 – **184)** 108 Highway 70 E #11, Glenwood, AR 71943-8800 – **185)** 3301 Barham Blvd #300, Los Angeles, CA 90068-1477 – **186)** 2821 S Parker Rd #1205, Aurora, CO 80014-2708 – **187)** 330 SW 27th Ave #207, Miami, FL 33135-2957 – **188)** 1419 W Bannock St, Boise, ID 83702-5234 – **189)** 180 N Stetson St #1250, Chicago, IL 60601-6732 – **190)**

3999 Las Vegas Blvd S #K, Las Vegas, NV 89119-1097 – **191)** 12½ E Market St, Lewistown, PA 17044-2123 – **192)** 6223 Old Mendenhall Rd, High Point, NC 27263-3940 – **193)** 55 Hawthorne St #1100, San Francisco, CA 94105-3932 – **194)** 780 Johnson Ferry Rd NE #500, Atlanta, GA 30342-1436 – **195)** 20 Guest St 3rd Flr, Brighton, MA 02135-2040 – **196)** 1726 Reisterstown Rd #117, Pikesville, MD 21208-2986 – **197)** Tower 14-21700 Northwestern Hwy #1190, Southfield, MI 48075-4923 – **198)** 604 Ludington St, Escanaba, MI 49829-3830 – **199)** 4104 Country Lane, Saint Joseph, MO 64506-4921 – **200)** 1400 11th Ave #3, Helena, MT 59601-7996 – **201)** 3012 Highwoods Blvd #201, Raleigh, NC 27604-1031 – **202)** 320 N Jensen Rd, Vestal, NY 13850-2111 – **203)** 1835 Moriah Woods Blvd, Memphis, TN 38117-7122 – **204)** 8122 Datapoint Dr #600, San Antonio, TX 78229-3446 – **205)** 320 Emery Dr, Omak, WA 98841-9237 – **206)** 2396 Hallie Rd, Chippewa Falls, WI 54729-7519 – **207)** 1111 Virginia St E, Charleston, WV 25301-2406 – **208)** 244 Goodwin Crest Dr #300, Birmingham, AL 35209-3700 – **209)** 261 Portsea St, New Haven, CT 06519-2104 – **210)** 8000 Belfort Parkway #100, Jacksonville, FL 32256-6971 – **211)** 306 W 8th St, Coffeyville, KS 67337-5829 – **212)** 8230 Summa Ave, Baton Rouge, LA 70809-3421 – **213)** Tower 14-21700 Northwestern Hwy #1190, Southfield, MI 48075-4923 – **214)** 4045 N Mesa St, El Paso, TX 79902-1526 – **215)** 11373 Wallace Pike, Bristol, VA 24202-2743 – **216)** 126 Kessel Rd, Fisher, WV 26818-4012 – **217)** 67 Garden Court, Monterey, CA 93940-5302 – **218)** 30 How St, Haverhill, MA 01830-6131 – **219)** 615 S Frederick Ave #300, Gaithersburg, MD 20877-1243 or PO Box 2195, Manassas, VA 20108-2195 – **220)** 8044 Montgomery Rd #650, Cincinnati, OH 45236-2959 – **221)** 196 Main St, Winston, OR 97496-ND – **222)** 11451 Katy Freeway #125, Houston, TX 77079-2004 – **223)** 50 W Broadway #200, Salt Lake City, UT 84101-2024 – **224)** 500 W Boone Ave, Spokane, WA 99201-2404 – **225)** 501 N 44th St #425, Phoenix, AZ 85008-6587 – **226)** 1425 River Park Dr #520, Sacramento, CA 95815-4524 – **227)** 800 W Olympic Blvd #A-200, Los Angeles, CA 90015-1360 – **228)** 3131 S Vaughn Way #601, Aurora, CO 80014-3516 – **229)** 8551 NM 30th Ter, Miami, FL 33122 – **230)** 855 College St, Eastman, GA 31023-6771 – **231)** 402 Main St, Williamsburg, KY 40769-1126 – **232)** 6341 W Port Ave, Shreveport, LA 71129-2415 – **233)** 5800 Foxridge Dr #600, Mission, KS 66202-2347 – **234)** 3228 S US Hwy 117, Rose Hill, NC 28458-8498 – **235)** 3500 E Rosser Ave, Bismarck, ND 58501-3398 – **236)** 32 Ave of the Americas 3 Floor, New York, NY 10013-2473 – **237)** 3505 Olsen Blvd #117, Amarillo, TX 79109-3096 – **238)** 7080 Lee Highway, Fairlawn, VA 24141-8416 – **239)** 1820 Eastlake Ave E, Seattle, WA 98102-3711 – **240)** 11 E Superior St #380, Duluth, MN 55802-3016 – **241)** 100 NW 76th Dr #2, Gainesville, FL 32607-6659 – **242)** 154 Boone Dr, Newman, GA 30263-2801 – **243)** 435 N Michigan Ave, Chicago, IL 60611-4076 – **244)** 3232 Hendersonville Hwy, Pisgah Forest, NC 28768-7806 – **245)** 2920 S Durango Dr, Las Vegas, NV 89117-4412 – **246)** 917 SE 19th Ave, Albany, OR 97322 – **247)** 4050 Eisenhauer Rd, San Antonio, TX 78218-3409 – **248)** 2194 US Hwy 319 S, Thomasville, GA 31792-1417 – **249)** 5660 E Franklin Rd # 200, Nampa, ID 83687-5133 – **250)** PO Box 1, Springfield, MA 01101-0001 – **251)** 2075 Central Ave, Billings, MT 59102-4956 – **252)** 201 West Morehead St #200, Charlotte, NC 28202 – **253)** 7 Parkway Center #625, Pittsburgh, PA 15220-3707 – **254)** 2 Beeco Rd, Greer, SC 29650-1004 – **255)** 11240 Waples Mill Rd #405, Fairfax, VA 22030-6078 – **256)** 1 Commerce St #300, Montgomery, AL 36104-3542 – **257)** 3183 Airway Ave #D, Costa Mesa, CA 92626-4611 – **258)** 865 Battery St, San Francisco, CA 94111-1503 – **259)** 6805 Corporate Dr #130, Colorado Springs, CO 80919-5903 – **260)** 1650 S Dixie Hwy, Boca Raton, FL 33432-7462 – **261)** 2500 Maitland Center Pkwy #401, Maitland, FL 32751-4179 – **262)** 5440 Moeller Ave, Cincinnati, OH 45212-1211 – **263)** 2147 Springs Rd, Mount Airy, NC 27030-2447 – **264)** 1020 S 25th St, Fargo, ND 58103-2312 – **265)** PO Box 2000012, Brooklyn, NY 11220-0012 – **266)** 7136 S Yale Ave #500, Tulsa, OK 74136-6325 – **267)** 2000 West Loop S #300, Houston, TX 77027-3510 – **268)** 300 St Croix Trail S, Lakeland, MN 55043-ND or PO Box 25130, Saint Paul, MN 55125-0130 – **269)** 1601 W Peachtree St NE, Atlanta, GA 30309-2663 – **270)** 5625 N Milwaukee Ave, Chicago, IL 60646-6221 – **271)** 18553 Gentry Rd, Lebanon, MO 65536-5748 – **272)** 36581 N Reservoir Rd, Polson, MT 59860-8677 – **273)** 128 S 4th St, O'Neill, NE 68763-1814 or PO Box 8, Aurora, NE 68818-0008 – **274)** 1211 SW 5th Ave 6 Flr, Portland, OR 97204-3735 – **275)** 2211 E Missiouri Ave # S-300, El Paso, TX 79903-3831 – **276)** 1899 Carbonville Rd, Helper, UT 84526-ND or PO Box 875, Price, UT 84501-0875 – **277)** 301 Brookswood Rd #208, Sherwood, AR 72120-4200 – **278)** 7677 Engineer Rd, San Diego, CA 92111-1582 – **279)** 4695 S Monaco St, Denver, CO 80237-3408 – **280)** 5211 W Laurel St #101, Tampa, FL 33607-1725 – **281)** 2090 Palm Beach Lake Blvd #801, West Palm Beach, FL 33409-6508 – **282)** 10550 Barkley St, Overland Park, KS 66212-1824 – **283)** 8 Lawrence Rd , Derry, NH 03038-4191 – **284)** 3011 W Grand Blvd #800, Detroit, MI 48202-3086 – **285)** 2828 NC 126, Morganton, NC 28655-8264 – **286)** 137 Rapids Rd, Champlain, NY 12919-4945 – **287)** 6222 West Interstate 10, San Antonio, TX 78201-2097 – **288)** 1717 US Hwy 72 E, Athens, AL 35611-4413 – **289)** 10948 Cleveland Ave, Oakdale, CA 95361-9709 – **290)** 20125 S Tamiami Trail, Estero, FL 33928-2117 – **291)** 330 21st Ave S #610, Minneapolis, MN 55455-4550 – **292)** 818 Main St, Miles City, MT 59301-3221 – **293)** 275 River Rd, Rockingham, NC 28380-1536 – **294)** 500 4th St NW, Albuquerque, NM 87102-2102 – **295)** 2 Penn Plaza #1700, New York, NY 10121-0085 – **296)** 904 Center St, Lewiston, NY 14092-1737 or 600 The East Mall #400, Toronto, ON M9B 4B1 – **297)** 3201 Royalty Row, Irving, TX 75062-4961 – **298)** 504 Middle Creek Rd, Cedar Bluff, VA 24609-ND – **299)** 1820 Eastlake Ave E, Seattle, WA 98102-3711 – **300)** 3400 W Highway 89a, Sedona, AZ 86336-4914 – **301)** 180 N Stetson St #1100, Chicago, IL 60601-6723 – **302)** 274 Britton Rd, Monticello, ME 04760-3110 – **303)** 265 Highpoint Dr, Ridgeland, MS 39157-6018 – **304)** 17336 US Highway 421 S, Dunn, NC 28334-5580 – **305)** 1381 W Main St, Forest City, NC 28043-2525 – **306)** 595 E Plumb Lane, Reno, NV 89502-3503 – **307)** 1735 North Lynn St, Arlington, VA 22209 – **308)** 142 Skyland Blvd E, Tuscaloosa, AL 35405-4096 – **309)** 113 E New Hope Rd, Rogers, AR 72758-6058 – **310)** 3202 N Oracle Rd, Tucson, AZ 85705-3820 – **311)** 1415 Fulton St, Fresno, CA 93721-1609 – **312)** 1101 Marsh Rd, Eureka, CA 95501-1574 – **313)** 8965 Lindblade St, Culver City, CA 90232 – **314)** 32900 Radio Road, Leesburg, FL 34788-3903 – **315)** 20450 NW 2nd Ave, Miami, FL 33169-2505 – **316)** 210 Interstate North Cir SE #100, Atlanta, GA 30339-2206 – **317)** 1065 S Range Ave, Colby, KS 67701-3505 – **318)** 4000 Radio Drive #1, Louisville, KY 40218-4568 – **319)** 1795 Tittabawassee Rd, Saginaw, MI 48604-9431 – **320)** 600 First Ave N, Billings, MT 59101-2654 – **321)** 4801 E Independence Blvd #815, Charlotte, NC 28212-5490 – **322)** 1020 S 25th St, Fargo, ND 58103-3212 – **323)** 1541 Alta Dr #400, Whitehall, PA 18052-5632 – **324)** 1502 Wampanoag Trail, Riverside, RI 02915-1075 – **325)** 2175 Highway 75 #6, Blountville, TN 37617 – **326)** 1835 Moriah Woods Blvd, Memphis, TN 38117-7122 – **327)** 2000 West Loop S #300, Houston, TX 77027-3510 – **328)** 4413 82nd St #300, Lubbock, TX 79424-3395 – **329)** 500 Dominion Tower - 999 Waterside Dr, Norfolk, VA 23510-3300 – **330)** 2219 Yew St Rd, Bellingham, WA 98229-8898 – **331)** 1601 E 57th Ave, Spokane, WA 99223-6623 – **332)** 944 Harlem St, Altoona, WI 54720-1127 – **333)** 213 E 2nd St, Soda Springs, ID 83276-1411 – **334)** 462 Merrimack St, Methuen, MA 01844-5804 – **335)** 1010 2nd St N, Sauk Rapids, MN 56379-2527 – **336)** 2775 Mt Ephraim Ave, Camden, NJ 08104-3295 – **337)** 1919 N Broadway Ave, Oklahoma City, OK 73103-4499 – **338)** 1032 Melody Lane, Crewe, VA 23930-ND – **339)** 200 Tower Rd, Waupaca, WI 54981-1699 – **340)** 134 4th Ave, Huntington, WV 25701-1253 – **341)** 188 John Turner Broadcast Blvd, Jacksonville, AL 36265-6659 or PO Box 8, Anniston, AL 36202-0008 – **342)** 750 Battery Street, 2nd Floor, San Francisco, CA 94111 – **343)** 999 Douglas Ave #3318, Altamonte Springs, FL 32714-5213 – **344)** 4198 Rebecca Circle, Valdosta, GA 31606-2201 – **345)** 1501 Hargis Lane, Jackson, KY 41339-1102 – **346)** 2422 Burton St SE, Grand Rapids, MI 49546-4806 – **347)** 6721 W 121st St, Overland Park, KS 66209-2003 – **348)** 1115 Honeysuckle Dr, Keene, TX 76059-2101 – **349)** 102 Taos St, Santa Fe, NM 87505-3832 – **350)** 1203 Troy-Schenectady Rd #201, Latham, NY 12110-1046 – **351)** 2 Beeco Rd, Greer, SC 29650-1004 – **352)** 1612 Junction Ave #1, Sturgis, SD 57785-2166 – **353)** 2514 Eugenia Ave, Nashville, TN 37211-2117 – **354)** 145 Jackson St NE, Blacksburg, VA 24060-3931 – **355)** 55 Alder St NW #3, Ephrata, WA 98823-1663 – **356)** 800 8th Ave SE, Largo, FL 33771-2162 – **357)** 5475 N Milwaukee Ave, Chicago, IL 60630-1249 – **358)** 3400 Idaho Ave NW #200, Washington, DC 20016-3000 – **359)** 17487 Driftwood Ln, Park Rapids, MN 56470-2739 – **360)** 2205 College Ave #3, Elmira, NY 14903-1223 – **361)** 160 Varick St, New York, NY 10013-1220 – **362)** 4673 Winterset Dr, Columbus, OH 43220-8113 – **363)** 3090 Olive St #400, Dallas, TX 75219-7640 – **364)** 460 West Century Dr, Salt Lake City, UT 84123-2534 – **365)** 4301 W Hundred Rd, Chester, VA 23831-1737 – **366)** 2201 6th Ave #1500, Seattle, WA 98121-1840 – **367)** 64 East Broadway, Tucson, AZ 85701 – **368)** 1255 E Main St #A, Grass Valley, CA 95945-5711 – **369)** 2000 E Gene Autry Way, Anaheim, CA 92806-6143 – **370)** 3500 N Causeway Blvd #830, Metairie, LA 70002-3561 – **371)** 276 Turnpike Rd, Westborough, MA 01581 – **372)** 625 2nd Ave S #200, Minneapolis, MN 55402-1961 – **373)** 4405 Providence Lane #D, Winston-Salem, NC 27106-3226 – **374)** 34 N 4th St, Reading, PA 19601-3996 – **375)** 230-2 Goodman Rd E #202, Southaven, MS 38671-5151 – **376)** 1423 S Beverly St, Casper, WY 82609-4131 – **377)** 6530 Spanish Fort Blvd #B, Spanish Fort, AL 36527-5014 or PO Box 1328, Mobile, AL 36633-1328 – **378)** 3256 Penryn Rd #100, Loomis, CA 95650-8052 – **379)** 221 Pall Bearer Rd, Thomasville, GA 31792-1101 – **380)** 4000 Radio Drive #1,

Louisville, KY 40218-4568 – **381)** 3735 Rigolette Rd, Pineville, LA 71360-7365 – **382)** 1011 N Lincoln St, West Point, NE 68788-1003 – **383)** 7255 S Tenaya Way #100, Las Vegas, NV 89113-1900 – **384)** 4801 E Independence Blvd #815, Charlotte, NC 28212-5490 – **385)** 1201 N Jackson Ave #900, McAllen, TX 78501-5764 – **386)** PO Box 7111, Charlottesville, VA 22906-7111 – **387)** 1114 N Almon St, Moscow, ID 83843-8507 – **388)** 120 Summit Pkwy #200, Birmingham, AL 35209-4741 – **389)** 4695 S Monaco St, Denver, CO 80237-3403 – **390)** 98 Mill Plain Rd, Danbury, CT 06811-6101 – **391)** 1200 Weimer Hall, Gainesville, FL 32611 – **392)** 2100 Park Central Blvd #100, Pompano Beach, FL 33064-2219 – **393)** 5625 N Milwaukee Ave, Chicago, IL 60646-6221 – **394)** 20 Guest St 3rd Flr, Brighton, MA 02135-2040 – **395)** 3434 W Kilbourn Ave, Milwaukee, MN 53208-3313 – **396)** 1333 S Kirkwood Rd St, Saint Louis, MO 63122-7266 – **397)** 3012 Highwoods Blvd #201, Raleigh, NC 27604-1031 – **398)** 1301 E 9th St #252, Cleveland, OH 44114-1800 – **399)** 104 S Center St #400, Ebensburg, PA 15931-1656 – **400)** 8828 N Stemmons Fwy #106, Dallas, TX 75247-3720 – **401)** 3000 Bering Dr, Houston, TX 77057-5708 – **402)** 500 Dominion Tower - 999 Waterside Dr, Norfolk, VA 23510-3300 – **403)** 645 Elliott Ave W #400, Seattle, WA 98119-3911 – **404)** 300 Broadway #8, San Francisco, CA 94133-4545 – **405)** 5211 W Laurel St #101, Tampa, FL 33607-1725 – **406)** 1465 Northside Dr NW #218, Atlanta, GA 30318-4239 – **407)** 601 W Roanoke Dr, Fitzgerald, GA 31750-3633 – **408)** 1162 E Hwy 126, Pittsburg, KS 66762-8712 – **409)** 425 Stockbridge Rd, Great Barrington, MA 01230-1233 – **410)** 260 Hegenberger Rd, Oakland, CA 94621-1491 – **411)** 6605 SE Lake Rd, Portland, OR 97222-2161 – **412)** 555 E City Ave #330, Bala Cynwyd, PA 19004-1137 – **413)** 8122 Datapoint Dr #600, San Antonio, TX 78229-3446 – **414)** 434 Bearcat Dr, Salt Lake City, UT 84115-2520 – **415)** 240 Central Ave, Oak Hill, WV 25901-3006 – **416)** 2278 Wortham Lane, Grovetown, GA 30813-5103 – **417)** 701 N Brand Blvd #550, Glendale, CA 91203-1235 – **418)** 400 Poydras St #800, New Orleans, LA 70130-3245 – **419)** PO Box 308, Bath, ME 04530-0308 – **420)** MSU - 404 Wilson Road Room 212, East Lansing, MI 48824-1212 – **421)** PO Box 49, Park Rapids, MN 56470-0049 – **422)** 1115 Honeysuckle Dr, Keene, TX 76059-2101 – **423)** 6767 W Tropicana Ave #102, Las Vegas, NV 89103-4755 – **424)** 1751 Hanshaw Rd, Ithaca, NY 14850-9105 – **425)** 2175 Highway 75 #6, Blountville, TN 37617 – **426)** 2621 West A St, Pasco, WA 99301-4702 – **427)** 2360 NE Coachman Rd, Clearwater, FL 33765-2216 – **428)** 30 E San Joaquin St #105, Salinas, CA 93901-2946 – **429)** 5757 Blue Lagoon Dr #450, Miami, FL 33126 – **430)** 2432 US Hwy 2 E, Kalispell, MT 59901-2310 – **431)** 13 Summerlin Rd, Asheville, NC 28806-2800 – **432)** 1007 Plum Creek Parkway , Lexington, NE 68850-2621 – **433)** PO Box 9090, Window Rock, AZ 86515-9090 – **434)** 345 Hudson St Flr 11, New York, NY 10014-4502 – **435)** 8101 N High St #360, Columbus, OH 43235-1442 – **436)** 1405 E Ellendale Ave, Dallas, OR 97338-1709 – **437)** 3715 N Natchez Ct, Nashville, TN 37211-3421 – **438)** 1600 Pasadena Blvd, Pasadena, TX 77502-2402 – **439)** 3650 131st SE #550, Bellevue, WA 98006-1334 – **440)** 619 Cameron St, Eau Claire, WI 54703-4700 – **441)** 1301 Central Pkwy SW, Decatur, AL 35601-4817 – **442)** 560 Higuera St #G, San Luis Obispo, CA 93401-3850 – **443)** 1442 Ethan Way #101, Sacramento, CA 95825-2232 – **444)** 965 S Irving St, Denver, CO 80219-3422 – **445)** 2800 Shallowford Rd NE, Atlanta, GA 30341-5217 – **446)** PO Box 490, Caldwell, ID 83606-0490 – **447)** 455 N Cityfront Plaza Dr, Chicago, IL 60611 – **448)** 122 Green St #2L, Worcester, MA 01604-4138 – **449)** 37 Ellisville Blvd, Laurel, MS 39440-4523 – **450)** 243 Riverchase Way #A, Lexington, SC 29072-9470 – **451)** 4501 N McColl Rd, McAllen, TX 78504-2431 – **452)** 10613 Bellaire Blvd #900, Houston, TX 77072-5221 – **453)** 750 Ridgeview Dr #204, Saint George, UT 84770-2665 – **454)** 145 Jackson St NE, Blacksburg, VA 24060-3931 – **455)** 747 E Green St #101, Pasadena, CA 91101 – **456)** 2320 NE 2nd St #5, Ocala, FL 34470-6992 – **457)** 214 Television Circle, Savannah, GA 31406-4519 – **458)** 1240 Radio Drive, Pikeville, KY 41501-4779 – **459)** 3003 Snelling Ave N, Saint Paul, MN 55113-1599 – **460)** 398 S Main St, Granite Falls, NC 28630-8535 – **461)** 801 E DuBois Ave, DuBois, PA 15801-3643 – **462)** 2514 Eugenia Ave, Nashville, TN 37211-2117 – **463)** 10613 Bellaire Blvd #900, Houston, TX 77072-5221 – **464)** 207 University Blvd #200, Harrisonburg, VA 22801-3752 – **465)** 4686 E Van Buren St #300, Phoenix, AZ 85008-6967 – **466)** 260 Hegenberger Rd, Oakland, CA 94621-1491 – **467)** 340 Townsend St #4, San Francisco, CA 94107-1698 – **468)** 200 S A St #400, Oxnard, CA 93030-5717 – **469)** 3455 W 83rd Ave, Westminster, CO 80030-4005 – **470)** 135 Burnside Ave, East Hartford, CT 06108-3466 – **471)** 5211 W Laurel St, Tampa, FL 33607-1736 – **472)** 710 S Clinton St, Iowa City, IA 52242-4214 – **473)** 184 Target Industrial Circle #207, Bangor, ME 04401-5718 – **474)** 20733 W 10 Mile Rd, Southfield, MI 48075-1086 – **475)** 3436 Highway 45N, Meridian, MS 39301 – **476)** PO Box 15400, Durham, NC 27704-0400 – **477)** 1000 20th Ave SW, Minot, ND 58701-6447 – **478)** 1301 N Main St, Roswell, NM 88201-5013 – **479)** 6006 Grand Central Ave, Parkersburg, WV 26105-9125 or PO Box 5559, Vienna, WV 26105-5559 – **480)** 114 S Jefferson St, Kittanning, PA 16201-2408 – **481)** 5989 Susquehanna Plaza Dr, Hellam, PA 17406-8910 – **482)** 225 S Pleasantburg Dr #3B, Greenville, SC 29607-2533 – **483)** 162 Freehill Rd, Gray, TN 37615-3144 – **484)** 105 N Ash Ave, South Pittsburg, TN 37380-1565 – **485)** 4300 S US Highway 281, Edinburg, TX 78539-9650 – **486)** 3245 Basie Rd, Richmond, VA 23228-3404 – **487)** 0700 SW Bancroft St, Portland, OR 97239-4226 – **488)** 16880 W US Highway 63, Hayward, WI 54843-7186 – **489)** 700 Wellington Hills Rd, Little Rock, AR 72211-2026 – **490)** 961 N Emerald Ave #A, Modesto, CA 95351-1556 – **491)** 2100 E Tahquitz Canyon Way, Palm Springs, CA 92262-7046 – **492)** 7350 US Hwy 50, Lamar, CO 81052-9563 – **493)** 1800 Turtle Mound Rd, Melbourne, FL 32934-8105 – **494)** 2970 Peachtree Rd NW #700, Atlanta, GA 30305-4919 – **495)** 290 Hegenberger Rd, Oakland, CA 94621-1436 – **496)** 712 3rd St, West Lafayette, IN 47907-2005 – **497)** PO Box 228, Mayking, KY 41837-0228 – **498)** 601 Central Ave N, Faribault, MN 55021-1307 – **499)** 1109 Tower Dr, Burlington, NC 27215-4425 – **500)** 8755 W Flamingo Rd, Las Vegas, NV 89147-8667 – **501)** 3256 Penryn Rd #100, Loomis, CA 95650-8052 – **502)** 75 Oxford St, Providence, RI 02905-4722 – **503)** 660 Flormann St #100, Rapid City, SD 57701-4679 – **504)** 7322 Southwest Frwy #500, Houston, TX 77074-2084 – **505)** 2495 N Vernal Ave, Vernal, UT 84078-ND – **506)** 1770 Van Buren Dr, Dumfries, VA 22025-2036 – **507)** 1700 SE Mile Hill Dr #243, Port Orchard, WA 98366-3507 – **508)** 500 W Boone Ave, Spokane, WA 99201-2497 – **509)** 12100 W Howard Ave, Greenfield, WI 53228-1851 – **510)** 450 Leonard Ave Extension, Fairmont, WV 26554-3878 – **511)** 1913 Barry St, Oxford, AL 36203-2319 – **512)** PO Box 1179, Douglas, AZ 85608-1179 – **513)** 1117 W Route 66, Flagstaff, AZ 86001-6213 – **514)** 1845 W Empire Ave, Burbank, CA 91504-3402 – **515)** 190 Turner Dr #G, Durango, CO 81303-8231 – **516)** PO Box 7069, Breckenridge, CO 80424-7069 – **517)** 11700 Central Pkwy, Jacksonville, FL 32224-2600 – **518)** 5211 W Laurel St, Tampa, FL 33607-1736 – **519)** 521 S Scott St, Bainbridge, GA 39819-4101 – **520)** 544 N Arthur Ave, Pocatello, ID 83204-3002 – **521)** 329 Maine St, Quincy, IL 62301-3928 – **522)** 1496 Bellevue St #202, Green Bay, WI 54311-4205 – **523)** 804 College St, Bowling Green, KY 42101-2133 – **524)** 5966 Grove Hill Rd, Frederick, MD 21703-6012 – **525)** 390 Golden Ave, Battle Creek, MI 49015-4598 – **526)** 37208 US Hwy 169, Aitkin, MN 56431-4195 – **527)** 1015 W Pine St, Poplar Bluff, MO 63901-4839 – **528)** 4908 Ridgewood Rd, Jackson, MS 39211-5422 – **529)** 3250 S Reserve St #200, Missoula, MT 59801-8236 – **530)** 11530 Carmel Commons Blvd, Charlotte, NC 28226-3976 – **531)** 525 Evans St, Greenville, NC 27858-2311 – **532)** 815 Lafayette Rd, Portsmouth, NH 03801-5406 – **533)** 27 William St 11th Flr, New York, NY 10005-2718 – **534)** 500 Corporate Parkway #200, Buffalo, NY 14226-1263 – **535)** 4045 NW 64th St #600, Oklahoma City, OK 73116-2615 – **536)** 1250 Siskiyou Blvd, Ashland, OR 97520-5010 – **537)** 3304 S Highway 281, Aberdeen, SD 57401-8792 – **538)** 430 State Highway 165 #C, Branson, MO 65616-3541 – **539)** 9601 McAllister Freeway #1200, San Antonio, TX 78216-4686 – **540)** 105 Whitehall Rd, Lynchburg, VA 24501-6706 – **541)** PO Box 31000, Spokane, WA 99223-3016 – **542)** 821 University Ave, Madison, WI 53706-1412 – **543)** 401 11th St #200, Huntington, WV 25701-2235 – **544)** 1716 KROE Lane, Sheridan, WY 82801-9681 – **545)** 1415 Fulton St, Fresno, CA 93721-1609 – **546)** 7601 Riviera Blvd, Miramar, FL 33023-6574 – **547)** 544 Mulberry St #500, Macon, GA 31201-8258 – **548)** 1416 Locust St, Des Moines, IA 50309-3014 – **549)** 3501 Broadway St, Mount Vernon, IL 62864-2202 – **550)** 929 Howard Ave, New Orleans, LA 70113-1148 – **551)** 7119 W M-68, Indian River, MI 49749-9472 – **552)** 1189 N Jackson St, Houston, MS 38851-8273 – **553)** 401 Saw Mill Hollow Rd, Burnsville, NC 28714-9789 – **554)** 126 W 3rd St, Valentine, NE 69201-1826 – **555)** 305 N Church St, Wartburg, TN 37887-3164 – **556)** 6214 W 34th Ave, Amarillo, TX 79109-4006 – **557)** 615 Olive St, Texarkana, TX 75501-5512 – **558)** 1011 Radio Drive, Grundy, VA 24614-6157 – **559)** 13379 Great Springs Rd, Smithfield, VA 23430-6930 – **560)** 501 E Broadway St, Forrest City, AR 72335-3801 – **561)** 985 Lincoln Way #103, Auburn, CA 95603-5255 – **562)** 720 S Colorado Ave, Denver, CO 80246 – **563)** 1188 Lake View Dr, Altamonte Springs, FL 32714-2713 – **564)** 2973 US Hwy 84 W, Valdosta, GA 31601 – **565)** 2502 S Frederick Ave, Oelwein, IA 50662-3116 – **566)** 624 3rd St S, Nampa, ID 83651-3840 – **567)** 2560 Snake River Ave, Lewiston, ID 83501-9685 – **568)** 1496 Bellevue St #202, Green Bay, WI 54311-4205 – **569)** 500 Victory Rd #2, Quincy, MA 02171-3132 – **570)** 7825 Tuckerman Ln #217, Potomac, MD 20854-3241 – **571)** 26495 American Dr, Southfield, MI 48034-6114 – **572)** 3109 S 10 Mile Dr, Jefferson City, MO 65109-1012 – **573)** 63 Braswell Rd, Hattiesburg, MS 39401-9730 – **574)** 100 W Lyndale Ave #B, Helena, MT 59601-2999 – **575)** 1560 N Corbin St, Silver City, NM

88061-6526 – **576)** 403 W Pueblo Dr, Española, NM 87532-2530 – **577)** 9418 River Rd, Marcy, NY 13403-2071 – **578)** 1250 Siskiyou Blvd, Ashland, OR 97520-5010 – **579)** 260 Hegenberger Rd, Oakland, PA 94621-1491 – **580)** 60 Markfield Dr #4, Charleston, SC 29407-7907 – **581)** 25 Garlington Rd, Greenville, SC 29615-4613 – **582)** 222 Mallory Station Rd, Franklin, TN 37067-0201 – **583)** 2000 West Loop S #300, Houston, TX 77027-3510 – **584)** 9800 University Ave, Lubbock, TX 79423-5302 – **585)** 701 German School Rd, Richmond, VA 23225-5357 – **586)** 351 Elliott Ave W #400, Seattle, WA 98119-3911 – **587)** 817 Suncrest Place, Charleston, WV 25303-2302 – **588)** 600 Beacon Parkway W #400, Birmingham, AL 35209-3118 – **589)** 6530 Spanish Fort Blvd #B, Spanish Fort, AL 36527-5014 or PO Box 1328, Mobile, AL 36633-1328 – **590)** 260 Battle St, Marshall, AR 72650-9440 – **591)** 2425 E Camelback Rd #570, Phoenix, AZ 85016-4250 – **592)** 12370 Hesperia Rd #16, Victorville, CA 92392-5808 – **593)** 340 Townsend St #4, San Francisco, CA 94107-1698 – **594)** 495 Benham St, Hamden, CT 06514-2009 – **595)** 809 S Westover Blvd, Albany, GA 31707-4953 – **596)** 1010 Tower Place, Bogart, GA 30622-3052 – **597)** 209 N Elm St, Shenandoah, IA 51601-1139 – **598)** 1301 E Douglas Rd, Mishawaka, IN 46545-1732 – **599)** 1240 Radio Drive, Pikeville, KY 41501-4779 – **600)** 356 Broad St, Fitchburg, MA 01420-3030 – **601)** 351 Tilghman Rd, Salisbury, MD 21804-1920 – **602)** PO Box 432, Elk Rapids, MI 46629 – **603)** 16405 Haven Rd, Little Falls, MN 56345-6400 – **604)** 324 Broadway St, Cape Girardeau, MO 63701-7331 – **605)** 3600 Highway 7 N, Baker, MT 59313-ND – **606)** 4405 Providence Lane #D, Winston-Salem, NC 27106-3226 – **607)** 1361 Colony Dr, New Bern, NC 28562-4129 – **608)** 1928 E Portal Place, Scottsbluff, NE 69361-2727 – **609)** 1515 W Main St, Farmington, NM 87401-3896 – **610)** 265 Hegeman Ave, Colchester, VT 05446-3174 – **611)** 404 Main St #4, Klamath Falls, OR 97601-6021 – **612)** 1703 Walnut Bottom Rd, Carlisle, PA 17015-9151 – **613)** 193 S Keystone Ave, Sayre, PA 18840-1330 – **614)** 1301 S Abe St, San Angelo, TX 76903-7245 – **615)** 50 W Broadway #200, Salt Lake City, UT 84101-2024 – **616)** 3934 Electric Rd, Roanoke, VA 24018-4513 – **617)** 4304 W 24th Ave Suite 200, Kennewick, WA 99338 – **618)** 67 W Court Square, Troy, AL 36081-2611 – **619)** 1838 Commerce Dr #A, Lakeside, AZ 85929-7007 – **620)** 1100 Mohawk St #280, Bakersfield, CA 93309-7417 – **621)** 1321 N Gene Autry Trail, Palm Springs, CA 92262-5473 – **622)** 1400 NE 42nd Terrace, Kansas City, MO 64116 – **623)** 4002 W Gandy Blvd #A, Tampa, FL 33611-3410 – **624)** 2970 Peachtree Rd NW #700, Atlanta, GA 30305-4919 – **625)** 1501 Mount Vernon Rd, Vidalia, GA 30474-3031 – **626)** 47 North 100 West, Jerome, ID 83338 – **627)** 125 S Main St, Harlan, KY 40831-2109 – **628)** 9960 Corporate Campus Dr #3600, Louisville, KY 40223-4070 – **629)** 420 Western Ave, South Portland, ME 04106-1704 – **630)** 121 N Front St, Marquette, MI 49855-4300 – **631)** 109 E Clark St, Albert Lea, MN 56007-2420 – **632)** 27 N 27th St, Billings, MT 59101-2357 – **633)** 1190 Patton Ave, Asheville, NC 28806-2706 – **634)** 301 8th St S, Fargo, ND 58103-1826 – **635)** 201 S Bailey Ave, North Platte, NE 69101-5406 – **636)** 111 Broadway, New York, NJ 10006-1901 – **637)** 3256 Penryn Rd #100, Loomis, CA 95650-8052 – **638)** 625 Delaware Ave #308, Buffalo, NY 14202-1007 – **639)** 3226 Jefferson Rd, Ashtabula, OH 44004-9112 – **640)** 5800 E Skelly Dr #150, Tulsa, OK 74135-6416 – **641)** 1211 SW 5th Ave 6th Fl, Portland, OR 97204-3735 – **642)** 200 Fleet St 4th Flr, Pittsburgh, PA 15220-2910 – **643)** 181 E Evans St #311, Florence, SC 29506-2512 – **644)** 207 University Blvd #200, Harrisonburg, VA 22801-3752 – **645)** PO Box 2482, Kirkland, WA 98083-2482 – **646)** 821 University Ave, Madison, WI 53706-1412 – **647)** 2705 E Parkway Dr, Russellville, AR 72802-2006 – **648)** 1101 Marsh Rd, Eureka, CA 95501-1574 – **649)** 5670 Wilshire Blvd #200, Los Angeles, CA 90036-5611 – **650)** 229 Pajaro St #205, Salinas, CA 93901-3499 – **651)** 1801 Rockville Pike #405, Rockville, MD 20852-5604 – **652)** 100 NW 76th Dr #2, Gainesville, FL 32607-6659 – **653)** 312 E Nine Mile Rd #29D, Pensacola, FL 32514-1475 – **654)** 1650 S Dixie Hwy, Boca Raton, FL 33432-7462 – **655)** 1691 Forsyth St, Macon, GA 31201-1407 – **656)** 854 Lindsay Blvd, Idaho Falls, ID 83402-1820 – **657)** 208 N Thomas Dr, Shreveport, LA 71107-6520 – **658)** 243 Central St, Lowell, MA 01852-2214 – **659)** 2110 Cliff Rd, St Paul, MN 55122-3522 – **660)** 7000 Squibb Rd, Mission, KS 66202-3233 – **661)** 3233 Burnt Mill Dr #4, Wilmington, NC 28403-2676 – **662)** 733 E Roosevelt Ave, Grants, NM 87020-2113 – **663)** 1155 Gummow Dr, Fallon, NV 89406-9453 – **664)** 1203 Troy-Schenectady Rd #201, Latham, NY 12110-1046 – **665)** 101 Pine St, Dayton, OH 45402-2925 – **666)** 305 Hwy 315, Pittston, PA 18640-3987 – **667)** 6223 Old Mendenhall Rd, High Point, NC 27263-3940 – **668)** 745 Main St, Deadwood, SD 57732-1015 – **669)** 11530 Carmel Commons Blvd, Charlotte, NC 28226-3976 – **670)** 1600 Pasadena Blvd, Pasadena, TX 77502-2404 – **671)** 390 E Annabella Rd, Richfield, UT 84701-2692 – **672)** 901 E Valley Dr, Bristol, VA 24201-4903 – **673)** 1200 Chesterly Dr #160, Yakima, WA 98902-7345 – **674)** 1915 Mirro Dr, Manitowoc, WI 54220-6715 – **675)** 300 Harrison Ave, Weston, WV 26452-2100 – **676)** 3871 N Commerce Dr, Tucson, AZ 85705-2983 – **677)** 44 Gough St #301, San Francisco, CA 94103-5424 – **678)** 414 E Cota St, Santa Barbara, CA 93101-1624 – **679)** 3131 S Vaughn Way #601, Aurora, CO 80014-3516 – **680)** 758 Colonel Ledyard Hwy, Ledyard, CT 06339 – **681)** 2150 W 68th St #202, Hialeah, FL 33016-1802 – **682)** 610 Sycamore St #220, Celebration, FL 34747-4996 – **683)** 239 Ezzard St, Lawrenceville, GA 30046-5396 – **684)** 24 Frank Lloyd Wright Dr, Ann Arbor, MI 48105-9755 – **685)** 1569 N Central Ave, Monett, MO 65708-1104 – **686)** 1650 Midland Rd, Southern Pines, NC 28387-2111 – **687)** 625 Delaware Ave #308, Buffalo, NY 14202-1007 – **688)** 117 Ridge Pike, Lafayette Hill, PA 19444-1900 – **689)** 109 Plaza Dr #2, Johnstown, PA 15905-1212 – **690)** 4711 Old Kingston Pike, Knoxville, TN 37919-5207 – **691)** 5495 Murray Rd, Memphis, TN 38119-3703 – **692)** 12900 Preston Rd #200, Dallas, TX 75230-1380 – **693)** 1535 Narrows Rd, Narrows, VA 24124-ND – **694)** 3256 Penryn Rd #100, Loomis, CA 95650-8052 – **695)** 20872 NE Kelley Ave, Blountstown, FL 32424-1115 – **696)** 190 N State St, Chicago, IL 60601-3302 – **697)** PO Box 1336, Yazoo, MS 39194-1336 – **698)** 309 Renard Place SE #206, Albuquerque, NM 87107-4848 – **699)** 3134 Lake Rd, Horseheads, NY 14845-3103 – **700)** 1900 NW Expressway St #1000, Oklahoma City, OK 73118-1854 – **701)** 728 N Hanover St, Carlisle, PA 17013-1534 – **702)** 5100 S Tennis Lane, Sioux Falls, SD 57108-2212 – **703)** 110 India Rd, Paris, TN 38242-7565 – **704)** 140 4th Ave N #340, Seattle, WA 98109-4932 – **705)** 2800 N 44th St #100, Phoenix, AZ 85008-1560 – **706)** 5100 Commerce Dr, Bakersfield, CA 93309-0684 – **707)** 44 Gough St #301, San Francisco, CA 94103-5424 – **708)** 75153 Merle Dr #D, Palm Desert, CA 92211-5197 – **709)** 220 State St #106, Fort Morgan, CO 80701-2116 – **710)** 9090 Hogan Rd, Jacksonville, FL 32216-4648 – **711)** 9721 Executive Center Dr N #200, St Petersburg, FL 33702-2439 – **712)** 3296 Summit Ridge Pkwy #910, Duluth, GA 30096 – **713)** 1300 Hampton Ave #100, Saint Louis, MO 63139 – **714)** 70 Adams Hill Rd, Asheville, NC 28806-3841 or PO Box 159, Black Mountain, NC 28711-0159 – **715)** 103 Hanover St, Newport, NH 03766-1098 or PO Box 2295, New London, NH 03257-2295 – **716)** 345 Hudson St Fl 11, New York, NY 10014-4502 – **717)** 5110 SE Stark St, Portland, OR 97215-1751 – **718)** 1625 Hwy 109 N, Gallatin, TN 37066-8135 – **719)** 3639 Wolfin Ave, Amarillo, TX 79102-2119 – **720)** 5100 Southwest Freeway, Houston, TX 77056-7308 – **721)** 1019 Washington Ave, Waco, TX 76701-1256 – **722)** 3256 Penryn Rd #100, Loomis, CA 95650-8052 – **723)** 2202 Jolliff Rd, Chesapeake, VA 23321-1416 – **724)** 5999 Center Dr, Los Angeles, CA 90045-8901 – **725)** 67 Main St, Sharon, CT 06069-2018 – **726)** 2555 Ponce De Leon Blvd #225, Coarl Gables, FL 33134-6033 – **727)** 5011 Capitol Ave, Omaha, NE 68132-2921 – **728)** 419 Broadway, Paterson, NM 07501-2104 – **729)** Foster Plaza 5, 651 Holiday Dr, Pittsburgh, PA 15220-2740 – **730)** 100 E Shockley Ferry Rd, Anderson, SC 29624-3746 – **731)** 706 Butterfield Rd, Yakima, WA 98901-2021 – **732)** 4209 N Frontage Rd, Fayetteville, AR 72703-5002 – **733)** 3222 S Richey Ave, Tucson, AZ 85704-7738 – **734)** 121 W Alvin Ave, Santa Maria, CA 93458-3002 – **735)** 1355 E Altamonte Dr, Altamonte Springs, FL 32701-5011 – **736)** 427 S Wall Sreet, Calhoun, GA 30701-2431 – **737)** 3656 W Belmont Ave, Chicago, IL 60618-5328 – **738)** 1402 E Kansas Ave, Garden City, KS 67846-5806 – **739)** 1170 Soldiers Field Rd, Allston, MA 02134-1092 – **740)** 6710 Oxon Hill Rd #100, Oxon Hill, MD 20745-1158 – **741)** 7355 N Orcale Rd #102, Tucson, AZ 85704-6353 – **742)** 900 Forestview Lane N, Plymouth, MN 55441-5934 – **743)** 18920 E Valley View Pkwy #C, Independence, MO 64055-7020 – **744)** 4405 Providence Lane #D, Winston-Salem, NC 27106-3226 – **745)** 4321 Stuart Andrew Blvd #E, Charlotte, NC 28217-1588 – **746)** 136 N 7th St, Reedsport, OR 97467-1503 – **747)** 3654 Park Ave, Memphis, TN 38111-5626 – **748)** 1602 S Brownlee Blvd, Corpus Christi, TX 78404-3134 – **749)** 210 W Cota St, Shelton, WA 98584-2264 – **750)** 303 8th St, Point Pleasant, WV 25550-1209 – **751)** 150 Nichols Ave, Casper, WY 82601-1816 – **752)** 5050 Edison Ave #218, Colorado Springs, CO 80915-3450 – **753)** 2555 Ponce De Leon Blvd #225, Coral Gables, FL 33134-6033 – **754)** 800 8th Ave SE, Largo, FL 33771-2162 – **755)** 3230 Steve Reynolds Blvd #219, Duluth, GA 30096-8833 – **756)** 2141 Grand Ave, Des Moines, IA 50312-5303 – **757)** 4321 Stuart Andrew Blvd #E, Charlotte, NC 28217-1588 – **758)** 619 Alexander Rd Fl 3, Princeton, NJ 08540-6000 – **759)** 5620 S Lima Rd, Avon, NY 14414-9791 – **760)** 151 E 1st Ave, Everett, PA 15537-1351 – **761)** 2340 Martin Luther King Jr Ave, Knoxville, TN 37915-1625 – **762)** 5787 S Hampton Rd #285, Dallas, TX 75232-2290 – **763)** 3256 Penryn Rd #100, Loomis, CA 95650-8052 – **764)** 55 Hawthorne St #1100, San Francisco, CA 94105-3914 – **765)** 506 W 1st Ave, Crestview, FL 32536-2420 – **766)** 5590 Rio Grande Ave, Jacksonville, FL 32254-1354 – **767)** 552 Laney-Walker Extension, Augusta, GA 30901-3014 – **768)** 3400 Idaho Ave NW #200, Washington, DC 20016-3000 – **769)** 1100 Victors Way #100, Ann

Arbor, MI 48108-5220 – **770)** 608 State Highway 30, Pipestone, MN 56164-1458 – **771)** 508 Main St, Miles City, MT 59301-3047 – **772)** 180 Radio Hill Road, Franklin, NC 28734-6927 – **773)** 96 Chestnut St, Cooperstown, NY 13326 – **774)** 125 West End Ave 6th Flr, New York, NY 10023-6387 – **775)** 2080 Laura St, Springfield, OR 97477-2197 – **776)** 11640 Highway 17 Bypass, Murrells Inlet, SC 29576-9332 – **777)** 539 Ragland Rd, Madison Heights, VA 24572-ND or PO Box 1079, Lynchburg, VA 24505-1079 – **778)** 700 Monticello Ave #301, Norfolk, VA 23510-2538 – **779)** PO Box 31000, Spokane, WA 99223-3016 – **780)** PO Box 2482, Kirkland, WA 98083-2482 – **781)** 5 Rosemar Circle, Parkersburg, WV 26104-1203 – **782)** 1900 W Carmen St, Guadalupe, AZ 85283-2559 – **783)** 40356 Oak Park Way, Oakhurst, CA 93612-8872 – **784)** 1400 NE 42nd Terrace, Kansas City, MO 64116 – **785)** 800 8th Ave SE, Largo, FL 33771-2162 – **786)** 1546 Golf Course Road, Tallapoosa, GA 30176 – **787)** 3303 E Chicago St, Caldwell, ID 83605-6904 – **788)** PO Box 818, Benton, IL 62812-0818 – **789)** 401 Whitney Ave #160, Gretna, LA 70056-2573 – **790)** 350 Mass Ave #145, Arlington, MA 02474-6713 – **791)** 2100 Fairplain Ave, Benton Harbor, MI 49022-6828 – **792)** 4801 E Independence Blvd #815, Charlotte, NC 28212-5490 – **793)** 3185 S Highland Dr #13, Las Vegas, NV 89109-1029 – **794)** 2900 Sutro St, Reno, NV 89512-1616 – **795)** 4365 Fulton Dr NW, Canton, OH 44718-2823 – **796)** 1555 Hamilton St Fl 6, Philadelphia, PA 19130-4085 – **797)** 214 W Pleasant Dr, Pierre, SD 57501-2472 – **798)** 2100 Trawood Dr, El Paso, TX 79935-3301 – **799)** 205 9th St, Farwell, TX 79325-ND – **800)** 3606 S 500 W, Salt Lake City, UT 84115-4208 – **801)** 244 Goodwin Crest Dr #300, Birmingham, AL 35209-3700 – **802)** 5670 Wilshire Blvd #200, Los Angeles, CA 90036-5611 – **803)** 2070 N Palafox St, Pensacola, FL 32501-2145 – **804)** 4015 N Monroe St, Tallahassee, FL 32303-2139 – **805)** 40 Monument Circle #600, Indianapolis, IN 46204-3011 – **806)** 4200 N Old Lawrence Rd, Wichita, KS 67219-3211 – **807)** 11 Bryant Ave SE, Wadena, MN 56482-1543 – **808)** 119 N 3rd St, Hannibal, MO 63401-0711 – **809)** 112 E 3rd Ave, Plentywood, MT 59254-2223 – **810)** 2929 Radio Station Road, Greenville, NC 27834-0864 – **811)** 372 S Dorset St, South Burlington, VT 05403-6363 – **812)** 235 Walton St, Syracuse, NY 13202-1533 – **813)** 1227 County Line Rd, Selinsgrove, PA 17870-8188 or PO Box 1070, Sunbury, PA 17801-0870 – **814)** 6304 White Horse Rd #B-5, Greenville, SC 29611-3203 – **815)** 621 O'Grady Dr, Chattanooga, TN 37419-1305 – **816)** 2650 Thousand Oaks Blvd #4100, Memphis, TN 38118-2451 – **817)** 6161 Savoy Dr #1200, Houston, TX 77036-3363 – **818)** 310 W Wall St #104, Midland, TX 79701-5123 – **819)** 1140 Rose Hill Dr, Charlottesville, VA 22903-5128 – **820)** 2651 S Fish Hatchery Rd, Fitchburg, WI 53711-5410 – **821)** 306 S Kanawha St, Beckley, WV 25801-5619 – **822)** 19245 Hwy 127, Athens, AL 35614-6805 – **823)** 2300 Portola Dr, Santa Cruz, CA 95062-4203 – **824)** 10 Executive Dr, Farmington, CT 06032-2841 – **825)** 2828 W Flagler St, Miami, FL 33135-1337 – **826)** 4300 W Cypress St, #1040, Tampa, FL 33607 4185 – **827)** 3490 Shallowford Rd NE #302, Atlanta, GA 30341-2934 – **828)** 500 W Boone Ave, Spokane, WA 99201-2404 – **829)** 934 W 138th St, Riverdale, IL 60827-1673 – **830)** 4000 Radio Drive #1, Louisville, KY 40218-1568 – **831)** 827 Fairview Dr SW, Lenoir, NC 28645-6023 – **832)** 0700 SW Bancroft St, Portland, OR 97239-4226 – **833)** 2652 Library Rd #3, Pittsburgh, PA 15234-3127 – **834)** 2440 Millwood Ave, Columbia, SC 29205-1128 or PO Box 2355, West Columbia, SC 29171-2355 – **835)** 4131 N Central Expressway #1000, Dallas, TX 75204-2121 – **836)** 6 E Main St, Price, UT 84501-3032 – **837)** 700 Wellington Hills Rd, Little Rock, AR 72211-2026 – **838)** 2200 Smith Lane, Fortuna, CA 95540-2771 or PO Box 109, Eureka, CA 95502-0109 – **839)** 1907 Mile High Stadium West Cir, Denver, CO 80204-1908 – **840)** 3737 Lake Ave, Fort Wayne, IN 46805-5554 – **841)** 500 Victory Rd, Quincy, MA 02171-3139 – **842)** 3800 Hooper Ave, Baltimore, MD 21211-1313 – **843)** 1400 NE 42nd Terrace, Kansas City, MO 64116 – **844)** 5445 Johnson Rd, Bozeman, MT 59718-8333 – **845)** PO Box 90, Smithfield, NC 27577-0090 – **846)** 210 Montague Ave, Greenwood, SC 29649-1935 – **847)** 2175 Highway 75 #6, Blountville, TN 37617 – **848)** 3218 Quincy St, Plainview, TX 79072-1906 – **849)** 1000 Dexter Ave N #100, Seattle, WA 98109-3582 – **850)** 1859 21st Ave, Rice Lake, WI 54868-9502 – **851)** 2001 N 3rd St #102, Phoenix, AZ 85004-1439 – **852)** 4043 Geer Rd, Hughson, CA 95326-9715 – **853)** 39650 Liberty Street, Fremont, CA 94538 – **854)** 1360 E Sherwood Dr, Grand Junction, CO 81501-7546 – **855)** 1465 Northside Dr NW #218, Atlanta, GA 30318-4220 – **856)** 714 Narrow Way, Saint Simons Island, GA 31522-9712 – **857)** 3301 University Dr S, Fargo, ND 58104-6289 – **858)** 1411 Locust St, Saint Louis, MO 63103-2332 – **859)** 8755 W Flamingo Rd, Las Vegas, NV 89147-8667 – **860)** 234 Airport Plaza Blvd #5, Farmingdale, NY 11735-3938 – **861)** 6200 Oak Tree Blvd 4th Flr, Independence, OH 44131-2510 – **862)** 16414 San Pedro Ave #575, San Antonio, TX 78232-2277 – **863)** 1047 Route 302, Wells River, VT 05081-9742 – **864)** 112 N Pearl St, Berlin, WI 54923-1570 – **865)** 2500 Battleship Pkwy, Mobile, AL 36602-8003 – **866)** 360 Main St, Clinton, AR 72031-6622 – **867)** 3800 W Alameda Ave, Burbank, CA 91505-4300 – **868)** 3463 Ramona Ave #15, Sacramento, CA 95826-3827 – **869)** 311 112th Ave NE, St Petersburg, FL 33716-3394 – **870)** 820 N LaSalle St, Chicago, IL 60610-3214 – **871)** 211 Jason St, Pittsfield, MA 01201-5998 – **872)** 120 West State St, Traverse City, MI 49684 – **873)** 1 Julian Price Place, Charlotte, NC 28208-5211 – **874)** 5010 Underwood Ave, Omaha, NE 68132-2297 – **875)** 462 Merrimack St, Methuen, MA 01844-5804 – **876)** 619 N Turner St, Hobbs, NM 88240-8232 – **877)** 8010 N Main St, Dayton, OH 45405-2249 – **878)** 63088 NE 18th St #200, Bend, OR 97701-7102 – **879)** 2311 Old Arch Rd, Norristown, PA 19401-2013 – **880)** 1270 Mineral Spring Ave, North Providence, RI 02904-4637 – **881)** 26321 Stateline Rd W, Ardmore, TN 38449-3083 – **882)** 6161 Savoy Dr #1200, Houston, TX 77036-3363 – **883)** 6545 Crown Forest Dr, Plano, TX 75024-7489 or PO Box 1629, Cleburne, TX 76033-1629 – **884)** 700 Monticello Ave #311, Norfolk, VA 23510-2523 – **885)** 1630 Oakland Rd #A109, San Jose, CA 95131-2450 – **886)** 1400 NE 42nd Terrace, Kansas City, MO 64116 – **887)** 2131 Crimmins Lane, Falls Church, VA 22043-1962 – **888)** 144 Gould St #155, Needham Heights, MA 02494-2338 – **889)** 1220 Olive St, 3rd Floor, Saint Louis, MO 63103-2324 – **890)** 4611 Terry Rd #C, Jackson, MS 39212-5646 – **891)** 410 New Bridge St #3B, Jacksonville, NC 28540-4759 – **892)** 1250 Riverfront Center, Saint Johnsville, NY 12010-4602 – **893)** 7700 S Lewis Ave, Tulsa, OK 74136-7701 – **894)** 1500 Valley River Dr #350, Eugene, OR 97401-2163 – **895)** 314 E Highland Mall Blvd #250, Austin, TX 78752-3725 – **896)** 2201 S 6th St, Las Vegas, NV 89104-2999 – **897)** 320 Barnett Blvd, Tallassee, AL 36078-1506 – **898)** 83 E Shaw Ave #150, Fresno, CA 93710-7622 – **899)** 136 S Oak Knoll Ave #300, Pasadena, CA 91101-2624 – **900)** 1130 Radio Road, Bartow, FL 33830-7600 – **901)** 5815 Westside Rd, Austell, GA 30106-3179 – **902)** 6341 W Port Ave, Shreveport, LA 71129-2415 – **903)** 27675 Halsted Rd, Farmington Hills, MI 48331-3511 – **904)** 1600 Utica Ave S #400, Minneapolis, MN 55416-1480 – **905)** 2234 Hodges Chapel Rd, Benson, NC 27504 – **906)** 3500 E Rosser Ave, Bismarck, ND 58501-3398 – **907)** 731 Lexington Ave, New York, NY 10022-1331 – **908)** 5110 SE Stark St, Portland, OR 97215-1751 – **909)** 2440 Millwood Ave, Columbia, SC 29205-1128 or PO Box 2355, West Columbia, SC 29171-2355 – **910)** 1302 N Shepherd Dr, Houston, TX 77008-3752 – **911)** 12100 W Howard Ave, Milwaukee, WI 53228-1851 – **912)** 2926 Huntsville Hwy #D, Fayetteville, TN 37334-6687 – **913)** 305 N 2nd St, Rogers, AR 72756 – **914)** 1321 N Gene Autry Trail, Palm Springs, CA 92262-5473 – **915)** 5244 Madison Ave, Sacramento, CA 95841-3004 – **916)** 301 Downing St, Brewton, AL 36426 – **917)** 8551 NW 30th Ter, Miami, FL 33122-1908 – **918)** 1355 E Altamonte Dr, Altamonte Springs, FL 32701-5011 – **919)** 5601 Cassia St, Boise, ID 83705-1836 – **920)** 120 Eaton St, Peoria, IL 61603-4217 – **921)** 2504 Ardmore St SE, Grand Rapids, MI 49506-4901 – **922)** 310 South Lafrenz Rd, Liberty, MO 64068-7944 – **923)** 7255 S Tenaya Way #100, Las Vegas, NV 89113-1900 – **924)** 3258 Merchant Rd, Warsaw, NY 14569-9320 – **925)** 5100 S Tennis Lane, Sioux Falls, SD 57108-2212 – **926)** 1302 N Shepherd Dr, Houston, TX 77008-3752 – **927)** 300 E. Bryant Rd, Conroe, TX 77301 – **928)** 3245 Basie Rd, Richmond, VA 23228-3404 – **929)** PO Box 1299, Lebanon, VA 24266-1299 – **930)** 1949 Mountain View Dr, Cody, WY 82414-4932 – **931)** 5455 Jug Factory Rd, Tuscaloosa, AL 35405-4213 – **932)** 1445 W Baseline Rd, Phoenix, AZ 85041-7010 – **933)** 3400 Olive Ave #550, Burbank, CA 91505-5544 – **934)** 1582 S Parker Rd #204, Denver, CO 80231-2716 – **935)** 777 River Rd, Middletown, CT 06457-3922 – **936)** 2727 Shipley Rd, Wilmington, DE 19810-3299 – **937)** 407 N Howard Ave #200, Tampa, FL 33606-1575 – **938)** 118 N Patterson St, Valdosta, GA 31601-5570 – **939)** 6626 Dubuque Trail, Norwalk, IA 50211-9645 or PO Box 838, Des Moines, IA 50304-0838 – **940)** 1801 E Main St, Marion, IL 62959-5115 – **941)** 131 N Santa Fe Ave, Salina, KS 67401-2615 – **942)** 22 W Main St, Mount Sterling, KY 40353-1314 – **943)** 5555 Hilton Ave #500, Baton Rouge, LA 70808-2564 – **944)** 500 Victory Rd #2, Quincy, MA 02171-3132 – **945)** 830 Oilfield Ave, Shelby, MT 59474-1641 – **946)** 2581 US Hwy 70 W, Goldsboro, NC 27530-9553 – **947)** 290 Hegenberger Rd, Oakland, CA 94621-1436 – **948)** 404 Main St, Klamath Falls, OR 97601-6021 – **949)** 5110 SE Stark St, Portland, OR 97215-1751 – **950)** 5732 N Tryon St, Charlotte, NC 28213-6802 – **951)** 11 Main St, Rapid City, SD 57701-2831 – **952)** 821 Pineville Rd, Chattanooga, TN 37405-2633 – **953)** 510 W Economy Rd, Morristown, TN 37814-3223 – **954)** 5426 N Mesa St, El Paso, TX 79912-5421 – **955)** 35 Eagle Rock Lane, Churchville, VA 24421 – **956)** 801 Old Wawawai Rd, Pullman, WA 99163-9002 – **957)** 3650 131st Ave #550, Bellevue, WA 98006-1334 – **958)** 944 Harlem St, Altoona, WI 54720-1127 – **959)** 2800 E College Ave, Appleton, WI 54915-3255 – **960)** 494 Blue Prince Rd, Bluefield, WV 24701-9577 – **961)** 9831 Beach Blvd #7, Jacksonville, FL 32207-7229 – **962)** PO Box 593642,

Orlando, FL 32859-3642 – **963)** 1100 Spring St #610, Atlanta, GA 30309-2828 – **964)** 25 NW Point Blvd #400, Elk Grove Village, IL 60007-1030 – **965)** 635 W 7th St #400, Cincinnati, OH 45203-1549 – **966)** 1115 Tamarack Rd #500, Owensboro, KY 42301-6988 – **967)** 8121 Georgia Ave #806, Silver Spring, MD 20910-4945 – **968)** 208 Middle Rd, Skowhegan, ME 04976-5023 – **969)** 15130 N Road, Fenton, MI 48430-1380 – **970)** 310 S La Frenz Rd, Liberty, MO 66105-2003 – **971)** 1338 Bragg Blvd, Fayetteville, NC 28301-4202 – **972)** PO Box 52, Greenville, SC 29602-0052 – **973)** 8 Robbins St #201, Toms River, NJ 08753-7668 – **974)** 1086 Teaneck Rd #4F, Teaneck, NJ 07666-4858 – **975)** 100 Saratoga Village Blvd #21, Malta, NY 12020-3703 – **976)** 3100 N Triphammer Rd #100, Lansing, NY 14882-8906 – **977)** 840 Philadelphia St #100, Indiana, PA 15701-3922 – **978)** 619 Alexander Rd, Princeton, NJ 08540-6000 – **979)** 15 Century Blvd #101, Nashville, TN 37214-3692 – **980)** 13725 Montfort Dr, Dallas, TX 75240-4455 – **981)** 9601 McAllister Fwy #1200, San Antonio, TX 78216-4695 – **982)** 55 N 300 W, Salt Lake City, UT 84180-1109 – **983)** 1675 Grandview Rd, Martinsville, VA 24112-2319 – **984)** 812 E Beale St, Kingman, AZ 86401-5925 – **985)** 9255 Towne Centre Dr #535, San Diego, CA 92121-3038 – **986)** 2905 King St, San Jose, CA 95122-1518 – **987)** 6360 SW 41st Place, Davie, FL 33314-3412 – **988)** 255 Cedardale Dr SE, Owatonna, MN 55060-4425 – **989)** 4321 Stuart Andrew Blvd #E, Charlotte, NC 28217-1588 – **990)** 118 E Main St, Clinton, NC 28328-4029 – **991)** 303 N. Boston Ave, Tulsa, OK 74103-1602 – **992)** 109 Old Chapin Rd #Q, Lexington, SC 29072-2065 – **993)** 2219 Yew St Rd, Bellingham, WA 98229-8855 – **994)** 1015 Main St, Wheeling, WV 26003-2782 – **995)** 230 Goodman Rd E #202, Southaven, TN 38671-5151 – **996)** 1400 Eon Dr #144B, Bakersfield, CA 93309-9404 – **997)** 4201 NW 77th Ave, Miami, FL 33166 – **998)** 10143 Commerce St, Summerville, GA 30747-1356 – **999)** 600 W Cavanaugh Rd, Lansing, MI 48910-5254 – **1000)** 1926 W Division St, St Cloud, MN 56301 – **1001)** 731 S Pear Orchard Rd #27, Ridgeland, MS 39157-4839 – **1002)** 317 First Ave E, Kalispell, MT 59901-9601 – **1003)** 122 Cinema Dr, Wilmington, NC 28403-1490 – **1004)** 5011 Capitol Ave, Omaha, NE 68132-2921 – **1005)** 2900 Sutro St, Reno, NV 89512-1616 – **1006)** 100 Chestnut St #1700, Rochester, NY 14604-2418 – **1007)** 470 Leadmine Rd, Gaffney, SC 29340-4037 – **1008)** 9040 Executive Dr #303, Knoxville, TN 37923-4639 – **1009)** 5353 W Alabama St #450, Houston, TX 77056-5922 – **1010)** 1903 S Lamesa Rd, Midland, TX 79701-1706 – **1011)** 10025 Lakewood Dr SW #B, Tacoma, WA 98499-3897 – **1012)** 2609 Jordan Lane NW, Huntsville, AL 35816-1030 – **1013)** 1780 W Holly St, Fayetteville, AR 72703-1307 – **1014)** 5183 N 35th St, Milwaukee, WI 53209-5399 – **1015)** 1601 N 7th St #310, Phoenix, AZ 85006-2481 – **1016)** 621 S Virgil Ave #400, Los Angeles, CA 90005-4043 – **1017)** 3260 Blume Dr #520 Plaza II, Richmond, CA 94806-5715 – **1018)** UMC Campus Box 207, Boulder, CO 80309-1001 – **1019)** 4300 W Cypress St, #1040, Tampa, FL 33607 4185 – **1020)** 2970 Peachtree Rd NW #700, Atlanta, GA 30305-4919 – **1021)** 6500 W Main St #315, Belleville, IL 62223-3700 – **1022)** 2915 Maples Rd, Fort Wayne, IN 46816-3199 – **1023)** 71991 US Hwy 71 S, Jackson, MN 56143-ND – **1024)** 1400 NE 42nd Terrace, Kansas City, MO 64116 – **1025)** 1190 Hollywood Blvd, Bay Saint Louis, MS 39520-1662 – **1026)** 1700 Buena Vista Dr, Monroe, NC 28112-6306 – **1027)** 2000 Randolph Rd SE #103, Albuquerque, NM 87106-2146 – **1028)** 395 Hudson St Fl 7, New York, NY 10014-7452 – **1029)** 13333 SW 68th Pkwy, Tigard, OR 97223-8304 – **1030)** 105 Ash Ave, South Pittsburg, TN 37380-1513 – **1031)** 14001 Dallas Pkwy #300, Dallas, TX 75240-7369 – **1032)** 2131 Crimmins Lane, Falls Church, VA 22043-1962 – **1033)** 5606 Medical Circle, Madison, WI 53719-1232 – **1034)** 132 Carubia Dr, Core, WV 26541-7137 – **1035)** 75-153 Merle Dr #D, Palm Desert, CA 92211-5197 – **1036)** 3256 Penryn Rd #100, Loomis, CA 95650-8052 – **1037)** 625 N Michigan Ave #300, Chicago, IL 60611-3163 – **1038)** 10 Cabot Rd #302, Medford, MA 02155-5173 – **1039)** 3250 Franklin St, Detroit, MI 48207-4219 – **1040)** 738 Blowing Rock Rd, Boone, NC 28607-4840 – **1041)** 875 W 5th St, Winston-Salem, NC 27101-2505 – **1042)** 5702 52nd Ave S, Fargo, ND 58104-5605 – **1043)** 1559 W 4th St, Williamsport, PA 17701-5650 – **1044)** 219 Savannah-Gardner Rd, New Castle, PA 16101-5546 – **1045)** 4337 Big Barn Dr, Little River, SC 29566-6802 – **1046)** 2514 Eugenia Ave, Nashville, TN 37211-2117 – **1047)** 6222 West Interstate 10, San Antonio, TX 78201-2097 – **1048)** 703 3rd Ave, Huntington, WV 25701-1421 – **1049)** 1359 Carmichael Way, Montgomery, AL 36106-3629 – **1050)** 2919 E Broadway Blvd #235, Tucson, AZ 85716-5301 – **1051)** 139 W Olive Ave, Fresno, CA 93728-3035 – **1052)** 4135 Northgate Blvd #1, Sacramento, CA 95834-1226 – **1053)** 9255 Towne Centre Dr #535, San Diego, CA 92121-3038 – **1054)** 1985 NW 88th Ct, Doral, FL 33172 – **1055)** 302 S Poplar St, Centralia, IL 62801-3900 – **1056)** 120 West State St, Traverse City, MI 49684 – **1057)** 2300 N Lelia St, Guymon, OK 73942-2840 – **1058)** 400 Market St Fl 10, Philadelphia, PA 19106-2530 – **1059)** 369 Tower Rd, Waynesburg, PA 15370-3663 or PO Box 990, Greensburg, PA 15601-0990 – **1060)** 1726 Dakota Ave S, Huron, SD 57350-4024 – **1061)** 6080 Mt Moriah Rd Ext, Memphis, TN 38115-2645 – **1062)** 1079 E Trinity Lane, Nashville, TN 37216-3043 – **1063)** 4501 N McColl Rd, McAllen, TX 78504-2431 – **1064)** 750 Ridgeview Dr #204, Saint George, UT 84770-2665 – **1065)** 1400 W Main St, Auburn, WA 98001-5230 – **1066)** 10399 State Hwy 238, Afton, WY 83110-ND – **1067)** 302 S 2nd St #204, Laramie, WY 82070-3650 – **1068)** 39138 Fremont Blvd 3rd Flr, Fremont, CA 94538-1305 – **1069)** 1308 E Hwy 56, Salem, IN 47167-9690 – **1070)** 104 Main St N, Stillwater, MN 55082-5076 – **1071)** 6223 Old Mendenhall Rd, High Point, NC 27263-3940 – **1072)** 108 Radio Station Rd, Whiteville, NC 28472-4906 – **1073)** 661 Little Britain Rd, Newburgh, NY 12553-6150 – **1074)** 4 Summit Park Dr #150, Independence, OH 44131-6921 – **1075)** 161 Hillwood Ave #B, Falls Church, VA 22046-2983 – **1076)** PO Box 680748, Fort Payne, AL 35968-1608 – **1077)** 2821 US Highway 231, Wetumpka, AL 36093-1222 – **1078)** 900 Patte Rd, Willcox, AZ 85643-3408 – **1079)** 200 South "A" St #400, Oxnard, CA 93030-5717 – **1080)** 140 N Main, Lakeport, CA 95453-4815 – **1081)** 4002 W Gandy Blvd, Tampa, FL 33611-3410 – **1082)** 1701 S 55th St, Kansas City, KS 66106-2241 – **1083)** 3 Converse St #101, Palmer, MA 01069-1538 – **1084)** PO Box 504, Ann Arbor, MI 48106-0504 – **1085)** 728 Western Ave, Fergus Falls, MN 56537-1095 – **1086)** 210 W Front St, Forsyth, MT 59327-ND – **1087)** 525 Evans St, Greenville, NC 27858-2311 – **1088)** 147 N Garden St, Marion, NC 28752-3709 – **1089)** 149 Main St #210, Nashua, NH 03060-2725 – **1090)** 55 Horsehill Rd, Cedar Knolls, NJ 07927-2003 – **1091)** 241 W 4th St, Emporium, PA 15834-1047 – **1092)** 7 Parkway Center #625, Pittsburgh, PA 15221-3019 – **1093)** 4230 Faber Place Dr #100, North Charleston, SC 29405-8512 – **1094)** 601 Washington St, Alexandria, LA 71301-8028 – **1095)** 4050 Eisenhauer Rd, San Antonio, TX 78218-3409 – **1096)** 2242 E 1000 S, Roosevelt, UT 84066-4554 – **1097)** 1 Radio Lane, Danville, VA 24541-5235 – **1098)** 1901 N Moore St #200, Arlngton, VA 22209-1746 – **1099)** Murrow Comm Cntr - WSU, Pullman, WA 99163-ND – **1100)** 200 1st Ave W #104, Seattle, WA 98119-4291 – **1101)** 11800 W Grange Ave, Hales Corners, WI 53130-1099 – **1102)** 714 Nicholas St, Rupert, WV 25984 – **1103)** 120 Summit Pkwy #200, Birmingham, AL 35209-4719 – **1104)** 4501 Broadway, Miami, AZ 85539-3800 – **1105)** 1500 Cotner Ave, Los Angeles, CA 90025-3303 – **1106)** 3256 Penryn Rd #100, Loomis, CA 95650-8052 – **1107)** 1901 N Moore St #200, Arlington, VA 22209-1706 – **1108)** 225 Hollywood Blvd NW, Fort Walton Beach, FL 32548-4725 – **1109)** 2100 Coral Way #200, Coral Gables, FL 33145-2639 – **1110)** 4005 Golden Isle W, Baxley, GA 31513-7972 – **1111)** 1410 Hwy 411 NE, Cartersville, GA 30121-5115 – **1112)** 1541 E Grand Ave, Des Moines, IA 50316-3542 – **1113)** 400 W Sunnyside Rd, Idaho Falls, ID 83402-4613 – **1114)** 5560 E Franklin Rd #200, Nampa, ID 83687 – **1115)** 12250 Weber Hill Rd #25, Belleville, MO 63127-1552 – **1116)** 6161 Fall Creek Rd, Indianapolis, IN 46220-5032 – **1117)** 2825 Government St, Baton Rouge, LA 70806-5412 – **1118)** 309 Waverly Oaks Rd #103, Waltham, MA 02452-8403 – **1119)** 425 Centerstone Ct #1, Zeeland, MI 49464-2249 – **1120)** 2330 W Grand St, Springfield, MO 65802-4900 – **1121)** 1119 Eastview Dr, Asheboro, NC 27203-4576 – **1122)** PO Box 7509, Trenton, NJ 08628-0509 – **1123)** 2502 Camino Entrada #C, Santa Fe, NM 87507-4911 – **1124)** 1064 James St, Syracuse, NY 13203-2704 – **1125)** 175 Ken Mar Industrial Pkwy, Broadview Heights, OH 44147-2950 – **1126)** 604 Chillicothe St #405, Portsmouth, OH 45662-4024 – **1127)** 471 Robison Rd W, Erie, PA 16509-5425 – **1128)** 315 S Atherton St, State College, PA 16801-4045 – **1129)** 6223 Old Mendenhall Rd, High Point, NC 27263-3940 – **1130)** 51 Commerce St, Sumter, SC 29150-5014 or PO Box 6344, Florence, SC 29501-6344 – **1131)** 346 S Main St, Winner, SD 57580-1832 – **1132)** 1108 Hendricks St, Chattanooga, TN 37406-3159 – **1133)** 108 W College St, Dickson, TN 37055-1936 – **1134)** 121 S Cotton Square, Lufkin, TX 75904-2933 – **1135)** 1150 Pepsi Place #300, Charlottesville, VA 22901-2865 – **1136)** 3520 Kingsbury Cir, Roanoke, VA 24014-1356 – **1137)** 328 100th St, Amery, WI 54001-4024 – **1138)** 912 Lane 11½, Powell, WY 82435-9222 – **1139)** 273 Azalea Rd #403, Mobile, AL 36609-1970 – **1140)** 1838 Commerce Dr #A, Lakeside, AZ 85929-7007 – **1141)** 1321 N Gene Autry Trail, Palm Springs, CA 92262-5473 – **1142)** 700 E Mineral King Ave, Visalia, CA 93292-6923 – **1143)** 6106 Hoffner Ave, Orlando, FL 32822-4906 – **1144)** 2824 Palm Beach Blvd, Ft Myers, FL 33916-1503 – **1145)** 325 John Knox Rd #G, Tallahassee, FL 32303-4161 – **1146)** 1501 13th Ave, Columbus, GA 31901-1908 – **1147)** 1801 N Elm St, Commerce, GA 30529-2347 – **1148)** 630 Falls Ave, Twin Falls, ID 83301-3300 – **1149)** 1035 Lincoln Rd #205, Bettendorf, IA 52722-4149 – **1150)** 25802 County Road 26, Elkhart, IN 46517-9132 – **1151)** 1410 N Western Ave, Liberal, KS 67901-2212 – **1152)** 758 Colonel Ledyard Hwy, Ledyard, CT 06339 – **1153)** 35 Baltimore St, Cumberland, MD 21502-3024 – **1154)** 2095 S US Highway 131, Petoskey, MI 49770-

9216 – **1155)** 26455 American Dr, Southfield, MI 48034-6114 – **1156)** 305 W Washington St, Brainerd, MN 56401-2923 – **1157)** 1530 Greenview Dr SW #200, Rochester, MN 55902-1080 – **1158)** 5732 N Tryon St, Charlotte, NC 28607-4835 – **1159)** 1270 Buffalo Rd, Smithfield, NC 27577-7443 – **1160)** 101 Back Rd, Dover, NH 03820-5012 – **1161)** 961 Matley Lane #120, Reno, NV 89502-2119 – **1162)** 50 James E Casey Dr, Buffalo, NY 14206-2367 – **1163)** 34 Chestnut St, Oneonta, NY 13820-2466 – **1164)** 5101 S Shields Blvd, Oklahoma City, OK 73129-3217 – **1165)** 888 Rogue River Highway, Grants Pass, OR 97527-5209 – **1166)** 440 Rebecca Lane, Lebanon, PA 17046-1734 – **1167)** 1816 Savannah Hwy, Hampton, SC 29924-6545 – **1168)** 4721 W. 71st St, Sioux Falls, SD 57108 – **1169)** 640 W Hwy 25/70, Newport, TN 37821-8068 – **1170)** 7700 Carpenter Freeway Fl2, Dallas, TX 75247-4829 – **1171)** 3824 Wayside Rd, Stuart, VA 24171-2506 – **1172)** 1130 14th Ave, Longview, WA 98632-3017 – **1173)** 2810 Southern Dr, Gillette, WY 82718-9369 – **1174)** 601 Greensboro Ave #507, Tuscaloosa, AL 35401-1795 – **1175)** 2800 N 44th St #100, Phoenix, AZ 85008-1559 – **1176)** 880 Via Esteban #C, San Luis Obispo, CA 93420-2462 – **1177)** 600 Grant St #600, Denver, CO 80203-3540 – **1178)** 500 Grand Ave #210, Destin, FL 32541-1410 – **1179)** 7080 Industrial Way, Macon, GA 31206-7538 – **1180)** 117 SE 5th St, Evansville, IN 47708-1639 – **1181)** 929 Howard Ave, New Orleans, LA 70113-1148 – **1182)** 762 Water St, Fitchburg, MA 01420-6481 – **1183)** PO Box 308, Bath, ME 04530-0308 – **1184)** 2110 Cliff Rd, Saint Paul, MN 55122-2347 – **1185)** 216 Belmont Rd, Grand Forks, ND 58201-4620 – **1186)** 25539 NC Hwy 125, Scotland Neck, NC 27874-ND – **1187)** 204 E Broadway, Farmington, NM 87401-6418 – **1188)** 150 Spectrum Blvd, Las Vegas, NV 89101-4860 – **1189)** 500 Frank W. Burr Buld #19, Teaneck, NY 07666 – **1190)** 100 Chestnut St #1700, Rochester, NY 14604-2418 – **1191)** 1574 Coburg Rd PMB 237, Eugene, OR 97401-4802 – **1192)** 275 Radio Road, Hanover, PA 17331-1140 – **1193)** 219 Savannah-Gardner Rd, New Castle, PA 16101-5546 – **1194)** 106 Assembly Dr, Piedmont, SC 29673 – **1195)** 3004 E Highway 76, Mullins, SC 29574-7396 or PO Box 1020, Marion, SC 29571-1020 – **1196)** 886 Mt Olivet Rd, Columbia, TN 38401-8031 – **1197)** 301 W South Temple, Salt Lake City, UT 84101-1216 – **1198)** 110 W Spiller Ave, Wytheville, VA 24382-1953 – **1199)** 808 E Sprague Ave, Spokane, WA 99202-2126 – **1200)** 4010 Summitview Ave, Yakima, WA 98908-2966 – **1201)** 491 S Washburn St #400, Oshkosh, WI 54904-6733 – **1202)** 1101 Cameron Rd, Opp, AL 36467-2407 – **1203)** 2250 W Sunset Ave #3, Springdale, AR 72762-5187 – **1204)** 2654 Cramer Lane, Chico, CA 95928-8838 – **1205)** 765 Story Rd, San Jose, CA 95122 – **1206)** 2030 Iowa Ave #A, Riverside, CA 92507-7412 – **1207)** 920 W Basin Rd #400, New Castle, DE 19720-1013 – **1208)** 3071 Continental Dr, West Palm Beach, FL 33407-3274 – **1209)** 1176 Satellite Blvd NW #200, Suwanee, GA 30024-2868 – **1210)** 245 Alfred St, Savannah, GA 31408-3205 – **1211)** 436 N Main St, Pocatello, ID 83204-3018 – **1212)** 331 Fulton St #1200, Peoria, IL 61602-1475 – **1213)** 30129 E US Hwy 54, Pratt, KS 67124-8304 – **1214)** 1039 Eggners Ferry Rd, Benton, KY 42025-8070 – **1215)** 219 Main St, Manchester, KY 40962-1259 – **1216)** 3250 S Reserve St #200, Missoula, MT 59801-8236 – **1217)** 526 Main Ave SE, Hickory, NC 28602-1103 – **1218)** 907 Lejeune Blvd, Jacksonville, NC 28540-5916 – **1219)** 5011 Capitol Ave, Omaha, NE 68132-2921 – **1220)** 69 Stanhope Ave, Keene, NH 03431-1577 – **1221)** 59 Court St #100, Binghamton, NY 13901-3293 – **1222)** 1611 S Main St, Dayton, OH 45409-2547 – **1223)** 2003 NW 56th St, Pendleton, OR 97801-4593 – **1224)** 1 Forever Dr, Holidaysburg, PA 16648-3029 – **1225)** 1246 Cranston St, Cranston, RI 02920-7318 – **1226)** 102 S 5th St, Crockett, TX 75835-2037 – **1227)** 2720 Highway 83, Weslaco, TX 78596-1225 – **1228)** 2525 Kell Blvd #200, Wichita Falls, TX 76308-1008 – **1229)** 2602 Whitehouse Rd #E, South Chesterfield, VA 23834-5398 – **1230)** N72 W12922 Good Hope Rd, Menomonee Falls, WI 53051-4441 – **1231)** 113 W Oak St, Sparta, WI 54656-1712 – **1232)** 204 Main St #201, Logan, WV 25601-3943 – **1233)** 3525 Soldier Springs Rd, Laramie, WY 82070-8903 – **1234)** 111 N Spring St, Searcy, AR 72143-7712 – **1235)** 44 Gough St #301, San Francisco, CA 94103-5424 – **1236)** 1250 Siskiyou Blvd, Ashland, OR 97520-5010 – **1237)** 747 E Green St #101, Pasadena, CA 91101 – **1238)** 6805 Corporate Dr #130, Colorado Springs, CO 80919-1977 – **1239)** 2355 Pluckebaum Rd, Cocoa, FL 32926-5179 – **1240)** 1 Boot Key, Marathon, FL 33050 – **1241)** PO Box 151300, Tampa, FL 33684-1300 – **1242)** 100 WMTM Road, Moultrie, GA 31788-4104 – **1243)** 341 S Yorktown Pike, Mason City, IA 50401-4533 – **1244)** 3110 Upper Fords Creek Rd, Orofino, ID 83544-9629 – **1245)** 401 N Michigan Ave #2010, Chicago, IL 60611-4206 – **1246)** 401 W Main St #301, Lexington, KY 40507-1646 – **1247)** 1526 Corporate Dr, Shreveport, LA 71107-6338 – **1248)** 1423 Clarkview Rd, Baltimore, MD 21209-2134 – **1249)** 77 Monroe Center NW #1000, Grand Rapids, MI 49503-2912 – **1250)** 2115 Washington Ave S, Bemidji, MN 56601-8918 – **1251)** 731 S Pear Orchard Rd #27, Ridgeland, MS 39157-4839 – **1252)** 2147 Springs Rd, Mount Airy, NC 27030-ND – **1253)** 1811 W O St, McCook, NE 69001-4264 – **1254)** 110 Babbitt Rd, Franklin, NH 03235-2105 – **1255)** 1842 S Broad St, Trenton, NJ 08610-6002 – **1256)** 1960 Idaho St, Carson City, NV 89701-5324 – **1257)** 5426 William St, Lancaster, NY 14086-9320 – **1258)** 51 S Pearl St, Albany, NY 12207-1500 – **1259)** 6555 Carnegie Ave #100, Cleveland, OH 44103-4619 – **1260)** 7136 S. Yale #500, Tulsa, OK 74136 – **1261)** 7590 Highway 238, Jacksonville, OR 97530-9728 – **1262)** 305 Hwy 315, Pittston, PA 18460-3987 – **1263)** 118 E 3rd St E, Mobridge, SD 57601-2511 – **1264)** 510 W Economy Rd, Morristown, TN 37814-3223 – **1265)** 1300 WWCR Ave, Nashville, TN 37218-3800 – **1266)** 3601 S Congress Ave #F, Austin, TX 78704-7280 – **1267)** 207 University Blvd #200 , Harrisonburg, VA 22801-3752 – **1268)** 2201 6th Ave #1500, Seattle, WA 98121-1840 – **1269)** 343 High St, Morgantown, WV 26505-5515 – **1270)** PO Box 1747, Foley, AL 36536-1747 – **1271)** 16 Martin Luther King St, Selma, AL 36703-3109 – **1272)** 3256 Penryn Rd #100, Loomis, CA 95650-8052 – **1273)** 650 S E St #H, San Bernadino, CA 92408-1946 – **1274)** 900 Front St, San Francisco, CA 94111-1427 – **1275)** 820 11th Ave, Greeley, CO 80631-3246 – **1276)** 40 Cuprak Rd, Norwich, CT 06360-2008 – **1277)** 316 E Taylor Rd, DeLand, FL 32724-7817 – **1278)** 1310 S Florida Ave, Wauchula, FL 33873-9479 – **1279)** 2215 Perimeter Park Dr, Atlanta, GA 30341-1307 – **1280)** 415 Park Ave, Twin Falls, ID 83301-7752 – **1281)** 21 E St Joseph St, Indianapolis, IN 46204-1025 – **1282)** 95 Jackson St, Prestonsburg, KY 41653-1010 – **1283)** 613 N 5th St, West Monroe, LA 71291-1726 – **1284)** 122 Green St #2L, Worcester, MA 01604-4138 – **1285)** 779 Warren Ave, Portland, ME 04103-1176 – **1286)** 23300 Goddard Rd, Taylor, MI 48180-4131 – **1287)** 436 W. Front St, Traverse City, MI 49684 – **1288)** 20132 Highway 15, Glencoe, MN 55350-5643 – **1289)** 2702 E 32nd St, Joplin, MO 64804-4307 – **1290)** 3313 15th St #F, Great Falls, MT 59405-ND – **1291)** 1190 Patton Ave, Asheville, NC 28806-2706 – **1292)** 4801 E Independence Blvd #815, Charlotte, NC 28212-5497 – **1293)** 707 Leon St, Durham, NC 27704-4125 – **1294)** 1185 9th St NE, Thompson, ND 58278-9343 – **1295)** 8 Robbins St #201, Toms River, NJ 08753-7668 – **1296)** 133 Jackson St. NE, Albuquerque, NM 87108 – **1297)** 419 Broadway, Paterson, NJ 07501-2104 – **1298)** 39 Kellogg Rd, New Hartford, NY 13413-2849 – **1299)** 906 SW Alder St, Newport, OR 97365-4712 – **1300)** 134 E Pitt St, Bedford, PA 15522-1311 – **1301)** 310 2nd Ave, Warren, PA 16365-2407 – **1302)** 51 Commerce St, Florence, SC 29501-6344 or PO Box 6344, Sumter, SC 29151-1269 – **1303)** 1 WDXI Drive, Jackson, TN 38305-4124 – **1304)** 3090 Olive St #400, Dallas, TX 75219-7640 – **1305)** 8023 Vantage Dr #840, San Antonio, TX 78230-4771 – **1306)** 3231 Old Lee Highway #506, Fairfax, VA 22030-1504 – **1307)** 5589 Greenwich Rd #200, Virginia Beach, VA 23462-6565 – **1308)** 152101 W County Road 12, Prosser, WA 99350-7265 – **1309)** 2651 S Fish Hatchery Rd, Madison, WI 53711 5400 – **1310)** 276 Seneca Trail, Ronceverte, WV 24970-1343 – **1311)** 2700 Corporate Dr #115, Birmingham, AL 35242-2735 – **1312)** 311 Lexington Ave, Fort Smith, AR 72901-3842 – **1313)** 5345 Madison Ave, Sacramento, CA 95841-3141 – **1314)** 1 Broadcast Ln, Waterbury, CT 06706 – **1315)** 1055 NE 125th St, North Miami, FL 33161-5804 – **1316)** 2360 St Johns Bluff Rd S #2, Jacksonville, FL 32246-2310 – **1317)** 1779 Independence Blvd, Sarasota, FL 34234-2106 – **1318)** 1000 Memorial Dr, Griffin, GA 30223-4446 – **1319)** 17525 Highway 1, Vivian, LA 71082-9526 – **1320)** 42 Union St, Attleboro, MA 02703 – **1321)** 600 W Cavanaugh Rd, Lansing, MI 48910-5254 – **1322)** 1009 W Ridge St #A, Marquette, MI 49855-3963 – **1323)** 507 SE 11th St, Grand Rapids, MN 55744-3950 – **1324)** 1750 S Brentwood Blvd #811, Saint Louis, MO 63144-1344 – **1325)** 2438 Highway 43 S, Picayune, MS 39466-7486 – **1326)** 875 W 5th St, Winston Salem, NC 27101-2505 – **1327)** 90 Tennessee St #B, Murphy, NC 28906-2958 – **1328)** 3600 County Road 19 S, Minot, ND 58701-ND – **1329)** 8 Lawrence Rd , Derry, NH 03038-4191 – **1330)** 900 Parish St 3rd FLR, Pittsburgh, PA 15220-3407 – **1331)** 1801 Charleston Hwy #J, Cayce, SC 29033-2019 or PO Box 5106, Columbia, SC 29250-0626 – **1332)** 500 S Phillips Ave, Sioux Falls, SD 57104-6825 – **1333)** 162 Free Hill Rd, Gray, TN 37615-3144 – **1334)** 1030 Oakdale St, Manchester, TN 37355-5618 – **1335)** 1782 W Sam Houston Pkwy N, Houston, TX 77043-2723 – **1336)** 306 W Broad St, Richmond, VA 23220-4219 – **1337)** 1308 Coolidge Rd, Aberdeen, WA 98520-6317 – **1338)** 645 25th Ave N, Wisconsin Rapids, WI 54495-3294 – **1339)** 1111 E Willow St, Scottsboro, AL 35768-2210 – **1340)** 4433 E Broadway Blvd #210, Tucson, AZ 85711-3536 – **1341)** 3301 Barham Blvd #201, Los Angeles, CA 90068-1477 – **1342)** 401 Pacheco Blvd, Los Banos, CA 93635-4227 – **1343)** 4100 Metzger Rd, Fort Pierce, FL 34947-1712 – **1344)** 7179 Printers Alley, Milton, FL 32583-5347 – **1345)** PO Box 866, Pensacola, FL 32591-0866 – **1346)** 514 Jefferson St, Waterloo, IA 50701-5422 – **1347)** 4320 Dundee Rd, Northbrook, IL 60062-1703 – **1348)** 4463 E County Road 1200S, Haubstadt, IN 47639 or PO Box 4164, Evansville, IN 47724 – **1349)** 2120 N Woodlawn St #352, Wichita, KS 67208-1881 – **1350)** 821 Adams Rd, Corbin, KY 40701-4708 – **1351)** PO Box 159, Carencro, LA 70520-0159 – **1352)** 552 Massachusetts Ave #201, Cambridge, MA 02139-4088 – **1353)** 13321 New Hampshire Ave #207, Silver Spring, MD 20904-3450 – **1354)** 6317 Taylor Dr, Flint, MI 48507-4683 – **1355)** 1496 Bellevue St #202, Green Bay, WI 54311-4205 – **1356)** 1399 E Reed Rd, Greenville, MS 38703-7234 – **1357)** 401 E Coal Ave, Gallup, NM 87301-6099 – **1358)** 419 Broadway, Paterson, NJ 07501-2104 – **1359)** 60 North Ave, Owego, NY 13827-1325 – **1360)** 9700 SE Eastview Dr, Happy Valley, OR 97086-6975 – **1361)** 1 Boston Store Place, Erie, PA 16501-2312 – **1362)** 1516 4th Ave #B, Conway, SC 29526-5032 – **1363)** 25 Garlington Rd, Greenville, SC 29615-4613 – **1364)** 1200 S Stockton Ave, Monahans, TX 79756-4060 – **1365)** 710 Grove St, Danville, VA 24541-1704 – **1366)** 22479 Front St, Accomac, VA 23301-1641 or PO Box 460, Onley, VA 23418-0460 – **1367)** 5408 S Freya St, Spokane, WA 99223-7114 – **1368)** 2100 Washington Ave, Sheboygan, WI 53081-7042 – **1369)** 1530 Main St, Lander, WY 82520-2658 – **1370)** 1913 Barry St, Oxford, AL 36203-2319 or PO Box 1350, Gadsden, AL 35902-1350 – **1371)** 2222 Main St, North Little Rock, AR 72114-2302 – **1372)** 2030 Iowa Ave #A, Riverside, CA 92507-7412 – **1373)** 1410 Neotomas Ave #200, Santa Rosa, CA 95405-7533 – **1374)** 45 Pomfret St, Putnam, CT 06260-1827 – **1375)** 436 Mall Blvd, Brunswick, GA 31525-1819 – **1376)** 6174 GA Hwy 57, Macon, GA 31217-3405 or PO Box 2127, Warner Robins, GA 31099-2127 – **1377)** 1416 Locust St, Des Moines, IA 50309-3014 – **1378)** 805 Stewart Ave, Lewiston, ID 83501-4709 – **1379)** 1419 W Bannock St, Boise, ID 83702-5234 – **1380)** 671 E County Road 400 S, Kokomo, IN 46902-8101 – **1381)** 400 Poydras St #800, New Orleans, LA 70130-3245 – **1382)** PO Box 1533, Black Mountain, NC 28771 – **1383)** 277 Union Ave #205, Laconia, NH 03246-3114 – **1384)** 27 Wiliam St 11th Flr, New York, NY 10005-2718 – **1385)** 5411 Jefferson St NE #100, Albuquerque, NM 87109-3485 – **1386)** 7755 Freedom Ave NW, North Canton, OH 44720-6905 – **1387)** 5 Brooks Robinson Way, York, PA 17401-2401 – **1388)** 1408 E Gibson St, Jasper, TX 75951-6123 – **1389)** 12451 Network Blvd #140, San Antonio, TX 78249-3445 – **1390)** 1035 Avalon Dr, Forest, VA 24551-2970 – **1391)** 214 Walnut Dr SE, Wise, VA 24293-ND – **1392)** 645 Church St #400, Norfolk, VA 23510-1712 – **1393)** PO Box 19123, Birmingham, AL 35219-9123 or PO Box 622, Jasper, AL 35502-0622 – **1394)** 316 East Taylor Rd., Deland, FL 32724 or PO Pox 63, Mobile, AL 36601-0063 – **1395)** 2425 E Camelback Rd #570, Phoenix, AZ 85016-4250 – **1396)** 2121 Lancey Dr, Modesto, CA 95355-3000 – **1397)** 9660 Granite Ridge Dr, San Diego, CA 92123-2657 – **1398)** 2 S Parish Ave, Johnstown, CO 80534-7800 – **1399)** 869 Blue Hills Ave, Bloomfield, CT 06002-3710 – **1400)** 1505 Dundee Rd, Winter Haven, FL 33884-1013 – **1401)** 3890 Dunn Ave #804, Jacksonville, FL 32218-6429 – **1402)** 2828 W Flagler St, Miami, FL 33135-1337 – **1403)** 2000 Indian Hills Dr, Sioux City, IA 51104-1602 – **1404)** 4154 Jennings Dr, Kalamazoo, MI 49048-1087 – **1405)** 2115 Washington Ave S, Bemidji, MN 56601-8918 – **1406)** 88 Vilcom Center Dr #130, Chapel Hill, NC 27514-1660 – **1407)** 123 Egg Harbor Rd #302, Sewell, NJ 08080-9406 – **1408)** 1096 Mechem Dr #G3, Ruidoso, NM 88345-7057 – **1409)** 59 Court St #100, Binghamton, NY 13901-3293 – **1410)** 8044 Montgomery Rd #650, Cincinnati, OH 45236-2959 – **1411)** 229 Broad St, Conneaut, OH 44030-2616 – **1412)** 80404 Cooney Lane, Hermiston, OR 97838-6613 – **1413)** 3355 NE Cornell Rd, Hillsboro, OR 97124-5018 – **1414)** 212 S Centre St, Pottsville, PA 17901-3532 – **1415)** 100 Cross Hill Way, Easley, SC 29640-8854 – **1416)** 701 S Pierce St #101, Amarillo, TX 79101-2428 – **1417)** 4638 Decker Dr, Baytown, TX 77520-1418 – **1418)** 5801 Marvin D Love Freeway #409, Dallas, TX 75237-2319 – **1419)** 325 Poplar Knob Rd, Galax, VA 24333-4106 – **1420)** 1820 Heritage Center Way, Harrisonburg, VA 22801-8451 – **1421)** 1040 S Henderson St, Seattle, WA 98108-4720 – **1422)** 1420 Bellevue St, Green Bay, WI 54311-5649 – **1423)** 527 Gibbs St, Ravenswood, WV 26164-1011 – **1424)** 2717 Yellowstone Rd, Rock Springs, WY 82901-2813 – **1425)** 210 Radio Road, Corona, CA 92879-1722 – **1426)** PO Box 669, Marysville, CA 95901-0018 – **1427)** 2347 Bering Dr, San Jose, CA 95131-1125 – **1428)** 1515 E Silver Springs Blvd #134, Ocala, FL 34470-6830 – **1429)** 6565 North W St #270, Pensacola, FL 32505-1797 – **1430)** 2420 Waycross Highway, Jesup, GA 31545-2332 – **1431)** 346 W 8th St, Dubuque, IA 52001-4649 – **1432)** 120 W 7th St #400, Bloomington, IN 47404-3869 – **1433)** 2601 Central Ave #C, Dodge City, KS 67801-6212 – **1434)** PO Box 487, Grayson, KY 41143-0487 – **1435)** 1726 Reisterstown Rd #117, Pikesville, MD 21208-2986 – **1436)** 49 Acme Rd, Brewer, ME 04412-1545 – **1437)** 1101 S Cass St, Traverse City, MI 49684-3235 – **1438)** 750 Dewey Blvd #1, Butte, MT 59701-3200 – **1439)** 910 E McNeill St, Lillington, NC 27546-7483 – **1440)** 9349 China Grove Church Rd, Pineville, NC 28134-8531 – **1441)** PO Box 127, Tabor City, NC 28463-0127 – **1442)** 216 Belmont Rd, Grand Forks, ND 58201-4620 – **1443)** 500 N Commercial St, Manchester, NH 03101-1151 – **1444)** 20 Tucker Dr, Poughkeepsie, NY 12603-1644 – **1445)** 280 State St, Rochester, NY 14614-1033 – **1446)** 125 S Superior St, Toledo, OH 43602-1790 – **1447)** 2513 6th Ave, Altoona, PA 16602-2129 – **1448)** 2615 Broad St, Chattanooga, TN 37408-3100 – **1449)** 4301 Westbank Dr #301, Austin, TX 78746-4400 – **1450)** 1285 W 2320 S, Salt Lake City, UT 84119-1448 – **1451)** 1129 Chatham Heights, Martinsville, VA 24112-2149 – **1452)** 26256 Highway 47, South Hill, VA 23970-ND – **1453)** 1201 E Division St, Neillsville, WI 54456-2123 – **1454)** RR1 Box 139, Dunmore, WV 24934-9712 – **1455)** 1201 Main St, Moundsville, WV 26003-2844 – **1456)** PO Box 630, Vernon, AL 35592-0630 – **1457)** 415 N McKinley St, Little Rock, AR 72205 – **1458)** 816 W 6th St, Parker, AZ 85344-4599 – **1459)** 1425 River Park Dr #520, Sacramento, CA 95815-4524 – **1460)** 175 Church St, Naugatuck, CT 06770-4180 – **1461)** 432 S Nova Rd, Ormond Beach, FL 32174-6121 – **1462)** 11300 4th St N #143, Saint Petersburg, FL 33716-2939 – **1463)** 1201 Peachtree Street, NE #800, Atlanta, GA 30361 – **1464)** 1 Parker Place #485, Janesville, WI 53545-4078 – **1465)** 2915 Maples Rd, Fort Wayne, IN 46816-3199 – **1466)** 4535 Metropolitan Ave, Kansas City, KS 66106-2599 – **1467)** 110 Dennis Dr, Lexington, KY 40503-2917 – **1468)** 8230 Summa Ave, Baton Rouge, LA 70809-3421 – **1469)** 808 Huron Ave, Port Huron, MI 48060-3705 – **1470)** 13225 Dogwood Dr, Baxter, MN 56425-8669 – **1471)** 12250 Weber Hill Rd #25, Saint Louis, MO 63127-1552 – **1472)** 70 Adams Hill Rd, Asheville, NC 28806-3841 – **1473)** 3720 Reynolda Rd, Winston-Salem, NC 27106-2232 – **1474)** 7035 E Washington St Ext, Bath, NY 14810 – **1475)** 27 Wiliam St 11th Flr, New York, NY 10005-2718 – **1476)** 1232 E 2nd St, Tulsa, OK 74120-2010 – **1477)** 786 Diamond Hill Rd, Woonsocket, RI 02895-1499 – **1478)** 445 Carolina Springs Rd, North Augusta, SC 29841-8801 – **1479)** 518 St Joseph St, Rapid City, SD 57701-2717 – **1480)** 1811 Carters Creek Pike, Franklin, TN 37064-6823 – **1481)** 3704 Whittier Rd, Millington, TN 38108-2649 – **1482)** 4045 N Mesa St, El Paso, TX 79902-1526 – **1483)** 3308 Broadway St #401, San Antonio, TX 78209-6550 – **1484)** 1600 Pasadena Blvd, Pasadena, TX 77502-2404 – **1485)** 2809 Emerywood Pkwy #540, Henrico, VA 23294-3745 – **1486)** 67 Merchants Row, Rutland, VT 05701-5910 – **1487)** 2707 Colby Ave #1380, Everett, WA 98201-3568 – **1488)** 1456 E Green Bay St, Shawano, WI 54166-2258 – **1489)** 801 Noble St #30, Anniston, AL 36201-5698 – **1490)** 1780 W Holly St, Fayetteville, AR 72703-1307 – **1491)** 136 S Oak Knoll Ave #300, Pasadena, CA 91101-2624 – **1492)** 4043 Geer Rd, Hughson, CA 95326-9715 – **1493)** 4700 Walnut St, Boulder, CO 80301-2548 – **1494)** 7120 SW 24th Ave, Gainesville, FL 32607-3705 – **1495)** 233 N Michigan Ave #2800, Chicago, IL 60601-5519 – **1496)** 516 Main St, Hazard, KY 41701-1775 – **1497)** 17 Columbus Rd, Plymouth, MA 02360-4810 – **1498)** 1325 G Street #750, Washington, DC 20005-3104 – **1499)** 28 Houlton Rd, Presque Isle, ME 04769-5206 – **1500)** 1613 Lawrence Hwy , Charlotte, MI 48813-8844 – **1501)** 640 Lincoln Ave SE, Saint Cloud, MN 56304-1024 – **1502)** 313 Old Route 66, Saint Robert, MO 65584-ND or PO Box D, Waynesville, MO 65583-0480 – **1503)** 10250 Lorraine Rd, Gulfport, MS 39503-6005 – **1504)** 315 A Street, Meridian, MS 39301-4512 – **1505)** 115 N Church St, Rocky Mount, NC 27804-5402 – **1506)** 1000 20th Ave SW, Minot, ND 58701-6447 – **1507)** 212 W Apache St, Farmington, NM 87401-6235 – **1508)** 3521 N Bensign Rd, Hobbs, NM 88240 – **1509)** 2 Pendell Rd, Poughkeepsie, NY 12601-1500 – **1510)** 8456 Smokey Hollow Rd, Baldwinsville, NY 13027-8222 – **1511)** 39540 Bradbury Rd, Middleport, OH 45760-9703 – **1512)** 7461 South Ave, Youngstown, OH 44512-5789 – **1513)** 285 Liberty St NE #365, Salem, OR 97301-0034 – **1514)** 2294 Clements Ferry Rd, Charleston, SC 29492-7729 – **1515)** 104 Cherry St, Athens, TN 37303-ND – **1516)** 122 Radio Road, Jackson, TN 38301-3465 – **1517)** 810 W 200 N, Logan, UT 84321-3726 – **1518)** 2043 10th St NE, Roanoke, VA 24012-5309 – **1519)** 372 Dorset St, South Burlington, VT 05403-6212 – **1520)** 17 N. 3rd Street #103, Yakima, WA 98901 – **1521)** 557 Scott St, Wausau, WI 54403-4829 – **1522)** 366 S Section St, Fairhope, AL 36532-ND – **1523)** 1605 Simpson Lane, Marysville, CA 95901-9747 – **1524)** 1950 S Sunwest Lane #302, San Bernadino, CA 92408-3227 – **1525)** 10 Columbus Blvd #24, Hartford, CT 06106-1973 – **1526)** 1575 McKee Rd #206, Dover, DE 19904-1382 – **1527)** 1061 Collier Center Way #9, Naples, FL 34110-8403 – **1528)** 3765 N John Young Pkwy, Orlando, FL 32804-3213 – **1529)** 3411 W Tharpe St, Tallahassee, FL 32303-1139 – **1530)** 940 Brownlee Rd, Jackson, GA 30233-2418 – **1531)** 1411 Locust St, Saint Louis, MO 63103-2332 – **1532)** 1632 S Maize Rd, Wichita, KS 67209-3912 – **1533)** 100 Eversole St #1 , Harlan, KY 40831-2346 – **1534)** 707 Leon St, Durham, NC 27704-4125 – **1535)** 1301 E 4th St, North Platte, NE 69101-4302 – **1536)** 1705 Lake St, Elmira, NY 14901-1299 – **1537)** 134 Mullin St, Watertown, NY 13601-3616 – **1538)** 717 E David Rd, Dayton, OH 45429-5218 – **1539)** 278 SW Arthur St, Portland, OR 97201-4745 – **1540)** 2147 Market St,

Nesquehoning, PA 18240-1422 or PO Box D, Lansford, PA 18232-0801 – **1541)** Centre City Towers - 650 Smithfield St #620, Pittsburgh, PA 15222-3913 – **1542)** 219 Luckett St NW, Roanoke, VA 24017-6812 – **1543)** 201 State St, La Crosse, WI 54601-3246 – **1544)** 100 Kanawha Terrace, Saint Albans, WV 25177-2771 – **1545)** 1716 KROE Lane, Sheridan, WY 82801-9681 – **1546)** 3900 11th Ave, Tuscaloosa, AL 35401-7056 – **1547)** 208 Buena Vista Rd, Hot Springs, AR 71913-8208 – **1548)** 500 E Tyler Pkwy, Payson, AZ 85541-3276 – **1549)** 2171 Ralph Ave, Stockton, CA 95206-3699 – **1550)** 777 River Rd, Middletown, CT 06457-3922 – **1551)** 2710 W Atlantic Ave, Delray Beach, FL 33445-4431 – **1552)** 1800 Northgate Blvd #A10, Sarasota, FL 34234-2157 – **1553)** 1820 Wynnton Rd, Columbus, GA 31906-2930 – **1554)** 12544 N Main St, Trenton, GA 30752-2227 – **1555)** 3535 E Kimberly Rd, Davenport, IA 52807-2583 – **1556)** PO Box 84, Jerome, ID 83338-0084 – **1557)** 685 E 1675 N, Michigan City, IN 46360-9503 – **1558)** 22 Sconticut Neck Rd, Fairhaven, MA 02719-1930 – **1559)** 59346 Madison Ave, Mankato, MN 56001-8518 – **1560)** 73 Varney Rd #A, Wolfeboro, NH 03894-ND – **1561)** 187 Vienna Rd, Newark, NY 14513-9124 – **1562)** 715 Route 52, Beacon, NY 12508-1047 – **1563)** 4 Summit Park Dr #150, Independence, OH 44131-6921 – **1564)** 40 Rickert Rd, Doylestown, PA 18901-2326 – **1565)** 12 W Long Ave, Du Bois, PA 15801-2100 – **1566)** 101 Riverview Rd, Erwin, TN 37650-8722 – **1567)** 7351 Hunton St, Warrenton, VA 20187-2222 – **1568)** 1133 Kresky Ave, Centralia, WA 98531-3789 – **1569)** 45 Campbell Rd, Walla Walla, WA 99362-9597 – **1570)** 134 4th Ave, Huntington, WV 25701-1220 – **1571)** 22 Cogswell Ave, Pell City, AL 35125-2438 – **1572)** 1415 Fulton St, Fresno, CA 93721-1609 – **1573)** 747 E Green St #101, Pasadena, CA 91101 – **1574)** 342 Day St, San Francisco, CA 94131-2313 – **1575)** 4700 S Syracuse St #1050, Denver, CO 80237-2713 – **1576)** 100 NW 76th Dr #2, Gainesville, FL 32607-6659 – **1577)** 13085 SW 133rd Ct, Miami, FL 33186-5850 – **1578)** 404 W Lime St, Lakeland, FL 33815-4651 – **1579)** 3100 E 15th St, Panama City, FL 32405-7421 – **1580)** PO Box 2419, Covington, GA 30015-7419 – **1581)** 613 Silver Circle, Dalton, GA 30721-4551 – **1582)** 9245 N Meridian St #300, Indianapolis, IN 46260-1832 – **1583)** 116 N 4th St, Williamsburg, KY 40769-1115 – **1584)** 10 Cabot Rd #302, Medford, MA 02155-5173 – **1585)** 236 Admiral Dr, Annapolis, MD 21401-3123 – **1586)** 1150 Haynor Rd, Ionia, MI 48846-8532 – **1587)** 6500 W Main St #315, Belleville, IL 62223-3700 – **1588)** 3216 Griffith Rd, Monroe, NC 28110 – **1589)** 1103 N Green St, Morganton, NC 28655-9003 – **1590)** 990 N Center St Extension, Mount Olive, NC 28365-2704 – **1591)** 3205 W North Front St, Grand Island, NE 68803-4024 – **1592)** 1496 Bellevue St #202, Green Bay, WI 54311-4205 – **1593)** 320 N Jensen Rd, Vestel, NY 13850-2111 – **1594)** 2625 S Memorial Dr, Tulsa, OK 74129-2600 – **1595)** 4205 Cherry Ave NE, Keizer, OR 97303-4856 or PO Box 1430, Salem, OR 97308-1430 – **1596)** 1 Forever Dr, Holidaysburg, PA 16648-3029 – **1597)** 2278 Wortham Lane, Grovetown, GA 30813-5103 or PO Box 510, Appling, GA 30802-0510 – **1598)** 230 Goodman Rd E #202, Southaven, MS 38671-5151 – **1599)** 630 Mainstream Dr, Nashville, TN 37228-1204 – **1600)** 4638 Decker Dr, Baytown, TX 77520-1418 – **1601)** 3308 Broadway St #401, San Antonio, TX 78209-6550 – **1602)** 257 E 200 S #400, Salt Lake City, UT 84111-2073 – **1603)** 2298 Rose Ridge, Clintwood, VA 24228-7738 – **1604)** 403 Capital St, Lewiston, ID 83501-1815 – **1605)** 2029 Freeway Dr, Mount Vernon, WA 98273-5470 – **1606)** 1 Commerce St #300, Montgomery, AL 36104-3549 – **1607)** 8211 Geyer Springs Rd #P6, Little Rock, AR 72209-4909 – **1608)** 1100 N. 52nd St, Phoenix, AZ 85008 – **1609)** 1124 Foster Rd, Napa, CA 94558-6520 – **1610)** 1101 S Broadway #C, Santa Maria, CA 93454-6660 – **1611)** 32992 US Highway 34, Wray, CO 80758-9161 – **1612)** 419 Broadway, Paterson, NJ 07501-2104 – **1613)** 222 Hazard St, Orlando, FL 32804-3030 – **1614)** 613 Tallapoosa St W, Bremen, GA 30110-1838 – **1615)** 3833 US Highway 82, Brunswick, GA 31523-7735 – **1616)** 513 Hampshire St, Quincy, IL 62301-2928 – **1617)** 3901 Brendenwood Rd, Rockford, IL 61107-2200 – **1618)** 825 S Kansas Ave #100, Topeka, KS 66612-1233 – **1619)** 1350 Main St #1206, Springfield, MA 01103-1667 – **1620)** 779 Warren Ave, Portland, ME 04103-1007 – **1621)** 24 Frank Lloyd Wright Dr, Ann Arbor, MI 48105-9755 – **1622)** 2244 Ravine Rd, Kalamazoo, MI 49004-3506 – **1623)** 1300 Godward St NE #1440, Minneapolis, MN 55413-3089 – **1624)** PO Box 1369, Pascagoula, MS 39568-1369 – **1625)** 512 Peanut Rd, Elizabethtown, NC 28337-8811 – **1626)** 200 Radio Drive, Lexington, NC 27292-8010 – **1627)** 101 S Main St, Gloversville, NY 12078-3820 – **1628)** 4 Summit Park Dr #150, Independence, OH 44131-6921 – **1629)** 3624 Avion Dr, Medford, OR 97504-4011 – **1630)** 1049 N Sekol Ave, Scranton, PA 18504-1098 – **1631)** 1210 Snyder Rd, Lansdale, PA 19446-4614 – **1632)** 101 N. Main St #1000, Greenville, SC 29601-4852 – **1633)** 540 Cumberland St W, Cowan, TN 37318-3115 – **1634)** 301 S Polk St #100, Amarillo, TX 79101-1404 – **1635)** 115 Radio Road, Livingston, TX 77351-7702 – **1636)** 6400 N Belt Line Rd #110, Irving, TX 75063-6065 – **1637)** 950 Kenbridge Rd, Blackstone, VA 23824-3105 – **1638)** 1420 Bellevue St, Green Bay, WI 54311-5649 – **1639)** 900 Bluefield Ave, Bluefield, WV 24701-2760 – **1640)** 1251 Earl L Core Rd, Morgantown, WV 26505-5881 – **1641)** 1707 Warnke Rd NW, Cullman, AL 35055-2231 – **1642)** 1501 13th Ave, Columbus, GA 31901-1908 – **1643)** 6803 West Blvd, Inglewood, CA 90302-1895 – **1644)** 903 N Main St, Salinas, CA 93906-3912 – **1645)** 7150 Campus Dr #150, Colorado Springs, CO 80920-3157 – **1646)** 1355 N Maple Ave, Bartow, FL 33830-3024 or PO Box 452905, Miami, FL 33245-2905 – **1647)** 449 N 12th St, Defuniak Springs, FL 32433-0411 – **1648)** 2824 Palm Beach Blvd, Fort Myers, FL 33916-1503 – **1649)** 1611 Atlantic Blvd, Atlantic Beach, FL 32233-2516 or PO Box 51585, Jacksonville Beach, FL 32240-1585 – **1650)** 5815 Westside Rd, Austell, GA 30106-3179 – **1651)** 2141 Grand Ave, Des Moines, IA 50312-5303 – **1652)** 930 E Lincoln Ave, Goshen, IN 46528-3504 – **1653)** 1240 Radio Drive, Pikeville, KY 41501-4779 – **1654)** 631 Main St, Baton Rouge, LA 70801-1911 – **1655)** 130 Enterprise Dr, Marshfield, MA 02050-2110 – **1656)** 18720 16 Mile Road, Big Rapids, MI 49307-9303 – **1657)** 1433 Main Ave N, Thief River Falls, MN 56701-1141 – **1658)** 4424 Hampton Ave, Saint Louis, MO 63109-2232 – **1659)** 1338 Bragg Blvd, Fayetteville, NC 28301-4202 – **1660)** 1055 Skyway Dr, Marshall, NC 28753-3809 – **1661)** 11291 39th St SW, Dickinson, ND 58601-9206 – **1662)** 403 E 25th St, Kearney, NE 68847-5515 – **1663)** 123 Egg Harbor Rd #302, Sewell, NJ 08080-9406 – **1664)** 8755 W Flamingo Rd, Las Vegas, NV 89147-8667 – **1665)** 105 Kenwood Ave, Bethlehem, NY 12148-ND or PO Box 89, Rexford, NY 12148-0089 – **1666)** 6325 Sheridan Dr, Williamsville, NY 14221-4801 – **1667)** 605 S Front St #300, Columbus, OH 43215-5626 – **1668)** 600 Corporate Cir #100, Harrisburg, PA 17110-9787 – **1669)** PO Box 701, Tunkhannock, PA 18657-0701 – **1670)** 919 N Main St, Cleburne, TX 76033-3853 – **1671)** 10614 Rockley Rd, Houston, TX 77099-3514 – **1672)** 11240 Waples Mill Rd #405, Fairfax, VA 22030-6078 – **1673)** 7080 Lee Highway , Fairlawn, VA 24141-8416 – **1674)** 290 Hegenberger Rd, Oakland, CA 94621-1436 – **1675)** 4010 Summitview Ave, Yakima, WA 98908-2966 – **1676)** 1065 Radio Park Dr, Mt. Clare, WV 26408-9516 – **1677)** 3051 S. White Mountain Rd., Show Low, AZ 85901-7435 – **1678)** 3222 S Richey Ave, Tucson, AZ 85713-5453 – **1679)** 570 E Avenue Q9, Palmdale, CA 93550-2354 – **1680)** 8265 Sierra College Blvd #312, Roseville, CA 95661-9403 – **1681)** 869 Blue Hills Ave, Bloomfield, CT 06002-3789 – **1682)** 800 8th Ave SE, Largo, FL 33771-2162 – **1683)** 1650 S Dixie Hwy, Boca Raton, FL 33432-7462 – **1684)** 20 John Davenport Dr NW, Rome, GA 30165-2536 – **1685)** 331 Fulton St #1200, Peoria, IL 61602-1475 – **1686)** 1036 Hwy 541, Jackson, KY 41339 or PO Box 577, Stanton, KY 40380-0577 – **1687)** 900 N Lake Shore Dr, Lake Charles, LA 70601-2120 – **1688)** 500 W Cummings Park #2600, Woburn, MA 01801-6503 – **1689)** 351 Tilghman Rd, Salisbury, MD 21804-1920 – **1690)** PO Box 308, Bath, ME 04530-0308 – **1691)** 3338 E Bristol Rd, Burton, MI 48529-1408 – **1692)** 3003 27th Ave S #400, Minneapolis, MN 55406-1914 – **1693)** 240 Moss Hill Dr, New Albany, MS 38652-3400 – **1694)** 4321 Stuart Andrew Blvd #E, Charlotte, NC 28217-1588 – **1695)** 401 Saw Mill Hollow Rd, Burnsville, NC 28714-9789 – **1696)** 1751 Hanshaw Rd, Ithaca, NY 14850-9105 – **1697)** 1541 Alta Dr #400, Whitehall, PA 18052-5622 – **1698)** 2440 Millwood Ave, Columbia, SC 29205-1128 or PO Box 2355, West Columbia, SC 29171-2355 – **1699)** 1320 Brick Church Pike, Nashville, TN 37207-5038 – **1700)** 3911 S 1st St, Abilene, TX 79605-1639 – **1701)** 1101 Kilgore Dr, Henderson, TX 75652-5129 – **1702)** 166 N Main St, Broadway, VA 22815-9702 – **1703)** 100 Bluefield Ave #3, Bluefield, WV 24701-2884 – **1704)** 1635 S Gold St, Centralia, WA 98531-8997 – **1705)** 2241 W Main St, Moses Lake, WA 98837-2826 – **1706)** 2410 S Main St #A, West Bend, WI 53095-5270 – **1707)** 40 Park Rd #B, Pleasant Grove, AL 35127-1910 – **1708)** 9 North Church St #C, Fairhope, AL 36532-2427 – **1709)** 1 Radio Drive, Berryville, AR 72616-ND – **1710)** 824 E Washington St, Phoenix, AZ 85034-1088 – **1711)** 5640 S Broadway St, Eureka, CA 95503-6997 – **1712)** 514 W. 19th St, Merced, CA 95340 – **1713)** 13749 Beach Blvd, Westminster, CA 92683-3204 – **1714)** 5230 W Highway 98, Panama City, FL 32401-1058 – **1715)** 1111 Boulevard SE, Atlanta, GA 30312-3895 – **1716)** PO Box 786, Jerome, ID 83338-5483 – **1717)** 3775 W Dugger Ave W, Terre Haute, IN 47885-9794 – **1718)** 1632 S Maize Rd, Wichita, KS 67209-3912 – **1719)** 486 Lakeside Dr, Jenkins, KY 41537-8917 – **1720)** 1 Home St, Somerset, MA 02720-5229 – **1721)** 301 Fulton St W, Grand Rapids, MI 49404-6492 – **1722)** 28084 Van Born Rd, Westland, MI 48186-5159 – **1723)** 35006 US Highway 2 E, Fosston, MN 56542-9268 – **1724)** 1100 S Tryon St #210, Charlotte, NC 28203-4297 – **1725)** 804 Perryman St, Fair Bluff, NC 36401-1902 – **1726)** 292 Old Clarkesville Rd, Toccoa Falls, NC 30577-ND – **1727)** 5942 County Route 64, Hornell, NY 14843-9730 – **1728)** 27 Wiliam St 11th Flr, New York, NY 10005-2718 – **1729)** 185 Genesee St #1501, Utica, NY 13501-2109 – **1730)** 550 Market Ave S, Canton,

OH 44702-2103 – **1731)** 635 W 7th St #201A, Cincinnati, OH 45203-1513 – **1732)** 111 Presidential Blvd #100, Bala Cynwyd, PA 19004-1009 – **1733)** 369 E GE Patterson Ave, Memphis, TN 38126-3301 – **1734)** 12900 Preston Rd #201, Dallas, TX 75230-1380 – **1735)** 6161 Savoy Dr #1140, Houston, TX 77036-3323 – **1736)** 1211 W Hein Rd, San Antonio, TX 78220-3301 – **1737)** 4415 39th Place, Brentwood, MD 20772-1106 – **1738)** 306 W Broad St, Richmond, VA 23220-4219 – **1739)** 504 23rd St NW, Roanoke, VA 24017-5414 – **1740)** 10 Clinton St #10, Springfield, VT 05156-3310 – **1741)** 601 Main St #400, Vancouver, WA 98660-3404 – **1742)** 730 Ray O Vac Lane, Madison, WI 53711-2472 – **1743)** 44 Gough St #301, San Francisco, CA 94103-5424 – **1744)** 90 Kay Ave, Milford, CT 06460-5495 – **1745)** 3400 Idaho Ave NW #200, Washington, DC 20016-3000 – **1746)** 8451 S Cherokee Blvd #B, Douglasville, GA 30134-8520 – **1747)** 4802 E 62nd St, Indianapolis, IN 46220-5296 – **1748)** 2 Radio Plaza St, Ferndale, MI 48220-2129 – **1749)** 3415 University Ave SE, Minneapolis, MN 55114-3327 – **1750)** 8145 E Evans Rd #8, Scottsdale, AZ 85260-3645 – **1751)** PO Box 6326, Santa Maria, CA 93456-6326 – **1752)** 8729 9th St #110, Rancho Cucamonga, CA 91730-4312 – **1753)** 2600 El Camino Real #224, Palo Alto, CA 94306-1721 – **1754)** 1032 S Union Blvd #100, Lakewood, CO 80228-3374 – **1755)** 1150 W King St, Cocoa, FL 32922-8618 – **1756)** 308 Victory Rd, Quincy, MA 02171-3129 – **1757)** 6721 W 121st St, Overland Park, KS 66209-2003 – **1758)** 1411 Locust St, Saint Louis, MO 63103-2332 – **1759)** 704 N King St #604, Wilmington, DE 19801-3535 – **1760)** 1213 San Pedro Dr NE, Albuquerque, NM 87110-6725 – **1761)** 277 Gravel Hill Rd, Palmyra, PA 17078-8535 – **1762)** 3660 Route 30 #D, Latrobe, PA 15650-4309 – **1763)** 15096 South Dakota Highway 15 , Milbank, SD 57252-5954 – **1764)** 55 Music Square W, Nashville, TN 37203-3207 – **1765)** 755 S 11th St #102, Beaumont, TX 77701-3723 – **1766)** 1601 E 57th Ave, Spokane, WA 99223-6623 – **1767)** 1224 E. Brady Street, Milwaukee, WI 53202 – **1768)** PO Box 2245, Watsonville, CA 95077-2245 – **1769)** 2284 S Victoria Ave #2-G, Ventura, CA 93003-6626 – **1770)** 1188 Lake View Dr, Altamonte Springs, FL 32714-2713 – **1771)** 412 W Oakland Park Blvd, Wilton Manors, FL 33311-1712 – **1772)** 8451 S Cherokee Blvd #B, Douglasville, GA 30134-8520 – **1773)** 2980 US Highway 51, Clinton, IL 61727-9479 – **1774)** PO Box 159, Carencro, LA 70520-0159 – **1775)** 369 Shelburne Rd, Greenfield, MA 01301-9653 – **1776)** 10 Radio Lane, Brunswick, MD 21788-1645 – **1777)** 122 4th Ave SW, Rochester, MN 55902-3339 – **1778)** 125 S Kingshighway St, Sikeston, MO 63801-2943 – **1779)** 431 Eaton Rd, Mocksville, NC 27028-8653 – **1780)** 824 US Hwy 158 W Bypass, Warrenton, NC 27589-9796 – **1781)** 500 Corporate Parkway #200, Buffalo, NY 14226-1265 – **1782)** 400 E Britton Rd, Oklahoma City, OK 73114-7507 – **1783)** 5110 SE Stark St, Portland, OR 97215-1751 – **1784)** 6161 Savoy Dr #1140, Houston, TX 77036-3323 – **1785)** 1211 W. Hein Rd, San Antonio, TX 78220 – **1786)** 2707 Colby Ave #1380, Snohomish, WA 98201-3568 – **1787)** 4317 E Broadway St, North Little Rock, AR 72117-4124 – **1788)** 1545 River Park Dr #500, Sacramento, CA 95815-4693 – **1789)** 6455 N. Union Dr. #200, Colorado Springs, CO 80918-5844 – **1790)** 5900 Pickettville Rd, Jacksonville, FL 32254-1172 – **1791)** PO Box 216, Dalton, GA 30722-0216 – **1792)** 123 Broadway, Taunton, MA 02780-2507 or PO Box 329, Middleborough Center, MA 02346-2329 – **1793)** 3338 E Bristol Rd, Burton, MI 48529-1408 – **1794)** 919 Lilac Dr N, Golden Valley, MN 55422-4615 – **1795)** 3025 Waughtown St #G, Winston-Salem, NC 27107-1634 – **1796)** 8044 Montgomery Rd #650, Cincinnati, OH 45236-2959 – **1797)** 5807 S Garnett St #K, Tulsa, OK 74146-6847 – **1798)** 501 E 38th St, Erie, PA 16546-0002 – **1799)** 9570 Pan American Dr, El Paso, TX 79927-2001 – **1800)** 200 S 10th #600, McAllen, TX 78501-4869 – **1801)** 1190 Daniels Chapel Rd, New Boston, TX 75570-ND – **1802)** 1445 W Baseline Rd, Phoenix, AZ 85041-7010 – **1803)** 3700 Wilshire Blvd #600, Los Angeles, CA 90010-3013 – **1804)** 869 Church St, Eatonton, GA 31024-6452 – **1805)** 514 Jefferson St, Waterloo, IA 50701-5422 – **1806)** 2730 University Blvd W #200, Wheaton, MD 20902-4658 – **1807)** 545 Fire Tower Rd, Yanceyville, NC 27379-ND – **1808)** PO Box 1540, Exeter, NH 03833-1540 – **1809)** PO Box 471, San Fernando, CA 91341 – **1810)** 200 Monument Rd #6, Bala Cynwyd, PA 19004-1726 – **1811)** 904 N Main St, Punxsutawney, PA 15767-2641 – **1812)** 3931 Whitehorse Rd, Greenville, SC 29611-5599 – **1813)** 6161 Savoy Dr #1140, Houston, TX 77036-3323 – **1814)** 1246 W Laurel #200, San Antonio, TX 78201-6431 – **1815)** 400 Las Colinas Blvd E #1033, Irving, TX 75039-5599 – **1816)** 114 Lakeside Ave, Seattle, WA 98122-6542 – **1817)** 1550 The Boardwalk #1, Huntsville, AL 35816-ND – **1818)** Univ of Arizona, Tucson, AZ 85721-0067 – **1819)** 15165 7th St #D, Victorville, CA 92392-3816 – **1820)** 139 W Olive Ave, Fresno, CA 93728-3035 – **1821)** 40931 Freemont Blvd, Freemont, CA 94538-4307 – **1822)** 8 Lawrence Rd , Derry, NH 03038-4191 – **1823)** 2405 E Moody Blvd #402, Bunnell, FL 32110-5994 – **1824)** 330 SW 27th Ave #207, Miami, FL 33135-2957 – **1825)** 4107 W Spruce St #250, Tampa, FL 33607-2327 – **1826)** 411 Radio Station Road, North Augusta, SC 29841-9411 – **1827)** 2460 Atlanta Rd, Smyrna, GA 30080 – **1828)** 7120 US Highway 41, Vienna, GA 31092-4605 – **1829)** 6943 Titian Dr, Baton Rouge, LA 70806-2767 – **1830)** 143 Rumford Ave, Auburndale, MA 02466-1311 – **1831)** 901 S Kingshighway, Cape Girardeau, MO 63703-8003 – **1832)** 4104 Country Lane, Saint Joseph, MO 64506-4921 – **1833)** 430-C State Highway 165 S, Branson, MO 65616-3541 – **1834)** 1213 San Pedro Dr NE, Albuquerque, NM 87110-6725 – **1835)** 5166 Meadowood Mall Circle, Reno, NV 89502-6502 – **1836)** 2448 E 81st St #5500, Tulsa, OK 74137-4201 – **1837)** 944 Exeter Ave, Exeter, PA 18643-1215 – **1838)** 101 Lee St, Bristol, VA 24201-4355 – **1839)** 314 S Redwood Rd, Salt Lake City, UT 84104-3536 – **1840)** 2043 10th St NE, Roanoke, VA 24012-5309 – **1841)** PO Box 3213, Ferndale, WA 98248-3213 – **1842)** 6605 SE Lake Rd, Portland, OR 97222-2161 – **1843)** 730 Ray O Vac Lane, Madison, WI 53711-2472 – **1844)** 510 Pegasus Court, Winchester, VA 22602-4596 – **1845)** 3561 Pegasus Dr #107, Bakersfield, CA 93308-0658 – **1846)** 1800 W Hibiscus Blvd #138, Melbourne, FL 32901-2624 – **1847)** 120 S 35th St #2, Council Bluffs, IA 51501-3203 – **1848)** 4200 W Main St, Kalamazoo, MI 49006-2766 – **1849)** 121 W Atkins St, Dobson, NC 27017-8709 – **1850)** 290 Hegenberger Rd, Oakland, CA 94621-1436 – **1851)** 8686 Michael Lane, Fairfield, OH 45014-3096 – **1852)** 202 Lawrence Rd, Clemson, SC 29631-1091 – **1853)** 1111 Westrac Dr #104, Fargo, ND 58103 – **1854)** 5353 W Alabama #415, Houston, TX 77056 – **1855)** 9434 Parkfield Dr, Austin, TX 78758-6227 – **1856)** PO Box 778, South Boston, VA 24592-0778 – **1857)** 9834 17th Ave SW, Seattle, WA 98106-2713 – **1858)** 2600 S Jackson St, Seattle, WA 98144-2499 – **1859)** 5181 N 35th St, Milwaukee, WI 53209-5399 – **1860)** 215 3rd Street S, Oneonta, AL 35121-2184 – **1861)** 6820 Pacific Ave #3A, Stockton, CA 95207-2604 – **1862)** 548 E Alisal St, Salinas, CA 93905-2760 – **1863)** 127 Glenn Rd, Auburndale, FL 33823-2401 – **1864)** 9831 Beach Blvd #7, Jacksonville, FL 32246-4703 – **1865)** 2424 Old Rex Morrow Rd, Ellenwood, GA 30294-3901 – **1866)** 834 N Tower Rd, Freeport, IL 61032-8650 – **1867)** 462 Merrimack St, Methuen, MA 01844-5804 – **1868)** 1550 Hart Rd, Towson, MD 21286-1697 – **1869)** 2110 Cliff Rd, Eagan, MN 55122-2347 – **1870)** PO Box 49, Park Rapids, MN 56470-0049 – **1871)** 1111 S Glenstone Ave #3-102,, Springfield, MO 65804 – **1872)** PO Box 1071, Bay Springs, MS 39422-1071 – **1873)** 17890 US Hwy 64 W, Siler City, NC 27344-1631 – **1874)** 3105 Evans St #E, Greenville, NC 27834-6899 – **1875)** 3568 Lenox Rd, Geneva, NY 14456-2058 – **1876)** 28 E Market St, Danville, PA 17821-1940 – **1877)** 40 Rickert Rd, Doylestown, PA 18901-2326 – **1878)** 1860 Executive Park NW #E, Cleveland, TN 37312-2743 – **1879)** 275 Glenwood Dr, Rocky Mount, VA 24151-2136 – **1880)** 3616 State Highway 47, Rhinelander, WI 54501-8819 – **1881)** 1215 Church St, Oxford, AL 36203-1639 – **1882)** 8145 E. Evans Road, #8, Scottsdale, AZ 85260 – **1883)** 747 E Green St #101, Pasadena, CA 91101 – **1884)** 5050 E Edison Ave #218, Colorado Springs, CO 80915-3540 – **1885)** 3765 N John Young Parkway, Orlando, FL 32804-3213 – **1886)** PO Box 2312, Quincy, FL 32353-2312 – **1887)** 1510 NE 162nd St, North Miami Beach, FL 33162-4716 – **1888)** 2601 Nicholasville Rd, Lexington, KY 40503-3307 – **1889)** 4200 Parliament Place #300, Lanham, MD 20706-1881 – **1890)** 5115 Telephone Rd, Pascagoula, MS 39567-1130 – **1891)** 41 Pennsylvania Ave, Medford, NY 11763-3717 – **1892)** 3360 E Livingston Ave #2A, Columbus, OH 43227-1961 – **1893)** 36991 KGAL Drive, Lebanon, OR 97355-9666 – **1894)** 4284 Memorial Dr Ste B, Decatur, GA 30032-1220 – **1895)** 236 Woodland Dr, Shelbyville, TN 37160-6759 – **1896)** 100 Stoddart St, Beaver Dam, WI 53916-1306 – **1897)** 509 N Main St, Tuscumbia, AL 35674-2048 – **1898)** 303 N Spring St, Fordyce, AR 71742-3317 – **1899)** 4209 N Frontage Rd, Fayetteville, AR 72703-5002 – **1900)** 750 Story Rd, San Jose, CA 95122-2604 – **1901)** 2284 Victoria Ave #2-G, Ventura, CA 93003-6626 – **1902)** 4100 Metzger Rd, Fort Pierce, FL 34947-1712 – **1903)** 3551 42nd Ave S #B106, Saint Petersburg, FL 33711-4369 – **1904)** 1104 W Broad Ave, Albany, GA 31707-4340 – **1905)** PO Box 746, LaFayette, GA 30728-0746 – **1906)** 2 Radio Loop, Swainsboro, GA 30401-5673 – **1907)** 2100 Lee St, Evanston, IL 60202-1539 – **1908)** 1800 N Meridian St #603, Indianapolis, IN 46202-1433 – **1909)** 1200 Baker Ave, Great Bend, KS 67530-4523 – **1910)** 16221 National Pike, Hagerstown, MD 21740-2150 – **1911)** 182 N Angola Rd, Coldwater, MI 49036-9554 – **1912)** 1185 9th St NE, Thompson, ND 58278-9343 or PO Box 13638, Grand Forks, ND 58208-3638 – **1913)** 1416 Shelby Highway, Cherryville, NC 28021-8356 – **1914)** 911 W Main St, Clayton, NC 27520-1620 – **1915)** 85592 574th Ave, Wayne, NE 68787-7043 – **1916)** 231 N Union St, Olean, NY 14760-2663 – **1917)** 1795 W Market St, Akron, OH 44313-7001 – **1918)** 170 3rd St, Netarts, OR 97141-9489 – **1919)** 12 Kent Rd, Aston, PA 19014-1498 – **1920)** 575 Grove St,

Honesdale, PA 18431-1041 – **1921)** 19 Luther Ave, Warwick, RI 02886-4615 – **1922)** 222 Commerce St, Kingsport, TN 37660-4319 – **1923)** 215 S Market St, Carthage, TX 75633-2623 – **1924)** 6900 Commerce Ave, El Paso, TX 79915-1102 – **1925)** 1600 Pasadena Blvd, Pasadena, TX 77502-2404 – **1926)** 5501 Bagby Ave, Waco, TX 76711-2300 – **1927)** 227 E Belt Blvd, Richmond, VA 23224-1205 – **1928)** 2201 6th Ave #1500, Seattle, WA 98121-1840 – **1929)** 1414 16th St, Two Rivers, WI 54241-3031 or PO Box 100, Denmark, WI 54208-0100 – **1930)** 125 E 3rd St, New Richmond, WI 54017-1800 – **1931)** 2609 Jordan Lane NW, Huntsville, AL 35816-1030 – **1932)** 912 S Perry St, Montgomery, AL 36104-5002 – **1933)** 1110 E Olive Ave, Fresno, CA 93728-3535 – **1934)** 747 E Green St #101, Pasadena, CA 91101 – **1935)** 1479 Sanborn Rd, Yuba City, CA 95993-6042 – **1936)** 7800 E Orchard Rd #400, Greenwood Village, CO 80111-2599 – **1937)** 4190 Belfort Rd #450, Jacksonville, FL 32233-2516 – **1938)** 2475 Mercer Ave #104, West Palm Beach, FL 33401-7447 – **1939)** 5815 Westside Rd SW , Austell, GA 30106-3179 – **1940)** 1110 26th Ave SW, Cedar Rapids, IA 52404-3430 – **1941)** 11603 Highway 308, Larose, LA 70373 – **1942)** 60 Temple Pl #200, Boston, MA 02111-1324 – **1943)** 15 Hampton Ave, Northampton, MA 01060-3809 – **1944)** 4230 Packard Rd, Ann Arbor, MI 48108-1597 – **1945)** 6500 Brooklyn Blvd, Brooklyn Center, MN 55429-1754 – **1946)** 1001 Highlands Plaza Dr W #100, Saint Louis, MO 63110-1339 – **1947)** 1338 Bragg Blvd, Fayetteville, NC 28301-4202 – **1948)** 418 Duncan Rd, Flat Rock, NC 28731-4712 or PO Box 462, Hendersonville, NC 28793-0462 – **1949)** 1213 San Pedro Dr NE, Albuquerque, NM 87110-6725 – **1950)** 1705 Lake St, Elmira, NY 14901-1299 – **1951)** 333 7th Ave #1401, New York, NY 10001-5021 – **1952)** 3818 E Main St, Cushing, OK 74023 – **1953)** 7140 SW Macadam Ave, Portland, OR 97219-3013 – **1954)** 134 E Pitt St, Bedford, PA 15522-1311 – **1955)** 2 Milledge Rd, Augusta, GA 30904-3063 – **1956)** 259 S Willow Ave #A, Cookeville, TN 38501-3140 – **1957)** 3704 Whittier Rd, Memphis, TN 38108-2649 – **1958)** PO Box 300901, Arlington, TX 76007-0901 – **1959)** 9434 Parkfield Dr, Austin, TX 78758-6227 – **1960)** 2722 S Redwood Rd #1, Salt Lake City, UT 84119-8410 – **1961)** 645 Church St #400, Norfolk, VA 23510-1712 – **1962)** 4840 Lincoln Rd, Blaine, WA 98230-9602 or PO Box 75150 RPO White Rock, White Rock, BC V4B 5L3 – **1963)** N7502 Radio Road, Ripon, WI 54971-9231 – **1964)** 134 4th Ave, Huntington, WV 25701-1253 – **1965)** 1201 Main St, Wheeling, WV 26003-2844 – **1966)** 3256 Penryn Rd #100, Loomis, CA 95650 8052 – **1967)** 7251 Plantation Rd, Pensacola, FL 32504-6334 – **1968)** 5011 Capitol Ave, Omaha, NE 68132-2921 – **1969)** 2700 Earl Rudder Freeway S #5000, College Station, TX 77845-5011 – **1970)** 2600 S Jackson St, Seattle, WA 98144-2499 – **1971)** 4404 Napoleon Street SE, Iowa City, IA 52240-8143 – **1972)** 5787 S Hampton Rd #108, Dallas, TX 75232-6377 – **1973)** PO Box 1531, Broomfield, CO 80038-1531 – **1974)** 3260 Blume Dr #520 Plaza II, Richmond, CA 94806-5715 – **1975)** 1909 East Pass Rd #D11, Gulfport, MS 39507-3778 – **1976)** 4045 NW 64th St #306, Oklahoma City, OK 73116-2616 – **1977)** 3030 SW Moody Ave #210, Portland, OR 97201-4868 – **1978)** 10348 South Redwood Rd, South Jordan, UT 84095 – **1979)** 1496 Bellevue St #202, Green Bay, WI 54311-4205 – **1980)** 333 S Kerr Blvd, Sallisaw, OK 74955-7212 – **1981)** 4525 Wilshire Blvd 3rd Flr, Los Angeles, CA 90010-3845 – **1982)** 3131 S Vaughn Way #601, Aurora, CO 80014-3516 – **1983)** 721 Shirley St, Cedar Falls, IA 50613-1513 – **1984)** 5426 N Mesa St, El Paso, TX 79912-5442 – **1985)** 2202 Mt Jolliff Rd, Chesapeake, VA 23321-1416 – **1986)** 1020 W Main St, Merced, CA 95340-4521 – **1987)** 1496 Bellevue St #202, Green Bay, FL 54311-4205 – **1988)** 7000 Squibb Rd, Mission, KS 66202-3233 – **1989)** 4200 W Main St, Kalamazoo, MI 49006-2749 – **1990)** 1520 South Blvd #300, Charlotte, NC 28203-3701 – **1991)** 2720 S 7th Ave SW, Fargo, ND 58103-8710 – **1992)** 27 Wiliam St 11th Flr, New York, NY 10005-2718 – **1993)** 5501 Bagby Ave, Waco, TX 76711-2300 – **1994)** 20720 Marilla St, Chatsworth, CA 91311-4407 – **1995)** 3360 Alta Mesa Dr, Redding, CA 96002-2831 – **1996)** 7080 Industrial Way, Macon, GA 31216-7538 – **1997)** 730 Ray O Vac Lane, Madison, WI 53711-2472 – **1998)** 139 W Olive Ave, Fresno, CA 93728-3035 – **1999)** 50 S Clarke Rd, Ocoee, FL 34761 – **2000)** 1109 Hudson Lane, Monroe, LA 71201-6003 – **2001)** 4417 Broadmoor Ave SE, Kentwood, MI 49512 – **2002)** 27 William St Fl 11, New York, NY 19125-4347 – **2003)** 705 5th Ave S #350, Seattle, WA 98104-4425 – **2004)** 3463 Ramona Ave #15, Sacramento, CA 95826-3827 – **2005)** 12136 Bayaud Ave #125, Lakewood, CO 80228-2115 – **2006)** 1100 Spring St #610, Atlanta, GA 30309-2828 – **2007)** 800 South Wells #300, Chicago, IL 60607 – **2008)** 28095 Three Notch Rd #2B, Mechanicsville, MD 20659-3373 – **2009)** 2609 Jordan Lane NW, Huntsville, AL 35816-1030 – **2010)** 75 NW 167th St, North Miami Beach, FL 33169-6017 – **2011)** 4143 109th St, Urbandale, IA 50322-7925 – **2012)** 5 Provident Bank Park Dr, Pomona, NY 10970-3540 – **2013)** 901 E Pike Blvd, Weslaco, TX 78596-4937 – **2014)** 11737 Nelon Dr, Corpus Christi, TX 78410-3028

FM STATIONS IN MAJOR METROPOLITAN AREAS

Scope: The listing shows FM stations (87.9-107.9MHz) with a City of License (CL) in the respective Metropolitan Statistical Area (MSA), plus other stations (marked °) - incl. fringe stations - with a CL in adjacent MSA's that may also be audible in the defining city/cities of each metro area (e.g. Atlanta in the Atlanta Metro Area or Houston and/ or Galveston in the Houston-Galveston Metro Area etc) and beyond.

Atlanta Metro Area (Atlanta–Sandy Springs–Roswell, GA MSA)

	MHz	kW	Sta	City of License	Station
	88.1	0.019	GA	Buford	W201CC (KAWZ)
#	88.1	100	GA	Warm Springs	WJSP-FM
	88.1	0.009	GA	Woodstock	W201DM (KAWZ)
#	88.5	50	GA	Atlanta	WRAS
	88.7	0.115	GA	Tallapoosa	WEYY
	88.9	5	GA	The Rock°	WKEU-FM
#	89.1	0.84	GA	Gainesville	WBCX
	89.3	65	GA	Atlanta	WRFG
	89.5	6	GA	Winder	WYFW
	89.7	0.01	GA	Atlanta	W209CD (WLOG)
	89.7	0.01	GA	Tallapoosa	W209CG (WCLK)
#	90.1	100	GA	Atlanta	WABE
	90.5	0.01	GA	Snellville	W213BE (KAWZ)
#	90.7	0.43	GA	Carrollton	WUWG
	90.7	18	GA	Griffin	WMVV
#	91.1	100	GA	Atlanta	WREK
	91.5	8.9	GA	Cumming	WWEV-FM
	91.7	7.3	GA	Cartersville	WCCV
	91.7	13	GA	Peachtree City	WMVW
#	91.9	6	GA	Atlanta	WCLK
	91.9	0.008	GA	Gainesville	W220EH (KAWZ)
	92.1	1.65	GA	Carrollton	WBTR-FM
	92.1	5.5	GA	Jackson	WJGA-FM
	92.1	0.01	GA	North Canton	W221AW (WCCV)
	92.3	0.25	GA	Marietta	W222AF (WAKL)
	92.5	0.25	GA	Lawrenceville	W223CQ (WLKQ-FM) (sp)
	92.5	0.12	GA	Lithia Springs	W223BP (WUBL-HD2)
	92.5	12	GA	Zebulon	WEKS
#	92.9	66	GA	Atlanta	WZGC
	93.3	38	GA	Greenville	WVFJ-FM
	93.3	0.235	GA	Norcross	W227DN (WTZA) (sp)
	93.5	0.18	GA	Smyrna	W228EA (WAZX) (viet)
	93.5	0.23	GA	Suwanee	W228CA (WSRV-HD2)
	93.7	0.25	GA	Atlanta	W229AG (WCNN)
	93.7	0.25	GA	Tallapoosa	W229CI (WKNG)
#	94.1	100	GA	Smyrna	WSTR
	94.5	0.166	GA	Atlanta	W233BF (WSTR-HD3)
	94.5	0.25	GA	Gainesville	W233CO (WGGA)
	94.5	0.022	GA	Suwanee	WAOO-LP (sp)
#	94.9	80	GA	Atlanta	WUBL
#	95.5	100	GA	Doraville	WSBB-FM
#	96.1	100	GA	Atlanta	WWPW
	96.5	0.1	GA	Atlanta	W243EE (WJZA)
	96.5	0.25	GA	Marietta	W243DQ (WFTD) (sp)
	96.5	0.25	GA	Winder	W243CE (WCHK) (sp)
	96.7	0.099	GA	Atlanta	W244EI (WQXI) (ko)
#	96.7	2.1	GA	Union City	WBZW
	96.9	0.055	GA	Griffin	W245CN (WYFK)
#	97.1	100	GA	Gainesville	WSRV
	97.3	0.23	GA	Manchester	W247CJ (WFDR)
#	97.5	8.5	GA	Fayetteville	WUMJ
	97.7	0.075	GA	Duluth	W249CK (WSRV-FM)
	97.9	0.25	GA	Atlanta	W250BC (WWWQ-HD3)
	98.1	0.022	GA	Duluth	WNRE-LP
#	98.5	100	GA	Atlanta	WSB-FM
	98.9	0.144	GA	Atlanta	W255CJ (WWWQ-HD2)
	98.9	1.85	GA	Tallapoosa	WWGA
	99.1	0.03	GA	Marietta	WIEH-LP (sp)
	99.1	0.02	GA	Newnan	WQEE-LP
	99.1	0.1	GA	Riverdale	WRGU-LP
	99.3	0.015	GA	Atlanta	W257DF (WCLK)
	99.3	100	GA	Cornelia°	WCON-FM
#	99.7	100	GA	Atlanta	WWWQ
	100.1	0.099	GA	Atlanta	W239AY (WPLO) (sp)
	100.1	0.005	GA	Morrow	W261BG (WCCV)
	100.3	0.25	GA	Cartersville	W262CD (WBHF)
	100.3	0.105	GA	Gainesville	W262AL (WCON-FM)

MHz	kW	Sta	City of License	Station
#100.5	13.5	GA	College Park	WNNX
100.9	0.105	GA	Woodstock	W265AV (WUBL-HD3)
#101.1	21.5	GA	Ellijay°	WLJA-FM
101.1	0.25	GA	Winder	W266BW (WJZA)
#101.5	100	GA	Marietta	WKHX-FM
101.9	0.1	GA	Atlanta	WATB-LP (ch)
101.9	0.01	GA	Carrollton	W270AS (WVFJ-FM)
101.9	0.25	GA	Griffin	W270DB (WHIR)
102.1	0.22	GA	Atlanta	W271CV (WWPW-HD4)
102.1	0.1	GA	Fayetteville	WGAF-LP
102.3	8.2	GA	Buford	WLKQ-FM (sp)
102.3	0.25	GA	Griffin	W272DM (WKEU)
102.5	0.055	GA	Canton	W273CT (WLVG)
#102.5	3	GA	Mableton	WPZE
102.9	0.015	GA	Canton	WPCG-LP
102.9	0.115	GA	Decatur	W275BK (WUMJ-HD2)
103.1	0.25	GA	Atlanta Junction	W276CL (WROM)
#103.3	100	GA	Atlanta	WVEE
103.7	0.02	GA	Atlanta	WRUX-LP
103.7	0.099	GA	Atlanta	W279CZ (WIFN)
103.9	0.25	GA	Lawrenceville	W280EZ (WISK) (sp)
#104.1	100	GA	Palmetto	WALR-FM
104.5	0.1	GA	Cartersville	WHLB-LP
104.5	0.18	GA	Douglasville	W283CT (WXJO)
#104.7	24	GA	Athens°	WFSH-FM
105.1	0.12	GA	Decatur	W286DN (WWSZ)
#105.3	61	GA	Bowdon	WBZY (sp)
#105.7	20	GA	Canton	WRDA
105.9	4.9	GA	Milner	WFAL
106.1	100	GA	Arcade	WNGC
106.3	0.19	GA	Carrollton	W292EW (WLBB)
106.3	0.25	GA	Marietta	W292EV (WFOM)
#106.7	77	GA	Gainesville	WAKL
107.1	100	GA	Aragon	WTSH-FM (sp)
107.1	0.25	GA	Jonesboro	W296BB (WSB-FM)
107.1	0.25	GA	Winder	W296CX (WJBB)
#107.5	33	GA	Roswell	WAMJ
107.9	0.1	GA	Gainesville	WJPV-LP
#107.9	35	GA	Hampton	WHTA

Baltimore Metro Area (Baltimore–Columbia–Towson, MD MSA)

MHz	kW	Sta	City of License	Station
# 88.1	15.5	MD	Baltimore	WYPR
# 88.5	50	DC	Washington°	WAMU
# 88.7	7	PA	Middletown°	WXPH
# 88.9	12.5	MD	Baltimore	WEAA
89.3	50	DC	Washington°	WPFW
# 89.7	10	MD	Towson	WTMD
# 90.1	24	DC	Washington°	WCSP-FM
90.3	12	PA	Lancaster°	WJTL
90.5	17.5	MD	Worton°	WKHS
# 90.9	75	DC	Washington°	WETA
91.1	1.1	MD	Bel Air	WHFC
# 91.5	50	MD	Baltimore	WBJC
# 91.9	23.5	MD	Takoma Park°	WGTS
# 92.3	37	MD	Baltimore	WERQ-FM
92.5	22	VA	Winchester°	WINC-FM
92.7	0.1	MD	Baltimore	WVTO-LP
92.7	2.15	MD	Prince Frederick°	WDCJ
# 93.1	16	MD	Baltimore	WPOC
93.5	0.004	MD	Baltimore	WTTZ-LP
# 93.9	24.5	DC	Washington°	WKYS
94.3	0.1	MD	Baltimore	W232CL (WRBS)
# 94.5	19	PA	Lancaster°	WDAC
# 94.7	20.5	MD	Bethesda°	WIAD
# 94.7	50	DE	Dover°	WDSD
95.1	50	MD	Baltimore	WRBS-FM
# 95.5	50	MD	Morningside°	WPGC-FM
# 95.9	3	MD	Glen Burnie	WWIN-FM
# 96.1	13.5	PA	Red Lion°	WSOX
# 96.3	16.5	DC	Washington°	WHUR-FM
96.7	0.08	MD	Baltimore	W244DA (WZBA)
96.7	12.5	MD	Easton°	WCEI-FM
96.9	50	PA	Lancaster°	WLAN-FM
# 97.1	17.5	DC	Washington°	WASH
97.5	0.25	MD	Baltimore	W248AO (WVBV)
# 97.9	13	MD	Baltimore	WIYY
98.3	0.005	MD	Edgemere	W252BR (WWIN-FM)
98.5	10.5	PA	York-Hanover°	WYCR
# 98.7	50	DC	Washington°	WMZQ-FM
99.1	45	MD	Bowie°	WDCH-FM
# 99.5	22	DC	Washington°	WIHT
99.9	0.22	MD	Aberdeen	W260BV (WQLL)
99.9	0.013	MD	Annapolis	W260BM (WNAV)
99.9	7.6	MD	Frederick°	WFRE
100.1	0.002	MD	Baltimore	W261CD (WZBA)
#100.3	50	DC	Washington°	WBIG-FM
100.7	25	MD	Westminster	WZBA
#101.1	22.5	DC	Washington°	WWDC
#101.3	7.4	PA	Lancaster°	WROZ
101.5	0.136	MD	Baltimore	W268BA (WBAL)
#101.9	13.5	MD	Baltimore	WLIF
102.3	0.099	MD	Baltimore	W272BJ (WOLB)
#102.3	2.9	MD	Bethesda°	WMMJ
102.3	0.205	MD	Westminster	W272CX (WTTR)
#102.7	50	MD	Baltimore	WQSR
103.1	6	MD	Grasonville	WRNR-FM
#103.3	6.4	PA	York°	WARM-FM
#103.5	44	DC	Washington°	WTOP-FM
103.7	39	MD	Havre de Grace	WXCY
#104.1	20	MD	Waldorf°	WPRS-FM
#104.3	13	MD	Baltimore	WZFT
104.7	0.057	MD	Annapolis	WYZT-LP
104.7	8.3	MD	Hagerstown°	WAYZ
104.7	0.25	MD	Havre de Grace	W284BE (WHGM)
104.9	0.01	MD	White Marsh	W285EJ (WWMX)
#105.1	33	VA	Arlington°	WAVA-FM
105.1	25	PA	Ephrata°	WIOV-FM
#105.7	50	MD	Catonsville	WJZ-FM
105.7	25	PA	York°	WQXA-FM
#105.9	28	VA	Woodbridge°	WMAL-FM
106.1	0.25	MD	Baltimore	W291BA (WLIF-HD2)
#106.5	10.3	MD	Baltimore	WWMX
106.7	14	PA	Hershey°	WWKL
#106.7	20	VA	Manassas°	WJFK-FM
106.9	0.25	MD	Baltimore	W295BX (WFSI)
#106.9	15.5	MD	Myersville°	WWEG
107.3	19.5	DC	Washington°	WLVW
107.5	0.25	MD	Bel Air	W298CG (WHGM)
107.7	16	PA	Gettysburg°	WGTY
#107.9	49	MD	College Park°	WLZL (sp)

Boston Metro Area (Boston-Cambridge-Newton, MA-NH MSA)

MHz	kW	Sta	City of License	Station
88.1	0.64	MA	Cambridge	WMBR
88.3	0.66	MA	Boxford	WBMT
88.3	0.1	MA	Concord	WIQH
88.3	0.175	MA	Franklin	WGAO
88.3	0.105	MA	Rockland	WRPS
88.5	2.7	MA	Rockport	WWRN
# 88.9	4	MA	Boston	WERS
89.1	0.008	MA	Acton	WHAB
89.3	0.014	MA	Lynn	WCDV-LP (sp)
# 89.3	7	RI	Newport°	WNPN
# 89.7	100	MA	Boston	WGBH
90.3	1	MA	Newton	WZBC
90.5	7.7	MA	Scituate	WSMA
90.5	1.1	MA	Worcester°	WICN
# 90.9	12	MA	Boston	WBUR-FM
91.3	0.1	MA	Framingham	WDJM-FM
91.5	0.18	MA	Bridgewater	WBIM-FM
91.5	0.1	MA	Gloucester	WUMZ
91.5	1.4	MA	Lowell	WUML
91.5	0.125	MA	Medford	WMFO
91.5	0.17	MA	Milton	WMLN-FM
91.5	0.007	MA	Wellesley	WZLY
91.7	1.1	MA	Marshfield	WUMT
91.7	0.5	MA	Maynard	WAVM
91.7	0.13	MA	Salem	WMWM
91.7	0.5	MA	Stow	WUMG
# 91.9	0.16	MA	Boston	WUMB-FM
92.3	39	RI	Providence°	WPRO-FM
# 92.5	25	MA	Andover	WXRV
92.5	0.099	MA	Framingham	WXRV-FM1
92.5	0.099	MA	Newton	WXRV-FM3
92.5	1.2	MA	Boston	WXRV-FM4
92.5	0.24	MA	Boston	WXRV-FM5
# 92.9	18.5	MA	Brookline	WBOS
# 93.3	31	MA	Taunton°	WSNE-FM
# 93.7	34	MA	Lawrence	WEEI-FM
# 94.1	50	RI	Providence°	WHJY
# 94.5	9.2	MA	Boston	WJMN
94.9	0.021	MA	Acton	WAEM-LP
94.9	0.04	MA	Dedham	W235CS (WAMG) (sp)

MHz	kW	Sta	City of License	Station
94.9	0.07	MA	East Boston	+ WZMR-LP
94.9	0.07	MA	East Boston	+ WZMW-LP
95.1	0.07	MA	Lowell	W236CU (WLLH) (sp)
95.3	1.45	MA	Cambridge	WHRB
95.5	18.5	RI	Providence°	WLVO
# 95.7	14.5	NH	Manchester°	WZID
95.9	1.6	MA	Marshfield	WATD-FM
96.1	0.015	NH	Portsmouth	WBUB-LP
# 96.1	16.5	MA	Worcester°	WSRS
96.3	0.005	MA	Beacon Hill	W242AA (WCRB)
96.5	0.01	MA	Needham	W243DC (WXRV)
96.7	0.01	MA	Plymouth	W244CF (WRYP)
# 96.9	22.5	MA	Boston	WBQT
97.3	50	MA	New Bedford°	WJFD-FM (por)
97.5	50	NH	Dover°	WOKQ
# 97.7	2.05	MA	Brockton	WKAF
97.7	0.004	MA	Sudbury	WYAJ
98.1	0.006	MA	Lawrence	WGUA-LP
‡ 98.1	0.148	MA	Medford	W251CR (WZBR)
# 98.1	44	MA	New Bedford°	WCTK
# 98.5	9	MA	Boston	WBZ-FM
99.1	50	MA	Plymouth	WPLM-FM
# 99.5	27	MA	Lowell	WCRB
99.9	50	MA	Barnstable°	WQRC
99.9	0.25	MA	Boston	W260DS (WJDR) (sp)
99.9	0.017	MA	Holliston	WHHB
99.9	0.01	MA	Lawrence	W260AS (WMSJ)
99.9	0.1	MA	Winchester	WQEB-LP (ch)
99.9	0.25	RI	Woonsocket°	W236CW (WNRI)
100.1	2.85	MA	Southbridge°	WWFX
100.1	0.025	MA	Waltham	WBRS
100.3	0.04	MA	Boston	W262CV (WROL)
#100.3	50	NH	Portsmouth	WHEB
#100.7	21.5	MA	Boston	WZLX
101.1	0.22	MA	Brockton	W247CB (WBMS)
101.1	11.5	NH	Manchester°	WGIR-FM
101.3	0.25	MA	Cambridge	W267CE (WJIB)
101.3	0.15	MA	Milford°	W267CD (WMRC)
101.5	0.038	MA	Gloucester	W268AM (WERS)
#101.7	13.5	MA	Lynn	WBWL
‡102.1	0.25	MA	Framingham	W271CU (WSRO)
102.1	3	NH	Hampton	WSAK
102.1	0.01	MA	Quincy	W271CG (WRYP)
#102.5	14	MA	Waltham	WKLB-FM
102.9	0.1	MA	Auburndale	WLAS-LP
102.9	0.014	MA	Boston	WBCA-LP
102.9	0.082	MA	Concord	W275CM (WBNW)
102.9	0.1	MA	Dorchester	WBPG-LP
102.9	0.008	MA	Framingham	WBNU-LP (sp)
102.9	0.019	MA	Franklin	WFPR-LP
102.9	0.215	MA	Lawrence	W275BH (WNNW) (sp)
#103.3	8.7	MA	Boston	WBGB
103.7	0.01	MA	Boston	W279BQ (WRYP)
#103.7	37	RI	Westerly°	WVEI-FM
103.9	0.25	NH	Portsmouth	W280DG (WEVO)
#104.1	21	MA	Boston	WBMX
104.5	37	MA	Fitchburg°	WXLO
104.5	0.01	MA	Boston	WXLO-FM1
104.5	0.7	MA	Waltham	WXLO-FM3
104.9	0.019	MA	Boston	WRBB
104.9	6	MA	Gloucester	WBOQ
#105.1	50	RI	Providence°	WWLI
105.3	0.25	MA	Methuen	W287CW (WUBG)
#105.7	23	MA	Framingham	WROR-FM
106.1	0.096	MA	Boston	W291CZ (WRCA)
106.1	50	MA	Hyannis°	WCOD-FM
106.1	0.1	NH	Portsmouth	WSCA-LP
106.3	6	NH	Nashua°	WFNQ
#106.3	1.15	RI	Woonsocket°	WWKX
#106.7	21.5	MA	Boston	WMJX
#107.3	9.6	MA	Westborough°	WKVB
#107.9	20.5	MA	Medford	WXKS-FM

Charlotte Metro Area (Charlotte-Concord-Gastonia, NC-SC MSA)

MHz	kW	Sta	City of License	Station
88.1	26.5	NC	Hickory°	WJYJ
88.1	0.17	NC	Monroe	W201DI (WOTJ)
88.3	50	NC	Boiling Springs°	WLXK
88.3	0.01	NC	Harrisburg	W202BW (WOGR-FM)
# 88.5	60	NC	Winston-Salem°	WFDD
88.9	97.9	SC	Rock Hill	WNSC-FM
89.3	50	SC	Chesterfield	WRFE
89.9	100	NC	Davidson	WDAV
90.3	7.5	SC	Richburg	WRBK
# 90.7	100	NC	Charlotte	WFAE
91.1	100	SC	Gaffney°	WYFG
91.3	98	SC	Columbia°	WLTR
91.3	0.25	NC	Harrisburg	W217AX (WDAV)
91.5	0.14	SC	Ft. Mill	WRFJ
91.7	7.5	NC	Dallas	WSGE
91.9	0.038	NC	Statesville	W220DL (WHPE-FM)
# 91.9	30	NC	Wingate	WRCM
92.1	0.013	SC	York	W221EO (WRBK)
92.3	100	NC	Asheboro°	WKRR
92.3	0.25	NC	Charlotte	W222CW (WTCG)
92.3	0.055	SC	Rock Hill	W222CV (WYFQ-FM)
# 92.5	100	SC	Greenville°	WESC-FM
# 92.7	10.5	NC	Harrisburg	WQNC
92.9	0.25	NC	Statesville	W225BD (WAME)
93.1	0.18	NC	Monroe	W226CD (WIXE)
93.1	0.035	SC	Rock Hill	WRHJ-LP
93.3	93	NC	Forest City°	WTPT
93.3	0.01	NC	Salisbury	WOGR-FM
93.5	0.25	SC	Rock Hill	W228EJ (WAVO)
93.5	8.7	NC	Wadesboro°	WYFQ-FM
93.7	0.095	NC	Charlotte	W229CF (WYFQ)
# 93.7	100	SC	Greenville°	WFBC-FM
93.9	8.9	SC	Winnsboro°	WSCZ
94.1	100	NC	Lexington°	WWLV
94.3	0.019	NC	Monroe	W232DI (WXRC)
94.3	0.054	SC	Rock Hill	W232AX (WRHM-FM)
94.5	100	SC	Greenville°	WGTK-FM
94.7	0.25	SC	Charlotte	W234BY (WBCN)
94.7	0.1	NC	Mooresville	WLYT-LP
# 95.1	100	NC	Charlotte	WNKS
95.5	100	NC	High Point°	WHPE-FM
95.7	100	NC	Hickory°	WXRC
# 96.1	100	NC	Shelby°	WHQC
96.5	0.25	NC	Charlotte	W243BY (WOSF)
# 96.9	100	NC	Statesville	WKKT
97.3	0.25	NC	Monroe	W247CV (WXNC) (sp)
97.3	100	NC	No. Wilkesboro°	WKBC-FM
97.5	0.25	NC	Charlotte	W248CO (WZGV)
# 97.5	100	SC	Columbia°	WCOS-FM
# 97.9	95	NC	Concord	WPEG
98.3	0.25	NC	Concord	W252DI (WEGO)
98.3	0.25	NC	Dallas	W252BU (WOSF)
98.5	0.095	NC	Davidson	W253CV (WCRU)
98.5	0.24	NC	Indian Trail	W253BA (WTJY)
98.5	0.088	SC	Rock Hill	WYTX-LP
98.7	0.18	NC	Belmont	W254AZ (WRFX-HD2)
# 98.7	100	NC	Greensboro°	WSMW
# 98.9	100	SC	Spartanburg°	WSPA-FM
99.1	0.25	NC	Charlotte	W256BP (WNOW) (sp)
99.1	0.067	NC	Monroe	WDZD-LP
99.1	0.08	NC	Statesville	WASQ-LP
# 99.3	7.7	SC	Chester	WBT-FM
99.3	0.25	NC	Kannapolis	W257EI (WRKB)
99.3	0.25	NC	Mooresville	W257EJ (WHIP)
# 99.5	100	NC	High Point°	WMAG
# 99.7	84	NC	Kannapolis	WRFX
100.1	0.25	NC	Huntersville	W261BZ (WHQC)
100.1	0.25	NC	Monroe	W261DW (WDEX)
100.1	0.085	SC	Rock Hill	W261CY (WRHI)
100.3	0.25	NC	Charlotte	W262BM (WHQC)
#100.3	100	NC	High Point°	WMKS
#100.5	100	SC	Gray Court°	WSSL-FM
100.7	0.25	NC	Statesville	W264CU (WSIC)
#100.9	6	NC	Indian Trail	WPZS
101.1	0.22	NC	Gastonia	W266DC (WGNC)
101.3	0.08	NC	Charlotte	W267BZ (WNCW)
101.3	0.038	NC	Salisbury	W267AG (WBFJ-FM)
101.3	100	SC	Sumter°	WWDM
101.5	0.1	NC	Belmont	WBAC-LP
101.5	0.024	NC	Charlotte	WMFB-LP
#101.9	100	NC	Gastonia	WBAV-FM
102.3	2.55	SC	Pageland	WGSP-FM (sp)
102.3	0.027	SC	York	WTPJ-LP
102.5	0.2	NC	Charlotte	W273DA (WFNZ)
102.5	0.027	NC	Statesville	WEZG-LP
#102.9	30.5	NC	Hickory°	WLKO
103.3	0.25	NC	Charlotte	W277CB (WGIV)

MHz	kW	Sta	City of License	Station
103.3	0.25	NC	Salisbury	W277DD (WSAT)
#103.7	100	NC	Charlotte	WSOC-FM
104.1	0.25	SC	Ft. Mill	W281BE (WRHM)
#104.1	100	NC	Winston-Salem°	WTQR
‡104.3	0.25	NC	Charlotte	W282BP (WHVN)
104.5	0.25	SC	Chester	W283CY (WGCD)
#104.7	96	NC	Charlotte	WKQC
#105.3	51	SC	Gaffney°	WOSF
105.7	0.25	NC	Pineville	W289BO (WCRU)
105.9	0.25	NC	Mooresville	W290DK (WSIC)
#106.1	21	NC	Waxhaw	WOLS (sp)
#106.5	84	NC	Salisbury	WEND
#106.9	36	NC	Black Mountain°	WMIT
107.1	0.05	NC	Charlotte	WJPK-LP
#107.1	2.4	SC	Lancaster	WRHM
107.1	0.084	NC	Salisbury	WLJZ-LP
107.3	4.5	SC	Chesterfield	WVSZ
107.5	0.25	NC	Charlotte	W298CF (WGSP) (sp)
#107.9	100	NC	Charlotte	WLNK

Chicago Metro Area (Chicago-Naperville-Elgin, IL-IN-WI MSA)

MHz	kW	Sta	City of License	Station
88.1	2	IL	Carpentersville	WWTG
88.1	0.1	IL	Chicago	WCRX
88.1	0.09	IL	Crete	WBMF
88.1	0.18	IL	La Grange	WLTL
88.1	0.15	IL	Lincolnshire	WAES
88.1	0.14	IL	Lockport	WLRA
88.1	0.3	IL	Rosemont	WTZI
88.1	0.25	IL	Wheaton	WAIW
‡ 88.1	0.054	IL	Winnetka	WNTH
88.3	0.4	IN	Chesterton	WDSO
88.3	0.1	IL	Chicago	WZRD
88.3	0.15	IL	Chicago	WXAV
‡ 88.3	0.25	IL	Downers Grove	WDGC-FM
88.3	0.1	IL	Palatine	WHCM
88.5	0.16	IL	Chicago	WHPK
88.5	1.5	IL	Flossmoor	WHFH
88.5	0.185	IL	Glenview	WGBK
88.5	0.125	IL	Hinsdale	WHSD
88.7	0.1	IL	Chicago	WLUW
88.7	0.32	IL	Elmhurst	WRSE
88.7	2.1	IN	Gary	WGVE-FM
88.7	0.1	IL	Joliet	WCSF
88.7	0.6	IL	Sugar Grove	WSRI
88.9	0.003	IL	Chicago	WIIT
88.9	0.74	IL	Elgin	WEPS
88.9	0.295	IL	Lake Forest	WMXM
88.9	0.1	IL	Monee	WGEN-FM
88.9	0.1	IL	River Grove	WRRG
88.9	0.5	IL	Summit	WARG
89.1	0.019	IL	DeKalb	W206CE (WGCN) (sp)
89.1	1.1	IN	Lowell	WLPR-FM
89.1	1.5	IL	Naperville	WONC
89.1	0.55	IL	Round Lake Beach	WOKL
# 89.3	0.28	IL	Chicago	WKKC
89.3	7.2	IL	Evanston	WNUR-FM
89.3	1.35	IL	Morris	WUON
# 89.5	4	IN	Chesterton	WBEW
# 89.5	50	IL	DeKalb	WNIJ
# 89.7	35	IL	Kankakee°	WONU
# 90.1	100	IL	Chicago	WMBI-FM
90.5	3.1	IN	Crown Point	WRTW
90.5	0.008	IL	Park Ridge	WMTH
90.7	50	MI	Berrien Springs°	WAUS
# 90.7	0.006	IL	Chicago	WRTE
# 90.7	1.45	IL	Morris	WBEQ
# 90.9	5	IL	Glen Ellyn	WDCB
91.1	0.099	IL	Chicago	W216CL (WBEZ)
# 91.5	5.7	IL	Chicago	WBEZ
91.7	0.01	IL	Elgin	W219CD (WWTG)
91.7	6.5	IL	Woodstock	WZKL
91.9	50	IL	Joliet	WJCH
# 92.3	50	IN	Hammond	WPWX
92.5	20	IL	DeKalb	WCLR
92.5	0.065	IL	Zion	W223CN (WPJX)
92.7	1.8	IL	Arlington Heights	WCPY
92.7	0.055	IN	Gary	W224EA (WLTH)
# 93.1	6.7	IL	Chicago	WXRT
93.5	3.5	IL	Lemont	WVIV-FM (sp)
93.5	0.051	IN	Valparaiso	WITW-LP
# 93.9	4	IL	Chicago	WLIT-FM
94.3	3.5	IL	Glendale Heights	WAWE
94.3	0.25	IL	Elmwood Park	WAWE-FM1
94.3	0.099	IL	Cicero	WAWE-FM2
94.3	0.099	IL	Chicago	WAWE-FM3
94.3	0.012	IN	Gary	W232CK (WFRN-FM)
# 94.7	4.4	IL	Chicago	WLS-FM
94.9	3	IL	DeKalb	WDKB
95.1	0.25	IL	Bolingbrook	W236CG (WLEY-FM-HD2)
95.1	0.06	IL	Chicago	W236CF (WLEY-FM-HD2)
95.1	0.25	IL	Plano	W236DB (WSPY-FM)
# 95.1	50	WI	Union Grove°	WIIL
95.1	0.036	IN	Valparaiso	WVUR-FM
# 95.5	5.3	IL	Chicago	WCHI-FM
# 95.9	2.85	IL	Aurora	WERV-FM
95.9	0.01	IN	Crown Point	W240BJ (WHLP)
95.9	0.08	IL	Evanston	W240DE (WKTA)
95.9	0.25	IL	Evanston	W240EH (WCGO)
95.9	3	IN	Michigan City°	WEFM
# 96.3	3.3	IL	Chicago	WBBM-FM
96.7	0.082	IL	Elgin	W244EJ (WRMN)
# 96.7	3.1	IL	Joliet	WSSR
96.7	0.099	IL	Park Ridge	W244BQ (WLEY-FM) (sp)
96.9	0.25	IL	Morris	W245CE (WCSJ)
# 96.9	50	IL	Zion	WWDV
# 97.1	8.3	IL	Chicago	WDRV
97.5	0.25	IL	Chicago	W248BB (WCKL-FM)
97.5	0.25	IL	Joliet	W248DH (WJOL)
97.5	0.25	IN	Valparaiso	W248AP (KLTH)
# 97.9	4	IL	Chicago	WCKL-FM
98.3	0.1	IL	Chicago	WQEG-LP (ch)
‡ 98.3	0.09	IL	Chicago	W252AW (WMBI-FM) (sp)
98.3	0.1	IL	Chicago	WGHC-LP
98.3	3	IL	Crest Hill	WCCQ
98.3	0.016	IL	Round Lake Heights	WRLR-LP
# 98.7	6	IL	Chicago	WFMT
98.9	0.25	IL	DeKalb	W255BN (WLBK)
99.1	0.1	IL	Cicero	WZQC-LP
99.1	0.01	IL	Joliet	W256CA (WJKL)
99.1	0.087	IL	Park Forest	W256CL (WLIT-FM)
99.3	1.15	IL	Zion	WXFM-FM
# 99.5	5.7	IL	Chicago	WUSN
99.9	50	IL	Park Forest	WYHI
99.9	0.01	IL	Waukegan	W260BL (WLGS-LP)
#100.3	5.7	IL	Chicago	WSHE-FM
100.5	0.25	IL	DeKalb	W263BM (WSQR)
100.7	2.45	IL	Coal City	WRXQ
100.7	0.006	IL	Englewood	W264BF (WHLP)
#100.7	50	WI	Racine°	WKKV-FM
#101.1	5.7	IL	Chicago	WKQX
101.5	0.1	IN	Gary	W268DI (WWCA)
101.5	0.032	IL	Huntley	WHRU-LP
101.5	0.05	IL	Lake Forest	W268DE (WNTD)
101.5	0.1	IL	Lake Villa	WLGS-LP
101.5	0.25	IL	Seward Township	W268AY (WMBI) (sp)
101.5	0.15	IL	Tinley Park	W268CY (WWHN)
#101.9	4.2	IL	Skokie	WTMX
#102.3	1.05	IL	Crete	WYCA
102.3	0.09	IL	Elmhurst	W272DQ (WCKG)
102.3	0.027	IN	Portage	W272BZ (WFRN-FM)
102.3	3	IL	Waukegan	WXLC
102.5	0.25	IL	Plano	W273CZ (WSQR)
#102.7	3.8	IL	Oak Park	WVAZ
103.1	6	IL	Highland Park	WPNA-FM (pol)
103.1	6	IL	Morris	WCSJ-FM
103.1	0.01	IL	Park Forest	W276BM (WRDZ) (pol)
103.1	0.1	IN	Valparaiso	WVLP-LP
#103.5	4.3	IL	Chicago	WKSC-FM
103.9	0.1	IL	Channahon	WLMM-LP
103.9	0.17	IL	Chicago	W280EM (WTMX-HD2)
103.9	1.35	IN	Crown Point	WXRD
103.9	2.55	IL	Dundee	WAWY
#104.3	4.1	IL	Chicago	WBMX
104.7	0.099	IL	Chicago	W284DA (WRDZ)
104.7	0.25	IN	Hammond	W284CY (WJOB)
104.7	50	IL	Morris	WCFL
#105.1	5.7	IL	Evanston	WOJO (sp)
105.3	0.027	IL	DeKalb	W287AU (WSRI)
105.5	0.075	IL	Aurora	W288EA (WBIG)
105.5	0.017	IL	Chicago	WLPN-LP
105.5	1.25	IN	Valparaiso	WLJE

MHz	kW	Sta	City of License	Station
#105.5	1.6	IL	Woodstock	WZSR
#105.9	4.1	IL	Elmwood Park	WCFS-FM
#106.3	3.8	IL	Genoa	WYRB
#106.3	4.1	IL	Lansing	WSRB
#106.7	50	IL	Des Plaines	WPPN (sp)
106.7	0.25	IN	Valparaiso	W294BA (WIMS)
106.9	0.25	IL	Lake Bluff	W295CG (WPPN) (sp)
107.1	0.018	IL	Chicago	WCPX-LP
107.1	2.65	IN	Lowell	WZVN
107.1	3.1	IL	Plano	WSPY-FM
107.1	0.07	IL	Vernon Hills	W296DA (WNVR) (pol)
#107.5	3.7	IL	Chicago	WGCI-FM
107.9	21	IL	Aurora	WLEY-FM (sp)
107.9	0.099	IL	Cicero	WLEY-FM2 (sp)
107.9	0.099	IL	Chicago	WLEY-FM3 (sp)
107.9	0.099	IL	Chicago	WLEY-FM4 (sp)
107.9	0.25	IN	Valparaiso	W300DM (WAKE)

Dallas - Fort Worth Metro Area (Dallas-Ft. Worth-Arlington, TX MSA)

MHz	kW	Sta	City of License	Station
88.1	100	TX	McKinney	KNTU
88.3	9.4	TX	Keene	KJRN
# 88.5	61	TX	Mesquite	KEOM
88.5	3.5	TX	Weatherford	KMQX
88.7	10	TX	Ft. Worth	KTCU-FM
# 88.9	100	TX	Commerce	KETR
89.1	47	TX	Springtown	KSQX
# 89.3	55	TX	Dallas	KNON
89.3	0.34	TX	Mineral Wells	KYQX
89.5	12	TX	Stephenville°	KEQX
89.7	95	TX	Sanger	KAWA
90.1	29.7	TX	Dallas	KERA
90.5	38	TX	Greenville	KTXG
90.5	0.25	TX	Mineral Wells	K213CS (KDKR)
90.5	4.7	TX	Stephenville°	KTRL
90.9	100	TX	Dallas	KCBI
91.3	0.35	TX	Commerce	KYJC
91.3	100	TX	Decatur	KDKR
91.5	0.25	TX	Greenville	K218EB (WYFQ-FM)
# 91.7	19.29	TX	Dallas	KKXT
92.1	0.1	TX	Dallas	KPVC-LP (sp)
92.1	0.015	TX	Denton	KXDE-LP (sp)
92.1	1.65	TX	Farmersville	KXEZ
92.1	25	TX	Glen Rose	KTFW-FM
# 92.5	99	TX	Dallas	KZPS
92.9	0.099	TX	Dallas	K225CM (KBFB)
92.9	0.067	TX	Denton	KUZU-LP
92.9	0.25	TX	Ft. Worth	K225BR (KBFB)
92.9	0.071	TX	Garland	KYYE-LP (sp)
92.9	0.1	TX	Grand Prairie	KGPJ-LP (sp)
93.1	0.1	TX	Cleburne	K226BM (KCLE)
93.3	50	TX	Haltom City	KLIF-FM
93.7	0.04	TX	Italy	K229DR (KBFB)
93.7	43	TX	Krum	KNOR (sp)
# 94.1	98	TX	Ft. Worth	KLNO (sp)
# 94.5	100	TX	Gainesville°	KZMJ
94.9	100	TX	Arlington	KLTY
95.3	0.15	TX	Ft. Worth	K237HD (KHVN)
95.3	17	TX	Howe°	KHYI
95.3	1.55	TX	Tolar	KOME-FM
95.5	0.058	TX	Arlington	KRQP-LP (sp)
95.5	0.024	TX	Dallas	KVWR-LP
95.5	0.25	TX	Dallas	K238CC (KVTT) (urdu)
95.5	0.027	TX	Seagoville	KSGV-LP
95.7	0.25	TX	Burleson	K239CC (KYQX)
95.9	0.115	TX	Garland	K240DS (KYFA-FM) (sp)
95.9	100	TX	Jacksboro°	KFWR
# 96.3	100	TX	Ft. Worth	KSCS
96.7	90	TX	Flower Mound	KTCK-FM
96.7	0.01	TX	Greenville	KCCG-LP
# 97.1	97	TX	Ft. Worth	KEGL
97.5	0.05	TX	Dallas	K248BC (KDKR)
97.5	0.1	TX	Ft. Worth	KFTW-LP
# 97.5	32	TX	Tom Bean°	KLAK
97.5	0.043	TX	Weatherford	K248BY (KYQX)
# 97.9	100	TX	Dallas	KBFB
98.3	93	TX	Bridgeport	KBOC (sp)
98.3	0.25	TX	Cleburne	K252EB (KPMA-FM) (sp)
98.3	0.1	TX	Greenville	KKVI-LP
# 98.7	100	TX	Dallas	KLUV
# 99.1	100	TX	Denton	KFZO (Sp)
99.1	0.25	TX	Waxahachie	K256DE (KBEC)
# 99.5	100	TX	Ft. Worth	KPLX
99.9	0.021	TX	Balch Springs	KYBS-LP (sp)
99.9	0.064	TX	Denton	KDVP-LP (sp)
99.9	0.25	TX	Irving	K260BP (KDKR)
99.9	0.25	TX	McKinney	K260CX (KFCD) (sp)
99.9	90	TX	Waco°	WACO-FM
#100.3	97	TX	Dallas	KJKK
100.7	98	TX	Highland Village	KWRD-FM
#101.1	98	TX	Dallas	WRR
101.5	0.25	TX	Cleburne	K268DQ (KHFX) (sp)
101.5	0.25	TX	Garland	K268CL (KGPF) (sp)
101.5	0.1	TX	Greenville	KYLP-LP (sp)
101.7	92	TX	Azle	KYDA
102.1	100	TX	Ft. Worth-Dallas	KDGE
102.5	0.25	TX	Dallas	K273BJ (KEXB)
102.5	0.1	TX	Denton	KOCQ-LP (sp)
102.5	0.01	TX	Ft. Worth	KEFW-LP (sp)
102.5	0.25	TX	Ft. Worth	K273CS (KFJZ) (sp)
102.5	100	TX	Hillsboro°	KBRQ
102.5	0.02	TX	Mineral Wells	K273CP (KYQX)
102.5	18	TX	Whitesboro°	KMAD-FM
#102.9	100	TX	Dallas	KDMX
103.3	98	TX	Allen	KESN
#103.7	100	TX	Highland Park-Dallas	KVIL
104.1	0.1	TX	Dallas	KEJC-LP (sp)
104.1	0.1	TX	Ft. Worth	KLEJ-LP (sp)
104.1	0.1	TX	Grand Prairie	KZGP-LP (sp)
104.1	0.1	TX	Mansfield	KYRE-LP
104.1	0.25	TX	McKinney	K281CS (KHSE) (as)
104.5	100	TX	Dallas	KKDA-FM
104.9	35	TX	Pilot Point	KZMP-FM
#105.3	97	TX	Dallas	KRLD-FM
105.7	93	TX	Decatur	KRNB
105.9	0.25	TX	Commerce	K290AP (KGVL)
#106.1	100	TX	Denton	KHKS
106.5	0.1	TX	Dallas	K293CM (KBFB-HD3) (sp)
106.7	75	TX	Muenster°	KZZA (sp)
106.9	0.14	TX	Royse City	K295BF (KYLP-LP) (sp)
#107.1	74	TX	Benbrook	KESS (sp)
107.1	0.013	TX	Garland	KYEB-LP (sp)
107.1	0.06	TX	Mesquite	KBPM-LP
#107.5	16.5	TX	Ft. Worth	KMVK (sp)
#107.9	100	TX	Lewisville	KDXX (sp)

Denver Metro Area (Denver-Aurora-Lakewood, CO MSA)

MHz	kW	Sta	City of License	Station
88.1	4.4	CO	Lakewood	KVOD
# 88.5	4	CO	Boulder°	KGNU-FM
# 88.7	12	CO	Manitou Springs°	KCME
88.9	3	CO	Ft. Collins°	KRFC
88.9	0.099	CO	Plainview	K205FV (KLDV)
# 89.3	12	CO	Denver	KUVO
89.7	80	CO	Loveland°	KXGR
# 90.1	52	CO	Denver	KCFR-FM
# 90.5	20	CO	Colorado Springs°	KTLF
90.5	0.003	CO	Littleton	K213EG (KTSG)
90.7	0.1	CO	Longmont°	KGUD
90.9	0.09	CO	Pleasant View	K215FI (KZET)
91.1	100	CO	Morrison	KLDV
# 91.5	36	CO	Greeley°	KUNC
91.7	0.026	CO	Idaho Springs	K219LF (KUNC)
92.1	42	CO	Castle Rock	KJMN (sp)
# 92.5	57	CO	Broomfield	KKSE-FM
92.9	60	CO	Colorado Springs°	KKPK
92.9	0.099	CO	Denver	K225BS (KUVO-HD3)
# 93.3	71	CO	Wheat Ridge	KTCL
93.7	0.099	CO	Lakewood	K229BS (KDSP)
93.9	0.1	CO	Aurora	KETO-LP
93.9	0.58	CO	Loveland°	KCWA
94.1	0.25	CO	Golden	K231BQ (KOA)
94.3	0.25	CO	Brighton°	K232FK (KLVZ)
94.3	79	CO	Colorado Springs°	KILO
94.7	100	CO	Lafayette°	KRKS-FM
95.1	72	CO	Colorado Springs°	KATC-FM
95.1	0.25	CO	Commerce City	K236CQ (KLTT)
95.3	0.065	CO	Denver	K237GG (KLDC)
# 95.7	100	CO	Denver	KPTT
96.1	0.099	CO	Englewood	K241CP (KNRV)
# 96.1	100	CO	Greeley°	KSME
96.5	100	CO	Evergreen	KXPK (sp)
96.9	0.073	CO	Golden	K245CM (KKLC)
# 96.9	72	CO	Pueblo°	KCCY-FM

MHz	kW	Sta	City of License	Station
# 97.3	100	CO	Boulder°	KBCO
97.7	0.25	CO	Denver	K249EX (KBNO) (sp)
97.7	25	CO	Strasburg	KPLS-FM
# 97.9	100	WY	Cheyenne°	KXBG
98.1	71	CO	Colorado Springs°	KKFM
# 98.5	100	CO	Denver	KYGO-FM
# 98.9	72	CO	Pueblo°	KKMG
99.1	0.06	CO	Denver	K256CT (KGNU-FM)
99.1	100	CO	Windsor°	KUAD-FM
# 99.5	100	CO	Denver	KQMT
99.9	0.099	CO	Denver	K260DQ (KDFD)
# 99.9	79	CO	Pueblo°	KVUU
#100.3	100	CO	Denver	KIMN
100.7	0.099	CO	Denver	K264BO (KLZ)
100.7	77	CO	Pueblo°	KGFT
#101.1	100	CO	Denver	KOSI
101.5	20	CO	Commerce City	KJHM-FM1
101.5	97	CO	Watkins	KJHM
101.7	0.035	CO	Evergreen	K269CL (KPTT)
101.9	9.5	CO	Centennial	KXWA
102.1	6	CO	Estes Park°	KGRE-FM (sp)
102.3	1	CO	Greenwood Vlg	KVOQ-FM
#102.5	17	CO	Loveland°	KTRR
102.7	0.25	CO	Denver	K274DF (KPOF)
102.7	0.1	CO	Idaho Springs	KYGT-LP
102.7	57	CO	Manitou Springs°	KBIQ
103.1	0.25	CO	Denver	K276FK (KYGO-FM)
#103.5	100	CO	Denver	KRFX
103.9	0.03	CO	Pleasant View	K280GB (KLDV)
103.9	1.75	CO	Pueblo West°	KRXP
103.9	16.5	CO	Severance°	KRKA
#104.3	100	CO	Longmont°	KKFN
104.7	0.25	CO	Denver	K284CI (KDCO)
#105.1	100	CO	Denver	KXKL-FM
#105.5	50	CO	Timnath°	KJAC
#105.9	100	CO	Denver	KALC
106.3	0.099	CO	Denver	K292FM (KTLF)
#106.3	1.6	CO	Widefield°	KKLI
#106.7	100	CO	Denver	KWBL
107.1	20	CO	Aurora	KFCO-FM3
107.1	97	CO	Bennett	KFCO
#107.5	100	CO	Lakewood	KQKS
107.9	0.25	CO	Denver	K300CP (KBPI)
#107.9	100	CO	Ft. Collins°	KBPI
#107.9	32	CO	Pueblo°	KBPL

Detroit Metro Area (Detroit-Warren-Dearborn, MI MSA)

MHz	kW	Sta	City of License	Station
88.1	0.36	MI	Bloomfield Hills	WBFH
88.1	0.044	MI	Highland Park	WHPR-FM
88.1	0.3	MI	Plymouth	WSDP
88.3	0.11	MI	Auburn Hills	WXOU
88.3	5.5	MI	Grosse Pte Shores	WDTE
88.3	1.3	MI	Port Huron	WNFA
88.3	0.105	MI	Southfield	WSHJ
88.9	7.4	MI	Imlay City	WDTR
89.1	0.1	MI	Warren	WPHS
# 89.1	15.5	MI	Ypsilanti°	WEMU
89.3	0.27	MI	Dearborn	WHFR
89.3	0.044	MI	Orchard Lake	WBLD
89.5	2.4	MI	Auburn Hills	WAHS
89.5	0.1	MI	Novi	WOVI
90.1	50	MI	Huron Township	WDTP
90.3	0.037	MI	Rochester Hills	KDTI
# 90.5	87	MI	East Lansing°	WKAR-FM
# 90.9	22.5	MI	Detroit	WRCJ-FM
91.3	0.12	MI	Port Huron	WRSX
91.3	13.5	OH	Toledo°	WGTE-FM
91.5	1.05	MI	China Township	WVMV
# 91.7	93	MI	Ann Arbor°	WUOM
91.9	0.18	MI	Port Huron	WORW
# 92.3	45	MI	Detroit	WMXD
92.3	0.01	MI	New Baltimore	W222AP (WESA)
# 92.5	50	OH	Toledo°	WVKS
92.7	0.099	MI	Detroit	W224CC (WLQV)
92.7	0.125	MI	Port Huron	W224DT (WHLX)
# 93.1	26.5	MI	Detroit	WDRQ
93.5	0.099	MI	Detroit	W228CJ (WDMK-HD2)
93.5	5.2	MI	Howell	WHMI-FM
93.5	0.2	MI	New Baltimore	W228DE (WNIC)
94.1	0.21	MI	Holly	W231CV (WUFL)
94.3	0.099	MI	Detroit	W232CA (WUFL)
# 94.7	13.5	MI	Birmingham	WCSX
95.1	0.099	MI	Detroit	W236DR (WMKM)
# 95.5	100	MI	Detroit	WKQI
# 96.3	20	MI	Detroit	WDVD
96.7	0.058	MI	Detroit	WNUC-LP
96.7	0.099	MI	Detroit	W244DL (WEXL)
# 97.1	15	MI	Detroit	WXYT-FM
97.5	0.088	MI	Ecorse	W248CC (WDTP)
# 97.9	50	MI	Detroit	WJLB
98.3	0.115	MI	Detroit	W252BX (WDMK-HD2)
98.3	0.013	MI	Holly	W252CP (WDKL)
# 98.7	50	MI	Detroit	WDZH
# 99.5	17.5	MI	Detroit	WYCD
99.9	0.25	MI	Detroit	W260CB (WDMK-HD2)
#100.3	32	MI	Dearborn	WNIC
100.7	0.1	MI	Ferndale	WFCB-LP
#101.1	27	MI	Detroit	WRIF
101.5	0.099	MI	Detroit	W268CN (WDTK)
#101.5	33	OH	Toledo°	WRVF
#101.9	48	MI	Detroit	WDET-FM
102.3	3	MI	Port Huron	WGRT
#102.7	50	MI	Mount Clemens	WDKL
102.9	50	MI	Ann Arbor°	WWWW-FM
103.1	0.089	MI	Farmington Hills	W276DR (WFDF)
103.1	2.6	MI	Lapeer	WQUS
103.1	0.25	MI	Rochester Hills	W276DB (WUFL)
#103.5	50	MI	Detroit	WMUZ-FM
103.9	0.01	MI	Yates°	W280EL (WVMV-FM)
#104.3	190	MI	Detroit	WOMC
104.7	0.25	MI	Detroit	W284BQ (WUFL)
#104.7	50	OH	Toledo°	WIOT
#105.1	50	MI	Detroit	WMGC-FM
105.5	0.038	MI	Rochester Hills	W288BK (WMXD-HD2)
105.5	0.099	MI	Southfield	W288DW (WDEO)
#105.9	20	MI	Detroit	WDMK
106.3	0.099	MI	Westland	W292DK (WMXD)
#106.7	61	MI	Detroit	WLLZ
106.9	0.25	MI	Lapeer	W295CT (WMPC)
107.1	3	MI	Ann Arbor°	WQKL
107.1	0.25	MI	Detroit	W296CG (WMXD-HD3)
107.1	0.099	MI	Detroit	W296DY (WRDT)
107.1	6	MI	Port Huron	WSAQ
#107.5	50	MI	Detroit	WGPR
107.9	0.085	MI	Dearborn	W300DI (WDTW) (sp)
#107.9	50	MI	Flint°	WCRZ

Houston - Galveston Metro Area (Houston-The Woodlands-Sugar Land, TX MSA)

MHz	kW	Sta	City of License	Station
88.1	0.05	TX	Freeport	K201FA (KCZO) (sp)
88.1	0.2	TX	Galveston	K201DZ (KFTG) (sp)
88.1	0.25	TX	Houston	K201IY (KJIC) (sp)
88.1	0.25	TX	Katy	K201EU (KFTG)
88.1	0.7	TX	Pasadena	KFTG (sp)
88.3	100	TX	Willis	KAFR
# 88.7	100	TX	Houston	KUHF
# 89.3	87	TX	Humble	KSBJ
89.3	5.6	TX	Humble	KSBJ-FM3
89.3	3	TX	Humble	KSBJ-FM4
89.3	4	TX	Humble	KSBJ-FM5
89.5	0.08	TX	Galveston	K208DG (KPFT)
89.7	5.6	TX	Alvin	KACC
# 90.1	100	TX	Houston	KPFT
90.5	36	TX	Santa Fe	KJIC-FM
90.7	0.1	TX	Hardin	KGBV
# 90.9	18.5	TX	Houston	KTSU
91.1	17.5	TX	Lake Jackson	KYBJ
91.3	0.099	TX	Houston	K217GB (KXNG)
# 91.3	31	TX	Prairie View	KPVU
‡ 91.5	0.099	TX	Houston	K218EJ (KJIC)
# 91.7	50	TX	Houston	KXNG
# 92.1	22	TX	Seabrook	KROI
92.3	0.25	TX	Houston	K222CX (KYOK)
92.3	32	TX	Livingston°	KEHH
92.5	0.15	TX	Houston	K223DH (KBRZ) (hindi)
92.5	0.032	TX	Houston	KHGF-LP (sp)
92.5	0.03	TX	Houston	K223CW (KCOH)
92.5	0.1	TX	South Houston	KJJG-LP
# 92.9	93.7	TX	Pasadena	KKBQ
93.3	97	TX	Port Arthur°	KQBU-FM
# 93.7	100	TX	Houston	KQBT
94.1	23.5	TX	Hempstead	KLTR

MHz	kW	Sta	City of License	Station
94.1	0.099	TX	Houston	K231CN (KJOZ) (sp)
94.1	0.1	TX	Houston	KBIH-LP (sp)
# 94.5	97	TX	Houston	KTBZ-FM
‡ 94.9	0.042	TX	Conroe	KKFH-LP (sp)
94.9	0.25	TX	Houston	K235CS (KLVL)
94.9	0.1	TX	Houston	KRUT-LP (sp)
94.9	0.1	TX	Pasadena	KPFG-LP (sp)
95.1	0.099	TX	Missouri City	K236AR (KFTG) (sp)
95.3	0.064	TX	Cleveland	KORG-LP
95.3	0.075	TX	Conroe	K237FS (KHJK)
95.3	0.088	TX	Friendswood	KEPH-LP
95.3	0.057	TX	Houston	KZLD-LP (sp)
# 95.7	100	TX	Houston	KKHH
96.1	0.041	TX	Houston	KTRU-LP
96.1	0.25	TX	Houston	K241CM (KTEK)
96.1	0.004	TX	Houston	KCDF-LP
96.1	0.25	TX	Houston	K241CO (KSHJ) (sp)
96.1	0.017	TX	Sugar Land	KIRP-LP (sp)
# 96.5	97	TX	Houston	KHMX
# 96.9	100	TX	El Campo°	KXBJ
96.9	0.05	TX	Houston	K245CQ (KWWJ) (sp)
# 97.1	100	TX	Cleveland	KTHT
97.3	0.2	TX	Houston	K247CP (KHPT)
97.5	2	TX	Houston	KFNC-FM1
# 97.5	100	TX	Mont Belvieu	KFNC
# 97.9	100	TX	Houston	KBXX
98.3	0.03	TX	Houston	K252FR (KMIC) (sp)
# 98.5	100	TX	Port Arthur°	KTJM (sp)
98.7	0.19	TX	Houston	K254BZ (KBXX) (sp)
# 99.1	96	TX	Houston	KODA
99.5	0.22	TX	Houston	KOHV-LP
99.5	0.12	TX	Houston	K258DA (KTBZ-FM)
99.5	0.025	TX	La Marque	KHEA-LP
99.5	0.099	TX	Sugar Land	K258BZ (KSBJ)
99.7	0.1	TX	Galveston	KLHG-LP (sp)
99.7	0.01	TX	Houston	K259DC (KREH) (viet)
99.7	0.1	TX	Houston	KOYM-LP (sp)
99.7	0.1	TX	Houston	KHGV-LP
99.9	0.1	TX	Houston	KNJC-LP (sp)
99.9	0.15	TX	Houston	K260DD (KRCM)
99.9	26	TX	Liberty	KHIH
#100.3	95	TX	Houston	KILT-FM
100.7	100	TX	Lumberton	KKHT-FM
100.7	0.1	TX	Richmond	K264CN (KQUE) (sp)
#101.1	96	TX	Houston	KLOL (sp)
101.5	0.09	TX	Cleveland	KZCL-LP
101.5	0.1	TX	Cypress	KOER-LP
101.5	0.25	TX	Houston	K268CW (KHCB) (sp)
101.5	0.1	TX	Houston	KHSX-LP
101.5	0.083	TX	Liberty	KXAQ-LP
#101.7	35	TX	Bay City°	KNTE (sp)
101.7	0.25	TX	Houston	K269GS (KGBC) (sp)
101.7	0.1	TX	Houston	KQEU-LP (ch)
101.7	0.06	TX	Houston	K269GT (KBXX)
#102.1	100	TX	Houston	KMJQ
102.5	50	TX	Beaumont°	KTCX
102.5	0.012	TX	Conroe	KJHJ-LP (sp)
102.5	0.099	TX	Houston	K273AL (KJOZ) (sp)
102.5	0.004	TX	Houston	KJFI-LP
102.5	0.001	TX	Houston	KMAZ-LP
#102.9	100	TX	Houston	KLTN (sp)
103.3	100	TX	Freeport	KJOJ (sp)
103.3	0.25	TX	Houston	K277DE (KNTH)
103.5	0.022	TX	Cypress	KCYB-LP
#103.7	100	TX	La Porte	KHJK
104.1	92.18	TX	Houston	KRBE
104.5	0.008	TX	Conroe	KZCW-LP
104.5	0.099	TX	Houston	K283CH (KQBT)
#104.5	100	TX	Orange°	KKMY
#104.9	10.5	TX	Deer Park	KAMA-FM (sp)
105.3	9.2	TX	Hempstead	KTWL
105.3	0.099	TX	Houston	K287BQ (KTBZ-FM-HD3)
#105.3	50	TX	Winnie	KXXF
105.7	100	TX	Houston	KHCB-FM
106.1	0.007	TX	Conroe	KZCC-LP
106.1	0.19	TX	Houston	K291CE (KGLK)
106.1	100	TX	Orange°	KIOC
106.5	100	TX	Galveston	KOVE-FM (sp)
#106.9	91.6	TX	Conroe	KHPT
107.1	0.12	TX	Richmond	K296HJ (KODA)

MHz	kW	Sta	City of License	Station
107.3	0.013	TX	Conroe	KCVE-LP (sp)
#107.5	95	TX	Lake Jackson	KGLK
#107.9	90	TX	Beaumont°	KQQK (sp)

Los Angeles Metro Area (Los Angeles-Long Beach-Anaheim, CA MSA)

MHz	kW	Sta	City of License	Station
# 88.1	30	CA	Long Beach	KKJZ
# 88.3	3.2	CA	Thousand Oaks°	KCLU-FM
# 88.5	0.37	CA	Northridge	KCSN
88.5	0.8	CA	West Los Angeles	KCSN-FM1
88.7	0.2	CA	Avalon	KISL
88.7	0.4	CA	Claremont	KSPC
# 88.7	12	CA	Santa Barbara°	KDRW
88.9	0.2	CA	Irvine	KUCI
88.9	5.8	CA	Lancaster	KTLW
88.9	2.9	CA	Los Angeles	KXLU
88.9	0.01	CA	Santa Clarita	K205EP (KTLW)
89.1	0.04	CA	Laguna Beach	K206AA (KSBR)
# 89.3	0.6	CA	Pasadena	KPCC
89.3	0.003	CA	Santa Clarita	KPCC-FM1
89.3	0.35	CA	West Los Angeles	KPCC-FM2
89.3	0.7	CA	West Los Angeles	KPCC-FM3
89.5	0.075	CA	Newport Beach	K208AM (KSBR)
89.7	2.75	CA	Riverside°	KSGN
# 89.9	6.9	CA	Santa Monica	KCRW
90.1	0.019	CA	Buena Park	KBPK
90.1	0.01	CA	Palmdale	K211EY (KHMS)
90.1	0.01	CA	Santa Ana	K211DK (KMRO) (sp)
90.1	0.0017	CA	Walnut	KSAK
90.3	10.5	CA	Camarillo°	KMRO (sp)
90.3	0.09	CA	Fountain Valley	KLIE-LP
90.3	0.01	CA	Temple City	K212FA (KHRI)
90.7	110	CA	Los Angeles	KPFK
90.7	1.5	CA	Malibu	KPFK-FM1
91.1	0.099	CA	Arcadia	K216EM (KKLQ)
91.1	0.25	CA	Inglewood	K216FM (KYLA)
91.1	0.01	CA	Quartz Hill	K216FA (KAWZ)
# 91.1	4.8	CA	Thousand Oaks°	KDSC
# 91.5	39	CA	Los Angeles	KUSC
91.5	0.2	CA	Santa Clarita	KUSC-FM1
# 91.9	3.2	CA	San Bernardino°	KVCR
91.9	0.2	CA	Studio City	K220HC (KKLQ)
# 92.3	42	CA	Los Angeles	KRRL
92.3	0.32	CA	Santa Clarita	KRRL-FM1
92.7	0.69	CA	Fountain Valley	KYLA
‡ 92.7	0.065	CA	San Marino	K224EY (KRRL)
92.7	1.4	CA	Thousand Oaks°	KYRA
# 93.1	27.5	CA	Los Angeles	KCBS-FM
# 93.5	0.1	CA	Laguna Niguel	KXRN-LP
93.5	5	CA	Ontario°	KDEY-FM
93.5	4.2	CA	Redondo Beach	KDAY
93.5	6	CA	Rosamond°	KQAV
93.7	12.5	CA	Santa Barbara°	KDB
# 93.9	18.5	CA	Los Angeles	KLLI (sp)
93.9	0.25	CA	Santa Clarita	KLLI-FM1 (sp)
94.3	6	CA	Garden Grove	KEBN (sp)
94.3	6	CA	San Fernando	KBUA (sp)
94.3	0.046	CA	Valencia & Newhall	KBUA-FM1 (sp)
# 94.7	52	CA	Los Angeles	KTWV
95.1	0.01	CA	Lancaster	K236AW (KOST)
# 95.1	50	CA	San Bernardino°	KFRG
95.1	12.5	CA	Ventura°	KBBY-FM
# 95.5	61	CA	Los Angeles	KLOS
95.9	1.2	CA	Camarillo°	KCAQ
95.9	6	CA	La Mirada	KFSH-FM
96.3	6.6	CA	Los Angeles	KXOL-FM (sp)
96.3	0.01	CA	Palmdale	K242CR (KMRO) (sp)
96.7	0.05	CA	Los Angeles	KGAP-LP
96.7	1.75	CA	Redlands°	KCAL
# 96.7	6	CA	Santa Ana	KWIZ (sp)
96.7	0.28	CA	Santa Paula°	KLJR-FM (sp)
96.9	0.25	CA	Lancaster	K245CL (KUTY) (sp)
# 97.1	21	CA	Los Angeles	KAMP-FM
97.5	0.1	CA	Castaic	KHUG-LP
# 97.5	16	CA	Goleta°	KLSB
# 97.5	72	CA	Riverside°	KLYY (sp)
# 97.9	33	CA	East Los Angeles	KLAX-FM (sp)
98.1	0.1	CA	Santa Clarita	K251CF (KHTS)
98.3	0.08	CA	Culver City	K252FK (KOCP)
98.3	0.1	CA	Lancaster	KFXM-LP
98.3	0.1	CA	Los Angeles	K252FO (KSUR)
98.3	1.5	CA	Oxnard°	KDAR

	MHz	kW	Sta	City of License	Station
#	98.3	6	CA	West Covina	KRCV (sp)
#	98.7	75	CA	Los Angeles	KYSR
	99.1	0.007	CA	Chatsworth	KWSV-LP-FM1
	99.1	0.1	CA	Long Beach	KLBP-LP
	99.1	0.1	CA	Los Angeles	+ KZUT-LP
	99.1	0.1	CA	Los Angeles	+ KFEP-LP
	99.1	0.1	CA	Los Angeles	+ KLDB-LP
	99.1	0.071	CA	Malibu	KBUU-LP
	99.1	0.01	CA	Palmdale	K256BS (KODV) (sp)
	99.1	0.25	CA	Pasadena	K256CX (KRDC)
#	99.1	2.55	CA	Riverside°	KGGI
	99.1	0.1	CA	Simi Valley°	KWSV-LP
	99.1	0.05	CA	Venice	KTPC-LP
	99.5	10	CA	Los Angeles	KKLA-FM
	99.9	29.5	CA	San Bernardino°	KOLA
	99.9	34	CA	Santa Barbara°	KTYD
#	100.3	5.4	CA	Los Angeles	KKLQ
	100.3	0.1	CA	Santa Clarita	KKLQ-FM2
	100.7	0.25	CA	Guasti°	K264AF (KRLD-FM)
	100.7	0.06	CA	Los Angeles	K264CQ (KWKW) (sp)
	100.7	0.01	CA	Palmdale	K264BQ (KTQX) (sp)
	100.7	39	CA	Ventura°	KHAY
#	101.1	51	CA	Los Angeles	KRTH
	101.5	0.1	CA	El Monte	KQSG-LP
	101.5	0.185	CA	Lake Los Angeles	K268CO (KTLW)
‡	101.5	0.05	CA	Los Angeles	KFQM-LP
	101.5	0.05	CA	Los Angeles	KQBH-LP
	101.5	0.025	CA	Los Angeles	KZKA-LP
	101.5	0.024	CA	Los Angeles	K268DD (KTYM)
	101.5	0.042	CA	Newport Beach	KOCI-LP
	101.5	0.05	CA	Panorama City	KROJ-LP
	101.5	0.1	CA	Pasadena	KHBG-LP (sp)
	101.5	0.1	CA	Santa Clarita	KZNQ-LP
	101.5	0.1	CA	West Covina	KQPV-LP (ch)
#	101.9	4.8	CA	Glendale	KSCA (sp)
	101.9	0.09	CA	Santa Clarita	KSCA-FM1 (sp)
	102.3	5.6	CA	Compton	KJLH
	102.3	0.008	CA	Lancaster	K272FI (KOSS)
#	102.7	8	CA	Los Angeles	KIIS-FM
	102.7	0.21	CA	Santa Clarita	KIIS-FM1
	102.9	5.5	CA	Oxnard°	KXLM (sp)
	103.1	0.3	CA	Newport Beach	KDLE (sp)
#	103.1	3.7	CA	Santa Monica	KDLD (sp)
	103.3	105	CA	Santa Barbara°	KRUZ
#	103.5	12.5	CA	Los Angeles	KOST
	103.5	0.5	CA	Santa Clarita	KOST-FM1
	103.7	0.95	CA	El Rio°	KMLA (sp)
#	103.9	4.1	CA	Inglewood	KRCD (sp)
#	104.3	65	CA	Los Angeles	KBIG
	104.3	0.38	CA	Santa Clarita	KBIG-FM1
	104.7	18	CA	Oxnard°	KOCP
	104.7	0.25	CA	Calabasas	KOCP-FM3
	104.7	1.9	CA	Granada Hills	KOCP-FM4
	104.7	2.3	CA	Las Flores Canyon	KOCP-FM5
	104.7	0.007	CA	Quartz Hill	K284CD (KODV) (sp)
	104.7	0.05	CA	Santa Ana	+ KSXA-LP
	104.7	0.05	CA	Santa Ana	+ KRQL-LP
	104.7	0.048	CA	Walnut	KQEV-LP (ch)
#	105.1	18	CA	Los Angeles	KKGO
	105.1	0.06	CA	Santa Clarita	KKGO-FM1
	105.5	6	CA	Hemet°	KXRS (sp)
	105.5	3	CA	Long Beach	KBUE (sp)
	105.5	0.31	CA	Ojai°	KFYV
	105.5	6	CA	Rosamond°	KVVS
#	105.9	25	CA	Los Angeles	KPWR
	106.3	3	CA	Lancaster	KGMX
	106.3	0.96	CA	Oak View°	KVYB
	106.3	6	CA	Santa Ana	KALI-FM
	106.7	0.18	CA	Lancaster	K294DA (KAVL)
	106.7	5.5	CA	Pasadena	KROQ-FM
	106.7	0.05	CA	Santa Clarita	KROQ-FM1
#	107.1	6	CA	Arcadia	KSSE (sp)
	107.1	0.02	CA	San Fernando	KSSE-FM1 (sp)
	107.1	0.1	CA	Lancaster	K296GX (KOSS)
	107.1	0.37	CA	Ventura°	KSSC (sp)
#	107.5	29.5	CA	Los Angeles	KLVE
	107.5	0.1	CA	Santa Clarita	KLVE-FM1 (sp)
	107.9	0.1	CA	Los Angeles	KSXS-LP
#	107.9	0.53	CA	San Clemente	KWVE-FM
	107.9	0.02	CA	San Clemente	KWVE-FM4
	107.9	0.1	CA	Santa Clarita	KQRU-LP

Miami - Fort Lauderdale Metro Area (Miami-Fort Lauderdale-West Palm Beach, FL MSA)

	MHz	kW	Sta	City of License	Station
	88.1	0.165	FL	Homestead	WRGP
	88.1	50	FL	West Palm Beach	WAYF
	88.3	6	FL	Pennsuco	WGNK (sp)
‡	88.5	7.7	FL	Florida City	WMFL
	88.5	3	FL	Sunrise	WKPX
#	88.9	7.4	FL	Miami	WDNA
	89.3	100	FL	Boynton Beach	WRMB
	89.7	100	FL	Miami	WMLV
	90.3	8	FL	Ft. Lauderdale	WYBP
	90.3	0.01	FL	West Palm Beach	W212CG (WCNO)
	90.5	5.9	FL	Coral Gables	WVUM
#	90.7	38	FL	West Palm Beach	WFLV
	90.9	100	FL	Cutler Bay	WLFE
#	91.3	47	FL	Miami	WLRN-FM
	91.9	50	FL	Hammocks	WMKL
#	92.1	7.2	FL	West Palm Beach	WZZR (sp)
	92.3	17	FL	Hialeah	WCMQ-FM (sp)
	92.5	0.25	FL	Belle Glade	W223AJ (WAFC)
	92.5	0.24	FL	West Palm Beach	W223CJ (WSVU)
	92.7	0.022	FL	Ft. Lauderdale	WZOP-LP
	92.7	0.1	FL	Miami	WMXR-LP
#	93.1	98	FL	Miami	WFEZ
	93.3	0.132	FL	North Palm Beach	W227CX (WRLX-HD2)
	93.5	15.5	FL	Belle Glade	WBGF
	93.5	50	FL	Islamorada°	WZFL
	93.5	0.25	FL	Miami	W228BY (WZFL)
	93.7	0.25	FL	West Palm Beach	W229DG (WJBW)
#	93.9	100	FL	Miami Beach	WMIA-FM
	94.3	0.045	FL	Miami	WQPN-LP
#	94.3	50	FL	Riviera Beach	WRLX (sp)
	94.5	0.031	FL	Key Biscayne	WSQF-LP
	94.5	0.1	FL	Miami	WVGK-LP (sp)
	94.5	0.099	FL	Oakland Park	W233AP (WZTU-HD3)
	94.7	0.099	FL	West Palm Beach	W234DA (WWRF) (sp)
#	94.9	100	FL	Miami Beach	WZTU (sp)
	95.3	0.25	FL	Boca Raton	W237BD (WWNN) (sp)
	95.3	0.031	FL	Miami	WJEW-LP (sp)
	95.3	0.07	FL	Miami	W237CP (WMLV)
	95.3	0.049	FL	Miami Beach	WLJM-LP
#	95.5	100	FL	Juno Beach	WLDI
#	95.7	17	FL	No. Miami Beach	WRMA (sp)
	95.9	0.25	FL	North Palm Beach	W240CI (WSVU)
	96.1	0.25	FL	Boca Raton	W241AX (WPBR) (ha)
	96.1	0.048	FL	Hollywood	WZPP-LP
	96.3	0.201	FL	Jupiter	W242CI (WMBX-HD2)
#	96.5	100	FL	Miami	WPOW
	96.9	0.25	FL	Lauderdale Lakes	W245BC (WSBR)
	96.9	0.095	FL	Miami	WWWO-LP (sp)
	96.9	0.099	FL	North Miami	W245BF (WRGP)
#	97.3	100	FL	Miami	WFLC
	97.7	0.02	FL	Homestead	WWPP-LP
	97.7	0.25	FL	Miami	W249DM (WOCN) (sp)
#	97.9	100	FL	Palm Beach	WRMF
#	98.3	100	FL	Goulds	WRTO-FM (sp)
	98.3	0.054	FL	Palm Beach	WPBV-LP
	98.3	0.045	FL	West Palm Beach	WPBE-LP (sp)
	98.7	0.014	FL	Miami	WPSI-LP
#	98.7	100	FL	Wellington	WKGR
#	99.1	93	FL	Miami	WEDR
	99.5	0.094	FL	Hialeah Gardens	WHIM-LP (sp)
	99.5	0.084	FL	Miami Shores	WBUJ-LP
	99.5	6	FL	Palm Beach Gardens	WLLY-FM (sp)
#	99.9	100	FL	Boca Raton	WKIS
	100.3	4	FL	Lake Park	WLML
	100.3	0.097	FL	Miami	WQNB-LP
#	100.7	100	FL	Ft. Lauderdale	WHYI-FM
	101.1	0.1	FL	Boca Raton	WRIZ-LP
	101.1	0.1	FL	Hollywood	WDKK-LP
	101.1	0.05	FL	Miami	WDVS-LP
	101.1	0.097	FL	West Palm Beach	WDZP-LP (ha)
#	101.5	100	FL	Miami	WLYF
	101.7	0.19	FL	North Palm Beach	W269DS (WSVU)
	101.9	0.1	FL	Miami	W270CV (WKAT) (sp)
	101.9	0.08	FL	Oakland Park	WOIB-LP
	101.9	0.25	FL	West Palm Beach	W270AD (WFLV-HD2)
	102.1	0.08	FL	Ft. Lauderdale	WNGK-LP
	102.3	0.07	FL	Hallandale	WEXI-LP

MHz	kW	Sta	City of License	Station
#102.3	100	FL	Jensen Beach°	WMBX
102.3	0.25	FL	Miami	W272DS (WQOS)
#102.7	100	FL	Pompano Beach	WMXJ
#103.1	90	FL	Indiantown	WIRK
103.1	0.045	FL	Miramar	WUGR-LP
#103.5	100	FL	Ft. Lauderdale	WMIB
103.7	0.013	FL	West Palm Beach	W279DG (WCNO)
103.9	0.25	FL	Boca Raton	W280DU (WWNN)
103.9	0.02	FL	Jupiter	WJUP-LP
103.9	0.099	FL	Miami	W280FV (WURN) (sp)
104.1	0.25	FL	West Palm Beach	W279DG (WPSP) (sp)
#104.3	100	FL	Miramar	WSFS
104.7	0.031	FL	Coconut Creek	WYUN-LP
104.7	0.099	FL	Miami	W284CS (WMIA-FM)
104.7	0.054	FL	Miami	WAYG-LP
104.7	0.25	FL	West Palm Beach	W284CR (WFLV-HD3)
#105.1	100	FL	Coral Gables	WHQT
#105.5	50	FL	Hobe Sound°	WOLL
105.5	50	FL	Islamorada°	WWWK (sp)
105.5	0.085	FL	Tamarac	W288DD (WZTU-HD3)
#105.9	100	FL	Ft. Lauderdale	WBGG-FM
#106.3	19	FL	Jupiter	WUUB
106.3	50	FL	Leisure City	WRAZ-FM (sp)
106.3	6	FL	Miramar Beach	WSBZ
106.3	0.067	FL	Pembroke Pines	WIPU-LP
#106.7	100	FL	Ft. Lauderdale	WXDJ (sp)
106.9	0.19	FL	Jupiter	W295BJ (WSVU)
107.1	0.25	FL	Belle Glade	W296DN (WSWN)
107.1	0.25	FL	Boynton Beach	W296EC (WLVJ) (sp)
107.1	0.099	FL	Ft. Lauderdale	W296DK (WFLL)
#107.1	50	FL	Key Largo	WURN-FM (sp)
107.1	0.1	FL	Pompano Beach	WAFG-LP
#107.5	95	FL	Miami	WAMR-FM (sp)
107.9	0.099	FL	No. Miami Beach	W300DF (WAVS)
#107.9	100	FL	West Palm Beach	WEAT

Minneapolis - St. Paul Metro Area (Minneapolis-St. Paul-Bloomington, MN-WI MSA)

MHz	kW	Sta	City of License	Station
88.1	5.52	MN	Newport	WAJC
# 88.3	70	WI	Menomonie°	WHWC
88.3	11	MN	Waconia	KJGT
88.5	2.9	MN	Minneapolis	KBEM-FM
88.7	0.1	MN	Cambridge	WUSG-LP
88.7	3	WI	River Falls	WRFW
# 89.3	100	MN	Northfield°	KCMP
89.7	40	MN	Princeton	KPCS
# 89.9	6.2	MN	Minneapolis	KMOJ
# 90.1	100	MN	Collegeville°	KSJR-FM
# 90.3	0.9	MN	Minneapolis	KFAI
90.3	15	MN	North Branch	KMKL
# 90.5	75	MN	St. Peter°	KNGA
90.7	0.099	MN	Golden Valley	K214DF (KTIS-FM)
# 91.1	100	MN	Minneapolis	KNOW-FM
91.5	0.216	MN	Bloomington	K218DK (KJLY)
91.7	0.05	MN	North Branch	W219DT (WAJC)
# 91.7	94	MN	Rochester°	KZSE
91.7	0.005	MN	St. Paul	WMCN
91.9	0.025	MN	Minneapolis	K220JP (KSJN)
92.1	0.25	MN	Albertville	K221ES (KHRI)
92.1	0.08	MN	St. Paul	W221BS (WDGY)
# 92.5	100	MN	Golden Valley	KQRS-FM
92.9	0.25	MN	St. Paul	W225AP (KTCZ-FM)
93.1	0.25	WI	River Falls	W226CK (WEVR-FM)
93.3	0.099	MN	Shoreview	W227BF (KQQL-HD2)
# 93.7	100	MN	Minneapolis	KXXR
94.1	0.002	MN	Minneapolis	K235BP (KSTP)
94.1	0.1	MN	St. Paul	WFNU-LP
# 94.5	100	MN	St. Paul	KSTP-FM
94.9	0.25	MN	St. Paul	W235CT (WREY) (sp)
95.3	0.9	MN	St. Paul	KZGO
95.5	25	MN	Mora°	KBEK
95.5	6	MN	New Prague	KCHK-FM
95.7	4	WI	Baldwin	WDMO
95.7	0.25	MN	St. Paul	K239CJ (KMNV) (sp)
95.9	3	MN	Faribault°	KQCL
95.9	3	MN	Forest Lake	WLKX-FM
# 96.3	19	MN	Edina	KQGO
96.7	0.17	MN	Calhoun Beach	K244FE (KFXN-FM)
# 97.1	100	MN	Minneapolis	KTCZ-FM
97.5	0.25	MN	Minneapolis	W248CU (KTIS)
97.5	100	MN	Rochester°	KNXR
97.5	0.1	MN	St. Louis Park	KPPS-LP
97.7	0.25	MN	Albertville	K249ED (KTCZ-FM)
97.9	0.1	MN	Lakeville	KEFE-LP (sp)
97.9	0.09	MN	St. Paul	KQEP-LP (ch)
98.1	97	MN	St. Cloud°	WWJO
98.1	0.1	MN	St. Paul	KENL-LP (sp)
98.5	100	MN	Minneapolis	KTIS-FM
98.9	0.1	MN	Minneapolis	KRSM-LP
99.1	0.1	MN	Maple Grove	KPJT-LP
# 99.5	100	MN	Minneapolis	KSJN
99.9	0.25	MN	Coon Rapids	K260BA (KFXN-FM-HD3)
#100.3	100	MN	Minneapolis	KFXN-FM
100.7	0.099	MN	Falcon Heights	W264BR (KUOM)
100.9	100	MN	Blooming Prairie°	KOWZ
#101.3	100	MN	Richfield	KDWB-FM
101.7	0.1	MN	Minneapolis	KALY-LP (som)
#102.1	100	MN	St. Paul	KEEY-FM
102.5	0.25	MN	Fridley	K273BH (KTCZ-FM-HD3)
#102.9	100	MN	Minneapolis	KMNB
103.3	0.25	WI	New Richmond	W277CW (WIXK) (hm)
103.5	0.175	MN	Cottage Grove	K278BP (KTLK)
103.5	100	MN	Mankato°	KYSM-FM
103.7	0.25	WI	Hudson	W279DD (WDGY)
#104.1	100	MN	St. Louis Park	KZJK
104.5	0.099	MN	Minneapolis	K283BG (KUOM)
104.7	100	MN	St. Cloud°	KCLD-FM
104.7	0.1	MN	St. Paul	WEQY-LP
104.9	0.25	MN	St. Paul	K285CQ (KFXN) (hm)
105.1	2.6	MN	Lakeville	WGVX
105.3	25	MN	Cambridge	WLUP
105.5	0.25	MN	Bayport	K288GR (KFXN-FM-HD3)
105.7	0.95	MN	Eden Prarie	WWWM-FM
105.9	12	MN	Red Wing°	KWNG
#106.1	9.1	MN	Elk River	KLCI
106.3	6	WI	River Falls	WEVR-FM
106.5	0.196	MN	Elko	K293BA (KJLY)
106.5	0.006	MN	St. Louis Park	KUOM-FM
106.7	0.25	MN	New Prague	K294DF (KCHK-FM)
106.7	0.17	MN	West St. Paul	K294AM (KFAI)
#107.1	22	MN	Coon Rapids	KTMY
107.5	48	MN	Faribault°	KBGY
107.5	0.25	MN	Minneapolis	K298CO (WWTC)
#107.9	100	MN	Anoka	KQQL

New York Metro Area (New York-Newark-Jersey City, NY-NJ-PA MSA)

MHz	kW	Sta	City of License	Station
88.1	0.78	NJ	Asbury Park	WYGG
88.1	0.18	NY	Brentwood	WXBA
88.1	0.1	NY	Brookville	WCWP
88.1	0.5	NJ	Hopatcong	WDNJ (sp)
88.1	0.042	NY	Valhalla	WARY
# 88.3	2.5	NJ	Newark	WBGO
88.5	0.125	NY	Plainview	WPOB
88.5	2	CT	Stamford°	WEDW-FM
88.5	0.45	NJ	Sussex	WNJP
88.5	0.125	NY	Syosset	WKWZ
88.7	0.47	NY	Hempstead	WRHU
88.7	1.35	NJ	New Brunswick°	WRSU-FM
88.7	0.01	NY	Nyack	WNYK
88.7	0.2	NJ	Wayne	WPSC-FM
‡# 88.9	0.2	NY	Mt Kisco	WWES
88.9	1.5	NY	Smithtown	WFRS
88.9	0.011	NY	Staten Island	WSIA
88.9	1	NJ	West Long Branch	WMCX
89.1	8.3	NY	New York	WNYU-FM
89.1	0.005	NY	New York	WNYU-FM1
# 89.1	3	NJ	Teaneck	WFDU
89.3	0.11	NY	Copiague	WGSS
89.3	15.2	NJ	Freehold	WFJS-FM
89.3	1.6	NY	Monroe	WLJP
89.3	0.52	NJ	Netcong	WNJY
89.5	10	CT	Bridgeport°	WPKN
# 89.5	2.4	NJ	South Orange	WSOU
89.7	1.6	NJ	Freehold Township	WRDR
‡ 89.7	0.038	NY	Mt Kisco	W209CJ (WMNR)
89.9	0.25	NJ	Manahawkin	WNJM
# 89.9	1.35	NY	New York	WKCR-FM
90.1	3.6	NY	Stony Brook	WUSB
90.3	0.01	NY	Brooklyn	WKRB
# 90.3	0.5	NY	Garden City	WHPC
90.3	0.1	NJ	Mahwah	WRPR
90.3	0.008	NY	New York	WHCR-FM

MHz	kW	Sta	City of License	Station
90.3	0.25	NY	Ossining	WQXW
90.3	0.1	NJ	Piscataway	WVPH
90.3	0.009	NJ	Union Township	WKNJ-FM
90.3	0.001	NJ	Upper Montclair	WMSC
# 90.5	0.9	NJ	Lincroft	WBJB-FM
90.5	0.125	NJ	Morristown	WJSV
# 90.7	15	NJ	Manahawkin	WYRS
# 90.7	46	NY	New York	WFUV
90.7	2.5	NY	New York	WFUV-FM3
91.1	1.25	NJ	East Orange	WFMU
# 91.1	20	CT	Fairfield°	WSHU-FM
91.1	0.015	NY	Ossining	WOSS
91.3	0.25	NY	Huntington Station	W217AF (WSHU-FM)
91.3	3.7	NY	Poughkeepsie°	WVKR-FM
# 91.5	2	NY	New York	WNYE
91.7	0.82	NY	Pomona	WLFR
# 91.9	5.4	NJ	Hackettstown°	WXPJ
91.9	6	NY	Lake Ronkonkoma	WSHR
91.9	0.01	NY	New City	W220EG (WMFU)
91.9	0.01	NJ	Parlin	W220AA (WRDR)
91.9	0.01	NJ	Weehawken	W220EJ (WFMU)
# 92.3	6	NY	New York	WNYL
92.7	0.105	NJ	Franklin Township	W224CW (WQHT-HD2) (as)
# 92.7	2	NY	Garden City	WQBU-FM (sp)
92.7	0.08	NY	New York	WQBU-FM1 (sp)
92.7	1.2	NY	Brooklyn	WQBU-FM2 (sp)
92.7	6	NY	Middletown°	WRRV
92.9	3.1	NY	Manorville	WEHM
92.9	0.08	NY	Pomona	W225BV (WYRS)
# 93.1	5.4	NJ	Paterson	WPAT-FM (sp)
# 93.5	1.75	NY	New Rochelle	WVIP
93.5	0.25	NY	Warwick	W228CG (WTBQ)
93.7	0.1	NY	Westbrookville	WQPU-LP
# 93.9	5.2	NY	New York	WNYC-FM
94.1	0.25	NY	Chester	W231BP (WLJP)
94.3	0.05	NJ	Alpine	W232AL (WNSH-HD4)
# 94.3	1.3	NJ	Asbury Park	WJLK
94.3	0.001	NY	Peekskill	W232DQ (WLNA)
94.3	2.6	NY	Smithtown	WWSK
94.3	0.058	NJ	Wood Ridge	WSBP-LP
94.5	50	NJ	Trenton°	WPST
# 94.7	40	NJ	Newark	WNSH
94.9	0.015	NY	Hauppauge	W235BB (WKLV)
# 95.1	30	PA	Bethlehem°	WZZO
95.1	29.5	CT	Brookfield°	WRKI
95.1	0.25	NJ	Edison	W236CT (WPST)
95.1	0.027	NY	Ft. Greene	W236CH (WNSH-HD4)
95.1	0.25	NY	Patchogue	W236DH (WLID)
# 95.5	6.7	NY	New York	WPLJ
95.9	0.06	NJ	Dover	W240EE (WTOC) (sp)
95.9	0.25	NY	Hempstead	W240DF (WGBB) (ch)
‡ 95.9	0.07	NJ	Kearney	WNJI-LP
‡ 95.9	0.039	NJ	Maplewood	WZYE-LP
95.9	0.01	NY	Peekskill	W240CR (WAMC)
# 95.9	4	NJ	Point Pleasant	WRAT
# 95.9	3	CT	Southport°	WFOX
95.9	0.027	NJ	Wayne	WYNE-LP
96.3	6	NY	New York	WXNY-FM (sp)
96.7	0.25	NJ	Asbury Park	W244EE (WADB)
96.7	0.09	NJ	Parsippany	W232CY (WXMC) [1]
# 96.7	3.1	NY	Port Chester	WARW
96.7	0.25	NY	Warwick	W244EA (WALL)
96.9	0.01	NY	Manorville	W245BA (WABC)
# 97.1	6.7	NY	New York	WQHT
97.5	0.25	NJ	Jersey City	W248CG (WXMC) (sp)
97.5	0.063	NJ	Newton	WRSK-LP
# 97.5	39	NY	Patchogue	WALK-FM
# 97.9	6	NY	New York	WSKQ-FM (sp)
98.1	0.25	NY	Patchogue	W251BY (WPTY-HD2)
98.3	0.01	NY	Brooklyn	W252CS (WVIP)
98.3	3	NY	Hempstead	WKJY
# 98.3	1.2	NJ	New Brunswick°	WMGQ
98.3	0.15	NJ	Sussex	W252DY (WYNY)
# 98.7	6	NY	New York	WEPN-FM
# 99.1	15	CT	New Haven°	WPLR
# 99.1	28	NJ	Zarephath	WAWZ
99.5	10	NY	New York	WBAI
# 99.9	27.5	CT	Bridgeport°	WEZN-FM
# 99.9	50	PA	Easton°	WODE-FM
#100.1	1.7	NJ	Manahawkin	WJRZ-FM
#100.3	6	NJ	Newark	WHTZ
100.7	0.125	NJ	Eatontown	W264DH (WHTG)
100.7	0.2	NJ	Edison	W264BT (WPRB)
100.7	50	NY	Peekskill	WHUD
100.9	0.046	NJ	Manahawkin	W265CS (WSJO)
#101.1	6.7	NY	New York	WCBS-FM
#101.3	12	CT	Hamden°	WKCI-FM
101.5	0.1	NY	Plainview	W268AN (WVIP-HD3)
101.5	0.038	NY	Queens	W268BY (WVIP)
#101.5	15.5	NJ	Trenton°	WKXW
#101.9	6	NY	New York	WFAN-FM
102.3	0.1	NJ	Arrowhead Village	WUPC-LP (sp)
#102.3	6	NY	Babylon	WBAB
102.3	0.01	NY	Brooklyn	WBQE-LP
102.3	0.59	NJ	Franklin	WSUS
102.3	0.015	NJ	Hazlet	WXDP-LP (sp)
102.3	0.25	NY	New York	W272DX (WMCA)
#102.7	6	NY	New York	WNEW-FM
103.1	1.55	NY	Bay Shore	WBZO
103.1	0.035	NJ	Ft. Lee	W276AQ (WNSH-HD4)
#103.3	14	NJ	Princeton°	WPRB
#103.5	6	NY	Lake Success	WKTU
103.7	2.3	NJ	Newton	WNNJ
#103.9	0.98	NY	Bronxville	WNBM
103.9	0.148	NJ	Edison	W280GA (WWRL) (as)
103.9	0.01	NJ	Hazlet	WCNM (sp)
104.1	0.225	NJ	Lakewood Township	W281CK (WOBM)
#104.3	6	NY	New York	WAXQ
104.5	0.01	NY	Selden	W283BA (WLIR-FM)
104.7	0.25	NY	Hempstead	W284DG (WHLI)
104.7	0.099	NY	New York	W284BW (WWRV) (sp)
104.7	7.4	NY	Poughkeepsie°	WSPK
#105.1	6	NY	New York	WWPR-FM
#105.5	1	NJ	Dover	WDHA-FM
105.5	0.019	NY	Flushing	WQEQ-LP
105.5	0.019	NY	Queens	WDMB-LP
105.7	13	NJ	Manahawkin	WCHR-FM
105.7	0.25	NY	Selden	W289AD (WSUF)
#105.9	0.61	NJ	Newark	WQXR-FM
#106.1	49	NY	Patchogue	WBLI
106.3	1.1	NJ	Eatontown	WKMK
106.3	0.98	NY	Mt Kisco	WFME
106.3	0.001	NY	New York	W292FV (WFME)
106.3	0.099	NY	New York	W292DV (WNYH) (sp)
#106.7	6	NY	New York	WLTW
107.1	1.9	NY	Briarcliff Manor	WXPK
107.1	0.1	NY	Hempstead	W296CQ (WKJI)
107.1	5	NJ	Long Branch	WWZY
107.1	0.01	NY	Warwick	W296BD (WAMC-FM)
107.3	0.006	NY	Stony Brook	W297BM (WUSB)
#107.5	4.2	NY	New York	WBLS
107.9	0.004	NJ	Dover	WCFT-LP
107.9	0.1	NJ	Lakewood	WMDI-LP
107.9	0.25	NJ	Manahawkin	W300AO (WJRZ-HD2)
#107.9	20.5	CT	Westport°	WEBE

Orlando Metro Area (Orlando-Kissimmee-Sanford, FL MSA)

MHz	kW	Sta	City of License	Station
# 88.3	100	FL	Orlando	WPOZ
# 88.7	35	FL	The Villages°	WMYZ
88.9	25	FL	Edgewater°	WKTO
89.1	5.2	FL	Kissimmee	WLAZ (sp)
89.3	7.1	FL	Titusville°	WPIO
89.5	22	FL	Cedar Creek°	WMFV
# 89.7	69	FL	Tampa°	WUSF
# 89.9	0.36	FL	Orlando	WUCF-FM
90.3	9.4	FL	Eustis	WIGW
90.3	0.75	FL	Haines City°	WLVF
# 90.7	100	FL	Orlando	WMFE-FM
91.1	100	FL	Lakeland°	WKES
91.5	0.9	FL	Winter Park	WPRK
91.9	25	FL	Lakeland°	WYFO
# 92.3	99	FL	Orlando	WWKA
92.7	0.028	FL	Kissimmee	WKIE-LP (sp)
92.7	0.027	FL	Winter Garden	W224CQ (WYFO)
92.7	0.027	FL	Winter Park	WRXW-LP
92.9	50	FL	Ocala°	WMFQ
93.1	0.25	FL	Orlando	W226BT (WFLF)
93.3	0.25	FL	Sanford	W227CP (WPOZ-HD3)
# 93.3	100	FL	Tampa°	WFLZ-FM
93.5	0.24	FL	Orlando	W228DF (WOCL-HD3)
93.5	0.038	FL	Union Park	W228BK (WYFO)

MHz	kW	Sta	City of License	Station
93.7	0.051	FL	Kissimmee	WNKQ-LP (sp)
93.7	100	FL	Ocala°	WOGK
93.9	0.085	FL	Orlando	WWRT-LP (sp)
# 94.1	100	FL	Lakeland°	WLLD
94.1	0.25	FL	Orlando	W231CT (WFLF)
94.9	0.225	FL	Orlando	W235CR (WTLN)
94.9	100	FL	Tampa°	WWRM
# 95.3	12	FL	Maitland	WYPO
95.7	0.1	FL	Christmas	WLPM-LP
95.7	48	FL	Ormond-By-The-S°	WHOG-FM
95.9	0.099	FL	Orlando	W240BV (WPOZ-HD2)
96.1	0.019	FL	Kissimmee	W241BP (WYFO)
96.1	0.068	FL	Orlando	WWID-LP (sp)
# 96.5	99	FL	Orlando	WOEX (sp)
96.9	0.25	FL	Deltona°	W245CL (WJRR-HD2)
97.1	0.027	FL	Clermont	W246BT (WRUM) (sp)
97.1	0.25	FL	Kissimmee	W246CK (WRUM-HD2) (sp)
97.1	0.1	FL	Mount Dora	WVGT-LP
# 97.9	100	FL	Clearwater°	WXTB
97.9	0.25	FL	Kissimmee	W250CE (WRSO) (sp)
# 98.1	50	FL	Deltona°	WNUE-FM (sp)
# 98.3	27	FL	Ft. Meade°	WWRZ
98.5	0.018	FL	Orlando	WHPB-LP
# 98.9	44	FL	Orlando	WMMO
# 99.3	50	FL	Cocoa°	WLRQ-FM
99.3	0.1	FL	Winter Garden	WGPD-LP (sp)
99.5	0.166	FL	Orlando	W258DD (WONQ) (sp)
99.7	0.016	FL	Kissimmee	WBVL-LP (sp)
99.7	0.1	FL	Lake Mary	WWRG-LP
99.9	0.067	FL	Apopka	WPKA-LP (sp)
99.9	0.1	FL	Orlando	WIME-LP (sp)
99.9	0.048	FL	Orlando	WOGJ-LP (ha)
99.9	0.019	FL	Winter Garden	WIDT-LP (sp)
#100.3	95	FL	Orlando	WRUM (sp)
100.7	0.01	FL	Orlando	WUOH-LP
#100.7	100	FL	Tampa°	WMTX
#101.1	95	FL	Cocoa Beach°	WJRR
101.5	0.225	FL	Orlando	W268CT (WTLN) (sp)
#101.5	100	FL	St. Petersburg°	WPOI
#101.9	90	FL	Daytona Beach°	WQMP
102.3	0.08	FL	Kissimmee	WMQV-LP (sp)
102.5	0.25	FL	Orlando	W273CA (WPOZ-HD4) (sp)
102.7	50	FL	Rockledge°	WHKR
103.1	22	FL	Windermere	WOTW
103.5	0.25	FL	Eatonville	W278CN (WURB) (sp)
#103.5	66	FL	Gulfport°	WFUS
103.7	0.25	FL	Clermont	W279CT (WPOZ)
103.7	0.191	FL	Kissimmee	W279DI (WURB) (sp)
#104.1	94	FL	Cocoa Beach°	WTKS-FM
104.5	0.221	FL	Altamonte Springs	W283AN (WTKS-HD2)
104.7	0.25	FL	Kissimmee	W284DM (WHOO)
#105.1	94	FL	Orlando	WOMX
105.5	0.08	FL	Kissimmee	WTMS-LP (sp)
105.5	0.25	FL	Oviedo	W288CJ (WDYZ)
#105.9	96	FL	DeLand°	WOCL
106.3	13.5	FL	Melbourne°	WCIF
106.3	0.215	FL	Orlando	W292DZ (WPOZ-HD3)
#106.7	100	FL	Tavares	WXXL
107.1	0.25	FL	Eustis	W296DO (WKIQ) (sp)
107.1	100	FL	Melbourne°	WAOA-FM
107.3	0.25	FL	Orlando	W297BB (WDBO)
#107.7	100	FL	Mount Dora	WMGF

Philadelphia Metro Area (Philadelphia-Camden-Wilmington, PA-NJ-DE-MD MSA)

MHz	kW	Sta	City of License	Station
88.1	0.08	NJ	Berlin	WNJS-FM
88.1	0.01	PA	Philadelphia	WPEB
88.1	0.088	DE	Pike Creek	WMHS
88.1	0.11	NJ	Trenton°	WNJT-FM
88.1	0.43	PA	Warwick	WZZD
# 88.5	2.65	PA	Philadelphia	WXPN
88.9	10	NJ	Pemberton°	WBZC
88.9	0.9	PA	Sellersville	WBYO
89.1	1.2	DE	Christiana	WXHL-FM
89.1	0.7	PA	Radnor	WYBF
# 89.1	1.15	NJ	Trenton°	WWFM
89.1	0.1	PA	Villanova	WXVU
89.3	2.5	NJ	Bridgeton°	WNJB-FM
89.3	0.46	PA	Coatesville	WRTJ
89.3	1.6	PA	Warminster	WRDV
# 89.5	1.9	NJ	Cherry Hill	WYPA
89.7	3.8	NJ	Delaware Township°	WDVR
89.7	0.75	NJ	Glassboro	WGLS-FM
# 90.1	7.7	PA	Philadelphia	WRTI
# 90.5	21	NJ	Medford Lakes°	WVBV
# 90.9	13.5	PA	Philadelphia	WHYY-FM
# 91.3	6.8	DE	Newark	WVUD
# 91.3	13.5	NJ	Ocean City°	WRTQ
91.3	1.5	NJ	Trenton°	WTSR
91.5	0.1	NJ	Blackwood	WDBK
91.5	0.11	PA	Swarthmore	WSRN-FM
91.7	0.1	PA	Bristol	WLBS
91.7	0.8	PA	Philadelphia	WKDU
91.7	0.5	PA	Telford	WBMR
91.7	0.1	PA	West Chester	WCUR
91.7	0.1	DE	Wilmington	WMPH
92.1	0.016	PA	Horsham	WEMQ-LP
92.1	6	NJ	Vineland°	WVLT
# 92.5	15	PA	Philadelphia	WXTU
92.9	0.24	NJ	Burlington°	W225DJ (WIFI)
92.9	0.1	PA	Philadelphia	WOOM-LP
92.9	0.015	PA	Philadelphia	+ WRLG-LP
92.9	0.015	PA	Philadelphia	+ WRGU-LP
92.9	0.015	PA	Philadelphia	+ WGGT-LP
# 93.3	16.5	PA	Philadelphia	WMMR
# 93.7	47.1	DE	Wilmington	WSTW
# 94.1	9.6	PA	Philadelphia	WIP-FM
# 94.5	19	PA	Lancaster°	WDAC
94.5	50	NJ	Trenton°	WPST
# 94.7	50	DE	Dover°	WDSD
94.9	0.004	PA	Coatesville	W235AT (WVBV)
94.9	0.014	PA	Folsom	WRSD
94.9	0.022	NJ	Marlton°	W235BZ (WVBV)
94.9	0.074	PA	Philadelphia	W235CE (WVBV)
94.9	0.002	PA	Radnor	W235AP (WBYO)
95.1	50	NJ	Atlantic City°	WAYV
# 95.1	30	PA	Bethlehem°	WZZO
95.1	0.007	PA	Philadelphia	W236CL (WPEB)
95.3	0.25	NJ	Pennsauken	W237EH (WSTW-HD2)
95.3	0.12	PA	West Chester	W237EW (WCHE)
95.3	0.05	DE	Wilmington	WHGE-LP
# 95.7	8.9	PA	Philadelphia	WBEN-FM
96.1	50	PA	Easton°	WCTO
96.1	0.25	PA	Philadelphia	W241CH (WURD)
# 96.5	9.6	PA	Philadelphia	WTDY-FM
96.9	50	NJ	Atlantic City°	WFPG
96.9	0.026	PA	Glenside	W245AG (WBYO)
96.9	0.175	DE	Wilmington	W245CJ (WVJJ)
97.1	0.074	PA	Bensalem	W246AR (WDVR)
97.1	0.01	NJ	Collingswood	W246AQ (WXHL-FM)
97.1	0.25	PA	Colmar	W246CN (WPAZ)
97.3	50	NJ	Millville°	WENJ
# 97.5	26	NJ	Burlington°	WPEN
# 98.1	9.6	PA	Philadelphia	WOGL
98.5	0.1	PA	No. Philadelphia	WJYN-LP
98.5	0.077	PA	Philadelphia	WQEW-LP (ch)
98.5	0.1	DE	Wilmington	W253CQ (WTMC)
# 98.9	27	PA	Philadelphia	WUSL
# 99.1	28	NJ	Zarephath°	WAWZ
# 99.5	50	DE	Wilmington	WJBR-FM
# 99.9	50	PA	Easton°	WODE-FM
99.9	0.01	PA	Havertown	WHHS
99.9	0.085	DE	Newark	WIZU-LP
99.9	0.05	PA	Philadelphia	W260CZ (WHAT)
#100.3	17	PA	Media	WRNB
#100.7	11	PA	Allentown°	WLEV
100.7	0.099	NJ	Mount Holly	W264BH (WJBR-HD3)
#101.1	14	PA	Philadelphia	WBEB
#101.5	15.5	NJ	Trenton°	WKXW
101.7	3.3	NJ	Canton°	WDEL-FM
101.7	0.003	PA	Coatesville	W269BL (WBYO)
101.7	0.015	PA	Pottstown	W269BT (WVBV)
#102.1	27	PA	Philadelphia	WIOQ
102.5	0.099	PA	Philadelphia	W273DO (WDAS)
102.5	10	PA	Reading°	WRFY-FM
#102.9	8.9	PA	Philadelphia	WMGK
#103.3	14	NJ	Princeton°	WPRB
103.5	0.2	PA	Pottstown	W278BR (WPAZ)
103.5	0.08	PA	Village Green	W278AK (WXHL-FM)
103.7	50	NJ	Atlantic City°	WMGM
103.7	39	MD	Havre de Grace°	WXCY

MHz	kW	Sta	City of License	Station
103.9	0.27	PA	Jenkintown	WPHI-FM
103.9	0.005	PA	Wagontown	W280CP (WDAC)
#104.1	50	PA	Allentown°	WAEB-FM
104.1	0.04	NJ	Cherry Hill	W281CL (WXHL-FM)
#104.5	11.5	PA	Philadelphia	WRFF
#104.9	10	NJ	Egg Harbor City°	WSJO
‡104.9	0.25	PA	Lansdale	W285EW
105.1	25	PA	Ephrata°	WIOV-FM
#105.3	16.5	PA	Philadelphia	WDAS-FM
105.7	0.25	NJ	Camden	W289AZ (WEMG) (sp)
105.7	13	NJ	Manahawkin°	WCHR-FM
105.7	0.024	PA	Plymouth°	WEMZ-LP
#106.1	22.5	PA	Philadelphia	WISX
106.5	0.007	PA	Eagleville	WRDY-LP
106.5	0.09	PA	Philadelphia	WPPM-LP
106.5	0.016	PA	Warminster	WHII-LP
#106.9	38	NJ	Camden	WKVP
107.3	0.02	PA	Philadelphia	W297AD (WRDV)
107.3	0.185	DE	Wilmington	W297CA (WSRY)
#107.5	30	PA	Boyertown°	WBYN-FM
107.7	0.25	DE	Marshallton	W299BH (WRTI)
107.9	0.78	NJ	Pennsauken	WPPZ-FM
Phoenix Metro Area (Phoenix-Mesa-Scottsdale, AZ MSA)				
88.3	22.5	AZ	Phoenix	+ KVCP
88.3	22.5	AZ	Phoenix	+ KPHF
88.7	15	AZ	Chandler	KPNG
88.9	0.01	AZ	Phoenix	K205CI (KEBR-FM)
89.1	30	AZ	Fountain Hills	KLVK
# 89.5	29.7	AZ	Phoenix	KBAQ
89.7	0.01	AZ	Scottsdale	K209DV (KBAQ-FM)
89.9	45	AZ	Superior	KLVA
90.3	100	AZ	Phoenix	KFLR-FM
90.7	2	AZ	Apache Junction	KVIT
90.7	0.075	AZ	Cave Creek	K214DN (KRKY-FM)
90.9	58	AZ	Prescott°	KLVH
91.1	0.075	AZ	Guadalupe	K216FO (KRUC) (sp)
91.1	0.25	AZ	Wickenburg	K216GP (KLVK)
# 91.5	100	AZ	Phoenix	KJZZ
91.7	0.01	AZ	Rio Verde	K219DZ (KJZZ)
# 92.3	100	AZ	Glendale	KTAR-FM
92.7	0.25	AZ	Phoenix	K224CJ (KAZG)
92.9	0.1	AZ	Desert Ridge	KDWR-LP
92.9	0.003	AZ	Paradise Valley	K225CT (KPHX)
# 93.3	100	AZ	Mesa	KDKB
93.7	0.25	AZ	Phoenix	K229DB (KOY) (sp)
93.9	0.002	AZ	Scottsdale	KWSS-LP
94.1	4.7	AZ	San Carlos°	KRDE
# 94.5	95.6	AZ	Phoenix	KOOL-FM
94.9	0.25	AZ	Chandler	K235CB (KOAI)
95.1	41	AZ	Sun City West	KOAI
# 95.5	100	AZ	Phoenix	KYOT
95.9	0.25	AZ	Buckeye	K240DC (KYOT)
95.9	21	AZ	Cottonwood°	KKLD
95.9	0.25	AZ	Tempe	K240EU (KQFN)
96.1	0.14	AZ	Ft. McDowell	K241BQ (KZON-HD3)
‡ 96.1	0.25	AZ	Phoenix	K241CS (KKFR)
96.3	5.3	AZ	Wickenburg	KSWG
# 96.5	30	AZ	Claypool°	KIKO-FM
96.5	0.25	AZ	Laveen	K243BN (KLVK)
# 96.9	100	AZ	Phoenix	KMXP
97.3	0.04	AZ	Goodyear	K247BH (KFLR-FM)
97.3	0.25	AZ	Payson°	K247CF (KBSZ)
# 97.5	42	AZ	Dewey-Humboldt°	KMVA
# 97.9	96	AZ	Tempe	KUPD
98.3	41	AZ	Mayer°	KKFR (sp)
# 98.7	97	AZ	Phoenix	KMVP-FM
99.3	17	AZ	Payson°	KEMP
99.3	0.25	AZ	Phoenix	K257CD (KQFN)
99.5	0.02	AZ	Mesa	KFXY-LP
99.5	7.9	AZ	Morristown	KRPH (sp)
‡ 99.5	0.625	AZ	Wittman	KRPH-FM1 (sp)
# 99.9	100	AZ	Phoenix	KESZ
#100.3	90	AZ	Globe°	KQMR (sp)
#100.7	100	AZ	Scottsdale	KSLX-FM
101.1	40	AZ	Cordes Lakes°	KNRJ
101.1	0.05	AZ	Florence	KOHF-LP
#101.5	100	AZ	Phoenix	KALV-FM
101.9	0.25	AZ	Phoenix	K270BZ (KNAI) (sp)
#102.1	58	AZ	Spring Valley°	KAHM
#102.5	100	AZ	Phoenix	KNIX-FM

MHz	kW	Sta	City of License	Station
102.9	0.19	AZ	Phoenix	K275CP (KIHP)
102.9	0.1	AZ	Phoenix	KDIF-LP
103.1	42	AZ	Florence	KCDX
103.1	0.1	AZ	Sun City West	KSCW-LP
#103.5	48	AZ	Glendale	KLNZ (sp)
#103.9	99.6	AZ	Gilbert	KZON
#104.3	40	AZ	Camp Verde°	KAJM
#104.7	100	AZ	Mesa	KZZP
105.1	46	AZ	Wickenburg	KHOV-FM (sp)
105.3	0.42	AZ	Constellation°	KHOV-FM1 (sp)
105.3	0.25	AZ	Mesa	K287BX (KFNN)
105.5	0.8	AZ	Avondale	KAIZ
105.9	7	AZ	Glendale	KHOT-FM1 (sp)
105.9	36	AZ	Paradise Valley	KHOT-FM (sp)
#106.3	23	AZ	Sun City	KOMR (sp)
106.5	0.86	AZ	Arizona City	KKMR
106.5	0.25	AZ	Phoenix	K283CO (KSUN) (sp)
106.7	0.25	AZ	Phoenix	K294CW (KASA)
106.7	3.7	AZ	Prescott Valley°	KPPV
106.9	6	AZ	Buckeye	KDVA (sp)
#107.1	17	AZ	Apache Junction	KVVA-FM (sp)
107.5	0.25	AZ	Phoenix	K298CK (KNUV) (sp)
#107.9	100	AZ	Chandler	KMLE
Riverside - San Bernadino Metro Area (Riverside-San Bernardino-Ontario, CA MSA)				
88.1	0.15	CA	Banning	KRTM
88.1	0.01	CA	Victorville	K201CD (KVCR)
88.3	0.01	CA	Barstow	K202DM (KHMS)
88.3	0.15	CA	Riverside	KUCR
# 88.5	1.6	CA	Palm Springs	KPSC
88.5	0.2	CA	Victorville	KHMS
88.7	0.014	CA	Banning	K204GG (KSGN)
88.7	0.145	CA	Big Bear City	KFHM
88.7	0.4	CA	Claremont°	KSPC
88.9	0.006	CA	Indio	K205DT (KAWZ)
88.9	0.27	CA	Temecula	KSDW
88.9	0.01	CA	Yucca Valley	K205DK (KODV) (sp)
89.1	5.8	CA	Barstow	KODV (sp)
# 89.1	0.35	CA	Redlands	KUOR-FM
# 89.3	3.2	CA	Indio	KCRI
# 89.3	0.6	CA	Pasadena°	KPCC
89.5	1.2	CA	Victorville	KLXD
89.7	0.01	CA	Palm Springs	K209AK (KSGN)
89.7	2.75	CA	Riverside	KSGN
89.9	0.01	CA	Apple Valley	K210DL (KEFX)
# 89.9	6.9	CA	Santa Monica°	KCRW
90.1	0.6	CA	Yucaipa	KLRD
90.3	0.006	CA	Barstow	K212BD (KAWZ)
# 90.3	0.34	CA	Coachella	KVLA-FM
90.3	0.01	CA	Victorville	K212EK (KAWZ)
90.5	3.5	CA	Yucca Valley	KNLM
90.7	110	CA	Los Angeles°	KPFK
90.9	0.01	CA	Barstow	K215ET (KNLB)
90.9	0.01	CA	Beaumont	K215BA (KCRW)
90.9	0.23	CA	Coachella	KPSH
91.1	0.285	CA	Perris	KKLP
91.1	0.056	CA	Yucca Valley	K216CX (KAWZ)
91.3	1.55	CA	Barstow	KWTH
91.3	0.04	CA	Coachella	K217EZ (KLXB) (sp)
# 91.5	39	CA	Los Angeles°	KUSC
91.7	0.01	CA	Victorville	K219DK (KMRO) (sp)
# 91.9	3.2	CA	San Bernardino	KVCR
92.1	0.027	CA	Barstow	K221GB (KLXD)
92.3	0.06	CA	Cathedral City	K222DA (KWXY)
92.3	42	CA	Los Angeles°	KRRL
92.5	0.1	CA	Yucaipa	KQLH-LP
92.7	0.285	CA	Adelanto	KYZA
92.7	0.005	CA	Fontana	K224DK (KLRD)
# 92.7	4.2	CA	Indio	KKUU
# 92.9	6	CA	Menifee	KXFG
93.1	0.039	CA	Indio	K226BT (KGAY)
# 93.1	27.5	CA	Los Angeles°	KCBS-FM
93.3	1.3	CA	Big Bear City	KBHR
93.3	0.01	CA	Palm Springs	K227BX (KVLA-FM)
93.5	0.006	CA	Barstow	K228CO (KODV) (sp)
93.5	5	CA	Ontario	KDEY-FM
93.7	26.5	CA	Coachella	KCLB-FM
# 93.7	6	CA	Newberry Springs	KIQQ-FM (sp)
93.9	0.01	CA	Barstow	K230AO (KNLB)
# 93.9	18.5	CA	Los Angeles°	KLLI (sp)

MHz	kW	Sta	City of License	Station
94.1	0.1	CA	Big Bear City	KSVB-LP
94.3	4.6	CA	Barstow	KDUC
94.3	0.1	CA	Redlands	KHSH-LP
94.3	0.1	CA	San Bernardino	KJVA-LP (sp)
94.5	0.099	CA	Big Bear Lake	KVBB-LP
94.5	0.54	CA	Temecula	KMYT
# 94.7	52	CA	Los Angeles°	KTWV
95.1	0.05	CA	Coachella	KWXZ-LP
# 95.1	50	CA	San Bernardino	KFRG
# 95.5	61	CA	Los Angeles°	KLOS
95.9	8.9	CA	Barstow	KXXZ (sp)
95.9	6	CA	La Mirada °	KFSH-FM
96.1	1.4	CA	San Jacinto	KRQB (sp)
96.3	0.01	CA	Indio	K242BR (KMRO) (sp)
96.3	6.6	CA	Los Angeles°	KXOL-FM (sp)
96.3	0.13	CA	Victorville	K242CS (KATJ-FM-HD2)
96.5	0.01	CA	Big Bear City	K243BQ (KNLM)
96.7	1.75	CA	Redlands	KCAL-FM
96.9	0.05	CA	Temecula	KPTL-LP
97.1	0.01	CA	Apple Valley	K246CL (KLXD)
# 97.1	21	CA	Los Angeles°	KAMP-FM
97.3	0.034	CA	Indio	K247CL (KLXB) (sp)
# 97.5	72	CA	Riverside	KLYY (sp)
97.9	33	CA	East Los Angeles°	KLAX-FM (sp)
98.1	0.008	CA	Beaumont	K251CC (KMET) (sp)
98.1	0.008	CA	Grand Terrace	K251AH (KMRO) (sp)
98.1	0.158	CA	Indio	K251BX (KRCK-FM)
98.1	0.07	CA	Victorville	KRXV-FM1
98.1	1.55	CA	Yermo	KRXV
98.3	0.003	CA	Temecula	K252BF (KSSD) (sp)
# 98.3	6	CA	West Covina°	KRCV (sp)
# 98.5	38	CA	Cathedral City	KDES-FM
# 98.7	75	CA	Los Angeles°	KYSR
98.7	0.001	CA	Victorville	KNVU-LP (sp)
99.1	0.054	CA	Palm Springs	K256CU (KKGX)
# 99.1	2.55	CA	Riverside	KGGI
99.5	0.19	CA	Apple Valley	K258DE (KWRN) (sp)
99.5	0.01	CA	Barstow	K258CK (KTQX) (sp)
99.5	10	CA	Los Angeles°	KKLA-FM
99.5	3	CA	Rancho Mirage	KMRJ
99.9	29.5	CA	San Bernardino	KOLA
100.1	0.003	CA	Rancho Mirage	KRAQ-LP (sp)
#100.3	5.4	CA	Los Angeles°	KKLQ
100.5	25	CA	Palm Springs	KPSI-FM
100.7	0.013	CA	Corona	K264CI (KBRT)
#100.7	0.26	CA	George	KATJ-FM
100.7	0.25	CA	Guasti	K264AF (KLRD)
100.9	1.5	CA	Beaumont	KAEH (sp)
100.9	0.19	CA	Cathedral City	K265FH (KPSF)
#101.1	51	CA	Los Angeles°	KRTH
101.3	2.25	CA	Hinkley	KWIE
101.3	1.55	CA	Idyllwild	KATY-FM
101.5	0.1	CA	Corona	KORM-LP (sp)
101.5	0.25	CA	Palm Springs	K268AH (KJJZ-HD2)
101.5	0.01	CA	Victorville	K268DU (KQTE)
101.5	0.1	CA	West Covina°	KQPV-LP (ch)
101.7	0.3	CA	Big Bear Lake	KXSB (sp)
101.9	0.095	CA	Cathedral City	K270AI (KLOV)
#101.9	4.8	CA	Glendale°	KSCA (sp)
102.3	6	CA	Apple Valley	KZXY-FM
102.3	2.6	CA	Indio	KRHQ
102.3	0.05	CA	Riverside	K272FQ (KCAA)
102.5	0.015	CA	Big Bear City	K273CO (KBHR)
102.5	4.3	CA	Hemet	KGGN
#102.7	8	CA	Los Angeles°	KIIS-FM
103.1	0.01	CA	Muscoy	K276EF (KEFX)
103.1	0.3	CA	Newport Beach°	KDLE (sp)
103.1	0.25	CA	Victorville	KXVV
103.3	1.25	CA	Temecula	KTMQ
103.5	1.9	CA	Coachella	KPST-FM (sp)
#103.5	12.5	CA	Los Angeles°	KOST
103.7	0.25	CA	Yucca Valley	K279CO (KNWH)
103.9	0.25	CA	Cathedral City	K280CV (KKUU-HD2)
103.9	0.022	CA	Coachella	K280FO (KYRM) (sp)
103.9	0.18	CA	Lake Arrowhead	KHTI
104.1	4.1	CA	Murrieta	KKLM
#104.3	65	CA	Los Angeles°	KBIG
104.7	0.175	CA	Palm Springs	K284CR (KNWZ)
104.7	4.1	CA	Redlands	KQIE
104.7	0.75	CA	Sunnymead Ranch	KQIE-FM1
#105.1	18	CA	Los Angeles°	KKGO
105.5	0.008	CA	Big Bear Lake	KWBB-LP
105.5	0.059	CA	Corona	KGIC-LP (sp)
105.5	6	CA	Hemet	KXRS (sp)
105.5	3	CA	Long Beach°	KBUE (sp)
105.5	0.01	CA	Victorville	K288DJ (KFSG)
#105.9	25	CA	Los Angeles°	KPWR
106.1	50	CA	Palm Springs	KPLM
106.1	0.25	CA	San Jacinto	KPLM-FM2
106.1	0.003	CA	Victorville	K291CM (KVTR) (sp)
106.3	0.07	CA	San Bernardino	K292GN (KJVA-LP) (sp)
106.3	6	CA	Santa Ana°	KALI-FM
106.5	0.56	CA	Lucerne Valley	KIXA
106.5	0.04	CA	Moreno Valley	K293CF (KCCA)
#106.7	5.5	CA	Pasadena°	KROQ-FM
106.9	0.007	CA	Muscoy	K295AI (KMRO) (sp)
106.9	2.7	CA	Palm Springs	KDGL-FM1
106.9	4	CA	Yucca Valley	KDGL
107.1	0.1	CA	Adelanto	KPTG-LP
#107.1	6	CA	Arcadia°	KSSE (sp)
107.3	0.25	CA	Palm Springs	K297BO (KDES-HD2)
107.3	0.1	CA	Redlands	KWRS-LP
#107.5	29.5	CA	Los Angeles°	KLVE (sp)
107.9	0.05	CA	Indio	K300CW (KLRD) (sp)
#107.9	0.53	CA	San Clemente°	KWVE-FM

San Diego Metro Area (San Diego-Carlsbad, CA MSA)

MHz	kW	Sta	City of License	Station
# 88.3	22	CA	San Diego	KSDS
88.9	0.27	CA	Temecula°	KSDW
89.1	0.33	CA	Descanso	KNSJ
89.1	0.004	CA	San Diego	K206AC (KPBS-FM)
# 89.5	25.7	CA	San Diego	KPBS-FM
89.9	0.001	CA	Lemon Grove	K210CL (KCRW)
90.7	110	CA	Los Angeles°	KPFK
91.3	0.19	CA	Borrego Springs	KKJD
91.3	0.1	CA	Pala	KPRI
91.9	0.05	CA	Borrego Springs	K220GJ (KAWZ)
# 92.1	0.47	CA	Escondido	KARJ
# 92.3	42	CA	Los Angeles°	KRRL
92.9	0.05	CA	Borrego Springs	K225BA (KCRI)
# 92.9	6	CA	Menifee°	KXFG
# 93.3	50	CA	El Cajon	KHTS-FM
93.7	0.01	CA	Rancho Bernardo	K229BO (KPFK)
93.7	0.05	CA	San Diego	KCZP-LP
# 94.1	77	CA	San Diego	KMYI
94.5	0.54	CA	Temecula°	KMYT
# 94.7	52	CA	Los Angeles°	KTWV
# 94.9	26.5	CA	San Diego	KBZT
# 95.1	50	CA	San Bernardino°	KFRG
# 95.5	63	CA	Los Angeles°	KLOS
95.7	0.004	CA	Borrego Springs	K239CE (KKJD) (sp)
# 95.7	28	CA	Carlsbad	KSSX
96.1	25	CA	Campo	KYDO
96.1	0.25	CA	Oceanside	K241CT (KCBQ)
96.1	0.011	CA	San Diego	K241CH (KSDW)
96.1	0.7	CA	Santee	KYDO-FM1
# 96.5	26.5	CA	San Diego	KYXY
96.9	0.25	CA	San Pasqual	K245AI (KSDW)
97.3	0.16	CA	Escondido	KWFN-FM4
# 97.3	50	CA	San Diego	KWFN
97.5	72	CA	Riverside°	KLYY (sp)
# 98.1	26.5	CA	San Diego	KXSN
98.5	0.25	CA	Oceanside	K253AD (KSSX-HD2)
99.3	0.25	CA	San Diego	K257FV (KLVJ)
99.5	0.05	CA	Fallbrook	KXFB-LP
99.9	29.5	CA	San Bernardino°	KOLA
100.1	0.11	CA	Julian	KKLJ
100.7	30	CA	San Diego	KFMB-FM
#101.1	51	CA	Los Angeles°	KRTH
101.1	0.05	CA	San Diego	KVIB-LP
#101.5	50	CA	San Diego	KGB-FM
102.1	30	CA	Encinitas	KLVJ
#102.9	30	CA	San Diego	KLQV (sp)
103.3	0.015	CA	San Diego	K277DG (KNSN)
103.3	0.25	CA	San Diego	K277DH (KLSD)
103.3	0.05	CA	San Diego	K277DI (KOGO)
103.3	1.25	CA	Temecula°	KTMQ
#103.7	26.5	CA	San Diego	KSON
104.1	4.1	CA	Murrieta°	KKLM
#104.3	65	CA	Los Angeles°	KBIG
#105.3	26	CA	San Diego	KIOZ

MHz	kW	Sta	City of License	Station
105.3	0.01	CA	San Diego	KIOZ-FM1
106.1	0.25	CA	Encinitas	K291CR (KPRZ)
106.1	50	CA	Palm Springs°	KPLM
#106.5	50	CA	San Diego	KLNV (sp)
106.7	0.001	CA	Fallbrook	K294CS (KSDW)
107.1	3	CA	Fallbrook	KSSD (sp)
107.9	0.004	CA	Alpine	KRLY-LP
#107.9	0.53	CA	San Clemente°	KWVE-FM

San Francisco Metro Area (San Francisco-Oakland-Hayward, CA MSA)

MHz	kW	Sta	City of License	Station
88.1	0.017	CA	El Cerrito	KECG
88.1	8.4	CA	Sacramento°	KEBR
88.1	0.007	CA	San Rafael	KSRH
# 88.5	110	CA	San Francisco	KQED-FM
88.9	0.25	CA	Oakland	K205BM (KLVS)
# 88.9	50	CA	Sacramento°	KXPR
89.1	0.1	CA	Atherton	KCEA
89.1	0.42	CA	Calistoga°	KBBF
89.3	0.46	CA	Berkeley	KPFB
89.3	0.01	CA	Concord	K207EP (KYCC)
89.3	0.145	CA	Fremont	KOHL
89.3	0.043	CA	Moss Beach	KMVS
89.3	0.1	CA	Pescadero	KPDO
89.5	0.8	CA	Moraga	KSMC
89.5	0.27	CA	San Francisco	KPOO
89.7	0.11	CA	Los Altos°	KFJC
89.9	0.8	CA	Angwin°	KOSC
89.9	0.01	CA	Bolinas	K210EH (KWMR)
89.9	0.018	CA	Hayward	KCRH
90.1	0.01	CA	Livermore	K211EZ (KYCC)
90.1	0.5	CA	Stanford°	KZSU
90.3	0.2	CA	Dublin	K212BJ (KYCC)
90.3	1	CA	San Francisco	KDFC
90.5	0.41	CA	Concord	KVHS
90.5	0.32	CA	Point Reyes Stn	KWMR
90.5	0.004	CA	Inverness Park	KWMR-FM2
90.5	1.5	CA	San Jose°	KSJS
90.7	0.5	CA	Berkeley	KALX
# 91.1	11	CA	San Mateo	KCSM
91.5	0.01	CA	Marshall	KXCF
# 91.7	1.9	CA	San Francisco	KALW
91.9	0.01	CA	Byron	K220JV (KAWZ)
92.1	3	CA	Walnut Creek	KKDV
92.1	0.253	CA	Martinez	KKDV-FM3
# 92.3	32	CA	San Jose°	KSJO
92.7	6	CA	Alameda	KREV
92.9	2.3	CA	Healdsburg°	KFGY
‡ 92.9	0.058	CA	Oakley	KLSN-LP
93.3	6	CA	San Francisco	KRZZ (sp)
93.3	0.19	CA	Pleasanton	KRZZ-FM1 (sp)
93.7	0.41	CA	Felton°	KXZM (sp)
93.7	0.099	CA	San Francisco	K229DD (KVTO) (ch)
94.1	59	CA	Berkeley	KPFA
94.1	0.045	CA	Oakley	KPFA-FM3
94.5	44	CA	Gilroy°	KBAY
# 94.9	30	CA	San Francisco	KYLD
94.9	0.186	CA	Pleasanton	KYLD-FM1
95.3	0.87	CA	Los Gatos°	KRTY
95.3	0.04	CA	San Francisco	K237GZ (KDOW)
95.3	0.49	CA	Vacaville°	KUIC
# 95.7	6.9	CA	San Francisco	KGMZ-FM
95.7	0.186	CA	Walnut Creek	KGMZ-FM2
96.1	0.1	CA	Alameda	+ KACR-LP
96.1	0.1	CA	Alameda	+ KJTZ-LP
96.1	4.7	CA	Morgan Hill°	KSQQ (por)
96.1	0.075	CA	Oakland	KEXU-LP
96.1	0.007	CA	San Francisco	KPEA-LP
96.5	3.3	CA	Martinez	KOIT-FM3
# 96.5	24	CA	San Francisco	KOIT
96.9	0.1	CA	Hayward	KEPT-LP
96.9	0.1	CA	Oakland	KGPC-LP
96.9	0.003	CA	San Francisco	KQEB-LP (ch)
96.9	0.001	CA	San Francisco	KQEA-LP (ch)
# 97.3	82	CA	San Francisco	KLLC
97.3	4.8	CA	Pleasanton	KLLC-FM2
# 97.7	4	CA	Los Altos°	KJLV
97.7	2.05	CA	Monte Rio°	KVRV
97.7	0.01	CA	San Pablo	K249DJ (KECG)
97.7	0.1	CA	Walnut Creek	KQWA-LP (ch)
# 98.1	75	CA	San Francisco	KISQ
98.1	10	CA	Pleasanton	KISQ-FM2
98.1	1	CA	Concord	KISQ-FM3
# 98.5	10	CA	San Jose°	KUFX
98.5	0.15	CA	Pleasanton	KUFX-FM3
# 98.9	6.1	CA	San Francisco	KSOL (sp)
98.9	0.15	CA	Sausalito	KSOL-FM2 (sp)
98.9	0.185	CA	Pleasanton	KSOL-FM3 (sp)
# 99.1	1.1	CA	Santa Cruz°	KSQL (sp)
99.3	0.01	CA	Los Gatos°	K257BE (KLVS)
‡ 99.3	0.05	CA	Muir Beach	KGXY-LP
99.3	0.099	CA	San Francisco	K257GE (KVMR)
99.3	6	CA	St. Helena°	KVYN
# 99.7	40	CA	San Francisco	KMVQ-FM
99.7	0.185	CA	Walnut Creek	KMVQ-FM3
100.1	6	CA	Santa Rosa°	KZST
#100.3	14.5	CA	San Jose°	KBRG (sp)
100.7	6	CA	San Rafael	KVVZ
100.9	0.008	CA	Fremont	K265CV (KLVR)
#101.3	125	CA	San Francisco	KIOI
101.3	0.9	CA	Pleasanton	KIOI-FM2
101.3	0.15	CA	Walnut Creek	KIOI-FM1
101.7	4.1	CA	Livermore	KKIQ
101.7	0.46	CA	Hayward	KKIQ-FM1
101.7	0.24	CA	San Francisco	K269FB (KSFB)
101.7	2.2	CA	Santa Rosa°	KHTH
#102.1	33	CA	San Francisco	KRBQ
102.1	1	CA	San Francisco	KRBQ-FM2
#102.5	15	CA	Salinas°	KDON-FM
102.5	0.002	CA	San Francisco	+ KSFP-LP
102.5	0.002	CA	San Francisco	+ KXSF-LP
#102.9	7.2	CA	Berkeley	KBLX-FM
102.9	0.185	CA	Pleasanton	KBLX-FM2
103.3	0.01	CA	San Francisco	K277CH (KLVS)
#103.7	6.4	CA	San Francisco	KOSF
103.7	0.185	CA	Pleasanton	KOSF-FM2
104.1	0.093	CA	San Francisco	K281BU (KLVS)
#104.5	7.1	CA	San Francisco	KNBR-FM
104.5	0.185	CA	Pleasanton	KNBR-FM3
104.9	2.3	CA	Rohnert Park°	KDHT
104.9	0.099	CA	Walnut Creek	K285FA (KSFB)
#105.3	15	CA	San Francisco	KITS
105.3	0.61	CA	Walnut Creek	KITS-FM1
105.3	0.044	CA	Pleasanton	KITS-FM2
105.3	0.33	CA	Antioch	KITS-FM4
#105.7	50	CA	Santa Clara°	KVVF (sp)
#106.1	69	CA	San Francisco	KMEL
106.1	6.5	CA	Walnut Creek	KMEL-FM2
106.5	42	CA	San Jose°	KEZR
#106.9	80	CA	San Francisco	KFRC-FM
106.9	4.8	CA	Pleasanton	KFRC-FM1
#107.3	4.1	CA	Livermore	KLVS
#107.7	8.9	CA	San Mateo	KSAN
107.7	0.185	CA	Pleasanton	KSAN-FM1

Seattle - Tacoma Metro Area (Seattle-Tacoma-Bellevue, WA MSA)

MHz	kW	Sta	City of License	Station
88.1	0.005	WA	Everett	K201EN (KWAO)
88.1	65	WA	Vashon	KWAO
# 88.5	68	WA	Tacoma	KNKX
88.9	0.002	WA	Enumclaw	K205DF (KAWZ)
88.9	0.03	WA	Mercer Island	KMIH
89.1	0.013	WA	Bremerton°	K206DM (KAWZ)
89.1	0.01	WA	Granite Falls	K206DL (KAWZ)
89.1	0.009	WA	Issaquah	K206CJ (KRQZ)
89.3	0.033	WA	Gig Harbor	K207AZ (KGHP)
# 89.3	1.25	WA	Olympia°	KAOS
89.3	0.07	WA	Sumner&Lake Tapps	K207AP (KGRG-FM)
# 89.5	8.5	WA	Seattle	KNHC
89.7	1	WA	Roy	KWFJ
# 89.9	0.23	WA	Auburn	KGRG-FM
89.9	0.06	WA	Bellevue	KASB
89.9	1.35	WA	Gig Harbor	KGHP
90.1	0.1	WA	Tacoma	KUPS
# 90.3	4.7	WA	Seattle	KEXP-FM
90.7	5.8	WA	Everett	KSER
90.9	51	WA	Tacoma	KVTI
91.1	1.15	WA	Port Townsend°	KROH
# 91.3	8	WA	Bellevue	KBCS
91.5	1.6	WA	Granite Falls	KQXI
# 91.7	4.3	WA	Tacoma	KYFQ
91.9	2.2	WA	Port Townsend°	KPTZ
92.1	0.15	WA	Tacoma	K221FJ (KNTB) (sp)
92.1	0.25	WA	West Seattle	K221FR (KNKX)

MHz	kW	Sta	City of License	Station
# 92.5	56.8	WA	Bellevue	KQMV
# 92.9	50	WA	Bellingham°	KISM
92.9	0.05	WA	Waller	KNLI-LP
# 93.3	100	WA	Seattle	KUBE
# 94.1	69	WA	Seattle	KSWD
94.5	0.099	WA	Seattle	K233BU (KTTH)
# 94.5	0.83	WA	Shelton°	KRXY
# 94.9	100	WA	Seattle	KUOW-FM
95.3	0.12	WA	Everett	K237GN (KRKO)
95.3	0.099	WA	Kent	K263BJ (KZIZ) (pun)
95.3	0.003	WA	Seattle	KDXB-LP
95.3	0.019	WA	Tacoma	KTQA-LP
95.3	0.22	WA	Tumwater°	K237FR (KYYO)
# 95.7	100	WA	Seattle	KJR-FM
96.1	37	WA	Olympia°	KXXO
# 96.5	70	WA	Seattle	KJAQ
# 96.9	11	WA	McCleary°	KYYO
96.9	0.038	WA	Seattle	KODX-LP
# 97.3	52	WA	Tacoma	KIRO-FM
97.7	69	WA	Oakville°	KOMO-FM
97.7	0.03	WA	Redmond	K249DX (KOMO-FM)
# 98.1	66	WA	Seattle	KING-FM
98.5	1.6	WA	Central Park°	KNBQ
98.5	0.25	WA	Redmond	K253CG (KARR)
# 98.9	68	WA	Seattle	KNUC
99.3	64	WA	Elma°	KDDS-FM (sp)
99.3	1	WA	Kent	KDDS-FM4 (sp)
99.3	0.5	WA	Seattle	KDDS-FM1 (sp)
99.5	0.09	WA	Everett	K258BJ (KEJI) (sp)
# 99.9	68	WA	Seattle	KISW
100.3	0.041	WA	Kent	KUCP-LP
100.3	0.23	WA	Shoreline	K262CX (KBLE)
100.3	0.01	WA	Tacoma	K262CI (KLSW)
#100.7	68	WA	Seattle	KKWF
101.1	0.12	WA	Everett	K266CJ (KKXA)
101.1	0.46	WA	Magnuson Park	KMGP-LP
101.5	100	WA	Seattle	KPLZ-FM
101.9	0.076	WA	Bellevue	KQES-LP (ch)
101.9	0.016	WA	Tacoma	KTAH-LP
101.9	0.007	WA	Vashon	KVSH-LP
102.1	0.1	WA	Auburn	K271BS (KOMO-FM)
102.1	0.007	WA	Seattle	KXSU-LP
#102.5	68	WA	Seattle	KZOK-FM
#102.9	70	WA	Centralia°	KZTM (sp)
103.3	1.4	WA	Oak Harbor°	KZNW (sp)
103.3	0.25	WA	Seattle	K277AE (KNDD)
103.3	0.25	WA	Shelton°	K277CZ (KMAS)
#103.7	68	WA	Tacoma	KHTP
#104.1	60	WA	Bellingham°	KAFE
104.1	0.06	WA	Lakewood	K281CI (KGHO-LP)
104.1	0.099	WA	Seattle	K281CQ (KGNW)
#104.3	2.35	WA	Chehalis°	KMNT
104.5	6.7	WA	Covington	KLSW
104.9	0.1	WA	Duvall	KAPY-LP
#104.9	17	WA	Eatonville	KTDD
104.9	0.015	WA	Seattle	KHUH-LP
#105.3	54	WA	Edmonds	KCMS
105.7	0.06	WA	Gig Harbor	K289BZ (KGHP)
105.7	0.009	WA	Orting	K289AK (KAWZ)
105.7	0.1	WA	Seattle	KVRU-LP
#106.1	73	WA	Tacoma	KBKS-FM
106.5	0.01	WA	Enumclaw	K293AY (KRQZ)
#106.5	63	WA	Lynden°	KWPZ
#106.9	49	WA	Bremerton°	KRWM
107.3	0.006	WA	Greenwater	K297BD (KAWZ)
‡107.3	0.1	WA	High Rock°	KWJZ-LP
107.3	0.009	WA	Seattle	KBFG-LP
#107.7	68	WA	Seattle	KNDD

St. Louis Metro Area (St. Louis, MO–IL MSA)

MHz	kW	Sta	City of License	Station
# 88.1	42	MO	St. Louis	KDHX
88.7	50	IL	Edwardsville	WSIE
# 88.9	20	MO	Ste. Genevieve°	KSEF
89.1	0.08	IL	Carlinville	W206AN (WYFG)
# 89.1	50	MO	St. Charles	KCLC
89.3	25	MO	Festus	KTBJ
89.5	0.068	MO	Cedar Hill	KNLH
89.5	0.1	MO	Ferguson	KCFV
89.5	0.3	IL	Greenville	WGRN
89.7	0.12	MO	Ballwin	KGNX
‡ 89.7	0.25	IL	East St. Louis	WCBW-FM
89.9	0.084	MO	Arnold	KGNA-FM
# 89.9	1.5	IL	Godfrey	WLCA
89.9	1	MO	Washington	KGNV
90.1	5	IL	Carlinville	WLLM-FM
90.1	0.06	IL	Granite City	W211AD (WBGL)
90.1	0.05	MO	Gray Summit	K211GB (WMSH)
90.1	0.01	MO	Overland	KRHS
90.3	0.009	MO	Clayton	KWUR
90.3	5.2	IL	Sparta°	WMSH
# 90.7	100	MO	St. Louis	KWMU
91.1	50	IL	Carlinville	WIBI
91.5	85	MO	St. Louis	KSIV-FM
91.9	0.17	IL	Carlyle	W220EN (WOLG)
91.9	0.099	MO	St. Louis	K220HT (KTBJ)
# 92.3	100	MO	St. Louis	WIL-FM
92.7	0.25	IL	Caseyville	W224DC (WRYT)
92.7	0.089	MO	Fenton	KFTN-LP
92.9	0.25	IL	Staunton	W225CX (WSMI)
92.9	0.036	MO	Webster Groves	KWRH-LP
93.1	36	MO	Perryville°	KBDZ
93.3	50	MO	Hermann°	KLUQ
# 93.7	74	MO	St. Louis	KSD
94.3	0.25	IL	Alton	W232CR (WIL-HD3)
# 94.7	100	MO	Crestwood	KSHE
95.1	0.099	MO	St. Louis	K236CS (WSDZ)
95.1	0.25	MO	Warrenton	K236CK (KWRE)
# 95.5	24.5	IL	Bethalto	WFUN-FM
95.7	0.25	MO	Crestwood	K244FO (KHOJ)
95.9	6	IL	Carlinville	WOLG
95.9	0.099	MO	St. Louis	K240ES (KSIV)
# 96.3	92	MO	St. Louis	KNOU
96.7	2.1	IL	Carlyle	WCXO
# 97.1	100	MO	Florissant	KFTK-FM
97.5	2.5	IL	Breese	WDLJ
97.5	0.025	MO	Florissant	KWAP-LP
97.7	26.5	MO	Potosi°	KHZR
# 98.1	90	MO	St. Louis	KYKY
98.5	100	MO	Farmington°	KTJJ
98.7	0.25	MO	St. Louis	K254CR (KFTK-FM)
99.1	100	MO	Clayton	KLJY
99.5	0.008	MO	St. Louis	KTGP-LP
99.7	50	IL	Hillsboro°	WXAJ
99.9	0.1	IL	Freeburg	WZJM-LP
99.9	10.5	MO	Warrenton	KFAV
100.1	2	MO	De Soto	KDJR
#100.3	17	MO	Bridgeton	KATZ-FM
100.7	6	MO	Troy	KFNS-FM
#101.1	100	IL	East St. Louis	WXOS
101.5	0.099	MO	St. Peters	K268CT (WHHL)
101.7	3.1	MO	Elsberry	KWUL
101.7	6	IL	Greenville	WGEL
101.9	0.25	MO	Bellefontaine°	K270BW (KLJY-HD2)
#102.5	100	MO	St. Louis	KEZK-FM
102.7	0.25	IL	Greenville	W274CE (WPMB)
102.9	0.25	MO	St. Charles	K275CI (KHOJ)
102.9	0.037	MO	St. Louis	KYGV-LP
102.9	0.075	MO	Washington	K275BU (WMSH)
#103.3	90	MO	St. Louis	KLOU
103.7	0.25	IL	Mascoutah	W279AQ (KATZ)
103.9	0.25	IL	Greenville	W280DR (WGEL)
#104.1	50	MO	Hazelwood	WHHL
104.5	0.099	MO	St. Louis	K283CI (KXEN)
104.5	3	MO	Washington	KSLQ-FM
#104.9	8.4	IL	Columbia	KMJM-FM
105.1	0.016	MO	Washington	K286BG (KFAV)
105.3	0.099	MO	St. Louis	K287BY (KXFN)
105.3	6	IL	Staunton	WAOX
105.3	0.25	MO	Wentzville	K287CM (KYRO)
#105.7	53.1	IL	Collinsville	KPNT
106.1	50	IL	Litchfield°	WSMI-FM
106.1	0.25	MO	St. Louis	K281CW (KTRS)
#106.5	90	IL	Granite City	WARH
106.9	0.099	MO	St. Louis	K295CQ (WGNU)
107.1	0.25	IL	Alton	W296DR (WBGZ)
107.1	0.25	MO	Washington	K296HA (KRAP)
107.3	0.25	MO	St. Louis	K297BI (KNOU-HD2)
#107.7	100	MO	St. Louis	KSLZ

Tampa - St. Petersburg Metro Area (Tampa–St. Petersburg–Clearwater, FL MSA)

MHz	kW	Sta	City of License	Station
# 88.1	100	FL	Bradenton°	WJIS

	MHz	kW	Sta	City of License	Station
#	88.5	6.65	FL	Tampa	WMNF
	88.9	60	FL	Tarpon Springs	WYFE
	89.1	54	FL	Sarasota°	WSMR
	89.3	3.9	FL	St. Catherine°	WKFA
#	89.7	69	FL	Tampa	WUSF
	90.1	0.023	FL	Brandon	WYPW-LP
#	90.1	21	FL	Inverness°	WJUF
#	90.5	100	FL	Tampa	WBVM
	90.9	0.025	FL	Tampa	W215CJ (WKES)
	91.1	100	FL	Lakeland°	WKES
#	91.5	75	FL	New Port Richey	WCIE
	91.9	25	FL	Lakeland°	WYFO
	91.9	0.03	FL	Oldsmar	W220EK (WCIE)
	92.1	0.099	FL	Tampa	W221DW (WHFS)
#	92.1	11.5	FL	Venice°	WCTQ
	92.3	0.25	FL	Brooksville	W222CI (WWJB)
#	92.5	50	FL	Safety Harbor	WYUU (sp)
	92.9	100	FL	Charlotte Harbour°	WIKX
	92.9	0.25	FL	Tampa	W246BY (WGES) (sp)
#	93.3	100	FL	Tampa	WFLZ-FM
	93.7	0.1	FL	Riverview	W229BM (WBTP)
#	94.1	100	FL	Lakeland°	WLLD
	94.5	0.25	FL	Brandon	W233CV (WHBO)
	94.5	0.25	FL	Gulfport	W233AV (WFLA)
#	94.9	100	FL	Tampa	WWRM
	95.3	0.25	FL	Pinellas Park	W237CW (WDAE)
#	95.7	100	FL	Clearwater	WBTP
	96.1	2.8	FL	Dade City	WTMP-FM (sp)
	96.3	0.024	FL	Clearwater	WPCQ-LP
	96.3	0.1	FL	St. Petersburg	WBPU-LP
	96.3	0.091	FL	Sun City Center	WSCQ-LP
‡	96.3	0.1	FL	Tampa	WURK-LP
	96.7	0.087	FL	Brandon	W244BE (WFLA)
	96.7	0.1	FL	Dade City	WZPH-LP
	96.7	0.026	FL	St. Petersburg	WMTB-LP
	96.7	0.099	FL	Tampa	W244EG (WWBA)
	96.9	100	FL	Ft. Myers°	WINK-FM
#	97.1	11.5	FL	Holiday	WSUN
	97.1	0.8	FL	St. Petersburg	WSUN-FM3
	97.1	1.3	FL	Pinellas Park	WSUN-FM4
	97.5	0.18	FL	St. Petersburg	W248CA (WTMP)
	97.5	100	FL	Winter Haven°	WPCV
#	97.9	100	FL	Clearwater	WXTB
#	98.3	27	FL	Ft. Meade°	WWRZ
	98.3	0.25	FL	Largo	W252DF (WWBA)
#	98.7	47	FL	Holmes Beach°	WPBB
	99.1	0.25	FL	Bayonet Point	W256CT (WFLA)
	99.1	0.06	FL	Seffner	WVVD-LP (sp)
	99.1	0.046	FL	St. Petersburg	WUJM-LP
#	99.5	100	FL	St. Petersburg	WQYK-FM
	100.1	0.1	FL	St. Petersburg	WUBP-LP
	100.1	0.1	FL	Sun City Center	WGGF-LP
	100.1	0.08	FL	Town 'n' Country	WVVF-LP (sp)
	100.3	0.25	FL	Bayonet Point	W262CP (WTBN)
#	100.7	100	FL	Tampa	WMTX
	101.1	0.235	FL	Tampa	W266CW (WTIS) (sp)
#	101.5	100	FL	St. Petersburg	WPOI
	101.9	0.1	FL	Brandon	WSDX-LP
	101.9	0.25	FL	New Port Richey	W270DH (WPSO)
	101.9	0.1	FL	Ruskin	WPHX-LP
	101.9	0.235	FL	Tampa	W270DU (WMGG) (sp)
	102.1	0.011	FL	Land O' Lakes	WWFH-LP
	102.1	0.015	FL	St. Petersburg	WPBW-LP
	102.3	0.25	FL	Dade City	W272EH (WDCF)
	102.5	0.25	FL	New Port Richey	W273CP (WSUN)
#	102.5	100	FL	Sarasota°	WHPT
	102.9	0.25	FL	Tampa	W275AZ (WFUS)
	103.1	0.25	FL	New Port Richey	W276CX (WRBQ-FM)
#	103.5	68	FL	Gulfport	WFUS
	103.9	0.065	FL	Largo	W280FD (WXYB) (gr)
	103.9	0.25	FL	Spring Hill	W280DK (WWJB)
	103.9	0.25	FL	Tampa	W280DW (WUSF)
	104.1	0.1	FL	Palm Harbor	WZIG-LP
	104.3	25	FL	Sarasota°	WKZM
	104.3	0.25	FL	Tampa	W282CI (WLCC) (sp)
#	104.7	100	FL	Tampa	WRBQ-FM
	105.1	0.25	FL	Sarasota°	W286CQ (WCTQ)
	105.1	0.048	FL	Tampa	WWZT-LP
#	105.5	33	FL	New Port Richey	WDUV
	105.9	0.25	FL	West Tampa	W290BJ (WFLA)
	106.1	0.25	FL	Clearwater	W291CW (WTAN)
	106.3	25	FL	Spring Hill	WGHR
#	106.5	13	FL	Sarasota°	WRUB (sp)
	106.7	0.25	FL	Tampa	W294CR (WQBN) (sp)
#	106.7	100	FL	Tavares°	WXXL
	106.9	0.25	FL	St. Petersburg	W295CF (WYUU-HD2) (sp)
‡	106.9	0.05	FL	Tampa	WQTA-LP
#	107.3	100	FL	St. Petersburg	WXGL
	107.7	0.25	FL	Tampa	W299CI (WAMA) (sp)
#	107.9	47	FL	Coral Cove°	WSRZ-FM
	107.9	0.1	FL	Spring Hill	WPHC-LP

Washington (DC) Metro Area (Washington-Arlington-Alexandria, DC-VA-MD-WV MSA)

	MHz	kW	Sta	City of License	Station
#	88.1	15.5	MD	Baltimore°	WYPR
	88.1	0.01	MD	College Park	WMUC-FM
	88.1	1	MD	Frederick	WYPF
#	88.5	50	DC	Washington	WAMU
	88.7	0.027	VA	Fredericksburg	W204CH (WYFJ)
#	88.9	12.5	MD	Baltimore°	WEAA
	88.9	0.2	MD	Frederick	W205BL (WETA)
	89.3	50	DC	Washington	WPFW
#	89.7	7.4	MD	Towson°	WTMD
	89.7	0.008	VA	Woodbridge	W209BY (WRVL)
	89.9	41	VA	Culpeper	WPIR
#	90.1	24	DC	Washington	WCSP-FM
	90.5	47	VA	Fredericksburg	WPER
#	90.9	75	DC	Washington	WETA
	91.1	0.006	MD	Frederick	W216CM (WCRH)
	91.3	13.5	VA	Culpeper	WARN
#	91.5	50	MD	Baltimore°	WBJC
	91.5	0.019	VA	Fredericksburg	W218CV (KAWZ)
#	91.9	23.5	MD	Takoma Park	WGTS
#	92.3	37	MD	Baltimore°	WERQ-FM
	92.5	22	VA	Winchester°	WINC-FM
	92.7	2.15	MD	Prince Frederick	WDCJ
#	93.1	16	MD	Baltimore°	WPOC
#	93.3	50	VA	Fredericksburg	WFLS-FM
	93.5	0.15	MD	Frederick	W228AM (WWEG)
	93.5	0.13	MD	Silver Spring	W228DI (WBQH) (sp)
#	93.9	24.5	DC	Washington	WKYS
	94.1	0.01	VA	Fredericksburg	W231BJ (WLMP-LP)
	94.3	2	VA	Buckland	WLZV
	94.3	0.16	MD	Frederick	W232WG (WWFD)
	94.3	0.02	MD	Takoma Park	WOWD-LP
#	94.7	20.5	MD	Bethesda	WIAD
	94.9	0.08	VA	Fredericksburg	W235BT (WQIQ)
#	95.1	50	MD	Baltimore°	WRBS-FM
	95.3	0.178	VA	Culpeper	W237CA (WCVA)
#	95.5	50	MD	Morningside	WPGC-FM
#	95.9	3	MD	Glen Burnie°	WWIN-FM
	95.9	0.25	DC	Washington	W240DJ (WOL)
#	96.3	16.5	DC	Washington	WHUR-FM
	96.5	0.25	VA	Fredericksburg	W243BS (WFLS-HD2)
	96.7	0.021	VA	Arlington°	WERA-LP
	96.7	12.5	MD	Easton°	WCEI-FM
	96.7	0.018	MD	Rockville	WQER-LP
#	97.1	17.5	DC	Washington	WASH
	97.5	0.25	VA	Alexandria	W248BN (WTNT) (sp)
	97.5	0.25	MD	Baltimore°	W248AO (WVWB)
	97.5	11.4	WV	Martinsburg°	WLTF
	97.7	0.05	VA	Reston	W249DX (WKDV) (sp)
#	97.9	13	MD	Baltimore°	WIYY
	98.1	0.25	VA	Manassas	W251CH (WURA)
	98.3	3	MD	Mechanicsville°	WSMD-FM
	98.3	0.15	VA	Reston	W252DC (WAMU)
#	98.7	50	DC	Washington	WMZQ-FM
	99.1	45	MD	Bowie	WDCH-FM
#	99.5	22	DC	Washington	WIHT
	99.9	7.6	MD	Frederick	WFRE
#	100.3	50	DC	Washington	WBIG-FM
	100.7	0.1	VA	Falls Church	W264DB (WFAX)
	100.7	25	MD	Westminster°	WZBA
#	101.1	22.5	DC	Washington	WWDC
	101.5	50	VA	Fredericksburg	WBQB
#	101.9	13.5	MD	Baltimore°	WLIF
	102.1	0.082	MD	Prince Frederick	WMJS-LP
#	102.3	2.9	MD	Bethesda	WMMJ
#	102.5	32	VA	Winchester°	WUSQ-FM
#	102.7	50	MD	Baltimore°	WQSR
	102.7	0.014	VA	Fredericksburg	WLMP-LP

MHz	kW	Sta	City of License	Station
102.9	4	MD	California°	WKIK-FM
102.9	0.05	VA	Reston	W275BO (WWWT-FM-HD2)[1]
#103.1	6	VA	Culpeper	WJMA
103.1	0.1	VA	Falls Church	W276DT (WMET)
103.1	6	MD	Grasonville°	WRNR-FM
103.1	1	MD	Middletown	WAFY
#103.5	44	DC	Washington	WTOP-FM
#103.9	0.35	MD	Braddock Heights	WTLP
#104.1	20	MD	Waldorf	WPRS-FM
#104.3	13	MD	Baltimore°	WZFT
104.7	8.3	MD	Hagerstown°	WAYZ
104.7	0.099	DC	Washington	W284CQ (WWDC-HD2)
#105.1	33	VA	Arlington°	WAVA-FM
105.5	0.099	VA	Reston	W288BS (WKYS-HD3) (rus)
#105.7	50	MD	Catonsville°	WJZ-FM
105.9	28	VA	Woodbridge	WMAL-FM
106.3	0.1	MD	Frederick	W292FR (WARK)
106.3	0.075	VA	Fredericksburg	W292EF (WJYJ-FM)
#106.5	10.3	MD	Baltimore°	WWMX
#106.7	20	VA	Manassas	WJFK-FM
#106.9	15.5	MD	Myersville	WWEG
#107.3	19.5	DC	Washington	WLVW
#107.7	29	VA	Manassas	WWWT-FM
#107.9	49	MD	College Park	WLZL (sp)

#) HD Radio (hybrid trs) ‡) Temporarily inactive at time of publication (FCC authorized "Silent STA" status) +) Time-shared allocation (shared tx). Languages other than English: (as) Asian languages, (ch) Chinese, (gr) Greek, (ha) Haitian, (hm) Hmong, (kor) Korean, (pol) Polish, (por) Portuguese, (pun) Punjabi, (rus) Russian, (som) Somali, (sp) Spanish, viet) Vietnamese, [1]) Hindi & other Indian languages.

URUGUAY

L.T: UTC -3h — **Pop:** 3.5 million — **Pr.L:** Spanish — **E.C:** 230V/50Hz — **ITU:** URG — **Int. dialling code:** +598

MINISTERIO DE EDUCACION Y CULTURA Servicios de Comunicación Audiovisual (SECAN)

✉ Sarandí 430, 11000 Montevideo ☎ 2916-1933 **E:** direcciongeneral@mu.uy **W:** mu.com.uy
L.P: Dir Ernesto Kreimerman

UNIDAD REGULADORA DE SERVICIOS DE COMUNICACIONES (URSEC)

✉ Avda. Uruguay 988, 11100 Montevideo ☎ 2902-8082 **E:** info@ursec.gub.uy **W:** gub.uy/unidad-reguladora-servicios-comunicaciones/ **L.P:** Pres: Mercedes Aramendía Falco

ASOCIACIÓN NACIONAL DE BROADCASTERS URUGUAYOS (ANDEBU)

✉ Carlos Quijano 1264, 11100 Montevideo ☎ 2902-1525 **E:** andebu@andebu.org **W:** andebu.org **L.P:** Pres: Eduaredo Ferrari

COOPERATIVA DE RADIO EMISORAS DEL INTERIOR (CORI)

✉ Av. 18 de Julio 948, 6° Piso, Esc 603, 11000 Montevideo ☎ 2902-9047
W: cori.com.uy **E:** coriamfm@adinet.com.uy

ASOCIACIÓN DE RADIOS INTERIOR (RAMI)

✉ Nueva York 1618, 11800 Montevideo ☎ 2924-6722 / 29241310 📠2924-7279 **E:** rami@adinet.com.uy

RED ORO

✉ Paz Idependencia 759, 8° Piso, Esc.852, 11100 Montevideo ☎ 2902-0111 **W:** radiosredoro.com.uy **E:** contacto@radiosredoro.com.uy

ASOCIACION MUNDIAL DE RADIOS COMUNITARIAS (AMARC URUGUAY)

✉ Germán Barbato 1480, 11000, Montevideo ☎ 2902-1236 **W:** amarcuruguay.org **E:** mesanacional@amarcuruguay.org

RADIODIFUSIÓN NACIONAL DEL URUGUAY (RNU) (Gov)

✉ Sarandí 430, 11000 Montevideo ☎ 2 1768 2 915 5378 **W:** rnu.com.uy **E:** web@rnu.uy **L.P.:** Dir:. Fabiana Conti

MW	Call	kHz	kW	Station, location, h. of tr.
CO01)	CW1	550	25	R. Colonia, Colonia: 24h
MO01)	CX58	580	2	R. Clarín, Montevideo: 24h
MO02)	CX4	610	50	R. Rural, Montevideo: 24h
MO03a)	CX6	650	25	R. Clásica, (Rdif. Nal. del Uruguay, Montevideo: 24h
RN01)	CW68	680	1/0.7	R. Young, Young: 09-03
MO04)	CX8	690	25	R. Sarandí, Montevideo: 24h
MO05)	CX10	730	5/2.5	R. Continente, Montevideo (IPDA)
SA01)	CW27	740	5/1.1	R. Tabaré, Salto: 0900-0300
MO06)	CX12	770	100	R. Oriental, Montevideo: 24h
MO07)	CX14	810	50	R. El Espectador, Montevideo: 24h
MO08)	CX16	850	50	R. Carve, Montevideo: 0825-0300
MO09)	CX18	890	50/10	R. Sport 890, Montevideo: 24h
AR01)	CW17	900	3/1	R. Frontera, Artigas: 0900-0300
MO10)	CX20	930	50	R. Monte Carlo, Montevideo: 24h
DU01)	CW96	960	2/1	R. Yi, Durazno: 1000-0200
MO11)	CX22	970	20/3	R. Universal, Montevideo: 0900-0400
MO12)	CX24	1010	25	R. 1010 AM, Montevideo: 0900-0400
SA03)	CW102E	1020	0.1	R. Libertadores, Salto: 0900-0300
MO03b)	CX26	1050	50	R. Uruguay, Montevideo: 24h
MO14)	CX28	1090	15	R. R.Maria, Montevideo: 24h
TA01)	CX111	1110	3	R. Paso de los Toros, Paso de los Toros: 1000-0300
SA04)	CW31	1120	10	R. Salto, Salto: 1000-0300
MO15)	CX30	1130	20	R. Nacional, Montevideo: 24h
TT05)	CW116	1160	2/1	R. Agraria , Cerro Chato: 0830-0100
MO16)	CX32	1170	10	Radiomundo, Montevideo: 1100-0300
AR02)	CX118	1180	10	R. LV de Artigas, Artigas: 0900-0300
FL01)	CW33	1200	1	La Nueva R., Florida: 24h
SO01)	CX121	1210	2/1	Difusora Soriano, Mercedes: 24h
MA01)	CV121	1210	2/1	Em. RBC, Piriápolis: 24h
TT02)	CW121	1210	0.25	R. El Libertador, Vergara: 0830-0300
RI05)	CX122	1220	1/0.5	R. Reconquista, Rivera: 0945-0300
PA01)	CW35	1240	5	R. Paysandú, Paysandú: 0900-0400
MO17)	CX36	1250	3	R. Centenario, Montevideo: 24h
AR03)	CW125	1250	5	R. Bella Unión, Bella Unión: 0900-0300
RO01)	CW37	1260	3	Dif. Rochense, Rocha: 24h
AR04)	CV127	1270	4/2	R. Cuareim, Artigas: 0900-0200
TA02)	CW64	1280	3/1	R. Tacuarembó, Tacuarembó: 0750-0200 Sun: 1000-0200
MO03c)	CX38	1290	50	Em del Sur, Montevideo: 1000-0300
PA02)	CW39	1320	1	R. LV de Paysandú, Paysandú: 0900-0400
RO02)	CW132	1320	1/0.5	R. Fortaleza, Rocha: 0900-0300
MO19)	CX40	1330	5	R. Fénix, Montevideo: 0900-0300
CL01)	CW53	1340	10/1	LV de Melo, Melo: 0800-0300
CL02)	CW136	1360	1	R. Río Branco, Río Branco: 0900-0300
SJ01)	CW41	1360	2.5	R. 41, San José de Mayo: 0900-0300
MO20)	CX42	1370	5.3/2.5	Em. Ciudad,Montevideo: 1100-0300
RI01)	CV137A	1370	0.5	R. Real, Minas de Corrales: 0930-0130
RN02)	CW137	1370	1/0.5	R. San Javier, San Javier: 0900-0030
TT03)	CW45	±1390	5	Dif. Treinta y Tres, Treinta y Tres: 0800-0300
TA03)	CX140	1400	25	R. Zorrilla de San Martín, Tacuarembó: 0900-0300
MO21)	CX44	1410	10/5	AM Libre "La Catorce 10", Montevideo: 24h
SA05)	CW141	1410	2/0.5	R. Turistica, Salto: 24h
LA01)	CW43	1420	5	R. Lavalleja, Minas: 00830-0300
PA03)	CX142	1420	1/0.5	R. Felicidad, Paysandú: 24h
DU02)	CW25	1430	20/5	R. Durazno, Durazno: 24h
RI02)	CX144	1440	3/0.5	R. Rivera, Rivera: 0830-0300)
MO22)	CX46	1450	10/5	R. América, Montevideo: (0900-0630)
SA06)	CW145	1450	1/0.25	R. Arapey, Salto: 24h
CO02)	CX146	1460	1	R. Carmelo, Carmelo: 0900-030
LA02)	CV146	1460	0.25	R. José Batlle y Ordoñez, José Batlle y Ordoñez: 1000-0200
CA01)	CX147	1470	2	R. Cristal del Uruguay,Las Piedras: 24h
CL03)	CW147	1470	1	R. Maria, Melo: 0830-0330
RO04)	CW148	1480	3	R. Universo, Castillos: 24h
RI03)	CW43B	1480	5/1.5	R. Internacional, Rivera: 0800-0300
RN03)	CX148	1480	1	Difusora Rio Negro, Young: 0900-0300
AR05)	CV149	1490	1/0.25	R. del Centro, Baltasar Brum: 1100-0300
CO03)	CX149	1490	5	R. del Oeste, Nueva Helvecia: 0930-0300
RN04)	CX151	1510	1/0.5	R. Rincón, Fray Bentos: 1000-0300
MA02)	CW57	1510	2/0.5	R. San Carlos, San Carlos: 0830-0300
TA04)	CW151	1510	0.5	R. Ibirapitá, San Gregorio de Polanco: 1000-0200

MW	Call	kHz	kW	Station, location, h. of tr.
CL04)	CX152	1520	2	R. Acuarela, Melo: 0900-0300
PA05)	CV152	1520	1/0.5	R. Paz, "La Nueva R.", Guichón: 1000-2300
CO04)	CW153	1530	0.25	Em. Cono Sur, Nueva Palmira: 0925-0100
PA04)	CW154	1540	0.1	R. Charrúa, Paysandú: 1000-0300
TT04)	CX154	1540	1	R. Patria, Treinta y Tres: 0800-0300
SO02)	CV154	1540	1	R. Centro, Cardona: 0900-0200
SO04)	CV155	1550	0.25	R. Agraciada, Mercedes: 24h
DU03)	CW155	1550	2/0.5	R. Sarandí del Yí, Sarandí del Yí: 1030-0130
FO01)	CX156	1560	2/0.5	Dif. Americana, Trinidad: 0930-0130
RI04)	CV156	1560	1	R. Vichadero: 1000-0200
CA02)	CX157	1570	2/0.5	R. Canelones: 0930-0230
AR06)	CW157A	1570	0..25	Em. Celeste, Tomás Gomensoro: 0830-0100
LA03)	CW54	1580	2/0.5	Em. del Este, Minas: 0800-0200
SO05)	CW158	1580	1/0.5	R. San Salvador, Dolores: 24h
RO05)	CW159	1590	1/0.25	R. Nueva R. Lascano, Lascano
CO06)	CX159	1590	1	R. Real, Colonia: 0930-0300
CA03)	CV160	1600	1	R. Continental, Pando: 0915-0300
RN05)	CX160	1600	1	R. Litoral, Fray Bentos: 0900-0300

‡ = inactive, ± = varying freq.

Addresses & other information:

AR00) ARTIGAS

AR01) Av Lecueder 803, 55000 Artigas ☎4772-2433 **W:** emisorasfrontera.uy **E:** emisorasfronter@hotmail.com - **FM:** 88.3MHz "Frontera FM" – **AR02)** Av Lecueder 483, 55000 Artigas ☎4772-2447 📠4772-4744 **W:** radioartigas.com **E:** radioartigas118@gmail.com - **FM:** 90.7MHz "Amatista FM" – **AR03)** Enrique Ferreira 1550, 55100 Bella Unión ☎4779 2058 **W:** radiobellaunion.com **E:** radiobellaunion@gmail.com or informativoradiobu@gmail.com - **FM:** 105.5MHz "Stereo Norte FM" – **AR04)** Av Lecueder 167, 55000 Artigas ☎4772 2867 **W:** radiocuareim.com **E:** racua@adinet.com.uy – **AR05)** Batlle y Ordóñez y 25 de Agosto, 55001 Baltasar Brum, ☎4776-2109 **W:** radiodelcentro.com **E:** radiodelcentro1490@gmail.com – **AR06)** 18 de Julio y 19 de Abril, Vivienda 8 55002 Tomás Gomensoro ☎4777 2157
E: radioceleste@hotmail.com

CA00) CANELONES

CA01) Treinta y Tres – 590 – y avenida José Gervasio Artigas 781, 90200 Las Piedras ☎2364-4775 **W:** radiocristaldeluruguay.com.uy **E:** cx147cristal@gmail.com – **CA02)** Gral. Fructuoso Rivera 216, 90000 Canelones ☎4332 1570 **W:** radiocanelones.com.uy **E:** 1570amsrl@gmail.com – **CA03)** Av Artigas 977, 91000 Pando ☎2292-2512 **W:** radiocontinental.com.uy **E:** administracion@radiocontinental.com.uy

CL00) CERRO LARGO

CL01) Remigio Castellanos 721, 37000 Melo ☎4642 2397 **W:** lavozdemelo.com **E:** lavozdemelo@gmail.com – **CL02)** Virrey Arredondo 986, 37100 Rio Branco ☎4675 2009 **W:** radioriobranco.com.uy **E:** am1360@adinet.com.uy – **CL03)** Avenida Brasil 829, 37000 Melo ☎4642-2386 **W:** radiomaria.org.uy **E:** coordinator.ury@radiomaria.org – **CL04)** José Pedro Varela 750, 37000 Melo ☎4642-2051 **W:** radioacuarela.blogspot.com **E:** acuarelaradio@yahoo.com.ar

CO00) COLONIA

CO01) Rivadavia 383, 70000 Colonia del Sacramento ☎4522-2006 **W:** radiocolonia.com **E:** publicidad@radiocolonia.com - **FM:** 93.5MHz "FM Mágica" – **CO02)** 19 de Abril 444, 70100 Carmelo ☎4542 7232 **W:** radiocarmelo.com **E:** radiocarmelo@adinet.com.uy – **CO03)** Calle Berna 1375, 70201 Nueva Helvecia ☎4554-4409 **W:** ro.com.uy **E:**1490@ro.com.uy - **FM:** 90.7MHz "Reflejos" – **CO04)** Del Medio s/n y Ruta Nacional N° 12,, 70101 Nueva Palmira ☎4544-6053 **W:**emisoraconosurpalmira.blogspot.com **E:** emisoraconosur@gmail.com / emisoraconosurventas@gmail.com – **CO06)** Av Gral. Flores 472, 70000 Colonia del Sacramento ☎4522-2030 **E:** radioreal@adinet.com.uy

DU00) DURAZNO

DU01) Brigadier General Fructuoso Rivera 501, 97000 Durazno ☎4362 2701 **W:** am960.com.uy **E:** radioyi960@gmail.com - **FM:** 95.1MHz R.City – **DU02)** Juan Zorilla de San Martin 875, 97000 Durazno ☎4362-2015 📠4362-2058 **W:** infodurazno.com **E:** director@radiodurazno.com – **DU03)** Sarandí 428, 97100 Sarandí del Yí ☎43679155 **W:**radiosarandidelyi.com **E:** norasan155@GMAIL.COM - **FM:** 89.5MHz "Scala FM"

FL00) FLORIDA

FL01) Antonio Maria Fernández 800, 94000 Florida ☎4352 2026 **W:** cw33florida.com.uy **E:** cw33@adinet.com.uy - **FM:** 88.7MHz "Claridad" –**FO00) FLORES**

FO01) 25 de Agosto 724, 85000 Trinidad ☎4364-2229 **W:** agenda.org.uy/difusoraamericana **E:** am1560@hotmail.com

LA00) LAVALLEJA

LA01) José E Rodó 530, 30000 Minas ☎4442-2304 – **W:** radiolavalleja.com **E:** cw43radiolavalleja@gmail.com – **LA02)** Camino Nacional s/n y Treinta y Tres, Mza 2, Padrón 25U 30200 José Batlle y Ordoñez ☎4469 2132 **E:** cerronicoperez@gmail.com - **FM:** 96.5 MHz – **LA03)** Treinta y Tres 632, 30000 Minas ☎4442 3092 **W:** cw54emisoradeleste.com **E:** federalfm@federalfm.com.uy - **FM:** 107.3MHz "Federal FM"

MA00) MALDONADO

MA01) Chacabuco y Moreno, PA, 20200 Piriápolis ☎4432 2771 **W:** radiorbc.com **E:** info@radirbc.com – **MA02)** Calle Sarandí 775, 20400 San Carlos ☎4266-9162 **E:** radiosancarlos@adinet.com.uy

MO00) MONTEVIDEO

MO01) Av. 18 de Julio 1516, 9° Piso, Apto. 7. 7, 11200 Montevideo ☎2400 6877 📠2400 5841 **W:** radioclarin.com **E:** radioclarin@vera.com.uy – **MO02)** Av. Joaquín Suarez 3409, 11700 Montevideo ☎2336-0610 **W:** radiorural.uy **E:** radiorural610@gmail.com – **MO03)** Sarandí 430, 1° piso, 11000 Montevideo ☎2902 5640 **W:** radionacional.com.uy **E:** info@radionacional.com.uy– Rpt. to Cas, 7011, 11000 Montevideo. **E:** lmoreira@montevideo.com.uy – **MO03a)** R. Clásica **W:** radioclasica.uy **E:** web@rnu.uy – **FM:** 97.1 MHz – **MO03b)** R. Uruguay **W:** radiouruguay.uy **E:** web@rnu.uy – **MO03c)** Em. Del Sur **W:** emisoradelsur.com.uy **E:** emisoradelsur947@gmail.com – **MO04)** Enriqueta Compte y Riquet 1250, 11800 Montevideo ☎2208 2612 📠2203 6906 **W:** sarandi690.com.uy **E:** contacto@sarandi.com.uy – **MO05)** Germán Barbato 1472, 11100 Montevideo ☎2902 4039 📠2902 4038 **E:** cx10.730.continente@adinet.com.uy – **MO06)** Cerrito 475, 11000 Montevideo ☎2916-1130 **W:** oriental770.com **E:** programacion@oriental.com.uy – **MO07)** Dr. Pablo de Mari 1015, 11200 Montevideo ☎ 2418-0151 **W:** espectador.com **E:** digital@espectador.com.uy – **MO08)** Mercedes 973, 11100 Montevideo ☎2902 6162 **W:** carve850.com.uy **E:** matiasreyesroque@gmail.com (Matías Reyes Roque, stn mgr) prensacarve@gmail.com – **MO09)** Enriqueta Compte y Riquet 1250, 11800 Montevideo ☎2208-2612 **W:** sport890.com.uy **E:** sport890@sport890.com.uy – Rpt. to: fgopar34@gmail.com – **MO10)** Av 18 de Julio 1224, 1° piso, 11100 Montevideo ☎2901 4433 **W:** radiomontecarlo.com.uy **E:** portal@radiomontecarlo.com.uy – **MO11)** Av 18 de Julio 1220, 3° piso, 11100 Montevideo ☎2902 6022 **W:** 970universal.com **E:** administracion@970universal.com / cx22@adinet.com.uy – **MO12)** Mercedes 973, 11100 Montevideo ☎2903-0146 **W:** radio1010.com.uy **W:** radio1010.uy **E:** contacto@sadrep.com.uy – **MO14)** Av. 18 de Julio 4° Piso, 11800 Montevideo ☎2903 0094**W:** radiomaria.org.uy **E:** info.ury@radiomaria.org – **MO15)** Palacio Salvo, Plaza Independencia 846, EP, 11100 Montevideo ☎2902 5640 **W:** radionacional.com.uy **E:** administracion@radionacional.com.uy – **MO16)** Rambla Armenia 1647, Apto. 13, 11300 Montevideo ☎2628 9240**W:** enperspectiva.net/radiomundo-1170-am – **MO17)** Av 18 de Julio 1357, Apto. 202, 11200 Montevideo ☎2903 0302 **W:** radio36.com.uy **E:** radio36@gmail.com – **MO19)** Canelones 1969, 11200 Montevideo ☎2408-3292 **W:** cx40radiofenix.com **E:** radiofenix@adinet.com.uy – **MO20)** Arenal Grande 2093, 11800 Montevideo ☎2929 1370 📠2924 0700 **W:** emisoraciudaddemontevideo.com.uy **E:** CX42@emisoraciudaddemontevideo.com.uy – **MO21)** Av. General José Garibaldi 2579, 11600 Montevideo ☎2487-3565 **W:** lacatorce10.com.uy **E:** gerencia@lacatorce10.com – **FM:**89.7 FM Libre – **MO22)** Emilio Frugoni 1312, 11200 Montevideo ☎2400-2121 **W:** cx46.com.uy **E:** correo@cx46.com

PA00) PAYSANDÚ

PA01) Av España 1629, 60000 Paysandú ☎4722 3980 **W:** radiopaysandu.com.uy **E:** am1240@adinet.com.uy or correo@radiocw39.com – **PA02)** 18 de Julio 614, 60000 Paysandú ☎4722 2267 **W:** paysandu.com/radiocw39/ **E:** cw39lavozdepaysandu@gmail.com – **PA03)** 33 Orientales 946,1° piso, Apt 1, 60000 Paysandú ☎4722 4020 **W:** radiofelicidad.com.uy **E:** radiofelicidad@radiofelicidad.com.uy – **PA04)** Rincon 1236, 60000 Paysandú ☎4722-1817 **W:** radiocharrua.com **E:** contacto@radiocharrua.com – **PA05)** Luis Alberto de Herrera 346, 60008 Guichón ☎4742-2053 **W:** pazlanuevaradio.online **E:** pazam1520@gmail.com

RI00) RIVERA

RI01) Av Dr. Davison s/n e/18 de Julio y DR. Ross, 40002 Rivera ☎44622-3807 **W:** radioreal.com.uy **E:** eduardo.andina@gmail.com — **RI02)** Dr Gabriel Anollés 441, 40000 Rivera ☎4622-3230 **W:** radiorivera.com.uy **E:** radiorivera@gmail.com –**RI03)** Av Sarandí 792, 40000 Rivera ☎4622-3259 **W:** internacionalamyfm.com **E:** internac@gmail.com - **FM:** 94.5MHz – **RI04)** Blvd. Gral. José Gervasio Artigas 160, 40003 Vichadero ☎4654 2018 **W:** radiovichadero.com **E:**

radiovichadero@gmail.com – **FM:** 102.9 MHz – FM de la Cumbre – **RI05)** Francisco Acuña de Figueroa 887, 40000 Rivera ☎🖷4622-5893 **W:** multimediadelnorte.com/reconquista **E:** cx122reconquista@gmail.com - **FM: FM:** 90.7 MHz – Acacia FM

RN00) RIO NEGRO

RN01) Rincón 1689, 65100 Young ☎4567-2071 **W:** radioyoung.net **E:** am680@adinet.com.uy - **FM:** 93.3MHz FM Luna – **RN02)** 27 de Julio s/n y Basilio Lubkov y Alberto Espalter, 65001 San Javier ☎4569 2005 **W:** 1370am.com.uy **E:** radiosanjavier@hotmail.com – **RN03)** Rincón 1811, 65100 Young ☎4567-3125 **E:** imagenfm@adinet.com.uy - **FM:** 89.1MHz "Imágen FM" – **RN04)** 25 de Mayo 3164, 65000 Fray Bentos ☎4562-2022 **W:** radiorincon.com.uy **E:** contacto@radiorincon.com.uy - **FM:** 107.7 MHz Rincón FM – **RN05)** 18 de Julio 1260, 65000 Fray Bentos ☎4562-3100 **E:** controlradiolitoral@gmail.com

RO00) ROCHA

RO01) José Pedro Ramírez 127, 27000 Rocha ☎4472 2250 **W:** difusorarochense.com.uy **E:** difusorarochense@gmail.com - **FM:** 91.5MHz & 106.3MHz – **RO02)** Zorrilla de San Martin 200, 27000 Rocha ☎4472 1198 **W:** radiofortaleza.uy **E:** fortaleza1320@gmail.com – **RO04)** 18 de Julio 1322, 27200 Castillos ☎44758054 **W:** radiouniverso.uy **E:** am1480@vera.com.uy or grupouniverso@vera.com.uy – **RO05)** Piedras – ex Dr. Nicolás Corbo 1152, 27300 Lascano ☎4456-8380 **W:** nuevaradiolascano.com **E:** lanuevaradio@adinet.com.uy ☎

SA00) SALTO

SA01) Lavalleja 22 Bis, 50000 Salto ☎4734 0298 **W:** radiotabare.com.uy **E:** info@radiotabare.com.uy or amtabare@adinet.com.uy – **SA03)** Uruguay 1416, 50000 Salto ☎4732-6272 **W:** amlibertadores.com **E:** amlibertadores@adinet.com.uy – **FM:** 101.5MHz "Siglo XXI" – **SA04)** Brasil 715, 50000 Salto ☎4733 2615 **W:** agenda.org.uy/radiosalto **E:** cw31salt@adinet.com.uy or radiosalto@adinet.com.uy - **FM:** 88.3MHz "Emisora del Lago" – **SA05)** Grito de Asencio 1014, 50000 Salto ☎4733-7290 **W:** 1410salto.com **E:** turisticaradio1410@gmail.com – **SA06)** Treinta y Tres Orientales 73, 50000 Salto ☎4732-6264 **W:** 10minutos.com.uy **E:** amarapey@adinet.com.uy - **FM:** 90.9 MHz FM Impacto **SJ00) SAN JOSÉ**

SJ01) Dr. Evaristo Ciganda 511, 80000 San José de Mayo ☎4342-6444 **W:** radio41.com.uy **E:** 1360am@radio41.com.uy

SO00) SORIANO

SO01) De Castro y Careaga 568, 75000 Mercedes ☎453-2948 **W:** difusorasoriano.com.uy **E:** difusorasoriano@adinet.com.uy – **FM:** 89.3 MHz **SO02)** Calle Joaquín Suárez y Lavalleja, 75200 Cardona ☎4536-9315 **W:** radiocentrocardona.blogspot.com **E:** radiocentro@adinet.com.uy – **SO04)** Cristobál Colón 319 Planta Alta, 75000 Mercedes ☎4532-8536 **W:** radioagraciada.agenda.org.uy **E:** radioagraciada1550@hotmail.com - **FM:** 100.3MHz "Galicia" – **SO05)** Av Grito de Asencio 1695, 75100 Dolores ☎4534 2110 **W:** radiosansalvador.com.uy **E:** administracion@radiosansalvador.com.uy - **FM:** 89.7MHz "Skorpio"

TA00) TACUAREMBÓ

TA01) 18 de Julio 743, 45100 Paso de los Toros ☎4664 2333 **W:** am.pasodelostoros.com **E:** radiopasodelostoros@pasodelostoros.com - **FM:** 91.9 MHz "Toros FM" – **TA02)** Ituzaingó 246, 45000 Tacuarembó ☎4632-2898 **W:** emisorastacuarembo.com - **FM:** 92.5MHz – Armonia FM – **TA03)** 18 de Julio 302/310, 45000 Tacuarembó ☎46322605 – **W:** radiozorrilla.com **E:** zsm@adinet.com - **FM:** 88.9MHz "Em de la Música" – **TA04)** Arturo J. Mollo 141, 45200 San Gregorio de Polanco ☎4639-4536 **W:** radioibirapita1510am.blogspot.com **E:**radioibirapita1510am@yahoo.com

TT00) TREINTA Y TRES

TT02) Cnl. Marcelo Barreto s/n, 33002 Vergara ☎4458 2917 **W:** ellibertador.com.uy **E:** ellibertador@adinet.com.uy – **TT03)** Pablo Zufriátegui 1076, 33000 Treinta y Tres ☎4452-2452 **W:** difusoratreintaytres.com.uy **E:** cw45@adinet.com.uy – **TT04)** Atanasio Sierra 1092, 33000 Treinta y Tres ☎4452-3532 **W:** radiopatria.com.uy **E:** radiopatria@gmail.com – **TT05)** Juan Muñoz (RN-7) s/n, 30204 Cerro Chato ☎4466 2200 **W:** radioagrariadeluruguay.com **E:** radioagraria@hotmail.com Rpts. to: cx2ua@hotmail.com

FM in Montevideo (MHz): all stns 10-100kW. 89.1 Uni-Radio (LP stn) – **MO21)** 89.7 La Catorce 10 – **MO22)** 90.3 FM Oldies – 91.1 R.Futura – 91.5 ZOE Gospel Music – **MO04)** 91.9 R.Disney – **MO7)** 92.5 Urbana FM - 93.9 Océano – **MO03)** 94.7 Emisora del Sur (SODRE) – 95.5 Em. Del Plata – 96.3 Alfa FM – **MO03a)** 97.1 Babel (R.Clasica) – 97.9 M24 – 98.7 Diamante FM – 99.5 Em. del Sol – 100.3 Aire FM – 101.3 Nuevo Tiempo – 101.9 Azul FM – 103.7 Latina FM – **MO10)** 104.3 Radio Cero – 105.9 Galaxia FM – 106.7 La Ley FM.

NB: In the rest of the country there are 165 FM outlets. There are also 156 authorised Community LPFM stns

UZBEKISTAN

L.T: UTC +5h — **Pop:** 33 million — **Pr.L:** Uzbek (official), Karakalpak (additional official regional language), Tajik — **E.C:** 220V/50Hz — **ITU:** UZB

O'ZBEKISTON RESPUBLIKASI AXBOROT TEXNOLOGIYALARI VA KOMMUNIKATSIYALARINI RIVOJLANTIRISH VAZIRLIGI

(Ministry for Development of Information Technologies & Communications)

✉ Amir Temur sho ko'chasi 4, 100047 Toshkent ☎ +998 71 2384107 🖷 +998 71 2398782 **E:** info@mitc.uz **W:** mitc.uz

L.P: Minister: Shuxrat Sadikov

O'ZBEKISTON MILLY TELERADIOKOMPANIYASI (Gov)

✉ A. Navoiy ko'chasi 69, 100011 Toshkent ☎ +998 71 2141250 **E:** info@mtrk.uz **W:** mtrk.uz

✉ Radio studios: Istiqlol ko'chasi 49, 100047 Toshkent; exc. O'zbekiston 24: Olmazor ko'chasi 2, 100047 Toshkent.

L.P: Pres: Alisher Xadjaev

FM	**1***	**2**	**3**	**kW**
Andijon	-	105.2	-	1
Buxoro	102.0c	103.9	105.4	2
Namangan	-	105.2	-	2
Navoi	106.6g	104.0	105.8	2
Nukus**	103.1f	104.6	-	2
Qarshi	102.3e	103.1	105.6	1
Toshkent	103.1	104.0	107.8	4
Samarqand	105.2i	101.9	-	1
Urganch	103.5l	101.5	-	4

+ translators *) incl. reg prgrs (see below) **) Located in Karakalpakstan (autonomous province)

D.Prgr: Prgr 1 (O'zbekiston): 0000-1900 – **Prgr 2 (Yoshlar):** 24h – **Prgr 3 (Mahalla):** 2200-1900 – **Prgr 4 (O'zbekiston 24):** 24h via webcasting – **Local Station: "Toshkent"** on Toshkent 87.9 (4kW): 0000-1900 in Uzbek, Russian.

O'zbekiston MTRK Regional Services

D.Prgr: via Prgr 1 txs. Some branches also transmit on exclusive freqs (see below). **a) Andijon TRK:** Istiqlol ko'chasi 9, 170120 Andijon **E:** andijon@mtrk.uz – **b) Buxoro TRK:** Eshanov ko'chasi 20, 200120 Buxoro **E:** buxorotv@mtrk.uz – **c) Farg'ona TRK:** 150100 Farg'ona **E:** fargona@mtrk.uz – **d) Jizzax TRK:** Rashidov maydon, 130100 Jizzax **E:** jizzaxtvr@mtrk.uz. "R. Sanzar" on 105.4MHz: 24h. – **e) Qashqadaryo TRK:** 180100 Qarshi **E:** qashqadaryo_trk@mtrk.uz – **f) Qoraqalpog'iston TRK:** Dustnazarov ko'chasi 20, 230100 Nukus – **g) Navoiy TRK:** Xalklar Do'stligi ko'chasi 32, 210100 Navoiy **E:** ntrk.nazorat@mtrk.uz – **h) Namangan TRK:** Holhanov ko'chasi 1, 160136 Namangan **E:** namangan@mtrk.uz – **i) Samarqand TRK:** 140100 Samarqand. "R. Jahon" on 105.2MHz: 24h. – **j) Sirdaryo TRK:** 120100 Guliston **E:** svtrk@mtrk.uz – **k) Surxondaryo TRK:** 190100 Termiz. – **l) Xorazm TRK:** 220100 Urganch. **E:** xorazmtvr@mtrk.uz.

OTHER STATIONS

FM	**MHz**	**kW**	**Location**	**Station**
8)	88.4	1	Toshkent	Navro'z FM
9)	100.4	2	Nukus*	Nukus-FM
1B)	100.5	2	Toshkent	Oriat FM
10)	100.5	1	Farg'ona	Ruxsor FM
3)	101.0	1	Toshkent[1]	O'zbegim taronasi
2)	101.5	1	Toshkent	R. Grand
5)	102.0	2	Toshkent	Avtoradio Hamroh
6)	102.7	1	Toshkent[1]	Vodiy sadosi
4A)	103.5	1	Toshkent	R. Poytaxt
4A)	104.5	1	Samarqand	R. Poytaxt
1A)	106.5	4	Toshkent	Oriat Dono
6)	106.9	1	Angren[1]	Vodiy sadosi
4B)	107.2	1	Toshkent	R. Poytaxt-Inform
7)	107.2	1	Samarqand	STV Radio

+ txs below 1kW. *) Located in Karakalpakstan (autonomous province) [1]) + txs in other towns on same freq. (synchr. network)

Addresses & other information:

1A,B) Istikbol ko'chasi 6, 100000 Toshkent. 1A) in Uzbek **E:** radio@oriatdono.uz; 1B) in Russian **E:** fm@oriat.uz – **2)** Bunyodkor ko'chasi 15, 100043 Toshkent **E:** radio@grand.uz – **3)** Shaxrisabz ko'chasi 16a, 100000 Toshkent **E:** ut101@mail.ru – **4A,B)** Movaraunnahr ko'chasi 14, 100000 Toshkent **E:** radio1072@rambler.ru 9B) in Russian. – **5)** Shayxontohur ko'chasi 36, 100007 Toshkent **E:** hamroh@mail.ru – **6)**

Mirobod ko'chasi 39/1A, 100000 Toshkent **E:** mtrk@intal.uz – **7)** Firdavskiy ko'chasi 1, 140100 Samarqand **E:** info@stv.uz – **8)** Muqumiy ko'chasi 178, 100096 Toshkent **E:** info@navruzfm.uz – **9)** Nukus – **10)** Marg'ilon ko'chasi 76, 150100 Farg'ona **E:** 100_5@inbox.ru.

VANUATU

L.T. UTC + 11h — **Pop:** 309,242 — **Pr.L:** Bislama, English, French — **E.C:** 50Hz, 220V — **ITU:** VUT

TELECOMMUNICATIONS AND RADIOCOMMUNICATIONS REGULATOR (TRR)

✉ PO Box 3547, Port Vila, Efate ☎ + 678 27621 **W:** www.trr.vu

VANUATU BROADCASTING & TELEVISION CORPORATION (VBTC) (Pub)

✉ PMB 9049, Port Vila ☎ +678 23615/22999 Ext 127/128 🖷 +678 22026 **L.P:** CEO: Francis Herman, Exec Producer Radio: Ms Marie-Noelle Kaltack, Mgr-Tech. Srvcs: Warren Roberts
W: vbtc.vu **E:** technical@vbtc.com.vu

MW	kHz	kW	Station
Emten Lagoon, Efate	1125	10	R. Vanuatu
SW	**kHz**	**kW**	**Station**
Emten Lagoon, Efate	*3945	1.5-2	R. Vanuatu 0530-0900
Emten Lagoon, Efate	5040	1.5-2	R. Vanuatu 0930-1130, 1730-2200
Emten Lagoon, Efate	7260	1.5-2	R. Vanuatu 1130-1730 †
FM	**MHz**	**kW**	**Station**
Port Vila, Efate	98.0	0.2	Paradise 98FM
Tanna	98.0	0.2	Paradise 98FM
Port Vila, Efate	99.0		Femme Pawa 99FM
Luganville, Espiritu Sto	100.0		R. Vanuatu
Port Vila, Efate	100.0	1	R. Vanuatu

*harmonics on 7890 and 11835.

National Radio Service: Radio Vanuatu D.Prgr: Mon-Sat 1815-0030, Sun 1815-1030 other times relay Paradise FM] **MW:** 24/7 including relay Paradise FM **FM: Paradise FM** Port Vila **Prgr:** commercial 24/7

Other Stations:

FM	MHz	Station
1) Port Vila	107.0	Capitol FM107
1) Santo	107.0	Capitol FM107
1) Tanna	107.0	Capitol FM107
1) Outer Islands	107.0	Capitol FM107
2) Port Vila, Efate	96.3	BUZZ FM

Addresses & other information:
1) Capitol FM Transpacific Haus, PO Box 369, Port Vila Vanuatu ☎ +678 25107 **E**: sales1@ vanuatufm107.com– **2)** PO Box 1292 Port Vila ☎ +678 24427 **LP:** Marc Neil-Jones **W:** buzzfm.vu **E:** info@buzzfm.vu **ID:** The All New Buzzfm 96.3. Switch your Dial. **Prgr:** 24/7
NB: No information available on infrastructure upgrade announced 2019 to install a MW and a SW transmitter at Emten Lagoon to improve radio and free to air TV services throughout Vanuatu, and to reopen Radio Vanuatu's MW transmission facilities at Luganville.

VATICAN CITY STATE

L.T: UTC +1h (28 Mar-31 Oct: +2h) — **Pop:** 450 — **Pr.L:** Italian — **E.C:** 230V/50Hz — **ITU:** CVA

RADIO VATICANA (Rlg.)

✉ Vatican Radio, Via della Conciliazione 5, 00120 Vatican City ☎ +39 06 698 83551 Int. Rel: ☎ +39 06 698 83551 🖷 +39 06 698 84565 **W:** vaticannews.va/it/rvi.html **E:** rei@spc.va
L.P: TD: Paolo Ruffini; CE: Maurizio Venuti; Head of Int. Rel: Giacomo Ghisani **E:** relint@spc.va Vatican Radio Museum, guided visiting tour c/o Palazzo Pio XII, Piazza Pia 3, 00120 Vatican City ☎ +39 06 698 83995 **E:** visitemuseorv@vatiradio.va
FM: 103.8mhZ 10Kw; 105.0MHz 15kW
Prgr: RV Italia: 103.8; 105.0MHz 24h. Also rel. Radio inBlu irr.
DAB+: Channel 12D 1kW (Roma) Channel 12D 1kW (Milano)
Ann: Before all transmissions: Latin: "Laudetur Jesus Christus" (Praised be Jesus Christ), repeated in the language of the broadcast, then stn identification. **IS:** "Christus Vincit". **V.** by QSL-card **E:** qsl.request@spc.va

EXTERNAL SERVICE: Vatican Radio see International Radio section

Other Stations:
FM (Tx in Vatican territory): 93.3MHz 10kw Radio Zeta **W:** radiozeta.it, 96.3MHz 10kW Radio inBLU **W:** radioinblu.it

VENEZUELA

L.T: UTC -4h — **Pop:** 28 million — **Pr.L:** Spanish — **E.C:** 110V/60Hz — **ITU:** VEN

COMISIÓN NACIONAL DE TELECOMUNICACIONES (CONATEL)

✉ Avenida Veracruz con Calle Cali, Edificio CONATEL, Urb. Las Mercedes, Caracas 1060 🖷 +58 212 993 8801 **W:** conatel.gob.ve **E:** conatel@conatel.gob.ve

CÁMARA VENEZOLANA DE LA INDUSTRIA DE LA RADIODIFUSIÓN

✉ Ap. 3955, Caracas 1060 ☎ +58 212 2634855, 2634528 🖷 +58 212 2614783 **E:** camradio@camradio.org

Hrs of tr: 24h unless shown. **Call:** YV—, ‡=inactive, (r)=repeater, ±=variable frequency. **NB:** Due to crisis, most stations operate on lower power and many have gone completely off the air. Only stations operational at editorial deadline are listed, but others may return.

MW	Call	kHz	kW	Station, location, h. of tr.
DC01)	KE	550	50	R. Mundial, Caracas
AN01)	XY	610	10	R. Centro, Cantaura
LA01)	SE	610	10	R. Cristal, Barquisimeto
AP01)	ZC	620	25	R. Fe y Alegría, Guasdualito
ZU01)	NO	620	5	R. Libertad, Cabimas
DC02)	KA	630	25	RNV Informativa, Caracas
DC03)	LL	670	100	R. Rumbos, Caracas
DC05)	KY	710	20	R. Capital, Caracas
FA01)	MN	780	15	R. Coro, Coro
DC07)	KC	‡790	10	R. Venezuela, Caracas
LA02)	XM	790	50	R. Minuto "La Barquisimetana", Barquisimeto
DC08)	LT	830	25	R. Sensación, Caracas
GU01)	YE	860	10	R. Enlace 860, Valle de la Pascua
TA01)	OL	860	10	R. Mundial, San Cristóbal
LA04)	MP	870	10	Unión R. Notícias, Barquisimeto
DC10)	RQ	910	20	RQ 910 AM, Caracas
NE01)	QX	920	20	R. Nueva Esparta, Porlamar
AN10)	QM	980	2	La Voz de El Tigre, El Tigre
DC12)	RT	990	20	R. Tropical, Caracas
AR01)	PC	1010	10	R. Aragua, Cagua
YA01)	TW	1020	25	R. Alegría, Chivacoa
CA01)	LB	1040	20	LV de Carabobo, Valencia
ME01)	ON	1040	10	Mundial Los Andes, Mérida
AR02)	NR	1080	10	Mundial 1080, Maracay
DC13)	SZ	1090	20	Unión Radio, Caracas
YA02)	PB	1090	10	R. Yaracuy, San Felipe
LA03)	KQ	1130	10	R. Popular, Barquisimeto
DC16)	RL	1130	10	R. Ideal, Maiquetía
TA02)	ZD	1190	10	R. Cultural del Táchira, San Cristóbal
DC14)	OZ	1200	10	R. Tiempo, Caracas
DC15)	RM	1260	10	BBN Radio, Caracas
GU02)	QS	1280	5	R. Zaraza, Zaraza
TR01)	OF	1280	10	R. Trujillo, Trujillo
DC10)	KH	1300	10	Deportiva 1300 AM Center, Caracas
AR03)	WP	1320	5	R. Apolo, Turmero
DC17)	NE	1340	10	R. Uno, Caracas
DC18)	ZA	1390	20	R. Fe y Alegría, Caracas
DC19)		1420	5	R. Sintonía, Caracas
VA01)	KJ	1450	8	R. María, Catia la Mar
DC20)	XD	1490	10	R. Dinámica, Caracas
SU01)	RZ	1500	5	R. 2000, Cumaná
DC20)	UD	1590	10	R. Deporte, Caracas

State abbreviations: AM = Amazonas, AN = Anzoátegui, AP = Apure, AR = Aragua, BA = Barinas, BO = Bolívar, CA = Carabobo, CO = Cojedes, DA = Delta Amacuro, DC = Distrito Capital, FA = Falcón, GU = Guárico, LA = Lara, ME = Mérida, MI = Miranda, MO = Monagas, NE = Nueva Esparta, PO = Portuguesa, SU = Sucre, TA = Táchira, TR = Trujillo, VA = Vargas, YA = Yaracuy, ZU = Zulia.
N.B: These abbreviations are not officially recognized by the Venezuelan Post Office. Letters should therefore carry the full name.

Addresses & other information:
AAN00) ANZOÁTEGUI

AN01) Av. Hospital cruce con Calle Freites, Edif.Radio Centro, Cantaura 6007 **W:** twitter.com/radiocentro610 – **AN10)** Av Francisco de Miranda N° 196, Al lado del Banco Provincial, El Tigre 6034
AP00) APURE
AP01) Carr. Nacional, Vía Elorza La Arenosa, Edif. Fe y Alegría, Guasdualito 5063 **W:** radios.feyalegrianoticias.com/guasdualito-am
AR00) ARAGUA
AR01) Calle Sucre, Edificio Comercial y Profesional Sucre, Piso 2, Oficina #3, Cagua 2122 **W:** facebook.com/radioaragu – **AR02)** Urb. Calicanto, Calle Coromoto, Norte 6, Detrás de la Maestranza Cesar Girón, Maracay 2101 **W:** facebook.com/Radio1080amdigitalmaracay – **AR03)** Av. Bermúdez, Torre Apolo, PB, entre Mariño y Bolívar, Turmero 2115 **W:** twitter.com/radioapoloam
CA00) CARABOBO
CA01) Av Rosarito, Torre Trebol, P1, Ofc 13, Urb Lomas del Este, Valencia 2001 **W:** facebook.com/lvc1040am
DC00) DISTRITO CAPITAL
DC01) Calle Nueva York Cruce con Av.Rio de Janeiro, Edif YVKE Mundial, P1, Las Mercedes, Caracas 1060, Edo.Miranda **W:** radiomundial.com.ve – **DC02)** Final Calle Las Marías, Edif. Radio Nacional de Venezuela, entre Chapellín y Country Club, La Frorida, Caracas 1050, Edo. Miranda **W:** facebook.com/RNVInformativa – **DC03)** Av.Francisco de Miranda, Multicentro Empresarial del Este, Edif.Libertador, P7, Núcleo A Chacao, Caracas 1060, Edo Miranda **W:** radiorumbos.net – **DC05)** Av.Francisco de Miranda, Centro Comercial Los Ruices, P3, Los Ruices, Caracas 1071, Edo Miranda **W:** radiocapital710.com – **DC07)** Av.Rómulo Gallegos, Edif.KLM, P12, Ofc CyD, Los Palos Grandes, Caracas 1062, Edo Miranda **W:** radiovenezuela.com.ve – **DC08)** Av Santiago de Chile, Quinta Radio Sensación, Los Caobos, Caracas 1050 – **DC10)** Centro Comercial Concresa, Nivel 1, Circuito Center, Prados del Este, Caracas 1080, Edo.Miranda **W:** facebook.com/rq910 facebook.com/deportiva1300am-115190646562992 – **DC12)** Puente Nuevo a Puerto Escondido, Edif.Torre del Oeste, P1, El Silencio, Caracas 1010, Distrito Capital (or Ap.3674, Caracas 1010-A) **W:** radiotropicalyvrt990.com.ve – **DC13)** Av.Mohedano, Entre Calle Los Granados y 1ª transversal, Edif. Splendor, La Castellana, Caracas 1060, Edo.Miranda **W:** unionradio.net – **DC14)** Av Los Mangos N° 49, Qta.Radio Tiempo, La Florida, Caracas 1050-A, Edo. Miranda **W:** www.radiotiempo1200.com – **DC15)** Av. Los Mangos con Av.Valencia Parpacén, Qta. Marisabel, La Florida, Caracas 1050, Edo. Miranda **W:** bbnradio.org/wcm4/spanish/Radio/Emisoras/tabid/646/StationID/236/Default.aspx – **DC16)** Centro Comercial Uslar, P15, Ofc 152, Montalbán, Caracas 1021, Distrito Capital **W:** radioideal.com.ve – **DC17)** Edif Mundial, Av Tamanaco, El Rosal, Caracas 1060 **W:** twitter.com/radiouno1340am – **DC18)** Calle 3B, Edif.C-207, P2, (detrás del McDonald's), La Urbina, Caracas 1070, Edo.Miranda **W:** radiofeyalegrianoticias.com – **DC19)** Calle La Joya, Torre Cosmos, P9, Ofc 9A, Chacao, Caracas 1060, Edo. Miranda (or Centro Comercial El Pichacho, P8, San António de los Altos 1204). **W:** radiosintonia1420.com.ve – **DC20)** Av.Boulevard Brasil N° 74, de Santa Ana a Providencia La Pastora, Caracas 1010, Distrito Capital **W:** radiodinamica.com.ve – **DC21)** Av Circunvalación del Sol, Centro Profesional Sta Paula, Torre A, P5 Ofc 51, Caracas 1061, Edo.Miranda. **W:** radiodeporte.com.ve
FA00) FALCÓN
FA01) Avenida Manaure esquina Maparari, Edificio Pepelupe, Coro 4101 **W:** radiocoro780.com
GU00) GUÁRICO
GU01) Av RómuloGallegos, Edif. Flor de Pascua, Loc 2, Valle de la Pascua 2307. **W:** enlace860am.tk – **GU02)** Calle Concordia, Qta Puerto Arturo N° 35, Zaraza 2332 **W:** circuitoz.com.ve/radio_zaraza.html
LA00) LARA
LA01) Av. Venezuela con Calles 13 y 14, Edif.Radio Cristal, Barquisimeto 3001 **W:** twitter.com/cristalam610 – **LA02)** Av.Pedro León Torres, Centro Comercial Venrol, locales 29 y 30, Barquisimeto 3001. **W:** radiominuto.net – **LA03)** Calle 29, Entre Calles 18 y 19, Casa N° 18-74, Barquisimeto 3001 **W:** radiopopular1130.wixsite.com/envivo – **LA04)** Av Los Leones, Centro Empresarial Caracas, P5, Ofc 5-2, Barquisimeto 3002 **W:** unionradio.net
ME00) MÉRIDA
ME01) Calle 44 N° 3-57, Diagonal al Colegio de Médicos, Mérida 5101 **W:** facebook.com/mundiallosandes **FM:** 106.3
NE00) NUEVA ESPARTA
NE01) Av Miranda, Edif.Best, P2, Porlamar 6301 **W:** nuevaesparta920am.com
SU00) SUCRE
SU01) Av Santa Rosa 18, Sector La Copita, frente a la Iglesia Santa Rosa de Lima, Cumaná 6101 **W:** radio2000.com.ve
TA00) TACHIRA
TA01) Av Las Lomas, Edif.Primo Centro, Locales 3-12 y 3-13, San Cristóbal 5001 **W:** mundial860am.com – **TA02)** Av 19 de Abril con Av 8, La Concordia, San Cristóbal 5001 **W:** facebook.com/LaCulturalFm - **FM:** 100.3MHz
TR00) TRUJILLO
TR01) Calle Independencia N° 10-11, Trujillo 3102 **W:** radiotrujillo1280.com.ve
VA00) VARGAS
VA01) 3era Norte Av Guaicaipuro, Quinta Mirna, Caracas **W:** radiomaria.org.ve
YA00) YARACUY
YA01) Av 10, Entre Calles 7y8, Edif.Alegría, Chivacoa 3202 **W:** twitter.com/alegria1020 – **YA02)** Prolongación 5ta Av.Urb.Andrés Eloy Blanco, Sector la Aduana, San Felipe 3201
ZU00) ZULIA
ZU01) Av El Muelle N° 1, Edif.Radio Libertad, frente a la Plaza Bolívar, Cabimas 4013 **W:** facebook.com/RadioLibertad620am

FM in Caracas (MHz): 88.1 Adulto Joven – 88.9 Romántica – 89.7 X FM – 90.3 Unión Radio Cultural – 90.7 Pacífica – 91.1 RNV Informativa – 91.5 Rebelde – 91.9 Candela Pura – 92.9 Corazón Llanero – 93.5 Melodía Stereo – 94.1 Hot FM – 94.5 Mundial – 94.9 Líder – 95.5 Play FM – 95.9 Miraflores – 96.3 Alba Ciudad – 96.9 Inolvidable – 97.7 Difusión Latina – 98.7 Advanta FM – 99.9 Éxitos – 100.7 Digital FM – 101.5 Kys – 101.9 Tiuna – 102.3 Salsa Caribe – 102.7 Baila – 103.3 Radiorama Stereo – 103.9 RNV Activa – 104.5 Musik FM – 105.3 Planeta – 105.5 RSD Stereo – 105.7 Fe y Alegría Noticias – 105.9 Pop – 106.1 Fiesta Latina – 106.5 Fiesta – 107.3 La Mega – 107.9 Onda

VIETNAM

L.T: UTC +7h — **Pop:** 97 million — **Pr.L:** Vietnamese — **E.C:** 220V/50Hz — **ITU:** VTN

AUTHORITY OF BROADCASTING AND ELECTRONIC INFORMATION
Ministry of Information and Communications (MIC)
✉ 9th Floor, 115 Tran Duy Hung, Cau Giay, Hanoi ☎ +84 24 39448034 🖷 +84 24 39448036 **E:** vanthucucqlptth@mic.gov.vn **W:** mic.gov.vn **L.P:** Minister: Nguyen Manh Hung

DÀI TIẾNG NÓI VIỆT NAM (VOV, RADIO THE VOICE OF VIETNAM) (Gov)
✉ 58 Quan Su Str, Hanoi ☎ +84 24 8255694 🖷 +84 24 8265875 **W:** vov.vn **E:** qhqt.vov@hn.vnn.vn
L.P: Pres: Nguyen The Ky. Dir Editorial Sce: Uong Ngoc Dau. Dir Tech Sce: Nguyen Xuan Huy

MW kHz	Net	kW	Station, location, h of tr
549	2	200	Hung Yen, (Site: My Hao): 2145-1700
576	2,P	50	Khanh Hoa, Nha Trang: 2145-1700
594	1	50	Danang, (Site: An Hai): 2145-1700
630	1	200	Quang Binh, Dong Hoi: 2145-1700
648	1	50	Binh Dinh, Quy Nhon, (Site: An Nhon): 2145-1700
657	1,C	100	Ho Chi Minh C., Quan Tre: 2145-1700
666	1	50	Khanh Hoa, Nha Trang: 2145-1700
675	1	500	Hung Yen, (Site: My Hao): 2145-1700
702	2,Q,D	50	Danang, (Site: An Hai): 2145-1700
711	1	500	Can Tho, Thoi Long: 2145-1700
729	2	200	Quang Binh, Dong Hoi: 2145-1700
740	2,P	50	Binh Dinh, Quy Nhon, (Site: An Nhon): 2145-1700
783	2	500	Can Tho, Thoi Long: 2145-1700
819	2	20	Dac Lac, Buon Ma Thuot: 2145-1700
873	4	500	Can Tho, Thoi Long: 2155-1700§
1242	E	500	Can Tho, Thoi Long: 1300-1600

‡) r. inactive ±) variable fq. §) split schedule

SW kHz	Net	kW	Location, h. of tr
6020	4	20	Buon Ma Thuot: 2200-1600
‡6165	4	50	Xuan Mai: 2200-2300, 2330-2400, 1130-1400
7210	1	20	Buon Ma Thuot: 2145-1700
9635	1	100	Son Tay: 2145-1700
9850	4	50	Xuan Mai: 0400-0600
11720	1	50	Xuan Mai: 1030-1500v

‡) r. inactive

SW Stations: Xuan Mai (also known as CK2) 50kW (GC: 105.36E 20.53N). Buon Me Thuot 2x20kW (G.C: 108.03E 12.41N). Son Tay (see Int Radio section)

Netw.: 1/2: Voice of Vietnam 1st/2nd national prgr – **4:** Voice of Vietnam minorities network – **C:** VOV Thanh Pho Ho Chi Minh **E:** Voice of Vietnam external sces – **P:** also carries Provincial sce (see separate Regional stations listings below for details).
FM (MHz): All FM powers shown are TRP.
Prgrs. from Hanoi
VOV1, news & current affairs: 2145-1700. **FM:** A Luoi 102.7, Ba Thuoc 93.1, Bach Long Vi 103.0, Ca Mau 95.9, Cao Bang 94.0, Cat Ba 95.8, Con Dao 101.0, Da Nang 100.0, Dac Lac 104.5, Dao Ly Son 89.9, Dien Bien Phu 96.3, Dong Van 101.0, Ha Giang 100.0, Ha Long 104.0, Ham Rong 105.1, Hanoi (Tam Dao) 100.0 10kW, Ho Chi Minh C. 94.0 10kW, Huang Su Phi 94.0, Kon Tum 91.5, Lai Chau 95.0, Lao Bao 101.0, Lao Cai 94.0, Meo Vac 100.0, Mong Cai 96.6, Muong Nhe 95.0, Muong Te 101.5, Nguyen Binh 97.0, Phu Quoc 95.0, Quan Ba 95.0, Quang Ngai 95.5, Quy Hop 101.5, Phu Quoc 95.0, Son La 93.5, Sop Cop 99.0, Thai Binh 97.0, Tra Vinh 102.5, Truong Sa 100.0, Tuy Hoa 102.7, Van Don 94.0, and also relayed in part by many regional sts. **N:** 2205, 2300, 0100, 0300, 0500, Mon-Sat 0630, 0700, Mon-Sat 0730, 0800, Mon-Sat 1000, 1100, 1230, MF 1330, 1430. SW freqs marked + relay VOV3 1700-2145
VOV2, economic, social, cultural & education prgrs: 2145-1700. **FM:** Bac Kan 99.5, Buon Ma Thuot 102.7 5kW, Cao Bang 103.5, Da Nang 89.0, Hanoi (Tam Dao) 96.5 10kW, Ho Chi Minh C. 96.5 10kW, Huang Su Phi 99.5, Kon Tum 92.5, Lai Chau 100.5, Lang Son (Mau Son) 93.5, Moc Chau 92.5, Muong Nhe 96.5, Phu Quoc 103.5, Quan Ba 96.5,Son La (Deo Pha Din) 93.5 20kW, Phu Yen 102.7 5kW, Tuong Duong 104,0, Van Don 99.5, Yen Bai 97.5. **LL:** English 0600, French 0615, Chinese/Japanese/Vietnamese through English 0630 (repeated Mon-Sat 1600-1645)
VOV3, news & music prgrs: 24h on FM (freqs in) An Giang (Nui Cam) 102.7, Dac Nong (Gia Nghia) 96.6 5kW, Da Nang (Ba Na) 102.5 10kW, Hanoi (Tam Dao) 102.7 20kW, Ho Chi Minh C. (Quan Tre) 104.5 10kW, Hue 106.1 10kW, Quang Binh 96.1 5kW, Qui Nhon 103.1 10kW, Son La 101.0, Tay Ninh (Nui Ba Den) 101.0 20kW, Thanh Hoa 94.9, Vinh (Thien Tuong) 102.7. Inc. **One Radio**: Mon-Sat 2300-0200, 0900-1600, Sun 0600-1600.
VOV4, prgrs for ethnic minorities: Bana, Ede, Giarai, Hmong, K'Hor (Koho), Sedang, Thai, M'Nong: 2200-1600 on 6020kHz, Bing Thuan (Phan Thiet) 102.0 5kW, Dac Lac (Buon Ma Thuot) 100.0 5kW, Da Lat 101.0, Dac Nong (Gia Nghia) 101.5 5kW, Ninh Thuan 102.7, Phu Yen (Tuy Hoa) 96.0 2.5kW, for Central Highlands. **Dao, H'Mong (Ho Mong), Thai:** 2150-2300, 0000-0030, 1145-1400 on 6165kHz, 0400-0530 on 9850kHz for Northern Vietnam, also in whole or in part on Bac Kan 97.8, Cao Bang (Phan Thanh) 97.0 10kW, Ba Thuoc 94.9, Dien Bien Phu 98.0 2kW, Ha Giang (Quan Ba) 103.2 10kW, Huang Su Phi 97.0, Lai Chau (Muong Te) 101.5 2kW, Lang Son (Mau Son) 101.0 10kW, Lao Cai 99.1, Muong Nhe 97.5, Quan Ba 90.5, Son La (Deo Pha Din) 104.3 10kW,. **Co Tu:** 2330-2400, 0420-0450, 1230-1300 on Danang (Ba Na) 100.0 10kW, Dong Giang 99.5. **Cham, Khmer (Kho Me), Vietnamese:** 2155-1330 on 873kHz, Can Tho 88.0, An Giang (Nui Cam) 91.5 20kW, Tay Ninh (Nui Ba Den) 101.0 20kW for the Mekong Delta. **FM:** most freqs relay VOV1, VOV3 or provincial stns at times.
VOV5, prgrs for foreigners: Hanoi 105.5, Ha Long 105.7, Ho Chi Minh City (Quan Tre) 105.7: **Cambodian:** 0800-0830. **Chinese:** 0400-0430, 1100-1130. **English:** 0030-0130, 0500-0600, 0900-1030, 1200-1300, 1400-1500, 1600-1730. **French:** 0130-0230, 0600-0700, 1300-1330. **German:** 0000-0030 **Indonesian:** 0730-0800. **Japanese:** 0430-0500, 1330-1400. **Lao:** 0700-0730. **Russian:** 0230-0300, 0830-0900. **Spanish:** 1030-1100. **Thai:** 1130-1200. **Vietnamese:** 0300-0400, 1500-1600
VOV6 Literature & Arts: Hanoi/Ho Chi Minh City 96.5
VOV Traffic Channel (VOV Giao Thông): 2230-1800. **FM:** Hanoi (Me Tri) 91.0 5kW, Ho Chi Minh C. (Quan Tre) 91.0 5kW, Quang Tri 88.5, Binh Dinh/Dak Lak/Da Nang (Son Tra)/Ha Tinh/Mong Cai/Nha Trang 91.0, Dong Hoi/Ha Long/Lang Son/Lao Cai/Ninh Thuan/Phan Thiet/ Phu Yen/Quang Ngai/Thanh Hoa 91.5
Mekong FM: 24h regional prgrs and relay VOV Traffic Channel in Vietnamese. **FM:** Can Tho 90.0
Xone FM: 24h music prgrs for young people ✉ 4th Floor, 100 Nguyen Luong Bang, District 7, Ho Chi Minh City. **FM:** Can Tho/Da Nang (Son Tra)/Hanoi/Ho Chi Minh C. 89.0
VOV 24/7: 24h in **English**. **FM:** Can Tho/Da Nang/Ha Long/Hanoi/Ho Chi Minh C./Nha Trang 104.0, Hue/Phu Quoc 104.5
Joy FM: 2300-1700 health and lifestyle prgrs in Vietnamese. **FM:** Hanoi 98.9, Binh Duong (Ho Chi Minh C. area) 101.7
VOV Thanh Pho Ho Chi Minh (TPHCM): opt-out programming in Vietnamese & Cham for Ho Chi Minh C. area on 657kHz: 2330-2400, 0330-0500, 0930-1100 (times vary).
Ann: 'Dây là Dai Tiếng Nói Việt Nam, Khmer: 'Thini Vithyu Samleng Vietnam'.

REGIONAL STATIONS

MW	kHz	Net	kW	Station, location, h of tr
1)	576	2,P	50	Khanh Hoa, Nha Trang: 2145-1700
2)	610	H	200	Ho Chi Minh City, Tang Nhon Phu: 2100-1700
3)	702	2,Q,D	50	Danang, (Site: An Hai): 2145-1700
4)	740	2,P	50	Binh Dinh, Quy Nhon, (Site: An Nhon): 2145-1700
5)	756	P	10	Long An, Tan An: 2200-1100§
6)	828	P	50	Son La: 2200-1400§
7)	±900	P	10	Ha Tinh: 2200-1200§
8)	909	P	10	Ca Mau: 2200-1330§
9)	1098	P	10	Thua Thien Hue, Hue: 2145-1145/1310§

±) variable fq. §) split schedule, see Reg. stns for details
Netw.: 1/2: Voice of Vietnam 1st/2nd national prgr (see VOV listings above) – **D:** Radio & TV Danang – **H:** Voice of the People of Ho Chi Minh City – **P:** Provincial sce – **Q:** Radio & TV Quang Nam (Hoi An, Quang Nam Province).
General remarks: Schedules shown are for provincial services on MW. Stns may also relay VOV1 at times, but relays of VOV as a rule are not included in the schedules below. Several hundred FM stns are operated by local gvnts of county-level admin. divisions (*huyen* or counties, *thi xa* or county-level towns, and *quan* or urban districts). These generally transmit with powers in the 50-500W range and with limited hours, and in many cases relay the provincial stn or Hanoi at times. **Ann:** Provincial sces usually identify as 'Radio & TV (name of province)", in Vietnamese: 'Dài Phát Thanh Truyên Hình (name)'
Addresses & other information:
1) 70 Tran Phu, Nha Trang. 2230-2200, 0430-0500, 1030-1100 - **FM:** 103.3MHz 0.1kW/106.5MHz 2kW + relays – **2)** 3 Nguyen Dinh Chieu, Dist. 1, Ho Chi Minh City. H: 2100-1700 in Vietnamese/Khmer - **FM:** 87.7/95.6 20kW/99.9MHz 20kW. Districts: Hoc Mon 93.0MHz, Nha Be 96.5MHz, Binh Chanh 103.4MHz, Can Gio 105.0MHz, Cu Chi 106.5MHz – **3)** Q: Tran Phu Road, Tan Thanh Ward, Tam Ky Town, Quang Nam: 2220-2245, 0400-0430, 1145-1215 - **FM:** 97.6MHz 2kW. D: 33 Le Loi, Hai Chau Ward, Da Nang. 2245-2300, 0430-0445, 1215-1315(SS 1400) - **FM:** 96.3MHz 5kW – **4)** 23 Mai Xuan Thuong, Quy Nhon City. 2230-2300, 0430-0500, 1145-1230 - **FM:** 97.0MHz 5kW, (Huai Nhon) 99.9MHz 1kW – **5)** 125 National Road 1A, Ward 4, Tan An City. 2200-0030(Sat 0100, Sun 0315), 0430-0530, 1000-1110/1210 - **FM:** 96.9MHz 3kW – **6)** Group 12, Quyet Thang Ward, Son La Town. 2200-2400, 0400-0600, 1200-1400 in Vietnamese/Hmong - **FM:** 96.0MHz 2kW + relays – **7)** 28 Phan Dinh Phung, Ha Tinh Town. 2200-2330, 0400-0600, 1100-1200 - **FM:** 93.6MHz 0.05kW – **8)** 413 Nguyen Trai, Phuoong 9, Ca Mau. - **FM:** 94.6MHz 5kW – **9)** 58 Huong Vong St, Hue. 2230-2300, 0400-0500, 0955-1100, occ. 1145-1310 - **FM:** 93.0MHz 2kW & 96.0MHz 0.02kW

Provincial sces operating on FM only (MHz):
An Giang (Long Xuyen) 90.1MHz; Bac Giang 98.4 5kW; Bac Kan 99.3 2kW; Bac Lieu 93.8 2kW; Bac Ninh 92.1 2kW; Ba Ria Vung Tau (Nui Nho) 92.0 5kW; Ben Tre 97.9 2kW; Bing Duong (Thu Dau Mot) 92.5 10kW; Binh Phuoc (Dong Xoai) 89.4 2kW; Binh Thuan (Phan Thiet) 92.3MHz 5kW; Cao Bang 99.0 5kW; Dac Lac (Buon Ma Thuot) 94.7 5kW; Ca Mau 94.6MHz 5kW; Can Tho 97.3MHz 5kW; Dac Nong (Gia Nghia) 88.8 2kW, (Dak Mil) 95.5 2kW; Dien Bien (Dien Bien Phu) 96.3 1kW; Dong Nai 97.5 5kW; Gia Lai (Pleiku) 93.7 2kW + relays; Ha Giang 92.0 2kW + relays; Hai Duong 104.5 5kW; Hai Phong 93.7 3kW; Ha Nam (Phu Ly) 93.3 2kW; Hanoi 90.0 10kW (+ 5 Huynh Thuc Khang, Dong Da District, Hanoi) + 96.0 2kW (Prgr 2, tr. In Ha Dong), Hau Giang 89.6 3kW; Hoa Binh 105.0 5kW; Hung Yen 92.7 2kW; Kien Giang (Rach Gia_ 99.4MHz 5kW; Kon Tum 95.1MHz 3kW; Lam Dong (Da Lat) 97.0 2kW + relays; Lang Son 88.2MHz 1kW, (Mau Son) 101.0MHz 10kW; Lao Cai 91.0 5kW, 95.2 1kW & 97.0 10kW; Nam Dinh 95.1 2kW; Nghe An (Vinh) 99.6 10kW + relays; Ninh Binh 98.1 2kW; Ninh Thuan (Phan Rang Thap Cham) 95.0 5kW & 99.6 2kW; Phu Tho (Viet Tri) 106.0 5kW; Phu Yen 96.0 2.5kW; Quang Binh (Dong Hoi) 94.1 1kW; Quang Ngai 102.9MHz 5kW; Quang Ninh (Ha Long) 97.8 10kW; Quang Tri (Dong Ha) 92.5 5kW;Soc Trang 100.4 2kW; Tay Ninh 103.1MHz 5kW; Thai Binh 91.7 3.3kW; Thanh Hoa 92.3 10kW; Tieng Giang (My Tho) 96.2 2kW; Thai Nguyen 106.5MHz 1kW; Tra Vinh 92.7 2kW; Tuyen Quang 95.6 2kW;Vinh Long 90.2 1kW; Vinh Phuc 102.7 2kW; Yen Bai 92.1 2kW + relays

VIRGIN ISLANDS, BRITISH (UK)

L.T: UTC -4h — **Pop:** 30,000 — **Pr.L:** English — **E.C:** 110V/60Hz — **ITU:** VRG

VIRGIN ISLANDS BROADCASTING LTD. (Comm.)
Baughers Bay, P.O. Box 78, Road Town, Tortola, BVI ☎ +1 284 494 2250/2430/6994 ▤ +1 284 494 1139 **E:** zbvi@surfbvi.com **W:** zbviradio.net **L.P:** MD: Delker Herbert Vardilos. GM: Harvey Herbert. Ops Mgr: Sandra Potter. Production Mgr: Iris Jones
MW: ZBVI 780kHz 10kW **D.Prgr:** MF 0930-0200, Sat 1000-0300, Sun 1100-0200. Local **N:** 1105, 1605, 2000. **Ann:** "This is ZBVI Radio from Tortola"

CARIBBEAN BROADCAST NETWORK LTD. (Comm.)
2nd Floor Chevelle Center, Road Town, Tortola ☎ +1 284 340 3461 **W:** cbnvirginislands.com **L.P:** Owner: Andrew A.B.B. Cox Sr.
CBN-Radio 90.9FM (CSS) The Caribbean Superstation: 90.9MHz (1.8kW)
CBN-Radio 92.3FM (ZCBN) The Breeze of the Virgin Islands: 92.3MHz (1.8kW)

OTHER STATIONS (FM in MHz):
ZCCR, Little Dicks Hill Rd, East End, PO Box 41, Tortola VG1110 ☎ +1 284 495 0461 **W:** caribbeanchristianradio.org FM 94.1 (8.5kW). Ann: CCR Your Caribbean Christian Station. Format: Gospel – **ZKING The Voice of the Virgin Islands,** Christian Broadcasting Network, Horsepath, Road Town, PO Box 2993, Tortola VG1110 ☎ +1 284 494 4600 **W**: zkingradio.com. FM 100.9 (5kW). Format: Rlg. – **ZVCR The Fuze,** Westend, Road Town, Tortola VG1130 ☎ +1 284 499 3893 **W:** letsfuzevi.com. FM 106.9

VIRGIN ISLANDS, US (USA)

L.T: UTC -4h — **Pop:** 100,000 — **Pr.L:** English (official), Virgin Island Creole, Spanish — **E.C:** 120V/60Hz — **ITU:** VIR

FEDERAL COMMUNICATIONS COMMISSION (FCC)
see main entry under USA

MW	Call	kHz	kW	MW	Call	kHz	kW
1)	WSTX	970	5/1	5)	WDHP	1620	10/1
2)	WVWI	1000	5/1	6)	WIGT	1690	0.9
4)	WSTA	1340	1				
FM	**Call**	**MHz**	**kW**	**FM**	**Call**	**MHz**	**kW**
7)	WIVH	89.9	1.4	12)	WVIQ	99.5	32
8)	WSKX	90.7	10	1)	WSTX	100.3	50
9)	WVSE	91.9	7.4	16)	WEVI	101.3	4.6
10)	WTJX	93.1	1.3	20)	WIVI	102.1	1.75
11)	WVVI	93.5	9.6	21)	WVJZ	103.1	0.17
12)	WJKC	95.1	15	5)	WAXJ	103.5	6
13)	WVIY	95.3	50	17)	WZIN	104.3	44
21)	WWKS	96.1	2.4	12)	WMNG	104.9	6
14)	WTJC	96.9	0.01	21)	WVJZ	105.3	30
3)	WUVI	97.3	0.1	18)	WVIE	107.3	1.7
6)	WGOD	97.9	50	19)	WLDV	107.9	3.6
15)	WMYP	98.3	1.9				

Addresses & other information:
1) Caledonia Communications Corp., 2111 Company St, Suite 3, Christiansted, St. Croix 00820 ☎ +1 340 332 1900 **E:** wstxradio@gmail.com **W:** wstxradio.com. Stns: WSTX-AM on 970kHz (news/sport/talk) & WSTX-FM on 100.3MHz (reggae) – **2)** PO Box 305678, Charlotte Amalie, St. Thomas 00803 ☎ +1 340 776 1000 Ann: "Radio One" (News/talk/sport) – **3)** Penha House 2nd floor, 2 John Brewers Bay, St. Thomas 00802 ☎ +1 340 693 1081 **E:** wuviradio@gmail.com & wuvi@uvi.edu **W:** wuvi.uvi.edu. Ann: "The Voice of the University" (College radio/rlg) – **4)** 121 Sub Base, St. Thomas 00801 ☎ +1 340 774 4500 **E:** info@wsta.com **W:** 1340wsta.com. Ann: "The People's Station" (Rlg) – **5)** Reef Broadcasting Inc., 6079A Castle Coakley, Christiansted, St. Croix 00820 ☎ +1 340 719 1620 ▤ +1 340 778 1686 **E:** reefbroadcasting@yahoo.com **W:** reefbroadcasting.com. Stns: WAXJ 'The Reef' on 103.5MHz (Urban AC/reggae) & WDHP on 1620kHz (Local Information/Music) – **6)** Three Angels Corp., 22A Estate Dorothea, PO Box 5012, Charlotte Amalie, St. Thomas 00803 ☎ +1 340 774 4498 **E:** wgod98@viaccess.net. Ann: "WGOD - The Word of God in The Caribbean". Relays 3ABN after 0200 – **7)** Good News For Life, 5007 Mt. Washington, Christiansted, St. Croix 00820 **W:** wivh.org. Ann: "WIVH The Voice Of Hope" (Rlg.) – **8)** Better Communications Group, PO Box 6867, Christiansted, St. Croix VI00823 (Reggae & salsa) – **9)** Ste. 101 Barren Spot, Village Mall, Christiansted, St. Croix 00823 ☎ +1 340 772 9090/226 0913 **W:** papiloveradio.com. Ann: "Latino 91.9 - Papi Love Radio" (Spanish) – **10)** 36-37 Estate Richmond, Christiansted VI00820 ☎ +1 340 718 3339 **W:** wtjx.org. Ann: "National Public Radio" – **11)** Gallows Bay, PO Box 25387, Christiansted, St. Croix 00824 ☎ +1 340 773 5935 Ann: "Caribbean Country" – **12)** JKC Communications, 5020 Anchors Way, PO Box 25680, Christiansted, St. Croix 00824 ☎ +1 340 773 0995 **W:** isle95.com. Stns: Isle 95 on 95.1MHz (Urban/reggae), Sunny 99.5 (A/C) & Mongoose 104.9 (Classic hits) – **13)** WVIY, Charlotte Amalie (planned; CP has expired) – **14)** PO Box 1045, St. Thomas 00804 ☎ +1 340 776 4531 (Rlg.) – **15)** PO Box 25387, Christiansted, St. Croix 00824 ☎ +1 340 772 0998. Ann: "La Nueva Rumba" (Spanish/Tropical/Variety) – **16)** Lifeline, 6215 Peter's Rest, Christiansted 00800 ☎ +1 340 227 5466 **W:** liferadiovi.weebly.com. Ann: "Life 101.3" (Rlg.) – **17)** Pan Caribbean Broadcasting de P.R., Aryuro Watlington Sta, PO Box 306117, Charlotte Amalie, St. Thomas 00803 ☎ +1 340 776 1043. Ann: "The Buzz" (Rock) – **18)** Virgin Islands Radio Entertainment Detroit, 929B Government Str., Baton Rouge, LA70802 **W:** talk1073.com. Ann: "Talk 107.3FM" – **19)** Creative Minds, 84 Kronprindsens Gade, Charlotte Amalie 00802 ☎ +1 340 774 8923/713 1079 **W:** davybe.com Ann: "Da Vybe" – **20)** Ackley Caribbean Enterprises, Cruz Bay, St. John. Ann: Pirate Radio – **21)** Gark LLC, PO Box 2179/8209, Charlotte Amalie, St. Thomas 00801 ☎ +1 340 776 1013. Stns: KISS on 96.1 (Urban Adult) & 105 JAMZ on 103.1/105.3

WAKE ISLAND (USA)

L.T: UTC +12h — **Pop:** 100 (military personnel & contractors) — **Pr.L:** English — **E.C:** 120V/60Hz — **ITU:** WAK

THE QUAKE (Mil)
USAF Detachment 3, 13AF, PACAF/Chugach Federal Solutions Inc. PO Box 187, Wake Island 96898 ☎ +1 808 424 2101 **E:** baseops@wakeisland.net **L.P:** Comms Mgr: Colin Bradley
FM: ‡104.5MHz (Probably currently inactive)
NB: American Forces Network (AFN) provides satellite radio/TV broadcasts via base cable system and internet radio (2019)

WALLIS & FUTUNA (France)

L.T: UTC +12h — **Pop:** 11,600 — **Pr.L:** French (official), Futunan, Wallisian — **E.C:** 220V/50Hz — **ITU:** WAL

COMITÉ TERRITORIAL DE L'AUDIOVISUEL DE NOUVELLE-CALÉDONIE ET DES ÎLES WALLIS-ET-FUTUNA see main entry under New Caledonia

WALLIS ET FUTUNA LA PREMIÈRE (Pub)
B.P.102, Pointe Matala, 98600 Mata-Utu, Uvea, Iles de Wallis et Futuna (par Nouméa, Nouvelle-Calédonie) ☎ +33 68 1721300 ▤ +33 68 1722346 **W:** la1ere.francetvinfo.fr/wallisfutuna (live streaming)
D.Prgr: 24h local and satellite relay from Paris

FM	MHz	kW	Station
Sigave/ Mt Utulimu, Futuna	88.0	0.3	W et F la 1ère
Sigave/ Leava, Futuna	89.0	0.1	W et F la 1ère
Sigave/ Apipi, Futuna	90.0	0.1	W et F la 1ère
Alo/Mont Mamati, Futuna	91.0	0.1	W et F la 1ère
Uvea/Pointe de Matala, Wallis	100.0		W et F la 1ère
Uvea/Mont Loka, Wallis	101.0	0.5	W et F la 1ère
Uvea/Pointe de Matalaa	103.0	0.2	France Inter

YEMEN

L.T: UTC +3h — **Pop:** 30 million — **Pr.L:** Arabic — **E.C:** 220V/50Hz — **ITU:** YEM

MINISTRY OF INFORMATION (under rebel control)
P.O. Box 19560, Al-Zubairy St, San'a ☎+967 1 215116/7/8 ▤ +967 1 207716 **W:** yemen-media.gov.ye **E:** yemen-info@y.net.ye

NB: All transmitters except 97.1, 98.1 and 104.1MHz below, operated by Houthi rebels, are reported inactive. Radio operation from San'a is under rebel control and Saudi Arabian & UAE backed government radio operates from Aden studio via Saudi Arabian & UAE transmitters, for more details see COTB section.

YEMEN GENERAL CORPORATION FOR RADIO & TV
San'a (under rebel control)

MW	kHz	kW	Netw.	Times
San'a	‡711	200	G	0700-1700
San'a	‡837	30	G	1700-0400

FM (MHz): Ad-Damigh 99.9 5kW, Al-Ashmur 92.6 5kW, Hudayda, 90.4 (L)/107.0 (G), Ibb 96.0 (G)/98.4 (L), Riam 92.4 5kW, San'a 97.1 (G)/89.9 (L)/96.5 (Y), Taiz 88.1 (G)/89.0 (L).
G=General prgr. from San'a: 24h. **Y=Youth prgr.** on 89.9/96.5MHz + 3 other trs. **L=Local prgr.** All r. inactive ‡

Other (rebel) Stations:
Grand FM, San'a: 93.9MHz **W:** facebook.com/RadioGrandFM
Voice of the People: Hodeida 91.1, Jizan 93.1, San'a 97.1, Aden 98.1, Imran 107.1MHz **W:** sawtalshaab.com
Voice of Yemen R, San'a: 98.1MHz **W:** yemen-voice-fm.com

VOICE OF THE REPUBLIC (SOWT AL-JUMHURIYA)
✉ Hudayda (in support of the internationally recognized government)
MW: relayed via Dhabbaya, UAE 1170kHz 1300-0300v.
FM: Al-Mukha 93.1Mhz, Hudayda 104.1MHz
See also COTB section under Target: Yemen.

Other Stations (in areas controlled by the internationally recognized government):
Aden Future R, Aden: 92.9MHz **W:** facebook.com/adenfuturefm
R. Al-Ghad al-Mashriq, Aden: 90.9MHz, Hudaydah 88.8MHz
W: alghadye.com
R. Bandaraden, Aden: 99.9MHz **W:** bandaraden.net
R. Belqees, Aden: 97.7MHz **W:** belqees.tv
R. Lana, Aden: 91.9MHz **W:** lanaradio.fm

ZAMBIA

L.T: UTC +2h — **Pop:** 18 million — **Pr.L:** English (official), Bemba, Nyanja, Tonga — **E.C:** 230V/50Hz — **ITU:** ZMB

MINISTRY OF INFORMATION AND BROADCASTING SERVICES (MIBS)
✉ P.O. Box 51025, 6th Floor, New Government Complex, Nassar Rd, Lusaka ☎+260 211 237150 🖷 +260 211 235410 **W:** www.mibs.gov.zm

ZAMBIA NATIONAL BROADCASTING CORPORATION (ZNBC, Pub)
✉ P.O. Box 50015, Mass Media Complex, Alick Nkhata Rd, Lusaka 10101 ☎+260 211 252005 🖷 +260 211 254920 **W:** myznbc.com **E:** sales2@znbc.co.zm **L.P:** DG: Chibamba Kanyama. Actg. Dir. Tech. Sces: Mr. Malolela Lusambo. PD: Kenneth Maduma. PR Officer: Masuzyo Ndhlovu.

SW	kHz	kW	Sce	Times
Lusaka	5995	100	R1	24h

FM(MHz)	R1	R2	N	R4	kW
Chipata	93.3	96.5	95.7	-	1
Choma	-	-	105.7	-	
Kabwe	-	-	-	92.1	0.5
Kapiri Mposhi	97.5	94.3	91.3	-	1
Kasama	88.3	92.3	91.5	-	1
Kitwe	98.5	95.7	94.1	88.1	2
Livingstone	89.3	97.3	100.5	95.7	1/0.5
Lusaka	102.9	95.7	92.5	88.1	2
Mansa	88.3	92.3	91.5	-	1
Mongu	94.9	91.7	98.1	-	1
Solwezi	95.3	91.3	93.3	-	1

R. One in 7 Zambian languages: 24h – **R. Two in English:** 0245-2205 – **N=Parliament Radio** (stream on **W:** streamer.parliament.gov.zm:8063/listen.pls – **R. Four (music channel) in English:** 0240-2205
Ann: E: "This is Radio Two of ZNBC broadcasting from Lusaka". Chichewa: "Kuno ndi ku Zambia National Broadcasting Corporation wa Lusaka." **IS:** Call of the Fish Eagle.

Other Stations (FM: MHz):
Breeze FM: Chipata 89.3, Petauke 89.7, Katete 98.9. **W:** breezefmchipata.com – **Chikuni R,** Monze: 91.9 0.5kW. **W:** chikuniradiozm.org – **Explorers R,** Petauke: 88.1 **W:** facebook.com/88.1fmPetauke – **Flava FM,** Kitwe: 87.7 **W:** flavafm.co.zm – **Hone FM,** Lusaka: 94.1 **W:** evelynhone.edu.zm – **Hot FM,** Lusaka: 87.7, Kapiri 88.7, Copper Belt 97.3. **W:** hot877.com – **Joy FM,** Lusaka: 92.1. **W:** facebook.com/JoyfmRadioZambia – **MAZ FM,** Luapula: 95.5/100.9 **W:** facebook.com/mazfm100.9 – **Money FM,** Lusaka: 93.7 **W:** moneyfmzambia.com – **Pan African R,** Lusaka: 105.1 **W:** panafricanfm.com – **Pasme R,** Petauke: 91.3 **W:** facebook.com/pasmeradiostations – **Q FM:** Lusaka 93.3, Kabwe 88.9, Choma 89.8, Mumbwa 89.1 **W:** www.qfmzambia.com – **R. Christian Voice**: FM: Ndola 98.9, Kapiri 101.5, Kitwe 105.3, Lusaka 106.1. **W:** rcvoice.co.zm – **R. Icengelo**: Kitwe 89.1, Kaloko 102.9 **W:** www.radioicengelo.org – **R. Liseli,** Mongu 105.3 **W:** facebook.com/oblateradioliseli – **R. Lyambai,** Mongu 101.3 **W:** en.unesco.org/radioict/radios/radio-lyambai – **R. Maria Zambia**: Kanjala 88.5 0.3kW, Katete 94.9. **W:** www.radiomaria.org.zm **Yatsani Voice**, Lusaka: 99.3 2kW. **W:** facebook.com/radiomariayatsanivoice – **R. Musi-o-Tunya,** Livingstone: 106.1 **W:** facebook.com/RadioMusiotunya106.1FM – **R. Phoenix**: Lusaka 89.5, Kabwe 100, Kitwe 100.5, Chingola 104, Kapiri/Mposhi 104.5, Ndola/Luanshya 107.6 **W:** radiophoenix.co.zm – **Sky FM:** Lusaka 88.5, Choma 88.8, Zimba 93.8, Monze 95.1, Livingstone 102.4 **W:** facebook.com/skyfm.zambia – **UNZA R**, Lusaka: 91.7 **W:** facebook.com/unzafm – **Yar FM,** Kitwe: 89.9 **W:** yarfm.co.zm – **Zambezi FM,** Livingstone: 94.1/107.7MHz **W:** facebook.com/zambezifm107.7 – **5 FM,** Lusaka: 89.9MHz 0.5kW **W:** 5fm.co.zm

BBC African Sce: Kitwe/Lusaka 98.1 2kW.
RFI Afrique: Kitwe 92.5, Lusaka 100.5 in English/French/Swahili

ZIMBABWE

L.T: UTC +2h — **Pop:** 15 million — **Pr.L:** Official languages: Chewa, Chibarwe, English, Kalanga, Koisan, Nambya, Ndau, Ndebele, Shangani, Shona, Sotho, Tonga, Tswana, Venda, Xhosa — **E.C:** 220V/50Hz — **ITU:** ZWE

BROADCASTING AUTHORITY OF ZIMBABWE (BAZ)
✉ 1 Pennefather , Media Centre, Rainbow Towers Grounds, P.O. Box CY496, Causeway, Harare ☎+263 4 797382-5 🖷 +263 4 797375 **W:** baz.co.zw **E:** baz@comone.co.zw

ZIMBABWE BROADCASTING CORPORATION (ZBC, Gov)
✉ P.O. Box HG 444, Broadcasting Centre, Pockets Hill, Highlands, Harare ☎+263 4 498610 **W:** zbc.co.zw **E:** onlinenewszbc@gmail.com

FM (MHz)	R1	R2	R3	R4	kW
Beithbridge	88.5	93.6	98.1	105.2	
Bulawayo	90.0	96.3	99.6	103.1	10
Chipinge	94.5	97.8	101.3	104.9	10
Chiredzi	93.3	95.5	98.8	102.3	10
Chivhu	93.3	96.5	103.3	106.8	
Gokwe	89.9	96.8	89.6	103.5	
Gwanda	105.8	95.4	98.7	102.2	20
Gweru	90.7	93.9	97.2	100.7	5
Harare	92.8	96.0	99.3	102.8	10
Hwange	91.5	98.2	94.7	101.5	10
Kadoma	88.5	94.8	98.1	101.6	10
Karoi	99.9	96.6	93.4	90.3	10
Kenmaur	90.4	93.5	97.5	103.5	
Masvingo	106.5	92.9	99.4	102.9	
Mount Darwin	92.0	95.2	98.5	102.0	10
Mutare	105.3	89.1	98.7	105.8	3
Mutorashanga	104.7	94.3	91.1	101.1	
Nyanga	105.5	91.7	94.9	101.7	3
Rutenga	101.1	88.0	91.1	94.3	
Victoria Falls	92.3	96.1	92.9	89.9	8

R1) Classic263: mainly in English: 24h – **R2) R. Zimbabwe:** in Shona/Ndebele/English: 24h – **R3) Power FM:** youth programme in English: 24h – **R4) National FM:** in 14 minority languages: 24h
Central Radio, Gweru: 95.8MHz in English, Ndebele, Shona.
Khulumani FM, Bulawayo: 95.0MHz.

Other Stations:
Breeze FM, Victoria Falls: 91.2MHz **W:** breezefm.co.zw
Capitalk, Harare: 100.4MHz **W:** capitalkfm.com
Diamond FM, Mutare: 103.8MHz **W:** diamondfm.co.zw
Hevoi FM, Masvingo: 100.2MHz **W:** facebook.com/hevoifm
Midlands FM, Gweru: 98.4MHz **W:** facebook.com/Midlands984
Nyaminyami FM, Kariba: 94.5MHz **W:** nyaminyamifm.co.zw
Star FM: Harare 89.7MHz, Bulawayo 93.1MHz **W:** starfm.co.zw
Skyz Metro FM, Bulawayo: 100.3MHz **W:** skyzmetroradio.co.zw
Ya FM, Zvishavane: 91.8MHz **W:** yafm.co.zw
Zi FM: Mutare 95.4MHz, Masvingo 96.1MHz, Mutorashanga 97.6MHz, Nyanga 98.2MHz, Beitbridge 101.6MHz, Gweru 104.3MHz, Kadoma 1052.MHz, Harare 106.4MHz, Victoria Falls 106.5MHz, Bulawayo 106.7MHz **W:** zifmstereo.co.zw

INTERNATIONAL RADIO

Section Contents

Initial entries for each letter, see Main Index for full details.

NB: The copy deadline for this section was 16 November 2020

Notes for the International Radio section

Country abbreviation codes are shown after the country name. The three-letter codes after each frequency are transmitter site codes. These, and the Area/Country codes in the Area column, can all be decoded by referring to the tables in the Reference Section.

Where a frequency has an asterisk (*) etc. after it, see the '**KEY**' section at the end of the schedule entry.

The following symbols are used throughout this section:
† = Irregular transmissions/broadcasts;
‡ = Inactive at editorial deadline;
± = variable frequency;
+ = DRM (Digital Radio Mondiale) transmission.

Where transmitter details are given for a particular entity, the number of units shown represents the installed capability of the site, but does not reflect any details of txs being coupled/bridged (to increase overall power output), run at reduced power or remaining unused.
Should a site become decommissioned or dismantled it is removed from the table, but if a site is merely dormant/inactive it is marked with the 'inactive' symbol shown above.

If **Webcast** is shown, the letter(s) after indicate the service(s) available: **D**=On Demand audio; **L**=Live audio; **P**=Podcast For international services we have shown, where possible, languages available only via the webcast. We do not include those broadcasters that have a foreign service only available via the internet and are no longer broadcasting via MW and or SW radio.

An alphabetical listing of **Religious Broadcasters**, cross-referenced by country, is given at the end of the section.

AFGHANISTAN (AFG)

RADIO TELEVISION AFGHANISTAN (RTA) (Gov)

13th Street, Wazir Mohammad Akhbar Khan, Kabul, Afghanistan.
☎ +92 20 2310147.
E: info@rta.org.af **W:** www.facebook.com/rtaworld
Webcast: L
L.P: DG: Zarin Anzor.
MW: [KAB] Kabul, Pol-e Charkhi: 1296kHz 400kW; [KHO] Khost, Tani: 621kHz 200kW. Both txs are operated on behalf of USAGM (USA).
SW: [KAB] Kabul, Yakatut: 1 x 100kW.
FM/DAB: FM: 93.0MHz (Kabul).
kHz: *6100*

Winter Schedule 2020/2021

English	Days	Area	kHz
1530-1600	daily	SAs	6100kab†
Urdu	**Days**	**Area**	**kHz**
1600-1630	daily	SAs	6100kab†

Key: † Irregular.
Ann: English: "Radio Afghanistan".
Notes: External Service of the state broadcasting company Radio Television Afghanistan (RTA). RTA also provides relay facilities on MW for USAGM (USA).

ALASKA (ALS)

KNLS INTERNATIONAL (Rlg)

P.O. Box 473, Anchor Point, AK 99556, USA. (Transmitting station)
☎ +1 907 2352326. 🖷 +1 907 2352326.
E: knls@aol.com **W:** www.knls.org (English); www.knls.net (Russian); www.smzg.org (Chinese)
Webcast: D
605 Bradley Court, Franklin, TN 37067, USA. (World Christian Broadcasting HQ & studios)
☎ +1 615 3718707. 🖷 +1 615 3718791.
L.P: SM: Dave Dvorak; WCB Vice Pres of Engineering (Franklin, TN): Kevin Chambers.
SW: [NLS] Anchor Point, AK: 2 x 100kW.
kHz: *5905, 6075, 6110, 6120, 7370, 7395, 9535, 9570, 9605, 9625, 9665, 9715, 9720, 9730*

Winter Schedule 2020/2021

Chinese	Days	Area	kHz
0800-1000	daily	EAs	7370nls
1000-1100	daily	EAs	9715nls
1100-1200	daily	EAs	9720nls
1300-1400	daily	EAs	5905nls, 7395nls
1400-1500	daily	EAs	9535nls
1500-1600	daily	EAs	9570nls
English	**Days**	**Area**	**kHz**
0800-0900	daily	EAs	6075nls
1000-1100	daily	EAs	9605nls
1200-1300	daily	EAs	9625nls, 9665nls
1400-1500	daily	EAs	6110nls
Russian	**Days**	**Area**	**kHz**
0900-1000	daily	RUS	6120nls
1100-1200	daily	RUS	9570nls
1500-1600	daily	RUS	9730nls

Ann: English: "This is Alaska calling. You're listening to station KNLS, Anchor Point, Alaska, United States of America", "This your New Life Station KNLS, Anchor Point, Alaska, broadcasting from the top of the world".
V: QSL-card.

Notes: On air since 23 July 1983. KNLS is a SW transmitting station owned by World Christian Broadcasting, Inc. (WCB). The stn retransmits prgrs produced in the Franklin, TN studios of WCB and WCB partner organisations. Further prgrs of WCB's language services in Chinese, English and Russian can be heard via its sister transmitting stn Madagascar World Voice (see under Madagascar for schedules).

ALBANIA (ALB)

RADIO TIRANA INTERNATIONAL (Pub)

Rruga "Ismail Qemali" nr. 11, 1001 Tirana, Albania.
☎ +355 42223650. 🖷 +355 42223650.
E: english@rtsh.al **W:** rti.rtsh.al
Webcast: L (Webcast languages: English, French, German, Greek, Italian, Serbian, Turkish).
L.P: DG (RTSH): Thoma Gëllçi.
SAT: Eutelsat 16A.
kHz: *3985, 6005, 7780, 15770*

Winter Schedule 2020/2021

English	Days	Area	kHz
1330-1400	mtwtfs.	CEu,WEu	6005kll
2030-2100	.t.....	Eu,ME,NAf	15770rmi
2230-2300	mtwt.s.	NAm,Eu	7780rmi
German	**Days**	**Area**	**kHz**
1600-1630	daily	CEu	3985kll

Ann: English: "Radio Tirana"; French: "Ici Tirana"; German: "Hier ist Tirana".
V: QSL-card.

Notes: Radio Tirana International is the international service of the public broadcaster Radio Televizioni Shqiptar (RTSH). RTSH ended SW & MW transmissions from txs in Albania in March 2017. The rebroadcasts via a 1kW SW tx at Kall (Germany) are an independent, personal initiative of the operator of the German relay platform "Shortwaveservice"; a project that is primarily targeting SWLs/DXers in Europe.

ALGERIA (ALG)

RADIO ALGÉRIENNE (Pub)

21 Boulevard des Martyrs, 16000 Algiers, Algeria.
☎ +213 21483790. Fax +213 21230823.
E: radioalgerie@gmail.com **W:** www.radioalgerie.dz
Webcast: L
L.P: (EPRS) DG: Chabane Lounakel; Dir, Technical Services: Mohamed Salah Saidi.
SAT: Alcomsat 1, Badr 6, Eutelsat 5WA/7WA/Hot Bird 13C, SES 4.
kHz: *5940, 6040, 6060, 6105, 6140, 7245, 7295, 7315, 7375*

Winter Schedule 2020/2021

Arabic	Days	Area	kHz
0400-0500	daily	CAf,WAf	6060iss*
0500-0600	daily	NAf,WAf	6105iss*
0500-0600	daily	CAf,WAf	7295iss*
0600-0700	daily	NAf,WAf	7245iss*
1800-2000	daily	CAf,WAf	7375iss*
1900-2000	daily	NAf,WAf	7315iss*
2000-2100	daily	NAf,WAf	6140iss*
2000-2200	daily	NAf,CAf	5940iss*
2100-2300	daily	NAf,WAf	6040iss*

Key: * Mainly Koran prgr. May include relays of R. Algérie Int., in Arabic and French.
Ann: Arabic: "Huna Al-Djazair".
V: QSL-card.

Notes: Relays of EPRS (Etablissement Public de Radiodiffusion Sonore) Home Sce 'Koran' prgr and Chaîne 1/3. Relays of Home Service 'Koran' prgr, may also include news in French.

ANTARCTICA (ATA)

RADIO NACIONAL "ARCÁNGEL SAN GABRIEL" (LRA36) (Pub)

Base Esperanza, Antártida Argentina 9411, Argentina.
☎ +54 2974 445304.
E: tranalra36@radionacional.gov.ar
L.P: Dir: TC Gustavo Quiroga.
SW: [LRA] Base Antártica Esperanza: 1 x 1, 1 x 10kW. The 10kW tx (when in use) is operated at around 1.2-1.5kW.
FM/DAB: FM: 96.7MHz (Esperanza Base)
kHz: *15476*

Winter Schedule 2020/2021

Spanish	Days	Area	kHz
1400-1600	..w....	SAm	15476lra†,*

Key: † Irregular; * USB/AM mode (H3E). Schedule is variable.
Ann: Spanish: "Desde Base Esperanza, transmite LRA36, Radio Nacional Arcángel San Gabriel".
V: QSL-card/letter (Rp. 1 IRC); Eqsl.

Notes: Local stn of the Argentinian national public service broadcaster Radio Nacional, launched on 20 October 1979. Operated by staff of the Argentinian Army (Comando antártico del Ejército). 24h on FM for the population of the Esperanza base. The SW trs are intended as a link between servicemen/scientists on the base and their families & friends on the Argentinian mainland.

ARGENTINA (ARG)

RAE – ARGENTINA AL MUNDO (Pub)

555 Maipú, C1006ACE, Buenos Aires, Argentina.
☎ +54 11 43256368. Fax +54 11 43259433.
E: rae@radionacional.gov.ar; argentinainternationalradio@gmail.com (English Sce)
W: www.radionacional.com.ar/rae-nueva-web
Webcast: D/L/P
L.P: Dir: Luis María Barassi.
SW: [BUE] Buenos Aires, General Pacheco ‡: 2 x 50, 1 x 100kW.
kHz: *5010, 5800, 5850, 5950, 7730, 7780, 9395, 15770*

Winter Schedule 2020/2021

Various	Days	Area	kHz
0200-0230	.twtfs.	NAm	9395rmi*
0200-0300	..twtfs	SAm	5800rmi*
0230-0300	.twtfs.	NAm,Eu	7780rmi*
0800-0900	.twtf..	NAm	5950rmi*
0800-0900	..w....	NAm	5850rmi*, 7730rmi*
0900-1000	.twtfs.	NAm	5950rmi*
1300-1330	m.....s	NAm,Eu	15770rmi*
1600-1700	mtwt...	NAm	7780rmi*
2200-2300	mtwtf..	NAm	9395rmi*
2200-2300	mtwtf..	Car	5010rmi*
2330-2400	mtwtf..	NAm,Eu	7780rmi*

Key: * All broadcasts have been replaced by multi-lingual transmissions, with short news bulletins in several languages, during the Coronavirus pandemic; ‡ Inactive at time of publication.
Ann: English: "RAE Argentina to the World".
V: QSL-card (Email rpt to qslrae@gmail.com).
Notes: External Sce of the national public-service broadcaster Radio y Televisión Argentina (RTA S.E.).

ARMENIA (ARM)

PUBLIC RADIO OF ARMENIA (Pub)

A. Manoogian Street 5, 0025 Yerevan, Armenia.
☎ +374 10 558010. Fax +374 10 551513.
E: info@armradio.am **W:** www.armradio.am
L.P: CEO: Arman Saghatelyan.
MW/SW: Via Gavar transmitting station.
kHz: *1395*

Winter Schedule 2020/2021

Azeri	Days	Area	kHz
1730-1745	daily	Cau	1395erv
Farsi	**Days**	**Area**	**kHz**
1645-1700	daily	IRN	1395erv
Kurdish (Kurmanji)	**Days**	**Area**	**kHz**
1600-1630	daily	Cau	1395erv
1630-1645	daily	Cau	1395erv*
Turkish	**Days**	**Area**	**kHz**
1700-1715	daily	TUR	1395erv

Key: * For the Yezidi ethnic minority in Armenia.
Ann: At beginning of each broadcast, in Armenian: "Yerevan khosum", followed by ID in the language of the prgr: Azeri: "Danisir Irävan", Farsi: "Inja Yerevane", Turkish: "Burasi Erivan".
IS: After IS, opens with National Anthem.
Notes: The schedule contains both Foreign Service trs and prgrs for ethnic minorities in Armenia.

AR RADIO INTERCONTINENTAL (Tx Operator)

A. Manoogian Street 5, 0025 Yerevan, Armenia.
☎ +374 10 551143. Fax +374 10 554600.
E: aa@arradio.am **W:** www.arradio.am
L.P: Pres: Armen Amiryan; CEO: Mher Margaryan.
MW: [ERV] Gavar, Noratus: 864/1350/1377kHz 1000kW.
Notes: AR Radio Intercontinental is the operator of high power MW txs at the Noratus transmitting site.

RADIO (CLOSED JOINT STOCK COMPANY) (Tx Operator)
1213 Noratus, Armenia.
☎ +374 264 62611.
L.P: Dir (acting): Vladimir Ghazanchyan.
MW: [ERV] Gavar, Noratus: 1314kHz 1000kW‡, 1395kHz 500kW.
SW: [ERV] Gavar, Noratus: 3 x 100, 3 x 1000kW
Key: ‡ Transmitter inactive at time of publication.
Notes: The Closed Joined Stock Company (CJSC) "Radio" is the operator of high power MW and SW txs at the Noratus transmitting site. CJSC "Radio", initially a state-run company, was owned by the (now liquidated) Swiss-registered Europress Group Sàrl until October 2016.

ASCENSION ISLAND (ASC)

BBC ATLANTIC RELAY STATION
English Bay, Ascension Island, ASCN 1ZZ.
☎ +247 64458. 🖷 +247 66117.
E: ops-asc@encompass.co.ac
L.P: Engineering Mgr: Jeff Francis.
SW: [ASC] English Bay: 6 x 250kW.
V: QSL-letter. (For direct report)
Notes: Owned by the BBC and operated by Encompass Digital Media Services Ltd (see under United Kingdom).

AUSTRALIA (AUS)

REACH BEYOND AUSTRALIA (Rlg)
P.O. Box 291, Kilsyth VIC 3137, Australia; 281-283 Colchester Road, Kilsyth VIC 3137, Australia.
☎ +61 3 87208000.
E: radio@reachbeyond.org.au **W:** www.reachbeyond.org.au
Transmitting site: P.O. Box 1339, Kununurra WA 6743, Australia; Lot 579, Packsaddle Road, Kununurra WA 6743, Australia
☎ +61 8 91669000.
L.P: CEO: Dale Stagg; Frequency Mgr: Ken Lingwood; Media Mgr: Jonas Santos.
SW: [KNX] Kununurra: 3 x 100kW.
kHz: *11825, 11865, 11875, 11905, 11945, 15410*

Winter Schedule 2020/2021

	Days	Area	kHz
Bengali	**Days**	**Area**	**kHz**
1245-1300	...t...	As	11825knx
1315-1330	....f..	As	11875knx
Bhojpuri	**Days**	**Area**	**kHz**
1300-1315	..w....	As	11875knx
Burmese	**Days**	**Area**	**kHz**
1145-1200	daily	As	11865knx
1200-1230	mt.tf..	As	11945knx
Chhattisgarhi	**Days**	**Area**	**kHz**
1300-1315	.....ss	As	11825knx, 11875knx
Dzongkha	**Days**	**Area**	**kHz**
1130-1145	.twt.ss	As	11825knx
1145-1200	......s	As	11825knx
English	**Days**	**Area**	**kHz**
1200-1230	......s	As	11825knx
1315-1330	m.w.f..	As	11825knx
1345-1400	daily	As	11875knx
Gujarati	**Days**	**Area**	**kHz**
1245-1300	..w....	As	11825knx
Himachali	**Days**	**Area**	**kHz**
1300-1315	...t...	As	11875knx
Hindi	**Days**	**Area**	**kHz**
1215-1245	mtwtf..	As	11825knx
1230-1300	......s	As	11825knx
1230-1300	daily	As	11875knx
1245-1300	.....s.	As	11825knx
1315-1330	..w....	As	11875knx
1330-1345	daily	As	11875knx
Japanese	**Days**	**Area**	**kHz**
1100-1130	daily	As	11905knx
2230-2300	....fs.	As	15410knx
Kannada	**Days**	**Area**	**kHz**
1200-1215	mtwtf..	As	11825knx
Kurukh	**Days**	**Area**	**kHz**
1245-1300	.t.....	As	11825knx
1300-1315	.t.....	As	11875knx
Malayalam	**Days**	**Area**	**kHz**
1315-1330	...t...	As	11825knx
Marathi	**Days**	**Area**	**kHz**
1300-1315	....f..	As	11875knx
1315-1330	...t...	As	11875knx
Marwari	**Days**	**Area**	**kHz**
1245-1300	....f..	As	11825knx
Matu	**Days**	**Area**	**kHz**
1200-1230	..w..ss	As	11945knx
Nepali	**Days**	**Area**	**kHz**
1130-1200	m...f..	As	11825knx
1315-1330	......s	As	11825knx
Oriya	**Days**	**Area**	**kHz**
1315-1330	......s	As	11875knx
Punjabi	**Days**	**Area**	**kHz**
1230-1245	....f..	As	11825knx
1300-1315	m......	As	11875knx
1315-1330	.....s.	As	11875knx
Rohingya	**Days**	**Area**	**kHz**
1130-1145	daily	As	11865knx
Tamil	**Days**	**Area**	**kHz**
1200-1230	.....s.	As	11825knx
1300-1315	mtwtf..	As	11825knx
1315-1330	.t...s.	As	11825knx
1315-1330	m......	As	11875knx
Telugu	**Days**	**Area**	**kHz**
1245-1300	m......	As	11825knx
1315-1330	.t.....	As	11875knx
Tsangla	**Days**	**Area**	**kHz**
1145-1200	.twt.s.	As	11825knx
Urdu	**Days**	**Area**	**kHz**
1245-1300	.....s.	As	11825knx

Ann: English: "This is Reach Beyond Australia - Life Changing Radio".
V: QSL-card.
Notes: Partner organisation of World Radio Missionary Fellowship, Inc (USA) and its media ministry Reach Beyond. Launched 2003 as "HCJB Australia", later rebranded "HCJB Global Australia", and in 2014 "Reach Beyond Australia".

HOBART RADIO INTERNATIONAL
Based in Lewisham, TAS 7173, Australia.
E: hriradio@gmail.com **W:** hriradio.org
Webcast: D
L.P: Host: Robb Wise.
SW: Via 3rd party facilities.
kHz: *5130, 5850, 5950, 7730, 7780, 9955*

Winter Schedule 2020/2021

English	Days	Area	kHz
0030-0100	......s	NAm	7730rmi
0430-0500	m......	NAm	5130bcq
0430-0500	......s	LAm	9955rmi
0830-0900	.....s.	NAm	5950rmi
0830-0900	......s	NAm	5850rmi, 7730rmi
2230-2300	......s	LAm	9955rmi
2330-2400	......s	Eu	7780rmi

Ann: English: "Hobart Radio International".
V: e-QSL.
Notes: "Hobart Radio International" (HRI) is a radio show produced by the Tasmanian DXer Robb Wise. HRI was founded 2004 and initially transmitted via various European pirate radio stns. Since 2015, HRI began hiring airtime via legal third party providers.

AUSTRIA (AUT)

RADIO Ö1 (ORF) (Pub)
See National Radio section.
Webcast: D/L/P

SW: Uses txs provided by ORS.
SAT: Astra 1N.
kHz: *6155*

Winter Schedule 2020/2021

German	**Days**	**Area**	**kHz**
0600-0710	.....ss	Eu,NAf,ME	6155mos
0600-0720	mtwtf..	Eu,NAf,ME	6155mos

V: QSL-letter.
Notes: Relay of the "Morgenjournal" news magazine on ORF's domestic channel "Ö1" ("Österreich 1"). ORF's External Service "R. Österreich International" (RÖI) was closed in 2003 and replaced by Home Service productions. ORF continued to transmit on SW the 15min "Report from Austria" in English until it was cancelled at the end of 2008.

ÖSTERREICHISCHE RUNDFUNKSENDER GMBH & CO KG (ORS) (Tx Operator)

✉ Würzburggasse 30, A-1136 Wien, Austria.
☎ +43 1 87012680. 🖷 +43 1 8704012773.
E: office@ors.at **W:** www.ors.at
L.P: CEO: Michael Wagenhofer, MD: Norbert Grill.
SW: [MOS] Moosbrunn: 2 x 100, 2 x 500kW.
Notes: ORS is the national transmitter network operator.

BANGLADESH (BGD)

BANGLADESH BETAR (Pub)

✉ 31 Syed Mahbub Morshad Avenue, Shah-e-Bangla Nagar, Dhaka-1207, Bangladesh.
☎ +880 2 9670657. (Ext. Sce); +880 2 44813062. (DG) 🖷 +880 2 44813063. (DG)
E: betar.external@yahoo.com (Dir, Ext Sce); dg@betar.gov.bd (DG)
W: www.betar.gov.bd
Webcast: D/L
✉ 121 Kazi Nazrul Islam Avenue, Shahbagh, Dhaka-1000, Bangladesh.
L.P: DG: Narayan Chandra Shil; Dir, External Sce: Kamal Ahmed; Senior Engineer, Research & Receiving Centre: Abu Tabib Md. Zia Hasan.
SW: [DKA] Dhaka, two sites: Kabirpur ‡: 2 x 250kW; Shavar: 1 x 100kW.
kHz: *4750*

Winter Schedule 2020/2021

Arabic	**Days**	**Area**	**kHz**
1600-1630	daily	SAs	4750dka
Bengali	**Days**	**Area**	**kHz**
1630-1730	daily	SAs	4750dka
1915-2000	daily	SAs	4750dka
English	**Days**	**Area**	**kHz**
1230-1300	daily	SAs	4750dka
1745-1900	daily	SAs	4750dka
Hindi	**Days**	**Area**	**kHz**
1515-1545	daily	SAs	4750dka
Nepali	**Days**	**Area**	**kHz**
1315-1345	daily	SAs	4750dka
Urdu	**Days**	**Area**	**kHz**
1400-1430	daily	SAs	4750dka

Ann: English: "This is the External Service of Bangladesh Betar".
IS: Local composition, played on violin and tanpura.
V: QSL-card. (Rpt to Senior Engineer, Research & Receiving Centre. Email rpt to: rrc@dhaka.net)
Notes: External service of the national public broadcaster Bangladesh Betar, launched on 1 Jan 1972.

BELARUS (BLR)

RADIO BELARUS INTERNATIONAL (Gov)

✉ Cyrvonaja Street 4, 220807 Minsk, Belarus.
☎ +375 17 2395852. 🖷 +375 17 2848574.
E: radio_belarus@tvr.by **W:** radiobelarus.by
Webcast: D/L (Webcast/Satellite languages: Arabic, Chinese, English, French, German, Polish, Russian, Spanish).
L.P: Dir: Navum Halpiarovic; Vice Dir: Vjacaslaŭ Lakcjušyn.
SW: Via Shortwaveservice (Germany).
FM/DAB: FM: See National Radio section.
kHz: *3985*

Winter Schedule 2020/2021

English	**Days**	**Area**	**kHz**
1800-1900	daily	CEu,WEu	3985kll
2000-2100	daily	CEu,WEu	3985kll
French	**Days**	**Area**	**kHz**
1540-1600	daily	CEu,WEu	3985kll
German	**Days**	**Area**	**kHz**
2100-2300	daily	CEu	3985kll
Spanish	**Days**	**Area**	**kHz**
1520-1540	daily	CEu,WEu	3985kll

Ann: German: "Hier ist Radio Belarus International".
Notes: International Service of the National State Radio-TV Company of Belarus. Short and mediumwave transmissions ended in spring 2016. The current rebroadcasts, via a 1kW SW tx at Kall, (Germany) are an independent, personal initiative of the operator of the German relay platform "Shortwaveservice". This is a project that target, primarily, SWLs/DXers in Europe.

BELGIUM (BEL)

RADIO ONDA

✉ Rue Stevens-Delannoy 22, 1020 Bruxelles, Belgium.
☎ +32 471 747293. (cell)
E: info@radioonda.be **W:** www.radioonda.be (English/French); ondaasbl.wixsite.com/home/a-radio (Portuguese).
L.P: Project coordinator: Julio Roth.
SW: [BOR] Borculo (Netherlands): 1 x 1kW (temporary installation, run at 0.1kW in accordance with current Dutch licence).
kHz: *6140*

Winter Schedule 2020/2021

English/French/ Portuguese	**Days**	**Area**	**kHz**
0000-2400	daily	Eu	6140bor†

Key: † Irregular.
Notes: Produced by the registered voluntary association "Onda pour le dévelopment de la communication sociale et culturelle de la communauté Brésilienne en Belgique". Plans to use a second, higher, frequency.

BROADCAST BELGIUM (Broker)

✉ P.O. Box 1, B-2310 Rijkevorsel, Belgium.
☎ +32 33 147800.
E: info@broadcast.be **W:** www.broadcast.be
✉ 5201 Blue Lagoon Drive, 8th Floor, Miami, FL 33126, USA. (Alyx & Yeyi, LLC)
☎ +1 305 5728070.
E: info@alyx-yeyi.com **W:** www.alyx-yeyi.com; www.airtime.org
L.P: MD: Ludo Maes.
Notes: Broadcast Belgium (and its U.S. branch Alyx & Yeyi, LLC) provides brokerage of SW airtime.

BENIN (BEN)

TWR WEST AFRICA TRANSMITTING STATION

✉ B.P. 1039, Parakou, Benin.
☎ +229 23102055.
E: 1566@twr.org
L.P: SM: Garth Kennedy.
MW: [PAR] Parakou: 1476kHz 200kW, 1566kHz 100kW.
Notes: Owned by TWR, For corporate details, see under TWR (USA). For schedule, see TWR Africa (South Africa).

BONAIRE (BES)

TWR BONAIRE (Rlg)

✉ P.O. Box 388, Kralendijk, Bonaire, Caribbean Netherlands.
☎ +599 7178800. 🖷 +599 7178808.
E: 800am@twr.org **W:** www.twrbonaire.com
Webcast: D/L
L.P: Dir: Bernard Oosterhoff.
MW: [TWB] Belnem: 800kHz 100kW, 400kW (run at 440kW).

FM/DAB: FM: 89.5MHz (Bonaire) with separate, local schedule.
kHz: *800*

Winter Schedule 2020/2021

English	Days	Area	kHz
2300-2400	daily	Car	800twb
Macushi	**Days**	**Area**	**kHz**
0945-1000	......s	B	800twb
Portuguese	**Days**	**Area**	**kHz**
0800-0945	.....ss	B	800twb
0800-1000	mtwtf..	B	800twb
Spanish	**Days**	**Area**	**kHz**
0000-0500	daily	Car,CUB	800twb
1000-1130	daily	Car	800twb
Wayampi	**Days**	**Area**	**kHz**
0945-1000	.....s.	B	800twb

Ann: English: "TWR Bonaire, in the Dutch Caribbean".
V: QSL-card.
Notes: Branch and transmitting station. Owned by TWR. For corporate details, see under USA.

BOTSWANA (BOT)

USAGM BOTSWANA TRANSMITTING STATION

✉ Private Bag 38, Selebi-Phikwe, Botswana.
☎ +267 2610932. 🖷 +267 2610185.
L.P: SM: Charles Shepard.
MW: [BOT] Selebi-Phikwe, Moepeng Hill: 909kHz 600kW. (Reserve tx: 50kW).
SW: [BOT] Selebi-Phikwe, Moepeng Hill: 4 x 100kW.
V: QSL-card. (Email rpt to manager_botswana@bot.usagm.gov)

BULGARIA (BUL)

SPACELINE LTD

✉ bul. James Bourchier 71, 6th Floor, 1407 Sofia, Bulgaria.
☎ +359 2 9625962.
E: info@spaceline.bg
W: www.spaceline.bg; www.facebook.com/shortwave.airtime
L.P: GM: Dimitar Todorov.
V: eQSL-card (for brokered stns).
Notes: Spaceline Ltd manages & brokers the operation of the NURTS-owned SW transmitting center Kostinbrod (see NURTS Bulgaria entry). Spaceline also brokers airtime on the Gavar SW/MW transmitting center in Armenia (see Radio CJSC entry under Armenia).

NURTS BULGARIA (Tx Operator)

✉ bul. Peyo K. Yavorov 2, 1164 Sofia, Bulgaria.
☎ +359 2 8069300. 🖷 +359 2 8069309.
E: ir@vivacom.bg **W:** www.vivacom.bg
L.P: CEO's: Emil Atanasov, Svilen Popov.
SW: [SOF] Sofia, Kostinbrod: 4 x 50, 3 x 100, 1 x 250kW (incl. 4 DRM capable txs, run at 70kW in DRM mode).
Notes: NURTS, a subsidiary of Bulgarian Telecommunications Company EAD (brand name: "Vivacom"), is the Bulgarian national transmitter operator. The operation of the SW transmitting center Kostinbrod is managed and brokered by Spaceline Ltd (see separate entry).

CANADA (CAN)

RADIO CANADA INTERNATIONAL (RCI) ‡ (Pub)

✉ 1400, boulevard René-Levesque Est, Montréal QC H2L 2M2, Canada.
☎ +1 514 5977461.
E: info@rcinet.ca **W:** www.rcinet.ca
Webcast: D/P
L.P: Editor-in-Chief: Soleïman Mellali.
SW: Via Shortwaveservice (Germany).
Key: ‡ The operator of the Shortwaveservice platform (Germany) has ceased rebroadcasting RCI webcasts on SW.
Notes: RCI is the External Service of the public service Canadian Broadcasting Corp. RCI ended shortwave transmissions in 2013. The rebroadcasts of selected RCI webcasts via a 1kW SW tx at Kall (Germany) were an independent, personal initiative of the operator of the German relay platform "Shortwaveservice". The project that targets, primarily, SWLs/DXers in Europe".

BIBLE VOICE BROADCASTING (BVB) (Rlg)

✉ P.O. Box 95561, Newmarket, ON L3Y 8J8, Canada.
☎ +1 905 8982500.
E: mail@bvbroadcasting.org **W:** www.bvbroadcasting.org
Webcast: D
✉ 350 Davis Drive, Newmarket, ON L3Y 2N7, Canada. (HAGCM)
☎ +1 905 8985447. 🖷 +1 905 8982500.
W: www.hagcm.org
L.P: International Ministry Coordinator: Mrs. Marty McLaughlin.
kHz: *5900, 5935, 5995, 6080, 6240, 7365, 7520, 7555, 9400, 9440, 9450, 9715, 11790, 11875, 11900, 17650, 21480*

Winter Schedule 2020/2021

Amharic	Days	Area	kHz
1630-1730	.t.....	EAf	11790nau
1700-1730	..wt...	EAf	11790nau
1730-1800	......s	EAf	11790nau
Arabic	**Days**	**Area**	**kHz**
0200-0230	daily	ME	5900sof
0500-0515	....f...	ME	9450nau
0600-0615	daily	NAf	9440nau
1715-1730	m.w....	ME	5995sof
1715-1745	...tfs.	ME	5995sof
1745-1800	daily	ME	5995sof
1800-1830	.....s.	WAs	7365nau
1930-1945	daily	NAf	5900sof
1945-2000	daily	NAf	9400sof
English	**Days**	**Area**	**kHz**
0200-0230	...t...	SAs	11790mdc
1200-1230	.....s.	EAs	17650mdc
1230-1245	......s	SEA	21480mdc**
1300-1330	mt.t..s	EAs	7555dsb
1400-1430	.....s.	SAs	11900nau*
1430-1500	.....s.	SAs	11900nau
1800-1815	....f..	ME	9715mos
1800-1830	...t...	ME	9715mos
1830-1930	.....ss	ME	9715mos
1915-1930	......s	ME	5935nau
1930-2015	......s	ME	6080nau
Korean	**Days**	**Area**	**kHz**
1300-1330	....fs.	EAs	7555dsb
1830-1845	.....ss	EAs	7520dsb
Nuer	**Days**	**Area**	**kHz**
1630-1700	daily	CAf	11875iss
Oromo	**Days**	**Area**	**kHz**
1600-1630	mt....s	EAf	11790nau
Persian	**Days**	**Area**	**kHz**
1800-1830	....f..	WAs	7365nau
1800-1900	...t...	WAs	7365nau
1830-1900	.t....s	WAs	7365nau
Somali	**Days**	**Area**	**kHz**
1630-1700	.....ss	EAf	11790nau
Tigrinya	**Days**	**Area**	**kHz**
1730-1800	.tw....	EAf	11790nau
Urdu	**Days**	**Area**	**kHz**
1200-1300	.....s.	SAs	6240tac

Key: * 1st Sat of month; ** 1st & 3rd Sun of month.
V: QSL-card.
Notes: BVB is a service of High Adventure Gospel Communication Ministries (Canada), in cooperation with Bible Voice (UK) and High Adventure Gospel Communication Ministries, Inc (USA). BVB's SW transmissions consist of religious paid programming, produced by small religious organisations, or individuals. Each prgr has its own brand. The schedule is subject to change without notice.

RADIO SADAYE ZINDAGI (Rlg)

☎ +1 450 3051354.
E: info@afghanradio.org **W:** afghanradio.org
Webcast: L

P.O.Box 322, Port Colborne, ON L3K SW1, Canada. (Pamir Productions).
+1 289 4781189.
E: info@pamirmedia.org **W:** pamirmedia.org
L.P: Associate Dir (Pamir Productions): Shoaib Ebadi.
kHz: *1467, 5130, 5940*

Winter Schedule 2020/2021

Dari	Days	Area	kHz
0000-0200	daily	AFG	5130bis
0230-0300	daily	AFG	5940dha
1500-1530	daily	AFG	1467bis
1500-1800	daily	AFG	5130bis

V: eQSL-card.
Notes: Sadaye Zindagi ("Sound of Life") is a 24h Internet radio station for listeners in Afghanistan, produced by Pamir Productions. Parts of the programming is distributed on MW/SW with assistance of global religious platforms like TWR (USA) and IBRA Media (Sweden). Pamir Productions is a partner ministry of TWR.

RED TELECOM (Broker)
522 Old Orchard Grove, Toronto, ON M5M 2G6, Canada.
+1 416 7311266. +1 416 3527539.
E: info@red-telecom.com
116 Main St., 2nd Floor, Road Town, Tortola, British Virgin Islands.
L.P: MD: Daniel Robinson.
Notes: Red Telecom Ltd brokers airtime for tx facilities of Teleradiokom in Tajikistan and RRTM in Uzbekistan.

CHINA (CHN)

CHINA RADIO INTERNATIONAL – VOICE OF THE SOUTH CHINA SEA (Gov)
See China Radio International for contact details.
W: vscs.cri.cn
Webcast: L
FM/DAB: FM: 89.1MHz (Sanya: 3kW); 96.6MHz (Wuzhishan: 3kW); 96.8MHz (Wenchang: 3kW); 101.0MHz (Sansha, Yongxing (Woody) Island, South China Sea: 3kW); 102.0MHz (Qionghai: 3kW), all in Hainan province.
kHz: *9720, 11640, 11700, 11805, 11895, 11955*

Winter Schedule 2020/2021

Chinese	Days	Area	kHz
0900-1000	daily	SEA	11895nnn
Filipino	**Days**	**Area**	**kHz**
1200-1230	daily	SEA	9720xia, 11955xuw
Indonesian	**Days**	**Area**	**kHz**
1330-1430	daily	SEA	11805xuw, 11955kun
Malay	**Days**	**Area**	**kHz**
1230-1330	daily	SEA	11700xuw, 11955kun
Vietnamese	**Days**	**Area**	**kHz**
1200-1300	daily	SEA	11640xia

Notes: Launched on 9 Apr 2013. The Voice of the South China Sea is a service produced by China Radio International (CRI), aimed at countries around the South China Sea.

CHINA RADIO INTERNATIONAL (CRI) (Gov)
16a, Shijingshan Rd, Beijing 100040, P.R. China.
+86 10 68891000, 68891001. +86 10 68892738, 68891582.
E: aboutcri@cri.com.cn; crieng@cri.com.cn **W:** www.cri.cn
Webcast: D/L
L.P: GD: Wang Gengnian; CE: Wang Lian; Dir, English Sce: Yang Lei.
MW/SW: See NRTA for tx information.
SAT: Apstar 6C, Intelsat 14/19/20, Superbird C2, Telstar 11N, Yamal 202.
kHz: *603, 684, 900, 963, 1017, 1044, 1080, 1188, 1269, 1296, 1323, 1341, 1422, 1521, 5905, 5910, 5915, 5955, 5965, 5970, 5975, 5980, 5985, 5990, 6010, 6020, 6025, 6040, 6055, 6060, 6065, 6070, 6075, 6080, 6090, 6095, 6100, 6105, 6110, 6115, 6135, 6140, 6145, 6150, 6155, 6160, 6165, 6175, 6180, 6185, 6190, 7205, 7210, 7215, 7220, 7225, 7235, 7240, 7245, 7250, 7255, 7260, 7265, 7275, 7285, 7290, 7295, 7300, 7305, 7315, 7320, 7325, 7330, 7335, 7340, 7345, 7350, 7360, 7365, 7370, 7380, 7385, 7390, 7395, 7400, 7405, 7410, 7415, 7420, 7425, 7430, 7435, 7440, 7445, 9410, 9415, 9440, 9450, 9455, 9460, 9470, 9490, 9515, 9520, 9525, 9535, 9540, 9550, 9555, 9560, 9565, 9570, 9585, 9590, 9600, 9610, 9615, 9620, 9630, 9640, 9645, 9655, 9665, 9675, 9685, 9690, 9695, 9705, 9710, 9720, 9730, 9745, 9760, 9765, 9770, 9785, 9795, 9800, 9825, 9855, 9860, 9865, 9870, 9875, 9880, 11610, 11635, 11640, 11650, 11680, 11690, 11700, 11710, 11720, 11730, 11750, 11760, 11770, 11780, 11785, 11790, 11795, 11820, 11840, 11860, 11870, 11875, 11880, 11885, 11895, 11900, 11910, 11945, 11955, 11975, 11980, 11990, 12015, 12035, 12070, 13570, 13580, 13590, 13600, 13610, 13630, 13640, 13645, 13650, 13655, 13660, 13685, 13720, 13730, 13740, 13750, 13770, 13780, 13790, 13800, 13810, 13850, 13855, 15110, 15120, 15125, 15130, 15135, 15145, 15160, 15170, 15180, 15185, 15190, 15210, 15220, 15225, 15250, 15260, 15335, 15340, 15350, 15425, 15430, 15435, 15440, 15445, 15465, 15505, 15525, 15550, 15560, 15620, 15665, 15700, 17485, 17490, 17510, 17520, 17540, 17560, 17570, 17615, 17630, 17640, 17650, 17670, 17680, 17690, 17710, 17720, 17730, 17735, 17740, 17750, 17855, 17880*

Winter Schedule 2020/2021

Albanian	Days	Area	kHz
1900-2000	daily	Eu	6020szg, 7385kas
Amoy	**Days**	**Area**	**kHz**
0100-0200	daily	SAs	9610kun
0100-0200	daily	SEA	9460kun, 9550kun, 9860jin, 11945kun, 11980kun
0100-0300	daily	SEA	15425xia, 17490bei
1200-1300	daily	SEA	11910bei
1400-1500	daily	SEA	9655kun, 11650kun
Arabic	**Days**	**Area**	**kHz**
0500-0700	daily	ME,NAf	17485kas
1600-1700	daily	EAf	15125bko
1600-1700	daily	NAf	17880bko
1600-1800	daily	ME,NAf	7300kas
1830-1930	daily	NAf	11640bko, 13685bko
2000-2200	daily	ME,NAf	6100xia
Bengali	**Days**	**Area**	**kHz**
0200-0300	daily	SAs	9655kun, 11640kun
1300-1400	daily	SAs	1188kun, 9600bji
1300-1500	daily	SAs	9490kun, 11610kun
1400-1500	daily	SAs	1269xuw
1500-1600	daily	SAs	9610kun, 9690kun
Bulgarian	**Days**	**Area**	**kHz**
1100-1200	daily	Eu	15180uru
1830-1900	daily	Eu	6020szg, 7265uru, 9695kun
2030-2100	daily	Eu	7320kun, 9720uru
Burmese	**Days**	**Area**	**kHz**
0200-0300	daily	BRM	900deh
0700-0800	daily	BRM	900deh
1100-1200	daily	SEA	1188kun, 9880kun
1300-1400	daily	SEA	9880kun
1300-1500	daily	SEA	7400kun
1400-1500	daily	BRM	900deh
Cantonese	**Days**	**Area**	**kHz**
0000-0100	daily	SEA	11820xia, 17490bei
0400-0500	daily	NAm	5910qvc
0400-0600	daily	EAs	13655xia, 15160jin
0700-0800	daily	EAs	11640jin, 13610xia
1000-1100	daily	Pac	15440kun, 17670kun
1100-1200	daily	Pac	9540bei, 13580kun
1100-1200	daily	SEA	603dof, 7370nnn, 9590kun, 9645bei
1200-1300	daily	NAm	9570qvc
1700-1800	daily	EAf	7220xia
1700-1800	daily	SAf	7325uru
1900-2000	daily	Eu	7215bei, 9770kas*
2300-2400	daily	SEA	6140kun, 6180kun, 7325kun, 9630jin, 11945kun
Chaozhou	**Days**	**Area**	**kHz**
0700-0800	daily	SEA	15145xia, 17750xia
1100-1200	daily	SEA	9440kun, 11875kun
1800-1900	daily	Eu	6010uru, 7285xia

Chinese	Days	Area	kHz
0000-0100	daily	EAs	11780jin, 11900bei
0000-0100	daily	SEA	9620kun, 11975kun, 12035xia
0000-0200	daily	SEA	13580bei
0000-0400	daily	EAs	13655xia
0100-0200	daily	SEA	9655nnn, 11640xia, 11770nnn
0100-0200	daily	SAs	7250uru, 7300kas
0100-0400	daily	EAs	15160jin
0200-0300	daily	NAm	6180qvc
0200-0300	daily	SAm	7330kas, 11780bei
0200-0300	daily	SAs	9825uru
0300-0400	daily	SAs	9450kas, 17540bei
0300-0600	daily	EAs	15130bei
0400-0500	daily	SAs	13640kas, 15170kas
0500-0600	daily	SAs	15110kas
0500-0700	daily	EAs	15120bei
0600-0700	daily	Eu	13720kas
0600-0700	daily	EAs	13655xia, 15160jin
0600-0800	daily	SEA	11710nnn, 13750kun, 17740xia
0700-0800	daily	SEA	11875nnn
0700-0800	daily	SAs	17520kas
0700-0900	daily	Eu	17650kas
0800-0900	daily	EAs	9880bei, 11640jin, 13610xia
0800-0900	daily	SAs	15550kas
0800-1000	daily	CAs,Cau	15560xia, 17560xia
0900-1000	daily	EAs	7430jin, 9440xia
0900-1000	daily	Pac	15440kun, 17670kun
0900-1100	daily	SEA	9460nnn, 11980kun, 13850bei, 15250kun, 15340xia
0900-1100	daily	EAs	5965bei
0900-1100	daily	SAs	13780kas, 15525uru
1000-1100	daily	EAs	7255xia, 9880bei
1000-1200	daily	Eu	17650kas
1100-1200	daily	EAs	7435bei
1100-1200	daily	Pac	11750bei, 15440kun
1100-1200	daily	SAs	9515kas, 11980kas
1200-1300	daily	EAs	7390bei
1200-1300	daily	Eu	13720kas
1200-1300	daily	SAs	7205kas, 9655kas
1200-1400	daily	ME,NAf	11790kas*, 13810kas*
1200-1400	daily	SAs	9540kun
1200-1400	daily	SEA	7440nnn, 9855bei
1200-1500	daily	ME	9520uru
1300-1400	daily	SEA	7215xia
1300-1400	daily	EAs	7205bei
1300-1400	daily	Eu	13855kas
1400-1500	daily	EAs	7210bei
1400-1500	daily	Eu	9590kas, 11785kas
1400-1500	daily	SAs	9730kas
1400-1500	daily	SEA	6040xia, 7410bei
1400-1600	daily	SAs	7235kas
1500-1600	daily	SEA	5910bei, 9455kun
1500-1600	daily	EAs	7255bei
1500-1600	daily	Eu	9590kas, 9705kas
1500-1600	daily	SAs	9560kas
1730-1830	daily	ME,NAf	7275uru, 7315kun, 9695kun
1730-1830	daily	Eu	6150szg, 7445uru
2000-2100	daily	Eu	7335szg, 7440bei
2000-2100	daily	ME,NAf	7245kas, 9865kun
2000-2100	daily	SAf	7205xia
2200-2300	daily	EAs	7305bei
2200-2300	daily	NAf,ME	7265kun, 7395uru
2200-2300	daily	SAf	5975bei, 7430jin
2200-2300	daily	SEA	6100kun, 6140kun, 6180kun, 7325kun
2230-2400	daily	NAf,WAf	11975bko, 15505bko
2300-2400	daily	EAs	9555bei
2300-2400	daily	Eu	7300uru
2300-2400	daily	WAf	7295bko

Croatian	Days	Area	kHz
1700-1800	daily	Eu	7335bei, 9410kas
2100-2200	daily	Eu	6135bei, 7225bei

Czech	Days	Area	kHz
1100-1200	daily	Eu	15225kas, 17570kas
1900-1930	daily	Eu	7325szg
1900-2000	daily	Eu	7415uru

English	Days	Area	kHz
0000-0100	daily	EAs	9560bei
0000-0100	daily	SAs	7425kas
0000-0200	daily	SAs	6075kas, 6180kas
0000-0200	daily	SEA	11885xia, 15125bei
0100-0200	daily	Eu	9675kas
0100-0200	daily	SAs	7370kas
0100-0200	daily	NAm	6180qvc
0200-0300	daily	SAs	9610kas
0200-0400	daily	SAs	11770kas
0300-0400	daily	NAm	5910qvc
0300-0400	daily	SAs	13800kas
0300-0500	daily	EAs	13590bei, 15120bei
0400-0600	daily	CAs	17855bei
0400-0600	daily	CAs,Eu	17730xia
0500-0700	daily	ME,NAf	17510kas
0500-0700	daily	SAs	15430kas
0500-0900	daily	SAs	11895kas, 15465kas
0500-1100	daily	SAs	15350kas
0600-0700	daily	SEA	13645xia
0600-0700	daily	ME	11870kas, 15145kas
0600-0800	daily	SEA	17710bei
0700-0800	daily	SEA	13660xia
0700-0900	daily	ME,NAf	17670kas
0700-1000	daily	SAs	15185kas
0700-1300	daily	Eu	17490kas
0800-1000	daily	EAs	9415xia
0900-1000	daily	Eu	17570uru, 17650kas
0900-1100	daily	Pac	15210kun, 17690jin
1000-1100	daily	EAs	5955xia, 7215xia, 11635bei
1000-1100	daily	SAs	15190kas
1000-1200	daily	SEA	13590bei, 13720xia
1100-1200	daily	SAs	11795kas
1100-1200	daily	SEA	9730bei
1100-1300	daily	SAs	7250kas, 11650uru, 12015kas
1100-1300	daily	SEA	1269xuw
1100-1600	daily	EAs	5955bei
1200-1300	daily	SEA	684dof, 1188kun, 9600kun, 9645bei, 9730kun
1200-1300	daily	CAs	11690xia
1200-1300	daily	Pac	9760kun
1200-1300	daily	SAs	9460kas
1200-1400	daily	SEA	1341hdu, 11980kun
1200-1400	daily	Eu	13790uru
1200-1400	daily	Pac	11760kun
1300-1400	daily	Eu	11640kas
1300-1400	daily	NAm	9570qvc
1300-1400	daily	Pac	11900kun
1300-1400	daily	SAs	7300kas, 9655kas
1300-1400	daily	SEA	9730bei, 11910bei
1300-1500	daily	CAs,Eu	9765bji
1300-1600	daily	SEA	9870xia
1400-1500	daily	ME	6100uru
1400-1500	daily	SAs	7300uru, 9460uru
1400-1500	daily	Eu	9795uru, 11880kas
1400-1600	daily	EAf	13685bko, 17630bko
1400-1600	daily	SEA	6135xia
1500-1600	daily	Eu	9525kas
1500-1600	daily	NAf,ME	6095kas, 9720uru
1500-1600	daily	NAm	15700qvc

English	Days	Area	kHz
1500-1600	daily	SAs	1188kun, 7395uru, 9785jin
1500-1600	daily	SEA	7325bei
1500-1700	daily	Eu	9675kas
1500-1800	daily	SAs	1323uru
1500-1800	daily	SEA	9880nnn
1600-1700	daily	Eu	9875kas
1600-1700	daily	NAf,ME	7420uru
1600-1700	daily	SEA	6060kun
1600-1800	daily	Eu	7255kas
1600-1800	daily	SAf	7435jin, 9570bei
1600-1800	daily	SAs	7235kas
1600-1800	daily	SEA	1080xuw, 6175nnn
1700-1800	daily	ME	6165bei
1700-1800	daily	SAs	6140kas, 7410kas
1700-1800	daily	SEA	6090kun, 7420kun
1700-1900	daily	Eu	6100bei
1800-1900	daily	Eu	7405bei
1830-1930	daily	NAf	11640bko
1900-2100	daily	ME,NAf	7295uru, 9440kun
2000-2100	daily	SAf	5985bei
2000-2130	daily	CAf	13630bko
2000-2130	daily	EAf	11640bko
2000-2200	daily	Eu	7285xia, 7415kas, 9600kas
2100-2200	daily	SAf	7205xia, 7325bei
2200-2300	daily	EAs	5915bei
2300-0100	daily	SEA	11790xia
2300-0200	daily	Eu	7350kas
2300-2400	daily	NAm,CAm	5990qvc
2300-2400	daily	SAs	5915kas, 7410kas
2300-2400	daily	EAs	6145bei
2300-2400	daily	SEA	9535kun
Esperanto	**Days**	**Area**	**kHz**
1100-1200	daily	EAs	7210uru, 9450uru
1300-1400	daily	SEA	9440nnn, 9695bei
1700-1800	daily	Eu	7205bei, 7420xia
1930-2030	daily	Eu	7265uru, 9745uru
2200-2300	daily	SAm	7315kas, 9860kas
Filipino	**Days**	**Area**	**kHz**
1130-1200	daily	SEA	1341hdu, 5910bei, 7410jin, 11955kun, 12070xia
1430-1500	daily	SEA	1341hdu, 7325bei, 11640bei
French	**Days**	**Area**	**kHz**
0600-0800	daily	Eu	15220kas
1200-1400	daily	Eu	13570kas
1300-1400	daily	EAf	13685bko
1300-1400	daily	NAf	17880bko
1300-1400	daily	Eu	13720kas
1600-1800	daily	Eu	7350kas
1800-2000	daily	Eu	7360xia
1800-2000	daily	NAf,WAf	7385kas
1830-2030	daily	WAf	7350kas, 9645kun
2030-2230	daily	Eu	6115bei, 7350uru
2130-2230	daily	CAf	13630bko
2130-2230	daily	NAf,WAf	11975bko
German	**Days**	**Area**	**kHz**
0600-0800	daily	Eu	17615uru, 17720kas
1600-1800	daily	Eu	5970xia, 7380bji
1800-2000	daily	Eu	6160xia, 7395kas, 9615uru
Hakka	**Days**	**Area**	**kHz**
0000-0100	daily	SEA	9460kun, 9550kun, 9610kun, 9860jin
0400-0500	daily	SEA	17510xia, 17710bei
0400-0500	daily	SAs	13740kas, 15350kas
1600-1700	daily	SAf	6090xia, 7325uru
Hausa	**Days**	**Area**	**kHz**
0800-0900	daily	WAf	7295bko
1630-1730	daily	WAf	9620kas, 9665kun
1730-1830	daily	WAf	9450kas, 9685kun
1800-1830	daily	WAf	11640bko, 13645bko
Hindi	**Days**	**Area**	**kHz**
0300-0400	daily	SAs	9695kas, 9870kas, 11640kas, 11700kas
1300-1400	daily	SAs	1269xuw, 1422kas, 7265uru, 9450kas
1500-1600	daily	SAs	7225uru, 7265kas
1600-1700	daily	SAs	1188kun, 1422kas, 5915kas, 7395kun
1600-1800	daily	SAs	1269xuw
Hungarian	**Days**	**Area**	**kHz**
1000-1100	daily	Eu	15220kas, 17570kas
1900-1930	daily	Eu	7435xia, 9560uru
2030-2100	daily	Eu	7390jin, 9585kas
2130-2200	daily	Eu	7445uru
Indonesian	**Days**	**Area**	**kHz**
0830-0930	daily	SEA	15135kun, 17735kun
1030-1130	daily	SEA	11700kun, 15135kun
Italian	**Days**	**Area**	**kHz**
0600 0700	daily	Eu	15620kas
1800-1900	daily	Eu	7340kas, 7435jin
2030-2130	daily	Eu	7265uru, 7345kas
Japanese	**Days**	**Area**	**kHz**
1000-1100	daily	EAs	9440xia
1000-1300	daily	EAs	7325jin
1100-1300	daily	EAs	7260xia
1100-1600	daily	EAs	1044hnl
1300-1400	daily	EAs	7325xia
1300-1500	daily	EAs	7410jin
1400-1500	daily	EAs	7395xia
1500-1600	daily	EAs	5980xia, 7220jin
2200-2300	daily	EAs	5985xia, 7440jin
2300-2400	daily	EAs	9695jin, 9720xia
Khmer	**Days**	**Area**	**kHz**
0000-0100	daily	SEA	11990nnn
1030-1130	daily	SEA	684dof, 15160nnn, 17680kun
1200 1300	daily	SEA	9440kun, 11680nnn
1400-1500	daily	SEA	684dof, 6055nnn, 9880nnn
2300-0100	daily	SEA	684dof, 9765nnn
2300-2400	daily	SEA	7430nnn
Korean	**Days**	**Area**	**kHz**
1000-1100	daily	EAs	1017cah**
1100-1500	daily	EAs	5965xia
1100-1600	daily	EAs	1017cah, 1323hdn
2100-2300	daily	EAs	1017cah, 1323hdn, 7290xia
Lao	**Days**	**Area**	**kHz**
1230-1330	daily	SEA	1080xuw, 7360kun, 9785kun
1430-1530	daily	SEA	1080xuw, 7360kun, 9675kun
Malay	**Days**	**Area**	**kHz**
0930-1030	daily	SEA	15135kun, 17680kun
Mongolian	**Days**	**Area**	**kHz**
0000-0100	daily	EAs	7205bei, 9470xia
1100-1200	daily	EAs	6100uru, 7390huh
1200-1300	daily	EAs	1323uru, 5915huh, 5990huh
1300-1400	daily	EAs	6100uru, 7285bei
1400-1500	daily	EAs	5915huh, 5990huh
2300-2400	daily	EAs	6185xia, 7205xia
Nepali	**Days**	**Area**	**kHz**
0130-0230	daily	SAs	11860kun
0130-0330	daily	SAs	13780kun
0230-0330	daily	SAs	11730kun
1400-1500	daily	SAs	1188kun, 7220xia, 7435kun

Nepali	Days	Area	kHz
1500-1600	daily	SAs	1269xuw, 7215kun, 9535xia

Pashto	Days	Area	kHz
0200-0230	daily	WAs	6065kas, 7350kas, 11840xia
1500-1600	daily	WAs	7435kun, 9665kas
1530-1600	daily	WAs	6165uru

Persian	Days	Area	kHz
1500-1530	daily	ME	6165uru, 9600kas
1800-1900	daily	ME	7325bei, 7415xia

Polish	Days	Area	kHz
2000-2100	daily	Eu	6020szg, 7305uru

Portuguese	Days	Area	kHz
0000-0100	daily	SAm	9710kas
1900-2000	daily	Eu	7335jin, 9730kas
1900-2000	daily	SAf	5985bei, 7205xia, 7365bei, 9535bji
1930-2000	daily	SAf	11640bko, 13630bko
2200-2300	daily	Eu	6175xia, 7260uru
2200-2300	daily	SAm	9410kas, 9685kas
2300-0100	daily	SAm	6100bei
2300-2400	daily	SAm	13650qvc

Romanian	Days	Area	kHz
0900-1000	daily	Eu	15260kas
1900-2000	daily	Eu	6090uru
1930-2000	daily	Eu	7435xia

Russian	Days	Area	kHz
0000-0200	daily	CAs	1521uru
0100-0200	daily	CAs	5905kas
0100-0200	daily	CAs,Eu	9440xia
0200-0300	daily	CAs	5915kas
0200-0300	daily	CAs,Eu	11980xia
0300-0400	daily	CAs	11710uru, 15435xia
0300-0400	daily	CAs,Eu	17710jin
0300-0500	daily	CAs	7325kas
0400-0500	daily	CAs,Eu	17640xia
0400-0600	daily	CAs,Eu	15445kas, 15665uru
0800-1000	daily	CAs,Eu	15335kas, 15665uru
1000-1100	daily	EAs	7390huh
1000-1200	daily	EAs	5915huh, 7290szg
1100-1200	daily	CAs	6080bei
1100-1200	daily	EAs	1323uru
1100-1600	daily	EAs	963hdn, 1323hei
1100-2000	daily	CAs	1521uru
1200-1300	daily	CAs,Eu	7215xia, 9590szg, 9685uru
1200-1300	daily	EAs	6100bei, 7410szg
1200-1700	daily	CAs	5905kas
1300-1400	daily	CAs,Eu	9665xia
1300-1400	daily	EAs	5915huh, 5990huh, 7255szg
1300-1500	daily	EAs	1323uru
1400-1500	daily	CAs,Eu	7330xia
1400-1500	daily	EAs	7435szg
1500-1600	daily	CAs,Eu	6025xia, 6105szg, 6180uru
1500-1600	daily	EAs	5915huh, 5965bei, 5990huh
1600-1700	daily	CAs,Eu	7215szg, 7265bei
1600-1800	daily	CAs,Eu	6040uru
1700-1800	daily	CAs,Eu	6070xia, 7265uru, 7410szg
1800-1900	daily	CAs,Eu	6070bei, 7210uru, 7255szg
1900-2000	daily	CAs,Eu	6100bei, 6110xia, 7245bji
2000-2100	daily	CAs,Eu	6155bei, 7255bji
2300-0100	daily	EAs	5990huh, 7415huh

Serbian	Days	Area	kHz
1200-1300	daily	Eu	15180uru
2000-2030	daily	Eu	7325uru, 7390xia, 9585kas
2100-2130	daily	Eu	7325xia, 7445kun

Sinhala	Days	Area	kHz
1400-1500	daily	SAs	7265kas, 9665jin
2330-0030	daily	SAs	6100kun, 7260kas

Spanish	Days	Area	kHz
0000-0100	daily	NAm,CAm	5990qvc
0000-0100	daily	SAm	15120qvc
0100-0300	daily	SAm	9710kas
0600-0800	daily	Eu	15135kas
2100-2300	daily	Eu	6020szg, 9640kas
2200-2300	daily	SAm	6100bei
2200-2400	daily	Eu	7250uru
2300-0100	daily	SAm	9800kas
2300-0300	daily	SAm	9590kas

Swahili	Days	Area	kHz
1600-1800	daily	EAf	5985bei, 7245xia
1700-1800	daily	CAf	13645bko
1700-1800	daily	EAf	15125bko

Tamil	Days	Area	kHz
0200-0300	daily	SAs	9800kas, 11870kas
0300-0400	daily	SAs	13600kun, 13730kas
1400-1500	daily	SAs	5965kas, 9610kas
1500-1600	daily	SAs	7360kas, 9490kas

Thai	Days	Area	kHz
1130-1230	daily	SEA	1080xuw, 7360kun, 9785kun
1330-1430	daily	SEA	1080xuw, 7360kun, 9785kun

Turkish	Days	Area	kHz
1500-1600	daily	ME	9565kun
1600-1700	daily	ME	6165uru, 7325kun
1900-2000	daily	ME	7255kun, 9655kun

Urdu	Days	Area	kHz
0100-0200	daily	SAs	7240kas
0100-0300	daily	SAs	6020kas
0200-0300	daily	SAs	7290kas
1400-1500	daily	SAs	7285kun
1400-1600	daily	SAs	1422kas, 6075kas
1500-1600	daily	SAs	7285kas

Vietnamese	Days	Area	kHz
0000-0100	daily	SEA	11770bei, 13770xia
0400-0600	daily	SEA	603dof, 684dof, 11650kun, 17740xia
1100-1200	daily	SEA	11785bji, 11990xia
1100-1500	daily	SEA	9550bei
1100-1700	daily	SEA	1296kun
1200-1300	daily	SEA	11720bji
1200-1700	daily	SEA	603dof
1300-1400	daily	SEA	684dof, 9685xia
1400-1500	daily	SEA	9685bji
1500-1600	daily	SEA	6190bei
1500-1700	daily	SEA	684dof
1600-1700	daily	SEA	6010bei, 7315kun
2300-0100	daily	SEA	603dof
2300-2400	daily	SEA	7220xia, 9415bei

Key: * Relay of CRI News Radio; ** CNR8 relay.

Ann: Arabic: "Idha'at as-Sin ad-Duwaliyah"; Chinese: "Zhongguo guoji guangbo diantai"; English: "This is China Radio International, broadcasting from Beijing"; French: "Ici Radio Chine Internationale"; German: "Hier ist Radio China International"; Indonesian: "Inilah Radio CRI, China Radio International"; Japanese: "Kochirawa Pekin Hoso, Chugoku Kokusai Hosokyoku desu"; Korean: "Jungguk gukje bangsonggugimnida"; Malay: "Inilah Radio Antarabangsa China, dalam bahasa Melayu"; Mongolian: "Hyatadyn Olon Ulsyn Radio"; Russian: "Govorit Mezhdunarodnoye Radio Kitaya"; Spanish: "Esta es Radio Internacional de China"; Swahili: "Hii ni Radio China kimataifa"; Vietnamese: "Day la dai phatthanh quoc te Trung quoc".

IS: First bars of the National Anthem.

V: QSL-card.

Notes: Founded on 3 Dec 1941. Since March 2018, China Radio International is produced under the umbrella of the state-owned China Media Group.

CHINA TIBET BROADCASTING (CTB) – HOLY TIBET (Gov)

41 Beijing Zhonglu, Lhasa, Xizang 850000, P.R. China.
+86 891 6834073.
E: holytibetprogram@163.com **W:** www.vtibet.com
Webcast: D
SW: See NRTA for tx information.
kHz: *4905, 4920, 6025, 6110, 6130, 6200, 7255, 7385, 9490, 9580*

Winter Schedule 2020/2021

English	Days	Area	kHz
0700-0800	daily	As	4905lha, 4920lha, 6025lha, 6110lha, 6130lha, 6200lha, 9490lha, 9580lha
1600-1700	daily	As	4905lha, 4920lha, 6025lha, 6110lha, 6130lha, 6200lha, 7255lha, 7385lha

Ann: English: "This is Holy Tibet, presented to you by China Tibet Broadcasting".
V: QSL-card.
Notes: "Holy Tibet" is an English language prgr produced by the provincial Xizang Radio and Terlevision Station (branded in English as China Tibet Broadcasting - CTB).

VOICE OF GUANGXI BEIBU WAN (BEIBU BAY RADIO) (Gov)

75 Minzu Dadao, Nanning, Guangxi 530022, P.R.China.
+86 771 5802999. +86 771 5802555.
E: bbrtv@bbrtv.com **W:** www.bbrtv.com
Webcast: L
SW: See NRTA for tx information.
FM/DAB: FM: 96.3MHz (Nan Shan, 10kW)
kHz: *5050, 9820*

Winter Schedule 2020/2021

Cantonese	Days	Area	kHz
1130-1200	daily	SEA	5050nnn, 9820nnn
1520-1530	daily	SEA	5050nnn, 9820nnn
Chinese	**Days**	**Area**	**kHz**
0945-1130	daily	SEA	5050nnn, 9820nnn
1300-1400	daily	SEA	5050nnn*, 9820nnn*
1500-1520	daily	SEA	5050nnn, 9820nnn
2240-0100	daily	SEA	5050nnn
2250-0100	daily	SEA	9820nnn
Thai	**Days**	**Area**	**kHz**
1530-1600	daily	SEA	5050nnn, 9820nnn
Vietnamese	**Days**	**Area**	**kHz**
1200-1300	daily	SEA	5050nnn, 9820nnn
1400-1500	daily	SEA	5050nnn**, 9820nnn**

Key: * 1330-1335 Mon: Khmer, Tue: Lao, Wed/Sat: Burmese, Thu/Sun: Tha, Fri: Vietnamese; ** Relay of CRI Vietnamese prgr.
Ann: Chinese: "Guangxi Bei-bu Wan zhi sheng"; Vietnamese: "Tiêng nói Vinh bac bô Quáng Táy".
V: QSL-letter.
Notes: The Voice of Guangxi Beibu Wan (English brand: "Beibu Bay Radio") is a joint External Service project of the provincial Guangxi Radio & Television Station and China Radio International. Beibu Bay, in the South China Sea, is also known as the Gulf of Tonkin.

XINJIANG BROADCASTING STATION (XJBS) – VOICE OF CHINA (Gov)

830 Tuanjie Lu, Ürümqi, Xinjiang 830044, P.R. China.
+86 991 2508509, +86 991 2578492.
W: kirgiz.acradio.cn; www.xjbs.com.cn
Webcast: D/L (D: kirgiz.acradio.cn/vod/zgzs.shtml)
L.P: Dir (XJBS): Shi Linjie.
MW/SW: See NRTA for tx information.
FM/DAB: FM: 98.2MHz (Ürümqi; relays the regional Kyrgyz network)
kHz: *1233, 7295, 9705*

Winter Schedule 2020/2021

Kyrgyz	Days	Area	kHz
1130-1230	daily	KGZ	1233uru, 7295uru, 9705uru
1400-1500	daily	KGZ	1233uru

Ann: Kyrgyz: "Jungo Shinjang radyyo tele ystansyyasy".
Notes: Launched in 2012. "Voice of China" (Kyrgyz: Jungo Ünü) is a daily one hour prgr for listeners in Kyrgyzstan produced by the regional Xinjiang Broadcasting Station (XJBS), and aired on the SW/MW/FM freqs of XJBS's ethnic minority language network in Kyrgyz (cf. National Radio section).

YUNNAN RADIO AND TELEVISION INTERNATIONAL – RADIO SHANGRI–LA (Gov)

182 Renmin Xi Lu, Kunming, Yunnan 650031, P.R. China.
+86 871 5310211. +86 871 5361744.
E: admin@ynradio.com **W:** yngradio.com
Webcast: L
SW: See NRTA for tx information.
FM/DAB: FM: 99.0MHz
kHz: *6035*

Winter Schedule 2020/2021

Chinese	Days	Area	kHz
1100-1630	daily	SEA	6035sha†
2200-2400	daily	SEA	6035sha†
Vietnamese	**Days**	**Area**	**kHz**
1630-1700	daily	SEA	6035sha†

Key: † Irregular.
Ann: Chinese: "Yunnan diantai, Xianggelila zhi sheng"; English: "Yunnan Radio and Television International, The Voice of Shangri-la", Vietnamese: "Đài lai tieng nói Shangri-La".
V: QSL-letter.
Notes: International Service of the provincial Yunnan Radio and Television Station, launched on 1 Oct 1986. Identified as "Yunnan People's Broadcasting Station - The Voice of Shangri-La", until 2018, when it adopted the current name.

NATIONAL RADIO AND TELEVISION ADMINISTRATION (NRTA) (Tx Operator)

2 Fuxingmenwai Street, Xicheng District, Beijing 100866, P.R.China.
+86 10 66092707. +86 10 68512174.
W: www.nrta.gov.cn
L.P: Minister/Dir: Nie Chenxi.
MW: [CAH] Changchun (Jilin prov.). 1017kHz 100kW; [DEH] Mangshi (Dehong auton. prefecture, Yunnan prov.): 900kHz 50kW; [DOF] Dongfang (Hainan prov.): 603/684kHz 600kW; [HDN] Huadian (Jilin prov.): 963/1323kHz 600kW; [HDU] Guangzhou, Liantang (Guangdong prov.): 1341kHz 200kW; [HEI] Shuangyashan (Heilongjiang prov.): 1323 kHz 200kW; [HNL] Changzhou, Henglin (Jiangsu prov.): 1044kHz 600kW; [KAS] Kashgar (Kashi), Sayibage (Xinjiang Uighur auton. region): 1422kHz 600kW; [KUN] Kunming, Anning (Yunnan prov.): 1188/1296kHz 300kW; [URU] Ürümqi (Wulumuqi) (Xinjiang Uighur auton. region), two sites: Hongyanchi: 1233kHz 10kW, Hutubi: 1323/1521kHz 500kW; [XUW] Xuanwei (Yunnan prov.): 1080/1269kHz 600kW.
SW: [BEI] Beijing, Doudian: 150/500kW; [BJI] Baoji, Uishan (Shaanxi prov.): 150kW; [HUH] Hohhot, Bikeqi (Nei Menggu auton. region): 4 x 100kW; [JIN] Jinhua, Lanxi (Zhejiang prov.): 2 x 100, 3 x 500kW; [KAS] Kashgar (Kashi), Sayibage (Xinjiang Uighur auton. region): 2 x 100, 8 x 500kW; [KUN] Kunming, Anning (Yunnan prov.): 4 x 150, 4 x 500kW; [LHA] Lhasa (Chengguan) (Xizang auton. region): 13 x 100kW; [NNN] Nanning (Guangxi Zhuang auton. region): 2 x 15; 2 x 100kW; [SHA] Kunming, Shalang (Yunnan prov.): 1 x 50kW; [SZG] Shijiazhuang, Nanpozhuan (Hebei prov.): 2 x 500kW; [URU] Ürümqi (Wulumuqi) (Xinjiang Uighur auton. region), two sites: Changji: 100kW, Hutubi: 9 x 100, 8 x 500kW; [XIA] Xi'an, Xianyang (Shaanxi prov.): 150/500kW.
Notes: NRTA is an executive branch under the State Council of the People's Republic of China. NRTA was formed in 2018 as the successor to the former State Administration for Press, Publication, Radio, Film and Television (SAPPRFT).

CUBA (CUB)

RADIO HABANA CUBA (RHC) (Gov)

Apartado 6240, La Habana 10600, Cuba.
+53 7 8775524. +53 7 8776531.
E: inforhc@enet.cu **W:** www.radiohc.cu

Webcast: L
L.P: DG: Tania Hernández Castellanos; Advisor Consultant to DG: Prof. Arnaldo Coro Antich; Chief Eng: Ing. Luis Pruna Amer.
SW: Uses txs operated by Radiocuba.
FM/DAB: FM: 91.7MHz (Isla de la Juventud); 102.5MHz (La Habana).
SAT: Hispasat 30W-4.
kHz: *5040, 6000, 6060, 6100, 9535, 9650, 9700, 11670, 11760, 11850, 11880, 11950, 13680, 13700, 13740, 15140, 15230, 15680, 15730*

Winter Schedule 2020/2021

Arabic	**Days**	**Area**	**kHz**
1900-1930	daily	NAm	15140hab
2130-2200	daily	Eu	13680hab
Creole	**Days**	**Area**	**kHz**
0000-0030	daily	SAm	15730bej
0100-0130	daily	Car	5040hab
1930-2000	daily	NAm	15140hab
English	**Days**	**Area**	**kHz**
0000-0100	daily	CAm	5040hab
0100-0700	daily	NAm	9700hab
0100-0800	daily	NAm	6000hab
0500-0700	daily	NAm	6060hab
0600-0700	daily	CAm	5040hab
0600-0800	daily	NAm	6100hab
2000-2100	daily	NAm	15140hab
2200-2300	daily	Af	11880hab
Esperanto	**Days**	**Area**	**kHz**
0800-0830	......s	NAm	6100hab
1600-1630	......s	Am	11760hab, 15140hab
2330-2400	......s	SAm	15730bej
French	**Days**	**Area**	**kHz**
0100-0130	daily	SAm	15730bej
0130-0200	daily	Car	5040hab
2030-2100	daily	Eu	13680hab
2100-2130	daily	Af	11880hab
2100-2130	daily	NAm	15140hab
2330-2400	mtwtfs.	SAm	15730bej
Portuguese	**Days**	**Area**	**kHz**
0030-0100	daily	SAm	15730bej
2100-2130	daily	Af	11880hab
2100-2130	daily	Eu	13680hab
2300-2400	daily	SAm	15230qvc
Spanish	**Days**	**Area**	**kHz**
0000-0100	.twtfs.	NAm	6000qvc*, 11950hab*
0000-0500	daily	NAm	6060hab
0000-0500	daily	SAm	11670hab
0000-0600	daily	SAm	15230qvc
0200-0600	daily	CAm	5040hab
1200-1400	daily	NAm	6100hab
1200-1500	daily	NAm	6000hab
1200-1500	daily	SAm	13740hab
1200-1600	daily	Car	9650bej
1200-1600	daily	SAm	15140hab
1200-1600	daily	CAm	9535hab
1200-1600	daily	Am	11760hab
1300-1600	daily	NAm	15230qvc
1400-1600	daily	NAm	13700hab
1600-1630	mtwtfs.	Am	11760hab, 15140hab
1630-1900	daily	Am	11760hab
1630-1900	daily	NAm	15140hab
2200-0000	daily	Eu	15680hab
2200-0300	daily	Am	11760hab
2200-0500	daily	Car	9650bej
2200-0500	daily	SAm	13740hab
2200-0600	daily	CAm	9535hab
2200-0600	daily	SAm	11850hab
2200-2400	daily	CAm	5040hab

Key: * Mesa Redonda TV talkshow audio (teleSUR)
Ann: English: "This is Radio Havana Cuba".
V: QSL-card and letter. (Email to: radiohc@enet.cu)
Notes: Radio Habana Cuba is the External Sce of the state-owned Instituto Cubano de Radio y Television (ICRT). Frequencies and schedule are variable.

EMPRESA DE RADIOCOMUNICACIÓN Y DIFUSIÓN DE CUBA (RADIOCUBA) (Tx Operator)

✉ Calle Habana No 406, e/ Obispo y Obrapía, Habana Vieja, La Habana 10100, Cuba.
☎ +53 7 8607181. 📠 +53 7 8603107.
E: atencion.poblacion@radiocuba.cu **W:** www.radiocuba.cu
L.P: DG: Justo Moreno García.
SW: La Habana, three sites: [BEJ] Bejucal, Casualidad 3 x 50, 1 x 100kW; [HAB] Bauta, Corralillo: 1 x 50, 6 x 100kW; [QVC] Quivicán, San Felipe (Transmitting centre "Titán"): 5 x 250kW.
Notes: Radiocuba, a state operated company that forms part of the Ministry of Information and Communications, is the national transmitter network operator.

CYPRUS (CYP)

BBC EAST MEDITERRANEAN RELAY STATION

✉ P.O. Box 54912, 3729 Limassol, Cyprus.
☎ +357 24332511. 📠 +357 24332595.
E: mgt.bemrs@cytanet.com.cy
L.P: Engineering Mgr: Andreas Themistocleous.
MW: [ZAK] Zakaki, Lady's Mile (Akrotiri Sovereign Base Area): 639/720kHz 500kW.
V: QSL-card. (For direct report)
Notes: Owned by the BBC and operated by Encompass Digital Media Services Ltd (see under United Kingdom).

CZECHIA (CZE)

RADIO PRAGUE INTERNATIONAL (Pub)

✉ Vinohradská 12, 120 99 Praha 2, Czechia.
☎ +420 221552933. 📠 +420 221552903.
E: cr@radio.cz **W:** www.radio.cz
Webcast: D/L/P. (Webcast/Satellite languages: Czech, English, French, German, Russian)
L.P: Editor-in-Chief: Miroslav Krupicka.
SW: Leases airtime on WRMI (See under USA).
SAT: Astra 3B.
kHz: *5010, 5800, 6005, 7780, 9955, 15770*

Winter Schedule 2020/2021

English	**Days**	**Area**	**kHz**
0130-0200	.twtfs.	Car,SAm	5800rmi
0400-0430	m.....s	LAm	9955rmi
1300-1330	mtwtfs.	LAm	9955rmi
2000-2030	.t.....	Eu,NAm	15770rmi
German	**Days**	**Area**	**kHz**
1030-1100	daily	WEu	6005kll
Spanish	**Days**	**Area**	**kHz**
0200-0230	daily	Eu,NAm	7780rmi
0300-0330	daily	LAm	9955rmi
1130-1200	daily	CAm	5010rmi

Ann: English: "You're listening to Radio Prague International, the international service of Czech Radio".
V: QSL-card.
Notes: R. Prague International (Ceský Rozhlas 7 - R. Praha) is the Int. Sce of the public service broadcaster Ceský Rozhlas. The relay of the German prgr via a SW 1kW tx at Kall (Germany) is an independent, personal initiative of the operator of the German relay platform "Shortwaveservice". The project is targeting, primarily, SWLs/DXers in Europe.

DENMARK (DNK)

RADIO 208

✉ See World Music Radio (WMR)
E: mail@radio208.dk **W:** www.radio208.dk
Webcast: L
MW: [ISH] Ishøj: 1440kHz 0.5kW
SW: [HVI] Hvidovre: 1 x 0.075kW (F.pl: 0.15kW)
kHz: *1440, 5805*

Winter Schedule 2020/2021

English	**Days**	**Area**	**kHz**
0000-2400	daily	Eu	1440ish, 5805hvi

Notes: Produced by Hartvig Media A/S (See National R. section); sister station of World Music Radio (see separate entry).

RADIO OZ–VIOLA

✉ Engparken 35, DK-3400 Hillerød, Denmark.
E: jansteendk@hotmail.com **W:** ozviola.dk
L.P: Project Coordinator: Jan Sørensen (a.k.a "Jan Steen") (OZ8AO).
SW: [HIL] Hillerød: 1 x 0.15kW.
kHz: *5825*

Winter Schedule 2020/2021

English	Days	Area	kHz
1200-1400	.....ss	Eu	5825hil
2100-2300	..w....	Eu	5825hil

Key: † Irregular.
Ann: Danish: "Velkommen til OZ-Viola".
V: eQSL-card.
Notes: Weekend leisure time operation by a group of SW enthusiasts with amateur radio background, based on a temporary test licence (to be renewed once a year). The tx is installed in a private home. Due to the hobby nature of the broadcasts, trs may not be aired each weekend. F.Pl: Move to 5980kHz.

WORLD MUSIC RADIO (WMR)

✉ P.O.Box 112, DK-8960 Randers SØ, Denmark.
E: hartvig@wmr.dk
W: wmr.dk; www.facebook.com/WorldMusicRadioWMR
Webcast: L
L.P: Dir (Hartvig Media): Stig Hartvig Nielsen.
MW: [HVI] Hvidovre: 927kHz 0.5kW (F.pl)
SW: [BRG] Bramming: 1 x 0.1kW (F.pl: 0.5kW); [RND] Randers: 1 x 0.2kW.
kHz: *5840, 15805*

Winter Schedule 2020/2021

English	Days	Area	kHz
0000-2400	daily	Eu	5840brg
0700-2000	.....ss	Eu	15805rnd†

Key: † Irregular.
V: eQSL-card.
Notes: WMR is an internet radio station produced by Hartvig Media A/S. Initially launched as a pirate radio station in 1967 and, later, as a licensed station with own SW transmitter from Karup, Denmark (until 2005). The current low power SW trs are a leisure time operation, based on temporary licences (renewed annually) and primarily aimed at listeners in the DX hobby/SWL community. The txs are installed in private homes.

DJIBOUTI (DJI)

USAGM DJIBOUTI TRANSMITTING STATION

✉ Radiodiffusion Télévision de Djibouti, 1 Rue Saint-Laurent du Var, PK 12, Djibouti.
MW: [DJI] Djibouti, Dorale: 1431kHz 600kW.
Notes: Transmitting centre of the state broadcaster Radiodiffusion Télévision de Djibouti (RTD), equipped and contracted by USAGM (USA) for transmitting USAGM funded services; managed by the USAGM Germany Transmitting Station.

ECUADOR (EQA)

VOZANDES MEDIA (Rlg)

✉ Casilla 17-17-691, Quito, Ecuador.
☎ +593 2 5101770.
E: vozandes@gmail.com; hcjb@andenstimme.org
W: andenstimme.org (in German)
✉ Pasaje Jacinto de la Cuava Oe4-33 y Av. Brasil, Quito, Ecuador.
☎ +593 2 2278831.
E: kichwa@hcjb.org (HCJB Quito Kichwa section) **W:** www.facebook.com/hcjbkichwa (HCJB Quito Kichwa section), radiohcjb.org (HCJB Ecuador)
L.P: Chmn: Horst Rosiak.
SW: [QUI] Quito, Mount Pichincha 1 x 1kW.
kHz: *6050*

Winter Schedule 2020/2021

Cha'palaa	Days	Area	kHz
2130-2200	daily	EQA	6050qui
Cofan	**Days**	**Area**	**kHz**
0000-0030	daily	EQA,CLM,PRU	6050qui
German	**Days**	**Area**	**kHz**
0400-0500	.....s.	Eu	6050qui*
Quichua (Kichwa)	**Days**	**Area**	**kHz**
0100-0230	m.....s	EQA,CLM,PRU	6050qui
0130-0145	.tw....	EQA,CLM,PRU	6050qui
0130-0230	...tfs.	EQA,CLM,PRU	6050qui
0200-0230	.tw....	EQA,CLM,PRU	6050qui
0925-1045	mt.....	EQA,CLM,PRU	6050qui
0925-1100	..wtf..	EQA,CLM,PRU	6050qui
0925-1130	.....ss	EQA,CLM,PRU	6050qui
2200-2315	mt.....	EQA,CLM,PRU	6050qui
2200-2330	..wtfss	EQA,CLM,PRU	6050qui
Shuar	**Days**	**Area**	**kHz**
2330-2400	daily	EQA,CLM,PRU	6050qui
Spanish	**Days**	**Area**	**kHz**
0100-0130	.twtfs.	EQA,CLM,PRU	6050qui
0145-0200	.tw....	EQA,CLM,PRU	6050qui
1045-1400	mt.....	EQA,CLM,PRU	6050qui
1100-1400	..wtf..	EQA,CLM,PRU	6050qui
1130-1400	.....ss	EQA,CLM,PRU	6050qui
2100-2130	daily	EQA,CLM,PRU	6050qui
2315-2330	mt.....	EQA,CLM,PRU	6050qui
Waorani	**Days**	**Area**	**kHz**
0030-0100	daily	EQA	6050qui

Key: * Outside of primary target area: Rebroadcast of a DX prgr produced by Arbeitsgemeinschaft Radio HCJB e.V. (Germany) as "DX catch" for DXers in Europe. Special eQSL available from deutsch@andenstimme.org
V: QSL-card. Rp (1 IRC).
Notes: HCJB (World Radio Missionary Fellowship, Inc - USA) stopped all SW operations in Ecuador the late 2000s, and in 2009 handed over their SW tx in Quito to the voluntary organisation Asociación Vozandes Media (AVM) which is not part of the HCJB organisation. AVM was founded by staff of the former, Quito-based HCJB German language service and cooperates with the local HCJB FM & MW station in Ecuador. The SW service (labeled "Indianerradio" in German) is targeting the indigenous population in Ecuador with transmissions in Cha'palaa, Cofan, Kichwa, Shuar and Waorani (there are speakers of Cofan, Kichwa and Shuar also in the border areas of neighbouring Columbia and Peru), as well as Spanish (mostly relay of HCJB FM). AVM provides the technical and administrative support for these prgrs that are produced by local, third-party partners & the local HCJB station.

EGYPT (EGY)

RADIO CAIRO (Gov)

✉ P.O. Box 1186, 11511 Cairo, Egypt.
☎ +20 2 25789461. 🖷 +20 2 25789461.
E: englisheuropeservice@gmail.com **W:** www.egradio.eg; dotnet.ertu.org; www.facebook.com/English-Europe-Service-501737149967656 (European Service)
Webcast: D/L (www.egradio.eg)
L.P: (NMA) Pres: Hussein Zein; Secretary Gen: Amgad Baleigh.
MW: [ABZ] Abu Zaabal: 1071kHz 100kW; [BTR] Batrah: 621kHz 1000kW; [ELA] El Arish: 1008kHz 100kW.
SW: [ABS] Abis ‡: 2 x 125kW; [ABZ] Abu Zaabal ‡: 13 x 100, 1 x 250, 4 x 500kW.
FM/DAB: FM: See National Radio section (NMA "European Programme" tx network.)
kHz: *621, 1008, 9440, 9510, 9540, 9545, 9650, 9810, 9885, 9900, 9940*

Winter Schedule 2020/2021

Albanian	Days	Area	kHz
1500-1600	daily	Eu	9440abs‡
Arabic	**Days**	**Area**	**kHz**
0000-2400	daily	ME	621btr*
2330-0045	daily	SAm	9650abs‡

English	Days	Area	kHz
2115-2245	daily	Eu	9900abs‡
French	**Days**	**Area**	**kHz**
2000-2115	daily	Eu	9885abs‡
German	**Days**	**Area**	**kHz**
1900-2000	daily	Eu	9810abs‡
Hebrew	**Days**	**Area**	**kHz**
1500-2200	daily	ME	1008ela
Italian	**Days**	**Area**	**kHz**
1800-1900	daily	Eu	9540abs‡
Portuguese	**Days**	**Area**	**kHz**
2215-2330	daily	SAm	9545abs‡
Russian	**Days**	**Area**	**kHz**
1900-2000	daily	Eu	9510abs‡
Spanish	**Days**	**Area**	**kHz**
0045-0200	daily	SAm	9900abs‡
Turkish	**Days**	**Area**	**kHz**
1700-1900	daily	ME	9940abs‡

Key: ‡ Inactive on SW at time of publication; * Voice of Arabs prgr.
Ann: English: "You are tuned to Radio Cairo"; Arabic: "Sowt il-Arab min al-Qahira"; VO Africa: "Sowt-il Afrikiy min al-Qahira".
V: QSL-card. (Send to: P.O. Box 566, 11511 Cairo, Egypt). Email rpt to freqmeg@yahoo.com
Notes: Radio Cairo is the External Sce of the National Media Authority (NMA) (previously known as "Egyptian Radio & TV Union (ERTU)"). There have been no trs on SW since 2019.

ESWATINI (SWZ)

TWR ESWATINI TRANSMITTING STATION

✉ P.O. Box 64, Manzini, Eswatini.
☎ +268 25052781. 📠 +268 25055333.
L.P: Chief Engineer: Mike Lambert.
MW: [MAN] Manzini, Mpangela Ranch: 1170kHz 100kW.
SW: [MAN] Manzini, Mpangela Ranch: 3 x 100kW.
Ann: English: "This is Trans World Radio, Eswatini".
V: eQSL-card.
Notes: Owned by TWR. For corporate details, see under TWR (USA). For schedule, see TWR Africa (South Africa).

FINLAND (FIN)

SCANDINAVIAN WEEKEND RADIO (SWR)

✉ Hollitie 1025, FI-34930 Liedenpohja, Finland.
☎ +358 3 4755776. (studio, during broadcast only)
E: info@swradio.net **W:** www.swradio.net
Webcast: L (www.radioverkko.fi, 0800-2200 only)
L.P: Chief Editor: Esa Saunamäki; QSL Mgr: Tapani Häkkinen.
MW: [VIR] Virrat, Liedenpohja: 1602kHz 0.4kW.
SW: [VIR] Virrat, Liedenpohja: 2 x 0.1kW.
FM/DAB: FM: 94.9MHz (Virrat, Liedenpohja, 0.5kW).
kHz: *1602, 5980, 6170, 11690, 11720*

Winter Schedule 2020/2021

English/Finnish	Days	Area	kHz
0000-0600	.....s.	Eu	6170vir*
0000-0800	.....s.	Eu	11690vir*
0000-2200	.....s.	Eu	1602vir*
0600-0900	.....s.	Eu	5980vir*
0800-1400	.....s.	Eu	11720vir*
0900-1500	.....s.	Eu	6170vir*
1400-1700	.....s.	Eu	11690vir*
1500-1900	.....s.	Eu	5980vir*
1700-1900	.....s.	Eu	11720vir*
1900-2200	.....s.	Eu	6170vir*, 11690vir*
2200-2300	....f..	Eu	11720vir*
2200-2400	....f..	Eu	1602vir*, 6170vir*
2300-2400	....f..	Eu	11690vir*

Key: * 1st Sat of month, local time (= UTC+2h).
Ann: English: "You are listening to Scandinavian Weekend Radio".
V: QSL-card (for rpt sent by mail; rpt form downloadable from website) Rp (2 IRCs/EUR/USD); eQSL-card (for online rpt via website).
Notes: On air since 1 July 2000. Leisure time operation by a group of SW enthusiasts and licenced to the amateur radio club Vaihtoehtoisen radiotoiminnan tukiyhdistys ry (callsign: OH6SWR). The stn is run on a series of temporary licences for 24h on the first Saturday Local Time (UTC: Fri 2200-Sat 2200 winter, Fri 2100-Sat 2100 summer) for three consecutive months (Feb-Apr, June-Aug, Oct-Dec). No transmissions in Jan, May, Sep as required by law, before the club is entitled to a new series of licences.

FRANCE (F)

RADIO FRANCE INTERNATIONALE (RFI) (Pub)

✉ 80 rue Camille Desmoulins, F-92130 Issy-les-Moulineaux, France.
☎ +33 184228484.
E: english.service@rfi.fr **W:** www.rfi.fr
Webcast: L/P
✉ B.P. 9516, F-75016 Paris Cedex 16, France.
L.P: Pres/DG (FMM): Marie-Christine Saragosse; Dir (RFI): Victor Rocaries.
SW: Leased from TDF & third-party foreign relays.
SAT: Anik F1R/F3, AsiaSat 7, Astra 1N, Badr 4, Eutelsat 7B/8WB/16A/36B/Hot Bird 13B, Hispasat 30W-5, Intelsat 11-Sky Brazil 1, Intelsat 18/20/21/30, SES 5/6/7, Superbird C2.
kHz: *3965, 5925, 6040, 7205, 7295, 7380, 7390, 9580, 9635, 9650, 9660, 9665, 9725, 9790, 9805, 9810, 11700, 11760, 11780, 11790, 11995, 13695, 13740, 15300, 15455, 17660, 17815, 17850, 21580, 21690*

Winter Schedule 2020/2021

French	Days	Area	kHz
0000-2400	daily	Eu	3965iss+
0400-0700	daily	EAf,CAf	7390iss
0400-0800	daily	Af	9790iss
0500-0600	daily	CAf	6040iss
0600-0700	daily	NAf,WAf	5925iss
0600-0800	daily	WAf,CAf	11700iss
0700-0800	daily	CAf	15300iss*, 17850iss**
0700-1100	daily	WAf	13695iss
0800-1100	daily	CAf	17850iss, 21580iss
0800-1100	daily	WAf	15300iss
1200-1300	daily	CAf	21580iss, 21690mdc
1200-1300	daily	NAf,WAf	15300iss
1200-1300	daily	WAf,CAf	17660iss
1700-1800	daily	CAf	15300iss
1700-1800	daily	WAf,CAf	11995iss, 13740iss
1800-1900	daily	WAf,CAf	9725iss
1800-1900	daily	CAf	9660iss*, 13740iss**
1800-1900	daily	NAf,WAf	9810iss
1800-2000	daily	WAf,CAf	11995iss
1900-2000	daily	WAf,CAf	9580iss, 9635iss
1900-2200	daily	NAf,WAf	7205iss
2000-2200	daily	NAf,WAf	9790iss
Fulani	**Days**	**Area**	**kHz**
1300-1330	.....ss	WAf	17660iss
1730-1800	.....ss	WAf	11780iss
Hausa	**Days**	**Area**	**kHz**
0600-0630	daily	WAf,CAf	7295iss, 9805iss
0700-0730	daily	WAf,CAf	11760iss, 13740iss
1600-1700	daily	WAf,CAf	15300iss
2000-2030	daily	WAf,CAf	7380iss
Mandinka	**Days**	**Area**	**kHz**
0800-0830	mtwtf..	WAf	15455iss
1200-1230	daily	WAf	17815iss
1700-1730	.....ss	WAf,CAf	11780iss
Swahili	**Days**	**Area**	**kHz**
0430-0500	daily	EAf,CAf	9665mdc
0530-0600	daily	EAf,CAf	11790mdc
1500-1600	daily	EAf,CAf	21690iss
Vietnamese	**Days**	**Area**	**kHz**
1300-1400	......s	SEA	9650pao

Key: + DRM; * Dec-Feb; ** March.
Ann: French: "Ici Paris, Radio France Internationale".
V: QSL-card.
Notes: RFI is produced under the umbrella of the External Services

holding France Médias Monde (FMM), formerly Audiovisuel Extérieur de la France (AEF).

RADIO FOR PEACE INTERNATIONAL (RFPI)

Produced in France.
E: contact@rfpi.eu **W:** www.rfpi.eu; www.facebook.com/radioforpeaceinternational
Webcast: D
kHz: *6070, 6160, 7780, 9955, 15770, 21525*

Winter Schedule 2020/2021

French	Days	Area	kHz
0200-0300	....f..	NAm,CAm	6160bcq
1300-1400	......s	Eu,ME,Af	15770rmi
1400-1500	...t....	Af	21525rmi
2000-2100	....f..	Eu,ME,Af	15770rmi
2100-2200	..w....	LAm	9955rmi
2100-2200	......s	NAm,Eu,ME	7780rmi
2100-2200	......s	Eu	6070rob

Ann: English: "You're listening to Radio For Peace International"; French: "Vous écoutez la Radio Pour La Paix Internationale".
V: E-QSL (Email rpts to qsl@rfpi.eu)
Notes: On SW since 11 May 2019. "Radio For Peace International" is a feature/music show presented by "Tiphanie", a radio personality of the prgr "Atlantic 2000 International" (a French pirate radio show which is also aired via third partly legal SW relays at times). The RFPI prgr has no connection with a SW radio station of the same name that was broadcasting from Costa Rica from 1987-2003.

TDF S.A.S. (Tx Operator)

106 Avenue Marx Dormoy, 92541 Montrouge Cedex, France.
☎ +33 149651000.
E: presse_tdf@tdf.fr **W:** www.tdf.fr; www.tdf-group.com
L.P: (TDF Group) Pres: Olivier Huart; DG: Benoit Mérel.
SW: [ISS] Issoudun: 12 x 500kW (2 are DRM capable).
V: QSL-card. (For RFI and other broadcaster relays via ISS)
Notes: TDF S.A.S., part of the TDF group, is the national French transmitter network operator.

GERMANY (D)

DEUTSCHER WETTERDIENST (DWD) (Gov)

DWD Seeschifffahrtsberatung, Bernhard Nocht-Str. 20, D-20359 Hamburg, Germany.
☎ +49 69 80626201. 🖷 +49 69 80626193.
E: seewetterfunk@dwd.de **W:** www.dwd.de
Transmitter site: DWD Wetterfunkstelle, Haidkamp 10, D-25421 Pinneberg, Germany.
L.P: Pres: Prof. Dr. Gerhard Adrian.
SW: [PIN] Pinneberg: 2 x 10kW.
kHz: *5905, 6180*

Winter Schedule 2020/2021

German	Days	Area	kHz
0600-0630	daily	BaS,NoS,Med	5905pin, 6180pin
1200-1230	daily	BaS,NoS,Med	5905pin, 6180pin
1600-1630	daily	Med	5905pin, 6180pin
2000-2030	daily	BaS,NoS,Med	5905pin, 6180pin

V: QSL-card.
Notes: Shipping forecasts for the Baltic Sea, North Sea and Mediterranean Sea, produced by DWD (Germany's National Meteorological Service).

DEUTSCHE WELLE (DW) (Pub)

Kurt-Schumacher-Str. 3, D-53113 Bonn, Germany.
☎ +49 228 4290. 🖷 +49 228 4293000.
E: info@dw.com **W:** www.dw.com
Webcast: D/L/P. Webcast-only languages (some of which may also be broadcast on local FM affiliate stns): Arabic, Bengali, Chinese, Dari, Croatian, Greek, Pashto, Persian, Portuguese, Spanish, Turkish, Urdu.
Voltastr. 6, D-13355 Berlin.
☎ +49 30 46460.
L.P: DG: Peter Limbourg; PD: Gerda Meuer; MD, Distribution, Marketing and Technology: Guido Baumhauer; Dir, Int Relations: Klaus Bergmann.
SAT: Eutelsat 7B/Hot Bird 13B, Intelsat 20, SES 5.
kHz: *7235, 9570, 9830, 11830, 11980, 15195, 15275, 15350, 17800*

Winter Schedule 2020/2021

Amharic	Days	Area	kHz
1600-1700	daily	ETH	11830iss, 15275iss
Hausa	**Days**	**Area**	**kHz**
0630-0700	daily	WAf	7235sao, 9570iss, 9830iss
1300-1400	daily	WAf	9830sao, 11980sao, 17800iss
1425-1630	.....s.	WAf	15195iss*, 15350iss*
1800-1900	daily	WAf	7235iss, 9570iss, 9830sao

Key: * Live coverage of German football league (Bundesliga) matches.
V: QSL-card. (Rpt to DW Customer Service; Email rpt to tb@dw.com)
Notes: Deutsche Welle is a public service External broadcaster.

EVANGELISCHE MISSIONS–GEMEINDEN (Rlg)

Lauenburger Strasse 12, D-51709 Marienheide, Germany.
☎ +49 2264 3625.
E: info@missionsbote.de **W:** www.missionsbote.de
Webcast: D
L.P: Head of missionary society: Andreas Herzog.
kHz: *6055*

Winter Schedule 2020/2021

German	Days	Area	kHz
1130-1200	.....ss	Eu	6055nau

V: QSL-card.
Notes: Produced by Missionswerk Evangelische Missions-Gemeinden in Deutschland e.V.

RADIO HCJB DEUTSCHLAND (Rlg)

Postfach 8025, D-32736 Detmold, Germany.
☎ +49 5232 7980816. 🖷 +49 30 61090010376.
E: info@hcjb.de **W:** www.hcjb.de
Webcast: L
L.P: Prgr Mgr: Marco Schaa.
SW: [WNM] Weenermoor: 2 x 1.5, 1 x 3kW.
SAT: Astra 1N.
kHz: *3995, 5920, 7365*

Winter Schedule 2020/2021

German	Days	Area	kHz
0500-0400	daily	CEu	3995wnm*
0700-1700	daily	CEu	5920wnm*
0900-1400	daily	CEu	7365wnm*
Russian	**Days**	**Area**	**kHz**
0400-0500	daily	CEu	3995wnm**

Key: * Incl. segment in Low German 0730-0800 (on 3995 repeated at 1930-2000) produced by SW-Radio ** Segment provided by SW-Radio (various producers incl Radio Studio "Otkroveniye", Russia).
V: QSL-card.
Notes: Run by Arbeitsgemeinschaft Radio HCJB e.V., a partner organisation of Vozandes Media (Ecuador) and the Reach Beyond media ministry of World Radio Missionary Fellowship, Inc. (USA). Most of the 24/7 programming is produced by various small religious German prgr producers, e.g. Lutherische Stunde, Missionswerk Heuckelbach, SW-Radio.The schedule includes prgrs in Low German and Russian for re-immigrated mennonites of German origin from Russia and Central Asia. The latest detailed schedule can be found on the station website. While the satellite & internet feed is aimed at a general audience, the SW txs (installed on private land) are owned and operated by a group of SW enthusiasts and aretargeting, primarily, listeners in the DX/SWL community.

CHANNEL 292

Eja 2, D-85276 Pfaffenhofen, Germany.
☎ +49 8441 4569988.
E: info@channel292.de **W:** www.channel292.de
L.P: Project coordinator/CEO (Intermedicom GmbH): Rainer Ebeling (DB8QC).
SW: [ROB] Rohrbach, Eja: 2 x 10kW.
kHz: *3955, 6070, 9670*

Winter Schedule 2020/2021

German/Various	Days	Area	kHz
0000-2400	daily	Eu	3955rob†, 6070rob†, 9670rob†

Key: † Irregular (highly flexible) schedule with breaks (esp. on 3955/9670), depending on airtime bookings (latest schedules see website).
Ann: English: "Radio Channel 2-9-2".
V: eQSL-card. For direct rpts to relayed prgrs: see www.channel292.de/stations-contact-data
Notes: Channel 292 (initially launched as R. 6150 in 2012, renamed in 2013) is a leisure time operation, run by a group of SW enthusiasts. Formally licensed to Intermedicom GmbH. The tx is installed on private land. Airtime is leased to third-party prgr producers. Schedule is variable (dependent on airtime bookings). Vacant tr hrs may be filled with rebroadcasts of vintage radio shows from the era of offshore radio.

EUROPA 24

✉ c/o Interessengemeinschaft Hochfrequenztechnik e.V., Johann-Strauß-Str. 22, D-45711 Datteln, Germany.
☎ +49 2363 3988986.
E: radioeuropa24@gmx.de
L.P: Project Coordinator: Bernd Feyock (DG2YID).
SW: [DAT] Datteln 1 x 0.2kW
kHz: *6150*

Winter Schedule 2020/2021

German	Days	Area	kHz
0830-1800	daily	CEu	6150dat

Ann: German: "Hier ist Europa 24 (vierundzwanzig)"
V: eQSL-card.
Notes: On the air since 2014. Leisure time operation by a group of SW enthusiasts (licensed to the registered voluntary association "Interessengemeinschaft Hochfrequenztechnik e.V."). The tx is installed in a residential house.

RADIO DARC

✉ c/o Rainer Englert, Dorfstrasse 14, D-85567 Bruck-Alxing, Germany.
E: radio@darc.de **W:** www.darc.de/nachrichten/radio-darc
Webcast: D (www.alximedia.de/radio)
✉ Lindenallee 4, D-34225 Baunatal, German. (DARC)
☎ +49 561 949880. 🖷 +49 561 9498850.
L.P: Editor: Rainer Englert (DF2NU).
FM/DAB: The weekly show is rebroadcast by a number of non-commercial community radio stns in Germany (also via R. Helsinki - Freies Radio Graz, Austria), see website for details.
kHz: *3955, 6070, 9670*

Winter Schedule 2020/2021

German	Days	Area	kHz
1000-1100	......s	Eu	6070mos, 9670rob
1600-1700	m......	Eu	6070rob, 9670rob
2000-2100	......s	Eu	3955rob

Ann: German: "Sie hören Radio DARC".
V: QSL-card.
Notes: Prgr produced by association of German radio amateurs, Deutscher Amateur-Radio-Club e.V. (DARC). On SW since 22 March 2015.

RADIO JOYSTICK

✉ Postfach 595, D-55529 Bad Kreuznach, Germany.
☎ +49 671 20278967.
E: radiojoystick@gmail.com
W: www.radiojoystick.de; www.facebook.com/radiojoystick
Webcast: L (24h rotation of the show)
L.P: Presenter: Jens F. Hofstadt. (a.k.a "Charlie Prince")
kHz: *7330*

Winter Schedule 2020/2021

German	Days	Area	kHz
1100-1200	......s	Eu	7330mos*

Key: * 1st Sunday of month.
V: QSL-card.
Notes: Monthly broadcast of the "Charlie-Prince-Show". R. Joystick was launched 1985 as a pirate radio prgr; the show has been relayed on SW via various (pirate and legal) rebroadcasters over the years.

RADIO ÖÖMRANG

✉ Tanenwai 24, D-25946 Nebel-Westerheide, Germany.
☎ +49 4682 2688. 🖷 +49 4682 2262.
E: familie-koelzow@t-online.de
L.P: Producer: Gernot Schrader.
FM/DAB: FM: 96.7/97.6/98.8/105.2MHz (Via Westküste FM)
kHz: *15215*

Winter Schedule 2020/2021

English/German	Days	Area	kHz
1600-1700	......s	NAm	15215iss*

Key: * 21 February 2021 only (tentative schedule, subject to confirmation)
Ann: English: "This is Radio Öömrang, the freedom voice of Öömrang".
V: Does not verify. Rpt can be sent to Media Broadcast Services GmbH.
Notes: The prgr "Radio Öömrang" ("Radio Amrum") is broadcast each year on 21 February, a major North Frisian holiday (Biikebrånen). The prgr was founded by radio amateur Arjan Kölzow on the island of Amrum in North Germany; the first SW broadcast was on 21 February 2006. The broadcast is aimed at the descendants of North Frisian immigrants in North America, and is presented bilingually in Standard German & English, incl. interviews in the North Frisian language (Öömrang dialect).

RADIO SE–TA2

✉ Katzenstr. 20B, D-08118 Hartenstein, Germany.
☎ +49 37605 696610.
E: se-ta@web.de
L.P: Project coordinator: Christoph Gerber.
SW: [HST] Hartenstein: 1 x 1kW.
kHz: *6095, 6115*

Winter Schedule 2020/2021

German	Days	Area	kHz
1000-1200	.....ss	CEu	6115hst
1100-1200	.....s.	Eu	6095nau*

Key: * 2 Jan 2021.
V: eQSL-card
Notes: R. SE-TA2 ("Sender Tannenberg 2") is a leisure-time operation of a group of shortwave enthusiasts. The group's radio show was first broadcast via Channel 292 (Germany) in late 2019. Own trs started on 1 September 2020; the tx is installed in a residential property.

SHORTWAVE RADIO

✉ D-29323 Wietze, Germany.
☎ +49 5146 9877007
E: 3975@shortwaveradio.de; 6160@shortwaveradio.de; studio@shortwaveradio.de **W:** shortwaveradio.de
✉ Freundeskreis Shortwaveradio e.V., c/o Christian Senne, Hagebuttenweg 7, D-61239 Ober-Mörlsen, Germany.
L.P: Project Coordinator: Kai-Frank Strehl (DJ9KAI).
SW: [WIS] Winsen an der Aller: 1 x 1, 1 x 2.5kW
kHz: *3975, 6160*

Winter Schedule 2020/2021

English	Days	Area	kHz
0700-2300	daily	WEu	3975wis
0800-1600	daily	WEu	6160wis

Ann: English: "This is Shortwave 3-9-7-5", "This is Shortwave 6-1-6-0".
V: eQSL-card (donation required, see website).
Notes: On the air since August 2017. Leisure time operation by a group of SW enthusiasts. The txs are installed in a private house. Programming is produced in the UK, Germany, Italy and elsewhere. Frequency usage is variable.

SHORTWAVESERVICE

✉ Kuchenheimer Str. 155, D-53881 Euskirchen, Germany.
☎ +49 2251 146085.
E: info@shortwaveservice.com **W:** www.shortwaveservice.com; classicbroadcast.de (Technical info); radio360.eu (Podcast portal)
Webcast: L/P (P: radio360.eu)
L.P: Project Coordinator: Christian Milling.

SW: [KLL] Kall, Krekel: 4 x 1kW.
Ann: German: "Sie hören Shortwaveservice".
V: QSL-card.
Notes: On the air since 24 November 2007. The SW relay service (initially branded "R. 700 Kurzwellendienst") is a leisure time operation by a group of radio enthusiasts, and primarily targeting listeners in the European DX/SWL community. The programming consists of relays of third-party prgrs & nonstop music. Shortwaveservice is transmitted via 1kW txs that are owned & operated by the radio amateur Burkhard Baumgartner (DF5XV), installed at a vintage utility radio site (formerly run by German police forces).

WELLE 370 (DAS FUNKERBERG RADIO)

Funkerberg 20, Senderhaus 1, D-15711 Königs Wusterhausen, Germany.
E: welle370@funkerberg.de **W:** www.welle370.de
Webcast: D (soundcloud.com/welle370)
E: verein@funkerberg.de
W: museum.funkerberg.de; rundfunkstadt.de; 100jahrerundfunk.de
L.P: Chmn (Förderverein Sender Königs Wusterhausen e.V.): Rainer Suckow.
MW: Funkerberg Museum, Königs Wusterhausen: 810kHz 0.009kW (broadcasts for local area, during special events); Not in parallel with SW.
kHz: *6140*

Winter Schedule 2020/2021

German	Days	Area	kHz
0900-1000	......s	Eu	6140mos*

Key: * 1st Sunday of month.
V: QSL-card.
Notes: Monthly prgr produced by the registered voluntary association "Förderverein Sender Königs Wusterhausen e.V.". The association is in charge of maintaining a museum at a historical transmitter site ("Funkerberg") in Königs Wusterhausen (owned by the town of Königs Wusterhausen).

USAGM GERMANY TRANSMITTING STATION

Wildbahn 6, D-68623 Lampertheim, Germany.
☎ +49 6206 1590. 🖷 +49 6206 159189.
E: swhite@usagm.gov
L.P: SM: Shannon White.
SW: [BIB] Biblis: 11 x 100kW; [LAM] Lampertheim: 9 x 100kW.
V: QSL-card.

MEDIA BROADCAST GMBH (Tx Operator)

Erna-Scheffler-Str. 1, D-51103 Köln, Germany.
☎ +49 221 71015000.
E: info@media-broadcast.com **W:** www.media-broadcast.com
L.P: CEO: Arnold Stender; Sales Consultant, Business Unit Radio: Uwe Ludwig.
SW: [NAU] Nauen: 2 x 100, 4 x 500kW.
V: QSL-card. (For relayed stns. Email rpts: qsl-shortwave@media-broadcast.com).
Notes: Media Broadcast GmbH, a subsidiary of Freenet AG, is a major transmitter network operator in Germany and owner of the SW transmitting centre in Nauen.

GREECE (GRC)

VOICE OF GREECE (I FONI TIS ELLADAS) (Pub)

Mesogeion Ave. 432, Office P 211, 15342 Agia Paraskevi, Greece.
☎ +30 2106066439.
E: thevoiceofgreece@ert.gr; ertinternational@ert.gr **W:** int.ert.gr
Webcast: L (webradio.ert.gr)
L.P: MD (ERT): Giorgios Gampritsos; Channel Dir (I Foni Tis Elladas): Mrs Gianna Triantafilli.
SW: [AVL] Vathy (Avlida municipality), Kalochori-Pantichi: 2 x 100kW, 1 x 250kW.
kHz: *9420*

Winter Schedule 2020/2021

Greek	Days	Area	kHz
1900-0800	daily	Eu,Am	9420avl†

Key: † Irregular, times variable.
Ann: Greek: "Edo Athina, I Foni tis Elladas".
V: eQSL-card. Email rpt to spanagiotou@ert.gr (Stelios Panagiotou)
Notes: International service produced by the Greek public broadcaster ERT, primarily serving the Greek communities abroad. The prgrs include relays of ERT Home Service channels and may include segments in Albanian, English, Polish, Romanian, Russian and Spanish. SW tr hours are highly variable.

GUAM (GUM)

KSDA (AWR ASIA/PACIFIC RELAY STATION)

P.O. Box 8990, Agat, Guam 96928. (Transmitting station)
☎ +1 671 5652000. 🖷 +1 671 5652983.
E: guam@awr.org
EIS Building B, Unit 1101, 71/15 Soi Pridi Banomyong 37, Sukhumvit 71 Road, Klongton Nua, Vadhana District, Bangkok 10110, Thailand. (AWR Asia/Pacific branch & studios)
☎ +66 223818869.
W: www.awr.org
L.P: SM: Victor Shepherd; Chief Engineer: Brook Powers.
SW: [SDA] Agat, Facpi Point: 5 x 100kW.
Ann: English: "This is Adventist World Radio - The Voice of Hope - KDSA, Agat, Guam".
V: QSL-card (Rpt to AWR Asia/Pacific Branch in Thailand).
Notes: Transmitting station owned by Adventist Broadcasting Service, Inc., see USA for corporate details. For schedules, see AWR Asia/Pacific (Thailand).

KTWR (TWR RELAY STATION)

P.O.Box 6095, Merizo, Guam 96916-0395. (Transmitting station)
☎ +1 671 8288637. 🖷 +1 671 8288636.
E: ktwrfcd@twr.org **W:** www.twr.asia/about/guam
85 Playfair Road #04-01, Tong Yuan Industrial Building, Singapore 368000. (TWR Asia branch & studios)
☎ +65 65015150. 🖷 +65 64443053.
E: info@twr.asia **W:** ktwrdrm.blogspot.com (technical blog)
L.P: Stn Dir: George Ross; Chief Engineer: Mike Sabin.
SW: [TWR] Merizo: 1 x 100, 2 x 250kW.
Ann: English: "Welcome to KTWR Agana, Guam".
IS: "We've a story to tell the Nations", played on an organ.
V: QSL-card. Rp. (3 IRCs)
Notes: Transmitting station owned by TWR, Inc. See USA for corporate details. For schedule, see TWR Asia (Singapore).

INDIA (IND)

ALL INDIA RADIO (AIR) (Pub)

External Services Division (ESD), P.O.Box 500, New Delhi 110001, India.
☎ +91 11 23421220. 🖷 +91 11 23421220.
E: esd@prasarbharati.gov.in; adg.esd@prasarbharati.gov.in (ESD)
W: www.allindiaradio.gov.in; airworldservice.org
Webcast: D/L/P (airworldservice.org)
Director, External services Divison, Room no 402, New Broadcasting House, All India Radio, 27 Mahadev Road, New Delhi 110001, India.
☎ +91 11 23421160; +91 11 23421192; +91 11 23421190.
E: directoresd@yahoo.co.in; gosesdair@yahoo.co.in (GOS)
W: newsonair.nic.in (AIR News Services Division Web Portal).
L.P: DG: Fayyaz Sheheryar; Additional DG (ESD): Raj Shekhay Vyas; Dir (ESD): Amlanjyoti Mazumdar; Engineer-in-Chief: Chandra Bhanu Singh.
MW: [JAL] Jalandhar: 702kHz 300kW; [KKT] Chinsurah: 594/603kHz 1000kW*; [RAJ] Rajkot 1062/1071kHz 1000kW*; [TUT] Tuticorin: 1053kHz 200kW. *) Reduced power applies to DRM freqs 603 & 1062kHz.
SW: [ALG] Aligarh: 2 x 250kW; [BGL] Bengalaru, Doddaballapur: 5 x 500kW; [DEL] Delhi, two sites: Khampur (G.C. 28N49 077E07): 1 x 250kW; Kingsway (G.C. 28N43 077E12): 2 x 100kW; [PAN] Panaji: 1 x 250kW.
FM/DAB: FM: 103.6MHz (Gharinda 20kW). "Des Punjab" channel: FM Rainbow Jalandhar relay & AIR External Service (ESD) 0025-0130, 0430-0830 & 0930-1230 Urdu, 1230-1300 Saraiki, 1300-1430 Punjabi, 1430-1830 Urdu.
kHz: *594, 7380, 7550, 9580, 9620, 9950, 11560, 11620, 15030, 15410, 17595*

Winter Schedule 2020/2021

Baluchi	Days	Area	kHz
1500-1600	daily	SAs	9620alg
Bengali	**Days**	**Area**	**kHz**
0130-0430	daily	SAs	594kkt
1130-1430	daily	SAs	594kkt
Chinese	**Days**	**Area**	**kHz**
1145-1155	daily	EAs	15030bgl+
1145-1315	daily	EAs	17595bgl*
Dari	**Days**	**Area**	**kHz**
0300-0345	daily	WAs	11560bgl
1315-1415	daily	WAs	11560bgl
English	**Days**	**Area**	**kHz**
1000-1010	daily	EAs	15410bgl+
1745-1755	daily	Eu	7550bgl+
Farsi	**Days**	**Area**	**kHz**
0400-0430	daily	ME	11560bgl
Nepali	**Days**	**Area**	**kHz**
0700-0800	daily	SAs	9950del, 11620del
Pashto	**Days**	**Area**	**kHz**
0215-0300	daily	WAs	11560bgl
1415-1530	daily	WAs	11560bgl
Sindhi	**Days**	**Area**	**kHz**
0100-0200	daily	SAs	7380bgl
Tibetan	**Days**	**Area**	**kHz**
1215-1330	daily	EAs	9580bgl*
Urdu	**Days**	**Area**	**kHz**
0830-1130	daily	SAs	9950del

Key: + DRM (may include simulcasts with Vividh Bharati on 2nd channel); * Jammed.

Ann: Dari: "Inja Delhi"; English: "This is the General Overseas Service of All India Radio"; Hindi: "Yeh Akashvani ki videsh prasaran sewa hai"; Nepali: "Yo All India Radio ho"; Sinhala: "Me All India Radio videshiya sevayai"; Tamil: "Idi Akashvani videsh sewai".

V: QSL-card. Email rpt to gosesdair@yahoo.co.in; spectrum-manager@prasarbharati.gov.in. Rpt by mail/fax to Director (Spectrum Management & Synergy), All India Radio, Room No. 204, Akashvani Bhawan, New Delhi-110001, India; Fax: +91 11 23421062.

Notes: External Sce of All India Radio (the radio division of the national public broadcaster Prasar Bharati Corporation). Established on 1 October 1939. AIR's External Sce in English is branded "General Overseas Service" (GOS). Some services in national languages of India are produced by AIR's regional stations. The services in Gujarati, Hindi, Makayam, Tamil and Telugu are directed at overseas Indians, while those in Bengali, Kannada, Punjabi, Urdu, Saraiki and Sindhi are meant for listeners in the Indian Sub-continent.

FEBA INDIA (Rlg)

✉ 7 Commissariat Road, Bengaluru 560025, India. (Head Office & Studio)
☎ +91 80 25328191; +91 80 25559063.
E: febaindia@vsnl.com **W:** febaonline.org
Webcast: L
✉ A-42-44, Manushri Building, Dr. Mukherji Nagar, New Delhi 110009, India. (Branch Office & Studio)
☎ +91 11 27652426; +91 11 27652084.
L.P: Dir: Christian Benjamin.
kHz: *873, 1548, 9540, 11580*

Winter Schedule 2020/2021

English	Days	Area	kHz
1400-1430	.....s.	IND	1548put‡
Hindi	**Days**	**Area**	**kHz**
1400-1430	....f.s	IND	1548put‡
1430-1500	..wtfss	IND	9540tac
Malayalam	**Days**	**Area**	**kHz**
1245-1315	...tfs.	IND	11580twr
Tamil	**Days**	**Area**	**kHz**
0130-0200	mt...ss	IND	873put
1300-1330	....f..	IND	873put

Key: ‡ Inactive at time of publication.

V: QSL-email. E-mail rpt to: kenneth@febaindia.org (Kenneth Edward)

Notes: Far East Broadcasting Associates of India (FEBA India) is regional partner of Far East Broadcasting Company, Inc (USA) (see USA for FEBC corporate details), targeting the Indian subcontinent.

TWR INDIA (Rlg)

✉ 1st Floor, 24/46 Aspiran Garden 1st St, Aspiran Garden Colony, Kilpauk, Chennai, Tamil Nadu-600010, India
☎ +91 44 26440161.
E: info@twr.in **W:** twr.in; radio882.com
Webcast: D/L
L.P: CEO: George Philip.
kHz: *882, 1467, 7280, 7505, 7590, 9290, 9910, 9950*

Winter Schedule 2020/2021

Awadhi	Days	Area	kHz
1345-1400	m......	SAs	9910erv
Bagri	**Days**	**Area**	**kHz**
1345-1400	....f..	SAs	1467bis
Banjara	**Days**	**Area**	**kHz**
1330-1345	.....s.	SAs	882put
Bengali	**Days**	**Area**	**kHz**
1315-1330	.....s.	SAs	9910erv
2230-2300	daily	SAs	882put
Bhatri	**Days**	**Area**	**kHz**
1315-1330	......s	SAs	9910erv
Bhojpuri	**Days**	**Area**	**kHz**
1400-1430	mtwtf..	SAs	9910erv
Bondo	**Days**	**Area**	**kHz**
1330-1345	..w....	SAs	9290erv
Bundelkhandi	**Days**	**Area**	**kHz**
1330-1345	.....s.	SAs	9910erv
Chhattisgarhi	**Days**	**Area**	**kHz**
1400-1415	......s	SAs	882put
1500-1530	mtwtf..	SAs	882put
1600-1615	......s	SAs	882put
Dari	**Days**	**Area**	**kHz**
1500-1530	daily	SAs	1467bis
Deccani	**Days**	**Area**	**kHz**
1630-1645	......s	SAs	882put
1630-1700	mtwtf..	SAs	882put
Dogri	**Days**	**Area**	**kHz**
1430-1445	.tw....	SAs	9910erv
Dzongkha	**Days**	**Area**	**kHz**
0045-0100	.....s.	SAs	7280kch
English	**Days**	**Area**	**kHz**
1415-1420	.....ss	SAs	9290erv
1420-1425	daily	SAs	9290erv
1425-1445	.....ss	SAs	9290erv
Gondi	**Days**	**Area**	**kHz**
1330-1400	mtwtf..	SAs	882put
1345-1400	......s	SAs	882put
Gujarati	**Days**	**Area**	**kHz**
1430-1515	.....s.	SAs	882put
1500-1530	......s	SAs	882put
2330-2400	mtwt.ss	SAs	882put
Hindi	**Days**	**Area**	**kHz**
0045-0100	......s	SAs	7280kch
0045-0115	mtwtf..	SAs	7280kch
1330-1345	......s	SAs	9910erv
1330-1345	...t...	SAs	1467bis
1345-1400	.twtf..	SAs	9910erv
1345-1415	daily	SAs	9290erv
1400-1430	.....ss	SAs	9910erv
1415-1420	mtwtf..	SAs	9290erv
1430-1445	m..tfss	SAs	9910erv
1430-1445	mtwtf..	SAs	9950kch
2300-2330	daily	SAs	882put
Ho	**Days**	**Area**	**kHz**
1330-1345	.....s.	SAs	9290erv
Kannada	**Days**	**Area**	**kHz**
1430-1445	......s	SAs	882put
1430-1500	mtwtf..	SAs	882put
Kashmiri	**Days**	**Area**	**kHz**
1330-1345	.....s.	SAs	1467bis

Kashmiri	Days	Area	kHz
1345-1400	.....ss	SAs	9910erv
1400-1430	......s	SAs	1467bis
Kharia	**Days**	**Area**	**kHz**
1330-1345	m......	SAs	9290erv
Konkani	**Days**	**Area**	**kHz**
1415-1430	.....s.	SAs	882put
Koya	**Days**	**Area**	**kHz**
1400-1415	.....s.	SAs	882put
Kui	**Days**	**Area**	**kHz**
1315-1330	.....s.	SAs	9290erv
Kukna	**Days**	**Area**	**kHz**
2330-2345	....f..	SAs	882put
Kumaoni	**Days**	**Area**	**kHz**
1345-1400	.....s.	SAs	1467bis
Kurukh	**Days**	**Area**	**kHz**
1315-1330	..wtf..	SAs	9290erv
1345-1400	......s	SAs	9950kch
Kutchi	**Days**	**Area**	**kHz**
2345-2400	....f..	SAs	882put
Maghai	**Days**	**Area**	**kHz**
1330-1345	...tf..	SAs	9290erv
Maithili	**Days**	**Area**	**kHz**
1315-1345	mtwtf..	SAs	9910erv
1330-1345	......s	SAs	9290erv
Malayalam	**Days**	**Area**	**kHz**
0000-0030	daily	SAs	882put
Marathi	**Days**	**Area**	**kHz**
1600-1630	mtwtfs.	SAs	882put
1630-1700	.....s.	SAs	882put
Marwari	**Days**	**Area**	**kHz**
1345-1400	..w....	SAs	9950kch
Mawachi	**Days**	**Area**	**kHz**
1345-1400	...tf..	SAs	9950kch
Mundari	**Days**	**Area**	**kHz**
1315-1330	mt.....	SAs	9290erv
Oriya	**Days**	**Area**	**kHz**
1415-1430	......s	SAs	882put
1515-1530	.....s.	SAs	882put
1530-1600	daily	SAs	882put
Pahari	**Days**	**Area**	**kHz**
1330-1345	....f..	SAs	1467bis
Punjabi	**Days**	**Area**	**kHz**
1330-1400	.tw....	SAs	1467bis
1430-1445	.t.....	SAs	1467bis
1445-1545	mtwtf..	SAs	7505kch
Pushto	**Days**	**Area**	**kHz**
1445-1500	....fss	SAs	1467bis
Sadri	**Days**	**Area**	**kHz**
1330-1345	.t.....	SAs	9290erv
Santhali	**Days**	**Area**	**kHz**
1315-1330	......s	SAs	9290erv
Saraiki	**Days**	**Area**	**kHz**
1430-1445	...t...	SAs	1467bis
Sindhi	**Days**	**Area**	**kHz**
1400-1430	mtwtf..	SAs	9950kch
Soura	**Days**	**Area**	**kHz**
1330-1345	......s	SAs	882put
Tamil	**Days**	**Area**	**kHz**
0030-0130	daily	SAs	882put
Telugu	**Days**	**Area**	**kHz**
1345-1400	.....s.	SAs	882put
1400-1430	mtwtf..	SAs	882put
Tulu	**Days**	**Area**	**kHz**
1615-1630	......s	SAs	882put
Urdu	**Days**	**Area**	**kHz**
1330-1400	m.....s	SAs	1467bis
1400-1430	mtwtfs.	SAs	1467bis
1430-1445	m.w..ss	SAs	1467bis
1600-1630	daily	SAs	7590kch
Varli	**Days**	**Area**	**kHz**
1445-1500	......s	SAs	882put

Vasavi	Days	Area	kHz
1345-1400	mt.....	SAs	9950kch

V: QSL-card.
Notes: TWR regional division, covering the Indian subcontinent. For corporate details, see under TWR (USA).

INDONESIA (INS)

VOICE OF INDONESIA (VOI) (Pub)

P.O. Box 1157, Jakarta 10110, Indonesia; Jl. Medan Merdeka Barat 4-5, Jakarta 10110, Indonesia.
☎ +62 21 3456811. Fax +62 21 3500990.
E: voi@voinews.id; english@voinews.id **W:** www.voinews.id
Webcast: D/L
L.P: Dir: Agung Susatyo, Head of Technique & Multimedia: Syafruddin Asb.
SW: [JAK] Jakarta (presumed/unconfirmed location): 1 x 10kW; [PGA] Palangkaraya 1 x 50kW.
kHz: *3325, 4750*

Winter Schedule 2020/2021

Arabic	Days	Area	kHz
1600-1700	daily	SEA	3325pga, 4750jak†
Chinese	**Days**	**Area**	**kHz**
1100-1200	daily	SEA	3325pga, 4750jak†
1500-1600	daily	SEA	3325pga, 4750jak†
Dutch	**Days**	**Area**	**kHz**
1900-2000	daily	SEA	3325pga, 4750jak†
English	**Days**	**Area**	**kHz**
1000-1100	daily	SEA	3325pga, 4750jak†
1300-1400	daily	SEA	3325pga, 4750jak†
2100-2200	daily	SEA	3325pga, 4750jak†
French	**Days**	**Area**	**kHz**
2000-2100	daily	SEA	3325pga, 4750jak†
German	**Days**	**Area**	**kHz**
1800-1900	daily	SEA	3325pga, 4750jak†
Indonesian	**Days**	**Area**	**kHz**
1400-1500	daily	SEA	3325pga, 4750jak†
Japanese	**Days**	**Area**	**kHz**
1200-1300	daily	SEA	3325pga, 4750jak†
Spanish	**Days**	**Area**	**kHz**
1700-1800	daily	SEA	3325pga, 4750jak†

Key: † Irregular.
Ann: English: "This is the Voice of Indonesia, in Jakarta"; Spanish: "La Voz de Indonesia en Jakarta".
V: QSL-card.
Notes: The Voice of Indonesia (RRI World Service) is the External Sce of the public service broadcaster Radio Republik Indonesia (RRI).

IRAN (IRN)

PARS TODAY (VOICE OF THE ISLAMIC REPUBLIC OF IRAN) (Gov)

P.O. Box 19395-6767, Tehran, Iran.
☎ +98 21 22013687; +98 21 22162731. Fax +98 21 22044287.
E: english@parstoday.com **W:** parstoday.com
Webcast: D/L
☎ +98 21 22013720.
L.P: Pres (IRIB): Mohammad Sarafraz; DG, Int. Affairs: Abbas Naseri Taheri.
MW: [AHW] Ahvaz, Bandar-e Mahshar: 576/1080kHz 750kW; [BNB] Bonab: 639kHz 400kW; [BNT] Bandar-e Torkaman: 1449kHz 400kW; [CHR] Chabahar: 765kHz 1000kW; [JOL] Jolfa 1323kHz 50kW; [KIA] Bandar-e Kiashahr: 702kHz 500kW; [KIH] Kish Island: 1224kHz 300kW; [QSH] Qasr-e Shirin: 612/1161kHz 600kW; [TYB] Tayebad: 720kHz 400kW; [ZAB] Zabol: 1098kHz 200kW.
SW: [AHW] Ahvaz, Bandar-e Mahshar: 2 x 250kW; [SIR] Sirjan: 10 x 500kW; [ZAH] Zahedan: 2 x 500kW.
SAT: Eutelsat 3B/Hot Bird 13E, Intelsat 902.
kHz: *576, 612, 639, 702, 720, 765, 1080, 1098, 1161, 1224, 1323, 1395, 1449, 5925, 5930, 5935, 5940, 5950, 5980, 6000, 6040, 6060, 6075, 6085, 6090, 6110, 6130, 6150, 6160, 7225, 7230, 7280, 7290, 7300, 7305, 7310, 7355, 7360, 7375, 7380, 7425, 7430, 7435, 7445, 9475, 9495, 9530, 9550, 9660, 9725, 9755, 9800, 9835, 9870, 11780,*

11870, 11875, 11880, 11930, 13680, 13690, 13710, 13790, 13820, 15140, 15200, 15240, 15360, 15440, 17630, 17665

Winter Schedule 2020/2021

Albanian	**Days**	**Area**	**kHz**
1820-1920	daily	Eu	5925sir, 7305sir
Arabic	**Days**	**Area**	**kHz**
0000-2400	daily	ME	1224kih***
0130-0320	daily	ME	1161qsh
0130-0330	daily	NAf,ME	6040sir
0220-1250	daily	ME	765chr
0230-0530	daily	ME	7380zah*
0320-0420	daily	ME	6085sir*
0330-0600	daily	NAf,ME	9725sir
0330-1630	daily	ME	576ahw
0420-1530	daily	ME	612qsh
0530-0730	daily	NAf,ME	13820zah
0600-0830	daily	ME	13790sir
0830-1030	daily	ME	13820sir
0930-1430	daily	NAf,ME	9800sir
1030-1430	daily	ME	9530zah
1430-1730	daily	ME	9800sir
1430-1730	daily	NAf,ME	7310zah
1530-2030	daily	ME	1161qsh**
1620-0120	daily	ME	765chr**
1700-0330	daily	ME	1080ahw****
1730-0230	daily	NAf,ME	6060zah**
Armenian	**Days**	**Area**	**kHz**
1620-1720	daily	Cau	7430sir
Azeri	**Days**	**Area**	**kHz**
0050-0520	daily	ME	1323jol
0100-0520	daily	Cau	702kia
1420-1650	daily	ME	702kia, 1323jol
Azeri (Aran)	**Days**	**Area**	**kHz**
0530-0930	daily	Cau	702kia
Bengali	**Days**	**Area**	**kHz**
1420-1520	daily	ME	9870ahw
1420-1520	daily	SAs	6150sir
1620-1650	daily	SAs	6150sir, 7375sir
Bosnian	**Days**	**Area**	**kHz**
1720-1820	daily	Eu	6110sir
Dari	**Days**	**Area**	**kHz**
0300-0630	daily	ME	1098zab
0300-1520	daily	WAs	720tyb
0550-0820	daily	WAs	13690sir
0820-1520	daily	WAs	1098zab
0920-1220	daily	WAs	9495sir
0920-1250	daily	WAs	11930sir
English	**Days**	**Area**	**kHz**
1020-1120	daily	ME	702kia
1520-1620	daily	SAs,SEA	7300sir
1920-2020	daily	Eu	6040sir
1920-2020	daily	SAf	11880sir
French	**Days**	**Area**	**kHz**
1820-1920	daily	Eu	6130sir
2320-0020	daily	WAf,CAf	7360sir, 9660sir
German	**Days**	**Area**	**kHz**
1720-1820	daily	Eu	5940sir, 6090sir, 7425sir
Hausa	**Days**	**Area**	**kHz**
0550-0650	daily	WAf,CAf	13710sir, 15360sir
1220-1250	daily	WAf,CAf	17665sir
1820-1920	daily	WAf,CAf	9475sir
2220-2320	daily	WAf,CAf	7225sir, 7280sir
Hebrew	**Days**	**Area**	**kHz**
0420-0450	daily	ME	9755sir, 11780sir
0650-0720	daily	ME	15440sir
1150-1220	daily	ME	15240sir
Hindi	**Days**	**Area**	**kHz**
1420-1520	daily	SAs	7445sir
Italian	**Days**	**Area**	**kHz**
1750-1820	daily	Eu	5930sir
Kurdish	**Days**	**Area**	**kHz**
0420-0520	daily	ME	639bnb
1320-1420	daily	ME	7355sir
1320-1620	daily	ME	639bnb
Pashto	**Days**	**Area**	**kHz**
0220-0320	daily	WAs	6075sir, 6160sir
0720-0820	daily	WAs	1098zab
1220-1320	daily	WAs	7360zah, 7435sir
1250-1320	daily	WAs	765chr
1620-1720	daily	WAs	5935zah
Russian	**Days**	**Area**	**kHz**
0320-0420	daily	Cau,CAs	9550sir
1320-1420	daily	Cau,CAs	1449bnt, 7290sir
1920-2020	daily	Eu,Cau	702kia
Spanish	**Days**	**Area**	**kHz**
0720-0820	daily	Eu	15200sir, 17630sir
2020-2120	daily	Eu	7360sir
2020-2120	daily	Eu,SAm	11870sir
2350-0120	daily	SAm	7230sir
2350-0250	daily	CAm,Eu	5980sir
Swahili	**Days**	**Area**	**kHz**
0450-0550	daily	CAf,EAf	13680sir, 15140sir
Tajik	**Days**	**Area**	**kHz**
0050-0220	daily	CAs	720tyb, 5950sir, 7360sir
1520-1720	daily	CAs	720tyb
1520-1720	daily	WAs	1098zab
Talysh	**Days**	**Area**	**kHz**
1720-1820	daily	ME	702kia
Turkish	**Days**	**Area**	**kHz**
0420-0550	daily	ME	11875sir
1550-1720	daily	ME	9870sir
1820-1920	daily	ME	639bnb, 702kia
Turkmen	**Days**	**Area**	**kHz**
1420-1820	daily	CAs	1395grg, 1449bnt
Urdu	**Days**	**Area**	**kHz**
0130-0230	daily	ME	1098zab
0130-0230	daily	SAs	765chr
1250-1420	daily	SAs	9835sir
1320-1420	daily	SAs	765chr
1520-1620	daily	SAs	765chr, 6000sir

Key: * "VO Palestine" prgr; ** Incl. "VO Palestine" prgr: 1930-2030; *** Incl. "Neda al-Bahrain" prgr: 0900-1200; **** Incl. "Neda al-Bahrain" prgr: 1700-2000 (W: nedaalbahrain.com).

Ann: Arabic: "Huna Tahran - Sawt al Jumhuriya al Islamiya fi Iran"; English: "IRIB English Radio", "This is the Voice of the Islamic Republic of Iran"; French: "Ici Tehran, la Voix de la République Islamique de l'Iran"; Russian: "Govorit Tegeran, Golos Islamskoy Respubliki Iran".

IS: "Love's Rainfall", by Nasser Cheshmazar.

V: QSL-card.

Notes: Pars Today / The Voice of the Islamic Republic of Iran is the External Sce of the state broadcaster IRIB. The prgr "Voice of Palestine" targets listeners in the territories under Palestinian Authority; the prgr "Neda al-Bahrain" (Call of Bahrain) targets listeners in Bahrain.

ISRAEL (ISR)

VOICE OF HOPE – MIDDLE EAST ‡ (Rlg)

✉ c/o Cultural & Social Center "Beit Gabriel on the Kinneret", Tzemah Junction, Route 90, 151320 Emeq HaYardan, Israel (studios). ☎ +972 54 6929952.

E: mail@voiceofhope.com; jacob@ivic.co.il

W: www.voiceofhope.com/station_middleeast.html

Webcast: L

✉ 543 Country Club Drive, Simi Valley, CA 93065, USA.

LP: Pres (SCG): John D. Tayloe; Vice Pres, Ops (SCG): Ray Robinson; CEO (Voice of Hope Ltd): Jacob Dayan; SM (VOH - Middle East): Gary Hull.

MW: Via own tx installed at Bezeq site (see Bezeq).

Key: ‡ Inactive on MW since Jan 2020.

Ann: Arabic: "Sawt al Amal"; English: "From the shores of the Sea of Galilee, this is the Voice of Hope".

V: QSL-card. (Email rpt to: reports@voiceofhope.com)
Notes: Produced by Voice of Hope Ltd (Israel), part of the Voice of Hope World Radio Network operated by Strategic Communications Group (SCG), USA (see KVOH - Voice of Hope entry under USA). On the air since 28 March 2017.

BEZEQ (THE ISRAEL TELECOMMUNICATIONS CORP. LTD) (Tx Operator)

132 Menachem Begin St, Azrieli Center 2, 671101 Tel Aviv, Israel.
☎ +972 3 6262600. 🖷 +972 3 6262609
E: dover@bezeq.co.il **W:** www.bezeq.co.il
L.P: Chmn (Bezeq Group): Shlomo Rodav.
MW: [SHE] She'ar Yashuv ‡: 1287kHz 50kW (tx owned by, and operated on behalf of Strategic Communications Group, USA).
Notes: Established in 1984. Bezeq is the national transmitter network operator in Israel.

ITALY (I)

IRRS–SHORTWAVE (NEXUS–IBA)

☎ +39 02 2666971.
E: info@nexus.org **W:** www.nexus.org (General); www.egradio.org (European Gospel Radio)
Webcast: L
34 Temple Hall, Mount Saint Annes, Milltown, Dublin 6, Ireland (Milano Ventures Ltd)
☎ +353 1 9069231.
E: info@mv.ie **W:** www.milanoventures.com
L.P: Chmn (NEXUS-IBA)/CEO (Milano Ventures Ltd): Alfredo E. Cotroneo
SW: Via tx leased from Radiocom (Romania) and/or NURTS Bulgaria.
kHz: *7290, 9510, 15515*

Winter Schedule 2020/2021

English	Days	Area	kHz
0900-1000	.....s	Eu,ME,NAf	9510tig
1030-1300	......s	Eu,ME,NAf	9510tig
1900-2000	daily	Eu,ME,NAf	7290sof
Oromo	**Days**	**Area**	**kHz**
1500-1530	.....s.	EAf	15515sof*

Key: * Relay of R. Wara Wangeelaa (Rlg) (W: www.facebook.com/Radiowarrawangeelaa).
Ann: English: "This is IRRS Shortwave in Milano, signing on".
IS: S/on: Triumphal Scene from Aida (Verdi); S/off: Prisoners' Chorus (Verdi).
V: E-QSL (Email rpt to: reports@nexus.org)
Notes: Relay services for prgr producers and broadcasters, via Internet (24/7) and via leased airtime on a third party SW tx in Romania and/or Bulgaria. Brands used for SW services are "Italian Radio Relay Service", "Irish Radio Relay Service", as well as "European Gospel Radio" (for religious relays). NEXUS-International Broadcasting Association (NEXUS-IBA) was founded 1990 in Italy as a non-commercial broadcasting association. While initially broadcasting via its own tx in Milan (Italy), NEXUS-IBA later began to rent airtime from SW providers in several European countries (Bulgaria, Romania, Slovakia). Milano Ventures Ltd (Ireland) was founded 2016 and is the commercial arm of the operation.

JAPAN (J)

RADIO JAPAN (NHK WORLD) (Pub)

2-1, Jinnan 2-chome, Shibuya-ku, Tokyo 150-8001, Japan.
☎ +81 3 34651111. 🖷 +81 3 34811350.
E: nhkworld@nhk.jp **W:** www.nhk.or.jp/nhkworld
Webcast: D/L/P
W: www.nhkint.or.jp (NHK International, Inc)
L.P: DG (NHK International, Inc): Takaaki Takai; Pres (NHK): Akinobu Maeda; DG, Broadcasting (NHK): Hideo Koike.
SW: Leased from KDDI & foreign relays.
SAT: Badr 4, Intelsat 19/20/21.
kHz: *927, 1386, 5985, 6075, 6090, 6105, 6155, 6165, 6190, 6195, 7245, 7265, 7445, 7450, 7565, 9560, 9580, 9625, 9680, 9750, 9765, 9795, 9855, 9895, 11630, 11685, 11740, 11790, 11815, 11825, 11895, 11910, 11925, 11945, 13650, 13725, 13730, 13840, 15130, 15195, 15280, 15290, 15325, 15720, 17810, 17830*

Winter Schedule 2020/2021

Arabic	Days	Area	kHz
0600-0630	daily	ME,NAf	6165iss
Bengali	**Days**	**Area**	**kHz**
1300-1345	daily	SAs	11685sng
Burmese	**Days**	**Area**	**kHz**
1030-1100	daily	SEA	11740sng
1430-1500	daily	SEA	11740sng
1445-1505	..w..s.	SEA	5985yan*
2340-2400	daily	SEA	13650yam
Chinese	**Days**	**Area**	**kHz**
0400-0430	daily	EAs	11825yam
1130-1200	daily	EAs	6090yam
1230-1300	daily	EAs	6190yam
1330-1400	daily	EAs	6190yam
1430-1500	daily	EAs	6190yam
2230-2250	daily	EAs	9560yam
English	**Days**	**Area**	**kHz**
0430-0500	mtwtf..	Eu	6155mos
0430-0500	mtwtf..	SAf	7445iss
0430-0500	mtwtf..	WAf	7245smg
0500-0530	.....ss	Eu	6155mos
0500-0530	.....ss	SAf	7445iss
0500-0530	.....ss	WAf	7245smg
1100-1130	daily	SEA	11825sng
1400-1430	daily	SAs	6165tac
1400-1430	daily	SEA	11925dha
1540-1600	...tf..	SEA	5985yan*
French	**Days**	**Area**	**kHz**
0530-0600	daily	CAf	13840mdc
0530-0600	daily	WAf	7450iss
2030-2100	daily	WAf	9855mdc
Hindi	**Days**	**Area**	**kHz**
0100-0120	daily	SAs	6155tac
1430-1500	daily	SAs	15720mdc
1530-1600	daily	SAs	7565tac
Indonesian	**Days**	**Area**	**kHz**
1115-1145	daily	SEA	17830dha
1315-1345	daily	SEA	11925dha
2130-2200	daily	SEA	6075yam
Japanese	**Days**	**Area**	**kHz**
0200-0300	daily	EAs	11790yam
0200-0400	daily	CAm	6105iss
0200-0400	daily	SAs	15325yam
0200-0500	daily	EAs	15195yam
0200-0500	daily	SEA	17810yam
0300-0500	daily	ME,NAf	7265nau
0700-0800	daily	EAs	11825yam
0700-0900	daily	SAm	7445yam
0700-1000	daily	SEA	15280yam
0800-1000	daily	WAf	15290iss
0800-1600	daily	EAs	9750yam
1000-1500	daily	SEA	11815yam
1300-1400	daily	SAs	9795yam
1500-1700	daily	SAs	9680yam
1700-1900	daily	ME,NAf	9765nau
1700-1900	daily	SAf	11945iss
1900-2100	daily	CAf	15130iss
1900-2100	daily	ME,NAf	9895yam
2000-2100	daily	Pac	9625yam
2100-2300	daily	SEA	11630yam
2100-2400	daily	EAs	11910yam
Korean	**Days**	**Area**	**kHz**
0415-0445	daily	EAs	11895yam
1100-1130	daily	EAs	6090yam
1200-1230	daily	EAs	6090yam
1300-1330	daily	EAs	6190yam
1400-1430	daily	EAs	6190yam
2210-2230	daily	EAs	9560yam

Persian	Days	Area	kHz
0400-0430	daily	ME	9855tac
1430-1500	daily	ME	13725iss
1630-1700	daily	ME	927dsb
Portuguese	**Days**	**Area**	**kHz**
0900-0930	daily	SAm	6195hri
Russian	**Days**	**Area**	**kHz**
0330-0400	daily	EEu	1386vst
0430-0500	daily	EEu	6165nau
0530-0600	daily	EAs	11790yam
1100-1130	daily	EAs	5985yam
1600-1630	daily	CAs	927dsb
1730-1800	daily	EEu	1386vst
Spanish	**Days**	**Area**	**kHz**
0400-0430	daily	SAm	6195hri
0400-0430	daily	CAm	5985rmi
0930-1000	daily	SAm	6195hri
Swahili	**Days**	**Area**	**kHz**
0330-0400	daily	EAf	9560mdc
1730-1800	daily	EAf	13730mdc
Thai	**Days**	**Area**	**kHz**
1130-1200	daily	SEA	11740sng
1230-1300	daily	SEA	11740sng
2300-2320	daily	SEA	13650yam
Urdu	**Days**	**Area**	**kHz**
1515-1545	daily	SAs	9580dha
1700-1730	daily	SAs	927dsb
Vietnamese	**Days**	**Area**	**kHz**
1100-1130	daily	SEA	11740sng
2320-2340	daily	SEA	13650yam

Key: * Via MRTV Yangon (also on 576 & 594kHz). Many broadcasts are replaced by NHK Newsline, in English, during the Coronvavirus emergency.
Ann: Chinese: "Zheli shi riben guoji guangbo diantai, NHK huanqiu guangbowang"; English: "This is NHK World, Radio Japan in Tokyo"; Indonesian: "Inilah Radio Jepang, NHK World, siaran bahasa Indonesia"; Japanese: "Kochirawa NHK Warudo, Rajio Nippon, NHK no kokusaihoso desu"; Korean: "Yeogineun NHK World, Radio Ilbonimnda".
IS: Melody "Kazoe Uta".
V: QSL-card.

Notes: Radio Japan is the External Sce of the public broadcaster NHK, produced by its subsidiary NHK International, Inc. The Japanese programmes include relays of NHK domestic Radio 1. Radio Japan's foreign language prgr's are also relayed by local stations in the following countries: Arabic, to IRQ: 2000-2030 via R. Dijla (Baghdad 88.3MHz + 4 cities) & to ISR (West Bank & Gaza): 2100-2130 via All for Peace Radio (Ramallah 87.8MHz), via Reehan FM (Jerico 95.6MHz); Bengali, to BGD: 1500-1545 via Bangladesh Betar (Dhaka 104.0MHz + 6 cities); Hindi, to IND: 1830-1900 via Big FM (New Delhi 92.7MHz + 4 cities); Indonesian, to INS: 1405-1435 via R. Elshinta (Jakarta 90.0MHz + 8 cities), 1400-1430 via R. Rasita (Simalungun 1170kHz) & via various local FM stns in 42 cities; Persian, to AFG: 1430-1500 via R. Khillid (Kabul & Herat 88.0MHz); Swahili, to TZA: 0330-0400 via R. Uhai (Tabora 94.1MHz), 1730-1800 via Tanzania Broadcasting Corp. (Dar es Salaam 90.0MHz + nationwide FM) & 1730-1800 via Hits FM (Zanzibar 92.5MHz); Thai, to THA: 0200-0230 via Naresuan Univ. R. (Phitsanulok 107.25MHz), 1230-1300 via Maejo Univ. R. (Chiang Mai 95.5MHz) & via Khon Kaen Univ. R. (Khon Kaen 103.0MHz), Mon-Fri 1230-1300 via Thammasat Univ. R. (Bangkok 981kHz 10kW) & via Mahasarakham Univ. R. (Maha Sarakham 102.25MHz); Vietnamese to VTN: Mon 1300-1320, Tue-Fri 1300-1315, Sat 1330-1345, Sun 1330-1350 via VOV Giao Thong on 91.0MHz (Hanoi, Ho Chi Minh City, Can Tho and Quang Binh).

KDDI CORPORATION (Tx Operator)
✉ Garden Air Tower, 10-10, Iidabashi 3-chome, Chiyoda-ku, Tokyo 102-8460, Japan.
☎ +81 3 33470077. 🖷 +81 3 33475845.
E: kmo-pr@kddi.com **W:** www.kddi.com
L.P: Chmn: Makoto Takahashi.
SW: [YAM] Tokyo, Yamata: 4 x 100, 7 x 300kW.
Notes: KDDI Corporation is a major national telecommunications provider.

KOREA, North (KRE)

PYONGYANG BROADCASTING STATION (PYONGYANG PANGSONG) (Gov)
✉ Pyongyang, Democratic People's Republic of Korea.
W: www.gnu.rep.kp
Webcast: D
MW/SW: Uses txs provided by the Ministry of Post & Telecommunications.
FM/DAB: FM: 91.2/92.9/93.3/93.9/94.5/96.7/97.3/97.7/98.1/99.6/101.8/106.5MHz (Locations unknown).
kHz: *621, 657, 801, 855, 873, 3220, 3320, 6400*

Winter Schedule 2020/2021

Korean	Days	Area	kHz
0300-0700	daily	EAs	621chj
1300-2000	daily	EAs	621chj
1800-2000	daily	EAs	873snu, 3220ham
2100-1800	daily	EAs	6400kng
2100-1900	daily	EAs	801kmk, 3320pyo
2100-2000	daily	EAs	657kan, 855swo

Ann: Korean: "Pyongyang Pangsong-imnida".
IS: Song of General Kim Il Sung. Opening & closing music: National Anthem.
V: QSL-card
Notes: External Sce of the Radio & TV Broadcasting Committee of the Democratic People's Republic of Korea for Korean listeners in South Korea, Japan and the P.R. China. Jammed in parts of the target area.

VOICE OF KOREA (VOK) (Gov)
✉ Pyongyang, Democratic People's Republic of Korea.
☎ +850 2 3816035. 🖷 +850 2 3814416.
E: vok@star-co.net.kp **W:** vok.rep.kp
Webcast: D
MW/SW: Uses txs provided by the Ministry of Post & Telecommunications.
SAT: Thaicom 5.
kHz: *621, 6070, 6170, 6185, 7210, 7220, 7235, 7570, 7580, 9425, 9435, 9445, 9650, 9730, 9850, 9875, 9890, 11635, 11645, 11710, 11735, 11910, 12015, 13650, 13760, 15105, 15180, 15245*

Winter Schedule 2020/2021

Arabic	Days	Area	kHz
1500-1600	daily	ME,NAf	9890kuj, 11645kuj
1700-1800	daily	ME,NAf	9890kuj, 11645kuj
Chinese	**Days**	**Area**	**kHz**
0300-0400	daily	SEA	13650kuj, 15105kuj
0500-0600	daily	EAs	7220kuj, 9445kuj, 9730kuj
0600-0700	daily	SEA	13650kuj, 15105kuj
0800-0900	daily	EAs	7220kuj, 9445kuj
1100-1200	daily	EAs	7220kuj, 9445kuj
1300-1400	daily	SEA	6185kuj, 9850kuj
2100-2300	daily	EAs	7235kuj, 9445kuj, 9875kuj, 11635kuj
English	**Days**	**Area**	**kHz**
0400-0500	daily	EAs	7220kuj, 9445kuj, 9730kuj
0400-0500	daily	LAm	11735kuj, 13760kuj, 15180kuj
0500-0600	daily	SEA	13650kuj, 15105kuj
0600-0700	daily	EAs	7220kuj, 9445kuj, 9730kuj
1000-1100	daily	LAm	6170kuj, 9435kuj
1000-1100	daily	SEA	6185kuj, 9850kuj
1300-1400	daily	NAm	9435kuj, 11710kuj
1300-1400	daily	Eu	7570kuj, 12015kuj
1500-1600	daily	Eu	7570kuj, 12015kuj
1500-1600	daily	NAm	9435kuj, 11710kuj
1600-1700	daily	ME,NAf	9890kuj, 11645kuj
1800-1900	daily	Eu	7570kuj, 12015kuj
1900-2000	daily	ME,NAf	9875kuj, 11635kuj

English	Days	Area	kHz
1900-2000	daily	SAf	7210kuj, 11910kuj
2100-2200	daily	Eu	7570kuj, 12015kuj
French	**Days**	**Area**	**kHz**
0400-0500	daily	SEA	13650kuj, 15105kuj
0600-0700	daily	LAm	11735kuj, 13760kuj, 15180kuj
1100-1200	daily	LAm	6170kuj, 9435kuj
1100-1200	daily	SEA	6185kuj, 9850kuj
1400-1500	daily	NAm	9435kuj, 11710kuj
1400-1500	daily	Eu	7570kuj, 12015kuj
1600-1700	daily	Eu	7570kuj, 12015kuj
1600-1700	daily	NAm	9435kuj, 11710kuj
1800-1900	daily	ME,NAf	9875kuj, 11635kuj
1800-1900	daily	SAf	7210kuj, 11910kuj
2000-2100	daily	Eu	7570kuj, 12015kuj
German	**Days**	**Area**	**kHz**
1600-1700	daily	Eu	6170kuj, 9425kuj
1800-2000	daily	Eu	6170kuj, 9425kuj
Japanese	**Days**	**Area**	**kHz**
0700-1300	daily	EAs	621chj, 7580kuj, 9650kuj
0900-1300	daily	EAs	6070kng
2100-2350	daily	EAs	621chj, 7580kuj, 9650kuj
Korean	**Days**	**Area**	**kHz**
0900-0950	daily	EAs	7220kuj, 9445kuj
1200-1250	daily	LAm	6170kuj, 9435kuj
1200-1250	daily	SEA	6185kuj, 9850kuj
1400-1450	daily	SEA	6185kuj, 9850kuj
1700-1750	daily	Eu	7570kuj, 12015kuj
1700-1750	daily	NAm	9435kuj, 11710kuj
2000-2050	daily	Eu	6170kuj, 9425kuj
2000-2050	daily	ME,NAf	9875kuj, 11635kuj
2000-2050	daily	SAf	7210kuj, 11910kuj
2300-2350	daily	EAs	7235kuj, 9445kuj, 9875kuj, 11635kuj
2300-2350	daily	Eu	7570kuj, 12015kuj
Russian	**Days**	**Area**	**kHz**
0700-0900	daily	EAs	9875kuj, 11735kuj
0700-0900	daily	Eu	13760kuj, 15245kuj
1400-1600	daily	Eu	6170kuj, 9425kuj
1700-1800	daily	Eu	6170kuj, 9425kuj
Spanish	**Days**	**Area**	**kHz**
0300-0400	daily	LAm	11735kuj, 13760kuj, 15180kuj
0500-0600	daily	LAm	11735kuj, 13760kuj, 15180kuj
1900-2000	daily	Eu	7570kuj, 12015kuj
2100-2300	daily	Eu	7570kuj, 12015kuj

Ann: Arabic: "Huna Sowt al Koriya"; Chinese: "Chaoxian zhi sheng guangbo diantai"; English: "This is Voice of Korea"; French: "La Voix de la Corée"; German: "Hier ist die Stimme Koreas"; Japanese: "Choson no koe hoso desu"; Korean: "Joson Jung-ang Pangsong-imnida"; Russian: "Govorit Golos Korei"; Spanish: "Aqui la Voz de Corea".
IS: Song of General Kim Il Sung. Opening music: National Anthem.
V: QSL-card.
Notes: Voice of Korea ("R. Pyongyang" until 2002) is the External Sce of the Radio & TV Broadcasting Committee of the Democratic People's Republic of Korea.

MINISTRY OF POST & TELECOMMUNICATIONS (Tx Operator)

✉ Oesong-dong, Central District, Pyongyang, Democratic People's Republic of Korea.
☎ +850 2 3813180. 🖷 +850 2 3814418.
E: mptird@star-co.net.kp
L.P: Minister: Kwang Chol Kim.
MW: [CHJ] Chongjin: 621kHz 500kW; [KAN] Kangnam: 657kHz 1500kW; [KMK] Kimchaek 801kHz 500kW; [SNU] Sinuiju: 873kHz 250kW; [SWO] Sangwon: 855kHz 500kW.
SW: [CHJ] Chongjin: 1 x 5kW; [KNG] Kanggye: 1 x 250kW; [KUJ] Kujang: 10 x 200kW; [PYO] Pyongyang: 1 x 100kW. The line-up reflects the situation before the installation of new Chinese-made txs (20/50/100/150kW) in recent years.
Notes: The Ministry of Post and Telecommunications owns and operates the transmitter network in the Democratic People's Republic of Korea.

KOREA, South (KOR)

KBS WORLD RADIO (Pub)

✉ 13, Yeouigongwon-ro, Yeongdeungpo-gu, Seoul, 07235, Rep. of Korea.
☎ +82 2 7813885. (English) 🖷 +82 2 7813694.
E: rki@kbs.co.kr; english@kbs.co.kr **W:** world.kbs.co.kr
Webcast: D/L/P
L.P: Pres/CEO (KBS): Yang Sung-dong; Exec. Producer (KBS World Radio): Paek Seung Yeop.
MW: [DAN] Dangjin (HLCA): 972kHz 1500kW; [KIM] Gimje (HLSR): 1170kHz 500kW.
SW: [KIM] Gimje: 8 x 100, 3 x 250kW; [HWA] Hwaseong: 1 x 100kW.
kHz: *972, 1170, 1557, 3955, 5950, 6015, 6040, 6045, 6090, 6095, 6155, 7215, 7275, 9515, 9570, 9580, 9605, 9630, 9640, 9645, 9740, 9770, 9805, 11795, 11810, 15160, 15575*

Winter Schedule 2020/2021

Arabic	Days	Area	kHz
2000-2100	daily	ME,NAf	6090wof
Chinese	**Days**	**Area**	**kHz**
1100-1200	daily	EAs	1557kou
1130-1230	daily	EAs,SEA	6095kim, 9770kim
1300-1400	daily	EAs	1170kim, 7275kim
2300-2400	daily	EAs,SEA	7215kim, 9805kim
English	**Days**	**Area**	**kHz**
0200-0300	daily	LAm	9580kim
0800-1030	daily	SEA	9770kim
1300-1400	daily	NAm	15575kim
1300-1400	daily	SEA	9570kim
1400-1600	daily	SAs	9630kim
1500-1700	daily	Eu	9515kim
1600-1700	daily	SEA	9640kim
2200-2300	daily	Eu	11810kim
French	**Days**	**Area**	**kHz**
2000-2100	daily	Af	5950iss
2100-2200	daily	Eu	3955wof
German	**Days**	**Area**	**kHz**
2000-2100	daily	Eu	3955wof
Indonesian	**Days**	**Area**	**kHz**
1200-1300	daily	SEA	9570kim
1400-1500	daily	SEA	9570kim
1600-1700	daily	SEA	9805kim
2200-2300	daily	SEA	9805kim
Japanese	**Days**	**Area**	**kHz**
0100-0200	daily	EAs	9580kim
0200-0300	daily	EAs,LAm	11810kim
0800-0900	daily	EAs	7275kim
0800-1000	daily	EAs	6155kim
1100-1200	daily	EAs	1170kim
Korean	**Days**	**Area**	**kHz**
0300-0400	daily	EAs,LAm	11810kim
0350-2400	daily	EAs	972dan*, 6015hwa*
0700-0800	daily	Eu	6045wof
0800-1000	daily	EAs,SEA	9570kim
0900-1000	daily	EAs,SEA	7275kim
0900-1000	daily	ME,Af	15160kim
1000-1100	daily	EAs	1170kim
1100-1200	daily	EAs,SEA	7275kim
1400-0400	daily	EAs	1170kim**
1400-1500	daily	NAm	15575kim
1600-1800	daily	Eu	7275kim
1600-1800	daily	ME,Af	9740kim
1700-1900	daily	Eu	9515kim
Russian	**Days**	**Area**	**kHz**
1200-1300	daily	EAs	1170kim

Russian	Days	Area	kHz
1300-1400	daily	CAs	9645kim
1800-1900	daily	Eu	6040wof
Spanish	**Days**	**Area**	**kHz**
0100-0200	daily	LAm	9605hri, 11810kim
0200-0300	daily	NAm	15575kim
1100-1200	daily	LAm	11795kim
1800-1900	daily	Eu,Af	9740kim
Vietnamese	**Days**	**Area**	**kHz**
1030-1100	daily	SEA	9770kim
1530-1600	daily	SEA	9640kim
2300-2330	daily	SEA	7275kim

Key: * 1st Global Korean Network; ** 2nd Global Korean Network.

Ann: Arabic: "Huna KBS World Radio min Si'ul"; Chinese: "Zheli shi Hanguo guoji guangbo diantai, zai Dahanminguo shoudu Shou'er wei nin boyin"; English: "This is KBS World Radio, the overseas service of the Korean Broadcasting System, coming to you from Seoul, the capital of the Republic of Korea"; German: "Hier ist KBS World Radio aus Seoul, der Auslandssender der Republik Korea"; Indonesian: "Inilah siaran bahasa Indonesia, KBS World Radio, yang dipancarkan langsung dari ibu kota Republik Korea, Seoul"; Japanese: "Kochirawa Kankoku Souru kara okurishiteimasu KBS no rajio kokusai hoso, KBS warudo rajio desu"; Korean: "Yeogineun Daehan Minguk Seoul-eseo bonaedeurineun KBS World Radio urimal bangsong-imnida"; Spanish: "Esto es KBS World Radio, emitiendo desde Seúl, Republica de Corea."; Vietnamese: "Day la chuong trinh phat thanh tieng Viet cua dai KBS World Radio phat thanh tu Seoul Han quoc". Global Korean Network 1: "Jungpa Gubaek-chilsib-i (972) kHz, Hanminjok Neteuwokeu Chaeneol, KBS Hanminjok Je-il Bangsong-imnida"; Global Korean Network 2: "Jungpa Cheonbaek-chilsip (1170) kHz, Daehan Mingook Seoureseo Bonae Deurineun Hanminjok Neteuwokeu Chaeneol, KBS Hanminjok Je-I Bangsong-imnida".
IS: Korean children's song "Dar-a Dar-a Balgeun Dar-a (Oh, Bright Moon)", played on a glockenspiel. Original music "Dawn" composed by Kim Hee Jyo, with KBS symphony orchestra.
V: QSL-card. Online-form available on website.
Notes: KBS World Radio is the External Sce of the public broadcaster Korean Broadcasting System (KBS). The channels of "KBS Global Korean Network" are aimed at ethnic Koreans living outside of the Republic of Korea. KBS World Radio prgrs are also distributed as part of the global (UK-based) WRN Satellite/Internet feed. Some prgrs are relayed by affiliated FM stns: Indonesian 1200-1300 via R. Camajaya FM on 102.6MHz in Jakarta & via GISA FM on 107.7MHz in Aceh Utara (Indonesia); Spanish M-F 1800-1855 via R. Palermo FM on 94.7MHz in Buenos Aires (Argentina).

FEBC KOREA (Rlg)

P.O. Box 88, Seoul 04067, Republic of Korea.
☎ +82 2 3200431. Fax +82 2 3200229.
E: febcadm@febc.net **W:** www.febc.net (Korean); english.febc.net (English)
Webcast: L
Yeongdeungpo-dong 6-ga 8-1, Yeongdeungpo-gu, Seoul 150-036, Republic of Korea.
L.P: Pres: Dr Billy Kim; Mgr, Int'l Relations: Chung Soo Kim.
MW: [JEJ] Jeju (HLAZ): 1566kHz 250kW; [SEO] Seoul, Daebu Isl (HLKX): 1188kHz 100kW.
FM/DAB: FM: See National Radio section.
kHz: *1188, 1566*

Winter Schedule 2020/2021

Chinese	Days	Area	kHz
1100-1230	daily	EAs	1566jej
1345-1630	daily	EAs	1566jej
Japanese	**Days**	**Area**	**kHz**
1230-1345	daily	J	1566jej
Korean	**Days**	**Area**	**kHz**
1800-1000	daily	EAs	1566jej
1900-1100	daily	EAs	1188seo
Russian	**Days**	**Area**	**kHz**
1630-1700	daily	RUS	1566jej

Ann: Chinese: "HLKX. Zheli shi zhongpo 1188 (yao yao ba ba) qianhe, Yiyou Diantai di 2 (er) dai.", "HLAZ. Zheli shi zhongbo 1566 (yao wu liu liu) qianhe, Yiyou Diantai di 1 (yi) dai"; English: "It's 8 o'clock and time for daily English segment on HLKX 1188 on your AM radio dial"; Japanese: "Kochirawa kirisutokyo hosokyoku FEBC desu"; Korean: Jungpa Cheonbaek-palsip-pal (1188) kHz, Pyojun FM Paeng-nyuk-jeom-gu (106.9) MHz, Areumdaun Chanyanggwa Gibbeun Sosigeul Jeonhaneun Geukdong Bangsong-imnida", "Jungpa Cheon-o-baeng-nyuk-sim-nyuk (1566) kHz, Pyojun FM Jeju Baek-sa-jeom-chil (104.7) MHz, Seogwipo Baeg-il-jeom-il (101.1) MHz, Daehan Minguk Seongyo Jungsim Jeju Geukdong Bangsong-imnida. HLAZ".
V: QSL-card.
Notes: FEBC Korea is a regional division of Far East Broadcasting Company, Inc (FEBC) (USA) with a nationwide tx network on MW & FM. FEBC Korea's MW txs also carry prgrs produced by other national studios of FEBC, targeting China, Japan and the Far Eastern part of Russia. The trs may include prgrs provided by small religious prgr producers and broadcast under own labels. Some airtime is leased to non-religious third-party broadcasters.

KUWAIT (KWT)

RADIO KUWAIT (Gov)

See National Radio section.
Webcast: L (www.media.gov.kw)
SW: [KBD] Kuwait, Kabd: 5 x 500kW (3 txs are DRM capable).
FM/DAB: FM: See National Radio section.
SAT: Arabsat 5C, AsiaSat 5, Badr 4, Eutelsat 8WB/Hot Bird 13C, Galaxy 19, Intelsat 19, Hispasat 30W-5.
kHz: *5960, 7250, 9750, 11630, 11970, 13650, 15110, 15515, 15530, 15540, 17550, 17760*

Winter Schedule 2020/2021

Arabic	Days	Area	kHz
0300-0630	daily	ME	5960kbd
0500-0900	daily	EAs	15515kbd
0945-1325	daily	Eu	15110kbd+
1100-1325	daily	NAf	9750kbd
1400-1600	daily	CAf	11630kbd*
1600-1800	daily	SAs	15540kbd
1700-2000	daily	NAm	13650kbd†
2000-2400	daily	NAm	17550kbd
English	**Days**	**Area**	**kHz**
0500-0800	daily	SAs	11970kbd+**
0500-0800	daily	Eu	15530kbd**
1800-2100	daily	Eu	15540kbd+†
Filipino	**Days**	**Area**	**kHz**
1000-1200	daily	SEA	17760kbd
Persian	**Days**	**Area**	**kHz**
0800-1000	daily	ME	7250kbd

Key: + DRM; † Irregular; * Koran prgr; ** In Arabic, at time of publication;
Ann: Arabic: "Huna al-Kuwait".
V: QSL-card. (Email rpt to kwtfreq@media.gov.kw)
Notes: Arabic prgrs are relays of Home Sce networks.

USAGM KUWAIT "GEORGE A. MOORE JR" TRANSMITTING STATION

USAGM Transmitting Station, c/o US Embassy, P.O. Box 77, Safat 13001, Kuwait City, Kuwait.
☎ +965 24562754. Fax +965 24562754.
L.P: SM: Gunter E. Schwabe.
MW: [KWT] Kuwait, Umm Al-Rimam: 1548kHz 600kW; 1593kHz 150kW.
SW: [KWT] Kuwait, Umm Al-Rimam: 6 x 250kW.
V: QSL-card. (Email to manager_kuwait@kuw.usagm.gov)

KYRGYZSTAN (KGZ)

KYRGYZTELECOM (Tx Operator)

Chui avenue 96, 720000 Bishkek, Kyrgyzstan.
☎ +996 312 681616. Fax +996 312 662424.
E: info@kt.kg **W:** www.kt.kg
L.P: DG: Salavat Iskakov.
MW: [BIS] Bishkek, Krasnaya Rechka: 612kHz 200kW (2x100kW), 1467kHz 500kW (both operated on behalf of TWR).
SW: [BIS] Bishkek, Krasnaya Rechka: 1 x 15kW. (Estimated power)

Notes: Kyrgyztelekom is the national tx operator.

LAOS (LAO)

LAO NATIONAL RADIO (Gov)

See National Radio Section.
Webcast: D/L (lnr.org.la)
MW: [VIE] Vientiane 567kHz 200kW.
SW: [VIE] Vientiane 1 x 50kW.
FM/DAB: FM: See National Radio section.
kHz: *567, 6130*

Winter Schedule 2020/2021

	Days	Area	kHz
Chinese	**Days**	**Area**	**kHz**
1400-1430	daily	SEA	567vie, 6130vie‡
English	**Days**	**Area**	**kHz**
1430-1500	daily	SEA	567vie, 6130vie‡
French	**Days**	**Area**	**kHz**
1500-1530	daily	SEA	567vie, 6130vie‡
Khmer	**Days**	**Area**	**kHz**
1330-1400	daily	SEA	567vie, 6130vie‡
Thai	**Days**	**Area**	**kHz**
1530-1600	daily	SEA	567vie, 6130vie‡
Vietnamese	**Days**	**Area**	**kHz**
1600-1630	daily	SEA	567vie, 6130vie‡

Key: ‡ Inactive on SW at time of publication, but is expected to return to the air.
Ann: English: "This is the Lao National Radio, broadcasting from Vientiane, capital - the Lao People's Democratic Republic".
V: QSL-card.
Notes: The foreign language trs are part of LNR's "National Channel" (see National Radio section).

LITHUANIA (LTU)

LIETUVOS RADIJO IR TELEVIZIJOS CENTRAS (LRTC) (Tx Operator)

Sausio 13-osios g. 10, LT-04347 Vilnius, Lithuania.
☎ +370 5 2040300. Fax +370 5 2040325.
E: info@telecentras.lt **W:** www.telecentras.lt
LP: GD: Remigijus Šeris.
MW: [VST] Anykščiai, Viešintos: 1386kHz 200kW (run at 75kW)
Notes: LRTC is the national transmitter network operator.

MADAGASCAR (MDG)

MADAGASCAR WORLD VOICE (Rlg)

World Christian Broadcasting, Immeuble Assist, 7ème etage, 101 Antananarivo, Madagascar.
E: mwvradio@gmail.com **W:** www.africanpathways.org (English); www.knls.net (Russian)
Webcast: D
605 Bradley Court, Franklin, TN 37067, USA. (World Christian Broadcasting)
☎ +1 615 3718707. (USA)
E: wcbctn@worldchristian.org **W:** www.worldchristian.org
LP: Pres/CEO (USA): Andy Baker; SM (Madagascar): Mahefa Rakotomamonjy.
SW: [MWV] Mahajanga II (Belobaka); Amparemahitsy: 2 x 100kW.
kHz: 6180, *9765, 9845, 9880, 11610, 11825, 11965, 13670, 13710, 13760, 17530*

Winter Schedule 2020/2021

	Days	Area	kHz
Arabic	**Days**	**Area**	**kHz**
1900-2000	daily	ME,NAf	13670mwv
2000-2100	daily	ME,NAf	13710mwv
Chinese	**Days**	**Area**	**kHz**
0400-0500	daily	EAs	17530mwv
2100-2200	daily	EAs	11610mwv
English	**Days**	**Area**	**kHz**
0300-0400	daily	As	13760mwv
0400-0500	daily	Af	11825mwv
1800-1900	daily	Af	13670mwv
2000-2100	daily	Af	11965mwv
Portuguese	**Days**	**Area**	**kHz**
2100-2200	daily	B	9765mwv
Russian	**Days**	**Area**	**kHz**
1800-1900	daily	RUS	9880mwv
1900-2000	daily	RUS	9845mwv
Spanish	**Days**	**Area**	**kHz**
0300-0400	daily	LAm	6180mwv

Ann: English: "Madagascar World Voice", "From the beautiful region of the Indian Ocean, this is your New Life Station", "African Pathways Radio".
IS: "Chariots of Fire", by Vangelis.
V: QSL-card. (rpt to USA address)
Notes: Transmitting station owned by World Christian Broadcasting, Inc (WCB), USA. The stn retransmits prgrs produced in the U.S. studios of WCB and WCB partner organisations. Further prgrs of WCB's language services in Chinese, English and Russian can be heard via its sister transmitting stn KNLS (see under Alaska for schedules).

MALAGASY GLOBAL BUSINESS S.A. (MGLOB) (Tx Operator)

P.O.Box 404, 101 Antananarivo, Madagascar.
☎ +261 202242222. Fax +261 202243184.
E: via website contact form on **W:** mglob.mg
Lot Bonnet 88, Ivandry, 101 Antananarivo, Madagascar.
LP: Dir: Tovonirina Razananaivo (Interim); Airtime Sales & Frequency Mgr: Rocus de Joode.
SW: [MDC] Talata Volonondry: 3 x 250kW. Backup tx 1 x 250kW
V: QSL-card (for relayed prgrs). Email rpt to qsl@mglob.mg
Notes: In 2012, Malagasy Global Business S.A. (MGLOB) took over the operation of the former Radio Netherlands Worldwide Relay Station at Talata Volonondry. The company was founded by former staff of the transmitting station.

MALI (MLI)

SOCIÉTÉ MALIENNE DE TRANSMISSION ET DET DIFFUSION S.A. (SMTD–SA) (Tx Operator)

Route de l'Aéroport, face Météo, (BP E5303), Bamako, Mali.
☎ +223 20708171. Fax +223 20708168.
E: info@smtd.ml **W:** www.smtd.ml
LP: Dir: Ismaila Togola.
SW: [BKO] Bamako, Kati: 2 x 100kW.
Notes: SMTD-SA was founded in 2015 as the national transmitter operator in Mali.

MOLDOVA (MDA)

Transnistria

PRIDNESTROVSKIY RADIOTELETSENTR (Tx Operator)

MD-4006 Maiac, Pridnestrovian Moldavian Republic, Moldova.
☎ +373 210 66500.
E: prtc@idknet.com
LP: DG: Vitaliy Kucherenko; Technical Dir: Sergey Omelchenko.
MW: [KCH] Grigoriopol, Maiac: 999/1413/1548kHz 1000kW.
SW: [KCH] Grigoriopol, Maiac: 5 x 1000kW.
V: eQSL-card. (For relayed stns)
Notes: Pridnestrovskiy Radioteletsentr (owned by RTRN, Russia) provides high power MW & SW transmitting facilities.

MONACO (MCO)

MONACO MEDIA DIFFUSION (MMD) (Tx Operator)

10-12 quai Antoine 1er, MC-98000 Monte Carlo, Monaco.
☎ +377 97974700. Fax +377 97974707.
E: contact@mmd.mc **W:** www.mmd.mc
LP: Chmn: Jean Pastorelli; Managing Dir: Pierre Medicin.
MW: [ROU] Roumoules (France): 1467kHz 1000kW.
Notes: MMD (formerly Monte Carlo Radiodiffusion/MCR) is majority-owned by the Principality of Monaco and a joint venture with the French transmitter operator TDF. MMD is the national transmitter network owner in Monaco and also maintains high power transmitting centres in France (at the border to Monaco).

MONGOLIA (MNG)

VOICE OF MONGOLIA (Pub)

P.O. Box 365, Ulaanbaatar 13, Mongolia.
☎ +976 1 1327900. Fax +976 1 1323096.
E: vom_en@yahoo.com **W:** www.vom.mn
Webcast: D (Webcast languages: Chinese (Mandarin), English, Japanese, Mongolian & Russian)
L.P: Dir, Foreign Sce: Mrs Narantuya B; Mail Editor: Bolorchimeg E.
SW: Leased from RTBN.
kHz: *6005, 12015, 12085*

Winter Schedule 2020/2021

Chinese	Days	Area	kHz
1000-1030	daily	EAs	12085uba
1430-1500	daily	EAs	12015uba
English	**Days**	**Area**	**kHz**
0900-0930	daily	EAs	12085uba
1300-1330	mtwtfs.	CEu,WEu	6005kll
1530-1600	daily	EAs	12015uba
Japanese	**Days**	**Area**	**kHz**
1030-1100	daily	EAs	12085uba
1500-1530	daily	EAs	12015uba
Mongolian	**Days**	**Area**	**kHz**
0930-1000	daily	EAs	12085uba
1400-1430	daily	EAs	12015uba

Ann: English: "Welcome to the Voice of Mongolia, in English".
V: QSL-card. Rp (2 IRCs or 1 USD) appreciated.
Notes: The Voice of Mongolia is the External Sce of the Mongolian National Radio & TV. Launched 1964 as "R. Ulaanbaatar", renamed "Voice of Mongolia" on 1 Jan 1997. The relay via a 1kW SW tx at Kall (Germany) is an independent, personal initiative of the operator of the German relay platform "Shortwaveservice"; a project that is primarily targeting SWLs/DXers in Europe.

RADIO AND TELEVISION BROADCASTING NETWORK (RTBN) (Tx Operator)

Bayangol district, 17th subdistrict, Amarsanaagiin St., Ulaanbaatar, Mongolia.
☎ +976 77 003111. Fax +976 77 003119.
E: info@rtbn.gov.mn **W:** rtbn.gov.mn
L.P: CEO: Ch. Oyuünbaatar.
SW: [UBA] Ulaanbaatar, Khonkhor: 1 x 250kW.
Notes: RTBN is the national transmitter operator in Mongolia.

NETHERLANDS (HOL)

MIKE RADIO

☎ +31 62 8973930 (cell)
E: mikeradio@live.nl **W:** mike-radio.nl
SW: [HEE] Heerde: 1 x 1kW.
kHz: *3940, 6195*

Winter Schedule 2020/2021

English/Dutch	Days	Area	kHz
0600-1100	......s	Eu	6195hee*
1700-2300	..w.fs.	Eu	3940hee*

Key: * Schedule variable.
V: eQSL-card
Notes: Former pirate radio station; licensed operation since 2020. The transmitter is installed in a residential house.

RADIO DELTA INTERNATIONAL ‡

E: radiodelta@icloud.com **W:** www.radiodelta.am
L.P: Dir: Aart Bosmans.
SW: [ELB] Elburg: 1 x1kW.
kHz: *6005, 6020*

Winter Schedule 2020/2021

English/Dutch	Days	Area	kHz
0700-1800	...tfs.	Eu	6020elb*
2100-0200	....fs.	Eu	6005elb*

Key: ‡ F. Pl. (Not on the air at time of publication)
Notes: Former pirate radio station; licenced since 2020. The transmitter is installed in a residential house.

RADIO PIEPZENDER

P.O.Box 2702, 6049 ZG Herten, The Netherlands.
☎ +31 65 5597513 (cell; text messages only)
E: radioqsl@hotmail.com **W:** piepzender.nl
SW: [ZWO] Zwolle: 1 x 1kW (run at 0.2kW)
kHz: *3920, 15880*

Winter Schedule 2020/2021

English/Dutch	Days	Area	kHz
0700-1600	.....ss	Eu	15880zwo*
1600-2400	daily	Eu	3920zwo

Key: * F.Pl.
V: eQSL-card.
Notes: The tx is a vintage utility transmitter, installed in a private home.

THE MIGHTY KBC

Argonstraat 6, NL-6718 WT Ede, Netherlands.
☎ +31 318 552491. Fax +31 318 437801.
E: themightykbc@gmail.com **W:** www.kbcradio.eu
Webcast: L
L.P: Producer: Eric van Willegen.
FM/DAB: DAB: See National Radio section.
kHz: *5960, 6080, 6095*

Winter Schedule 2020/2021

English	Days	Area	kHz
0000-0200	......s	NAm	5960nau
0900-1600	......s	Eu	6095nau**
2000-2200	....f..	Eu	6080erv*

Key: * 25 Dec 2020; ** 27 Dec 2020.
V: QSL-card. Rp. (2 EUR/2 USD/2 IRCs or equivalent PayPal donation); eQSL-letter.
Notes: Relay of KBC Import/Export-sponsored KBC Radio. Occasionally, the airtime is subleased to third-party prgr producers.

NEW ZEALAND (NZL)

RNZ PACIFIC (RNZI) (Pub)

P.O. Box 123, Wellington, New Zealand.
☎ +64 4 4741437. Fax +64 4 4741433.
E: news@rnzi.com **W:** www.rnz.co.nz/international
Webcast: D/L/P
L.P: Mgr: Moera Tuilaepa-Taylor; Technical Mgr: Adrian Sainsbury; Transmission Engineer: Andy Anderson.
SW: [RAN] Rangitaiki: 1 x 100kW. Backup tx: 1 x 100kW.
kHz: *5975, 6115, 7285, 11690, 11725, 13840, 15720*

Winter Schedule 2020/2021

English/Pacific Languages	Days	Area	kHz
0400-0700	daily	Pac	13840ran
0700-1000	daily	Pac	11725ran
1000-1300	daily	Pac	11725ran
1300-1650	daily	Pac	6115ran
1300-1900	.....s.	Pac	6115ran
1650-1735	mtwtf.s	Pac	5975ran+
1735-1835	mtwtf.s	Pac	7285ran+
1835-2000	mtwtf.s	Pac	11690ran+
1900-2000	.....s.	Pac	11725ran
2000-2300	daily	Pac	13840ran
2300-0400	daily	Pac	15720ran

Key: + DRM
Ann: English: "RNZ Pacific".
IS: Call of the New Zealand bellbird.
V: eQSL-card for rpt by email or via online form on website. Rpts received by postal mail are no longer processed.
Notes: RNZ Pacific (until 2017 branded "R. New Zealand International" - RNZI) is a 24/7 service produced by the public broadcaster R. New Zealand (RNZ) for listeners in the Pacific region. The SW prgrs are in English, with news in various Pacific languages (and

a press review in French on Tue 0520 New Zealand Time = 1720 UTC; 1h earlier when DST is in effect in NZL). There is a maintenance day at the tx site every 1st Wednesday (UTC) from 2230 to Thursday 0600. During this period there may be interruptions to the transmissions or maintenance tests. Schedule is subject to frequent change, see RNZ Pacific website for latest frequencies and programming.

NIGERIA (NIG)

VOICE OF NIGERIA (VON) (Gov)

✉ 7th Floor, Radio House, Herbert Macaulay Way, Area 10, Garki, 900001 Abuja, Nigeria. (Headquarters).
☎ +234 9 2344016. 🖷 +234 9 2346970.
E: info@von.gov.ng **W:** von.gov.ng
Webcast: L
✉ Broadcasting House, Plot no 345, Ikoyi Rd, 40003 Lagos, Nigeria. (Main studio building)
☎ +234 1 2693076. 🖷 +234 1 2691944.
L.P: DG: Osita Okechukwu.
SW: [AJA] Abuja, Lugbe: 2 x 250kW.
kHz: *7255, 11770, 15120*

Winter Schedule 2020/2021

	Days	Area	kHz
Arabic	**Days**	**Area**	**kHz**
1600-1615	daily	NAf,ME	11770aja** 15120aja+†
English	**Days**	**Area**	**kHz**
0800-1000	daily	WAf	7255aja*
1630-1900	daily	Af,Eu	11770aja** 15120aja+†
French	**Days**	**Area**	**kHz**
1000-1030	daily	WAf	7255aja*
Fulfulde	**Days**	**Area**	**kHz**
0700-0800	daily	WAf	7255aja*
1900-2000	daily	WAf	11770aja** 15120aja+†
Hausa	**Days**	**Area**	**kHz**
0600-0700	daily	WAf	7255aja*
2000-2100	daily	WAf	11770aja** 15120aja+†
Igbo	**Days**	**Area**	**kHz**
1045-1100	daily	WAf	7255aja*
1615-1630	daily	WAf	11770aja** 15120aja+†
Yoruba	**Days**	**Area**	**kHz**
1030-1045	daily	WAf	7255aja*

Key: + DRM; † Irregular; Alternative frequencies: * 9690 or 11770kHz; ** 7255 or 9690kHz.
Ann: English: "You're listening to the Voice of Nigeria, Abuja".
V: QSL-card.
Notes: The External Sce The Voice of Nigeria was initially produced by the national broadcaster Federal Radio Corporation of Nigeria (FRCN), but became an autonomous broadcasting entity in 1990.

MANARA RADIO (Rlg)

✉ Based in Abuja, Nigeria.
☎ +234 706 7575751.
E: manaratv1@gmail.com **W:** www.facebook.com/ManaraRadio; www.manaratv.com
Webcast: L
✉ Plot 528, T.O.S. Benson Crescent, Abuja, Nigeria. (JIBWIS)
☎ +234 705 8050605.
E: jibwisnigeria@gmail.com **W:** www.jibwisnigeria.org; www.facebook.com/JibwisNig
L.P: Chmn (Manara Radio & TV): Abdullahi Bala Lau.
kHz: *13710, 15285*

Winter Schedule 2020/2021

Hausa	Days	Area	kHz
0700-0800	daily	WAf	13710iss
1600-1700	daily	WAf	15285iss

Ann: Hausa: "Manara Rediyo International".
Notes: Manara Radio ("Minaret Radio") is a sunni muslim station, produced by the religious broadcasting company Manara Radio & Television, and targeting Hausa speakers in West Africa and the Middle East. Initiated by the Nigerian Islamic organization JIBWIS (Jama'atu Izalatul Bidah Wa Iqamatis Sunnah). On air since 12 June 2015.

NORTH MACEDONIA (MKD)

RADIO MAKEDONIJA (Pub)

✉ blvd. Goce Delcev 18, 1000 Skopje, North Macedonia.
☎ +389 2 5119874.
E: radiomakedonija@mrt.com.mk **W:** mrt.com.mk
Webcast: L ("MR Sat").
MW: Leased from Nacionalna Radiodifuzija.
kHz: *810*

Winter Schedule 2020/2021

	Days	Area	kHz
Albanian	**Days**	**Area**	**kHz**
2000-2030	mtwtf..	SEu	810sko
Bulgarian	**Days**	**Area**	**kHz**
1900-1930	mtwtf..	SEu	810sko
Greek	**Days**	**Area**	**kHz**
1930-2000	mtwtf..	SEu	810sko
Macedonian	**Days**	**Area**	**kHz**
1830-0400	.....s.	SEu	810sko
2100-0400	mtwtf..	SEu	810sko
Music	**Days**	**Area**	**kHz**
1830-1900	mtwtf..	SEu	810sko
Serbian	**Days**	**Area**	**kHz**
2030-2100	mtwtf..	SEu	810sko

Ann: Macedonian: "Radio Makedonija - programa za sdranstvo".
V: QSL-letter.
Notes: International Sce of the public service broadcaster Nacionalna Radio Televizija - NRT (formerly Makedonska Radio Televizija - MRT). Initially launched in 1993 as "R. Biljana"; re-branded "R. Makedonija" in 1999. When MRT launched the 24/7 satellite audio channel "MR Sat" in 2003, R. Makedonija became a prgr block on this channel, together with a relay of domestic Prgr 1 of Macedonian Radio ("R. Skopje"). While this channel has not been transmitted on satellite for a number of years due to budget restraints, the audio stream on the NRT (MRT) website continues to be labelled "MR Sat". NB: Although MRT was renamed NRT in 2019, the old brand may still be used during a transition period.

NACIONALNA RADIODIFUZIJA (Tx Operator)

✉ blvd. Goce Delcev 18, 1000 Skopje, North Macedonia.
☎ +389 2 3297100.
E: makedonska.radiodifuzija@jpmrd.gov.mk **W:** jpmrd.gov.mk
L.P: Dir: Admirim Aliti
MW: [SKO] Skopje, Sveti Nikole: 810kHz 100kW.
Notes: Nacionalna Radiodifuzija is the national transmitter network provider.

NORTHERN MARIANA ISL. (MRA)

USAGM NORTHERN MARIANAS "ROBERT E. KAMOSA" TRANSMITTING STATION (REKTS)

✉ P.O. Box 504969, Saipan, MP 96950, USA.
☎ +1 670 2331624. 🖷 +1 670 2331614.
L.P: SM: Mica F. Cochran.
SW: [SAI] Saipan, Agingan Point: 3 x 100kW; [TIN] Tinian: 2 x 250, 6 x 500kW.
V: QSL-card (Email rpt to manager_mariana@mar.usagm.gov)
Notes: USAGM owned transmitting station; operation & maintenance is contracted to Rome Research Corporation (RRC).

NORWAY (NOR)

LKB/LLE BERGEN KRINGKASTER

✉ P.O.Box 100, N-5331 Rong, Norway.
☎ +47 56141270.
E: styret@bergenkringkaster.no **W:** www.bergenkringkaster.no; www.la1ask.no; www.facebook.com/groups/bergenkringkaster
✉ Grensedalen 59, N-5306 Erdal, Norway. (Museum Tx site & Studio)
L.P: Chmn: Per Dagfinn Green (LA1TNA); Chief Eng: Øystein Ask (LA7CFA); Chief Editor: Svenn Martinsen.
MW: [ERD] Bergen, Erdal: 1314kHz 1kW (run at 0.7kW).
SW: [ERD] Bergen, Erdal: 1 x 0.1kW (run at 0.05kW).‡
FM/DAB: FM: 93.8MHz (Erdal, 0.1kW)
kHz: *1314*

Winter Schedule 2020/2021

English/ Norwegian	Days	Area	kHz
0855-1600	daily	NEu	1314erd

Ann: English: "You are listening to LKB/LLE Bergen Broadcasting Station"; Norwegian: "Du lytter til LKB LLE Bergen Kringkaster".
IS: "MacGyver in Space" by Øyvind Ask.
V: QSL-card/letter (Rp: 3 USD) or eQSL-card (Email to report@bergenkringkaster.no)
Notes: LKB/LLK Bergen Kringkaster is a stn operated by the registered voluntary association "Foreningen Bergen Kringkaster" (FBK), a group of enthusiasts with background in amateur radio, and run with vintage and/or amateur radio equipment on the premises of a radio museum owned by the Askøy municipality near Bergen. The stn is run on the basis of a temporary license that has to be renewed within certain intervals. Due to the leisure time nature of the operation, trs may be irregular at times. The programming consist of a mix of own prgrs and/or a relay of the Internet radio stns R. Northern Star/The Ferry (see separate entry).

RADIO NORTHERN STAR / THE FERRY

✉ P.O.Box 100, N-5331 Rong, Norway.
☎ +47 56324985.
E: 1000@northernstar.no; 2000@theferry.cc
W: www.northernstar.cc; www.theferry.cc
Webcast: L
✉ c/o P7 Kristen Riksradio, Idrettsvegen 10, N-5353 Straume, Norway. (Studio)
L.P: MD: Svenn Martinsen.
MW: [ERD] Bergen, Erdal: 1611kHz 2kW (run at 0.3kW). Additional site nearby, for occasional test purposes only: Toftøy 630kHz 1kW (run at 0.01kW)
SW: [ERD] Bergen, Erdal: 1 x 1kW (run at 0.3kW)
FM/DAB: FM: 91.8MHz (Erdal, 0.1kW)
kHz: *1314, 1611, 5895*

Winter Schedule 2020/2021

English/ Norwegian	Days	Area	kHz
0420-2310	daily	NEu	1611erd
1600-2310	daily	NEu	1314erd
Norwegian	**Days**	**Area**	**kHz**
1400-2310	daily	NEu	5895erd*

Key: * USB/AM mode (H3E).
Ann: English: R. Northern Star: "This is Radio Northern Star - Your Radio Heartland of Music"; The Ferry: "You're on The Ferry - Your Beautiful Music Connection - theferry.cc".
IS: R. Northern Star: "Northern Star" by Ann Reed; The Ferry: "Water Music - Suite in D major - Alla Hornpipe" by Georg Friedrich Händel
V: QSL-email or letter. Rp.
Notes: R. Northern Star (launched 2013) & The Ferry (launched 2017) are two Internet radio stns produced by Northern Star Media Services AS in a studio leased from the Norwegian Christian radio station P7 Kristen Riksradio. Both prgrs carry religious segments during certain times of the day. The txs are co-located with the txs of Bergen Kringkaster (see separate entry).

OMAN (OMA)

RADIO SULTANATE OF OMAN (Pub)

✉ See National Radio section.
Webcast: L
SW: [THU] Thumrait: 1 x 100kW (presumed to be run at 50kW).
SAT: Arabsat 5C, AsiaSat 5, Badr 6, Eutelsat 7WA/Hot Bird 13C, Galaxy 19, Hellas Sat 3, Hispasat 30W-4.
kHz: *13600, 15140*

Winter Schedule 2020/2021

Arabic	Days	Area	kHz
0400-1000	daily	EAf	13600thu†
1500-1800	daily	Eu,ME	15140thu†
English	**Days**	**Area**	**kHz**
1400-1500	daily	Eu,ME	15140thu†

Key: † Irregular.
Ann: Arabic: "Idha'atu Saltanat Oman min Muscat"; English: "This is Radio Sultanate of Oman FM".
V: QSL-folder.
Notes: On air since 30 July 1970. Relays of Home Sce programmes in Arabic and English.

BBC EASTERN RELAY STATION

✉ P.O. Box 40, 422 Al Ashkarah, Oman.
E: opsaseela@yahoo.com
L.P: Senior Transmitter Engineer: Khalid Nasser.
MW: [SLA] A'Seela: 702/1413kHz 800kW.
SW: [SLA] A'Seela: 3 x 250kW.
V: QSL-card. (For direct report)
Notes: Owned by the BBC and operated by Encompass Digital Media Services Ltd (see under United Kingdom).

PAKISTAN (PAK)

FEBA PAKISTAN (Rlg)

✉ P.O.Box 318, Rawalpindi, Pakistan.
☎ +92 51 5166621.
E: fctp74@gmail.com **W:** www.febapak.org; www.feba-radio.org
Webcast: L (awazdost.org)
L.P: Dir: Saleem Shazaad.
kHz: *6170*

Winter Schedule 2020/2021

Pashto	Days	Area	kHz
0230-0300	....f..	PAK	6170dha
Punjabi	**Days**	**Area**	**kHz**
0215-0230	m......	PAK	6170dha
Sindhi	**Days**	**Area**	**kHz**
0215-0230	.twt...	PAK	6170dha
Urdu	**Days**	**Area**	**kHz**
0200-0215	mtwt...	PAK	6170dha
0200-0230	....fss	PAK	6170dha

Notes: Produced by the charitable Feba Communications Trust, associated with Far East Broadcasting Company, Inc (USA).

PALAU (PLW)

T8WH – HOPE RADIO (Rlg)

✉ 300 Highland Eve, Morgantown, WV 26505, USA.
☎ +1 304 2414211.
E: contact@hoperadio.net **W:** hoperadio.net
Webcast: L
✉ P.O. Box 66, Koror, PW 96940, Republic of Palau (Transmitting Site).
W: www.mfcministries.org
L.P: CEO/Pres: Joe Perozich; Media Coordinator: Scott Reppert; Chief Engineer (T8WH): Gary Shirk.
SW: [HBN] Medorm (Babeldaob Island): 3 x 100kW
FM/DAB: FM: 102.5MHz (KRST-FM Koror, 0.75kW)
kHz: *9930, 9965, 15680*

Winter Schedule 2020/2021

English	Days	Area	kHz
0115-0230	......s	SEA	15680hbn
0800-0900	mtwtf..	EAs	9965hbn
0800-0915	......s	SEA	15680hbn
0800-0945	.....s.	SEA	15680hbn
0800-0945	.....s.	EAs	9965hbn
0800-1145	......s	EAs	9965hbn
0800-1200	.....s.	SEA	9930hbn‡

Key: ‡ Inactive at time of publication.
V: eQSL-card (Online rpt form available on website)
Notes: Transmitting station owned by MFC Ministries, Inc (USA); the stn was purchased in 2020 from Family Broadcasting Corp. (USA). Historical callsigns (licensed to previous owners): T8BZ, KHBN. T8WH transmits paid religious programming.

PHILIPPINES (PHL)

RADYO PILIPINAS OVERSEAS SERVICE (DZRP) (Gov)

✉ 4th floor, Government Media Center Bldg. (PIA), Visayas Ave,

Vasra, 1128 Quezon City, Metro Manila, Philippines.
☎ +63 2 7727716.
E: dzrp.radyopilipinas@gmail.com **W:** www.pbs.gov.ph
Webcast: L
L.P: Acting SM: Remigio L. Sampang.
SW: Uses facilities provided by USAGM (USA).
kHz: *9475, 9925, 12120, 15190, 15640, 17820*

Winter Schedule 2020/2021

	Days	Area	kHz
English	**Days**	**Area**	**kHz**
0200-0330	daily	ME	9475pht, 15640pht, 17820pht
Filipino	**Days**	**Area**	**kHz**
1730-1930	daily	ME	9925pht, 12120pht, 15190pht

Ann: English: "This is Radyo Pilipinas, the Overseas Service of the Philippines Broadcasting Service, PBS. Radyo Pilipinas is reaching you from Manila, Philippines"; "Radyo Pilipinas Overseas Service, The Voice of the Philippines".
V: QSL-card. Rp (2 IRCs). Rec. acc.
Notes: Radyo Pilipinas is the External Sce of the Philippine Broadcasting Service (PBS), organised under the Philippine government Bureau of Broadcast Services (BBS). Broadcasts include relays of PBS's domestic services Radyo ng Bayan and Radyo Magasin.

FEBC PHILIPPINES (Rlg)

✉ P.O.Box 14205, Ortigas Center Post Office, Pasig City 1605, Philippines.
☎ +63 2 6543322. 🖷 +63 2 6540894.
E: info@febc.ph **W:** febc.ph
✉ 46/F One Corporate Centre, Dona Julia Vargas cor. Meralco Avenues, Ortigas Center, Pasig City 1605, Philippines.
L.P: Pres: Dan Andrew S. Cura.
SW: [BOC] Bocaue (Bulacan prov.): 5 x 100kW; [IBA] Iba (Zambales prov.): 4 x 100kW.
kHz: *9450, 9795, 9920, 11650, 11750, 12055, 12095, 12120, 13870, 15215, 15330, 15420, 15435, 15560, 15580, 15620, 15640*

Winter Schedule 2020/2021

	Days	Area	kHz
Achang	**Days**	**Area**	**kHz**
1230-1245	daily	SEA	12095boc
Akha	**Days**	**Area**	**kHz**
1215-1230	daily	SEA	12120boc
Bahnar	**Days**	**Area**	**kHz**
1230-1300	m.w.f..	SEA	9920iba
Buginese	**Days**	**Area**	**kHz**
0930-1000	daily	SEA	15580boc
Burmese	**Days**	**Area**	**kHz**
1330-1400	daily	SEA	12120boc
2330-0030	daily	SEA	15640boc
Chin (Daai)	**Days**	**Area**	**kHz**
1245-1300	daily	SEA	12120boc
Chin (Mro)	**Days**	**Area**	**kHz**
0030-0045	daily	SEA	15640boc
Hmong (Black)	**Days**	**Area**	**kHz**
1300-1330	daily	SEA	12095boc
Hmong (Blue - Njua)	**Days**	**Area**	**kHz**
1100-1130	.....ss	SEA	12095boc
2300-2330	.....ss	SEA	12095boc
Hmong (White - Daw)	**Days**	**Area**	**kHz**
1100-1130	mtwtf..	SEA	12095boc
2300-2330	mtwtf..	SEA	12095boc
Hre	**Days**	**Area**	**kHz**
1230-1300	.t.t.ss	SEA	9920iba
Iu Mien	**Days**	**Area**	**kHz**
1030-1100	daily	SEA	13870boc
1200-1230	daily	SEA	12095boc
2300-2330	daily	SEA	9450boc
Jarai	**Days**	**Area**	**kHz**
1200-1230	...tfs.	SEA	9920iba
Javanese	**Days**	**Area**	**kHz**
0100-0130	daily	SEA	15560boc
1400-1430	daily	SEA	15620boc
Jingpho	**Days**	**Area**	**kHz**
0045-0100	daily	SEA	15640boc
Karen (Pa'o)	**Days**	**Area**	**kHz**
1145-1200	daily	SEA	15330boc
Khmer	**Days**	**Area**	**kHz**
1100-1300	daily	SEA	13870boc
Khmu	**Days**	**Area**	**kHz**
0000-0015	daily	SEA	9795iba
1330-1400	daily	SEA	12095boc
Koho	**Days**	**Area**	**kHz**
1300-1330	daily	SEA	9920iba
Lahu	**Days**	**Area**	**kHz**
0015-0045	daily	SEA	12055boc
1400-1430	daily	SEA	11750boc
Lao	**Days**	**Area**	**kHz**
1130-1200	daily	SEA	12095boc
2330-2400	daily	SEA	9795iba
Lu	**Days**	**Area**	**kHz**
1030-1100	daily	SEA	12095boc
2345-0015	daily	SEA	12055boc
Makassarese	**Days**	**Area**	**kHz**
0900-0930	daily	SEA	15580boc
Minangkabau	**Days**	**Area**	**kHz**
0930-1000	daily	SEA	15420boc
Mon	**Days**	**Area**	**kHz**
1115-1145	daily	SEA	15330boc
2300-2330	daily	SEA	9795iba
Naga	**Days**	**Area**	**kHz**
1230-1245	daily	SEA	12120boc
Palaung (Palc)	**Days**	**Area**	**kHz**
2330-2345	daily	SEA	12055boc
Rade	**Days**	**Area**	**kHz**
1200-1230	mtw...s	SEA	9920iba
Rawang	**Days**	**Area**	**kHz**
1200-1215	daily	SEA	12120boc
Russian	**Days**	**Area**	**kHz**
1500-1600	daily	RUS	9920boc, 11650boc
Sasak	**Days**	**Area**	**kHz**
1030-1100	daily	SEA	15580boc
Shan	**Days**	**Area**	**kHz**
0000-0045	daily	SEA	15435boc
Sundanese	**Days**	**Area**	**kHz**
1000-1030	daily	SEA	15580boc
Tai (Dam)	**Days**	**Area**	**kHz**
1245-1300	daily	SEA	12095boc
Tai (Nua)	**Days**	**Area**	**kHz**
0045-0100	daily	SEA	15435boc
Tibetan	**Days**	**Area**	**kHz**
1200-1230	mt....s	EAs	15215dha
Ukrainian/ Russian	**Days**	**Area**	**kHz**
1530-1600	......s	RUS	9920boc
Vietnamese	**Days**	**Area**	**kHz**
1100-1200	daily	SEA	9795iba
Wa	**Days**	**Area**	**kHz**
0045-0100	daily	SEA	12055boc

Ann: English: "This is FEBC Radio, broadcasting from Manila, Philippines".
V: QSL-card. Rp. preferred (3 IRCs)
Notes: Far East Broadcasting Company (Philippines), Inc is a regional division of Far East Broadcasting Company, Inc (FEBC) (USA), see USA for corporate details. FEBC Philippines runs a network of local FM/MW stns in the country and operates the SW transmitting stations Bocaue and Iba. The prgrs on SW (targeting Asia and Russia) are produced by FEBC partner organisations around the world and may include broadcasts under their own labels.

RADIO VERITAS ASIA (Rlg)
Buick St., Fairview Park, Quezon City, Metro Manila 1106, Philippines.
☎ +63 2 9390011. 🖷 +63 2 9390011.
E: via website **W:** rvasia.org
L.P: GM: Fr. Carlos S. Lariosa; PD: Rev. Msgr. Gabriel Htun Myint; Technical Dir: Engr. Alex M. Movilla.
Relayed Via: 3rd party transmitting facilities.
kHz: *9700*

Winter Schedule 2020/2021

Kachin	Days	Area	kHz
0000-0030	daily	SEA	9700smg

V: QSL-card.
Notes: Catholic station, on air since 11 April 1969. Owned by the "Philippine Radio Educational and Information Center" (PREIC), composed of Filipino bishops and professionals.

USAGM PHILIPPINES TRANSMITTING STATION
P.O.Box 151, CPO 1099, 1050 Manila, Philippines.
☎ +63 45 9820254. 🖷 +63 45 9821402.
L.P: Acting SM: Derek L. Gifford.
SW: [PHT] Tinang: 12 x 250kW.
V: QSL-card. (Email rpt to manager_philippines@usagm.gov)

POLAND (POL)

RADIO POLAND (Pub)
Al. Niepodleglosci 77/85, 00-977 Warszawa, Poland.
☎ +48 226453302. 🖷 +48 226453952.
E: zagranica@polskieradio.pl; ru@polskieradio.pl (Russian)
W: www.polskieradio.pl
Webcast: D/L/P. Additional languages on Web/DAB/SAT/local FM affiliates: English, Polish, Ukrainian.
L.P: Dir: Andrzej Rybalt.
FM/DAB: DAB: See National Radio section.
SAT: Eutelsat Hot Bird 13C.
kHz: *1386, 6005*

Winter Schedule 2020/2021

	Days	Area	kHz
Belarusian	**Days**	**Area**	**kHz**
0400-0500	daily	BLR	1386vst
English	**Days**	**Area**	**kHz**
1300-1400	daily	Eu	1386vst
German	**Days**	**Area**	**kHz**
1600-1630	daily	CEu	6005kll
1630-1700	daily	CEu	1386vst
Polish	**Days**	**Area**	**kHz**
1530-1600	daily	LTU,BLR,UKR	1386vst
Russian	**Days**	**Area**	**kHz**
1600-1630	daily	RUS	1386vst
Ukrainian	**Days**	**Area**	**kHz**
0500-0530	daily	UKR	1386vst

Ann: Russian: "Radio Polsha - zarubezhnaya sluzhba Polskogo radio", "V efire Radio Polsha".
V: QSL-card.
Notes: International Sce of the public broadcaster Polskie Radio. The current SW relay via a 1kW tx at Kall (Germany) is an independent, personal initiative of the operator of the German relay platform "Shortwaveservice"; a project that is primarily targeting SWLs/DXers in Europe.

SPW RADIO WARSZAWA (F.pl)
Stowarzyszenie Park Kulturowy TRCN, ul. Gen. Tadeusza Kutrzeby 52, 05-082 Stare Babice, Poland.
E: stowarzyszenie@radiostacjababice.org
W: trcn.pl; www.facebook.com/radiostacjababice
L.P: Pres (Stowarzyszenie Park Kulturowy TRCN): Jaroslaw Chrapek; Vice Pres: Tomasz Mis.
SW: [BAC] Warszawa, Stare Babice: 1 x 10kW (F.pl; site is not yet constructed).
Notes: Planned SW heritage radio station; a project of the association Stowarzyszenie Park Kulturowy TRCN (with members from the amateur radio community) in cooperation with Warsaw University of Technology, in memory of the historical SW transmitting centre "Transatlantic Radio Station" (TRCN) that was situated in Babice-Boernerowo (demolished in 1945).

ROMANIA (ROU)

RADIO ROMANIA INTERNATIONAL (RRI) (Pub)
P.O. Box 1-111, 014700 Bucuresti, Romania.
☎ +40 213031357; +40 213031465. 🖷 +40 212232613.
E: rri@rri.ro **W:** www.rri.ro
Webcast: D/L
L.P: Secretary General: Eugen Cojocariu.
SW: Leased from Radiocom.
kHz: *5910, 5920, 5925, 5930, 5935, 5940, 5945, 5955, 5990, 6020, 6025, 6030, 6040, 6130, 6145, 6150, 6170, 6175, 6180, 7210, 7220, 7235, 7290, 7310, 7320, 7325, 7330, 7345, 7350, 7360, 7370, 7375, 7410, 7420, 9490, 9600, 9610, 9620, 9740, 9810, 9820, 11660, 11780, 11790, 11800, 11820, 11825, 11945, 11960, 11975, 13630, 13730, 13750, 15255, 15260, 15380, 15430, 15450, 15460, 15600, 17640, 17780, 17800, 17810, 17850*

Winter Schedule 2020/2021

	Days	Area	kHz
Arabic	**Days**	**Area**	**kHz**
0730-0800	daily	NAf	9610gal, 11660gal
0730-0800	daily	ME	11960tig, 13630tig
1300-1330	daily	ME	11945gal, 13630tig
1300-1330	daily	NAf	15460gal, 17810tig
1630-1700	daily	ME	5925gal, 7290tig
1630-1700	daily	NAf	9610gal, 11975gal
Aromanian	**Days**	**Area**	**kHz**
1530-1600	daily	Eu	5955tig
1730-1800	daily	Eu	5955tig
1930-2000	daily	Eu	5955tig
Chinese	**Days**	**Area**	**kHz**
0500-0530	daily	EAs	11820tig, 13730tig+
1330-1400	daily	EAs	9610tig, 11825tig
English	**Days**	**Area**	**kHz**
0100-0200	daily	NAm	6130gal, 7325gal
0400-0500	daily	NAm	6020gal, 7410tig
0400-0500	daily	SAs	9820tig+, 11790gal
0630-0700	daily	AUS,NZL	15450tig+, 17780gal
0630-0700	daily	Eu	6040gal+, 7345tig
1200-1300	daily	EAf	15600tig, 17800gal
1200-1300	daily	Eu	13750tig, 15460tig
1800-1900	daily	Eu	5935tig, 7350tig+
2130-2200	daily	Eu	6030gal+, 7375gal
2130-2200	daily	NAm	6170tig, 7310tig
2300-2400	daily	Eu	6040gal+, 7220gal
2300-2400	daily	EAs	7325tig, 9620tig
French	**Days**	**Area**	**kHz**
0200-0300	daily	NAm	6130gal, 7410gal
0600-0630	daily	WAf	11790tig, 13730tig
0600-0630	daily	Eu	6040gal+, 7360gal
1100-1200	daily	Eu	11780gal, 15255gal, 15430tig
1100-1200	daily	NAf	17640tig
1700-1800	daily	Eu	6025tig+, 7325tig
2100-2130	daily	Eu	6030gal+, 7375gal
German	**Days**	**Area**	**kHz**
0700-0730	daily	Eu	6175tig+, 7345tig
1500-1600	daily	Eu	6040tig, 7330tig
1900-2000	daily	Eu	6180tig, 7235tig+
Italian	**Days**	**Area**	**kHz**
1500-1530	daily	Eu	5955tig
1700-1730	daily	Eu	5955tig
1900-1930	daily	Eu	5955tig+
Romanian	**Days**	**Area**	**kHz**
0100-0300	daily	NAm	5910tig, 7420tig
0500-0600	daily	Eu	6145gal, 7220gal+
0800-0900	......s	WAs	15430gal, 17850gal
0800-1000	......s	ME	11960tig, 13630tig
0900-1000	......s	EAf	15380gal
0900-1000	......s	Eu	11780gal
1000-1100	......s	Eu	15260gal

Romanian	Days	Area	kHz
1000-1100	......s	NAf	15430tig, 17640tig
1300-1400	daily	Eu	7320tig
1400-1600	daily	Eu	9810gal, 11975gal
1700-1800	daily	ME	7370gal, 9810gal
1800-2100	daily	Eu	5990gal, 7375gal
Russian	**Days**	**Area**	**kHz**
0530-0600	daily	RUS	5940tig, 7330tig
1400-1500	daily	RUS	5945tig+, 7210tig
1600-1700	daily	RUS	6030tig+, 7290tig
Serbian	**Days**	**Area**	**kHz**
1630-1700	daily	Eu	5955tig
1830-1900	daily	Eu	5955tig
2030-2100	daily	Eu	5930tig
Spanish	**Days**	**Area**	**kHz**
0000-0100	daily	SAm	6040gal, 7325tig, 9600tig, 11800tig
0300-0400	daily	SAm	9740tig, 11800tig
0300-0400	daily	CAm	6150gal, 7410gal
2000-2100	daily	Eu	5920tig, 7235tig
2200-2300	daily	SAm	9490tig+, 11800tig
Ukrainian	**Days**	**Area**	**kHz**
1600-1630	daily	Eu	5955tig
1800-1830	daily	Eu	5955tig
2000-2030	daily	Eu	5930tig

Key: + DRM.
Ann: English: "This is Radio Romania International".
V: QSL-card. (Online reception report form available)
Notes: Radio Romania International is the External Sce of the public broadcaster Radio Romania. Romanian language prgrs include relays of Home Sce networks.

RADIOCOM (Tx Operator)

sos. Oltenitei nr. 103, sector 4, 041303 Bucuresti, Romania.
☎ +40 315003013. +40 315003013.
E: office@radiocom.ro **W:** www.radiocom.ro
L.P: DG: Gabriel Grecu.
SW: [GAL] Bacau, Galbeni: 2 x 300kW; [TIG] Bucuresti, two sites: Tiganesti (G.C. 44N45 026E06): 3 x 300kW; Saftica (G.C. 44N38 026E05): 1 x 100kW.
Notes: Radiocom is the national transmitter network owner.

RUSSIA (RUS)

GTRK "ADYGEYA" – RADIOKANAL SOOTECHESTVENNIKI (Gov)

ul. Zhukovskogo 24, 385000 Maykop, Russia.
☎ +7 8772 522615.
E: adigradio@mail.ru **W:** www.adygtv.ru/radio
Webcast: D
L.P: Dir: Vyacheslav Zhachemuk.
SW: Leased from RTRN.
kHz: *6000*

Winter Schedule 2020/2021

Adyghe	Days	Area	kHz
1800-1900	m...f..	ME	6000arm*
1900-2000	......s	ME	6000arm

Key: * Mondays also in Arabic and Turkish.
V: Email rpt may be sent to the tx operator RTRN, see separate entry.
Notes: Prgr for the Circassian communities in the Near East, produced by the state broadcasting company GTRK "Adygeya" (a regional branch of the national broadcasting company VGTRK). The prgr is licensed under the brand Radiokanal "Sootechestvenniki" (Radio channel "Compatriots"). Prgrs for domestic audience: See National Radio section.

VESTI FM (Gov)

Contact details see National Radio Section.
kHz: *1413*

Winter Schedule 2020/2021

Russian	Days	Area	kHz
0000-2400	daily	UKR	1413kch

Notes: Relay of domestic prgr, produced by the national broadcasting company VGTRK.

RADIOAGENCY–M (Broker)

123308 Moskva, ul. Demyana Bednogo 24, Russia.
☎ +7 499 1919161. +7 499 1918591.
E: abat@radioagency.ru
L.P: Dir: Aleksey A. Titov.
V: QSL-card. (For brokered stns)
Notes: Radioagency-M brokers air time for SW txs in Moldova (Pridnestrovian Moldavian Republic) and Uzbekistan.

RUSSIAN TELEVISION AND RADIO BROADCASTING NETWORK (RTRN) (Tx Operator)

ul. Nikolskaya 7, 109012 Moscow, Russia.
☎ +7 495 6480111. +7 495 6480111.
E: press@rtrn.ru **W:** www.rtrs.ru
L.P: DG: Andrey Romanchenko.
SW: [ARM] Krasnodar, Tbilisskaya: 1 x 100kW.
V: eQSL-card (Email rpt to vsamay@rtrn.ru)
Notes: RTRN is the national transmitter network operator in Russia. RTRN also owns the transmitting centre Maiac in Moldova (Transnistria).

SÃO TOMÉ E PRÍNCIPE (STP)

USAGM SÃO TOMÉ TRANSMITTING STATION

CP 522, São Tomé, São Tomé e Príncipe.
☎ +239 2223406. +239 2223406.
L.P: SM: Sinisa Kurtic.
MW: [SAO] Pinheira: 1530kHz 600kW.
SW: [SAO] Pinheira: 5 x 100kW.
V: eQSL-letter. (Email rpt to Secretary of SM, Helena de Menezes: hmenezes@usagm.gov)

SAUDI ARABIA (ARS)

SAUDI RADIO INTERNATIONAL (SAUDI BROADCASTING AUTHORITY – SBA) (Gov)

P.O. Box 60059, Riyadh-11545, Saudi Arabia.
☎ +966 11 4425170. +966 11 4041692.
E: vinfo@sbc.sa **W:** www.sbc.sa
Webcast: L
W: www.media.gov.sa (Ministry of Media)
L.P: Minister of Media: Turki Abdullah Al-Shabana; Chmn/Pres (SBA): Dawood Bin Abdulaziz Al-Shiryan.
SW: [JED] Jeddah, Al-Khumra: 4 x 250kW (Tx site may be operated directly by the Engineering Dept of the Ministry of Media. Exact no of txs unconfirmed; additional txs may be installed); [RIY] Riyadh: 8 x 500kW.
SAT: Al Yah 1, Arabsat 5A/C, AsiaSat 5, Badr 4/7, Eutelsat Hot Bird 13C, Galaxy 19, Hellas Sat 3, Hispasat 30W-4, Nilesat 201.
kHz: *7240, 9555, 9650, 9675, 9695, 9790, 9870, 9885, 11820, 11915, 11935, 13610, 13710, 13720, 13775, 13780, 15120, 15170, 15205, 15225, 15285, 15380, 15435, 17560, 17615, 17705, 17730, 17740, 17805, 17895, 21505, 21670*

Winter Schedule 2020/2021

Arabic	Days	Area	kHz
0300-0600	daily	Eu,CAs	15170riy*
0300-0800	daily	CAs,EAs	17895riy*
0500-1100	daily	YEM	13780riy**
0500-1400	daily	YEM	13610riy**
0600-0900	daily	Eu	17740riy**
0600-0900	daily	ME	15380riy*
0600-0900	daily	NAf	17730riy**
0900-1200	daily	ME	11935riy*
0900-1200	daily	NAf	17805riy**
0900-1200	daily	SAs,SEA	17615riy*
0900-2100	daily	YEM	9650riy**
1200-1400	daily	ME	15380riy*
1200-1500	daily	Eu	17705riy**
1200-1500	daily	NAf	17895riy*, 21505riy**
1300-1600	daily	SAf	17615riy*

Arabic	**Days**	**Area**	**kHz**
1400-1800	daily	YEM	9790riy**
1500-1800	daily	Eu	15435riy**
1500-1800	daily	NAf	13710riy*, 15225riy**
1600-1800	daily	Eu	15205riy*
1600-1800	daily	WAf,CAf	17560riy*
1800-2300	daily	Eu	9870riy**, 11820riy*
1800-2300	daily	NAf	9555riy**, 11915riy
Bengali	**Days**	**Area**	**kHz**
0900-1200	daily	SAs	15120riy
Indonesian	**Days**	**Area**	**kHz**
0900-1200	daily	SEA	21670riy
Pashto	**Days**	**Area**	**kHz**
1400-1600	daily	WAs	9695riy
Persian	**Days**	**Area**	**kHz**
1200-1800	daily	ME	7240riy
Somali	**Days**	**Area**	**kHz**
0700-0900	daily	EAf	13720riy
Swahili	**Days**	**Area**	**kHz**
0400-0700	daily	EAf	15285riy*
Turkish	**Days**	**Area**	**kHz**
1800-2100	daily	ME	9675riy
Urdu	**Days**	**Area**	**kHz**
1200-1500	daily	SAs	13775riy
Uzbek/Turkmen	**Days**	**Area**	**kHz**
1600-1800	daily	CAs	9885riy

Key: * Koran prgr; ** General prgr.
Ann: Arabic: "Idha'at ar-Riyadh" (General Prgr); "Idha-atu'l-Koran al-Kareem min al-mamlakah al-arabiyah t'il-saudiah"(Koran Prgr).
IS: 'Ud' (Oriental Lute). Opens and closes with National Anthem.
V: Does not verify reception reports.
Notes: The Saudi Broadcasting Authority (SBA) is a government entity operating under the Ministry of Media. The prgrs in Arabic are relays of Home Sce prgrs.

SINGAPORE (SNG)

TWR ASIA (Rlg)

85 Playfair Road #04-01, Tong Yuan Industrial Building, Singapore 368000.
☎ +65 65015150. Fax +65 64443053.
E: asiafeedback@twr.org **W:** www.twr.asia
Webcast: D
L.P: Dir: Sebastian Chan.
SW: Via TWR relay station KTWR (Guam).
kHz: *7500, 7510, 9910, 9975, 11965, 11995, 12040, 13800*

Winter Schedule 2020/2021

Assamese	**Days**	**Area**	**kHz**
1215-1245	mtwtf..	SEA	9910twr
Burmese	**Days**	**Area**	**kHz**
1145-1215	mtwtfs.	SEA	12040twr
Cantonese	**Days**	**Area**	**kHz**
1345-1400	mtwtf..	CHN	9975twr
Chinese	**Days**	**Area**	**kHz**
1100-1130	.....s.	CHN	9910twr+
1145-1200	......s	CHN	9910twr
1200-1215	daily	CHN	9975twr
1200-1215	mtwtf.s	CHN	9910twr
1315-1330	.....s.	CHN	9975twr
1315-1350	mtwtf.s	CHN	9975twr
1330-1345	......s	CHN	9975twr
1345-1400	.....s.	CHN	9975twr
English	**Days**	**Area**	**kHz**
1000-1015	......s	SEA	11965twr
1000-1020	mtwtf..	AUS,NZL,Pac	11995twr
1000-1045	.....s.	SEA	11995twr
1025-1055	......s	SAs	13800twr+
1100-1130	......s	EAs	9910twr
1100-1130	mtwtf.s	SEA	11965twr
1130-1145	......s	EAs	9910twr
1130-1145	.t.tf..	SEA	11965twr
English	**Days**	**Area**	**kHz**
1315-1345	.....s.	EAs	7510twr
Hakka	**Days**	**Area**	**kHz**
1145-1200	daily	CHN	9975twr
1315-1330	mtwtf..	CHN	9975twr
Hui-Zu	**Days**	**Area**	**kHz**
1115-1145	daily	CHN	9975twr
Indonesian	**Days**	**Area**	**kHz**
1030-1100	.....ss	SEA	11965twr
Japanese	**Days**	**Area**	**kHz**
1217-1245	......s	EAs	7500twr
1245-1315	......s	EAs	7500twr+
Karen (Sgaw)	**Days**	**Area**	**kHz**
1215-1230	......s	SEA	12040twr
1215-1245	mtwtf..	SEA	12040twr
Kokborok	**Days**	**Area**	**kHz**
1245-1315	mtwtf..	SAs	9910twr
Korean	**Days**	**Area**	**kHz**
1315-1345	mtwtf..	EAs	7510twr
1345-1515	daily	EAs	7510twr
1515-1545	.....s.	EAs	7510twr
1515-1615	m.....s	EAs	7510twr
Madurese	**Days**	**Area**	**kHz**
1000-1030	mtwtf..	SEA	11965twr
Manipuri	**Days**	**Area**	**kHz**
1300-1315	......s	SAs	9910twr
Mongolian	**Days**	**Area**	**kHz**
1100-1115	daily	EAs	9975twr
Nepali	**Days**	**Area**	**kHz**
1300-1315	.....s.	SAs	9910twr
Sundanese	**Days**	**Area**	**kHz**
1030-1100	mtwtf..	SEA	11965twr
Vietnamese	**Days**	**Area**	**kHz**
1245-1300	......s	SEA	9975twr
1245-1315	.....s.	SEA	9975twr
Yi	**Days**	**Area**	**kHz**
1215-1230	mtwtfs.	CHN	9975twr

Key: + DRM
V: QSL-card. (Online form on website)
Notes: TWR regional branch for Asia. For corporate details, see under TWR (USA).

BBC FAR EASTERN RELAY STATION

51 Turut Track, Singapore 718930.
☎ +65 67937511. Fax +65 67937834.
L.P: Stn Mgr: Cindy Yao; Chief Eng: Tam Lam Soon.
SW: [SNG] Singapore: 4 x 100, 5 x 250kW.
V: QSL-card. (For direct report)
Notes: Owned by the BBC and operated by Encompass Digital Media Services Ltd (see under United Kingdom).

SLOVAKIA (SVK)

RADIO SLOVAKIA INTERNATIONAL (Pub)

Mýtna 1, P.O. Box 55, 817 55 Bratislava 15, Slovakia.
☎ +421 2 57273734. Fax +421 2 52496282.
E: rsi@slovakradio.sk; englishsection@slovakradio.sk **W:** rsi.rtvs.sk
Webcast: L. Webcast languages: English, French, German, Russian, Slovak, Spanish.
L.P: Chief Script Adviser: Mária Mikušová.
SW: Leases airtime on WRMI (See under USA).
SAT: Astra 3B.
kHz: *3985, 5010, 5850, 6005, 7780, 9395, 9955*

Winter Schedule 2020/2021

English	**Days**	**Area**	**kHz**
0030-0100	daily	NAm	5850rmi
0030-0100	daily	Eu,NAm	7780rmi
0330-0400	daily	NAm	9395rmi
1000-1030	daily	WEu	6005kll
1530-1600	daily	WEu	6005kll
1630-1700	daily	WEu	6005kll

French	Days	Area	kHz
1230-1300	daily	WEu	6005kll
1430-1500	daily	WEu	6005kll
1630-1700	daily	WEu	3985kll
1930-2000	daily	WEu	3985kll
German	**Days**	**Area**	**kHz**
1100-1130	daily	WEu	6005kll
1200-1230	daily	WEu	6005kll
1400-1430	daily	WEu	6005kll
1900-1930	daily	WEu	3985kll
Slovak	**Days**	**Area**	**kHz**
0000-0030	daily	Eu,NAm	7780rmi
0000-0030	daily	NAm	5850rmi
Spanish	**Days**	**Area**	**kHz**
0030-0100	daily	CAm	5010rmi
0030-0100	daily	NAm	9395rmi
0330-0400	daily	LAm	9955rmi
1330-1400	mtwtf..	LAm	9955rmi
1500-1530	daily	WEu	6005kll

Ann: English: "You are listening to Radio Slovakia International".
V: QSL-card.
Notes: International service of the public service Slovak Radio (Slovenský Rozhlas), launched 1993. The relay via a SW 1kW tx at Kall (Germany) is an independent, personal initiative of the operator of the German relay platform "Shortwaveservice"; a project that is primarily targeting SWLs/DXers in Europe.

TWR EUROPE AND CAMENA (Rlg)

P.O. Box 12, 820 02 Bratislava 22, Slovakia.
☎ +421 2 48209220
E: twre@twr.org **W:** www.twreurope.org
Webcast: D
The head office of TWR Europe and CAMENA is located in Cyprus. Other European branch: P.O. Box 176, 3780 BD Voorthuizen, The Netherlands
L.P: Dir: Daryl Van Dyken.
kHz: *612, 864, 999, 1350, 1377, 1467, 1548, 6240*

Winter Schedule 2020/2021

Arabic	Days	Area	kHz
1830-2050	.....ss	ME	1350erv
1830-2055	mtwtf..	ME	1350erv
2045-2200	daily	NAf	1467rou
Belarusian	**Days**	**Area**	**kHz**
1945-2000	m......	Eu	999kch
Bosnian	**Days**	**Area**	**kHz**
2040-2055	......s	Eu	1548kch
2040-2110	.....s.	Eu	1548kch
Bulgarian	**Days**	**Area**	**kHz**
1930-1945	.....s.	Eu	1548kch
Farsi	**Days**	**Area**	**kHz**
1815-1830	mtw..ss	ME	1377erv
1830-2000	...tf..	ME	1377erv
Gilaki	**Days**	**Area**	**kHz**
1815-1830	...t...	ME	1377erv
Hungarian	**Days**	**Area**	**kHz**
2015-2040	.....ss	Eu	1548kch
2015-2100	mtwtf..	Eu	1548kch
Kabyle	**Days**	**Area**	**kHz**
2115-2145	mtwtfs.	NAf	1467rou
Karakalpak	**Days**	**Area**	**kHz**
1640-1655	.....ss	CAs	864erv
1655-1710	.....s.	CAs	864erv
Kazakh	**Days**	**Area**	**kHz**
1500-1545	daily	CAs	612bis
1545-1600	daily	CAs	6240tac
1625-1640	daily	CAs	864erv
1700-1715	....fss	CAs	612bis
Kurdish (Kurmanji)	**Days**	**Area**	**kHz**
1745-1800	daily	ME	1350erv
Kurdish (Sorani)	**Days**	**Area**	**kHz**
1800-1815	.twtfss	ME	1377erv
Kyrgyz	**Days**	**Area**	**kHz**
1715-1730	....fss	CAs	612bis
Montenegrin	**Days**	**Area**	**kHz**
2055-2110	......s	Eu	1548kch
Polish	**Days**	**Area**	**kHz**
2045-2115	mtwtf..	Eu	1467rou
Qashqai	**Days**	**Area**	**kHz**
1815-1830	....f..	ME	1377erv
Romanian	**Days**	**Area**	**kHz**
1945-2015	.....ss	Eu	1548kch
Romany (Balkan)	**Days**	**Area**	**kHz**
1930-1945	mtwtf.s	Eu	1548kch
Romany (Vlax)	**Days**	**Area**	**kHz**
1945-2015	mtwtf..	Eu	1548kch
Russian	**Days**	**Area**	**kHz**
1545-1600	......s	CAs	612bis
1545-1630	mtwtfs.	CAs	612bis
1640-1710	mtwtf..	CAs	864erv
1745-1800	......s	RUS	999kch
1800-1845	mtw....	RUS	999kch
1815-1830	.....s.	RUS	999kch
1815-1900	.....s.	RUS	999kch
1830-1845	...t...	RUS	999kch
1830-1900	mt..f.s	RUS	999kch
1845-1900	.twtf..	RUS	999kch
Serbian	**Days**	**Area**	**kHz**
2100-2130	mtwtf..	Eu	1548kch
2110-2125	.....ss	Eu	1548kch
Tajik	**Days**	**Area**	**kHz**
1630-1645	daily	CAs	1467bis
Turkish	**Days**	**Area**	**kHz**
1800-1830	daily	ME	1350erv
Turkmen	**Days**	**Area**	**kHz**
1610-1625	daily	CAs	864erv
Uighur	**Days**	**Area**	**kHz**
1700-1730	mtwt...	CAs	612bis
Ukrainian	**Days**	**Area**	**kHz**
1830-1845	......s	Eu	999kch
1830-1900	mtwtf..	Eu	999kch
1830-1915	.....s.	Eu	999kch
1900-1930	.t....s	Eu	999kch
1900-1945	....f..	Eu	999kch
1900-2000	..wt...	Eu	999kch
Uzbek	**Days**	**Area**	**kHz**
1600-1700	......s	CAs	612bis
1630-1700	mtwtfs.	CAs	612bis
1655-1710	......s	CAs	864erv
1710-1740	daily	CAs	864erv

Ann: English: "This is Trans World Radio. The following programme is in the ... language".
V: QSL-card.
Notes: TWR regional division, covering Europe, Russia, and CAMENA (Central Asia, Middle East, North Africa). For corporate details, see under TWR (USA).

SOUTH AFRICA (AFS)

TWR AFRICA (Rlg)

P.O. Box 4232, Kempton Park, 1620, South Africa.
☎ +27 11 9742885. 🖷 +27 11 9749960.
E: info@twrafrica.org **W:** www.twrafrica.org
Webcast: D/L/P
San Croy Business Park, Die Agora Rd., Kempton Park, 1619, South Africa.
L.P: Dir: Steve Stavropoulos; CE: Mike Lambert.
MW: Via TWR Benin & TWR Swaziland relay stations.
SW: Via TWR Swaziland relay station & leased foreign relays.
SAT: Intelsat 20.
kHz: *1170, 1476, 1566, 4760, 6100, 6130, 7245, 7455, 9380, 9500, 9585, 11660, 11780, 13580, 15105*

Winter Schedule 2020/2021

	Days	Area	kHz
Amharic	**Days**	**Area**	**kHz**
1630-1645	m......	EAf	11660man
1700-1730	daily	EAf	11660man
1730-1800	......s	EAf	11660man
Arabic (Juba)	**Days**	**Area**	**kHz**
1530-1545	mtwtf..	EAf	13580man
Bambara	**Days**	**Area**	**kHz**
2040-2200	......s	WAf	1566par
Bete/Baoule/Senoufo	**Days**	**Area**	**kHz**
2130-2215	m......	WAf	1566par
Chokwe	**Days**	**Area**	**kHz**
1850-1905	.....s.	SAf	6130man
Ditammari	**Days**	**Area**	**kHz**
1925-1940	.....s.	WAf	1566par
English	**Days**	**Area**	**kHz**
0320-0330	mtwtf..	WAf	1566par
0430-0500	.....s.	WAf	1566par
0445-0515	......s	WAf	1476par
0530-0545	mtwtf..	WAf	1566par
1420-1455	daily	SAf	7455man
1725-1750	.....s.	WAf	1476par
1725-1820	mtwtf.s	WAf	1476par
1745-1825	mtwtfs.	WAf	1566par
1800-1850	.....s.	EAf	9500man
1800-1900	mtwtf.s	EAf	9500man
1800-2015	daily	SAf	1170man
1805-1825	......s	WAf	1566par
English/French/Baoule	**Days**	**Area**	**kHz**
2200-2215	.t.....	WAf	1566par
English/Igbo/Twi	**Days**	**Area**	**kHz**
0430-0445	......s	WAf	1566par
Ewe	**Days**	**Area**	**kHz**
0515-0530	.....s.	WAf	1566par
Fiote	**Days**	**Area**	**kHz**
1905-1920	....f..	SAf	6130man
Fongbe	**Days**	**Area**	**kHz**
1725-1745	daily	WAf	1566par
1940-2010	mtwtf..	WAf	1566par
Fongbe/Bambara	**Days**	**Area**	**kHz**
1745-1805	......s	WAf	1566par
French	**Days**	**Area**	**kHz**
1455-1525	.....ss	WAf	9585man
1935-1950	.....ss	WAf	15105man
2040-2100	mtwtf..	WAf	1566par
2100-2130	mtwtf..	WAf	1566par
2130-2200	..wtfs.	WAf	1566par
2200-2215	..wtfss	WAf	1566par
French/Mina	**Days**	**Area**	**kHz**
2040-2100	.....s.	WAf	1566par
Fulfulde	**Days**	**Area**	**kHz**
1910-1925	.....ss	WAf	1566par
1915-1930	mtwtf..	WAf	1476par
1915-1945	.....ss	WAf	1476par
1940-2010	.....ss	WAf	1566par
Hadiyya	**Days**	**Area**	**kHz**
1645-1700	....fs.	EAf	11660man
Hausa	**Days**	**Area**	**kHz**
0320-0430	mtwtf..	WAf	1476par
0330-0430	mtwtf..	WAf	1566par
0345-0430	.....ss	WAf	1566par
Igbo	**Days**	**Area**	**kHz**
0430-0445	mtwtf.s	WAf	1476par
0430-0500	mtwtf..	WAf	1566par
0445-0520	mtwtf..	WAf	1476par
1750-1820	.....s.	WAf	1476par
Kambaata	**Days**	**Area**	**kHz**
1630-1645	....fs.	EAf	11660man
Kanuri	**Days**	**Area**	**kHz**
1855-1915	daily	WAf	1476par
Kanuri	**Days**	**Area**	**kHz**
1910-1925	mtwtf..	WAf	1566par
KiKongo	**Days**	**Area**	**kHz**
1905-1920	......s	SAf	6130man
Kimbundu	**Days**	**Area**	**kHz**
1950-2005	mtwtf..	SAf	6130man
Kinyarwanda/Kirundi	**Days**	**Area**	**kHz**
1600-1615	......s	CAf	13580man
1600-1630	mtwtf..	CAf	13580man
Kotokoli	**Days**	**Area**	**kHz**
1925-1940	mtwtf..	WAf	1566par
Kuanyama	**Days**	**Area**	**kHz**
1920-1935	......s	SAf	6130man
Kunama	**Days**	**Area**	**kHz**
1800-1830	......s	EAf	7245kch
Lingala	**Days**	**Area**	**kHz**
1905-1935	daily	CAf	15105man
1935-2005	mtwtf..	CAf	15105man
Luchazi	**Days**	**Area**	**kHz**
1905-1920	..w....	SAf	6130man
Lukpa	**Days**	**Area**	**kHz**
1925-1940	......s	WAf	1566par
Luvale	**Days**	**Area**	**kHz**
1905-1920	...t...	SAf	6130man
Makua	**Days**	**Area**	**kHz**
1420-1450	.....s.	SAf	9585man
Malagasy	**Days**	**Area**	**kHz**
1455-1525	mtwtf..	SAf	9585man
Oromo	**Days**	**Area**	**kHz**
1630-1645	.t....s	EAf	11660man
1630-1700	..wt...	EAf	11660man
1730-1800	mtwtfs.	EAf	11660man
Oromo/Borana	**Days**	**Area**	**kHz**
1645-1700	mt....s	EAf	11660man
Portuguese	**Days**	**Area**	**kHz**
1630-1645	.....s.	SAf	4760man
1905-1920	mt.....	SAf	6130man
1920-1950	mtwtf..	SAf	6130man
1920-2005	.....s.	SAf	6130man
1935-2005	......s	SAf	6130man
Portuguese/Lomwe	**Days**	**Area**	**kHz**
1420-1450	mtwtf..	SAf	9585man
Senoufo/Goun	**Days**	**Area**	**kHz**
2130-2200	.t.....	WAf	1566par
Shangaan	**Days**	**Area**	**kHz**
1630-1645	.t.....	SAf	4760man
Shona	**Days**	**Area**	**kHz**
1455-1525	daily	SAf	7455man
1525-1555	mtwtf..	SAf	7455man
2115-2200	daily	SAf	1170man
Shona/Ndebele	**Days**	**Area**	**kHz**
0330-0415	daily	SAf	4760man
Somali	**Days**	**Area**	**kHz**
1500-1530	daily	EAf	11780man
1530-1545	.....ss	EAf	11780man
Swahili	**Days**	**Area**	**kHz**
1745-1815	mtwtf..	EAf	9380man
1745-1825	......s	EAf	9380man
1800-1840	.....s.	EAf	9380man
Tamasheq	**Days**	**Area**	**kHz**
2100-2130	.....s.	WAf	1566par
Tigre	**Days**	**Area**	**kHz**
1800-1830	.....s.	EAf	7245kch
Tigrinya	**Days**	**Area**	**kHz**
1800-1845	mtwf...	EAf	7245kch
1815-1845	....f..	EAf	7245kch
Turkana	**Days**	**Area**	**kHz**
1745-1800	.....s.	EAf	9380man
Twi	**Days**	**Area**	**kHz**
0500-0515	.....s.	WAf	1566par

Twi	**Days**	**Area**	**kHz**
0500-0530	mtwtf..	WAf	1566par
Umbundu	**Days**	**Area**	**kHz**
1820-1850	mtwtf..	SAf	6130man
1850-1905	mtwtf.s	SAf	6130man
1905-1920	.....s.	SAf	6130man
Various	**Days**	**Area**	**kHz**
1855-1910	daily	WAf	1566par
2010-2040	daily	WAf	1566par
Yao	**Days**	**Area**	**kHz**
1700-1730	daily	SAf	6100man
Yoruba	**Days**	**Area**	**kHz**
1820-1855	daily	WAf	1476par
1825-1855	daily	WAf	1566par
Zulu	**Days**	**Area**	**kHz**
1745-1800	......s	SAf	1170man
2015-2115	daily	SAf	1170man

Ann: English: "Trans World Radio", "TWR".
IS: Last bar of "We've a story to tell the Nations", played on hand bells.
V: QSL-folder. Rp. (3IRCs appreciated)
Notes: TWR regional division covering most parts of Africa (except North Africa, which is served by TWR Europe). For corporate details, see under TWR (USA). TWR Africa administrates the TWR transmitting stations in Benin and Eswatini.

SPAIN (E)

RADIO EXTERIOR DE ESPAÑA (REE) (Pub)

✉ Casa de la Radio, Avenida de la Radio y la Televisión 4, Pozuelo de Alarcón, 28223 Madrid, Spain.
☎ +34 91 5817000.
E: secretariatecnica.ree@rtve.es
W: www.rtve.es/radio/radio-exterior
Webcast: D/L/P (Webcast languages: Arabic, English, Ladino, Portuguese, Russian, Spanish)
L.P: Dir: Antonio Buitrago.
SW: [NOB] Noblejas: 4 x 300kW.
SAT: AsiaSat 5, Astra 1M, EchoStar 9-Galaxy 23, Eutelsat 8WB.
kHz: *9690, 11685, 11940, 12030*

Winter Schedule 2020/2021

Arabic	**Days**	**Area**	**kHz**
1730-1800	mtwtf..	WAf,Atl	11685nob
1730-1800	mtwtf..	ME,IOc	12030nob
2230-2300	mtwtf..	ME,IOc	12030nob
2230-2300	mtwtf..	WAf,Atl	11685nob
English	**Days**	**Area**	**kHz**
2300-2330	m.w.f..	ME,IOc	12030nob
2300-2330	m.w.f..	NAm	9690nob
2300-2330	m.w.f..	SAm	11940nob
2300-2330	m.w.f..	WAf,Atl	11685nob
French	**Days**	**Area**	**kHz**
2330-2400	m.w.f..	WAf,Atl	11685nob
2330-2400	m.w.f..	ME,IOc	12030nob
2330-2400	m.w.f..	NAm	9690nob
2330-2400	m.w.f..	SAm	11940nob
Ladino	**Days**	**Area**	**kHz**
1800-1830	.t.....	ME,IOc	12030nob
2230-2300	......s	NAm	9690nob
2230-2300	......s	SAm	11940nob
2230-2300	......s	WAf,Atl	11685nob
2230-2300	......s	ME,IOc	12030nob
2300-2330	.t.....	ME,IOc	12030nob
2300-2330	.t.....	NAm	9690nob
2300-2330	.t.....	SAm	11940nob
2300-2330	.t.....	WAf,Atl	11685nob
Portuguese	**Days**	**Area**	**kHz**
0000-0030	.twtfs.	NAm	9690nob
0000-0030	.twtfs.	SAm	11940nob
1800-1830	mtwtf..	WAf,Atl	11685nob
Russian	**Days**	**Area**	**kHz**
1800-1830	m..tf..	ME,IOc	12030nob
Spanish	**Days**	**Area**	**kHz**
0030-0300	.twtfs.	SAm	11940nob
0030-0300	.twtfs.	NAm	9690nob
1500-2230	......s	ME,IOc	12030nob
1500-2230	......s	NAm	9690nob
1500-2230	......s	SAm	11940nob
1500-2230	......s	WAf,Atl	11685nob
1500-2300	.....s.	ME,IOc	12030nob
1500-2300	.....s.	NAm	9690nob
1500-2300	.....s.	SAm	11940nob
1500-2300	.....s.	WAf,Atl	11685nob
1600-1730	mtwtf..	WAf,Atl	11685nob
1600-1730	mtwtf..	ME,IOc	12030nob
1800-1830	...tf..	ME,IOc	12030nob
1830-2300	mtwtf..	WAf,Atl	11685nob
1830-2300	mtwtf..	ME,IOc	12030nob
1900-2300	mtwtf..	NAm	9690nob
1900-2300	mtwtf..	SAm	11940nob
2300-2330	...t...	NAm	9690nob
2300-2400	...t...	ME,IOc	12030nob
2300-2400	...t...	SAm	11940nob
2300-2400	...t...	WAf,Atl	11685nob
2330-2400	.t.....	WAf,Atl	11685nob
2330-2400	.t.....	ME,IOc	12030nob
2330-2400	.t.....	NAm	9690nob
2330-2400	.t.....	SAm	11940nob

V: QSL-card.
Notes: REE is the Int. Sce of the public broadcaster Radio Nacional de España (RNE).

RADIO MI AMIGO INTERNATIONAL

✉ Avenida de Europa 85, Urb. La Marina, 03177 San Fulgencio, Spain.
E: studio@radiomiamigo.international **W:** www.radiomiamigo.international
Webcast: L
kHz: *6085*

Winter Schedule 2020/2021

English/Dutch/ French/German	**Days**	**Area**	**kHz**
0800-1700	daily	CEu,WEu	6085kll

Ann: English: "Welcome to Radio Mi Amigo International".
V: QSL-card.
Notes: Radio Mi Amigo International is a 24/7 Internet radio channel; the prgr consists of 60s/70s orientated music shows in English, Dutch, French and German.

SRI LANKA (CLN)

SRI LANKA BROADCASTING CORPORATION (SLBC) (Pub)

✉ P.O. Box 574, Colombo 00700, Sri Lanka; Independence Square, Colombo 00700, Sri Lanka.
☎ +94 11 2697491. 🖷 +94 11 2691568.
E: chmnslbc@slbc.lk (Chairman); ddge@slbc.lk (Dir, Engineering)
W: www.slbc.lk
Webcast: L
✉ SLBC Trincomalee Relay Station, Kuchchavali, Trincomalee, Sri Lanka. (MW Transmitting Station)
☎ +94 26 2222699. 🖷 +94 26 2222097.
L.P: Chmn: Siddi Mohamed Farook; DG: Erananda Hettiarachchi; Dir, Engineering: M.G.W. Priyadarshana.
MW: [PUT] Puttalam: 873/882kHz 400kW, 1125kHz 50kW; [TRM] Trincomalee, Perkara: 1548kHz 400kW.
SW: [TRM] Trincomalee, Perkara: 3 x 300kW.
kHz: *1125, 11750, 11905*

Winter Schedule 2020/2021

Bengali/Hindi	**Days**	**Area**	**kHz**
0030-0100	daily	SAs	11905trm
Sinhala	**Days**	**Area**	**kHz**
1700-1830	daily	ME	11750trm*
Tamil	**Days**	**Area**	**kHz**
0715-0815	....f..	SAs	1125put

Key: * Relay of domestic prgr: City FM.
Ann: Sinhala: "Sri Lanka Guwan Viduliye Mada Peradiga Sevaya"; Tamil " Sri Lanka Vanoli".
IS: Melody on drums.
V: QSL-card. Rp.
Notes: SLBC's External Service ("Asian Service") for listeners in Asia and expatriates in Asia & the Middle East. SLBC is also leasing airtime on its transmitting facilities to third party customers, both from the Puttalam MW site and the Trincomalee MW/SW site (in 2012, SLBC took over the former Deutsche Welle Relay Station in Trincomalee).

SUDAN (SDN)

VOICE OF AFRICA – SUDAN RADIO (Pub)

P.O.Box 572, Omdurman, Sudan.
☎ +249 1 87572956. 🖷 +249 1 87556006.
E: Via website. **W:** www.sudanradio.gov.sd
E: info@mininfo.gov.sd (Ministry of Information) **W:** mininfo.gov.sd (Ministry of Information)
L.P: DG (Sudan National Public Radio Corp.): Mutasim Fadul.
SW: Via tx provided by SGCRTVT (Sudanese General Corporation for Radio & TV Transmission).
kHz: *9505*

Winter Schedule 2020/2021

English	**Days**	**Area**	**kHz**
1715-1800	daily	CAf	9505alf
French	**Days**	**Area**	**kHz**
1630-1715	daily	CAf	9505alf
Swahili	**Days**	**Area**	**kHz**
1800-1900	daily	CAf	9505alf

Ann: English: "This is the Voice of Africa, broadcasting from Sudan Radio"; French: "La Voix d' Afrique, Radio National de Soudan".
Notes: The Voice of Africa is the External Service of the Sudan National Public Radio Corp. ("Sudan Radio"). First transmissions in October 2012.

SUDANESE GENERAL CORPORATION FOR RADIO & TV TRANSMISSION (SGCRTVT) (Tx Operator)

Omdurman, Sudan.
E: info@mininfo.gov.sd **W:** mininfo.gov.sd
L.P: Dir: Nabigh Khogali.
SW: [ALF] Omdurman, Al Fitahab: 1 x 100kW.
Notes: SGCRTVT, under the roof of the Ministry of Information, is the national transmitter operator in Sudan.

SWEDEN (S)

IBRA MEDIA (Rlg)

P.O.Box 15144, SE-16715 Bromma, Sweden.
☎ +46 8 6089680.
E: info@ibra.se **W:** ibra.se
L.P: Mgr, IBRA Media: Pontus Fridolfsson; Public Relations: Birger Thureson.
kHz: *5895, 6180, 7510, 9515, 9540, 9775, 11655, 15260*

Winter Schedule 2020/2021

Afar	**Days**	**Area**	**kHz**
1600-1630	daily	EAf	11655dha
Amharic	**Days**	**Area**	**kHz**
1615-1630	..wtf.s	EAf	9540erv
1630-1700	daily	EAf	9540erv
Arabic	**Days**	**Area**	**kHz**
0800-0830	daily	ME	15260wof
1700-1800	daily	ME	9775wof
1730-1900	daily	EAf	9515wof
Bengali	**Days**	**Area**	**kHz**
1500-1530	daily	SAs	5895tac
Guragena	**Days**	**Area**	**kHz**
1615-1630	mtw....	EAf	9540erv
Oromo	**Days**	**Area**	**kHz**
1700-1730	daily	EAf	9540dha
Silte	**Days**	**Area**	**kHz**
1730-1800	daily	EAf	7510erv
Somali	**Days**	**Area**	**kHz**
1730-1800	daily	EAf	6180dha
Tigrinya	**Days**	**Area**	**kHz**
1730-1757	daily	EAf	9540dha

V: QSL-card.
Notes: IBRA Media is a multimedia ministry of the Swedish Pentecostal Movement. IBRA radio prgrs (formerly branded "IBRA Radio") are on air since July 1955.

SWITZERLAND (SUI)

SRG SSR (SWISS BROADCASTING CORP.) (Pub)

See National Radio section.
Webcast: D/L
SW: Via Shortwaveservice (Germany).
kHz: *3985, 6005*

Winter Schedule 2020/2021

German	**Days**	**Area**	**kHz**
1130-1200	daily	CEu	6005kll*
1700-1800	daily	CEu	3985kll*

Key: * Relay of R. SRF1.
Notes: The Swiss Broadcasting Corp. ended shortwave transmissions in 2004. The current relay via a 1kW SW tx at Kall (Germany) is an independent, personal initiative of the operator of the German relay platform "Shortwaveservice"; a project that is primarily targeting SWLs/DXers in Europe. The prgrs consist of selected relays of R. SRF1 (a domestic channel produced by SRG SSR's German language unit Schweizer Rundfunk und Fernsehen - SRF).

SYRIA (SYR)

RADIO DAMASCUS (Gov)

Ommayad Square, Damascus, Syria
☎ +963 11 2720700. 🖷 +963 11 2234930.
E: en@ortas.online **W:** en.ortas.online/?f=Radio-Damascus
Webcast: D/L (D also at soundcloud.com/SyrianForeignRadios). Web languages: English, French, German, Spanish, Turkish, Russian.
MW: [TTS] Tartus: 783kHz 300kW.
kHz: *783*

Winter Schedule 2020/2021

French	**Days**	**Area**	**kHz**
0600-0700	daily	ME	783tts
Hebrew	**Days**	**Area**	**kHz**
0400-0530	daily	ME	783tts
Russian	**Days**	**Area**	**kHz**
0530-0600	daily	ME	783tts

Ann: Russian: "Govorit Damask, radioveshchatelnaya stantsiya Siriyskoy Arabskoy Respubliki".
V: QSL-card.
Notes: Radio Damascus is the International Sce of the state broadcaster General Organization of Radio & TV - Syria (ORTAS).

TAIWAN (Rep. of China) (TWN)

RADIO TAIWAN INTERNATIONAL – RTI (CHUNGYANG KUANGPO TIANTAI) (Gov)

P.O. Box 123-199, Taipei 11199, Taiwan; 55 Pei An Road, Taipei 10462, Taiwan.
☎ +886 2 28856168. 🖷 +886 2 28862382.
E: rti@rti.org.tw **W:** www.rti.org.tw
Webcast: D/L/P
L.P: Chmn: Lu Ping; Pres: Chang Cheng.
MW: [KOU] Kouhu: 1098/1557kHz 300kW; [MIN] Minhsiung: 1422kHz 50kW.
SW: [KOU] Kouhu: 3 x 100kW; [PAO] Paochung: 4 x 100, 6 x 300kW; [TSH] Tanshui: 4 x 300kW.
kHz: *1098, 1422, 1557, 5010, 5800, 5900, 5955, 5990, 6005, 6075, 6105, 6145, 6180, 6185, 7300, 7430, 7780, 9400, 9415, 9425, 9430, 9490, 9525, 9545, 9555, 9610, 9625, 9660, 9680, 9735, 9740, 9745,*

9885, 9900, 11695, 11840, 11915, 12100, 15270, 15320, 15465

Winter Schedule 2020/2021

Amoy	**Days**	**Area**	**kHz**
0900-1000	daily	EAs	9400kou
Cantonese	**Days**	**Area**	**kHz**
0400-0430	daily	EAs	15320pao
1000-1030	daily	EAs	9735pao, 15270pao
1200-1230	daily	EAs	9735pao
1200-1230	daily	EAs,SEA	6105kou
1500-1530	daily	EAs	9545pao
Chinese	**Days**	**Area**	**kHz**
0400-0600	daily	EAs	11840pao
0730-0900	daily	EAs	11840pao
0900-1000	daily	EAs	15465pao
0900-1100	daily	EAs	1557kou
1000-1100	daily	EAs	7300tsh
1000-1200	daily	EAs	6105kou
1000-1300	daily	EAs	9555pao, 9885pao
1000-1600	daily	EAs	9660kou
1000-1600	daily	SAs,Af	6180tsh
1100-1200	daily	EAs	11840pao
1100-1400	daily	EAs	9680tsh
1200-1400	daily	EAs	7430pao
1200-1705	daily	EAs	1557kou
1300-1400	daily	EAs	6105kou
1300-1705	daily	EAs	1098kou
1400-1700	daily	EAs	6145kou
1400-1730	daily	EAs	6075kou
1500-1705	daily	EAs	7300tsh
2200-2400	daily	EAs	6075kou, 6105kou, 9900pao
English	**Days**	**Area**	**kHz**
0300-0400	daily	EAs	15320pao
1120-1140	daily	SEA	12100pao
1600-1700	daily	SAs,Af	6185tsh
2200-2230	daily	Eu,NAm	7780rmi
French	**Days**	**Area**	**kHz**
1900-1930	daily	Eu	6005sof
1900-2000	......s	Af	9680iss
German	**Days**	**Area**	**kHz**
1900-1930	daily	Eu	5900sof
Hakka	**Days**	**Area**	**kHz**
0430-0500	daily	EAs	15320pao
1030-1100	daily	EAs	9735pao, 15270pao
1230-1300	daily	EAs	9735pao
1230-1300	daily	EAs,SEA	6105kou
1530-1600	daily	EAs	9545pao
Hokkien	**Days**	**Area**	**kHz**
1100-1120	daily	EAs	12100pao
Indonesian	**Days**	**Area**	**kHz**
0000-0100	....f..	SEA	1422min
1000-1100	daily	SEA	11915pao
1140-1200	daily	SEA	12100pao
1200-1300	daily	SEA	11915pao
1200-1300	...t...	SEA	1422min
1400-1500	daily	SEA	9735pao
Japanese	**Days**	**Area**	**kHz**
0800-0900	daily	EAs	11695pao
1100-1200	daily	EAs	9740pao
Korean	**Days**	**Area**	**kHz**
1030-1100	daily	EAs	9610pao
2200-2230	daily	EAs	5955tsh
2300-2330	daily	EAs	9430pao
Russian	**Days**	**Area**	**kHz**
1100-1200	daily	CAs	9490tsh
1700-1730	daily	Eu	5990sof
Spanish	**Days**	**Area**	**kHz**
0100-0130	daily	LAm	5800rmi
0200-0230	daily	LAm	5010rmi
Taiwanese	**Days**	**Area**	**kHz**
1200-1300	daily	EAs	1098kou
Thai	**Days**	**Area**	**kHz**
0000-0100	daily	SEA	9745pao
0100-0200	..t....	SEA	1422min
1200-1300	..w....	SEA	1422min
1300-1400	daily	SEA	9525pao
1400-1500	daily	SEA	9415pao
Vietnamese	**Days**	**Area**	**kHz**
0100-0200	..w....	SEA	1422min
1100-1200	.t.....	SEA	1422min
1100-1200	daily	SEA	9425pao
1400-1500	daily	SEA	9625pao
2300-2400	daily	SEA	9745pao

Ann: Chinese: "Cheli shih Chungyang Kuangpo Tiantai, Taiwan chih Yin"; English: "This is Radio Taiwan International"; Indonesian: "Inilah Radio Taiwan Internasional"; Japanese: "Kochirawa Taiwan Kokusai Hoso, RTI, Chukaminkoku Chuohosokyoku no nihongobangumi desu".
V: QSL-card.
Notes: Formed in 1998, when the former Central Broadcasting System (owned by the Ministry of Defense) was joined with the international section of the Broadcasting Corporation of China (Voice of Free China). Programmes to mainland China are jammed by "China National Radio (CNR)" 1st programme transmissions (usually).

TAJIKISTAN (TJK)

VOICE OF TAJIK (OVOZI TOJIK) (Gov)

Sheroz St. 31, 734025 Dushanbe, Tajikistan.
☎ +992 37 2277417.
E: ovozitojik2016@mail.ru, info@ktr.tj
W: ktr.kj; radiotoj.tj; www.facebook.com/safhaimusicol
Webcast: L (radiotoj.tj)
L.P: Chmn (State Committee for Radio & TV): Asadulloi Rahmon.
MW/SW: Leased from Teleradiokom.
SAT: Al Yah 1, NSS12.
kHz: *1143, 7245*

Winter Schedule 2020/2021

Arabic	**Days**	**Area**	**kHz**
1200-1300	daily	ME	1143dsb, 7245dsb
Dari	**Days**	**Area**	**kHz**
0600-0800	daily	WAs	1143dsb, 7245dsb
English	**Days**	**Area**	**kHz**
1300-1400	daily	WAs	1143dsb, 7245dsb
Farsi	**Days**	**Area**	**kHz**
0400-0600	daily	ME	1143dsb, 7245dsb
1600-1800	daily	ME	1143dsb, 7245dsb
Hindi	**Days**	**Area**	**kHz**
1100-1200	daily	SAs	1143dsb, 7245dsb
Russian	**Days**	**Area**	**kHz**
0800-1000	daily	CAs	1143dsb, 7245dsb
Tajik	**Days**	**Area**	**kHz**
0200-0400	daily	CAs	1143dsb, 7245dsb
1400-1600	daily	CAs	1143dsb, 7245dsb
Uzbek	**Days**	**Area**	**kHz**
1000-1100	daily	CAs	1143dsb, 7245dsb

V: eQSL-letter.
Notes: External Sce of the State Committee for TV and Radio Broadcasting.

TELERADIOKOM (Tx Operator)

Safarov St. 85, 734001 Dushanbe, Tajikistan.
☎ +992 37 2210912. Fax +992 37 2217974.
E: info@teleradiocom.tj **W:** www.teleradiocom.tj
L.P: DG: Suhrob Aliyev.
MW: [DSB] Two sites: Dushanbe, Yangiyul (G.C: 38N29 068E48): 1143kHz 150kW, 1251kHz 100kW; Orzu (G.C: 37N32 068E48): 801kHz 1000kW, 927kHz 300kW. Operated on behalf of USAGM (USA): 972kHz 800kW.
SW: [DSB] Two sites: Dushanbe, Yangiyul (G.C: 38N29 068E48): 1 x 50, 5 x 100kW; Orzu (G.C: 37N32 068E48): 2 x 1000kW. Operated on behalf of USAGM (USA): 1 x 250, 1 x 500kW.
Notes: Teleradiokom, operating under the roof of the State Committee for Radio & Television, is the national transmitter network owner.

TANZANIA (TZA)

ZANZIBAR BROADCASTING CORPORATION (Pub)

P.O. Box 314, Zanzibar, Tanzania.
☎ +255 24 2330000. 🖷 +255 24 2330000.
E: zanzibarbroadcasting@zbc.co.tz **W:** zbc.co.tz
Webcast: L
L.P: DG: Hassan Abdallah Massawi; Dir (Radio): Rafi Haji Makame.
SW: [DOL] Zanzibar City; Dole: 1 x 50kW.
kHz: *6015, 11735*

Winter Schedule 2020/2021

English	**Days**	**Area**	**kHz**
1800-1810	daily	EAf,ME	11735dol†
Swahili	**Days**	**Area**	**kHz**
0330-0600	daily	EAf	6015dol
1500-1800	daily	EAf,ME	11735dol†
1810-2100	daily	EAf,ME	11735dol†

Key: † Irregular.
Ann: English: "Zanzibar Broadcasting Corporation"; "ZBC".
Notes: Relay of domestic services (see National Radio section).

THAILAND (THA)

RADIO SARANROM (Gov)

443 Sri Ayudhya Road, Bangkok 10400, Thailand.
☎ +66 26435094. 🖷 +66 26435093.
E: radio_saranrom@mfa.go.th; information05@mfa.go.th
W: saranrom.mfa.go.th
Webcast: D
L.P: Dir, Broadcasting Division (Information Dept): Jesda Katavetin.
MW: Uses tx operated by USAGM (USA).
kHz: *1575*

Winter Schedule 2020/2021

English	**Days**	**Area**	**kHz**
1100-1130	m......	SEA	1575bph
Thai	**Days**	**Area**	**kHz**
1030-1100	daily	SEA	1575bph
1100-1130	.twtf..	SEA	1575bph
1200-1230	mtwtf..	SEA	1575bph
1500-1530	daily	SEA	1575bph
2230-2400	mtwt..s	SEA	1575bph

V: QSL-card.
Notes: Service for Thai's living in South East Asia, produced by the Information Department of the Thai Ministry of Foreign Affairs.

RADIO THAILAND WORLD SERVICE (HSK9) (Gov)

Public Relations Department, Royal Thai Government, 236 Vibhavadi Rangsit Road, Ding Daeng, Bangkok 10400, Thailand.
☎ +66 22771814. 🖷 +66 22776139.
E: radiothailand@prd.go.th
W: nbt.prd.go.th; www.facebook.com/RadioThailandWorldService
Webcast: D/L
L.P: Dir: Mrs Kasemsiri Pengpis.
SW: Uses txs operated by USAGM (USA).
FM/DAB: FM: 88.3MHz (Bangkok 10kW)
SAT: Thaicom 5.
kHz: *5875, 7475, 9940, 13750, 17630, 17640*

Winter Schedule 2020/2021

Chinese	**Days**	**Area**	**kHz**
1115-1130	daily	SEA	5875udo
1315-1330	daily	EAs	9940udo
English	**Days**	**Area**	**kHz**
0000-0100	daily	NAm	13750udo
0200-0230	daily	NAm	13750udo
0530-0600	daily	Eu	17640udo
1145-1200	daily	SEA	5875udo
1230-1300	daily	SEA,Pac	9940udo
1400-1430	daily	SEA,Pac	9940udo
1900-2000	daily	Eu	7475udo
2030-2045	daily	Eu	7475udo
German	**Days**	**Area**	**kHz**
2000-2015	daily	Eu	7475udo*
Japanese	**Days**	**Area**	**kHz**
1300-1315	daily	SEA,Pac	9940udo*
Malay	**Days**	**Area**	**kHz**
1200-1215	daily	SEA	9940udo
Thai	**Days**	**Area**	**kHz**
0100-0200	daily	NAm	13750udo
0230-0330	daily	NAm	13750udo
1000-1100	daily	ME	17630udo
1130-1145	daily	SEA	5875udo
1330-1400	daily	EAs	9940udo
1800-1900	daily	Eu	7475udo
2045-2115	daily	Eu	7475udo
Vietnamese	**Days**	**Area**	**kHz**
1100-1115	daily	SEA	5875udo

Key: * May be replaced with English.
Ann: English: "Broadcasting from Bangkok, this is Radio Thailand's World Service".
IS: Gongs and chimes.
V: QSL-card.
Notes: Radio Thailand World Service is the External Sce and is produced by the Thai Government Public Relations Department.

AWR ASIA/PACIFIC (Rlg)

EIS Building B, Unit 1101, 71/15 Soi Pridi Banomyong 37, Sukhumvit 71 Road, Klongton Nua, Vadhana District, Bangkok 10110, Thailand.
☎ +66 23818869.
E: asia@awr.org
L.P: Dir, Asia/Pacific Region: Surachet Insom.
kHz: *1548, 5905, 5955, 6155, 7360, 7410, 9450, 9460, 9470, 9510, 9610, 9645, 9740, 9765, 9785, 9800, 9875, 9930, 11610, 11620, 11690, 11870, 11955, 11980, 11990, 12030, 12040, 12085, 12105, 15210, 15215, 15255, 15330, 15360, 15365, 15430, 15445, 15450, 15480, 15500, 15550, 15610, 15625, 15680, 15705, 17525, 17540, 17650, 17770*

Winter Schedule 2020/2021

Amoy	**Days**	**Area**	**kHz**
0100-0130	mtwt..s	EAs	15625trm‡, 17650trm
1200-1230	mtwt..s	EAs	9610sda, 9800dsb, 12030sda
Assamese	**Days**	**Area**	**kHz**
1330-1400	..w...s	SAs	15550tac
Bengali	**Days**	**Area**	**kHz**
1300-1330	daily	SAs	15255trm
Burmese	**Days**	**Area**	**kHz**
0000-0030	daily	SEA	17650sda
1430-1500	daily	SEA	11620sda
Cantonese	**Days**	**Area**	**kHz**
0130-0200	mtwtf.s	EAs	15625trm‡, 17650trm
1230-1300	mtwt.ss	SEA	9800dsb
1230-1300	mtwt.ss	EAs	9610sda, 12030sda
Chin (Asho)	**Days**	**Area**	**kHz**
1400-1430	daily	SAs	11870sda
2330-2400	daily	SAs	15330sda
Chinese	**Days**	**Area**	**kHz**
0000-0100	daily	EAs	15625sda
0100-0130	....fs.	EAs	15625trm‡, 17650trm
0130-0200	.....s.	EAs	15625trm‡, 17650trm
1000-1100	daily	EAs	11690sda, 15450sda
1100-1200	daily	EAs	9610sda, 11690sda, 15210sda
1200-1230	....fs.	EAs	9610sda, 9800dsb, 12030sda
1230-1300	....f..	EAs	9610sda, 9800dsb, 12030sda
1300-1330	mtwtf..	EAs	9470sda
1330-1400	daily	EAs	9930trm‡
1400-1500	daily	EAs	9450trm‡, 15705trm
2100-2200	daily	EAs	9785trm
2200-2300	daily	EAs	11870sda, 11980sda
2300-2400	daily	EAs	15215sda, 15625sda
English	**Days**	**Area**	**kHz**
1530-1600	daily	SAs	12040trm‡

English	Days	Area	kHz
2200-2230	.t.t..s	SEA	11990sda
Hindi	**Days**	**Area**	**kHz**
1500-1600	daily	SAs	15215trm‡
1530-1600	daily	SAs	1548trm, 7410tac
Hmong	**Days**	**Area**	**kHz**
1330-1400	...tf..	SEA	15550tac
Ilocano	**Days**	**Area**	**kHz**
1030-1100	....f.s	SEA	17540sda
Indonesian	**Days**	**Area**	**kHz**
1100-1130	daily	SEA	15500sda
1330-1400	mt...s.	SEA	15550tac
2230-2300	daily	SEA	11955sda
Javanese	**Days**	**Area**	**kHz**
1130-1200	m.w.f..	SEA	15500sda
2230-2300	daily	SEA	11990sda
Kachin	**Days**	**Area**	**kHz**
1300-1330	daily	SEA	12105sda
Kannada	**Days**	**Area**	**kHz**
1500-1530	daily	SAs	9765erv
Karen	**Days**	**Area**	**kHz**
0030-0100	daily	SEA	17525sda
1430-1500	daily	SEA	11955sda, 12085sda
Khasi	**Days**	**Area**	**kHz**
1330-1400	daily	SAs	15480sda
Khmer	**Days**	**Area**	**kHz**
1300-1330	daily	SEA	15550trm‡
2300-2330	daily	SEA	15365sda
Kokborok	**Days**	**Area**	**kHz**
1330-1400	daily	SAs	15255sda
Korean	**Days**	**Area**	**kHz**
1200-1300	daily	EAs	9460tac, 9875sda
1300-1400	daily	EAs	9740sda
1400-1500	daily	EAs	9645sda
2100-2200	daily	EAs	5955sda
Lao	**Days**	**Area**	**kHz**
1330-1400	...t.s.	SEA	12085sda
2330-2400	...t.s.	SEA	15365sda
Malayalam	**Days**	**Area**	**kHz**
1530-1600	daily	SEA	15680mdc
Meitei	**Days**	**Area**	**kHz**
1230-1300	daily	SAs	15430trm
Mizo	**Days**	**Area**	**kHz**
1500-1530	daily	SAs	12085sda
Mon	**Days**	**Area**	**kHz**
1200-1230	daily	SEA	15610trm
Mongolian	**Days**	**Area**	**kHz**
1030-1100	daily	EAs	15500sda‡
Nepali	**Days**	**Area**	**kHz**
1300-1330	daily	SAs	15610sda
1500-1530	daily	SAs	9740trm
Ngaju	**Days**	**Area**	**kHz**
2200-2230	daily	SEA	11955sda
Oriya	**Days**	**Area**	**kHz**
1530-1600	daily	EAs	9740trm
Russian	**Days**	**Area**	**kHz**
1100-1130	daily	RUS	5905sda
2000-2030	daily	RUS	7360sda
Shan	**Days**	**Area**	**kHz**
1130-1200	daily	SEA	15610trm
Sindhi	**Days**	**Area**	**kHz**
1630-1700	.t.t.ss	SAs	15360trm
Sinhala	**Days**	**Area**	**kHz**
1400-1430	daily	SEA	15255mdc
Sundanese	**Days**	**Area**	**kHz**
1130-1200	.t.t.ss	SEA	15500sda
2200-2230	m.w.fs.	SEA	11990sda
Tagalog	**Days**	**Area**	**kHz**
1030-1100	mtwt.s.	SEA	17540sda
Tamil	**Days**	**Area**	**kHz**
1500-1530	daily	SEA	1548trm, 7410tac
Telugu	**Days**	**Area**	**kHz**
1430-1500	daily	SAs	1548trm
Thai	**Days**	**Area**	**kHz**
0000-0030	daily	SEA	9510trm
1330-1400	daily	SEA	15450trm‡
2330-2400	mtw.f.s	SEA	15365sda
Thai (Isan)	**Days**	**Area**	**kHz**
1330-1400	mtw.f.s	SEA	12085sda
Tibetan	**Days**	**Area**	**kHz**
1530-1600	...tf..	EAs	6155dsb
Uighur	**Days**	**Area**	**kHz**
1300-1330	.....ss	EAs	9470sda
Vietnamese	**Days**	**Area**	**kHz**
0100-0200	.....s.	SEA	15445tsh
1300-1400	daily	SEA	17770mdc
2200-2300	daily	SEA	11610sda
2300-2330	daily	SEA	15330sda

Key: ‡ Inactive at time of publication.
V: QSL-card.
Notes: Regional branch of Adventist Broadcasting Service, Inc (USA), see USA for corporate details. In 2014, this branch was moved to Thailand after having been based in Indonesia in earlier years. The individual AWR prgrs are produced by a large number of partner studios within the region.

USAGM THAILAND TRANSMITTING STATION

P.O. Box 99, Amphur Muang, Udon Thani 41000, Thailand.
Bangkok MW Transmitter Plant: Rangsit-Bangpoon Road, Bangkok, Thailand.
L.P: Acting SM: William Martin.
MW: [BPH] Bangkok, Rasom: 1575kHz 1000kW.
SW: [UDO] Udon Thani, Ban Dung: 7 x 500kW.
V: QSL-card. (Email to manager_thailand@tha.usagm.gov)

TURKEY (TUR)

VOICE OF TURKEY (VOT) (Pub)

P.O. Box 333, Yenisehir, Ankara 06443, Turkey; TRT Sitesi, A Blok No: 427, Ankara 06109, Turkey.
☎ +90 312 4909809. 🖷 +90 312 4909845.
E: tsrturkce@trt.net.tr (Turkish); englishdesk@trt.net.tr (English)
W: trtvotworld.com; www.turkiyeninsesiradyosu.com
Webcast: D/L/P
☎ +90 312 4633372. (English Desk)
L.P: Head (TRT External Services Department): Süleyman Erdal.
SW: [EMR] Emirler: 5 x 500kW.
FM/DAB: FM: TRT World: 94.1MHz (Izmir), 105.6MHz (Ankara), 106.8MHz (Istanbul); TRT Arabi TV audio: 91.6MHz (Istanbul).
SAT: Astra 1N, Eutelsat Hot Bird 13D, Galaxy 19, Optus D2, Türksat 3A/4A.
kHz: *5945, 5960, 5965, 5970, 5980, 5985, 6000, 6050, 6070, 6120, 6125, 6185, 7240, 7245, 7265, 7280, 9410, 9495, 9505, 9595, 9610, 9620, 9625, 9660, 9700, 9840, 11660, 11710, 11795, 11815, 11925, 11955, 11965, 12035, 13590, 13655, 13685, 15235, 15270, 15350, 15360, 15390, 15480, 17530, 17720*

Winter Schedule 2020/2021

Arabic	Days	Area	kHz
1000-1100	daily	ME,NAf	11955emr
1500-1600	daily	ME	5985emr
1500-1600	daily	NAf	17720emr
Azeri	**Days**	**Area**	**kHz**
0800-0900	daily	ME	11710emr
1630-1730	daily	ME	5965emr
Bulgarian	**Days**	**Area**	**kHz**
1200-1230	daily	Eu	7245emr
Chinese	**Days**	**Area**	**kHz**
1200-1300	daily	EAs	13590emr
Dari	**Days**	**Area**	**kHz**
1600-1630	daily	WAs	9595emr
English	**Days**	**Area**	**kHz**
0400-0500	daily	Eu,NAm	6125emr

English	Days	Area	kHz
0400-0500	daily	ME	7240emr
1330-1430	daily	Eu	12035emr
1730-1830	daily	CAs,SAs	9660emr
1930-2030	daily	Eu	6050emr
2130-2230	daily	SEA,Pac	9610emr
2300-2400	daily	Eu,NAm	5960emr
Farsi	**Days**	**Area**	**kHz**
0930-1100	daily	ME	11795emr
1600-1700	daily	ME	6070emr
French	**Days**	**Area**	**kHz**
1830-1930	daily	CAf	9620emr
2030-2130	daily	Eu	5970emr
2030-2130	daily	NAf,WAf	9625emr
Georgian	**Days**	**Area**	**kHz**
1100-1200	daily	Cau	9840emr
German	**Days**	**Area**	**kHz**
1230-1330	daily	Eu	15270emr
1830-1930	daily	Eu	5945emr
Hausa	**Days**	**Area**	**kHz**
0600-0700	daily	WAf	15235emr
Italian	**Days**	**Area**	**kHz**
1500-1530	daily	Eu	6185emr
Kazakh	**Days**	**Area**	**kHz**
1430-1500	daily	CAs	9505emr
Malay	**Days**	**Area**	**kHz**
0500-0600	daily	SEA	17530emr
Pashto	**Days**	**Area**	**kHz**
1630-1700	daily	WAs	9595emr
Russian	**Days**	**Area**	**kHz**
1400-1500	daily	CAs,Eu	9410emr
Spanish	**Days**	**Area**	**kHz**
0200-0300	daily	CAm,Eu	7265emr
0200-0300	daily	SAm,Eu	7280emr
1730-1830	daily	Eu	9495emr
Swahili	**Days**	**Area**	**kHz**
0700-0800	daily	CAf	15235emr
Tatar	**Days**	**Area**	**kHz**
1100-1130	daily	Eu,CAs	15360emr
Turkish	**Days**	**Area**	**kHz**
0100-0300	daily	CAs	6000emr
0400-0700	daily	Eu	9700emr
0500-0700	daily	ME	11660emr
0700-1000	daily	ME	11925emr
0700-1300	daily	ME	15480emr
0700-1400	daily	Eu	15350emr
1400-1700	daily	Eu	11815emr
1700-2200	daily	Eu	5980emr
1700-2200	daily	ME	6120emr
Turkmen	**Days**	**Area**	**kHz**
1300-1330	daily	CAs	11965emr
Urdu	**Days**	**Area**	**kHz**
1300-1400	daily	SAs	15390emr
Uyghur	**Days**	**Area**	**kHz**
0300-0400	daily	CAs	7240emr
1330-1430	daily	CAs	13685emr
Uzbek	**Days**	**Area**	**kHz**
1130-1200	daily	CAs	13655emr
1700-1730	daily	CAs	9595emr

Ann: English: "This is the Voice of Turkey's English transmission"; German: "Hier ist der Kurzwellensender Die Stimme der Türkei"; Spanish: "Esta es La Voz de Turquia"; Turkish: "Burasi Türkiye'nin Sesi Radyosu".
V: QSL-card.
Notes: The Voice of Turkey is the External Sce of the public service Turkish Radio-TV Corporation, TRT (Türkiye Radyo Televizyon Kurumu).

UKRAINE (UKR)

RADIO UKRAINE INTERNATIONAL (RUI) (Pub)

✉ vul. Kreshchatyk 26, 01001 Kyiv, Ukraine.
☎ +380 44 2791757.
E: inoradio@nrcu.gov.ua **W:** nrcu.gov.ua
Webcast: L
L.P: Dir: Zhanna Mishcherska.
SAT: Amos 3.
kHz: *6005*

Winter Schedule 2020/2021

German	Days	Area	kHz
0900-1000	daily	CEu	6005kll

V: QSL-card.
Notes: Produced by the National Public Broadcasting Company of Ukraine. The relay of the German prgr via a SW 1kW tx at Kall (Germany) is an independent, personal initiative of the operator of the German relay platform "Shortwaveservice"; a project that is primarily targeting SWLs/DXers in Europe.

UNITED ARAB EMIRATES (UAE)

ABU DHABI MEDIA (Tx Operator)

✉ 4th St, sector 18, Abu Dhabi, United Arab Emirates.
☎ +971 2 4144000. 🖷 +971 2 4144001.
E: communications@admedia.ae **W:** www.admedia.ae
☎ +971 2 4144999. 🖷 +971 2 4144990.
E: info@livehd.ae **W:** www.livehd.ae
L.P: Chmn/MD: Mohamed Ebraheem Al Mahmod; Dir, Radio: Abdulrahman Awadh Al Harti.
MW: [DHA] Dhabbaya: 1170kHz 800kW ‡
SW: [DHA] Dhabbaya: 4 x 500kW.
Notes: Abu Dhabi Media is a state media company and transmitter operator.

UNITED KINGDOM (G)

BBC WORLD SERVICE (Pub)

✉ Broadcasting House, Portland Place, London W1A 1AA, United Kingdom.
☎ +44 20 72403456. 🖷 +44 20 75571258.
E: worldservice.letters@bbc.co.uk **W:** www.bbc.co.uk/worldserviceradio (English); www.bbc.co.uk/ws/languages (all languages)
Webcast: L/P (P: www.bbc.co.uk/podcasts/worldserviceradio)
L.P: Dir (World Service Group): Jamie Angus.
MW/SW: Via BBC-owned overseas relay stations (operated by Encompass Digital Media Services) & third party foreign relays. Also domestically via txs of the BBC R. 4 network (operated by Arqiva).
FM/DAB: FM: See National Radio section (0100-0530 winter / 0000-0430 summer via BBC R. 4 txs).
SAT: Al Yah 1, AsiaSat 5, Astra 1N, Badr 4, Eutelsat 7A/36B/Hot Bird 13B, Intelsat 19/10-02/19/34, Koreasat 6, Nilesat 201, Optus 10, SES 7, Superbird C2, Thaicom 5, XM3/4.
kHz: *198, 639, 702, 720, 1251, 1413, 3915, 3955, 5845, 5875, 5890, 5895, 5930, 5960, 5970, 5975, 5995, 6005, 6010, 6070, 6080, 6090, 6095, 6135, 6150, 6170, 6180, 6195, 7220, 7265, 7285, 7300, 7305, 7325, 7335, 7355, 7445, 7465, 7485, 9410, 9510, 9545, 9560, 9580, 9585, 9600, 9750, 9820, 9900, 9915, 11660, 11750, 11810, 11825, 11850, 11905, 11945, 11995, 12015, 12065, 12095, 13680, 13750, 13790, 13860, 15310, 15315, 15400, 15420, 15490, 15620, 17640, 17745, 17765, 17780, 17830, 21630*

Winter Schedule 2020/2021

Amharic	Days	Area	kHz
1730-1750	mtwtf..	EAf	7335smg, 9600sla, 12095dha
1830-1850	mtwtf..	EAf	7335smg, 9600sla
Arabic	**Days**	**Area**	**kHz**
0200-0600	daily	ME	639zak, 720zak
0300-0400	daily	NAf	5995dha
0300-0500	daily	NAf	5875wof
0500-0600	daily	NAf	12015dha
0600-0700	daily	NAf	15315sla
1500-2100	daily	ME	702sla
1700-1900	daily	NAf	9585dha
1700-2100	daily	ME	720zak

Arabic	Days	Area	kHz
1800-2100	daily	ME	639zak
1900-2000	daily	NAf	6150dha
2000-2100	daily	NAf	6150sla
Bengali	**Days**	**Area**	**kHz**
1330-1400	daily	SAs	9510sng, 9900trm, 11750sla
1630-1700	daily	SAs	7265sla, 9585sng
Burmese	**Days**	**Area**	**kHz**
0000-0030	daily	SEA	7465sng, 9560sng, 15310pht
1330-1400	daily	SEA	7485sng, 9560pht, 11995sng
Dari	**Days**	**Area**	**kHz**
0030-0100	daily	WAs	1413sla, 5930mos, 7445wof
0130-0200	daily	WAs	5930mos, 6195sla, 7445wof
0230-0300	daily	WAs	5875erv, 6195sla, 7445wof
0830-0900	daily	WAs	12065sla, 15310sla
0930-1000	daily	WAs	12065sla, 15310sla
1030-1100	daily	WAs	12065sla, 15310sla
1400-1500	daily	WAs	5975sng, 7465sla
1600-1630	daily	WAs	5975sla, 7465sng
1630-1700	.....ss	WAs	5975sla, 7465sng
1700-1800	daily	WAs	5875erv, 6070sla, 7465sng
English	**Days**	**Area**	**kHz**
0000-0100	daily	SAs	5875erv, 5970sla
0100-0200	daily	SAs	5970erv, 12095sng
0100-0230	daily	SAs	1413sla
0100-0520	daily	Eu	198dro
0300-0400	daily	ME	6195sla
0300-0500	daily	ME	7285sla
0400-0500	daily	EAf	9915mdc
0400-0500	daily	ME	12095sla
0500-0600	daily	CAf	6195asc
0500-0600	daily	EAf	13860dha
0500-0600	daily	SAf	12095mdc
0500-0600	daily	WAf	5875smg
0500-0700	daily	WAf	6005asc
0600-0700	daily	WAf	7325wof
0600-0700	daily	SAf	9410sao
0600-0700	daily	CAf	7445asc, 12095smg
0600-0700	daily	Eu	3955wof+
0600-0800	daily	EAf	13680mdc
0600-0800	daily	SAf	15400mdc
0700-0800	daily	SAf	12095sao
0700-0800	daily	WAf	7325sao, 9915asc
0700-0800	daily	CAf	9410sao, 15490smg
0800-0900	daily	SAs	15620sng+
1000-1030	.twtfs.	CAs	1251dsb
1000-1200	daily	EAs,SEA	9580sng
1000-1200	daily	SEA	6195sng, 11945sng
1200-1300	daily	EAs	11850sng
1200-1300	daily	SAs	12065sla, 15310sla
1300-1330	daily	CAs	1251dsb
1300-1400	daily	SAs	9410sla, 12065sng
1300-1800	daily	SAs	1413sla
1500-1600	daily	EAf	9410sla
1500-1900	daily	ME	7485sng
1600-1700	daily	SAf	12095dha, 17640asc
1600-1800	daily	CAf	17830asc
1600-2000	daily	EAf	7445mdc
1700-1800	daily	WAf	17780asc
1700-1800	daily	CAs	1251dsb
1700-1900	daily	ME	6195sla
1700-1900	daily	WAf	15400asc
1700-2000	daily	SAf	7265mdc
1800-1900	daily	CAf	11810asc
English	**Days**	**Area**	**kHz**
1800-1900	daily	WAf	9915wof
1800-2000	daily	EAf	9410dha
1900-2000	daily	SAf	6195sao
1900-2100	daily	CAf	11810wof
1900-2100	daily	ME	1413sla
1900-2100	daily	WAf	12095asc
2100-2200	mtwtf..	CAf	11810asc
2100-2200	mtwtf..	WAf	12095asc
2200-2300	daily	EAs	5960sla
2200-2300	daily	SEA	6150pht, 7300sla
2200-2400	daily	SEA	3915sng, 5890sng
2200-2400	daily	EAs,SEA	6195sng
2300-2400	daily	SEA	11825pht
Farsi	**Days**	**Area**	**kHz**
0330-0430	daily	CAs	1251dsb
0330-0430	daily	ME	1413sla, 6010tac, 6095sla, 7485kch
0430-0530	daily	ME	9410dha, 11905sla, 13750tac
1600-1700	daily	ME	5875sof, 6195sla
1830-1930	daily	ME	6170sof
French	**Days**	**Area**	**kHz**
0600-0630	daily	NAf	6135smg, 7265wof
0600-0630	daily	WAf	5875asc
0600-0630	daily	CAf	7305asc
0700-0730	daily	WAf	7305asc
0700-0730	daily	CAf	17830dha
1200-1230	daily	CAf	17765asc
1200-1230	daily	NAf	15490wof
1200-1230	daily	WAf	17640asc
1800-1830	daily	SAf	9750smg
1800-1830	daily	WAf	7220smg, 15490asc
1800-1830	daily	CAf	6180sof
1800-1830	daily	NAf	6080wof
Hausa	**Days**	**Area**	**kHz**
0530-0600	daily	WAf	5975wof, 6135asc, 7305asc
0630-0700	daily	WAf	5975asc, 7305asc, 17830dha
1400-1430	mtwtf..	WAf	15400asc, 17780asc, 21630dha
1930-2000	daily	WAf	9545wof, 11660asc, 15490asc
2000-2030	....f..	WAf	9545wof, 11660asc, 15490asc
Kinyarwanda/ Kirundi	**Days**	**Area**	**kHz**
0500-0600	.....s.	EAf	13790dha, 15490erv
0530-0600	......s	EAf	13790dha, 15490erv
1630-1700	mtwtf..	EAf	9820dha, 15420mdc
Korean	**Days**	**Area**	**kHz**
1530-1830	daily	EAs	5845pht, 5895dsb, 7355sng
Oromo	**Days**	**Area**	**kHz**
1750-1810	mtwtf..	EAf	7335smg, 9600sla, 12095dha
1850-1910	mtwtf..	EAf	7335smg, 9600sla
Pashto	**Days**	**Area**	**kHz**
0100-0130	daily	WAs	5930mos, 6195sla, 7445wof
0200-0230	daily	WAs	5875erv, 6195sla, 7445wof
0300-0330	daily	WAs	7300dha, 7445erv, 9410dha
0900-0930	daily	WAs	12065sla, 15310sla
1000-1030	m.....s	CAs	1251dsb
1000-1030	daily	WAs	12065sla, 15310sla
1100-1130	daily	WAs	12065sla, 15310sla
1500-1600	daily	WAs	5975sla, 7465sng
1630-1700	mtwtf..	WAs	5975sla, 7465sng

Pashto	Days	Area	kHz
1800-1900	daily	WAs	1413sla, 5875erv, 6090sla, 7465sng
1830-1900	daily	CAs	1251dsb
Somali	**Days**	**Area**	**kHz**
0400-0430	daily	EAf	11995mdc, 13790dha
1100-1130	daily	EAf	15420dha, 17745mdc
1400-1500	daily	EAf	12095mdc, 15420sof, 17745dha
Tajik	**Days**	**Area**	**kHz**
0200-0230	daily	CAs	1251dsb
0930-1000	daily	CAs	1251dsb
1400-1500	daily	CAs	1251dsb
1800-1830	daily	CAs	1251dsb
Tigrinya	**Days**	**Area**	**kHz**
1810-1830	mtwtf..	EAf	7335smg, 9600sla, 12095dha
1910-1930	mtwtf..	EAf	7335smg, 9600sla
Uzbek	**Days**	**Area**	**kHz**
1330-1400	daily	CAs	1251dsb

Key: + DRM.
Ann: English: "BBC World Service"; "This is the BBC".
V: Does not verify reception reports.
Notes: BBC World Service is produced by the Global News division of the British Broadcasting Corp. The English service is available 24/7 on local FM/MW relays in many countries, as well as part-time relayed on national domestic channels, esp. in countries of the British Commonwealth. Many language services are relayed by local affiliates. Transmissions in some Asian languages are jammed.

AWR AFRICA (Rlg)

1 Milbanke Court, Milbanke Way, Bracknell, Berkshire RG12 1RP, United Kingdom.
☎ +44 1344 401401. Fax +44 1344 401419.
E: africa@awr.org
L.P: Dir, Africa Region: Ray Allen.
kHz: *5950, 6055, 6065, 6120, 6155, 7225, 7270, 7275, 7325, 7350, 9515, 9580, 9630, 9780, 9800, 9850, 9860, 11640, 11720, 11800, 11870, 11880, 11955, 11980, 11985, 12040, 12065, 15145, 15410, 15490, 17570, 17730, 17790*

Winter Schedule 2020/2021

Amharic	Days	Area	kHz
0400-0430	daily	EAf	12065trm‡
1630-1700	daily	EAf	12040nau
Arabic	**Days**	**Area**	**kHz**
0500-0600	daily	NAf,ME	17790trm
0600-0700	daily	NAf	11880mos
0700-0800	daily	NAf	11980nau
1800-1900	daily	EAf	11955mos
1900-2000	daily	NAf	6120nau
1900-2000	daily	NAf,ME	11985mdc
Dyula	**Days**	**Area**	**kHz**
2000-2030	daily	WAf	7270mos
English	**Days**	**Area**	**kHz**
1530-1600	mtw..ss	SAs	6155dsb
1600-1630	daily	ME	9580erv, 17730mdc
French	**Days**	**Area**	**kHz**
0430-0500	daily	WAf	5950nau
0600-0630	daily	NAf	9860nau, 11640nau
0700-0730	daily	NAf	11880mos
0800-0830	daily	NAf	15145mos
1930-2000	daily	CAf	9780mos
2000-2030	daily	WAf	7225nau, 9515mdc
2030-2100	daily	WAf	7270mos
Hausa	**Days**	**Area**	**kHz**
0500-0530	daily	WAf	9630mos
1900-1930	daily	WAf	7275mos
Ibo	**Days**	**Area**	**kHz**
1930-2000	daily	WAf	9850iss
Maasai	**Days**	**Area**	**kHz**
1730-1800	daily	EAf	11955mos
Malagasy	**Days**	**Area**	**kHz**
0300-0400	daily	SAf	6065mdc
1400-1500	daily	SAf	6055mdc
Mossi	**Days**	**Area**	**kHz**
2000-2030	daily	WAf	17570mdc
Nigerian Pidgin	**Days**	**Area**	**kHz**
2100-2130	daily	WAf	11985mdc
Oromo	**Days**	**Area**	**kHz**
0300-0330	daily	EAf	15410trm
1730-1800	daily	EAf	11870nau
Somali	**Days**	**Area**	**kHz**
1630-1700	daily	EAf	15490nau
Swahili	**Days**	**Area**	**kHz**
1700-1730	daily	EAf	11720mdc, 11800mos
Tachelhit	**Days**	**Area**	**kHz**
0830-0900	daily	NAf	15145nau
1930-2000	daily	NAf	7325nau
Tigrinya	**Days**	**Area**	**kHz**
0300-0330	daily	EAf	7350nau
1630-1700	daily	EAf	11955nau
Twi	**Days**	**Area**	**kHz**
2130-2200	daily	WAf	9800nau
Yoruba	**Days**	**Area**	**kHz**
2030-2100	daily	WAf	11985mdc

Key: ‡ Inactive at time of publication.
V: QSL-card.
Notes: Regional branch of Adventist Broadcasting Service, Inc (USA), covering Africa. The individual AWR prgrs are produced by a large number of partner studios within the region. Earlier, this branch also managed transmissions to Europe and prgrs in Persian, Punjabi, Turkish, Urdu, they are now administered by the HQ in the USA (see USA entry for schedules and corporate details).

ENCORE (CLASSICAL MUSIC ON RADIO TUMBRIL)

Based in Scotland, United Kingdom.
E: encoretumbril@gmail.com **W:** www.tumbril.co.uk
L.P: Producer/Host: Brice Avery.
kHz: *3955, 5010, 5800, 5850, 6070, 9455, 9670, 15770*

Winter Schedule 2020/2021

English	Days	Area	kHz
0100-0200	......s	NAm	5010rmi, 5850rmi
0300-0400	m......	NAm	9455rmi
0300-0400	...t...	SAm,Car	5800rmi
1100-1200	.....s.	Eu	6070rob, 9670rob
1300-1400	.t.t...	Eu	15770rmi
1700-1800	......s	Eu	9670rob
2000-2100	....f..	Eu	6070rob
2200-2300	......s	Eu	3955rob

V: eQSL-card.
Notes: On SW since March 2019. "Encore" (a.k.a "Classical Music on Radio Tumbril") is a weekly classical music show produced by Brice Avery.

ENCOMPASS DIGITAL MEDIA SERVICES LTD (Tx Operator)

610 Chiswick High Road, London W4 5RU, United Kingdom.
☎ +44 20 71316131.
E: via website. **W:** www.encompass.tv
E: jodi.joshua@encompass.co.ac (Jodi Joshua/BBC Relay Stations)
W: World Radio Network (WRN): www.encompass.tv/world-radio-network
L.P: CEO: Bill Tillson.
SW: [WOF] Woofferton: 6 x 250, 4 x 300kW.
V: Does not verify. See Encompass Digital Media Services operated BBC Relay Stations (Ascension, Cyprus, Oman and Singapore) for direct QSLs.
Notes: After acquiring Babcock Media Services in September 2018, Encompass Digital Media Services Ltd is the new owner and operator of the shortwave transmitting centre Wooferton in the UK; it also operates the BBC overseas relay stations, under a management contract.

UNITED STATES OF AMERICA (USA)

U.S. AGENCY FOR GLOBAL MEDIA (USAGM) (Gov)

330 Independence Avenue SW, Washington, D.C 20237, USA.
☎ +1 202 2034000.
E: publicaffairs@usagm.gov **W:** usagm.gov
L.P: Chmn: Kenneth Weinstein; CEO: Michael Pack; Dir (Office of Technology, Services & Innovation - TSI): Terry Balazs.
V: QSL-card (for all USAGM funded services; Email rpt to qsl@usagm.gov)
Notes: USAGM (until August 2018: BBG - Broadcasting Board of Governors) is the independent, autonomous agency responsible for all U.S. government and government sponsored, non-military, international broadcasting. USAGM funded services are produced by the following entities: Voice of America (VOA), Office of Cuba Broadcasting (OCB), Middle East Broadcasting Networks Inc (MBN), R. Free Asia Inc (RFA) and RFE/RL Inc (see separate entries for schedules). The USAGM Office of Technology, Services & Innovation (TSI) manages, operates, and maintains a network of overseas SW and MW transmitting stations in Botswana, Germany, Kuwait, Philippines, São Tomé & Príncipe and Thailand. TIS also manages USAGM supplied SW/MW transmitting equipment installed at sites operated by foreign partners in Afghanistan (RTA), Djibouti (RTD) and Tajikistan (Teleradiokom). In addition, TSI oversees the activities of the USAGM owned domestic "Robert E. Kamosa" SW transmitting station in the Northern Mariana Islands which is currently operated by Rome Research Corporation.

RADIO AZADI (Gov)

1201 Connecticut Avenue NW, Washington, DC 20036, USA.
☎ +1 202 4576900. 🖷 +1 202 4576992.
E: azadiweb@rferl.org **W:** www.azadiradio.org; pa.azadiradio.org (Pashto); da.azadiradio.org (Dari)
Webcast: L
Vinohradská 159A, 100 00 Prague 10, Czechia. (Studio)
☎ +420 2 21122370. 🖷 +420 2 21123245.
L.P: Dir: Hashem Mohmand.
MW/SW: Via txs on sites operated by (or on behalf of) USAGM.
FM/DAB: FM: See National Radio section. (Afghanistan)
SAT: Eutelsat Hot Bird 13B.
kHz: *1296, 12070, 12140, 13860, 15640*

Winter Schedule 2020/2021

Dari	Days	Area	kHz
0300-0330	daily	AFG	1296kab, 12140udo, 13860udo
0430-0530	daily	AFG	1296kab, 12070kwt, 12140kwt
0630-0730	daily	AFG	1296kab, 12140kwt, 15640kwt
0830-0930	daily	AFG	1296kab, 12140kwt, 15640kwt
1030-1130	daily	AFG	1296kab, 12140kwt, 15640kwt
1230-1330	daily	AFG	1296kab, 12140kwt, 15640dha
1400-1430	daily	AFG	1296kab, 12140kwt, 15640smg
Pashto	**Days**	**Area**	**kHz**
0230-0300	daily	AFG	1296kab, 12140udo, 13860udo
0330-0430	daily	AFG	1296kab, 12140kwt, 13860kwt
0530-0630	daily	AFG	1296kab, 12070kwt, 12140kwt
0730-0830	daily	AFG	1296kab, 12140kwt, 15640kwt
0930-1030	daily	AFG	1296kab, 12140kwt, 15640kwt
1130-1230	daily	AFG	1296kab, 12140kwt, 15640kwt
1330-1400	daily	AFG	1296kab, 12140kwt, 15640smg

Ann: Dari: "Inja Radyoi Azadi"; Pashto: "Da Azadi Radyo".
V: QSL-card.
Notes: USAGM funded service for listeners in Afghanistan, launched in January 2002 as "R. Free Afghanistan". Produced by RFE/RL, Inc in studios in Prague, Czechia.

RADIO FARDA (Gov)

1201 Connecticut Avenue NW, Washington, D.C. 20036, USA.
☎ +1 202 8287220. 🖷 +1 202 8287235.
E: comment@radiofarda.com; info@radiofarda.com
W: www.radiofarda.com
Webcast: D/L/P
Vinohradská 159A, 100 00 Prague 10, Czechia. (Studio)
☎ +420 2 21124113. 🖷 +420 2 21122622.
L.P: Dir: Armand Mostofi.
SW: Via txs on sites operated by USAGM, plus other relays.
SAT: AsiaSat 7, Eutelsat Hot Bird 13B, NSS 12.
kHz: *5860, 7580, 7585, 9895, 9990, 11695, 12005, 12025, 13765, 15690, 17560*

Winter Schedule 2020/2021

Farsi	Days	Area	kHz
0230-0830	daily	IRN	7585kwt
0400-0530	daily	IRN	13765udo
0400-0730	daily	IRN	12025lam
0430-0730	daily	IRN	9895bib
0530-0730	daily	IRN	13765lam
0630-1800	daily	IRN	12005bib
0730-1330	daily	IRN	17560udo
0730-1530	daily	IRN	13765lam, 15690lam
0830-1230	daily	IRN	9990kwt
1230-1430	daily	IRN	9990udo
1330-1630	daily	IRN	11695lam
1430-0530	daily	IRN	5860kwt
1530-1730	daily	IRN	7580lam
1730-2130	daily	IRN	7580udo

Ann: Farsi: "Radyo Farda".
V: QSL-card.
Notes: USAGM funded service for listeners in Iran, launched in December 2002. Produced by RFE/RL, Inc in studios in Prague, Czechia.

RADIO FREE ASIA (RFA) (Gov)

2025 M Street NW, Suite 300, Washington, DC 20036, USA.
☎ +1 202 5304900. 🖷 +1 202 5307794.
E: contact@rfa.org; info@rfa.org **W:** www.rfa.org
Webcast: D/L/P
L.P: Chmn (RFA): Kenneth Weinstein; Pres (acting): Parameswaran Ponnudurai; Vice Pres, Communications & External Relations: Rohlt Mahajan; Dir, Programme & Ops Support: A.J. Janitschek.
MW/SW: Via txs on sites operated by USAGM, plus other relays.
SAT: AsiaSat 7, Eutelsat Hot Bird 13B, NSS 12, Telstar 18 Vantage.
kHz: *1188, 1557, 1566, 5890, 5970, 7415, 7420, 7470, 7480, 7510, 7520, 7540, 7545, 7565, 7580, 7665, 9315, 9350, 9380, 9390, 9410, 9450, 9455, 9510, 9535, 9670, 9690, 9700, 9720, 9790, 9860, 9905, 9910, 9940, 9985, 11520, 11530, 11540, 11550, 11590, 11725, 11750, 11765, 11775, 11780, 11795, 11800, 11805, 11850, 11855, 11885, 11890, 11895, 11935, 11945, 11950, 11980, 12010, 12050, 12055, 12065, 12125, 13650, 13685, 13740, 13795, 13830, 15110, 15155, 15255, 15340, 15665, 15745, 17580, 17660, 17675, 17730, 17760, 17815, 17820, 17830, 17840, 21480, 21700*

Winter Schedule 2020/2021

Burmese	Days	Area	kHz
0030-0130	daily	BRM	7510dsb, 7540dsb, 9510tin
1230-1330	daily	BRM	9350dsb, 11795sai, 15110kwt
1330-1400	daily	BRM	13740tin
1330-1430	daily	BRM	9380dsb, 11795kwt, 12055tin
Cantonese	**Days**	**Area**	**kHz**
1400-1500	daily	CHN	9390tin
Chinese	**Days**	**Area**	**kHz**
0300-0400	daily	CHN	11980kwt
0300-0700	daily	CHN	15340sai, 17660sai
0400-0600	daily	CHN	11980tin
0500-0600	daily	CHN	21700tin

Chinese	Days	Area	kHz
0600-0700	daily	CHN	11980dsb, 17760tin
1500-1600	.....ss	CHN	11590kwt
1500-1600	.t.t...	CHN	11725kwt
1500-1600	daily	CHN	7420dsb, 9790sai
1500-1600	m.w.f..	CHN	11765kwt
1500-1700	daily	CHN	7665dsb
1600-1700	.....ss	CHN	9905sai
1600-1700	m.w.f..	CHN	9455sai
1600-1700	daily	CHN	7415tin
1600-1700	.t.t...	CHN	9720sai
1600-1900	daily	CHN	11590tin
1700-2000	daily	CHN	9860sai
1900-2100	daily	CHN	5890kwt, 9455sai
1900-2200	daily	CHN	1557kou, 7520kwt
2000-2100	daily	CHN	11520tin
2000-2200	daily	CHN	9410sai
2100-2200	daily	CHN	9455kwt
2300-2400	daily	CHN	9860tin, 11520tin, 11775sai

Khmer	Days	Area	kHz
1230-1300	daily	CBG	9390sai
1230-1330	daily	CBG	15155tin
1300-1330	daily	CBG	9390tin
1430-1500	daily	CBG	9720sai, 11750tin
2230-2330	daily	CBG	9390sai, 11850tin

Korean	Days	Area	kHz
1000-1100	daily	KRE	1566jej
1500-1700	daily	KRE	11520tin
1500-1900	daily	KRE	1188seo, 9985sai, 11550sai
2100-2200	daily	KRE	9940tin, 9985sai, 11945sai

Lao	Days	Area	kHz
0000-0100	daily	LAO	9910kwt
1100-1200	daily	LAO	13685tin

Tibetan	Days	Area	kHz
0100-0200	daily	CHN	9670dsb, 11895dsb, 13795sai
0100-0300	daily	CHN	11950kwt
0200-0300	daily	CHN	9455kwt, 11540tin, 11895sai, 12010tin
0600-0700	daily	CHN	15255dha, 15665dsb, 17675bib, 21480tin
1000-1100	m......	CHN	17830tin
1000-1100	.....s.	CHN	17660tin
1000-1100	....f..	CHN	17840tin
1000-1100	...t...	CHN	17820tin
1000-1100	..w....	CHN	17815tin
1000-1100	.t.....	CHN	17580tin
1000-1100	daily	CHN	9690dsb, 15665tin
1000-1100	......s	CHN	17730tin
1100-1300	daily	CHN	12050kwt, 15745tin
1100-1400	daily	CHN	9315dsb
1200-1230	daily	CHN	11935tin
1200-1400	daily	CHN	13830dsb
1230-1300	daily	CHN	11935sai
1300-1400	daily	CHN	11855sai, 13650kwt, 15745dsb
1500-1600	daily	CHN	9315dsb, 11805kwt, 12125tin
2200-2300	daily	CHN	7480kwt, 9790kwt, 12050tin
2300-2400	daily	CHN	5970dsb, 7470dsb, 7540kwt, 9535kwt

Uyghur	Days	Area	kHz
0100-0200	daily	CHN	7580dsb, 9450sai, 9700kwt, 11530tin, 12065kwt
1600-1700	m......	CHN	11800kwt
1600-1700	.....s.	CHN	11890kwt
1600-1700	....f..	CHN	11885kwt
1600-1700	...t...	CHN	11780kwt
1600-1700	...t..s	CHN	11775kwt
1600-1700	..w....	CHN	11805kwt
1600-1700	daily	CHN	7545dsb, 7565kwt

Ann: At the start of each transmission (language) block, in English: "You are listening to Radio Free Asia", followed by ID in the language of the broadcast.

V: QSL-card. Rpt to 'Reception Reports', Radio Free Asia, 2025 M Street NW, Washington, DC 20036, USA (Email rpt to qsl@rfa.org). Online rpt form available at techweb.rfa.org (registration required).

Notes: USAGM funded service for listeners in East & South East Asia. Initially launched in 1951 by the "Committee for Free Asia". Produced by Radio Free Asia, Inc. Transmissions are jammed in parts of the target area. In case of jamming, some SW freqs may temporarily be shifted up to ± 5 kHz during the broadcast by the tx operator. Burmese and Tibetan language broadcasts include segments in various local languages/dialects.

RADIO FREE EUROPE/RADIO LIBERTY (RFE/RL) (Gov)

✉ 1201 Connecticut Avenue NW, Washington, DC 20036, USA. (Corporate Office)
☎ +1 202 4576900. 🖷 +1 202 4576992.
E: zvanersm@rferl.org **W:** www.rferl.org
Webcast: D/L. Web-only languages (some of which may also be broadcast on local FM affiliate stns): Albanian (Kosovo), Armenian, Azeri, Bosnian, Crimean Tatar, Georgian, Kyrgyz, Hungarian, Macedonian, Montenegrin, Romanian, Serbian, Ukrainian.
✉ Vinohradská 159A, 100 00 Prague 10, Czechia. (HQ/Studios)
☎ +420 2 21121111. 🖷 +420 2 21123013.
E: hokuvovaj@rferl.org **W:** All language services have own dedicated websites, see www.rferl.org for details.
L.P: Pres (acting); Daisy Sindelar; Vice Pres/Editor-in-Chief: Nenad Pejic; Dir of Media & Public Affairs (Prague): Joanna Levison; Deputy Dir of Media & Public Affairs (Washington, DC): Martins Zvaners.
MW/SW: Via txs on sites operated by USAGM, plus other relays.
SAT: AsiaSat 7, Eutelsat Hot Bird 13B, Intelsat 907, NSS 12.
kHz: *1386, 6060, 7475, 9470, 9490, 9940, 11965, 12045, 15490*

Winter Schedule 2020/2021

Russian	Days	Area	kHz
1800-2100	daily	EEu	1386vst
Tajik	**Days**	**Area**	**kHz**
1400-1700	daily	CAs	7475udo, 9470lam
Turkmen	**Days**	**Area**	**kHz**
1400-1600	daily	CAs	6060kwt, 11965bib
Uzbek	**Days**	**Area**	**kHz**
1400-1500	daily	CAs	12045bib, 15490lam
1600-1700	daily	CAs	9490bib, 9940udo

Ann: English: "This is Radio Free Europe, Radio Liberty, Praha"; Radio Liberty: Belarusian: "Havoryc Radyjo Svaboda"; Russian: "Govorit Radio Svoboda"; Tajik: "Injo Radioi Ozodi"; Turkmen: "Gepleýär Azatlyk Radiosy"; Uzbek: "Ozodlik Radiosidan gapiramiz".

V: QSL-card.

Notes: USAGM funded station for listeners in Eastern Europe and the successor states to the former USSR. Radio Free Europe (launched 1949, targeting Eastern Europe incl. Prgrs in Baltic languages) and Radio Liberty (launched 1953, targeting the USSR) merged into a single broadcaster, RFE/RL Inc, in 1976. Since the 1990s, the task of RFE/RL has been expanded to produce services targeting Afghanistan, Iran and Pakistan, see Radio Azadi, Radio Farda, Radio Mashaal.

RADIO MARTÍ (Gov)

✉ 4201 NW 77th Avenue, Miami, FL 33166, USA.
☎ +1 305 4377000. 🖷 +1 305 4377016.
E: editor@martinoticias.com **W:** www.radiotelevisionmarti.com
Webcast: L/P
✉ 3919 VOA Site B Road, Grimesland, NC 27837, USA (SW tx site - "Edward R. Murrow" Transmitting Station); US Government Rd, Marathon, FL 33050, USA (MW tx site)
L.P: Dir (acting) (OCB): Jeffrey Scott Shapiro.
MW: [MTH] Marathon, FL: 1180kHz 100kW.
SW: [GRV] Greenville, NC: 3 x 250, 5 x 500kW.
kHz: *1180, 5980, 6030, 6125, 7345, 7355, 7365, 7375, 7435, 9565, 11860, 11930, 13820*

Winter Schedule 2020/2021

Spanish	Days	Area	kHz
0000-0200	daily	CUB	7365grv
0000-0400	.twtfs.	CUB	6125grv
0000-0400	daily	CUB	6030grv
0000-2400	daily	CUB	1180mth
0200-0400	daily	CUB	7355grv
1000-1200	daily	CUB	6030grv
1000-1300	daily	CUB	5980grv
1000-1400	daily	CUB	7355grv
1200-1400	daily	CUB	7435grv
1300-2200	daily	CUB	11930grv
1400-2000	daily	CUB	13820grv
1400-2200	daily	CUB	11860grv
1700-0200	daily	CUB	7345grv+
2000-2400	daily	CUB	9565grv
2200-2300	daily	CUB	7355grv
2200-2400	daily	CUB	7375grv
2300-0400	daily	CUB	7435grv
2300-2400	mtwtf..	CUB	6125grv

Key: + DRM.

Ann: Spanish: "Aquí Radio Martí, servicio de información para Cuba, transmitiendo desde Miami, Estados Unidos".

V: QSL-card.

Notes: USAGM funded service for listeners in Cuba, launched in May 1985. Produced by Office of Cuba Broadcasting (OCB). Transmissions on SW are jammed. OCB operates the MW transmitting station Marathon, FL and (since 2014) the SW transmitting station Greenville, NC.

RADIO MASHAAL (Gov)

1201 Connecticut Avenue NW, Washington, DC 20036, USA.
☎ +1 202 4576900. 🖷 +1 202 4576992.
W: www.mashaalradio.com
Webcast: L/D/P
Vinohradská 159A, 100 00 Prague 10, Czechia. (Studio)
☎ +420 2 21121111. 🖷 +420 2 21123013.
L.P: Dir: Amanullah Ghilzai.
LW/MW/SW: Via txs on sites operated by (or on behalf of) USAGM, plus other relays.
MW/SW: Via txs provided by USAGM (USA).
FM/DAB: FM: See National Radio section. (Afghanistan)
SAT: Eutelsat Hot Bird 13B.
kHz: *621, 12110, 13500, 15760, 17880*

Winter Schedule 2020/2021

Pashto	Days	Area	kHz
0400-0500	daily	AFG,PAK	13580udo
0400-1300	daily	AFG,PAK	621kho, 12110kwt, 15760udo
0500-1000	daily	AFG,PAK	13580kwt
1000-1300	daily	AFG,PAK	17880bib

Ann: Pashto: "Daa Mashaal Radyo".

V: QSL-card.

Notes: USAGM funded service for Pashto speaking listeners in Pakistan (Khyber Pakhtunkhwa & Pashtun areas of Balochistan) and Pashtun areas of Afghanistan along the border with Pakistan, launched on 15 January 2010. Produced by RFE/RL, Inc in studios in Prague, Czechia.

RADIO SAWA (Gov)

7600 Boston Boulevard, Springfield, VA 22153, USA.
☎ +1 703 6885200. 🖷 +1 703 6885255.
E: comments@alhurra.com **W:** www.radiosawa.com
Webcast: L
L.P: Pres (MBN): Alberto M. Fernandez; Managing Editor: Maha Rabie.
MW: Via txs on transmitting site, operated by USAGM.
FM/DAB: See National Radio section (Iraq, Jordan, Lebanon, Palestinian Territories).
SAT: Badr 4, Eutelsat 7WA/Hot Bird 13B, Intelsat 907, Nilesat 201, NSS 12.
kHz: *1548, 1593*

Winter Schedule 2020/2021

Arabic	Days	Area	kHz
0000-2400	daily	ME	1548kwt, 1593kwt‡

Key: ‡ Inactive at time of publication.

Ann: Arabic: "Radio Sawa".

V: QSL-card.

Notes: USAGM funded service for young Arab listeners in the Middle East, launched on 23 March 2002. Produced by Middle East Broadcasting Networks, Inc (MBN)

VOA ASHNA RADIO (Gov)

330 Independence Avenue SW, Washington, DC 20237, USA.
☎ +1 202 6193136. (Dari); +1 202 3027619. (Pashto) 🖷 +1 202 3825193. (Dari); +1 202 2125260. (Pashto)
E: dari@voanews.com (Dari); pashto@voanews.com (Pashto)
W: www.darivoa.com; www.pashtovoa.com
Webcast: L/P
L.P: Chief (VOA Afghanistan Service): Beth Mendelson.
MW/SW: Via txs on sites operated by (or on behalf of) USAGM.
FM/DAB: FM: See National Radio section. (Afghanistan)
kHz: *1296, 7290, 7495, 9975, 12075, 12140, 13860*

Winter Schedule 2020/2021

Dari	Days	Area	kHz
0100-0130	daily	WAs	1296kab, 7290kwt, 7495udo
0200-0230	daily	WAs	1296kab, 7495kwt, 12140udo
1500-1530	daily	WAs	1296kab, 12075udo, 12140kwt, 13860wof
Dari/Pashto	**Days**	**Area**	**kHz**
1530-1630	daily	WAs	1296kab, 12075udo, 12140kwt, 13860wof
Pashto	**Days**	**Area**	**kHz**
0030-0100	daily	WAs	1296kab, 7290kwt, 7495udo
0130-0200	daily	WAs	1296kab, 7290bib, 7495kwt
1430-1500	daily	WAs	1296kab, 12075kwt, 12140kwt, 13860wof
1630-1730	daily	WAs	1296kab, 9975lam, 12075udo, 12140kwt

Ann: Dari: "Inja VOA Radyoi Ashna"; Pashto: "Da VOA Ashna Radyo".

V: QSL-card.

Notes: USAGM funded service for listeners in Afghanistan, launched in April 2004. Produced in the VOA studios.

VOA DEEWA RADIO (Gov)

330 Independence Avenue SW, Washington, DC 20237, USA.
☎ +1 202 2050403. 🖷 +1 202 3825218.
E: deewaradio@voanews.com **W:** voadeewanews.com
Webcast: L/P
L.P: Managing Editor: Nafees Talkar.
MW/SW: Via txs on sites operated by (or on behalf of) USAGM, plus other relays.
FM/DAB: FM: See National Radio section. (Afghanistan)
SAT: Eutelsat Hot Bird 13B
kHz: *621, 7470, 7495, 7530, 9355, 9370, 9765, 13590*

Winter Schedule 2020/2021

Pashto	Days	Area	kHz
0100-0400	daily	AFG,PAK	621kho, 7470lam, 7530kwt, 9765udo
1300-1400	daily	AFG,PAK	13590dha
1300-1600	daily	AFG,PAK	7495udo
1300-1900	daily	AFG,PAK	621kho, 9355kwt, 9370udo
1400-1500	daily	AFG,PAK	13590kwt
1500-1700	daily	AFG,PAK	13590lam
1600-1900	daily	AFG,PAK	7495bib
1700-1900	daily	AFG,PAK	7530kwt

Ann: Pashto: "Deewa Radio".

V: QSL-card.

Notes: USAGM funded service for Pashto speaking listeners in northwestern Pakistan along the border with Afghanistan, launched on 29 September 2006. Produced in the VOA studios. Some Deewa R. prgrs are also carried as part of VOA's Urdu service feed (see under Voice of America - VOA).

VOA STUDIO 7 (Gov)

✉ Voice of America, Africa Division, 330 Independence Avenue SW, Washington, DC 20237, USA.
☎ +1 202 2059942. (Then select #11) 🖷 +1 202 2034230.
E: studio7@voanews.com **W:** www.voazimbabwe.com
Webcast: D/P
L.P: Dir (Africa Division): Negussie Mengesha.
MW/SW: Via txs on transmitting site operated by USAGM.
kHz: *909, 4930, 6175, 7255, 13860, 15460*

Winter Schedule 2020/2021

English/Ndebele/ Shona	Days	Area	kHz
0400-0500	mtwtf..	ZWE	909bot, 6175bot, 7255sao
1700-1800	daily	ZWE	909bot, 4930bot, 13860sao, 15460sao
1800-1900	mtwtf..	ZWE	909bot, 4930bot, 13860sao, 15460sao

Ann: English: "You're listening to Studio 7 for Zimbabwe, coming to you live from the Voice of America in Washington".
V: QSL-card.
Notes: Service for listeners in Zimbabwe, launched on 7 April 2003. Produced in the VOA studios.

VOICE OF AMERICA (VOA) (Gov)

✉ 330 Independence Avenue SW, Washington, D.C. 20237, USA.
☎ +1 202 2034000.
E: audiencemail@voanews.com
W: www.voanews.com; www.insidevoa.com
Webcast: D/L/P. Web-only audio languages: Creole, Indonesian, Spanish, Thai.
W: All language services have own dedicated websites, see www.voanews.com for details.
L.P: Dir (acting): Elez Biberaj; PD: Kelu Chao.
MW/SW: Via txs provided by USAGM, plus other relays.
SAT: AsiaSat 7, Eutelsat Hot Bird 13B, Intelsat 907, NSS 12, Superbird C2.
kHz: *600, 909, 972, 1188, 1431, 1530, 1566, 1575, 4930, 4960, 5880, 5885, 5890, 5930, 6020, 6040, 6080, 6150, 6170, 6195, 7225, 7275, 7445, 7455, 7460, 7465, 7470, 7475, 7485, 7515, 7525, 7545, 7560, 7580, 9335, 9340, 9355, 9380, 9390, 9485, 9490, 9510, 9550, 9575, 9585, 9605, 9620, 9670, 9750, 9760, 9765, 9775, 9795, 9800, 9825, 9880, 9885, 9975, 9985, 11570, 11610, 11650, 11660, 11670, 11675, 11720, 11760, 11820, 11850, 11870, 11875, 11900, 11905, 11910, 11945, 11965, 11975, 12030, 12040, 12070, 12075, 12080, 12120, 12125, 13580, 13590, 13630, 13740, 13750, 13765, 13830, 13865, 15110, 15120, 15150, 15180, 15260, 15270, 15425, 15450, 15460, 15560, 15580, 15600, 15610, 15620, 15715, 15730, 17585, 17600, 17655, 17680, 17700, 17720, 17850, 17865, 17885, 17895, 21600, 21620, 21760, 21795*

Winter Schedule 2020/2021

Amharic	Days	Area	kHz
1700-1730	mtwtf..	EAf	12040sao
1700-1730	mtwtf..	Af	15580bot
1800-1900	daily	EAf	9485wof, 12040dha, 13765kwt
Bambara	**Days**	**Area**	**kHz**
2130-2200	mtwtf..	WAf	5885kwt, 5930sao, 12075bot, 15120asc
Bengali	**Days**	**Area**	**kHz**
1130-1200	mtwtf..	SEA	12030pht, 12125udo, 15715udo
1300-1330	mtwtf..	SEA	1575bph
1600-1630	daily	SAs	1575bph
Burmese	**Days**	**Area**	**kHz**
0000-0030	daily	BRM	1575bph
0130-0230	daily	BRM	9355udo, 11820pht, 15110pht
1200-1230	daily	BRM	11965pht, 15560pht, 17680pht
1430-1500	daily	BRM	1575bph
1430-1530	daily	BRM	15450pht
1430-1630	daily	BRM	9335pht, 11870pht

Burmese	Days	Area	kHz
1530-1600	daily	BRM	1575bph
2330-0030	daily	BRM	6150udo, 9335pht, 9380pht
Cantonese	**Days**	**Area**	**kHz**
1300-1500	daily	EAs	7545pht
Chinese	**Days**	**Area**	**kHz**
0000-0100	daily	EAs	7560udo, 9880udo, 11945pht, 15425pht
0900-1000	daily	EAs	17720udo
0900-1100	daily	EAs	9795pht, 11650udo, 13740udo
0900-1200	daily	EAs	15150udo
1000-1500	daily	EAs	9825pht
1100-1200	daily	EAs	11660pht, 12080pht
1200-1300	daily	EAs	7515udo, 11660udo, 11900pht
1300-1400	daily	EAs	7470udo, 9585pht
1300-1430	daily	EAs	11660pht
1400-1500	daily	EAs	9605pht, 12120pht
1430-1500	daily	EAs	11660udo
2200-2300	daily	EAs	7445udo, 9620pht
English	**Days**	**Area**	**kHz**
0300-0400	daily	Af	909bot
0300-0430	daily	Af	1530sao
0300-0500	daily	Af	9775bot
0300-0600	daily	Af	4930bot
0300-0700	daily	Af	6080sao
0400-0500	.....ss	Af	909bot
0400-0500	daily	Af	4960sao
0500-0700	daily	Af	909bot, 15580bot
0600-0700	daily	Af	1530sao, 9550sao
1130-1200	.....ss	SEA	12030pht, 12125udo, 15715udo
1300-1330	.....ss	SEA	1575bph
1400-1500	daily	SEA	17885bot
1400-1630	daily	Af	15580bot
1400-1700	daily	Af	4930bot
1500-1600	daily	Af	7455bot, 17895sao
1530-1700	daily	EAf	1431dji
1600-1630	daily	Af	6080sao
1600-1700	daily	Af	909bot, 1530sao
1600-1800	daily	Af	17895bot
1630-1700	.....ss	Af	6080sao, 15580bot
1630-1700	mtwtf..	Af	11850dha*, 13865wof*, 15180sao*
1630-1700	daily	SAs,SEA	1575bph
1700-1730	.....ss	Af	15580bot
1700-1730	daily	Af	11850kwt
1700-1800	daily	Af	6080sao
1730-1800	daily	Af	11850sao
1730-2100	daily	Af	15580bot
1800-1830	daily	EAf	1431dji
1800-1900	.....ss	Af	909bot, 4930bot
1800-1900	daily	Af	11610udo
1900-2000	daily	Af	13590sao
1900-2100	daily	Af	909bot, 4930bot
2000-2100	daily	Af	6195bot
2000-2200	daily	Af	1530sao
2030-2100	daily	EAf	1431dji
2100-2130	.....ss	EAf	1431dji
2100-2200	daily	Af	6195sao, 11720grv
2130-0330	daily	EAf	1431dji
French	**Days**	**Area**	**kHz**
0530-0600	mtwtf..	Af	1530sao
0530-0630	mtwtf..	Af	4960sao, 6020sao, 9885smg, 13830bot
0830-0900	..w..s.	Af	12030sao, 15715smg, 17700bot
1100-1130	.....s.	Af	12030sao, 13750bot, 15715bot, 17850smg
1830-1930	daily	Af	12075smg, 15730bot
1830-2000	daily	Af	1530sao

French	Days	Area	kHz
1830-2030	daily	EAf	1431dji
1900-2000	daily	Af	17700grv
1930-2030	daily	Af	11900sao, 12075bot, 15730grv
2000-2030	daily	Af	9485kwt
2030-2100	......s	Af	11900sao, 11975smg
2030-2100	.....ss	Af	9485kwt, 12075bot
2100-2130	mtwtf..	EAf	1431dji
2100-2130	mtwtf..	Af	5930sao, 9485kwt, 12075bot

Hausa	Days	Area	kHz
0500-0530	daily	WAf	1530sao, 4960sao, 6020sao, 6170asc
0700-0730	daily	WAf	4960sao, 12070smg, 15580bot
1500-1530	daily	WAf	9575sao, 11850sao, 15460bot
1530-1600	mtwtf..	WAf	9575sao, 11850sao, 15460bot
2030-2100	.....s.	WAf	11900sao, 11975smg
2030-2100	mtwtfs.	WAf	4960sao, 6040sao, 9765wof, 11850sao, 13750sao

Khmer	Days	Area	kHz
1330-1430	daily	CBG	1575bph, 9335pht, 11675pht
2200-2230	daily	CBG	1575bph, 5880pht, 7460pht, 9340pht

Kinyarwanda/ Kirundi	Days	Area	kHz
0330-0430	daily	EAf	7275sao, 7460bot, 9885sao
0430-0530	mtwtf..	EAf	7275sao, 7460bot, 9885sao
1400-1500	.....ss	EAf	9885sao, 13630bot, 15460smg
1600-1630	daily	EAf	11850bot, 13630smg, 15460sao
1830-1900	mtwtf..	EAf	11850bot, 13630sao
1930-2000	mtwtf..	EAf	9885bot, 11850sao, 12040kwt

Korean	Days	Area	kHz
1100-1500	daily	EAs	1188seo
1200-1300	daily	EAs	7465pht, 9490pht
1200-1400	daily	EAs	11570pht
1300-1500	daily	EAs	9800pht, 9985sai
1400-1500	daily	EAs	11570sai
1700-1800	daily	EAs	1566jej
1900-2100	daily	EAs	7465pht, 9800pht, 9975udo

Kurdish	Days	Area	kHz
1400-1500	daily	ME	15270bib, 15600wof
1700-1800	daily	ME	7475bib, 9390bib, 9750lam
1900-2000	daily	ME	7225bib, 7485lam, 9750bib

Lao	Days	Area	kHz
1230-1300	daily	LAO	1575bph

Oromo	Days	Area	kHz
1730-1800	mtwtf..	EAf	9485wof, 12040lam, 13765kwt

Portuguese	Days	Area	kHz
1630-1700	....f..	Af	13630bot, 17655sao
1700-1800	daily	Af	1530sao, 13630bot, 17655grv
1800-1830	mtwtf..	Af	13630bot, 17655grv

Somali	Days	Area	kHz
0330-0400	daily	EAf	9510smg, 9825lam, 11875dha
1030-1100	daily	EAf	13580kwt, 15620bot, 17600udo
1300-1400	daily	EAf	15620smg, 17600kwt
1600-1800	daily	EAf	11610wof, 11905lam
1700-1800	daily	EAf	1431dji

Spanish	Days	Area	kHz
0000-0200	.....ss	LAm	600hjh
0000-0300	mtwtf..	LAm	600hjh

Swahili	Days	Area	kHz
1630-1700	daily	EAf	13750kwt, 15260wof, 15460sao

Tibetan	Days	Area	kHz
0000-0030	daily	EAs	5890kwt
0000-0100	daily	EAs	7580kwt, 9670udo
0030-0100	daily	EAs	5890udo
0300-0400	daily	EAs	21600pht, 21795pht
0300-0600	daily	EAs	17865pht
0400-0500	daily	EAs	15610udo, 21620pht
0500-0600	daily	EAs	15560udo, 21760pht
1400-1500	daily	EAs	11760pht, 11910udo, 13830udo, 17585bib
1600-1700	daily	EAs	7525pht, 9760udo, 11670pht

Tigrinya	Days	Area	kHz
1900-1930	mtwtf..	EAf	9485bot, 12040dha, 13765kwt

Urdu	Days	Area	kHz
1400-0200	daily	ME	972dsb

Vietnamese	Days	Area	kHz
2130-2200	daily	SEA	1575bph

Key: * Special service for South Sudan: "South Sudan in Focus".
Ann: English: Before the start of all foreign language programs: "Welcome to the Voice of America in... (language)"; at the end of the transmission period on each frequency before tx s/off: "This program has come to you from the Voice of America, Washington".
V: QSL-card. (Email rpt to: audiencemail@voanews.com)
Notes: Launched in 1942, under the roof of the U.S. Foreign Information Service (FIS). From 1953-1994 financed by the U.S. Information Agency (USIA), 1994-2018 by Broadcasting Board of Governors (BBG), and by U.S. Agency For Global Media (USAGM) since August 2018. Some transmissions in Asian languages are jammed.

ADVENTIST WORLD RADIO (AWR) (Rlg)

12501 Old Columbia Pike, Silver Spring, ML 20904-6600, USA.
☎ +1 301 6806304. +1 301 6806303.
E: info@awr.org **W:** www.awr.org
Webcast: D/L/P
W: eu.awr.org (European services)
L.P: Pres: Duane McKey; Freq Manager: Claudius Dedio.
kHz: *5010, 5950, 5980, 6120, 6185, 9610, 9770, 9830, 11955, 11985, 12015, 12025, 15150, 15360, 15410*

Winter Schedule 2020/2021

Bulgarian	Days	Area	kHz
0400-0430	daily	Eu	5950nau
1600-1630	daily	Eu	9830nau

Dari	Days	Area	kHz
0230-0300	daily	WAs	15410trm

Farsi	Days	Area	kHz
0330-0400	daily	WAs	6120mos
0430-0500	daily	WAs	15410trm
1630-1700	daily	WAs	9770mos

Italian	Days	Area	kHz
1000-1100	......s	Eu	9610nau

Kazakh	Days	Area	kHz
0200-0230	daily	CAs	15410trm

Kyrghyz	Days	Area	kHz
0400-0430	daily	CAs	15410trm

Oriya	Days	Area	kHz
1500-1530	daily	WAs	15150mdc

Pashto	Days	Area	kHz
1630-1700	m.w.f..	WAs	15360trm

Punjabi	Days	Area	kHz
0230-0300	daily	SAs	5980mos
1530-1600	daily	WAs	11955mos

Spanish	Days	Area	kHz
0000-0030	daily	CAm	5010rmi
Turkish	**Days**	**Area**	**kHz**
0400-0430	daily	ME	6185mos
1500-1530	daily	ME	11955mos
Urdu	**Days**	**Area**	**kHz**
0200-0230	daily	SAs	5980mos
1400-1430	daily	SAs	12025mos
1600-1630	daily	SAs	11985trm, 12015mos
Uzbek	**Days**	**Area**	**kHz**
0330-0400	daily	CAs	15410trm

IS: Various arrangements of the melody "Lift Up the Trumpet".
V: QSL-card; eQSL-card (Email rpt to qsl@awr.org for all AWR transmissions)
Notes: AWR the international broadcast ministry of the Seventh-day Adventist Church. Produced by Adventist Broadcasting Service, Inc. which also is the owner of the SW transmitting station KSDA in Guam. The schedule contains transmissions of AWR Americas & AWR Europe which are administered by the U.S. headquarters. For schedules of other regional divisions, see AWR Africa (United Kingdom) and AWR Asia/Pacific (Thailand).

ALAMEDA BIBLE FELLOWSHIP (Rlg)

2203 Central Ave, Alameda, CA 94501, USA.
☎ +1 510 5223990.
E: oneaccordonemouth@gmail.com **W:** searchinghisword.com
Webcast: D (unrelated to radio broadcasts)
kHz: *5010, 5850, 5985, 7245, 7730, 7780, 9955, 13660, 15770*

Winter Schedule 2020/2021

English	Days	Area	kHz
0030-0100	.t.t.s.	LAm	9955rmi
0100-0130	m.w.f..	NAm	5850rmi
0100-0130	m...f..	Car	5010rmi
0830-0900	m....s.	NAm,Pac	7730rmi
0830-0900	m....s.	NAm	5850rmi
1330-1400	m.w.f..	Eu,NAf,ME	15770rmi
1700-1730	m.w.f..	EAf	13660iss
1900-1930	m...f..	NAf,WAf	7245iss
2030-2100	mt..f..	NAm,Eu,ME	7780rmi
Spanish	**Days**	**Area**	**kHz**
0000-0030	.t.t.s.	NAm,Pac	7730rmi
0100-0130	.t.t.s.	NAm	5850rmi
0100-0130	.t....s	Car	5010rmi
0330-0400	.t.t..s	CAm	5985rmi
2230-2300	m.w.f..	LAm	9955rmi

Notes: Bible study prgr produced by Alameda Bible Fellowship.

FAMILY RADIO (Rlg)

1360 South Loop Rd., Ste. 130, Alameda, CA 94502, USA.
☎ +1 800 5431495.
E: info@familyradio.org **W:** www.familyradio.org
Webcast: D/L/P
L.P: Pres: Tom Evans.
kHz: *5010, 5950*

Winter Schedule 2020/2021

Spanish	Days	Area	kHz
0700-0800	daily	NAm	5950rmi
2300-2400	daily	CAm	5010rmi

Ann: English: "You are listening to Family Radio".
V: QSL-card.
Notes: Produced by Family Stations, Inc. Launched in 1959, first SW broadcasts in 1973.

FAR EAST BROADCASTING COMPANY INC (FEBC) (Rlg)

P.O. Box 1, La Mirada, CA 90637-0001, USA; 15700 Imperial Hwy, La Miranda, CA 90638-2500, USA.
☎ +1 562 9474651. 🖷 +1 562 9430160.
E: info@febc.org **W:** www.febc.org; febcintl.org
Webcast: D
L.P: Chmn/CEO: Ed Cannon.
V: QSL-email for transmissions by FEBC branches. Printed QSL-cards are available only directly from the FEBC branches in South Korea and the Philippines.
Notes: Far East Broadcasting Company, Inc (FEBC) is a global evangelical media enterprise. For schedules, see India (FEBA India), Pakistan (FEBA Pakistan), Philipines (FEBC Philippines) and South Korea (FEBC Korea). FEBC owns transmitting stations in several countries, incl. the Philippines and South Korea.

FOLLOW THE BIBLE MINISTRIES (Rlg)

P.O.Box 1332, Alameda, CA 94501, USA.
☎ +1 510 7480504.
E: followthebibleministries@yahoo.com **W:** www.followthebibleministries.com; www.isannihilationtrue.com/ftbm
Webcast: D
3374 Washington Court, Alameda, CA 94501, USA.
L.P: Host: David Hoff.
kHz: *6180, 11660, 12005*

Winter Schedule 2020/2021

Arabic	Days	Area	kHz
1830-1900	......s	NAf,ME	6180wof
English	**Days**	**Area**	**kHz**
1900-1930	......s	WAf	11660asc
1900-1930	......s	SAf	12005asc

V: QSL-email.
Notes: Bible Study prgr produced by the Christian organisation "Follow The Bible Ministries".

KVOH – VOICE OF HOPE (Rlg)

543 Country Club Drive, Simi Valley, CA 93065, USA.
☎ +1 805 3380075. 🖷 +1 805 2736905.
E: mail@voiceofhope.com (general); studio@voiceofhope.com (prgr feedback) **W:** www.voiceofhope.com
Webcast: L
L.P: Pres (SCG): John D. Tayloe; Vice Pres, Ops (SCG): Ray Robinson; CE (KVOH): Jim Shoffner.
SW: [VOH] Rancho Simi, CA: 1 x 50, 1 x 100kW.
kHz: *17775*

Winter Schedule 2020/2021

English	Days	Area	kHz
1600-2100	.....s.	CAm,SAm	17775voh
Spanish	**Days**	**Area**	**kHz**
1500-2200	mtwtf..	CAm,SAm	17775voh

Ann: English: "From Los Angeles to all of the Americas, this is the Voice of Hope".
V: QSL-card. (Email rpt to: reports@voiceofhope.com)
Notes: Owned by the charitable organisation Strategic Communications Group (SCG). Part of the Voice of Hope World Radio Network; sister stations operated by SCG outside of the U.S.: Voice of Hope - Africa (see under Zambia) and Voice of Hope - Middle East (see under Israel). KVOH Initially began broadcasting in November 1986 under the ownership of High Adventures Ministries. The network broadcasts both own and paid religious programming.

LIVING WATER MINISTRY BROADCASTING (Rlg)

308 Shadow Lane, Euless, TX 76039, USA.
☎ +1 817 9836527.
E: bill.byers@yahoo.com **W:** www.lwmintl.org
L.P: Dir (Living Water Ministries International, Inc): Bill Byers.
kHz: *7515*

Winter Schedule 2020/2021

Korean	Days	Area	kHz
1515-1615	..wtf..	EAs	7515twr
1545-1615	.....s.	EAs	7515twr

Ann: Korean: "Saengmyeong-ui Gang Bangsong".
Notes: Produced by Living Water Ministries International, Inc.

PAN AMERICAN BROADCASTING (Rlg)

5424 Sunol Blvd, Ste #10-258, Pleasanton, CA 94566-7705, USA.
☎ +1 925 4629800.
E: info@panambc.com **W:** www.radiopanam.com
Webcast: L
L.P: Pres: Jeff Bernald.
kHz: *5945, 6060, 6120, 11800, 21525*

Winter Schedule 2020/2021

English	Days	Area	kHz
1400-2100	daily	Af	21525rmi*

English	Days	Area	kHz
1430-1500	......s	ME	11800nau
1600-1700	......s	EAf	6120nau**
1630-1730	......s	SAs	6060tac**
1630-1730	......s	EAs	5945tac**
Japanese	**Days**	**Area**	**kHz**
1300-1400	.....s.	EAs	5945tac

Key: * R. Africa Network; ** Tony Alamo Ministry prgrs.
V: QSL-card.
Notes: Pan American Broadcasting, Inc. sells air time for religious paid programming, broadcast via international tx providers, and via Radio Miami International ("Radio Africa Network").

REACH BEYOND (Rlg)

1065 Garden of the Gods Road, Colorado Springs, CO 80907, USA.
☎ +1 719 5909800. 🖷 +1 719 5909801.
E: info@reachbeyond.org **W:** reachbeyond.org
L.P: Pres/CEO: Wayne Pederson; Frequency Mgr: Douglas Weber.
kHz: *7300, 9500*

Winter Schedule 2020/2021

Chechen	Days	Area	kHz
1600-1630	.....s.	RUS	9500nau
Russian	**Days**	**Area**	**kHz**
1530-1600	.....s.	RUS	9500nau*
Tachelhit	**Days**	**Area**	**kHz**
2100-2115	daily	NAf	7300wof

Key: * Produced by Radio Studio "Otkroveniye" (Russia), see also R. HCJB Deutschland (Germany).
V: QSL-card.
Notes: Reach Beyond (previously known as HCJB Global Voice) is the media ministry of World Radio Missionary Fellowship, Inc. See Australia and Germany for shortwave stations run by Reach Beyond partner organisations.

SUPREME MASTER TV (Rlg)

P.O.Box 730247, San Jose, CA 95173-0247, USA
☎ +1 626 4444385. 🖷 +1 626 4444386.
E: peace@suprememastertv.com **W:** suprememastertv.com
Webcast: L
P.O.Box 9, Xihu, Miaoli 36899, Taiwan. (HQ)
W: www.godsdirectcontact.org
kHz: *5800, 5850, 5950, 7570, 7780, 9395, 15770*

Winter Schedule 2020/2021

English	Days	Area	kHz
0000-0100	daily	NAm	5950rmi
0200-0700	daily	NAm	5950rmi
0900-1000	daily	NAm	5850rmi
1000-1100	daily	NAm	5950rmi
1100-1400	daily	NAm	7570rmi
1400-1500	......s	NAm,Eu,ME	7780rmi
1400-2000	daily	Eu,ME,Af	15770rmi
2000-2200	daily	NAm	9395rmi
2100-0100	daily	Car,SAm	5800rmi

Notes: Audio relay of "Supreme Master TV", a spiritual web-TV channel produced by the U.S. branch of the Taiwan-based, worldwide operating "The Supreme Master Ching Hai International Association", led by Vietnamese-born Mrs. Ching Hai.

THE OVERCOMER MINISTRY (Rlg)

P.O.Box 691, Walterboro, SC 29488, USA; 12680 Augusta Hwy, Walterboro, SC 29488, USA.
☎ +1 843 7015053.
E: lastime@overcomerministry.org **W:** www.overcomerministry.org
Webcast: L
L.P: Owner (Faith Cathedral Fellowship, Inc) & Radio Host: Ralph G. Stair. (a.k.a. "Brother Stair")
SAT: Eutelsat Hot Bird 13B, Galaxy 19, Optus D2, Thaicom 5.
kHz: *3215, 4840, 5800, 5850, 5890, 5935, 6115, 7315, 7490, 7730, 7780, 9265, 9350, 9395, 9400, 9455, 11600, 12160, 13845, 15770, 15825*

Winter Schedule 2020/2021

English	Days	Area	kHz
0000-0200	daily	NAm	9455rmi
0100-0800	daily	NAm	7730rmi
0200-0300	......s	NAm	3215wcr
0300-0800	daily	NAm	5850rmi
0300-1300	.....ss	Af	5890wcr
0300-1400	daily	NAm,ME,Eu	7780rmi
0400-0800	daily	NAm	9395rmi
0400-2100	daily	NAm	9455rmi
0500-0600	mtwtf..	NAm	3215wcr
0500-1300	mtwtf..	Af	5890wcr
0600-1200	daily	NAm	3215wcr
0700-1000	mtwtf..	Eu,NAm	7315inb+
0700-1000	.....ss	Eu,NAf	9265inb+
0700-1300	mtwtf..	NAm	4840wcr
1000-1200	mtwtf..	Eu,NAf	9265inb+
1000-1300	.....s.	NAm	4840wcr
1000-1600	.....s.	NAm	5850rmi, 7730rmi
1000-2000	daily	NAm	9395rmi
1200-1300	daily	Eu,ME,Af	15770rmi
1400-1500	daily	ME	9400sof
1400-2000	.....s.	NAm,Eu,NAf	13845wcr
1400-2100	.....s.	Car,SAm	5800rmi
1500-1600	......s	NAm	7490wcr
1500-1700	daily	Eu	11600sof
1500-1700	mtwtf..	ME	9400sof
1600-1700	......s	NAm,ME,Eu	7780rmi
1600-1900	..w....	NAm	7490bcq
1600-2000	.t.tf..	NAm	7490bcq
1600-2000	mtwtf..	NAm,Eu,NAf	13845wcr
1600-2100	m.....s	NAm	7490bcq
1600-2200	.....s.	NAm	7490bcq
1700-2000	daily	NAm,ME,Eu	7780rmi
1800-1900	......s	Af	12160wcr
1800-1900	mtwtf..	NAm,Eu,NAf	15825wcr
1900-2100	.....s.	Af	12160wcr
2100-2400	daily	Eu,ME,Af	15770rmi
2200-2300	.....s.	Af	9350wcr
2300-2400	mtwtf..	NAm,Eu	6115wcr
2300-2400	daily	NAm	5850rmi, 7730rmi, 9455rmi
2300-2400	mtwtf..	Af	5935wcr

Key: + DRM.
Ann: English: "You are listening to The Overcomer radio broadcast".
V: QSL-card.
Notes: Evangelistic radio based ministry of Ralph G. Stair and his religious organisation - Faith Cathedral Fellowship, Inc. Schedule is subject to change without notice.

TRANS WORLD RADIO (TWR) (Rlg)

P.O. Box 8700, Cary, NC 27512, USA.
☎ +1 919 4603700. 🖷 +1 919 4603702.
E: info2@twr.org **W:** www.twr.org; www.twr360.org
Webcast: D/L
L.P: Chmn: Dr Thomas J. Lowell; Pres/CEO: Lauren Libby.
V: QSL-card.
Notes: Trans World Radio, Inc (TWR) is a global Christian media enterprise. For TWR's regional divisions and schedules, see under Austria (TWR Europe), India (TWR India), Singapore (TWR Asia) and South Africa (TWR Africa). TWR owns transmitting facilities in Benin, Bonaire, Eswatini and Guam.

UNIVERSITY NETWORK (Rlg)

1615 S. Glendale Av, Glendale, CA 91205, USA.
☎ +1 818 2408151.
E: pastor@pastormelissascottvideos.com
W: www.pastormelissascott.com; www.drgenescott.com
Webcast: L (TV audio)
L.P: Pres/CEO: Melissa Scott.
SAT: Galaxy 19.
kHz: *5935, 13845*

Winter Schedule 2020/2021

English	Days	Area	kHz
0100-1300	daily	NAm,Eu	5935wcr

English	Days	Area	kHz
1800-0100	......s	NAm,Eu	13845wcr
2000-0100	mtwtfs.	NAm,Eu	13845wcr

Ann: English: "You're watching the University Network".
V: Does not verify reception reports.
Notes: Run by (Pastor) Melissa Scott, who took over the operation in 2005 after the death of her husband, (Pastor) Dr. William Eugene "Gene" Scott. The transmissions are a relay of the "University Network" satellite TV channel audio and consist of sermons by Melissa Scott and archived material from the period of Gene Scott.

WEWN – EWTN SHORTWAVE RADIO (Rlg)

5817 Old Leeds Rd, Irondale, AL 35210-2164, USA.
☎ +1 205 2712900. 🖷 +1 205 2712926.
E: radio@ewtn.com **W:** www.ewtn.com
Webcast: D/L/P
High Rd, Vandiver, AL 35176, USA. (Tx Site)
L.P: Chmn/CEO: Michael P. Warsaw; Pres/COO: Doug Keck; Vice Pres, Engineering: Terry L Borders; Freq Mgr: Glen Tapley.
SW: [EWN] Vandiver, AL: 4 x 500kW.
SAT: Galaxy 15, Intelsat 19/20/21, XM3/4.
kHz: *5970, 9385, 9470, 12050, 15610*

Winter Schedule 2020/2021

English	Days	Area	kHz
0000-0900	daily	Af	9385ewn
0900-1300	daily	EAs	9470ewn‡
1900-2400	daily	Af	15610ewn
Spanish	**Days**	**Area**	**kHz**
0000-1400	daily	LAm	5970ewn
1400-2400	daily	LAm	12050ewn

Key: ‡ Inactive at time of publication.
Ann: English: "This is EWTN Global Catholic Radio Network - WEWN, Birmingham, Alabama, USA".
V: QSL-card.
Notes: Owned by the Eternal Word Television Network, Inc. Catholic station, began broadcasting on 28 December 1992.

WINB (Rlg)

P.O. Box 88, Red Lion, PA 17356, USA; 2900 Windsor Road, Red Lion, PA 17356-8534, USA.
☎ +1 717 2445360. 🖷 +1 717 2460363.
E: sally@winb.com **W:** www.winb.com
Webcast: D/L
L.P: Pres (World International Broadcasters, Inc): John H. Norris; Airtime Sales/Frequency Mgr: Hans Johnson.
SW: [INB] Red Lion, PA: 1 x 15, 1 x 50kW.
kHz: *7315, 9265, 13655*

Winter Schedule 2020/2021

English	Days	Area	kHz
0000-0330	......s	CAm	9265inb
0000-0400	mtwtfs.	CAm	9265inb
0700-1000	mtwtf..	CAm	7315inb+
1000-1200	mtwtf..	CAm	9265inb+
1200-1400	......s	CAm	9265inb
1200-1700	mtwtf..	Eu,NAf	13655inb+
1400-2400	.....ss	CAm	9265inb
2000-2400	mtwtf..	CAm	9265inb

Key: + DRM.
Ann: English: "This is WINB, Red Lion, Pennsylvania, USA".
V: QSL-card.
Notes: Owned by World International Broadcasters, Inc. Operational since October 1962. The station transmits religious and other programming. Schedule varies, depending on airtime sales.

WJHR RADIO INTERNATIONAL (Rlg) ‡

5920 Oak Manor Drive, Milton, FL 32570, USA.
☎ +1 850 6235405.
E: wjhr@usa.com
L.P: Owner: George Scott Mock.
SW: [JHR] Milton, FL: 1 x 0.25kW (run at 1kW PEP).
kHz: *15555*

Winter Schedule 2020/2021

English	Days	Area	kHz
1400-2200	daily	NAm	15555jhr‡

Key: ‡ Inactive on SW at time of publication.
Ann: English: "You're listening to WJHR Radio International. WJHR Radio is located in the city of Milton, Florida".
V: QSL-email.
Notes: WJHR ("John Hill Radio") is owned by George Scott Mock (dba "Hill Radio International"), and operated by members of the Mt. Calvary Baptist Church. On the air since November 2009. Very occasional test transmissions may be heard on 15810.

WLC RADIO (Rlg)

221 E 21st St, Cheyenne, WY 82001, USA.
☎ +1 869 4692529.
E: galal@worldslastchance.com **W:** www.worldslastchance.com
Webcast: D
L.P: Pres (World's Last Chance, LLC): Galal P. Doss
kHz: *5910, 9330, 17520*

Winter Schedule 2020/2021

Arabic	Days	Area	kHz
0700-1000	daily	NAf	17520sof
1800-2100	daily	NAf,ME	5910wof
English	**Days**	**Area**	**kHz**
0100-0300	daily	NAm	9330bcq
0300-0600	daily	NAm	9330bcq
0600-0800	daily	NAm	9330bcq
0800-0900	daily	NAm	9330bcq
1400-1600	daily	NAm	9330bcq
1600-1900	daily	Eu	9330bcq
French	**Days**	**Area**	**kHz**
1000-1100	daily	Eu	9330bcq
German	**Days**	**Area**	**kHz**
1900-2200	daily	Eu	9330bcq
Portuguese	**Days**	**Area**	**kHz**
0900-1000	daily	Eu	9330bcq
2200-0100	daily	B,Af	9330bcq
Spanish	**Days**	**Area**	**kHz**
1100-1300	daily	LAm	9330bcq
1300-1400	daily	LAm	9330bcq

V: E-QSL (online reception report form available)
Notes: On SW since 8 July 2019. Produced by World's Last Chance, LLC.

WMLK ‡ (Rlg)

P.O. Box C, Bethel, PA 19507, USA; 190 Frantz Rd, Bethel, PA 19507, USA.
☎ +1 717 9334518.
E: wmlkradio7@gmail.com **W:** www.wmlkradio.net
W: www.assembliesofyahweh.com
L.P: Operating Engineer: Gary A. McAvin.
SW: [MLK] Bethel, PA ‡: 1 x 250kW (tx yet to be installed).
Key: ‡ Inactive on SW at time of publication.
Ann: English: "This is Radio Station WMLK".
V: QSL-card. Rp.
Notes: Owned by the Assemblies of Yahweh. In 2017, a fire destroyed the transmitter building. At editorial deadline, WMLK was awaiting a new 250kW transmitter to be shipped from Switzerland.

WRNO WORLDWIDE (Rlg)

P.O. Box 895, Fort Worth, TX 76101, USA; 777 Main St., Suite 1235, Fort Worth, TX 76102, USA.
☎ +1 817 8509990. 🖷 +1 817 8509994.
E: info@wrnoworldwide.com **W:** www.wrnoworldwide.com
Webcast: L
3711 Barataria Blvd, Marrero, LA 70072, USA. (Tx Site)
L.P: Chmn, Good News World Outreach: Robert E. Mawire.
SW: [RNO] New Orleans, LA: 1 x 50kW.
kHz: *7505*

Winter Schedule 2020/2021

English	Days	Area	kHz
0200-0500	daily	NAm	7505rno†

Key: † Irregular (flexible) schedule (dependent on airtime bookings).
Ann: English: "You're listening to WRNO Worldwide".
V: QSL-card. Rp. (2 IRCs).

Notes: Owned by Good News World Outreach. The station transmits religious paid programming.

WTWW (Rlg)

P.O.Box 102, Lebanon, TN 37088, USA; 2115 Leeville Pike, Lebanon, TN 37090, USA.
☎ +1 615 7245225.
E: email@wtww.us **W:** wtww.us
Webcast: L
131 Hiwassee Rd, Lebanon, TN 37087, USA (Tx Site); 6611 Ormond Dr, Nashville, TN 37205, USA (Studio).
☎ +1 615 3528682.
L.P: Pres (Leap of Faith, Inc): George V. McClintock; Engineer: Ted Randall.
SW: [TWW] Lebanon, TN: 1 x 50, 2 x 100kW.
kHz: *5085, 5830, 9475, 9930, 15810*

Winter Schedule 2020/2021

English	Days	Area	kHz
0200-0600	daily	NAm	5830twwt*
1400-0200	......s	NAm	9475twwt
1400-2200	daily	CAm	9930tww‡
1400-2400	daily	NAm	15810tww‡
2200-0800	daily	NAm	5085tww*

Key: † Irregular; ‡ Inactive at time of publication.
Ann: English: "This is WTWW, Lebanon, Tennessee, USA".
V: QSL-card.
Notes: Owned by Leap of Faith, Inc. Initially licensed as WBWW while under construction; on the air since 19 Feb 2010 (tests from Jan 2010). While WTWW ("We Transmit World Wide") transmits mainly paid religious programming, one tx is used to carry a secular music format (oldies) at times.

WWCR SHORTWAVE – WORLD WIDE CHRISTIAN RADIO (Rlg)

1300 WWCR Avenue, Nashville, TN 37218, USA.
☎ +1 615 2551300. 🖷 +1 615 2551311.
E: wwcr@wwcr.com **W:** www.wwcr.com
Webcast: L
L.P: GM: Eric Westenberger; Chief Engineer: Phil Patton; Ops Mgr: Brady Murray; Frequency Mgr: Dr Jerry Plummer.
SW: [WCR] Nashville, TN: 4 x 100kW.
kHz: *3215, 4840, 5890, 5935, 6115, 7490, 7520, 9350, 9980, 12160, 13845, 15025*

Winter Schedule 2020/2021

English	Days	Area	kHz
0000-0100	daily	Af	5935wcr
0000-0300	daily	CAm,Af	7520wcr
0100-0700	daily	NAm,Eu	4840wcr
0200-0300	mtwtfs.	NAm,NAf	3215wcr
0300-0500	mtwtf.s	CAm,Af	5890wcr
0300-0600	daily	NAm,NAf	3215wcr
0700-1000	.....ss	NAm,Eu	4840wcr
1000-1100	......s	NAm,Eu	4840wcr
1100-1300	mtwtf.s	NAm,Eu	4840wcr
1200-1700	daily	NAm,Eu,NAf	15825wcr
1230-1300	mtwtf..	NAm,Eu,NAf	15825wcr
1300-1330	.....s.	NAm,Eu,NAf	15825wcr
1300-1400	daily	NAm,Eu	13845wcr
1300-1500	daily	Af	7490wcr
1300-2400	daily	CAm,Af	9980wcr
1400-1500	mtwtf..	NAm,Eu	13845wcr
1500-1600	mtwtfs.	Af	7490wcr
1500-1800	......s	NAm,Eu	13845wcr
1600-1800	daily	Af	12160wcr
1800-1900	mtwtfs.	Af	12160wcr
1900-2000	mtwtf.s	Af	12160wcr
1900-2200	daily	NAm,Eu,NAf	15825wcr
2100-2300	mtwtf.s	Af	9350wcr
2200-0200	.....ss	NAm,Eu	6115wcr
2200-2215	m...f..	NAm,Eu	6115wcr
2300-2400	.....s.	NAm,Eu	6115wcr
2300-2400	.....ss	Af	5935wcr

Spanish	Days	Area	kHz
2215-2230	.t.t...	NAm	6115wcr
2230-2245	.t.....	NAm	6115wcr
2245-2300	.t.tf..	NAm	6115wcr

Ann: English: "This is World Wide Christian Radio-WWCR, Nashville, Tennessee, USA".
V: QSL-card. Rp. preferred (1 USD). Email rpt to qsl@wwcr.com
Notes: Owned by F.W. Robbert Broadcasting Co., Inc. The station transmits religious paid programming.

FROM THE ISLE OF MUSIC / UNCLE BILL'S MELTING POT

5713 N St Louis Ave, Chicago, IL 60659-4405, USA.
☎ +1 773 2676548.
E: tilfordproductions@gmail.com; bill@tilfordproductions.com
W: www.facebook.com/fromtheisleofmusic; www.facebook.com/UncleBillsMeltingPot
W: www.tilfordproductions.com
L.P: Owner (Tilford Productions)/Host: William "Bill" Tilford.
kHz: *6070, 7490, 9400, 9670*

Winter Schedule 2020/2021

English	Days	Area	kHz
0800-0900	......s	Eu	9670rob*
2000-2100	.t.....	Eu	6070rob*
2300-2400	......s	NAm	7490bcq*
English/Spanish	**Days**	**Area**	**kHz**
0100-0200	.t.....	NAm	7490bcq
1300-1400	.....s.	Eu	6070rob
1500-1600	......s	Eu	9400sof
1900-2000	.t.....	Eu	6070rob

Key: * 'Uncle Bill's Melting Pot'
Notes: Weekly music shows, produced by Tilford Productions LLC. "From the Isle of Music" is dedicated to the music of Cuba (aka 'The Isle of Music'). Uncle Bill's Melting Pot is a programme of world music and comedy.

SHORTWAVE RADIOGRAM

E: radiogram@verizon.net **W:** swradiogram.net
W: www.facebook.com/groups/567099476753304 (SW Radiogram Facebook group; Facebook account required)
L.P: Presenter: Dr Kim Andrew Elliott (KD9XB).
kHz: *5050, 7730, 7780, 9265, 13655, 15770*

Winter Schedule 2020/2021

English	Days	Area	kHz
0030-0100	....f..	NAm	9265inb*
0330-0400	.....s.	NAm	9265inb*
0800-0830	......s	NAm	5850rmi*, 7730rmi*
1300-1330	....f..	NAm	15770rmi*
1330-1400	.....s.	NAm	15770rmi*
1500-1530	....f..	NAm	13655inb*,+
2330-2400	......s	NAm	7780rmi*

Key: + DRM; * Text and images are broadcast in various soundcard generated digital modes, such as MFSK32/64, Olivia 64-2000, SSTV, and others.
V: eQSL-card.
Notes: Shortwave Radiogram (initially VOA Radiogram 2013-2017) is a weekly prgr for the technical-minded enthusiast, created & produced by Dr Kim Andrew Elliott. It transmits experimental digital test & images via analogue SW txs, using sound card produced digital signals that are superimposed on the audio feed, in modes like Olivia, MFSK, Thor, IKFP and decodable with freeware like Fldigi. SW Radiogram is the successor to VOA Radiogram which Elliot launched in March 2013 while working for Voice of America; it was aired each weekend via the IBB transmitting stn Greenville until his retirement in June 2017.

VORW RADIO INTERNATIONAL

Produced in Lynchburg, VA, USA.
E: vorwinfo@gmail.com
W: www.patreon.com/TheReportOfTheWeek
Webcast: D (subscription required)
kHz: *5800, 5850, 7730, 7780, 9955, 15770*

Winter Schedule 2020/2021

English	Days	Area	kHz
0100-0200	....f..	NAm,Eu,ME	7780rmi
0200-0300	m...fss	NAm	5850rmi
0300-0400	....f..	Car,SAm	5800rmi
0800-0900	.t.....	NAm,Pac	7730rmi
0800-0900	.t.....	NAm	5850rmi
1300-1400	...t...	Eu,ME,Af	15770rmi
2000-2100	...t...	NAm,Eu,ME	7780rmi
2100-2200	....f..	LAm	9955rmi
2100-2200	......s	NAm,Eu,ME	7780rmi
2200-2300	...t...	LAm	9955rmi

V: eQSL-card.
Notes: VORW ("Voice of The Report of the Week") is a weekly radio show hosted by John Jurasek, the author of the (food-related) Youtube channel "The Report of the Week". Sporadically on SW since 2015; regularly since 2016 (via rebroadcasters).

WBCQ – THE PLANET

274 Britton Road, Monticello, ME 04760, USA.
☎ +1 207 5389180.
E: wbcq@wbcq.com **W:** www.wbcq.com
Webcast: D/L
L.P: Owner/GM: Allan Weiner; Chief Engineer: Tim Smith.
SW: [BCQ] Monticello, ME: 4 x 50kW, 1 x 500kW.
kHz: *6160, 7490*

Winter Schedule 2020/2021

English	Days	Area	kHz
0000-0100	m....ss	NAm,CAm	7490bcq†±
0000-0100	.....s.	NAm,CAm	6160bcq†±
0000-0130	..w....	NAm,CAm	6160bcq†±
0000-0200	.t.tf..	NAm,CAm	6160bcq†±
0200-0300	.....s.	NAm,CAm	6160bcq†±
2000-2100	mtwtf..	NAm,CAm	7490bcq†±
2300-2330	m......	NAm,CAm	7490bcq†±
2300-2400	.t.....	NAm,CAm	7490bcq†±
2330-2400	m..t...	NAm,CAm	7490bcq†±
Spanish	**Days**	**Area**	**kHz**
0030-0100	..w....	NAm,CAm	7490bcq†±

Key: ± Frequency variable; † Flexible/Irregular schedule, dependent on airtime bookings (may have breaks).
Ann: English: "You are listening to WBCQ, Monticello, Maine, The United States of America - The Planet".
V: QSL-card. (SASE)
Notes: Owned by Allan H. Weiner/Becker Broadcast Systems, Inc. Leases air time to religious and non-religious prgr producers. Schedule is subject to daily variation (according to bookings) and start/end times are approximate. On air since 8 September 1998.

WHRI

274 Britton Road, Monticello, ME 04760, USA.
☎ +1 207 5389180.
L.P: Owner/GM: Allan H. Weiner.
SW: [HRI] Furman, SC: 3 x 100, 2 x 500kW.
kHz: *5920, 7315, 7385, 7520, 9605, 9840, 11825, 15530, 17815, 21610*

Winter Schedule 2020/2021

English	Days	Area	kHz
0000-0100	daily	NAm,Eu	5920hri
0000-0100	daily	NAm	7385hri
0100-0200	.twtfs.	NAm,Eu	5920hri
0100-0200	m.....s	NAm	7385hri
0200-0300	daily	NAm,Eu	5920hri
0200-0300	m.....s	LAm	7315hri
0200-0400	.twtfs.	LAm	7315hri
0200-0900	daily	NAm	7385hri
0300-0400	daily	NAm,Eu	5920hri
0300-0400	......s	LAm	7315hri
0300-0400	......s	NAm,Eu	7520hri
0400-0430	m.....s	LAm	7315hri
0400-0600	.twtfs.	NAm,Eu	5920hri
0430-0600	m.....s	LAm	7315hri
0600-0900	daily	NAm,Eu	5920hri
0600-0900	daily	LAm	7315hri
0900-1000	.....ss	LAm	7315hri
0900-1000	mtwtf..	NAm	7385hri
0900-1000	mtwtf.s	AUS,NZL,Pac	11825hri
0900-1000	.....ss	NAm,Eu	5920hri
1000-1100	......s	AUS,NZL,Pac	11825hri
1000-1100	mtwtfs.	LAm	7315hri
1000-1200	daily	NAm,Eu	5920hri
1000-1400	daily	NAm	7385hri
1100-1300	daily	LAm	7315hri
1200-2300	daily	NAm	9840hri
1300-1400	......s	NAm,Eu	9605hri
1400-1800	daily	Af	21610hri
1800-2000	daily	NAm,Eu	17815hri
2200-2300	......s	AUS,NZL,Pac	15530hri
2300-2400	mtwtf..	NAm,Eu	5920hri
2300-2400	.....ss	NAm	7385hri
2300-2400	daily	LAm	7315hri

Notes: Owned by Allan H. Weiner since August 2020; previously owned by Family Broadcasting Corporation.

WORLD OF RADIO (WOR)

P.O. Box 1684, Enid, OK 73702, USA.
E: woradio@yahoo.com
W: www.worldofradio.com; www.angelfire.com/ok/worldofradio
Webcast: D/P
L.P: Producer and host: Glenn Hauser.
SW: Via WRMI (USA), WBCQ (USA).
kHz: *5010, 5800, 5850, 6160, 7290, 7490, 7730, 7780, 9955, 15770*

Winter Schedule 2020/2021

English	Days	Area	kHz
0030-0100	m......	NAm	7730rmi
0100-0130	.t.t...	Eu,ME,NAf	7780rmi
0130-0200	m.....s.	Eu,ME,NAf	7780rmi
0130-0200	....f..	NAm	5850rmi*, 9955rmi*
0130-0200	....f..	Car, CAm	5010rmi*
0200-0230	.t.....	Eu,ME,NAf	9955rmi
0230-0300	m......	LAm	5800rmi
0230-0300	.....s.	Eu,ME,NAf	7780rmi
0330-0400	.t.....	LAm	5800rmi
0400-0430	m......	NAm	6160bcq±**
0430-0500	m......	LAm	9955rmi
1300-1330	.....s.	Eu,ME,NAf	15770rmi
1900-1930	m......	Eu	7290sof***
2200-2230	..w....	NAm	7490bcq±
2300-2330	..w....	LAm	9955rmi

Key: * 1st play of new episode; ** Times variable; *** Also relayed via Challenger R. in Italy, on 594kHz (Villa Estense 1kW); ± Variable frequency. Schedule is subject to change without notice; latest schedule at: www.worldofradio.com/radioskd.html
V: QSL-card (A dedicated WOR QSL-card is only available for bcasts via WRMI, issued by WRMI for direct rpt)
Notes: World of Radio is a weekly non-commercial listener-supported, public service program about communications around the world, especially shortwave. Has been on the air since 1982, first via WRNO, and since via several US SW stations. It summarizes extensive DX and other news published in the WOR news and discussiongroup (groups.io/g/WOR)

WRMI – RADIO MIAMI INTERNATIONAL

175 Fontainebleau Blvd., Suite 1N4, Miami, FL 33172, USA.
☎ +1 305 5599764. Fax +1 305 5598186.
E: info@wrmi.net **W:** www.wrmi.net
Webcast: L (only trs on 9955kHz)
L.P: GM: Jeff White; Dir, Technical: Jose Raul Mena.
SW: [RMI] Okeechobee, FL: 1 x 50, 12 x 100kW.
kHz: *5010, 5800, 5850, 5950, 5985, 7570, 7730, 7780, 9395, 9455, 9955, 15770, 21525*

Winter Schedule 2020/2021

English	Days	Area	kHz
0000-1000	daily	NAm,Pac	7730rmi
0000-1100	daily	NAm	5850rmi

English	Days	Area	kHz
0000-1400	daily	NAm	7570rmi
0000-2400	daily	NAm	5950rmi, 9455rmi
0330-0600	daily	CAm	5985rmi
1000-1700	.....s.	NAm,Pac	7730rmi
1100-1200	......s	Eu,ME,Af	15770rmi
1100-1700	.....s.	NAm	5850rmi
1200-2400	daily	Eu,ME,Af	15770rmi
1400-2100	.....s.	NAm	7570rmi
1400-2100	daily	Af	21525rmi
1400-2400	daily	Car,SAm	5800rmi
2100-2400	daily	NAm	7570rmi
2230-2400	....f..	NAm	5850rmi
2300-2400	daily	NAm	7570rmi
English/Spanish	**Days**	**Area**	**kHz**
0000-0230	daily	Car	5010rmi
1100-1200	daily	Car	5010rmi
1100-1300	.....ss	Car,SAm	9955rmi
1200-1230	....fs.	Car	5010rmi
1230-1700	.....s.	Car	5010rmi
1300-1500	daily	Car,SAm	9955rmi
1530-1700	daily	Car,SAm	9955rmi
2200-0500	daily	Car,SAm	9955rmi
English/Various	**Days**	**Area**	**kHz**
0000-0400	daily	Car,SAm	5800rmi
0000-2400	daily	NAm,Eu,ME	7780rmi, 9395rmi
Spanish	**Days**	**Area**	**kHz**
2300-2400	daily	Car	5010rmi

Ann: English: "Your're listening to WRMI, Radio Miami International, Okeechobee, Florida, USA".
V: QSL-card.
Notes: Owned by Radio Miami International, Inc. On air since June 1994. WRMI provides air time for prgrs by various production companies and rebroadcasts international radio stations. Some programme blocks are relays of World Radio Network (WRN). See WRMI web site for detailed schedule. Some prgrs aimed at a Cuban audience are jammed. Detailed schedule: see www.wrmi.net

WWRB

Airline Transport Communications Inc., Listener Services, P.O. Box 7, Manchester, TN 37349-0007, USA.
☎ +1 931 7286087. Fax +1 931 7286087.
E: dfrantz@wwrb.org **W:** www.wwrb.org
Webcast: L
6755 Shady Grove Road, Morrison, TN 37355, USA. (Tx Site & Studio)
L.P: Owner & CE: Dave Frantz.
SW: [WRB] Morrison, TN: 1 x 100kW.
kHz: *3185, 3215*

Winter Schedule 2020/2021

English	Days	Area	kHz
0200-0500	m.....s	NAm	3185wrb
2300-0200	.....ss	NAm	3215wrb

Ann: English: "This is radio station WWRB - Worldwide Radio Broadcasting".
V: QSL-card. (Email rpts not accepted)
Notes: A subsidiary operation of Airline Transport Communications, Inc. The station transmits religious paid programming. Freq usage/schedule varies, depending on airtime sales. Times variable. Alternative frequency: 5050kHz (used mainly in the spring/summer broadcast season).

UZBEKISTAN (UZB)

RADIOALOQA, RADIOESHITTIRISH VA TELEVIDENIYE MARKAZI (RRTM) (Tx Operator)

Amir Timur Street 109a, 100202 Toshkent, Uzbekistan.
☎ +998 71 2356516. Fax +998 71 2344517.
E: qabulhona@crrt.uz **W:** www.crrt.uz
L.P: GD: Emir R. Gaziyev.
SW: [TAC] Toshkent: 11 x 100kW.
Notes: RRTM, a division of the State Communications and Information Agency of Uzbekistan, is the national transmitter network operator in Uzbekistan.

VATICAN CITY STATE (CVA)

VATICAN RADIO (Rlg)

Piazza Pia 3, I-00120 Vatican City.
☎ +39 06 69883945. Fax +39 06 69883463.
E: english@vaticannews.va **W:** www.vaticannews.va
Webcast: D/L/P
W: www.comunicazione.va
L.P: DG (Dicastery for Communication): Paolo Nusiner.
SW: [SMG] Santa Maria di Galeria: 4 x 100, 5 x 500kW.
FM/DAB: FM: See National Radio section.
SAT: Eutelsat 5WA/12WB/Hot Bird 13B.
kHz: *3985, 5920, 6010, 6115, 6145, 6185, 7230, 7235, 7250, 7305, 7320, 7360, 7365, 7410, 7420, 7445, 7485, 9580, 9645, 9705, 9720, 11620, 11935, 13830, 15595, 17790*

Winter Schedule 2020/2021

Amharic	Days	Area	kHz
1530-1600	daily	EAf	11935smg, 13830smg
Amharic (Liturgy)	**Days**	**Area**	**kHz**
0930-1050	......s	EAf	15595smg, 17790smg
Arabic	**Days**	**Area**	**kHz**
0710-0730	mtwtfs.	NAf	11620smg
1630-1700	daily	ME	7230smg
1630-1700	daily	NAf,ME	9705smg
Arabic (Liturgy)	**Days**	**Area**	**kHz**
0930-1050	......s	NAf,ME	15595smg, 17790smg
Armenian	**Days**	**Area**	**kHz**
1600-1620	daily	Eu	6185smg, 7360smg
Armenian (Liturgy)	**Days**	**Area**	**kHz**
0930-1050	......s	Eu	15595smg, 17790smg
Belarusian	**Days**	**Area**	**kHz**
1700-1720	daily	BLR	6185smg
Chinese	**Days**	**Area**	**kHz**
1230-1300	.....s.	EAs	6115pht, 7485pht, 9720pht
2200-2230	daily	EAs	9580sai
2200-2230	daily	Eu	6185smg, 7410smg
English	**Days**	**Area**	**kHz**
1630-1700	daily	Af	11935mdc, 13830smg
1715-1730	daily	ME	7230smg
2000-2030	daily	Af	6010smg, 7365smg
English (Liturgy)	**Days**	**Area**	**kHz**
1130-1200	....f..	Af	15595smg, 17790smg
French	**Days**	**Area**	**kHz**
0730-0745	mtwtfs.	NAf	11620smg
1700-1715	daily	ME	7230smg
1700-1728	daily	NAf	11935smg
1700-1730	daily	Af	9705smg
2030-2100	daily	Af	6010smg, 7365smg
German	**Days**	**Area**	**kHz**
1500-1520	daily	CEu	3985kll
Hindi	**Days**	**Area**	**kHz**
1430-1450	daily	As	5920pht, 7320pht
Italian	**Days**	**Area**	**kHz**
0700-0710	mtwtfs.	NAf,ME	11620smg
Latin (Liturgy)	**Days**	**Area**	**kHz**
1940-2000	daily	Af	6010smg, 7235smg, 7365smg
Latin (Mass)	**Days**	**Area**	**kHz**
0620-0700	daily	NAf,ME	11620smg
Malayalam	**Days**	**Area**	**kHz**
1510-1530	daily	As	5920pht, 7320pht
Portuguese	**Days**	**Area**	**kHz**
0100-0130	daily	Af	7305grv
1800-1830	daily	Af	9705smg
2100-2130	daily	Af	7365smg
Romanian (Liturgy)	**Days**	**Area**	**kHz**
0810-0925	......s	Eu	7250smg, 9645smg

Russian	**Days**	**Area**	**kHz**
1230-1300	daily	RUS	6145pht, 7445pht
1620-1640	daily	RUS	6185smg, 7360smg
Russian (Liturgy)	**Days**	**Area**	**kHz**
0930-1050	......s	RUS	15595smg, 17790smg
Somali	**Days**	**Area**	**kHz**
1615-1630	.....s.	EAf	11935mdc, 13830smg
Spanish	**Days**	**Area**	**kHz**
0130-0200	daily	SAm	7305grv
1230-1245	daily	SAm	7305grv
Swahili	**Days**	**Area**	**kHz**
1600-1615	.....s.	Af	11935mdc, 13830smg
1600-1630	mtwtf.s	Af	11935mdc, 13830smg
Tamil	**Days**	**Area**	**kHz**
1450-1510	daily	As	5920pht, 7320pht
Tigrinya	**Days**	**Area**	**kHz**
1730-1800	daily	EAf	9705smg, 11935smg
Ukrainian	**Days**	**Area**	**kHz**
1740-1800	daily	UKR	6185smg, 7360smg
Ukrainian (Liturgy)	**Days**	**Area**	**kHz**
0705-0800	......s	UKR	9645smg, 11620smg
Vietnamese	**Days**	**Area**	**kHz**
2315-2400	daily	SEA	7420pht, 9580pht

Ann: Before all transmissions: Latin: "Laudetur Jesus Christus" (Praised be Jesus Christ), repeated in the language of the broadcast, then station identification. English: "This is the English program of Vatican Radio".

V: QSL-card. Email rpt to qsl.request@spc.va

Notes: On air since 12 Feb 1931. Produced by the Vatican Secretariat for Communications. Certain schedule variations apply on Catholic Holy Days. The rebroadcast of the German webcast via a 1kW SW tx at Kall (Germany) is an independent, personal initiative of the operator of the German relay platform "Shortwaveservice"; a project that targets, primarily, SWLs/DXers in Europe.

VIETNAM (VTN)

VOICE OF VIETNAM (OVERSEAS SERVICE) (VOV) (Gov)

45 Ba Trieu Street, Hanoi, Vietnam.
☎ +84 24 38266809. +84 24 38266707..
E: vovworld@vov.vn **W:** vovworld.vn; vov.vn
Webcast: D/L
L.P: Dir (VOV5): Nguyen Tien Long.
MW: [OMO] Can Tho, Thoi Hung: 1242kHz 2000kW (assumed to be run at 500kW).
SW: [VNI] Son Tay: 11 x 100kW.
FM/DAB: FM: 105.5MHz (Hanoi); 105.7MHz (Ho Chi Minh City).
SAT: Vinasat 1.
kHz: *1242, 7220, 7280, 7285, 9730, 9840, 12020*

Winter Schedule 2020/2021

Chinese	**Days**	**Area**	**kHz**
1100-1130	daily	As	7220vni
1200-1230	daily	As	7220vni
1300-1330	daily	As	7220vni
2200-2230	daily	As	7220vni
2230-2300	daily	As	9840vni‡±, 12020vni‡±
English	**Days**	**Area**	**kHz**
1000-1030	daily	As	9840vni±, 12020vni‡±
1130-1200	daily	As	9840vni±, 12020vni±
1230-1300	daily	As	9840vni±, 12020vni±
1330-1400	daily	As	9840vni±, 12020vni±
1500-1530	daily	As	9840vni±, 12020vni±
1600-1630	daily	Eu	7280vni, 9730vni
1600-1630	daily	ME	7220vni
1900-1930	daily	Eu	7280vni, 9730vni
2030-2100	daily	ME	7220vni
2130-2200	daily	Eu	7280vni, 9730vni
2330-2400	daily	As	9840vni±, 12020vni‡±
French	**Days**	**Area**	**kHz**
1200-1230	daily	As	7285vni
1300-1330	daily	As	7285vni
1630-1700	daily	ME	7220vni
1930-2000	daily	Eu	7280vni, 9730vni
2030-2100	daily	Eu	7280vni, 9730vni
2100-2130	daily	ME	7220vni
German	**Days**	**Area**	**kHz**
1830-1900	daily	Eu	7280vni, 9730vni
2000-2030	daily	Eu	7280vni, 9730vni
Indonesian	**Days**	**Area**	**kHz**
1030-1100	daily	As	9840vni±, 12020vni±
1300-1330	daily	As	9840vni±, 12020vni±
1430-1500	daily	As	9840vni±, 12020vni±
2300-2330	daily	As	9840vni±, 12020vni±
Japanese	**Days**	**Area**	**kHz**
1100-1130	daily	As	9840vni±, 12020vni±
1200-1230	daily	As	9840vni±, 12020vni±
1400-1430	daily	As	9840vni±, 12020vni±
2200-2230	daily	As	9840vni‡±, 12020vni‡±
Khmer	**Days**	**Area**	**kHz**
1600-1630	daily	As	1242omo
Lao	**Days**	**Area**	**kHz**
1100-1200	daily	As	7285vni
1330-1430	daily	SEA	1242omo
Russian	**Days**	**Area**	**kHz**
1130-1200	daily	As	7220vni‡
1230-1300	daily	As	7220vni‡
1630-1700	daily	Eu	7280vni, 9730vni
Spanish	**Days**	**Area**	**kHz**
1800-1830	daily	Eu	7280vni, 9730vni
2100-2130	daily	Eu	7280vni, 9730vni
Thai	**Days**	**Area**	**kHz**
1230-1300	daily	As	7285vni
1430-1500	daily	SEA	1242omo
Vietnamese	**Days**	**Area**	**kHz**
1500-1600	daily	ME	7220vni
1500-1600	daily	SEA	1242omo
1700-1800	daily	Eu	7280vni, 9730vni

Key: ‡ Inactive at time of publication; ± Frequency variable, up to 1.0kHz, or more, below nominal.

Ann: English: "This is the Voice of Vietnam".

V: QSL-card.

Notes: External Sce (also branded VOV5) of the national state broadcaster Đài Tiềng Nói Viet Nam (R. Voice of Vietnam). The Chinese programming includes segments in Cantonese.

ZAMBIA (ZMB)

VOICE OF HOPE – AFRICA (Rlg)

543 Country Club Drive, Simi Valley, CA 93065, USA. (SCG)
E: mail@voiceofhope.com (general); studio@voiceofhope.com (prgr feedback) **W:** www.voiceofhope.com/station_africa.html
Webcast: L
L.P: Pres (SCG): John D. Tayloe; Vice Pres, Operations (SCG): Ray Robinson; Vice Pres (VO Hope - Africa): Chela Silwamba; CE (VO Hope - Africa): Fancis Musonda.
SW: [LUV] Lusaka, Makeni Ranch: 2 x 100kW.
kHz: *4965, 6065, 9680, 11680*

Winter Schedule 2020/2021

English	**Days**	**Area**	**kHz**
0400-0800	daily	WAf	11680luv
0400-0800	daily	CAf,EAf,SAf	9680luv
1400-1600	daily	WAf	6065luv
1400-1600	daily	CAf,EAf,SAf	9680luv
1600-2100	daily	WAf	6065luv
1600-2100	daily	CAf,EAf,SAf	4965luv
Swahili	**Days**	**Area**	**kHz**
1200-1400	daily	EAf,CAf	9680luv

Ann: English: "From Zambia to Africa with love, this is the Voice of Hope".

V: QSL-card. (Email rpt to: reports@voiceofhope.com)

Notes: Run by Strategic Communications Group (SCG), USA. Sister station to KVOH (see under USA) and Voice of Hope - Middle East (see under Israel).

CLANDESTINE AND OTHER TARGET BROADCASTS

Clandestine Broadcasts (Clan) are politically-motivated broadcasts produced by groups opposed to the government of the target country.

Other Target Broadcasts can be produced by either governmental or non-governmental organisations and are targetted at zones of regional or local conflict.

Most COTBs are transmitted via the facilities of international transmitter operators.

The following symbols are used in this section: † Irregular transmsission; ‡ Inactive at editorial deadline. ± Variable frequency.

Where a station is no longer broadcasting, the inactive symbol (‡) appears next to the station name. If a station has been inactive for a second consecutive season it will be removed from the listing.

Target: AZERBAIJAN (AZE)

VOICE OF FREE TALYSHISTAN

✉ c/o Modus Vivendi Center, Agatangeghos St. 2, 0010 Yerevan, Armenia.
E: tolishstonisado@gmail.com **W:** www.facebook.com/tolishstonisado
Webcast: D (not directly related to MW broadcast)
E: modusvivendicenter@gmail.com
W: www.modusvivendicenter.org
kHz: *1395*

Winter Schedule 2020/2021

Talysh	Days	Area	kHz
1715-1730	daily	Cau	1395erv

Ann: Talysh: "Ozodä Tollsstoni Sädo".
Notes: Produced by the NGO "Modus Videndi Center".

Target: CHAD (TCD)

RADIO NDARASON INTERNATIONALE

✉ Based in N'Djamena, Chad.
☎ +235 65078648.
E: Via website. **W:** www.ndarason.com
Webcast: L
✉ 5 Winchester St, Westdene, Johannisburg, 2092, South Africa. (Okapi Consulting)
☎ +27 72 3788235. (cell)
E: info@okapi.cc **W:** www.okapi.cc
L.P: Project Dir (Dir, Okapi Consulting): David Smith.
FM/DAB: See National Radio section. (Cameroon, Chad)
kHz: *7425, 9535, 9635, 12050*

Winter Schedule 2020/2021

French/Kanuri/ Kanembu	Days	Area	kHz
0500-0600	daily	TCD	7425wof
0600-0700	daily	TCD	9535wof
0700-0800	daily	TCD	9535asc
1800-1900	daily	TCD	9635wof
1900-2100	daily	TCD	12050asc

Ann: French: "Radio Ndarason Internationale".
Notes: On SW since 24 Feb 2018. Produced by the Chad branch of South Africa based Okapi Consulting in partnership with the intergovernmental "Lake Chad Commission". The stn has studios in N'Djaména (Chad) and Maiduguri (Nigeria) and targets the Kanuri, Kanembu and Buduma speaking populations in areas under influence of Boko Haram in the Chad Basin region (esp. Northern Nigeria and Chad). The Kanuri word "ndarason" translates as "Everywhere You Go" ("This radio station is with you, wherever you go"). Former sister stn, and successor project of the Nigeria-based Dandal Kura Radio International. The project receives government funding from the Netherlands, Germany and the UK.

Target: CHINA (CHN)

SOUND OF HOPE (XI WANG ZHI SHENG)

✉ 6-4, Lane 84, Guotai St, North District, Taichung 404, Taiwan.
E: soh.soundofhope1990@gmail.com **W:** www.soundofhope.org
Webcast: D/L/P
✉ 333 Kearny St, San Francisco, CA 94108, USA. (HQ)
☎ +1 415 3988009. 📠 +1 415 2765861.
E: editor@bayvoice.net **W:** www.bayvoice.net;
L.P: Pres (Sound of Hope Radio Network, Inc): Allen Yong Zeng.
kHz: *6215, 6230, 6280, 6370, 6730, 6870, 6900, 6970, 7210, 7280, 7310, 7460, 7600, 7650, 7730, 7810, 9080, 9120, 9155, 9180, 9200, 9215, 9230, 9255, 9280, 9320, 9540, 9635, 9730, 9850, 9920, 9970, 9990, 10160, 10820, 10870, 10920, 10960, 11070, 11100, 11120, 11160, 11410, 11440, 11460, 11500, 11530, 11580, 11600, 11715, 11765, 11775, 11970, 12150, 12170, 12190, 12230, 12345, 12370, 12430, 12500, 12550, 12800, 12870, 12880, 12910, 12950, 12980, 13020, 13130, 13160, 13530, 13620, 13640, 13680, 13775, 13870, 13890, 13920, 13980, 14370, 14430, 14500, 14560, 14600, 14640, 14690, 14725, 14775, 14800, 14820, 14850, 14870, 14900, 14920, 14940, 14980, 15070, 15285, 15340, 15580, 15740, 15775, 15800, 15840, 15870, 15920, 15940, 15970, 16100, 16160, 16250, 16300, 16350, 16600, 16680, 16770, 16790, 16980, 17080, 17150, 17170, 17200, 17400, 17440, 17760, 18180, 18870, 19840, 21530, 21800*

Winter Schedule 2020/2021

Chinese	Days	Area	kHz
0000-2400	daily	CHN	6215ust±,*, 6230ust±,*, 6280ust±,*, 6370ust±,*, 6730ust±,*, 6870ust±,*, 6900ust±,*, 6970ust±,*, 7210ust±,*, 7280ust±,*
0100-1600	daily	CHN	9320ust±,**, 9635ust±,**, 9730ust±,**, 10960ust±,**, 12430ust±,*, 13640ust±,**, 14430ust±,**, 14800ust±,*, 14900ust±,**, 15340ust±,**,

Chinese	Days	Area	kHz
			16300ust±,**,
			17440ust±,**
1100-2300	daily	CHN	7600ust±,**
2100-1700	daily	CHN	7310ust±,*,
			7460ust±,*,
			7650ust±,*,
			7730ust±,*,
			7810ust±,*,
			9080ust±,*,
			9120ust±,*,
			9155ust±,*,
			9180ust±,*,
			9200ust±,*,
			9215ust±,*,
			9230ust±,*,
			9255ust±,*,
			9280ust±,*,
			9540ust±,*,
			9850ust±,*,
			9920ust±,*,
			9970ust±,*,
			9990ust±,*,
			10160ust±,*,
			10820ust±,*,
			10870ust±,*,
			10920ust±,*,
			11070ust±,*,
			11100ust±,*,
			11120ust±,*,
			11160ust±,*,
			11410ust±,*,
			11440ust±,*,
			11460ust±,*,
			11500ust±,*,
			11530ust±,*,
			11580ust±,*,
			11600ust±,*,
			11715ust±,*,
			11765ust±,*,
			11775ust±,*,
			11970ust±,*,
			12150ust±,*,
			12170ust±,*,
			12190ust±,*,
			12230ust±,*,
			12345ust±,*,
			12370ust±,*,
			12500ust±,*,
			12550ust±,*,
			12800ust±,*,
			12870ust±,*,
			12880ust±,*,
			12910ust±,*,
			12950ust±,*,
			12980ust±,*,
			13020ust±,*,
			13130ust±,*,
			13160ust±,*,
			13530ust±,*,
			13620ust±,*,
			13680ust±,*,
			13775ust±,*,
			13870ust±,*,
			13890ust±,*,
			13920ust±,*,
			13980ust±,*,
			14370ust±,*,
			14500ust±,*,
			14560ust±,*,
			14600ust±,*,
			14640ust±,*,
2300-1100	daily	CHN	11410ust±,**

Key: ± Variable frequency; * Includes segments in Cantonese (times variable); ** Relay of R. Free Asia (RFA), Includes Cantonese 1400-1500 (times variable).

Ann: Chinese: "Xiwang zhi sheng guoji guangbo diantai".
V: QSL-card. Email rpt to joanna.xia@bayvoice.net
Notes: Established on 20 June 2003 in San Francisco, USA. Falun Gong-related Sound of Hope Radio International is the shortwave service of Sound of Hope Radio Network, Inc (USA). The organisation is a provider of Chinese language news and cultural programming for the worldwide Chinese community. The SW transmissions are part funded by the U.S. Agency for Global Broadcasting (USAGM), see under United States. Some frequencies are jammed. The site code "ust" refers to "Unknown Site in Taiwan". All transmissions are believed to be broadcast from txs with a few kW output. The International Telecommunication Union (ITU) have reported their direction finding has concluded that the following frequencies are from South Korea: 6970, 7650, 9080, 9155, 9200, 9215, 9230, 9340, 10160, 10920, 11120, 11530, 11535, 12150, 12345, 12430, 12820, 12870, 12950, 13550, 13870, 13890, 14430, 14560, 14600, 14800, 14820, 14850, 15840, 15920, 16100, 16600, 16680 and 18200kHz. 9155, 9255, 9990, 11070, 11410, 13980 and 17400kHz are transmitted from Mongolia and 15070kHz is from Thailand, as noted in ITU 'International Monitoring' editions 361 to 367.

VOICE OF TIBET

✉ Stiftelsen Voice of Tibet, Kirkegata 5, 0153 Oslo, Norway. (Administration)
☎ +47 22111209.
E: oystalme@gmail.com **W:** www.vot.org
Webcast: D
✉ Ratoe Chuwar Labrang, Phuntsok Gyatsal House, Session Road, Dharamsala 176215, Distt Kangra H.P., India (Main Editorial Office)
☎ +91 1892 228179; +91 1892 222384. 🖷 +91 1892 224913.
L.P: Dir: Øystein Alme; Editor-in-Chief: Tenzin Paldon.
SAT: AsiaSat 7.
kHz: *7488, 9888*

Winter Schedule 2020/2021

Tibetan	Days	Area	kHz
1230-1400	daily	CHN	9888dsb±
2300-2400	daily	CHN	7488dsb±

Key: ± Frequency variable to escape jamming.
Ann: Tibetan: "Di nor we bod kyi rlung 'phrin khang yin".
IS: Opening Music: National Anthem of Tibet, "Gyallu".
V: QSL-card.
Notes: On the air since 14 May 1996. Produced by the Norwegian foundation "Voice of Tibet". 24/7 on satellite and relayed on SW as per schedule above. SW freqs are often changed to counter jamming.

Target: CUBA (CUB)

WRMI – RADIO MIAMI INTERNATIONAL

✉ See International Radio section, under "USA".
SW: See International Radio section, under USA.
Notes: WRMI relays a number of anti-Government broadcasts to Cuba, in Spanish, from various programmme producers. For full programme details, see www.wrmi.net

RADIO REPÚBLICA (Clan)

✉ P.O. Box 110235, Hialeah, FL 33011-0235, USA.
☎ +1 305 2794416.
Webcast: D/P (P: radiorepublica.us)
✉ 730 NW 107th Ave, Ste 117, Miami, FL 33155, USA (Directorio Democrático Cubano).
☎ +1 305 2202713.
L.P: National Secretary (Directorio Democrático Cubano): Orlando Gutierrez-Boronat.
kHz: *9490*

Winter Schedule 2020/2021

Spanish	Days	Area	kHz
0200-0300	.twt...	CUB	9490iss
0200-0400	m...fss	CUB	9490iss

Ann: Spanish: "Esta es Radio República, voz del Directorio Democrático Cubano, transmitiendo para Cuba".
V: QSL-email. Rpt to Maria Lima (Special Assistant to Program

Coordinator) marialima@directorio.org
Notes: On air since August 2005. Produced by Directorio Democrático Cubano. Jammed.

Target: DJIBOUTI (DJI)

LA VOIX DE DJIBOUTI ‡
Produced in Belgium.
+253 77854946 (Djibouti)
E: info@lavoixdedjibouti.info
W: lavoixdedjibouti.info; www.facebook.com/lavoixdedjibouti
Webcast: D
Key: ‡ Inactive on SW at time of publication.
Ann: French: "Radio LVD"
Notes: Produced by a group of activists in the Djibouti diaspora. Initially on SW 2010-2012; resumed transmission in summer 2020.

Target: ERITREA (ERI)

RADIO ERENA
3, rue Henri Becque, F-75013 Paris, France.
+33 145896451. +33 145896451.
E: radioerena@gmail.com; radioerena@yahoo.com **W:** erena.org
Webcast: D/L (D: www.shekortet.com)
+49 7161 3541614. (Germany)
SAT: Eutelsat 8WB.
kHz: *9720*

Winter Schedule 2020/2021

Arabic	**Days**	**Area**	**kHz**
1730-1800	m.w.f..	ERI	9720sof
Tigrinya	**Days**	**Area**	**kHz**
1700-1730	daily	ERI	9720sof
1730-1800	.t.t.ss	ERI	9720sof

Ann: Tigrinya: "Radio Erena".
Notes: Radio Erena (Radio Erythrée Internationale) is a satellite/online radio station run by Eritrean journalists abroad, supported by "Reporters Without Borders". Produced in Paris/France and Göppingen/Germany. On SW since November 2012.

VOICE OF YIAKL (DIMTSI YIAKL)
10501 Polk Square Ct, North Potomac, MD 20878, USA.
+1 540 4217802 (Bayto Yiakl USA)
E: mfesehaye82@gmail.com (Bayto Yiakl USA)
W: baytoyiakl.org; www.facebook.com/yiaklusa (Bayto Yiakl USA)
Webcast: D
kHz: *17545*

Winter Schedule 2020/2021

Arabic/Tigrinya	**Days**	**Area**	**kHz**
1530-1600	.....s.	ERI	17545iss

Ann: Tigrinya: "Dimtsi Yiakl".
Notes: Oppositional prgr produced by the NGO Bayto Yiakl USA, Inc.

Target: ETHIOPIA (ETH)

RADIO OMN (OROMIA MEDIA NETWORK)
1144 Larpenteur Ave W, Saint Paul, MN 55113-6320, USA.
+1 612 2946770.
E: info@oromiamedia.com **W:** www.facebook.com/OromiaMedia
L.P: Exec. Dir (OMN): Jawar Mohammed.
kHz: *11990*

Winter Schedule 2020/2021

Oromo	**Days**	**Area**	**kHz**
1630-1730	m.w..s.	EAf	11990sof

Ann: Oromo: "Raadiyoo OMN".
Notes: Produced by U.S. based NGO Oromia Media Network, Inc. (OMN).

VOICE OF OROMO LIBERATION (Clan)
Postfach 510620, D-13366 Berlin, Germany.
+49 30 4943372. +49 30 4943372.
E: sbo.radio88@gmail.com
W: www.oromoliberationfront.org/sbo.html
Webcast: D (2014-2015 archive only)
kHz: *9610*

Winter Schedule 2020/2021

Amharic	**Days**	**Area**	**kHz**
1730-1800	..w....	ETH	9610nau
Oromo	**Days**	**Area**	**kHz**
1700-1730	..w.f.s	ETH	9610nau

Ann: Amharic: "Radio Bilisummaa Oromoo"; Oromo: "Kun Sagalee Bilisummaa Oromoo".
V: QSL-letter.
Notes: On air since 6 July 1988. Produced by the "Oromo Liberation Front" (OLF).

Target: IRAN (IRN)

RADIO IRAN INTERNATIONAL
Based in London, United Kingdom.
E: info@iranintl.com **W:** iranintl.com
Webcast: L
Building 11, Chiswick Park, Chiswick High Rd, Chiswick, London W4 5XR, United Kingdom. (Volant Media)
+44 20 39113000.
E: info@volantmedia.net **W:** volantmedia.net
L.P: Dir (Volant Media): Adel Al-Abdulkarim; Dir (Iran International TV): Mahmood Enayat.
SAT: Iran International TV: Al Yah 1, Astra 2G, Badr 6, Eutelsat 7B / Hot Bird 13C, Express AM6, Galaxy 19, TurkmenÄlem / MonacoSat.
kHz: *6270, 11550*

Winter Schedule 2020/2021

Farsi	**Days**	**Area**	**kHz**
0430-1200	daily	IRN	11550erv
1200-0430	daily	IRN	6270erv

Ann: Farsi: "Radyo Iran International".
Notes: R. Iran International is the brand of the audio feed of the satellite TV station "Iran International TV", produced by Volant Media UK Ltd. SW/MW transmissions of the TV audio started on 19 November 2019.

RADIO RANGINKAMAN ‡
Based in Los Angeles, California, USA.
+1 818 6499406.
E: radioranginkaman@gmail.com **W:** radioranginkaman.org
Webcast: D
SAT: Eutelsat Hot Bird 13B (via Encompass Digital Media "WRN Persian" Sat-Feed "R. Jahani").
Key: ‡ Inactive on SW at time of publication.
Notes: Prgr targetting the LGBT (lesbian, gay, bisexual and transgender) communities in Iran, Afghanistan and Tajikistan. The name translates in English as 'Radio Rainbow'. On SW since 24 September 2012. Also carried by KIRN Simi Valley, CA 670kHz (USA).

Target: KOREA, North (KRE)

FURUSATO NO KAZE/ILBON–UI BARAM (WIND FROM JAPAN) (Gov)
Policy Planning Division, Headquarters for the Abduction Issue, Cabinet Secretariat, 6-1 Nagata-cho 1-chome, Chiyoda-ku, Tokyo 100-8968, Japan.
+81 3 52532111. +81 3 3592 2300, +81 3 3581 6011.
E: info@rachi.go.jp
W: www.rachi.go.jp/jp/shisei/radio; www.rachi.go.jp/en (English)
Webcast: D
kHz: *5895, 5945, 6045, 6155, 7290, 7295, 9560, 9690, 9705, 9800*

Winter Schedule 2020/2021

Japanese	Days	Area	kHz
1330-1400	daily	KRE	5895tac, 7295tsh, 9705pao
1430-1500	daily	KRE	5895tac, 7290tsh, 9560pao
1600-1630	daily	KRE	5945tac, 6045tsh, 9690pao
1700-1730	daily	KRE	6155tsh
Korean	**Days**	**Area**	**kHz**
1300-1330	daily	KRE	5895tac, 7295tsh, 9705pao
1500-1600	daily	KRE	5945tac, 7290tsh, 9800pao
1630-1700	daily	KRE	6155tsh

Ann: Japanese: "Furusato no Kaze"; Korean: "Ilbon-ui Baram".
V: QSL-letter.
Notes: On the air since 9 July 2007. Produced by the Japanese government agency "Headquarters for the Abduction Issue", targeting Japanese citizens that are believed to have been abducted to North Korea between 1977 and 1983. Jammed. "Furusato no Kaze" (English: "Wind from the Homeland") is the name of the Japanese broadcast; "Ilbon-ui Baram" is the name of the Korean broadcast (English: "Wind from Japan", Japanese: "Nippon no Kaze").

VOICE OF WILDERNESS (Rlg)

✉ P.O.Box 8, Nonhyeon-dong, Seoul 06104, Rep. of Korea.
☎ +82 2 7968846. 🖷 +82 2 7927567.
E: main@cornerstone.or.kr **W:** www.cornerstone.or.kr; uscornerstone.org
Webcast: D/L
✉ Cornerstone Ministries Int., P.O. Box 4002, Tustin, CA 92781, USA.
☎ +1 714 4840042. 🖷 +1 714 4840046.
E: info@cornerstoneusa.org (USA) **W:** cornerstoneusa.org
L.P: Principle (Cornerstone Ministries Int.): Isaac Lee.
kHz: *7625*

Winter Schedule 2020/2021

Korean	Days	Area	kHz
1400-1500	mtwtfs.	EAs	7625tac
1400-1530	......s	EAs	7625tac

Ann: Korean: "Gwangya-ui Sori Bangsong-imnida".
V: QSL-letter.
Notes: Produced by the South Korean branch of Cornerstone Ministries International (USA). On SW since 2 October 1993. Jammed.

NATIONAL UNITY RADIO

✉ Unification Media Group, 2F, 59, Donggyo-ro, Mapo-gu, Seoul, 04018, Rep. of Korea.
☎ +82 2 63542012. 🖷 +82 505 8712012.
E: umg@uni-media.net **W:** www.uni-media.net (Korean); www.unificationmediagroup.org (English)
Webcast: D
L.P: Pres (UMG): Lee Gwang Baek.
kHz: *5985, 7200*

Winter Schedule 2020/2021

Korean	Days	Area	kHz
1100-1300	daily	KRE	7200tsh
2100-2200	daily	KRE	5985tsh

Ann: Korean: "Jigeum yeoleobunkkeseoneun gugmintong-ilbangsong-eul deudgo gyesibnida".
V: QSL-email.
Notes: On air since 10 December 2005, initially launched as "Radio Free Chosun" (RFC). Re-branded "National Unity Radio" on 22 October 2015. A project of the U.S. Congress-funded NGO "Unification Media Group" (UMG), which was co-founded by RFC together with Open R. for North Korea (and two other South Korean media outlets) on 26 November 2014. Jammed. The 1800-2000 broadcast on 774kHz was in parallel with 92.3MHz FM, but ceased on April 30, 2019. F.Pl: Reactivation of MW broadcast.

SHIOKAZE (SEA BREEZE)

✉ c/o COMJAN, Dairoku Matsuya Building 301, 3-8, Koraku 2-chome, Bunkyo-ku, Tokyo 112-0004, Japan.
☎ +81 3 56845058. 🖷 +81 3 56845059.
E: comjansite2003@chosa-kai.jp **W:** www.chosa-kai.jp/siokaze
L.P: Dir, COMJAN & Producer/Editor: Tatsuru Murao.
kHz: *5990, 6045, 6085, 6145, 7270, 7295*

Winter Schedule 2020/2021

Chinese	Days	Area	kHz
1300-1330	m......	KRE	6145yam*, 7295yam*
1600-1630	m......	KRE	5990yam**, 6085yam**
English	**Days**	**Area**	**kHz**
1300-1400	...t...	KRE	6145yam*, 7295yam*
1600-1700	...t...	KRE	5990yam**, 6085yam**
Japanese	**Days**	**Area**	**kHz**
1300-1330	.....s.	KRE	6145yam*, 7295yam*
1300-1400	.t.....	KRE	6145yam*, 7295yam*
1330-1400	......s	KRE	6145yam*, 7295yam*
1405-1435	daily	KRE	6045yam***, 7270yam***
1600-1630	.....s.	KRE	5990yam**, 6085yam**
1600-1700	.t.....	KRE	5990yam**, 6085yam**
1630-1700	......s	KRE	5990yam**, 6085yam**
Korean	**Days**	**Area**	**kHz**
1300-1330	......s	KRE	6145yam*, 7295yam*
1300-1400	..w.f..	KRE	6145yam*, 7295yam*
1330-1400	m....s.	KRE	6145yam*, 7295yam*
1600-1630	......s	KRE	5990yam**, 6085yam**
1600-1700	..w.f..	KRE	5990yam**, 6085yam**
1630-1700	m....s.	KRE	5990yam**, 6085yam**
1630-1700	.....s.	KRE	5990yam**, 6085yam**

Key: Alt frequencies: * 5935/5980; ** 7325/7345; *** 6070/6165kHz. Other frequencies, between 5930-7435kHz, may be used as necessary.
Ann: English: "This is JSR Shiokaze, Sea Breeze, from Tokyo, Japan"; Japanese: "Kochirawa Shiokaze desu"; Korean: "Yeogineun Shiokaze, Badatbaramimnida".
V: QSL-card. Rp (1 USD).
Notes: On SW since 30 October 2005. JSR Shiokaze (JSR = callsign of the prgr) is produced by the private "Investigation Commission on Missing Japanese Probably Related to North Korea" (COMJAN) and is aimed at reaching Japanese citizens believed to have been abducted to North Korea between 1977 and 1983. Jammed. Frequencies subject to change, usually around 1st of month.

756AM (Clan)

✉ c/o National Intelligence Service (NIS), Naegok-dong, Seocho-gu, Seoul, 06796, Rep. of Korea.
W: www.nis.go.kr (NIS); eng.nis.go.kr (NIS, English)
MW: [MSN] Jeongok, Misan (South Korea): 756kHz 100kW (presumed power).
kHz: *756*

Winter Schedule 2020/2021

Korean	Days	Area	kHz
0000-2400	daily	KRE	756msn

Notes: On air since 1 May 2019. Operated by the South Korean National Intelligence Service (NIS). Programming consists of a 4 hour news and cultural program, which is repeated. No official name/ID. Jammed.

ECHO OF HOPE (VOH) (Clan)

✉ c/o National Intelligence Service (NIS), Naegok-dong, Seocho-gu, Seoul, 06796, Rep. of Korea.

W: www.nis.go.kr (NIS); eng.nis.go.kr (NIS, English)
SW: [JNM] Hwaseong, Jeongnam (South Korea); 4 x 100kW; [NWN] Seoul, Taereung (South Korea): 2 x 10, 1 x 100kW (presumed power).
kHz: *3985, 4880, 5995, 6245, 6350, 9095*

Winter Schedule 2020/2021

Korean	Days	Area	kHz
0300-2300	daily	KRE	3985jnm±, 5995jnm±, 6350jnm±
0700-0300	daily	KRE	4880nwn±, 6245nwn±, 9095nwn±

Key: ± Times and frequencies variable.
Ann: Korean: "Huimang-ui meari pangsong-imnida, VOH (vee-oh-aitch)".
Notes: Initially launched as "Voice of Reunification", re-named "Echo of Hope" in 1973. Operated by the South Korean National Intelligence Service (NIS), though claiming to be a prgr of the (non-existent) "General Union of Overseas Compatriots". Since 2008, the stn been using the English abbreviation "VOH" (="Voice of Hope") in the ID. Jammed.

FREE NORTH KOREA RADIO (Clan)

P.O.Box 117-12-226, Magok-dong, Gangseo-gu, Seoul, Rep. of Korea.
☎ +82 2 64119333. Fax +82 2 64119334.
E: mini6915@hanmail.net **W:** www.fnkradio.com
Webcast: D
E: suzanne@defenseforumfoundation.org
W: www.defenseforumfoundation.org
L.P: Pres: Kim Seong Min.
kHz: *7550, 7600*

Winter Schedule 2020/2021

Korean	Days	Area	kHz
1300-1400	daily	KRE	7600tac
2000-2100	daily	KRE	7550tac

Ann: Korean: "Daehan Minguk Seoul-eso bonaeneun Jayu Bukhan Bangsong-imnida".
V: QSL-letter.
Notes: On SW since 15 Dec 2005. Produced by FNK Media and funded by the U.S. "Defense Forum Foundation" (U.S. Congress grants). Launched in December 2003, as an internet-based radio prgr by Kim Seong Min, a defector from North Korea. The service is sponsored, in part, by paid religious programmes. These may be broadcast at various times throughout the programme and include a 30-minute religious segment (without an official programme name), that begins with a statement in Korean, that translates as: "We send a broadcast for the members of the underground, whose ability to keep faith in the midst of persecution and harsh control to the authorities". Jammed.

FREEDOM FM RADIO (Clan)

c/o National Intelligence Service (NIS), Naegok-dong, Seocho-gu, Seoul, 06796, Rep. of Korea.
W: www.nis.go.kr (NIS); eng.nis.go.kr (NIS, English)
FM/DAB: FM: 94.5MHz/97.7MHz/100.6MHz/103.1MHz. Txs are located in South Korea, near the North Korean border.
Notes: First heard in May 1999. Operated by the South Korean National Intelligence Service (NIS), though until around 2014 claiming to be a prgr of the (non-existent) "Young Men's Hangyeore Fellowship Association" (Hangyeore Sarang Cheongnyeon Moim). On the air 24h. Jammed.

NORTH KOREA REFORM RADIO (Clan)

11, Cheonggu-ro 14-gil, Jung-gu (Songwon Buiding) floor 3, Seoul 04613, Republic of Korea.
☎ +82 2 22426512. Fax +82 2 22426512.
E: nkreform@naver.com **W:** nkreform.com
Webcast: D
L.P: Pres: Kim Seung Chul.
kHz: *7590*

Winter Schedule 2020/2021

Korean	Days	Area	kHz
1430-1530	daily	KRE	7590tac
2030-2130	daily	KRE	7590tac

Ann: Korean: "Inmini baraneun saeroun sesang-ul hamgge ggumg-guneun Joseon Gyaehyeok Bangsong-imnida".
V: QSL-card.
Notes: On SW since December 2007. Produced by the NGO "North Korea Development Institute" (NKDI), funded by the U.S. foundation "National Endowment for Democracy" (U.S. Congress grants). Jammed.

RADIO FREE KOREA (Clan)

c/o National Intelligence Service (NIS), Naegok-dong, Seocho-gu, Seoul, 06796, Rep. of Korea.
W: www.nis.go.kr (NIS); eng.nis.go.kr (NIS, English)
MW: [GOY] Seoul, Goyang (South Korea): 1143kHz 100kW.
kHz: *1143*

Winter Schedule 2020/2021

Korean	Days	Area	kHz
0250-0100	daily	KRE	1143goy

Ann: Korean: "Jayu Koria Bangsong-imnida. RFK"; "Koria Mirae Yeondae-eseo bonae deurineun Radio Free Korea, Jayu Koria Bangsong-imnida".
Notes: On air since 25 June 2014. Operated by the South Korean National Intelligence Service (NIS), though claiming to be a prgr of the (non-existent) organisation "Korea Future Solidarity". Jammed. Also relays programmes produced by KBS and SBS.

VOICE OF FREEDOM (Clan)

c/o Ministry of National Defence (MND), 1, Yongsan-dong 3-ga, Yongsan-gu, Seoul, 04383, Rep. of Korea.
☎ +82 2 7484662.
W: www.mnd.go.kr (MND)
SW: [JAN] Hwaseong, Jangan (South Korea): 1 x 10kW. (presumed power)
FM/DAB: FM: 101.7MHz (Baengnyeongdo Island); 103.1MHz (Ganghwado Island & Mt. Daeamsan); 107.3MHz (Mt. Hwaaksan). Txs are located in South Korea, near the North Korean border.
kHz: *5920*

Winter Schedule 2020/2021

Korean	Days	Area	kHz
0300-0800	daily	KRE	5920jan*
0900-1400	daily	KRE	5920jan*
1500-2000	daily	KRE	5920jan*
2100-0200	daily	KRE	5920jan*

Key: * Alt. freqs: 5940/6020/6045/6135kHz.
Ann: Korean: "Yeogineun Daehan Minguk Seoul-eseo bonae deurineun Jayu-ui Sori Bangsong-imnida".
V: QSL-letter.
Notes: Launched on FM on 24 May 2010 and on SW in August 2014 (tests since May 2014). Operated by the Ministry of National Defense. Jammed. Schedule on FM: as SW.

VOICE OF THE PEOPLE (Clan)

c/o National Intelligence Service (NIS), Naegok-dong, Seocho-gu, Seoul, 06796, Rep. of Korea.
W: www.nis.go.kr (NIS); eng.nis.go.kr (NIS, English)
SW: [GOY] Seoul, Goyang (South Korea): 6 x 50kW. (presumed power)
kHz: *3480, 3910, 3930, 4450, 6520, 6600*

Winter Schedule 2020/2021

Korean	Days	Area	kHz
0300-2300	daily	KRE	3480goy±, 3910goy±, 6520goy±
0700-0300	daily	KRE	3930goy±, 4450goy±, 6600goy±

Key: ± Frequency and times variable.
Ann: Korean: "Joseon Nodongja Chongdongmaeng-eseo bonae deurineun Inmin-ui Sori pangsong-imnida".
Notes: On air since 25 June 1985. Operated by the South Korean National Intelligence Service (NIS), although claiming to be a prgr of

the "Korean Workers Union". Jammed.

Target: KOREA, North & South (KOA)

VOICE OF THE MARTYRS KOREA (Rlg)

✉ Duksung Building 236-1, Mapo-dong, Mapo-gu, Seoul 04176, Rep. of Korea.
☎ +82 2 20650703. 📠 +82 2 20650704.
E: tfoley@vomkorea.kr **W:** www.vomkorea.kr
✉ 1815 SE Bison Rd, Bartlesville, OK 74006, USA. (The Voice of the Martyrs, Inc)
☎ +1 918 3378016.
E: thevoice@vom-usa.org **W:** www.persecution.com
L.P: CEO: Eric Foley.
kHz: *7530, 9930*

Winter Schedule 2020/2021

Korean	Days	Area	kHz
1200-1230	daily	EAs	9930tac
1530-1600	daily	EAs	7530tac
2100-2130	daily	EAs	7530tac

Ann: Korean: "I-bangsong-oen Daehan-Minguk Seoul-eseo bonaedeurineun Sungyo sori Tansaeng sori bangsong-imnida" (Translation: "This is a broadcast from the Republic of Korea, Seoul. This is the Voice of Martyrdom - The Voice of Birth").
V: QSL-email.
Notes: On shortwave since 31 October 2009, initially as "Voice of Freedom". Produced by the South Korean branch of the world-wide operating ministry The Voice of the Martyrs, Inc (USA), and targeting Korean listeners both on the Korean Peninsula, and in Japan. Jammed in parts of the target area.

Target: KOREA, South (KOR)

VOICE OF THE MARTYRS KOREA (Rlg)

✉ Duksung Building 236-1, Mapo-dong, Mapo-gu, Seoul 04176, Rep. of Korea.
☎ +82 2 20650703. 📠 +82 2 20650704.
E: tfoley@vomkorea.kr **W:** www.vomkorea.kr
✉ 1815 SE Bison Rd, Bartlesville, OK 74006, USA. (The Voice of the Martyrs, Inc)
☎ +1 918 3378016.
E: thevoice@vom-usa.org **W:** www.persecution.com
L.P: CEO: Eric Foley.
kHz: *7530, 9930*

Winter Schedule 2020/2021

Korean	Days	Area	kHz
1200-1230	daily	EAs	9930tac
1530-1600	daily	EAs	7530tac
2100-2130	daily	EAs	7530tac

Ann: Korean: "I-bangsong-oen Daehan-Minguk Seoul-eseo bonaedeurineun Sungyo sori Tansaeng sori bangsong-imnida" (Translation: "This is a broadcast from the Republic of Korea, Seoul. This is the Voice of Martyrdom - The Voice of Birth").
V: QSL-email.
Notes: On shortwave since 31 October 2009, initially as "Voice of Freedom". Produced by the South Korean branch of the world-wide operating ministry The Voice of the Martyrs, Inc (USA), and targeting Korean listeners both on the Korean Peninsula, and in Japan. Jammed in parts of the target area.

ECHO OF UNIFICATION (TONG–IL–E MEARI PANGSONG) (Clan)

✉ Pyongyang, Democratic People's Republic of Korea.
E: webmaster@tongilvoice.com **W:** www.tongilvoice.com
Webcast: D/P
SW: Uses txs provided by the North Korean Ministry of Post & Telecommunications.
FM/DAB: FM: 89.4/97.0/97.8MHz (Haeju, North Korea, 10kW).
kHz: *3945, 3970, 6250*

Winter Schedule 2020/2021

Korean	Days	Area	kHz
0400-0600	daily	KOR	3945pyo, 3970chj±†, 6250pyo
1200-1400	daily	KOR	3945pyo, 3970chj±†, 6250pyo
2200-0000	daily	KOR	3945pyo, 3970chj±†, 6250pyo

Key: ± Variable frequency; † Irregular.
Ann: Korean: "Yeogineun Tong-il-e Meari Pangsong-imnida".
IS: "We Are One".
Notes: On the air since 1 Dec 2012. Produced by the "Committee for the Peaceful Reunification of the Fatherland". The FM txs follow the same schedule as SW. Jammed.

Target: NIGERIA (NIG)

DANDAL KURA RADIO INTERNATIONAL

✉ 37 Cemetery Road, Maiduguri, Borno State, Nigeria.
☎ +234 809 4818092.
E: info@dandalkura.com
W: www.dandalkura.com; www.facebook.com/dandalkuraradio
Webcast: L
L.P: MD/CEO: Faruk Dalhatu.
kHz: *9850, 13590*

Winter Schedule 2020/2021

English/Kanuri	Days	Area	kHz
0700-0800	daily	NIG	13590nau
1800-1830	daily	NIG	9850iss

Notes: Funded by the USAID and established with support of Freedom Radio (an independent local radio network in Northern Nigeria and VOA affiliate, owned by Film Lab & Production Services Ltd). Target audience is the Kanuri and Hausa speaking population in areas under influence of Boko Haram in and around the Lake Chad Basin (parts of Nigeria, Chad, Niger and Cameroon). On SW since January 2015. Dandal Kura translates as "meeting place".

Target: PAKISTAN (PAK)

RADIO SEDAYEE KASHMIR (Clan)

✉ c/o All India Radio (AIR), Akashvani Bhavan, Sansad Marg, New Delhi-110001, India.
SW: Via txs of All India Radio (AIR).
kHz: *6030, 6100*

Winter Schedule 2020/2021

Dogri	Days	Area	kHz
0310-0330	daily	PAK	6030del
0810-0830	daily	PAK	6100del
1510-1530	daily	PAK	6030del
Kashmiri	**Days**	**Area**	**kHz**
0230-0310	daily	PAK	6030del
0730-0810	daily	PAK	6100del
1430-1510	daily	PAK	6030del

Ann: Urdu: "Ye Radio Sedayee Kashmir".
Notes: On air since early 2003. Radio Sedayee Kashmir is a prgr representing the views of the Indian government in the dispute with Pakistan over Kashmir.

Target: RWANDA (RRW)

RADIO ITAHUKA (Clan)

✉ 1200 G St, Suite 800, Washington, DC 20005, USA.
☎ +1 202 5096774. (Cell)
E: radioitahuka@gmail.com
W: www.blogtalkradio.com/radioitahuka
Webcast: D
☎ +1 508 3358771. (Cell, RNC)
E: jpturayishimye@yahoo.com (RNC)

W: rwandanationalcongress.org (RNC)
kHz: *15420*

Winter Schedule 2020/2021

Kinyarwanda	Days	Area	kHz
1800-1900	.....s.	RRW	15420mdc

Notes: Produced by the U.S. based oppositional group "Rwanda National Congress" (RNC). On SW since November 2016.

Target: SOMALIA (SOM)

RADIO ERGO

P.O.Box 2234, 00621 Nairobi, Kenya.
+254 20 4002102.
E: info@radioergo.org **W:** www.radioergo.org
Webcast: D/P
Nørregade 18, DK-1165 København K, Denmark. (IMS)
+45 88327000. +45 33120099.
E: info@mediasupport.org **W:** www.mediasupport.org
L.P: Prgr Mgr: Louise Tunbridge.
kHz: *17845*

Winter Schedule 2020/2021

Somali	Days	Area	kHz
1200-1300	daily	SOM	17845dha

Ann: Somali: "Halkani waa Radio Ergo".
V: QSL-card
Notes: Produced by IMS Productions Aps (a branch of IMS - International Media Support). Originally aired under the name "IRIN Radio" by the UN Office for the Coordination of Humanitarian Affairs (OCHA) since 2008. IMS Productions took over the operation on 1 July 2011 and rebranded the service "Radio Ergo".

Target: SOUTH SUDAN (SSD)

EYE RADIO

P.O. Box 425, Plot 48, Block 1 Korok, Juba, South Sudan.
+211 922486980.
E: eyemediahr@eyeradio.org **W:** www.eyeradio.org
Webcast: L
L.P: Chmn (Eye Media): Tombura Michael Renzi; CEO (Eye Media): Stephen Omiri.
FM/DAB: FM: See National Radio section (South Sudan).
kHz: *7340, 15410*

Winter Schedule 2020/2021

English/Arabic/ Others	Days	Area	kHz
0400-0500	mtwtf..	SSD	7340smg
1600-1800	mtwtf..	SSD	15410iss

Notes: Eye Radio began in 2010 as "SRS FM", a local FM stn set up in Juba by the U.S.-funded, originally Nairobi-based Sudan Radio Service (SRS). It was re-branded "Eye Radio" in August 2012. Since then it is produced by the U.S.-funded NGO "Eye Media". The stn can be heard 24/7 on FM in large parts of the country; complementing SW trs began in April 2016. The SW broadcasts are in Arabic, Bari, Dinka, Lotuhu, Nuer, Shilluk, Zande, as well as in English.

RADIO TAMAZUJ

c/o Free Press Unlimited, Witte Kruislaan 55, 1217 AM Hilversum, The Netherlands
+31 35 6254340.
E: radiotamazuj@gmail.com **W:** radiotamazuj.org
Webcast: D
E: info@freepressunlimited.org **W:** www.freepressunlimited.org
L.P: Dir: Hildebrand Bijleveld.
kHz: *7315, 11650, 11705, 15400*

Winter Schedule 2020/2021

Arabic (Juba)	Days	Area	kHz
0330-0430	daily	SSD	7315iss*, 11650mdc*
1500-1600	daily	SSD	11705mdc*, 15400iss*

Key: * Includes 10 minute news in English on Tuesday and Friday.
Ann: Arabic (Juba): "Radio Tamazuj".
V: QSL-card.
Notes: Radio Tamazuj (Tamazuj meaning "intermingling" or "mixing" in Arabic) was launched in November 2011 as broadcast within the timeslot of the sister prgr R. Dabanga (which is targeting Sudan); on air as separate prgr since January 2012. Produced by the Dutch foundation "Free Press Unlimited". The prgr targets audiences in South Sudan and the southern states of Sudan, with particular focus on the border areas between both countries. Jammed.

Target: SUDAN (SDN)

RADIO DABANGA

c/o Free Press Unlimited, Weesperstraat 3, 1018 DN Amsterdam, The Netherlands.
+31 20 8000470.
E: radiodabanga@gmail.com **W:** www.dabangasudan.org
Webcast: D
E: info@freepressunlimited.org **W:** www.freepressunlimited.org
L.P: Editor-in-chief: Kamal Elsadig.
kHz: *7315, 11640, 11650, 15550*

Winter Schedule 2020/2021

Arabic (Darfuri)	Days	Area	kHz
0430-0500	daily	SDN	7315smg, 11650mdc
1530-1630	daily	SDN	11640sof, 15550smg

Ann: All languages: "Radio Dabanga".
V: QSL-card.
Notes: On air since 15 November 2008, produced by the Dutch foundation "Free Press Unlimited". Radio Dabanga is aimed at listeners in the Darfur area in Western Sudan. The broadcasts are in Standard Arabic, Darfuri Arabic, Fur, Masalit and Zaghawa. Occasionally Jammed.

Target: TURKEY (TUR)

DENGÊ WELAT

Based in Belgium.
+32 53 415717.
E: radyo@welat.info **W:** denge-welat.org; radyowelat.com
Webcast: D/L
SAT: Eutelsat 7WA/Hot Bird 13C.
kHz: *7350, 9525, 11530*

Winter Schedule 2020/2021

Kurdish	Days	Area	kHz
0330-0600	daily	ME	7350iss±
0600-1500	daily	ME	11530kch±
1500-1600	daily	ME	11530iss±
1600-2200	daily	ME	9525iss±

Key: ± Frequency may varied, to escape Turkish jamming.
Ann: Kurdish: "Era Dengê Welat".
Notes: Dengê Welat ("Voice of Homeland") replaced Dengê Kurdistanê on 1 Oct 2017. Originally launched as Dengê Mezopotamya on 1 Sep 2012 (on shortwave since 7 Sep). The station broadcasts (in various Kurdish dialects) in support of "Partiya Karkerên Kurdistanê" (PKK) - the Kurdistan Worker's Party - which strives for the establishment of an independent state of Kurdistan (consisting of territories that are currently part of Eastern Turkey, Northern Iraq, Western Iran, Northern Syria). Since 2019, the SW trs are jammed.

Target: VIETNAM (VTN)

RADIO DLSN

Vietnam Democracy Radio, P.O. Box 612882, San Jose, CA 95161, USA.
+1 408 6639860.
E: lienlac.dlsn@gmail.com
W: radiodlsn.com; www.facebook.com/radiodlsn
Webcast: D
kHz: *9670*

Winter Schedule 2020/2021

Vietnamese	Days	Area	kHz
1230-1300	daily	VTN	9670pao

Ann: Vietnamese: "Đây là dây phát thanh Đáp Lòi Sông Núi".
Notes: Radio DLSN (Đáp Lòi Sông Núi - "Fatherland") was launched on 15 May 2011. Produced by the "Foundation for Democracy in Vietnam".

Target: WESTERN SAHARA (AOE)

NATIONAL RADIO OF THE SAHRAWI ARAB DEMOCRATIC REPUBLIC

Based in Rabouni, Algeria.
W: rasdradio.info
Webcast: D/L
c/o Ambassade du République Arabe Sahraouie Démocratique, 1, Rue Franklin Roosevelt, 16000 Algiers, Algeria.
L.P: DG: Mohamed Salem Laabeid.
MW: [RBN] Rabouni (Algeria): 1550kHz 100kW (presumed to be run on reduced power).
kHz: *1550*

Winter Schedule 2020/2021

Arabic	Days	Area	kHz
0700-1300	daily	NAf	1550rbn†
1700-2300	daily	NAf	1550rbn

Key: † Irregular.
Ann: Arabic: "Huna el-estudiohaay al-markaziya al-wataniya, Sowt al-sha'ab a-Sahraui al-mukafa".
V: QSL-letter.
Notes: On air since 28 December 1975, founded by the "Polisario Front". Operated by the Ministry of Information of the government-in-exile of the Sahrawi Arab Democratic Republic, with approval by the Algerian authorities. Jammed.

Target: YEMEN (YEM)

RADIO AL-AZM (Gov)

See National Radio section (Saudi Arabia).
MW: See National Radio section. (Saudi Arabia)
SW: Via tx of SBA/Ministry of Media (Saudi Arabia). Location presumed to be Jeddah, but not confirmed at time of publication.
FM/DAB: FM: See National Radio section. (Saudi Arabia)
SAT: Arabsat 5A.
kHz: *11745*

Winter Schedule 2020/2021

Arabic	Days	Area	kHz
0300-0700	daily	YEM	11745jed
0900-2200	daily	YEM	11745jed

Notes: On the air since 11 September 2017. Produced by the Saudi Broadcasting Authority (SBA), for Saudi military personnel serving in Yemen and Southern Saudi Arabia.

REPUBLIC OF YEMEN RADIO (RADIO SANA'A) (Gov)

kHz: *11860*

Winter Schedule 2020/2021

Arabic	Days	Area	kHz
0200-2200	daily	YEM	11860jed

Notes: Broadcasts in support of Yemeni president Hadi and the Aden-based provisional government. Appears to be a relocated service, formerly produced by the Yemen General Corp. for Radio&TV in Sana'a (after that the Sana'a broadcasting house came under rebel control). Possibly produced in state radio studios in Aden, or in Saudi Arabia. Assumed to be aired via a transmitter in Saudi Arabia.

VOICE OF THE REPUBLIC (Clan)

Reported to be based in Al Mukha, Taiz Governorate, Yemen.
L.P: Founder: Brig. Gen. Tariq Mohammed Abdullah Saleh.
MW: Via tx provided by Abu Dhabi Media (United Arab Emirates).
FM/DAB: FM: 93.1MHz (Al Mukha), 104.1MHz (Al Hudaydah).
SAT: Eutelsat 7WA.
kHz: *1170*

Winter Schedule 2020/2021

Arabic	Days	Area	kHz
1400-0300	daily	YEM	1170dha*

Key: * Times variable.
Ann: Arabic: "Idh'at Sowt-il Jumhuriya".
Notes: Launched in May 2018. Operated by the military organiation "Yemeni National Resistance", in support of the internationally recognized Yemeni government. 24h on FM & satellite.

INTERNATIONAL & CLANDESTINE UPDATES

Pdfs containing updates of the B20 schedules in this edition will be uploaded to *www.wrth.com* in early February 2021.

The A21 schedules will be uploaded in early May 2021, and an A21 update in mid-July 2021.

Notes

Religious Broadcasters Cross Reference Table

This cross reference table of religious broadcasters in the International Radio and COTB sections can be used to look up a station and/or schedule by country. If a station is shown as not having a schedule under its entry, marked '×', (because it is a relay station or similar), look in the '**Schedule Location**' and '**Schedule Country**' columns, where you will find the name of the broadcaster and country where the schedule can be found (usually a parent broadcaster or station HQ).

Broadcaster/ Station	Broadcaster Country	Has own Schedule?	Schedule Location (if different)	Schedule Country	WRTH Section
Adventist World Radio (AWR)	USA	✓		USA	International
Almeda Bible Fellowship	USA	✓		USA	International
AWR Africa	G	✓		G	International
AWR Asia/Pacific	THA	✓		THA	International
Bible Voice Broadcasting (BVB)	CAN	✓		CAN	International
Evangelische Missions-Gemeinden	D	✓		D	International
Family Radio	USA	✓		USA	International
Far East Broadcasting Company Inc (FEBC)	USA	×	HQ, no schedule	—	International
FEBA India	IND	✓		IND	International
FEBA Pakistan	PAK	✓		PAK	International
FEBC Korea	KOR	✓		KOR	International
FEBC Philippines	PHL	✓		PHL	International
Follow the Bible Ministries	USA	✓		USA	International
Ibra Media	S	✓		S	International
KNLS International	ALS	✓		ALS	International
KSDA (AWR Asia/Pacific Relay Station)	GUM	×	Adventist World R	USA	International
KTWR (TWR Relay Station)	GUM	×	TWR Asia/Pacific	USA	International
KVOH - Voice of Hope	USA	✓		USA	International
Living Water Ministry Broadcasting	USA	✓		USA	International
Madagascar World Voice	MDG	✓		MDG	International
Manara Radio	NIG	✓		NIG	International
Pan American Broadcasting	USA	✓		USA	International
Radio HCJB Deutschland	D	✓		D	International
Radio Sadaye Zindagi	CAN	✓		CAN	International
Radio Veritas Asia	PHL	✓		PHL	International
Reach Beyond	USA	✓		USA	International
Reach Beyond Australia	AUS	✓		AUS	International
Supreme Master TV	USA	✓		USA	International
T8WH - Hope Radio	PLW	✓		PLW	International
The Overcomer Ministry	USA	✓		USA	International
Trans World Radio (TWR)	USA	×	HQ, no schedule	—	International
TWR Africa	AFS	✓		AFS	International
TWR Asia	SNG	✓		SNG	International
TWR Bonaire	BES	✓		BES	International
TWR Eswatini Transmitting Station	SWZ	×	TWR Africa	AFS	International
TWR Europe and CAMENA	AUT	✓		AUT	International
TWR India	IND	✓		IND	International
TWR West Africa Transmitting Station	BEN	×	TWR Africa	AFS	International
University Network	USA	✓		USA	International
Vatican Radio	CVA	✓		CVA	International
Voice of Hope - Africa	ZMB	✓		ZMB	International
Voice of Hope - Middle East ‡	ISR	✓		ISR	International
Voice of the Martyrs Korea	KOA	✓		KOA	C&OTB
Voice of Wilderness	KRE	✓		KRE	C&OTB
Vozandes Media	EQA	✓		EQA	International
WEWN - EWTN Shortwave Radio	USA	✓		USA	International
WHRI	USA	✓		USA	International
WINB	USA	✓		USA	International
WJHR Radio International ‡	USA	✓		USA	International
WLC Radio	USA	✓		USA	International
WMLK ‡	USA	×	No Schedule	—	International
World Christian Broadcasting Inc.	USA	×	HQ, no schedule	—	International
WRNO Worldwide	USA	✓		USA	International
WTWW	USA	✓		USA	International
WWCR Shortwave - World Wide Christian R.	USA	✓		USA	International
WWRB	USA	✓		USA	International

Key: ‡ Station inactive on MW/SW at time of publication

FREQUENCY LISTS

Section Contents

(For country codes and transmitter codes, please see the decode tables in the Reference section)

Please note that the North America MW listing has been removed in order to increase the number of MW stations in the main USA listing

EUROPE, AFRICA & MIDDLE EAST

kHz	kW	Ctry	Station, location
25	300	BLR	STFT Station, Vileyka (CW)
	900	RUS	STFT Station, 3 stns (CW)
60	15	G	STFT Station, Anthorn (CW)
66.66	10	RUS	STFT Station, Moscow (AM)
77.5	50	D	STFT Station, Mainflingen (CW/PSK)
153	200	ROU	Antena Satelor, Brasov
162	800	F	STFT Station, Allouis
171	1600	MRC	Medi 1, Nador
189	150	ISL	RUV Rás 1/2, Gufuskálar
198	50	G	BBC R4, Burghead
	500	G	BBC R4, Droitwich
	50	G	BBC R4, Westerglen
207	75	ISL	RUV Rás 1/2, Eidar
225	1200/700	POL	Polskie R. 1, Solec Kujawski
234	750/375	LUX	RTL, Beidweiler
243	50	DNK	DR P4 news & weather, Kalundborg
252	1500/750	ALG	R. Algérienne 3, Tipaza
	300/150	IRL	RTE Radio 1, Summerhill (Clarkstown)
531	600	ALG	R. Algérienne Jil FM, F'Kirina
	10	ARS	SBA Quran prgr, Bisha
	50	BOT	R. Botswana, Maun
	10	E	RNE R. 5, Córdoba
	20	E	RNE R. 5, Oviedo
	10	E	RNE R. 5, Pamplona
	10	E	RNE R. 5, Pontevedra
	10	FRO	Kringvarp Føroya Útvarpið, Akraberg
	15	ROU	Antena Satelor, Urziceni
	15	ROU	R. România Actualitati, Petrosani
540	50	E	Onda Cero Catalunya, Barcelona
	1000	HNG	MR Kossuth R, Solt
	600	KWT	R. Kuwait Main prgr, Kabd
	600	MRC	SNRT National Netw./Reg, Sidi Bennour
	10	MWI	MBC R. 1, Mangochi
	50	NIG	Sokoto State BC "Rima R. ", Sokoto
	50	SDN	South Darfur State R, Nyala
549	600	ALG	R. Algérienne Jil FM, Sidi Hamadouche
	1	ARS	SBA R. Al-Azm, Jizan
	30	ARS	SBA R. Riyadh, 2 stns
	2000	ARS	SBA R. Riyadh, Qurayyat
	20	GAB	RTG 2, Oyem
	25	IRL	Spirit R, Carrickroe
	50	NIG	Manoma R, Kano (F.Pl.)
	1	RKS	R. Kosova 1, Prištinë
	15	SVN	R. Koper, Beli Kriz
558	10	ALG	R. Algérienne 1/R. Ouargla, Touggourt
	50	BOT	R. Botswana, Muchenje
	20	E	RNE R. 5, A Coruña
	20	E	RNE R. 5, San Sebastián
	50	E	RNE R. 5, Valencia
	100	EGY	NMA Educational prgr, Cairo (Abu Zaabal)
	1	G	Panjab Radio, London
	200	IRN	R. Iran, Ardakan
	500	IRN	R. Iran, Azarshahr
	150	IRN	R. Iran, Bojd
	200	IRN	R. Iran, Bushehr
	300	IRN	R. Iran, Gonbad-e Kavus
	200	IRN	R. Iran, Habibabad (Isfahan)
	100	IRN	R. Iran, Hamadan
	600	IRN	R. Iran, Iranshahr
	100	IRN	R. Iran, Kiashahr
	200	IRN	R. Iran, Mashhad

kHz	kW	Ctry	Station, location
	50	IRN	R. Iran, Sefiddasht (Shahrekord)
	400	IRN	R. Iran, Shiraz (Dehnow)
	400	IRN	R. Iran, Shushtar
	400	IRN	R. Iran, Sirjan
	600	IRN	R. Iran, Tehran (Goldashteh)
	50	IRN	R. Iran, Yazd
	50	IRN	R. Iran, Zahedan
	50	IRN	R. Iran, Zanjan
	10	MWI	MBC R. 1, Karonga
	400	ROU	R. România Actualitati, Târgu Jiu
	12	SVN	MMR/R. Slovenija 1, Nemcavci
567	25	AFS	Cape Talk, Cape Town (Klipheuwel)
	20	ARS	SBA Quran prgr, Abha/Afif
	200	ARS	SBA Quran prgr, Jeddah (Bahrah)
	50	E	RNE R. 5, Murcia
	50	KEN	KBC R. Taifa, Garissa
	100	ROU	R. România Actualitati, Brasov/Satu Mare
	300	SYR	Syrian R. Main prgr, Damascus
576	50	AFS	R. Veritas, Meyerton
	400/200	ALG	R. Béchar, Béchar
	20	ARS	SBA Quran prgr, Jizan
	200	BUL	Horizont, Vidin Gramada
	20	CNR	RNE R. Nacional, Las Palmas
	100	E	RNE R. 5, Barcelona
	50	IRN	R. Chichest, Maku
	400/150	IRN	VOIRI, Bandar-e Mahshahr
	100	OMA	R. Sultanate of Oman, Haima
585	1200	ARS	SBA R. Riyadh, Riyadh
	600	E	RNE R. Nacional, Madrid
	1000	IRN	R. Farhang, Tehran (Gheslagh)
	200	TUN	ERTT National prgr, Gafsa
	50	TZA	Zanzibar BC, Chumbuni
594	50	ARS	SBA Call of Islam, Makkah
	2000	ARS	SBA R. Riyadh, Duba
	10	ARS	SBA R. Riyadh, Hofuf
	5/1	I	Challenger R, Villa Estense
	30	MWI	MBC R. 1, Lilongwe (inactive)
	200	NIG	FRCN Kaduna, Jaji
596	50	MRC	SNRT A/R, Oujda (nominal 594kHz)
603	100	CYP	CyBC 3, Nicosia
	10	E	RNE R. 5, Palencia
	50	E	RNE R. 5, Sevilla
	50	EGY	NMA Koran prgr, Sohag
	2	G	BBC R. 4, Newcastle
	0.4	G	Smooth R, Littlebourne
	10	IRN	R. Mashhad, Bajgiran
	25	NIG	Ogun State BC, Abeokuta
	500	OMA	R. Sultanate of Oman, Bidiya
	30	ROU	Antena Satelor, Bucuresti
	15	ROU	R. Oltenia Craiova, Drobeta-Turnu Severin
	100	ROU	R. România Actualitati, Botosani/Oradea
612	5	ARS	SBA R. Jeddah, Hail
	15	ARS	SBA R. Riyadh, Aflaj
	100	BHR	R. Bahrain Quran prgr, Manama
	10	E	RNE R. Nacional, Lleida
	10	E	RNE R. Nacional, Vitoria
	600	IRN	VOIRI, Qasr-e-Shirin
	100	JOR	R. Jordan Main prgr, Shobak
	300	MRC	SNRT National Netw, Sebaa-Aioun
	50	NIG	Kwara State BC, Ilorin
621	200	AFG	BBG Deewa R. /R. Mashal, Khost

kHz	kW	Ctry	Station, location
	100	BOT	R. Botswana, Selebi-Phikwe
	100	CNR	RNE R. Nacional, Santa Cruz de Tenerife
	10	E	RNE R. Nacional, Avila
	10	E	RNE R. Nacional, Jaén
	10	E	RNE R. Nacional, Palma de Mallorca
	300	EGY	NMA Vo Arabs, Batra (Al-Mansura)
	50	IRN	R. Khalij e Fars, Bandar Abbas
	150	MDA	PGTRK R. 1 Plyus, Grigoriopol
	50/10	TZA	TBC Taifa, Mbeya (irregular)
630	10	ARS	SBA Quran prgr, Najran
	20	ARS	SBA R. Jeddah, Jizan
	10	KWT	R. Kuwait Quran prgr, Magwa
	50	MDG	RNM, Antananarivo (irreg.)
	0.01	NOR	The Ferry, Bergen (irr.)
	12	POR	RTP Antena 1, Montemor-o-Velho/ Miranda do D.
	50	ROU	Antena Satelor, Voinesti
	400	ROU	R. Timisoara/R. R. Act, Ortisoara
	300	TUN	ERTT National prgr, Tunis Djedeida
	300	TUR	TRT 1/Reg, Mersin Kazanli
639	250	CYP	BBC Arabic Sce, Zakaki (Ladies Mile)
	300	E	RNE R. Nacional, A Coruña
	10	E	RNE R. Nacional, Albacete
	20	E	RNE R. Nacional, Almeria
	50	E	RNE R. Nacional, Bilbao
	50	E	RNE R. Nacional, Zaragoza
	400	IRN	VOIRI, Bonab
	50	KEN	KBC R. Taifa, Garissa
	100	LSO	LNBS R. Lesotho, Lancer's Gap
	50	NIG	Kaduna State Media Corp, Katabu
	100	OMA	R. Sultanate of Oman, Buraimi
	10	SDN	North Kordofan State R, Al-Ubayyid
648	2000	ARS	SBA R. Riyadh, Jeddah (Khumra)
	50	BOT	R. Botswana, Mopipi
	10	E	RNE R. Nacional, Badajoz
	1	G	R. Caroline, Orfordness
	10	SVN	R. Murski Val, Nemcavci
	25	UKR	R. Krym Roalii, Chonhar
657	50	AFS	R. Pulpit/R. Kansel, Meyerton
	20	ARS	SBA Quran prgr, Rafha
	50	E	RNE R. 5, Madrid
	2	G	BBC R. Wales, Wrexham
	100	I	RAI Radiouno/Reg, Pisa
	100	IRN	R. Gilan, Kiashahr
666	10	ALG	R. Algérienne 1/R. Tindouf
	50	E	SER R. Barcelona, Barcelona
	50	IRN	R. Fars, Abadeh
	60	IRN	R. Fars, Darab
	10	IRN	R. Fars, Kazerun
	150	IRN	R. Fars, Lamerd/Lar/Qir
	400	IRN	R. Fars, Shiraz (Dehnow)
	44	POR	RTP Antena 1, 5 stns
	10	SDN	Kassala State R, Kassala
	100	SYR	Syrian R. Youth prgr, Damascus
675	25	ARS	SBA R. Riyadh, Abha/Afif
	0.1	HOL	Alfa Radio, Haaksbergen
	0.05	HOL	Citrus AM, Emst
	0.1	HOL	Groeistad R. /Studio 675/ Hofstad R., Wassenaar
	0.1	HOL	R. Calypso, Oostwold
	0.1	HOL	Radio Nostalgie, Kollumerzwaag
	0.1	HOL	Unique AM, Wijchen
	50	KEN	KBC R. Taifa, Marsabit
	100	LBY	Vo Homeland, Benghazi (inactive)
	600	QAT	Qatar RTC, Al Arish
684	200	ARS	SBA R. Jeddah, Jeddah (Bahrah)
	10	ARS	SBA R. Jeddah, Riyadh

kHz	kW	Ctry	Station, location
	200	E	RNE R. Nacional, Sevilla
	100	ETH	R. Ethiopia, Metu
	50	IRN	R. Mashhad, Kashmar
	100	IRN	R. Mashhad, Mashhad
	10	MAU	MBC R. Maurice, Malherbes
	50	NIG	Yobe BC, Damaturu
	10	RUS	R. Radonezh, Olgino (Sankt-Peterburg)
	50	TUN	ERTT National prgr, Medenine
693	10	ALG	R. Algérienne 1/R. Adrar, Reggane
	5	ALG	R. Algérienne 2, Aboudid (inactive)
	25	BOT	R. Botswana, Shakawe
	5	E	RNE R. Nacional, Boal
	20	E	RNE R. Nacional, Toledo
	10	E	RNE R. Nacional, Tortosa
	141	G	BBC R. 5 Live, 10 stns
	150	G	BBC R. 5 Live, Droitwich
		GRC	Diavlos 1, Athína
	0.5	I	R. Zai.net, Siziano
	100	IRN	R. Khalij e Fars, Bandar Lengeh
	40	SSD	South Sudan BC, Juba (inactive)
702	50	AFS	LM Radio, Springs (Johannesburg)
	25	ALG	R. Algérienne 1/R. Laghouat
	50	ARS	SBA R. Jeddah, Bisha/Duba
	10	EGY	NMA Reg./Koran prgr, Asswan
	10	EGY	NMA Reg./Koran prgr, El-Kharga
	500	IRN	VOIRI, Kiashahr
	800	OMA	BBC Arabic Service, A'Seela
	5	SVK	SR R. Patria/Devín, Kosice
711	25	E	COPE Murcia
	100	EGY	NMA Youth & Sports prgr, Tanta
	0.5	I	Media R. Castellana, Castel San Pietro Terme
	0.05	I	R. King Italia, Cerveteri
	600/200	IRN	R. Ahvaz, Ahvaz
	300	MRC	SNRT National Netw./R, Laâyoune
	50	ROU	R. România Actualitati, Sighetu Marmatiei
	100/10	TZA	TBC Taifa, Kigoma
720	10	CNR	RNE R. 5, Santa Cruz de Tenerife
	250	CYP	BBC Arabic Sce, Zakaki (Ladies Mile)
	10/0.3	G	BBC R. 4, Lisnagarvey + 2 stns
	400	IRN	R. Mashhad/VOIRI, Taybad
	40	POR	RTP Antena 1, 4 stns
	40	ROU	R. România Actualitati, 3 sites
729	25	AFS	Cape Pulpit/Kaapse Kansel, Cape Town
	10	E	RNE R. Nacional, Alicante
	10	E	RNE R. Nacional, Cuenca
	20	E	RNE R. Nacional, Logroño
	20	E	RNE R. Nacional, Málaga
	100	E	RNE R. Nacional, Oviedo
	10	E	RNE R. Nacional, Valladolid
	0.2	G	BBC Essex, Manningtree
	70	GRC	ERT1, Athína
	50	NIG	Kano State BC, Jogana
738	5	ALG	R. Algérienne 1/R. Illizi, In Amenas
	600	E	RNE R. Nacional, Barcelona
	0.4	G	BBC Hereford & W., Worcester
	50	IRN	R. Bushehr, Dayyer
	50	MOZ	Antena Nacional, Maputo (Joannisse)
	100	OMA	R. Sultanate of Oman, Salalah
747	10	ARS	SBA R. Al-Azm, Najran
	10	ARS	SBA R. Jeddah, Buraidah
	25	CNR	RNE R. 5, Las Palmas
	10	E	RNE R. 5, Cádiz
	0.1	HOL	Cupra Radio, Emmer-Compascuum
	0.05	HOL	Different R. 747 AM, Nijkerk
	0.1	HOL	MCB Radio, Alphen an den Rijn
	0.1	HOL	R. 0511/Seagull, Harlingen

kHz	kW	Ctry	Station, location
	0.1	HOL	R. Vrij Zwolle, Zwolle
	0.1	HOL	Radio 4 Brainport, Waalre
	100	IRN	R. Arbayeen, Ilam (Sept./Oct. Only)
	100	IRN	R. Yazd, Yazd
	60	NIG	Nagarta R, Kaduna
	10	SDN	Khartoum State R, Khartoum
	5	SDN	Red Sea State R, Port Sudan
756	10	EGY	NMA Reg./Koran prgr, Qena
	2	G	BBC R 4, Redruth
	1	G	R. Cumbria, Carlisle
	200/50	IRN	R. Jahanbin, Shahr-e-Kord
	10	MWI	MBC R. 1, Blantyre
	100	NIG	R. Oyo, Ibadan
	2	POR	RTP Antena 1, Lamego (inactive)
	400	ROU	R. România Actualitati, Lugoj (Boldur)
765	50	ARS	SBA Quran prgr, 3 stns
	0.5	G	BBC Essex, Chelmsford
	600	IRN	R. Iran/VOIRI, Chabahar
	50	MOZ	EP de Nampula, Nampula
	50	SDN	SRTC General prgr, Khartoum Soba
774	40	E	RNE R. Nacional, 4 stns
	60	E	RNE R. Nacional, Cáceres
	20	E	RNE R. Nacional, Ourense
	50	E	RNE R. Nacional, San Sebastián
	100	E	RNE R. Nacional, Valencia
	400	EGY	NMA Middle East prgr, Alexandria (Abis)
	1	G	BBC R4, Enniskillen/Plymouth
	0.5	G	R. Leeds/BBC Asian Network, Farnley
	0.1	G	Smooth R, Gloucester
	0.5	I	R. Zai.net, Milano (inactive)
	1	I	Viva La Radio, Firenze
	100	IRN	R. Markazi, Arak
783	5	ALG	R. Algérienne 1/R. Illizi, Djanet
	10	ALG	R. Algérienne 1/R. Souf, El Oued
	100	ARS	SBA Call of Islam, Ras al-Khair
	50	E	COPE, Barcelona
	150	IRN	R. Zahedan, Iranshahr
	50	MTN	R. Mauritanie, Nouakchott (inactive)
	5	SDN	River Nile State R, Atbara
	300	SYR	Syrian R. 1/FS, Tartus Besira
792	50	ARS	SBA Quran prgr, Jeddah (An-Nuziah)
	10	CZE	R. Dechovka, Hradec Králové (St žery)
	50	E	SER R. Sevilla
	1	G	BBC R. Foyle, Londonderry
	50	IRN	R. Zanjan, Zanjan
	20	IRQ	IMN Republic of Iraq R, Baghdad
801	100	BHR	R. Bahrain General prgr, Manama (inactive)
	10	E	RNE R. Nacional, Burgos
	10	E	RNE R. Nacional, Castello
	25	E	RNE R. Nacional, Ciudad Real
	10	E	RNE R. Nacional, Girona
	20	E	RNE R. Nacional, Lugo
	10	E	RNE R. Nacional, Zamora
	100	ETH	Vo Amhara State, Bahir Dar (Zege)
	2	G	R. Devon, Barnstaple
		GRC	Studio 1, Athína
	0.1	HOL	R. Jong Europa, Alphen aan den Rijn
	0.1	HOL	Stem van Drenthe, Hogeveen (irreg.)
	100	IRN	R. Zahedan, Zahedan
810	20	ARS	SBA Quran prgr, Hafar al-Batin
	5	ARS	SBA R. Jeddah, Abha
	20	E	SER R. Madrid
	100	G	BBC R. Scotland, Burghead
	100	G	BBC R. Scotland, Westerglen
	100	IRN	R. Lorestan, Khorramabad
	100	MKD	MR Sat (R. Makedonija), Sveti Nikole
	50	MOZ	EP de Gaza, Xai-Xai
	200/50	UAE	Pravasi Bharathi, Al-Dhabbaya (AM/DRM)
819	300	EGY	NMA General prgr, Batra (al-Mansura)
	0.1	HOL	Keukenduin, Wassenaar
	0.1	HOL	Studio Denakker, Klazienaveen
	1	I	Radio Diffusione Europea, Trieste (inactive)
	60	IRN	R. Tabaristan, Chalus (Darya)
	30	IRN	R. Tabaristan, Sari
	10	MAU	MBC R. Mauritius, Malherbes
	10	SDN	Northern State R, Dongola
828	25	AFS	Magic 828, Cape Town (Klipheuwel)
	1	AZR	RDP Açores, Monte das Cruzes
	100	ETH	R. Ethiopia, Arba Minch
	0.2	G	BBC Asian Network, Sedgley
	0.1	G	Greatest Hits R. West Yorkshire, Leeds
	0.3	G	Smooth R, Bournemouth
		GRC	Studio 54, Athína
	0.1	HOL	R. 4 Brainport/R. Nederwetten, Nuenen
	0.1	HOL	Stichting Middengolf, Utrecht (F.Pl.)
	50	IRN	R. Birjand, Tabas
	100	NIG	FRCN Enugu
	10	RUS	Rgazeta Slovo/Pravoslavnoye R, Skt-P.
837	10	CNR	COPE Las Palmas, Gran Canaria
	10	E	COPE, Burgos
	5	E	COPE, El Ferrol
	10	E	COPE, Sevilla
	100	ETH	R. Oromiya, Robe (Bale)
	0.5	G	BBC Asian Network, Freemen's Common
	1	G	R. Cumbria, Barrow
	300	IRN	R. Isfahan, Habibabad
840	100	ERI	Vo the Broad Masses 2, Asmara (nom. fq 837kHz)
846	20	ARS	SBA Quran prgr, Buraida
	0.3	DNK	NB24, København (F.Pl.)
		GRC	R. Alfa Mike, Athína
	0.05	HOL	Album AM, Uden
	0.01	HOL	Fryskeheide, Twijzelerheide
	0.1	HOL	Haaglanden R. Internationaal, Voorburg
	0.1	HOL	R. Mebo 2, Westerlee
	0.1	HOL	Veluws Genot, Oldebroek
	3	IRL	R. North, Redcastle
	50	IRN	R. Tabriz, Miyaneh
	20	UAE	Holy Quran R, Umm al-Quwain
855	100	ARS	SBA Quran prgr, Ras al-Khair
	50	E	RNE R. Nacional, 5 stns
	300	E	RNE R. Nacional, Murcia
	20	E	RNE R. Nacional, Pontevedra
	50	E	RNE R. Nacional, Santander
	20	E	RNE R. Nacional, Tarragona
	100	ETH	R. Ethiopia, Harar
	1	G	BBC R. Lancashire, Preston
	0.2	G	Sunshine R, Ludlow
	20	JOR	R. Jordan Main prgr, Amman (inactive)
	400	ROU	R. România Actualitati, Tancabesti
864	1000	ARM	TWR relay, Gavar
	10	E	RNE R. Nacional, Socuellamos
	400	EGY	NMA Koran prgr, Santah
	50	IRN	R. Kermanshah, Qasr-e Shirin
873	10	ALG	R. Algérienne 1/R. Ghardaïa
	10	ARS	SBA Quran prgr, Ar-Rass
	10	E	SER R. Galicia, Stgo. de Compostela
	25	E	SER R. Zaragoza
	100	ETH	R. Ethiopia, Addis Ababa
	0.3	G	BBC R. Norfolk, West Lynn
	1	G	BBC R. Ulster, Enniskillen
	40	HNG	Magyar R. 4, Lakihegy/Pécs
	50	IRN	R. Bojnurd, Bojnurd
	50	MDA	R. Moldova Actualitati, Chisinau

kHz	kW	Ctry	Station, location
	50	MOZ	EP de Sofala, Beira (Dondo)
	10	SDN	Al-Gezira State R, Wad Madani
	5	SDN	Northern State R, Wadi Halfa
	25	UKR	UR1, Chasiv Yar
882	100	ARS	SBA Quran prgr, Dammam
	20	CNR	COPE Tenerife, La Laguña
	5	E	COPE, Alicante
	5	E	COPE, Gijón
	5	E	COPE, Málaga
	5	E	COPE, Valladolid
	10	EGY	NMA General prgr, Matruh
	10	G	BBC Wales, Penmon
	100	G	BBC Wales, Washford
		GRC	R. Ita-Vita, Athína
	60	IRN	R. Mahabad, Mahabad
891	600/300	ALG	R. Algérienne 1, Ouled Fayet (irregular)
	100	ETH	R. Ethiopia, Dese
	0.1	HOL	Hotradio Hits, Huissen
	0.1	HOL	Polderpop Radio, Veldhoven
	50	IRN	R. Dena, Dehdasht/Yasouj
	50	LSO	LNBS Ultimate FM, Lancer's Gap
	2.5	POR	R. Renascença, Vilamoura
	5	SDN	Sennar State R, Singa
	300	TUR	TRT 1/Reg, Antalya
900	1000	ARS	SBA R. Riyadh, Qurayyat
	5	E	COPE, Granada
	5	E	COPE, Vigo
	10	E	R. Popular, Bilbao
	0.1	HOL	Sitara FM, Vianen
	0.1	HOL	Theonex AM, Hoogeveen
	100/50	I	RAI Radiouno/Reg, Milano
	600	IRN	R. Quran, Tehran (Goldastoh)
909	10	ALG	R. Algérienne 1, Tamanrasset
	600	BOT	VOA, Mopeng Hill (Selebi-Phikwe)
	5	E	RNE R. 5, Palma de Mallorca
	118	G	BBC R. 5 Live, 9 stns
	150	G	BBC R. 5 Live, Brookmans Park
	200	G	BBC R. 5 Live, Moorside Edge
	150	IRN	R. Kerman, Sirjan
	200	ROU	R. Cluj, Jucu
	25	ROU	R. Constanta, Valu lui Traian
	50	ROU	R. România Actualitati, Timisoara
917	50	NIG	R. Gotel, Yola
918	20	E	R. Inter, Madrid (inactive)
	10	EGY	NMA General prgr, Bawiti
		GRC	Studio 7-40, Athína
	0.1	HOL	Citrus AM, Emst
	0.1	HOL	R. Monique 918, Velsen-Noord
	0.05	HOL	R. President, Hoogvliet
	0.1	HOL	R. T-Pot, Gasselternijveen
	50	IRN	R. Kerman, Jiroft
	30	NIG	R. Benue, Makurdi
927	10	ALG	R. Algérienne 1/R. Adrar, Timimoun
	20	ARS	SBA R. Jeddah, Hofuf
	0.3	DNK	World Music R, København (F.Pl.)
		GRC	Black & White, Athína
	50	IRN	R. Lorestan, Dorud
	100	TUR	TRT 1, Izmir
936	100	ARS	SBA Quran prgr, Makkah/Riyadh
	20	E	RNE R. 5, Alicante
	20	E	RNE R. 5, Valladolid
	20	E	RNE R. 5, Zaragoza
	10	EGY	NMA General prgr, Salum
	50	EGY	NMA Om Kalthoum prgr, Cairo
	0.15	G	Dales R, Hawes
	0.2	G	Smooth R, Naish Hill
	10/5	I	RAI Radiouno/Reg, Venezia
	300	IRN	R. Chichest, Miandoab
	50	IRN	R. Chichest, Urmia
	200	MRC	SNRT A/R, Agadir
	100	SYR	Syrian R. Main prgr, Homs
945	10/2.5	AFG	R. Talwaza, Sharana
	25	AGL	RNA N'Gola Yetu, Mulenvos (inactive)
	50	ARS	SBA R. Riyadh, Hail
	0.2	G	Gold, Derby
	0.7	G	Smooth R, Bexhill
		GRC	R. Galatsi, Athína
	100	IRN	R. Kordestan, Dehgolan
	10	NIG	R. Kebbi, Birnin Kebbi
	15	ROU	R. România Actualitati, Miercurea Ciuc
	5	SDN	South Kordofan State R, Al-Fulah
	20	STP	R. Nacional, Pinheira
950	100	ERI	VO the Broad Masses 1, Asmara (nom. fq 945kHz)
954	50	E	Onda Cero, Madrid
	2.5	ETH	R. Sidama, Yirga Alem
	300	TUR	TRT 1/Reg, Trabzon
963	100	CYP	CyBC 1, Nicosia
	0.2	G	Asian Sound R, Haslingden
	1	G	Sunrise R, East London
		GRC	R. Polytechnic, Athína
	200	IRN	R. Birjand, Bojd (Birjand)
	20	KWT	R. Kuwait Multilingual/Main prgr, Magwa
	50	MOZ	EP de Tete, Tete
	0.1	POL	Twoje Radio Lipsko, Lipsko
	1	POR	R. Renascença, Seixal (Lisboa)
	100	SDN	SRTC Peace R. /Koran prgr, Khartoum Soba
	100	TUN	ERTT International ch, Tunis Djedeida
972	50	BOT	R. Botswana, Takatokwane
	5	E	RNE R. Nacional, Cabra
	2	E	RNE R. Nacional, Monforte de Lemos
	100	ETH	R. Ethiopia, Robe (Bale)
	1	G	Sunrise R, West London
		GRC	R. Takis A5, Athína
	100	IRN	R. Ilam, Ilam
	5	MEL	RNE R. Nacional, Mellilla
	25	NIG	Katsina State R, Dutsin-Ma
981	100	ALG	R. Algérienne 2, Ouled Fayet (Algér)
	20	ARS	SBA Quran prgr, Madinah
	15	CZE	R. Český Impuls, Praha (Líbeznice)/Domamil
	2	EGY	NMA General prgr, Abu Simbel/Baris
	10	EGY	NMA Reg./Koran prgr, Assiut
	20/10	I	RAI Reg. "Trst A", Trieste
	1	IRL	R. Star Country, Emmyvale
	100	IRN	R. Hamadan, Hamadan
	3	POR	R. Renascença, Coimbra
990	10	E	SER R. Bilbao
	5	E	SER R. Cádiz
	1	G	BBC R. 5 Live, Tywyn
	1	G	BBC R. Devon, Exeter
	0.3	G	Greatest Hits R. South Yorkshire, Doncaster
	1	I	Z100, Zinasco (inactive)
	50	NIG	Bauchi R. Corp, Bauchi
999	20	ARS	SBA Quran prgr, Duba
	50	E	COPE, Madrid
	0.3	G	Gold, Nottingham
	0.8	G	Greatest Hits R. Lancashire, Preston
	50/10	I	RAI Radiouno/Reg, Torino
	50	IRN	R. Sanandaj, Baneh
	20	IRQ	R. Al-Bilad/Al-Amal, Baghdad
	500	MDA	TWR, Grigoriopol
	5	MLT	R. Malta, Bizbizja
1008	10	CNR	esRadio, Las Palmas (special events)
	5	E	SER R. Alicante

kHz	kW	Ctry	Station, location
	5	E	SER R. Extremadura, Badajoz
	10	E	SER R. Girona
	50	EGY	NMA Palestine/Hebrew prgr, El Arish
	10	EGY	NMA Reg. prgr, El Fayoum
	50	GRC	ERT1/Reg, Kerkira
	0.1	HOL	Impact AM, Wassenaar
	0.1	HOL	R. Babylona, Lauwersoog (F.Pl.)
	0.1	HOL	R. Babylona, Musselkanaal
	0.1	HOL	R. Experience, Wageningen
	0.1	HOL	R. Transparant, Creil
	0.1	HOL	United AM, Neede
	100	IRN	R. Semnan, Semnan
	50	MOZ	EP de Maputo, Maputo
1017	10	E	RNE R. 5, Burgos
	10	E	RNE R. 5. Granada
	0.5	I	Amica Radio Veneta, Vigonza
	50	IRN	R. Iran, Bandar Abbas
1026	10	ALG	RA 1/R. Ouargla, Hassi Messaoud
	5	E	SER R. Asturias, Oviedo
	5	E	SER R. Jaén
	5	E	SER R. Jerez, J. de la Frontera
	10	E	SER R. Reus
	5	E	SER R. Salamanca
	5	E	SER R. Vigo
	0.5	G	BBC R. Cambrigeshire, Chesterton Fen
	1	G	BBC R. Jersey, Trinity
	1.7	G	Downtown R. /Downtown Country, Belfast
	200	IRN	R. Tabriz, Azarshahr
	50	MOZ	EP de Manica, Chimoio
	25	NIG	Jigawa BC, Dutse
	5	SDN	Blue Nile State R, Al-Damazin
1035	20	ARS	SBA R. Jeddah, Rafha
	100/200	EST	Semeynoye Radio Eli/TWR, Tartu
	10	ETH	R. Oromiya, Adama (Nazret)
	1	G	BBC R. Sheffield/Asian Netw, Sheffield
	1	G	Lyca Dilse, Southall (London)
	0.3	G	Westsound, Ayr
		GRC	R. Vinylio, Athína
	0.1	HOL	Neverland AM, Venlo (irreg.)
1044	20	ARS	SBA R. Jeddah, Afif
	10	E	SER R. San Sebastian, Donostia-S.S.
	5	E	SER R. Valladolid
	200	ETH	R. Ethiopia, Mekele
		GRC	R. Daffy, Athína
	50	IRN	R. Ilam, Dehloran
1053	5	E	COPE, Vila Real
	25	E	COPE, Zaragoza
	100	ETH	R. Oromiya, Nekemte
	38	G	TalkSport, 8 stns
	500	G	TalkSport, Droitwich
	100	IRN	R. Iran, Khorramabad
	30	IRN	R. Zahedan, Saravan
	100	LBY	Vo Homeland, Tripoli (inactive)
	400	ROU	R. Iasi, Uricani
	10	RUS	R. Mariya, Sankt-Peterburg
1062	20/1	CZE	Country R, Praha (Zbraslav)
	10/6	I	RAI Radiouno/Reg, Ancona
	60/10	I	RAI Radiouno/Reg, Cagliari
	20/2	I	RAI Radiouno/Reg, Catania
	200	IRN	R. Kerman, Kerman
	300	TUR	TRT 1/Reg, Diyarbakir
1071	5	ALG	R. Algérienne 1, Illizi
	50	ARS	SBA R. Riyadh, Bisha
	100	EGY	NMA Adults/Wadi al Nil, Cairo (Abu Zaabal)
	2	G	TalkSport, Clipstone/Newcastle
		GRC	R. Mesogeia, Athína
	100	IRN	R. Ma'aref, Qom (Alborz)
	100	SYR	R. Al-Nour (LBN) relay, Tartus Amrit
1080	10	ARS	SBA R. Jeddah, Najran
	10	E	Onda Cero, Toledo
	5	E	SER R. Coruña, A Coruña
	5	E	SER R. Granada
	10	E	SER R. Huesca
	5	E	SER R. Mallorca, Palma de M.
	20	EGY	NMA General prgr, El Minya/Luxor
	3	ETH	R. Fana, Addis Ababa
	600/400	IRN	VOIRI, Mahshahr
1089	10	ALG	R. Algérienne 1/R. Adrar
	20	ARS	SBA R. Jeddah, Qurayyat
	13	G	TalkSport, 2 stns
	400	G	TalkSport, Brookmans Park
	50/100	G	TalkSport, Moorside Edge
	80	G	TalkSport, Washford
	125	G	TalkSport, Westerglen
	50	IRN	R. Semnan, Shahrud
1098	100	ARS	SBA R. Jeddah, Dammam
	25	E	RNE R. 5, Almeria
	10	E	RNE R. 5, Avila
	5	E	RNE R. 5, Huelva
	20	E	RNE R. 5, Lugo
	0.1	HOL	Milano Team, Punthorst
	0.05	HOL	R. Gasselte, Gasselte
	0.5	I	Media R. Castellana, Castel San Pietro Terme
	200	IRN	VOIRI, Zabol
	25	SVK	SR R. Patria/Devín, Nitra
1107	400	AFG	RTV Afghanistan, Pol-e-Charkhi
	20	E	RNE R. 5, Caceres
	20	E	RNE R. 5, Camargo
	25	E	RNE R. 5, Logroño
	10	E	RNE R. 5, Ponferrada
	10	E	RNE R. 5, Teruel
	1.5	G	MFR 2, Inverness
	6	G	TalkSport, 5 stns
		GRC	R. 322, Athína
	10	I	RAI Radiouno/Reg, Roma
	50	IRN	R. Mashhad, Sabzevar
	25	NIG	FRCN Kaduna, Jaji
1116	20	ARS	SBA R. Jeddah, Madinah
	5	E	SER R. Albacete
	5	E	SER R. Pontevedra
	1	G	BBC R Derby, Burnaston Lane
	0.5	G	BBC R. Guernsey, Rohais
	20	HNG	MR Dankó Rádió, Miskolc/ Mosonmagyaróvár
	10	I	RAI Radiouno/Reg, Palermo
	20	IRQ	R. Dar as-Salam, Baghdad
1125	5	E	RNE R. 5, Badajoz
	10	E	RNE R. 5, Castelló
	10	E	RNE R. 5, Soria
	10	E	RNE R. 5, Toledo
	10	E	RNE R. 5, Vitoria
		GRC	Mini Watt, Athína
	50	IRN	R. Qazvin, Qazvin
1134	5	E	COPE, Jerez de la Frontera
	5	E	COPE, Pamplona
	10	E	COPE, Salamanca
	0.003	G	BFBS Gurkha R, 3 sites
	0.001	G	LPAMs
		GRC	R. Asimatos, Athína
	0.1	HOL	Eye AM, Alkmaar
	0.1	HOL	Japie de Portier, Buitenpost
	10	IRN	R. Tabriz, Kaleybar

kHz	kW	Ctry	Station, location
	100	KWT	R. Kuwait Main prgr, Kabd
1143	5	E	COPE, Jaén
	2	E	COPE, Ourense
	50	IRN	R. Iran, Yasuj
1152	10	E	RNE R. 5, Albacete
	10	E	RNE R. 5, Cartagena
	10	E	RNE R. 5, Lleida
	20	E	RNE R. 5, Málaga
	10	E	RNE R. 5, Zamora
	4	G	Clyde 2, Glasgow
	1.5	G	Greatest Hits R. Manchester, Manchester
	2	G	Greatest Hits R. NE (Tyne & Wear), Newcastle
	24	G	LBC News, London
	0.8	G	Smooth R, Norwich
	0.3	G	Smooth R, Plymouth
	400	ROU	R. România Actualitati, Cluj (Jucu)
1161	5	ALG	RA 1/R. Tamanrasset, In Salah
	100	EGY	NMA Reg. prgr, Tanta
	0.4	G	Magic, Hull
	0.2	G	Smooth R, Swindon
	1.4	G	Tay 2, Dundee
	600	IRN	VOIRI, Qasr-e Shirin
1170	0.2	G	GHR Staffordshire & Cheshire, Stoke-on-Trent
	0.3	G	Greatest Hits R. NE (Teesside), Stockton
	0.6	G	Greatest Hits R. South Wales, Swansea
	0.3	G	Smooth R, Ipswich
	0.1	G	Smooth R, Portsmouth
	15	SVN	R. Capodistria, Beli Kriz
	100	SWZ	TWR, Mpangela Ranch (Manzini)
	800	UAE	Vo the Republic of Yemen, Al-Dhabbaya
1179	25	CNR	SER R. Club Tenerife, Santa Cruz
	2	E	SER R. Rioja, Logroño
	50	E	SER R. València
	10	EGY	NMA General prgr, Qena
	0.1	HOL	Antenne Domstad, Utrecht
	0.1	HOL	Luth, Nieuw Amsterdam (F.Pl.)
	50	IRN	R. Iran, Chabahar
	50	MOZ	EP da Zambézia, Quelimane (Namacata)
	400	ROU	R. România Actualitati, Bacau (Galbeni)
	10	ROU	R. România Actualitati, Resita
	0.005	S	Hörby Radioförening, Hörby
1188		GRC	R. Nikolaos Elata, Athína
	300	HNG	Magyar R. 4, Marcali
	100	HNG	Magyar R. 4, Szolnok
	300	IRN	R. Payam, Tehran
1197	2.4	G	Absolute R, 5 stns
	50	IRN	R. Ardabil, Parsabad-Moghan
	15	ROU	Brasov FM, Brasov
1206	20	ARS	SBA R. Jeddah, Aflaj
	2.5	GRC	R. 9, Athína
		GRC	R. Sex Machine, Athína
	10	IRN	R. Birjand, Nehbandan
	50	MOZ	EP de Inhambane, Inhambane
	1	ROD	Mauritius BC R. Rodrigues, Citronelle
1215	20	ARS	SBA R. Jeddah, Hafar al-Barin
	20	ARS	SBA R. Riyadh, Madinah
	50	BOT	R. Botswana, Mahalapye
	5	E	COPE, Córdoba
	5	E	COPE, Léon
	5	E	COPE, Santander
	2.5	ETH	Gimbi Educational Radio, Gimbi
	20	G	Absolute R, 5 stns
	63	G	Absolute R, Brookmans Park
	53	G	Absolute R, Droitwich
	50	G	Absolute R, Moorside Edge
	50	G	Absolute R, Washford
	50	G	Absolute R, Westerglen
1224	5	E	COPE, Almería
	5	E	COPE, Huelva
	5	E	COPE, Lleida
	5	E	COPE, Lugo
	5	E	COPE, Palma de Mallorca
	0.1	HOL	Amplivier Radio, Damwoude
	0.1	HOL	De Rode Adelaar, Waalwijk
	0.05	HOL	Piratensound, Lemele
	0.1	HOL	R. 1224, Lunteren
	0.1	HOL	R. Emmeloord, Emmeloord
	50	IRN	R. Iran, Kerman
	400	IRN	VOIRI, Kish Island
	50	MOZ	EP de Cabo Delgado, Pemba
1233	20	CZE	R. Dechovka, Praha (Líbeznice) + 4 stns
	1	G	Absolute R, 2 stns
	50	KEN	KBC Northeastern Sce, Marsabit
1242	3.5	G	Absolute R, 3 stns
	0.3	G	Smooth R, Maidstone
		GRC	R. Apollon, Athína
	500	OMA	R. Sultanate of Oman, Barka (Seeb)
1251	0.001	G	BFBS Gurkha R, York
	0.001	G	LPAMs
	0.8	G	Smooth R, Bury St. Edmunds
	50	HNG	MR Dankó Rádió, Nyíregyháza/Szombathely
	0.1	HOL	Memories AM, Geffen
	2	POR	R. Renascença, Castelo Branco/Chaves
1260	500	ARS	SBA R. Riyadh, Dammam
	5	E	SER R. Algeciras
	5	E	SER R. Murcia
	1	G	Absolute R, Lydd
	0.2	G	Sabras R, Leicester
	0.6	G	Smooth R, Wrexham
	10	IRN	R. Isfahan, Khur
	50	MOZ	EP do Niassa, Lichinga
1269	2	AFS	Arrowline Chinese R, Edenvale (Johannesburg)
	5	E	COPE, Badajoz
	5	E	COPE, Zamora
		GRC	R. FBI, Athína
	50	IRN	R. Ardabil, Khalkhal
	100	KWT	R. Kuwait Classical music, Kabd
	10	NIG	Taraba State BS, Jalingo
1278	10	EGY	NMA General prgr, Asswan
	0.002	G	BFBS Gurkha R, Folkestone/Stafford
	0.4	G	Greatest Hits R. West Yorkshire, Bradford
	300	IRN	R. Kermanshah, Kermanshah
	100	OMA	R. Sultanate of Oman, Bahla
1287	5	E	SER R. Castilla, Burgos
	10	E	SER R. Lleida
	5	E	SER R. Lugo
	0.001	G	BFBS Gurkha R, 6 sites
	0.001	G	BFBS UK, Bovington
	0.001	G	LPAMs
	0.1	HOL	Hotradio Hits, Bornebroek
	0.1	HOL	Kilrock, 's-Gravendeel
	0.1	HOL	R. 0511/Seagull, Ternaard
	0.05	HOL	Radio Daewa AM, Nunspeet
	0.1	HOL	Stichting Audiovisuelle Faciliteiten, Malden (F.Pl.)
	50	ISR	Vo Hope Middle East, She'ar Yashuv (inactive)
	2	POR	RTP Antena 1, Portalegre
1290	1	AGL	EP do Zaire, Soyo (inactive)
1296	400	AFG	Azadi/Ashna R, Pol-e-Charkhi

kHz	kW	Ctry	Station, location
	50	E	COPE, Valencia
	10	G	R. XL, Birmingham
	1	I	Viva La Radio, Milano (inactive)
	50	IRN	R. Zabol, Zabol
1305	10	AFG	R. Kandahar
	20	E	RNE R. 5, Bilbao
	20	E	RNE R. 5, Ciudad Real
	10	E	RNE R. 5, León
	25	E	RNE R. 5, Ourense
	10	EGY	NMA General prgr, Assiut
	0.2	G	Greatest Hits R. South Yorkshire, Barnsley
	1	G	Premier Christian R, Chingford/Epsom
	1	GRC	ERT1/Reg, Tripoli
	1	I	R. Monterosa, Coltano (inactive)
	50	IRN	R. Bushehr, Bushehr
1314	1000	ARM	Public R. of Armenia FS, Gavar
	20	E	RNE R. 5, Cuenca
	10	E	RNE R. 5, Salamanca
	10	E	RNE R. 5, Tarragona
	1	EGY	NMA General prgr, Nag Hamadi
	1	EGY	NMA Reg./Koran prgr, Abu Simbel
	50	IRN	R. Iran, Ardabil
	1	NOR	R. Northern Star, Bergen Erdal (irr.)
	50	ROU	Antena Satelor, Constanta (Valu lui Traian)
	25	ROU	Antena Satelor, Timisoara
	15	ROU	R. Oltenia Craiova, Craiova
1323	0.02	G	Akash R, Leeds
	0.5	G	Smooth R, Brighton
	50	IRN	VOIRI/R. Tabriz, Jolfa
	15	ROU	R. Târgu Mures, Târgu Mures
	10	TZA	R. One Swahili channel, Moshi
1332	0.6	G	Gold, Peterborough
	0.1	G	R. Warrington
	0.1	HOL	De Parel van Twente, Goor
	0.1	HOL	Extra AM, Amsterdam
	0.1	HOL	R. Beilen AM, Beilen
	0.1	HOL	Telecom, Bennekom (F.Pl.)
	300	IRN	Tehran Province Radio, Tehran (Goldasteh)
	50	ROU	R. România Actualitati, Galati
1341	10	E	Onda Cero, Almeria
	5	E	Onda Cero, Ciudad Real
	5	E	SER R. León
	100	EGY	NMA Cult./Songs prgr, Cairo (Abu Zaabal)
	20	EGY	NMA General prgr, Idfu/Siwa
	10	EGY	NMA Koran/Educ./Sports prgr, Bawiti
	100	G	BBC R. Ulster, Lisnagarvey
	20	IRN	R. Kerman, Bam
	100	KWT	R. Kuwait Quran/2nd prgr, Magwa
1350	1000	ARM	TWR relay, Gavar
	50	BOT	R. Botswana, Tshapong (irregular)
	10	EGY	NMA General prgr, Quseir
	0.001	G	LPAMs
	30	GEO	Abkhaz State R, Sokhumi
	5	HNG	Magyar R. 4, Györ
1359	100	ETH	VO Tigray Revolution, Mekele
	0.3	G	Smooth R, Chelmsford
		GRC	LMG, Athína
1368	1	AFS	Eden Radio, Edenvale (inactive)
	10	EGY	NMA General prgr, El Kharga
	20	G	Manx Radio, Foxdale
		GRC	Halastra R, Athína
	150	IRN	R. Golestan, Gonbad-e Kavus
	10	SEY	SBC Radio, Victoria
1377	1000	ARM	TWR relay, Gavar
	0.1	G	Asian Sound R, Ashton Moss
		GRC	Supersonic, Athína
	50	IRN	R. Kermanshah, Paveh
	50	IRN	R. Zahedan, Chabahar
	50	TZA	R. Free Africa, Mwanza

kHz	kW	Ctry	Station, location
1386	10	EGY	NMA Reg./Koran prgr, Luxor
	0.001	G	LPAMs
		GRC	R. Makedonia, Thessaloniki
	50	KEN	KBC English/Northeastern Sce, Maralal
	75	LTU	Relays via R. Baltic Waves Int, Viešintos
1395	0.1	HOL	Columbia AM, Aalst
	0.1	HOL	Haaglanden R. Internationaal, Voorburg
	0.1	HOL	Happy AM, Nieuw- en Sint Joosland
	0.1	HOL	Loostad Radio, Apeldoorn
	0.1	HOL	Nostalgie AM, Siddeburen
	0.1	HOL	R. Seabreeze AM, Grou
	0.1	HOL	Sterrekijker AM, Elim
	0.3	IRL	Energy Power AM, Dublin (wwekends)
	50	IRN	R. Khalij e-Fars, Hajiabad
	50	IRN	VOIRI, Gorgan
1404	50	GRC	ERT1/Reg, Komotini
	0.1	I	R. 106, Casalgrande
	10	IRN	R. Iran, Qir
	10	MWI	MBC R. 1, Chitipa
	50	ROU	R. Cluj/R. Sighet, Sighetu Marmatiei
	15	ROU	R. România Actualitati, Sibiu
1413	5	E	RNE R. 5, Girona
	10	E	RNE R. 5, Jaén
	20	E	RNE R. 5, Vigo
	1	G	BBC R. Gloucestershire, 2 stns
	0.04	G	Bradford Asian R, Bradford
	1	G	Premier Christian R, 2 stns
	10	IRN	R. Fars, Estahban
	500	MDA	Vesti FM, Grigoriopol
	800	OMA	BBC World Sce, A'Seela
1422	1	AFS	Hellenic R, Bedfordview (Johannesburg)
	50	ALG	R. Multichaîne, Ouled Fayet (Algér)
	20	ARS	SBA Call of Islam, Riyadh
	10	EGY	NMA Reg./Koran prgr, Salum
	10	MWI	MBC R. 1, Matiya
	10	ROU	R. România Actualitati, Olanesti
1431	600	DJI	Voice of America, Djibouti (Pk 12)
	0.001	G	LPAMs
	0.35	G	Smooth R, Southend
	0.35	GRC	1431 AM, Thessaloniki
	5/2	I	RAI Radiouno/Reg, Foggia
1440	1600	ARS	SBA R. Riyadh, Ras al-Khair
	0.5	DNK	R. 208, København
	10	NIG	Adamawa BC, Yola
1449	200	ARS	SBA R. Riyadh, Jeddah (Bahrah)
	0.2	G	BBC Asian Network, Gunthorpe
	2	G	BBC R. 4, Redmoss
	0.001	G	LPAMs
	2	I	RAI Radiouno/Reg, Belluno
	400	IRN	VOIRI, Bandar Torkaman
1458	10	BHR	R. Bahrain General prgr, Manama
	5	G	BBC Asian Network, Langley Mill
	5	G	Gold, Manchester
	125	G	Lyca R. 1458, London
	4	GIB	GBC R. Gibraltar, Wellington Front
	10	IRN	R. Birjand, Ghayen
	100	ROU	R. România Actualitati, Constanta
1467	50	ARS	SBA R. Riyadh, Hafar Al-Batin
	1000	F	Trans World R, Roumoules
	0.1	HOL	R. Eldorado, Damwâld
	0.1	HOL	R. Paradijs, Utrecht
	0.1	HOL	R. Piepzender, Zwolle
	0.1	HOL	Zuidwest Brabant AM, Heerle (weekends)
	0.1	HOL	Zwartemeer (F.Pl.)
	50	IRN	R. Qom, Alborz (Qom)
1476	0.4	AUT	Museumsradio AM, Bad Ischl
	100	BEN	TWR Africa, Parakou
	10	EGY	NMA Reg./Koran prgr, El Minya
	0.25	G	Carillon Wellbeing Radio, Coalville

kHz	kW	Ctry	Station, location
		GRC	R. Veteranos, Athína
	50	IRN	R. Kurdistan, Marivan
1485	1	AFS	R. Today, Honeydew (Johannesburg)
	0.003	D	Funklust, Erlangen
	5	E	SER R. Alcoi
	10	E	SER R. Santander
	10	E	SER R. Zamora
	10	ETH	R. Ethiopia, Negele Borana
	1	G	BBC R. 4, Carlisle
	0.001	HOL	approx. 30 stations
	0.02	I	R. Briscola, Lenta (irreg.)
	1	I	R. Studio X, Livorno
	0.2	I	Regional Radio, Otricoli (irreg.)
	400/100	IRN	R. Abadan, Jamshidabad
	10	IRN	R. Chichest, Khoy
	10	IRN	R. Fars, Jahrom
	10	IRN	R. Iran, Damghan
	0.3	LVA	R. Merkurs, Riga Daugavriva
	1	MEL	SER R. Melilla, Melilla
	1	NOR	NRK P1/Troms og Finnmark, Longyearbyen
	3	ROU	R. Vocea Sperantei, 3 sites
	12	SDN	Al-Qadarif State R, Al-Qadarif
1494	10	IRN	R. Mashhad, Taybad
	50	MDA	R. Moldova Actualitati, Cahul/Edinet
1500	0.001	D	Radio Eule, München
1503	1	BIH	R. 1503 Zavidovici/R. FBiH, Zavidovici
	5	E	RNE R. 5, La Linea
	2	E	RNE R. 5, Monforte de Lemos
	25	EGY	NMA Koran prgr, El Arish (inactive)
	1	G	BBC R. Stoke, Sideway
1512	1000	ARS	SBA Quran prgr, Jeddah (Khumra)
	0.2	I	Mini Radio, Castano Primo (inactive)
	50	IRN	R. Ardabil, Ardabil
1521	2000	ARS	SBA R. Riyadh, Duba
	10	BHR	Bahrain TV audio, Manama
	5	E	SER R. Castelló
	0.07	G	Flame Christian & Community R, Wirral
	0.1	G	R. Panj, Coventry
	10	SVK	SR R. Patria/Devín, Rimavská Sobota
1530	0.7	G	Greatest Hits R. West Yorkshire, Huddersfield
	0.04	G	R. Ramadhan, Glasgow
	0.25	I	R. Milano Centrale, Milano (irreg.)
	3	MDR	Posto Emissor do Funchal, Poiso
	15	ROU	R. Constanta, Nufăru
	15	ROU	R. România Actualitati, Radauti (Mihaileni)
	600	STP	VOA, Pinheira
1539	6	E	SER R. Elche, Elx
	5	E	SER R. Manresa (irregular)
		GRC	Voreios Ihos, Thessaloniki
	50	IRN	R. Golestan, Gorgan
	200/50	UAE	Pravasi Bharathi, Al-Dhabbaya (temp. frequency)
1548	10	AFS	R. Islam, Lenasia (Johannesburg)
	2	G	Forth 2, Edinburgh
	98	G	Gold, London
	0.7	G	Greatest Hits R. South Yorkshire, Sheffield
	10	IRN	R. Birjand, Ferdows
	15	IRN	R. Dena, Gachsaran
	10	IRN	R. Iran, Larijan
	600	KWT	R. Sawa, Kuwait
	500	MDA	TWR, Grigoriopol
1550	50	ALG	R. Nacional de la RASD, Rabouni (inactive)
1557	0.8	G	Gold, Northampton
	0.5	G	Smooth R, Southampton
	0.25	I	R. Milano XR, Magenta (irreg.)
	50	IRN	R. Iran, Zabol
1566	100	BEN	TWR Africa, Parakou
	0.6	G	BBC Somerset, Taunton
	0.8	G	Premier Christian R, Guildford
	0.06	G	Salaam BCR, Bury
	1	HOL	Vahon Hindustani Radio, Haag
	0.5	I	R. Kolbe, Schio
	50	IRN	R. Iran, Bam
1575	2	AFG	R. Kunar, Asadabad
	5	E	SER R. Córdoba
	10	EGY	NMA Koran/Educ./Sports, Quseir
	0.003	G	R. Seerah, Leicester
	50/30	I	RAI Radiouno/Reg, Genova
	2	MAU	BBC WS, Bigara
1584	0.25	AFS	R. 1584, Pretoria (Laudium)
	1	BHR	R. Bahrain English prgr, Manama
	5	CEU	SER Radiolé, Ceuta
	5	E	SER R. Gandía
	5	E	SER R. Ourense
	11	EGY	NMA Reg./Koran prgr, Idfu/Baris
	0.2	G	Asian FX, N. London
	0.3	G	BBC Hereford & Worcester, Woofferton
	0.2	G	Tay 2, Perth
	1	GRC	Ilida R, Kastro
	0.1	HOL	Fidelio Radio, Driebergen-Rijsenburg
	2.5	I	R. Diffusione Europea, Trieste
		I	R. Studio X, Arezzo
	2	I	Regional Radio, Otricoli
	50	IRN	R. Semnan, Biyarjomand
	10	IRN	R. Semnan, unk. loc.
	0.1	POL	R. Andrychów, Andrychów
	1	ROU	ALT FM, Timisoara
	4	ROU	R. Vocea Sperantei, 4 sites
	0.03	RUS	R. Chistaya Volna, Belorechensk
	5	SDN	White Nile State R, Kosti
1593	10	EGY	NMA Reg./Koran prgr, Matruh
	5	F	Bretagne 5, Saint-Gouéno
	150	KWT	R. Sawa, Kuwait
	10	ROU	Brasov FM, Sibiu
	15	ROU	R. Cluj, Oradea
	15	ROU	R. România Actualitati, Ion Corvin
	15	ROU	R. Târgu Mures, Miercurea Ciuc
	0.005	TUR	AFN Incirlik (Adana)
1597	0.1	I	Galaxy Radio, Posillipo (irreg.)
1602	5	E	SER R. Cartagena
	5	E	SER R. Linares
	5	E	SER R. Ontinyent
	5	E	SER R. Segovia
	10/1	EGY	NMA Reg./Koran prgr, Nag Hamadi
	10	EGY	NMA Reg./Koran/Sports, Siwa
	0.4	FIN	Scandinavian Weekend R, Virrat
	0.1	G	Desi R, Southall (London)
	0.1	HOL	R. Flandria, Hemelum
	0.02	I	Dot Radio, Spello
	0.1	I	R. a Colori, Bologna
	0.1	I	R. Jeans, Savona (inactive)
	1	I	R. Milano 1602, Milano (inactive)
	0.05	I	R. Tre Network, Poggibonsi
	0.5	I	RTV R. Treviso, Pordenone
	10	IRN	R. Dezful, Dezful
	20	IRN	R. Semnan, Damghan/Garmsar
	10	IRN	R. Yazd, Bahabad
	1	LVA	R. Tsentr, Riga Daugavriva
	0.8	POL	R. AM, Kraków
	1	ROU	ALT FM, Arad
	1	ROU	R. Vocea Sperantei, Piatra Neamt
	5	SDN	South Kordofan State R, Kadugli
	0.5	SRB	RTS Beograd 1, Sjenica
1611	0.1	NOR	R. Northern Star, Bergen Erdal (irr.)

EAST ASIA & PACIFIC

Abbreviations peculiar to the E.Asia/Pacific section of MW freq. lists: AF = allocated freq; C. = City; PO = Present operation on; Proj. = Projected station; (t) = translator.
Australia: The numeral preceding the call letters indicates the state: 2 = New South Wales. 3 = Victoria. 4 = Queensland. 5 = South Australia. 6 = Western Australia. 7 = Tasmania. 8 = Northern Territory. ACT = Australian Capital Territory. **China, P.R:** If several locations are listed for one frequency, the power listed applies to the first entry. For full details see country section. **Indonesia:** Only RRI stns included. For details of other stns see country section. **Philippines:** Province Abbreviations: Ag Nte = Agusan del Norte; Ag Sur = Agusan del Sur; Ant = Antique; Boh = Bohol; Bat = Batangas; Buk = Bukidnon; Bul = Bulacan; Cag = Cagayan; Cam Nte = Camarines Norte; Cam Sur = Camarines Sur; Dvo Nte = Davao del Norte; Dvo Sur = Davao del Sur; Isa = Isabela; I.Nte = Ilocos Norte; I.Sur = Ilocos Sur; LU = La Union; Lanao Nte = Lanao del Norte; Lanao Sur = Lanao del Sur; Mag = Maguindanao; Mas = Masbate; M Octal = Mindoro Occidental; Mind Or = Mindoro Oriental; Mis Octal = Misamis Occidental; Mis Or = Misamis Oriental; Mt Prov = Mountain Province; Neg Occ = Negros Occidental; Neg Or = Negros Oriental; Nva Viz = Nueva Vizcaya; Pam = Pampanga; Pang = Pangasinan; Que = Quezon; Riz = Rizal; S Cot = South Cotabato; S Leyte = Southern Leyte; S Sur = Surigao del Sur; Sor = Sorsogon; Tar = Tarlac; Z Nte = Zamboanga del Norte; Z Sib = Zamboanga Sibugay; Z Sur = Zamboanga del Sur; Zamb = Zambales.
Russia: Regions in the Asian parts of Russia: Sib. = Siberia. FE = Far East.

kHz	kW	Ctry	Call	Station, location
164	250	MNG		MRT (1), Ulaanbaatar
209	40	MNG		MRT (1) + Goviin Dolgion Büsiin Public R., Dalanzadgad
	40	MNG		MRT (1) + Reg., Ölgii
	40	MNG		MRT (1), Choibalsan
227	40	MNG		MRT (1) + Govi-Altai Public R., Altai
279	150	TKM		Turkmen Radio (1), Asgabat
531	10	AUS	6DL	ABC (L), Dalwallinu
	5	AUS	4KZ	Innisfail
	5	AUS	2PM	Kempsey
	0.5	AUS	5RTI	R. Italiana, Adelaide (HPON)
	5	AUS	3GG	Warragul
	10	CHN		ZJ
	300	IND		AIR, Jodhpur A
	10	J	JOQG	NHK (1), Morioka
	1	J		NHK (1), Nago
	5	NZL		531pi, Auckland
	2	NZL		More FM, Alexandra
	10	PHL	DZBR	Allied Bc. Center, Batangas C, Bat.
	25	THA		R. Thailand, Maha Sarakham
	10	TWN	BED57	BCC (L), Taipei (Tucheng)
540	10	AUS	4QL	ABC (L), Longreach
	5	AUS	7SD	Scottsdale
	50	CHN		AH (CNR1); LN (CNR1)
	10	CHN		QH
	20	IND		AIR, Aizawl
	10	INS		RRI, Bandung (4)
	1	J	JOSK	NHK (1), Kitakyushu
	1	J		NHK (1), Matsumoto
	5	J	JOMG	NHK (1), Miyazaki
	1	J		NHK (1), Nanao/Ishigaki
	5	J	JOJG	NHK (1), Yamagata
	1	NZL		Rhema, Christchurch
	2	NZL		Rhema, New Plymouth
	5	NZL		Rhema, Tauranga
	1	PHL	DYRB	DWRL Radio, Inc., Cebu C
	10	PHL	DZWT	Mt. Province BC, Baguio C, Benguet
	5	PHL	DXGH	Pacific Bc. System, Gen. Santos C, S Cot
	5	SMO		National Radio 2AP, Apia (repl.mast)
	5	THA		Yaan Kraw, Bangkok
549	50	AUS	2CR	ABC (L), Orange
	25	CHN		EN
	1200	CHN		FJ (CNR5)
	100	IND		AIR, Ranchi A
	10	J	JOAP	NHK (1), Okinawa
	1	NZL		Gold AM, Nelson
	2	NZL		Rhema, Kaitaia
	5	PHL	DXHM	Catholic Media Netw., Madong, Mind Or
	10	PHL	DWRB	Philippine Bc. Sce., Naga C, Cam. Sur
	10	THA		R. Thailand, Mukdahan
	100	THA		Sor.Wor.Sor, Lampang
	40	TJK		TR (2), Yangiyul
	200	VTN		Hung Yen (2) (My Hao)
550	5	HWA	KNUI	Kahului, Maui
558	50	AUS	6WA	ABC (L), Wagin
	5	AUS	4AM	Atherton
	5	AUS	4GY	Gympie
	100	BGD		Bangladesh Betar, Khulna
	120	CHN		XJ + 9 stns
	10	FJI		Fiji Bc. Corp. Ltd. (RF1), Suva
	100	IND		AIR, Mumbai B
	20	J	JOCR	CRK, Kobe
	250	KOR	HLQH	KBS, Daegu (2)
	5	NZL		Gold AM, Invercargill
	40	PHL	DZXL	R. Mindanao Netw., Pasig C, NCR
	10	THA		R. Thailand, Kanchanaburi
567	10	AUS	4JK	ABC (L), Julia Creek
	0.1	AUS	6...	ABC (L), W. A., 4 stns
	0.5	AUS	2BH	Broken Hill
	10	CHN		JS (CNR1)
	20	CHN		TJ; EN
	10	GUM	KGUM	Agana
	20	HKG		RTHK (3), Golden Hill
	300	IND		AIR, Dibrugarh
	100	J	JOIK	NHK (1), Sapporo
	100	KOR	HLKF	KBS, Jeonju
	200	LAO		Lao National Radio (N), Vientiane (kM 49)
	50	NZL		RNZ (N), Wellington
	300	PAK		PBC, Khuzdar
	5	PHL	DXCH	Pacific Bc. System, Cotabato C, Mag.
	5	THA		Jor. Sor. 5, Chaiyaphum
570	1	HWA	KUAI	Eleele, Kauai
576	50	AUS	2RN	ABC (N), Sydney
	200	BRM		Myanma Radio (N), Yangon
	200	CHN		YN; ZJ(v); EN; FJ
	200	IND		AIR, Alappuzha
	1	J	JODG	NHK (1), Hamamatsu
	10	J	JOHG	NHK (1), Kagoshima
	1	KOR		KBS, Suncheon (3)
	100	NPL		R. Nepal, Surkhet
	2.5	NZL		Star, Hamilton
	5	PHL	DZHR	Cebu Bc. Co., Tuguegarao, Cag.
	10	PHL	DXMF	People's Bc. Sce., Davao C, Dvo Sur
	10	PHL	DYMR	Philippine Bc. Sce., Cebu C
	10	PHL	DZMQ	Philippine Bc. Sce., Dagupan C, Pang.
	5	THA		Tor. Chor. Dor., Bangkok
	50	VTN		Khanh Hoa (2/P), Nha Trang
585	10	AUS	7RN	ABC (N), Hobart
	10	AUS	6PB	ABC (P), Perth
	10	AUS	2WEB	Bourke (CRS)

kHz	kW	Ctry	Call	Station, location
	50	CHN		JS + 11 stns
	200	CHN		Southeast BC, FJ
	300	IND		AIR, Nagpur A
	50	INS		RRI, Surabaya (4)
	10	J	JOPG	NHK (1), Kushiro
	20	LAO		Lao National Radio (P), Khantabouly
	2	NZL		R. Ngâti Porou, Ruatoria
	500	PAK		PBC, Islamabad
	5	PHL	DXCP	Catholic Media Netw., Gen. Santos C, S Cot
	1	PHL	DYLL	Philippine Bc. Sce., Iloilo C
	10	PNG		NBC National, Port Moresby
	5	THA		Thor. Phor. 3, Phrae
	5	THA		Wor. Por. Tho. 15, Chumphon
590	7.5	HWA	KSSK	Honolulu, Oahu
594	50	AUS	3WV	ABC (L), Horsham
	400	BRM		Myanma Radio (N), Naypyidaw
	300	CHN		XZ; SD (2 stns)
	1000	IND		AIR, Chinsurah, FS
	300	J	JOAK	NHK (1), Tokyo
	5	NZL		Star, Timaru
	2	NZL		Star, Wanagnui
	5	PHL	DXDB	Catholic Media Netw., Malaybalay, Buk.
	20	PHL	DZBB	GMA Network, Inc., Quezon C, NCR
	5	THA		Phon. Por. Thor. Or., Bangkok
	10	TWN	BEH44	Fu Hsing BS (1), Kaohsiung
	5	TWN	BEH38	Fu Hsing BS (2), Taichung
	10	TWN	BEH2	Fu Hsing BS (2), Taipei
	50	VTN		Danang (1) (An Hai)
603	10	AUS	4CH	ABC (L), Charleville
	2	AUS	6PH	ABC (L), Port Hedland
	10	AUS	2RN	ABC (N), Nowra
	100	CHN		EN + 35 stns
	10	CHN		GD (CNR1)
	600	CHN		HA (CRI)
	200	IND		AIR, Ajmer
	5	J	JOOG	NHK (1), Obihiro
	5	J	JOKK	NHK (1), Okayama
	500	KOR	HLSA	KBS, Namyang (Seoul)
	5	NZL		R. Waatea, Auckland
	10	PHL	DZLL	Bicol Bc. System, Naga C, Cam Sur
	5	PHL	DZVV	Consolidated Bc. Syst., Inc., Vigan, I. Sur
	5	PHL	DXPR	R. Mindanao Netw., Pagadian C, Z Sur (v)
	5	THA		Wor. Por. Tho. 12, Khon Kaen
610	200	VTN		Ho Chi Minh C. (H), Tang Nhon Phu
612	50	AUS	4QR	ABC (L), Brisbane
	10	AUS	6RN	ABC (N), Dalwallinu
	100	CHN		FJ; GD (2stns); LN (2stns); SC (2stns)
	200	IND		AIR, Bengaluru
	100	J	JOLK	NHK (1), Fukuoka
	100/200	KGZ		Kyrgyz R. (1)/TWR relay, Bishkek
	2	NZL		Star, Christchurch
	2	NZL		Star, Nelson
	5	NZL		Star, New Plymouth
	5	PHL	DWSP	Philippine Bc. Corp., Itogon, Benguet
	10	PHL	DYHP	R. Mindanao Netw., Cebu C
	5	THA		Mor. Kor., Chiang Mai
	5	THA		Wor. Sor. Por., Lop Buri
621	50	AUS	3RN	ABC (N), Melbourne
	2	AUS	6EL	Bunbury
	200	CHN		HL; HB; QH; SC; SD
	20	HKG		RTHK (P), Golden Hill
	100	IND		AIR, Patna
	3	J	JOCG	NHK (1), Asahikawa
	1	J		NHK (1), Iida/Nobeoka
	500	KRE		Pyongyang BS/VoK, Chongjin
	2	NZL		Rhema, Dunedin
	2	NZL		Rhema, Whangarei
	1	PHL	DWJS	Philippine Bc. Sce., Legazâi C, Albay
	1	PHL	DZVC	Philippine Bc. Sce., Virac, Catanduanes
	10	PHL	DXDC	R. Mindanao Netw., Davao C, Dvo Sur
	5	PHL	DZTG	R. Philippines Netw., Tuguegarao, Cag.
	100	THA		Sor.Wor.Sor, Khon Kaen
	5	TUV		R. Tuvalu, Funafuti
	1	TWN		Taiwan BC, Tahsi
630	5	AUS	6AL	ABC (L), Albany
	50	AUS	4QN	ABC (L), Townsville
	0.4	AUS	7RN	ABC (N), Queenstown
	10	AUS	2PB	ABC (P), Sydney
	100	BGD		Bangladesh Betar, Dhaka
	200	CHN		JX (CNR2); EN (CNR2)
	1	CKH		R. Cook Is. AM, Rarotonga
	10	GUM	KUAM	Agana
	100	IND		AIR, Thrissur
	50	INS		RRI, Makassar
	10	KOR		KBS, Yeosu
	10	NZL		RNZ (N), Napier
	100	PAK		PBC (1), Lahore
	50	PHL	DZMM	ABS-CBN Bc. Corp., Quezon C, NCR (r.inactive)
	10/5	PHL	DYWB	Consolidated Bc. Syst., Inc., Bacolod C, Neg. Occ.
	5	THA		Mor. Thor. Bor. 11, Bangkok
	10	TWN	BED65	BCC (N), Ilan
	10	TWN		Taiwan BC, Sungling
	200	VTN		Quang Binh (1), Dong Hoi
639	1	AUS	4MS	ABC (L), Mossman
	10	AUS	5CK	ABC (L), Port Pirie
	2	AUS	8RN	ABC (N), Katherine
	5	AUS	2HC	Coff's Harbour
	400	BRM		Thazin Radio (M), Thin Village
	200/400	CHN		BJ (CNR1); SC (CNR1)
	100	IND		AIR, Kohima
	5	J	JOIP	NHK (1), Oita
	10	J	JOPB	NHK (2), Shizuoka
	5	J	JOWN	STV, Hakodate
	10	PAK		PBC, Karachi (Landhi)
	5	PHL	DXKR	R. Mindanao Netw., Koronadal, Cot. Sur
	1	PHL	DZRL	R. Philippines Netw., Batac, I. Nte
	10	THA		R. Thailand, Chiang Mai
	20	THA		R. Thailand, N. Si Thammarat
648	2	AUS	6GF	ABC (L), Kalgoorlie
	10	AUS	2NU	ABC (L), Tamworth
	50	CHN		GD + 4 stns
	200	IND		AIR, Indore
	10	J		AFN, Okinawa C.
	5	J	JOIG	NHK (1), Toyama
	100	NPL		R. Nepal, Dhankuta
	5	PHL	DYRC	Manila Bc. Co., Cebu C
	10	PHL	DWRH	Pacific Bc. System, Santiago C, Isa.
	10	PHL	DWRM	Philippine Bc. Sce., Pto. Princesa, Palawan
	3	PHL	DXMB	R. Mindanao Netw., Malaybalay, Buk.
	25	THA		R. Thailand, Khon Kaen
	20	TWN	BED34	BCC (N), Taipei (Tucheng)
	50	VTN		Binh Dinh (1), Quy Nhon (An Nhon)
650	10	HWA	KPRP	Honolulu, Oahu
657	10	AUS	2BY	ABC (L), Byrock
	2	AUS	8RN	ABC (N), Darwin
	2	AUS		SEN Track, Perth (HPON)
	300	CHN		EN; JL; ZJ
	5	CHN		FJ (CNR1)
	200	IND		AIR, Kolkata A
	50	KOR	HLKM	KBS, Chuncheon
	1500	KRE		Pyongyang BS, Kangnam
	10	NZL		RNZ (AM)/Star, Tauranga
	50	NZL		RNZ (AM)/Star, Wellington
	5	PHL	DXDD	Dan-ag sa Dakbayan Bc. Corp., Ozamis C, Mis. Occ.
	1	PHL	DYES	Philippine Bc. Sce., Borongan, E. Samar
	5	PHL	DWRN	Philippine R. Corp., Naga C, Cam. Sur
	5	PHL	DYVR	R. Mindanao Netw., Roxas C, Capiz
	1	PHL	DZLU	Satellite Bc. Corp., S. Fernando C, LU
	5	THA		Jor. Sor. 1, Bangkok
	20	TWN	BEV59	Cheng Sheng BC (2), Taichung
	100	VTN		Ho Chi Minh C. (1/C), Quan Tre
666	5	AUS	2CN	ABC (L), Canberra
	2	AUS	4CC	Biloela (t)
	1	AUS	6LN	Carnarvon (F.PI FM)
	2	AUS	4LM	Mt. Isa

kHz	kW	Ctry	Call	Station, location
	200	CHN		QH + 8 stns
	600	CHN		VO Strait, FJ
	100	IND		AIR, New Delhi B
	100	J	JOBK	NHK (1), Osaka
	35	PHL	DZRH	Manila Bc. Co., Makati C, NCR
	5	THA		Thor. Phor. 2, Surin
	50	VTN		Khanh Hoa (1), Nha Trang
670	5	HWA	KPUA	Hilo, Hawaii
675	10	AUS	2CO	ABC (L), Albury
	5	AUS	6BE	ABC (L), Broome
	200	CHN		NM; XJ; YN (2 stns); ZJ
	10	HKG		RTHK (6), Peng Chau
	20	IND		AIR, Bhadravathi
	20	IND		AIR, Chhatarpur
	100	IND		AIR, Itanagar
	5	J	JOVK	NHK (1), Hakodate
	5	J	JOUG	NHK (1), Yamaguchi
	10	KOR		KBS, Jeonju (3)
	10	NZL		RNZ (N), Christchurch
	5	PHL	DYKC	R. Philippines Netw., Mandaue, Cebu
	1	PHL	DXGD	Sulu Tawi-Tawi Bc. Found., Bongao, Tawi-Tawi
	5	THA		Sor. Thor. Ror. 2, Bangkok
	5	TWN		Cheng Sheng BC, Peikang
	500	VTN		Hung Yen (1) (My Hao)
684	5	AUS	6BS	ABC (L), Busselton
	10	AUS	2KP	ABC (L), Kempsey
	1	AUS	8RN	ABC (N), Tennant Creek
	1200	CHN		FJ (CNR6)
	200	CHN		GS + 9 stns
	600	CHN		HA (CRI)
	200	IND		AIR, Kargil A
	100	IND		AIR, Kozhikode
	100	IND		AIR, Port Blair
	5	J	JODF	IBC, Morioka
	1	J	JOLO	IBC, Ofunato
	5	J	JOAG	NHK (1), Nagasaki
	100	NPL		R. Nepal, Pokhara
	5	PHL	DZCV	Filipinas Bc. Netw,., Tuguegarao, Cag.
	5	PHL	DWJJ	Kaissar Bc. Netw., Cabanatuan, Nva. Ecija
	10	PHL	DYEZ	Manila Bc. Co., Bacolod, Neg. Occ.
	5	THA		Thor. Phor. 4, N. Si Thammarat
	5	THA		Yaan Kraw, Udon Thani
	10	TWN	BEC22	VO Han Bc. Netw., Taipei
690	10	HWA	KHNR	Honolulu, Oahu
693	2	AUS	5SY	ABC (L), Streaky Bay
	10/5	AUS	4KQ	Brisbane
	1	AUS	4LM	Cloncurry (t)
	5	AUS	6WR	Kununurra (CRS)
	5	AUS	3AW	Melbourne
	0.5	AUS	4KZ	Tully (t)
	1000	BGD		Bangladesh Betar (A), Dhaka
	300	CHN		SN; HL
	500	J	JOAB	NHK (2), Tokyo
	5	NZL		Gold AM, Dunedin
	1	PHL	DYKX	Manila Bc. Co., Kalibo, Aklan
	10	PHL	DYPH	Manila Bc. Co., Pto. Princesa, Palawan
	10	PHL	DXBC	R. Mindanao Netw., Butuan, Ag. Nte
	1	PHL	DXDX	R. Philippines Netw., Gen. Santos C, S. Cot.
	10/5	PHL	DZTP	Tirad Pass R/TV Bc. Netw., Candon, I. Sur
	5	THA		Siang Adison, Saraburi
	8	TWN	BEC32	VO Han Bc. Netw., Tainan
	10	TWN	BEC25	VO Han Bc. Netw., Taoyuan
702	10	AUS	6KP	ABC (L), Karratha
	50	AUS	2BL	ABC (L), Sydney
		CHN		GD (CRI DS)
	200	CHN		JS + 6 stns
	200	IND		AIR, Jalandhar A, FS
	10	INS		RRI, Manokwari
	10	J	JOFB	NHK (2), Hiroshima
	10	J	JOKD	NHK (2), Kitami
	50	KRE		Korean Central BS (C/R), Chongjin (r.inactive)
	1	NZL		Gold AM, Ashburton
	10	NZL		Magic Talk, Auckland
	50	PHL	DZAS	FEBC, Valenzuela, NCR
	150	TJK		TR (1), Orzu
	50	VTN		Danang (2/Q/D) (An Hai)
705	10	LAO		Lao National Radio (P), Luang Prabang
711	10	AUS	4QW	ABC (L), Roma/St. George
	10	CHN		QH + 7 stns
	200	IND		AIR, Siliguri
	500	KOR	HLKA	KBS, Sorae (Seoul)
	100	PAK		PBS, Dera Ismail Khan
	5	PHL	DZVR	Newsounds Bc. Netw., Laoag, I. Nte
	5	PHL	DXIC	R. Mindanao Netw., Iligan C, Lanao Nte
	5	PHL	DXRD	Swara Sug Media Corp., Davao C, Dvo. Sur
	5	PHL	DZYI	Swara Sug Media Corp., Ilagan, Isa.
	20	THA		Sor.Wor.Sor, U. Ratchathani
	5	THA		Wor. Por. Thor., Chiang Mai
	5	THA		Wor. Sor. Por., Lop Buri
	10	TWN	BED92	BCC (C), Tainan
	250	TWN		VO Kuanghua, Hsinfeng
	500	VTN		Can Tho (1), Thoi Long
720	4	AUS	4AT	ABC (L), Atherton
	0.4	AUS	2ML	ABC (L), Murwillumbah
	2	AUS	3MT	ABC (L), Omeo
	50	AUS	6WF	ABC (L), Perth
	0.05	AUS	2RN	ABC (N), Armidale
	200	CHN		BJ (CNR16)
	50	CHN		FJ (CNR2) (2 stns)
	10	CHN		JL(CNR8)
	1	CHN		SC; AH (2 stns)
	10	CHN		XJ (CNR13) (2 stns)
	200	IND		AIR, Chennai A
	10	INS		RRI, Ambon
	1	J	JOIL	KBC, Kitakyushu
	500	KRE		Korean Central BS (C/R), Wiwon (Kanggye) (r.inactive)
	10	NZL		RNZ (N), Invercargill
	5	PHL	DZJO	Bayanihan Bc. Corp., San Juan, NCR
	1	PHL	DYOK	Manila Bc. Co., Iloilo C
	5	PHL	DZSO	Newsounds Bc. Netw., San Fernando, LU
	5/10	THA		R. Thailand, Krabi
	5	THA		Sor. Thor. Ror. 5, Chon Buri
	10	TWN	BED58	BCC (N), Taichung
729	50	AUS	5RN	ABC (N), Adelaide
	100	BRM		Myanma Radio (Y), Yangon
	200	CHN		JX; EN
	100	IND		AIR, Guwahati A
	10	INS		RRI, Nabire
	50	J	JOCK	NHK (1), Nagoya
	3	NZL		Gold AM, Whangarei
	2.5	NZL		RNZ (N), Tokoroa
	10	PHL	DXIF	Newsounds Bc. Netw., Cagayan de Oro C, Mis. Or.
	5	PHL	DXOR	Pedro N. Roa Bc., Cagayan de Oro C, Mis. Or.
	5	PHL	DZGB	People's Bc. Netw., Legaspi C, Albay
	10	PHL	DWPE	Philippine Bc. Sce., Tuguegarao, Cag.
	5	PHL	DXMY	R. Mindanao Netw., Cotabato C, Mag.
	25	THA		R. Thailand, N. Ratchasima
	0.5	TWN	BEE43	Shih Hsin BS, Taipei
	200	VTN		Quang Binh (2), Dong Hoi
738	50	AUS	2NR	ABC (L), Grafton
	5	AUS	6MJ	ABC (L), Manjimup
	200	CHN		HN + 5 stns
	200	IND		AIR, Hyderabad A
	1	J		KNB, Takaoka
	5	J	JOLR	KNB, Toyama
	10	J	JORR	RBC, Naha, Okinawa
	100	KOR	HLKG	KBS, Daegu
	5	NZL		Magic Talk, Christchurch
	60	PHL	DZRB	Philippine Bc. Sce., Quezon C, NCR
	5	THA		Wor. Por. Tho. 2, Chiang Mai
	5	THA		Wor. Por. Tho. 5, Songkhla
	100	TWN	BEL2	Yuyeh BS, Penghu

kHz	kW	Ctry	Call	Station, location
740	5	HWA	KCIK	Kihei, Maui
	50	VTN		Binh Dinh (2/P), Quy Nhon (An Nhon)
747	0.2	AUS	8JB	ABC (L), Jabiru
	10	AUS	4QS	ABC (L), Toowoomba
	3.5	AUS	7PB	ABC (P), Hobart
	5/1	AUS	6SE	Esperance (F.PI FM)
	10	CHN		GD (CNR1/12)
	200	CHN		SC + 31 stns
	300	IND		AIR, Lucknow
	10	INS		RRI, Bengkulu
	500	J	JOIB	NHK (2), Sapporo
	100	KOR	HLKH	KBS, Gwangju
	0.4	NZL		NewstalkZB, Rotorua
	10	PHL	DZJC	Manila Bc. Co., Laoag C, I. Nte
	5	PHL	DXND	Notre Dame Bc. Corp., Kidapawan, N. Cot.
	10	PHL	DYHB	R. Mindanao Netw., Bacolod, Neg. Occ.
	5	SMO		National Radio 2AP, Apia (repl.mast)
	5	THA		Ror. Dor., Bangkok
	5	THA		Thor. Phor. 2, Udon Thani
750	1	CHN		SX
756	2	AUS	2TR	ABC (L), Taree
	10	AUS	3RN	ABC (N), Wangaratta
	2	AUS	6TZ	Margaret River
	50	CHN		GD (CNR1) (3 stns); SD (CNR1)
	150	CHN		HL (CNR1)
	100	IND		AIR, Jagdalpur
	10	INS		RRI, Purwokerto
	10	J	JOGK	NHK (1), Kumamoto
	0.8	NZL		Puketapu R., Palmerston
	10	NZL		RNZ (N), Auckland
	100	PAK		PBC (1), Quetta (Yaru)
	10	PHL	DXBZ	Baganian Bc. Corp., Pagadiani, Z Sur
	1	PHL	DWHL	Beta Bc. Syst., Olongapo C, Zamb.
	10	PHL	DWRS	Philippine Bc. Sce., Tayug, Pang.
	2	PHL	DXJM	R. Corp. of the Philippines, Butuan C, Ag. Nte
	5	THA		Kor. Wor. Sor. 1, Surin
	5	THA		Nor. Thor. Phor., Narathiwat
	1	TWN		Sheng Li chih Sheng BC, Makung
	10	VTN		Long An (P), Tan An
760	10	HWA	KGU	Honolulu, Oahu
765	5	AUS	2EC	Bega
	0.5	AUS	4GC	Hughenden (t)
	0.5	AUS	8HOT	Katherine (t)
	5	AUS	5CC	Port Lincoln
	10	CHN		EN + 3 stns
	600	CHN		FJ (CNR5)
	200	IND		AIR, Dharwad
	1	INS		RRI, Tual
	5	J	JOPF	KRY, Shunan
	5	J	JOJF	YBS, Kofu
	10	KOR	HLCQ	MBC, Daejeon
	2.5	NZL		R. Kahungungu, Hawkes Bay
	5	PHL	DXGS	DWRL Radio, Inc., Gen. Santos C, S. Cot.
	10	PHL	DYAP	Palawan Bc. Corp., Pto. Princesa, Palawan (r.inactive)
	5	PHL	DYAR	Swara Sug Media Corp., Cebu C
	5	PHL	DZYT	Swara Sug Media Corp., Tuguegarao, Cag.
	5	RUS		R. Vostok Rossii, Berezovyy, FE + 9 stns
	20	RUS		R. Vostok Rossii, Khabarovsk, FE + 1 stn
	5	THA		Neung. Por. Nor., Lampang
	5	THA		Thor. Or. 2, Lop Buri
774	50	AUS	3LO	ABC (L), Melbourne
	10	CHN		BJ (Bejing Int.)
	200	CHN		HB; LN; SX; XJ
	100	IND		AIR, Shimla
		INS		RRI, Fak-Fak
	500	J	JOUB	NHK (2), Akita
	10	KOR	HLAN	MBC, Chuncheon
	10	KOR	HLAJ	MBC, Jeju
	5	NZL		Gold AM, New Plymouth
	25	PHL	DWWW	Interactive Bc. Media, Inc., Quezon C, NCR
	10	PHL	DXSM	Philippine Bc. Sce., Jolo, Sulu
	10	PHL	DXSO	Philippine Bc. Sce., Marawi C, Lanao Sur
	10	PHL	DYRI	R. Mindanao Netw., Iloilo C
	5	THA		Phon. Mor. 2, Rayong
	5	THA		Sor. Sor. Sor., Udon Thani
	20	TWN	BEV88	Hsien Sheng BC, Taoyuan
	1	TWN	BEV56	Sheng Li chih Sheng BC (1), Tainan
	20	TWN	BEV94	Taiwan BC, Taichung
783	2	AUS	8AL	ABC (L), Alice Springs
	2	AUS	6VA	Albany (F.PI FM)
	100	CHN		EB (4 stns); GD
	600	CHN		VO Strait, FJ
	20	HKG		RTHK (5), Golden Hill
	10	INS		RRI, Ende
	5	PHL	DYME	Masbate Comm. Bc. Co., Masbate C
	5	PHL	DZNL	Philippine Bc. Corp., San Fernando, LU
	10	PHL	DXRA	RMC Bc. Co., Inc., Davao C, Dvo Sur
	10	THA		R. Thailand, Ranong
	5	THA		Thor. Phor. 3, Kamphaeng Phet
	500	VTN		Can Tho (2), Thoi Long
792	25	AUS	4RN	ABC (N), Brisbane
	200	CHN		GX +11 stns
	100	IND		AIR, Pune
	1	J		NHK (1), Takada/Naze
	1	J		NHK (1), Takayama/Enbetsu
	50	KOR	HLSQ	Seoul Bc. System, Goyang (Seoul)
	100	NPL		R. Nepal, Kathmandu
	5	NZL		Gold AM, Hamilton
	5	PHL	DWGV	GV Bc. System, Angeles C, Pampanga
	5	PHL	DYRR	Ormoc Bc. Co., Ormoc C, Leyte
	5	PHL	DXPD	People's Bc. Sce., Pagadian, Z. Sur
	10	PHL	DXBN	Philippine Bc. Sce., Butuan, Ag. Nte
	5	PHL	DWES	Rolin Bc. Enterprises, Narra, Palawan
	5	THA		Wor. Por. Thor., Bangkok
	1	TWN	BEV79	Keelung BS, Keelung
	10	TWN	BEC33	VO Han Bc. Netw., Hualien
801	2	AUS	4QY	ABC (L), Cairns
	2	AUS	5RM	Berri
	5	AUS		SEN Track, Gosford
	50	CHN		GD + 27 stns
	10	GUM	KTWG	Agana
	200	IND		AIR, Jabalpur
	10	INS		RRI, Semarang
	500	KRE		Pyongyang BS, Kimchaek
	1.5	NZL		Rhema, Nelson
	5	PHL	DYKA	Catholic Media Netw., San José, Ant.
	5	PHL	DXES	Consolidated Bc. Syst., Inc., Gen. Santos C, S. Cot.
	5	PHL	DYWC	Franciscan Bc. Corp., Dumaguete, Neg. Or.
	10	PHL	DZNC	Newsounds Bc. Netw., Cauayan, Isa.
	1	PHL	DXBL	Swara Sug Media Corp., Bislig, Surigao S.
	5	THA		Mor. Thor. Bor. No. 31, N. Sawan
	5	THA		Thor. Or. 15, Chiang Rai
	5	THA		Thor. Or. 8, U. Ratchathani
	1	TWN		Chien Kuo BS, Hsinhua
	250	TWN		VO Kuanghua, Kuanyin (r.inactive)
810	10	AUS	2BA	ABC (L), Bega
	20	AUS	6RN	ABC (N), Perth
	200	CHN		ZJ + 6 stns
	300	IND		AIR, Rajkot A
	7.5	INS		RRI, Merauke
	50	J		AFN, Tokyo
	20	KOR	HLCT	MBC, Daegu (r.inactive)
	50	KRE		Korean Central BS (C/R), Kaesong
	10	NPL		R. Nepal, Dipayal
	2	NZL		BBC WS NZ, Auckland
	10	NZL		RNZ (N), Dunedin
	1	PHL	DXRG	Philippine Bc. Sce., Gingoog C, Mis. Or.
	10	PHL	DZRJ	Rajah Bc. Netw., Manila, NCR
	10	PNG		NBC Morobe, Lae
	2	PNG		NBC Rabaul
	20	THA		R. Thailand, Nong Khai
	10	THA		R. Thailand, Sangkhlaburi
	10	THA		R. Thailand, Trang

kHz	kW	Ctry	Call	Station, location
	10	TWN	BEV54	Kuo Sheng BC, Changhua
819	10	AUS	2GL	ABC (L), Glen Innes
	5	AUS	6KW	ABC (L), Kununurra
	100	BGD		Bangladesh Betar (B), Dhaka
	200	CHN		SX; SD; XJ(2 stns)
	200	IND		AIR, New Delhi A
	5	J	JONK	NHK (1), Nagano
	20	KOR	HLCN	MBC, Gwangju
	500	KRE		Korean Central BS (C), Pyongyang
	10	NZL		RNZ (N), Tauranga
	10	PHL	DYVL	Manila Bc. Co., Tacloban, Leyte
	5	PHL	DWAR	Swara Sug Media Corp., Laoag C, I. Nte
	10	PHL	DXUM	Univ. of Mindanao Bc. Netwk, Davao C, Dvo Sur
	1	PHL	DWMG	Vanguard R. Netw., Solano, Nva Viz
	10	THA		R. Thailand, Bangkok (Pathum Thani)
	15	TJK		TR (1), Khujand
	10	TWN	BED28	BCC (N), Taitung
	5	TWN	BEV35	Cheng Sheng BC, Taipei
	20	VTN		Dac Lac (2), Buon Ma Tuhot
828	10	AUS	6GN	ABC (L), Geraldton
	10	AUS	3GI	ABC (L), Sale
	1	AUS	4GC	Charters Towers
	50	CHN		BJ + 7 stns
	10	CHN		HL (CNR2)
	20	IND		AIR, Panaji B
	20	IND		AIR, Silchar
	300	J	JOBB	NHK (2), Osaka
	1	PHL	DZTC	Govt of Tarlac Prov., Tarlac C
	5	PHL	DWZR	Hypersonic Bc. Center, Legaspi C, Albay
	10	PHL	DXCC	R. Mindanao Netw., Cagayan de Oro C, Mis. Or.
	5	THA		Thor. Phor. 3, Sukhothai
	5	THA		Wor. Por. Tho. 4, N. Si Thammarat
	50	VTN		Son La (P)
830	10	HWA	KHVH	Honolulu, Oahu
837	1	AUS	6ED	ABC (L), Esperance
	10	AUS	4RK	ABC (L), Rockhampton
	1000	CHN		FJ (CNR5)
	50	CHN		HL + 4 stns
	100	IND		AIR, Vijayawada
	1	J		NHK (1), Nayoro
	10	J	JOQK	NHK (1), Niigata
	50	KOR	HLKY	CBS, Seoul
	2	NZL		RNZ (N), Kaitaia
	2.5	NZL		RNZ (N), Whangarei
	10	PHL	DYFM	Consolidated Bc. Syst., Inc., Iloilo C
	10	PHL	DXJS	Philippine Bc. Sce., Tandag, S Sur
	5	PHL	DXRE	Swara Sug Media Corp., Gen. Santos C, S. Cotab.
	5	THA		Nor. Thor. Phor., Sakon Nakhon
	10	THA		R. Thailand, Bangkok (Pathum Thani)
846	2.5	AUS	6CA	ABC (L), Carnarvon
	10	AUS	2RN	ABC (N), Canberra
	5	AUS	4EL	Cairns
	100	BGD		Bangladesh Betar, Rajshahi (Bogra)
	10	CHN		BJ (CRI DS4)
	30	CHN		HB + 32 stns
	200	IND		AIR, Ahmedabad
	5	J		NHK (1), Koriyama
	1	J		NHK (1), Uwajima/Hitoyoshi
		KIR		R. Kiribati, Kiritimati Is
	10	KOR	HLAU	MBC, Ulsan
	2	NZL		NewstalkZB, Masterton
	50	PHL	DZRV	R. Veritas, Quezon C, NCR
	10	THA		R. Thailand, Phetchabun
	10	TWN	BEC38	VO Han Bc. Netw., Penghu
	250	TWN		VO Kuanghua, Kuanyin (r.inactive)
850	5	HWA	KHLO	Hilo, Hawaii
855	10	AUS	4QO	ABC (L), Eidsvold
	10	AUS	4QB	ABC (L), Pialba
	3.5	AUS	3CR	Melbourne (CRS)
	50	CHN		YN (CNR2); XJ
	10	INS		RRI, Mataram (r.inactive)
	10	KOR	HLCX	MBC, Jeonju
	500	KRE		Pyongyang BS, Sangwon
	2	NZL		Rhema, Hamilton
	5	PHL	DXZH	Cebu Bc. Co., Zamboanga C, Z. Sur
	10	PHL	DZGE	Filipinas Bc. Netw,., Naga C, Cam. Sur
	5	PHL	DXGO	Pacific Bc. System, Davao C, Dvo Sur
	5	THA		Mor. Thor. Bor. 12, Prachin Buri
	4.6	TWN	BED27	BCC (N), Hualien
	1	TWN	BEV72	Cheng Sheng BC, Chia-i
	1	TWN	BEV24	Min Pen BC (2), Taipei
864	2	AUS	7RPH	Hobart (CRS)
	2	AUS	6AM	Northam
	2	AUS	4GR	Toowoomba
	50	CHN		AH; EB; EN; SD; ZJ (2 stns)
	10	HKG		Hong Kong Comm. Bc. Co., Peng Chau
	100	IND		AIR, Shillong
	10	INS		RRI, Cirebon
	1	J	JOXN	CRT, Nasu
	5	J	JOPR	FBC, Fukui
	3	J	JOHE	HBC, Asahikawa
	1	J		HBC, Enbetsu
	3	J	JOQF	HBC, Muroran
	10	J	JOXR	ROK, Naha, Okinawa
	1	J	JOSO	SBC, Matsumoto
	100	KOR	HLKR	KBS, Gangneung
	10	NZL		NewstalkZB, Invercargill
	5	PHL	DZWM	Alaminos City Bc. Corp., Alaminos, Pang.
	10	PHL	DYHH	Philippine Air Force, Bogo, Cebu
	10	PHL	DZIP	R. Palaweño, Pto. Princesa, Palawan
	5	PHL	DWSI	Swara Sug Media Corp., Santiago, Isa.
	10	THA		R. Thailand, Si Sa Ket
	10	THA		R. Thailand, Tak
	10	TWN	BED25	BCC (N), Kaohsiung
873	2	AUS	6DB	ABC (L), Derby
	2	AUS	4AY	Innisfail (HPON)
	6	AUS	2GB	Sydney
	100	BGD		Bangladesh Betar, Chittagong
	200	CHN		China Huayi BC, FJ
	100	CHN		HL + 7 stns
	300	IND		AIR, Jalandhar B
	500	J	JOGB	NHK (2), Kumamoto
	250	KRE		Pyongyang BS (C/R), Sinuiju (r.inactive)
	1	NZL		Newstalk ZB, Ashburton
	5	PHL	DZPA	Abra Comm. Bc. Corp., Bangued, Abra
	5	PHL	DZRC	Filipinas Bc. Netw,., Legaspi C, Albay
	5	PHL	DXRB	Swara Sug Media Corp., Butuan C, Ag. Nte
	5	PHL	DYUP	Univ. of the Philippines in the Visyas, Miagao, Iloilo
	5	THA		Wor. Kor. Thor. Mor., Bangkok
	500	VTN		Can Tho (4), Thoi Long
880	2	HWA	KHCM	Honolulu, Oahu
882	5	AUS	4BH	Brisbane
	10	AUS	6PR	Perth
	2	AUS	3RPH	Warrnambool (CRS)
	200	CHN		FJ (3 stns) + 10 stns
	400	CLN		TWR relay, Puttalam
	300	IND		AIR, Imphal
	10	J	JOPK	NHK (1), Shizuoka
	1	J		STV, Esashi
	3	J	JOWS	STV, Kushiro
	20	KOR	HLKI	KBS, Daejeon
	40	MNG		MRT (1), Mörön
	10	NZL		RNZ (AM)/Star, Auckland
	50	PHL	DWIZ	Aliw Bc. Corp., Navotas, NCR
	10	PHL	DXMS	Notre Dame Bc. Corp., Cotabato C, Mag.
	10	PHL	DYOG	Philippine Bc. Sce., Calbayog, W. Samar
	10	TWN	BEG77	BCC (N), Hsinchu
	1	TWN		Feng Ming BC, Penghu
891	50	AUS	5AN	ABC (L), Adelaide
	5	AUS	4TAB	R. TAB, Townsville (HPON)
	200	CHN		NX; LN; SD; XJ
	20	IND		AIR, Rampur
	10	INS		RRI, Malang (4)
	10	INS		RRI, Ternate
	20	J	JOHK	NHK (1), Sendai

kHz	kW	Ctry	Call	Station, location
	250	KOR	HLKB	KBS, Busan
	5	NZL		Magic Music, Wellington
	5	PHL	DZGR	People's Bc. Sce., Tuguegarao, Cag.
	400	THA		R. Thailand, Bangkok (Sara Buri)
	10	TWN	BED24	BCC (L), Tainan
900	2	AUS	8HA	Alice Springs
	2	AUS	6BY	Bridgetown
	5	AUS	2LM	Lismore (F.PI FM)
	5	AUS	2LT	Lithgow (F.PI FM)
		CHN		BJ (CRI DS5)
	10	CHN		QH (CNR2)
	50	CHN		YN (CRI)
	100	CHN		YN + 38 stns
	5	HWA	KMVI	Kahului, Maui
	100	IND		AIR, Kadapa
	5	J	JOHF	BSS, Yonago
	5	J	JOHO	HBC, Hakodate
	5	J	JOZR	RKC, Kochi
	50	KOR	HLKV	MBC, Seoul
	2.5	NZL		Coast, Whangarei
	6	NZL		RNZ (AM)/Star, Dunedin
	5	PHL	DYOW	Consolidated Bc. Syst., Inc., Roxas, Capiz
	5	PHL	DWNE	Nueva Ecija Prov. Gov., Cabanatuan C, Nva Viz.
	5	PHL	DXRZ	R. Mindanao Netw., Zamboanga C, Z. Sur
	2	PNG		NBC Eastern Highlands, Goroka
	10	VTN		Ha Tinh (v) (P)
909	300	CHN		FJ (CNR6)
	50	CHN		SC + 6 stns
	100	IND		AIR, Gorakhpur
	10	INS		RRI, Sorong
	10	J	JOCB	NHK (2), Nagoya
	5	J	JOVX	STV, Abashiri
	5	NZL		RNZ (AM)/Star, Napier
	5	NZL		Star, Hawkes Bay
	5	PHL	DZEA	Catholic Media Netw., Laoag C, I. Nte
	5	PHL	DYSP	Republic Bc. System, Pto. Princesa, Palawan
	5	PHL	DYLA	Visayas Mindanao C. of TU, Cebu C
	10	THA		R. Thailand, Dansai (Loei)
	25	THA		R. Thailand, Surin
	10	VTN		Ca Mau (P)
918	2/2.5	AUS	4VL	Charleville
	2	AUS	6NA	Narrogin
	600	CBG		Nat. Radio of Kampuchea, Phnom Penh (Kandal Steung)
	200	CHN		SD
	300	IND		AIR, Suratgarh
	1	J	JOPN	KRY, Iwakuni
	1	J	JOPM	KRY, Shimonoseki
	1	J		YBC, Tsuruoka/Yonezawa/Shinjo
	5	J	JOEF	YBC, Yamagata
	2.5	NZL		RNZ (N), Timaru
	50	PHL	DZSR	Philippine Bc. Sce., Quezon C, NCR
	5	PHL	DXRS	R. Mindanao Netw., Surigao C, S. Nte
	10	THA		R. Thailand, Bangkok (Pathum Thani)
	10	THA		Sor. Wor. Phor. 1, Chiang Mai
927	5	AUS	4CC	Gladstone
	5	AUS	3UZ	Melbourne
	100	CHN		FJ (CNR6)
	200	CHN		GZ + 27 stns
	100	IND		AIR, Visakhapatnam
	25	INS		RRI, Pekanbaru (4)
	5	J	JOFG	NHK (1), Fukui
	5	J	JOKG	NHK (1), Kofu
	1	J		NHK (1), Wakkanai/Tsuyama
	2	NZL		NewstalkZB, Palmerston N.
	5	PHL	DXDA	Office of the Governor, San Francisco, Ag. Sur
	5	PHL	DZLG	People's Bc. Sce., Legaspi, Albay
	5	PHL	DXMD	R. Mindanao Netw., Gen. Santos C, S. Cot.
	5	PHL	DWRS	Solidnorth Bc.Syst., Vigan, I. Sur
	5	PHL	DXMM	Sulu Tawi-Tawi Bc. Found., Jolo,Sulu
	300	TJK		Relays
	10	TWN	BED43	BCC (C), Taichung
930		CHN		ZJ
936	10	AUS	7ZR	ABC (L), Hobart
	10	AUS	4PB	ABC (P), Brisbane
	5	AUS	6FX	Fitzroy Crossing (CRS)
	200	CHN		AH
	100	IND		AIR, Tiruchirapalli
	5	J	JOTR	ABS, Akita
	1	J		MRT, 4 stns
	5	J	JONF	MRT, Miyazaki
	10	KOR		KBS, Changwon (3)
	1	NZL		AM936 Chinese R., Auckland
	5	PHL	DWIM	Insular Bc. System, Calapan, Mind. Or.
	10	PHL	DXIM	Philippine Bc. Sce., Cagayan de Oro C, Mis. Or.
	1	PHL	DZXT	R. Corp. of the Philippines, Tarlac C
	1	PHL	DYCC	R. Mindanao Netw., Calbayog C, W. Samar
	1	PHL	DYKW	R. Philippines Netw., Binalgaban, Neg. Occ.
	5	PHL	DXDN	Univ. of Mindanao, Tagum C, Dvo Nte
	50	THA		Sor.Wor.Sor, N. Sawan
	10	THA		Thor. Phor. 4, Pattani
	1	TWN	BEV98	Cheng Kung BS, Kaohsiung
	5	TWN		VO Han Bc. Netw., Taoyuan
940	10	HWA	KKNE	Honolulu, Oahu
945	1	AUS	4HI	Dysart (t)
	2	AUS	3UZ	RSN, Bendigo (HPON)
	50	CHN		HL (2 stns); HB (2 stns); NM (5 stns)
	400	CHN		JL (CNR 1)
	10	CHN		XJ (CNR13) (2 stns)
	100	IND		AIR, Sambalpur
	1	J		NHK (1), Fukue
	1	J	JOQP	NHK (1), Hikone
	3	J	JOIQ	NHK (1), Muroran
	5	J	JOXK	NHK (1), Tokushima
	2	NZL		NewstalkZB, Gisborne
	5	PHL	DXRO	Swara Sug Media Corp., Cotabato C, Mag.
	10	PHL	DXDV	Vismin R. and TV Bc. Net, Butuan C, Ag. Nte
	10	THA		Thor. Or. 1, Bangkok
	10	THA		Thor. Phor. 2, Kalasin
954	0.35	AUS	4EL	Gordonvale (t)
	5	AUS	2UE	Sydney
	50	CHN		NM (2 stns) + 7 stns
	200	IND		AIR, Najibabad
	10	INS		RRI, Kendari
	100	J	JOKR	TBS Radio, Tokyo
	1	NZL		Coast, Dunedin
	40	PHL	DZEM	Christian Era Bc. Sce., Quezon City, NCR
	10	PHL	DWFB	Philippine Bc. Sce., Laoag C, I. Nte
	1	PHL	DXJT	Philippine Bc. Sce., Tangub C, Mis Octal
	10	THA		Thor. Or. 10, Phitsanulok
	10	THA		Thor. Or. 16, Chantaburi
	10	TWN	BEV85	Chien Kuo BS, Hsinying
963	2	AUS	6TZ	Bunbury
	5	AUS	2RG	Griffith
	5	AUS	5SE	Mt. Gambier
	5	AUS	4WK	Warwick
	20	BGD		Bangladesh Betar, Sylhet
	600	CHN		JL (CRI)
	50	CHN		LN; EB; HB; XJ (2 stns)
	20	IND		AIR, Jalgaon
	5	J	JOTG	NHK (1), Aomori
	5	J	JOZK	NHK (1), Matsuyama
	1	J	JOSP	NHK (1), Saga
	1	J		NHK (1), Yonago/Hagi
	10	KOR	HLCR	KBS, Andong
	10	KOR	HLKS	KBS, Jeju
	10	NZL		RNZ (AM)/Star, Christchurch
	5	PHL	DZNS	Archdiocese of Nueva Segovia, Vigan, I. Sur
	10	PHL	DXOM	Notre Dame Bc. Corp., Koronadal C, S. Cot.

kHz	kW	Ctry	Call	Station, location
	10	PHL	DYMF	People's Bc. Sce., Cebu C
	5	PHL	DXYZ	Swara Sug Media Corp., Zamboanga C, Z. Sur
	10	THA		Phon Mor. 2, Bangkok
	25	THA		Sor.Wor.Sor, Krabi
	20	TWN	BED55	BCC (C), Taipei (Tucheng)
	10	TWN	BEV84	Taiwan BC, Chunghsing
972	2	AUS	5PB	ABC (P), Adelaide
	0.3	AUS	2DU	Cobar (t)
	5	AUS	2MW	Murwillumbah
	150	CHN		EN; HL; XJ
	300	IND		AIR, Cuttack
	50	INS		RRI, Surakarta
	1500	KOR	HLCA	KBS, Dangjin
	5	NZL		Rhema, Wellington
	5	PHL	DXKH	Cebu Bc. Co., Cagayan de Oro C, Mis. Or.
	1	PHL	DYSM	Cebu Bc. Co., Catarman, N. Samar
	5	PHL	DWTI	Katigbak Enterprises, Lucena C, Que.
	5	PHL	DWFR	Philippine Bc. Sce., Bontoc, Mt. Prov.
	10	THA		Nor. Thor. Phor., Phetchabun
	800	TJK		VOA relay, Orzu
981	2	AUS	3HA	Hamilton
	2	AUS	6KG	Kalgoorlie
	5	AUS	2NM	Muswellbrook
	200	CHN		JL/ JX/ XJ (CNR1); GD (CNR1) (3 stns)
	5	CHN		SD
	100	IND		AIR, Raipur
	1	J		NHK (1), Kisofukushima/Sasebo
	2	NZL		RNZ (N), Kaikohe
	100	PAK		PBC, Turbat
	10	PHL	DXBR	Consolidated Bc. Syst., Inc., Butuan C, Ag. Nte
	10	PHL	DYBQ	Intercontinental Bc. Corp., Iloilo C
	5	PHL	DWMT	Philippine Bc. Corp., Naga C, Cam. Sur
	5	PHL	DXDR	R. Mindanao Netw., Dipolog, Z. Nte
	10	PHL	DXOW	R. Pilipino Corp., Davao C, Dvo Sur
	5	PHL	DZRD	Swara Sug Media Corp., Dagupan C, Pang.
	10	THA		Mahaawittayalai Thammasat, Pathum Thani
	25	THA		R. Thailand, Mae Hong Son
	20	THA		R. Thailand, Nakhon Phanom
	25	THA		R. Thailand, Yala
	2	TWN	BEV68	Feng Ming BC (2), Kaohsiung
	250	TWN		VO Kuanghua, Hsinfeng
990	0.5	AUS	8GO	ABC (L), Nhulunbuy
	0.5	AUS	3RN	ABC (N), Albury-Wodonga
	5.5	AUS	6RPH	Perth (CRS)
	5	AUS	4RO	Rockhampton
	100	CHN		SH; EB; YN (4 stns)
	10	FJI		Fiji Bc. Corp. Ltd. (RFGold), Suva
	5	HWA	KIKI	Honolulu, Oahu
	300	IND		AIR, Jammu
	10	J	JORK	NHK (1), Kochi
	10	KOR	HLAP	MBC, Changwon (r.inactive)
	1	NZL		Apna 990, Auckland
	5	PHL	DZMT	Pacific Bc. System, Laoag, I. Nte
	5	PHL	DYTH	Pacific Bc. System, Tacloban C, Leyte
	5	PHL	DXBM	Republic Bc. System, Cotabato C, Mag.
	10	PHL	DZIQ	Trans-Radio Bc. Corp., Makati C, NCR
	10	THA		Sor. Wor. Phor. 2, N. Ratchasima
	20	TWN	BEV58	Cheng Sheng BC (1), Taichung
999	2	AUS	2NB	ABC (L), Broken Hill
	5	AUS	2ST	Nowra (F.PI FM)
	10	BGD		Bangladesh Betar, Thakurgaon
	200	CHN		LN + 8 stns
	1	FSM	V6AF	Baptist R. Pohnpei, Kolonia
	1	IND		AIR, Almora
	20	IND		AIR, Coimbatore
		INS		RRI, Bandung (3)
		INS		RRI, Cirebon (3)
	150	INS		RRI, Jakarta (3) (r.inactive)
	1	J		NHK (1), Fukuyama/Hachinoe
	1	J		NHK (1), Nakamura
	10	KOR	HLCL	CBS, Gwangju
	1.5	NZL		Manawatu Peoples R., Palmerston N.
	5	PHL	DWMI	Katigbak Enterprises, Calapan, Mind. Or.
	5	PHL	DZEQ	Philippine Bc. Sce., Baguio C, Benguet
	1	PHL	DXPT	Philippine Bc. Sce., Bongao, Tawi-Tawi
	1	PHL	DXHP	R. Mindanao Netw., Bislig, S. Sur
	5	PHL	DYSS	Republic Bc. System, Cebu C
	10	THA		Phon. Neung Ror. Or., Bangkok
	10	THA		Thor. Phor. 3, Chiang Rai
	1	TWN	BEV92	Tien Nan BS, Taipei
1008	10	AUS	4TAB	Brisbane
	5	AUS	7TAB	R. TAB, Launceston (HPON)
	0.3	AUS	2TAB	Sky Sports R., Canberra (HPON)
	2	AUS	6TAB	TAB R. (WA), Geraldton (HPON)
	1	CHN		BJ (CNR DS3)
	50	CHN		TJ + 24 stns
	1	CHN		XJ (CNR 13)
	200	CHN		YN (CNR1)
	100	IND		AIR, Kolkata B
	10	INS		RRI, Gorontalo
	10	INS		RRI, Madiun
	50	J	JONR	ABC, Osaka
	10	NZL		NewstalkZB, Tauranga
	100	PAK		PBC, Hyderabad
	5	PHL	DWBS	Catholic Media Netw., Sto. Domingo, Albay
	10	PHL	DXXX	R. Philippines Netw., Zamboanga C, Z. Sur (v)
	5	PHL	DWGO	Subic Bc. Corp., Olongapo C, Zamb.
	10	THA		Wor. Por. Tho 3, N. Ratchasima
	10	TWN	BED88	BCC (C), Taitung
	1	TWN	BEV60	Cheng Sheng BC, Kaohsiung
1017	0.5	AUS	6WH	ABC (L), Wyndham
	5	AUS	2KY	Sydney
	1	AUS	6TAB	Vision Chr.R., Bunbury (HPON)
	50	CHN		GD (2 stns); EB; QH
	100	CHN		JL (CRI)
	1	CHN		ZJ (CNR1)
	20	IND		AIR, Chennai B
	50	J	JOLB	NHK (2), Fukuoka
	10	KOR	HLAW	MBC, Andong
	10	NZL		NewstalkZB, Christchurch
	10	PHL	DWDC	Intercontinental Bc. Corp., Dagupan C, Pang.
	10	PHL	DXRR	Kalayaan Bc. System, Davao C, Dvo Sur
	10	PHL	DWLC	Philippine Bc. Sce., Lucena C, Que.
	5	PHL	DXSN	Silangan Bc. Corp., Surigao C, S. Nte
	10	THA		Thor. Or. 5, Prachuap KK
	10	TON	A3Z	Tonga Bc. Comm., Nuku'alofa
	10	TWN	BED53	BCC (C), Hsinchu
1026	14.5	AUS	3PB	ABC (P), Melbourne
	5	AUS	4AA	Mackay
	200	CHN		GZ; BJ + 4 stns
	20	IND		AIR, Prayagraj
	5	INS		RRI, Serui
	2	NZL		Newstalk ZB, Kaitaia/Whangarei
	2.5	NZL		Star, Invercargill
	5	PHL	DXMC	People's Bc. Sce., Koronadal, S. Cot.
	10	PHL	DZAR	Swara Sug Media Corp., Quezon C, NCR
	10	THA		R. Thailand, Betong (Yala)
	25	THA		R. Thailand, Phitsanulok
	1	TWN	BEV51	Chung Hua BC (2), Sanchung
	1	TWN		Tien Sheng BS, Yuanli
1035	2	AUS	2EA	Wollongong (SBS)
	50	CHN		HB (CNR1); LN (CNR1)
	20	IND		AIR, Guwahati B
	5	INS		RRI, Bandar Lampung
		INS		RRI, Palu
	1	J	JOHD	NHK (2), Takamatsu
	1	J	JOIC	NHK (2), Toyama
	1	J		NHK (2), Tsuruoka
	10	KOR	HLCP	KBS, Pohang
	20	NZL		Newstalk ZB, Wellington
	100	PAK		PBC, Multan
	5	PHL	DZWX	Consolidated Bc. Syst., Inc., Baguio C, Benguet

kHz	kW	Ctry	Call	Station, location
	10	PHL	DYRL	R. Pilipino Corp., Bacolod C, Neg. Occ.
	5/1	PHL	DXUZ	Univ. de Zamboanga, Ipil, Z. Sib (v)
	6	SLM		SIBC, Honiara
	10	THA		Phaak Phiset, Bangkok
	10	TWN	BED26	BCC (C), Chia-i
1040	10	HWA	KLHT	Honolulu, Oahu
1044	1	AUS	6BR	ABC (L), Bridgetown
	2	AUS	2UH	ABC (L), Muswellbrook
	0.5	AUS	4WP	ABC (L), Weipa
	2	AUS	5AU	Port Pirie (t)
	600	CHN		JS (CRI)
	10	CHN		NM; XJ (2 stns); YN
	10	HKG		Metro Bc. Corp., Peng Chau
	100	IND		AIR, Mumbai A
	2	INS		RRI, Biak
	10	INS		RRI, Sibolga
	1	KOR		AFNK, Chuncheon
	10	NZL		NewstalkZB, Dunedin
	5	PHL	DYMS	Cebu Bc. Co., Catbalogan, W. Samar (v)
	10	PHL	DZNG	Newsounds Bc. Network, Naga C, Cam. Sur (v)
	5	PHL	DXCO	R. Pilipino Corp., Cayagan de Oro, Mis. Or.
	5	PHL	DXLL	R. T. Bc. Specialists Phil., Zamboanga C, Z. Sur
	10	THA		Kor. Wor. Sor. 5, Khon Kaen
	5	TWN	BEV64	Yen Sheng BS (1), Hualien
1050		CHN		ZJ
1053	5	AUS	2CA	Canberra, ACT
	0.5	AUS	4RF	SEN Track, Brisbane (HPON)
	10	BGD		Bangladesh Betar, Rangpur
	10	CHN		BJ (CNR 10)
	50	CHN		LN + 15 stns
	20	IND		AIR, Leh
	200	IND		AIR, Tuticorin, FS
	50	J	JOAR	CBC, Nagoya
	100	PAK		PBC, Larkana
	10	PHL	DXKD	R. Philippines Netw., Dipolog, Z. Nte
	5	PHL	DYSA	Univ. of San Agustin, Iloilo C
	10	THA		Mor. Thor. Bor. 11, Bangkok
1060	5	HWA	KIPA	Hilo, Hawaii
1062	2	AUS	5MV	ABC (L), Renmark/Loxton
	2	AUS	4TI	ABC (L), Thursday Isl.
	150	CHN		Zhujiang EBS, GD; GD;HL
	100	IND		AIR, Passighat
	50	KOR	HLKQ	KBS, Cheongju
	1	NZL		Gold AM, Wanganui
	40	PHL	DZEC	Eagle Bc. Corp., Quezon C, NRC
	5	PHL	DXKI	FEBC, Koronadal C, S. Cot.
	10/5	PHL	DYEC	Puerto Princesa Bc.Co., Pto Princesa C, Palawan
	10	THA		R. Thailand, Phuket
	10	THA		Thor. Or. 9, Udon Thani
	10	TWN	BED77	BCC (L), Taichung
	1	TWN	BEV82	Cheng Sheng BC, Ilan
	5	TWN	BEV74	Min Li BS, Pingtung
	1	TWN		Taiwan BC, Tahsi
1071	2	AUS	6WB	Katanning
	2	AUS	4SB	Kingaroy
	5	AUS	3EL	Maryborough
	100	CHN		XJ + 8 stns
	1000	IND		AIR, Rajkot, FS
	20	J	JOFK	NHK (1), Hiroshima
	5	J	JOWM	STV, Obihiro
	2.5	NZL		RNZ (N), Masterton
	5	PHL	DXKT	R. Philippines Netw., Davao C, Dvo Sur
	1	PHL	DZSL	S. O. L. Telebc. Station, Talisay, Cam Nte
	1	PHL	DYXT	Universal Bc. System, Tagbilaran C, Bohol
	10	THA		SW Rattasapha, Bangkok
	1	TWN	BEV96	Tien Sheng BS, Tainan
1080	2	AUS	2MO	Gunnedah
	2	AUS	6IX	Perth
	5	AUS	7TAB	R. TAB, Hobart (HPON)
	10	BGD		Bangladesh Betar, Rajshahi
	10	CHN		JS + 4 stns
	600	CHN		YN (CRI)
	5	HWA	KWAI	Honolulu, Oahu (temp.inactive)
	10	INS		RRI, Singaraja (r.inactive)
	10	KOR	HLAT	MBC, Yeosu
	1.1	MRA	KCNM	Choice Bc. Comp., Chalan Kiya, Saipan
	10	NZL		NewstalkZB, Auckland
	5	PHL	DWRL	DWRL Radio, Inc., Legaspi C, Albay
	5	PHL	DWIN	Eagle Bc. Corp., Dagupan C, Pang.
	5	PHL	DYBH	Pacific Bc. System, Bacolod C, Neg Occ
	1	PHL	DXKS	R. Philippines Netw., Surigao, S. Nte
	10	THA		Wor. Por. Tho. 10, Chiang Rai
	10	THA		Wor. Por. Tho. 16, Yala
	10	THA		Wor. Por. Tho. 9, N. Sawan
1089	5	AUS	3WM	Horsham
	5	AUS	2EL	Orange
	600	CHN		FJ (CNR6)
	200	CHN		LN; HN
	20	IND		AIR, Naushera
	20	IND		AIR, Udipi
	10	J	JOHB	NHK (2), Sendai
	2.5	NZL		Gold AM, Palmerston N.
	10	PHL	DXCM	Univ. of Mindanao, Cotabato C, Mag.
	10	TWN	BEG28	Kaohsiung BS, Kaohsiung
1098	0.2	AUS	2RN	ABC (N), Goulburn
	2	AUS	4LG	Longreach
	2	AUS	6MD	Merredin
	1000	CHN		QH (CNR1/11)
	50	CHN		TJ + 27 stns
	10	INS		RRI, Jambi
	10	INS		RRI, Sumenep
	1	J	JOMF	NBC, Sasebo
	5	J	JOGF	OBS, Oita
	5	J	JOWO	RFC, Koriyama
	1	J	JOSW	SBC, Iida
	5	J	JOSR	SBC, Nagano
		KAZ		Qazaq Radiosy, Jetisai + 1 stn
	20	KOR	HLCJ	KBS, Jinju
	25	MHL	V7AB	R. Marshall Islands, Majuro
	5	NZL		NewstalkZB, Christchurch
	10	PHL	DWAD	Crusaders Bc. System, Mandaluyong C, NCR
	5	PHL	DXCL	Swara Sug Media Corp., Cagayan de Oro C, Mis. Or.
	10	THA		R. Thailand, Mae Sot
	10	THA		Sor. Wor. Phor. 3, Songkhla
	300	TWN		RTI, Kouhu
	10	VTN		Thua Tien Hue (P), Hue
1107	5	AUS	2EA	Sydney (SBS)
	100	CHN		XJ + 8 stns
	20	IND		AIR, Kalaburgi
	5	INS		RRI, Kupang
	10	INS		RRI, Yogyakarta (4)
	1	J		MBC, Akune/Oguchi/Sendai
	20	J	JOCF	MBC, Kagoshima
	5	J	JOMR	MRO, Kanazawa
	1	J		MRO, Nanao
	10	KOR	HLAV	MBC, Pohang
	3	NZL		Magic Talk, Rotorua
	5	NZL		Magic Talk, Tauranga
	1	PHL	DZOM	Ben Viduya, Calapan C, Mind. Or.
	5	PHL	DYIN	Inter-Island Broadc. Corp., Kalibo, Aklan
	10	PHL	DWDY	Northeastern Bc. Sce., Cauayan, Isa.
	5	PHL	DXBB	Sarangani Bc. Network, Gen. Santos C, S. Cot.
	10	THA		Mor. Kor., Bangkok (Samut Sakhon)
	10	THA		Thor. Phor. 2, Khon Kaen
1110	5	HWA	KAOI	Kihei, Maui
1116	6.3/17	AUS	4BC	Brisbane
	5	AUS	3AK	Melbourne
	600	CHN		FJ (CNR5)
	120	CHN		HL (CNR2)
	200	CHN		SC; AH; HA; SD
	300	IND		AIR, Srinagar A
	5	J	JODR	BSN, Niigata
	5	J	JOAF	RNB, Matsuyama

kHz	kW	Ctry	Call	Station, location
	1	J	JOAL	RNB, Niihama
	1	J	JOAM	RNB, Uwajima
	2.5	NZL		RNZ (N), Nelson
	5	PHL	DYAG	Cadiz R. And TV Netw., Cadiz C, Neg. Occ.
	5	PHL	DXAS	FEBC, Zamboanga C, Z. Sur
	10	PHL	DYTR	Tagbilaran Bc. Corp., Tagbilaran C, Bohol
	5	PHL	DZLB	Univ. of the Philippines, Los Banos, Laguna
	10	THA		Thor. Phor. 3, Phitsanulok
	3.5	TWN	BED72	BCC (N), Yuli
	10	TWN	BEC30	VO Han Bc. Netw., Ilan
	10	TWN	BEC22	VO Han Bc. Netw., Taipei
1125	2	AUS	1RPH	Canberra (CRS)
	5	AUS	5MU	Murray Bridge
	50	CHN		HB (2 stns); EB
	50	CLN		WRN relay, Puttalam
	20	IND		AIR, Tezpur
	20	IND		AIR, Udaipur
	1	J		NHK (2), Hagi/Nayoro
	1	J	JOIZ	NHK (2), Muroran
	10	J	JOAD	NHK (2), Naha, Okinawa
	1	J	JOOC	NHK (2), Obihiro
	1	J		NHK (2), Takayama
	1	J	JOLC	NHK (2), Tottori
	1	NZL		Gold AM, Hawkes Bay
		NZL		R. Hauraki, Dunedin
	10	PHL	DZWN	Consolidated Bc. Syst., Inc., Dagupan C, Pang.
	10	PHL	DXGL	PEC Bc. Corp., Butuan C, Ag. Nte
	5	PHL	DXGM	Republic Bc. System, Davao C, Dvo. Sur
	25	THA		R. Thailand, Chanthaburi
	5	TWN	BEV36	Cheng Sheng BC, Yunlin
	10	VUT		R. Vanuatu (VBTC), Efate
1130	1	HWA	KPHI	Honolulu, Oahu
1134	2	AUS	2AD	Armidale (F.PI FM)
	5	AUS	3CS	Colac
	2	AUS	6TZ	Collie(t)
	10	CHN		SN; GS; XJ; ZJ
	1000	IND		AIR, Chinsurah (Mogra) (FS)
	100	J	JOQR	NCB, Tokyo
	500	KOR	HLKC	KBS, Hwaseong
	100	PAK		PBC (2), Quetta
	10	PHL	DWDD	Dept. of Nat. Defence, Quezon C, NCR
	1	PHL	DWBT	Philippine Bc. Sce., Basco, Batanes
	1	PHL	DYRM	Philippine R. Corp., Dumaguete, Neg. Or. (v)
	10	PHL	DXOS	Publ.Affairs Service, AFP, Basilan Isl., Basilan
	5	PHL	DWJS	Rolin Bc. Enterprises, Roxas, Palawan
	5	PHL	DXMV	Univ. of Mindanao, Valencia, Buk.
	10	THA		R. Thailand, Lampang
	10	THA		Thor. Phor. 2, N. Ratchasima
	10	TWN	BEG26	Taipei BS, Taipei
1143	5	AUS	4HI	Emerald
	2	AUS	2HD	Newcastle
	10	CHN		BJ (CNR8)
	50	CHN		EN + 31 stns
	20	IND		AIR, Ratnagiri
	20	IND		AIR, Rohtak
	20	J	JOBR	KBS, Kyoto
	100	KOR		R. Free Korea, Gyeonggi-do
	10	NPL		R. Nepal, Bardibas
	2.5	NZL		RNZ (N), Hamilton
	10	PHL	DYAF	Diocese of Bacolod, Bacolod, Neg. Occ.
	10	PHL	DZMR	FEBC, Santiago C, Isa
	10	THA		Or. Sor. Mor. Thor., Bangkok
	150	TJK		TR (FS), Yangiyul
	100	TWN	BEL3	Yuyeh BS, Penghu
1152	10	AUS	6PB	ABC (P), Busselton
	2	AUS	2WG	Wagga Wagga
	150	CHN		HN; LN
	10	IND		AIR, Kavaratti
	10	J	JORB	NHK (2), Kochi
	10	J	JOPC	NHK (2), Kushiro
	10	KOR	HLCW	KBS, Wonju
	2	NZL		Newstalk ZB, Timaru
	100	PAK		PBC, Rawalpindi
	5	PHL	DYCM	Masbate Comm. Bc. Co., Bogo, Cebu
	10	THA		Ror. Dor., Chiang Mai
	10	THA		Ror. Dor., Khon Kaen
	1	TWN	BED68	BCC (C), Puli
	5	TWN	BEV70	Hua Sheng BC (1), Taipei
1161	1	AUS	7FG	ABC (L), Fingal
	10	AUS	5PA	ABC (L), Naracoorte
	2	AUS	4FC	Maryborough
	10	BGD		Bangladesh Betar, Rangamati
		CHN		CNR1
	10	CHN		HB; JS; SD; GX (2 stns)
	20	IND		AIR, Trivandrum
	0.25	KOR		AFNK, Uijeongbu
	20	KOR	HLKU	MBC, Busan
	5	NZL		Te Ūpoko o te Ika, Wellington
	5	PHL	DYRD	Bohol Chronicle R. Corp., Tagbilaran C, Bohol
	5	PHL	DZMD	People's Bc. Netw., Daet, Cam. Nte
	10	PHL	DWCM	Philippine Bc. Corp., Dagupan C, Pang.
	5	PHL	DYKR	R. Mindanao Netw., Kalibo, Aklan
	1	PHL	DXDS	Univ. of Mindanao, Davao C, Dvo. Sur
	10	THA		Sor. Thor. Ror. 9, U. Ratchathani
	20	THA		Wor. Sor. Sor., Bangkok
	40	TJK		TR (2), Orzu
	10	TWN	BED86	BCC (C), Ilan
	10	TWN	BED89	BCC (C), Miaoli
	1.2	TWN	BEV67	Feng Ming BC (1), Kaohsiung
1170	5	AUS	2CH	Sydney
	20	BGD		Bangladesh Betar (C), Dhaka
	600	CHN		JX (CNR1); GD (CNR1)
	10	CHN		NM (8 stns) + 9 stns
	500	KOR	HLSR	KBS, Gimje
	5	MHL		Eagle Christian Radio, Majuro (r.inactive)
	100	PAK		PBS (3), Peshawar
	10	PHL	DYSL	FEBC, Sogod, S Leyte
	10	PHL	DXMR	Philippine Bc. Sce., Zamboanga C, Z. Sur
	10	THA		Sor. Thor. Ror. 4, Chantaburi
	10	THA		Sor. Thor. Ror. 8, Phitsanulok
1179	5	AUS	3RPH	Melbourne (CRS)
	100	CHN		HB; HL; JS; XJ
	20	IND		AIR, Rewa
	10	INS		RRI, Padang
	50	J	JOOR	MBS, Osaka
	5	NZL		Ake 1179, Auckland
	10	PHL	DWET	End-Time Mission Bc.Sce., Santiago C, Isa.
	5	PHL	DYSB	GMA Netw., Inc., Bacolod C, Neg. Occ
	5	PHL	DYCX	Newsounds Bc. Netw., S. J. de Buenavista, Antique
	1	PHL	DZRS	R. Sorsogon Netw., Inc., Sorsogon C
	5	PHL	DXYK	Republic Bc. System, Butuan C, Ag. Nte
	10	THA		Nor. Thor. Phor, Chiang Rai
	10	THA		Sor. Sor. Sor., Bangkok
	2.5	TWN		Kuo Sheng BC, Erhlin
1188	2	AUS	6XM	ABC (L), Exmouth
	2	AUS	2NZ	Inverell
	10	CHN		EB(2 stns); JL
	300	CHN		YN (CRI)
	50	IND		AIR, Mumbai C
	10	INS		RRI, Manado (4)
	10	J	JOKP	NHK (1), Kitami
	100	KOR	HLKX	FEBC, Seoul
	0.4	NZL		RNZ (N), Rotorua
	5	PHL	DXLX	Consolidated Bc. Syst., Inc., Iligan, Lanao Nte
	5	PHL	DZLT	R. Corp. of the Philippines, Lucena C, Que.
	5	PHL	DZXO	Vanguard R. Netw., Cabanatuan, Nva. Ecija
	10	THA		Kor. Wor. Sor. 3, Sakon Nakhon
	10	THA		Thor. Phor. 1, Sa Kaeo
	10	THA		Thor. Phor. 3, Phitsanulok
	5	TWN	BED32	BCC (C), Hualien

kHz	kW	Ctry	Call	Station, location
	1	TWN	BEV57	Sheng Li chih Sheng BC (2), Tainan
	1	TWN	BEV46	Taiwan BC (2), Taipei
1197	2	AUS	5RPH	Adelaide (CRS)
	0.5	AUS	4YB	Brisbane (CRS)
	10	CHN		HL; FJ; SD; SH
	20	IND		AIR, Tirunelveli
	10	INS		RRI, Palangkaraya
	5	J	JOYF	IBS, Mito
	1	J	JOFO	RKB, Kitakyushu
	1	J		RKC, Nakamura
	1	J		RKK, 3 stns
	10	J	JOBF	RKK, Kumamoto
	1	J		STV, 3 stns
	3	J	JOWL	STV, Asahikawa
	1	KOR		AFNK, Dongducheon
	2	NZL		NewstalkZB, Wanganui
	5	PHL	DXFE	FEBC, Davao C, Dvo Sur
	5	PHL	DWBA	Satellite Bc. Corp., Bangued, Abra
	10	THA		Jor. Tor. Lor, Lop Buri
1206	5/5	AUS	2CC	Canberra
	5	AUS	2GF	Grafton
	2	AUS	6TAB	TAB R. (WA), Perth (HPON)
	10	CHN		FJ (CNR2)
	200	CHN		JL + 11 stns
	200	IND		AIR, Bhawanipatna
	10	INS		RRI, Denpasar
	10	THA		Thor. Phor. 1, Prachuap KK
	10	TWN	BEV62	Taiwan BC, Hsinchu
1210	1	HWA	KZOO	Honolulu, Oahu
1215	0.5	AUS	6NM	ABC (L), Northam
	0.25	AUS	4HI	Moranbah (t)
	50	CHN		GD (CNR7)
	50	CHN		HL; HB (2 stns)
	20	CHN		LN (CNR2)
	20	IND		AIR, Pudducherri
	10	INS		RRI, Samarinda
	1	J	JOBW	KBS, Hikone
	2	J	JOBO	KBS, Maizuru
	10	KOR	HLAK	MBC, Jinju
	2	NZL		NewstalkZB, Kaikohe
	10	PHL	DYRF	Word Bc. Corp., Cebu C
	10	THA		Kor. Wor. Sor. 2, Phrae
	25	THA		R. Thailand, Surat Thani
	10	THA		Thor. Phor. 2, U. Ratchathani
	1	TWN		Tien Sheng BS, Pengshan
1224	5	AUS	3EA	Melbourne (SBS)
	5	AUS	2RPH	Sydney (CRS)
	100	CHN		FJ (CNR6)
	100	CHN		GX (s stns); JS
	10	IND		AIR Srinagar C
	10	J	JOJK	NHK (1), Kanazawa
	10	PHL	DXED	Eagle Bc. Corp., Davao C, Dvo Sur
	5	PHL	DWSR	Manila Bc. Co., Lucena, Que.
	10	PHL	DZAG	Philippine Bc. Sce., Agoo, LU
	10	THA		Thor. Or. 15, Chiang Rai
	10	THA		Thor. Or. 4, N. Sawan
	10	TWN	BED52	BCC (C), Kaohsiung
	1	TWN	BEV71	Hua Sheng BC (2), Taipei
1233	10	AUS	2NC	ABC (L), Newcastle
	120	CHN		XJ (3 stns); HN (2 stns); JS
	20	IND		AIR, Tura
	5	INS		RRI, Pontianak
	5	J	JOUR	NBC, Nagasaki
	5	J	JOGR	RAB, Aomori
	2	NZL		Magic Talk, Wellington
	5	PHL	DYVS	FEBC, Bacolod, Neg. Occ.
	5	PHL	DWRV	R. Veritas, Bayombong, Nva Viz.
	10	THA		Thor. Or. 1, Bangkok
	10	THA		Wor. Por. Tho. 7, Udon Thani
	1	TWN		Chung Hua BC, Juifang
1240	5	HWA	KEWE	Wailuku, Maui
1242	2	AUS	5AU	Port Augusta
	2	AUS	8TAB	R. TAB, Darwin (HPON)
	5	AUS	3GV	Sale
	2	AUS	4AK	Toowoomba/Oakey
	100	CHN		YN; HB (2 stns); JX; LN
	100	IND		AIR, Varanasi
	10	INS		RRI, Bogor
	100	J	JOLF	NBS, Tokyo
	10	KOR	HLSB	MBC, Wonju
	2	NZL		One Double X, Whakatane
	5	PHL	DXZB	DXZB/TV13 Coop., Inc., Zamboanga C, Z. Sur
	20	PHL	DWBL	FBS R. Netw., Pasig C, NCR
	5	PHL	DXSY	Times Bc. Corp., Ozamis C, Mis. Occ.
	1	TWN		Yen Sheng BS (2), Hualien
	500	VTN		Can Tho (E), Thoi Long
1250	1	CHN		ZJ
1251	2	AUS	2DU	Dubbo
		CHN		BJ (CRI DS1)
	200	CHN		QH + 27 stns
	20	IND		AIR, Sangli
	10	INS		RRI, Banda Aceh (4)
	10	KOR	HLKT	CBS, Daegu
	5	NZL		Rhema, Auckland
	10	PAK		PBC, Loralai
	1	PHL	DYRG	Intercontinental Bc. Corp., Kalibo, Aklan
	2.5	PHL	DZMS	People's Bc. Netw., Sorsogon C
	10	THA		Jor. Sor. 3, Roi Et
	5	THA		Thor. Or. 6, Bangkok
	100	TJK		Various relays, Yangiyul
	10	TWN	BEC29	VO Han Bc. Netw., Kaohsiung
1260	2	AUS	3SR	Shepparton
	2	AUS	4MW	Thursday Island (CRS)
	10	CHN		LN; HN; XZ
	1	FSM	V6AG	Joy Family R., Colonia, Yap
	20	IND		AIR, Ambikapur
	20	J	JOIR	TBC, Sendai
	400	PAK		PBS (2), Peshawar
	5	PHL	DZEL	Eagle Bc. Corp., Lucena C, Que
	5	PHL	DWMC	Magiliw Comm. Bc. Co., Rosales, Pang.
	5	PHL	DXRF	Manila Bc. Co., Davao C, Dvo Sur
	10	PHL	DYDD	Siam Bc. Netw. Corp., Lapu-Lapu C, Cebu
	25	THA		R. Thailand, Chiang Rai
	1	TWN		Cheng Sheng BC, Taipao
1269	5	AUS	6RN	ABC (N), Busselton
	5	AUS	2SM	Sydney
	10	CHN		SX (2 stns); JL; JS
	600	CHN		YN (CRI)
	20	IND		AIR, Agartala
	20	IND		AIR, Madurai
	1	J	JOFM	HBC, Esashi
	5	J	JOHW	HBC, Obihiro
	1	J		JRT, Ikeda
	5	J	JOJR	JRT, Tokushima
		NZL		The Hits, Takaka
	10	PHL	DWRC	Republic Bc. System, San Nicolas, I. Nte
	10	THA		Kho. Sor. Thor. Bor., Bangkok
	10	THA		Mor. Kor, Songkhla
	1	TWN	BEV37	Cheng Sheng BC, Taitung
	10	TWN	BEC44	VO Han Bc. Netw., Penghu
1270	5	HWA	KNDI	Honolulu, Oahu
1278	5	AUS	3EE	Melbourne
	100	CHN		EB (2 stns); FJ; HL; JX
	50	J	JOFR	RKB, Fukuoka
	2	NZL		Newstalk ZB, Napier-Hastings
	10	PHL	DZRM	Philippine Bc. Sce., Quezon C, NCR
	1	TWN		Fuhsingkang BS, Peitou
1287	2	AUS	2TM	Tamworth (F.PI FM)
	10	BGD		Bangladesh Betar, Barishal
	10	CHN		FJ (CNR1)
	25	CHN		GD + 8 stns
	100	IND		AIR, Panaji A
	25	INS		RRI, Palembang
	50	J	JOHR	HBC, Sapporo
	10	KOR	HLAX	MBC, Cheongju
	10	KOR	HLAF	MBC, Gangneung
	2	NZL		Newstalk ZB, Westport
	5	PHL	DZZH	Manila Bc. Co., Sorsogon C
	10	THA		Sor. Or. Thor., Bangkok (Samut Prakan)

kHz	kW	Ctry	Call	Station, location
	10	THA		Thor. Phor. 3, Uttaradit
	10	THA		Wor. Por. Tho. 6, U. Ratchathani
	10	TWN	BEC27	VO Han Bc. Netw., Taichung
1296	10	AUS	6RN	ABC (N), Wagin
	5	AUS	4RPH	Brisbane (CRS)
	25	CHN		SH + 5 stns
	300	CHN		YN (CRI)
	10	IND		AIR, Darbhanga
	10	J	JOTK	NHK (1), Matsue
	2.5	NZL		NewstalkZB, Hamilton
	10	PHL	DXAB	ABS-CBN Bc. Corp., Davao C, Dvo Sur (r.inactive)
	5	PHL	DYJJ	Intercontinental Bc. Corp., Roxas C, Capiz
	5	PHL	DWPR	Multipoint Broadc. Netwk., Dagupan C, Pang.
	10	THA		R. Thailand, Pattani
	10	TWN	BED47	BCC (N), Tainan
	1	TWN	BEV23	Min Pen BC (1), Taipei
1305	2	AUS	5RN	ABC (N), Renmark/Loxton
		CHN		NM (CNR8)
	10	CHN		QH (CNR2)
	10	CHN		SD
	20	IND		AIR, Parbhani
	2.5	NZL		R. Dunedin
	10	THA		Yaan Kraw, Sara Buri
	5	AUS	3BT	Ballarat
1314	5	AUS	2TAB	Sky Sports R., Wollongong (HPON)
	10	BGD		Bangladesh Betar, Cox's Bazar
	50	CHN		CQ + 6 stns
	20	IND		AIR, Bhuj
	50	J	JOUF	OBC, Osaka
	10	KOR	HLCM	CBS, Jeonbuk
	2	NZL		RNZ (N), Gisborne
	10	PHL	DWXI	Delta Bc. System, Parañaque, NCR
	10	THA		Mor. Kor., Khon Kaen
	1	TWN	BEP33	Ching Cha BS, Tainan
	10	TWN	BEV76	Tien Sheng BS, Chunan
1322	5	PHL	DXAD	Mindanao DMPC, Marawi, Lanao Sur (v)
1323	3.3	AUS	5DN	Adelaide
	0.4	AUS	1--	Star AM, Canberra (HPON)
	200	CHN		HL(CRI)
	600	CHN		JL (CRI)
	500	CHN		XJ (CRI)
	10	CHN		ZJ + 5 stns
	20	IND		AIR, Kolkata C
	1	J	JOFP	NHK (1), Fukushima
	1	J		NHK (1), Yamada
	3	NZL		Coast, Hawera
	10	PHL	DXHR	Gateway UHF Bc., Butuan C, Ag. Nte. (v)
	10	PHL	DYSI	GMA Netw., Inc., Iloilo C
	10	PHL	DZRK	Philippine Bc. Sce., Tabuk, Kalinga
	10	THA		Thor. Or. 13, Chiang Mai
	10	THA		Thor. Or. 7, Surat Thani
	7	TJK		Tajik R1, Dushanbe
	1	TWN	BEV45	Taiwan BC (1), Taipei
1332	5	AUS	4BU	Bundaberg
	2	AUS	3SH	Swan Hill
	10	CHN		EN (4 stns) + 4 stns
	10	IND		AIR, Tezu
	10	INS		RRI, Jakarta (4) (r.inactive)
	50	J	JOSF	Tokai R., Nagoya
	10	KOR	HLAO	MBC, Chungju (r.inactive)
	10	NZL		Gold AM, Auckland
	100	PAK		PBC (2), Lahore
	1	PHL	DZKI	R. Philippines Netw., Iriga C, Cam. Sur
	5	PHL	DWAY	Swara Sug Media Corp., Cabanatuan, Nva. Ecija
	10	THA		Or. Sor., Bangkok
	10	THA		Thor. Or. 14, Maha Sarakham
	1	TWN		Taiwan BC, Puli
	10	TWN	BEC36	VO Han Bc. Netw., Kaohsiung
1341	5	AUS	3CW	3CW 1341, Geelong (HPON)
	5	AUS	2TAB	Sky Sports R., Newcastle (HPON)
	300	CHN		GD (CRI/CNR 1)
	100	CHN		HL + 6 stns
	1	IND		AIR, Kohima
	1	J		NHK (1), Iwaki/Minamata
	25	KAZ		Qazaq Radiosy, Aqtaý
	2	NZL		NewstalkZB, Nelson
	10	PAK		PBC, Bhawalpur
	20	THA		R. Thailand, Loei
	10	THA		R. Thailand, Phangnga
	25	THA		R. Thailand, Ubon Ratchathani
1350	5	AUS	2LF	Young
	50	CHN		YN + 5 stns
	1	FSM	V6A	Baptist Mid-Missions, Weno, Chuuk (r.inactive)
	0.09	GUM	KUSG	Agana
	20	IND		AIR, Kupwara
	10	INS		RRI, Tarakan (r.inactive)
	20	J	JOER	RCC, Hiroshima
	10	KOR	HLAQ	MBC, Samcheok
	1	NZL		Gold AM, Rotorua
	50	PHL	DWUN	Prog.Bc.Corp., Quezon, C, NCR
	10	THA		Phon. Neung Ror. Or., Bangkok
	10	THA		Wor. Por. Tho. 17, Trang
	10	TWN	BED63	BCC (N), Chia-i
	2.5	TWN	BEV50	Chung Hua BC (1), Sanchung
1359	0.2	AUS	3UZ	RSN, Mildura (HPON)
		CHN		FJ / JS (CNR1)
	1	NZL		More FM, Queenstown
	1	PHL	DYSJ	Inter-Island Broadc. Corp., S. J. de Buenavista, Antique
	5	PHL	DZYR	Philippine R. Corp., S. Fernando, LU
	10	THA		Thor. Phor. 2, Sakhon Nakhon
	5	TWN	BEC40	VO Han Bc. Netw., Hualien
1368	2	AUS	2GN	Goulburn (F.PI FM)
	10	CHN		HL; FJ (v); HB (2 stns)
	1	J	JOTS	HBC, Wakkanai
	5	J	JOHP	NHK (1), Takamatsu
	1	J	JOLG	NHK (1), Tottori
	1	J		NHK (1), Tsuruoka
	2	KRE		Korean Central BS (E), Pyongyang
	1	NZL		Magic Talk, Hawkes Bay
	0.8/0.1	NZL		Village R., Tauranga
	1	PHL	DZRA	Catanduanes State College, Virac, Catanduanes
	2.5	PHL	DZBS	R. Philippines Netw., Baguio C, Benguet
	10	PHL	DXKO	R. Philippines Netw., Cagayan de Oro C, Mis. Or.
	10	THA		R. Thailand, Buri Ram
	25	THA		R. Thailand, Nan
	10	THA		Thor. Or. 12, N. Pathom
	1	TWN		Min Li BC, Fangliao
1370	6.2	HWA	KUPA	Pearl City, Oahu (temp.inactive)
1377	5	AUS	3MP	Melbourne
	600	CHN		EN (CNR1)
	100	CHN		XZ + 5 stns
	20	IND		AIR, Hyderabad B
	10	INS		RRI, Tolitoli (r.inactive)
	1	J		NHK (2), Hachinohe
	1	J	JOAC	NHK (2), Nagasaki
	5	J	JOUC	NHK (2), Yamaguchi
	2	NZL		Star, Dunedin
	10	PHL	DXKP	R. Philippines Netw., Pagadian C, Z. Sur
	10	THA		R. Thailand, Chumphon
	10	THA		Wor. Phon 4, Phitsanulok
	10	TWN	BEC31	VO Han Bc. Netw., Yunlin
1386	50	CHN		TJ + 6 stns
	20	IND		AIR, Gwalior
	10	J	JOHC	NHK (2), Kagoshima
	10	J	JOJB	NHK (2), Kanazawa
	10	J	JOQC	NHK (2), Morioka
	5	J	JOKB	NHK (2), Okayama
	10	KOR	HLAM	MBC, Mokpo
	10	NZL		R. Tarana, Auckland
	5	PHL	DYVW	Catholic Media Netw., Borongan, E. Samar
	10	PHL	DXCR	Mt. View College, Valencia, Buk.
	3.5	TWN	BED74	BCC (C), Yuli

kHz	kW	Ctry	Call	Station, location
1395	0.2	AUS	2LG	ABC (L), Lithgow
	5	AUS	5AA	Adelaide
	50	CHN		AH (3 stns) + 2 stns
	20	IND		AIR, Bikaner
	1	INS		RRI, Wamena
	1	J	JOCE	CRK, Toyooka
	1	J	JOWE	RFC, Wakamatsu
	2	NZL		NewstalkZB, Oamaru
	5	PHL	DZVT	Apostolic Vicariate of S. J., San Jose, Min. Occ.
	10	PHL	DYCH	Cebu Bc. Co., Talisay C, Cebu
	10	THA		Nor. Thor. Phor., Chiang Rai
	1	TWN		Cheng Sheng BC, Tafa
1404	2	AUS	2PK	Parkes/Forbes
	4	AUS	6TAB	TAB R. (WA), Busselton (HPON)
	50	CHN		FJ (2 stns); HB (3 stns); LN
	20	IND		AIR, Gangtok
	5	J	JOQL	HBC, Kushiro
	1	J	JOVO	SBS, Hamamatsu
	10	J	JOVR	SBS, Shizuoka
	10	KOR	HLKP	CBS, Busan
	5	NZL		Rhema, Invercargill
	1	PHL	DYKB	R. Philippines Netw., Bacolod, Neg. Occ.
	10	THA		Jor. Sor. 4, Yasothon
	25	THA		R. Thailand, Songkhla
	10	THA		Thor. Phor. 1, Suphan Buri
	10	TWN	BEV78	Yi Shih BS, Keelung
1413	5	AUS	2EA	Newcastle (SBS)
	0.5	AUS	3UCB	Vison Chr.R., Shepparton (HPON)
	10	BGD		Bangladesh Betar, Comilla
	10	CHN		XJ + 6 stns
	20	IND		AIR, Kota
	5	INS		RRI, Sungai Liat
	50	J	JOIF	KBC, Fukuoka
	2	NZL		NewstalkZB, Tokoroa
	1	NZL		R. Ferrymead, Christchurch
	5	PHL	DYXW	Filipinas Bc. Netw,., Tacloban C, Leyte
	5	PHL	DWRA	Republic Bc. System, Bauio C, Benguet
	10	TWN	BED54	BCC (N), Miaoli
	1	TWN	BED67	BCC (N), Puli
1420	5	HWA	KKEA	Honolulu, Oahu
1422	5	AUS	3XY	3XY R. Hellas, Melbourne (HPON)
	1	AUS	4AM	Port Douglas (t)
	2	AUS	6GS	R. Great Southern, Wagin (HPON)
	20	CHN		SH; SX (2 stns); SC; FJ (2 stns)
	600	CHN		XJ (CNR1/13/CRI)
	0.5	CHR	6ABCRN	ABC Radio National, Phosphate Hill
	50	J	JORF	RF, Yokohama
	10	THA		Phon. Neung Ror. Or., Bangkok
	10	THA		R. Thailand, Amnat Charoen
	10	THA		Sor. Wor. Phor. 4, Phitsanulok
	1	TWN		Chien Kuo BS, Kuanyin
	50	TWN		RTI, Minhsiung
1431	2	AUS	2RN	ABC (N), Wollongong
	2	AUS		Vision Chr.R., Kalgoorlie (HPON)
	10	BGD		Bangladesh Betar, Bandorban
	10	CHN		EB + 7 stns
	1	J		BSS, Izumo
	1	J	JOHL	BSS, Tottori
	5	J	JOZF	GBS, Gifu
	1	J		NBC, Fukue
	1	J	JOWW	RFC, Iwaki
	5	J	JOVF	WBS, Wakayama
	2	NZL		R. Kidnappers, Hawkes Bay
	5	THA		Sor. Thor. Ror. 6, Songkhla
	10	THA		Thor. Or. 3, N. Ratchasima
1440	2	AUS	1EA	Canberra (SBS)
	10	CHN		FJ (CNR1)
	50	CHN		GX (4 stns); LN
	3	J		STV, Muroran
	50	J	JOWF	STV, Sapporo
	1	J		STV, Tomakomai
	10	KIR		R. Kiribati, Bairiki, Tarawa Is
	1	KOR		AFNK, Gunsan
	5	KOR		AFNK, Pyeongtak/Waegwan

kHz	kW	Ctry	Call	Station, location
	1.1	MRA	KKMP	Blue Continent Comm., Saipan
	0.2	NZL		Moana Radio, Tauranga
	10	PHL	DWDH	Manila Bc. Co., Dagupan C, Pang.
	0.01	PHL	DXSI	So. Inst. of Tech., Cagayan de Oro C, Mis. Or.
	10	THA		Thor. Phor. 2, N. Phanom
	10	THA		Wor. Por. Tho. 8, Samut Sakhon
1449	5	AUS	2MG	Mudgee
	2	AUS	6TAB	TAB R. (WA), Mandurah (HPON)
	20	CHN		SD (2 stns)
	10	FSM	V6AH	FSMBS R. Pohnpei, Kolonia
	5	J	JOQM	HBC, Abashiri
	1	J		RNC, Marugame
	5	J	JOKF	RNC, Takamatsu
	10	KOR	HLQB	KBS, Ulsan
	10	MLD		Divehi Raajjeyge Adu, Thilafushi
	2	NZL		RNZ (N), Palmerston N.
	5	PHL	DXSA	Mindanao Bc. Co., Inc., Marawi C, Lanao Sur
	10	THA		Thor. Phor. 3, Phichit
	10	THA		Wor. Sor. Por., Chumphon
1458	2	AUS	2PB	ABC (P), Newcastle
	200	CHN		NM; EN; JS; LN
	20	IND		AIR, Barmer
	20	IND		AIR, Bhagalpur
	1	J		IBS, Sekijo
	1	J	JOYL	IBS, Tsuchiura
	1	J	JOUO	NBC, Saga
	1	J		RCC, Shobara
	1	J	JOWR	RFC, Fukushima
	2.5	NZL		RNZ (N), Westport
	10	PHL	DYZZ	Siam Bc. Netw. Corp., Gihulngan, Neg. Occ.
	10	PHL	DZJV	ZOE Bc. Netw., Calamba, Laguna
	10	THA		Jor. Sor. 6, Si Sa Ket
	10	THA		Sor. Thor. Ror. 3, Phuket
	1	TWN		Fushing BC, Kaohsiung
1467	2	AUS	3ML	Mildura
	10	CHN		EB; FJ; JX; SD
	100	IND		AIR, Jeypore
	10	INS		RRI, Ranai
	1	J	JOVB	NHK (2), Hakodate
	1	J	JOMC	NHK (2), Miyazaki
	1	J	JONB	NHK (2), Nagano
	1	J	JOID	NHK (2), Oita
	1	J		NHK (2), Wakkanai
	500	KGZ		TWR relay, Bishkek
	50	KOR	HLKN	KBS, Mokpo
	1	PHL	DWVR	R. Veritas, San Jose C, Nva Ecija
	5	PHL	DXVP	RCA-ZBN, Zamboanga C, Z. Sur
	100	THA		Sor.Wor.Sor, Pathum Thani
1476	1	AUS	5MG	ABC (L), Mt. Gambier
	2	AUS	4ZR	Roma
	50	CHN		HL (2 stns) + 8 stns
	1	J		NHK (2), Iida
	10	PAK		PBC, Faisalabad
	1	PHL	DZYA	R. Pilipino Corp., Angeles C, Pamp.
	10	PHL	DXRJ	Rajah Bc. Netw., Iligan C, Lanao Nte
	1	PHL	DWRB	Ribbon Bc. Netw., Lipa C, Bat
	50	THA		R. Thailand, Chiang Mai
1485	0.1	AUS	2RN	ABC (N), Wilcannia
	0.05-0.2	AUS		ABC (L), 2 stns
	0.15	AUS	2EA	Wollongong (SBS)
	10	CHN		HB + 16 stns
	1	IND		AIR, 8 stns
	1	J	JOPL	KRY, Hagi
	1	J	JOGO	RAB, Hachinohe
	5	PHL	DYDH	Pacific Bc. System, Iloilo C
1494	2	AUS	2AY	Albury
	1	CHN		XJ (2stns) + 2 stns
	5	FSM	V6AI	FSMBS R. Yap, Colonia
	1	J	JOTL	HBC, Nayoro
	1	J		RSK, 5 stns
	10	J	JOYR	RSK, Okayama
	2.5	NZL		Gold AM, Timaru

kHz	kW	Ctry	Call	Station, location
	3	NZL		RNZ (AM)/Star, Hamilton
	5	PHL	DXOC	DWRL Radio, Inc., Ozamis C, Mis. Occ.
	10	PHL	DWSS	Supreme Bc. Systems DWSS, Pasig C, NCR
	10	THA		Or. Sor. Mor. Thor., Bangkok
	5	TWN	BEE34	Chiao Yu Bc. System, Changhua
	10	TWN	BEE32	Chiao Yu Bc. System, Taipei
1500	5	HWA	KHKA	Honolulu, Oahu
1503	5	AUS	3KND	Melbourne (CRS)
	10	CHN		HN; AH; SX (2 stns)
	1	FSM	V6AJ	FSMBS R. Kosrae, Tofol
	10	J	JOUK	NHK (1), Akita
	1	J		NHK (1), Aso
	2.5	NZL		Gold AM, Christchurch
	5	NZL		Gold AM, Wellington
	10	THA		Jor. Sor. 2, Surat Thani
1512	10	AUS	2RN	ABC (N), Newcastle
	10	CHN		GS; SD
	20	IND		AIR, Kokrajhar
	10	INS		RRI, Bukittinggi
	1	J		NHK (2), Koriyama/Matsumoto
	5	J	JOZB	NHK (2), Matsuyama
	0.25	KOR		AFNK, Pohang/Jinhae
	10	PAK		PBC, Gilgit
	10	PHL	DYAB	ABS-CBN Bc. Corp., Cebu C (r.inactive)
	10	PHL	DZAT	End Time Mission, Lucena C, Que
	10	THA		Kor. Wor. Sor. 4, Phayao
	10	THA		Thor. Or. 11, Songkhla
	10	TWN		Ching Cha BS, Hsinchu
1521	2	AUS	2QN	Deniliquin
	25	CHN		EB (2 stns) + 20 stns
	500	CHN		XJ (CRI)
	20	IND		AIR, Tawang
	1	J	JOTC	NHK (2), Aomori
	1	J	JOFC	NHK (2), Fukui
	1	J	JODC	NHK (2), Hamamatsu
	1	J		NHK (2), Ishigaki/Nakamura
	1	J	JOJC	NHK (2), Yamagata
	1	J		NHK (2), Yonago
	1	NZL		Gold AM, Tauranga
	10	THA		Nor. Thor. Phor, Bangkok
1530	2	AUS	2VM	Moree
	50	CHN		ZJ; JL; SX
	0.25	GUM	KVOG	Agana
	20	IND		AIR, Agra
	1	J	JODO	BSN, Joetsu
	5	J	JOXF	CRT, Utsunomiya
	1	J	JOEO	RCC, Fukuyama
	1	J		RCC, Mihara
	1	NZL		The Wireless Station, Hawkes Bay
	25	PHL	DZME	Capitol Bc. Center, Quezon C, NCR
	10	THA		Thor. Phor. 1, Chanthaburi
	10	THA		Wor. Por. Tho. 14, Uttaradit
	1	AUS	2RF	Niche R. Netw., Sydney (HPON)
1539	5	AUS	5TAB	R. TAB, Adelaide (HPON)
	100/300	CHN		QH (CNR1); ZJ
	5	PHL	DZYM	Philippine R. Corp., San José, Mind. Occ.
	10	THA		Phon Ror. Kao, Kanchanaburi
1540	5	HWA	KREA	Honolulu, Oahu
1548	50	AUS	4QD	ABC (L), Emerald
	200	CHN		SD
	400	CLN		Gospel for Asia, Trincomalee
		KAZ		Qazaq Radiosy, Sapaq
	1	NZL		Coast, Palmerston N.
	5	PHL	DYDM	Catholic Media Netw., Maasin C, So. Leyte
	10	PHL	DZSD	GMA Netw., Inc., Dagupan C, Pang.
1557	0.5	AUS	5TAB	KIX Country, Renmark/Loxton (HPON)
	2	AUS	2RE	Taree (F.PI FM)
	25	CHN		EB (2 stns)
		KAZ		Qazaq Radiosy, Lepsi
	2	NZL		Hokonui R., Hawera
	10	PAK		PBC, Skardu
	10	THA		R. Thailand, Trat
	10	THA		Siang Adison, Phetchabun
	300	TWN		RTI, Kouhu
1566	0.2	AUS	4GM	ABC (L), Gympie
	5	AUS	3NE	Wangaratta
	10	CHN		EB + 5 stns
	250	KOR	HLAZ	FEBC, Jeju
	0.1	NFK	VL2NI	R. Norfolk
		NZL		AM936 Chinese R., Wellington (Fpl)
	10	PHL	DXID	Ass. of Islamic Dev. Coop., Pagadian C, Z. Sur
1570	15	HWA	KUAU	Haiku, Maui
1575	5	AUS		KIX Country, Renmark/Loxton (HPON)
	5	AUS		SEN Track, Wollongong
	2	CHN		LN; GX; JL
	1	J		AFN, Iwakuni
	1	J		AFN, Misawa
	0.3	J		AFN, Sasebo
	2.5	NZL		OAR FM, Dunedin
	10	PHL	DXJR	Cagayan de Oro Media Corp., Manolo Fortich, Buk.
	1000	THA		R. Saranrom/BBG, Ayutthaya
1584	0.2	AUS	4VL	Cunnamulla (t)
	0.2	AUS	2EC	Narooma (t)
	0.5	AUS	4CC	Rockhampton (t)
	0.05-0.1	AUS		ABC (L), 3 stns
	10	CHN		SX (2 stns) + 8 stns
	0.1	HKG		RTHK (3), Chung Hom Kok
	1	IND		AIR, 6 stns
	1	NZL		R. Hauraki, Hawkes Bay
	0.25	PAK		PBC, Sibi
	1	PHL	DWBR	Dawnbreaker's Found., Talavera, Nva Ecija
1593	5	AUS	3RG	SEN Track, Melbourne (HPON)
	0.2	AUS	2TAB	Sky Sports R., Murwillumbah (HPON)
	10	CHN		HL; XJ
	600	CHN		JS (CNR1)
	5	FSM	V6AK	FSMBS R. Chuuk, Weno
	10	IND		AIR, Bhopal A
	10	J	JOTB	NHK (2), Matsue
	10	J	JOQB	NHK (2), Niigata
	2.5	NZL		Coast, Christchurch
	5	NZL		R. Samoa, Auckland
	10	PHL	DXSK	Ranao Radio & TV Bc. Sys. Corp, Marawi C, Lanao Sur
	10	THA		R. Thailand, Ratchaburi
	1	TWN		Yuyeh BS, Ilan
1602	0.2-0.4	AUS		ABC (L), 3 stns
	1	CHN		JS
	1	IND		AIR, 8 stns
	1	J		NHK (2), 6 stns
	1	J	JOCC	NHK (2), Asahikawa
	1	J	JOFD	NHK (2), Fukushima
	1	J	JOSB	NHK (2), Kitakyushu
	1	J	JOKC	NHK (2), Kofu
	0.25	PAK		PBC, Abbotabad
	1	PHL	DZUP	Univ. of the Philippines, Quzon C, NCR
1611	0.05-0.4	AUS		17 stns (MFNAS)
	10	PHL	DWNX	R. Mindanao Netw., Naga C, Cam Sur
1620	0.4	AUS		8 stns (MFNAS)
1629	0.1-0.4	AUS		10 stns (MFNAS)
1638	0.4	AUS		4 stns (MFNAS)
	0.6	PHL	DWGI	Guzman Inst. Of Tech., Manila, NCR
1647	0.4	AUS		2 stns (MFNAS)
1656	0.4	AUS		4 stns (MFNAS)
1665	0.4	AUS		2 stns (MFNAS)
1674	0.4	AUS		R. Hanji, Melbourne/Sydney (MFNAS)
	1	PHL	DZBF	Mun. of Marikina, Marikina C, NCR
1683	0.4	AUS		R. Club AM, Melbourne/Sydney (MFNAS)
1692	0.06-0.4	AUS		3 stns (MFNAS) + 2 f.pl.
1701	0.1-0.4	AUS		3 stns (MFNAS)

NORTH AMERICA

The North American MW frequency listing is now shown in each respective country: Alaska, Canada, Hawaii and the United States. This change allowed for the addition of over 1000 extra US MW stations in the National Radio section.

CENTRAL AMERICA, CARIBBEAN, & MEXICO

Abbreviations: Broadc.=Broadcasting, Corp.=Corporation, Em=Emisora, LV=La Voz, Nal=Nacional, Nat=National, Sce=Service.
Call signs: Costa Rica TI_, Cuba CM_, Dominican Republic HI_, El Salvador YS_, Guatemala TG_, Honduras HR_, Mexico XE_, Nicaragua YN_, Panama HO_

kHz	kW	Ctry	Call	Station, location
530	10	CUB	BQ	R. Enciclopedia, Villa María
		CUB	BA	R. Rebelde, Caribe
	1	CUB	BA	R. Rebeldeantánamo-R.Reloj
540	1	CUB	BA	R. Rebelde, Sancti Spíritus-Progreso
	10	CUB	BA	R. Rebelde, Santa Ritaisí
	5	DOM	B20	R. ABC, Santo Domingo
	20/2.5	MEX	WF	Heraldo R. Estado de México, Tlalmanalco
	5/2.5	MEX	HS	La Mejor, Los Mochis
	4/1	MEX	TX	La Ranchera de Paquimé, Nuevo Casas Grandes
	1. 5/1	MEX	WA	Los 40, Monterrey
	150	MEX	WA	Los 40, San Luis Potosí
	5/1	MEX	MIT	R. IMER, LV de Balún Canán, Comitán
	25/3.5	MEX	SURF	R. Zion, Tijuana
	25	NCG	A3OW	R. Corporación, Managua
	5	SLV	HV	La Estación de la Palabra, San Salvador
550	5	CTR	SCL	R. Santa Clara, Cd. Quesada
	12	CUB	BA	R. Rebelde, Pinar del Río-San Juan
	1	HND	XT	ABC R., Tegucigalpa
	0.5	HND	XD	R. Manantial, San Marcost
	5/0.15	MEX	PL	La Super Estación, Cd. Cuauhtémoc
	2.5/0.15	MEX	GNAY	R. Aztlán, Tepic
	5	PTR	WPAB	WPAB 550, Ponce
560	10	CUB	BA	R. Rebeldeego de Avila-Rebelde/Reloj
		GTM	RV	R. Poder y Unción/R. 5-60, Guatemala
	1	GTM		R. Quetzal, Malacatán
	1	HND	KL	R. Reloj, San Pedro Sula
	1.4/0.25	MEX	GIK	La Acerera, Monclova
	10/1	MEX	SRD	La Tremenda, Santiago Papasquiaro
	1.5/0.5	MEX	OC	R. Chapultepec, México
	10/1	MEX	MZA	Sol FM, Manzanillo
570	5	CTR	ELR	R. Libertad, San José
	1	CUB	BA	R. Rebelde, Pilón-Siguanea
	25	CUB	BD	R. Reloj, Santa Clara-Reloj
	10/5	DOM	B22	R. Cristal/LV de la Liberación, Santo Domingo
	1	GTM	PA	R. Palmeras, Escuintla
	5/2	MEX	BJB	BJB Regional Mexicana, Monterrey
	2/1.7	MEX	LQ	Candela, Morelia
	5/2.5	MEX	OA	La Mexicana, Oaxaca
	10	SLV	KT	Nonstop music, San Salvador
580	2.5	CUB	BA	R. Rebeldebujabo
	5	GTM	Y	R. Progreso, Guatemala
	3	HND	ZQ	R. Cadena Voces, Tegucigalpa
	3	HND	EO	Super Estrella de Occidente, S. Rosa de Copán
	10/1	MEX	AV	Canal 58, Guadalajara
	5/0.7	MEX	FI	Fiesta Mexicana, Chihuahua
	5/2.5	MEX	LRDA	La Rancherita del Aire, Piedras Negras
	1/0.25	MEX	YI	Mix FM, Cancún
	10	NCG	A3LP	R. 580, Managua
	4.5	PTR	WKAQ	R. KAQ, San Juan
590	25	CUB	BF	R. Musical Nacional, La Julia
	10	CUB	BA	R. Rebeldeantánamo-Burenes
	10/5	DOM	B24	R. Santa María, La Vega
	5	GTM	RQ	R. Quiché, Sta Cruz del Quiché
	10	HND	LP3	R. América, San Pedro Sula
	1	HND		R. América, Tela
	10/0.25	MEX	GTO	Éxtasis Digital, León
	5/0.5	MEX	FD	La Mejor, Reynosa
	1	MEX	E	R. Fórmula Durango, Durango
	25/10	MEX	PH	Sabrosita 590, México
600	50	CUB	BA	R. Rebelde, San Germán
	1/0.5	MEX	MN	Acustik R., Monterrey
	10/0.5	MEX	OCH	K'in R., Ocosingo
	5/1	MEX	BB	La Comadre, Puros Éxitos, Acapulco
	5/1	MEX	HW	La Mejor, Chametla
	10	NCG	A3MD	La Nueva R. Ya, Managua
	5	PTR	WYEL	Mayagüez
	3	SLV	NK	Vox 94.5 FM, San Salvador
610	10	CUB	BA	R. Rebelde, Bueycito
	10	CUB	BA	R. Rebeldeane
	1	CUB	BA	R. Rebeldeenfuegos-Malecón
	1	CUB	BD	R. Reloj, Trinidad- R. Trinidad
	5	GTM	GA	R. Alianza, Guatemala
	1	HND		R. América, Gracias
	3	HND	LP4	R. América, Santa Rosa de Copán

kHz	kW	Ctry	Call	Station, location
	6/1	MEX	GS	Chavez R. GS, Guasave
	10/0.2	MEX	UM	La Nueva Candela, Valladolid
	5/1	MEX	UF	La Z, Uruapan
	1	MEX	SORN	Viva Saltillo, Saltillo
	1/0.25	PTR	WEXS	X-61, Patillas
620	25	CUB	BA	R. Rebelde, Colón
	10	DOM	B28	R. Santo Domingo, Santo Domingo
	5	GTM	PQ	R. 6-20, San Cristóbal
	10	HND		R. América, Siguatepeque
	2.5	MEX	GMSR	620 AM, La R. Que Se Ve, Villahermosa
	1/0.25	MEX	GH	La Lupe, Río Bravo
		MEX	PBSD	Origen R., Soledad Diez Gutiérrez
	50/5	MEX	NK	R. 6.20, México
	5	MEX	SS	Unánimo Deportes, Ensenada
	50	NCG	N	R. Nicaragua, Managua
630	5	CUB	BC	R. Progreso, Camagüey-Isabel Hortensia
	3.5	HND	LP	R. América, Choluteca
	5	HND	LP7	R. América, La Ceiba
	1/0.25	MEX	FX	Amor 101, Guaymas
	10/0.75	MEX	FU	F-U, LV Amiga de la Cuenca, Cosamaloapan
	10/0.5	MEX	PBGJ	Jalisco R. AM, Guadalajara
	10	MEX	FB	La FB 6-30, Monterrey
	0.5	MEX	CCQ	La Z, Cancún
	1/0.15	MEX	ERO	R. Tamaulipas, Esteros
	2	PNR	J35	R. Provincias, Chitré
	5	PTR	WUNO	NotiUno 6-30, San Juan
	10	SLV	LN	Voz Evangélica Santa Sion, San Salvador
640	10	CUB	BC	R. Progreso, Las Tunas-Progreso
	50	CUB	BC	R. Progresoanabacoa-Progreso
	5	MEX	JUA	La Lupe Chihuahua, Cd.Juárez
	50/25	MEX	NQ	NQ R., Tulancingo
	5/1	MEX	TAM	Romántica, Cd.Victoria
650	10	CUB	BC	R. Progresoego de Avila-Surco/Progreso
	5	CUB	BA	R. Rebelde, Santiago de Cuba-Eide
	15/5	DOM	B31	R. Universal, Santo Domingo
	1	HND	LP	R. América, Danlí
	2.5	HND		R. América, Olanchito
	1	HND		R. América, Tocoa
	2.5	HND	VS	R. Católica de Olancho, Juticalpa
	1/0.1	MEX	HEEP	Acustik R., Hermosillo
	5/1	MEX	TNT	Chavez R. 65, Los Mochis
	5/0.2	MEX	PX	LV del Ángel, Puerto Ángel
	10/2.5	MEX	CSBK	Puerto Vallarta
	2.5/0.02	MEX	VG	R. Fórmula Yucatán, Mérida
	5	PNR	S22	R. Mía, Panamá
660	12	CUB	BC	R. Progreso, Jovellanos
	3	DOM	B32	R. Visión Cristiana, Santiago
	3	GTM	Q	LV de Quetzaltenango
	3	HND	NN18	LV de Honduras, La Ceiba
	1	HTI		R. Lumière, Port-au-Prince
	10/1	MEX	FZ	ABC R., Monterrey
	1	MEX	DGEP	Acustik R., Durango
	50/1	MEX	DTL	Ciudadana 6-60, México
	2.5/0.25	MEX	SJC	KVOZ, San José del Cabo
	50/10	MEX	EY	La Kaliente, Aguascalientes
	30d	MEX	CPR	R. Chan Santa Cruz, Felipe Carrillo Puerto
	5	NCG		R. Máxima, Managua
670	1	CUB	BQ	R. Enciclopedia, Cárdenas-2
	5	CUB	BA	R. Rebelde, Bahía Honda
	10	CUB	BA	R. Rebelde, Camagüey-Villa Rosita
		CUB	BA	R. Rebelde, Caribe
	10	CUB	BA	R. Rebelde, Central Brasil, Jaronú
	10	CUB	BA	R. Rebelde, El Coco
	10	CUB	BA	R. Rebelde, Las Tunas-Rebelde
	1	CUB	BA	R. Rebelde, Los Palacios
	5	CUB	BA	R. Rebelde, Morón
	1	CUB	BA	R. Rebelde, Pinar del Río-Coloma
	50	CUB	BA	R. Rebelde, Santa Clara-Rebelde
	1	CUB	BA	R. Rebelde, Santa Lucía
	50	CUB	BA	R. Rebelderoyo Arenas
	5	CUB	BA	R. Rebeldetanzas-Circunvalación
		CUB	BA	R. Rebeldeyarí
	5	DOM	B33	R. Dial, San Pedro de Macorís
	1	HND	NN20	LV de Honduras, Sta Rosa de Copán
	10	HND	NN	LV de Honduras, Tegucigalpa
	1	PNR	LY	R. Hogar, Panamá
680	3	DOM	B38	R. Zamba, S. Ignacio de Sabaneta
	1	HND	NN7	LV de Honduras, Danlí
	10	HND	NN8	LV de Honduras, San Pedro Sula
	10	HND	NN2	LV de Honduras, Siguatepeque
	5/2.5	MEX	CHG	Súper 102.7, Chilpancingo
	10/2	NCG	AM	R. La Primerísima, Managua
	10	PTR	WAPA	Cadena WAPA R., San Juan
690	10	CUB	BC	R. Progreso, Santa Clara-Progreso
	5	CUB	BC	R. Progreso, Santiago de Cuba-Sta. María
	10	DOM	B39	R. Guarachita, Sto Domingo
	1	GTM	VB	R. Tamazulapa, Jutiapa
	1	HND	NN3	LV de Honduras, Choluteca
	100/5	MEX	N	R. Centro y El Fonógrafo, México
	10/1	MEX	RG	RG La Deportiva, Monterrey
	78/50	MEX	WW	U R., Tijuana
	10/5	NCG	RH	R. Hermanos, Matagalpa
	5	PNR		R. Evangelio Vivo, Panamá
	10	PNR	R43	R. Veraguas AM, Santiago
700	10	CTR	JC	R. Sonora, San José
	1	GTM	AJ	R. Inspiración, Escuintla
	5	MEX	LX	La Grande de Michoacán, Zitácuaro
	10/0.15	MEX	DKR	La Octava y Universal, Guadalajara
	5d	MEX	ETCH	LV de los Tres Ríos, Etchojoa
	5	MEX	XPUJ	LV del Corazón de la Selva, X'pujil
710	10	CUB	AM	R. Guamá, La Palma
	50	CUB	BA	R. Rebelde, Cacocúm
	25	CUB	BA	R. Rebelde, Camagüey-Tagarro
	50	CUB	BA	R. Rebelde, La Julia
	50	CUB	BA	R. Rebelde, Santa Clara-Reloj
	1	CUB	BA	R. Rebelde, Yaguajay
	200	CUB	BA	R. Rebeldeambas-Centro 6
	50	CUB	BA	R. Rebeldertí-Centro 5
		DOM	B41	Ondas del Caribe, San Cristóbal
		DOM		Red Nacional Cristiana, Santo Domingo
	2.5	HND	SG	R. LV de la Libertad, Catacamas
	1	MEX	MAR	98.5 FM, Acapulco
	5/0.5	MEX	OAEP	Acustik R., Oaxaca
	1/0.25	MEX	SLEP	Acustik R., San Luis Potosì
	10/1	MEX	MP	R. 710, México
	10	PNR	Q51	KW Continente, Panamá
	10/0.75	PTR	WKJB	KJB, Mayagüez
720	2.5	CUB	BC	R. Progresobujabo
	5	DOM	B48	R. Cayacoa, Higüey
	1.5	DOM	B42	R. Norte, Santiago
	2	MEX	JAGC	La Bonita del Norte, Juan Aldama
	8/0.25	MEX	DE	La Kaliente, Saltillo
	5d	MEX	KN	La Ke Buena, Huetamo
	1	MEX	JCC	La Zeta, Cd. Juárez
		NCG		R. Asunción, Juigalpa
	25	NCG	A3RC	R. Católica, Managua
	10	PNR	B50	R. República, Chitré
	1	SLV	RA	R. Qué Buena, San Salvador
730	10	CUB	BC	R. Progreso, La Fe-Progreso
	1	HND	NN4	R. Centro, Tegucigalpa
	5/1	MEX	GDL	Arroba FM, Guadalajara
	50/1	MEX	HB	La Mexicana, Hidalgo del Parral
	10d	MEX	PET	LV de los Mayas, Peto
	60	MEX	X	W Deportes, México
740	10	CUB	KO	R. Angulo, Sagua de Tánamo
	5	HND	IH	La Super Grande, Juticalpat
	2.5	HND	VC	LV Evangélica, Olanchito
	1	HND	QQ	R. Intibucá, La Esperanzat
	1	HND	TG2	R. Satélite, San Pedro Sulat
	1	MEX	VAY	Amor FM, Puerto Vallarta
	10/1	MEX	KV	Exa FM, Villahermosa
	20/10	MEX	CAQ	R. Fórmula QR, Cancún
	10/1	MEX	QN	R. Fórmula, Torreón

kHz	kW	Ctry	Call	Station, location
	5/1	MEX	POR	TPrende, Putla de Guerrero
	50	NCG	A3LS	La Sandino, Managua
	5	PNR	N26	R. Cristal, David
	10	PTR	WIAC	WIAC 740, San Juan
750	10	CUB	BC	R. Progreso, Palmira
	5	DOM	B44	R. Jesús es el Señor, Santiago
	5	MEX	ACEP	Acustik R., Acapulco
	10d	MEX	JMN	LV de los Cuatro Pueblos, Jesús María
	10	MEX	UORN	Media Group R. Michoacán, Uruapan
	5/0.25	MEX	CSI	Romántica, Culiacán
	5	PNR		R. Amistad, Los Pozos
760	5	CTR	LX	R. Columbia, San José
	10	CUB	BC	R. Progresoane
		CUB	BC	R. Progresoyarí Arriba-II Frente1
	5	GTM	HB	R. 760 AM, Guatemala
	2.5	HND	XW	R. Comayagüela, Tegucigalpa
	5/1	HTI		R. Lumière, Les Cayes
	70/10	MEX	ABC	ABC R., México
	5/1	MEX	ZZ	R. Gallito, Guadalajara
	5/0.5	MEX	RA	R. Uno, San Cristóbal de las Casas
	5/0.1	MEX	NY	R. Xeny, Nogales
	5	PNR	XO	LV del Istmo, Panamá
	5	PTR	WORA	NotiUno, Mayagüez
	5	SLV	KL	KL La Poderosa, San Miguel
770	10	CUB	CW	R. Artemisa, La Salud
	10	CUB	BA	R. Rebelde, Las Tunas-Victoria
	1	HND	RD	R. Majestad, Juticalpa
	5/1.5	MEX	ML	La Ranchera, Apatzingán
	10	MEX	ANT	LV de las Huastecas, Tancanhuitz de Santos
	2.5/1	MEX	ACH	R. Fórmula Monterrey 770, Monterrey
	2.5/1	MEX	FRTM	XEFRTM, Fresnillo
	10	SLV	KL	KL La Poderosa, San Salvador
780	10	CTR	RA	R. América, San José
	0.5	DOM	B47	R. Constanza, Constanza
	1	GTM	CK	Sultana La Cristiana, Zacapa
	1/0.25	MEX	TMEP	Acustik R., Tampico
	2.5/1	MEX	XY	La Poderosa Voz del Balsas, Cd.Altamirano
	5/1	MEX	SFT	La Poderosa, San Fernando
	10d	MEX	GLO	LV de la Sierra Juárez, Guelatao de Juárez
	5/0.5	MEX	LD	R. Costa, Autlán
	5	PNR		MQV R., Panamá
	10	VRG	ZBVI	ZBVI, Tortola
790	25	CUB	BD	R. Reloj, Pinar del Río-Politécnico
	10	CUB	BD	R. Relojlguín
	3	HND	TG	R. Satélite, Tegucigalpa
	0.25	MEX	GAJ	Fórmula Jalisco 7-90 AM, Guadalajara
	1/0.25	MEX	SU	La Dinámica, Mexicali
	5/0.75	MEX	NT	R. Fórmula, La Paz
800	440	BES	PJB	Trans World R., Kralendijk
	3	CTR	SD	R. La Gigante, San José
	1	DOM	B50	R. Bonao Bendición, Bonao
	1	HND	DL	R. Corporación, Comayaguat
	3	HND	XS2	R. Moderna, San Pedro Sula
	0.5/0.25	MEX	SPN	Cadena 800, Tijuana
	1	MEX	QT	La Poderosa, Veracruz
	5d	MEX	ZV	LV de la Montaña, Tlapa de Comonfort
	50	MEX	ROK	R. Cañón, Cd.Juárez
	10/2.5	MEX	ERG	RG La Deportiva 92.9 FM, Montemorelos
	50	NCG	A3RO	R. Cadena 800, Managua
	12	SLV	AX	La Voz del Buen Pastor, San Salvador
810	10	BAH		ZNS, The National Voice, Nassau
	10	CUB	BC	R. Progresoantánamo-Burenes
	5	DOM	B52	R. Salvación Internacional, Baní
		GTM		R. Circuito San Juan, San Juan
		GTM	END	R. Constelación, Totonicapán
		GTM		R. Moapán, Sta Elena
	6	HND	VC	LV Evangélica, La Ceiba
	3	HND	LP24	R. Valle, Cholutecat
	7/0.6	MEX	AGR	R. Fórmula, Acapulco
	5/1	MEX	HT	R. Huamantla, Huamantla
	5/0.1	MEX	RI	R. Rey, Reynosa
	1/0.5	MEX	EMM	Salmantina, Salamanca
	2.5/0.25	MEX	RB	Sol Estéreo, Cozumel
	5d	MEX	RSV	Tribuna R., Cd. Obregón
	25	PTR	WKVM	R. Paz 810, San Juan
820	10	CUB	BU	R. Ciudad Habanaroyo Arenas
	1	CUB	BC	R. Progreso, Moa-Rolo Monterrey
	10	CUB	BD	R. Relojego de Ávila-Rebelde/Reloj
	10	GTM	TO	R. El Maestro en Casa, Guatemala
	5	HND	LP16	R. Moderna, Tegucigalpa
	7/3	HND	KW	R. Sultana, Sta Rosa de Copánt
	3.5/0.5	MEX	ABCA	ABC R. Canal 820, Mexicali
	10/1	MEX	BM	Ke Buena, San Luis Potosí
	10/1	MEX	BA	R. Cañón, Guadalajara
	1d	MEX	GRC	RTG Más R., Coyuca de Catalán
830		CUB	J	CMKC R. Revolucionyarí Arriba-II Frente2
	10	DOM	B54	Emisora HIJB, Santo Domingo
	5	GTM	AV	R. Satélite, Mazatenango
	1	HND	JB	Cadena Radial Impacto, Comayagua
	1	HND	RU	R. Uno, San Pedro Sula
	5/0.25	MEX	LN	La Caliente, Linares
	1/0.5	MEX	TLX	La Poderosa, Tlaxiaco
	8d	MEX	PUR	LV de los P'urhépechas, Cheran
	25/5	MEX	ITE	R. Capital, México
	5	PNR	R56	R. Península, Macaracas
840	1	CUB	J	CMKC R. Revolución, Palma Soriano
	10	CUB	E	R. CMHW, Santa Clara-CMHW
	1	GTM		R. Idea Maranatha, Jutiapa
	2.5	GTM		R. Luz, San Pedro Carchá
	3	HND	QW	LV Evangélica, Tela
	10	HTI		R. 4VEH, Cap Haitien
	1/0.25	MEX	TEY	Fiesta l a Más Picuda, Tepic
	5/1	MEX	XXX	Fiesta Mexicana, Tamazula
	5	NCG	A3NT	R. Fe 840, Managua
	10	PNR	L80	Nacional FM, Panamá
	5/1	PTR	WXEW	R. Victoria, Yabucoa
	10	SLV	FB	R. Santa Biblia, San Salvador
850	2	CTR	RDR	R. Cartago, Cartago
	1	CUB	BC	R. Progreso, Trinidad-Tetraplexer
	1	CUB	BD	R. Reloj, Nueva Gerona
	5/1	PTR	WABA	WABA, Aguadilla
860		CUB	BD	R. Reloj, Bolondrón
	10	CUW	PJZ-86	Z-86 R. Curom, Willemstad
	1.5	HND	BV	R. Piedra Blanca, Catacamas
	0.5	HND		R. Río de Dios, Olanchito
	5	MEX	MO	La Poderosa/UniR., Tijuana
	10/1	MEX	CTL	R. Chetumal, Chetumal
	1/0.5	MEX	ZOL	R. Noticias 860, Cd. Juárez
	5/1.5	MEX	NL	R. Recuerdo, Monterrey
	45/10	MEX	UN	R. UNAM AM, México
	10	PNR	L55	R. Reforma, Chitré
	10	SCN		Voice of Nevis, Nevis
870	10	CTR	UCR	R. 870 UCR, San Pedro Montes de Oca
	10	CUB	BD	R. Reloj, Baracoa-Van Van
	10	CUB	BD	R. Reloj, Bueycito
	1	CUB	BD	R. Reloj, Sancti Spíritus-Reloj
	4	DOM	B59	R. La Vega, La Vega
	0.5	GTM	L	R. Victoria, Mazatenango
	10d	MEX	TAR	LV de la Sierra Tarahumara, Guachochi
	10/0.25	MEX	ACC	LV del Puerto, Pto. Escondido
	1	MEX	GRO	RTG Más R., Chilpancingo
	10	NCG	CD	R. Centro, Juigalpa
	1.25	PTR	WQBS	WQBS R., San Juan
	2	SLV	AR	R. Renacer, San Salvador
880	12	CUB	BC	R. Progreso, Pinar del Río-San Juan
	10	HND	H	R. Nacional de Honduras, Tegucigalpa
	5/0.25	MEX	CHEP	XECHEP, Chihuahua
	10	NCG	A3EP	R. El Pensamiento, Managua
	1/0.5	PTR	WYKO	La Poderosa 880, Sabana Grande
890		CUB	J	CMKC R. Revolución, Santiago de Cuba
	200	CUB	BC	R. Progresoambas-Centro 6

kHz	kW	Ctry	Call	Station, location
	3	DOM		Consentida, Mao
	1	GTM	HU	R. Escuintla, Escuintla
	5	PNR	Q62	R. Ritmo Stereo, Chitré
	0.25	PTR	WFAB	R. Unidad Cristiana, Ceiba
	3	SLV	LA	R. Elohim, Santa Ana
900	5	BRB		CBC R. 94.7, St Michael
	50	CUB	BC	R. Progreso, San Germán
	1	GTM	MA	R. Amatique, Puerto Barrios
	1	HND	UP6	R. Satélite, La Ceiba
	10/2.5	MEX	OK	Amor FM, Monterrey
	100	MEX	W	W R., México
	2	SLV	QJ	R. Tiempo, San Salvador
910	10	CTR	UM	BBN R. 9-10, San José/Quesada
	25	CUB	HA	R. Cadena Agramonte, Camagüey-Tagarro
	5	CUB	BL	R. Metropolitana, Villa María
	5	CUB	BD	R. Reloj, Bolondrón
	10	GTM	KL	R. Fe y Esperanza, Guatemala
	10	HND	VS	La Voz de Suyapa, Tegucigalpa
	5/0.1	MEX	LNEP	Acustik R., León
	0.25	MEX	AO	R. Mexicana, Mexicali
	5	NCG		R. Jinotega, Jinotega
	10	PNR	L81	Nacional FM, David
	4.4	PTR	WPRP	NotiUno, Ponce
920	1	CUB	BC	R. Progreso, Pilón-Siguanea
	5	HND	SK	R. Catacamas, Catacamast
	1	HND	RM	R. Sistema, Comayagua
	1	MEX	ZAR	Arroba FM, Puebla
	5/1	MEX	RE	La Comadre, Celaya
	5/2.5	MEX	LCM	La Poderosa, Lázaro Cárdenas
	10/1	MEX	LT	R. María México, Tlaquepaque
	1.5/0.5	MEX	STRC	Voces, Campeche
	10	NCG	W	R. Mundial, Managua
	5	PNR	S56	R. Mía, Los Santos
930	5	CTR	RCR	R. Costa Rica, San José
	1	CUB	BD	R. Reloj, La Jaiba
	1	CUB	BD	R. Reloj, Stgo de Cuba-Sta.María
	1	CUB	BD	R. Relojenfuegos-Malecón
	4	HND	CQ	Cadena Radial Samaritano, La Ceiba
	5d	MEX	TLA	LV de la Mixteca, Tlaxiaco
	1	MEX	SAME	SJ 103.3 FM, Saltillo
	2	PNR	K85	R. Mi Preferida,Pto. Armuelles
	2.5	PTR	WYAC	WIAC 740, Cabo Rojo
	3	SLV	TG	R. San José, San Salvador
940	1	CUB	BC	R. Progreso, Sancti Spíritus-Progreso
	10	GTM	LV	Eventos Católicos R., Guatemala
	1	HND	CR	DCR, Tegucigalpa
	1/0.1	MEX	MMM	940 AM Oldies, Mexicali
	30	MEX	Q	Ke Buena, México
	10/1	MEX	RLA	R. Surcalifornia, Santa Rosalía
	1d	MEX	RKS	Romántica, Reynosa
	10/2.5	PTR	WIPR	Máxima 940 AM, San Juan
950	1	CUB	KC	R. R. Relojyarí Arriba-II Frente1
	10	CUB	BD	R. Reloj, Camagüey-Isabel Hortensia
	10	CUB	BD	R. Relojroyo Arenas, HA
	10	DOM	B68	R. Popular, Santo Domingo
	1	GTM	AF	R. Indiana, Mazatenango
	5	HND	QL	R. Centro de Honduras, Siguatepeque
	3/0.9	MEX	MAB	Heraldo R, Cd. del Carmen
	5/0.5	MEX	MEX	La Mexicana, Cd.Guzmán
	1/0.5	MEX	FA	La Poderosa, Chihuahua
	10d	MEX	OJN	LV de la Chinantla, San Lucas Ojitlán
	20/5	MEX	KAM	R. Fórmula BC Tijuana, Tijuana
	1	SLV	HG	R. Chaparrastique, San Miguel
960	5	CTR	CS	R. Actual, San José
	10	CUB	BD	R. Relojantánamo-La Piña
	1/0.25	MEX	OZ	Amor FM, Xalapa
	10/2.5	MEX	HK	HK 9-60, LV de Guadalajara, Guadalajara
	5d	MEX	TPH	Las Tres Voces de Durango, Santa Maríade Ocotán
	2.5	NCG	ACTH	R. Trópico Húmedo, San Carlos
	1/1.7	PTR	WDNO	Cima Norte, Quebradillas
970	5	CUB	AM	R. Guamá, Los Palacios
	1	CUB	BA	R. Rebelde, Trinidad-Tetraplexer
	5/1	DOM	B72	R. Barahona, Barahona
	6	DOM	B71	R. Olímpica, La Vega
	5	GTM	AX	R. Continental, Guatemala
	2	HND	LY	R. Millenium, Tegucigalpa
	50/4	MEX	RFR	Fórmula 970, México
	5	MEX	J	La Jota Mexicana, Cd.Juárez
	1/0.25	MEX	CJ	Los 40, Apatzingán
	1	MEX	O	NotiGAPE, Matamoros
	1/0.5	MEX	SW	R. Madera, Cd. Madera
	1	MEX	UG	R. Universidad de Guanajuato, Guanajuato
	3	PNR	S97	Ondas Centrales, Santiago
	5/1	VIR	WSTX	WSTX, St Croix
980	10	CTR	TNT	R. Managua, San José
	2.5	CUB	B	R. COCO, El Sapo
	1	CUB	BD	R. Reloj, Moa-Rolo Monterrey
	5	HND	VC	LV Evangélica, Comayagua
	2	HND	ZC	R. Rhema, San Pedro Sula
	1	HND	AO	R. Tocoa, Tocoa
	5/0.2	MEX	LC	R. Pía, La Piedad
	5	MEX	LFFS	XELFFS Mi Gente, Izúcar de Matamoros
990	25	CUB	AM	R. Guamá, Pinar del Río-Politécnico
	5/1	DOM	C84	R. Eternidad, Sto Domingo
	1	GTM	AL	R. Perla de Oriente, Chiquimula
	3.5	HND	PR	R. Paz, Cholutecat
	1.4/3	MEX	CL	La Rocola 9-90, Mexicali
	50	MEX	T	La T Grande, Monterrey
	2.5/1	MEX	IU	Stereo Cristal, Oaxaca
	5	PNR		COC R., Panamá
	0.91	PTR	WPRA	La Primera, Mayagüez
1000	1	CTR	MIL	R. 2 Rock, San José
	10	CUB	CW	R. Artemisatemisa
	5	CUB	NM	R. Granma, Media Luna
		GTM		R. Cultural y Educativa, Patzún
		GTM		R. Revelación y Verdad, Guatemala
	1	HND	XZ	HCH R., Tegucigalpa
	3	HND	CY	R. Congolón, Graciast
	1	MEX	FV	La Rancherita, Cd.Juárez
	50/20	MEX	OY	Mil AM, México
	5/0.35	MEX	MYL	So Good, Mérida
	10	NCG	FF	R. Hosanna, Managua
	5/1	VIR	WVWI	WVWI, R. One, St Thomas
1010	1	GTM		R. Caribe, Izabal
	1	GTM	XI	R. Ixil, Nebaj
	1	HND	CD	R. Constelación. Juticalpat
	1	HND	LL	R. Visión Cristiana, Tocoa
	1d	MEX	HGO	Hidalgo R., Huejutla
	20/2	MEX	PA	Ke Buena, Puebla
	5d	MEX	TUX	LV de la Sierra Oriente, Tuxpan
	50/5	MEX	HL	R. Cañón, Guadalajara
	0.5/0.2	MEX	XN	Toño, Ures
	5	NCG	FAVP	R. LV del Pinar, Ocotal
1020		CTR		R. Metrópoli, Cartago
	10	CUB	M	CMKS R. Trinchera Antiimp., Baracoa-Van Van
	5	CUB	CW	R. Artemisa, Bahía Honda AR
	1	CUB	AM	R. Guamá, Santa Lucía
	5	GTM	CM	R. Frontera, Pajapita
	3	HND	PN	R. Visión Cristiana Internacional, Marcovia
	1	MEX	COEP	Acustik R., Colima
	5/0.5	MEX	PR	Éxtasis Digital, Poza Rica
	1/0.25	MEX	WO	Sol Stereo, Chetumal
	5	PNR		R. Ancón, Panamá
	1/0.3	PTR	WOQI	R. Casa Pueblo, Adjuntas
	5	SLV	CA	La Voz de la Liberación, San Salvador
1030		HTI		R. Ginen, Port-au-Prince
	5	MEX	SDD	La Tremenda/PSN R., Puerto Nuevo
	10/0.25	MEX	VFS	LV de la Frontera Sur, Las Margaritas
	5d	MEX	FEL	LV del Gran Pueblo, Felipe Carrillo Puerto

kHz	kW	Ctry	Call	Station, location
	5/1	MEX	IE	Oye Digital, Matehuala
	50/5	MEX	QR	R. Centro y El Fonógrafo, México
	10/1	MEX	ROPJ	W R. Bajío, Lagos de Moreno
	1	SLV	RM	R. Frontera, Ahuachapán
1040	10	CUB	CL	R. Mayabeque, Güines
	1	HND	VC	LV Evangélica, Danlí
	5	HND	VC	LV Evangélica, Juticalpa
	10/1	MEX	BBB	ESNE R, Guadalajara
	5/0.25	MEX	SAG	R. Lobo Bajío, Irapuato
	5/0.5	MEX	PLE	R. Palenque, Palenque
	2.5	PNR	J2	Canajagua AM Stereo, Las Tablas
	9/0.25	PTR	WNVI	R. Nueva Vida, Moca
1050	10	CUB	LL	R. Victoria, Las Tunas-Victoria
	1.5	DOM	B80	R. Hispaniola, Santiago
	5/1	GTM	SL	LV de los Cuchumatanes, Huehuetenango
	10d	MEX	D	La Poderosa, Mexicali
	1	MEX	IP	La Poderosa, Uruapán
	10/1	MEX	BCS	La R. de Sudcalifornia, La Paz
	100	MEX	G	La Ranchera 1050, Monterrey
	10	SLV	U	R. Evangélica Sinaí, San Miguel
1060	25	CUB	DL	CMGW R. 26, Jovellanos
		HND	KT	R. La Catracha, Tegucigalpa
	7/2.5	MEX	RDO	La Raza 1060, Reynosa
	100/20	MEX	EP	R. Educación, México
	5/0.5	PTR	WCGB	Rock R. Network, Juana Díaz
1070	10	CUB	M	CMKS R. Trinchera Antiimp.ant.-Burenes
	10	CUB	AM	R Guamáane
	5/1	DOM	B83	HIBI R., S. Francisco de Macorís
	3/2	GTM	D	LV de Occidente, Quetzaltenango
	1	HND	LE	R. Unica, San Pedro Sula
	3	HND	BB	R. Unidad Evangélica, Catacamas
	1/0.2	MEX	AGS	Estéreo Pop, Acapulco
	1/0.25	MEX	IT	Exa FM, Cd. del Carmen
	3	PNR		R. Mi Favorita, Penonomé
	0.5/2.5	PTR	WMIA	Cadena WAPA R., Arecibo
1080	1	CTR	FC	Faro del Caribe, San José
	5	CUB	CH	R. Cadena Habana, Villa María
	10	CUB	IP	R. Surcoego de Ávila-Surco/Progreso
	1	DOM	B84	RPQ, Santo Domingo
	1	GTM	LU	R. Novedad, Zacapa
	3	HND	IE	R. Senda de Vida, San Lorenzot
	5d	MEX	PBPV	Jalisco R. AM, Puerto Vallarta
	5/0.25	MEX	TUL	R. Mexiquense Valle de México, Tultitlán
	0.25	PTR	WLEY	R. Ley, Cayey
	1	SLV	IM	R. CRET, San Miguel
	6	SLV	ME	R. CRET, San Salvador
1090	1	CUB	LL	R. Victoria, Amancio
	2.5	DOM	B85	R. Amistad, Santiago
	10	HND	CQ	Cadena Radial Samaritano, Tegucigalpa
	50	MEX	PRS	KJAV Ultra 104.9, Rosarito
	1	MEX	HR	La HR, Puebla
	5/0.5	MEX	AU	Milenio R, Monterrey
	1d	MEX	WL	Xtrema, Nuevo Laredo
	0.2/0.7	PTR	WSOL	R. Sol, San Germán
	1	SLV	MG	R. Cadena CRET, Atiquizaya
1100	5	CTR	SCR	R. Chorotega, Santa Cruz
	1	CUB	KO	R. Anguloyarí
	1	DOM	B86	Aliento FM, San Pedro de Macorís
	1	GTM	SR	R. Superior, Coatepeque
	1	HND	AJ	R. Gualaco, Gualaco
	1.5	HND	ND	R. La Esperanza, La Esperanzat
	1	HND	VA	R. Tiempo, San Pedro Sula
	5	MEX	BV	R. Alegría, Moroleón
	5/0.5	MEX	TGO	R. Cañón, Tlaltenango
	1d	MEX	GRM	RTG R. Guerrero, Ometepec
	5	PNR	M92	LV de la Liberación, Panamá
	6	SLV	RF	R. Cristo Viene, San Salvador
1110	10	CUB	KO	R. Angulolguín
	1/0.5	DOM	B91	R. Marién, Dajabón
	1/0.5	MEX	WR	Cristo Rey R., Ciudad Juarez
	1/0.2	MEX	PVJ	Fiesta Mexicana, Pto Vallarta
	0.25	MEX	PU	La P-U, Monclova
	1/0.25	MEX	VS	Maxima 96-3, Hermosillo
	1	MEX	OQ	NotiGAPE, Reynosa
	2.5/0.5	PTR	WVJP	Z101 Digital, Caguas
1120	1	CTR	ACE	R. Alajuela, Alajuela
	0.5	GTM	C	R. Dios es Amor, Guatemala
	2	HND	TL	R. Fiesta, Tegucigalpa
	0.5	MEX	UNO	Acustik R., Guadalajara
	5	MEX	POP	Fórmula 11-20 AM, Puebla
	5/0.5	MEX	TQE	La R. de Tabasco, Tenosique
	0.4/0.1	MEX	MX	Noticias 1120, Mexicali
	1d	MEX	RUY	R. Universidad, Mérida
	5	NCG	A3CP	R. CEPAD, Managua
	5	PNR	M21	R. Sonora, Panamá
	2.6/5	PTR	WMSW	R. Once, Hatillo
	3	SLV	LR	R. Elohim, San Salvador
1130		CUB	BA	R. Rebelde, Imías
	1	GTM	VR	Em. Unidas LV de la Costa Sur, Retalhuleu
	2	HND	HP	Estéreo Pinares, Siguatepeque
	1	HND	BT	Ritmo 1130, Juticalpa
	1/0.1	MEX	FN	Candela, Uruapan
	1	MEX	HN	Los 40, Nogales
	5	MEX	CHAP	R. Chapingo, Chapingo
	1d	MEX	LUP	R. Lupita, Las Varas
	0.2/0.7	PTR	WOIZ	R. Antillas, Guayanilla
	1	SLV	GL	R. Misionera Voz de Alerta, San Miguel
1140	5	CTR	DKN	R. Nueva, Guápiles
	1	CUB	NL	R. Bayamo, Media Luna
	1	CUB	BQ	R. Camagüey, Camagüey-Isabel Hortensia
	1	CUB	DP	R. Ciudad Bandera, Cárdenas-2
		CUB	FL	R. Ciudad del Marenfuegos-Malecón
	25	CUB	CL	R. Mayabeque, La Salud
	10	CUB	BF	R. Musical Nacional, Santa Clara-Progreso
	10	CUB	BA	R. Rebelde, Aguada
		CUB	BA	R. Rebelde, Caribe
		CUB	BA	R. Rebeldeantánamo-La Piña
	5	CUB	BA	R. Rebeldetanzas-Circunvalación
	25	CUB	IP	R. Surco, Morón
	3	HND	VC	LV Evangélica, Choluteca
	1	HND	UL	R. Pico Bonito, La Ceiba
	50	MEX	MR	R. Esperanza, Monterrey
	1	MEX	PEC	R. San Bartolo, San Bartolo Tutotepec
	1/0.5	MEX	TEC	R Tecpatán, Tecpatán
	5	PNR	B49	R. Panamericana, Panamá
	10	PTR	WQII	Once Q Cadena Nac., San Juan
	10	SLV	TS	LV del Rey de Gloria, San Salvador
1150	10	CUB	NL	R. Bayamo, Entronque Bueycito
	5	DOM	B96	Onda Musical, Sto Domingo
	10	GTM	T	R. Cadena Sonora, Guatemala
	1	HND	LP12	R. Universal, Tegucigalpa
	50/10	MEX	JP	Acustik R., México
	10/1	MEX	XP	La Mejor, Tuxtepec
	1	MEX	RM	R. Fórmula BC Mexicali, Mexicali
	50/1	MEX	AD	R. Metrópoli, Guadalajara
	10/0.15	MEX	UAS	R. UAS, Culiacán
	1.5/0.5	MEX	TVR	Vida Azul, Tuxpan
1160	10	ATG		Caribbean R. Lighthouse, St John's
	1	CUB	NL	R. Bayamo, Pilón-Siguanea
	1	HND	VZ	R. Juan Pablo II, Siguatepeque
		HND		R. Nueva Palestina, Nueva Palestina
	10	MEX	QIN	LV del Valle, San Quintín
	5/2.5	PTR	WBQN	R. Borinquén, Barceloneta-Manatí
1170	10	CUB	M	CMKS R. Trinchera Antiimp., Sta. Ritaisí
	5	GTM	RL	R. Cadena Landívar, Quetzaltenango
	2	HND	AF	La Campeonísima, Choluteca
	5d	MEX	RT	Ke Buena, Reynosa
	5/0.1	MEX	FEM	R. Disney, Hermosillo
	0.2	PTR	WLEO	R. Leo, Ponce
1180	5	CTR	PJ	R. Victoria, Heredia
	1	CUB	DX	CMDX R. Baracoa, Bujabo

kHz	kW	Ctry	Call	Station, location
	5	CUB	BA	R. Rebelde, Bahía Honda
	1	CUB	BA	R. Rebelde, Banes
		CUB	BA	R. Rebelde, Bolondrón
	50	CUB	BA	R. Rebelde, Cacocúm
	50	CUB	BA	R. Rebelde, Camagüey-Villa Rosita
	5	CUB	BA	R. Rebelde, Cárdenas-1
	10	CUB	BA	R. Rebelde, Central Brasil, Jaronú
	25	CUB	BA	R. Rebelde, Colón
		CUB	BA	R. Rebelde, Corralillo
	10	CUB	BA	R. Rebelde, Güines
		CUB	BA	R. Rebelde, Hectométrico
	10	CUB	BA	R. Rebelde, La Palma
	10	CUB	BA	R. Rebelde, Las Tunas-Rebelde
	10	CUB	BA	R. Rebelde, Los Palacios
	1	CUB	BA	R. Rebelde, Moa-Rolo Monterrey
	5	CUB	BA	R. Rebelde, Nueva Gerona
		CUB	BA	R. Rebelde, Pinar del Río-Coloma
	1	CUB	BA	R. Rebelde, Puerto Padre
	5	CUB	BA	R. Rebelde, Sagua de Tánamo
	10	CUB	BA	R. Rebelde, Sagua la Grande
	1	CUB	BA	R. Rebelde, San Cristóbal
	1	CUB	BA	R. Rebelde, Sancti Spíritus-Progreso
	10	CUB	BA	R. Rebelde, Santa Catalina
	10	CUB	BA	R. Rebelde, Santa Clara-CMHW
	1	CUB	BA	R. Rebelde, Santa Lucía
		CUB	BQ	R. Rebelde, Santiago de Cuba-Eide
	10	CUB	BA	R. Rebelde, Sta Cruz del Norte-La Sierrita
		CUB	BA	R. Rebeldeáimaro
	50	CUB	BA	R. Rebeldeambas-Centro 6
	50	CUB	BA	R. Rebeldeanabacoa
	1	CUB	BA	R. Rebeldeantánamo-R. Reloj
	1	CUB	BA	R. Rebeldeego de Avila-Rebelde/Reloj
	5	CUB	BA	R. Rebeldeenfuegos-1ra Tulipán
	10	CUB	BA	R. Rebelderoyo Arenas
	200	CUB	BA	R. Rebeldertí-Centro 5
	5	CUB	BA	R. Rebeldetanzas-La Jaiba
	10	CUB	BA	R. Rebeldetemisa
	1	CUB	BA	R. Rebeldeyarí Arriba-II Frente1
	1	HND	AZ	R. El Tigre, Tegucigalpa
	1	HND		R. Río de Dios, Belén
	5/1.5	MEX	DCH	Ke Buena, Cd. Delicias
	3 1/5	MEX	FR	R. Felicidad, México
	10	MEX	UBS	R. Universidad Autonoma de Baja California Sur, La Paz
	10	PNR	U	AM Original, Santiago
	10	PNR		R. Chinavisión, Panamá
1190	10	CUB	JD	R. Coral/R. Revoluciónivirico
	1	CUB	GL	R. Sancti Spíritus, Trinidad-Tetraplexer
	5	HND	VW3	R. Cadena Voces, El Progreso
	5	MEX	JOEP	Acustik R., Jojutla
	0.25/0.1	MEX	MBC	Cadena 1190 AM, Mexicali
	10/0.1	MEX	CT	Contacto 11-90, Monterrey
	1/0.1	MEX	PZ	R. Centro 11-90, Cd.Juárez
	2.5/1	MEX	XQ	R. Universidad, San Luís Potosí
	50/10	MEX	WK	W R., Guadalajara
	10-May	PTR	WBMJ	Rock R. Netw., San Juan
1200	5	CTR	TQ	R. Cucu, San José
	1	CUB	GL	R. Sancti Spíritus, Yaguajay
	5	DOM	C23	R. VEN/RTM RD, Sto Domingo
	12	GTM	RJ	R. Unción, Jutiapa
	1	HND	SI	R. Impacto, Telat
	2.5	MEX	QY	La Bestia Grupera, Toluca
	1	MEX	PAS	R. Punta Abreojos, Punta Abreojos
	5	MEX	CPAC	RTQ, Jalpan
	0.25/1	PTR	WGDL	La Mejor AM, Lares
1210		CUB	BA	R. Rebelde, Las Tunas-Progreso
	10	CUB	GL	R. Sancti Spíritus, Sancti Spíritus-Reloj
	5	DOM		R. Merengue, San Francisco de Macorís
	10/5	GTM	MX	R. Miel Central, Guatemala
	5/1	MEX	PUE	92.1 FM, Puebla
	5d	MEX	COPA	LV de los Vientos, Copainalá
	5	PTR	WHOY	R. Hoy, Salinas

kHz	kW	Ctry	Call	Station, location
	1	SLV	CG	R. Salem, Zacatecoluca
1220	1	CTR	Q	R. Fe y Poder, Limón
	10	CUB	BY	R. Caribe, La Fe-Progreso
	1	HND		R. Destellos de Luz, Sabá
	3	HND	SD	R. Destellos de Luz, Sabá
	1	HND	OP	R. Sintonía, Juticalpa
	1	HND	YS	R. Suari, Marcala
	1	HND	ZB	Una Voz Que Clama en el Desierto, S. P. S.
	100	MEX	B	La B Grande, México
	4.5d	MEX	SAL	R. Universidad Agraria, Saltillo
1230		CUB	BC	R. Progreso, Bayamo
		GTM		R. América, Cuyotenango
	1	GTM	AT	R. Atlántida, Puerto Barrios
	3	HND	CQ	Cad. R. Samaritano, San Marcos de Colón
	10	MEX	CSEP	Acustik R., Culiacán
	0.5	MEX	DKN	Fórmula Jalisco 12-30 AM, Guadalajara
	20/1	MEX	TVH	La R. de Tabasco, Villahermosa
	10/1	MEX	IZ	R. Fórmula Monterrey 1230, Monterrey
	1	PTR	WNIK	Única R., Arecibo
1240	1	DOM		Red Nacional Cristiana, Puerto Plata
	1	HND	ZC	R. Vanguardia, Tegucigalpa
	1	MEX	WG	Bengala 1240/R. Guadalupana, Cd.Juárez
	1	MEX	CG	Ke Buena, Nogales
	1	MEX	RD	La Comadre, Pachuca
	25	MEX	MEFM	MG R. Michoacán, Morelia
	5	NCG	A3RR	R. Vida, Managua
	1/5	PTR	WALO	Walo R., Humacao
	1	SLV	QN	R. Norteña, San Miguel
1250	1	CUB	M	CMKS R. Trinchera Antimperialista, Imías
	5	DOM	C29	R. Juventud, La Romana
	1	GTM		LV Cristiana, Totonicapán
	1	GTM	PY	R. Payakí, Esquipulas
	1	HND	KF	R. Garzel, Juticalpa
	1	HND	YF	R. Renacimiento, Comayagua
	1	MEX	VREP	Acustik R., Veracruz
	10/1	MEX	DK	DK 12-50, Guadalajara
	5/0.5	MEX	ZT	La Magnífica 1250 AM, Puebla
	1/0.25	MEX	TEJ	R. Mexiquense, Tejupilco
	0.25/1	PTR	WJIT	R. Hit, Sabana
1260	5	CTR	DIO	R. Emaús, San Vito de Coto Brus
	2.5	CUB	BC	R. Progreso, Media Luna
	1	HND	FP	R. Amistad, San Marcos de Colón
	1	MEX	MTV	El Lobo de Mina, Minatitlán
	50/35	MEX	L	La Comadre, México
	1/0.25	MEX	ZH	La Estación que se Escucha, Salamanca
	5/1	MEX	JY	La Mejor, Autlán
	10d	MEX	JAM	LV de la Costa Chica, Santiago Jamiltepec
	1/0.25	MEX	MW	Río Digital 93.9, San Luis Río Colorado
	5/0.25	MEX	OG	XEOG La Primera, Ojinaga
	2.5/2	PTR	WISO	Cadena WAPA R, Ponce
	12	SLV	AA	R. Abba, San Salvador
1270	1	DOM	C32	R. Ambiente, Baní
	2.5	GTM	CQ	R. Exclusiva, Guatemala
	1/0.25	MEX	RRR	La Huasteca, Papantla
	10/0.15	MEX	RPL	La Poderosa RPL, León
	1/0.5	MEX	GL	La Verdad R., Navojoa
	0.5	MEX	AZ	La Z, Tijuana
	10	MEX	TGME	XETGME, Torreón
	3.5	SLV	QZ	R. Visión, San Miguel
1280		CUB	BQ	R. Enciclopedia, Trinidad - R., Trinidad
	1	CUB	JN	R. Mambí, Santiago de Cuba-Sta.María
	1	HND	OW	LV de la Victoria, Juticalpa
	1	HND	BN	R. San Miguel, Marcalat
	1/0.5	MEX	EG	ABC R., Puebla
	10/1	MEX	AW	La Gran AW, Monterrey
	2.5/1	MEX	SQ	R. San Miguel, S. M. de Allende
	1d	MEX	TUT	R. Tamaulipas, Tula
	5/1	PTR	WCMN	NotiUno, Arecibo
	1	SLV	MQ	R. Emaús, San Vicente
1290		GTM		R. Miramundo, Zacapa
	1/0.5	MEX	IX	La Pantera, Sahuayo

kHz	kW	Ctry	Call	Station, location
	1/0.25	MEX	AP	Romántica, Cd.Obregón
	5	PNR		La Nueva 1290 AM, Las Tablas
	1	SLV	MA	R. Chalatenango, Chalatenango
1300	1	CTR	GL	R. La Fuente Musical, Cartago
		CUB	JB	R. Titán, Palma Soriano
	5	HND	IV	CCI R., Tegucigalpa
	5	HND	LR	Estéreo Emaus, Santa Rosa de Copán
	1/0.25	MEX	AWL	El Corazón de la Sierra,Jacala
	1/0.1	MEX	XW	La Bestia Grupera, Nogales
	10/0.75	MEX	XV	La Z, León
	38/1	MEX	P	R. Mexicana Nuestras Noticias, Cd. Juárez
	-	MEX	CPAD	R. UV, Xalapa
	1	NCG	A2CC	Canal 130 AM, Managua
	1	PNR	I417	R. Baha'í, Boca del Monte
	5/1	PTR	WTIL	Cadena WAPA R., Mayagüez
		SLV	KG	R. Unción y Presencia de Dios, San Miguel
	1	SXM	PJD-2	The Voice of St Maarten, Philipsburg
1310	1	CUB	BQ	R. Enciclopedia, Nueva Gerona
	1	DOM	C36	R. Real AM, La Vega
	1	GTM	AN	R. LV de los Altos, Quetzaltenango
	2.5	HND	VC	LV Evangélica, San Pedro Sula
	5	HND	CM	R. Universidad de Agricultura, Catacamas
	1/0.25	MEX	AM	La R. de Matamoros, Matamoros
	5/0.25	MEX	VB	R. 13 Más Vallenata, Monterrey
	1	MEX	RAM	R. Amanecer, LV Indígena, Betania
	1	MEX	C	R. Enciso/PSN R., Tijuana
	10/1	MEX	TIA	R. Vital, Guadalajara
	1d	MEX	GRT	RTG Más R. Taxco, Taxco de Alarcón
1320	1	CUB	DL	CMGW R. 26tanzas-La Jaiba
		CUB	KA	Ecos de Sagua, Sagua de Tánamo
		CUB	CW	R. Artemisa, San Cristóbal
	0.5	GTM	ME	R. Quezada, Jutiapa
	10	MEX	PNME	XEPNME, Piedras Negras
	5/2.3	PTR	WSKN	R. Isla 1320, San Juan
1330	3	DOM	C38	R. Visión Cristiana, Santo Domingo
	5	GTM	MU	Unión R, Guatemala
	1.5	PTR	WENA	La Buena 1330, Yauco
		SLV	TG	R. Cristo Te Llama, San Salvador
1340	5	CTR	HR	R. Sideral, San Ramón
	0.25	CUB		AFN, Talk R., Guantánamo Bay
	10	CUB	FL	R. Ciudad del Mar, Palmira
	5	HND	CQ	Cadena Radial Samaritano, Comayagua
	10	HND	TQ	R. Adventista Maranatha, San Pedro Sula
	1	MEX	APM	Candela, Apatzingán
	1	MEX	BK	La BK, Nuevo Laredo
	1	MEX	CR	La Zeta, Morelia
	0.6	MEX	MT	R. Diamante, Matamoros
	1	MEX	AA	R. Variedades, Mexicali
	5/1	MEX	DKT	Radiorama 13-40, Frecuencia Deportiva, Guadalajara
	1	MEX	NV	Romántica 1340, Monterrey
	1	MEX	QB	Super Stereo Miled, Tulancingo
	0.95	PTR	WWNA	R. Una, Aguadilla
	1	VIR	WSTA	WSTA, St Thomas
1350	10	CUB	FL	R. Ciudad del Mar, Aguada
	1	CUB	LM	R. Libertad, Puerto Padre
	1	DOM	C41	Ondas del Yuna, Bonao
	0.25	MEX	ZD	La Mandona, Camargo
	5/1	MEX	CAH	La Popular, LV de Soconusco, Cacahoatán
	10d	MEX	CTZ	LV de la Sierra Norte, Cuetzalán
	8d	MEX	LBL	R. Centro, San Luis Río Colorado
	5/0.5	MEX	TB	R. Laguna, Torreón
	5/1	MEX	QK	Tropicalísima 13-50, México
	5	PNR	Z38	BBN R., Panamá
	2.5	PTR	WEGA	Candelita 7, Vega Baja
1360		CTR	CA	R. Tica, San José
	10	GTM	LK	R. Tic Tac, Guatemala
	1	HND	BS	R. San Pedro, Tegucigalpat
	1/0.4	MEX	DI	@FM, Chihuahua
	-	MEX	IGEP	Acustik R., Iguala

kHz	kW	Ctry	Call	Station, location
	10d	MEX	ZON	LV de la Sierra de Zongolica, Zongolica
1370	1	CUB	MA	R. Playita, Imías
	1	GTM	AC	LV de Colomba, Colomba
	5	HND	UN	LVC R., Catacamas
	5/0.5	MEX	GNK	La La Ranchera Norteña, Nuevo Laredo
	1/0.25	MEX	RPU	La Lupe, Durango
	10/1	MEX	PJ	R. Ranchito, Guadalajara
	0.5	MEX	HG	Vida 13-70, Mexicali
	5/1.2	PTR	WIVV	Rock R. Network,Vieques Island
	1	SLV	KO	R. Lluvias de Bendición, San Miguel
1380	1	CTR	MS	R. Guanacaste, Liberia
	1	CUB	KO	R. Angulo, Banes
		DOM		Antena 13-80, Santo Domingo
	1	DOM	C47	R. Nacional, Santiago
	0.5	GTM	EB	R. Momostenango Educativa, Momostenango
	50/5	MEX	CO	Romántica 13-80, México
	10/1	MEX	TP	Sensación FM, Xalapa
	10	PNR		Bendición R., Panamá
	1	PTR	WOLA	R. Prócer, Barranquitas
1390	6	GTM	YC	R. Fe y Esperanza, Guatemala
	1	HND	VC	LV Evangélica, Santa Rosa de Copán
	10/5	HND	VC	LV Evangélica, Tegucigalpa
	10/2.5	MEX	TY	@FM, Tecomán
	1	MEX	CTAM	IMRyT Señal de Identidad, Cuautla
	5/1	MEX	XO	La Super Buena, Cd.Mante
	1	MEX	OR	NotiGAPE, Reynosa
	10/2.5	MEX	ZG	R. Mezquital, Ixmiquilpan
	1	PTR	WISA	La Voz del Noroeste, Isabela
	1	SLV	JU	R. Getsemani, La Unión
		SLV		R. LV de la Palabra Que Cambia, Chalchuapa
	1	SLV	JS	Sinaí R, LV del Rey de Gloria, Soyapango
1400	1	CUB	ES	R. Sagua, Sagua La Grande
	5	GRD		Harbour Light of the Windwards, Carriacou
	1	HND	UV	R. Cristo Eterno, Catacamas
	2.5/1	MEX	XI	Lokura FM, Ixtapan de la Sal
	51	MEX	SH	R. Sabinas, Cd.Sabinas
	1	MEX	UBJ	R. Universidad, Oaxaca
	1	PTR	WIDA	R. Vida, Carolina
	1	SLV	JI	LV del Litoral, Usulután
1410	5	GTM	GH	Nueva R. Xelajú, Quetzaltenango
	2.5/10	MEX	KB	Alfa FM, Guadalajara
	2.5/1	MEX	BS	Bandolera 14-10, México
	1/0.25	MEX	AS	Fiesta Mexicana, Nuevo Laredo
	1/0.25	MEX	CUA	R. Universidad, Campeche
	5	PNR	H779	R. Mensabé, Las Tablas
	1	PTR	WRSS	R. Progreso, San Sebastián
1420	1	CTR	RPN	R. Pampa, Liberia
	1	GTM	RP	R. FGER, Guatemala
	5/0.5	MEX	F	Activa 14-20, Cd.Juárez
	5/0.4	MEX	H	Antología Vallenata, Monterrey
	10/2	MEX	XX	TUDN R., Tijuana
	1	MEX	EW	W1420/LV del Bajo Bravo, Matamoros
	1	PTR	WUKQ	Ponce
1430	3	CTR	RDVC	R. San Carlos, Cd. Quesada
	5	DOM	C54	R. Emanuel, Santiago
	1.2	GTM	AG	LV de Huehuetenango
	1	HND	FO	LV Evangélica, Puerto Cortés
	1	HND	VM	R. Maranatha, La Paz
	5/1	MEX	TT	R. Tlaxcala, La Doble T, Tlaxcala
	5/0.15	MEX	WD	R. X, Cd. Miguel Alemán
	5	PTR	WNEL	NotiUno, Caguas
1440	5	DOM	C55	R. Impactante, Sto Domingo
	0.5	GTM	MS	R. Nacional, Mazatenango
	5	HND	RD	R. Belén, La Ceiba
	25/5	MEX	EST	Ondas de Paz, México
	25	NCG	A3MR	R. Maranatha, Managua
1450	1	CUB	LN	R. Maboas, Amancio Rodríguez
	1	CUB	CL	R. Mayabeque, Sta. Cruz del Norte-La Sierrita

kHz	kW	Ctry	Call	Station, location
	1	GTM	LG	R. Hosanna, Guatemala
	1	MEX	PREP	Acustik R., Poza Rica
	2/1	MEX	RY	La Poderosa Voz del Sur, Arcelia
	1	MEX	RNB	R. Impacto, Sahuayo y Jiquilpan
	1	PTR	WCPR	Coamomall R., Coamo
	1	SLV	KR	R. Restauración, San Miguel
1460		CUB	JL	R. 8SFyarí Arriba-II Frente2
	2.5	GTM	RN	R. Petén, Flores
	1	HND	MS2	La Voz del Patuca, Campamento
	2.5	HND	GC	R. Reino, San Pedro Sula
	5/0.5	MEX	KC	Planeta, Oaxaca
	1	MEX	YC	R. Fórmula Juárez, Cd.Juárez
	10/0.25	MEX	CB	R. Ranchito, San Luis Río Colorado
	1	MEX	GRA	RTG R., Acapulco
	0.5/0.3	PTR	WRRE	Maranatha R. Ministries, Juncos
	0.5	PTR	WLRP	R. Raíces, San Sebastián
1470	1	CUB	LB	R. Chaparra, Puerto Padre
		DOM		R. Barahona, Duvergé
	1	DOM	C60	Red Nacional. Cristiana, San Francisco de Macorís
	50/5	MEX	AI	Fórmula 1470, México
	1/0.5	MEX	IND	Hidalgo R., Tlanchinol
	10/0.25	MEX	HI	La Consentida, Ciudad Miguel Alemán
	1/0.1	MEX	ACE	R. Fórmula, Mazatlán
	2.5/0.5	MEX	BAL	R. Voz Maya de México, Bécal
	10/5	MEX	RCN	RCN/UniR. 14-70, Tijuana
	5	PNR		La Primerísima, Panamá
	2/4	PTR	WKUM	Cumbre, Orocovis
1480	1	HND	EZ	R. Misiones Int., Comayagüela
	20/1	MEX	ZJ	14-80 Simplemente Supérate, Guadalajara
	10/1	MEX	TKR	La TKR, Rancherita y Regional, Monterrey
	5	MEX	CARH	LV del Pueblo Hña-hñu, Cárdonal
	5/0.15	MEX	VIC	R. Tamaulipas, Cd.Victoria
	1/0.25	MEX	NS	Z107.1, Navojoa
	5	PTR	WMDD	El 14-80, Fajardo
1490	1	CUB	KN	R. Mayaríyarí
	1	GTM	RE	R. Modelo, Retalhuleu
	1	HND	HY	R. Boquerón, Juticalpa
	1	MEX	MS	R. Mexicana, Matamoros
	1	MEX	CJC	R. Net, Cd.Juárez
	1	MEX	YTM	R. Teocelo, Teocelo
	5/1	PTR	WDEP	R. Isla, Ponce
1500	1	CTR	RC	R. Cima, Ciudad Quesada
	50/5	MEX	DF	Fórmula 1500, México
	1/0.5	MEX	FL	La FL, Guanajuato
	1/0.25	PTR	WMNT	R. Atenas, Manatí
	1	SLV	DA	R. Peniel, San Salvador
	1	SLV	CS	R. Pentecostal Bethel, Usulután
1510	10/3	DOM	C67	R. Pueblo, Sto Domingo
		GTM	DX	R. Centroamericana, Guatemala
	1	HND	EM	R. Emmanuel, Nueva Ocotepequet
	10d	MEX	QI	Opus 1510, Monterrey
	0.25	MEX	HUI	R. Huichapan, Huichapan
	10	MEX	PBGR	R. Miled, Guadalajara
	1	PTR	WBSG	Super 15-10, Lajas
1520		CUB	KZ	R. Baraguá, Palma Soriano
		GTM		R. Taysal, Sta Elena de la Cruz
	5	HND	MQ	R. Manantial de Vida Eterna, Juticalpa
	1	HND	DF	R. Ríos de Agua Viva, Siguatepeque
	1d	MEX	VUC	La Norteñita, Allende
	1d	MEX	EH	La Primera, San Luis Río Colorado
	1/0.25	MEX	ATL	R. Mexiquense, Atlacomulco
	25	PTR	WRSJ	Activa 15-20/IBC News Network, San Juan
1530	10/0.1	MEX	SD	Arroba FM León, Silao
	50/1	MEX	UR	Éxtasis Digital, México
	0.5	NCG	A4TS	R. LV de Teresa, Santa Teresa
	10	PNR		R. Avivamiento, Panamá
	1/0.25	PTR	WUPR	Exitos 1530, Utuado
1540	50	BAH		ZNS, The Light, Freeport
	5	MEX	HOS	La Invasora, Hermosillo
	5/0.5	MEX	STN	La Octava y Universal, Monterrey
	4	PNR		Festival 1540 AM, Santiago
	1d	PTR	WIBS	Caribe 1540 AM, Guayama
1550		CUB		R. Guaímaroáimaro
		CUB	BC	R. Progreso, La Palma
	1	CUB	BA	R. Progreso, Sagua La Grande
	5	CUB	BA	R. Rebelde, Cárdenas-2
		CUB	BA	R. Rebelde, Corralillo
		CUB	BA	R. Rebelde, Hectométrico
		CUB	BA	R. Rebelde, Jayamá
		CUB	BA	R. Rebelde, San Cristóbal
	10	CUB	BA	R. Rebelde, Santa Catalina
	10	CUB	BA	R. Rebelde, Santa Clara-Rebelde
	1	CUB	BA	R. Rebelde, Yaguajay
	1	CUB	BA	R. Rebeldeantánamo-La Piña
	5	CUB	BA	R. Rebeldeenfuegos-1ra Tulipán
	5	CUB	BA	R. Rebeldetanzas-Circunvalación
	1	HND		R. Miel, Sabá
	1	MEX	BG	Cadena 1550 AM, Tijuana
	1	MEX	REL	La 15-50, Morelia
	5/0.25	MEX	NU	La Rancherita, Nuevo Laredo
	0.25	PTR	WKFE	R. Café Dinámica, Yauco
	5	SLV	CZ	R. Sanidad Divina, San Salvador
1560	5	CTR	OAR	R. Nicoya, Nicoya
	1	DOM		R. Única, Santiago
		GTM		R. Inspiración, Quetzaltenango
	1/0.25	MEX	MAS	La Estación Familiar, Salamanca
	1d	MEX	JPV	R. Deportiva 15-60, Cd. Juárez
	10	PNR		R. Adventista, Panamá
	5/0.75	PTR	WBYM	La Mas Z R., Bayamón
1570	10	GTM	VE	R. VEA, Guatemala
	100	MEX	RF	La Poderosa, Cd.Acuña
	1/0.1	PTR	WPPC	R. Felicidad, Peñuelas
1580	1	DOM	C76	R. Neyba, Neyba
	1/0.25	MEX	LI	Máxima, Chilpancingo
	10	MEX	DM	Mix, Hermosillo
	5/2	PTR	WVOZ	Cadena WAPA R, Morovis
1590	1.5	CTR	LGJ	R. 16, Grecia
	1	DOM	C73	R. Libertad, Santiago
	1	GTM	XC	R. Triunfadora, Chimaltenango
	5	HND	BX	R. Perla, El Progreso
	20/1	MEX	VOZ	Arroba FM CDMX, México
	1	PTR	WXRF	Cadena WAPA R, Guayama
1600	2	CTR	CH	R. Buenísima, Golfito
	1.5	CTR	MQ	R. Pococí, Guápiles
	5	DOM	C78	R. Revelación en América, Santo Domingo
	5	MEX	GEM	R. Mexiquense, Metepec
	5	PTR	WCMA	Cima 103.7, Bayamón
		SLV	MV	R. Maya Visión, San Salvador
1620		CUB	NL	R. Bayamo, Bayamo
		CUB	BA	R. Rebelde, Amancio Rodríguez
		CUB	BA	R. Rebelde, El Coco
		CUB	BA	R. Rebelde, El Sapo
	1	CUB	BA	R. Rebeldeantánamo-R.Reloj
	1	MEX	CSCGU	Creo R., Guachochi
	10/1	VIR	WDHP	WDHP, St Croix
1630	10/1	MEX	UT	UABC R., Tijuana
		SLV		R. Elohim, San Salvador
1640	1/0.5	DOM		R. Juventus Don Bosco, Boca
	1/0.5	DOM		R. Juventus Don Bosco, Romana
	1/0.5	DOM	C80	R. Juventus Don Bosco, Santo Domingo
1650	5	MEX	ARZ	ZER R. 16-50, México
1660	10/1	PTR	WGIT	Faro de Santidad, Canóvanas
1670	3	DOM	C81	LV del Yuna, Bonao
	1	MEX	ANAH	R. Anáhuac, Huixquilucan
	10/1	MEX	FCR	Reynosa
1680	1	DOM	C82	R. Senda, San Pedro de Macorís
1690	0.9	VIR	WIGT	WIGT, St Thomas
1700	10	MEX	PE	Heraldo R. Tijuana, Tecate

SOUTH AMERICA

(including Brazil)

Abbreviations: Dif=Difusora, Em=Emisora, LV=La Voz, Nal=Nacional, SF=Santafé.

kHz	kW	Ctry	Call	Station, location
530	1/0.25	ARG		Somos R. AM 530, Buenos Aires
	15	FLK		Falklands R., Stanley
540	10/5	ARG	LU17	R. Golfo Nuevo, Pto. Madryn
		ARG		R. Italia, Villa Martelli
	25/1	ARG	LRA14	R. Nacional, Santa Fé
	10/5	ARG	LRA25	R. Nacional,Tartagal
	1	ARG		R. Pasión, Buenos Aires
	25/5	ARG		Ushuaia
	10/2.5	B	J450	Feliz FM, Niterói
	1/0.25	B	H894	R. Guajajara, Barra do Corda
	1/0.5	B	L331	R. Ipanema, Ipanema
	1/0.25	B	H610	R. Jornal, Canindé
	10/1	B	J778	R. Mirador, Rio do Sul
	1/0.25	B	J322	R. Nova Era, Borrazópolis
	1/0.25	B	I914	R. Primeiro de Julho, Agua Branca
	10/1	B	H755	R. Riviera, Goiânia
	10/1	B	K322	R. Sepé, Santo Ângelo
	1/0.25	B	K734	R. Wolf Sumaré, Sumaré
		BOL		Radiodifusora Victoria, La Paz
	1	CHL	CB54	R. Serrano, Melipilla
	10	CLM	KA	R. Auténtica, Bogotá
	25	EQA	FA2	R. Santiago, Guayaquil
	10	PRU	OBX4E	R. Inca del Perú, Lima
	1	PRU	OCX2D	R. San Antonio, El Porvenir
550	2.5/0.5	ARG	LRG206	La Primera, Neuquen
	5/1	B	I796	R. Aleluia, Garanhuns
	10/0.5	B	J331	R. Banda B, Curitiba
	5/0.5	B	L225	R. Cataguases, Cataguases
	10/5	B	I429	R. Mais, Sinop
	5/0.5	B	K578	R. Mantiqucira, Cruzeiro
	2.5/0.25	B	K287	R. Santa Cruz, Santa Cruz do Sul
	1/0.25	B	I902	R. Serra da Capivara, São Raimundo Nonato
	1/0.25	B	H644	R. Vale do Quincoê, Acopiara
	20/5	B	L263	Super Rede Boa Vontade
	5/0.5	B	K700	Super Rede Boa Vontade, Sertãozinho
	2	CHL	CC55	R. Corporación, Concepción
	1	CHL	CD55	R. Voz de la Tierra, Angol
	50	CLM	HF	R. Nacional. de Colombia, Medellín
	20/12	PRG	ZP16	R. Parque, Ciudad del Este
	1	PRU	OBU6W	R. Bacan Sat // 750, Pocollay
	25	URG	CW1	R. Colonia, Colonia
	50	VEN	KE	R. Mundial, Caracas
560	25/5	ARG	LV1	R. Colón, San Juan
	10/3	ARG	LT15	R. del Litoral, Concordia
	25/5	ARG	LRA13	R. Nacional, Bahia Blanca
	25/1	ARG	LRA9	R. Nacional, Esquel
	25/1	ARG	LRA16	R. Nacional, La Quiaca
	1/0.25	B	H289	R. Coari, Coari
	1/0.25	B	H604	R. Educ. Jaguaribana, Limoeiro do Nte.
	25/5	B	H887	R. Educadora do Maranhão, São Luís
	5/1	B	H456	R. Jornal, Itabuna
	1/0.5	B	J214	R. Londrina Londrina
	35/1	B	K761	R. Paulista, Santa Isabel
	5/0.25	B	H769	R. Sul Goiana, Quirinópolis
	5/1	B	K231	Tua Rádio São Francisco, Caxias do Sul
	15	BOL		R. El Mundo, La Paz
	10	CLM	GS	R. Nac. de Colombia, Tunja
	10	EQA	AK2	CRE Satelital, Guayaquil
	10	GUY		V. of Guyana, Georgetown
	1	PRU	OBU4M	R. Bacan Sat, Sicaya
	5	PRU	OBZ4L	R. Oriente, Lima
	5	PRU	OBX1H	Radiomar, Chiclayo
570	5	ARG		R. Argentina, Buenos Aires
	1/0.25	B	K717	Bariri R. Clube, Bariri
	25/5	B	L261	R. Capital, Belo Horizonte
	1/0.5	B	J349	R. Continental, Palotina
	1/0.5	B	K267	R. Diario Gospel 570, Passo Fundo
	5/0.5	B	J735	R. Eldorado, Criciúma
	1/0.25	B	J794	R. Fronteira, Dionísio Cerqueira
	1/0.25	B	K698	R. Jornal, Nhandeara
	1/0.25	B	N407	R. Jornal, São José dos Quatro Marcos
	1/0.25	B	H614	R. Uirapuru, Itapipoca
	5/0.25	B	H613	R. Verde Vale, Juazeiro do Norte
	5/1	B	K672	R.Difusora, Taubaté
		CHL	CB57	R. Salud 570, Santiago
	100	CLM	ND	R. Nac. de Colombia, Bogotá
	1	PRG	ZP15	R. LV del Amambay, Pedro Juan Caballero
	12	PRG	ZP39	R. San Roque Gonzáles, Ayolas
	3	PRU	OAM2M	R. Antena 9, Huamachuco
	1	PRU	OAM5I	R. OAM5I, Salas
	3	PRU	OAU1M	R. Univ. Nal. Pedro Ruiz Gallo, Lambayeque
580	3	ARG		R. Andina, San Rafael
	20	ARG	LU20	R. Chubut, Trelew
	25/5	ARG	LW1	R. Univ. Nal. de Córdoba, Córdoba
	7/0.5	B	L328	R. América, Uberlândia
	1/0.25	B	K540	R. Clube, Americana
	2.5/0.25	B	J330	R. Grande Lago, Santa Helena
	25/1	B	I387	R. Imaculada Conceição, Campo Grande
	2/0.25	B	J327	R. Pitanga, Pitanga
	20/10	B	I776	R. Rede Brasil, Recife
	1/0.25	B	K724	R. Regional, Palmital
	50/5	B	J465	R. Relógio, Sao Gonçalo
	1/0.25	B	H799	R. Serra Azul, Caiapônia
	2/0.5	B	K299	R. Thê São Gabriel, São Gabriel
	10	BOL		R. Panamericana, La Paz
	50/10	CLM	HP	R. Nac. de Colombia, Cali
	10	EQA	FC2	Unión R., Guayaquil
	1	PRU	OAM7N	R&TV Aswanqhari, Azángaro
	1	PRU	OCY2L	R. El Sol, La Esperanza
	10	PRU	OAX2E	R. Marañón, Jaén
	12	PRU	OAX4M	R. Maria, Lima
	2	URG	CX58	R. Clarín, Montevideo
590	100	ARG	LS4	R. Continental, Buenos Aires
	25/10	ARG	LV12	R. Independencia, San Miguel de Tucumán
	25/1	ARG	LRA30	R. Nacional, San Carlos de Bariloche
	5/1	B	K643	R. 79, Ribeirão Preto
	5/0.5	B	K210	R. Alegrete, Alegrete
	10/1	B	K534	R. Atlântica, Santos
	1/0.25	B	K612	R. Clube, Mirandópolis
	10/5	B	H445	R. Cruzeiro da Bahia, Salvador
	10	B	O700	R. Dif. de Roraima, Boa Vista
	2.7/0.75	B	J240	R. Dif. Regional, Cruzeiro do Oeste
	10/5	B	J234	R. Difusora AM 590, Curitiba
	2/1	B	J901	R. Progresso, Descanso
	5/0.25	B	I692	R. Serrana, Araruna
	1	CHL	CC59	CARACOL 590, Concepción
	10	CHL	CD59	R. Pingüino, Punta Arenas
	50	CLM	CR	Impacto R., Medellín
	5	EQA	RF1	R. Super K800, Quito
	5	PRG	ZP32	R. Ycuámandyjú, San Pedro
	1	PRU	OCX6V	NSE R., Arequipa
	1	PRU	OCU6P	R. OCU6P, Candarave
	1	PRU	OAM5E	R. Sembrador, Chincha

kHz	kW	Ctry	Call	Station, location
600	25/1	ARG	LU5	R. Neuquén, Neuquén
	1/0.25	B	H627	R. Cultura, Aracati
	1/0.25	B	H...	R. Dif.de Rio Real, Rio Real
	100	B	K278	R. Gaúcha, Porto Alegre
	10/1	B	H920	R. Mirante, São Luís
	10	B	H287	R. Municipal, São Gabriel da Cachoeira
	10/1	B	H486	R. Vale do Rio Grande, Barreiras
	10	BOL		R. ACLO, Sucre
		BOL		R. Familiar, Santa Cruz
	1	BOL		Radioemisoras del Recobro, La Paz
	10	CHL	CB60	R. Vida Nueva, Santiago
	50	CLM	HJ	R. Libertad, Barranquilla
	40	EQA	XY2	R. Ciudadana, Guayaquil
	10	PRU	OBZ4W	R. Cora, Lima
	1	PRU	OCU1K	R. Frias, Frias
	1	PRU	OCU6S	R. OCU6S, Marsical Nieto
	1	PRU	OBX2B	R. Onda de Paz
610	5	ARG		R. General San Martin, San Martin
	1	ARG	LRK201	R. Solidaridad, Añatuya
	10/2	B	H249	R. Imperial, Marechal Deodoro
	100/25	B	L268	R. Itatiaia, Belo Horizonte
	1/0.25	B	I678	R. Progresso, Sousa
	10/0.5	B	J746	R. Super Condá, Chapecó
	1/0.25	B	K532	R. Transertaneja, Mogi Mirim
	10	B	H321	Super Rede Boa Vontade, Manaus
	30	CLM	KL	La Cariñosa, Bogotá
	50	CLM	D90	R. Nac. de Colombia, Riohacha
	10	EQA	MJ1	R. Caravana, Quito
	50	PRG	ZP30	R. ZP30, Filadelfia
	1	PRU	OAM7M	R. Continental, Ayaviri
	1	PRU	OBU6V	R. OBU6V, Pocollay
	6	PRU	OCY2I	R. Santa Monica, Chota
	50	URG	CX4	R. Rural, Montevideo
	10	VEN	XY	R. Centro, Cantaura
	10	VEN	SE	R. Cristal, Barquisimeto
620	25/5	ARG	LRA28	R. Nacional, La Rioja
	25/5	ARG	LRA18	R. Nacional, Río Turbio
	25/5	ARG	LV4	R. Nacional, San Rafael
	25/5	ARG	LRA26	R. Nacional. Resistencia
	25/5	ARG	LT17	R. Provincia de Misiones, Posadas
	10	B	H590	R. Assunção Cearense, Fortaleza
	2.5/0.25	B	J332	R. Jandaia, Jandaia do Sul
	50/10	B	K521	R. Jovem Pan, São Paulo
	1/0.25	B	K315	R. Municipal, Tenente Portela
	10/1	B	K270	R. Pelotense, Pelotas
	5/0.25	B	J779	Super-R. Dif., Rio do Sul
	10	BOL		R. San Gabriel, El Alto
	10	CHL	CC62	R. Bío-Bío, Concepción
	1	CHL	CA62	R. Norte Verde, Ovalle
	50/20	CLM	EL	Colmundo R., Cali
	10	CLM	VP	Colmundo R., Cartagena
	7	EQA	XY3	R. Ciudadana, Loja
	5	PRG	ZP40	R. Ñasaindý, San Estanislao
	0.4	PRU	OAX2M	R. Chepen, Chepen
	1	PRU	OCX6K	R. Maria, Uchumayo, Aqp
	10	PRU	OBU4B	R. Ovación, San Isidro
	25	VEN	ZC	R. Fe y Alegría, Guasdualito
	5	VEN	NO	R. Libertad, Cabimas
630	25/5	ARG	LRF201	R. Nacional Patagonia, Comodoro Rivadavia
	50/5	ARG	LS5	R. Rivadavia, Buenos Aires
	25/5	ARG	LW8	R. San Salvador de Jujuy
	10/5	B	J920	R. Aperipe, Aracaju
	1/0.5	B	H636	R. Cidade, Campos Sales
	5/0.25	B	K635	R. Cidade, Presidente Prudente
	10/5	B	I384	R. Dif. Bom Jesús, Cuiabá
	10	B	H422	R. Dif. de Macapá, Macapá
	1/0.5	B	I904	R. Dif., Barras
	1/0.25	B	J800	R. Doze de Maio, São Lourençod'Oeste
	5/0.25	B	J300	R. Educadora, Marechal Cândido Rondón
	10/0.5	B	H924	R. Macaru, Viana
	10/0.5	B	J284	R. Parana Educativa, Curitiba
	1/0.25	B	K289	R. Santamariense, Santa Maria
	10	CHL	CB63	R. Stela Maris, Valparaíso
	1	PRU	OBU7I	Chaski R., Urubamba
	18	PRU	OBX1U	R. Cutivalú, Castilla
	25	VEN	KA	RNV Informativa, Caracas
640	10/5	ARG	LU18	R. El Valle, General Roca
	25/5	ARG	LRA24	R. Nacional, Río Grande
	10/5	ARG	LV15	R. Villa Mercedes, Villa Mercedes
	50/10	B	K277	R. Bandeirantes, Porto Alegre
	50/5	B	H757	R. Dif. Pai Eterno. Goiânia, Goiânia
	10/0.5	B	H458	R. Dif. Sul da Bahia, Itabuna
	10/0.25	B	L320	R. Educadora, Porteirinha
	10/1	B	I424	R. Tangará, Tangará da Serra
	20/1	B	J262	Super R. Deus é Amor, Londrina
		BOL		R. ACLO, Tarija
	1	CHL	CD64	R. Cooperativa, Temuco
	0.25	CHL	CC64	R. Portales, Curico
	10	CLM	BJ	RCN R., Santa Marta
	10	EQA	BI2	R. Morena, Guayaquil
	15	PRG	ZP19	R. Caaguazú, Coronel Oviedo
	10	PRU	OAZ4K	R. Del Pacifico, Lima
	3	PRU	OAU1Y	R. La Luz, José Leonardo Ortiz
	10	PRU	OBX7B	R. Onda Azul, Puno
650	3	ARG		Belgrano AM 650, Buenos Aires
	5/0.5	B	I672	R. Alto Piranhas, Cajazeiras
	1/0.25	B	K508	R. Andradina, Andradina
	1/0.5	B	J202	R. Banda B Norte Pioneiro, Cambará
	5/0.5	B	H462	R. Clube, Valença
	8/1	B	J250	R. Colméia, Cascavel
	5/1	B	K518	R. da Cidade, Santos
	5/0.8	B	K524	R. Dif., Piracicaba
	5/0.5	B	K238	R. Difusão Sul Riograndense, Erechim
	1/0.25	B	H790	R. Kompleta, Jussara
	1/0.25	B	I925	R. Tapuio, Miguel Alves
	10/1	B	I540	R. Tropical, Santarém
	5/0.5	B	L309	R. Veredas, Unaí
	10/0.5	B	L200	R. Vitoriosa, Lagoa Formosa
	15	BOL		R. Dif. Integración, El Alto
	50	CLM	KH	Antena 2, Bogotá
	5	EQA	FD4	R. Visión, Manta
	50	PRG	ZP4	R. Uno, Chaco
	1.5	PRU	OBU2P	R. Bendición Cristiana, Huambos
		PRU	OAU9D	R. Kampagkis, Nieva
	1	PRU	OBM7C	R. OBM7C, Sandia
	1	PRU	OCU5Q	R. OCU5Q, Pueblo Nuevo
	1	PRU	OCU6L	R. OCU6L, Alto de la Alianza
	1	PRU	OAX2N	R. Regional del Norte, Trujillo
	25	URG	CX6	R. Clásica
660	1	ARG		Amplitud 660, Ciudad Evita
	1/0.25	ARG	LT41	R. LV del Sur Entrerriano, Gualeguaychú
	10/5	B	J673	R. Boas Novas AM, Porto Velho
	1/0.25	B	K319	R. Canção Nova, Vacaria
	10/0.5	B	K639	R. Clube 1, Ribeirão Preto
	10/0.25	B	L206	R. Clube, Curvelo
	5/1	B	J472	R. Friburgo, Nova Friburgo
	5/1	B	I787	R. Jornal, Limoeiro
	1/0.25	B	K286	R. Marajá, Rosário do Sul
	20/0.5	B	K777	R. Mundial, São Paulo
	5/0.25	B	H465	R. Nova Jornal, Itapetinga
	1/0.25	B	H518	R. Planalto, Euclides da Cunha
	1/0.25	B	I925	R. Tacarijus, São Miguel do Tapuio
	1/0.25	B	I552	R. Xinguara, Xinguara
	1	BOL		R. ABC, Santa Cruz
		BOL		R. Taller de Historia Oral Andina, La Paz
	50	CHL	CB66	R. Colo Colo, Santiago
	10	CLM	EZ	R. Auténtica, Cali
	5	PRG	ZP26	R. Itapirú, Ciudad del Este
	10	PRG	ZP74	R. Regional, Concepción
	3	PRU	OCX1U	R. J.H.C., Chiclayo
	10	PRU	OCX4R	R. La Inolvidable, Lima
	3	PRU	OAZ7J	R. Santa Monica, Wanshaq
670	1	ARG	LT4	R. LT4 Digital, Posadas - CNN
	25/5	ARG	LRI209	R. Mar del Plata, Mar del Plata
	10/3	ARG	LRA52	R. Nacional, Chos Malal
	25/5	ARG	LRA11	R. Nacional, Comodoro Rivadavia
	4	ARG		R. Republica, Ciudad Evita
	5/1	ARG		R. Universidad, La Rioja
	5/0.25	B	I539	R. Atalaia, Óbidos

kHz	kW	Ctry	Call	Station, location
	3/0.25	B	J231	R. Canção Nova Esperança, Nova Esperança
	10/2	B	J248	R. Cidade, Curitiba
	1/0.5	B	K598	R. Convenção, Itu
	2.5/0.25	B	K296	R. Cult. Jaguarão, Santa. Vitória do Palmar
	10/5	B	J921	R. Cultura de Sergipe, Aracaju
	0.25	B	H208	R. Dif., Sena Madureira
	10/0.5	B	K370	R. Gazeta, Carazinho
	10/1	B	H420	R. Jovem Pan News - Equatorial, Macapá
	1/0.25	B	I927	R. Livramento, José de Freitas
	1/0.25	B	L347	R. Montanhesa, Ponte Nova
	1	B	H288	R. Nac. do Alto Solimões, Tabatinga
	1/0.25	B	I537	R. Rural, Altamira
	6/1	B	I422	R. Transpantaneira, Poconé
	1/0.25	B	H297	R. Vale do Rio Madeira, Humaitá
	5/0.25	B	L361	R. Vitoriosa, Uberaba
		BOL		R. Comunitaria Cadena Provincial, Jihuacuta
	25	CLM	PL	Antena 2, Medellín
	10	CLM	R33	UIS AM, Bucaramanga
	10	PRU	OAX7H	R. Nal. del Perú, Puno
	100	VEN	LL	R. Rumbos, Caracas
680	10/5	ARG	LT3	R. Cerealista, Rosario
	2	ARG		R. Magna, Villa Martelli
	25/5	ARG	LV6	R. Nihuil, Mendoza
	25/5	ARG	LU12	R. Río Gallegos, Río Gallegos
	20/5	B	J452	R. Copacabana, Rio de Janeiro
	10/0.5	B	H765	R. Difusora, Jataí
	50	B	K275	R. Farroupilha, Porto Alegre
	1/0.25	B	L348	R. Futura, Ibiá
	10/1	B	I793	R. Grande Rio, Petrolina
	5/0.25	B	J362	R. Poema, Pitanga
	1/0.25	B	L326	R. União, João Pinheiro
		BOL		R. ACLO, Potosí
	5	BOL		R. Andina, La Paz
	10	BOL		R. Jallalla Coca, Chulumani
	10	CHL	CC68	R. Cooperativa, Concepción
	50	CLM	ZO	R. Nacional de Colombia, Barranquilla
	10	EQA	VP2	R. Atalaya, Guayaquil
	50	PRG	ZP11	R. Caritas, Ñemby
	5	PRU	OAX5E	Emisora del Pacifico, Ica
	0.5	PRU	OBX2L	R. Amauta, Chócope
		PRU	OCU6Q	R. Americana, Moquegua
	5	PRU	OAM4B	R. OAM4B, Chaupimarca
	20	PRU	OBX4A	R. RBC, San Isidro
	5	PRU	OCY2Y	R. San Luis, Jaén
	1	PRU	OBU7G	R. Vida, Cusco
	1/0.7	URG	CW68	R. Young, Young
690	2	ARG		K-24 en R., Virrey del Pino
	10/5	ARG	LU19	R. LV de Comahue, Cipolletti
	50/5	ARG	LRA4	R. Nacional, Salta
	10/1	B	I201	R. América, Vitoria
	1/0.25	B	K646	R. Brasil, Santa Bárbara d'Oeste
	1/0.25	B	K625	R. Cidade, Pereira Barreto
	20/5	B	I532	R. Clube do Pará, Belém
	1/0.25	B	K588	R. Clube, Guaratinguetá
	10/1	B	H453	R. Cultura, Ilhéus
	5/1	B	J229	R. Dif. de Londrina, Londrina
	50/5	B	L228	R. Mineira, Belo Horizonte
	25/10	B	H587	R. Shalom, Fortaleza
	50/1	B	H780	R. Sociedade Ceres, Ceres
	10	CHL	CD69	R. Estrella del Mar, Ancud
	10	CHL	CB69	R. Santiago, Santiago
	35	CLM	CZ	W R., Bogotá
	1	PRU	OAM7C	R. Altiva, Yanaoca
	25	URG	CX8	R. Sarandí, Montevideo
700	25/5	ARG	LV3	Cadena 3 - R. Córdoba
	50	B	K686	Nossa Radio, São Paulo
	5/0.4	B	J507	R. Aliança, Italva
	1/0.25	B	K356	R. Batovi, São Gabriel
	25/0.5	B	H801	R. Pouso Alto, Piracanjuba
		BOL		R. Pacha Kamasa, El Alto
	1	CHL	CD70	Nueva R. Valdivia, Valdivia
	5	CHL	CD70A	R. Magallanes, Punta Arenas
	30	CLM	CX	W R., Cali
	50	EQA	RS2	R. Sucre, Guayaquil
	12	PRG	ZP12	R. Nacional, Pilar
	3	PRU	OBU4J	R. La Luz, El Tambo
	1	PRU	OBU7K	R. La Salle, Maras
	10	PRU	OAU9A	R. Maria, Moyobamba
	25	PRU	OBZ4H	R. R. Integridad, San Miguel
	1	PRU	OBU2T	R. Sausal Superior, Ascope
710	50	ARG	LRL202	R. Diez, Buenos Aires
	25/5	ARG	LRA19	R. Nacional, Pto. Iguazú
	25/1	ARG	LRA17	R. Nacional, Zapala
	10/0.25	B	H490	R. 21 News, Eunápolis
	10/0.25	B	K559	R. 710, Bauru
	10/2.5	B	H710	R. Aliança, Brasília
	1/0.25	B	J328	R. Alternativa, Cândido de Abreu
	1/0.25	B	I901	R. Alvorada do Sertão, São João do Piauí
	10/0.5	B	L219	R. Cancella, Ituiutaba
	1/0.5	B	I933	R. Clube, Barras
	2/0.25	B	L333	R. Dif. HD, Pouso Alegre
	5/1	B	H240	R. Jornal, Maceió
	20/0.5	B	L258	R. Manhuaçu, Manhuaçu
	2/0.25	B	L319	R. Planeta, Carmo do Paranaíba
	25/5	B	I534	R. Rural, Santarém
	10	B	J451	R. Sucesso AM, Rio de Janeiro
	1/0.5	B	H910	R. Verdes Vales, Grajaú
	10	BOL		R. Pío XII, Siglo Veinte
	1	CLM	YD	R. La Paz, Paipa
	10	CLM	NX	R. Red RCN, Medellín
	1	PRU	OAU6L	R. Amor, Socabaya, Aqp
	10	PRU	OCX7I	R. Nacional del Peru, Puerto Maldonado
	5	PRU	OBX5Q	R. Programas del Perú, Ica
	5	PRU	OCU2X	R. TurboMix, Cajamarcal
	20	VEN	KY	R. Capital, Caracas
720	1	ARG	LRA59	R. Nacional, Gobernador Gregores
	50/5	ARG	LV10	R.de Cuyo, Mendoza
	1	B	H281	CBN, Itacoatiara
	100	B	I770	R. Cl de Pernambuco, Recife
	5/1	B	I390	R. Clube, Dourados
	1/0.25	B	K575	R. Difusora, Casa Branca
	1/0.25	B	K722	R. Espaço Livre, Olímpia
	100	B	K276	R. Guaíba, Porto Alegre
	10	B	H202	R. Integração, Cruzeiro do Sul
	1/0.25	B	K718	R. RC Vale, Cruzeiro
	1/0.25	B	K701	R. Sentinela, Ourinhos
	10	BOL		R. La Cruz del Sur, La Paz
	1	CHL	CC72	R. Interamericana, Concepción
	1	CHL	CA72	R. Portales, Iquique
	25	CLM	VO	Transmisora Quindío, Armenia
	5	EQA	IC1	R. Municipal, Quito
	10	EQA	PR2	R. Única, Machala
	50	PRG	ZP17	R. Pai Puku, Teniente M.I. Fernández
	3	PRU	OBU7D	NSE R., Santiago
	0.5	PRU	OAU1O	R. Frecuencia Oceánica, San José
	25	PRU	OAX2J	R. Nal.. del Perú, Trujillo
	2	PRU	OCU7J	R. Noticias, Puno
	10	PRU	OAU4E	R. Sideral, La Oroya
730	10/5	ARG		R. Concepto, Gonzales Catán
	25/5	ARG	LRA27	R. Nacional, Catamarca
	25/5	ARG	LRA3	R. Nacional, Santa Rosa
	20/1	ARG	LU23	R. Nal - R. Lago Argentino, El Calafate
	10/0.25	B	K523	R. Cidade, Jundiaí
	10/1	B	K610	R. Dirceu, Marília
	1/0.25	B	H896	R. Eldorado, Codó
	5/0.25	B	J353	R. Integração Metropolitana, Corbélia
	5/1	B	L287	R. JM 730, Uberaba
	10/2.5	B	I410	R. Jornal, Cáceres
	10/1	B	L297	R. Manchester, Juiz de Fora
	7/0.6	B	J208	R. Marumby, Curitiba
	10/0.5	B	I217	R. Novo Tempo, Vitória
	1/0.25	B	J323	R. Objetiva, Campo Mourão
	50/5	B	H759	R. Sagres 730 AM, Goiânia
	5/1	B	J787	R. Tubá, Tubarão
	2.5	BOL		R. Yungas, Chulumani
	1	CHL	CD73	R. Angelina, Los Angeles
	10	CHL	CB73	R. Cooperativa AM, Valparaíso

kHz	kW	Ctry	Call	Station, location
	10	CLM	CU	Melodía Estéreo, Bogotá
	50	PRG	ZP7	R. ABC Cardinal, Nueva Italia
	1	PRU	OAM7X	R. Altura, Macusani
	10	PRU	OAX1D	R. del Pacifico, Piura
	2.5	PRU	OBU2Q	R. Maria, Cajamarca
	1	PRU	OCU6G	R. OCU6G, Tacna
	50	PRU	OAX4G	R. Programas del Perú, San Isidro
	5/2.5	URG	CX10	R. Continente, Montevideo
740	10	ARG		AM 740 La Carretera, Allen
	3	ARG	LRI200	R. Municipal, Puerto Deseado
	1	ARG	LRA55	R. Nacional, Alto Río Senguer
	5/1	ARG	LRH251	R. Provincia del Chaco, Resistencia
	5	ARG		R. Rebelde, Valentin Alsina
	10/1	B	J753	CBN Diário, Florianópolis
	5/0.25	B	K283	R. Cultura Riograndina, Rio Grande
	1/0.25	B	K553	R. Cultura, Bariri
	2.5/0.25	B	K265	R. Palmeira, Palmeira das Missões
	100	B	H446	R. Soc. da Bahia, Salvador
	25/0.5	B	K650	R. Trianon, São Paulo
		BOL		R. Pueblo de Dios, La Paz
	10	CLM	HB	Ecos de Pasto, Pasto
	50	CLM	NS	R. Guatapurí, Valledupar
	1/0.5	PRG	ZP38	R. Hechizo, Caazapá
	10	PRU	OAX6C	R. Continental, Paucarpat Aqp
	1	PRU	OCX2X	R. El Puerto, Pascamayo
	5	PRU	OBX2U	R. Ilucan, Cutervo
	1	PRU	OAM7R	R. Publica, Juliaca
	1	PRU	OBU7C	R. Rede, Cusco
	3	PRU	OCU4X	R. Vision, Huancayo
	5/1.1	URG	CW27	R. Tabaré, Salto
750	1/0.5	ARG	LRL203	R. AM 7-50, Llavallol
	100	ARG	LRA7	R. Nacional, Córdoba
	5/0.25	B	J815	R. Aliança, Concórdia
	100/5	B	L213	R. América, Belo Horizonte
	5/0.5	B	K696	R. Atual, Registro
	1/0.25	B	K516	R. Clube, Osvaldo Cruz
	12/0.5	B	K642	R. CMN, Ribeirão Preto
	50/25	B	H709	R. Jovem Pan, Brasília
	1/0.25	B	I897	R. Liberdade, Campo Maior
	1.5/0.25	B	K661	R. Super Piratininga, São José dos Campos
	1/0.25	B	H792	R. Tocantins, Tocantinópolis
	1/0.25	B	I541	R. Ximango, Alenquer
	50	CLM	DK	Caracol R., Medellín
	5	CLM	LH	LV de Yopal, Yopal
	30	EQA	RC2	R. Caravana, Guayaquil
	5	PRG	ZP42	R. LV de la Policía Nacional,San Lorenzo
	1	PRU	OBU6I	R. Bacan Sat, Pocollay
	10	PRU	OCX4X	R. Los Andes, Cerro de Pasco
	1	PRU	OAM5D	R. OAM5D, Chincha
	5	PRU	OAU9G	R. OAU9G, Bellavista
	1	PRU	OCU7Q	R. Tupac Anaru/FM, Yanaoca Canas
760	18/4	ARG	LU6	Emisora Atlántica, Mar del Plata
	5/0.5	B	H461	R. Cidade, Vitória da Conquista
	1/0.25	B	H252	R. Delmiro, Delmiro Gouveia
	2.5/0.25	B	L257	R. Difusora, Machado
	25/1	B	J478	R. Manchete AM, Niterói
	25/2	B	J742	R. Nereu Ramos, Blumenau
	10/0.5	B	L360	R. Terra, Monte Claros
	25/10	B	H588	R. Uirapuru, Fortaleza
	1/0.25	B	K541	R. Urubupungá, Andradina
	50	BOL		R. Fides, La Paz
	50	CHL	CB76	R. Cooperativa, Santiago
	25	CLM	AJ	RCN R., Barranquilla
	10	EQA	QE1	R. Quito, Quito
	25/10	PRG	ZP80	R. Encarnación, Encarnación
	0.5	PRU	OBX2K	R. Andino, Otuzco
	1	PRU	OAM7Q	R. Azángaro, Azángaro
	10	PRU	OCU4G	R. Bienstar, Chorillos
		PRU	OCX7V	R. Cadena Los Andes, Chaski
	1	PRU	OBU5B	R. Municipal, Chincheros
	1	PRU	OBM7K	R. OBM7K, Mazuku
770	5/1	ARG		R. Cooperativa, Tapiales
	5/0.5	B	I412	R. Caiuás, Dourados
	5/0.25	B	J344	R. Cidade, Cambé
	10/0.25	B	I560	R. Clube, Marabá
	2.5/0.25	B	L209	R. Cultura d'Oeste, Lavras
	1/0.25	B	L337	R. Itabira, Itabira
	5/0.5	B	K506	R. Mix, Limeira
	1/0.25	B	H922	R. Vitória, Coelho Neto
	5	BOL		R. Cosmos, Cochabamba
	5	CHL	CD127	R. Agricultura, Temuco
	1	CHL	CD77	R. Cooperativa, Castro
	100	CLM	JX	RCN R., Bogotá
	25/12	EQA	MF2	R. Revolución, Guayaquil
	2.5	PRU	OBX6H	R. La Inolvidable, Caiama, Aqp
	2.5	PRU	OAU7D	R. LV de Allincapac, Macusani
	1	PRU	OCU7K	R. LV Evangelica, Urcos
	3	PRU	OCX1T	R. Vision, José Leonardo Ortiz
	100	URG	CX12	R. Oriental, Montevideo
780	25/5	ARG	LV8	R. Libertador, Mendoza
	25/5	ARG	LRA12	R. Nacional, Santo Tomé
	10/5	ARG	LRF210	R. Tres, Trelew
	25/5	ARG	LRA10	R.Nacional, Ushuaia
	10/5	B	H919	R. Alvorada, Zé Doca
	50/25	B	K691	R. America, Sao Paulo
	5/2	B	K229	R. Diário da Manhã, Carazinho
	30/10	B	I771	R. Jornal do Comércio, Recife
	10/1	B	L259	R. Manhumirim, Manhumirim
	25	B	K279	R. Princesa AM, Porto Alegre
	10	CHL	CD78	R. Sago, Osorno
	10	CLM	ZG	LV de Dios, Cali
	5	CLM	FV	R. Viva, Pasto
	30	PRG	ZP70	R. Primero de Marzo, Asunción
	1	PRU	OBU2N	R. Coremarca, Bambamarca
	10	PRU	OAX1K	R. Nal. del Perú, Tumbes
	10	PRU	OAZ7S	R. Nuevo Tiempo, Juliaca
	2	PRU	OCU5L	R. OCU5L, Ayacucho
	3	PRU	OAX4X	R. Victoria,Lima
	15	VEN	MN	R. Coro, Coro
790	5	ARG	LV19	R. Malargüe
	100	ARG	LR6	R. Mitre, Buenos Aires
	25/5	ARG	LRA22	R. Nacional, San Salvador de Jujuy
	2.5/0.25	B	J316	R. Clube, Faxinal
	5/0.25	B	K674	R. Cultura, Taubaté
	1/0.25	B	I931	R. Mafrense, Simplício Mendes
	10/0.25	B	J337	R. RCC, Curitiba
	1/0.25	B	H505	R. Regional, Serrinha
	1/0.25	B	H899	R. Rio Flores, Tuntum
	1/0.25	B	J789	R. Videira, Videira
	1	CLM	NC	Ecos del Combeima, Ibagué
	15	CLM	DC	Múnera Eastman R, Medellín
	3	PRU	OAZ7H	R. La Luz, Cusco
	10	PRU	OAX2I	R. Programas del Perú, Trujillo
	2.5	PRU	OBU6D	R. Uno, Tacna
	50	VEN	XM	R. Minuto, Barquisimeto
	10	VEN	KC	R. Venezuela, Caracas
800	1/0.25	ARG	LV23	R. Andina - R. Rio Atuel, General Alvear
	5	ARG	LT43	R. Mocoví, General Pinedo
	25/2	ARG	LU15	R. Viedma, Viedma
	10	B	I921	R. Antares, Teresina
	10/1	B	H705	R. MEC, Brasília
	100	B	J457	R. MEC, Rio de Janeiro
	10	B	K292	R. Universidade, Santa Maria
	5	BOL		R. Play, La Paz
	5/1	CHL	CB80	R. Maria, Viña del Mar
	100	CLM	BW	RCN R., Bucaramanga
	10	EQA	ML2	R. Super K800, Guayaquil
	5	PRG	ZP73	La Union R.800, Asunción
	5/3	PRG	ZP27	R. Mbaracayú, Salto del Guairá
	0.3	PRU	OBX6A	Contacto Sur, Cerro Colorado, Aqp
	0.5	PRU	OAU4H	R. La Luz, Huaral
	0.5	PRU	OBX5B	R. Sur, Ica
	1	PRU	OBU4D	R. Vida, Huancayo
	3	PRU	OCU2Y	R. Vision, Cajamarca
	1	PRU	OCX1P	Telecom del Norte, Piura
810	5/1	ARG		R. Federal, CF Buenos Aires
	10/1	ARG		R. Mitre AM 810, Córdoba
	5/0.5	B	K732	R. Canção Nova do Coração de Maria, São José do Rio Preto

kHz	kW	Ctry	Call	Station, location
	1/0.25	B	L354	R. Cidade, Capinópolis
	1.9/0.25	B	K324	R. Cinderela, Campo Bom
	5/0.25	B	K604	R. Dif. Jundiaiense, Jundiaí
	1/0.25	B	L252	R. Educadora, Ubá
	5/0.5	B	J336	R. Esperança, Prudentópolis
	1/0.5	B	K655	R. Universal, Santos
	50/5	B	H589	R. Verdes Mares, Fortaleza
	2/0.25	B	J261	Rede Terra Nativa, Cornélio Procópio
	60	CLM	CY	Caracol R., Bogotá
	1.5	PRU	OBU5E	ABC R. TV, Huamanga
	1	PRU	OAU2G	R. Apocali, Trujillo
	3	PRU	OCU5Z	R. Asociación Cultural Tintaya, Cotabambas
	5	PRU	OAM7E	R. Jerusalen, Cusco
	1	PRU	OCU6R	R. OCU6R, General Sanchec
	1	PRU	OCU2V	R. Onda Popular, Jaen
	10	PRU	OAX7T	R. Programas del Perú, Juliaca
	2	PRU	OCU6Q	R. R.Santa Cruz, Moquegua
	50	URG	CX14	R. El Espectador, Montevideo
820	2/0.5	ARG	LRI208	Estacion 820, Glew
	25/5	ARG	LRA8	R. Nacional, Formosa
	5/1	ARG	LU24	R. Tres Arroyos, Tres Arroyos
	10/5	B	J738	CBN, Blumenau
	50/5	B	H752	R. Bandeirantes, Goiânia
	5/0.25	B	I912	R. Cacique Bruenque, Regeneração
	0.5/0.25	B	K622	R. Clube, Ourinhos
	10/5	B	J238	R. Cultura, Foz do Iguaçu
	20/1	B	H534	R. Cultura, Utinga
	1/0.25	B	L291	R. da Familia, São Sebastião do Paraíso
	0.25	B	H207	R. Dif. de Tarauacá, Tarauacá
	5/1	B	K241	R. do Vale, Estrela
	1/0.25	B	H...	R. Educ. 6 de Agosto, Xapuri
	1/0.25	B	K602	R. Jauense, Jaú
	5/1	B	I775	R. Paulo Frei, Recife
	1/0.25	B	J357	R. Princesa, Roncador
	10	BOL		R. Altiplano Advenir, La Paz
		CHL	CB82	R. Carabineros, Santiago
	1	CHL	CD82	R. Concordia, La Unión
	10/1	CHL	CA82B	R. La Serena, La Serena
	1	CHL	CC82	R. UCSC, Concepción
	50	CLM	ED	Caracol R., Cali
	5	EQA	VI5	R. LV de Ingapirca, Cañar
	20	PRU	OAX4O	R. Libertad, Lima
	0.5	PRU	OBX2J	R. Nuevo Continente, Cajamarca
		PRU	OBU1X	R. Vision, Piura
830	10/5	ARG	LT8	La Ocho AM 830, Rosario
	5	ARG		R. Del Pueblo, Villa Luzuriaga
	1/0.5	ARG	LT21	R. Municipal, Alvear
	10/1	ARG	LV18	R. Municipal, San Rafael
	25/5	ARG	LU14	R. Provincia de Santa Cruz, Río Gallegos
	1/0.25	B	H925	R. Boa Esperança, Esperantinópolis
	5/0.6	B	K346	R. Cassino, Rio Grande
	15/5	B	L244	R. Cultura, Belo Horizonte
	5/0.25	B	H506	R. Extremo Sul da Bahia, Itamaraju
	10/1	B	I556	R. Guarany de Marajó, Soure
	7.5/0.75	B	J224	R. Iguassu, Araucária
	5/0.25	B	K332	R. Independente, Cruz Alta
	10/1	B	H905	R. Mirante do Maranhão, Imperatriz
	5/1	B	K746	R. Novo Tempo, Nova Odessa
	1/0.25	B	H659	R. Pioneira, Forquilha
	1/0.25	B	I906	R. Primeira Capital, Oeiras
	20/1	B	J926	R. Princesa da Serra, Itabaiana
	1/0.25	B	J311	R. Progresso, Clevelândia
	10/0.5	B	J488	R. Tropical AM, Rio de Janeiro
	15	CLM	DM	Q'hubo R. AM/R. Reloj, Medellín
	10	EQA	RM2	R. Huancavilca, Guayaquil
	10	PRU	OAU4C	R. Capital, El Tambo
	5	PRU	OAM2A	R. Educacion, Trujillo
	1	PRU	OAZ7U	R. Inti Raymi, Santiago
	10	PRU	OAX6D	R. Nacional del Perú, Tacna
	1	PRU	OAM7W	R. OAM7W, Macusani
	1	PRU	OCU2M	R. Universo, Bambamarca
	25	VEN	LT	R. Sensación, Caracas
840	25/10	ARG	LU2	R. Bahía Blanca, Bahía Blanca
	5	ARG		R. General Belgrano, Ciudad Evita
	10/5	ARG	LT12	R. General Madariaga - R.Nal, Paso de los Libres
	25/5	ARG	LV9	R. Salta AM 840, Salta
	100/50	B	K687	R. Bandeirantes, São Paulo
	1/0.5	B	H648	R. Campo Maior, Quixeramobim
	10/0.25	B	H253	R. Canaviero, União dos Palmares
	10	B	K248	R. Cultura, Porto Alegre
	25/5	B	H447	R. Excelsior da Bahia, Salvador
	10/1.2	B	J320	R. Inconfidência, Umuarama
	1/0.25	B	H298	R. Rio Madeira, Manicoré
	10/1	B	J750	R. Rural, Concórdia
	1/0.25	B	I937	R. Vitória, Batalha
	3	BOL		R. Atipiri, El Alto
	10	CHL	CB84	R. Portales, Valparaíso
	10	CHL	CD84	R. Santa María, Coyhaique
	30	CLM	KK	HJ Doble K Sistema INRAI, Neiva
	5	CLM	NA	R. Robledo, Cartago
	25	EQA	PN1	R. Vigía, Quito
	5	PRG	ZP6	R. Guairá, Villarrica
	1	PRU	OBX6Y	R. Azul, Cayama Aqp
	1	PRU	OCU1C	R. Campesina de Ayabaca, Ayabaca
		PRU		R. Campesina, Huari
	1	PRU	OAU2E	R. Nuevo Continente, San Ignacio
	1	PRU	OCU5N	R. OCU5N, Abancay
	1	PRU	OCU7I	R. Santa Cruz, Kunturkanki
	1	PRU	OAU3Q	R. Vision, Casma
850	1	ARG		AM 850 La Gauchita, Merlo
	1/0.25	B	J807	R. Atalaia, Campo Erê
		B	J470	R. Campos Difusora, Campos dos Goytacazes
	5/0.25	B	H474	R. Caraiba, Senhor do Bonfim
	2.5/0.25	B	J808	R. Cidade, Brusque
	2.5/0.25	B	K644	R. Clube AM, Rio Claro
	1/0.25	B	I909	R. Grande Picos, Picos
	5/1	B	I693	R. Rural, Guarabira
	1/0.25	B	I555	R. Tocantins, Cametá
	5/1	B	H776	R.Tropical, Porangatu
	5	BOL		R. María, Montero
	35	CLM	KC	Candela 8-50, Bogotá
	20	EQA	YS2	R. San Francisco, Guayaquil
	5	PRU	OAM7I	R. Lorena, San Sebastian
	1	PRU	OBU1M	R. Nal. del Peru, Ayabaca
	40	PRU	OAX4A	R. Nal. del Perú, Lima
		PRU	OAU6S	R. Nal. del Peru, Tarata
	1	PRU	OAM5L	R. OAM5L, Acori
	1	PRU	OBU3B	R. OBU3B. Cerro Jactay
	1	PRU	OBX9W	R. OBX9W, Chachapoyas
	1	PRU	OCU1Y	R. OCU1Y, Chiclayo
		PRU	OBU7Z	R. Pachamama, Puno
	50	URG	CX16	R. Carve, Montevideo
860	0.5	ARG		R. Digital, Lanus
	1	ARG	LRA56	R. Nacional, Perito Moreno
		ARG		San Carlos de Bariloche
	25/10	B	H592	R. Cidade de Fortaleza, Maracanaú
	10/1	B	K288	R. Guarathan, Santa Maria
		BOL		R. FM Colores, Cochabamba
	10	BOL		R. Nueva America, La Paz
	10	CHL	CC86	R. Inés de Suárez, Concepción
	50	CLM	NJ	LV del Cañaguate/W R., Valledupar
	10	CLM	DV	Voces de Occidente, Buga
	10	EQA	PC1	R. Positiva, Quito
	1	PRG	ZP28	LV de la Cordillera, Caacupé
	3	PRU	OCX1M	R. Nuevo Norte, Sullana
		PRU	OBM7B	R. OBM7B, Sandia
	10	VEN	YE	R. Enlace 860, Valle de la Pascua
	10	VEN	OL	R. Mundial, San Cristóbal
870	100	ARG	LRA1	R. Nacional, Buenos Aires
	5/0.25	B	L349	R. Atividade, Muriaé
	5/1	B	K705	R. Central, Campinas
	5/1	B	H499	R. Cidade, Juazeiro
	1/0.5	B	L318	R. Cultura, Diamantina
	1/0.5	B	N409	R. Garça Branca, Guiratinga
	5/0.5	B	H749	R. Lago Dourado, Uruaçu
	1/0.25	B	H591	R. Liberdade, Iguatu
	1/0.25	B	I547	R. Marajó, Breves

kHz	kW	Ctry	Call	Station, location
	10/0.5	B	H906	R. Mirante, Codó
	12/0.25	B	H457	R. Nacional, Itabuna
	5/0.25	B	J243	R. Nova Ingá, Maringá
	12/0.25	B	J784	R. São Francisco, São Francisco do Sul
	10/0.5	B	H754	R. Universitária, Goiânia
	1	CLM	GD	Em. Reina de Colombia, Chiquinquirá
	5	CLM	ZH	R. Verdad y Vida, Medellín
	10	CLM	LA	Uniminuto R. Tolima, Ibagué
	16	EQA	LY2	R. Cristal, Guayaquil
	2.5	PRU	OCX4D	R. Huancayo, El Tambo
	2.5	PRU	OCX6F	R. Impacto Universal, Uchumayo Aqp
	5	PRU	OAU7O	R. Libertad, Puno
	1	PRU	OCX7R	R. Mundo, Wanchaq
	10	PRU	OBX1F	R. Programas del Perú, Chiclayo
	10	VEN	MP	Unión R. Notícias, Barquisimeto
880	10/5	ARG	LU14	R. Provincia de Santa Cruz, Las Heras
	1/0.25	ARG		R. Provincial de Sierra Colorada, Sierra Colorada
	100	B	L275	AM 880 R. Inconfidência, Belo Horizonte
	25/2.5	B	K249	R. Itaí, Porto Alegre
	1/0.25	B	I680	R. Maringá, Pombal
	2.5/0.25	B	K317	R. São Miguel, Uruguaiana
	8/0.25	B	K363	R. Seberi, Seberirel
		BOL		R. Inca, El Alto
		BOL		Rdif. Oriente, Santa Cruz
	10	CHL	CB88	R. Universal, Santiago
	20	CLM	GE	Caracol R., Bucaramanga
	10	EQA	FJ1	R. Católica Nacional, Quito
	5	PRU	OCU4S	R. Cumbre, Chaupimarca
	1	PRU	OBU5W	R. OBU5W
	2	PRU	OAX2P	R. Sintonia, Trujillo
	50	PRU	OBZ4N	R. Union, Lima
890	25/5	ARG	LV11	Em. Santiago del Estero, Rubia Moreno
	20/1	ARG	LU33	Emisora Pampeana, Santa Rosa
	10	ARG		R. Libre, Villa Caraza
	5/0.25	B	L370	R. Clube, Inhapim
	5/0.25	B	K215	R. Difusora, Bento Gonçalves
	10/0.5	B	I453	R. Guaicurus, Fátima do Sul
	1/0.25	B	K562	R. Imaculada Conceição, Bilac
	5/0.25	B	J338	R. Itapuã, Pato Branco
	1/0.25	B	H642	R. Itatiaia, Santa Quitéria
	50/2.5	B	H706	R. Planalto, Brasília
	5/1	B	I536	R. Ponta Negra, Santarém
	1/0.25	B	J755	R. Santa Catarina, Florianópolis
	10/1	B	L250	R. Santa Cruz, Almenara
	20/10	B	I772	R. Tamandaré, Olinda
	2.5/0.25	B	J287	R. Ubá, Ivaiporã
	1	CHL	CC89	R. Nuevo Mundo, Concepcion
	20	CLM	PM	R. Galeón/Caracol R., Santa Marta
	10	CLM	CE	Vida 890, Bogotá
	5/0.5	PRG	ZP33	R. Tres de Febrero, Itá
	3	PRU	OBX7S	R. Bahá´í del Lago Titicaca, Chiucuito
	1	PRU	OCU5J	R. Cielo, San Pedro de Cachora
	1	PRU	OCU7C	R. Laramani, Espinar
	1	PRU	OAU2N	R. Nor Andina, Celendin
	1	PRU	OCU5W	R. OCU5W, Ica
	50/10	URG	CX18	R. Sport 890, Montevideo
900	10/1	ARG		R. Municipal, 25 de Mayo
	25/2.5	ARG	LT7	R. Provincia de Corrientes, Corrientes
	5/0.5	B	K263	R. ABC 900, Nôvo Hamburgo
	2.5/0.5	B	K211	R. Aratiba, Aratiba
	1/0.25	B	K742	R. Clube de Itapetininga, Itapetininga
	10/2.5	B	I455	R. Dif. Arco-Íris, Araputanga
	5/0.25	B	K511	R. Difusora, Presidente Prudente
	10/0.8	B	K664	R. Jovem Pan, São José do Rio Preto
	25/5	B	I533	R. Liberal, Belém
	1/0.25	B	K301	R. Municipal, São Pedro do Sul
	1	B	H488	R. Sisal, Conceição do Coité
	50/10	B	J454	R. Tamoio, Rio de Janeiro
	5/0.25	B	J295	R. União, Toledo
	1/0.25	B	L338	R. Vinícola, Andradas
	2.5/0.25	B	L311	Rede Gerais, Carangola
	5/0.1	BOL		La Popular, La Paz
	1	BOL		R. Central Misionera, Cochabamba
		BOL		R. Dios es Amor Universal, Potosi
	0.25	BOL		R. LV Nacional, Tarija
		BOL		R. Tomina la Frontera, Villa Tomina
	1	CHL	CB90	R. Corporacion, Viña del Mar
	1	CHL	CD90	R. LV de la Costa, Osorno
	1	CHL	CC90	R. Nuble, Chillán
	10	CLM	EY	LV de Cali, Cali
	10	CLM	DD	RCN Fiesta, Cúcuta
	10	PRU	OBX4X	R. Felicidad, Lima
	1	PRU	OCU1P	R. Huarmaca, Huarmaca
	3	PRU	OBX6K	R. Nevada, Uchumayo, Aqp
	1	PRU	OBM7M	R. OBM7M, Inambari
		PRU	OAX3E	R. Ribereña, Aucaycu
	3/1	URG	CW17	R. Frontera, Artigas
910	150	ARG	LR5	R. La Red, Ituzaingó
	25/5	ARG	LRA23	R. Nacional, San Juan
	10/0.5	B	H804	R. Cidade, Jaraguá
	7.5/0.25	B	K536	R. Jovem Pan News, Piracicaba
	1/0.25	B	J207	R. Nova AM, Apucarana
	5/1	B	N206	R. Play Hits, Juiz de Fora
	1/0.25	B	L292	R. Teófilo Otoni, Teófilo Otoni
	5/0.5	B	K320	R. Venâncio Aires, Venâncio Aires
	1	CHL	CC91	R. Tropical Latina
	10	CLM	DO	LV del Río Grande, Medellín
	1	CLM	TT	Ondas del Porvenir, Samacá
	30	CLM	MY	RCN R., San Andrés
	10	EQA	BO2	La R. Redonda, Guayaquil
	1	PRU	OAU5M	R. Estacion Wari, Ayacucho
	1	PRU	OAU7G	R. Frontera, Juliaca
	1	PRU	OAU7M	R. Regional - R.Quechua, Sicuani
	20	VEN	RQ	RQ 910 AM, Caracas
920	5/0.5	B	I697	João Pessoa
	5/0.5	B	L271	R. Cultura, Visconde do Rio Branco
	1/0.25	B	I895	R. Dif. Grande, Picos
	10/0.5	B	I893	R. Educadora, Parnaíba
	10/0.25	B	K584	R. Imperador, Franca
	40/1	B	K775	R. Nacional Gospel, Cotia
	25/2	B	H519	R. Novo Tempo, Salvador
	5/1	B	H788	R. Vale da Serra, São Luís de Monte Belos
	20/2	B	K348	R.Tramandaí, Tramandaí
		BOL		R. Bartolina Sisa, El Alto
		BOL		R. Dios es Amor Universal, Cochabamba
	3	BOL		R. Encuentro, Sucre
	1	BOL		R. San Andres de Topohoco, Topohoco
	1	CHL	CD92	R. 920, Temuco
	10	CLM	AA	Em. Fuentes, Cartagena
	10	CLM	JN	HSB R., Pasto
	10	CLM	SJ	LV del Pueblo/R. María, Ibagué
	10	EQA	RU3	CRO, Machala
	10	EQA	AB1	R. Democracia, Quito
	20/100	PRG	ZP1	R. Nacional del Paraguay, Chaco-i
	1	PRU	OAM7H	CVC La Voz, Cusco
		PRU		R. Campesina, Juli
	1	PRU	OAX9V	R. Marginal, Tocache
	1	PRU	OBX2S	R. Ollantay, Virú
	10	PRU	OBX1J	R. Programas del Peru, Piura
	1	PRU	OCU7W	R. R.Red Andina, Tambopata
	1	PRU	OCX5C	R. Stelar, Chinca Alta
	2.5	PRU	OBU6M	R. Uno, Tacna
	3	PRU	OAM2G	R. Vision, Samangay
	20	VEN	QX	R. Nueva Esparta, Porlamar
930	5	ARG		R. Nativa, Ciudad Evita
	25/1	ARG	LV7	R. Tucumán, San Miguel de Tucumán
	5/0.5	ARG	LV28	R. Villa María, Villa María
	20/2.5	B	K230	R. Caxias, Caxias do Sul
	1/0.25	B	K503	R. Clube, Itapira
	10/0.5	B	I423	R. Clube, Rondonópolis
	10/1	B	J232	R. Cultura, Curitiba
	1/0.25	B	J227	R. Cultura, Rolândia
	7/0.25	B	H646	R. Metropolitana, Caucaia
	10/1	B	J235	R. Princesa, Francisco Beltrão
	10/0.5	B	K298	R. Santo Ângelo, Santo Ângelo
	10/5	B	L229	R. Vitoriosa, Araguari
	10	CHL	CB93	R. Nuevo Mundo, Santiago
	10	CHL	CD93	R. Reloncaví

kHz	kW	Ctry	Call	Station, location
	5	CLM	IA	Bésame/ W R., Manizales
	10	CLM	CS	LV de Bogotá, Bogotá
	5	EQA	BA6	R. Ambato, Ambato
	5	PRU	OAX4E	Moderna - R.Papa, Lima
	3	PRU	OBU7T	R. Cadena Colca, Juliaca
	1	PRU	OAM7J	R. Cadena Sur, Espinar
	1	PRU	OCX2V	R. Inti, Chepén
	3	PRU	OCU1O	R. Nor Andina, Olmos
	1	PRU	OBU5S	R. OBU5S, Pucar del Sara Sara
	5	PRU	OBX9V	R. OBX9V, Huambo
	5	PRU	OBX6T	R. Yaravi, Cerro Colorado, Aqp.
	50	URG	CX20	R. Monte Carlo, Montevideo
940	3/0.5	ARG	LRH200	R. Chajarí, Chajarí
	20/5	ARG	LRJ241	R. Dimensión, San Luís
	100	B	J453	Super Rede Boa Vontade, Rio de Janeiro
	1	BOL		R. Chuquisaca XXI, Sucre
		BOL		R. Metropolitana, La Paz
		BOL		R. Pan de de Vida, Santa Cruz
	1	CHL	CB94	R. Valentín Letelier, Valparaíso
	5	CLM	A76	Frecuencia U, Medellín
	10	CLM	GB	R. Calima, Cali
	25	CLM	TL	RCN R., Cúcuta
	3	EQA	CP5	R. Caravana, Cuenca
	10	EQA	BZ1	R. CCE, Quito
		PRU	OBX2G	R. Cutervo, Cutervo
	1.5	PRU	OBX7P	R. Las Vegas - W R., Wanchaq
	1	PRU	OBU4E	R. Luz, Jauja
	1	PRU	OBU6G	R. OBU6G, Cotahuasi
	1	PRU	OBU1Y	R. Studio Satelite, Tambo Grande
950	25/5	ARG	LR3	CNN - R.Argentina, Buenos Aires
	25/5	ARG	LT16	RSP - R. Sáenz Peña, Roque Saénz Peña
	25/10	B	L212	R. Atalaia, Belo Horizonte
	1/0.25	B	I923	R. Boa Esperança, Padre Marcos
	10/0.25	B	H916	R. Dif. Karajás, João Lisboa
	10/1	B	H593	R. Educadora do Nordeste, Sobral
	10/0.25	B	K260	R. Independente, Lajeado
	7/0.5	B	L281	R. Indy, Bueno Brandão
	1/0.25	B	I681	R. Jornal, Sousa
	25/5	B	I782	R. Planalto, Carpina
	10/0.25	B	I932	R. São José dos Altos, Altos
	1/0.25	B	J736	R. Vale, Tijucas
	5/0.25	B	K510	Super R. 950, Vera Cruz
	5	CLM	UJ	Armonias Boyacenses, Tunja
	15	CLM	FN	Caracol R., Pereira
	3	EQA	UE5	LV de AIIECH, Colta
	3	EQA	AV1	R. Chaskis del Norte, Ibarra
	1.5	PRU	OAM2H	Onda Popular, Bambamarca
		PRU		R. Campesina, Tarata
	1	PRU	OAM7S	R. OAM7S, Juliaca
	1.5	PRU	OAU9K	R. OAU9K, Shucshuyacu
	1	PRU	OBU5N	R. OBU5N, Paucar del Sara Sara
	1	PRU	OBX3S	R. Programas del Perú, Chimbote
	1	PRU	OBU5R	Radio y TV Mallmanya, Callhuahuacho
960	25/5	ARG	LRA6	R. Nacional,Mendoza
	10/1	ARG	LU13	R. Necochea, Necochea
	50/1	B	H802	R. Caraiba, Aparecida de Goiânia
	1/0.25	B	I551	R. Clube, Itaituba
	1/0.25	B	H618	R. Cultura dos Inhamuns, Tauá
	10	B	H241	R. Difusora de Alagôas, Maceió
	5/0.25	B	J733	R. Guarujá, Orleans
	1/0.25	B	J257	R. Mais, Maringá
	50/10	B	K689	R. São Paulo, São Paulo
	8/0.25	B	J813	R. Super Difusora, Xanxerê
	1	BOL		R. Huayna Potosí, Milluni
	1	BOL		R. Kollasuyo, Potosí
	10	BOL		R. Santa Cruz, Santa Cruz
	10	CHL	CB96	Dossil Radio Chile, Santiago
	10	CHL	CD96	R. Polar, Punta Arenas
	5	CLM	HX	Blu R., Bucaramanga
	10	CLM	HN	Caracol R., Magangué
	1.5	EQA	SA5	R. Sononda Int., Cuenca
	1	PRU	OBU7P	R. Concierto Santa Monica, Espinar
	18	PRU	OBX6S	R. El Pueblo 960, Mariano Melgar, Aqp
	1	PRU	OCY4V	R. Manantial, Chilca
	10	PRU	OAX4D	R. Panamericana, Lima
	3	PRU	OBX1Y	R. WSP, Chiclayo
	2/1	URG	CW96	R. Yi, Durazno
970	3	ARG		R. Génesis, Valentin Alsina
	5/1	ARG	LT25	R. Guaraní, Curuzú Cuatiá
	25	ARG	LRA43	R. Nacional, Neuquén
	7. 5/1	B	J260	R. Alvorada, Londrina
	5/0.25	B	J730	R. Araguaia, Brusque
	5/0.25	B	L243	R. Caratinga, Caratinga
	10/0.25	B	J277	R. Difusora do Paraná, Marechal Cândido Rondón
	5/0.25	B	K684	R. Hertz, Franca
	50/10	B	K201	R. Liberdade, Porto Alegre
	5/0.25	B	H612	R. Monólitos, Quixadá
	1/0.25	B	K529	R. Piratininga, São João da Boa Vista
		B	L264	R. São João del Rei, São João del Rei
	1	CHL	CD97	R. Austral, Valdivia
	1	CHL	CC97	R. Lautaro, Talca
	1	CHL	CD97A	R. Patagonia Chilena, Coyhaique
	15	CLM	VK	Armonías del Caquetá, Florencia
	1	CLM	HKX59	Ecos del Cacique, Calarcá
	10	CLM	CI	R. Red RCN, Bogotá
	1	EQA	MB1	R. Imperio, Ibarra
	80	PRG	ZP9	Universo 970 AM, Villa Hayes
	1	PRU	OBX5A	R. Comericial Sonora, Ica
	1.5	PRU	OBX1V	R. La Capullana, Sullana
	1	PRU	OAU2K	R. Lider del Norte, Cajamarca
	5	PRU	OAU7A	R. Tropicana, Wanchaq
	1	PRU	OBU7B	R. Union Qollasuyo, Juliaca
	20/3	URG	CX22	R. Universal, Montevideo
980	3/1	ARG	LU37	R. General, Pico
	25/1	ARG		R. Luján Valcheta, Valcheta
	5/1	ARG	LT39	R. Victoria, Victoria
	25/5	ARG		Rio Gallegos
	5/1	ARG		San Salvador de Jujuy
	50/300	B	H707	R. Nacional, Brasília
	3	BOL		R. Esperanza, Aiquile
		BOL		R. La Bohemia, Sucre
	2.5	BOL		R. Mar, La Paz
		BOL		R.dif. Concordia, Oruro
	10	CHL	CB98	R. Corporacion, Valparaíso
	100	CLM	ES	RCN R., Cali
	15	CLM	JV	Tropicana, Cúcuta
	1	EQA	JI5	R. El Prado, Riobamba
	5	PRG	ZP31	R. Mburucuyá, Pedro Juan Caballero
	1	PRU	OCX2R	Andina R., Chota
	1	PRU	OCU7X	R. Caden Sur, Sicuani
	1	PRU	OBU1N	R. Campesina, Huancabamba
		PRU		R. Comercial Cosmos, La Peca
	1	PRU	OBU5K	R. LV de Huamanga, Huamanga
	1	PRU	OBU4H	R. OBU4H, Huancayo
	1	PRU	OAU1N	R. Primavera, Lambayeque
	1.5	PRU	OAU6F	R. Universidad, Arequipa
	2	VEN	QM	La Voz de El Tigre, El Tigre
990	25/5	ARG	LR4	AM 990 - R. de Verdad, Villa Dominico
	25/5	ARG	LRH203	R. AM 990, Formosa
	1	ARG	LRJ201	R. Calingasta, Tamberías
	1/0.25	B	K360	R. Clube, Pedro Osório
	100/10	B	J461	R. Contemporânea, Rio de Janeiro
	10/0.25	B	K579	R. Cultura Regional, Dois Córregos
	2/0.25	B	J763	R. Itapiranga, Itapiranga
	10/1	B	J596	R. Rural, Mossoró
	1/0.25	B	I922	R. Vale do Canindé, Oeiras
		BOL		R. Municipal de Colcha
	5	CLM	HI	LV de Garagoa, Garagoa
	50	CLM	CH	RCN R., Medellín
	3	PRU	OCU1H	R. Bendicion Cristiana, Piura
	10	PRU	OAX6K	R. Continental, Tacna
	0.5	PRU	OBX2M	R. Contumaza, Contumaza
	12	PRU	OBX4J	R. Latina, Miraflores
	2.5	PRU	OCU7T	R. Milagros, Juliaca
		PRU	OCU4A	R. Oro, Huayllay
		PRU	OBX3L	R. Peruana, Chimbote
	20	VEN	RT	R. Tropical, Caracas
1000	5/1	ARG		Comodoro Rivadavia
	10/1	ARG		La Rioja

kHz	kW	Ctry	Call	Station, location
	1/0.25	ARG	LT42	R. Del Iberá, Mercedes
	5/1	ARG	LU16	R. Río Negro, Villa Regina
	1	ARG		R. Sintonia, José C.Paz
	2.5/0.5	B	I698	R. Oeste da Paraíba, Cajazeiras
	1/0.25	B	I791	R. Princesa Serrana, Timbaúba
	200	B	K522	R. Record, São Paulo
		BOL		FM Unica, Cochabamba
		BOL		R. LV del Arrebatamiento, Guaqui
	1	BOL		R. Taypi, La Paz
	1	BOL		Rdif. del Oriente, Santa Cruz
	10	CHL	CB100	BBN R., Santiago
	10	CLM	JG	R. Nac. de Colombia, Manizales
	15	CLM	AQ	RCN R., Cartagena
	5	PRG	ZP36	R. Mil, Chaco-i
	2.5	PRU	OBX6R	R. Edesa, Cerro Colorado, Aqp
	1	PRU	OBX3V	R. Huanuco
	1	PRU	OBX5W	R. Lircay, Lircay
	1	PRU	OAM4N	R. OAM4N, Barranca
	1	PRU	OBU4Z	R. OBU4Z, Pariahuanaca
	7	PRU	OCU1N	R. OCU1N, San José
	2	PRU	OAZ7P	R. Prensa al Dia, Cusco
1010	4	ARG		R. Onda Latina, Valentin Alsina
	20/5	ARG	LV16	R. Rio Cuarto, Rio Cuarto
	25/5	B	H448	R. Bahia, Salvador
	25/5	B	J263	R. Celinauta, Pato Branco
	5/0.25	B	K611	R. Diário, Martinópolis
	5/0.5	B	K507	R. Dif., Lençóis Paulista
	10/1	B	L230	R. Educadora, Coronel Fabriciano
	3/1	B	K344	R. Missioneira, São Luiz Gonzaga
	12.5/2.5	B	H625	R. O´Povo CBN, Fortaleza
	10/0.5	B	H772	R. Santelenense, Sta. Helena de Goiás
	7/0.75	B	K232	R. Tua Voz, Caxias do Sul
	10	BOL		R. Bahá'í de Bolivia, Oruro
	10	CHL	CD101	R. Nielol, Temuco
	10	CLM	CC	Acuario Estéreo, Bogotá
	15	CLM	JR	Caracol R., Neiva
	10/5	CLM	BN	LV del Galeras, Pasto
	5	CLM	ZD	R. Panzenú, Montería
	10	CLM	OP	Sistema Cardenal, Barranquilla
	10	EQA	NR6	R. Líder TSB, Ambato
	1	PRU	OBU1L	LV de las Huaringas, Huancabamba
		PRU		R. Cajamarca, Cajamarca
	10	PRU	OAX4U	R. Cielo, Lima
	1	PRU	OBX9T	R. Fé, Bagua Grande
	1	PRU	OCU7P	R. Nac. del Peru, Juli
	1	PRU	OBU5T	R. OBU5T, Cotabambas
	1	PRU	OBU6L	R. Orcopampa, Orcopampa
	1.5	PRU	OBX2P	R. San Francisco, Cajamarca
	1	PRU	OBZ1C	R. Sonora, Tumbes
	25	URG	CX24	R. 1010 AM, Montevideo
	10	VEN	PC	R. Aragua, Cagua
1020	25/2.5	ARG	LRJ214	AM Mil 20, San Juan
	1/0.5	ARG	LRA58	R. Nacional, Río Mayo
	10/5	ARG	LT10	R. Univ. Nal. del Litoral, Santa Fé
	10/0.5	B	H781	R. Boas Novas, Firminópolis
	10/0.25	B	J244	R. Colombo, Curitiba
	5/0.25	B	K515	R. Cultura, Assis
	2.5/0.5	B	K531	R. Educadora, Limeira
	25/5	B	K202	R. Eldorado, Porto Alegre
	1/0.25	B	J307	R. Independência, Medianeira
	1/0.25	B	H664	R. Macambira, Ipueiras
	25/1	B	H247	R. Maceio, Rio Largo
	1/0.25	B	H423	R. Porto, Santana
		BOL		R. Illimani - R. Patria Nueva, Azurduy
		BOL		R. Illimani - R. Patria Nueva, Bermejo
		BOL		R. Illimani - R. Patria Nueva, Camiri
		BOL		R. Illimani - R. Patria Nueva, Caracolla
		BOL		R. Illimani - R. Patria Nueva, Caranavi
		BOL		R. Illimani - R. Patria Nueva, Catavi
		BOL		R. Illimani - R. Patria Nueva, Challapata
		BOL		R. Illimani - R. Patria Nueva, Chapare
		BOL		R. Illimani - R. Patria Nueva, Chulumani
		BOL		R. Illimani - R. Patria Nueva, Cobija
		BOL		R. Illimani - R. Patria Nueva, Cochabamba
		BOL		R. Illimani - R. Patria Nueva, Colomi
		BOL		R. Illimani - R. Patria Nueva, Copacabana
		BOL		R. Illimani - R. Patria Nueva, Coro Coro
		BOL		R. Illimani - R. Patria Nueva, Desaguadero
		BOL		R. Illimani - R. Patria Nueva, Entre Rios
		BOL		R. Illimani - R. Patria Nueva, Escoma
		BOL		R. Illimani - R. Patria Nueva, Guaqui
		BOL		R. Illimani - R. Patria Nueva, Huanuni
		BOL		R. Illimani - R. Patria Nueva, Ichoca-Quime
		BOL		R. Illimani - R. Patria Nueva, Independencia
		BOL		R. Illimani - R. Patria Nueva, Kami
		BOL		R. Illimani - R. Patria Nueva, La Asunta
	10	BOL		R. Illimani - R. Patria Nueva, La Paz
		BOL		R. Illimani - R. Patria Nueva, Llica
		BOL		R. Illimani - R. Patria Nueva, Machareti
		BOL		R. Illimani - R. Patria Nueva, Oruro
		BOL		R. Illimani - R. Patria Nueva, Potosi
		BOL		R. Illimani - R. Patria Nueva, Pucarani
		BOL		R. Illimani - R. Patria Nueva, Puerto Quijarro
		BOL		R. Illimani - R. Patria Nueva, Qhurpa
		BOL		R. Illimani - R. Patria Nueva, Riberalta
		BOL		R. Illimani - R. Patria Nueva, San Borja
		BOL		R. Illimani - R. Patria Nueva, Santa Cruz
		BOL		R. Illimani - R. Patria Nueva, Sopachuy
		BOL		R. Illimani - R. Patria Nueva, Sucre
		BOL		R. Illimani - R. Patria Nueva, Tapichullo
		BOL		R. Illimani - R. Patria Nueva, Taraco
		BOL		R. Illimani - R. Patria Nueva, Tarija
		BOL		R. Illimani - R. Patria Nueva, Tiawanaku
		BOL		R. Illimani - R. Patria Nueva, Tiraque
		BOL		R. Illimani - R. Patria Nueva, Topohoco
		BOL		R. Illimani - R. Patria Nueva, Trinidad
		BOL		R. Illimani - R. Patria Nueva, Tupiza
		BOL		R. Illimani - R. Patria Nueva, Unica
		BOL		R. Illimani - R. Patria Nueva, Uyuni
		BOL		R. Illimani - R. Patria Nueva, Valle Alto
		BOL		R. Illimani - R. Patria Nueva, Vallegrande
		BOL		R. Illimani - R. Patria Nueva, Vilaque
		BOL		R. Illimani - R. Patria Nueva, Villamontes
		BOL		R. Illimani - R. Patria Nueva, Villazon
		BOL		R. Illimani - R. Patria Nueva, Yacuiba
		BOL		R. Illimani - R. Patria Nueva, Yapacani
		BOL		R. Illimani - R. Patria Nueva. Tarata
	5	CHL	CC102	R. Amiga,Talca
	10	CLM	DQ	Emisora Claridad, Medellín
	10	CLM	KS	La Cariñosa, Villavicencio
	10	CLM	FT	La FM, Ibagué
	15	CLM	DZ	R. Primavera, Bucaramanga
	10	CLM	FQ	RCN R., Pereira
	5	EQA	GO3	R. Estelar, Santa Rosa
	25	PRG	ZP14	R. Ñandutí,San Lorenzo
	0.5	PRU	OBU5M	R. AM Vida, Huamanga
	2	PRU	OAU2P	R. Bambamarca, Bambamarca
	1	PRU	OBU4F	R. Cristo Vive, Huancayo
	1	PRU	OBU7O	R. Informes, Sicuani
	1	PRU	OAU6J	R. Internacional, Tacna
	5	PRU	OAM7Y	R. Kinsachata Tintaya, Espinar
	1	PRU	OBU1D	R. La Luz, Piura
	1	PRU	OCU1M	R. OCU1M, José Leonardo Ortiz
	0.1	URG	CW102E	R. Libertadores, Salto
	25	VEN	TW	R. Alegría, Chivacoa
1030	100	ARG	LS10	R. del Plata, Buenos Aires
	5/0.25	B	J271	R. Atalaia, Londrina
	100/5	B	J467	R. Capital, Rio de Janeiro
	2.5/0.25	B	J312	R. Clube, Realeza
	1/0.25	B	H791	R. Colinas, Colinas do Tocantins
	1/0.25	B	K224	R. Cultura, Canguçu
	5/0.25	B	K525	R. Difusora, Franca
	1/0.25	B	K554	R. Em. da Barra, Barra Bonita
		B	I441	R. Itai do Rio Claro, Rondonopolis
	10/1	B	H892	R. Jainara, Bacabal
	20/5	B	I777	R. Olinda, Olinda
	5/1	B	J683	R. Rondônia, Ariquemes

kHz	kW	Ctry	Call	Station, location
		BOL		R. 24 de Junio, Totora
	3	BOL		R. Comunitaria Riberalte, Riberalta
	3	BOL		R. de los Pueblos Originarios, Orinaca
		BOL		R. Illimani - R. Patria Nueva, Coripata
		BOL		R. Illimani - R. Patria Nueva, Coroico
		BOL		R. Illimani - R. Patria Nueva, San Pablo de Lipez
		BOL		R. Illimani - R.Patria Nueva, Camargo
	3	BOL		R. Independencia, Independencia
		BOL		R. Mojocoya AM, Mojocoya
	10	CHL	CC103	R. Chilena, Concepción
	1	CHL	CD103	R. Chiloé, Castro
	1	CHL	CD103A	R. Payne AM, Puerto Natales
	1	CHL	CB103	R. Progreso, Talagante
	30	CLM	DT	Antena 2, Cali
	10	CLM	DJ	La Cariñosa, Duitama
	15	CLM	RF	Ondas del Cesar, Aguachica
	5	CLM	GX	RPC Lorica R., Lorica
	5	EQA	RF2	R. Ecuantena, Guayaquil
	1	PRU	OCX6L	R. Cumbia, Arequipa
	1	PRU	OCX7O	R. HG-AM, Cusco
	5	PRU	OAM2E	R. La Beta Cajamarca
	5	PRU	OAU2U	R. Los Andes, Huamachuco
	1	PRU	OAX7N	R. LV del Altiplano, Puno
	1	PRU	OBX9Z	R. OBX9Z, San Ramon
1040	10/1	ARG	LRG203	R. Capital, Santa Rosa
	200/100	B	K537	R. Capital, São Paulo
		BOL		R. 12 de Marzo, Tarabuco
	0.25	BOL		R. Atlántida, Oruro
	1	BOL		R. Bolivianíssima, La Paz
		BOL		R. San Julián, San Julián
	15	CLM	CJ	Colmundo R., Bogotá
	15	CLM	UB	Colmundo R., Pasto
	15	CLM	FM	LV de Armenia, Armenia
	15	CLM	BF	LV del Norte/Blu R., Cúcuta
	10	CLM	SY	R. 1040, Popayán
	15	CLM	AI	R. Tropical, Barranquilla
	1	EQA	GB6	R. Colosal, Ambato
	5	PRG	ZP43	R. Arapysandú, San Ignacio
	1	PRU	OBX5U	R. La Luz, Ica
	1	PRU	OAU7H	R. Los Andes, Espinar
	10	PRU	OBX4O	R. Metropolitiana, Miraflores
	1	PRU	OAU3P	R. Nueva Vida, Chimbote
	1	PRU	OAM2L	R. OAM2L, Pomahuaca
	1	PRU	OAZ1D	R. Vecinal, Piura
	20	VEN	LB	LV de Carabobo, Valencia
	10	VEN	ON	Mundial Los Andes, Mérida
1050	1.3	ARG		R. General Güemes, Villa Lynch
	10/1	ARG	LV27	R. San Francisco, San Francisco
	10/0.5	B	J497	R. Angra, Angra dos Reis
	100/1	B	I203	R. Capixaba, Vitória
	1/0.25	B	L236	R. Rural, Tupaciguara
	10/0.5	B	K601	R. Show Jardinópolis
		BOL		R. Caiza D, Caiza D
		BOL		R. Comunitaria, Huacaya
	3	BOL		R. Sabaya, Sabaya
	10	CLM	FZ	La Cariñosa Voz del Centro, Espinal
	10	CLM	E73	LV del Cinaruco/Caracol, Arauca
	10	CLM	GU	R. Bucarica, Bucaramanga
	5	CLM	NG	R. Palmira, Palmira
	10	CLM	AW	RCN R., Montería
	10	CLM	BB	Sistema Cardenal, Valledupar
	5	EQA	RQ2	R. Águila Sport, Guayaquil
	1	PRU	OBZ4J	Bethel R., Huancayo
	3	PRU	OBX6B	Bethel R., Uchumayo, Aqp
	3	PRU	OCU1E	R. Bendición Cristiana, Chiclayo
	1	PRU	OAZ7Q	R. Noticias, Juliaca
	1	PRU	OCX2B	R. San Sebastian, Chepen
	1	PRU	OAZ1C	R. Superior, Chulucanas
		PRU		R. Tigre, Rejopampa, Sorochuco
	50	URG	CX26	R. Uruguay, Montevideo
1060	1.5	ARG		R. Excelsior, Monte Grande
	25	B	L278	R. 880, Belo Horizonte
	5/0.25	B	K220	R. Camaqüense, Camaquã
	30/1	B	J495	R. Canção Nova, Nova Iguaçu
	5/1	B	H460	R. Cl. de Conquista, Vitória da Conquista
	10/0.5	B	J306	R. Educadora, Francisco Beltrão
	5/0.25	B	K533	R. Educadora, Piracicaba
	10/0.5	B	J246	R. Evangelizar, Curitiba
	5/1	B	N604	R. Imaculada Conceição, Dourados
	2/0.4	B	J830	R. Mais Alegria, Florianópolis
	2/0.25	B	K302	R. São Luiz, São Luiz Gonzaga
	5	B	H807	R. Serra Dourada, Minacu
	5	B	J597	R. Tapuyo, Mossoró
	5/0.25	B	K765	R. Universitária, Garça
	1	BOL		R. Dif. Colosal, Sucre
	1.5	BOL		R. Noticias, Oruro
		BOL		R. Qhana Amazonía, Caranavi
	100	CHL	CB106	R. Inolvidable, Santiago
	1	CLM	YX	R. Caracolí, Sincelejo
	10	CLM	LY	R. Delfín, Riohacha
	10	CLM	MV	R. Furatena, Chiquinquirá
	1	CLM	MG	R. Litoral, Turbo
	15	CLM	OV	R. Surcolombiana, Neiva
	15	CLM	FJ	RCN R., Manizales
	3	EQA	CH2	R. Fiesta, Machala
	1	PRU	OAU5P	Estacion Wari, Huamanga
	1	PRU	OAU7U	R. Estudio 1060, Cusco
	1	PRU	OCY4D	R. Exito, Lima
	1	PRU	OBU6O	R. Municipilidad, Omate
	2	PRU	OCU1V	R. OCU1V, Tumbes
	3	PRU	OAU3S	R. R.Cielo, Chimbote
	2	PRU	OBU5Q	R. Restauracion, Andahuaylas
		PRU	OBU1F	R. Studio 1060. Piura
	5	PRU	OCY2O	R. Sudamerica, Cutervo
	1	PRU	OCU7V	Tambopata
1070	25/1	ARG		Paseo de Indios
	10/1	B	K633	Prudente AM, Presidente Prudente
	2/0.25	B	K218	R. Caçapava, Caçapava do Sul
	20/2.5	B	I673	R. Cajazeiras, Cajazeiras
	1/0.25	B	L316	R. do Povo, Muzambinho
	1/0.25	B	K758	R. Jornal, Barretos
	1/0.25	B	K343	R. Metrópole, Crissiumal
	10/0.25	B	K615	R. Metropolitana, Mogi das Cruzes
	1/0.25	B	K603	R. Piratininga de Jaú, Jaú
	5/0.5	B	H492	R. Rural 'R. Tropical', Ipiaú
	2/0.25	B	K357	R. Serrana, Bento Gonçalves
	20	CLM	AH	Em. Atlántico, Barranquilla
	30	CLM	CG	R. Santa Fe/R. Reloj, Bogotá
	15	CLM	VR	R. Súper, Popayán
	5	EQA	CJ5	LV del Tomebamba, Cuenca
	3	PRU	OBX9J	R. Andes, Tarapoto
	1	PRU	OAM5K	R. OAM5K, Huancavelica
	1	PRU	OAU3N	R. OAU3N, Huánuco
	0.2	PRU	OAX5A	R. San Juan, San Juan de Marcona
	1	PRU	OAU6K	R. Trinidad, Paucarpata, Aqp.
	1	PRU	OAU1J	R. Vida, José Leonardo Ortiz
	1	PRU	OBX4G	R. Visión, San Ramón
1080	10/1	ARG		AM 1080, Paso de los Libres
	25/5	ARG	LU3	Ondas del Sur, Bahía Blanca:
	0.25	ARG	LW4	R. Orán, Argentina
	10/1	B	K669	R. Boa Nova, Sorocaba
	25/5	B	H708	R. Capital - Rede Aleliua, Brasília
	25/0.7	B	L251	R. Capital, Juiz de Fora
	2.5/0.5	B	L232	R. Cultura, Dores do Indaiá
	10	B	K280	R. da Universidade, Porto Alegre
	5/1	B	K557	R. Difusora, Batatais
	1/0.25	B	H485	R. Fascinação, Itapetinga
	10/0.5	B	I784	R. Jornal do Comercio, Caruaru
	3/0.25	B	K254	R. Marabá, Iraí
	1/0.25	B	K704	R. Monumental, Aparecida
	15/5	B	I540	R. Novo Tempo, Belém
	10/0.5	B	H470	R. Subaé, Feira de Santana
		BOL		R. Comunitaria, Juana Azurduy
		BOL		R. Comunitaria, Sopachuy
		BOL		R. Comunitario Carama, Machareti
		BOL		R. Comunitario Carama, Sucre
		BOL		R. Espiritu Santo, La Paz
	1	CHL	CD108	R. Los Confines, Angol
	1	CHL	CA108	Vicuña

kHz	kW	Ctry	Call	Station, location
	10	CLM	JF	Cadena Radial Vida, Cali
	10	CLM	AX	LV de Antioquia, Medellín
	10	CLM	AW	LV de Montería, Montería
	10	CLM	KT	R. Auténtica, Villavicencio
	10	CLM	MH	R. Melodía, Bucaramanga
	1	EQA	AB4	R. Contacto, Manta
	10	EQA	BH6	R. Latacunga AM, Latacunga
	10	EQA	KD2	Sistema 2, Guayaquil
	10	PRG	ZP25	R. Monumental, Chaco-i
	1	PRU	OBU4W	R. Cielo, Huancayo
	10	PRU	OAU4I	R. La Luz, Lima
	1.5	PRU	OBX1D	R. La Luz, Piura
	1	PRU	OBU6H	R. LV del Sur, Moquegua
	5	PRU	OCU4O	R. Mineria, Chaupimarca
	1	PRU	OCU7O	R. Nacional, Ayaviri
	1	PRU	OAU2L	R. Nueva Vida, Cajamarca
	2.2	PRU	OAX7S	R. Salkantay, Cusco
	10	VEN	NR	Mundial 1080, Maracay
1090	1	ARG		AM Libertad , Rosario
	3	ARG		R. Décadas, José León Suárez
	25/1	B	H758	R. Aliança, Aparecida de Goiânia
	1/0.25	B	J345	R. Banda 1, Sarandi
	5/0.5	B	J786	R. Bandeirantes, Tubarão
	1/0.25	B	K768	R. Canção Nova, Paulina
	5/0.25	B	L357	R. Catuaí, Manhuaçu
	3/0.5	B	K609	R. Clube, Marília
	1/0.25	B	J732	R. Colón, Joinville
	3/0.25	B	K618	R. Cultura, Monte Alto
	5/0.5	B	H254	R. Gazeta, Pão de Açucar
	1/0.25	B	K341	R. Giruá, Giruá
	50/5	B	J468	R. Metropolitana, Rio de Janeiro
	10	B	H893	R. Rio Balsas, Balsas
	1/0.25	B	K262	R. Salette, Marcelino Ramos
	1/0.25	B	H455	R. Santa Cruz, Ilhéus
	2.5/0.25	B	J283	R. Vicente Palotti, Coronel Vivida
		BOL		R. Comunitaria Pachakuti, Achocalla
	5	CHL	CD109	Castro
	5/1	CHL	CC109	R. Chilena del Maule, Talca
	5	CLM	OM	Blu R., Cartagena
	15	CLM	BC	Caracol R., Cúcuta
	10	CLM	JB	Click R. /Blu R., Guamo
	8	CLM	IH	R. Reloj Boyacá, Sogamoso
	3	EQA	VC1	R. Irfeyal, Quito
	1	PRU	OBX6X	R. Amistad, Arequipa
	1	PRU	OAU5F	R. Inti Andina, Aucara
	2	PRU	OCU1Z	R. Vision, Tumbes
	15	URG	CX28	R. R.Maria, Montevideo
	10	VEN	PB	R. Yaracuy, San Felipe
	20	VEN	SZ	Unión R., Caracas
1100	1	ARG		R. Estilo, Glew
	10/0.5	ARG		R. Mitre, Corrientes
	5/0.5	ARG	LRG204	Red Pampeana, General Pico
	1/0.25	B	H638	R. Dif. dos Inhamuns, Tauá
	1/0.25	B	J607	R. Seridó, Caicó
		BOL		R. Chaka, Pucarani
	1	BOL		R. Universidad de Oruro
		BOL		Universal R. Concienia, El Alto
	10	CHL	CB110	BBN R. Viña del Mar
	15	CLM	AT	Caracol R., Barranquilla
	5	CLM	GI	Em. José Antonio Galán, Socorro
	10	CLM	CN	Emisora BBN, Bogotá
	15	CLM	YZ	La FM, Neiva
	5	CLM	GQ	Transmisora Surandes/Todelar, Andes
	1	EQA	GR6	R. Novedades, Latacunga
	1	EQA	LE7	R. Oriental, Tena
	5	PRG	ZP71	R. Ñú Verá, Capitán Bado
		PRU	OCU2E	R. 1000, Julcan
	1	PRU	OBX7Z	R. LTC, Juliaca
	1	PRU	OCU4N	R. OCU4N, Cañete
	1	PRU	OBX1L	R. Ondas de Paz, Chiclayo
	1	PRU	OAZ4W	R. Programas del Peru, Barranca
	1	PRU	OCY4G	Sonorama R., Huancayo
1110	25/5	ARG	LS1	R. de la Ciudad, Dique Luján
	1	B	L267	R. Aurilândia, Nova Lima
	2.5/0.25	B	K325	R. Cruzeiro do Sul, Itaqui
	2.5/0.25	B	K257	R. Cultura Jaguarão, Jaguarão
	1/0.5	B	J752	R. Cultura, Florianópolis
	1/0.25	B	L205	R. Planalto, Araguari
	25/2	B	H782	R. Redentor, Sto. Antônio do Escoberto
	2/0.25	B	K306	R. Sobradinho, Sobradinho
	20/10	B	I689	R. Tabajara, João Pessoa
	1	B	I392	R. Transamérica, Ponta Porã
	1	B	H464	R. Vox, Muritiba
	1/0.25	B	K617	Transamérica Hits, Mogi Mirim
		BOL		R. Raqaypampa, Raqaypampa
	10	CHL	CD111	R. La Frontera, Temuco
	5	CLM	GP	LV del Río Arauca, Arauca
	9	CLM	DI	R. Bolivariana AM, Medellín
	10	CLM	EW	R. Reloj, Cali
	10	CLM	JP	RCN R., Villavicencio
	1	PRU	OBU6F	R. Austral, Ilo
	0.5	PRU	OCX1R	R. Centro Popular, La Union
	3	PRU	OAU3R	R. Cielo, Huánuco
	1	PRU	OAU4J	R. Feliz, Lima
	1	PRU	OCX2U	R. Jaén, Jaén
	5	PRU	OCX7T	R. Machupicchu, Cusco
	3	URG	CX111	R. Paso de los Toros, Paso de los Toros
1120	1	ARG		Em. Santiago y Copla, Ciudad Evita
	1/0.5	ARG	LRK204	R. 21, San Miguel
	25/5	ARG	LV5	R. Sarmiento, San Juan
	1	ARG		R. Sudamericana, San Andrés
	5/0.5	B	H513	R. Belo Campo, Belo Campo
	10/1	B	K660	R. Cidade, São José dos Campos
	1/0.25	B	K671	R. Clube Imperial, Taquaritinga
	10	B	H257	R. Estrela, Valenta
	0.3	B	H511	R. Jornal, Souto Soares
	25/1	B	J253	R. Mais, São José dos Pinhais
	5/1	B	I778	R. Relógio, Paulista
		BOL		R. Celestial el Milagro, El Alto
		BOL		R. El Porvenir, Tiquipaya
		BOL		R. Illimani - R. Patria Nueva, Huarina
		BOL		R. Wiñay Khantatt, Tiawuanaku
	10	CLM	TI	Emisora Vox Dei, Cúcuta
	15	CLM	GH	R. Reloj, Bucaramanga
	10	CLM	KQ	Tropicana Boyacá, Tunja
	10	PRG	ZP24	La Deportiva, San Lorenzo
	1	PRU	OCU4E	R. Bendición, Barranca
	1.5	PRU	OBX2I	R. Dinamica, Trujillo
	0.5	PRU	OAU5W	R. Huayllahuara
	1	PRU	OCX6U	R. Municipal, Cerro Colorado, Aqp
	5	PRU	OAX8A	R. Nacional, Iquitos
	3	PRU	OAM2F	R. Paz, Chota
	1	PRU	OAU5H	R. Quispillaccta, Ayacucho
		PRU		R. San Bartolome, Junin
	10	URG	CW31	R. Salto, Salto
1125	1	PRU	OBX8R	R. Nuevo Tiempo, Campoverde
1130	25/5	ARG	LRA21	R. Nacional, Santiago del Estero
	5	ARG		R. Show, Francisco Alvarez
	5/1	B	I783	R. Cultura do Nordeste, Caruaru
	5/0.25	B	J333	R. Ingamar, Marialva
	10	B	I531	R. Marajoara, Belém
	100/50	B	J460	R. Nacional, Rio de Janeiro
	10/0.25	B	H667	R. Patu, Senador Pompeu
	5/1	B	J790	R. Princesa d'Oeste, Xanxerê
		BOL		R. Illimani - R. Patria Nueva, Montero
	15	CLM	VA	Cadena Radial Vida, Bogotá
	10	CLM	QQ	R. Reloj, Pasto
	3	EQA	PV6	R. Centro, Ambato
	1	EQA	CC3	R. Romántica, Machala
	2.6	PRU	OAX4N	R. Bacán Sat., Lima
	3	PRU	OBU6Q	R. Cielo, Moquegua
		PRU	OAM4K	R. OAM4K, Junin
	1	PRU	OCU1R	R. OCU1
	1	PRU	OCU6I	R. OCU6I, Camaná
	1.2	PRU	OAX2V	R. Onda Popular, Cajamarca
	1	PRU	OAU7B	R. Onda Popular, Juliaca
	5	PRU	OAM7F	R. Ondas de Paz, Cuzco
	20	URG	CX30	R. Nacional, Montevideo
	10	VEN	RL	R. Ideal, Maiquetía
	10	VEN	KQ	R. Popular, Barquisimeto

kHz	kW	Ctry	Call	Station, location
1140	1	ARG		R. La Luna, El Palomar
	10/1	ARG	LU22	R. Tandil, Tandil
	5/0.7	B	K316	R. Charrua, Uruguaiana
	5/0.25	B	K709	R. Costa Azul, Ubatuba
	2/0.25	B	K228	R. Cruz Alta, Cruz Alta
	10	B	H449	R. Cultura da Bahia, Salvador
	1/0.25	B	K645	R. Cultura, Rio Claro
	1/0.25	B	J352	R. Dif. América, Chopinzinho
	10/0.5	B	K550	R. Difusora, Assis
	1/0.25	B	L248	R. Doicesana, Campanha
	2/0.5	B	K330	R. Jornal Sobral, Butiá
	1/0.25	B	K708	R. Nova Regional, Registro
	10/1	B	H607	R. Progresso, Russas
	10/0.5	B	I398	R. Regional, Fátima do Sul
		BOL		R. San Isidro, Colomi
		BOL		R. Sol Poder de Dios, Huancane
		BOL		R. Sol Poder de Dios, La Paz
	100	CHL	CB114	R. Nacional, Santiago
	10	CLM	E67	LV de los Centauros/Caracol, Villavicencio
	10	CLM	KO	R. Esperanza, Cartagena
	10	CLM	DL	R. Paisa/RCN La Cariñosa, Medellín
	10	CLM	CL	R. Panamericana/Blu R., Girardot
	10	CLM	RN	RCN R., Barbosa
	1	EQA	AZ5	R. Alpha Musical, Cuenca
	5/2	PRG	CP22	R. Central de Notícias, Atyrá
		PRU	OCU2D	Chami R., Otuzco
	1	PRU	OAU3C	R. Bahia, Chimbote
	1	PRU	OAX6L	R. Capital, Cerro Colorado, Aqp
	0.5	PRU	OAX5W	R. Chinchaysuyo, Chinca Alta
	5	PRU	OAU1T	R. Fraternal, Ferreñafe
	5	PRU	OAM2O	R. Maria, Chota
	1.5	PRU	OBX1W	R. Piura, Piura
	1	PRU	OCY4C	R. Programas del Perú, Pilcomayo
1150	10/1	ARG	LT9	R. Brigadier López, Santa Fé
	5/1	ARG	LRA51	R. Nacional, Jáchal
	25/5	ARG	LRA2	R. Nacional, Viedma
	0.1	ARG		R. Sagrada Familia, Ciudad Madero
	50/5	ARG	LRH202	R. Tupámbaé, Posadas
	5/0.5	B	J617	R. Cabugi do Seridó, Jardim do Seridó
	20/1	B	H250	R. Cultura, Arapiraca
	10/0.5	B	J456	R. Três Rios, Três Rios
	100/50	B	K656	Super Radio, São Paulo
	0.3	BOL		R. Guaqui, Puerto de Guaqui
	15	CLM	FI	Caracol R., Armenia
	1	CLM	TE	LV del Chocó/RCN R., Quibdó
	10	CLM	BT	R. Catatumbo/Blu R., Ocaña
	10	CLM	FP	RCN R., Neiva
	1	CLM	GJ	W R., Duitama
	0.5	PRU	OCY2E	R. Chasquillacta, Pedro Galvez
	2.5	PRU	OAU7X	R. La Sureña, Juliaca
	5	PRU	OBU4K	R. Mineria, Cerro de Pasco
	1	PRU	OAM4R	R. OAM4R, Huayllay
	2.5	PRU	OCX7Q	R. Universal, Wanchaq
1160	5/0.5	ARG	LRH253	R. Cataratas, Pto. Iguazú
	5/2.5	ARG	LU32	R. Coronel Olavarría, Olavarría
	1	ARG		R. Independencia, Remedios de Escalada
	5/1	ARG	LRA57	R. Nacional, El Bolsón
	5/1	ARG		Salta
	30/0.5	B	H714	Brasília
	10/5	B	I385	R. A Voz Do Oeste, Cuiabá
	2. 5/1	B	K558	R. Bandeirantes, Bauru
	5/0.5	B	K517	R. Cacique, Sorocaba
	4/0.25	B	K673	R. Cacique, Taubaté
	5/0.25	B	K582	R. Difusora, Fernandópolis
	50/10	B	I202	R. Espírito Santo, Vitória
	5/1	B	I558	R. Guamá, São Miguel do Guamá
	9/0.7	B	J741	R. Itaberá, Blumenau
	5/1	B	K245	R. Luz e Alegria, Frederico Westphalen
	9/1	B	K242	R. Miriam, Farroupilha
	1/0.25	B	H660	R. Montevidéo, Cedro
	1/0.25	B	H323	R. Soc. TV Manauara, Boca do Acre
	2. 5/1	B	K273	R. Universidade Católica, Pelotas
	1/0.25	B	H652	R. Vale do Coreaú, Granja
	5	BOL		R. Centenario, Sta. Cruz
	10	BOL		R. Continental, La Paz

kHz	kW	Ctry	Call	Station, location
	1	BOL		R. Nuevo Mundo, Sucre
	3/1	BOL		R. RTC Deportiva, Cochabamba
	1	CHL	CC116	R. Ancoa, Linares
	1	CHL	CD116A	R. Baha'i, Temuco
	5	CLM	AZ	Em. Frecuencia Bolivariana, Montería
	15	CLM	OC	Fuego AM, Bogotá
	15	CLM	AU	Ondas del Orteguaza, Florencia
	10	CLM	EV	R. Eco, Cali
	10	CLM	EC	R. San José de Cúcuta, Cúcuta
	5	CLM	ZV	RCN R. Las Lajas, Ipiales
	3	EQA	CY5	LV del Pueblo, Azogues
	1	EQA	UR6	R. Runatacuyac, Latacunga
	1	EQA	VR3	R. Vía, Machala
	10	PRG	ZP72	R. Antena Dos, Asunción
	5	PRU	OAX4C	R. 1160/R.Onda Cero Lima
	1	PRU	OCX7Z	R. del Sur, Tambopata
	1	PRU	OBX5O	R. Huanta 2000, Huanta
	0.3	PRU	OAX2C	R. Libertad Mundo, Trujillo
	1	PRU	OCU1Q	R. LV Campesino, Huarmaca
	1	PRU	OCU4V	R. Maranatha, Huancayo
	1	PRU	OBX6G	R. Nac. del Perú, Moquegua
	1	PRU	OCX1S	Radiales Nor Oriental del Marañon, Chiclayo
	2/1	URG	CW116	R. Agraria , Cerro Chato
1170	5	ARG		La R. de Mi País, Hurlingham
	10/5	ARG	LRA29	R. Nacional, San Luis
	20/10	B	J273	R. Aleluia, Curitiba
	10/5	B	K569	R. Bandeirantes, Campinas
	5/0.25	B	J498	R. Bom Jesus, Bom Jesus de Itabapoana
	1/0.25	B	H205	R. Dif. de Feijó, Feijó
	10/1	B	J598	R. Difusora, Mossoró
	2.5/0.45	B	J334	R. Entre Rios, Sto. Antônio do Sudoeste
	5/2.5	B	H284	R. Guaranópolis, Maués
	1/0.25	B	K207	R. Itapuí, Santo Antônio da Patrulha
	5/0.25	B	H473	R. Jornal, Eunápolis
	1.5	B	K380	R. Pitangueira, Itaqui
	10/0.25	B	L327	R. Vanguarda, Ipatinga
	5	CHL	CD117	R. Natales, Puerto Natales
	10	CLM	NW	Caracol R., Cartagena
	10	CLM	GA	Lluvias R., Tunja
	10	CLM	E74	Meridiano 70, Arauca
	10	CLM	BX	Ondas del Meta, Villavicencio
	10	CLM	FW	R. Nutibara, Medellín
	1	CLM	JE	RCN R., Tuluá
	5	EQA	RV2	R. Filadelfia, Guayaquil
	1	PRU	OBU7F	Bethel R., Cusco
	0.5	PRU	OCX7Y	R. Constelación, Puno
	1	PRU	OAM4I	R. COSAT, Satlpo
	1	PRU	OAU4N	R. Horizonte La Voz del Agro, Pueblo Nuevo
	1	PRU	OAU2M	R. Jerusalen, Cajamarca
	1	PRU	OAZ3K	R. Nor Peruana Chimbote
	1	PRU	OAM7A	R. OAM4E, Paramonga
	2	PRU	OAM5B	R. OAM5B, Acobamba
	10	PRU	OBX6L	R. Programas del Perú, Uchumayo, Aqp
	10	URG	CX32	Radiomundo, Montevideo
1180	0.25	ARG		AM San Ponciano, Abasto
	1/0.5	ARG	LRI230	R. de la Sierra, Tandil
	10/5	B	H889	R. Capital, São Luís
	1/0.25	B	H248	R. Correio do Sertão, Santana do Ipanema
	10/0.25	B	L203	R. Cultura, Alfenas
	2.5/0.25	B	J314	R. Educadora, São João do Ivaí
	10/0.5	B	J237	R. Guaçu, Toledo
	5/0.25	B	J737	R. Integração d'Oeste, São José do Cedro
	1/0.25	B	I797	R. Jornal, Vitória de Sto. Antão
	50/10	B	J463	R. Mundial, Rio de Janeiro
	5/0.25	B	K749	R. Nova, Bebedouro
	1	BOL		R. Ingavi, Viacha
		BOL		R. Sajama Estero, Oruro
	50	CHL	CB118	R. Portales, Santiago
	15	CLM	FX	Caracol R., Manizales
	20	CLM	GK	La Cariñosa, Bucaramanga
	10/5	CLM	JT	RCN R., Ibagué
	2	EQA	DP5	R. Cuenca, Cuenca -2400v

kHz	kW	Ctry	Call	Station, location
	5/1	PRG	ZP52	R. Coronel Oviedo, Coronel Oviedo
	1	PRU	OAM2K	Municipalidad Provincial de Jaen, Jaen
	10	PRU	OCU4K	NSE R., Lima
	1	PRU	OCU6N	R. Bacan Sat 2, Pocollay
	1	PRU	OCY4Z	R. Libertad Junin
	1	PRU	OAU2T	R. Siglo 21, Chota
	2.5	PRU	OAZ1H	R. Vencinal, Piura
	10	URG	CX118	R. LV de Artigas, Artigas
1190		ARG		R. La Más Santiagueña, Gregorio de Laferrere
	50/5	ARG	LRA15	R. Nacional, San Miguel de Tucumán
		ARG	LR9	R. Perfil, Buenos Aires
	10/0.25	B	K729	R. 31 de Março, Sta. Cruz das Palmeiras
	5/0.5	B	K234	R. Cerro Azul, Cerro Largo
	50/1	B	L221	R. Guarani, Belo Horizonte
	10/1	B	H459	R. Juazeiro, Juazeiro
	2.5/0.25	B	K512	R. Marconi, Paraguaçu Paulista
	1/0.5	B	K741	R. Regional, Taquarituba
	2.5/0.25	B	K301	R. São Lourenço, São Lourenço do Sul
		BOL		R. Comunitaria, Guaqui
	1	CLM	CT	LV de la Costa, Barranquilla
	10	CLM	CV	R. Cordillera, Bogotá
	10	CLM	KG	R. Mira, Tumaco
	1	EQA	RF6	R. El Sol Sol, Pujilí
	2	EQA	DE2	UCSG R., Guayaquil
	5	PRG	ZP45	LV de la Libertad, Henendarias
	10	PRU	OAX1E	Bravasa R., Chiclayo
	5	PRU	OBX3D	R. Ancash, Huaraz
	1	PRU	OCX6G	R. Central de Noticias, Miraflores Aqp
	3	PRU	OAM7V	R. Cielo, Tambopata
	3	PRU	OCU1S	R. Cielo. Tumbes
	2	PRU	OBU5U	R. OBU5U, Huamanga
	2	PRU	OAX7B	R. Tawantinsuyo, Cusco
	3	PRU	OAU9J	R. Vision, Nueva Cajamarca
	10	VEN	ZD	R. Cultural del Táchira, San Cristóbal
1200	5/1	ARG	LRF203	R. 3 Andina, Esquel
	5/1.5	ARG	LT6	R. Goya, Goya
		ARG		R. Juventud, Florencia Varela
	5/1	ARG		Rio Grande
	1/0.5	ARG		Uspallata
	10	B	H585	R. Clube AM 1200, Fortaleza
	10/0.5	B	H482	R. Clube Rio do Ouro, Jacobina
	50/1	B	H251	R. Correio, Pilar
	100/20	B	K520	R. Cultura Brasil, São Paulo
	5/1	B	K239	R. Erechim, Erechim
	1/0.5	B	K342	R. Fundação Cotrisel, São Sepé
		BOL		Cuarzo Comunicaciones, La Paz
	0.25	BOL		R. 24 de Noviembre, Valle Alto
		BOL		R. Capital, Oruro
	5	BOL		R. Oriental, Santa Cruz
	10	CHL	CD120	R. Agricultura, Los Angeles
	1	CLM	CD	Em. Nueva Época, Fusagasugá
	15	CLM	IJ	LV de la Raza, Medellín
	10	CLM	BV	R. Principe, Cartagena
	10	CLM	NF	R. Red RCN, Cali
	10	CLM	GC	RCN R., Sogamoso
	3	EQA	CS1	R. Super K 1200, Sangolquí
	10	PRG	ZP44	R. Libre, Luque
	3	PRU	OAX4B	Cadena R. 1200, Lima
	1	PRU	OAU2A	LV de Cumbe, Cajamarca
	3	PRU	OAU4G	R. Andes, Huancayo
	1	PRU	OBX5X	R. Comercial, Abancay
		PRU	OCX7S	R. Continental, Juliaca
	1	PRU	OCU1A	R. Fe, Piura
	3	PRU	OAU6P	R. La Luz, Tacna
		PRU		R. Master Mix, Huancavelica
	1	PRU	OAM7O	R. Universidad, Puno
	1	URG	CW33	La Nueva R., Florida
	10	VEN	OZ	R. Tiempo, Caracas
1210		ARG		R. del Promesero, José C. Paz
	1/0.5	ARG	LRI229	R. Las Flores, Las Flores
	1.5	ARG		R. Mailin, Gregorio de Laferrere
	10/0.25	B	H498	R. Canção Nova, Vitória da Conquista
	10/1	B	I786	R. Jornal, Garanhuns
	5/0.5	B	J620	R. Potengi, São Paulo do Potengi

kHz	kW	Ctry	Call	Station, location
	5/0.25	B	H637	R. Principe Imperial, Crateús
	10/0.5	B	J785	R. Super Santa, Tubarão
	10/5	B	K240	R. Transcontinental, Porto Alegre
	5/0.25	B	K668	R. Vanguarda, Sorocaba
	10/1	B	K509	R. Vida Nova, Jaboticabal
	25/5	B	J219	Super R. Deus é Amor, Curitiba
	50/2.5	B	H711	Super Rede Boa Vontade, Brasília
	1	CHL	CD121	Puerto Montt
	1	CHL	CC121	R. Universidad de Talca, Talca
		CHL	CB121	R. Valparaiso, Valparaiso
	10	CLM	FR	Bésame / W R., Neiva
	10	CLM	E65	La Cariñosa, Cúcuta
	10	CLM	BQ	La Cariñosa, Pereira
	1	EQA	JM6	R. SIRA, Ambato
	1	PRU	OCY4T	R. Galaxia, Satipo
	1	PRU	OBU3D	R. OBU3D, Chimbote
	1	PRU	OCU2W	R. OCU2W, Querocoto
	1	PRU	OBX3X	R. Ondas de Paz, Huanuco
	1	PRU	OCU7B	R. Qorilazo, Chumbivilcas
	1	PRU	OAX7M	R. Quillabamba, Quillabamba
	1	PRU	OAX2Q	R. Universo, Trujillo
	2/1	URG	CX121	Difusora Soriano, Mercedes
	2./1	URG	CV121	Em. RBC, Piriápolis
	0.25	URG	CW121	R. El Libertador, Vergara
1220	5/1	ARG		Eco R. AM 1210, Buenos Aires
	1	ARG		Precidencia Roque Sáenz Peña
	10/5	ARG	LRI224	R. Onda Marina, Mar del Plata
	1	BOL		R. Batallión Topátar, Oruro
		BOL		R. La Asunta, Asunta
		BOL		R. La Voz Cristiana, Achacachi
		BOL		R. Progreso La Luz del Alba, Cochabamba
	1	BOL		R. Splendid, La Paz
	10	CHL	CD122	R. Maria, Temuco
	10	CLM	KR	R. María Colombia, Bogotá
	10	CLM	NM	R. Viva, Ipiales
	10	CLM	AV	RCN R. Uno, Montería
	10	CLM	MT	RCN R., San Gil
	5	EQA	PA1	R. Marañón, Quito
		PRU	OBU5I	R. Bethel, San Clemente
	1.5	PRU	OCU4W	R. Cora, Huancayo
		PRU	OCU4H	R. Fe, Lima
	3	PRU	OCX1X	R. Libertad, Chiclayo
	10	PRU	OAX6X	R. Melodia, Hunter, Aqp
	1	PRU	OAU7N	R. Universidad de San Antonio Abad, Cusco
	1/0.5	URG	CX122	R. Reconquista, Rivera
1230		ARG		R. Claridad, Monte Grande
	1	ARG		R. Creativa, Lanus
	25/5	ARG	LT2	R. Gen. San Martín, Rosario
	5/1	ARG	LW5	R. Libertador, General San Martin
	1	ARG		R. Litoral, Isidro Casanova
	5/0.5	B	K716	Jovem Pan News, Campinas
	1/0.25	B	K573	R. Cacique, Capão Bonito
	2/0.25	B	K326	R. Clube Nonoai, Nonoai
	5/0.25	B	L208	R. Correio da Serra, Barbacena
	10/1	B	I670	R. Correio Jovem Pan, João Pessoa
	10/2.5	B	H756	R. Daqui, Goiânia
	5/0.65	B	J776	R. Dif. Colméia, Porto União
	10/0.25	B	K637	R. Difusora, Rancharia
	1/0.25	B	K352	R. Encruzilhadense, Encruzilhada do Sul
	10/0.7	B	N203	R. Estrela de Ibiúna, Campina Verde
	1/0.25	B	H532	R. Povo, Ubatã
	2.3/0.35	B	K333	R. Prata, Nova Prata
	1/0.25	B	H...	R. Veneza, Caxias
	50/10	B	R699	Super Rede Boa Vontade, São Paulo
	15	CLM	EH	Colmundo R., Bucaramanga
	10	CLM	IL	Em. Minuto de Dios, Medellín
	6	CLM	BR	Em. R. Recuerdos, Tunja
	10	CLM	LK	R. Calidad, Cali
	1	CLM	TP	R. Colina Caracol, Girardot
	5	EQA	FV2	R. Galáctica, Guayaquil
	3	PRG	ZP21	Fénix AM, Caaguazú
	1	PRU	OAM2B	R. Fé, Cajamarca
		PRU		R. Frecuencia Amistad, Juliaca
		PRU	OCU4C	R. La Luz, Huacho

kHz	kW	Ctry	Call	Station, location
	1	PRU	OBX4Z	R. LV de Oxapampa, Oxapampa
	1	PRU	OBU6T	R. OBU6T, Moquequa
	1	PRU	OBZ4Y	R. Selecciones,Tarma
	1	PRU	OAU7V	R. Surupana, Caminca
	2.5	PRU	OAM7T	R. Tambopata, Tambopata
1240	1	ARG		R. Cadena Uno, Ciudadela
	10/1	ARG	LRI218	R. Universidad Nal. del Sur, Bahia Blanca
	5/0.25	B	K621	Orlândia R. Clube, Orlândia
	1/0.25	B	K200	R. Aparados da Serra, Bom Jesus
	1/0.25	B	J215	R. Arapongas, Arapongas
	5	B	I774	R. Capibaribe, Recife
	10/2.5	B	K653	R. Clube, Santos
	5/0.25	B	K251	R. Ibirubá, Ibirubá
	2.2	B	J810	R. Iracema, Cunhae Porã
	2/0.25	B	J280	R. Matelândia, Matelândia
	10/0.25	B	K565	R. Municipalista, Botucatu
	5/0.25	B	L317	R. Pirapora AM, Pirapora
	10/0.35	B	L303	R. Platina/Jovem Pan News, Ituiutaba
	1/0.25	B	H654	R. São Francisco, Canindé
	1/0.25	B	K355	R. São Jerônimo, São Jerônimo
	5/0.25	B	L294	R. Três Pontas, Três Pontas
		BOL		R. Lider Zaráte Willka, La Paz
	2	BOL		R. Los Andes, Tarija
		BOL		R. Nueva Generación, Qhurpa
	0.25	CHL	CA124	R. Club Chuquicamate, Calma
	25	CHL	CB124	R. Universidad de Santiago, Santiago
	3	CLM	JA	R. Buenaventura, Buenaventura
	10	CLM	FG	RCN R., Armenia
	1	EQA	PA1	R. Metropolitana, Yaruquí
	1	PRU	OAU9B	R. Bagua Grande, Chachapoyas
		PRU	OCX1C	R. Campesina, Ayaviri
	12	PRU	OAU4V	R. Cumbre, Huancayo
	1	PRU	OAU5U	R. Eco, Ica
	1	PRU	OAZ1A	R. Ferreñafe, Ferrañafe
	1	PRU	OAU3L	R. La Luz, Chimbote
	15	PRU	OAU6D	R. Lider, Socabaya, Aqp
	1	PRU	OAU2Y	R. Nor Andino, Santiago de Chuco
	5	PRU	OCU7Z	R. Pachatusán, Sicuani
	1	PRU	OCX1C	R. Sechura, Sechura
	5	URG	CW35	R. Paysandú, Paysandú
1250	10	ARG		R. Estirpe Nacional, San Justo
	50	B	L367	Nossa Radio, Belo Horizonte
	5/0.5	B	I412	R. Caiuás, Dourados
	2.5/0.25	B	J313	R. Danúbio Azul, Sta. Isabel do Oeste
	15/0.5	B	K233	R. Dif. Caxiense, Caxias do Sul
	1	B	H594	R. Educadora, Crateús
	5/0.25	B	J766	R. Jovem Pan News, Joinville
	15/0.5	B	J500	R. Litoral, Casimiro de Abreu
	1/0.25	B	I701	R. Sociedade de Soledade, Soledade
	1	B	K272	R. Tupanci, Pelotas
		BOL		R. Amboro, Santa Cruz
		BOL		R. Comunitaria Compi, Capilaya
		BOL		R. Indoamerica, Potosi
	2.5	BOL		R. La Plata, Sucre
		BOL		R. Sararenda, Camiri
		BOL		Rdif. Achocalla, Achocalla
	10	CHL	CD125	R. Pilmaiquen, Valdivia
	10	CLM	CA	Capital R., Bogotá
	10	CLM	OK	Em. ABC, Barranquilla
	15	CLM	HS	W R., Cúcuta
	2	EQA	EM1	R. Ondas Carchenses, Tulcán
	5	PRG	ZP3	R. Asunción, Asunción
	1	PRU	OAX9C	R. Americana, Nueva Cajamarca
	1	PRU	OAU6I	R. Campesina, Omate
	3	PRU	OBX8S	R. Cielo, Calleria
	5	PRU	OAX4L	R. Cora, Lima
	1.5	PRU	OBZ1B	R. Dif. BNS, Talara Alta
	1	PRU	OAU2V	R. HGV, Santa Cruz
	3	PRU	OBX7A	R. Solar, Cusco
	5	URG	CW125	R. Bella Unión, Bella Unión
	3	URG	CX36	R. Centenario, Montevideo
1260		ARG		AM 1260-Somos Parte de Tu Vida, Temperly
	0.5	ARG		R. Amor, Villa Tesel
	10/5	ARG	LT14	R. Nacional General Urquiza, Paraná
		ARG		R. y Television del Neuquén, Neuquén
	1/0.25	B	K629	Pirajau R. Clube, Pirajuí
	10/0.5	B	J740	R. Arca da Aliança, Blumenau
	1/0.25	B	K204	R. Cultura, São Borja
	100/40	B	K688	R. Morada do Sol, São Paulo
		BOL		R. Dios es Amor Universal, Tarija
		BOL		R. LV de la Esperanca, Quillacollo
	10	BOL		R. Nacional de Huanuni, Hunanuni
		BOL		R. SERVIR, Caranavi
		BOL		Red de Com. Nueva Imagen Para Bolivia
	1	CHL	CC126	R. Condell, Curicó
	10	CHL	CD126	R. Maria, Punta Arenas
	5	CLM	CO	Caracol R., Ibagué
	1	CLM	HU	Caracol R., San Andrés
	5	CLM	LX	Emisora Lux Dei, Villavicencio
	5	CLM	NO	Lluvias R., Duitama
	5	CLM	DA	R. Auténtica, Medellín
	5	CLM	ET	R. María Colombia, Cali
	5	CLM	TM	R. Sonar, Ocaña
	5	CLM	OH	RCN R., Valledupar
	1	EQA	RO6	R. Calidad, Ambato
	2	EQA	CL3	R. Contacto XG, Cuenca
	5	PRG	ZP34	R. Panambi Vera, Villarrica
		PRU		R. Cielo, Trujullo - relay of R.Cielo, Lima
	1	PRU	OCU4F	R. Corazón Andino, El Tambo
	3	PRU	OAU3G	R. El Pregonero, Chimbote
	1	PRU	OAU3F	R. La Luz, Huanuco
	3	PRU	OCU4B	R. La Luz, San Vicente de Cañete
	1	PRU	OBX6D	R. Manahaim, Uchumayo Aqp
	0.3	PRU	OBX5S	R. Nal. del Perú, Ayacucho
	1	PRU	OCX10	R. Nova, Chiclayo
		PRU	OBX2C	R. Otuzco, Otuzco
	3	URG	CW37	Dif. Rochense, Rocha
	10	VEN	RM	BBN R., Caracas
1270	25/5	ARG	LRA20	R. Nacional, Las Lomitas
	100/25	ARG	LS11	R. Provincia de Buenos Aires, La Plata
	5/0.5	B	K206	R. América, Montenegro
	2/0.5	B	K640	R. Bandeirantes, Ribeirão Preto
	10/2.5	B	I530	R. Boas Novas, Belém
	100/10	B	H753	R. Brasil Central, Goiânia
	5/0.5	B	K678	R. Brasil, Campinas
	10/1	B	J236	R. Capital, Curitiba
	5/0.5	B	J593	R. Clube AM 1270, Natal
	2.5/0.5	B	L300	R. Estância, São Lourenço
	5/0.5	B	J222	R. Guairacá, Mandaguari
	5/0.5	B	K250	R. Vera Cruz, Horizontina
	5	CHL	CB127	R. Festival, Viña del Mar
		CHL	CD134A	R.Mirador, Temuco
	1	CLM	IM	Colmundo R., Pereira
	2	CLM	AR	La Cariñosa, Cartagena
	1	CLM	XQ	R. Auténtica, Ubaté
	5	CLM	TX	W R., Bucaramanga
	2	EQA	LD4	R. Junín, Junín
	10	EQA	UM2	R. Universal, Guayaquil
	3	PRU	OBU6N	R. Cielo, Tacna
	1	PRU	OCX2Z	R. Estacion Latina, Cepén
	2	PRU	OAU7S	R. Horizonte, Cusco
	0.4	PRU	OAZ4H	R. Huacho, Huacho
	0.4	PRU	OBZ4T	R. La Merced, Chanchamayo
	1	PRU	OAU1S	R. Nor Peru, Paita
	2	PRU	OAM5A	R. OAM5A, Huancavelica
	1	PRU	OBU6P	R. San Antonio, Callalli
	4/2	URG	CV127	R. Cuareim, Artigas
1280	5	ARG		AM 1280 La R.,Gregorio de Laferrere
	6	ARG		R. Cadena. Eco, CA Buenos Aires
	7/1.5	ARG	LU11	R. Trenque Lauquén, Tr. Lauquén
	10/5	B	I688	R. Sanhauá, Bayeux
	100	B	J455	R. Tupi, Rio de Janeiro
		BOL		R. Altar de Dios, Achacachi
		BOL		R. Comunitaria Ondas del Titicaca, Huarina
		BOL		R. Cristiana Comunidad del Sur, Cochabamba
		BOL		R. Fronera, Yacuiba
	1	CHL	CD128	R. la Palabra, Osorno

kHz	kW	Ctry	Call	Station, location
	5	CLM	KN	Aviva2, Bogotá
	5	CLM	LR	Caracol R., Pasto
	5	CLM	CM	HJ Doble K Sistema INRAI, Pitalito
	5	CLM	HO	Impacto Popular, San Juan del Cesar
	1	CLM	NQ	LV del Río Suárez, Barbosa
	5	CLM	MB	R. Suroeste, Concordia
		PRU		R. Bethel, Chaquimarca
	1	PRU	OAU1R	R. Bethel, San Jose
	2.5	PRU	OCU7S	R. Continental, Macusani
		PRU	OBX3C	R. El Puerto, Chimbote
	1	PRU	OCU7R	R. Fé, Sicuani
	0.5	PRU	OBX6P	R. Fénix, Camaná
	1	PRU	OAX3Y	R. La Selva, Rupa-Rupa
	1	PRU	OBX2F	R. Moderna, Cajamarca
	3	PRU	OBU5J	Yeshua R., Chinca Alta
	3/1	URG	CW64	R. Tacuarembó, Tacuarembó
	10	VEN	OF	R. Trujillo, Trujillo
	5	VEN	QS	R. Zaraza, Zaraza
1290	1/0.5	ARG	LRI371	R. Amanecer, Reconquista
	1	ARG		R. Interactiva, Ciudad Madero
	5/1	ARG	LRJ212	R. Murialdo, Villa Nueva de Guaymallén
	1	ARG		R. Provinciana, San Miguel
	5/1	B	J734	R. Araranguá, Araranguá
	25/0.5	B	J310	R. Brasil Sul, Londrina
	5/1	B	J804	R. Camboriú, Balneário Camboriú
	1/0.5	B	K745	R. Estadão, São José dos Campos
	10/1	B	H450	R. Metropole, Salvador
	5/1	B	K663	R. Novo Tempo, São José do Rio Preto
	10/5	B	H888	R. Timbira, São Luís
		BOL		R. Comunitaria Alaxpacha, Canaviri
		BOL		R. Tomas Katari de America, Ocuri
	1	BOL		Radiodifusoras Minería, Oruro
	0.25	CHL	CA129	R. Coya, Los Angeles
	5	CLM	OI	ConecZión R., Sampués
	5	CLM	TH	LV de las Estrellas, Medellín
	5	CLM	MC	R. Viva 12-90, Cali
	5	CLM	KY	RCN R., Girardot
	3	EQA	JA5	LV del Río Tarqui, Cuenca
	5	PRU	OCX6B	R. Cielo, Cerro Colorado Aqp
	1	PRU	OAM2C	R. Estelar, Chota
	1	PRU	OBU4S	R. Exito, La Oroya
	1	PRU	OBU5V	R. OBU5V, Ayacucho
	1	PRU	OCX1Q	R. Programas del Perú, Tumbes
	1	PRU	OBU2D	R. Sonorama, Trujillo
	1	PRU	OBU4Q	S & RD, Hualmay
	1	PRU	OCU4P	San Vicente de Cañete
	50	URG	CX38	Em del Sur, Montevideo
1300	2	ARG		R. La Salada - RLS, Buenos Aires
	5/1	ARG		R. Mitre, San Rafael
	10/1	ARG	LRA5	R. Nacional, Rosario
	5/0.25	B	J288	R. Educadora, Dois Vizinhos
	5/1	B	L339	R. Eldorado, Sete Lagoas
	1/0.25	B	I799	R. Guarany, Camaragibe
	10	B	H586	R. Iracema, Fortaleza
	30/0.25	B	K649	R. Onda Viva, Santo Anastácio
	2/0.25	B	K762	R. Real AM 1300, São Carlos
	1/0.25	B	K337	R. Regional, Santo Cristo
	50/1	B	K535	R. Universo, São Paulo
	80/13	B	K203	Super Rede Boa Vontade, Porto Alegre
	5	BOL		R. Bandera Beniana, Trinidad
	1	BOL		R. Fuerzas Armadas, Sta. Cruz
	2.5	BOL		R. Loyola, Sucre
	15/6	BOL		R. Sol Poder de Diós, El Alto
		BOL		R. Voz de Dios y No del Hombre, Cochabamba
		BOL		Sistem de Comuncacion, Oruro
	1	CHL	CB130	R. Conexiones, Santiago
	5	CLM	OG	Aviva2, Cartagena
	5	CLM	RB	CRB-Cadena Radial Boyacense, Tunja
	5	CLM	NB	Onda 5, Bucaramanga
	5	CLM	EA	R. Lumbí, Mariquita
	5	CLM	LD	R. Reloj, Pereira
	2.5	EQA	RU1	R. Festival, Sto Domingo de los Colorados
	3.5	EQA	AK6	R. La Paz, Guaranda
	5	PRG	ZP53	R. Fe y Alegria, Villa Hayes
	3	PRU	OBU6X	R. Candarave, Ilabaya
		PRU		R. Chumpiwilkas, Santo Tomas Chumbivilcas
	0.5	PRU	OAX3O	R. Cielo, Independencia
	5	PRU	OAX4S	R. Comas, Comas
	1	PRU	OAU1U	R. Frecuencia Lider, Morro
	0.35	PRU	OAX7X	R. La Decana - R. Juliaca, Juliaca
	1	PRU	OBX9P	R. La Luz, Tarapoto
	1	PRU	OAZ8B	R. Nuevo Mundo, Pucallapa
	2.5	PRU	OCU4R	R. OCU4R, Ahuac
	1	PRU	OCU6W	R. OCU6W, Mariscal Cáceres
	5	PRU	OAX7P	R. Onda Imperial, Cusco
	1	PRU	OAU2I	R. Paraiso, Cajabamba
	10	VEN	KH	Deportiva 1300 AM Center, Caracas
1310	0.8	ARG		AM Renecar,Moreno
	0.25	ARG		Gesell Radio, Villa Gesell
	0.5	ARG		R. Dr. Gregorio Alvarez, Piedra del Aguila
		ARG		R. Imagen, Castelar
	10/5	ARG	LRA42	R. Nacional, Gualeguaychú
	5/0.25	B	K566	Bragança AM, Bragança Paulista
	10/0.5	B	J274	R. Atalaia, Maringá
	1/0.25	B	H454	R. Bahiana, Ilhéus
	10/0.5	B	I691	R. Cidade Esperança, Esperança
	1/0.25	B	J504	R. Coroados, São Fidélis
	2/1	B	K596	R. Difusora, Itápolis
	10/0.25	B	L351	R. Difusora, Salinas
	1/0.25	B	H656	R. Liberdade, Boa Viagem
	1/0.25	B	H422	R. Nova Mazagão, Mazagão
	10/1	B	K305	R. Sarandi, Sarandi
	5	CLM	DG	Caracol R., Montería
	5	CLM	JZ	R. 3
	5	CLM	LM	R. Santa Bárbara, Santa Bárbara
	5	CLM	AK	Voz de la Patria Celestial, Barranquilla
	0.5	EQA	CP3	LV de El Oro, Pasaje
	3	EQA	CI5	R. Internacional TVO, Biblián
	10/0.5	PRG	ZP53	LV del Este, J.E. Estgarribia
	3	PRU	OBU5X	Ayacucho
	3	PRU	OCU1D	Bethel R., Piura
	1	PRU	OBX2D	R. Chota, Chota
	1	PRU	OBX4L	R. Irvisa, Huacho
	6	PRU	OAU6N	R. Libertad, Alto Selva Alegre Aqp
	5	PRU	OAU3T	R. OAU3T, Rupa Rupa
	12	PRU	OBX8L	R. Vision Amazonia, Iquitos
1320		ARG		Plus R., Lanús
	5/1	ARG	LV24	R. Andina, Tunuyán
		ARG		R. Area Uno, Caseros
	5/3	ARG	LU10	R. Azul, Azul
	1	ARG		R. Máster, Luján
	0.5	ARG		R. Sintonia, Canning
		ARG		R.Santa Catalina, José C. Paz
	50/5	B	J475	R. Boas Novas, Petropôlis
	1/0.25	B	K223	R. Clube, Canela
	5/1	B	K271	R. Cultura, Pelotas
	1/0.25	B	I823	R. Cultura, São José do Egito
		B	H809	R. Liberdade, Uruaçu
	5/0.25	B	L322	R. Mucuri, Teófilo Otoni
	5/0.5	B	J351	R. RCI, Foz do Iguaçu
	3/0.25	B	K266	R. Sulbrasileira, Panambi
	12/0.5	B	J255	R. Tropical Gospel, Curitiba
	5/0.45	B		R. Vitôria, Videira
	3	BOL		R. Comunitaria La Lumbrera, La Paz
		BOL		R. Comunitaria Tawantinsuyo, Taraco
		BOL		R. Em. Septima Voz, Achocalla
	10	BOL		R. San Rafael, Cochabamba
		BOL		R. Sucre, Sucre
	1	CHL	CD132	R. Lincoyan, Mulchén
	5	CLM	NK	Hope R., Palmira
	5	CLM	MS	La Cariñosa, Barrancabarmeja
	5	CLM	NV	La Cariñosa, Girardot
	5	CLM	HT	R. Guateque Stereo, Guateque
	5	CLM	TA	R. María, Medellín
	3	EQA	JD6	R. Continental, Ambato
	1	EQA	FR2	R. Guayaquil, Babahoyo
	1	PRU	OBU5L	La Luz del Mundo, Pueblo Nuevo
	2.5	PRU	OCU4T	R. Bacan Sat., Huancayo

kHz	kW	Ctry	Call	Station, location
	5	PRU	OCU5V	R. Cultural Tintaya, Cotabambas
	1	PRU	OBU1S	R. Frecuencia Popular, Olmos
		PRU	OAX4I	R. La Cronica, Lima
	0.5	PRU	OBU6B	R. Majes
	5	PRU	OAU3W	R. OAU3W, La Caleta
	1	PRU	OBU6A	R. OBU6A, Tacna
	3	PRU	OAU7W	R. TV Peru, Juliaca
	1/0.5	URG	CW132	R. Fortaleza, Rocha
	1	URG	CW39	R. LV de Paysandú, Paysandú
	5	VEN	WP	R. Apolo, Turmero
1330	10/1	ARG	LRI237	AM Rosario, Rosario
	5/1	B	J749	R. Chapecó, Chapecó
	10/0.5	B	J739	R. Clube, Blumenau
	1	B	H468	R. Continental, Serrinha
	10/0.5	B	J621	R. Eldorado, Natal
	10/0.5	B	J264	R. Jaguariaíva, Jaguariaiva
	30/0.25	B	K638	R. Paulista, Regente Feijó
	50/10	B	K736	R. Terra, Osasco
	5/1	B	K641	R. Terra, Ribeirão Preto
	1/0.25	B	K236	R. Upacaraí, Dom Pedrito
	3	CHL	CB133	R. Romance, Santiago
	3/1.5	CHL	CD133	R. Vicente Pérez Rosales, Puerto Montt
	5	CLM	LS	Caracol R., Popayán
	5	CLM	NR	La Caliente 13-30, San Gil
	5	CLM	AP	R. Auténtica, Cartagena
	1	CLM	RD	R. Fénix, El Peñol
	10	PRG	ZP13	R. Chaco Boreal, Asunción
	1	PRU	OVX6E	Frequencia 1330, Arequipa
	1	PRU	OAU1A	R. Amistad, Chiclayo
	0.5	PRU	OBU5P	R. Bethel, Huamanga
	1	PRU	OAM2D	R. Fé, La Esperanza
	1	PRU	OBX9Y	R. Fé, Tarapoto
	1	PRU	OCU1J	R. Frecuencia Ideal, Frias
	2	PRU	OAM4L	R. OAM4L, Tarma
	1	PRU	OCX7K	R. San Miguel, Wanchaq
	5	URG	CX40	R. Fénix, Montevideo
1340	1/0.25	ARG		Goya
	1	ARG		R. Mediterránea, Rosario del Tala
	0.8	ARG		R. Renacer, Moreno
	25/4	B	K227	CBN, Porto Alegre
	5/1	B	I671	R. Correio, João Pessoa
	5/0.25	B	J249	R. Cultura, Arapongas
	10/5	B	L241	R. Cultura, Itabirito
	2.5/0.25	B	J205	R. Difusora, Rio Negro
	5/0.5	B	J490	R. Jornal, Rio Bonito
	10/4	B	K374	R. Journal da Manhã, Ijui
	20/0.25	B	J368	R. Nacional News, Cascavel
	2.5/0.25	B	H661	R. Pitaguary, Maracanaú
	10/2	B	H886	R. São Luís, São Luís
	0.5	BOL		R. Comunitaria Jach'a Suyu, Corocoro
		BOL		R. Comunitaria La Voz de Valle, Sococoni
	0.5	BOL		R. Copacabana, Copacabana
		BOL		R. La Mision, La Paz
		BOL		TV Sist. de Comunicacione Mundial, Cochabama
	10	CHL	CB134	R. Colo Colo, Valparaíso
	1	CHL	CC134	R. La Discusión, Chillán
	1	CHL	CD134	R. Vida Nueva, Panguipulli
	5	CLM	FB	Amor, Bogotá
	5	CLM	KD	La Cariñosa, Neiva
	1	CLM	NP	LV de Nariño, Nariño
	5	CLM	FA	LV del Caribe, Barranquilla
	5	CLM	PY	R. Lemas, Cúcuta
	5	CLM	IS	RCN R., Buenaventura
	5	CLM	HA	RCN R., Pasto
	5	CLM	HY	RCN R., Sincelejo
	5	EQA	CO4	LV de su Amigo, Esmeraldas
	1	EQA	RG3	Ondas de Esperanza, Loja
	10	PRU	OAU4Q	R. Alegria, Pucasana
	0.5	PRU	OAX5D	R. Chincha, Chincha Alta
		PRU		R. Choque, Chumbivilcas
	1	PRU	OAU4N	R. Jauja, Jauja
	1	PRU	OBU3C	R. OBU3C, Casma
	1	PRU	OCU6U	R. OCU6U, Mejia Sur
	1	PRU	OBX1K	R. San Francisco, Piura
	1	PRU	OAU2S	R. Shalom, Cajamarca
	1	PRU	OBU7V	R. Sudamericana, Juliaca
	10/1	URG	CW53	LV de Melo, Melo
	10	VEN	NE	R. Uno, Caracas
1350	1/0.25	ARG		Juan José Castelli, Chaco
	25/5	ARG	LS6	R. Buenos Aires, Burzaco
	5/1	ARG		R. Sucesos, Villa Carlos Paz
	1/0.25	B	J760	R. Bandeirantes, Itajaí
	50/5	B	H201	R. Capital, Rio Branco
	5/1	B	K313	R. Difusora, Três Passos
	1/0.25	B	H662	R. Liberal Jagoaribana, Morada Nova
	50/0.25	B	K692	RBC AM, Ibiuna
	50/10	B	H520	Super Rede Boa Vontade, Salvador
		BOL		R. America, Sucre
		BOL		R. Comunitario Inti, Contorno/Viacha
		BOL		R. Llacxa, Achocalla
		BOL		R. TV Salesiana, Yapacani
	0.02	CHL	CD135	Puerto Montt
	1	CHL	CA135	R. Riquelme, Coquimbo
	5	CLM	HL	Bésame, Ibagué
	5	CLM	DS	Ondas de la Montaña, Medellín
	5	CLM	EN	R. Armonía, Cali
	5	CLM	OA	RCN R. Uno, Santa Marta
	1	EQA	SF5	San Fernando R., San Fernando
	3	EQA	VR2	Teleradio 1350 AM , Guayaquil
	1	PRU	OBU5O	R. Atlantis, Huamanga
	1	PRU	OCU1I	R. Fé, Tumbes
	3	PRU	OCU6D	R. Municipal, Ichuña
	1	PRU	OAU3X	R. OAU3X, Pillco Marca
	1	PRU	OAM4H	R. Paraiso, Huacho
		PRU	OBX8D	R. Super, Pucallpa
	1	PRU	OAU1H	R. Vision, Chiclayo
1355	0.25	BOL		R. Armonía, Cliza
1360	0.25	ARG		AM 1360 - R. Coop. Estirpe Entrerriana, Maria Grande
	0.4	ARG		R. Nuestra Señore de Itatí, Morón
	50/10	B	J464	R. Bandeirantes, Rio de Janeiro
	10/0.25	B	J265	R. Cidade, Pato Branco
	10/1	B	H469	R. Cultura, Paulo Afonso
	5/0.25	B	H650	R. Iracema, Ipu
	1/0.25	B	K759	R. Luzes da Ribalta, Santa Bárbara d'Oeste
	3/0.25	B	K281	R. Navegantes, Porto Lucena
	1/0.25	B	K739	R. Regional, Dracena
	1/0.25	B	J268	Rede Terra Nativa, Assaí
		BOL		R. 24 de Septiembre, Santa Cruz
	2.5	BOL		R. Cochabamba, Cochabamba
		BOL		R. La Cruz del Sur, Potosí
	5	CHL	CC136	R. Universidad Bio Bio, Concepcion
	5	CLM	RA	Ecos 1360 R./R. María, Pereira
	1	CLM	KV	R. Zapatoca, Zapatoca
	5	CLM	UO	Sistema Cardenal, Cartagena
	1	PRG	ZP37	R. Yby Yaú, Yby Yaú
	10	PRU	OCU4I	R. Bienestar, Lima
	1	PRU	OBZ1A	R. Cielo, Piura
	1	PRU	OBZ5Z	R. Cruz del Sur, Palpa
	1	PRU	OAU3A	R. Intercontinental, Yungay
	2	PRU	OCU2Z	R. Las Palmas, Querocotillo
	7.5	PRU	OCX6T	R. Popular, Mariano Melgar
	2.5	PRU	OAX7R	R. Sicuani, Sicuani
	1	PRU	OAU4O	R. Sudamericana, Tarma
	2.5	URG	CW41	R. 41, San José de Mayo
	1	URG	CW136	R. Río Branco, Río Branco
1370	1/0.25	ARG		ADN R., Rafaela
	3	ARG		AM Trece-70, González Catan
	0.25	ARG		Junin
	10/5	ARG	LRA54	R. Nacional, Ingeniero Jacobacci
	50/7	B	J267	R. Canção Nova, Curitiba
	2.5/0.25	B	J618	R. Dif., São Miguel
	2.5	B	I892	R. Difusora, Teresina
	1/0.25	B	K334	R. Gazeta, Alegrete
	0.25	B	H555	R. Jornal Grande, Monte Santo
	25/0.5	B	K243	R. Mãe de Deus, Flores da Cunha
	1/0.25	B	H628	R. Vanguarda, Caridade
		BOL		R. Coral, Oruro

kHz	kW	Ctry	Call	Station, location
	0.15	BOL		R. Libertad, Cliza
	1	CHL	CD137	R. Vida Nueva, Temuco
	5	CLM	BO	Em. Minuto de Dios, Barranquilla
	1	CLM	BD	Frecuencia F, Cúcuta
	5	CLM	KI	R. Mundial, Bogotá
	1	CLM	NI	R. Sabanas/Blu R., Sincelejo
	5	CLM	EQ	RCN R., Popayán
	2.5	CLM	NU	RCN R., Rionegro
	5	EQA	VO2	LV de Milagro, Milagro
	7	EQA	AO5	R. El Rocio, Biblián
	1	PRU	OCX5A	Inti R., Abanacy
	3	PRU	OCU5Y	R. Chalhuahuacho, Chalhuahuacho
	10	PRU	OCU4U	R. Los Andes, Cerro de Pasco
		PRU	OAX6T	R. Moquegua, Moquegua
	5	PRU	OAU9E	R. OAU9E, Moyobamba
	1	PRU	OBU6Y	R. OBU6Y, Viraco
	3	PRU	OAM7G	R. Qosqo Wayra, Cusco
	5.3/2.5	URG	CX42	Em. Ciudad,Montevideo
	0.5	URG	CV137A	R. Real, Minas de Corrales
	1/0.5	URG	CW137	R. San Javier, San Javier
1380	5/1	ARG	LRI231	AM 1380 R.Necochea, Necochea
	0.5	ARG		R. AM Súper Sport, Temperley
	2	ARG		R. Buenas Nuevas, Merlo
	5/1	B	H283	R. Alvorada, Parintins
	6/0.25	B	J827	R. Barriga Verde, Capinzal
	6/0.25	B	K372	R. Chiru, Palmitinho
	10/5	B	I773	R. Continental, Recife
	1/0.25	B	K293	R. Cultura, Sant´Aana do Livramento
	6/0.25	B	K350	R. Cultura, Tapera
	1/0.5	B	K616	R. Difusora, Mogi Guaçu
	1/0.25	B	J831	R. Freguencia, Garopaba
	5/0.25	B	K751	R. Fronteira, Presidente Prudente
	1/0.25	B	L323	R. Gorutubana, Janaúba
	1/0.25	B	J367	R. Integração, Toledo
	10/1	B	I…	R. Itaí de Rio Claro, Iúna
	1/0.25	B	H909	R. Tropical, Caixas
	5/0.25	B	H495	R. União, Gandu
	1/0.25	B	L218	Rede Gerais, Brasópolis
		BOL		LV del Espiritu Santo, El Alto
	1.5	BOL		R. Bandera Tricolor, Cochabamba
		BOL		R. Em. Tunupa, Tianawaku
		BOL		R. Global, Sucre
		BOL		R. Horizontes, Huanuni
	0.5	BOL		R. Luis de Fuentes, Tarija
		BOL		R. Maria, La Paz
		BOL		R. Maria, Santa Cruz
		BOL		R. TV Minera Matilde, Carabuco
	50	CHL	CB138	R. Plenitud, Santiago
	1	CLM	EJ	Armonías del Palmar, Palmira
	5	CLM	ID	Em. Potencia Latina, La Plata
	5	CLM	MM	La Nota, Valledupar
	3	CLM	LG	LV de La Dorada, La Dorada
	3	CLM	JD	NSE R., Medellín
	5	CLM	EE	RCN R., Tunja
	5	EQA	CV1	R. Cristal, Quito
	1	EQA	JR6	R. Mera, Ambato
	1	PRG	ZP8	R. Concepción, Concepción
	2.5	PRU	OUA7L	R. Andina, Juliaca
	1	PRU	OAX2W	R. Atahualpa, Cajamarca
	1	PRU	OAU2H	R. Campesina, Cajamarca
	1	PRU	OCY4U	R. Nuevo Tiempo, Lima
	1	PRU	OAM5E	R. OAM5E, Salas
	1	PRU	OCU7U	R. OCU7U, Tambopata
	1	PRU	OBX3I	R. Pilco Mozo, Huanuco
	1	PRU	OAU3U	R. R.dif San Juan, Chimbote
		PRU	OBU4L	R. Rescate,Huancayo
	3	PRU	OAX6O	R. San Martin, Arequipa
	1	PRU	OBZ1D	RB - R. Bellavista, Bellavista
1390		ARG		La Rocha Azul AM 1390, Libertad
	12/3	ARG	LR11	R. Univ. Nacional, La Plata
		ARG		R.General Paz,José C Paz
	1/0.25	ARG	LRJ217	R.Municipal. Malargü
	25	B	K570	Campinas
	2.5	B	K594	R. Anchieta, Itanhaém
	10/1	B	J242	R. Cultura, Maringá
	10/1	B	I535	R. Educadora, Bragança
	25	B	K209	R. Esperança, Porto Alegre
	5/0.25	B	J599	R. Farol, Touros
	10/5	B	O701	R. Roraima, Caracaraí
	5/0.5	B	J473	R. Sul Fluminense AM, Barra Mansa
		BOL		R. Andina, Pongo Khasa
	5	CLM	FO	LV de los Andes, Manizales
	5	CLM	FY	Olímpica Espinal, El Espinal
	5	CLM	YW	R. Auténtica, Pacho
	1	CLM	ZY	R. María Colombia, Bucaramanga
	1.5	EQA	EA5	R. Tropicana, Cuenca
		PRU		Corp. R. TV Continental Ayaviri, Umachiri
	0.5	PRU	OBU2U	Frequencia del Norte, Santa Cruz
	2.5	PRU	OCU5C	R. Cielo, Ayacucho
	1	PRU	OAU7T	R. Enlace, Kunturkanki
	3	PRU	OAM7A	R. Exitosa, Sicuani
		PRU	OCU1G	R. Fe, Pimentel
	3	PRU	OAU2Z	R. La Luz, Trujillo
	5	URG	CW45	Dif. Treinta y Tres, Treinta y Tres
	20	VEN	ZA	R. Fe y Alegría, Caracas
1400	1/0.25	ARG	LRH207	AM del NEA, Charata
	1	ARG		R. Carandá, Gregorio de Laferrerè
	5/1	ARG	LRG202	R. Cumbre, Neuquén
		ARG		R.Salavina, Moron
	1/0.25	ARG	LRI216	Universidad de Villa Maria
	10/1	B	J339	R. Ágape, Balsa Nova
	1/0.25	B	I926	R. Cantagalo, Jaicós
	10/1	B	H200	R. Dif. Acreana, Rio Branco
	5/0.35	B	J775	R. Entre Rios, Palmitos
	2/0.45	B	J346	R. Jornal São Miguel, São Migueldo Iguaçu
	5/0.25	B	K682	R. Metrópole, São José do Rio Preto
	50/5	B	J462	R. Rio de Janeiro, Rio de Janeiro
	1	B	N660	Radiodifusão Guaraí, Guaraí
		BOL		R. Antena 2000, Sucre
	5	BOL		R. Nacional de Bolivia, La Paz
	5	CHL	CD140	R. La Amistad, Los Angeles
	5	CHL	CD140A	R. Maria, Puerto Montt
	1	CLM	JJ	Caracol R. Ipiales, Ipiales
	1	CLM	ER	Ecos del Atrato/W R., Quibdó
	5	CLM	KM	Em. Mariana, Bogotá
	5	CLM	HM	La Cariñosa Armenia, Calarcá
	5	CLM	AS	La Cariñosa, Barranquilla
	1	CLM	BK	LV de la Gran Colombia, Cúcuta
	3	EQA	FL2	R. Z Uno, Guayaquil
	1	PRU	OAU2H	R. Agricultura, Cajamarca
	1	PRU	OCU6F	R. Candaravena, Candaravna
	2.5	PRU	OBX4W	R. Ecco, Lima
	1	PRU	OAX7I	R. La Hora, Cuzco
	1	PRU	OBX4H	R. Luz, Tarma
	1	PRU	OAM5G	R. OAM5G, Ica
	1	PRU	OBU3E	R. OBU3E, Chimbote
	1	PRU	OCU5S	R. OCU5S, Preov
	25	URG	CX140	R. Zorrilla de San Martín, Tacuarembó
1410	1/0.25	ARG		Godoy Cruz
	1	ARG		La Mil 1410, Chivilcoy
	5/1	ARG		R. Folclorismo, José León Suárez
	0.5	ARG		R. Fundacion, Rafael Calzada
	0.5	ARG		R. María de La Paz, Villa Mercedes
	1/0.25	B	K683	Jovem Pan News, Rio Claro
	5/1	B	I382	Nova R. Clube, Corumbá
	5/1	B	K246	R. Garibaldi, Garibaldi
	30/0.85	B	H803	R. JK AM, Sto Antônio do Descoberto
	1/0.25	B	K284	R. Minuano, Rio Grande
	10/0.5	B	H467	R. Planeta, São Gonçalo dos Campos
	5/0.5	B	J614	R. Santa Cruz, Santa Cruz
	5	B	K294	R. Santa Rosa, Santa Rosa
	0.25	BOL		R. Atlantida, Oruro
	5	CHL	CB141	R. Amor, Valparaiso
	1	CHL	CD141	R. Loncoche, Loncoche
	5	CLM	DU	Em. Cultural Univ. de Antioquia, Medellín
	1	CLM	TY	LV del Carare, Vélez
	5	CLM	EI	R. Guadalajara, Buga
	1	EQA	KD5	R. Centro Gualaceo, Gualaceo
	1	EQA	VE1	R. El Tiempo, Quito

kHz	kW	Ctry	Call	Station, location
	1	PRU	OBX8I	Dif. Comercial, Pucallapa
	1	PRU	OBZ4V	R. Bethel, Huacho
	1	PRU	OBU7A	R. Corporacion Wayra, Juliaca
	3	PRU	OCU5G	R. Genesis, Huanta
	1	PRU	OCU2Q	R. Huracana, Pedro Galvez
	1	PRU	OAU3Y	R. Ke Buena, Paucarbambilia
	3	PRU	OBU1H	R. La Luz, Tumbes
	1	PRU	OBU1G	R. Olmos, Olomos
	10/5	URG	CX44	AM Libre, Montevideo
	2/0.5	URG	CW141	R. Turistica, Salto
1420	1/0.25	ARG	LRI220	AM 1420 Con Vos, Villa Martelli
	1/0.25	ARG	LRK221	R. Ciudad Perico, Perico
	1	ARG		R. General Conesa, General Conesa
		ARG		R. Grandero Puntanos, San Luis
	2.5/0.5	B	K597	C.R.N., Itatiba
	5/1	B	L288	R. Cultura, Sete Lagoas
	5/0.25	B	J269	R. Cultura, Umuarama
	1/0.25	B	J609	R. Farol, Alexandria
	10/2.5	B	J754	R. Guarujá, Florianópolis
	1/0.25	B	L313	R. Montanhês Botelhos, Botelhos
	1/0.25	B	K733	R. Nova, São Manuel
	3	B	K308	R. Tapense, Tapes
	1	BOL		R. Centro, Cochabamba
		BOL		R. Comunitaria, José Ballivian
		BOL		R. Creo en Milagros, Murillo
	1.5	BOL		R. Guadalquivir, Tarija
		BOL		R. Luz del Mundo, Santa Cruc
		BOL		R. Omasuyos Andina, Achacachi
	1	BOL		R. Real Audiencia, Sucre
	1	CHL	CB142	R. Panamcricana, Santiago
	5	CLM	HK	Cadena Radial Vida, Manizales
	1	CLM	D23	Ecos de Frontino, Frontino
	1	CLM	LE	La Cariñosa, Ibagué
	2	CLM	SN	R. Lenguerke, Zapatoca
	5	CLM	BH	R. Magdalena, Santa Marta
		EQA		R. Integración, Salcedo
	5	PRG	ZP42	R. Güyrá Campana, Horqueta
	1	PRU	OBU6C	R. Fe, Arequipa
	0.5	PRU	OBU5H	R. la Luz, Salas
	5	PRU	OAM2P	R. La Positiva, Bambamarca
	2	PRU	OCU1F	R. OCU1F, Tambo Grande
	1	PRU	OBZ4G	R. San Isidro, Lima
	1.5	PRU	OAM7K	R. San Luis, Pallpata
	1/0.5	URG	CX142	R. Felicidad, Paysandú
	5	URG	CW43	R. Lavalleja, Minas
	5	VEN		R. Sintonía, Caracas
1430	1	ARG		R. Cunumi Guasú, Rafael Castillo
	1/0.25	ARG	LV26	R. Rio Tercero, Río Tercero
	1/0.25	ARG	LT24	R. San Nicolas, San Nicolás
	5/1	ARG		San Fernando del Valle
	5	B	K379	Estação Portão, Portão
	50/10	B	J200	R. Evangelizar, Curitiba
	1/0.25	B	K366	R. Guarita, Coronel Bicaco
	25/0.25	B	K707	R. Imaculada Conceição, São Roque
	5/0.25	B	I826	R. Independência, Goiana
	1/0.25	B	K666	R. Serra Negra, Serra Negra
	1	CHL	CC143	R. Rumbos,Rancagua
	5	CLM	QX	R. Majagual, Sincelejo
	1	CLM	CK	R. Sensación, Yarumal
	5	CLM	PW	R. Ya, Barranquilla
	5	CLM	KU	Uniminuto R., Bogotá
	3.5	EQA	GF1	R. Futura, Quito
	2	PRG	ZP35	R. Mangoré, San Juan Bautista
	1	PRU	OCU4L	Chilca, Cañete
	1	PRU	OAZ3H	R. Chavin, Chimbote
	1	PRU	OAU6M	R. Lider, Tacna
	1	PRU	OCU2U	R. LV de Salvación, Jaén
	1	PRU	OAZ7M	R. Programas Peru, Cusco
	3	PRU	OBU7U	R. Red Andina, Juliaca
	0.5	PRU	OAZ4V	R. Universal, El Tambo
	1	PRU	OBX9H	R. Utcubamba, Bagua Grande
	20/5	URG	CW25	R. Durazno, Durazno
1440		ARG		R. AM 1440, Mar de Ajó
	0.25	ARG	LU36	R. Coronel Suárez, Coronel Suárez
	1/0.25	ARG	LRI221	R. General Obligado, Reconquista
	2	ARG		R. Impacto, Ciudad Madero
	1/0.25	ARG	LV20	R. Laboulaye, Laboulaye
	5/1	ARG	LRA53	R. Nacional San Martín de los Andes
	5/1	ARG		Santiago del Estero
	0.25	ARG		Villa Gesell
	1/0.25	B	K752	R. Azul, Americana
	2.5/0.5	B	K221	R. Ceres, Naõ Me Toque
	2.5/0.5	B		R. Clarim AM, Itai
	10/0.25	B	K634	R. Comercial, Presidente Prudente
	1/0.25	B	K568	R. Eldorado Centro Norte Paulista, Cajuru
	5/0.3	B	K328	R. Excelsior, Gramado
	50/1	B	H466	R. Independência, Santo Amaro
	20/5	B	J469	R. Livre, Rio de Janeiro
		BOL		LV de Juno, Tiraque
	1	BOL		R. Batallón Colorados, La Paz
	0.25	BOL		R. Bolivia, Cochabamba
		BOL		R. Comunitaria Eco Saywani, Carabuco
		BOL		R. Dif. Tropico, Trinidad
	2/1	BOL		R. Yaguary, Vallegrande
		BOL		Sistema de Comunicaciones Horizontes, Sucre
	1	CHL	CC144	R. El Sembrador, Chillán
	1	CHL	C144A	Tu R. Popular, La Serene
	5	CLM	NZ	Colmundo R., Medellín
	5	CLM	EK	R. Tuluá, Tuluá
	2	EQA	OV5	Ondas del Volante, Azogues
	1	EQA	BA1	R. Panorama, Ibarra
	3	PRU	OCU5P	R. Cielo, Ica
	2	PRU	OAU2O	R. Frecuencia VH, Celendin
	1	PRU	OAX4K	R. Imperial 2, Lima
	1	PRU	OBU1Z	R. OBU1Z, Vice
	2.5	PRU	OCU5K	R. OCU5K, Ayacucho
	2.5	PRU	OAX6R	R. Santa Monica, Hunter, Aqp
	3	PRU	OAM7L	R. Solar, Espinar
	2	PRU	OBX1T	R. Tumán, Tumán
	3/0.5	URG	CX144	R. Rivera, Rivera
1450	5	ARG		AM Banderas, Moreno
	1/0.25	ARG		Ceres
	1/0.25	ARG		General Acha
	1/0.25	ARG	LRJ211	R. AM Las 40, Villa Aberastain
	5/1	ARG	LRI213	R. El Sol, Don Bosco
	5/1	ARG		R. Epoca, Corrientes
	10/0.25	B	J822	Jovem Pan News AM, Criciúma
	1/0.25	B	H900	R. Boa Esperança, São João dos Patos
	50/5	B	K591	R. Boa Nova, Guarulhos
	1/0.25	B	J279	R. Cabiúna, Bandeirantes
	1/0.25	B	I699	R. Certão, Patos
	1/0.25	B	I908	R. Cultura do Gurguéia, Bom Jesus
	1/0.25	B	K338	R. Cultura, Arvorezinha
	2.5/0.25	B	K526	R. Cultura, Ituverava
	1/0.25	B	I794	R. Cultura, Palmares
	1/0.25	B	H901	R. Cultura, Pedreiras
	3/0.25	B	L312	R. Diamante, Coromandel
	1/0.25	B	J301	R. Dif. Ubiratanense, Ubiratã
	1/0.25	B	H601	R. Difusora Cristal, Quixeramobim
	1/0.25	B	H531	R. Ipirá, Ipirá
	1/0.25	B	I559	R. Juruá, São Felix do Xingu
	1/0.25	B	H623	R. Pinto Martins, Camocim
	1/0.25	B	J317	R. Rainha de Altônia, Altônia
	1/0.25	B	K657	R. São Carlos, São Carlos do Pinhal
	1/0.25	B	O701	R. Transamérca Hits, Alto Alegre
	1/0.25	B	J674	R. Vilhena, Vilhena
	1	BOL		R. Em. Bolivia, Oruro
	0.5	BOL		R. Magnal, Capinota
	4	CHL	CC145	R. Tropical Latina - RTL, Curicó
	1	CHL	CB145	R. Universidad Técnica, Valparaíso
	5	CLM	NL	Antena 2/La Cariñosa, Manizales
	5	CLM	BY	Olímpica Girardot, Flandes
	5	CLM	HH	R. Católica Metropolitana, Bucaramanga
	1	CLM	E20	R. María Colombia, Urrao
	5	PRG	ZP29	Mercedita AM, Vallemi
	1	PRU	OBU4Y	R. Andina, Huancayo
	1	PRU	OBX4K	R. Fortaleza, Barranca
		PRU		R. Libertad, Bambamarca
		PRU	OAU2W	R. Manantial de Vida, Cajamarca

kHz	kW	Ctry	Call	Station, location
	1	PRU	OBU6K	R. OBU6K, Chivay
	1	PRU	OCX2J	R. San Juan, Trujillo
		PRU	OCU6E	R. Santa Cruz, Ichuña
	1	PRU	OAM4A	R. Vida, Tinyahuarco
	10/5	URG	CX46	R. América, Montevideo
	1/0.25	URG	CW145	R. Arapey, Salto
	8	VEN	KJ	R. María, Catia la Mar
1460	1	ARG		R. Contacto, San Antonio de Padua
	0.25	ARG		R. Jerusalén, Monte Grande
	0.25	ARG	LU30	R. Maipú
	0.1	ARG	LU34	R. Pigüé, Pigüé
	1/0.25	ARG	LT29	R. Venado Tuerto, Venado Tuerto
	10/0.25	B	J615	R. Agreste, Santo Antônio
	5/0.25	B	J308	R. Ampere, Ampere
	1/0.25	B	K373	R. Campinas, Campinas do Sul
	1/0.25	B	J228	R. Central do Paraná, Ponta Grossa
	5/0.5	B	K548	R. Clube Ararense, Araras
	1/0.25	B	L201	R. Cul. do Porto Novo, Além Paraíba
	1/0.25	B	I903	R. Cultura, Amarante
	1/0.25	B	K214	R. Cultura, Bagé
	1/0.25	B	H523	R. Ferro Doido, Morro do Chapéu
	1/0.25	B	L363	R. Gerais AM, Raul Soares
	1/0.25	B	H774	R. Independência do Tocantins, Paraíso do Tocantins
	1/0.25	B	H595	R. Ressurreição, Massapé
	2.5	B	J756	R. Sentinela do Vale, Gaspar
	1/0.25	B	H616	R. Uirapuru, Morada Nova
	1/0.25	B	H917	R. Vanguarda, Santa Luzia
	10/0.5	B	J932	TransBRasil AM, Estância
		BOL		R. Canal de Television Quillacollo
		BOL		R. Jiwasa, Carabuco
		BOL		R. Plenitud de Vida, El Alto
	1	CHL	CC146	R. Armonía, Talcahuano
		CHL	CD146B	R. Ona Porvinir
	1	CHL	CB146	R. Palabra Viva, Santiago
	5	CLM	JW	ENC R.
	5	CLM	ZU	La Cariñosa, Pasto
	1	CLM	MU	LV de Amalfi
	1	CLM	E26	R. Capiro, La Ceja
	5	CLM	TN	R. María Colombia, Turbo
	1	CLM	AL	R. Sincelejo, Sincelejo
	3	EQA	IC6	R. Nuevos Horizontes, Latacunga
	1	PRU	OBU6R	R. Bahia, Mollendo
	0.5	PRU	OCY4I	R. Imperial, Junin
	1	PRU	OAZ4F	R. La Oroya, La Oroya
	2.5	PRU	OAU3V	R. Municipal, Cabana
		PRU	OBU7M	R. OBU7M, Marcapata
	10	PRU	OAX7W	R. Sol de los Andes, Juliaca
	1	PRU	OAX1V	R. Sullana, Sullana
	1	PRU	OCU4Y	R. Voz Cristiana, Chongo Bajo
	1	PRU	OAM5C	Rdif. Disaga, Pueblo Nuevo
	1	URG	CX146	R. Carmelo, Carmelo
	0.25	URG	CV146	R. José Batlle y O., José Batlle y Ordoñez
1470	1/0.5	ARG	LU26	La Dorrego AM 1470, Coronel Dorrego
	0.7	ARG		R. Cad. AM 1470, Remedios de Escalada
	1/0.25	ARG	LT20	R. Junín, Junin
		ARG		R. Lider, Mariano Acosta
	1	ARG		R. Municipal, Luis Beltrán
	1/0.5	ARG	LT26	R. Nuevo Mundo, San José
	2/0.5	ARG	LT28	R. Rafaela, Rafaela
	1/0.25	B	J476	R. Absoluta, Campos dos Goytacazes
	1/0.25	B	I413	R. Alvorada, Itaporã
	1/0.25	B	J481	R. Barra do Pirai, Barra do Piraí
	1/0.25	B	K771	R. Bastos AM, Bastos
	1/0.25	B	H779	R. Cidade, Goiás
	1	B		R. Cidade, Turiaçu
	1/0.25	B	L247	R. Dif., Ituiutaba
	1/0.25	B	I900	R. Difusora Vale do Uruçuí, Uruçuí
	1/0.25	B	H665	R. Guanancés de Itapajé, Itapajé
	1/0.25	B	I913	R. Ingazeira, Paulistana
	1/0.25	B	K712	R. Jornal, Indaiatuba
	5/0.25	B	K599	R. Mensagem, Jacareí
	0.25	B	H509	R. Morro Verde, Mairi
	3/0.25	B	J798	R. Nova Líder, Herval d'Oeste
	1/0.25	B	H908	R. Paranoá, Presidente Dutra
	1/0.25	B	K632	R. Primavera, Porto Ferreira
	1/0.25	B	J676	R. Rondônia, Cacoal
	1/0.25	B	J616	R. Rural de Parelhas, Parelhas
	3/0.25	B	ZYJ374	R. Tradição, Rio Branco de Sul
	1/0.25	B	H901	R. Urbano Santos,Urbano Santos
		BOL		R. Em. Ayni, Corapata
	1	BOL		R. Integración, Padilla
	1	CHL	CB147	R. Sargento Aldea, San Antonio
	5	CLM	II	Esperanza Colombia R., Medellín
	5	CLM	TB	Ondas de Ibagué, Ibagué
	5	CLM	HQ	R. Futurama, Pacho
	5	CLM	NT	R. Huellas, Cali
	1.5	EQA	LD2	R. Ecos de Naranjito, Naranjito
	1	EQA	ED1	Rdif. Ecos de Cayambe, Cayambe
	1	PRU	OCY2G	R. Amistad, Quiruvilca
	1	PRU	OAU1P	R. California, Lambayeque
	1	PRU	OAX7G	R. Cusco, Cusco
	20	PRU	OAU4B	R. Felicidad, Lima
	0.8	PRU	OAX6M	R. Tacna, Tacna
	2.5	PRU	OAU6E	R. Victoria, Alto Selva Alegre Aqp
	1	PRU	OCU4Y	R. Voz Cristiana, Chongo Bajo
	2	URG	CX147	R. Cristal del Uruguay,Las Piedras
	1	URG	CW147	R. Maria, Melo
1480	1	ARG		Tu Voz En R., Tapiales
	1/0.25	B	J731	R. Arca da Aliança, Joinville
	1/0.25	B	K551	R. Atibaia, Atibaia
	0.5	B	K767	R. Boituva, Boituva
	1/0.25	B	H795	R. Cultura, Miracema do Tocantins
	5/0.25	B	L265	R. Difusora, Nanuque
	10	B	H897	R. Itapecuru, Colinas
	1/0.25	B	J370	R. Pérola, Pérola d'Oeste
	10/0.5	B	J485	R. Popular, Duque de Caxias
	1/0.25	B	H671	R. Princesa do Norte, Morrinhos
	1/0.25	B	J681	R. Rondônia, Pimenta Bueno
	1/0.25	B	H524	R. Santana, Santana
		BOL		LV de los Andes, Carabuco
		BOL		R. Amor de Diós, El Alto
		BOL		R. Bendita Trinidad y Espirito Santo, Cobija
		BOL		R. Bendita Trinidad y Espirito Santo, Cochabamba
		BOL		R. Bendita Trinidad y Espirito Santo, Santa Cruz
	0.1	BOL		R. Cadena Sur, Potosi
		BOL		R. Charcas-Mundial, Sucre
	1/0.8	BOL		R. Chiwalakii, Vacas
		BOL		R. Comunitaria Waley, Desaguadero
		BOL		R. Domingo Savio, Independencia
	1	CHL	CA148	R. Comunicativa, Ovalle
	1	CHL	CC148	R. La Amistad de Tomé, Tomé
	5	CLM	OD	R. Rodadero, Santa Marta
	1	CLM	TC	R. Sonsón, Sonsón
	1	EQA	HV4	R. LV de Jipijapa, Jipijapa
	5	PRG	ZP20	R. América, Villeta
	1	PRG	ZP23	R. Dos Fronteras, Bella Vista Norte
	0.6	PRU	OCX2C	R. Comercial San Pedro, Virú
	1	PRU	OAZ7G	R. Espinar, Yauri
	1	PRU	OAU4A	R. Mineria, Santa Rosa de Sacco
	1	PRU	OAM4F	R. OAM4F, Barranca
		PRU	OBM7F	R. OBM7F, Tambopata
	0.2	PRU	OBU2H	R. Santa Ana, Cutervo
	1	URG	CX148	Difusora Rio Negro, Young
	5/1.5	URG	CW43B	R. Internacional, Rivera
	3	URG	CW148	R. Universo, Castillos
1490	1	ARG		R. AM Vida, Córdoba
		ARG		R. Ciudad de Caá Cati, Maquinista Savio
		ARG		R. Dif. Emanuel, Partido de Ezieza
	1.5	ARG		R. Gama, Lanús
	1/0.25	ARG	LV22	R. Huinca Renancó, Huinca Renancó:
	1/0.25	ARG		Rivadavia
	5/1	B	H246	Em. Rio São Francisco, Penedo
	25/0.25	B	K208	R. Assisense, São Francisco de Assis
	1/0.25	B	J210	R. Cornélio, Cornélio Procópio

kHz	kW	Ctry	Call	Station, location
	1/0.25	B	K680	R. Cult., Vargem Grande do Sul
	2.5/0.25	B	J791	R. Cultura, Xaxim
	1/0.25	B	K530	R. Difusora, Olímpia
	1/0.25	B	K583	R. Educadora, Fernandópolis
	25/0.5	B	K764	R. Imaculada Conceição, Mauá
	0.25	B	L231	R. Onda Viva, Araguari
	1/0.25	B	L274	R. Paraisópolis, Paraisópolis
	1/0.25	B	L353	R. Pirapetinga, Pirapetinga
	0.25	B	H512	R. Planalto d'Oeste, Correntina
	3/0.25	B	K309	R. Taquara, Taquara
	1	BOL		R. Jacinto Rodriguez, San José, Oruro
	0.25	CHL	CB149	La Mexicana, San Bernardo
	1	CHL	CA149	R. Alicanto, El Salvador
	4	CLM	BS	Em. Punto Cinco, Bogotá
	5	CLM	ZB	LV de los Robles, Tuluá
	5	CLM	AY	R. Vida Nueva, Barranquilla
	3	EQA	MV1	La Nueva R. Pasión, Quito
	2	EQA	AM5	R. Santa María, Azogues
	2.5	PRU	OCU7Y	Cadena Sur del Peru, Cusco
	1	PRU	OAX8F	R. Atlántiada, Iquitos
	1.3	PRU	OAX6Q	R. Fidelidad, Cerro Colorado, Aqp
	1	PRU	OAX1L	R. Imperio, Chiclayo
	0.5	PRU	OCX4P	R. La Luz, Cerro de Pasco
	1	PRU	OAX5N	R. Nazca, Nazca
	1	PRU	OAM7P	R. OAM7P, Capachica
		PRU		R. Patron Santiago, Challhuacho
	2.5	PRU	OBU5C	Rdif. los Chankas, Andahuaylas
	1/0.25	URG	CV149	R. del Centro, Baltasar Brum
	5	URG	CX149	R. del Oeste, Nueva Helvecia
	10	VEN	XD	R. Dinámica, Caracas
1500		ARG		AM Entre Mares, San Clemente del Tuyú
	5/1	ARG		Mendoza
	0.25	ARG	LT34	R. Nuclear, Zárate
	0.25	ARG		R. Olivera, General Rodriguez
		ARG		R. Tres Fronteras, Isidro Casanova
		ARG		R. Vida, Río Cuarto
	1/0.25	B	L340	R. Aparecida do Sul, Ilicínea
	2.5/0.25	B	K549	R. Cidade das Arvores, Araras
	1/0.25	B	K773	R. Cumbica, Guarulhos
	0.5	B	H487	R. Jacuípe, Riachão do Jacuípe
	5/0.25	B	K225	R. Liberdade, Canguçu
	1/0.25	B	K706	R. Vale do Rio Grande, Miguelópolis
	1/0.25	B	I919	R. Voz do Longa, Esperantina
	2	BOL		R. Comunitaria Tawantinsuyo, Laja
		BOL		R. Litoral, Cochabamba
	1	BOL		R. Sagrado Corazón, Mineros
		BOL		R. Universidad Juan Misael Saracho, Villamontes
	1	CHL	CD150	R. Tierra del Fuego, Porvenir
	1	CHL	CB150	R. Trasandina, Los Andes
	5	CLM	TW	Kirios R, Fusagasugá
	5	CLM	UW	R. María Colombia, Manizales
	5	CLM	LJ	Sonora 1500 AM, Cali
	1	PRU	OCU4Q	LV Liberacion, Huancayo
	1	PRU	OAU6B	R. Bulevar, Tacna
	0.5	PRU	OBX2X	R. Comercial, Trujillo
	1	PRU	OBX3J	R. Luz y Sonido, Huanuco
	2	PRU	OBU2J	R. San Pablo, San Pablo
	18	PRU	OBX4I	R. Santa Rosa, Lima
	1	PRU	OAM7B	R. TV Cristiana, Sicuani
	5	VEN	RZ	R. 2000, Cumaná
1510		ARG		LV del Oeste, Libertad
	1	ARG		R. Alabanza, Guernica
	1/0.25	ARG	LRI253	R. Belgrano, Suardi
	1	ARG		R. RBN, Banfield Oeste
	2/0.25	ARG		Villa Angela
	1/0.25	B	K719	R. Athenas Paulista, Jaboticabal
	10/1	B	K654	R. Cacique, Santos
	1/0.25	B	J602	R. Centenário, Caraúbas
	0.25	B		R. Central, Jaru
	1/0.25	B	K665	R. Cl. Regional, São Manuel
	5/0.5	B	H493	R. Dif. do Descobrimento, Porto Seguro
	1/0.25	B	I936	R. Nordeste, Picos
	10/0.25	B	I544	R. Oriente de Redenção, Redenção
	1/0.25	B	H608	R. Planalto, São Benedito
	1/0.25	B	I896	R. Progresso, Corrente
	1/0.25	B	K...	R. Rural, Rinópolis
	1/0.25	B	J492	R. Teresópolis, Teresópolis
	0.25	B	H630	R. Trapiá, Pedra Branca
	0.5/0.25	B	K770	R. Vale - Aleluia Musica, Salto
		BOL		R. Wiñay Jatha, El Alto
	1/0.5	CHL	CA151	R. Luís Alvarez Sierra, Illapel
	1	CHL	CC151	R. Rancagua, Rancagua
	5	CLM	D24	LV de La Unión, La Unión
	1	CLM	A22	LV de San Luis, San Luis de Gaceno
	3	EQA	BD1	R. Monumental, Quito
	0.5	EQA	IO2	R. Naval, Guayaquil 1030-0100
	1	EQA	RY6	R. Runacunapac Yachana, Simiátug
	3	PRU	OCX6Q	R. Alegria, Mariano Melgar, Aqp
	1	PRU	OBX8K	R. Centro de los Medios, Sepahua
	1	PRU	OBX7P	R. Las Vegas, Wanchaq
	1	PRU	OAM4Q	R. OAM4Q, Supe Puerto
	1	PRU	OCU4M	R. OCU4M, San Vicente de Cañete
	1	PRU	OBU1B	R. Super Real, Olmos
	1	PRU	OCX4J	R. Tarma, Tarma
	1	PRU	OCX1V	R. Tumbes, Tumbes
	1	PRU	OAM1C	R. TV Motupe, Motupe
	0.5	URG	CW151	R. Ibirapitá, San Gregorio de Polanco
	1/0.5	URG	CX151	R. Rincón, Fray Bentos
	2/0.5	URG	CW57	R. San Carlos, San Carlos
1516	1	PRU	OAM2Q	R. Charles, Bambamarca
1520	2	ARG		LV del Sur, Luis Guillón
	5/0.5	ARG		R. Chascomus, Chascomús
	3	ARG		R. Cielo Nuevo, Isidro Casanova
	0.25	ARG	LT38	R. Gualeguay, Gualeguay
	2	ARG		R. Norteña, Los Polvorines
		ARG		R. Palabra de Vida, La Matanza
	1/0.25	B	K627	Pinhal R. Cl., Espírito Sto. do Pinhal
	1/0.25	B	H653	R. Cachoeira, Solonópole
	1/0.25	B	K760	R. Catedral, Sorocaba
	10/0.5	B	J491	R. Continental, São João do Meriti
	1/0.25	B	H797	R. Cristal, Cristalândia
	10/1	B	K614	R. da Cidade, Mogi das Cruzes
	10/0.5	B	J931	R. Ilha AM, Tobias Barreto
	0.25	B	K...	R. Legal, Viradouro
	1/0.25	B	H928	R. Mirante AM, Chapadinha
	1/0.25	B	H899	R. Mirante, Pindaré-Mirim
	1/0.25	B	J292	R. Nova Cultura, Palotina
	1/0.25	B	H806	R. Nova RCB, Campos Belos
	1/0.25	B	H635	R. Regional, Ipu
	1/0.25	B	I801	R. Surubim, Surubim
	1	BOL		R. la Chiwana, Cochabamba
		BOL		R. La Luz del Tiempo, El Alto
		BOL		R. Rural, Tarata
		BOL		R. San Pedro, Tiawuanaku
		BOL		R. Universidad Juan Misael Saracho, Sucre
	1	CHL	CB152	R. Integración, San Antonio
	1	CHL	CC152	R. Soberanía, Linares
	1	CLM	RL	Antena de los Andes/Reloj, Sta Rosa de Cabal
	5	CLM	LQ	La R. del Príncipe de Paz, Barranquilla
	1	CLM	MA	LV del Suroeste, Jericó
	5	CLM	LI	Su Presencia R., Bogotá
	0.5	EQA	RI5	LV de Guamote, Guamote
		PRU		R. Andina, Lampa
	1	PRU	OBU7X	R. Avance - Voz Evangelica, Espinar
	1	PRU	OAX1C	R. Cristal, Chiclayo
	1	PRU	OCU1T	R. LV del Campesino, Ayabacha
	3	PRU	OBU5Z	R. Municipal, Castrovirreyna
		PRU	OAM4C	R. OAM4C, San Juan
	6	PRU	OBU6Z	R. OBU6Z, Mascal Nieto
	2	PRU	OCU5F	R. OCU5F, Huanta
	2	URG	CX152	R. Acuarela, Melo
	1/0.5	URG	CV152	R. Paz, Guichón
1530	5	ARG		LV del Futuro, Merlo
	0.25	ARG	LRJ200	R. Centro Morteros, Morteros
	1.5	ARG		R. Esencia, San Miguel Oeste

kHz	kW	Ctry	Call	Station, location
	1/0.25	B	L280	R. Clube, Pouso Alegre
	1/0.25	B	J761	R. Dif., Itajaí
	2.5	B	J796	R. Porto Feliz, Mondaí
	0.25	B	L262	R. Progresso, Monte Santo de Minas
	5/0.25	B	K300	R. Progresso, São Leopoldo
	1/0.25	B	K235	R. Sulina, Dom Pedrito
	1/0.25	B	H666	R. Tres Fronteiras, Campos Sales
	1/0.25	B	K755	R. Universal, Teodoro Sampaio
	0.25	BOL		R. Litoral, Llica
		BOL		R. Salesiana, Kami
	1	CHL	CB153	R. Nexo, Quillota
	1	CHL	CA153	R. Vida Nueva, Copiapó
	1	CHL	CC153	R.Patagual, Coronel
	1	CLM	EU	Caracol R. Sevilla, Sevilla
	5	CLM	OZ	LV de la Prov. de Padilla, San Juan del Cesar
	5	CLM	DN	Yeshu'a LV de Jesucristo, Medellín
	5	EQA	CC5	Ondas Cañaris AM, Azogues
	3	EQA	MZ6	R. Dorado Deportes, Pelileo
	1	PRU	OBZ4S	R. 15-50, Huancayo
	1	PRU	OAM2Q	R. Charles, Bambamarca
		PRU	OCX1Y	R. La Jefa, Sullana
	10	PRU	OBU4C	R. Milenia, Lima
	1	PRU	OBU7N	R. Ondas del Sur Oriente, Quillabamba
	3	PRU	OBX2R	R. Oriental, Jaén
	1	PRU	OAU5R	R. Universidad San Juan Bautista, Subtanjalla
	0.5	PRU	OAZ7F	Rdif. Espinar, Yauri
	0.25	URG	CW153	Em. Cono Sur, Nueva Palmira
1540	1	ARG		R. AM Lider, Benavidez
		ARG		R. Luminares al Mundo, Maximo Paz
	0.25	ARG	LT35	R. Mon, Pergamino
	0.25	ARG	LU28	R. Tuyú
		ARG		R. Zorobabel, Monte Grande
		ARG		Rio Gallegos
	2/0.5	B	K564	Jovem Pan News, Botucatu
	1/0.25	B	J611	R. Baixa Verde, João Câmara
	1/0.25	B	I545	R. Boa Vista, São Sebastião da Boa Vista
	5/0.25	B	J803	R. Capinzal, Capinzal
	1/0.25	B	J508	R. Clube, Paraíba do Sul
	1/0.25	B	K514	R. Cultura, Leme
	50/1	B	K723	R. Nova Difusora, Osasco
		B		R. Novo Milenio, Ribeirão Preto
	1/0.25	B	K282	R. Quaraí, Quaraí
	1/0.25	B	H921	R. Santa Maura, Lago da Pedra
	0.25	B	H...	R. Sociedade, Itiruçu
	1/0.25	B	L217	Super Difusora Bomdespachense, Bom Despacho
		BOL		R. Bendita Trinidad y Espirito Santo, El Alto
		BOL		R. Comunitaria Rio Chico, Sucre
		BOL		R. Comunitario Tutuka, Vilaque
	0.8	BOL		R. Sariri, Escoma
	1	CHL	CC154	R. Portales, Chillán
	1	CHL	CD154	R. San José de Alcudia, Río Bueno
		CHL	CB144	R. Sudamerica, Santiago
	1	CLM	A26	Em. Brisas del Río Chico, Belmira
	1	CLM	HD	LV del Petróleo/Caracol, Barrancabermeja
	5	CLM	ZF	R. Cóndor, Manizales
	3	EQA	FM2	R. Cristal de Ventanas, Babahoyo
	1	PRU	OAM4G	R. Angie@Net, Barranca
	0.3	PRU	OBX4N	R. Corporacion, Cerro de Pasco
	1	PRU	OCX7V	R. Los Andes, Cusco
	1	PRU	OBX1B	R. LV de la Frontera, Tumbes
	1	PRU	OAU6A	R. Milenio Universal, Alto Selva Alegre
	2	PRU	OBU2A	R. Mundial, Trujillo
	1	PRU	OCU6H	R. OCU6H, Pocollay
	1	URG	CV154	R. Centro, Cardona
	0.1	URG	CW154	R. Charrúa, Paysandú
	1	URG	CX154	R. Patria, Treinta y Tres
1550	1	ARG		Estacion Quince Cincuenta, Villa Florito
	0.25	ARG	LT32	R. Chivilcoy, Chivilcoy
		ARG		R. La Amistad, José C. Paz
	5/0.25	ARG	LT23	R. Regional, San Genaro
	1/0.25	B	I550	R. Cabano, Maracanã
	1/0.25	B	K572	R. Cacique, Capivari
	1/0.25	B	K377	R. Cidade AM, Capão do Leão
	1/0.25	B	K501	R. Clube, Itararé
	1/0.25	B	L211	R. Cultura, Monte Carmelo
	1/0.25	B	L222	R. Difusora, Carmo do Rio Claro
	10/1	B	K590	R. Guarujá AM, Guarujá
	1/0.25	B	J479	R. Imperial, Petrópolis
	5/0.25	B	H518	R. Independencia do São Francisco, Juazeiro
	1/0.25	B	J606	R. Ivipanin, Areia Branca
	10/0.25	B	I700	R. Jardim da Borborema, Areia
	1/0.25	B	K375	R. Soledad, Soledade
	10/1	B	H926	Sist. Janaina de Rdif, Vargem Grande
	10	BOL		R. Caranavi, Caranavi
	1	CHL	CC155	R. Manuel Rodríguez, San Fernando
	1	CHL	CB155	R. Provincial AM, Putaendo
	5	CLM	LT	Em. Revivir en Cristo, Cali
	5	CLM	ZI	G12 R., Bogotá
	5	CLM	QD	R. Auténtica, Calarcá
	1	EQA	AD2	LV de El Triunfo, El Triunfo
	1	PRU	OAU3D	R. Cruz, Chimbote
	5	PRU	OBX4P	R. Independencia, Independencia
		PRU		R. Integracion, Cutervo
	1	PRU	OCU1B	R. La Clave, Castilla
	3	PRU	OAU5Z	R. La Luz del Mundo, Subtanjalla
	1	PRU	OBX5J	R. Maria, Huamanaga
	1	PRU	OCU1W	R. OCU1W, Monsefú
	1	PRU	OAM7D	R. San Sebastian, Livitaca
	0.25	URG	CV155	R. Agraciada, Mercedes
	2/0.5	URG	CW155	R. Sarandí del Yí, Sarandí del Yí
1560	0.25	ARG	LT33	Cadena Nueve, 9 de Julio
	0.5/0.25	ARG		LV de Tandil, Tandil
	1/0.25	ARG		Mendoza
		ARG		R. Antena, Lobos
	1.5	ARG		R. Castañares, Ituzaingó
	10/5	ARG	LT11	R. Gral. Franc. Ramírez, Concepción del Uruguay
	2.5/0.25	B	K310	R. Açoriana, Taquari
	1/0.25	B	H903	R. Agua Branca, Vitorino Freire
	10/0.25	B		R. Barigui, Almirante Tamandaré
	0.25	B	K725	R. Cidade, Pedreira
	1/0.25	B	J364	R. Clube, Mallet
	0.25	B	J361	R. Cultura Serpin, Ribeirão do Pinhal
	1/0.25	B	H622	R. Difusora Vale de Curu, Pentecoste
	5/0.25	B	J501	R. Grande Rio, Itaguaí
	1/0.25	B	L256	R. Jornal, Leopoldina
	1/0.25	B	I...	R. Paranaita, Paranaita
	1/0.25	B	K593	R. Show, Igarapava
	15	BOL		R. Luz del Mundo, La Paz
	1	BOL		R. Occidental, Oruro
	0.5	BOL		R. Urkupiña, Quillacollo
	1	CHL	CB156	R. Manantial, Talagante
	1	CHL	CD156	R. Parque, Villarrica
	5	CLM	LP	La Cariñosa, Tuluá
	5	CLM	XZ	Santa María de la Paz, Medellín
	5	CLM	HE	Voces Rovirenses, Málaga
	1.5	EQA	ZD1	R. Ecos Culturales de Urcuquí, Urcuquí
	1	PRU	OAZ7N	R. Maria, Wanchaq
	1	PRU	OAM1B	R. Moderna, Olmos
	1	PRU	OCU6K	R. OCU6K, Alto de la Alianza
	1	PRU	OAM2I	R. R. Antena Norte, Cajabamba
	2.5	PRU	OCU4Z	R. Rumba, Hualhuas
	1	PRU	OCX6N	R. Sabor, Arequipa
	2/0.5	URG	CX156	Dif. Americana, Trinidad
	1	URG	CV156	R. Vichadero
1570	5/1	ARG	LRI223	Lomas de Zamora
	1	ARG		R. AM Rocha, Tolosa
	0.5	ARG		R. Eben-Ezer, Ezeiza
		ARG		R. La Morena de Itati, Grand Bourg
		ARG		R. La Region, Luis Palacio
	2.5	ARG		R. Melody, Remedios de Escalada

kHz	kW	Ctry	Call	Station, location
	10/0.25	B	K651	R. ABC, Santo André
	1/0.25	B	K552	R. Avaré, Avaré
	1/0.25	B	J341	R. Clube, Nova Aurora
	10/0.5	B	H907	R. Cultura do Rio Jordão, Coroatá
	1/0.25	B	J493	R. Cultura, Valença
	1/0.25	B	K605	R. Junqueirópolis, Junqueirópolis
	5/0.25	B	K358	R. Metrópole, Gravataí
	1/0.25	B	N665	R. Nossa R., Gurupi
	1/0.25	B	H621	R. Sertão Central,Senador Pompeu
	1/0.25	B	K667	R. Socorro, Socorro
	1/0.25	B	J832	R. Tanagrá, Tangará
	0.25	B	L242	R. Unifei, Itajubá
	1/0.25	B	K648	R. Zequinha de Abreu, Santa Rita do Passa Quatro
		BOL		R. Pedro Ignacio Muiba
	1	CHL	CC157	R. Cristo Llama Al Pecador, Rancagua
	1	CHL	CC157A	R. Familia del Maule, Talca
	1	CLM	E70	R. Auténtica, Manizales
	0.5	EQA	CC4	R. La Voz, Manta
	25	PRU	OCU4J	R. Bethel, Lima
	1	PRU	OAU7Z	R. Carraviz, Juliaca
		PRU	OBU2L	R. Jesus es la Vida, Granja Porcón
	1	PRU	OCX1Z	R. La Nueva Esperanza, Tambo Grande
	2.5	PRU	OCU5O	R. Musuq Chaski R., Huamanga
	1	PRU	OAM5H	R. OAM5H, Chinca Alta
	1	PRU	OBU3A	R. OBU3A. Cerro Jactay
	1	PRU	OCU7L	R. Vilcanota, Sicuani
	1	PRU	OCU2C	Rdif. Julcan, Otuzco
	0.25	URG	CW157A	Em. Celeste, Tomás Gomensoro
	2/0.5	URG	CX157	R. Canelones
1580	2	ARG		AM Tradición, San Martín
		ARG		Charata
	1	ARG		R. 26. de Julio, Longchamps
	0.25	ARG	LT36	R. Chacabuco, Chacabuco
		ARG		R. Cóndor, Moreno
	1	ARG		R. La Cueva, 25 de Mayo
	0.25	ARG	LT27	R. LV del Montiel, Villaguay
	1/0.25	B	H502	R. Atalaia, Canavieiras
	2.5/0.25	B	H497	R. Barra de Mendes, Barra do Mendes
	1/0.25	B	L290	R. Cultura, Santos Dumont
	1/0.25	B	K504	R. Difusora, Amparo
	1/0.25	B	N611	R. Difusora, Ivinhema
	1/0.25	B	L329	R. Educadora, Espinosa
	9/0.25	B	K237	R. Encantado AM, Encantado
	0.25	B	J505	R. Geração 2000, Teresópolis
	0.25	B		R. Grande Vale, Paraibuna
	1/0.25	B	L210	R. Liberdade, Itapecirica
	1/0.25	B	L335	R. Nova Guaranésia, Guaranésia
	1/0.25	B	J613	R. Novos Tempos, Ceará Mirim
	1/0.5	B	J487	R. Popular Fluminense, Conceição de Macabu
	5/0.25	B	J506	R. Resende AM, Resende
	1/0.25	B	I898	R. Santa Clara, Floriano
	0.25	B	K743	R. São João Batista, Itaporanga
	2.5/0.25	B	J342	R. São João do Sudoeste, São João
		BOL		LV del Valle, Valle Alto
	1	BOL		R. Adonai, Santa Cruz
	3	BOL		R. Bermejo, Bermejo
		BOL		R. Comunitaria Jacinto Rodrìguez, Caracolla
		BOL		R. Contacto, Sucre
		BOL		R. El Fuego del Espíritu Santo, El Alto
		BOL		R. Magazine Tarija, Tarija
	1	CHL	CC158	R. Colchagua, Santa Cruz
	5	CLM	QT	Candela 8-50, Bogotá
	5	CLM	QZ	R. María Colombia, Barranquilla
	5	CLM	RM	Sistema Cardenal, Sincelejo
	2.5	PRU	OAM4O	R. Andina, Huacho
		PRU	OCU6M	R. Bacan Sat., Tacna
	1	PRU	OBX1M	R. Naylamp, Lambayeque
		PRU	OAM2R	R. OAM2R, Jaen
	1	PRU	OBU6S	R. OBU6S, Orcopampa
	1	PRU	OAU4P	R. San Juan, Tarma
	1	PRU	OAU5J	R. Virgen del Carmen, Huancavelica
	2/0.5	URG	CW54	Em. del Este, Minas
	1/0.5	URG	CW158	R. San Salvador, Dolores
1590		ARG		R. Americana, Villa Fiorito
	1	ARG		R. Dolores, Dolores
		ARG		R. Stentor, Buenos Aires
	0.25	B	N207	Lambari
	1/0.25	B	L368	R. Cidade Carinho, Ubá
	10/0.5	B	J823	R. Clube, Joinville
	1/0.25	B	I703	R. Correio do Vale, Itaporanga
	1/0.25	B	J290	R. Cultura, Andirá
	10/1	B	L369	R. Guaicuí, Várzea da Palma
	1/0.25	B	I403	R. Independência, Eldorado
	10/0.5	B	K774	R. Japi, Cabreúva
	1	B	ZYI802	R. Restauração, Bezerros
	0.3	B	H...	R. Vale do Jiquiriçá, Jiquiriça
	1	B	H...	R. Veneza, Eusébio
		BOL		R. Kollasuyo Marka, Tiawanaku
	1	BOL		R. Wayana Songo, Pongo K´asa
	0.1	CHL	CC159A	Parral
	1	CHL	CB159	R. Aconcagua, San Felipe
	5	CLM	IP	Emisora BBN, Envigado
	5	CLM	WB	R. Nuestra Señora/R. María, Socorro
	1	EQA	RZ1	R. Mensaje, Cayambe
	1	EQA	QT6	R. Panamericana, Quero
	1	PRU	OAU7C	R. Asillo, Azangaro
	1	PRU	OBU2C	R. Bendicion, Trujillo
	1	PRU	OCX6S	R. Mundo, Arequipa
		PRU	OAM2S	R. Municipal, San Marcos
	3	PRU	OAM5J	R. OAM5J, Ica
	1	PRU	OBU5F	R. OBU5F, Lucanas
	1.5	PRU	OAZ4Z	R. Vida, Lima
	1/0.25	URG	CW159	R. Nueva R. Lascano, Lascano
	1	URG	CX159	R. Real, Colonia
	10	VEN	UD	R. Deporte, Caracas
1600	1	ARG		R. Armonia, Caseros
	0.25	ARG		R. EME Centro, Montes de Oca
	100/20	B	K779	R. Nove de Julho, São Paulo
		BOL		LV del Campesino, Cochabamba
	0.5	BOL		R. P.C.A., Valle Alto
	0.25	CHL	CD160	R. Alternativa, Temuco
	0.25	CHL	CB160A	R. Fe, Viña del Mar
	0.25	CHL	CC160	R. Llacolén, Concepción
	0.25	CHL	CB160	R. Nuevo Tiempo, Santiago
	0.25	CLM	HKO63	R. Jardín, Jardín
	3	PRU	OBM7A	R. Antena 5, Wanchaq
	2.5	PRU	OBU4R	R. Nuevo Tiempo, Huancayo
	3	PRU	OCU6C	R. OCU6C Moquequa
	1	URG	CV160	R. Continental, Pando
	1	URG	CX160	R. Litoral, Fray Bentos
1610	1	ARG		R. Luz del Mundo, Rafael Calzada
	0.5	ARG		R. Magica, Laboulaye
	0.5	PRU	OAU6O	R. El Sol, Arequipa
		PRU		R. Inka, Acora
1620	10/1	ARG		AM 16-20 La Radio, Mar del Plata
		ARG		R. Mitre, Cañada de Gómez
		ARG		R. Sentires,Merlo
	5/1	ARG		Universidad de Buenos Aires
		PRU		R. Choquechamaca, Chamaca
1630	10/1	ARG	LRI222	R. America, San José
	1	ARG		R. Unidad, Alejandro Korn
1640		ARG		General Madariaga
	1	ARG		R. Hosanna 1640, Isidro Casanova
1650		ARG		R. Estrellas, Longchamps
		PRU		R. Santa Roas, San Ignacio, Otuzco
1660	0.25	ARG		Junin
	1/0.25	ARG		Paso de los Libres
	5/0.25	ARG	LRI232	R. Ciudad de Nogoyá, Nogoyá
	1	ARG		R. Revivir, Gregorio de la Ferrere
1680	0.2	ARG		R. G, Quilmes
	1/0.5	ARG		Universidad Tecnlógica Nacional
1710		ARG		R. Selva, Gonzáles Catán

SHORTWAVE STATIONS OF THE WORLD

For country and site codes, see relevant tables in the reference section. Stations marked as '***dom***' in the site column are domestic/national broadcasts. Stations marked with '**STF**' in the site column are Standard Time/Frequency transmissions. The column '**N**' indicates Notes. Symbols used in the '**N**' column are '**+**', indicating DRM transmissions; '**±**' which indicates variable frequency; '**†**' for irregular transmissions and **‡** for frequencies that were inactive at the editorial deadline. The '**Ctry**' column shows the location of the transmitter site. The country code shown after international entries denotes the country the station is listed under in the International or COTB sections of WRTH.

kHz	N	kW	Ctry	Site	Station, location
2485	†	5	VUT	*dom*	R. Vanuatu, Port Vila
2500		10	CHN	STF	BPM, Pucheng
		5	HWA	STF	WWVH NIST, Kauai, HI
		2.5	USA	STF	WWV NIST, Fort Collins, CO
3185		100	USA	wrb	WWRB, USA
3205	+	50	KRE	*dom*	KCBS, Pyongyang
3215		100	USA	wcr	The Overcomer Ministry, USA
		100	USA	wcr	WWCR, USA
		100	USA	wrb	WWRB, USA
3220		5	KRE	*dom*	KCBS/Reg., Hamhung
		5	KRE	ham	Pyongyang Broadcasting Station, KRE
3250		100	KRE	*dom*	KCBS, Pyongyang
3260	†	4	PNG	*dom*	NBC Madang, Madang
3310		10	BOL	*dom*	R. Mosoj Chaski, Cochabamba
3320		50	KRE	pyo	Pyongyang Broadcasting Station, KRE
3325		20	INS	pga	Voice of Indonesia, INS
	†	10	PNG	*dom*	NBC Bougainville, Buka
3330		3	CAN	STF	CHU, Ottawa
3345	†	10	INS	*dom*	RRI, Ternate
3365	†	3.5	B	*dom*	107.5 FM, Araraquara
3375	†	1	B	*dom*	R. Municipal, São Gabriel Cach.
3480	±	50	KOR	goy	Voice of the People, KRE
3900		5	CHN	*dom*	Hulun Buir PBS, Hailar
3910	±	50	KOR	goy	Voice of the People, KRE
3915		250	SNG	sng	BBC World Service, G
3920		0.2	HOL	zwo	R.Piepzender, HOL
	†	5	KRE	*dom*	KCBS/Reg., Hyesan
3925		10	J	*dom*	R. Nikkei 1, Sapporo
3930	±	50	KOR	goy	Voice of the People, KRE
3940		1	HOL	hee	Mike Radio, HOL
3945		10	J	*dom*	R. Nikkei 2, Tokyo
		100	KRE	pyo	Echo of Unification, KOR
		5	VUT	*dom*	R. Vanuatu, Port Vila
3950		100	CHN	*dom*	Xinjiang PBS, Urumqi
3955	†	8	D	rob	Channel 292, D
		8	D	rob	Encore Classical Music, G
		8	D	rob	R. DARC, D
	+	250	G	wof	BBC World Service, G
		250	G	wof	KBS World R., KOR
3959	†	5	KRE	*dom*	KCBS/Reg., Kanggye
3965	+	1	F	iss	R. France International (RFI), F
3970	±†	5	KRE	chj	Echo of Unification, KOR
3975		1	D	wis	Shortwave Radio, D
3985		100	CHN	*dom*	CNR2 Business R., Golmud
		1	D	kll	R. Belarus International, BLR
		1	D	kll	R. Slovakia International, SVK
		1	D	kll	R. Tirana International, ALB
		1	D	kll	SRG SSR Swiss B'casting Corp., SUI
		1	D	kll	Vatican R., CVA
	±	100	KOR	jnm	Echo of Hope (VOH), KRE
3990	†	15	CHN	*dom*	Gannan PBS, Hezuo
		100	CHN	*dom*	Xinjiang PBS, Urumqi
3995		1.5	D	wnm	R. HCJB Deutschland, D
4010		100	KGZ	*dom*	KGR1, Bishkek
4055	†	0.7	GTM	*dom*	R. Verdad, Chiquimula
4450	±	50	KOR	goy	Voice of the People, KRE
4500		50	CHN	*dom*	Xinjiang PBS, Urumqi
4750		100	BGD	dka	Bangladesh Betar, BGD
	†	100	BGD	*dom*	Bangladesh Betar, Savar
		100	CHN	*dom*	CNR1 VO China, Hailar
	†	10	INS	jak	Voice of Indonesia, INS
4760		2.5	IND	*dom*	AIR, Leh
		50	SWZ	man	TWR Africa, AFS
4764	±	0.5	PRU	*dom*	R. Huanta 2000, Huanta
4765		50	CUB	*dom*	R. Progreso, Bejucal
		50	TJK	*dom*	Tajik R., Yangiyul
4775	†	1	B	*dom*	R. Congonhas, Congonhas
	†	1.4	PRU	*dom*	R. Tarma Internacional, Tarma
4800		100	CHN	*dom*	CNR1 VO China, Golmud
4810	‡	1	PRU	*dom*	R. Logos, Chazuta
4820		100	CHN	*dom*	Xizang PBS, Lhasa
		15	KGZ	*dom*	KGR1, Bishkek
4835	‡	10	IND	*dom*	AIR, Gangtok
4840		100	USA	wcr	The Overcomer Ministry, USA
		100	USA	wcr	WWCR, USA
4850		100	CHN	*dom*	Xinjiang PBS, Urumqi
4862	±	5	B	*dom*	R. Alvorada, Londrina
4875	†	10	B	*dom*	R. Roraima, Boa Vista
4880	±	100	KOR	nwn	Echo of Hope (VOH), KRE
4885		2	B	*dom*	R. Clube do Pará, Belém
		5	B	*dom*	Rdif. Acreana, Rio Branco
4895	†	5	B	*dom*	R. Novo Tempo, Campo Grande
	†	10	MNG	*dom*	Mongolian R. 1, Mörön
4900		50	CHN	*dom*	VO Strait Dialect Sce, Fuzhou
4905		5	B	*dom*	R. Relógio, Rio de Janeiro
		100	CHN	lha	CTB - Holy Tibet, CHN
		100	CHN	*dom*	Xizang PBS, Lhasa
4920		100	CHN	lha	CTB - Holy Tibet, CHN
		100	CHN	*dom*	Xizang PBS, Lhasa
	‡	1	PRU	*dom*	R. LV del Pueblo, Santiago de Chuco
4925	†	5	B	*dom*	R. Rural, Tefé
4930		100	BOT	bot	VO America (VOA), USA
		100	BOT	bot	VOA Studio 7, USA
	‡	1	PRU	*dom*	R. Sur Andina, Pitumarca
4940		50	CHN	*dom*	VO Strait News Ch, Fuzhou
		1	CLM	*dom*	La Montana Colombia, Maicao
	†	1	PRU	*dom*	R. San Antonio, Villa Atalaya
4950	†	25	AGL	*dom*	R. Nal de Angola, Mulenvos
		50	IND	*dom*	AIR, Kashmir, Srinagar
4955	†	5	PRU	*dom*	R. Amauta, Huanta
4960		100	STP	sao	VO America (VOA), USA
4965		100	ZMB	luv	Voice of Hope - Africa, ZMB
4975		10	CHN	*dom*	Fujian PBS, Fuzhou
4980		100	CHN	*dom*	Xinjiang PBS, Urumqi
4985		10	B	*dom*	R. Brasil Central, Goiânia
4990		10	CHN	*dom*	Hunan PBS, Xiangtan
		1	SUR	*dom*	R. Apintie, Paramaribo
4996		5	RUS	STF	RWM, Moscow
5000		20	CHN	STF	BPM, Pucheng
		10	HWA	STF	WWVH NIST, Kauai, HI

kHz	N	kW	Ctry	Site	Station, location
		2	KOR	STF	HLA, Daejeon
		10	USA	STF	WWV NIST, Fort Collins, CO
5005	†	50	GNE	*dom*	Rdif Guinea Ecuatorial, Bata
5010	†±	10	MDG	*dom*	R. Nal Malagasy, Ambohidrano
		100	USA	rmi	Adventist World R. (AWR), USA
		100	USA	rmi	Alameda Bible Fellowship, USA
		100	USA	rmi	Encore Classical Music, G
		100	USA	rmi	Family R., USA
		100	USA	rmi	R. Prague International, CZE
		100	USA	rmi	R. Slovakia International, SVK
		100	USA	rmi	R. Taiwan International (RTI), TWN
		100	USA	rmi	RAE - Argentina Al Mundo, ARG
		100	USA	rmi	World of Radio, USA
		100	USA	rmi	WRMI - R. Miami International, USA
5020		5	SLM	*dom*	Solomon Islands BC, Honiara
5025		100	CUB	*dom*	R. Rebelde, Bauta
		5	PRU	*dom*	R. Quillabamba, Quillabamba
5035	†	10	B	*dom*	R. Aparecida, Aparecida
	†	5	B	*dom*	R. Educação Rural, Coari
5040		100	CUB	hab	R. Habana Cuba, CUB
		50	IND	*dom*	AIR, Jeypore
		5	VUT	*dom*	R. Vanuatu, Port Vila
5050		50	CHN	nnn	Beibu Bay R., CHN
	‡	4.5	IND	*dom*	AIR, Aizawl
5055		1	AUS	*dom*	4KZ, Innisfail Qld
5060		100	CHN	*dom*	Xinjiang PBS, Urumqi
5085		100	USA	tww	WTWW, USA
5130		15	KGZ	bis	R. Sadaye Zindagi, CAN
		100	USA	bcq	Hobart R. International, AUS
5800		100	USA	rmi	Encore Classical Music, G
		100	USA	rmi	R. Prague International, CZE
		100	USA	rmi	R. Taiwan International (RTI), TWN
		100	USA	rmi	RAE - Argentina Al Mundo, ARG
		100	USA	rmi	Supreme Master TV, USA
		100	USA	rmi	The Overcomer Ministry, USA
		100	USA	rmi	VORW R. International, USA
		100	USA	rmi	World of Radio, USA
		100	USA	rmi	WRMI - R. Miami International, USA
5805		0.25	DNK	hvi	Radio 208, DNK
5825		0.1	CHL	*dom*	R. Triunfal Evangélica, Talagante
		0.15	DNK	hil	R. Oz-Viola, DNK
5830	†	100	USA	tww	WTWW, USA
5840		0.1	DNK	brg	World Music Radio (WMR), DNK
5845		250	PHL	pht	BBC World Service, G
5850		100	USA	rmi	Alameda Bible Fellowship, USA
		100	USA	rmi	Encore Classical Music, G
		100	USA	rmi	Hobart R. International, AUS
		100	USA	rmi	R. Slovakia International, SVK
		100	USA	rmi	RAE - Argentina Al Mundo, ARG
		100	USA	rmi	Shortwave Radiogram, USA
		100	USA	rmi	Supreme Master TV, USA
		100	USA	rmi	The Overcomer Ministry, USA
		100	USA	rmi	VORW R. International, USA
		100	USA	rmi	World of Radio, USA
		100	USA	rmi	WRMI - R. Miami International, USA
5860		250	KWT	kwt	R. Farda, USA
5875		300	ARM	erv	BBC World Service, G
		250	ASC	asc	BBC World Service, G
		250	BUL	sof	BBC World Service, G
		250	CVA	smg	BBC World Service, G
		250	G	wof	BBC World Service, G
		250	THA	udo	R. Thailand World Service, THA
5880		250	PHL	pht	VO America (VOA), USA
5885		250	KWT	kwt	VO America (VOA), USA
5890		250	KWT	kwt	R. Free Asia (RFA), USA
		250	KWT	kwt	VO America (VOA), USA
		250	SNG	sng	BBC World Service, G
		250	THA	udo	VO America (VOA), USA
		100	USA	wcr	The Overcomer Ministry, USA
		100	USA	wcr	WWCR, USA
5895		0.3	NOR	erd	R. Northern Star/The Ferry, NOR

kHz	N	kW	Ctry	Site	Station, location
		250	TJK	dsb	BBC World Service, G
		100	UZB	tac	Furusato no Kaze/Ilbon-u Baram, KRE
		300	UZB	tac	Furusato no Kaze/Ilbon-u Baram, KRE
		100	UZB	tac	IBRA Media, S
5900		100	BUL	sof	Bible Voice Broadcasting (BVB), CAN
		50	BUL	sof	Bible Voice Broadcasting (BVB), CAN
		50	BUL	sof	R. Taiwan International (RTI), TWN
5905		100	ALS	nls	KNLS International, ALS
		100	CHN	kas	China R. International (CRI), CHN
		10	D	pin	Deutscher Wetterdienst (DWD), D
		100	GUM	sda	AWR Asia/Pacific, THA
5910		500	CHN	bei	China R. International (CRI), CHN
		250	CUB	qvc	China R. International (CRI), CHN
		250	G	wof	WLC Radio, USA
		300	ROU	tig	R. Romania International, ROU
5915		50	BRM	*dom*	Myanma R., Naypyitaw
		500	CHN	bei	China R. International (CRI), CHN
		100	CHN	huh	China R. International (CRI), CHN
		100	CHN	kas	China R. International (CRI), CHN
5920		1.5	D	wnm	R. HCJB Deutschland, D
		10	KOR	jan	Voice of Freedom, KRE
		250	PHL	pht	Vatican R., CVA
		300	ROU	tig	R. Romania International, ROU
		100	USA	hri	WHRI, USA
		250	USA	hri	WHRI, USA
5925		100	CHN	*dom*	CNR5 Vo Zhonghua, Beijing
		500	F	iss	R. France International (RFI), F
		500	IRN	sir	Pars Today (VOIRI), IRN
		300	ROU	gal	R. Romania International, ROU
		50	VTN	*dom*	VO Vietnam 2, Xuan Mai
5930		300	AUT	mos	BBC World Service, G
		500	IRN	sir	Pars Today (VOIRI), IRN
		100	ROU	tig	R. Romania International, ROU
		100	STP	sao	VO America (VOA), USA
5935	†	1	BOL	*dom*	R. Yura, Yura
		100	CHN	*dom*	Xizang PBS, Lhasa
		250	D	nau	Bible Voice Broadcasting (BVB), CAN
		500	IRN	zah	Pars Today (VOIRI), IRN
		300	ROU	tig	R. Romania International, ROU
		100	USA	wcr	The Overcomer Ministry, USA
		100	USA	wcr	University Network, USA
		100	USA	wcr	WWCR, USA
5940		10	B	*dom*	R. Voz Missionária, Camboriú
	‡	20	ETH	*dom*	Ethiopian Somali Regional State Radio, Jigjiga
		500	F	iss	R. Algeriénnne, ALG
		500	IRN	sir	Pars Today (VOIRI), IRN
		90	ROU	tig	R. Romania International, ROU
		250	UAE	dha	R. Sadaye Zindagi, CAN
5945		100	CHN	*dom*	CNR1 VO China, Beijing
	+	300	ROU	tig	R. Romania International, ROU
		250	TUR	emr	Voice of Turkey (VOT), TUR
		100	UZB	tac	Furusato no Kaze/Ilbon-u Baram, KRE
		100	UZB	tac	Pan American Broadcasting, USA
5950		125	D	nau	Adventist World R. (AWR), USA
		125	D	nau	AWR Africa, G
		100	ETH	*dom*	VO Tigray Revolution, Geja
		250	F	iss	KBS World R., KOR
		500	IRN	sir	Pars Today (VOIRI), IRN
		100	USA	rmi	Family R., USA
		100	USA	rmi	Hobart R. International, AUS
		100	USA	rmi	RAE - Argentina Al Mundo, ARG
		100	USA	rmi	Supreme Master TV, USA
		100	USA	rmi	WRMI - R. Miami International, USA
5952	†	5	BOL	*dom*	R. Pío XII, Siglo Veinte
5955		150	CHN	bei	China R. International (CRI), CHN
		500	CHN	xia	China R. International (CRI), CHN
		100	GUM	sda	AWR Asia/Pacific, THA
		100	ROU	tig	R. Romania International, ROU
	+	40	ROU	tig	R. Romania International, ROU
		300	TWN	tsh	R. Taiwan International (RTI), TWN

kHz	N	kW	Ctry	Site	Station, location
5960		100	CHN	*dom*	Xinjiang PBS, Urumqi
		125	D	nau	The Mighty KBC, HOL
		250	KWT	kbd	R. Kuwait, KWT
		250	OMA	sla	BBC World Service, G
		500	TUR	emr	Voice of Turkey (VOT), TUR
5965		500	CHN	bei	China R. International (CRI), CHN
		100	CHN	kas	China R. International (CRI), CHN
		500	CHN	xia	China R. International (CRI), CHN
		500	TUR	emr	Voice of Turkey (VOT), TUR
5970		300	ARM	erv	BBC World Service, G
		500	CHN	xia	China R. International (CRI), CHN
		15	CHN	*dom*	Gannan PBS, Hezuo
		250	OMA	sla	BBC World Service, G
		200	TJK	dsb	R. Free Asia (RFA), USA
		500	TUR	emr	Voice of Turkey (VOT), TUR
		100	USA	ewn	WEWN - EWTN Shortwave, USA
5975		250	ASC	asc	BBC World Service, G
		500	CHN	bei	China R. International (CRI), CHN
		100	CHN	*dom*	CNR8, Beijing
		125	G	wof	BBC World Service, G
	+	50	NZL	ran	RNZ Pacific (RNZI), NZL
		125	OMA	sla	BBC World Service, G
		250	SNG	sng	BBC World Service, G
		50	VTN	*dom*	VO Vietnam 1, Hanoi
5980		300	AUT	mos	Adventist World R. (AWR), USA
		500	CHN	xia	China R. International (CRI), CHN
		0.1	FIN	vir	Scandinavian Weekend R., FIN
		500	IRN	sir	Pars Today (VOIRI), IRN
		1	PRU	*dom*	R. Chaski, Urubamba
		500	TUR	emr	Voice of Turkey (VOT), TUR
		250	USA	grv	R. Martí, USA
5985		50	BRM	*dom*	Myanma R., Yangon
		50	BRM	yan	R. Japan (NHK World), J
		500	CHN	bei	China R. International (CRI), CHN
		500	CHN	xia	China R. International (CRI), CHN
		300	J	yam	R. Japan (NHK World), J
		250	TUR	emr	Voice of Turkey (VOT), TUR
		200	TWN	tsh	National Unity R., KRE
		100	USA	rmi	Alameda Bible Fellowship, USA
		100	USA	rmi	R. Japan (NHK World), J
		100	USA	rmi	WRMI - R. Miami International, USA
5990		50	BUL	sof	R. Taiwan International (RTI), TWN
		100	CHN	huh	China R. International (CRI), CHN
	†	50	CHN	*dom*	Qinghai PBS, Xining
		250	CUB	qvc	China R. International (CRI), CHN
		300	J	yam	Shiokaze, KRE
		300	ROU	gal	R. Romania International, ROU
5995		50	BUL	sof	Bible Voice Broadcasting (BVB), CAN
	±	100	KOR	jnm	Echo of Hope (VOH), KRE
	†	50	MLI	*dom*	R. Mali, Bamako (Kati)
		250	UAE	dha	BBC World Service, G
	†	35	ZMB	*dom*	ZNBC R. One, Lusaka
6000		100	CHN	*dom*	CNR1 VO China, Beijing
		100	CUB	hab	R. Habana Cuba, CUB
		250	CUB	hab	R. Habana Cuba, CUB
		250	CUB	qvc	R. Habana Cuba, CUB
		500	IRN	sir	Pars Today (VOIRI), IRN
		100	RUS	arm	GTRK "Adygeya", RUS
		500	TUR	emr	Voice of Turkey (VOT), TUR
6005		125	ASC	asc	BBC World Service, G
		50	BUL	sof	R. Taiwan International (RTI), TWN
		1	D	kll	R. Poland, POL
		1	D	kll	R. Prague International, CZE
		1	D	kll	R. Slovakia International, SVK
		1	D	kll	R. Tirana International, ALB
		1	D	kll	R. Ukraine International (RUI), UKR
		1	D	kll	SRG SSR Swiss B'casting Corp., SUI
		1	D	kll	Voice of Mongolia, MNG
		1	HOL	elb	R. Delta International, HOL
6010	†	5	B	*dom*	R. Inconfidência, Belo Horizonte
		500	CHN	bei	China R. International (CRI), CHN
		500	CHN	uru	China R. International (CRI), CHN
		100	CHN	*dom*	CNR11 Tibetan Sce, Baoji-Sifan
		250	CVA	smg	Vatican R., CVA
		100	UZB	tac	BBC World Service, G
6015		100	CHN	*dom*	Xinjiang PBS, Urumqi
		100	KOR	hwa	KBS World R., KOR
		50	TZA	dol	Zanzibar Broadcasting Corp., TZA
6020		100	CHN	kas	China R. International (CRI), CHN
		500	CHN	szg	China R. International (CRI), CHN
		1	HOL	elb	R. Delta International, HOL
		300	ROU	gal	R. Romania International, ROU
		100	STP	sao	VO America (VOA), USA
		20	VTN	*dom*	VO Vietnam 1, Buôn Ma Thuôt
6025		500	CHN	xia	China R. International (CRI), CHN
		100	CHN	lha	CTB - Holy Tibet, CHN
		100	CHN	*dom*	Xizang PBS, Lhasa
	+	90	ROU	tig	R. Romania International, ROU
6030		1	CAF	*dom*	R. Ndeke Luka, Boali
		1	CAF	*dom*	R. Water for Good, Boali
	†	0.1	CAN	*dom*	CFVP Calgary, AB
	+	30	CHN	*dom*	CNR1 VO China, Beijing
	†	100	ETH	*dom*	R. Oromia, Geja
	†	250	IND	*dom*	AIR, Delhi
		250	IND	*dom*	AIR, Delhi (Radio Sadayee Kashmir)
		250	IND	del	R. Sedayee Kashmir, PAK
	+	90	ROU	gal	R. Romania International, ROU
	+	90	ROU	tig	R. Romania International, ROU
		250	USA	grv	R. Martí, USA
6035	†	30	BTN	*dom*	Bhutan BS, Thimpu
	†	50	CHN	sha	Yunnan RTV International, CHN
6040	‡	7.5	B	*dom*	R. Evangelizar AM, Curitiba
		500	CHN	uru	China R. International (CRI), CHN
		500	CHN	xia	China R. International (CRI), CHN
		150	CHN	*dom*	CNR2 Business R., Beijing
		50	CHN	*dom*	Nei Menggu-Mo, Hohhot
		500	F	iss	R. Algeriénnne, ALG
		500	F	iss	R. France International (RFI), F
		250	G	wof	KBS World R., KOR
		500	IRN	sir	Pars Today (VOIRI), IRN
		300	ROU	gal	R. Romania International, ROU
	+	90	ROU	gal	R. Romania International, ROU
		300	ROU	tig	R. Romania International, ROU
		100	STP	sao	VO America (VOA), USA
6045		300	G	wof	KBS World R., KOR
		300	J	yam	Shiokaze, KRE
		300	TWN	tsh	Furusato no Kaze/Ilbon-u Baram, KRE
6050		100	CHN	*dom*	Xizang PBS, Lhasa
		1	EQU	qui	Vozandes Media, EQA
		1	LBR	*dom*	ELWA R., Monrovia
		250	TUR	emr	Voice of Turkey (VOT), TUR
6055		100	CHN	nnn	China R. International (CRI), CHN
		125	D	nau	Ev. Missions-Gemeinden, D
		50	J	*dom*	R. Nikkei 1, Tokyo
		100	MDG	mdc	AWR Africa, G
6060		150	CHN	kun	China R. International (CRI), CHN
		15	CHN	*dom*	Sichuan Ethnic R, Chengdu
		100	CUB	hab	R. Habana Cuba, CUB
		500	F	iss	R. Algeriénnne, ALG
		500	IRN	zah	Pars Today (VOIRI), IRN
		250	KWT	kwt	RFE/RL, USA
		100	UZB	tac	Pan American Broadcasting, USA
6065		100	CHN	kas	China R. International (CRI), CHN
		150	CHN	*dom*	CNR2 Business R., Beijing
		100	MDG	mdc	AWR Africa, G
		100	ZMB	luv	Voice of Hope - Africa, ZMB
6070		100	AUT	mos	R. DARC, D
	†	1	CAN	*dom*	CFRX Toronto, ON
		500	CHN	bei	China R. International (CRI), CHN
		500	CHN	xia	China R. International (CRI), CHN
	†	8	D	rob	Channel 292, D
		8	D	rob	Encore Classical Music, G

kHz	N	kW	Ctry	Site	Station, location
		8	D	rob	Isle of Music/Melting Pot, USA
		8	D	rob	R. DARC, D
		8	D	rob	R. For Peace Int. (RFPI), F
		200	KRE	kng	Voice of Korea, KRE
		250	OMA	sla	BBC World Service, G
		500	TUR	emr	Voice of Turkey (VOT), TUR
6075		100	ALS	nls	KNLS International, ALS
		100	CHN	kas	China R. International (CRI), CHN
		15	CHN	*dom*	CNR1 VO China, Yushu
		500	IRN	sir	Pars Today (VOIRI), IRN
		300	J	yam	R. Japan (NHK World), J
		100	TWN	kou	R. Taiwan International (RTI), TWN
6080		100	ARM	erv	The Mighty KBC, HOL
		10	B	*dom*	R. Marumby, Curitiba
		500	CHN	bei	China R. International (CRI), CHN
		100	CHN	*dom*	CNR1 VO China, Golmud
		7	CHN	*dom*	Hulun Buir PBS, Hailar
		125	D	nau	Bible Voice Broadcasting (BVB), CAN
		250	G	wof	BBC World Service, G
		100	STP	sao	VO America (VOA), USA
6085		1	D	kll	R. Mi Amigo International, E
	‡	10	IND	*dom*	AIR, Gangtok
		500	IRN	sir	Pars Today (VOIRI), IRN
		300	J	yam	Shiokaze, KRE
6090		150	CHN	kun	China R. International (CRI), CHN
		500	CHN	uru	China R. International (CRI), CHN
		500	CHN	xia	China R. International (CRI), CHN
		100	CHN	*dom*	CNR2 Business R., Golmud
		100	ETH	*dom*	Amhara R., Geja
		250	G	wof	KBS World R., KOR
		500	IRN	sir	Pars Today (VOIRI), IRN
		300	J	yam	R. Japan (NHK World), J
		250	OMA	sla	BBC World Service, G
6095		500	CHN	kas	China R. International (CRI), CHN
		100	D	nau	R. SE-TA2, D
		100	D	nau	The Mighty KBC, HOL
		250	KOR	kim	KBS World R., KOR
		250	OMA	sla	BBC World Service, G
6100	†	100	AFG	kab	R.Television Afghanistan (RTA), AFG
		500	CHN	bei	China R. International (CRI), CHN
		150	CHN	kun	China R. International (CRI), CHN
		100	CHN	uru	China R. International (CRI), CHN
		500	CHN	uru	China R. International (CRI), CHN
		500	CHN	xia	China R. International (CRI), CHN
		100	CUB	hab	R. Habana Cuba, CUB
		250	IND	*dom*	AIR, Delhi (Radio Sadayee Kashmir)
		250	IND	del	R. Sedayee Kashmir, PAK
	†	125	KRE	*dom*	KCBS, Kanggye
		100	SWZ	man	TWR Africa, AFS
6105	‡	6	BOL	*dom*	R. Panamericana, La Paz
		500	CHN	szg	China R. International (CRI), CHN
		500	F	iss	R. Algeriénne, ALG
		500	F	iss	R. Japan (NHK World), J
		100	TWN	kou	R. Taiwan International (RTI), TWN
6110		100	ALS	nls	KNLS International, ALS
		500	CHN	xia	China R. International (CRI), CHN
		100	CHN	lha	CTB - Holy Tibet, CHN
		100	CHN	*dom*	Xizang PBS, Lhasa
		100	ETH	*dom*	R. Fana, Geja
		50	IND	*dom*	AIR, Kashmir, Srinagar
		500	IRN	sir	Pars Today (VOIRI), IRN
6115		500	CHN	bei	China R. International (CRI), CHN
	†	50	COG	*dom*	R. Congo, Brazzaville
		1	D	hst	R. SE-TA2, D
		50	J	*dom*	R. Nikkei 2, Tokyo
		50	NZL	ran	RNZ Pacific (RNZI), NZL
		250	PHL	pht	Vatican R., CVA
		100	USA	wcr	The Overcomer Ministry, USA
		100	USA	wcr	WWCR, USA
6120		100	ALS	nls	KNLS International, ALS
		300	AUT	mos	Adventist World R. (AWR), USA
		100	CHN	*dom*	Xinjiang PBS, Urumqi
		250	D	nau	AWR Africa, G
		125	D	nau	Pan American Broadcasting, USA
		500	TUR	emr	Voice of Turkey (VOT), TUR
6125		100	CHN	*dom*	CNR1 VO China, Beijing
		100	CHN	*dom*	CNR1 VO China, Shijiazhuang
		500	TUR	emr	Voice of Turkey (VOT), TUR
		250	USA	grv	R. Martí, USA
6130		100	CHN	lha	CTB - Holy Tibet, CHN
		100	CHN	*dom*	Xizang PBS, Lhasa
		500	IRN	sir	Pars Today (VOIRI), IRN
	‡	50	LAO	vie	Lao National R., LAO
	‡	50	LAO	*dom*	R. Nationale Lao, Vientiane
		300	ROU	gal	R. Romania International, ROU
		100	SWZ	man	TWR Africa, AFS
6135		250	ASC	asc	BBC World Service, G
	†	10	B	*dom*	R. Aparecida, Aparecida
	‡	10	BOL	*dom*	R. Santa Cruz, Santa Cruz
		500	CHN	bei	China R. International (CRI), CHN
		100	CHN	xia	China R. International (CRI), CHN
		250	CVA	smg	BBC World Service, G
	†	30	MDG	*dom*	R. Nal Malagasy, Ambohidrano
6140		100	AUT	mos	Welle 370, D
		100	CHN	kas	China R. International (CRI), CHN
		100	CHN	kun	China R. International (CRI), CHN
		500	F	iss	R. Algeriénne, ALG
	†	0.5	HOL	bor	R. Onda, BEL
6145		150	CHN	bei	China R. International (CRI), CHN
		100	CHN	*dom*	CNR17 Kazakh Sce, Lingshi
	†	50	CHN	*dom*	Qinghai PBS, Xining
		300	J	yam	Shiokaze, KRE
		300	ROU	gal	R. Romania International, ROU
		100	TWN	kou	R. Taiwan International (RTI), TWN
		250	PHL	pht	Vatican R., CVA
6150		500	CHN	szg	China R. International (CRI), CHN
		0.2	D	dat	Europa 24, D
		500	IRN	sir	Pars Today (VOIRI), IRN
		125	OMA	sla	BBC World Service, G
		250	PHL	pht	BBC World Service, G
		300	ROU	gal	R. Romania International, ROU
		250	THA	udo	VO America (VOA), USA
		250	UAE	dha	BBC World Service, G
6155		300	AUT	mos	R. Japan (NHK World), J
		300	AUT	mos	R. Ö1 (ORF), AUT
		500	CHN	bei	China R. International (CRI), CHN
		150	CHN	*dom*	CNR2 Business R., Beijing
		100	KOR	kim	KBS World R., KOR
		100	TJK	dsb	AWR Africa, G
		100	TJK	dsb	AWR Asia/Pacific, THA
		300	TWN	tsh	Furusato no Kaze/Ilbon-u Baram, KRE
		100	UZB	tac	R. Japan (NHK World), J
6160		1	B	*dom*	Rádio Rio Mar, Manaus
	†	1	B	*dom*	Rede Boa Vontade, Porto Alegre
		500	CHN	xia	China R. International (CRI), CHN
		1	D	wis	Shortwave Radio, D
		500	IRN	sir	Pars Today (VOIRI), IRN
		50	USA	bcq	R. For Peace Int. (RFPI), F
	†±	50	USA	bcq	WBCQ, USA
	±	50	USA	bcq	World of Radio, USA
6165		50	BRM	*dom*	Thazin R., Pyin U Lwin
		250	CHN	bei	China R. International (CRI), CHN
		500	CHN	uru	China R. International (CRI), CHN
		100	CHN	*dom*	CNR6 VO Shenzhou, Beijing
		125	D	nau	R. Japan (NHK World), J
		500	F	iss	R. Japan (NHK World), J
	‡	100	TCD	*dom*	ONRTV, N'Djamena-Gredia
		100	UZB	tac	R. Japan (NHK World), J
		50	VTN	*dom*	VO Vietnam Min, Xuan Mai
6170		250	ASC	asc	VO America (VOA), USA
		250	BUL	sof	BBC World Service, G
		0.1	FIN	vir	Scandinavian Weekend R., FIN

kHz	N	kW	Ctry	Site	Station, location
		200	KRE	kuj	Voice of Korea, KRE
		300	ROU	tig	R. Romania International, ROU
		250	UAE	dha	FEBA Pakistan, PAK
6174		1	PRU	*dom*	R. Tawantinsuyo, Cusco
6175		100	BOT	bot	VOA Studio 7, USA
		100	CHN	nnn	China R. International (CRI), CHN
		500	CHN	xia	China R. International (CRI), CHN
		100	CHN	*dom*	CNR1 VO China, Beijing
	+	90	ROU	tig	R. Romania International, ROU
6180		100	B	*dom*	R. Nac. da Amazônia, Brasília
		250	BUL	sof	BBC World Service, G
		100	CHN	kas	China R. International (CRI), CHN
		100	CHN	kun	China R. International (CRI), CHN
		150	CHN	kun	China R. International (CRI), CHN
		500	CHN	uru	China R. International (CRI), CHN
		100	CHN	*dom*	CNR17 Kazakh Sce, Lingshi
		250	CUB	qvc	China R. International (CRI), CHN
		10	D	pin	Deutscher Wetterdienst (DWD), D
		300	G	wof	Follow The Bible Ministries, USA
		100	MDG	mwv	Madagascar World Voice (MWV), MDG
		300	ROU	tig	R. Romania International, ROU
		300	TWN	tsh	R. Taiwan International (RTI), TWN
		250	UAE	dha	IBRA Media, S
6185		300	AUT	mos	Adventist World R. (AWR), USA
		15	CHN	*dom*	China Huayi BC, Fuzhou
		500	CHN	xia	China R. International (CRI), CHN
		250	CVA	smg	Vatican R., CVA
		200	KRE	kuj	Voice of Korea, KRE
		1.5	MEX	*dom*	Señal Cultura México, México
		500	TUR	emr	Voice of Turkey (VOT), TUR
		300	TWN	tsh	R. Taiwan International (RTI), TWN
6190		500	CHN	bei	China R. International (CRI), CHN
		100	CHN	*dom*	CNR2 Business R., Golmud
		50	CHN	*dom*	Xinjiang PBS, Urumqi
		300	J	yam	R. Japan (NHK World), J
6195		125	ASC	asc	BBC World Service, G
		100	BOT	bot	VO America (VOA), USA
		1	HOL	hee	Mike Radio, HOL
		125	OMA	sla	BBC World Service, G
		250	OMA	sla	BBC World Service, G
		250	SNG	sng	BBC World Service, G
		100	STP	sao	BBC World Service, G
		100	STP	sao	VO America (VOA), USA
		100	USA	hri	R. Japan (NHK World), J
		250	USA	hri	R. Japan (NHK World), J
6200		100	CHN	lha	CTB - Holy Tibet, CHN
		50	CHN	*dom*	VO Jinling, Nanjing
		100	CHN	*dom*	Xizang PBS, Lhasa
6210		1	COD	*dom*	R. Kahuzi, Bukavu
6215	±	1	TWN	ust	Sound of Hope, CHN
6230	±	1	TWN	ust	Sound of Hope, CHN
6240		100	UZB	tac	Bible Voice Broadcasting (BVB), CAN
		100	UZB	tac	TWR Europe & CAMENA, SVK
6245	±	10	KOR	nwn	Echo of Hope (VOH), KRE
6250	‡	20	GNE	*dom*	Rdif Guinea Ecuatorial, Malabo
		100	KRE	pyo	Echo of Unification, KOR
6270		100	ARM	erv	Radyo Iran International, IRN
6280	±	1	TWN	ust	Sound of Hope, CHN
6350	±	100	KOR	jnm	Echo of Hope (VOH), KRE
6370	±	1	TWN	ust	Sound of Hope, CHN
6400		50	KRE	kng	Pyongyang Broadcasting Station, KRE
6520	±	50	KOR	goy	Voice of the People, KRE
6600	±	50	KOR	goy	Voice of the People, KRE
6730	±	1	TWN	ust	Sound of Hope, CHN
6870	±	1	TWN	ust	Sound of Hope, CHN
6900	±	1	TWN	ust	Sound of Hope, CHN
6970	±	1	TWN	ust	Sound of Hope, CHN
7120	‡	100	SOM	*dom*	R. Hargeisa
		0.1	SOM	*dom*	Warsan Radio, Baidoa
7140	†	100	ERI	*dom*	VO Broad Masses 1, Asmara
7180	†	100	ERI	*dom*	VO Broad Masses 2, Asmara
7200		200	TWN	tsh	National Unity R., KRE
7205		150	CHN	bei	China R. International (CRI), CHN
		500	CHN	bei	China R. International (CRI), CHN
		100	CHN	kas	China R. International (CRI), CHN
		500	CHN	xia	China R. International (CRI), CHN
		100	CHN	*dom*	Xinjiang PBS, Urumqi
		500	F	iss	R. France International (RFI), F
	†	100	SDN	*dom*	SRTC, Al-Fitahab
7210		150	CHN	bei	China R. International (CRI), CHN
		100	CHN	uru	China R. International (CRI), CHN
		500	CHN	uru	China R. International (CRI), CHN
		20	CHN	*dom*	Yunnan PBS, Kunming
		200	KRE	kuj	Voice of Korea, KRE
		300	ROU	tig	R. Romania International, ROU
	±	1	TWN	ust	Sound of Hope, CHN
		20	VTN	*dom*	VO Vietnam 1, Buôn Ma Thuôt
7215		500	CHN	bei	China R. International (CRI), CHN
		500	CHN	kun	China R. International (CRI), CHN
		500	CHN	szg	China R. International (CRI), CHN
		500	CHN	xia	China R. International (CRI), CHN
		100	CHN	*dom*	CNR1 VO China, Shijiazhuang
		250	KOR	kim	KBS World R., KOR
7220	‡	10	CAF	*dom*	R. Centrafrique, Bangui
		500	CHN	jin	China R. International (CRI), CHN
		500	CHN	xia	China R. International (CRI), CHN
		100	CHN	*dom*	CNR2 Business R., Golmud
		100	CVA	smg	BBC World Service, G
		200	KRE	kuj	Voice of Korea, KRE
		300	ROU	gal	R. Romania International, ROU
	+	90	ROU	gal	R. Romania International, ROU
		100	VTN	vni	Voice of Vietnam (VOV), VTN
	‡	100	VTN	vni	Voice of Vietnam (VOV), VTN
7225		500	CHN	bei	China R. International (CRI), CHN
		500	CHN	uru	China R. International (CRI), CHN
		10	CHN	*dom*	Sichuan Ethnic R, Chengdu
		250	D	nau	AWR Africa, G
		100	D	bib	VO America (VOA), USA
		500	IRN	sir	Pars Today (VOIRI), IRN
7230		100	CHN	*dom*	CNR1 VO China, Xianyang
		50	CHN	*dom*	Xinjiang PBS, Urumqi
		100	CVA	smg	Vatican R., CVA
		500	IRN	sir	Pars Today (VOIRI), IRN
7235		100	CHN	kas	China R. International (CRI), CHN
		500	CHN	kas	China R. International (CRI), CHN
		100	CVA	smg	Vatican R., CVA
		500	F	iss	Deutsche Welle, D
		200	KRE	kuj	Voice of Korea, KRE
		300	ROU	tig	R. Romania International, ROU
	+	90	ROU	tig	R. Romania International, ROU
		100	STP	sao	Deutsche Welle, D
7240		500	ARS	riy	Saudi R. International (SBA), ARS
		100	CHN	kas	China R. International (CRI), CHN
		100	CHN	*dom*	Xizang PBS, Lhasa
		500	TUR	emr	Voice of Turkey (VOT), TUR
7245		150	CHN	bji	China R. International (CRI), CHN
		500	CHN	kas	China R. International (CRI), CHN
		500	CHN	xia	China R. International (CRI), CHN
		150	CHN	*dom*	CNR2 Business R., Beijing
		250	CVA	smg	R. Japan (NHK World), J
		250	F	iss	Alameda Bible Fellowship, USA
		500	F	iss	R. Algeriénne, ALG
		300	MDA	kch	TWR Africa, AFS
		100	TJK	dsb	Voice of Tajik (Ovozi Tojik), TJK
		250	TUR	emr	Voice of Turkey (VOT), TUR
7250		100	CHN	kas	China R. International (CRI), CHN
		500	CHN	uru	China R. International (CRI), CHN
		250	CVA	smg	Vatican R., CVA
	†	100	IND	*dom*	AIR, Delhi
		250	KWT	kbd	R. Kuwait, KWT
7255		150	CHN	bei	China R. International (CRI), CHN

kHz	N	kW	Ctry	Site	Station, location
		150	CHN	bji	China R. International (CRI), CHN
		500	CHN	kas	China R. International (CRI), CHN
		500	CHN	kun	China R. International (CRI), CHN
		500	CHN	szg	China R. International (CRI), CHN
		500	CHN	xia	China R. International (CRI), CHN
		100	CHN	*dom*	CNR2 Business R., Baoji
		100	CHN	lha	CTB - Holy Tibet, CHN
		100	CHN	*dom*	Xizang PBS, Lhasa
		250	NIG	aja	Voice of Nigeria, NIG
		100	STP	sao	VOA Studio 7, USA
7260		100	CHN	kas	China R. International (CRI), CHN
		500	CHN	uru	China R. International (CRI), CHN
		500	CHN	xia	China R. International (CRI), CHN
		100	CHN	*dom*	Xinjiang PBS, Urumqi
	†	50	MNG	*dom*	Mongolian R. 3, Ulaanbaatar
7265		500	CHN	bei	China R. International (CRI), CHN
		100	CHN	kas	China R. International (CRI), CHN
		500	CHN	kun	China R. International (CRI), CHN
		500	CHN	uru	China R. International (CRI), CHN
	†	100	CHN	*dom*	CNR2 Business R., Baoji-Sifan
		250	D	nau	R. Japan (NHK World), J
		250	G	wof	BBC World Service, G
		125	MDG	mdc	BBC World Service, G
		125	OMA	sla	BBC World Service, G
		500	TUR	emr	Voice of Turkey (VOT), TUR
7270		300	AUT	mos	AWR Africa, G
		50	CHN	*dom*	Nei Menggu-Mo, Hohhot
	†	100	IND	*dom*	AIR, Chennai (FM Gold)
		300	J	yam	Shiokaze, KRE
7275		300	AUT	mos	AWR Africa, G
		500	CHN	uru	China R. International (CRI), CHN
		100	CHN	*dom*	CNR1 VO China, Beijing
		7	CHN	*dom*	Guizhou PBS, Guiyang
		100	CHN	*dom*	Xinjiang PBS, Urumqi
		100	KOR	kim	KBS World R., KOR
		250	KOR	kim	KBS World R., KOR
		100	STP	sao	VO America (VOA), USA
7280		500	IRN	sir	Pars Today (VOIRI), IRN
		300	MDA	kch	TWR India, IND
		500	TUR	emr	Voice of Turkey (VOT), TUR
	±	1	TWN	ust	Sound of Hope, CHN
		100	VTN	vni	Voice of Vietnam (VOV), VTN
7285		500	CHN	bei	China R. International (CRI), CHN
		100	CHN	kas	China R. International (CRI), CHN
		500	CHN	kun	China R. International (CRI), CHN
		500	CHN	xia	China R. International (CRI), CHN
	+	50	NZL	ran	RNZ Pacific (RNZI), NZL
		250	OMA	sla	BBC World Service, G
		100	VTN	vni	Voice of Vietnam (VOV), VTN
7290		100	BUL	sof	IRRS Shortwave, I
		50	BUL	sof	World of Radio, USA
		100	CHN	kas	China R. International (CRI), CHN
		500	CHN	szg	China R. International (CRI), CHN
		500	CHN	xia	China R. International (CRI), CHN
		100	CHN	*dom*	CNR1 VO China, Beijing
		100	D	bib	VOA Ashna R., USA
	†	10	INS	*dom*	RRI, Nabire
		500	IRN	sir	Pars Today (VOIRI), IRN
		250	KWT	kwt	VOA Ashna R., USA
		300	ROU	tig	R. Romania International, ROU
		300	TWN	tsh	Furusato no Kaze/Ilbon-u Baram, KRE
7295		500	CHN	uru	China R. International (CRI), CHN
		100	CHN	uru	Xinjiang BC Station - VO China, CHN
		100	CHN	*dom*	Xinjiang PBS, Urumqi
		500	F	iss	R. Algeriénnne, ALG
		500	F	iss	R. France International (RFI), F
	‡	4.5	IND	*dom*	AIR, Aizawl
		300	J	yam	Shiokaze, KRE
		100	MLI	bko	China R. International (CRI), CHN
		300	TWN	tsh	Furusato no Kaze/Ilbon-u Baram, KRE
7300		100	CHN	kas	China R. International (CRI), CHN
		500	CHN	kas	China R. International (CRI), CHN
		500	CHN	uru	China R. International (CRI), CHN
		250	G	wof	Reach Beyond, USA
		500	IRN	sir	Pars Today (VOIRI), IRN
		250	OMA	sla	BBC World Service, G
		300	TWN	tsh	R. Taiwan International (RTI), TWN
		250	UAE	dha	BBC World Service, G
7305		250	ASC	asc	BBC World Service, G
		150	CHN	bei	China R. International (CRI), CHN
		500	CHN	uru	China R. International (CRI), CHN
		100	CHN	*dom*	CNR1 VO China, Shijiazhuang
		500	IRN	sir	Pars Today (VOIRI), IRN
		250	USA	grv	Vatican R., CVA
7310		100	CHN	*dom*	Xinjiang PBS, Urumqi
		500	IRN	zah	Pars Today (VOIRI), IRN
		300	ROU	tig	R. Romania International, ROU
	±	1	TWN	ust	Sound of Hope, CHN
7315		500	CHN	kas	China R. International (CRI), CHN
		100	CHN	kun	China R. International (CRI), CHN
		500	CHN	kun	China R. International (CRI), CHN
		150	CHN	*dom*	CNR2 Business R., Xianyang
		250	CVA	smg	R. Dabanga, SDN
		500	F	iss	R. Algeriénne, ALG
		250	F	iss	R. Tamazuj, SSD
	+	15	USA	inb	The Overcomer Ministry, USA
		250	USA	hri	WHRI, USA
	+	50	USA	inb	WINB, USA
7320		500	CHN	kun	China R. International (CRI), CHN
		250	PHL	pht	Vatican R., CVA
		100	ROU	tig	R. Romania International, ROU
7325		500	CHN	bei	China R. International (CRI), CHN
		500	CHN	jin	China R. International (CRI), CHN
		100	CHN	kas	China R. International (CRI), CHN
		150	CHN	kun	China R. International (CRI), CHN
		500	CHN	kun	China R. International (CRI), CHN
		500	CHN	szg	China R. International (CRI), CHN
		500	CHN	uru	China R. International (CRI), CHN
		500	CHN	xia	China R. International (CRI), CHN
		250	D	nau	AWR Africa, G
		300	G	wof	BBC World Service, G
	†	1	PNG	*dom*	Wantok R. Light, Mount Hagen
		300	ROU	gal	R. Romania International, ROU
		300	ROU	tig	R. Romania International, ROU
		100	STP	sao	BBC World Service, G
7330		100	AUT	mos	R. Joystick, D
		500	CHN	kas	China R. International (CRI), CHN
		500	CHN	xia	China R. International (CRI), CHN
		300	ROU	tig	R. Romania International, ROU
7335		500	CHN	bei	China R. International (CRI), CHN
		500	CHN	jin	China R. International (CRI), CHN
		500	CHN	szg	China R. International (CRI), CHN
		100	CHN	*dom*	CNR2 Business R., Baoji-Sifan
		250	CVA	smg	BBC World Service, G
7340		500	CHN	kas	China R. International (CRI), CHN
		100	CHN	*dom*	Xinjiang PBS, Urumqi
		250	CVA	smg	Eye R., SSD
7345		50	BRM	*dom*	Thazin R., Pyin U Lwin
		500	CHN	kas	China R. International (CRI), CHN
		100	CHN	*dom*	CNR1 VO China, Beijing
		300	ROU	tig	R. Romania International, ROU
	+	50	USA	grv	R. Martí, USA
7350		100	CHN	kas	China R. International (CRI), CHN
		500	CHN	kas	China R. International (CRI), CHN
		500	CHN	uru	China R. International (CRI), CHN
		100	CHN	*dom*	CNR11 Tibetan Sce, Baoji-Sifan
		250	D	nau	AWR Africa, G
	±	250	F	iss	Dengê Welat, TUR
	+	90	ROU	tig	R. Romania International, ROU
7355		500	IRN	sir	Pars Today (VOIRI), IRN
		250	SNG	sng	BBC World Service, G
		250	USA	grv	R. Martí, USA

kHz	N	kW	Ctry	Site	Station, location
7360		100	CHN	kas	China R. International (CRI), CHN
		100	CHN	kun	China R. International (CRI), CHN
		500	CHN	xia	China R. International (CRI), CHN
		100	CHN	*dom*	CNR11 Tibetan Sce, Baoji-Sifan
		250	CVA	smg	Vatican R., CVA
		100	GUM	sda	AWR Asia/Pacific, THA
		500	IRN	sir	Pars Today (VOIRI), IRN
		250	IRN	zah	Pars Today (VOIRI), IRN
		300	ROU	gal	R. Romania International, ROU
7365		500	CHN	bei	China R. International (CRI), CHN
		100	CHN	*dom*	CNR1 VO China, Shijiazhuang
		250	CVA	smg	Vatican R., CVA
		100	D	nau	Bible Voice Broadcasting (BVB), CAN
		3	D	wnm	R. HCJB Deutschland, D
		250	USA	grv	R. Martí, USA
7370		100	ALS	nls	KNLS International, ALS
		100	CHN	kas	China R. International (CRI), CHN
		100	CHN	nnn	China R. International (CRI), CHN
		150	CHN	*dom*	CNR2 Business R., Beijing
		300	ROU	gal	R. Romania International, ROU
7375		150	CHN	*dom*	CNR2 Business R., Beijing
		500	F	iss	R. Algeriénnne, ALG
		500	IRN	sir	Pars Today (VOIRI), IRN
		300	ROU	gal	R. Romania International, ROU
		250	USA	grv	R. Martí, USA
7380		150	CHN	bji	China R. International (CRI), CHN
		500	F	iss	R. France International (RFI), F
		500	IND	bgl	All India R. (AIR), IND
		500	IRN	zah	Pars Today (VOIRI), IRN
7385		500	CHN	kas	China R. International (CRI), CHN
		100	CHN	*dom*	CNR5 Vo Zhonghua, Beijing
		100	CHN	lha	CTB - Holy Tibet, CHN
		100	CHN	*dom*	Xizang PBS, Lhasa
		100	USA	hri	WHRI, USA
7390		150	CHN	bei	China R. International (CRI), CHN
		100	CHN	huh	China R. International (CRI), CHN
		500	CHN	jin	China R. International (CRI), CHN
		500	CHN	xia	China R. International (CRI), CHN
		500	F	iss	R. France International (RFI), F
7395		100	ALS	nls	KNLS International, ALS
		500	CHN	kas	China R. International (CRI), CHN
		500	CHN	kun	China R. International (CRI), CHN
		500	CHN	uru	China R. International (CRI), CHN
		500	CHN	xia	China R. International (CRI), CHN
		150	CHN	*dom*	CNR2 Business R., Xianyang
7400		100	CHN	kun	China R. International (CRI), CHN
7405		500	CHN	bei	China R. International (CRI), CHN
7410		500	CHN	bei	China R. International (CRI), CHN
		500	CHN	jin	China R. International (CRI), CHN
		100	CHN	kas	China R. International (CRI), CHN
		500	CHN	szg	China R. International (CRI), CHN
		250	CVA	smg	Vatican R., CVA
		300	ROU	gal	R. Romania International, ROU
		300	ROU	tig	R. Romania International, ROU
		100	UZB	tac	AWR Asia/Pacific, THA
7415		100	CHN	huh	China R. International (CRI), CHN
		500	CHN	kas	China R. International (CRI), CHN
		500	CHN	uru	China R. International (CRI), CHN
		500	CHN	xia	China R. International (CRI), CHN
		250	MRA	tin	R. Free Asia (RFA), USA
7420		150	CHN	kun	China R. International (CRI), CHN
		500	CHN	uru	China R. International (CRI), CHN
		500	CHN	xia	China R. International (CRI), CHN
		100	CHN	*dom*	Nei Menggu-Ch, Hohhot
		250	PHL	pht	Vatican R., CVA
		300	ROU	tig	R. Romania International, ROU
		250	TJK	dsb	R. Free Asia (RFA), USA
7425		100	CHN	kas	China R. International (CRI), CHN
		150	CHN	*dom*	CNR2 Business R., Xianyang
		250	G	wof	R. Ndarason Internationale, TCD
		500	IRN	sir	Pars Today (VOIRI), IRN

kHz	N	kW	Ctry	Site	Station, location
7430		500	CHN	jin	China R. International (CRI), CHN
		100	CHN	nnn	China R. International (CRI), CHN
		500	IRN	sir	Pars Today (VOIRI), IRN
		100	TWN	pao	R. Taiwan International (RTI), TWN
7435		500	CHN	bei	China R. International (CRI), CHN
		500	CHN	jin	China R. International (CRI), CHN
		500	CHN	kun	China R. International (CRI), CHN
		500	CHN	szg	China R. International (CRI), CHN
		500	CHN	xia	China R. International (CRI), CHN
		500	IRN	sir	Pars Today (VOIRI), IRN
		250	USA	grv	R. Martí, USA
7440		500	CHN	bei	China R. International (CRI), CHN
		500	CHN	jin	China R. International (CRI), CHN
		100	CHN	nnn	China R. International (CRI), CHN
7445		300	ARM	erv	BBC World Service, G
		125	ASC	asc	BBC World Service, G
		500	CHN	kun	China R. International (CRI), CHN
		500	CHN	uru	China R. International (CRI), CHN
		500	F	iss	R. Japan (NHK World), J
		250	G	wof	BBC World Service, G
		500	IRN	sir	Pars Today (VOIRI), IRN
		300	J	yam	R. Japan (NHK World), J
		250	MDG	mdc	BBC World Service, G
		250	PHL	pht	Vatican R., CVA
		250	THA	udo	VO America (VOA), USA
7450		100	CHN	*dom*	Xizang PBS, Lhasa
		500	F	iss	R. Japan (NHK World), J
7455		100	BOT	bot	VO America (VOA), USA
		100	SWZ	man	TWR Africa, AFS
7460		100	BOT	bot	VO America (VOA), USA
		250	PHL	pht	VO America (VOA), USA
	±	1	TWN	ust	Sound of Hope, CHN
7465		125	OMA	sla	BBC World Service, G
		250	PHL	pht	VO America (VOA), USA
		250	SNG	sng	BBC World Service, G
7470		100	D	lam	VOA Deewa R., USA
		250	THA	udo	VO America (VOA), USA
		250	TJK	dsb	R. Free Asia (RFA), USA
7475		100	D	bib	VO America (VOA), USA
		250	THA	udo	R. Thailand World Service, THA
		250	THA	udo	RFE/RL, USA
7480		250	KWT	kwt	R. Free Asia (RFA), USA
7485		100	D	lam	VO America (VOA), USA
		300	MDA	kch	BBC World Service, G
		250	PHL	pht	Vatican R., CVA
		250	SNG	sng	BBC World Service, G
7488	±	100	TJK	dsb	Voice of Tibet, CHN
7490		50	USA	bcq	Isle of Music/Melting Pot, USA
		50	USA	bcq	The Overcomer Ministry, USA
		100	USA	wcr	The Overcomer Ministry, USA
	†±	50	USA	bcq	WBCQ, USA
	±	50	USA	bcq	World of Radio, USA
		100	USA	wcr	WWCR, USA
7495		100	D	bib	VOA Deewa R., USA
		250	KWT	kwt	VOA Ashna R., USA
		250	THA	udo	VOA Ashna R., USA
		250	THA	udo	VOA Deewa R., USA
7500		200	GUM	twr	TWR Asia, SNG
	+	90	GUM	twr	TWR Asia, SNG
7505		100	IND	*dom*	AIR, Delhi
		300	MDA	kch	TWR India, IND
	†	50	USA	rno	WRNO Worldwide, USA
7510		300	ARM	erv	IBRA Media, S
		200	GUM	twr	TWR Asia, SNG
		200	TJK	dsb	R. Free Asia (RFA), USA
7515		200	GUM	twr	Living Water Ministry, USA
		250	THA	udo	VO America (VOA), USA
7520		250	KWT	kwt	R. Free Asia (RFA), USA
		100	TJK	dsb	Bible Voice Broadcasting (BVB), CAN
		250	USA	hri	WHRI, USA
		100	USA	wcr	WWCR, USA

kHz	N	kW	Ctry	Site	Station, location
7525		250	PHL	pht	VO America (VOA), USA
7530		250	KWT	kwt	VOA Deewa R., USA
		100	UZB	tac	VO the Martyrs Korea, KOR
7540		250	KWT	kwt	R. Free Asia (RFA), USA
		200	TJK	dsb	R. Free Asia (RFA), USA
7545		250	PHL	pht	VO America (VOA), USA
		200	TJK	dsb	R. Free Asia (RFA), USA
7550	+	200	IND	bgl	All India R. (AIR), IND
		100	UZB	tac	Free North Korea R., KRE
7555	†	100	IND	*dom*	AIR, Delhi
		100	TJK	dsb	Bible Voice Broadcasting (BVB), CAN
7560		250	THA	udo	VO America (VOA), USA
7565		250	KWT	kwt	R. Free Asia (RFA), USA
		100	UZB	tac	R. Japan (NHK World), J
7570		200	KRE	kuj	Voice of Korea, KRE
		100	USA	rmi	Supreme Master TV, USA
		100	USA	rmi	WRMI - R. Miami International, USA
7580		100	D	lam	R. Farda, USA
		200	KRE	kuj	Voice of Korea, KRE
		250	KWT	kwt	VO America (VOA), USA
		250	THA	udo	R. Farda, USA
		200	TJK	dsb	R. Free Asia (RFA), USA
7585		250	KWT	kwt	R. Farda, USA
7590		300	MDA	kch	TWR India, IND
		100	UZB	tac	North Korea Reform R., KRE
7600	±	1	TWN	ust	Sound of Hope, CHN
		100	UZB	tac	Free North Korea R., KRE
7625		100	UZB	tac	Voice of Wilderness, KRE
7650	±	1	TWN	ust	Sound of Hope, CHN
7665		200	TJK	dsb	R. Free Asia (RFA), USA
7730	±	1	TWN	ust	Sound of Hope, CHN
		100	USA	rmi	Alameda Bible Fellowship, USA
		100	USA	rmi	Hobart R. International, AUS
		100	USA	rmi	RAE - Argentina Al Mundo, ARG
		100	USA	rmi	Shortwave Radiogram, USA
		100	USA	rmi	The Overcomer Ministry, USA
		100	USA	rmi	VORW R. International, USA
		100	USA	rmi	World of Radio, USA
		100	USA	rmi	WRMI - R. Miami International, USA
7780		100	USA	rmi	Alameda Bible Fellowship, USA
		100	USA	rmi	Hobart R. International, AUS
		100	USA	rmi	R. For Peace Int. (RFPI), F
		100	USA	rmi	R. Prague International, CZE
		100	USA	rmi	R. Slovakia International, SVK
		100	USA	rmi	R. Taiwan International (RTI), TWN
		100	USA	rmi	R. Tirana International, ALB
		100	USA	rmi	RAE - Argentina Al Mundo, ARG
		100	USA	rmi	Shortwave Radiogram, USA
		100	USA	rmi	Supreme Master TV, USA
		100	USA	rmi	The Overcomer Ministry, USA
		100	USA	rmi	VORW R. International, USA
		100	USA	rmi	World of Radio, USA
		100	USA	rmi	WRMI - R. Miami International, USA
7810	±	1	TWN	ust	Sound of Hope, CHN
7850		5	CAN	STF	CHU, Ottawa
9080	±	1	TWN	ust	Sound of Hope, CHN
9095	±	10	KOR	nwn	Echo of Hope (VOH), KRE
9120	±	1	TWN	ust	Sound of Hope, CHN
9155	±	1	TWN	ust	Sound of Hope, CHN
9180	±	1	TWN	ust	Sound of Hope, CHN
9200	±	1	TWN	ust	Sound of Hope, CHN
9215	±	1	TWN	ust	Sound of Hope, CHN
9230	±	1	TWN	ust	Sound of Hope, CHN
9255	±	1	TWN	ust	Sound of Hope, CHN
9265		50	USA	inb	Shortwave Radiogram, USA
	+	15	USA	inb	The Overcomer Ministry, USA
	+	50	USA	inb	WINB, USA
		50	USA	inb	WINB, USA
9280	±	1	TWN	ust	Sound of Hope, CHN
9290		300	ARM	erv	TWR India, IND
9315		200	TJK	dsb	R. Free Asia (RFA), USA

kHz	N	kW	Ctry	Site	Station, location
9320	±	1	TWN	ust	Sound of Hope, CHN
9330		250	USA	bcq	WLC Radio, USA
		500	USA	bcq	WLC Radio, USA
9335		250	PHL	pht	VO America (VOA), USA
9340		250	PHL	pht	VO America (VOA), USA
9350		200	TJK	dsb	R. Free Asia (RFA), USA
		100	USA	wcr	The Overcomer Ministry, USA
		100	USA	wcr	WWCR, USA
9355		250	KWT	kwt	VOA Deewa R., USA
		250	THA	udo	VO America (VOA), USA
9370		250	THA	udo	VOA Deewa R., USA
9380		250	PHL	pht	VO America (VOA), USA
		100	SWZ	man	TWR Africa, AFS
		200	TJK	dsb	R. Free Asia (RFA), USA
9385		250	USA	ewn	WEWN - EWTN Shortwave, USA
9390		100	D	bib	VO America (VOA), USA
		100	MRA	sai	R. Free Asia (RFA), USA
		250	MRA	tin	R. Free Asia (RFA), USA
9395		100	USA	rmi	R. Slovakia International, SVK
		100	USA	rmi	RAE - Argentina Al Mundo, ARG
		100	USA	rmi	Supreme Master TV, USA
		100	USA	rmi	The Overcomer Ministry, USA
		100	USA	rmi	WRMI - R. Miami International, USA
9400		100	BUL	sof	Bible Voice Broadcasting (BVB), CAN
		100	BUL	sof	Isle of Music/Melting Pot, USA
		100	BUL	sof	The Overcomer Ministry, USA
		300	TWN	kou	R. Taiwan International (RTI), TWN
9410		500	CHN	kas	China R. International (CRI), CHN
		100	MRA	sai	R. Free Asia (RFA), USA
		125	OMA	sla	BBC World Service, G
		250	OMA	sla	BBC World Service, G
		100	STP	sao	BBC World Service, G
		500	TUR	emr	Voice of Turkey (VOT), TUR
	†	10	TWN	*dom*	Fu Hsing BS
		250	UAE	dha	BBC World Service, G
9415		500	CHN	bei	China R. International (CRI), CHN
		500	CHN	xia	China R. International (CRI), CHN
		300	TWN	pao	R. Taiwan International (RTI), TWN
9420		100	CHN	*dom*	CNR13 Uyghur Sce, Lingshi
		100	CHN	*dom*	CNR6 VO Shenzhou, Beijing
	†	170	GRC	avl	Voice of Greece, GRC
9425		200	KRE	kuj	Voice of Korea, KRE
		300	TWN	pao	R. Taiwan International (RTI), TWN
9430		300	TWN	pao	R. Taiwan International (RTI), TWN
9435		200	KRE	kuj	Voice of Korea, KRE
9440		150	CHN	kun	China R. International (CRI), CHN
		500	CHN	kun	China R. International (CRI), CHN
		100	CHN	nnn	China R. International (CRI), CHN
		500	CHN	xia	China R. International (CRI), CHN
		125	D	nau	Bible Voice Broadcasting (BVB), CAN
	‡	125	EGY	abs	R. Cairo, EGY
9445		200	KRE	kuj	Voice of Korea, KRE
9450		100	CHN	kas	China R. International (CRI), CHN
		500	CHN	kas	China R. International (CRI), CHN
		100	CHN	uru	China R. International (CRI), CHN
	‡	125	CLN	trm	AWR Asia/Pacific, THA
		250	D	nau	Bible Voice Broadcasting (BVB), CAN
		100	MRA	sai	R. Free Asia (RFA), USA
		100	PHL	boc	FEBC Philippines, PHL
9455		150	CHN	kun	China R. International (CRI), CHN
		100	CHN	*dom*	CNR1 VO China, Lingshi
		250	KWT	kwt	R. Free Asia (RFA), USA
		100	MRA	sai	R. Free Asia (RFA), USA
		100	USA	rmi	Encore Classical Music, G
		100	USA	rmi	The Overcomer Ministry, USA
		100	USA	rmi	WRMI - R. Miami International, USA
9460		100	CHN	kas	China R. International (CRI), CHN
		150	CHN	kun	China R. International (CRI), CHN
		100	CHN	nnn	China R. International (CRI), CHN
		500	CHN	uru	China R. International (CRI), CHN
		100	UZB	tac	AWR Asia/Pacific, THA

kHz	N	kW	Ctry	Site	Station, location
9470		100	CHN	xia	China R. International (CRI), CHN
		100	CHN	*dom*	CNR1 VO China, Beijing
		100	CHN	*dom*	Xinjiang PBS, Urumqi
		100	D	lam	RFE/RL, USA
		100	GUM	sda	AWR Asia/Pacific, THA
	‡	250	USA	ewn	WEWN - EWTN Shortwave, USA
9475		500	IRN	sir	Pars Today (VOIRI), IRN
		250	PHL	pht	R. Pilipinas (DZRP), PHL
	†	100	USA	tww	WTWW, USA
9480		100	CHN	*dom*	CNR11 Tibetan Sce, Baoji-Sifan
9485		100	BOT	bot	VO America (VOA), USA
		300	G	wof	VO America (VOA), USA
		250	KWT	kwt	VO America (VOA), USA
9490		100	CHN	kas	China R. International (CRI), CHN
		150	CHN	kun	China R. International (CRI), CHN
		100	CHN	lha	CTB - Holy Tibet, CHN
		100	CHN	*dom*	Xizang PBS, Lhasa
		100	D	bib	RFE/RL, USA
		150	F	iss	R. República, CUB
		250	PHL	pht	VO America (VOA), USA
	+	90	ROU	tig	R. Romania International, ROU
		300	TWN	tsh	R. Taiwan International (RTI), TWN
9495		500	IRN	sir	Pars Today (VOIRI), IRN
		250	TUR	emr	Voice of Turkey (VOT), TUR
9500		100	CHN	*dom*	CNR1 VO China, Shijiazhuang
		100	D	nau	Reach Beyond, USA
		100	SWZ	man	TWR Africa, AFS
9505		100	SDN	alf	VO Africa - Sudan R., SDN
		500	TUR	emr	Voice of Turkey (VOT), TUR
9510		50	CHN	*dom*	Xinjiang PBS, Urumqi
		125	CLN	trm	AWR Asia/Pacific, THA
		250	CVA	smg	VO America (VOA), USA
	‡	125	EGY	abs	R. Cairo, EGY
		250	MRA	tin	R. Free Asia (RFA), USA
		100	ROU	tig	IRRS Shortwave, I
		250	SNG	sng	BBC World Service, G
9515		100	CHN	kas	China R. International (CRI), CHN
		150	CHN	*dom*	CNR2 Business R., Beijing
		250	G	wof	IBRA Media, S
		100	KOR	kim	KBS World R., KOR
		250	KOR	kim	KBS World R., KOR
		250	MDG	mdc	AWR Africa, G
9520		500	CHN	uru	China R. International (CRI), CHN
		50	CHN	*dom*	Nei Menggu-Ch, Hohhot
9525		500	CHN	kas	China R. International (CRI), CHN
	±	250	F	iss	Dengê Welat, TUR
		300	TWN	pao	R. Taiwan International (RTI), TWN
9530		100	CHN	*dom*	CNR11 Tibetan Sce, Baoji-Sifan
		500	IRN	zah	Pars Today (VOIRI), IRN
		50	VTN	*dom*	VO Vietnam 1, Xuan Mai
9535		100	ALS	nls	KNLS International, ALS
		250	ASC	asc	R. Ndarason Internationale, TCD
		150	CHN	bji	China R. International (CRI), CHN
		100	CHN	kun	China R. International (CRI), CHN
		500	CHN	xia	China R. International (CRI), CHN
		100	CUB	hab	R. Habana Cuba, CUB
		250	G	wof	R. Ndarason Internationale, TCD
		250	KWT	kwt	R. Free Asia (RFA), USA
9540		300	ARM	erv	IBRA Media, S
		500	CHN	bei	China R. International (CRI), CHN
		500	CHN	kun	China R. International (CRI), CHN
	‡	125	EGY	abs	R. Cairo, EGY
	±	1	TWN	ust	Sound of Hope, CHN
		250	UAE	dha	IBRA Media, S
		100	UZB	tac	FEBA India, IND
9545	‡	125	EGY	abs	R. Cairo, EGY
		250	G	wof	BBC World Service, G
		300	G	wof	BBC World Service, G
		5	SLM	*dom*	Solomon Islands BC, Honiara
		300	TWN	pao	R. Taiwan International (RTI), TWN
9550		10	B	*dom*	R. Boa Vontade, Porto Alegre
		500	CHN	bei	China R. International (CRI), CHN
		150	CHN	kun	China R. International (CRI), CHN
		500	IRN	sir	Pars Today (VOIRI), IRN
		100	STP	sao	VO America (VOA), USA
9555		500	ARS	riy	Saudi R. International (SBA), ARS
		150	CHN	bei	China R. International (CRI), CHN
		200	TWN	pao	R. Taiwan International (RTI), TWN
9560		150	CHN	bei	China R. International (CRI), CHN
		100	CHN	kas	China R. International (CRI), CHN
		500	CHN	uru	China R. International (CRI), CHN
		100	CHN	*dom*	Xinjiang PBS, Urumqi
		300	J	yam	R. Japan (NHK World), J
		250	MDG	mdc	R. Japan (NHK World), J
		250	PHL	pht	BBC World Service, G
		125	SNG	sng	BBC World Service, G
		300	TWN	pao	Furusato no Kaze/Ilbon-u Baram, KRE
9565		500	CHN	kun	China R. International (CRI), CHN
		250	USA	grv	R. Martí, USA
9570		100	ALS	nls	KNLS International, ALS
		500	CHN	bei	China R. International (CRI), CHN
		100	CHN	*dom*	CNR2 Business R., Golmud
		250	CUB	qvc	China R. International (CRI), CHN
		500	F	iss	Deutsche Welle, D
		100	KOR	kim	KBS World R., KOR
9575		100	STP	sao	VO America (VOA), USA
9580		300	ARM	erv	AWR Africa, G
		100	CHN	lha	CTB - Holy Tibet, CHN
		100	CHN	*dom*	Xizang PBS, Lhasa
		500	F	iss	R. France International (RFI), F
		500	IND	bgl	All India R. (AIR), IND
		250	KOR	kim	KBS World R., KOR
		250	MRA	sai	Vatican R., CVA
		250	PHL	pht	Vatican R., CVA
		250	SNG	sng	BBC World Service, G
		250	UAE	dha	R. Japan (NHK World), J
9585		500	CHN	kas	China R. International (CRI), CHN
		250	PHL	pht	VO America (VOA), USA
		205	SNG	sng	BBC World Service, G
		100	SWZ	man	TWR Africa, AFS
		250	UAE	dha	BBC World Service, G
9590		50	BRM	*dom*	Thazin R., Pyin U Lwin
		500	CHN	kas	China R. International (CRI), CHN
		150	CHN	kun	China R. International (CRI), CHN
		500	CHN	szg	China R. International (CRI), CHN
9595		500	TUR	emr	Voice of Turkey (VOT), TUR
9600		150	CHN	bji	China R. International (CRI), CHN
		500	CHN	kas	China R. International (CRI), CHN
		150	CHN	kun	China R. International (CRI), CHN
		125	OMA	sla	BBC World Service, G
		300	ROU	tig	R. Romania International, ROU
9605		100	ALS	nls	KNLS International, ALS
		250	PHL	pht	VO America (VOA), USA
		250	USA	hri	KBS World R., KOR
		250	USA	hri	WHRI, USA
9610		100	CHN	kas	China R. International (CRI), CHN
		100	CHN	kun	China R. International (CRI), CHN
		150	CHN	kun	China R. International (CRI), CHN
		100	CHN	*dom*	CNR8, Beijing
		100	D	nau	Adventist World R. (AWR), USA
		100	D	nau	Voice of Oromo Liberation, ETH
		100	GUM	sda	AWR Asia/Pacific, THA
		300	ROU	gal	R. Romania International, ROU
		250	ROU	tig	R. Romania International, ROU
		500	TUR	emr	Voice of Turkey (VOT), TUR
		300	TWN	pao	R. Taiwan International (RTI), TWN
9615		500	CHN	uru	China R. International (CRI), CHN
9620		500	CHN	kas	China R. International (CRI), CHN
		100	CHN	kun	China R. International (CRI), CHN
		150	CHN	*dom*	CNR2 Business R., Beijing
		250	IND	*dom*	AIR, Aligarh
		250	IND	alg	All India R. (AIR), IND

kHz	N	kW	Ctry	Site	Station, location
		250	PHL	pht	VO America (VOA), USA
		300	ROU	tig	R. Romania International, ROU
		500	TUR	emr	Voice of Turkey (VOT), TUR
9625		100	ALS	nls	KNLS International, ALS
		300	J	yam	R. Japan (NHK World), J
		500	TUR	emr	Voice of Turkey (VOT), TUR
		300	TWN	pao	R. Taiwan International (RTI), TWN
9630		300	AUT	mos	AWR Africa, G
	†	10	B	*dom*	R. Aparecida, Aparecida
		500	CHN	jin	China R. International (CRI), CHN
		100	CHN	*dom*	CNR1 VO China, Golmud
		100	CHN	*dom*	CNR17 Kazakh Sce, Lingshi
		250	KOR	kim	KBS World R., KOR
9635		500	F	iss	R. France International (RFI), F
		250	G	wof	R. Ndarason Internationale, TCD
	†	50	MLI	*dom*	R. Mali, Bamako (Kati)
	±	1	TWN	ust	Sound of Hope, CHN
9636	±	100	VTN	*dom*	VO Vietnam 1, Son Tay
9640		500	CHN	kas	China R. International (CRI), CHN
		100	KOR	kim	KBS World R., KOR
9645		500	CHN	bei	China R. International (CRI), CHN
		500	CHN	kun	China R. International (CRI), CHN
		100	CHN	*dom*	CNR1 VO China, Beijing
		100	CVA	smg	Vatican R., CVA
		250	CVA	smg	Vatican R., CVA
		100	GUM	sda	AWR Asia/Pacific, THA
		100	KOR	kim	KBS World R., KOR
9650		100	ARS	riy	Saudi R. International (SBA), ARS
		50	CUB	bej	R. Habana Cuba, CUB
	‡	125	EGY	abs	R. Cairo, EGY
	†	50	GUI	*dom*	RTG, Conakry
		200	KRE	kuj	Voice of Korea, KRE
		300	TWN	pao	R. France International (RFI), F
9655		100	CHN	kas	China R. International (CRI), CHN
		100	CHN	kun	China R. International (CRI), CHN
		150	CHN	kun	China R. International (CRI), CHN
		500	CHN	kun	China R. International (CRI), CHN
		100	CHN	nnn	China R. International (CRI), CHN
	+	30	CHN	*dom*	CNR1 VO China, Urumqi
9660		500	F	iss	R. France International (RFI), F
		500	IRN	sir	Pars Today (VOIRI), IRN
		500	TUR	emr	Voice of Turkey (VOT), TUR
		100	TWN	kou	R. Taiwan International (RTI), TWN
9665		100	ALS	nls	KNLS International, ALS
		10	B	*dom*	R. Voz Missionária, Camboriú
		500	CHN	jin	China R. International (CRI), CHN
		100	CHN	kas	China R. International (CRI), CHN
		500	CHN	kun	China R. International (CRI), CHN
		500	CHN	xia	China R. International (CRI), CHN
		100	CHN	*dom*	CNR5 Vo Zhonghua, Beijing
	†	50	KRE	*dom*	KCBS, Pyongyang
		250	MDG	mdc	R. France International (RFI), F
9670	†	8	D	rob	Channel 292, D
		8	D	rob	Encore Classical Music, G
		8	D	rob	Isle of Music/Melting Pot, USA
		8	D	rob	R. DARC, D
		250	THA	udo	VO America (VOA), USA
		250	TJK	dsb	R. Free Asia (RFA), USA
		300	TWN	pao	R. DLSN, VTN
9675		500	ARS	riy	Saudi R. International (SBA), ARS
		500	CHN	kas	China R. International (CRI), CHN
		150	CHN	kun	China R. International (CRI), CHN
		100	CHN	*dom*	CNR1 VO China, Beijing
9680		500	F	iss	R. Taiwan International (RTI), TWN
		300	J	yam	R. Japan (NHK World), J
		300	TWN	tsh	R. Taiwan International (RTI), TWN
		100	ZMB	luv	Voice of Hope - Africa, ZMB
9685		150	CHN	bji	China R. International (CRI), CHN
		500	CHN	kas	China R. International (CRI), CHN
		500	CHN	kun	China R. International (CRI), CHN
		500	CHN	uru	China R. International (CRI), CHN

kHz	N	kW	Ctry	Site	Station, location
		500	CHN	xia	China R. International (CRI), CHN
		100	CHN	*dom*	CNR5 Vo Zhonghua, Beijing
9690		150	CHN	kun	China R. International (CRI), CHN
		100	E	nob	R. Exterior de España (REE), E
		200	TJK	dsb	R. Free Asia (RFA), USA
		300	TWN	pao	Furusato no Kaze/Ilbon-u Baram, KRE
9695		500	ARS	riy	Saudi R. International (SBA), ARS
		500	CHN	bei	China R. International (CRI), CHN
		500	CHN	jin	China R. International (CRI), CHN
		100	CHN	kas	China R. International (CRI), CHN
		500	CHN	kun	China R. International (CRI), CHN
9700		100	CUB	hab	R. Habana Cuba, CUB
		250	CVA	smg	R. Veritas Asia, PHL
		250	KWT	kwt	R. Free Asia (RFA), USA
		500	TUR	emr	Voice of Turkey (VOT), TUR
9705		500	CHN	kas	China R. International (CRI), CHN
		100	CHN	uru	Xinjiang BC Station - VO China, CHN
		100	CHN	*dom*	Xinjiang PBS, Urumqi
		250	CVA	smg	Vatican R., CVA
		300	TWN	pao	Furusato no Kaze/Ilbon-u Baram, KRE
9710		500	CHN	kas	China R. International (CRI), CHN
		100	CHN	*dom*	CNR1 VO China, Shijiazhuang
9715		100	ALS	nls	KNLS International, ALS
		100	AUT	mos	Bible Voice Broadcasting (BVB), CAN
9720		100	ALS	nls	KNLS International, ALS
		50	BUL	sof	R. Erena, ERI
		500	CHN	uru	China R. International (CRI), CHN
		500	CHN	xia	China R. International (CRI), CHN
		150	CHN	*dom*	CNR2 Business R., Baoji-Xinjie
		500	CHN	xia	CRI - VO South China Sea, CHN
		100	MRA	sai	R. Free Asia (RFA), USA
		250	PHL	pht	Vatican R., CVA
9725		500	F	iss	R. France International (RFI), F
		500	IRN	sir	Pars Today (VOIRI), IRN
9730		100	ALS	nls	KNLS International, ALS
		50	BRM	*dom*	Myanma R., Yangon
		500	CHN	bei	China R. International (CRI), CHN
		100	CHN	kas	China R. International (CRI), CHN
		500	CHN	kas	China R. International (CRI), CHN
		100	CHN	kun	China R. International (CRI), CHN
		200	KRE	kuj	Voice of Korea, KRE
	±	1	TWN	ust	Sound of Hope, CHN
		100	VTN	vni	Voice of Vietnam (VOV), VTN
9735		300	TWN	pao	R. Taiwan International (RTI), TWN
9740		125	CLN	trm	AWR Asia/Pacific, THA
		100	GUM	sda	AWR Asia/Pacific, THA
		250	KOR	kim	KBS World R., KOR
		300	ROU	tig	R. Romania International, ROU
		300	TWN	pao	R. Taiwan International (RTI), TWN
9745		500	CHN	uru	China R. International (CRI), CHN
		300	TWN	pao	R. Taiwan International (RTI), TWN
9750		50	CHN	*dom*	Nei Menggu-Mo, Hohhot
		250	CVA	smg	BBC World Service, G
		100	D	bib	VO America (VOA), USA
		100	D	lam	VO America (VOA), USA
		300	J	yam	R. Japan (NHK World), J
		250	KWT	kbd	R. Kuwait, KWT
9755		100	CHN	*dom*	CNR2 Business R., Baoji-Sifan
		500	IRN	sir	Pars Today (VOIRI), IRN
9760		500	CHN	kun	China R. International (CRI), CHN
		250	THA	udo	VO America (VOA), USA
9765		300	ARM	erv	AWR Asia/Pacific, THA
		150	CHN	bji	China R. International (CRI), CHN
		100	CHN	nnn	China R. International (CRI), CHN
		250	D	nau	R. Japan (NHK World), J
		250	G	wof	VO America (VOA), USA
		100	MDG	mwv	Madagascar World Voice (MWV), MDG
		250	THA	udo	VOA Deewa R., USA
9770		300	AUT	mos	Adventist World R. (AWR), USA
		500	CHN	kas	China R. International (CRI), CHN

kHz	N	kW	Ctry	Site	Station, location
		100	KOR	kim	KBS World R., KOR
9774	†	10	TWN	*dom*	Fu Hsing BS
9775		100	BOT	bot	VO America (VOA), USA
		150	CHN	*dom*	CNR2 Business R., Beijing
		250	G	wof	IBRA Media, S
9780		300	AUT	mos	AWR Africa, G
	†	50	CHN	*dom*	Qinghai PBS, Xining
9785		500	CHN	jin	China R. International (CRI), CHN
		150	CHN	kun	China R. International (CRI), CHN
		100	CHN	*dom*	CNR8, Beijing
		125	CLN	trm	AWR Asia/Pacific, THA
9790		100	ARS	riy	Saudi R. International (SBA), ARS
		500	F	iss	R. France International (RFI), F
		250	KWT	kwt	R. Free Asia (RFA), USA
		100	MRA	sai	R. Free Asia (RFA), USA
9795		500	CHN	uru	China R. International (CRI), CHN
		300	J	yam	R. Japan (NHK World), J
		100	PHL	iba	FEBC Philippines, PHL
		250	PHL	pht	VO America (VOA), USA
9800		100	CHN	kas	China R. International (CRI), CHN
		500	CHN	kas	China R. International (CRI), CHN
		250	D	nau	AWR Africa, G
		500	IRN	sir	Pars Today (VOIRI), IRN
		250	PHL	pht	VO America (VOA), USA
		100	TJK	dsb	AWR Asia/Pacific, THA
		300	TWN	pao	Furusato no Kaze/Ilbon-u Baram, KRE
9805		500	F	iss	R. France International (RFI), F
		100	KOR	kim	KBS World R., KOR
9810		100	CHN	*dom*	CNR1 VO China, Nanning
		100	CHN	*dom*	CNR2 Business R., Baoji-Sifan
	‡	125	EGY	abs	R. Cairo, EGY
		500	F	iss	R. France International (RFI), F
		300	ROU	gal	R. Romania International, ROU
9819		10	B	*dom*	R. Nove de Julho, São Paulo
9820		15	CHN	nnn	Beibu Bay R., CHN
		150	CHN	*dom*	CNR2 Business R., Xianyang
	+	90	ROU	tig	R. Romania International, ROU
		250	UAE	dha	BBC World Service, G
9825		100	CHN	uru	China R. International (CRI), CHN
		100	D	lam	VO America (VOA), USA
		250	PHL	pht	VO America (VOA), USA
9830		100	CHN	*dom*	CNR1 VO China, Beijing
		125	D	nau	Adventist World R. (AWR), USA
		500	F	iss	Deutsche Welle, D
		100	STP	sao	Deutsche Welle, D
9835		100	CHN	*dom*	Xinjiang PBS, Urumqi
		500	IRN	sir	Pars Today (VOIRI), IRN
	‡	100	MLA	*dom*	RTM Sarawak FM, Kajang
9840		250	TUR	emr	Voice of Turkey (VOT), TUR
		250	USA	hri	WHRI, USA
	±	100	VTN	vni	Voice of Vietnam (VOV), VTN
	‡±	100	VTN	vni	Voice of Vietnam (VOV), VTN
9845		100	CHN	*dom*	CNR1 VO China, Beijing
		100	MDG	mwv	Madagascar World Voice (MWV), MDG
9850	†	50	CHN	*dom*	Qinghai PBS, Xining
		250	F	iss	AWR Africa, G
		100	F	iss	Dandal Kura R. International, NIG
		200	KRE	kuj	Voice of Korea, KRE
	+†	20	RUS	*dom*	R. Purga, Komsomolsk-na-Amure
	±	1	TWN	ust	Sound of Hope, CHN
		100	VTN	*dom*	VO Vietnam Min, Xuan Mai
9855		500	CHN	bei	China R. International (CRI), CHN
		250	MDG	mdc	R. Japan (NHK World), J
		100	UZB	tac	R. Japan (NHK World), J
9860		500	CHN	jin	China R. International (CRI), CHN
		500	CHN	kas	China R. International (CRI), CHN
		100	CHN	*dom*	CNR1 VO China, Beijing
		250	D	nau	AWR Africa, G
		100	MRA	sai	R. Free Asia (RFA), USA
		250	MRA	tin	R. Free Asia (RFA), USA
9865		500	CHN	kun	China R. International (CRI), CHN
9870		500	ARS	riy	Saudi R. International (SBA), ARS
		100	CHN	kas	China R. International (CRI), CHN
		500	CHN	xia	China R. International (CRI), CHN
	+	30	CHN	*dom*	CNR1 VO China, Qiqihar
		500	IRN	ahw	Pars Today (VOIRI), IRN
		500	IRN	sir	Pars Today (VOIRI), IRN
9875		500	CHN	kas	China R. International (CRI), CHN
		100	GUM	sda	AWR Asia/Pacific, THA
		200	KRE	kuj	Voice of Korea, KRE
9880		500	CHN	bei	China R. International (CRI), CHN
		100	CHN	kun	China R. International (CRI), CHN
		100	CHN	nnn	China R. International (CRI), CHN
		100	MDG	mwv	Madagascar World Voice (MWV), MDG
		250	THA	udo	VO America (VOA), USA
9885		500	ARS	riy	Saudi R. International (SBA), ARS
		100	BOT	bot	VO America (VOA), USA
		250	CVA	smg	VO America (VOA), USA
	‡	125	EGY	abs	R. Cairo, EGY
		100	STP	sao	VO America (VOA), USA
		100	TWN	pao	R. Taiwan International (RTI), TWN
9888	±	100	TJK	dsb	Voice of Tibet, CHN
9890		100	CHN	*dom*	CNR13 Uyghur Sce, Lingshi
		200	KRE	kuj	Voice of Korea, KRE
9895		100	D	bib	R. Farda, USA
		300	J	yam	R. Japan (NHK World), J
9900		125	CLN	trm	BBC World Service, G
	‡	125	EGY	abs	R. Cairo, EGY
		300	TWN	pao	R. Taiwan International (RTI), TWN
9905		100	MRA	sai	R. Free Asia (RFA), USA
9910		300	ARM	erv	TWR India, IND
		100	GUM	twr	TWR Asia, SNG
		200	GUM	twr	TWR Asia, SNG
		250	GUM	twr	TWR Asia, SNG
	+	90	GUM	twr	TWR Asia, SNG
		250	KWT	kwt	R. Free Asia (RFA), USA
9915		125	ASC	asc	BBC World Service, G
		250	G	wof	BBC World Service, G
		250	MDG	mdc	BBC World Service, G
9920		100	PHL	boc	FEBC Philippines, PHL
		100	PHL	iba	FEBC Philippines, PHL
	±	1	TWN	ust	Sound of Hope, CHN
9925		250	PHL	pht	R. Pilipinas (DZRP), PHL
9930	‡	125	CLN	trm	AWR Asia/Pacific, THA
	‡	100	PLW	hbn	T8WH - Hope R., PLW
	‡	100	USA	tww	WTWW, USA
		100	UZB	tac	VO the Martyrs Korea, KOR
9940	‡	125	EGY	abs	R. Cairo, EGY
		250	MRA	tin	R. Free Asia (RFA), USA
		250	THA	udo	R. Thailand World Service, THA
		250	THA	udo	RFE/RL, USA
9950		100	IND	*dom*	AIR, Delhi
		100	IND	del	All India R. (AIR), IND
		300	MDA	kch	TWR India, IND
9955		100	USA	rmi	Alameda Bible Fellowship, USA
		100	USA	rmi	Hobart R. International, AUS
		100	USA	rmi	R. For Peace Int. (RFPI), F
		100	USA	rmi	R. Prague International, CZE
		100	USA	rmi	R. Slovakia International, SVK
		100	USA	rmi	VORW R. International, USA
		100	USA	rmi	World of Radio, USA
		100	USA	rmi	WRMI - R. Miami International, USA
9965		100	PLW	hbn	T8WH - Hope R., PLW
9970	±	1	TWN	ust	Sound of Hope, CHN
9975		100	D	lam	VOA Ashna R., USA
		100	GUM	twr	TWR Asia, SNG
		200	GUM	twr	TWR Asia, SNG
		250	THA	udo	VO America (VOA), USA
9980		100	USA	wcr	WWCR, USA
9985		100	MRA	sai	R. Free Asia (RFA), USA

kHz	N	kW	Ctry	Site	Station, location
		100	MRA	sai	VO America (VOA), USA
9990		250	KWT	kwt	R. Farda, USA
		250	THA	udo	R. Farda, USA
	±	1	TWN	ust	Sound of Hope, CHN
9996		5	RUS	STF	RWM, Moscow
10000		2	ARG	STF	LOL, Buenos Aires
		1	B	STF	PPE Observatório Nal, Rio de Janeiro
		20	CHN	STF	BPM, Pucheng
		10	HWA	STF	WWVH NIST, Kauai, HI
		10	USA	STF	WWV NIST, Fort Collins, CO
10160	±	1	TWN	ust	Sound of Hope, CHN
10820	±	1	TWN	ust	Sound of Hope, CHN
10870	±	1	TWN	ust	Sound of Hope, CHN
10920	±	1	TWN	ust	Sound of Hope, CHN
10960	±	1	TWN	ust	Sound of Hope, CHN
11070	±	1	TWN	ust	Sound of Hope, CHN
11100	±	1	TWN	ust	Sound of Hope, CHN
11120	±	1	TWN	ust	Sound of Hope, CHN
11160	±	1	TWN	ust	Sound of Hope, CHN
11410	±	1	TWN	ust	Sound of Hope, CHN
11440	±	1	TWN	ust	Sound of Hope, CHN
11460	±	1	TWN	ust	Sound of Hope, CHN
11500	±	1	TWN	ust	Sound of Hope, CHN
11520		250	MRA	tin	R. Free Asia (RFA), USA
11530	±	250	F	iss	Dengê Welat, TUR
	±	300	MDA	kch	Dengê Welat, TUR
		250	MRA	tin	R. Free Asia (RFA), USA
	±	1	TWN	ust	Sound of Hope, CHN
11540		250	MRA	tin	R. Free Asia (RFA), USA
11550		100	ARM	erv	Radyo Iran International, IRN
		100	MRA	sai	R. Free Asia (RFA), USA
11560		500	IND	bgl	All India R. (AIR), IND
11570		100	MRA	sai	VO America (VOA), USA
		250	PHL	pht	VO America (VOA), USA
11580		200	GUM	twr	FEBA India, IND
	±	1	TWN	ust	Sound of Hope, CHN
11590		250	KWT	kwt	R. Free Asia (RFA), USA
		250	MRA	tin	R. Free Asia (RFA), USA
11600		100	BUL	sof	The Overcomer Ministry, USA
	±	1	TWN	ust	Sound of Hope, CHN
11610		150	CHN	kun	China R. International (CRI), CHN
		150	CHN	*dom*	CNR2 Business R., Beijing
		250	G	wof	VO America (VOA), USA
		100	GUM	sda	AWR Asia/Pacific, THA
		100	MDG	mwv	Madagascar World Voice (MWV), MDG
		250	THA	udo	VO America (VOA), USA
11620		100	CHN	*dom*	CNR5 Vo Zhonghua, Beijing
		250	CVA	smg	Vatican R., CVA
		100	GUM	sda	AWR Asia/Pacific, THA
		100	IND	del	All India R. (AIR), IND
11630		100	CHN	*dom*	CNR17 Kazakh Sce, Lingshi
		300	J	yam	R. Japan (NHK World), J
		250	KWT	kbd	R. Kuwait, KWT
11635		500	CHN	bei	China R. International (CRI), CHN
		200	KRE	kuj	Voice of Korea, KRE
11640		100	BUL	sof	R. Dabanga, SDN
		500	CHN	bei	China R. International (CRI), CHN
		500	CHN	jin	China R. International (CRI), CHN
		100	CHN	kas	China R. International (CRI), CHN
		500	CHN	kas	China R. International (CRI), CHN
		150	CHN	kun	China R. International (CRI), CHN
		500	CHN	xia	China R. International (CRI), CHN
		500	CHN	xia	CRI - VO South China Sea, CHN
		250	D	nau	AWR Africa, G
		100	MLI	bko	China R. International (CRI), CHN
11645		200	KRE	kuj	Voice of Korea, KRE
11650		100	CHN	kun	China R. International (CRI), CHN
		150	CHN	kun	China R. International (CRI), CHN
		500	CHN	uru	China R. International (CRI), CHN
		250	MDG	mdc	R. Dabanga, SDN
		250	MDG	mdc	R. Tamazuj, SSD
		100	PHL	boc	FEBC Philippines, PHL
		250	THA	udo	VO America (VOA), USA
11655		250	UAE	dha	IBRA Media, S
11660		125	ASC	asc	BBC World Service, G
		250	ASC	asc	Follow The Bible Ministries, USA
		150	CHN	*dom*	CNR2 Business R., Xianyang
		250	PHL	pht	VO America (VOA), USA
		300	ROU	gal	R. Romania International, ROU
		100	SWZ	man	TWR Africa, AFS
		250	THA	udo	VO America (VOA), USA
		250	TUR	emr	Voice of Turkey (VOT), TUR
11665	†	100	MLA	*dom*	RTM Wai FM, Kajang
11670		150	CHN	*dom*	CNR2 Business R., Beijing
		100	CUB	hab	R. Habana Cuba, CUB
		250	PHL	pht	VO America (VOA), USA
11675		250	PHL	pht	VO America (VOA), USA
11680		100	CHN	nnn	China R. International (CRI), CHN
	†	100	KRE	*dom*	KCBS, Kanggye
		100	ZMB	luv	Voice of Hope - Africa, ZMB
11685		100	CHN	*dom*	CNR11 Tibetan Sce, Baoji-Sifan
		100	E	nob	R. Exterior de España (REE), E
		250	SNG	sng	R. Japan (NHK World), J
11690		500	CHN	xia	China R. International (CRI), CHN
		0.1	FIN	vir	Scandinavian Weekend R., FIN
		100	GUM	sda	AWR Asia/Pacific, THA
	+	50	NZL	ran	RNZ Pacific (RNZI), NZL
11695	+	30	CHN	*dom*	CNR1 VO China, Dongfang
		100	D	lam	R. Farda, USA
		300	TWN	pao	R. Taiwan International (RTI), TWN
11700		100	CHN	kas	China R. International (CRI), CHN
		150	CHN	kun	China R. International (CRI), CHN
		100	CHN	xuw	CRI - VO South China Sea, CHN
		500	F	iss	R. France International (RFI), F
11705		250	MDG	mdc	R. Tamazuj, SSD
11710		100	CHN	nnn	China R. International (CRI), CHN
		500	CHN	uru	China R. International (CRI), CHN
		100	CHN	*dom*	CNR1 VO China, Beijing
		200	KRE	kuj	Voice of Korea, KRE
		250	TUR	emr	Voice of Turkey (VOT), TUR
11715	±	1	TWN	ust	Sound of Hope, CHN
11720		150	CHN	bji	China R. International (CRI), CHN
		100	CHN	*dom*	CNR1 VO China, Shijiazhuang
		0.1	FIN	vir	Scandinavian Weekend R., FIN
		250	MDG	mdc	AWR Africa, G
		250	USA	grv	VO America (VOA), USA
		100	VTN	*dom*	VO Vietnam 1, Xuan Mai
11725		250	KWT	kwt	R. Free Asia (RFA), USA
		50	NZL	ran	RNZ Pacific (RNZI), NZL
11730		500	CHN	kun	China R. International (CRI), CHN
11735		200	KRE	kuj	Voice of Korea, KRE
	†	50	TZA	dol	Zanzibar Broadcasting Corp., TZA
11740		100	CHN	*dom*	CNR2 Business R., Lingshi
		250	SNG	sng	R. Japan (NHK World), J
11745		250	ARS	jed	R. Al-Azm, YEM
11750		500	CHN	bei	China R. International (CRI), CHN
		100	CHN	*dom*	CNR1 VO China, Shijiazhuang
		125	CLN	trm	Sri Lanka Broadcasting Corp., CLN
		250	MRA	tin	R. Free Asia (RFA), USA
		125	OMA	sla	BBC World Service, G
		100	PHL	boc	FEBC Philippines, PHL
11760		500	CHN	kun	China R. International (CRI), CHN
		100	CHN	*dom*	CNR1 VO China, Shijiazhuang
		100	CUB	hab	R. Habana Cuba, CUB
		500	F	iss	R. France International (RFI), F
		250	PHL	pht	VO America (VOA), USA
11765		250	KWT	kwt	R. Free Asia (RFA), USA
	±	1	TWN	ust	Sound of Hope, CHN
11770		500	CHN	bei	China R. International (CRI), CHN
		100	CHN	kas	China R. International (CRI), CHN
		100	CHN	nnn	China R. International (CRI), CHN

kHz	N	kW	Ctry	Site	Station, location
		100	CHN	*dom*	Xinjiang PBS, Urumqi
		250	NIG	aja	Voice of Nigeria, NIG
11775		250	KWT	kwt	R. Free Asia (RFA), USA
		100	MRA	sai	R. Free Asia (RFA), USA
	±	1	TWN	ust	Sound of Hope, CHN
11780		100	B	*dom*	R. Nac. da Amazônia, Brasília
		500	CHN	bei	China R. International (CRI), CHN
		500	CHN	jin	China R. International (CRI), CHN
		500	F	iss	R. France International (RFI), F
		500	IRN	sir	Pars Today (VOIRI), IRN
		250	KWT	kwt	R. Free Asia (RFA), USA
		300	ROU	gal	R. Romania International, ROU
		100	SWZ	man	TWR Africa, AFS
11785		150	CHN	bji	China R. International (CRI), CHN
		500	CHN	kas	China R. International (CRI), CHN
11790		100	CHN	kas	China R. International (CRI), CHN
		500	CHN	xia	China R. International (CRI), CHN
		250	D	nau	Bible Voice Broadcasting (BVB), CAN
		300	J	yam	R. Japan (NHK World), J
		125	MDG	mdc	Bible Voice Broadcasting (BVB), CAN
		250	MDG	mdc	R. France International (RFI), F
		300	ROU	gal	R. Romania International, ROU
		300	ROU	tig	R. Romania International, ROU
11795		100	CHN	kas	China R. International (CRI), CHN
		250	KOR	kim	KBS World R., KOR
		250	KWT	kwt	R. Free Asia (RFA), USA
		100	MRA	sai	R. Free Asia (RFA), USA
		250	TUR	emr	Voice of Turkey (VOT), TUR
11800		300	AUT	mos	AWR Africa, G
		150	CHN	*dom*	CNR2 Business R., Beijing
		250	D	nau	Pan American Broadcasting, USA
		250	KWT	kwt	R. Free Asia (RFA), USA
		300	ROU	tig	R. Romania International, ROU
11805		100	CHN	xuw	CRI - VO South China Sea, CHN
		250	KWT	kwt	R. Free Asia (RFA), USA
11810		125	ASC	asc	BBC World Service, G
		100	CHN	*dom*	CNR8, Beijing
		250	G	wof	BBC World Service, G
		250	KOR	kim	KBS World R., KOR
11815	†	10	B	*dom*	R. Brasil Central, Goiânia
		300	J	yam	R. Japan (NHK World), J
		250	TUR	emr	Voice of Turkey (VOT), TUR
11820		500	ARS	riy	Saudi R. International (SBA), ARS
		500	CHN	xia	China R. International (CRI), CHN
		250	PHL	pht	VO America (VOA), USA
		250	ROU	tig	R. Romania International, ROU
11825		100	AUS	knx	Reach Beyond Australia, AUS
		300	J	yam	R. Japan (NHK World), J
		100	MDG	mwv	Madagascar World Voice (MWV), MDG
		250	PHL	pht	BBC World Service, G
		250	ROU	tig	R. Romania International, ROU
		250	SNG	sng	R. Japan (NHK World), J
		250	USA	hri	WHRI, USA
11830		500	F	iss	Deutsche Welle, D
11835		150	CHN	*dom*	CNR2 Business R., Xianyang
11840		500	CHN	xia	China R. International (CRI), CHN
		100	TWN	pao	R. Taiwan International (RTI), TWN
11845		150	CHN	*dom*	CNR2 Business R., Xianyang
11850		100	BOT	bot	VO America (VOA), USA
		100	CUB	hab	R. Habana Cuba, CUB
		250	KWT	kwt	VO America (VOA), USA
		250	MRA	tin	R. Free Asia (RFA), USA
		250	SNG	sng	BBC World Service, G
		100	STP	sao	VO America (VOA), USA
		250	UAE	dha	VO America (VOA), USA
11855	†	10	B	*dom*	R. Aparecida, Aparecida
		100	MRA	sai	R. Free Asia (RFA), USA
11860		250	ARS	jed	Rep. of Yemen R. (R. Sana'a), YEM
		500	CHN	kun	China R. International (CRI), CHN
		100	CHN	*dom*	Xizang PBS, Lhasa
		250	USA	grv	R. Martí, USA
11865		100	AUS	knx	Reach Beyond Australia, AUS
11870		100	CHN	kas	China R. International (CRI), CHN
		250	D	nau	AWR Africa, G
		100	GUM	sda	AWR Asia/Pacific, THA
		500	IRN	sir	Pars Today (VOIRI), IRN
		250	PHL	pht	VO America (VOA), USA
11875		100	AUS	knx	Reach Beyond Australia, AUS
		500	CHN	kun	China R. International (CRI), CHN
		100	CHN	nnn	China R. International (CRI), CHN
		100	F	iss	Bible Voice Broadcasting (BVB), CAN
		500	IRN	sir	Pars Today (VOIRI), IRN
		250	UAE	dha	VO America (VOA), USA
11880		300	AUT	mos	AWR Africa, G
		500	CHN	kas	China R. International (CRI), CHN
		100	CUB	hab	R. Habana Cuba, CUB
		500	IRN	sir	Pars Today (VOIRI), IRN
11885		500	CHN	xia	China R. International (CRI), CHN
		100	CHN	*dom*	Xinjiang PBS, Urumqi
		250	KWT	kwt	R. Free Asia (RFA), USA
11890		250	KWT	kwt	R. Free Asia (RFA), USA
11895		10	B	*dom*	R. Boa Vontade, Porto Alegre
		100	CHN	kas	China R. International (CRI), CHN
		100	CHN	nnn	CRI - VO South China Sea, CHN
		300	J	yam	R. Japan (NHK World), J
		100	MRA	sai	R. Free Asia (RFA), USA
		200	TJK	dsb	R. Free Asia (RFA), USA
11900		500	CHN	bei	China R. International (CRI), CHN
		150	CHN	kun	China R. International (CRI), CHN
		250	D	nau	Bible Voice Broadcasting (BVB), CAN
		250	PHL	pht	VO America (VOA), USA
		100	STP	sao	VO America (VOA), USA
11905		75	AUS	knx	Reach Beyond Australia, AUS
		100	CHN	*dom*	CNR6 VO Shenzhou, Beijing
		125	CLN	trm	Sri Lanka Broadcasting Corp., CLN
		100	D	lam	VO America (VOA), USA
		250	OMA	sla	BBC World Service, G
11910		500	CHN	bei	China R. International (CRI), CHN
		300	J	yam	R. Japan (NHK World), J
		200	KRE	kuj	Voice of Korea, KRE
		250	THA	udo	VO America (VOA), USA
11915		500	ARS	riy	Saudi R. International (SBA), ARS
		100	CHN	*dom*	CNR2 Business R., Baoji-Sifan
		300	TWN	pao	R. Taiwan International (RTI), TWN
11925		100	CHN	*dom*	CNR1 VO China, Lingshi
		500	TUR	emr	Voice of Turkey (VOT), TUR
		100	UAE	dha	R. Japan (NHK World), J
		250	UAE	dha	R. Japan (NHK World), J
11930		500	IRN	sir	Pars Today (VOIRI), IRN
		250	USA	grv	R. Martí, USA
11935		500	ARS	riy	Saudi R. International (SBA), ARS
		100	CHN	*dom*	CNR5 Vo Zhonghua, Beijing
		250	CVA	smg	Vatican R., CVA
		250	MDG	mdc	Vatican R., CVA
		100	MRA	sai	R. Free Asia (RFA), USA
		250	MRA	tin	R. Free Asia (RFA), USA
11940		100	E	nob	R. Exterior de España (REE), E
11945		100	AUS	knx	Reach Beyond Australia, AUS
		100	CHN	kun	China R. International (CRI), CHN
		150	CHN	kun	China R. International (CRI), CHN
		500	F	iss	R. Japan (NHK World), J
		100	MRA	sai	R. Free Asia (RFA), USA
		250	PHL	pht	VO America (VOA), USA
		300	ROU	gal	R. Romania International, ROU
		250	SNG	sng	BBC World Service, G
11950		100	CHN	*dom*	Xizang PBS, Lhasa
		100	CUB	hab	R. Habana Cuba, CUB
		250	KWT	kwt	R. Free Asia (RFA), USA
11955		300	AUT	mos	Adventist World R. (AWR), USA
		300	AUT	mos	AWR Africa, G
		100	CHN	kun	China R. International (CRI), CHN

kHz	N	kW	Ctry	Site	Station, location
		500	CHN	kun	CRI - VO South China Sea, CHN
		100	CHN	xuw	CRI - VO South China Sea, CHN
		250	D	nau	AWR Africa, G
		100	GUM	sda	AWR Asia/Pacific, THA
		500	TUR	emr	Voice of Turkey (VOT), TUR
11960		100	CHN	*dom*	CNR1 VO China, Beijing
		300	ROU	tig	R. Romania International, ROU
11965		100	D	bib	RFE/RL, USA
		100	GUM	twr	TWR Asia, SNG
		100	MDG	mwv	Madagascar World Voice (MWV), MDG
		250	PHL	pht	VO America (VOA), USA
		250	TUR	emr	Voice of Turkey (VOT), TUR
11970	+	200	KWT	kbd	R. Kuwait, KWT
	±	1	TWN	ust	Sound of Hope, CHN
11975		500	CHN	kun	China R. International (CRI), CHN
		100	CHN	*dom*	Xinjiang PBS, Urumqi
		250	CVA	smg	VO America (VOA), USA
		100	MLI	bko	China R. International (CRI), CHN
		300	ROU	gal	R. Romania International, ROU
11980		100	CHN	kas	China R. International (CRI), CHN
		100	CHN	kun	China R. International (CRI), CHN
		150	CHN	kun	China R. International (CRI), CHN
		500	CHN	xia	China R. International (CRI), CHN
		250	D	nau	AWR Africa, G
		100	GUM	sda	AWR Asia/Pacific, THA
		250	KWT	kwt	R. Free Asia (RFA), USA
		250	MRA	tin	R. Free Asia (RFA), USA
		100	STP	sao	Deutsche Welle, D
		200	TJK	dsb	R. Free Asia (RFA), USA
11985		125	CLN	trm	Adventist World R. (AWR), USA
		250	MDG	mdc	AWR Africa, G
11990		100	BUL	sof	R. OMN (Oromia Media Netw.), ETH
		100	CHN	nnn	China R. International (CRI), CHN
		500	CHN	xia	China R. International (CRI), CHN
	+	30	CHN	*dom*	CNR1 VO China, Qiqihar
		100	GUM	sda	AWR Asia/Pacific, THA
11995		500	F	iss	R. France International (RFI), F
		100	GUM	twr	TWR Asia, SNG
		250	MDG	mdc	BBC World Service, G
		250	SNG	sng	BBC World Service, G
12005		250	ASC	asc	Follow The Bible Ministries, USA
		100	D	bib	R. Farda, USA
12010		250	MRA	tin	R. Free Asia (RFA), USA
12015		300	AUT	mos	Adventist World R. (AWR), USA
		100	CHN	kas	China R. International (CRI), CHN
		200	KRE	kuj	Voice of Korea, KRE
		250	MNG	uba	Voice of Mongolia, MNG
		250	UAE	dha	BBC World Service, G
12020	±	100	VTN	vni	Voice of Vietnam (VOV), VTN
	‡±	100	VTN	vni	Voice of Vietnam (VOV), VTN
12025		300	AUT	mos	Adventist World R. (AWR), USA
		100	D	lam	R. Farda, USA
	+†	20	RUS	*dom*	R. Purga, Komsomolsk-na-Amure
12030		100	E	nob	R. Exterior de España (REE), E
		100	GUM	sda	AWR Asia/Pacific, THA
		250	PHL	pht	VO America (VOA), USA
		100	STP	sao	VO America (VOA), USA
12035		500	CHN	xia	China R. International (CRI), CHN
		500	TUR	emr	Voice of Turkey (VOT), TUR
12040	‡	125	CLN	trm	AWR Asia/Pacific, THA
		250	D	nau	AWR Africa, G
		100	D	lam	VO America (VOA), USA
		100	GUM	twr	TWR Asia, SNG
		250	KWT	kwt	VO America (VOA), USA
		100	STP	sao	VO America (VOA), USA
		250	UAE	dha	VO America (VOA), USA
12045		100	CHN	*dom*	CNR1 VO China, Beijing
		100	D	bib	RFE/RL, USA
12050		250	ASC	asc	R. Ndarason Internationale, TCD
		250	KWT	kwt	R. Free Asia (RFA), USA

kHz	N	kW	Ctry	Site	Station, location
		250	MRA	tin	R. Free Asia (RFA), USA
		100	USA	ewn	WEWN - EWTN Shortwave, USA
12055		100	CHN	*dom*	CNR17 Kazakh Sce, Lingshi
		250	MRA	tin	R. Free Asia (RFA), USA
		100	PHL	boc	FEBC Philippines, PHL
12065	‡	125	CLN	trm	AWR Africa, G
		250	KWT	kwt	R. Free Asia (RFA), USA
		125	OMA	sla	BBC World Service, G
		250	OMA	sla	BBC World Service, G
		250	SNG	sng	BBC World Service, G
12070		500	CHN	xia	China R. International (CRI), CHN
		250	CVA	smg	VO America (VOA), USA
		250	KWT	kwt	RFE/RL - R. Azadi, USA
12075		100	BOT	bot	VO America (VOA), USA
		250	CVA	smg	VO America (VOA), USA
		250	KWT	kwt	VOA Ashna R., USA
		250	THA	udo	VOA Ashna R., USA
12080		100	CHN	*dom*	CNR2 Business R., Baoji-Sifan
		250	PHL	pht	VO America (VOA), USA
12085		100	GUM	sda	AWR Asia/Pacific, THA
		250	MNG	uba	Voice of Mongolia, MNG
12095		125	ASC	asc	BBC World Service, G
		250	CVA	smg	BBC World Service, G
		250	MDG	mdc	BBC World Service, G
		250	OMA	sla	BBC World Service, G
		100	PHL	boc	FEBC Philippines, PHL
		125	SNG	sng	BBC World Service, G
		100	STP	sao	BBC World Service, G
		250	UAE	dha	BBC World Service, G
12100		300	TWN	pao	R. Taiwan International (RTI), TWN
12105		100	GUM	sda	AWR Asia/Pacific, THA
12110		250	KWT	kwt	R. Mashaal, USA
12120		100	PHL	boc	FEBC Philippines, PHL
		250	PHL	pht	R. Pilipinas (DZRP), PHL
		250	PHL	pht	VO America (VOA), USA
12125		250	MRA	tin	R. Free Asia (RFA), USA
		250	THA	udo	VO America (VOA), USA
12140		250	KWT	kwt	RFE/RL - R. Azadi, USA
		250	KWT	kwt	VOA Ashna R., USA
		250	THA	udo	RFE/RL - R. Azadi, USA
		250	THA	udo	VOA Ashna R., USA
12150	±	1	TWN	ust	Sound of Hope, CHN
12160		100	USA	wcr	The Overcomer Ministry, USA
		100	USA	wcr	WWCR, USA
12170	±	1	TWN	ust	Sound of Hope, CHN
12190	±	1	TWN	ust	Sound of Hope, CHN
12230	±	1	TWN	ust	Sound of Hope, CHN
12345	±	1	TWN	ust	Sound of Hope, CHN
12370	±	1	TWN	ust	Sound of Hope, CHN
12430	±	1	TWN	ust	Sound of Hope, CHN
12500	±	1	TWN	ust	Sound of Hope, CHN
12550	±	1	TWN	ust	Sound of Hope, CHN
12800	±	1	TWN	ust	Sound of Hope, CHN
12870	±	1	TWN	ust	Sound of Hope, CHN
12880	±	1	TWN	ust	Sound of Hope, CHN
12910	±	1	TWN	ust	Sound of Hope, CHN
12950	±	1	TWN	ust	Sound of Hope, CHN
12980	±	1	TWN	ust	Sound of Hope, CHN
13020	±	1	TWN	ust	Sound of Hope, CHN
13130	±	1	TWN	ust	Sound of Hope, CHN
13160	±	1	TWN	ust	Sound of Hope, CHN
13530	±	1	TWN	ust	Sound of Hope, CHN
13570		500	CHN	kas	China R. International (CRI), CHN
13580		500	CHN	bei	China R. International (CRI), CHN
		500	CHN	kun	China R. International (CRI), CHN
		250	KWT	kwt	R. Mashaal, USA
		250	KWT	kwt	VO America (VOA), USA
		100	SWZ	man	TWR Africa, AFS
		250	THA	udo	R. Mashaal, USA
13590		500	CHN	bei	China R. International (CRI), CHN
		125	D	nau	Dandal Kura R. International, NIG

kHz	N	kW	Ctry	Site	Station, location
		100	D	lam	VOA Deewa R., USA
		250	KWT	kwt	VOA Deewa R., USA
		100	STP	sao	VO America (VOA), USA
		500	TUR	emr	Voice of Turkey (VOT), TUR
		250	UAE	dha	VOA Deewa R., USA
13600		150	CHN	kun	China R. International (CRI), CHN
	†	50	OMA	thu	R. Sultanate of Oman, OMA
13610		100	ARS	riy	Saudi R. International (SBA), ARS
		500	CHN	xia	China R. International (CRI), CHN
		100	CHN	*dom*	CNR1 VO China, Nanning
13620	±	1	TWN	ust	Sound of Hope, CHN
13630		100	BOT	bot	VO America (VOA), USA
		250	CVA	smg	VO America (VOA), USA
		100	MLI	bko	China R. International (CRI), CHN
		300	ROU	tig	R. Romania International, ROU
		100	STP	sao	VO America (VOA), USA
13640		100	CHN	kas	China R. International (CRI), CHN
	±	1	TWN	ust	Sound of Hope, CHN
13645		500	CHN	xia	China R. International (CRI), CHN
		100	MLI	bko	China R. International (CRI), CHN
13650		250	CUB	qvc	China R. International (CRI), CHN
		300	J	yam	R. Japan (NHK World), J
		200	KRE	kuj	Voice of Korea, KRE
		250	KWT	kwt	R. Free Asia (RFA), USA
	†	250	KWT	kbd	R. Kuwait, KWT
13655		500	CHN	xia	China R. International (CRI), CHN
		500	TUR	emr	Voice of Turkey (VOT), TUR
	+	50	USA	inb	Shortwave Radiogram, USA
	+	15	USA	inb	WINB, USA
13660		500	CHN	xia	China R. International (CRI), CHN
		500	F	iss	Alameda Bible Fellowship, USA
13670		100	CHN	*dom*	Xinjiang PBS, Urumqi
		100	MDG	mwv	Madagascar World Voice (MWV), MDG
13680		100	CUB	hab	R. Habana Cuba, CUB
		500	IRN	sir	Pars Today (VOIRI), IRN
		250	MDG	mdc	BBC World Service, G
	±	1	TWN	ust	Sound of Hope, CHN
13685		100	MLI	bko	China R. International (CRI), CHN
		250	MRA	tin	R. Free Asia (RFA), USA
		500	TUR	emr	Voice of Turkey (VOT), TUR
13690		500	IRN	sir	Pars Today (VOIRI), IRN
13695		500	F	iss	R. France International (RFI), F
13700		100	CHN	*dom*	CNR13 Uyghur Sce, Lingshi
		100	CUB	hab	R. Habana Cuba, CUB
13710		500	ARS	riy	Saudi R. International (SBA), ARS
		100	F	iss	Manara R., NIG
		500	IRN	sir	Pars Today (VOIRI), IRN
		100	MDG	mwv	Madagascar World Voice (MWV), MDG
13720		500	ARS	riy	Saudi R. International (SBA), ARS
		500	CHN	kas	China R. International (CRI), CHN
		500	CHN	xia	China R. International (CRI), CHN
13725		500	F	iss	R. Japan (NHK World), J
13730		100	CHN	kas	China R. International (CRI), CHN
		250	MDG	mdc	R. Japan (NHK World), J
		300	ROU	tig	R. Romania International, ROU
	+	90	ROU	tig	R. Romania International, ROU
13740		100	CHN	kas	China R. International (CRI), CHN
		100	CUB	hab	R. Habana Cuba, CUB
		500	F	iss	R. France International (RFI), F
		250	MRA	tin	R. Free Asia (RFA), USA
		250	THA	udo	VO America (VOA), USA
13750		100	BOT	bot	VO America (VOA), USA
		500	CHN	kun	China R. International (CRI), CHN
		250	KWT	kwt	VO America (VOA), USA
		300	ROU	tig	R. Romania International, ROU
		100	STP	sao	VO America (VOA), USA
		250	THA	udo	R. Thailand World Service, THA
		100	UZB	tac	BBC World Service, G
13760		200	KRE	kuj	Voice of Korea, KRE
		100	MDG	mwv	Madagascar World Voice (MWV), MDG
13765		100	D	lam	R. Farda, USA
		250	KWT	kwt	VO America (VOA), USA
		250	THA	udo	R. Farda, USA
13770		500	CHN	xia	China R. International (CRI), CHN
13775		500	ARS	riy	Saudi R. International (SBA), ARS
	±	1	TWN	ust	Sound of Hope, CHN
13780		100	ARS	riy	Saudi R. International (SBA), ARS
		100	CHN	kas	China R. International (CRI), CHN
		500	CHN	kun	China R. International (CRI), CHN
13790		500	CHN	uru	China R. International (CRI), CHN
		500	IRN	sir	Pars Today (VOIRI), IRN
		250	UAE	dha	BBC World Service, G
		300	UAE	dha	BBC World Service, G
13795		100	MRA	sai	R. Free Asia (RFA), USA
13800		100	CHN	kas	China R. International (CRI), CHN
	+	90	GUM	twr	TWR Asia, SNG
13810		100	CHN	kas	China R. International (CRI), CHN
13820		500	IRN	sir	Pars Today (VOIRI), IRN
		500	IRN	zah	Pars Today (VOIRI), IRN
		250	USA	grv	R. Martí, USA
13825	+	30	CHN	*dom*	CNR1 VO China, Beijing
13830		100	BOT	bot	VO America (VOA), USA
		250	CVA	smg	Vatican R., CVA
		250	THA	udo	VO America (VOA), USA
		250	TJK	dsb	R. Free Asia (RFA), USA
13840		250	MDG	mdc	R. Japan (NHK World), J
		50	NZL	ran	RNZ Pacific (RNZI), NZL
13845		100	USA	wcr	The Overcomer Ministry, USA
		100	USA	wcr	University Network, USA
		100	USA	wcr	WWCR, USA
13850		500	CHN	bei	China R. International (CRI), CHN
13855		500	CHN	kas	China R. International (CRI), CHN
13860		300	G	wof	VOA Ashna R., USA
		250	KWT	kwt	RFE/RL - R. Azadi, USA
		100	STP	sao	VOA Studio 7, USA
		250	THA	udo	RFE/RL - R. Azadi, USA
		250	UAE	dha	BBC World Service, G
13865		300	G	wof	VO America (VOA), USA
13870		100	CHN	*dom*	Xizang PBS, Lhasa
		100	PHL	boc	FEBC Philippines, PHL
	±	1	TWN	ust	Sound of Hope, CHN
13890	±	1	TWN	ust	Sound of Hope, CHN
13920	±	1	TWN	ust	Sound of Hope, CHN
13980	±	1	TWN	ust	Sound of Hope, CHN
14370	±	1	TWN	ust	Sound of Hope, CHN
14430	±	1	TWN	ust	Sound of Hope, CHN
14500	±	1	TWN	ust	Sound of Hope, CHN
14560	±	1	TWN	ust	Sound of Hope, CHN
14600	±	1	TWN	ust	Sound of Hope, CHN
14640	±	1	TWN	ust	Sound of Hope, CHN
14670		3	CAN	STF	CHU, Ottawa
14690	±	1	TWN	ust	Sound of Hope, CHN
14725	±	1	TWN	ust	Sound of Hope, CHN
14775	±	1	TWN	ust	Sound of Hope, CHN
14800	±	1	TWN	ust	Sound of Hope, CHN
14820	±	1	TWN	ust	Sound of Hope, CHN
14850	±	1	TWN	ust	Sound of Hope, CHN
14870	±	1	TWN	ust	Sound of Hope, CHN
14900	±	1	TWN	ust	Sound of Hope, CHN
14920	±	1	TWN	ust	Sound of Hope, CHN
14940	±	1	TWN	ust	Sound of Hope, CHN
14980	±	1	TWN	ust	Sound of Hope, CHN
14996		5	RUS	STF	RWM, Moscow
15000		20	CHN	STF	BPM, Pucheng
		10	HWA	STF	WWVH NIST, Kauai, HI
		10	USA	STF	WWV NIST, Fort Collins, CO
15030	+	200	IND	bgl	All India R. (AIR), IND

kHz	N	kW	Ctry	Site	Station, location
15070	±	1	TWN	ust	Sound of Hope, CHN
15105		200	KRE	kuj	Voice of Korea, KRE
		100	SWZ	man	TWR Africa, AFS
15110		100	CHN	kas	China R. International (CRI), CHN
		250	KWT	kwt	R. Free Asia (RFA), USA
	+	250	KWT	kbd	R. Kuwait, KWT
		250	PHL	pht	VO America (VOA), USA
15120		500	ARS	riy	Saudi R. International (SBA), ARS
		250	ASC	asc	VO America (VOA), USA
		500	CHN	bei	China R. International (CRI), CHN
		250	CUB	qvc	China R. International (CRI), CHN
	+†	250	NIG	aja	Voice of Nigeria, NIG
15125		500	CHN	bei	China R. International (CRI), CHN
		100	MLI	bko	China R. International (CRI), CHN
15130		150	CHN	bei	China R. International (CRI), CHN
		500	F	iss	R. Japan (NHK World), J
15135		500	CHN	kas	China R. International (CRI), CHN
		100	CHN	kun	China R. International (CRI), CHN
		500	CHN	kun	China R. International (CRI), CHN
15140		100	CUB	hab	R. Habana Cuba, CUB
		500	IRN	sir	Pars Today (VOIRI), IRN
	†	50	OMA	thu	R. Sultanate of Oman, OMA
15145		300	AUT	mos	AWR Africa, G
		100	CHN	kas	China R. International (CRI), CHN
		500	CHN	xia	China R. International (CRI), CHN
		125	D	nau	AWR Africa, G
15150		250	MDG	mdc	Adventist World R. (AWR), USA
		250	THA	udo	VO America (VOA), USA
15155		250	MRA	tin	R. Free Asia (RFA), USA
15160		500	CHN	jin	China R. International (CRI), CHN
		100	CHN	nnn	China R. International (CRI), CHN
		250	KOR	kim	KBS World R., KOR
15170		500	ARS	riy	Saudi R. International (SBA), ARS
		100	CHN	kas	China R. International (CRI), CHN
15180		500	CHN	uru	China R. International (CRI), CHN
	+	30	CHN	*dom*	CNR1 VO China, Kunming
		200	KRE	kuj	Voice of Korea, KRE
		100	STP	sao	VO America (VOA), USA
15185		100	CHN	kas	China R. International (CRI), CHN
15190	†	5	B	*dom*	R. Inconfidência, Belo Horizonte
		500	CHN	kas	China R. International (CRI), CHN
		250	PHL	pht	R. Pilipinas (DZRP), PHL
15195		500	F	iss	Deutsche Welle, D
		300	J	yam	R. Japan (NHK World), J
15200		500	IRN	sir	Pars Today (VOIRI), IRN
15205		500	ARS	riy	Saudi R. International (SBA), ARS
15210		500	CHN	kun	China R. International (CRI), CHN
		100	GUM	sda	AWR Asia/Pacific, THA
15215	‡	125	CLN	trm	AWR Asia/Pacific, THA
		500	F	iss	R. Öömrang, D
		100	GUM	sda	AWR Asia/Pacific, THA
		250	UAE	dha	FEBC Philippines, PHL
15220		500	CHN	kas	China R. International (CRI), CHN
15225		500	ARS	riy	Saudi R. International (SBA), ARS
		500	CHN	kas	China R. International (CRI), CHN
15230		250	CUB	qvc	R. Habana Cuba, CUB
15235		500	TUR	emr	Voice of Turkey (VOT), TUR
15240		500	IRN	sir	Pars Today (VOIRI), IRN
15245		200	KRE	kuj	Voice of Korea, KRE
15250		100	CHN	kun	China R. International (CRI), CHN
15255		125	CLN	trm	AWR Asia/Pacific, THA
		100	GUM	sda	AWR Asia/Pacific, THA
		250	MDG	mdc	AWR Asia/Pacific, THA
		300	ROU	gal	R. Romania International, ROU
		250	UAE	dha	R. Free Asia (RFA), USA
15260		500	CHN	kas	China R. International (CRI), CHN
		300	G	wof	IBRA Media, S
		300	G	wof	VO America (VOA), USA
		300	ROU	gal	R. Romania International, ROU
15270		150	CHN	*dom*	CNR2 Business R., Beijing
		100	D	bib	VO America (VOA), USA
		500	TUR	emr	Voice of Turkey (VOT), TUR
		100	TWN	pao	R. Taiwan International (RTI), TWN
15275		500	F	iss	Deutsche Welle, D
15280		300	J	yam	R. Japan (NHK World), J
15285		500	ARS	riy	Saudi R. International (SBA), ARS
		150	F	iss	Manara R., NIG
	±	1	TWN	ust	Sound of Hope, CHN
15290		250	F	iss	R. Japan (NHK World), J
15300		500	F	iss	R. France International (RFI), F
15310		125	OMA	sla	BBC World Service, G
		250	OMA	sla	BBC World Service, G
		250	PHL	pht	BBC World Service, G
15315		250	OMA	sla	BBC World Service, G
15320		300	TWN	pao	R. Taiwan International (RTI), TWN
15325		300	J	yam	R. Japan (NHK World), J
15330		100	GUM	sda	AWR Asia/Pacific, THA
		100	PHL	boc	FEBC Philippines, PHL
15335		500	CHN	kas	China R. International (CRI), CHN
15340		500	CHN	xia	China R. International (CRI), CHN
		100	MRA	sai	R. Free Asia (RFA), USA
	±	1	TWN	ust	Sound of Hope, CHN
15350		100	CHN	kas	China R. International (CRI), CHN
		500	F	iss	Deutsche Welle, D
		500	TUR	emr	Voice of Turkey (VOT), TUR
15360		125	CLN	trm	Adventist World R. (AWR), USA
		125	CLN	trm	AWR Asia/Pacific, THA
		500	IRN	sir	Pars Today (VOIRI), IRN
		500	TUR	emr	Voice of Turkey (VOT), TUR
15365		100	GUM	sda	AWR Asia/Pacific, THA
15370		100	CHN	*dom*	CNR1 VO China, Shijiazhuang
15375	‡	10	TWN	*dom*	Fu Hsing BS
15380		500	ARS	riy	Saudi R. International (SBA), ARS
		100	CHN	*dom*	CNR1 VO China, Beijing
		300	ROU	gal	R. Romania International, ROU
15390		100	CHN	*dom*	CNR13 Uyghur Sce, Lingshi
		500	TUR	emr	Voice of Turkey (VOT), TUR
15400		125	ASC	asc	BBC World Service, G
		250	ASC	asc	BBC World Service, G
		250	F	iss	R. Tamazuj, SSD
		250	MDG	mdc	BBC World Service, G
15410		75	AUS	knx	Reach Beyond Australia, AUS
		125	CLN	trm	Adventist World R. (AWR), USA
		125	CLN	trm	AWR Africa, G
		250	F	iss	Eye R., SSD
	+	200	IND	bgl	All India R. (AIR), IND
15420		250	BUL	sof	BBC World Service, G
		125	MDG	mdc	BBC World Service, G
		250	MDG	mdc	R. Itahuka, RRW
		100	PHL	boc	FEBC Philippines, PHL
		250	UAE	dha	BBC World Service, G
15425		500	CHN	xia	China R. International (CRI), CHN
		250	PHL	pht	VO America (VOA), USA
15430		100	CHN	kas	China R. International (CRI), CHN
		125	CLN	trm	AWR Asia/Pacific, THA
		300	ROU	gal	R. Romania International, ROU
		300	ROU	tig	R. Romania International, ROU
15435		500	ARS	riy	Saudi R. International (SBA), ARS
		500	CHN	xia	China R. International (CRI), CHN
		100	PHL	boc	FEBC Philippines, PHL
15440		500	CHN	kun	China R. International (CRI), CHN
		500	IRN	sir	Pars Today (VOIRI), IRN
15445		500	CHN	kas	China R. International (CRI), CHN
		100	TWN	tsh	AWR Asia/Pacific, THA
15450	‡	125	CLN	trm	AWR Asia/Pacific, THA
		100	GUM	sda	AWR Asia/Pacific, THA
		250	PHL	pht	VO America (VOA), USA
	+	90	ROU	tig	R. Romania International, ROU
15455		500	F	iss	R. France International (RFI), F
15460		100	BOT	bot	VO America (VOA), USA

kHz	N	kW	Ctry	Site	Station, location
		250	CVA	smg	VO America (VOA), USA
		300	ROU	gal	R. Romania International, ROU
		300	ROU	tig	R. Romania International, ROU
		100	STP	sao	VO America (VOA), USA
		100	STP	sao	VOA Studio 7, USA
15465		100	CHN	kas	China R. International (CRI), CHN
		100	TWN	pao	R. Taiwan International (RTI), TWN
15476	†	1	ATA	lra	RN Arcángel S.Gabriel (LRA36), ATA
15480		100	CHN	*dom*	CNR1 VO China, Beijing
		100	GUM	sda	AWR Asia/Pacific, THA
		500	TUR	emr	Voice of Turkey (VOT), TUR
15490		250	ARM	erv	BBC World Service, G
		300	ARM	erv	BBC World Service, G
		250	ASC	asc	BBC World Service, G
		250	CVA	smg	BBC World Service, G
		250	D	nau	AWR Africa, G
		100	D	lam	RFE/RL, USA
		250	G	wof	BBC World Service, G
15500		150	CHN	*dom*	CNR2 Business R., Beijing
	‡	100	GUM	sda	AWR Asia/Pacific, THA
		100	GUM	sda	AWR Asia/Pacific, THA
15505		100	MLI	bko	China R. International (CRI), CHN
15515		100	BUL	sof	IRRS Shortwave, I
		250	KWT	kbd	R. Kuwait, KWT
15525		500	CHN	uru	China R. International (CRI), CHN
15530		250	KWT	kbd	R. Kuwait, KWT
		250	USA	hri	WHRI, USA
15540		100	CHN	*dom*	CNR2 Business R., Lingshi
	+†	250	KWT	kbd	R. Kuwait, KWT
		250	KWT	kbd	R. Kuwait, KWT
15550		100	CHN	kas	China R. International (CRI), CHN
		100	CHN	*dom*	CNR1 VO China, Beijing
	‡	125	CLN	trm	AWR Asia/Pacific, THA
		250	CVA	smg	R. Dabanga, SDN
		100	UZB	tac	AWR Asia/Pacific, THA
15555	‡	1	USA	jhr	WJHR R. International, USA
15560		500	CHN	xia	China R. International (CRI), CHN
		100	PHL	boc	FEBC Philippines, PHL
		250	PHL	pht	VO America (VOA), USA
		250	THA	udo	VO America (VOA), USA
15570		100	CHN	*dom*	CNR11 Tibetan Sce, Baoji-Sifan
15575		250	KOR	kim	KBS World R., KOR
15580		100	BOT	bot	VO America (VOA), USA
		100	PHL	boc	FEBC Philippines, PHL
	±	1	TWN	ust	Sound of Hope, CHN
15595		100	CVA	smg	Vatican R., CVA
		250	CVA	smg	Vatican R., CVA
15600		250	G	wof	VO America (VOA), USA
		300	ROU	tig	R. Romania International, ROU
15610		125	CLN	trm	AWR Asia/Pacific, THA
		100	GUM	sda	AWR Asia/Pacific, THA
		250	THA	udo	VO America (VOA), USA
		250	USA	ewn	WEWN - EWTN Shortwave, USA
15620		100	BOT	bot	VO America (VOA), USA
		500	CHN	kas	China R. International (CRI), CHN
		250	CVA	smg	VO America (VOA), USA
		100	PHL	boc	FEBC Philippines, PHL
	+	100	SNG	sng	BBC World Service, G
15625	‡	125	CLN	trm	AWR Asia/Pacific, THA
		100	GUM	sda	AWR Asia/Pacific, THA
15640		250	CVA	smg	RFE/RL - R. Azadi, USA
		250	KWT	kwt	RFE/RL - R. Azadi, USA
		100	PHL	boc	FEBC Philippines, PHL
		250	PHL	pht	R. Pilipinas (DZRP), PHL
		250	UAE	dha	RFE/RL - R. Azadi, USA
15665		500	CHN	uru	China R. International (CRI), CHN
		250	MRA	tin	R. Free Asia (RFA), USA
		200	TJK	dsb	R. Free Asia (RFA), USA
15680		100	CUB	hab	R. Habana Cuba, CUB
		250	MDG	mdc	AWR Asia/Pacific, THA
		100	PLW	hbn	T8WH - Hope R., PLW
15690		100	D	lam	R. Farda, USA
15700		250	CUB	qvc	China R. International (CRI), CHN
15705		125	CLN	trm	AWR Asia/Pacific, THA
15710		100	CHN	*dom*	CNR6 VO Shenzhou, Beijing
15715		100	BOT	bot	VO America (VOA), USA
		250	CVA	smg	VO America (VOA), USA
		250	THA	udo	VO America (VOA), USA
15720		250	MDG	mdc	R. Japan (NHK World), J
		50	NZL	ran	RNZ Pacific (RNZI), NZL
15730		100	BOT	bot	VO America (VOA), USA
		50	CUB	bej	R. Habana Cuba, CUB
		250	USA	grv	VO America (VOA), USA
15735	+†	20	RUS	*dom*	R. Purga, Komsomolsk-na-Amure
15740	±	1	TWN	ust	Sound of Hope, CHN
15745		250	MRA	tin	R. Free Asia (RFA), USA
		200	TJK	dsb	R. Free Asia (RFA), USA
15760		250	THA	udo	R. Mashaal, USA
15770		100	USA	rmi	Alameda Bible Fellowship, USA
		100	USA	rmi	Encore Classical Music, G
		100	USA	rmi	R. For Peace Int. (RFPI), F
		100	USA	rmi	R. Prague International, CZE
		100	USA	rmi	R. Tirana International, ALB
		100	USA	rmi	RAE - Argentina Al Mundo, ARG
		100	USA	rmi	Shortwave Radiogram, USA
		100	USA	rmi	Supreme Master TV, USA
		100	USA	rmi	The Overcomer Ministry, USA
		100	USA	rmi	VORW R. International, USA
		100	USA	rmi	World of Radio, USA
		100	USA	rmi	WRMI - R. Miami International, USA
15775	±	1	TWN	ust	Sound of Hope, CHN
15800	±	1	TWN	ust	Sound of Hope, CHN
15805	†	0.2	DNK	rnd	World Music Radio (WMR), DNK
15810	‡	100	USA	tww	WTWW, USA
15825		100	USA	wcr	The Overcomer Ministry, USA
		100	USA	wcr	WWCR, USA
15840	±	1	TWN	ust	Sound of Hope, CHN
15870	±	1	TWN	ust	Sound of Hope, CHN
15880		0.2	HOL	zwo	R.Piepzender, HOL
15920	±	1	TWN	ust	Sound of Hope, CHN
15940	±	1	TWN	ust	Sound of Hope, CHN
15970	±	1	TWN	ust	Sound of Hope, CHN
16100	±	1	TWN	ust	Sound of Hope, CHN
16160	±	1	TWN	ust	Sound of Hope, CHN
16250	±	1	TWN	ust	Sound of Hope, CHN
16300	±	1	TWN	ust	Sound of Hope, CHN
16350	±	1	TWN	ust	Sound of Hope, CHN
16600	±	1	TWN	ust	Sound of Hope, CHN
16680	±	1	TWN	ust	Sound of Hope, CHN
16770	±	1	TWN	ust	Sound of Hope, CHN
16790	±	1	TWN	ust	Sound of Hope, CHN
16980	±	1	TWN	ust	Sound of Hope, CHN
17080	±	1	TWN	ust	Sound of Hope, CHN
17150	±	1	TWN	ust	Sound of Hope, CHN
17170	±	1	TWN	ust	Sound of Hope, CHN
17200	±	1	TWN	ust	Sound of Hope, CHN
17400	±	1	TWN	ust	Sound of Hope, CHN
17440	±	1	TWN	ust	Sound of Hope, CHN
17485		500	CHN	kas	China R. International (CRI), CHN
17490		500	CHN	bei	China R. International (CRI), CHN
		500	CHN	kas	China R. International (CRI), CHN
17510		500	CHN	kas	China R. International (CRI), CHN
		500	CHN	xia	China R. International (CRI), CHN
17520		250	BUL	sof	WLC Radio, USA
		100	CHN	kas	China R. International (CRI), CHN
17525		100	GUM	sda	AWR Asia/Pacific, THA
17530		100	MDG	mwv	Madagascar World Voice (MWV), MDG

kHz	N	kW	Ctry	Site	Station, location
		500	TUR	emr	Voice of Turkey (VOT), TUR
17540		500	CHN	bei	China R. International (CRI), CHN
		100	GUM	sda	AWR Asia/Pacific, THA
17545		150	F	iss	VO Yiakl, ERI
17550		100	CHN	*dom*	CNR1 VO China, Beijing
		250	KWT	kbd	R. Kuwait, KWT
17560		500	ARS	riy	Saudi R. International (SBA), ARS
		500	CHN	xia	China R. International (CRI), CHN
		250	THA	udo	R. Farda, USA
17565		100	CHN	*dom*	CNR1 VO China, Beijing
17570		500	CHN	kas	China R. International (CRI), CHN
		500	CHN	uru	China R. International (CRI), CHN
		250	MDG	mdc	AWR Africa, G
17580		100	CHN	*dom*	CNR1 VO China, Lingshi
		250	MRA	tin	R. Free Asia (RFA), USA
17585		100	D	bib	VO America (VOA), USA
17595		100	CHN	*dom*	CNR1 VO China, Shijiazhuang
		500	IND	bgl	All India R. (AIR), IND
17600		250	KWT	kwt	VO America (VOA), USA
		250	THA	udo	VO America (VOA), USA
17605		100	CHN	*dom*	CNR1 VO China, Beijing
17615		500	ARS	riy	Saudi R. International (SBA), ARS
		500	CHN	uru	China R. International (CRI), CHN
17625		150	CHN	*dom*	CNR2 Business R., Beijing
17630		500	IRN	sir	Pars Today (VOIRI), IRN
		100	MLI	bko	China R. International (CRI), CHN
		250	THA	udo	R. Thailand World Service, THA
17640		125	ASC	asc	BBC World Service, G
		250	ASC	asc	BBC World Service, G
		500	CHN	xia	China R. International (CRI), CHN
		300	ROU	tig	R. Romania International, ROU
		250	THA	udo	R. Thailand World Service, THA
17650		500	CHN	kas	China R. International (CRI), CHN
		125	CLN	trm	AWR Asia/Pacific, THA
		100	GUM	sda	AWR Asia/Pacific, THA
		125	MDG	mdc	Bible Voice Broadcasting (BVB), CAN
17655		100	STP	sao	VO America (VOA), USA
		250	USA	grv	VO America (VOA), USA
17660		500	F	iss	R. France International (RFI), F
		100	MRA	sai	R. Free Asia (RFA), USA
		250	MRA	tin	R. Free Asia (RFA), USA
17665		500	IRN	sir	Pars Today (VOIRI), IRN
17670		500	CHN	kas	China R. International (CRI), CHN
		500	CHN	kun	China R. International (CRI), CHN
17675		100	D	bib	R. Free Asia (RFA), USA
17680		100	CHN	kun	China R. International (CRI), CHN
		150	CHN	kun	China R. International (CRI), CHN
		250	PHL	pht	VO America (VOA), USA
17690		500	CHN	jin	China R. International (CRI), CHN
		100	CHN	*dom*	CNR1 VO China, Nanning
17700		100	BOT	bot	VO America (VOA), USA
		250	USA	grv	VO America (VOA), USA
17705		500	ARS	riy	Saudi R. International (SBA), ARS
17710		500	CHN	bei	China R. International (CRI), CHN
		500	CHN	jin	China R. International (CRI), CHN
17720		500	CHN	kas	China R. International (CRI), CHN
		250	THA	udo	VO America (VOA), USA
		500	TUR	emr	Voice of Turkey (VOT), TUR
17730		500	ARS	riy	Saudi R. International (SBA), ARS
		500	CHN	xia	China R. International (CRI), CHN
		250	MDG	mdc	AWR Africa, G
		250	MRA	tin	R. Free Asia (RFA), USA
17735		100	CHN	kun	China R. International (CRI), CHN
17740		500	ARS	riy	Saudi R. International (SBA), ARS
		500	CHN	xia	China R. International (CRI), CHN
17745		125	MDG	mdc	BBC World Service, G
		250	UAE	dha	BBC World Service, G
17750		500	CHN	xia	China R. International (CRI), CHN
17760		250	KWT	kbd	R. Kuwait, KWT

kHz	N	kW	Ctry	Site	Station, location
		250	MRA	tin	R. Free Asia (RFA), USA
	±	1	TWN	ust	Sound of Hope, CHN
17765		250	ASC	asc	BBC World Service, G
17770	+	30	CHN	*dom*	CNR1 VO China, Dongfang
		250	MDG	mdc	AWR Asia/Pacific, THA
17775		100	USA	voh	KVOH - Voice of Hope, USA
17780		125	ASC	asc	BBC World Service, G
		250	ASC	asc	BBC World Service, G
		300	ROU	gal	R. Romania International, ROU
17790		250	CLN	trm	AWR Africa, G
		250	CVA	smg	Vatican R., CVA
17800	+	30	CHN	*dom*	CNR1 VO China, Kunming
		500	F	iss	Deutsche Welle, D
		300	ROU	gal	R. Romania International, ROU
17805		500	ARS	riy	Saudi R. International (SBA), ARS
17810		300	J	yam	R. Japan (NHK World), J
		300	ROU	tig	R. Romania International, ROU
17815		500	F	iss	R. France International (RFI), F
		250	MRA	tin	R. Free Asia (RFA), USA
		250	USA	hri	WHRI, USA
17820		250	MRA	tin	R. Free Asia (RFA), USA
		250	PHL	pht	R. Pilipinas (DZRP), PHL
17830		125	ASC	asc	BBC World Service, G
	+	30	CHN	*dom*	CNR1 VO China, Urumqi
		250	MRA	tin	R. Free Asia (RFA), USA
		250	UAE	dha	BBC World Service, G
		250	UAE	dha	R. Japan (NHK World), J
17840		250	MRA	tin	R. Free Asia (RFA), USA
17845		100	CHN	*dom*	CNR1 VO China, Shijiazhuang
		250	UAE	dha	R. Ergo, SOM
17850		250	CVA	smg	VO America (VOA), USA
		500	F	iss	R. France International (RFI), F
		300	ROU	gal	R. Romania International, ROU
17855		500	CHN	bei	China R. International (CRI), CHN
17865		250	PHL	pht	VO America (VOA), USA
17880		100	D	bib	R. Mashaal, USA
		100	MLI	bko	China R. International (CRI), CHN
17885		100	BOT	bot	VO America (VOA), USA
17890		100	CHN	*dom*	CNR1 VO China, Beijing
17895		500	ARS	riy	Saudi R. International (SBA), ARS
		100	BOT	bot	VO America (VOA), USA
		100	STP	sao	VO America (VOA), USA
18180	±	1	TWN	ust	Sound of Hope, CHN
18870	±	1	TWN	ust	Sound of Hope, CHN
19840	±	1	TWN	ust	Sound of Hope, CHN
20000		2	USA	STF	WWV NIST, Fort Collins, CO
21480		125	MDG	mdc	Bible Voice Broadcasting (BVB), CAN
		250	MRA	tin	R. Free Asia (RFA), USA
21505		500	ARS	riy	Saudi R. International (SBA), ARS
21525		100	USA	rmi	Pan American Broadcasting, USA
		100	USA	rmi	R. For Peace Int. (RFPI), F
		100	USA	rmi	WRMI - R. Miami International, USA
21530	±	1	TWN	ust	Sound of Hope, CHN
21580		500	F	iss	R. France International (RFI), F
21600		250	PHL	pht	VO America (VOA), USA
21610		250	USA	hri	WHRI, USA
21620		250	PHL	pht	VO America (VOA), USA
21630		250	UAE	dha	BBC World Service, G
21670		500	ARS	riy	Saudi R. International (SBA), ARS
21690		500	F	iss	R. France International (RFI), F
		250	MDG	mdc	R. France International (RFI), F
21700		250	MRA	tin	R. Free Asia (RFA), USA
21760		250	PHL	pht	VO America (VOA), USA
21795		250	PHL	pht	VO America (VOA), USA
21800	±	1	TWN	ust	Sound of Hope, CHN
25000		0.1	FIN	STF	Centre for Metrology, Espoo
		2.5	USA	STF	WWV NIST, Fort Collins, CO
26060	+	0.01	HNG	*dom*	Budapesti Muszaki Egyetem, Budapest

International Broadcasts in English, French, German, Portuguese and Spanish

ENGLISH

0000	English	Area	kHz
0000-0100	BBC World Sce	SAs	5875erv, 5970sla
0000-0100	CRI	SAs	7425kas
0000-0100	CRI	EAs	9560bei
0000-0100	R. Habana Cuba	CAm	5040hab
0000-0100	R. Thailand WS	NAm	13750udo
0000-0100	Supreme Master	NAm	5950rmi
0000-0100	WBCQ	NAm,CAm	6160bcq †±
0000-0100	WBCQ	NAm,CAm	7490bcq †±
0000-0100	WHRI	NAm,Eu	5920hri
0000-0100	WHRI	NAm	7385hri
0000-0100	WWCR	Af	5935wcr
0000-0130	WBCQ	NAm,CAm	6160bcq †±
0000-0200	CRI	SEA	11885xia, 15125bei
0000-0200	CRI	SAs	6075kas, 6180kas
0000-0200	The Mighty KBC	NAm	5960nau
0000-0200	Overcomer Min.	NAm	9455rmi
0000-0200	WBCQ	NAm,CAm	6160bcq †±
0000-0300	WWCR	CAm,Af	7520wcr
0000-0330	WINB	CAm	9265inb
0000-0400	WINB	CAm	9265inb
0000-0900	WEWN	Af	9385ewn
0000-1000	WRMI	NAm,Pac	7730rmi
0000-1100	WRMI	NAm	5850rmi
0000-1400	WRMI	NAm	7570rmi
0000-2400	R. 208	Eu	1440ish, 5805hvi
0000-2400	World Music R.	Eu	5840brg
0000-2400	WRMI	NAm	5950rmi, 9455rmi
0030-0100	Alameda Bible	LAm	9955rmi
0030-0100	Hobart R. Int.	NAm	7730rmi
0030-0100	R. Slovakia Int	NAm	5850rmi
0030-0100	R. Slovakia Int	Eu,NAm	7780rmi
0030-0100	SW Radiogram	NAm	9265inb*
0030-0100	World of Radio	NAm	7730rmi
0100	**English**		
0100-0130	Alameda Bible	Car	5010rmi
0100-0130	Alameda Bible	NAm	5850rmi
0100-0130	World of Radio	Eu,ME,NAf	7780rmi
0100-0200	BBC World Sce	SAs	5970erv, 12095sng
0100-0200	CRI	NAm	6180qvc
0100-0200	CRI	SAs	7370kas
0100-0200	CRI	Eu	9675kas
0100-0200	Encore ClassMus	NAm	5010rmi, 5850rmi
0100-0200	R. Romania Int.	NAm	6130gal, 7325gal
0100-0200	VORW R. Int.	NAm,Eu,ME	7780rmi
0100-0200	WHRI	NAm,Eu	5920hri
0100-0200	WHRI	NAm	7385hri
0100-0230	BBC World Sce	SAs	1413sla
0100-0300	WLC Radio	NAm	9330bcq
0100-0520	BBC World Sce	Eu	198dro
0100-0700	R. Habana Cuba	NAm	9700hab
0100-0700	WWCR	NAm,Eu	4840wcr
0100-0800	R. Habana Cuba	NAm	6000hab

0100	English	Area	kHz
0100-0800	Overcomer Min.	NAm	7730rmi
0100-1300	University Net.	NAm,Eu	5935wcr
0115-0230	T8WH - Hope R.	EAs	15680hbn
0130-0200	R. Prague Int.	Car,SAm	5800rmi
0130-0200	World of Radio	Car, CAm	5010rmi*
0130-0200	World of Radio	NAm	5850rmi*, 9955rmi*
0130-0200	World of Radio	Eu,ME,NAf	7780rmi
0200	**English**		
0200-0230	BVB	SAs	11790mdc
0200-0230	R. Thailand WS	NAm	13750udo
0200-0230	World of Radio	Eu,ME,NAf	9955rmi
0200-0300	CRI	SAs	9610kas
0200-0300	KBS World R.	LAm	9580kim
0200-0300	Overcomer Min.	NAm	3215wcr
0200-0300	VORW R. Int.	NAm	5850rmi
0200-0300	WBCQ	NAm,CAm	6160bcq †±
0200-0300	WHRI	NAm,Eu	5920hri
0200-0300	WHRI	LAm	7315hri
0200-0300	WWCR	NAm,NAf	3215wcr
0200-0330	R. Pilipinas	ME	9475pht, 15640pht, 17820pht
0200-0400	CRI	SAs	11770kas
0200-0400	WHRI	LAm	7315hri
0200-0500	T8WH - Hope R.	SEA	15680hbn
0200-0500	WRNO	NAm	7505rno †
0200-0500	WWRB	NAm	3185wrb
0200-0600	WTWW	NAm	5830tww †*
0200-0700	Supreme Master	NAm	5950rmi
0200-0900	WHRI	NAm	7385hri
0230-0300	World of Radio	LAm	5800rmi
0230-0300	World of Radio	Eu,ME,NAf	7780rmi
0300	**English**		
0300-0400	BBC World Sce	ME	6195sla
0300-0400	CRI	SAs	13800kas
0300-0400	CRI	NAm	5910qvc
0300-0400	Encore ClassMus	SAm,Car	5800rmi
0300-0400	Encore ClassMus	NAm	9455rmi
0300-0400	Madagascar W.V.	As	13760mwv
0300-0400	R. Taiwan Int.	EAs	15320pao
0300-0400	VOA	Af	909bot
0300-0400	VORW R. Int.	Car,SAm	5800rmi
0300-0400	WHRI	NAm,Eu	5920hri
0300-0400	WHRI	LAm	7315hri
0300-0400	WHRI	NAm,Eu	7520hri
0300-0430	VOA	Af	1530sao
0300-0500	BBC World Sce	ME	7285sla
0300-0500	CRI	EAs	13590bei, 15120bei
0300-0500	VOA	Af	9775bot
0300-0500	WWCR	CAm,Af	5890wcr
0300-0600	VOA	Af	4930bot
0300-0600	WLC Radio	NAm	9330bcq
0300-0600	WWCR	NAm,NAf	3215wcr
0300-0700	VOA	Af	6080sao
0300-0800	Overcomer Min.	NAm	5850rmi
0300-1300	Overcomer Min.	Af	5890wcr

0300	English	Area	kHz
0300-1400	Overcomer Min.	NAm,ME,Eu	7780rmi
0320-0330	TWR Africa	WAf	1566par
0330-0400	R. Slovakia Int	NAm	9395rmi
0330-0400	SW Radiogram	NAm	9265inb*
0330-0400	World of Radio	LAm	5800rmi
0330-0600	WRMI	CAm	5985rmi
0400	**English**		
0400-0430	R. Prague Int.	LAm	9955rmi
0400-0430	WHRI	LAm	7315hri
0400-0430	World of Radio	NAm	6160bcq±**
0400-0500	BBC World Sce	ME	12095sla
0400-0500	BBC World Sce	EAf	9915mdc
0400-0500	Madagascar W.V.	Af	11825mwv
0400-0500	R. Romania Int.	NAm	6020gal, 7410tig
0400-0500	R. Romania Int.	SAs	9820tig +, 11790gal
0400-0500	VOA	Af	4960sao
0400-0500	VOA	Af	909bot
0400-0500	VO Korea	LAm	11735kuj, 13760kuj, 15180kuj
0400-0500	VO Korea	EAs	7220kuj, 9445kuj, 9730kuj
0400-0500	VO Turkey	Eu,NAm	6125emr
0400-0500	VO Turkey	ME	7240emr
0400-0600	CRI	CAs,Eu	17730xia
0400-0600	CRI	CAs	17855bei
0400-0600	WHRI	NAm,Eu	5920hri
0400-0800	Overcomer Min.	NAm	9395rmi
0400-0800	VO Hope-Africa	WAf	11680luv
0400-0800	VO Hope-Africa	CAf,EAf,SAf	9680luv
0400-2100	Overcomer Min.	NAm	9455rmi
0430-0500	Hobart R. Int.	NAm	5130bcq
0430-0500	Hobart R. Int.	LAm	9955rmi
0430-0500	R. Japan	Eu	6155mos
0430-0500	R. Japan	WAf	7245smg
0430-0500	R. Japan	SAf	7445iss
0430-0500	TWR Africa	WAf	1566par
0430-0500	World of Radio	LAm	9955rmi
0430-0600	WHRI	LAm	7315hri
0445-0515	TWR Africa	WAf	1476par
0500	**English**		
0500-0530	R. Japan	Eu	6155mos
0500-0530	R. Japan	WAf	7245smg
0500-0530	R. Japan	SAf	7445iss
0500-0600	BBC World Sce	SAf	12095mdc
0500-0600	BBC World Sce	EAf	13860dha
0500-0600	BBC World Sce	WAf	5875smg
0500-0600	BBC World Sce	CAf	6195asc
0500-0600	Overcomer Min.	NAm	3215wcr
0500-0600	VO Korea	SEA	13650kuj, 15105kuj
0500-0700	BBC World Sce	WAf	6005asc
0500-0700	CRI	SAs	15430kas
0500-0700	CRI	ME,NAf	17510kas
0500-0700	R. Habana Cuba	NAm	6060hab
0500-0700	VOA	Af	909bot, 15580bot
0500-0800	R. Kuwait	SAs	11970kbd +**
0500-0800	R. Kuwait	Eu	15530kbd**
0500-0900	CRI	SAs	11895kas, 15465kas
0500-1100	CRI	SAs	15350kas
0500-1300	Overcomer Min.	Af	5890wcr
0530-0545	TWR Africa	WAf	1566par
0530-0600	R. Thailand WS	Eu	17640udo
0600	**English**		
0600-0700	BBC World Sce	Eu	3955wof +
0600-0700	BBC World Sce	WAf	7325wof
0600-0700	BBC World Sce	CAf	7445asc, 12095smg
0600-0700	BBC World Sce	SAf	9410sao
0600-0700	CRI	ME	11870kas, 15145kas
0600-0700	CRI	SEA	13645xia
0600-0700	R. Habana Cuba	CAm	5040hab
0600-0700	VOA	Af	1530sao, 9550sao

0600	English	Area	kHz
0600-0700	VO Korea	EAs	7220kuj, 9445kuj, 9730kuj
0600-0800	BBC World Sce	EAf	13680mdc
0600-0800	BBC World Sce	SAf	15400mdc
0600-0800	CRI	SEA	17710bei
0600-0800	R. Habana Cuba	NAm	6100hab
0600-0800	WLC Radio	NAm	9330bcq
0600-0900	WHRI	NAm,Eu	5920hri
0600-0900	WHRI	LAm	7315hri
0600-1200	Overcomer Min.	NAm	3215wcr
0630-0700	R. Romania Int.	AUS,NZL	15450tig+, 17780gal
0630-0700	R. Romania Int.	Eu	6040gal+, 7345tig
0700	**English**		
0700-0800	BBC World Sce	SAf	12095sao
0700-0800	BBC World Sce	WAf	7325sao, 9915asc
0700-0800	BBC World Sce	CAf	9410sao, 15490smg
0700-0800	CRI	SEA	13660xia
0700-0800	CTB-Holy Tibet	As	4905lha, 4920lha, 6025lha, 6110lha, 6130lha, 6200lha, 9490lha, 9580lha
0700-0900	CRI	ME,NAf	17670kas
0700-1000	CRI	SAs	15185kas
0700-1000	Overcomer Min.	Eu,NAm	7315inb +
0700-1000	Overcomer Min.	Eu,NAf	9265inb +
0700-1000	WINB	CAm	7315inb +
0700-1000	WWCR	NAm,Eu	4840wcr
0700-1300	CRI	Eu	17490kas
0700-1300	Overcomer Min.	NAm	4840wcr
0700-2000	World Music R.	Eu	15805rnd †
0700-2300	Shortwave R.	WEu	3975wis
0800	**English**		
0800-0830	SW Radiogram	NAm	5850rmi*, 7730rmi*
0800-0900	BBC World Sce	SAs	15620sng +
0800-0900	IsleOfM/MeltPot	Eu	9670rob*
0800-0900	KNLS Int.	EAs	6075nls
0800-0900	VORW R. Int.	NAm	5850rmi
0800-0900	VORW R. Int.	NAm,Pac	7730rmi
0800-0900	WLC Radio	NAm	9330bcq
0800-0945	T8WH - Hope R.	EAs	15680hbn
0800-1000	CRI	EAs	9415xia
0800-1000	VO Nigeria	WAf	7255aja*
0800-1030	KBS World R.	SEA	9770kim
0800-1145	T8WH - Hope R.	SEA	9965hbn
0800-1200	T8WH - Hope R.	SEA	9930hbn ‡
0800-1600	Shortwave R.	WEu	6160wis
0830-0900	Alameda Bible	NAm	5850rmi
0830-0900	Alameda Bible	NAm,Pac	7730rmi
0830-0900	Hobart R. Int.	NAm	5850rmi, 7730rmi
0830-0900	Hobart R. Int.	NAm	5950rmi
0900	**English**		
0900-0930	VO Mongolia	EAs	12085uba
0900-1000	CRI	Eu	17570uru, 17650kas
0900-1000	IRRS Shortwave	Eu,ME,NAf	9510tig
0900-1000	Supreme Master	NAm	5850rmi
0900-1000	WHRI	AUS,NZL,Pac	11825hri
0900-1000	WHRI	NAm,Eu	5920hri
0900-1000	WHRI	LAm	7315hri
0900-1000	WHRI	NAm	7385hri
0900-1100	CRI	Pac	15210kun, 17690jin
0900-1300	WEWN	EAs	9470ewn ‡
0900-1600	The Mighty KBC	Eu	6095nau**
1000	**English**		
1000-1010	All India R.	EAs	15410bgl+
1000-1015	TWR Asia	SEA	11965twr
1000-1020	TWR Asia	AUS,NZL,Pac	11995twr
1000-1030	BBC World Sce	CAs	1251dsb
1000-1030	R. Slovakia Int	WEu	6005kll
1000-1030	VO Vietnam	As	9840vni ±, 12020vni‡±
1000-1045	TWR Asia	SEA	11995twr

1000	English	Area	kHz
1000-1100	CRI	SAs	15190kas
1000-1100	CRI	EAs	5955xia, 7215xia, 11635bei
1000-1100	KNLS Int.	EAs	9605nls
1000-1100	Supreme Master	NAm	5950rmi
1000-1100	VO Indonesia	SEA	3325pga, 4750jak †
1000-1100	VO Korea	LAm	6170kuj, 9435kuj
1000-1100	VO Korea	SEA	6185kuj, 9850kuj
1000-1100	WHRI	AUS,NZL,Pac	11825hri
1000-1100	WHRI	LAm	7315hri
1000-1100	WWCR	NAm,Eu	4840wcr
1000-1200	BBC World Sce	SEA	6195sng, 11945sng
1000-1200	BBC World Sce	EAs,SEA	9580sng
1000-1200	CRI	SEA	13590bei, 13720xia
1000-1200	Overcomer Min.	Eu,NAf	9265inb +
1000-1200	WHRI	NAm,Eu	5920hri
1000-1200	WINB	CAm	9265inb +
1000-1300	Overcomer Min.	NAm	4840wcr
1000-1400	WHRI	NAm	7385hri
1000-1600	Overcomer Min.	NAm	5850rmi, 7730rmi
1000-1700	WRMI	NAm,Pac	7730rmi
1000-2000	Overcomer Min.	NAm	9395rmi
1020-1120	Pars Today	ME	702kia
1025-1055	TWR Asia	SAs	13800twr+
1030-1300	IRRS Shortwave	Eu,ME,NAf	9510tig
1100	**English**		
1100-1130	R. Japan	SEA	11825sng
1100-1130	R. Saranrom	SEA	1575bph
1100-1130	TWR Asia	SEA	11965twr
1100-1130	TWR Asia	EAs	9910twr
1100-1200	CRI	SAs	11795kas
1100-1200	CRI	SEA	9730bei
1100-1200	Encore ClassMus	Eu	6070rob, 9670rob
1100-1200	WRMI	Eu,ME,Af	15770rmi
1100-1300	CRI	SEA	1269xuw
1100-1300	CRI	SAs	7250kas, 11650uru, 12015kas
1100-1300	WHRI	LAm	7315hri
1100-1300	WWCR	NAm,Eu	4840wcr
1100-1400	Supreme Master	NAm	7570rmi
1100-1600	CRI	EAs	5955bei
1100-1700	WRMI	NAm	5850rmi
1120-1140	R. Taiwan Int.	SEA	12100pao
1130-1145	TWR Asia	SEA	11965twr
1130-1145	TWR Asia	EAs	9910twr
1130-1200	VOA	SEA	12030pht, 12125udo, 15715udo
1130-1200	VO Vietnam	As	9840vni ±, 12020vni ±
1145-1200	R. Thailand WS	SEA	5875udo
1200	**English**		
1200-1230	BVB	EAs	17650mdc
1200-1230	RchBeyondAUS	As	11825knx
1200-1300	BBC World Sce	EAs	11850sng
1200-1300	BBC World Sce	SAs	12065sla, 15310sla
1200-1300	CRI	CAs	11690xia
1200-1300	CRI	SEA	684dof, 1188kun, 9600kun, 9645bei, 9730kun
1200-1300	CRI	SAs	9460kas
1200-1300	CRI	Pac	9760kun
1200-1300	KNLS Int.	EAs	9625nls, 9665nls
1200-1300	R. Romania Int.	Eu	13750tig, 15460tig
1200-1300	R. Romania Int.	EAf	15600tig, 17800gal
1200-1300	Overcomer Min.	Eu,ME,Af	15770rmi
1200-1400	CRI	Pac	11760kun
1200-1400	CRI	SEA	1341hdu, 11980kun
1200-1400	CRI	Eu	13790uru
1200-1400	R. Oz-Viola	Eu	5825hil
1200-1400	WINB	CAm	9265inb
1200-1700	WINB	Eu,NAf	13655inb +
1200-1700	WWCR	NAm,Eu,NAf	15825wcr
1200-2300	WHRI	NAm	9840hri
1200-2400	WRMI	Eu,ME,Af	15770rmi
1230-1245	BVB	SEA	21480mdc**
1230-1300	BangladeshBetar	SAs	4750dka
1230-1300	R. Thailand WS	SEA,Pac	9940udo
1230-1300	VO Vietnam	As	9840vni ±, 12020vni ±
1230-1300	WWCR	NAm,Eu,NAf	15825wcr
1300	**English**		
1300-1330	BBC World Sce	CAs	1251dsb
1300-1330	BVB	EAs	7555dsb
1300-1330	R. Prague Int.	LAm	9955rmi
1300-1330	SW Radiogram	NAm	15770rmi*
1300-1330	VOA	SEA	1575bph
1300-1330	VO Mongolia	CEu,WEu	6005kll
1300-1330	World of Radio	Eu,ME,NAf	15770rmi
1300-1330	WWCR	NAm,Eu,NAf	15825wcr
1300-1400	BBC World Sce	SAs	9410sla, 12065sng
1300-1400	CRI	Eu	11640kas
1300-1400	CRI	Pac	11900kun
1300-1400	CRI	SAs	7300kas, 9655kas
1300-1400	CRI	NAm	9570qvc
1300-1400	CRI	SEA	9730bei, 11910bei
1300-1400	Encore ClassMus	Eu	15770rmi
1300-1400	KBS World R.	NAm	15575kim
1300-1400	KBS World R.	SEA	9570kim
1300-1400	R. Poland	Eu	1386vst
1300-1400	Shiokaze	KRE	6145yam*, 7295yam*
1300-1400	VO Indonesia	SEA	3325pga, 4750jak †
1300-1400	VO Korea	Eu	7570kuj, 12015kuj
1300-1400	VO Korea	NAm	9435kuj, 11710kuj
1300-1400	VO Tajik	WAs	1143dsb, 7245dsb
1300-1400	VORW R. Int.	Eu,ME,Af	15770rmi
1300-1400	WHRI	NAm,Eu	9605hri
1300-1400	WWCR	NAm,Eu	13845wcr
1300-1500	CRI	CAs,Eu	9765bji
1300-1500	WWCR	Af	7490wcr
1300-1600	CRI	SEA	9870xia
1300-1800	BBC World Sce	SAs	1413sla
1300-2400	WWCR	CAm,Af	9980wcr
1315-1330	RchBeyondAUS	As	11825knx
1315-1345	TWR Asia	EAs	7510twr
1330-1400	Alameda Bible	Eu,NAf,ME	15770rmi
1330-1400	R. Tirana Int.	CEu,WEu	6005kll
1330-1400	SW Radiogram	NAm	15770rmi*
1330-1400	VO Vietnam	As	9840vni ±, 12020vni ±
1330-1430	VO Turkey	Eu	12035emr
1345-1400	RchBeyondAUS	As	11875knx
1400	**English**		
1400-0200	WTWW	NAm	9475tww †
1400-1430	BVB	SAs	11900nau*
1400-1430	FEBA India	IND	1548put
1400-1430	R. Japan	SEA	11925dha
1400-1430	R. Japan	SAs	6165tac
1400-1430	R. Thailand WS	SEA,Pac	9940udo
1400-1500	CRI	ME	6100uru
1400-1500	CRI	SAs	7300uru, 9460uru
1400-1500	CRI	Eu	9795uru, 11880kas
1400-1500	KNLS Int.	EAs	6110nls
1400-1500	R. Sult.of Oman	Eu,ME	15140thu †
1400-1500	Supreme Master	NAm,Eu,ME	7780rmi
1400-1500	Overcomer Min.	ME	9400sof
1400-1500	VOA	SEA	17885bot
1400-1500	WWCR	NAm,Eu	13845wcr
1400-1600	CRI	EAf	13685bko, 17630bko
1400-1600	CRI	SEA	6135xia
1400-1600	KBS World R.	SAs	9630kim
1400-1600	VO Hope-Africa	WAf	6065luv
1400-1600	VO Hope-Africa	CAf,EAf,SAf	9680luv
1400-1600	WLC Radio	NAm	9330bcq

1400	English	Area	kHz
1400-1630	VOA	Af	15580bot
1400-1700	VOA	Af	4930bot
1400-1800	WHRI	Af	21610hri
1400-2000	Supreme Master	Eu,ME,Af	15770rmi
1400-2000	Overcomer Min.	NAm,Eu,NAf	13845wcr
1400-2100	PanAm Bcasting.	Af	21525rmi*
1400-2100	Overcomer Min.	Car,SAm	5800rmi
1400-2100	WRMI	Af	21525rmi
1400-2100	WRMI	NAm	7570rmi
1400-2200	WJHR	NAm	15555jhr ‡
1400-2200	WTWW	CAm	9930tww ‡
1400-2400	WINB	CAm	9265inb
1400-2400	WRMI	Car,SAm	5800rmi
1400-2400	WTWW	NAm	15810tww ‡
1415-1420	TWR India	SAs	9290erv
1420-1425	TWR India	SAs	9290erv
1420-1455	TWR Africa	SAf	7455man
1425-1445	TWR India	SAs	9290erv
1430-1500	BVB	SAs	11900nau
1430-1500	Lao National R.	SEA	567vie, 6130vie ‡
1430-1500	PanAm Bcasting.	ME	11800nau
1500	**English**		
1500-1530	SW Radiogram	NAm	13655inb*,+
1500-1530	VO Vietnam	As	9840vni ±, 12020vni ±
1500-1600	BBC World Sce	EAf	9410sla
1500-1600	CRI	SAs	1188kun, 7395uru, 9785jin
1500-1600	CRI	NAm	15700qvc
1500-1600	CRI	NAf,ME	6095kas, 9720uru
1500-1600	CRI	SEA	7325bei
1500-1600	CRI	Eu	9525kas
1500-1600	Overcomer Min.	NAm	7490wcr
1500-1600	VOA	Af	7455bot, 17895sao
1500-1600	VO Korea	Eu	7570kuj, 12015kuj
1500-1600	VO Korea	NAm	9435kuj, 11710kuj
1500-1600	WWCR	Af	7490wcr
1500-1700	CRI	Eu	9675kas
1500-1700	KBS World R.	Eu	9515kim
1500-1700	Overcomer Min.	Eu	11600sof
1500-1700	Overcomer Min.	ME	9400sof
1500-1800	CRI	SAs	1323uru
1500-1800	CRI	SEA	9880nnn
1500-1800	WWCR	NAm,Eu	13845wcr
1500-1900	BBC World Sce	ME	7485sng
1520-1620	Pars Today	SAs,SEA	7300sir
1530-1600	AWR Africa	SAs	6155dsb
1530-1600	AWR As/Pacific	SAs	12040trm ‡
1530-1600	R. Slovakia Int	WEu	6005kll
1530-1600	RTV Afghanistan	SAs	6100kab†
1530-1600	VO Mongolia	EAs	12015uba
1530-1700	VOA	EAf	1431dji
1540-1600	R. Japan	SEA	5985yan*
1600	**English**		
1600-1630	AWR Africa	ME	9580erv, 17730mdc
1600-1630	VOA	Af	6080sao
1600-1630	VO Vietnam	ME	7220vnl
1600-1630	VO Vietnam	Eu	7280vni, 9730vni
1600-1700	BBC World Sce	SAf	12095dha, 17640asc
1600-1700	CRI	SEA	6060kun
1600-1700	CRI	NAf,ME	7420uru
1600-1700	CRI	Eu	9875kas
1600-1700	CTB-Holy Tibet	As	4905lha, 4920lha, 6025lha, 6110lha, 6130lha, 6200lha, 7255lha, 7385lha
1600-1700	KBS World R.	SEA	9640kim
1600-1700	PanAm Bcasting.	EAf	6120nau**
1600-1700	R. Taiwan Int.	SAs,Af	6185tsh
1600-1700	Shiokaze	KRE	5990yam**, 6085yam**

1600	English	Area	kHz
1600-1700	Overcomer Min.	NAm,ME,Eu	7780rmi
1600-1700	VOA	Af	909bot, 1530sao
1600-1700	VO Korea	ME,NAf	9890kuj, 11645kuj
1600-1800	BBC World Sce	CAf	17830asc
1600-1800	CRI	SEA	1080xuw, 6175nnn
1600-1800	CRI	SAs	7235kas
1600-1800	CRI	Eu	7255kas
1600-1800	CRI	SAf	7435jin, 9570bei
1600-1800	VOA	Af	17895bot
1600-1800	WWCR	Af	12160wcr
1600-1900	Overcomer Min.	NAm	7490bcq
1600-1900	WLC Radio	Eu	9330bcq
1600-2000	BBC World Sce	EAf	7445mdc
1600-2000	Overcomer Min.	NAm,Eu,NAf	13845wcr
1600-2000	Overcomer Min.	NAm	7490bcq
1600-2100	KVOH - VO Hope	CAm,SAm	17775voh
1600-2100	Overcomer Min.	NAm	7490bcq
1600-2100	VO Hope-Africa	CAf,EAf,SAf	4965luv
1600-2100	VO Hope-Africa	WAf	6065luv
1600-2200	Overcomer Min.	NAm	7490bcq
1630-1700	R. Slovakia Int	WEu	6005kll
1630-1700	Vatican R.	Af	11935mdc, 13830smg
1630-1700	VOA	Af	11850dha*, 13865wof*, 15180sao*
1630-1700	VOA	SAs,SEA	1575bph
1630-1700	VOA	Af	6080sao, 15580bot
1630-1730	PanAm Bcasting.	EAs	5945tac**
1630-1730	PanAm Bcasting.	SAs	6060tac**
1630-1900	VO Nigeria	Af,Eu	11770aja**, 15120aja+,†
1700	**English**		
1700-1730	Alameda Bible	EAf	13660iss
1700-1730	VOA	Af	11850kwt
1700-1730	VOA	Af	15580bot
1700-1800	BBC World Sce	CAs	1251dsb
1700-1800	BBC World Sce	WAf	17780asc
1700-1800	CRI	SEA	6090kun, 7420kun
1700-1800	CRI	SAs	6140kas, 7410kas
1700-1800	CRI	ME	6165bei
1700-1800	Encore ClassMus	Eu	9670rob
1700-1800	VOA	Af	6080sao
1700-1900	BBC World Sce	WAf	15400asc
1700-1900	BBC World Sce	ME	6195sla
1700-1900	CRI	Eu	6100bei
1700-2000	BBC World Sce	SAf	7265mdc
1700-2000	Overcomer Min.	NAm,ME,Eu	7780rmi
1715-1730	Vatican R.	ME	7230smg
1715-1800	VO Africa	CAf	9505alf
1725-1750	TWR Africa	WAf	1476par
1725-1820	TWR Africa	WAf	1476par
1730-1800	VOA	Af	11850sao
1730-1830	VO Turkey	CAs,SAs	9660emr
1730-2100	VOA	Af	15580bot
1745-1755	All India R.	Eu	7550bgl +
1745-1825	TWR Africa	WAf	1566par
1745-1900	BangladeshBetar	SAs	4750dka
1800	**English**		
1800-0100	University Net.	NAm,Eu	13845wcr
1800-1810	Zanzibar BC	EAf,ME	11735dol†
1800-1815	BVB	ME	9715mos
1800-1830	BVB	ME	9715mos
1800-1830	VOA	EAf	1431dji
1800-1850	TWR Africa	EAf	9500man
1800-1900	BBC World Sce	CAf	11810asc
1800-1900	BBC World Sce	WAf	9915wof
1800-1900	CRI	Eu	7405bei
1800-1900	Madagascar W.V.	Af	13670mwv
1800-1900	R. Belarus Int.	CEu,WEu	3985kll
1800-1900	R. Romania Int.	Eu	5935tig, 7350tig +

1800	English	Area	kHz
1800-1900	Overcomer Min.	Af	12160wcr
1800-1900	Overcomer Min.	NAm,Eu,NAf	15825wcr
1800-1900	TWR Africa	EAf	9500man
1800-1900	VOA	Af	11610udo
1800-1900	VOA	Af	909bot, 4930bot
1800-1900	VO Korea	Eu	7570kuj, 12015kuj
1800-1900	WWCR	Af	12160wcr
1800-2000	BBC World Sce	EAf	9410dha
1800-2000	WHRI	NAm,Eu	17815hri
1800-2015	TWR Africa	SAf	1170man
1800-2100	R. Kuwait	Eu	15540kbd +†
1805-1825	TWR Africa	WAf	1566par
1830-1930	BVB	ME	9715mos
1830-1930	CRI	NAf	11640bko
1900	**English**		
1900-1930	Alameda Bible	NAf,WAf	7245iss
1900-1930	FollowTheBible	WAf	11660asc
1900-1930	FollowTheBible	SAf	12005asc
1900-1930	VO Vietnam	Eu	7280vni, 9730vni
1900-1930	World of Radio	Eu	7290sof***
1900-2000	BBC World Sce	SAf	6195sao
1900-2000	IRRS Shortwave	Eu,ME,NAf	7290sof
1900-2000	R. Thailand WS	Eu	7475udo
1900-2000	VOA	Af	13590sao
1900-2000	VO Korea	SAf	7210kuj, 11910kuj
1900-2000	VO Korea	ME,NAf	9875kuj, 11635kuj
1900-2000	WWCR	Af	12160wcr
1900-2100	BBC World Sce	CAf	11810wof
1900-2100	BBC World Sce	WAf	12095asc
1900-2100	BBC World Sce	ME	1413sla
1900-2100	CRI	ME,NAf	7295uru, 9440kun
1900-2100	Overcomer Min.	Af	12160wcr
1900-2100	VOA	Af	909bot, 4930bot
1900-2200	WWCR	NAm,Eu,NAf	15825wcr
1900-2400	WEWN	Af	15610ewn
1915-1930	BVB	ME	5935nau
1920-2020	Pars Today	SAf	11880sir
1920-2020	Pars Today	Eu	6040sir
1930-2015	BVB	ME	6080nau
1930-2030	VO Turkey	Eu	6050emr
2000	**English**		
2000-0100	University Net.	NAm,Eu	13845wcr
2000-2030	R. Prague Int.	Eu,NAm	15770rmi
2000-2030	Vatican R.	Af	6010smg, 7365smg
2000-2100	CRI	SAf	5985bei
2000-2100	Encore ClassMus	Eu	6070rob
2000-2100	IsleOfM/MeltPot	Eu	6070rob*
2000-2100	Madagascar W.V.	Af	11965mwv
2000-2100	R. Belarus Int.	CEu,WEu	3985kll
2000-2100	R. Habana Cuba	NAm	15140hab
2000-2100	VOA	Af	6195bot
2000-2100	VORW R. Int.	NAm,Eu,ME	7780rmi
2000-2100	WBCQ	NAm,CAm	7490bcq †±
2000-2130	CRI	EAf	11640bko
2000-2130	CRI	CAf	13630bko
2000-2200	CRI	Eu	7285xia, 7415kas, 9600kas
2000-2200	Supreme Master	NAm	9395rmi
2000-2200	The Mighty KBC	Eu	6080erv*
2000-2200	VOA	Af	1530sao
2000-2400	WINB	CAm	9265inb
2030-2045	R. Thailand WS	Eu	7475udo
2030-2100	Alameda Bible	NAm,Eu,ME	7780rmi
2030-2100	R. Tirana Int.	Eu,ME,NAf	15770rmi
2030-2100	VOA	EAf	1431dji
2030-2100	VO Vietnam	ME	7220vni
2100	**English**	**Area**	**kHz**
2100-0100	Supreme Master	Car,SAm	5800rmi

2100	English	Area	kHz
2100-2130	VOA	EAf	1431dji
2100-2200	BBC World Sce	CAf	11810asc
2100-2200	BBC World Sce	WAf	12095asc
2100-2200	CRI	SAf	7205xia, 7325bei
2100-2200	VOA	Af	6195sao, 11720grv
2100-2200	VO Indonesia	SEA	3325pga, 4750jak †
2100-2200	VO Korea	Eu	7570kuj, 12015kuj
2100-2200	VORW R. Int.	NAm,Eu,ME	7780rmi
2100-2200	VORW R. Int.	LAm	9955rmi
2100-2300	R. Oz-Viola	Eu	5825hil
2100-2300	WWCR	Af	9350wcr
2100-2400	Overcomer Min.	Eu,ME,Af	15770rmi
2100-2400	WRMI	NAm	7570rmi
2115-2245	R. Cairo	Eu	9900abs ‡
2130-0330	VOA	EAf	1431dji
2130-2200	R. Romania Int.	Eu	6030gal +, 7375gal
2130-2200	R. Romania Int.	NAm	6170tig, 7310tig
2130-2200	VO Vietnam	Eu	7280vni, 9730vni
2130-2230	VO Turkey	SEA,Pac	9610emr
2200	**English**		
2200-0200	WWCR	NAm,Eu	6115wcr
2200-0800	WTWW	NAm	5085tww*
2200-2215	WWCR	NAm,Eu	6115wcr
2200-2230	AWR As/Pacific	SEA	11990sda
2200-2230	R. Taiwan Int.	Eu,NAm	7780rmi
2200-2230	World of Radio	NAm	7490bcq ±
2200-2300	BBC World Sce	EAs	5960sla
2200-2300	BBC World Sce	SEA	6150pht, 7300sla
2200-2300	CRI	EAs	5915bei
2200-2300	Encore ClassMus	Eu	3955rob
2200-2300	KBS World R.	Eu	11810kim
2200-2300	R. Habana Cuba	Af	11880hab
2200-2300	Overcomer Min.	Af	9350wcr
2200-2300	VORW R. Int.	LAm	9955rmi
2200-2300	WHRI	AUS,NZL,Pac	15530hri
2200-2400	BBC World Sce	SEA	3915sng, 5890sng
2200-2400	BBC World Sce	EAs,SEA	6195sng
2230-2300	Hobart R. Int.	LAm	9955rmi
2230-2300	R. Tirana Int.	NAm,Eu	7780rmi
2230-2400	WRMI	NAm	5850rmi
2300	**English**		
2300-0100	CRI	SEA	11790xia
2300-0200	CRI	Eu	7350kas
2300-0200	WWRB	NAm	3215wrb
2300-2330	REE	WAf,Atl	11685nob
2300-2330	REE	SAm	11940nob
2300-2330	REE	ME,IOc	12030nob
2300-2330	REE	NAm	9690nob
2300-2330	WBCQ	NAm,CAm	7490bcq †±
2300-2330	World of Radio	LAm	9955rmi
2300-2400	BBC World Sce	SEA	11825pht
2300-2400	CRI	SAs	5915kas, 7410kas
2300-2400	CRI	NAm,CAm	5990qvc
2300-2400	CRI	EAs	6145bei
2300-2400	CRI	SEA	9535kun
2300-2400	IsleOfM/MeltPot	NAm	7490bcq*
2300-2400	R. Romania Int.	Eu	6040gal +, 7220gal
2300-2400	R. Romania Int.	EAs	7325tig, 9620tig
2300-2400	Overcomer Min.	NAm	5850rmi, 7730rmi, 9455rmi
2300-2400	Overcomer Min.	Af	5935wcr
2300-2400	Overcomer Min.	NAm,Eu	6115wcr
2300-2400	TWR Bonaire	Car	800twb
2300-2400	VO Turkey	Eu,NAm	5960emr
2300-2400	WBCQ	NAm,CAm	7490bcq †±
2300-2400	WHRI	NAm,Eu	5920hri
2300-2400	WHRI	LAm	7315hri
2300-2400	WHRI	NAm	7385hri
2300-2400	WRMI	NAm	7570rmi
2300-2400	WWCR	Af	5935wcr

2300	English	Area	kHz
2300-2400	WWCR	NAm,Eu	6115wcr
2330-2400	Hobart R. Int.	Eu	7780rmi
2330-2400	SW Radiogram	NAm	7780rmi*
2330-2400	VO Vietnam	As	9840vni ±, 12020vni‡±
2330-2400	WBCQ	NAm,CAm	7490bcq †±

ENGLISH/VARIOUS

0400	**English/Arabic/Others**		
0400-0500	Eye R.	SSD	7340smg
1600	**English/Arabic/Others**		
1600-1800	Eye R.	SSD	15410iss
0600	**English/Dutch**		
0600-1100	Mike R.	Eu	6195hee*
0700	**English/Dutch**		
0700-1600	R.Piepzender	Eu	15880zwo*
0700-1800	R. Delta Int	Eu	6020elb*
1600	**English/Dutch**		
1600-2400	R.Piepzender	Eu	3920zwo
1700	**English/Dutch**		
1700-2300	Mike R.	Eu	3940hee*
2100	**English/Dutch**		
2100-0200	R. Delta Int	Eu	6005elb*
0800	**English/Dutch/French/German**		
0800-1700	R. MiAmigo Int.	CEu,WEu	6085kll
0000	**English/Finnish**		
0000-0600	Scan.Weekend R.	Eu	6170vir*
0000-0800	Scan.Weekend R.	Eu	11690vir*
0000-2200	Scan.Weekend R.	Eu	1602vir*
0600	**English/Finnish**		
0600-0900	Scan.Weekend R.	Eu	5980vir*
0800	**English/Finnish**		
0800-1400	Scan.Weekend R.	Eu	11720vir*
0900	**English/Finnish**		
0900-1500	Scan.Weekend R.	Eu	6170vir*
1400	**English/Finnish**		
1400-1700	Scan.Weekend R.	Eu	11690vir*
1500	**English/Finnish**		
1500-1900	Scan.Weekend R.	Eu	5980vir*
1700	**English/Finnish**		
1700-1900	Scan.Weekend R.	Eu	11720vir*
1900	**English/Finnish**		
1900-2200	Scan.Weekend R.	Eu	6170vir*, 11690vir*
2200	**English/Finnish**		
2200-2300	Scan.Weekend R.	Eu	11720vir*
2200-2400	Scan.Weekend R.	Eu	1602vir*, 6170vir*
2300	**English/Finnish**		
2300-2400	Scan.Weekend R.	Eu	11690vir*
2200	**English/French/Baoule**		
2200-2215	TWR Africa	WAf	1566par
0000	**English/French/Portuguese**		
0000-2400	R. Onda	Eu	6140bort
1600	**English/German**		
1600-1700	R. Öömrang	NAm	15215iss*
0400	**English/Igbo/Twi**		
0430-0445	TWR Africa	WAf	1566par
0700	**English/Kanuri**		
0700-0800	Dandal Kura R.	NIG	13590nau
1800	**English/Kanuri**		
1800-1830	Dandal Kura R.	NIG	9850iss
1100	**English (Liturgy)**		
1130-1200	Vatican R.	Af	15595smg, 17790smg
0400	**English/Ndebele/Shona**		
0400-0500	VOA Studio 7	ZWE	909bot, 6175bot, 7255sao
1700	**English/Ndebele/Shona**		
1700-1800	VOA Studio 7	ZWE	909bot, 4930bot, 13860sao, 15460sao
1800	**English/ Ndebele/Shona**	**Area**	**kHz**
1800-1900	VOA Studio 7	ZWE	909bot, 4930bot, 13860sao, 15460sao
0400	**English/Norwegian**		
0420-2310	R. N.Star/Ferry	NEu	1611erd
0800	**English/Norwegian**		
0855-1600	LKB/LLE Bergen	NEu	1314erd
1600	**English/Norwegian**		
1600-2310	R. N.Star/Ferry	NEu	1314erd
0400	**English/Pacific Languages**		
0400-0700	RNZ Pacific	Pac	13840ran
0700	**English/Pacific Languages**		
0700-1000	RNZ Pacific	Pac	11725ran
1000	**English/Pacific Languages**		
1000-1300	RNZ Pacific	Pac	11725ran
1300	**English/Pacific Languages**		
1300-1650	RNZ Pacific	Pac	6115ran
1300-1900	RNZ Pacific	Pac	6115ran
1600	**English/Pacific Languages**		
1650-1735	RNZ Pacific	Pac	5975ran +
1700	**English/Pacific Languages**		
1735-1835	RNZ Pacific	Pac	7285ran +
1800	**English/Pacific Languages**		
1835-2000	RNZ Pacific	Pac	11690ran +
1900	**English/Pacific Languages**		
1900-2000	RNZ Pacific	Pac	11725ran
2000	**English/Pacific Languages**		
2000-2300	RNZ Pacific	Pac	13840ran
2300	**English/Pacific Languages**		
2300-0400	RNZ Pacific	Pac	15720ran
0000	**English/Spanish**		
0000-0230	WRMI	Car	5010rmi
0100	**English/Spanish**		
0100-0200	IsleOfM/MeltPot	NAm	7490bcq
1100	**English/Spanish**		
1100-1200	WRMI	Car	5010rmi
1100-1300	WRMI	Car,SAm	9955rmi
1200	**English/Spanish**		
1200-1230	WRMI	Car	5010rmi
1230-1700	WRMI	Car	5010rmi
1300	**English/Spanish**		
1300-1400	IsleOfM/MeltPot	Eu	6070rob
1300-1500	WRMI	Car,SAm	9955rmi
1500	**English/Spanish**		
1500-1600	IsleOfM/MeltPot	Eu	9400suf
1530-1700	WRMI	Car,SAm	9955rmi
1900	**English/Spanish**		
1900-2000	IsleOfM/MeltPot	Eu	6070rob
2200	**English/Spanish**		
2200-0500	WRMI	Car,SAm	9955rmi
0000	**English/Various**		
0000-0400	WRMI	Car,SAm	5800rmi
0000-2400	WRMI	NAm,Eu,ME	7780rmi, 9395rmi

FRENCH

0000	**French**		
0000-2400	RFI	Eu	3965iss +
0100	**French**		
0100-0130	R. Habana Cuba	SAm	15730bej
0130-0200	R. Habana Cuba	Car	5040hab
0200	**French**		
0200-0300	R. ForPeaceInt.	NAm,CAm	6160bcq
0200-0300	R. Romania Int.	NAm	6130gal, 7410gal
0400	**French**		
0400-0500	VO Korea	SEA	13650kuj, 15105kuj
0400-0700	RFI	EAf,CAf	7390iss
0400-0800	RFI	Af	9790iss
0430-0500	AWR Africa	WAf	5950nau

0500	French	Area	kHz
0500-0600	RFI	CAf	6040iss
0530-0600	R. Japan	CAf	13840mdc
0530-0600	R. Japan	WAf	7450iss
0530-0600	VOA	Af	1530sao
0530-0630	VOA	Af	4960sao, 6020sao, 9885smg, 13830bot
0600	**French**		
0600-0630	AWR Africa	NAf	9860nau, 11640nau
0600-0630	BBC World Sce	WAf	5875asc
0600-0630	BBC World Sce	NAf	6135smg, 7265wof
0600-0630	BBC World Sce	CAf	7305asc
0600-0630	R. Romania Int.	WAf	11790tig, 13730tig
0600-0630	R. Romania Int.	Eu	6040gal+, 7360gal
0600-0700	R. Damascus	ME	783tts
0600-0700	RFI	NAf,WAf	5925iss
0600-0700	VO Korea	LAm	11735kuj, 13760kuj, 15180kuj
0600-0800	CRI	Eu	15220kas
0600-0800	RFI	WAf,CAf	11700iss
0700	**French**		
0700-0730	AWR Africa	NAf	11880mos
0700-0730	BBC World Sce	CAf	17830dha
0700-0730	BBC World Sce	WAf	7305asc
0700-0800	RFI	CAf	15300iss*, 17850iss**
0700-1100	RFI	WAf	13695iss
0730-0745	Vatican R.	NAf	11620smg
0800	**French**		
0800-0830	AWR Africa	NAf	15145mos
0800-1100	RFI	WAf	15300iss
0800-1100	RFI	CAf	17850iss, 21580iss
0830-0900	VOA	Af	12030sao, 15715smg, 17700bot
1000	**French**		
1000-1030	VO Nigeria	WAf	7255aja*
1000-1100	WLC Radio	Eu	9330bcq
1100	**French**		
1100-1130	VOA	Af	12030sao, 13750bot, 15715bot, 17850smg
1100-1200	R. Romania Int.	Eu	11780gal, 15255gal, 15430tig
1100-1200	R. Romania Int.	NAf	17640tig
1100-1200	VO Korea	LAm	6170kuj, 9435kuj
1100-1200	VO Korea	SEA	6185kuj, 9850kuj
1200	**French**		
1200-1230	BBC World Sce	NAf	15490wof
1200-1230	BBC World Sce	WAf	17640asc
1200-1230	BBC World Sce	CAf	17765asc
1200-1230	VO Vietnam	As	7285vni
1200-1300	RFI	NAf,WAf	15300iss
1200-1300	RFI	WAf,CAf	17660iss
1200-1300	RFI	CAf	21580iss, 21690mdc
1200-1400	CRI	Eu	13570kas
1230-1300	R. Slovakia Int	WEu	6005kll
1300	**French**		
1300-1330	VO Vietnam	As	7285vni
1300-1400	CRI	EAf	13685bko
1300-1400	CRI	Eu	13720kas
1300-1400	CRI	NAf	17880bko
1300-1400	R. ForPeaceInt.	Eu,ME,Af	15770rmi
1400	**French**		
1400-1500	R. ForPeaceInt.	Af	21525rmi
1400-1500	VO Korea	Eu	7570kuj, 12015kuj
1400-1500	VO Korea	NAm	9435kuj, 11710kuj
1430-1500	R. Slovakia Int	WEu	6005kll
1455-1525	TWR Africa	WAf	9585man
1500	**French**		
1500-1530	Lao National R.	SEA	567vie, 6130vie ‡
1540-1600	R. Belarus Int.	CEu,WEu	3985kll

1600	French	Area	kHz
1600-1700	VO Korea	Eu	7570kuj, 12015kuj
1600-1700	VO Korea	NAm	9435kuj, 11710kuj
1600-1800	CRI	Eu	7350kas
1630-1700	R. Slovakia Int	WEu	3985kll
1630-1700	VO Vietnam	ME	7220vni
1630-1715	VO Africa	CAf	9505alf
1700	**French**		
1700-1715	Vatican R.	ME	7230smg
1700-1728	Vatican R.	NAf	11935smg
1700-1730	Vatican R.	Af	9705smg
1700-1800	RFI	WAf,CAf	11995iss, 13740iss
1700-1800	RFI	CAf	15300iss
1700-1800	R. Romania Int.	Eu	6025tig +, 7325tig
1800	**French**		
1800-1830	BBC World Sce	NAf	6080wof
1800-1830	BBC World Sce	CAf	6180sof
1800-1830	BBC World Sce	WAf	7220smg, 15490asc
1800-1830	BBC World Sce	SAf	9750smg
1800-1900	RFI	CAf	9660iss*, 13740iss**
1800-1900	RFI	WAf,CAf	9725iss
1800-1900	RFI	NAf,WAf	9810iss
1800-1900	VO Korea	SAf	7210kuj, 11910kuj
1800-1900	VO Korea	ME,NAf	9875kuj, 11635kuj
1800-2000	CRI	Eu	7360xia
1800-2000	CRI	NAf,WAf	7385kas
1800-2000	RFI	WAf,CAf	11995iss
1820-1920	Pars Today	Eu	6130sir
1830-1930	VOA	Af	12075smg, 15730bot
1830-1930	VO Turkey	CAf	9620emr
1830-2000	VOA	Af	1530sao
1830-2030	CRI	WAf	7350kas, 9645kun
1830-2030	VOA	EAf	1431dji
1900	**French**		
1900-1930	R. Taiwan Int.	Eu	6005sof
1900-2000	RFI	WAf,CAf	9580iss, 9635iss
1900-2000	R. Taiwan Int.	Af	9680iss
1900-2000	VOA	Af	17700grv
1900-2200	RFI	NAf,WAf	7205iss
1930-2000	AWR Africa	CAf	9780mos
1930-2000	R. Slovakia Int	WEu	3985kll
1930-2000	VO Vietnam	Eu	7280vni, 9730vni
1930-2030	VOA	Af	11900sao, 12075bot, 15730grv
1935-1950	TWR Africa	WAf	15105man
2000	**French**		
2000-2030	AWR Africa	WAf	7225nau, 9515mdc
2000-2030	VOA	Af	9485kwt
2000-2100	KBS World R.	Af	5950iss
2000-2100	R. ForPeaceInt.	Eu,ME,Af	15770rmi
2000-2100	VO Indonesia	SEA	3325pga, 4750jak †
2000-2100	VO Korea	Eu	7570kuj, 12015kuj
2000-2115	R. Cairo	Eu	9885abs ‡
2000-2200	RFI	NAf,WAf	9790iss
2030-2100	AWR Africa	WAf	7270mos
2030-2100	R. Habana Cuba	Eu	13680hab
2030-2100	R. Japan	WAf	9855mdc
2030-2100	Vatican R.	Af	6010smg, 7365smg
2030-2100	VOA	Af	11900sao, 11975smg
2030-2100	VOA	Af	9485kwt, 12075bot
2030-2100	VO Vietnam	Eu	7280vni, 9730vni
2030-2130	VO Turkey	Eu	5970emr
2030-2130	VO Turkey	NAf,WAf	9625emr
2030-2230	CRI	Eu	6115bei, 7350uru
2040-2100	TWR Africa	WAf	1566par
2100	**French**		
2100-2130	R. Habana Cuba	Af	11880hab
2100-2130	R. Habana Cuba	NAm	15140hab
2100-2130	R. Romania Int.	Eu	6030gal +, 7375gal
2100-2130	TWR Africa	WAf	1566par
2100-2130	VOA	EAf	1431dji

2100	French	Area	kHz
2100-2130	VOA	Af	5930sao, 9485kwt, 12075bot
2100-2130	VO Vietnam	ME	7220vni
2100-2200	KBS World R.	Eu	3955wof
2100-2200	R. ForPeaceInt.	Eu	6070rob
2100-2200	R. ForPeaceInt.	NAm,Eu,ME	7780rmi
2100-2200	R. ForPeaceInt.	LAm	9955rmi
2130-2200	TWR Africa	WAf	1566par
2130-2230	CRI	NAf,WAf	11975bko
2130-2230	CRI	CAf	13630bko
2200	**French**		
2200-2215	TWR Africa	WAf	1566par
2300	**French**		
2320-0020	Pars Today	WAf,CAf	7360sir, 9660sir
2330-2400	REE	WAf,Atl	11685nob
2330-2400	REE	SAm	11940nob
2330-2400	REE	ME,IOc	12030nob
2330-2400	REE	NAm	9690nob
2330-2400	R. Habana Cuba	SAm	15730bej

FRENCH/VARIOUS

2200	**French/Baoule/English**		
2200-2215	TWR Africa	WAf	1566par
0800	**French/Dutch/English/German**		
0800-1700	R. MiAmigo Int.	CEu,WEu	6085kll
0000	**French/English/Portuguese**		
0000-2400	R. Onda	Eu	6140bor †
0500	**French/Kanuri/Kanembu**		
0500-0600	R. Ndarason Int	TCD	7425wof
0600	**French/Kanuri/Kanembu**		
0600-0700	R. Ndarason Int	TCD	9535wof
0700	**French/Kanuri/Kanembu**		
0700-0800	R. Ndarason Int	TCD	9535asc
1800	**French/Kanuri/Kanembu**		
1800-1900	R. Ndarason Int	TCD	9635wof
1900	**French/Kanuri/Kanembu**		
1900-2100	R. Ndarason Int	TCD	12050asc
2000	**French/Mina**		
2040-2100	TWR Africa	WAf	1566par

GERMAN

0400	**German**		
0400-0500	Vozandes Media	Eu	6050qui*
0500	**German**		
0500-2300	R. HCJB DeuLand	CEu	3995wnm*
0600	**German**		
0600-0630	DWD	BaS,NoS,Med	5905pin, 6180pin
0600-0710	R. Ö1 (ORF)	Eu,NAf,ME	6155mos
0600-0720	R. Ö1 (ORF)	Eu,NAf,ME	6155mos
0600-0800	CRI	Eu	17615uru, 17720kas
0700	**German**		
0700-0730	R. Romania Int.	Eu	6175tig +, 7345tig
0700-1700	R. HCJB DeuLand	CEu	5920wnm
0800	**German**		
0830-1800	Europa 24	CEu	6150dat
0900	**German**		
0900-1000	R. Ukraine Int.	CEu	6005kll
0900-1000	Welle 370	Eu	6140mos*
0900-1400	R. HCJB DeuLand	CEu	7365wnm
1000	**German**		
1000-1100	R. DARC	Eu	6070mos, 9670rob
1000-1200	R. SE-TA2	CEu	6115hst
1030-1100	R. Prague Int.	WEu	6005kll
1100	**German**		
1100-1130	R. Slovakia Int	WEu	6005kll
1100-1200	R. Joystick	Eu	7330mos*

1100	German	Area	kHz
1100-1200	R. SE-TA2	Eu	6095nau*
1130-1200	Ev.MissionsGem	Eu	6055nau
1130-1200	SRG SSR	CEu	6005kll*
1200	**German**		
1200-1230	DWD	BaS,NoS,Med	5905pin, 6180pin
1200-1230	R. Slovakia Int	WEu	6005kll
1230-1330	VO Turkey	Eu	15270emr
1400	**German**		
1400-1430	R. Slovakia Int	WEu	6005kll
1500	**German**		
1500-1520	Vatican R.	CEu	3985kll
1500-1600	R. Romania Int.	Eu	6040tig, 7330tig
1600	**German**		
1600-1630	DWD	Med	5905pin, 6180pin
1600-1630	R. Poland	CEu	6005kll
1600-1630	R. Tirana Int.	CEu	3985kll
1600-1700	R. DARC	Eu	6070rob, 9670rob
1600-1700	VO Korea	Eu	6170kuj, 9425kuj
1600-1800	CRI	Eu	5970xia, 7380bji
1630-1700	R. Poland	CEu	1386vst
1700	**German**		
1700-1800	SRG SSR	CEu	3985kll*
1720-1820	Pars Today	Eu	5940sir, 6090sir, 7425sir
1800	**German**		
1800-1900	VO Indonesia	SEA	3325pga, 4750jak †
1800-2000	CRI	Eu	6160xia, 7395kas, 9615uru
1800-2000	VO Korea	Eu	6170kuj, 9425kuj
1830-1900	VO Vietnam	Eu	7280vni, 9730vni
1830-1930	VO Turkey	Eu	5945emr
1900	**German**		
1900-1930	R. Slovakia Int	WEu	3985kll
1900-1930	R. Taiwan Int.	Eu	5900sof
1900-2000	R. Cairo	Eu	9810abs ‡
1900-2000	R. Romania Int.	Eu	6180tig, 7235tig +
1900-2200	WLC Radio	Eu	9330bcq
2000	**German**		
2000-2015	R. Thailand WS	Eu	7475udo*
2000-2030	DWD	BaS,NoS,Med	5905pin, 6180pin
2000-2030	VO Vietnam	Eu	7280vni, 9730vni
2000-2100	KBS World R.	Eu	3955wof
2000-2100	R. DARC	Eu	3955rob
2100	**German**		
2100-2300	R. Belarus Int.	CEu	3985kll
2300	**German**		
2300-0400	R. HCJB DeuLand	CEu	3995wnm

GERMAN/VARIOUS

0800	**German/Dutch/English/French**		
0800-1700	R. MiAmigo Int.	CEu,WEu	6085kll
1600	**German/English**		
1600-1700	R. Öömrang	NAm	15215iss*
0000	**German/Various**		
0000-2400	Channel 292	Eu	3955rob †, 6070rob †, 9670rob †

PORTUGUESE

0000	Portuguese	Area	kHz
0000-0030	REE	SAm	11940nob
0000-0030	REE	NAm	9690nob
0000-0100	CRI	SAm	9710kas
0030-0100	R. Habana Cuba	SAm	15730bej
0100	**Portuguese**		
0100-0130	Vatican R.	Af	7305grv

0800	Portuguese	Area	kHz
0800-0945	TWR Bonaire	B	800twb
0800-1000	TWR Bonaire	B	800twb
0900	**Portuguese**		
0900-0930	R. Japan	SAm	6195hri
0900-1000	WLC Radio	Eu	9330bcq
1600	**Portuguese**		
1630-1645	TWR Africa	SAf	4760man
1630-1700	VOA	Af	13630bot, 17655sao
1700	**Portuguese**		
1700-1800	VOA	Af	1530sao, 13630bot, 17655grv
1800	**Portuguese**		
1800-1830	REE	WAf,Atl	11685nob
1800-1830	Vatican R.	Af	9705smg
1800-1830	VOA	Af	13630bot, 17655grv
1900	**Portuguese**		
1900-2000	CRI	SAf	5985bei, 7205xia, 7365bei, 9535bji
1900-2000	CRI	Eu	7335jin, 9730kas
1905-1920	TWR Africa	SAf	6130man
1920-1950	TWR Africa	SAf	6130man
1920-2005	TWR Africa	SAf	6130man
1930-2000	CRI	SAf	11640bko, 13630bko
1935-2005	TWR Africa	SAf	6130man
2100	**Portuguese**		
2100-2130	R. Habana Cuba	Af	11880hab
2100-2130	R. Habana Cuba	Eu	13680hab
2100-2130	Vatican R.	Af	7365smg
2100-2200	Madagascar W.V.	B	9765mwv
2200	**Portuguese**		
2200-0100	WLC Radio	B,Af	9330bcq
2200-2300	CRI	Eu	6175xia, 7260uru
2200-2300	CRI	SAm	9410kas, 9685kas
2215-2330	R. Cairo	SAm	9545abs ‡
2300	**Portuguese**		
2300-0100	CRI	SAm	6100bei
2300-2400	CRI	SAm	13650qvc
2300-2400	R. Habana Cuba	SAm	15230qvc

PORTUGUESE/VARIOUS

0000	Portuguese/English/French		
0000-2400	R. Onda	Eu	6140bor †
1400	**Portuguese/Lomwe**		
1420-1450	TWR Africa	SAf	9585man

SPANISH

0000	Spanish	Area	kHz
0000-0030	AWR	CAm	5010rmi
0000-0030	Alameda Bible	NAm,Pac	7730rmi
0000-0100	CRI	SAm	15120qvc
0000-0100	CRI	NAm,CAm	5990qvc
0000-0100	R. Habana Cuba	NAm	6000qvc*, 11950hab*
0000-0100	R. Romania Int.	SAm	6040gal, 7325tig, 9600tig, 11800tig
0000-0200	R. Martí	CUB	7365grv
0000-0200	VOA	LAm	600hjh
0000-0300	VOA	LAm	600hjh
0000-0400	R. Martí	CUB	6030grv
0000-0400	R. Martí	CUB	6125grv
0000-0500	R. Habana Cuba	SAm	11670hab
0000-0500	R. Habana Cuba	NAm	6060hab
0000-0500	TWR Bonaire	Car,CUB	800twb
0000-0600	R. Habana Cuba	SAm	15230qvc
0000-1400	WEWN	LAm	5970ewn
0000-2400	R. Martí	CUB	1180mth
0000	**Spanish**	**Area**	**kHz**
0030-0100	R. Slovakia Int	CAm	5010rmi
0030-0100	R. Slovakia Int	NAm	9395rmi
0030-0100	WBCQ	NAm,CAm	7490bcq †±
0030-0300	REE	SAm	11940nob
0030-0300	REE	NAm	9690nob
0045-0200	R. Cairo	SAm	9900abs ‡
0100	**Spanish**		
0100-0130	Alameda Bible	Car	5010rmi
0100-0130	Alameda Bible	NAm	5850rmi
0100-0130	R. Taiwan Int.	LAm	5800rmi
0100-0130	Vozandes Media	EQA,CLM,PRU	6050qui
0100-0200	KBS World R.	LAm	9605hri, 11810kim
0100-0300	CRI	SAm	9710kas
0130-0200	Vatican R.	SAm	7305grv
0145-0200	Vozandes Media	EQA,CLM,PRU	6050qui
0200	**Spanish**		
0200-0230	R. Prague Int.	Eu,NAm	7780rmi
0200-0230	R. Taiwan Int.	LAm	5010rmi
0200-0300	KBS World R.	NAm	15575kim
0200-0300	R. República	CUB	9490iss
0200-0300	VO Turkey	CAm,Eu	7265emr
0200-0300	VO Turkey	SAm,Eu	7280emr
0200-0400	R. Martí	CUB	7355grv
0200-0400	R. República	CUB	9490iss
0200-0600	R. Habana Cuba	CAm	5040hab
0300	**Spanish**		
0300-0330	R. Prague Int.	LAm	9955rmi
0300-0400	Madagascar W.V.	LAm	6180mwv
0300-0400	R. Romania Int.	CAm	6150gal, 7410gal
0300-0400	R. Romania Int.	SAm	9740tig, 11800tig
0300-0400	VO Korea	LAm	11735kuj, 13760kuj, 15180kuj
0330-0400	Alameda Bible	CAm	5985rmi
0330-0400	R. Slovakia Int	LAm	9955rmi
0400	**Spanish**		
0400-0430	R. Japan	CAm	5985rmi
0400-0430	R. Japan	SAm	6195hri
0500	**Spanish**		
0500-0600	VO Korea	LAm	11735kuj, 13760kuj, 15180kuj
0600	**Spanish**		
0600-0800	CRI	Eu	15135kas
0700	**Spanish**		
0700-0800	Family R.	NAm	5950rmi
0720-0820	Pars Today	Eu	15200sir, 17630sir
0900	**Spanish**		
0930-1000	R. Japan	SAm	6195hri
1000	**Spanish**		
1000-1130	TWR Bonaire	Car	800twb
1000-1200	R. Martí	CUB	6030grv
1000-1300	R. Martí	CUB	5980grv
1000-1400	R. Martí	CUB	7355grv
1045-1400	Vozandes Media	EQA,CLM,PRU	6050qui
1100	**Spanish**		
1100-1200	KBS World R.	LAm	11795kim
1100-1300	WLC Radio	LAm	9330bcq
1100-1400	Vozandes Media	EQA,CLM,PRU	6050qui
1130-1200	R. Prague Int.	CAm	5010rmi
1130-1400	Vozandes Media	EQA,CLM,PRU	6050qui
1200	**Spanish**		
1200-1400	R. Habana Cuba	NAm	6100hab
1200-1400	R. Martí	CUB	7435grv
1200-1500	R. Habana Cuba	SAm	13740hab
1200-1500	R. Habana Cuba	NAm	6000hab
1200-1600	R. Habana Cuba	Am	11760hab
1200-1600	R. Habana Cuba	SAm	15140hab
1200-1600	R. Habana Cuba	CAm	9535hab
1200-1600	R. Habana Cuba	Car	9650bej
1230-1245	Vatican R.	SAm	7305grv

1300	Spanish	Area	kHz
1300-1400	WLC Radio	LAm	9330bcq
1300-1600	R. Habana Cuba	NAm	15230qvc
1300-2200	R. Martí	CUB	11930grv
1330-1400	R. Slovakia Int	LAm	9955rmi
1400	**Spanish**		
1400-1600	R. Habana Cuba	NAm	13700hab
1400-1600	LRA36	SAm	15476lra †,*
1400-2000	R. Martí	CUB	13820grv
1400-2200	R. Martí	CUB	11860grv
1400-2400	WEWN	LAm	12050ewn
1500	**Spanish**		
1500-1530	R. Slovakia Int	WEu	6005kll
1500-2200	KVOH - VO Hope	CAm,SAm	17775voh
1500-2230	REE	WAf,Atl	11685nob
1500-2230	REE	SAm	11940nob
1500-2230	REE	ME,IOc	12030nob
1500-2230	REE	NAm	9690nob
1500-2300	REE	WAf,Atl	11685nob
1500-2300	REE	SAm	11940nob
1500-2300	REE	ME,IOc	12030nob
1500-2300	REE	NAm	9690nob
1520-1540	R. Belarus Int.	CEu,WEu	3985kll
1600	**Spanish**		
1600-1630	R. Habana Cuba	Am	11760hab, 15140hab
1600-1730	REE	WAf,Atl	11685nob
1600-1730	REE	ME,IOc	12030nob
1630-1900	R. Habana Cuba	Am	11760hab
1630-1900	R. Habana Cuba	NAm	15140hab
1700	**Spanish**		
1700-0200	R. Martí	CUB	7345grv +
1700-1800	VO Indonesia	SEA	3325pga, 4750jak †
1730-1830	VO Turkey	Eu	9495emr
1800	**Spanish**		
1800-1830	REE	ME,IOc	12030nob
1800-1830	VO Vietnam	Eu	7280vni, 9730vni
1800-1900	KBS World R.	Eu,Af	9740kim
1830-2300	REE	WAf,Atl	11685nob
1830-2300	REE	ME,IOc	12030nob
1900	**Spanish**		
1900-2000	VO Korea	Eu	7570kuj, 12015kuj
1900-2300	REE	SAm	11940nob
1900-2300	REE	NAm	9690nob
2000	**Spanish**		
2000-2100	R. Romania Int.	Eu	5920tig, 7235tig
2000-2400	R. Martí	CUB	9565grv
2020-2120	Pars Today	Eu,SAm	11870sir
2020-2120	Pars Today	Eu	7360sir
2100	**Spanish**		
2100-2130	VO Vietnam	Eu	7280vni, 9730vni
2100-2130	Vozandes Media	EQA,CLM,PRU	6050qui
2100-2300	CRI	Eu	6020szg, 9640kas
2100-2300	VO Korea	Eu	7570kuj, 12015kuj
2200	**Spanish**		
2200-0000	R. Habana Cuba	Eu	15680hab
2200-0300	R. Habana Cuba	Am	11760hab
2200-0500	R. Habana Cuba	SAm	13740hab
2200-0500	R. Habana Cuba	Car	9650bej
2200-0600	R. Habana Cuba	SAm	11850hab
2200-0600	R. Habana Cuba	CAm	9535hab
2200-2300	CRI	SAm	6100bei
2200-2300	R. Martí	CUB	7355grv
2200-2300	R. Romania Int.	SAm	9490tig +, 11800tig
2200-2400	CRI	Eu	7250uru
2200-2400	R. Habana Cuba	CAm	5040hab
2200-2400	R. Martí	CUB	7375grv
2215-2230	WWCR	NAm	6115wcr
2230-2245	WWCR	NAm	6115wcr
2230-2300	Alameda Bible	LAm	9955rmi
2245-2300	WWCR	NAm	6115wcr
2300	**Spanish**		
2300-0100	CRI	SAm	9800kas
2300-0300	CRI	SAm	9590kas
2300-0400	R. Martí	CUB	7435grv
2300-2330	REE	NAm	9690nob
2300-2400	Family R.	CAm	5010rmi
2300-2400	REE	WAf,Atl	11685nob
2300-2400	REE	SAm	11940nob
2300-2400	REE	ME,IOc	12030nob
2300-2400	R. Martí	CUB	6125grv
2300-2400	WRMI	Car	5010rmi
2315-2330	Vozandes Media	EQA,CLM,PRU	6050qui
2330-2400	REE	WAf,Atl	11685nob
2330-2400	REE	SAm	11940nob
2330-2400	REE	ME,IOc	12030nob
2330-2400	REE	NAm	9690nob
2350-0120	Pars Today	SAm	7230sir
2350-0250	Pars Today	CAm,Eu	5980sir

SPANISH/VARIOUS

0000	Spanish/English		
0000-0230	WRMI	Car	5010rmi
0100	**Spanish/English**		
0100-0200	IsleOfM/MeltPot	NAm	7490bcq
1100	**Spanish/English**		
1100-1200	WRMI	Car	5010rmi
1100-1300	WRMI	Car,SAm	9955rmi
1200	**Spanish/English**		
1200-1230	WRMI	Car	5010rmi
1230-1700	WRMI	Car	5010rmi
1300	**Spanish/English**		
1300-1400	IsleOfM/MeltPot	Eu	6070rob
1300-1500	WRMI	Car,SAm	9955rmi
1500	**Spanish/English**		
1500-1600	IsleOfM/MeltPot	Eu	9400sof
1530-1700	WRMI	Car,SAm	9955rmi
1900	**Spanish/English**		
1900-2000	IsleOfM/MeltPot	Eu	6070rob
2200	**Spanish/English**		
2200-0500	WRMI	Car,SAm	9955rmi

NB: Not all broadcasts are daily, please check main schedules under the appropriate country for full details. Language combinations are only shown for broadcasts where English, French, German, Portuguese or Spanish is listed as the first language in the combination. English etc. may appear in parts of other language combinations not shown here, (see full schedule under main station entries).

For *, ** and *** please see '**Key**' under the individual entry for that station in the International Radio section

Key: + = DRM broadcast; † = irregular; ‡ = inactive at time of publication; .± = variable frequency

DRM International Broadcasts

0000	Language	Area	Station	kHz, site
0000-2400	French	Eu	RFI	3965iss+
0000-2400	French	Eu	RFI	3965iss+
0400				
0400-0500	English	SAs	R. Romania Int.	9820tig+
0500				
0500-0530	Chinese	EAs	R. Romania Int.	13730tig+
0500-0800	English	SAs	R. Kuwait	11970kbd+
0500-0600	Romanian	Eu	R. Romania Int.	7220gal+
0600				
0600-0700	English	Eu	BBC World Sce	3955wof+
0630-0700	English	AUS,NZL	R. Romania Int.	15450tig+
0630-0700	English	Eu	R. Romania Int.	6040gal+
0600-0630	French	Eu	R. Romania Int.	6040gal+
0700				
0700-1000	English	Eu,NAf	Overcomer Min.	9265inb+
0700-1000	English	Eu,NAm	Overcomer Min.	7315inb+
0700-1000	English	CAm	WINB	7315inb+
0700-0730	German	Eu	R. Romania Int.	6175tig+
0800				
0800-0900	English	SAs	BBC World Sce	15620sng+
0900				
0945-1325	Arabic	Eu	R. Kuwait	15110kbd+
1000				
1000-1010	English	EAs	All India R.	15410bgl+
1000-1200	English	Eu,NAf	Overcomer Min.	9265inb+
1000-1200	English	CAm	WINB	9265inb+
1025-1055	English	SAs	TWR Asia	13800twr+
1100				
1100-1130	Chinese	CHN	TWR Asia	9910twr+
1145-1155	Chinese	EAs	All India R.	15030bgl+
1200				
1200-1700	English	Eu,NAf	WINB	13655inb+
1245-1315	Japanese	EAs	TWR Asia	7500twr+
1400				
1400-1500	Russian	RUS	R. Romania Int.	5945tig+
1500				
1500-1530	English	NAm	SW Radiogram	13655inb+
1600				
1600-1615	Arabic	NAf,ME	VO Nigeria	15120aja+†
1630-1900	English	Af,Eu	VO Nigeria	15120aja+†
1650-1735	English/ Pacific Languages	Pac	RNZ Pacific	5975ran+
1615-1630	Igbo	WAf	VO Nigeria	15120aja+†
1600-1700	Russian	RUS	R. Romania Int.	6030tig+
1700				
1745-1755	English	Eu	All India R.	7550bgl+
1735-1835	English/ Pacific Languages	Pac	RNZ Pacific	7285ran+
1700-1800	French	Eu	R. Romania Int.	6025tig+
1700-0200	Spanish	CUB	R. Martí	7345grv+
1800				
1800-2100	English	Eu	R. Kuwait	15540kbd+†
1800-1900	English	Eu	R. Romania Int.	7350tig+
1835-2000	English/ Pacific Languages	Pac	RNZ Pacific	11690ran+
1900				
1900-2000	Fulfulde	WAf	VO Nigeria	15120aja+†
1900-2000	German	Eu	R. Romania Int.	7235tig+
1900-1930	Italian	Eu	R. Romania Int.	5955tig+
2000				
2000-2100	Hausa	WAf	VO Nigeria	15120aja+†
2100				
2130-2200	English	Eu	R. Romania Int.	6030gal+
2100-2130	French	Eu	R. Romania Int.	6030gal+
2200				
2200-2300	Spanish	SAm	R. Romania Int.	9490tig+
2300				
2300-2400	English	Eu	R. Romania Int.	6040gal+

Key:
† Irregular.
+ DRM (Digital Radio Mondiale)

Some DRM broadcasts from All India Radio consist of a DRM Simulcast, with Hindi (Vividh Bharati prgrs) on 2nd channel

NB: Not all broadcasts are daily. Please refer to individual schedules under the main station entry in the International Radio section for full details.

Some DRM transmissions may be test broadcasts and subject to change or interruption during the broadcast.

Further information on DRM broadcasts, including low power test transmissions, can be found online.

NATIONAL TELEVISION

Section Contents

Initial entries for each letter, see Main Index for full details

CHARACTERISTICS OF ANALOGUE TELEVISION SYSTEMS (Recommendation ITU-R BT.470-6, Revision 2005)

System	Number of lines	Channel width MHz.	Vision band-width MHz.	Vision/Sound separation MHz.	Vestigial side-band MHz.	Vision mod.	Sound mod.
B	625	7	5	+5.5	0.75	Neg.	FM
B1	625	8	5	+5.5	0.75	Neg.	FM
D	625	8	6	+6.5	0.75	Neg.	FM
D1	625	8	5	+6.5	0.75	Neg.	FM
G	625	8	5	+5.5	0.75	Neg.	FM
H	625	8	5	+5.5	1.25	Neg.	FM
I	625	8	5.5	+5.996	1.25	Neg.	FM
I1	625	8	5.5	+5.996	1.25	Neg.	FM
K	625	8	6	+6.5	0.75	Neg.	FM
K1	625	8	5	+6.5	0.75	Neg.	FM
L	625	8	6	+6.5	1.25	Pos.	AM
M	525	6	4.2	+4.5	0.75	Neg.	FM
N	625	6	4.2	+4.5	0.75	Neg.	FM

DIGITAL TERRESTRIAL TELEVISION SYSTEMS (DTT)

ATSC (**A**dvanced **T**elevision **S**ystems **C**ommittee)
(North America, parts of Central America & Asia))

DTMB (**D**igital **T**errestrial **M**ultimedia **B**roadcast) i
(P.R. China, Cuba, Laos)

DVB-T/DVB-T2 (**D**igital **V**ideo **B**roadcasting - **T**errestrial)
(Europe, Africa, parts of Asia, Pacific)

ISDB-T/ISDB-TB (**I**ntegrated **S**ervices **D**igital **B**roadcasting - **T**errestrial)
(ISDB-T: Japan, parts of Asia; ISDB-TB: Parts of So. America, Botswana)

DIGITAL/ANALOGUE CHANNEL INFORMATION

Digital: Centre carrier frequencies in MHz
Analogue: Vision carrier frequencies in MHz
(**NB:** Not all assigned channels are in use)

VHF CHANNELS

[A] Channels (Digital & Analogue)
(Americas, parts of Asia & Pacific)

	Dig	Analg		Dig	Analg		Dig	Analg
A2 =	57	55.25	A6 =	85	83.25	A10 =	195	193.25
A3 =	63	61.75	A7 =	177	175.25	A11 =	201	199.25
A4 =	69	67.25	A8 =	183	181.25	A12 =	207	205.25
A5 =	79	77.25	A9 =	189	187.25	A13 =	213	211.25

[E] Channels (Digital & Analogue)
(Most of Europe, Greenland, Africa, most of Asia & Pacific)

	Dig	Analg		Dig	Analg		Dig	Analg
E2 =	(*)	48.25	E6 =	184.5	182.25	A10 =	212.5	210.25
E3 =	(*)	55.75	E7 =	191.5	189.25	A11 =	219.5	217.25
E4 =	(*)	62.25	E8 =	198.5	196.25	E12 =	226.5	224.25
E5 =	177.5	175.25	E9 =	205.5	203.25			

*) Analogue only

[K] Channels (Analogue only)
(Parts of Africa)

K4 = 175.25 K7 = 199.25 K10 = 223.25
K5 = 183.25 K8 = 207.25
K6 = 191.25 K9 = 215.25

[R] Channels (Analogue only)
(Parts of Europe, Russia, parts of Asia)

R1 = 49.75 R5 = 93.25 R9 = 199.25
R2 = 59.25 R6 = 175.25 R10 = 207.25
R3 = 77.25 R7 = 183.25 R11 = 215.25
R4 = 85.25 R8 = 191.25 R12 = 223.25

Specific National Parameters:

South Africa & Namibia (Analogue only)

SA4 = 175.25 SA7 = 199.25 SA10 = 223.25
SA5 = 183.25 SA8 = 207.25 SA11 = 231.25
SA6 = 191.25 SA9 = 215.25 SA13 = 247.43

China (P.R.) (Analogue only)

DS1 = 49.75 DS5 = 85.25 DS9 = 192.25
DS2 = 57.75 DS6 = 168.25 DS10 = 200.25
DS3 = 65.75 DS7 = 176.25 DS11 = 208.25
DS4 = 77.25 DS8 = 184.25 DS12 = 216.25

Australia & parts of Pacific (Digital & Analogue)

	Dig	Analg		Dig	Analg
AU0 =	48.5	46.25	AU7 =	184.5	182.25
AU1 =	59.5	57.25	AU8 =	191.5	189.25
AU2 =	66.5	64.25	AU9 =	198.5	196.25
AU3 =	88.5	86.25	AU9A =	205.5	203.25
AU4 =	97.5	95.25	AU10 =	212.5	209.25
AU5 =	104.5	102.25	AU11 =	219.5	216.25
AU5A =	140.5	138.25	AU12 =	226.5	224.25
AU6 =	177.5	175.25			

UHF CHANNELS

[A] Channels (Digital & Analogue)
(Americas, parts of Asia & Pacific)

Ch	Dig	Analg	Ch	Dig	Analg	Ch	Dig	Analg
14 =	473	471.25	33 =	587	585.25	52 =	701	699.25
15 =	479	477.25	34 =	593	591.25	53 =	707	705.25
16 =	485	483.25	35 =	599	597.25	54 =	713	711.25
17 =	491	489.25	36 =	605	603.25	55 =	720	717.25
18 =	497	495.25	37 =	611	609.25	56 =	725	723.25
19 =	503	501.25	38 =	617	615.25	57 =	731	729.25
20 =	509	507.25	39 =	623	621.25	58 =	737	735.25
21 =	515	513.25	40 =	629	627.25	59 =	743	741.25
22 =	521	519.25	41 =	635	633.25	60 =	749	747.25
23 =	527	525.25	42 =	641	639.25	61 =	755	753.25
24 =	533	531.25	43 =	647	645.25	62 =	761	759.25
25 =	539	537.25	44 =	653	651.25	63 =	767	765.25
26 =	545	543.25	45 =	659	657.25	64 =	773	771.25
27 =	551	549.25	46 =	665	663.25	65 =	779	777.25
28 =	557	555.25	47 =	671	669.25	66 =	785	783.25
29 =	563	561.25	48 =	677	675.25	67 =	791	789.25
30 =	569	567.25	49 =	683	681.25	68 =	797	795.25
31 =	575	573.25	50 =	689	687.25	69 =	803	801.25
32 =	581	579.25	51 =	695	693.25			

[E] Channels (Digital & Analogue), [R] Channels (Analogue)
(Europe, Greenland, Russia, Africa, most of Asia & Oceania)

Ch	Dig	Analg	Ch	Dig	Analg	Ch	Dig	Analg
21 =	474	474.25	38 =	610	607.25	55 =	746	743.25
22 =	482	479.25	39 =	618	615.25	56 =	754	751.25
23 =	490	487.25	40 =	626	623.25	57 =	762	759.25
24 =	498	495.25	41 =	634	631.25	58 =	770	767.25
25 =	506	503.25	42 =	642	639.25	59 =	778	775.25
26 =	514	511.25	43 =	650	647.25	60 =	786	783.25
27 =	522	519.25	44 =	658	655.25	61 =	794	791.25
28 =	530	527.25	45 =	666	663.25	62 =	802	799.25
29 =	538	535.25	46 =	674	671.25	63 =	810	807.25
30 =	546	543.25	47 =	682	679.25	64 =	818	815.25
31 =	554	551.25	48 =	690	687.25	65 =	826	823.25
32 =	562	559.25	49 =	698	695.25	66 =	834	831.25
33 =	570	567.25	50 =	706	703.25	67 =	842	839.25
34 =	578	575.25	51 =	714	711.25	68 =	850	847.25
35 =	586	583.25	52 =	722	719.25	69 =	858	855.25
36 =	594	591.25	53 =	730	727.25			
37 =	602	599.25	54 =	738	735.25			

[DS] Channels (Digital & Analogue)
(China, P.R., exc. SAR Macau, SAR Hong Kong)

Ch	Dig	Analg	Ch	Dig	Analg	Ch	Dig	Analg
13 =	474	471.25	28 =	634	631.25	43 =	754	751.25
14 =	482	479.25	29 =	642	645.25	44 =	762	759.25
15 =	490	487.25	30 =	650	647.25	45 =	770	767.25
16 =	498	493.25	31 =	658	655.25	46 =	778	775.25
17 =	503	503.25	32 =	666	663.25	47 =	786	783.25
18 =	514	517.25	33 =	674	671.25	48 =	794	791.25
19 =	522	519.25	34 =	682	679.25	49 =	802	799.25
20 =	530	527.25	35 =	690	687.25	50 =	810	807.25
21 =	538	535.25	36 =	698	695.25	51 =	818	815.25
22 =	549	546.25	37 =	706	703.25	52 =	826	823.25
23 =	554	551.25	38 =	714	711.25	53 =	834	831.25
24 =	562	559.25	39 =	722	719.25	54 =	842	839.25
25 =	610	607.25	40 =	730	727.25	55 =	850	847.25
26 =	618	615.25	41 =	738	735.25	56 =	856	855.25
27 =	626	623.25	42 =	746	743.25	57 =	866	863.25

[J] Channels (Digital only)
(Japan)

Ch		Dig	Ch		Dig	Ch		Dig
13	=	473	30	=	575	47	=	677
14	=	479	31	=	581	48	=	683
15	=	485	32	=	587	49	=	689
16	=	491	33	=	593	50	=	695
17	=	497	34	=	599	51	=	701
18	=	503	35	=	605	52	=	707
19	=	509	36	=	611	53	=	713
20	=	515	37	=	617	54	=	720
21	=	521	38	=	623	55	=	725
22	=	527	39	=	629	56	=	731
23	=	533	40	=	635	57	=	737
24	=	539	41	=	641	58	=	743
25	=	545	42	=	647	59	=	749
26	=	551	43	=	653	60	=	755
27	=	557	44	=	659	61	=	761
28	=	563	45	=	665	62	=	767
29	=	569	46	=	671			

[AU] Channels (Digital only)
(Australia & parts of Oceania)

Ch		Dig	Ch		Dig	Ch		Dig
28	=	529.5	42	=	627.5	56	=	732.5
29	=	536.5	43	=	641.5	57	=	739.5
30	=	543.5	44	=	648.5	58	=	746.5
31	=	550.5	45	=	655.5	60	=	753.5
32	=	557.5	46	=	662.5	61	=	760.5
33	=	565.5	47	=	669.5	62	=	767.5
34	=	571.5	48	=	676.5	63	=	774.5
35	=	578.5	49	=	683.5	64	=	781.5
36	=	585.5	50	=	690.5	65	=	788.5
37	=	592.5	51	=	697.5	66	=	795.5
38	=	599.5	52	=	704.5	67	=	802.5
39	=	606,5	53	=	711.5	68	=	809.5
40	=	613.5	54	=	718.5	69	=	816.5
41	=	620.5	55	=	725.5			

[NZ] Channels (Digital only)
(New Zealand & parts of Oceania)

Ch		Dig	Ch		Dig	Ch		Dig
25	=	506	34	=	578	43	=	650
26	=	514	35	=	586	44	=	658
27	=	522	36	=	594	45	=	666
28	=	530	37	=	602	46	=	674
29	=	538	38	=	610	47	=	682
30	=	546	39	=	618	48	=	690
31	=	554	40	=	626	49	=	698
32	=	562	41	=	634			
33	=	570	42	=	642			

INTRODUCTION

The TV section contains information about terrestrial TV stations (and ⌘ radio prgrs via DTT), in a compact format. If applicable, each country entry is devided into subsections: "National Stations", "Regional Stations", "Local Stations", "Foreign TV Relays", "Foreign Military Stations". The subsection "DTT Tx Networks" contains details of DTT transmitter operators or licensees, and DTT transmitters. Contact info for domestic prgrs included in the DTT multiplexes is found in the subsections mentioned above.
Keys: "Systems": # = txs to be phased out, § = analogue or digital txs are being phased out (tx details no longer listed) ⇩= analogue shutdown date; [A], [DS], [E], [J], [K], [R], [AU], [NZ], [SA] refer to the channel characteristics as shown in the "Channel Information" table. Tx networks for national stations are listed either with main txs (power limit applied) or with key tx(s). Local Stations (if included) are listed in full; if no tx location is given, the site refers to the city of the station's headquarters. (-) = tx details not received at editorial deadline.

AFGHANISTAN

Systems: DVB-T2 (MPEG4) [E]; § PAL-B/G [E]; BFBS-TV: DVB-T (MPEG4) [E]

National Stations ([a]=analogue)
RTA TV (Gov) ✉ Street #13, Wazir Mohammad Akbar Khan, Kabul ☎ +93 20 2102487 **E:** info@rta.org.af **W:** www.rta.org.af **L.P:** DG (RTA): Zarin Anzor **Chs:** RTA, RTA News **Txs: RTA:** Kabul [a]ch11 (2kW) & relay txs. NB: Local stations in Herat, Kandahar, Khost. – **AFGHAN TV (Comm)** ✉ Kabul ☎ +93 777 555566 **L.P:** DG: Ahmed Shah Afghanzai **Txs:** Kabul [a]ch24 & relay txs – **ARIANA TELEVISION NETWORK (ATN) (Comm)** ✉ 318, Darulaman Rd, Kabul ☎ +93 700 111113 **E:** marketing@arianatelevision.com **W:** www.arianatelevision.com **L.P:** MD: Arral Azizullah **Txs:** Kabul [a]ch4 & relay txs. – **TOLO TV (Comm)** ✉ P.O.Box 225, Kabul **E:** info@tolo.tv **W:** www.tolo.tv **L.P:** Dir: Saad Mohseni **Txs:** Kabul [a]ch9 & relay txs.

Local Stations not shown.

DTT Tx Network (DVB-T2)
Tx Operator: Oqaab **W:** www.oqaab.af **M1-4✪:** 1TV, 3 Sport, AAA Family, AAA Music, Afghan TV, Al Jazeera Arabic, Al Jazeera English, Anaar TV, Aria TV, ARY TV, ATV, BBC Persian, BBC World News, CCTV, CNBC Europe, CNNi, DD News, DD Urdu, Dubai Sport 3, DW TV, Emrooz TV, Family 1, France 24, GEM Bollywood, GEM Junior, GEM Life, GEM Travel, GEM TV, Hum TV, iMovie, IRINN, Jahonnamo, Kabul News, Khawar, Khurshid, Maiwand, Manoto 1, MBC 2, MBC 3 Cartoon, MBC 4, MBC Action, MBC Ballywood, MBC Max, Mitra, My Cartoon, Onyx, Parliament, Pashto 1, Peace TV HD, Persian Movie, Persian Music, Pigham TV, Press TV HD, Quran TV, Rah-e Farda, River TV, RTA, RTA News, Rubix, Russia Today English, Shamshad, Sunnah TV, Tamadoon, TV Bokhoristan, TV Safina, TVT 1 Tajikistan, VOA Persian, Watan, Yas Sport, Zhowandoon **Txs:** (Kabul); nationwide netw. planned.

Foreign Military Station
BFBS-TV Relay (Serving British Mil) ✉ Chalfont Grove, Narcot Lane, Chalfont St Peter, Buckinghamshire, SL9 8TN, United Kingdom. **Mux✪(DVB-T):** BBC One, BBC One (d), BBC Two, BBC Two (d), ITV, ITV (d), BFBS Extra, BFBS Extra (d), Sky Sports, BT Sport, BFBS Sport, Sky News, Nepali TV (d=delayed, i.e. time-shifted) ⌘ Forces R. BFBS (Afghanistan), BFBS R.2, BFBS Gurkha R. **Txs:** ch27 (SFN).

ALASKA (USA)

System: ATSC [A]

LOCAL STATIONS IN MAJOR TV MARKETS

Anchorage, AK Area

Ch	kW	State	City of License	Callsign
3	0.04	AK	King Mountain	K03GL
7	50	AK	Anchorage	KYES-TV
8	50	AK	Anchorage	KAKM
10	50	AK	Anchorage	KTUU-TV
12	41	AK	Anchorage	KYUR
14	0.26	AK	Anchorage	KYES-TV
17	0.1	AK	Anchorage	KACN-LD
20	234	AK	Anchorage	KTBY
22	15	AK	Anchorage	K22HN-D
24	1.31	AK	Trapper Creek	K24AG-D
25	1.5	AK	Anchorage	K25QK-D
28	28.9	AK	Anchorage	KTVA
31	15	AK	Anchorage	KLDY-LD
32	15	AK	Anchorage	KBLT-LD
33	17.2	AK	Anchorage	KDMD
35	15	AK	Anchorage	KCFT-CD

Fairbanks, AK Area

Ch	kW	State	City of License	Callsign
4	0.3	AK	Delta Junction	K04RP-D
7	0.56	AK	Delta Junction	K11WZ-D
8	0.3	AK	Nenana	K08OV-D
9	30	AK	Fairbanks	KUAC-TV
11	1.6	AK	Fairbanks	KTVF
12	0.36	AK	Healy	K12RF-D
13	3	AK	Fairbanks	KXDF-CD
13	0.3	AK	Healy	K13AAE-D
17	1.01	AK	Delta Junction	K17AF-D
18	16	AK	Fairbanks	KATN
20	30.9	AK	North Pole	KJNP-TV
22	15	AK	Fairbanks	KFXF-LD
26	27	AK	Fairbanks	KTVF

ALBANIA

Systems: DVB-T (MPEG4); DVB-T2 (MPEG4) [E]

National Stations
RADIOTELEVISIONI SHQIPTAR (RTSH) (Pub) ✉ Rr. Ismail Qemali nr. 11, 1001 Tiranë ☎ +355 42230842 **E:** marketing@rtsh.al **W:** www.rtsh.al **L.P:** DG: Thoma Gëllçi **Chs:** RTSH 1, RTSH 2, RTSH Sport – **TOP CHANNEL (Comm)** ✉ Rr. 5 Dëshmorët nr. 20, Mëzez, 150 Tiranë ☎ +355 42253177 **E:** info@top-channel.tv **W:** top-channel.tv – **TV KLAN (Comm)** ✉ Rr. Aleksandër Moisiu nr. 97, 1007 Tiranë ☎ +355 42347805 **E:** info@tvklan.al **W:** tvklan.al.

Local Stations not shown.

DTT Tx Networks (DVB-T exc. where noted)
Licensee: RTSH **Mux (DVB-T2):** RTSH 1 HD, RTSH 2 HD, RTSH Sport, RTK1 ⌘ R. Tirana 1-3, R. Tirana International, R. Tirana Jazz, R. Tirana Klasik **Txs:** MFN – **Licensee:** DigitALB **W:** www.digitalb.al **M1✪(exc.*):** Top News*, Top Channel, Bang Bang, Çufo, Junior TV, My Music, Serial Stinët, EXP Histori, EXP Natyra, EXP Shkencë **M2✪(exc.*):** BCTV Europe*, Film Aksion, Film Autor, Film Drame, Film Hits, Film Komedi, Film Thriller, Film Gold, Dorcel TV, Stars XXX TV **M3✪:** RTSH1, TV Klan, ABC News, News 24, IN TV, Supersport 1-5 **M4✪:** Report TV, Alpha TV, Music AI, T, Mega, Rai Uno, Rai Due, Italia 1, Canale 5, BBC World News, CNN int., Euronews, Fashion TV, Supersport 6 **M5✪(exc.*):** Ndihma e Klientit*, City TV, IN TV, Baby TV, Family HD, Film Nje HD, Film Dy HD, Supersport 1-4 HD, Travel Channel HD **Txs: M1:** ch62 (SFN), **M2:** ch64 (SFN), **M3:** ch67 (SFN), **M4:** ch69 (SFN). **M5 (DVB-T2):** ch29 (Dajt) – **Licensee:** Tring Digital **W:** www.tring.al **M1✪(exc.*):** RTV 21, Fax News*, National Geographic Channel, Tip TV, Tring Tring, Tring Kids, Tring Fantasy, Rai Uno, Italia 1, Canale 5, Ant1 Europe, Tring Jolly HD **M2✪(exc.*):** Vision+*, Living HD, Tring Super, Tring Comedy, Tring Planet, Tring Life, Tring Action, Tring Shqip, Tring World, 3 Plus, Folk+ **M3✪:** Fox, Fox Life, Fox Crime, Smile TV, Tring Sport News HD, Tring Sport 1-4 HD, Desire **Txs: M1:** ch47 (Dajt) **M2:** ch59 (Dajt) **M3:** ch56 (Dajt).
Local Licensees not shown.

ALGERIA

System: DVB-T (MPEG2) [E]. Sahrawi Refugee Camps: PAL-B [E]

ÉTABLISSEMENT PUBLIC DE TÉLÉVISION (EPTV) (Pub) ✉ 21, Boulevard des Martyrs, Alger ☎ +213 21 602300 **E:** alger-contact@entv.dz **W:** www.entv.dz **L.P:** DG: Ahmed Bensabane **Chs:** TV1 (El Oula), Canal Algérie, TV3 (El Ekhbaria), TV4 (Tamazight), TV5 (Kannat El Coraän), TV6, TV7 (El Mâarifa).

DTT Tx Network
Tx Operator: Télédiffusion d'Algérienne (TDA) **W:** www.tda.tz **M:** TV1, Canal Algérie, TV3, TV4, TV5, TV6, TV7 ⌘ Chaîne 1, R. Algérie Internationale, Chaîne 3.

Location	ch	kW	Location	ch	kW
Adrar	21	1.5	Djebel Bouderga	29	1
Tamanrasset	21	1.5	Bouzaréah	32	1.5
Filfila	22	1.2	Zerga	32	1.5
Timimoun	22	1.5	Akfadou	33	2
Ain Salah	22	1.5	Mécheria	35	1.5
Doukhane	22	1.5	Bechar	37	1.5
El Oued	22	1.5	Meghress	41	1.5
Djebel Khar	23	1.5	Ain N'sour	41	1.5
Hassi R'Mel	23	1.5	M'Cid	42	1.5
Ouargla	23	1.5	Hassi Messaoud	42	1.5
Bordj El Bahri	24	1.5	Chrea	43	1.2
In Amenas	24	1.5	Tessala	43	1.2
Dirah	25	1.5	Mahouna	44	1.5
Nador	25	1.5	Bouzizi	45	1.5
Mezghitane	27	1.5	Sbaa Mokrane	49	1.2
Kef Lekhel	28	1.5	+ txs below 1kW.		

Sahrawi Refugee Camps

RASD TV (Gov) ✉ BP 470, 37000 Tindouf ☎ +213 49 923525 **W:** rasd.tv **Tx:** Rabouni ªch22 (10kW). Rel. Al Aoula (Morocco) & own prgrs (ª=analogue)

ANDORRA

System: DVB-T (MPEG2) [E]

RÀDIO I TELEVISIÓ D'ANDORRA (Pub)✉ Baixada del Molí 24, AD500 Andorra la Vella ☎ +376 873777 **E:** rtva@rtva.ad **W:** www.andorradifusio.ad **L.P:** DG: Xavier Mujal Closa **Ch:** ATV.

DTT Tx Networks
Licensee: Andorra Telecom **W:** www.andorratelecom.ad **M1:** 8TV, C8, Teledeporte, TVI Internacional ⌘ RAC1, R. Comercial, RNE R. Exterior **M2:** 3/24, Arte, BBC World News, RTPi, Telecinco ⌘ COPE, Antena 1 **M3:** Esport3, Euronews, Pirineus TV, TV5 Monde ⌘ R. Valira, RTBF La Première, RTS La Première **M4:** CNN Int., Cuatro, La Sexta, NRJ12, SIC ⌘ NRJ, CNN R., Cadena SER **M5:** ATV HD, ATV (SD), La 2, M6, TF1, TV3 ⌘ RNA, RNA Andorra Música, Catalunya R. **M4:** Antena 3, France 2, France 3, La 1, Super3/33 ⌘ RNE R.4, RFI, Onda Cero.

Location	M1	M2	M3	M4	M5	M6
SFN	25	28	34	36	42	45

ANGOLA

Systems: ISDB-TB [E]; § PAL-I [E]

TV ZIMBO (Gov) ✉ Avenida de Talatona, Luanda Sul ☎+244 222 636900 **W:** www.facebook.com/OficialTVZimbo – **TELEVISÃO PÚBLICA DE ANGOLA (Pub)** ✉ CP 2604, Luanda ☎ +244 222 320326 **W:** tpa.sapo.ao **L.P:** Pres: Francisco José Mendes **Chs:** TPA1, TPA2.

DTT Tx Networks
Tx Operator: TPA **M:** TPA1, TPA2, TV Zimbo **Txs:** ch31 (Luanda) & nationwide MFN under construction

ANGUILLA (UK)

System: NTSC-M [A]

KREATIVE COMMUNICATIONS NETWORK (KCN) (Comm)✉ P.O.Box 154, The Valley ☎ +1 264 5843519 **E:** info@kcntv4.com **W:** kcntv4.com **L.P:** CEO: Carlton Pickering **Stns:** ZJF-TV3 ch3 (0.003kW), ZJF-TV9 ch9 (0.03kW). V2C-TV 10 (

ANTARCTICA

NB: No terrestrial TV station.

ANTIGUA & BARBUDA

System: NTSC-M [A]

ABS-TV (Gov) ✉ Cross St., St. John's, Antigua ☎ +1 268 4620010 **E:** abstvradio@ab.gov.ag **W:** abstvradio.com **L.P:** SM: Trevor Parker. **Tx:** ch10V (5kW).

ARGENTINA

Systems: ISDB-TB [A]; § PAL-N [A] ⇩2021

National Stations
TV PÚBLICA (Pub) ✉Avenida Figueroa Alcorta 2977, 1425 Buenos Aires ☎+54 11 8026001 **W:** www.tvpublica.com.ar – **EL NUEVE (Comm)**✉Av. Dorrego 1708, 1414 Buenos Aires ☎ +54 11 50936838 **W:** www.elnueve.com.ar – **EL TRECE (Comm)**✉ Lima 1261, Constitucion, Capital Federal ☎ +54 11 3050013 **W:** www.eltrecetv.com.ar – **TELEFE (Comm)**✉ Pavón 2495, 1248 Buenos Aires ☎ +54 11 43080145 **W:** telefe.com.

Local Stations not shown.

DTT Tx Networks
Licensee: Radio y Televisión Argentina **M1:** Encuentro, Encuentro Movil, Paka Paka, TaTeTi **Txs:** ch22 (Buenos Aires) & MFN. **M2:** TV Pública HD, TV Pública Movil, Construir TV **Txs:** ch23 (Buenos Aires) & MFN. **M3:** Gol TV, Go TV Movil, V!vra, Suri TV, Video Éxito **Txs:** ch24 (Buenos Aires) & MFN. **M4:** CN23, C5N, Telesur, 360 TV **Txs:** ch25 (Buenos Aires) & MFN. – **Licensee:** Telefe **M:** Telefe HD, Telefe (SD) **Tx:** ch34 (Buenos Aires) & MFN. – **Licensee:** El Trece **M:** El Trece **Tx:** ch33 (Buenos Aires) & MFN. – **Licensee:** El Nueve **M:** El Nueve HD, El Nueve, (SD), El Nueve Movil **Txs:** ch35 (Buenos Aires) & MFN. **Local licensees** not shown.

ARMENIA

System: DVB-T2 (MPEG4) [E]

National Stations
ARMENIAN PUBLIC TELEVISION (Pub)✉ 26, G. Hovsepyan St., Nork 47, 0047 Yerevan ☎ +374 10 650015 **E:** International@armtv.com **W:** www.1tv.am **L.P:** CEO (acting): Armen Amirian **Ch:** H1 – **ARMENIA TV (Comm)**✉ 1, Yeghvard Highway, 0054 Yerevan ☎ +374 10 369344 **E:** info@armeniatv.am **W:** armeniatv.am – **H2 (Comm)**✉ 3/1, Quarter # G-3, 0088 Yerevan ☎ +374 10 398831 **E:** lraber@tv.am **W:** www.tv.am **L.P:** DG: Samvel Mayrapetyan.

Local Stations not shown.

DTT Tx Network
Tx Operator: Television and Radio Broadcasting Network of Armenia **W:** tna.am **M1:** H1, H2, Shant TV, Kentron TV, Shoghakat TV, Armenia TV, Yerkir Media, RTR Planeta **M2:** Mir TV Armenia, AR TV, Arm News, Dari 21, ATV, 5 Kanal, MO TV, CNN International, Pervyy kanal, Rossiya K **M3:** Local stns

Location	M1	M2	M3	M4*
Yerevan	23	28	35	43

+ nationwide MFN *) F.pl

ARUBA (Netherlands)

Systems: # NTSC-M [A]; DVB-T (MPEG2) planned

ARUBA BROADCASTING CO. N.V. (ATV) (Comm)✉ P.O.Box 5040, Oranjestad ☎+297 5838150 **Tx:** Oranjestad ch15 – **CANAL 22 (Comm)** ✉ Oranjestad. ☎+297 5859500 **W:** www.facebook.com/Canal22aruba **Tx:** Oranjestad ch22 – **TELEARUBA (Comm)**✉ P.O.Box 392, Oranjestad ☎ +297 5857302 **E:** info@telearuba.aw **W:** telearuba.aw **Tx:** Oranjestad ch13 (3kW).

ASCENSION ISLAND (UK)

System: PAL-I [E]

BFBS-TV Relay (Serving British Mil)✉ Chalfont Grove, Narcot Lane, Chalfont St Peter, Buckinghamshire, SL9 8TN, United Kingdom. **Txs: BBC One:** Travellers Hill ch64, Cross Hill ch50 & ch61 **ITV:** Travellers Hill ch64, Cross Hill ch46.

AUSTRALIA

System: DVB-T (MPEG2) [AU]

National Stations
AUSTRALIAN BROADCASTING CORPORATION (ABC) (Pub)✉ ABC Ultimo Centre, 700 Harris St, Ultimo, NSW 2007 ☎ +61 2 83331500 **E:** comments@your.abc.net.au **W:** www.abc.net.au

L.P: MD: David Anderson **Chs (terr.):** ABC, ABC Me, ABC Comedy/ABC Kids, ABC News – **SPECIAL BROADCASTING SERVICE (SBS) (Pub)** Locked bag 028, Crows Nest, NSW 1585 ☎ +61 2 94302828 **E:** comments@sbs.com.au **W:** www.sbs.com.au **L.P:** MD: James Taylor – **NATIONAL INDIGIOUS TELEVISION (NITV) (Pub)** 5 Parsons Street, Alice Springs, NT 0870 ☎ +61 8 89534763 **E:** admin@nitv.org.au **W:** www.nitv.org.au.

Major Regional Stations
IMPARJA TELEVISION (Pub) P.O.Box 2924, Alice Springs, NT 0871 ☎ +61 89 523744 **W:** www.imparja.com.au – **NETWORK TEN (Comm)** P.O. Box 10, Lane Cove, NSW 2066 ☎ +61 2 8870222 **W:** tenplay.com.au **L.P:** CEO: Paul Anderson – **NINE NETWORK (Comm)** P.O.Box 27, Willoughby, NSW 2068 ☎ +61 2 99069999 **W:** www.nine.com.au **L.P:** CEO: Hugh Marks – **PRIME TELEVISION (Comm)** PO Box 878, Dickson, ACT 2602 ☎ +61 2 62423700 **W:** www.prime7.com.au – **SEVEN NETWORK (Comm)** Television Centre, Mobbs Lane, Epping, NSW 2121 ☎ +61 2 8587777 **W:** www.sevenwestmedia.com.au **L.P:** CEO: James Warburton – **SOUTHERN CROSS AUSTEREO (Comm)** 257 Clarendon St, South Melbourne, VIC 3205 ☎ +61 3 92432100 **W:** www.southerncrossaustereo.com.au – **WIN TELEVISION (Comm)** Television Ave, Mt St Thomas, Wollongong, NSW 2500 ☎ +61 2 42234199 **W:** www.wintv.com.au.

Local Stations not shown.

DTT Tx Networks (National Stations & Major Regional Stns)
National Licensee: ABC **M:** ABC, ABC HD, ABC Comedy/ABC Kids, ABC Me, ABC News 24 ⌘ ABC Radio National, ABC Local Radio, ABC Classic, ABC Double J, ABC Jazz, ABC Triple J, ABC Triple J Unearthed, ABC Kids Listen, ABC Country, ABC News on Radio – **National Licensee:** SBS **M:** SBS, SBS HD, SBS Viceland HD, SBS World Movies, SBS Food, NITV ⌘ SBS Radio 1-3, SBS Arabic24, SBS Pop Desi, SBS Chill, SBS Pop Asia – **Regional Licensee:** Seven Network **M:** Seven, 7HD, 7Two, 7mate, 7mate HD, Open Shop, 7flix,. Racing.com – **Regional Licensee:** Nine Network **M:** Nine Regional, 9HD, 9Gem, 9Gem, 9Go!, 9Life, SBN, Aspire TV – **Regional Licensee:** Network Ten **M:** 10, 10 HD, 10 Bold, 10 Peach, 10 Shake, TVSN, Spree TV.

Location	ABC	7N	9N	10N	SBS	kW
Sydney	12	6	8	11	34	50
+ MFN						

AUSTRIA

System: DVB-T2 (MPEG4) [E]; § DVB-T (MPEG2)

National Stations
ÖSTERREICHISCHER RUNDFUNK (ORF) (Pub) Würzburgasse 30, 1136 Wien ☎ +43 1 878780 **E:** presse@orf.at **W:** orf.at **L.P:** DG: Alexander Wrabetz **Chs:** ORF eins, ORF2 incl. reg. stns: a) ORF Burgenland (Buchgraben 51, 7000 Eisenstadt), b) ORF Kärnten (Sponheimer Straße 13, 9020 Klagenfurt), c) ORF Niederösterreich (Radioplatz 1, 3109 St.Pölten), d) ORF Oberösterreich (Europaplatz 3, 4010 Linz), e) ORF Salzburg (Nonntaler Hauptstraße 49d, 5020 Salzburg), f) ORF Steiermark (Marburgerstr. 20, 8042 Graz), g) ORF Tirol (Rennweg 14, 6010 Innsbruck), h) ORF Vorarlberg (Höchsterstraße 38, 6850 Dornbirn), i) ORF Wien (Argentinierstr. 30a, 1040 Wien), ORF III – **ATV (Comm)** Aspernbrückengasse 2, 1020 Wien ☎ +43 1 213640 **E:** atv@atv.at **W:** atv.at **L.P:** MD: Thomas Gruber – **OE24.TV (Comm)** Friedrichstrasse 10, 1010 Wien ☎ +43 1 588110 **E:** online-feedback@oe24.at **W:** www.oe24.at **L.P:** CEO: Nikolaus & Wolfgang Fellner – **PULS 4 (Comm)** Maria Jacobi Gasse 1, 1030 Wien ☎ +43 1 999880 **W:** www.puls4.com **L.P:** CEO: Markus Breitenecker – **SERVUS TV (Comm)** Ludwig-Bieringer-Platz 1, 5073 Wals ☎ +43 662 842244 **E:** kontakt@servustv.at **W:** www.servus.com **L.P:** CEO: Ferdinand Wegscheider.

Local Stations not shown (via Mux 3 txs).

DTT Tx Networks
Tx Operator: Österreichische Sender GmbH & Co KG (ORS) **W:** www.ors.at **M1✪:** ORF 1, ORF 1 HD, ORF2 Wien, ORF2 HD incl. reg. prgrs, ORF III HD, ORF Sport+ HD ⌘ Ö1, Ö3, FM4 **M2✪:** HGTV, RTL, ZDFinfo, 3sat HD, ATV2, ATV HD, PULS 4, RTL HD, ServusTV HD **M3:** Comedy Central, gotv, HopeTV, Kabel eins Doku, Ländle TV, oe24.TV, ProSiebenMAXX, SRF1, SRF zwei, Welt, Regional/Local stns **M4✪:** Arte HD, BR Süd HD, DMAX, Nickelodeon, NITRO, n-tv, ONE, Phoenix, RTLplus, SAT.1 Gold, Super RTL **M5✪:** Das Erste HD, Eurosport 1, Kabel eins, KiKa, Playboy TV, RTL 2, Sixx, Sport 1, ZDF HD, ZDF_neo HD **M6✪:** NDR, CNN, Deluxe Music, Disney Channel, Pro 7, Puls 24, Puls 4 HD, Sat.1 HD, Vox HD ⌘ R. Maria.

Location	M1	M2	M3	M4	M5	M6	kW
Bregenz (Pfänder*)	24	21	41	31	25	22	2x56/20/3x50
Bruck a.d.M. (Mugel)	41	25	-	47	-	-	45/56/45
Graz (Schöckl*)	26	23	-	47	39	50	24/24/3x25
Innsbruck (Patscherkofel*)	24	27	36	37	23	22	63
Klagenfurt (Dobratsch)	24	23	-	48	30	51	(**)
Linz (Lichtenberg*)	43	37	44	41	45	24	50
Mattersburg (Heuberg)	52V	34V	-	36V	30V	53V	20
Rechnitz (Hirschenstein)	43V	23V	-	47V	39V	50V	25
Salzburg (Gaisberg*)	32	29	-	47	38	42	2x40/32/2x25
St.Pölten (Jauerling*)	31	21	-	38	55	58	2x50/3x40
Schärding (Schardenberg)	43	-	-	-	-	-	16
Schladming (Hauser Kaibling)	34	29	-	47	38	42	30/3x40
Viktring (Stifterkogel)	24	23	-	48	30	51	15/4x14
Waidhofen/Ybbs (Sonntagbg.)	43	37	-	41	45	24	12/9/3x12
Weitra (Wachberg)	31	-	-	-	-	-	14
Wien (Kahlenberg*)	24	34	41V	36	60	53	2x63/5/3x63

+ sites with txs below 10kW. *) + SFN **) 80/66/50/66/50/63/50
NB: Some txs with multiplexes 1 and 3 are still broadcasting in DVB-T during a transition pertiod to DVB-T2

AZERBAIJAN

System: DVB-T2 (MPEG4) [E]

National Stations
AZÄRBAYCAN TELEVIZIYA VÄ RADIO VERISLÄRI (Gov) Mehdi Hüseyn St. 1, AZ 1011 Bakı ☎ +994 12 4984720 **E:** info@aztv.az **W:** www.aztv.az **L.P:** Chmn: Rövşän Mämmädov **Chs:** AzTV, Idman Azärbaycan, Mädäniyyät TV – **ICTIMAI TELEVIZIYA (ITV) (Pub)** Şärifzadä St. 241, AZ 1012 Bakı ☎ +994 12 4335525 **E:** info@itv.az **W:** www.itv.az **L.P:** DG: Balakişi Qasımov – **AZAD AZÄRBAYCAN TV (ATV) (Comm)** Şärifzadä St. 2, AZ 1012 Bakı ☎ +994 12 4977274 **E:** info@atv.az **W:** news.atv.az – **LIDER TV (Comm)** Ä.Äläkbärov St. 83/23, AZ 1141 Bakı ☎ +994 12 4978899 **E:** lidertvonline@gmail.com **W:** www.facebook.com/lidertvazerbaijan – **SPACE TV (Comm)** Hüseyn Cavid Ave. 8, AZ 1073 Bakı ☎ +994 12 4921256 **E:** info@spacetv.az **W:** www.spacetv.az.

Local Stations not shown.

DTT Tx Network
Tx Operator: RITN Teleradio IB **W:** teleradio.az **M:** AzTV, Idman Azärbaycan, Mädäniyyät TV, Lider TV, Space TV, ATV, Xäzär TV, TRT1, local stns **Local licensees** not shown.

Location	M	kW
Bakı	37	1.2

+ nationwide MFN.

MOUNTAINOUS KARABAGH

LERNAYIN GHARABAGH HANRAYIN HERUSTARADIOYIN KERUTYUN Tigran Mets St. 23a, Stepanakert (mail via Armenia) ☎ +374 47 945261 **E:** artv_or@ktsurf.net **W:** www.artsakh.tv **L.P:** Chmn: Norek A. Gasparyan

DTT Tx Networks
Tx Operator Mux 1: Television and Radio Broadcasting Network of Armenia **W:** tna.am **M:** H1, H2, Shant TV, Kentron TV, Shoghakat TV, Armenia TV, Yerkir Media, RTR Planeta **Txs:** (-) – **Tx Operator Mux 2:** Arsakh TV **M:** Artsakh TV **Txs:** (-)

AZORES (Portugal)

System: DVB-T (MPEG4) [E]

RTP AÇORES (Pub) Rua Ernesto do Canto 40, 9500-312 Ponta Delgada ☎ +351 296202700 **E:** rtpa@rtp.pt **W:** www.rtp.pt/acores **L.P:** Dir: Lorina Bernardo.

DTT Tx Network
Licensee: Altice Portugal **M:** RTP1, RTP2, RTP3/RTP Açores, RTP Memória, SIC, TVI, ARTV

Location	ch	kW	Location	ch	kW
Santa Barbara	45	3.2	Barrosa	48	6.4
Pico Alto	46	3.3	+ txs below 3kW		

BAHAMAS

System: ATSC [A]

ZNS TV (Pub) P.O.Box N-1347, Nassau ☎ +1 242 5023800 **E:**

znsnews@gmail.com **W:** znsbahamas.com **L.P:** GM (Broadcasting Corp. of the Bahamas): Kayleaser Devaux-Isaacs **Chs:** ZNS TV, The Parliament Channel **Tx:** Nassau ch13 (50kW).

BAHRAIN

System: DVB-T2 (MPEG4) [E]

BAHRAIN TELEVISION (BTV) (Pub)✉ P.O.Box 1075, Bahrain ☎ +973 17686000 **L.P:** Dir: Yousef Mohammed **Chs:** BTV Arabic, BTV English, BTV Sports Channel 1, BTV Sports Channel 2, BTV Quran Channel, BTV International

DTT Tx Network
Tx Operator: BTV **M:** BTV Arabic, BTV English, BTV Sports Channel 1, BTV Sports Channel 2, BTV Quran Channel, BTV International, BBC World Service News **Txs:** (-)

BANGLADESH

Systems: DVB-T2 (MPEG4) [E]; # PAL-B [E]

SANGSAD BANGLADESH TV (Gov)✉ Dhaka **W:** www.parliament.gov.bd **Tx:** Dhaka [a]ch6 (20kW) – **BANGLADESH TELEVISION (BTV) (Pub)**✉ TV Bhaban, Rampura, Dhaka 1219 ☎ +880 2 8618606 **W:** www.btv.gov.bd **L.P:** DG: SM Haroon-or-Rashid **Txs:** Dhaka [a]ch9 (20kW) & netw. ([a]=analogue)

DTT Tx Networks (under construction)
Tx Operator: BTV **M:** BTV, BTV World, Sangsad Bangladesh TV **Txs:** ch(-) Dhaka, Chittagong, Khulna (3.5kW)

BARBADOS

System: NTSC-M [A]

CARIBBEAN BROADCASTING CORP. (CBC TV8) (Pub)✉ P.O. Box 900, Pine Hill, Bridgetown ☎ +1 246 4675400 **W:** www.cbc.bb **L.P:** CEO: Sanka Price **Txs:** Bridgetown ch8 (60kW).

BELARUS

Systems: DVB-T (MPEG4), DVB-T2 (MPEG4) [E]

National Stations
BELARUSKAJE TELEBACANNE (BT) (Gov) ✉ Makaionka St. 9, 220807 Minsk ☎ +375 17 2634301 **E:** pr@tvr.by **W:** www.tvr.by **Chs (terr.):** Belarus 1, Belarus 2, Belarus 3, Belarus 4 (Regional Stns), Belarus 5 – **OBSHCHENATSIONALNOYE TELEVIDENIYE (ONT) (Gov)**✉ Kamunistyčny St. 6, 220029 Minsk ☎ +375 17 2170124 **E:** w@ont.by **W:** ont.by **L.P:** Pres: Grigoriy L. Kisel – **STOLICHNOYE TV (STV) (Gov)** ✉ Kamunistyčny St. 6, 220029 Minsk ☎ +375 17 2906272 **E:** reklama@ctv.by **W:** www.ctv.by **L.P:** DG: Yuriy Koziyatko.

DTT Tx Networks (DVB-T2 exc. where noted)
Tx Operator: Beltelekom **W:** beltelecom.by **M1 (DVB-T):** Belarus 1, Belarus 2, Belarus 3, ONT, STV, NTV-Belarus, RTR-Belarus, TV Mir **M2✪(exc.*)** Belarus 5*, 8 Kanal Belarus, Russkiy Illusion, Kinomiks, VTV, TV3 Belarus, TNT International, RU TV Belarus, Karusel, Shanson TV, Moya Planeta, Rossiya K, Ohota i Rybalka, Usadba Telekanal, Setanta Sport, Doma TV, Evrokino, Kinopremiera, Oruzhiye **M3✪:** Soyuz TV, Kuhnya TV, BelMuz, RTVi, Muzhskoe Kino, Kinosemya, Tiji, Gulli Girl, Multimania TV, Kinomiks, Kinokomediya, Kinohit, Rodnoye Kino, BelRos TV, Match! Premier, V gostyah u skazki, O!, Yasnaye TV, Dom Kino, Virtualniy Kinozal. **Regional/Local muxes:** not shown.

Location	1	2	3	kW	Location	1	2	3	kW
Asipovičy	49	51	38	2	Drahičyn	57	58	35	2
Astryna	42	37	51	1	Dryčyn	44	51	38	2
Asvieja	33	30	42	1	Hara	33	30	42	2
Aziareck	25	36	38	1	Hieraniony	49	29	33	2
Babrujsk	47	52	40	2	Homiel	51	30	38	2
Baranavičy	39	26	31	2	Hrodna	42	37	51	1
Barysaŭ	48	23	57	1	Ivanava Slabada	42	35	37	2
Bierazino	41	46	58	2	Kapyl	34	43	47	1
Biahoml	40	47	50	1	Kašalioŭ	41	26	31	1
Biaroza	43	58	35	1	Kasciukovičy	50	51	39	2
Brahin	43	39	21	2	Kreva	59	25	23	1
Braslaŭ	43	53	21	1	Krupski	41	46	58	2
Ciachcin	43	46	58	2	Kryčaŭ	50	59	39	1

Location	1	2	3	kW	Location	1	2	3	kW
Kuplin	51	53	47	2	Sianno	25	36	38	2
Liuban	44	51	34	1	Sinkievičy	58	35	37	2
Luki	41	26	31	1	Slaŭharad	50	59	39	2
Mahilioŭ	49	56	33	2	Slonim	41	36	31	2
Masty	21	25	36	1	Smiataničy	46	41	31	1
Mazyr	48	41	31	1	St. Darohi	44	51	38	2
Miadziel	44	51	34	2	Stoŭbcy	34	43	47	1
Minsk	48	32	57	1	Strelčyki	59	25	23	1
Mscislaŭl	49	56	33	2	Svislač	21	25	36	2
Myta	49	29	33	2	Ušačy	40	47	50	1
Navasielle	48	32	57	1	V. Čučavičy	56	50	33	1
Orša	25	36	38	1	Valosavičy	46	41	31	2
Pinsk	56	50	52	2	Viciebsk	43	31	48	1
Radaškavičy	48	32	57	1	Zaščobje	43	39	31	1
Rakitnica	51	53	47	2	Žitkavičy	42	35	37	2
Salihorsk	34	43	47	2	Žlobin	57	52	40	2
Saltanoŭ	51	30	38	1	+ sites with txs below 1kW				

Local licensee: Kosmos TV **W:** www.cosmostv.com **M✪(exc.*) (DVB-T):** Belarus 5*, TLC, Discovery Channel, Animal Planet, Eurosport, Karusel, Ohota i Rybalka, TNT International, Usadba, BBK (BelBiznesKanal), Muzhskoe Kino, Kinokomedia, Kinohit, Nashe Novoe Kino, Kinomiks, Cinema TV, Dom Kino, Zhara TV, Viasat History, Shanson TV **Tx:** ch29 (Minsk 1kW).

BELGIUM

Systems: DVB-T (MPEG2) [E], DVB-T2 (MPEG4) [E]

Flanders

National Station
VLAAMSE RADIO EN TELEVISIEOMROEP (VRT) (Pub)✉ A. Reyerslaan 52, 1043 Brussel ☎ +32 2 7413111 **E:** info@vrt.be **W:** www.vrt.be **L.P:** CEO: Frederik Delaplace **Chs (terr.):** (in Flemish) Één, Canvas, Ketnet.

DTT Tx Network (DVB-T2)
Licensee: M7 Group **M1✪:** Één, Canvas, Ketnet, CAZ2, VIER, Vijf, Zes, VTM, VTM2, VTM3, VTM4, Penthouse **M2✪:** Club-RTL, VTM Kids, Plug RTL, RTL-TVi.

Location	M1	M2	kW	Location	M1	M2	kW
Antwerpen	44V	47V	10	St.Pieters-Leew	43V	46V	20
Brussel	43	46	10	Schoten	44V	47V	20
Egem	43V	46V	20	Veltem	43V	46V	20
Genk	44	47	20				

+ txs below 10kW

Wallonia

National Stations
RADIO TÉLÉVISION BELGE DE LA COMMUNAUTÉ FRANÇAISE (RTBF) (Pub)✉ Boulevard Reyers 52, 1044 Bruxelles ☎ +32 2 7372111 **W:** www.rtbf.be **L.P:** CEO: Jean-Paul Philippot **Chs:** (in French) La Une, Tipik, La Troix – **BELGISCHER RUNDFUNK (BRF) (Pub)**✉ Kehrweg 11, 4700 Eupen ☎ +32 87 591111 **E:** info@brf.be **W:** brf.be **L.P:** Dir: Toni Wimmer. **Ch:** (News-magazine in German) Blickpunkt.

DTT Tx Network (DVB-T)
Tx Operator: RTBF **M:** La Une, Tipik, La Troix, Euronews (via Liège tx: Euronews/BRF Blickpunkt) ⌘ RTBF La Première, VivaCité, Musiq3, Classic 21, Tipik, BRF1.

Location	Ch	kW	Location	Ch	kW
Liège	45	100	Wavre	56	80
Anderlues	56	80	Léglise	57	100
Profondville	56	50	Marche-en-Famene	57	13
Tournai	56V	40			

+ txs below 10kW

Local Licensee: BX1 ✉ rue Gabrielle Petit 32/34, 1080 Bruxelles ☎ +32 2 4212121 **E:** pv@bx1.be **W:** bx1.be **M:** BX1 **Tx:** ch55V (Bruxelles 8kW).

BELIZE

Systems: NTSC-M [A]

BELIZE BROADCASTING NETWORK (BBN) (Comm) ✉ Belize City ☎ +501 2232008 **E:** ramon@bbn9.com **W:** www.facebook.com/BBNbelize **L.P:** Chmn/CEO: Ramon Vasquez **Tx:** ch9 – **CHANNEL 5 (Comm)**✉ P.O.Box 679, Belize City ☎ +501 2277781 **E:** gbtz@btl.net **W:** www.channel5belize.com **Tx:** ch5 – **CHANNEL 7 (Comm)**✉ P.O.Box 89, Belize City ☎ +501 2277246 **E:** tvseven@btl.net **W:**

www.7newsbelize.com **Tx:** ch7 – **TBN (Rlg)** ✉ Belize City **Tx:** ch13.

BENIN

System: DVB-T2 (HEVC) [E]

National Stations
OFFICE DE RADIODIFFUSION ET TÉLÉVISION DU BÉNIN (ORTB) (Gov) ✉ BP 366, Cotonou ☎+229 21301096 **E:** ortb@intnet.bj **W:** ortb.bj – **LC2 (Comm)** ✉ 05 BP 427 Cotonou. ☎+229 21334749 **E:** lc2@intnet.bj **W:** www.facebook.com/LC2Television.

Local Stations
Canal 3: 02 BP 371, Cotonou **Carrefour TV:** 01BP 440, Bohicon **Golfe TV:** 06 BP 1624, Cotonou **Imalè Africa:** Puerto-Novo.

DTT Tx Network
Licensee: StarTimes **M1+2(partly✪):** multiprgr **Txs:** MFN

BERMUDA (UK)

System: DVB-T (MPEG4) [A]

BERMUDA BROADCASTING CO. LTD (BBC) (Comm)✉ P.O.Box HM 452, Hamilton HMBX ☎ +1 441 2952828 **E:** contactus@bermudabroadcasting.com **W:** bermudabroadcasting.com **L.P:** CEO: Patrick Singleton **Chs:** ZFB-TV (ABC affiliate), ZBM-TV (CBS affiliate).

DTT Tx Networks
Licensee: BBC **M:** ZFB-TV, ZBM-TV **Tx:** ch20 (Hamilton) – **Licensee:** World On Wireless Ltd **W:** www.wow.bm **M✪:** multiprgr **Txs:** (-).

BHUTAN

System: DVB-T2 (MPEG4) [E]

BHUTAN BROADCASTING SERVICE (BBS) (Pub)✉ P.O.Box 101, Thimphu ☎ +975 2 323580 **E:** md@bbs.bt **W:** www.bbs.bt **L.P:** CEO: Kaka Tshering **Chs:** BBS 1, BBS 2.

DTT Tx Network
Tx Operator: BBS **M:** BBS 1, BBS 2 **Txs:** MFN

BOLIVIA

Systems: ISDB-TB [A]; § NTSC-M [A] ⇩2022

National Stations
BOLIVIA TV (BTV) (Gov)✉ Av. Camacho 1485, Ed. La Urbana, La Paz ☎ +591 2 2203404 **W:** www.boliviatv.bo **Txs:** La Paz ch16 & relay txs. – **TELEVISIÓN UNIVERSITARIA (Educ)** ✉ Av. 6 de Agosto No. 2170, 13383 La Paz ☎ +591 2 359297 **E:** canal13@umsa.bo **W:** www.tvu.umsa.bo. **Txs:** La Paz ch14 & relay txs – **ATB (ASOCIACIÓN TELEVISIÓN BOLIVIANO) (Comm)**✉ Av. Argentina 2057, La Paz ☎ +591 2 2229922 **E:** atbcbb@atb.com.bo **W:** www.atb.com.bo **Tx:** La Paz ch40 & relay txs – **BOLIVISIÓN (Comm)**✉ Av Santa Cruz esq, Tres pasos al frente, Santa Cruz ☎ +591 3 3524544 **W:** www.redbolivision.tv.bo **Txs:** La Paz ch33 & relay txs. – **RED UNO DE BOLIVIA (Comm)**✉ Romecin Campos 592, Sopocachi, 14976 La Paz ☎ +591 2 2203339 **E:** notivision@reduno.com.bo **W:** www.reduno.com.bo **Txs:** La Paz ch42 & relay txs – **RTP (Comm)**✉ Calle Juán de la Riva 1527, La Paz ☎ +591 2 2421111 **E:** rtp@rtpbolivia.com.bo **W:** www.rtpbolivia.com.bo **Txs:** La Paz ch31 & relay txs – **UNITEL (UNIVERSAL DE TELEVISIÓN) (Comm)**✉ Av. Carrasco Pje. Carrasco 1388, La Paz ☎ +591 2 359297 **W:** www.unitel.tv. **Txs:** La Paz ch28 & relay txs.

Local Stations not shown.

BONAIRE (Netherlands)

System: DVB-T (MPEG2) [E]

TELECURAÇAO RELAY (Curaçao): ch(-).

BOSNIA & HERZEGOVINA

Systems: DVB-T2 (MPEG4) [E]; § PAL-B/G [E]

National (Federal) Station
RADIO TELEVIZIJA BOSNE I HERCEGOVINE (BHRT) (Pub)✉ Bulevar Meše Selimovića 12, 71000 Sarajevo ☎ +387 33 455124 **E:** sptrgov@bhrt.ba **W:** www.bhrt.ba **L.P:** DG: Belmin Karamehmedović **Ch:** BHT1.

Federacija Bosna i Hercegovina

National Station
FTV (Pub)✉ Bulevar Meše Selimovića 12, 71000 Sarajevo ☎ +387 33 461539 **E:** press@rtvfbih.ba **W:** www.rtvbih.ba **L.P:** DG (RTVFBiH): Džemal Šabić.

Local Stations not shown.

DTT Tx Network (under construction)
Licensee: BHRT **M:** BHT1, FTV, RTRS

Location	ch	Location	ch
Bjelašnica	30	Tušenica	38
Majevica	25	Velez	26
Plješevica	24	Vlašić	22
Trovrh	38		

Republika Srpska

National Station
RADIO TELEVIZIJA REPUBLIKE SRPSKE (RTRS) (Pub) ✉ ul. Kralja Petra I Karađorđevića 129, 78000 Banja Luka ☎ +387 51 301660 **E:** tv@rtrs.tv **W:** www.rtrs.tv **L.P:** DG: Mladen Branković.

Local Stations not shown.

DTT Tx Network (under construction)
Licensee: BHRT **M:** BHT1, FTV, RTRS

Location	ch	Location	ch
Kozara	32	Leotar	46

BOTSWANA

Systems: ISDB-TB [E]; § PAL-I [E]

BOTSWANA TV (BTV) (Gov) ✉ P.O.Box 0060, Gaborone ☎ +267 3658000 **E:** marketing@btv.gov.bw **W:** www.facebook.com/Botswana-Television-BW-260382237810321 **L.P:** GM: Bontle Mogotllwana – **E-BOTSWANA (Comm)** ✉P.O.Box 921, Gaborone **E:** info@ebotswana.co.bw **L.P:** GM: David Coles.

DTT Tx Network
Licensee: StarTimes **M(partly✪):** multiprgr **Txs:** MFN

BRAZIL

System: ISDB-TB [A]

National Stations
TV BRAZIL (Pub) ✉ An. Gomes Freire 474, Centro, 20231-010 Rio de Janeiro, RJ ☎ +55 21 21176208 **W:** tvbrasil.ebc.com.br – **TV CULTURA (Pub)** ✉ Rua Vladimir Herzog 75, Agua Branca, SP 05036-900 São Paulo, SP ☎ +55 11 38743122 **E:** dirprog@tvcultura.com.br **W:** tvcultura.cmais.com.br – **CENTRAL NACIONAL DE TELEVISÃO (CNT) (Comm)** ✉ Rua Francisco Caron 29, Pilarzinho, 82120-200 Curitiba, PR ☎ +55 41 3383377 **E:** cnt@cnt.com.br **W:** www.cnt.com.br – **REDE BRASIL DE TELEVISÃO (RBTV) (Comm)** ✉ Alameda dos Uapés, 313 - Saúde, 04067-030 São Paulo, SP **W:** rbtv.com.br – **REDE GLOBO (Comm)** ✉ Rua Lopes Quintas 303, Jardim Botanico, 22460-010 Rio de Janeiro, RJ ☎ +55 21 25402000 **E:** wm@redeglobo.com.br **W:** redeglobo.globo.com – **REDE RECORD (Comm)** ✉ Rua da Várzea 240, 01140-080 São Paulo, SP ☎ +55 11 36604761 **E:** tvrecord@rederecord.com.br **W:** rederecord.r7.com – **SISTEMA BRASILEIRO DE TELEVISÃO (SBT) (Comm)** ✉ Av. das Comunicações 4, Vila Jaraguá, 06278-905 Osasco, SP ☎ +55 11 70873000 **E:** marketing@sbt.com.br **W:** www.sbt.com.br.

Local Stations not shown.

DTT Tx Networks
Nationwide & local multiprgr MFNs.

BRITISH INDIAN OCEAN TERRITORY

Systems: BFBS-TV: DVB-T (MPEG4) [E]; AFN-TV: NTSC [A]

Diego Garcia

BFBS-TV Relay (Serving British Mil) ✉ BFBS Diego Garcia **M:** BBC One (d), BBC Two (d), ITV (d), BFBS Extra (d), Sky News (d=delayed, i.e. time-shifted) ⌘ Forces R. BFBS, BFBS R.2, BFBS Gurkha R. **Tx:** ch27.

Foreign Military Station
AFN-TV Relay (U.S. Mil) ✉ AFN Diego Garcia, APO, AP 96595-0014, USA **Chs:** AFN Pacific line-up **Txs:** Diego Garcia ch6/8/10/12 (0.2kW)

BRUNEI

System: DVB-T (MPEG4), DVB-T2 (MPEG4) [E]

RADIO TELEVISYEN BRUNEI (RTB) (Gov) ✉ Bandar Seri Begawan, BS8610, Negara ☎ +673 2243111 **E:** rtbdir@rtb.gov.bn **W:** www.rtb.gov.bn **L.P:** Dir: Hj Muhd. Suffian Bin Hj. Bungsu **Chs:** RTB1, RTB2, RTB3, RTB4, RTB News, Aneka, Perdana, Sukmaindera

DTT Tx Network (DVB-T2 exc. *=DVB-T)
Tx Operator: RTB **Mux:** RTB1, RTB2, RTB3, RTB4, RTB News, Aneka, Perdana, Sukmaindera **Txs:** ch28* (Bt. Subok), ch30 (Bt. Subok 5kW, Bt. Andulau 5kW).

BULGARIA

System: DVB-T (MPEG4) [E]

BALGARSKA NATSIONALNA TELEVIZIA (BNT) (Pub) ✉ ul. San Stefano 29, 1504 Sofia ☎ +359 2 9661149 5 **E:** press@bnt.bg **W:** www.bnt.bg **L.P:** DG: Emil Koshlukov **Chs (terr.):** BNT1, BNT2, BNT3 & reg. studios – **BTV (Comm)** ✉ Natsionalen Dvorets na Kulturata, 1463 Sofia ☎ +359 2 9176800 **E:** pr@btv.bg **W:** www.btv.bg **L.P:** DG (bTV Media Group): Florian Skala – **BULGARIA ON AIR (Comm)** ✉ bul. Bryuksel 1, 1540 Sofia ☎ +359 2 4484070 **E:** office@bulgarionair.bg **W:** bgonair.bg – **FOLKLOR TV (Comm)** ✉ ul. Gyueshevo 85, 1330 Sofia ☎ +359 2 9201640 **E:** office@folklor-tv.bg **W:** folklor.tv – **NOVA TELEVIZIA (Comm)** ✉ bul. Hristofor Kolumb 41, 1592 Sofia ☎ +359 2 805000 **E:** office@novatv.bg **W:** novatv.bg **L.P:** CEO: Iva Stoyanova – **TV EVROPA (Comm)** ✉ bul. Tsarigradsko shose 101, 1113 Sofia ☎ +359 2 9797044 **E:** office@tvevropa.com **W:** www.tvevropa.com.

DTT Tx Networks
Licensee: NURTS Digital **W:** www.nurts.bg **M1:** Kanal 3, Bulgaria On Air, The Voice, TV Evropa, Fan Folk TV, Folklor TV **M2:** BNT1 & reg. prgrs, BNT2, BNT3, bTV, Nova Televizia.

Location	M1	M2	kW	Location	M1	M2	kW
Belogradchik	32	49	5	Smolyan	34	49	5
Dobrich	22	29	5	Sofia	27	40	5
Gotse Delchev	31	29	5	St. Zagora	22	37	5
Kardzhali	26	42	5	Shumen	28	40	5
Plovdiv	25	35	5	Varna	22	29	5
Ruse	26	49	5	Vidin	32	49	2
Sliven	22	37	5	+ sites with txs below 2kW.			

NB. Local muxes not shown.

BURKINA FASO

System: DVB-T2 (MPEG4) [E]

National Station
RADIODIFFUSION TÉLÉVISION DU BURKINA (RTB) (Pub) ✉ 01 BP 2530, Ouagadougou 01 ☎ +226 50318353 **E:** television@rtb.bf **W:** www.rtb.bf **L.P:** DG: Pascal Yemboini Thiombiano **Chs:** RTB, RTB2 (Regional).
Local Stations not shown.

DTT Tx Network
Tx Operator: RTB **M:** RTB, RTB2 (Regional) **Txs:** MFN

BURUNDI

System: DVB-T2 (MPEG4) [E]

National Station
RADIO TÉLÉVISION NATIONALE DU BURUNDI (RTNB) (Pub) ✉ BP 1900, Bujumbura ☎ +257 22224760 **E:** rtnb@cbinf.com **W:** www.rtnb.bi **L.P:** DG: Eric Nshimirimana

Local stations
Héritage TV: BP 4251, Bujumbura. **Rema TV:** 29, Rue de la Mission, Bujumbara. **Télé Renaissance:** BP 2986, Bujumbura. **TV Salama:** BP 2607, Bujumbura.

DTT Tx Network
Tx Operator: StarTimes **M(partly✪):** multiprgr **Txs:** MFN.

CABO VERDE

System: DVB-T2 (MPEG2) [E]

TELEVISÃO DE CABO VERDE (TCV) (Pub) ✉ Rua 13 de Janeiro, 1-A, Achada Santo António, Praia ☎ +238 2605200 **E:** tcv@rtc.cv **W:** www.rtc.cv **L.P:** Dir (TV): António Teixeira.

DTT Tx Network
Licensee: CV Telecom **W:** www.cvtelecom.cv **M:** Televisão de Cabo Verde, SIC Noticias, TV Record, Rai Uno, BBC World, TV5, TV Galicia, Infinito, Fox Life, Fashion TV, Euronews, Eurosport, Extreme Sport, TVE Internacional, CNBC, MCM, RTP África, Lusomundo Premium, Lusomundo Gallery, Playboy, SportTv, RTP1, RTP2, SIC, TVI. **Txs:** MFN

CAMBODIA

Systems: DVB-T2 (MPEG4) [E], DTMB [E]; § PAL-B [E]

National Stations
NATIONAL TELEVISION OF CAMBODIA (TVK) (Gov) ✉ 62 Preah Monivong Boulevard, Sangkat Sras Chork, Khan Daun Penh, Phnon Penh 12202 ☎ +855 23 430827 **E:** info@tvk.gov.kh **W:** www.tvk.gov.kh – **BAYON TV (Comm)** ✉ National Road No 1, Boeung Snoa, Chbar Ampeou, Phnon Penh 12357 ☎ +855 23 363695 **E:** bayontv@camnet.gov.kh **W:** bayontv.com.kh – **CAMBODIAN TV NETWORK (CTN) (Comm)** ✉ National Highway 5, Phum Krol Ko, Sangkat Kilomet 6, Khan Russei Keo, Phnom Penh 12104 ☎ +855 12 800800 **E:** wmaster@ctncambodia.com **W:** www.ctn.com.kh (CTN); mytv.com.kh (MyTV) **Chs:** CTN, MyTV.

Local Stations not shown.

DTT Tx Network
Licensee: PPCTV **W:** www.ppctv.com.kh **M(partly✪):** multiprgr **Txs:** MFN.

CAMEROON

System: DVB-T2 (MPEG4) [E]

National Stations
CAMEROON RADIO AND TELEVISION (CRTV) (Pub) ✉ BP 1634, Yaoundé ☎ +237 2214088 **E:** infos@crtv.cm **W:** crtv.cm **L.P:** DG: Charles Ndongo – **SPECTRUM TÉLÉVISION (STV) (Comm)** ✉ BP 4883, Douala ☎ +237 3433045 **E:** spectrum1@camnet.cm **W:** www.facebook.com/StvCameroon **Chs:** STV1, STV2.

Local Stations not shown.

DTT Tx Network
Tx Operator: StarTimes **M(partly✪):** multiprgr **Txs:** MFN

CANADA

Systems: ATSC [A]; § NTSC-M [A] (small markets only)

National Networks ([a]=analogue; O&O = owned-and-operated)
CANADIAN BROADCASTING CORP. (CBC/RADIO-CANADA) (Pub) ✉ 181 Queen St, Box 3220 Stn C, Ottawa ON K1Y 1E4 ☎ +1 613 2886000 **W:** www.cbc.ca **L.P:** Pres/CEO: Catherine Tait. **Networks:** CBC Television (English), ICI Radio-Canada Télé (French). **CBC Television:** ✉ 250 Front St W, Box 500 Stn A, Toronto ON M5W 1E6 ☎ +1 416 2053311 **W:** www.cbc.radio-canada.ca **L.P:** Exec. Vice Pres. (English Networks): Barbara Williams **O&O Stations:** CBAT-DT Fredericton NB ch31 (7.4kW), CBCT-DT Charlottetown PE ch13 (13kW), CBET-DT Windsor ON ch9 (26kW), CBHT-DT Halifax NS ch39 (157.5kW), CBKT-DT Regina SK ch9 (60kW), CBLT-DT Toronto ON ch20 (106.9kW), CBMT-DT Montréal QC ch21 (107kW), CBNT-DT St. John's NF ch8 (14.5kW), CBOT-DT Ottawa ON ch25 (165kW), CBRT-DT Calgary AB ch21 (23.5kW), CBUT-DT Vancouver BC ch43

(103.3kW), CBWT-DT Winnipeg MB ch27 (42kW), CBXT-DT Edmonton AB ch42 (131.7kW), CFYK-DT Yellowknife NT ch8 (2.4kW) & translators. Affiliates: 1. **ICI Radio-Canada Télé:** ✉ 1400 René-Lévesque Boul. E, Box 6000, Montréal QC H3C 3A8 ☎ +1 514 5976000 **W:** ici.radio-canada.ca **L.P:** Exec. Vice Pres. (French Networks): Louis Lalande. **O&O Stations:** CBAFT-DT Moncton NB ch11 (17.7kW), CBFT-DT Montréal QC ch19 (250kW), CBKFT-DT Regina SK ch13 (27.1kW), CBLFT-DT Toronto ON ch25 (106.2kW), CBOFT-DT Ottawa ON ch9 (3.5kW), CBUFT-DT Vancouver BC ch26 (27.5kW), CBVT-DT Québec QC ch25 (2.5kW), CBWFT-DT Winnipeg MB ch51 (7.6kW), CBXFT-DT Edmonton AB ch47 (15.2kW), CJBR-DT Rimouski QC ch45 (167.5kW), CKSH-DT Sherbrooke QC ch9 (36.3kW), CKTM-DT Trois-Rivières QC ch28 (38.9kW), CKTV-DT Saguenay QC ch12 (7.4kW) & translators. Affiliates: 2. – **CTV INC. (Comm)** (Div. of Bell Media Inc) ✉ 9 Channel Nine Court, Scarborough ON M1S 4B5 ☎ +1 416 3325000 **W:** www.ctv.ca **L.P:** Pres (Bell Media): Randy Lennox. **Networks:** CTV, CTV Two **O&O Stations: CTV:** CFCF-DT Montréal QC ch12 (10.6kW), CFCN-DT Calgary AB ch29 (220kW), CFCN-DT-5 Lethbridge AB ch13 (139kW), CFQC-DT Saskatoon SK ch8 (13kW), CFRN-DT Edmonton AB ch12 (25kW), CFRN-TV-6 Red Deer AB ch12 (25kW), CFTO-DT Toronto ON ch9 (10.2kW), CHBX-TV Sault Ste. Marie ON [a]ch2 (100kW), CICC-TV Yorkton SK [a]ch10 (56kW), CICI-TV Sudbury ON [a]ch5 (100kW), CIPA-TV Prince Albert SK [a]ch9 (325kW), CITO-TV Timmins ON [a]ch3 (100kW), CIVT-DT Vancouver BC ch32 (33kW), CJCB-TV Sydney NS [a]ch4 (180kW), CJCH-DT Halifax NS ch48 (400kW), CJOH-DT Ottawa ON ch13 (19kW), CKCK-DT Regina SK ch8 (23kW), CKCO-DT Kitchener ON ch13 (12kW), CKCW-DT Moncton NB ch29 (390kW), CKLT-DT St. John NB ch9 (7.6kW), CKNY-TV North Bay ON [a]ch10 (132.6kW), CKY-DT Winnipeg MB ch7 (24kW) & translators. Affiliates: 5. **CTV Two:** CFPL-DT London ON ch10 (45kW), CFTK-TV Terrace/Kitimat BC [a]ch3 (13.8kW), CHRO-DT-43 Ottawa ON ch43 (60kW), CHRO-TV Pembroke ON [a]ch5 (100kW), CHWI-DT Windsor ON ch16 (3.4kW), CIVI-DT Victoria BC ch23 (1.5kW), CJDC-TV Dawson Creek BC [a]ch5 (9.5kW), CKVR-DT Barrie ON ch10 (11kW) & translators. – **GLOBAL TV NETWORK INC. (Comm)** (Div. of Corus Entertainment Inc) ✉ 81 Barber Greene Road, Toronto, ON M3C 2A2 ☎+1 416 4465311 **W:** www.globaltv.com **L.P:** Pres/CEO (Corus Entertainment): Doug Murphy **Network:** Global. **O&O Stations:** CFRE-DT Regina SK ch11 (17.3kW), CFSK-DT Saskatoon SK ch42 (30kW), CHAN-DT Vancouver BC ch22 (40kW), CHBC-DT Kelowna BC ch27 (32.6kW), CHNB-DT St. John NB ch12 (6kW), CICT-DT Calgary AB ch41 (50kW), CIHF-DT Halifax NS ch8 (1kW), CIII-DT Toronto ON ch41 (100kW), CISA-DT Lethbridge AB ch7 (19.7kW), CITV-DT Edmonton AB ch13 (25kW), CKMI-DT Québec QC ch20 (18kW), CKND-DT Winnipeg MB ch40 (25.1kW) & translators. Affiliates: 2

Major Regional Networks ([a]=analogue)
ONTARIO EDUCATIONAL COMMUNICATIONS AUTHORITY (Pub) ✉ 2180 Yonge Street, Toronto, ON M4S 2B9 ☎ +1 416 4842600 **W:** www.tvo.org **L.P:** Chmn (TVO): Chris Day **Network:** TVOntario (TVO). **O&O Stations:** CICA-DT Toronto ch19 (106.5kW) & translators (ON). – **SOCIÉTÉ DE TÉLÉDIFFUSION DU QUEBEC (Pub)** ✉ 1000 rue Fullum, Montréal QC H2K 3L7 ☎ +1 514 5212424 **W:** www.telequebec.tv **L.P:** Pres/CEO: Marie Collin **Network:** Télé-Québec (French). **O&O Stations:** CIVA-DT Val-d'Or QC ch12 (22kW), CIVB-DT Rimouski QC ch22 (136kW), CIVC-DT Trois-Rivières QC ch45 (290kW), CIVF-DT Baie-Trinité QC ch12 (46kW), CIVG-DT Sept-Îles QC ch9 (19kW), CIVK-DT Carleton QC ch15 (140kW), CIVM-DT Montréal QC ch26 (269kW), CIVO-DT Gatineau QC ch30 (300kW), CIVP-DT Chapeau QC ch23 (0.76kW), CIVQ-DT Québec QC ch15 (194kW), CIVS-DT Sherbrooke QC ch24 (31kW), CIVV-DT Saguenay QC ch8 (84.9kW) & translators (QC). – **2190015 ONTARIO INC. (Comm)** ✉Box 6143 Stn A, Toronto ON M5W 1P6 ☎ +1 416 4921595 **W:** www.chz.com; www.chch.com **L.P:** Chmn/CEO: Romen Podzyhun. **Network:** Channel Zero. **O&O Stations:** CHCH-DT Hamilton ON ch15 (132kW) & translators (ON). – **NOVOO (Comm)** (Div. of Bell Media Inc) ✉ 85 Rue Saint-Paul Ouest, Montréal QC H2Y 3V4 ☎ +1 514 3906035 **W:** noovo.ca **L.P:** Pres (Bell Media): Randy Lennox **Network:** Noovo (French). **O&O Stations:** CFAB-DT Québec QC ch39 (98kW), CFJP-DT Montréal QC ch35 (13.9kW), CFRS-DT Saguenay QC ch38 (4.3kW), CFKS-DT Sherbrooke QC ch30 (4.6kW), CFKM-DT Trois-Rivières QC ch34 (9.4kW). Affiliates: 4 (QC). – **GROUPE TVA INC. (Comm)** (Div. of Québecor Media Inc) ✉ 1600 boul. de Maisonneuve Est, Montréal QC H2L 4P2 ☎ +1 514 5269251 **W:** tva.canoe.com **L.P:** Pres/CEO (Québecor Media): France Lauzière **Network:** TVA (French). **O&O Stations:** CFCM-DT Québec QC ch17 (210kW), CFER-DT Rimouski QC ch11 (3.3kW), CFTM-DT Montréal QC ch10 (11kW), CHEM-DT Trois-Rivières QC ch8 (11.5kW), CHLT-DT Sherbrooke QC ch7 (4kW), CJPM-DT Saguenay QC ch46 (200kW). Affiliates: 4 – **JIM PATTISON BROADCAST GROUP LP (Comm)** ✉ 460 Pemberton Terrace, Kamloops BC V2C 1T5 ☎ +1 250 3723322 **W:** jpbroadcast.com **L.P:** Pres: Rod Schween **O&O Stations (City Affiliates):** CFJC-TV Kamloops BC [a]ch4 (3.7kW), CHAT-TV Medicine Hat AB [a]ch6 (58kW), CKPG-TV Prince George BC [a]ch2 (8.3kW) & translators (AB & BC). – **ROGERS MEDIA INC. (Comm)** (Div. of Rogers Communications Inc) ✉ 333 Bloor St. E, 7th flr, Toronto ON M4W 1G9 ☎ +1 416 9358200 **W:** www.rogersmedia.com; www.citytv.com; www.omnitv.ca **L.P:** Pres/CEO: Joseph Natale **Networks:** City, OMNI Television (OMNI 1, OMNI 2). **O&O Stations: City:** CHMI-DT Portage la Prairie MB ch13 (8.3kW), CITY-DT Toronto ON ch44 (15kW), CJNT-DT Montréal QC ch49 (4kW), CKAL-DT Calgary AB ch49 (100kW), CKEM-DT Edmonton AB ch17 (107kW), CKVU-DT Vancouver BC ch33 (8.3kW) & translators. Affiliates: 3 (see Jim Pattison Broadcast Group) **OMNI 1:** CFMT-DT Toronto ON ch47 (22.2kW), CHNM-DT Vancouver BC ch20 (8.3kW), CJCO-DT Calgary AB ch38 (25kW), CJEO-DT Edmonton AB ch44 (58kW) & translators. **OMNI 2:** CJMT-DT Toronto ON ch40 (18.1kW) & translators.

Other Regional Networks & Local Stations not shown.

CANARY ISLANDS (Spain)

System: DVB-T (MPEG2, MPEG4) [E]

National (Regional) Stations
TELEVISIÓN ESPAÑOLA EN CANARIAS (TVE) (Pub) ✉ Plazoleta de Milton 1, 35005 Las Palmas de Gran Canaria ☎ +34 928 293096 – **RADIOTELEVISIÓN CANARIA (RTCV) (Pub)** ✉Mariucha 2, 35012 Las Palmas de Gran Canaria ☎ +34 928 280188 **W:** www.rtvc.es. **Ch:** TV Canaria.

Local Stations not shown.

DTT Tx Networks
Tx Operator: Cellnex Telecom **National Muxes 1-7:** see Spain; **Regional Mux (R):** TV Canaria, TV Canaria HD ⌘ Canarias R., R. Ecca **Local muxes** not shown.

Location	M1	M2	M3	M4	M5	M6	M7	R
SFN	28	36	35	32	34	31	25	30*

*) exc. Fuerteventura & Lanzarote ch22

CAYMAN ISLANDS (UK)

System: NTSC-M [A]

CAYMAN ISLANDS GOVERNMENT TV (CIGTV) (Gov) ✉ 113 Elgin Ave., George Town, Grand Cayman KY1-9005 ☎ +1 345 2442092 **W:** www.facebook.com/CIGTV-Cayman-387996724618019 **Tx:** ch23 – **CAYMAN ADVENTIST TELEVISION NETWORK (CATN) (Rlg)** ✉ P.O.Box 515, George Town, Grand Cayman KY1-1106. **E:** mission@candw.ky **Tx:** ch30. Rel. 3ABN (USA) – **CAYMAN CHRISTIAN TV LTD (CCT) (Rlg)** ✉ Northward, P.O. Box 964, Grand Cayman KY1-1102 ☎ +1 345 9472599 **Tx**: ch21. Rel. TBN (USA).

CENTRAL AFRICAN REPUBLIC

Systems: DVB-T2 (MPEG4) [E]; § SECAM-K1 [VHF=K]

National Stations
TÉLÉVISION CENTRAFRICAINE (TVCA) (Gov) ✉ BP 940, Bangui ☎ +236 75501412 – **VISION 4TV-RCA (Comm)** ✉ Bangui.

DTT Tx Network
Tx Operator: StarTimes **M(partly✪):** multiprgr **Txs:** MFN

CHAD

Systems: DVB-T2 (HEVC) [E]; § SECAM-K1 [VHF=K, UHF=E]

TÉLÉ TCHAD (Gov) ✉ BP 5123, N'Djamena ☎ +235 22522923 **E:** tele.tchad@intnet.td **W:** www.onrtv.org **L.P:** DG (ONRTV): Boukar Sanda.

DTT Tx Network
Tx Operator: StarTimes **M(partly✪):** multiprgr **Txs:** MFN

CHILE

Systems: ISDB-TB [A]; § NTSC-M [A] ⇩2024

National Stations ([a]=analogue)
TVN CHILE (Pub) ✉ Bellavista 0990, Providencia, Santiago ☎

+56 2 7077130 **E:** tvngprog@tvn.cl **W:** www.tvchile.cl **Txs:** Santiago ch33 & relay txs – **CANAL 13 (Rlg, Comm)** ✉ Inés Matte Urrejola 0825, Providencia, Santiago ☎ +56 2 6302356 **E:** mailbag@13.cl **W:** www.13.cl **Txs:** Santiago ch24 & relay txs – **CHILEVISIÓN (CHV) (Comm)** ✉ Inés Matte Urrejola 0890, Providencia, Santiago ☎ +56 2 4615100 **E:** rcarmi@chilevision.cl **W:** www.chilevision.cl **Txs:** Santiago ch30 & relays txs – **LA RED (Comm)** ✉ Avenida Quilín 3750, Macul, Santiago ☎ +56 2 23854000 **E:** lared@lared.cl **W:** lared.cl **Txs:** Santiago ch28 & relay txs – **MEGA (Comm)** ✉ Av. Vicuña Mackenna 1348, Santiago ☎ +56 2 8108000 **E:** mega@mega.cl **W:** www.mega.cl **Txs:** Santiago ch27 & relays – **TELECANAL (Comm)** ✉ Nueva Tajamar 481, Oficina 201, Torre Central, Las Condes, Santiago ☎ +56 2 4115600 **E:** telecanal@telecanal.cl **W:** www.telecanal.cl **Tx:** Santiago ªch2 & relays txs – **TV+ (Comm)** ✉ Av. Presidente Kennedy #9070, Oficina 601, Vitacura, Santiago ☎ +56 2 26167400 **E:** direccion@ucv.cl **W:** www.tvmas.tv **Txs:** Santiago ch29 & relay txs.

Local Stations not shown.

CHINA (People's Rep. of)

Systems: DTMB [DS]; § PAL-D [DS]

National Stations
CHINA MEDIA GROUP (Gov) ✉ 11 Fuxing Lu, Haidian Qu, Beijing 100859 ☎ +86 10 68500114 **L.P:** Pres: Shen Haixiong **Networks:** China Central Television (CCTV) **W:** www.cctv.com; China Global Television Network (CGTN) (✉ 13rd Ring North Road, Chaoyang Qu, Beijing 100020) **W:** www.cgtn.com – **CHINA EDUCATION TELEVISION (CETV) (Gov)** ✉ 160 Fuxingmennei Dajie, Xicheng Qu, Beijing 100031 ☎ +86 10 66419055 **L.P:** Pres: Yuan Xiaoping **W:** www.centv.cn.

Provincial Stations (all Gov)
AH) Anhui TV: 666 Longtu Lu, Shushan Qu, Hefei, Anhui 230071 **W:** www.ahrtv.cn **BJ)** Beijing TV: 98 Jianguo Lu, Chaoyang Qu, Beijing 100022 **W:** www.bmn.net.cn **CQ)** Chongqing TV: 333 Longshan Dadao, Chongqing 401147 **W:** www.cbg.cn **EB)** Hebei TV: 100 Jianshe Dajie, Shijiazhuang, Hebei 050021 **W:** www.hebtv.com **EN)** Henan TV: 18 Zhenghua Lu, Jinshui Qu, Zhengzhou, Henan 450008 **W:** www.hntv.tv **FJ)** Fujian TV: 128 Xihuan Nanlu, Taijiang Qu, Fuzhou, Fujian 350004 **W:** www.fjtv.net **GD)** Guangdong TV: 686 Renmin Beilu, Guangzhou, Guangdong 510012 **W:** www.gdtv.cn **GS)** Gansu TV: 561 Zhangsutan, Chengguan Qu, Lanzhou, Gansu 730010 **W:** www.gstv.com.cn **GX)** Guangxi TV: 73 Minzu Dadao, Nanning, Guangxi 530022 **W:** www.gxtv.cn **GZ)** Guizhou TV: 25 Ruijin Nanlu, Guiyang, Guizhou 550001 **W:** www.gzstv.com **HA)** Hainan TV: 71 Nansha Lu, Haikou, Hainan 570206 **W:** www.bluehn.com **HB)** Hubei TV: 1 Zhongbei Lu, Liangdao Jie,Wuchang Qu, Wuhan, Hubei 430071 **W:** news.hbtv.com.cn **HL)** Heilongjiang TV: 333 Hanshui Lu, Harbin, Heilongjiang 150090 **W:** www.hljtv.com **HN)** Hunan TV: Liuyang He Daqiao Dong, Changsha, Hunan 410003 **W:** zixun.hunantv.com **JL)** Jilin TV: 2066 Weixing Lu, Changchun, Jilin 130033 **W:** www.jilintv.cn **JS)** Jiangsu TV: 4 Beijing Donglu, Xuanwu Qu, Nanjing, Jiangsu 210008 **W:** www.jstv.com **JX)** Jiangxi TV: 207 Hongdu Zhong Dadao, Nanchang, Jiangxi 330046 **W:** www.jxntv.cn **LN)** Liaoning TV: 79 Wenhua Lu, Heping Qu, Shenyang, Liaoning 110003 **W:** www.lntv.com.cn **NM)** Nei Menggu TV: 1 Chengjisihan Xijie, Hohhot, Nei Menggu 010050 **W:** www.nmtv.com.cn **NX)** Ningxia TV: 66 Beijing Zhonglu, Jinfeng Qu, Yinchuan, Ningxia 750004 **W:** www.nxtv.cn **QH)** Qinghai TV: 81 Xiguan Dajie, Xining, Qinghai 810008 **W:** www.qhbtv.com **SD)** Shandong TV: 81 Jingshi Lu, Jinan, Shandong 250062 **W:** www.sdtv.cn **SC)** Sichuan TV: 66 Shiji Cheng Lu, Chengdu, Sichuan 610041 **W:** www.sctv.com **SH)** Shanghai TV: 298 Weihai Lu, Shanghai 200041 **W:** www.smg.cn **SN)** Shaanxi TV: 336 Chang'an Nanlu, Xi'an, Shaanxi 710061 **W:** www.sxtvs.com **SX)** Shanxi TV: 318 Yingze Dajie, Taiyuan, Shanxi 030001 **W:** www.sxgdcm.com **TJ)** Tianjin TV: 143 Weijin Lu, Heping Qu, Tianjin 300070 **W:** tjtv.enorth.com.cn **XJ)** Xinjiang TV: 830 Tuanjie Lu, Urumqi, Xinjiang 830044 **XZ)** Xizang TV: 41 Beijing Zhonglu, Chengguan Qu, Lhasa, Xizang 850004 **W:** www.vtibet.com/ds **YN)** Yunnan TV: 182 Renmin Xilu, Kunming, Yunnan 650031 **W:** www.yntv.cn **ZJ)** Zhejiang TV: 111 Moganshan Lu, Hangzhou, Zhejiang 310005 **W:** www.cztv.com.
NB: Keys to regional codes - see National radio section.

DTT Tx Networks
Tx Operator: NRTA **W:** www.nrta.gov.cn **M1:** CCTV1, CCTV2, CCTV4, CCTV10, CCTV12, CCTV13, CCTV14, CCTV15 **M2:** CCTV1 HD, CCTV7, CCTV9, CCTV11, CGTN, CETV3 **R1+R2:** various provincial/local stations

Location	M1	M2	R1	R2
Beijing	45	46	22	40

+ nationwide MFN
Local muxes not shown.

CHRISTMAS ISLAND (Australia)

NB: No terrestrial TV station.

COCOS (Keeling) ISLANDS (Australia)

NB: No terrestrial TV station.

COLOMBIA

System: DVB-T2 (MPEG4) [A]

National Stations
RADIO TELEVISIÓN NACIONAL DE COLOMBIA (RTVC) (Pub) ✉ Avenida El Dorado No. 46-76, Bogotá ☎+57 1 2200700 **E:** info@rtvc.gov.co **W:** www.rtvc.gov.co – **CARACOL TELEVISIÓN (Comm)** ✉ Calle 103 #69 B 43, Bogota ☎ +57 1 6430430 **E:** serviciocliente@caracol.com.co **W:** www.caracoltv.com – **RCN TELEVISIÓN (Comm)** ✉ Av Americas 65-82, Bogotá ☎ +57 1 4269292 **W:** www.canalrcn.com.

Local Stations not shown.

DTT Tx Networks

Location	RTVC	Caracol	RCN	R	L1	L2
SFN	16	14	15	17	27	28

Multiplexes: RTVC: Señal Colombia HD, Canal Institucional HD, Canal 1 HD ⌘ R. Nacional de Colombia, Radiónica, Canal Educativo RTVC **Caracol:** Caracol HD, Caracol HD2, La Kalle HD, Caracol Móvil, ⌘ Blue R. **RCN:** RCN HD, RCN HD2, NTN24, RCN Móvil ⌘ RCN R., La FM, R. Uno **R:** Regional Stations **L1+L2:** Local stns (Bogotá area only).

COMOROS

Systems: DTMB [E]; § SECAM-K1 [VHF=K]

National Station
OFFICE DE RADIO ET TÉLÉVISION DES COMORES (ORTC) (Pub) ✉ BP 250, Moroni ☎ +269 7744045 **W:** www.ortc.fr **L.P:** DG: Mohamoud Salim.

Local Stations (all Comm)
Djabal TV: Iconi. **Kartala RTV:** Moroni. **TV-Sha:** Moroni. **MTV:** Moroni. **RTV Anjouanaise (RTA):** Mbouyoujou-Ouani, Ile Autonome d'Anjouan.

DTT Tx Network
Tx Operator: n/a **M:** multiprgr **Txs:** MFN

CONGO (Dem. Rep.)

System: DVB-T2 (MPEG4) [E]

National Station
RADIOTÉLÉVISION NATIONALE CONGOLAISE (RTNC) (Pub) ✉ BP 3164, Gombe, Kinshasa ☎ +243 1 5260601 **W:** www.facebook.com/RTNCofficielle1 **Chs:** RTNC1, RTNC2, RTNC3.

Local Stations not shown.

DTT Tx Network
Tx Operator: StarTimes **M (partly✪):** RTNC3, Tropicana TV, La chaîne du Sénat, Télé 50, Raga TV, B-Ones **Txs:** ch26 (Kinshasa 0.5kW) & netw. under constr. – **Local Tx Operators** not shown.

CONGO (Rep.)

System: DVB-T2 (MPEG4) [E]

TÉLÉ CONGO (Gov) ✉ BP 1046, Brazzaville ☎ +242 222810116 **W:** telecongo.com **L.P:** DG: Jean Obambi – **DRTV (Comm)** ✉ BP 1974, Brazzaville **W:** www.facebook.com/DRTV-International-230828793639419.

DTT Tx Network
Tx Operator: StarTimes **M(partly✪):** multiprgr **Txs:** MFN

COOK ISLANDS

System: PAL-B [NZ]

COOK ISLANDS TV (CITV) (Comm) ✉ P.O.Box 126, Avarua, Rarotonga ☎ +682 29460 **E:** watchus@citv.co.ck **W:** www.citv.co.ck **L.P:** CEO: Jeane Matenga **Txs:** Airport ch4, Works Depot, TV studio, Mauke ch5, Matavera ch6, Titikaveka ch7, Aitutaki & Rarotonga ch9, Tu Papa ch10, Hospital & Ngatangiia ch11.

COSTA RICA

Systems: ISDB-TB [A]; § NTSC-M [A] ⇩2021

National Stations
SISTEMA NACIONAL DE RADIO Y TELEVISIÓN S.A. (SINART) (Pub) ✉ Apt 7-1908-1000, San José ☎ +506 22313333 **E:** digital@sinart.go.cr **W:** costaricamedios.cr **L.P:** Pres: Lorna Chacón **Txs:** San José ch13 & relay txs – **REPRETEL (Comm)** ✉ Apartado 2860, 1000 San José ☎ +506 22906665 **E:** info@repretel.com **W:** www.repretel.com **Chs:** Canal 4, 6, 11. **Txs:** San José ch26 – **TELETICA (Comm)** ✉Sabana Oeste, San José ☎ +506 22101201 **E:** info@teletica.com **W:** www.teletica.com **Tx:** San José ch14.

Local Stations not shown.

CÔTE D'IVOIRE

System: DVB-T2 (MPEG4) [E]

RADIODIFFUSION TÉLÉVISION IVOIRIENNE (RTI) (Pub) ✉ 08 BP 883, Abidjan 08 ☎ +225 22449039 **E:** dgrti@aviso.ci **W:** www.rti.ci **L.P:** DG: Fousseny Dembélé **Chs:** RTI1, RTI2.

DTT Tx Network
Tx Operator: StarTimes **M(partly✪):** multiprgr **Txs:** MFN

CROATIA

System: DVB-T2 (HEVC) [E]; § DVB-T (MPEG4) [E]

National Stations
HRVATSKA RADIO-TELEVIZIJA (HRT) (Pub) ✉ Prisavlje 3, 10000 Zagreb. ☎ + 385 1 6163366 **W:** www.hrt.hr **L.P:** DG: Kazimir Bačić. **Chs:** HRT1, HRT2, HRT3, HRT4 – **NOVA TV (Comm)** ✉ Remetinecka cesta 139, 10000 Zagreb ☎ +385 1 6008300 **E:** novatv@novatv.hr **W:** novatv.dnevnik.hr **L.P:** DG: Dražen Mavrić **Chs:** Nova TV, Doma TV – **RTL TELEVIZIJA (Comm)** ✉ Krapinska 45, 10000 Zagreb ☎ +385 1 3660000 **E:** rtl@rtl.hr **W:** www.rtl.hr **L.P:** Pres/CEO: Marc Puškarić. **Chs (terr.):** RTL, RTL2, RTL Klockica.

Local Stations (via Mux 4, DTT regions: a-i)
Gradska TV: Molatska bb, 23000 Zadar (g) **Kanal RI:** Trg Riječke rezolucije 3, 51000 Rijeka (e). **Nezavisna Istarska Televizija (NIT):** Trg pod lipom 1, 52000 Pazin (e). **RI-TV:** Užarska 17/3, 51000 Rijeka (e). **Slavonskobrodska Televizija:** Mile Budaka 1/IV, 35 000 Slavonski Brod (b). **TV Cakovec:** Kralja Tomislava 6, 40000 Čakovec (c). **TV Jadran:** Split (h). **TV Nova:** M. Laginje 5, 52100 Pula (e). **TV Slavonije i Baranje:** Hrvatske republike 20, 31000 Osijek (a). **Varaždinska Televizija (VTV):** Kralja P. Krešimira IV 6a, 42000 Varaždin (c). **Vinkovacka Televizija (VKTV):** Trg dr.F.Tuđmana 2, 32100 Vinkovci (a).

DTT Tx Networks (DVB-T2 exc. where stated otherwise*)
Licensee M1,M2,M4: OIV **W:** www.oiv.hr **M1:** HRT1 HD, HRT2 HD, HRT3 HD, HRT4 HD, RTL HD, RTL2 HD, Doma TV HD, Nova TV **M2:** HRT3, HRT4, RTL2, Doma TV, local stns **M4 (DVB-T):** CMC, RTL Klockica, SPTV, local stns. **Licensee Mux 3:** HT d.d. **W:** www.evotv.hr **M3✪:** N1, Al Jazeera Balkans, CNN, National Geographic, NatGeo Wild, Viasat Explore, Viasat History, Epic Drama, Doku TV HD, Viasat Nature HD, HBO HD, HBO2 HD, HBO3 HD, Cinemax, Cinemax 2, Klasik TV, TV1000, AXN, Movie Generation, RTL Living, Kino TV, Cinestar TV, FOX, FOX Life, M1 Film, M1 Gold. *) Not all txs of M1&M2 are DVB-T2 yet **Local multiplexes** not shown.

Location	M1	M2	M3	M4*
Belje	36	44	38	21a
Biokovo	33	53	23	34h
Borinci	38	44	38	21a
Brač	33	53	23	53h
Ćelevac	51	59	21	31g
Drenovci	36	-	-	-
Gruda	51	59	-	-
Ivanščica	44V	48V	28	36Vc
Kalnik	44	48	28	-
Krk	28	53	57	45
Labinštica	33	53	23	34h
Lastovo	33	-	-	-
Lička Plješevica	30	44	-	54
Mali Losinj	28	53	-	-
Mirkovica	30	44	-	54
Moslavačka Gora	23	39	28	-
Pag	51	59	21	-
Papuk	23	39	38	58
Petrova Gora	25	48	-	-
Promina	51	59	21	31g
Psunj	23	39	28	58
Pula	28	53	-	45e
Razromir	28	53	-	-
Rota	33	53	-	-
Sljeme	25	48	28	42d
Srđ	51	59	22	28i
Stipanov Grič	30	44	36	54
Sveta Gera	25	48	-	-
Sveta Nedjelja	25	48	28	42
Šibenik	51	59	-	31g
Učka	28	53	57	29e
Ugljan	51	59	21	31g
Uljenje	51	59	-	-
Zagreb (HRT HQ)	25	48	-	-

+ repeaters. *) DTT regions a-i, see under "Local Stations" (stns are being moved to M2 of DVB-T2 txs)
NB: OIV is converting the tx networks from DVB-T to DVB-T2. During the transition, txs and multiplexes are subject to changes not reflected in this chart.

CUBA

Systems: DTMB [A]; § NTSC-M [A] ⇩2024

National Station (ª=analogue)
INSTITUTO CUBANO DE RADIO Y TELEVISIÓN (ICRT) (Gov) ✉ Televisión Cubana, Calle 23 #258 e/L y M, Vedado, La Habana 10400 ☎ +53 7 8309705 **E:** tvcubana@icrt.cu **W:** www.tvcubana.icrt.cu **L.P:** Pres: Alfonso Noya **Chs:** Canal Educativo, Canal Educativo 2, Cubavisión, Tele Rebelde, Multivisión, Canal Clave, Canal Infantil, Regional stns. **Txs: Canal Educativo:** La Habana ªch4 (309kW) & netw.; **Canal Educativo 2:** La Habana ªch15 (631kW) & netw.; **Cubavisión:** La Habana ªch6 (129kW) & netw.; **Tele Rebelde:** La Habana ªch2 (132kW) & netw. **Multivisión:** La Habana ªch21 (3.2kW) & netw.

Local Stations not shown.

DTT Tx Network (under construction)
Tx Operator: Radiocuba **M1:** Canal Educativo, Canal Educativo 2, Cubavisión, Cubavisión Internacional, Multivisión, Tele Rebelde, Canal Clave, Canal Infantil ⌘ R.Rebelde, R.Progreso, R.Taíno, R. Enciclopedia, R. CMBF, R.Reloj **M2:** HD-mux **R:** Regional stns

Location	M1	M2	R	kW
Baracoa	38	-	-	12.6
Bartolome Maso	51	-	-	63
Ciego de Avila	33	-	-	12.6
Cienfuegos	27	42	-	4/10
Isla de la Juventud	41	-	-	12.6
Jacan	45	51	20	200/4/200
La Capitana	39	-	-	12.6
La Habana	38	36	-	79.4/39.8
La Palma	28	-	-	20
Las Tunas	33	-	-	12.6
Matanzas	31	-	-	15.8
Moa	43	-	-	12.6
Pinar del Rio	36	-	-	50
San Pedro de Alamar	51	-	-	12.6
Sancti Spiritus	29	-	-	40
Santa Clara	13	32	-	100/40
Santiago de Cuba	33	-	-	1000
Tabacal	29	-	-	15.8
Trinidad	46	-	-	12.6

+ sites with txs below 10kW.

CURAÇAO (Netherlands)

System: DVB-T (MPEG2) [E]

TELECURAÇAO (Gov) ✉ Berg Ararat zn., Willemstad ☎ +599 9 7771688 **E:** info@telecuracao.com **W:** telecuracao.com **M:** TeleCuraçao 1, TeleCuraçao 2 ⌘ TCFM 93.3 **Txs:** ch26 (SFN) – **NOS PAIS (Comm)** ✉ Handelskade 24, Willemstad ☎ +599 9 5277008 **E:** mavis@nospais.com **W:** www.facebook.com/NosPaisTV **M:** multiprgr **Txs:** SFN.

CYPRUS

System: DVB-T (MPEG4) [E]

National Stations
RADIOFONIKO IDRYMA KYPROU (RIK) (Pub) ✉ P.O.Box 24824, 1397 Lefkosia ☎ +357 22862000 **E:** info@cybc.com.cy **W:** cybc.com.cy **L.P:** DG: Michalis Maratheftis **Chs (terr.):** RIK1, RIK2, RIK HD – **ANT1 (Comm)** ✉ P.O.Box 20923, 1665 Lefkosia ☎+357 22200200 **W:** www.ant1iwo.com – **CAPITAL TV (Comm)** ✉ P.O.Box 55633, 3781 Limassol ☎ +357 25577577 **W:** www.capitaltv.com.cy – **EXTRA TV (Comm)** ✉ P.O.Box 70651, 3801 Limassol ☎ +357 25715111 **W:** www.facebook.com/Extra-Tv-Cyprus-Channel-192069144189665 – **OMEGA TV (Comm)** ✉ P.O.Box 27400, 1644 Lefkosia ☎ +357 22477777 **E:** info@omegatv.com.cy **W:** www.omegatv.com.cy – **PLUS TV (Comm)** ✉ Neas Engomis St. 8, 2409 Lefkosia ☎ +357 22600600 **W:** www.facebook.com/PlusChannelCy – **SIGMA TV (Comm)** ✉ P.O.Box 21836, 1513 Lefkosia ☎ +357 22580100 **E:** info@sigmatv.com **W:** www.sigmatv.com.

Local stations not shown.

DTT Tx Networks
Tx Operator Mux 1: RIK **M1:** RIK1, RIK2, RIK HD, ERT World, Euronews **Tx Operator Mux 2+3:** Velister **W:** www.velister.com.cy **M2:** ANT1, Sigma TV, Omega TV, Plus TV, Extra TV, Capital TV **M3:** Prime Tel, Alpha TV, Smile TV, CBC TV Mall.

Location	M1	M2	M3
SFN1	49	50	54
SFN2	39	41	30

NORTHERN CYPRUS

National Station
BAYRAK RADIO TELEVISYON KURUMU (BRTK) (Gov) ✉ Dr. Fazıl Küçük Bulvarı, Lefkoşa (mail: via Mersin 10, Turkey) ☎ +90 392 2254577 **E:** info@brtk.net **W:** www.brtk.net **L.P:** Chair: Meryem Özkurt **Chs:** BRT1, BRT2, BRT3.

Local Stations not shown.

DTT Tx Networks
Tx Operator: BRTK **M1:** BRT1 HD, BRT2 HD, BRT3. Kanal T, KTV (Kıbrıs TV), Kıbrıs Genç TV, Kanal SIM, Ada, Diyalog TV **M2:** currently duplicates M1 **Txs: M1:** ch41 (SFN) **M2:** ch33 (SFN).

AKROTIRI & DHEKELIA (UK)

NB: No terrestrial TV station.

CZECHIA

System: DVB-T2 (HEVC) [E]; § DVB-T (MPEG2, MPEG4) [E]

National Stations
CESKÁ TELEVIZE (CT) (Pub) ✉ Kavcí Hory, 14070 Praha 4 ☎ +420 261131111 **E**: info@ceskatelevize.cz **W:** www.ceskatelevize.cz **L.P:** DG: Petr Dvořák **Chs:** ČT1, ČT2, Reg prgrs, ČT3, ČT24, ČT Art/Déčko, ČT Sport – **PRIMA TV (Comm)** ✉ Na Zertvách 24, 18000 Praha 8 ☎ +420 266700111 **E**: informace@iprima.cz **W:** www.iprima.cz **Chs:** TV Prima, Prima COOL, Prima Family, Prima Love, Prima Zoom, Prima Krimi, CNN-Prima News – **TV NOVA (Comm)** ✉ Kříženeckého nám. 5, 15252 Praha 5 ☎ +420 233100111 **E**: info@nova.cz **W:** tv.nova.cz **L.P:** DG: Klára Brachtlová **Chs:** Nova, Nova 2, Nova Action, Nova Cinema, Nova Gold – **TV BARRANDOV (Comm)** ✉ Kříženeckého nám. 322, 15200 Praha 5 **W:** www.barrandov.tv **Chs (terr.):** TV Barrandov, Barrandov Kino, Barrandov Krimi – **TV ÓCKO (Comm)** ✉ Vrchlického 29, 15000 Praha ☎ +420 257222256 **E**: ocko@ocko.tv **W:** ocko.tv. **Chs:** Óčko, Óčko Star.

Regional & Local Stations not shown.

DTT Tx Networks (DVB-T2)
Tx Operator: České Radiokomunikace a.s. **W:** www.radiokomunikace.cz **M1:** ČT1 HD, ČT2 HD (incl. reg. prgrs), ČT3, ČT24, ČT Sport HD, ČT Art HD/Déčko HD **M2:** Nova Cinema, Prima Family, Nova, Prima Cool, Prima Love, Óčko, Prima Zoom, Óčko Star, Barrandov Kino, Barrandov Krimi, Prima Max, Barrandov TV, Prima Krimi, CNN-Prima News **M3:** Nova Cinema, Nova, TV Noe, Barrandov Kino, Barrandov Krimi, Seznam.cz TV, Barrandov TV, NASA TV (UHD) **M4:** Nova, Šlágr TV, Relax, Rebel, TV JOJ, Retro, Comedy Central, JOJ Family, Nova 2, Nova Gold, Nova Action.
DVB-T Networks/Licensees not shown: all still existing DVB-T txs will be gradually switched off until 2021.

Location	M1	M2	M3	M4	kW
Benešov (Kozmice)	-	-	-	44	40
Brno (Barvičova ul.)	26V	40V	33V	46V	10
Brno (Hády)	26	40	33	-	10
Brno (Jihlavská)	-	-	-	46	10
Brno (Kojál)	26	40	33	-	100
Č. Budějovice (Kleť)	39	27	33	30	3x100/63
Cheb (Zelená hora)	26	38	31	-	20
Chomutov (Jedlová hora)	33	38	31	-	32
Domažlice (Vraní vrch)	26	34	31	-	10
Frenštát pod Radhoštěm	-	-	-	45	10
Frýdek-Místek (Lysá hora)	26	28	31	45	3x25/10
Hlubočec	-	-	-	45	10
Hodonín	-	-	-	46	10
Hradec Králové	-	-	-	45	10
Jablonec nad Nisou	-	-	-	43	10
Jáchymov (Klínovec)	39	38	31	45	3x20/40
Jeseník (Praděd)	26	28	31	-	100
Jihlava (Javořice)	26	28	35	-	100
Karlovy Vary (Tři Kříže)	26	34	31	-	0.025/25/0.025
Liberec (Ještěd)	26	28	-	-	25/32
Mariánské Lázně (Dyleň)	-	-	-	45	50
Mikulov (Děvín)	26	38	-	-	25
Olomouc (Slavonín)	-	-	-	44	10
Ostrava	-	-	-	45	10
Ostrava (Hošťálkovice)	26	28	31	-	100
Pardubice (vrch Krásný)	26	28	-	-	100
Pardubice (Slatiňany)	-	-	-	-	20
Plzeň	-	-	-	43	32
Plzeň (Krašov)	26	34	-	-	100
Praha	26	40	23	-	32
Praha (Cukrák)	-	40	23	-	100
Praha (Ládví)	-	-	-	42	20
Praha (Novodvorská)	-	-	-	42	10
Praha (Olšanská)	-	-	-	42	10
Rakovník (Louštín)	-	-	-	44	63
Sušice (Svatobor)	26	34	-	42	2x100/20
Teplice	-	-	-	21	10
Trutnov (Černá hora)	26	28	-	-	100
Uherské Hradište (Rovnina)	-	-	-	42	10
Ústí n.L. (Buková hora)	33	38	-	-	100
Ústí n.L. (Krušnohorská)	-	-	-	21	10
Valašské Klobouky	26	22	-	-	25
Vimperk	39	27	22	-	20
Votice (Mezivrata)	26	40	22	-	32
Zlín (Jižní svahy)	-	-	-	42	10
Zlín (Tlustá hora)	26	22	33	-	100
Znojmo (Deblínek)	-	-	-	46	10

+ sites with txs below 10kW.

DENMARK

Systems: DVB-T2 (MPEG4) [E]; # DVB-T (MPEG4)

National Stations
DR (Pub) ✉ TV Byen, Emil Holms Kanal 20, 0999 København C ☎ +45 35203040 **E**: presse@dr.dk **W:** www.dr.dk **L.P:** DG: Maria Rørbye Rønn **Chs (terr.):** DR1, DR2, DR Ramasjang – **TV2 DANMARK (Pub)** ✉ Rugaardsvej 25, 5100 Odense C ☎ +45 65919191 **E**: tv2@tv2.dk **W:** tv2.dk **L.P:** CEO: Anne Engdal Stig Christensen. Regional stns (**W:** www.tv2regionerne.dk): a) TV2/Bornholm (Brovangen 1, 3720 Aakirkeby), b) TV2/Fyn (Olfert Fischers Vej 31, 5220 Odense SØ), c) TV2/Lorry (Allégade 7-9, 2000 Frederiksberg), d) TV/Midt-Vest (Søvej 2, 7500 Holstebro), e) TV2/Nord (Søparken 4, 9440 Åbybro), f) TV Syd (Media Park 1, 6000 Kolding), g) TV2 Øst (Kildemarksvej 7, 4760

Vordingborg), h) TV2/Østjylland (Skejbyparken 1, 8200 Århus N) **Chs (terr.):** TV2, TV2 Regional Stations, TV2 Charlie, TV2 Fri, TV2 News, TV2 Sport, TV2 Sport X, TV2 Zulu – **Nordic Entertainment Group (Comm)** ✉ Strandlodsvej 30, 2300 København S ☎ +45 77305500 **W:** nentgroup.dk **L.P:** Pres/CEO: Anders Jensen **Chs (terr.):** TV3, TV3+, TV3 Puls, TV3 Sport 1&2, TV3 MAX.

Local Stations (via Mux 1, see below)
a) Ø-TV: Sendesamvirke Bornholm, Åbogade 9, 3760 Gudhjem; **b) Fynboen TV:** Sendesamvirke FYN 2014-19, Banevænget 24, 5270 Odense N; **c) Kanal Hovedstaden:** Sendesamvirket for Kanal Hovedstaden, Lyrskovgade 2-4, 1758 København V; **d) Kanal Midt-Vest:** Sendesamvirke Kanal Midt-Vest, Søvej 2, 7500 Holstebro; **e) Kanal Nord:** Sendesamvirke Kanal Nord, Søparken 2, 9440 Aabybro; **f) Kanal Syd:** Sendesamvirke Syd, c/o Gunnar Thomsen, Østerbrogade 30, 6000 Kolding; **g) Lokalkanalen:** NFMK (Nykøbing Falster Multimedie Klub), Voldgade 1, 4800 Nykøbing F; **h) Kanal Østjylland:** Sendesamvirke Kanal Østjylland, c/o Aarhus Global Media, Bjørnholms Allé 6, 8260 Viby J.

DTT Tx Networks (DVB-T2 exc. where indicated)
Licensee Mux 1+2: DIGI-TV I/S **W:** www.digi-tv.dk **M1:** DR1 HD, DR2 HD, DR Ramasjang HD, TV2 Regional Stations HD, Folketinget HD, Local stns **M2:** TV2 HD (incl. reg. prgrs), TV3 HD, Kanal 5 HD, TV3+ HD, dk4 HD, VH1, SVT1, NRK1 – **Licensee Mux 3-6:** Boxer TV A/S **W:** www.boxertv.dk **M3✪:** TV2 News HD, TV2 Charlie HD, TV2 Fri HD, TV2 Zulu HD, TV2 Sport HD, TV2 Sport X HD, Nickelodeon, Disney Channel, Disney Jr, ZDF **M4✪:** TV3 Puls HD, Paramount Network HD, TV3 Sport HD, TV3 MAX HD, Xee, National Geographic HD **M5✪:** Kanal 4 HD, 6'eren HD, Canal 9 HD, Eurosport 1 HD, Eurosport 2 HD, Discovery, Animal Planet HD, TLC HD – **Licensee Local Mux L:** Sendesamvirket for Kanal Hovedstaden **M:** various.

Location	M1*	M2	M3*	M4	M5	L	kW
Hadsten	24h	44	36h	46	26	-	50
Hedensted	41f	43	36f	46	30	-	50
Jyderup	34g	48	23g	42	31	-	50
København (1)	40c	33	23c	42	31	-	50
København (2)	40c	33	23c	42	31	35	5x10/4
København (2)	-	-	-	-	-	39	4
Nakskov	34g	48	38g	42	31	-	10
Nibe	39e	37	35e	29	26	-	50
Rø	40a	33	39a	32	45	-	25
Svendborg	35b	37	22b	25	30	-	25
Thisted	31dV	22V	21dV	45V	27V	-	25
Tolne	39e	37	35e	29	26	-	10
Tommerup	35b	37	22b	25	30	-	50
Varde	41f	32	33f	34	23	-	50
Viborg	38d	28	21d	45	27	-	50
Videbæk	48d	47	42d	34	23	-	50
Vordingborg	34g	48	38g	42	31	-	50
Åbenrå	40f	32	22f	25	30	-	50

+ sites with txs below 10kW. (1) Søborg (2) Gladsaxe *) incl. Local stns (Mux 1 a-h) & TV 2 Reg stns (Mux 1+3 a-h)

DJIBOUTI

Systems: DVB-T2 (MPEG4) [E]; § SECAM-B [E]

RADIODIFFUSION TÉLÉVISION DJIBOUTI (RTD) (Gov) ✉ BP 97, Djibouti ☎ +253 21352294 **E:** rtd@intnet.dj **W:** www.rtd.dj **L.P:** DG: Abdoulkader Ahmed Idriss **Ch:** Télé Djibouti 1-4

DTT Tx Network
Tx Operator: Djibouti Télécom **M:** Télé Djibouti 1-4 **Txs:** MFN.

DOMINICA

NB: No terrestrial TV stations.

DOMINICAN REPUBLIC

System: ATSC [A]

National Station
CORPORACIÓN ESTATAL DE RADIO Y TV (CERTV) (Pub) ✉ Av. Dr. Tejeda Florentino 8, Sto. Domingo ☎ +1 809 6892121 **E:** info@certv.gob.do **W:** www.certv.gob.do **L.P:** DG: Ramón Tejeda Read. **Txs:** ch4 (SFN).

Local Stations not shown.

EASTER ISLAND (Chile)

System: # NTSC-M [A]; ISDB-TB [A] planned

TV RAPA NUI ✉ Hanga Roa, Isla de Pascua. **Tx:** ch13.

ECUADOR

Systems: ISDB-TB [A]; § NTSC-M [A] ⇩2023

National Stations
SISTEMA ECUATORIANA DE RADIO Y TELEVISIÓN (Pub) ✉ San Salvador E6-49 y Eloy Alfaro, Edificio Medias Públicos, Quito. **W:** www.rtvecuador.ec; www.tctelevision.com; www.gamavision.com.ec **Chs:** Ecuador TV, TC Televisión, Gama TV. **Txs: TC Televisión:** Quito ch36 & relay txs, **Gama TV:** Quito ch30 & relay txs, **Ecuador TV:** Quito ch26 & relay txs. – **CANAL UNO (Comm)** ✉ Av. del Bosque Mz 112, Ciudadela Kennedy Norte, Guayaquil ☎ +593 4 2680200 **W:** www.facebook.com/canalunotvecuador **Txs:** Quito ch12 & relay txs – **ECUAVISA (Comm)** ✉ Bosmediano 447, José Carb, Quito 1 ☎ +593 2 2995300 **W:** www.ecuavisa.com **Txs:** Quito ch36 & relay txs – **RTS (RED TELESISTEMA) (Comm)** ✉ Av. de los Shyris y Suecia, Edificio Renazzo Plaza #202, Quito ☎ +593 2 2272086 **E:** rts@rts.com.ec **W:** www.rts.com.ec **Txs:** Quito ch34 & relay txs – **RTU (RADIO Y TELEVISIÓN UNIDAS) (Comm)** ✉ Carrión E555 y Juan León Mera, Quito. **E:** noticias@canalrtu.tv **W:** www.canalrtu.tv **Txs:** Quito ch46 & relay txs – **TELEAMAZONAS (Comm)** ✉ Av. A. Granda C. 529 y Av. Brasil, Quito ☎ +593 2 2430350 **E:** contactenos@teleamazonas.com **W:** www.teleamazonas.com. **Txs:** Quito ch32 & relay txs.

Local Stations not shown.

EGYPT

Systems: DVB-T2 (MPEG4) [E]; § PAL-B/G [E] ⇩2021

NATIONAL MEDIA AUTHORITY (Gov) ✉ TV Bldg, Corniche El Nil, Cairo 11511 ☎ +20 2 25757155 **E:** tvinfo@ertu.org **W:** ertu.org **L.P:** Chmn: Hussein Zein **Chs (terr.):** Channel 1 & Channel 2 (National), Regional stns, Nile TV, Nile Comedy, Nile Culture, Nile Drama, Nile Family, Nile Life, Nile News, Nile Sport, Maspero Zaman

DTT Tx Networks (under construction)
Tx Operator: ERTU **M1&2:** multiprgr

Location	M1	M2	kW	Location	M1	M2	kW
Alexandria	34	27	2/1	Ismailia	27V	-	2.5
Beni Suef	33	31	2	Luxor	45	28	2/0.5
Cairo	32	36	4	Matruh	6	8	2.2
Dumyat	23	31	2/0.6	Minya	45V	32V	2
El Amain	40	-	2	Sallum	9	-	1
El Arish	23V	-	2	Sohag	37	29	2/0.5
El Mahalla	42	47	4/2	Tanta	25	39	2/0.5
El Negila	33	-	2	Zagazig	21	37	2
El Tur	26	-	2	+ sites with txs below 1kW.			

EL SALVADOR

Systems: ISDB-T [A]; § NTSC-M [A] ⇩2022

National Stations
TELEVISION EL SALVADOR (TVES) (CANAL 10) (Pub) ✉ Ap. Postal No. 104, Neuva San Salvador ☎ +503 2280499 **E:** tydiez@es.com.sv **W:** www.tencanal10.tv **Txs:** ch10 (SFN). – **CANAL 12 (Comm)** ✉ Carretera Panaméricana #12, Antiguo Custatlan, La Libertad, San Salvador ☎ +503 25601212 **E:** canal12@canal12.com.sv **W:** www.canal12.com.sv **Txs:** ch12 (SFN). – **TELECORPORACIÓN SALVADOREÑA (TCS) (Comm)** ✉ Alameda Manuel Enrique Araújo, Edifício Canales 2, 4 y 6, San Salvador ☎ +503 22092000 **W:** www.tcs.com.sv **L.P:** CEO: Boris Eserski. **Chs:** Teledos, Canal Cuatro, Canal Seis. **Txs:** Teledos ch2 (SFN), Canal Cuatro ch4 (SFN), Canal Seis ch6 (SFN). – **AGAPE TV (CANAL 8) (Rlg)** ✉ Calle Gerardo Barrios No. 1511, Col. Cucumacayán, Santa Salvador ☎ +503 22812828 **E:** info@agapetv8.com **W:** www.agapetv8.com **Txs:** ch8 (SFN).

Local Stations not shown.

EQUATORIAL GUINEA

Systems: DVB-T2 (MPEG4); § PAL-B/G [E]

TELEVISIÓN GUINEA ECUATORIAL (TVGE) (Pub) ✉ Calle 3 Augusto, Malabo ☎ +240 222515335 **E:** info@rtvge.tv **W:** www.tvgelive.gq – **ASONGA TELEVISIÓN (Comm)** ✉ Bata **W:** www.facebook.com/radiotelevisionasonga.

DTT Tx Network
Tx Operator: StarTimes **M(partly✪):** multiprgr **Txs:** MFN

ERITREA

System: PAL-B/G [E]

ERITREA TELEVISION (ERI-TV) (Gov) ✉ Asmara ☎ +291 1 116033 **E:** aslmelashe@yahoo.com **W:** www.eri.tv **Chs:** ERI-TV1, ERI-TV2, ERI-TV3 **Txs: ERI-TV1:** Asmara ch5 (5kW), Assab ch11 (5kW) & relay txs. **ERI-TV2:** (-). **ERI-TV3:** (-).

ESTONIA

System: DVB-T (MPEG4), DVB-T2 (MPEG4), DVB-T2 (HEVC) [E]

EESTI TELEVISIOON (ETV) (Pub) ✉ Faehlmanni 12, 15029 Tallinn ☎ +372 6284133 **E:** etv@etv.ee **W:** etv.err.ee **L.P:** Chmn (ERR): Rein Veidemann. **Chs:** ETV, ETV2, ETV+ – **ALL MEDIA EESTI (Comm)** ✉ Peterburi tee 81, 11415 Tallinn ☎ +372 6220200 **L.P:** CEO: Priit Leito **Chs:** TV3, TV6 – **POSTIMEES GRUPP (Comm)** ✉ Maakri 23a, 10145 Tallinn ☎ +372 6662350 **E:** eestimeedia@eestimeedia.ee **W:** www.eestimeedia.ee **L.P:** CEO: Andrus Raudsalu **Chs:** Kanal 2, Kanal 11, Kanal 12, MyHits.

DTT Tx Networks (DVB-T except where indicated)
Tx Operator: Levira AS **W:** www.levira.ee **M1:** ETV, ETV2, ETV+ **M2✪:** Kanal 12, TV6, Sony Channel, Sony Turbo, Discovery, Animal Planet, History, Kidzone TV, Eurosport, Setana Sports, TV3+, PBK Estonia, NTV Mir **M3✪:** Kanal 11, Euronews, Fox Life, Fox, Filmzone, Filmzone+, ID Xtra, National Geographic, Eurosport 2, MyHits, TLC, Hustler TV **M4 (DVB-T2/MPEG4)✪:** Kanal 2 HD, TV3 HD, Kanal 12 HD, TV6 HD, Kanal 11 HD, Sony Channel HD, Filmzone HD, Sony Turbo HD, Filmzone+ HD, TV3+ HD **M6(✪exc.*):** Kanal 2, TV3, France 24*, Viasat History, RTL Television, Travel Channel, Dom Kino, RTR Planeta, REN TV Estonia **M7 (DVB-T2/HEVC):** ETV HD, ETV2 HD ETV+ HD.

Location	M1	M2	M3	M4	M6	M7	kW
Ellamaa	28	-	-	-	-	42	8.8/3.6
Koeru	39	27	43	47	44	41	5/2x1.6/8.5/6/2.5
Kohtla-Nõmme	33	34	31	46	29	48	15/2x2/1/2x2
Pehka	28V	-	-	37V	-	42V	6.6/2x3.6
Pärnu	26	34	36	46	32	24	18/3x20/19/7
Tallinn (TV-tower)	28	25	45	37	30	42	19/3x15/20/8.5
Valgjärve	23	40	43	47	44	35	20/2x14/2x19/8

+ sites with txs below 5kW **NB:** Mux 5 not assigned.

ESWATINI

System: DVB-T2 (MPEG4) [E]

ESWATINI TELEVISION AUTHORITY (ETVA) (Pub) ✉ Private Bag A146, Mbabane ☎ +268 24043036 **E:** info@swazitv.co.sz **W:** www.swazitv.co.sz **L.P:** Chair: Carol Ngcobo.

DTT Tx Network
Tx Operator: Multichoice Eswatini **M(partly✪):** multiprgr **Txs:** MFN

ETHIOPIA

Systems: DVB-T2 (MPEG4) [E]; § PAL-B/G [E] ⇩2021

National Station
ETHIOPIAN BROADCASTING CORP. (EBC) (Pub) ✉ P.O.Box 5544, Addis Ababa ☎ +251 11 5505483 **W:** www.facebook.com/EBCzena **L.P:** GM: Nigussie Mitiku **Chs (terr.):** EBC1, EBC2, EBC3, reg. stns.

Local Stations
Dire TV: Dire Dawa. **Harari TV:** Harar. **Oromia Radio & TV (ORTV):** P.O.Box 2919, Adama. **Somali TV:** Jijiga.

DTT Tx Network
Tx Operator: EBC **Mux:** EBC1, EBC2, EBC3, EBC4 **Txs:** ch42 (Addis Ababa 10kW) & MFN.

FALKLAND ISLANDS (UK)

System: DVB-T (MPEG4) [E]

BFBS-TV Relay (Serving British Military) ✉ BFBS Falkland Islands, Mt. Pleasant, BFPO 655 ☎ +500 32179 **E:** falklands@bfbs.com **M(✪exc.*)** BBC One, BBC One (d)*, BBC Two, BBC Two (d)*, ITV, ITV (d)*, BFBS Extra, BFBS Extra (d)*, Sky Sports, BT Sport, BFBS Sport, Sky News* (d=delayed, i.e. time-shifted) ⌘ Forces R. BFBS (Falkland Islands)*, BFBS R.2*, BFBS Gurkha R.* **Txs:** ch27 (SFN).
NB: The FTA time-shifted editions of BBC One, BBC Two, ITV, BFBS Extra are also serving the civilian population.

FAROE ISLANDS (Denmark)

System: DVB-T (MPEG4) [E]

KRINGVARP FØROYA - SJÓNVARP (KVF) (Pub) ✉ P.O.Box 1299, 110 Tórshavn ☎ +298 347500 **E:** kringvarp@kvf.fo **W:** kvf.fo **L.P:** CEO: Ivan Hentze Niclasen – **IKTUS (Rlg)** ✉ c/o Anja Hansen, Landsvegur 9, 511 Gøtugjógv **E:** iktus@iktus.fo **W:** iktus.fo.

DTT Tx Networks
Licensee Mux 1-4: Televarpið **W:** tv.fo **M1✪:** TV3+ HD, Kanal 4, Kanal 5, Visjon Norge, National Geographic, BBC Brit, BBC World News **M2(✪exc.*):** KVF*, DR1 HD, DR2 HD, NRK1, TV3, TV3 Puls, TV2 Charlie **M3✪:** RUV, DR Ramasjang/Viasat Film Family, Viasat Film Premiere HD, Viasat Film Action, Viasat Series, Discovery, MTV, Nickelodeon/VH1 **M4(✪exc.*):** Rás 1*, TV2 HD, 6'eren, TV3 Sport 1, TV3 Max, Disney Channel, Animal Planet, Europort 1 – **Licensee Mux 5:** R2 Net **W:** r2net.fo **M5:** 10'arin, IKTUS HD.

Location	M1	M2	M3	M4	M5	kW
Klakkur	22	24	26	28	31	0.25
Knúkur	37	39	41	43	31	0.04
Stongin	52	50	48	46	34	0.04
Støðlafjall	52	50	48	46	-	0.04
Velbastaður	52V	50V	48V	46V	-	0.04

+ repeaters.

FIJI

System: DVB-T2 (MPEG4) [E]

National Stations
FIJI BROADCASTING CORP. (FBC) (Pub) ✉ 69 Gladstone Rd, Suva ☎ +679 3314333 **E:** infocenter@fbc.com.fj **W:** www.fbc.com.fj **L.P:** CEO: Riyaz Sayed-Khaiyum. **Ch:** FBC TV – **FIJI TV (Comm)** ✉ 20 Gorrie Street, Suva ☎ +679 3305100 **E:** fijitv@is.com.fj **W:** fijione.tv **L.P:** CEO (Fiji TV Ltd): Karen Lobendahn – **MAI TV (Comm)** ✉ Grantham Rd, Suva ☎ +679 3275051 **E:** info@tv.com.fj **W:** www.facebook.com/maitvfiji **L.P:** CEO: Richard Broadbridge.

Local Stations not shown.

DTT Tx Network
Tx Operator: Walesi Ltd **W:** www.walesi.com.fj **M:** FBC TV, Fiji TV, Mai TV; Sky Pacific channels✪**Txs:** MFN

FINLAND

Systems: DVB-T2 (MPEG4) [E]; DVB-T (MPEG2)

National Stations
YLEISRADIO OY (Pub) ✉ Uutiskatu 5, 00240 Helsinki ☎ +358 9 14801 **W:** www.yle.fi **L.P:** CEO: Merja Ylä-Anttila **Chs:** Yle TV1, Yle TV2, Yle Teema & Fem – **ALFA TV (Comm)** ✉ Ratapellonkuja 4, 04250 Kerava ☎ +358 10 3273000 **E:** info@alfatv.fi **W:** alfatv.fi **L.P:** Chmn/CEO: Hannu Haukka – **CANAL DIGITAL (Comm)** ✉ P.O.Box 2, 00381 Helsinki ☎ +358 9 54264200 🖷 +358 9 54264270 **E:** asiakaspalvelu@canaldigital.fi **W:** www.canaldigital.fi – **MTV OY (Comm)** ✉ Ilmalankatu 2, 00033 MTV ☎ +358 10 300300 **W:** www.mtv3.fi **L.P:** CEO (MTV3 Media): Johannes Leppänen **Chs (terr.):** MTV3, AVA, Sub – **NELONEN (Comm)** ✉ Töölönlahdenkatu 2, 00100 Helsinki ☎ +358 9 4545414 **W:** www.nelonen.fi **L.P:** Pres (Nelonen Media): Kari Laakso. **Chs (terr.):** Nelonen, Jim, Liv, Hero – **DISCOVERY NETWORKS FINLAND OY (Comm)** ✉ Mechelininkatu 1a, 00180 Helsinki ☎ +358 20 7870850 **W:** discoveryfinland.fi **Chs:** TV5, Kutonen, Frii.

DTT Tx Networks (DVB-T2 except where noted)

Tx Operator: Digita Oy **W:** www.digita.fi **M1 (DVB-T):** Yle TV1, Yle TV2, Yle Teema & Fem, AVA, MTV3, Nelonen **M2✪:** Yle TV1 HD, Yle TV2 HD, MTV3, Yle Teema & Fem HD **M3 (DVB-T):** TV 5, Kutonen, TLC, FOX, Frii, Rex TV, National Geographic **M4✪:** C More Max, C More Juniori, Discovery, Paramount Network, NatGeo Wild, Animal Planet, C More First HD, C More Series, C More Sport 1 HD, C More Sport 2 HD, C More Hits, Nick Jr, V Film Premiere HD, V Sport Live 1-5 **M5 (DVB-T):** Sub, Liv, Jim, Hero, Alfa TV, MT, INEZ, One Way TV, C More Max **M6✪:** Eurosport 1, Eurosport 2, Investigation Discovery, Disney Jr, Disney XD, Disney Channel, V Film Action HD, V Sport Jääkiekko HD, V Sport Hockey, V Sport Urheilu, V Sport Golf, AdultTV.fi.

Location	M1	M2	M3	M4	M5	M6	kW
Anjalankoski	22	27	26	44	39	41	50
Espoo	32	44	46	43	26	39	50
Eurajoki	38	45	42	36	37	33	50
Fiskars	32	24	46	43	23	39	10
Haapavesi	34	42	44	40	24	33	50
Iisalmi	26	22	-	-	38	-	30
Inari	48	25	-	-	-	-	12
Joutseno	47	35	36	44	32	41	50
Jyväskylä	30	35	28	27	22	41	50
Kerimäki	30	42	33	26	37	41	50
Kiihtelysvaara	32	38	-	-	-	-	30
Koli	25	40	47	48	29	41	60
Kruunupyy	30	22	41	40	28	25	50
Kuopio	24	36	39	32	46	41	50
Lahti	33	37	40	37	48	42	50
Lapua	38	37	33	40	48	25	50
Mikkeli	29	43	25	44	38	41	50
Oulu	41	22	28	25	37	33	50
Pernaja	23	24	-	43	36	41	10
Pihtipudas	23	29	43	-	45	-	80
Posio	31	23	-	-	-	-	14
Pyhätunturi	24	42	-	-	41	-	16
Pyhävuori	28	41	-		35	-	50
Rovaniemi	43	38	-	-	46	-	10
Ruka	33	48	28	-	-	-	10
Taivalkoski	32	42	-	-	38	-	14
Tammela	22	27	25	31	30	35	60
Tampere	34	23	44	43	46	24	50
Tervola	40	42	-	-	44	-	18
Turku	29	44	47	36	41	33	100
Vaasa	38	37	-	40	48	25	10
Vuokatti	30	23	27	48	35	36	80
Ylläs	30	28	-	-	36	-	14
Ähtäri	26	39	-	-	-	-	50

+ sites with txs below 10kW.

Licensee Local Mux: Elisa **W:** elisa.fi **Mux✪:** SVT1, SVT2, SVT Barnkanalen/SVT24, SVT Kunskapskanalen, TV3, TV4, När-TV, KRS-TV **Txs:** ch31 (Vaasa 3.5kW + SFN), ch33 (SFN), ch35 (SFN).

Åland

ÅLANDS RADIO/TV AB (Pub) ✉ Ålandsvägen 24, 22101 Mariehamn ☎ +358 18 26060 **E:** info@radiotv.ax **W:** www.radiotv.ax **L.P:** Editor-in-Chief: Camilla Karlsson-Henderson **Ch:** Ålandskanalen.

DTT Tx Network (DVB-T exc. where stated)
Licensee: Ålands Radio/TV AB **M1:** SVT1, SVT2, SVT Barnkanalen/SVT24, SVT Kunskapskanalen, Ålandskanalen **M2:** Yle TV1, Yle TV2, Yle Teema & Fem, TV4, Ålandskanalen Extra **M3:** SVT1 HD, SVT2 HD, Yle 1 HD, Yle 2 HD, Yle Teema & Fem HD. **Txs: M1:** ch25 (Smedsböle 30kW) **M2:** ch35 (Smedsböle 30kW) **M3 (DVB-T2):** ch28 (Smedsböle 30kW).

FRANCE

System: DVB-T (MPEG4) [E]

National Stations
ARTE (Pub) ✉ 8 rue Marceau, 92785 Issy-les-Moulineaux CEDEX 9 ☎ +33 155007777 **W:** www.arte.tv **L.P:** Pres: Bruno Patino – **FRANCE 24 (Pub)** ✉ 80 rue Camille Desmoulins, 92130 Issy-les-Moulineaux ☎ +33 184228484 **W:** www.france24.com **L.P:** Chair/CEO (France Médias Monde): Marie-Christine Saragosse **NB:** Terrestrially available via Mux 15 in Paris. – **FRANCE TÉLÉVISIONS (Pub)** ✉ (HQ/France 2-4/Franceinfo) 7 esplanade Henri-de-France, 75907 Paris CEDEX 15 ☎ +33 156226000 **W:** www.francetelevisions.fr; www.france.tv; france3-regions.francetvinfo.fr (France 3 regional stns); www.la1ere.fr (La 1ère) **L.P:** CEO: Delphine Ernotte Cunci **Chs:** France 2-5, France 3 regional stns, Franceinfo, La 1ère (for French overseas territories) **France 5:** ✉10 rue Horace Vernet, 92123 Issy-les-Moulineaux CEDEX 9 ☎ +33 156229191. **La 1ère:** ✉35-37 rue Danton, 92240 Malakoff ☎ +33 155227100 **NB:** France 4 is scheduled to cease in 2021. – **LA CHAÎNE PARLEMENTAIRE - ASSEMBLÉE NATIONALE (LCP-AN) (Pub)** ✉ 106 rue de l'Université, 75007 Paris ☎ +33 140639050 **W:** www.lcp.fr **L.P:** Pres: Bertrand Delais – **PUBLIC SÉNAT (Pub)** ✉ 92 boulevard Raspail, 75006 Paris ☎ +33 142344400 **W:** www.publicsenat.fr/direct **L.P:** Chmn/CEO: Emmanuel Kessler – **GROUPE ALTICE MÉDIA (BFM TV/RMC DÉCOUVERTE/RMC STORY) (Comm)** ✉16 rue du General Alain de Boissieu, 75015 Paris ☎ +33 171191181 **W:** www.alticefrance.com; www.bfmtv.com; rmcdecouverte.bfmtv.com; www.rmcstory.fr **L.P:** DG: Alain Weill. – **GROUPE CANAL+ (C8/ CANAL+*/CNEWS/CSTAR/PLANÈTE+) (Comm)** ✉ 1 place du spectacle, 92863 Issy-les-Moulineaux CEDEX 9 ☎ +33 171353535 **L.P:** Chmn: Maxime Saada **W:** www.vivendi.com; www.canalplus.com (*=Chs (terr.): Canal+, Canal+ Cinéma, Canal+ Sport) – **GROUPE M6 (6TER/GULLI/M6/PARIS PREMIÈRE/W9) (Comm)** ✉ 89-91 avenue Charles de Gaulle, 92200 Neuilly-sur-Seine CEDEX ☎ +33 141926666 **W:** www.groupem6.fr; www.6play.fr; www.gulli.fr **L.P:** Chmn: Nicolas de Tavernost – **GROUPE NRJ (CHERIE 25/NRJ12) (Comm)** ✉ 46-50 avenue Théophile Gautier, 75016 Paris ☎ +33 140713929 **W:** www.nrjgroup.fr; www.nrj-play.fr **L.P:** CEO: Jean-Paul Baudecroux – **GROUPE TF1 (LCI/TF1/TF1 SÉRIES FILM/TFX/TMC) (Comm)** ✉ 1 quai du Point-du-Jour, 92656 Boulogne-Billancourt CEDEX ☎ +33 141411234 **W:** www.groupe-tf1.fr; www.tf1.fr; www.lci.fr **L.P:** Chmn/CEO: Gilles Pélisson – **L'ÉQUIPE (Comm)** ✉ 4 cours de l'Île Seguin, 92102 Boulogne-Billancourt CEDEX ☎ +33 140932020 **W:** www.lequipe.fr/lachainelequipe.

Local/Regional Stations (~ =time-shared on Paris ch28)
Txs: (a-u) or (1) = via txs of Mux 1 ("a-u" via txs of 10kW & above, see main tx table; "-" via txs below 10kW, txs not shown); (15) = via txs of Regional Mux 15 (see main tx table; only txs at main sites shown).
Alsace 20 (a): 333A avenue de Colmar, 67100 Strasbourg. **Azur TV** (q) **/ Province Azur** (s) **/ Var Azur** (t): 16 avenue Edouard Grinda, 06200 Nice. **BDM TV** (15^{2}~): 51 avenue de Flandre, 75019 Paris. **BFM Grand Lille TV** (-)/ **BFM Grand Littoral TV** (r): 9 rue Archimède, 59200 Villeneuve-d'Ascq. **BFM Lyon Métropole** (-): 227 cours Lafayette, 69006 Lyon CEDEX 7. **BFM Paris** (n): 2 rue du Général André de Boissieu, 75015 Paris. **BIP TV** (-): Rue des Noués Chaudes, 36100 Issoudun. **Canal 32** (15^{3}): 7 rue Raymond Aron, 10120 Saint-André-les-Verger. **D!CI TV** (-): ZA La Grande Île Nord, 05230 Chorges. **Demain IDF** (15^{2}): 90 rue du Ranelagh, 75016 Paris. **IDF1** (15^{2}~): 7 rue des Bretons, 93210 La Plaine Saint-Denis. **LDVTV (Léonard De Vinci Télévision)** (-): Lycée Léonard de Vinci, Le Mazel, 43120 Monistrol-sur-Loire. **Matélé** (o): Espace Créatis, 6 avenue Archimède, 02100 Saint-Quentin. **Mirabelle TV** (d): 2 rue Saint-Vincent, 57140 Woipp. **Tébéo** (f): 19 rue Jean Macé, 29200 Brest. **TébéSud** (j): 8 rue Auguste Nayel, 56100 Lorient. **Télé Bocal** (15^{2}~): 1/3 rue Frédéric Le Maître, 75020 Paris. **TéléGrenoble** (-): 109 rue Hilaire de Chardonnet, 38000 Grenoble. **Télé Paese** (-): 36 chemin de Palazzi, 20220 Sant-Reparata-di-Balagn. **Télénantes** (e): 10 rue Voltaire, 44000 Nantes. **TL7 (Télévision Loire 7)** (-): Rue Jules Verne, 42530 Saint-Genest-Lerpt. **TLC (Télévision Locale du Choletais)** (15^{1}): ZI la Bergerie, rue Ampère, 49280 La Séguinière. **TV Tours Val de Loire** (h): 232 avenue de Grammont, 37019 Tours CEDEX. **TV Vendée** (15^{1}): ZI le Séjour, 13 rue Thomas Edison, 85170 Dompierre-sur-Yon. **TVPI** (m): Route de Bayonne, 64210 Bidart. **TV7 Bordeaux** (i): 23 quai des Queyries, 33100 Bordeaux. **TV8 Mont-Blanc** (-): 170 impasse des Lys Gillon, 74330 Épagny. **TVR** (g): 19 rue de la Quintaine, 35000 Rennes. **Via Angers** (-): 3 rue de la Rame, 49100 Angers. **Via Grand Paris** (15^{2}): 4, rue de la Prairie, 95000 Cergy. **Via LMTV Sarthe** (c): 21 rue Pasteur, 72000 Le Mans. **Via Normandie** (b): 4 passage de la Luciline, 76000 Rouen. **Vià Occitanie Montpellier** (p) **/ Vià Occitanie Pays Catalan** (-) **/ Vià Occitanie Pays Gardois** (-) **/ Vià Occitanie Toulouse** (-): 14 allée du Piot, 30660 Gallargues-le-Montueux. **Vosges Télévision Images Plus** (k): 2 rue de la Chipotte, 88007 Épinal. **Wéo Nord Pas de Calais** (l) **/ Wéo Picardie** (u): 8 place du Général de Gaulle, 59023 Lille CEDEX.

DTT Tx Networks (HD except where noted)
Licensee Mux 1: Société de gestion du réseau R1 ✉ 7 esplanade Henri-de-France, 75015 Paris ☎ +33 156226000 **M:** France 2, France 3 incl. reg prgrs, France 4, Franceinfo, local/regional stns (SD) – **Licensee Mux 2:** Nouvelles télévisions numériques ✉ 1 place du Spectacle, 92130 Issy-les-Moulineaux ☎ +33 171354839 **M:** C8, BFM TV, CNEWS, CStar, Gulli – **Licensee Mux 3:** Compagnie du numérique hertzien ✉1 place du Spectacle, 92863 Issy-les-Moulineaux ☎ +33 171350151 **M✪:** Canal+, LCI (SD), Paris Première (SD), Canal+ Sport, Canal+ Cinéma, Planète+ – **Licensee Mux 4:**

Multi 4 ✉ 89 avenue Charles de Gaulle, 92200 Neuilly-sur-Seine ☎ +33 141926666 **M:** France 5, M6, Arte, W9, 6ter – **Licensee Mux 6:** SMR6 ✉ 1 quai du Point-du-Jour, 92100 Boulogne-Billancourt ☎ +33 141411234 **M:** TF1, TMC, TFX, NRJ12, LCP-AN/Public Sénat – **Licensee Mux 7:** MHD7 ✉1 quai du Point-du-Jour, 92100 Boulogne-Billancourt ☎ +33 141411234 **M:** TF1 Séries Film, L'Équipe, RMC Story, RMC Découverte, Chérie 25 – **Licensees Mux 15 (Local/Regional):** various local/regional licensees **M:** various local/regional stns (SD) (depending on region, cf. chapter "Local/Regional Stations" 15[123]).

Location	1	2	3	4	6	7	15	kW
Abbeville	35u	25	22	45	39	28	-	79
Ajaccio	21	37	34	44	31	24	-	65
Amiens	41u	31	34	47	44	37	-	40/30/4x40
Aurillac	37	45	43	42	48	39	-	40
Autun	48	42	32	35	37	39	-	40
Auxerre	29	47	26	31	44	23	-	40
Avignon	45	36	33	47	42	39	-	50/32/4x50
Bar-le-Duc	48	30	44	22	35	34	-	3x13/9.5/2x13
Bastia	21	37	34	44	31	24	-	32/2x36/32/36/32
Bayonne	42m	46	45	39	30	43	33°	6x25/1
Bergerac	33	41	22	31	28	35	-	40
Besançon (Lomont)	43	44	41	23	47	26	-	50
Besançon (Montf.)	43	44	41	23	47	26	-	25
Bordeaux	23i	37	45	39	30	26	-	63/36/4x63
Bourges	21	27	43	24	36	40	-	63
Brest	43f	35	30	39	34	46	-	191/145/107/141/145/100
Caen	25	42	22	29	28	45	-	100/50/100/94/2x100
Carcassonne	32	31	43	42	46	41	-	50/28/6x50
Chambéry	47	29	27	25	26	39	-	13
Charleville-Méz.	44	36	26	34	23	40	-	100/27/50/54/2x50
Chartres	47	21	43	40	44	31	-	25
Cherbourg-Octev.	31	42	30	39	37	45	-	13
Clermont-Ferrand	25	47	22	30	28	29	-	50
Corte	21	37	34	44	31	24	-	10/6/4x10
Dijon	29	21	27	33	37	39	-	32
Dunkerque	28r	31	27	45	21	25	-	13/6/4x13
Gex	45	21	27	28	24	39	-	63
Hirson	48o	32	27	25	35	39	-	80/2x22/3x80
Laval	33	34	43	37	41	35	-	9/14/3x10/8
Le Havre	43	44	41	32	46	47	-	20/16/6/2x20/13
Le Mans	26c	27	22	46	36	35	-	3x79/66/79/32
Lille	24l	23	27	26	21	29	-	79/20/79/14/2x79
Limoges	46	47	32	34	29	44	-	100/69/4x100
Longwy	25d	31	47	22	33	39	-	20/10/5/3x10
Lyon	43	44	41	40	46	23	-	126
Marseille	23s	38	30	35	26	29	-	2x100/32/3x100
Metz	36d	31	47	22	29	34	-	100/87/79/2x85/65
Montpellier	40p	31	43	48	46	41	-	100/32/4x100
Mulhouse	24a	21	41	37	27	45	-	100
Nancy	28	26	43	22	33	34	-	50/31/4x50
Nantes	47e	23	30	45	29	32	38[1]	98/2x65/83/2x65/30
Niort	25	27	22	40	36	43	-	71
Paris	35n	25	22	30	32	42	28[2]	50/51/50/51/2x50/5
Parthenay	48	31	33	21	39	43	-	13
Reims	29	36	43	46	45	40	-	79
Rennes	21g	40	27	36	24	46	-	79
Rouen	26b	36	34	33	23	37	-	40/26/10/3x40
Saint-Raphaël	39q	22	28	25	48	45	-	63
Sarrebourg	23d	26	47	22	25	34	-	50/47/4x50
Sens	37	47	26	31	44	23	38*	5x10/0.65
Strasbourg	48a	26	47	22	25	43	-	50/2x20/10/2x20
Toulon	43t	22	28	25	48	29	-	10
Toulouse	21	38	24	27	36	34	-	50
Tours	42h	23	45	24	29	37	-	50/42/4x50
Troyes	41	21	28	24	25	23	27[3]	6x100/2
Ussel	23	27	24	21	36	40	-	10
Vannes	22j	25	42	48	33	28	-	20/23/2x20/22/20
Verdun	25d	31	47	22	33	39	-	100/4x65/100
Vittel	42k	39	29	37	27	45	-	2x10/7/3x10

+ sites with txs below 10kW; 1-7=National Muxes 1-4/6/7; °=rel. Euskal Telebista (ETB) Spain (ETB1-3, ETB SAT) *) France 3 Île de France – **DVB-T2 (HEVC) technical UHD trial:** ch24 (Paris/Tour Eiffel 1kW), ch35 (Nantes) (Licensee: TDF). **M:** UHD1, UHD2, UHD3.

FRENCH GUIANA

System: DVB-T (MPEG4) [E]

GUYANE LA 1ÈRE (Pub) ✉ Boulevard du docteur Lama, F-97354 Rémire-Montjoly ☎ +594 594256700 **W:** la1ere.francetvinfo.fr/guyane **L.P:** Dir: Gérard Guillaume – **KVT (Comm)** ✉ 100, avenue Auguste Boudinot, F-97310 Kourou ☎ +594 594321541 **E:** ktv.tnt@gmail.com **W:** www.facebook.com/KTV-Guyane-937513049694276 **L.P:** Pres: Emmanuel Toko.

DTT Tx Networks
Tx Operator: TDF **Mux:** Guyane la 1ère HD, France 2-5*, Franceinfo, Arte, KVT **Txs:** MFN. *) France 4 will cease in 2021

FRENCH POLYNESIA

System: DVB-T (MPEG4) [E]

POLYNÉSIE LA 1ÈRE (Pub) ✉ BP 60125, F-98702 Faa'a ☎ +33 689861616 **W:** la1ere.francetvinfo.fr/polynesie **L.P:** Dir: Gérard Hoarau – **TAHITI NUI TV (TNTV) (Comm)** ✉ BP 348, F-98713 Papeete ☎ +33 689473636 **E:** tntv@tntv.pf **W:** www.tntv.pf **L.P:** DG: Mateata Maamaatuaiahutapu.

DTT Tx Networks
Tx Operator: TDF **Mux:** Polynésie la 1ère, France 2-5*, Franceinfo, Arte, TNTV **Txs:** MFN. *) France 24 will cease in 2021

FRENCH SO. & ANTARTIC LANDS

NB: No terrestrial TV station.

GABON

System: DVB-T2 (MPEG4)

GABON TÉLÉVISION (Pub) ✉ BP 10150, Libreville ☎ +241 01732152 **E:** ggabontelevisions@gmail.com **W:** www.facebook.com/Nfiubane **Chs:** RTG1, RTG2 – **LABEL TV (Comm)** ✉Complexe Audiovisuel Nelson Mandela, Route du stade, Rond point Heliconia, (BP 8991), Libreville ☎ +241 01453833 **E:** info@alabeltv.com **W:** www.facebook.com/alabeltv.

DTT Tx Networks
Tx Operator: StarTimes **Mux(partly ✪):** multiprgr **Txs:** MFN

GALAPAGOS ISLANDS (Ecuador)

System: NTSC-M [A]

CANAL MUNICIPAL (Pub) ✉ San Cristóbal **W:** www.facebook.com/canalmunicipal98 **Tx:** ch7. – **TELE INSULAR (Comm)** ✉ San Cristóbal **Tx:** ch9. – **TELE GALÁPAGOS (Rlg)** ✉ Misión Franciscana, Puerto Baquerizo Moreno, Isla San Cristóbal, Galapagos, Ecuador ☎ +593 5 2520144 **Tx:** ch13.

GAMBIA

System: DVB-T2 (MPEG4) [E]

GAMBIA RADIO & TELEVISION SERVICES (GRTS) (Gov) ✉ P.O.Box 2380, Serekunda ☎ +220 4374251 **E:** grts@gamtel.gm **W:** www.facebook.com/grts.gm **L.P:** DG: Abdou MK Touray

DTT Tx Network
Tx Operator: StarTimes **Mux(partly ✪):** multiprgr **Txs:** MFN

GEORGIA

Systems: DVB-T2 (MPEG4) [E]

National Stations
GEORGIAN PUBLIC BROADCASTER (Pub) ✉ M. Kostava St. 68, 0171 Tbilisi ☎ +995 32 2362294 **E:** info@gpb.ge **W:** www.gpb.ge **L.P:** DG: vacant **Chs:** GPB TV1, GPB TV2. **Regional Station: Ajara Radio & TV,** Memed Abashidze Ave. 41, 6000 Batumi – **IMEDI TV (Comm)** ✉ Lubliana St. 5, 0159 Tbilisi ☎+995 32 2463041 **E:** contact@imedi.ge **W:** www.imedi.ge **Chs:** Imedi TV, GDS TV – **KOMEDIA TV (Comm)** ✉ Tbilisi – **RUSTAVI 2 (Comm)** ✉ Sandro Euli St., Sa, 0186 Tbilisi ☎ +995 32 2201111 **E:** tv@rustavi2.com **W:** rustavi2.com.

Local Stations not shown.

DTT Tx Networks
Licensee Mux 1: Georgian Teleradio Center **W:** www.tvrcenter.ge **M1:** GPB TV1 HD, GPB TV2, GPB Ajara TV HD – **Licensee Mux 2-4** Stereo+ Ltd **M2:** Imedi TV HD, Rustavi 2, Marao Arkhi, Maestro TV, GDS, Pirveli TV, Obiektivi TV, Komedi Arkhi, Palitra News, Pormula TV

M3 (✪exc.*): Starvision TV*, Ertsulovneba*, Silk*, Pirveli Gasartobi TV*, Ragbi TV*, Stereo+*, Mtavari TV*, Digital TV Info Channel*, Pirveli Arkhi (1 TV Georgia), Basti Bubu, Mult, TV 3, Pyatnitsa!, Perec, Ren TV, STS, TNT, Ru TV, Telekanal Oruzhe, Cinema, Nauka 2.0, NST, Viasat Histor **M4✪:** Pervyy Kanal, RTR Planeta, Ohota i Rybalka, VIP HD, VIP Hit, VIP Family, Viasat Sport, TV 1000, TV 1000 Action, FOX, Food Network, Setanta Sports HD, Setanta Sports+ HD, Eurosport 1, VH1, Baby TV, Nickelodeon, Discovery Channel, National Geographic, Nat Geo Wild, FightBox HD, Eroxxx, Erox HD, Euronews, BBC World News, Bollywood TV, Amedia Premium HD **Txs: M1:** ch36 (Tbilisi) & MFN. **M2-4:** ch(-) (Tbilisi) & nationwide MFN. **Local licensees/muxes** not shown.

ABKHAZIA

APSUA XÖYNTKARRATÄ TELERADIOKOMPANIA ✉ V.Ardzinba St. 16, Sokhumi (mail via Russia) ☎ +7 840 2266144 **E:** info@apsua.tv **W:** www.apsua.tv **L.P:** DG: Ronald Bganba

DTT Tx Network
Licensee: Ekran ABK **M1:** Apsua TV, Abaza TV, Pervyy Kanal, Rossiya 1, NTV, TV Tsentr, 5 Kanal, TV Zvezda, Rossiya K, Rossiya 24, Kuban 24V: **M2✪:** STS, TNT, Match!, Karusel, Che, Kinopokaz, Ohotnik i Rybolov, Teleputeshestviya, Match!Boets, Discovery Channel, Kanal Disney, HD Life **M3✪:** Sport 1, Ren TV, TV 3, Domashniy, RU TV, National Geographic, Nat Geo Wild.

SOUTH OSSETIA

PTRK "IR" ✉ Geroev St. 48, Tskhinvali (mail via Russia) ☎ +7 9974 451218 **E:** radio-ir@yandex.ru **L.P:** Dir: Robert Kulumbegov

DTT Tx Network
Licensee: RTRS **M1:** Rossiya 1, Rossiya 24, Rossiya K, Karusel, Match TV, Pervyy kanal, NTV, OTR, 5-kanal, TV Tsentr **M2:** Domashniy, TV Zvezda, Mir TV, Muz-TV, Pyatnitsa, REN TV, Spas, STS, TNT, TV-3 **M3:** PTRK "Ir" **Txs**:(-).

GERMANY

System: DVB-T2 (HEVC) [E]; DVB-T (MPEG2)

National Stations
ARBEITSGEMEINSCHAFT DER ÖFFENTLICH-RECHTLICHEN RUNDFUNKANSTALTEN DEUTSCHLANDS (ARD) (Pub) ✉ Arnulfstrasse 42, 80335 München ☎ +49 89 590001 **L.P:** Chair: Tom Buhrow **W:** www.ard.de; www.daserste.de **Chs (terr.):** Das Erste, regional stns, tagesschau24, One, Phoenix, KIKA (KIKA is produced jointly with ZDF). **NB.** ARD is the head organisation for the regional public service broadcasters: **Bayerischer Rundfunk (BR)**: Rundfunkplatz 1, 80335 München ☎ +49 89 59002433 **W:** www.br.de **Hessischer Rundfunk (HR)**: Bertramstrasse 8, 60320 Frankfurt ☎ + 49 69 1551 **W:** www.hr-online.de **Mitteldeutscher Rundfunk (MDR)**, Kantstrasse 71-73, 04275 Leipzig ☎ +49 341 22760 **W:** www.mdr.de **Norddeutscher Rundfunk (NDR)**, Rothenbaumchaussee 132, 20149 Hamburg ☎ +49 40 4131 **W:** www.ndr.de **Rundfunk Berlin-Brandenburg (RBB)** Masurenallee 8-14, 14057 Berlin ☎ +49 30 9799330141 **W:** www.rbb-online.de **Radio Bremen Fernsehen (RB)**, Diepenau 10, 28195 Bremen ☎ +49 421 2460 **W:** www.radiobremen.de **Saarländischer Rundfunk (SR)**, Funkhaus Halberg, 66100 Saarbrücken ☎ +49 681 6020 **W:** www.sr.de **Südwestrundfunk (SWR)**, Neckarstrasse 230, 70190 Stuttgart ☎ +49 711 92910001 **W:** www.swr.de **Westdeutscher Rundfunk (WDR)**, Appellhoffplatz 1, 50667 Köln ☎ +49 221 2202100 **W:** www.wdr.de – **ZWEITES DEUTSCHES FERNSEHEN (ZDF) (Pub)** ✉ Postfach 4040, 55030 Mainz ☎ +49 6131 701 **E:** info@zdf.de **W:** www.zdf.de **L.P:** DG: Thomas Bellut **Chs (terr.):** ZDF, ZDF_neo, ZDFinfo, 3sat (3sat is produced jointly with ARD) – **MEDIENGRUPPE RTL DEUTSCHLAND GMBH (Comm)** ✉ Picassoplatz 1, 50679 Köln ☎ +49 221 45600 **E:** info@mediengruppe-rtl.de **W:** www.mediengruppe-rtl.de **L.P:** CEO: Bernd Reichart **Chs (terr.):** RTL, RTL II, SuperRTL, RTL NITRO, Vox, n-tv – **PROSIEBENSAT.1 MEDIA SE (Comm)** ✉ Medienallee 7, 85774 Unterföhring ☎ +49 89 950710 **W:** www.prosiebensat1.com **L.P:** CEO: Rainer Beaujean **Chs (terr.):** ProSieben, ProSieben Maxx, Sat1, Sat1 Gold, Kabel eins, Sixx – **TELE 5** ✉ Bavariafilmplatz 7, 82031 Grünwald ☎ +49 89 6495680 **E:** info@tele5.de **W:** www.tele5.de **L.P:** CEO: Alberto Horta – **WELT (Comm)** ✉ Axel-Springer-Straße 65, 10888 Berlin ☎ +49 30 20902400 **E:** info@n24.de **W:** www.welt.de **L.P:** Editor-in-Chief: Ulf Poschard.

Local Stations not shown.

DTT Tx Networks (DVB-T2)
Licensee M1+2: ARD **M1:** Das Erste HD, arte HD, Phoenix HD, One HD, Tagesschau24 HD **M2:** Regional public service stns (HD) – **Licensee M3:** ZDF **M:** ZDF HD, 3Sat HD, ZDFinfo HD, ZDF_neo HD, KIKA HD – **Licensee M4-6:** Freenet **W:** www.freenet-group.de **M4✪:** RTL HD, RTL II HD, Vox HD, SuperRTL HD, NITRO HD, n-tv HD, Tele 5 HD **M5✪:** Sat1 HD, ProSieben HD, Kabel eins HD, Sixx HD, ProSieben Maxx HD, Sat 1 Gold HD, Sport 1 HD **M6 ✪:** Disney Channel HD, Welt HD, DMAX HD, Comedy Central HD, Eurosport 1 HD, Nick HD, 1.2.3.TV HD, QVC HD, QVC2 HD, HSE24 HD, Bibel TV HD.
NB: The content of the muxes is licensed individually by each federal state and may vary in certain cases.

RE	Location	M1	M2	M3	M4	M5	M6	kW
NW	Aachen (SFN)	26V	35V	29V	40V	43V	36V	(-)
BW	Aalen	32	28	23	-	-	-	50
BY	Amberg	23	47	37	-	-	-	50
BY	Augsburg	41	22	44	33	39	25	50
NI	Aurich	29	43	35	-	-	-	79
BW	Baden-Baden	36	39	33	35	44	29	50
BY	Bamberg	40	30	37	-	-	-	50
BE	Berlin (SFN)[1]	25	40	33	27	31	42	(-)
NW	Bonn	26V	35V	29V	40V	43V	36V	20
NI	Braunschweig (SFN)[1]	23V	40V	36V	44V	21V	47V	(-)
SH	Bredstedt	26	24	31	-	-	-	25
	Bregenz*	45	46	-	-	-	-	10
HB	Bremen	29	46	35	42	48	22	20/10/32/3x50
HB	Bremen	-	30	-	-	-	-	20
ST	Brocken	45V	34V	37V	-	-	-	50
BY	Brotjacklriegel	28V	40V	-	-	-	-	100
SH	Bungsberg	47V	39V	21V	-	-	-	2x100/50
BY	Büttelberg	42	29	-	-	-	-	50
BB	Cottbus	23	44	36	-	-	-	100
NS	Dannenberg	32	43	-	-	-	-	10
HE	Darmstadt	42V	34V	22V	31V	25V	47V	10
BY	Dillberg	42V	29V	34V	-	-	-	50
BW	Donaueschingen	43	47	37	-	-	-	50
RP	Donnersberg	30	46	-	-	-	-	50
NW	Dortmund	25V	35V	29V	40V	43V	48V	50
SN	Dresden	34V	39V	36V	46V	29V	42V	3x100/3x50
NW	Düsseldorf	46V	35V	29V	40V	43V	48V	50
NW	Essen	25V	35V	29V	40V	43V	48V	20/5x50
SL	Felsberg	32V	-	-	-	-	-	20
SH	Flensburg	47V	39V	21V	-	-	-	79
HE	Frankfurt/M.	42V	34V	22V	31V	25V	47V	50
BB	Frankfurt/O.	25V	40V	33V	-	-	-	50
BW	Freiburg	36	39	33	28	42	29	50
MV	Garz	36	29	46		-	-	2x40/20
BY	Gelbelsee	41	22	44	-	-	-	50
SL	Göttelborner Höhe	32V	42V	55V	-	-	-	50
NI	Göttingen (SFN)[1]	23	40	35	-	-	-	(-)
HE	Großer Feldberg	42V	34V	22V	31V	25V	47V	50
BY	Grünten	45	46	40	-	-	-	100
HE	Habichtswald	46	29	35	28	25	48	20
NW	Hagen	25V	35V	29V	40V	43V	48V	10
ST	Halle	38V	24V	49V	43V	28V	26V	50
HH	Hamburg (SFN)	23	40	33	27	28	45	(-)
HH	Hamburg (SFN)	-	41	-	-	-	-	(-)
NI	Hannover	23	41	36	44	21	47	40/5x50
SH	Heide	26	24	31	-	-	-	32
BW	Heidelberg	27	21	41	35	44	24	50
BY	Heidelstein	-	-	26	-	-	-	50
MV	Helpterberg	36	22	23	-	-	-	20
NI	Hildesheim	23V	40V	36V	-	-	-	40/50/40
BY	Hohe Linie	27V	21V	36V	-	-	-	100
HE	Hohe Wurzel	42V	34V	22V	31V	25V	47V	100
BY	Hohenpeissenberg	45	46	40	-	-	-	50
BY	Hoher Bogen	28V	21V	-	-	-	-	100
HE	Hoher Meißner	46	29	35	-	-	-	50
TH	Inselsberg	27V	39V	41V	-	-	-	50
TH	Jena	39V	56V	41V	44V	33V	47V	2x10/5/3x10
RP	Kaiserslautern	30	46	37	35	44	40	20
BW	Karlsruhe	27V	21V	41V	35V	44V	24V	10
HE	Kassel	46V	29V	35V	28V	25V	48V	10
SH	Kiel	47	39	21	27	28	45	3x50/3x20
RP	Koblenz	23	33	28	31	25	47	3x50/3x20
NW	Köln	26V	35V	29V	40V	43V	36V	20
BY	Kreuzberg	36	43	-	-	-	-	100
BY	Landshut	28	40	46	-	-	-	20

RE	Location	M1	M2	M3	M4	M5	M6	kW
NW	Langenberg	25V	35V	29V	40V	43V	48V	50
BW	Langenbrand	27	21	33	35	44	29	50
SN	Leipzig	35V	24V	49V	43V	28V	26V	3x100/3x50
SN	Löbau	34V	39V	36V	-	-	-	50
SH	Lübeck (SFN)[1]	23	41	33	27	28	45	(-)
ST	Magdeburg	45V	34V	37V	46V	29V	48V	2x100/4x50
BY	München	31V	30V	34V	35V	26V	48V	100
BY	Nürnberg	42V	47V	34V	35V	24V	25V	50
BY	Ochsenkopf	40	30	37	-	-	-	100
BY	Pfaffenberg	36	43	26	-	-	-	50
BY	Pfarrkirchen	28	40	46	-	-	-	50
BY	Pfaffenhofen	41	22	44	-	-	-	2x5/50
HE	Rimberg	42	29	22	-	-	-	50
BW	Ravensburg	43	47	37	-	-	-	50
MV	Rostock	36V	29V	46V	44V	24V	26V	40
SL	Saarbrücken	32V	46V	37V	35V	44V	45V	10
RP	Scharteberg	30	46	37	-	-	-	50
NI	Schiffdorf	29	30	35	42	48	22	2x10/5/3x20
NI	Schiffdorf	-	46	-	-	-	-	2
SH	Schleswig	47V	39V	21V	-	-	-	10
MV	Schwerin	36	29	46	44	24	26	32
SL	Spiesen	32V	-	-	-	-	-	25
NI	Steinkimmen	29	30	35	-	-	-	2x79/5
NI	Steinkimmen	-	46	-	-	-	-	4
BW	Stuttgart	32	28	23	42	25	45	50
NI	Torfhaus	23V	40V	-	-	-	-	32
RP	Trier	30	46	37	35	44	40	10
NS	Visselhövede	32	43	25				50
BW	Ulm	43	47	37	-	-	-	50
BW	Waldenburg	32	28	23	-	-	-	50
SH	Wedel	23	41	-	-	-	-	10
BY	Wendelstein	31V	30V	34V	35V	26V	48V	100
NW	Wesel	46V	35V	29V	40V	43V	48V	50
ST	Wittenberg	38V	24V	37V	-	-	-	50
NI	Wolfsburg	22V	42V	36V	-	-	-	25
NW	Wuppertal	46	35	29	40	43	48	20
HE	Würzberg	48	34	41	-	-	-	50
BY	Würzburg	36	43	26	-	-	-	50

+ sites with txs below 10kW. *) Located in Austria [1]) SFN txs have H or V polarisation

Regional & Local Licensees (DVB-T) not shown.

RE) Region codes (federal states): BB=Brandenburg, BE=Berlin, BW=Baden-Württemberg, BY=Bayern, HB=Bremen, HE=Hessen, HH=Hamburg, MV=Mecklenburg-Vorpommern, NI=Niedersachsen, NW=Nordrhein-Westfalen, RP=Rheinland-Pfalz, SH=Schleswig-Holstein, SL=Saarland, ST=Sachsen-Anhalt, SN=Sachsen, TH=Thüringen.

GHANA

System: DVB-T2 (MPEG4) [E]

GHANA BROADCASTING CORP. (GBC) (Gov) ✉ P.O. Box 1633, Accra ☎ +233 30 2221161 **E:** info@gbcghana.comh **W:** www.gbc-ghana.com **L.P:** CEO: Kwame Akuffo Anoff-Ntow **Chs:** GTV, GBC 24, GBC Life, GTV Sports+ – **E.TV GHANA (Comm)** ✉ P.O.Box CT 5976, Accra ☎ +233 30 2912071 **E:** info@etvghana.com **W:** etvghana.com – **METRO TV (Semi-Gov, Comm)** 59 Josiah Tongogara Street, Labone, Accra 🖷 +233 30 2765701 **E:** info.metrotvgh@gmail.com **W:** www.metrotvonline.com **L.P:** CEO: Talal Fattal – **TV3 (Comm)** ✉ Box M83, Accra ☎ +233 30 2763458 **E:** info@tv3network.com **W:** 3news.com **L.P:** CEO: Santokh Singh.

DTT Tx Networks
Tx Operator: StarTimes **M1:** GTV, GBC 24, GBC Life, GTV Sports+,TV3, Kwese Free Sports, NET2, BBC World News, God TV, FOX Entertainment✪, Showtime✪, Hi Nolly✪, Homebase✪, Setanta Africa✪, Kiss✪, KidsCo✪ **M2✪:** Skyy One, Music World, Channel D, Sports24, Cinimax, Heaven, Planet Kidz, Fiesta, Skyy World, e.TV Ghana ⌘ Skyy Power FM, Citi FM **Txs:** MFN.

GIBRALTAR (UK)

Systems: DVB-T (MPEG2), DVB-T2 (MPEG4) [E]

GBC TELEVISION (Pub) ✉ Broadcasting House, 18 So. Barrack Rd, Gibraltar ☎ +350 20048990 **E:** television@gbc.gi **W:** www.gbc.gi **L.P:** CEO (Gibraltar Broadcasting Corp): Gerard Teuma.

DTT Tx Networks
Tx Operator: Arqiva **M1:** GBC TV ⌘ R. Gibraltar 1 **M2:** GBC TV HD, Al Jazeera **Txs: M1 (DVB-T):** ch56 (Upper Rock) **M2 (DVB-T2):** ch30 (Upper Rock).

GREECE

System: DVB-T (MPEG4) [E]

National Stations
ELLINIKI RADIOFONIA TILEORASI A.E. (ERT) (Pub) ✉ TV studios: Leoforos Mesogeion 136, 11527 Athina ☎+30 2106066000 **E:** info@ert.gr **W:** www.ert.gr **L.P:** MD: Christos Leontis **Chs:** ERT1, ERT2, ERT3, ERT Sports HD – **VOULI TILEORASI (Pub)** ✉ Leoforos Vasilisis Sofias 11, 10671 Athina ☎ +30 2103735320 **E:** kanali@parliament.gr **W:** www.hellenicparliament.gr/Enimerosi/Vouli-Tileorasi – **ALPHA TV (Comm)** ✉ Ambelakion, Biomichaniko Parko, 15351 Pallini ☎ +30 2122124000 **E:** pr@alphatv.gr **W:** www.alphatv.gr **L.P:** Pres/CEO: Dimitris Kontominas – **ANTENNA TV (ANT1) (Comm)** ✉ Leoforos Kifisias 10-12, 15125 Marousi ☎ +30 2106886100 **E:** pr@antenna.gr **W:** www.antenna.gr **L.P:** CEO: Tasos Michalakis – **MAKEDONIA TV (m.) (Comm)** ✉ 26is Oktovriou 90, 54627 Thessaloniki ☎ +30 2310504300 **E:** info@maktv.gr **W:** www.maktv.gr **L.P:** GM: Georgios Zois – **MEGA CHANNEL (Comm)** ✉ Syggrou 340, 17673 Kallithea ☎ +30 2107547000 **W:** www.megatv.com **L.P:** GM: Evangelos Marinakis – **OPEN TV (Comm)** ✉ 2o chlm Leoforos Paianias-Markopoulou, 19400 Koropi ☎ +30 2112122000 **E:** info@tvopen.gr **W:** www.tvopen.gr **L.P:** CEO: Dimitris Michalelis – **SKAI TV (Comm)** ✉ Ethnarchou Makariou & Falireos 2, 18547 Neo Faliro ☎ +30 2104800170 **E:** technicaltv@skai.gr **W:** www.skai.gr **L.P:** CEO (Skai Group): Giannis Alafouzos – **STAR CHANNEL (Comm)** ✉ Viltanioti 36, 14564 Kifisia ☎ +30 2111891000 **E:** info@star.gr **W:** www.star.gr **L.P:** GM: Karolos Alkalai.

Regional & Local Stations not shown.

DTT Tx Networks
Licencee M1+4: ERT **M1:** ERT1, ERT2, ERT3, ERT Sports HD, Vouli ⌘ ERA Radio 1-3, ERA Sport, Kosmos, I Foni tis Elladas **M4:** BBC World News, DW-TV, RIK Sat, TV5 Monde Europe – **Licensee M2+3,5+6, R1-R3:** Digea **W:** www.digea.gr **M2:** Alpha TV, ANT1, Open Beyond TV **M3:** m. (Makedonia TV), Skai TV, Star Channel **M5:** ANT1 HD, Star Channel HD, Skai TV HD, m.HD **M6:** Alpha TV HD, Mega Channel HD, Open TV HD **Muxes R1-3:** Regional muxes with various regional/local stns **Additional muxes (+):** [1]) (Transitional) Egnatia TV, Pella TV, Time TV; Digea: [2]) Ena Channel, Epsilon TV, Star Kentrikis Elladas

Location	M1	M2	M3	M4	M5	M6	R1	R2	R3	(+)	kW
Achendrias	24	25	37	-	-	-	55	-	-	-	3.2
Aigina	21	22	27	28	30	40	45	52	54	-	6.3
Ainos	21	22	33	36	-	-	59	60	52	-	10
Ainos	-	-	-	-	-	-	-	-	56	-	10
Akarnanika	23	27	28	32	-	-	46	51	-	-	25
Aroi	24	25	31	34	35	42	44	53	-	-	6.3
Avlonas	21	22	27	28	30	40	45	52	54	-	3.2
Axonas	39	24	26	32	-	-	41	-	-	-	1.6
Chlomo	39	33	35	-	-	-	53	-	-	-	6.3
Chortiatis	24	27	30	36	43	48	55	56	-	51[1]	25
Doliana	21	23	24	-	42	45	50	60	-	-	6.3
Dovroutsi	22	35	38	40	42	45	52	-	-	-	6.3
Kelli	44	26	32	-	-	-	47	52	-	-	3.2
Kleisoura	44	26	32	-	-	-	47	52	-	-	1.6
Lichada	46	33	35	-	-	-	53	-	-	-	3.2
Ligkiades	24	25	30	31	-	-	52	54	-	-	6.3
Malaxa	21	31	34	-	-	-	54	-	-	-	6.3
Metaxas	41	28	29	-	-	-	50	54	-	-	3.2
Monte Smith	21	24	26	32	-	-	43	-	-	-	1.6
Monte Smith	39	-	-	-	-	-	-	-	-	-	1.6
Osios Patapios	26	29	41	-	-	-	51	56	-	-	1.6
Pantokratoras	37	30	34	-	-	-	54	56	-	-	6.3
Parnitha	21	22	27	28	30	40	45	52	54	53[2]	16
Paros	42	33	39	-	-	-	53	-	-	-	6.3
Petalidi	29	31	32	37	43	44	48	51	-	-	6.3
Pilio	21	26	29	37	-	-	47	-	-	-	16
Plaka	24	27	30	31	33	36	43	48	-	-	6.3
Polygyros	25	31	34	38	46	49	50	54	-	-	1.6
Pythio	25	32	35	46	47	50	51	56	-	-	3.2
Rogdia	39	25	37	-	-	-	55	-	-	-	6.3
Soros	21	26	29	37	-	-	47	-	-	-	1.6
Soros	44	-	-	-	-	-	-	-	-	-	1.6
Styra	23	24	31	32	34	36	38	49	50	-	6.3

Location	M1	M2	M3	M4	M5	M6	R1	R2	R3	(+)	kW
Syros	46	29	37	-	-	-	48	-	-	-	3.2
Thasos	22	23	37	39	41	44	47	51	-	-	16
Xylokastro	26	29	41	43	47	48	51	56	-	-	3.2
Ymittos	21	22	27	28	30	40	45	52	54	-	32

+ sites with txs below 1kW.
NB: In preparation for the re-assignment of the 700MHz band to mobile services, txs on chs 49-60 are gradually being moved to lower chs.

GREENLAND (Denmark)

System: DVB-T (MPEG2, MPEG4) [E]

National Station
KNR-TV (Pub) ✉ P.O.Box 1007, 3900 Nuuk ☎ +299 361500 **E:** knr@knr.gl **W:** knr.gl **L.P:** Dir (KNR): Karl Henrik Simonsen **Chs:** KNR1, KNR2.

DTT Tx Networks
Tx Operator: TELE-POST **M (MPEG4):** KNR1, KNR2, DR1 +4, DR2 +4, DR Ultra +4 **Txs:** MFN – **Local Licencees:** not shown.

GRENADA

System: NTSC-M [A]

GBN-TV (Gov) ✉ P.O.Box 535, St. George's ☎ +1 473 4445521 **E:** grenadabroadcastingnetwork@gmail.com **W:** gbn.gd **Txs:** North/East ch7 (4kW), St. George's ch11 (5kW) – **MEANINGFUL TELEVISION (MTV) (Comm)** ✉Lagoon Road, St. George ☎ +1 473 4408442 **E:** mtvgrenada@gmail.com **W:** www.facebook.com/MTVNEWSGRENADA **Txs:** Saint George's ch9 & netw. – **GFN-TV (Rlg)** ✉ P.O.Box 2747, St. Paul's, St. George ☎ +1 473 4354297 **W:** www.globalfamilynetwork.net **L.P:** Project Dir: John Bartels **Tx:** St. George's ch4.

GUADELOUPE (France)

System: DVB-T (MPEG4) [E]

GUADELOUPE LA 1ÈRE (Pub) ✉ BP 180, F-97122 Baie-Mahault ☎ +590 590939696 **E:** secretariaguadir@francetv.fr **W:** la1ere.francetvinfo.fr/guadeloupe **L.P:** Dir: Sylvie Gengoul – **ALIZÉS TV (Comm)** ✉ Tour Sécid, Place de la Rénovation, F-97110 Pointe-à-Pitre ☎ +590 590572600 **E:** contact@alizes.com **W:** www.facebook.com/alizes.guadeloupe – **CANAL 10 (Comm)** ✉ 21, Bd Marquisart De Houelbourg, F-97122 Baie-Mahault ☎ +590 590267303 **E:** contact@canal10-tv.com **W:** www.canal10-tv.com **L.P:** Pres: Lisa Rodriguez – **ÉCLAIR TV (ETV) (Comm)** ✉ 12, rue Alfred Lumière, Bureau n° 6, F-97122 Baie-Mahaut. ☎ +590 590328080 **W:** www.etv.gp **L.P:** Pres: Mario Constant Moradel.

DTT Tx Networks
Tx Operator: TDF **M:** Guadeloupe la 1ère HD, France 2-5*, Franceinfo, Arte, Canal 10 **Txs:** MFN – **Local Mux:** Alizes TV HD, ETV HD **Txs:** MFN. *) France 4 will cease in 2021

GUAM (USA)

System: ATSC [A]

Local Stations

ch	kW	Territory	City of License	Callsign
8	3.5	GU	Hagatna	KUAM-TV
12	54.7	GU	Agana	KGTF
14	12.5	GU	Tamuning	KTGM
22	1.95	GU	Dededo	KEQI-LP
26	1.4	GU	Tamuning	KTKB-LD

GUATEMALA

Systems: ISDB-TB [A]; # NTSC-M [A] ⇩2022

National Stations ([a]=analogue)
GUATEVISIÓN (Pub) ✉ Calzada Roosevelt 22-43, Zona 11, Edificio Tikal Futura, Torre Sol 4o, Nivel, Guatemala ☎ +502 23286000 **E:** info@guatevision.com **W:** www.guatevision.com **Txs:** [a]ch25 – **RADIO Y TELEVISIÓN DE GUATEMALA (Comm)** ✉ 30, Av. 3-40, Zona 11, 01011 Guatemala ☎ +502 25945320 **Chs:** Canal 3, Canal 7, Teleonce, Trecevisión **W:** www.chapintv.com **Txs: Canal 3:** [a]ch3 (240kW); **Canal 7:** [a]ch7 (180kW), **Teleonce:** ch11 (316kW); **Trecevisión:** [a]ch13 (25kW) – **AZTECA GUATEMALA (Comm)** ✉ 12 Avenida 1-96, Zona 2 de Mixco, Colonia Alvarado, Guatemala ☎ +502 24111140 🖷 +502 24111200 **E:** festrada@tvaguatemala.tv **W:** www.azteca.com.gt **Tx:** [a]ch31 – **MAZATELEVISIÓN (Comm)** ✉ Suchitepequez.**Tx:** [a]ch58 – **TV USAC (Educ)** ✉ Paraninfo universitario 2a. Av. 12-40, Zona 1. Guatemala ☎ +502 22536791 **W:** www.tvusac.com **Tx:** [a]ch33 – **CANAL 27 (Rlg)** ✉ Carretera Vieja a Antigua 2 Calle 23-70, Zona 1 de Mixco, Guatemala ☎ +502 24213434 **E:** canal27@motivacioncristiana.org **W:** www.canal27.org **Tx:** [a]ch27 – **CANAL 63 (Rlg)** ✉ Guatemala **W:** www.canalcatolico.tv **Tx:** [a]ch63 – **CANAL 65 (Rlg)** ✉ Guatemala **Tx:** [a]ch65. Rel. ETWN (USA) – **ENLACE CANAL 21 (Rlg)** ✉ Guatemala **E:** guatemala@enlace.org **Tx:** [a]ch21. Rel. TBN (USA).

Local Stations not shown.

GUINEA

System: DVB-T2 (MPEG4) [E]

RADIO TÉLÉVISION GUINÉENNE (RTG) (Pub) ✉ BP 391, Conakry. ☎ +224 30452786 **W:** rtgkoloma.info **L.P:** DG: Sékouba Savané **Chs:** RTG1, RTG2

DTT Tx Network
Tx Operator: StarTimes **M(partly✪):** multiprgr **Txs:** MFN.

GUINEA-BISSAU

System: DVB-T2 (MPEG4) [E]

TELEVISÃO DA GUINÉ-BISSAU (TGB) (Gov) ✉ CP 178, Bissau **W:** www.facebook.com/TGB-Televisão-da-Guiné-Bissau-105117960878805 **L.P:** DG: Catouplin Mendes da Costa.

DTT Tx Network
Tx Operator: StarTimes **M(partly✪):** multiprgr **Txs:** MFN.

GUYANA

Systems: # NTSC-M [A]; ATSC [A] planned

National Station
NATIONAL COMMUNICATIONS NETWORK (NCN) (Gov) ✉ Homestretch Ave, Durban Backland, Georgetown ☎ +592 2235162 **E:** ceo@ncnguyana.com **W:** ncnguyana.com **Tx:** ch11.

Local Stations not shown.

HAITI

System: DVB-T2 (MPEG4)

National Station
RADIO TÉLÉVISION NATIONALE D'HAÏTI (RTNH) (Pub) ✉ BP 13400, Delmas 33, Port-au-Prince ☎ +509 2460200 **W:** www.rtnh.ht **L.P:** DG: Gamal Augustin.

Local Stations not shown.

DTT Tx Networks
Tx Operator: RTNH **M:** RTNH **Txs:** ch8 (Port-au-Prince) & nationwide MFN – **Tx Operator:** NUtv **W:** www.nu-tv.com **M1-6✪:** multiprgr **Txs:** MFN.

HAWAII (USA)

System: ATSC [A]

LOCAL STATIONS IN MAJOR TV MARKETS

Honolulu, HI Area

ch	kW	State	City of License	Callsign
8	7.2	HI	Honolulu	KHON-TV
11	15.7	HI	Honolulu	KHET
15	12	HI	Waimanalo	KUPU
18	74	HI	Honolulu	KALO
19	60.7	HI	Honolulu	KIKU
20	41.1	HI	Honolulu	KITV
22	40	HI	Honolulu	KHII

ch	kW	Sta	City of License	Callsign
23	23	HI	Honolulu	KGMB
26	4.58	HI	Honolulu	KWBN
27	262	HI	Honolulu	KAAH-TV
29	2.6	HI	Kailua	KKAI
31	20.1	HI	Honolulu	KWHE
32	17	HI	Kaneohe	KPXO-TV
33	40.6	HI	Honolulu	KBFD-DT
35	25	HI	Honolulu	KHNL

HONDURAS

System: ISDB-TB [A]

National Stations
TELEVISIÓN NACIONAL DE HONDURAS (TNH) (Gov) ✉ Edificio Ejecutivo #2 - 4 nivel Frente Casa Presidencial Tegucigalpa, M.D.C., Tegucigalpa **E:** info@tnh.gob.hn **W:** tnh.gob.hn **L.P:** Chmn: Víctor G. Hémela **Txs:** Tegucigalpa ch20 & relays. – **CANAL 6 (Comm)** ✉ 5ta Cll, 26 y 27 Ave., Bo. Río de Piedras, San Pedro Sula ☎ +504 25505009 **W:** canal6.com.hn **Tx:** Tegucigalpa ch19 & relays. – **CANAL 11 (Comm)** ✉ 5ta Cll, 26 y 27 Ave., Bo. Río de Piedras, San Pedro Sula **W:** canal11.hn **Tx:** Tegucigalpa ch11 & relays. – **HONDURED (Comm)** ✉ Casilla 3424, Tegucigalpa. **W:** www.hondured.tv **Txs:** Tegucigalpa ch13 & relays. – **TELEPROGRESO (Comm)** ✉ 9 Ave 12 St. N, Edificio Turiplaza, El Progreso 23201 ☎ +504 26482222 **E:** micanal@teleprogreso.tv **W:** www.teleprogreso.tv **Txs:** Tegucigalpa ch48 & relays – **TELEVICENTRO (TVC) (Comm)** ✉ Boulevard Suyapa, Tegucigalpa ☎ +504 22327835 **W:** televicentro.hn **Chs:** Canal Cinco, Canal 3, Cadena 7/4 **Txs:** Tegucigalpa ch7 & relays.– **VTV (Comm)** ✉ 9 Cll. 10 Ave, N.O. Bo. Guamalito, San Pedro Sula **W:** www.vtv.com.hn **Txs:** Tegucigalpa ch9 & relays.

Local Stations not shown.

HONG KONG (China, SAR)

System: DTMB [E]

RADIO TELEVISION HONG KONG (RTHK) (Pub) ✉ 30 Broadcast Drive, Kowloon, Hong Kong ☎ +852 23396330 **E:** ccu@rthk.hk **W:** www.rthk.hk **L.P:** Dir of Broadcasting: Ka-wing Leung. **Chs:** RTHK TV31, RTHK TV32, RTHK TV33 – **HK TELEVISION ENTERTAINMENT CO. LTD (HKTE) (Comm)** ✉ 39/F, PCCW Tower, Taikoo Place, 979 King's Road, Quarry Bay, Hong Kong ☎ +852 22398899 **E:** enquiry@viu.tv **W:** viu.tv **Chs:** ViuTVsix, ViuTV – **TELEVISION BROADCASTS LTD. (TVB) (Comm)** ✉ TVB City, 77 Chun Choi Street, Tseung Kwan O Industrial Estate, Kowloon, Hong Kong ☎ +852 23359123 **E:** tvbpr@tvb.com.hk **W:** www.tvb.com **L.P:** Chmn: Kwok Keung Chan **Chs:** Jade, J2, TVB News, Pearl, TVB Finance & Information.

DTT Tx Networks
Tx Operator: n/a **M1:** RTHK TV31, RTHK TV32, RTHK TV33 **M2:** TVB **M:** J2, TVB News, Pearl, TVB Finance & Information **M3:** ViuTVsix, ViuTV, Jade.

Location	M1	M2	M3
SFN	62	35	(MFN)

HUNGARY

System: DVB-T (MPEG4) [E]; DVB-T2 (HEVC) [E]

National Stations
DUNA MÉDIASZOLGÁLTATÓ NONPROFIT ZRT. (DMN) (Pub) ✉ Naphegy tér 8, 1016 Budapest ☎ +36 1 7595050 **E: E:** international@dunamsz.hu **W:** www.dunamsz.hu **L.P:** DG: Menyhért Dobos. Studios: ✉ Szabadság tér 17, 1810 Budapest 5; Mészáros u. 48-54, 1016 Budapest (Duna). **Chs:** M1, M2, M4 Sport, M4 Sport+, M5, reg. prgrs: a) Budapesti stúdió, b) Debreceni stúdió, c) Miskolci stúdió, d) Pécsi stúdió, e) Soproni stúdió, f) Szegedi stúdió; Duna, Duna World – **RTL KLUB (Comm)** ✉ Nagytétényi út 29, 1222 Budapest ☎ +36 1 3828283 **E:** rtlklub@rtl.hu **W:** rtl.hu **L.P:** CEO: Gabriella Vidus – **TV2 (Comm)** ✉ Róna u. 174, 1145 Budapest ☎ +36 1 4676400 **E:** info@tv2.hu **W:** tv2.hu **L.P:** CEO: Pavel Stantchev.

Local Stations not shown.

DTT Tx Networks (DVB-T2 exc.*)
Tx Operator: Antenna Hungária **W:** ahrt.hu **M1*:** M1 HD (incl. reg prgrs), M4 Sport HD, Duna HD, Duna World/M4 Sport+ ⌘ Kossuth R., Petőfi R., Bartók R., Dankó R. **M3*:** M2 HD, M5 HD, TV2, RTL Klub, Izaura TV, Dikh TV, Pesti TV, Spektrum Home, MinDig TV Pluzs Info **M2✪:** AXN, Viasat 3, RTL+, Prime, Moziverzum, Comedy Central, Nickelodeon, Cartoon Network, National Geographic, Life TV, Hir TV, Mozi+, Spektrum, ATV, Sport 2 HD, Arena 4 HD, Sorozat+ **M4✪:** Film+, Spiler TV 2, Spiler 1, RTL2, Super TV2, TV2 Kids, Disney Channel, AMC, Paramount Channel, Discovery Channel, TV2 Comedy, Jocky TV, Cool, Ozone Network, TV4, Sport 1 HD, TV Paprika **M5✪:** Fit HD, TLC, RTL Gold, Fishing & Hunting, Brazzers TV, Animal Planet, Discovery Science, NatGeo Wild, Viasat History, Filmbox Premium, Minimax, Sláger TV, Pax TV, Bonum TV, LiChi TV, SuperOne, Boomerang, Heti TV, FiX TV, D1 TV, Nick Jr, NickToons, JimJam, Baby TV, HEVC Test card.

Location	M1	M2	M3	M4	M5	kW
Aggtelek	45c	35	28	31	48	50
Budapest	24a	41	38	29	34	42/57.5/100/89
Csávoly	25f	28	42	45	27	66/50/2x69
Csengőd	25f	28	42	45	27	38/42/40/39
Debrecen	40b	32	38	46	29	12/13.5/12/13
Fehérgyarmat	24b	41	38	31	34	32/76/62/51
Gerecse	26e	41	38	29	22	14/11.5/91/81
Győr	35e	46	25	42	22	29.5/36/32/35.5
Kabhegy	35e	46	32	29	22	100/2x98/56
Kékes	38c	36	44	46	34	79/74/2x83
Komádi	40b	32	38	46	29	60/51/37/79
Nagykanizsa	41e	24	32	29	31	55/50/2x55
Pécs	37d	47	32	45	27	42/78/51/55
Salgótarján	24e	36	38	46	34	13.5/14/13.5/18
Sopron	40e	33	32	42	22	81/74/72/83
Szeged	26f	31	42	23	22	20/19/2x20
Szentes	26f	31	42	23	22	87/95.5/79/83
Szolnok	30c	36	44	46	34	19/18/19/19.5
Szombathely	41e	33	32	29	22	12/2x11/12
Tokaj	26c	35	43	31	29	65/66/52.5/54
Úzd	37d	47	32	45	27	50/52/54/51
Vásvar	41e	33	32	29	22	55/69/65/55

+ site with txs below 10kW. °) incl. reg prgrs (a-f), see above
Local Licensees (DVB-T) not shown.

ICELAND

Systems: DVB-T (MPEG4) [E], DVB-T2 (MPEG4) [E]

National Stations
RÚV (Pub) ✉ Efstaleiti 1, 103 Reykjavík ☎ +354 5153000 **E:** istv@ruv.is **W:** www.ruv.is **L.P:** DG: Stefán Eiríksson **Chs:** RÚV, RÚV2 – **SÍMINN HF (Comm)** ✉ Ármúla 25, 108 Reykjavík ☎ +354 5956000 **W:** www.siminn.is **Ch:** Sjónvarp Símans – **SÝN HF (Comm)** ✉ Suðurlandsbraut 8, 108 Reykjavík ☎ +354 599900 **E:** syn@syn.is **W:** syn.is **L.P:** CEO: Heiðar Guðjónsson **Chs:** Stöð 2, Stöð 2 Bíó, Stöð 2 Fjölskylda, Stöð 2 Sport 1-5, Stöð 2 Esport, Stöð 2 Golf.

Local Station
Kristniboðskirkja Omega (Rlg): Grensásvegi 8, 108 Reykjavík; **DVB-T2:** ch41 (Vatnssendi 0.3kW, Mosfellsbær 0.05kW, Straumsvik 0.05kW, Kópavogur 0.01kW).

DTT Tx Networks (DVB-T exc. where noted)
Licensee: Sýn hf **W:** syn.is **M1✪(exc.*):** RÚV*, Stöð 2, Stöð 2 Sport, Stöð 2 Sport 2, Stöð 2 Bíó, Stöð 2 Fjölskylda **M2✪(exc.*) (DVB-T2):** RÚV HD*, RÚV2 HD*, N4*, Hringbraut*, Sjónvarp Símans, DR1, BBC Brit, National Geographic, Food Network **M3✪:** Stöð 2 Golf, Stöð 2 Sport 3, Stöð 2 Sport 4, Discovery Channel, Animal Planet, CNN International.

Location	M1	M2	M3	kW
Borgarland	22	21		1
Gagnheiði	26	28	-	1
Skálafell	34	35	-	1

+ sites with txs below 1kW (M3=only txs below 1kW)

INDIA

Systems: DVB-T2 (MPEG4) [E]; § PAL-B/G [E] ⇩2023

DOORDARSHAN (DD) (Pub) ✉ Doordarshan Bhawan, Copernicus Marg, New Delhi-110001 ☎ +91 11 23114599 **E:** dgdd@doordarshan.gov.in **W:** doordarshan.gov.in **L.P:** DG: Mayank Agarwal **Chs (terr.):** National chs: DD National, DD News, DD Sports, DD Bharati, DD Urdu, DD Kisan, DD India, DD Retro; Regional chs: DD Arun Prabha, DD Bangla, DD Bihar, DD Chandana, DD Girnar, DD Madhya Pradesh, DD Malayalam, DD North East, DD Oriya, DD Podhigai, DD Punjabi, DD Rajasthan, DD Sahyadri, DD Saptagiri, DD Uttar Pradesh, DD Yadagiri, DD Kashir.

DTT Tx Networks
Tx Operator: Doordardshan **M1:** DD National, DD News, DD Sports, DD Bharati, DD Kisan, DD Regional chs ⌘ AIR radio chs **M2:** DD HD, DD Urdu, DD India, DD Retro.

Location	M1	M2	kW	Location	M1	M2	kW
Ahmedabad	32	-	6	Kolkata	22	-	6
Aurangabad	23	-	6	Lucknow	32	-	6
Bangalore	24	-	6	Mumbai	21	27	6
Bhopal	23	-	6	New Delhi	34	26	6
Chennai	29	-	6	Patna	24	-	6
Cuttack	29	-	6	Raipur	23	-	6
Guwahati	29	-	6	Ranchi	23	-	6
Hyderabad	24	-	6	Srinagar	24	-	6
Indore	26	-	6	Thiruvananthapuram	28	-	6
Jalandhar	33	-	6				

+ nationwide MFN under construction

INDONESIA

Systems: DVB-T2 (MPEG4) [E]; § PAL-B/G [E] ⇩2023

National Stations ([a]=analogue)
TELEVISI EDUKASI (TVE) (Gov) 🖃 Jl. RE. Martadinata Km. 5.5 Ciputat, Tangerang 15411. ☎ +62 21 7418808 **W:** tve.kemdikbud.go.id **Chs:** Channel 1, Channel 2 **Txs:** via DTT & relays in provinces – **TELEVISI REPUBLIK INDONESIA (TVRI) (Pub)** 🖃 Jalan Gerbang Pemuda, Senayan, Jakarta 10270 ☎ +62 21 3846740 **E:** wmaster@tvri.co.id **W:** tvri.co.id **L.P:** MD: Farhat Syukri **Chs:** TVRI Nasional, TVRI Sumut. **Txs:** TVRI1: Jakarta [a]ch6 (5kW) & netw.; TVRI2: Jakarta [a]ch9. – **ANTV (PT CAKRAWALA ANDALAS TELEVISI) (Comm)** 🖃 Mulia Center Building, 19th Floor, Jl. HR Rasuna Said Kav. X-6 No.8, Jakarta 12940 ☎ +62 21 5222084 **E:** sales@anteve.co.id **W:** www.antvklik.com **Txs:** Jakarta [a]ch47 (40kW) & netw. – **GTV (PT GLOBAL INFORMASI BERMUTU) (Comm)** 🖃Wisma Indovision Lantai 17, Jalan Raya Panjang Z/III, Green Garden, Jakarta 11520 ☎ +62 21 5828555 **W:** www.gtv.id **Txs:** Jakarta [a]ch51 (120kW) & netw. – **INDOSIAR (PT. INDOSIAR VISUAL MANDIRI) (Comm)** 🖃 Jl. Damai No 11, Daan Mogot, Jakarta 11510 ☎ +62 21 5672222 **E:** program@indosiar.com **W:** www.indosiar.com **Txs:** Jakarta [a]ch41 (120kW) & netw. – **METRO TV (PT MEDIA TELEVISI INDONESIA)** 🖃 Jl. Pilar Mas Raya Kav. A-D., Kedoya, Kebon Jeruk, Jakarta 11520 ☎ +62 21 58300077 **E:** info@metrotvnews.com **W:** www.metrotvnews.com **Txs:** Jakarta [a]ch57 & netw. – **MNC TV (PT MEDIA NUSANTARA CITRA TV) (Comm)** 🖃 Jalan Pintu II, Taman Mini Indonesia Indah, Pondok Gede, Jakarta Timur 13810 ☎ +62 21 8412473 **E:** info@mnctv.com **W:** www.mnctv.com **Txs:** Jakarta [a]ch37 (80kW) & netw. – **RCTI (PT RAJAWALI CITRA TELEVISI INDONESIA) (Comm)** 🖃 Jl. Raya Perjuangan No. 3, kb. Jeruk, Jakarta 11000 ☎ +62 21 5303540 **E:** pr@rcti.tv **W:** www.rcti.tv **Txs:** Jakarta [a]ch43 & netw. – **SCTV (PT SURYA CITRA TELEVISI) (Comm)** 🖃 Graha SCTV 2nd floor, Jl. Gatot Subroto Kav 21, Jakarta 12930 ☎ +62 21 5225555 **E:** pr@sctv.co.id **W:** www.sctv.co.id **Txs:** Jakarta [a]ch45 (120kW) & netw. – **TRANS TV (PT TELEVISI TRANSFORMASI INDONESIA) (Comm)** 🖃 Jl. Kapten Tendean Kav. 12-14A, Jakarta 12790 ☎ +62 21 7944240 **E:** wmaster@transtv.co.id **W:** www.transtv.co.id **Txs:** Jakarta [a]ch29 (80kW) & netw. – **TRANS 7 (PT DUTA VISUAL NUSANTARA TIVI TUJUH) (Comm)** 🖃 Menara Bank Mega Lt. 20, Jl. Kapt. P. Tendean Kav.12-14A, Jakarta 12790 ☎ +62 21 79177000 **E:** info@trans7.co.id **W:** www.trans7.co.id **Txs:** Jakarta [a]ch49 (60kW) & network. – **TVONE (PT LATIVI MEDIA KARYA (Comm)** 🖃 Kawasan Industri Pulo Gadung, Jl Rawa Teratai II No 2, Jakarta Timur 13260 ☎ +62 21 4613545 **E:** info@tvone.co.id **W:** www.tvonenews.tv **Txs:** Jakarta [a]ch53 & netw.

Local Stations not shown.

DTT Tx Networks
Licensee: TVRI/PT Telekom **Mux 1:** TVRI Nasional, TVRI Sumut, TV Edukasi, MNC TV/GTV – **Licensee:** Televisi Digital Indonesie **W:** tvdigital.kominfo.go.id **Mux 2:** SCTV, ANTV, tvOne, Trans TV, Trans7, Metro TV

Location	M1	M2	kW
Jakarta	42	46	1.5/5

+ nationwide MFN under construction

IRAN

Systems: DVB-T2 (MPEG4) [E]; § PAL-B/G [E]
ISLAMIC REPUBLIC OF IRAN BROADCASTING (IRIB) (Gov) 🖃 P.O.Box 19395-3333, 19395 Tehran ☎ +98 21 22041093 **E:** tv@irib.ir **W:** www.iribtv.ir **L.P:** Pres: Abdolali Ali Asgari **Chs (terr.):** IRIB TV1-TV5, IRIB Provincial stations, Amoozesh, IFilm, Iran Kala, IRINN, Mostanad, Namayesh, Nasim, Ofogh, Omid, Pooya/Nahal, Quran, Salamat, Shoma, Tamasha, Varzesh, Al-Alam, Al-Khawtar, Press TV.

DTT Tx Network
Tx Operator: IRIB **M1:** IRIB TV1-TV5, Amoozesh, IRINN, Nasim, Quran, Salamat ⌘ IRIB radio channels **M2:** IFilm, Mostanad HD, Namayesh, Ofogh, Pooya/Nahal, Press TV, Varzesh, IRIB Provincial stations, Al-Alam, Al-Khawtar ⌘ IRIB radio channels **M3:** IRIB TV3 HD, IFilm HD, Iran Kala, Omid, Press TV HD, Shoma, Tamasha HD ⌘ IRIB radio channels.

Location	M1	M2	M3
Tehran (Jamaran)	37	43	34

+ nationwide MFN

IRAQ

Systems: PAL-B/G [E]; DVB-T2 (MPEG4) [E]

National Station
IRAQI MEDIA NETWORK (IMN) (Pub) 🖃 Salhiya, Baghdad ☎ +964 1 8844412 **W:** imn.iq **L.P:** DG: Mujahid Abu al-Hill **Chs:** Al-Iraqiya TV, Al-Iraqiya News **Txs: Al-Iraqiya TV:** Baghdad ch9 & netw.

Local Stations not shown.

Iraqi Kurdistan

DTT Tx Network
Tx Operator: United Mix Media 🖃 House No 635, Italian City Compound, Erbil ☎ +964 750 6421919 **E:** info@mixmedia.tv **W:** www.mixmedia.tv **Mux:** Ala TV, Amozhgary, Ankawa TV, Asman TV, Aso Sports TV, Astera TV, Babylon TV, Bangawaz TV, Best HD, Biaban Family, Biaban Movies, Biaban Music, Biaban Sport, BMC TV, Chare TV, Cihan TV, Dahen TV, Duhok TV, Effect HD, Esta, Falcon Eye, Falcon Family, GK Sulejmania, GK Hawler, GK Satellite, GK Sport, I Movies, I Baby, Jamawar, Jojo Mama TV, Judi TV, K24 TV, Kanal 6, Key House, Khak TV, Khezan TV, KNN TV, Komall TV, Kurdistan Sport, Kurdistan TV, Kurdmax, Kurdmax Pepule, Kurdsat TV, Kurdsat News TV, Law TV, Max TV, Mnara TV, Net TV, New Line TV, New Art HD, Niga Family, Niga Kids, Niga Movies, NRT, NRT 2, One World TV, Parwarda TV, Payam TV, Pelistank TV, Qellat TV, Rasan TV, Rudaw, Speda TV, Sport HD, Srusht, Suly, U2 HD, UTV Suleymania, X FM TV, Xezan TV, Zagros **Txs:** MFN.

IRELAND

System: DVB-T (MPEG4) [E]

RTÉ (Pub) 🖃 Nutley Ln, Donnybrook, Dublin 4 ☎ +353 1 2083111 **E:** info@rte.ie **W:** www.rte.ie **L.P:** DG: Dee Forbes **Chs:** RTÉ One, RTÉ2, RTÉ News Now, RTÉjr. – **TG4 (Pub)** 🖃 Baile na hAbhann, Co. Galway H91 X4TO ☎ +353 91 505050 **E:** info@tg4.ie **W:** www.tg4.ie **L.P:** DG: Alan Esslemont – **VIRGIN MEDIA (Comm)** 🖃 Building P2, EastPoint Business Park, Clontarf, Dublin 3 ☎ +353 1 2458000 **W:** www.virginmedia.ie **L.P:** CEO: Tony Hanway **Chs:** Virgin Media 1-3.

DTT Tx Networks
Tx Operator: RTÉ Network Ltd (2RN) **W:** www.2rn.ie **M1:** RTÉ2 HD, Virgin Media 1, TG4, RTÉ News Now, Tithe an Oireachtais **M2:** RTÉ One HD, Virgin Media 2, Virgin Media 3, RTÉjr, RTÉ One +1, RTÉ2 +1.

Location	M1	M2	kW	Location	M1	M2	kW
Cairn Hill	47	44	160	Mount Leinster	23	39	160
Clermont Carn	42V	45V	160	Mullaghanish	21	24	200
Dungervan	32	34	10	Spur Hill	45	39	50
Holywell Hill	22	25	20	Three Rock	30	33	63
Kildruff	31	37	25	Truskmore	42	45	160
Kippure	34	35	63	Woodcock Hill	47	44	10
Maghera	48	46	160	+ sites with txs below 10kW.			

ISRAEL

Systems: DVB-T2 (MPEG4), # DVB-T (MPEG4) [E]

ISRAELI PUBLIC BROADCASTING CORP. (IPBC) (Pub) 🖃161 Jaffa Road, Jerusalem 91280 **E:** info@kan.org.il **W:** www.kan.org.il **L.P:** CEO: Eldad Koblenz **Chs:** KAN 11, KAN Educational, MAKAN 33 (in Arabic) **KAN 11** 🖃 P.O.Box 7139, Jerusalem 91071 ☎ +972

2 5301333 **MAKAN 33** ✉ P.O.Box 13172, Jerusalem 91131 ☎ +972 2 5013800 – **THE SECOND AUTHORITY FOR TELEVISION AND RADIO (SATR) (Pub)** ✉ P.O.Box 3445, Jerusalem ☎+972 2 6556222 **E:** rashut@rashut2.org.il **W:** www.rashut2.org.il **L.P:** Chair: Yulia Shamalov Berkovich. **NB:** SATR supervises the commercial TV channels Keshet 12 and Reshet 13. **Keshet 12 (Comm)** ✉Ramat HaHayal, Tel Aviv **W:** www.mako.co.il/tv; **Reshet 13 (Comm)** ✉Ramat HaHayal, Tel Aviv **W:** 13tv.co.il – **CHANNEL 20 (Comm)** ✉ Tel Aviv **E:** news20@ch-20.tv **W:** www.20il.co.il – **CHANNEL 99 (KNESSET CHANNEL) (Gov)** ✉ Kiryat Ben-Gurion, Jerusalem 91950 ☎ +972 2 6541636 **E:** feedback@knesset.gov.il **W:** www.knesset.gov.il.

DTT Tx Networks (incl. coverage of West Bank & Gaza Strip)
Tx Operator: Bezeq **W:** www.bezeq.co.il **Mux:** KAN 11 HD, KAN 11 4K, KAN Educational, MAKAN 33, MAKAN 33 HD, Channel 99, Keshet 12, Reshet 13, Channel 20, Music 24 **Txs:** ch26 (DVB-T)/ch28 (DVB-T2) (SFN, Central Israel), ch29 (DVB-T)/ch32 (DVB-T2) (SFN, Northern/Southern Israel).

WEST BANK & GAZA STRIP
(Palestinian Authority/State of Palestine)

Systems: # PAL-B/G [E]; DVB-T2 (MPEG4) [E]

National Station
PALESTINE PUBLIC BROADCASTING CORP. ✉ P.O.Box 984, Ramallah Albereih, West Bank ☎ +970 2 2987903 **E:** pbcinfo@pbc.ps **W:** www.pbc.ps **L.P:** Chmn: Ahmad Hazoury **Txs:** Nablus ch5, Khan Yunis ch21, Ariha (Jericho) ch21, Kasser-Elhakim (Gaza) ch23, Ramallah ch25, Halhul ch30, Jenin ch31, Betjala ch34.

Local Stations not shown.

DTT Tx Network
Tx Operator: Starcom **W:** www.facebook.com/starcom.dvbt2 **M:** Star Mix, Star Sport 1-3, Star Movies, Star Kids, Star Drama, others **Tx:** ch34 (Gaza)

ITALY

Systems: # DVB-T (MPEG2), # DVB-T2 (MPEG4) [E], DVB-T2 (HEVC) [E]

National Stations
RADIOTELEVISIONE ITALIANA (RAI) (Pub) ✉ Direzione Centrale TV, Viale Mazzini 14, 00195 Roma ☎ +39 06 36864046 **E:** portale@rai.it **W:** www.rai.it **L.P:** CEO: Fabrizio Salini **Chs (terr.):** Rai 1-5, Rai Gulp, Rai Movie, Rai News 24, Rai Sport, Rai Scuola, Rai Storia, Rai YoYo – **CANALE ITALIA (Comm)** ✉ Via Aosta 1, 35142 Padova ☎ +39 049 8733111 **E:** canaleitalia@canaleitalia.it **W:** canaleitalia.it – **LA 7 (Comm)** ✉ Via della Pineta Sacchetti 229, 00166 Roma ☎ +39 06 35584800 **E:** la7@la7.tv **W:** www.la7.tv – **MEDIASET (Comm)** ✉ Viale Europa 48, Palazzo dei Cigni, 20093 Cologno Monzese MI ☎ +39 02 25149301 **W:** www.mediaset.it **L.P:** CEO: Pier Silvio Berlusconi – **RETE ORO (Comm)** ✉ Via Accademia degli Agiati 47, 00147 Roma ☎ +39 06 5964971 **W:** www.reteoro.tv – **SKY ITALIA (Comm)** ✉ Via Monte Penice 7, 20138 Milano ☎ +39 06 454732 **W:** www.sky.it **L.P:** CEO: Maximo Ibarra.

Local Stations not shown.

DTT Tx Networks (DVB-T except where noted)
Licensee: Rai **M1:** Rai 1, Rai 2, Rai 3 + regional prgrs, Rai News 24, Rete Oro, HEVC Test card ⌘ Rai R.1-3 **M2:** Rai 5, Rai Scuola, Rai Sport, Rai Storia ⌘ Rai R.Tutta Italiana, Rai R.3 Classica, Rai R.Techetè, Rai R.Live, Rai R.Kids, Rai Isoradio, Rai Gr Parlamento, Rai R.1 Sport, Rai R.2 Indie **M3:** Rai 1 HD, Rai 4, Rai Gulp, Rai Movie, Rai Premium, Rai YoYo **M4:** Rai 2 HD, Rai 3 HD, Rai Sport+ HD **M5 (DVB-T2):** Rai 4 HD, Rai Premium HD **M6:** Rai 1, Rai 2, Rai 3, Rai News 24, Rai Storia, Rete Oro.

Location	M1	M2	M3	M4	M5	M6[1]
SFN	(MFN)	30	26	40	(MFN)	25
SFN (Sardegna 1)	(MFN)	49	43	41	45	-
SFN (Sardegna 2)	(MFN)	49	43	47	45	-

[1]) Lazio only

Licensee: Mediaset **M1✪:** Premium Action, Premium Crime, Premium Stories, Premium Emotion, Sky Sport 24 HD, Sky Sport Mondiali HD, Sky Sport Mondiali (SD), Sky Sport **M2:** 20 Mediaset, QVC, Food Network, Mediaset Extra, Focus, TOPcrime, Boing, Cartoonito **M3✪:** Rete 4 HD, Canale 5 HD, Italia 1 HD, 20 Mediaset HD **M4:** Rete 4, Canale 5, Italia 1, Iris, La 5, TGCOM24 **M5✪:** Sky Uno, Sky Atlantic, Fox, National Geographic, Sky Sport Uno HD, Sky Sport Uno (SD), Sky Sport, Sky Sport 24.

Location	M1	M2	M3	M4	M5
Roma	52	36	38	49	56

+ nationwide SFN (SFN channels differ in some regions)
Licensee: Persidera **W:** www.persidera.it **M1:** Real Time, RTL 102.5 TV, HSE24. Giallo, Super!, DMAX, Radiofreccia, RTL 102.5 TV HD, HSE24 HD, Radiofreccia HD ⌘ R.Capital, R.Deejay, R.m2o, RTL 102.5, RTL102.5 News, R.Freccia **M2:** TV2000, Motor Trend, Canale 63, Alma TV, BOM Channel, R. Kiss Kiss TV, Mediatext.it, Alice, Marcopolo, Casedesignstili, PopEconomy, Babel-Romit TV, Parole di Vita, Sfera TV, Cusano Italia TV, RDS Social TV, R. Zeta ⌘ R.Vaticano Italia **M3:** K2, frisbee, Boing Plus, Spike, Supertennis, VH1, RadioItaliaTV, TV8, VH1 ⌘ R.Italia SMI **M4:** Nove, Paramount Network, HGTV, Deejay TV, Nove, Deejay TV HD, Cielo, Sky TG24 ⌘ R. Maria **M5:** Canale 61, Donna Sport TV, Italia Channel, Gold TV Italia, La 4 Italia, Channel 24, Rete Italia, Lineagem, Juwelo, HSE24 Donna, Air Italia, Linea Italia, Orler TV, Fire TV, Mondo Calcio, Canale 162, Donna Shopping, Canale 165, ILIKE TV, Canale 232, Rainbow, HSE24 Beauty, Pianeta TV.

Location	M1	M2	M3	M4	M5
Roma	47	55	48	44	33

+ nationwide SFN (SFN channels differ in some regions)
Licensee: Dfree **W:** www.dfree.tv **M:** Sportitalia, Padre Pio TV, TV 153, R. 105, R101 TV, TV 243, Donnashopping, Virgin R., Premium Cinema 1, Premium Cinema 2 ⌘ R. 101, R. Monte Carlo, R. 105, Virgin R. **Txs:** Roma ch50 & SFN/MFN – **Licensee:** H3G **W:** www.tre.it **M (DVB-T2):** Sportitalia HD **Txs:** Roma ch37 & SFN/MFN – **Licensee:** Cairo Communication **W:** www.cairocommunication.it **M:** La7, La7 HD, La7d, La7d HD **Txs:** Roma ch25 & SFN/MFN – **Licensee:** Canale Italia **W:** www.canaleitalia.it **M1:** Italia 53/83/84/121/124/125/127/134/135/136/141/142/148/150/154/156/159/160, Cantando Ballando, Italia TV 2 ⌘ RPL - La Tua R. **Txs:** Roma ch39 & MFN. **M2:** Italia 143/148/154/155/160, Canale Italia 3 Extra/6/11/83/84, Shopping Italia, Galaxy TV2, France 24, Serenissima ⌘ R.Canale Italia, Volami Nel Cuore **Txs:** Roma ch22 & MFN.
Regional/Local licensees not shown (except below).

South Tyrol

Regional Licensee: Rundfunk-Anstalt Südtirol (RAS) **W:** www.ras.bz.it **M1:** ORF eins, ORF2 Tirol, ORF III, Das Erste, ZDF, 3Sat **M2:** SRF1, SRF zwei, BR Fernsehen Süd, Kika, Arte, RSI LA1 **M3*:** ZDF HD, SRF1 HD, SRF zwei HD **M4*:** ORF eins HD, ORF2 Tirol HD, Das Erste HD **M5 (DVB-T2/HEVC):** ORF III HD, BR Süd HD, arte HD, RSI La1 HD **Txs:** **M1:** Bolzano ch34 & MFN **M2:** Bolzano ch51 & MFN **M3:** Bolzano ch27 & MFN **M4:** Bolzano ch59 & MFN **M5:** MFN.

JAMAICA

Systems: ATSC [A]; § NTSC-M [A] ⇩2021

PUBLIC BROADCASTING CORP. OF JAMAICA (Pub) ✉ 5-9 South Odeon Avenue, Kingston ☎ +1 876 7549123 **E:** info@pbcjamaica.org **W:** pbcjamaica.org **Txs:** (-) – **CVM TELEVISION LTD (Comm)** ✉ 69 Constant Spring Rd, Kingston 10 ☎ +1 876 9319400 🖷 +1 876 9311573 **E:** customerservice@cvmtv.com **W:** www.cvmtv.com **L.P:** CEO: Andre McGlone **Txs:** Kingston ch4 (3.2kW) & Netw. – **TELEVISION JAMAICA LTD (TVJ) (Comm)** ✉ P.O.Box 100, Kingston 10 ☎ +1 876 9265620 **E:** tvjadmin@cwjamaica.com **W:** www.televisionjamaica.com **L.P:** GM: Claire C. Grant **Txs:** Kingston [a]ch11 (3.2kW) & netw. – **LOVE TV (Rlg)** ✉ 12 Carlton crescent, Kingston ☎ +1 876 9689596 **W:** www.facebook.com/lovetvja **L.P:** GM: Moya Thomas **Txs:** Kingston [a] ch6 (2.5kW) & netw. ([a]=analogue)

JAPAN

System: ISDB-T [J]

National Stations
NIPPON HOSO KYOKAI (NHK) (Pub) ✉ 2-1, Jinnan 2-chome, Shibuya-ku, Tokyo 150-8001 ☎ +81 3 34651111 **W:** www.nhk.or.jp **Chs:** NHK General TV, NHK Educational TV **L.P:** Pres: Terunobu Maeda – **ALL-NIPPON NEWS NETWORK (ANN) (Comm)** ✉ 9-1, Roppongi 6-chome, Minato-ku, Tokyo 106-8001 ☎ +81 3 64061111 **W:** www.tv-asahi.co.jp **L.P:** Chmn/CEO: Hiroshi Hayakawa– **FUJI TELEVISION NETWORK (FTN) (Comm)** ✉ 4-8, Daiba 2-chome, Minato-ku, Tokyo 137-8088 ☎ +81 3 55008888 **W:** www.fujitv.co.jp; www.fnn-news.com **L.P:** Chmn: Masaki Miyauchi – **JAPAN NEWS NETWORK (JNN) (Comm)** ✉ 3-6, Akasaka 5-chome, Minato-ku, Tokyo 107-8006. ☎ +81 3 37461111 **W:** www.tbs.co.jp **L.P:** Chmn: Shinji Takeda – **NIPPON NEWS NETWORK (NNN) (Comm)** ✉

6-1, Higashi Shimbashi 1-chome, Minato-ku, Tokyo 105-7444 ☎ +81 3 62154444 **W:** www.ntv.co.jp; www.news24.jp **L.P:** Chmn: Yoshio Okubo – **TV TOKYO NETWORK (TXN) (Comm)** ✉ 3-12, Toranomon 4-chome, Minato-ku, Tokyo 105-8012 ☎ +81 3 54707777 **W:** www.tv-tokyo.co.jp **L.P:** Chmn: Ichiro Ishikawa.
NB. Commercial stns are relayed nationwide via local affiliates.

Local Stations not shown.

DTT Tx Networks (National Stations)

Location	NHK[1]	NHK[2]	ANN	FTN	JNN	NNN	TXN
Tokyo (Tokyo Skytree)	27	26	24	21	22	25	23

+ nationwide tx networks [1]) NHK General TV [2]) NHK Educational TV

JORDAN

System: DVB-T2 (MPEG4) [E]

JORDAN RADIO & TELEVISION (JRTV) (Pub) ✉ P.O.Box 1041, 11118 Amman ☎ +962 6 4749171 **E:** tv@jrtv.gov.jo **W:** www.jrtv.jo **L.P:** DG: Mohammad Balqar **Chs:** Jordan TV, Jordan TV Sports

DTT Tx Network
Tx Operator: JRTV **Mux:** Jordan TV **Txs:** MFN

KAZAKHSTAN

Systems: DVB-T2 (MPEG4) [E]; § SECAM-D/K [R], § PAL-D/K [R] ⇩2021

National Stations
QAZAQSTAN RTRK (Gov) ✉ Qonaev k. 4, 010000 Nur-Sultan ☎ +7 7172 757161 **W:** kaztrk.kz **Chs:** Qazaqstan, Qazsport, Balapan, Regional stations – **HABAR (Gov)** ✉ Jeltoqsan k. 185, 050013 Almaty ☎ +7 727 2700001 **E:** khabar@khabar.kz **W:** khabar.kz **Chs:** Habar, Habar 24, Kazakh TV – **KTK (Comm)** ✉ Respýblika alany 13, 050013 Almaty ☎ +7 727 2583657 **E:** ktk@ktk.kz **W:** www.ktk.kz **L.P:** DG: Arman Shuraev – **NTK (Comm)** ✉ Respýblika alany 13, 050013 Almaty ☎ +7 727 2672750 **E:** office@ntk.kz **W:** www,ntk.kz **L.P:** GD: Saida Igenbek – **31 KANAL (Comm)** ✉ Tajibaev k. 155, 050060 Almaty ☎ +7 727 3153131.

Local Stations not shown.

DTT Tx Networks (under construction)
Tx Operator: Kazteleradio **W:** www.kazteleradio.kz **M1:** Pervyy kanal Eurasia, Qazaqstan, Balapan, Qazsport, Habar, Habar 24, Kazakh TV, 7 Kanal, KTK, 31 Kanal, Astana TV, Mir **M2:** Asyl Arna, NTK, ON TV, Almaty TV, STV Kazakhstan, Qazaqstan RTRK Regional stns, Novoe Televidenye, Tvoyo TV, TDK 42, Gakku TV, Muzzone, Muzlife, Local stns **Txs: M1:** ch47 (Almaty) + MFN under construction. **M2:** ch33 (Almaty) + MFN under construction.

KENYA

System: DVB-T2 (MPEG4) [E]

National Stations
KENYA BROADCASTING CORP. (KBC) (Gov) ✉ P.O.Box 30456, Harry Thuku Road, 00100 Nairobi ☎ +254 20 334567 **E:** kbctv@swift-kenya.com **W:** www.kbc.co.ke **L.P:** MD: Naim Bilal **Chs:** Channel 1, Heritage TV – **CITIZEN TV (Comm)** ✉ P.O.Box 7468, 00300 Nairobi ☎ +254 20 2721415 **E:** news@royalmedia.co.ke **W:** citizentv.co.ke – **KENYA TELEVISION NETWORK (KTN) (Comm)** ✉ P.O.Box 56985, 00100 Nairobi ☎ +254 20 227122 **E:** admin@ktnkenya.com **W:** www.standardmedia.co.ke – **K24 (Comm)** ✉ 3rd Floor, Longonot Place, Kijabe St., 00100 Nairobi ☎ +254 21 248000 **W:** www.news24.co.ke – **NATION TV (NTV) (Comm)** ✉ P.O.Box 49010, Nairobi 00100 GPO ☎ +254 20 3208000 **E:** tvnews@nation.co.ke **W:** ntv.nation.co.ke – **FAMILY TV (Rlg)** ✉ P.O.Box 2330 KNH, Nairobi ☎ +254 20 4200000 **E:** info@familykenya.com **W:** familymedia.tv

Local Stations not shown.

DTT Tx Networks
Licensee: Signet Ltd (KBC) **M:** KBC Channel One, Heritage TV, NTV, KTN, CNBC Africa, K24, EATN, EATV, Family TV, God TV, Kiss TV, Classic TV, Citizen TV, GBS ⌘ KBC English Service, KBC Idha FM, Metro FM, Coro FM **Txs:** ch57 (Nairobi 2.5kW) & nationwide MFN – **Licensee:** StarTimes **M✪:** multiprgr **Txs:** MFN.

KIRIBATI

System: DVB-T2 (MPEG4) [E]

KIRI 1 TV (WAVE TV) (Comm) ✉ TK Plaza, Bairiki **E:** taotinkiribati@gmail.com **W:** www.facebook.com/kiriOneTv

DTT Tx Network
Tx Operator: Click Pacific **W:** clickpacific.com **M:** Kiri 1 TV, 22 prgrs✪ **Txs:** SFN.

KOREA, North

Systems: DVB-T2 (MPEG4) [E]; # PAL-D/K [R]

RADIO AND TELEVISION BROADCASTING COMMITTEE (Gov) ✉ Jonsung-dong, Moranbong District, Pyongyang ☎ +850 2 816035 🖷 +850 2 812100 **L.P:** Chmn: Yong Bo Hwang **Chs:** Korean Central Television (KCTV), Mansudae Television (MTV), Ryongnamsan Television (RTV), Sports Television (STV).

Txs: KCTV:

Location	ch	kW	Location	ch	kW
Sangmasan	1	10	Ripbong	8	10
Chayubong	2	30	Chaedoksan	9	30
Suryongsan	2	30	Sepo	9	70
Hamhung	3	70	Sinyang	9	30
Pagaebong	3	30	Unjubong	9	70
Chaedoksan	4	30	Wangjaesan	9	30
Songjinsan	4	20	Wonsan	10	70
Wonsan	4	10	Chonchon	11	10
Chajiryong	5	30	Haeju	11	70
Paekam	5	10	Sambongsan	11	10
Kangtyong	5	30	Chajiryong	12	30
Kumgangsan	5	30	Chonchon	12	10
Sambongsan	5	10	Chongjin	12	70
Tokusan	5	20	Haksongsan	12	20
Chongjin	6	70	Kaesong	12	70
Hyangsan	6	10	Pyongyang	12	70
Sepo	6	70	Ripbong	12	10
Sinuiju	6	70	Sobaeksan	12	30
Sariwon	7	30	Songsan	12	10
Chayubong	8	30	Tokusan	12	20
Haksongsan	8	20	Wangjaesan	12	30
Kanggye	8	70	+ relay txs below 10kW		

MTV: Pyongyang ch5 (350kW); **RTV/STV:** Kaesong ch9 (30kW), Pyongyang ch9 (140kW).

DTT Tx Network (under construction)
Tx Operator: Ministry of Post and Telecommunication **M:** KCTV, MTV, RTV, STV **Txs:** ch25 (Pyongyang), ch31 (Pyongyang) + nationwide MFN under construction.

KOREA, South

System: ATSC [A]

National Stations
EDUCATIONAL BROADCASTING SYSTEM (EBS) (Pub) ✉ 281, Hallyu world-ro, Ilsandong-gu, Goyang-si, Gyeonggi-do 10393 ☎ +82 2 5262562 **W:** www.ebs.co.kr **L.P:** Pres/CEO: Kim Myeong-jung. **Chs:** EBS1, EBS2 – **KOREAN BROADCASTING SYSTEM (KBS) (Pub)** ✉ 113, Yeouigongwon-ro, Yeoungdeungpo-gu, Seoul 07235 ☎ +82 2 7812001 **W:** www.kbs.co.kr **L.P:** Pres: Yang Sung-Dong **Chs:** KBS1, KBS2 – **MUNHWA BROADCASTING CORP. (MBC) (Comm)** ✉ 267, Seongam-ro, Mapo-gu, Seoul 03925 ☎ +82 2 7890011 **W:** www.imbc.com **L.P:** Pres/CEO: Park Seong-Je – **SEOUL BROADCASTING SYSTEM (SBS) (Comm)** ✉ 161, Mokdongseo-ro, Yangcheon-gu, Seoul 07996 ☎ +82 2 20610006 **W:** www.sbs.co.kr **L.P:** Pres: Park Jung-Hoon.

Regional/Local Stations (all Comm)
Regional Station: O Broadcasting System (OBS): 233, Ojeong-ro, Bucheon-si, Gyeonggi-do 14442; ch25 + translators (MFN) – **Local Stations: CJB** (Cheongju), **G1** (Chuncheon), **JIBS** (Jeju), **JTV** (Jeonju), **KBC** (Gwangju), **KNN** (Busan), **TBC** (Daegu), **TJB** (Daejeon), **UBC (Ulsan)** are SBS affiliates and carry the SBS network outside of local programming (key txs see below).

DTT Tx Networks

Location	E*	E*[1]	K1	K1[1]	K2	K2[1]	M	M[1]	S/L°	S[1]	LOCAL
Andong	36	-	32	-	34	-	22	-	24	-	(TBC)
Busan	18	-	14	52	16	56	17	55	15	53	(KNN)
Changwon	32	-	22	-	25	-	26	-	33	-	(KNN)
Cheongju	35	-	23	52	34	56	20	-	23	-	(CJB)
Chuncheon	48	-	32	-	41	-	33	-	40	-	(G1)

Location	E*	E*[1]	K1	K1[1]	K2	K2[1]	M	M[1]	S/L°	S[1]	LOCAL
Chungju	49	-	39	-	47	-	40	-	43	-	(CJB)
Daegu	18	-	14	52	16	56	17	55	15	53	(TBC)
Daejeon	38	-	26	52	32	56	17	55	15	53	(TJB)
Gangneung	18	-	15	52	17	56	14	53	16	55	(G1)
Gwangju	32	-	17	52	18	56	14	55	15	53	(KBC)
Jeju	35	-	27	-	29	-	31	-	33	-	(JIBS)
Jeonju	46	-	27	-	44	-	41	-	33	-	(JTV)
Jinju	31	-	20	-	23	-	21	-	19	-	(KNN)
Mokpo	38	-	44	-	46	-	37	-	16	-	(KBC)
Pohang	51	-	42	-	50	-	46	-	41	-	(TBC)
Seoul	18	54	15	52	17	56	14	55	16	53	(SBS)
Suncheon	24	-	44	-	46	-	16	-	38	-	(KBC)
Ulsan	48	-	28	49	40	56	34	29	30	39	(UBC)
Wonju	51	-	44	19	45	56	46	22	40	34	(G1)

+ translators (MFN) E=EBS, K1=KBS1, K2=KBS2, M=MBC, S=SBS L=Local *) Multiplex includes EBS1, EBS2 °) Local stns (SBS affiliates) [1]) UHD (**W:** uhdkorea.org)
NB: T-DMB (VHF) networks with radio & TV services for mobile devices not shown (see National Radio section).

KOSOVO

Systems: DVB-T (MPEG4) [E], DVB-T2 (MPEG4) [E]; § PAL-B/G [E]

National Stations
RADIOTELEVIZIONI I KOSOVËS (RTK) (Pub) ✉ Rr. Xhemail Prishtina nr. 12, 10000 Prishtinë ☎+383 38 230102 **E:** post@rtklive.com **W:** www.rtklive.com **L.P:** Chmn: Ismet Bexheti **Chs (terr.):** RTK1-4 – **KOHAVISION TV (KTV) (Comm)** ✉ Rr. Nene Tereza, 10000 Prishtinë ☎ +381 38 248014 **E:** kohavision@koha.net **W:** www.kohavision.tv – **RTV 21 (Comm)** ✉ Pallati i Mediave, Aneks II, 10000 Prishtinë ☎ +381 38 241526 **E:** lajmet@rtv21.tv **W:** rtv21.tv.

Local Stations ([a]=analogue)
TV Ballkan: Rr. Adem Jashari 8, 20000 Prizereni; [a]ch53. **TV Besa:** Rr. Kater Kullat n.n., 20000 Prizereni; [a]ch30. **TV Dukagjini:** Rr. Fehmi Agani 16, 30000 Pejë; [a]ch36. **TV Festina:** Rr. Deshmoret e Kombit n.n., Ferizaj; [a]ch40. **TV Herc:** 73000 Shterpcë; ch35. **TV Iliria:** Rr. Hoxhë Jonuzi n.n., 61000 Viti; [a]ch28. **TV Liria:** Rr. Reçak n.n., Ferizaj; [a]ch29. **TV Mir:** Rr. Vojske Jugoslavije n.n., Leposaviq; [a]ch23. **TV Mitrovica:** 40000 Mitrovicë; [a]ch42. **TV Most:** Rr. Nemanjica 14, Zveqan; [a]ch61. **TV Opinion:** Rr. Marin Barleti, n.n, Zym; [a]ch28. **TV Prizren:** Rr. Papa Gjon Pali II 1A, 20000 Prizereni; [a]ch60. **TV Puls:** Shillovë; 60000 Gjilan [a]ch36. **TV Syri Vision:** Rr. Sadik Pozhegu 28, 50000 Gjakovë; [a]ch33. **TV Tema:** Rr. Sadik Bega n.n., Ferizaj; ch50. **TV Vali:** Pasjak; 60000 Gjilan [a]ch39. **TV Zoom:** Kuvcë e Epërme; [a]ch43.

DTT Tx Networks (DVB-T2 exc. where noted)
Licensee Mux 1: RTK **M (DVB-T):** RTK1 HD, RTK 2-4, RTSH1, Klan Kosova HD, Rrokum HD – **Licensee Mux 2:** RTV 21 Media **M:** TV 21 HD, RTV 21 Plus HD, RTV 21 Mix HD, RTV 21 Popullore HD, RTV 21 Junior HD, RTV 21 NewsBiz HD, RTV 21 Maqedoni HD, Klan Kosova – **Licensee Mux 3:** Kohavision **M:** KTV HD, Arta HD. **Txs:** nationwide MFN under construction.

KUWAIT

System: DVB-T2 (MPEG4) [E]

KUWAIT TELEVISION (Gov) ✉ P.O. Box 621, 13007 Safat ☎ +965 22415300 **W:** www.media.gov.kw **Chs:** KTV1, KTV2, KTV Al Arabi, KTV Ethraa, KTV Sport, KTV Sport Plus, KTV Kids, KTV Al Qurain, KTV Al Majlis.

DTT Tx Network
Tx Operator: Ministry of Information **M:** KTV1, KTV2, KTV Al Arabi, KTV Ethraa, KTV Sport, KTV Sport Plus, KTV Kids, KTV Al Qurain, KTV Al Majlis **Txs:** MFN (ch30, ch34, ch56).

KYRGYZSTAN

System: DVB-T2 (MPEG4) [E]

National Stations
KOOMDUK TELERADIO BERÜÜ KORPORATSIYASY (KTRK) (Pub) ✉ Jash Gvardiya blvd. 59, 720010 Bishkek ☎ +996 312 392059 **E:** public@ktrk.kg **W:** www.ktrk.kg **L.P:** DG: Usen Jaynak **Ch:** Kyrgyzstan, Balastan, Madaniyat, Muzyka, Sport – **ELTR (Pub)** ✉ blvd. Erkindik 122, 720040 Bishkek ☎ +996 312 906144 **L.P:** Dir: Shayyrbek Abdrakhmanov **W:** www.facebook.com/elkanaly – **5 KANAL (Pub)** ✉ Ibraimov St 24, 720000 Bishkek ☎ +996 312 592066 **E:** koordinator@5tv.kg **W:** 5tv.kg.

Local Stations not shown.

DTT Tx Networks
Tx Operator: Kyrgyztelecom **W:** www.kt.kg **M1:** KTRK, Madaniyat, Balastan, KTRK Muzyka, KTRK Sport, Ala-Too 24, 5 Kanal, Piramida, ELTR, ELTR Ilim Jana Bilim, Mir, Pervyy kanal, Mir, RTR Planeta, Intimak TV, Local stns **M2:** Mir 24, TNT Kyrgyzstan, Domashniy Telekanal, Sanat TV, Tumar TV, 312 Kino, 312 Muzika, Semieyniy, NTS HD, Lyubimiy TV, TV1.KG, Aziya TV, Osh TV, Osh Pirim, Marva, TRT Avaz, Cinemax HD **M3:** Rossiya 24, Ren TV Kyrgyzstan, NTV Kyrgyzstan, ON 1, NTS Sport HD, Pyatnitsa!. Ayan TV, NBT, Keremet TV, Kyrgyz TV, Echo Manas, Ya!, 8 Kanal, Anten TV **M4:** Kyrgyzstan TV, Nur TV, Next TV, 24 TV, 7 Kanal, Life TV, New TV, Aprel TV, Cholpon Plus **Txs: M1:** ch25 (Bishkek) & nationwide netw. **M2-4:** MFN

LAOS

Systems: DTMB [E]; § PAL-B [E] ⇩2021

National Station
LAO NATIONAL TELEVISION (LNTV) (Gov) ✉ P.O.Box 5635, Vientiane ☎ +856 21 710643 **E:** info@lntv.gov.la **W:** www.lntv.gov.la **L.P:** DG: Bounchao Phichit **Chs:** LNTV1, LNTV3.

Provincial/Local Stations not shown.

DTT Tx Networks
Licensee: Lao Digital TV Co. Ltd **W:** www.facebook.com/VientianeCapital021454446 **Mux 1-6(partly✪):** multiprgr

Location	M1	M2	M3	M4	M5	M6[1]
Vientiane	21	25	37	41	45	49

+ nationwide MFN

LATVIA

System: DVB-T (MPEG4) [E]

National Stations
LATVIJAS TELEVIZIJA (LTV) (Pub) ✉ Zaķusalas krastmala 3, LV-1509 Rīga ☎ +371 67200316 **E:** ltv@ltv.lv **W:** ltv.lsm.lv **L.P:** Chmn: Ivars Priede **Chs:** LTV1, LTV7 – **ALL MEDIA LATVIA (Comm)** ✉ Dzelzavas iela 120g, LV-1021 Rīga ☎ +371 67479100 **E:** pasts@skaties.lv. **W:** skaties.lv **L.P:** CEO: Pierre Danon **Chs:** TV3, TV3 Life, TV3 Mini, TV6, 3+ – **LATVIJAS REGIONU TELEVIZIJA (RE:TV) (Comm)** ✉ Purva iela 12a, LV-4201 Valmiera ☎ +371 64219043 **E:** redakcija@retv.lv **W:** www.retv.lv **L.P:** Dir: Elīna Leimane – **LATVIJAS ŠLAGERKANALS (Comm)** ✉ Elizabetes iela 57a-22, LV-1050 Rīga ☎ +371 67296345 **E:** info@slageris.lv **W:** slageris.lv – **RIGATV 24 (Comm)** ✉ Blaumaņa iela 32, LV-1011 Rīga ☎ +371 67630301 **E:** reklama@rigatv24.lv **W:** rigatv24.lv **L.P:** Dir: Klāvs Kalniņš.

Local Station
Vidusdaugavas Televizija (Comm): Jaunā iela 16, LV-5201 Jēkabpils; ch55 (0.5 kW).

DTT Tx Networks
Licensee: SIA Tet **W:** www.tet.lv **M1:** LTV1, LTV7, RE:TV, Riga TV24, Sportacentrs.com **M2✪:** 3+, Eurosport 1, National Geographic, PBK, REN Baltija, RTR Planeta, STV, TV1000, TV3, TV3 Life, TV6 **M3✪:** 360TV, Best4Sport TV, Euronews, Muz TV, Nickelodeon, NTV Mir, Okhotnik i Ribolov, Pyatnitsa, Star Family, TV3 Mini, VIP Comedy **M4✪:** Animal Planet, BBC Earth, CNN International, Discovery Channel, Discovery Science, DTX, Investigation Discovery, MTV Europe, Nick Jr, TLC, Travel Channel **M5✪:** STS Baltics, FilmZone, Fox, Fox Life, Hustler TV, Kinokomediya, Sony Channel, Sony Turbo, TNT, TV1000 Russkoye Kino, VH1 Europe **M6✪:** Disney Channel, Disney Junior, Disney XD, Eurosport 2, Jim Jam, KHL, KidZone, Kinomiks, Latvijas Šlāgerkanāls, Setanta Sports **M7✪:** Discovery HD Showcase, Eurosport HD, MTV Live HD.

Location	M1	M2	M3	M4	M5	M6	M7	kW
Cesvaine	22	46	41	58	30	24	-	75/2x120/110/2x100
Daugavpils	27	50	44	47	39	40	-	65/80/65/100/2x80
Dundaga	30	-	-	-	-	-	-	15
Kuldīga	30	40	47	52	25	35	-	65/5x80
Liepāja	21	23	39	26	33	35	-	50
Limbaži	21	-	-	-	-	-	-	13

Location	M1	M2	M3	M4	M5	M6	M7	kW
Rēzekne	27	50	44	47	39	37	-	5x100/5
Rīga	28	31	43	45	48	44	59	5x85/74/80
Valmiera	21	51	54	50	33	37	-	65/3x80/65/25
Viesīte	38	46	60	53	26	23	-	16

+ sites with txs below 10kW.

LEBANON

Systems: # PAL-B/G [E]; DVB-T2 (MPEG4) [E] planned

TÉLÉ-LIBAN (Pub) ✉ Tallet El Khayat, Corniche canal 7, P.O.Box 4848, Beirut ☎ +961 1 786930 **W:** www.teleliban.com.lb **L.P:** CEO: Talal El Makdessi **Chs:** Channel 1, Channel 2 **Txs: Channel 1:** Beirut ch7 (50kW) & netw., **Channel 2:** Beirut ch9 & netw. – **AL-JADEED TV (Comm)** ✉ BP 110, 5958 Beirut ☎ +961 1 303300 **E:** info@aljadeed.tv **W:** www.aljadeed.tv **Txs:** (-). – **AL-MANAR TV** ✉ BP 354/25, Beirut ☎ +961 1 276000 **E:** info@almanar.com.lb **W:** almanar.com.lb **Txs:** (-). – **FUTURE TELEVISION (Comm)** ✉ BP 13-6052, Sanayeh, Beirut ☎ +961 1 355355 **W:** www.futuretvnetwork.com **Txs:** (-). – **LEBANESE BROADCASTING CORP. (LBC) (Comm)** ✉ BP 165853, Zouk 111, Beirut ☎ +961 9 850850 **E:** info@lbcgroup.tv **W:** www.lbcgroup.tv **L.P:** SM: Pierre Al Daher. **Txs:** (-). – **MURR TELEVISION (MTV) (Comm)** ✉ Ashrafieh Fouad Chehab Street, RML Building, Beirut ☎ +961 1 841020 **W:** www.mtv.com.lb **L.P:** Chmn/CEO: Michel El Murr. **Txs:** (-). – **NATIONAL BROADCASTING NETWORK (NBN) (Comm)** ✉ BP 13-6633 Chouran, Beirut ☎ +961 1 841020 **E:** info@nbn.com.lb **W:** www.nbn.com.lb **Txs:** (-).

LESOTHO

System: DVB-T2 (MPEG4) [E]

LESOTHO TELEVISION (LTV) (Gov) ✉ P.O.Box 552, Maseru 0100 ☎ +266 22323808 **W:** www.facebook.com/LNBS-Lesotho-tv-407313100120153.

DTT Tx Network
Tx Operator: StarTimes **M(partly✪):** multiprgr **Txs:** MFN

LIBERIA

System: DVB-T2 (MPEG4) [E]

LIBERIA BROADCASTING SYSTEM (LBS) (Pub) ✉ P.O.Box 594, Paynesville ☎ +231 886669808 **E:** ledgeehood@elbcradio.com **W:** elbcradio.com **L.P:** DG: Ledgerhood J. Rennie – **CLAR TV (Comm)** ✉ Pegasus Building, Mechlin St. 231, Monrovia ☎ +231 776016778 **E:** thissong2050@yahoo.com **W:** www.facebook.com/ClarTv **L.P:** SM: Ahmed Pabai – **DCTV (Comm)** ✉ P.O.Box 1312, Monrovia ☎ +231 777130958 **W:** www.facebook.com/Voicetvliberia – **POWER TV (Comm)** ✉ Broad & Gurley St., Monrovia ☎ +231 886518418 **W:** www.facebook.com/power9tv – **REAL TV (Comm)** ✉ Duport St., Paynesville ☎ +231 770142319 **E:** abkollie2002@yahoo.com **W:** www.facebook.com/RealTV3 **L.P:** SM: Aaron Kollie.

DTT Tx Network
Tx Operator: StarTimes **M(partly✪):** multiprgr **Txs:** MFN

LIBYA

Systems: PAL-B/G [E] ; DVB-T2 (MPEG4) [E] planned

National Station
LIBYA NATIONAL CHANNEL (LNC) (Gov) ✉ Al Ashat Street, Tripoli ☎ +218 21 3402160 **E:** info@ltv.ly **W:** www.ltv.ly **Txs:** (pol.H) Tripoli ch6 (20kW) & network.

Local Stations not shown.

LIECHTENSTEIN

NB: No terrestrial TV station.

LITHUANIA

System: DVB-T (MPEG4) [E]

National Stations
LIETUVOS NACIONALINIS RADIJAS IR TELEVIZIJA (LRT) (Pub) ✉ Konarskio g. 49, 03123 Vilnius ☎ +370 5 2363100 **E:** lrt@lrt.lt **W:** www.lrt.lt **L.P:** DG: Monika Garbačiauskaitė-Budrienė. **Chs (terr.):** LRT Televizija, LRT Plius– **ALL MEDIA LITHUANIA (Comm)** ✉ P. Lukšio g. 23, LT-09132 Vilnius ☎ +370 5 2030101 **E:** info@@tv3.lt **W:** www.tv3.lt **L.P:** CEO: Laura Blaževičiūtė **Chs:** TV3, TV6, TV8 – **DELFI TV (Comm)** ✉ Gynėjų g. 16, 01109 Vilnius ☎ +370 5 2045400 **E:** info@delfi.lt **W:** www.delfi.lt **L.P:** Dir: Vytautas Benokraitis – **LIETUVOS RYTAS TV (Comm)** ✉ Gedimino pr. 12 A, 01103 Vilnius ☎ +370 5 2743718 **E:** tv@lrytas.lt **W:** tv.lrytas.lt **L.P:** Dir: Audrius Siaurusevičius – **UAB LAISVAS IR NEPRIKLAUSOMAS KANALAS (Comm)** ✉ Šeškinės g. 20, 07156 Vilnius ☎ +370 5 2431058 **E:** lnk@lnk.lt **W:** lnk.lt **L.P:** DG: Zita Sarakienė **Chs**: LNK, TV1, BTV, Info TV, 2TV.

Local Stations (all Comm)
Balticum TV: Taikos pr. 101d, 94198 Klaipėda; ch40✪ (Plungė 1.66kW), ch45✪ (Girulai 0.05kW). **Dzukijos televizija:** Rotušės a. 2, 62141 Alytus; ch30 (2.5kW). **FMT TV:** Vilniaus g. 31, 01402 Vilnius; ch24 (Papliauškos 1kW, Trakai 0.93kW). **Marijampoles televizija:** Gedimino g. 11, 68307 Marijampolė; ch41 (1kW). **Pukas-TV:** Ringuvos g. 61, 45242 Kaunas; ch54 (Juragiai 0.8kW). **Roventos TV:** Draugystės g. 18-1, 89168 Mažeikiai; ch58 (Mažeikiai 1.6kW). **Šiauliu televizija:** Liejyklos g. 10, 78147 Šiauliai; ch30 (Bubai 3.2kW). **TV7:** Chemikų g. 138a, 55218 Jonava; ch40 (0.3kW). **TVP Wilno:** Naugarduko g. 76, 03202 Vilnius (via DTT mux "R"). **Ventos regionine televizija:** Ventos g. 32a, Venta, 85316 Akmenės r.; ch37 (Venta 2kW).

DTT Tx Networks
Tx Operator: Lietuvos radijo ir televizijos centras (LRTC) **W:** www.telecentras.lt **M1:** LRT Televizija HD, LRT Plius HD, LRT Televizija (SD), LRT Plius (SD) **M2:** LNK, TV3, TV1, BTV, TV6, TV8, Info TV, Lietuvos rytas TV, 2TV, Delfi TV, Nastoyashcheye Vremya (RFE/RL) **Regional Mux (R):** TVP Info, TVP Historia, TVP Polonia, TVP Wilno, Nuta TV, Power TV.

Location	M1	M2	R	kW
Bubiai	34	22	-	32/21
Druskininkai	40	47	-	7.6/3.5
Giruliai	29	60	-	30/19
Ignalina	35	28	-	5.1/4.7
Juragiai	21	44	-	37/19
Moletai	48	57	-	7/3.6
Nida	29	60	-	5
Pažagieniai	32	29	-	25/9
Rokiškis	32	49	-	8/2
Švekšna	29	60	-	10/1
Švenčionys	35	28	33	8/6/1
Tauragė	29	60	-	35/40
Utena	35	28	-	11/6
Varena	40	47	-	7/4
Viešintos	32	49	-	7
Vilnius	48	57	31	120/32/5
Visaginas	35	28	-	5.1/4.7

+ sites with only txs below 5kW

LORD HOWE ISLAND (Australia)

NB: No terrestrial TV station.

LUXEMBOURG

System: DVB-T (MPEG2) [E]

RTL GROUP (Comm) ✉ 43, blvd Pierre Frieden, 1543 Luxembourg ☎ +352 24861 **W:** www.rtlgroup.com; www.rtl.lu **L.P:** CEO (RTL Group): Thomas Rabe. **NB:** RTL Group is the company holding for several radio & TV enterprises. Channel distributed terrestrially via txs in Luxembourg: **RTL Télé Lëtzebuerg, den 2ten RTL** (in Luxembourgish); **RTL4, RTL5, RTL7, RTL8** (in Dutch, for viewers in the Netherlands); **Club RTL** (in Flemish, for viewers in Belgium); **Plug RTL, RTL TVI** (in French, for viewers in Belgium).

DTT Tx Networks
Tx Operator: BCE **W:** www.bce.lu **M1:** Club RTL, Plug RTL, RTL TVI, RTL4, RTL5, RTL7 **Tx:** ch24 (Dudelange 40kW) **M2:** RTL Télé Lëtzebuerg, RTL Télé Lëtzebuerg HD, den 2ten RTL, den 2ten RTL HD **Tx:** ch27 (Dudelange 145kW) **M3:** RTL8, Luxe TV **Tx:** ch21 (Dudelange 200kW).

MACAU (China, SAR)

System: DTMB [E]

TELEDIFUSÃO DE MACAU S.A. (TDM) (Pub) CP 446, Macau ☎ +853 28520206 **E:** tdmadm@tdm.com.mo **W:** www.tdm.com.mo **L.P:** Chmn: Lo Song Man.

DTT Tx Networks
Tx Operator: TDM **M1:** TDM Ou Mun, Canal Macau, TDM Informação, TDM Entretenimento ⌘ R. Macau **M2:** CCTV-1, CCTV-5, CCTV-13, CGTN, CGTN Documentary, FJTV, HBS World, SETV, GRT World **M3:** TDM HD, TDM Vida.

Location	M1	M2	M3
SFN	24	43	48

MADAGASCAR

Systems: DVB-T2 (MPEG4) [E]; § SECAM-K1 [VHF=K]

National Station
TELEVISIONA MALAGASY (TVM) (Pub) BP 271, 101 Antananarivo ☎ +261 20 2221784 **E:** webtvmalagasy@gmail.com **W:** www.facebook.com/tvm.malagasy.officiel.

Local Stations not shown.

DTT Tx Network
Licensee: StarTimes **M(partly✪):** multiprgr **Txs:** MFN.

MADEIRA (Portugal)

System: DVB-T (MPEG4) [E]

RTP MADEIRA (Pub) Rua Caminho de Santo António 145, 9020-002 Funchal ☎ +351 291709100 **E:** martim.santos@rtp.pt **W:** www.rtp.pt/rtpmadeira **L.P:** Dir: Martim Santos.

DTT Tx Network
Licensee: Altice Portugal **Mux:** RTP1, RTP2, RTP3/RTP Madeira, RTP Memória, SIC, TVI, ARTV **Txs:** ch47 (SFN), exc. Porto Santo ch46.

MALAWI

System: DVB-T2 (MPEG4) [E]

National Station
MALAWI BROADCASTING CORP. (Pub) P.O.Box 30133, Chichiri, Blantyre 3 ☎ +265 1871971 **E:** tvmalawi@malawi.net **W:** www.mbc.mw **L.P:** DG: Aubrey Edward Sumbuleta.

Local Stations not shown.

DTT Tx Network
Licensee: Multichoice Malawi **M(partly✪):** MBC TV, Luso, God News Broadcasting Services (GBS), Timveni, Luntha, Channel for All Africa (CAN), Calvary (CFC), Times, Hope, Zodiak, Joy, Matindi, Ufulu, Beta, Ufulu, Angaliba, African Bible College (ABC), Laura TV **Txs:** MFN.

MALAYSIA

System: DVB-T2 (MPEG4) [E]

RADIO TELEVISYEN MALAYSIA (RTM) (Gov) Dept. of Broadc, Angkasapuri, Kuala Lumpur 50614 ☎ +60 3 22825333 **E:** aduan@rtm.gov.my **W:** www.rtm.gov.my **L.P:** DG: Datuk Abu Bakar Ab Rahim **Chs:** TV1, TV2, TV Okey, RTM HD Sports, RTM BES – **PERTUBUHAN BERITA NASIONAL MALAYSIA (BERNAMA) (BERNAMA NEWS CHANNEL) (Gov)** No 28, Jalan BERNAMA, Off Jalan Tun Razak, 50400 Kuala Lumpur ☎ +60 3 26939933 **E:** helpdesk@bernama.com **W:** bernama.com – **MEASAT BROADCAST NETWORK SYSTEMS SDN BHD (ASTRO) (Comm)** All Asia Broadcast Centre, Technology Park Malaysia, L/Raya Puchong-Sg.Besi,Bukit Jalil, 57000 Kuala Lumpur ☎ +60 3 95433838 **E:** wecare@astro.com.my **W:** www.astro.com.my – **MEDIA PRIMA BERHAD (Comm)** Balai Berita, Anjung Riong 31, Jalan Riong, Bangsar, 59100 Kuala Lumpur ☎ +60 3 22820353 **E:** communications@mediaprima.com.my **W:** www.mediaprima.com.my **Chs:** 8TV (**W:** www.8tv.com.my), NTV7 (**W:** www.ntv7.com.my), TV3 (**W:** www.facebook.com/TV3MALAYSIA), TV9 (**W:** www.tv9.com.my) – **ALHIJRAH MEDIA CORP. (TV ALHIJRAH) (Rlg)** Pusat Penyiaran Digital TV AlHijrah,, Kompleks Pusat Islam, Jalan Perdana, 50480 Kuala Lumpur ☎ +60 3 20281500 **E:** info@tvalhijrah.com **W:** www.tvalhijrah.com.

DTT Tx Networks
Licensee: RTM **Mux**: TV1, TV2, TV Okey, RTM HD Sports, RTM BES **Txs:** ch44 (Kuala Lumpur) & nationwide MFN. – **Licensee:** U Television **Mux✪**: multiprgr. **Txs:** MFN.

MALDIVES

System: ISDB-T [E]

PUBLIC SERVICE MEDIA (PSM) (Pub) Radio Building, Ameenee Magu, Malé, 20331 ☎ +960 3000300 **E:** info@psm.mv **W:** www.psm.mv; psmnews.mv **L.P:** Chmn: Ibrahim Hilmee **Chs:** TVM, Maldives TV, Yes TV, PSM News, Majlis.

DTT Tx Network
Licensee: PSM **Mux**: TVM, TV Maldives, Yes TV, PSM News, Majlis **Txs:** (-)

MALI

Systems: DVB-T2 (MPEG2) [E]; § SECAM-B/G [VHF=K, UHF=E]

RADIODIFFUSION TÉLÉVISION DU MALI (ORTM) (Pub) BP 171, Bamako ☎ +223 20210737 **E:** info@ortm.ml **W:** ortm.ml **L.P:** CEO: Sidiki N'fa Konaté **Chs:** ORTM, TM2 – **AFRICABLE TV (Comm)** Avenue de l'OUA - Immeuble Bemba Bagayoko, (B.P: E2498), Bamako ☎ +223 20209191 **E:** info@africabletelevision.com **W:** www.africabletelevision.com – **ENERGIE TV (Comm)** Immeuble Mhlogistique - Sotelco face a Bougouba, route de la zone industrielle, Bamako ☎ +223 77606242 **E**; mhlogistique@gmail.com **W:** www.facebook.com/etelevision – **SÉGOU TV (Comm)** Ségou – **DAMBE TV (Rlg)** Bamako ☎ +223 20800910 **E:** dambetv2018@yahoo.com.

DTT Tx Network
Tx Operator: Société Malienne de Transmission et de Diffusion (SMTD-SA) **W:** www.smtd.ml **M:** ORTM, TM2, Africable TV, Dambe TV, Energie TV, Ségou TV, France 24, TV5 Monde **Txs:** MFN.

MALTA

System: DVB-T (MPEG4) [E]

TELEVIXIN MALTA (TVM) (Pub) 75, Triq San Luqa, Gwardamanġia, Tal-Pietà, PTA 1022 ☎ +356 21225051 **E:** info@tvm.com.mt **W:** www.tvm.com.mt **L.P:** CEO (Public Broadcasting Services): Charles Dalli **Chs:** TVM, TVM2, Parlament ta' Malta TV – **F LIVING CHANNEL (Comm)** BME Studios, Triq il-Gudja, Luqa, LQA 2022 ☎ +356 21664566 **E:** flivingchannel@gmail.com **W:** fliving.tv **L.P:** Dir's (Bonaci Media Entertainment): Karl & Romina Bonaci – **NET TV (Comm)** Media.Link Communications, Dar Ċentrali, Triq Herbert Ganado, Tal-Pietà, PTA 1450 ☎ +356 21243641 **W:** netnews.com.mt **L.P:** Chmn: Joe Saliba – **ONE TV (Comm)** ONE Productions Ltd., A28b, Qasam Industrijali, Marsa, MRS 3000 ☎ +356 25682568 9 **E:** info@one.com.mt **W:** www.one.com.mt **L.P:** Chmn: Jason Micallef – **SMASH TV (Comm)** SMASH Communications Ltd., 4, Triq Tax-Xewk, Raħal Ġdid, PLA 1341 ☎ +356 21697829 **E:** smashnewsroom@gmail.com **W:** smash.godaddysites.com **L.P:** Dir: Joseph Baldacchino – **XEJK TV (Comm)** 28, T/G fi Triq Valetta, Luqa, LQA 1559 ☎ +356 21578022 **E:** info@xejkmalta.com **W:** www.xejkmalta.com.

DTT Tx Networks
Licensee: PBS **M:** TVM HD, TVM2 HD ⌘ Radju Malta, Radju Malta 2, Magic Malta, R.4 **Tx:** ch5 (Gharghur) – **Licensee:** GO PLC **W:** www.go.com.mt **M1✪:** TV2000, Fox, BBC Entertainment, MyZen TV, Nickelodeon, MTV, VH1, TSN 3 **M2✪:** Boomerang, Discovery Channel, Discovery Science, TLC, Discovery Family, National Geographic, TSN 5 **M3✪:** La 5, BBC World News, Sky News, Bloomberg, Lifetime, Travel Channel, History Channel, Trace TV **M4✪:** Mediaset Italia, FOX Life, Cartoonito, JimJam, Animal Planet, AMC, Eurosport 2 **M5✪:** GO Stars, ITV Choice, CBS Reality, Food Network, Cartoon Network, Nat Geo Wild, H2, TSN 4 **M6✪:** Rai 1, Rai 2, Rai 3, Disney Channel, Nick Jr, Crime & Investigation, TSN 6 **M7✪:** Italia 1, Canale 5, Rete 4, Fine Living Network, E! Entertainment, Baby TV, TSN 1 **M8✪:** Weather & Info, Euronews, CNN International, CNBC Europe, Eurosport, TSN 2 **M9:** TVM, TVM 2, One TV,

Net TV, Smash TV, F Living, Xejk TV, Parlament ta' Malta TV.

Location	M1	M2	M3	M4	M5	M6	M7	M8	M9
SFN	35	28	31	38	45	56	58	60	43

MARSHALL ISLANDS (USA associated)

NB: No terrestrial TV station.

MARTINIQUE (France)

System: DVB-T (MPEG4) [E]

MARTINIQUE LA 1ÈRE (Pub) 1 rue Loulou Boislaville, Pointe-Simon Tour Lumina, F-97263 Fort-de-France ☎ +596 596595200 **W:** la1ere.francetvinfo.fr/martinique – **KANAL MARTINIQUE TÉLÉVISION (KMT) (Comm)** Voie n° 7, Renéville, F-97200 Fort-de-France ☎ +596 596718604 **E:** webmaster@kmttelevision.com **W:** kmttelevision.com **L.P:** Pres: Roland Laouchez – **ZITATA TV (Comm)** quartier Sud Batelière, F-97233 Schoelcher **W:** www.facebook.com/Zitata.mq **L.P:** Dir: Max Monrose – **VIAATV (Comm)** 2 Habitation la Trompeuse, F-97232 Le Lamentin ☎ +596 596754444 **E:** contact@viaatv.tv **W:** viaatv.tv **L.P:** DG: Patrick Jean-Pierre.

DTT Tx Network
Tx Operator: TDF **M:** Martinique la 1ère HD, France 2-5*, Franceinfo, Arte, viàATV, KMT **Txs:** MFN. **Local Mux:** Zitata TV **Txs:** MFN *) France 4 will cease in 2021

MAURITANIA

System: DVB-T2 (MPEG4) [E]

TÉLÉDIFFUSION DE MAURITANIE (TDM) (Pub) Ilot A lot Nr 627/TV-Zeina, BP 5176, Nouakchott ☎ +222 45255548 **E:** tdm@tdm.mr **W:** www.tdm.mr **L.P:** DG: Mohamed Dieh Sidaty **Chs:** El Mouritania, El Mouritania 2.

DTT Tx Network
Tx Operator: TDM **M:** El Mahdara, Al Mouritania, El Mouritania 2, Arriadia, Athagavia, El Barlemania, Sahel TV, El Watania, Chinguitt TV, El Mourabitoune, Chaine Promotionnelle TDM **Txs:** MFN

MAURITIUS

System: DVB-T (MPEG2) [E]

MAURITIUS BROADCASTING CORP. (MBC) (Pub) BP 48, Curepipe ☎ +230 6755001 **E:** dirgen@mbc.intnet.mu **W:** www.mbcradio.tv **L.P:** DG (acting): Anooj Ramsurrun.

DTT Tx Networks
Licensee: Multi Carrier Mauritius Ltd Clement Charoux Street, Malherbes, Curepipe ☎ +230 6753234 **E:** mcml@multi-carrier.net **W:** www.multi-carrier.net **M1:** MBC1, MBC2, MBC3, MBC Digital 4, Cine 12, TV5 Monde, Zoom TV ⌘ RM1, RM2, Kool FM **M2:** Sports 11, CCTV-9, France 24, MBC Knowledge, Bhojpuri Channel, BBC World News **M3:** Senn Kreol, DD Podhigai, DD Sahyadri, DD Saptagiri, DD Urdu Channel ⌘ Best FM **Txs:** MFN

MAYOTTE (France)

System: DVB-T (MPEG4) [E]

MAYOTTE LA 1ÈRE (Pub) Piste de la Carrière, Les Hauts-Vallons, F-97600 Mamoudzou ☎ +262 269601017 **W:** la1ere.francetvinfo.fr/mayotte – **KWEZI TÉLÉVISION (KTV) (Comm)** F-97610 Dzaoudzi, Ile de Mayotte **E:** tv@kwezi.fr **W:** www.linfokwezi.fr **L.P:** Patrick Millan – **TÉLÉMANTE (Comm)** 1, Bahoni Ld Pamandzi, F-97615 Dzaoudzi, Ile de Mayotte ☎ +262 639694792 **E:** telemante@gmail.com **W:** telemante.fr **L.P:** Pres: Thierry Mac-Luckie.

DTT Tx Network
Tx Operator: TDF **Mux:** Mayotte la 1ère HD, France 2-5*, Franceinfo, Arte, KTV, Télémante **Txs:** MFN. *) France 4 will cease in 2021

MEXICO

System: ATSC [A]

National Stations
AZTECA, SA DE C.V. (Comm) Periférico Sur 4121, Col. Fuentes del Pedregal, México, D.F. 14140 ☎ +52 55 30991313 **E:** webtv@tvazteca.com **W:** www.tvazteca.com **L.P:** CEO: Benjamin Salinas Sada. **Chs:** Azteca 7, Azteca Trece. **Txs: Azteca 7:** XHIMT-TDT Ciudad de México ch24 (464kW) & relay txs; **Azteca Trece:** XHDF-TDT Ciudad de México ch25 (468kW) & relay txs. – **CADENA TRES I, SA DE C.V. (Comm)** Mariano Escobedo #700, Col. Anzures, Delegación Miguel Hidalgo, Ciudad de México, D.F. 11590 ☎ +52 55 51283000 **W:** www.imagentv.com **Ch:** Imagen Televisión **Txs:** XHCTMX-TDT Ciudad de México ch29 (295kW) & relay txs. – **TELEVISA, SA DE C.V. (Comm)** 2000 Avenida Vasco De Quiroga Santa Fe, México, D.F. 01210 ☎ +52 55 52612000 **W:** www.televisa.com **Chs:** Las Estrellas, Canal 5, Galavisión, FOROtv. **Txs: Las Estrellas:** XEW-TDT Ciudad de México ch32 (270kW) & relay txs; **Canal 5:** XHGC-TDT Ciudad de México ch31 (270kW) & relay txs; **FOROtv:** XHTV-TDT Ciudad de México ch49 (270kW) & relay txs; **Galavisión:** XEQ-TDT Ciudad de México ch22 (270kW) & relay txs.

Regional/Local Stations not shown.

MICRONESIA (USA associated)

Systems: NTSC-M [A]; DVB-T (MPEG2)

WAAB-TV (Gov) Department of Youth and Civic Affairs, P.O.Box 30, Colonia, Yap, FM 96943 ☎ +1 691 3502502 **Tx:** ch7 (1kW) – **KPON-TV (Comm)** Central Micronesia Communications Inc, P.O.Box 460, Kolonia, Pohnpei, FM 96941. **Tx:** Pohnpei ch7 (1kW) – **TTTK-TV (Comm)** Chuuk, FM 96942. **Tx:** Moen ch7 (0.1kW).

MOLDOVA

Systems: DVB-T2 (MPEG4) [E]; § SECAM-D/K [R], § PAL-D/K

National Stations
TELERADIO-MOLDOVA (Pub) str. Hâncești nr. 64, 2018 Chișinău ☎ +373 22 723380 **E:** tvdir@trm.md **W:** www.trm.md **L.P:** Pres: Olga Bordeianu **Ch:** Moldova 1, Moldova 2 – **CANAL 2 (Comm)** bd. D.Cantemir nr. 1/1, 2001 Chișinău ☎+373 22 809112 **W:** www.canal2.md – **CANAL 3 (Comm)** str. Bănulescu-Bodoni nr. 57/1, 2102 Chișinău ☎ +373 22 854615 **E:** info@mediaproduction.md **W:** www.canal3.md – **JURNAL TV (Comm)** str. Vlaicu Pârcalab 63, 2012 Chișinău ☎ +373 22 235008 **E:** contact@jurnaltv.md **W:** jurnaltv.md – **N4 (Comm)** str. Mihai Eminescu, 41/1, 2012 Chișinău ☎ +373 22 821801 **E:** office@n4.md **W:** n4.md – **PRIME (Comm)** str. Bănulescu-Bodoni nr. 57/1, 2005 Chișinău ☎ +373 22 244746 **E:** info@prime.md **W:** www.prime.md – **PRIMUL IN MOLDOVA (Comm)** str. A. Sciusev, nr. 76. 2012 Chișinău ☎+373 22 929394 **W:** primul.md – **PUBLIKA TV (Comm)** str. Ghioceilor nr. 1, 2071 Chișinău ☎+373 22 815555 **W:** www.publika.md.

Local Stations (all analogue)
Drochia TV: str. Gudanov, nr. 57/1, 5201 Drochia; ch28 (0.3kW). **Media TV:** str. Ștefan cel Mare nr. 14, 4101 Cimișlia; ch43 (0.4kW). **Sor-TV:** str. Calea Baltului 100a, 3000 Soroca; ch43 (0.3kW). **Studio-L:** bd. M. Eminescu nr. 23, 4301 Căușeni; ch35 (0.2kW). **TV Prim:** str. Suveranității nr. 5, of. 94, 4901 Glodeni; ch35 (0.4kW).

DTT Tx Networks
Tx Operator: Radiocomunicatii **W:** www.radiocom.md **M1:** Moldova 1, Primul în Moldova, TVR Moldova, Jurnal TV, Prime, TV8, NTV Moldova, Publika TV, STS (Mega), Canal 2, Canal 3, Pro TV Chișinău, ⌘ R. Moldova, R. Micul Samaritean **M2:** tbd

Location	M1	M2	Location	M1	M2
Cahul	36	28*	Mîndreștii Noi	22	24*
Căușeni	21	29*	Strășeni	31	26*
Chisinau	56	58	Trifești	28	36*
Cimișlia	36	28*	Ungheni	22	24*
Edineț	30	37*	+ translators *) F.pl		

Gagauzia

GRT (Pub): str. Lenin nr. 134, 3802 Comrat; Vulcănești ch24 (0.2kW), Comrat ch36 (0.2kW), Copceac ch47 (0.03kW) – **ATV:** str. Tretiacov nr. 4, of. 36, 3801 Comrat; ch40 (0.2kW).

TRANSNISTRIA

PRIDNESTROVSKAYA GTRK (PGTRK) per. Khristoforovo 5,

3300 Tiraspol ☎ +373 533 25708 **W:** tv.pgtrk.ru **L.P:** Dir: Igor Nikitenko **Ch:** Pervyy Pridnestrovskiy.

Local Stations not shown.

DTT Tx Networks
Licensee: Interdnestrkom **W:** www.idc.md **M1:** tbd **M2✪:** TSV, Russkiy Bestseller, Rossiya 24, Moslva 24, Moskva Doveriye, Disney Channel, Yu, TVTs International, RU.TV, ⌘ R. DFM, Russkoye R., Hit FM, R. Maksimum **M3✪:** Rossiya 1, NTV, Pervyy Kanal, STS, Ren TV, TV3, Pervyy Pridnestrovskiy, Match TV, TNT ⌘ R. Sputnik

Location	M1	M2	M3
SFN	59	61	38

Local muxes not shown.

MONACO

System: DVB-T (MPEG4) [E]

MONACO INFO (Gov) 6 Quai Antoine 1er, 98000 Monaco ☎ +377 97983939 **E:** contact@monacobroadcast.mc **W:** monacoinfo.com; www.monacobroadcast.mc.

DTT Tx Network
Tx Operator: Monaco Media Diffusion **W:** www.mmd.mc **M:** Monaco Info HD, MMD-2 HD **Tx:** ch30 & 35 (Mont Agel).

MONGOLIA

System: DVB-T2 (MPEG4) [E]

MONGOLYN ÜNDESNII OLON NIITIYN RADIO TELEVIZ (MÜONRT) (Pub) Bayangol district, 11th subdistrict, Khuvisgalyn Rd. 3, Ulaanbaatar ☎ +976 1 1325802 **E:** info@mnb.mn **W:** www.mnb.mn **L.P:** DG: Ninjjamts Luvsandash.

Local Stations not shown.

DTT Tx Networks
Tx Operator: MRTBN **Mux 1-3 (partly✪):** multiprgr **Local Muxes L1-L4 (Ulaanbaatar) (partly✪):** multiprgr.

Location	M1	M2	M3	L1	L2	L3	L4
Ulaanbaatar	39	49	51	31	33	35	37

+ nationwide MFN

MONTENEGRO

System: DVB-T2 (MPEG4) [E]

National Stations
RADIO I TELEVIZIJA CRNE GORE (RTCG) (Pub) Bul. Džordža Vašingtona bb, 81000 Podgorica ☎ +382 20 225999 **E:** kontakt@rtcg.me **W:** www.rtcg.me **L.P:** DG: Božidar Šundić **Chs (terr.):** TVCG1, TVCG2 – **NOVA M (Comm)** Bul. Ivana Crnojevića 97, 81000 Podgorica ☎ +382 20 403505 **E:** redakcija@novam.tv **W:** novam.tv **L.P:** CEO: Ivana Sebek – **TV PRVA (Comm)** Bul. Džordža Vašingtona 56/6, 81000 Podgorica ☎ +382 20 234840 **E:** info@prvatv.me **W:** www.facebook.com/PRVACG **L.P:** Dir: Aleksandar Bošković – **TV VIJESTI (Comm)** Trg Republike bb, 81000 Podgorica ☎ +382 20 404601 **E:** desk@vijesti.me **W:** www.vijesti.me **L.P:** Dir: Slavoljub Šćekić.

Local Stations
TV Boin: Dušici bb, 81206 Tuzi; ch21 (Velja Gora). **TV Budva:** 13. jula bb, 85310 Budva; ch46 (Spas). **TV Glas Plava:** Čaršijska bb, 84325 Plav; ch38 (Kofiljača). **TV Nikšic:** Novice Cerovića 30a, 81400 Nikšić; ch23 (SFN). **TV Pljevlja:** Zekerijaha Cinare bb, 84210 Pljevlja; ch26 (Tvrdaš). **TV Sun:** Partizanska 9, 84000 Bijelo Polje; ch40 (Obrov).

DTT Tx Networks
Tx Operator: Radio difuzni centar d.o.o. **W:** rdc.co.me **M1✪(exc.*):** TVCG1*, TVCG2*, Nova M*, TV Prva*, TV Vijesti*, Nat. Geographic, 24 Kitchen, Pink 2, Nickelodeon, Arenasport 1, RTS1, RTS Sat, Happy TV, Studio B, DM Sat, Hayat Plus, Al Jazeera Balkans ⌘ R. Crne Gore*, R. 98* **M2✪(exc.*):** Fox Crime, Fox Movies, Fox Life, Arenasport 2-5, Nick Jr, Pink Film, Pink Kids, Pink Music, Elta 1 HD*, DW-TV, RTV1, O2 TV, Fashion TV.

Location	M1	M2	kW	Location	M1	M2	kW
Bjelasica	43	25	78	Tović	35	27	11.5
Lovćen	35	27	100	Tvrdaš	49	22	2.9
Sjenica	24	27	17.5				

+ sites with txs below 2kW. *) Local stns a+b: see above

MONTSERRAT (UK)

System: NTSC-M [A]

ZJB-TV (Gov) Sweeney's, Montserrat ☎ +1 664 4912885 **E:** zjb@gov.ms **W:** zjb.gov.ms **Tx:** Chance Pic ch13 – **ANTILLES TV LTD (Comm)** P.O. Box 342, Plymouth, Montserrat ☎ +1 664 4912226 **Tx:** Chance Pic ch7 (48kW).

MOROCCO

System: DVB-T (MPEG2) [E]

SOCIÉTÉ NATIONALE DE RADIODIFFUSION ET DE TÉLÉVISION (SNRT) (Pub) BP 1042, Rabat ☎ +212 537700319 **W:** www.snrt.ma **Chs (terr.):** Al Aoula, Arriyadia, Arrabia, Assadissa, Aflam, Al Maghrabia, Tamazight, Laayoune TV – **TÉLÉVISION 2M (Semi-Gov, Comm)** Km 7,3 route de Rabat Ain Sebaa, Casablanca 20250 ☎ +212 522354444 **W:** 2m.ma **L.P:** DG: Salim Cheikh – **MEDI 1 TV (Comm)** Zone Franche de Tanger, Lot 31BP, Tangier 90100 ☎ +212 539399800 **W:** medi1tv.com.

DTT Tx Networks
Tx Operator: SNRT **M1:** Al Aoula, 2M, Arriyadia, Arrabia, Al Maghribia, Assadissa, Medi 1 TV **M2:** Al Aoula HD, Arradiya HD, Assadissa HD, Aflam HD, Tamazight, Laayoune TV

Location	M1	M2
Rabat	30	23

+ nationwide MFN

CEUTA (Spain)

System: DVB-T (MPEG2, MPEG4) [E]

Local Stations
Radio Televisión Ceuta (RTVCE) (Pub): Alcalde Sanchez Prados nº 5, 51001 Ceuta.

DTT Tx Networks
Operator: Cellnex Telecom **National Muxes 1-7:** see Spain; **Local Mux Ceuta (L):** RTVCE, Canal Sur ⌘ Radio Ceuta.

Location	M1	M2	M3	M4	M5	M6	M7	L
Ceuta	28	45	21	27	25	43	32	37

MELILLA (Spain)

System: DVB-T (MPEG2, MPEG4) [E]

Local Stations
TV Melilla (TVM) (Pub): General Macías 11, 52001 Melilla. **Popular TV (Comm)**: Calle Pablo Vallescá, s/n Edif. Ánfora, 2ª Planta, 52001 Melilla .

DTT Tx Networks
Operator: Cellnex Telecom **National Muxes 1-7:** see Spain; **Local Mux Melilla (L):** TV Melilla, Popular TV, Canal Sur, Canal Sur 2.

Location	M1	M2	M3	M4	M5	M6	M7	L
Melilla	21	24	27	41	45	38	36	43

MOZAMBIQUE

System: DVB-T2 (MPEG4) [E]

TELEVISÃO DE MOÇAMBIQUE (TVM) (Pub) CP 2675, Maputo ☎ +258 21 308117 **E:** tvm@tvm.co.mz **W:** www.tvm.co.mz **L.P:** Chmn: Armando Inroga **Chs:** TVM, TVM2 – **KTV (Comm)** Av. Julius Nyerere 390, Maputo ☎ +258 21 491744 **E:** comercialktv@sapo.mz **L.P:** DG: Izilda Kayroniss Mussa – **SOICO TELEVISÃO (STV) (Comm)** Rua de Timor Leste 108, Maputo ☎ +258 21 315117 📠 +258 21 301865 **E:** stv@soico.co.mz **W:** stv.co.mz **L.P:** DG: Daniel David – **TELEVISÃO MIRAMAR (Comm)** 25 de Setembro Av., Maputo ☎ +258 21 498440 **E:** comercial@miramar.co.mz **W:** miramar.co.mz.

DTT Tx Networks
Licensee: TVM **M:** TVM, TVM2, RTP África **Txs:** MFN – **Licensee:** Multichoice Moçambique SA **M✪:** multiprgr **Txs:** MFN – **Licensee:** StarTimes **M✪:** multiprgr. **Txs:** MFN.

MYANMAR

System: DVB-T2 (MPEG4) [E]

MYANMA RADIO AND TELEVISION (MRTV) (Gov) ⌧ Naypyidaw ☎ +95 67 79483 **E:** mrtv@mptmail.net.mm **W:** www.mrtv.gov.mm – **MYAWADY TV (Mil)** ⌧ Yangon **W:** myawady.net.mn.

DTT Tx Networks
Licensee M1: MRTV **M:** MRTV HD, MRTV Hluttaw, MRTV NRC, MRTV Farmer, MRTV Sport, MITV, Education Channel, MRTV Entertainment, MRTV-4, Channel 7, 5 Plus, MNTV, Channel 9, Mizzima TV, Democratic Voice of Burma (DVB), Channel K, YTV,Fortune TV ⌘ Myanma Radio, Upper Tineyinthar, Lower Tineyinthar – **Licensee M2:** Myawady TV **M:** MWD Variety HD, MWD Movies HD, MWD Education, Knowledge and Sports HD, MWD HD, MWD Family HD, MWD Documentary HD, MWD Shopping HD ⌘ Thazin FM R. – **Licensee M3:** Forever Group **M:** MRTV-4, Channel 7, Mahabawdi Channel, Readers Channel ⌘ Teen R. Pyinsawadi FM1, Teen R. Pyinsawadi FM2, Mandalay FM R.

Location	M1	M2	M3	kW
Yangon	31	42	27	3
+ nationwide MFN				

NAMIBIA

System: DVB-T2 (MPEG4) [E]

NAMIBIAN BROADCASTING CORP. (NBC) (Pub) ⌧ Cullinan St. Northern Industrial, Windhoek 9000 ☎ +264 61 2913111 **E:** pr@nbc.na **W:** www.nbc.na **L.P:** DG: Stanley Similo **Chs:** NBC1, NBC2, NBC3, NBC4, NBC5 – **ONE AFRICA TV (Comm)** ⌧ Storch House, Storch St., Windhoek ☎ +264 61 253190 **E:** paul@mac.com.na **W:** www.oneafrica.tv **L.P:** MD: Paul van Schalkwyk – **THIS TV (Rlg)** ⌧ Windhoek **W:** www.facebook.com/thistvnamibia – **TBN NAMIBIA (Rlg)** ⌧ P.O.Box 1587, Swakopmund ☎ +264 64 401100 **E:** comments@tbnnamibia.tv **W:** www.tbnnamibia.tv.

DTT Tx Networks
Licensee: NBC **M:** NBC1, NBC2, NBC3, NBC4, NBC5, One Africa TV, TBN, Edu-TV, This TV ⌘ 10 NBC Radio prgrs **Txs:** MFN – **Licensee:** MultiChoice Namibia Pty **M✪:** M-Net, SuperSport 1, SABC Africa, Discovery, Channel O. **Txs:** MFN.

NAURU

System: DVB-T2 (MPEG4) [E]

NAURU TELEVISION (NTV) (Gov) ⌧ Government Offices, Yaren District ☎ +674 4443113.

DTT Tx Network
Licensee: Digicel **M:** multiprgr **Txs:** SFN

NEPAL

System: DVB-T2 (MPEG4) [E]

National Stations
NEPAL TELEVISION (Pub) ⌧ P.O.Box 3826, Singha Durbar, Kathmandu ☎ +977 1 4200348 **E:** info@ntv.org.np **W:** ntv.org.np **Chs:** NTV, NTV Plus, NTV News – **KANTIPUR TELEVISION (Comm)** ⌧ P.O.Box 7368, Subidhanagar, Kathmandu ☎ +977 1 4466300 **E:** info@kantipurtv.com **W:** kantipurtv.com **L.P:** MD: Kailash Sirohiya.

Local Stations not shown.

DTT Tx Network
Tx Operator: Prabhu TV **W:** www.prabhutv.com.np **M:** multiprgr **Txs:** MFN.

NETHERLANDS

System: DVB-T2 (HEVC) [E]

National Stations
NEDERLANDSE PUBLIEKE OMROEP (NPO) (Pub) ⌧ P.O.Box 26444, 1202 JJ Hilversum ☎ +31 35 6779222 **E:** voorlichting@npo.nl **W:** www.npo.nl **L.P:** Chmn: Shula Rijxman. **Chs (terr.):** NPO1, NPO2, NPO3. Prgrs for the NPO are provided by **Nederlandse Omroep Stichting (NOS):** Sumatralaan 45, 1217 GP Hilversum; **NTR:** P.O.Box 29000, 1202 MA Hilversum; and the following broadcasting organizations: **AVROTROS:** P.O.Box 2, 1200 JA Hilversum; **BNNVARA:** P.O.Box 175 1200 AD Hilversum; **EO:** P.O.Box 21000, 1202 BB Hilversum; **Human:** P.O.Box 135, 1200 AC Hilversum; **KRO-NCRV:** P.O.Box 200, 1200 AE Hilversum; **MAX:** P.O.Box 554, 2700 AM Hilversum; **PowNed:** P.O.Box 92109, 1090 AC Amsterdam; **VPRO:** P.O.Box 11, 1200 JC Hilversum; **WNL:** P.O.Box 23620, 1100 EC Amsterdam – **RTL NEDERLAND (Comm)** ⌧ P.O.Box 15016, 1200 TV Hilversum ☎ +31 35 6718718 **E:** info@rtl.nl **W:** www.rtl.nl **Chs (terr.):** RTL4, RTL5, RTL7, RTL8 – **TALPA TV (Comm)** ⌧ P.O.Box 18179, 1001 ZB Amsterdam ☎ +31 20 8007000 **E:** mediasolutions@talpanetwork.com **W:** tv.talpanetwork.com **Chs (terr.):** NET5, SBS6, Veronica TV.

Regional Stations (Pub) (via DTT Mux 1)
a) L1TV: P.O.Box 31, 6200 AA Maastricht; **b) Omroep Brabant TV:** Postbus 108, 5600 AC Eindhoven; **c) Omroep Fryslân:** P.O.Box 7600, 8903 JP Leeuwarden; **d) Omroep Zeeland TV:** P.O.Box 1090, 4388 ZH Oost-Souburg; **e) RTV Utrecht:** P.O.Box 9043, 3506 GA Utrecht; **f) RTV Drenthe:** P.O.Box 999, 9400 AZ Assen; **g) Omroep Flevoland:** P.O.Box 567, 8200 AN Lelystad; **h) Omroep Gelderland:** P.O.Box 747, 6800 AS Arnhem; **i) TV Noord:** P.O.Box 30101, 9701 BH Groningen; **j) RTV Noord Holland:** P.O.Box 9823, 1006 AM Amsterdam; **k) TV Oost:** P.O.Box 1000, 7550 BA Hengelo; **l) TV Rijmond:** P.O.Box 350, 3000 AJ Rotterdam; **m) TV West:** P.O.Box 24012, 2490 AA Den Haag.

Local Station
AT5: P.O.Box 3976, 1001 AT Amsterdam; time-shared via DTT Mux 3.

DTT Tx Networks
Licensee M1: NPO **M1:** NPO1, NPO2, NPO3, Public Regional Stations (a-m) ⌘ NPO R.1, 2, 3FM, 4, 5, Soul & Jazz, FunX, Public reg. radio stns – **Licensee M2-M5:** KPN **W:** www.kpn.com **M2✪:** RTL4, RTL5, RTL7, NET5, SBS6 ⌘ Classic FM, R. 10, Q-Music, R.Veronica, Sky R. 101 FM, Slam!FM, 100%NL **M3✪:** BBC One, BBC Two, MTV, NGC, TLC, FOX Sports 1, Fox Sports 2/ONS/Cartoon Netw./AT5, 24Kitchen ⌘ Arrow Classic Rock, BNR Nieuwsradio, R.538 **M4✪:** Één, Canvas, Discovery Channel, Eurosport, Comedy Central, RTL8, Veronica TV/Disney XD, Pornhub TV **M5✪:** CNN, Nickelodeon/Spike, Xite, FOX, Investigation Discovery, RTL Z, Ketnet/OP12 ⌘ BBC Radio 1-4, SubLime FM, VRT R.1, R.2, Klara, Studio Brussel, MNM.

Location	M1*	M2	M3	M4	M5	kW
Alkmar	34j	36	23	47	44	40/20/16/20/19
Almere	26g	32	45	24	27	5/2x10/2x5
Alphen a.d.R.	39m	32	45	24	27	12/3x15/10
Amsterdam (Zuidas)	34j	32	45	24	27	5/9/10/8/7
Apeldoorn	26h	42	31	30	28	20
Arnhem	26h	42	31	30	28	20/2x40/2x20
Breda	33b	32	31	30	35	15/20/15/20/15
Den Bosch	33b	42	31	30	28	5/20/2x5/20
Den Haag (Bezuidenh.)	39m	32	45	24	27	3x15/2x10
Den Haag (Zichtenb.)	39m	32	45	24	27	4x10/5
Deventer	22k	36	23	47	44	10
Doetinchem	26h	42	31	30	28	2x20/40/2x20
Eindhoven (Croy)	30b	42	31	30	28	15
Enschede	22k	36	23	47	44	20/19/2x20/10
Goes	21d	32	29	48	35	2x10/9/2x10
Groningen	40i	46	21	33	25	20
Haarlem	34j	32	45	24	27	2x10/20/2x13
Heerlen	33a	21	31	24	27	2x20/40/2x20
Helmond	33b	42	31	30	28	15
Hengelo	22k	36	23	47	44	2x20/3x40
Hilversum	34j	32	45	24	27	3x15/2x10
Hoogersmilde	22f	46	21	33	25	3x40/29/40
IJsselstein	39e	32	45	24	27	2x15/14/10/5
Krimpen a.d.IJ.	21l	32	45	24	27	10
Leeuwarden	40c	46	21	33	25	20
Lelystad	26g	36	23	47	44	2x20/10/2x20
Loon op Zand	33b	42	31	30	28	20/4x15
Maarssen	39e	32	45	24	27	10/13/12/9/8
Maastricht	33a	21	31	24	27	2x10/15/10/9
Nijmegen	26h	42	31	30	28	10/20/2x14/20
Oegstgeest	39m	32	45	24	27	15/2x12/2x10
Oss	26h	42	31	30	28	19/4x10
Oss	33b	-	-	-	-	10
Roermond	33a	21	31	24	27	10
Rotterdam (Waalhaven)	21l	32	45	24	27	10
Sittard	33a	21	31	24	27	20/17/20/18/17
Sliedrecht	21l	32	45	24	27	10/2x8/2x6
Utrecht	39e	32	45	24	27	10/4x5

Location	M1*	M2	M3	M4	M5	kW
Veenendal	39e	42	31	30	28	15/17/2x16/21
Veenendal	26h	-	-	-	-	15
Venlo	33a	21	31	30	28	3x20/5/40
Zoetermeer	39m	32	45	24	27	10/6/7/5/2
Zwolle	22k	36	23	47	44	2x19/20/19/18

+ sites with txs below 10kW. Pol=V. *) incl. regional stns a-m (see above).

NEW CALEDONIA (France)

System: DVB-T (MPEG4) [E]

NOUVELLE CALEDONIE LA 1ÈRE (Pub) 1, rue Maréchal Leclerc, F-98848 Nouméa CEDEX ☎ +687 687274327 **W:** la1ere.francetvinfo.fr/nouvellecaledonie **L.P:** Dir: Walles Kotra – **CALEDONIA (Comm)** BP 2086, F-98860 Koné ☎ +687 687299040 **E:** redaction@caledonia.nc **W:** www.caledonia.nc.

DTT Tx Networks
Tx Operator: TDF **Mux:** Nouvelle Caledonie la 1ère, France 2-5*, Franceinfo, Arte, Caledonia **Txs:** MFN *) France 4 will cease in 2021

NEW ZEALAND

System: DVB-T (MPEG4) [NZ]

National Stations
MAORI TELEVISION (Pub) P.O.Box 113-017, Newmarket, Auckland 1149 ☎ +64 9 5397000 **W:** www.maoritelevision.com – **TELEVISION NEW ZEALAND (TVNZ) (Pub)** P.O.Box 3819, Auckland ☎ +64 9 9167000 **W:** tvnz.co.nz **L.P:** CEO: Kevin Kenrick **Chs:** TVNZ 1, TVNZ 2, TVNZ Duke – **MEDIAWORKS TV (Comm)** P.O.Box 92624, Symonds St., Auckland 1150 ☎ +64 9 9289000 **E:** replies@mediaworks.co.nz **W:** www.mediaworks.co.nz **Chs:** TV3, TV3+, Bravo, The Edge TV, The Breeze TV – **PRIME TELEVISION (Comm)** 1 John Glenn Ave., North Harbour, Auckland ☎ +64 9 4140700 **E:** info@primetv.co.nz **W:** www.primetv.co.nz.

Local Stations not shown.

DTT Tx Networks
Tx Operator: Kordia **W:** kordiasolutions.com **M1:** TVNZ 1 HD, TVNZ +1, TVNZ 2 HD, TVNZ +1, TVNZ Duke HD **M2:** TV3 HD, TV3+, Bravo, Bravo +1, The Edge TV **M3:** Parliament TV, Māori Television, CTV8, Prime, TV29, Apna, Al Jazeera, Hope Channel, HGTV, Choice TV ⌘ R. NZ National, R. NZ Concert, BaseFM.

Location	M1	M2	M3
Auckland (Waiatarua)	29	33	45

+ nationwide MFN

NICARAGUA

System: ISDB-TB [A]; § NTSC [A] ⇩2021

National Stations ([a]=analogue)
CANAL 15 NICARAGÜENSE (Gov) Managua **Txs:** Managua [a]ch15 & MFN – **CANAL 6 (Comm)** 3 1/2 Carretera Sur Contigo Shell, Managua ☎ +505 22660118 **E:** info@canal6.com.ni **W:** canal6.com.ni **Txs:** ch20 (Managua) + MFN – **CANAL 10 (Comm)** Hotel Mansión Teodolinda, 2c, Abajo ☎ +505 22227788 **W:** www.canal10.com.ni **Tx:** Managua [a]ch10 – **CANAL DE NOTICIAS DE NICARAGUA (CDNN) (Comm)** Carretera a Masaya Km. 4½, Motorama ½c al Su, Managua ☎ +505 22670170 **W:** www.cdnn23.com **Tx:** Managua [a]ch23 – **MULTINOTICIAS (CANAL 4)** Del Montoya, 1c al Sur, 1c al Este, Managua ☎ +505 22663420 **W:** www.canal4.com.ni **Tx:** Managua [a]ch4 – **NICAVISIÓN (CANAL 12) (Comm)** Apdo 2766, Managua ☎ +505 22660691 **W:** www.canal12.com.ni **Tx:** [a]ch12 – **TELENICA (CANAL 8) (Comm)** Apdo Postal 3611, Hotel Mansión Teodolinda 1c al Sur, y ½ Abajo ☎ +505 22665021 **W:** www.tn8.tv **Tx:** Managua [a]ch8 – **TELEVICENTRO (CANAL 2) (Comm)** Apdo Postal 688, Managua ☎ +505 22682222 **E:** canal2@canal2.com.ni **W:** www.canal2.com.ni **Tx:** Managua [a]ch2 (25kW) – **ENLACE NICARAGUA (CANAL 21) (Rlg)** 12 Avenida SO, Distrito II, Managua ☎ +505 22512000 **E:** nicaragua@enlace.org **W:** www.enlace.org/nicaragua **Tx:** Managua [a]ch21. Rel. TBN (USA).

Local Stations not shown.

NIGER

System: DVB-T2 (MPEG4) [E]

OFFICE DE RADIODIFFUSION TELEVISION DU NIGER (ORTN) (Gov) BP 309, Niamey ☎ +227 20723686 **E:** ortny@intnet.net **W:** www.ortn.ne **L.P:** DG: Loïc Crespin. **Chs:** Télé-Sahel, Tal-TV – **TÉNÉRÉ TV (Comm)** BP 13600, Niamey ☎ +227 20736576 **E:** tenerefm@intnet.net **W:** www.facebook.com/TENERE-TV-176221962941923.

DTT Tx Network)
Tx Operator: ORTN **M:** Télé-Sahel, Tal-TV, Ténéré TV **Txs:** MFN.

NIGERIA

Systems: DVB-T2 (MPEG4) [E]; § PAL-B [E] ⇩2021

National Station
NIGERIAN TELEVISION AUTHORITY (NTA) (Pub) P.M.B 113, Garki, Abuja ☎ +234 9 2346907 **E:** info@nta.ng **W:** www.nta.ng **L.P:** DG: Yakubu Ibn Mohammed **Chs:** NTA, NTA2, reg. stns.

Local Stations
DBN Television (Comm): The Dream Centre, Durosinmi etti Drive, Lekki Phase 1, Lagos. **Galaxy TV (Comm):** Lagos. **Lagos TV (Comm)** Lagos. **Minaj Broadcast International (MBI) (Comm):** P.O.Box 3975, Mushin, Lagos.

DTT Tx Network
Tx Operator: StarTimes **M(partly✪):** multiprgr **Txs:** MFN.

NIUE

Systems: # PAL-B [NZ]; DTT planned

TV NIUE (Gov) P.O.Box 68, Alofi ☎ +683 4026 **E:** gm.bcn@mail.gov.nu **W:** www.facebook.com/tvniue **L.P:** GM: Trever Tiakia **Txs:** Makefu ch4 (0.01kW), Alofi ch6 (0.75kW), Mutulau ch8 (0.04kW).

NORFOLK ISLAND (Australia)

System: DVB-T (MPEG2) [AU]

TV NORFOLK ISLAND (TVNI) Taylors Road, Norfolk Island 2899, Australia ☎ +672 3 52500 **Txs:** **TVNI:** ch10 (Mt. Pitt); **Rel. Hope Channel (USA):** ch7V (Mt. Pitt 0.02kW).

DTT Tx Network
Tx Operator: Norfolk Telecom **M1:** ABC HD, ABC2, ABC News 24 ⌘ ABC Jazz R., ABC Double J. **M2:** Seven, Imparja, SBS One, SBS Two **Txs: M1:** ch25 (Mt. Pitt 0.02kW), **M2:** ch32 (Mt. Pitt 0.02kW)

NO. MARIANA IS (USA associated)

NB: No terrestrial TV station.

NORTH MACEDONIA

System: DVB-T (MPEG4) [E]

National Stations
NACIONALNA RADIO TELEVIZIJA (NRT) (Pub) bul. Goce Delčev bb, 1000 Skopje ☎ +389 2 5119899 **W:** www.mtv.com.mk **L.P:** DG: Marjan Cvetkovski **Chs (terr.):** MRT1, MRT2, Sobranski kanal – **ALFA (Comm)** Gradski stadion, 1000 Skopje ☎ +389 2 3217170 **W:** www.alfa.mk – **ALSAT-M (Comm)** ul. Krste Misirkov 7, 1000 Skopje ☎ +389 2 3290364 **W:** alsat-m.tv – **KANAL 5 (Comm)** ul. Skupi bb, 1000 Skopje ☎ +389 2 3091551 **E:** kanal5@kanal5.com.mk **W:** kanal5.com.mk – **TV SITEL (Comm)** ul. Gradski stadion bb, 1000 Skopje ☎ +389 2 3116566 **E:** marketing@sitel.com.mk **W:** sitel.com.mk – **TV TELMA (Comm)** ul. Nikola Parapunov bb, 1000 Skopje ☎ +389 2 3076677 **E:** telma@telma.com.mk **W:** telma.com.mk.

Local Stations not shown.

DTT Tx Networks
Licensee M1-3+6: A1 Makedonija **W:** www.a1.mk **M1✪(exc.*):** MRT 1*, MRT 2*, MRT Sobraniski Kanal*, Nasha TV, DM Sat, Cine Star Premiere 1, Cine Star Action TV, Sport Klub 3, Da Vinci Learning, Baby TV, HBO, HBO 2, Shenja TV, Viasat Explore, TV1000 **M2✪:** TV 24, N1 Srbija, Sport Klub, Sport Klub 4, Viasat History, Viasat Nature,

National Geographic, 24 Kitchen, Cine Star TV, FOX Life, FOX Crime, Pikaboo, Magic TV, Cinemania, Cinestar Action, CNN International **M3✪:** 1TV, RTV21 Maqedoni, Grand TV, Cine Star Premiere 2, Sport Klub 2, Sport Klub 5, FOX, FOX Movies, HBO 3, E!, Cartoon Network, Boomerang, VH 1 Adria, Hustler TV, Private TV, Top Channel, Klan HD **M6:** Alfa, Alsat-M, Kanal 5, TV Telma, TV Sitel, Local stns – **Licensee M4+5:** NRT **M4:** MRT1, MRT2, Sobraniski kanal, Sobraniski kanal HD **M5:** MRT1 HD, MRT 2 HD.

Location	M1	M2	M3	M4	M5	M6
Boskija	21	37	49	34	41	50
Crn Vrv	26	28	30	23	52	40
Mali Vlaj	32	39	41	26	36	44
Pelister	25	29	33	22	37	38
Popova Šapka	24	34	38	27	36	41
Stracin	21	41	46	37	42	50
Turtel	22	32	43	24	39	38

+ translators

NORWAY

System: DVB-T (MPEG4) [E]

National Stations
NORSK RIKSKRINGKASTING (NRK) (Pub) 🖃 0340 Oslo ☎ +47 23047000 **E:** info@nrk.no **W:** www.nrk.no **L.P:** DG: Thor Gjermund Eriksen **Chs:** NRK1 (incl. regional prgrs), NRK2, NRK3/NRK Super – **CANAL DIGITAL (Comm)** 🖃4896 Grimstad ☎ +47 81559600 **E:** kundeservice@canaldigital.no **W:** www.canaldigital.no – **DISCOVERY NETWORKS NORWAY (Comm)** 🖃 Postboks 4800, 0422 Oslo ☎ +47 21022000 **E:** resepsjon@discovery.com **W:** www.discovery.no – **TV2 (Comm)** 🖃 Postboks 7222, 5020 Bergen ☎ +47 55908070 **E:** info@tv2.no **W:** www.tv2.no **L.P:** CEO: Olav T. Sandnes.

Local Stations (all Comm) (via Mux 3)
a) TKTV: P.O.Box 8, 6501 Kristiansund; **b) TV Haugaland:** P.O.Box 408, 5501 Haugesund; **c) TV Nord:** P.O.Box 1193, 9504 Alta; **d) TV Telemark:** P.O.Box 2833, 3702 Skien; **e) TV Vest:** Lervigsveien 16, 4095 Stavanger; **f) TV Øst:** Hjellumveien 89, 2322 Ridabu.

DTT Tx Networks
Licensee: Norges televisjon AS **W:** www.ntv.no **M1:** NRK1 HD (incl. reg prgrs), NRK2 HD, NRK3/NRK Super HD **M2✪:** TV2 HD, TV2 Livsstil, TV2 Nyhetskanalen, TV2 Sport 1, TV2 Sport 2, SVT1, Eurosport Norge, BBC Brit, Disney Channel **M3✪:** TV Norge HD, MAX, FEM, VOX, TV2 Zebra HD, Frikanalen/Local Stations, Eurosport 1, Disney Jr, Viasport 1, Viasport+ **M4✪:** TV3, Viasat 4, TV6, FOX, Discovery Channel, National Geographic, TLC, History Channel, Visjon Norge, TV2 Sport Premium, BBC World News.

Location	M1	M2	M3*	M4	kW
Bagn	32	39	23f	26	50
Bergen	33	41	39	43	50
Bjerkreim	23	26	30e	27	50
Bokn	36	40	35b	44	50
Bremanger	25	28	31	46	50
Førde	35	45	32	22	10
Gamlemsveten	37	38	34a	24	50
Gausta	29	27	35	32	10
Greipstad	44	41	47	24	50
Grong	21	31	35	24	50
Gulen	37	42	26	29	50
Hadsel	45	48	38	25	50
Halden	32	45	21	38	60
Hammerfest	33	37	26c	41	50
Hemnes	42	45	48	29	50
Hovdefjell	23	33	48	36	50
Jetta	36	48	38f	21	50
Kistefjell	26	48	38	21	50
Kongsberg	41	34	44	24	50
Kongsvinger	29	48	43	28	50
Kopparen	26	40	45	23	50
Lyngdal	25	41	47	32	50
Lønahorgi	31	25	40	46	50
Melhus	33	28	25	30	50
Mosvik	44	47	46	37	50
Narvik	21	27	37	24	50
Nordfjordeid	40	44	33	27	10
Nordhue	37	31	45f	27	50
Nordkapp	30	40	43c	23	50
Oslo	33	42	30	30	50
Reinsfjell	39	42	35a	29	50
Salten	23	43	33	30	50
Skien	41	34	44d	24	50
Sogndal	21	24	34	38	50
Steigen	31	41	44	47	50
Stord	32	38	48b	47	50
Trolltind	27	39	42	34	50
Tron	26	34	40f	23	50
Varanger	28	33	41c	35	50
Vega	25	32	37	22	50

+ sites with txs below 10kW. *) incl. local stns (see above)

OMAN

Systems: DVB-T2 (MPEG4); § PAL-B/G [E]

PUBLIC AUTHORITY FOR RADIO TV (PART) 🖃 P.O.Box 1130, 113 Madinat Al Ilam, Oman ☎ +968 24603888 **E:** feedback@part.gov.om **W:** www.part.gov.om **Chs:** Oman TV General, Oman TV Sport, Oman TV Mobashir, Oman TV Cultural.

DTT Tx Network
Tx Operator: Ministry of Transport and Communications **M:** multiprgr **Txs:** MFN

PAKISTAN

Systems: # PAL-B/G [E]; DTMB [E] planned

PAKISTAN TELEVISION CORP. LTD (PTV) (Gov) 🖃 P.O.Box 1221, Islamabad 44000 ☎ +92 51 9208651 6 **E:** ptvhq@hotmail.com **W:** ptv.com.pk **Chs (terr.):** PTV Home, PTV News, regional stns, AJK TV **Txs: PTV Home:** Islamabad ch6 (50kW) & network; **PTV News:** (-) **AJK TV:** Rawlakot ch27 (5kW) & network – **ATV (Comm)** 🖃 11 -F, Model Town, Lahore ☎ +92 42 5853669 **E:** info@atv.com.pk **W:** atv.com.pk **Txs:** (-).

PALAU (USA associated)

NB: No terrestrial TV station.

PANAMA

System: DVB-T (MPEG2) [A]

National Stations
SYSTEMA ESTATAL DE RADIO Y TELEVISIÓN (SERT) (Pub) 🖃 Apt. 0843-0256, Curundu, diagonal al Ministerio de Obras Públicas, Panamá ☎ +507 5071500 **E:** administracion@sertv.gob.pa **W:** sertv.gob.pa **Chs:** SERTV – **FETV (Educ)** 🖃Ave Ricardo J. Alfaro Contiguo al Gimnasio de la USMA, Apdo.6-7295, El Dorado, Panamá ☎ +507 2308000 **W:** www.fetv.org **L.P:** DG: Manuel Santiago Blanquer i Planells – **COMPAÑÍA DIGITAL DE TELEVISIÓN, S.A (NEXT TV) (Comm)** 🖃 Via Espana Sector de Carrasquilla, Apdo. postal 87-1989, Zona 7, Panamá **W:** www.nextvpanama.com – **RPC TELEVISIÓN (Comm)** 🖃Ave 12 de Octubre, Apartado 1-1425, Panamá 8 ☎ +507 2104104 **W:** www.rpctv.com – **TELEMETRO (TLM) (Comm)** 🖃 Ave 12 de Octubre, Apartado 0827-00116, Panamá ☎ +507 2106845 **W:** www.telemetro.com **L.P:** Pres: Fernando Eleta Almarán – **TELEVISORA NACIONAL S.A (TVN) (Comm)** 🖃 Apt. 0819-07129, El Dorado, Panamá ☎ +507 2793700 **E:** tvn@tvn-2.com **W:** www.tvn-2.com **L.P:** DG: Agustin De La Guardia **Chs:** TVN, TVMAX.

Local Stations not shown.

DTT Tx Networks
Tx Operator: n/a **M1:** Tu Canal TV **M2:** Enlace, Enlace Juvenil **M3:** SERTV ⌘ R. Nacional, Crisol FM **M4:** RPC HD, TLM HD, Mall TV **M5:** TVN HD, TVN+, TVMAX HD **M6:** Hosanna Vision HD ⌘ Hosanna R. **M7:** FETV **M8:** NEXT TV, +23 ⌘ RCM R. **M9:** ATV

Location	M1	M2	M3	M4	M5	M6	M7	M8	M9
SFN	26	30	41	42	45	47	48	49	51

PAPUA NEW GUINEA

Systems: DVB-T2 (MPEG4) [E]; § PAL-B/G [NZ]

NATIONAL BROADCASTING CORP. (NBC) (Gov) 🖃 P.O.Box 1359, Boroko NCD 111 ☎ +675 3255233 **W:** www.facebook.com/NBCNewsPNG **L.P:** Chmn: Timothy Tala – **EMTV (Comm)** 🖃 P.O.Box

443, Boroko NCD 111 ☎ +675 3257322 **E:** online@emtv.com.pg **W:** emtv.com.pg **L.P:** CEO (Media Niugini Ltd): Ken Clark.

DTT Tx Network
Tx Operator: Digicel **M:** NBC TV, EMTV **Txs:** MFN

PARAGUAY

Systems: ISDB-TB [A]; § PAL-N [A] ⇩2021

National Stations
PARAGUAY TV (Gov) ✉ Avda. Alberdi 633 c/Gral Díaz, Asunción ☎ +595 21 494000 **E:** contacto@paraguaytv.gov.py **W:** www.paraguaytv.gov.py **Txs:** Asunción ch15 & relays – **LATELE (Comm)** ✉ Av. Eusebio Ayala 2995, Esq. Pasaje Tembetary, Asunción ☎ +595 21 4157400 **E:** info@latele.com.py **W:** www.latele.com.py **Txs:** Asunción ch28 & relays – **PARAVISIÓN (Comm)** ✉ Av. Mariscal López esq. Bélgica, Asunción ☎ +595 21 664380 **E:** info@paravision.com.py **W:** www.paravision.com.py **Txs:** Asunción ch19 & relays – **RED GUARANÍ (Comm)** ✉ Gral. Santos 1024 c/Concordia, Asunción ☎ +595 21 205444 **Txs:** Asunción ch17 & relays – **RED PARAGUAYA DE COMUNICACIÓN (RPC) (Comm)** ✉ Calles Comendador Nicolás Bó y Guaranies, Lambaré, Asunción ☎ +595 21 332823 **E:** commercial@rpc.com.py **W:** rpc.com.py **Txs:** Asunción ch27 & relays – **SISTEMA NACIONAL DE TELEVISIÓN (SNT) (Comm)** ✉ Av. Carlos Antonio Lopez 572, Asunción ☎ +595 21 424222 **E:** snt@snt.com.py **W:** www.snt.com.py **Txs:** Asunción ch20 & relays – **TELEFUTURO (Comm)** ✉ Andrade c/ O'Higgins, Villa Morra, Asunción ☎ +595 21 608756 **W:** telefuturo.com.py **Txs:** Asunción ch18 & relays.

Local Stations not shown.

PERU

Systems: ISDB-TB [A]; § NTSC-M [A] ⇩2021

National Stations
TV PERÚ (Pub) ✉ Av. Jose Galvez 1040, Santa Beatriz, Líma ☎ +51 1 6190707 **W:** www.tvperu.gob.pe **Txs:** ch16 (SFN) – **AMÉRICA TELEVISIÓN (Comm)** ✉ Montero Rosas 1099, Santa Beatriz, Líma ☎ +51 1 2657361 **E:** americanoticias@americatv.com.pe **W:** www.americatv.com.pe **L.P:** CEO: Erjc Jurgensen **Txs:** ch24 (SFN) – **ATV (ANDINA DE RADIODIFUSIÓN) (Comm)** ✉ Arequipa 3570, San Isidro, Apartado 270077, Líma ☎ +51 1 2212261 **W:** www.atv.pe **Txs:** ch18 (SFN) – **LATINA TELEVISIÓN (Comm)** ✉ Av. San Felipe 968, Jesús Mariá, Líma 11 ☎ +51 1 4707272 **E:** info@latina.pe **W:** www.latina.pe **Txs:** ch20 (SFN) – **PANAMÉRICANA TELEVISIÓN (Comm)** ✉ Av. Arequipa 1110, Líma ☎ +51 1 4113200 **W:** panamericana.pe **Txs:** ch26 (SFN) – **VIVA TV (Comm)** ✉ Manco Capac 333, La Victoria, Líma ☎ +51 1 4337674 **W:** www.vivatv.pe **Txs:** ch38 (SFN).

Local Stations not shown.

PHILIPPINES

Systems: ISDB-TB [A]; § NTSC-M [A] ⇩2023

National Stations
INTERCONTINENTAL BROADCASTING CORP. (IBC) (Gov) ✉ Broadcast City, Capitol Hills, Diliman, Quezon City ☎ +63 2 9318781 **L.P:** Pres/CEO: Manolito Ocampo-Cruz. **Txs:** DZTV-TV Manila ch26 & relay stns. – **PEOPLE'S TELEVISION NETWORK, INC (PTV) (Gov)** ✉ Broadcast Complex, Visayas Ave, Quezon City 1100 ☎ +63 2 9206521 **W:** www.ptv.ph **L.P:** GM: Dino Apolonio. **Txs:** DWGT-TV Manila ch42 & relay stns – **PROGRESSIVE BROADCASTING CORP. (UNTV) (Pub)** ✉ #907 ESDA Philam, Quezon City. **W:** www.untvweb.com **L.P:** Pres: Alfredo L. Henares. **Txs:** DWAO-TV Manila ch38 & relay stns – **ABC DEVELOPMENT CORP. (TV5) (Comm)** ✉ AMPC Bldg., 136 Amorsolo cor. Gamboa Sts., Legaspi Village, Makati City ☎ +63 2 8923801 **W:** www.tv5.com.ph **L.P:** Chmn: Manny V. Pangilinan. **Txs:** DWET-TV Manila ch18 & relay stns – **BROADCAST ENTERPRISES AND AFFILIATED MEDIA, INC (BEAM TV) (Comm)** ✉ 3/F The Globe Plaza 1, Pioneer Highlands South Condominiun Corp., Pioner St, Metro Manila ☎ +63 2 5864747 **W:** beam.com.ph **L.P:** Chmn: Steve Macion. **Txs:** DWKC-TV Manila ch50 & relay stns – **GMA NETWORK, INC (Comm)** ✉ EDSA, Diliman, Quezon City, Metro Manila ☎ +63 2 9285041 **W:** www.gmanetwork.com **L.P:** Chmn/CEO: Filipe Gozon. **Txs:** DZBB-TV Manila ch15 & relay stns – **NINE MEDIA CORP, INC. (Comm)** ✉ Broadcast City, Capitol Hills, Quezon City ☎ +63 2 9315080 **L.P:** Pres/CEO: Reggie Galura **Txs:** DZKB-TV Manila ch19 & relay stns – **RAJAH BROADCASTING NETWORK, INC. (2ND AVENUE) (Comm)** ✉ 3/F Save-A-Lot Mall, 2284 Pasong Tamo Ext., Makati City ☎ +63 2 8933404 **E:** rjofc@compass.com.ph **W:** www.rjplanet.com **L.P:** Owner: Ramon Jacinto **Txs:** DZRJ-TV Manila ch29 & relay stns – **SOUTHERN BROADCASTING NETWORK, INC. (ETC) (Comm)** ✉ Suite 2901 Jollibee Plaza, Emerald Ave., Ortigas Center, Pasig City ☎ +63 2 6363286 **E:** genceo@sbnphilippines.net **W:** www.solarentertainmentcorp.com **L.P:** Pres/CEO: Teofilo A. Henson **Txs:** DWCP-TV Manila ch21 & relay stns – **GATEWAY UHF BROADCASTING (3ABN) (Rlg)** ✉ Sumulong Highway, Block 5, Brgy. Sta. Cruz, Antipolo City **Txs:** DWVN-TV Manila ch45 & relay stns – **SONSHINE MEDIA NETWORK INTERNATIONAL (SMNI) (Rlg)** ✉ Suite 3102 31/F Jollibee Plaza, F. Ortigas Jr. Road, Ortigas Center, Pasig City, 1600 ☎ +63 2 6830772 **E:** sonshine@sonshinemedia.com **W:** www.smni.com **Txs:** DWAQ-TV Manila ch40 & relay stns – **ZOE BROADCASTING NETWORK, INC. (LIGHT NETWORK) (Rlg)** ✉ 22F Strata 2000 Bldg., F. Ortigas Road, Ortigas Ctr, Pasig City ☎ +63 6383469 **W:** lightnetwork.ph **L.P:** Chmn: Eddie Villanueva. **Txs:** DZOZ-TV Manila ch33 & relay stns.

Local Stations not shown.

PITCAIRN ISLANDS (UK)

System: PAL-G [E]

Foreign TV Relay
Hope Channel (USA): ch29 (0.0035kW).

POLAND

System: DVB-T2 (HEVC); # DVB-T (MPEG4) ⇩2022

National Stations
TELEWIZJA POLSKA S.A. (TVP) (Pub) ✉ ul. Woronicza 17, 00-999 Warszawa ☎ +48 225478000 **E:** tvp@tvp.pl **W:** www.tvp.pl **L.P:** Pres: Jacek Kurski **Chs (terr.):** TVP1, TVP2, TVP3 + regional stns, TVP INFO, TVP ABC, TVP Historia, TVP Kultura, TVP Rozrywka, TVP Sport – **TVN S.A. (Comm)** ✉ ul. Wiertnicza 166, 02-952 Warszawa ☎ +48 228566060 **E:** widzowie@tvn.pl **W:** www.tvn.pl **L.P:** Chmn: Piotr Korycki – **TELEVIZJA POLSAT SP.Z.O.O. (Comm)** ✉ ul. Ostrobramska 77, 04-175 Warszawa ☎ +48 225145533 **E:** poczta@polsat.pl **W:** www.polsat.pl **L.P:** Chmn (Group Polsat): Mirosław Blaszczyk. **Chs (terr.):** TV Polsat, TV4, Polsat Cafe, Polsat Film, Polsat News, Polsat Play, Polsat Sport – **TV PULS (Comm)** ✉ ul. Chełmska 21, 00-724 Warszawa ☎ +48 225597300 **E:** recepcja@pulstv.pl **W:** tvpuls.pl **L.P:** Chmn: Dariusz Dabski.

Local Stations (all Comm)
MWE Teleport: ul. Błękitna 3, 55-040 Kobierzyce **M:** TVN HD, Polsat HD, Eska TV Extra, TVR, Gold TV, Mango 24, Power TV, Nuta TV, Junior Music, Echo24, NTL, TV Okazje, Biznes24, TV Regionalna, Ultra TV 4K (SD); ch27 (Wrocław 2kW, Świdnica 1kW, Kobierzyce 1kW). **NTL:** ul. 11-go Listopada 2, 97-500 Radomsko **M:** NTL, 4fun.tv, Eska TV Extra, STARS.TV, Junior Music, Power TV, Nuta TV, TVR, Gold TV, TV Okazje, Red Carpet, Biznes24, Mango 24, Ultra 4K (SD); ch36 (Kamieńsk 1.5kW, Łódź 0.79kW, Częstochowa 0.36kW, Tomaszów Maz. 0.01kW). **TVL:** ul. Tysiąclecia 2, 59-300 Lubin **M:** TV Regionalna, Nuta TV, Power TV, Junior Music; ch43 (Glogów 1kW, Lubin SFN, Ornontowice 1.5kW, Rybnik 1kW).

DTT Tx Networks (DVB-T exc. where indicated)
Tx Operator: EmiTel **W:** www.emitel.pl **M1:** TVP ABC, TV Trwam, Stopklatka TV, Fokus TV, TTV, ATM Rozrywka, Eska TV, Polo TV **M2:** Polsat, TVN, TV4, TV Puls, TVN7, Super Polsat, TV 6, TV Puls 2 **M3:** TVP1 HD, TVP2 HD, TVP3 (Regional stations), TVP INFO, TVP Historia, TVP Sport HD **M4✪ (DVB-H):** Polsat Sport, Polsat Sport Extra, Polsat News, Polsat Play, Polsat Film, Polsat Cafe, Tele5, TVP Seriale, Kino Polska, Comedy Central, Comedy Central Family, Nickelodeon ⌘ R.RMF FM, R.RMF MAXXX, R.ZET, Antyradio, R.Plus, TOK FM, Złote Przeboje, Eska Rock, R. MUZO FM, R. VOX FM, Rock R. **M8:** Nowa TV, Metro, WP, ZOOM TV, TVP Rozrywka, TVP Kultura HD **Test Mux "TVP" (T) (DVB-T2/HEVC):** TVP Polonia HD, TVP Kultura HD, TVP Rosrywka HD **Test Mux "Polsat": (DVB-T2/HEVC):** TVN HD, TVN7 HD, TTV HD **Txs:** ch29 (Warszawa PKiN 2.4kW), ch42 (Katowice 0.8kW) **Local Mux "LRT":** LRT Lituanica **Tx:** ch23 (Suwalki/Góra Krzemianucha 0.1kW).

Location	1	2	3	4	8	T	kW
Białogard (Sławoborze)	21	35	38	-	7	37	3x50/25/10
Białystok (Krynice)	46	49	22	38	8	35	58/67/2x100/24/10
Bydgoszcz (Trzeciewiec)	41	32	36	34	8	40	4x100/20/50
Ciechanów	25	57	39	-	12V	44	2x5/10/16/10

Location	1	2	3	4	8	T	kW
Częstochowa (Wręczyca)	35	39	41	32	9V	-	2x100/80/50/8
Człuchów	-	-	48	-	8V	-	20/2
Elbląg (Jagodnik)	27	21	26	39V	6	44	2x10/7.5/100/2.8/10
Gdańsk (Chwaszczyno)	37	35	22	25	6V	44	3x100/26/20/100
Giżycko (Miłki)	43	48	50	-	9V	24	2x100/90/2/25
Gołańcz (Chojna)	42	43	31	-	9V	44	2x20/23/40/10
Gorlice	-	-	34	-	-	-	20
Iława (Kisielice)	38	24	26	-	8	-	2x100/35/6
Iława (Kisielice)	-	-	36	-	-	-	3
Iława (Kisielice)	-	-	29	-	-	-	50
Jelenia Góra (Śn. Kotły)	30	35	49	-	6V	-	3x100/8
Kalisz (Mikstat)	38	44	31	-	-	37	3x100/20
Kalisz (Mikstat)	-	-	26	-	-	-	35
Kamieńsk	-	-	26	-	9	-	12/5
Kartuzy	-	-	22	-	6V	-	15/7
Katowice (Bytków)	-	-	41V	24	-	-	8/10
Katowice (Kosztowy)	21	40	41	24	6	27	50/63/100/10/20/30
Katowice (Kosztowy)	-	-	34	-	-	-	5
Kielce (Święty Krzyż)	30	37	47	-	8V	44	2x100/150/10/25
Kłodzko (Czarna Góra)	46	33	25	-	6V	37	3x50/0.5/20
Kluczbork (Wierzbica Górna)	-	-	34	-	-	-	12
Kobyla Góra	-	-	-	-	8	-	15
Konin (Żółwieniec)	55	45	27	-	7V	22	2x100/15/14/50
Konin (Żółwieniec)	-	-	36	-	-	-	40
Koronowo (Okole)	-	-	-	34V	-	-	10
Koszalin (Gołogóra)	23	47	38	-	7	44	2x100/71/15/50
Koszalin (Gołogóra)	-	-	48	-	-	-	100
Kraków (Chorągwica)	25	23	22	33	7V	27	3x100/7.2/10/80
Kraków (Chorągwica)	-	-	47	-	-	-	35
Krosno (Sucha Góra)	48	32	29	-	6V	24	3x100/18/40
Lębork (Skórowo Nowe)	37	35	48	-	6V	24	10
Legnica	-	-	24-47		-	-	2.8/10
Leżajsk (Giedlarowa)	43	31	26	-	6V	24	2x100/71/20/15
Leżajsk (Giedlarowa)	-	-	36	-	-	-	15
Lódz	46	24	43	-	49V	33	2x100/170/5/40
Lódz (Zygry)	-	-	-	-	9	-	25
Luban (Nowa Karczma)	-	-	24	-	-	-	20
Lublin (Boży Dar)	-	-	23	-	12	-	20/30
Lublin (Komin EC Wrotków)	-	-	-	-	35V	-	11.3
Lublin (Piaski)	33	21	23	-	12	25	3x100/35/50
Nowy Tomyśl (Bolewice)	-	-	27	-	-	-	33
Nowy Tomyśl (Bolewice)	-	-	32	-	-	-	3
Olsztyn (Komin MPEC)	-	-	-	44V	-	-	10
Olsztyn (Pieczewo)	28	33	26	23	9	45	3x100/22/60/50
Opole (Chrzelice)	29	23	34	-	-	-	3x100
Opole (Góra Św. Anny)	-	-	-	-	6	27	10/5
Ostrołęka (Kopernika)	-	-	-	-	12V	11	
Ostrołęka (Ławy)	40	41	42	-	-	31	3x60/50
Płock (Komin b. mleczarni Mitex)	-	-	39	35	12V	-	15/5/25
Płock (Rachocin)	25	57	39	-	12V	44	3x100/10/50
Płock (Rachocin)	-	-	36	-	-	-	3
Poznań (Komin EC Karolin)	-	-	-	28V	-	-	10
Poznań (Piątkowo)	-	-	27	-	-	-	20
Poznan (Śrem)	23	39	27	-	7	29	2x100/110/22/40
Przemyśl (Tatarska Góra)	43	31	26	-	6V	24	3x20/8/10
Przysucha (Kozlowiec)	30	37	26	-	8V	44	2x50/10/15.5/10
Rabka (G. Lubon Wielki)	43	36	34	-	7V	-	2x10/9.8/0.2
Radom (Wacyn)	-	-	42	28	8V	-	50/8/8.5
Ryki	22	24	52	-	7V	38	3x20/8/10
Ryki	-	-	42	-	-	-	4
Siedlce (Łosice)	36	43	56	-	9V	39	20/50/40/10/40
Siedlce (Łosice)	-	-	52	-	-	-	100
Sokołów Podlaski	36	-	56	-	9V	-	5/10/7
Solina (Góra Jawor)	48	32	29	-	6V	24	3x20/1.1/10
Suwałki (G. Krzemianucha)	43	29	58	-	7V	24	3x20/9.5/20
Świnoujście (Chrobrego)	21	34	-	-	-	-	10
Szczawnica (G. Prehyba)	45	36	34	-	7V	27	2x20/22/1.6/10
Szczecin (Kołowo)	41	34	48	30	6	37	3x100/15/20/100
Szczecin (Warszewo)	-	-	48	-	-	-	14
Tarnobrzeg	43	31	26	-	8	-	2x5/30/15
Tarnów (G. Św. Marcin)	45	23	22	33	7	21	3x50/4/3/5
Tarnów (G. Św. Marcin)	-	-	26V	-	-	-	5
Toruń (Komin PGE Toruń)	-	-	36	34V	8	-	12/2.5/15
Wałbrzych (G. Chełmiec)	-	-	25	47	6V	-	20/3/0.3
Wałcz (Rusinowo)	42	43	33	-	9V	44	2x100/25/40/50
Wałcz (Rusinowo)	-	-	31	-	-	-	100
Warszawa (PKiN)	58	48	27	34V	7	31	2x3/10/2.2/17/3
Warszawa (Raszyn)	58	48	27	34	7	31	2x100/130/100/2/50
Wisła (G. Skrzyczne)	21	40	41	-	7V	27	2x100/60/1.5/10
Wrocław (Góra Ślęża)	46	33	25	-	6V	37	3x100/16/100
Wrocław (Żórawina)	-	-	25	42V	-		30/8
Żagań (Wichów)	45	21	32	-	8V	37	3x50/20/25
Zakopane (G. Gubalówka)	43	36	34	-	7V	28	3x20/0.5/10
Zamość (Tarnawatka)	34	32	36	-	12	34	3x50/40/50
Zielona Góra (Jemiolów)	45	21	32	-	8V	38	2x80/100/22/30

+ sites with txs below 10kW. Pol.=H exc. where stated otherwise

PORTUGAL

System: DVB-T (MPEG4) [E]

RÁDIO E TELEVISÃO DE PORTUGAL, S.A. (RTP) (Pub) Av. Marechal Gomes da Costa 37, 1849-030 Lisboa ☎ +351 217947000 **E:** rtp@rtp.pt **W:** www.rtp.pt **L.P:** Pres: António Maria Maciel de Castro Feijó **Chs (terr.):** RTP1, RTP2, RTP3, RTP Memória, RTP Açores and RTP Madeira (see Azores, Madeira), RTP África (see Cabo Verde, Guinea-Bissau, Mozambique, São Tomé e Príncipe). – **SOCIEDADE INDEPENDENTE DE COMUNICAÇÃO, S.A. (SIC) (Comm)** Estrada da Outurela 119, 2794-052 Carnaxide ☎ +351 214179550 **E:** contacto@siconline.pt **W:** sic.pt **L.P:** Pres: Francisco Pedro Balsemão – **TELEVISÃO INDEPENDENTE, S.A. (TVI) (Comm)** R. Mário Castelhano, 40, Queluz de Baixo, 2749-502 Barcarena ☎ +351 214347500 **E:** relacoes.exteriores@iol.pt **W:** tvi.iol.pt **L.P:** DG: Luís Cabral – **ARTV (CANAL PARLAMENTO)** Palácio de S. Bento, 1249-068 Lisboa ☎ +351 213919663 **E:** canal.parlamento@ar.parlamento.pt **W:** www.canal.parlamento.pt

DTT Tx Networks

Licensee: Altice Portugal **W:** www.telecom.pt **Mux:** RTP1, RTP2, RTP3, RTP Memória, SIC, TVI, ARTV

Location	ch	kW	Location	ch	kW
Beja	30	5.9	Palmela	45	8.7
Évora Centro	30	5	Lousã (Trevim)	46	5.8
Lisboa (Restelo)	35	5	Miranda do Douro	46	5
Almada	37	8.6	São Mamede	47	7.6
Mendro	40	8.7	Marofa	48	7.9
Porto (Monte da Virgem)	42	7.5	Montejunto	48	6.6

+ txs below 5kW

PUERTO RICO (USA Commonwealth)

System: ATSC [A]

LOCAL STATIONS IN MAJOR TV MARKETS

San Juan, PR Area

ch	kW	Territory	City of License	Callsign
3	2.7	PR	Guaynabo	WZNA-LD
4	1	PR	Naranjito	W24EI-D
4	1	PR	Carolina	WVDO-LD
6	2	PR	San Juan	WWXY-D
7	25	PR	Ponce	WSTE-DT
9	0.4	PR	Fajardo	W09AT-D
9	21.6	PR	Ponce	WSUR-DT
10	3	PR	San Juan	W10DD-D
11	38	PR	Caguas	WLII-DT
13	38	PR	Fajardo	WORO-DT
14	200	PR	Ponce	WTIN-TV
14	4	PR	Isabel Segunda	WVQS-LD
15	174	PR	Fajardo	WMTJ
18	18	PR	Naranjito	WECN
20	15	PR	San Juan	W20EJ-D
21	1000	PR	San Juan	+ WJPX
21	1000	PR	San Juan	+ WTCV
22	10	PR	San Juan	+ WSJN-CD
22	10	PR	Toa Baja	+ WELU
23	50	PR	Humacao	WVSN
24	10	PR	Bajamon	+ WDWL
24	10	PR	Caguas	+ WUJA
26	250	PR	San Juan	WIPR-TV
27	584	PR	San Juan	WAPA-TV
28	925	PR	San Juan	WKAQ-TV
28	0.5	PR	Utuado	W28EQ-D
29	15	PR	San Lorenzo	W29EE-D
30	15	PR	Guayama	W30ED-D
30	40	PR	Carolina	WRFB
34	40.3	PR	Guayama	WIDP
35	50	PR	Arecibo	WCCV-TV
36	15	PR	Guayama	WXWZ-LD

+) Shared transmitter (multiplex)

QATAR

System: DVB-T2 (MPEG4) [E]

QATAR MEDIA CORP. (Pub) ✉ P.O.Box 1944, Doha ☎ +974 44894444 **E:** contact@qna.org.qa **W:** www.qtv.qa **Chs:** Qatar TV, Al Rayan TV, Al Dawri/Al Kass, Jeem TV, Baraem TV, Al Bidda TV.

DTT Tx Networks
Tx Operator: Qatar Media Corp. **M:** Qatar TV, Al Rayan TV, Al Dawri/Al Kass, Jeem TV, Baraem TV, Al Bidda TV **Txs:** ch53 (Doha) & nationwide MFN – **Local Licensees** not shown.

RÉUNION (France)

System: DVB-T (MPEG4) [E]

RÉUNION LA 1ÈRE (Pub) ✉ 12 rue René Demarne F-97490 Saint Denis ☎ +262 262406767 **W:** la1ere.francetvinfo.fr/reunion **L.P:** Dir: Gora Patel – **ANTENNE RÉUNION (Comm)** ✉ BP 80001, F-97801 Saint-Denis CEDEX 009 ☎ +262 262482828 **W:** www.antennereunion.fr **L.P:** DG: Christophe Ducasse.

DTT Tx Network
Tx Operator: TDF **Mux:** Réunion la 1ère HD, France 2-5*, Franceinfo, Arte, Antenne Réunion **Txs:** MFN. *) France 4 will cease in 2021

ROMANIA

System: DVB-T2 (MPEG4) [E]

National Station
TELEVIZIUNEA ROMÂNA (TVR) (Pub) ✉ Calea Dorobanţilor nr. 191, sector 1, 010565 Bucureşti ☎ +40 21 3199112 **E:** office@tvr.ro **W:** www.tvr.ro **L.P:** DG: Doina Gradea. **Chs (terr.):** TVR1, TVR2, TVR3, Regional stns.

Local Stations not shown.

DTT Tx Network
Tx Operator: Radiocom **W:** www.radiocom.ro **M:** TVR1 HD, TVR2 HD, TVR3, TVR Cluj, TVR Craiova, TVR Iaşi, TVR Timişoara, TVR Târgu Mureş.

Location	ch	kW	Location	ch	kW
Arad (Şiria)	21	90	Iaşi (Pietrăria)	43	70
Bacău	39	60	Magura Boiu	21	65
Baia Mare (Mogoşa)	21	32	Măgura Odobeşti	38	75
Balota	40	55	Nasaud (Dej)	30	10
Băneasa (Călăraşi)	36	62	Negreşti-Oaş	21	11
Bârlad	39	50	Olteniţa (Hotarele)	30	20
Bihor	30	60	Oradea	44	70
Bistriţa (Heniu)	40	80	Petroşani (Parâng)	29	20
Botoşani (Săveni)	31	30	Piatra Neamţ	26	17
Braşov (Tampa)	34	20	Piteşti	27	11
Bucegi (Coştila)	22	150	Rarău	38	805
Bucureşti (CNCR)	30	10	Semenic	44	800
Bucureşti	30	60	Sibiu (Paltiniş)	37	95
Buzău (Istriţa)	28	13	Suceava	38	50
Calafat (Pleniţa)	21	10	Târgu Mureş	24	12
Cerbu (Novaci)	29	130	Timişoara (Urseni)	21	160
Cluj (Feleac)	26	40	Topliţa (Borsec)	32	15
Comăneşti	40	85	Topolog	38	60
Constanţa	30	55	Tulcea	38	10
Cozia	27	30	Varatec	32	42
Craiova (Simnic)	28	11	Vaslui	39	45
Galaţi (Văcăreni)	24	70	Zalău	30	15
Harghita	32	80	+ sites with txs below 10kW		

Local Licensees not shown.

RUSSIA

System: DVB-T2 (MPEG4) [E]

National Stations
VSEROSSIYSKAYA GOSUDARSTVENNAYA TELEVIZIONNAYA I RADIOVESHCHATELNAYA KOMPANIYA (VGTRK) (Gov) ✉ 125040 Moskva, 5-ya Yamskogo Polya ul. 19/21 ☎ +7 495 2326333 **W:** www.vgtrk.com **L.P:** DG: Oleg B. Dobrodeyev. ✉Studios: Rossiya 1, Rossiya 24, Match TV: 15162 Moskva, ul. Shabolovka 37; Rossiya K: 119902 Moskva, ul. Zubovskiy bul. 4; Karusel: 127427 Moskva, ul. Ak. Korolyova 19. **Chs:** Rossiya 1, Rossiya K, Rossiya 24, Karusel, Match TV; Regional Stations (see chapter below).

VGTRK Regional Services: AD) GTRK "Adygeya": 385000 Maykop, ul. Zhukovskogo 24. **AK)** GTRK "Altay": 656045 Barnaul, Zmeinogorskiy trakt 27a. **AM)** GTRK "Amur": 675000 Blagoveshchensk, per. Svyatitelya Innokentiya 15. **AR)** GTRK "Pomorye": 163069 Arkhangelsk, ul. Troitskiy 73. **AS)** GTRK "Lotos": 414040 Astrakhan, ul. Lyakhova 4. **BA)** GTRK "Bashkortostan": 450076 Ufa, ul. Gafuri 9/1. **BE)** GTRK "Belgorod": 308000 Belgorod, pr. Slavy 60. **BR)** GTRK "Bryansk": 241033 Bryansk, ul. Stanke Dimitrova 77. **BU)** GTRK "Buryatiya": 670000 Ulan-Ude, ul. Erbanova 7. **CB)** GTRK "Yuzhnyy Ural": 454000 Chelyabinsk, ul. Ordzhonikidze 54b. **CC)** GTRK "Vaynakh": 364000 Groznyy, ul. B.Khmelnitskogo 147, korpus 5. **CK)** GTRK "Chukotka": 686710 Anadyr, ul. Lenina 18. **CV)** GTRK "Chuvashiya": 428003 Cheboksary, ul. Nikolayeva 4. **DA)** GTRK "Dagestan": 367032 Makhachkala, ul. Magomeda Gadzhieva 182. **IN)** GTRK "Ingushetiya": 366720 Nazran, pr. Bazorkina 72. **IR)** GTRK "Irkutsk": 664003 Irkutsk, ul. Gorkogo 15. **IV)** GTRK "Ivteleradio": 153647 Ivanovo, ul. Teatralnaya 31. **KA)** GTRK "Kaliningrad": 236016 Kaliningrad, ul. Klinicheskaya 19. **KB)** GTRK "Kabardino-Balkariya": 360000 Nalchik, pr. Lenina 3. **KC)** GTRK "Karachayevo-Cherkesiya": 357100 Cherkessk, ul. Krasnoarmeyskaya 51. **KD)** GTRK "Kuban": 350038 Krasnodar, ul. Radio 5. **KE)** GTRK "Kuzbass": 650000 Kemerovo, ul. Teletsentr 3. **KG)** GTRK "Kurgan": 640018 Kurgan, ul. Sovetskaya 105. **KH)** GTRK "Dalnevostochnaya": 682632 Khabarovsk, ul. Lenina 4. **KL)** GTRK "Kaluga": 248021 Kaluga, Pole Svobody 40a. **KM)** GTRK "Kamchatka": 683000 Petropavlovsk-Kamchatskiy, ul. Sovetskaya 62. **KN)** GTRK "Krasnoyarsk": 660028 Krasnoyarsk, ul. Mechnikova 44a. **KO)** GTRK "Komi Gor": 167610 Syktyvkar, Oktyabrskiy pr. 164. **KS)** GTRK "Kostroma": 156005 Kostroma, ul. Nikitskaya 10. **KT)** GTRK "Kareliya": 185630 Petrozavodsk, ul. Pirogova 2. **KU)** GTRK "Kursk": 305016 Kursk, ul. Sovetskaya 32. **KV)** GTRK "Vyatka": 610002 Kirov, ul. Uritskogo 34. **KX)** GTRK "Kalmykiya": 358000 Elista, ul. M. Gorkogo 34. **KY)** GTRK "Yugoriya": 626200 Khanty-Mansiysk, ul. Mira 7. **LI)** GTRK "Lipetsk": 398050 Lipetsk, pl. Plekhanova 1. **MA)** GTRK "Magadan": 685024 Magadan, ul. Kommuny 8/12. **MD)** GTRK "Mordoviya": 430000 Saransk, ul. Dokuchayeva 29. **ME)** GTRK "Mariy-El": 424014 Yoshkar-Ola, ul. Osipenko 50. **MU)** GTRK "Murman": 183032 Murmansk, ul. Varnichnaya Sopka 1. **NE)** Territorialnoye otdeleniya GTRK "Pomorye", 164700 Naryan-Mar, ul. Smidovicha 19. **NN)** GTRK "Nizhniy Novgorod": 603600 Nizhniy Novgorod, ul. Belinskogo 9a. **NO)** GTRK "Slaviya": 173620 Velikiy Novgorod, ul. B.Moskovskaya 106. **NS)** GTRK "Novosibirsk", 630048 Novosibirsk, ul. Rimskogo-Korsakova 9. **OB)** GTRK "Orenburg": 460024 Orenburg, per. Televizionnyy 3. **OL)** GTRK "Oryol": 302028 Oryol, ul. 7 Noyabrya 43. **OM)** GTRK "Irtysh": 644050 Omsk, pr. Mira 2. **PM)** GTRK "Vladivostok": 690091 Vladivostok, ul. Uborevicha 20a. **PR)** GTRK "Perm": 614070 Perm, ul. Tekhnicheskaya 7. **PS)** GTRK "Pskov": 180000 Pskov, ul. Nekrasova 50. **PZ)** GTRK "Penza": 440602 Penza, ul. Lermontova 39. **RA)** GTRK "Gornyy Altay": 659700 Gorno-Altaysk, ul. Choros-Gurkina 38. **RK)** GTRK "Khakasiya": 662000 Abakan, ul. Vyatkina 12. **RO)** GTRK "Don-TR": 344101 Rostov-na-Donu, ul. 1-ya Barrikadnaya 18. **RS)** GTRK "Sakha": 677007 Yakutsk, ul. Ordzhonikidze 48. **RT)** GTRK "Tyva": 667003 Kyzyl, ul. Gornaya 31. **RY)** GTRK "Oka": 390006 Ryazan, ul. Skomoroshinskaya 20. **SA)** GTRK "Samara": 443011 Samara, ul. Sovetskoy Armii 205. **SL)** GTRK "Sakhalin": 693000 Yuzhno-Sakhalinsk, ul. Komsomolskaya 209. **SM)** GTRK "Smolensk": 214000 Smolensk, ul. Dzerzhinskogo 17. **SO)** GTRK "Alaniya": 362007 Vladikavkaz, Osetinskaya gorka 2. **SP)** GTRK "Sankt-Peterburg": 197022 St.Peterburg, nab. reki Karpovki 43. **SR)** GTRK "Saratov": 410004 Saratov, 2-ya Sadovaya ul. 7. **ST)** GTRK "Stavropolye": 355000 Stavropol, ul. Dzerzhinskogo 149-151. **SV)** GTRK "Ural": 620026 Yekaterinburg, ul. Lunacharskogo 212. **TA)** GTRK "Tambov": 392720 Tambov, ul. Michurinskaya 8a. **TL)** GTRK "Tula": 300600 Tula, Staronikitskaya ul. 1. **TO)** GTRK "Tomsk": 634045 Tomsk, ul. Yakovleva 5.. **TS)** GTRK "Tatarstan": 420015 Kazan, ul. M. Gorkogo 15. **TV)** GTRK "Tver": 170000 Tver, ul. Vagzhanova 9. **TY)** GTRK "Region-Tyumen": 625013 Tyumen, ul. Permyakova 6. **UD)** GTRK "Udmurtiya": 426069 Izhevsk, ul. Pesochnaya 9. **UL)** GTRK "Volga": 432030 Ulyanovsk, ul. Narimanova 62. **VG)** GTRK "Volgograd-TRV": 400005 Volgograd, ul. Marshala Rokossovskogo 100. **VL)** GTRK "Vladimir": 600000 Vladimir, ul. Bol. Moskovskaya 62. **VN)** GTRK "Voronezh": 394625 Voronezh, ul. Karl Marksa 114. **VO)** GTRK "Vologda": 160000 Vologda, ul. Predtecheskaya 32. **YA)** GTRK "Yaroslaviya": 150014 Yaroslavl, ul. Bogdanovicha 20. **YN)** GTRK "Yamal": 626600 Salekhard, ul. Lambinykh 3. **YV)** GTRK "Bira": 679016 Birobidzhan, ul. Oktyabrskaya 15. **ZB)** GTRK "Chita": 672090 Chita, ul. Kostyushko-Grigorovicha 27. **NB:** Keys to region codes: see

National Radio section. – **MIR TV (Gov)** ✉ 107076 Moskva, ul. Krasnobogatyrskaya 44 ☎ +7 495 6480792 **E:** mir24@mirtv.ru **W:** mirtv.ru **L.P:** Chief Editor: Radik Batyrshin – **TV ZVEZDA (Mil)** ✉ 129164 Moskva, pr. Mira 126 ☎ +7 495 6459289 **E:** info@tvzvezda.ru **W:** tvzvezda.ru **L.P:** Chief Editor: A. Kharkov – **PERVYY KANAL (Semi-Gov)** ✉ 127000 Moskva, ul. Ak. Korolyova 12 ☎ +7 495 2179838 **E:** dip@1tv.ru **W:** www.1tv.ru **L.P:** DG: Konstantin Ernst – **TV TSENTR (Municipal)** ✉ 115184 Moskva, ul. Bolshaya Tatarskaya 33-1 ☎ +7 495 9593900 **E:** press@tvc.ru **W:** www.tvc.ru **L.P:** DG: Yuliya Bystritskaya – **OBSHCHESTVENNOYE TELEVIDENIYE ROSSII (OTR) (Pub)** ✉ 127427 Moskva, ul. Ak. Korolyova 19 **E:** press@otr-online.ru **W:** otr-online.ru **L.P:** Chief Editor: Anatoliy Lysenko – **5 KANAL (Comm)** ✉ 197376 St.Peterburg, ul. Chapygina 6 ☎ +7 812 3351560 **E:** trk@spbtv.ru **W:** www.5-tv.ru **L.P:** Chief Editor: N.V. Ilyina – **GAZPROM MEDIA (Comm)** ✉ 123022 Moskva, ul. Rochdelskaya 20 ☎ +7 495 7896800 **E:** info@gazprom-media.com **W:** www.gazprom-media.com; www.ntv.ru (NTV), tv3.ru (TV3), tnt-online.ru (TNT), friday.ru (Pyatnitsa!) **L.P:** Chmn: Aleksey Miller **Chs (terr.):** NTV, TV3, TNT, Pyatnitsa! – **MUZ-TV (Comm)** ✉ 105066 Moskva, ul. Olkhovskaya 4 ☎ +7 495 2131888 **E:** info@muz-tv.ru **W:** muz-tv.ru **L.P:** DG: Arman Davletyarov – **REN-TV (Comm)** ✉ 115093 Moskva, Partiyniy per. 1 ☎ +7 495 9376170 **E:** pressa@ren-tv.com **W:** ren.tv **L.P:** DG: Vladimir Tyulin – **STS MEDIA (Comm)** ✉ 125254 Moskva, Leningradskiy pr. 31 ☎ +7 495 7856347 **W:** www.ctcmedia.ru; ctc.ru (STS), domashniy.ru (Domashniy) **L.P:** CEO: Vyachislav Murugov **Chs (terr.):** Domashniy, STS – **SPAS (Rlg)** ✉ 129075 Moskva, P.O.Box 79 ☎ +7 495 6510829 **E:** office@spas-tv.ru **W:** spastv.ru **L.P:** DG: Boris Korchevnikov.

Other Regional & Local Stations not shown.

DTT Tx Networks
Tx Operator: RTRS **W:** www.rtrs.ru **M1:** Rossiya 1, Rossiya 24, Rossiya K, Karusel, Match TV, Pervyy kanal, NTV, OTR, 5-kanal, TV Tsentr, VGTRK Regional TV stns ⌘ R. Rossii, Mayak, Vesti FM. **M2:** Domashniy, TV Zvezda, Mir TV, Muz-TV, Pyatnitsa, REN TV, Spas, STS, TNT, TV3

Re	Location	M1	M2	kW	Re	Location	M1	M2	kW
AD	Maykop	45	22	5	NN	N.Novgorod	28	53	5
AK	Barnaul	27	58	5	NO	V.Novgorod	30	58	2
AM	Blagoveshchensk	34	36	0.5	NS	Novosibirsk	29	24	2
AR	Arkhangelsk	33	44	5	OB	Orenburg	22	28	5
AS	Astrakhan	26	36	5	OL	Oryol	26	41	5
BA	Ufa	25	43	2	OM	Omsk	31	49	2
BE	Belgorod	43	46	5	PM	Vladivostok	37	56	5
BR	Bryansk	39	23	2	PR	Perm	23	49	10
BU	Ulan-Ude	30	32	2	PS	Pskov	49	56	2
CB	Chelyabinsk	24	40	2	PZ	Penza	57	44	5
CC	Groznyy	32	59	2	RA	Gorno-Altaysk	24	32	1
CK	Anadyr	21	26	0.25	RK	Abakan	24	32	1
CV	Cheboksary	46	57	0.25	RO	Rostov-na-Donu	37	38	5
DA	Makhachkala	22	52	2	RS	Yakutsk	33	46	5
IN	Nazran	38	36	2	RT	Kyzyl	33	37	1
IR	Irkutsk	38	57	5	RY	Ryazan	43	27	1
IV	Ivanovo	59	57	1	SA	Samara	27	57	5
KA	Kaliningrad	47	30	1	SL	Yu-Sakhalinsk	21	51	1
KB	Nalchik	34	21	5	SM	Smolensk	39	46	1
KC	Cherkessk	58	59	1	SO	Vladikavkaz	35	50	5
KD	Krasnodar	39	60	5	SP	Sankt-Peterburg	35	45	5
KE	Kemerovo	23	43	2	SR	Saratov	36	40	2
KH	Khabarovsk	38	30	5	ST	Stavropol	57	32	1
KL	Kaluga	46	44	5	SV	Yekaterinburg	46	60	5
KM	Petropavlovsk-K.	22	26	2	TA	Tambov	46	56	10
KN	Krasnoyarsk	25	45	5	TL	Tula	34	60	5
KO	Syktyvkar	26	34	2	TO	Tomsk	21	44	5
KS	Kostroma	46	43	2	TS	Kazan	36	53	5
KT	Petrozavodsk	25	39	2	TV	Tver	37	58	2
KU	Kursk	24	53	5	TY	Tyumen	35	44	5
KV	Kirov	32	36	5	UD	Izhevsk	36	57	5
KX	Elista	46	39	2	UL	Ulyanovsk	56	59	5
KY	Khanty-Mansiysk	38	44	2	VG	Volgograd	37	39	5
LI	Lipetsk	30	40	1	VL	Vladimir	36	50	5
MA	Magadan	27	29	5	VN	Voronezh	52	43	5
MD	Saransk	43	46	2	VO	Vologda	34	35	5
ME	Yoshkar-Ola	38	56	2	YA	Yaroslavl	39	36	5
MO	Moskva	30	24	10	YN	Nakhodka	35	59	5
MU	Murmansk	44	55	1	YV	Birobidzhan	34	37	2
NE	Naryan-Mar	26	30	0.25	ZB	Chita	24	34	5

NB: Only txs in top-level administrative capitals shown.
Regional/Local licensees not shown.

CRIMEA

NB: The station listing can be found at the end of the Ukraine entry.

RWANDA

System: DVB-T2 (MPEG4) [E]

RWANDA BROADCASTING AGENCY (RBA) (Pub) ✉ P.O.Box 83, Kigali ☎ +250 252576540 **E:** info@rba.co.rw **W:** www.rba.co.rw – **TV10 (Comm)** ✉ Plot 1187, Kigali Road, Kigali ☎ +250 784444444 **E:** radiotv10rwanda@gmail.com **W:** www.radiotv10.rw **L.P:** CEO: Eugene Nyagahene.

DTT Tx Networks
Licensee: StarTimes **M(partly✪):** RTV, TV10, CNN, TV5 Monde, France 24 Français, France 24 English, Al Jazeera, True Movies **Txs:** MFN – **Licensee:** TV10 **M✪:** multiprgr **Txs:** MFN

SABA (Netherlands)

Systems: # NTSC-M [A]; DVB-T (MPEG2) planned

ATV RELAY (Aruba Broadcasting Co., Aruba): ch11

SAMOA

System: DVB-T2 (MPEG4) [E]

TV1 (Comm) ✉ P.O.Box 3691, Apia ☎ +685 24790 **W:** www.tv1samoa.tv **L.P:** GM: Galumalemana Faiesea Matafeo – **TV3 (Comm)** ✉ Taufusi, Apia ☎ +685 33330 **E:** tvsamoa3@ipasifika.net **W:** www.facebook.com/tv3samoa **L.P:** CEO: Atanoa Herbert Crichton – **EKFS TV2 (Rlg)** ✉ P.O.Box 96, Apia ☎ +685 27882 **W:** www.facebook.com/EFKSTV2 **L.P:** CEO: Tofilau Elijah Ryan – **KINGDOM TV (KTV) (Rlg)** ✉ Sogi, Apia ☎ +685 21447 **E:** worshipcentre@samoa.ws **L.P:** GM: Rev. Afereti Lui – **UPUMANA TV (Rlg)** ✉ Apia **L.P:** Dir: Spa Silva.

DTT Tx Network
Tx Operator: Samoa Digital Company Ltd **W:** www.facebook.com/SamoaDigitalCommunications **M:** multiprgr **Txs:** MFN

SAMOA, AMERICAN (USA)

System: ATSC [A]

Local Stations

ch	kW	Territory	City of License	Callsign
5	60	AS	Pago Pago	KVZK-5
11	0.03	AS	Pago Pago	K11UU-D

SAN MARINO

System: DVB-T (MPEG2) [E]

SAN MARINO RTV (Pub) ✉ Viale J.F.Kennedy 13, SM-47890 San Marino ☎ +378 0549 882000 **E:** amministrazione@sanmarinortv.sm **W:** www.smtvsanmarino.sm **L.P:** Pres: Davide Gasperoni **M:** San Marino RTV HD, San Marino RTV (SD), San Marino RTV2-4, San Marino RTV Sport ⌘ R. San Marino Classic **Txs:** ch51 (SFN).

SÃO TOMÉ & PRÍNCIPE

System: DVB-T2 (MPEG4) [E]

TELEVISÃO SANTOMENSE (TVS) (Pub) ✉ CP 420, Bairro da Quinta do Santo António, 420 São Tomé ☎ +239 2221041 **E:** tvs@cstome.net **W:** www.tvs.st.

DTT Tx Network
Tx Operator: StarTimes **M:** TVS, RTP África **Txs:** MFN

SAUDI ARABIA

System: DVB-T2 (MPEG4) [E]

SAUDI BROADCASTING AUTHORITY (Gov) ✉ P.O.Box 570, Riyadh 11421 ☎ +966 1 4014440 **W:** www.sba.sa **Chs (Terr.):** Saudia

TV, Saudi 2TV, Al-Riyadih, Al-Ekhbariya, Al-Eqtisadiyah, Al-Sunna, Al-Quran.

DTT Tx Networks
Tx Operator: Ministry of Culture and Information **M1:** TV1, TV2, Al-Riyadih, Al-Ekhbariya, Al-Eqtisadiyah, Al-Sunna, A-Quran ⌘ General prgr, Second prgr, R.Quran, European prgr **M2:** Sindo TV, B Channel **M3:** O Channel, Kompas TV), **M4:** MBC1, MBC4, MBC Action **M5:** Fox **M6:** LBC Sat **M7:** n/a **M8:** ITV1, ITV2 **M9:** OSN First, OSN News, Al Yawm, Series Channel **M10:** ABP News, ABP Majha, ABP Ananda. (NB: Local variations may apply)

Location	M1	M2	M3	M4	M5	M6	M7	M8	M9	M10
Jeddah	30	21	23	25	29	31	35	41	43	45

+ nationwide network.

SENEGAL

System: DVB-T2 (MPEG4) [E]

RADIODIFFUSION TÉLÉVISION SÉNÉGALAISE (Pub) ✉ BP 1765, Dakar ☎ +221 338217801 **E:** rts@rts.sn **W:** www.rts.sn **L.P:** DG: Racine Talla **Chs:** RTS1, SN2 – **TÉLÉ FUTURS MÉDIAS (TFM) (Comm)** ✉ BP 17795, Dakar ☎ +221 338491644 **W:** www.igfm.sn.

DTT Tx Network
Tx Operator: Excaf Telecom Group **W:** www.excaf.com **M(partly✪):** RTS1, SN2, multiprgr **Txs:** MFN.

SERBIA

System: DVB-T2 (MPEG4) [E]

National Stations
RADIO-TELEVIZIJA SRBIJE (RTS) (Pub) ✉ Takovska 10, 11000 Beograd ☎ +381 11 3212000 **E:** kontaktcentar@rts.rs **W:** www.rts.rs **L.P:** DG: Kristijan Golubović **Chs (terr.):** RTS1, RTS2, RTS3 – **KOPERNIKUS CORP. (Comm)** ✉ Autoput 22, 11080 Zemun ☎ +381 11 3012000 **W:** www.prva.rs (Prva TV); www.b92.net (TV B92) **L.P:** CEO (Kopernikus Corp.): Srđan Milovanović **Chs (terr.):** Prva TV, TV B92 – **NACIONALNA TELEVIZIJA HAPPY (Comm)** ✉ Aleksandra Dubčeka 14, 11080 Zemun ☎ +381 11 3778373 **E:** office@happytv.rs **W:** www.happytv.rs **L.P:** DG: Aleksandra Krstić – **TV PINK (Comm)** ✉ Neznanog junaka 1, 11000 Beograd ☎ +381 11 3063400 **E:** marketing@rtvpink.com **W:** www.rtvpink.com **L.P:** DG (Pink Media Group): Željko Mitrović.

Local Stations (via Mux 2 - DTT regions a-i*)
K::CN K: Dimitrija Tucovića 17, 11550 Lazarevac (a,h). **K::CN 1:** Cara Dušanova 45, 18000 Niš (e). **K::CN Raška:** Dušanova 6, 36350 Raška (f). **KA TV:** Ibarska 10, 36000 Kraljevo (e,g). **Mostnet:** Jug Bogdanova 94, 18400 Prokuplje (e). **NTV:** Vojvode Mišića 50/I, 18300 Niš (e). **RTV Branicevo:** Bate Bulića bb, 12300 Petrovac na Mlavi (d). **RTV Novi Pazar:** Stane Bačanin 29, 36300 Novi Pazar (f,g). **Sandžak TV:** Dimitrija Tucovića bb, 36300 Novi Pazar (f). **Sandžacka TV Mreža:** Bogoljuba Čukića 9, 36320 Tutin (f). **Sat TV:** Bože Dimitrijevića 130a, 12000 Požarevac (d,h,l). **Sportska TV:** Mićuna Pavlovića 1, 37000 Kruševac (f). **Studio B:** Masarikova 5, 11000 Beograd (a). **T1:** Zmaj Jovina 3, 19250 Majdanpek (d,i). **Televizija Plus:** Balkanska 71, 37000 Kruševac (f). **Televizija 5 plus:** Mihajla Pupina 1, 31000 Užice (g). **TV 4S:** Stojana Ljubića bb, 16205 Bojnik (f). **TMS Televizija Telemark:** Sinđelićeva bb, 32000 Čačak (g). **TV Aldi:** Maršala Tita 19, 17523 Preševo (b). **TV AS:** Kralja Milana 9, 15000 Šabac (c). **TV Belle Amie:** Trg Kralja Milana 6-8, 18000 Niš (b,e,i). **TV Bor:** Moše Pijade 19, 19210 Bor (d,i). **TV Bujanovac:** Karađorđev trg bb, 17520 Bujanovac (b). **TV Caribrod:** Trg dr Zorana Đinđića 2, 18320 Dimitrovgrad (i). **TV Diskos:** Kruševacka 22, 37230 Aleksandrovac (f). **TV F Kanal:** Trg oslobođenja bb, 19000 Zaječar (d,i). **TV Galaksija 32:** PTC Vavilon, Železnička bb, 32000 Čačak (g). **TV Gem:** Dimitrija Tucovića 1, 11550 Lazarevac (a). **TV Golija:** Milinka Kušića 23, 32250 Ivanjica (g). **TV Istok:** Jasikovacka petlja bb, 19224 Salaš (d,i). **TV Jasenica:** Francuska 9/9, 11420 Smederevska Palanka (h). **TV Jedinstvo:** AVNOJ-a d, sprat 2, stan 7, 11090 Novi Pazar (f). **TV Jefimija:** Birčaninova 10, 37000 Kruševac (f). **TV K-1:** Radanska 66, 16000 Leskovac (e). **TV Kanal M:** Nemanjina bb, 35250 Paraćin (h). **TV Kladovo:** Vinogradarska 15, 19320 Kladovo (d). **TV Kraljevo:** Konarevo bb, 36000 Kraljevo (e). **TV Kragujevac:** Branka Radičevića 9, 34000 Kragujevac (h). **TV Kruševac:** Trg kosovskih junaka 6, 37000 Kruševac (e). **TV Kuršumlija:** Palih boraca 79, 18430 Kuršumlija (f). **TV Laser:** Momčila Miloševića bb, 18360 Svrljig (e). **TV Lav Plus:** Skadarska 7, 32000 Čačak (g). **TV Leskovac:** Bulevar oslobođenja 9, 16000 Leskovac (e). **TV Lotel Plus:** Maksima Gorkog 2, 15300 Loznica (c). **TV Melos:** Hajduk Veljkova 2, 36000 Kraljevo (e,g). **TV Mlava:** Bate Bulića bb, 12300 Petrovac na Mlavi (d). **TV Palma Plus:** Železnička bb, 35000 Jagodina (h). **TV Pi Kanal:** Mite Gage 10, 18300 Pirot (i). **TV Podrinje:** Kneza Miloša 3, 15300 Loznica (c). **TV Požega:** Vojvode Mišića bb, 31210 Požega (g). **TV Pirot:** Branka Radičevića bb, 18300 Pirot (i). **TV Preševo:** Petnaestog novembra 90, 17523 Preševo (b). **TV Priboj:** Trg FAPA-a bb, 31330 Priboj (g). **TV Prima:** Vuka Karadžića bb, 31250 Bajina Bašta (g). **TV Ritam:** Pere Mačkatovca 2, 17500 Vranje (b). **TV Sezam:** Moše Pijade 23, 19210 Bor (d). **TV Sunce:** Ilije Garašanina 36, 34300 Aranđelovac (h). **TV Šabac:** Kneza Lazara 1, 15000 Šabac (c). **TV Trans:** Badnjevska bb, 19300 Negotin (d). **TV Trstenik:** Knjeginje Milice bb, 37240 Trstenik (e). **TV Vranje:** Partizanska 17a, 17500 Vranje (b). **TV Vrnjacka Banja:** Vrnjačka 1, 36210 Vrnjačka Banja (f). **TV Vujic:** Užicka 25, 14104 Valjevo (c). **TV Zona plus:** Branka Radičevića 30, 18000 Niš (e). **VA Plus:** Norveških Interniraca 23, 14000 Valjevo (c). **Vranjska plus:** Oca Justina Popovica 3/3, 17500 Vranje (b).
*) local stns transmitted exclusively in lp DTT regions not listed

DTT Tx Networks
Tx Operator: JP Emisiona Technika i Veze (ETV) **W:** etv.rs **M1:** RTS1, RTS2, RTS3, Happy TV, ETV Info, TV B92, Prva TV, TV Pink ⌘ R. Beograd 1, R. Beograd 2, R. Beograd 202 **M2:** Local stations **M3✪:** Arena Sport 1-5, Minimax, Nickelodeon, Film Klub, Agro TV, Ženska TV, Kitchen TV, Hram TV, Info na dlanu, Sve na dlanu, Pink 2, Pink 3 Info, Pink Kids, Pink Serije, Pink Premium, Pink Movies, Pink Action, Pink Comedy, Pink Pedia, Pink Reality, Pink Western, Pink Thriller.

Location	M1	M2*	M3	kW
Avala	22	28a	45	100
Besna Kobila	35	39b	43	50
Deli Jovan	23	43d	41	10
Jastrebac	27	38e	42	50
Kopaonik	24	32f	34	50
Maljen	32	34c	37	10
Ovčar	23	36g	39	80
Rudnik	26	29h	35	32
Tupižnica	22	25i	28	50

+ sites with txs below 10kW *) Local stns a-i, see above

Vojvodina

RADIO-TELEVIZIJA VOJVODINE (RTV) (Pub) ✉ Ignjata Pavlasa 3, 21101 Novi Sad ☎ +381 21 2101420 **E:** office@rtv.rs **W:** www.rtv.rs **L.P:** DG: Miodrag Koprivica **Chs:** RTV1, RTV2

Local Stations (via Mux 2 - DTT regions j-m)
KTV Televizija: Heroja Pinkija 75, 21000 Novi Sad (m). **Novosadska TV:** Trg slobode 3, 21000 Novi Sad (k). **OK TV:** Janošikova 127, 26210 Kovačica (l). **RTV Panonija:** Hajduk Veljkova 11, 21000 Novi Sad (j). **Sremska TV:** Zlatka Šnajdera 2, 22240 Šid (k). **Televizija SD:** Goranska 12, 11300 Smederevo (l). **TV Banat:** Omladinski trg 17, 26300 Vršac (l). **TV Delta:** Milana Simina 16, 21000 Novi Sad (k). **TV K9:** Dimitrije Bugarskog, 21000 Novi Sad (k). **TV Kanal 25:** Vidovdanska 12a, 25250 Odžaci (k), **TV Lav:** Stepe Stepanovića 6, 26300 Vršac (l). **TV Most:** Arse Teodorovića 5, 21000 Novi Sad (j,k). **TV Pancevo:** Nikole Đurkovića 1, 26101 Pančevo (l). **TV Petrovec:** Industrijska zona bb, 21470 Bački Petrovac (k). **TV Rubin:** Svetosavska 43, 23300 Kikinda (m). **TV Santos:** Koče Kolarova 29, 23000 Zrenjanin (m). **TV Viminacium:** Koste Abraševića 30, 12000 Požarevac (l). **TV YuEco:** Magnetna polja bb, 24000 Subotica (j).

DTT Tx Networks
Tx Operator: JP Emisiona Technika i Veze (ETV) **W:** etv.rs **M1:** RTS1, RTS2, RTS3, RTV1, RTV2, Happy TV, ETV Info, TV B92, Prva TV, TV Pink ⌘ R. Beograd 1, R. Beograd 2, R. Beograd 202 **M2:** Local stations **M3✪:** Arena Sport 1-5, Minimax, Nickelodeon, Film Klub, Agro TV, Ženska TV, Kitchen TV, Hram TV, Info na dlanu, Sve na dlanu, Pink 2, Pink 3 Info, Pink Kids, Pink Serije, Pink Premium, Pink Movies, Pink Action, Pink Comedy, Pink Pedia, Pink Reality, Pink Western, Pink Thriller.

Location	M1	M2*	M3	kW
Crveni Cot	24	30k	41	100
Kikinda	32	55m	29	10
Sombor	40	43j	34	10
Subotica	40	43j	29	50
Vršac	25	31l	37	50

*) Local stns j-l, see above

SEYCHELLES

System: DVB-T2 (HEVC) [E]

SEYCHELLES BROADCASTING CORP. (SBC) (Pub) ✉ P.O.Box

321, Victoria, Mahé ☎ +248 4289600 **E:** tv@sbc.sc **W:** www.sbc.sc **L.P:** CEO: Antoine Onezime **Chs:** SBC1, SBC2.

DTT Tx Network
Tx Operator: StarTimes **M(currently FTA, but to be partly✪ later):** SBC1, SBC2, TV5 Monde, TiVi5, TV5 Lifestyle, CGTN News, CGTN Français, France 24, RT TV ⌘ Radyo Sesel, Paradise FM, BBCWS, RFI **Txs:** MFN

SIERRA LEONE

System: DVB-T2 (MPEG4) [E]

SIERRA LEONE BROADCASTING CORP. (SLBC) (Pub) ✉ New England Ville, Freetown ☎ +232 22 240123 **E:** slbc.slnews@gmail.com **W:** www.facebook.com/slbcnews.sl **L.P:** DG: Joseph Egbenda Simon Kapuwa.

DTT Tx Network
Tx Operator: StarTimes **M(partly✪):** multiprgr **Txs:** MFN

SINGAPORE

System: DVB-T2 (MPEG4) [E]

MEDIACORP PTE. LTD (Comm) ✉ 1 Stars Avenue, Singapore 138507 ☎ +65 63333888 **W:** www.mediacorp.sg **L.P:** CEO: Tham Loke Kheng.

DTT Tx Networks
Tx Operator: Mediacorp **M1:** Channel 5 HD, Suria HD **M2:** Channel 8 HD, Vasantham HD **M3:** Channel U HD, CNA HD.

Location	M1	M2	M3
SFN	29	31	33

SLOVAKIA

Systems: DVB-T (MPEG2, MPEG4) [E]; DVB-T2 (MPEG4) [E]

National Stations
ROZHLAS A TELEVÍZIA SLOVENSKÁ (RTVS) (Pub) ✉ Mlynská Dolina 28, 84545 Bratislava ☎ +421 2 60611111 **E:** press@rtvs.sk **W:** www.rtvs.sk; www.rtvs.org **L.P:** DG: Jaroslav Rezník **Chs (terr.):** STV1, STV2, reg prgrs – **TA3 (Comm)** ✉ Gagarinova 12, 82015 Bratislava 215 ☎ 421 2 48203511 **E:** ta3@ta3.com **W:** www.ta3.com **L.P:** DG: Mirjana Hron Sikimič– **TV JOJ (Comm)** ✉ P.O.Box 33, 83007 Bratislava 37 ☎ +421 2 59888111 **E:** joj@joj.sk **W:** www,joj.sk **L.P:** CEO: Marcel Grega **Chs:** TV JOJ, Plus, WAU – **TV MARKÍZA (Comm)** ✉ Bratislavská 1/a, 84356 Bratislava 48 ☎ +421 2 68274111 **E:** sekretariatgr@markiza.sk **W:** www.markiza.sk **L.P:** DG: Matthias Settele **Chs:** TV Markíza, Dajto, Doma.

Local Stations not shown.

DTT Tx Networks (DVB-T exc. where stated)
Tx Operator: Towercom, a.s. **W:** www.towercom.sk **M1:** STV2 HD, TV Lux, TV Osem, ČT1✪, ČT2✪, JOJ Cinema HD✪, Sport 1✪, Sport 2✪ **M2:** TV JOJ, Plus, WAU, TA3 **M3:** STV1 HD, STV1 (SD), STV2 HD, STV2 (SD) **M4✪(DVB-T2):** TV Markiza, Dajto, Doma, Prima Prime, Prima Cool, Eurosport 1, Eurosport 2, Film+, Nickelodeon, VH1, Viasat Explore, Viasat History, Viasat Nature, RIK/Minimax ⌘ R. Slovensko, R. Devín, Rádio_FM, R. Patria, R. Slovakia International, R. Pyramida, R. Litera, R. Junior – **Local Tx Operators:** not shown.

Location	M1	M2	M3	M4	kW
Banská Bystrica (Laskomer)	47	51	33	40	25/2x26/25
Banská Štiavnica (Sitno)	50	21	48	31	32/50/35/25
Bardejov (Magura)	47	40	54	46	13/3x16
Borský Mikuláš (Dubník)	-	56	27	-	20/22
Bratislava (Kamzík)	44	56	27	39	32/3x50
Košice (Dubník)	23	59	25	22	13/16/31/10
Košice (Heringeš)	23	59	25	21	13/20/17/20
Kráľovský Chlmec	57	59	25	-	10
Lučenec (Blatný vrch)	49	60	33	32	20/16/2x20
Námestovo (Magurka)	44	59	26	-	23/22/31
Nitra (Zobor)	28	21	48	31	25/44/40/16
Nové Mesto n.V. (V.Javorina)	55	56	57	23	3x50/25
Poprad (Hranovnica)	41	55	24	39	16/50/2x20
Rožňava	57	27	54	-	20
Ružomberok (Úložisko)	44	59	26	46	20/50/3x20
Snina (Magurica)	57	59	25	-	25/21/20
Stará Ľubovňa (Kolník)	41	55	24	-	23/25/20
Trenčín	55	52	57	-	30/40/50
Žilina (Krížava)	35	52	32	39	6/18/2x10

+ sites with txs below 10kW. Pol=V.

SLOVENIA

System: DVB-T (MPEG4) [E]

National Stations
RADIOTELEVIZIJA SLOVENIJA (RTVSLO) (Pub) ✉ Kolodvorska 2-4, 1000 Ljubljana ☎ +386 1 4752121 **E:** info@rtvslo.si **W:** www.rtvslo.si **L.P:** DG: Igor Kadunc **Chs:** SLO1, SLO2, SLO3, TV Koper/Capodistria, Tele M – **NOVA24TV (Comm)** ✉ Linhartova 13, 1000 Ljubljana ☎ +386 1 2355293 **E:** info@nova24tv.si **W:** nova24tv.si – **TV3 MEDIAS (Comm)** ✉ Šmartinska cesta 152, 1000 Ljubljana ☎ +386 8 3874404 🖷 +386 8 3874402 **E:** info@tv3-medias.si **W:** tv3m.si.

Local Stations not shown.

DTT Tx Networks
Licensee: RTVSLO **M1:** SLO1 HD, SLO2 HD, SLO3 HD, TV Koper/Capodistria, Tele M, Vaš kanal **M3:** SLO1, SLO2, SLO3, TV3, Golica TV, Sponka Gold TV, Nova24TV, TV Petelin, Obvestilo C. **NB:** M2 not assigned.

Location	M1	M3	kW	Location	M1*	M3	kW
Beli Križ	27	33	5	Pečarovci	27	37	5
Boč	27	37	5	Plešivec	27	37	25
Golo Brdo	27	22	5	Pohorje	27	37	100
Kambreško	27	22	5	Skalnica	27	33	5
Krim	32	38	5	Slavnik	27	22	5
Krvavec	32	38	100	Tinjan	27	33	5
Kuk	27	22	5	Trdinov vrh	32	38	20
Kum	32	38	5	Trstelj	27	33	25
Nanos	27	22	200	+ sites with txs below 5kW			

Local licensees not shown.

SOLOMON ISLANDS

Systems: DVB-T (MPEG2) [AU], PAL-B [AU]

TELEKOM TELEVISION LTD (TTV) (Comm) ✉ Cnr Mendana Ave & Mud Ave, Point Cruz, (PO Box 148), Honiara ☎ +677 28882 **E:** info@ttv.sb **W:** www.ttv.sb **L.P:** CEO: Arthur Yen **Txs: TTV1:** Honiara ch7 (1kW) & netw. **TTV2:** Honiara ch9A (1W) & netw. **TTV3:** Honiara ch11 (1kW).

DTT Tx Network
Tx Operator: TTV **M1:** TTV1, Al Jazeera, ESPN, ABC Australia **M2:** TTV2, BBC World News, Edge Sport **M3:** TTV3, NHK World TV, EWTN, CGTN **M4:** DW-TV, ESPN2, Channel News Asia, France 24.

Location	M1	M2	M3	M4	kW
Honiara	29	28	8	6	2x1.8/0.25/0.35

SOMALIA

System: DVB-T2 (MPEG4) [E]

National Station
SOMALI NATIONAL TELEVISION (SNTV) (Pub) ✉ Mogadishu **E:** info@sntv.so **W:** sntv.so.

Regional/Local Stations not shown.

DTT Tx Network
Tx Operator: SNTV **M:** multiprgr **Txs:** MFN.
Local licensees not shown.

SOUTH AFRICA

Systems: DVB-T2 (MPEG4) [SA]; § PAL-I [VHF=SA, UHF=E] ⇩2021

SOUTH AFRICAN BROADCASTING CORP. (SABC) (Pub) ✉ Private Bag XI, Auckland Park 2006 ☎ +27 11 7149111 **E:** info@sabc.co.za **W:** www.sabc.co.za **L.P:** Chmn: Bongumusa Makhathini. **Chs:** SABC1, SABC2, SABC3, SABC News, SABC Encore – **E.TV (Comm)** ✉ Private Bag x9944, Sandton 2146 ☎ +27 21 4814500 **E:** info@etv.co.za **W:** www.etv.co.za – **M-NET (Comm)** ✉ P.O.Box 4950, Randburg 2125 ☎ +27 11 2893000 **E:** inquiries@mnet.co.za **W:** m-net.dstv.com **L.P:** CEO: Yolisa Phahle.

DTT Tx Networks
Licensee: Sentech **W:** www.sentech.co.za **M:** SABC1, SABC2, SABC3, SABC News, SABC Encore, e.tv **Txs:** MFN – **Licensee:** Multichoice **W:** www.multichoice.co.za **M✪:** multiprgr. **Txs:** MFN

SOUTH SUDAN

System: DVB-T2 (MPEG4) [E]

National Station
SOUTH SUDAN BROADCASTING CORP. (SSBC) (Pub) ✉ Juba ☎ +211 912 452275 **L.P:** Dir: Suzan Alphonse.

Local Stations not shown.

DTT Tx Network
Tx Operator: SSBC **Mux:** multiprgr **Txs:** MFN

SPAIN

System: DVB-T (MPEG2, MPEG4) [E]

National Stations
TELEVISION ESPAÑOLA (TVE) (Pub) ✉ Avenida de Radiotelevision, 4 , Prado del Rey, 28223 Pozuelo de Alarcon (Madrid) ☎ +34 91 5817000 **E:** direccion.comunicacion@rtve.es **W:** www.rtve.es **L.P:** Pres (RTVE): Rosa María Mateo **Chs:** La 1, La 2, 24h, Clan, TDP – **ANTENA 3 (Comm)** ✉ Carretera San Sebastian de los Reyes, 28700 Madrid ☎ +34 1 6320500 **W:** www.antena3.com – **CUATRO (Comm)** ✉ Avenida de los Artesanos 6, 28760 Madrid ☎ +34 91 7367000 **E:** internet@cuatro.com **W:** www.cuatro.com – **LA SEXTA (Comm)** ✉ C/ Virgilio, 2 Edificio 4, 28223 Pozuelo de Alarcón☎ +34 91 8382966 **E:** rr.hh@lasexta.com **W:** www.lasexta.com – **TELECINCO (Comm)** ✉ Ctra de Irún, Km 11,700, 28049 Madrid ☎ +34 902 155555 **E:** inversores@telecinco.es **W:** www.telecinco.es.

Regional Stations (Pub) (available on Multiplex "R"))
AN) Radio y Televisión de Andalucía (RTVA): Edificio Cana Sur, Avda. Josó Gálvez 1, 41092 Isla de la Cartuja (Sevilla) **W:** www.canalsur.es. Chs: Canal Sur, Canal Sur 2, Andalusía TV. **AR)** Corporación Aragonesa de Radio y Televisión (CARTV): Avda. Maria Zambrano 2, 50018 Zaragoza. **W:** www.cartv.es. Chs: Aragón TV. **AS)** Radioelevisión del Principado de Asturias (RTPA): Edificio RTPA, Parque Cientifico y Tecnológico de Gijon, c/ Luis Blanco 82, 33203 Gijon. **W:** www.rtpa.es. Chs: TPA7, TPA8. **BA)** Ente Público de Radiotelevisión de la Islas Baleares (EPRTVIB): c/ Madalena, 21 Polígon Son Bugadelles, 07180 Santa Ponça **W:** www.ib3tv.com. Ch: IB3 TV. **CA)** Corporació Catalana de Mitjans Audivisuals (CCMA): HQ: Via Augusta 252, 4a planta, 08817 Barcelona; Televisió de Catalunya: Carrer de la TV3, s/n, 08970 Sant Joan Despi (Barcelona) **W:** www.ccma.cat. Chs: TV3, TV3 HD, 33, Canal Super3, 324, Canal 3XL, Esport 3. **CL)** Radio Televisión de Castilla y León: c/Monasterio San Millán de la Cogolla 30, 47015 Valladoid **W:** www.rtvcyl.es Chs: CyLTV, La 8. **CM)** Castilla-La Mancha Media (CMM): C/ Río Alberche, s/n Polígono Santa Mª de Benquerencia, 45007 Toledo **W:** www.cmmedia.es. Chs: CMT, CMT 2. **EU)** Euskal Irrati Telebista (EITB): Capuchinos de Basurto 2, 48013 Bilbao **W:** www.eitb.eus Chs: ETB1, ETB2, ETB3. **GA)** Compañía de Radio-Televisión de Galicia (CRTVG): Bando - San Marcos s/n, 15820 Santiago de Compostela **W:** www.crtvg.es. Chs: TVG, tvG2. **MA)** Ente Público Radio Televisión Madrid (EPRTVM): Paseo del Príncipe 3, 28223 Pozuelo de Alarcón (Madrid). **W:** www.telemadrid.es. Chs: Telemadrid, Telemadrid HD, LaOtra. **MU)** Radiotelevisión de la Región de Murcia (RTRM): Plaza de San Agustín 5, 30005 Murcia. **W:** www.rtrm.es Chs: 7RM, 7RM HD. **VA)** Ràdiotelevisió Valenciana (RTVV): Polígon Accés Ademús s/n, 46100 Burjassot, València. **W:** www.rtvv.es. Chs: Canal Nou, Canal Nou Dos, Canal Nou 24.
NB. Keys to region codes see National Radio section.

Local Stations not shown.

DTT Tx Networks
Operator: Cellnex Telecom **W:** www.cellnextelecom.com **M1:** La 1 HD, La 1 (SD), La 2 HD, La 2 (SD), 24h, Clan ⌘ RNE R. Nacional, RNE R.5 **M2:** TDP HD, TDP (SD), Clan HD, Clan (SD), DKISS, TEN ⌘ RNE R. Clásica HQ, RNE R.3 HQ, RNE R. Exterior, SER, Los40, Dial, Kiss FM, Hit FM, esRadio **M3:** GOL, DMAX, Disney Channel, Paramount Network ⌘ Cadena 100, R. Maria, R. Marca, Vaughn R. **M4:** Antena 3 HD, Antena 3 (SD), laSexta HD, laSexta (SD), Neox, Nova, TVE 4K **M5:** Telecinco HD, Telecinco (SD), Cuatro HD, Cuatro (SD), FDF, Divinity **M6:** Boing, Energy, Mega, TRECE ⌘ Onda Cero, Europa FM, Melodia FM, Cope, Rock FM **M7:** Atreseries HD, BeMad TV HD, RealMadrid TV HD, TEN ⌘ Los40 Classic, Los40 Urban, Radiolé **R:** Regional Muxes (see Regional Stations) **Local Muxes** not shown.

Location	M1	M2	M3	M4	M5	M6	M7	R
Madrid	33	41	32	34	25	26	22	38

+ nationwide MFN

SRI LANKA

Systems: ISDB-TB [E]; # PAL-B/G [E]

National Stations ([a]=analogue)
SRI LANKA RUPAVAHINI CORP. (SLRC) (Pub) ✉ P.O. Box 2204, Colombo 7 ☎ +94 11 2697491 **L.P:** CEO: Gamini Somachandra Rasaputhra **E:** dg@rupavahini.lk **W:** www.rupavahini.lk **Chs:** Rupavahini, Channel Eye/Nethra TV. **Txs: Rupavahini:** Pidurutalagala [a]ch5 (20kW), Kokavil [a]ch8 (20 kW) & relay txs; **Channel Eye/ Nethra TV:** Pidurutalagala [a]ch7 (20kW) & network – **INDEPENDENT TELEVISION NETWORK (ITN) (Comm)** ✉ Wickramasinghepura, Battaramulla ☎ +94 11 2774424 **E:** itnadm@slt.lk **W:** www.itn.lk **L.P:** Chmn: Rosmund Senaratne **Chs:** ITN, Vasantham TV **Txs Vasantham TV:** Deniyaya [a]ch9 (20kW), Colombo [a]ch12 (100kW), Yatiyantota [a]ch12 (100kW), Nayabedde [a]ch12 (3kW) – **MTV CHANNEL (PVT) LTD. (Comm)** ✉ 7, Braybrook Pl., Colombo 2 ☎ +94 11 4792600 **E:** info@media.maharaja.lk **W:** tv1.lk (TV1); shakthitv.lk (Shakhti TV); sirasatv.lk (Sirasa TV) **L.P:** CEO: Gayirika Perusignhe. **Chs:** TV1 (English), Shakthi TV (Tamil), Sirasa TV (Singalese). **Txs: TV1/ Shakthi:** Colombo [a]ch25 (5kW) & network; **Sirasa:** Colombo [a]ch23 (5kW) & netw. – **SWARNAVAHINI (EAP BROADCASTING CO. LTD.) (Comm)** ✉ 676 Galle Rd, Colombo 3 ☎ +94 11 2599642 **E:** admin@swarnavahini.lk **W:** www.facebook.com/swarnavahini **L.P:** Chmn: Dayanath Jayasuriya. **Txs:** Colombo [a]ch34 (5kW) & netw. – **TELSHAN NETWORK (PVT) LTD. (TNL) (Comm)** ✉ Innagale Estate Dampe-Piliyandala ☎ +94 11 2501681 **E:** info@tnltv.lk **W:** tnltv.lk **L.P:** Chmn/MD: Shantilal Nilkant Wickremesinghe **Txs:** Piliyandala [a]ch3 (20kW), Polgahawela [a]ch3 (1kW), Nuweraeliya [a]ch4 (40kW), Colombo [a]ch21 (22kW), Hantana (Kandy) [a]ch21 (22kW), Piliyandala [a]ch26 (22kW), Ratnapura [a]ch26 (1kW).

Local Stations not shown.

ST BARTHÉLEMY (France)

System: DVB-T (MPEG4) [E]

DTT Tx Networks
Tx Operator: TDF **Mux:** Guadeloupe La 1ère, France 2-5*, Franceinfo, Arte **Txs:** ch41 (SFN). *) France 4 will cease in 2021

ST EUSTATIUS (Netherlands)

NB: No terrestrial TV station.

ST HELENA (UK)

System: DVB-T2 (MPEG4) [E]

DTT Tx Network
Tx Operator: Sure South Atlantic Ltd. ✉ P.O.Box 2, Bishop's Rooms, Jamestown, St. Helena Island, South Atlantic Ocean STHL 1ZZ **E:** service@sure.co.sh **W:** www.sure.co.sh **Mux✪:** M-Net, M-Net Movies Premiere, M-Net Movies Drama & Romance, M-Net Movies Action, Super Sport One, Super Sport Two, Super Sport Three, Super Sport Five, Super Sport Six, Super Sport Seven, BBC Entertainment, BBC World News, Discovery, Cartoon Network, Disney, BBC Lifestyle (+ Local Channel 1), National Geographic (+ Local Channel 2) ⌘ Two radio prgrs **Txs:** (-).

ST KITTS & NEVIS

NB: No terrestrial TV station.

ST LUCIA

System: NTSC-M [A]

HELEN TELEVISION (HTS) (Comm) ✉ P.O. Box 621, The Morne, Castries ☎ +1 758 4524982 **E:** news@htsstlucia.org **W:** www.

htsstlucia.org **L.P:** MD: Linford Fevrier **Txs:** Castries ch4 (20kW H) & ch5 (20kW H).

ST MAARTEN (Netherlands)

System: DVB-T (MPEG2) [E]

LEEWARD BROADCASTING CORP. (LBC) ✉ P.O.Box 375, Philipsburg. **Tx:** (-).

ST MARTIN (France)

System: DVB-T (MPEG4) [E]

IOTV (Comm) ✉ 7, route de Friar's Bay, F-97150 Saint-Martin ☎ +690 690343464 **W:** www.facebook.com/io.tvsxm.

DTT Tx Network
Tx Operator: TDF **Mux:** Guadeloupe la 1ère HD, France 2-5*, Franceinfo, Arte, IOTV **Txs:** ch41 (Terre Basse), ch43 (Pic Paradis). *) France 4 will cease in 2021

ST PIERRE & MIQUELON (France)

System: DVB-T (MPEG4) [E]

SAINT-PIERRE ET MIQUELON LA 1ÈRE (Pub) ✉ BP 4227, F-97500 Saint-Pierre et Miquelon ☎ +508 411111 **W:** la1ere.francetvinfo.fr/saintpierremiquelon **L.P:** Dir: Gilles Derouet.

DTT Tx Network
Tx Operator: TDF **Mux:** Saint-Pierre et Miquelon la 1ère, France 2-5*, Franceinfo, Arte **Txs:** ch35 (Phare de Galantry), ch37 (Cap à l'Aigle), ch41 (Pointe au Cheval). *) France 4 will cease in 2021

ST VINCENT & THE GRENADINES

System: NTSC-M [A]

SVGTV (Gov) ✉ P.O.Box 705, Kingstown, St. Vincent ☎ +1 784 4561078 **E:** svgbc@vincysurf.com **W:** www.svg-tv.com **L.P:** MD: R. Paul MacLeish. **Txs:** (pol.H) Dorsetshirehill ch9 (0.4kW), Layouhill ch7 (0.04kW), Maroonhill ch7 (0.04kW), Belleislehill ch11 (0.06kW), Mustique ch11 (0.06kW), Bequia ch13 (0.06kW).

Foreign TV Relay
TBN (USA): Kingstown ch4.

SUDAN

System: DVB-T2 (MPEG4) [E]

SUDAN TELEVISION (Gov) ✉ P.O.Box 1094, Omdurman ☎ +249 183557398 **E:** sudantvlive@sudanmail.net **Chs:** Sudan TV, Blue Nile TV, Spacetoons.

DTT Tx Network
Licensee: Multichoice Sudan **M(partly✪):** multiprgr **Txs:** MFN

SURINAME

System: ATSC

National Stations
ALGEMENE TELEVISIE VERZORGING (ATV) (Gov) ✉ Van het Hogerhuysstraat 58-60, Paramaribo ☎ +597 404611 📠 +597 402660 **E:** info@atv.sr **W:** www.atv.sr **Chs:** ATV, TV2 **Txs:** Paramaribo ch12 (0.4kW) & netw. – **SURINAAMSE TELEVISIE STICHTING (STVS) (Pub)** ✉ Stadiumlaan, Paramaribo ☎ +597 473032 **E:** info@stvs.sr **W:** stvs.sr **Txs:** Paramaribo ch8 (1kW) & netw.

Local Stations (all Comm)
Ampies Broadcasting Corp: P.O.Box 885, Paramaribo; ch4 (1kW). **Garuda TV:** Goudstraat 20, Paramaribo; ch23. **Radika TV:** P.O.Box 1083, Paramaribo; ch14 (1kW). **Rapar Broadcasting Network (RBN):** P.O.Box 975, Paramaribo; ch5 (2kW). **Rasonic:** Bataviastraat 2, Nickerie; ch7 (1kW). **TV Apinti:** P.O.Box 595, Paramaribo; ch10 (1kW). **TV Sookha:** Batavaiastraat 25, Nickerie; tx:(-).

DTT Tx Network
Licensee: Wise NV **W:** www.wise.sr **M✪:** multiprgr **Txs:** MFN.

SWEDEN

Systems: DVB-T (MPEG2), DVB-T2 (MPEG4) [E]

National Stations
SVERIGES TELEVISION AB (SVT) (Pub) ✉ Oxenstiernsgatan 26-34, 105 10 Stockholm ☎ +46 8 7840000 **E:** info@svt.se **W:** www.svt.se **L.P:** MD: Hanna Stjärne **Chs:** SVT1, SVT2, Kunskapskanalen, SVT Barnkanalen/SVT24, regional prgrs – **CANAL DIGITAL SVERIGE AB (Comm)** ✉ Tegeluddsvägen 3, 115 80 Stockholm ☎ +46 8 7722700 **E:** kundservice@canaldigital.se **W:** www.canaldigital.se – **NORDIC ENTERTAINMENT GROUP AB (NENT) (Comm)** ✉ Ringvägen 52, 118 67 Stockholm ☎ +46 8 56202500 **W:** www.nent-group.com **L.P:** CEO: Anders Jensen – **TV4 MEDIA AB (Comm)** ✉ Tegeluddsvägen 3-5, 115 79 Stockholm ☎ +46 8 4594000 **E:** info@tv4.se **W:** www.tv4.se **L.P:** CEO: Casten Almqvist.

Local Stations not shown.

DTT Tx Networks (DVB-T2 except where stated)
Licensee: Boxer TV Access AB **W:** www.boxer.se **M1 (DVB-T):** SVT1 (incl. reg. prgrs), SVT2 (incl. reg. prgrs), SVT Kunskapskanalen, SVT Barnkanalen/SVT24 **M2✪(exc.*) (DVB-T):** TV3, TV4*, Sjuan, TV6*, Kanal 5, Kanal 9, Kanal 11; Stockholm region only: Yle TV Finland **M3✪(DVB-T):** TV8, Nickelodeon/MTV, Paramount Network, TV10, Discovery Channel, TLC, TV12, Eurosport 1 **M5✪:** Axess TV, BBC World News, C More Series, Nick Jr/BBC Earth, Fox, CNN, C More First, Eurosport 2, SF-kanalen/C More Golf, Investigation Discovery, V Series, V Film Premiere, V Sport Premium, V Sport 1, V Motor **M6✪(exc.*):** SVT1 HD (incl. reg. prgrs)*, SVT2 HD (incl. reg. prgrs)*, TV3 HD, TV4 HD, Kanal 5 HD, Animal Planet HD **M7✪:** C More Live HD/C More Hits, Sportkanalen HD, National Geographic HD, C More Hockey, C More Football/Stars, V Sport Extra, Al Jazeera, Fight Sports.

Location	M1	M2	M3	M5	M6	M7[1]	kW[1]
Arvidsjaur (Julträsk)	34	24	30	42	25	37	50
Bollnäs	29	23	34	31	39	6	50
Borlänge (Idkerberget)	47	32	43	41	45	28	50
Borås (Dalsjöfors)	44	29	46	42	36	41	50
Bäckefors	35	22	31	26	25	5	50
Emmaboda (Bälshult)	21	28	46	45	47	8	50
Filipstad (Klockarhöjden)	42	30	33	23	46	40	50
Finnveden (Bredaryd)	26	48	31	35	38	7	50
Gällivare	33	28	40	46	43	22	50
Gävle (Skogmur)	27	24	26	30	46	9	50
Göteborg (Brudaremossen)	30	27	46	43	40	9	50
Halmstad (Oskarström)	21	28	45	47	32	7	10
Helsingborg (Olympia)	27	43	25	41	22	30	10
Hudiksvall (Forsa)	29	23	34	31	39	44	50
Hörby (Sallerup)	33	43	25	41	22	10	50
Jönköping (Bondberget)	28	23	33	35	40	6	50
Kalix	29	27	21	35	48	45	50
Karlshamn	27	24	42	41	30	8	50
Karlskrona (Vämö)	27	24	42	41	30	8	50
Karlstad (Sörmon)	42	30	44	26	46	40	50
Kiruna (Kirunavaara)	39	35	44	42	29	32	50
Kisa	29	38	30	43	42	6	50
Lycksele (Knaften)	45	28	22	38	48	35	50
Malmö (Jägersro)	33	43	25	41	22	10	50
Mora (Eldris)	22	25	35	44	42	38	50
Motala (Ervasteby)	27	45	41	43	39	21	50
Norrköping (Krokek)	36	46	47	32	28	5	50
Nässjö	22	23	33	35	25	6	50
Pajala	34	23	31	37	47	32	50
Skellefteå	23	26	46	43	31	6	50
Skövde	37	24	32	34	47	21	50
Sollefteå (Multrå)	46	44	31	24	21	26	50
Stockholm (Nacka)	23	42	39	32	45	21	50
Storuman	33	43	36	46	26	35	50
Sundsvall (S Stadsberget)	47	27	30	24	43	26	50
Sunne (Blåbärskullen)	36	39	47	26	34	7	50
Sveg (Brickan)	21	24	46	36	41	32	50
Trollhättan	23	22	31	28	25	9	50
Tåsjö (Hoting)	32	40	30	25	41	37	50
Uddevalla (Herrestad)	23	22	31	28	25	9	50
Uppsala (Vedyxa)	40	29	33	30	43	21	50
Varberg (Grimeton)	21	28	45	47	32	7	10
Visby (Follingbo)	31	44	48	48	37	22	50
Vislanda (Nydala)	40	44	37	39	34	8	50

Location	M1	M2	M3	M5	M6	M7[1]	kW[1]
Vännäs (Granlundsberget)	47	36	29	43	27	39	50
Västervik (Fårhult)	26	34	30	43	40	24	50
Västerås (Lillhärad)	44	22	34	38	31	35	50
Ånge (Snöberg)	42	37	40	35	28	38	50
Älvsbyn	36	39	47	38	32	45	50
Örebro (Lockhyttan)	29	25	33	38	48	35	50
Örnsköldsvik (Ås)	23	34	31	24	21	39	50
Östersund (Brattåsen)	27	45	48	36	22	38	50
Östhammar (Valö)	40	48	26	30	43	6	50
Överkalix	26	27	21	35	48	45	50

+ sites with txs below 10kW. 1) Power refers to UHF chs

SWITZERLAND

System: DVB-T (MPEG2) [E]

DTT Tx Network
Tx Operator: Swisscom **W:** www.swisscom.ch **M:** SRF1, SRF Zwei **Tx:** ch34 (Altstätten/Hoher Kasten 1.8kW).

NB: All domestic distribution of TV prgrs via DTT in Switzerland ceased in June 2019. However, in 2020 a private cable TV company from Austria (Kabel-TV Lampert GmbH & Co KG) obtained a licence from the Swiss regulator to lease a tx on Swiss territory for the re-transmission of two German language channels of the Swiss public broadcaster SRG SSR so that they can be received on the Austrian side for re-transmission in cable TV networks (start: June 2020).

SYRIA

System: DVB-T2 (MPEG4)

National Stations
ORGANIZATION OF RADIO & TELEVISION - SYRIA (ORTAS) (Gov) ✉ Ommayad Square, Damascus ☎ +963 11 2720700 **E:** srtv@ortas.online **W:** ortas.online **Chs:** Syria 1, Syria Sat, Syria News, Drama, Sport 24 – **ADDOUNIA TV (Comm)** ✉ Damascus **W:** www.facebook.com/addouniach.

Local Station
Ugarit TV (Gov), Latakia.

DTT Tx Network
Tx Operator: ORTAS **M:** Syria 1, Syria Sat, Syria News, Drama, Sport 24 **Txs:** MFN.

TAIWAN (Rep. of China)

System: DVB-T (MPEG2, MPEG4) [A]

TAIWAN BROADCASTING SYSTEM (TBS) (Pub) ✉ 50, Lane 75, Kang-Ning Rd., Section 3, Taipei 114 ☎ +886 2 26332000 **W:** www.tbs.org.tw **L.P:** Chair: Yaly Chao **NB:** TBS is the holding for the public service broadcasters CTS and PTS. **Chinese Television System (CTS)** ✉ 100, Kuang Fu South Rd, Taipei 106 ☎ +886 2 27510321 **E:** wwwpub@mail.cts.com.tw **W:** www.cts.com.tw **Chs:** CTS HD, CTS Education & Culture, CTS News Channel, CTS Variety. **Public Television Service (PTS)** ✉ as TBS ☎ +886 2 26339122 **E:** pub@mail.pts.org.tw **W:** www.pts.org.tw **L.P:** Pres/CEO: Sunshine Kuang **Chs:** PTS, PTS2, PTS3, Hakka TV – **CHINA TELEVISION CO., LTD (CTV) (Comm)** ✉ 120, Chung-Yang Rd, Taipei 115 ☎ +886 2 27838308 **E:** pubr@mail.chinatv.com.tw **W:** www.ctv.com.tw **L.P:** Chmn: Chiu Chia-Yu **Chs:** CTV HD, CTV News Channel, CTV Bravo, CTV Classic. – **FORMOSA TELEVISION, INC. (FTV) (Comm)** ✉ 24/F, 30, Pa Te Road, Section 3, Tapei 105 ☎ +886 2 25702570 **E:** service@ftv.com.tw **W:** www.ftv.com.tw **Chs:** FTV HD, FTV News, Follow Me TV, Four Seasons TV. **L.P:** Chairman: Kuo Bei-hong – **TAIWAN TELEVISION ENTERPRISE CO., LTD (TTV) (Comm)** ✉ 10, Pa Te Rd, Section 3, Taipei 10560 ☎ +886 2 25781515 **E:** ref@email.ttv.com.tw **W:** www.ttv.com.tw **Chs:** TTV HD, TTV Finance, TTV News Channel, TTV Variety.

DTT Tx Networks (MPEG2 exc. *=MPEG4)
Licensee: CTS **M:** CTS HD*, CTS Education & Culture, CTS News Channel, CTS Variety – **Licensee:** PTS **M1:** PTS, PTS2, PTS3, Hakka TV **M2*:** PTS HD – **Licensee:** CTV **M:** CTV HD*, CTV News Channel, CTV Bravo, CTV Classic – **Licensee:** FTV **M:** FTV HD*, FTV News, Follow Me TV, Four Seasons TV ⌘ Formosa Network – **Licensee:** TTV **M:** TTV HD*, TTV Finance, TTV News Channel, TTV Variety.

Location	PTS M1	PTS M2	CTS	CTV	FTV	TTV
SFN	26	30	34	24	28	32

TAJIKISTAN

Systems: DVB-T2 (MPEG4) [E]; § SECAM-D/K [R], § PAL-D/K [R]

National Station
KUMITAI TELEVIZION VA RADIOI (Gov) ✉ TV studios: Bekhzod St. 7a, 734013 Dushanbe ☎ +992 37 2224357 **E:** info@ktr.tj **W:** www.ktr.tj **L.P:** Chmn: Asadulloi Rahmon **Chs:** TV Tojikiston, TV Safina, Jahonnamo, Bahoriston, TV Sinamo, Varzish Sport, Futbol, Shahnavoz.

Local Stations not shown.

DTT Tx Network
Tx Operator: Teleradiokom **M:** TV Tojikiston HD, TV Safina HD, Jahonnamo, Bahoriston, TV Sinamo HD, Varzish Sport HD, Futbol HD, Shahnavoz, Regional Stns **Txs:** ch46 (Dushanbe 2.5kW), ch49 (Khujand) + nationwide MFN.

TANZANIA

System: DVB-T2 (MPEG4) [E]

National Stations
TANZANIA BROADCASTING CORP. (TBC) (Pub) ✉ P.O.Box 31519, Dar es Salaam ☎ +255 22 2700062 **E:** info@tbc.go.tz **W:** tbc.go.tz **L.P:** DG: Ayub Rioba **Chs:** TBC1, TBC2 – **CHANNEL TEN (Comm)** ✉ P.O.Box 19045, Dar es Salaam ☎ +255 22 2116341 **E:** info@channelten.co.tz **W:** channelten.co.tz – **INDEPENDENT TELEVISION (ITV) (Comm)** ✉ P.O.Box 4374, Dar es Salaam ☎ +255 22 2775914 5 **E:** info@itv.co.tz **W:** www.itv.co.tz – **STAR TV (Comm)** ✉ P.O.Box 1732, Mwanza ☎ +255 28 2503262 **W:** www.startv.co.tz.

Local Stations not shown.

DTT Tx Networks
Licensee: Basic Transmissions Ltd **M:** multiprgr **Txs:** MFN – **Licensee:** Star Media Tanzania Ltd (StarTimes) **M✪:** multiprgr **Txs:** MFN – **Licensee:** Agape Associates Limited **M✪:** multiprgr **Txs:** MFN.

THAILAND

Systems: DVB-T2 (MPEG4) [E]

MCOT PLC (MODERNINE TV) (Gov) ✉ 63/1 Rama IX Road, Huay Khwang, Bangkok 10320 ☎ +66 2 22016000 **W:** www.mcot.net – **NATIONAL BROADCASTING SERVICES OF THAILAND (NBT) (Gov)** ✉ 90 91 New Phetchaburi Road, Huay Khwang, Bangkok 10320 ☎ +66 2 3182110 **W:** nbt2hd.prd.go.th – **ROYAL ARMY TELEVISION (TV5) (Mil)** ✉ 210 Phaholyothin Rd, Sanam Pao, Bangkok 10400 ☎ +66 2 22710060 **E:** army@tv5.co.th **W:** www.tv5.co.th – **THAI PUBLIC BROADCASTING SERVICE (TPBS) (Pub)** ✉ 1010 Shinawatra Tower III, 13 Vibhavadi Rangsit Road, Chatchuchak, Bangkok 10900 ☎ +66 2 27911000 **E:** webmaster@thaipbs.or.th **W:** www.thaipbs.or.th – **BANGKOK BROADCASTING & TELEVISION (BBTV) (Comm)** ✉ P.O.Box 4-56, Bangkok 10900 ☎ +66 2 2720010 **E:** marketing@ch7.com **W:** www.ch7.com – **BANGKOK ENTERTAINMENT CO. LTD. (CHANNEL 3) (Comm)** ✉ Floors 7, 15, 16, The Emporium Tower, Sukhumvit Road, Khlong Tan, Khlong Toey, Bangkok 10110 ☎ +66 2 22623333 **W:** www.thaitv3.com.

DTT Tx Networks
Tx Operator: MCOT **M1 (PRD):** PRD HD, NBT HD **M2 (RTA1):** TV5 HD, Channel 7 HD, One HD, TNN, Workpoint TV, True4U **M3 (MCOT):** GMM 25 HD, MCOT HD, TV8, Thairath TV **M4 (TBPS):** TPBS HD, Channel 3 HD, Channel 8 **M5 (RTA2):** Amarin TV, PPTV HD, Mono 29, Nation TV

Location	M1	M2	M3	M4	M5
Bangkok (SFN)	26	36	40	44	48

+ nationwide MFN

TIMOR-LESTE

System: PAL-G [E]; DTMB [E] planned

RADIO TELEVISAUN TIMOR-LESTE (RTTL) (Pub) ✉ Estrada Mercado Municipal, Caicoli. Dili **E:** info@rttlep.tl **W:** rttlep.tl ☎ +670 3321827 **L.P:** Pres:Tomada de Posse **Txs:** Dili ch23 & netw.

TOGO

System: DVB-T2 (MPEG4) [E]

National Stations
TÉLÉVISION TOGOLAISE (Gov) ✉ BP 3286, Lomé ☎ +228 22215357 **E:** televisiontogolaise@yahoo.fr **W:** tvt.tg **L.P:** DG: Kuessan Yovodévi – **TV2 (Comm)** ✉ Lomé ☎ +228 22514993 **W:** www.facebook.com/Tv2-TOGO-1439012189648666 **L.P:** DG: Eudoxie Théophane.

Local Station
TV7: BP 81104, Lomé.

DTT Tx Network
Tx Operator: StarTimes **M(partly✪):** multiprgr **Txs:** MFN

TOKELAU (New Zealand)

NB: No terrestrial TV station.

TONGA

System: DVB-T2 (MPEG4) [E]

TONGA BROADCASTING COMMISSION (Gov) ✉ P.O.Box 36, Nuku'alofa ☎ +676 23555 **E:** info@tonga-broadcasting.net **W:** www.tonga-broadcasting.net **Chs:** TV Tonga, TV Tonga 2 (incl. relay CCTV-9), TV Vava'u – **DOULOS BROADCASTING NETWORK (Rlg)** ✉ P.O.Box 91, Nuku'alofa ☎ +676 23314 **W:** www.facebook.com/DoulosTVTonga **L.P:** Dir: Gerhard Taukolo Taukolo.

DTT Tx Networks
Tx Operator: Digicel **W:** www.digicelgroup.com **Mux✪:** multiprgr **Tx:** ch45V (Nuku'alofa 1kW).

TRINIDAD & TOBAGO

Systems: DVB-T (MPEG4) [A]; # NTSC-M [A]

National Stations
CCN-TV6 (Comm) ✉ 35 Independence Sq, Port-of-Spain, Trinidad ☎ +1 868 6278806 **W:** www.tv6tnt.com **L.P:** CEO: Dawn Thomas **Txs:** [a]ch6 (25kW) & [a]ch18 (1kW) (Trinidad), [a]ch19 (Tobago) – **C TELEVISION (CNMG) (Comm)** ✉ 11A Maraval Road, Port-of-Spain, Trinidad **W:** ctvtt.com **L.P:** CEO (acting): Julian Rogers **Txs:** [a]ch9, [a]ch13 – **GAYELLE TV (Comm)** ✉ 13 Southern Main Road, Curepe, Trinidad and Tobago, Curepe Village, Saint George, Trinidad ☎ +1 868 2906880 **E:** gayelletv@gmail.com **W:** www.facebook.com/GayelleTheCaribbean **Tx:** [a]ch23 & [a]ch27 (Trinidad).

Local Stations not shown.

DTT Tx Networks
Licensee: Green Dot Ltd **W:** www.gd.tt **Mux 1-4:** multiprgr **Txs:** SFN.

TRISTAN DA CUNHA (UK)

System: PAL-I [E]

NB: Terrestrial relay of a BFBS feed consisting of BBC One, BBC Two, ITV, BFBS Extra.

TUNISIA

System: DVB-T (MPEG4) [E]

TÉLÉVISION TUNISIENNE (Pub) ✉ Avenue de la Ligue Arabe, 1002 Tunis ☎ +216 71800844 **E:** info@watania1.tn; info@.watania2.tn **W:** www.watania1.tn; www.watania2.tn **Chs:** Watanya 1; Watanya 2 – **ATTESSIA (Comm)** ✉ 12 Rue de l'Energie. 2035 Ariana **E:** digital@attessia.tv **W:** www.attessia.tv – **CHARTAGE PLUS (Comm)** ✉ Tunis **E:** communication@carthageplus.tv **W:** www.facebook.com/carthageplustv – **EL HIWAR ETTOUNSI (Comm)** ✉ Avenue Habib Bourguiba, 1000 Tunis ☎ +216 71844855 **E:** contact@elhiwarettounsi.tv **W:** www.elhiwarettounsi.com – **HANNIBAL TV (HTV) (Comm)** ✉ 885 Rue du 13 Août Choutrana II, 2036 Ariana ☎ +216 70944944 **E:** info@hannibaltv.com.tn **W:** www.hannibaltv.com.tn – **TELVZA TV (Comm)** ✉ 42 Rue 8603, 2035 Ariana ☎ +216 56716123 **E:** commercial@telvza-tv.tn **W:** www.telvza-tv.tn – **TUNISNA TV (Comm)** ✉ ☎ +216 25226500 **E:** chaine.tunisna@gmail.com **W:** www.tunisna.tv – **AL INSEN (Rlg)** ✉ Route de Sidi Mansour, 3000 Sfax **W:** www.alinsen.tv.

DTT Tx Networks
Tx Operator: Office National de la Télédiffusion (ONT) **W:** www.telediffusion.net.tn **M:** Watanya 1, Watanya 2, Al Janoubia, Tunisna TV, Telvza TV, Attesia, Al Insen, El Hiwar Ettounsi, Hannibal TV, Chartage Plus ⌘ R. Nationale, R. Culturelle, R. Tunisie Chaîne Internationale, R. Jeunes.

Location	ch	Location	ch
Trozza	21	Zarzis	28
Kchabta	23	Nefta	28
Ain Draham	28	Chaambi	29
Kef Errand	30	Souk Ejomaa	44
Zaghouan	36	Boukornine	45
Remada	36	Brourmet	51
Biadha	37	Goraa	52
Ksour Essaf	38	Tozeur	55
Ghraba	41		

TURKEY

Systems: DVB-T2 (HEVC) [E]; § PAL-B/G [E]

National Stations
TÜRKIYE RADYO TELEVIZYON KURUMU (TRT) (Pub) ✉ TRT-TV Department, TRT Sitesi A, Blok 427, Oran, 06109 Ankara ☎ +90 312 4901058 **E:** genel.sekreterlik@trt.net.tr **W:** www.trt.net.tr **Chs (terr.):** TRT1, TRT2, TRT Haber, TRT Spor, TRT Spor 2, TRT Çocuk, TRT Kurdî, TRT Avaz, TRT Türk, TRT Belgesel, TRT Müzik, TRT Diyanet, Regional stns. – **ATV (Comm)** ✉ Barbaros Bulvarı 125, Cam Han, Beşiktaş, 34349 İstanbul ☎ +90 216 4742020 **E:** editor@atv.com.tr **W:** www.atv.com.tr – **CNN TÜRK (Comm)** ✉ Hürriyet Media Towers, Evren Mah. Güneşli, Bağcilar, 34204 İstanbul ☎ +90 212 4785856 **E:** info@cnnturk.com.tr **W:** www.cnnturk.com – **FLASH TV (Comm)** ✉ Çatma Mescit Mah., Tepebaşı Cad. & Elektrik Sok. 11, Beyoğlu, 34430 İstanbul ☎ +90 212 2568282 **E:** flashtv-w@flashtv.com.tr **W:** www.flashtv.com.tr – **HABER TÜRK (Comm)** ✉ Tevfik Bey Mah., 20 Temmuz Cad 24, Sefaköy, Küçükçekmece, 34295 İstanbul ☎ +90 212 5805267 **W:** www.haberturk.com – **KANAL D (Comm)** ✉ Kanal D TV Center, 100. Yil Mah., Bağcılar, 34204 İstanbul ☎ +90 212 4135111 **E:** bizeyazin@kanald.com.tr **W:** www.kanald.com.tr – **KANAL 7 (Comm)** ✉ Otakçılar Cad. 78, Eyüp, 34030 İstanbul ☎ +90 212 4378080 **E:** kanal7@kanal7com **W:** www.kanal7.com – **MELTEM TV (Comm)** ✉ Inönü Cad. 96, Beşyol, Küçükçekmece, 34295 İstanbul ☎ +90 212 6240999 **E:** bilgi@meltemtv.com.tr **W:** www.meltemtv.com.tr – **NTV (Comm)** ✉ Eskibüyükdere Cad. 61, Uso Center, Maslak, Şişli, 34381 İstanbul ☎ +90 212 3350000 **W:** www.ntv.com.tr **Chs:** NTV, NTV Spor – **SHOW TV (Comm)** ✉ AKS Televizyon, Yapi Kredi Plaza, E Blok 1, Levent, Beşiktaş, 34330 İstanbul ☎ +90 212 3550101 **E:** info@showtvnet.com **W:** www.showtv.com.tr – **STAR TV (Comm)** ✉ Doğan TV Center, 100. Yil Mah., Bağcilar, 34204 İstanbul ☎: +90 212 4135000 **E:** izleyicitemsilcisi@startv.com.tr **W:** www.startv.com.tr – **TV8 (Comm)** ✉ Ihlamurdere Cad., Yeşil Çimen Sok. 5, OTIM, Beşiktaş, 34353 İstanbul ☎ +90 212 2885152 **E:** tv8@tv8.com.tr **W:** www.tv8.com.tr.

Local Stations not shown.

DTT Tx Networks
Tx Operator: Anten A. Ş. **Mux 1-6:** multiprgr.

Location	M1	M2	M3	M4	M5	M6
Ankara (Çankaya)	7	24	28	34	37	38

+ nationwide MFN

TURKMENISTAN

System: DVB-T2 (MPEG4) [E]

TELEWIDENIÝE, RADIOGEPLESIKLER WE KINEMATOGRAFIÝA BARAKDY DÖWLET KOMITET (Gov) ✉ Magtymguly köçesi 89, 744000 Aşgabat ☎ +993 12 351515 **L.P:** Chmn: Arslan Aşirow **TV Studios:** ✉ 2003 St. 3, 744000 Aşgabat **Chs:** Altyn Asyr, Miras, Ýaşlyk, Türkmenistan Sport, Türkmen Owazy, Aşgabat.

DTT Tx Networks
Tx Operator: Ministry of Communications **M1**:Altyn Asyr HD, Miras HD, Ýaşlyk HD, Türkmenistan Sport HD, Türkmen Owazy HD, Aşgabat **M2**: Altyn Asyr, Miras, Ýaşlyk, Türkmenistan Sport, Türkmen Owazy.

Location	M1	M2	kW
Aşgabat	43	48	1.3

+ nationwide MFN

TURKS & CAICOS ISLANDS (UK)

NB: No terrestrial TV station.

TUVALU

System: PAL-B [E]

TUVALU MEDIA CORP. (TMC) (Pub) ✉ Private Mail Bag, Funafuti ☎ +688 20139 **E:** media@tuvalu.tv **Tx:** Funafuti ch n/a (0.02kW).

UGANDA

System: DVB-T2 (MPEG4) [E]

National Stations
UGANDA BROADCASTING CORP. (UBC) (Pub) ✉ P.O.Box 2038, Kampala ☎ +256 41 4257034 **E:** info@ubc.go.ug **W:** www.ubc.go.ug **L.P:** Chmn: James Tumusiime.

Local Stations not shown.

DTT Tx Networks
Licensee: Multichoice Uganda **M:** KBC, NTV, QTV, KTN, Citizen, K24, Kiss TV **Txs:** MFN – **Licensee:** StarTimes **M✪:** multiprgr **Txs:** MFN.

UKRAINE

Systems: DVB-T2 (MPEG4) [E]; DVB-T (MPEG2, MPEG4) [E]

National Stations
NATSIONALNA SUSPILNA TELERADIOKOMPANIA UKRAINY (NSTU) (Pub) ✉ vul. Melnykova 42, 04119 Kyiv ☎ +380 44 2413909 **W:** 1tv.com.ua **L.P:** GD: Zurab Alasania. **Chs (terr.):** UA:Pershyi, UA:Kultura – **1+1 (Comm)** ✉ vul. Kyrylivska 23, 04080 Kyiv ☎ +380 44 4900101 **E:** feedback@1plus1.ua **W:** www.1plus1.ua – **INTER (Comm)** ✉ vul. Dmytrivska 30, 01601 Kyiv ☎ +380 44 4906765 **E:** program@inter.ua **W:** inter.ua – **5 KANAL (Comm)** ✉ vul. Elektrykiv 26, 04176 Kyiv ☎ +380 44 3517720 **E:** box@5.ua **W:** www.5.ua.

Local Stations not shown.

DTT Tx Networks (DVB-T2)
Licensee Mux 1-3, 5: Zeonbud **W:** www.zeonbud.com.ua **M1:** Inter, Ukraina, 1+1, NTN, K1, UA:Pershyi, ICTV, Enter-Film **M2:** Zoom, Indigo, STB, TET, K2, Novyi kanal, M1, Priamyi **M3:** Mega, Piksel TV, XSport, NLO, 2+2, Zik, Espreso, PlusPlus **M5:** 5 Kanal, UA:Kultura, Rada, NTSU Regional stns, Local stns. – **Local licensees** (DVB-T/MPEG2, MPEG4) not shown. **NB:** M4 not assigned.

Location	M1	M2	M3	M5	kW
Andriivka	50	40	43	42	3x4.9/4.9
Bershad	35	53	54	51	4.9
Bilopillia	55	42	51	33	5.5x
Buky	62	61	29	37	1.26/2x0.4/1
Cherkasy	48	28	21	53	5.5
Chernihiv	22	34	35	61	5.7
Dnipro	26	35	25	40	5.5
Ivano-Frankivsk	42	41	31	58	0.9/2x2.8/
Izium	26	39	25	43	2.7
Kamianets-Podilskyi	22	29	51	44	2x1.1/2x2.3
Kamianske	22	40	55	28	0.5/2x1.1/1.1
Kharkiv	31	35	48	58	4.9
Kherson	34	58	39	44	3x2.6/1
Khmelnytskyi	22	29	51	50	5.2
Kholmy	22	49	54	61	2.4
Khust	39	53	56	61	2.7
Kovel	44	27	59	52	4.9/2.5/2x4.9
Krasnohorivka	26	37	41	51	3/2/2x1
Krasnoperekopsk	24	31	43	53	1.1
Kropyvnytskyi	49	53	22	47	5.4
Kryvyi Rih	41	51	54	38	5.5
Kyiv	26	31	49	29	12
Lviv	22	28	40	33	6.4
Mariupol	39	42	34	24	5
Melitopol	33	26	28	50	5.4/3x5.9
Mykolaiv	34	58	39	48	1.25/5.3/2x1
Novodnistrovsk	60	34	64	25	2.7/0.5/2x2.7
Odesa	43	32	39	23	4.5
Olevsk	51	52	53	43	2.8
Petrovirivka	35	41	47	33	3x5.4/5.4
Podilsk	62	43	54	40	5.4
Pryluky	52	27	56	32	5.1
Rivne	38	42	40	33	4.9
Shostka	24	59	58	60	5.2
Starobilsk	32	55	62	58	2.4
Ternopil	25	39	23	37	4.8
Trostianets	54	49	51	30	5.2
Vasylivka	29	41	57	36	4.7
Vinnytsia	39	32	31	49	3.6
Zaporizhzhia	43	31	49	57	3x3.1/2.9

+ sites with only txs below 1kW.

NB: Txs in **Donets Basin** not shown.

CRIMEA
(under Russian administration)

System: DVB-T2 (MPEG4) [E]

TRK "KRYM" (Gov) ✉ 295001 Simferopol, ul. Studencheskaya 14 ☎ +7 652 546406 **W:** 1tvcrimea.ru **Ch:** 1 Krym – **OBSHCHESTVENNAYA KRYMSKO-TATARSKAYA TRK (OKTT) (Pub)** ✉ 295011 Simferopol, ul. Kozlova 45a ☎ +7 978 9809009 **E:** ok_trk@mail.ru **W:** trkmillet.ru **L.P:** DG: Ervin Musayev **Ch:** Millet.

Other Regional Stations/Local Stations not shown.

DTT Tx Networks
Tx Operator: RTRS **M1:** Rossiya 1, Rossiya 24, Rossiya K, Karusel, Match TV, Pervyy kanal, NTV, OTR, 5-kanal, TV Tsentr ⌘ R. Rossii, Mayak, Vesti FM **M2:** Domashniy, TV Zvezda, Mir TV, Muz-TV, Pyatnitsa, REN TV, Spas, STS, TNT, TV-3 **M3:** 1 Krym, 1 Krym HD, Krym 24 HD, Millet, Mir 24, Moskva 24, Local stns

Location	M1	M2	M3	kW
Simferopol	36	37	58	0.2

+ MFN

UNITED ARAB EMIRATES

System: DVB-T2 (MPEG4) [E]

ABU DHABI MEDIA (Gov) ✉ P.O.Box 637, Abu Dhabi ☎ +971 2 44451111 **E:** adtv@emi.co.ae **W:** www.adtv.ae **Chs:** Abu Dhabi TV, Emirate TV, AD Drama, AD Sports, YasTV – **DUBAI MEDIA INC (Gov)** ✉ P.O.Box 835, Dubai ☎ +971 4 3077000 **W:** www.dmi.gov.ae – **SHARJAH TV (Gov)** ✉ P.O.Box 111, Sharjah ☎ +971 6 5011111 **W:** www.facebook.com/shjtv – **AJMAN TV (Comm)** ✉ P.O.Box 422, Ajman ☎ +971 6 7465000 **E:** progajtv@ajmantv.com **W:** www.facebook.com/AjmanTelevision.

DTT Tx Networks
Tx Operator: Abu Dhabi Media **M:** multiprgr **Txs:** (-) **Tx Operator:** Ajman TV **M:** multiprgr **Tx:** ch26 (Ajman) **Tx Operator:** Dubai Media Inc **M:** multiprgr **Txs:** (-) **Tx Operator:** Sharjah TV **M:** multiprgr **Txs:** (-).

UNITED KINGDOM

Systems: DVB-T (MPEG2), DVB-T2 (MPEG4) [E]

National Stations
BRITISH BROADCASTING CORP. (BBC) (Pub) ✉ BBC Television Centre, 80 Wood Lane, London W12 4RJ ☎ +44 20 87438000 **W:** www.bbc.com **L.P:** DG: Tim Davie **Chs (terr.):** BBC One (incl. regional prgrs), BBC Two, BBC Four, CBBC, CBeebies, BBC News, BBC Parliament, Alba **Reg: a) BBC Cambridgeshire:** Broadcasting House, Cambridge Business Park, Cowley Rd, Cambridge, CB4 0WZ; **b) BBC Channel Islands:** 18-21 Parade Rd, St Helier JE2 3PL; **c) BBC East:** The Forum, Millennium Plain, Norwich NR2 1BH; **d) BBC East Midlands:** London Rd, Nottingham NG2 4UU; **e) BBC East Yorkshire & Lincolnshire:** Queen's Court, Hull HU1 3RH; **f) BBC London:** Marylebone High St., London W1A 6FL; **g) BBC North East & Cumbria:** Broadcasting Centre, Barrack Rd, Newcastle upon Tyne NE99 2NE; **h) BBC North**

West: New Broadcasting House, Oxford Rd, Manchester M60 1SJ; **i) BBC Northern Ireland:** Ormeau Avenue, Belfast BT2 8HQ; **j) BBC Oxford:** 269 Banbury Rd, Summertown, Oxford, OX2 7DW; **k) BBC Scotland:** 40 Pacific Quay, Glasgow G51 1DA; **l) BBC South:** Broadcasting House, 10 Havelock Rd, Southampton SO14 7PU; **m) BBC South East:** The Great Hall, Mount Pleasant Rd, Tunbridge Wells TN1 1QQ; **n) BBC South West:** Broadcasting House, Seymour Rd, Plymouth PL3 5BD; **o) BBC Wales:** Llantrisant Rd, Cardiff CF5 2YQ; **p) BBC West:** Broadcasting House, Whiteladies Rd, Bristol BS8 2LR; **q) BBC West Midlands:** Level 7, The Mailbox, Birmingham B1 1RF; **r) BBC Yorkshire:** 2 St Peter's Square, Leeds LS9 8AH – **CHANNEL FOUR TELEVISION CORP. (Pub)** ✉ 124 Horseferry Rd, London SW1P 2TX ☎ +44 20 73964444 **W:** www.channel4.com **L.P:** CEO: Alexandra Mahon – **S4C AUTHORITY (Pub)** ✉ Park Ty Glas, Llanishen, Caerdydd/Cardiff CF14 5DU ☎ +44 2920 747444 **E:** gwifren@s4c.cymru **W:** www.s4c.cymru **L.P:** CEO: Owen Evans – **ITV PLC (Comm)** ✉ London Television Centre, Upper Ground, London SE1 9LT ☎ +44 20 76201620 **W:** www.itv.com **L.P:** CEO: Carolyn McCall. **Chs:** ITV (incl. regional prgrs), ITV2, ITV3, ITV4, ITV Be, CITV. **Reg: a) ITV Anglia:** Anglia House, Norwich NR1 3JG; **b) ITV Border:** 1 Clifford Court, Cooper Way, Parkhouse, Carlisle CA3 0JG; **c) ITV Central:** Central Court, Gas Street, Birmingham B1 2JT; **d) ITV Channel Islands:** The Television Centre, St Helier, Jersey, Channel Islands JE1 3ZD; **e) ITV Cymru Wales:** T3 Assembly Square, Britannia Quay, Cardiff Bay CF10 4PL; **f) ITV Granada:** Quay St., Manchester M60 9EA; **g) ITV London:** 200 Gray's Inn Rd, London WC1X 8HF; **h) ITV Meridian:** New Cut Road, Vinters Park, Maidstone, Kent ME14 5NZ; **i) ITV Tyne Tees:** Television House, The Watermark, Gateshead, NE11 9SZ; **j) ITV West Country:** 470 Bath Rd, Bristol BS4 3HG; **k) ITV Yorkshire:** The Television Centre, 104 Kirkstall Rd, Leeds LS3 1JS; **l) STV:** STV Group PLC, Pacific Quay, Glasgow G51 1PQ **W:** www.stv.tv; **m) UTV:** City Quays 2, Clarendon Dock, Belfast BT1 3YD **W:** www.itv.com/news/utv – **CHANNEL 5 BROADCASTING LTD (Comm)** ✉ 22 Long Acre, London WC2E 9LY ☎ +44 20 75505555 **W:** www.channel5.com – **SKY PLC (Comm)** ✉ Grant Way, Isleworth, London TW7 5QD ☎ +44 20 77053000 **W:** www.sky.com **L.P:** CEO: Jeremy Darroch.

DTT Tx Networks (DVB-T except where indicated otherwise)
Licensee Mux 1+3: BBC **M1:** BBC One (incl. reg. prgrs a-r), BBC Two, CBBC, CBeebies/BBC Four, BBC Alba, BBC News, BBC Parliament, BBC RB ⌘ BBC R.1, 1Xtra, R.2, R.3, R.4, R.4 Extra, R.5 Live, R.5 Live Sports Extra, R.6 Music, BBC Asian Network, BBCWS, BBC Local stations **M3 (DVB-T2):** TBN, Shopping Quarter, BBC One HD, BBC Two HD, ITV HD, Channel 4 HD, Channel 5 HD, CBBC HD – **Licensee Mux 2:** Digital 3&4 Ltd. **M2:** ITV (incl. reg. prgrs a-k), Channel 4, Channel 5, ITV 2, ITV3, E4, Film4, Channel 4 +1, More4, ITV4, ITVBe, ITV +1 – **Licensee Mux 4:** SDN Ltd. **M4:** QVC, Drama, 5USA, CCXTV, ITV2 +1, E4, 5STAR, Paramount Network, Sony Movies Action, Channel 5 +1, TJC, ITV3 +1, ITV4 +1, Blaze, CBS Reality, Horror Channel, TCC, Blaze +1, Create & Craft, ITVBe +1, CITV, Ketchup, SonLife, Arise News, ADULT section, ADULT Expanded ⌘Capital FM London, Absolute R., Heart – **Licensee Mux 5-7:** Arqiva **W:** www.arqiva.com **M5:** Sky Arts, Really, Dave, E4 +1, 4Music, pick, Quest Red, Food Network, Gems TV, Film4 +1, Challenge, 4seven, Smithsonian Channel, Yesterday +1, Quest +1, Hochanda, Together TV, Sky News ADULT smileTV3, ADULT Xpanded TV ⌘talkSPORT, RNIB Connect, Classic FM, LBC, TWR.**M6:** Ideal World, Yesterday, Sony Movies , QVC Beauty, QVC Style, DMAX, CBS Justice, HGTV, CBS Drama, Jewellery Maker, Dave ja vu, Talking Pictures TV, PBS America, Pop, RT, Aljazeera English, ADULT Babestation, ADULT Studio 66, ADULT Section ⌘Hits R., KISS FRESH, Kiss FM, KISSTORY, Magic, Greatest Hits R., Kerrang!, Smooth R., Premier R. **M7 (DVB-T2):** Merit, FreeSports, Quest Red +1, NOW 80s, More4 +1, Together TV +1, PBS America +1, Forces TV, CBeebies HD/BBC Four HD, BBC News HD, QVC HD, QVC Beauty HD, RT HD, Quest HD. **NB:** Some regional variations may apply (e.g. ITV is replaced by STV in Scotland and by UTV in Northern Ireland). – **Local/regional muxes** not shown.

Location	1°	2°	3	4	5	6	7	kW
Angus	39k	42l	45	33	36	48	55	3x20/3x10/5
Beacon Hill	44n	41j	47	42	45	40	33	3x20/3x10/7.3
Belmont	22e	25k	28	30	23	26	55	3x150/50/2x100/37
Bilsdale	26g	29i	23	43	46	40	31	3x100/3x50/18.5
Black Hill	46k	43l	40	41	44	47	55	6x100/43
Blaenplwyf	27o	24e	21	25	22	28	-	3x40/3x10
Bluebell Hill	32m	34h	45	40	43	46	55	6x20/7.5
Brougher Mt.	29i	31m	37	21	24	27	-	3x20/3x2
Caldbeck	25g	28b	22	23	26	30	-	3x100/3x50
Caldbeck	27k	24l	-	-	-	-	-	50/100
Caradon Hill	28n	25j	22	21	24	27	31	3x100/3x50/11.6
Carmel	23o	26e	29	33	36	48	-	3x20/3x10
Chatton	45g	42i	39	41	44	47	-	3x20/3x10
Craigkelly	27k	24l	21	29	31	38	55	3x20/3x10/11
Crystal Palace	23f	26g	48	25	22	28	55	6x200/43

Location	1°	2°	3	4	5	6	7	8	kW
Darvel	22k	25l	28	32	34	35	55		3x20/3x10/7.5
Divis	27i	21m	24	23	26	30	51		3x100/3x50/12
Dover	33m	35h	36	39	42	48	-		3x80/3x40
Durris	28k	25l	22	23	26	30	55		3x100/3x50/14.5
Emley More	47r	44k	41	51	52	48	55		5x174/87/55
Hannington	45l	42h	39	40	43	46	55		4x50/3x25/37
Heathfield	41m	44h	47	40	43	46	-		20
Huntshaw Cross	30n	31j	37	32	34	35	-		3x20/3x10
Keelylang Hill	46k	43l	40	42	45	39	-		3x20/3x10
Knockmore	31k	37l	29	33	36	46	-		3x20/3x10
Limavady	41i	44m	47	40	43	45	-		3x20/3x10
Llanddona	40o	43e	46	41	44	47	-		3x20/3x10
Mendip	32p	34j	35	48	33	36	55		6x100/72
Midhurst	48l	54h	36	33	34	29	-		3x20/3x10
Moel-y-Parc	45o	39e	42	51	36	48	55		3x20/3x10
Oxford	41l	44h	47	29	37	31	55		3x100/3x50/16.5
Pontop Pike	39g	42i	45	32	34	35	55		3x100/3x50/34
Preseli	43o	46e	40	42	45	39	-		3x20/3x10
Redruth	44n	41j	47	48	33	32	-		3x20/3x10
Ridge Hill	28q	25c	22	21	24	27	55		3x20/4x10
Ridge Hill	-	29j	-	-	-	-	-		20
Rosemarkie	45k	39l	42	43	46	40	-		3x20/3x10
Rowridge	24l	27h	21	25	22	28	55		3x200/3x50/24
Rumster Forest	27k	24l	21	32	34	35	-		3x20/3x10
Sandy Heath	27a	24a	21	51	36	48	55		3x180/3x170/50
Selkirk	32k	34l	35	33	35	48	-		3x10/3x5
Stockland Hill	26n	23j	29	25	22	28	-		3x50/3x25
Sudbury	44c	41a	47	29	31	37	-		100
Sutton Coldfield	43q	46c	40	42	45	39	55		6x200/89
Talconeston	40c	43a	36	42	45	39	55		6x100/27
The Wrekin	26q	23c	30	41	44	47	-		3x20/3x10
Waltham	32d	34c	35	29	37	31	55		3x50/3x25/10
Wenvoe	41o	44e	47	42	45	39	55		3x100/3x50/47
Winter Hill	32h	34f	35	29	31	37	55		6x100/26

+ sites with txs below 10kW. Pol=H °) incl. reg. prgrs (subregional prgrs not indicated)
NB: In preparation for the re-assignment of the 700MHz band to mobile services, txs on chs 49-60 are gradually being moved to lower chs.

UNITED STATES OF AMERICA

Systems: ATSC [A]; § NTSC-M [A] (some LPs only)

Main National Networks
(O&O = owned-and-operated) (*= Spanish-language networks)
PUBLIC BROADCASTING SERVICE (PBS) (Pub) ✉ 1320 Braddock Place, Alexandria, VA 22314-1698 ☎ +1 703 7395000 **W:** www.pbs.org **L.P:** Pres/CEO: Paula A. Kerger. **Member Stations:** ca 350 – **ABC, INC (Comm)** (Subsidiary of Walt Disney Co.) ✉ 77 W 66th St., New York, NY 10023-6298 ☎ +1 212 4567777 **W:** abc.go.com **L.P:** Pres: John Hare. **O&O Stations:** KABC-TV Los Angeles CA ch7 (28.7kW); KFSN-TV Fresno CA ch30 (260kW); KGO-TV San Francisco CA ch7 (23.8kW); KTRK-TV Houston TX ch13 (32.4kW); WABC-TV New York, NY ch7 (34kW); WLS-TV Chicago IL ch22 (908kW); WPVI-TV Philadelphia PA ch6 (34kW); WTVD Durham NC ch11 (45kW). **Full Power Affiliates:** ca 220 – **CBS TELEVISION STATIONS (Comm)** (Division of ViacomCBS, Inc) ✉ 51 W 52nd St, New York, NY 10019-6119 ☎ +1 212 9754321 **W:** www.cbs.com **L.P:** Pres/CEO (ViacomCBS) Bob Bakish. **O&O Stations:** KCBS-TV Los Angeles CA ch31 (485kW); KCNC-TV Denver CO ch35 (1000kW); KDKA-TV Pittsburgh PA ch25 (1000kW); KOVR-TV Sacramento CA ch25 (1000kW); KPIX-TV San Francisco CA ch29 (1000kW); KTVT-TV Dallas TX ch19 (1000kW); KYW-TV Philadelphia PA ch30 (790kW); WBBM-TV Chicago IL ch12 (8kW); WBZ-TV Boston MA ch20 (922kW); WCBS-TV New York NY ch36 (321kW); WCCO-TV Minneapolis MN ch32 (1000kW); WFOR-TV Miami FL ch22 (1000kW); WJZ-TV Baltimore MD ch13 (33.8kW); WWJ-TV Detroit MI ch44 (425kW). **Full Power Affiliates:** ca 210 – **ESTRELLA TV* (Comm)** ✉ 1845 Empire Avenue, Burbank, CA 91504 **W:** www.estrellatv.com **L.P:** CEO (Estrella Media, Inc): Peter Markham **O&O Stations:** KETD Denver CO ch45 (100kW); KMPX Dallas TX ch30 (1000kW); KPNZ Salt Lake City UT ch24 (450kW); KRCA Los Angeles CA ch7 (28.7kW); KSDX-LD San Diego CA ch9 (0.275kW); KVPA-LD Phoenix AZ ch34 (15kW); KZJL Houston TX ch21 (880kW); WASA-LD New York NY ch25 (15kW); WESV-LD Chicago IL ch40 (6kW); WGEN-TV Key West ch8 (7kW) **Affiliates:** ca 53 – **FOX TELEVISION STATIONS, LLC (Comm)** (Fox Broadcasting Co. - a subsidiary of Fox Corp.) ✉ 10201 W. Pico Blvd., Los Angeles, CA 90035 ☎ +1 310 3693716 **W:** www.fox.com **L.P:** CEO: Jack Abernethy **O&O Stations:** KCPQ Tacoma WA ch13 (50kW); KDFW Dallas TX ch35 (857kW); KMSP-TV Minneapolis MN ch9

(30kW); KRIV Houston TX ch26 (1000kW); KSAZ-TV Phoenix AZ ch10 (48kW); KTBC Austin TX ch7 (98.6kW); KTTV Los Angeles CA ch11 (115kW); KTVU Oakland CA ch44 (1000kW); WAGA Atlanta GA ch27 (1000kW); WFLD Chicago IL ch24 (737kW); WITI-TV Milwaukee WI ch31 (1000kW); WJBK Detroit MI ch7 (27kW); WJZY Charlotte NC ch25 (1000kW); WOFL Orlando FL ch22 (607kW); WOGX Ocala FL ch31 (500kW); WNYW New York NY ch27 (151kW); WTTG Washington DC ch36 (1000kW); WTVT Tampa FL ch12 (72.3kW); WTXF-TV Philadelphia PA ch31 (1000kW). **Full Power Affiliates:** ca 220 – **ION TELEVISION (Comm)** (ION Media Networks, Inc) ✉ 601 Clearwater Park Road, West Palm Beach, FL 33401 **W:** www.iontelevision.com **L.P:** Chmn/CEO (ION Media Networks): Brandon Burgess **NB:** In 2020, ION Media Network, Inc was acquired by E.W. Scripps Company. **O&O Stations:** 60 **Affiliates:** ca 48 – **LATV* (Comm)** (LATV Networks, LLC) ✉ 2323 Corinth Avenue, Los Angeles, CA 90064 **W:** latv.com **L.P:** COO: Luca Bentivoglio **Affiliates:** ca 37 – **MYNETWORKTV, INC (Comm)** (Fox Broadcasting Co. - a subsidiary of Fox Corp.) ✉ 110201 W Pico Blvd Los Angeles, CA 90064-2606 **W:** www.mynetworktv.com **O&O Stations:** KCOP-TV Los Angeles CA ch13 (120kW); KDFI-TV Dallas TX ch27 (1000kW); KUTP Phoenix AZ ch26 (1000kW); KTXH Houston TX ch19 (421kW); WDCA Washington D.C ch36 (1000kW); WFTC Minneapolis MI ch29 (1000kW); WMYT-TV Charlotte NC ch25 (1000kW); WPWR-TV Gary IN ch24 (737kW); WRBW Orlando FL ch41 (763kW); WWOR-TV Secaucus NJ ch25 (57.8kW). **Full Power Affiliates:** ca 200 – **NBCUNIVERSAL MEDIA, LLC (Comm)** (Division of Comcast Corp.) ✉ 30 Rockefeller Plaza, New York, NY 10112 ☎ +1 212 6644444 **W:** www.nbc.com **L.P:** CEO: Jeff Shell. **O&O Stations:** KNBC Los Angeles CA ch36 (665kW); KNSD San Diego CA ch17 (387kW); KNTV San Francisco CA ch12 (103.1kW); KXAS-TV Fort Worth, TX ch24 (825kW); WBTS-CD Nashu NH (15kW); WCAU Philadelphia PA ch28 (700kW); WMAQ-TV Chicago IL ch33 (398kW); WNBC New York, NY ch35 (408.8kW); WRC-TV Washington DC ch34 (1000kW); WTVJ Miami FL ch31 (1000kW); WVIT Hartford CT ch31 (374kW); WYCN-LD Boston MA ch36 (12.1kW). **Full Power Affiliates:** ca 220 – **NBCU TELEMUNDO ENTERPRISES (TELEMUNDO*) (Comm)** (Division of NBCUniversal Media, LLC) ✉ 2290 West 8th Avenue, Hialeah, FL 33010 ☎ +1 305 8848200 **W:** www.telemundo.com **L.P:** Chmn: Beau Ferrari. **O&O Stations:** KBLR Las Vegas NV ch20 (1000kW); KDEN-TV Denver CO ch29 (800kW); KHRR Tucson AZ ch16 (396kW); KNSO Fresno CA ch11 (45kW); KSTS San Jose CA ch19 (500kW); KTAZ Phoenix AZ ch29 (595kW); KTDO Las Cruces NM ch26 (132kW); KTMD Galveston TX ch22 (1000kW); KUAN-LD Poway CA ch17 (387kW); KVEA Corona CA ch25 (620kW); KVDA San Antonio TX ch38 (1000kW); KXTX-TV Dallas TX ch36 (925kW); WNEU Merrimack NH ch29 (700kW); WNJU Linden NJ ch35 (575kW); WRMD-CD Tampa FL ch30 (15kW); WSNS-TV Chicago IL ch33 (398kW); WSCV Fort Lauderdale FL ch30 (1000kW); WTMO Orlando FL ch31 (15kW; WWSI Atlantic City NJ ch28 (700kW); WZDC-CD Washington DC ch34 (1000kW). **Full Power Affiliates:** ca 45 – **THE CW NETWORK, LLC (Comm)** (Subsidiary of CBS Entertainment Group and Warner Media) ✉ 4000 Warner Blvd., Burbank, CA 91522 ☎ +1 818 9775000 **W:** www.cwtv.com **L.P:** Chmn/CEO: Mark Pedowitz. **O&O Stations:** KBCW San Francisco CA ch45 (1000kW); KMAX-TV Sacramento CA ch21 (725kW); KSTW Tacoma WA ch11 (100kW); WKBD-TV Detroit MI ch34 (285kW); WPCW Jeannette PA ch11 (30kW); WPSG Philadelphia PA ch33 (440kW); WTOG St. Petersburg FL ch19 (700kW); WUPA Atlanta GA ch36 (1000kW). **Full Power Affiliates:** ca 200 – **UNIMÁS* (Comm)** (Subsidiary of Univision Communications, Inc) ✉ 9405 NW 41st Street, Miami, FL 33178-2301 ☎ +1 305 4713900 **W:** www.unimas.com **L.P:** Pres/CEO (Univision Communications, Inc.): Vincent Sadusky. **O&O Stations:** KFPH-DT Phoenix AZ ch13 (33kW); KFSF-DT Vallejo CA ch34 (370kW); KFTH-DT Alvin TX ch36 (1000kW); KFTR-DT Los Angeles CA ch29 (370kW); KFTU-DT Douglas AZ ch36 (5kW); KNIC-DT Blanco TX ch18 (1000kW); KSTR-DT Irving TX ch34 (1000kW); KTFD-DT Boulder CO ch28 (400kW); KFTB-CA Bakersfield CA ch31 (14.9kW); KTFF-DT Porterville CA ch23 (330kW); KTFK-DT Stockton CA ch26 (850kW); KTFO-CD Austin, TX ch36 (15kW); KTFQ-DT Albuquerque NM ch16 (350kW); WAMI-DT Hollywood FL ch24 (775kW); WFPA-CA Philadelphia PA ch35 (5.7kW); WFTT-DT Tampa FL ch25 (750kW); WFUT-DT Newark NJ ch26 (195kW); WOTF-DT Melbourne FL ch15 (130kW); WTNC-LD Raleigh NC ch19 (15kW); WUTF-DT Marlborough MA ch19 (50kW); WUVG-DT Athens GA ch17 (15kW); WXFT-DT Aurora IL ch22 (908kW). **Full Power Affiliates:** ca 35. – **UNIVISION* (Comm)** (Subsidiary of Univision Communications, Inc) ✉ 9405 NW 41 St., Miami, FL 33178-2301 ☎ +1 305 4713900 **W:** www.univision.com **L.P:** Pres/CEO (Univision Communications, Inc.): Vincent Sadusky. **O&O Stations:** KABE-CD Bakersfield CA ch35 (13kW); KAKW-DT Killeen TX ch13 (39kW); KDTV-DT San Francisco CA ch20 (475kW); KFTV-DT Hanford CA ch20 (350kW); KMEX-DT Los Angeles CA ch34 (500kW); KTVW-DT Phoenix AZ ch33 (470kW); KUTH-DT Provo UT ch32 (194kW); KUVE-DT Green Valley AZ ch34 (185kW); KUVN-DT Garland TX ch33 (1000kW); KUVS-DT Modesto CA ch18 (500kW); KWEX-DT San Antonio TX ch24 (785kW); KXLN-DT Rosenberg TX ch30 (1000kW); WFDC-DT Arlington VA ch15 (1000kW); WGBO-DT Joliet IL ch35 (290kW); WQHS-DT Cleveland OH ch36 (780kW); WLTV-DT Miami FL ch23 (535kW); WXTV-DT Paterson NJ ch26 (195kW); WUVC-DT Fayetteville NC ch22 (480kW); WUVG-DT Athens GA ch18 (1000kW); WUVP-DT Vineland NJ ch17 (645kW). **Full Power Affiliates:** ca 45 – **TRINITY BROADCASTING NETWORK, INC (TBN) (Rlg)** ✉2442 Michelle Drive, Tustin, CA 92780 **W:** www.tbn.org **LP:** Chmn: Matthew W. Crouch **O&O Stations:** KAAH-TV Honolulu HI ch27 (262kW); KDOR-TV Bartlesville OK ch36 (1000kW); KDTX-TV Dallas TX ch21 (735kW); KETH-TV Houston TX ch24 (1000kW); KHCE-TV San Antonio TX ch16 (850kW); KITU-TV Beaumont TX ch29 (920kW); KLUJ-TV Harlingen TX ch34 (45kW); KNAT-TV Albuquerque NM ch24 (320kW); KNMT Portland OR ch32 (777kW); KPAZ-TV Phoenix AZ ch20 (1000kW);KPJR-TV Greeley CO ch17 (633kW); KTAJ-TV St. Joseph MO ch21 (1000kW); KTBN-TV Santa Ana CA ch33 (1000kW); KTBO-TV Oklahoma City OK ch15 (700kW); KTBW-TV Tacoma WA ch21 (107kW); WBUY-TV Holly Springs MS ch26 (950kW); WDLI-TV Canton OH ch22 (950kW); WELF-TV Dalton GA ch16 (360kW); WGTW-TV Burlington NJ ch36 (205kW); WHFT-TV Miami FL ch28 (701kW); WHLV-TV Cocoa FL ch51 (1000kW); WHSG-TV Monroe GA ch22 (1000kW); WJEB-TV Jacksonville FL ch21 (622kW); WKOI-TV Richmond, IN ch31 (1000kW); WMCF-TV Montgomery AL ch46 (851kW); WMPV-TV Mobile AL ch18 (275kW); WMWC-TV Galesburg IL ch8 (23kW); WPGD-TV Hendersonville TN ch33 (1000kW); WRBJ-TV Magee MS ch34 (968kW); WSFJ-TV Newark OH ch19 (15kW); WTBY-TV Poughkeepsie NY ch22 (/kW);WTCE-TV Fort Pierce FL ch18 (730kW); WTJP-TV Gadsden AL ch26 (1000kW); WTPC-TV Virginia Beach VA ch7 (85kW); WWRS-TV Mayville WI ch34 (504kW); WWTO-TV La Salle IL ch35 (15kW). **Affiliates:** ca 11.

Other Networks (*= Spanish-language networks)
CREATE (Pub) ✉ American Public Television: 55 Summer St., 4th Floor, Boston, MA 02110 **W:** createtv.com – **MHZ WORLDVIEW (Pub)** ✉8101A Lee Highway, Falls Church, VA 22042 **W:** mhznetworks.org – **Vme* (Pub)** ✉ Vme Media, Inc: 1001 Brickell Bay Drive Suite 1208 Miami, FL 33131 **W:** www.vmetv.com – **WORLD (Pub)** ✉ American Public Television: 55 Summer St., 4th Floor, Boston, MA 02110 **W:** worldchannel.org – **ACCUWEATHER CHANNEL (Comm)** ✉ AccuWeather, Inc: 385 Science Park Road, State College, PA 16803 **W:** www.accuweather.com – **ANTENNA TV (ATV) (Comm)** ✉ Tribune Broadcasting: 435 N. Michigan Ave., 6th Floor, Chicago, IL 60611 **W:** antennatv.tv – **AZTECA AMÉRICA* (Comm)** ✉ 601 Clearwater Park Road, West Palm Beach, FL 33401 **W:** aztecaamerica.com – **BOUNCE (Comm)** ✉ Bounce Media, LLC: P.O. Box 673252, Marietta, GA 30006 **W:** www.bouncetv.com – **COMET (Comm)** (Joint-venture of Metro-Goldwyn-Mayer and Sinclair Television Group, Inc) ✉ Sinclair Television Group, Inc.: 10706 Beaver Dam Rd, Cockeysville, MD 21030 **W:** www.comettv.com – **COZI TV (Comm)** ✉ NBCUniversal Media, LLC: 30 Rockefeller Plaza, New York, NY 10112 **W:** www.cozitv.com – **DABL** ✉ CBS Television Distribution, Inc: 825 Eighth Ave, 30th Floor, New York, NY 10019 **W:** www.dabl.com– **DECADES (Comm)** (Joint-venture of CBS Television Studios and Weigel Broadcasting Co) ✉ Weigel Broadcasting Co.: 26 North Halsted, Chicago, IL 60661 **W:** www.decades.com – **COURT TV/COURT TV MYSTERY (Comm)** ✉ Court TV Media, LLC: 3500 Piedmont Road, Suite 400, Atlanta, GA 30305 **W:** www.courttv.com – **GET TV (Comm)** ✉ CPE US Networks, Inc: 10202 West Washington Boulevard, Culver City, CA 90232 **W:** www.get.tv – **GRIT (Comm)** ✉ GRIT Media, LLC: 1080 West Peachtree St, #309 Atlanta, GA 30309 **W:** www.grittv.com – **HEARTLAND (Comm)** ✉Luken Communications, LLC: 225 E 8th St, Chattanooga, TN 37402 **W:** www.watchheartlandtv.com – **H&I TV (Comm)** ✉H&I National Limited Partnership: 26 North Halsted, Chicago, IL 60661 **W:** www.handitv.com – **HSN (Comm)** ✉ HSN, Inc: 2501 118th Ave N, St Petersburg, FL 33716 **W:** www.hsn.com – **ION PLUS (Comm)** ✉ ION Media Networks, Inc: 601 Clearwater Park Road, West Palm Beach, FL 33401 **W:** ionplustv.com – **JUSTICE NETWORK (Comm)** ✉ Justice Network, LLC: 318 E Bond Ave, West Memphis, AR 72301 **W:** www.justicenetworktv.com – **LAFF (Comm)** ✉ Laff Media, LLC: Suite 400, 3500 Piedmont Road NE, Atlanta, GA 30305 **W:** www.laff.com – **LIGHT TV (Comm)** ✉ Allen Media Group, LLC: 1925 Century Park East 10th Floor, Los Angeles, CA 90067 **W:** www.lighttv.com – **LIVE WELL NETWORK (Comm)** ✉ ABC, Inc (Subsidiary of Walt Disney Co.): 77 W. 66th St., New York, NY 10023-6298 **W:** livewellnetwork.com – **ME-TV NETWORK (Comm)** ✉ Weigel Broadcasting Co: 26 North Halsted, Chicago, IL 60661 **W:** www.metv.com – **MOVIES! (Comm)** (Joint-venture of Weigel Broadcasting Co and Twenty-First Century Fox, Inc) ✉ Weigel Broadcasting Co.: 26 North

Halsted, Chicago, IL 60661 **W:** moviestvnetwork.com – **QUBO (Comm)** Qubo Venture, LLC: 601 Clearwater Park Road, West Palm Beach, FL 33401 **W:** qubo.com – **QVC (Comm)** QVC, Inc: 1200 Wilson Drive, West Chester, PA 19380 **W:** www.qvc.com – **RETRO TV (Comm)** Retro Television, Inc: P.O.Box 11409, Chattanooga, TN 37401 **W:** www.myretrotv.com – **START TV (Comm)** Start TV, LLC: 26 North Halsted, Chicago, IL 60661 **W:** www.starttv.com – **TELEXCITOS* (Comm)** Telemundo Network Group: 2290 West 8th Avenue, Hialeah, FL, 33010. **W:** www.telexitos.com – **THE FAMILY CHANNEL (Comm)** ValCom, Inc: 429 Rockaway Valley Road, Boonton Township, NJ 07005 **W:** www.famchannel.com – **THIS TV (Comm)** Allen Media Group, LLC: 1925 Century Park East 10th Floor, Los Angeles, CA 900671 **W:** thistv.com – **TUFF TV (Comm)** TUFF TV Network, LLC: 55 Marietta Street, N.W. Suite 1000, Atlanta, GA 30303 **W:** www.tufftv.com – **WEATHER NATION (Comm)** WeatherNation, Inc.: 8101 E. Prentice Ave #700, Greenwood Village, CO 80111 **W:** www.weathernationtv.com – **YOUTOO AMERICA (Comm)** Center Post Networks, LLC: 808 E Abram St, Arlington, TX 76010-1209 **W:** youtooamerica.com – **ALMAVISION* (Rlg)** Almavision TV, Inc: P. O.Box 26590. Santa Ana, CA 92799 **W:** almavision.com – **CORNERSTONE TV (Rlg)** Cornerstone Television, Inc: 1 Signal Hill Dr, Wall, PA 15148 **W:** www.ctvn.org – **DAYSTAR TV (Rlg)** God Fellowship, Inc: 3901 Hwy 121, Bedford, TX 76021 **W:** www.daystar.com – **ENLACE* (Rlg)** Trinity Broadcasting Network, Inc: 2823 West Irving Blvd., Irving, TX 75061 **W:** www.enlace.org – **HILLSONG CHANNEL (Rlg)** Trinity Broadcasting Network, Inc: 14171 Chambers Rd., Tustin, CA 92780 **W:** hillsong.com – **JUCE TV (Rlg)** Trinity Broadcasting Network, Inc: 2442 Michelle Dr, Tustin, CA 92780 **W:** www.jucetv.com – **SMILE OF A CHILD TV (Rlg)** AMC Networks, Inc: P.O.Box 10700, Santa Ana, CA 92711-0700 **W:** www.smileofachildtv.org – **THREE ANGELS BROADCASTING NETWORK (3ABN) (Rlg)** Three Angels Broadcasting, Inc: 17466 Route 37, Johnston City, IL 62951 **W:** 3abn.org.

Local Stations

There are more than 3,600 local TV stns operating. As of September 30, 2020: (Full Power) Commercial stns: 1,368 - (Full power) Educational stns: 390 - Low power stns: 1,860. There are also 3,543 translators.

LOCAL STATIONS IN MAJOR TV MARKETS

Atlanta, GA Area

ch	kW	State	City of License	Callsign
2	3	GA	Atlanta	WUVM-LP
3	3	GA	Atlanta	WTHC-LD
7	48	GA	Athens	WGTV
8	3	GA	Athens	WIGL-LD
8	0.15	GA	Toccoa	W08EG-D
9	3	GA	Atlanta	WEQT-LD
10	80	GA	Atlanta	WXIA-TV
11	3	GA	Macon	WUEO-LD
12	3	GA	Atlanta	WDNV-LD
13	0.14	GA	Carrollton	W13DJ-D
14	15	GA	Atlanta	WSKC-CD
15	15	GA	Gainesville	WGGD-LD
16	687	GA	Rome	WPXA-TV
18	1000	GA	Athens	WUVG-DT
19	1000	GA	Atlanta	WGCL-TV
20	11.4	GA	Atlanta	WANN-CD
21	55	GA	Atlanta	WPBA
22	1000	GA	Monroe	WHSG-TV
23	15	GA	Norcross	WKTB-CD
24	240	GA	Toccoa	WGTA
25	500	GA	Atlanta	WATL
26	2	GA	Atlanta	WLVO-LD
27	1000	GA	Atlanta	WAGA-TV
28	12	GA	Cleveland	WDWW-LD
29	15	GA	Atlanta	WYGA-CD
30	15	GA	Atlanta	WTBS-LD
31	805	GA	Atlanta	WPCH-TV
32	305	GA	Atlanta	WSB-TV
34	288	GA	Atlanta	WATC-DT
35	15	GA	Atlanta	WDTA-LD
36	1000	GA	Atlanta	WUPA

Boston, MA Area

ch	kW	Sta	City of License	Callsign
5	6.7	MA	Boston	+ WGBH-TV
5	6.7	MA	Boston	+ WFXZ-CD
9	6.5	NH	Manchester	WMUR-TV
10	5	MA	Norwell	+ WWDP
10	5	MA	Foxborough	+ WMFP
11	30	NH	Durham	WENH-TV
19	50	MA	Worcester	WUTF-TV
20	850	MA	Boston	WBZ-TV
21	163	MA	Boston	WSBK-TV
22	150	MA	Boston	+ WBPX-TV
22	150	MA	Woburn	+ WDPX-TV
23	80.6	NH	Concord	+ WPXG-TV
23	80.6	MA	Lowell	+ WYDN
27	400	MA	Marlborough	+ WUNI
27	400	NH	Derry	+ WWJE-DT
29	700	NH	Merrimack	WNEU
30	15	MA	Boston	WCRN-LD
31	15	NH	Concord	WLEK-LD
32	300	MA	Boston	+ WGBX-TV
32	300	NH	Nashua	+ WBTS-CD
33	922	MA	Boston	WCVB-TV
34	1000	MA	Boston	WFXT
35	900	MA	Boston	+ WHDH
35	900	MA	Cambridge	+ WLVI
38	15	MA	Boston	WHDT-LD
40	3.5	MA	Boston	W40BO-D
45	15	MA	Boston	WCEA-LD

Chicago. IL Area

ch	kW	Sta	City of License	Callsign
4	0.3	IL	Chicago	WOCK-CD
9	3	IN	Wolcott	KPDS-LD
11	0.4	IL	Arlington Heights	WRJK-LP
12	8	IL	Chicago	WBBM-TV
16	14	IN	Valparaiso	WAAA-LD
17	300	IN	Gary	WYIN
18	15	IL	Chicago	WMEU-CD
19	645	IL	Chicago	WGN-TV
20	15	IL	Chicago	WWME-CD
21	140	IN	Hammond	WJYS
22	908	IL	Chicago	+ WLS-TV
22	908	IL	Aurora	+ WXFT-DT
23	130	IL	Chicago	WCIU-TV
24	737	IL	Chicago	+ WFLD
24	737	IN	Gary	+ WPWR-TV
25	110	IL	Chicago	+ WTTW
25	110	IL	Chicago	+ WYCC
26	15	IL	Chicago	WPVN-CD
28	1	IL	Arlington Heights	WEDE-CD
29	15	IL	Aurora	WAUR-LD
30	15	IL	Chicago	WDCI-LD
30	10.8	IL	Earlville	WSPY-LD
31	15	IL	Chicago	WDCI-LD
31	15	IL	Chicago	W25DW-D
32	15	IL	Plano	+ WLPD-CD
32	15	IL	Naperville	+ WWTO-TV
33	380	IL	Chicago	+ WMAQ-TV
33	380	IL	Chicago	+ WSNS-TV
34	400	IL	Chicago	WCPX-TV
35	290	IL	Joliet	WGBO-DT

Dallas - Fort Worth, TX Area

ch	kW	Sta	City of License	Callsign
3	2.5	TX	Britton	KODF-LD
5	3	TX	Dallas	KPFW-LD
5	3	TX	Garland	KXDA-LD
7	1.4	TX	Fort Worth	K07AAD-D
8	45.6	TX	Dallas	WFAA
9	26	TX	Fort Worth	KFWD
10	3	TX	De Soto	KHPK-LD
11	2.2	TX	Fort Worth	KUVN-CD
12	2.5	TX	Dallas	KJJM-LD
14	975	TX	Dallas	KERA-TV
18	465	TX	Fort Worth	KTXA
19	1000	TX	Fort Worth	KTVT
20	15	TX	Dallas-ft Worth	KBOP-LD
21	735	TX	Dallas	KDTX-TV
22	7	TX	Keene	KGSW-LD
22	15	TX	De Soto	KNAV-LP
22	15	TX	Stephenville	K22NR-D
23	1000	TX	Greenville	KTXD-TV
24	925	TX	Fort Worth	KXAS-TV
25	1000	TX	Arlington	KPXD-TV
26	15	TX	Dallas	K26KC-D
26	15	TX	Mineral Wells	KNMW-LD
27	1000	TX	Dallas	KDFI
29	415	TX	Denton	+ KDTN
29	415	TX	Paris	+ KPTD-LP
30	1000	TX	Decatur	KMPX
31	1000	TX	Lake Dallas	KAZD

ch	kW	Sta	City of License	Callsign
32	780	TX	Dallas	KDAF
33	1000	TX	Garland	KUVN-DT
34	1000	TX	Irving	KSTR-DT
35	1000	TX	Dallas	KDFW
36	925	TX	Dallas	KXTX-TV
Denver, CO Area				
3	3	CO	Denver	K03IY-D
5	1.5	CO	Cripple Creek	KRDH-LD
7	54	CO	Denver	KMGH-TV
9	45	CO	Denver	KUSA
11	16	WY	Cheyenne	KQCK
13	33.6	CO	Broomfield	KBDI-TV
14	15	CO	Denver	KZDN-LD
15	200	CO	Castle Rock	KETD
16	2	CO	Denver	KQDK-CD
17	317	CO	Greeley	KPJR-TV
18	330	CO	Denver	KPXC-TV
19	13.8	CO	Denver	KSBS-CD
20	84	CO	Denver	+ KRMT
20	84	CO	Arvada	+ KDNF-LD
21	50	CO	Fort Collins	KFCT
21	2	CO	Denver	KDEO-LD
22	15	CO	Boulder	K22NW-D
23	1000	CO	Sterling	KCDO-TV
24	7.5	CO	Fort Collins	KMLN-LD
24	0.25	CO	Boulder	K24HQ-D
25	15	CO	Fort Collins	KPXH-LD
28	400	CO	Denver	KTFD-TV
29	800	CO	Longmont	KDEN-TV
30	15	CO	Denver	+ KLPD-LD
30	15	CO	Denver	+ KZCO-LD
31	960	CO	Denver	KTVD
32	650	CO	Boulder	KCEC
33	1000	CO	Denver	KRMA-TV
34	1000	CO	Denver	KWGN-TV
35	1000	CO	Denver	KCNC-TV
36	1000	CO	Denver	KDVR
Detroit, MI Area				
3	6.5	MI	Detroit	WHNE-LD
7	27	MI	Detroit	WJBK
15	15	MI	Detroit	WHPS-CD
20	345	MI	Detroit	WTVS
21	380	MI	Detroit	WWJ-TV
22	15	MI	Detroit	WDWO-CD
24	370	MI	Ann Arbor	WPXD-TV
25	765	MI	Detroit	WXYZ-TV
27	605	MI	Mount Clemens	WADL
28	4	MI	Redford	WLPC-CD
31	935	MI	Detroit	WMYD
32	720	MI	Detroit	WDIV-TV
34	285	MI	Detroit	WKBD-TV
35	10	MI	Detroit	WUDT-LD
Houston, TX Area				
3	0.3	TX	Houston	KZHO-LD
5	3	TX	Dayton	KTDJ-LD
7	0.3	TX	Houston	KDHU-LD
8	65	TX	Houston	KUHT
9	3	TX	Houston	KBMN-LD
11	60	TX	Houston	KHOU
13	32	TX	Houston	KTRK-TV
14	15	TX	Houston	KVQT-LD
15	15	TX	Houston	KVVV-LD
19	1000	TX	Houston	KTXH
20	15	TX	Missouri City	KUVM-CD
21	880	TX	Houston	KZJL
22	15	TX	Victoria	K22JW-D
22	1000	TX	Galveston	KTMD
23	350	TX	Galveston	KLTJ
24	1000	TX	Houston	KETH-TV
25	1000	TX	Katy	KYAZ
26	800	TX	Houston	KRIV
27	15	TX	Houston	+ KBPX-LD
27	15	TX	Houston	+ KQHO-LD
28	15	TX	Houston	KUGB-CD
29	15	TX	Houston	KEHO-LD
30	1000	TX	Rosenberg	KXLN-DT
31	1000	TX	Baytown	KUBE-TV
32	1000	TX	Conroe	KPXB-TV
33	1000	TX	Conroe	KTBU
34	1000	TX	Houston	KIAH
35	1000	TX	Houston	KPRC-TV

ch	kW	Sta	City of License	Callsign
36	1000	TX	Alvin	KFTH-DT
Los Angeles, CA Area				
2	3	CA	Los Angeles	KHIZ-LD
2	0.9	CA	Los Angeles	KYAN-LD
3	3	CA	Agoura Hills	KVTU-LD
3	3	CA	Temecula	K12PO
4	35	CA	Los Angeles	+ KWHY-TV
4	35	CA	Garden Grove	+ KBEH
5	25.8	CA	San Bernardino	KVCR-DT
7	29	CA	Los Angeles	+ KABC-TV
7	29	CA	Riverside	+ KRCA
8	3	CA	Los Angeles	KFLA-LD
9	25	CA	Los Angeles	KCAL-TV
10	3	CA	Los Angeles	KIIO-LD
10	3	CA	Riverside	KZSW-LD
11	115	CA	Los Angeles	KTTV
12	110	CA	Anaheim	KDOC-TV
13	120	CA	Los Angeles	KCOP-TV
18	700	CA	Long Beach	+ KSCI
18	700	CA	Huntington Beach	+ KOCE-TV
21	2	CA	Los Angeles	KTAV-LD
22	15	CA	Los Angeles	+ KHTV-CD
22	15	CA	Avalon	+ KAZA-TV
23	150	CA	Twentynine Palms	KVMD
23	1.5	CA	Ventura	KIMG-LD
23	15	CA	Los Angeles	KSMV-LD
24	1000	CA	San Bernardino	+ KPXN-TV
24	1000	CA	Inglewood	+ KILM
25	620	CA	Corona	KVEA
26	15	CA	Van Nuys	KSKJ-CD
27	14.4	CA	Ontario	+ KPOM-CD
27	14.4	CA	Ontario	+ KSFV-CD
28	155	CA	Los Angeles	+ KCET
28	155	CA	Los Angeles	+ KLCS
29	370	CA	Ontario	KFTR-DT
30	0.5	CA	Ontario	KCIO-LD
30	670	CA	Rancho Palos Verdes	+ KXLA
30	670	CA	Ventura	+ KJLA
31	485	CA	Los Angeles	KCBS-TV
32	15	CA	Los Angeles	+ KNLA-CD
32	15	CA	Los Angeles	+ KNET-CD
32	6.63	CA	Riverside	KRMV-LD
33	1000	CA	Santa Ana	KTBN-TV
34	500	CA	Los Angeles	KMEX-DT
35	1000	CA	Los Angeles	KTLA
36	665	CA	Los Angeles	KNBC
Miami, FL Area				
4	3	FL	Miami	WMDF-LD
8	3	FL	Miami	WVFW-LD
9	158	FL	Miami	WSVN
10	128	FL	Miami	WPLG
11	3	FL	Miami	WDFL-LD
16	3	FL	West Gate	W16CC-D
17	15	FL	Miami	WBEH-CD
18	15	FL	Miami	W17DG-D
18	15	FL	Miami	WTXI-LD
19	15	FL	Miami	WSBS-CD
21	225	FL	Miami	WPXM-TV
22	1000	FL	Miami	WFOR-TV
23	1000	FL	Miami	WLTV-DT
24	775	FL	Hollywood	WAMI-DT
25	415	FL	Boca Raton	WBEC-TV
26	765	FL	Miami	WLRN-TV
27	1000	FL	Miami	WSFL-TV
28	701	FL	Miami	WHFT-TV
29	1000	FL	Miami	+ WPBT
29	1000	FL	Miami	+ WURH-CD
29	1000	FL	Boynton Beach	+ WXEL-TV
30	1000	FL	Fort Lauderdale	WSCV
31	1000	FL	Miami	WTVJ
32	1000	FL	Miami	WBFS-TV
33	15	FL	Miami	WJAN-CD
45	15	FL	Miami	WGEN-LD
Minneapolis, MI Area				
9	30	MN	Minneapolis	KMSP-TV
11	45	MN	Minneapolis	KARE
14	15	MN	St. Paul	K14RB-D
15	15	MN	Minneapolis	KWJM-LD
16	470	MN	St. Cloud	KPXM-TV
17	15	MN	Minneapolis	WUMN-LD

ch	kW	Sta	City of License	Callsign
19	6	WI	River Falls	W19EN-D
20	3	MN	Minneapolis	KMBD-LD
22	1000	MN	Minneapolis	WUCW
23	325	MN	St. Paul	KTCI-TV
24	1.5	WI	Grantsburg	W24CL-D
25	1	MN	Minneapolis	KJNK-LD
27	291	WI	Menomonie	WHWC-TV
28	5	MN	St. Cloud	K28PQ-D
29	1000	MN	Minneapolis	WFTC
30	1000	MN	Minneapolis	KSTC-TV
31	15	MN	Minneapolis	WDMI-LD
32	1000	MN	Minneapolis	WCCO-TV
33	15	MN	Minneapolis	K33LN-D
34	662	MN	St. Paul	KTCA-TV
35	755	MN	St. Paul	KSTP-TV
New York, NY Area				
2	0.3	NY	New York	WKOB-LD
3	7	NJ	Middletown Township	+ WJLP
3	7	NY	New York	+ WNWT-LD
4	0.3	NJ	East Orange	WPXO-LD
7	34	NY	New York	WABC-TV
8	41	NJ	New Brunswick	+ WNJB
8	41	NJ	Montclair	+ WNJN
10	0.27	NY	New York	WNXY-LD
11	7.5	NY	New York	WPIX
12	6.5	NJ	Newark	+ WNET
12	6.5	NY	Manhattan	+ WNDT-CD
12	6.5	NY	New York	+ WMBQ-CD
18	1000	NJ	Newton	WMBC-TV
20	15	NY	Hempstead	W20CQ-D
20	1.6	NJ	Teaneck	W20EF-D
21	200	CT	Stamford	+ WEDW
21	200	CT	Bridgeport	+ WZME
22	7	NJ	Edison	+ WDVB-CD
22	7	NJ	Jersey City	+ WTBY-TV
23	11	NY	Poughkeepsie	W23ER-D
23	3.87	NJ	Sussex	W23EX-D
23	655	NY	Smithtown	WFTY-DT
24	151	NY	New York	WNYE-TV
25	57.8	NJ	Secaucus	+ WWOR-TV
25	57.8	NY	New Rochelle	+ WRNN-TV
26	200	NJ	Newark	+ WFUT-DT
26	200	NJ	Paterson	+ WXTV-DT
27	92.8	NY	New York	WNYW
27	1.5	NJ	Belvidere	W27EC-D
28	15	NY	New York	WNYJ-LD
29	1000	NY	Riverhead	WLNY-TV
29	1.5	NJ	Hackettstown	W29EV-D
30	0.8	NY	New York	WNYN-LD
31	15	NY	Highland	WZPK-LD
32	72	NY	Garden City	WLIW
34	170	NY	New York	WPXN-TV
35	575	NJ	Linden	+ WNJU
35	575	NY	New York	+ WNBC
36	548	NY	New York	WCBS-TV
Philadelphia, PA Area				
2	34	DE	Wilmington	WDPN-TV
4	10	NJ	Atlantic City	WACP
6	34	PA	Philadelphia	WPVI-TV
7	0.025	PA	Allentown	W07DC-D
9	81	PA	Bethlehem	+ WBPH-TV
9	81	PA	Philadelphia	+ WPPT
9	81	PA	Allentown	+ WLVT-TV
9	81	PA	Allentown	+ WFMZ-TV
10	3	NJ	Atlantic City	WSJT-LD
13	30	DE	Wilmington	+ WHYY-TV
13	30	NJ	Princeton	+ WMCN-TV
16	5	NJ	Springville	WDUM-LD
17	645	PA	Philadelphia	+ WPHL-TV
17	645	NJ	Vineland	+ WUVP-DT
22	15	NJ	Trenton	+ WPHY-CD
22	15	PA	Willow Grove	+ WTVE
23	60.7	NJ	Camden	+ WNJS
23	60.7	NJ	Trenton	+ WNJT
24	15	PA	Philadelphia	WPHA-CD
24	80.6	PA	Allentown	WFMZ-AB
24	5	PA	Reading	W24CS-D
25	2.5	PA	Darby	W36DO-D
26	15	NJ	Glassboro	WQAV-CD
27	8.5	NJ	Hammonton	WPSJ-CD
27	1.5	NJ	Belvidere	W27EC-D
28	745	PA	Philadelphia	+ WCAU
28	745	NJ	Mount Laurel	+ WWSI
29	15	PA	Philadelphia	WELL-LD
29	15	NJ	Atlantic City	W29FF-D
30	420	PA	Philadelphia	KYW-TV
31	1000	PA	Philadelphia	WTXF-TV
32	15	PA	Philadelphia	WZPA-LD
33	440	PA	Philadelphia	WPSG
34	131	DE	Wilmington	WPPX-TV
35	15	PA	Philadelphia	WFPA-CD
36	205	NJ	Wildwood	+ WMGM-TV
36	205	NJ	Millville	+ WGTW-TV
Phoenix, AZ Area				
8	40	AZ	Phoenix	KAET
10	48	AZ	Phoenix	KSAZ-TV
12	39	AZ	Mesa	KPNX
14	15	AZ	Phoenix	K14RK-D
15	458	AZ	Phoenix	KNXV-TV
16	15	AZ	Phoenix	KPHE-LD
17	1000	AZ	Phoenix	KPHO-TV
18	3	AZ	Phoenix	K18JL-D
19	15	AZ	Gila River Indian Co	KGRF-LD
20	1000	AZ	Phoenix	KPAZ-TV
21	4.5	AZ	Gila River Indian Co	KGRQ-LD
22	12.5	AZ	Phoenix	KPDF-CD
23	15	AZ	Phoenix	KTVP-LD
24	1000	AZ	Phoenix	KTVK
25	5.5	AZ	Globe	KFPB-LD
26	1000	AZ	Phoenix	KUTP
27	445	AZ	Phoenix	KASW
29	595	AZ	Phoenix	KTAZ
31	645	AZ	Tolleson	KPPX-TV
32	15	AZ	Phoenix	KEJR-LD
33	470	AZ	Phoenix	KTVW-DT
34	15	AZ	Phoenix	KVPA-LD
35	15	AZ	Phoenix	KFPH-CD
36	15	AZ	Phoenix	KAZT-CD
Sacramento, CA Area				
2	3	CA	Middletown	KFTY-LD
2	0.55	CA	Planada	K02QP-D
3	5	CA	Sacramento	KCSO-LD
4	0.3	CA	Esparto	K04QR-D
4	1	CA	Turlock	KBIS-LD
9	33	CA	Sacramento	KVIE
10	28.6	CA	Sacramento	KXTV
11	0.1	CA	Mariposa	K11XT-D
12	2	CA	Modesto	K12XJ-D
14	15	CA	Sacramento	KSAO-LD
14	5.9	CA	Stockton	KMMW-LD
15	0.5	CA	Ceres	KBSV
15	0.125	CA	Yuba City	KYUB-LD
18	500	CA	Modesto	KUVS-DT
19	15	CA	Sacramento	KMUM-CD
20	4.7	CA	Sacramento	K20JX-D
21	1000	CA	Sacramento	KSPX-TV
22	1000	CA	Sacramento	KTXL
23	425	CA	Stockton	KQCA
24	1000	CA	Sacramento	KMAX-TV
25	1000	CA	Stockton	KOVR
26	800	CA	Stockton	KTFK-DT
27	15	CA	Sacramento	KBTV-CD
28	15	CA	Yuba City	KKPM-CD
30	15	CA	Sacramento	KAHC-LD
31	15	CA	Keyes	KFMS-LD
32	15	CA	Sacramento	KSTV-LD
32	10	CA	Stockton	KFKK-LD
34	10	CA	Modesto	KACA-LP
34	15	CA	Sacramento	KEZT-CD
35	1000	CA	Sacramento	KCRA-TV
42	15	CA	Sacramento	KMSX-LD
San Francisco, CA Area				
2	3	CA	Morgan Hill	KQRO-LD
2	3	CA	Middletown	KFTY-LD
3	2.5	CA	San Francisco	KURK-LD
4	3	CA	San Rafael	KQSL-LD
5	18.6	CA	Cotati	KRCB
6	0.1	CA	Petaluma	KFMY-LD
7	50	CA	San Francisco	KRON-TV
8	0.2	CA	San Francisco	KDTS-LD
11	0.039	CA	San Francisco	KPJC-LD
12	47	CA	San Francisco	KGO-TV

ch	kW	Sta	City of License	Callsign
13	103	CA	San Jose	KNTV
19	500	CA	San Jose	KSTS
20	475	CA	San Francisco	+ KDTV-DT
20	475	CA	San Francisco	+ KTSF
21	15	CA	San Francisco	+ KOFY-TV
21	15	CA	San Francisco	+ KCNZ-CD
21	15	CA	San Francisco	+ KMTP-TV
21	15	CA	Petaluma	+ KQRM-LP
22	15	CA	San Franciso	+ KAXT-CD
22	15	CA	Palo Alto	+ KTLN-TV
21	11	CA	Santa Rosa	KDTV-CD
22	3	CA	Santa Rosa	KZHD-LD
23	15	CA	San Jose	KSCZ-LD
24	0.55	CA	San Jose	KAAP-LD
26	1	CA	Santa Rosa	KUKR-LD
27	465	CA	San Mateo	KPJK
28	1000	CA	San Francisco	KBCW
29	1000	CA	San Francisco	KPIX-TV
30	1000	CA	San Francisco	+ KQED
30	1000	CA	San Jose	+ KQEH
31	1000	CA	Oakland	KTVU
32	1000	CA	San Francisco	+ KCNS
32	1000	CA	Concord	+ KTNC-TV
32	1000	CA	Fremont	+ KEMO-TV
33	510	CA	San Jose	KKPX-TV
34	370	CA	Vallejo	KFSF-DT
36	550	CA	San Jose	KICU-TV
Seattle, WA Area				
6	3	WA	Seattle	KYMU-LD
8	0.25	WA	Seattle	K08OU-D
9	22	WA	Seattle	KCTS-TV
11	100	WA	Tacoma	KSTW
12	3	WA	Seattle	KUSE-LD
13	30	WA	Tacoma	KCPQ
14	535	WA	Bellingham	KVOS-TV
16	260	WA	Seattle	KFFV
18	2.2	WA	Point Pulley	K18NI-D
18	4.4	WA	Puyallup	K18NH-D
19	187	WA	Centralia	KCKA
19	165	WA	Bellingham	KBCB
21	107	WA	Tacoma	KTBW-TV
23	715	WA	Seattle	KIRO-TV
24	504	WA	Bellevue	KUNS-TV
25	715	WA	Seattle	KING-TV
26	1	WA	Bremerton	K26IC-D
26	4	WA	Everett	K26OZ-D
27	100	WA	Tacoma	KBTC-TV
29	2	WA	Everett	K29ED-D
30	915	WA	Seattle	KOMO-TV
31	700	WA	Everett	KONG
33	400	WA	Bellevue	KWPX-TV
34	123	WA	Tacoma	KWDK
36	115	WA	Seattle	KZJO
Tampa, FL Area				
9	41	FL	Tampa	+ WFLA-TV
9	41	FL	St. Petersburg	+ WTTA
10	69	FL	St. Petersburg	WTSP
12	72	FL	Tampa	WTVT
13	25	FL	Tampa	+ WEDU
13	25	FL	Tampa	+ WEDQ
14	3.5	FL	Largo.	WPDS-LD
15	0.425	FL	Oldsmar	WZRA-CD
16	15	FL	Lealman	W16DQ-D
17	1000	FL	Tampa	WFTS-TV
18	1000	FL	Lakeland	WMOR-TV
19	500	FL	St. Petersburg	WTOG
20	1000	FL	Tampa	WVEA-TV
21	1000	FL	Clearwater	WCLF
24	90	FL	Sarasota	WWSB
25	750	FL	Venice	WFTT-TV
26	5.9	FL	Clearwater	WXAX-CD
26	14.9	FL	Sarasota	WSNN-LD
27	6	FL	Tampa	WBKH-LD
29	218	FL	Bradenton	WXPX-TV
30	14	FL	Tampa	WRMD-CD
31	13	FL	Orient City	W15CM-D
33	15	FL	Tampa	WGCT-LD
35	15	FL	Tampa	WTAM-LD
36	15	FL	St. Petersburg	WSPF-CD
36	5.2	FL	Sebring	W23CN-D
Washington, DC Area				
7	52	DC	Washington	WJLA-TV
9	52	DC	Washington	+ WUSA
9	52	MD	Silver Spring	+ WJAL
13	4.2	WV	Martinsburg	WWPX-TV
14	15	DC	Washington	WWTD-LD
15	1000	VA	Arlington	+ WFDC-DT
15	1000	DC	Washington	+ WDCW
20	15	VA	Vienna	WAZT-CD
20	7	MD	Lake Shore	WQAW-LP
21	1000	MD	Annapolis	WMPT
23	10	DC	Washington	WDDN-LD
23	15	VA	Damascus	WDWA-LD
24	5.1	VA	Woodstock	WDCO-CD
28	41	MD	Frederick	WFPT
30	48	DC	Washington	+ WMDO-CD
30	48	DC	Washington	+ WIAV-CD
31	240	DC	Washington	WETA-TV
32	15	DC	Washington	WRZB-LD
33	152	DC	Washington	WHUT-TV
34	1000	DC	Washington	+ WRC-TV
34	1000	DC	Washington	+ WZDC-CD
35	16.5	VA	Manassas	WPXW-TV
36	1000	DC	Washington	+ WTTG
36	1000	DC	Washington	+ WDCA
45	15	DC	Washington	W45DN-D

+ = Shared transmitter (multiplex).

NB: A number of stns is still being relocated to new channels, as part of a major freq reshuffle in connection with the assignment of the 700MHz band to mobile services.

URUGUAY

System: ISDB-TB [A]

National Station
TELEVISIÓN NACIONAL URUGUAY (TNU) (Gov) 🖃 Bvrd. Artigas 2552,11600 Montevideo ☎ +598 2 4871129 **E:** contacto@tnu.com.uy **W:** www.tnu.com.uy **Tx:** Montevideo ch30 & MFN.

Key Local Stations
CANAL 4 (Comm) 🖃 Paraguay 2253, 11800 Montevideo ☎ +598 2 9247924 **W:** www.canal4.com.uy **Tx:** Montevideo ch29 – **CANAL 10 (Comm)** 🖃 Lorenzo Carnelli 1234, 11200 Montevideo ☎ +598 2 4002120 **W:** www.canal10.com.uy **Tx:** Montevideo ch31 – **TELEDOCE (Comm)** 🖃 Enriqueta Compte y Rique 1276, 11800 Montevideo ☎ +598 2 2083363 **E:** teledoce@teledoce.com **W:** www.teledoce.com **Tx:** Montevideo ch28.

Other Local Stations not shown.

UZBEKISTAN

System: DVB-T2 (MPEG4) [E]; § DVB-T [E]

National Stations
UZBEK TELEVISION (Gov) 🖃 Navoiy St. 69, 100011 Toshkent ☎+998 71 1141250 **E:** info@mtrk.uz **W:** www.mtrk.uz **L.P:** Chmn: Alisher Xadjayev **Chs:** O'zbekiston, Yoshlar, Toshkent, Sport TV, Madaniyat va ma'rifat, Dunyo bo'ylab, Bolajon, Oilaviy, Kinoteatr, Navo, Sport, O'zbekiston 24, regional stns.

Local Stations not shown.

DTT Tx Networks (DVB-T2)
Licensee: Uzdigital TV **W:** uzdtv.uz **M1:** O'zbekiston, Toshkent, Sport, Dunyo bo'ylab, Bolajon, Madaniyat va ma'rifat, Kinoteatr, Oilaviy, Mahalla, Yoshlar, Navo, Milliy TV, UzReport TV HD, Mening Yurtim, Z'or TV HD, Sevimli HD, Futbol TV HD, O'zbekiston 24 HD **M2✪:** Pervyy Kanal, Rossiya 1, NTV, Match TV, Zvezda Telekanal, TV Centr, TV 3, Rossiya 24, Karusel, Euronews, Ohkota i Rybalka, Discovery Channel, National Geographic, Eurosport 1, Kinohit, Kinopremiera **M3✪:** Disney Kanal, Kinosvidanye, Muz TV, RuTV, Telekafe, Match! Arena, Match! Futbol 1, Animmal Planet, Rossiya K, Dom Kino, Match! Futbol 2, Indinskoye Kino, TV 1000, TV 1000 Russkoye Kino, Viasat History, Viasat Explore **M4✪(exc.*):** UzReport TV*, Mening Yutim*, Sevimli TV*, Futbol TV*, Rossiya K, Dom Kino, Match! Futbol 2, Indinskoye Kino, TV 1000, TV 1000 Russkoye Kino, Viasat History, Viasat Explore **M5✪:** Discovery Science, Retro, Auto Plus, Nashe Novoe Kino, Rodnoe Kino, Detskiy Mir, Tehno 24, Fashion TV, Match! Igra, National Geographic HD, Nat Geo Wild HD,

Travel Channel HD, Match! Futbol 1 HD

Location	M1	M2	M3	M4	M5	kW
Toshkent	42	41	37	29	(-)	2

+ national MFN

VANUATU

Systems: DTMB [E]; DVB-T2 (MPEG4) [E]

National Station
TV BLONG VANUATU (TBV) (Gov) P.M.B. 049, Port Vila **E:** reception@vbtc.vu **W:** www.vbtc.vu **L.P:** Pres (VBTC): Johnety Jerette.

Local Stations not shown.

DTT Tx Network
Tx Operator: Telsat Pacific **W:** www.telsatbb.vu **M✪ (DVB-T2)** multiprgr (incl. local channels 1NOMO and KAM) **Txs:** (-) – **Tx Operator:** Vanuamadia Digital Media Ltd **M(✪ exc.*) (DTMB):** VBTC* + multiprgr **Txs:** ch48 (SFN).

VATICAN CITY STATE

System: DVB-T (MPEG4) [E]

VATICAN MEDIA (Rlg) Via della Conciliazione 5, I-00120 Città del Vaticano ☎ +39 06 69845050 **E:** spc@spc.va **W:** www.comunicazione.va **Mux:** Vatican Media HD (CTV HD), Vatican Media Feed (CTV Feed)✪ ⌘ R. Vaticana Italia, R. Vaticana Europa/America, R. Vaticana Africa/Asia **Tx:** ch45 (Castel Gandolfo).

VENEZUELA

Systems: ISDB-TB [A]; # NTSC-M [A] ⇩2021

National Stations
TVES (TELEVISORA VENEZOLANA SOCIAL) (Gov) Caracas **W:** www.tves.gob.ve – **VIVE (VISIÓN VENEZUELA) (Gov)** Final Av. Panteón, Foro Libertador, Edf. Biblioteca Nacional, AP-4, Altagracia, Caracas ☎+58 212 5051611 **E:** atencionciudadana@vive.gob.ve **W:** www.vive.gob.ve – **VTV (VENEZOLANA DE TELEVISION) (Gov)** Ap. 2979, Caracas 1050. ☎ +58 212 2349581 **E:** atencionciudadano@vtv.gob.ve **W:** www.vtv.gob.ve – **TELESUR (Pub)** Calle Vargas con Calle Santa Clara, edificio TeleSUR, Boleita Norte, Caracas ☎ +58 212 6000202 **E:** contactenos@telesurtv.net **W:** www.telesurtv.net – **GLOBOVISIÓN (Comm)** av. Los Pinos, cruce con Calle Alameda, Qta. Globovisión, Urb. Alta Florida, Caracas ☎ +58 212 7301134 **E:** info@globovision.com **W:** www.globovision.com – **MERIDIANO TELEVISÓN (Comm)** Final av. San Martin con Av. La Paz, Edificio Bloque De Armas, Caracas ☎ +58 212 4064516 **E:** meridianotv@internet.ve **W:** www.meridiano.com.ve – **TELEVEN (Comm)** Av. Romulo Gallegos con 4ta. transversal de horizonte, Edificio Televen, Caracas 1071 ☎ +58 212 2800151 **E:** webmaster@televen.com **W:** www.televen.com – **VENEVISIÓN (Comm)** Av. La Salle, Edif, Venevision,Colinas de Los Caobos, Caracas 1050 ☎ +58 212 7089444 **W:** www.venevision.net – **VALE TV (Rlg)** Final Av. La Salle, Quinta ValeTV, Colinas de los Caobos, Caracas ☎ +58 212 7939215 **W:** www.facebook.com/ValeTV.

Local Stations not shown.

DTT Tx Networks
Tx Operator: n/a **M1:** VTV, TeleSUR, HispanTV, RT Español, Canal Uno (Argentina), VTV móvil **M2:** TVes, TLT La Tele Tuya, Meridiano TV, Venevisión, Televen, TVes móvil **M3:** Corazón Llanero, CGTN Español, 123TV, TV ConCiencia, Ávila TV, Ávila TV móvil **M4:** Vive, Alba TV, Colombeia, ANTV, TVFANB, PDVSA TV, TeleSUR móvil.

Location	M1	M2	M3	M4
SFN	22	23	24	25

VIETNAM

System: DVB-T2 (MPEG2) [E]

National Stations
VIETNAM TELEVISION (Gov) 43 Nguyen Chi Thanh, Ba Dinh District, Hanoi ☎ +84 438355931 **E:** toasoan@vtv.vn **W:** vtv.vn **L.P:** DG: Tran Binh Minh **Chs (terr.):** VTV1-9.

Regional and Local Stations not shown.

DTT Tx Networks
Licensee: Vietnam Multimedia Corporation (VCT) **W:** tvnet.gov.vn **M:** VTV1-9, VTV3 HD, VTV6 HD, VTC1-4✪, VTC5, VTC6✪, VTC7, VTC9, VTC11-14✪, VCT16✪, Hanoi TV 1, HTV1 **Txs:** ch26 (Hanoi 1.3kW) & nationwide MFN.

VIRGIN ISLANDS, BRITISH (UK)

System: NTSC-M [A]

CARIBBEAN BROADCAST NETWORK (BVI) LTD (Comm) 2nd Floor, Chevelle Center Main Street, Road Town, Tortola VG 1110 ☎ +1 284 3463633 **E:** carribeanbroadcasting@gmail.com **W:** www.cbnvirginislands.com **Tx:** ch51.

VIRGIN ISLANDS, US (USA)

System: ATSC [A]

Local Stations

ch	kW	Territory	City of License	Callsign
5	2.8	VI	Charlotte Amalie	WFIG-LD
5	0.3	VI	Christiansted	W05AW-D
17	4.2	VI	Charlotte Amalie	WVXF
19	3.25	VI	Charlotte Amalie	WVGN-LD
20	1	VI	Christiansted	WSVI
21	6	VI	Charlotte Amalie	WZVI
22	3.75	VI	Charlotte Amalie	WMNS-LD
23	23.7	VI	Christiansted	WCVI-TV
36	52.3	VI	Charlotte Amalie	WTJX-TV

WAKE ISLAND (USA)

NB: No terrestrial TV station.

WALLIS & FUTUNA (France)

System: DVB-T (MPEG4) [E]

WALLIS ET FUTUNA LA 1ÈRE (Pub) BP 102, Pointe Matala, F-98600 Mata Utu ☎ +33 681722020 **W:** la1ere.francetvinfo.fr/wallisfutuna.

DTT Tx Network
Tx Operator: TDF **M:** Wallis et Futuna la 1ère HD, France 2-5*, Franceinfo, Arte **Txs:** ch34 (SFN). *) France 4 will cease in 2021

YEMEN

System: PAL-B [E]

YEMEN GENERAL CORP. FOR RADIO & TV (Gov) P.O.Box 1140, al-Guraf, Sana'a. **Txs:**(-).

ZAMBIA

System: DVB-T2 (MPEG4) [E]

National Stations
ZAMBIA NATIONAL BROADCASTING CORP. (ZNBC) (Gov) P.O.Box 50015, Lusaka 10101☎ +260 21 1254989 **E:** znbctv@znbc.co.zm **W:** www.znbc.co.zm **Chs:** ZNBC TV1, ZNBC TV2, ZNBC TV3, ZNBC TV4 – **MUVI TV (Comm)** P.O.Box 33932, Lusaka 10101 ☎ +260 21 1253271 **E:** frontoffice@muvitv.com **W:** www.muvitv.com.

Local Stations not shown.

DTT Tx Network
Licensee: Multichoice Zambia **M(partly✪):** multiprgr **Txs:** MFN.

ZIMBABWE

System: DVB-T2 (MPEG4) [E]

ZIMBABWE TELEVISION (ZTV) (Gov) P.O.Box HG 444, Highlands, Harare ☎ +263 4 498610 **E:** zbc@zbc.co.zw **W:** www.zbc.co.zw **Chs:** ZTV1, ZTV2.

DTT Tx Network
Licensee: Multichoice Zimbabwe **M(partly✪):** multiprgr **Txs:** MFN.

REFERENCE

Section Contents

MAIN COUNTRY INDEX

GEOGRAPHICAL AREA CODES USED IN WRTH

Codes assigned by the International Telecommunications Union ITU (except * = WRTH code)

Code	Country
ABW	Aruba
AFG	Afghanistan
AFS	South Africa
AGL	Angola
AIA	Anguilla
ALB	Albania
ALG	Algeria
ALS	Alaska
AMS	St Paul & Amsterdam Is
AND	Andorra
AOE	Western Sahara
ARG	Argentina
ARM	Armenia
ARS	Saudi Arabia
ASC	Ascension Island
ATA	Antarctica
ATG	Antigua & Barbuda
AUS	Australia
AUT	Austria
AZE	Azerbaijan
AZR	Azores
B	Brazil
BAH	Bahamas
BDI	Burundi
BEL	Belgium
BEN	Benin
BER	Bermuda
BES	Bonaire / Saba / St Eustatius
BFA	Burkina Faso
BGD	Bangladesh
BHR	Bahrain
BIH	Bosnia & Herzegovina
BIO	British Indian Ocean Territory
BLM	St Barthélemy
BLR	Belarus
BLZ	Belize
BOL	Bolivia
BOT	Botswana
BRB	Barbados
BRM	Myanmar
BRU	Brunei
BTN	Bhutan
BUL	Bulgaria
CAF	Central African Republic
CAN	Canada
CBG	Cambodia
CEU*	Ceuta
CHL	Chile
CHN	China (People's Rep. of)
CHR	Christmas Island
CKH	Cook Islands
CLM	Colombia
CLN	Sri Lanka
CME	Cameroon
CNR	Canary Islands
COD	Congo (Dem. Rep. of the)
COG	Congo (Rep. of the)
COM	Comoros
CPV	Cabo Verde
CRO	Crozet Islands
CTI	Côte d'Ivoire
CTR	Costa Rica
CUB	Cuba
CUW	Curaçao
CVA	Vatican City State
CYM	Cayman Islands
CYP	Cyprus
CZE	Czechia
D	Germany
DGA	Diego Garcia
DJI	Djibouti
DMA	Dominica
DNK	Denmark
DOM	Dominican Republic
E	Spain
EGY	Egypt
EQA	Ecuador
ERI	Eritrea
EST	Estonia
ETH	Ethiopia
F	France
FIN	Finland
FJI	Fiji
FLK	Falkland Islands
FRO	Faroe Islands
FSM	Micronesia
G	United Kingdom
GAB	Gabon
GAL*	Galapagos Islands
GEO	Georgia
GHA	Ghana
GIB	Gibraltar
GLP	Guadeloupe
GMB	Gambia
GNB	Guinea-Bissau
GNE	Equatorial Guinea
GRC	Greece
GRD	Grenada
GRL	Greenland
GTM	Guatemala
GUF	French Guiana
GUI	Guinea
GUM	Guam
GUY	Guyana
HKG	Hong Kong
HND	Honduras
HNG	Hungary
HOL	Netherlands
HRV	Croatia
HTI	Haiti
HWA	Hawaii
I	Italy
ICO	Cocos (Keeling) Islands
IND	India
INS	Indonesia
IRL	Ireland
IRN	Iran
IRQ	Iraq
ISL	Iceland
ISR	Israel
J	Japan
JMC	Jamaica
JOR	Jordan
KAZ	Kazakhstan
KEN	Kenya
KER	Kerguelen Islands
KGZ	Kyrgyzstan
KIR	Kiribati
KOR	Korea, South
KRE	Korea, North
KWT	Kuwait
LAO	Laos
LBN	Lebanon
LBR	Liberia
LBY	Libya
LCA	St Lucia
LHW*	Lord Howe Island
LIE	Liechtenstein
LSO	Lesotho
LTU	Lithuania
LUX	Luxembourg
LVA	Latvia
MAC	Macao
MAF	St Martin
MAU	Mauritius
MCO	Monaco
MDA	Moldova
MDG	Madagascar
MDR	Madeira
MEL*	Melilla
MEX	Mexico
MHL	Marshall Islands
MKD	North Macedonia
MLA	Malaysia
MLD	Maldives
MLI	Mali
MLT	Malta
MNE	Montenegro
MNG	Mongolia
MOZ	Mozambique
MRA	Northern Mariana Is
MRC	Morocco
MRT	Martinique
MSR	Montserrat
MTN	Mauritania
MWI	Malawi
MYT	Mayotte
NCG	Nicaragua
NCL	New Caledonia
NFK	Norfolk Island
NGR	Niger
NIG	Nigeria
NIU	Niue
NMB	Namibia
NOR	Norway
NPL	Nepal
NRU	Nauru
NZL	New Zealand
OCE	French Polynesia
OMA	Oman
PAK	Pakistan
PAQ	Easter Island
PHL	Philippines
PLW	Palau
PNG	Papua New Guinea
PNR	Panama
POL	Poland
POR	Portugal
PRG	Paraguay
PRU	Peru
PSE*	Palestine[1]
PTC	Pitcairn Islands
PTR	Puerto Rico
QAT	Qatar
REU	Réunion
RKS*	Kosovo
ROD	Rodrigues
ROU	Romania
RRW	Rwanda
RUS	Russia
S	Sweden
SCN	St Kitts & Nevis
SDN	Sudan
SEN	Senegal
SEY	Seychelles
SHN	St Helena
SLM	Solomon Islands
SLV	El Salvador
SMA	American Samoa
SMO	Samoa
SMR	San Marino
SNG	Singapore
SOM	Somalia
SPM	St Pierre & Miquelon
SRB	Serbia
SRL	Sierra Leone
SSD	South Sudan
STP	São Tomé & Príncipe
SUI	Switzerland
SUR	Suriname
SVK	Slovakia
SVN	Slovenia
SWZ	Eswatini
SXM	St Maarten
SYR	Syria
TCA	Turks & Caicos Islands
TCD	Chad
TGO	Togo
THA	Thailand
TJK	Tajikistan
TKM	Turkmenistan
TKL	Tokelau
TLS	Timor-Leste
TON	Tonga
TRC	Tristan da Cunha
TRD	Trinidad & Tobago
TUN	Tunisia
TUR	Turkey
TUV	Tuvalu
TWN*	Taiwan (Rep. of China)
TZA	Tanzania
UAE	United Arab Emirates
UGA	Uganda
UKR	Ukraine
URG	Uruguay
USA	United States of America
UZB	Uzbekistan
VCT	St Vincent & the Grenadines
VEN	Venezuela
VIR	Virgin Islands
VRG	British Virgin Islands
VTN	Vietnam
VUT	Vanuatu
WAL	Wallis & Futuna
WAK	Wake Island
XGZ	Gaza Strip[1]
XWB	West Bank[1]
YEM	Yemen
ZMB	Zambia
ZWE	Zimbabwe

1) The code "PSE" is used as target designation in the "COTB" section of International Radio; otherwise the codes "XGZ"/"XWB" are used.

ABBREVIATIONS & SYMBOLS USED IN WRTH

🖃	Address
☎	Telephone
🖷	Fax
✪	encrypted
⌘	Radio via DTT
†	irrregular
‡	inactive
±	variable frequency
acc.	accepted
Admin.	Administration
alt.	alternate, alternative
AM	Amplitude Modulation
Ann.	Announcement
Ap.	Apartado
approx.	approximate(ly)
Assoc.	Association
Asst.	Assistant
Ave	Avenue, Avenida
B.P.	Boîte Postale
B'caster	Broadcaster
Bldg	Building
Bo	Barrio/Bairro
Broadc.	Broadcast(ing)
BS	Broadc. Stn/Sce
C	Chinese
C.P.	Case/Caixa Postal, Construction Permit
Ca	Calle
Cad.	Cadena
Cas.	Casilla
Cd.	Ciudad
Ce.	Central
CEO	Chief Exec. Officer
cf.	refer to
Ch.	Channel
Chmn.	Chairman/Chair
Cl.	Club(e)
Clan.	Clandestine
Co.	Company
Com.	Comunicações
comm.	commercial
Contr.	Controller
Corp.	Corporation
Cra.	Carrera
Cult.	Cultura, Cultural
D	Daily, On Demand audio
d	directional antenna
D.Prgr	Daily Programme(s)
DAB	Digital Audio Broadc.
DMB	Digital Multimedia Broadcasting
Dem.	Democratic
Dep.	Deputy
Dept.	Department
Depto.	Departamento
Desp.	Despacho
DG	Director General
Dif.	Difusora, Difusão
Diff.	Diffusion
Dir.	Director
Div.	Division
dom	domestic
DRM	Digital Radio Mondiale
DSB	Double Side Band
DST	Daylight Saving Time
DTT	Digital Terrestrial TV
DVB	Digital Video Broadc.
DX	Long Distance (Reception)
E	English
E:	Email
E.C	Electric Current
Ea.	East(ern)
Edif.	Edificio
Educ.	Education(al), Educación
e.g.	for example
Em.	Emis(s)ora
Eng.	Engineer(ing)
ERP	Effective Radiated Power
Esq.	Esquina
E-QSL	electronic QSL
est.	estimated
Est.	Estado
exc.	except
excl.	excluding
exec.	executive
ext.	external
F	French
F.Pl.	Future Plan(s)
fed.	federal
FM	Frequency Modulation
Fr.	Father
Freq.	Frequency
Fri	Friday
FS	Foreign Service
Ft.	Fort
G	German
G.C	Geographical Coordinates
GD	General Director
gen.	general
GM	General Manager
Gov.	Government(al)
Gte.	Gerente
H	Horizontal Pol.
h(rs)	hour(s)
HD	High Definition
HQ	Headquarters
HS	Home Service
I	Italian
ID	(Station) Identification
i.e.	that is
Inc.	Incorporated
incl.	including
Inf.	Information
int.	international
IRC	Int. Reply Coupon
irr.	irregular
IS	Interval Signal
I./Is	Island/Islands
kHz	kiloHertz
L	Local, Live audio
L.P	Leading Personnel
L.T	Local Time
Langs.	Languages
Lp.	Low power (transmitter)
LSB	Lower Side Band
Ltd	Limited
LV	La Voz, La Voce
LW	Longwave
max.	maximum
M:	Multiplex
MD	Managing Director
MF	Mondays-Fridays
MFN	Multi Freq. Netw.
Mgr	Manager
MHz	MegaHertz
mil.	military
Min.	Ministry, Ministerio, Ministério
min(s)	minute(s)
Mon	Monday
Mpal.	Municipal
Mpo.	Município
Mt	Mount, Mountain
MW	Mediumwave
N.	News
NB	Note (Nota Bene)
n.f.	nominal frequency
n/a	not available, not applicable
nal.	nacional
nat.	national
nd	nondirectional antenna
NE	North East(ern)
Netw.	Network
No.	North(ern), Number
nom.	nominal
Nte	Norte
NW	North West(ern)
occ.	occasional(ly)
Op(s)	Operation(s)
Org.	Organisation
Ote.	Oeste
P	Portuguese, Podcast
P.O.	Post Office
P.R.	Public Relations, People's Republic
PD	Programme Director
pl.	planned
Pol.	Polarisation
Pop.	Population
Pr.	Praça
Pr.L	Principal Language(s)
Pres.	President
Priv.	Private
Prgr(s).	Programme(s)
Prod.	Production
Prov.	Province, Provincial
Pt.	Point
Pte.	Presidente
Pto.	Puerto
Pub	Public service
Pub(s)	Publication(s)
QSL	Reception Confirmation
R.	Radio, Rádio, Rádíó Radyjo, Radyo
r.	reported, repeater
Rdif.	Radiodifusion
R. Dif.	Radio Difusora
Rec.	Recording(s)
Reg.	Region(al)
Rel.	Relay(s), Relations
Rep.	Republic
Rev.	Reverend
rlg	religious
Rp.	Return Postage
Rpt.	(Reception) Report
S.	San(ta), Sán, Santo
s/off	sign off
s/on	sign on
SAE	Self Addressed Envelope
SAR	Special Administrative Region
Sat	Saturday, satellite
Sce.	Service
Sched.	Schedule
SE	South East(ern)
Secr.	Secretary
Sen.	Senior
SFN	Single Freq. Netw.
Sist.	Sistema
SM	Station Manager
So.	South(ern)
Soc.	Sociedad(e)
Sp.	Spanish
SS	Sat/Sun
SSB	Single Side Band
St	Saint, Street
Stn	Station
Str.	Street, Straße
Su.	Summer
Sun	Sunday
Superv.	Supervisor
SW	Shortwave South West(ern)
Syst.	System
tbd	to be defined
TD	Technical Director
techn.	technical
terr.	terrestrial
Thu	Thursday
tr(s)	transmission(s)
TRP	Transmitter Power
Tue	Tuesday
tx(s)	transmitter(s)
ul.	ulitsa, ulica
u.c.	under construction
Univ.	University
unk.	unknown
UHF	Ultra High Frequency
USB	Upper Side Band
UTC	Coordinated Universal Time
V	Vertical Pol.
V.	Verification
v.	varying/variable
VHF	Very High Frequency
VO	Voice of
W	Weekdays (Mon-Sat)
W:	Web
We.	West(ern)
Wed	Wednesday
Wi.	Winter
Wrp.	Weather Report

TRANSMITTER SITES

Location & Decode Tables

INTERNATIONAL TRANSMITTER SITES

The columns marked '**SW**' and '**MW**' have a '✓' or '×' to indicate if the site has the capability to transmit on Mediumwave (and/or Longwave) or Shortwave as appropriate. Where the symbol '**‡**' is shown after a transmitter site name this indicates that the site is not currently being used in our schedules. This may be because the site is inactive or not being used for international broadcasting at the time of publication. Some inactive sites are in the process of being constructed, or repaired, while others are simply dormant and could possibly be used again.

If a site on the list is known to have been decommissioned or dismantled it will be removed.

Code	Site	Ctry	Lat	Long	SW	MW
abs	Abis ‡	EGY	31N08	030E04	✓	×
abz	Abu Zaabal	EGY	30N16	031E22	✓	×
ahw	Ahvaz, Bandar-e Mahshar	IRN	30N37	049E12	✓	✓
aia	The Valley ‡	AIA	18N13	063W01	✓	✓
aja	Abuja, Lugbe	NIG	08N58	007E22	✓	×
alf	Omdurman, Al Fitahab	SDN	15N35	032E27	✓	×
alg	Aligarh	IND	28N00	078E06	✓	×
arm	Krasnodar, Tbilisskaya	RUS	45N28	040E06	✓	×
asc	English Bay	ASC	07S54	014W23	✓	×
avl	Vathy (Avlida municipality)	GRC	38N23	023E36	✓	×
bac	Warszawa, Stare Babice (F.PI)	POL	52N15	020E51	✓	×
bcq	Monticello, ME	USA	46N20	067W49	✓	×
bei	Beijing, Doudian	CHN	39N38	116E06	✓	×
bej	La Habana, Bejucal	CUB	22N52	082W20	✓	×
bgl	Bengaluru, Doddaballapur	IND	13N15	077E29	✓	×
bib	Biblis	D	49N41	008E29	✓	×
bis	Bishkek, Krasnaya Rechka	KGZ	42N53	074E59	✓	✓
bji	Baoji, Qishan (Shaanxi prov.)	CHN	34N42	106E56	✓	×
bko	Bamako, Kati	MLI	12N45	008W03	✓	×
bnb	Bonab	IRN	37N18	046E03	×	✓
bnt	Bandar-e Torkaman	IRN	36N54	054E03	×	✓
boc	Bocaue (Bulacan prov.)	PHL	14N48	120E55	✓	×
bor	Borculo	HOL	52N07	006E31	✓	×
bot	Selebi-Phikwe, Moepeng Hill	BOT	21S57	027E38	✓	✓
bph	Bangkok, Rasom	THA	14N24	100E47	×	✓
brg	Bramming	DNK	55N29	008E39	✓	×
btr	Batrah	EGY	31N10	031E26	×	✓
bue	Buenos Aires, General Pacheco ‡	ARG	34S26	058W37	✓	×
cah	Changchun (Jilin prov.)	CHN	43N44	125E24	×	✓
cer	Cërrik, Shtërmen	ALB	41N00	020E00	✓	×
chc	Chuncheon (HLAN)	KOR	37N56	127E43	×	✓
chj	Chongjin	KRE	41N46	129E42	✓	✓
chr	Chabahar	IRN	25N29	060E32	×	✓
cni	Chennai	IND	13N08	080E07	✓	×
dan	Dangjin (HLCA)	KOR	36N58	126E37	×	✓
dat	Datteln	D	51N39	007E20	✓	×
deh	Mangshi (Dehong auton. prefecture, Yunnan prov.)	CHN	24N27	098E36	×	✓
del	Delhi	IND	28N43	077E12	✓	×
dha	Dhabbaya	UAE	24N10	054E15	✓	✓
dji	Djibouti, Dorale	DJI	11N34	043E04	×	✓
dka	Dhaka, two sites: Kabirpur ‡; Shavar	BGD	24N00	090E15	✓	×
dof	Dongfang (Hainan prov.)	CHN	18N53	108E39	×	✓
dol	Dole	TZA	06S06	039E15	✓	×
dro	Droitwich	G	52N18	002W06	×	✓
dsb	Dushanbe	TJK	38N29	068E48	✓	✓
ela	El Arish	EGY	31N07	033E42	×	✓
elb	Elburg	HOL	52N26	005E52	✓	×
emr	Emirler	TUR	39N24	032E51	✓	×
erd	Bergen, Erdal	NOR	60N27	005E13	✓	×
erv	Gavar, Noratus	ARM	40N25	045E11	✓	✓
ewn	Vandiver, AL	USA	33N30	086W29	✓	×
gal	Bacau, Galbeni	ROU	46N45	026E51	✓	×
goy	Seoul, Goyang	KOR	37N36	126E51	✓	✓
grg	Gorgan (Tentative location)	IRN	36N51	056E26	×	✓
grv	Greenville, NC	USA	35N28	077W12	✓	×
hab	La Habana, Bauta	CUB	22N57	082W33	✓	×
ham	Hamhung	KRE	39N55	127E31	✓	×

Code	Site	Ctry	Lat	Long	SW	MW
hbn	Medorm, Babeldaob Island	PLW	07N27	134E29	✓	×
hdn	Huadian (Jilin prov.)	CHN	43N07	126E31	×	✓
hdu	Guangzhou, Liantang (Guangdong prov.)	CHN	23N24	113E14	×	✓
hee	Heerde	HOL	52N40	006E03	✓	×
hei	Shuangyashan (Heilongjiang prov.)	CHN	46N43	131E13	×	✓
hil	Hillerød	DNK	55N53	012E16	✓	×
hjh	Barranquilla (HJHJ Radio Libertad)	CLM	11N00	074W48	×	✓
hnl	Changzhou, Henglin (Jiangsu prov.)	CHN	31N42	120E07	×	✓
hri	Furman, SC	USA	32N41	081W08	✓	×
hst	Hartenstein	D	50N40	012E41	✓	×
huh	Hohhot, Bikeqi (Nei Menggu auton. reg.)	CHN	40N48	111E12	✓	×
hvi	Hvidovre (F.pl)	DNK	55N39	012E28	✓	✓
hwa	Hwaseong	KOR	37N13	126E47	✓	×
iba	Iba (Zambales prov.)	PHL	15N22	119E57	✓	×
inb	Red Lion, PA	USA	39N54	076W35	✓	×
ish	Ishøj	DNK	55N37	012E21	×	✓
iss	Issoudun	F	46N56	001E53	✓	×
jak	Jakarta (Uncomfirmed location)	INS	06S24	106E52	✓	×
jal	Jalandhar	IND	31N09	075E47	×	✓
jan	Hwaseong, Jangan	KOR	37N18	126E58	✓	×
jed	Jeddah, Al Khumra	ARS	21N15	039E10	✓	×
jej	Jeju (HLAZ)	KOR	33N29	126E23	×	✓
jhr	Milton, FL	USA	30N39	087W05	✓	✓
jin	Jinhua, Lanxi (Zhejiang prov.)	CHN	29N07	119E19	✓	×
jnm	Hwaseong, Jeongnam	KOR	37N09	127E00	✓	×
jol	Jolfa	IRN	38N56	045E36	×	✓
kab	Kabul	AFG	34N32	069E20	✓	✓
kan	Kangnam	KRE	38N50	125E40	×	✓
kas	Kashgar (Kashi), Sayibage (Xinjiang Uighur auton. reg.)	CHN	39N21	075E46	✓	✓
kbd	Kuwait, Kabd	KWT	29N09	047E46	✓	×
kch	Grigoriopol, Maiac	MDA	47N17	029E25	✓	✓
kho	Khost, Tani	AFG	33N20	069N56	×	✓
kia	Bandar e-Kiashahr	IRN	37N25	050E01	×	✓
kih	Kish Island	IRN	26N34	053E56	×	✓
kim	Gimje	KOR	35N49	126E52	✓	✓
kkt	Chinsurah	IND	23N02	088E21	×	✓
kll	Kall, Krekel	D	50N29	006E31	✓	×
kmk	Kimchaek	KRE	40N41	129E12	×	✓
kng	Kanggye	KRE	41N01	126E39	✓	×
knx	Kununurra	AUS	15S49	128E40	✓	×
kou	Kouhu	TWN	23N32	120E10	✓	✓
kuj	Kujang	KRE	40N05	126E07	✓	×
kun	Kunming, Anning (Yunnan prov.)	CHN	24N53	102E30	✓	✓
kwt	Kuwait, Umm Al-Rimam	KWT	29N31	047E40	✓	✓
lam	Lampertheim	D	49N36	008E32	✓	×

Code	Site	Ctry	Lat	Long	SW	MW
lha	Lhasa (Chengguan) (Xizang auton. reg.)	CHN	29N39	091E15	✓	×
lra	Base Antártica Esperanza	ATA	63S24	057W00	✓	×
luv	Lusaka, Makeni Ranch	ZMB	15S32	028E00	✓	×
man	Manzini, Mpangela Ranch	SWZ	26S20	031E36	✓	✓
mdc	Talata Volonondry	MDG	18S45	047E37	✓	×
min	Minhsiung	TWN	23N34	120E26	×	✓
mlk	Bethel, PA ‡	USA	40N29	076W17	✓	×
mos	Moosbrunn	AUT	48N00	016E28	✓	×
msn	Jeongok, Misan	KOR	38N01	126E59	×	✓
mth	Marathon Key, FL	USA	24N42	081W05	×	✓
mwv	Mahajanga II (Belobaka), Amparemahitsy	MDG	15S43	046E26	✓	×
nau	Nauen	D	52N39	012E55	✓	×
nls	Anchor Point, AK	ALS	59N45	151W44	✓	×
nnn	Nanning (Guangxi Zhuang auton. reg)	CHN	22N48	108E11	✓	×
nob	Noblejas	E	39N57	003W26	✓	×
nwn	Seoul, Taereung	KOR	37N38	127E07	✓	×
omo	Can Tho, Thoi Hung	VTN	10N07	105E34	×	✓
pan	Panaji	IND	15N27	073E51	✓	×
pao	Paochung	TWN	23N43	120E18	✓	×
par	Parakou	BEN	09N21	002E37	×	✓
pga	Palangkaraya	INS	02S13	113E55	✓	×
pht	Tinang	PHL	15N22	120E37	✓	×
pin	Pinneberg	D	53N40	009E48	✓	×
put	Puttalam	CLN	07N58	079E48	×	✓
pyo	Pyongyang	KRE	39N03	125E42	✓	×
qsh	Qasr-e Shirin	IRN	34N27	045E37	×	✓
qui	Quito, Mount Pichincha	EQU	00S10	078W32	✓	×
qvc	La Habana, Quivicán	CUB	22N49	082W18	✓	×
raj	Rajkot	IND	22N30	070E31	×	✓
ran	Rangitaiki	NZL	38S51	176E26	✓	×
rbn	Rabouni	ALG	27N33	008W06	×	✓
riy	Riyadh	ARS	24N49	046E52	✓	×
rmi	Okeechobee, FL	USA	27N27	080W56	✓	×
rnd	Randers	DNK	56N27	010E02	✓	×
rno	New Orleans, LA	USA	29N50	090W07	✓	×
rob	Rohrbach, Eja	D	48N36	011E33	✓	×
rou	Roumoules	F	43N48	006E10	×	✓
sai	Saipan, Agingan Point	MRA	15N07	145E42	✓	×
sao	Pinheira	STP	00N18	006E45	✓	✓
sda	Agat, Facpi Point	GUM	13N20	144E39	✓	×
seo	Seoul, Daebu Isl (HLKX)	KOR	37N13	126E33	×	✓
sha	Kunming, Shalang (Yunnan prov.)	CHN	25N41	102E41	✓	×
she	She'ar Yashuv	ISR	33N13	035E39	×	✓
sir	Sirjan	IRN	29N36	055E47	✓	×
sko	Skopje, Sveti Nikole	MKD	41N47	021E53	×	✓
sla	A'Seela	OMA	21N55	059E37	✓	✓
smg	Santa Maria di Galeria	CVA	42N03	012E19	✓	×
sng	Singapore	SNG	01N25	103E43	✓	×
snu	Sinuiju	KRE	40N05	124E27	×	✓

Code	Site	Ctry	Lat	Long	SW	MW
sof	Sofia, Kostinbrod	BUL	42N49	023E11	✓	×
swo	Sangwon	KRE	38N53	126E06	×	✓
szg	Shijiazhuang, Nanpozhuan (Hebei prov.)	CHN	38N13	114E06	✓	×
tac	Toshkent	UZB	41N13	069E09	✓	×
thu	Thumrait	OMA	17N38	053E56	✓	×
tig	Bucuresti	ROU	44N45	026E06	✓	×
tin	Tinian	MRA	15N03	145E36	✓	×
trm	Trincomalee, Perkara	CLN	08N45	081E08	✓	✓
tsh	Tanshui	TWN	25N11	121E25	✓	×
tts	Tartus	SYR	34N57	035E53	×	✓
tut	Tuticorin	IND	08N49	078E05	×	✓
twb	Bonaire, Belnem	BES	12N06	068W17	×	✓
twr	Merizo	GUM	13N17	144E40	✓	×
tww	Lebanon, TN	USA	36N17	086W06	✓	×
tyb	Tayebad	IRN	34N44	060E48	×	✓
uba	Ulaanbaatar, Khonkhor	MNG	47N48	107E11	✓	×
udo	Udon Thani, Ban Dung	THA	17N40	103E12	✓	×
uru	Ürümqi (Wulumuqi), (Xinjiang Uighur auton. reg.),	CHN	44N09	086E54	✓	✓
ust	Taiwan (exact site unknown)	TWN	—	—	✓	✓
vie	Vientiane	LAO	18N00	102E38	✓	×
vir	Virrat, Liedenpohja	FIN	62N23	023E37	✓	✓
vni	Son Tay	VTN	21N12	105E22	✓	×
voh	Rancho Simi, CA	USA	34N15	118W39	✓	×
vst	Anykšciai, Viešintos	LTU	55N42	024E59	×	✓
wcr	Nashville, TN	USA	36N12	086W54	✓	×
wis	Winsen an der Aller	D	52N40	009E52	✓	×
wnm	Weenermoor	D	53N12	007E19	✓	×
wof	Woofferton	G	52N19	002W43	✓	×
wrb	Morrison, TN	USA	35N37	086W01	✓	×
xia	Xi'an, Xianyang (Shaanxi prov.)	CHN	34N22	108E37	✓	×
xuw	Xuanwei (Yunnan prov.)	CHN	26N08	104E01	✓	✓
yam	Tokyo, Yamata	J	36N10	139E49	✓	×
yan	Yangon (Mayangon) - (Myanma R.)	BRM	16N52	096E10	✓	×
zab	Zabol	IRN	31N02	061E33	×	✓
zah	Zahedan	IRN	29N28	060E52	✓	×
zak	Zakaki, Lady's Mile (Akrotiri Sovereign Base Area)	CYP	34N37	033E00	×	✓
zwo	Zwolle	HOL	52N29	006E06	✓	×

TARGET AREA CODES

Code	Target Area	Code	Target Area	Code	Target Area	Code	Target Area
Af	Africa	CAs	Central Asia	LAm	Latin America	Pac	Pacific
Am	Americas	Cau	Caucasia	ME	Middle East	SAf	Southern Africa
As	Asia	CEu	Central Europe	Med	Mediterranean	SAm	South America
Atl	Atlantic Ocean	EAf	Eastern Africa	NAf	Northern Africa	SAs	Southern Asia
BaS	Baltic Sea	EAs	Eastern Asia	NAm	North America	SEA	South East Asia
CAf	Central Africa	EEu	Eastern Europe	NAs	Northern Asia	SEu	Southern Europe
CAm	Central America	Eu	Europe	NEu	Northern Europe	WAf	Western Africa
Car	Caribbean	IOc	Indian Ocean	NoS	North Sea	WAs	West Asia

DOMESTIC SW TRANSMITTER SITES

Coordinate System: WGS84 (rounded)

NB: For coordinates of sites that are jointly used for National and International/COTB services, see the International Transmitter Sites table

Ctry	Site	Lat	Long
AUS	Gunnedah	30S58	150E15
AUS	Innisfail	17S31	146E01
AGL	Luanda	08S51	013E19
B	Araraquara	21S47	048W10
B	Belém	01S27	048W29
B	Belo Horizonte	19S55	043W56
B	Boa Vista	02N51	060W43
B	Brasilía	15S36	048W08
B	Cachoeira Paulista	22S40	045W01
B	Camboriú	26S59	048W38
B	Campo Grande	20S24	054W35
B	Coari	04S05	063W08
B	Congonhas	20S30	043W53
B	Curitiba	25S23	049W10
B	Foz do Iguaçu	25S31	054W34
B	Goiânia	16S43	049W18
B	Ibitinga	21S43	048W47
B	Londrina	23S18	051W13
B	Manaus	03S04	060W00
B	Parintins	02S38	056W44
B	Porto Alegre	30S03	051W10
B	Rio Branco	09S58	067W49
B	São Gonçalo	22S49	043W04
B	S. Gabriel da Cachoeira	00S09	067W03
B	São Paulo	23S33	046W39
B	Tefé	03S24	064W45
BOL	Cochabamba	17S23	066W11
BOL	La Paz	16S30	068W08
BOL	S. José de Chiquitos	17S53	060W45
BOL	Santa Cruz	17S46	063W11
BOL	Siglo Veinte	18S23	066W38
BOL	Yura	20S02	066W10
BRM	Naypyitaw	19N45	096E11
BRM	Pyin U Lwin	22N01	096E33
BRM	Yangon	16N52	096E09
BTN	Thimphu	27N29	089E37
CAF	Boali	04N53	018E01
CAN	Calgary	50N54	113W53
CAN	Toronto	43N30	079W38
CHN	Fuzhou	25N45	117E11
CHN	Hailar	49N11	119E43
CHN	Hezuo	34N58	102E55
CHN	Lingshi	36N52	111E56
CHN	Xichang	27N49	102E14
CHN	Xining	36N39	101E36
CLM	Puerto Lleras	03N16	073W22
COD	Bukavu	02S30	028E52
COD	Bunia	01N32	030E11
ERI	Asmara	15N13	038E53
ETH	Addis Ababa	08N47	038E39
GNE	Bata	01N49	009E47
GUI	Conakry	09N41	013W32
IND	Aizawl	23N43	092E43
IND	Gangtok	27N20	088E40
IND	Jaipur	26N55	075E45
IND	Jeypore	18N55	082E34
IND	Leh	34N07	077E35
IND	Srinagar	34N02	074E54
J	Nagara	35N28	140E12
J	Nemuro	43N17	145E34
KRE	Hamhung	39N55	127E31
LBR	Monrovia	06N14	010W42
MDG	Ambohidrano	18S47	047E29
MEX	México	19N26	099W08
MNG	Altai	46N19	096E15
MNG	Mörön	49N37	100E10
PNG	Buka	05S25	154E40
PNG	Mt. Hagen	05S51	144E14
PRU	Chazuta	06S34	076W08
PRU	Atalaya	10S44	073W45
PRU	Cusco	13S32	071W57
PRU	Huanta	12S54	074W13
PRU	Iquitos	03S51	073W13
PRU	Quillabamba	12S49	072W41
PRU	Pitumarca	13S58	071W25
PRU	Santiago de Chuco	08S09	078W10
PRU	Urubamba	13S18	072W07
RUS	Komsomolsk-na-Amure	50N39	136E55
SLM	Honiara	09S25	160E03
SOM	Baydhabo	03N07	043E39
SUR	Panamaribo	05N51	055E12
VTN	Buôn Mê Thuôt	12N40	108E12
VTN	Xuân Mai	20N53	105E34
VUT	Port-Vila	17S45	168E22

Notes

CLUBS FOR DXERS & INTERNATIONAL LISTENERS

This section lists non-commercial hobby clubs serving international radio enthusiasts. Most clubs are orientated to DXing, the reception of distant radio stations, some are oriented to programme listening. Many clubs produce bulletins on a regular basis. Sample copies of club periodicals are often available in pdf-format, or mailed upon request per post for return postage (contact the club for payment details). For officially multilingual countries, the language(s) used in club publications (and/or activities) is indicated when known; for non-English speaking countries also if a publication is partly or entirely in English: EE = English, FF = French, GG = German, II = Italian, JJ = Japanese, PP=Portuguese, RR = Russian, SS = Spanish. This list does not include clubs run by commercial publications or by individual broadcasters. °) Website not updated for more than a year

EUROPE

European DX Council (EDXC) (Umbrella organization of DX Clubs in Europe) General Secretary: Chrissy Brand (**E:** chrissylb@hotmail.co.uk), Assistant General Secretary: Christian Ghibaudo (**E:** chr.ghibaudo@gmail.com) **W:** edxcnews.wordpress.com

AUSTRIA: Austrian DX Board (ADXB) (Club der Freunde elektronischer Medien - Rundfunk global), c/o Musisches Zentrum, Zeltgasse 7, 1080 Wien. **E:** adxbsuess@aon.at **W:** www.adxb-oe.org Pub: *Rundbrief* (quarterly, pdf). Annual DX camp. Member of AGDX (Germany); club members receive the monthly AGDX publication *Radio-Kurier - weltweit hören.*

CZECHIA/SLOVAKIA: Ceskoslovenský DX Klub (CSDXK), Lorencova 5424, 76001 Zlín, Czechia. **E:** mail@dx.cz **W:** www.dx.cz Pub: *Radio* (pdf)

DENMARK: Dansk DX Lytter Klub (DDXLK), P.O.Box 112, 8960 Randers SØ. **E:** ddxlk@ddxlk.dk **W:** www.ddxlk.dk Pub: *DX-AKTUELLT* (Swedish/Danish, joint publication with SDXF [Sweden]; bimonthly, printed & pdf)

FINLAND: Finlands Svenska DX-Förbund rf (FSDXF), P.O.Box 9, 68601 Jakobstad (Umbrella organization of Swedish language DX clubs in Finland) – **Suomen DX-liitto ry (SDXL)**, Annankatu 31-33, C 49 c, 00100 Helsinki (Umbrella organization of Finnish language DX clubs) **E:** toimisto@sdxl.fi **W:** sdxl.fi Pub (Finnish/EE): *Radiomaailma* (8 times per year, pdf), *DXclusive* (pdf)

FRANCE: Radio Club des Écouteurs Lorrains, 19 rue des Jeux, 54570 Foug. **E:** alinco54@orange.fr **W:** www.rcdel.fr° – **Radio Club du Perche**, 82 bis, Coat Canton, 29140 Rosporden. **E:** g.lelouet@orange.fr **W:** radioclub.perche.free.fr – **Radio DX Club d'Auvergne et Francophonie**, Centre Municipal P. et M. Curie, 2 bis rue du Clos Perret, 63100 Clermont-Ferrand. ☎ +33 6 89077976 **E:** radiodxclub63@gmail.com **W:** www.radiodx63.fr

GERMANY: Arbeitsgemeinschaft DX e.V. (AGDX), Postfach 1214, 61282 Bad Homburg (Umbrella organization for the German DX clubs adxb-DL, UKW/TV Arbeitskreis der AGDX, Worldwide DX Club, and for the Austrian DX-Board) **E:** mail@agdx.de **W:** www.agdx.de Pub: see ADDX. – **Assoziation Deutschsprachiger Kurzwellenhörer e.V. (ADDX)**, Scharsbergweg 14, 41189 Mönchengladbach. **E:** kurier@addx.de **W:** www.addx.de Pub (jointly for members of ADDX & AGDX, and ADXB-OE in Austria): *Radio-Kurier - weltweit hören* (monthly; printed & pdf) – **Assoziation Junger DXer e.V. (adxb-DL)**, c/o Thomas Schubaur, Neufnachstr. 30, 86850 Fischach. **E:** dl1ts@t-online.de **W:** www.adxb-dl.de° – **Hamburger Freunde des Rundfunkfernempfangs**, c/o Dieter Schäfer, Am Sportplatz 18, 24629 Kisdorf. **E:** dl1lad@darc.de – **Kurzwellenclub Schwalmtal e.V.**, c/o Helmut Reitzer Jr, Willy-Rösler-Str. 41, 41366 Schwalmtal. **E:** dk0kws@qsl.net **W:** www.qsl.net/dk0kws° – **Kurzwellenfreunde Rhein/Ruhr e.V.**, c/o U. Schnelle, Kurfürstenstr. 37, 45883 Gelsenkirchen – **Kurzwellenfreunde Wuppertal (KWFW)**, c/o Werner Kortmann, Postfach 220342, 42373 Wuppertal – **Oldenburger Kurzwellenfreunde**, c/o Olaf C. Hänßler, Sandweg 98, 26135 Oldenburg **E:** olaf.haenssler@gmail.com – **Radiofreunde NRW**, c/o Christof Proft, Kurfürstenstr. 15, 52066 Aachen **E:** info@radiofreunde-nrw.de **W:** www.radiofreunde-nrw.de – **Rhein-Main-Radio-Club e.V. (RMRC)**, Postfach 700849, 60558 Frankfurt **E:** mail@rmrc.de **W:** www.rmrc.de. **UKW/TV Arbeitskreis der AGDX**, c/o H.-J. Kuhlo, Wilhelm-Leuschner-Str. 293B, 64347 Griesheim (FM/TV only) **E:** sekretariat@ukwtv.de **W:** www.ukwtv.de Pub: *Reflexion* (printed & pdf) – **Worldwide DX Club (WWDXC)**, Postfach 1214, 61282 Bad Homburg **E:** mail@wwdxc.de **W:** www.wwdxc.de. Pub: *DX Magazine* (EE; printed & pdf)

HUNGARY: Hungarian DX Club, c/o Tibor Szilagyi **E:** tiszi2035@yahoo.com.

IRELAND: Irish DX Club, c/o Edward Dunne, 17 Anville Drive, Kilmacud, Stillorgan, Co. Dublin **E:** irishdxclub@live.ie Pub: *MediaWatch* (by email)

ITALY: Associazione Italiana Radioascolto (AIR), C.P. 1338, 10100 Torino (AD). **E:** redazione@air-radio.it **W:** www.air-radio.it Pub: *Radiorama* (monthly, pdf) – **BCL Sicilia Club**, c/o Roberto Scaglione, C.P. 119, Succursale 34, 90144 Palermo (PA). **E:** info@bclnews.it **W:** www.bclnews.it – **Coordinamento del Radioascolto (Co.Rad)**, c/o Dario Monferini (Web-based umbrella organisation of various Italian DX clubs) **E:** info@corad.net **W:** www.corad.net° – **DX FANZINE** c/o Antonello Napolitano, Taranto. **E:** dxf@dxfanzine.com. **W:** www.dxfanzine.com, www.dxfanzine.org Pub: *DX Fanzine* (Monthly, EE, pdf). **FM-DX Italy**, c/o Fabrizio Carnevalini (Web-based, FM-TV DX only) **E:** fabrizio58it@yahoo.it **W:** www.fmdx.altervista.org – **Gruppo d'Ascolto Radio Televisivo della Sicilia**, c/o Gioacchino Stallone, Via G.Falcone 11, Lotto 27, interno 3, 91025 Marsala (TP). **E:** gsicilia2013@libero.it **W:** www.radiolondra.me – **Play-DX**, c/o Dario Monferini, Via Davanzati 8, 20158 Milano (MI). (II/EE/SS) (specialises in difficult DX) **E:** info@playdx.com **W:** www.playdx.com°; playdxblog.blogspot.com Pub: *PLAY-DX* (weekly)

NETHERLANDS: Benelux DX Club (BDXC), Rietdekkerstraat 40, 1445 KG Purmerend. **E:** secretaris@bdxc.nl **W:** www.bdxc.nl Pub: *BDXC-Bulletin* (Dutch/EE, printed & pdf)

RUSSIA: Club of DX-ers, c/o Vadim Alexeew, Moscow **E:** rtscenter@mtu-net.ru – **Russian DX League**, c/o Anatoly Klepov, Moscow **E:** rusdx@yandex.ru **W:** rusdx.narod.ru Pub: *RUS-DX* (separate RR/EE versions, by email) – **St. Petersburg DX Club**, c/o Alexander Beryozkin, P.O.Box 13, 192007 St. Petersburg **E:** dxspb@nrec.spb.ru Pub: *Broadcasting in Russian* (RR, biennial, printed)

SPAIN: Asociación DX Barcelona (ADXB), P.O. Box 335, 08080 Barcelona. **E:** info@mundodx.net **W:** www.mundodx.net Pub: *MundoDX-Mundimedia* (SS/Catalan, DVD published 11 times per year with text, images & videos) – **Asociación Española de Radioescucha (AER)**, Apartado 10014, 50080 Zaragoza. **E:** general@aer.org.es **W:** aer.org.es Pub: *El Dial (d), El Dial (e), El Dial (fm)* (all pdf

SWEDEN: Arctic Radio Club (ARC), c/o Tore Larsson, Frejagatan 14A, 52 143 Falköping (MW/LW only) **E:** torelarsson.dx@gmail.

com **W:** arcticradioclub.blogspot.com Pub: *MV-Eko* (Swedish/EE, pdf) – **Sveriges DX Förbund (SDXF)**, P.O.Box 1097, 40 523 Göteborg (Umbrella organization). **E:** registrator@sdxf.se **W:** www.sdxf.se Pub: *DX-aktuellt* (Swedish/Danish, joint publication with DDXLD, Denmark; bimonthly, printed & pdf). Local member clubs: **Northern Sweden: Sundsvalls Radioamatörer (SK3BG)**, c/o Christer Byström, P.O.Box 173, 851 03 Sundsvall ☎ +46 60 561285 **W:** sk3bg.se **Central Sweden: Aros DX Club**, c/o Rolf Berglund, Flisavägen 22, 723 53 Västerås. Contact: Magnus Jespersson ☎ +46 21 180505 **W:** 123minsida.se/cadsy/29301960 – **Delsbo Radioklubb (SK3PH)**, c/o Håkan Johansson, Storgatan 54, 824 70 Delsbo. Contact: Dan Andersson ☎ +46 65 310320 **E:** drak_ph@hotmail.com **W:** sk3ph.se – **Mälardalens Radiosällskap**, c/o Lars Skoglund, Radarvägen 22, 183 59 Täby ☎ +46 8 7563292 **W:** hem.bredband.net/mrsdxing – **Norrköpings Distanslyssnare**, c/o Claes Olsson, Guldringen 68, 603 68 Norrköping ☎ +46 11 182223 **W:** ndl-dx.se **Southern Sweden: Malmö Kortvågsklubb**, c/o Dan Olsson, Högalidsvägen 77C, 244 36 Kävlinge ☎ +46 73 3115998 **W:** www.mkvk.se – **Tibro DX-Klubb**, c/o Börje Sahlén, V. Långgatan 139A, 543 33 Tibro ☎ +46 70 2276053 **W:** www.ugglenatt.cyber-site.nu/Tibro-DX-klubb – **Västkustens DX-Klubb**, c/o Alf Persson, Malörtsvägen 3, 449 33 Nödinge ☎ +46 30 396463 **W:** www.facebook.com/vdxkgbg; wordpress.radiomuseet.se/vdxk

UNITED KINGDOM: British DX Club (BDXC), 10 Hemdean Hill, Caversham, Reading RG4 7SB. **E:** bdxc@bdxc.org.uk **W:** www.bdxc.org.uk Pub: *Communication* (printed & pdf) – **International Shortwave League (ISWL)**, c/o Peter Lewis, 18 Bittaford Wood, Ivybridge, Devon, PL21 0ET. **E:** vfgnsu@yahoo.co.uk **W:** www.iswl.org.uk Pub: *Monitor* (pdf) – **Medium Wave Circle (MWC)**, c/o Herman Boel, Papeveld 3, 9320 Erembodegem-Aalst, Belgium (LW/MW only) **E:** herman@hermanboel.eu **W:** www.mwcircle.org Pub: *Medium Wave News* (pdf)

AFRICA

CÔTE D'IVOIRE: DX-Ivoire, c/o Jibirila Liasu, B.P. 197, Abidjan 20. (FF)

KENYA: DX Listeners' Club, c/o Oscar Machuki, PO Box 646, Kisii 4-0200. (EE/Swahili) (SW only) ☎ +254 721 534171 **E:** oscarmogire@yahoo.com

NIGERIA: Africa DX Association, c/o Mr. Friday I. Okoloise, NITEL, P.M.B. 23, Lafia, Plateau State. (EE) – **International DX Club**, Emmanuel Ezeani, P.O.Box 1633, Sokoto, Sokoto State. (EE) **E:** emmanuel_ezeani@yahoo.com

RÉUNION: Club DX de La Réunion, E: contest@rallye-dx.com **W:** www.rallye-dx.com° (FF/EE, SW only)

SÃO TOMÉ & PRÍNCIPE: Clube DX-STP, c/o Petter Leal Bouças, Av. 12 de Julho, Vila Maria (C.P. 490), São Tomé. **E:** petterboudx@hotmail.com

TANZANIA: Kemogemba DX Listeners Club, c/o Ras Franz Manko Ngogo, P.O.Box 71, Tarime, Mara. (EE/Swahili) ☎ + 255 75 5814704 **E:** kemogemba@yahoo.com

TOGO: Club Inter Amitié Radio, CCF, B.P. 2090, Lomé. (FF) – **Groupe Endoc**, B.P. 2667, Lomé. (FF)

TUNISIA: Club des Auditeurs et de l'Amitié, c/o De Riadh Sakka, Route de Gremda Merkez Sahnoun, 3012 Sfax. (FF)

UGANDA: International DX Club of East Africa, c/o Samuel Ouma, P.O. Box 565, Iganga. (EE) ☎ +256 772 444201 **E:** samuel.ouma@talk21.com **W:** www.facebook.com/idxeastafrica

ASIA

BANGLADESH: Aurora Listeners' Club, c/o Miss Kakali Rani, Harida Khalsi-6403, Madhnagar-Natore-6400 – **Wave Surfers' Association**, c/o Ashik Eqbal Tokon, Mohammadpur, Dhaka. **E:** rosedwlc@yahoo.com **W:** wsabd.webs.com; rosedwlc.webs.com°. Pub: *DX-Net* (Bengali, quarterly)

INDIA: Apollo DX International, c/o Deepak Kumar Das, Dholi Sakra 843105, Dist. Muzaffarpur, Bihar – **Ardic DX Club**, c/o Jaisakthivel, T., Dept of Communication, Manonmaniam Sundranar University, Abishekapatti Post, Tirunelveli 627012, Tamil Nadu. ☎ +91 98413 66086 Pub: *DXers Guide* (EE quartely), *Sarvadesa Vanoli* (Tamil monthly). DX Prgr: Vaanoli Ulagam on AIR (Tamil). **E:** ardicdxclub@yahoo.co.in **W:** dxersguide.blogspot.com – **Asian DX League**, c/o Partha Sarathi Goswami, Kishalaya Book Stall, College Road, Siliguri 734001, West Bengal **E:** dxing@india.com – **Chaudhary Srota Sangh**, c/o Santosh Kumar (President), Kharauna Jairam, Kharauna Dih 843113, Dist. Muzaffarpur, Bihar – **Chaitak Listeners Club**, PO-BELDA, Naboday Pally, Dt-Paschim Medinipur 721424, WB **E:** sbchanu@gmail.com – **Chennai DX Club**, c/o K. Raja, 21 JP Koil St, Old Washermenpet, Chennai 600021, Tamil Nadu. **E:** chennaidxclub@gmail.com – **Foreign Radio Listeners' Club,** c/o Prasenjit Bhakat, 313/8 Ghoradhara, P.O Jhargram 721507, West Bengal. ☎ +91 3221 256084 **E:** frlclub@gmail.com – **Globe Radio DX Club (GRDXC)**, c/o Harjot Singh Brar, P.O.Box 158, Chandigarh 160017, Chandigarh. **E:** grdxc@yahoo.co.in – **Indian DX Club International (IDXCI)**, GPO Box 646, Kolkata 700001, West Bengal. **E:** idxc.international@gmail.com **W:** www.idxci.in, www.idxciexpedition.blogspot.com, facebook.com/groups/idxcintl (Facebook group), Chat group: t.me/IDXCI Pub: *Asian DX Review* (Monthly, EE, pdf) – **International DX Association**, c/o Bedanta Das, 1-No,Galiahati, Near Night School, Barpeta 781301, Assam. ☎ +91 3665 236267 **E:** das884@gmail.com Pub: *DX Times* (EE) – **Metali Listeners' Club**, c/o Mr Shivendu Paul, 49/36, Dr SG Dhar Lane, P.O. Khagra, Dist. Murshidabad 742103, West Bengal. **E:** metalilistenersclub@gmail.com ☎ +91 94348 58497 – **Minnakkal Kurinji DX Club**, c/o E. Selvaraj, Choolaimedu Street, Minnakkal Post, Dist. Namakkal 637505, Tamil Nadu. **E:** selvarajminnakkal@gmail.com – **Paribar Bandhu SWL Club**, c/o Mr Anand Mohan Bain, UCO Bank, 47/6, Nehru Nagar, P.O. Nehru Nagar, Bhilai, Dist. Durg 490020, Chattisgarh. **E:** anand_mohan10@yahoo.com ☎ +91 94255 21083, +91 78840 31648. – **Pollachi DX Club**, c/o Mr. N. Lakshmanan, Sri Mugha Bhavan, 44/77 Lac Colony, Dr Ansari Street, Pollachi 642001, Tamil Nadu. ☎ +91 98650 16402 **W:** pollachiradioclub.blogspot.com° – **Span Radio Listeners' Club**, c/o A Ragu, Nandavankula Theru, Vedaraniam 614810, Tamil Nadu. ☎ +91 4369 318808 – **Utkarna Shrota Sangha**, c/o Mr. Rajib Bandopadhyay, Amrita Bhaban, P.O. Makardah 711409, Dist. Howrah, West Bengal ☎ +91 94334 28609, **E:** ussrajib@gmail.com – **World DX Club & Library**, c/o Baidyanath Upadhyaya, At Khairabarigaon, P.O. Khawrang, Udalguri 784509, Darrang, Assam. – **World DXing Club**, c/o Mr Madhab Ch. Sagour, 93/1, Mitrapara Road, P.O. Naihati 743 165, 24 Parganas (North), West Bengal. – **World Radio Club**, c/o Mr. Biswanath Mandal, Chak Harharia, P.O. Islampur 742304, Dist. Murshidabad, West Bengal ☎ +91 3481 236534 **E:** bmandalwrc@rediffmail.com – **Young Stars Radio Club**, c/o Mr Hari Madugula, 40 Hastinapura Colony, Raghavendra Residency-FF4, Sainikpuri, Hyderabad 500094, Andhra Pradesh. **W:** ysrc.webs.com – **Youth International Radio Listeners' Club**, c/o Mr. Pranab Kumar Roy, Shyamnagar, 741 155, Nadia, West Bengal. ☎ +91 3471 252163 **E:** etherbarta@gmail.com Pub: *Etherbarta* (Bengali), *Radio Monitors' Guide* (EE)

INDONESIA: Borneo Listeners Club, Jalan Penjajap Timur 3A, Pemangkat, Kalimantan Barat 79453. (Indonesian/EE). **E:** h.rudi@yahoo.co.id **W:** bielsiklub.blogspot.com° Pub: *Mediator* – **Indonesian DX Club (IDXC)**, P.O.Box 50, Kutoarjo 54201. (EE/Indonesian).

JAPAN: Asian Broadcasting Institute (ABI), P.O.Box 2334, Ginza Branch, Japan Post, Tokyo 100-8698. **E:** info@abiweb.jp **W:** www.abiweb.jp – **Japan Short Wave Club (JSWC)**, P.O.Box 44, Kamakura 248-8691. (JJ/EE) ☎🖷 +81 467 432167 **W:** www5a.biglobe.ne.jp/~BCLSWL/jswc.html **E:** jswchq@live.jp Pub: *SW DX Guide* (JJ/EE) – **Nagoya DXers Circle (NDXC)**, c/o Shigenori Aoki, 2-51 Kasumori-cho, Nakamura-ku, Nagoya 453-0855. **W:** www.ndxc.starfree.jp

KOREA, SOUTH: Northeast Asian Broadcasting Institute (NEABI), c/o SeKyung Park, #103-302, Geumho Apt, 240-32 Yeomchang-dong, Gangseo-gu, Seoul 157-861. **E:** neabipress@gmail.com **W:** www.neabi.com Pub: *Reports* (Korean, monthly)

NEPAL: Friendship Radio Club, c/o Mr Umesh Regmi, Tanki Sinuwari 5, District Morang, Biratnagar. **E:** friendshipradioclub@yahoo.com – **Listeners' Club of Nepal** (Reg. No.144), P.O.Box 126, Biratnagar-4 – **Small Giant Radio Listener Club** (Reg. No.17), P.O.Box 21110, Kathmandu

PAKISTAN: International Radio Listeners Club, Karachi. **E:** irlclub@hotmail.com **W:** sites.google.com/site/irlclub° – **National Society of Pakistani DXers**, c/o Liaqat Ali, E-161/1, Iqbal Park, opposite Adil Hospital, Defence Housing Society Rd, Lahore Cantt. – **Pakistani Shortwave Listeners' Association**, c/o Muhammad Imran Mehr, 38/2 Habib Colony, Bahawalpur 63108, Punjab. ☎ +92 334 6865847, +92 300 6801719. **E:** imran.mehr@gmail.com Pub: *Radio World* (bi-monthly, pdf) – **Shortwave Listeners Club**, c/o Israr Ahmad Chaudhary, Street #2, Madina Park, Sheikhupura 39350, Punjab. **E:** pals_swlc@yahoo.com – **Wonderful World of Shortwave (WWSW)**, c/o Baber Shehzad, 43 Habib Colony, Bahawalpur 63108, Punjab. **E:** baber73@yahoo.com. Pub: *News Letter of Pakistani DX-ers* (by email)

SRI LANKA: Union of Asian DXers (UADX), c/o Victor Goonetilleke, "Shangri-La" 298 Kolamunne, Piliyandala. **E:** victor.goonetileke@gmail.com **W:** dxasia-uadx.blogspot.com° (EE)

PACIFIC

AUSTRALIA: Australian Radio DX Club (ARDXC), c/o John Wright, 71 Hilton Avenue, Roselands NSW 2196. **E:** dxer1234@gmail.com **W:** www.facebook.com/ARDXC.Inc Pub: *Australian DX News* (printed & pdf)

NEW ZEALAND: New Zealand Radio DX League, P.O. Box 178, Mangawhai 0540. **E:** secretary@radiodx.com **W:** www.radiodx.com Pub: *NZ DX Times* (monthly, pdf)

NORTH AMERICA

CANADA: Canadian International DX Club (CIDX), P.O.Box 67063-Lemoyne, St. Lambert, QC J4R 2T8. **E:** cidxclub@yahoo.com **W:** www.cidx.ca Pub: *The Messenger* (pdf, monthly) – **Club d'Ondes Courtes du Québec**, 5120, 35ème rue, Grand Mere, PO G9T 3N6 – **Ontario DX Association (ODXA)**, 3211 Centennial Drive, Apt. 23, Vernon, BC V1T 2T8. **E:** odxa@rogers.com **W:** www.facebook.com/groups/ontariodx (private Facebook group) – **Vancouver Shortwave Association**, P.O.Box 500, Vancouver, BC V5L 1C.

MEXICO: Audio Pico DX Club, c/o César Granillo, Ap. Postal 309, 94301 Orizaba, Veracruz – **Club DX Miguel Auza**, c/o Luis Antero Aguilar, Ap. Postal 38, 98330 Miguel Auza, Zacatecas – **Consultorio DX**, c/o Miguel Angel Rocha Gámez, Ap. Postal 31, 31820 Ascensión, Chihuahua – **Sociedad de Ingenieros Radioescuchas**, c/o Rafael Gustavo Grajeda Rosado, Ap. Postal 203, Admon. No.1, 91701 Veracruz, Veracruz. **E:** rggr681121@hotmail.com

USA: Boston Area DXers, c/o Paul Graveline, 9 Stirling St., Andover, MA 01810-1408 **W:** www.naswa.net/badx – **Central Indiana Shortwave Club,** c/o Steve Hammer, 2517 E. DePauw Road, Indianapolis, IN 46227-4404. – **DecalcoMania**, c/o Phil Bytheway, 9705 Mary NW, Seattle, WA 98117-2334. (Club for collectors of station promo, items and airchecks). **E:** phil_tekno@yahoo.com **W:** www.anarc.org/decal° Pub: *DecalcoMania* – **Hampton Roads DX Association**, c/o Dr. Marc Fink, P.O.Box 2681, Chesapeake, VA 23327-2681. ☎ +1 757 547 3668 **E:** familyfoot@msn.com (LW, MW, SW, FM/TV) – **Indiana Recording Club,** c/o Bill Davies, 1729 E. 77th St., Indianapolis, IN 46240. (Club for airchecks and recordings of mediumwave stations). – **International Radio Club of America (IRCA)**, P.O.Box 60241, Lafayette, LA 70596. (MW only) **E:** ircamember@ircaonline.org **W:** www.ircaonline.org Pub: *DX Monitor* (printed & pdf) – **Longwave Club of America (LWCA)**, c/o Kevin Carey, 9213 State Route 5 & 20, Bloomfield, NY 14469 **E:** hq.lwca@gmail.com **W:** www.lwca.org Pub: *The Lowdown* – **Miami Valley DX Club (MVDXC)**, P.O.Box 292132, Columbus, OH 43229. **W:** www.anarc.org/mvdxc° Pub: *DX World*. – **Michigan Area Radio Enthusiasts Inc**, P.O.Box 200, Manchester, MI 48158. **E:** mare.radio@gmail.com – **Minnesota DX Club (MDXC)** c/o James Dale, 16330 Germane Ct W, Rosemount, MN 55068. **E:** mndxclub@charter.net Pub: *MDXC Newsletter* – **National Radio Club Inc (NRC)**, P.O.Box 473251, Aurora, CO 80047-3251. (MW only) **E:** via website contact page **W:** nationalradioclub.org Pub (bi-weekly in winter, monthly in summer): *DX News (DXN)* (printed), *e-DXN* (pdf version of DXN) – **North American Shortwave Association (NASWA)**, P.O. Box 3292, Allentown, PA 18104 **E:** hq@naswa.net **W:** www.naswa.net Pub: *The Journal* (monthly, printed) and *Flashsheet* (weekly, pdf) – **Pacific Northwest/British Columbia DX Club**, c/o Bruce Portzer, 6546 19th Ave NE, Seattle WA 98115. **E:** phil_tekno@yahoo.com **W:** www.anarc.org/pnbcdxc° Pub: *PNBCDXC newsletter* (every one or two months) – **Puna DX Club,** c/o Jerry Witham, P.O.Box 596, Keaau, HI 96749 – **Rocky Mountain Radio Listeners,** c/o Mike Curta, P.O.Box 470776, Aurora, CO 80047-0776. – **Southern California Area DXerS (SCADS)**, c/o Bill Fisher Sr., 6398 Pheasant Drive, Buena Park, CA 90620-1356. ☎ +1 714 522 6434 **E:** williamfishersr@gmail.com – **Worldwide TV-FM DX Association (WFTDA)**, P.O.Box 501, Somersville, CT 06072 (FM/TV only). **E:** sales@wtfda.org **W:** www.wtfda.org Pub: *VUD* (pdf).

SOUTH AMERICA

ARGENTINA: Grupo DX Suquia (GDXS), c/o Oscar H. González, Padre Vila 195, 5127 Río Primero, Córdoba. **E:** contacto@grupodx-suquia.com.ar **W:** grupodxsuquia.com.ar, www.facebook.com/groups/GrupoDXSuquia (Facebook group) Pub: *Circular DX* (SS, pdf) – **Grupo Radioescucha Argentino (GRA)**, c/o Marcelo A. Cornachioni, Alvarez Thomas 248, B1832DNF Lomas de Zamora, Buenos Aires. **E:** info@conexiongra.com.ar **W:** gruporadioescuchaar-gentino.wordpress.com

BRAZIL: Associação DX do Brasil, C.P. 4, 58300-970 Santa Rita, Paraiba. **E:** cartas@adxb.com.br **W:** www.adxb.com.br – **DX Clube do Brasil (DXCP)**, C.P. 1594, 09571-970 São Caetano do Sul (SP). **E:** dxcb@bol.com.br **W:** www.ondascurtas.com – **DX Clube Sem Fronteiras**, C.P. 77, 55002-970 Caruaru, Pernambuco. ☎ +55 81 992571734 **E:** dxclubesemfronteiras@gmail.com, dxcsf@dxclubesemfronteiras.com **W:** www.dxclubesemfronteiras.com Pub: *DX Sem Fronteiras* (Quartely, PP, printed & pdf)

CHILE: Federación de Clubes de Radioaficionados de Chile (FEDERACHI), c/o Héctor Frías Jofre, Dr. Eduardo Cruz Coke 389, Oficina C, Casilla 9570, Santiago 21. **E:** federachi@federachi.cl **W:** www.federachi.cl

COLOMBIA: Grupo Internacional de Diexistas y Radioaficionados, c/o Miguel Bayona. **E:** m-bayona@hotmail.com

URUGUAY: Grupo DX Internacional, Calle Batovi 2068, CP 11800, Montevideo. **E:** grupodxinternacional@yahoo.com **W:** www.facebook.com/groups/grupodxinternacional Pub: *Bitacora DX* (global)

VENEZUELA: Asociación Diexista de Venezuela, Ap. Postal 65657, Caracas 1066-A. **E:** marl1@hotmail.com – **Club Diexistas de la Amistad Internacional (CDXA)**, c/o San Gil Gonzáles Santiago, Ap. Postal 202, Barinas, Estado Barinas 5201-A. **E:** 40cdxainternacional@yahoo.com **W:** venezueladx.blogspot.com°; www.facebook.com/groups/531629043622500 (public Facebook group "Cadena DX")

STANDARD TIME & FREQUENCY TRANSMISSIONS

What are STFTs?

Standard Time and Frequency Transmissions (STFTs) are transmissions aimed at testing and calibrating radio receivers and synchronizing clocks. When broadcast on shortwave, STFTs usually consist of continuous AM and/or SSB transmissions of 'beeps' or 'pips' every second (often referred to as 'Time Signals'), with the time in UTC (or local time) announced at certain intervals. Some stations broadcast for 24 hours a day while other stations run for up to a few hours daily or on certain days of the week.

Also listed in this chapter is a selection of standard broadcast and VLF utility stations that broadcast regular timechecks in modes other than AM/SSB. The VLF transmitters of the maritime navigation networks Loran-C/Chayka on 100kHz and similar VLF txs primarily used for navigation purposes, except for txs of the "Beta" system of the Russian Navy and BPL in P.R. China, are not included.

Using STFTs

STFTs are invaluable aids for the SW radio user. Not only do they allow listeners to synchronise clocks to UTC but they are also a handy tool for checking propagation and reception paths. Their most useful role for serious shortwave listeners, however, is for checking that equipment is performing as it should and to test for receiver frequency calibration errors.

Checking Performance

It is possible to carry out tests on a variety of frequencies ranging from 2500 to 20000kHz. First select an appropriate set of STFTs, perhaps by saving them into a set of memory channels if your radio has the facility. A quick check can be made for the characteristic ticks and pulses to ensure that there is a good reception path and that the STFT is currently active, before moving on to the tests themselves. Don't forget that it is essential to allow the radio to warm up for at least one hour before starting these tests.

The object of the exercise is to mix the incoming STFT signal with an internally generated signal from the radio's Beat Frequency Oscillator (BFO) and then tune the radio until the resulting whistle, or heterodyne as it is known, drops down to zero. This process of tuning for 'zero beat' then ensures that the radio is on exactly the same frequency as the transmission – any error shown on the dial will be the receiver error and any drift in tone will be receiver drift.

For most radios it will suffice to select either upper or lower sideband mode with a wide filter setting and use a loudspeaker or pair of headphones with a good low frequency audio performance. Many SW receivers have internal speakers which are not good when it comes to reproducing low notes so are useless for this procedure.

As you carefully tune down and hear the note drop, you should find that the S-meter needle starts to fluctuate. This means that you are very close to 'zero beat'. The lower the rate of S-meter needle movement, the nearer you are to the end point. At this stage you will probably not be able to hear much in the headphones apart from a near silent carrier, and the meter will be your best guide as it will be indicating the 'phase error' between the STFT and your BFO. When your needle moves at its slowest rate, you have reached zero beat. Make a note of the dial reading as this will show the receiver error.

For those radios with particularly good filters, which may prevent a 'zero beat' approach, a similar technique can be used by switching to CW mode. This method requires the use of an audio digital frequency meter – ask around at your radio club and you will probably find one. First of all, refer to the manual and find the 'CW offset' frequency. This is the audio frequency which the receiver will produce when it is exactly tuned to the carrier of the STFT. Common values are 600Hz to 800Hz. Some radios allow the user to programme the CW offset, so make sure that it has not been changed before you start the tests.

The procedure is essentially the same as has just been described, except that you will be tuning the radio until the DFM reads 600Hz exactly, then the receiver dial will show you any error. By repeating this test on a number of frequencies, you can be confident that your radio is accurate, or at least be aware of any errors or developing problems, and of course these are handy techniques for testing a radio you are considering buying.

STFT Stations, Schedules and Contact Information

ARGENTINA

✉ Servicio de Hidrografía Naval, Observatorio Naval, Av. Montes de Oca 2124, C1270ABV Buenos Aires, Argentina ☎ +54 11 43611162
E: onba@hidro.gov.ar **W**: www.hidro.gov.ar

Location	Call	kHz	kW	Mode	Schedule
Buenos Aires	LOL	10000	2	AM	1400-1500 (MF)

BELARUS

✉ 43-y uzel svyazi Voenno-morskogo Flota RF, Vileyka, Belarus.

Location	Call	kHz	kW	Mode	Schedule
Vileyka	RJH69	*25	300	CW	0706-0747

Key: *) :06-:25 on 25.0, :27-:30 on 25.1, :32-:35 on 25.5, :38-:41 on 23.0, :44-:47 on 20.5kHz.
NB: Site is operated by Russian Navy; see Russia for HQ.

BRAZIL

✉ Divisão Serviço da Hora (DSHO), Observatório Nacional, R. Gal. José Cristino 77, São Cristóvão, Rio de Janeiro, CEP 20921-400, Brazil ☎ +55 21 35049100
E: dsh@on.br **W**: www.horalegalbrasil.mct.on.br

Location	Call	kHz	kW	Mode	Schedule
Rio de Janeiro	PPE	10000	1	H3E*	24h

Key: *) USB/AM

CANADA

✉ National Research Council Canada (NRC), 1200 Montreal Road, Bldg M-58, Ottawa, ON, K1A 0R6, Canada ☎ +1 613 9935698
E: radio.chu@nrc-cnrc.gc.ca **W:** nrc.canada.ca

Location	Call	kHz	kW	Mode	Schedule
Ottawa	CHU	3330	3	H3E*	24h
	CHU	7850	5	H3E*	24h
	CHU	14670	3	H3E*	24h

Key: *) USB/AM

CHINA (P.R.)

✉ National Time Service Center (NTSC), Chinese Academy of Sciences, P.O.Box 18, Lintong 710600, Shaanxi, P.R.China ☎ +86 29 83890326
E: kyc@ntsc.cas.cn **W:** www.ntsc.cas.cn

Location	Call	kHz	kW	Mode	Schedule
Shangqiu	BPC	68.5	90	CW	0000-2100
Pucheng	BPL	100	800	-	0530-1330

Location	Call	kHz	kW	Mode	Schedule
Pucheng	BPM	2500	10	AM	0730-0100
	BPM	5000	20	AM	24h
	BPM	10000	20	AM	24h
	BPM	15000	20	AM	0100-0900

FRANCE

Systèmes de Référence Temps-Espace (SYRTE), L'Observatoire de Paris, 61 avenue de l'Observatoire, 75014 Paris, France ☎+33 140512067
E: info.syrte@obspm.fr **W:** syrte.obspm.fr

Location	Call	kHz	kW	Mode	Schedule
Allouis	(none)	162	800	PSK	24h

NB: Tx is leased from TDF

GERMANY

Physikalisch-Technische Bundesanstalt (PTB), Bundesallee 100, 38116 Braunschweig, Germany ☎ +49 531 59230
E: time@ptb.de **W:** www.ptb.de

Location	Call	kHz	kW	Mode	Schedule
Mainflingen	DCF77	77.5	50	CW/PSK	24h

NB: Tx is leased from Media Broadcast.

HAWAII (USA)

NIST radio station WWVH, P.O.Box 417, Kekaha, HI 96752, USA
E: wwvh@boulder.nist.gov

Location	Call	kHz	kW	Mode	Schedule
Kekaha, HI	WWVH	2500	5	AM	24h
	WWVH	5000	10	AM	24h
	WWVH	10000	10	AM	24h
	WWVH	15000	10	AM	24h

NB: Time announced in female voice. NIST HQ: see USA.

JAPAN

Japan Standard Time Group, Applied Electromagnetic Research Institute, National Institute of Information and Communications Technology (NICT), 4-2-1, Nukui-Kitamachi, Koganei, Tokyo 184-8795, Japan ☎ +81 42 3277567
E: horonet@ml.nict.go.jp **W:** jjy.nict.go.jp

Location	Call	kHz	kW	Mode	Schedule
Mt. Ohtakadoya	JJY	40	10	CW	24h
Mt. Hagane	JJY	60	10	CW	24h

KOREA, SOUTH

Center for Time and Frequency, Korea Research Institute of Standards & Science (KRISS), 267 Gajeong-ro, Yuseong-gu, Daejeon 34113, Rep. of Korea ☎ +82 42 8685145
E: dhyu@kriss.re.kr **W:** www.kriss.re.kr

Location	Call	kHz	kW	Mode	Schedule
Yeoju*	-	65	10	CW	24h
Daejeon	HLA	5000	2	AM	24h

Key: *) Tx for test purposes only (installed at KBS tx site)

KYRGYZSTAN

Sukhoputnyy uzel svyazi Tikhookeanskogo flota VMF RF, Chaldybar, Kyrgyzstan.

Location	Call	kHz	kW	Mode	Schedule
Chaldybar	RJH66	*25	300	CW	0406-0447,1006-1047

Key: *) :06-:25 on 25.0, :27-:30 on 25.1, :32-:35 on 25.5, :38-:41 on 23.0, :44-:47 on 20.5kHz.
NB: Site is operated by Russian Navy; see Russia for HQ.

RUSSIA

Generalniy Shtab Voenno-morskogo Flota RF (Russian Navy), St.Petersburg, Russia **W:** flot.com

Location	Call	kHz	kW	Mode	Schedule
Arkhangelsk	RJH77	*25	300	CW	0906-0947
Khabarovsk	RAB99	**25	300	CW	0206-0236, 0606-0636
Krasnodar	RJH63	**25	300	CW+	1106-1140
N.Novgorod	RJH90	*25	300	CW	0806-0847

Key: *) :06-:25 on 25.0, :27-:30 on 25.1, :32-:35 on 25.5, :38-:41 on 23.0, :44-:47 on 20.5kHz; **) :06-:20 on 25.0, :21-:23 on 25.1, :24-:26 on 25.5, :27-:31 on 23.0, :32-:36(40) on 20.5kHz; +) also in FSK mode :36-:40 on 20.5kHz.

Main Metrological Center of the State Service of Time, Frequency and Determination of the Parameters of the Earth Rotation (MMC SSTF), Russian Metrological Institute of Technical Physics and Radio Engineering (FSUE "VNIIFTRI"), Moscow Region, 141570 Mendeleevo, Russia ☎+7 495 5350836
E: office@vniiftri.ru **W:** www.vniiftri.ru

Location	Call	kHz	kW	Mode	Schedule
Taldom	RBU	66.6	50	CW	24h
Taldom	RWM	4996	10	CW	24h
Taldom	RWM	9996	10	CW	24h
Taldom	RWM	14996	10	CW	24h

NB: Txs are leased from RTRS.

East Siberian Branch of FSUE "VNIIFTR", 664056 Irkutsk, ul. Borodina 57, Russia ☎+7 3952 468303
E: office@vniiftri-irk.ru **W:** www.vniiftri-irk.ru

Location	Call	kHz	kW	Mode	Schedule
Angarsk	RTZ	50	10	CW	2000-1900

NB: Tx is leased from RTRS.

TAIWAN

National Time and Frequency Standard Laboratory, Chunghwa Telecom Co. Ltd, P.O.Box 71, Zhongli 320, Rep. of China ☎+886 3 4244066
E: stdtime@gmail.com **W:** www.stdtime.gov.tw

Location	Call	kHz	kW	Mode	Schedule
Chung-Li	BSF	77.5	1	CW	24h

UNITED KINGDOM

National Physical Laboratory, Hampton Road, Teddington, Middlesex, TW11 0LW, United Kingdom ☎ +44 20 89773222
E: time@npl.co.uk **W:** www.npl.co.uk

Location	Call	kHz	kW	Mode	Schedule
Anthorn*	MSF	60	15	CW	24h
Droitwich**	(none)	198	500	PSK	24h

Key: *) Tx is leased from Encompass Digital Media; **) Tx is provided by Arqiva and carries BBC Radio 4/BBCWS prgrs.

UNITED STATES OF AMERICA

National Institute of Standards and Technology (NIST), Physical Masurement Laboratory (PML), Time & Frequency Division, 325 Broadway, M/S 847, Boulder, CO 80305-3328, USA ☎ +1 303 4973295
E: inquiries@nist.gov **W:** www.nist.gov

NIST radio stations WWV/WWVB, 2000 East County Rd. 58, Ft. Collins, CO 80524 **E:** nist.radio@boulder.nist.gov **W:** wwv@nist.gov

Location	Call	kHz	kW	Mode	Schedule
Ft. Collins, CO	WWVB	60	50	CW	24h
	WWV	2500	2.5	AM	24h
	WWV	5000	10	AM	24h
	WWV	10000	10	AM	24h
	WWV	15000	10	AM	24h
	WWV	20000	2.5	AM	24h
	WWV	25000	2.5	AM	24h*

Key: *) Experimental broadcast, trs may be interrupted or suspended without notice

NB: WWV: Time announced in male voice. See also under Hawaii.

INTERNATIONAL BROADCASTING ORGANISATIONS & INSTITUTES

ARAB STATES BROADCASTING UNION (ASBU)
CP 250, 1080 Tunis Cedex, Tunisia. Street address: Rue 8840, centre urban nord, Tunis, Tunisia
☎ +216 71849000
E: asbu@asbu.net **W:** www.asbu.net
L.P: DG: Suleiman Abderrehim

ASIA-PACIFIC BROADCASTING UNION (ABU)
P.O.Box 12287, 50772 Kuala Lumpur, Malaysia
☎ +60 3 22823592
E: info@abu.org.my **W:** www.abu.org.my
L.P: Pres (acting): Ibrahim Eren; Secr. General: Javad Mottaghi

ASIA-PACIFIC INSTITUTE FOR BROADCASTING DEVELOPMENT (AIBD)
P.O.Box 12066, 50766 Kuala Lumpur, Malaysia. Street address: Angkasapuri, Jalan Pantai Dalam, 50614 Kuala Lumpur, Malaysia
☎ +60 3 22824618
E: info@aibd.org.my **W:** www.aibd.org.my
L.P: Dir: Philomena Gnanapragasam

ASIA-PACIFIC SATELLITE COMMUNICATIONS COUNCIL (APSCC)
Suite T-1602 Poonglim Iwantplus, 255-1 Seohyun-dong, Bundang-gu, Seongnam, Gyeonggi-do 463-862, Republic of Korea
☎ +82 31 7836244
E: info@apscc.or.kr **W:** www.apscc.or.kr
L.P: Pres: Gregg Daffner

ASOCIACIÓN INTERNACIONAL DE RADIODIFUSIÓN (AIR)
Carlos Quijano 1264, 11100 Montevideo, Uruquay
☎ +598 2 9011319
E: mail@airiab.com **W:** www.airiab.com
L.P: Pres: José Louis Saca; DG: Juan Andres Lerena

CARIBBEAN BROADCASTING UNION (CBU)
Caribbean Media Centre, Suite 1B, Building #6A, Harbour Industrial Estate, Harbour Road, St. Michael, 11145, Barbados
☎ +1 246 4301007
E: info@caribroadcastunion.org **W:** caribroadcastunion.org
L.P: Pres: Gary Allen

DIGITAL RADIO MONDIALE (DRM)
DRM Project Office, P.O.Box 360, CH-1218 Grand-Saconnex, Switzerland
E: projectoffice@drm.org **W:** www.drm.org
L.P: Chair (DRM Consortium)/Pres (DRM Association): Ruxandra Obreja

EUROPEAN BROADCASTING UNION (EBU)
L'Ancienne-Route 17A, CH-1218 Grand-Saconnex, Switzerland
☎ +41 22 7172111 Fax +41 22 7474000
E: ebu@ebu.ch **W:** www.ebu.ch
L.P: DG: Noel Curran

HIGH FREQUENCY CO-ORDINATION CONFERENCE (HFCC)
E: info@hfcc.org **W:** www.hfcc.org
L.P: Chmn: Jeff White

INTERNATIONAL INSTITUTE OF COMMUNICATIONS (IIC)
Highlands House, 165 The Broadway, London, SW19 1NE, United Kingdom
☎ +44 20 85448076
E: enquiries@iicom.org **W:** www.iicom.org
L.P: Pres: Chris Chapman

INTERNATIONAL TELECOMMUNICATIONS UNION (ITU)
Place des Nations, 1211 Genève 20, Switzerland
☎ +41 22 7305111
E: itumail@itu.int **W:** www.itu.int
L.P: Secr. General: Houlin Zhao; Deputy Secr. General: Malcolm Johnson

NORTH AMERICAN BROADCASTERS ASSOCIATION (NABA)
c/o CBC, 205 Wellington St West, Suite 9C200, Toronto, ON M5V 3G7, Canada
☎ +41 22 7305111
E: contact@nabanet.com **W:** nabanet.com
L.P: Pres: Richard Friedel; DG: Michael McEwen

PUBLIC MEDIA ALLIANCE
Arts 1.80, DEV, University of East Anglia, Norwich NR4 7TJ, United Kingdom
☎ +44 1603 592335
E: info@publicmediaalliance.org **W:** publicmediaalliance.org
L.P: CEO: Sally-Ann Wilson

SOUTHERN AFRICAN BROADCASTING ASSOCIATION (SABA)
c/o NBC, Pettenkoffer St., Windhoek North, Windhoek, Namibia
E: dantagonanuses@gmail.com **W:** www.saba-news.org
L.P: Pres: Stanley Similo; Secr. General: Ellen Nanuses

UNION AFRICAINE DE RADIODIFFUSION (UAR)
BP 3237, Dakar, Senegal. Street address: Avenue Carde, Immeuble CSS, Dakar, Senegal
☎ +221 338211625
W: contact@uar-aub.org **W:** www.uar-aub.org
L.P: CEO: Grégoire Ndjaka

WORLD ASSOCIATION OF COMMUNITY RADIO BROADCASTERS (AMARC)
International Secretariat, 2 rue Sainte-Catherine Est, suite 102, Montréal, Quebec, H2X 1K4, Canada
☎ +1 514 9820351
W: www.amarceurope.eu; amarc-ap.org

WORLD DAB
WorldDAB Project Office, 6th Floor, 55 New Oxford Street, London, WC1A 1BS, United Kingdom
☎ +44 20 70100742
E: info@worlddab.org **W:** www.worlddab.org
L.P: Pres: Patrick Hannon

SELECTED INTERNET RESOURCES FOR DXERS & RADIO LISTENERS

GENERAL & LINK PAGES:

BCL News: bclnews.it
Bruce's AM Log: bamlog.com
DX Central: dxcentralonline.com
DX Info Centre: dxinfocentre.com
DXing.com: dxing.com
DXing.info: dxing.info
Canada's Original Radio website: dxer.ca
Hard-Core-DX: hard-core-dx.com
History of SW: ontheshortwaves.com
History of WRTH: wrthhistory.com
Radio Communication Archive: dokufunk.org
Radio Logs and Station Lists - 20's to today: worldradiohistory.com/Radio_Log_Master_Page.htm
Radio Portal: radio-portal.org
Radio Heritage Foundation: radioheritage.net
World of Radio: worldofradio.com
World Radio Map: worldradiomap.com

DATABASES & SCHEDULES:

ADDX Foreign Frequency List: addx.de/Hfpdat/plaene.php
AM Query: fcc.gov/media/radio/am-query
Asian Broadcasting Institute: abiweb.jp
Broadcasting in South & SE Asia: asiawaves.net
Canada & US AM Station Info: topazdesigns.com/ambc
DXAsia: dxasia.in
EiBi Shortwave Schedules: eibispace.de
FM List: fmlist.org
MW List: mwlist.org
Pacific Asian Log: radiohcritage.net/PAL_searchD.asp
Short-wave Info: short-wave.info

NEWS SOURCES AND BULLETINS:

BC-DX Top News: wwdxc.de/topnews.htm
Biener's DX-Digest: biener-media.de
DX-Fanzine: dxfanzine.com
DX-Listening Digest: worldofradio.com/dxldmid.html
Shortwave Bulletin: hard-core-dx.com/swb
Ydun's Mediumwave Info: mediumwave.info

ONLINE RADIO:

directory.shoutcast.com – live365.com – multilingualbooks.com/online-radio.html – publicradiofan.com – radio.garden – radiosure.com – tunein.com – vtuner.com
Web DX-listening: globaltuners.com – remotehams.com/online.html – rx.linkfanel.net – websdr.org

RECEIVERS, ANTENNAS:

Dave's Radio Receiver page: n9ewo.angelfire.com/
Receiver Test Data: sherweng.com/table.html
RF Circuit Building Blocks Page: qsl.net/wa1ion

STATION IDENTIFICATION:

Interval Signals Online: intervalsignals.net
Interval Signal Database: intervalsignals.org
National Anthems: national-anthems.net – nationalanthems.info

PROPAGATION:

Solar Terrestrial Activity Report: solen.info/solar
Space Weather Prediction Center: swpc.noaa.gov

MAILING LISTS, ETC:

A-DX Mailingliste (G): ratzer.at/a-dx
Hard-Core-DX mailing list: hard-core-dx.com/mailman/listinfo/hard-core-dx
Google groups at groups.google.com: rrusdx (Eng) – rusdxplus (Ru) – fr.rec.radio (F)
Lists at groups.io: dxrad (F) – SDR-Radio
Lists at Mailman.qth.net: AMFMTVDX – SWL
Lists at Yahoogroups.com: ABDX – ASWLC – ausS-WDXgroup – bangladx – bclnews (It.) – condiglist (S) – BCDX2 – conexiondigital (S) – cumbre_dx – dexismo (Port.) – DRM-shortwave-dx – drmna – dxld – dxingwithcumbre – dxplorer – dx_india – dx_sasia – fmdxitalia (It.) – harmonics – LatinMWDX – longwaveradiostation-listening – media_dx (Ru.) – mwdx – mw-br (Port.) – mwmasts – NORDX (Sw.) – NoticiasDX (S) – ondescourtes (F) – open_dx (Ru.) – PakistanDXers playdx2003 (It.) – ptdx (Port.) – RadioBroadcasting – radioescutas (Port.) – RealDX – recradioshortwave – SDRlist – sdr-users – shortwave – ShortwaveBasics – shortwavedxing – shortwavelistening – ShortWaveRadio – ShortwaveRadios – shortwave-radio – shortwaves – shortwavesites – Shortwave-SWL-Antenna –skywavesdx – skywavesmw – soft_radio – SWPirates – SWR-Wordwide – thebasicsofshortwave – UDXF – UKQRM – webreceivers
NB: Yahoo groups have now closed and many ex-Yahoo groups have moved to groups.io or elsewhere.
Facebook.com: Cumbre DX – I Love AM Radio – India DXing Cooperation Forum – Indian DX Club International – Mittelwellenfreunde (G) – No Mundo do Dexismo (Port.) – Radio Listening Interest Group – Shortwave Radio Station Listening – SWL for Shortwave Listeners – World DX – World Shortwave Forum – WRTH – World Radio TV Handbook

ADVERTISERS' INDEX

ADVERTISING SALES

Advertising sales manager:

Advertising Sales Manager
PO Box 290
Oxford OX2 7FT
UK
Tel: +44 1865 339355
Fax: +44 1865 339301
Email: wrth@wrth.com